Standard Edition

BUSINESS LAW

and the Legal Environment

FOURTH EDITION

Jeffrey F. Beatty
Boston University

Susan S. Samuelson
Boston University

THOMSON

™

WEST

Australia · Brazil · Canada · Mexico · Singapore · Spain · United Kingdom · United States

THOMSON

WEST

Business Law and the Legal Environment: Standard Edition, 4e
Jeffrey F. Beatty, Susan S. Samuelson

VP/Editorial Director:
Jack W. Calhoun

Publisher:
Rob Dewey

Acquisitions Editor:
Steve Silverstein, Esq.

Sr. Developmental Editor:
Bob Sandman

Executive Marketing Manager:
Lisa Lysne

Production Project Manager:
Tamborah Moore

Technology Project Editor:
Pam Wallace

Web Coordinator:
Scott Cook

Sr. Manufacturing Coordinator:
Charlene Taylor

Production House:
Lachina Publishing
Services

Printer:
QuebecorWorld-Versailles
Versailles, KY

Art Director:
Michelle Kunkler

Internal Designer:
Kim Torbeck, Imbue Design

Cover Designer:
Kim Torbeck, Imbue Design

Cover Images:
© Philip Coblentz/Brand X Pictures

Photography Manager:
John Hill

Photo Researcher:
Jan Seidel, Seidel Associates

Library of Congress Control Number:
2005935131

For more information about our
products, contact us at:

Thomson Learning Academic
Resource Center 1-800-423-0563

Thomson Higher Education
5191 Natorp Boulevard
Mason, Ohio 45040
USA

The study guide includes the following pertinent features:

- A Chapter Outline

- Chapter Objectives

- Matching Exercises

- True-False Questions

- Multiple Choice Questions

- Short Essays

- Case Problems

- Answers for Self-Study

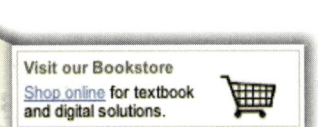
If your bookstore does not carry this study guide (0-324-37519-0), you can order it directly by visiting the "bookstore" at this text's companion Web site http://beatty.westbuslaw.com.

Contents: Overview

UNIT 5

Business Organizations 753

UNIT 6

Government Regulation 925

UNIT 7

Property and Cyberlaw 1001

Contents

UNIT 2

Contracts   229

Unit 4

Agency and Employment Law   649

UNIT 7

Property and Cyberlaw   1001

Preface

It has been more than a decade since we began work on the first edition of this textbook. At the time, publishers warned us that our undertaking was risky because there were already so many business law texts. Despite these warnings, we were convinced that there was a market for a business law book that was different from all the others. Our goal was to capture the passion and excitement, the sheer enjoyment, of the law. Business law is notoriously complex, and as authors we are obsessed with accuracy. Yet this intriguing subject also abounds with human conflict and hard-earned wisdom, forces that can make a law book sparkle.

Now, as the fourth edition goes to press, we look back over the past decade and think of the students who have said to us, "This is the best textbook I have ever read," or "I had no idea business law could be so interesting," or the faculty who have told us, "Until I read your book I never really understood UCC 2-207" or "With your book, we have great class discussions." Comments such as these never cease to thrill us and to make us grateful that we persisted in writing a business law text like no other—a book that is precise and authoritative *yet a pleasure to read.*

Comprehensive. Staying comprehensive means staying current. This fourth edition contains over 150 new cases. Almost all were reported within the last two or three years, and many within the last 12 months. We never include a new court opinion merely because it is recent; but the law evolves continually, and our willingness to toss out old cases and add important new ones insures that this book—and its readers—remain on the frontier of legal developments.

Look, for example, at the important field of corporate governance. All texts cover cumulative voting, and so do we. Yet a future executive is far likelier to face conflicts over Sarbanes-Oxley, executive compensation, and shareholder proposals. We present a clear path through this thicket of new issues, including comprehensive coverage of the Enron case and its more recent progeny. We want tomorrow's business leaders to anticipate the challenges that await them and then use their knowledge to avert problems.

We have greatly rewritten many chapters for this fourth edition, to insure full coverage of rapidly evolving issues such as cyberlaw, securities law, UCC revisions, and countless other topics. For example, Chapter 27 provides extensive coverage of the Bankruptcy Abuse Prevention and Consumer Protection Act of 2005 (page 624). However, we have kept the strong narrative flow from the earlier editions. Like you, we are here to teach. We do not use boxes because, in our experience, they disrupt the flow of the text. Students inform us that a box indicates peripheral material, that is, material they routinely skip; we prefer to give them an uncluttered whole. Each chapter contains several **Internet addresses,** offering students a quick link to additional knowledge. These addresses, however, are woven into the body of the text, to reinforce the point that new technology and research methods are an integral part of a lively discipline. For example, page 695 in

Chapter 30 on employment law contains the address of the Web site where the Labor Department answers questions about the Family and Medical Leave Act. We believe that a well written chapter is seamless and cohesive.

Strong Narrative. The law is full of great stories, and we use them. Your students and ours should come to class excited. In Chapter 3, on dispute resolution (page 43), we explain litigation by tracking a double-indemnity lawsuit. An executive is dead. Did he drown accidentally, obligating the insurance company to pay? Or did the businessman commit suicide, voiding the policy? The student follows the action from the discovery of the body, through each step of the lawsuit, to the final appeal. The chapter offers a detailed discussion of dispute resolution, but it does so by exploiting the human drama that underlies litigation.

Students read stories and remember them. Strong narratives provide a rich context for the remarkable quantity of legal material presented. When students care about the material they are reading, they persevere. We have been delighted to find that they also arrive in class eager to question, discuss, and learn.

Precise. The great joy of using English accurately is the power it gives us to attack and dissect difficult issues, rendering them comprehensible to any lay reader. This text takes on the most complex legal topics of the day, yet it is appropriate for *all college and graduate level students.* Accessible prose goes hand in hand with legal precision. We take great pride in walking our readers through the most serpentine mazes this tough subject can offer. UCC section 2-207, on "battle of forms" conflicts, is hardly sexy material, but it is important. We spotlight the real-world need for section 2-207, and then use pin-point directions to guide our readers through its many switchbacks, arriving at a full understanding with sanity and good humor intact. (See page 262.)

As we explore this extraordinary discipline, we lure readers along with quirky anecdotes and colorful diagrams. (Notice the color displays throughout chapter 16 that clarify complex third party transactions.) However, before the trip is over we insist that students:

- gauge policy and political considerations,
- grapple with legal and social history,
- spot the nexus between disparate doctrines, and
- confront tough moral choices.

Beyond that, we ask students to figure out how to avoid the very problems that have generated our law.

Authoritative. We insist, as you do, on a lawbook that is indisputably accurate. A professor must teach with assurance, confident that every paragraph is the result of exhaustive research and meticulous presentation. Dozens of tough-minded people spent thousands of hours reviewing this book, and we are delighted with the stamp of approval we have received from trial and appellate judges, working attorneys, scholars, and teachers.

We reject the cloudy definitions and fuzzy explanations that can invade judicial opinions and legal scholarship. To highlight the most important rules, we use bold print, and then follow with vivacious examples written in clear, forceful English. (See, for example, the discussion of factual cause on page 159.) We cheerfully venture into contentious areas, relying on very recent appellate decisions. (Can computer software be patented? See page 1026.) Where there is doubt about the current (or future) status of a doctrine, we say so. In areas of particularly heated debate, we footnote our work: we want you to have absolute trust in this book.

A Book for Students. We have written this book as if we were speaking directly to our students. We provide black letter law, but we also explain concepts in terms that hook students. Over the years, we have learned how much more successfully we can teach when our students are intrigued. No matter what kind of a show we put on in class, *they are only learning when they want to learn.*

Every chapter begins with a story, either fictional or real, to illustrate the issues in the chapter and provide context. Chapter 7, on negligence (page 152), opens with a drunken student who staggers from a fraternity party and causes a serious automobile accident while driving home. The intoxicated student is obviously liable. Are other fraternity members? Students want to know—right away.

Most of today's college students were not yet born when Jimmy Carter was president. They come to college with varying levels of preparation; many now arrive from foreign countries. We have found that to teach business law most effectively we must provide its context. The chapter on securities law begins with a brief but graphic description of the 1929 stock market crash and the Great Depression (page 871). Only with this background do students grasp the importance and impact of our securities laws.

At the same time, we enjoy offering "nuts and bolts" information that grab students: how much money corporate directors earn; how scam artists create car accidents in order to file fraudulent insurance claims; how to create a living will. In Chapter 40, on consumer law, we bring home the issue of credit history by providing Web sites that students can use to check their own credit reports (page 965).

Students respond enthusiastically to this approach. One professor asked a student to compare our book with the one that the class was then using. This was the student's reaction: "I really enjoy reading the [Beatty & Samuelson] textbook, and I have decided that I will give you this memo ASAP, but I am keeping the book until Wednesday so that I may continue reading. Thanks! :-)"

Along with other professors, we have used this text in courses for undergraduates, MBAs and executive MBAs, the students ranging in age from 18 to 55. This book works, as some unsolicited comments indicate:

- An undergraduate wrote, "This is the best textbook I have had in college, on any subject."

- A business law professor stated that the "clarity of presentation is superlative. I have never seen the complexity of contract law made this readable."

- An MBA student commented, "I think the textbook is great. The book is relevant, easy to understand, and interesting."

- A state supreme court justice wrote that the book is "a valuable blend of rich scholarship and easy readability. Students and professors should rejoice with this publication."

- A Fortune 500 vice-president, enrolled in an Executive MBA program, commented, "I really liked the chapters. They were crisp, organized, and current. The information was easy to understand and enjoyable."

- An undergraduate wrote, "The textbook is awesome. A lot of the time I read more than what is assigned—I just don't want to stop."

Humor. Throughout the text we use humor—judiciously—to lighten and enlighten. Not surprisingly, students have applauded—but is wit appropriate? How dare we employ levity in this venerable discipline? We offer humor because we take law seriously. We revere the law for its ancient traditions, its dazzling intricacy, its relentless though imperfect attempt to give order and decency to our world. Because we are confident of our respect for the law, we are not afraid to employ some levity. Leaden prose masquerading as legal scholarship does no honor to the field.

Humor also helps retention. We have found that students remember a contract problem described in an original setting, and from that setting recall the underlying principle. By contrast, one widget is hard to distinguish from another.

FEATURES

We chose the features for our book with great care. As mentioned above, all features are considered an essential part of the text and are woven into its body. Also, each feature responds to an essential pedagogical goal. Here are some of those goals and the matching feature.

New Feature: Devil's Advocate

GOAL: Challenge the court's conclusions. In this feature we provide short critical commentary on the decision just reported. We are reminding students that the court's holding is the work of mortals. There is generally a very respectable counter-argument, which at least some people will find more persuasive. Students should consider the opposing view, and should practice formulating their own positions, independent of the judges' reasoning. A student who concludes, after analyzing alternative views, that the court got it right, understands the holding more comprehensively than one who never considered the other side.

For example, in chapter 8, on Criminal Law, we include the famous *Ewing* case (page 197) on cruel and unusual punishment, but follow it with a Devil's Advocate feature arguing against a sentence of 25 years to life in a recidivist shoplifting case.

New Feature: Public Policy

GOAL: Provide context for understanding the law. What are the policies underlying this case or statute? Why is the law this way? What is the impact of the law? In Chapter 36 on Shareholders, we explain why Sarbanes-Oxley was passed but then provide data about the cost of compliance. Is this statute worth the cost? (page 862).

For cases, we assume that the court's decision wisely allocated compensation between the parties, but then ask: was it the best ruling for the rest of us? This feature reminds students that a decision prompted by one dispute between two litigants may have dramatic consequences for local communities, companies, families, employees, voters and many others. What are the financial implications of the holding? Will business costs be passed on to unsuspecting citizens? Who is harmed, who is helped? Is this the *best* possible decision? How would you improve it?

In chapter 15 on written contracts, a court refuses to enforce an oral agreement for the sale of land even though the defendant, in court when the agreement was announced, promptly put the property up for sale, then changed her mind. Public Policy (page 338) forces students to question whether the statute of frauds is now routinely abused.

You Be The Judge

GOAL: Get them thinking independently. When reading case opinions, students tend to accept the court's "answer." Judges, of course, try to write decisions that appear indisputable, when in reality they may be controversial—or wrong. From time to time we want students to think through the problem and reach their own answer. Virtually every chapter contains a You Be The Judge feature, providing the facts of the case and conflicting appellate arguments. The court's decision, however, appears only in the Instructor's Manual.

Since students do not know the result, discussions tend to be more free-flowing. For instance, many commentators feel that *Smith v. Van Gorkom*, the landmark case on the business judgment rule, was wrongly decided. However, when students read the court's opinion they rarely consider the opposing side. Now, with the case presented as You Be the Judge in Chapter 35 (page 834), the students disagree with the court at least half the time. They are thinking.

Economics & the Law

Goal: Understand the economic impact of the law. This feature helps students understand how laws do (or, in some cases, do not) make economic sense. For example, in Chapter 37 on securities (page 871) we explain why insider trading causes harm, and therefore, why the law prohibits it. Conversely, Chapter 41 on environmental law (page 974) explains why political considerations often interfere with the most rational environmental decisions.

Newsworthy

GOAL: Prove that the law touches each of us every day. Students are intrigued to see the relevancy of what they are learning. Each chapter contains at least one Newsworthy feature—a newspaper or magazine article illustrating the legal issue under discussion. Thus, in Chapter 28 on agency law (page 650), an article about an American diplomat killed by terrorists demonstrates that an agency relationship exists only when the principal has control over its agent.

Cyberlaw

GOAL: Master the present and anticipate the future. The computer has changed all of our lives forever, and the courts and statute books are full of fascinating cyberlaw issues. Do employers have the right to read workers' e-mail? When does an electronic signature satisfy the statute of frauds? Can a company hold its shareholder meetings in cyberspace? Cyberlaw discussions are woven throughout the chapters, highlighted with an icon.

At Risk

GOAL: Help managers stay out of court. As every lawyer knows, the best lawsuit is the one that never happens. Some of our students are already in the workforce, and the rest soon will be, so we offer ideas on avoiding legal disputes. Sometimes we provide detailed methods to avoid the particular problem; other times we challenge the students to formulate their own approach to dispute prevention.

Ethics

GOAL: Make ethics real. We ask ethical questions about cases, legal issues, and commercial practices. Is it fair for one party to void a contract by arguing, months after the fact, that there was no consideration? Do managers have ethical obligations to older workers for whom employment opportunities may be limited? What is wrong with bribery? What is the ethical obligation of developed nations to dispose of toxic waste from computers? We do not have definitive answers but believe that asking the questions, and encouraging discussion, reminds students that ethics is an essential element of justice, and of a satisfying life.

Update

Goal: To keep students current. As we go to press, this book is accurate and up to date. Inevitably, however, during the book's three-year life span some laws will change.

Courts will decide cases, legislatures will pass statutes. When we can foresee that the law is likely to change in a particular area, we ask the students to research the latest developments. For example, in Chapter 47 on estates and insurance, we reported that Congress was considering legislation to reduce or eliminate the estate tax and ask students to research the status of this law (p. 1117).

Cases

GOAL: Let the judges speak. Each case begins with a summary of the facts and a statement of the issue. Next comes a tightly edited version of the decision, in the court's own language, so that students "hear" the law developing in the diverse voices of our many judges. We cite cases using a modified bluebook form. In the principal cases in each chapter, we provide the state or federal citation, the regional citation, and the LEXIS or Westlaw citation. We also give students a brief description of the court. Because many of our cases are so recent, some will have only a regional reporter and a LEXIS or Westlaw citation.

Practice Tests

GOAL: Encourage students to practice! At the end of the chapters we challenge the students with ten or more problems, including the following:

- *Internet Research Problem.* This question sends students to the Beatty & Samuelson *Business Law (Standard Edition)* Web site. There they will find an Internet link where they can explore issues from the chapter.

- *You Be The Judge Writing Problem.* The students are given appellate arguments on both sides of the question and must prepare a written opinion.

- *Ethics.* This question highlights the ethical issues of a dispute and calls upon the student to formulate a specific, reasoned response.

- *CPA Questions.* For topics covered by the CPA exam, administered by the American Institute of Certified Public Accountants, the practice tests include questions from previous CPA exams.

- *Role Reversal.* Students are asked to formulate their own test questions. Crafting questions is a good way to reinforce what they already understand and recognize areas that they need to review.

TEACHING MATERIALS

For more information about any of these ancillaries, contact your Thomson Learning/West Legal Studies Sales Representative for more details, or visit the Beatty & Samuelson Business Law (Standard Edition) Web site at http://beatty.westbuslaw.com/.
Student Study Guide. (ISBN: 0-324-37519-0) Students may purchase a study guide that includes a chapter outline, chapter objectives, and practice questions. Students can find further practice problems in the Online Quiz at http://beatty.westbuslaw.com.
Instructor's Manual. (ISBN: 0-324-37532-8) This manual includes special features to enhance class discussion and student progress:

- Dialogues. These are a series of questions-and-answers on pivotal cases and topics. The questions provide enough material to teach a full session. In a pinch, you could walk into class with nothing but the manual and use the Dialogues to conduct an exciting class.

- Action learning ideas: interviews, quick research projects, drafting exercises, classroom activities, commercial analyses, and other suggested assignments that get students out of their chairs and into the diverse settings of business law.

- Skits. Various chapters have lively skits that students can perform in class, with no rehearsal, to put legal doctrine in a real-life context.

- A chapter theme and a quote of the day.

- Current Focus. This feature offers updates of text material.

- Additional cases and examples.

- Answers to You Be the Judge cases from the text and to the Practice Test questions found at the end of each chapter.

Test Bank. (ISBN: 0-324-37531-X) The test bank offers hundreds of essay, short answer, and multiple choice problems and may be obtained in hard copy or electronic format.

ExamView Testing Software—Computerized Testing Software. This testing software contains all of the questions in the printed test bank. This program is an easy-to-use test creation software compatible with Microsoft Windows. Instructors can add or edit questions, instructions, and answers; and select questions by previewing them on the screen, selecting them randomly, or selecting them by number. Instructors can also create and administer quizzes online, whether over the Internet, a local area network (LAN), or a wide area network (WAN). The ExamView testing software is available on the Instructor's Resource CD.

Instructor's Resource CD (IRCD). (ISBN: 0-324-37528-X) The IRCD contains the ExamView testing software files, the test bank in Microsoft Word files, the Instructor's Manual in Microsoft Word files, and the Microsoft PowerPoint Lecture Review Slides.

Microsoft PowerPoint Lecture Review Slides. PowerPoint slides are available for use by students as an aid to note-taking and by instructors for enhancing their lectures. Download these slides at at http://beatty.westbuslaw.com. The PowerPoint slides are also available on the IRCD.

West's Digital Video Library. Featuring 60+ segments on the most important topics in Business Law, West's Digital Video Library helps students make the connection between their textbook and the business world. Access to West's Digital Video Library is free when bundled with a new text, and students with used books can purchase access to the video clips online. New to this edition are LawFlix, twelve scenes from Hollywood movies with instructor materials for each film clip. The accompanying instructor materials include elements such as goals for the clips, questions for students (with answers for the instructor), background on the film and the scene, and fascinating trivia about the film, its actors and its history. For more information about West's Digital Video Library, visit: http://digitalvideolibrary.westbuslaw.com.

West Legal Studies in Business Resource Center. This Web site offers a unique, rich and robust online resource for instructors and students. The address http://www.westbuslaw.com provides customer service and product information, links to all text-supporting Web sites, and other cutting-edge resources such as *NewsEdge* and **Court Case Updates.**

LegalTrac. An excellent resource for research and writing assignments, *LegalTrac*™ provides indexing for approximately 875 titles including major law reviews, legal newspapers, bar association journals and international legal journals, and also contains law-related articles from over 1,000 additional business and general interest titles. *LegalTrac*™ is available as an optional package with a new text.

The Business and Company Resource Center. The Business & Company Resource Center (BCRC) is a premier online business research tool that allows you to seamlessly search thousands of periodicals, journals, references, financial information, industry reports, company histories and much more. Visit http://bcrc.swlearning.com to learn more about this powerful tool. BCRC is available as an optional package with a new text.

The Wall Street Journal. For a nominal additional cost, any new West Legal Studies in Business text can be packaged with a card entitling students to a 15-week subscription to both the print and online versions of *The Wall Street Journal*. Instructors who have at least seven students activate their subscriptions will automatically receive their own free subscription.

A Handbook of Basic Law Terms, Black's Law Dictionary Series. This paperback dictionary, prepared by the editor of the popular Black's Law Dictionary, can be packaged for a small additional cost with any new West Legal Studies in Business text.

Student Guide to the Sarbanes-Oxley Act. This brief overview for business students explains the Sarbanes-Oxley Act, what is required of whom, and how it might affect students in their business life. Available as an optional package with the text.

West Legal Studies in Business VHS Video Library. Qualified adopters using this text have access to the entire library of West videos, a vast selection of videos covering most business law issues. There are some restrictions, and if you have questions, please contact your local Thomson Learning/ West Legal Studies in Business sales representative or visit http://www.westbuslaw.com/video_library.html.

Interaction with the Authors. This is our standard: Every professor who adopts this book must have a superior experience. We are available to help in any way we can. Adopters of this text often call us or e-mail us to ask questions, obtain a syllabus, offer suggestions, share pedagogical concerns, or inquire about ancillaries. One of the pleasures of working on this project has been this link to so many colleagues around the country. We value those connections, are eager to respond, and would be happy to hear from you.

TO THE STUDENT

Each Practice Test contains one **Role Reversal** feature, in which we challenge you to create your own exam question. Your professor may ask you to submit the questions in writing or electronically or to prepare an overhead slide. The goal is to think creatively and accurately. The question should be challenging enough that the average student will need to stop and think but clear enough that there is only one answer. Questions can be formatted as essay, short answer, or multiple choice.

For a multiple choice question, the first step is to isolate the single issue that you want to test. For example, in the unit on contract law, you do not want to ask a question that concerns five different aspects of forming an agreement. A good question will focus exclusively on one issue, for example, whether a job offer has to be in writing (some do, others do not). Create a realistic fact pattern that raises the issue. Provide one answer that is clearly correct. Add additional answers that might seem plausible but are definitely incorrect.

Some exam questions are very direct and test whether a student knows a definition. Other questions require deeper analysis. Here are two multiple choice questions. The first is direct.

Question: Which contract is governed by the Uniform Commercial Code?

a. An agreement for an actor to appear in a movie for a $600,000 fee.
b. An agreement for an actor to appear in a movie for a fee of $600,000 plus 2% of box office.
c. An agreement for the sale of a house.
d. An agreement for the sale of 22,000 picture frames.
e. An agreement for the rental of an apartment.

As you will learn later on, the correct answer is (d) because the Code applies to the sale of goods, not to employment contracts or real estate deals.

The next question is more difficult, requiring the student to spot the issue of law involved (product liability), remember how damages are awarded in such cases (generally, without regard to fault), and make a simple calculation.

Question: Lightweight Corp. manufactures strings of Christmas tree lights and sells 3.5 million sets per year. Every year, between 10 and 20 of the company's strings have a manufacturing defect that causes a consumer injury. Maxine receives a severe shock from a Lightweight string of lights. She sues. The evidence at trial is that: 1) Lightweight's safety record is the best in the industry; 2) all competing companies have a higher rate of injuries; 3) the lights that injured Maxine arrived at her house in the factory box, untouched by anyone outside of Lightweight; 4) Maxine operated the lights properly. Maxine's medical bills amount to $200,000; her lost income is $100,000; and her pain and suffering amounts to $600,000. What is the probable outcome at trial?

a. Maxine will win $200,000.
b. Maxine will win $100,000.
c. Maxine will win $900,000.
d. Maxine will win nothing.
e. Lightweight might win damages for a frivolous lawsuit.

As you will learn, the correct answer is (c). Lightweight is responsible under product liability law regardless of its careful work and excellent record. Maxine is entitled to all of her damages. Notice that the same question could be used in essay format, simply by deleting the multiple choice answers.

Jeffrey F. Beatty
Phone: (617) 353-6397
E-mail: jfbeatty@bu.edu

Susan S. Samuelson
Phone: (617) 353-2033
E-mail: ssamuels@bu.edu

Boston, Massachusetts

ACKNOWLEDGMENTS

We are grateful to the following reviewers who gave such helpful comments on the first three editions:

Weldon Blake
Bethune Cookman College

Karl Boedecker
University of San Francisco

Brad Childs
Belmont University

Philip E. DeMarco
Mission Community College

Julia Derrick
Brevard Community College

Carol Docan
California State University, Northridge

Kiren Dosanjh
California State University Northridge

Rafi Efrat
California State University, Northridge

Mary Kay Finn
The University of Akron

Edward Gac
University of Colorado

Randall K. Hanson
University of North Carolina
  at Wilmington

Charles Hartmann
Wright State University

Thomas Higgins
Illinois Central College

Charles E. King
Colorado Christian University

Richard L. Kohn
Southeast Community College

Greg McCann
Stetson University

Linda Moran
Santa Rosa Jr. College

Carol L. Nielsen
Bemidji State University

Cynthia Phillips
Moorehead State University

Vivica Pierre
California State University, Long Beach

Linda Samuels
The University of Akron

Minna Schiller
Bellevue Community College

Lara Short
Middle Tennessee State University

Charles Soos
Rutgers School of Business

Ben Thompson
Georgia Southern University

Scott White
University of Wisconsin–Platteville

Dexter Woods
Ohio Northern University

For Annabel, *semper laetans*
j.f.b.

For Bill, *valens atque benevolus*
s.s.s.

The Legal Environment

Introduction to Law

The Pagans were a motorcycle gang with a reputation for violence. Two of its rougher members, Rhino and Backdraft, entered a tavern called the Pub Zone, shoving their way past the bouncer. The pair wore gang insignia, in violation of the bar's rules. For a while, all was quiet, as the two sipped drinks at the bar. Then they followed an innocent patron toward the men's room, and things happened fast.

"Wait a moment," you may be thinking. "Are we reading a chapter on business law or one about biker crimes in a roadside tavern?" Both.

Law is powerful, essential, and fascinating. We hope this book will persuade you of all three ideas. Law can also be surprising. Later in the chapter we will return to the Pub Zone (with armed guards) and follow Rhino and Backdraft to the back of the pub. Yes, the pair engaged in street crime, which is hardly a focus of this text. However, their criminal acts will enable us to explore one of the law's basic principles, negligence. Should a pub owner pay money damages to the victim of gang violence? The owner herself did nothing aggressive. Should she have prevented the harm? Does her failure to stop the assault make her liable?

We place great demands on our courts, asking them to make our large, complex, and sometimes violent society into a safer, fairer, more orderly place. The Pub Zone case is a good example of how judges reason their way through the convoluted issues involved. What began as a gang incident ends up as a matter of commercial liability. We will traipse after Rhino and Backdraft because they have a lesson to teach anyone who enters the world of business. ■

THREE IMPORTANT IDEAS ABOUT LAW

Power

The strong reach of the law touches us all. To understand something that powerful is itself power. Suppose, some years after graduation, you are a mid-level manager at Sublime Corp., which manufactures and distributes video games and related hardware and software. You are delighted with this important position in an excellent company—and especially glad you bring legal knowledge to the job. Sarah, an expert at computer-generated imagery, complains that Rob, her boss, is constantly touching her and making lewd comments. That is sexual harassment and your knowledge of *employment law* helps you respond promptly and carefully. You have dinner with Jake, who has his own software company. Jake wants to manufacture an exciting new video game in cooperation with Sublime, but you are careful not to create a binding deal. (*Contract law.*) Jake mentions that a similar game is already on the market. Do you have the right to market one like it? That answer you already know. (*Intellectual property law.*)

The next day a letter from the Environmental Protection Agency asks how your company disposes of toxic chemicals used to manufacture computer drives. You can discuss it efficiently with in-house counsel, because you have a working knowledge of *environmental law* and *administrative law*. You may think your corporation is about to surge ahead in its field, and you would like to invest in its stock. But wait! Are you engaging in insider trading? Your training in *securities law* will distinguish the intelligent investment from the felony.

It is not only as a corporate manager that you will confront the law. As a voter, investor, juror, entrepreneur, and community member, you will influence and be affected by the law. Whenever you take a stance about a legal issue, whether in the corporate office, in the voting booth, or as part of local community groups, you help to create the social fabric of our nation. Your views are vital. This book will offer you knowledge and ideas from which to form and continually reassess your legal opinions and values.

Importance

Law is also essential. Every society of which we have any historical record has had some system of laws. Naturally, the systems have varied enormously.

An extraordinary example of a detailed written law comes from the Visigoths, a nomadic European people who overran much of present-day France and Spain during the fifth and sixth centuries A.D. Their code admirably required judges to be "quick of perception, clear in judgment, and lenient in the infliction of penalties." It detailed dozens of crimes. For example, a freeman who kidnapped the slave of another had to repay the owner with four slaves and suffer 100 lashes. If he did not have four slaves to give, the kidnapper was himself reduced to slavery. Sadly, the code explicitly permitted torture of slaves and lower-class freemen, while prohibiting it for nobles.[1] The Iroquois Native Americans, disregarded by many historians, in fact played a role in the creation of our own government. Five major nations made up the Iroquois group: the Mohawk, Cayuga, Oneida, Onondaga, and Seneca. Each nation governed itself as to domestic issues. But each nation also elected "sachems" to a League of the Iroquois. The league had authority over any matters that were common to all, such as relations with outsiders. Thus, by the fifteenth century, the Iroquois had solved the problem of *federalism:* how to have two levels of government, each with specified powers. Their system impressed Benjamin Franklin and others and influenced the drafting of our Constitution, with its powers divided between state and federal governments.[2] As European nations today seek to create a more united Europe, they struggle with the same problem.

The greatest of all Chinese lawgivers disliked written law altogether. Confucius, who lived from 551 to 479 B.C.E., understood law within a broader social perspective. He considered good rulers, strong family ties, and an enlightened nobility to be the surest methods to a good society. "As a judge, I decide disputes, for that is my duty; but the best thing that could happen would be to eliminate the causes for litigation!" Although he spoke 2,500 years ago, the distinction Confucius described is still critically important in our society: Which do we trust more—a written law or the people who enforce it?

Fascination

In 1835, the young French aristocrat Alexis de Tocqueville traveled through the United States, observing the newly democratic people and the qualities that made them unique. One of the things that struck de Tocqueville most forcefully was the American tendency to file suit: "Scarcely any political question arises in the United States that is not resolved, sooner or later, into a judicial question."[3] De Tocqueville got it right: For better or worse, we do expect courts to solve many problems.

Not only do Americans litigate—they watch each other do it. Every television season offers at least one new courtroom drama to a national audience breathless for more cross-examination. Almost all of the states permit live television coverage of real trials. The most heavily viewed event in the history of the medium was the O.J. Simpson murder trial, although as this book goes to press, that honor may be assumed by the trial of a certain pop star. Nonetheless, cameras in the courthouse are still controversial. Federal courts generally prohibit them. Only a small (but growing) number of foreign countries allows coverage of some judicial proceedings, including Australia, Canada, France, Hong Kong, Israel, Italy, the Netherlands, Norway, the Philippines, and Spain. Proponents urge that televising trials increases awareness of social ills and reduces the chances of judicial unfairness. Opponents argue that the camera transforms a dignified search for truth into a carnival show of publicity gimmicks.

Regardless of where we allow cameras, it is an undeniable benefit of the electronic age that we can obtain information so quickly. From time to time we will mention Web sites of interest. Some of these are for nonprofit groups while others are commercial sites. We do not endorse or advocate on behalf of any group or company, but simply wish to alert you to what is out there. The commercial site of a cable television company devoted to trial broadcasts, http://www.courttv.com/, includes up-to-the-minute information on current cases, often including trial testimony, appeal briefs, and other timely data.

---

[1]   S.P. Scott, *Visigothic Code (Forum Judicum)* (Littleton, CO: Fred B. Rothman & Co., 1982), pp. 3, 45.
[2]   Jack Weatherford, *Indian Givers* (New York: Fawcett Columbine, 1988), pp. 133–150.
[3]   Alexis de Tocqueville, *Democracy in America* (1835), Vol. 1, Ch. 16.

The law is a big part of our lives, and it is wise to know something about it. Within a few weeks, you will probably find yourself following legal events in the news with keener interest and deeper understanding. In this chapter we develop the background for our study. We look at where law comes from: its history and its present-day institutions. In the section on jurisprudence, we examine different theories about what "law" really means. And finally we see how courts—and students—analyze a case.

ORIGINS OF OUR LAW

It would be nice if we could look up "the law" in one book, memorize it, and then apply it. But the law is not that simple, and *cannot* be that simple, because it reflects the complexity of contemporary life. In truth, there is no such thing as "the law." Principles and rules of law actually come from many different sources. Why is this so? In part because we inherited a complex structure of laws from England. We will see that by the time of the American Revolution, English law was already an intricate system.

Additionally, ours is a nation born in revolution and created, in large part, to protect the rights of its people from the government. The Founding Fathers created a national government but insisted that the individual states maintain control in many areas. As a result, each state has its own government with exclusive power over many important areas of our lives. To top it off, the Founders guaranteed many rights to the people alone, ordering national *and* state governments to keep clear. This has worked, but it has caused a multilayered system, with 50 state governments and one federal government all creating and enforcing law.

A summary of English legal history will show the origin of our legal institutions. This brisk survey will also demonstrate that certain problems never go away. Anglo-Saxon England, about 1,000 years ago, was a world utterly different from our own. Yet we can see uncanny foreshadowings of our own unfinished efforts to create a peaceful world.

English Roots

England in the tenth century was a rustic agricultural community with a tiny population and very little law or order. Danes and Swedes invaded repeatedly, terrorizing the Anglo-Saxon peoples. Criminals were hard to catch in the heavily forested, sparsely settled nation. The king used a primitive legal system to maintain a tenuous control over his people.

England was divided into shires, and daily administration was carried out by a "shire reeve," later called a sheriff. The shire reeve collected taxes and did what he could to keep peace, apprehending criminals and acting as mediator between feuding families. Two or three times a year, a shire court met; lower courts met more frequently.

Contemporary law: Mediation lives on. As we discuss in Chapter 3, on dispute resolution, lawsuits have grown ever more costly. Increasingly, companies are turning to mediation to settle disputes. The humble shire reeve's work is back in vogue.

Because there were so few officers to keep the peace, Anglo-Saxon society created an interesting method of ensuring public order. Every freeman (nonslave) belonged to a group of 10 freemen known as a "tithing," headed by a "tithingman." If anyone injured a person outside his tithing or interfered with the king's property, all 10 men of the tithing could be forced to pay.

Contemporary law: Today, we still use this idea of collective responsibility. In a business partnership, all partners are personally responsible for the debts of the partnership. They could potentially lose their homes and all assets because of the irresponsible

Medieval tenants in demesne *harrowing, plowing, and seeding a field.*

conduct of one partner. That liability has helped create new forms of business organization, including limited liability companies, which we discuss in Chapter 32 on business organizations.

When cases did come before an Anglo-Saxon court, the parties would often be represented either by a clergyman, by a nobleman, or by themselves. There were few professional lawyers. Each party produced "oath helpers," usually 12, who would swear that one version of events was correct. The court explicitly gave greater credence to oath helpers from the nobility.

Contemporary law: The Anglo-Saxon oath helpers are probably forerunners of our modern jury of 12 persons. But as to who is telling the truth, that is a question that will never disappear. We deny giving a witness greater credence because of his or her status. But is that accurate? Some commentators believe that jurors are overly impressed with "expert witnesses," such as doctors or engineers, and ignore their own common sense when faced with such "pedigreed" people.

In 1066, the Normans conquered England. William the Conqueror made a claim never before made in England: that he owned all of the land. The king then granted sections of his lands to his favorite noblemen, as his tenants in chief, creating the system of feudalism. These tenants in chief then granted parts of their land to *tenants in demesne,* who actually occupied a particular estate. Each tenant in demesne owed fidelity to his lord (hence "landlord"). So what? Just this: land became the most valuable commodity in all of England, and our law still reflects that.

Contemporary law: One thousand years later, American law still regards land as special. The statute of frauds, which we study in the section on contracts, demands that contracts for the sale or lease of property be in writing. And landlord-tenant law, vital to students and many others, still reflects its ancient roots. Some of a landlord's rights are based on the 1,000-year-old tradition that land is uniquely valuable.

In 1250, Henry de Bracton (d. 1268) wrote a legal treatise that still influences us. *De Legibus et Consuetudinibus Angliae* (*On the Laws and Customs of England*), written in Latin, summarized many of the legal rulings in cases since the Norman Conquest. De Bracton was teaching judges to rule based on previous cases. He was helping to establish the idea of *precedent.* **The doctrine of precedent, which developed gradually over centuries, requires that judges decide current cases based on previous rulings.**

Contemporary law: This vital principle is the heart of American common law. Precedent ensures predictability. Suppose a 17-year-old student promises to lease an apartment from a landlord, but then changes her mind. The landlord sues to enforce the lease. The student claims that she cannot be held to the agreement because she is a minor. The judge will look for precedent, i.e., older cases dealing with the same issue, and he will find many holding that a contract generally may not be enforced against a minor. That precedent is binding on this case, and the student wins. The accumulation of precedent, based on case after case, makes up the **common law.**

During the next few centuries, judges and lawyers acquired special training and skills. Some lawyers began to plead cases full-time and gained unique skill—and power. They represented only those who could pay well.

Parliament passed an ever greater number of laws, generally called **statutes,** the word we still use to mean a law passed by a legislative body. Parliament's statutes swelled in number and complexity until they were unfathomable to anyone but a lawyer.

Contemporary law: Our society still struggles with unequal access to legal talent. Rich people often fare better in court than poor. And many Americans regard law as byzantine and incomprehensible. A primary purpose of this text is to remove the mystique from the law and to empower you to participate in legal matters.

As lawyers became more highly skilled, they searched ever wider for ways to defeat the other side. One method was by attacking the particular writ in the case. The party bringing the case was called the plaintiff. His first task was to obtain a **writ,** which was a letter from the central government ordering a court to hear the case. Each type of lawsuit required a different writ. For example, a landlord's lawsuit against a tenant required one kind of writ, while a claim of assault needed a different one. If a court decided that the plaintiff's lawyer had used the wrong writ, it would dismiss the lawsuit. This encouraged lawyers for the defendant to attack the writ itself, claiming it was inappropriate. By doing that, they could perhaps defeat the case without ever answering who did what to whom.

Contemporary law: This is the difference between procedure and substance, which will become clear during the course. **Substantive** rules of law state the rights of the parties. For example, it is substantive law that if you have paid the purchase price of land and accepted the deed, you are entitled to occupy the property. **Procedural** rules tell how a court should go about settling disputes. For example, what evidence can be used to establish that you *did* pay for the property? How much evidence is necessary? Who may testify about whether you paid? Those are all issues of procedural law. To this day, lawyers attack procedural aspects of an opponent's case before dealing with the substantive rights.

Here is an actual case from more than six centuries ago, in the court's own language. The dispute illustrates that some things have changed but others never do. The plaintiff claims that he asked the defendant to heal his eye with "herbs and other medicines." He says the defendant did it so badly that he blinded the plaintiff in that eye.

THE OCULIST'S CASE (1329)

LI MS. Hale 137 (1), fo. 150, Nottingham*

Attorney Launde [for defendant]: Sir, you plainly see how [the plaintiff claims] that he had submitted himself to [the defendant's] medicines and his care; and after that he can assign no trespass in his person, inasmuch as he submitted himself to his care: but this action, if he has any, sounds naturally in breach of covenant. We demand [that the case be dismissed].

Excerpts from Judge Denum's Decision: I saw a Newcastle man arraigned before my fellow justice and me for the death of a man. I asked the reason for the indictment, and it was said that he had slain a man under his care, who died within four days afterwards. And because I saw that he was a [doctor] and that he had not done the thing feloniously but [accidentally] I ordered him to be discharged. And suppose a blacksmith, who is a man of skill, injures your horse with a nail, whereby you lose your horse: you shall never have recovery against him. No more shall you here.

Afterwards the plaintiff did not wish to pursue his case any more. ■

This case from 1329 is an ancient medical malpractice case. Defendant's lawyer makes a procedural argument. Attorney Launde does not deny that his client blinded the plaintiff. He claims that the plaintiff has brought the wrong kind of lawsuit. Launde argues that the plaintiff should have brought a case of "covenant," i.e., a lawsuit about a contract.

---

* J. Baker and S. Milsom, *Sources of English Legal History* (London: Butterworth & Co., 1986).

Judge Denum decides the case on a different principle. He gives judgment to the defendant because the plaintiff voluntarily sought medical care. He implies that the defendant would lose only if he had attacked the plaintiff. As we will see when we study negligence law, this case might have a different outcome today. Note also the informality of the judge's ruling. He rather casually mentions that he came across a related case once before and that he would stand by that outcome. The idea of precedent is just beginning to take hold.

Sometimes a judge refused to hear a case, ruling that no such claims were legal. The injured party might then take his case to the Chancellor, in London, whose status in the king's council gave him unique, flexible powers. This *Court of Chancery* had no jury. The court's duty was to accomplish what "good conscience" required, that is, an *equitable* result, and so this more creative use of a court's power became known as **equity.**

Contemporary law: In present-day America, judges still exercise equity powers, based on those cases the Chancery court accepted. For example, a court today might issue an injunction requiring a factory owner to stop polluting the air. The injunction (order to stop) is an equitable remedy. Only a judge can exercise equitable powers because, historically, Chancery had no jury. If a judge grants an injunction, she is said to be exercising equitable powers.

Parliament added statutes on more and more matters, at times conflicting with common law rulings of the various judges. What should a court do when faced with a statute that contradicts well-established precedent? In the seventeenth century, one of England's greatest judges, Lord Coke, addressed the problem. In *Dr. Bonham's Case,*[4] Lord Coke ruled that "when an Act of Parliament is against Common right and reason, or repugnant, or impossible to be performed, the Common Law will control it and adjudge such Act to be void."

Audacious man! In a decision of breathtaking strength, Lord Coke declared that a single judge could overrule the entire Parliament, based on what the judge might consider "common right and reason." This same tension carries on today between elected officials, such as state legislators, and courts, which sometimes declare acts of the legislatures void.

Of course, by the time Lord Coke was on the bench, in the seventeenth century, English common law had also spread across the ocean to the newly created colonies. We will pick up the story in America.

Law in the United States

The colonists brought with them a basic knowledge of English law, some of which they were content to adopt as their own. Other parts, such as religious restrictions, were abhorrent to them. Many had made the dangerous trip to America precisely to escape persecution, and they were not interested in recreating their difficulties in a new land. Finally, some laws were simply irrelevant or unworkable in a world that was socially and geographically so different. American law ever since has been a whitewater river created from two strong currents: One carries the ancient principles of English common law, the other, a zeal and determination for change.

During the nineteenth century, the United States changed from a weak, rural nation into one of vast size and potential power. Cities grew, factories appeared, and sweeping movements of social migration changed the population. Changing conditions raised new legal questions. Did workers have a right to form industrial unions? To what extent should a manufacturer be liable if its product injured someone? Could a state government invalidate an employment contract that required 16-hour workdays? Should one company be permitted to dominate an entire industry?

---

4   Eng. Rep. 638 (C.P. 1610).

In the twentieth century, the rate of social and technological change increased, creating new legal puzzles. Were some products, such as automobiles, so inherently dangerous that the seller should be responsible for injuries even if no mistakes were made in manufacturing? Who should clean up toxic waste if the company that had caused the pollution no longer existed? If a consumer signed a contract with a billion-dollar corporation, should the agreement be enforced even if the consumer never understood it? As we venture into this millennium, new and startling questions are certain to confront us. Before we can begin to examine the answers, we need to understand the sources of contemporary law.

SOURCES OF CONTEMPORARY LAW

During the colonial period there were few trained lawyers and fewer law books in America. After the Revolution that changed, and law became a serious, professional career. The first great legal achievement was the adoption of the United States Constitution.

Constitutions

United States Constitution

The United States Constitution, adopted in 1789 by the original 13 colonies, is the supreme law of the land.[5] Any law that conflicts with it is void. This Federal Constitution, as it is also known, does three basic things. First, it establishes the national government of the United States, with its three branches. The Constitution creates the Congress, with a Senate and a House of Representatives, and prescribes what laws Congress may pass. The same document establishes the office of the president and the duties that go with it. And it creates the third branch of government, the federal courts, describing what cases they may hear.

Second, the Constitution ensures that the states retain all power not given to the national government. This simple idea has meant that state governments play an important role in all of our lives. Major issues of family law, criminal law, property law, and many other areas are regulated predominantly by the various states.

Third, the Constitution guarantees many basic rights to the American people. Most of these rights are found in the amendments to the Constitution. The First Amendment guarantees the rights of free speech, free press, and the free exercise of religion. The Fourth, Fifth, and Sixth Amendments protect the rights of any person accused of a crime. Other amendments ensure that the government treats all people equally and that it pays for any property it takes from a citizen. Merely by creating a limited government of three branches and guaranteeing basic liberties to all citizens, the Constitution became one of the most important documents ever written.

State Constitutions

In addition to the Federal Constitution, each state has a constitution that establishes its own government. All states have an executive (the governor), a legislature, and a court system. Thus there are two entire systems of government affecting each of us: a federal government, with power over the entire country, and a state government, exercising those powers that the United States Constitution did not grant to the federal government. This is federalism at work.

---

[5] The complete text of the Constitution appears in Appendix A.

Statutes

The second important source of law is statutory law. The Constitution gave to the United States Congress the power to pass laws on various subjects. These laws are statutes, like those passed by the English Parliament. For example, the Constitution allows Congress to pass statutes about the military: to appropriate money, reorganize divisions, and close bases. You can find any federal statute, on any subject, at the Web site of the United States House of Representatives, which is **http://www.house.gov/**.

State legislatures also pass statutes. Each state constitution allows the legislature to pass laws on a wide variety of subjects. All state legislatures, for example, may pass statutes about family law issues such as divorce and child custody.

Common Law

As we have seen, the common law originated in England as lawyers began to record decisions and urge judges to follow earlier cases. As judges started to do that, the earlier cases, called *precedent*, took on steadily greater importance. Eventually, judges were *obligated* to follow precedent. **The principle that precedent is binding on later cases is *stare decisis*, which means "let the decision stand."** *Stare decisis* makes the law predictable, and this in turn enables businesses and private citizens to plan intelligently.

Equity

Principles of equity, created by the Chancellor in England, traveled to the colonies along with the common law rules. All states permit courts to use equitable powers. An example of a contemporary equitable power is an *injunction*, a court order that someone stop doing something. Suppose a music company is about to issue a new compact disc by a well-known singer, but a composer claims that the recording artist has stolen his song. The composer, claiming copyright violation, could seek an injunction to prevent the company from issuing the compact disc. Every state has a trial court that can issue injunctions and carry out other equitable relief. As was true in medieval England, there is no jury in an equity case.

Administrative Law

In a society as large and diverse as ours, the executive and legislative branches of government cannot oversee all aspects of commerce. Congress passes statutes about air safety, but U.S. senators do not stand around air traffic towers, serving coffee to keep everyone awake. The executive branch establishes rules concerning how foreign nationals enter the United States, but presidents are reluctant to sit on the dock of the bay, watching the ships come in. **Administrative agencies** do this day-to-day work.

Most administrative agencies are created by Congress or by a state legislature. Familiar examples at the federal level are the Federal Communications Commission (FCC), which regulates most telecommunications; the Federal Trade Commission (FTC), which oversees interstate trade; and the Immigration and Naturalization Service (INS), which controls our nation's borders. At the state level, regulators set insurance rates for all companies in the state, control property development and land use, and regulate many other issues.

Other Sources of Law

Treaties

The Constitution authorizes the president to make treaties with foreign nations. These must then be ratified by the United States Senate. When they are ratified, they are as

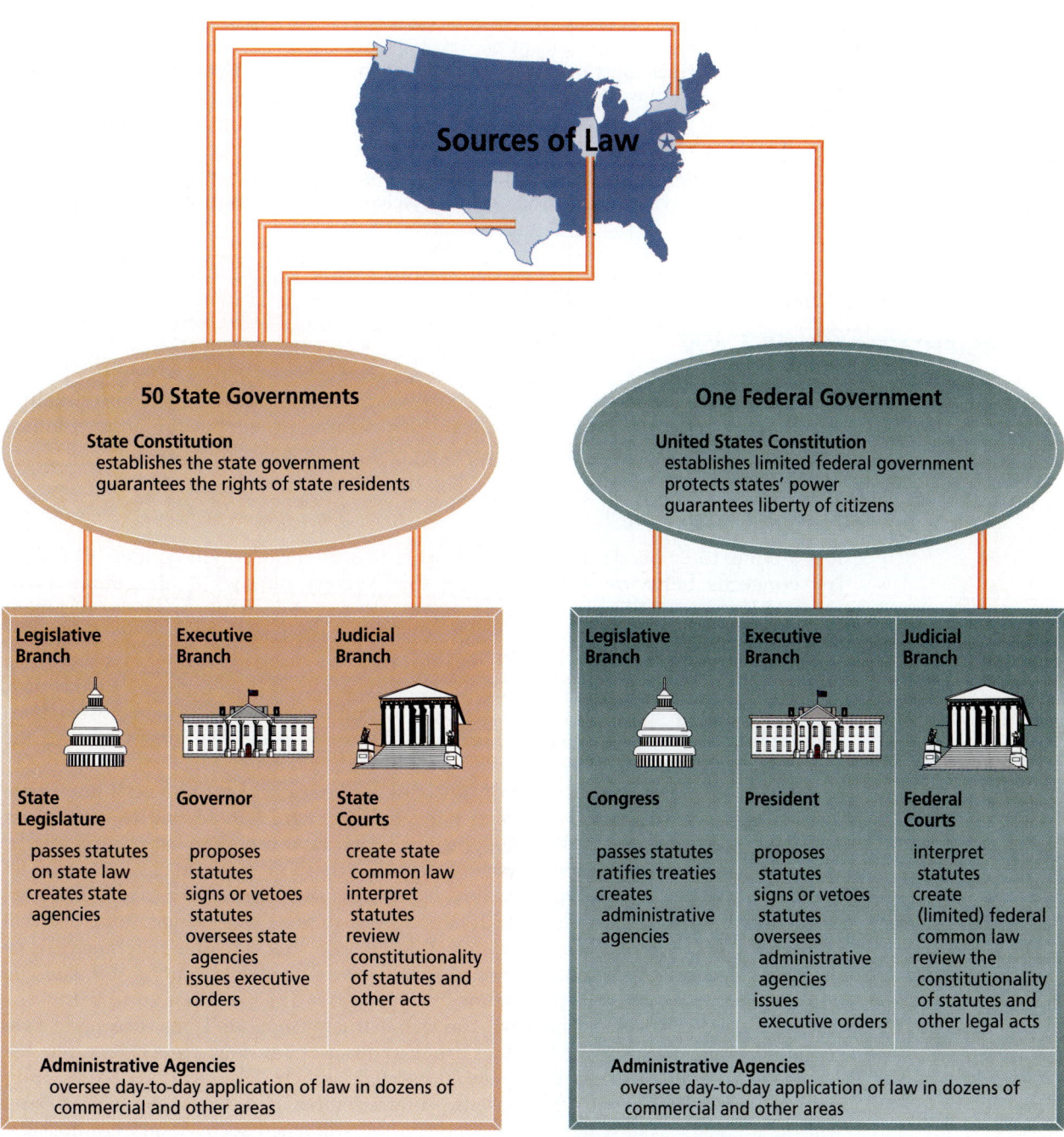

Sources of Law

50 State Governments

State Constitution
establishes the state government
guarantees the rights of state residents

One Federal Government

United States Constitution
establishes limited federal government
protects states' power
guarantees liberty of citizens

Legislative Branch

State Legislature
passes statutes on state law
creates state agencies

Executive Branch

Governor
proposes statutes
signs or vetoes statutes
oversees state agencies
issues executive orders

Judicial Branch

State Courts
create state common law
interpret statutes
review constitutionality of statutes and other acts

Administrative Agencies
oversee day-to-day application of law in dozens of commercial and other areas

Legislative Branch

Congress
passes statutes
ratifies treaties
creates administrative agencies

Executive Branch

President
proposes statutes
signs or vetoes statutes
oversees administrative agencies
issues executive orders

Judicial Branch

Federal Courts
interpret statutes
create (limited) federal common law
review the constitutionality of statutes and other legal acts

Administrative Agencies
oversee day-to-day application of law in dozens of commercial and other areas

Federal Form of Government. Principles and rules of law come from many sources. The government in Washington creates and enforces law throughout the nation. But 50 state governments exercise great power in local affairs. And citizens enjoy constitutional protection from both state and federal government. The Founding Fathers wanted this balance of power and rights, but the overlapping authority creates legal complexity.

binding upon all citizens as any federal statute. In 1994 the Senate ratified the North American Free Trade Agreement (NAFTA) with Mexico and Canada. NAFTA was controversial then and remains so today—but it is now the law of the land.

Executive Orders

In theory all statutes must originate in Congress or a state legislature. But in fact executives also legislate by issuing executive orders. For example, in 1970 Congress authorized President Nixon to issue wage-price controls in an effort to stabilize the economy. This was a colossal grant of power, allowing the president personally to regulate the nation's economy. Critics charge that Congress should not give away the powers that the people have granted to it, and such delegations of authority have led to extensive lawsuits.

CLASSIFICATIONS OF LAW

We have seen where law comes from. Now we need to classify the law into different types. There are three main classifications that we use throughout the book: criminal and civil law, substantive and procedural law, and public and private law.

Criminal and Civil Law

It is a crime to embezzle money from a bank, to steal a car, to sell cocaine. **Criminal law concerns behavior so threatening that society outlaws it altogether.** Most criminal laws are statutes, passed by Congress or a state legislature. The government itself prosecutes the wrongdoer, regardless of what the bank president or car owner wants. A district attorney, paid by the government, brings the case to court. The injured party, for example the owner of the stolen car, is not in charge of the case, although she may appear as a witness. The government will seek to punish the defendant with a prison sentence, a fine, or both. If there is a fine, the money goes to the state, not to the injured party.

Civil law is different, and most of this book is about civil law. **The civil law regulates the rights and duties between parties.** Tracy agrees in writing to lease you a 30,000-square-foot store in her shopping mall. She now has a *legal duty* to make the space available. But then another tenant offers her more money, and she refuses to let you move in. Tracy has violated her duty, but she has not committed a crime. The government will not prosecute the case. It is up to you to file a civil lawsuit. Your case will be based on the common law of contract. You will also seek equitable relief, namely, an injunction ordering Tracy not to lease to anyone else. You should win the suit, and you will get your injunction and some money damages. But Tracy will not go to jail.

Some conduct involves both civil and criminal law. Suppose Tracy is so upset over losing the court case that she becomes drunk and causes a serious car accident. She has committed the crime of driving while intoxicated, and the state will prosecute. Tracy may be fined or imprisoned. She has also committed negligence, and the injured party will file a lawsuit against her, seeking money. We will again see civil and criminal law joined together when we return to the *Pub Zone* case, later in the chapter.

Substantive and Procedural Law

We saw the distinction between substantive and procedural law in *The Oculist's Case* and it remains important today. **Substantive law defines the rights of people.** Substantive law requires that a landlord who has signed a lease must deliver the store to her tenant. Most of this book concerns substantive law. **Procedural law establishes the processes for settling disputes.** Procedural law requires that to get an injunction against Tracy, you must first notify her in writing of your claims and the time and place of the hearing on the injunction.

Public and Private Law

Public law refers to the rights and obligations of governments as they deal with the nation's citizens. For example, when the Federal Trade Commission prohibits deceptive advertising, that is public law. **Private law** regulates the duties between individuals. Landlord-tenant law is private law.

JURISPRUDENCE

We have had a glimpse of legal history and a summary of the present-day sources of American law. But what *is* law? That question is the basis of a field known as **jurisprudence.** How do we distinguish a moral rule from a legal rule? What is the real nature of law? Can there be such a thing as an "illegal" law?

Law and Morality

Law is different from morality, yet the two are obviously linked. There are many instances when the law duplicates what all of us would regard as a moral position. It is negligence to drive too fast in a school district, and few would dispute the moral value of that law. And similarly with contract law: If the owner of land agrees in writing to sell property to a buyer at a stated price, the seller must go through with the deal, and the legal outcome matches our moral expectations.

On the other hand, we have had laws that we now clearly regard as immoral. At the turn of the century, a factory owner could typically fire a worker for any reason at all—including, for example, his religious or political views. Today, we would say it is immoral to fire a worker because she is Jewish—and the law prohibits it.

Finally, there are legal issues where the morality is not so clear. You are walking down a country lane and notice a three-year-old child playing with matches near a barn filled with hay. Are you obligated to intervene? No, says the law, though many think that is preposterous. (See Chapter 4, on common law, for details.) A company buys property and then discovers, buried under the ground, toxic waste that will cost $300,000 to clean up. The original owner has gone bankrupt. Should the new owner be forced to pay for the cleanup? If the new owner fails to pay for the job, who will? (See Chapter 41, on environmental law.)

Legal Positivism

This philosophy can be simply stated: Law is what the sovereign says it is. The **sovereign** is the recognized political power whom citizens obey, so in the United States, both state and federal governments are sovereign. A legal positivist holds that whatever the sovereign declares to be the law *is* the law, whether it is right or wrong.

The primary criticism of legal positivism is that it seems to leave no room for questions of morality. A law permitting a factory owner to fire a worker because she is Catholic is surely different from a law prohibiting arson. Do citizens in a democracy have a duty to consider such differences?

Most states allow citizens to pass laws directly at the ballot box, a process called voter referendum. California voters often do this, and during the 1990s, they passed one of the state's most controversial laws. Proposition 187 was designed to curb illegal immigration into the state by eliminating social spending for undocumented aliens. Citizens debated the measure fiercely but passed it by a large margin. One section of the new law forbade public schools from educating illegal immigrants. The law obligated a principal to inquire into the immigration status of all children enrolled in the school and to report undocumented students to immigration authorities. Several San Diego school principals rejected the new rules, stating that they would neither inquire into immigration status nor report undocumented aliens. Their statements produced a heated response. Some San Diego residents castigated the school officials as lawbreakers, claiming that

- A school officer who knowingly disobeyed a law was setting a terrible example for students, who would assume they were free to do the same

- The principals were advocating permanent residence and a free education for anyone able to evade our immigration laws; and

- The officials were scorning grass-roots democracy by disregarding a law passed by popular referendum.

Others applauded the principals' position, asserting that

- The referendum's rules would transform school officials from educators into border police, forcing them to cross-examine young children and their parents

- The new law was foolish because it punished innocent children for violations committed by their parents; and

- Our nation has long respected civil disobedience based on humanitarian ideals, and these officials were providing moral leadership to the whole community.

Ultimately, no one had to decide whether to obey Proposition 187. A federal court ruled that only Congress had the power to regulate immigration and that California's attempt was unconstitutional and void. The debate over immigration reform—and ethics—did not end, however. Congress periodically considers proposals to cut social benefits for illegal immigrants. ◆

Natural Law

St. Thomas Aquinas (1225–1274) answered the legal positivists even before they had spoken. In his *Summa Theologica*, he argued that an unjust law is no law at all and need not be obeyed. It is not enough that a sovereign makes a command. The law must have a moral basis.

Where do we find the moral basis that would justify a law? Aquinas says that "good is that which all things seek after." Therefore, the fundamental rule of all laws is that "good is to be done and promoted, and evil is to be avoided." This sounds appealing, but also vague. Exactly which laws promote good and which do not? Is it better to have a huge corporation dominate a market or many smaller companies competing? Did the huge company get that way by being better than its competitors? If Wal-Mart moves into a rural area, establishes a mammoth store, and sells inexpensive products, is that "good"? Yes, if you are a consumer who cares only about prices. No, if you are the owner of a Main Street store driven into bankruptcy. Maybe, if you are a resident who values small town life but wants lower prices.

Natural law debates are eternal. One of the greatest of the ancient Greek dramatists, Sophocles (496–406 B.C.E.), touches upon the subject in one of his famous plays, *Antigone*. Oedipus's two sons, Eteocles and Polyneices, have arranged to rule Thebes in rotation, but when Eteocles refuses to give up the throne, Polyneices and his many supporters attack the city. Both brothers are killed in the battle. Creon, who inherits the crown, declares that Eteocles will receive a hero's burial but that Polyneices must lie exposed in the dust. Anyone attempting to bury him will be executed. Antigone, the sister of the dead men, is horrified. Declaring that religious beliefs compel her to rescue her brother's soul from perpetual torment, she attempts to bury Polyneices. Antigone admits to Creon that she understood his ruling, but retorts, in the language of natural law:

> [Your] order did not come from God. Justice,
> That dwells with the gods below, knows no such law.
> I did not think your edicts strong enough
> To overrule the unwritten unalterable laws
> Of God and heaven, you being only a man.
> They are not of yesterday or to-day, but everlasting,
> Though where they came from, none of us can tell.[6]

Creon, a legal positivist, responds simply and forcefully that "Our country is our life." Any attack upon the city-state warrants death, as does any disobedience of its laws. Ultimately, he orders Antigone to her death and then, inevitably, regrets his decision.

Two thousand five hundred years later, we still debate the meaning and significance of natural law. Court cases and political debates about abortion, stem cell research, school prayer, evolution, and euthanasia all echo the themes disputed by Creon and Antigone.

What does natural law tell us about abortion? Abortion supporters, or those advocating free choice, will say that natural law protects a woman's reproductive rights and that it is violent and unnatural for any government to tell a woman what to do with her body. Opponents of abortion reach the opposite conclusion, arguing that no good can come from terminating the life of a fetus and that a law permitting abortion is no law at all. What do you think?

Legal Realism

Legal realists take a very different tack. They claim it does not matter what is written as law. What counts is who enforces that law and by what process. All of us are biased by issues such as income, education, family background, race, religion, and many other factors. These personal characteristics, they say, determine which contracts will be enforced and which ignored, why some criminals receive harsh sentences while others get off lightly, and so on.

Judge Jones hears a multimillion dollar lawsuit involving an airplane crash. Was the airline negligent? The law is the same everywhere, but legal realists say that Jones's background will determine the outcome. If she spent 20 years representing insurance companies, she will tend to favor the airline. If her law practice consisted of helping the "little guy," she will favor the plaintiff.

Other legal realists argue, more aggressively, that those in power use the machinery of the law to perpetuate their control. The outcome of a given case will be determined by the needs of those with money and political clout. A court puts "window dressing" on a decision, they say, so that society thinks there are principles behind the law. A problem with legal realism, however, is its denial that any lawmaker can overcome personal bias. Yet clearly some do act unselfishly.

---

[6] Sophocles, *Antigone,* translated by E.F. Watling in *Sophocles, The Theban Plays* (New York: Penguin, 1964).

Summary of Jurisprudence	
Legal Positivism	Law is what the sovereign says.
Natural Law	An unjust law is no law at all.
Legal Realism	Who enforces the law counts more than what is in writing.

No one school of jurisprudence is likely to seem perfect. We urge you to keep the different theories in mind as you read cases in the book. Ask yourself which school of thought is the best fit for you.

WORKING WITH THE BOOK'S FEATURES

In this section we introduce a few of the book's features and discuss how you can use them effectively. We will start with *cases*.

Analyzing a Case

A law case is the decision a court has made in a civil lawsuit or criminal prosecution. Cases are the heart of the law and an important part of this book. Reading them effectively takes practice. Let us return to the Pub Zone tavern, which we visited in the chapter's opener, and see what we can learn about courts and the law.

KUEHN V. PUB ZONE

364 N.J. Super. 301, 835 A.2d 692
Superior Court of New Jersey, Appellate Division, 2003

Facts: Maria Kerkoulas owned the Pub Zone bar. She knew that several motorcycle gangs frequented the tavern. From her own experience tending bar, and conversations with city police, she knew that some of the gangs, including the Pagans, were dangerous and prone to attack customers for no reason. Kerkoulas posted a sign prohibiting any motorcycle gangs from entering the bar while wearing "colors," that is, insignia of their gangs. She believed that gangs without their colors were less prone to violence, and experience proved her right.

Rhino, Backdraft, and several other Pagans, all wearing colors, pushed their way past the tavern's bouncer and approached the bar. Although Kerkoulas saw their colors, she allowed them to stay for one drink. They later moved towards the back of the pub, and Kerkoulas believed they were departing. In fact, they followed a customer named Karl Kuehn to the men's room, where without any provocation they savagely beat him. Kuehn was knocked unconscious and suffered brain hemorrhaging, disc herniation, and numerous fractures of facial bones. He was forced to undergo various surgeries, including eye reconstruction.

Although the government prosecuted Rhino and Backdraft for their vicious assault, our case does not concern that prosecution. Kuehn sued the Pub Zone, and that is the case we will read. The jury awarded him $300,000 in damages. However, the trial court judge overruled the jury's verdict. He granted a judgment for the Pub Zone, meaning that the tavern owed nothing. The judge ruled that the pub's owner could not have foreseen the attack on Kuehn, and had no duty to protect him from an outlaw motorcycle gang. Kuehn appealed, and the appeals court's decision follows:

Issue: **Did the Pub Zone have a duty to protect Kuehn from the Pagans' attack?**

▼

Excerpts from Judge Payne's Decision: Whether a duty exists depends upon an evaluation of a number of factors including the nature of the underlying risk of harm, that is, its foreseeability and severity, the opportunity and ability to exercise care to prevent the harm, the comparative interests of and the relationships between or among the parties, and, ultimately, based on considerations of public policy and fairness, the societal interest in the proposed solution.

Since the possessor [of a business] is not an insurer of the visitor's safety, he is ordinarily under no duty to exercise any care until he knows or has reason to know that the acts of the third person are occurring, or are about to occur. He may, however, know or have reason to know, from past experience, that there is a likelihood of conduct on the part of third persons in general which is likely to endanger the safety of the visitor, even though he has no reason to expect it on the part of any particular individual.

We find the totality of the circumstances presented in this case give rise to a duty on the part of the Pub Zone to have taken reasonable precautions against the danger posed by the Pagans as a group. In this case, there was no reason to suspect any particular Pagan of violent conduct. However, the gang was collectively known to Kerkoulas to engage in random violence. Thus, Kerkoulas had knowledge as the result of past experience and from other sources that there was a likelihood of conduct on the part of third persons in general that was likely to endanger the safety of a patron at some unspecified future time. A duty to take precautions against the endangering conduct thus arose.

We do not regard our recognition of a duty in this case to give rise to either strict or absolute liability on the part of the Pub Zone. To fulfill its duty in this context, the Pub Zone was merely required to employ "reasonable" safety precautions. It already had in place a prohibition against bikers who were wearing their colors, and that prohibition, together with the practice of calling the police when a breach occurred, had been effective in greatly diminishing the occurrence of biker incidents on the premises. The evidence establishes that the prohibition was not enforced on the night at issue, that three Pagans were permitted entry while wearing their colors, and the police were not called. Once entry was achieved, the Pub Zone remained under a duty to exercise reasonable precautions against an attack.

The jury's verdict must therefore be reinstated. ■

Analysis

Let's take it from the top. The case is called *Kuehn v. Pub Zone*. Karl Kuehn is the **plaintiff**, the person who is suing. The Pub Zone is being sued, and is called the **defendant**. In this example, the plaintiff's name happens to appear first but that is not always true. When a defendant loses a trial and files an appeal, *some* courts reverse the names of the parties.

The next line gives the legal citation, which indicates where to find the case in a law library. We explain in the footnote how to locate a book if you plan to do research.[7]

---

[7] If you want to do legal research, you need to know where to find particular legal decisions. A case citation guides you to the correct volume(s). The full citation of our case is *Kuehn v. Pub Zone*, 364 N.J. Super. 301, 835 A.2d 692. The string of numbers identifies two different books in which you can find the full text of this decision. The first citation is to "N.J. Super," which means the official court reporter of the state of New Jersey. New Jersey, like most states, reports its law cases in a series of numbered volumes. This case appears in volume 364 of the New Jersey Superior Court reporters. If you go to a law library and find that book, you can then turn to page 301 and—*voila!*—you have the case. The decision is also reported in another set of volumes, called the regional reporters. This series of law reports is grouped by geographic region. New Jersey is included in the Atlantic region, so our case appears in reporters dedicated to that region. The "A" stands for Atlantic. After a series of reporters reaches volume 999, a second set begins. Our case appears in volume 835 of the second set of the Atlantic reporters ("A.2d"), at page 692. In addition, most cases are now available online, and your professor or librarian can show you how to find them electronically.

The *Facts* section provides a background to the lawsuit, written by the authors of this text. The court's own explanation of the facts is often many pages long, and may involve complex matters irrelevant to the subject covered in this book, so we relate only what is necessary. This section will usually include some mention of what happened at the trial court. Lawsuits always begin in a trial court. The losing party often appeals to a court of appeals, and it is usually an appeals court decision that we are reading. The trial judge ruled in favor of Pub Zone, but later, in the decision we are reading, Kuehn wins.

The *Issue* section is very important. It tells you what the court had to decide—and also why you are reading the case. In giving its decision, a court may digress. If you keep in mind the issue and relate the court's discussion to it, you will not get lost.

Excerpts from Judge Payne's Decision begins the court's discussion. This is called the *holding*, meaning a statement of who wins and who loses. The holding also includes the court's *rationale*, which is the reasoning behind the decision.

The holding that we provide is an edited version of the court's own language. Some judges write clear, forceful prose, others do not. Either way, their words give you an authentic feel for how judges think and rule, so we bring it to you in the original. Occasionally we use brackets [ ] to substitute our language for that of the court, either to condense or to clarify. Notice the brackets in the second paragraph of the Pub Zone decision. Judge Payne explains the point at much greater length, so we have condensed some of his writing into the phrase "of a business."

We omit a great deal. A court's opinion may be three pages or it may be 75. We do not use ellipses (. . .) to indicate these deletions, because there is more taken out than kept in, and we want the text to be clean. When a court quotes an earlier decision verbatim but clearly adopts those words as its own, we generally delete the quotation marks, as well as the citation to the earlier case. If you are curious about the full holding, you can always look it up.

Let us look at a few of Judge Payne's points. The holding begins with a discussion of *duty*. The court explains that whether one person (or bar) owes a duty to protect another depends upon several factors, including whether the harm could be foreseen, how serious the injury could be, and whether there was an opportunity to prevent it.

Judge Payne then points out that the owner of a business is not an insurer of a visitor's safety. Typically, the owner has a duty to a visitor *only* if he has a reason to know that some harm is likely to occur. How would a merchant know that? Based on the character of the business, suggests the judge, or the owner's experience with particular people.

The judge then applies this general rule to the facts of this case. He concludes that the Pub Zone did in fact have a duty to protect Kuehn from the Pagans' attack. Based on Kerkoulas's experience, and warnings received from the police, she knew that the gang was dangerous and should have foreseen that admitting them in their "colors" greatly increased the chance of an attack.

Next, the court points out that it is not requiring the Pub Zone to *guarantee* everyone's safety. The bar was merely obligated to do a *reasonable* job. The prohibition on colors was a good idea, and calling the police had also proven effective. The problem of course was that in this case, Kerkoulas ignored her own rule about gang insignia, and failed to call the police.

Based on all the evidence, the jury's finding of liability was reasonable, and its verdict must be reinstated. In other words, Kuehn, who lost at the trial, wins on appeal. What the court has done is to *reverse* the lower court's decision, meaning to turn the loser into the winner. In other cases we will see an appellate court *remand* the case, meaning to send it back down to the lower court for additional steps. Or the appellate judges could *affirm* the lower court's decision, meaning to leave it unchanged.

Devil's Advocate

Each chapter has several cases. After some of them, a "Devil's Advocate" feature offers you a contrasting view of the legal issue. This is not part of the case, but is instead a suggestion of another perspective on the problem discussed. The authors take no position for or against the court's decision, but merely want you to consider an alternate view, and decide which analysis of the law makes more sense to you—that of the court or the Devil's Advocate. Is the following view persuasive?

Devil's Advocate

A court should not force small businesses to guarantee their customers' safety. Two or three violent men, whether motorcycle gang members or frustrated professors, could enter a grocery store or clothing retailer at any time and mindlessly attack innocent visitors. Random attacks are just that—random, unforeseeable. No merchant should be required to anticipate them. Send the criminals to jail, but do not place the burden on honest business people. ◆

Update

In this feature we ask students to find a current article on an issue discussed in the text. The goal is for you to apply the principles of this course to current events—this material is very real! You may use periodicals from the library or articles from any electronic database. The article should be dated within the past two months.

Update

Find an article online concerning a tavern's liability for a criminal assault. What did the bar allegedly do or fail to do? Is this a civil or criminal case? What outcome do you anticipate? How could the owner have avoided the problem? ◆

You Be the Judge

Many cases involve difficult decisions for juries and judges. Often both parties have legitimate, opposing arguments. Most chapters in this book will have a feature called "You Be the Judge," in which we present the facts of a case but not the court's holding. We offer you two opposing arguments based on the kinds of claims the lawyers made in court. We leave it up to you to debate and decide which position is stronger or to add your own arguments to those given. The following case is another negligence lawsuit, with issues similar to those in the Pub Zone case. A suicide caused a distraught family to sue a rock singer and music producer. Once again the defendants asked the judge to dismiss the case. They pointed out, correctly, that a negligence case requires a plaintiff to prove that the defendant *could have foreseen the type of harm that occurred*. Could Ozzy Osbourne have foreseen this sad outcome to one of his songs? You be the judge.

YOU Be The Judge

MCCOLLUM V. CBS, INC.

202 Cal. App. 3d 989, 249 Cal. Rptr. 187, 1988 Cal. App. LEXIS 909, California Court of Appeal, 1988

Facts: John McCollum, 19 years old, was an alcoholic with serious emotional problems. He listened over and over to music recorded by Ozzy Osbourne on CBS records, particularly two albums called *Blizzard of Oz* and *Diary of a Madman*. He usually listened to the music on the family stereo in the living room because the sound was most intense there. One Friday evening, though, he went to his bedroom and lay on his bed, listening to more

Osbourne music. He placed a loaded .22-caliber handgun to his right temple and pulled the trigger.

McCollum's parents sued Osbourne and CBS records, claiming that they negligently aided and encouraged John to commit suicide. The parents' argument was that Osbourne's songs were designed to appeal to unstable youths and that the message of some of his music explicitly urged death. One of the songs John had listened to before his death was "Suicide Solution," which included these lyrics:

> Wine is fine but whiskey's quicker
> Suicide is slow with liquor
> Take a bottle drown your sorrows
> Then it floods away tomorrows
> Now you live inside a bottle
> The reaper's travelling at full throttle
> It's catching you but you don't see
> The reaper is you and the reaper is me
> Breaking law, knocking doors
> But there's no one at home
> Made your bed, rest your head
> But you lie there and moan
> Where to hide, Suicide is the only way out
> Don't you know what it's really about.*

The trial court dismissed the lawsuit, ruling that the plaintiff had not made out a valid negligence claim. The court ruled that the First Amendment's free speech provision protected the rights of Osbourne and CBS to publish any music they wanted. In addition, the court found that the defendants could not have foreseen that anyone would respond to the lyrics by taking his own life. With no foreseeability, the court ruled, the plaintiffs' case must fail. The parents appealed.

You Be the Judge: Was McCollum's suicide foreseeable?

Argument for the Parents: Your honors, for years Ozzy Osbourne has been well known as the "madman" of rock 'n' roll. The words and music of his songs revolve around bizarre, antisocial beliefs, emphasizing death and satanic worship. Many of his songs suggest that life is hopeless and that suicide is not only acceptable but desirable. Now one

of his devoted fans has acted on Osbourne's advice and killed himself. The defendants share responsibility for this tragic death.

Osbourne and CBS knew that many of Osbourne's fans struggled with self-identity, alienation, and substance abuse. Both defendants aggressively targeted this market and reaped enormous profits. They realized that the confused youths who adored Osbourne were precisely those most vulnerable to vicious advice. Yet in spite of their knowledge, both defendants churned out songs such as "Suicide Solution," urging troubled, chemically addicted young people to kill themselves. Not only was it *foreseeable* that one of Osbourne's fans would sooner or later take his life, it was *inevitable*. The only way to ensure that this doesn't occur again is to permit a jury to hear the parents' case and, if it is persuaded by the evidence, to award the grieving parents damages.

Argument for Osbourne and CBS: Your honors, we all agree that this death was tragic and unnecessary. But the plaintiffs delude themselves if they think that Mr. Osbourne and CBS bear any responsibility. The fact is that John McCollum was deeply troubled and alcoholic. He was responsible for his life—and for his own death. Next to the young man himself, of course, those who bear the greatest responsibility for his sad life and gruesome end are his parents, the plaintiffs in this case. Mr. Osbourne and CBS sympathize with the parents' bereavement, but not with their attempt to foist responsibility onto others.

If the plaintiffs' far-fetched foreseeability argument were the law—which it is not—every singer, writer, and film and television producer would be at risk of several thousand lawsuits every year. Under their theory, a producer who made a bank robbery movie would be liable for every robbery that took place afterward, as would every author or singer who ever mentioned the subject. The First Amendment was written to ensure that we *do* have access to arts and entertainment, and to prohibit efforts at silencing artists with outlandish lawsuits. This death was never foreseeable and no jury should ever hear the case. ▪

---

* Words and music by John Osbourne, Robert Daisley, and Randy Rhoads. TRO © Copyright 1981 Essex Music International, Inc., New York, New York and Blizzard Music Ltd., London England. Used by permission.

Chapter Conclusion

We depend upon the law to give us a stable nation and economy, a fair society, a safe place to live and work. These worthy goals have occupied Anglo-Saxon kings and twenty-first-century lawmakers alike. But while law is a vital tool for crafting the society we want, there are no easy answers about how to create it. In a democracy, we all participate in the crafting. Legal rules control us, yet *we* create *them*. A working knowledge of the law can help build a successful career—and a solid democracy.

Chapter Review

1. Our federal system of government means that law comes from a national government in Washington, D.C., and from 50 state governments.

2. The history of law foreshadows many current legal issues, including mediation, partnership liability, the jury system, the role of witnesses, the special value placed on land, the idea of precedent, and the difference between substantive and procedural law.

3. The primary sources of contemporary law are

   - United States Constitution and state constitutions

   - Statutes, which are drafted by legislatures

   - Common law, which is the body of cases decided by judges, as they follow earlier cases, known as precedent; and

   - Administrative law, the rules and decisions made by federal and state administrative agencies.

4. Other sources of contemporary law include

   - Treaties

   - Executive orders

5. Criminal law concerns behavior so threatening to society that it is outlawed altogether. Civil law deals with duties and disputes between parties, not with outlawed behavior.

6. Substantive law defines the rights of people. Procedural law describes the processes for settling disputes.

7. Jurisprudence is concerned with the basic nature of law. Three theories of jurisprudence are

   - Legal positivism: The law is what the sovereign says it is.

   - Natural law: An unjust law is no law at all.

   - Legal realism: Who enforces the law is more important than what the law says.

Practice Test

1. Can one person really understand all of the legal issues mentioned at the beginning of this chapter? For example, can a business executive know about insider trading and employment law and environmental law and tort law and all of the others? Will a court really hold one person to such knowledge?

2. Why does our law come from so many different sources?

3. The stock market crash of 1929 and the Great Depression that followed were caused in part because so many investors blindly put their money into stocks they knew nothing about. During the 1920s it was often impossible for an investor to find out what a corporation was planning to do with its money, who was running the corporation, and many other vital things. Congress responded by passing the Securities Act of 1933, which required a corporation to divulge more information about itself before it could seek money for a new stock issue. What kind of law did the Congress create? Explain the relationship between voters, Congress, and the law.

4. Union organizers at a hospital wanted to distribute leaflets to potential union members, but hospital rules prohibited leafleting in areas of patient care, hallways, cafeterias, and any areas open to the public. The National Labor Relations Board (NLRB) ruled that these restrictions violated the

law and ordered the hospital to permit the activities in the cafeteria and coffee shop. The NLRB cannot create common law or statutory law. What kind of law was it creating?

5. Leslie Bergh and his two brothers, Milton and Raymond, formed a partnership to help build a fancy saloon and dance hall in Evanston, Wyoming. Later, Leslie met with his friend and drinking buddy, John Mills, and tricked Mills into investing in the saloon. Leslie did not tell Mills that no one else was investing cash or that the entire enterprise was already insolvent. Mills mortgaged his home, invested $150,000 in the saloon—and lost every penny of it. Mills sued all three partners for fraud. Milton and Raymond defended on the ground that they didn't commit the fraud, only Leslie did. The defendants lost. Was that fair? By holding them liable, what general idea did the court rely on? What Anglo-Saxon legal custom did the ruling resemble?

6. **ETHICS** Confucius did not esteem written laws, believing instead that good rulers were the best guarantee of justice. Does our legal system rely primarily on the rule of law or the rule of people? Which do you instinctively trust more? Legal realists argue that the "rule of law" is a misleading term. What point are they making, and how does it relate to Confucius's principles? Confucius himself was an extraordinarily wise man, full of wisdom about life and compassion for his fellow citizens. Since he was extraordinary, what does that tell us about other rulers by contrast? How does that affect Confucius's own views?

7. Tommy Parker may have been involved in some unsavory activities as an officer in a failed savings and loan institution. A federal agency, the Office of Thrift Supervision (OTS), ordered Tommy not to spend or waste any of his own assets while it was investigating him. Later, Tommy and his wife, Billie, got divorced and divided their property. On February 18, the OTS filed papers in court asking for an order that *Billie* not spend any of her assets. Billie received a copy of the papers on February 20, and the hearing took place on February 24, without Billie in attendance. The court ordered Billie not to spend any assets except for essential living expenses. Billie appealed, claiming that under court rules she was entitled to five days' notice before the hearing took place and that weekend days are not counted. She had had only two business days'

notice. Assume that her counting of the days was correct (which it was). Explain the difference between procedural law and substantive law. Which type of law was Billie relying on? Should her appeal be granted?

8. Plaintiff Miss Universe, Inc., owns the trademark "Miss U.S.A." For decades, the company has produced the Miss U.S.A. beauty pageant, seen by many millions of people in the United States. William Flesher and Treehouse Fun Ranch began to hold a nude beauty pageant in California. They called this the "Miss Nude U.S.A." pageant. Most of the contestants were from California; the majority of states were not represented in the contest. Miss Universe sued Flesher and Treehouse, claiming that the public would be confused and misled by the similar names. The company sought an *equitable remedy* in this lawsuit. What does "equitable" mean? What equitable remedy did Miss Universe seek? Should it win?

9. Bill and Diane are hiking in the woods. Diane walks down a hill to fetch fresh water. Bill meets a stranger, who introduces herself as Katrina. Bill sells a kilo of cocaine to Katrina, who then flashes a badge and mentions how much she enjoys her job at the Drug Enforcement Agency. Diane, heading back to camp with the water, meets Freddy, a motorist whose car has overheated. Freddy is late for a meeting where he expects to make a $30 million profit; he's desperate for water for his car. He promises to pay Diane $500 tomorrow if she will give him the pail of water, which she does. The next day, Bill is in jail and Freddy refuses to pay for Diane's water. Explain the criminal law/civil law distinction and what it means to Bill and Diane. Who will do what to whom, with what results?

10. **YOU BE THE JUDGE** WRITING PROBLEM Should trials be televised? Here are a few arguments to add to those in the chapter. You be the judge. **Arguments against Live Television Coverage:** We have tried this experiment and it has failed. Trials fall into two categories: Those that create great public interest and those that do not. No one watches dull trials, so we do not need to broadcast them. The few that are interesting have all become circuses. Judges and lawyers have shown that they cannot resist the temptation to play to the camera. Trials are supposed to be about justice, not entertainment. If a

citizen seriously wants to follow a case, she can do it by reading the daily newspaper. **Arguments for Live Television Coverage:** It is true that some televised trials have been unseemly affairs, but that is the fault of the presiding judges, not the media. Indeed, one of the virtues of television coverage is that millions of people now understand that we have a lot of incompetent people running our courtrooms. The proper response is to train judges to run a tight trial by prohibiting the grandstanding in which some lawyers may engage. Access to accurate information is the foundation on which a democracy is built, and we must not eliminate a source of valuable data just because some judges are ill-trained.

11. In his most famous novel, *The Red and the Black*, the French author Stendhal (1783–1842) wrote: "There is no such thing as 'natural law': this expression is nothing but old nonsense. Prior to laws, what is natural is only the strength of the lion, or the need of the creature suffering from hunger or cold, in short, need." What do you think?

12. ***ROLE REVERSAL*** Each Practice Test contains one Role Reversal feature, in which we challenge you to create your own exam question. The goal is to think creatively and accurately. Crafting questions is a good way to reinforce what you understand and recognize the areas you need to review. Your professor may ask you to submit the questions in writing or electronically or to prepare an overhead slide.

The question should be challenging enough that the average student will need to stop and think, but clear enough that there is only one answer. Useful questions can be formatted as essay, short answer, or multiple choice. Notice that some exam questions are very direct, while others require deeper analysis. Here are two examples. The first focuses on a definition.

Question: Legal positivism is:

a. A decision by an appeals court *affirming* the trial court.

b. A decision by an appeals court *reversing* a trial court.

c. A theory of jurisprudence insisting that the law is what the sovereign says it is.

d. A theory of law requiring that current cases be decided based on earlier decisions.

e. A theory of law requiring that current cases be decided by a majority vote of the judges.

As you know, the correct answer is "c."

The next question demands that the student spot the issue of law involved (foreseeability) and correctly apply it to the facts provided.

Question: Marvin asks Sheila, a qualified auto mechanic, to fix his engine, which constantly stalls (stops) while driving. When Marvin returns, Sheila informs him that the engine is now "Perfect—runs like a top." Marvin drives home along Lonesome Highway. Suddenly the car stalls. Sheila has not fixed it. Marvin pulls over and begins the long walk to the nearest telephone. A blimp flies overhead, advertising "Top" brand tires. Tragically, the blimp suddenly plummets to earth and explodes 20 feet from Marvin, seriously injuring him. Marvin sues Sheila. Sheila's best defense is that:

a. The falling blimp is so bizarre that Sheila could never have foreseen it.

b. Sheila made *reasonable efforts* to fix the engine.

c. Marvin should have checked the engine himself.

d. Marvin should have carried a cell phone with him in case of emergencies.

e. Sheila is a qualified mechanic and her work is presumptively sufficient.

The correct answer is "a." Notice that the same facts could be used as an essay question, simply by deleting the multiple-choice answers. Now it is your turn for Role Reversal: draft a multiple-choice question focusing on *legal realism*.

Internet Research Problem

Go to **http://beatty.westbuslaw.com** to find two current cases that interest you: one civil, one criminal. Explain the different roles played by each type of law, and summarize the issues in the respective cases.

> **You can find further practice problems at http://beatty.westbuslaw.com or in the Study Guide that accompanies this text.**

Business Ethics and Social Responsibility

Arthur Haupt is a 79-year-old retired waiter who lives with his black cat, Max, in a tidy 650-square-foot apartment in Chicago's Rienzi Plaza apartment building. He works 20 hours a week, shelving books at Loyola University's law library, earning $6.95 an hour. He also gets Social Security and two modest pensions. His total income last year was $18,713. His monthly rent in this federally subsidized apartment is $352. Market rent for an equivalent apartment would be as high as $1,644.

Last fall, Haupt's landlord notified him that he might be evicted. Nationally, landlords have taken about 125,000 units out of the federal subsidy program. At the same time, demand for subsidized housing is rising, in part because big cities such as Chicago are tearing down their old public-housing projects and telling residents to find subsidized apartments instead. Where will Arthur Haupt go?

The landlord, Sheldon Baskin, is not a bad guy. Twenty years ago, he and his partners signed a contract with the federal government, promising to build and maintain an apartment building for low-income Chicagoans. In exchange, the government guaranteed a steady stream of rent. But now the contract on Rienzi Plaza is set to expire. Baskin could make a larger profit on the building, by either

© MEL CURTIS/PHOTODISC/GETTY IMAGES

selling it, converting it to condominiums, or renting to unsubsidized tenants who could pay more. What does Baskin owe to his investors?

The Rienzi tenants and community groups have begun looking for a white knight—someone who could buy the building and preserve its low-income housing. Two for-profit organizations that specialize in investing in "affordable" housing expressed interest in buying Rienzi, but neither has made an offer.

Meanwhile, Baskin asked government officials how much more rent they would pay if he extended his contract for five years. Officials said they would have to hire an outside consultant to do a market study, a task that would take months—long past the deadline by which federal regulations require Baskin to announce his decision.[1] ■

Business is an enormously powerful tool that corporate managers can use to accomplish many goals. They may wish to earn a good living, even to become wealthy, but they can also use their business skills to cure the ill, feed the hungry, entertain the bored, and in many other ways affect their community, their country, and their world.

This book is primarily about the impact of law on business. But law is only one set of rules that governs business; ethics is another. **Ethics is the study of how people ought to act.** Law and ethics are often in harmony. Most reasonable people agree that murder should be prohibited. But law and ethics are not always compatible. In some cases, it might be *ethical* to commit an *illegal* act; in others, it might be *unethical* to be *legal.* Here are two examples in which law and ethics might conflict:

> George Hart, a 75-year-old man confined to a wheelchair, robbed a bank in San Diego of $70 so that he could buy heart medicine. He entered a branch of the HomeFed Bank, where he had $4 in his account, and apologized while demanding $70 from a teller, threatening to blow up the bank if she did not comply. Hart was arrested minutes later when he tried to buy a $69 bottle of heart medicine at a nearby drugstore. Hart said he "hated to have to go to this extreme," but insisted he had tried every other way to find money to buy the medicine.[2]

In 1963, Martin Luther King, Jr., was arrested in Birmingham, Alabama, for leading illegal sit-ins and marches to protest laws that discriminated against African Americans. When eight local clergymen criticized his activities, King offered this defense:

> We know through painful experience that freedom is never voluntarily given by the oppressor; it must be demanded by the oppressed. . . . Perhaps it is easy for those who have never felt the stinging darts of segregation to say "Wait.". . . [W]hen you see the vast majority of your 20 million Negro brothers smothering in an air-tight cage of poverty in the midst of an affluent society; when you suddenly find your tongue twisted as you seek to explain to your six-year-old daughter why she can't go to the public amusement park that has just been advertised on television, and see tears welling up when she is told that Funtown

---

[1] Based on Jonathan Eig, "Landlord's Dilemma: Help Poor Tenants or Seek More Profits," *Wall Street Journal,* July 17, 2001, p. 1. Republished with permission of *The Wall Street Journal;* permission conveyed through the Copyright Clearance Center, Inc.

[2] "Bank Robber in Wheelchair Has an Alibi: His Medicine," *New York Times,* Jan. 18, 1991, p. A16.

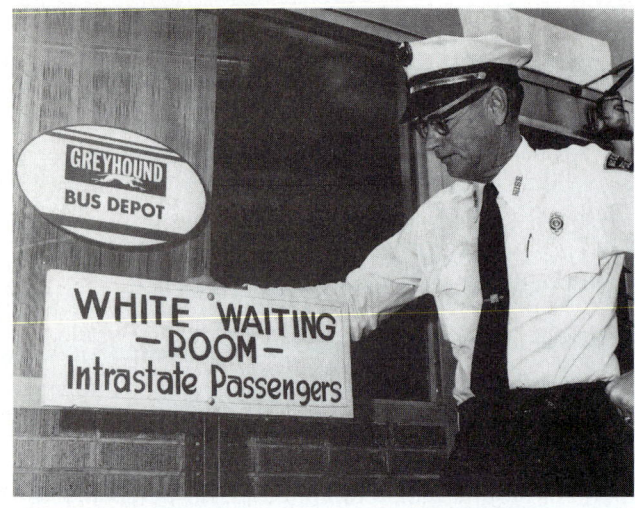

Is this law ethical?

is closed to colored children. . . . [W]hen you take a cross-country drive and find it necessary to sleep night after night in the uncomfortable corners of your automobile because no motel will accept you. . . . How can [we] advocate breaking some laws and obeying others? The answer lies in the fact that there are two types of laws: just and unjust. I agree with St. Augustine that "an unjust law is not law at all."[3]

Could one argue in the case of the bank robber that his actions, while illegal, were ethical? Would the argument be stronger if he had been stealing the money to help someone else? In the case of Martin Luther King, Jr., would it be reasonable to conclude not only that breaking the law was ethical, but also that *obeying* the law would have been *unethical?* Were the eight clergymen who criticized King behaving unethically by upholding these odious laws?

The other chapters of this book focus on legal issues, but this chapter concentrates on ethics. In all of the examples in this chapter, the activities are *legal*, but are they *ethical?*

WHY BOTHER WITH ETHICS?

Business schools teach students how to maximize the profitability of an enterprise, large or small. Does ethical behavior maximize profitability? Some people argue that, in the long run, ethical behavior does indeed pay. But they must mean the very long run, because to date there is little evidence that ethical behavior *necessarily* pays financially, either in the short or the long run.

For instance, when a fire destroyed the Malden Mills factory in Lawrence, Massachusetts, its 70-year-old owner, Aaron Feuerstein, could have shut down the business, collected the insurance money, and sailed off into retirement. But a layoff of the factory's 3,000 employees would have been a major economic blow to the region. So instead Feuerstein kept the workers on the payroll while he rebuilt the factory. These actions gained him a national reputation as a business hero. Many consumers promised to buy more of the company's patented Polartec fabric. In the end, however, the story did not have a fairy-tale ending: Five years after the fire, Malden Mills filed bankruptcy papers. The company was not able to pay off the loans it had incurred to keep the business going.

In contrast, unethical companies may perform well financially. Mutuals.com offers shares in Vice Funds, a mutual fund that invests in "booze, bets, bombs, and butts" (alcohol, gambling, defense contractors, and cigarettes.) Over the past five years, these industries have earned better returns than the Standard & Poor's 500. Even for individuals, unethical behavior is no bar to financial success. The first antitrust laws in America were designed, at least in part, to restrain John D. Rockefeller's unethical activities.

---

[3]   Martin Luther King, Jr., "Letter from Birmingham Jail," *The Christian Century*, June 12, 1963.

Yet, four generations later, his name is still synonymous with wealth and his numerous heirs can live comfortably on their inheritance from him.[4]

If ethical behavior does not necessarily pay and unethical behavior sometimes does, why bother with ethics?

Society as a Whole Benefits from Ethical Behavior

John Akers, the former chairman of IBM, argues that without ethical behavior, a society cannot be economically competitive. He puts it this way:

> Ethics and competitiveness are inseparable. We compete as a society. No society anywhere will compete very long or successfully with people stabbing each other in the back; with people trying to steal from each other; with everything requiring notarized confirmation because you can't trust the other fellow; with every little squabble ending in litigation; and with government writing reams of regulatory legislation, tying business hand and foot to keep it honest. That is a recipe not only for headaches in running a company, it is a recipe for a nation to become wasteful, inefficient, and noncompetitive. There is no escaping this fact: the greater the measure of mutual trust and confidence in the ethics of a society, the greater its economic strength.[5]

People Feel Better When They Behave Ethically

Every businessperson has many opportunities to be dishonest. Consider how one person felt when he resisted temptation:

> Occasionally a customer forgot to send a bill for materials shipped to us for processing. . . . It would have been so easy to rationalize remaining silent. After all, didn't they deserve to lose because of their inefficiency? However, upon instructing our staff to inform the parties of their errors, I found them eager to do so. They were actually bursting with pride. . . . Our honesty was beneficial in subtle ways. The "inefficient" customer remained loyal for years. . . . [O]ur highly moral policy had a marvelously beneficial effect on our employees. Through the years, many an employee visited my office to let me know that they liked working for a "straight" company.[6]

Profitability is generally not what motivates managers to care about ethics. Managers want to feel good about themselves and the decisions they have made; they want to sleep at night. Their decisions—to lay off employees, install safety devices in cars, burn a cleaner fuel—affect peoples' lives. When two researchers asked businesspeople why they cared about ethics, the answers had little to do with the profitability:

> The businesspeople we interviewed set great store on the regard of their family, friends, and the community at large. They valued their reputations, not for some nebulous financial gain but because they took pride in their good names.[7]

The Web site **http://www.yourtruehero.org** offers examples of ordinary people who have inspired others with their ethical behavior.

---

[4] Chapter 39, on antitrust, discusses Rockefeller's career at greater length.

[5] David Grier, "Confronting Ethical Dilemmas," unpublished manuscript of remarks at the Royal Bank of Canada, Sept. 19, 1989.

[6] Hugh Aaron, "Doing the Right Thing in Business," *Wall Street Journal,* June 21, 1993, p. A10.

[7] Amar Bhide and Howard H. Stevenson, "Why Be Honest if Honesty Doesn't Pay?" *Harvard Business Review,* Sept.–Oct. 1990, pp. 121–129, at 127.

Unethical Behavior Can Be Very Costly

Unethical behavior is a risky business strategy—it may lead to disaster. An engaged couple made a reservation, and put down a $1,500 deposit, to hold their wedding reception at a New Hampshire restaurant. Tragically, the bride died of asthma four months before the wedding. Invoking the terms of the contract, the restaurant owner refused to return the couple's deposit. In a letter to the groom, he admitted, "Morally, I would of course agree that the deposit should be returned." When newspapers reported this story, customers deserted the restaurant and it was forced into bankruptcy—over a $1,500 disagreement.[8] Unethical behavior does not always damage a business, but it certainly has the potential of destroying a company overnight. So why take the risk?

Even if unethical behavior does not devastate a business, it can cause other, subtler damage. In one survey, a majority of those questioned said that they had witnessed unethical behavior in their workplace and that this behavior had reduced productivity, job stability, and profits. Unethical behavior in an organization creates a cynical, resentful, and unproductive workforce.

So why bother with ethics? Because society benefits when managers behave ethically. Because ethical managers have happier, more satisfying lives. And because unethical behavior can destroy a business faster than a snake can bite.

WHAT IS ETHICAL BEHAVIOR?

It is one thing to decide, in theory, that being ethical is good; in practice, it can be much more difficult to make the right decisions. Supreme Court Justice Potter Stewart once said that he could not define pornography, but he knew it when he saw it. Many people feel the same way about ethics—that somehow, instinctively, they know what is right and wrong. In real life, however, ethical dilemmas are often not black and white, but many shades of gray. The purpose of this section is to analyze the following ethics checklist as an aid to managers in making tough decisions:

- What are the facts?
- What are the critical issues?
- Who are the stakeholders?
- What are the alternatives?
- What are the ethical implications of each alternative?
  - Is it legal?
  - How would it look in the light of day?
  - What are the consequences?
  - Does it violate important values?
  - Does it violate the Golden Rule?
  - Is it just?
  - Has the process been fair?
- Is more than one alternative right?

---

8   John Milne, "N.H. Restaurant Goes Bankrupt in Wake of Wedding Refund Flap," *Boston Globe*, Sept. 9, 1994, p. 25.

- Which values are in conflict?
- Which of these values are most important?
- Can you find an alternative that is consistent with your values?

Analyzing the Ethics Checklist

What Are the Facts?

Although this question seems obvious, people often forget in the heat of battle to listen to (and, more importantly, to *hear*) all the different viewpoints. Instead of relying on hearsay and rumor, it is crucial to discover the facts, firsthand, from the people involved. There is always another side to the story. It may be easy to condemn a bank robber, until learning the money was needed to buy medicine.

What Are the Critical Issues?

In analyzing ethical dilemmas, expand your thinking to include *all* the important issues. Avoid a narrow focus that encompasses only one or two aspects. In the case of the New Hampshire restaurant that refused to refund a deposit, the owner focused on the narrow legal issue. His interpretation of the *contract* was correct. But if the owner had expanded his thinking to include consideration for his customers, he might have reached a different decision.

Who Are the Stakeholders?

Stakeholders are all the people potentially affected by the decision. That list might include subordinates, bosses, shareholders, suppliers, customers, members of the community in which the business operates, society as a whole, or even more remote stakeholders, such as future generations. The interests of these stakeholders often conflict. Current shareholders may benefit from a company's decision to manufacture a product that contributes to global warming, while future generations are left to contend with a potential environmental nightmare.

What Are the Alternatives?

The next step is to list the reasonable alternatives. A creative manager may find a clever solution that is a winner for everyone. What alternatives might be available to Sheldon Baskin, the landlord who faced a dilemma in the opening scenario?

What Are the Ethical Implications of Each Alternative?

Is the Alternative Legal? Illegal may not always be synonymous with unethical, but, as a general rule, you need to think long and hard about the ethics of any illegal activities. **How Would the Alternative Look in the Light of Day?** If your activities were reported on the evening news, how would you feel? Proud? Embarrassed? Horrified? Undoubtedly, sexual harassment would be virtually eliminated if people thought that their parents, spouse, or partner would shortly see a video replay of the offending behavior. **What Are the Consequences of This Alternative?** Ask yourself: Am I hurting anyone by this decision? Which alternative will cause the greatest good (or the least harm) to the most people? For example, you would like to fire an incompetent employee. That decision will clearly have adverse consequences for him. But the other employees in your division will benefit and so will the shareholders of your company. Overall, your decision will cause more good than harm.

You should look with a particularly critical eye if an alternative benefits you while harming others. Suppose that you become CEO of a company whose headquarters are located in a distant suburb. You would like to move the headquarters closer to your home to cut your commuting time. Of course, such a decision would be expensive for shareholders and inconvenient for other employees. Do you simply impose your will on the company or consider the consequences for everyone?

This approach to decision making was first developed by two nineteenth-century English philosophers, Jeremy Bentham and John Stuart Mill. They argued that all decisions should be evaluated according to how much happiness they create. This philosophy is called **utilitarianism.** Some commentators have criticized utilitarianism on practical grounds—benefit and harm are difficult to measure. Others also argue that not all happiness is equal. A band of robbers may receive more benefit from stealing money than the victim suffers harm, but most people would nonetheless argue that the decision to steal is wrong. Despite these criticisms, it is wise at least to consider the costs and benefits of a decision.

Does the Alternative Violate Important Values? In addition to consequences, consider fundamental values. It is possible to commit an act that does not harm anyone else, but is still the wrong thing to do. Suppose, for instance, that you are away from home and have the opportunity to engage in a temporary sexual liaison. You are absolutely certain that your spouse will never find out and your partner for the night will have no regrets or guilt. There would be no negative consequences, but you believe that infidelity is wrong, *regardless of the consequences,* so you resist temptation.

Some people question whether, as a diverse, heterogeneous society (not to mention, world), we have common values. But throughout history, and across many different cultures, common values do appear. The following values are almost universal:

- *Consideration* means being aware of and concerned about other people's feelings, desires, and needs. The considerate person is able to imagine how he would feel in someone else's place.

- *Courage* is the strength to act in the face of fear and danger. Courage can require dramatic action (saving a buddy on a battlefield) or quiet strength (doing what you think is right, despite opposition from your boss).

- *Integrity* means being sincere, honest, and loyal. If you have integrity, you do not criticize others behind their back or take credit for their ideas and efforts.

- *Responsibility* means being trustworthy and dependable. The responsible person meets her commitments and lives up to her promises. If you promise to finish a project by a certain date, your colleagues can count on that pledge.

- *Self-control* is the ability to resist temptation. The person with self-control does not drink or eat too much, party too hard, watch too much television, or spend too much money.

Although reasonable people may disagree about a precise list of important values, most would agree that values matter. Try compiling your own list of values and then check it periodically to see if you are living up to it in your business and personal life. In one survey, business executives reported that the values they respected most were responsibility and honesty.

Does the Alternative Violate the Golden Rule? We all know the Golden Rule: Do unto others as you would have them do unto you. If one of the alternatives you are considering would be particularly unpleasant when done to you, reconsider.

Immanuel Kant, an eighteenth-century German philosopher, took the Golden Rule one step further with a concept he called the **categorical imperative.** According to Kant, you should not do something unless you would be willing for everyone else to do it, too (and not just to you). Imagine that you could cheat on an exam without getting caught. You might gain some short-term benefit—a higher grade. But what would happen if everyone cheated? The professor would have to make the exams harder or curve everyone's grade down. If your school developed a reputation for cheating, you might not be able to find a job after graduation. Cheating works only if most people are honest. To take advantage of everyone else's honesty is contemptible.

Is the Alternative Just? Are you respecting individual rights such as liberty (privacy, free speech, and religious freedom), welfare (employment, housing, food, education), and equality? Would it be just to fire an employee because her political views differ from your own?

Has the Process Been Fair? Unequal outcomes are acceptable, provided they are the result of a fair process. At the end of a poker game, some players have won and others lost, but no one can complain that the result was unfair, unless players cheated. In a business context, a fair process means applying the same set of rules to everyone. If three of your subordinates are vying for the same promotion, it would be unfair to let one state her case to you but not the others.

Is More than One Alternative Right?

Thus far, the ethics checklist has served two purposes. It helps to clarify the issues at stake. It also filters out decisions that are downright wrong. Have you considered lying to a customer about product specifications? For a start, such an action violates principles of integrity, not to mention the Golden Rule. Nor would you want your activity to be revealed on the front page of the local newspaper.

Often, the most difficult decisions arise not in cases of right versus wrong but in situations of right versus right.[9] President Harry Truman's decision to drop atomic bombs on two Japanese cities is a classic example of right versus right. He argued that if he had not ended the war by using nuclear weapons, more Americans and Japanese would have died during a land invasion. Looking simply at the consequences, he concluded that the terrible suffering by the Japanese people was justified because, ultimately, fewer people died overall. At the same time, Truman's decision violated the Golden Rule and Kant's categorical imperative. Indeed, since the end of World War II, the United States has worked hard to ensure that no one else ever deploys nuclear weapons. The ethics checklist presents no clear-cut answer. In the end, Truman decided that the most right (or least wrong) choice was to end the war quickly.

Nuclear weapons make a dramatic example, but what about a more typical business decision? AT&T adopted a policy of cutting costs to maximize its stock price. To implement this policy, the company laid off 40,000 people, despite record profits. Even as workers suffered, shareholders benefited because the company's stock price rose in response to the layoff announcement. But is stock price the only issue? Does the company have an obligation to protect employee jobs? Is one right more important than another?

Which Values Are in Conflict? There are many ways to justify a decision to lay off workers, even 40,000 of them. If managers avoid layoffs, then profits suffer, stock prices fall, companies merge, and executives lose their own jobs. In business school and on the job, managers learn how to analyze, compete, and win. Competing—and winning—are important. But what about other values, such as compassion and caring? Do the individual people affected by this decision matter, too?

Which of These Values Are Most Important? Suppose that, growing up, you had seen family members or neighbors suffering through bouts of unemployment. That experience might have taught you that compassion is a high priority. Managers must determine which values are important in their own lives.

---

9   For a thoughtful discussion of right versus right, see Joseph L. Badaracco, Jr., *Defining Moments: When Managers Must Choose between Right and Right* (Boston: Harvard Business School Press, 1997).

Can You Find an Alternative That Is Consistent with Your Values? The decision you make not only determines the kind of person you are now, but also sets your course for the future. Can you reach a decision that is consistent with the kind of person you are or want to be? Instead of announcing massive layoffs, some companies offer generous severance packages, retraining programs, and other voluntary methods of reducing the workforce. Shareholders may receive less benefit, but employees suffer less harm.

The following article discusses the importance of values in achieving personal fulfillment.

ECONOMICS
& the LAW

Once upon a time, there was a game that Wall Street traders and investment bankers liked to play—often on the commute home to Greenwich, Connecticut, or Short Hills, New Jersey, after a particularly profitable or trying day. It was called "What's Your Number?" The answer—in millions of dollars—was the amount you would want to have socked away before you could ditch your high-pressure job and lead the life you really wanted.

The breathtaking part of this game was not the numbers. And it was not that the question was asked by men and women in their 20s, 30s, and 40s. No, the remarkable part of this diversion was that the players kept increasing their numbers. There never seemed to be a high enough answer to "How much is enough?"

And there was a price to pay for all this money. "If your sense of accomplishment is all wrapped up in a bank account, it's going to affect your relationships," said Dr. Stephen Goldbart, a codirector of the Money, Meaning & Choices Institute, a consulting and training firm in San Francisco. "Absorption with money is going to make the human side of you unavailable. Our society has mixed up what it means to feel fulfilled and successful with making a lot of money."

As you might have guessed, this fable seems to have a moral. After the World Trade Center attacks, many of Wall Street's gold hoarders said they then realized what was really important: family, friends, and health. But meaningful work and personal fulfillment can't be ordered like pizza. They don't come conveniently attached to certain jobs or careers. The hardest thing about abandoning money as a scorecard for success and fulfillment is that there is no handy replacement, no way to advertise your newfound virtue. The second hardest thing is realizing that if your fulfillment needs to be advertised, you have simply traded one game for another.[10] ◆

APPLYING THE ETHICS CHECKLIST: MAKING DECISIONS

An organization has responsibilities to customers, employees, shareholders, and society generally, both here and overseas. Employees also have responsibilities to their organizations. The purpose of this section is to apply the ethics checklist to actual business dilemmas. The checklist does not lead to one particular solution; rather it is a method to use in thinking through ethics problems. The goal is for you to reach a decision that satisfies you.

Organization's Responsibility to Society

Facts. In the United States, teenagers routinely list alcohol commercials among their favorite advertisements. Adolescents who frequently see ads for alcohol are more likely to believe that drinkers are attractive, athletic, and successful. They are also more likely to drink, drink excessively, and drink in hazardous situations such as driving a car.

---

[10] Ellyn Spragins, "When Numbers Cease to Matter," New York Times, Oct. 7, 2001, §4, p. 8. Copyright © 2001 by The New York Times Co. Reprinted by permission.

While Secretary of Health and Human Services, Louis W. Sullivan publicly denounced the test marketing of Uptown, a high-tar cigarette targeted at African Americans. He called it "contemptible that the tobacco industry has sought to increase their market" among minorities because this population was "already bearing more than its fair share of smoking-related illness and mortality." Comedian Jay Leno joked that R. J. Reynolds named the cigarette Uptown "because the word 'Genocide' was already taken."[11]

A promotion for Request Jeans shows a man pinning a naked woman against a shower wall. Another advertisement featured childlike model Kate Moss lying naked on a couch. Above the couch was a picture of the product being promoted—Calvin Klein's Obsession for Men. Or how about the ad for a stereo that has a picture of a woman with these words, "She's terrific in bed, she's witty and intelligent, but she didn't have a Linn hi-fi. Her sister did and I married her sister."

Critical Issues. What are the obligations of advertising executives and marketing managers to those who see their ads? Is it ethical to sell jeans by glorifying rape? Are men more likely to commit rape as a result of seeing one of these advertisements? Is it ethical to entice teenagers into drinking or African Americans into smoking? If these ads sell product, is that justification enough?

Stakeholders. Ad designers are primarily responsible to their firms and the firms' clients. After all, designers are paid to sell product, not to make the world a better place. But what about the people who see the advertisements? Do the designers have any responsibility to them? Or to society as a whole?

Alternatives. Firms have at least four alternatives in dealing with issues of ethics in advertising. They can

- Ignore ethics and simply strive to create promotions that sell the most product, whatever the underlying message;

- Try, in a general way, to minimize racism, sexism, and other exploitation;

- Include, as part of the development process, a systematic, focused review of the underlying messages contained in their advertisements; or

- Refuse to create any ads that are potentially demeaning, insensitive, or dangerous, recognizing that such a stand may lead to a loss of clients.

Ethical Implications. All of these alternatives are perfectly legal. And, far from the ad executives being embarrassed if the ads see the light of day, the whole purpose of ads is to be seen. As for the consequences, the ads may help clients sell their products. But the ads may also harm those who see them by encouraging, among other things, drinking, smoking, sexual assault, and promiscuity. A manager might question whether these ads violate fundamental values. Are they showing consideration for others? Do they encourage self-control? As for the Golden Rule, how would an advertising executive feel about an ad in which he was being sexually assaulted? Or a promotion in which he was assumed to be less valuable than a

Is this ad unethical?

---

[11] Richard W. Pollay, Jung S. Lee, and David Carter-Whitney, "Separate, But Not Equal: Racial Segmentation in Cigarette Advertising," *Journal of Advertising*, Mar. 1992, vol. 21, no. 1, p. 45.

stereo system? Are these ads just? Do they violate principles of equality? Is the process by which they have been created fair? Have those who may be adversely affected by them had an opportunity to be heard?

Right versus Right. In a country with rampant anorexia among teenage girls, is it ethical to run ads with emaciated girls as role models? Is it ethical to run ads for lottery tickets when these tickets are largely purchased by those who can least afford to gamble? If you worked in an advertising agency or marketing department, you might feel a strong sense of loyalty to your company. But what about consideration for those who could be harmed by your ads? You must decide which values are important to you and look for solutions that enable you to live by these values.

Some of the ads described in this section appear stunningly tasteless. They could have been worse, however. The Ad Graveyard (**http://zeldman.com/ad.html**) offers examples of proposed ads that never saw the light of day, for very obvious reasons.

Organization's Responsibility to Its Customers

In this chapter's opening scenario, Sheldon Baskin faces a dilemma: Now that his contract with the federal government has expired, he can raise rents by as much as 500 percent at Rienzi Plaza, home to 140 poor and elderly tenants. Moving would be difficult for the elderly tenants, especially since they are unlikely to find another apartment in the neighborhood. They might end up in homeless shelters. But what about Baskin's partners? Is it fair to them if he decides to subsidize the rents of low-income tenants? Does he owe his partners the highest return on their investment?

What would you do if you were Sheldon Baskin? He is concerned about several important stakeholders—his partners and his tenants. What about the community? Does it benefit from having elderly members? Will the community be harmed if some of these elderly become homeless? How will Baskin feel about himself if he puts these elderly tenants out on the street? Or if *The Wall Street Journal* runs a front-page article about his eviction plans? On the other hand, could he argue that it is the government's responsibility to house the poor and elderly? What decision would be best for Baskin? The tenants? His partners? The community?

Organization's Responsibility to Its Employees

Enron

Which deal would you rather have?

- *Plan A:* Your company has a 401(k) pension plan. Federal law permits you to contribute a certain amount tax free each year. You can then invest that money in a choice of mutual funds. In addition, for every dollar you put in, your employer will contribute a dollar of company stock. The good news is that, if the stock market—and your company—prosper, your retirement years will indeed be golden. The downside is that if the stock market or your company declines, you could be like one of the tenants in Rienzi Plaza, unable to pay your rent.

- *Plan B:* The amount of your annual pension is guaranteed by the company, regardless of how the market performs. This guarantee is backed up by a federal agency. In addition to your regular pension plan, you have the right to invest in a special 401(k) plan, for which the company guarantees a minimum annual return of 12 percent.

Enron Corp. offered Plan A to its rank-and-file employees; Plan B was reserved for top executives. At one point, 60 percent of the assets in the Plan A 401(k) was invested in Enron stock. Then the stock plummeted in value from $80 a share to under $1. As the stock price sank, the company imposed a month-long "blackout" prohibiting all employees from selling any stock in the 401(k) while a new plan administrator took over. Less than a month after the blackout ended, the company filed for bankruptcy. As a result, the 401(k) plans lost $1.3 billion of their $2.1 billion worth.

The fate of Enron raises two issues:

1. *Equality of treatment within the company.* Is it ethical for top executives to set up two such different pension/savings plans for company employees? Should top executives be entitled to guaranteed retirement pay while rank-and-filers are at the mercy of stock market fluctuations?

   Alternatively, could one argue that offering top executives a better pension is no more unfair than paying them higher wages? What difference does it make if the difference in pay between the top and bottom takes the form of higher current compensation, a better pension, or a fancier executive dining room?

2. *The ethics of pension plans versus 401(k) plans.* A traditional pension plan (such as top Enron officials had) guarantees a certain annual payment for the life of the employee. Under federal law, companies must set aside money to meet these promises. If, for whatever reason, the company fails to do so, a federal agency guarantees the payments (up to certain limits). These traditional pension plans are more expensive for companies to operate. To avoid this financial commitment, many companies have switched to 401(k) plans in which all the risk is borne by the employee.

   Supporters of 401(k) plans argue that these plans are better than nothing, which is what companies would offer if 401(k) plans were not available. These plans are good for employees: The matching employer contributions entice many workers into saving money that they might otherwise just spend. And the plans are good for employers: In some circumstances, companies even receive extra tax breaks for contributing their own stock to their 401(k) plans. The younger employees whom companies want to attract rarely object to a 401(k) pension plan because they do not appreciate the significant disadvantages (and companies have not been eager to educate them).

What will you do when you become a top executive in a large company? Is it enough just to meet the minimum requirements of the pension laws? Should the employee plan look like yours? Does your obligation to shareholders require you to save money by offering the cheapest possible pension plan to employees? Would a generous pension plan for all employees benefit the company by attracting valuable workers, or harm the company by decreasing its profits?

Gillette

When James Kilts became CEO of Gillette Co., the consumer products giant had been a mainstay of the Boston community for a hundred years. But the organization was going through hard times: Its stock was trading at less than half its peak price and some of its storied brands of razors were wilting under intense competitive pressure. In four short years, Kilts turned Gillette around—strengthening its core brands, cutting jobs, and paying off debt. With its stock up 61 percent, Kilts had added $20 billion in shareholder value.

Then suddenly Kilts sold Gillette to Procter & Gamble Co. for $57 billion. So short was Kilts's stay in Boston that he never moved his family from their home in Rye, New York. The deal was sweet for Gillette shareholders—the company's stock price went up 13 percent in one day. And tasty also for Kilts—his payoff was $153 million, including a $23.9 million reward from P&G for having made the deal and a "change in control" clause in his employment contract that was worth $12.6 million. In addition, P&G agreed to pay him $8 million a year to serve as vice chairman after the merger. When he retires, his pension will be $1.2 million per year. Moreover, two of his top lieutenants were offered payments totaling $57 million.

Any downside to this deal? Four percent of the Gillette workforce—6,000 employees—were to be fired. If the payouts to the top three Gillette executives were divided among these 6,000, each unemployed worker would receive $35,000. The loss of this many employees (4,000 of whom live in New England) will have a ripple effect throughout the area economy. Although Gillette shareholders have certainly benefited in the short run from the sale, their profit would have been even greater without this $210 million payout to the executives. Moreover, about half the increase in Gillette revenues during the time that Kilts was running the show are attributable to currency fluctuations. A cheaper dollar increased revenue overseas. If the dollar had moved in the opposite direction, there might not have been any increase in revenue. Indeed, for the first two years after Kilts joined Gillette, the stock price declined. It wasn't until the dollar turned down that the stock price improved.

Some commentators have asked: (1) Do CEOs who receive sweeteners have too strong an incentive to sell their companies; and (2) Is it unseemly for them to be paid so much when many employees will lose their jobs? As one observer put it, "People think they are joining a company for the long haul and boom, the rug is pulled out from under them because the CEO wants a quick payday."[12] One study found that CEOs who receive sweeteners negotiate a lower sale price than those who do not.[13] But another commentator said of Kilts, "His incentives were based on performance, and he performed. Look at his track record. There's a market for CEOs and he's one of the best."[14]

Organization's Responsibility to Its Shareholders

Ford Motor Company was founded by William C. Ford Jr.'s great-grandfather Henry. The younger Ford is an avid environmentalist and also head of the company that bears his name. He shares the concern of many environmentalists that automobile exhaust contributes to global warming. Under the younger Ford's leadership, the company decided to increase the fuel economy of its sports utility vehicles (SUVs) by 25 percent (about five miles per gallon). This decision came shortly after Congress, partly in response to lobbying by automobile manufacturers, refused to increase national fuel economy standards.

Ford Motor was a leader in the development of SUVs, which comprised about a fifth of its output each year. Because these heavy cars are gas inefficient, Ford was barely able to meet existing federal standards. To achieve higher fuel economy, the company had to make more auto parts out of lighter aluminum and redesign the SUV engines. The cost of implementing these changes was substantial, but the company decided not to pass the costs on to consumers. The plan was controversial within the company itself, because some insiders believe that consumers would prefer more powerful cars to more gas-efficient ones.

---

12 Mark Maremont, "No Razor Here: Gillette Chief to Get A Giant Payday," *Wall Street Journal*, Jan. 31, 2005, p. 1.
13 *Ibid.*
14 *Ibid.*

Milton Friedman, a Nobel Laureate in economics, famously observed, "The one and only social responsibility of business is to increase its profits."[15] He argued that an executive should act for the benefit of the owners of the company. His primary responsibility is to them. If an individual wishes to support other responsibilities, such as a charity, a church, a city, or a country, let him do so with his own time and money, not that of the shareholders.

If you were a shareholder of Ford Motor Company, would you support the fuel efficiency initiative? Perhaps you would prefer to earn higher returns on your stock so that you could give money to other projects you consider more compelling (finding an AIDS vaccine, for example). Should William Ford, who inherited his company stock, have the right to spend company funds to support his pet projects? If the air needs to be cleaner or the schools richer, why shouldn't private donors or public institutions be responsible, not one company's shareholders?[16]

Do executives have an obligation to be socially responsible? Ford officials argued that their fuel economy initiative might be profitable—it might increase sales enough to make up for the lower profit per car. Moreover, an environmentally friendly image might help sales on all of its cars, not just SUVs. By voluntarily increasing its own fuel standards, Ford might head off tighter federal regulation.

*up*date   **Find a current news article about fuel economy standards. Have other automobile manufacturers (here and abroad) followed Ford's lead? Did Ford sales increase enough to offset the cost of making these design changes?** ◆

Organization's Responsibility Overseas

An American company's ethical obligations do not end at the border. What ethical duties does an American manager owe to stakeholders in countries where the culture and economic circumstances are very different?

Here is a typical story from Guatemala:

My father left home a long time ago. My mother supported me and my five brothers and sisters by selling tortillas and corn. Our house was a tin shack on the side of the road. We were crowded with all of us in one room, especially when it rained and the roof and sides leaked. There were hundreds of squatters in the neighborhood, but one day the police came and cleared us all out. The owners of the land said we couldn't come back unless we paid rent. How could we afford that? I was 12 and my mother said it was time for me to work. But most people won't hire children. Lots of other kids shine shoes or beg, but I heard that the maquila [clothing factory] was willing to hire children if we would work as hard as older people.

I can keep up with the grown-ups. We work from 6:00 in the morning to 6:30 at night, with half an hour break at noon. We have no other breaks the whole rest of the day. If I don't work fast enough, they hit me, not too hard, and threaten to fire me. Sometimes, if there is too much work to do, they'll lock the doors and not let us out until everything is finished.

---

[15] Milton Friedman, "The Social Responsibility of Business Is to Increase Its Profits," *New York Times Magazine*, Sept. 13, 1970, p. 32.

[16] See, for instance, David Henderson, "Misguided Virtue: False Notions of Corporate Social Responsibility," Hobart Paper 142, Institute of Economic Affairs, London, cited in *The Economist*, Nov. 17, 2001, p. 70.

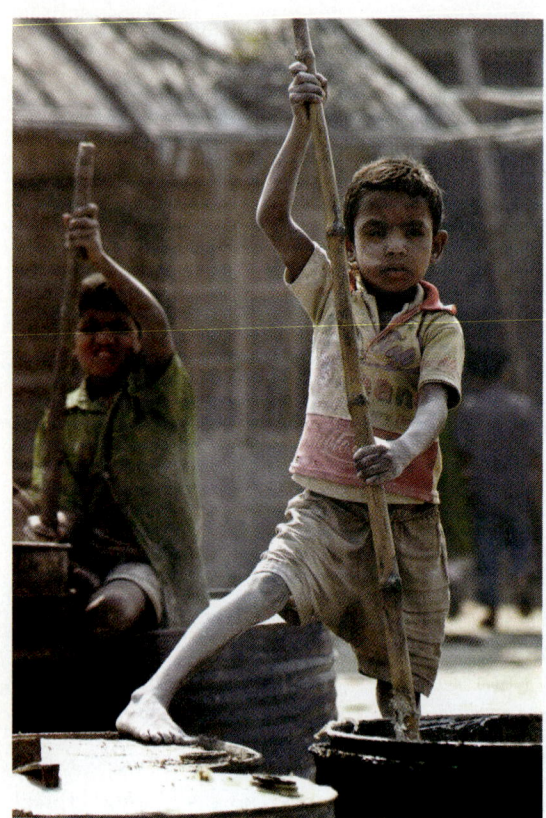

What are the ethical obligations of a company that uses foreign workers?

I'm always really tired at the end of the day and in the morning, too. But I earn $30 a week and without that money, we would not have enough to eat. My mother hopes all of my brothers and sisters can get jobs in the factory, too.

Of course, I'd rather be in school where I could wear a uniform and have friends. Then I could get a job as a clerk at the medical clinic. I would find people's files and tell them how long before the doctor could see them.

This description paints a distasteful picture indeed: children being beaten as they work 12-hour days. Should American companies (and consumers) buy goods that are produced in sweatshop factories? Jeffrey Sachs, a leading economist and adviser to developing nations, says, "My concern is not that there are too many sweatshops but that there are too few."[17] Why would he support sweatshops and child labor?

Historically, poor children have worked. Indeed, for many people and for many centuries, the point of having children was to create a supply of free labor to help support the family. In England in 1860, almost 40 percent of 14-year-old boys worked, and that was not just a few hours at Burger Box, but more likely 60 hours a week. That percentage is higher than in Africa or India today. For a child in a desperately poor family, the choice is not work or school, it is work, starvation, or prostitution. (For a history of sweatshops in America, work your way over to **http://americanhistory.si.edu/sweatshops/**.)

Industrialization has always been the first stepping stone out of dire poverty—it was in England, it is now in the Third World. Eventually, higher productivity leads to higher wages. In China, factory managers have complained that their employees want to work even longer hours to earn more money. The results in China have been nothing short of remarkable—if each of China's provinces were counted as a separate country, then 20 of the world's fastest growing economies between 1978 and 1995 would have been Chinese. During the Industrial Revolution in England, per capita output doubled in 58 years. In China, it took only 10 years.

During the past 50 years, Taiwan and South Korea welcomed sweatshops. During the same period, India resisted what it perceived to be foreign exploitation. Although all three countries started at the same economic level, Taiwan and South Korea today have much lower levels of infant mortality and much higher levels of education than India.[18]

When governments or customers try to force Third World factories to pay higher wages, the factory owners typically either relocate to lower wage countries or mechanize, thereby reducing the need for workers. In either case, the local economy suffers.

The difference, however, between the twenty-first and the nineteenth centuries is that now there are wealthy countries able to help their poorer neighbors. In the nineteenth century, England was among the richest countries, so it was on its own to solve

[17] Allen R. Meyerson, "In Principle, A Case for More 'Sweatshops,'" *New York Times,* June 22, 1997, p. E5.

[18] The data in this and the preceding paragraph are from Nicholas D. Kristof and Sheryl WuDunn, "Two Cheers for Sweatshops," *New York Times Magazine,* Sept. 24, 2000, p. 70.

its economic problems. Is America ethically obligated to assist the people around the world who live in abject poverty? Already, owing to pressure from activists, many companies have introduced better conditions in their factories. Workers are less likely to be beaten. They can go to the bathroom without asking permission. They might even receive rudimentary medical care. Manufacturing processes use fewer dangerous chemicals. Factories are cleaner, with better lighting and more ventilation. But hours are still long and wages low.

Companies argue that higher wages lead to increased prices, which, in their turn, drive away customers. Many of these sweatshops produce clothing. As a consumer, how much would be you willing to pay in higher clothing prices to eliminate sweatshops and child labor? As a taxpayer, how much are you willing to pay in taxes to subsidize Third World incomes so that sweatshops and child labor are no longer necessary?

Employees' Responsibility to Their Organization

Darby has been working for 14 months at Holden Associates, a large management consulting firm. She is earning $65,000 a year, which *sounds* good, but does not go very far in New York City. It turns out that her peers at competing firms are typically paid 20 percent more and receive larger annual bonuses. Darby works about 60 hours a week, more if she is traveling. A number of times she has had to reschedule her vacation or cancel personal plans to meet client deadlines. She hopes to go to business school in a year and has already begun the application process.

Holden has a policy that permits any employee who works as late as 8:00 P.M. to eat dinner at company expense. The employee can also take a taxi home. Darby is in the habit of staying until 8:00 P.M. every night, whether or not her workload requires it. Then she orders enough food for dinner, with leftovers for lunch the next day. She has managed to cut her grocery bill to virtually nothing. Sometimes she invites her boyfriend to join her for dinner. As a student, he is always hungry and broke. Darby often uses the Holden taxi to take them back to his apartment, although the cab fare is twice as high as to her own place.

Sometimes Darby stays late to work on her business school applications. Naturally she uses Holden equipment to print out and photocopy the finished applications. Darby has also been known to return catalog purchases through the Holden mailroom on the company dime. Many employees do that and the mailroom staff do not seem to mind.

Is Darby doing anything wrong? How would you behave in these circumstances?

Chapter Conclusion

Even employees who are ethical in their personal lives may find it difficult to uphold their standards at work if those around them behave differently. Managers wonder what they can do to create an ethical environment in their companies. To help foster a sense of ethics within their organizations, many U.S. companies have developed their own formal ethics codes. For instance, Johnson & Johnson's corporate credo states that managers must take actions that are "just and ethical" and all employees must be "good citizens." (For a closer look at this credo, go to **http://www.jnj.com/our_company/ our_credo/credo_heading.htm**.) Many companies have also instituted formal ethics training programs for their employees.

In the end, however, the surest way to infuse ethics throughout an organization is for top executives to behave ethically themselves. Few employees will bother to "do the right thing" unless they observe that their bosses value and support such behavior. To ensure a more ethical world, managers must be an example for others, both within and outside their organizations.

For further discussion and updates on ethical issues, check in at **http://ethics.acusd .edu/index.html**.

Chapter Review

1. There are at least three reasons to be concerned about ethics in a business environment:

   - Society as a whole benefits from ethical behavior.

   - People feel better when they behave ethically.

   - Unethical behavior can be very costly.

2. The ethics checklist:

   - What are the facts?

   - What are the critical issues?

   - Who are the stakeholders?

   - What are the alternatives?

   - What are the ethical implications of each alternative?

   - Is it legal?

   - How would it look in the light of day?

   - What are the consequences?

   - Does it violate important values?

   - Does it violate the Golden Rule?

   - Is it just?

   - Has the process been fair?

   - Is more than one alternative right?

     - Which values are in conflict?

     - Which of these values are most important?

     - Can you find an alternative that is consistent with your values?

Practice Test

1. A Harvard Business School alumna told this story about her life as an MBA student in the 1980s:

   > During the spring of my first year, I took a Business Policy class. One of the young men in the class hung a bigger than life-size poster in the back of the room. It was a naked woman chained to a tree next to a Paul Bunyan-type man, fully clothed in a flannel jacket, with a chain saw. He was starting to de-limb her. The class broke up. The professor was standing there doubled over in laughter. There were 85 men guffawing away as if it were the funniest thing they'd ever seen. The women just sat there with their mouths open.

   Did this professor and these students behave ethically? What would you consider to be ethical behavior in this circumstance for the men, the women, and the professor?

2. Joya is the head of the personal insurance division of a large insurance company. Six months before, she was almost promoted to vice-president, but she lost out to Bill, a colleague from another division. Bill has now called a meeting to discuss who should be promoted to head the marine insurance division. In Joya's opinion, Ichiro is the most qualified person. However, she knows that Bill will not support him because he is Japanese and a relatively recent immigrant to the United States. Nonetheless, Joya is astonished at the meeting when Bill announces that the staff in the marine insurance division strongly object to Ichiro because of his drinking problem. Joya knows that Ichiro does not have a drinking problem and that the staff in his department think he would be a terrific choice. Based on Bill's false information, those at the meeting agree that the promotion should go to Jim, who happens to be a friend of Bill's. Joya knows that Jim is unpopular in his division because of his harsh, demanding style. She thinks that his appointment as department head will be disastrous. At the end of the meeting, Bill says that he will report the sense of the meeting to the CEO. Joya knows the CEO (they exchange pleasantries when passing in the hallways), but they have no regularly scheduled meetings. Nor is Joya likely to have the opportunity to mention Bill's behavior in a casual way. She is concerned that if she reports Bill is lying, the CEO will think she is causing trouble out of jealousy that Bill got the job she wanted. What should Joya do?

3. Executives were considering the possibility of moving their company to a different state. They wanted to determine if employees would be willing to relocate, but they did not want the employ-

ees to know the company was contemplating a move because the final decision had not yet been made. Instead of asking the employees directly, the company hired a firm to carry out a telephone survey. When calling the employees, these "pollsters" pretended to be conducting a public opinion poll and identified themselves as working for the new state's Chamber of Commerce. Has this company behaved in an ethical manner? Would there have been a better way to obtain this information?

4. Mark is an executive for a multinational office equipment company that would like to enter the potentially vast Chinese market. The official tariffs on office equipment imported into China are so high that these goods are uncompetitive in the local market. Mark discovers, however, that many companies sell their goods to importers offshore. These importers then negotiate "special" tariff rates with Chinese officials. Because these custom officials are under pressure to meet revenue targets, sometimes they are willing to negotiate lower, unofficial rates. What would you do if you were Mark?

5. Rap artist Ice-T and his band, Body Count, recorded a song called *Cop Killer* in which the singer gleefully anticipates slitting a policeman's throat. (The lyrics to this song are available at **http://www.cleat.org/remember/TimeWarner/ lyrics.html**.) Time Warner, Inc., produced this song and other gangsta rap recordings with violent and sexually degrading lyrics. Recorded music was an important source of profits for the company, which was struggling with a $15 billion debt and a depressed stock price. If Time Warner renounced rap albums, its reputation in the music business—and future profits—might have suffered. This damage could spill over into the multimedia market, which is crucial to Time Warner's future. The company was concerned about several important stakeholders—shareholders, consumers, suppliers (rap musicians). What decision would you have made if you had been CEO of Time Warner?

6. H. B. Fuller Co. of St. Paul is a leading manufacturer of industrial glues. Its mission statement says the company "will conduct business legally and ethically." It has endowed a university chair in business ethics and donates 5 percent of its profits to charity. But now it is under attack for selling its shoemakers' glue, Resistol, in Central America. Many homeless children in these countries have become addicted to Resistol's fumes. So widespread is the problem that glue-sniffers in Central America are called "resistoleros." Glue manufacturers in Europe have added a foul-smelling oil to their glue that discourages abusers. Fuller fears that the smell may also discourage legitimate users. What should Fuller do?

7. According to the Electronic Industries Association, questionable returns have become the toughest problem plaguing the consumer electronics industry. Some consumers purchase electronic equipment to use once or twice for a special occasion and then return it—a radar detector for a weekend getaway or a camcorder to record a wedding. Or a customer might return a cordless telephone because he cannot figure out how it works. The retailer's staff lacks the expertise to help, so they refund the customer's money and ship the phone back to the manufacturer labeled as defective. Excessive and unwarranted returns force manufacturers to repackage and reship perfectly good products, imposing extra costs that squeeze their profits and raise prices to consumers. One retailer returned a cordless telephone that was two years old and had been chewed up by a dog. What ethical obligations do consumers and retailers have in these circumstances?

8. Consider this complaint from an ethics professor:

> I make my living teaching and writing about ethics. . . . But in our own world—in our departments of philosophy and religious studies and medical humanities and ethics institutes—what happens?
>
> - Job openings [for instructors] are announced for positions that are already earmarked for specific persons. . . . [O]ver half the positions announced in the official employment newsletter for the American Academy of Religion were not "real."
>
> - It is extremely common for letters of application, even those responding to announced openings, to go without acknowledgment.
>
> - There are numerous instances of candidates who are brought to campus for interviews and who wait in vain to hear anything from their prospective employers.

When the candidates finally call, embarrassed but desperate, they are told, "Oh, that position has been filled."

Do recruiters have any ethical obligations to job candidates?

9. Six months ago, Todd, David, and Stacey joined a large, prestigious accounting firm in Houston. On paper, these three novices look similar and each graduated from a top MBA program. All three were assigned to work for the same client, a national restaurant chain. They quickly became friends and often lunched together. One day, a senior manager in the firm stopped by the conference room where Todd and David were working to ask if they would like to join him for lunch at the posh Hunter Club nearby. David said, "Thanks, that'd be great, but we usually eat lunch with Stacey. Could she come, too?" The manager hemmed and hawed for a minute, shifted his weight from one foot to the other, and finally said, "The Hunter Club doesn't allow women at lunch." What should Todd and David do?

10. Genentech, Inc., manufactured Protropin, a genetically engineered version of the human growth hormone. This drug's purpose was to enhance the growth of short children. Protropin was an important product for Genentech, accounting for more than one-third of the company's total revenue of $217 million. Although the drug was approved for the treatment of children whose bodies made inadequate quantities of growth hormone, many doctors prescribed it for children with normal amounts of growth hormone who simply happened to be short. There was no firm evidence that the drug actually increased growth for short children with normal growth hormone. Moreover, many people questioned whether it is appropriate to prescribe such a powerful drug for cosmetic reasons, especially when the drug might not work. Nor was there proof that it was safe over the long term. Was Genentech behaving ethically? Should it have discouraged doctors from prescribing the drug to normal, short children?

11. **ROLE REVERSAL** Write one or two paragraphs that could be used as an essay question describing an ethical dilemma that you have faced in your own life.

Internet Research Problem

Go to http://beatty.westbuslaw.com and click on "Ethics Tools: Resolving Ethical Dilemmas (with Real-to-Life Examples)." Outline the steps you would take to resolve one of these dilemmas. Use the ethics checklist in this chapter to guide you.

> **You can find further practice problems at http://beatty.westbuslaw.com or in the Study Guide that accompanies this text.**

Dispute Resolution

Tony Caruso had not returned for dinner, and his wife, Karen, was nervous. She put on some sandals and hurried across the dunes, a half mile to the ocean shore. She soon came upon Tony's dog, Blue, tied to an old picket fence. Tony's shoes and clothing were piled neatly nearby. Karen and friends searched frantically throughout the evening. A little past midnight, Tony's body washed ashore, his lungs filled with water. A local doctor concluded he had accidentally drowned.

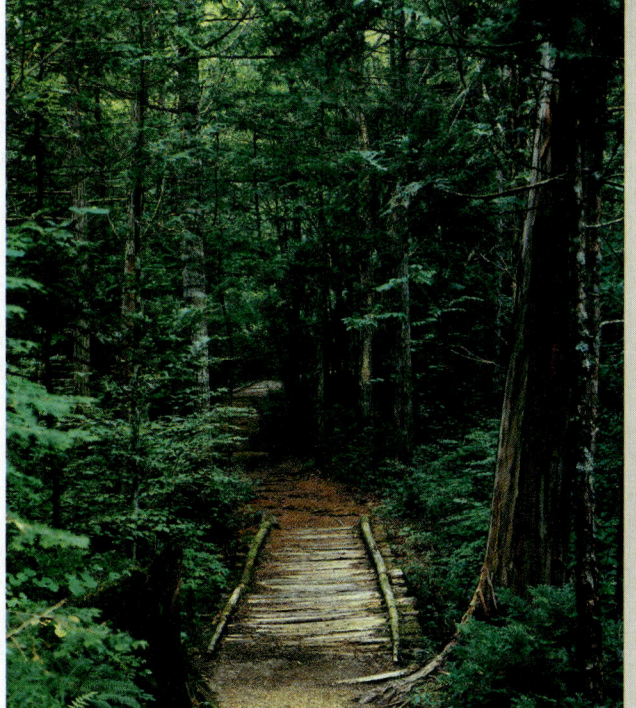

© AKIRA KAEDE/PHOTODISC/GETTY IMAGES

Karen and her friends were not the only ones distraught. Tony had been partners with Beth Smiles in an environmental consulting business, Enviro-Vision. They were good friends, and Beth was emotionally devastated. When she was able to focus on business issues, Beth filed an insurance claim with the Coastal Insurance Group. Beth hated to think about Tony's death in financial terms, but she was relieved that the struggling business would receive $2 million on the life insurance policy.

Several months after filing the claim, Beth received this reply from Coastal: "Under the policy issued to Enviro-Vision, we are conditionally liable in the amount of $1 million in the event of Mr. Caruso's death. If his death is accidental, we are conditionally liable to pay double indemnity of $2 million. But pursuant to section H(5) death by suicide is not covered. After a thorough investigation, we have concluded that Anthony Caruso's death was an act of suicide, as defined in section B(11) of the policy. Your claim is denied in its entirety." Beth was furious. She was convinced Tony was incapable of suicide. And her company could not afford the $2 million loss. She decided to consult her lawyer, Chris Pruitt. ■

THREE FUNDAMENTAL AREAS OF LAW

This case is a fictionalized version of several real cases based on double indemnity insurance policies. In this chapter we follow Beth's dispute with Coastal from initial interview through appeal, using it to examine three fundamental areas of law: alternative dispute resolution, the structure of our court systems, and civil lawsuits. But first we need to look at the best sort of dispute—the kind that is avoided.

Dispute Prevention

Over the years, one of the important services attorney Chris Pruitt has done for Enviro-Vision is *prevent disputes*. It is vital to understand and apply this concept in business and professional work and in everyday life. There is an old saying that you have a chance to go broke twice in your life: once when you lose a lawsuit, the other time when you win. The financial and emotional costs of litigation are extraordinarily high.

at **RISK**

You can avoid disputes in many different ways. Throughout the text we specify an array of preventive steps as they relate to the different legal problems posed. Here we can mention a few of the potential disputes Enviro-Vision avoided by thinking ahead.

When Beth and Tony started Enviro-Vision, Chris pointed out that, as business partners, the best way to protect both their friendship and their business was with a detailed partnership agreement. Although Beth and Tony found it tedious to create, the agreement helped them avoid problems such as those concerning capital contributions to the partnership, about who owns what, and about hiring and firing employees. Further, Enviro-Vision avoids unjustified firings by giving all employees written job descriptions. It educates employees about sexual harassment. When drafting a contract, Beth has learned to be sure that the client knows exactly what it is getting, when the work is due, what the risks are, and how much it will cost. Each of these practices has prevented potential lawsuits. ◆

When Beth Smiles meets with her lawyer, Chris Pruitt brings a second attorney from his firm, Janet Booker, who is an experienced **litigator,** that is, a lawyer who handles court cases. If they file a lawsuit, Janet will be in charge, so Chris wants her there for the first meeting. Janet probes about Tony's home life, the status of the business, his personal finances, everything. Beth becomes upset that Janet doesn't seem sympathetic, but Chris explains that Janet is doing her job: she needs all the information, good and bad.

Litigation versus Alternative Dispute Resolution

Janet starts thinking about the two methods of dispute resolution: litigation and alternative dispute resolution. **Litigation** refers to lawsuits, the process of filing claims in court, and ultimately going to trial. **Alternative dispute resolution** is any other formal or informal process used to settle disputes without resorting to a trial. It is increasingly popular with corporations and individuals alike because it is generally cheaper and faster than litigation.

ALTERNATIVE DISPUTE RESOLUTION

Janet Booker knows that even after expert legal help, vast expense, and years of work, litigation may leave clients unsatisfied. If she can use alternative dispute resolution (ADR) to create a mutually satisfactory solution in a few months, for a fraction of the cost, she is glad to do it. We will look at different types of ADR and analyze their strengths and weaknesses.

Negotiation

In most cases the parties negotiate, whether personally or through lawyers. Fortunately, the great majority of disputes are resolved this way. Negotiation often begins as soon as a dispute arises and may last a few days or several years.

Mediation

Mediation is the fastest growing method of dispute resolution in the United States. Here, a neutral person, called a mediator, attempts to coax the two disputing parties toward a voluntary settlement. (In some cases, there may be two or more mediators, but we will use the singular.) Generally, the two disputants voluntarily enter mediation, although some judges order the parties to try this form of ADR before allowing a case to go to trial.

A mediator does not render a decision in the dispute, but uses a variety of skills to prod the parties toward agreement. Often a mediator will shuttle between the antagonists, hearing their arguments, sorting out the serious issues from the less important, prompting the parties and lawyers alike to consider new perspectives, and looking for areas of agreement. Mediators must earn the trust of both parties, listen closely, try to diffuse anger and fear, and build the will to settle. Good mediators do not need a law degree, but they must have a sense of humor and low blood pressure.

Mediation has several major advantages. Because the parties maintain control of the process, the two antagonists can speak freely. They need not fear conceding too much, because no settlement takes effect until both parties sign. All discussions are confidential, further encouraging candid talk. This is particularly helpful in cases involving proprietary information that might be revealed during a trial.

Of all forms of dispute resolution, mediation probably offers the strongest "win–win" potential. Since the goal is voluntary settlement, neither party needs to fear that it will end up the loser. This is in sharp contrast to litigation, where one party is very likely to lose. Removing the fear of defeat often encourages thinking and talking that are more open and realistic than negotiations held in the midst of a lawsuit. Studies show that over 75 percent of mediated cases do reach a voluntary settlement. Such an agreement is particularly valuable to parties that wish to preserve a long-term relationship. Consider two companies that have done business successfully for 10 years but now are in the midst of a million dollar trade dispute. A lawsuit could last three or more years and destroy any chance of future trade. However, if the parties mediate the disagreement, they might reach an amicable settlement within a month or two and could quickly resume their mutually profitable business.

This form of ADR works for disputes both big and small. Two college roommates who cannot get along may find that a three-hour mediation session restores tranquillity in the apartment. On a larger scale, consider the work of former United States Senator George Mitchell, who mediated the Anglo-Irish peace agreement, setting Northern Ireland on the path to peace for the first time in three centuries. Like most good mediators, Mitchell was remarkably patient. In an early session, Mitchell permitted the head of one militant party to speak without interruption—for seven straight hours. The diatribe yielded no quick results, but Mitchell believed that after Northern Ireland's tortured history, any nonviolent discussions represented progress.

Arbitration

In this form of ADR, the parties agree to bring in a neutral third party, but with a major difference: the arbitrator has the power to impose an award. The arbitrator allows each side equal time to present its case and, after deliberation, issues a binding decision, generally without giving reasons. Unlike mediation, arbitration ensures that there will be a final result, although the parties lose control of the outcome. Arbitration is generally faster and cheaper than litigation.

Parties in arbitration give up many rights that litigants retain, including discovery and class action. *Discovery*, as we see below, allows the two sides in a lawsuit to obtain, before trial, documentary and other evidence from the opponent. Arbitration permits both sides to keep secret many files that would have to be divulged in a court case, potentially depriving the opposing side of valuable evidence. A party may have a stronger case than it realizes, and the absence of discovery may permanently deny it that knowledge. A *class action* is a suit in which one injured party represents a large group of people who have suffered similar harm. For example, in an employment discrimination case, a large group of employees who claim similar injury might band together to bring the case, giving themselves much greater clout. Arbitration eliminates this possibility, since injured employees face the employer one at a time. Finally, the fact that an arbitrator may not provide a written, public decision bars other plaintiffs, and society generally, from learning what happened.

Mandatory Arbitration

This variation contains one big difference: the parties agree *in advance* to arbitrate any disputes that may arise. For example, a consumer who purchases a computer or hires a real estate agent may sign an agreement requiring arbitration of any disputes; a customer opening an account with a stockbroker or bank—or health plan—may sign a similar form, often without realizing it. The good news is fewer lawsuits; the bad news is you might be the person kept out of court.

Assume that you live in Miami. Using the Internet, you order a $2,000 ThinkLite laptop computer, which arrives in a carton, loaded with six fat instructional manuals and many small leaflets. You read some of the documents and ignore others. For four weeks you struggle to make your computer work, to no avail. Finally, you telephone ThinkLite and demand a refund, but the company refuses. You file suit in your local court, at which time the company points out that buried among the hundreds of pages it mailed you was a *mandatory arbitration form.* This document prohibits you from filing suit against the company and states that if you have any complaint with the company, you must fly to Chicago; pay a $2,000 arbitrator's fee; plead your case before an arbitrator selected by the Laptop Trade Association of America; and, in the event you lose, pay ThinkLite's attorney's fees, which could be several thousand dollars. Is that mandatory arbitration provision valid? It is too early to say with finality, but thus far the courts that have faced such clauses have enforced them.[1]

To return to our hypothetical case, Janet Booker proposes to Coastal Insurance that they use ADR to expedite a decision in their dispute. Coastal rejects the offer. Coastal's lawyer, Rich Stewart, says that suicide is apparent. He does not want a neutral party to split the difference and award $1 million to Enviro-Vision. Janet reports this explanation to Beth, but adds that she does not believe it. She thinks that Coastal wants the case to drag on as long as possible in the hopes that Enviro-Vision will ultimately settle cheap.

It is a long way to go before trial, but Janet has to prepare her case. The first thing she thinks about is where to file the lawsuit.

COURT SYSTEMS

The United States has over 50 *systems* of courts. One nationwide system of *federal* courts serves the entire country. In addition, each *state* has its court system. The state and federal courts are in different buildings, have different judges, and hear different kinds of cases. Each has special powers and certain limitations.

State Courts

The typical state court system forms a pyramid, as Exhibit 3.1 shows. You may use the Internet to learn the exact names and powers of the courts in your state. Go to **http://www.state.[two-letter abbreviation for state].us/**, and click on "agencies," "courts," or a similar link.

Trial Courts

Almost all cases start in trial courts, the ones endlessly portrayed on television and in film. There is one judge and there will often (but not always) be a jury. This is the only court to hear testimony from witnesses and receive evidence. **Trial courts determine the facts of a particular dispute and apply to those facts the law given by earlier appellate court decisions.**

In the Enviro-Vision dispute, the trial court will decide all important facts that are in dispute. Did Tony Caruso die? Did he drown? Assuming he drowned, was his death accidental or suicide? Once the jury has decided the facts, it will apply the law to those facts. If Tony Caruso died accidentally, contract law provides that Beth Smiles is entitled to double indemnity benefits. If the jury decides he killed himself, Beth gets nothing.

Facts are critical. That may sound obvious, but in a course devoted to legal principles, it is easy to lose track of the key role that factual determinations play in the resolution of any dispute. In the Enviro-Vision case, we will see that one bit of factual evidence goes undetected, with costly consequences.

Jurisdiction refers to a court's power to hear a case. In state or federal court, a plaintiff may start a lawsuit only in a court that has jurisdiction over that kind of case.

---

[1] See, e.g., Hill v. Gateway 2000, 105 F.3d 1147, 1997 U.S. App. LEXIS 1877 (7th Cir. 1997), upholding a similar clause.

State Supreme Court

Appellate Courts

Appeal Courts

General Civil Division

General Criminal Division

Small Claims Division

Municipal Division

Juvenile Division

Probate Division

Land Division

Domestic Relations Division

Trial Courts of General Jurisdiction   Trial Courts of Limited Jurisdiction

Exhibit 3.1

Some courts have very limited jurisdiction, while others have the power to hear almost any case.

Trial Courts of Limited Jurisdiction. These courts may hear only certain types of cases. Small claims court has jurisdiction only over civil lawsuits involving a maximum of, say, $2,500 (the amount varies from state to state). Municipal court has jurisdiction over traffic citations and minor criminal matters. A juvenile court hears only cases involving minors. Probate court is devoted to settling the estates of deceased persons, though in some states it will hear certain other cases as well. Land court focuses on disputes about title to land and other real property issues. Domestic relations court resolves marital disputes and child custody issues.

Trial Courts of General Jurisdiction. Trial courts of general jurisdiction, however, can hear a very broad range of cases. The most important court, for our purposes, is the

A trial court determines facts, while an appeals court ensures that the lower court correctly applied the law to those facts.

general civil division. This court may hear virtually any civil lawsuit. In one day it might hear a $450 million shareholders' derivative lawsuit, an employment issue involving freedom of religion, and a foreclosure on a mortgage. Most of the cases we study start in this court.[2] If Enviro-Vision's case against Coastal goes to trial in a state court, it will begin in the trial court of general jurisdiction.

Appellate Courts

Appellate courts are entirely different from trial courts. Three or more judges hear the case. There are no juries, ever. These courts do not hear witnesses or take new evidence. They hear appeals of cases already tried below. **Appeals courts generally accept the facts given to them by trial courts and review the trial record to see if the court made errors of law.**

Generally, an appeals court will accept a factual finding unless there was *no evidence at all* to support it. If the jury decides that Tony Caruso committed suicide, the appeals court will normally accept that fact, even though the appeals judges consider the jury's conclusion dubious. On the other hand, if a jury concluded that Tony had been murdered, an appeals court would overturn that finding if neither side had introduced any evidence of murder during the trial.

An appeals court reviews the trial record to make sure that the lower court correctly applied the law to the facts. If the trial court made an **error of law,** the appeals court may require a new trial. Suppose the jury concludes that Tony Caruso committed suicide, but votes to award Enviro-Vision $1 million because it feels sorry for Beth Smiles. That is an error of law: if Tony committed suicide, Beth is entitled to nothing. An appellate court will reverse the decision. Or suppose that the trial judge permitted a friend of Tony's to state that he was certain Tony would never commit suicide. Normally, such opinions are not permissible in trial, and it was a legal error for the judge to allow the jury to hear it.

Court of Appeals. The party that loses at the trial court may appeal to the intermediate court of appeals. The party filing the appeal is the **appellant.** The party opposing the appeal (because it won at trial) is the **appellee.**

This court allows both sides to submit written arguments on the case, called **briefs.** Each side then appears for oral argument, usually before a panel of three judges. The appellant's lawyer has about 15 minutes to convince the judges that the trial court made serious errors of law, and that the decision should be **reversed,** that is, nullified. The appellee's lawyer has the same time to persuade the court that the trial court acted correctly, and that the result should be **affirmed,** that is, permitted to stand.

State Supreme Court. This is the highest court in the state, and it accepts some appeals from the court of appeals. In most states, there is no absolute right to appeal to

---

[2] Note that the actual name of the court will vary from state to state. In many states it is called superior court, because it has power superior to the courts of limited jurisdiction. In New York it is called supreme court (anything to confuse the layperson); in some states it is called court of common pleas; in Oregon and other states it is a circuit court. They are all civil trial courts of general jurisdiction. Within this branch, some states are beginning to establish specialized business courts, to hear complex commercial disputes. At least one state has created a cybercourt, for high-tech cases. Lawyers will argue their cases by teleconference and present evidence via streaming video.

the Supreme Court. If the high court regards a legal issue as important, it accepts the case. It then takes briefs and hears oral argument just as the appeals court did. If it considers the matter unimportant, it refuses to hear the case, meaning that the court of appeals' ruling is the final word on the case.[3]

In most states seven judges, often called justices, sit on the Supreme Court. They have the final word on state law.

Federal Courts

As discussed in Chapter 1, federal courts are established by the United States Constitution, which limits what kinds of cases can be brought in any federal court. See Exhibit 3.2. For our purposes, two kinds of civil lawsuits are permitted in federal court: federal question cases and diversity cases.

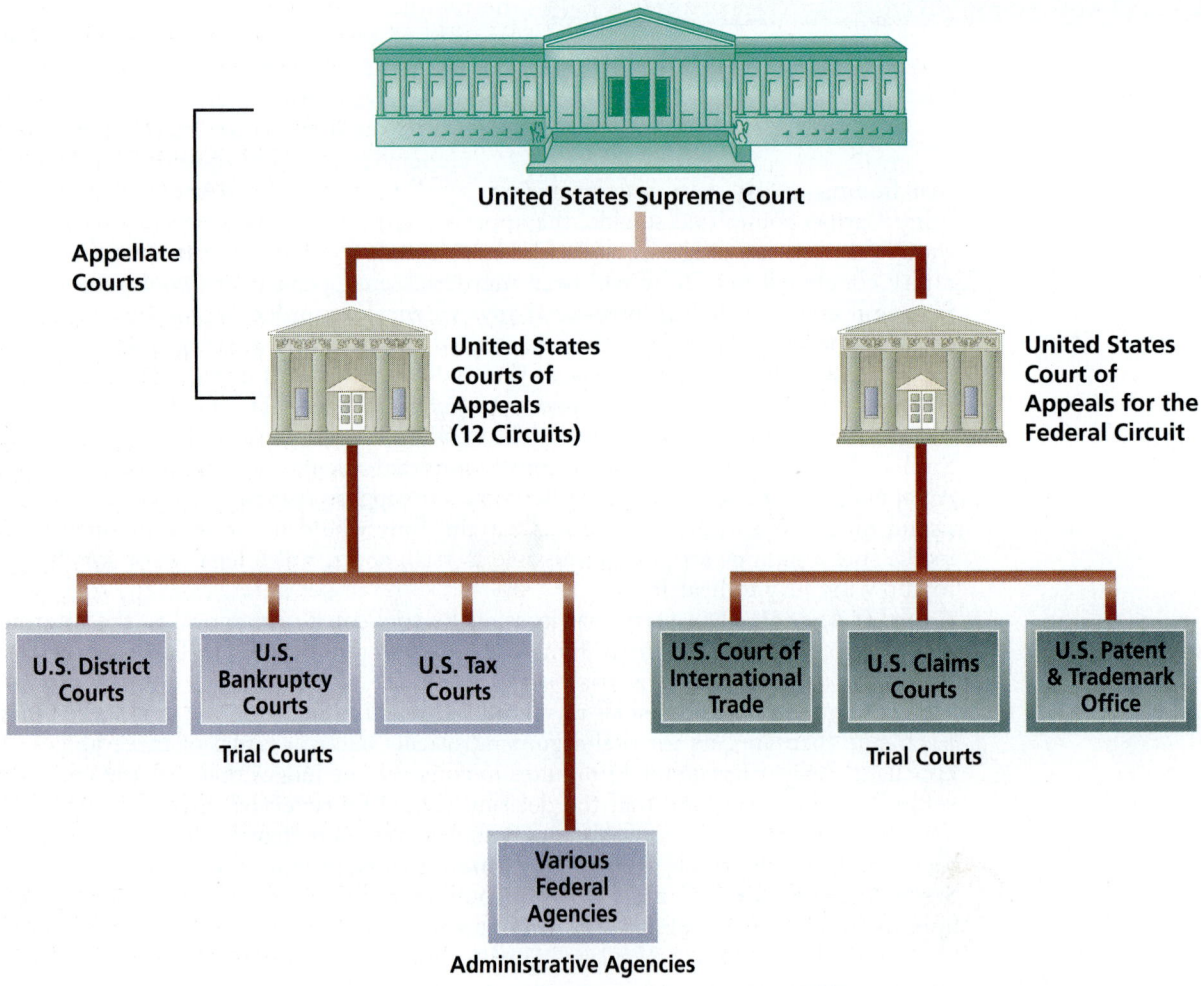

United States Supreme Court

Appellate Courts

United States Courts of Appeals (12 Circuits)

United States Court of Appeals for the Federal Circuit

U.S. District Courts	U.S. Bankruptcy Courts	U.S. Tax Courts

Trial Courts

U.S. Court of International Trade	U.S. Claims Courts	U.S. Patent & Trademark Office

Trial Courts

Various Federal Agencies

Administrative Agencies

Exhibit 3.2

---

3   In some states with smaller populations, there is no intermediate appeals court. All appeals from trial courts go directly to the state supreme court.

Federal Question Cases

A claim based on the United States Constitution, a federal statute, or a federal treaty is called a federal question case.[4] Federal courts have jurisdiction over these cases. If the Environmental Protection Agency orders Logging Company not to cut in a particular forest, and Logging Company claims that the agency has wrongly deprived it of its property, that suit is based on a federal statute and is thus a federal question. If Little Retailer sues Mega Retailer, claiming that Mega has established a monopoly, that claim is also based on a statute—the Sherman Antitrust Act—and creates federal question jurisdiction. Enviro-Vision's potential suit merely concerns an insurance contract. The federal district court has no federal question jurisdiction over the case.

Diversity Cases

Even if no federal law is at issue, federal courts have **diversity jurisdiction** when (1) the plaintiff and defendant are citizens of different states *and* (2) the amount in dispute exceeds $75,000. The theory behind diversity jurisdiction is that courts of one state might be biased against citizens of another state. To ensure fairness, the parties have the option of federal court.

Enviro-Vision is located in Oregon and Coastal Insurance is incorporated in Georgia.[5] They are citizens of different states and the amount in dispute far exceeds $75,000. Janet could file this case in United States District Court based on diversity jurisdiction.

Trial Courts

United States District Court. This is the primary trial court in the federal system. The nation is divided into about 94 districts, and each has a district court. States with smaller populations have one district. States with larger populations have several districts; Texas is divided geographically into four districts.

Other Trial Courts. There are other, specialized trial courts in the federal system. Bankruptcy Court, Tax Court, and the United States Court of International Trade all handle name-appropriate cases. The United States Claims Court hears cases brought against the United States, typically on contract disputes.

Judges. The president of the United States nominates all federal court judges, from district court to Supreme Court. The nominees must be confirmed by the Senate.

Appellate Courts

United States Courts of Appeals. These are the intermediate courts of appeals. As the map below shows, they are divided into "circuits," which are geographical areas. There are 11 numbered circuits, hearing appeals from district courts. For example, an appeal from the Northern District of Illinois would go to the Court of Appeals for the Seventh Circuit. You will find an interactive map of the District and Circuit Courts at http://www.uscourts.gov/links.html.

A twelfth court, the Court of Appeals for the District of Columbia, hears appeals only from the district court of Washington, D.C. This is a particularly powerful court because so many suits about federal statutes begin in the district court for the District

---

4 28 U.S.C. §1331 governs federal question jurisdiction and 28 U.S.C. §1332 covers diversity jurisdiction.
5 For diversity purposes, a corporation is a citizen of the state in which it is incorporated and the state in which it has its principal place of business.

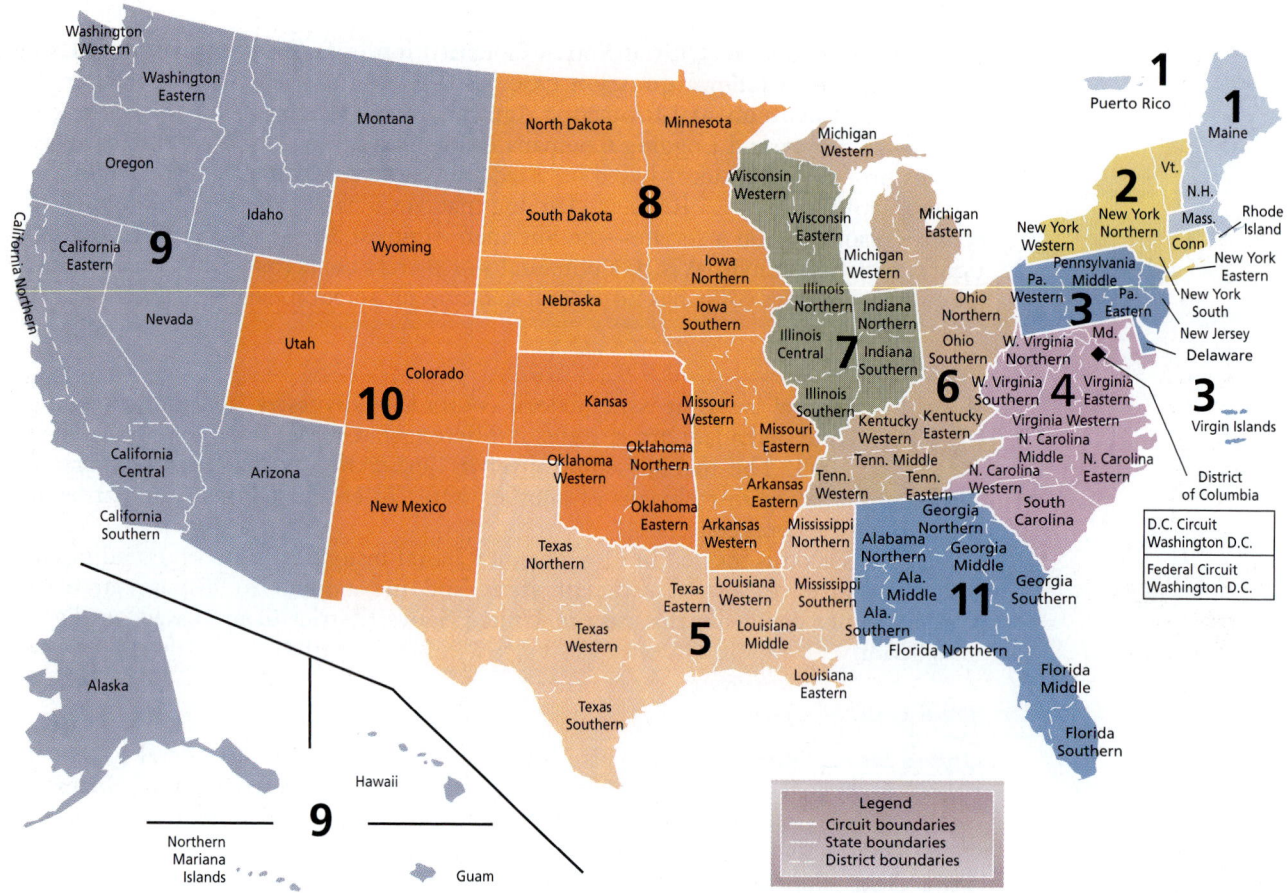

Legend
Circuit boundaries
State boundaries
District boundaries

of Columbia. Also in Washington is the thirteenth Court of Appeals, known as the Federal Circuit. It hears appeals from specialized trial courts, as shown in Exhibit 3.2.

Within one circuit there are many circuit judges, up to about 30 judges in the largest circuit, the Ninth. When a case is appealed, three judges hear the appeal, taking briefs and hearing oral argument.

United States Supreme Court. This is the highest court in the country. There are nine justices on the Court. One justice is the chief justice and the other eight are associate justices. When they decide a case, each justice casts an equal vote. The chief justice's special power comes from his authority to assign opinions to a given justice. The justice assigned to write an opinion has an opportunity to control the precise language and thus to influence the voting by other justices. For a face-to-face meeting with Supreme Court justices, past and present, introduce yourself to http://www.oyez.org.

The Supreme Court has the power to hear appeals in any federal case and in certain cases that began in state courts. Generally, it is up to the Court whether or not it will accept a case. A party that wants the Supreme Court to review a lower court ruling must file a petition for a **writ of certiorari,** asking the Court to hear the case. The Court receives about 8,000 of these requests every year but currently accepts fewer than 100. Most cases accepted involve either an important issue of constitutional law or an interpretation of a major federal statute.

LITIGATION

Janet Booker decides to file the Enviro-Vision suit in the Oregon trial court. She thinks that a state court judge may take the issue more seriously than a federal district court judge.

Pleadings

The documents that begin a lawsuit are called the **pleadings.** These consist of the complaint, the answer, and sometimes a reply.

Complaint

The plaintiff files in court a **complaint,** which is a short, plain statement of the facts she is alleging and the legal claims she is making. The purpose of the complaint is to inform the defendant of the general nature of the claims and the need to come into court and protect his interests.

Janet Booker files the complaint, as shown below. Since Enviro-Vision is a partnership, she files the suit on behalf of Beth, personally.

STATE OF OREGON
CIRCUIT COURT

Multnomah County   Civil Action No. _____

_____

Elizabeth Smiles,
Plaintiff

JURY TRIAL DEMANDED

v.

Coastal Insurance Company, Inc.,
Defendant

_____

COMPLAINT

Plaintiff Elizabeth Smiles states that:

1. She is a citizen of Multnomah County, Oregon.
2. Defendant Coastal Insurance Company, Inc., is incorporated under the laws of Georgia and has as its usual place of business 148 Thrift Street, Savannah, Georgia.
3. On or about July 5, 2006, plaintiff Smiles ("Smiles"), Defendant Coastal Insurance Co, Inc. ("Coastal") and Anthony Caruso entered into an insurance contract ("the contract"), a copy of which is annexed hereto as Exhibit "A." This contract was signed by all parties or their authorized agents, in Multnomah County, Oregon.
4. The contract obligates Coastal to pay to Smiles the sum of two million dollars ($2 million) if Anthony Caruso should die accidentally.
5. On or about September 18, 2006, Anthony Caruso accidentally drowned and died while swimming.
6. Coastal has refused to pay any sum pursuant to the contract.
7. Coastal has knowingly, willingly and unreasonably refused to honor its obligations under the contract.

WHEREFORE, plaintiff Elizabeth Smiles demands judgment against defendant Coastal for all monies due under the contract; demands triple damages for Coastal's knowing, willing, and unreasonable refusal to honor its obligations; and demands all costs and attorney's fees, with interest.

ELIZABETH SMILES,
By her attorney,
[Signed]
Janet Booker
Pruitt, Booker & Bother
983 Joy Avenue
Portland, OR
October 18, 2006

Service

When she files the complaint in court, Janet gets a summons, which is a paper ordering the defendant to answer the complaint within 20 days. A sheriff or constable then *serves* the two papers by delivering them to the defendant. Coastal's headquarters are in Georgia, so the state of Oregon has required Coastal to specify someone as its agent for receipt of service in Oregon.

Answer

Once the complaint and summons are served, Coastal has 20 days in which to file an answer. Coastal's answer, shown below, is a brief reply to each of the allegations in the complaint. The answer tells the court and the plaintiff exactly what issues are in dispute. Since Coastal admits that the parties entered into the contract that Beth claims they did, there is no need for her to prove that in court. The court can focus its attention on the disputed issue: whether Tony Caruso died accidentally.

STATE OF OREGON
CIRCUIT COURT

Multnomah County   Civil Action No. 06-5626

Elizabeth Smiles,
Plaintiff
v.
Coastal Insurance Company, Inc.,
Defendant

ANSWER

Defendant Coastal Insurance Company, Inc., answers the complaint as follows:
1. Admit.
2. Admit.
3. Admit.
4. Admit.
5. Deny.
6. Admit.
7. Deny.
COASTAL INSURANCE COMPANY, INC.,
By its attorney,
[Signed]
Richard B. Stewart

Kiley, Robbins, Stewart & Glote
333 Victory Boulevard
Portland, OR
October 30, 2006

If the defendant fails to answer in time, the plaintiff will ask for a **default judgment,** meaning a decision that the plaintiff wins without a trial.

Counter-Claim

Sometimes a defendant does more than merely answer a complaint, and files a **counter-claim,** meaning a second lawsuit by the defendant against the plaintiff. Suppose that after her complaint was filed in court, Beth had written a letter to the newspaper, calling Coastal a bunch of "thieves and scoundrels who spend their days mired in fraud and larceny." Coastal would not have found that amusing. The company's answer would have included a counter-claim against Beth for libel, claiming that she falsely accused the insurer of serious criminal acts. Coastal would have demanded money damages.

If Coastal counter-claimed, Beth would have to file a **reply,** which is simply an answer to a counter-claim. Beth's reply would be similar to Coastal's answer, admitting or denying the various allegations.

Class Actions

Suppose Janet uncovers evidence that Coastal denies 80 percent of all life insurance claims, calling them suicide. She could ask the court to permit a **class action.** If the court granted her request, she would represent the entire group of plaintiffs, including those who are unaware of the lawsuit or even unaware they were harmed. Class actions can give the plaintiffs much greater leverage, since the defendant's potential liability is vastly increased. In the back of her mind, Janet has thoughts of a class action, *if* she can uncover evidence that Coastal has used a claim of suicide to deny coverage to a large number of claimants.

NEWS*worthy*

From his small town in Maine, Ernie decides to get rich quickly. On the Internet he advertises "Energy Breakthrough! Cut your heating costs 15 percent for only $25." One hundred thousand people send him their money. In return, they receive a photocopied graph, illustrating that if you wear two sweaters instead of one, you will feel 15 percent warmer. Ernie has deceitfully earned $2,500,000 in pure profit. What can the angry homeowners do? Under the laws of fraud and consumer protection, they have a legitimate claim to their $25, and perhaps even to treble damages ($75). But few will sue, because the time and effort required would be greater than the money recovered.

Economists analyze such legal issues in terms of *efficiency*. The laws against Ernie's fraud are clear and well intended, but they will not help in this case because it is too expensive for 100,000 people to litigate such a small claim. The effort would be hugely *inefficient*, both for the homeowners and for society generally. The economic reality may permit Ernie to evade the law's grasp.

That is one reason we have class actions. A dozen or so "heating plan" buyers can all hire the same lawyer. This attorney will file court papers in Maine on behalf of *everyone*, nationwide, who has been swindled by Ernie—including the 99,988 people who have yet to be notified that they are part of the case. Now the con artist, instead of facing a few harmless suits for $25, must respond to a multimillion-dollar claim being handled by an experienced lawyer. Treble damages become menacing: three times $25 times 100,000 is no joke, even to a cynic like Ernie. He may also be forced to pay for the plaintiffs' attorney, as well as all costs of notifying class members and disbursing money to them. With one lawyer representing an entire class, the legal system has become fiercely efficient.

Congress recently passed a statute designed to force large, multi-state class actions out of state courts, into federal. Proponents of the new law complained that state courts often gave excessive verdicts, even for frivolous lawsuits. They said the cases hurt businesses while enriching lawyers. Opponents argued that the new law was designed to shield large corporations from paying for the harm they cause, by sending the cases into a federal system that is often hostile to them. ◆

Judgment on the Pleadings

A party can ask the court for a judgment based simply on the pleadings themselves, by filing a motion to dismiss. **A motion is a formal request to the court** that the court take some step or issue some order. During a lawsuit the parties file many motions. A **motion to dismiss** is a request that the court terminate a case without permitting it to go further. Suppose that a state law requires claims on life insurance contracts to be filed within three years, and Beth files her claim four years after Tony's death. Coastal would move to dismiss based on this late filing. The court might well agree, and Beth would never get into court.

Discovery

Few cases are dismissed on the pleadings. Most proceed quickly to the next step. **Discovery is the critical, pre-trial opportunity for both parties to learn the strengths and weaknesses of the opponent's case.**

The theory behind civil litigation is that the best outcome is a negotiated settlement and that parties will move toward agreement if they understand the opponent's case. That is likeliest to occur if both sides have an opportunity to examine most of the evidence the other side will bring to trial. Further, if a case does go all the way to trial, efficient and fair litigation cannot take place in a courtroom filled, like a piñata, with surprises. On television dramas, witnesses say astonishing things that amaze the courtroom (and keep viewers hooked through the next commercial). In real trials the lawyers know in advance the answers to practically all questions asked because discovery has allowed them to see the opponent's documents and question its witnesses. The following are the most important forms of discovery.

Interrogatories. These are written questions that the opposing party must answer, in writing, under oath.

Depositions. These provide a chance for one party's lawyer to question the other party, or a potential witness, under oath. The person being questioned is the **deponent.** Lawyers for both parties are present. During depositions, and in trial, good lawyers choose words carefully and ask

A deposition provides a chance for one party's lawyer to question the other party, or a potential witness, under oath.

questions calculated to advance their cause. A fine line separates ethical, probing questions from those that are tricky, and a similar line divides answers that are merely unhelpful from perjury.

Production of Documents and Things. Each side may ask the other side to produce relevant documents for inspection and copying; to produce physical objects, such as part of a car alleged to be defective; and for permission to enter on land to make an inspection, for example, at the scene of an accident.

Physical and Mental Examination. A party may ask the court to order an examination of the other party, if his physical or mental condition is relevant, for example, in a case of medical malpractice.

Requests for Admission. Either party can insist that the opposing party admit or deny certain facts, to avoid wasting time on points not in dispute. In a medical malpractice case, the plaintiff would request that the doctor admit he performed the surgery and admit what would be the normal level of care a surgeon would provide for such a case (while not expecting the surgeon to admit that he erred).

Janet Booker begins her discovery with interrogatories. Her goal is to learn Coastal's basic position and factual evidence and then follow up with more detailed questioning during depositions. Her interrogatories ask for every fact Coastal relied on in denying the claim. She asks for the names of all witnesses, the identity of all documents, the description of all things or objects that they considered. She requests the names of all corporate officers who played any role in the decision and of any expert witnesses Coastal plans to call. Interrogatory No. 18 demands extensive information on all *other* claims in the past three years that Coastal has denied based on alleged suicide. Janet is looking for evidence that would support a class action.

Beth remarks on how thorough the interrogatories are. "This will tell us what their case is." Janet frowns and looks less optimistic: she's done this before.

Coastal has 30 days to answer Janet's interrogatories. Before it responds, Coastal mails to Janet a notice of deposition, stating its intention to depose Beth Smiles. Beth and Janet will go to the office of Coastal's lawyer, and Beth will answer questions under oath. But at the same time Coastal sends this notice, it sends *25 other notices of deposition.* The company will depose Karen Caruso as soon as Beth's deposition is over. Coastal also plans to depose all seven employees of Enviro-Vision; three neighbors who lived near Tony and Karen's beach house; two policemen who participated in the search; the doctor and two nurses involved in the case; Tony's physician; Jerry Johnson, Tony's tennis partner; Craig Bergson, a college roommate; a couple who had dinner with Tony and Karen a week before his death; and several other people.

Beth is appalled. Janet explains that some of these people might have relevant information. But there may be another reason that Coastal is doing this: the company wants to make this litigation hurt. Janet will have to attend every one of these depositions. Costs will skyrocket.

Janet files a **motion for a protective order.** This is a request that the court limit Coastal's discovery by decreasing the number of depositions. Janet also calls Rich Stewart and suggests that they discuss what depositions are really necessary. Rich insists that all of the depositions are important. This is a $2 million case and Coastal is entitled to protect itself. As both lawyers know, **the parties are entitled to discover anything that could reasonably lead to valid evidence.**

Before Beth's deposition date arrives, Rich sends Coastal's answers to Enviro-Vision's interrogatories. The answers contain no useful information whatsoever. For example, Interrogatory No. 10 asked, "If you claim that Anthony Caruso committed suicide, describe every fact upon which you rely in reaching that conclusion." Coastal's answer simply says, "His state of mind, his poor business affairs, and the circumstances of his death all indicate suicide."

Janet calls Rich and complains that the interrogatory answers are a bad joke. Rich disagrees, saying that it is the best information they have so early in the case. After they debate it for 20 minutes, Rich offers to settle the case for $100,000. Janet refuses and makes no counteroffer.

Janet files a **motion to compel answers to interrogatories,** in other words, a formal request that the court order Coastal to supply more complete answers. Janet submits a **memorandum** with the motion, which is a supporting argument. Although it is only a few pages long, the memorandum takes several hours of library research and writing to prepare—more costs. Janet also informs Rich Stewart that Beth will not appear for the deposition, since Coastal's interrogatory answers are inadequate.

Rich now files *his* motion to compel, asking the court to order Beth Smiles to appear for her deposition. The court hears all of the motions together. Janet argues that Coastal's interrogatory answers are hopelessly uninformative and defeat the whole purpose of discovery. She claims that Coastal's large number of depositions creates a huge and unfair expense for a small firm.

Rich claims that the interrogatory answers are the best that Coastal can do thus far and that Coastal will supplement the answers when more information becomes available. He argues against Interrogatory No. 18, the one in which Janet asked for the names of other policyholders whom Coastal considered suicides. He claims that Janet is engaging in a fishing expedition that would violate the privacy of Coastal's insurance customers and provide no information relevant to this case. He demands that Janet make Beth available for a deposition.

These discovery rulings are critical because they will color the entire lawsuit. A trial judge has to make many discovery decisions before a case reaches trial. At times the judge must weigh the need of one party to see documents against the other side's need for privacy. One device a judge can use in reaching a discovery ruling is an **in camera inspection,** meaning that the judge views the requested documents alone, with no lawyers present, and decides whether the other side is entitled to view them. The following case illustrates a common discovery problem: refusal by one side to provide answers. The decision also demonstrates why such aggressive conduct can backfire disastrously.

AMERICAN CASH CARD CORP. V. AT&T CORP.

210 F.3d 354, 2000 WL 357670
United States Court of Appeals for the Second Circuit, 2000

Facts: The American Cash Card Corp. ("Amcash") sued AT&T, claiming that AT&T had promised to provide a long distance service at a special low rate, but had in fact charged much more. AT&T filed a counterclaim, saying that it had provided the promised telephone service but that Amcash had failed to pay its (very large) bills.

The trial court ordered that all discovery be finished by August 16, 1996. AT&T served its first request for documents and its first interrogatories in May of that year. Amcash requested two extensions of its response deadline, but then failed to produce documents or answers. In August, the court ordered Amcash to respond promptly or face sanctions. Amcash produced only a few answers to interrogatories. The court issued a second order, requiring a full response by October 8, 1996, threatening to dismiss Amcash's case if it failed to answer. Amcash withheld all papers concerning finances and other key issues.

In January 1997, the trial judge ordered Amcash to produce the financial records, including customer information, no later than January 31. The court also ordered Amcash to pay $7,500 to AT&T for that company's expenses in obtaining discovery orders.

▼

Amcash produced a few records, but retained many more. The company's general manager, Vicki Zakaria, admitted in a deposition that Amcash's attorney had never asked her to look for documents concerning AT&T, or to conduct an electronic search for relevant information, even though her computer contained substantial data relating to the phone company. She even mentioned that she had additional AT&T documents in her home, which she had never furnished.

In February, the trial court dismissed Amcash's claims and awarded AT&T $108,394,969 on its counterclaims. Amcash appealed.

Issue: Did the trial court abuse its discretion by dismissing Amcash's claims and allowing AT&T's claims?

Excerpts from the Court's Summary Order: Although entry of a default judgment is an extreme measure, discovery orders are meant to be followed. When we review a district court's entry of default judgment as a sanction, the question is not whether the Court of Appeals would as an original matter have entered such a judgment; it is whether the district court abused its discretion in so doing.

First, [Amcash contends,] the district court abused its discretion because of the severity of the effects of entering default judgment in this case. But here, as in other areas of the law, the most severe in the spectrum of sanctions provided by statute or rule must be available to the district court in appropriate cases, not merely to penalize those whose conduct may be deemed to warrant such a sanction, but to deter those who might be tempted to such conduct in the absence of such a deterrent.

Second, Appellants seem to maintain that the district court abused its discretion because its finding of bad faith was incorrect. The district court's finding in this respect is, however, a factual determination, subject to reversal only upon a showing of clear error. The district court's conclusions concerning Appellant's bad faith is, instead, amply supported by the facts in the record. Appellants try to avoid responsibility for their failure to obey the district court's discovery orders by shifting the blame to the incompetence of their trial counsel. But even if this were the case, the defense would not be availing. For a litigant chooses counsel at his peril, and here, as in countless other contexts, counsel's disregard of his professional responsibilities can lead to extinction of his client's claim.

Affirmed. ■

Public Policy

Public policy refers to the interest that society has in any dispute. In appellate cases, judges routinely consider not only the interests of the two parties, but also the effect that their ruling will have on the general population. Notice two public policy concerns in the *American Cash Card* case. First, the judges dismiss the plaintiff's suit partly for deterrent effect. What does that mean? Is that motive wise? Second, the judges decide the case based on *procedural,* rather than *substantive,* issues. Is it proper to decide a $100 million dispute without holding a trial? What is the public policy effect of this ruling? As you answer, take into account the importance of discovery in resolving disputes. ◆

In the Enviro-Vision case, the judge rules that Coastal must furnish more complete answers to the interrogatories, especially as to the factual basis of its denial. However, he rules against Interrogatory No. 18, the one concerning other claims Coastal has denied. This simple ruling kills Janet's hope of making a class action of the case. He orders Beth to appear for the deposition. As to future depositions, Coastal may take any 10, but then may take additional depositions only by demonstrating to the court that the deponents have useful information.

Rich proceeds to take Beth's deposition. It takes two full days. He asks about Enviro-Vision's past and present. He learns that Tony appeared to have won their biggest contract ever from Rapid City, Oregon, but that he then lost it when he had a fight with Rapid City's mayor. He inquires into Tony's mood, learns that he was depressed, and probes in every direction he can to find evidence of suicidal motivation. Janet and Rich argue frequently over questions and whether Beth should have to answer them. At times Janet is persuaded and permits Beth to answer; other times she instructs Beth not to answer. For example, toward the end of the second day, Rich asks

Beth whether she and Tony had been sexually involved. Janet instructs Beth not to answer. This fight necessitates another trip into court to determine whether Beth must answer. The judge rules that Beth must discuss Tony's romantic life only if Coastal has some evidence that he was involved with someone outside his marriage. The company lacks any such evidence.

Crucial Clue. Now limited to 10 depositions, Rich selects his nine other deponents carefully. For example, he decides to depose only one of the two nurses; he chooses to question Jerry Johnson, the tennis partner, but not Craig Bergson, the former roommate; and so forth. When we look at the many legal issues this case raises, his choices seem minor. In fact, unbeknownst to Rich or anyone else, his choices may determine the outcome of the case. As we will see later, Craig Bergson has evidence that is possibly crucial to the lawsuit. If Rich decides not to depose him, neither side will ever learn the evidence and the jury will never hear it. A jury can only decide a case based on the evidence presented to it. *Facts are elusive—and often controlling.*

In each deposition, Rich carefully probes with his questions, sometimes trying to learn what he actually does not know, sometimes trying to pin down the witness to a specific version of facts so that Rich knows how the witness will testify at trial. Neighbors at the beach testify that Tony seemed tense; one testifies about seeing Tony, unhappy, on the beach with his dog. Another testifies he had never before seen Blue tied up on the beach. Karen Caruso admits that Tony had been somewhat tense and unhappy the last couple of months. She reluctantly discusses their marriage, admitting there were problems.

Other Discovery. Rich sends Requests to Produce Documents, seeking medical records about Tony. Once again, the parties fight over which records are relevant, but Rich gets most of what he wants. Rich sends Requests for Admission, forcing Beth to commit herself to certain positions, for example, that Tony had lost the Rapid City contract and had been depressed about it.

Plaintiff's Discovery. Janet does less discovery than Rich because most of the witnesses she will call are friendly witnesses. She can interview them privately without giving any information to Coastal. With the help of Beth and Karen, Janet builds her case just as carefully as Rich, choosing the witnesses who will bolster the view that Tony was in good spirits and died accidentally.

She deposes all of the officers of Coastal who participated in the decision to deny insurance coverage. She is particularly aggressive in pinning them down as to the limited information they had when they denied Beth's claim.

Summary Judgment

When discovery is completed, both sides may consider seeking summary judgment. **Summary judgment is a ruling by the court that no trial is necessary because there are no** essential **facts in dispute.** The purpose of a trial is to determine the facts of the case, that is, to decide who did what to whom, why, when, and with what consequences. If there are no relevant facts in dispute, then there is no need for a trial.

Suppose Joe sues EZBuck Films, claiming that the company's new movie, Lover Boy, violates the copyright of a screenplay that he wrote, called Love Man. Discovery establishes that the two stories are suspiciously similar. But EZBuck's lawyer also learns that Joe sold the copyright for *Love Man* to HotShot Pix. EZBuck may or may not have violated a copyright, but there is no need for a trial because Joe *cannot win* even if there is a copyright violation. He does not own the copyright. The court will grant summary judgment for EZBuck.

In the following case, the defendant won summary judgment, meaning that the case never went to trial. And yet, this was only the beginning of trouble for that defendant, William Jefferson Clinton.

JONES V. CLINTON

990 F. Supp. 657, 1998 U.S. Dist. LEXIS 3902
United States District Court for the Eastern District of Arkansas, 1998

Facts: In 1991, Bill Clinton was governor of Arkansas. Paula Jones worked for a state agency, the Arkansas Industrial Development Commission (AIDC). When Clinton became president, Jones sued him, claiming that he had sexually harassed her. She alleged that, in May 1991, the governor arranged for her to meet him in a hotel room in Little Rock, Arkansas. When they were alone, he put his hand on her leg and slid it toward her pelvis. She escaped from his grasp, exclaimed, "What are you doing?" and said she was "not that kind of girl." She was upset and confused, and sat on a sofa near the door. She claimed that Clinton approached her, "lowered his trousers and underwear, exposed his penis and told her to kiss it." Jones was horrified, jumped up and said she had to leave. Clinton responded by saying, "Well, I don't want to make you do anything you don't want to do," and pulled his pants up. He added that if she got in trouble for leaving work, Jones should "have Dave call me immediately and I'll take care of it." He also said, "You are smart. Let's keep this between ourselves." Jones remained at AIDC until February 1993, when she moved to California because of her husband's job transfer.

President Clinton denied all of the allegations. He also filed for summary judgment, claiming that Jones had not alleged facts that justified a trial. Jones opposed the motion for summary judgment.

Issue: Was Clinton entitled to summary judgment or was Jones entitled to a trial?

Excerpts from Judge Wright's Decision: [To establish this type of a sexual harassment case, a plaintiff must show that her refusal to submit to unwelcome sexual advances resulted in a tangible job detriment, meaning that she suffered a specific loss. Jones claims that she was denied promotions, given a job with fewer responsibilities, isolated physically, required to sit at a workstation with no work to do, and singled out as the only female employee not to be given flowers on Secretary's Day.]

There is no record of plaintiff ever applying for another job within AIDC, however, and the record shows that not only was plaintiff never downgraded, her position was reclassified upward from a Grade 9 classification to a Grade 11 classification, thereby increasing her annual salary. Indeed, it is undisputed that plaintiff received every merit increase and cost-of-living allowance for which she was eligible during her nearly two-year tenure with the AIDC and consistently received satisfactory job evaluations.

Although plaintiff states that her job title upon returning from maternity leave was no longer that of purchasing assistant, her job duties prior to taking maternity leave and her job duties upon returning to work both involved data input. That being so, plaintiff cannot establish a tangible job detriment. A transfer that does not involve a demotion in form or substance and involves only minor changes in working conditions, with no reduction in pay or benefits, will not constitute an adverse employment action, otherwise every trivial personnel action that an irritable employee did not like would form the basis of a discrimination suit.

Finally, the Court rejects plaintiff's claim that she was subjected to hostile treatment having tangible effects when she was isolated physically, made to sit in a location from which she was constantly watched, made to sit at her workstation with no work to do, and singled out as the only female employee not to be given flowers on Secretary's Day. Plaintiff may well have perceived hostility and animus on the part of her supervisors, but these perceptions are merely conclusory in nature and do not, without more, constitute a tangible job detriment. Although it is not clear why plaintiff failed to receive flowers on Secretary's Day in 1992, such an omission does not give rise to a federal cause of action.

In sum, the Court finds that a showing of a tangible job detriment or adverse employment action is an essential element of plaintiff's sexual harassment claim and that plaintiff has not demonstrated any tangible job detriment or adverse employment action for her refusal to submit to the Governor's alleged advances. The President is therefore entitled to summary judgment [on this claim]. ∎

In other words, the court acknowledged that there were factual disputes, but concluded that even if Jones proved each of her allegations, she would *still* lose the case, because her allegations fell short of a legitimate case of sexual harassment. Jones appealed the case. Later the same year, as the appeal was pending and the House of Representatives was considering whether to impeach President Clinton, the parties settled the dispute. Clinton, without acknowledging any of the allegations, agreed to pay Jones $850,000 to drop the suit.

Janet and Rich each consider moving for summary judgment, but both correctly decide that they would lose. There is one major fact in dispute: Did Tony Caruso commit suicide? Only a jury may decide that issue. As long as there is *some evidence* supporting each side of a key factual dispute, the court may not grant summary judgment.

Final Preparation

Well over 90 percent of all lawsuits are settled before trial. But the parties in the Enviro-Vision dispute cannot seem to compromise, so each side gears up for trial. The attorneys make lists of all witnesses they will call. They then prepare each witness very carefully, rehearsing the questions they will ask. It is considered ethical and proper to rehearse the questions, provided the answers are honest and come from the witness. It is unethical and illegal for a lawyer to tell a witness what to say. The lawyers also have colleagues cross-examine each witness, so that the witnesses are ready for the questions the other side's lawyer will ask.

This preparation takes hours and hours, for many days. Beth is frustrated that she cannot do the work she needs to for Enviro-Vision, because she is spending so much time preparing the case. Other employees have to prepare as well, especially for cross-examination by Rich Stewart, and it is a terrible drain on the small firm. More than a year after Janet filed her complaint, they are ready to begin trial.

TRIAL

Adversary System

Our system of justice assumes that the best way to bring out the truth is for the two contesting sides to present the strongest case possible to a neutral factfinder. Each side presents its witnesses and then the opponent has a chance to cross-examine. The adversary system presumes that by putting a witness on the stand and letting both lawyers "go at" her, the truth will emerge.

The judge runs the trial. Each lawyer sits at a large table near the front. Beth, looking tense and unhappy, sits with Janet. Rich Stewart sits with a Coastal executive. In the back of the courtroom are benches for the public. On one bench sits Craig Bergson. He will watch the entire proceeding with intense interest and a strange feeling of unease. He is convinced he knows what really happened.

Janet has demanded a jury trial for Beth's case, and Judge Rowland announces that they will now impanel the jury.

Right to Jury Trial

Not all cases are tried to a jury. As a general rule, both plaintiff and defendant have a right to demand a jury trial when the lawsuit is one for money damages. For example, in a typical contract lawsuit, such as Beth's insurance claim, both plaintiff and defendant have a jury trial right whether they are in state or federal court. Even in such a case, though, the parties may *waive* the jury right, meaning they agree to try the case to a judge.

If the plaintiff is seeking an equitable remedy, such as an injunction, there is no jury right for either party. Equitable rights come from the old Court of Chancery in England, where there was never a jury. Even today, only a judge may give an equitable remedy.

Voir Dire

The process of selecting a jury is called **voir dire,** which means "to speak the truth."[6] The court's goal is to select an impartial jury; the lawyers will each try to get a jury as favorable to their side as possible.

Potential jurors are questioned individually, sometimes by the judge and sometimes by the two lawyers, as each side tries to ferret out potential bias. Each lawyer may make any number of **challenges for cause,** claiming that a juror has demonstrated probable bias. For example, if a prospective juror in the Enviro-Vision case works for an insurance company, the judge will excuse her on the assumption that she would be biased in favor of Coastal. If the judge perceives no bias, the lawyer may still make a limited number of **peremptory challenges,** entitling him to excuse that juror for virtually any reason, which need not be stated in court. For example, if Rich Stewart believes that a juror seems hostile to him personally, he will use a peremptory challenge to excuse that juror, even if the judge sensed no animosity. The process continues until 14 jurors are seated. Twelve will comprise the jury; the other two are alternates who hear the case and remain available in the event one of the impaneled jurors is taken ill. For a discussion of the jury's responsibility, see **http://www.placer.ca.gov/ courts/** and click on "Jury Duty," then on "General Information."

Although jury selection for a case can sometimes take many days, in the Enviro-Vision case the first day of the hearing ends with the jury selected. In the hallway outside the court, Rich offers Janet $200,000 to settle. Janet reports the offer to Beth and they agree to reject it. Craig Bergson drives home, emotionally confused. Only three weeks before his death, Tony had accidentally met his old roommate and they had had several drinks. Craig believes that what Tony told him answers the riddle of this case.

Opening Statements

The next day, each attorney makes an opening statement to the jury, summarizing the proof he or she expects to offer, with the plaintiff going first. Janet focuses on Tony's successful life, his business and strong marriage, and the tragedy of his accidental death.[7]

Rich works hard to establish a friendly rapport with the jury. He expresses regret about the death. Nonetheless, suicide is a clear exclusion from the policy. If insurance companies are forced to pay claims never bargained for, everyone's insurance rates will go up.

---

[6]   Students of French note that *voir* means "to see" and assume that *voir dire* should translate, "to see, to speak." However, the legal term is centuries old and derives not from modern French but from Old French, in which *voir* meant "truth."

[7]   Janet Booker has dropped her claim for triple damages against Coastal. To have any hope of such a verdict, she would have to show that Coastal had no legitimate reason at all for denying the claim. Discovery has convinced her that Coastal will demonstrate some rational reasons for what it did.

Exhibit 3.3
Burden of Proof. **In a civil lawsuit, a plaintiff wins with a mere preponderance of the evidence. But the prosecution must persuade a jury beyond a reasonable doubt in order to win a criminal conviction.**

Burden of Proof

In civil cases, the plaintiff has the burden of proof. That means that the plaintiff must convince the jury that its version of the case is correct; the defendant is not obligated to disprove the allegations.

The plaintiff's burden in a civil lawsuit is to prove its case by a **preponderance of the evidence.** It must convince the jury that its version of the facts is at least *slightly more likely* than the defendant's version. Some courts describe this as a "51–49" persuasion, that is, that plaintiff's proof must "just tip" credibility in its favor. By contrast, in a criminal case, the prosecution must demonstrate **beyond a reasonable doubt** that the defendant is guilty. The burden of proof in a criminal case is much tougher because the likely consequences are, too. See Exhibit 3.3.

Plaintiff's Case

Since the plaintiff has the burden of proof, Janet puts in her case first. She wants to prove two things. First, that Tony died. That is easy, since the death certificate clearly demonstrates it and since Coastal does not seriously contest it. Second, in order to win double indemnity damages, she must show that the death was accidental. She will do this with the testimony of the witnesses she calls, one after the other. Her first witness is Beth. When a lawyer asks questions of her own witness, it is **direct examination.** Janet brings out all the evidence she wants the jury to hear: that the business was basically sound, though temporarily troubled, that Tony was a hard worker, why the company took out life insurance policies, and so forth.

Then Rich has a chance to **cross-examine** Beth, which means to ask questions of an opposing witness. He will try to create doubt in the jury's mind. He asks Beth only questions for which he is certain of the answers, based on discovery. Rich gets Beth to admit that the firm was not doing well the year of Tony's death; that Tony had lost the best client the firm ever had; that Beth had reduced salaries; and that Tony had been depressed about business.

Rules of Evidence

The lawyers are not free simply to ask any question they want. The law of **evidence** determines what questions a lawyer may ask and how the questions are to be phrased, what answers a witness may give, and what documents may be introduced. The goal is to get the best evidence possible before the jurors so they can decide what really happened. In general, witnesses may only testify about things they saw or heard.

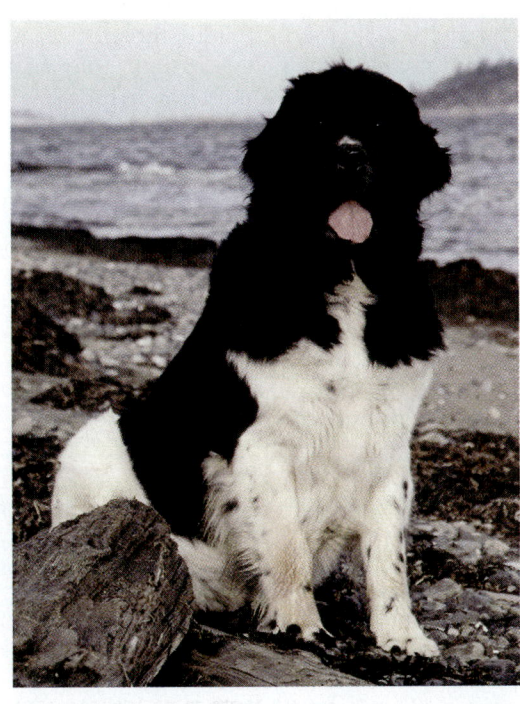

Is the pedigree relevant?

These rules are complex, and a thorough explication of them is beyond the scope of this chapter; however, they can be just as important in resolving a dispute as the underlying substantive law. Suppose a plaintiff's case depends upon the jury hearing about a certain conversation, but the rules of evidence prevent the lawyer from asking about it. That conversation might just as well never have occurred.

Janet calls an expert witness, a marine geologist, who testifies about the tides and currents in the area where Tony's body was found. The expert testifies that even experienced swimmers can be overwhelmed by a sudden shift in currents. Rich objects strenuously that this is irrelevant, because there is no testimony that there *was* such a current at the time of Tony's death. The judge permits the testimony.

Karen Caruso testifies that Tony was in "reasonably good" spirits the day of his death, and that he often took Blue for walks along the beach. Karen testifies that Blue was part Newfoundland. Rich objects that testimony about Blue's pedigree is irrelevant, but Janet insists it will show why Blue was tied up. The judge allows the testimony. Karen says that whenever Blue saw them swim he would instinctively go into the water and pull them to shore. Does that explain why Blue was tied up? Only the jury can answer.

Cross-examination is grim for Karen. Rich slowly but methodically questions her about Tony's state of mind and brings out the problems with the company, his depression, and tension within the marriage. Janet's other witnesses testify essentially as they did during their depositions.

Motion for Directed Verdict

At the close of the plaintiff's case, Rich moves for a **directed verdict,** that is, a ruling that the plaintiff has entirely failed to prove some aspect of her case. Rich is seeking to win without even putting in his own case. He argues that it was Beth's burden to prove that Tony died accidentally and that she has entirely failed to do that.

A directed verdict is permissible only if the evidence so clearly favors the defendant that reasonable minds could not disagree on it. If reasonable minds could disagree, the motion must be denied. Here, Judge Rowland rules that the plaintiff has put in enough evidence of accidental death that a reasonable person could find in Beth's favor. The motion is denied.

Defendant's Case

Rich now puts in his case, exactly as Janet did, except that he happens to have fewer witnesses. He calls the examining doctor, who admits that Tony could have committed suicide by swimming out too far. On cross-examination, Janet gets the doctor to acknowledge that he has no idea whether Tony intentionally drowned. Rich also questions several neighbors as to how depressed Tony had seemed and how unusual it was that Blue was tied up. Some of the witnesses Rich deposed, such as the tennis partner Jerry Johnson, have nothing that will help Coastal's case, so he does not call them.

Craig Bergson, sitting in the back of the courtroom, thinks how different the trial would have been had he been called as a witness. When he and Tony had the fateful drink, Tony had been distraught: business was terrible, he was involved in an extramarital affair that he could not end, and he saw no way out of his problems. He had no one to talk to and had been hugely relieved to speak with Craig. Several times Tony had said, "I just can't go on like this. I don't want to, anymore." Craig thought Tony seemed suicidal and urged him to see a therapist Craig knew and trusted. Tony had said that it was good advice, but Craig is unsure whether Tony sought any help.

This evidence would have affected the case. Had Rich Stewart known of the conversation, he would have deposed Craig and the therapist. Coastal's case would have been far stronger, perhaps overwhelming. But Craig's evidence will never be heard. Facts are critical. Rich's decision to depose other witnesses and omit Craig may influence the verdict more than any rule of law.

Closing Argument

Both lawyers sum up their case to the jury, explaining how they hope the jury will interpret what they have heard. Janet summarizes the plaintiff's version of the facts, claiming that Blue was tied up so that Tony could swim without worrying about him. Rich claims that business and personal pressures had overwhelmed Tony. He tied up his dog, neatly folded his clothes, and took his own life.

Jury Instructions

Judge Rowland instructs the jury as to its duty. He tells them that they are to evaluate the case based only on the evidence they heard at trial, relying on their own experience and common sense.

He explains the law and the burden of proof, telling the jury that it is Beth's obligation to prove that Tony died. If Beth has proven that Tony died, she is entitled to $1 million; if she has proven that his death was accidental, she is entitled to $2 million. However, if Coastal has proven suicide, Beth receives nothing. Finally, he states that if they are unable to decide between accidental death and suicide, there is a legal presumption that it was accidental. Rich asks Judge Rowland to rephrase the "legal presumption" part but the judge declines.

Verdict

The jury deliberates informally, with all jurors entitled to voice their opinion. Some deliberations take two hours; some take two weeks. Many states require a unanimous verdict; others require only, for example, a 10–2 vote in civil cases.

This case presents a close call. No one saw Tony die. Yet even though they cannot know with certainty, the jury's decision will probably be the final word on whether he took his own life. After a day and a half of deliberating, the jury notifies the judge that it has reached a verdict. Rich Stewart quickly makes a new offer: $350,000. Beth hesitates but turns it down.

The judge summons the lawyers to court, and Beth goes as well. The judge asks the foreman if the jury has reached a decision. He states that it has: the jury finds that Tony Caruso drowned accidentally, and awards Beth Smiles $2 million.

Motions after the Verdict

Rich immediately moves for a **judgment** *non obstante veredicto* (JNOV), meaning a judgment notwithstanding the jury's verdict. He is asking the judge to overturn the jury's verdict. Rich argues that the jury's decision went against all of the evidence. He also claims that the judge's instructions were wrong and misled the jury.

Judge Rowland denies the JNOV. Rich immediately moves for a new trial, making the same claim, and the judge denies the motion. Beth is elated that the case is finally over—until Janet says she expects an appeal. Craig Bergson, leaving the courtroom, wonders if he did the right thing. He felt sympathy for Beth and none for Coastal. Yet now he is neither happy nor proud.

APPEALS

Two days later, Rich files an appeal to the court of appeals. The same day, he phones Janet and increases his settlement offer to $425,000. Beth is tempted but wants Janet's advice. Janet says the risks of an appeal are that the court will order a new trial, and they would start all over. But to accept this offer is to forfeit over $1.5 million. Beth is unsure what to do. The firm desperately needs cash now. Janet suggests they wait until oral argument, another eight months.

Rich files a brief arguing that there were two basic errors at the trial: first, that the jury's verdict is clearly contrary to the evidence; and second, that the judge gave the wrong instructions to the jury. Janet files a reply brief, opposing Rich on both issues. In her brief, Janet cites many cases that she claims are **precedent:** earlier decisions by the state appellate courts on similar or identical issues. Although the following case is from a different jurisdiction, it is an example of the kind of case that she will rely on.

HERNANDEZ V. MONTVILLE TOWNSHIP BOARD OF EDUCATION

354 N.J. Super. 467, 808 A.2d 128
Superior Court of New Jersey, Appellate Division, 2002

Facts: Victor Hernandez had worked for more than 20 years as a custodian at a public power plant. He had received training in health and safety rules from the Occupational Safety and Health Administration (OSHA).

Hernandez took a second job as night custodian at an elementary school. Shortly after he started work, the school board fired him for alleged poor job performance. Hernandez filed suit, claiming that the real reason for his termination was that he had repeatedly notified his superiors of health and safety violations in the schools, including missing bulbs in emergency exit lights and toilets that backed up for long periods, spilling foul matter on the floor. He argued that his termination violated the state's Conscientious Employee Protection Act (CEPA), which is designed to protect whistleblowers who report violations of health laws.

The jury awarded Hernandez $44,000 for lost wages and $150,000 for emotional distress. The jury had not been permitted to hear his claim for punitive damages (those designed to punish a defendant for exceptionally bad conduct). The trial judge then granted a judgment notwithstanding the verdict (JNOV) to the school board, meaning that Hernandez won nothing. The trial judge stated:

"Talk about trivial. By the time the jury went out, I should have concluded that the plaintiff simply had not made out a case, under the CEPA law, because he never disclosed or threatened to disclose to his supervisor an activity, policy, practice of an employer that the employee reasonably believed was in violation of law or a rule. There simply was none. But in addition to that, there isn't any other evidence adduced by anyone in the case that these things that he's complaining about ever occurred. I didn't believe anything [plaintiff] said. [This is] trivialization beyond belief."

Hernandez appealed.

Issue: Did the trial court err by rejecting punitive damages, or by granting the JNOV?

Excerpts from Judge Axelrad's Decision: Plaintiff knew there were regulations and policies against exposing schoolchildren to urine and feces and against unlit exit signs, particularly in an elementary school setting. Plaintiff was informed by defendant's safety representative that OSHA's general standards require washing facilities to be maintained in a sanitary condition. Moreover, the staff handbook provided to plaintiff stressed the importance of safety.

Contrary to the court's finding in granting JNOV, it is irrelevant to plaintiff's CEPA claim whether there was independent corroboration of the overflowing toilets. Under the JNOV standard the court must accept as true plaintiff's testimony, which the jury clearly found credible. Moreover, [Facilities Manager] Vandeneulebroeke acknowledged that on more than one occasion if parts were not in stock it took a week to repair a toilet.

▼

Until plaintiff began complaining, he had a good work record. There was ample evidence in the record for the jury to conclude defendant's proffered reason for termination was a pretext and that the whistleblowing itself was a substantial factor in the termination. Thus, this was not a "runaway jury" as categorized by the court. Accordingly, it was error for the court to substitute its judgment for that of the jury and reverse the jury verdict.

Furthermore, the punitive damage claim should have been submitted to the jury. Plaintiff claims that [all of his superiors] lied in their testimony. He further testified that Foschini, the other janitor, warned him "to keep [his] mouth shut" because if he said anything about unsafe conditions and health hazards, he would get fired. Based upon the compensatory damage verdict, it appears that the jury agreed. Our Supreme Court [has] made it clear that "punitive damages, which are available under CEPA against public entities, should be determined by a jury as the trier of fact." There is no reason to remove this issue from the jury.

Because plaintiff presented sufficient evidence to sustain the jury verdict, we reverse the trial court's grant of a JNOV and reinstate the verdict on compensatory damages. We remand for a new trial on punitive damages and consideration of interest, attorney's fees and costs. ■

Eight months later, the lawyers representing Coastal and Enviro-Vision appear in the court of appeals to argue their case. Rich, the appellant, goes first. The judges frequently interrupt his argument with questions. Relying on decisions like *Hernandez,* they show little sympathy for his claim that the verdict was against the facts. They seem more sympathetic with his second point, that the instructions were wrong.

When Janet argues, all of their questions concern the judge's instructions. It appears they believe the instructions were in error. The judges take the case under advisement, meaning they will decide some time in the future—maybe in two weeks, maybe in five months.

Appeals Court Options

The court of appeals can **affirm** the trial court, allowing the decision to stand. The court may **modify** the decision, for example, by affirming that the plaintiff wins but decreasing the size of the award. (That is unlikely here; Beth is entitled to $2 million or nothing.) The court might **reverse and remand,** nullifying the lower court's decision and returning the case to the lower court for a new trial. Or it could simply **reverse,** turning the loser (Coastal) into the winner, with no new trial.

What will it do here? On the factual issue it will probably rule in Beth's favor. There *was* evidence from which a jury could conclude that Tony died accidentally. It is true that there was also considerable evidence to support Coastal's position, but that is probably not enough to overturn the verdict. As we saw in the *Hernandez* case, if reasonable people could disagree on what the evidence proves, an appellate court generally refuses to change the jury's factual findings. The court of appeals is likely to rule that a reasonable jury *could* have found accidental death, even if the appellate judges personally suspect that Tony may have killed himself.

The judge's instructions raise a more difficult problem. Some states would require a more complex statement about "presumptions."[8]

What does a court of appeals do if it decides the trial court's instructions were wrong? If it believes the error rendered the trial and verdict unfair, it will remand the case, that is, send it back to the lower court for a new trial. However, the court may

---

[8] Judge Rowland probably should have said, "The law presumes that death is accidental, not suicide. So if there were no evidence either way, the plaintiff would win because we presume accident. But if there is competing evidence, the presumption becomes irrelevant. If you think that Coastal Insurance has introduced some evidence of suicide, then forget the legal presumption. You must then decide what happened based on what you have seen and heard in court, and on any inferences you choose to draw." Note that the judge's instructions were different, though similar.

conclude that the mistake was **harmless error.** A trial judge cannot do a perfect job, and not every error is fatal. The court may decide the verdict was fair in spite of the mistake.

Janet and Beth talk. Beth is very anxious and wants to settle. She does not want to wait four or five months, only to learn that they must start all over. Janet urges that they wait a few weeks to hear from Rich: they don't want to seem too eager.

A week later, Rich telephones and offers $500,000. Janet turns it down, but says she will ask Beth if she wants to make a counter-offer. She and Beth talk. They agree that they will settle for $1 million. Janet then calls Rich and offers to settle for $1.7 million. Rich and Janet debate the merits of the case. Rich later calls back and offers $750,000, saying he doubts that he can go any higher. Janet counters with $1.4 million, saying she doubts she can go any lower. They argue, both predicting that they will win on appeal.

Rich calls, offers $900,000 and says, "That's it. No more." Janet argues for $1.2 million, expecting to nudge Rich up to $1 million. He doesn't nudge, instead saying, "Take it or leave it." Janet and Beth talk it over. Janet telephones Rich and accepts $900,000 to settle the case.

If they had waited for the court of appeals decision, would Beth have won? It is impossible to know. It is certain, though, that whoever lost would have appealed. Months would have passed waiting to learn if the state supreme court would accept the case. If that court had agreed to hear the appeal, Beth would have endured another year of waiting, brief writing, oral argument, and tense hoping. The high court has all of the options discussed: to affirm, modify, reverse and remand, or simply reverse.

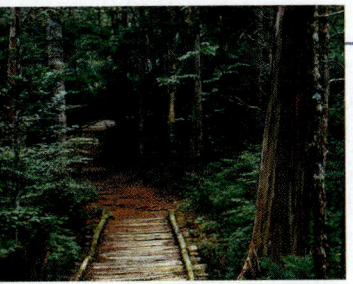

© PHOTODISC/GETTY IMAGES

Chapter Conclusion

No one will ever know for sure whether Tony took his own life. Craig Bergson's evidence might have tipped the scales in favor of Coastal. But even that is uncertain, since the jury could have found him unpersuasive. After two years, the case ends with a settlement and uncertainty—both typical lawsuit results. The missing witness is less common but not extraordinary. The vaguely unsatisfying feeling about it all is only too common and indicates why litigation is best avoided—by dispute prevention.

Chapter Review

1. Alternative dispute resolution (ADR) is any formal or informal process to settle disputes without a trial. Mediation, arbitration, and other forms of ADR are growing in popularity.

2. There are many *systems* of courts, one federal and one in each state. A federal court will hear a case only if it involves a federal question or diversity jurisdiction.

3. Trial courts determine facts and apply the law to the facts; appeals courts generally accept the facts found by the trial court and review the trial record for errors of law.

4. A complaint and an answer are the two most important pleadings, that is, documents that start a lawsuit.

5. Discovery is the critical pre-trial opportunity for both parties to learn the strengths and weaknesses of the opponent's case. Important forms of discovery include interrogatories, depositions, production of documents and objects, physical and mental examinations, and requests for admission.

6. A motion is a formal request to the court.

7. Summary judgment is a ruling by the court that no trial is necessary because there are no essential facts in dispute.

8. Generally, both plaintiff and defendant may demand a jury in any lawsuit for money damages.

9. Voir dire is the process of selecting jurors in order to obtain an impartial panel.

10. The plaintiff's burden of proof in a civil lawsuit is preponderance of the evidence, meaning that its version of the facts must be at least slightly more persuasive than the defendant's. In a criminal prosecution, the government must offer proof beyond a reasonable doubt in order to win a conviction.

11. The rules of evidence determine what questions may be asked during trial, what testimony may be given, and what documents may be introduced.

12. The verdict is the jury's decision in a case. The losing party may ask the trial judge to overturn the verdict, seeking a judgment *non obstante veredicto* or a new trial. Judges seldom grant either.

13. An appeals court has many options. The court may affirm, upholding the lower court's decision; modify, changing the verdict but leaving the same party victorious; reverse, transforming the loser into the winner; and/or remand, sending the case back to the lower court.

Practice Test

1. You plan to open a store in Chicago, specializing in beautiful rugs imported from Turkey. You will work with a native Turk who will purchase and ship the rugs to your store. You are wise enough to insist on a contract establishing the rights and obligations of both parties and would prefer an ADR clause. But you want to be sensitive to different cultures and do not want a clause that will magnify a problem or alienate the parties. Is there some way you can accomplish all of this?

2. Solo Serve Corp. signed a lease for space in a shopping center. The lease contained this clause: "Neither Landlord nor tenant shall engage in or permit any activity at or around the Demised Premises which violates any applicable law, constitutes a nuisance, or is likely to bring discredit upon the Shopping Center, or discourage customers from patronizing other occupants of the Shopping Center by other than activities customarily engaged in by reputable businesses." Westowne Associates, the landlord, later leased other space in the center to The Finish Line, an off-track betting business that also had a license to sell food and liquor. Solo Serve sued, claiming that Westowne had breached the lease. Solo Serve requested either a permanent injunction barring The Finish Line from using the center or that The Finish Line pay the cost of relocating its own business.

   The case raises two questions. The minor one is, did Westowne violate the lease? The major one is, how could this dispute have been prevented? It ultimately went to the United States Court of Appeals, costing both sides much time and money.

3. State which court(s) have jurisdiction as to each of these lawsuits:

   a. Pat wants to sue his next-door neighbor Dorothy, claiming that Dorothy promised to sell him the house next door.

   b. Paula, who lives in New York City, wants to sue Dizzy Movie Theatres, whose principal place of business is Dallas. She claims that while she was in Texas on holiday, she was injured by their negligent maintenance of a stairway. She claims damages of $30,000.

   c. Phil lives in Tennessee. He wants to sue Dick, who lives in Ohio. Phil claims that Dick agreed to sell him 3,000 acres of farmland in Ohio, worth over $2 million.

   d. Pete, incarcerated in a federal prison in Kansas, wants to sue the United States government. He claims that his treatment by prison authorities violates three federal statutes.

4. Probationary schoolteachers sued the New Madrid, Missouri, school district, claiming that the school district refused to give them permanent jobs because of their union organizing activity. The defendant school district claimed that each plaintiff was refused a permanent job because of inferior teaching. During discovery, the plaintiffs asked for the personnel files of probationary teachers who *had* been offered permanent jobs. The school district refused to provide them, arguing that the personnel files did not indicate the union status of the teachers and therefore would not help the plaintiffs. The trial court ruled that the school district need not release the files. On appeal, the plaintiffs argue that this hindered their ability to prove the real reasons they had been fired. How should the appeals court rule?

5. Students are now suing schools for sexual harassment. The cases raise important issues about the limits of discovery. In a case in Petaluma, California, a girl claimed that she was harassed for years and that the school knew about it and failed to act. According to press reports, she alleges that a boy stood up in class and asked, "I have a question. I want to know if [Jane Doe] has sex with hot dogs." In discovery, the school district sought the parents' therapy records, the girl's diary, and a psychological evaluation of the girl. Should they get those things?

6. British discovery practice differs from that in the United States. Most discovery in Britain concerns documents. The lawyers for the two sides, called solicitors, must deliver to the opposing side a list of all relevant documents in their possession. Each side may then request to look at and copy those it wishes. Depositions are rare. What advantages and disadvantages are there to the British practice?

7. *ETHICS* Trial practice also is dramatically different in Britain. The parties' solicitors do not go into court. Courtroom work is done by different lawyers, called barristers. The barristers are not permitted to interview any witnesses before trial. They know the substance of what each witness intends to say, but do not rehearse questions and answers, as in the United States. Which approach do you consider more effective? More ethical? What is the purpose of a trial? Of pretrial preparation?

8. Claus Scherer worked for Rockwell International and was paid over $300,000 per year. Rockwell fired Scherer for alleged sexual harassment of several workers, including his secretary, Terry Pendy. Scherer sued in United States District Court, alleging that Rockwell's real motive in firing him was his high salary.

   Rockwell moved for summary judgment, offering deposition transcripts of various employees. Pendy's deposition detailed instances of harassment, including comments about her body, instances of unwelcome touching, and discussions of extramarital affairs. Another deposition, from a Rockwell employee who investigated the allegations, included complaints by other employees as to Scherer's harassment. In his own deposition, which he offered to oppose summary judgment, Scherer testified that he could not recall the incidents alleged by Pendy and others.

He denied generally that he had sexually harassed anyone. The district court granted summary judgment for Rockwell. Was its ruling correct?

9. Lloyd Dace worked for ACF Industries as a supervisor in the punchpress department of a carburetor factory. ACF demoted Dace to an hourly job on the assembly line, and Dace sued, claiming that ACF discriminated on the basis of age. At trial, Dace showed that he had been 53 years old when demoted and had been replaced by a man aged 40. He offered evidence that ACF's benefits supervisor had attended the meeting at which his demotion was decided, and that the benefits supervisor was aware of the cost savings of replacing Dace with a younger man.

   At the end of Dace's case, ACF moved for a directed verdict and the trial court granted it. The judge reasoned that Dace's entire case was based on circumstantial evidence. He held that it was too speculative for the jury to infer age discrimination from the few facts that Dace had offered. Was the trial court correct?

10. *YOU BE THE JUDGE* WRITING PROBLEM Apache Corp. and El Paso Exploration Co. operated a Texas gas well that exploded, burning out of control for over a year. More than 100 plaintiffs sued the two owners, claiming damage to adjoining gas fields. The plaintiffs also sued Axelson, Inc., which manufactured a valve whose failure may have contributed to the explosion. Axelson, in turn, sued Apache and El Paso. Axelson sought discovery from both companies about an internal investigation they had conducted, before the blowout, concerning kickbacks (illegal payments) at the gas field. Axelson claimed that the investigation could shed light on what caused the explosion, but the trial court ruled that the material was irrelevant, and denied discovery. Axelson appealed. Is the investigation discoverable? **Argument for Axelson:** If the companies investigated kickbacks, they were concerned about corruption and mismanagement—both of which can cause employees to cut corners, ignore safety concerns, fabricate reports, and so forth. All of those activities have the potential to cause a serious accident. All parties are entitled to discover material that may lead to relevant evidence, and that could easily happen here. **Argument for Apache and El Paso:** This is a fishing expedition. The investigation was completed

before the explosion and is completely unrelated. Any internal investigation has the potential (a) to reveal valuable business or trade secrets and (b) to prove embarrassing to the companies investigated. Axelson's motive is to force the two owners to settle in order to avoid such revelations. Discovery is not supposed to be a weapon.

11. Imogene Williams sued the U.S. Elevator Corp. She claimed that when she entered one of the company's elevators, it went up three floors but failed to open, fell several floors, stopped, and then continued to erratically rise and fall for about 40 minutes. She claimed physical injuries and emotional distress. At trial, U.S. Elevator disputed every allegation. When the judge instructed the jury, he asked them to decide whether the company had been negligent. If it had, the jury was to decide what physical injuries Williams had suffered. The judge also instructed them that she could receive money for emotional damages only if the emotional damages resulted from her physical injury. The jury found for U.S. Elevator, deciding that it had not been negligent.

On appeal, Williams argues that the judge was wrong in stating that the emotional injuries had to result from the physical injuries. The court of appeals agreed that the instruction was incorrect. There could be emotional damages even if there were no physical injuries. What appellate remedy is appropriate?

12. ***ROLE REVERSAL*** Write a multiple-choice question that illustrates the unique significance of summary judgment: that there is no need for a trial because there are no essential facts in dispute.

Internet Research Problem

You may be called for jury duty before long. Read the summary of the juror's responsibilities at http://beatty.westbuslaw.com. Some people try hard to get out of jury duty. Why is that a problem in a democratic society?

> **You can find further practice problems at http://beatty.westbuslaw.com or in the Study Guide that accompanies this text.**

Common Law, Statutory Law, and Administrative Law

Jason observes a toddler wander onto the railroad tracks and hears a train approaching. He has plenty of time to pull the child from the tracks with no risk to himself, but chooses to do nothing. The youngster is killed. The child's family sues Jason for his callous behavior, and a court determines that Jason owes—nothing.

"Why can't they just fix the law?" students and professionals often ask, in response to Jason's impunity and countless other legal oddities. Their exasperation is understandable. This chapter cannot guarantee intellectual tranquillity, but it should diminish the sense of bizarreness that law can instill. We will look at three sources of law: common law, statutory law, and administrative law. Most of the law you learn in the course comes from one of these sources. The substantive law will make more sense when you have a solid feel for how it was created. ■

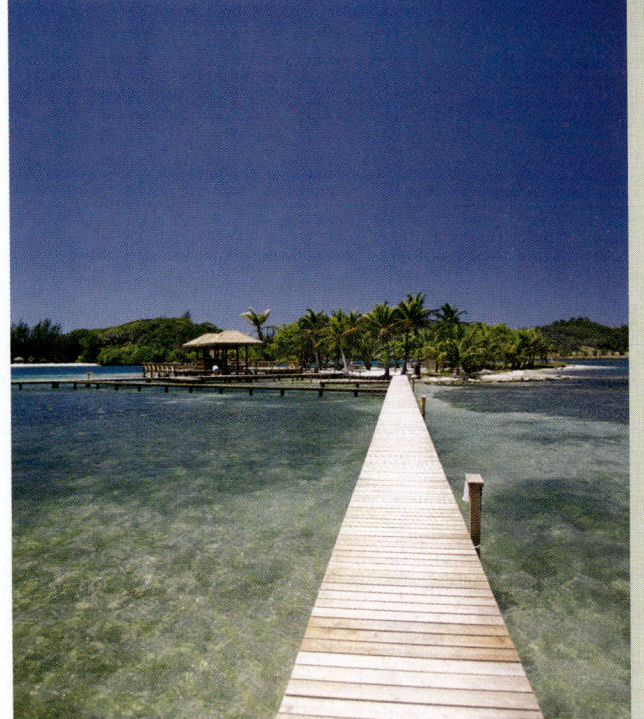

© PHILIP COBLENTZ/PHOTODISC/GETTY IMAGES

COMMON LAW

Jason and the toddler present a classic legal puzzle: What, if anything, must a bystander do when he sees someone in danger? We will examine this issue to see how the common law works.

The common law is judge-made law. It is the sum total of all the cases decided by appellate courts. The common law of Pennsylvania consists of all cases decided by appellate courts in that state. The Illinois common law of bystander liability is all of the cases on that subject decided by Illinois appellate courts. Two hundred years ago, almost all of the law was common law. Today, most new law is statutory. But common law still predominates in tort, contract, and agency law, and it is very important in property, employment, and some other areas.

We focus on appellate courts because they are the only ones to make rulings of law, as discussed in Chapter 3. In a bystander case, it is the job of the state's highest court to say what legal obligations, if any, a bystander has. The trial court, on the other hand, must decide *facts:* Was this defendant able to see what was happening? Was the plaintiff really in trouble? Could the defendant have assisted without peril to himself?

Stare Decisis

Nothing perks up a course like Latin. *Stare decisis* means "let the decision stand." It is the essence of the common law. The phrase indicates that once a court has decided a particular issue, it will generally apply the same rule in future cases. Suppose the highest court of Arizona must decide whether a contract for a new car, signed by a 16-year-old, can be enforced against him. The court will look to see if there is **precedent,** that is, whether the high court of Arizona has already decided a similar case. The Arizona court looks and finds several earlier cases, all holding that such contracts may not be enforced against a minor. The court will apply that precedent and refuse to enforce the contract in this case. Courts do not always follow precedent but they generally do: *stare decisis.*

Two words explain why the common law is never as easy as we might like: *predictability* and *flexibility.* The law is trying to accommodate both goals. The need for predictability is apparent: people must know what the law is. If contract law changed daily, an entrepreneur who leased factory space and then started buying machinery would be uncertain if the factory would actually be available when she was ready to move in. Will the landlord slip out of the lease? Will the machinery be ready on time? The need for predictability created the doctrine of *stare decisis.*

Yet there must also be flexibility in the law, some means to respond to new problems and changing social mores. In this new millennium, we cannot be encumbered by ironclad rules established before electricity was discovered. These two ideas may be obvious but they also conflict: the more flexibility we permit, the less predictability we enjoy. We will watch the conflict play out in the bystander cases.

Bystander Cases

This country inherited from England a simple rule about a bystander's obligations: you have no duty to assist someone in peril unless you created the danger. In *Union Pacific Railway Co. v. Cappier,*[1] through no fault of the railroad, a train struck a man, severing an arm and a leg. Railroad employees saw the incident happen but did nothing to assist

---

[1] 66 Kan. 649, 72 P. 281 (1903).

him. By the time help arrived, the victim had died. In this 1903 case the court held that the railroad had no duty to help the injured man:

> With the humane side of the question courts are not concerned. It is the omission or negligent discharge of legal duties only which come within the sphere of judicial cognizance. For withholding relief from the suffering, for failure to respond to the calls of worthy charity, or for faltering in the bestowment of brotherly love on the unfortunate, penalties are found not in the laws of men but in [the laws of God].

As harsh as this judgment might seem, it was an accurate statement of the law at that time in both England and the United States: bystanders need do nothing. Contemporary writers found the rule inhumane and cruel, and even judges criticized it. But—*stare decisis*—they followed it. With a rule this old and well established, no court was willing to scuttle it. What courts did do was seek openings for small changes.

Eighteen years after the Kansas case of *Cappier*, the court in nearby Iowa found the basis for one exception. Ed Carey was a farm laborer, working for Frank Davis. While in the fields, Carey fainted from sunstroke and remained unconscious. Davis simply hauled him to a nearby wagon and left him in the sun for an additional four hours, causing serious permanent injury. The court's response:

> It is unquestionably the well-settled rule that the master is under no legal duty to care for a sick or injured servant for whose illness or injury he is not at fault. Though not unjust in principle, this rule, if carried unflinchingly and without exception to its logical extreme, is sometimes productive of shocking results. To avoid this criticism [we hold that where] a servant suffers serious injury, or is suddenly stricken down in a manner indicating the immediate and emergent need of aid to save him from death or serious harm, the master, if present is in duty bound to take such reasonable measures as may be practicable to relieve him, even though such master be not chargeable with fault in bringing about the emergency.[2]

If this tranquil canoe trip turns perilous, a bystander has no obligation to respond. Is the common law rule a moral one?

And this is how the common law changes: bit by tiny bit. In Iowa, a bystander could now be liable *if* he was the employer and *if* the worker was suddenly stricken and *if* it was an emergency and *if* the employer was present. That is a small change but an important one.

For the next 50 years, changes in bystander law came very slowly. Consider *Osterlind v. Hill*, a case from 1928.[3] Osterlind rented a canoe from Hill's boatyard, paddled into the lake, and promptly fell into the water. For *30 minutes* he clung to the side of the canoe and shouted for help. Hill heard the cries but did nothing; Osterlind drowned. Was Hill liable? No, said the court: a bystander has no liability. Not until half a century later did that same state supreme court reverse its position and begin to require assistance in extreme cases—a long time for Osterlind to hold on.[4]

In the 1970s, changes came more quickly.

---

2   Carey v. Davis, 190 Iowa 720, 180 N.W. 889 (1921).
3   263 Mass. 73, 160 N.E. 301 (1928).
4   Pridgen v. Boston Housing Authority, 364 Mass. 696, 308 N.E.2d 467 (1974).

TARASOFF V. REGENTS OF THE UNIVERSITY OF CALIFORNIA

17 Cal. 3d 425, 551 P.2d 334, 131 Cal. Rptr. 14
Supreme Court of California, 1976

Facts: On October 27, 1969, Prosenjit Poddar killed Tatiana Tarasoff. Tatiana's parents claimed that two months earlier Poddar had confided his intention to kill Tatiana to Dr. Lawrence Moore, a psychologist employed by the University of California at Berkeley. They sued the university, claiming that Dr. Moore should have warned Tatiana and/or should have arranged for Poddar's confinement.

Issue: Did Dr. Moore have a duty to Tatiana Tarasoff, and did he breach that duty?

Excerpts from Justice Tobriner's Decision: Although under the common law, as a general rule, one person owed no duty to control the conduct of another, nor to warn those endangered by such conduct, the courts have carved out an exception to this rule in cases in which the defendant stands in some special relationship to either the person whose conduct needs to be controlled or in a relationship to the foreseeable victim of that conduct. Applying this exception to the present case, we note that a relationship of defendant therapists to either Tatiana or Poddar will suffice to establish a duty of care.

We recognize the difficulty that a therapist encounters in attempting to forecast whether a patient presents a serious danger of violence. Obviously we do not require that the therapist, in making that determination, render a perfect performance; the therapist need only exercise that reasonable degree of skill, knowledge, and care ordinarily possessed and exercised by members of [the field] under similar circumstances.

In the instant case, however, the pleadings do not raise any question as to failure of defendant therapists to predict that Poddar presented a serious danger of violence. On the contrary, the present complaints allege that defendant therapists did in fact predict that Poddar would kill, but were negligent in failing to warn.

In our view, once a therapist does in fact determine, or under applicable professional standards reasonably should have determined, that a patient poses a serious danger of violence to others, he bears a duty to exercise reasonable care to protect the foreseeable victim of that danger.

[The Tarasoffs have stated a legitimate claim against Dr. Moore.] ∎

The *Tarasoff* exception applies when there is some special relationship, such as therapist–patient. What if there is no such relationship? The 1983 case of *Soldano v. O'Daniels*[5] arose when a patron in Happy Jack's bar saw Villanueva threaten Soldano with a gun. The patron dashed next door, into the Circle Inn bar, told the bartender what was happening, and urged him to call the police. The bartender refused. The witness then asked to use the phone to call the police himself, but the bartender again refused. Tragically, the delay permitted Villanueva to kill Soldano.

As in the earlier cases we have seen, this case presented an emergency. But the exception created in *Carey v. Davis* applied only if the bystander was an employer, and that in *Tarasoff* only for a doctor. In *Soldano* the bystander was neither. Should the law require him to act, that is, should it carve a new exception? Here is what the California court decided:

> Many citizens simply "don't want to get involved." No rule should be adopted [requiring] a citizen to open up his or her house to a stranger so that the latter may use the telephone to call for emergency assistance. As Mrs. Alexander in Anthony Burgess' *A Clockwork Orange* learned to her horror, such an action may

---

[5]   141 Cal. App. 3d 443, 190 Cal. Rptr. 310, 1983 Cal. App. LEXIS 1539 (1983).

be fraught with danger. It does not follow, however, that use of a telephone in a public portion of a business should be refused for a legitimate emergency call.

We conclude that the bartender owed a duty to [Soldano] to permit the patron from Happy Jack's to place a call to the police or to place the call himself. It bears emphasizing that the duty in this case does not require that one must go to the aid of another. That is not the issue here. The employee was not the good samaritan intent on aiding another. The patron was.

Do these exceptions mean that the bystander rule is gone? *Parra v. Tarasco*[6] provides a partial answer. Ernesto Parra was a customer at the Jiminez Restaurant when food became lodged in his throat. The employees did not use the Heimlich maneuver or any other method to try to save him. Parra choked to death. Was the restaurant liable? No, said the Illinois Appeals Court. The restaurant had no obligation to do anything.

The bystander rule, that hardy oak, is alive and well. Various initials have been carved into its bark—the exceptions we have seen and a variety of others—but the trunk is strong and the leaves green. Perhaps someday the proliferating exceptions will topple it, but the process of the common law is slow and that day is nowhere in sight. In the meantime, it is nice to be reminded that even without a legal obligation, some citizens do choose to get involved.

NEWS*worthy*

As the freight train rumbled through rural Indiana, conductor Robert Mohr looked ahead and saw what seemed to be a puppy. Then the "puppy" sat up straight and shook her blond curls. Nineteen-month-old Emily Marshall had wandered away from her mother and was playing on the tracks, dead ahead. Engineer Rodney Lindley jammed on the brakes, but could not possibly stop the 96-car, 6,000-ton train. There was no time to jump off and sprint ahead to the girl. Mohr, aged 49, hustled onto the engine's catwalk and clambered forward, as Lindley slowed the train to 10 miles per hour. Gripping a guard rail, Mohr leaned perilously far forward, waited until the engine loomed directly above the child—and deftly booted her to safety. Emily bounced up with nothing worse than a chipped tooth and forehead cuts, and Mohr, the merrier, was a Hoosier hero. ◆

STATUTORY LAW

Most new law is statutory law. Statutes affect each of us every day, in our business, professional, and personal lives. When the system works correctly, this is the one part of the law over which we the people have control. We elect the local legislators who pass state statutes; we vote for the senators and representatives who create federal statutes. If we understand the system, we can affect the largest source of contemporary law. If we live in ignorance of its strengths and pitfalls, we delude ourselves that we participate in a democracy.

As we saw in Chapter 1, there are many systems of government operating in the United States: a national government and 50 state governments. Each level of government has a legislative body. In Washington, D.C., Congress is our national legislature. Congress passes the statutes that govern the nation. In addition, each state has a legislature, which passes statutes for that state only. In this section we look at how Congress

---

[6]   230 Ill. App. 3d 819, 595 N.E.2d 1186.

does its work creating statutes. State legislatures operate similarly, but the work of Congress is better documented and obviously of national importance.[7]

Bills

Congress is organized into two houses, the House of Representatives and the Senate. Either house may originate a proposed statute, which is called a **bill.** The bill must be voted on and approved by both houses. Once both houses pass it, they will send it to the president. If the president signs the bill, it becomes law and is then a statute. If the president opposes the bill, he will **veto** it, in which case it is not law.[8]

Committee Work

If you visit either house of Congress, you will probably find half a dozen legislators on the floor, with one person talking and no one listening. This is because most of the work is done in committees. Both houses are organized into dozens of committees, each with special functions. The House currently has about 27 committees (further divided into about 150 subcommittees) and the Senate has approximately 20 committees (with about 86 subcommittees). For example, the armed services committee of each house oversees the huge defense budget and the workings of the armed forces. Labor committees handle legislation concerning organized labor and working conditions. Banking committees develop expertise on financial institutions. Judiciary committees review nominees to the federal courts. There are dozens of other committees, some very powerful, because they control vast amounts of money, and some relatively weak.

When a bill is proposed in either house, it is referred to the committee that specializes in that subject. Why are bills proposed in the first place? For any of several reasons:

- *New Issue, New Worry.* If society begins to focus on a new issue, Congress may respond with legislation. We consider below, for example, the congressional response to employment discrimination.

- *Unpopular Judicial Ruling.* If Congress disagrees with a judicial interpretation of a statute, the legislators may pass a new statute to modify or "undo" the court decision. For example, if the Supreme Court misinterprets a statute about musical copyrights, Congress may pass a new law correcting the Court's error. However, the legislators have no such power to modify a court decision based on the Constitution. When the Supreme Court ruled that lawyers had a right *under the First Amendment* to advertise their services, Congress lacked the power to change the decision.

---

[7] See the chart of state and federal governments in Chapter 1. A vast amount of information about Congress is available on the Internet. The House of Representatives has a Web page at http://www .house.gov/. The Senate's site appears at http://www.senate.gov. Each page provides links to current law, pending legislation, votes, committees, and more. If you do not know the name of your representative or senator (shame!), the Web page will provide that information. Most state legislatures have Web sites, which you can reach from links found at http://www.ncsl.org/public/sitesleg .htm. These sites typically permit you to read statutes, research legislative history, examine the current calendar, and note upcoming events. For example, the Web site http://housegop.state.il.us/ brings you to the Republican caucus in the Illinois House of Representatives, while the site http:// www.housedem.state.il.us/ will take you to the same body's Democratic caucus. Many of these Web sites enable you to e-mail your local representatives.

[8] Congress may, however, attempt to override the veto. See the discussion below.

A civil rights demonstrator being arrested by the police.

- *Criminal Law.* Statutory law, unlike common law, is prospective. Legislators are hoping to control the future. And that is why almost all criminal law is statutory. A court cannot retroactively announce that it *has been* a crime for a retailer to accept kickbacks from a wholesaler. Everyone must know the rules in advance because the consequences— prison, a felony record—are so harsh.

Discrimination: Congress and the Courts

The civil rights movement of the 1950s and 1960s convinced most citizens that African Americans continued to suffer relentless discrimination in jobs, housing, voting, schools, and other basic areas of life. Demonstrations and boycotts, marches and counter-marches, church bombings and killings persuaded the nation that the problem was vast and urgent.

In 1963 President Kennedy proposed legislation to guarantee equal rights to African Americans in these areas. The bill went to the House Judiciary Committee, which heard testimony for weeks. Witnesses testified that blacks were often unable to vote because of their race, that landlords and home sellers adamantly refused to sell or rent to blacks, that education was still grossly unequal, and that blacks were routinely denied good jobs in many industries. Eventually, the Judiciary Committee approved the bill and sent it to the full House.

The bill was dozens of pages long and divided into "titles," with each title covering a major issue. Title VII concerned employment. We will consider the progress of Title VII in Congress and in the courts. Here is one section of Title VII, as reported to the House floor:[9]

> Sec. 703(a). It shall be an unlawful employment practice for an employer—
> (1) to fail or refuse to hire or to discharge any individual, or otherwise to discriminate against any individual with respect to his compensation, terms, conditions, or privileges of employment, because of such individual's race, color, religion, or national origin; or
> (2) to limit, segregate, or classify his employees in any way which would deprive or tend to deprive any individual of employment opportunities or otherwise adversely affect his status as an employee, because of such individual's race, color, religion, or national origin.

Debate

The proposed bill was intensely controversial and sparked angry argument throughout Congress. Here are some excerpts from one day's debate on the House floor, on February 8, 1964:[10]

> MR. WAGGONNER. I speak to you in all sincerity and ask for the right to discriminate if I so choose because I think it is my right. I think it is my right to choose my social companions. I think it is my right if I am a businessman to run it as I please, to do with my own as I will. I think that is a right the Constitution

---

9 The section number in the House bill was actually 704(a); we use 703 here because that is the number of the section when the bill became law and the number to which the Supreme Court refers in later litigation.
10 The order of speakers is rearranged, and the remarks are edited.

gives to every man. I want the continued right to discriminate and I want the other man to have the right to continue to discriminate against me, because I am discriminated against every day. I do not feel inferior about it.

I ask you to forget about politics, forget about everything except the integrity of the individual, leaving to the people of this country the right to live their lives in the manner they choose to live. Do not destroy this democracy for a Socialist government. A vote for this bill is no less.

MR. CONTE. If the serious cleavage which pitted brother against brother and citizen against citizen during the tragedy of the Civil War is ever to be justified, it can be justified in this House and then in the other body with the passage of this legislation which can and must reaffirm the rights to all individuals which are inherent in our Constitution.

The distinguished poet Mark Van Doren has said that "equality is absolute or no, nothing between can stand," and nothing should now stand between us and the passage of strong and effective civil rights legislation. It is to this that we are united in a strong bipartisan coalition today, and when the laws of the land proclaim that the 88th Congress acted effectively, judiciously, and wisely, we can take pride in our accomplishments as free men.

Other debate was less rhetorical and aimed more at getting information. The following exchange anticipates a 30-year controversy on quotas:

MR. JOHANSEN. I have asked for this time to raise a question and I would ask particularly for the attention of the gentleman from New York [MR. GOODELL] because of a remark he made—and I am not quarreling with it. I understood him to say there is no plan for balanced employment or for quotas in this legislation. . . . I am raising a question as to whether in the effort to eliminate discrimination—and incidentally that is an undefined term in the bill—we may get to a situation in which employers and conceivably union leaders, will insist on legislation providing for a quota system as a matter of self-protection.

Now let us suppose this hypothetical situation exists with 100 jobs to be filled. Let us say 150 persons apply and suppose 75 of them are Negro and 75 of them are white. Supposing the employer . . . hires 75 white men and 25 Negroes. Do the other 50 Negroes or anyone of them severally have a right to claim they have been discriminated against on the basis of color?

MR. GOODELL. It is the intention of the legislation that if applicants are equal in all other respects there will be no restriction. One may choose from among equals. So long as there is no distinction on the basis of race, creed, or color it will not violate the act.

The debate on racial issues carried on. Later in the day, Congressman Smith of Virginia offered an amendment that could scarcely have been smaller—or more important:

Amendment offered by MR. SMITH of Virginia: On page 68, line 23, after the word "religion," insert the word "sex."

In other words, Smith was asking that discrimination on the basis of sex also be outlawed, along with the existing grounds of race, color, national origin, and religion. Congressman Smith's proposal produced the following comments:

MR. CELLER. You know, the French have a phrase for it when they speak of women and men. They say "vive la difference." I think the French are right. Imagine the upheaval that would result from adoption of blanket language requiring total equality. Would male citizens be justified in insisting that women share with them the burdens of compulsory military service? What would become of traditional family relationships? What about alimony? What would become of the crimes of rape and statutory rape? I think the amendment seems illogical, ill timed, ill placed, and improper.

MRS. ST. GEORGE. Mr. Chairman, I was somewhat amazed when I came on the floor this afternoon to hear the very distinguished chairman of the Committee on the Judiciary [MR. CELLER] make the remark that he considered the amendment at this point illogical. I can think of nothing more logical than this amendment at this point.

There are still many States where women cannot serve on juries. There are still many States where women do not have equal educational opportunities. In most States and, in fact, I figure it would be safe to say, in all States—women do not get equal pay for equal work. That is a very well known fact. And to say that this is illogical. What is illogical about it? All you are doing is simply correcting something that goes back, frankly to the Dark Ages.

The debate continued. Some supported the "sex" amendment because they were determined to end sexual bias. But politics are complex. Some *opponents* of civil rights supported the amendment because they believed that it would make the legislation less popular and cause Congress to defeat the entire Civil Rights bill.

That strategy did not work. The amendment passed, and sex was added as a protected trait. And, after more debate and several votes, the entire bill passed the House. It went to the Senate, where it followed a similar route from Judiciary Committee to full Senate. Much of the Senate debate was similar to what we have seen. But some senators raised a new issue, concerning §703(2), which prohibited *segregating or classifying* employees based on any of the protected categories (race, color, national origin, religion, or sex). Senator Tower was concerned that §703(2) meant that an employee in a protected category could never be given any sort of job test. So the Senate amended §703 to include a new subsection:

Sec. 703(h). Notwithstanding any other provision of this title, it shall not be an unlawful employment practice for an employer . . . to give and to act upon the results of any professionally developed ability test provided that such test . . . is not designed, intended or used to discriminate because of race, color, religion, sex or national origin.

With that amendment, and many others, the bill passed the Senate.

Conference Committee

Civil rights legislation had now passed both houses, but the bills were no longer the same due to the many amendments. This is true with most legislation. The next step is for the two houses to send representatives to a House–Senate Conference Committee. This committee examines all of the differences between the two bills and tries to reach a compromise. With the Civil Rights bill, Senator Tower's amendment was left in; other Senate amendments were taken out. When the Conference Committee had settled every difference between the two versions, the new, modified bill was sent back to each house for a new vote.

The House of Representatives and the Senate again angrily debated the compromise language reported from the Conference Committee. Finally, after years of violent public demonstrations and months of debate, each house passed the same bill. President Johnson promptly signed it. The Civil Rights Act of 1964 was law. See Exhibit 4.1.

Title VII of the Civil Rights Act obviously prohibited an employer from saying to a job applicant, "We don't hire blacks." In some parts of the country, that had been common practice; after the Civil Rights Act passed, it became rare. Employers who routinely hired whites only, or promoted only whites, found themselves losing lawsuits.

Exhibit 4.1

The two houses of Congress are organized into dozens of committees, a few of which are shown here. The path of the 1964 Civil Rights Act (somewhat simplified) was as follows: (1) The House Judiciary Committee approved the bill and sent it to the full House; (2) the full House passed the bill and sent it to the Senate, where it was assigned to the Senate Judiciary Committee; (3) the Senate Judiciary Committee passed an amended version of the bill and sent it to the full Senate; (4) the full Senate passed the bill with additional amendments. Since the Senate version was now different from the bill the House passed, the bill went to a Conference Committee. The Conference Committee (5) reached a compromise and sent the new version of the bill back to both houses. Each house passed the compromise bill (6 and 7) and sent it to the president, who signed it into law (8).

A new group of cases arose, those in which some job standard was set that appeared to be racially neutral, yet had a discriminatory effect. In North Carolina, the Duke Power Co. required that applicants for higher paying, promotional positions meet two requirements: they must have a high school diploma, and they must pass a standardized written test. There was no evidence that either requirement related to successful job performance. Blacks met the requirements in lower percentages than whites, and consequently whites obtained a disproportionate share of the good jobs.

Title VII did not precisely address this kind of case. It clearly outlawed overt discrimination. Was Duke Power's policy overt discrimination, or was it protected by Senator Tower's amendment, §703(h)? The case went all the way to the Supreme Court, where the Court had to interpret the new law.

Statutory Interpretation

Courts are often called upon to interpret a statute, that is, to explain precisely what the language means and how it applies in a given case. There are three primary steps in a court's statutory interpretation:

- *Plain Meaning Rule.* When a statute's words have ordinary, everyday significance, the court will simply apply those words. Section 703(a)(1) of the Civil Rights Act prohibits firing someone because of her religion. Could an employer who had fired a Catholic because of her religion argue that Catholicism is not really a religion, but more of a social group? No. The word "religion" has a plain meaning and courts apply its commonsense definition.

- *Legislative History and Intent.* If the language is unclear, the court must look deeper. Section 703(a)(2) prohibits classifying employees in ways that are discriminatory. Does that section prevent an employer from requiring high school diplomas, as Duke Power did? The explicit language of the statute does not answer the question. The court will look at the law's history to determine the intent of the legislature. The court will examine committee hearings, reports, and the floor debates that we have seen.

- *Public Policy.* If the legislative history is unclear, courts will rely on general public policies, such as reducing crime, creating equal opportunity, and so forth. They may include in this examination some of their own prior decisions. Courts assume that the legislature is aware of prior judicial decisions, and if the legislature did not change those decisions, the statute will be interpreted to incorporate them.

Here is how the Supreme Court interpreted the 1964 Civil Rights Act.

GRIGGS V. DUKE POWER CO.

401 U.S. 424, 91 S. Ct. 849, 1971 U.S. LEXIS 134
United States Supreme Court, 1971

Excerpts from Mr. Chief Justice Burger's Decision: The objective of Congress in the enactment of Title VII is plain from the language of the statute. It was to achieve equality of employment opportunities and remove barriers that have operated in the past to favor an identifiable group of white employees over other employees. Under the Act, practices, procedures, or tests neutral on their face, and even neutral in terms of intent, cannot be maintained if they operate to "freeze" the status quo of prior discriminatory employment practices.

The Act proscribes not only overt discrimination but also practices that are fair in form, but discriminatory in operation. The touchstone is business necessity. If an employment practice which operates to exclude Negroes cannot be shown to be related to job performance, the practice is prohibited.

On the record before us, neither the high school completion requirement nor the general intelligence test is shown to bear a demonstrable relationship to successful performance of the jobs for which it was used.

Senator Tower offered an amendment which was adopted verbatim and is now the testing provision of section 703(h). Speaking for the supporters of Title VII, Senator Humphrey endorsed the amendment, stating: "Senators on both sides of the aisle who were deeply interested in Title VII have examined the text of this amendment and have found it to be in accord with the intent and purpose of that title." The amendment was then adopted. From the sum of the legislative history relevant in this case, the conclusion is inescapable that the . . . requirement that employment tests be job related comports with congressional intent. ∎

And so the highest Court ruled that if a job requirement had a discriminatory impact, the employer could use that requirement only if it was related to job performance. Many more cases arose. For almost two decades courts held that, once workers showed that a job requirement had a discriminatory effect, the employer had the burden to prove that the requirement was necessary for the business. The requirement had to be essential to achieve an important goal. If there was any way to achieve that goal without discriminatory impact, the employer had to use it.

Changing Times

But things changed. In 1989, a more conservative Supreme Court decided *Wards Cove Packing Co. v. Atonio.*[11] The plaintiffs were nonwhite workers in salmon canneries in Alaska. The canneries had two types of jobs, skilled and unskilled. Nonwhites (Filipinos and native Alaskans) invariably worked as low-paid, unskilled workers, canning the fish. The higher paid, skilled positions were filled almost entirely with white workers, who were hired during the off-season in Washington and Oregon.

There was no overt discrimination. But plaintiffs claimed that various practices led to the racial imbalances. The practices included failing to promote from within the company, hiring through separate channels (cannery jobs were done through a union hall, skilled positions were filled out of state), nepotism, and an English language requirement. Once again the case reached the Supreme Court, where Justice White wrote the Court's opinion.

If the plaintiffs succeeded in showing that the job requirements led to racial imbalance, said the Court, the employer now only had to demonstrate that the requirement or practice "serves, in a significant way, the legitimate employment goals of the employer. . . . [T]here is no requirement that the challenged practice be 'essential' or 'indispensable' to the employer's business." In other words, the Court removed the "business necessity" requirement of *Griggs* and replaced it with "legitimate employment goals."

Voters' Role

The response to *Wards Cove* was quick. Liberals decried it; conservatives hailed it. Everyone agreed that it was a major change that would make it substantially harder for plaintiffs to bring successful discrimination cases. Why had the Court changed its interpretation? Because the *Court* was different. The Court of the 1980s was more conservative, with a majority of justices appointed by Presidents Nixon and Reagan. And so, the voters' political preference had affected the high Court, which in turn changed the interpretation of a statute passed in response to voter concerns of the 1960s. See Exhibit 4.2.

Democrats introduced bills to reverse the interpretation of *Wards Cove*. President George H.W. Bush strongly opposed any new bill. He said it would lead to "quotas," that is, that employers would feel obligated to hire a certain percentage of workers from all racial categories to protect themselves from suits. This was the issue that Congressman Johansen had raised in the original House debate in 1964, but it had not been mentioned since.

Both houses passed bills restoring the "business necessity" holding of *Griggs*. Again there were differences, and a Conference Committee resolved them. After acrimonious debate, both houses passed the compromise bill in October 1990. Was it therefore law? No. President Bush immediately vetoed the bill. He said it would compel employers to adopt quotas.

---

[11] 490 U.S. 642, 109 S. Ct. 2115, 1989 U.S. LEXIS 2794 (1989).

Exhibit 4.2
Statutory interpretation can be just as volatile as the common law, because voters, politicians, and courts all change over time.

Congressional Override

When the president vetoes a bill, Congress has one last chance to make it law: an override. If both houses repass the bill, each by a two-thirds margin, it becomes law over the president's veto. Congress attempted to pass the 1990 Civil Rights bill over the Bush veto, but it fell short in the Senate by one vote.

Civil rights advocates tried again, in January 1991, introducing a new bill to reverse the *Wards Cove* rule. Again both houses debated and bargained. The new bill stated that, once an employee proves that a particular employment practice causes a discriminatory impact, the employer must "demonstrate that the challenged practice is job related for the position in question and consistent with business necessity."

Now the two sides fought over the exact meanings of two terms: "job related" and "business necessity." Each side offered definitions, but they could not reach agreement. It appeared that the entire bill would founder over those terms. So Congress did what it often does when faced with a problem of definition: it dropped the issue. Liberals and conservatives agreed not to define the troublesome terms. They would leave that task to courts to perform through statutory interpretation.

With the definitions left out, the new bill passed both houses. In November 1991, President Bush signed the bill into law. The president stated that the new bill had been improved and no longer threatened to create racial quotas. His opponents charged he had reversed course for political reasons, anticipating the 1992 presidential election.

And so, the Congress restored the "business necessity" interpretation to its own 1964 Civil Rights Act. No one would say, however, that it had been a simple process.

The Other Player: Money

No description of the legislative process would be complete, or even realistic, without mentioning money. Campaign contributions and spending have aroused controversy for decades. In 1971, Congress passed the Federal Election Campaign Act (FECA), which limited how much of his own money a federal candidate could spend. Three years later, the statute was amended to place two more limitations on federal campaigns: how much a campaign as a whole could spend, and how much anyone else could spend to promote a candidate. One goal was to reduce the power and influence of donors, who gave money expecting favors in return; another purpose was to permit candidates of modest means to compete with millionaire office seekers.

In 1976, the Supreme Court unsettled things in *Buckley v. Valeo,*[12] by ruling that mandatory *spending* limits violate the First Amendment. The Court permitted Congress to limit campaign *contributions*, from individuals and groups, but not to cap the amount that a candidate could spend. This decision was a windfall for wealthy candidates, who could now spend as much of their own money as they chose. It is no coincidence that most members of Congress are very rich.

In 1979, Congress amended the FECA to permit unlimited donations to *political parties* for use in "party building." Initially, party building meant only minor activities like get-out-the-vote drives and distribution of bumper stickers and buttons. Both parties, however, eventually discovered that it was easy to use party-building money in ways that would directly benefit candidates. These funds came to be known as *soft money*. Since the law placed no limit on soft money, the parties went after it feverishly, raising and spending hundreds of millions of dollars every election, effectively destroying any distinction between party building and campaigning.

ᵘᴾdate

In 2002, Congress passed legislation designed to curtail the influence of campaign donations by eliminating soft money and regulating campaign advertising. However, it is already apparent that the legislation did not eliminate soft money. During the 2004 election cycle, both parties exploited a new device, so-called "527" committees. These are tax-exempt groups, named after section 527 of the Internal Revenue Code, that raise enormous sums attempting to influence elections. Generally speaking they may not advocate for or against a federal candidate. Instead, they spend their money advocating positions on volatile topics, criticizing selected candidates on those same issues, and mobilizing voters they deem sympathetic to their cause. The 2004 presidential election was the most expensive in history, and 527s raised a total of $434 million, with the two largest groups spending over $70 million each. Soft money is proving hard to uproot.

Senators John McCain and Russ Feingold, authors of the original effort to reduce influence peddling, have already sponsored new legislation to clamp down on 527s. The non-profit Center for Public Integrity has brought to light many money scandals in Washington. To see what a sharp spotlight will reveal, glance at the center's Web page, http://www .publicintegrity.org. Common Cause, which you can visit at http://www.commoncause.org, works hard for campaign finance reform. The Center for Responsive Politics, at http:// www.crp.org/, includes in its Web site a dollar-by-dollar description of recent elections, demonstrating which candidates took how much from whom. ◆

ECONOMICS
& the LAW

When a contributor gives money to a congressman or senator, what is she hoping to accomplish? Does she merely want to assist an incumbent whose views match her own, in the hope of securing his reelection? Or is she attempting to influence the office holder's position on a particular issue? Economists agree that this is an important question, but disagree on the answer. One study concluded that campaign donors do hope to influence votes on particular issues. This economist charted the timing of donations. He discovered that disproportionate sums were donated, not during election campaigns, but during leg-

---

[12] 424 U.S. 1, 96 S. Ct. 612, 1976 U.S. LEXIS 16 (1976).

islative sessions, as important bills were coming up for vote. The donors tended to be those directly affected by the proposed legislation. The author of the study concluded that a substantial number of campaign donors attempt to influence a legislator's vote on a particular bill—regardless of whether they succeed.[13]

A second study reached a different conclusion. The authors compared how a legislator voted after he had announced his retirement (but still held office) with his voting pattern while he was an incumbent seeking reelection. These economists reasoned that if campaign donations influence a politician's views, then once the office holder announces his retirement and stops fund raising, his votes should shift back to his own, honest positions. But they discovered no such voting shift. The authors concluded that most politicians vote their conscience.[14] Which study do you find more persuasive? ◆

ADMINISTRATIVE LAW

Before beginning this section, please return your seat to its upright position. Stow the tray firmly in the seatback in front of you. Turn off any radios, CD players, or other electronic equipment. Sound familiar? Administrative agencies affect each of us every day in hundreds of ways. They have become the fourth branch of government. Supporters believe that they provide unique expertise in complex areas; detractors regard them as unelected government run amok.

Many administrative agencies are familiar. The Federal Aviation Agency, which requires all airlines to ensure that your seats are upright before takeoff and landing, is an administrative agency. The Internal Revenue Service haunts us every April 15. The Environmental Protection Agency regulates the water quality of the river in your town. The Federal Trade Commission oversees the commercials that shout at you from your television set.

Other agencies are less familiar. You may never have heard of the Bureau of Land Management, but if you go into the oil and gas industry, you will learn that this powerful agency has more control over your land than you do. If you develop real estate in Palos Hills, Illinois, you will tremble every time the Appearance Commission of the City of Palos Hills speaks, since you cannot construct a new building without its approval. If your software corporation wants to hire an Argentine expert on databases, you will get to know the complex workings of the Immigration and Naturalization Service: no one lawfully enters this country without its nod of approval.

Background

By the 1880s, the amazing iron horse crisscrossed America. But this technological miracle became an economic headache. Congress worried that the railroads' economic muscle enabled a few powerful corporations to reap unfair profits. The railroad industry needed closer regulation. Who would do it? Courts decide individual cases, they do not regulate industries. Congress itself passes statutes, but it has no personnel to oversee the day-to-day working of a huge industry. For example, Congress lacks the expertise to establish rates for freight passing from Kansas City to Chicago, and it has no personnel to enforce rates once they are set.

---

[13] Stratman, "The Market for Congressional Votes: Is Timing of Contributions Everything?" *Journal of Law and Economics,* 1998, vol. 41, p. 85.

[14] Bronars and Lott, "Campaign Donations," *Journal of Law and Economics,* 1997, vol. 40, p. 317.

A new entity was needed. Congress passed the Interstate Commerce Act, creating the Interstate Commerce Commission (ICC), the first administrative agency. The ICC began regulating freight and passenger transportation over the growing rail system and continued to do so for over 100 years. Congress gave the ICC power to regulate rates and investigate harmful practices, to hold hearings, issue orders, and punish railroads that did not comply.

The ICC was able to hire and develop a staff that was expert in the issues that Congress wanted controlled. The agency had enough flexibility to deal with the problems in a variety of ways: by regulating, investigating, and punishing. And that is what has made administrative agencies an attractive solution for Congress: one entity, focusing on one industry, can combine expertise and flexibility. However, the ICC also developed great power, which voters could not reach, and thereby started the great and lasting conflict over the role of agencies.

During the Great Depression of the 1930s, the Roosevelt administration and Congress created dozens of new agencies. Many were based on social demands, such as the need of the elderly population for a secure income. Political and social conditions dominated again in the 1960s, as Congress created agencies, such as the Equal Employment Opportunity Commission, to combat discrimination.

Then during the 1980s the Reagan administration made an effort to decrease the number and strength of the agencies. For several years some agencies declined in influence, though others did not. As we begin a new millennium, there is still controversy about how much power agencies should have, but there is no doubt that administrative agencies are a permanent part of our society.

Classification of Agencies

Agencies exist at the federal, state, and local level. We will focus on federal agencies because they have national impact and great power. Most of the principles discussed apply to state and local agencies as well. Virtually any business or profession you choose to work in will be regulated by at least one administrative agency, and it may be regulated by several.

Executive-Independent

Some federal agencies are part of the executive branch while others are independent agencies. This is a major distinction. The president has much greater control of executive agencies for the simple reason that he can fire the agency head at any time. An executive agency will seldom diverge far from the president's preferred policies. Some familiar executive agencies are the Internal Revenue Service (part of the Treasury Department); the Federal Bureau of Investigation (Department of Justice); the Food and Drug Administration (Department of Health and Human Services); and the Nuclear Regulatory Commission (Department of Energy).

The president has no such removal power over independent agencies. The Federal Communications Commission (FCC) is an independent agency. For many corporations involved in broadcasting, the FCC has more day-to-day influence on their business than Congress, the courts, and the president combined. Other powerful independent agencies are the Federal Trade Commission, the Securities and Exchange Commission, the National Labor Relations Board, and the Environmental Protection Agency.

Enabling Legislation

Congress creates a federal agency by passing **enabling legislation.** The Interstate Commerce Act was the enabling legislation that established the ICC. Typically, the

© GETTY IMAGES

An agency's interpretation of an environmental statute may be obscure, but the consequences affect us all.

enabling legislation describes the problems that Congress believes need regulation, establishes an agency to do it, and defines the agency's powers.

Critics argue that Congress is delegating to another body powers that only the legislature or courts are supposed to exercise. This puts administrative agencies above the voters. But legal attacks on administrative agencies invariably fail. Courts acknowledge that agencies have become an integral part of a complex economy. As long as there are some limits on an agency's discretion, a court will uphold its powers.

The Administrative Procedure Act

This act is a major limitation on how agencies do their work. Congress passed the Administrative Procedure Act (APA) in 1946 in an effort to bring uniformity and control to the many federal agencies. The APA regulates how federal agencies make rules, conduct investigations, hold meetings and hearings, reach decisions, and obtain and release information. How much power should agencies have? How much control should we impose on them? These are two of the major questions that businesses and courts face as we enter a new century.

Power of Agencies

Administrative agencies use three kinds of power to do the work assigned to them: they make rules, they investigate, and they adjudicate.

Rulemaking

One of the most important functions of an administrative agency is to make rules. In doing this, the agency attempts, prospectively, to establish fair and uniform behavior for all businesses in the affected area. **To create a new rule is to promulgate it.** Agencies promulgate two types of rules: legislative and interpretive.

Legislative Rules. These are the most important agency rules, and they are much like statutes. Here, an agency creates law by requiring businesses or private citizens to act in a certain way. Suppose you operate a Web site for young shoppers, aged 10 to 18. Like most online merchants, you consider yourself free to collect as much data as possible about consumers. Wrong. The Federal Trade Commission, a federal agency, has promulgated detailed rules governing any site directed to young children. Before obtaining private data from these immature consumers, you must let them know exactly who you are, how to contact site operators, precisely what you are seeking, and how it will be used. You must also obtain verifiable parental consent before collecting, using, or disclosing any personal information. Failure to follow the rules can result in a substantial civil penalty. This modest legislative rule, in short, will be more important to your business than most statutes passed by Congress.

Interpretive Rules. These rules do not change the law. They are the agency's interpretation of what the law already requires. But they can still affect all of us.

In 1977, Congress passed the Clean Air Act in an attempt to reduce pollution from factories. The act required the Environmental Protection Agency (EPA) to impose emission standards on "stationary sources" of pollution. But what did "stationary source" mean? It was the EPA's job to define that term. Obscure work, to be sure, yet the results could be seen and even smelled, because the EPA's definition would determine the quality of air entering our lungs every time we breathe. Environmentalists wanted the term defined to include every smokestack in a factory so that the EPA could regulate each one. The EPA, however, developed the "bubble concept," ruling that "stationary source" meant an entire factory, but not the individual smokestacks. As a result, polluters could shift emission among smokestacks in a single factory to avoid EPA regulation. Environmentalists howled that this gutted the purpose of the statute, but to no avail. The agency had spoken, merely by interpreting a statute.[15]

How Rules Are Made. Corporations fight many a court battle over whether an agency has the right to issue a particular rule and whether it was promulgated properly. The critical issue is this: How much participation is the public entitled to before an agency issues a rule? There are two basic methods of rulemaking.[16]

Informal Rulemaking. On many issues, agencies may use a simple "notice and comment" method of rulemaking. The agency must publish a proposed rule in advance and permit the public a comment period. During this period, the public may submit any objections and arguments, with supporting data. The agency will make its decision and publish the final rule.

For example, the Department of Transportation may use the informal rulemaking procedure to require safety features for all new automobiles. The agency must listen to objections from interested parties, notably car manufacturers, and it must give a written response to the objections. The agency is required to have rational reasons for the final choices it makes. However, it is not obligated to satisfy all parties or do their bidding.

Formal Rulemaking. In the enabling legislation, Congress may require that an agency hold a hearing before promulgating rules. Congress does this to make the agency more accountable to the public. After the agency publishes its proposed rule, it must hold a public hearing. Opponents of the rule, typically affected businesses, may cross-examine the agency experts about the need for the rule and may testify against it. When the agency makes its final decision about the rule, it must prepare a formal, written response to everything that occurred at the hearing.

When used responsibly, these hearings give the public access to the agency and can help formulate sound policy. When used irresponsibly, hearings can be manipulated to stymie needed regulation. The most famous example concerns peanut butter. The Food and Drug Administration (FDA) began investigating peanut butter content in 1958. It found, for example, that Jif peanut butter, made by Procter & Gamble, had only 75 percent peanuts and 20 percent of a Crisco-type base. P&G fought the investigation, and any changes, for years. Finally, in 1965, the FDA proposed a minimum of 90 percent peanuts in peanut butter; P&G wanted 87 percent. The FDA wanted no more than 3 percent hydrogenated vegetable oil; P&G wanted no limit.

The hearings dragged on for months. One day, the P&G lawyer objected to the hearing going forward because he needed to vote that day. Another time, when an FDA official testified that consumer letters indicated the public wanted to know what was really in peanut butter, the P&G attorney demanded that the official bring in and identify the letters—all 20,000 of them. Finally, in 1968, a decade after beginning its investigation, the FDA promulgated final rules requiring 90 percent peanuts but eliminating the 3 percent cap on vegetable oil.[17]

---

[15] An agency's interpretation can be challenged in court, and this one was.

[16] Certain rules may be made with no public participation at all. For example, an agency's internal business affairs and procedures can be regulated without public comment, as can its general policy statements. None of these directly affect the public, and the public has no right to participate.

[17] For an excellent account of this high-fat hearing, see Mark J. Green, *The Other Government* (New York: W. W. Norton & Co., 1978), pp. 136–150.

Hybrid Rulemaking. In an effort to avoid the agency paralysis made famous in the peanut butter case, some agencies use hybrid rulemaking, following the informal model but adding a few elements of the formal. The agency may give notice and a comment period, deny the right to a full hearing, but allow limited cross-examination on one or two key issues.

Investigation

Agencies do an infinite variety of work, but they all need broad factual knowledge of the field they govern. Some companies cooperate with an agency, furnishing information and even voluntarily accepting agency recommendations. For example, the U.S. Consumer Product Safety Commission investigates hundreds of consumer products every year and frequently urges companies to recall goods that the agency considers defective. Many firms comply. (For an up-to-the-minute report on dangerous products and company compliance, proceed carefully to **http://www.cpsc.gov/index.html**.)

Other companies, however, jealously guard information, often because corporate officers believe that disclosure would lead to adverse rules. To force disclosure, agencies use *subpoenas* and *searches*.

Subpoenas. A **subpoena** is an order to appear at a particular time and place to provide evidence. A **subpoena** *duces tecum* requires the person to appear and bring specified documents. Businesses and other organizations intensely dislike subpoenas and resent government agents plowing through records and questioning employees. What are the limits on an agency's investigation? The information sought:

- Must be *relevant* to a lawful agency investigation. The FCC is clearly empowered to investigate the safety of broadcasting towers, and any documents about tower construction are obviously relevant. Documents about employee racial statistics might indicate discrimination, but the FCC lacks jurisdiction on that issue and thus may not demand such documents.

- Must not be *unreasonably burdensome*. A court will compare the agency's need for the information with the intrusion on the corporation.

- Must not be *privileged*. The Fifth Amendment privilege against self-incrimination means that a corporate officer accused of criminal securities violations may not be compelled to testify about his behavior.

In the following case, an agency's subpoena power conflicted with an important right of confidentiality.

DOE V. MARYLAND BOARD OF SOCIAL WORKERS

384 Md. 161, 862 A.2d 996
Maryland Court of Appeals, 2004

Facts: "Ms. F." was a licensed social worker in Maryland. One of her clients, "John Doe," was convicted of child abuse and sex offenses involving his minor granddaughter. The Board of Social Work Examiners, an administrative agency, learned that Ms. F. had likely violated the law by failing to report the abuse. The agency began an investigation, and issued a subpoena *duces tecum* to Ms. F., demanding all treatment records for John Doe and his wife Jane Doe, for the year in which the abuse occurred.

The Does ("Petitioners") sued, asking the court to quash the subpoena, that is, to nullify it. They claimed that a social worker–client privilege prohibited disclosure of their records. The intermediate court of appeals declared the subpoena valid. The Does appealed to the state's highest court. ▼

Issue: Was the subpoena valid?

Excerpts from Judge Cathell's Decision: [A state statute] affords social workers and their clients similar protections that have long been applicable to other relationships where privacy issues and the need for open communication are of paramount importance, e.g., marital privilege, attorney–client privilege, psychiatrist/psychologist–patient privilege, clergyman–communicant privilege, etc. We consider the information contained in those treatment records to be both confidential *and* privileged. Therefore, we must examine the Board's claim that its subpoena power and obligation to oversee the conduct of the licensed social workers of this State provides an exception to petitioners' privilege and confidentiality rights as provided by law.

We agree with the intermediate appellate court that the Board's interests in obtaining Ms. F.'s treatment records of petitioners are clearly compelling. Of great importance is the fact that the Board itself was established by the Legislature "to protect the public by: (1) Setting minimum qualification, education, training, and experience standards for the licensing of individuals to practice social work; and (2) Promoting and maintaining high professional standards for the practice of social work." As the Court of Special Appeals stated in this regard: "To

deny the Board access to patient files is to deny it the ability to carry out its legislative mandate. If the Social Worker Board receives a complaint that a social worker failed to notify the appropriate agency of his/her reason to believe that a child had been subjected to abuse, a lack of access to the worker's records would effectively foreclose any meaningful investigation into that conduct and any basis for disciplinary action."

We hold that neither the social worker–client privilege nor any claim concerning petitioners' constitutional right to privacy automatically prevents the Board from subpoenaing petitioners' treatment records. While the Board is required by law to protect the petitioners' treatment records from further disclosure, the Board must be allowed to have access to those treatment records in order to fulfill its statutory mandate to protect the public by conducting a full investigation and, where appropriate, disciplining those licensed social workers who are found to be in violation of the [law]. This mandate cannot be carried out if clients are automatically allowed, after claiming either a social worker–client privilege or a constitutional privacy right, to block from disclosure records that the Board determines are necessary to its investigations.

Affirmed. ∎

PublicPolicy

The court is comparing two important public policy concerns. What are they? How does the court attempt to limit the intrusion into confidential records? What would happen if the administrative agency, reviewing the treatment notes, discovered evidence that the Does had committed additional crimes—or were planning to do so? Could the agency act on its knowledge? ◆

Search and Seizure. At times an agency will want to conduct a surprise **search** of an enterprise and **seize** any evidence of wrongdoing. May an agency do that? Yes, although there are limitations. When a particular industry is *comprehensively regulated*, courts will assume that companies know they are subject to periodic, unannounced inspections. In those industries, an administrative agency may conduct a search without a warrant and seize evidence of violations. For example, the mining industry is minutely regulated, with strict rules covering equipment, mining depths, transport and safety structures, air quality, and countless other things. Mining executives know that they are closely watched, and for good reason: mine safety is a matter of life and death, and surprise is an essential element of effective inspection. Accordingly, the Bureau of Mines may make unannounced, warrantless searches to ensure safety.[18] Today, it is a rare case that finds a warrantless search by an administrative agency to have been illegal.

---

[18] Donovan v. Dewey, 452 U.S. 594, 101 S. Ct. 2534, 1980 U.S. LEXIS 58 (1981).

Adjudication

To **adjudicate** a case is to hold a hearing about an issue and then decide it. Agencies adjudicate countless cases. The FCC adjudicates which applicant for a new television license is best qualified. The Occupational Safety and Health Administration (OSHA) holds adversarial hearings to determine whether a manufacturing plant is dangerous.

Most adjudications begin with a hearing before an **administrative law judge** (ALJ). There is no jury. An ALJ is an employee of the agency but is expected to be impartial in her rulings. All parties are represented by counsel. The rules of evidence are informal, and an ALJ may receive any testimony or documents that will help resolve the dispute.

After all evidence is taken, the ALJ makes a decision. The losing party has a right to appeal to an appellate board within the agency. The appellate board has the power to make a *de novo* **decision,** meaning it may ignore the ALJ's decision. A party unhappy with that decision may appeal to federal court.

LIMITS ON AGENCY POWER

There are four primary methods of reining in these powerful creatures: statutory, political, judicial, and informational.

Statutory Control

As discussed, the enabling legislation of an agency provides some limits. It may require that the agency use formal rulemaking or investigate only certain issues. The APA imposes additional controls by requiring basic fairness in areas not regulated by the enabling legislation.

Political Control

The president's influence is greatest with executive agencies. Congress, though, controls the purse. No agency, executive or independent, can spend money it does not have. An agency that angers Congress risks having a particular program defunded or its entire budget cut. Further, Congress may decide to defund an agency as a cost-cutting measure. In its effort to balance the budget, Congress abolished the Interstate Commerce Commission, transferring its functions to the Transportation Department.

Congress has additional control because it must approve presidential nominees to head agencies. Before approving a nominee, Congress will attempt to determine her intentions. And, finally, Congress may amend an agency's enabling legislation, limiting its power.

Judicial Review

An individual or corporation directly harmed by an administrative rule, investigation, or adjudication may generally have that action reviewed in federal court.[19] The party seeking review, for example, a corporation, must have suffered direct harm; the courts

---

[19] In two narrow groups of cases, a court may not review an agency action. In a few cases, courts hold that a decision is "committed to agency discretion," a formal way of saying that courts will keep hands off. This happens only with politically sensitive issues, such as international air routes. In some cases, the enabling legislation makes it absolutely clear that Congress wanted no court to review certain decisions. Courts will honor that.

will not listen to theoretical complaints about an agency action.[20] And that party must first have taken all possible appeals within the agency itself.[21]

Standard on Review

Suppose OSHA promulgates a new rule limiting the noise level within steel mills. Certain mill operators are furious because they will have to retool their mills in order to comply. After exhausting their administrative appeals, they file suit seeking to force OSHA to withdraw the new rule. How does a court decide the case? Or, in legal terms, what standard does a court use in reviewing the case? Does it simply substitute its own opinion for that of the agency? No, it does not. The standard a court uses must take into account:

Facts. Courts generally defer to an agency's factfinding. If OSHA finds that human hearing starts to suffer when decibels reach a particular level, a court will probably accept that as final. The agency is presumed to have expertise on such subjects. As long as there is *substantial evidence* to support the fact decision, it will be respected.

Law. Courts often—but not always—defer to an agency's interpretation of the law. This is due in part to the enormous range of subjects that administrative agencies monitor. Consider the following examples. "Chicken catchers" work in large poultry operations, entering coops, manually capturing broilers, loading them into cages, and driving them to a processing plant where they . . . well, never mind. On one farm, the catchers wanted to organize a union, but the company objected, pointing out that *agricultural* workers had no right to do so. Were chicken catchers agricultural workers? The National Labor Relations Board, an administrative agency, declared that chicken catchers were in fact *ordinary* workers, entitled to organize. The Supreme Court ruled that courts were obligated to give deference to the agency's decision about chicken catchers. If the agency's interpretation was *reasonable* it was binding, even if the court itself might not have made the same analysis. The workers were permitted to form a union—though the chickens were not.

The killer whales (Orcas) who live in Puget Sound are a threatened group. But are they a *separate population* from those that live in the ocean? If so, that would make them an *endangered species*, entitled to major protections from the federal government. The National Marine Fisheries Services (NMFS), an administrative agency, ruled that the Puget Sound whales were not a separate population, and therefore not endangered. However, a reviewing court disagreed, and refused to defer to the NMFS decision. The agency, said the court, reached its conclusion without using the best available scientific data. The judge ordered the NMFS to reconsider differences between the various whales, this time taking into account the animals' language (clicks, calls, and whistles), rituals, and culture. The Puget Sound Orcas may still obtain protected status.

In the case that follows, the agency determination is again very technical—but of profound significance to one frightened man.

---

[20] The law describes this requirement by saying that a party must have standing to bring a case. A college student who has a theoretical belief that the EPA should not interfere with the timber industry has no standing to challenge an EPA rule that prohibits logging in a national forest. A lumber company that was ready to log that area has suffered a direct economic injury: it has standing to sue.

[21] This is the doctrine of exhaustion of remedies. A lumber company may not go into court the day after the EPA publishes a proposed ban on logging. It must first exhaust its administrative remedies by participating in the administrative hearing and then pursuing appeals within the agency before venturing into court.

AMADOR-PALOMARES V. ASHCROFT

382 F.3d 864
United States Court of Appeals for the Eighth Circuit, 2004

Facts: Abelardo Amador-Palomares illegally entered the United States from Mexico as a 13-year-old boy, along with his family. He lived in this country continuously for about 20 years except for one four-month period when he returned to his native country. He had a young son, a United States citizen who suffered from tuberculosis and asthma.

The Immigration and Naturalization Service, an administrative agency, began deportation proceedings against Amador-Palomares, who admitted he was in the country illegally but requested a discretionary form of relief called "suspension of deportation." Under the Immigration and Naturalization Act (INA), suspension is potentially available to those (1) who have been in the nation at least seven years, (2) who are of good moral character, and (3) whose deportation would result in extreme hardship.

The Board of Immigration Appeals (BIA), part of the INS, rejected his claim for suspension, finding that he was not of good moral character. While awaiting a decision on his claim of suspension, Amador-Palomares was convicted of soliciting a prostitute and fined $350. The BIA noted that a different section of the INA, section 1182(a)(2)(D), prohibited admission into the United States of anyone who

> ii) directly or indirectly procures or attempts to procure or to import, prostitutes or persons for the purpose of prostitution, or receives the proceeds of prostitution.

The BIA interpreted this section of the law to mean that anyone convicted of soliciting a prostitute could not be a person of good moral character, for purposes of suspension of deportation. Amador-Palomares appealed.

Issue: Did the BIA improperly interpret immigration law and wrongfully deny suspension of deportation to Amador-Palomares?

Excerpts from Judge Melloy's Decision: If congressional intent is clear from the plain meaning of the statute, our inquiry ends. However, if we conclude that congressional intent is not obvious from the plain meaning, we must defer to the Board's interpretation of the statute, provided its construction is reasonable. Because the BIA is charged with administering the INA, its interpretation of the INA's provisions must be granted deference. We need not conclude that the agency construction was the only one it permissibly could have adopted to uphold the construction, or even the reading the court would have reached if the question initially had arisen in a judicial proceeding.

The [BIA] found that Mr. Amador-Palomares's single conviction for attempting to solicit for immoral purposes was a crime falling within the scope of §212(a)(2)(D). The petitioner may well be correct that Congress did not foresee the consequences that would attach to a single conviction of solicitation, but the Board's interpretation of the INA is entitled to deference, and we cannot say its interpretation was unreasonable. Therefore, we affirm the Board's decision and deny Mr. Amador-Palomares's petition for review. ■

Devil's Advocate

Why bow down to an agency decision that is harsh and poorly reasoned? The statutory section focuses on people who attempt to run a prostitution ring, not those caught soliciting. Surely a man who has lived in this country for 20 years should not be thrown out for one moral slip. ◆

Informational Control and the Public

We started this section describing the pervasiveness of administrative agencies. We should end it by noting one way in which all of us have some direct control over these ubiquitous authorities: information.

> A popular government, without popular information, or the means of acquiring it, is but a Prologue to a Farce or a Tragedy—or perhaps both. Knowledge will

forever govern ignorance, and a people who mean to be their own Governors must arm themselves with the power which knowledge gives.
James Madison, President, 1809–1817

Two federal statutes arm us with the power of knowledge.

Freedom of Information Act

Congress passed this landmark statute (known as "FOIA") in 1966. It is designed to give all of us, citizens, businesses, and organizations alike, access to the information that federal agencies are using. The idea is to avoid government by secrecy.

Any citizen or executive may make a "FOIA request" to any federal government agency. It is simply a written request that the agency furnish whatever information it has on the subject specified. Two types of data are available under FOIA. Anyone is entitled to information about how the agency operates, how it spends its money, and what statistics and other information it has collected on a given subject. People routinely obtain records about agency policies, environmental hazards, consumer product safety, taxes and spending, purchasing decisions, and agency forays into foreign affairs. A corporation that believes that OSHA is making more inspections of its textile mills than it makes of the competition could demand all relevant information, including OSHA's documents on the mill itself, comparative statistics on different inspections, OSHA's policies on choosing inspection sites, and so forth.

Second, all citizens are entitled to any records the government has *about them*. You are entitled to information that the Internal Revenue Service, or the Federal Bureau of Investigation, has collected about you.

FOIA does not apply to Congress, the federal courts, or the executive staff at the White House. Note also that, since FOIA applies to federal government agencies, you may not use it to obtain information from state or local governments or private businesses. For a step-by-step guide explaining how to make a FOIA request, see **http://www .aclu.org/library/foia.html**. For dramatic proof of FOIA's power, see **http://www.gwu.edu/ ~nsarchiv/nsa/foia.html**, a Web site devoted to government documents that have been declassified as a result of FOIA requests.

Exemptions. An agency officially has 10 days to respond to the request. In reality, most agencies are unable to meet the deadline but are obligated to make good faith efforts. FOIA exempts altogether nine categories from disclosure. The most important exemptions permit an agency to keep confidential information that relates to national security, criminal investigations, internal agency matters such as personnel or policy discussions, trade secrets or financial institutions, or an individual's private life.

Privacy Act

This 1974 statute prohibits federal agencies from giving information about an individual to other agencies or organizations without written consent. There are exceptions, but overall this act has reduced the government's exchange of information about us "behind our back."

Chapter Conclusion

"Why can't they just fix the law?" They can, and sometimes they do—but it is a difficult and complex task. "They" includes a great many people and forces, from common law courts to members of Congress to campaign donors to administrative agencies. The courts have made the bystander rule slightly more humane, but it has been a long and bumpy road. Congress managed to restore the legal interpretation of its own 1964 Civil Rights Act, but it took months of debate and compromising. The FDA squeezed more peanuts into a jar of Jif, but it took nearly a decade to get the lid on.

A study of law is certain to create some frustrations. This chapter cannot prevent them all. However, an understanding of how law is made is the first step toward controlling that law.

Chapter Review

1. *Stare decisis* means "let the decision stand," and indicates that once a court has decided a particular issue, it will generally apply the same rule in future cases.

2. The common law evolves in awkward fits and starts because courts attempt to achieve two contradictory purposes: predictability and flexibility.

3. The common law bystander rule holds that, generally, no one has a duty to assist someone in peril unless the bystander himself created the danger. Courts have carved some exceptions during the last 100 years, but the basic rule still stands.

4. Bills originate in congressional committees and go from there to the full House of Representatives or Senate. If both houses pass the bill, the legislation normally must go to a Conference Committee to resolve differences between the two versions. The compromise version then goes from the Conference Committee back to both houses, and if passed by both, to the president. If the president signs the bill, it becomes a statute; if he vetoes it, Congress can pass it over his veto with a two-thirds majority in each house.

5. Courts interpret a statute by using the plain meaning rule; then, if necessary, legislative history and intent; and finally, if necessary, public policy.

6. Campaign contributions and spending are largely uncontrolled.

7. Congress creates federal administrative agencies with enabling legislation. The Administrative Procedure Act controls how agencies do their work.

8. Agencies may promulgate legislative rules, which generally have the effect of statutes, or interpretive rules, which merely interpret existing statutes.

9. Agencies have broad investigatory powers and may use subpoenas and, in some cases, warrantless searches to obtain information.

10. Agencies adjudicate cases, meaning that they hold hearings and decide issues. Adjudication generally begins with a hearing before an administrative law judge and may involve an appeal to the full agency or ultimately to federal court.

11. The four most important limitations on the power of federal agencies are statutory control in the enabling legislation and the APA; political control by Congress and the president; judicial review; and the informational control created by the Freedom of Information Act and the Privacy Act.

Practice Test

1. **ETHICS** Suppose you were on a state supreme court and faced with a restaurant-choking case. Should you require restaurant employees to know and employ the Heimlich maneuver to assist a choking victim? If they do a bad job, they could cause additional injury. Should you permit them to do nothing at all? Is there a compromise position? What social policies are most important?

2. **YOU BE THE JUDGE** WRITING PROBLEM An off-duty, out-of-uniform police officer and his son purchased some food from a 7-Eleven store and were still in the parking lot when a carload of teenagers became rowdy. The officer went to speak to them and the teenagers assaulted him. The officer shouted to his son to get the 7-Eleven clerk to call for help. The son entered the store, told the clerk that a police officer needed help, and told the clerk to call the police. He returned 30 seconds later and repeated the request, urging the clerk to say it was a Code 13. The son claimed that the clerk laughed at him and refused to do it. The policeman sued

the store. **Argument for the Store:** We sympathize with the policeman and his family, but the store has no liability. A bystander is not obligated to come to the aid of anyone in distress unless the bystander created the peril, and obviously the store did not do so. The policeman should prosecute *and* sue those who attacked him. **Argument for the Police Officer:** We agree that in general a bystander has no obligation to come to the aid of one in distress. However, when a business that is open to the public receives an urgent request to call the police, the business should either make the call or permit someone else to do it.

3. You sign a two-year lease with a landlord for an apartment. The rent will be $1,000 per month. A clause in the lease requires payment on the first of every month. The clause states that the landlord has the right to evict you if you are even one day late with the payment. You forget to pay on time and deliver your check to the landlord on the third day of the month. He starts an eviction case against you. Who should win? If we enforce the contract, what social result does that have? If we ignore the clause, what effect does that have on contract law?

4. Federal antitrust statutes are complex, but the basic goal is straightforward: to prevent a major industry from being so dominated by a small group of corporations that they destroy competition and injure consumers. Does Major League Baseball violate the antitrust laws? Many observers say that it does. A small group of owners not only dominate the industry, but actually *own* it, controlling the entry of new owners into the game. This issue went to the United States Supreme Court in 1922. Justice Holmes ruled, perhaps surprisingly, that baseball is exempt from the antitrust laws, holding that baseball is not "trade or commerce." Suppose that a congressman dislikes this ruling and dislikes the current condition of baseball. What could he do?

5. Until recently, every state had a statute outlawing the burning of American flags. But in *Texas v. Johnson*,[22] the Supreme Court declared such statutes unconstitutional, saying that flag burning is symbolic speech, protected by the First Amendment. Does Congress have the power to overrule the Court's decision?

6. Whitfield, who was black, worked for Ohio Edison. Edison fired him, but then later offered to rehire him. At about that time, another employee, representing Whitfield, argued that Edison's original termination of Whitfield had been race discrimination. Edison rescinded its offer to rehire Whitfield. Whitfield sued Edison, claiming that the rescission of the offer to rehire was in retaliation for the other employee's opposition to discrimination. Edison defended by saying that Title VII of the 1964 Civil Rights Act did not protect in such cases. Title VII prohibits, among other things, an employer from retaliating against *an employee who has opposed* illegal discrimination. But it does not explicitly prohibit an employer from retaliating against one employee based on *another employee's* opposition to discrimination. Edison argued that the statute did not protect Whitfield. Outcome?

Background for Questions 7 through 9. The following three questions begin with a deadly explosion. In 1988, terrorists bombed Pan Am Flight 103 over Lockerbie, Scotland, killing all passengers on board. Congress sought to remedy security shortcomings by passing the Aviation Security Improvement Act of 1990, which, among other things, ordered the Federal Aviation Authority (FAA) to prescribe minimum training requirements and minimum staffing levels for airport security. The FAA promulgated rules according to the informal rulemaking process. However, the FAA refused to disclose certain rules, concerning training at specific airports. *Public Citizen, Inc. v. FAA.*[23]

7. Explain what "promulgated rules according to the informal rulemaking process" means.

8. A public interest group called Public Citizen, Inc., along with family members of those who had died at Lockerbie, wanted to know the details of airport security. What steps should they take to obtain the information? Are they entitled to obtain it?

9. The Aviation Security Improvement Act (ASIA) states that the FAA can refuse to divulge information about airport security. The FAA inter-

---

[22] 491 U.S. 397, 109 S. Ct. 2533, 1989 U.S. LEXIS 3115 (1989).
[23] 988 F.2d 186, 1993 U.S. App. LEXIS 6024 (D.C. Cir. 1993).

prets this to mean that it can withhold the data in spite of FOIA. Public Citizen and the Lockerbie family members interpret FOIA as being the controlling statute, requiring disclosure. Is the FAA interpretation binding?

10. Hiller Systems, Inc., was performing a safety inspection on board the M/V *Cape Diamond*, an ocean-going vessel, when an accident occurred involving the fire extinguishing equipment. Two men were killed. The Occupational Safety and Health Administration (OSHA), a federal agency, attempted to investigate, but Hiller refused to permit any of its employees to speak to OSHA investigators. What could OSHA do to pursue the investigation? What limits were there on what OSHA could do?

11. *ROLE REVERSAL* Draft a multiple-choice question that highlights the path of legislation from the first congressional committee to the president's desk.

Internet Research Problem

Research some pending legislation in Congress. Go to http://beatty.westbuslaw.com, and click on "bills." Choose some key words that interest you, and see what your government is doing. Read the summary of the bill, if one is provided, or go to the text of the bill, and scan the introduction. What do the sponsors of this bill hope to accomplish? Do you agree or disagree with their goals?

> **You can find further practice problems at** http://beatty.westbuslaw.com **or in the Study Guide that accompanies this text.**

Constitutional Law

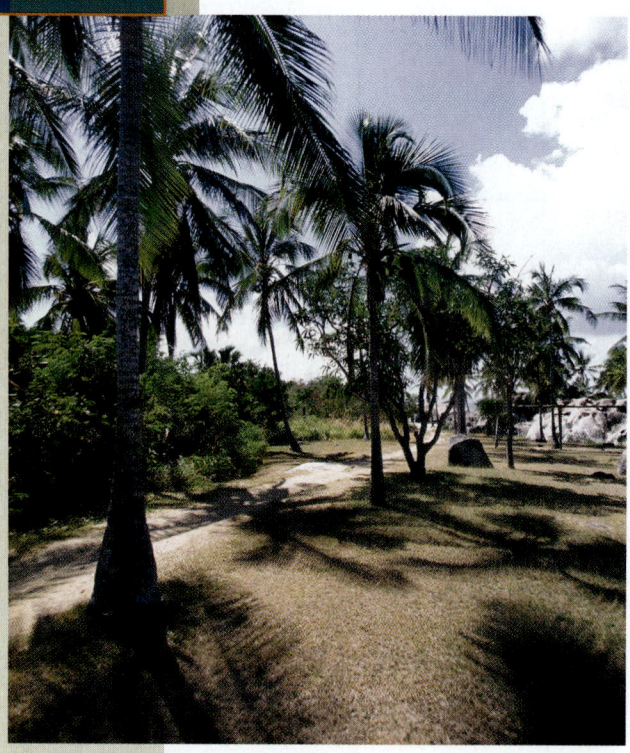

Suppose you want to dance naked in front of 75 strangers. Do you have the right to do it? May the police interrupt your show and insist that you don a few garments? You may consider these odd questions, as relatively few business law students contemplate a career as a nude dancer. Yet the answers to these questions will affect you every day of your life, even if you choose a more prosaic line such as investments or retailing (it is good to have a backup plan).

Consider a very different—yet related—question. A state government wants to reduce the number of children who get hooked on tobacco. The government prohibits most advertising aimed at youngsters, although the effect is to eliminate many ads that reach adults. The regulations are well intended, but are they fair? May a state forbid any conduct that it regards as harmful to its citizens? What if the same state passes a law preventing new construction along the coastline? This measure will protect the environment, but in the process it may render some very expensive beachfront property worthless. Whose interest is more important, that of the public or the property owners?

© PHILIP COBLENTZ/PHOTODISC/GETTY IMAGES

These seemingly unrelated questions all involve the same critical issue: power. Does your state have the power to prohibit nude dancing? If so, does that mean it could outlaw a campaign poster on your front lawn? Prohibit political protest? Is the state entitled to abolish tobacco ads, for a well-intended purpose? Outlaw beachfront development?

Questions about regulating nude dancing affect all of us because the answers reveal how much control the government may exercise. Constitutional law is a series of variations on one vital theme: government power. ■

GOVERNMENT POWER

One in a Million

The Constitution of the United States is the greatest legal document ever written. No other written constitution has lasted so long, governed so many, or withstood such challenge. This amazing work was drafted in 1787, when two weeks were needed to make the horseback ride from Boston to Philadelphia, a pair of young cities in a weak and disorganized nation. Yet today, when that trip requires less than two hours by jet, the same Constitution successfully governs the most powerful country on earth. This longevity is a tribute to the wisdom and idealism of the Founding Fathers.

The Constitution is not perfect. The original document contained provisions that were racist.[1] Other sections were unclear, and some needed early amendment. Overall, however, the Constitution has worked astonishingly well and has become the model for many constitutions around the world.

The Constitution is short and relatively easy to read. This brevity is potent. The Founding Fathers, also called the **Framers,** wanted it to last for centuries, and they understood that would happen only if the document permitted interpretation and "fleshing out" by later generations. The Constitution's versatility is striking, as we can see from the fact that the document can be used to resolve the crazy quilt of questions posed above. The *First Amendment* governs the two issues of nude dancing and tobacco advertising. Courts will use the *Takings Clause* to decide when a state's efforts to protect the environment have unfairly injured property owners.

This chapter is organized around the issue of power. The first part provides an overview of the Constitution, discussing how it came to be and how it is organized. The second part describes the power given to the three branches of government. The third part is the flip side of power, explaining what individual rights the Constitution guarantees to citizens.

---

[1] Two provisions explicitly endorsed slavery, belying the proposition that all people are created equal. The "Three-Fifths Clause," in Article I, section 2, required that for purposes of taxation and representation, a slave must be counted as three-fifths of a person. Article I, section 9, ensured that southern states would be permitted to continue importing slaves into the country at least until 1808.

OVERVIEW

Thirteen American colonies gained independence from Great Britain in 1783. The new status was exhilarating. This was the first nation in modern history founded on the idea that the people could govern themselves, democratically. The idea was daring, brilliant, and fraught with difficulties. The states were governing themselves under the Articles of Confederation, but these articles gave the central government no real power. The government could not tax any state or its citizens and had no way to raise money. A government without the ability to raise money does not govern, it panhandles. The national government also lacked the power to regulate commerce between the states or between foreign nations and any state. This was disastrous. States began to impose taxes on goods entering from other states. The young "nation" was a collection of poor relations, threatening to squabble themselves to death.

By 1787 the articles were largely deemed a failure, and the states sent a group of 55 delegates to Philadelphia to amend them. These delegates—the Framers of our Constitution—were not a true cross section of the populace. There were no women or blacks, artisans or small farmers. Most were wealthy; all were powerful within their states.

Rather than amend the old document, the Framers set out to draft a new one, to create a government that had never existed before. It was hard going. What structure should the government have? How much power? Representatives like Alexander Hamilton urged a strong central government. They were the *federalists*. The new government must be able to tax and spend, regulate commerce, control the borders, and do all things that national governments routinely do. But Patrick Henry and other *anti-federalists* feared a powerful central government. They had fought a bitter war precisely to get rid of autocratic rulers; they had seen the evil that a distant government could inflict. The anti-federalists insisted that the states retain maximum authority, keeping political control closer to home.

Another critical question was how much power the *people* should have. Most of the aristocratic delegates had little love for the common people and feared that extending this idea of democracy too far would lead to mob rule. Anti-federalists again disagreed. The British had been thrown out, they insisted, to guarantee individual liberty and a chance to participate in the government. Power corrupted. It must be dispersed amongst the people to avoid its abuse.

How to settle these basic differences? By compromise, of course. **The Constitution is a series of compromises about power.** We will see many provisions granting power to one branch of the government while at the same time restraining the authority given.

Separation of Powers

One method of limiting power was to create a national government divided into three branches, each independent and equal. Each branch would act as a check on the power of the other two, avoiding the despotic rule that had come from London. Article I of the Constitution created a Congress, which was to have legislative power. Article II created the office of president, defining the scope of executive power. Article III established judicial power by creating the Supreme Court and permitting additional federal courts.

Consider how the three separate powers balance one another: Congress was given the power to pass statutes, a major grant of power. But the president was permitted to veto legislation, a nearly equal grant. Congress, in turn, had the right to override the veto, ensuring that the president would not become a dictator. The president was allowed to appoint federal judges and members of his cabinet, but only with a consenting vote from the Senate.

Federalism

The national government was indeed to have considerable power, but it would still be *limited power.* Article I, section 8, enumerates those issues on which Congress may pass statutes. If an issue is not on the list, Congress has no power to legislate. Thus Congress may create and regulate a post office because postal service is on the list. But Congress may not pass statutes regulating child custody in a divorce: that issue is not on the list. Only the states may legislate child custody issues.

Individual Rights

The original Constitution was silent about the rights of citizens. This alarmed many who feared that the new federal government would have unlimited power over their lives. So in 1791 the first 10 amendments, known as the **Bill of Rights,** were added to the Constitution, guaranteeing many liberties directly to individual citizens.

In the next two sections, we look in more detail at the two sides of the great series of compromises: power granted and rights protected.

POWER GRANTED

Congressional Power

Article I of the Constitution creates the Congress with its two houses. Representation in the House of Representatives is proportionate with a state's population, but each state elects two senators. The article establishes who is qualified to serve in Congress, setting only three requirements: age, citizenship, and residence.

Congress may perform any of the functions enumerated in Article I, section 8, such as imposing taxes, spending money, creating copyrights, supporting the military, declaring war, and so forth. None of these rights is more important than the authority to raise and spend money (the *power of the purse*), because every branch of government is dependent upon Congress for its money. One of the most important items on this list of congressional powers concerns trade.

Interstate Commerce

"The Congress shall have power to regulate commerce with foreign nations, and among the several states." This is the **Commerce Clause.** With it, the Framers were accomplishing several things in response to the commercial chaos that existed under the Articles of Confederation:

1. ***International Commerce—Exclusive Power.*** As to international commerce, the Commerce Clause is clear: only the federal government may regulate it. The federal government must speak with one voice when regulating commercial relations with foreign governments.[2]

2. ***Domestic Commerce—Concurrent Power.*** As to domestic commerce, the clause gives *concurrent power,* meaning that both Congress and the states may regulate it. Congress is authorized to regulate trade between states; each state regulates business

---

[2] *Michelin Tire Corp. v. Wages, Tax Commissioner,* 423 U.S. 276, 96 S. Ct. 535, 1976 U.S. LEXIS 120 (1976).

within its own borders. Conflicts are inevitable, and they are important to all of us: *how* business is regulated depends upon *who* does it.

- *Positive Aspect: Congressional Power.* The Framers wanted to give power to Congress to bring coordination and fairness to trade between the states. This is the positive aspect of the Commerce Clause: **Congress is authorized to regulate interstate commerce.**

- *Negative or Dormant Aspect: A Limit on the States.* The Framers also wanted to stop the states from imposing the taxes and regulations that were wrecking the nation's domestic trade. This is the negative, or dormant, aspect of the Commerce Clause: **the power of the states to regulate interstate commerce is severely restricted.**

Substantial Effect Rule

An early test of the Commerce Clause's positive aspect came in the depression years of the 1930s, in *Wickard v. Filburn.*[3] The price of wheat and other grains had fluctuated wildly, severely harming farmers and the national food market. Congress sought to stabilize prices by limiting the bushels per acre that a farmer could grow. Filburn grew more wheat than federal law allowed and was fined. In defense, he claimed that Congress had no right to regulate him. None of his wheat went into interstate commerce. He sold some locally and used the rest on his own farm as food for livestock and as seed. The Commerce Clause, Filburn claimed, gave Congress no authority to limit what he could do.

The Supreme Court disagreed and held that **Congress may regulate any activity that has a substantial economic effect on interstate commerce.** Filburn's wheat affected interstate commerce because the more he grew for use on his own farm, the less he would need to buy in the open market of interstate commerce. Congress could regulate his farm. Since this ruling, most federal statutes based on the Commerce Clause have been upheld. Congress has used the Commerce Clause to regulate such diverse issues as the working conditions in a factory, discrimination in a motel, and the environmental aspects of coal mining.[4] Each of these has substantial effect on interstate commerce.

In *United States v. Lopez,*[5] however, the Supreme Court ruled that Congress had exceeded its power under the Commerce Clause. Congress had passed a criminal statute called the "Gun-Free School Zones Act," which forbade any individual from possessing a firearm in a school zone. The goal of the statute was obvious: to keep schools safe. Lopez was convicted of violating the act and appealed his conviction all the way to the high Court, claiming that Congress had no power to pass such a law. The government argued that the Commerce Clause gave it the power to pass the law, but the Supreme Court was unpersuaded.

> The possession of a gun in a local school zone is in no sense an economic activity that might, through repetition elsewhere, substantially affect any sort of interstate commerce. [Lopez] was a local student at a local school; there is no indication that he had recently moved in interstate commerce, and there is no requirement that his possession of the firearm have any concrete tie to interstate

---

[3] 317 U.S. 111, 63 S. Ct. 82, 1942 U.S. LEXIS 1046 (1942).

[4] *Maryland v. Wirts,* 392 U.S. 183, 88 S. Ct. 2017, 1968 U.S. LEXIS 2981 (1968); *Heart of Atlanta Motel v. United States,* 379 U.S. 241, 85 S. Ct. 348, 1964 U.S. LEXIS 2187 (1964); *Hodel v. Indiana,* 452 U.S. 314, 101 S. Ct. 2376, 1981 U.S. LEXIS 34 (1981).

[5] 514 U.S. 549, 115 S. Ct. 1624, 1995 U.S. LEXIS 3039 (1995).

commerce. To uphold the Government's contentions here, we would have to pile inference upon inference in a manner that would bid fair to convert congressional authority under the Commerce Clause to a general police power of the sort retained by the States. [The statute was unconstitutional and void.]

Congress's power is great—but still limited.

State Legislative Power

The "dormant" or "negative" aspect of the Commerce Clause governs state efforts to regulate interstate commerce. **The dormant aspect holds that a state statute that discriminates against interstate commerce is invariably unconstitutional.** The following case looks at interstate wine sales, so please do not read it if you plan to drive later today.

GRANHOLM V. HEALD

2005 WL 1130571
United States Supreme Court, 2005

Facts: Michigan and New York permitted in-state wineries to sell directly to consumers. They both denied this privilege to out-of-state producers, who were required to sell to wholesalers, who offered the wine to retailers, who sold to consumers. This created an impossible barrier for many small vineyards, which did not produce enough wine to attract wholesalers.

Local residents and out-of-state wineries sued, claiming that the state regulations violated the dormant Commerce Clause. The Sixth Circuit Court of Appeals found that the regulations violated the Commerce Clause, but the Second Circuit declared the statutes valid. Because of this "split in the circuits," the Supreme Court accepted the case.

Issue: Did the direct-sales regulations violate the dormant Commerce Clause?

Excerpts from Justice Kennedy's Decision: Time and again this Court has held that, in all but the narrowest circumstances, state laws violate the Commerce Clause if they mandate differential treatment of in-state and out-of-state economic interests that benefits the former and burdens the latter. This rule is essential to the foundations of the Union. The mere fact of nonresidence should not foreclose a producer in one State from access to markets in other States. States may not enact laws that burden out-of-state producers or shippers simply to give a competitive advantage to in-state businesses. This mandate reflects a central concern of the Framers that was an immediate reason for calling the Constitutional Convention: the conviction that in order to succeed, the new Union would have to avoid the tendencies toward economic Balkanization that had plagued relations among the Colonies and later among the States under the Articles of Confederation.

The discriminatory character of the Michigan system is obvious. The differential treatment requires all out-of-state wine, but not all in-state wine, to pass through an in-state wholesaler and retailer before reaching consumers. These two extra layers of overhead increase the cost of out-of-state wines to Michigan consumers. The cost differential, and in some cases the inability to secure a wholesaler for small shipments, can effectively bar small wineries from the Michigan market.

We have no difficulty concluding that [the laws of both states discriminate] against interstate commerce through direct-shipping laws.

We still must consider whether either State regime advances a legitimate local purpose that cannot be adequately served by reasonable nondiscriminatory alternatives. The States claim that allowing direct shipment from out-of-state wineries undermines their ability to police underage drinking. Minors, the States argue, have easy access to credit cards and the Internet and are likely to take advantage of direct wine shipments as a means of obtaining alcohol illegally.

▼

The States provide little evidence that the purchase of wine over the Internet by minors is a problem. Indeed, there is some evidence to the contrary. A recent study by the staff of the FTC found that the 26 States currently allowing direct shipments report no problems with minors' increased access to wine. This is not surprising. Minors are less likely to consume wine, as opposed to beer, wine coolers, and hard liquor. Minors who decide to disobey the law have more direct means of doing so. [Finally,] minors want instant gratification. Without concrete evidence that direct shipping of wine is likely to increase alcohol consumption by minors, we are left with the States' unsupported assertions. This is not enough.

[The Court struck down the regulations, leaving it to lower courts to fashion an appropriate remedy.] ■

Devil's Advocate

Underage drinking is a serious problem. The Court should allow states wide leeway in their efforts to limit the harm. Even if the regulations are imperfect, they may help reduce the damage. ◆

Supremacy Clause

What happens when both the federal and state governments pass regulations that are permissible, but conflicting? For example, Congress passed the federal Occupational Safety and Health Act (OSHA) establishing many job safety standards, including those for training workers who handle hazardous waste. Congress had the power to do so under the Commerce Clause. Later, Illinois passed its own hazardous waste statutes, seeking to protect both the general public and workers. The state statute did not violate the Commerce Clause because it imposed no restriction on interstate commerce.

Each statute specified worker training and employer licensing. But the requirements differed. Which statute did Illinois corporations have to obey? Article VI of the Constitution contains the answer. **The Supremacy Clause states that the Constitution, and federal statutes and treaties, shall be the supreme law of the land.**

- If there is a conflict between federal and state statutes, the federal law **preempts** the field, meaning it controls the issue. The state law is void.

- Even in cases where there is no conflict, if Congress demonstrates that it intends to exercise exclusive control over an issue, federal law preempts.

Thus state law controls only when there is no conflicting federal law *and* Congress has not intended to dominate the issue. In the Illinois case, the Supreme Court concluded that Congress intended to regulate the issue exclusively. Federal law therefore preempted the field, and local employers were obligated to obey only the federal regulations.

Executive Power

Article II of the Constitution defines the executive power. Once again the Constitution gives powers in general terms. The basic job of the president is to enforce the nation's laws. Three of his key powers concern appointment, legislation, and foreign policy.

Appointment

Administrative agencies play a powerful role in business regulation, and the president nominates the heads of most of them. These choices dramatically influence what issues the agencies choose to pursue and how aggressively they do it. For example, a president who believes that it is vital to protect our natural resources may appoint a forceful environmentalist to run the Environmental Protection Agency, whereas a president who dislikes federal regulations will choose a more passive agency head.[6]

---

[6]   For a discussion of administrative agency power, see Chapter 4, on administrative law.

The president's use of troops overseas without a formal declaration of war can cause tension with Congress.

© ED KASHI/CORBIS

Legislation

The president and his advisers propose bills to Congress. During the last 50 years, a vast number of newly proposed bills have come from the executive branch. Some argue that *too many* proposals come from the president and that Congress has become overly passive. When a president proposes controversial legislation on a major issue, such as Social Security reform, the bill can dominate the news—and Congress—for months or even years. The president, of course, also has the power to veto bills.[7]

Foreign Policy

The president conducts the nation's foreign affairs, coordinating international efforts, negotiating treaties, and so forth. The president is also the commander in chief of the armed forces, meaning that he heads the military. But Article II does not give him the right to declare war—only the Senate may do that. Thus a continuing tension between president and Congress has resulted from the president's use of troops overseas *without* a formal declaration of war. Once again, the Founding Fathers' desire to create a balanced government leads to uncertain application of the law.

Judicial Power

Article III of the Constitution creates the Supreme Court and permits Congress to establish lower courts within the federal court system.[8] Federal courts have two key functions: adjudication and judicial review.

Adjudicating Cases

The federal court system hears criminal and civil cases. All prosecutions of federal crimes begin in United States District Court. That same court has limited jurisdiction to hear civil lawsuits, a subject discussed in Chapter 3, on dispute resolution.

Judicial Review

One of the greatest "constitutional" powers appears nowhere in the Constitution. In 1803 the Supreme Court decided *Marbury v. Madison.*[9] Congress had passed a relatively minor statute that gave certain powers to the Supreme Court, and Marbury wanted the Court to use those powers. The Court refused. In an opinion written by Chief Justice John Marshall, the Court held that the statute violated the Constitution because Article III of the Constitution did not grant the Court those powers. The details of the case were insignificant, but the ruling was profound: because the statute violated the Constitution, said the Court, it was void. **Judicial review refers to the power of federal courts to declare a statute or governmental action unconstitutional and void.**

---

[7] For a discussion of the president's veto power and Congress's power to override a veto, see Chapter 4, on statutory law.

[8] For a discussion of the federal court system, see Chapter 3, on dispute resolution.

[9] 5 U.S. (1 Cranch) 137 (1803).

This formidable grab of power has produced two centuries of controversy. The Court was declaring that it alone had the right to evaluate acts of the other two branches of government—the Congress and the executive—and to decide which were valid and which void. The Constitution nowhere grants this power. Undaunted, Marshall declared that "[I]t is emphatically the province and duty of the judicial department to say what the law is." In later cases, the Supreme Court expanded on the idea, holding that it could also nullify state statutes, rulings by state courts, and actions by federal and state officials. In this chapter we have already encountered an example of judicial review, for example, in the *Lopez* case, where the justices declared that Congress lacked the power to pass local gun regulations.

Is judicial review good for the nation? Those who oppose it argue that federal court judges are all appointed, not elected, and that we should not permit judges to nullify a statute passed by elected officials because that diminishes the people's role in their government. Those who favor judicial review insist that there must be one cohesive interpretation of the Constitution and the judicial branch is the logical one to provide it. This dispute about power simmers continuously beneath the surface and occasionally comes to the boil.

YOUNGSTOWN SHEET & TUBE CO. V. SAWYER

343 U.S. 579, 72 S. Ct. 863, 1952 U.S. LEXIS 2625
United States Supreme Court, 1952

Facts: During the Korean War, steel companies and the unions were unable to reach a contract. The union notified the companies that they would strike, beginning April 9, 1952. President Truman declared steel essential to the war effort and ordered his Secretary of Commerce, Sawyer, to take control of the steel mills and keep them running. Sawyer immediately ordered the presidents of the various companies to serve as operating managers for the United States.

On April 30, the federal district court issued an injunction to stop Sawyer from running the mills. That same day the United States Court of Appeals "stayed" the injunction, i.e., it permitted Sawyer to keep operating the mills. The Supreme Court quickly granted *certiorari*, heard argument May 12, and issued its decision June 2 (at least five years faster than most cases reach final decision).

Issue: Did President Truman have the constitutional power to seize the steel mills?

Excerpts from Justice Black's Decision: It is clear that if the President had authority to issue the order he did, it must be found in some provision of the Constitution. And it is not claimed that express constitutional language grants this power to the President. The contention is that presidential power should be implied from the aggregate of his powers under the Constitution [including the clauses stating that "the executive power shall be vested in a President," that "he shall take care that the laws be faithfully executed," and that he "shall be Commander in Chief."]

The order cannot properly be sustained as an exercise of the President's military power as Commander in Chief. We cannot with faithfulness to our constitutional system hold that the Commander in Chief has the ultimate power as such to take possession of private property in order to keep labor disputes from stopping production. This is a job for the Nation's lawmakers, not for its military authorities.

Nor can the seizure order be sustained because of the several constitutional provisions that grant executive power to the President. In the framework of our Constitution, the President's power to see that the laws are faithfully executed refutes the idea that he is to be a lawmaker. The Constitution limits his functions in the lawmaking process to the recommending of laws he thinks wise and the vetoing of laws he thinks bad. And the Constitution is neither silent nor equivocal about who shall make laws which the President is to execute. The first section of the first article says that "All legislative powers herein granted shall be vested in a Congress of the

▼

United States." The Constitution did not subject this lawmaking power of Congress to presidential or military supervision or control.

The Founders of this Nation entrusted the law-making power to the Congress alone in both good and bad times. It would do no good to recall the his-torical events, the fears of power and the hopes for freedom that lay behind their choice. Such a review would but confirm our holding that this seizure order cannot stand.

[The district court's injunction is *affirmed.*] ∎

President Truman disliked anyone telling him what to do, and he disliked even more having the Supreme Court limit his powers during wartime. But he obeyed the Court's order.

Judicial Activism/Judicial Restraint. The power of judicial review is potentially dictato-rial. The Supreme Court nullifies statutes passed by Congress (*Marbury v. Madison*, *United States v. Lopez*) and executive actions (*Youngstown Sheet & Tube*). May it strike down any law it dislikes? In theory, no. The Court should nullify only laws that violate the Constitution. But of course that is circular, since it is the Court that will tell us which laws are violative.

Judicial activism refers to a court's willingness, or even eagerness, to become involved in major issues and to decide cases on constitutional grounds. **Judicial restraint** is the opposite, an attitude that courts should leave lawmaking to legislators and nullify a law only when it unquestionably violates the Constitution.

From the 1950s through the 1970s, the Supreme Court took an active role, decid-ing many major social issues on constitutional grounds. The landmark 1954 decision in *Brown v. Board of Education*[10] ordered an end to racial segregation in public schools, not only changing the nation's educational systems but altering forever its expectations about race. The Court also struck down many state laws that denied minorities the right to vote. Beginning with *Miranda v. Arizona*,[11] the Court began a sweeping reap-praisal of the police power of the state and the rights of criminal suspects during searches, interrogations, trials, and appeals. And in *Roe v. Wade*[12] the Supreme Court established certain rights to abortion, most of which remain after 30 years of continu-ous litigation and violence.

Beginning in the late 1970s, and lasting to the present, the Court has pulled back from its activism. Some justices believe that the Founding Fathers never intended the judicial branch to take so prominent a role in sculpting the nation's laws and its social vision. Simple numbers tell part of the story of a changing Court. Every year roughly 8,000 requests for review are made to the Court. In the early 1970s, the Supreme Court accepted almost 200 of these cases, but by the new millennium, it was taking fewer than 100. The Court's practice of judicial restraint means that major social issues will increas-ingly be left to state legislatures and Congress. For a look at the current justices, the full text of famous cases, and a calendar of pending cases, see **http://supct.law.cornell .edu/supct/**. You can tour the Court itself and even hear some of the justices read their opinions at **http://www.oyez.org**.

Exhibit 5.1 illustrates the balance among Congress, the president, and the Court.

up~date~

Find an article that describes a recent Supreme Court decision declaring a statute uncon-stitutional. What was the purpose of the statute? Why did the justices nullify the law? Do you agree with the Court's decision? ◆

---

[10] 347 U.S. 483, 74 S. Ct. 686, 1954 U.S. LEXIS 2094 (1954).
[11] 384 U.S. 436, 86 S. Ct. 1602, 1966 U.S. LEXIS 2817 (1966).
[12] 410 U.S. 113, 93 S. Ct. 705, 1973 U.S. LEXIS 159 (1973).

The Constitution established a federal government of checks and balances. Congress may pass statutes; the president may veto them; and Congress may override the veto. The president nominates cabinet officers, administrative heads, and Supreme Court justices, but the Senate must confirm his nominees. Finally, the Supreme Court (and lower federal courts) exercise judicial review over statutes and executive actions. Unlike the other checks and balances, judicial review is not provided for in the Constitution, but is a creation of the Court itself in *Marbury v. Madison*.

PROTECTED RIGHTS

The amendments to the Constitution protect the people of this nation from the power of state and federal government. The First Amendment guarantees rights of free speech, free press, and religion; the Fourth Amendment protects against illegal searches; the Fifth Amendment ensures due process; the Sixth Amendment demands fair treatment for defendants in criminal prosecutions; and the Fourteenth Amendment guarantees equal protection of the law. We consider the First, Fifth, and Fourteenth Amendments in this chapter and the Fourth, Fifth, and Sixth Amendments in Chapter 8, on crime.

The "people" who are protected include citizens and, for most purposes, corporations. Corporations are considered persons and receive most of the same protections. The great majority of these rights also extend to citizens of other countries who are in the United States.

Constitutional rights generally protect only against governmental acts. The Constitution generally does not protect us from the conduct of private parties, such as corporations or other citizens.

Incorporation

Constitutional protections apply to federal, state, and local governments. Yet that is not what the Bill of Rights explicitly states. The First Amendment declares that *Congress* shall not abridge the right of free speech. The Fourteenth Amendment explicitly limits the power only of *state* governments. But a series of Supreme Court cases has extended virtually all of the important constitutional protections to all levels of national, state, and local government. This process is called **incorporation** because rights explicitly guaranteed at one level are incorporated into rights that apply at other levels.

First Amendment: Free Speech

The First Amendment states that "Congress shall make no law . . . abridging the freedom of speech. . . ." In general, we expect our government to let people speak and hear whatever they choose. The Founding Fathers believed democracy would only work if the members of the electorate were free to talk, argue, listen, and exchange viewpoints in any way they wanted. The people could only cast informed ballots if they were informed. "Speech" also includes symbolic conduct, as the following case flamingly illustrates.

TEXAS V. JOHNSON

491 U.S. 397, 109 S. Ct. 2533, 1989 U.S. LEXIS 3115
United States Supreme Court, 1989

Facts: Outside the Republican National Convention in Dallas, Gregory Johnson participated in a protest against policies of the Reagan administration. Participants gave speeches and handed out leaflets. Johnson burned an American flag. He was arrested and convicted under a Texas statute that prohibited desecrating the flag, but the Texas Court of Criminal Appeals reversed on the grounds that the conviction violated the First Amendment. Texas appealed to the United States Supreme Court.

Issue: Does the First Amendment protect flag burning?

Excerpts from Justice Brennan's Decision: The First Amendment literally forbids the abridgment only of "speech," but we have long recognized that its protection does not end at the spoken or written word. While we have rejected the view that an apparently limitless variety of conduct can be labeled "speech," we have acknowledged that conduct may be sufficiently imbued with elements of communication to fall within the scope of the First and Fourteenth Amendments.

In deciding whether particular conduct possesses sufficient communicative elements to bring the First Amendment into play, we have asked whether an intent to convey a particularized message was present, and [whether] the likelihood was great

that the message would be understood by those who viewed it. Hence, we have recognized the expressive nature of students' wearing of black armbands to protest American military involvement in Vietnam; of a sit-in by blacks in a "whites only" area to protest segregation; of the wearing of American military uniforms in a dramatic presentation criticizing American involvement in Vietnam; and of picketing about a wide variety of causes.

[The Court concluded that burning the flag was in fact symbolic speech.]

It remains to consider whether the State's interest in reserving the flag as a symbol of nationhood and national unity justifies Johnson's conviction. Johnson was prosecuted because he knew that his politically charged expression would cause "serious offense."

If there is a bedrock principle underlying the First Amendment, it is that the Government may not prohibit the expression of an idea simply because society finds the idea itself offensive or disagreeable. Nothing in our precedents suggests that a State may foster its own view of the flag by prohibiting expressive conduct relating to it.

Could the Government, on this theory, prohibit the burning of state flags? Of copies of the Presidential seal? Of the Constitution? In evaluating these choices under the First Amendment, how would we decide which symbols were sufficiently special to warrant this unique status? To do so, we would be forced to consult our own political preferences, and impose them on the citizenry, in the very way that the First Amendment forbids us to do.

The way to preserve the flag's special role is not to punish those who feel differently about these matters. It is to persuade them that they are wrong. We can imagine no more appropriate response to burning a flag than waving one's own, no better way to counter a flagburner's message than by saluting the flag that burns, no surer means of preserving the dignity even of the flag that burned than by—as one witness here did—according its remains a respectful burial. We do not consecrate the flag by punishing its desecration, for in doing so we dilute the freedom that this cherished emblem represents.

The judgment of the Texas Court of Criminal Appeals is therefore *affirmed*. ■

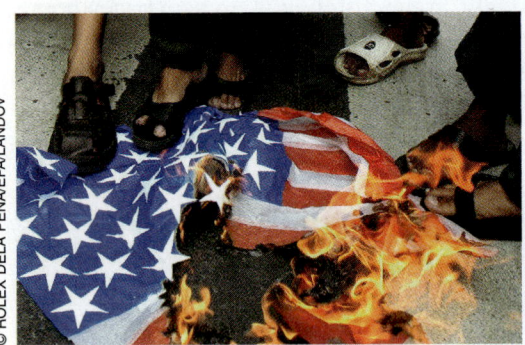

A flag burner.

© ROLEX DELA PENA/EPA/LANDOV

Flag burning is an issue that will not go away. For additional thoughts on the subject, ignite http://www.esquilax.com/flag/, an irreverent page that strongly supports the rights of free speech. To read an anti-flag burning Web page, extinguish all matches and go to http://www.cfa-inc.org/.

Political Speech

Because the Framers were primarily concerned with enabling democracy to function, political speech has been given an especially high degree of protection. Such speech may not be barred even when it is offensive or outrageous. A speaker, for example, could accuse a U.S. senator of being insane and could use crude, violent language to describe him. The speech is still protected. The speech lacks protection only if it is *intended and likely to create imminent lawless action*.[13] For example, suppose the speaker said, "The senator is inside that restaurant. Let's get some matches and burn the place down." Speech of this sort is not protected. The speaker could be arrested for attempted arson or attempted murder.

Time, Place, and Manner

Even when speech is protected, the government may regulate the *time*, *place*, and *manner* of such speech. A town may require a group to apply for a permit before using a public park for a political demonstration. The town may insist that the demonstration take place during daylight hours and that there be adequate police supervision and sanitation provided. However, the town may not prohibit such demonstrations outright.

The Supreme Court is frequently called upon to balance the rights of the general public with the rights of those seeking to publicize their causes. In *Madsen v. Women's Health Center, Inc.*,[14] the Court ruled that a local judge could limit protesters' access to a family planning clinic. The protesters, opposed to abortion, had repeatedly blocked access to the clinic, harassed patients and doctors at the clinic and at their homes, and paraded with graphic signs and bullhorns. The Court upheld the order prohibiting the protesters from coming within 36 feet of the clinic and also the order that prohibited excessive noise. But the Court overturned a part of the order that had forbidden protesters from displaying graphic images that could be seen inside the clinic. The Court said that the proper remedy was for the clinic to close its curtains.

---

13 *Brandenburg v. Ohio*, 395 U.S. 444, 89 S. Ct. 1827, 1969 U.S. LEXIS 1367 (1969).
14 511 U.S. 1016, 114 S. Ct. 1395, 1994 U.S. LEXIS 2671 (1994).

Morality and Obscenity

The regulation of morality and obscenity presents additional problems. Obscenity has never received constitutional protection. The Supreme Court has consistently held that it does not play a valued role in our society and has refused to give protection to obscene works. That is well and good, but it merely forces the question: What is obscene? (For a list of books that have been—and in some cases still are—banned by local, state, or foreign governments, go to **http://onlinebooks.library.upenn.edu** and click on "Banned Books."

In *Miller v. California*,[15] the Court created a three-part test to determine if a creative work is obscene. The basic guidelines for the factfinder are

- Whether the average person, applying contemporary community standards, would find that the work, taken as a whole, appeals to the prurient interest

- Whether the work depicts or describes, in a patently offensive way, sexual conduct specifically defined by the applicable state law; and

- Whether the work, taken as a whole, lacks serious literary, artistic, political, or scientific value.

If the trial court finds that the answer to all three of those questions is "yes," it may judge the material obscene; the state may then prohibit the work. If the state fails to prove any one of the three criteria, though, the work is not obscene.[16] A United States District Court ruled that "As Nasty As They Wanna Be," recorded by 2 Live Crew, was obscene. The appeals court, however, reversed, finding that the state had failed to prove lack of artistic merit.[17]

What if sexual conduct is not obscene? Let's go back to the chapter's starting point, nude dancing.

you Be The Judge

BARNES V. GLEN THEATRE, INC.

**501 U.S. 560, 111 S. Ct. 2456,
1991 U.S. LEXIS 3633**
United States Supreme Court, 1991

Facts: Indiana's public indecency statute prohibits any person from appearing nude in a public place. State courts have interpreted this to mean that a dancer in a theater or bar must wear pasties and a G-string. A nightclub called the Kitty Kat Lounge and several dancers who wished to perform nude filed suit, seeking an order that the statute was unconstitutional. The United States District Court ruled that the dancing was not expressive conduct and therefore was not entitled to First Amendment protection. The Court of Appeals reversed, declaring that it was nonobscene expressive conduct and thus protected by the First Amendment.

Indiana did not argue that the dancing was obscene. (If that were the issue, the *Miller* test would have determined the outcome.) Instead, Indiana claimed that its general police powers, including the power to protect social order, allowed it to enforce such a statute.

You Be the Judge: Does Indiana's public indecency statute violate the First Amendment?

▼

---

[15] 413 U.S. 15, 93 S. Ct. 2607, 1973 U.S. LEXIS 149 (1973).

[16] *Penthouse Intern Ltd. v. McAuliffe,* 610 F.2d 1353 (5th Cir. 1980).

[17] *Luke Records, Inc. v. Navarro,* 960 F.2d 134, 1992 U.S. App. LEXIS 9592 (11th Cir. 1992).

Argument for Indiana: Your honors, the State of Indiana has no wish to suppress ideas or censor speech. We are not trying to outlaw eroticism or any other legitimate form of expression. We are simply prohibiting nudity in public. We have outlawed all public nudity, not just nightclub performances. Nudity on the beach, in the park, or anywhere in public is prohibited.

We do this to protect societal order, to foster a stable morality. It is well established that the police power of the state includes the right to regulate the public health, safety, and morals. Our citizens disapprove of people appearing in the nude in public places. The citizens of virtually all states feel the same. Decent dress has been a part of good society since time immemorial. Our voting public is entitled to have that standard upheld.

We also enforce this statute because experience has shown that nightclubs such as these are often associated with criminal behavior. Prostitution, illegal drugs, and violence appear too frequently in the vicinity. It is a reasonable step for the State to maintain control over the performances and the people they will attract.

Argument for Kitty Kat: It is apparent beyond debate that dance is expressive conduct. As an art form it has existed for at least several thousand years. Eroticism, also, is not exactly news.

Erotic dance is clearly expressive conduct. Indeed, the present dancing derives its strength from its eroticism. If the State did not consider it erotic, doubtless it would have left the dancers alone. This dancing is expressive conduct and deserves the full protection of the First Amendment.

Indiana is choosing a certain type of expression and outlawing it. The state has not outlawed all nudity, since quite obviously nudity in private is beyond the State's reach. Nor has it prohibited all nude performances. Testimony of police at trial indicated that no arrests have ever been made for nudity as part of a play or ballet. Nudity is no longer anything novel in musicals, ballets, stage plays, or film. Indiana permits nudity in all of them and enforces its moralizing law only against nightclubs.

This is an obvious value judgment on the part of the State. The State is saying that if you can afford to pay for a Broadway show that happens to have nudity, you are free to enjoy it; if your taste or pocketbook leads you to the Kitty Kat Lounge, we deny your right to witness nudity. If the State is allowed to make that appraisal, then it is free to censor any expression—artistic, political, or any other—that it finds inferior. It was *precisely* to prevent states from outlawing unpopular expression that the Founding Fathers added the First Amendment. ■

cyberLaw

Concerned that pornography on the Internet was easily available to minors, Congress passed the Communications Decency Act (CDA), making it illegal for any person or company to send "obscene or indecent" communications to anyone under 18. Various plaintiffs, including library associations, booksellers, Internet service providers, and others, filed suit, claiming that the law would diminish the extraordinary opportunities for research and education that the Internet provides. The Supreme Court agreed, striking down the law as a violation of the First Amendment. The justices declared that the law failed to define "indecent." The CDA ignored the obscenity standard provided in *Miller v. California* and outlawed material that *did* have socially redeeming value. The Court noted that the law would deny adults access to a vast amount of material that they were legally entitled to obtain. Finally, the Court pointed out that concerned parents could purchase software to screen out objectionable items, avoiding the need for such far-reaching censorship.[18]

Congress has made additional attempts to protect minors from online pornography, but thus far each effort has been struck down as an overly broad restriction on free speech. ◆

[18] *Reno v. American Civil Liberties Union*, 521 U.S. 844, 117 S. Ct. 2329, 1997 U.S. LEXIS 4037 (1997).

Commercial Speech

This refers to speech that has a **dominant theme to propose a commercial transaction.** For example, most advertisements on television and in the newspapers are commercial speech. This sort of speech is protected by the First Amendment, but the government is permitted to regulate it more closely than other forms of speech. **Commercial speech that is false or misleading may be outlawed altogether.** However, regulations on commercial speech must be reasonable and directed to a legitimate goal, as the following case shows.

LORILLARD TOBACCO CO. V. REILLY

533 U.S. 525, 121 S. Ct. 2404, 150 L. Ed. 2d 532
United States Supreme Court (2001)

Facts: The Massachusetts government was convinced that advertising caused ever greater numbers of children to use tobacco products. The state crafted four regulations, which

1. restricted most cigarette advertising;

2. prohibited outdoor advertising of smokeless tobacco and cigars within 1,000 feet of schools or playgrounds;

3. prohibited indoor, point-of-sale advertising of smokeless tobacco and cigars placed less than five feet from the retailer's floor; and

4. required retailers to put all tobacco products behind a counter.

Tobacco manufacturers and sellers sued, and the case reached the United States Supreme Court.

The Supreme Court ruled that the first restriction violated the Supremacy Clause. Congress had passed a statute regulating cigarette warnings and advertising, and the federal law clearly stated that no states could pass any additional requirements. Congress had *pre-empted* the field and the Massachusetts regulation was void.

The plaintiffs next argued that the other three regulations violated their free speech rights.

Issue: Did the three Massachusetts regulations violate the First Amendment?

Excerpts from Justice O'Connor's Decision: We must determine whether the regulation directly advances the governmental interest asserted, and whether it is not more extensive than is necessary to serve that interest.

[The court acknowledged that advertising played a major role in a child's decision to use tobacco.] For instance, children smoke fewer brands of cigarettes than adults, and those choices directly track the most heavily advertised brands, unlike adult choices, which are more dispersed and related to pricing. Another study revealed that 72% of 6-year-olds and 52% of children ages 3 to 6 recognized "Joe Camel," the cartoon anthropomorphic symbol of R.J. Reynolds' Camel brand cigarettes. The FDA also made specific findings with respect to smokeless tobacco. The FDA concluded that "[t]he recent and very large increase in the use of smokeless tobacco products by young people and the addictive nature of these products has persuaded the agency that these products must be included in any regulatory approach that is designed to help prevent future generations of young people from becoming addicted to nicotine-containing tobacco products."

Whatever the strength of the Attorney General's evidence to justify the outdoor advertising regulations, however, we conclude that the regulations [are not] a reasonable fit between the means and ends of the regulatory scheme.

The outdoor advertising regulations prohibit any smokeless tobacco or cigar advertising within 1,000 feet of schools or playgrounds. In the District Court, petitioners maintained that this prohibition would prevent advertising in 87% to 91% of Boston, Worcester, and Springfield, Massachusetts. In some geographical areas, these regulations would constitute nearly a complete ban on the communication of truthful information about smokeless tobacco and cigars to adult consumers.

The State's interest in preventing underage tobacco use is substantial, and even compelling, but it is no less true that the sale and use of tobacco products by adults is a legal activity. We must consider that tobacco retailers and manufacturers have an interest in conveying truthful information about their products to adults, and adults have a corresponding interest in receiving truthful information about tobacco products.

A regulation cannot be sustained if it provides only ineffective or remote support for the government's purpose, or if there is "little chance" that the restriction will advance the State's goal. As outlined above, the State's goal is to prevent minors from using tobacco products and to curb demand for that activity by limiting youth exposure to advertising. The 5-foot rule does not seem to advance that goal. Not all children are less than 5 feet tall, and those who are certainly have the ability to look up and take in their surroundings.

[The court struck down the restrictions on outdoor advertising and the "five-foot" rule. The justices upheld the regulation that required all tobacco products to be placed behind a counter, declaring that the rule was a sensible way to stop youngsters from using unmonitored vending machines, and that the restriction had no effect on free speech.] ■

Devil's Advocate

If 72 percent of six-year-olds know who Joe Camel is, something is wrong. Which is more important, the health of our children, or the "right" of tobacco manufacturers to pander their goods to youngsters? The court made the wrong choice. ◆

Fifth Amendment: Due Process and the Takings Clause

You are a third-year student in a combined business/law program at a major state university. You feel great about a difficult securities exam you took in Professor Watson's class. The Dean's Office sends for you, and you enter curiously, wondering if your exam was so good that the dean is awarding you a prize. Not quite. The exam proctor has accused you of cheating. Based on the accusation, Watson has flunked you. You protest that you are innocent and demand to know what the accusation is. The dean says that you will learn the details at a hearing, if you wish to have one. She reminds you that if you lose the hearing you will be expelled from the university. Three years of work and your entire career are suddenly on the line.

The hearing is run by Professor Holmes, who will make the final decision. Holmes is a junior faculty member in Watson's department. (Next year, Watson will decide Holmes's tenure application.) At the hearing the proctor accuses you of copying from a student sitting in front of you. Both Watson and Holmes have already compared the two papers and concluded that they are strongly similar. Holmes tells you that you must convince him the charge is wrong. You examine the papers, acknowledge that there are similarities, but plead as best you can that you never copied. Holmes doesn't buy it. The university expels you, placing on your transcript a notation of cheating.

Have you received fair treatment? To answer that, we must look to the Fifth Amendment, which provides several vital protections. We will consider two related provisions, the Due Process Clause and the Takings Clause. Together, they state: "No person shall be . . . deprived of life, liberty, or property without due process of law; nor shall private property be taken for public use, without just compensation." These clauses prevent the government from arbitrarily taking the most valuable possessions of a citizen or corporation. We will discuss the civil law aspects of these clauses, but due process also applies to criminal law. The reference to "life" refers to capital punishment. The criminal law issues of this subject are discussed in Chapter 8, on crime.

In civil law proceedings, the government does have the right to take a person's liberty or property. But there are three important limitations:

- *Procedural Due Process.* Before depriving anyone of liberty or property, the government must go through certain procedures to ensure that the result is fair.

- *The Takings Clause.* When the government takes property for public use, such as to build a new highway, it has to pay a fair price.
- *Substantive Due Process.* Some rights are so fundamental that the government may not take them from us at all.

Procedural Due Process

The government deprives citizens or corporations of their property in a variety of ways. The Internal Revenue Service may fine a corporation for late payment of taxes. The Customs Service may seize goods at the border. As to liberty, the government may take it by confining someone in a mental institution or by taking a child out of the home because of parental neglect. **The purpose of procedural due process is to ensure that before the government takes liberty or property, the affected person has a fair chance to oppose the action.**

There are two steps in analyzing a procedural due process case:

- Is the government attempting to take liberty or property?
- If so, how much process is due? (If the government is *not* attempting to take liberty or property, there is no due process issue.)

Is the Government Attempting to Take Liberty or Property? Liberty interests are generally easy to spot: confining someone in a mental institution and taking a child from her home are both deprivations of liberty. A property interest may be obvious. Suppose that, during a civil lawsuit, the court **attaches** a defendant's house, meaning it bars the defendant from selling the property at least until the case is decided. This way, if the plaintiff wins, the defendant will have assets to pay the judgment. The court has clearly deprived the defendant of an important interest in his house, and the defendant is entitled to due process. However, a property interest may be subtler than that. A woman holding a job with a government agency has a "property interest" in that job, because her employer has agreed not to fire her without cause, and she can rely on it for income. If the government does fire her, it is taking away that property interest, and she is entitled to due process. A student attending any public school has a property interest in that education. If a public university suspends a law/business student, as described above, it is taking her property, and she, too, should receive due process.

How Much Process Is Due? Assuming that a liberty or property interest is affected, a court must decide how much process is due. Does the person get a formal trial, or an informal hearing, or merely a chance to reply in writing to the charges against her? If she gets a hearing, must it be held before the government deprives her of her property, or is it enough that she can be heard shortly thereafter? **What sort of hearing the government must offer depends upon how important the property or liberty interest is and on whether the government has a competing need for efficiency.** The more important the interest, the more formal the procedures must be.

Neutral Factfinder. Regardless of how formal the hearing, one requirement is constant: the factfinder must be neutral. Whether it is a superior court judge deciding a multimillion dollar contract suit or an employment supervisor deciding the fate of a government employee, the factfinder must have no personal interest in the outcome. In *Ward v. Monroeville*,[19] the plaintiff was a motorist who had been stopped for traffic offenses in a small town. He protested his innocence and received a judicial hearing. But the "judge" at the hearing was the town mayor. Traffic fines were a significant part

---

[19] 409 U.S. 57, 93 S. Ct. 80, 1972 U.S. LEXIS 11 (1972).

of the town's budget. The motorist argued that the town was depriving him of procedural due process because the mayor had a financial interest in the outcome of the case. The United States Supreme Court agreed and reversed his conviction.

Attachment of Property. As described above, a plaintiff in a civil lawsuit often seeks to *attach* the defendant's property. This protects the plaintiff, but it may also harm the defendant if, for example, he is about to close a profitable real estate deal. Attachments used to be routine. In *Connecticut v. Doehr*, the Supreme Court required more caution.[20] Based on *Doehr*, when a plaintiff seeks to attach at the beginning of the trial, a court must look at the plaintiff's likelihood of winning. Generally, the court must grant the defendant a hearing *before* attaching the property. The defendant, represented by a lawyer, may offer evidence as to how attachment would harm him and why it should be denied.

Government Employment. A government employee must receive due process before being fired. Generally, this means some kind of hearing, but not necessarily a formal court hearing. The employee is entitled to know the charges against him, to hear the employer's evidence, and to have an opportunity to tell his side of the story. He is not entitled to have a lawyer present. The hearing "officer" need only be a neutral employee. Further, in an emergency, where the employee is a danger to the public or the organization, the government may suspend with pay, before holding a hearing. It then must provide a hearing before the decision becomes final.

Academic Suspension. There is still a property interest here, but it is the least important of those discussed. When a public school concludes that a student has failed to meet its normal academic standards, such as by failing too many courses, it may dismiss him without a hearing. Due process is served if the student receives notice of the reason and has some opportunity to respond, such as by writing a letter contradicting the school's claims.

In cases of disciplinary suspension or expulsion, courts generally require schools to provide a higher level of due process. In the hypothetical at the beginning of this section, the university has failed to provide adequate due process.[21] The school has accused the student of a serious infraction. The school must promptly provide details of the charge and cannot wait until the hearing to do so. The student should see the two papers and have a chance to rebut the charge. Moreover, Professor Holmes has demonstrated bias. He appears to have made up his mind in advance. He has placed the burden on the student to disprove the charges. And he probably feels obligated to support Watson's original conclusion, since Watson will be deciding his tenure case next year.

The Takings Clause

Florence Dolan ran a plumbing store in Tigard, Oregon. She and her husband wanted to enlarge it on land they already owned. But the city government said that they could expand only if they dedicated some of their own land for use as a public bicycle path and for other public use. Does the city have the right to make them do that? For an answer we must look to a different part of the Fifth Amendment.

The Takings Clause is closely related to the Due Process Clause. **The Takings Clause prohibits a state from taking private property for public use without just compensation.** A town wishing to build a new football field may boot you out of your house. But the town must compensate you. The government takes your land through the power of **eminent domain.** Officials must notify you of their intentions and give

---

[20] 501 U.S. 1, 111 S. Ct. 2105, 1991 U.S. LEXIS 3317 (1991).

[21] See, e.g., *University of Texas Medical School at Houston v. Than*, 901 S.W.2d 926, 1995 Tex. LEXIS 105 (Tex. 1995).

you an opportunity to oppose the project and to challenge the amount the town offers to pay. But when the hearings are done, the town may write you a check and grind your house into goalposts, whether you like it or not.

More controversial issues arise when a local government does not physically take the property but passes regulations that restrict its use. Tigard is a city of 30,000 in Oregon. The city developed a comprehensive land use plan for its downtown area in order to preserve green space, to encourage transportation other than autos, and to reduce its flooding problems. Under the plan, when a property owner sought permission to build in the downtown section, the city could require some of her land to be used for public purposes. This has become a standard method of land use planning throughout the nation. States have used it to preserve coastline, urban green belts, and many environmental features.

When Florence Dolan applied for permission to expand, the city required that she dedicate a 15-foot strip of her property to the city as a bicycle pathway and that she preserve, as greenway, a portion of her land within a floodplain. She sued, and though she lost in the Oregon courts, she won in the United States Supreme Court. The Court held that Tigard City's method of routinely forcing all owners to dedicate land to public use violated the Takings Clause. The city was taking the land, even though title never changed hands.[22]

The Court did not outlaw all such requirements. What it required was that, **before a government may require an owner to dedicate land to a public use, it must show that this owner's proposed building requires this dedication of land.** In other words, it is not enough for Tigard to have a general plan, such as a bicycle pathway, and to make all owners participate in it. Tigard must show that it needs *Dolan's* land *specifically for a bike path and greenway.* This will be much harder for local governments to demonstrate than merely showing a city-wide plan. Some observers consider the decision a major advance for the interests of private property. They say that now the government cannot so easily demand that you give up land for public use. Property you have purchased with hard-earned money should truly be yours. Others decry the Court's ruling. In their view it harms our nation's effort to preserve the environment and gives a freer hand to those who value short-term profit over long-term planning.

In the following case, state regulations prohibited commercial development of a large waterfront property. However, the owner knew about the regulations when he obtained the land. Does his awareness of the regulations prevent him from raising the Takings Clause? Has he lost the entire value of his property?

PALAZZOLO V. RHODE ISLAND

533 U.S. 606, 121 S. Ct. 2448, 150 L. Ed. 2d 592, 2001 U.S. LEXIS 4910, 69 U.S.L.W. 4605
Supreme Court of the United States, 2001

Facts: In 1959, Shore Gardens, Inc. (SGI), bought a large parcel of waterfront property in Westerly, Rhode Island, a popular vacation area. The land was almost entirely salt marsh, subject to tidal flooding. SGI failed in its early efforts to develop the parcel. In the 1970s, Rhode Island created a Coastal Resources Management Council, to protect the state's extensive shoreline. The council published regulations that sharply limited development of coastal wetlands such as SGI's property. Later, SGI transferred the property to Anthony Palazzolo. In the 1980s, the new owner proposed a 74-lot residential subdivision and private beach club.

The council rejected his plan, and Palazzolo filed suit, claiming a violation of the Takings Clause. He sought $3,150,000, the value of the parcel if it

22 *Dolan v. City of Tigard,* 512 U.S. 374, 114 S. Ct. 2309, 1994 U.S. LEXIS 4826 (1994).

were developed. The Rhode Island Supreme Court held that he could not even raise such claims, because when he took the property he had notice of the restrictive regulations. The state court also held that Palazzolo had not been deprived of the land's use, because he was permitted to build a large, single-family house on an upland portion of the property worth about $200,000. Palazzolo appealed.

Issues: Was Palazzolo barred from making the claim because he took the property with notice of the development regulations? Was he entirely deprived of the use of his property?

Excerpts from Justice Kennedy's Decision: The Takings Clause of the Fifth Amendment prohibits the government from taking private property for public use without just compensation. The clearest sort of taking occurs when the government encroaches upon or occupies private land for its own proposed use. In [a 1922 case] the Court recognized that there will be instances when government actions do not encroach upon or occupy the property yet still affect and limit its use to such an extent that a taking occurs. In Justice Holmes' well-known, if less than self-defining, formulation, "while property may be regulated to a certain extent, if a regulation goes too far it will be recognized as a taking."

Since [then], we have given some, but not too specific, guidance to courts confronted with deciding whether a particular government action goes too far and effects a regulatory taking. First, we have observed that a regulation which "denies all economically beneficial or productive use of land" will require compensation under the Takings Clause. Where a regulation places limitations on land that fall short of eliminating all economically beneficial use, a taking nonetheless may have occurred, depending on a complex of factors including the regulation's economic effect on the landowner, the extent to which the regulation interferes with reasonable investment-backed expectations, and the character of the government action. [This is known as the "Penn Central" analysis, based on a case of that name.]

The state court held the postregulation acquisition of title was fatal to the claim for deprivation of all economic use, and to the Penn Central claim. Were we to accept the State's rule, the postenactment transfer of title would absolve the State of its obligation to defend any action restricting land use, no matter how extreme or unreasonable. A State would be allowed, in effect, to put an expiration date on the Takings Clause. This ought not to be the rule. Future generations, too, have a right to challenge unreasonable limitations on the use and value of land.

[The Rhode Island Supreme Court held] that all economically beneficial use was not deprived because the uplands portion of the property can still be improved. On this point, we agree with the court's decision. Petitioner accepts the Council's contention and the state trial court's finding that his parcel retains $200,000 in development value under the State's wetlands regulations. He asserts, nonetheless, that he has suffered a total taking and contends the Council cannot sidestep [earlier cases] by the simple expedient of leaving a landowner a few crumbs of value.

Assuming a taking is otherwise established, a State may not evade the duty to compensate on the premise that the landowner is left with a token interest. This is not the situation of the landowner in this case, however. A regulation permitting a landowner to build a substantial residence on an 18-acre parcel does not leave the property "economically idle."

The court did not err in finding that petitioner failed to establish a deprivation of all economic value, for it is undisputed that the parcel retains significant worth for construction of a residence. The claims under the Penn Central analysis were not examined, and for this purpose the case should be remanded. The judgment of the Rhode Island Supreme Court is affirmed in part and reversed in part, and the case is remanded for further proceedings not inconsistent with this opinion. ∎

Substantive Due Process

This doctrine is part of the Due Process Clause, but it is entirely different from procedural due process and from government taking. During the first third of the twentieth century, the Supreme Court frequently nullified state and federal laws, asserting that they interfered with basic rights. For example, in a famous 1905 case, *Lochner v. New York*,[23] the Supreme Court invalidated a New York statute that had limited the number

---

[23] 198 U.S. 45, 25 S. Ct. 539, 1905 U.S. LEXIS 1153 (1905).

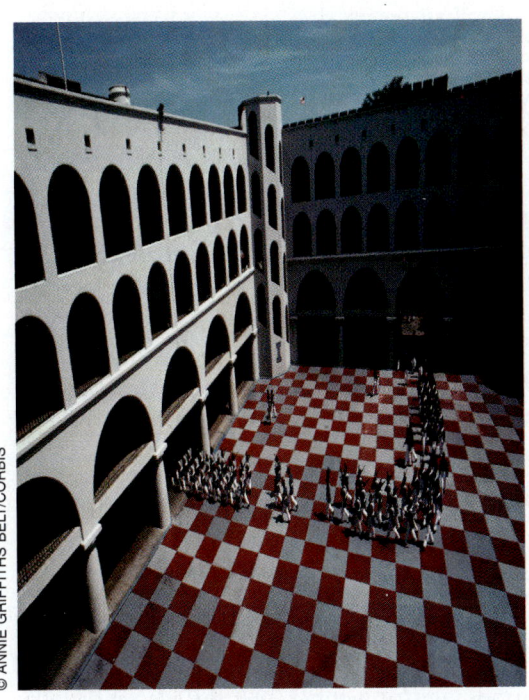

The Citadel.

of hours that bakers could work in a week. New York had passed the law to protect employee health. But the Court declared that private parties had a basic constitutional right to contract. In this case, the statute interfered with the rights of the employer and the baker to make any bargain they wished. Over the next three decades, the Court struck down dozens of state and federal laws that were aimed at working conditions, union rights, and social welfare generally. This was called **substantive due process** because the Court was looking at the substantive rights being affected, such as the right to contract, not at any procedures.

Critics complained that the Court was interfering with the desires of the voting public by nullifying laws that the justices personally disliked (judicial activism). During the Great Depression, however, things changed. Beginning in 1934, the Court completely reversed itself and began to uphold the types of laws it earlier had struck down. How does the Court now regard substantive due process issues? It treats economic and social regulations differently from cases involving fundamental rights.

Economic and Social Regulations. Generally speaking, the Court will now *presume valid* any statute that regulates economic or social conditions. If the *Lochner* case were heard today, the legislation would be upheld. State or federal laws regulating wages, working conditions, discrimination, union rights, and any similar topics are presumed valid. The Court will invalidate such a law only if it is *arbitrary or irrational.* Almost all statutes have some minimal rationality, and most are now upheld.

Fundamental Rights. The standard of review is different for laws that affect **fundamental rights.** The Constitution expressly provides some of these rights, such as the right of free speech, the right to vote, and the right to travel. Other rights do not explicitly appear in the Constitution, but the Supreme Court has determined that they are implied. One of the most important of these is the right to privacy. The Court has decided that the Bill of Rights, taken together, implies a right of privacy for all persons. This includes the right to contraception, to marriage, and, most controversially, to abortion.

Any law that infringes upon a fundamental right is presumed invalid and will be struck down unless it is necessary to a compelling government interest. For example, because it is a fundamental right, no state may outlaw abortion altogether. But the state may require a minor to obtain the consent of a parent or a judge. Although this infringes upon a fundamental right, the government has a compelling interest in regulating the welfare of minors, and this regulation is necessary to achieve that goal.

Fourteenth Amendment: Equal Protection Clause

Shannon Faulkner wanted to attend The Citadel, a state-supported military college in South Carolina. She was a fine student who met every admission requirement that The Citadel set except one: she was not a male. The Citadel argued that its long and distinguished history demanded that it remain all male. The state government claimed that Ms. Faulkner had no need to attend this particular school. Faulkner responded that she was a citizen of the state and ought to receive the benefits that others got, including the right to a military education. Could the school exclude her on the basis of gender?

The Fourteenth Amendment provides that "No State shall . . . deny to any person within its jurisdiction the equal protection of the laws." This is the **Equal Protection Clause,** and it means that, generally speaking, **governments must treat people equally.** Unfair classifications among people or corporations will not be permitted. A notorious example of unfair classification would be race discrimination: permitting only white children to attend a public school violates the Equal Protection Clause.

Yet clearly, governments do make classifications every day. Rich people pay a higher tax rate than poor people; some corporations are permitted to deal in securities, others are not. To determine which classifications are constitutionally permissible, we need to know what is being classified. There are three major groups of classifications. The outcome of a case can generally be predicted by knowing which group it is in.

- *Minimal Scrutiny: Economic and Social Relations.* Government actions that classify people or corporations on these bases are almost always upheld.
- *Intermediate Scrutiny: Gender.* Government classifications are sometimes upheld.
- *Strict Scrutiny: Race, Ethnicity, and Fundamental Rights.* Classifications based on any of these are almost never upheld.

Minimal Scrutiny: Economic and Social Regulation

Just as with the Due Process Clause, laws that regulate economic or social issues are presumed valid. They will be upheld if they are *rationally related to a legitimate goal.* This means a statute may classify corporations and/or people and the classifications will be upheld if they make any sense at all. The New York City Transit Authority excluded all methadone users from any employment. The United States District Court concluded that this violated the Equal Protection Clause by unfairly excluding all those who were on methadone. The court noted that even those who tested free of any illegal drugs and were seeking non-safety-sensitive jobs, such as clerks, were turned away. That, said the district court, was irrational.

Not so, said the United States Supreme Court. The Court admitted that the policy might not be the wisest. It would probably make more sense to test individually for illegal drugs rather than automatically exclude methadone users. But, said the Court, it was not up to the justices to choose the best policy. They were only to decide if the policy was rational. Excluding methadone users related rationally to the safety of public transport and therefore did not violate the Equal Protection Clause.[24]

Intermediate Scrutiny: Gender

Classifications based on sex must meet a tougher test than those resulting from economic or social regulation. Such laws must *substantially relate to important government objectives.* Courts have increasingly nullified government sex classifications as societal concern with gender equality has grown.

At about the same time Shannon Faulkner began her campaign to enter The Citadel, another woman sought admission to the Virginia Military Institute, an all-male state school. The Supreme Court held that Virginia had violated the Equal Protection Clause by excluding women from VMI. The Court ruled that gender-based government discrimination requires an "exceedingly persuasive justification," and that Virginia had failed that standard of proof. The Citadel promptly opened its doors to women.[25]

Today over 800 high school girls wrestle competitively. Some join female clubs but others have no such opportunity and compete with boys—or seek to. Some schools

---

[24] *New York City Transit Authority v. Beazer,* 440 U.S. 568, 99 S. Ct. 1355, 1979 U.S. LEXIS 77 (1979).
[25] *United States v. Virginia,* 518 U.S. 515, 116 S. Ct. 2264, 1996 U.S. LEXIS 4259 (1996).

allow girls to join the boys' wrestling team, but others refuse, citing moral reasons, concern for the girls' safety, and the possibility of sexual harassment. If a particular school has no female team, should girls be permitted to wrestle boys? Do they have an equal protection right to do so?

Strict Scrutiny: Race, Ethnicity, and Fundamental Rights

Any government action that intentionally discriminates against racial or ethnic minorities, or interferes with a fundamental right, is presumed invalid. In such cases, courts will look at the statute or policy with *strict scrutiny;* that is, courts will examine it very closely to determine whether there is compelling justification for it. The law will be upheld only if it is *necessary to promote a compelling state interest.* Very few meet that test.

- **Racial and Ethnic Minorities.** Any government action that intentionally discriminates on the basis of race or ethnicity is presumed invalid. For example, in *Palmore v. Sidoti,*[26] the state had refused to give child custody to a mother because her new spouse was racially different from the child. The practice was declared unconstitutional. The state had made a racial classification, it was presumed invalid, and the government had no *compelling need* to make such a ruling.

- **Fundamental Rights.** A government action interfering with a fundamental right also receives strict scrutiny and will likely be declared void. For example, New York State gave an employment preference to any veteran who had been a state resident when he entered the military. Newcomers who were veterans were less likely to get jobs, and therefore this statute interfered with the right to travel, a fundamental right. The Supreme Court declared the law invalid.[27]

Private Regulations

All of the rights discussed thus far offer protection only from government action, not from the conduct of private citizens or corporations. Suppose it is Sunday morning. You are happily reading the newspaper, sipping coffee, while your nine-year-old niece, visiting for the weekend, plays hopscotch on your front walk. There is a knock at the front door. The Neighborhood Association has arrived with a stern message: "Get the kid out of the neighborhood; she's not allowed." Astonished and enraged, you call your lawyer. But her answer leaves you dazed: You may not have children in your house. "But this is America!" you shout. "The Constitution," she replies, "does not apply."

Like 50 million other Americans, you live in a *common interest development (CID).* Yours happens to be a gated community of single-family homes, all of which were built by a developer. When you bought the house, you automatically joined the Neighborhood Association. Other CIDs take different forms: condominiums, co-ops, or retirement or vacation communities. They are increasingly common, and some observers predict that, soon, about 25 percent of all Americans will live in one.

Some CIDs ban children from living in the development or even visiting. Some prohibit signs on the lawns or windows; others outlaw pets, certain flowers, laundry drying in the sun, day-care centers, or pickup trucks. But various features make CIDs attractive to prospective residents. CIDs are often gated or locked in other ways, so they may be safer than surrounding neighborhoods. The community collects its own fees and operates many services, such as water and sewer, road maintenance, garbage

---

[26] 466 U.S. 429, 104 S. Ct. 1879, 1984 U.S. LEXIS 69 (1984).
[27] *Attorney General of New York v. Soto-Lopez,* 476 U.S. 898, 106 S. Ct. 2317, 1986 U.S. LEXIS 59 (1986).

collection, and other work traditionally done by towns and cities. Because they are privately managed by boards elected by the residents, CIDs often do this work more promptly and efficiently than public agencies.

However, the price residents pay is more than cash: they do indeed forfeit constitutional rights. The Constitution protects citizens from government action, and the local CID is not a government. As the law currently stands, you are probably giving up constitutional protections when you enter a CID. If the Neighborhood Association demands that your niece leave, you will probably have to drive her home. Suppose the nasty Neighborhood Association official also notices that your cat looks heavy. "No cats over 20 pounds," he snarls. "Read the rules." The pet-weight rule is also probably enforceable: get that cat off the sofa and onto a treadmill, fast.

© PHOTODISC/GETTY IMAGES

Chapter Conclusion

The legal battle over power never stops. The obligation of a state to provide equal educational opportunity for both genders relates to whether Tigard, Oregon, may demand some of Ms. Dolan's store lot for public use. Both issues are governed by one amazing document. That same Constitution determines what tax preferences are permissible, and even whether a state may require you to wear clothing. As social mores change in step with broad cultural developments, as the membership of the Supreme Court changes, the balance of power between federal government, state government, and citizens will continue to evolve. There are no easy answers to these constitutional questions because there has never been a democracy so large, so diverse, or so powerful.

Chapter Review

1. The Constitution is a series of compromises about power.

2. Article I of the Constitution creates the Congress and grants all legislative power to it. Article II establishes the office of president and defines executive powers. Article III creates the Supreme Court and permits lower federal courts; the article also outlines the powers of the federal judiciary.

3. Under the Commerce Clause, Congress may regulate any activity that has a substantial effect on interstate commerce.

4. A state may not regulate commerce in any way that will interfere with interstate commerce.

5. Under the Supremacy Clause, if there is a conflict between federal and state statutes, the federal law preempts the field. Even without a conflict, federal law preempts if Congress intended to exercise exclusive control.

6. The president's key powers include making agency appointments, proposing legislation, conducting foreign policy, and acting as commander in chief of the armed forces.

7. The federal courts adjudicate cases and also exercise judicial review, which is the right to declare a statute or governmental action unconstitutional and void.

8. Freedom of speech includes symbolic acts. Political speech is protected unless it is intended and likely to create imminent lawless action.

9. The government may regulate the time, place, and manner of speech.

10. Obscene speech is not protected.

11. Commercial speech that is false or misleading may be outlawed; otherwise, regulations on this speech must be reasonable and directed to a legitimate goal.

12. Procedural due process is required whenever the government attempts to take liberty or property. The amount of process that is due depends upon the importance of the liberty or property threatened.

13. The Takings Clause prohibits a state from taking private property for public use without just compensation.

14. A substantive due process analysis presumes that any economic or social regulation is valid, and presumes invalid any law that infringes upon a fundamental right.

15. The Equal Protection Clause generally requires the government to treat people equally. Courts apply strict scrutiny in any equal protection case involving race, ethnicity, or fundamental rights; intermediate scrutiny to any case involving gender; and minimal scrutiny to an economic or social regulation.

16. Generally, constitutional rights protect citizens only from the action of the government, not from actions of private organizations such as common interest developments.

Practice Test

1. Michigan's Solid Waste Management Act (SWMA) generally prohibited Michigan counties from accepting for disposal solid waste that had been generated outside that county. Fort Gratiot operated a sanitary landfill in St. Clair County, Michigan. The county denied Fort Gratiot permission to bring in solid waste from out of state, and Fort Gratiot sued. This case involves the negative, or dormant, aspect of the Commerce Clause. What is the difference between that aspect and the positive aspect? What is the evil that the dormant aspect is designed to avoid? How would you rule in this case?

2. *YOU BE THE JUDGE* WRITING PROBLEM Scott Fane was a CPA licensed to practice in New Jersey and Florida. He built his New Jersey practice by making unsolicited phone calls to executives. When he moved to Florida, the Board of Accountancy there prohibited him (and all CPAs) from personally soliciting new business. Fane sued. Does the First Amendment force Florida to forgo foreclosing Fane's phoning? **Argument for Fane:** The Florida regulation violates the First Amendment, which protects commercial speech. Fane was not saying anything false or misleading, but was just trying to secure business. This is an unreasonable regulation, designed to keep newcomers out of the marketplace and maintain steady business and high prices for established CPAs. **Argument for the Florida Board of Accountancy:** Commercial speech deserves—and gets—a lower level of protection than other speech. This regulation is a reasonable method of ensuring that the level of CPA work in our state remains high. CPAs who personally solicit clients are obviously in need of business. They are more likely to bend legal and ethical rules to obtain clients and keep them happy, and will lower the standards throughout the state.

3. Dairy farming in Massachusetts became more expensive than in other states. In order to help its dairy farmers, the state began taxing all milk sales in the state, whether the milk was produced in state or out of state. The money went into a fund that was then distributed among Massachusetts milk producers as a subsidy for their milk. Discuss.

4. President George H.W. Bush insisted that he had the power to send American troops into combat in the Middle East, without congressional assent. Yet before authorizing force in Operation Desert Storm, he secured congressional authorization. President Clinton stated that he was prepared to invade Haiti without a congressional vote. Yet he bargained hard to avoid an invasion, and ultimately American troops entered without the use of force. Why the seeming double talk by both presidents?

5. In the early 1970s, President Nixon became embroiled in the Watergate dispute. He was accused of covering up a criminal break-in at the national headquarters of the Democratic Party. Nixon denied any wrongdoing. A United States District Court judge ordered the president to

produce tapes of conversations held in his office. Nixon knew that complying with the order would produce damaging evidence, probably destroying his presidency. He refused, claiming executive privilege. The case went to the Supreme Court. Nixon strongly implied that even if the Supreme Court ordered him to produce the tapes, he would refuse. What major constitutional issue did this raise?

6. **ETHICS** In the landmark 1965 case of *Griswold v. Connecticut*, the Supreme Court examined a Connecticut statute that made it a crime for any person to use contraception. The majority declared the law an unconstitutional violation of the right of privacy. Justice Black dissented, saying, "I do not to any extent whatever base my view that this Connecticut law is constitutional on a belief that the law is wise or that its policy is a good one. [It] is every bit as offensive to me as it is to the majority. [There is no criticism by the majority of this law] to which I cannot subscribe—except their conclusion that the evil qualities they see in the law make it unconstitutional." What legal doctrines are involved here? Why did Justice Black distinguish between his personal views on the statute and the power of the Court to overturn it? Should a federal court act as a "superlegislature," nullifying statutes with which it disagrees? If a court aggressively takes on social issues, what dangers—and what advantages—does that present to society?

7. You begin work at Everhappy Corp. at the beginning of November. On your second day at work, you wear a political button on your overcoat, supporting your choice for governor in the upcoming election. Your boss glances at it and says, "Get that stupid thing out of this office or you're history, chump." You protest that his statement (a) violates your constitutional rights and (b) uses a boring cliché. Are you right?

8. Gilleo opposed American participation in the war in the Persian Gulf. She displayed a large sign on her front lawn that read, "Say No to War in the Persian Gulf, Call Congress Now." The city of Ladue prohibited signs on front lawns and Gilleo sued. The city claimed that it was regulating "time, place, and manner." Explain that statement, and decide who should win.

9. A federal statute prohibits the broadcasting of lottery advertisements, except by stations that broadcast in states permitting lotteries. The purpose of the statute is to support efforts of states that outlaw lotteries. Edge Broadcasting operated a radio station in North Carolina (a nonlottery state) but broadcast primarily in Virginia (a lottery state). Edge wanted to advertise Virginia's lottery but was barred by the statute. Did the federal statute violate Edge's constitutional rights?

10. Fox's Fine Furs claims that Ermine owes $68,000 for a mink coat on which she has stopped making payments. Fox goes to court, files a complaint, and also asks the clerk to *garnish* Ermine's wages. A garnishment is a court order to an employer to hold an employee's wages, or a portion of them, and pay the money into court so that there will be money for the plaintiff, if she wins. What constitutional issue does Fox's request for garnishment raise?

11. David Lucas paid $975,000 for two residential lots on the Isle of Palms near Charleston, South Carolina. He intended to build houses on them. Two years later the South Carolina legislature passed a statute that prohibited building seaward of a certain line, and Lucas's property fell in the prohibited zone. Lucas claimed that his land was now useless and that South Carolina owed him its value. Explain his claim. Should he win?

12. This case concerns unequal taxes on property. In Pennsylvania, a county tax commissioner appraises land, meaning that he sets a value for the land, and the owner then pays real estate taxes based on that value. A commissioner valued land at its sales price, whenever it was sold. If land did not sell for many years, he made little or no adjustment in its appraised value. As a result, some property was assessed at 35 times as much as neighboring land. A corporate landowner sued. What constitutional issue is raised? What should the outcome be?

13. **ROLE REVERSAL** Write an exam question that distinguishes between these three important Fifth Amendment protections: procedural due process, the Takings Clause, and substantive due process.

Internet Research Problem

Visit http://beatty.westbuslaw.com. Find a book that was formerly censored. Find another volume that is currently banned, either in the United States or elsewhere. How have changing mores affected censorship? Will the book that is currently outlawed someday be legal?

> **You can find further practice problems at http://beatty.westbuslaw.com or in the Study Guide that accompanies this text.**

Intentional Torts and Business Torts

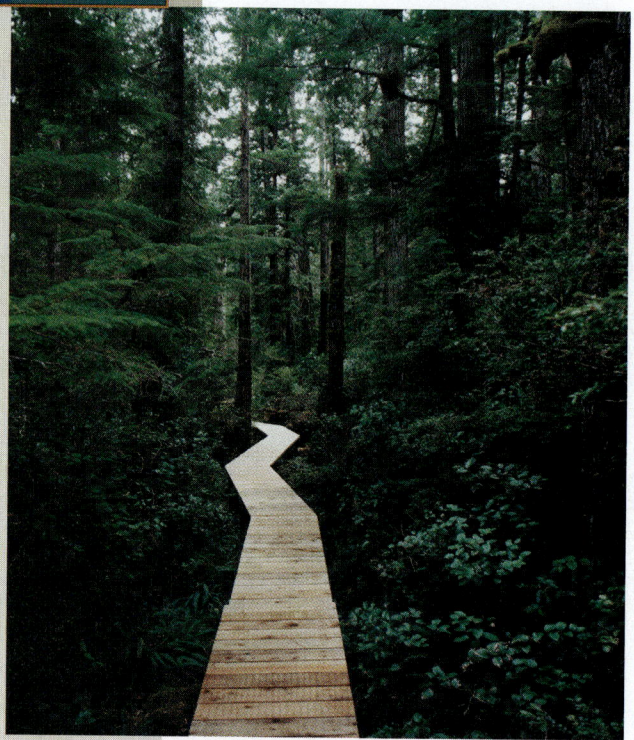

In a small Louisiana town, Don Mashburn ran a restaurant called Maison de Mashburn. The *New Orleans States-Item* newspaper reviewed his eatery, and here is what the article said:

"'Tain't Creole, 'tain't Cajun, 'tain't French, 'tain't country American, 'tain't good. I don't know how much real talent in cooking is hidden under the mélange of hideous sauces which make this food and the menu a travesty of pretentious amateurism but I find it all quite depressing. Put a yellow flour sauce on top of the duck, flame it for drama and serve it with some horrible multi-flavored rice in hollowed-out fruit and what have you got? A well-cooked duck with an ugly sauce that tastes too sweet and thick and makes you want to scrape off the glop to eat the plain duck. [The stuffed eggplant was prepared by emptying] a shaker full (more or less) of paprika on top of it. [One sauce created] trout à la green plague [while another should have been called] yellow death on duck."

Mashburn sued, claiming that the newspaper had committed libel, damaging his reputation and hurting his business.[1] Trout à la green plague will

---
[1]   *Mashburn v. Collin*, 355 So. 2d 879 (La. 1977).

be the first course on our menu of tort law. Mashburn learned, as you will, why filing

such a lawsuit is easier than winning it. ■

This odd word "tort" is borrowed from the French, meaning "wrong." And that is what it means in law: a tort is a wrong. More precisely, **a tort is a violation of a duty imposed by the civil law.** When a person breaks one of those duties and injures another, it is a tort. The injury could be to a person or her property. Libel is one example of a tort where, for example, a newspaper columnist falsely accuses someone of being an alcoholic. A surgeon who removes the wrong kidney from a patient commits a different kind of tort, called negligence. A business executive who deliberately steals a client away from a competitor, interfering with a valid contract, commits a tort called interference with a contract. A con artist who tricks money out of you with a phony offer to sell you a boat commits fraud, yet another tort.

Because tort law is so broad, it takes a while—and two chapters—to understand its boundaries. To start with, we must distinguish torts from two other areas of law: criminal law and contract law.

It is a crime to steal a car, to embezzle money from a bank, to sell cocaine. As discussed in Chapter 1, society considers such behavior so threatening that the government itself will prosecute the wrongdoer, whether or not the car owner or bank president wants the case to go forward. A district attorney, who is paid by the government, will bring the case to court, seeking to send the defendant to prison and/or to fine him. If there is a fine, the money goes to the state, not to the victim.

In a tort case, it is up to the injured party, the plaintiff, to seek compensation. She must hire her own lawyer, who will file a lawsuit. Her lawyer must convince the court that the defendant breached some legal duty and ought to pay money damages to the plaintiff. The plaintiff has no power to send the defendant to jail. Bear in mind that a defendant's action might be both a crime *and* a tort. The con artist who tricks money out of you with a fake offer to sell you a boat has committed the tort of fraud. You may file a civil suit against him and will collect money damages if you can prove your case. The con artist has also committed the crime of fraud. The state will prosecute, seeking to imprison and fine him.

A tort is also different from a contract dispute. A contract case is based on an agreement two people have already made. For example, Deirdre claims that Raul promised to sell her 10,000 pairs of sneakers at a good price but has failed to deliver them. She files a contract lawsuit. In a tort case, there is usually no "deal" between the parties. Don Mashburn had never met the restaurant critic who attacked his restaurant and obviously had never made any kind of contract. The plaintiff in a tort case claims that *the law* itself creates a duty that the defendant has breached.

Tort law is divided into categories. In this chapter we consider **intentional torts,** that is, harm caused by a deliberate action. The newspaper columnist who wrongly accuses someone of being a drunk has committed the intentional tort of libel. The con artist who tricks money from you has committed the intentional tort of fraud. In the next chapter we examine **negligence and strict liability,** which are injuries caused by neglect and oversight rather than by deliberate conduct.

When we speak of intentional torts, we do not mean that the defendant intended to *harm* the plaintiff. The intentional part of these torts is simply the physical act. If the defendant does something deliberately and it ends up injuring somebody, she is probably liable even if she meant no harm. Intentionally throwing a snowball at a friend is a deliberate act; if the snowball permanently damages his eye, the harm is unintended, but the defendant is liable for the intentional tort of battery. We look first at the most important intentional torts and then at the most important business torts.

Differences between Contract, Tort, and Criminal Law			
Type of Obligation	**Contract**	**Tort**	**Criminal Law**
How the obligation is created	The parties agree on a contract, which creates duties for both.	The civil law imposes duties of conduct on all persons.	The criminal law prohibits certain conduct.
How the obligation is enforced	Suit by plaintiff.	Suit by plaintiff.	Prosecution by government.
Possible result	Money damages for plaintiff.	Money damages for plaintiff.	Punishment for defendant, including prison and/or fine.
Example	Raul contracts to sell Deirdre 5,000 pairs of sneakers at $50 per pair, but fails to deliver them. Deirdre buys the sneakers elsewhere for $60 per pair and receives $50,000, her extra expense.	A newspaper falsely accuses a private citizen of being an alcoholic. The plaintiff sues and wins money damages to compensate for her injured reputation.	Leo steals Kelly's car. The government prosecutes Leo for grand theft, and the judge sentences him to two years in prison. Kelly gets nothing.

INTENTIONAL TORTS

Defamation

The First Amendment guarantees the right to free speech, a vital freedom that enables us to protect other rights. But that freedom is not absolute. Courts have long recognized that we cannot permit irresponsible speech to harm another's reputation. Free speech should not include the right to falsely accuse your neighbor of selling drugs. That sounds sensible enough, yet once we say that free speech and personal reputation both deserve protection, we have guaranteed perpetual conflict.

The law of defamation concerns false statements that harm someone's reputation. Defamatory statements can be written or spoken. Written defamation is *libel*. Suppose a newspaper accuses a local retail store of programming its cash registers to overcharge customers, when the store has never done so. That is libel. Oral defamation is *slander*. If Professor Wisdom, in class, refers to Sally Student as a drug dealer, and Sally has never sold anything stronger than Arm & Hammer, he has slandered her.

There are four elements to a defamation case. **An element is a fact that a plaintiff must prove to win a lawsuit.** The plaintiff in *any* kind of lawsuit must prove *all* of the elements to prevail. The elements in a defamation case are

- *Defamatory Statement.* This is a statement likely to harm another person's reputation. When Professor Wisdom accuses Sally of dealing drugs, that will clearly harm her reputation.

- *Falseness.* The statement must be false to be defamatory. If Sally Student actually sold marijuana to a classmate, then Professor Wisdom has a defense to slander.

- *Communicated.* The statement must be communicated to at least one person other than the plaintiff. If Wisdom speaks only to Sally and accuses her of dealing drugs, there is no slander. But there is if he shouts the accusation in a crowded hall.

- *Injury.* In slander cases, the plaintiff generally must show some injury. Sally's injury would be lower reputation in the school, embarrassment, and humiliation. But in libel cases, the law is willing to assume injury. Since libel is written, and more permanent, courts award damages even without proof of injury.[2]

Slander Per Se

Society has considered some statements to be so harsh that the plaintiff is not required to prove injury. These four kinds of slander are called *slander per se:* accusing the plaintiff of committing a serious crime, having a sexually transmitted disease, incompetence in her profession, or being an unchaste woman. (The sexual bias of the law caused it historically to assume that a reputation for promiscuity would hurt a woman's reputation but not a man's.) A plaintiff who proves slander per se will win, even if she cannot prove damages.

Opinion

Thus far, what we have seen is uncontroversial. If a television commentator refers to Frank Landlord as a "vicious slumlord who rents uninhabitable units," and Frank actually maintains his buildings perfectly, Frank will be compensated for the harm. But what if the television commentator states a harsh *opinion* about Frank? Remember that the plaintiff must demonstrate a "false" statement. **Opinion is generally a valid defense in a defamation suit because it cannot be proven true or false.**

Suppose that the television commentator says, "Frank Landlord certainly does less than many rich people do for our community." Is that defamation? Probably not. Who are the "rich people"? How much do they do? How do we define "does less"? These vague assertions indicate the statement is one of opinion. Even if Frank works hard feeding homeless families, he will probably lose a defamation case.

A related defense involves cases where a supposed statement of fact should not be taken literally. "Reverend Wilson's sermons go on so long, many parishioners suffer brain death before receiving communion." Brain death is a tragic fact of medical science, but this speaker obviously exaggerates to express his opinion. No defamation.

Mr. Mashburn, who opened the chapter suing over his restaurant review, lost his case. The court held that a reasonable reader would have understood the statements to be opinion only. "A shaker full of paprika" and "yellow death on duck" were not to be taken literally but were merely the author's expression of his personal dislike.

The following case features a word that is shocking to many but humorous to some. Is it defamatory?

you Be The Judge

KNIEVEL V. ESPN

393 F.3d 1068
Ninth Circuit Court of Appeals, 2005

Facts: Evel Knievel was a motorcycle stuntman who had built an international reputation through decades of daredevil feats. He rode through fire walls, flew over rattlesnakes, set world records for blasting over 14 parked buses, and spent 30 days in a coma when his 151-foot jump over the fountains of Caesar's Palace hotel came up a few feet short. The Smithsonian Institute honored his deeds, and he built a solid reputation as a community activist ▼

---

2 When defamation by radio and television became possible, the courts chose to consider it libel, analogizing it to newspapers because of the vast audience. This means that in broadcasting cases, a plaintiff generally does not have to prove damages.

and advocate for young people, using his fame to promote anti-drug programs and motorcycle safety.

ESPN held an awards program honoring winners in extreme sports (skateboarding, surfing, and motorcycle racing), and photographed many attending celebrities. On its Web site, EXPN.com, the network featured photos from the event, including one that depicted Knievel with his right arm around his wife, Krystal, and his left arm around a young woman. The caption read, "Evel Knievel proves that you're never too old to be a pimp."

The Knievels sued for defamation, claiming that the word "pimp" subjected them to hatred, contempt, and ridicule, and caused several of Evel's former clients to stop working with him. The district court dismissed the case without a jury trial, ruling that the photo and caption could not be defamatory because no reasonable viewer would have taken the phrase in its literal, criminal sense. The Knievels appealed.

Issue: **Should a jury have decided whether the photo and caption were defamatory?**

Argument for the Knievels: The issue is whether reasonable viewers (and reasonable jurors) might consider the material defamatory. Of course they could. A pimp is a criminal, and a particularly disgusting one at that. We can easily prove that Evel Knievel has never had anything to do with such revolting conduct. Let the Knievels make their case to a jury. If a dozen fair-minded people find the phrase funny, we will accept the verdict. We suspect they will conclude that an arrogant

sports network has gone too far with insulting language, and injured a hardworking man who has spent a lifetime building a marvelous reputation.

Argument for ESPN: Lighten up. This is a web site for young, hip people who watch extreme sports, use contemporary language, and possess what is known as a sense of humor. In the series of photographs on this site, one showed two men grasping hands; the caption read, "Colin McKay and Cary Hart share the love." Another shows a woman in a black dress, captioned, "Tara Dakides lookin' sexy, even though we all know she is hardcore."

The term pimp was not intended as a criminal accusation, nor would any reasonable viewer take it literally. Other photo captions, such as "hardcore," "scooping," "hottie of the year," and "thowing down a pose," indicate that all of the descriptions were loose, figurative, and humorous.

The Knievels' Rebuttal: Is broadcast vocabulary to be nothing more than a race to the gutter? And even if it is, who appointed ESPN as the referee in that ugly contest? Journalists owe us a higher standard.

ESPN's Rebuttal: If the Knievels want to take part in extreme events, and enjoy the attendant publicity, they have to be willing to take a joke. Everyone else does. We are a good judge of our audience, and are certain that no one but the Knievels took the phrase seriously. ■

Public Personalities

The rules of the game change for those who play in the open. Public officials and public figures receive less protection from defamation. An example of a **public official** is a police chief. A **public figure** is a movie star, for example, or a multimillionaire playboy constantly in the news. In the landmark case *New York Times Co. v. Sullivan*,[3] the Supreme Court ruled that the free exchange of information is vital in a democracy and is protected by the First Amendment to the Constitution. If the information wounds public people, that may just be tough luck.

The rule from the *New York Times* case is that a public official or public figure can win a defamation case only by proving actual malice by the defendant. **Actual malice means that the defendant knew the statement was false or acted with reckless disregard of the truth.** If the plaintiff merely shows that the defendant newspaper

---

3   376 U.S. 254, 84 S. Ct. 710, 1964 U.S. LEXIS 1655 (1964).

printed incorrect statements, even very damaging ones, that will not suffice to win the suit. In the *New York Times* case, the police chief of Birmingham, Alabama, claimed that the *Times* falsely accused him of racial violence in his job. He lost because he could not prove that the *Times* had acted with actual malice. If he had shown that the *Times* knew the accusation was false, he would have won.

cyberLaw

Kenneth Zeran awoke one day to learn he had become notorious. An unidentified person had posted a message on an AOL bulletin board advertising "Naughty Oklahoma T-Shirts." The shirts featured deeply offensive slogans relating to the 1995 bombing of a federal building in Oklahoma City, in which hundreds of innocent people died. Those interested in purchasing such a t-shirt were instructed to call "Ken" at Zeran's home telephone number. Zeran had nothing to do with the posting or the t-shirts. He was quickly inundated with phone messages from furious callers, some of whom made death threats.

Zeran could not change his number because he ran his business from his home. A radio station in Oklahoma City learned of the alleged offer, and angrily urged its listeners to call Zeran, which they did. Over the next few days, additional similar messages were posted, and before long Zeran was receiving an abusive call every two minutes. Zeran phoned AOL on the first day. The company promised to remove the messages immediately, but did not promptly delete the postings or close the responsible account. Zeran sued AOL for defamation—and lost.

The court held that AOL was immune from a defamation suit based on a third-party posting, based on the Communications Decency Act (CDA). Section 230 of the CDA creates this immunity for any Internet service provider, the court declared, adding:

> Lawsuits seeking to hold a service provider liable for its exercise of a publisher's traditional editorial functions, such as deciding whether to publish, withdraw, postpone or alter content, are barred. . . . Congress' purpose in providing the §230 immunity was thus evident. Interactive computer services have millions of users. The amount of information communicated via interactive computer services is therefore staggering. The specter of tort liability in an area of such prolific speech would have an obvious chilling effect. It would be impossible for service providers to screen each of their millions of postings for possible problems. Faced with potential liability for each message republished by their services, interactive computer service providers might choose to severely restrict the number and type of messages posted. Congress considered the weight of the speech interests implicated and chose to immunize service providers to avoid any such restrictive effect.[4]

What if the defamatory speech is posted not by an anonymous Internet user but by a paid contributor to the Internet service provider? Does the ISP become liable? For a full discussion of this rapidly evolving area, see Chapter 42 on cyberlaw. ◆

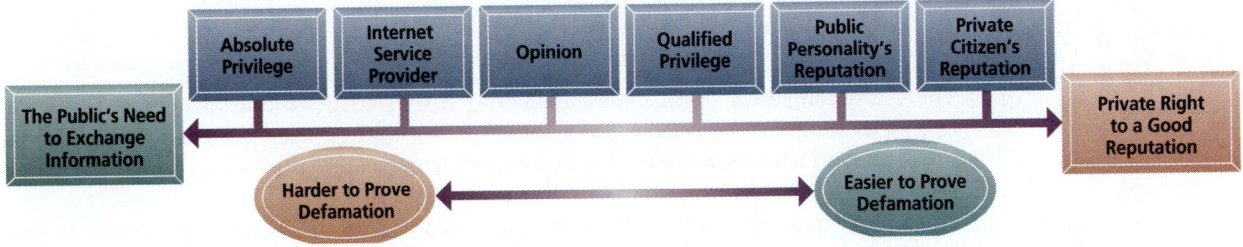

Defamation cases show a tension between the public's need for information and a citizen's right to protect his reputation.

---

4   *Zeran v. America Online, Inc.*, 129 F.3d 327, 1997 U.S. App. LEXIS 31791 (4th Cir. 1997).

How much discretion should we permit in false imprisonment cases?

Privilege

Defendants receive additional protection from defamation cases when it is important for them to speak freely. **Absolute privilege** exists in courtrooms and legislative hearings. Anyone speaking there, such as a witness in court, can say anything at all and never be sued for defamation. If Walter testifies that Ernestine had insider knowledge when she traded stock, he cannot be sued for slander even if he is wrong. (If the testimony is false and Walter knows it, that would be perjury, but still not slander.) Courts extend an absolute privilege in those few instances when candor is essential to a functioning democracy.

Qualified privilege exists when two people have a legitimate need to exchange information. Suppose Trisha Tenant lives in a housing project. She honestly believes that her neighbor is selling guns illegally. She reports this to the manager of the project, who investigates and discovers the guns were toys, being sold legally. The report was false but Trisha is not liable for slander. As long as Trisha acts in good faith and talks only to someone who ought to know about the activity, she is protected by qualified privilege.

False Imprisonment

False imprisonment is the intentional restraint of another person without reasonable cause and without consent. Suppose a bank teller becomes seriously ill and wants to go to the doctor, but the bank will not permit her to leave until she makes a final tally of her accounts. Against her wishes, company officials physically bar her from leaving the bank. That is false imprisonment. The restraint was unreasonable because her accounts could have been verified later.[5]

False imprisonment cases most commonly arise in retail stores, which sometimes detain employees or customers for suspected theft. Most states now have statutes governing the detention of suspected shoplifters. **Generally, a store may detain a customer or worker for alleged shoplifting provided there is a reasonable basis for the suspicion and the detention is done reasonably.** To detain a customer in the manager's office for 20 minutes and question him about where he got an item is lawful. To chain that customer to a display counter for three hours and humiliate him in front of other customers is unreasonable, and false imprisonment.

at RISK

Assume that you are a junior vice president of a chain of 15 retail clothing stores, all located in your state. The president has asked you to outline a sensible plan, to be given to all employees, for dealing with suspected shoplifters. Here are some ideas to consider:

- There are competing social values. Shoplifting is very costly to our society, causing businesses to lose anywhere from $5 billion to $25 billion annually. On the other hand, no one wants to shop in a "police state" environment.

---

5   *Kanner v. First National Bank of South Miami*, 287 So. 2d 715, 1974 Fla. App. LEXIS 8989 (Fla. Dist. Ct. App. 1974).

- What is a "reasonable" suspicion of shoplifting? What if a clerk sees a customer hurry out, wearing a sweater identical to those on display? Must the clerk have seen the customer pick up the sweater? Put it on?

- What is "reasonable" detention? Can you tackle someone running through the parking lot? Can you shoot him?

- How much questioning do you want to do, and how much would you prefer to leave to police?

- Some people in our society are biased against others, based on race or gender, while others are entirely free of such prejudices. How do you take that into account?

- Some states have passed "civil fine" statutes, which allow stores to demand, in writing, a fine from the shoplifter of up to three times the value of the goods taken. Often the shoplifter pays up immediately to avoid criminal prosecution. Should you lobby the state legislature to pass such a statute?

There are no perfect answers to these questions, but a manager clearly needs to consider them and to craft an approach that meets the legal standard: reasonable suspicion of shoplifting and reasonable detention. ◆

Intentional Infliction of Emotional Distress

What should happen when a defendant's conduct hurts a plaintiff emotionally but not physically? Historically, not much did happen. Courts once refused to allow recovery, assuming that if they awarded damages for mere emotional injury, they would be inviting a floodgate of dubious claims. But gradually judges reexamined their thinking and reversed this tendency. The law of emotional distress has been upsetting people ever since. Today, most courts allow a plaintiff to recover for emotional injury that a defendant intentionally caused. As we see in the next chapter, some courts will also permit recovery when a defendant's *negligent* conduct caused the emotional injury.

The intentional infliction of emotional distress results from extreme and outrageous conduct that causes serious emotional harm. A credit officer was struggling vainly to locate Sheehan, who owed money on his car. The officer phoned Sheehan's mother, falsely identified herself as a hospital employee, and said she needed to find Sheehan because his children had been in a serious auto accident. The mother provided Sheehan's whereabouts, which enabled the company to seize his car. But Sheehan spent seven hours frantically trying to locate his supposedly injured children, who in fact were fine. The credit company was liable for the intentional infliction of emotional distress.[6]

By contrast, a muffler shop, trying to collect a debt from a customer, made six phone calls over three months, using abusive language. The customer testified that this caused her to be upset, to cry, and to have difficulty sleeping. The court ruled that the muffler shop's conduct was neither extreme nor outrageous and sent the customer home for another sleepless night.[7] The following case arose in a setting that guarantees controversy—an abortion clinic.

---

[6]   *Ford Motor Credit Co. v. Sheehan*, 373 So. 2d 956, 1979 Fla. App. LEXIS 15416 (Fla. Dist. Ct. App. 1979).
[7]   *Midas Muffler Shop v. Ellison*, 133 Ariz. 194, 650 P.2d 496, 1982 Ariz. App. LEXIS 488 (Ariz. Ct. App. 1982).

JANE DOE AND NANCY ROE V. LYNN MILLS

212 Mich. App. 73, 536 N.W.2d 824, 1995 Mich. App. LEXIS 313
Michigan Court of Appeals, 1995

Facts: Late one night, an anti-abortion protestor named Robert Thomas climbed into a dumpster located behind the Women's Advisory Center, an abortion clinic. He found documents indicating that the plaintiffs were soon to have abortions at the clinic. Thomas gave the information to Lynn Mills. The next day, Mills and Sister Lois Mitoraj created signs, using the women's names, indicating that they were about to undergo abortions, and urging them not to "kill their babies."

Doe and Roe (not their real names) sued, claiming intentional infliction of emotional distress (as well as breach of privacy, discussed later in this chapter). The trial court dismissed the lawsuit, ruling that the defendants' conduct was not extreme and outrageous. The plaintiffs appealed.

Issue: Have the plaintiffs made a valid claim of intentional infliction of emotional distress?

Excerpts from the Court's *Per Curiam* Decision: Liability for the intentional infliction of emotional distress has been found only where the conduct complained of has been so outrageous in character, and so extreme in degree, as to go beyond all possible bounds of decency, and to be regarded as atrocious and utterly intolerable in a civilized community. Liability does not extend to mere insults, indignities, threats, annoyances, petty oppressions, or other trivialities. It has been said that the case is generally one in which the recitation of the facts to an average member of the community would arouse his resentment against the actor, and lead him to exclaim, "Outrageous!"

The conduct in this case involved defendants identifying plaintiffs by name and publicizing the fact of their abortions by displaying such information on large signs that were held up for public view.

In ruling that defendants' conduct was not sufficiently extreme and outrageous so as to permit recovery, the trial court was influenced in part by its conclusion that the information disclosed did not concern a private matter, inasmuch as it was obtained from a document that had been discarded into the trash. [But the plaintiffs themselves never placed their names on the discarded papers, and even if they had, such an act would not have indicated consent to such publicity.] The trial court also observed that defendants have a constitutional right to "protest peaceably against abortion." However, the objectionable aspect of defendants' conduct does not relate to their views on abortion or their right to express those views, but, rather, to the fact that defendants gave unreasonable or unnecessary publicity to purely private matters involving plaintiffs. Finally, the trial court observed that there is no statute prohibiting the kind of activity engaged in by defendants. It is not necessary, however, that a defendant's conduct constitute a statutory violation in order for it to be found extreme and outrageous.

We are of the opinion that the trial court erred in granting the defendants' motion for summary disposition of plaintiffs' claim of intentional infliction of emotional distress. Defendants' conduct involved more than mere insults, indignities, threats, annoyances, or petty oppressions. We believe this is the type of case that might cause an average member of the community, upon learning of defendants' conduct, to exclaim, "Outrageous!" Because reasonable men may differ with regard to whether defendants' conduct may be considered sufficiently outrageous and extreme so as to subject them to liability for intentional infliction of emotional distress, this matter should be determined by the trier of fact.

[Summary judgment for the defendants is reversed, and the case is remanded for trial.] ■

Battery and Assault

These two torts are related, but not identical. **Battery is an intentional touching of another person in a way that is unwanted or offensive.** As mentioned earlier, there need be no intention to *hurt* the plaintiff. If the defendant intended to do the physical act, and a reasonable plaintiff would be offended by it, battery has occurred.

Suppose an irate parent throws a chair at a referee during his daughter's basketball game, breaking the man's jaw. It is irrelevant that the father did not intend to injure the referee. But a parent who cheerfully slaps the winning coach on the back has not committed battery, because a reasonable coach would not be offended. An executive who gives an unwanted sexual caress to a secretary also commits this tort, even if he assumed that any normal female would be ecstatic over his attentions. (This is also sexual harassment, discussed in Chapter 30, on employment law.)

Assault occurs when a defendant does some act that makes a plaintiff fear an imminent battery. It is assault even though the battery never occurs. Suppose Ms. Wilson shouts "Think fast!" at her husband and hurls a toaster at him. He turns and sees it flying at him. His fear of being struck is enough to win a case of assault, even if the toaster misses. If the toaster happens to strike him, Ms. Wilson has also committed battery.

Recall the shoplifting problem. Assume that a store guard pulls an unloaded pistol on Sandra Shopper, suspecting her of theft. Sandra faints and strikes her head on a counter. When sued for assault, the store defends by claiming the guard never touched her and the gun was unloaded. Obviously, the store did not have the benefit of this law course. A reasonable shopper would have feared imminent battery, and the store is liable for assault.

Trespass, Conversion, and Fraud

Trespass

Trespass is intentionally entering land that belongs to someone else or remaining on the land after being asked to leave. It is also trespass if you have some object, let's say a car, on someone else's property and refuse to remove it. "Intentionally" means that you deliberately walk onto the land. If you walk through a meadow, believing it to be a public park, and it belongs to a private owner, you have trespassed.

This shows that the law strongly values the rights of private property owners. How strongly? Heather installs a springloaded rifle in her house, aimed at the front door and tripped by a wire connected to the door. Bruno breaks in at night, planning to steal, and is shot. Bruno, now serving time for breaking and entering, sues. Is Heather liable? In many states, no, she is not. Many courts hold that a homeowner may use a springloaded rifle to prevent a major felony, like entering a dwelling at night.[8]

Ethics

A few states disagree. Saying that we should not place a higher value on property than on human life, they make it unlawful to install a springloaded rifle. Who are the stakeholders? Which values are in conflict? Do the reasonable fear and anger of a homeowner justify a springloaded weapon, even if it costs a human life? Should it matter whether the home is occupied? That is, should a homeowner be entitled to set up such a weapon in her vacation home, even when she is hundreds of miles away? What if someone entered the home for an innocent reason, seeking shelter from a storm or intending to repair a gas leak?   ◆

Conversion

Conversion is taking or using someone's personal property without consent. Personal property is any possession other than land. Priceless jewels, ratty sneakers, and a

---

8   See, e.g., Restatement (Second) of Torts §85, permitting springloaded weapons wherever an actor himself could have used deadly force were he present, which, according to §143, includes defending a home from a breaking and entering during the nighttime. Compare the opposite result in *Katko v. Briney,* 183 N.W.2d 657, 1971 Iowa Sup. LEXIS 717 (Iowa 1971).

sailboat are all personal property. If Stormy sails away in Jib's sailboat and keeps it all summer, that is conversion. Stormy owes Jib the full value of the boat. This, of course, is similar to the crime of theft. The tort of conversion enables a plaintiff to pursue the case herself, without awaiting a criminal prosecution, and to obtain compensation.

Fraud

Fraud is injuring another person by deliberate deception. It is fraud to sell real estate knowing that there is a large toxic waste deposit underground of which the buyer is ignorant. Later in this chapter, a plaintiff claims that for many years a cigarette manufacturer fraudulently suggested its product was safe, knowing its assurances were deadly lies. Fraud is a tort, but it typically occurs during the negotiation or performance of a contract, and it is discussed in detail in Unit 2, on contracts.

DAMAGES

Compensatory Damages

Mitchel Bien, who is deaf and mute, enters the George Grubbs Nissan dealership, where folks sell cars aggressively. *Very* aggressively. Maturelli, a salesman, and Bien communicate by writing messages back and forth. Maturelli takes Bien's own car keys, and the two then test drive a 300ZX. Bien says he does not want the car, but Maturelli escorts him back inside and fills out a sales sheet. Bien repeatedly asks for his keys, but Maturelli only laughs, pressuring him to buy the new car. Minutes pass. Hours pass. Bien becomes frantic, writing a dozen notes, begging to leave, threatening to call the police. Maturelli mocks Bien and his physical disabilities. Finally, after four hours, the customer escapes.

Bien sues for the intentional infliction of emotional distress. Two former salesmen from Grubbs testify they have witnessed customers cry, yell, and curse as a result of the aggressive tactics. Doctors state that the incident has traumatized Bien, dramatically reducing his confidence and self-esteem and preventing his return to work even three years later.

The jury awards Bien damages. But how does a jury calculate the money? For that matter, why should a jury even try? Money can never erase pain or undo a permanent injury. The answer is simple: money, however inexact and ineffective, is the only thing a court has to give.

A successful plaintiff generally receives **compensatory damages,** meaning an amount of money that the court believes will restore him to the position he was in before the defendant's conduct caused injury. Here is how damages are figured.

First, a plaintiff receives money for medical expenses that he has proven by producing bills from doctors, hospitals, physical therapists, and psychotherapists. Bien receives all the money he has paid. If a doctor testifies that he needs future treatment, Bien will offer evidence of how much that will cost. The **single recovery principle** requires a court to settle the matter once and for all, by awarding a lump sum for past and future expenses. A plaintiff may not return in a year and say, "Oh, by the way, there are some new bills."

Second, the defendants are liable for lost wages. The court takes the number of days or months that Bien missed work and multiplies that times his salary. If Bien is currently unable to work, a doctor estimates how many more months he will miss work, and the court adds that to his damages.

Third, a plaintiff is paid for pain and suffering. Bien testifies about how traumatic the four hours were and how the experience has affected his life. He may state that he now fears shopping, suffers nightmares, and seldom socializes. To bolster the case, a plaintiff uses expert testimony, such as the psychiatrists who testified for Bien. Awards for pain and suffering vary enormously, from a few dollars to many millions, depending on the injury and depending on the jury. In some lawsuits, physical and psychological pain are momentary and insignificant; in other cases, the pain is the biggest part of the verdict. In this case, the jury awarded Bien $573,815, calculated as in the following table.[9]

Past medical	$ 70.00
Future medical	6,000.00
Past rehabilitation	3,205.00
Past lost earning capacity	112,910.00
Future lost earning capacity	34,650.00
Past physical symptoms and discomfort	50,000.00
Future physical symptoms and discomfort	50,000.00
Past emotional injury and mental anguish	101,980.00
Future emotional injury and mental anguish	200,000.00
Past loss of society and reduced ability to socially interact with family, former fiancee, and friends, and hearing (i.e., nondeaf) people in general	10,000.00
Future loss of society and reduced ability to socially interact with family, former fiancee, and friends, and hearing people	5,000.00
TOTAL	$573,815.00

Punitive Damages

Here we look at a different kind of award, one that is more controversial and potentially more powerful: punitive damages. The purpose is not to compensate the plaintiff for harm, because compensatory damages will have done that. **Punitive damages are intended to punish the defendant for conduct that is extreme and outrageous.** Courts award these damages in relatively few cases. When an award of punitive damages is made, it is generally in a case of intentional tort, although they occasionally appear in negligence suits.

---

[9] The compensatory damages are described in *George Grubbs Enterprises v. Bien*, 881 S.W.2d 843, 1994 Tex. App. LEXIS 1870 (Tex. Ct. App. 1994). In addition to the compensatory damages described, the jury awarded $5 million in punitive damages. The Texas Supreme Court reversed the award of punitive damages, but not the compensatory. *Id.*, 900 S.W.2d 337, 1995 Tex. LEXIS 91 (Tex. 1995). The high court did not dispute the appropriateness of punitive damages, but reversed because the trial court failed to instruct the jury properly as to how it should determine the assets actually under the defendants' control, an issue essential to punitive damages but not compensatory.

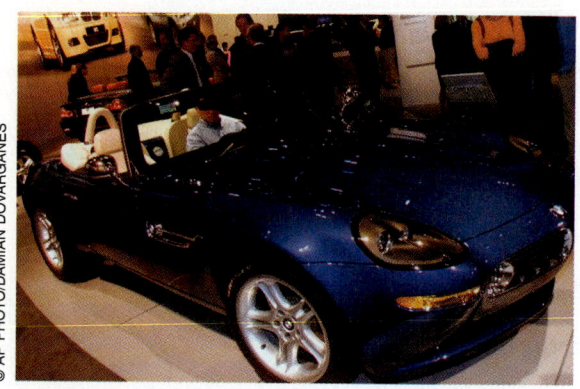

Do you need to know everything about your new car?

The idea behind punitive damages is that certain behavior is so unacceptable that society must make an example of it. A large award of money should deter the defendant from repeating the mistake and others from ever making it. This is social engineering in an extreme form. Predictably, some believe punitive damages represent the law at its most avaricious while others attribute to them great social benefit.

Although a jury has wide discretion in awarding punitive damages, the Supreme Court has ruled that a verdict must be reasonable. Ira Gore purchased a new BMW automobile from an Alabama dealer and then discovered that the car had been repainted. He sued. At trial, BMW acknowledged a nationwide policy of not informing customers of predelivery repairs when the cost was less than 3 percent of the retail price. The company had sold about 1,000 repainted cars nationwide. The jury concluded that BMW had engaged in gross, malicious fraud and awarded Gore $4,000 in compensatory damages and $4 million in punitive damages. The Alabama Supreme Court reduced the award to $2 million, but the United States Supreme Court ruled that even that amount was grossly excessive. The Court held that in awarding punitive damages, a court must consider three "guideposts":

- The reprehensibility of the defendant's conduct
- The ratio between the harm suffered and the award; and
- The difference between the punitive award and any civil penalties used in similar cases.

The Court concluded that BMW had shown no evil intent and that Gore's harm had been purely economic (as opposed to physical). Further, the Court found the ratio of 500 to 1, between punitive and compensatory damages, to be excessive, although it offered no definitive rule about a proper ratio. On remand, the Alabama Supreme Court reduced the punitive damages award to $50,000.[10] The U.S. Supreme Court has refused to provide a definitive ratio between compensatory and punitive damages, but has given additional guidance to lower courts:

- A trial court generally should not permit a punitive award more than nine times greater than the compensatory damages.
- The trial court may not use the defendant's wealth as an excuse to award an unreasonably high award.

When an insurance company intentionally deceived a vulnerable married couple, a Utah jury was so outraged it awarded $1 million compensatory and $145 million punitive damages. The Supreme Court reversed, ruling that the pair had suffered only economic harm and that the 145:1 ratio was irrational and intolerable.[11] Despite the Supreme Court guidelines, dramatic cases may still lead to very large awards, as the following case illustrates.

---

[10] *BMW of North America, Inc. v. Gore,* 517 U.S. 559, 116 S. Ct. 1589, 1996 U.S. LEXIS 3390 (1996).
[11] *State Farm Mutual Automobile Insurance Co. v. Campbell,* 538 U.S. 408, 123 S. Ct. 1513, 2003 WL 1791206 (2003).

WILLIAMS V. PHILIP MORRIS INCORPORATED

93 Or. App. 527, 92 P.3d 126
Court of Appeals of Oregon, 2004

Facts: Jesse Williams smoked three packs of Marlboros a day—and died of lung cancer. Philip Morris sold Marlboros, and controlled about one-half the cigarette market in the United States. Mayola Williams, Jesse's widow, sued the tobacco company, claiming fraud. She argued that for decades Philip Morris knew its cigarettes were addictive and knew they caused illness and death, but deceived the public to boost its profits. The jury awarded her $21,485 in economic damages, $800,000 in pain and suffering—and $79.5 million in punitive damages. Then the Supreme Court established the guidelines described above, and the case was sent back to the Oregon appellate court for reconsideration.

Issue: Was the punitive damage award excessive?

Excerpts from Judge Edmonds's Decision: [Jesse Williams] was highly addicted to tobacco, both physiologically and psychologically. Although, at the urging of his wife and children, he made several attempts to stop smoking, each time he failed, in part because of his addiction. When his family told him that cigarettes were dangerous to his health, he replied that the cigarette companies would not sell them if they were as dangerous as his family claimed. When one of his sons tried to get him to read articles about the dangers of smoking, he responded by finding published assertions that cigarette smoking was not dangerous. However, when Williams learned that he had inoperable lung cancer he felt betrayed, stating "those darn cigarette people finally did it. They were lying all the time." He died about six months after his diagnosis.

The jury could have found the following facts from the evidence before it. Defendant sold a product that it knew would cause death or serious injury to its customers when they used it as defendant intended them to use it. Despite that knowledge, defendant, together with the rest of the tobacco industry, engaged in an extensive campaign to convince smokers that the issue of cigarette safety was unresolved. It insisted that more research was necessary at the very time that it was carefully avoiding doing the very research for which it called, although it had an extensive program of research into other issues. Rather, it used its research to determine the optimum dose of nicotine in each cigarette, knowing of, but publicly denying, nicotine's highly addictive properties. Defendant also knew that, because of those addictive properties, it would be

difficult for smokers to quit smoking, and it relied on its fraudulent message to discourage them from doing so. The result, as defendant hoped, was that addicted smokers remained addicted and purchased more of its product. In short, defendant used fraudulent means to continue a highly profitable business knowing that, as a result, it would cause death and injury to large numbers of Oregonians.

Defendant's conduct not only shows a reckless disregard of the safety of others but conduct with knowledge that others would be harmed by its actions. Moreover, defendant's fraud was motivated by economic considerations. In other words, the jury could have found that defendant misrepresented the safety of its product for its own pecuniary gain, gain that it would not otherwise have achieved but for the misrepresentation.

We are mindful that the [Supreme Court has declared] that "few awards exceeding a single-digit ratio will satisfy due process." But even if the $79 million award is deemed to exceed a single-digit ratio, it is difficult to conceive of more reprehensible misconduct for a longer duration of time on the part of a supplier of consumer products to the Oregon public than what occurred in this case. We think the unique facts in this case, when compared to the circumstances considered by the Supreme Court and this court in other cases, would justify more than a single-digit award under the Due Process Clause.

Finally, we consider the subject of defendant's wealth and the profitability of its conduct. The evidence was that, at the time of trial, defendant's net worth was over $17 billion and defendant's profit for the most recent year for which figures were available was $1.6 billion. The jury could have found that a large award was necessary in order to punish defendant adequately because it would treat a small award as no more than an insignificant nuisance and part of the cost of doing business.

We conclude that an award of punitive damages in the amount of $79.5 million does not violate the Due Process Clause under the [Supreme Court] guidelines because the amount of the award is reasonable and proportionate to the wrong inflicted on decedent and the public of this state. We reinstate the award of punitive damages as originally found by the jury. ■

Tort Reform

Some people believe that jury awards are excessive and need statutory reform. For example, critics claim that large medical malpractice awards can drive doctors out of business. In medical cases and others, they argue, unrestrained juries harm hospitals, corporations, and communities with massive verdicts. About one-half of the states have passed some limits on tort awards. The laws vary, but many work this way. A jury is permitted to award whatever it considers fair for *economic* damages, meaning lost wages and medical expenses. However, *noneconomic* damages (pain and suffering), together with any punitive award, may not exceed a prescribed limit, such as three times the economic damages, or sometimes a flat cap, such as $250,000 total. These restrictions can drastically lower the total verdict. Congress has proposed and debated similar bills, but thus far none of these federal revisions have been enacted into law.

Opponents consider tort reform misplaced. They offer evidence that medical malpractice costs account for less than 2 percent of our astronomical health care costs. A report on 720 malpractice suits in two allegedly litigious counties showed only six verdicts for plaintiffs, and only one that would have been affected by a cap. Other studies indicate that punitive damages in general are rare and generally modest. One showed, for example, that courts award them in about 6 percent of those cases that plaintiffs win. When compensatory damages are $10,000, punitive damages (when given) average $10,000; when the compensatory award is $100,000, the punitive award, if any, averages $66,000.

Do punitive damages present the revolting specter of money-grubbing lawyers convincing gullible juries to award preposterous verdicts to avaricious clients? Or do they demonstrate that idealistic lawyers, working with no guarantee of a payday,[12] can use the humane instincts of a jury to force callous corporations to consider something other than the fabled bottom line? Is tort reform a necessary step to control runaway juries, or is it a gift to large corporations that do not wish to pay for the harm they cause?

*up*date

Although most plaintiffs never obtain one dollar in punitive damages, the verdicts can be large in toxic tort cases. When Captain Joseph Hazelwood's negligence caused the *Exxon Valdez* to run aground off the coast of Alaska, the ship dumped 11 million gallons of oil into the sea, damaging 3,000 square miles of vulnerable ecosystem. The oil spill forced fishermen into bankruptcy, disrupted entire communities, and killed hundreds of thousands of birds and marine animals. A decade later, many of the damaged species had not recovered. The jury decided that Exxon had been reckless by allowing Hazelwood to pilot the ship when the company knew he was an alcoholic. The jury awarded compensatory damages of $286 million and punitive damages of *$5 billion*. Exxon appealed, claiming that the company had voluntarily spent over $2 billion to clean up the spill and $1.3 billion in civil settlements. The appellate court reversed, declaring the punitive damages excessive under the *BMW* standard, and remanded the case with instructions to set a lower judgment. On remand, the trial court concluded that the harm was so appalling, the entire punitive award ought to be enforced. However, bowing to the appellate court's instructions, the trial judge reluctantly lowered the punitive damages ... to $4.5 billion.[13] Further appeals were certain. What is the status of the case? Do you agree that $5 billion was exorbitant? What *is* a fair figure?   ◆

---

[12] Lawyers normally take personal injury cases on a contingency basis, meaning that they receive no money up-front from their client. Their fee will be a percentage of the plaintiff's judgment *if* she wins. Lawyers often take about one-third of the award. But if the defendant wins, the plaintiff's lawyer will have worked several years for no pay.

[13] *In re the Exxon Valdez*, 296 F. Supp. 2d 1071 (U.S. Dist. Ct., D. Ala, 2004).

ECONOMICS
& the LAW

We know that damages should be based on such issues as medical expenses, lost wages, and so forth. Is it important whether the judge who presided over the trial was elected or appointed? Yes, it probably does matter, according to economists.

Judges are elected in 23 states and appointed in 27. Injured plaintiffs generally sue in the state where they reside; defendants are frequently out-of-state companies. Substantial data indicate that tort damages against out-of-state defendants are much higher in states where judges are elected than they are in states with appointed judges. Why would that be? Elected judges keep their jobs at the pleasure of local voters. A large tort award against a foreign company will bring money into the state. Voters may perceive such a judgment as a valuable redistribution of wealth. Also, elected judges need to raise money to run for office—and lawyers are generally their largest campaign contributors. One study found that in states with elected judges, verdicts against out-of-state defendants averaged $240,000 more than similar verdicts in states with appointed judges.[14] ◆

BUSINESS TORTS

In this section we look at four intentional torts that occur almost exclusively in a commercial setting: interference with a contract, interference with a prospective advantage, the rights to privacy and publicity, and Lanham Act violations. Note that several business torts are discussed elsewhere in the book:

- Patents, copyrights, and trademarks are discussed in Chapter 43, on intellectual property.

- False advertising, discussed in part under the Lanham Act section below, is considered more broadly in Chapter 40, on consumer law.

- Consumer issues are also covered in Chapter 40. The material in the present chapter focuses not on consumer claims but on disputes between businesses.

Tortious Interference with Business Relations

Competition is the essence of business. Successful corporations compete aggressively, and the law permits and expects them to. But there are times when healthy competition becomes illegal interference. This is called tortious interference with business relations. It can take one of two closely related forms—interference with a contract or interference with a prospective advantage.

Tortious Interference with a Contract

Tortious interference with a contract exists only if the plaintiff can establish the following four elements:

- There was a contract between the plaintiff and a third party;
- The defendant knew of the contract;
- The defendant improperly induced the third party to breach the contract or made performance of the contract impossible; and
- There was injury to the plaintiff.

---

[14] Tabarrok and Helland, "Court Politics: The Political Economy of Tort Awards," *Journal of Law and Economics*, 1999, vol. 42, p. 157.

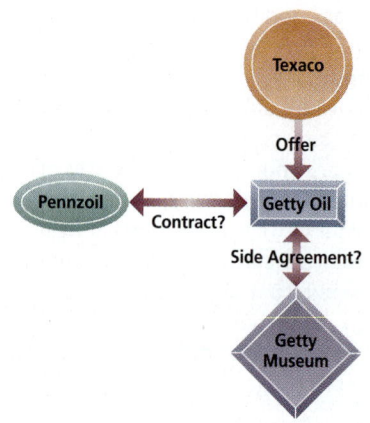

The $10 *billion* question. Texaco offered to pay $125 per share for Getty stock. The key issue was this: When Texaco made the offer, did a contract exist between Pennzoil and Getty? If, as the jury decided, there was a binding agreement, then Texaco committed tortious interference with a contract. If, however, Getty Corp. had a side agreement with the Getty Museum (one of its owners), then arguably there could be no contract between Getty and Pennzoil, and Texaco would have committed no tort at all.

Because businesses routinely compete for customers, employees, and market share, it is not always easy to identify tortious interference. There is nothing wrong with two companies bidding against each other to buy a parcel of land, and nothing wrong with one corporation doing everything possible to convince the seller to ignore all competitors. But once a company has signed a contract to buy the land, it is improper to induce the seller to break the deal. The most commonly disputed issues in these cases concern elements one and three: Was there a contract between the plaintiff and another party? Did the defendant *improperly* induce a party to breach it? Defendants will try to show that the plaintiff had no contract.

A defendant may also rely on the defense of **justification,** that is, a claim that special circumstances made its conduct fair. To establish justification, a defendant must show that:

- It was acting to protect *an existing economic interest*, such as its own contract with the third party

- It was acting in the *public interest*, for example, by reporting to a government agency that a corporation was overbilling for government services; or

- The existing contract could be *terminated* at will by either party, meaning that although the plaintiff had a contract, the plaintiff had no long-term assurances because the other side could end it at any time.

Texaco v. Pennzoil

One of the largest verdicts in the history of American law came in a case of contract interference. *Texaco, Inc. v. Pennzoil Co.* illustrates the two key issues: Did a contract exist, and was the defendant's behavior improper? In December 1983, Pennzoil made an unsolicited bid to buy 20 percent of Getty Oil at $100 per share. This offer was too low to satisfy the Getty board of directors, but it got the parties talking. The price increased to $110 per share, and the two sides began to put together pieces of a complicated deal: Gordon Getty would control four-sevenths of the Getty Oil stock, and Pennzoil would control three-sevenths. The J. Paul Getty Museum, which owned 11.8 percent of Getty stock, agreed to sell its shares *provided it was paid immediately*. Talks continued, the price moved up to $112.50 a share, and finally the Getty board voted to approve the deal. A press release announced an agreement in principle between Pennzoil and Getty.

Before the lawyers for both sides could complete the paperwork for the deal, Texaco appeared and offered Getty stockholders $125 per share for the entire company and later upped that offer to $128. Getty turned its attention to Texaco, leaving Pennzoil the jilted lover. This lover, though, decided to sue. In Texas state court, Pennzoil claimed that Texaco had interfered with a Pennzoil–Getty contract, costing Pennzoil vast amounts of money.

Pennzoil's strategy at trial was to vilify Texaco, depicting every move of the defendant as part of a strategy to wreck the Pennzoil–Getty deal. Texaco argued that there was no malice on its part because in fact there was no binding contract between the other two. All they had was an understanding in principle.

But the jury bought Pennzoil's argument, and they bought it big: $7.53 billion in actual damages, plus $3 billion more in punitive damages. The total of $10.53 billion is one of the highest verdicts in any law case. Texaco did not happen to have $10 billion it could spare, and the verdict threatened to destroy the oil company. Texaco appealed, but Texas appeals courts require a bond, in this case a $10 billion bond, meaning that the money must be paid into court while the appeal goes forward. Instead, Texaco filed for bankruptcy. While Texaco pursued its appeal, the two sides discussed a possible settlement but appeared far apart.

In the state appeals court, Texaco continued to claim that Pennzoil and Getty never had a valid contract. It based its argument on an obscure rule of the Securities and Exchange Commission (SEC), Rule 10B-13. This rule prevents the parties in a takeover negotiation from arranging a "side deal" while an offer is pending. Texaco's argument thus became: Pennzoil's original $100 per share offer was still pending when the two sides came up with their $112.50 per share, "three-sevenths/four-sevenths" deal. That deal involved a side arrangement with the Getty Museum, which would get its money faster than any other shareholders would. Because it would get about $1 billion, early receipt was a major financial advantage. The deal violated Rule 10B-13 and was therefore invalid. There was no contract and Texaco could not legally have interfered.

Pennzoil responded by saying that it had planned all along to equalize any benefits that the Getty Museum got by paying additional money to the other shareholders. Further, said Pennzoil, even if a technical violation of Rule 10B-13 had occurred, Pennzoil would have applied to the SEC and obtained an exemption from the rule. The Court of Appeals in Texas was unpersuaded by most of Texaco's arguments. The court did lower the punitive damages by $2 billion, but it otherwise affirmed. The court did not accept the argument that Rule 10B-13 destroyed the contract.

Texaco appealed to the Texas Supreme Court, all the while continuing to negotiate with Pennzoil over a possible settlement. Texaco decided to concentrate its final appeal on the Rule 10B-13 argument. In other words, a $10 billion case would be decided on the classic "interference" issue of whether a contract existed. Texaco spent months trying to convince the SEC to enter the case and explain to the Texas Supreme Court precisely what the little-known rule meant. Texaco received a huge boost when the SEC announced that it would in fact file a brief in the case. The brief it wrote seemed strongly to advance Texaco's argument. Pennzoil could sense that the tide was turning. And so, in December 1987, Pennzoil announced that the two parties had reached an agreement: Texaco would pay Pennzoil $3 billion as settlement for having wrongfully interfered with Pennzoil's agreement to buy Getty.

Tortious Interference with a Prospective Advantage

"Interference with a prospective advantage" is an awkward name for a tort that is simply a variation on interference with a contract. The difference is that, for this tort, there need be no contract; the plaintiff is claiming outside interference with an expected economic relationship. Obviously, the plaintiff must show more than just the hope of a profit. **A plaintiff who has a definite and reasonable expectation of obtaining an economic advantage may sue a corporation that maliciously interferes and prevents the relationship from developing.**

The defense of justification, discussed above, applies here as well. A typical example of justification is that the defendant is simply competing for the same business that the plaintiff seeks. There is nothing wrong with that.

To demonstrate interference with a prospective advantage, most courts require a plaintiff to show that the defendant's conduct was *independently* unlawful. Suppose Pink manufactures valves used in heart surgery. Pink is about to sign a deal for Rabbit to distribute the products. Zebra then says to Pink, "*I* want that deal. If you sign with Rabbit, I'll spread false rumors that the valves are unreliable." Pink gives in and signs a contract with Zebra. Zebra has committed interference with a prospective advantage because slander is independently illegal.[15] The ice cream fight that follows demonstrates why plaintiffs often file but seldom win these cases.

CARVEL V. NOONAN

3 N.Y. 3d 182, 785 N.Y.S.2d 359, 818 N.E.2d 1100
New York Court of Appeals, 2004

Facts: For decades, Carvel sold its ice cream only through franchised stores. However, a decline in revenues caused the company to begin selling its product in supermarkets. That effort expanded quickly, but many of the franchised stores (franchisees) went out of business. Franchisees filed suit, claiming tortious interference with a prospective advantage. In particular, the plaintiffs argued that Carvel undersold them in supermarkets, and issued coupons only redeemable there. The case reached New York's highest court.

Issue: Had Carvel committed tortious interference with a prospective advantage?

Excerpts from Justice Smith's Decision: The franchisees' tort claim is that Carvel unlawfully interfered with the relationships between the franchisees and their customers. The franchisees do not claim that the customers had binding contracts that Carvel induced them to breach; they allege only that, by implementing its supermarket program, Carvel induced the customers not to buy Carvel products from the franchisees. The juries have found that Carvel did so induce customers, and the question for us is whether that inducement was tortious interference under New York law.

We have recognized that inducing breach of a binding agreement and interfering with a nonbinding "economic relation" can both be torts, but that the elements of the two torts are not the same. Where there has been no breach of an existing contract, but only interference with prospective contract rights, however, plaintiff must show more culpable conduct on the part of the defendant. The implication is that, as a general rule, the defendant's conduct must amount to a crime or an independent tort.

The franchisees claim that Carvel did use wrongful "economic pressure" but that argument is ill-founded for two independent reasons. First, it is ill-founded because the economic pressure that must be shown is not, as the franchisees assume, pressure on the franchisees, but on the franchisees' customers. Conduct constituting tortious interference with business relations is, by definition, conduct directed not at the plaintiff itself, but at the party with which the plaintiff has or seeks to have a relationship.

Here, all Carvel did to the franchisees' customers was to make Carvel goods available in supermarkets at attractive prices; this was not "pressure" on these third parties but legitimate "persuasion," and thus tortious interference with economic relations was not established.

The franchisees' argument is also ill-founded because the Carvel activities they complain of do not amount to the sort of extreme and unfair "economic pressure" that might be "wrongful." The crux of the franchisees' complaint is that Carvel distributed its products through competitive channels, to an extent and in a way that was inconsistent with the franchisor-franchisee relationship. But the relationship between franchisors and franchisees is a complex

▼

---

[15] For a more detailed explanation, see *Wal-Mart Stores, Inc. v. Sturges*, 52 S.W.3d 711, 2001 Tex. LEXIS 18 (Tex. 2001).

one; while cooperative, it does not preclude all competition; and the extent to which competition is allowed should be determined by the contracts between the parties, not by courts or juries seeking after the fact to devise a code of conduct.

Apart from attacking the supermarket program in general as excessively and destructively competitive, the franchisees also attack the coupon-redemption element of that program as excessive "economic pressure." The essence of the coupon program was to give customers who used coupons a better price when they shopped in supermarkets. The mere institution of a coupon program was not "economic pressure" rising to the level of "wrongful" or "culpable" conduct.

[Carvel's conduct was not tortious interference with a prospective advantage.] ∎

Privacy and Publicity

We live in a world of dazzling technology, and it is easier than ever—and more profitable—to spy on someone. For example, the Web page http://www.thesmokinggun.com specializes in publishing revealing data about celebrities. Does the law protect us? What power do we have to limit the intrusion of others into our lives and to prohibit them from commercially exploiting information about us?

Intrusion

Intrusion into someone's private life is a tort if a reasonable person would find it offensive. Peeping through someone's windows or wiretapping his telephone are obvious examples of intrusion. In a famous case involving a "paparazzo" photographer and Jacqueline Kennedy Onassis, the court found that the photographer had invaded her privacy by making a career out of photographing her. He had bribed doormen to gain access to hotels and restaurants she visited, had jumped out of bushes to photograph her young children, and had driven power boats dangerously close to her. The court ordered him to stop.[16] Nine years later the paparazzo was found in contempt of court for again taking photographs too close to Ms. Onassis. He agreed to stop once and for all—in exchange for a suspended contempt sentence.

cyberLaw

Robert Konop, a pilot for Hawaiian Airlines, was distressed with the demands his company was making on employees, and also with his union's response. On a private Web site he criticized both parties and urged fellow pilots to switch to a different union. Konop gave his colleagues passwords to the site, while denying access to management and union officials. Hawaiian Airlines Vice-President James Davis surreptitiously visited the site by using the name and password of two pilots, with their consent. Davis entered the site at least 20 times in this fashion. Konop sued, claiming a violation of two important statutes:

- The **Electronic Communications Privacy Act,** which prohibits the unauthorized interception or disclosure of wire and electronic communications;[17] and

- The **Stored Communications Act,** which prohibits unauthorized access to a facility through which an electronic service is provided.[18]

The district court dismissed the claims, but the appellate court reversed, holding that Konop had raised legitimate—and novel—issues under both statutes. He deserved a trial to demonstrate that Davis had in fact violated these two laws.[19]

---

[16]   *Galella v. Onassis,* 487 F.2d 986, 1973 U.S. App. LEXIS 7901 (2d Cir. 1973).
[17]   18 U.S.C. § 2511.
[18]   18 U.S.C. § 2701.
[19]   *Konop v. Hawaiian Airlines, Inc.,* 236 F.3d 1035, 2001 U.S. App. LEXIS 191 (9th Cir. 2001).

The explosive growth of electronic commerce inevitably fosters a burgeoning docket of novel litigation. For a more detailed look at the statutes and issues involved, see Chapter 42 on cyberlaw. ◆

Commercial Exploitation

This right prohibits the use of someone's likeness or voice for commercial purposes. This business tort is the flip side of privacy and covers the right to make money from publicity. For example, it would be illegal to run a magazine ad showing actress Gwyneth Paltrow holding a can of soda, without her permission. The ad would imply that she endorses the product. Someone's identity is her own, and it cannot be exploited unless she permits it. Ford Motor Co. hired a singer to imitate Bette Midler's version of a popular song. The imitation was so good that most listeners were fooled into believing that Ms. Midler was endorsing the product. That, ruled a court, violated her right to commercial exploitation.[20]

The Lanham Act

The Lanham Act, a federal statute, was passed in 1946 and amended in 1988. Section 43(a) of the statute provides broad protection against false statements intended to hurt another business. In order to win a case under this section, a plaintiff must prove three things:

- That the defendants made *false or misleading fact statements* about the plaintiff's business. This could be a false comparative ad, showing the plaintiff's product to be worse than it is, or it could be a misleading ad, which, though literally accurate, is misleading about the defendant's own product.

- That the defendants used the statements *in commercial advertising or promotion.* In order to protect First Amendment rights of free speech, particularly political and social commentary, this act covers only commercial speech. A radio ad for beer could violate the Lanham Act; but a radio ad urging that smoking be abolished in public places is not a commercial statement and cannot violate the act.

- That statements created the *likelihood of harm* to the plaintiff.[21]

"Knock It Off brand food supplement will help you lose weight and gain muscle faster than any competing supplement," says the excited television commercial. A sculpted muscle-man flexes his pecs as the voice continues, "In tests with five leading competitors, Knock It Off users lost more pounds and added more strength than users of any other food supplement." A graph then shows that Knock It Off users did at least 30 percent better than users of the named competitors. Executives at CrunchTime supplement are unhappy when Knock It Off knocks CrunchTime out of the market lead. CrunchTime also believes the tests are fraudulent, and it sues.

At trial, the evidence indicates that Knock It Off did test its product against all others. An independent testing company established five groups of 100 supplement eaters, then weighed them all and measured them for strength, before and after the testing period. But during the test, Knock It Off offered all 100 of its users certain benefits: free use of a health club with a personal trainer, and three low-fat gourmet meals per day for the entire family. None of the other groups received such benefits. At the end of the trial period, the Knock It Off group was healthier. But at the end of the *trial,* CrunchTime is healthier—period.

---

[20] *Midler v. Ford Motor Co.,* 849 F.2d 460, 1988 U.S. App. LEXIS 8424 (9th Cir. 1988).
[21] 15 U.S.C. § 1125.

Knock It Off has violated the Lanham Act. The television commercial was literally true because Knock It Off users did better than those who took the competing products. But the ads were misleading because viewers were never told about the extra benefits that one group received. The court issues an injunction, prohibiting Knock It Off from showing the commercial, and also awards damages, based on the profits CrunchTime lost.

© PHOTODISC/GETTY IMAGES

Chapter Conclusion

This chapter has been a potpourri of sin, a bubbling cauldron of conduct best avoided. Although tortious acts and their consequences are diverse, two generalities apply. First, the boundaries of intentional torts are imprecise, the outcome of a particular case depending to a considerable extent upon the factfinder who analyzes it. Second, the thoughtful executive and the careful citizen, aware of the shifting standards and potentially vast liability, will strive to ensure that his or her conduct never provides that factfinder an opportunity to give judgment.

Chapter Review

1. A tort is a violation of a duty imposed by the civil law.

2. Defamation involves a defamatory statement that is false, uttered to a third person, and causes an injury. Opinion and privilege are valid defenses.

3. Public personalities can win a defamation suit only by proving actual malice.

4. False imprisonment is the intentional restraint of another person without reasonable cause and without consent.

5. The intentional infliction of emotional distress involves extreme and outrageous conduct that causes serious emotional harm.

6. Battery is an intentional touching of another person in a way that is unwanted or offensive. Assault involves an act that makes the plaintiff fear an imminent battery.

7. Compensatory damages are the normal remedy in a tort case. In unusual cases, the court may award punitive damages, not to compensate the plaintiff but to punish the defendant.

8. Tortious interference with business relations involves the defendant harming an existing contract or a prospective relationship that has a definite expectation of success.

9. The related torts of privacy and publicity involve unreasonable intrusion into someone's private life and unfair commercial exploitation by using someone's name, likeness, or voice without permission.

10. The Electronic Communications Privacy Act prohibits the unauthorized interception or disclosure of wire and electronic communications, and the Stored Communications Act bars unauthorized access to a facility through which an electronic service is provided.

11. The Lanham Act prohibits false statements in commercial advertising or promotion.

Practice Test

1. Benzaquin had a radio talk show in Boston. On the program, he complained about an incident earlier in the day, in which state trooper Fleming had stopped his car, apparently for lack of a proper license plate and safety sticker. Even though Benzaquin explained that the license plate had been stolen and the sticker had fallen onto the dashboard, Fleming refused to let him drive the car away, and Benzaquin and his daughter and two young grandsons had to find other transportation. On the show, Benzaquin angrily recounted the incident, then made the

following statements about Fleming and troopers generally: "arrogants wearing trooper's uniforms like tights"; "little monkey, you wind him up and he does his thing"; "we're not paying them to be dictators and Nazis"; "this man is an absolute barbarian, a lunkhead, a meathead." Fleming sued Benzaquin for defamation. Comment.

2. You are a vice-president in charge of personnel at a large manufacturing company. In-house detectives inform you that Gates, an employee, was seen stealing valuable computer equipment. Gates denies the theft, but you believe the detectives and fire him. The detectives suggest that you post notices around the company, informing all employees what happened to Gates and why. This will discourage others from stealing. While you think that over, a phone call from another company's personnel officer asks for a recommendation for Gates. Should you post the notices? What should you say to the other officer?

3. Caldwell was shopping in a K-Mart store, carrying a large purse. A security guard observed her look at various small items such as stain, hinges, and antenna wire. On occasion she bent down out of sight of the guard. The guard thought he saw Caldwell put something in her purse. Caldwell removed her glasses from her purse and returned them a few times. After she left, the guard approached her in the parking lot and said that he believed she had store merchandise in her pocketbook but was unable to say what he thought was put there. Caldwell opened the purse, and the guard testified he saw no K-Mart merchandise in it. The guard then told Caldwell to return to the store with him. They walked around the store for approximately 15 minutes, while the guard said six or seven times that he saw her put something in her purse. Caldwell left the store after another store employee indicated she could go. Caldwell sued. What kind of suit did she file, and what should the outcome be?

4. Fifteen-year-old Terri Stubblefield was riding in the back seat of a Ford Mustang II when the car was hit from behind. The Mustang was engulfed in a ball of fire, and Terri was severely burned. She died. Terri's family sued Ford, alleging that the car was badly designed—and that Ford knew it. At trial, Terri's family introduced evidence that Ford knew the fuel tank was dangerous and that it could have taken measures to make the

tank safe. There was evidence that Ford consciously decided not to remedy the fuel tanks in order to save money. The family sought two different kinds of damages from Ford. What were they?

5. **ETHICS** In the *Stubblefield* case in Question 4, the jury awarded $8 million in punitive damages to the family. Ford appealed. Should the punitive damages be affirmed? What are the obligations of a corporation when it knows one of its products may be dangerous? Is an automobile company ethically obligated to make a *totally safe* car? Should we require a manufacturer to improve the safety of its cars if doing so will make them too expensive for many drivers? What would you do if you were a mid-level executive and saw evidence that your company was endangering the lives of consumers to save money? What would you do if you were on a *jury* and saw such evidence?

6. Tata Consultancy of Bombay, India, is an international computer consulting firm. It spends considerable time and effort recruiting the best personnel from India's leading technical schools. Tata employees sign an initial three-year employment commitment, often work overseas, and agree to work for a specified additional time when they return to India. Desai worked for Tata, but then quit and formed a competing company, which he called Syntel. His new company contacted Tata employees by phone, offering more money to come work for Syntel, bonuses, and assistance in obtaining permanent resident visas in the United States. At least 16 former Tata employees left their work without completing their contractual obligations and went to work for Syntel. Tata sued. What did it claim, and what should be the result?

7. Pacific Express began operating as an airline in 1982. It had routes connecting western cities with Los Angeles and San Francisco and by the summer of 1983 was beginning to show a profit. In 1983, United Airlines tried to enter into a cooperative arrangement with Pacific in which United would provide Pacific with passengers for some routes so that United could concentrate on its longer routes. Negotiations failed. Later that year, United expanded its routes to include cities that only Pacific had served. United also increased its service to cities in which the two airlines were already competing. By early 1984,

Pacific Express was unable to compete and sought protection under bankruptcy laws. It also sued United, claiming interference with a prospective advantage. United moved for summary judgment. Comment.

8. ***YOU BE THE JUDGE*** WRITING PROBLEM Johnny Carson was for many years the star of a well-known television show, *The Tonight Show.* For about 20 years, he was introduced nightly on the show with the phrase, "Here's Johnny!" A large segment of the television watching public associated the phrase with Carson. A Michigan corporation was in the business of renting and selling portable toilets. The company chose the name "Here's Johnny Portable Toilets," and coupled the company name with the marketing phrase, "The World's Foremost Commodian." Carson sued, claiming that the company's name and slogan violated his right to commercial exploitation. **Argument for Carson:** The toilet company is deliberately taking advantage of Johnny Carson's good name. He worked hard for decades to build a brilliant career and earn a reputation as a creative, funny, likable performer. No company has the right to use his name, his picture, or anything else closely identified with him, such as the phrase "Here's Johnny." The pun is personally offensive and commercially unfair. **Argument for Here's Johnny Portable Toilets:** Johnny Carson doesn't own his first name. It is available for anyone to use for any purpose. Further, the popular term "john," meaning toilet, has been around much longer than Carson or even television. We are entitled to make any use of it we want. Our corporate name is amusing to cus-

tomers who have never heard of Carson, and we are entitled to profit from our brand recognition.

9. A Quaker State motor oil television commercial stated: "Warning: Up to half of all engine wear can happen when you start your car. At this critical time, tests prove Quaker State 10W-30 flowed faster to all vital parts. In all size engines tested, Quaker State protected faster, so it protected better." In fact, Quaker State's tests showed that its oil did flow much faster. Contrary to expectations, however, this did not translate into reduced engine wear. Castrol, a competing motor oil, sued, seeking an injunction. What law is the suit based on? What does "seeking an injunction" mean in this context? What result?

10. Caudle worked at Betts Lincoln-Mercury dealer. During an office party, many of the employees, including president Betts, were playing with an electric auto condenser, which gave a slight electric shock when touched. Some employees played catch with the condenser. Betts shocked Caudle on the back of his neck and then chased him around, holding the condenser. The shock later caused Caudle to suffer headaches, to pass out, and eventually to require surgery on a nerve in his neck. Even after surgery, Caudle had a slight numbness on one side of his head. He sued Betts for battery. Betts defended by saying that it was all horseplay and that he had intended no injury. Please rule.

11. ***ROLE REVERSAL*** Write a multiple-choice question about defamation in which one and only one element is missing from the plaintiff's case. Choose a set of answers that forces the student to isolate the missing element.

Internet Research Problem

Using the Internet, find a recent case in which a court awarded punitive damages for the intentional tort of either assault, battery, intentional infliction of emotional distress, or false imprisonment. What facts led to the punitive damages award? Make your own award of punitive damages, and then compare your judgment with the court's.

You can find further practice problems at http://beatty.westbuslaw.com or in the Study Guide that accompanies this text.

Negligence and Strict Liability

Party time! A fraternity at the University of Arizona welcomed new members, and the alcohol flowed freely. Several hundred people danced and shrieked and drank, and no one checked for proof of age. A common occurrence—but one that ended tragically. A minor student drove away, intoxicated, and slammed into another car. The other driver, utterly innocent of wrongdoing, was gravely injured.

The drunken student was obviously liable, but his insurance did not cover the huge medical bills. The injured man also sued the fraternity. Should that organization be legally responsible? The question leads to other, similar issues. Should a restaurant that serves alcohol to a minor be liable for harm that the youth might cause? Should the restaurant be responsible for serving an intoxicated adult who causes damage? If you give a party, should you be responsible for any damage caused by your guests?

These are all practical questions—worth considering before you entertain—and moral ones as well. They are typical issues of negligence law. In this contentious area, courts continually face one question: *When someone is injured, how far should responsibility extend?* ■

© IMAGE 100/GETTY IMAGES

NEGLIGENCE

We might call negligence the "unintentional" tort because it concerns harm that arises by accident. A person, or perhaps an organization, does some act, neither intending nor expecting to hurt anyone, yet someone is harmed. Should a court impose liability? The fraternity members who gave the party never wanted—or thought—that an innocent man would suffer terrible damage. But he did. Is it in society's interest to hold the fraternity responsible?

Before we can answer this question, we need some background knowledge. Things go wrong all the time, and people are hurt in large ways and small. Society needs a means of analyzing negligence cases consistently and fairly. We cannot have each court that hears such a lawsuit extend or limit liability based on an emotional response to the facts. One of America's greatest judges, Benjamin Cardozo, offered an analysis more than 75 years ago. His decision still dominates negligence thinking today, so we will let him introduce us to Helen Palsgraf.

PALSGRAF V. LONG ISLAND RAILROAD CO.

248 N.Y. 339, 162 N.E. 99, 1928 N.Y. LEXIS 1269
New York Court of Appeals, 1928

Facts: Ms. Palsgraf was waiting on a railroad platform. As a train began to leave the station, a man carrying a package ran to catch it. He jumped aboard but looked unsteady, so a guard on the car reached out to help him as another guard, on the platform, pushed from behind. The man dropped the package, which struck the tracks and exploded—since it was packed with fireworks. The shock knocked over some heavy scales at the far end of the platform, and one of them struck Palsgraf. She sued the railroad.

The jury found that the guards had acted negligently, and held the railroad liable. The company appealed.

Issue: Assuming the guards did a bad job assisting the passenger, was the railroad liable for the injuries to Ms. Palsgraf?

Excerpts from Justice Cardozo's Decision: The conduct of the defendant's guard, if a wrong in its relation to the holder of the package, was not a wrong in its relation to the plaintiff, standing far away. Relatively to her it was not negligence at all. Nothing in the situation gave notice that the falling package had in it the potency of peril to persons thus removed. Negligence is not actionable unless it involves the invasion of a legally protected interest, the violation of a right. Proof of negligence in the air, so to speak, will not do.

In every instance, before negligence can be predicated of a given act, back of the act must be sought and found a duty to the individual complaining, the observance of which would have averted or avoided the injury. What the plaintiff must show is a "a wrong" to herself; i.e., a violation of her own right, and not merely a wrong to someone else, nor conduct "wrongful" because unsocial.

There was nothing in the situation to suggest to the most cautious mind that the parcel wrapped in newspaper would spread wreckage through the station. If the guard had thrown it down knowingly and willfully, he would not have threatened the plaintiff's safety, so far as appearances could warn him. Liability can be no greater where the act is inadvertent. ∎

To win a negligence case, plaintiff must prove five elements:

- *Duty of Due Care*. The defendant had a duty of due care *to this plaintiff*. This is Judge Cardozo's point.
- *Breach*. The defendant breached her duty.
- *Factual Cause*. The defendant's conduct actually caused the injury.

- *Foreseeable Harm.* It was foreseeable that conduct like the defendant's might cause *this type of harm.*

- *Injury.* The plaintiff has actually been hurt.

Duty of Due Care

The first issue may be the most difficult in all of tort law: Did the defendant have a duty of due care to the injured person? Most courts accept Cardozo's viewpoint. Today, judges draw an imaginary line around the defendant and say that she owes a duty to the people within this circle, but not to those outside it. The test is generally "foreseeability." If the defendant could have foreseen injury to a particular person, she has a duty to him. If she could not have foreseen the harm, there is usually no duty.

Some cases are easy. Suppose Glorious University operates a cafeteria. Does the school have a duty of due care to its diners? Absolutely. Management knows that a grimy kitchen can cause serious illness, so the university has a duty to each of its patrons. On the other hand, assume the school bookstore sells a road map of Greece to a student. During spring break, the student drives recklessly along a narrow country lane in Greece, injuring a farmer. The university could never have foreseen harm to a Greek farmer merely from selling a map, so it never had a duty to the man.

Let us apply these principles to the fraternity case.

HERNANDEZ V. ARIZONA BOARD OF REGENTS

177 Ariz. 244, 866 P.2d 1330, 1994 Ariz. LEXIS 6
Arizona Supreme Court, 1994

Facts: At the University of Arizona, the Epsilon Epsilon chapter of Delta Tau Delta fraternity gave a welcoming party for new members. The fraternity's officers knew that the majority of its members were under the legal drinking age, but permitted everyone to consume alcohol. John Rayner, who was under 21 years of age, left the party. He drove negligently and caused a collision with an auto driven by Ruben Hernandez. At the time of the accident, Rayner's blood alcohol level was .15, exceeding the legal limit. The crash left Hernandez blind, severely brain damaged, and quadriplegic.

Hernandez sued Rayner, who settled the case, based on the amount of his insurance coverage. The victim also sued the fraternity, its officers and national organization, all fraternity members who contributed money to buy alcohol, the university, and others. The trial court granted summary judgment for all defendants and the court of appeals affirmed. Hernandez appealed to the Arizona Supreme Court.

Issue: Did the fraternity and the other defendants have a duty of due care to Hernandez?

Excerpts from Justice Feldman's Decision: Before 1983, this court arguably recognized the common-law rule of non-liability for tavern owners and, presumably, for social hosts. Traditional authority held that when "an able-bodied man" caused harm because of his intoxication, the act from which liability arose was the consuming not the furnishing of alcohol.

However, the common law also provides that:

> One who supplies [a thing] for the use of another whom the supplier knows or has reason to know to be likely because of his youth, inexperience, or otherwise to use it in a manner involving unreasonable risk of physical harm to himself and others is subject to liability for physical harm resulting to them.

We perceive little difference in principle between liability for giving a car to an intoxicated youth and liability for giving drinks to a youth with a car. A growing number of cases have recognized that one of the very hazards that makes it negligent to furnish liquor to a minor is the foreseeable prospect that the [youthful] patron will become drunk and injure himself or others. Accordingly, modern authority has increasingly recognized that one who furnishes

▼

liquor to a minor breaches a common law duty owed to innocent third parties who may be injured.

Furnishing alcohol to underaged drinkers violates numerous statutes. The conduct in question violates well-established common-law principles that recognize a duty to avoid furnishing dangerous items to those known to have diminished capacity to use them safely. We join the majority of other states and conclude that as to Plaintiffs and the public in general, Defendants had a duty of care to avoid furnishing alcohol to underage consumers.

Arizona courts, therefore, will entertain an action for damages against [one] who negligently furnishes alcohol to those under the legal drinking age when that act is a cause of injury to a third person. [Reversed and remanded.] ■

Ethics

As the Arizona court notes, its decision agrees with the majority of courts that have considered the issue. In most (but not all) states, anyone serving alcohol to a minor is liable for injuries that result to a third party. The case raises other important issues. As you examine them, focus on these ethical issues: What are the consequences? Which values are in conflict? Which of these values are most important?

- Should a social host who serves alcohol to an *adult* be liable for resulting harm? New Jersey has answered this question "yes." In the Garden State, if a social host pours drinks for a friend, aware that he is becoming drunk, and the friend injures a third party, the host is fully liable. The great majority of states to consider this issue have reached the opposite conclusion, holding that a social host is not liable for harm caused by an adult drinker. Why do most states distinguish between adult and underage guests, holding a social host liable only for serving minors? Is the distinction persuasive?

- Many states now have some type of **dram act,** making liquor stores, bars, and restaurants liable for serving drinks to intoxicated customers who later cause harm. Why might a state create such responsibility while refusing to hold social hosts liable?

- There are many signs that society is fed up with drunk drivers. Who should make the decision about social host liability, a court or a legislature? ◆

Economics & the Law

Economists often analyze legal issues by looking at **externalities: costs or benefits of one person's activity that affect someone else.** For example, a factory that pollutes the air imposes *negative externalities,* because the sullied atmosphere makes life unpleasant and unhealthy for those who live nearby. By contrast, a corporation that landscapes its headquarters to include a duck pond with waterfall creates *positive externalities,* by making the neighborhood more attractive for local residents.

Bars and restaurants can generate negative externalities because innocent people may be injured or killed by drivers who become intoxicated in those establishments. Dram shop laws force a financial dilemma on such firms. The more a tavern or café encourages its customers to drink, the greater its revenue—but also the larger its risk of a liability lawsuit. The goal of dram shop laws is to force businesses serving liquor to consider these externalities. In states without a dram shop law, the threat of a lawsuit is removed, and the establishment has an incentive to maximize alcohol consumption, despite the external costs.

Do dram shop laws work? Yes, answer the authors of one economic study. In states with such statutes, bars monitor underage drinking more aggressively, refuse drinks earlier to an intoxicated customer, check the references of their own employees more carefully, and prohibit their workers from drinking on the job. These economists conclude that dram shop laws are a promising way to reduce drunk driving accidents.[1] ◆

---

[1] Sloan, Liang, Stout, and Whetten-Goldstein, "Liability, Risk Perceptions, and Precautions at Bars," *Journal of Law and Economics,* 2000, vol. 43, p. 473.

Could the owner of the pond be liable?

Affirmative Duty to Act

In general, the common law does not require a bystander to come to the assistance of a person in danger, assuming that the bystander did not create the danger. Henrietta, sitting in a café, watches as a piano, wrapped in a rope harness, rises majestically above the sidewalk. She notices that the frayed rope is about to snap, just as kindly Mr. Good approaches. Henrietta is not legally obligated to call out to him and incurs no liability if the piano crashes down with a lethal cacophony. This rule is discussed in detail in Chapter 4.

Landowner's Duty

The common law applies special rules to a landowner for injuries occurring on her property. In most states, the owner's duty depends on the status of the person injured.

Lowest Liability: Trespasser. A **trespasser** is anyone on the property without consent. A landowner is only liable to a trespasser for intentionally injuring him or for some other gross misconduct. The landowner has no liability to a trespasser for mere negligence. Jake is not liable if a vagrant wanders onto his land and is burned by defective electrical wires.

Occasional Liability: Children. The law makes exceptions when the trespassers are **children**. If there is some man-made thing on the land that may attract children, the landowner is probably liable for any harm. Daphne lives next door to a day-care center and builds a goldfish pond on her property. She is probably liable if a child wanders onto her property and drowns, unless she has fenced off the dangerous area.

Higher Liability: Licensee. A **licensee** is anyone on the land for her own purposes but with the owner's permission. A social guest is a typical licensee. A licensee is entitled to a warning of hidden dangers that the owner knows about. If Juliet invites Romeo for a late supper on the balcony and fails to mention that the wooden railing is rotted, she is liable when her hero plunges to the courtyard.

Highest Liability: Invitee. An **invitee** is someone on the property as of right because it is a public place or a business open to the public. The owner has a duty of reasonable care to an invitee. Perry is an invitee when he goes to the town beach. If riptides have existed for years and the town fails to post a warning, it is liable if Perry drowns. Perry is also an invitee when he shops at Daphne's Boutique. Daphne is liable if she ignores spilled coffee that causes Perry to slip.

The courts of some states have modified these distinctions, and a few have eliminated them altogether. California, for example, requires "reasonable care" as to all people on the owner's property, regardless of how or why they got there. But most states still use the classifications outlined above.

Crime and Tort: Landowner's Liability

Law shows us trends in social issues. Regrettably, a major concern of tort law today is how to respond to injury caused by criminals. If a criminal assaults and robs a pedestrian in a shopping mall, that act is a crime and may be prosecuted by the state. But prosecution leaves the victim uncompensated. The assault is also an intentional tort (discussed in Chapter 6), and the victim could file a civil lawsuit against the criminal. But most violent criminals have no assets. Given this economic frustration and the flexibility of the common law, it is inevitable that victims of violence look elsewhere for compensation, as they did in the following tragic case.

WIENER V. SOUTHCOAST CHILDCARE CENTERS, INC.

32 Ca.4th 1138, 88 P.3d 517, 12 Cal. Rptr. 3d 615
Supreme Court of California, 2004

Facts: Southcoast operated a child-care facility on a busy street corner property that it leased from First Baptist Church. A four-foot-high chain link fence enclosed the playground located adjacent to the sidewalk and street. Steven Abrams intentionally drove his large Cadillac through the fence, onto the playground, and into a group of children, causing horrific carnage. He killed two children and injured many others. Abrams was convicted of first-degree murder.

Parents of killed and injured youngsters sued Southcoast and the church, alleging that the defendants knew the fence was inadequate to protect the children. The trial judge granted summary judgment for the defendants, ruling that Southcoast and the others owed no duty to prevent such harm. The appellate court reversed, and Southcoast appealed.

Issue: Did Southcoast have a duty to the plaintiffs to prevent this kind of harm?

Excerpts from Justice Chin's Decision: [Plaintiffs alleged] that defendants were aware the chain link fence in front of the property provided inadequate protection, and that Shirley Hawkinson, owner of Southcoast, had previously requested that church provide funds to erect a higher fence. In the past, before Southcoast operated the child care center, a few noninjury traffic accidents happened near the property next to the sidewalk.

One freak accident [had] occurred, of which Hawkinson testified she had no knowledge. According to a neighbor, [a mail truck driver had fallen out of his truck.] The truck took off and bounced over the curb and went through the fence before coming to a stop at a tree inside the yard. No one was injured in the incident. Neighbors testified that other traffic incidents occurred near the premises involving vehicles that hit the curb.

Plaintiffs argued that it did not matter whether the driver of the vehicle that killed the children acted negligently or with criminal intent, because the risk of harm from an unsafe fence was the same, and that defendants owed a duty to make the fence stronger.

The Court of Appeal below placed particular emphasis on the "kind of harm" plaintiffs' children suffered rather than the criminal act itself. The court observed that the nature of the harm—being struck by an automobile driven onto the playground—was not dependent on the driver's criminal state of mind. The court opined that defendants' conduct in failing to erect a sturdier barrier that would have withstood the assault from the car or defendants' failure to move the children to a more protected part of the child care center, resulted in the kind of harm for which negligence liability attaches.

[Our cases] analyze third-party criminal acts differently from ordinary negligence, and require us to apply a heightened sense of foreseeability before we can hold a defendant liable for the criminal acts of third parties. There are two reasons for this: first, it is difficult if not impossible in today's society to predict when a criminal might strike. Also, if a criminal decides on a particular goal or victim, it is extremely difficult to remove his every means for achieving that goal. A criminal can commit a crime anywhere. The burden of requiring a landlord to protect against crime everywhere has been considered too great in comparison with the foreseeability of crime occurring at a particular location to justify imposing an omnibus duty on landowners to control crime.

We conclude defendants owed no duty to plaintiffs because Abrams's brutal criminal act was unforeseeable. No evidence indicated defendants' child care facility had ever been the target of violence in the past and no hint existed that either defendants or any other similar business establishment had ever been the target of any criminal acts. Indeed, here, the foreseeability of a perpetrator's committing premeditated murder against the children was impossible to anticipate, and the particular criminal conduct so outrageous and bizarre, that it could not have been anticipated under any circumstances.

[Reversed. Summary judgment for the defendants.] ■

This decision is bad public policy. The court is giving the day care center (and everyone who cares for children) one free pass. Do nothing to make the premises safer because, even if you foresee the harm, you cannot be sued. Then, after the first tragedy, get busy and improve the place. We ought to use the law to protect our children. ◆

Tort liability (or lack of liability) for criminal acts is a major policy issue because someone will pay for the harm done. It may be the victim, the property owner, the employer, or society generally. If the law denies all liability, as in Southcoast, it is the victim who "pays" by remaining uncompensated. If a court holds a property owner or employer liable, the victim will feel better, but the defendant will probably pass on the expense to others. Society itself could reimburse crime victims directly, through state government, but only a few legislatures have voted such compensation.

Breach of Duty

The second element of a plaintiff's negligence case is **breach of duty.** Courts apply the *reasonable person* standard: **a defendant breaches his duty of due care by failing to behave the way a reasonable person would under similar circumstances.** Reasonable "person" means someone of the defendant's occupation. A taxi driver must drive as a reasonable taxi driver would. A heart surgeon must perform bypass surgery with the care of a trained specialist in that field.

Two medical cases illustrate the reasonable person standard. A doctor prescribes a powerful drug without asking his 21-year-old patient about other medicines she is currently taking. The patient suffers a serious drug reaction from the combined medications. The physician is liable for the harm. A reasonable doctor *always* checks current medicines before prescribing new ones.

On the other hand, assume that an 84-year-old patient dies on the operating table in an emergency room. The physician followed normal medical procedures at every step of the procedure, and acted with reasonable speed. In fact, the man had a fatal stroke. The surgeon is not liable. A doctor must do a reasonable professional job, but cannot guarantee a happy outcome.

Crime and Tort Revisited: Negligent Hiring and Retention

In a recent one-year period, more than 1,000 homicides and 2 million attacks occurred in the workplace. Companies must beware because they can be liable for hiring or retaining violent employees. A mailroom clerk with a previous rape and robbery conviction followed a secretary home after work and fatally assaulted her. Even though the murder took place off the company premises, the court held that the defendant would be liable if it knew or should have known of the mail clerk's criminal history.[2] In other cases, companies have been found liable for failing to check an applicant's driving record, to contact personal references, and to search criminal records.

Courts have also found companies negligent for *retaining* dangerous workers. If an employee threatens a coworker, the organization is not free to ignore the menacing conduct. If the employee acts on his threats, the company may be liable.[3]

What can an employer do to diminish the likelihood of workplace violence? Many things.

- Evaluate the workplace for unsafe physical features. Install adequate lighting in parking lots and common areas, hire security guards if necessary, and use closed-circuit television and identification cards. The judicial trend is toward greater liability. Two decades

---

[2] *Gaines v. Monsanto*, 655 S.W.2d 568, 1983 Mo. LEXIS 3439 (Mo. Ct. App. 1983).
[3] *Yunker v. Honeywell*, 496 N.W.2d 419, 1993 Minn. App. LEXIS 230 (Minn. Ct. App. 1993).

ago, the victim of a parking lot assault could rarely recover from the store; today, such lawsuits are common and frequently successful.

- Ensure that the company uses thorough pre-hire screening, contacts all former employers, and checks all references and criminal records. Nursing homes have been among the most delinquent at this, too often hiring convicted assailants who have later attacked elderly residents. The financial liability for such cruel assaults can be enormous.

- Respond quickly to dangerous behavior. In many cases of workplace violence, the perpetrator had demonstrated repeated bizarre, threatening, or obsessive behavior on the job, but his supervisors had not taken it seriously. Offer counseling where appropriate and fire employees when necessary. ◆

Negligence Per Se

In certain areas of life, courts are not free to decide what a "reasonable" person would have done, because the state legislature has made the decision for them. **When a legislature sets a minimum standard of care for a particular activity, in order to protect a certain group of people, and a violation of the statute injures a member of that group, the defendant has committed negligence per se.** A plaintiff who can show negligence per se need not prove breach of duty.

In Minnesota, the state legislature became alarmed about children sniffing glue, which they could easily purchase in local stores. The legislature passed a statute prohibiting the sale to a minor of any glue containing toluene or benzene. About one month later, 14-year-old Steven Zerby purchased Weldwood Contact Cement from the Coast-to-Coast Store in his hometown. The glue contained toluene. Steven inhaled the glue and died from injury to his central nervous system.

The store clerk had not realized that the glue was dangerous. Irrelevant: he violated the statute. Perhaps a reasonable person would have made the same error. Irrelevant. The legislature had passed the statute to protect children; the sale of the glue violated the statute; and a child was injured. The store was liable.[4]

Factual Cause and Foreseeable Harm

A plaintiff must also show that the defendant's breach of duty caused the plaintiff's harm. Courts look at two issues to settle causation: Was the defendant's behavior the *factual cause* of the harm? Was *this type of harm foreseeable?*[5]

Factual Cause

Nothing mysterious here. **If the defendant's breach physically led to the ultimate harm, it is the factual cause.** Suppose that Dom's Brake Shop tells Customer his brakes are now working fine, even though Dom knows that is false. Customer drives out of the shop, cannot stop at a red light, and hits Bicyclist crossing at the intersection. Dom is liable to Bicyclist. Dom's unreasonable behavior was the factual cause of the harm. Think of it as a row of dominoes. The first domino (Dom's behavior) knocked over the next one (failing brakes), which toppled the last one (the cyclist's injury).

Suppose, alternatively, that just as Customer is exiting the repair shop, Bicyclist hits a pothole and tumbles off her cycle, avoiding Customer's auto. Bicyclist's injuries stem

---

[4] *Zerby v. Warren*, 297 Minn. 134, 210 N.W.2d 58 (1973).

[5] Courts often refer to these two elements, grouped together, as *proximate cause* or *legal cause*. But, as many courts acknowledge, those terms have created legal confusion, so we use *factual cause* and *foreseeable types of harm*, the issues on which most decisions ultimately focus.

from her fall, not from the auto. Customer's brakes still fail, and Dom has breached his duty to Customer, but Dom is not liable to Bicyclist. She would have been hurt anyway. This is a row of dominoes that veers off to the side, leaving the last domino (cyclist's injury) untouched. No factual causation.

Foreseeable Type of Harm

For the defendant to be liable, the *type of harm* must have been reasonably foreseeable. In the case above, Dom could easily foresee that bad brakes would cause an automobile accident. He need not have foreseen exactly what happened. He did not know there would be a cyclist nearby. What he could foresee was this *general type* of harm involving defective brakes. Because the accident that occurred was of the type he could foresee, he is liable.

By contrast, assume the collision of car and bicycle produces a loud crash. Two blocks away, a pet pig, asleep on the window ledge of a twelfth-story apartment, is startled by the noise, awakens with a start, and plunges to the sidewalk, killing a veterinarian who was making a house call. If the vet's family sues Dom, should it win? Dom's negligence was the factual cause: it led to the collision, which startled the pig, which flattened the vet. Most courts would rule, though, that Dom is not liable. The type of harm is too bizarre. Dom could not reasonably foresee such an extraordinary chain of events, and it would be unfair to make him pay for it. See Exhibit 7.1. Another way of stating that Dom is not liable to the vet's family is by calling the falling pig a *superseding cause*. When one of the "dominoes" in the row is entirely unforeseeable, courts will call that event a superseding cause, letting the defendant off the hook.

Was the following accident too freakish to make a (former) friend liable?

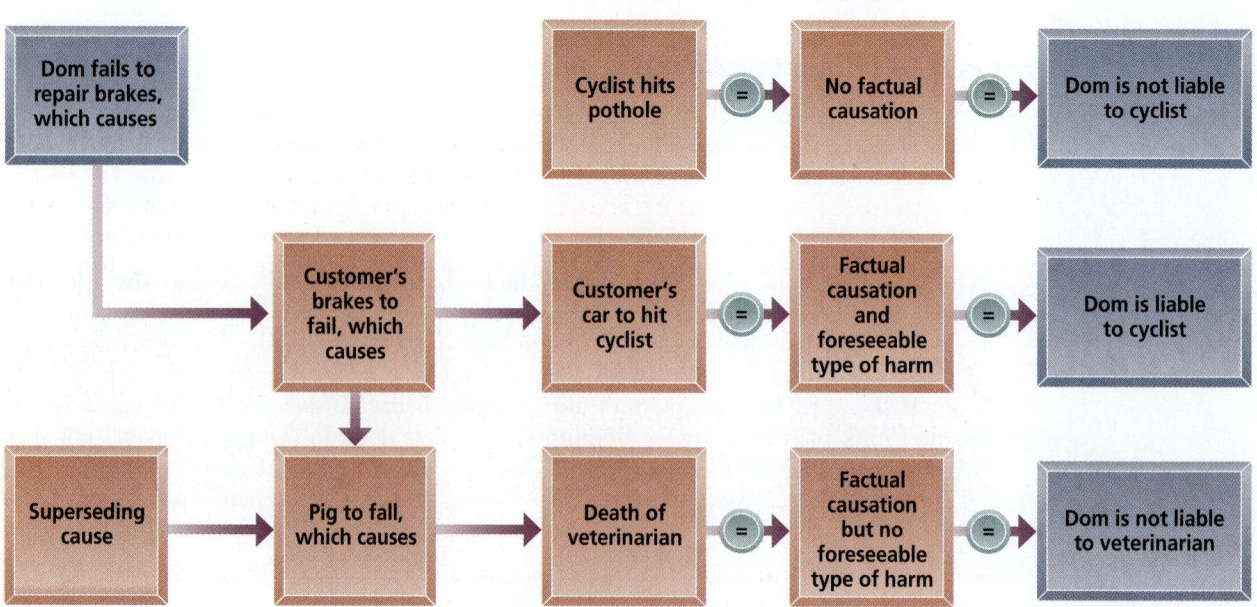

Exhibit 7.1

HEBERT V. ENOS

60 Mass. App. Ct. 817, 806 N.E.2d 452
Appeals Court of Massachusetts, 2004

Facts: Enos asked Hebert to water his flowers while he was on vacation. For three days, the agreeable neighbor did this without incident, but on the fourth day, when Hebert touched the outside faucet, he received a violent electric shock that shot him through the air, melted his sneakers and glasses, set his clothes on fire, and left him seriously injured. Hebert sued, claiming that Enos had caused the damage when he negligently repaired a second-floor toilet. Water from the steady leak had flooded through the walls, soaking wires and eventually causing the faucet to become electrified. The trial court granted summary judgment for Enos, ruling that even if he had done a bad job with the plumbing, this kind of injury was unforeseeable. Hebert appealed.

Issue: Was this type of injury foreseeable?

Excerpts from Judge Kafker's Decision: [One] is bound to anticipate and provide against what usually happens and what is likely to happen, but is not bound in like manner to guard against what is only remotely and slightly probable. We look to determine whether the general character and probability of the injury were foreseeable. We also recognize that there must be limits to the scope or definition of reasonable foreseeability based on considerations of policy and pragmatic judgment.

When we consider the likelihood, character, and location of the harm, we conclude as matter of law that the injuries sustained by Hebert were a highly extraordinary consequence of a defective second-floor toilet. Although we can envision a variety of foreseeable injuries arising out of a defective toilet, the electric shock to a neighbor when he touches a faucet outside the house is well beyond the range of reasonable apprehension and therefore not foreseeable. We therefore conclude that Hebert's severe and unfortunate injuries were the consequence of the type of unforeseeable accident for which we do not hold the defendant responsible in tort.

Affirmed. ■

Res Ipsa Loquitur

Normally, a plaintiff must prove factual cause and foreseeable type of harm in order to establish negligence. But in a few cases, a court may be willing to *infer* that the defendant caused the harm, under the doctrine of ***res ipsa loquitur*** ("the thing speaks for itself"). Suppose a pedestrian is walking along a sidewalk when an air conditioning unit falls on his head from a third-story window. The defendant, who owns the third-story apartment, denies any wrongdoing, and it may be difficult or impossible for the plaintiff to prove why the air conditioner fell. In such cases, many courts will apply *res ipsa loquitur* and declare that **the facts imply that the defendant's negligence caused the accident.** If a court uses this doctrine, then the defendant must come forward with evidence establishing that it did *not* cause the harm.

Because *res ipsa loquitur* dramatically shifts the burden of proof from plaintiff to defendant, it applies only when (1) the defendant had exclusive control of the thing that caused the harm, (2) the harm normally would not have occurred without negligence, and (3) the plaintiff had no role in causing the harm. In the air conditioner example, most states would apply the doctrine and force the defendant to prove she did nothing wrong.

The following case illustrates several of the elements of negligence that we have examined so far.

you Be The Judge

GRIFFITH V. VALLEY OF SUN RECOVERY, INC.

126 Ariz. 227, 613 P.2d 1283
Arizona Court of Appeals, 1980

Facts: Don Gorney was a "repo man." A repossession person is someone authorized to find and take cars whose owners are behind on payments. A repossessor is allowed to drive away in such a car, provided he can do it peacefully. Gorney worked for Valley of Sun Recovery. He sought a car belonging to Linda Marsalek and Bob Williams. Gorney knew that there had been other, failed efforts to repossess the Marsalek car, including a violent confrontation involving attack dogs. He thought he could do better.

Gorney went to the car at 4:00 in the morning. He unscrewed the bulb in an overhead street lamp. He unlocked the car, setting off its alarm, and quickly hid. The alarm aroused the neighborhood. Williams and a neighbor, Griffith, investigated and concluded it was an attempted theft. They called the police. Gorney watched all of this from his hiding place. When everyone had gone, Gorney entered the car, again setting off the alarm and arousing the neighborhood. Williams and Griffith again emerged, as did another neighbor, dressed in his underwear and carrying a shotgun. They all believed they had caught a thief. Williams shouted for the gun and the neighbor passed it to him, but it went off accidentally and severely injured Griffith.

Griffith sued Valley of Sun. The trial court granted summary judgment for Valley of Sun, and Griffith appealed.

You Be the Judge:
- Did Valley of Sun have a duty to Griffith?
- If so, did the company breach its duty?
- If so, was the breach the factual cause of the injury?
- If so, was this type of injury foreseeable?

Argument for Griffith: Your honors, Mr. Griffith should be allowed to make his case to a jury and let it decide whether Valley of Sun's repossession led to his injury. Mr. Griffith has demonstrated every element of negligence. Valley of Sun had a duty to everyone in the area when it attempted to repossess a car. It could easily have foreseen injury. Car repossessions always involve antagonism between the car owner and the repo company.

Obviously, Gorney breached his duty. He was caught up in some fantasy, dreaming that he was Harrison Ford in an adventure film. He knew from previous repossession attempts that trouble was certain. But rather than minimizing the danger, he exacerbated it. He unscrewed a lightbulb, guaranteeing poor visibility and confusion. He set off the car alarm twice, making the whole neighborhood jittery.

Factual causation is indisputable. Had it not been for his preposterous game playing, no neighbors would have been outside, no guns present—and no accidental shooting. And this type of harm is easily foreseeable. We should have a chance to take our case to a jury.

Argument for Valley of Sun Recovery: Your honors, there are three good reasons to end this case today: no duty, no breach, no causation.

It is preposterous to suggest that Valley of Sun has a legal duty to an entire neighborhood. Car owners behind on their payments live in all parts of all communities. Is a repossession company to become an insurer of the entire city?

Yes, some danger is involved because delinquent owners are irresponsible and sometimes dangerous. Should we therefore allow them to keep their cars? Of course not. We must act, and that is what Valley of Sun does.

They do it safely, your honors. Even if there had been a duty, there was no breach. Mr. Gorney attempted to repossess when it was least likely anyone would see him. What should Mr. Gorney have done, asked for permission to take the car? *That* is a recipe for violence. If the owner were reasonable, there would be no repossession in the first place.

Factual causation? Valley of Sun did not create this situation. The car owner did. He bought the car and failed to pay for it. Even if there were factual causation, Valley of Sun is not liable because there is a superseding cause: the negligent use of a firearm by one of Mr. Griffith's neighbors. No jury should hear this case, your honors, because there is no case. ■

Injury

Finally, a plaintiff must prove that he has been injured. In some cases injury is obvious. For example, Ruben Hernandez suffered grievous harm when struck by a drunk driver. But in other cases, injury is unclear. **The plaintiff must persuade the court that he has suffered a harm that is genuine, not speculative.**

up$_{date}$

A federal judge awarded $4 million to a California man who suffered severe brain damage after merchandise fell on him at a Wal-Mart store. Todd Caranto, a former Air Force medical corpsman, was Christmas shopping when more than a dozen heavy boxes of toys tumbled off high shelves and knocked him to the floor. The accident resulted in permanent brain damage and left the 26-year-old father of two unable to take care of himself. Caranto will require total care, 24 hours a day, for the rest of his life. He can walk but is unable to speak or communicate with anyone around him.

Find a current case that resulted in a multimillion-dollar plaintiff's verdict. How large was the award? What factors do you think most affected the jury's decision? How could the harm have been avoided? Are there lessons that a business can take from the case? ◆

Other cases raise tougher questions. Among the most vexing are suits involving *future* harm. Exposure to toxins or trauma may lead to serious medical problems down the road—or it may not. A woman's knee is damaged in an auto accident, causing severe pain for two years. She is clearly entitled to compensation for her suffering. After two years, all pain may cease for a decade—or forever. Yet there is also a chance that in 15 or 20 years the trauma will lead to painful arthritis. A court must decide today the full extent of present *and future* damages; the single recovery principle, discussed in Chapter 6, prevents a plaintiff from returning to court years later and demanding compensation for newly arisen ailments. The challenge to our courts is to weigh the possibilities and percentages of future suffering and decide whether to compensate a plaintiff for something that might never happen.

The following lawsuit concerns a couple's fear of developing AIDS, a worry that can be overwhelming. The court must still decide, however, whether the cause of the unhappiness is genuine injury or speculation.

COLE V. QUIRK

2001 Mass. App. Div. 139, 2001 WL 705730
Massachusetts Appellate Division, 2001

Facts: The Coles bought a used car from a dealership owned by Quirk. The dealer agreed to thoroughly clean the interior before delivery. Dissatisfied with the car's appearance, Timothy Cole began to clean the interior. As he reached into the pocket behind the driver's seat, a pair of surgical tweezers cut his finger, drawing blood. Cole feverishly washed his hands, and phoned his doctor, who told him he was at risk of contracting Hepatitis B and HIV. The Coles found prescriptions in the car, and learned that its former owner was a doctor. Terrified that Timothy might have contracted Hepatitis B or HIV, the Coles abstained from sex for over a year, and then practiced safe sex. Mr.

Cole suffered from diarrhea, nausea, and vomiting, based on this fear of HIV. He never tested positive for the disease. The tweezers were never tested.

The Coles sued Quirk. At the close of the Coles' case, the trial judge directed a verdict for Quirk. The Coles appealed.

Issue: Have the Coles demonstrated an injury?

Excerpts from Judge Winslow's Decision: Claims for HIV/AIDS-phobia have been described as an "uneasy class of cases in which bad news is worse than no news at all." Courts in other states have ▼

expressed two competing views regarding the proof of causation necessary to establish a claim for HIV/AIDS-phobia: (1) Actual Exposure: in order to maintain a cause of action for damages due to the fear of contracting HIV/AIDS, the plaintiff, who has not tested seropositive, must offer proof of actual exposure, meaning proof of both a scientifically accepted method of transmission of the virus *and* that the source of the allegedly transmitted blood or fluid was in fact HIV-positive; and (2) Reasonable Fear: the plaintiff, not tested seropositive, must prove a specific incident of potential exposure sufficient to create a reasonable fear of having contracted the AIDS virus, even in the absence of a proven source and channel of exposure.

We adopt the objective Actual Exposure standard of causation in reviewing the directed verdict in this action. Today, although much more is known about how HIV in fact is spread than was known at the beginning of the epidemic, many lay persons continue to believe that HIV can be transmitted through food, silverware, handshakes, and toilet seats.... If persons can obtain compensation for their fear of AIDS, it must be decided which fears are compensable. Should a person be compensated for fears which, although entirely unrealistic from a

scientific perspective, in fact affect the person very significantly? A person who truly believes HIV may be communicated through a handshake may suffer significant physical and emotional trauma as a result of shaking hands with a person whom he subsequently learns was HIV-infected. The objective standard of causation guards against claims for HIV/AIDS-phobia that are trivial, evanescent, temporary, feigned, or imagined.

Moreover, as a matter of public policy, adoption of the subjective standard holds the potential of stigmatizing persons infected with HIV and making them subject to claims for fear of HIV/AIDS that are not capable of readily being addressed by summary judgment. We agree that the widespread ignorance about the nature of this disease and the accompanying prejudices against persons suffering from it or, as here, merely alleged to suffer from it, pose dangers to the accuracy and fairness of the legal process in many ways. To prove their claim for HIV/AIDS-phobia, the Coles were required to prove both a scientifically accepted method of transmission of the virus *and* that the source of the allegedly transmitted blood or fluid was in fact HIV-positive. They did not meet this burden at trial.

Affirmed. ■

Public Policy

This is a dispute between a car dealer and purchaser, yet the court goes beyond the parties' arguments, and examines society's attitude towards infectious diseases generally. What is the court concerned about? Is it good for the judges to broaden their focus? ◆

Claims of emotional distress become more compelling when the HIV virus appears. At the Honolulu airport, several baggage workers discovered their hands dripping with blood that had leaked from a medical shipment. The blood tested HIV-positive. The workers were distraught, claiming that because their hands had open wounds, they were at risk of developing AIDS. The Hawaii court allowed their case to go forward, even though the baggage handlers had never acquired the disease. Because the blood was in fact contaminated, the workers' fear was foreseeable and reasonable—but only from the time of the incident to their receipt of a negative diagnosis. Once they knew they had not contracted the disease, fear was no longer reasonable.[6]

Bystander Cases

What if a defendant injures one person but someone *else* sues for emotional suffering? In a landmark California case,[7] a driver negligently caused the death of a child. The child's mother was nearby and witnessed the accident, though the mother was never in danger from the car. The driver was clearly liable for the wrongful death. Was he additionally liable to the mother for her purely emotional suffering? Yes, said the California

---

[6] *Roes v. FHP, Inc.*, 91 Haw. 470, 985 P.2d 661, 1999 Haw. LEXIS 317 (Hawaii, 1999).
[7] *Dillon v. Legg*, 68 Cal. 2d 728, 441 P.2d 912, 1968 Cal. LEXIS 201 (1968).

court. A bystander is entitled to damages for negligent infliction of emotional distress if (1) she was near the scene of the accident *and* (2) seeing the accident caused an immediate shock to her *and* (3) she is a close relative of the victim. Many but not all states now follow that rule.

Damages

The plaintiff's damages in a negligence case are generally **compensatory damages,** meaning an amount of money that the court believes will restore him to the position he was in before the defendant's conduct caused an injury. In unusual cases, a court may award **punitive damages,** that is, money intended not to compensate the plaintiff but to punish the defendant. We discussed both forms of damages in Chapter 6.

DEFENSES

Contributory and Comparative Negligence

Sixteen-year-old Michelle Wightman was out driving at night, with her friend Karrie Wieber in the passenger seat. They came to a railroad crossing, where the mechanical arm had descended and warning bells were sounding, in fact, *had been* sounding for a long time. A Conrail train, SEEL-7, had suffered mechanical problems and was stopped 200 feet from the crossing, where it had stalled for roughly an hour. Michelle and Karrie saw several cars ahead of them go around the barrier and cross the tracks. Michelle had to decide whether she would do the same.

Long before Michelle made her decision, the train's engineer had seen the heavy Saturday night traffic crossing the tracks, and realized the danger. A second train, TVLA, had passed the crossing at 70 miles per hour, without incident. SEEL-7's conductor and brakeman also understood the peril, but rather than posting a flagman, who could have stopped traffic when a train approached, they walked to the far end of their train to repair the mechanical problem. A police officer had come upon the scene, told his dispatcher to notify Conrail of the danger, and left.

Michelle decided to cross the tracks. She slowly followed the cars ahead of her. Seconds later both girls were dead. TV-9, a freight train traveling at 60 miles per hour, struck the car broadside, killing both girls instantly.

Michelle's mother sued Conrail for negligence. The company claimed that it was Michelle's foolish risk that led to her death. Who wins when both parties are partly responsible? It depends on whether the state uses a legal theory called contributory negligence. **Under contributory negligence, if the plaintiff is even slightly negligent she recovers nothing.** If Michelle's death occurred in a contributory negligence state, and the jury considered her even minimally responsible, her estate would receive no money.

Critics attacked this rule as unreasonable. A plaintiff who was 1 percent negligent could not recover from a defendant who was 99 percent responsible. So most states threw out the contributory negligence rule, replacing it with comparative negligence. **In a comparative negligence state, a plaintiff may generally recover even if she is partially responsible.** The jury will be asked to assess the relative negligence of the two parties.

Michelle died in Ohio, which is a comparative negligence state. The jury concluded that reasonable compensatory damages were $1 million. It also concluded that Conrail was 60 percent responsible for the tragedy and Michelle 40 percent. See Exhibit 7.2. The girl's mother received $600,000 in compensatory damages.

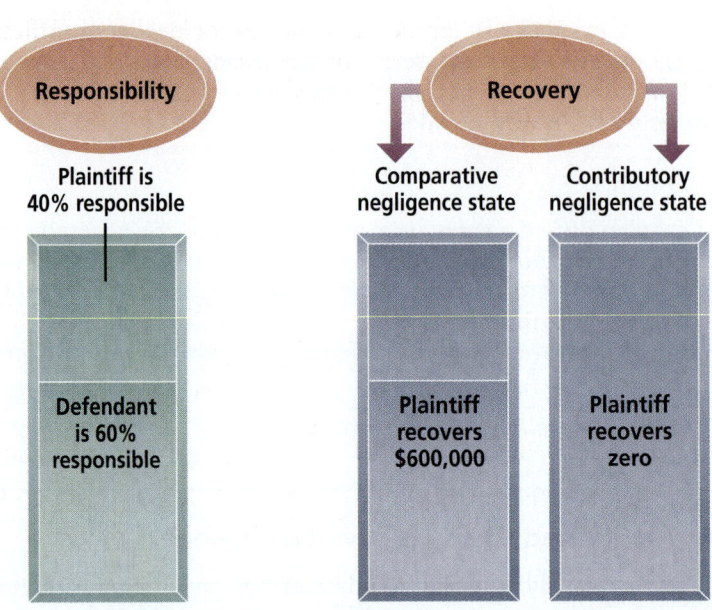

Exhibit 7.2
Defendant's negligence injures plaintiff, who suffers $1 million in damages.

Today, most but not all states have adopted some form of comparative negligence. Critics claim that this principle rewards a careless plaintiff. If Michelle had obeyed the law, she would still be alive. Why should the estate be compensated for her recklessness? In response to this complaint, many comparative negligence states do *not* permit a plaintiff to recover anything if he was more than 50 percent responsible for his own injury.

In the Conrail case, the jury decided that the rail company was extraordinarily negligent. Expert witnesses testified that similar tragedies occurred every year around the nation and the company knew it. Employees realized that the TV-9 train was approaching. Conrail could easily have prevented the loss of life by posting a flagman on the road. The jury awarded the estate $25 million in punitive damages. The trial judge reduced the verdict to $15 million, and the state supreme court approved it. Notice that, in Ohio and many states, a punitive award is *not* subject to the compensatory damages rule—all of the money goes to the plaintiff.[8]

Assumption of the Risk

Quick, duck! That was a close call—the baseball nearly knocked your ear off. If it had, the team would owe you ... nothing. Here at the ballpark, there is always a slight chance of injury, and you are expected to realize it. Wherever there is an obvious hazard, a special rule applies. **Assumption of the risk: a person who voluntarily enters a situation that has an obvious danger cannot complain if she is injured.** If you are not willing to tolerate the risk of being hurt by a batted ball, stay home and watch the game on television. And while you are here—pay attention, will you?!

Suppose that Good Guys, a restaurant, holds an ice-fishing contest on a frozen lake, to raise money for accident victims. Margie grabs a can full of worms and strolls

---

[8]   *Wightman v. Consolidated Rail Corporation*, 86 Ohio St. 3d 431, 715 N.E.2d 546, 1999 Ohio LEXIS 2924 (Ohio 1999).

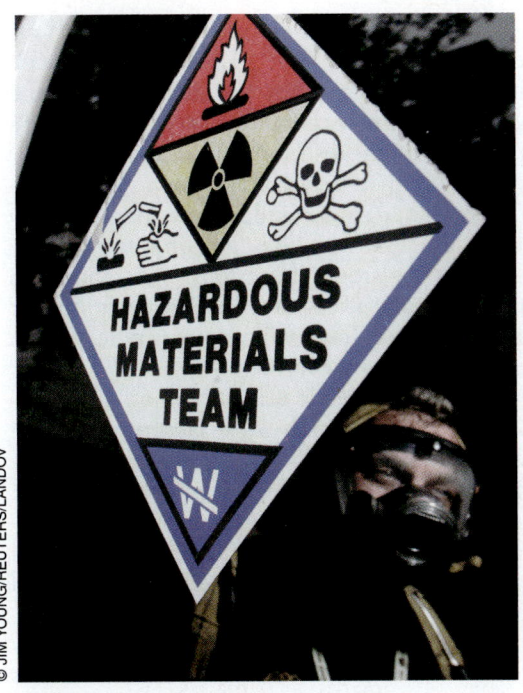

An ultrahazardous activity exposes a company to strict liability if anything goes wrong.

to the middle of the lake to try her luck, but slips on the ice and suffers a concussion. When she returns to consciousness, Margie should not bother filing suit—she assumed the risk.

STRICT LIABILITY

Some activities are so naturally dangerous that the law places an especially high burden on anyone who engages in them. A corporation that produces toxic waste can foresee dire consequences from its business that a stationery store cannot. This higher burden is **strict liability.** There are two main areas of business that incur strict liability: *ultrahazardous activity* and *defective products.* Defective products are discussed in Chapter 21, on product liability.

Ultrahazardous Activity

Ultrahazardous activities include using harmful chemicals, operating explosives, keeping wild animals, bringing dangerous substances onto property, and a few similar activities where the danger to the general public is especially great. **A defendant engaging in an ultrahazardous activity is virtually always liable for any harm that results.** Plaintiffs do not have to prove duty or breach or foreseeable harm. Recall the deliberately bizarre case we posed earlier of the pig falling from a window ledge and killing a veterinarian. Dom, the mechanic whose negligence caused the car crash, could not be liable for the veterinarian's death because the plunging pig was a superseding cause. But if the pig was jolted off the window ledge by Sam's Blasting Co., which was doing perfectly lawful blasting for a new building down the street, Sam is liable. Even if Sam took extraordinary care, it will do him no good at trial. The "reasonable person" rule is irrelevant in a strict liability case.

NEW JERSEY DEPARTMENT OF ENVIRONMENTAL PROTECTION V. ALDEN LEEDS, INC.

153 N.J. 272, 708 A.2d 1161, 1998 N.J. LEXIS 212, 46 ERC (BNA) 1447
Supreme Court of New Jersey, 1998

Facts: The Alden Leeds company packages, stores, and ships swimming pool chemicals. The firm does most of its work at its facility in Kearns, New Jersey. At any given time, about 21 different hazardous chemicals are present.

The day before Easter, a fire of unknown origin broke out in "Building One" of the company's site, releasing chlorine gas and other potentially dangerous by-products into the air. There were no guards or other personnel on duty. The fire caused $9 mil-

lion in damage to company property. Because of the potentially dangerous gas, the Department of Environmental Protection (DEP) closed the New Jersey Turnpike along with half a dozen other major highways, halted all commuter rail and train service in the area, and urged residents to stay indoors with windows closed. An unspecified number of residents went to local hospitals with respiratory problems.

Based on New Jersey's Air Pollution Control Act (APCA), the DEP imposed a civil fine on Alden

▼

Leeds for releasing the toxic chemicals. The appellate court reversed, finding that there was no evidence the company had caused the fire or the harm, and the case reached the state's high court.

Issue: Did the company cause the harm?

Excerpts from Justice Coleman's Decision: In 1962, this Court adopted the proposition that "an ultrahazardous activity which introduces an unusual danger into the community should pay its own way in the event it actually causes damage to others." In 1983, the Court expressly recognized "that the law of liability has evolved so that a landowner is strictly liable to others for harm caused by toxic wastes that are stored on his property and flow onto the property of others." The Court explained "that those who use, or permit others to use, land for the conduct of abnormally dangerous activities are strictly liable for resultant damages." The same rationale applies to pollution that is released into the air from chemicals stored at a chemical facility.

An actor who chooses to store dangerous chemicals should be responsible for the release of those chemicals into the air. That Alden Leeds lawfully and properly stored chemicals does not alter that conclusion. The risks attendant to the storage of dangerous substances counsel in favor of precautions to prevent their release. Alden Leeds took no such precautions. On the day of the fire, there was no one stationed at the plant to alert the authorities as soon as a fire or other unforeseen calamity erupted. Nor was there any other early warning system in place. A burglar or smoke alarm sounded, but there was no response to that alarm. The law imposes a duty upon those who store hazardous substances to ensure that the substances on their property do not escape in a manner harmful to the public. Alden Leeds failed to meet that burden.

Although Alden Leeds was not found responsible for the fire, the company's facility caused a release of air pollutants. The required nexus is satisfied by the knowing storage of hazardous chemicals. Regardless of what started the fire, it was the knowing storage of chemicals by Alden Leeds that caused the release of air contaminants once the fire reached the chemicals.

[Affirmed that the APCA is a strict liability statute and that there must be a causal nexus between the defendant and the harm. Reversed that the storing of hazardous chemicals by Alden Leeds does not satisfy that nexus. The DEP does *not* have to prove that the chemical operator started the fire.] ∎

As mentioned, maintaining a wild animal is also an ultrahazardous activity. If you own an elephant, beware. In one English case, a peaceable circus elephant was pestered by a small dog. It finally lunged for the dog and accidentally squashed a performing midget. The circus had to pay tall damages.[9] Interestingly, the same case in India would yield the opposite result, since in its native land an elephant is regarded as a domestic animal, imposing no strict liability.

Because "strict liability" translates into "defendant is liable," parties in tort cases often fight over whether the defendant was engaged in an ultrahazardous activity. If the court rules that the activity was ultrahazardous, the plaintiff is assured of winning. If the court rules that it was not ultrahazardous, the plaintiff must prove all elements of negligence.

Selling used batteries to a recycling company is *not* an ultrahazardous act, even if the processing later pollutes the earth. Pile driving is ultrahazardous. A lawful fireworks display does not incur strict liability, but crop dusting does. Cutting timber is generally not abnormally dangerous but hauling logs might be. The enormous diversity of business activities in our nation insures continual disputes over this important principle.

---

[9] *Behrens v. Bertram Mills Circus, Ltd.,* 2 Q.B. 1, 14–15 (1957).

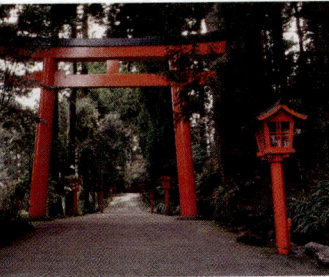

Chapter Conclusion

Tort issues necessarily remain in flux, based on changing social values and concerns. There is no final word on what is an ultrahazardous activity, or how much security a day care center must provide, or whether a social host can be liable for the destruction caused by a guest. What is clear is that a working knowledge of these issues and pitfalls can help everyone—business executive and ordinary citizen alike.

Chapter Review

1. The five elements of negligence are duty of due care, breach, factual causation, foreseeable type of harm, and injury.

2. If the defendant could foresee that misconduct would injure a particular person, he probably has a duty to her.

3. In most states, a landowner's duty of due care is lowest to trespassers; often higher to children; higher still to a licensee (anyone on the land for her own purposes but with the owner's permission); and highest of all to an invitee (someone on the property as of right).

4. A defendant breaches his duty of due care by failing to behave the way a reasonable person would under similar circumstances.

5. Employers may be liable for negligent hiring or negligent retention of employees.

6. If a legislature sets a minimum standard of care for a particular activity in order to protect a certain group of people, and a violation of the statute injures a member of that group, the defendant has committed negligence per se.

7. If one event physically led to the ultimate harm, it is the factual cause.

8. For the defendant to be liable, the type of harm must have been reasonably foreseeable.

9. The plaintiff must persuade the court that he has suffered a harm that is genuine, not speculative.

10. In a contributory negligence state, a plaintiff who is even slightly responsible for his own injury recovers nothing; in a comparative negligence state, the jury may apportion liability between plaintiff and defendant.

11. A defendant is strictly liable for harm caused by an ultrahazardous activity or a defective product. Ultrahazardous activities include using harmful chemicals, blasting, and keeping wild animals. Strict liability means that if the defendant's conduct led to the harm, the defendant is liable, even if she exercises extraordinary care.

Practice Test

1. Irving was a notary public who prepared income tax returns for Maroevich. Irving agreed to draft a will for Maroevich, leaving all of the property to Maroevich's sister, Biakanja. When Maroevich died, the probate court refused to accept the will because Irving had failed to have the signatures properly witnessed. As a result, Biakanja inherited only one-eighth of the estate. She sued Irving. Irving defended by saying that he had no duty of due care to Biakanja because all of his dealings were with Maroevich and none were with her. Discuss.

2. Jason Jacque was riding as a passenger in a car driven by his sister, who was drunk and driving 19 mph over the speed limit. She failed to negotiate a curve, skidded off the road, and collided with a wooden utility pole erected by the Public Service Company of Colorado (PSC). Jacque suffered severe brain injury. He sued PSC for negligently installing the pole too close to the highway at a dangerous curve where an accident was likely to happen. The trial court gave summary judgment for PSC, ruling that PSC owed no duty to Jacque. He appealed. Please rule.

3. At approximately 7:50 PM bells at the train station rang and red lights flashed, signaling an express train's approach. David Harris walked onto the tracks, ignoring a yellow line painted on

the platform instructing people to stand back. Two men shouted to Harris, warning him to get off the tracks. The train's engineer saw him too late to stop the train, which was traveling at approximately 99 mph. The train struck and killed Harris as it passed through the station. Harris's widow sued the railroad, arguing that the railroad's negligence caused her husband's death. Evaluate her argument.

4. A supervisor reprimanded an employee for eating in a restaurant when he should have been at work. Later, the employee showed up at the supervisor's office and shot him. Although the employee previously had been violent, management withheld this information from supervisory personnel. Discuss.

5. Ryder leased a truck to Florida Food Service; Powers, an employee, drove it to make deliveries. He noticed that the door strap used to close the rear door was frayed, and he asked Ryder to fix it. Ryder failed to do so in spite of numerous requests. The strap broke, and Powers replaced it with a nylon rope. Later, when Powers was attempting to close the rear door, the nylon rope broke and he fell, sustaining severe injuries to his neck and back. He sued Ryder. The trial court found that Powers's attachment of the replacement rope was a superseding cause, relieving Ryder of any liability, and granted summary judgment for Ryder. Powers appealed. How should the appellate court rule?

6. A new truck, manufactured by General Motors Corp., stalled in rush hour traffic on a busy interstate highway because of a defective alternator, which caused a complete failure of the truck's electrical system. The driver stood nearby and waved traffic around his stalled truck. A panel truck approached the GMC truck, and immediately behind the panel truck, Davis was driving a Volkswagen fastback. Because of the panel truck, Davis was unable to see the stalled GMC truck. The panel truck swerved out of the way of the GMC truck, and Davis drove straight into it. The accident killed him. Davis's widow sued GMC. GMC moved for summary judgment, alleging (1) no duty to Davis, (2) no factual causation, and (3) no foreseeable harm. Comment.

7. A prison inmate bit a hospital employee. The employee sued the state for negligence and lack of supervision, claiming a fear of AIDS. The plaintiff had tested negative for the AIDS virus three times, and there was no proof that the inmate had the virus. Comment on the probable outcome.

8. *ETHICS* Swimming pools in private homes often have diving boards, but those in public parks, hotels, and clubs rarely do. Why is that? Is it good or bad?

9. There is a collision between cars driven by Candy and Zeke, and both drivers are partly at fault. The evidence is that Candy is about 25 percent responsible, for failing to stop quickly enough, and Zeke about 75 percent responsible, for making a dangerous turn. Candy is most likely to win:

   a. A lawsuit for battery

   b. A lawsuit for negligence, in a comparative negligence state

   c. A lawsuit for negligence, in a contributory negligence state

   d. A lawsuit for strict liability; or

   e. A lawsuit for assault.

10. *YOU BE THE JUDGE* WRITING PROBLEM When Thomas and Susan Tamplin were shopping at Star Lumber with their six-year-old daughter Ann Marie, a 150-pound roll of vinyl flooring fell on the girl, seriously injuring her head and pituitary gland. Ann was clearly entitled to recover for the physical harm, such as her fractured skull. The plaintiffs also sought recovery for potential future harm. Their medical expert was prepared to testify that, although Ann would probably develop normally, he could not rule out the slight possibility that her pituitary injury might prevent her from sexually maturing. Is Ann entitled to damages for future harm? **Argument for Ann:** This was a major trauma, and it is impossible to know the full extent of the future harm. Sexual maturation is a fundamental part of life; if there is a possibility that Ann will not develop normally, she is entitled to present her case to a jury and receive damages. **Argument for Star Lumber:** A plaintiff may not recover for speculative harm. The "slight possibility" that Ann could fail to develop is not enough for her to take her case to the jury.

11. Van Houten owned a cat and allowed it to roam freely outside. In the three years he had owned it, it had never bitten anyone. The cat entered Pritchard's garage. Pritchard attempted to move it outside his garage, and the cat bit him. As a direct result of the bite, Pritchard underwent four surgeries, was fitted with a plastic finger joint, and spent more than $39,000 in medical bills. He sued Van Houten, claiming both strict liability and ordinary negligence. Please evaluate his claims.

12. *ROLE REVERSAL* Create a question that distinguishes between ordinary negligence and strict liability.

Internet Research Problem

Everyone knows that drunk driving is bad, but many people still do it. Proceed to http://beatty.westbuslaw .com. Find something that you did not know about drunk driving. What role should the law play in this problem, and what role should parents, students, and schools play?

> **You can find further practice problems at http://beatty.westbuslaw.com or in the Study Guide that accompanies this text.**

Crime

Crime can take us by surprise. Stacey tucks her nine-year-old daughter, Beth, into bed. Promising her husband, Mark, that she will be home by 11:00 PM, she jumps into her car and heads back to Be Patient, Inc. She puts a compact disc in the player of her $85,000 sedan and tries to relax. Be Patient is a health care organization that owns five geriatric hospitals. Most of its patients use Medicare, and Stacey supervises all billing to their largest client, the federal government.

She parks in a well-lighted spot on the street and walks to her building, failing to notice two men, collars turned up, watching from a parked truck. Once in her office she goes straight to her computer and works on billing issues. Tonight's work goes more quickly than she expected, thanks to new software she helped develop. At 10:30 she emerges from the building with a quick step and a light heart, walks to her car—and finds it missing.

A major crime has occurred during the 90 minutes Stacey was at her desk, but she will never report it to the police. It is a crime that costs Americans countless dollars each year, yet Stacey will not even mention it to friends or family. Stacey is the criminal. ◼

When we think of crime, we imagine the drug dealers and bank robbers endlessly portrayed on television. We do not picture corporate executives sitting at polished desks. "Street crimes" are indeed serious threats to our security and happiness. They deservedly receive the attention of the public and the law. (For a look at the FBI's 10 most wanted list, see http://www.fbi.gov.) But when measured only in dollars, street crime takes second place to white-collar crime, which costs society *tens of billions* of dollars annually.

The hypothetical about Stacey is based on many real cases and is used to illustrate that crime does not always dress the way we expect. Her car was never stolen; it was simply towed. Two parking bureau employees, watching from their truck, saw Stacey park illegally and did their job. It is Stacey who committed a crime—Medicare fraud. Stacey has learned the simple but useful lesson that company profits rise when she charges the government for work Be Patient has never done. For months she billed the government for imaginary patients. Then she hired a computer hacker to worm into the Medicare computer system and plant a "Trojan horse," a program that seemed useful to Medicare employees but actually contained a series of codes opening the computer to Stacey. Stacey simply entered the Medicare system and altered the calculations for payments owed to Be Patient. Every month, the government paid Be Patient about $10 million for imaginary work. Stacey's scheme was quick and profitable—and a distressingly common crime.

What do we do about cases like these? These questions involve multifarious fact issues and important philosophical values. In this chapter, we look first at the big picture of criminal law and then focus on that part of it that most affects business—white-collar crime. We examine four major issues:

- *Crime, Society, and Law.* What makes conduct criminal? We enumerate the basic elements that the prosecution must establish to prove that a crime has been committed, and also some of the most common defenses.

- *Crimes That Harm Business.* We look at specific crimes, such as fraud and embezzlement, that cost businesses enormous sums every year.

- *Crimes Committed by Business.* We analyze "white-collar crimes," which are generally committed by businesspeople and may be directed at consumers, other businesses, or the government.

- *Criminal Process and Constitutional Protections.* We examine how the Bill of Rights protects citizens subjected to search, interrogation, and trial. And we pay a final visit to Stacey.

CRIME, SOCIETY, AND LAW

Civil Law/Criminal Law

Most of this book concerns the civil law—the rights and liabilities that exist between private parties. As we have seen, if one person claims that another has caused her a civil injury, she must file a lawsuit and convince a court of her damages.

The criminal law is different. Conduct is **criminal** when society outlaws it. When a state legislature or Congress concludes that certain behavior threatens the population generally, it passes a statute forbidding that behavior, in other words, declaring it criminal. Medicare fraud, which Stacey committed, is a crime because Congress has outlawed it. Money laundering is a crime because Congress concluded it was a fundamental part of the drug trade and prohibited it.

Prosecution

Suppose the police arrest Roger and accuse him of breaking into a video store and stealing 25 video cameras, videos, and other equipment. The owner of the video store is the one harmed, but **it is the government that prosecutes crimes.** The local prosecutor will decide whether or not to charge Roger and bring him to trial.

Jury Right

The facts of the case will be decided by a judge or jury. A criminal defendant has a right to a trial by jury for any charge that could result in a sentence of six months or longer. The defendant may demand a jury trial or may waive that right, in which case the judge will be the factfinder.

Punishment

In a civil lawsuit, the plaintiff seeks a verdict that the defendant is liable for harm caused to her. But in a criminal case, the government asks the court to find the defendant **guilty** of the crime. The government wants the court to **punish** the defendant. If the judge or jury finds the defendant guilty, the court will punish him with a fine and/or a prison sentence. The fine is paid to the government, not to the injured person (although the court will sometimes order **restitution,** meaning that the defendant must reimburse the victim for harm suffered). It is almost always the judge who imposes the sentence. If the jury is not persuaded of the defendant's guilt, it will **acquit** him, that is, find him not guilty.

Felony/Misdemeanor

A **felony** is a serious crime, for which a defendant can be sentenced to one year or more in prison. Murder, robbery, rape, drug dealing, money laundering, wire fraud, and embezzlement are felonies. A **misdemeanor** is a less serious crime, often punishable by a year or less in a county jail. Public drunkenness, driving without a license, and simple possession of one marijuana cigarette are considered misdemeanors in most states.

Punishment

Why punish a defendant? Sometimes the answer is obvious. If a defendant has committed armed robbery, we want that person locked up. Other cases are not so apparent.

You are the judge in charge of sentencing Jason. He is a 61-year-old minister who has devoted 40 years to serving his community, leading his church, and helping to rehabilitate schools. Fifteen years ago he founded a children's hospital and has raised enormous sums to maintain it. He has labored with local government to rebuild abandoned housing and established a center for battered women. Jason suffers from a terminal illness and will die in three to four years. But the jury has just found that in his zeal to get housing built, Jason took kickbacks from construction firms run by gangsters. The construction companies padded their bills, some of which were paid with state and city money. They kicked back a small amount of this illegal profit to Jason, who gave the money to his charities. Jason thought of himself as Robin Hood, but the law regards him as a felon. You can fine Jason and/or sentence him to prison for a maximum of five years.

A flood of letters urges you to allow Jason to continue raising money and helping others. You need to understand the rationale of punishment. Over the past several centuries, philosophers in many countries—and judges in this country—have proposed various reasons for punishing the guilty.

Restraint

A violent criminal who appears likely to commit more crimes must be physically restrained. Here there is no pretense of prison being anything but a cage to protect the rest of society. (An online group that sees little good and much evil in our system of incarceration gives examples of perceived abuses at http://www.prisonactivist.org.) In Jason's case, there is clearly no reason to restrain him.

Deterrence

Imprisonment may deter future crimes in two ways. **Specific deterrence** is intended to teach *this defendant* that crime carries a heavy price tag, in the hope that he will never do it again. **General deterrence** is the goal of demonstrating to *society generally* that crime must be shunned. Notice that both ideas of deterrence are utilitarian; that is, they are means to an end. Specific and general deterrence both assume that by imprisoning someone, the law achieves a greater good for everyone. Jason almost certainly requires no specific deterrence. Is general deterrence a reason to imprison him?

Retribution

The German philosopher Immanuel Kant (1724–1804) rejected the idea of deterrence. He argued that human beings were supremely important and as a result must always be treated as ends in themselves, *never as a means to an end.* Kant would argue that, if deterrence were legitimate, then it would be all right to torture prisoners—even innocent prisoners—if this deterred massive amounts of crime.

For Kant, there is only one valid reason to punish: the prisoner deserves it. This is the idea of **retribution**—giving back to the criminal precisely what he deserves. A moral world, said Kant, requires that the government administer to all prisoners a punishment exactly equal to the crime they committed. A murderer must be put to death (even if he is dying from an illness and would live only a few days); an executive who bribes a government official must suffer a punishment equal to the harm he caused. To Kant, all of Jason's good deeds would be irrelevant, as would his terminal illness. If three years is the appropriate imprisonment for the crime of fraud, then he must serve three years, even if he dies in prison, even if it stops him from raising $10 million for charity.

Related to the idea of retribution is **vengeance.** When a serious crime has occurred, society wants the perpetrator to suffer. If we punish no one, people lose faith in the power and effectiveness of government and may take the law into their own hands.

Rehabilitation

To rehabilitate someone is to provide training so that he may return to a normal life. Most criminal justice experts believe that little or no rehabilitation occurs in a prison, though other forms of punishment may achieve this worthy goal.

Jason's Case. What is your decision? Restraint and specific deterrence are unnecessary. You may imprison him for general

Inside a prison. Which rationale for punishment do you find most persuasive?

deterrence or for retribution. Should you let him go free so that he can raise more money for good causes? In a similar case, a federal court judge decided that general deterrence was essential. To allow someone to go free, he said, would be to send a message that certain people can get away with crime. The judge sentenced the defendant to a prison term, though he shortened the sentence based on the defendant's age and ill health.[1]

The Prosecution's Case

In all criminal cases, the prosecution faces several basic issues.

Conduct Outlawed

Virtually all crimes are created by statute. The prosecution must demonstrate to the court that the defendant's alleged conduct is indeed outlawed by a statute. Returning to Roger, the alleged video thief, the state charges that he stole video cameras from a store, a crime clearly defined by statute as burglary.

Burden of Proof

In a civil case, the plaintiff must prove her case by a preponderance of the evidence.[2] But in a criminal case, the government must prove its case **beyond a reasonable doubt.** This is because the potential harm to a criminal defendant is far greater. Roger, the video thief, can be fined and/or sent to prison. The stigma of a criminal conviction will stay with him, making it more difficult to obtain work and housing. Therefore, in all criminal cases, if the jury has any significant doubt at all that Roger stole the video cameras, it *must* acquit him. This high standard of proof in a criminal case reflects a very old belief, inherited from English law, that it is better to set 10 guilty people free than to convict a single innocent one. We will see that our law offers many protections for the accused.

Actus Reus

Actus reus means the "guilty act." **The prosecution must prove that the defendant voluntarily committed a prohibited act.** Suppose Mary Jo files an insurance claim for a stolen car, knowing that her car was not stolen. That is insurance fraud, and mail fraud if she sent documents through the Post Office. Filing the claim is the *actus reus:* Mary Jo voluntarily filled out the insurance claim and mailed it. At a bar, Mary Jo describes the claim to her friend, Chi Ling, who laughs and replies, "That's great. It'll serve the company right." Has Chi Ling committed a crime? No. There is no *actus reus,* because Chi Ling has done nothing illegal. Her cynical attitude may contribute to higher premiums for all of us, but criminal law punishes acts, not thoughts or omissions.

Mens Rea

The prosecution must also show *mens rea,* a "guilty state of mind," on the defendant's part. This is harder to prove than *actus reus*—it requires convincing evidence about something that is essentially psychological. Precisely what "state of mind" the prosecution must prove varies, depending on the crime. We will discuss the exact *mens rea* requirement for various crimes later in the chapter. In general, however, there are four mental states that a prosecutor may be required to prove, depending on the crime: **General Intent.** Most crimes require a showing of general intent, meaning that the defendant intended to do the prohibited physical action (the *actus reus*). Suppose Miller,

---

[1]   *United States v. Bergman,* 416 F. Supp. 496, 1976 U.S. Dist. LEXIS 14577 (S.D.N.Y. 1976).

[2]   See the earlier discussion in Chapter 3, on dispute resolution.

a customer in a bar, picks up a bottle and smashes it over the head of Bud. In a trial for criminal assault, the *mens rea* would simply be the intention to hit Bud. The prosecution need not show that Miller intended serious harm, only that he intended the blow.

How will a prosecutor prove what was in Miller's mind? By circumstantial evidence: a witness will describe how Miller picked up the bottle and what he did with it. A jury is free to conclude that Miller intended physical contact since there would be no other reason for his action.

Specific Intent. Some crimes require the prosecution to prove that the defendant willfully intended to do something beyond the physical act. For example, burglary requires proof that the defendant entered a building at night and intended to commit a felony inside, such as stealing property.

Reckless or Negligent Conduct. For a few crimes, the prosecution is concerned more with the defendant's irresponsible conduct than with what the defendant was thinking. **Criminal recklessness** means consciously disregarding a substantial risk of injury. A pedestrian who jokingly points a gun at another commits criminal recklessness. The danger of the gun going off is obvious, and the defendant is guilty even if no shot is fired. A slightly lesser crime, **criminal negligence,** refers to gross deviations from reasonable conduct. A hunter who sees movement and shoots at it, without bothering to determine whether the target is a turkey or a professor, commits criminal negligence.

Strict Liability. In strict liability cases, the prosecution must only prove *actus reus.* If the defendant committed the act, he is guilty, regardless of mental state or irresponsibility. For example, in an effort to improve the environment, many states now hold corporate defendants strictly liable for discharging certain pollutants into the air. If an oil refinery discharges toxic fumes, it is strictly liable, regardless of what efforts it may have taken to control emissions. Thus, strict liability crimes are the easiest for a prosecutor to prove and potentially the most dangerous to corporations.

Defenses

A criminal defendant will frequently dispute the facts that link her to the crime. For example, she might claim mistaken identity (that she merely resembles the real criminal) or offer an alibi (that she can prove she was elsewhere when the crime was committed). In addition, a defendant may offer **legal defenses.** Many of these are controversial, as we will see.

Insanity

A defendant who can prove that he was **insane** at the time of the criminal act will be declared not guilty. This reflects the moral basis of our criminal law. Insane people, though capable of great harm, historically have not been considered responsible for their acts. A defendant found to be insane will generally be committed to a mental institution. If and when that hospital determines he is no longer a danger to society, he will, in theory, be released. Some people applaud this as deeply humane, while others see it as muddled thinking that allows guilty people to walk free. The most common test for insanity is the M'Naghten Rule.

M'Naghten Rule. The defendant must show (1) that he suffered a serious, identifiable mental disease and that because of it (2) he did not understand the nature of his act or did not know that it was wrong. Suppose Jerry, a homeless man, stabs Phil. At trial, a psychiatrist testifies that Jerry suffers from chronic schizophrenia, that he does not know where he is or what he is doing, and that when he stabbed Phil he believed he was sponging down his pet giraffe. If the jury believes the psychiatrist, it may find Jerry not guilty by reason of insanity.

What if the alleged mental defect is a result of the defendant's own behavior? You be the judge.

you Be The Judge

BIEBER V. PEOPLE

856 P.2d 811, 1993 Colo. LEXIS 630
Supreme Court of Colorado, 1993

Facts: Donald Bieber walked up to a truck in which William Ellis was sitting and shot Ellis, whom he did not know, in the back of his head. He threw Ellis's body from the truck and drove away. Shortly before and after the killing, Bieber encountered various people in different places. He sang "God Bless America" and the "Marine Hymn" to them and told them he was a prisoner of war and was being followed by communists. He told people he had killed a communist on "War Memorial Highway." The police arrested him.

Bieber had a long history of drug abuse. As a teenager, he began using drugs, including amphetamines. As an adult, he continued his heavy drug use, while making money selling drugs. Several years before the homicide, Bieber voluntarily sought treatment for mental impairment, entering a hospital and saying he thought he was going to hurt someone. He was later released into a long-term drug program.

Bieber was charged with first degree murder. He pleaded not guilty by reason of insanity. An expert witness testified that he was insane, suffering from "amphetamine delusional disorder" (ADD), a recognized psychiatric illness resulting from long-term use of amphetamines and characterized by delusions. At trial, Bieber's attorney argued that he was not intoxicated at the time of the crime but that he was insane due to ADD. The trial court refused to instruct that Bieber could be legally insane due to ADD, and the jury found Bieber guilty of first degree murder. He appealed.

You Be the Judge: May a jury find that a defendant with ADD is legally insane?

Argument for Bieber: Your honors, Mr. Bieber acknowledges the rule that someone who becomes voluntarily intoxicated and commits an offense is liable for the crime. That rule is irrelevant here, since Mr. Bieber was not intoxicated at the time of this homicide. He was insane.

The state of Colorado has long held that insanity is a valid defense to a criminal charge. It is morally and legally proper to distinguish between people who commit a crime out of viciousness and those who suffer serious mental illness. Mr. Bieber suffered from amphetamine delusional disorder, a serious psychotic illness recognized by the American Psychiatric Association. There was overwhelming evidence that he was out of control and did not know what he was doing at the time of the homicide.

The fact that ADD is brought about by years of amphetamine use should make no difference in an insanity case. This man's reason was destroyed by a serious illness. He should not be treated the same as a cold-blooded killer.

Argument for the State: Your honors, there is no qualitative difference between a person who drinks or takes drugs knowing that he or she will be momentarily "mentally defective" as an immediate result and one who drinks or takes drugs knowing that he or she may be "mentally defective" as an eventual, long-term result. In both cases, the person is aware of the possible consequences of his or her actions. We do not believe that in the latter case, such knowledge should be excused simply because the resulting affliction is more severe.

It is a matter of common knowledge that the excessive use of liquor or drugs impairs the perceptual, judgmental, and volitional faculties of the user. Also, because the intoxication must be "self-induced," the defendant necessarily must have had the conscious ability to prevent this temporary incapacity from coming into being at all. Self-induced intoxication by its very nature involves culpability.

As a matter of public policy, therefore, we must not excuse a defendant's actions, which endanger others, based upon a mental disturbance or illness that he or she actively and voluntarily contracted. There is no principled basis to distinguish between the short-term and long-term effects of voluntary intoxication by punishing the first and excusing the second. If anything, the moral blameworthiness would seem to be even greater with respect to the long-term effects of many, repeated instances of voluntary intoxication occurring over an extended period of time. We ask that you affirm. ■

Jury Role. The insanity defense creates fear and confusion in the public, but most experts believe the concern is unwarranted. A Connecticut study showed that the defense was invoked in only one-tenth of 1 percent of criminal prosecutions in that state, and that in over 90 percent of *those* cases it still failed. Juries are reluctant to acquit based on insanity, probably fearing that the defendant will soon be back on the streets. But just the opposite is true. Most defendants acquitted by reason of insanity spend more time in a mental hospital than convicts spend in prison for the same act.

Entrapment

You go to a fraternity party where you meet a friendly new frat member, Joey. After a drink or two, Joey asks if you can get him some marijuana. You tell him you never use drugs. A week later you accidentally meet Joey in the cafeteria and he repeats the question, promising a very large profit if you will supply him with an ounce. You again say "no thanks." About once a week Joey bumps into you, in the school hallways, in the bookstore, at parties. He continues to ask you to "get him some stuff," and his offers grow more lucrative. Finally, after six requests, you speak to someone who is reputed to deal in drugs. You buy an ounce, then offer it to Joey at a large markup. Joey gratefully hands over the money, takes your package—and flashes his badge in your face, identifying himself as an undercover agent of the State Police. You are speechless, which is fine, since Joey informs you that you have the right to remain silent.

Drugs are a deadly serious problem in our society, involved directly or indirectly in more than half of all street crime. We need creative police efforts. Has this one gone too far? The issue is entrapment. **When the government induces the defendant to break the law, the prosecution must prove beyond a reasonable doubt that the defendant was predisposed to commit the crime.**

If the government cannot prove predisposition, the defendant is not guilty. In other words, the goal is to separate the cases where the defendant was innocent before the government tempted him from those where the defendant was only too eager to break the law.

Most courts would agree that the state police officer entrapped the student. The seller said "no" five times. Unless the government has other evidence that the defendant was involved in dealing drugs, there appears to be no predisposition, and the entrapment defense is valid.

Duress

A defendant may plead duress if she can show that a threat by a third person caused her fear of imminent serious physical harm. The threatened harm must be physical. If Roger, the video thief, could show that a drug addict threatened to kill him if he did not steal the videos, he would have a valid duress defense.

By contrast, assume that Roger, a former accountant, stole the videos because he had been out of work for 14 months. A bank foreclosed his suburban home, and he had exhausted his savings during his job search. He and his two children were subsisting in an abandoned station wagon as his wife lay in a sanatorium, weak with tuberculosis. Roger was desperate for money to make a deposit on an apartment. His claim—and all claims—of *economic* duress will fail because there is no imminent physical harm.

CRIMES THAT HARM BUSINESS

Three major crimes involve taking money from businesses: larceny, fraud, and embezzlement. In each case the criminal ends up with money or property that belongs to someone else.

Larceny

It is holiday season at the mall, the period of greatest profits—and the most crime. At the Foot Forum, a teenager limps in wearing ragged sneakers and sneaks out wearing Super Rags, valued at $145. Down the aisle at a home furnishing store, a man is so taken by a $375 power saw that he takes it. Sweethearts swipe sweaters, pensioners pocket produce. All are committing larceny.

Larceny is the trespassory taking of personal property with the intent to steal it. "Trespassory taking" means that someone else originally has the property. The Super Rags are personal property (not real estate), they were in the possession of the Foot Forum, and the teenager deliberately left without paying, intending never to return the goods. That is larceny. By contrast, suppose Fast Eddie leaves Bloomingdale's in New York, descends to the subway system, and jumps over a turnstile without paying. Larceny? No. He has "taken" a service—the train ride—but not personal property.

Every day in the United States, over $25 million in merchandise is stolen from retail stores. Economists estimate that *12 cents out of every dollar* spent in retail stores covers the cost of shoplifting. Some criminal experts believe that drug addicts commit over half of all shoplifting to support their habits. Stores have added electronic surveillance, security patrols, and magnetic antitheft devices, but the problem will not disappear. We revisit this issue later, in the Ewing case, where we examine the heavy penalty one state has imposed on repeat offenders.

Fraud

Robert Dorsey owned Bob's Chrysler in Highland, Illinois. He ordered cars from the manufacturer, the First National Bank of Highland paid Chrysler, and Dorsey—supposedly—repaid the loans as he sold autos. Dorsey, though, began to suffer financial problems, and the bank suspected he was selling cars without repaying his loans. A state investigator notified Dorsey that he planned to review all dealership records. One week later a fire engulfed the dealership. An arson investigator discovered that an electric iron, connected to a timer, had been placed on a pile of financial papers doused with accelerant.

The saddest part of this true story is that it is only too common. Some experts suggest that 1 percent of corporate revenues are wasted on fraud alone. Dorsey was convicted and imprisoned for committing two crimes that cost business billions of dollars annually—fraud and arson.[3]

Fraud refers to various crimes, all of which have a common element: **the deception of another person for the purpose of obtaining money or property from him.** Robert Dorsey's precise violation was bank fraud, a federal crime. It is bank fraud to use deceit to obtain money, assets, securities, or other property under the control of any financial institution. The maximum penalty is a fine of $1 million and/or a prison term of 30 years.[4]

Wire fraud and **mail fraud** are additional federal crimes, involving the use of interstate mail, telegram, telephone, radio, or television to obtain property by deceit.[5] For example, if Marsha makes an interstate phone call to sell land that she does not own, that is wire fraud.

Insurance fraud is another common crime. A Ford suddenly swerves in front of a Toyota, causing it to brake hard. A Mercedes, unable to stop, slams into the Toyota, as

---

[3] *United States v. Dorsey,* 27 F.3d 285, 1994 U.S. App. LEXIS 15010 (7th Cir. 1994).
[4] 18 U.S.C. §1344.
[5] 18 U.S.C. §§1341–1346.

the Ford races away. Regrettable accident? No: a "swoop and squat" fraud scheme. The Ford and Toyota drivers were working together, hoping for an accident. The "injured" Toyota driver now goes to a third member of the fraud team—a dishonest doctor—who diagnoses serious back and neck injuries and predicts long-term pain and disability. The driver files a claim against the Mercedes's driver, whose insurer may be forced to pay tens or even hundreds of thousands of dollars for an accident that was no accident. Insurance companies investigate countless cases like this each year, trying to distinguish the honest victim from the criminal.

Finally, Stacey, the hospital executive described in the chapter's introduction, committed a fourth type of fraud. **Medicare fraud** includes using false statements, bribes, or kickbacks to obtain Medicare payments from the federal or state government.[6]

*up*date

Find a current news article describing a case of *wire, mail, or insurance fraud.* What did the perpetrator do? Was the scheme subtly crafted or crudely executed? How did authorities discover the crime? What was the outcome of the case? Were there steps that a concerned businessperson or insurance executive should have taken to avoid the problem? Now be fiendishly clever: If you were a criminal, how would you "improve" on this scheme to avoid detection? What should a business executive learn from your scheming? ◆

Tragic accident . . . or felony?

© AP PHOTO/THE EXPRESS, JASON CLARKE

Arson

Robert Dorsey, the Chrysler dealer, committed a second serious crime. **Arson** is the malicious use of fire or explosives to damage or destroy any real estate or personal property. It is both a federal and a state crime. Dorsey used arson to conceal his bank fraud. Most arsonists hope to collect on insurance policies. Every year thousands of buildings burn, particularly in economically depressed neighborhoods, as owners try to make a quick kill or extricate themselves from financial difficulties. We involuntarily subsidize their immorality by paying higher insurance premiums.

Embezzlement

This crime also involves illegally obtaining property, but with one big difference: the culprit begins with legal possession. **Embezzlement is the fraudulent conversion of property already in the defendant's possession.**

Professor Beach, in North Dakota, asks his work-study student, Sandy, to drive his car to the repair shop. Sandy drives halfway and then hears on the car radio a forecast of snow. "I don't like snow," she thinks. Sandy turns south and never stops until she reaches Key West, Florida. "This is nicer," she murmurs. Sandy is innocent of larceny because she took the car keys with Beach's permission, but guilty of embezzlement because she converted the auto to her own use.

Wherever money abounds, embezzlement tempts. Banks are prime targets. A loan officer embezzled money simply by creating false loans and taking the money for himself. He paid off earlier loans by taking out new ones and managed to stay ahead of the game until he had embezzled over $5 million. He was eventually caught by a suspicious teller.[7]

---

6   18 U.S.C. §§1320 et seq. (1994).

7   *Peoples State Bank v. American Casualty Co. of Reading, Mich.,* No. Ed-8425-11, *Lawyers Weekly,* May 17, 1993, p. 6A.

Computer Crime

cyberLaw

A 29-year-old computer whiz stole a car—using his keyboard. The man infiltrated a tele-phone company network and rigged a radio station's call-in promotion, winning himself a splendid new Porsche. He also damaged court-ordered wiretaps of alleged gangsters and may even have jammed the phones on an *Unsolved Mysteries* television episode in which *he was the featured fugitive!* In another case, a teenage boy crippled the airport control tower in Worcester, Massachusetts, by breaking into a telephone network and causing a computer crash that eliminated all power at the airport. ◆

The ascent of the Internet inevitably brings with it new forms of crime. Various federal statutes criminalize this behavior.

- The **Computer Fraud and Abuse Act** prohibits using a computer to commit theft, espionage, trespass, fraud, and damage to another computer.[8] This statute is the focal point of the case below.

- The **Access Device Fraud Act** outlaws the fraudulent use of cards, codes, account numbers, and other devices to obtain money, goods, or services.[9] For example, it is a violation of this act to reprogram a cellular telephone so that calls are charged to an improper account.

- The **Identity Theft and Assumption Deterrence Act** bars the use of false identifi-cation to commit fraud or other crime.[10] A waiter who uses stolen credit card num-bers to buy airline tickets has violated this act. The Federal Trade Commission receives about 100,000 complaints of identity theft every year, so you should guard identifying data carefully.

- The **Wire and Electronic Communications Interception Act** makes it a crime to intercept most wire, oral, and electronic communications.[11] (This law does not pro-hibit recording your own conversations.) We *warned* you not to tape your room-mate's conversations!

Identity Theft

Identity theft is growing explosively. How do thieves get personal information?

- Steal records at work by hacking into company files or bribing coworkers.
- Rummage through trash or mailboxes.
- Pose as a landlord or employer with a valid interest in your credit.
- "Skim," which means to use an electronic device to record your personal information when you are using a credit card for a proper purpose, such as paying at a retail store.
- "Phish," which means to contact you by phone or e-mail, posing as a legitimate company attempting to correct a problem with your account.

What do thieves do with private data?

- Open new credit card accounts and purchase "big ticket" items.
- Open a new bank account and write bad checks.
- Use credit cards and checks to drain your bank account.

---

[8] 18 U.S.C. §1030.
[9] 18 U.S.C. §1029.
[10] 18 U.S.C. §1028.
[11] 18 U.S.C. §2511.

- Give your name to police during an investigation, meaning that when the thieves fail to appear in court, a warrant will issue for *your* arrest.

How should an identity theft victim respond?

- Place a fraud alert on your credit reports, by phoning one of three credit companies (Equifax, 800-525-6285; Experian, 888-397-3742; TransUnion, 800-680-7289).

- Close any account that is potentially affected.

- Notify the local police.

- File a complaint with the Federal Trade Commission. You may do this online, at http://www.consumer.gov/idtheft.

The following case illustrates the type of simple scam that can blight the credit rating of innocent victims.

UNITED STATES V. AMURE

83 Fed. Appx. 52, 2003 WL 22905306
Sixth Circuit Court of Appeals, 2003

Facts: Femi Amure was convicted of identity theft in the sale of automobiles. He was sentenced to 26 months incarceration and two years of supervised release, and ordered to pay restitution of $73,817. Amure appealed, claiming that there was no credible evidence he had committed this crime.

Issue: Was there sufficient evidence that Amure committed identity theft?

Excerpts from the Court's *Per Curiam* Decision: Amure's sole argument on appeal centers on the purported lack of credibility of Anthony Davis ("Davis"). As a cooperating co-defendant, Davis testified at trial, describing how he obtained the credit histories and social security numbers of various individuals using credit software, then used—or had others use—the information to buy vehicles at several dealerships in Tennessee and Mississippi.

Davis explained that he wanted to help a friend, Kevin Walsh ("Walsh"), buy a Lexus automobile. Walsh contacted the Herrin-Gear Lexus dealership in Jackson and asked that a credit application be faxed to Davis's office. When Davis received the fax from the Jackson dealership, he called the salesman who had sent the fax. That salesman was Amure. According to Davis, Amure was told about, and agreed to go along with, Davis's scheme. Davis and Walsh thereafter traveled to Herrin-Gear where they purchased a 1998 Lexus LS400 using the identifying information of a person who, unlike Walsh, had a good credit history.

Davis next explained that he helped Winfred Boyd ("Boyd") buy a 2001 Lexus GS430 from Amure.

The car was intended for someone to whom Boyd owed money. According to Davis, Amure was paid $1,000.00 for his part in the Boyd sale.

Davis also testified that Amure processed the sale of a 2001 Chevrolet Tahoe for a "Sean Kearney." "Sean Kearney" was, in fact, Sylvester Kearney ("Kearney"), a co-defendant in this case. Because Kearney did not have insurance, Davis made up an insurance certificate for Kearney that he faxed to Amure. Kearney (who pleaded guilty in the case) testified that he paid Amure $1,000.00 when Amure delivered the car to him.

Davis finally testified that he purchased from Amure a 1998 Chevrolet Corvette for a friend of his, Deadrick Clayborn ("Clayborn"). Davis negotiated the deal in the name of John C. Davis, using a Social Security number that he obtained using his credit software. The car was delivered by Amure to Davis and Clayborn at an exit ramp on the expressway outside of Jackson.

Amure contends that, if the jurors had been rational, they would have disbelieved Davis and acquitted him on all counts. The jurors, however, observed Davis on the witness stand; they heard defense counsel's attacks on Davis's credibility during cross-examination and closing arguments; they were instructed as to their role in assessing witness credibility; and they chose to believe at least part of what Davis said. It is not our role to question the jury's assessment of Davis's credibility.

We affirm. ∎

CRIMES COMMITTED BY BUSINESS

A corporation can be found guilty of a crime based on the conduct of any of its **agents,** who include anyone undertaking work on behalf of the corporation. An agent can be a corporate officer, an accountant hired to audit a statement, a sales clerk, or almost any other person performing a job at the company's request.

If an agent commits a criminal act within the scope of his employment and with the intent to benefit the corporation, the company is liable.[12] This means that the agent himself must first be guilty. The normal requirements of *actus reus* and *mens rea* apply. If the agent is guilty, the corporation is, too.

Critics believe that the criminal law has gone too far. It is unfair, they argue, to impose *criminal* liability on a corporation, and thus penalize the shareholders, unless high-ranking officers were directly involved in the illegal conduct. The following case concerns a corporation's responsibility for an employee's death.

WISCONSIN V. KNUTSON, INC.

196 Wis. 2d 86, 537 N.W.2d 420, 1995 Wis. App. LEXIS 1223
Wisconsin Court of Appeals, 1995

Facts: Richard Knutson, Inc. (RKI) was constructing a sanitary sewer line for the city of Oconomowoc. An RKI crew attempted to place a section of corrugated metal pipe in a trench in order to remove groundwater. The backhoe operator misjudged the distance from the backhoe's boom to the overhead power lines and failed to realize he had placed the boom in contact with the wires. A crew member attempted to attach a chain to the backhoe's bucket and was instantly electrocuted.

The state charged RKI with negligent vehicular homicide under a statute that says: "Whoever causes the death of another human being by the negligent operation or handling of a vehicle is guilty of a Class E felony." The jury convicted, and RKI appealed, claiming that a corporation could not be held guilty under the statute.

Issue: May a corporation be guilty of vehicular homicide under the statute?

Excerpts from Judge Anderson's Decision: Here, the statute does not provide a definition of "whoever." We will thus employ extrinsic aids to uncover the legislature's intent.

LaFave and Scott [authors of a leading treatise] summarize the persuasive policy considerations supporting corporate criminal liability. Among those considerations is the factor that the corporate business entity has become a way of life in this country and the imposition of criminal liability is an essential part of the regulatory process. Another consideration centers on the premise that it would be unjust to single out one or more persons for criminal punishment when it is the corporate culture that is the origin of the criminal behavior. Also, the size of many corporations makes it impossible to adequately allocate responsibility to individuals.

An additional consideration is the indirect economic benefits that may accrue to the corporation through crimes against the person. To get these economic benefits, corporate management may shortcut expensive safety precautions, respond forcibly to strikes, or engage in criminal anticompetitive behavior. It has also been suggested that the free market system cannot be depended upon to guide corporate decisions in socially acceptable ways, and the threat of imposition of criminal liability is needed to deter inappropriate (criminal) corporate behavior. We agree that if a penal statute is intended to inhibit an act, a corporation is included within the class of perpetrators if to do so is within the spirit and purpose of the act. [The court concluded that a corporation may be guilty of vehicular homicide.]

Sufficiency of the Evidence: Homicide by negligent use of a vehicle has three elements: (1) that the defendant cause death (2) by criminal negligence (3)

▼

---

[12] *New York Central & Hudson River R.R. Co. v. United States,* 212 U.S. 481, 29 S. Ct. 304, 1909 U.S. LEXIS 1832 (1909). And note that what counts is the intention to benefit, not actual benefit. A corporation will not escape liability by showing that the scheme failed.

in the operation of a vehicle. Criminal negligence differs from ordinary negligence in two respects. First, the risk is more serious—death or great bodily harm as opposed to simple harm. Second, the risk must be more than an unreasonable risk—it must also be substantial.

RKI's management took no action to have the power lines de-energized or barriers erected; rather, management elected to merely warn employees about the overhead lines.

The evidence supports the conclusion that if RKI had enforced the written safety regulations of OSHA, had abided by its own written safety pro-gram and had complied with the contract requirements for construction on Wisconsin Electric's property, the electrocution death would likely not have happened. The finder of fact was justified in concluding that RKI operated vehicles in close proximity to the overhead power lines without recognizing the potential hazard to its employees in the vicinity of the vehicles. The jury could reasonably find that RKI's failure to take elementary precautions for the safety of its employees was a substantial cause of the electrocution death.

Judgment *affirmed*. ■

Punishing a Corporation

Fines

The most common punishment for a corporation is a fine. This makes sense in that the purpose of a business is to earn a profit, and a fine, theoretically, hurts. But most fines are modest by the present standards of corporate wealth.

Odwalla, Inc., sold fruit juices and nutritional shakes throughout much of the United States. A batch of its apple juice, which contained the highly toxic *E. coli* bacteria, killed a 16-month-old girl and seriously harmed 70 other people. Federal officials prosecuted, charging the company with violating food safety laws. Eventually, the company pleaded guilty, agreed to pay a $1.5 million fine, and submitted to a court-supervised probation for five years. Some public interest law groups applauded the punishment. Critics, though, complained that a million dollar fine is petty change for a large corporation and may have no deterrent effect on other companies. Odwalla has also paid millions of dollars to settle civil lawsuits brought by the injured consumers.

Compliance Programs

The **Federal Sentencing Guidelines** are the detailed rules that judges must follow when sentencing defendants convicted of crimes in federal court. The guidelines instruct judges to determine whether, at the time of the crime, the corporation had in place a serious **compliance program,** that is, a plan to prevent and detect criminal conduct at all levels of the company. A company that can point to a detailed, functioning compliance program may benefit from a dramatic reduction in the fine or other punishment meted out. Indeed, a tough compliance program may even convince federal investigators to curtail an investigation and to limit any prosecution to those directly involved, rather than attempting to get a conviction against high-ranking officers or the company itself.

at RISK

To persuade prosecutors or judges that it seriously intended to follow the law, a company must demonstrate a thorough and effective compliance plan:

- The program must be reasonably capable of reducing the prospect of criminal conduct.

- Specific, high-level officers must be responsible for overseeing the program.

- The company must not place in charge any officers it knows or should have known, from past experience, that are likely to engage in illegal conduct.

- The company must effectively communicate the program to all employees and agents.

- The company must ensure compliance by monitoring employees in a position to cheat and by promptly disciplining any who break the law. ◆

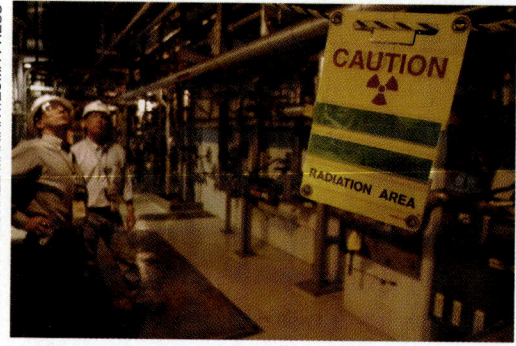

Is this business committing a crime?

Selected Crimes Committed by Business

Workplace Crimes

The workplace can be dangerous. Working on an assembly line exposes factory employees to fast-moving machinery. For a roofer, the first slip may be the last. The invisible radiation in a nuclear power plant can be deadlier than a bullet. The most important statute regulating the workplace is the federal **Occupational Safety and Health Act of 1970 (OSHA)**,[13] which sets safety standards for many industries.[14] May a state government go beyond standards set by OSHA and use the criminal law to punish dangerous conditions? In *People v. O'Neill*,[15] the courts of Illinois answered that question with a potent "yes," permitting a *murder prosecution* against corporate executives. Notice that whereas Wisconsin prosecuted RKI *Corporation* for vehicular homicide, Illinois brought this case against the corporate executives themselves.

NEWS*worthy*

Film Recovery Systems was an Illinois corporation in business to extract silver from used X-ray film and then resell it. Steven O'Neill was president of Film Recovery, Charles Kirschbaum was its plant manager, and Daniel Rodriguez the foreman. To extract the silver, workers at Film Recovery soaked the X-ray film in large, open, bubbling vats that contained sodium cyanide.

A worker named Stefan Golab became faint. He left the production area and walked to the lunchroom, where workers found him trembling and foaming at the mouth. He lost consciousness. Paramedics were unable to revive him. They rushed him to a hospital where he was pronounced dead on arrival. The Cook County medical examiner determined that Golab died from acute cyanide poisoning caused by inhalation of cyanide fumes in the plant.

Illinois indicted Film Recovery and several of its managers for murder. The indictment charged that O'Neill and Kirschbaum committed murder by failing to disclose to Golab that he was working with cyanide and other potentially lethal substances and by failing to provide him with appropriate and necessary safety equipment.

The case was tried to a judge without a jury. Workers testified that O'Neill, Kirschbaum, and other managers never told them they were using cyanide or that the fumes they inhaled could be harmful; that management made no effort to ventilate the factory; that Film Recovery gave the workers no goggles or protective clothing; that the chemicals they worked with burned their skin; that breathing was difficult in the plant because of strong, foul orders; and that workers suffered frequent dizziness, nausea, and vomiting.

The trial judge found O'Neill, Kirschbaum, and others guilty of murder. Illinois defines murder as performing an act that the defendant *knows will create a strong probability of death* in the victim, and the judge found they had done that. He found Film Recovery guilty of involuntary manslaughter. Involuntary manslaughter is *recklessly* performing an act that causes death. He sentenced O'Neill, Kirschbaum, and Rodriguez to 25 years in prison.

---

[13] 29 U.S.C. §§651 et seq. (1982).

[14] See Chapter 30, on employment law.

[15] 194 Ill. App. 3d 79, 550 N.E.2d 1090, 1990 Ill. App. LEXIS 65 (Ill. App. Ct. 1990).

The defendants appealed, contending that the verdicts were inconsistent. They argued, and the Illinois Court of Appeals agreed, that the judge had made contradictory findings. Murder required the specific intent of *knowing there was a strong probability of death,* whereas the manslaughter conviction required *reckless* conduct. The appeals court reversed the convictions and remanded for a new trial.

Moments before the new trial was to start, O'Neill, Kirschbaum, and Rodriguez all pleaded guilty to involuntary manslaughter. They received sentences of three years, two years, and four months, respectively. ◆

RICO

The **Racketeer Influenced and Corrupt Organizations Act (RICO)**[16] is one of the most powerful and controversial statutes ever written. Congress passed the law primarily to prevent gangsters from taking money they earned illegally and investing it in legitimate businesses. But RICO has expanded far beyond the original intentions of Congress and is now used more often against ordinary businesses than against organized criminals. Some regard this wide application as a tremendous advance in law enforcement, but others view it as an oppressive weapon used to club ethical companies into settlements they should never have to make.

RICO creates both criminal and civil law liabilities. The government may prosecute both individuals and organizations for violating RICO. For example, the government may prosecute a mobster, claiming that he has run a heroin ring for years. It may also prosecute an accounting firm, claiming that it lied about corporate assets in a stock sale to make the shares appear more valuable than they really were. If the government proves its case, the defendant can be hit with large fines and a prison sentence of up to 20 years. RICO also permits the government to seek forfeiture of the defendant's property. A court may order a convicted defendant to hand over any property or money used in the criminal acts or derived from them.

RICO creates civil liability as well. The government, organizations, and individuals all have the right to file civil lawsuits, seeking damages and, if necessary, injunctions. For example, shareholders claiming that they were harmed by the accounting firm's lies could sue the firm for money lost in buying and selling the stock. RICO is powerful (and for defendants, frightening) in part because a civil plaintiff can recover **treble damages,** that is, a judgment for three times the harm actually suffered, and can also recover attorney's fees.

What is a violation of this law? **RICO prohibits using two or more racketeering acts to accomplish any of these goals: (1) investing in or acquiring legitimate businesses with criminal money; (2) maintaining or acquiring businesses through criminal activity; or (3) operating businesses through criminal activity.**

What does that mean in English? It is a two-step process to prove that a person or an organization has violated RICO. We will assume that this is a criminal prosecution, though the steps are similar in a civil lawsuit.

- The prosecutor must show that the defendant committed two or more **racketeering acts,** which are any of a long list of specified crimes: embezzlement, arson, mail fraud, wire fraud, and so forth. Thus, if a gangster ordered a building torched in January and then burned a second building in October, that would be two racketeering acts. If a stockbroker told two customers that Bronx Gold Mines was a promising stock, when she knew that it was worthless, that would be two racketeering acts.

---

[16] 18 U.S.C. §§1961–1968.

- The prosecutor must show that the defendant used these racketeering acts to accomplish one of the three *purposes* listed above. If the gangster committed two arsons and then used the insurance payments to buy a dry cleaning business, that would violate RICO. If the stockbroker gave fraudulent advice and used the commissions to buy advertising for her firm, that would violate RICO.

Money Laundering

Money laundering consists of taking the proceeds of certain criminal acts and either (1) using the money to promote crime, or (2) attempting to conceal the source of the money.[17]

Money laundering is an important part of major criminal enterprises. Successful criminals earn enormous sums, and they strive to filter their profits back into the flow of commerce so that their crimes go undetected. Laundering is an essential part of the corrosive traffic in drugs. Profits, all in cash, mount so swiftly that the most difficult step for a successful dealer can be to use the money without attracting the government's attention. However, as the following case illustrates, it is not only drug dealers who seek to launder their wrongfully obtained cash. Why don't you stop by the clinic and let us have a look at that knee?

UNITED STATES V. BIEGANOWSKI

313 F.3d 264
Fifth Circuit Court of Appeals, 2002

Facts: Dr. Arthur Bieganowski operated five health clinics in El Paso, Texas. Richard Goldberg was his accountant. The government charged the pair with mail fraud and money laundering, in a three-part conspiracy. First, the defendants used a telemarketer, Richard Griego, to solicit patients, mostly auto-accident victims. Second, the pair submitted false invoices to insurance companies, billing for services that were unnecessary or never performed. Third, the two laundered the proceeds. Their billing service, called Servicio de Facturacion (Servicio) and located in Ciudad Juarez, Mexico, mailed invoices, then deposited insurance company reimbursements in clinic accounts at Bank of the West, in El Paso. From there the money was transferred to a Servicio account at the same bank, then to an account called UTM Professional Management (same bank), then to a different UTM account at Barclays Bank in New York, and finally to a Barclays bank in the Cayman Islands.

Both Bieganowski and Goldberg were convicted of mail fraud and money laundering. In this part of the case, Goldberg appeals his conviction and eight-year sentence, claiming there was insufficient evidence.

Issue: Was there sufficient evidence to convict Goldberg of mail fraud and money laundering?

Excerpts from Judge Garwood's Decision:

Mail Fraud
Goldberg's affiliation with Dr. Bieganowski's practice far exceeded the limits of an ordinary professional relationship, and involved him in nearly every aspect of the operation of the clinics. He spent almost every afternoon at Dr. Bieganowski's clinic and attended multiple meetings with the clinic staff, including meetings addressing such mundane administrative matters as employee dress codes.

The record also indicates that Goldberg was closely involved with Dr. Bieganowski's solicitation efforts. He not only attended meetings with Robert Griego, Bieganowski's telemarketer, but also reviewed the script that Griego used to solicit new patients. Goldberg knew that Griego told reluctant patients that they could increase their automobile-insurance settlements by generating higher medical bills, and he knew that Griego advised patients to obtain medical examinations even when those same patients told Griego that they were not injured.

Further, Goldberg's extensive efforts in setting up and overseeing an elaborate virtual labyrinth of bank accounts for Dr. Bieganowski's clinics, which concealed both the clinics' and Dr. Bieganowski's rela-

▼

---

[17] 18 U.S.C. §§1956 et seq.

tionship to the accounts and the ultimate disposition of the funds, is plainly suggestive of guilty knowledge. Goldberg correctly points out that each piece of evidence against him, viewed separately, may admit of an innocent explanation. That, however, is not determinative. The cumulative effect of this evidence is sufficient to support the inference that Goldberg was aware of the fraudulent billing practices.

Money Laundering

Agent Hivic of the IRS testified that over six million dollars of insurance company reimbursements were deposited in the various clinics' accounts. All of that six million dollars was then transferred from the clinics' accounts at the Bank of the West to the Servicio account, also located at the Bank of the West. Of that six million dollars, a little over two million was eventually transferred to the Cayman Islands.

Goldberg's argument proceeds from the premise that the Government failed to prove that *all* of Dr. Bieganowski's billings were fraudulent. If *some* billings were legitimate, then at least *some* of the money that was deposited into the clinic accounts at the Bank of the West and then consolidated in the Servicio account was also legitimate.

The entire six million dollars deposited into the clinics' accounts was thereafter transferred to the Servicio account. Therefore, even assuming that the Government only proved that a portion of those six million dollars represented the proceeds of fraudulent activity, the prosecution nevertheless satisfied its burden of demonstrating that the transfer involved the proceeds of specified unlawful activity.

There is also little doubt that the transfers from the clinics' accounts to the Servicio account were designed to conceal the source of the unlawful funds. A casual observer would not have immediately linked the contents of the Servicio account to Bieganowski as neither Dr. Bieganowski nor Goldberg were listed as shareholders (or officers or directors or authorized agents or account signatories) of Servicio.

[Affirmed as to mail fraud and money laundering convictions.] ■

PublicPolicy

Some people describe financial scams as "victimless crimes." Clearly this court, by imposing an eight-year sentence on Goldberg, sees the harm as real. Who is hurt by an insurance scheme like this? Was the punishment appropriate? ◆

Other Crimes

Additional crimes that affect business appear elsewhere in the text. An increasing number of federal and state statutes are designed to punish those who harm the environment. (See Chapter 41, on environmental law.) Antitrust violations, in which a corporation establishes a monopoly, can lead to criminal prosecutions. (See Chapter 39, on antitrust law.) Finally, securities fraud is a crime and can lead to severe prison sentences. (See Chapter 37, on securities regulation.)

Economics
& the Law

Reputational Penalty. Businesses convicted of criminal conduct often pay more than just a fine. Many economists have concluded that companies suffer significant reputational penalties as well. Studies indicate that several negative consequences generally follow a criminal conviction.

First, stock prices fall significantly, reducing shareholder wealth. The angry shareholders may seek compensation from the executives who committed the crime. Second, executives are often forced out of the offending company.

Finally, business relationships often suffer, especially for crimes such as fraud or overcharging in a contract. Suppose that Integrity Motors promises to sell to PlaneMaker 1,000 aircraft engines that have been tested for quality control. When too many of the engines fail, the state government convicts Integrity of falsifying test results. PlaneMaker will never buy another engine from Integrity, and other aircraft manufacturers may also turn away from the convicted company. One study concluded that these reputational penalties are much more likely to occur when the crime is committed against customers, as in the fraud case, rather than against the general public, as in a case of environmental damage.[18] ◆

---

[18] Alexander, "On the Nature of the Reputational Penalty for Corporate Crime: Evidence," *Journal of Law and Economics,* 1999, vol. 42, p. 489.

CONSTITUTIONAL PROTECTIONS

The police arrest Jake and charge him with armed robbery and rape. They claim that he entered a convenience store, took all the money from the cash register, robbed the clerk of her wristwatch, and then raped her. Jake refuses to talk, but the police are absolutely certain he is guilty. The community is outraged and wants a conviction. Should the police be allowed to question Jake for hours without stopping? May they lock him in a walk-in freezer? Beat him? After 5 hours of interrogation, followed by 10 hours in a freezer and a severe beating, Jake confesses. He tells the police where to find the money and the clerk's watch. Does his guilt render the police conduct acceptable?

These are issues of **criminal procedure.** We are no longer looking at the elements of particular crimes, as we have thus far, but at the *process of investigating, interrogating, and trying* a criminal defendant. The first 10 amendments to the United States Constitution, known as the Bill of Rights, control the behavior of all law enforcement officers.[19] In this section we look at some of the protections these amendments offer.

The Criminal Process

In order to understand constitutional safeguards, we need to know how the police do their work. The exact steps will vary from case to case, but the summary in Exhibit 8.1 highlights the important steps.

Informant

Yasmin is a secretary to Stacey, the Be Patient executive who opened this chapter. On her lunch break, Yasmin gets up the courage to telephone an FBI office and speaks to Moe, an agent. She reports that Stacey routinely charges the government for patients who do not exist. Moe arranges to interview Yasmin at her apartment that evening. He tape-records everything she says, including her own job history, her duties at Be Patient, and how she knows about the fraud. Yasmin has not only seen the false bills, she has entered some of them on computers. The next day, Moe prepares an **affidavit** for Yasmin to sign, detailing everything she told him. An affidavit is simply a written statement signed under oath.

Warrant

Moe takes Yasmin's affidavit to a United States magistrate, an employee of the federal courts who is similar to a judge. Moe asks the magistrate to issue search warrants for Be Patient's patient records. A search warrant is written permission from a neutral official, such as the magistrate, to conduct a search. **A warrant must specify with reasonable certainty the place to be searched and the items to be seized.** This warrant application names all five of Be Patient's hospitals and asks to look through their admission notes, surgery and doctor reports, and discharge data. It states that the records will be copied so that they can be compared with the bills the government has received.

Probable Cause

The magistrate will issue a warrant only if there is probable cause. **Probable cause** means that based on all of the information presented **it is likely that evidence of**

---

[19] As discussed in Chapter 5, on constitutional law, most of the protections as written apply only to state government or the federal government. But through the process of incorporation, almost all important criminal procedure rights have been expanded to apply to federal, state, and local governments.

Exhibit 8.1

crime will be found in the place mentioned. The magistrate will look at Yasmin's affidavit to determine (1) whether the informant (Yasmin) is reliable and (2) whether she has a sound basis for the information. If Yasmin is a five-time drug offender whose information has proven wrong in the past, the warrant should not issue. Here, Yasmin's career record is good, she has no apparent motive to lie, and she is in an excellent position to know what she is talking about. The magistrate issues the warrant, specifying exactly what records may be examined.

Search and Seizure

Armed with the warrants, Moe and other agents arrive at the various hospitals, show the warrants, and take away the appropriate records. The **search** may not exceed what is described in the warrant. Even if Moe suspects that Dr. Narkem is illegally drugging certain patients, he may not seize test tube samples from the lab. He may take only the records described in the warrant.

The agents cart the records back to headquarters and enter the data on a computer. The computer compares the records of actual patients with the bills submitted to the government and indicates that 10 percent of all bills are for fictional patients. Moe summarizes the new data on additional affidavits and presents the affidavits to the magistrate, who issues **arrest warrants,** authorizing the FBI to arrest Stacey and others involved in the overbilling.

Arrest

Moe arrives at Be Patient and informs Stacey that she is under arrest. He reads her the *Miranda* warnings, discussed below. He drives Stacey to FBI headquarters where she is **booked;** that is, her name, photograph, and fingerprints are entered in a log, along with the charges. She is entitled to a prompt **bail hearing.** A judge or magistrate will set an amount of bail that she must pay in order to go free pending the trial. The purpose of bail is to ensure that Stacey will appear for all future court hearings.

Indictment

Moe turns all of his evidence over to Larry, the local prosecutor for the United States. Larry presents the evidence to a **grand jury,** which is a group of ordinary citizens, like a trial jury. But the grand jury holds hearings for several weeks at a time, on many different cases. It is the grand jury's job to determine whether there is probable cause that this defendant committed the crime with which she is charged. Larry shows the computer comparison of the bills with the actual patient lists, and the grand jury votes to indict Stacey. An **indictment** is the government's formal charge that the defendant has committed a crime and must stand trial. The grand jury is persuaded that there is probable cause that Stacey billed for 1,550 nonexistent patients, charging the government for $290 million worth of services that were never performed. The grand jury indicts her for (1) Medicare fraud, (2) mail fraud, (3) several computer crimes, and (4) RICO violations.[20] It also indicts Be Patient, Inc., and other employees.

Arraignment

Stacey is ordered back to court. A clerk reads her the formal charges of the indictment. The judge asks whether Stacey has a lawyer, and of course she does. If she did not, the judge would urge her to get one quickly. If a defendant cannot afford a lawyer, the court will appoint one to represent her free of charge. The judge now asks the lawyer how Stacey pleads to the charges. Her lawyer answers that she pleads not guilty to all charges.

Discovery

During the months before trial, both prosecution and defense will prepare the most effective case possible. There is less formal discovery than in civil trials. The prosecution is obligated to hand over any evidence favorable to the defense that the defense attorney requests. The defense has a more limited obligation to inform the prosecution. In most states, for example, if the defense will be based on an alibi, counsel must explain the alibi to the government before trial. In Stacey's case most of the evidence is data that both sides already possess.

Motion to Suppress

If the defense claims that the prosecution obtained evidence illegally, it will move to suppress it. A **motion to suppress** is a request that the court exclude certain evidence because it was obtained in violation of the Constitution. We look at those violations later.

---

[20] In federal court, when the defendant is charged with a felony, formal charges may be made only by indictment. In many state court cases, the prosecutor is not required to seek an indictment. Instead, she may file an **information,** which is simply a formal written accusation. In state courts, most cases now begin by information.

Plea Bargaining

Sometime before trial the two attorneys will meet to consider a plea bargain. A **plea bargain** is an agreement between prosecution and defense that the defendant will plead guilty to a reduced charge, and the prosecution will recommend to the judge a relatively lenient sentence. Based on the RICO violations alone, Stacey faces a possible 20-year prison sentence, along with a large fine and a devastating forfeiture order. The government makes this offer: Stacey will plead guilty to 100 counts of mail fraud; Be Patient will repay all $290 million and an additional $150 million in fines; the government will drop the RICO and computer crime charges and recommend to the judge that Stacey be fined only $1 million and sentenced to three years in prison. In the federal court system, about 75 percent of all prosecutions end in a plea bargain. In state court systems the number is often higher.

Stacey agrees to the government's offer. The judge accepts the plea, and Stacey is fined and sentenced accordingly. A judge need not accept the bargain, but usually does.

Trial and Appeal

When there is no plea bargain, the case must go to trial. The mechanics of a criminal trial are similar to those for a civil trial, described in Chapter 3, on dispute resolution. It is the prosecution's job to convince the jury beyond a reasonable doubt that the defendant committed every element of the crime charged. The defense counsel will do everything possible to win an acquittal. In federal courts, prosecutors obtain a conviction in about 80 percent of cases; in state courts, the percentage is slightly lower. Convicted defendants have a right to appeal, and again, the appellate process is similar to that described in Chapter 3.

The Fourth Amendment

The Fourth Amendment prohibits the government from making illegal searches and seizures. This amendment protects individuals, corporations, partnerships, and other organizations.

In general, the police must obtain a warrant before conducting a search. There are six exceptions to this rule, in which the police may **search without a warrant:**

- *Plain View.* Police may search if they see a machine gun, for example, sticking out from under the front seat of a parked car.

- *Stop and Frisk.* If police have an articulable reason for suspecting that someone may be armed and dangerous, they may pat him down.

- *Emergencies.* If police pursue a store robber and catch him, they may search.

- *Automobiles.* If police have lawfully stopped a car and observe evidence of other crimes in the car, such as burglary tools, they may search.

- *Lawful Arrest.* Police may always search a suspect they have arrested.

- *Consent.* If someone in lawful occupancy of a home gives consent to a search, the police may do so.

Apart from those six cases, a warrant is required. If the police search without one, they have violated the Fourth Amendment. Even a search conducted with a warrant can violate the amendment. **A search with a warrant violates the Fourth Amendment if:**

- There was no probable cause to issue the warrant

- The warrant does not specify the place to be searched and the things sought; or

- The search extends beyond what is specified in the warrant.

Exclusionary Rule

Under the exclusionary rule, evidence obtained illegally may not be used at trial against the victim of the search. If the police conduct a warrantless search that is not one of the six exceptions, any evidence they find will be excluded from the trial.

Suppose when Yasmin called the FBI, Moe simply drove straight to one of Be Patient's hospitals and grabbed patient records. Moe lacked a warrant, and his search would be illegal. Stacey's lawyer would file a **motion to suppress** the evidence. Before the trial starts, the judge would hold a hearing. If he agreed that the search was illegal, he would **exclude** the evidence, that is, refuse to allow it in trial. The government could go forward with the prosecution only if it had other evidence.[21]

Is the exclusionary rule a good idea? The Supreme Court created the exclusionary rule to ensure that police conduct legal searches. The theory is simple: if police know in advance that illegally obtained evidence cannot be used in court, they will not be tempted to make improper searches.

Opponents of the rule argue that a guilty person may go free because one police officer bungled. They are outraged by cases like *Coolidge v. New Hampshire.*[22] Pamela Mason, a 14-year-old babysitter, was brutally murdered. Citizens of New Hampshire were furious, and the state's attorney general personally led the investigation. Police found strong evidence that Edward Coolidge had done it. They took the evidence to the attorney general who personally issued a search warrant. The search of Coolidge's car uncovered incriminating evidence, and he was found guilty of murder and sentenced to life in prison. But the United States Supreme Court reversed the conviction. The warrant had not been issued by a neutral magistrate. A law officer may not lead an investigation and simultaneously decide what searches are permissible.

After the Supreme Court reversed Coolidge's conviction, New Hampshire scheduled a new trial, attempting to convict him with evidence lawfully obtained. Before the trial began, Coolidge pleaded guilty to second degree murder. He was sentenced and remained in prison until his release 27 years later.

In fact, very few people do go free because of the exclusionary rule. For example, a study by the General Accounting Office showed that suppression motions were filed in 10.5 percent of all federal prosecutions. But in 80 to 90 percent of those motions, the judge declared that the search was legal. Evidence was actually excluded in only 1.3 percent of all prosecutions. And in about one-half of *those* cases, the court convicted the defendant on other evidence. Only in 0.7 percent of all prosecutions did the defendant go free after the evidence was suppressed. Other studies reveal similar results.[23]

---

[21] There are two important exceptions to the exclusionary rule:

Inevitable Discovery Exception. Suppose that Moe's search of Be Patient is declared illegal. But then officials in the Medicare office testify that they were already aware of Be Patient's fraud, had already obtained some proof, and were about to seek a search warrant for the same records that Moe took. If the court believes the testimony, it will allow the evidence to be used. The inevitable discovery exception permits the use of evidence that would inevitably have been discovered even without the illegal search.

Good Faith Exception. Suppose the police use a search warrant believing it to be proper, but it later proves to have been defective. Is the search therefore illegal? No, said the Supreme Court in *United States v. Leon,* 468 U.S. 897, 104 S. Ct. 3405, 1984 U.S. LEXIS 153 (1984). As long as the police reasonably believed the warrant was valid, the search is legal. It would violate the Fourth Amendment if, for example, it was later shown that the police knew the affidavit used to obtain the warrant was filled with lies. In such a case, the search would be illegal and the evidence obtained would be excluded.

[22] 403 U.S. 443, 91 S. Ct. 2022, 1971 U.S. LEXIS 25 (1971).

[23] See the discussion in *United States v. Leon* (Justice Brennan, dissenting), cited at footnote 21.

The Patriot Act of 2001

In response to the devastating attacks of September 11, 2001, Congress passed a sweeping anti-terrorist law known as the Patriot Act. The statute was designed to give law enforcement officials greater power to investigate and prevent potential terrorist assaults. The bill raced through Congress nearly unopposed. Proponents hailed it as a vital weapon for use against continuing lethal threats. Opponents argued that the law was passed in haste and threatened the liberties of the very people it purported to shield. They urged that the statute gave law officers too much power, permitting them to conduct searches, intercept private Internet communications, and examine financial and academic records—all with little or no judicial oversight. Supporters of the law responded that its most controversial sections were scheduled to expire in four years. In the meantime, they said, constitutional protections governed the law as they did all others.

As this book goes to press, it is difficult to assess the full impact of the Patriot Act. In an early legal test, a federal judge permitted the government to use secret evidence in its effort to freeze the assets of Global Relief Foundation, a religious organization suspected of terrorist activity. The group, which claimed to be purely humanitarian, asserted that it could hardly defend itself against unseen evidence. Finding "acute national security concerns," the judge allowed the government to introduce the evidence in private, without the foundation ever seeing it.

However, a different court struck down a controversial provision of the Patriot Act. The statute permits the FBI to issue a **national security letter** (NSL) to communications firms such as Internet service providers and telephone companies. An NSL typically demands that the recipient furnish to the government its customer records, and that the recipient never divulge to anyone what it has done. Under the Patriot Act, the FBI may issue an NSL, without court approval, anytime it believes the records are relevant to a terrorist investigation. A federal judge declared this section of the Patriot Act unconstitutional, because it authorized "coercive searches effectively immune from any judicial process, in violation of the Fourth Amendment." The court also declared that the section's nondisclosure requirement violated the free speech protections of the First Amendment.[24]

Public Policy

Terrorism is frightening. Freedom is vital. These competing dynamics shape the debate over the Patriot Act. In your view, where does the proper balance lie? ◆

The Fifth Amendment

The Fifth Amendment includes three important protections for criminal defendants: due process, double jeopardy, and self-incrimination.

Due Process

Due process requires fundamental fairness at all stages of the case. The basic elements of due process are discussed in Chapter 5, on constitutional law. In the context of criminal law, due process sets additional limits. The requirement that the prosecution disclose evidence favorable to the defendant is a due process rule. Similarly, if a witness says that a tall white male robbed the liquor store, it would violate due process for the police to place the male suspect in a lineup with four short women and two rabbits.

---

[24] *Doe v. Ashcroft,* 334 F. Supp. 2d 471 (S.D.N.Y. 2004).

Double Jeopardy

The prohibition against **double jeopardy** means that a criminal defendant may be prosecuted only once for a particular criminal offense. The purpose is to guarantee that the government may not destroy the lives of innocent citizens with repetitive prosecutions. Assume that Roger, the video thief, goes to trial. But the police officer cannot remember what the suspect looked like, and the jury acquits. Later, the prosecutor learns that a second witness actually *videotaped* Roger hauling VCRs from the store. Too late. The Double Jeopardy Clause prohibits the state from retrying Roger for the same offense.

Self-Incrimination

The Fifth Amendment bars the government from forcing any person to testify against himself. In other words, the police may not use mental or physical coercion to force a confession out of someone. (This clause applies only to people; corporations and other organizations are not protected.) Society does not want a government that engages in torture. Such abuse might occasionally catch a criminal, but it would grievously injure innocent people and make all citizens fearful of the government that is supposed to represent them. Also, confessions that are forced out of someone are inherently unreliable. The defendant may confess simply to end the torture. So Jake, the rape-robbery suspect who confessed at the beginning of this section, will never hear his confession used against him in court. Unless the police have other evidence, he will walk free.

When the FBI arrests Stacey for Medicare fraud, she may refuse to answer any questions. The privilege against self-incrimination covers any statement that might help to prosecute her. So, if the FBI agent asks Stacey, "Did you commit Medicare fraud?" she will refuse to answer. If the agent asks, "What are your duties here?" she will also remain silent.

Miranda

In *Miranda v. Arizona*,[25] the Supreme Court ruled that a confession obtained from a custodial interrogation may not be used against a defendant unless he was first warned of his Fifth Amendment rights. A "custodial interrogation" means that the police have prevented the defendant from leaving (usually by arresting him) and are asking him questions. If they do that, and obtain a confession from the defendant, they may use that confession in court only if they first warned him of his Fifth Amendment rights. He must be told that:

- He has the right to remain silent
- Anything he says can be used against him at trial
- He has the right to a lawyer; and
- If he cannot afford a lawyer, the court will appoint one for him.

Exclusionary Rule (Again). If the police fail to give these warnings before interrogating a defendant, the exclusionary rule prohibits the prosecution from using any confession. The rationale is the same as for Fourth Amendment searches: suppressing the evidence means that the police will not attempt to get it illegally. But remember that the confession is void only if it results from custodial questioning. Suppose a policeman, investigating a bank robbery, asks a pedestrian if he noticed anything peculiar. The pedestrian says, "You mean after I robbed the bank?" Result? No custodial questioning, and the confession *may* be used against him.

---

[25] 384 U.S. 436, 86 S. Ct. 1602, 1966 U.S. LEXIS 2817 (1966).

The Sixth Amendment

The Sixth Amendment guarantees the **right to a lawyer** at all important stages of the criminal process. Stacey, the hospital administrator, is entitled to have her lawyer present during custodial questioning and all court hearings. Because of this right, the government must **appoint a lawyer** to represent, free of charge, any defendant who cannot afford one.

The Eighth Amendment

The Eighth Amendment prohibits cruel and unusual punishment. The most dramatic issue litigated under this clause is the death penalty. The Supreme Court has ruled that capital punishment is not inherently unconstitutional. Most state statutes bifurcate a capital case, so that the jury first considers only guilt or innocence, and then, if the defendant is found guilty, deliberates on the death penalty. As part of that final decision, the jury must consider aggravating and mitigating circumstances that may make the ultimate penalty more or less appropriate.[26] However, other "cruel and unusual" issues are now coming to the forefront.

EWING V. CALIFORNIA

538 U.S. 11, 123 S. Ct. 1179, 155 L. Ed. 2d 108
United States Supreme Court, 2003

Facts: California passed a "three strikes" law, dramatically increasing sentences for repeat offenders. A defendant with two or more serious convictions, who was convicted of a third felony, had to receive an indeterminate sentence of life imprisonment. Such a sentence required the defendant to actually serve a minimum of 25 years, and in some cases much more.

Gary Ewing, on parole from a nine-year prison term, stole three golf clubs worth $399 each, and was prosecuted. Because he had prior convictions, the crime, normally a misdemeanor, was treated as a felony. Ewing was convicted and sentenced to 25 years to life. He appealed, claiming that the sentence violated the Eighth Amendment.

Issue: Did Ewing's sentence violate the Eighth Amendment?

Excerpts from Justice O'Connor's Decision: When the California Legislature enacted the three strikes law, it made a judgment that protecting the public safety requires incapacitating criminals who have already been convicted of at least one serious or violent crime. Nothing in the Eighth Amend-ment prohibits California from making that choice. To the contrary, our cases establish that States have a valid interest in deterring and segregating habitual criminals.

California's justification is no pretext. Recidivism is a serious public safety concern in California and throughout the Nation. According to a recent report, approximately 67 percent of former inmates released from state prisons were charged with at least one "serious" new crime within three years of their release. In particular, released property offenders like Ewing had higher recidivism rates than those released after committing violent, drug, or public-order offenses.

To be sure, California's three strikes law has sparked controversy. Critics have doubted the law's wisdom, cost-efficiency, and effectiveness in reaching its goals. This criticism is appropriately directed at the legislature, which has primary responsibility for making the difficult policy choices that underlie any criminal sentencing scheme. We do not sit as a "superlegislature" to second-guess these policy choices.

In imposing a three strikes sentence, the State's interest is not merely punishing the offense

▼

---

[26] *Gregg v. Georgia*, 428 U.S. 153, 96 S. Ct. 2909, 1976 U.S. LEXIS 82 (1976).

of conviction, or the "triggering" offense: It is in addition the interest in dealing in a harsher manner with those who by repeated criminal acts have shown that they are simply incapable of conforming to the norms of society as established by its criminal law.

Ewing's sentence is justified by the State's public-safety interest in incapacitating and deterring recidivist felons, and amply supported by his own long, serious criminal record. Ewing has been convicted of numerous misdemeanor and felony offenses, served nine separate terms of incarceration, and committed most of his crimes while on probation or parole. His prior "strikes" were serious felonies including robbery and three residential burglaries. To be sure,

Ewing's sentence is a long one. But it reflects a rational legislative judgment, entitled to deference, that offenders who have committed serious or violent felonies and who continue to commit felonies must be incapacitated. The State of California was entitled to place upon Ewing the onus of one who is simply unable to bring his conduct within the social norms prescribed by the criminal law of the State.

We hold that Ewing's sentence of 25 years to life in prison, imposed for the offense of felony grand theft under the three strikes law, is not grossly disproportionate and therefore does not violate the Eighth Amendment's prohibition on cruel and unusual punishments. ■

Devil's Advocate

Are we really going to send Ewing to prison for a minimum of 25 years—for *shoplifting*? It is true that Ewing is a recidivist, and undoubtedly a state is entitled to punish chronic troublemakers more harshly than first-time offenders. However, this still seems excessive. In California, a first-time offense of "arson causing *great bodily injury*" incurs a maximum nine-year sentence. A first-time offender convicted of voluntary manslaughter receives a sentence of no more than 11 years. Only a first-time murderer receives a penalty equal to Ewing's—25 years to life. It is unfair to Ewing to equate his property crimes with a homicide, and foolish for society to spend this much money locking him up. ◆

The Eighth Amendment also outlaws excessive fines. Forfeiture is the most controversial topic under this clause. **Forfeiture** is a *civil* law proceeding that is permitted by many different *criminal* statutes. Once a court has convicted a defendant under certain criminal statutes—such as RICO or a controlled substance law—the government may seek forfeiture of property associated with the criminal act. *How much* property can the government take? To determine if forfeiture was fair, courts generally look at three factors: whether the property was used in committing the crime, whether it was purchased with proceeds from illegal acts, and whether the punishment is disproportionate to the defendant's wrongdoing. Neal Brunk pleaded guilty to selling 2.5 ounces of marijuana, and the government promptly sought forfeiture of his house on 90 acres, worth about $99,000. The court found forfeiture was legitimate, because Brunk had used drug money to buy the land, and then sold narcotics from the property.[27] By contrast, Hosep Bajakajian attempted to leave the United States without reporting $375,000 cash to customs officials as the law requires. The government demanded forfeiture of the full sum, but the Supreme Court ruled that seizure of the entire amount would be grossly disproportionate to the minor crime of failing to report cash movement.[28]

---

[27] *U.S. v. Brunk*, 2001 U.S. App. LEXIS 7566 (4th Cir. 2001).
[28] *U.S. v. Bajakajian*, 524 U.S. 321, 118 S. Ct. 2028, 1998 U.S. LEXIS 4172 (1998).

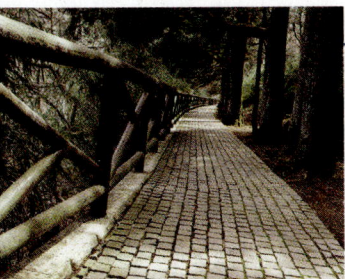
© IMAGE 100/GETTY IMAGES

Chapter Conclusion

Business crime appears in unexpected places, with surprising suspects. A corporate executive aware of its protean nature is in the best position to prevent it. Classic fraud and embezzlement schemes are often foiled with commonsense preventive measures. Federal Sentencing Guidelines make it eminently worthwhile for corporations to establish aggressive compliance programs. Sophisticated computer and money laundering crimes can be thwarted only with determination and the cooperation of citizens and police agencies. We can defeat business crime if we have the knowledge and the will.

Chapter Review

1. The rationales for punishment include restraint, deterrence, retribution, and rehabilitation.

2. In all prosecutions, the government must establish that the defendant's conduct was outlawed, that the defendant committed the *actus reus*, and that he had the necessary *mens rea*.

3. In addition to factual defenses, such as mistaken identity or alibi, a defendant may offer various legal defenses, including insanity, entrapment, and duress.

4. Larceny is the trespassory taking of personal property with the intent to steal.

5. Fraud refers to a variety of crimes, all of which involve the deception of another person for the purpose of obtaining money or property.

6. Arson is the malicious use of fire or explosives to damage or destroy real estate or personal property.

7. Embezzlement is the fraudulent conversion of property already in the defendant's possession.

8. Computer crime statutes prohibit computer trespass and fraud; wrongful use of cards, codes, and identification; and most intercepting or taping of conversations.

9. If a company's agent commits a criminal act within the scope of her employment and with the intent to benefit the corporation, the company is liable.

10. RICO prohibits using two or more racketeering acts to invest in legitimate business or carry on certain other criminal acts. RICO permits civil lawsuits as well as criminal prosecutions.

11. Money laundering consists of taking profits from a criminal act and either using them to promote crime or attempting to conceal their source.

12. The Fourth Amendment prohibits the government from making illegal searches and seizures.

13. The Fifth Amendment requires due process in all criminal procedures and prohibits double jeopardy and self-incrimination.

14. The Sixth Amendment guarantees criminal defendants the right to a lawyer.

15. Information obtained in violation of the Fourth, Fifth, or Sixth Amendment is generally excluded from trial.

16. The Eighth Amendment prohibits excessive fines and cruel and unusual punishments.

Practice Test

1. Arnie owns a two-family house in a poor section of the city. A fire breaks out, destroying the building and causing $150,000 damage to an adjacent store. The state charges Arnie with arson. Simultaneously, Vickie, the store owner, sues Arnie for the damage to her property. Both cases are tried to juries, and the two juries hear identical evidence of Arnie's actions. But the criminal jury acquits Arnie, while the civil jury awards Vickie $150,000. How did that happen?

2. **YOU BE THE JUDGE** WRITING PROBLEM An undercover drug informant learned from a mutual friend that Philip Friedman "knew where to get marijuana." The informant asked Friedman three times to get him some marijuana, and Friedman

agreed after the third request. Shortly thereafter Friedman sold the informant a small amount of the drug. The informant later offered to sell Friedman three pounds of marijuana. They negotiated the price and then made the sale. Friedman was tried for trafficking in drugs. He argued entrapment. Was Friedman entrapped? **Argument for Friedman:** The undercover agent had to ask three times before Friedman sold him a small amount of drugs. A real drug dealer, predisposed to commit the crime, leaps at an opportunity to sell. If the government spends time and money luring innocent people into the commission of crimes, all of us are the losers. **Argument for the Government:** Government officials suspected Friedman of being a sophisticated drug dealer, and they were right. When he had a chance to buy three pounds, a quantity only a dealer would purchase, he not only did so, but bargained with skill, showing a working knowledge of the business. Friedman was not entrapped—he was caught.

3. *ETHICS* Nineteen-year-old David Lee Nagel viciously murdered his grandparents, stabbing them repeatedly and slitting their throats, all because they denied him use of the family car. He was tried for murder and found not guilty by reason of insanity. He has lived ever since in mental hospitals. In 1994 he applied for release. The two psychiatrists who examined him stated that he was no longer mentally ill and was a danger neither to society nor to himself. Yet the Georgia Supreme Court refused to release him, seemingly because of the brutality of the killings. Comment on the court's ruling. What is the rationale for treating an insane defendant differently from others? Do you find the theory persuasive? If you do, what result must logically follow when psychiatrists testify that the defendant is no longer a danger? Should the brutality of the crime be a factor in deciding whether to prolong the detention? If you do not accept the rationale for treating such defendants differently, explain why not.

4. National Medical Enterprises (NME) is a large for-profit hospital and health corporation. One of its hospitals, Los Altos Hospital, in Long Beach, California, paid one doctor $219,275, allegedly for consulting work. In fact, the government claimed, the payment was in exchange for the doctor's referring to the hospital a large number of Medicare patients. Other NME hospitals engaged in similar practices, said the government. What crime is the government accusing NME of committing?

5. Kathy Hathcoat was a teller at a Pendleton, Indiana, bank. In 1990 she began taking home money that belonged in her cash drawer. Her branch manager, Mary Jane Cooper, caught her. But rather than reporting Hathcoat, Cooper joined in. The two helped cover for each other by verifying that their cash drawers were in balance. They took nearly $200,000 before bank officials found them out. What criminal charge did the government bring against Hathcoat?

6. Federal law requires that all banks file reports with the IRS any time a customer engages in a cash transaction in an amount over $10,000. It is a crime for a bank to "structure" a cash transaction, that is, to break up a single transaction of more than $10,000 into two or more smaller transactions (and thus avoid the filing requirement). In *Ratzlaf v. United States*, 510 U.S. 135, 114 S. Ct. 655, 1994 U.S. LEXIS 936 (1994), the Supreme Court held that in order to find a defendant guilty of structuring, the government must prove that he specifically intended to break the law, that is, that he knew what he was doing was a crime and meant to commit it. Congress promptly passed a law "undoing" Ratzlaf. A bank official can now be convicted on evidence that he structured a payment, even with no evidence that he knew it was a crime. The penalties are harsh. (1) Why is structuring so serious? (2) Why did Congress change the law about the defendant's intent?

7. Conley owned video poker machines. They are outlawed in Pennsylvania, but he placed them in bars and clubs. He used profits from the machines to buy more machines. Is he guilty of money laundering?

8. Northwest Telco Corp. (Telco) provides long-distance telephone service. Customers dial a general access number, then enter a six-digit access code and then the phone number they want to call. A computer places the call and charges the account. On January 10, 1990, Cal Edwards, a Telco engineer, noticed that Telco's general access number was being dialed exactly every 40 seconds. After each dialing, a different six-digit

number was entered, followed by a particular long-distance number. This continued from 10 PM to 6 AM. Why was Edwards concerned?

9. Under a new British law, a police officer must now say the following to a suspect placed under arrest: "You do not have to say anything. But if you do not mention now something which you later use in your defense, the court may decide that your failure to mention it now strengthens the case against you. A record will be made of anything you say and it may be given in evidence if you are brought to trial." What does a police officer in the United States have to say, and what difference does it make at the time of an arrest?

10. After graduating from college, you work hard for 15 years, saving money to buy your dream prop-

erty. Finally, you spend all your savings to buy a 300-acre farm with a splendid house and pool. Happy, an old college friend, stops by. She is saving her money to make a down payment on a coffee shop in town. You let her have a nice room in your big house for a few months, until she has the funds to make her down payment. But odd acquaintances stop by almost daily for short visits, and you realize that Happy is saving money from marijuana sales. You are unhappy with this, but out of loyalty you permit it to go on for a month. Why is that a big mistake?

11. ***ROLE REVERSAL*** Write a short-answer question that focuses on the elements of a RICO violation.

Internet Research Problem

Go to **http://beatty.westbuslaw.com** to find a Web site devoted to Internet crime. Find a current crime that might victimize you. What steps should you take to avoid harm?

> **You can find further practice problems at http://beatty.westbuslaw.com or in the Study Guide that accompanies this text.**

International Law

The day after Anfernee graduates from business school, he opens a shop specializing in sports caps and funky hats. Sales are brisk, but Anfernee is making little profit because his American-made caps are expensive. Then an Asian company offers to sell him identical merchandise for 45 percent less than the American suppliers charge. Anfernee is elated, but quickly begins to wonder. Why is the new price so low? Are the foreign workers paid a living wage? Could the Asian company be using child labor? The sales representative expects Anfernee to sell no caps except his. Is that legal? He also requests a $50,000 cash "commission" to smooth the export process in his country. That sounds suspicious. The questions multiply without end. Will the contract be written in English or a foreign language? Must Anfernee pay in dollars or some other currency? The foreign company wants a letter of credit. What does that mean? What law will govern the agreement? If the caps are defective, how will disputes be resolved—and where?

Anfernee should put this lesson under his cap: the world is now one vast economy, and negotiations quickly cross borders. Transnational business grows with breathtaking speed. The United States now exports more than $800 billion worth of goods each year, and an additional $330 billion worth of services. Leading exports include industrial machinery, computers, aircraft and other transportation equipment, electronic equipment, and chemicals.

Here are the nations that trade the most goods with the United States:

Rank	Country	Total Trade in Goods (exports plus imports), 2004, in billions of dollars
1	Canada	446
2	Mexico	267
3	China	231
4	Japan	184
5	Federal Republic of Germany	109
6	United Kingdom	82
7	South Korea	73
8	Taiwan	56
9	France	53
10	Malaysia	39
11	Italy	39
12	Netherlands	37
13	Ireland	36
14	Brazil	35
15	Singapore	35

Source: United States Census Bureau, **http://census.gov**.

The end is nowhere in sight. By 2010, a dozen developing countries with a total population 10 times that of the United States will account for 40 percent of all export opportunities. In China alone roughly 300 million people are entering the economic middle class—and the rank of potential consumers.

Who are the people who do all of this trading? Anfernee's modest sports cap concern is at one end of the spectrum. At the other are multinational enterprises (MNEs), that is, companies doing business in several countries simultaneously. ■

MNEs and Power

An MNE can take various forms. It may be an Italian corporation with a wholly owned American subsidiary that manufactures electrical components in Alabama and sells them in Brazil. Or it could be a Japanese company that licenses a software company in India to manufacture computer programs for sale throughout Europe. One thing is constant: the power of these huge enterprises. Each of the top 10 MNEs earns annual revenue greater than the gross domestic product of *two-thirds of the world's nations.* Over 200 MNEs have annual sales exceeding $1 billion and more cash available at any one time than the majority of countries do. Money means power. This corporate might can be used to create jobs, train workers, and build life-saving medical equipment. Such power can also be used to corrupt government officials, rip up the environment, and exploit already impoverished workers. International law is vital.

Trade Regulation

Nations regulate international trade in many ways. In this section we look at export and import controls that affect trade out of and into the United States. **Exporting** is shipping goods or services out of a country. The United States, with its huge farms, is the world's largest exporter of agricultural products. **Importing** is shipping goods and services into a country. The United States suffers trade deficits every year because the value of its imports exceeds that of its exports, as the following table demonstrates.

U.S. International Trade in Goods and Services (in millions of dollars)

Year	BALANCE			EXPORTS			IMPORTS		
	Total	Goods	Services	Total	Goods	Services	Total	Goods	Services
1980	-19,407	-25,500	6,093	271,834	224,250	47,584	291,241	249,750	41,491
1990	-80,864	-111,037	30,173	535,233	387,401	147,832	616,097	498,438	117,659
2000	-378,344	-452,414	74,070	1,070,980	771,994	298,986	1,449,324	1,224,408	224,916
2004	-617,725	-666,183	48,458	1,146,137	807,584	338,553	1,763,863	1,473,768	290,095

Source: United States Census Bureau, http://census.gov.

Export Controls

You and a friend open an electronics business, intending to purchase goods in this country for sale abroad. A representative of Interlex stops in to see you. Interlex is a Latin American electronics company, and the firm wants you to obtain for it a certain kind of infrared dome. The representative explains that this electronic miracle helps helicopters identify nearby aircraft. You find a Pennsylvania company that manufactures the domes, and you realize that you can buy and sell them to Interlex for a handsome profit. Any reason not to? As a matter of fact, there is.

All nations limit what may be exported. In the United States, several statutes do this. The **Export Administration Act of 1985**[1] is one. This statute balances the need for free trade, which is essential in a capitalist society, with important requirements of

---

[1]   50 U.S.C. §2402 (1994).

national security. The statute permits the federal government to restrict exports if they endanger national security, harm foreign policy goals, or drain scarce materials.

The Secretary of Commerce makes a **Controlled Commodities List** of those items that meet any of these criteria. No one may export any commodity on the list without a license, and the license may well be denied. A second major limitation comes from the **Arms Export Control Act.**[2] This statute permits the president to create a second list of controlled goods, all related to military weaponry. Again, no person may export any listed item without a license.

The Arms Export Control Act (AECA) will prohibit you from exporting the infrared domes to the overseas company. They are used in the guidance system of one of the most sophisticated weapons in the American defense arsenal. Foreign governments have attempted to obtain the equipment through official channels, but the American government has placed the domes on the list of restricted military items. When a U.S. citizen did send such goods overseas, he was convicted and imprisoned.[3]

Import Controls

Tariffs

Tariffs are the most widespread method of limiting what may be imported into a nation. **A tariff is a duty (a tax) imposed on goods when they enter a country.** Nations use tariffs primarily to protect their domestic industries. Because the company importing the goods must pay this duty, the importer's costs increase, making the merchandise more expensive for consumers. This renders domestic products more attractive. High tariffs unquestionably help local industry, but they proportionately harm local buyers. Consumers benefit from zero tariffs, because the unfettered competition drives down prices.

Tariffs change frequently and vary widely from one country to another. Even within one nation, tariffs may be low on some products and high on others, as the following table demonstrates.

Country	AVERAGE TARIFFS IMPOSED ON …		
	Manufactured Goods	**Clothing**	**Agricultural Produce**
Brazil	16.8%	22.9%	25–49%
China	9.6	16.1	100–200
European Union	4.4	11.4	25–49
Egypt	22.3	39.7	50–99
India	34.1	40	50–99
Japan	2.9	11	25–49
Sub-Saharan Africa	16.8	34.5	50–200
Turkey	5.9	11.8	25–49
United States	4	11.4	0–24

Sources: Economic Research Service, USDA; UNCTAD; the World Bank.

---

2   22 U.S.C. §2778 (1994).

3   *United States v. Tsai,* 954 F.2d 155, 1992 U.S. App. LEXIS 601 (3d Cir. 1992).

As we will see later in the chapter, regional trade treaties have changed the tariff landscape. Two-thirds of all U.S. products entering Mexico are duty free. Almost all trade between Canada and the United States is done with zero tariffs, which is partly why the two nations do more bilateral commerce than any others in the world.

Classification. The U.S. Customs Service imposes tariffs at the point of entry into the United States. A customs official inspects the merchandise as it arrives and **classifies** it, in other words, decides precisely what the goods are. This decision is critical because the tariff will vary depending on the classification.

Disputes at this stage typically involve an importer claiming that the Customs Service has imposed the wrong classification. The company seeks a different classification and lower tariff. The following case involves an unusual twist: The company argues that the tariff is *too low*. Now why would a sensible merchant do that?

RUBIE'S COSTUME COMPANY V. UNITED STATES

337 F.3d 1350
United States Court of Appeals for the Federal Circuit, 2003

Facts: The Customs Service examined five Halloween costumes, including "Witch of the Webs," "Pirate Boy," and "Cute and Cuddly Clown." The Service declared that "Cute and Cuddly Clown" was a baby's *garment*, with a duty rate of 16 percent; it ruled that all of the other outfits were *festive articles* permitted to enter duty-free.

Rubie's Costume Company filed suit, asking for a declaration that the costumes were *fancy dress*, which, under Customs regulations, are garments. Why? Because, of course, Rubie's was the largest *domestic* manufacturer of costumes in the United States. It was a different company that wanted to import the costumes. Rubie's hoped to cause two major problems for importers. First, if the costumes were garments, they would be subject to *quotas*, beyond which a company could bring in none at all. Second, each costume that did enter would cost an importer an additional 16 percent, a potentially fatal price difference in the cutthroat world of holiday fun.

The Court of International Trade ruled that the costumes were fancy dress garments, subject to the quotas and duties. The government and various importers appealed.

Issue: Were the costumes taxable fancy-dress garments or duty-free festive articles?

Excerpts from Judge Bryson's Decision: Wearing apparel refers to clothes or coverings for the human body worn for decency or comfort. Cognizant of these definitions, Customs' classification ruling is supported by a logical and well-reasoned explanation. [The Service] presents the correct classification as "festive articles" of flimsy, non-durable costumes having utility and used as well for festive occasions, based on functional or structural deficiencies as compared with the standard counterpart articles (e.g., wearing apparel). Customs focused on the texture and quality of the materials as "flimsy and non-durable textile costumes whose principal intended use is for a one time festive occasion [which] are distinct from 'wearing apparel' which the courts have held to be used for decency, comfort, adornment or protection." Customs reasons that the texture and quality of the materials is to be determined by such factors as the extent of styling features such as zippers, inset panels, darts or hoops, and whether the edges of the materials had been left raw or finished.

While the imports may simulate the structural features of wearing apparel, and have some incidents of clothes or coverings for the human body worn for decency or comfort, they are not practical articles which are ordinarily worn. Rather, the Halloween costumes for consumers have enormous "make believe" or festive value during appropriate occasions such as Halloween and incidentally afford the element of covering for decency or comfort. To the extent that such elements have any characteristics similar to "wearing apparel" to consumers of Halloween costumes, such features are clearly secondary to the costumes' festive value.

▼

In addition to the festive value fostered by the imports' features of styling, and of course, the simulation of fictitious characters, the subject merchandise such as the "one-size-fits-all" Scream Robe Costume has accessories such as a hood, belt, and "ghost-face" mask that further serve to enhance the festive value of imitating a character during Halloween or at a costume party. While an adult or child might wear a "one-size-fits-all" costume with its attendant accessories for decency or comfort, such benefits are incidental and the imports are primarily created for Halloween fun, strongly promoting festive value rather than cognitive association as wearing apparel. Such costumes are generally recognized as not being normal articles of apparel.

Mindful of Customs' specialized expertise in classifying imported articles, we conclude that textile costumes of a flimsy nature and construction, lacking in durability, and generally recognized as not being normal articles of apparel are classifiable as "festive articles." The decision of the Court of International Trade holding that the subject merchandise be classified as "wearing apparel" is reversed. ■

Valuation. After classifying the imported goods, customs officials impose the appropriate duty *ad valorem,* meaning "according to the value of the goods." In other words, the service must determine the value of the merchandise before it can tax a percentage of that value. This step can be equally contentious, since goods will have different prices at each stage of manufacturing and delivery. The question is supposed to be settled by the **transaction value** of the goods, meaning the price actually paid for the merchandise when sold for export to the United States (plus shipping and other minor costs). But there is often room for debate, so importers use customs agents to help negotiate the most favorable valuation.

Duties for Dumping and Subsidizing

Dumping means selling merchandise at one price in the domestic market and at a cheaper, unfair price in an international market. Suppose a Singapore company, CelMaker, makes cellular telephones for $20 per unit and sells them in the United States for $12 each, vastly undercutting domestic American competitors. CelMaker may be willing to suffer short-term losses in order to drive out competitors for the American market. Once it has gained control of that market, it will raise its prices, more than compensating for its initial losses. And CelMaker may get help from its home government. Suppose the Singapore government prohibits foreign cellular phones from entering Singapore. CelMaker may sell its phones for $75 at home, earning such high profits that it can afford the temporary losses in America.

In the United States, the Commerce Department investigates suspected dumping. If the Department concludes that the foreign company is selling items at **less than fair value,** and that this harms an American industry, it will impose a **dumping duty** sufficiently high to put the foreign goods back on fair footing with domestic products.

Subsidized goods are also unfair. Suppose the Singapore government permits CelMaker to pay no taxes for 10 years. This enormous benefit will enable the company to produce cheap phones and undersell competitors. Again, the United States imposes a tariff on subsidized goods, called **countervailing duties.** If CelMaker sells phones for $15 that would cost an unsubsidized competitor $21 to make, it will pay a $6 countervailing duty on every phone entering the United States.

Nontariff Barriers

All countries use additional methods to limit imports. A **quota** is a limit on the quantity of a particular good that may enter a nation. For example, the United States, like most importing nations, has agreements with many developing nations, placing a quota on imported textiles. In some cases, textile imports from a particular country may grow by only a small percentage each year. Without such a limit, textile imports from the developing world would increase explosively because costs are so much lower there. As part of the GATT treaty (discussed below), the wealthier nations pledged to increase textile imports from the developing countries, but whether that has occurred is open to dispute.

An **import ban** means that particular goods are flatly prohibited. Some nations prohibit alcohol imports for religious reasons. The United States bars the importation of narcotic drugs. Virtually all countries from time to time halt certain goods for political purposes, for example, to protest the behavior of the exporting country. The United States has increasingly used economic sanctions in an effort to advance its foreign policy goals. During one three-year period, it threatened or imposed sanctions 60 times, against 35 nations. Sanctions were aimed at Colombia for permitting drug trafficking; the Netherlands, Switzerland, and other European nations for trading with Cuba; and Taiwan for environmental violations. Proponents of such sanctions consider them essential components of an ethical foreign policy. Opponents regard them as hypocritical attempts at moral superiority.

Money and politics are a volatile mix, as demonstrated by all recorded history from 3000 B.C.E. to the present. As long as nations have existed, they have engaged in disputes about quotas and import bans. And that is why more than 100 countries negotiated and signed the GATT treaty, the subject of the next section.

General Agreement on Tariffs and Trade (GATT)

What is GATT? The greatest boon to American commerce in a century. The worst assault on the American economy in 200 years. It depends on whom you ask. Let's start where everyone agrees.

GATT is the General Agreement on Tariffs and Trade. This massive international treaty has been negotiated on and off since the 1940s to eliminate trade barriers and bolster commerce. GATT has already had considerable effect. In 1947 the worldwide average tariff on industrial goods was about 40 percent. Now it is about 4 percent (although agricultural duties still average over 40 percent). The world's economies have exploded over that half century. Proponents of GATT applaud the agreement. Opponents scoff that both lower duties and higher trade would have arrived without GATT.

The most recent round of bargaining took seven hard years. Finally, in 1994, the United States and 125 other countries signed the treaty. A **signatory,** that is, a nation that signs a treaty, is still not bound by the agreement until it is **ratified,** that is, until the nation's legislature votes to honor it. In the United States, Congress voted to ratify GATT. If the latest round of cuts is fully implemented, average duties in all signatories should drop to about 3.7 percent. Further, nearly half of all trade in industrial goods will be duty free, at least in developed countries. That must be good—or is it?

Trade

Leading supporters of GATT suggest that its lower tariffs vastly increase world trade. The United States is one of the biggest beneficiaries because for decades this country has imposed lower duties than most other nations. American companies for once compete on equal footing. A typical American family's annual income has increased due to the more vigorous domestic economy, and at the same time many goods are less expensive because they enter with low duties.

But opponents claim that the United States now competes against nations with unlimited pools of exploited labor. These countries dominate labor-intensive industries such as textiles, clothing, and manufacturing, and are steadily taking jobs from millions of American workers. It is unfair for U.S. companies to struggle against competitors in countries with no labor standards and dirt-cheap pay. Because domestic job losses come in low-end employment, those put out of work are precisely those least able to find a new job. The chasm between rich and poor is widening, leaving us all the losers.

World Trade Organization and the Environment

GATT created the **World Trade Organization (WTO)** to stimulate international commerce and resolve trade disputes. The WTO is empowered to hear arguments from any signatory nation about tariff violations or nontariff barriers. This international "court" may order compliance from any nation violating GATT and may penalize countries by imposing trade sanctions. Proponents say that it is high time to have one international body to resolve complex issues impartially and create an international body of trade law that corporations can rely on when planning business.

Here is how the WTO decides a trade dispute. Suppose that the United States believes that Brazil is unfairly restricting trade. The United States uses the WTO offices to request a consultation with Brazil's trade representative. In the majority of cases, these discussions lead to a satisfactory settlement. If the consultation does not resolve the problem, the United States asks the WTO's Dispute Settlement Body (DSB) to form a panel, which consists of three nations uninvolved in the dispute. After the panel hears testimony and arguments from both countries, it releases its report. The DSB generally approves the report, unless either nation appeals. If there is an appeal, the WTO Appellate Body hears the dispute and generally makes the final decision, subject to approval by the entire WTO. No single nation has the power to block final decisions. If a country refuses to comply with the WTO's ruling, affected nations may retaliate by imposing punitive tariffs. (The official Web site of the WTO, http://www.wto.org/, includes libraries on all sorts of international trade topics, from goods and services to dispute settlement and legal texts.)

The following case forced the WTO to weigh the merits of two important, competing goals: environmental protection and trade growth.

UNITED STATES—IMPORT PROHIBITION OF CERTAIN SHRIMP AND SHRIMP PRODUCTS

WT/DS58/R15
WTO Panel, 1998

Facts: Sea turtles are migratory animals that live throughout the world. The United States recognizes the animals as an endangered species. Studies showed that the greatest threat to the turtles, around the world, came from shrimp fishermen inadvertently catching the animals in their nets. The federal government responded by requiring any importers to certify that shrimp had been caught using Turtle Excluder Devices (TEDs), which keep the animals out of the nets.

India, Pakistan, Malaysia, and Thailand filed complaints with the WTO, claiming that the United States had no right to impose its environmental concerns on world trade. The United States argued that

Article XX of the WTO Agreement permitted trade restrictions based on environmental concerns. Article XX states in part:

> Nothing in this Agreement shall be construed to prevent the adoption or enforcement by any Member of measures:
> (b) necessary to protect human, animal or plant life or health;
> (g) relating to the conservation of exhaustible natural resources if such measures are made effective in conjunction with restrictions on domestic production or consumption;

The Dispute Settlement Body appointed a panel to hear the dispute and make recommendations.

▼

Issue: Did Article XX permit the United States to impose environmental restrictions on shrimp importers?

Excerpts from the Panel's Report: The WTO Agreement acknowledges that the optimal use of the world's resources must be pursued "in accordance with the objective of sustainable development, seeking both to protect and preserve the environment and to enhance the means of doing so in a manner consistent with [Members'] respective needs and concerns at different levels of economic development." On the other hand, [different sections of the Agreement] refer to "entering into reciprocal and mutually advantageous arrangements directed to the substantial reduction of tariffs and other barriers to trade and to the elimination of discriminatory treatment" in international trade relations. The central focus of that agreement remains the promotion of economic development through trade.

If one WTO Member were allowed to adopt such measures [as the shrimp regulation], then other Members would also have the right to adopt similar measures on the same subject but with differing, or even conflicting, requirements. If that happened, it would be impossible for exporting Members to comply at the same time with multiple conflicting policy requirements.

The United States claims that sea turtles are a shared global resource and that, therefore, it has an interest and a right to impose the measures at issue. Even assuming that sea turtles were a shared global resource, we consider that the notion of "shared" resource implies a common interest in the resource concerned. If such a common interest exists, it would be better addressed through the negotiation of international agreements than by measures taken by one Member conditioning access to its market to the adoption by other Members of certain conservation policies.

The Panel recommends that the Dispute Settlement Body request the United States to bring this measure into conformity with its obligations under the WTO Agreement. ■

The United States appealed the panel's decision to the WTO's Appellate Body.

UNITED STATES—IMPORT PROHIBITION OF CERTAIN SHRIMP AND SHRIMP PRODUCTS

AB-1998-4
WTO Appellate Body, 1998

Excerpts from the Appellate Body's Report: The [shrimp policy] requires other WTO Members to adopt a regulatory program that is not merely comparable, but rather essentially the same, as that applied to the United States shrimp trawl vessels. The effect is to establish a rigid and unbending standard by which United States officials determine whether or not countries will be certified, thus granting or refusing other countries the right to export shrimp to the United States.

The United States requires the use of approved TEDs at all times by domestic, commercial shrimp trawl vessels. It may be quite acceptable for a government to adopt a single standard applicable to all its citizens throughout that country. However, it is not acceptable, in international trade relations, for one WTO Member to use an economic embargo to require other Members to adopt essentially the same comprehensive regulatory program, without taking into consideration different conditions which may occur in the territories of those other Members.

The United States [failed] to engage other Members exporting shrimp to the United States, in serious, across-the-board negotiations with the objective of concluding bilateral or multilateral agreements for the protection and conservation of sea turtles.

We have not decided that the protection and preservation of the environment is of no significance to the Members of the WTO. Clearly, it is. We have not decided that the sovereign nations that are Members of the WTO cannot adopt effective measures to protect endangered species, such as sea turtles. Clearly, they can and should.

What we have decided in this appeal is simply this: although the measure of the United States in dispute in this appeal serves an environmental objective that is recognized as legitimate, this measure has been applied by the United States in a manner which constitutes arbitrary and unjustifiable discrimination between Members of the WTO. ■

Public Policy

Environmental groups attacked the ruling, declaring that the WTO paid lip service to the environment but ensured further killing of an important endangered species. Trade supporters applauded it. In addition to the trade versus environment tension, there is a second conflict: rich versus poor. Critics of the shrimp regulations claim that it is unseemly for a wealthy nation to punish subsistence fishermen because of environmental concerns. Their opponents argue that we all share this planet, and long term growth for each of us depends upon living in harmony with limited resources and fragile ecosystems. Which of the competing goals is more important to you? ◆

Is this right? Who should decide?

© GETTY IMAGES

Child labor is an even more wrenching issue. The practice exists to some degree in all countries and is common throughout the developing world. The International Labor Organization, an affiliate of the United Nations, estimates that 120 million children between the ages of 5 and 14 work full time, and 130 million more labor part time. As the world generally becomes more prosperous, this ugly problem has actually increased. Children in developing countries typically work in agriculture and domestic work, but many toil in mines and others in factories, making rugs, glass, clothing, and other goods.

The rug industry illustrates the international nature of this tragedy. In the 1970s, the Shah of Iran banned child labor in rug factories, but many manufacturers simply packed up and moved to southern Asia. Today, in India and Pakistan, tens of millions of children, some as young as four, toil in rug workrooms, seven days a week, 12 hours a day. Many, shackled to the looms they operate, are essentially slaves, working for pennies a day or, in some cases, for no money at all.

Ethics

Child labor raises compelling moral questions—and economic ones as well. No American company can compete with an industry that uses slave labor. As discussed above, the United States is relatively quick to impose trade sanctions in response to moral issues. In 1997, Congress passed a statute prohibiting the import of goods created by forced or indentured child labor. The first suit under the new law targeted the carpet factories of southern Asia and sought an outright ban on most rugs from that area. Is this statute humane legislation or cultural imperialism dressed as a nontariff barrier? Should the voters of this country or the WTO decide the issue? In answering such difficult questions, we must bear in mind that child labor is truly universal. The United Farm Workers union estimates that 800,000 underage children help their migrant parents harvest U.S. crops—work that few Americans are willing to do.

Our response to such a troubling moral issue need not take the form of a statute or lawsuit. Duke University is one of the most popular names in sports apparel, and the school sells about $20 million worth of T-shirts, sweatshirts, jackets, caps, and other sportswear bearing its logo. To produce its clothing, the university licenses about 700 companies in the United States and 10 foreign countries. In response to the troubling issue of child labor, Duke adopted a code of conduct that prohibits its manufacturers from using forced or child labor and requires all of the firms to pay a minimum wage, permit union organizing, and maintain a safe workplace. The university plans to monitor the companies producing its apparel and terminate the contract for any firm that violates its rules. ◆

Intellectual Property

Some foreign countries, particularly developing nations, have long ignored U.S. copyrights and patents. GATT changes things. It allows this country to halt duty-free imports from, and assess tariffs against, a nation that refuses to honor American copyrights or patents.

WTO Summary

It will be many years before we can fairly evaluate GATT and the WTO. In all likelihood, some of the most extreme claims will prove false, and the agreement's effects will evolve somewhere in the middle. Unquestionably, some industries will suffer, forcing workers into unemployment. Others will discover and exploit lucrative opportunities. Perhaps the final cost/benefit analysis of the WTO will be decided not by the letter of its rulings but by the spirit and goodwill of those who implement them.

Regional Agreements

Many regional agreements also regulate international trade. We will briefly describe some that affect the United States.

The EU (European Union Countries)

The European Union

The **European Union (EU)** used to be known as the Common Market. The original six members—Belgium, France, Luxembourg, the Netherlands, West Germany, and Italy—have been joined by nineteen additional countries. See the map on this page.

The EU is one of the world's most powerful associations, with a prosperous population of over 460 million. Its sophisticated legal system sets Union-wide standards for tariffs, dumping, subsidies, antitrust, transportation, and many other issues. The first goals of the EU were to eliminate trade barriers between member nations, establish common tariffs with respect to external countries, permit the free movement of citizens across its borders, and coordinate its agricultural and fishing policies for the collective good. The EU has largely achieved these goals. Most but not all of the EU countries have adopted a common currency, the euro. During the next decade the union will focus on further economic integration and effective coordination of foreign policy.

NAFTA

In 1993, the United States, Canada, and Mexico signed the **North American Free Trade Agreement (NAFTA).** The principal goal was to eliminate almost all trade barriers, tariff and nontariff, between the three nations. Like GATT, this trilateral (three-nation) compact has been controversial, and there will probably never be agreement on NAFTA's value because the treaty has enriched some while impoverishing others. Unquestionably, trade between the three nations has increased enormously. Mexico now exports more goods to the United States than do Germany, Britain, and Korea combined. Opponents of the treaty argue that NAFTA costs the United States jobs and lowers the living standards of American workers by forcing them to compete with low-paid labor. For example, Swingline Staplers closed a factory in Queens, New York, after 75 years of operation and moved to Mexico. Instead of paying its American workers $11.58 per hour, Swingline will pay Mexican workers 50 cents an hour to do the same job. Proponents contend that although some jobs are lost, many others are gained, especially in fields with a future, such as high technology. They claim that as new jobs invigorate the Mexican economy, consumers there will be able to afford American goods for the first time, providing an enormous new market. Both Canadian and Mexican law are available online at **http://www.lawsource.com/also/**.

ASEAN

The Association of Southeast Asian Nations consists of 10 countries: Brunei Darussalam, Cambodia, Indonesia, Laos, Malaysia, Myanmar, the Philippines, Singapore, Thailand, and Vietnam. The group's population of about 500 million produces a combined gross domestic product of $737 billion and total trade of $720 billion. ASEAN seeks to eliminate tariffs, accelerate economic growth, and promote peace and stability in the region.

Mercosur

Brazil, Argentina, Uruguay, and Paraguay formed Mercosur to improve commerce among the four South American nations. The organization represents the fourth largest economic entity in the world, after the EU, the United States, and Japan. The Mercosur nations have a combined population of over 200 million, and a GDP of more than $1 trillion. Almost all trade barriers between the nations have been eliminated, and the organization has established a broad social agenda focusing on education, labor, culture, the environment, justice, and consumer protection.

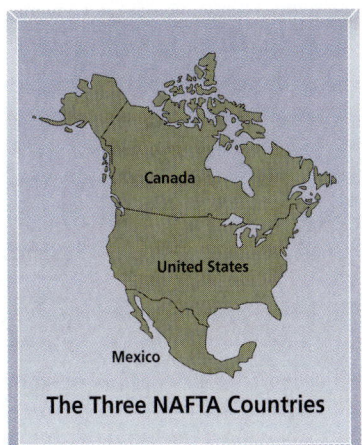

The Three NAFTA Countries

INTERNATIONAL SALES AGREEMENTS

Cowboy boots are hot in France. Big Heel, Inc., your small company in Tucson, Arizona, makes superb boots with exquisite detailing, and you realize that France could be a bonanza. Your first decision is how to produce and sell the boots in France. For our purposes, Big Heel has three choices:

- *Direct Sales.* You can continue to manufacture the boots in Tucson and sell them directly to French retailers.
- *Indirect Sales.* You can manufacture the boots in Tucson and use a French distributor to wholesale them to French stores.
- *Licensing.* You can license a French manufacturer to make Big Heel boots in France and wholesale them.

Direct Sales

You decide to sell the boots directly. Le Pied D'Or, a new, fast-growing French chain of shoe stores, is interested in buying 10,000 pairs of your boots, at about $300 per pair. You must focus on two principal issues: the sales contract and letters of credit. You are wise enough to know that you must have a written contract—$3 million is a lot of money for Big Heel.

This is a contract for the sale of goods. **Goods** are things that can be moved, such as boots, airplanes, pencils, and computers. A sale of goods is governed by different law than the sale of real estate (e.g., a house) or securities (e.g., a share of stock) or services (e.g., accounting).

What Law Governs the Sale of Goods?

Potentially, three conflicting laws could govern your boot contract: Arizona law, French law, and an international treaty. Each is different, and it is therefore essential to negotiate which law will control.

Because this contract is for the sale of goods, your local law is the Arizona **Uniform Commercial Code (UCC).** The UCC is discussed throughout Units 2 and 3, on contracts and commercial transactions. This statute has taken the common law principles of contract and modified them to meet the needs of contemporary business. Article 2 of the UCC governs the sale of goods. American business lawyers are familiar with the UCC and will generally prefer that it govern. French law is based on **Roman law** and the **Napoleonic Code** and is obviously different. French lawyers and business executives are naturally partial to it. How to compromise? Perhaps by using a neutral law.

The **United Nations Convention on Contracts for the International Sale of Goods (CISG)** is the result of 50 years of work by various international groups, all seeking to create a uniform, international law on this important subject. Finally, in 1980, a United Nations conference adopted the CISG, though it became the law in individual nations only if and when they adopted it. The United States and most of its principal trading partners have adopted this important treaty.

The CISG applies automatically to any contract for the sale of goods between two parties, from different countries, each of which is a signatory. France and the United States have both signed. Thus the CISG automatically applies to the Big Heel–Pied D'Or deal unless the parties *specifically opt out*. If the parties want to be governed by other law, they must state very clearly that they exclude the CISG and elect, for example, the UCC.

at RISK

Should the parties allow the CISG to govern? They can make an intelligent choice by first understanding how the CISG differs from other law. Here are a few key differences between the CISG and the UCC:

- **Must the contract be written?** Under the UCC, a contract for the sale of goods valued at over $500 generally must be written to be enforceable. But the CISG does not require a writing for any contract. Be advised that discussions you consider informal or preliminary might create a contract under the CISG.

- **When is an offer irrevocable?** The UCC declares that an offer is irrevocable only if it is in writing and states that it will be held open for a fixed period. But the CISG makes some offers irrevocable even if unwritten.

- **What if an acceptance includes new terms?** Under the UCC, an acceptance generally creates a contract, even if it uses new terms. But the CISG insists on an acceptance that is a "mirror image" of the offer. Almost anything else constitutes a rejection.

- **What remedies are available?** The UCC entitles a plaintiff only to money damages for breach of a sales contract. But the CISG permits many plaintiffs to seek specific performance of the contract, that is, to force the other party to perform the contract. ◆

Choice of Forum

The parties must decide not only what law governs, but where disagreements will be resolved. The French and American legal systems are dramatically different. In a

French civil lawsuit, generally neither side is entitled to depose the other or to obtain interrogatories or even documents, in sharp contrast to the American system where such discovery methods dominate litigation. American lawyers, accustomed to discovery to prepare a case and advance settlement talks, are unnerved by the French system. Similarly, French lawyers are dismayed at the idea of spending two years taking depositions, exchanging paper, and arguing motions, all at great expense. At trial, the contrasts grow. In a French civil trial, there is generally no right to a jury. The rules of evidence are more flexible (and unpredictable), neither side employs its own expert witnesses, and the parties themselves never appear as witnesses.

Choice of Language and Currency

The parties must select a language for the contract and a currency for payment. Language counts because legal terms seldom translate literally. Currency is vital because the exchange rate may alter between the signing and payment. Suppose the Argentine peso falls 30 percent against the dollar in one week. An Argentine company that contracted on Monday to pay $1 million for U.S. aircraft engines will suddenly have to pay 30 percent more in pesos to meet its contractual obligations. To avoid such calamities, companies engaged in international commerce often purchase from currency dealers a guarantee to obtain the needed currency at a future date for a guaranteed price. Assuming that Big Heel insists on being paid in U.S. dollars, Pied D'Or could obtain a quote from a currency dealer as to the present cost of obtaining $3 million at the time the boots are to be delivered. Pied D'Or might pay a 5 percent premium for this guarantee, but it will have insured itself against disastrous currency changes.

Choices Made. The parties agree that the contract price will be paid in U.S. dollars. Pied D'Or is unfamiliar with the UCC and absolutely refuses to make a deal unless either French law or the CISG governs. Your lawyer, Susan Fisher, recommends accepting the CISG, provided that the contract is written in English and that any disputes will be resolved in Arizona courts. Pied D'Or balks at this, but Fisher presses hard, and ultimately those are the terms agreed upon. Fisher is delighted with the arrangement, pointing out that the CISG provisions can all be taken into account as the contract is written, and that by using Arizona courts to settle any dispute, Big Heel has an advantage in terms of familiarity and location.

Letter of Credit

Because Pied D'Or is new and fast growing, you are not sure it will be able to foot the bill. Pied D'Or provides a letter of reference from its bank, La Banque Bouffon, but this is a small bank in Pleasanterie, France, unfamiliar to you. You need greater assurance of payment, and Fisher recommends that payment be made by **letter of credit.** Here is how the letter will work.

Big Heel demands that the contract include a provision requiring payment by confirmed, irrevocable letter of credit. Le Pied D'Or agrees. The French company now contacts its bank, La Banque Bouffon, and instructs Bouffon to issue a letter of credit to Big Heel. The letter of credit is a promise *by the bank itself* to pay Big Heel, if Big Heel presents certain documents. Banque Bouffon, of course, expects to be repaid by Pied D'Or. The bank is in a good position to assess Pied D'Or's creditworthiness, since it is local and can do any investigating it wants before issuing the credit. It may also insist that Pied D'Or give Bouffon a mortgage on property, or that Pied D'Or deposit money in a separate Bouffon account. Pied D'Or is the **account party** on the letter of credit, and Big Heel is the **beneficiary.**

But at Big Heel you are still not entirely satisfied about getting paid because you don't know anything about Bouffon. That is why you have required a *confirmed* letter of credit. Bouffon will forward its letter of credit to Big Heel's own bank, the Bandito Trust Company of Tucson. Bandito examines the letter and then *confirms* the letter. This is *Bandito's own guarantee* that it will pay Big Heel. Bandito will do this only if it knows, through international banking contacts, that Bouffon is a sound bank. The risk has now been spread to two banks, and at Big Heel you are confident of payment.

You get busy, make excellent boots, and pack them. When they are ready, you truck them to Galveston, where they are taken alongside a ship, *Le Fond de la Mer.* Your agent presents the goods to the ship's officials, along with customs documents that describe the goods. *Le Fond de la Mer's* officer in turn issues your agent a **negotiable bill of lading.** This document describes *exactly* the goods received—their quantity, color, quality, and anything else important.

You now take the negotiable bill of lading to Bandito Trust. You also present to Bandito a **draft,** which is simply a formal order to Bandito to pay, based on the letter of credit. Bandito will look closely at the bill of lading, which must specify *precisely* the goods described in the letter of credit. Why so nitpicky? Because the bank is dealing only in paper. It never sees the boots. Bandito is exchanging $3 million of its own money based on instructions in the letter of credit. The bank should pay only if the bill of lading indicates that *Le Fond de la Mer* received exactly what is described in the letter of credit. Bandito will decide whether the bill of lading is *conforming* or *nonconforming.* If the terms of both documents are identical, the bill of lading is conforming and Bandito must pay. If the terms vary, the bill of lading is nonconforming and Bandito will deny payment. Thus, if the bill of lading indicated 9,000 pairs of boots and 1,000 pairs of sneakers, it is nonconforming and Big Heel would get no money.

Bandito concludes that the documents are conforming, so it issues a check to Big Heel for $3 million. In return, you endorse the bill of lading and other documents over to the Bandito Bank, which endorses the same documents and sends them to Banque Bouffon. Bouffon makes the same minute inspection and then writes a check to Bandito. Bouffon then demands payment from Le Pied D'Or. Pied D'Or pays its bank, receiving in exchange the bill of lading and customs documents. Note that payment in all stages is now complete, though the boots are still rolling on the high seas. Finally, when the boots arrive in Le Havre, Pied D'Or trucks roll up to the wharf and, using the bill of lading and customs documents, collect the boots. See Exhibit 9.1.

Good news: They fit! Not all customers walk away in such comfort, as the following case indicates.

CENTRIFUGAL CASTING MACHINE CO., INC. V. AMERICAN BANK & TRUST CO.

966 F.2d 1348, 1992 U.S. App. LEXIS 13089
Tenth Circuit Court of Appeals, 1992

Facts: Centrifugal Casting Machine Co. (CCM) entered into a contract with the State Machinery Trading Co. (SMTC), an agency of the Iraqi government. CCM agreed to manufacture cast iron pipe plant equipment for a total price of $27 million. The contract specified payment of the full amount by confirmed irrevocable letter of credit. The Central Bank of Iraq then issued the letter, on behalf of SMTC (the "account party") to be paid to CCM (the "beneficiary"). The Banca Nazionale del Lavorov (BNL) confirmed the letter.

Following Iraq's invasion of Kuwait on August 2, 1990, President George H.W. Bush issued two executive orders blocking the transfer of property in the United States in which Iraq held any interest. In other words, no one could use, buy, or sell any Iraqi property or cash. When CCM attempted to draw upon the letter of credit, the United States government intervened. The government claimed that like all Iraqi money in the United States, this money was frozen by the executive order. The United States

▼

Exhibit 9.1

District Court rejected the government's claim, and the government appealed.

Issue: Is CCM entitled to be paid pursuant to the letter of credit?

Excerpts from Judge Sentelle's Decision: The United States contends on appeal that the freeze of Iraq's assets furthers national policy to punish Iraq by preventing it from obtaining economic benefits from transactions with American citizens, and by preserving such assets both for use as a bargaining chip in resolving this country's differences with Iraq and as a source of compensation for claims Americans may have against Iraq. We agree that these policy considerations are compelling and that we are therefore required to construe Iraqi property interests broadly. However, we are not persuaded these policies would be furthered by [creating] a property interest on behalf of Iraq that would not otherwise be cognizable under governing legal principles.

Two interrelated features of the letter of credit provide it with its unique value in the marketplace and are of critical importance in our consideration of the United States' claim here. First, the simple result [of a letter of credit] is that the issuer [i.e., the bank] substitutes its credit, preferred by the beneficiary, for that of the account party. Second, the issuer's obligation to pay on a letter of credit is completely independent from the underlying commercial transaction between the beneficiary and the account party. Significantly, the issuer must honor a proper demand even though the beneficiary has breached the underlying contract; even though the insolvency of the account party renders reimbursement impossible; and notwithstanding supervening illegality, impossibility, war or insurrection. This principle of independence is universally viewed as essential to the proper functioning of a letter of credit and to its particular value, i.e., its certainty of payment.

This assurance of payment gives letters of credit a central role in commercial dealings, and gives them a particular value in international transactions, in which sophisticated investors knowingly undertake such risks as political upheaval or contractual breach in return for the benefits to be reaped from international trade. Law affecting such an essential instrument of the economy must be shaped with sensitivity to its special characteristics. Accordingly, courts have concluded that the whole purpose of a letter of credit would be defeated by examining the merits of the underlying contract dispute to determine whether the letter should be paid.

Because of the nature of a letter of credit, we conclude that Iraq does not have a property interest in the money CCM received under the letter. The United States contends in essence that Iraq has a property interest in this money because it was allegedly a contract payment made by Iraq, which Iraq should recover because CCM breached the contract. In so arguing, the United States makes a breach of contract claim on behalf of Iraq that Iraq has never made, creates a remedy for the contracting parties in derogation of the remedy they themselves provided and, most importantly, disregards the controlling legal principles with respect to letters of credit.

Affirmed. ∎

Indirect Sales through a Distributor

You might also have decided that Big Heel would be better off doing business through a French shoe distributor, on the theory that the local company would have superior market knowledge and easier access to valuable retailers. The questions you face regarding choice of law, forum, and method of payment are identical to those you face in direct sales; they must be worked out in advance. But there is one additional problem that deserves close attention.

Suppose you choose Voleurs Freres, a French fashion distributor, to do all of Big Heel's work in France. Voleurs Freres will be an **exclusive dealer,** meaning that it will take on no other accounts of cowboy boots. In return you will give it an **exclusive distributorship,** indicating that no other French distributors will get a chance at Big Heel boots. This is a common method of working. Voleurs Freres benefits because no one else in France may distribute the valuable boots. Big Heel in turn need not worry that Voleurs Freres will devote more energy to a competing boot. It is a tidy relationship, but does it violate antitrust laws?

Antitrust laws make it illegal to destroy competition and capture an entire market. The United States and the EU both have strong antitrust laws that can potentially be applied domestically and in foreign countries.

EU Antitrust Law

The European Union law is found in Articles 85 and 86 of the Treaty of Rome. From the American point of view, the former is more important. **Article 85 outlaws any agreement, contract, or discussion that distorts competition within EU countries.** In other words, any attempt to gain a market edge by *avoiding* competition is going to be suspect. Suppose three Italian cosmetic firms agree to act in unison to increase earnings. They set common prices for makeup and agree that none will undersell the others. This greatly reduces competition, leaving the consumer with fewer options and more expensive products. Their deal violates Article 85.

Will Big Heel's contract with Voleurs Freres violate Article 85? There is no quick answer. You will need to do a careful market analysis and consult with French lawyers, who undoubtedly will have many questions. How popular are Big Heel boots in Europe? How many competitors would like to distribute them? How many other boot companies want Voleurs Freres to sell *their* products? Does the exclusive arrangement between Big Heel and Voleurs Freres diminish competition? Will consumers pay more because of the contract? These questions are a nuisance and an expense, but it is easier and cheaper to make the inquiry now than to face years of antitrust litigation.

American Antitrust Law

In the United States, the primary antitrust law is the **Sherman Act.**[4] This statute controls anticompetitive conduct that harms the American market. It will probably not affect the Big Heel–Voleurs Freres contract, since that deal is likely to have consequences only in Europe. But it is important to understand the Sherman Act when facing foreign competition. In effect, this statute is the American counterpart to Article 85. Any conduct that eliminates competition in the United States and enables one company, or group of companies, to control a market probably violates this law. And "any conduct" means that anticompetitive acts taking place in a foreign country may still violate the Sherman Act. A company doing business in the United States **may sue a competitor based on its conduct in a foreign country,** provided the local firm can show (1) that the foreign competitor *intends* to affect the U.S. market, and (2) that the foreign conduct has a *direct and substantial effect* on the U.S. market.

Let's look again at the Italian cosmetics makers. Suppose they decide to act in unison in the United States. They set common prices and agree not to compete with each other. That agreement is illegal. It violates the Sherman Act *even if all arrangements were made in Milan.* The companies intend to affect the U.S. market. When an American cosmetics firm demonstrates that the agreement caused it direct and substantial harm, the company may file suit in the United States against all three Italian corporations and expect to recover large damages.

International Comity

But what if the foreign corporation is doing business in a way that is entirely legal in its native country? May U.S. antitrust law still penalize the company's conduct if it harms American business? That was the question presented in the following case, which raises the issue of **international comity.** The word "comity" in this context means "concomitant jurisdiction," meaning that two courts have the right to hear a particular case. When those two courts are in different nations, the laws of the two countries may conflict. **In the event of a conflict, international comity requires one court to respect the other legal system and decline to hear a suit if it would more logically be resolved in the foreign country.** Does that principle govern the following case? The plaintiffs wanted the case heard in the United States under the Sherman Act, while the defendants wanted any dispute settled in Britain, where they believed British law would find them innocent of any wrongdoing.

you Be The Judge

HARTFORD FIRE INSURANCE CO. V. CALIFORNIA

509 U.S. 764, 113 S. Ct. 2891, 1993 U.S. LEXIS 4404
United States Supreme Court, 1993

Facts: Nineteen states and many private plaintiffs sued various insurance companies, alleging Sherman Act violations. The conspiracies related to commercial general liability (CGL) insurance, which covers the insured against accident and damage claims by customers, other companies, or the general public. The defendants were "reinsurance" companies. When a primary insurer issues a CGL policy to a corporation, it usually obtains for itself insurance to cover at least a portion of the risk it is assuming.

---
[4] See Chapter 39, on antitrust law.

Lloyd's of London is a major reinsurance center. Various English syndicates, working through Lloyd's, provide reinsurance for companies throughout the world. The plaintiffs alleged that reinsurers at Lloyd's forced American primary insurers to change the terms of their standard CGL insurance. These changes shortened the time during which a customer could file a claim under its policy, and eliminated certain claims altogether. These changes made CGL less valuable to the insured and more profitable to the reinsurers. The reinsurers were able to impose these changes because (1) there are only a few reinsurers worldwide and (2) all of the reinsurers worked in collusion to limit the coverage.

The United States District Court concluded that since the reinsurers' conduct was legal in Britain, international comity prevented an American court from hearing the claims. The court dismissed the case. The Court of Appeals reversed, and the London reinsurers appealed to the United States Supreme Court.

You Be the Judge: Does the principle of international comity prevent an American court from hearing these antitrust claims against London reinsurers?

Argument for the London Reinsurers: Lloyd's of London has been one of the world's most respected insurance organizations since 1688. Beginning in 1879, Parliament has directly regulated Lloyd's, and continues to control it today, pursuant to the Insurance Companies Act of 1982 and appropriate regulations. Under British law, insurance companies and reinsurance companies are *expressly exempt* from antitrust regulation. Everything that the defendants are alleged to have done in this case is *entirely legal* in Britain. It is an extraordinarily dangerous idea to permit the courts of one nation to subject foreign nationals to phenomenally expensive litigation for alleged conduct that was absolutely legal and proper where it was done.

Further, even though plaintiffs allege that the defendants' conduct technically violated American laws, there can be no suggestion that any of the reinsurers intended to harm any American corporation or citizen. This is not some shady conspiracy forged on a foggy night in an abandoned shack. The London reinsurers simply attempted to limit their own liability. They chose a lawful means to do it. They were doing, in other words, precisely what the plaintiffs in this case do when they buy insurance!

Argument for the Plaintiffs: Your honors, the defendants all engaged in conduct that they knew violated American antitrust laws. They did it for one reason: to increase their profits. That, of course, is why any corporation attempts to control a market. Here, by fixing deals with other major reinsurers, the Lloyd's syndicates were able to dictate the terms of American primary insurance and reduce coverage to the plaintiffs.

The defendants argue that they have obeyed British law, and that a so-called conflict in the laws requires American courts to stay away. But there is in fact no conflict between American and British law. It may be true that the reinsurers' monopolistic practices do not *violate* British law. But that does not mean that British law *requires* them to behave this way. It is black letter law that American antitrust laws may be applied against conduct that is lawful in a foreign nation. There would be a conflict only if British insurance law *required* Lloyd's firms to act collusively and attempt to control the American market. Obviously, it does not. The Lloyd's reinsurers are free to obey American law and British law, and that is what they ought to have done. They didn't, and we ask a chance to prove that in court.

These reinsurers are some of the most sophisticated business people in the world. They entered the American insurance market to make a profit and have stayed here many decades because they *are* earning money. They can't have it both ways. If they enter this market, they must be governed by its laws the same as anyone else. ∎

Licensing a Foreign Manufacturer

Big Heel has a third option when selling abroad, which is to license a French manufacturer to produce Big Heel boots. It should do this only if it is convinced the manufacturer will maintain sufficiently high standards. Even so, there are two major issues.

First, Big Heel must ensure that all of its patents and trademarks are protected. In fact, France will honor both forms of American intellectual property, and there should be no problems. But some nations may ignore American intellectual property rights, and no company should establish a licensing arrangement without investigating. As mentioned above, the WTO should increase respect worldwide for the intellectual property rights created by all nations.

Second, if Big Heel grants an exclusive license to any French manufacturer, it could encounter exactly the same antitrust problems as those discussed above. It must analyze both EU and American antitrust law before taking the risk.

INVESTING ABROAD

Foreign investment is another major source of international commerce. Assume that Ambux is an American communications corporation that decides to invest in a growing overseas market. The president of Ambux is particularly interested in building telephone systems in the former republics of the Soviet Union, reasoning that these economies offer great opportunity for growth. She wants you to report to her on the most important issues concerning possible investment in Uzbekistan and other former Soviet republics. You quickly realize that such an investment presents several related issues:

- Repatriation of profits
- Expropriation
- Sovereign immunity
- Act of State doctrine
- Foreign corrupt practices

Repatriation of Profits

Repatriation of profits occurs when an investing company pulls its earnings out of a foreign country and takes them back home. If Ambux builds a telephone system in Uzbekistan, it will plan to make money and then repatriate the profit to its headquarters in the United States. But Ambux must not assume an automatic right to do so. Many countries impose a much higher tax on repatriated profits than on normal income in order to keep the money in domestic commerce. Others bar repatriation altogether. Developing countries in particular want the money for further growth, and they tend to regard repatriation of rapidly earned profit as a close relative of exploitation. Thus, before Ambux invests anywhere, it must ensure that it can repatriate profits or be prepared to live with any limitations the foreign country might impose.

Fortunately, investing in Uzbekistan is relatively secure. Uzbekistan and the United States have signed a trade treaty guaranteeing unlimited repatriation for American investors. This treaty should suffice. But Ambux might still feel cautious. Uzbekistan is a new nation, and the mechanisms for actually getting the money out of Uzbekistan banks may be slow or faulty. The solution is to get a written agreement from the Minister of Commerce explicitly permitting Ambux to repatriate all profits and providing a clear mechanism to do it through the local banks.

Expropriation

Many nations, both developed and developing, **nationalize** property, meaning that they declare the national government to be the new owner. For example, during the

1940s and 1950s, Great Britain nationalized its coal, steel, and other heavy industries. The state assumed ownership and paid compensation to the previous owners. In the United States, nationalization is rare, but local governments often take land by eminent domain, to be used for roads or other public works. The United States Constitution requires that the owners be fairly compensated.

When a government takes property owned by foreign investors, it is called **expropriation.** Again, this practice is common and legal, provided there is adequate compensation. The U.S. government historically has acknowledged that the expropriation of American interests is legal, provided the host government pays the owners *promptly and fully, in dollars.* But if compensation is inadequate or long delayed, or made in a local currency that is hard to exchange, the taking is **confiscation.**

The courts of almost all nations concede that confiscation is illegal. But it can be difficult or impossible to prevent because courts of the host country may be partial to their own government. And any attempt to obtain compensation in an American court will encounter two separate problems: sovereign immunity and the Act of State doctrine.

Sovereign Immunity

Sovereign immunity holds that the courts of one nation lack the jurisdiction (power) to hear suits against foreign governments. Most nations respect this principle. In the United States, the **Foreign Sovereign Immunities Act (FSIA)** states that American courts generally cannot entertain suits against foreign governments. This is a difficult hurdle for a company to overcome when seeking compensation for foreign expropriation. There are three exceptions.

Waiver. A lawsuit is permitted against a foreign country that waives its immunity, that is, voluntarily gives up this protection. Suppose the Czech government wishes to buy fighter planes from an American manufacturer. The manufacturer might insist on a waiver in the sales contract, and the Czech Republic might be willing to grant one to get the weapons it desires. If the planes land safely but the checks bounce, the manufacturer may sue.

Commercial Activity. A plaintiff in the United States can sue a foreign country engaged in commercial activity, as opposed to political. Suppose the government of Iceland hires an American ecology-consulting firm to help its fishermen replenish depleted fishing grounds. Since fishing is a for-profit activity, the contract is commercial, and if Iceland refuses to pay, the company may sue in American courts.

Violation of International Law. A plaintiff in this country may sue a foreign government that has confiscated property in violation of international law, provided that the property either ends up in the United States or is involved in commercial activity that affects someone in the United States. Suppose a foreign government confiscates a visiting American ship, with no claim of right, and begins to use it for shipping goods for profit. Later, the ship carries some American produce. The taking was illegal, and it now affects American commerce. The original owner may sue.

He still has the sugar.

Act of State Doctrine

A second doctrine, annoyingly similar to sovereign immunity, could also affect Ambux or any company whose property is confiscated. The **Act of State doctrine** requires an American court to **abstain from any case in which a court order would interfere with the ability of the president or Congress to conduct foreign affairs.**

In the 1960s, Cuba expropriated American sugar interests, providing little or no compensation to the previous owners. The American owners sued, but in *Banco Nacional de Cuba v. Sabbatino*,[5] the United States Supreme Court refused to permit such suits in American courts. The Court ruled that even where there was strong evidence that the expropriation was illegal, American courts should not be involved because the executive and legislative branches must be free to conduct our foreign policy.

Investment Insurance

Companies eager to do business abroad but anxious about expropriation should consider publicly funded insurance. In 1971, Congress established the **Overseas Private Investment Corporation (OPIC)** to insure U.S. investors against overseas losses due to political violence and expropriation. OPIC insurance is available to investors at relatively low rates for investment in almost any country. The agency has had remarkable success at no cost to the U.S. government. Every year, OPIC participates in overseas ventures worth many billions of dollars, earning insurance fees that have paid the agency's entire budget and left a substantial surplus.

Should Ambux investigate OPIC insurance before investing in Uzbekistan? Absolutely. While the Uzbekistan government has the best of intentions with respect to foreign investment, the nation is young and the government has no track record. A government can change course as quickly as a gnat, and often with less planning. Why take unnecessary risks?

Foreign Corrupt Practices Act

The Foreign Corrupt Practices Act (FCPA)[6] makes it illegal for an American businessperson to give "anything of value" to any foreign official in order to influence an official decision. It is sad but true that in many countries bribery is routine and widely accepted. When Congress investigated foreign bribes to see how common they were, more than 300 U.S. companies admitted paying hundreds of millions of dollars in bribes to foreign officials. Legislators concluded that such massive payments distorted competition between American companies for foreign contracts, interfered with the free market system, and undermined confidence everywhere in our way of doing business. The statutory response was simple: foreign bribery is illegal, plain and simple. The FCPA has two principal requirements:

- *Bribes.* The statute makes it illegal for U.S. companies and citizens to bribe foreign officials to influence a governmental decision. The statute prohibits giving anything of value and also bars using third parties as a conduit for such payments.

- *Record Keeping.* All publicly traded companies—whether they engage in international trade or not—must keep detailed records that prevent hiding or disguising bribes. These records must be available for U.S. government officials to inspect.

Not all payments violate the FCPA. A **grease or facilitating payment is legal,** provided the company is paying a foreign official only to expedite performance of a routine function. Grease payments are common in many foreign countries to obtain a permit, process governmental papers, or obtain utility service. For example, the cost of a permit to occupy an office building might be $100, but the government clerk suggests that you will receive the permit faster (within this lifetime) if you pay $150,

---

[5]   376 U.S. 398, 84 S. Ct. 923, 1964 U.S. LEXIS 2252 (1964).

[6]   15 U.S.C. §§78 et seq.

one-third of which he will pocket. Such small payments are legal. Further, a payment **does not violate the FCPA if it was legal under the written laws** of the country in which it was made. Since few countries establish written codes *permitting* officials to receive bribes, this defense is unlikely to help many Americans who hand out gifts.

The following case is a classic example of bribery. Not much loyalty within Owl Securities. Why is that? What does it teach us?

UNITED STATES V. KING

354 F.3d 859
Eighth Circuit Court of Appeals, 2004

Facts: Owl Securities and Investments, Ltd., hoped to develop a large port in Limon, Costa Rica. The project included docks, housing, recreational facilities, an airport, and more. Richard King was one of Owl's largest investors, and Stephen Kingsley its CEO. The government charged King with attempting to bribe Costa Rican officials to obtain land and other concessions needed for their project. At trial, several of Owl's officers, including Kingsley, Richard Halford, and Albert Reitz, testified against King. A jury convicted King of violating the FCPA. He received a 30-month sentence and a fine of $60,000. He appealed.

Issue: Was there sufficient evidence that King had violated the FCPA?

Excerpts from Judge Beam's Decision: Viewing the evidence in the light most favorable to the verdict, there was ample evidence in the record to support the jury's convictions. The tape recordings, alone, support the jury's verdict. There was sufficient evidence to prove King's knowledge of the proposed payment long before Kingsley became an informant for the government.

For example, the following exchanges are just a small sample of what the jury heard:

Kingsley: Well you've always known about the closing cost fees and that.
King: I've known what?
Kingsley: You've known about the closing costs.
King: The one million dollars?
Kingsley: Yeah.
King: I've known about that for five years, yeah, . . .
[A later tape recording:]
Kingsley: Yeah, what, um, what Pablo had said, was why just pay, pay off the current politicians. Pay off the future ones.

King: That's right. Because we're gonna have to work with them anyway.
Kingsley: And so what he was saying was double, you know, give them more money. Buy the opposition. If you buy the current party and the opposition, then it doesn't matter who's in because there's only two parties.
King: The thing that really worries me is that, uh, if the Justice Department gets a hold of. Finds out how many people we've been paying off down there. Uh, or even if they don't. Are we gonna have to spend the rest of our lives paying off these petty politicians to keep them out of our hair? I can just see us, every, every day some politician on our doorstep down there wanting a hand out for this or that. . . . Think we could pay the top people enough, that the rest of the people won't bother us any. That's what I'm hoping this million and a half dollars does. I'm hoping it pays enough top people . . .
[A later recording:]
Kingsley: Now Pablo's continued to talk to the politicians. They know about the toll, closing costs call it what you will.
King: Does everybody agree to what we talked about recently?
Kingsley: Yeah, a million into escrow for the toll.
King: And then we get the property and then we do the (unintelligible)?
Kingsley: Um hum. Yeah now let me I'll, I'll, I'll come on to that because I'll explain how we work through that. Uh, essentially once the politicians see the money in escrow, they'll move. That's what it comes down to [clears throat]. Pablo's gonna send a list, an e-mail with a list of politicians already paid off and the ones he's gonna pay off.
King: Isn't that awfully dangerous?
Kingsley: No, e-mail's probably the most secure form of communication.
King: From what I read it's not, number one and number two, there's got to be a better way.

We affirm the judgment of the district court. ■

Transparency International, a nonprofit agency based in Germany, publishes a "Corruption Perception Index," gauging how much dishonesty businesspeople and scholars encounter in different nations. In 2004 the agency listed 145 nations on its index. The highest-ranking countries (perceived *least* corrupt) were Finland, New Zealand, Denmark, Iceland, Singapore, Sweden, Switzerland, Norway, Australia, and the United Kingdom. The agency listed the United States as the 17th least corrupt. The countries ranking lowest (perceived *most* corrupt) were Cote d'Ivoire, Georgia, Indonesia, Tajikstan, Turkmenistan, Azerbaijan, Paraguay, Chad, Myanmar, Nigeria, Bangladesh, and Haiti. The full index is available from Transparency International at **http://www.transparency.org**.

But corruption is a two-sided coin. Of the more than 200 nations in the world, very few aggressively prevent their nationals from bribing foreign officials. Further, in some countries, a bribe paid to a foreign official may be treated as a tax deduction!

American executives have long complained that the FCPA puts their companies at a competitive disadvantage, and political leaders have lobbied for an international agreement. Finally, the efforts are reaching fruition. The Organization for Economic Cooperation and Development (OECD) produced a "Convention of Combatting Bribery of Foreign Public Officials in International Business Transactions." About 36 of the world's largest trading nations have ratified the Convention.

The Convention requires signatories to enact criminal penalties for offering or giving bribes to foreign officials. The Convention also compels signatories to enact record-keeping laws that will prevent companies from disguising bribes. The Convention has various weaknesses, and it remains to be seen whether signatories will implement it aggressively, but the agreement is clearly a bold step on an ethical path.

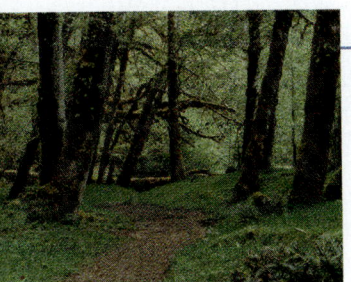

Chapter Conclusion

Overseas investment, like sales abroad, offers potentially great rewards but significant pitfalls. A working knowledge of international law is essential to any entrepreneur or executive seriously considering foreign commerce. Issues such as choice of law, currency protection, antitrust statutes, and expropriation can mean the difference between profit and loss. As the WTO lowers barriers, international trade will increase, and your awareness of these principles will grow still more valuable.

Chapter Review

1. Several statutes restrict exports from the United States that would harm national security, foreign policy, or certain other goals.

2. A tariff is a duty (tax) imposed on goods when they enter a country. The U.S. Customs Service classifies goods when they enter the United States and imposes appropriate tariffs.

3. Most countries, including the United States, impose duties for goods that have been dumped (sold at an unfairly low price in the international market) and for subsidized goods (those benefiting from government financial assistance in the country of origin).

4. The General Agreement on Tariffs and Trade (GATT) is lowering the average duties worldwide. Proponents see it as a boon to trade; opponents see it as a threat to workers and the environment.

5. GATT created the World Trade Organization (WTO), which resolves disputes between signatories to the treaty.

6. A sales agreement between an American company and a foreign company may be governed by the UCC, by the law of the foreign country, or by the United Nations Convention On Contracts For The International Sale Of Goods (CISG). The CISG differs from the UCC in several important respects.

7. A confirmed, irrevocable letter of credit is an important means of facilitating international sales contracts, because the seller is assured of payment by a local bank as long as it delivers the specified goods.

8. Antitrust laws exist in the United States, the European Union (EU), and other countries. International merchants must be careful not to make agreements that would distort competition.

9. International comity requires a local court to respect the legal system of a foreign country and dismiss a lawsuit if the dispute would more logically be resolved in the other nation.

10. A foreign government may restrict repatriation of profits.

11. Expropriation refers to a government taking property owned by foreign investors. U.S. courts regard this as lawful, provided the country pays the American owner promptly and fully, in dollars.

12. Sovereign immunity means that, in general, American courts lack jurisdiction to hear suits against foreign governments, unless the foreign nation has waived immunity, is engaging in commercial activity, or has violated international law.

13. The Act of State doctrine requires an American court to abstain from any case in which a court order would interfere with the ability of the president or Congress to conduct foreign affairs.

14. The Foreign Corrupt Practices Act (FCPA) makes it illegal for an American business person to bribe foreign officials.

Practice Test

1. Arnold Mandel exported certain high-technology electronic equipment. Later, he was in court arguing that the equipment he shipped should not have been on the Department of Commerce's Commodity Control List. What items may be on that list, and why does Mandel care?

2. Sports Graphics, Inc., imports consumer goods, including "Chill" brand coolers, which come from Taiwan. Chill coolers have an outer shell of vinyl, with handles and pockets, and an inner layer of insulation. In a recent federal lawsuit, the issue was whether "Chill" coolers were technically "luggage" or "articles used for preparing, serving or storing food or beverages." Who were the parties to this dispute likely to be, and why did they care about such a technical description of these coolers?

3. **ETHICS** Hector works in Zoey's importing firm. Zoey overhears Hector on the phone say, "O.K., 30,000 ski parkas at $80 per parka. You've got yourself a deal. Thanks a lot." When Hector hangs up, Zoey is furious, yelling, "I told you not to make a deal on those Italian ski parkas without my permission! I think I can get a better price elsewhere." "Relax, Zoey," replies Hector. "I wanted to lock them in, to be sure we had some in case your deal fell through. It's just an oral contract, so we can always back out if we need to." Is that ethical? How far can a company go to protect its interests? Does it matter that another business might make serious financial plans based on the discussion? Apart from the ethics, is Hector's idea smart?

4. **YOU BE THE JUDGE** WRITING PROBLEM Continental Illinois National Bank issued an irrevocable letter of credit on behalf of Bill's Coal Co. for $805,000, with the Allied Fidelity Insurance Co. as beneficiary. Bill's Coal Co. then went bankrupt. Allied then presented to Continental documents that were complete and conformed to the letter of credit. Continental refused to pay. Since Bill's Coal was bankrupt, there was no way Continental would collect once it had paid on the letter. Allied filed suit. Who should win? **Argument for Allied Fidelity:** An irrevocable letter of credit serves one purpose: to

assure the seller that it will be paid if it performs the contract. Allied has met its obligation. The company furnished documents demonstrating compliance with the agreement. Continental *must* pay. Continental's duty to pay is an independent obligation, unrelated to the status of Bill's Coal. The bank issued this letter knowing the rules of the game and expecting to make a profit. It is time for Continental to honor its word. **Argument for Continental Bank:** In this transaction, the bank was merely a middleman, helping to facilitate payment of a contract. Allied has fulfilled its obligations under the contract, and we understand the company's desire to be paid. Regrettably, Bill's Coal is bankrupt. No one is going to be paid on this deal. Allied should have researched Bill's financial status more thoroughly before entering into the agreement. While we sympathize with Allied's dilemma, it has only itself to blame and cannot expect the bank to act as some sort of insurance company for a deal gone awry.

5. Jean-François, a French wine exporter, sues Bob Joe, a Texas importer, claiming that Bob Joe owes him $2 million for wine. Jean-François takes the witness stand to describe how the contract was created. Where is the trial taking place?

6. Zenith and other American manufacturers of television sets sued Matsushita and 20 other Japanese competitors, claiming that the Japanese companies had conspired to drive Zenith and the Americans out of the American market. Supposedly, the Japanese companies agreed to maintain artificially high prices in Japan and artificially low prices in the United States. The goal of the low prices in the United States was to destroy American competition, and the goal of the high prices in Japan was to earn sufficient profits at home so that the companies could tolerate the temporary losses in the United States. Is the conduct of Matsushita in Japan subject to the Sherman Act?

7. The Kyrgyz Republic is another of the new nations that broke away from the old Soviet Union. In September 1994, the government of Kyrgyzstan made two independent announcements: (1) it was abolishing all taxes on repatriation; (2) the government was resigning and would shortly be replaced. Explain the significance of these announcements for an American

company considering a major investment in Kyrgyzstan.

8. The Instituto de Auxilios y Viviendas is a government agency of the Dominican Republic. Dr. Marion Fernandez, the general administrator of the Instituto and Secretary of the Republic, sought a loan for the Instituto. She requested that Charles Meadows, an American citizen, secure the Instituto a bank loan of $12 million. If he obtained a loan on favorable terms, he would receive a fee of $240,000. Meadows secured a loan on satisfactory terms, which the Instituto accepted. He then sought his fee, but the Instituto and the Dominican government refused to pay. He sued the government in United States District Court. The Dominican government claimed immunity. Comment.

9. Environmental Tectonics Corp. and W. S. Kirkpatrick & Co. were both competing for a valuable contract with the Nigerian government. Kirkpatrick got it. Tectonics then sued Kirkpatrick in the United States, claiming that Kirkpatrick got the contract only because it bribed Nigerian officials. Kirkpatrick acknowledged that the district court had jurisdiction but argued that it should abstain from hearing the case. What doctrine does Kirkpatrick rely on, and what should the trial court do?

10. Blondek and Tull were two employees of an American company called Eagle Bus. They hoped that the Saskatchewan provincial government would award Eagle a contract for buses. To bolster their chances, they went to Saskatchewan and paid $50,000 to two government employees. Back in the United States, they were arrested and charged with a crime. Suppose they argue that even if they did something illegal, it occurred in Canada, and that is the only nation that can prosecute them. Comment on the defense.

11. Richard Johnson, an American citizen, was a highly trained electrical engineer who had worked for Hughes Aircraft and Norcroft Corp. He strongly believed in the cause of the Provisional Irish Republican Army (PIRA), which at the time was attacking British civilian and military targets in Northern Ireland and England. Johnson researched and developed explosives to be exported to Ireland and used by the PIRA.

Christina Reid, an electrical engineer, worked with Johnson on IRA projects. She served as a courier of electronic components for remote-control bombs that the two sent to Northern Ireland. What legal problems did they risk by engaging in these transactions?

Internet Research Problem

At http://beatty.westbuslaw.com, read about the worldwide problem of sweatshops. Is this a serious problem? If so, what role should the law play in its resolution? What can one student do about it?

12. **ROLE REVERSAL** Draft an essay or short-answer question that involves a dispute brought to the WTO on one of these issues: dumping, nontariff barriers, or intellectual property.

You can find further practice problems at http://beatty.westbuslaw.com or in the Study Guide that accompanies this text.

Contracts

Introduction to Contracts

In Marina del Rey, California, Cassandra sits on the sunny deck of her waterside condominium, sipping a mocha latte while watching spinnakers fill with the warm Pacific wind. She has just received an offer of $1.7 million to buy her condominium. Cassandra has decided to counteroffer for $1.9 million. She is in high spirits because she assumes that at the very worst she has $1.7 million guaranteed, and that represents a huge profit to her. Cassandra plans to buy a cheaper house in North Carolina and invest her profits so that she can retire early. She opens the newspaper, notices a headline "Hard Body Threatens Suit," and turns the page, thinking that a corporate lawsuit in Ohio is of no concern to her. She is mistaken and may learn some hard lessons about contract law.

A year earlier, Jerusalem Steel had signed a contract with Hard Body, a manufacturer of truck and bus bodies. Jerusalem was to deliver 20,000 tons of steel to Hard Body's plant in Joy, Ohio. Hard Body relied on the contract, hiring 300 additional workers even before the steel was delivered, so that the plant would be geared up and ready to produce buses when the metal arrived. To help deal with the new workers, Hard Body offered a mid-level personnel job to Nicole. Hard Body told

Nicole, "Don't worry, we expect your job to last forever." Nicole, in turn, relied on that statement to quit her old job in Minneapolis, move to Joy, and sign an agreement with Jasper to purchase his house for $450,000. Based on that sales contract, Jasper phoned his offer to Cassandra's real estate agent for $1.7 million. See Exhibit 10.1.

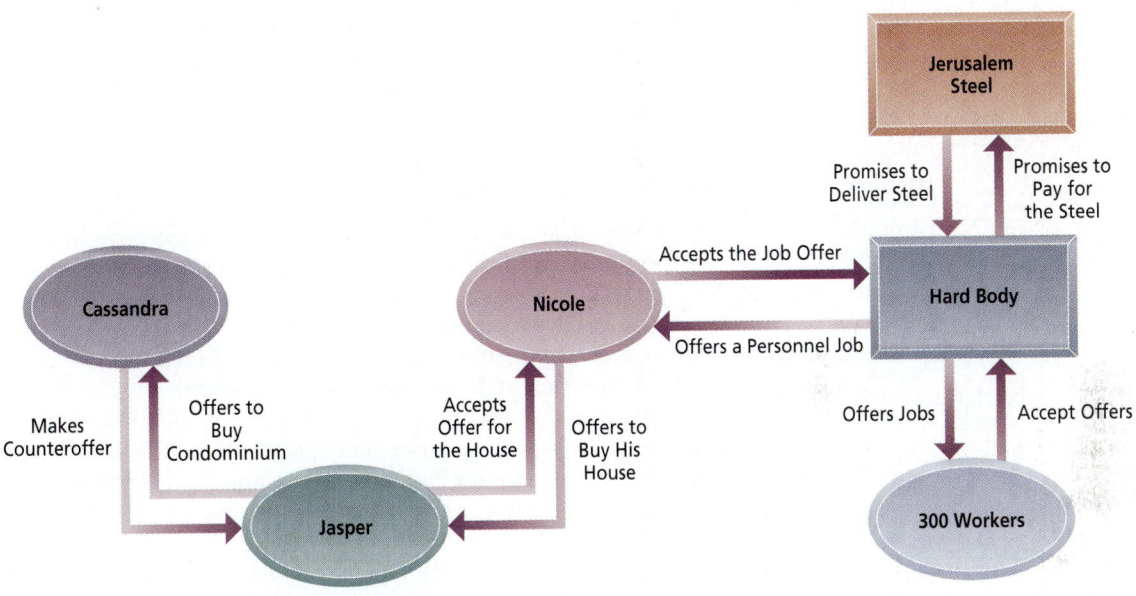

Exhibit 10.1
Contracts are intended to make business matters more predictable. Frequently, a series of contracts becomes mutually dependent.

But in the year since Jerusalem signed its contract, the price of the specified steel has gone up 60 percent. Jerusalem now refuses to deliver the steel unless the price is renegotiated. Hard Body has insisted on the original contract price. Hard Body cannot afford to buy steel at the current price, which would make its deal to produce buses unprofitable. If Hard Body receives no steel, does it have a valid lawsuit against Jerusalem? May the company force Jerusalem to deliver the steel? If it cannot get steel, may Hard Body lay off the newly hired workers? May the company fire Nicole, or does she have a job for life? If Nicole loses her paycheck, will the law force her to buy a house she no longer wants? Jasper will never get such a good price from anyone else, because with no work at Hard Body property prices in Joy will plummet. May Jasper refuse to buy Cassandra's condo, or is he committed for $1.7 million? ◼

CONTRACTS _____

The Purpose of a Contract

Throughout this unit on contracts, we will consider issues like those raised in the Cassandra–Hard Body story. This long chain of mutually dependent people and companies exemplifies not only the law of contracts but the *purpose* of contracts. Parties enter into contracts attempting to control their future. **Contracts exist to make business matters more predictable.** Most contracts work out precisely as the parties intended because the parties fulfill their obligations. Most—but not all. In this unit we will study contracts that have gone wrong. We look at these errant deals to learn how to avoid the problems they manifest.

Judicial Activism versus Judicial Restraint

We will see that courts *generally but not always do what we expect.* In most contract cases, judges do their best simply to enforce whatever terms the parties have agreed to. Even if the contract results in serious harm to one party, a court will typically enforce it. This is **judicial restraint**—a court taking a passive role and requiring the parties to fulfill whatever obligations they agreed to, whether the deal was wise or foolish. Judges often say that it is not their job to rewrite a deal that the parties crafted. For example, if a real estate developer contracts with a builder to erect 10 expensive homes, but the housing market collapses before construction begins, the developer is still obligated to pay the builder for the houses, even though the expense will cause him devastating losses. Judicial restraint makes the law **less flexible but more predictable.**

On the other hand, courts sometimes practice **judicial activism.** In contract law, this means that a court will ignore certain provisions of a contract, or an entire agreement, if the judge believes that enforcing the deal would be unjust. Further, a court may be willing to artificially create a contract where none existed, if the judge believes that is the only way to avoid injustice. Since judicial activism is always phrased in terms of "doing justice," it has an initial appeal. For example, when one party deceives the other with a misleading contract, it may be appropriate for a court to rewrite the agreement. But when a court practices judicial activism, it may diminish our ability to control our own future—which is the whole point of creating a contract. Judicial activism makes the law **more flexible but less predictable.** In this unit on contracts we look at many examples of both judicial activism and restraint.

Issues (and Answers)

The chain of contracts connecting Jerusalem Steel and Cassandra illustrates various contract problems. We consider each problem in detail in this unit, but here we briefly identify the issues and summarize the answers. A contract has four elements:

- *Agreement.* One party must make a valid offer, and the other party must accept it.
- *Consideration.* There has to be bargaining that leads to an exchange between the parties.
- *Legality.* The contract must be for a lawful purpose.
- *Capacity.* The parties must be adults of sound mind.

The chapters that follow cover each of the elements in sequence. Contract cases often raise several other important issues, which we examine in later chapters:

- *Consent.* Neither party may trick or force the other into the agreement.
- *Written Contracts.* Some contracts must be in writing to be enforceable.
- *Third Party Interests.* Some contracts affect people other than the parties themselves.
- *Performance and Discharge.* If a party fully accomplishes what the contract requires, his duties are discharged.
- *Remedies.* A court will award money or other relief to a party injured by a breach of contract.

When we apply these principles to the problem at this chapter's beginning, we see that Jerusalem Steel is almost certainly bound by its agreement. A rise in price is generally no excuse to walk away from a contract. Hard Body has made the bargain precisely to protect itself in case of a price rise. These are issues of offer and acceptance, consideration, and discharge. Can Hard Body force Jerusalem to deliver the steel? Probably not, as we learn in Chapter 18, on remedies. But Hard Body might be able to block Jerusalem from delivering the steel anywhere else. And Hard Body almost certainly is entitled to money damages if it is forced to buy steel at higher prices. If Hard Body is unable to obtain steel in the rising market, may it lay off its workers? Very likely, as Chapter 11, on agreement, indicates. Can it fire Nicole? The statement about expecting her job to last forever almost certainly creates no lifetime employment. In fact, even if Nicole has begun her job, the company can probably terminate her. What about the fact that she quit her job in reliance on this one? That raises an issue called promissory estoppel, which we discuss later in this chapter; it may or may not help Nicole, depending on the facts.

Must Nicole go through with her purchase of Jasper's house? Probably, as Chapters 15 and 18, on written contracts and remedies, will demonstrate. Do Jasper and Cassandra have a contract? No, because the agreement must be in writing to be enforceable. Even if there is no settled price, is Cassandra safe in assuming she has $1.7 million guaranteed? Not at all, as Chapter 11, on agreement, shows. If Cassandra had read this unit, she would be faxing a written contract to Jasper rather than waiting for her latte to cool.

All Shapes and Sizes

Some contracts are small. If you agree to sell your bicycle to your roommate for $75 at the end of the academic year, that is an enforceable agreement. But contracts can also be large. Lockheed Martin and Boeing spent years of work and millions of dollars competing for a Defense Department aircraft contract. Why the fierce effort? The deal was potentially good for 25 years and *$200 billion*. Lockheed won. The company earned the right to build the next generation of fighter jets—3,000 planes, with different varieties of the aircraft to be used by each of the American defense services and some allied forces as well. (Boeing promptly set to work designing and building unpiloted aircraft, which it believes will soar to the cutting edge of flight.)

Many contracts involve public issues. The Lockheed agreement concerns government agencies deciding how to spend taxpayer money for national defense. Other contracts concern intensely private matters. Mary Beth Whitehead signed a contract with William and Elizabeth Stern, of New Jersey. For a fee of $10,000, Whitehead agreed to be impregnated with Mr. Stern's sperm, carry the baby to term, and then deliver it to the Sterns for adoption. But when little Melissa was born, Whitehead changed her mind and fled to Florida with the baby. The Sterns sued for breach of contract.

Surrogacy contracts now lead to over 500 births per year. Are the contracts immoral? Should they be illegal? Are there limits to what one person may pay another to do? The New Jersey Supreme Court, the first to rule on the issue, declared the contract illegal and void. The court nonetheless awarded Melissa to the Sterns, saying that it was in the child's best interest to live with them. Inevitably, legislators disagree about this emotional issue. Some states have passed statutes permitting surrogacy. Others prohibit the enforcement of some or all surrogacy contracts. A few states have gone further, making paid surrogacy a crime. As usual, the law will develop more slowly than technology. Two Web sites report on current surrogacy laws: http://www.surrogacy.com and http://www.surrogatemothers.com.

At times we enter contracts without knowing it. Suppose you try to book a flight using your frequent flyer miles, but the airline tells you the terms of the frequent flyer program have changed and you must earn more mileage. According to the Supreme Court, you may well have an enforceable agreement based on the terms the airline quoted when you earned the miles.[1] At other times we may be stunned to learn that a contract we are relying on does not exist. Jerome Howard was the agent for rap recording star Domino. Howard was delighted that his contract gave him a long-term relationship with an artist whose most recent album sold at "platinum" levels. But Domino was unhappy with the arrangement and walked away from it—legally. Howard was not licensed by the state of California to work as a music agent. His contract with Domino was void.

Societal interests can shape contract law. For example, federal law requires that landowners clean up toxic waste on their property, a process that can cost millions of dollars. Suppose Klene Corp. wants to sell land that might have toxic chemicals underground. May Klene include a provision in its sales contract shifting the cost of any cleanup to the buyer? No, and yes. Regardless of what the contract says, federal statutes prohibit Klene from abandoning its own responsibility to clean up the waste. Yet the contract could make the buyer equally liable.

In turn, contract law can shape society. For example, some states cap the interest rate that a mortgage company may charge. Because of the cap, mortgage companies may not find it profitable to lend money to the most credit-risky customers, meaning that those people will be unable to borrow money. Other states place no cap at all on mortgage rates. This enables low-income borrowers to obtain funds. But it also means they pay astronomical interest rates, sometimes over 50 percent. The result? Many end up losing their homes. This is a typical problem at the intersection of public policy and contract law.

Contracts Defined

Contract law is a study in promises. Is Nicole entitled to a lifetime job at Hard Body? Is Jasper obligated to buy Cassandra's condominium? Contract law determines which promises to enforce. **A contract is a promise that the law will enforce.**

As we look more closely at the elements of contract law, we will encounter some intricate issues. This is partly because we live in a complex society, which conducts its business in an infinite variety of ways. It is also due to the constant tug between predictability and fairness, described above. Remember, though, that we are usually interested in answering three basic questions of common sense, all relating to promises:

- Is it certain that the defendant promised to do something?

- If she did promise, is it fair to make her honor her word?

- If she did not promise, are there unusual reasons to hold her liable anyway?

---

[1] *American Airlines, Inc. v. Wolens,* 513 U.S. 219, 115 S. Ct. 817, 1995 U.S. LEXIS 690 (1995).

DEVELOPMENT OF CONTRACT LAW

Courts have not always assumed that promises are legally significant. As English judges were developing the common law in the twelfth and thirteenth centuries, they seldom used the term "contract," focusing instead on other issues in the case. Suppose a farmer and a horse dealer orally agreed that the dealer would deliver two draught horses to the farmer by April 1, and the farmer agreed to pay £100 for each. If the horse dealer never made any effort to fulfill his promise, the farmer could *not* sue. Even if he lost a year's crop because of the dealer's incompetence, he recovered nothing. The dealer's promise was never binding unless he made it *in writing and affixed a seal* to the document. This was seldom done, and therefore most promises were unenforceable.

The common law changed very slowly, but by the fifteenth century courts began to allow some suits based on a broken promise. There were still major limitations. Suppose a merchant hired a carpenter to build a new shop, and the carpenter failed to start the job on time. Now courts would permit the suit but only if the merchant had paid some money to the carpenter. If the merchant made a 10 percent down payment, the contract would be enforceable. But if the merchant merely *promised* to pay when the building was done, and the carpenter never began work, the merchant could recover nothing.

In 1602, English courts began to enforce *mutual promises*, that is, deals in which neither party gave anything to the other but both promised to do something in the future. Thus, if a farmer promised to deliver a certain quantity of wheat to a merchant and the merchant agreed on the price, both parties were now bound by their promise, even though there had been no down payment. This was a huge step forward in the development of contract law, but many issues remained. Consider the following employment case from 1792, which raises issues of public policy that still challenge courts today.

Times change, but contract issues do not.

© THE BRIDGEMAN ART LIBRARY/GETTY IMAGES

DAVIS V. MASON

Court of King's Bench
Michaelmas Term, 33d George III, p. 118 (1792)

Facts: Mason was a surgeon/apothecary in the English town of Thetford. Davis wished to apprentice himself to Mason. The two agreed that Davis would work for Mason and learn his profession. They further agreed that if Davis left Mason's practice, he would not set up a competing establishment within 10 miles of Thetford at any time within 14 years. Davis promised to pay £200 if he violated the agreement not to compete.

Davis began working for Mason in July 1789. In August 1791, Mason dismissed Davis, claiming misconduct, though Davis denied it. Davis then established his own practice within 10 miles of Thetford. Mason sued for the £200.

Davis admitted promising to pay the money. But he claimed that the agreement should be declared illegal and unenforceable. He argued that 14 years was unreasonably long to restrict him from the town of Thetford, and that 10 miles was too great a distance. (Ten miles in those days might take the better part of a day to travel.) He added an additional policy argument, saying that it was harmful to the public health to restrict a doctor from practicing his profession: if the people needed his service, they

▼

should have it. Finally, he said that his "consideration" was too great for this deal. In other words, it was unfair that he should pay £200, because he did not receive anything of that value from Mason.

Issue: Was the contract too unreasonable to enforce?

Excerpts from Lord Kenyon's Decision: Here, the plaintiff being established in business as a surgeon at Thetford, the defendant wished to act as his assistant with a view of deriving a degree of credit from that situation; on which the former stipulated that the defendant should not come to live there under his auspices and steal away his patients: this seems to be a fair consideration. Then it was objected that the limits within which the defendant engaged not to practise are unreasonable: but I do not see that they are necessarily unreasonable, nor do I know how to draw the line. Neither are the public likely to be injured by an agreement of this kind, since every other person is at liberty to practise as a surgeon in this town.

Judgment for the Plaintiff. ■

The contract between Davis and Mason is called a **noncompetition agreement.** Today they are more common than ever, and frequently litigated. The policy issues that Davis raised have never gone away. Two hundred years later, a group of stockbrokers brought a class action suit, alleging that their employer had forced them to pay an excessive fee for taking their skills elsewhere.

You may well be asked to sign a noncompetition agreement sometime in your business or professional life. We look at the issue in detail in Chapter 12, on consideration. But note that in 1792 the court did in fact enforce the contract. In other words, the mutual promises seemed reasonable, and the court ordered the parties to live up to the deal.

That outcome was typical of contract cases for the next 100 years. Contracts were generally bargained between business people of roughly equal knowledge and power, and the law expected them to know what they were doing. Courts took a *laissez-faire* approach, declaring that parties had *freedom to contract* and would have to live with the consequences. Lord Kenyon saw Davis and Mason as equals, entering a bargain that made basic sense, and he had no intention of rewriting it. After 500 years of evolution, courts had come to regard promises as almost sacred. The law had gone from ignoring most promises to enforcing nearly all.

By the early twentieth century, bargaining power in business deals had changed dramatically. Farms and small businesses were yielding place to huge corporations in a trend that accelerated throughout the century. Today multinational corporations span many continents, wielding larger budgets and more power than many of the nations in which they do business. When such a corporation contracts with a small company or an individual consumer, the latter may have little or no leverage. Courts increasingly looked at the basic fairness of contracts. In other words, they were more willing to play an *activist* role.

Noncompetition agreements are no longer automatically enforced. Courts may alter them or ignore them entirely because the parties have such unequal power and because the public may have an interest in letting the employee go on to compete. Davis's argument—that the public is entitled to as many doctors as it needs—is frequently more successful in court today than it was before Lord Kenyon.

It is not only the unequal bargaining power that causes courts to look closely at contracts. The issue of toxic waste illustrates how the public interest may be "read into" a contract. Environmental statutes assume that the public interest requires holding all owners of property liable to clean up toxic waste. So even when the seller of polluted land writes a contract placing cleanup responsibility on the buyer, the courts will simply ignore the provision, holding that the seller remains liable. This is socially sensible, because it ensures that our world will be cleaned up, but it diminishes a party's ability to control its future.

Legislatures and the courts limit the effect of promises in other ways. Suppose you purchase a lawn mower with an attached tag, warning you that the manufacturer is not responsible in the event of any malfunction or injury. You are required to sign a form acknowledging that the manufacturer has no liability of any kind. That agreement is clear enough—but a court will not enforce it. The law holds that the manufacturer *has* warranted the product to be good for normal purposes, regardless of any language included in the sales agreement. If the blade flies off and injures a child, the manufacturer is liable. This is socially responsible, but again, it interferes with a private agreement.

The law has not come full circle back to the early days of the common law. Courts still enforce the great majority of contracts. But the possibility that a court will ignore an agreement means that any contract is a little less certain than it would have been a century ago. That is all the more reason to understand contract principles and avoid agreements that fall afoul of the law.

TYPES OF CONTRACTS

Bilateral and Unilateral Contracts

In a bilateral contract, both parties make a promise. A producer says to Gloria, "I'll pay you $2 million to star in my new romantic comedy, *A Promise for a Promise*, which we are shooting three months from now in Santa Fe." Gloria says, "It's a deal." That is a bilateral contract. Each party has made a promise to do something. The producer is now bound to pay Gloria $2 million, and Gloria is obligated to show up on time and act in the movie. The vast majority of contracts are bilateral contracts. They can be for services, such as this acting contract; they can be for the sale of goods, such as 1,000 tons of steel, or for almost any other purpose. When the bargain is a promise for a promise, it is a bilateral agreement.

In a unilateral contract, one party makes a promise that the other party can accept only by doing something. These contracts are less common. Suppose the movie producer says to Leo, "I'll give you a hundred bucks if you mow my lawn this weekend." Leo is not promising to do it. If he mows the lawn, he has accepted the offer and is entitled to his hundred dollars. If he spends the weekend at the beach, neither he nor the producer owes anything.

Express and Implied Contracts

In an express contract, the two parties explicitly state all important terms of their agreement. The vast majority of contracts are express contracts. The contract between the producer and Gloria is an express contract, because the parties explicitly state what Gloria will do, where and when she will do it, and how much she will be paid. Some express contracts are oral, as that one was, and some are written. They might be bilateral express contracts, as Gloria's was, or unilateral express contracts, as Leo's was. Obviously, it is good business sense always to make express contracts, and wise to put them in writing. We emphasize, however, that many oral contracts are fully enforceable.

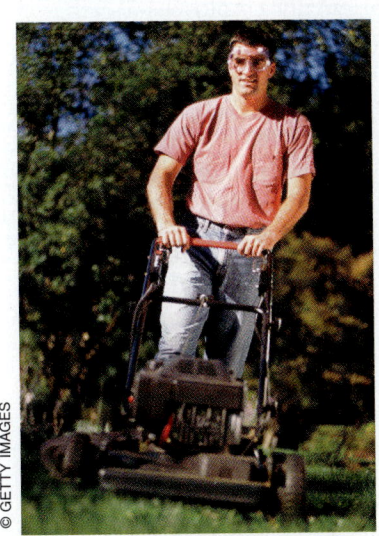

Does Leo have an implied contract to mow the lawn?

In an implied contract, the words and conduct of the parties indicate that they intended an agreement. Suppose every Friday, for two months, the producer asks Leo to mow his lawn, and loyal Leo does so each weekend. Then for three more weekends, Leo simply shows up without the producer asking, and the producer continues to pay for the work done. But on the twelfth weekend, when Leo rings the doorbell to collect, the producer suddenly says, "I never asked you to mow it. Scram." The producer is correct that there was no express contract, because the parties had not spoken for several weeks. But a court will probably rule that the conduct of the parties has *implied* a contract. Not only did Leo mow the lawn every weekend, but the producer even paid on three weekends when they had not spoken. It was reasonable for Leo to assume that he had a weekly deal to mow and be paid. Naturally, there is no implied contract thereafter.

Today, the hottest disputes about implied contracts continue to arise in the employment setting. Many corporate employees have at-will contracts with their companies. This means that the employees are free to quit at any time and the company has the right to fire them at any time, for virtually any reason. Courts routinely enforce at-will contracts. But often a company provides its workers with personnel manuals that guarantee certain rights. The legal issue is whether the handbook implies a contract guaranteeing the specified rights. That is the issue in the following case.

you Be The Judge

DEMASSE V. ITT CORPORATION

194 Ariz. 500, 984 P.2d 1138
Supreme Court of Arizona, 1999

Facts: Roger DeMasse and five others were employees-at-will at ITT Corporation, where they started working at various times between 1960 and 1979. Each was paid an hourly wage.

ITT issued an employee handbook, which it revised four times over two decades.

The first four editions of the handbook stated that within each job classification, any layoffs would be made in reverse order of seniority. The fifth handbook made two important changes. First, the document stated that "nothing contained herein shall be construed as a guarantee of continued employment. ITT does not guarantee continued employment to employees and retains the right to terminate or layoff employees."

Second, the handbook stated that "ITT reserves the right to amend, modify or cancel this handbook, as well as any or all of the various policies [or rules] outlined in it." Four years later, ITT notified its hourly employees that layoff guidelines for hourly employees would be based not on seniority but on ability and performance. About ten days later, the six employees were laid off, though

less senior employees kept their jobs. The six employees sued.

You Be The Judge: Did ITT have the right to unilaterally change the layoff policy?

Argument for the workers: It is true that all of the plaintiffs were originally employees-at-will, subject to termination at the company's whim. However, things changed when the company issued the first handbook. ITT chose to include a promise that layoffs would be based on seniority. Long-term workers and new employees all understood the promise and relied on it. The company put it there to attract and retain good workers. The policy worked. Responsible employees understood that the longer they remained at ITT, the safer their job was. Company and employees worked together for many years with a common understanding, and that is a textbook definition of an implied contract.

Once a contract is formed, whether express or implied, it is binding on both sides. That is the whole point of a contract. If one side could simply change the terms of an agreement on its own, what value would any contract have? The company's legal argument is a perfect symbol of its

▼

arrogance: It believes that because these workers are mere hourly workers, they have no rights, even under contract law. The company is mistaken. Implied contracts are binding, and ITT should not make promises it does not intend to keep.

Argument for ITT: Once an at-will employee, always one. ITT had the right to fire any of its employees at any time—just as the workers had the right to quit whenever they wished. That never changed, and in case any workers forgot it, the company reiterated the point in its most recent handbook. If the plaintiffs thought layoffs would happen in any particular order, that is their error, not ours.

All workers were bound by the terms of whichever handbook was then in place. For many years, the company had made a seniority-layoff promise. Had we fired a senior worker during that period, he or she would have had a legitimate complaint—and that is why we did not do it. Instead, we gave everyone four years' notice that things would change. Any workers unhappy with the new policies should have left to find more congenial work.

Why should an employee be allowed to say, "I prefer to rely on the old, outdated handbooks, not the new one"? The plaintiffs' position would mean that no company is ever free to change its general work policies and rules. Since when does an at-will employee have the right to dictate company policy? That would be disastrous for the whole economy—but fortunately it is not the law. ■

Ethics Besides the workers and the company, who are the other stakeholders? What *alternatives* were available to DeMasse? What are the most important *values* involved in this dispute? If there are conflicting values, which are most important? ◆

Executory and Executed Contracts

A contract is **executory** when one or more parties has not fulfilled its obligations. Recall Gloria, who agrees to act in the producer's film beginning in three months. The moment Gloria and the producer strike their bargain, they have an executory bilateral express contract.

A contract is **executed** when all parties have fulfilled their obligations. When Gloria finishes acting in the movie and the producer pays her final fee, their contract will be fully executed.

Valid, Unenforceable, Voidable, and Void Agreements

A **valid contract** is one that satisfies all of the law's requirements. A court will therefore enforce it. The contract between Gloria and the producer is a valid contract, and if the producer fails to pay Gloria, she will win a lawsuit to collect the unpaid fee.

An **unenforceable agreement** occurs when the parties intend to form a valid bargain but a court declares that some rule of law prevents enforcing it. Suppose Gloria and the producer orally agree that she will star in his movie, which he will start filming in 18 months. The statute of frauds requires that this contract be in writing, because it cannot be completed within one year. If the producer signs up another actress two months later, Gloria has no claim against him.

A **voidable contract** occurs when the law permits one party to terminate the agreement. This happens, for example, when the other party has committed fraud or misrepresentation. Suppose that Klene Corp. induces Smart to purchase 1,000 acres of land by telling Smart that there is no underground toxic waste, even though Klene knows that just under the topsoil lies an ocean of bubbling purple sludge. Klene is committing fraud. Smart may void the contract, that is, terminate it and owe nothing. If, for some reason, Smart still considers the land a bargain, he may go through with the sale. Klene has no power to void the contract.

A **void agreement** is one that neither party can enforce, usually because the purpose of the deal is illegal or because one of the parties had no legal authority to make a contract. When Jerome Howard agreed to represent the rapper Domino, the agreement was void from the start because Howard was not a licensed agent. He had no legal right to obtain employment for entertainers and therefore no lawful ability to sign a contract saying he would.

REMEDIES CREATED BY JUDICIAL ACTIVISM

Now we turn away from true contracts and consider two remedies created by judicial activism: promissory estoppel and quasi-contract. We emphasize that these remedies are exceptions. Most of the agreements that courts enforce are the express contracts that we have already studied. Nonetheless, the next two remedies have grown in importance over the last 100 years. In each case, a sympathetic plaintiff can demonstrate an injury. The harm has occurred in a setting where a contract might well have been made. But the crux of the matter is this: *there is no contract*. The plaintiff cannot claim that the defendant breached the contract, because none ever existed. The plaintiff must hope for more "creative" relief.

The two remedies can be confusingly similar. The best way to distinguish them is this:

- In promissory estoppel cases, the defendant made a promise that the plaintiff relied on.

- In quasi-contract cases, the defendant did not make any promise, but did receive a *benefit* from the plaintiff.

Promissory Estoppel

A fierce fire swept through Dana and Derek Andreason's house in Utah, seriously damaging it. The good news was that agents for Aetna Casualty promptly visited the Andreasons and helped them through the crisis. The agents reassured the couple that all of the damage was covered by their insurance, instructed them on which things to throw out and replace, and helped them choose materials for repairing other items. The bad news was that the agents were wrong: the Andreasons' policy had expired six weeks before the fire. When Derek Andreason presented a bill for $41,957 worth of meticulously itemized work that he had done under the agents' supervision, Aetna refused to pay.

The Andreasons sued—but not for breach of contract. There *was* no contract, that was exactly the problem. The insurance contract had expired. So they sued Aetna under the legal theory of promissory estoppel: **Even when there is no contract, a plaintiff may use promissory estoppel to enforce the defendant's promise if he can show that:**

- The defendant made a promise knowing that the plaintiff would likely rely on it

- The plaintiff did rely on the promise; and

- The only way to avoid injustice is to enforce the promise.

Aetna made a promise to the Andreasons, namely, its assurance that all of the damage was covered by insurance. The company knew that the Andreasons would rely on that promise, which they did by ripping up a floor that might have been salvaged, throwing out some furniture, and buying materials to repair the house. Is enforcing the promise the only way to avoid injustice? Yes, ruled the Utah Court of Appeals.[2] The Andreasons' conduct was reasonable and based entirely on what the Aetna agents told them. Under promissory estoppel, the Andreasons received virtually the same amount they would have obtained had the insurance contract been valid.

Promissory estoppel is an important development of twentieth-century law. The doctrine provides opportunities for a court to do justice where no contract exists. Clearly, this is judicial activism, helping people by crafting new remedies. But, as is true whenever the rules are "bent," it means that the outcome of a particular case is less predictable.

There was plenty of romance in the following case. Was there an enforceable promise?

NORTON V. HOYT

278 F. Supp. 2d 214
United States District Court for the District of Rhode Island, 2003

Facts: Gail Norton sued Russell Hoyt, and this is what she alleged. The two met when Norton, who was single, worked as an elementary school teacher. Hoyt told her he was also single, and they began an affair. She later learned that he was married, but he assured her he was getting a divorce, and they continued their relationship.

Six years later, Hoyt, who was rich, convinced Norton to quit her job so that they could travel together. The couple lived lavishly, spending time in Newport, Rhode Island, where Hoyt was part of the yachting crowd, in London, the Bahamas, and other agreeable places. Hoyt rented Norton an apartment, bought her cars, and repeated his promises to divorce his wife and marry his lover. He never did either.

After 23 years, Hoyt ended the relationship. Norton became ill, and saw various doctors for anxiety, depression, headaches, stomach maladies, and weight loss. During one joint therapy session, Hoyt told Norton and the psychiatrist that he would continue to support her with $80,000 a year. But he did not.

Norton sued, claiming promissory estoppel. Hoyt moved for summary judgment. In ruling on the motion, the court assumed that Norton's allegations were true.

Issue: Was Norton entitled to support, based on promissory estoppel?

Excerpts from Judge Lageux's Decision: Even viewed most favorably to the Plaintiff, the record fails to reveal a clear, unconditional, and unambiguous promise. Plaintiff's vacillations have not helped her cause. First, she claimed that Hoyt promised to divorce his wife, marry her, and provide lifetime support to her. Then she changed her mind and the promise became one to provide lifetime support to her regardless of whether Hoyt divorced his wife or not. Finally at the hearing on this motion, counsel argued that Hoyt had simply promised to take care of Norton for life. However, there can be many interpretations of the phrase "take care of for life." It could refer to care in a social, emotional, or financial context. As other courts have recognized, this is certainly not a clear and unambiguous promise.

Even assuming, *arguendo*, that there was a clear and unambiguous promise, Norton's reliance upon that promise was unreasonable. Though the couple had discussions about their life together and even discussed potential wedding plans, Plaintiff knew that Hoyt was married, and that he spent time at the marital domicile with his wife and children. Norton and Hoyt never openly associated as husband and wife, their friends and family knew that they were

▼

---

[2]   *Andreason v. Aetna Casualty & Surety Co.,* 848 P.2d 171, 1993 Utah App. LEXIS 26 (Utah App. 1993).

not married, and they did not exclusively cohabitate. Furthermore, Norton knew that Hoyt had lied in the past, was in an adulterous relationship, and apparently had made little effort to fulfill the terms of the promise. Reliance upon an unclear and ambiguous promise made by an apparently unreliable man was imprudent.

In any event, whatever form her reliance took, it is insufficient to overcome the other fatal flaws in her claim. Any promise for support that Hoyt made prior to the breakup is ambiguous at best, and, considering the source, was not a reasonable basis upon which to ground reliance. Sometime between year one and year 23 of the affair, it should have become clear to Norton that her reliance on Hoyt's promise to divorce his wife and marry her was misplaced.

[The defendant's motion for summary judgment is granted.] ■

Devil's Advocate

Why should one person be able to make repeated promises over two decades and escape all responsibility? Even if Hoyt's precise words varied, each of his promises involved long-term emotional and financial security for Norton. Norton was naïve, but Hoyt was dishonest. The law should be a tool for teaching people like him a lesson. ◆

Public Policy

Why have we chosen to illustrate an important point of law—promissory estoppel—with a case that fails? Because that is the typical outcome. Plaintiffs allege promissory estoppel very frequently, but seldom succeed. They do occasionally win, as the Andreasons demonstrated above, but courts are skeptical of these claims. The lesson is clear: Before you rely on a promise, negotiate a binding contract. ◆

Quasi-Contract

Don Easterwood leased over 5,000 acres of farmland in Jackson County, Texas, from PIC Realty for one year. The next year he obtained a second one-year lease. During each year, Easterwood farmed the land, harvested the crops, and prepared the land for the following year's planting. Toward the end of the second lease, after Easterwood had harvested his crop, he and PIC began discussing the terms of another lease. While they negotiated, Easterwood prepared the land for the following year, cutting, plowing, and disking the soil. But the negotiations for a new lease failed, and Easterwood moved off the land. He sued PIC Realty for the value of his work preparing the soil.

Easterwood had neither an express nor an implied contract for the value of his work. How could he make any legal claim? By relying on the legal theory of a quasi-contract: **Even when there is no contract, a court may use quasi-contract to compensate a plaintiff who can show that**

- The plaintiff gave some benefit to the defendant
- The plaintiff reasonably expected to be paid for the benefit and the defendant knew this; and
- The defendant would be unjustly enriched if he did not pay.

If a court finds all of these elements present, it will generally award the value of the goods or services that the plaintiff has conferred. The damages awarded are called *quantum meruit,* meaning that the plaintiff gets "as much as he deserved." The court is awarding money that it believes the plaintiff *morally ought to have,* even though there was no valid contract entitling her to it. This again is judicial activism, with the courts inventing a "quasi" contract where no true contract exists. The purpose is justice, the term is contradictory.

Don Easterwood testified that in Jackson County, it was quite common for a tenant farmer to prepare the soil for the following year but then be unable to farm the land.

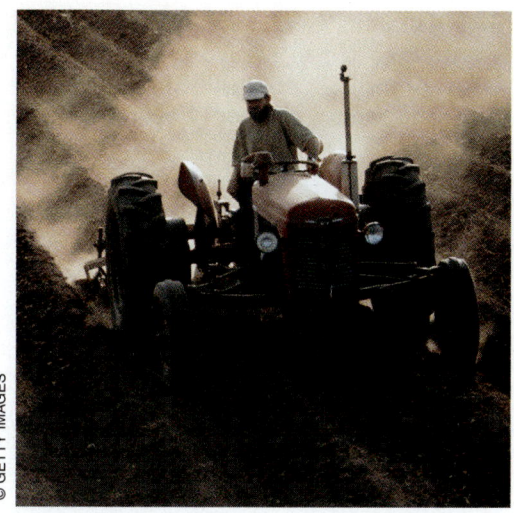

Quasi-contract may require compensation even when no contract exists.

In those cases, he claimed, the landowner compensated the farmer for the work done. Other witnesses agreed that this was the local custom. The court ruled that indeed there was no contract, but that all elements of quasi-contract had been satisfied. Easterwood gave a benefit to PIC because the land was ready for planting. Jackson County custom caused Easterwood to assume he would be paid, and PIC Realty knew it. Finally, said the court, it would be unjust to let PIC benefit without paying anything. The court ordered PIC to pay the fair market value of Easterwood's labors.

Almost all courts would agree with the result in the Easterwood case. But once again, if a court "invents" a contract where none existed, it may have opened the door to an infinite variety of claims. When would a defendant "reasonably know that the plaintiff expects compensation"? When is the enrichment "unjust"? The following case, from the same state, raises quasi-contract in the high stakes world of oil exploration. Notice that even within one court, judges can disagree about how far this doctrine should go.

VORTT EXPLORATION CO. V. CHEVRON U.S.A., INC.

33 Tex. Sup. J. 409, 787 S.W.2d 942, 1990 Tex. LEXIS 49
Supreme Court of Texas, 1990

Facts: A 160-acre tract of land in Texas contained valuable minerals. Both Vortt Exploration Co. and Chevron U.S.A. had rights to various sections of the land. Vortt's president proposed that the two companies enter a joint operating agreement to develop the minerals, and Chevron expressed some interest. For the next four years, the two companies negotiated but never reached an agreement. During the negotiations, Vortt provided Chevron with confidential seismic services, graphics, and maps, in an attempt to prod an agreement. Chevron used Vortt's information to locate and drill a producing well. Chevron then sued to invalidate Vortt's claim to mineral rights, and Vortt counterclaimed, seeking quasi-contract damages for the information it had provided Chevron.

The trial court found in favor of Vortt and awarded *quantum meruit* damages. But the court of appeals reversed, stating that Chevron could not know that Vortt expected to be paid for the information it divulged. Vortt appealed to the Texas Supreme Court.

Issue: Is Vortt entitled to *quantum meruit* damages based on quasi-contract?

Excerpts from Justice Hightower's Decision: *Quantum meruit* is an equitable remedy which does not arise out of a contract, but is independent of it. Generally, a party may recover under *quantum meruit* only when there is no express contract covering the services or materials furnished. This remedy is based upon the promise implied by law to pay for beneficial services rendered and knowingly accepted. Recovery in *quantum meruit* will be had when nonpayment for the services rendered could result in an unjust enrichment to the party benefited by the work.

Chevron knew that Vortt furnished the information with the expectation that a joint operating agreement would be reached. The parties had negotiated for over four years trying to achieve this end. At trial, Vortt's president testified that he shared the confidential seismic services, graphics, maps and other seismic information in the spirit of cooperation and that he would not have done so if he had not believed that a joint operating agreement would be reached. We hold that the trial court's findings of fact reflect that Chevron was reasonably notified that Vortt expected to be paid for the services and assistance which were rendered. [Vortt is entitled to money damages based on quasi-contract.]

▼

Excerpts from Justice Hecht's Dissenting Opinion: Vortt tried for years to persuade Chevron to agree to develop jointly certain mineral interests, but Chevron refused to make such an agreement. At one point in the negotiations, Vortt decided to "share" seismic information with Chevron "in the spirit of cooperation," in hopes that Chevron would agree to jointly develop the mineral interests. Chevron's representatives never asked to see the information. Vortt's representative never told Chevron that Vortt expected anything in return for the information. Indeed, Vortt's representative never expected Vortt to be paid for the information, and absolutely the only thing Vortt expected to gain by giving the information to Chevron was favorable consideration of the proposed agreement. Under these circumstances, the Court says, Chevron should reasonably have expected to pay Vortt for the information. The information cost Vortt roughly $18,000. The trial court ordered Chevron to pay Vortt $178,750 for it.

Was ever fainter hope more richly rewarded? For not refusing to look at Vortt's information, Chevron must pay ten times its cost. The court's ruling today should be a tremendous encouragement to benefaction. A frustrated negotiator should never overlook this tactic in attempting to induce agreement. The recipient of such charity, however, should beware.

I would hold that Chevron could not reasonably have expected to pay when Vortt did not expect to be paid. Accordingly, I would affirm the judgment of the court of appeals. ■

Public Policy

The dissent is concerned that unscrupulous companies will exploit this decision by revealing information during negotiations in the hope of later winning a case of quasi-contract. How might the court have limited its ruling to make that less likely? ◆

Four Theories of Recovery

Theory	Did the Defendant Make a Promise?	Is There a Contract?	Description
Express Contract	Yes	Yes	The parties intend to contract and agree on explicit terms.
Implied Contract	Not explicitly	Yes	The parties do not formally agree, but their words and conduct indicate an intention to create a contract.
Promissory Estoppel	Yes	No	There is no contract, but the defendant makes a promise that she can foresee will induce reliance; the plaintiff relies on it; and it would be unjust not to enforce the promise.
Quasi-Contract	No	No	There is no intention to contract, but the plaintiff gives some benefit to the defendant, who knows that the plaintiff expects compensation; it would be unjust not to award the plaintiff damages.

SOURCES OF CONTRACT LAW

Common Law

We have seen the evolution of contract law from the twelfth century to the present. Express and implied contracts, promissory estoppel, and quasi-contract were all crafted, over centuries, by appellate courts deciding one contract lawsuit at a time. In this country, the basic principles are similar from one state to another, but there have been significant differences concerning most important contract doctrines.

In part because of these differences, the twentieth century saw the rise of two major new sources of contract law: the Uniform Commercial Code and the Restatement of Contracts.

Uniform Commercial Code

Business methods changed quickly during the first half of the last century. Executives used new forms of communication, such as telephone and wire, to make deals. Transportation speeded up. Corporations routinely conducted business across state borders and around the world. Executives, lawyers, and judges wanted a body of law for commercial transactions that reflected modern business methods and provided uniformity throughout the United States. That desire gave birth to the Uniform Commercial Code (UCC), created in 1952. The drafters intended the UCC to facilitate the easy formation and enforcement of contracts in a fast-paced world. The Code governs many aspects of commerce, including the sale and leasing of goods, negotiable instruments, bank deposits, letters of credit, investment securities, secured transactions, and other commercial matters. Every state has adopted at least part of the UCC to govern commercial transactions within that state. For our purposes in studying contracts, the most important part of the Code is Article 2. The entire UCC is available online at **http://www.law.cornell.edu/ucc/ucc.table.html**.

UCC Article 2 governs the sale of goods. "Goods" means anything movable, except for money, securities, and certain legal rights. Goods include pencils, commercial aircraft, books, and Christmas trees. Goods do not include land or a house, because neither is movable, nor do they include a stock certificate. A contract for the sale of 10,000 sneakers is governed by the UCC; a contract for the sale of a condominium in Marina del Rey is governed by the California common law and its statute of frauds. Thus, when analyzing any contract problem as a student or business executive, you must note whether the agreement concerns the sale of goods. Most of the time the answer is clear, and you will immediately know whether the UCC or the common law governs. In some cases, as in a mixed contract for goods and services, it is not so obvious. **In a mixed contract, Article 2 governs only if the primary purpose was the sale of goods.** In the following case, the court had to decide the primary purpose.

FALLSVIEW GLATT KOSHER CATERERS, INC. V. ROSENFELD

2005 WL 53623
Civil Court, City of New York, 2005

Facts: During the Jewish holidays, Fallsview Glatt Kosher Caterers organized programs at Kutcher's Country Club, where it provided all accommodations, food, and entertainment.

Fallsview sued Willie Rosenfeld, alleging that he had requested accommodations for 15 members of his family, agreeing to pay $24,050, and then failed to appear or pay.

▼

Rosenfeld moved to dismiss, claiming that even if there had been an agreement, it was never put in writing. Under UCC section 2-201, any contract for the sale of goods worth $500 or more can be enforced only if it is in writing and signed. Fallsview argued that the agreement was not for the sale of goods, but for services. The company claimed that because the contract was not governed by the UCC, it should be enforced even with no writing.

Issue: Was the agreement one for the sale of goods, requiring a writing, or for services, enforceable with no writing?

Excerpts from Judge Battaglia's Decision: Mr. Rosenfeld contends that the "predominant purpose" and "main objective" of the agreement alleged by Fallsview was the "service of Kosher food," while the hotel accommodations and entertainment were merely "incidental or collateral" services.

Defendant's contention that the "predominant purpose" of the alleged agreement is the sale of food is said to be compelled by the very nature of the Passover holiday. [He argues that] "the essential religious obligation during this eight-day period and the principal reason why people attend events similar to the Program sponsored by plaintiff is in order to facilitate their fulfillment of the requirement to eat only food which is prepared in strict accordance with the mandate of Jewish law for Passover, i.e., food which is 'Kosher for Passover.' It is the desire to obtain these 'goods' and not the urge for 'entertainment' or 'accommodations' that motivates customers to subscribe to such 'Programs.' "

[Fallsview submitted] ten sheets, designated "Kutcher's Country Club Daily Activities" for Sunday, April 4, through Tuesday, April 13, 2004. The activities possible include tennis, racquetball, swimming, Swedish massage, "make over face lift show," "trivia time," aerobics, bingo, ice skating, dancing, "showtime," "power walk," arts and crafts, day camp, ping-pong, Yiddish theater, board games, horse racing, horseback riding, wine tasting, and indoor baci and that is only through Wednesday. These activities are provided, together with accommodations and food, for an "all inclusive" price that is apparently determined by the size and location of the room(s) and the numbers and ages of the persons in each party.

A review of the characteristics of the "program," which is the subject matter of the alleged agreement, leads the Court to conclude that the "essence" of the family and communal "experience" is defined primarily by "services" and not by "goods."

The intended scope of UCC section 2-201 is also indicated by its provision that "[a] writing is not insufficient because it omits or incorrectly states a term agreed upon but the contract is not enforceable under this paragraph beyond the quantity of goods shown in the writing." For the Code, quantity is even more important than price. A contract of the type involved here would rarely, if ever, specify the "quantity" of the "goods" to be provided. Nor would, for example, a contract for a week's stay at a weight-loss spa, or a zen-vegetarian retreat, or a cruise of the islands.

Plaintiff argues that "Defendant's proposition that a hotel reservation is a sale of goods would render all reservations made via telephone or the Internet unenforceable and would leave hotels in a precarious economic position." That may or may not be true, but the argument does highlight the importance of ensuring that a Statute of Frauds structured and outfitted by the Legislature for a particular transactional context not be casually applied to a very different commercial segment and model. The structure and terms of section 2-201 tell us that it was not intended to cover the agreement alleged in this Complaint.

Defendant's motion to dismiss is denied. ■

The common law governs contracts for services, employment, real estate and certain other things, and so each chapter in this unit will analyze the relevant common law principles—of offer and acceptance, consideration, and so forth. But the sale of goods is obviously a major element in business nationwide, and therefore each chapter will also discuss appropriate aspects of the Code.

Article 2 Alert. For more than a decade, the drafters of the UCC analyzed and debated significant revisions to Article 2 (and other articles). In 2003, they completed their work on Article 2, and the new version has many significant changes. However, the proposed changes will not become law until state legislatures choose to adopt them. As this book goes to press, no state has adopted the recommended changes. All references in this text are to the existing Article 2.

Restatement (Second) of Contracts

In 1932 the American Law Institute (ALI), a group of lawyers, scholars, and judges, drafted the Restatement of Contracts, attempting to codify what its members regarded as the best rulings of contract law. Where courts had disagreed, for example, about when to enforce promissory estoppel, the drafters of the Restatement chose what they considered the wisest decisions. The Restatement was a treatise and never became the law anywhere. But because of the eminence of those who wrote it, the Restatement influenced many courts as they decided contract cases.

In 1979, the ALI issued a new version, the Restatement (Second) of Contracts. This revised version naturally reflects the changes in society, business, and judicial decisions in the half century since the first edition. Like its predecessor, the Restatement (Second) is not the law anywhere, and in this respect it differs from the common law and the UCC. But the Restatement (Second) influences lawyers as they draft contracts and judges as they decide cases; we, too, will seek its counsel throughout the chapters on contracts.

© PHOTODISC/GETTY IMAGES

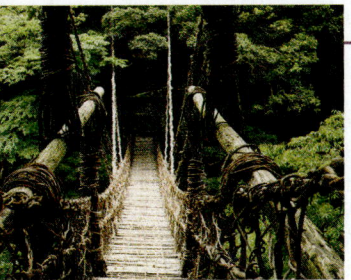

Chapter Conclusion

Contracts govern countless areas of our lives, from intimate family issues to multibillion dollar corporate deals. Understanding contract principles is essential for a successful business or professional career and is invaluable in private life. This knowledge is especially important because courts no longer rubber-stamp any agreement that two parties have made. If we know the issues that courts scrutinize, the agreement we draft is likelier to be enforced. We thus achieve greater control over our affairs—the very purpose of a contract.

Chapter Review

A contract is a promise that the law will enforce. Contracts are intended to make business matters more predictable. Analyzing a contract generally involves inquiring into some or all of these issues:

1. What is the subject of the agreement?

   - If the contract is for the sale of goods, UCC Article 2 governs.

   - If the contract is for services, employment, or real estate, the common law governs.

2. Did the parties intend to contract?

   - If the parties formally agreed and stated explicit terms, there is probably an express contract.

   - If the parties did not formally agree but their conduct, words, or past dealings indicate they intended a binding agreement, there may be an implied contract.

3. If there is an agreement, is there any reason to doubt its enforceability?

   - An unenforceable agreement is one with a legal defect, such as an oral agreement that the law requires to be in writing.

   - A voidable contract occurs when one party has committed fraud, giving the other party the right to terminate the agreement, or when one party lacks capacity to make the contract and may escape liability.

- A void agreement means that the law will ignore the deal regardless of what the parties want, typically because the purpose of the deal is illegal.

4. If there is no contract, are there other reasons to give the plaintiff damages?

   - A claim of promissory estoppel requires that the defendant made a promise knowing that

the plaintiff would likely *rely*, and the plaintiff did so. It would be wrong to deny recovery.

- A claim of quasi-contract requires that the defendant received a benefit, knowing that the plaintiff would expect compensation, and it would be unjust not to grant it.

Practice Test

1. What is the purpose of a contract?

2. Pennsylvania contracted with Envirotest Systems, Inc., an Arizona company, to build 86 automobile emissions inspection stations in 25 counties, and operate them for seven years. This contract is worth hundreds of millions of dollars to Envirotest. But suddenly Pennsylvania legislators opposed the entire system, claiming that it would lead to long delays and high expenses for motorists. These lawmakers urged that Pennsylvania simply stop construction of the new system. Was Pennsylvania allowed to get out of the contract because its legislators concluded the whole system is unwise?

3. Central Maine Power Co. made a promotional offer in which it promised to pay a substantial sum to any homeowner or builder who constructed new housing heated with electricity. Motel Services, Inc., which was building a small housing project for the city of Waterville, Maine, decided to install electrical heat in the units in order to qualify for the offer. It built the units and requested payment for the full amount of the promotional offer. Is Central Maine obligated to pay? Why or why not?

4. Interactive Data Corp. hired Daniel Foley as an assistant product manager at a starting salary of $18,500. Over the next six years Interactive steadily promoted Foley until he became Los Angeles branch manager at a salary of $56,116. Interactive's officers repeatedly told Foley that he would have his job as long as his performance was adequate. In addition, Interactive distributed an employee handbook that specified "termination guidelines," including a mandatory seven-step pre-termination procedure. Two years later Foley learned that his recently hired supervisor, Robert Kuhne, was under investigation by the

FBI for embezzlement at his previous job. Foley reported this to Interactive officers. Shortly thereafter, Interactive fired Foley. He sued, claiming that Interactive could only fire him for good cause, after the seven-step procedure. What kind of a claim is he making? Should he succeed?

5. The Hoffmans owned and operated a successful small bakery and grocery store. They spoke with Lukowitz, an agent of Red Owl Stores, who told them that for $18,000 Red Owl would build a store and fully stock it for them. The Hoffmans sold their bakery and grocery store and purchased a lot on which Red Owl was to build the store. Lukowitz then told Hoffman that the price had gone up to $26,000. The Hoffmans borrowed the extra money from relatives, but then Lukowitz informed them that the cost would be $34,000. Negotiations broke off and the Hoffmans sued. The court determined that there was no contract because too many details had not been worked out—the size of the store, its design, and the cost of constructing it. Can the Hoffmans recover any money?

6. **ETHICS** You want to lease your automobile to a friend for the summer but do not want to pay a lawyer to draw up the lease. Joanna, a neighbor, is in law school. She is not licensed to practice law. She offers to draft a lease for you for $100, and you unwisely accept. Later, you refuse to pay her fee and she sues to collect. Who will win the lawsuit, and why? Apart from the law, was it morally right for the law student to try to help out by drafting the lease? Was she acting helpfully, or foolishly, or fraudulently? Is it just for you to agree to her fee and then refuse to pay it? What is society's interest in this dispute? Should a court be more concerned with the ethical issue

raised by the conduct of the two parties or with the social consequences of this agreement?

7. Describe the role each of the following plays in contract law: the common law, the UCC, and the Restatement (Second) of Contracts.

8. *YOU BE THE JUDGE* WRITING PROBLEM John Stevens owned a dilapidated apartment that he rented to James and Cora Chesney for a low rent. The Chesneys began to remodel and rehabilitate the unit. Over a four-year period, they installed two new bathrooms, carpeted the floors, installed new septic and heating systems, and rewired, replumbed, and painted. Stevens periodically stopped by and saw the work in progress. The Chesneys transformed the unit into a respectable apartment. Three years after their work was done, Stevens served the Chesneys with an eviction notice. The Chesneys counterclaimed, seeking the value of the work they had done. Are they entitled to it? **Argument for Stevens:** Mr. Stevens is willing to pay the Chesneys exactly the amount he agreed to pay: nothing. The parties never contracted for the Chesneys to fix up the apartment. In fact, they never even discussed such an agreement. The Chesneys are making the absurd argument that anyone who chooses to perform certain work, without ever discussing it with another party, can finish the job and then charge it to the other person. If the Chesneys expected to get paid, obviously they should have said so. If the court were to allow this claim, it would be inviting other tenants to make improvements and then bill the landlord. The law has never been so foolish. **Argument for the Chesneys:** The law of quasi-contract was crafted for cases exactly like this. The Chesneys have given an enormous benefit to Stevens by transforming the apartment and enabling him to rent it at greater profit for many years to come. Stevens saw the work being done and understood that the Chesneys expected some compensation for these major renovations. If Stevens never intended to pay the fair value of the work, he should have stopped the couple from doing the work or notified them that there would be no compensation. It would be unjust to allow the landlord to seize the value of the work, evict the tenants who did it, and pay nothing.

9. Honeywell, Inc., and Minolta Camera Co. had a contract providing that Honeywell would give to Minolta various technical information on the design of a specialized camera lens. Minolta would have the right to use the information in its cameras provided that Minolta also used certain Honeywell parts in its cameras. Honeywell delivered to Minolta numerous technical documents, computer software, and test equipment, and Honeywell engineers met with Minolta engineers at least 20 times to discuss the equipment. Several years later, Honeywell sued, claiming that Minolta had taken the design information but failed to use Honeywell parts in its cameras. Minolta moved to dismiss, claiming that the UCC required lawsuits concerning the sale of goods to be filed within four years of the breach and that this lawsuit was too late. Honeywell answered that the UCC did not apply and that therefore Minnesota's six-year statute of limitations governed. Who is right?

10. Explain the difference between judicial restraint and judicial activism in contract law.

11. *ROLE REVERSAL* Write a multiple-choice question that requires use of the predominant factor test to determine whether a contract is one for goods or services.

Internet Research Problem

Visit **http://beatty.westbuslaw.com**. Select a state. Then click on judicial opinions. Search for a case concerning "quasi-contract." What are the details of the quasi-contract dispute? Who won and why?

> **You can find further practice problems at http://beatty.westbuslaw.com or in the Study Guide that accompanies this text.**

Agreement

Interior. A glitzy café, New York. Evening. Bob, a famous director, and Katrina, a glamorous actress, sit at a table, near a wall of glass looking onto a New York sidewalk that is filled with life and motion. Bob sips a margarita while carefully eyeing Katrina. Katrina stares at her wine glass.

BOB (smiling confidently): *Body Work* is going to be huge—for the right actress. I know a film that's gonna gross a hundred million when I'm holding one. I'm holding one.

KATRINA (perking up at the mention of money): It is quirky. It's fun. And she's very strong, very real.

BOB: She's you. That's why we're sitting here. We start shooting in seven months.

KATRINA (edging away from the table): I have a few questions. That nude scene.

BOB: The one on the toboggan run?

KATRINA: *That* one was O.K. But the one in the poultry factory—very explicit. I don't work nude.

BOB: It's not really nude. Think of all those feathers fluttering around.

KATRINA: It's nude.

BOB: We'll work it out. This is a romantic comedy, not tawdry exploitation.

Katrina, we're talking $2.5 million. A little accommodation, please. $600,000 up front, and the rest deferred, the usual percentages.

KATRINA: Bob, my fee is $3 million. As you know. That hasn't changed.

Katrina picks up her drink, doesn't sip it, places it on the coaster, using both hands to center it perfectly. He waits, as she stares silently at her glass.

BOB: We're shooting in Santa Fe, the weather will be perfect. You have a suite at the Excelsior plus a trailer on location.

KATRINA: I should talk with my agent. I'd need something in writing about the nude scene, the fee, percentages—all the business stuff. I never sign without talking to her.

Bob shrugs and sits back.

KATRINA (made anxious by the silence): I love the character, I really do.

BOB: You and several others love her. (That jolts her.) Agents can wait. I have to put this together fast. We can get you the details you want in writing. *Body Work* is going to be bigger than *Shakespeare in Love*.

That one hooks her. She looks at Bob. He nods reassuringly. Bob sticks out his hand, smiling. Katrina hesitates, lets go of her drink, and SHAKES HANDS, looking unsure. Bob signals for the check. ■

Do Bob and Katrina have a deal? *They* seem to think so. But is her fee $2.5 million or $3 million? What if Katrina demands that all nude scenes be taken out, and Bob refuses? Must she still act in the film? Or suppose her agent convinces her that *Body Work* is no good even with changes. Has Katrina committed herself? What if Bob auditions another actress the next day, likes her, and signs her? Does he owe Katrina her fee? Or suppose Bob learns that the funding has fallen apart and there will be no film. Is Katrina entitled to her money?

Bob and Katrina have acted out a classic problem in *agreement*, one of the basic issues in contract law. Their lack of clarity means that disputes are likely and lawsuits possible. Similar bargaining goes on every day around the country and around the world, and the problems created are too frequently resolved in court. Some of the negotiating is done in person; more is done over the phone, by fax, by e-mail—or all of them combined. This chapter highlights the most common sources of misunderstanding and litigation so that you can avoid making deals you never intended—or "deals" that you cannot enforce.

There almost certainly is no contract between Bob and Katrina. Bob's offer was unclear. Even if it was valid, Katrina counteroffered. When they shook hands, it is impossible to know what terms each had in mind.

MEETING OF THE MINDS

As courts dissect a negotiation that has gone awry, they examine the intent of the parties. **The parties can form a contract only if they had a meeting of the minds.** This requires that they (1) understood each other and (2) intended to reach an agreement.

Keep in mind that judges must make *objective assessments* of the respective intent of each party. A court will not try to get inside Katrina's head and decide what she was thinking as she shook hands. It will look at the handshake *objectively*, deciding how a reasonable person would interpret the words and conduct. Katrina may honestly have meant to conclude a deal for $3 million with no nude scenes, while Bob might in good faith have believed he was committing himself to $2.5 million and absolute control of the script. Neither belief will control the outcome. A reasonable person observing their discussion would not have known what terms they agreed to, and hence there is no agreement.

OFFER

Bargaining begins with an offer. An offer is a serious matter because it permits the other party to create a contract by accepting. **An offer is an act or statement that proposes definite terms and permits the other party to create a contract by accepting those terms.**

The person who makes an offer is the **offeror.** The person to whom he makes that offer is the **offeree.** The terms are annoying but inescapable because, like handcuffs, all courts use them. In most contract negotiations, two parties bargain back and forth, maybe for minutes, perhaps for months. Each may make several offers, revoke some proposals, suggest counteroffers, and so forth. For our purposes, the offeror remains the one who made the first offer, and the offeree is the one who received it.

Two questions determine whether a statement is an offer:

- Did the offeror *intend* to make a bargain?
- Are the terms of the offer definite?

Problems with Intent

Zachary says to Sharon, "Come work in my English language center as a teacher. I'll pay you $500 per week for a 35-hour week, for six months starting Monday." This is a valid offer. Zachary intends to make a bargain and his offer is definite. If Sharon accepts, the parties have a contract that either one can enforce. By contrast, we will consider several categories of statements that are *generally not* valid offers.

Invitations to Bargain

An invitation to bargain is not an offer. Suppose Martha telephones Joe and leaves a message on his answering machine, asking if Joe would consider selling his vacation condo on Lake Michigan. Joe faxes a signed letter to Martha saying, "There is no way I could sell the condo for less than $150,000." Martha promptly sends Joe a cashier's check for that amount. Does she own the condo? No. Joe's fax was not an offer. It is merely an invitation to bargain. Joe is indicating that he would be happy to receive an offer from Martha. He is not promising to sell the condo for $150,000 or for any amount.

Exhibit 11.1
The Litton case demonstrates why it is important to distinguish a valid offer from a mere price quote. Leviton's price list (including a limited warranty) was *not* an offer. When Litton ordered goods (with no limit to the warranty), it was making an offer, which Leviton accepted by delivering the goods. The resulting contract did not contain the limited warranty that Leviton wanted, costing that company a $4 million judgment.

Price Quotes

A price quote is generally not an offer. If Imperial Textile sends a list of fabric prices for the new year to its regular customers, the list is not an offer. Once again, the law regards it merely as a solicitation of offers. Suppose Ralph orders 1,000 yards of fabric, quoted in the list at $40 per yard. Ralph is making the offer, and Imperial may decline to sell at $40, or at any price, for that matter.

This can be an expensive point to learn. Leviton Manufacturing makes electrical fixtures and switches. Litton Microwave manufactures ovens. Leviton sent a price list to Litton, stating what it would charge for specially modified switches for use in Litton's microwaves. The price letter included a statement greatly limiting Leviton's liability in the event of any problem with the switches. Litton purchased thousands of the switches and used them in manufacturing its microwaves. But consumers reported fires due to defects in the switches. Leviton claimed that under the contract it had no liability. But the court held that the price letter was not an offer. It was a request to receive an offer. Thus the contract ultimately formed did not include Leviton's liability exclusion. Litton won over $4 million.[1] See Exhibit 11.1.

Letters of Intent

In complex business negotiations, the parties may spend months bargaining over dozens of interrelated issues. Because each party wants to protect itself during the discussions, ensuring that the other side is serious without binding itself to premature commitments, it may be tempting during the negotiations to draft a **letter of intent.** The letter *might* help distinguish a serious party from one with a casual interest, summarize the progress made thus far, and assist the parties in securing necessary financing. But a letter of intent contains a built-in danger: one party may not consider it binding. Yet if it is not a contract, what is it? That is exactly what you must decide in the following case.

---

[1] *Litton Microwave Cooking Products v. Leviton Manufacturing Co., Inc.,* 15 F.3d 790, 1994 U.S. App. LEXIS 1876 (8th Cir. 1994).

you Be The Judge

EVERGREEN INVESTMENTS, LLC V. FCL GRAPHICS, INC.

334 F.3d 750
Eighth Circuit Court of Appeals, 2003

Facts: Evergreen Investments, a Montana company, was negotiating to buy FCL Graphics, a commercial printing firm located in Illinois. After two years of discussions Evergreen's CFO, Larry Weis, and FCL's president, Frank Calabrese, signed a letter of intent. The letter included a purchase price of $53 million, payment terms, and the precise assets involved. The letter continued:

> The above-referenced terms are intended to form the basis and general understanding of the proposed acquisition. Binding terms and conditions for a potential transaction will depend on a number of factors, including but not limited to, the satisfactory completion of legal, business and financial due diligence investigations, and negotiation and execution of definitive legal documentation.
>
> Any proposed transaction will be subject to Evergreen's ability to arrange financing, on terms satisfactory to Evergreen, sufficient to consummate the acquisition and provide adequate working capital to meet the Company's on-going liquidity requirements and other obligations. In addition, any proposed transaction will be subject to certain legal, regulatory and other necessary third party approvals.
>
> Subject to the above conditions, both parties agree to use all their best efforts in good faith to close this transaction under the terms materially and substantially outlined herein within a reasonable time. In addition, by executing this Letter of Intent, Seller agrees to grant Evergreen a 90-day exclusivity period to consummate the proposed transaction. During such exclusivity period, Seller will not, directly or indirectly, engage in, conduct or entertain offers or discussions with any other person or party regarding a transaction of any kind involving the Company.

One month later, FCL notified Evergreen that it was terminating the discussions. Evergreen filed suit for breach of contract. The trial court granted summary judgment for FCL, ruling that the letter of intent (LOI) was not a binding agreement. Evergreen appealed.

You Be the Judge: Was the letter of intent a binding agreement?

Argument for Evergreen: Principal executives approved the agreement, knowing they were obligating their companies. After all, if the letter of intent was not binding, why bother to sign it—and why insist the other side do so?

All of the key terms were included in the letter of intent, including price, payment terms, and exact assets. The parties agreed to use their best efforts, in good faith, to quickly close the deal, and allotted themselves 90 days to wrap things up.

There was nothing left to do but finish certain legal paper work. The "due diligence" investigations were last-minute formalities that no one expected to cause any delay. After two years of hard bargaining, neither party expected the deal to fall apart while they obtained rubber-stamp approvals.

This is a clear breach of contract by FCL. Evidently, the company had a change of heart. It is now focusing on the label of this document—letter of intent—in hopes of evading its responsibilities. However, FCL cannot do that, because the name of the document is irrelevant—this is a binding contract.

Argument for FCL: The letter of intent makes it clear that the parties never reached a final agreement, and did not consider themselves bound by the letter itself. "Binding terms . . . will depend on a number of factors." In other words, the terms in the LOI are *not* binding. "Any proposed transaction will be subject to Evergreen's ability to arrange financing." In other words, there will be later proposals for a final contract, and even those will be contingent on Evergreen obtaining financing it is comfortable with.

The 90-day exclusivity period is the nail in the coffin. Why do parties need three months to negotiate? Because they have not reached an agreement. In this letter of intent, the parties merely noted the progress they had made thus far in discussions, while highlighting the reservations each side still had, and the work to be done before there was a final agreement.

Try as it might, Evergreen cannot transform its disappoint into a contract. ■

Advertisements

Mary Mesaros received a notice from the United States Bureau of the Mint, announcing a new $5 gold coin to commemorate the Statue of Liberty. The notice contained an order form stating:

> VERY IMPORTANT—PLEASE READ: YES, Please accept my order for the U.S. Liberty Coins I have indicated. I understand that all sales are final and not subject to refund. Verification of my order will be made by the Department of the Treasury, U.S. Mint. If my order is received by December 31, 1985, I will be entitled to purchase the coins at the Pre-Issue Discount price shown.

Mesaros ordered almost $2,000 worth of the coins. But the Mint was inundated with so many requests for the coin that the supply was soon exhausted. Mesaros and thousands of others never got their coins. This was particularly disappointing because the market value of the coins doubled shortly after their issue. Mesaros sued on behalf of the entire class of disappointed purchasers. Like most who sue based on an advertisement, she lost.[2] **An advertisement is generally not an offer.** An advertisement is merely a request for offers. The consumer makes the offer, whether by mail, as above, or by arriving at a merchant's store ready to buy. The seller is free to reject the offer.

Note that while the common law regards advertisements as mere solicitations, consumers do have protection from those shopkeepers intent upon deceit. Almost every state has some form of **consumer protection statute.** These statutes outlaw false advertising. For example, an automobile dealer who advertises a remarkably low price but then has only one automobile at that price has probably violated a consumer protection statute because the ad was published in bad faith, to trick consumers into coming to the dealership. The United States Mint did not violate any consumer protection statute because it acted in good faith and simply ran out of coins.

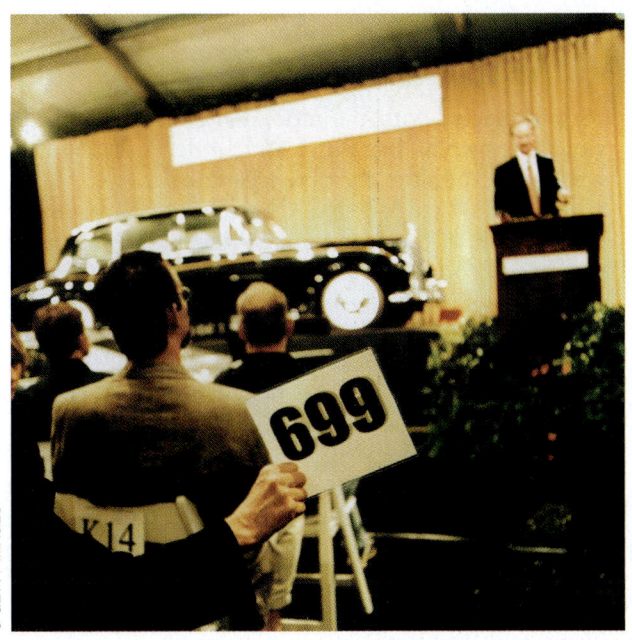

You have the high bid—but you may not have the property.

Auctions

It is the property you have always dreamed of owning—and it is up for auction! You arrive bright and early, stand in front, bid early, bid often, bid higher, bid highest of all—it's yours! For five seconds. Then, to your horror, the auctioneer announces that none of the bids were juicy enough and he is withdrawing the property. Robbery! Surely he cannot do that? But he can. Auctions are exciting and useful, but you must understand the rules.

Every day auctions are used to sell exquisite works of art, real estate, property confiscated from drug dealers, and many other things. Auctions for the sale of goods are governed by UCC §2-328; auctions for real estate are governed by the common law. The rules are similar and straightforward. **Placing an item up for auction is *not* an offer, it is merely a request for an offer.** The *bids* are the offers. If and when the hammer falls, the auctioneer has accepted the offer.

The important thing to know about a particular auction is whether it is conducted with or without

---

2 *Mesaros v. United States*, 845 F.2d 1576, 1988 U.S. App. LEXIS 6055 (Fed. Cir. 1988).

reserve. Most auctions are *with reserve*, meaning that the items for sale have a minimum price. The law assumes that an auction is with reserve unless the auctioneer clearly states otherwise. The auctioneer will not sell anything for less than its reserve (minimum price). So when the bidding for your property failed to reach the reserve, the auctioneer was free to withdraw it.

The rules are different in an auction *without reserve*. Here there is no minimum. Once the first bid is received, the auctioneer must sell the merchandise to the highest bidder.

Problems with Definiteness

It is not enough that the offeror intends to enter into an agreement. **The terms of the offer must be definite.** If they are vague, then even if the offeree "accepts" the deal, a court does not have enough information to enforce it and there is no contract.

You want a friend to work in your store for the holiday season. This is a definite offer: "I offer you a job as a sales clerk in the store from November 1 through December 29, 40 hours per week at $10 per hour." But suppose, by contrast, you say: "I offer you a job as a sales clerk in the store from November 1 through December 29, 40 hours per week. We will work out a fair wage once we see how busy things get." Your friend replies, "That's fine with me." This offer is indefinite and there is no contract. What is a fair wage? $5 per hour? $15 per hour? How will the determination be made? There is no binding agreement.

The following case presents a problem with definiteness, concerning a famous television show. You want to know what happened? Go to the place. See the guy. No, not the guy in hospitality. Our friend in waste management. Don't say nothing. Then get out.

BAER V. CHASE

392 F.3d 609
Third Circuit Court of Appeals, 2004

Facts: David Chase was a television writer-producer with many credits, including a detective series called *The Rockford Files.* He became interested in a new program, set in New Jersey, about a "mob boss in therapy," a concept he eventually developed into *The Sopranos.* Robert Baer was a prosecutor in New Jersey who wanted to write for television. He submitted a *Rockford Files* script to Chase, who agreed to meet with Baer.

When they met, Baer pitched a different idea, concerning "a film or television series about the New Jersey Mafia." He did not realize Chase was already working on such an idea. Later that year, Chase visited New Jersey. Baer arranged meetings for Chase with local detectives and prosecutors, who provided the producer with information, material, and personal stories about their experiences with organized crime. Detective Thomas Koczur drove Chase and Baer to various New Jersey locations, and introduced Chase to Tony Spirito. Spirito shared stories about loan sharking, power struggles between family members connected with the mob, and two colorful individuals known as Big Pussy and Little Pussy, both of whom later became characters on the show.

Back in Los Angeles, Chase wrote and sent to Baer a draft of the first *Sopranos* teleplay. Baer called Chase and commented on the script. The two spoke at least four times that year, and Baer sent Chase a letter about the script.

When *The Sopranos* became a hit television show, Baer sued Chase. He alleged that on three separate occasions Chase had agreed that if the program succeeded, Chase would "take care of" Baer, and would "remunerate Baer in a manner commensurate to the true value of his services." This happened twice on the phone, Baer claimed, and once during Chase's visit to New Jersey. The understanding was that if the show failed, Chase would owe nothing. Chase never paid Baer anything.

The district court dismissed the case, holding that the alleged promises were too vague to be enforced. Baer appealed. ▼

Issue: Was Chase's promise definite enough to be enforced?

Excerpts from Judge Greenberg's Decision: A contract arises from offer and acceptance, and must be sufficiently definite so that the performance to be rendered by each party can be ascertained with reasonable certainty. Therefore parties create an enforceable contract when they agree on its essential terms and manifest an intent that the terms bind them. If parties to an agreement do not agree on one or more essential terms of the purported agreement courts generally hold it to be unenforceable.

New Jersey law deems the price term, i.e., the amount of compensation, an essential term of any contract. An agreement lacking definiteness of price, however, is not unenforceable if the parties specify a practicable method by which they can determine the amount. However, in the absence of an agreement as to the manner or method of determining compensation the purported agreement is invalid. Additionally, the duration of the contract is deemed an essential term and therefore any agreement must be sufficiently definitive to allow a court to determine the agreed upon length of the contractual relationship.

Baer premises his argument on his view that New Jersey should disregard the well-established requirement of definiteness in its contract law when the subject-matter of the contract is an "idea submission." [However,] New Jersey precedent does not support Baer's attempt to carve out an exception to traditional principles of contract law for submission-of-idea cases. The New Jersey courts have not provided even the slightest indication that they intend to depart from their well-established requirement that enforceability of a contract requires definiteness with respect to the essential terms of that contract.

Nothing in the record indicates that the parties agreed on how, how much, where, or for what period Chase would compensate Baer. The parties did not discuss who would determine the "true value" of Baer's services, when the "true value" would be calculated, or what variables would go into such a calculation. There was no discussion or agreement as to the meaning of "success" of *The Sopranos*. There was no discussion how "profits" were to be defined. There was no contemplation of dates of commencement or termination of the contract. And again, nothing in Baer's or Chase's conduct, or the surrounding circumstances of the relationship, shed light on, or answers, any of these questions.

Affirmed. ∎

Ethics

Was it fair for Chase to use Baer's services without compensation? Did Baer really *expect* to get paid, or was he simply hoping that his work would land him a job? Has either party violated the Golden Rule? What are the most important *values* involved? ◆

Generally, vague terms creep into negotiations unobserved, because the parties want to conclude the deal and get to work. What happens when ambiguity is deliberate?

NEWS*worthy*

Jodee Berry was ecstatic. The 26-year-old, who waited tables at a Hooter's restaurant in Panama City, Florida, had won a promotional contest to sell the most beer. The restaurant manager had promised the winner a splendid prize, which Berry understood to be a new Toyota automobile. She alleges that she was blindfolded and led to the restaurant's parking lot, where she discovered not a new car, but a toy Yoda doll. She claims that the restaurant's manager stood inside laughing as he witnessed her disappointment. Berry saw no humor in the stunt and filed suit for breach of contract. The restaurant owner moved to dismiss, claiming that a company handbook required employee disputes to be settled by mediation or arbitration. The trial judge ruled that the handbook did not create a binding contract, and permitted the case to go forward.

The parties then settled. Berry's lawyer declined to disclose the amount of the settlement but did say that Berry could go to a local car dealership and "pick out whatever type of Toyota she wants." Does this case prove that all of us should strive to pronounce the letter *t* distinctly from *d*? ◆

UCC and Open Terms

Throughout this unit, we witness how the Uniform Commercial Code makes the law of sales more flexible. There are several areas of contract law where imperfect negotiations may still create a binding agreement under the Code, even though the same negotiations under the common law would have yielded no contract. "Open terms" is one such area.

Yuma County Corp. produced natural gas. Yuma wanted a long-term contract to sell its gas so that it could be certain of recouping the expenses of exploration and drilling. Northwest Central Pipeline, which operated an interstate pipeline, also wanted a deal for 10 or more years so it could make its own distribution contracts, knowing it would have a steady supply of natural gas in a competitive market. But neither Yuma nor Northwest wanted to make a long-term *price* commitment, because over a period of years the price of natural gas could double—or crash. Each party wanted a binding agreement without a definitive price. If their negotiations had been governed by the common law, they would have run smack into the requirement of definiteness—no price, no contract. But because this was a sale of goods, it was governed by the UCC.

> **UCC §2-204(3).** Even though one or more terms are left open, a contract for sale does not fail for indefiniteness if the parties have intended to make a contract and there is a reasonably certain basis for giving an appropriate remedy.

Thus a contract for the sale of goods may be enforced when a key term is missing. Business executives may have many reasons to leave open a delivery date, a price, or some other term. But note that the parties must still have *intended* to create a contract. The UCC will not create a contract where the parties never intended one.

In some cases the contract will state how the missing term is to be determined. Yuma County and Northwest drafted a contract with alternative methods of determining the price. In the event that the price of natural gas was regulated by the Federal Energy Regulatory Commission (FERC), the price would be the highest allowed by the FERC. If the FERC deregulated the price (as it ultimately did), the contract price would be the average of the two highest prices paid by different gas producers in a specified geographic area.

If the contract lacks a method for determining missing terms, the Code itself contains **gap-filler provisions,** which are rules for supplying missing terms. Some of the most important gap-filler provisions of the Code follow.

Open Price

In general, if the parties do not settle on a price, the Code establishes a *reasonable price.* This will usually be the market value or a price established by a neutral expert or agency. (UCC §2-305.)

Output and Requirements Provisions

An **output contract** obligates the seller to sell all of his output to the buyer, who agrees to accept it. For example, a cotton grower might agree to sell all of his next crop to a textile firm. A **requirements contract** obligates a buyer to obtain all of his needed goods from the seller. A vineyard might agree to buy all of its wine bottles from one supplier. Output and requirements contracts are by definition incomplete, since the exact quantity of the goods is unspecified. The Code requires that in carrying out such contracts, both parties act in good faith. Neither party may suddenly demand a quantity of goods (or offer a quantity of goods) that is disproportionate to their past dealings or their reasonable estimates. (UCC §2-306.)

Delivery, Time, and Payment

The Code provides terms for each of these issues. In general, the place of delivery is the seller's business. The time for shipping goods is usually a reasonable time, based on the normal trade practice. And payment is normally due when and where the buyer receives the goods. For each of these issues, the Code offers alternative provisions for cases with unusual facts. (UCC §§2-308 through 2-310.)

Warranties

Warranties are a source of frequent conflict between the parties because when something goes wrong, the costs can be enormous. Parties frequently enter a contract without agreeing on the warranty provisions, so the Code often supplies the terms. We consider warranty in detail in Chapter 21, on warranties and products liability. To summarize here, we can mention two important warranties that the Code implies. One is an **implied warranty of merchantability,** which means that the goods must be of at least average, passable quality in the trade. Ten thousand pairs of sneakers must be such that a typical shoe store would accept them. The other is an **implied warranty of fitness for a particular purpose.** If the seller knows that the buyer plans to use the goods for a particular purpose, the seller generally is held to warrant that the goods are in fact fit for that purpose. If an engine manufacturer knows that the buyer is going to use 10,000 engines in outboard motors, the Code normally considers that the manufacturer is warranting the engines for that purpose. (UCC §§2-312 through 2-317.)

Termination of Offers

As we have seen, the great power that an offeree has is to form a contract by accepting an offer. But this power is lost when the offer is terminated, which can happen in four ways: revocation, rejection, expiration, or operation of law.

Termination by Revocation

In general, the offeror may revoke the offer any time before it has been accepted. **Revocation is effective when the offeree receives it.** Douglas County, Oregon, sought bids on a construction job involving large quantities of rock. The Taggart Co. discovered a local source of supply with cheap rock and put in a bid. Shortly thereafter, Taggart discovered that the local rock was no longer for sale. Taggart hand delivered a written revocation of its bid. Later, the county opened all bids and accepted Taggart's low offer—but lost the case. By delivering its revocation, Taggart terminated the county's power to accept.[3]

Firm Offers and Revocability

Some offers cannot be revoked. A **firm offer** is one that by its own terms will be held open for a given period. Bonnie writes Clyde on January 2 and says, "I offer to sell you X for $1 million. This offer will be valid until February 2." Suppose Bonnie changes her mind on January 5 and wants to revoke. May she? It depends on "X."

Common Law Rule. Under the common law, revocation of a firm offer is effective if the offeree receives it before he accepts. Suppose Bonnie was offering to sell her ranch for that sum. Real estate is governed by the common law. On January 5 she faxed Clyde a revocation. On January 10 he mailed her an acceptance. Result? No contract—the revocation was effective.

---

[3] *R. J. Taggart, Inc. v. Douglas County,* 31 Or. App. 1137, 572 P.2d 1050, 1977 Ore. App. LEXIS 2868 (Or. Ct. App. 1977).

Option Contract. With an option contract, an interested purchaser buys the right to have the offer held open. **The offeror may not revoke an offer during the option period.** Suppose Clyde is interested in Bonnie's ranch, but needs three weeks to learn whether he can finance the purchase. They agree that Clyde will pay $25,000 for Bonnie to hold open her offer until February 2. Clyde arranges financing on January 20, but later that day Bonnie notifies him she is selling to someone else. Result? Clyde can enforce *his* contract. Bonnie had no power to revoke because Clyde had purchased an option.

Sale of Goods. Once again, the UCC has changed the law on the sale of goods. A writing, signed by a *merchant*, offering to hold open an offer for a stated period, may not be revoked. The open period may not exceed three months. Thus, if Bonnie is a merchant, and the "X" she is offering to sell Clyde is 10,000 theatrical costumes, she may not revoke any time before February 2. (UCC §2-205.)

Termination by Rejection

If an offeree rejects an offer, the rejection immediately terminates the offer. Suppose a major accounting firm telephones you and offers a job, starting at $80,000. You respond, "Nah. I'm gonna work on my surfing for a year or two." The next day you come to your senses and write the firm, accepting its offer. No contract. Your rejection terminated the offer and ended your power to accept.

Counteroffer. Frederick faxes Kim, offering to sell a 50 percent interest in the Fab Hotel in New York for only $135 million. Kim faxes back, offering to pay $115 million. Moments later, Kim's business partner convinces her that Frederick's offer was a bargain, and she faxes an acceptance of his $135 million offer. Does Kim have a binding deal? No. **A counteroffer is a rejection.** When Kim offered $115 million, she rejected Frederick's offer. Her original fax created a new offer, for $115 million, which Frederick never accepted. The parties have no contract at any price.

Termination by Expiration

Quentin calls you and offers you a job as best boy on his next motion picture. He tells you, "I've got to know by tomorrow night." If you call him in three days to accept, you are out of the picture. **When an offer specifies a time limit for acceptance, that period is binding.**

If the offer specifies no time limit, the offeree has a reasonable period in which to accept. A reasonable period varies, depending upon the type of offer, previous dealings between the parties, and any normal trade usage. "Trade usage" means the customary practices in a particular industry. When the parties are bargaining face to face, any offer made will normally be valid only during that discussion. Neither party may call the next day to accept. Similarly, if the offer concerns a speculative item, such as commodities futures, the offer will be open very briefly. On the other hand, if a used car wholesaler faxes an offer to sell 50 used cars for $5,000 each, and the local custom is to respond within three days, an acceptance faxed within two days creates a contract.

Termination by Operation of Law

In some circumstances, the law itself terminates an offer. **Death or mental incapacity of the offeror terminates an offer, whether the offeree knows of the change or not.** Arnie offers you a job as an assistant in his hot-air balloon business. Before you can even accept, Arnie tumbles out of a balloon at 3,000 feet. The offer terminates along with Arnie.

Destruction of the subject matter terminates the offer. A used car dealer offers to sell you a rare 1938 Bugatti for $75,000 if you bring cash the next day. You arrive, suitcase stuffed with century notes, just in time to see Arnie drop 3,000 feet through the air and crush the Bugatti. The dealer's offer is terminated.

ACCEPTANCE

As we have seen, when there is a valid offer outstanding, the offeree can create a contract by accepting. **The offeree must say or do something to accept.** Silence, though golden, is not acceptance. Marge telephones Vick and leaves a message on his answering machine: "I'll pay $75 for your law textbook from last semester. I'm desperate to get a copy, so I will assume you agree unless I hear from you by 6:00 tonight." Marge hears nothing by the deadline and assumes she has a deal. She is mistaken. Vick neither said nor did anything to indicate that he accepted.

When the offer is for a bilateral contract, the offeree generally must accept by making a promise. An employer calls you and says, "If you're able to start work two weeks from today, we can pay you $5,000 per month. Can you do it?" That is an

If it arrives at your front door, consider your offer accepted.

offer for a bilateral contract. You must accept by promising to start in two weeks. If you make the promise, both sides are contractually bound from the moment you agree. You do not, however, have the option to think it over for two weeks and then show up.

When the offer is for a unilateral contract, the offeree must accept by performing. A newspaper telephones you: "If you write us a 5,000-word article on iguanas that can play bridge, and get it to us by Friday at noon, we'll pay you $750." The newspaper does not want a promise, it wants the article. If your work is ready on time, you get paid. If you never write a word, neither party owes the other anything.

With some offers it is unclear whether the offeror wants acceptance by promise or performance. **If the offer is ambiguous, the offeree may accept by either a promise or performance.** A contractor offered to lease a Link-Belt construction crane from a dealer for two months for $6,500 per month. The contractor signed and mailed a written lease that required him to insure the crane. The dealer read the lease,

did not sign it, but delivered the crane. The crane was promptly destroyed. Was the contractor liable? Yes. The written lease invited acceptance by promise or by performance. The dealer accepted by delivering the crane, and the liability clause (requiring the contractor to obtain insurance) was part of their contract.[4] The rule is the same in cases involving the sale of goods. (UCC §2-206.)

Mirror Image Rule

If only he had known! A splendid university, an excellent position as department chair—gone. And all because of the mirror image rule.

Ohio State University wrote to Philip Foster offering him an appointment as a professor and chair of the art history department. His position was to begin July 1, and he had until June 2 to accept the job. On June 2, Foster telephoned the Dean and left a message accepting the position, *effective July 15*. Later, Foster thought better of it and wrote the university, accepting the school's starting date of July 1. Too late! Professor Foster never did occupy that chair at Ohio State. The court held that since his acceptance varied the starting date, it was a counteroffer. And a counteroffer, as we know, is a rejection.[5]

---

4   *Anderson Excavating v. Certified Welding,* 769 P.2d 887, 1988 Wyo. LEXIS 185 (Wyo. 1988).

5   *Foster v. Ohio State University,* 41 Ohio App. 3d 86, 534 N.E.2d 1220, 1987 Ohio App. LEXIS 10761 (Ohio Ct. App. 1987).

Was it sensible to deny the professor a job over a mere 14-day difference? Sensible or not, that is the law. **The common law mirror image rule requires that acceptance be on precisely the same terms as the offer.** If the acceptance contains terms that add or contradict the offer, even in minor ways, courts generally consider it a counteroffer. The rule worked reasonably well in the nineteenth century, when parties would write an original contract and exchange it, penciling in any changes. But now that businesses use standardized forms to purchase most goods and services, the rule creates enormous difficulties. Sellers use forms they have prepared, with all conditions stated to their advantage, and buyers employ their own forms, with terms they prefer. The forms are exchanged in the mail or electronically, with neither side clearly agreeing to the other party's terms.

The problem is known as the "battle of forms." Once again, the UCC has entered the fray, attempting to provide flexibility and common sense for those contracts involving the sale of goods. But for contracts governed by the common law, such as Professor Foster's, the mirror image rule is still the law.

UCC and the Battle of Forms

UCC §2-207 dramatically modifies the mirror image rule for the sale of goods. Under this provision, an acceptance that adds additional or different terms will often create a contract. The rule is intricate, but it is important to understand its basic features because most goods are bought and sold with standardized forms. Exhibit 11.2 illustrates UCC §2-207.[6]

Additional or Different Terms

One basic principle of the common law of contracts remains unchanged: the key to creation of a contract is a valid offer that the offeree *intends* to accept. If there is no intent to accept, there is no contract. The big change brought about by UCC §2-207 is this: **an offeree who accepts may include in the acceptance terms that are additional to or different from those in the offer.** Thus, even with additional or different terms, the acceptance may well create a contract.

> *Example A.* Wholesaler writes to Manufacturer, offering to buy "10,000 wheelbarrows at $50 per unit. Payable on delivery, 30 days from today's date." Manufacturer writes back, "We accept your offer of 10,000 wheelbarrows at $50 per unit, payable on delivery. Interest at normal trade rates for unpaid balances." Manufacturer clearly intends to form a contract. The company has added a new term, but there is still a valid contract.

However, if the offeree states that her acceptance is *conditioned on the offeror's assent* to the new terms, there is no contract.

> *Example B.* Same offer as above. Manufacturer adds the interest rate clause and states, "Our acceptance is conditional upon your agreement to this interest rate." Manufacturer has made a counteroffer. There is no contract, yet. If Wholesaler accepts the counteroffer, there is a contract; if Wholesaler does not accept it, there is no contract.

---

6 *Article 2 Alert.* There has been great dissatisfaction with §2-207, because it is hard to understand and even harder to apply. Under the proposed revisions, §2-206 would determine whether a contract exists. If the parties did make an enforceable deal, a simplified §2-207 would determine its provisions, based primarily on any terms that both parties explicitly agreed to, along with Code gap-filler terms. Some of the confusing concepts, such as "material alteration," will probably be deleted.

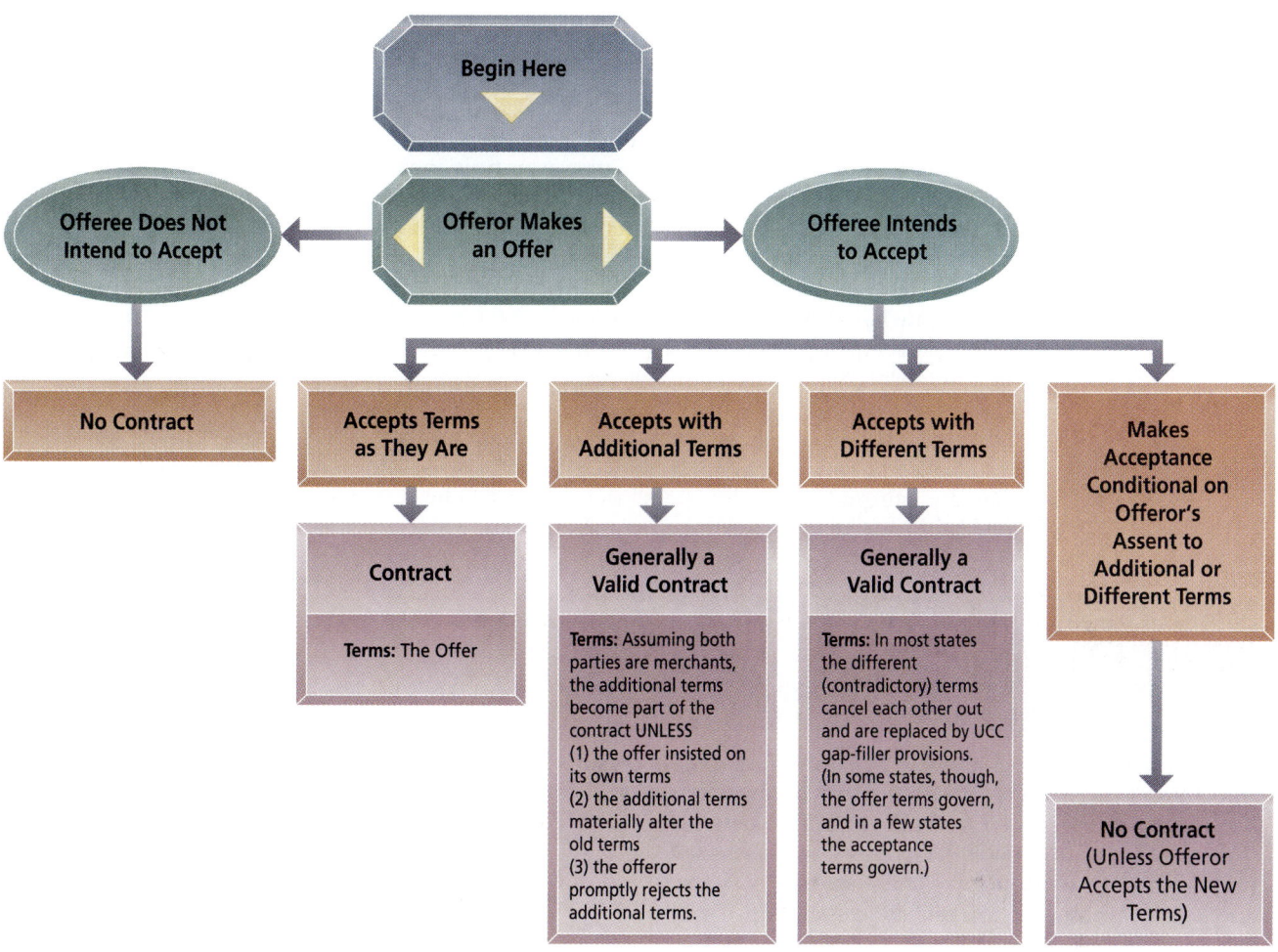

**Exhibit 11.2
UCC §2-207**

Additional terms are those that bring up new issues, such as interest rates, not contained in the original offer. Additional terms in the acceptance are considered proposals to add to the contract. Assuming that both parties are merchants, **the additional terms will generally become part of the contract.** Thus, in Example A, above, the interest rate will become a part of the binding deal. If Wholesaler is late in paying, it must pay whatever interest rate is current.

In three circumstances, the additional terms in the acceptance *do not* become part of the contract:

- If the original offer *insisted on its own terms.* In other words, if Wholesaler wrote, "I offer to buy them on the following terms and *no other terms,*" then the Manufacturer is not free to make additions.

- If the additional terms *materially alter* the original offer. Suppose Manufacturer wrote back, "We accept your offer for 10,000 wheelbarrows. Delivery will be made within 180 days, unless we notify you of late delivery." Manufacturer has changed the time from 30 days to 180 days, with a possible extension beyond that. That is a material alteration, and it will not become part of the contract. By contrast, Manufacturer's new language concerning "interest at normal trade rates" was not a material alteration, and therefore that interest rate becomes part of the contract.

- If the offeror receives the additional terms and *promptly objects* to them.

Different terms are those that contradict terms in the offer. For example, if the seller's form clearly states that no warranty is included, and the buyer's form says the seller warrants all goods for three years, the acceptance contains different terms. An acceptance may contain different terms and still create a contract. But in these cases, courts have struggled to decide what the terms of the contract are. **The majority of states hold that different (contradictory) terms cancel each other out.** Neither term is included in the contract. Instead, the neutral terms from the Code itself are "read into" the contract. These are the gap-filler terms discussed above. If, for example, the forms had contradictory warranty clauses (as they almost always do), the different terms would cancel each other out, and the warranty clauses from the UCC would be substituted.[7]

Here is a typical UCC §2-207 case in which the court must decide whether additional language "materially alters" the contract. The result is very different from what it would have been under the common law.

BAYWAY REFINING CO. V. TOSCO CORP.

215 F.3d 219
Second Circuit Court of Appeals, 2000

Facts: Bayway Refining and Oxygenated Marketing and Trading A.G. (OMT) were both in the business of buying and selling petroleum products. Bayway agreed to sell OMT 60,000 barrels of gasoline, and OMT faxed a confirmation letter stating that the document represented the full understanding of the parties. The next day, Bayway faxed its own confirmation letter, which stated that the document canceled and superseded any other correspondence. Bayway's fax *incorporated by reference* the company's own "General Terms and Conditions." Those general terms did not accompany the fax, but were available for OMT to examine if it wished. One of those terms stated that the buyer would be responsible for any federal taxes.

OMT, which never objected to the "general terms," received the gasoline but refused to reimburse Bayway for the federal taxes, which amounted to $464,035. Bayway sued. OMT claimed that the tax clause *materially altered* the contract and, under §2-207, never became part of the agreement. The district court gave summary judgment for Bayway, and OMT appealed.

Issue: Was the tax clause a material alteration or was it part of the contract?

Excerpts from Judge Jacobs's Decision: We hold that under §2-207(2)(b) the party opposing the inclusion of additional terms shoulders the burden of [proving that the new terms were a "material alteration."] A material alteration is one that would result in surprise or hardship if incorporated without express awareness by the other party. Surprise, within the meaning of the material alteration exception of §2-207(2)(b), has both the subjective element of what a party actually knew and the objective element of what a party should have known. A profession of surprise and raised eyebrows are not enough: Conclusory statements, conjecture, or speculation by the party resisting the motion will not defeat summary judgment. To carry the burden of showing surprise, a party must establish that, under the circumstances, it cannot be presumed that a reasonable merchant would have consented to the additional term.

OMT has adduced evidence that the Tax Clause came as an amazement to OMT's executives, who described the term's incorporation as "contract by

▼

---

[7] Not all states follow this rule, however. Some courts have held that when the acceptance contains terms that contradict those in the offer, the language in the offer should be final. A few courts have ruled that the terms in the acceptance should control.

ambush" and a "sleight-of-hand proposal." Thus OMT has sufficiently exhibited its subjective surprise. As to objective surprise, however, OMT has alleged no facts and introduced no evidence to show that a reasonable petroleum merchant would be surprised by the Tax Clause.

We conclude that Bayway has adduced compelling proof that shifting tax liability to a buyer is the custom and practice in the petroleum industry. Two industry experts offered unchallenged testimony that it is customary for the buyer to pay all the taxes resulting from a petroleum transaction. One expert stated that "this practice is so universally understood among traders in the industry, that I cannot recall an instance, in all my years of trading and overseeing trades, when the buyer refused to pay the seller for excise or sales taxes."

Moreover, common sense supports Bayway's evidence of custom and practice. The federal excise tax is imposed when taxable fuels are sold to any person who is not registered under [the appropriate tax code provision]. The buyer thereby controls whether any tax liability is incurred in a transaction. A trade practice that reflects a rational allocation of incentives (as trade practices usually do) would place the burden of the tax on the party that is in the position to obviate it—here, on OMT as the buyer.

OMT's only evidence of hardship is (generally) that it is a small business dependent on precarious profit margins, and it would suffer a loss it cannot afford. That does not amount to hardship in the present circumstances. Typically, courts that have relied on hardship to find that an additional term materially alters a contract have done so when the term is one that creates or allocates an open-ended and prolonged liability. The Tax Clause places on a buyer a contractual responsibility that bears on a specific sale of goods, that is (at least) not uncommon in the industry, and that the buyer could avoid by registration. The cry of hardship rings hollow, because any loss that the Tax Clause imposed on OMT is limited, routine and self-inflicted.

OMT failed to raise a factual issue as to hardship or surprise. Affirmed. ■

---

cyberLaw

Clickwraps and Shrinkwraps. You want to purchase Attila brand software and download it to your computer. You type in your credit card number and other information, agreeing to pay $99. Attila also requires that you "read and agree to" all of the company's terms. You click "I agree," without having read one word of the terms. Three frustrating weeks later, tired of trying to operate defective Attilaware, you demand a refund and threaten to sue. The company breezily replies that you are barred from suing, because the terms you agreed to included an arbitration clause. To resolve any disputes, you must travel to Attila's hometown, halfway across the nation, use an arbitrator that the company chooses, pay one-half the arbitrator's fee, and also pay Attila's legal bills if you should lose. The agreement makes it financially impossible for you to get your money back. Is that contract enforceable?

You have entered into a "clickwrap" agreement. Similar agreements, called "shrinkwraps," are packaged inside many electronic products. A shrinkwrap notice might require that before inserting a purchased CD into your computer, you must read and agree to all terms in the brochure. Clickwraps and shrinkwraps often include arbitration clauses. They frequently limit the seller's liability if anything goes wrong, saying that the manufacturer's maximum responsibility is to refund the purchase price (even if the software destroys your hard drive).

Many courts that have analyzed these issues have ruled that clickwrap and shrinkwrap agreements are indeed binding, even against consumers. The courts have emphasized that sellers are entitled to offer a product on any terms they wish, and that shrinkwrap and clickwrap are the most efficient methods of including complicated terms in a small space. Think before you click![8] ◆

---

[8] *ProCD, Inc. v. Zeidenberg,* 86 F.3d 1447 (7th Cir. 1996), is the leading case to enforce shrinkwrap agreements (and, by extension, clickwraps). *Klocek v. Gateway,* 104 F. Supp. 1332 (D. Kan. 2000), is one of the few cases to reject such contracts. *Klocek,* however, was dismissed for failure to reach the federal court $75,000 jurisdictional level.

However, some courts have *refused* to enforce such contracts against a consumer, stating that the buyer never understood or agreed to the shrinkwrapped terms. The court in the following case works hard to balance the competing interests, and in the process demonstrates that this new area of law is very much in flux.

SPECHT V. NETSCAPE COMMUNICATIONS CORPORATION

306 F.3d 17
Second Circuit Court of Appeals, 2002

Facts: A group of plaintiffs sued Netscape, claiming that two of the company's products illegally captured private information about files that they downloaded from the Internet. The plaintiffs alleged that this was electronic eavesdropping, in violation of two federal statutes.

From Netscape's Web page, the plaintiffs had downloaded SmartDownload, a software plug-in that enabled them to download the company's Communicator software. The web page advertised the benefits of SmartDownload, and near the bottom of the screen was a tinted button labeled "Download." The plaintiffs clicked to download. If, instead of downloading, they had scrolled further down, they would have seen an invitation to "review and agree to the terms of the Netscape SmartDownload software license agreement." By clicking the appropriate button, they would have been sent to a series of linked pages, and finally arrived at a license agreement. Among the terms was an agreement to arbitrate any dispute. In other words, a consumer downloading SmartDownload was in theory giving up the right to file suit if anything went wrong, and agreeing to settle the dispute by arbitration. However, the plaintiffs never reviewed the license terms.

In the district court, Netscape moved to dismiss the case and compel arbitration. Netscape claimed that the plaintiffs had forfeited any right to sue based on the license agreement. The district court denied the company's motion, ruling that the plaintiffs had not agreed to the terms of the license. Netscape appealed.

Issue: Had the plaintiffs agreed to arbitrate their claims?

Excerpts from Judge Sotomayor's Decision: Defendants argue that plaintiffs must be held to a standard of reasonable prudence and that, because notice of the existence of SmartDownload license terms was on the next scrollable screen, plaintiffs were on "inquiry notice" of those terms. We disagree with the proposition that a reasonably prudent offeree in plaintiffs' position would necessarily have known or learned of the existence of the SmartDownload license agreement prior to acting, so that plaintiffs may be held to have assented to that agreement with constructive notice of its terms.

Receipt of a physical document containing contract terms or notice thereof is frequently deemed, in the world of paper transactions, a sufficient circumstance to place the offeree on inquiry notice of those terms. These principles apply equally to the emergent world of online product delivery, pop-up screens, hyperlinked pages, clickwrap licensing, scrollable documents, and urgent admonitions to "Download Now!" What plaintiffs saw when they were being invited by defendants to download this fast, free plug-in called SmartDownload was a screen containing praise for the product and, at the very bottom of the screen, a "Download" button. Defendants argue that a fair and prudent person using ordinary care would have been on inquiry notice of SmartDownload's license terms.

We are not persuaded that a reasonably prudent offeree in these circumstances would have known of the existence of license terms. Plaintiffs were responding to an offer that did not carry an immediately visible notice of the existence of license terms or require unambiguous manifestation of assent to those terms. Thus, plaintiffs' apparent manifestation of consent was to terms contained in a document whose contractual nature was not obvious. Moreover, the fact that, given the position of the scroll bar on their computer screens, plaintiffs may have been aware that an unexplored portion of the Netscape Web page remained below the download button does not mean that they reasonably should have concluded that this portion contained a notice of license terms.

▼

We conclude that in circumstances such as these, where consumers are urged to download free software at the immediate click of a button, a reference to the existence of license terms on a submerged screen is not sufficient to place consumers on inquiry or constructive notice of those terms. There is no reason to assume that viewers will scroll down to subsequent screens simply because screens are there.

For the foregoing reasons, we affirm the district court's denial of defendants' motion to compel arbitration and to stay court proceedings. ■

Communication of Acceptance

The offeree must communicate his acceptance for it to be effective. The questions that typically arise concern the medium, the manner, and the time of acceptance.

Medium and Manner of Acceptance

The "medium" refers to whether acceptance is done in person or by mail, telephone, e-mail, or fax. The "manner" refers to whether the offeree accepts by promising, by making a down payment, by performing, and so forth. **If an offer demands acceptance in a particular medium or manner, the offeree must follow those requirements.** Suppose a newly incorporated town offers a power company the right to provide electrical service to the residents. The offer states that the power company must accept in writing, and the writing must be delivered to the town's offices by a given date. If the power company orally notifies the town of its acceptance and begins its preparations for delivering electrical service, it has no contract.

If the offer does not specify a type of acceptance, the offeree may accept in any reasonable manner and medium. We have already seen that an offer generally may be accepted by performance or by a promise, unless it specifies a particular method. The same freedom applies to the medium. If Masako faxes Eric an offer to sell 1,000 acres in Montana for $800,000, Eric may accept by mail or fax. Both are routinely used in real estate transactions, and either is reasonable. The same rule applies for the sale of goods.[9] If Masako e-mails Eric an offer to sell 20,000 pairs of jeans for $20 each, he may write, fax, or e-mail his reply.

Time of Acceptance: The Mailbox Rule

An acceptance is generally effective upon dispatch, meaning the moment it is out of the offeree's control. When Masako faxes her offer to sell land to Eric, and he mails his acceptance, the contract is binding the moment he puts the letter into the mail. In most cases, this **mailbox rule** is just a detail. But it becomes important when the offeror revokes her offer at about the same time the offeree accepts. Who wins? Suppose Masako's offer has one twist:

- On Monday morning, Masako faxes her offer to Eric.
- On Monday afternoon, Eric writes "I accept" on the fax.
- On Tuesday morning, Eric mails his acceptance.
- On Tuesday afternoon, Masako faxes Eric a revocation of her offer.
- On Thursday morning, Eric's acceptance arrives at Masako's office.

---

[9]   UCC §2-206(1)(a).

Outcome? Eric has an enforceable contract. Masako's offer was effective when it reached Eric. His acceptance was effective on Tuesday morning, when he mailed it. Nothing that happens later, such as Masako's attempt to revoke, can "undo" the contract.

SOLDAU V. ORGANON, INC.

860 F.2d 355, 1988 U.S. App. LEXIS 14757
United States Court of Appeals for the Ninth Circuit, 1988

Facts: Organon fired John Soldau. Then the company sent to him a letter offering to pay him double the normal severance pay, provided Soldau would sign a full release, that is, a document giving up any and all claims he might have against Organon. The release was included with the letter. Soldau signed it, dated it, and took it to the nearest post office, where he deposited it in the mailbox. When he returned home, Soldau discovered in the mail a check from Organon for the double severance pay. He hustled back to the post office, where he persuaded a postal clerk to open the mailbox and retrieve the release he had posted. He then cashed Organon's check and finally filed a suit against the company, alleging that his firing was age discrimination.

The federal district court gave summary judgment for Organon, ruling that Soldau's acceptance of the proposed release was effective when he mailed it, creating a contract. He appealed.

Issue: Did Soldau create a contract by mailing the release?

Excerpts from the *Per Curiam* Decision: The district court was clearly correct under California law. Soldau does not argue to the contrary. Instead, he contends that the formation and validity of the release are governed by federal law, and would not have been effective unless and until it had been received by Organon. We need not decide which body of law controls. Under federal as well as California law, Soldau's acceptance was effective when it was mailed.

The so-called "mailbox" or "effective when mailed" rule was adopted and followed as federal common law by the Supreme Court [at the beginning of the twentieth century]. We could not change the rule, and there is no reason to believe the Supreme Court would be inclined to do so. It is almost universally accepted in the common law world. It is enshrined in the Restatement (Second) of Contracts and endorsed by the major contract treatises.

Commentators are also virtually unanimous in [supporting the "effective upon dispatch" rule,] pointing to the long history of the rule; its importance in creating certainty for contracting parties; its essential soundness, on balance, as a means of allocating the risk during the period between the making of the offer and the communication of the acceptance or rejection to the offeror; and the inadequacy of the rationale offered by the Court of Claims for the change.

Since Soldau's contractual obligation to release Organon in return for Organon's obligation to make the enhanced severance payment arose when Soldau deposited his acceptance in the post office mailbox, his subsequent withdrawal of the acceptance was ineffectual.

Affirmed. ∎

PROMISSORY ESTOPPEL

Donald Moore and Clifford Garrett were interested in purchasing a small Michigan business called Winamac Plastics. They approached Max Brandt, a senior vice-president and loan officer at the First National Bank of Logansport, Indiana. Brandt already knew that Winamac had high debt and poor management, but he believed the company could be turned around. Brandt agreed that the bank would finance the purchase if Garrett and Moore moved Winamac to Logansport. Brandt also told the two that his personal lending authority was limited to $100,000. They expected to spend over $500,000 in restarting the company, and a loan for the remaining money would require committee approval.

Brandt approved a personal loan to Garrett and Moore of $100,000, most of which they used to acquire a two-thirds interest in Winamac. Later, Brandt prepared a loan application on behalf of Winamac itself, for $540,000. But the bank's committee turned down the loan because Winamac had such high debt.

Brandt assured the two entrepreneurs that the bank would approve a revised application, which he himself made. Garrett and Moore spent their remaining money setting up the company in Logansport. Months later, the bank turned down the second loan application. Garrett and Moore sued. Did they have any rights?

The trial court thought so, declaring that the various conversations created an oral contract to finance Winamac. The court awarded the plaintiffs $726,532, which included over $500,000 in lost profits. The appeals court affirmed. Were the two courts correct? No, ruled the Indiana Supreme Court. Here are the basic principles.

Did the parties intend to create a contract? Almost certainly. Clearly, the two entrepreneurs wanted a deal and thought they had one. Brandt was equally determined to finance the purchase.

Can we identify the terms of the contract? No. The "agreement" was fatally indefinite. Exactly how much money was to be loaned? What was the rate of interest? The loan's duration? The terms of repayment? The security for the loan? The parties never agreed on a single term. Perhaps if one item had been missing, the court might have supplied it. But since all key terms were absent, there could be no contract.

But Garrett and Moore had another possibility. **Under the doctrine of promissory estoppel, even if there is no contract, a promise may be enforceable if:**

- The offeror makes a promise knowing the offeree is likely to rely

- The offeree does in fact rely; and

- The only way to avoid injustice is to enforce the promise.

Here is how the court applied the doctrine to this case. Brandt did promise that the bank would lend whatever money was necessary to get Winamac back on its feet, although the amount was too indefinite to create a contract. Brandt knew the two men would rely on his promise, sinking their money into Winamac and moving it to Logansport. The Indiana Supreme Court concluded that the only way to avoid injustice was to enforce the promise, to a limited extent. Because there was no contract, the court refused to award lost profits. Instead, the plaintiffs received $73,000 in compensation for the money they spent relying on Brandt's promise. That was better than nothing, but far less than they would have obtained had there been a contract.[10]

Promissory estoppel is often a plaintiff's last-ditch argument. Frequently, judges reject such claims, ruling that no contract means no money. At other times, as Garrett and Moore discovered, a court enforces a promise but grants much less compensation than it would have if the parties had reached a clear agreement.

at RISK

How could Garrett and Moore have protected themselves? ◆

---

[10] *Garrett v. First National Bank of Logansport*, 577 N.E.2d 949, 1991 Ind. LEXIS 130 (Ind. 1991).

Chapter Conclusion

The law of offer and acceptance can be complex and even baffling. Yet for all its fault, the law is not the principal source of dispute between parties unhappy with negotiations. Most litigation concerning offer and acceptance comes from *lack of clarity* on the part of the people negotiating. Letters of intent are often an effort to "have it both ways," that is, to ensure the other side's commitment without accepting a corresponding obligation. Similarly, the "battle of the forms" is caused by corporate officers seeking to make a deal and hurry things forward without settling details. These, and the many other examples discussed, are all understandable given the speed and fluidity of the real world of business. But the executive who insists on clarity is likelier in the long run to spend more time doing business and less time in court.

Chapter Review

1. The parties can form a contract only if they have a meeting of the minds, which requires that they understand each other and intend to reach an agreement.

2. An offer is an act or statement that proposes definite terms and permits the other party to create a contract by accepting those terms.

3. Invitations to bargain, price quotes, and advertisements are generally not offers. A letter of intent may or may not be an offer, depending upon the exact language and whether it indicates that the parties have reached an agreement.

4. The terms of the offer must be definite, although under the UCC the parties may create a contract that has open terms.

5. An offer may be terminated by revocation, rejection, expiration, or operation of law.

6. The offeree must say or do something to accept. Silence is not acceptance.

7. The common law mirror image rule requires acceptance on precisely the same terms as the offer. Under the UCC, an offeree may often create a contract even when the acceptance includes terms that are additional to or different from those in the offer.

8. Clickwrap and shrinkwrap agreements are generally enforceable.

9. If an offer demands acceptance in a particular medium or manner, the offeree must follow those requirements. If the offer does not specify a type of acceptance, the offeree may accept in any reasonable manner and medium.

10. An acceptance is generally effective upon dispatch, meaning from the moment it is out of the offeree's control.

11. Under the doctrine of promissory estoppel, even without a contract a promise may be enforceable if the offeror knows the offeree is likely to rely, the offeree does rely, and the only way to avoid injustice is to enforce the promise.

Practice Test

1. Arnold owned a Pontiac dealership and wanted to expand by obtaining a Buick outlet. He spoke with Patricia Roberts and other Buick executives on several occasions. He now claims that those discussions resulted in an oral contract that requires Buick to grant him a franchise, but the company disagrees. His strongest evidence of a contract is the fact that Roberts gave him forms on which to order Buicks. Roberts answered that it was her standard practice to give such forms to prospective dealers, so that if the franchise were approved, car orders could be processed quickly. Is there a contract?

2. The town of Sanford, Maine, decided to auction off a lot it owned. The town advertised that it would accept bids through the mail, up to a specified date. Arthur and Arline Chevalier mailed in a bid that turned out to be the highest. When the town refused to sell them the lot, they sued. Result?

3. Arturo hires Kate to work in his new sporting goods store. "Look," he explains, "I can only pay you $9.00 an hour. But if business is good a year from now, and you're still here, I'm sure I can pay you a healthy bonus." Four months later Arturo terminates Kate. She sues.

   a. Kate will win her job back, plus the year's pay and the bonus.

   b. Kate will win the year's pay and the bonus.

   c. Kate will win only the bonus.

   d. Kate will win only her job back.

   e. Kate will win nothing.

4. The Tufte family leased a 260-acre farm from the Travelers Insurance Co. Toward the end of the lease, Travelers mailed the Tuftes an option to renew the lease. The option arrived at the Tuftes' house on March 30, and gave them until April 14 to accept. On April 13, the Tuftes signed and mailed their acceptance, which Travelers received on April 19. Travelers claimed there was no lease and attempted to evict the Tuftes from the farm. May they stay?

5. Northrop is a huge defense firm, and Litronic manufactures electronic components such as printed wire boards. Northrop requested Litronic to submit an offer on certain printed boards. Litronic sent its offer form, stating a price and including its pre-printed warranty clause, which limited its liability to 90 days. Northrop orally accepted the offer, then sent its own purchase order form, which contained a warranty clause holding the seller liable with no time limit. Six months after the goods were delivered Northrop discovered they were defective. Northrop sued, but Litronic claimed it had no liability. Was there a contract? If not, why not? If there was a contract, what were its warranty terms?

6. "Huge selection of Guernsey sweaters," reads a newspaper ad from Stuffed Shirt, a clothing retailer. "Regularly $135, today only $65." Waldo arrives at Stuffed Shirt at 4:00 that afternoon, but the shop clerk says there are no more sweaters. He shows Waldo a newly arrived Shetland sweater that sells for $145. Waldo sues, claiming breach of contract and violation of a consumer protection statute. Who will prevail?

   a. Waldo will win the breach of contract suit and the consumer protection suit.

   b. Waldo will lose the breach of contract suit but might win the consumer protection suit.

   c. Waldo will lose the consumer protection suit but should win the breach of contract suit.

   d. Waldo will win the consumer protection suit only if he wins the contract case.

   e. Waldo will lose both the breach of contract suit and the consumer protection suit.

7. Consolidated Edison Co. of New York (Con Ed) sought bids from General Electric Co. (GE) and others to supply it with two huge transformers. Con Ed required that the bids be held open for 90 days. GE submitted a written bid and included a clause holding the bid open for 90 days. During that period, Con Ed accepted GE's bid, but GE refused to honor it. Is there a contract?

8. The Dukes leased land from Lillian Whatley. Toward the end of their lease, they sent Ms. Whatley a new contract, renewing the lease for three years and giving themselves the option to buy the land at any time during the lease for $50,000. Ms. Whatley crossed out the clause giving them an option to buy. She added a sentence at the bottom, saying, "Should I, Lillian Whatley, decide to sell at end [sic] of three years, I will give the Dukes the first chance to buy." Then she signed the lease, which the Dukes accepted in the changed form. They continued to pay the rent until Ms. Whatley sold the land to another couple for $35,000. The Dukes sued. Are the Dukes entitled to the land at $50,000? At $35,000?

9. **ETHICS** Bill Brown Trucking specializes in hauling oversize loads, those that cannot fit on ordinary tractor-trailers. Brown met with James Wofford, an agent for Glens Falls Insurance, and asked Wofford for a "full coverage" policy. Brown showed Wofford photos of the kinds of loads his trucks hauled. Wofford issued Brown a policy, telling him, "You've got full coverage." One of Brown's trucks was hauling a large "asphalt dryer" on a tractor-trailer. The dryer itself struck a bridge overpass, but the truck was unhurt. Glens Falls refused coverage, pointing out that the policy was limited to accidents involving the "conveyance," meaning the truck. Brown sued. Assume that the policy clearly limited coverage to the "conveyance." Did Brown

have a case? Regardless of the legal issues, does the insurance company have an ethical obligation to help one of its insured, or is it free to dispute any claim if the company believes it has a chance to win? Insurance contracts are drafted by the company, not the insured. Does that affect ethical considerations?

10. *YOU BE THE JUDGE* WRITING PROBLEM Academy Chicago Publishers (Academy) approached the widow of author John Cheever about printing some of his unpublished stories. She signed a contract, which stated:

2. The Author will deliver to the Publisher on a mutually agreeable date one copy of the manuscript of the Work as finally arranged by the editor and satisfactory to the Publisher in form and content. . . .

5. Within a reasonable time and a mutually agreeable date after delivery of the final revised manuscript, the Publisher will publish the Work at its own expense, in such style and manner and at such price as it deems best, and will keep the Work in print as long as it deems it expedient.

Within a year, Academy had located and delivered to Mrs. Cheever more than 60 unpublished stories. But she refused to go ahead with the project. Academy sued for the right to publish the book. The trial court ruled that the agreement was valid; the appeals court affirmed;

Internet Research Problem

Search the Internet for an auction with a ring selling for over $500. Is the site reliable? Who is actually selling the item? If you were to pay for the ring, would you receive it? If you were unhappy with your purchase, what remedies would you have? How can you ascertain the Web site's reliability?

and the case went to the Illinois Supreme Court. Was Academy's offer valid, and was the contract enforceable? **Argument for Mrs. Cheever:** The agreement is too vague to be enforceable. None of the essential terms are specified: the number of stories, their length, who selects them, the date of publication, the size or cost of the book, or anything else. There is no contract. **Argument for Academy:** Mrs. Cheever wanted to publish this book and agreed in writing to help Academy do so. Both parties understood the essential nature of the book and were willing to permit some flexibility, to ensure a good edition. She has no right to back out now.

11. Rebecca, in Honolulu, faxes a job offer to Spike, in Pittsburgh, saying, "We can pay you $55,000 per year, starting June 1." Spike faxes a reply, saying, "Thank you! I accept your generous offer, though I will also need $3,000 in relocation money. See you June 1. Can't wait!" On June 1 Spike arrives, to find that his position is filled by Gus. He sues Rebecca.

   a. Spike wins $55,000.

   b. Spike wins $58,000.

   c. Spike wins $3,000.

   d. Spike wins restitution.

   e. Spike wins nothing.

12. *ROLE REVERSAL* Write a multiple-choice question focusing on the mailbox rule.

You can find further practice problems at http://beatty.westbuslaw.com **or in the Study Guide that accompanies this text.**

Consideration

We have all made promises that we soon regretted. Mercifully, the law does not hold us accountable for everything we say. Yet some promises must be enforced. Which ones? The doctrine of consideration exists for one purpose: to distinguish promises that are binding from those that are not. Which of these four promises should a court enforce?

PROMISE ONE. In a delirious burst of affection, Professor Parsley says to a class of 50 students, "You've been a great class all semester. Next week I'm going to mail each of you a check for $1,000." But that night, the professor reconsiders and decides that her class is actually a patch full of cabbage heads whose idea of work is getting out of bed before noon. The following day, in class, Parsley announces that she has changed her mind. Mike, a student, sues for his $1,000. Should a court enforce the professor's promise?

PROMISE TWO. After class, Parsley promises a student, Daisy, a part-time job as a researcher for the rest of the semester. "You can start on Monday," she says, "and we'll work out pay and all the details then." "You mean I can give up my job at Burger Bucket?" asks an elated Daisy. "Sure thing," chirps the prof. But on Monday, Parsley informs Daisy that she has lost the funding for her research and can offer no job. Daisy is unable to get back her position at Burger Bucket and sues Parsley.

273

PROMISE THREE. Professor Parsley announces in class that she will be selling her skis at the end of the semester for $450. After class, Arabella says she would like to buy the skis but can only afford to pay $250. Parsley frowns and mutters, "They're worth a lot more than that." But Arabella looks so heartbroken that Parsley adds, "OK, what the heck. You can have them May 15." On that date Arabella shows up with the cash, but Parsley explains that another student offered her the full $450 for the skis and she sold them. Arabella purchases a nearly identical pair for $475 and sues Parsley.

PROMISE FOUR. The professor makes no promise at all. In fact, she announces in class that she will be unable to attend the next session because her favorite racehorse, Preexisting Duty, is running in the third race at the local track and she wants to be there. The students are crushed at the idea of missing a class. Sam wails, "Don't do this to us, Professor! I'll pay you twenty bucks if you'll be here to teach us." Other students chime in, and in a groundswell of tears and emotion, the students promise a total of $1,000 if Parsley will do her job. She agrees. When she arrives to teach the next class, 50 suddenly sullen students refuse to pay, and she sues. ■

Society could enforce *all* promises in the interests of simple morality. Or should it enforce only those where the two sides engaged in some bargaining? Does it matter whether someone relied on a promise? Should the outcome be different if someone is promising to do what she is already obligated to do? These are important policy questions, affecting promises for a hundred dollars and deals for a billion; their answers lie in the law of consideration.

A BARGAIN AND AN EXCHANGE

Consideration is a required element of any contract. **Consideration means that there must be bargaining that leads to an exchange between the parties.** "Bargaining" indicates that each side is obligating itself in some way *to induce the other side to agree.* Generally, a court will enforce one party's promise only if the other party did something or promised something in exchange. Without an exchange of mutual obligations, there is usually no deal.

How would the four Parsley examples in the introduction work out? In the first case, Mike loses. There is no consideration because the students neither bargained for Parsley's promise nor gave anything in exchange for it. In the second case, there is also no contract because none of the terms were definite. What were Daisy's hours, her salary, her duties? Daisy cannot sue on a contract, but she does have a claim of promissory estoppel, the one major exception to the rule of consideration. Because Daisy relied on Parsley's promise, a court may give her some compensation. In case three,

Arabella should win. A bargain and an exchange occurred. The professor promised to sell the skis at a given price, then broke her promise. Arabella will probably recover $225, the difference between the contract price and what she was forced to pay for substitute skis. Finally, in the fourth case, the professor loses. Clearly, bargaining and an exchange took place, but the professor only promised to do something that she was already obligated to do. The law does not respect such a promise.

We will look more deeply into these issues. First, a case to demonstrate the basic rule: there must be bargaining and an exchange.

KELSOE V. INTERNATIONAL WOOD PRODUCTS, INC.

588 So. 2d 877, 1991 Ala. LEXIS 1014
Supreme Court of Alabama, 1991

Facts: Carol Kelsoe worked at International Wood Products. One day her supervisor, Rene Hernandez, promised Kelsoe 5 percent of the company's stock. But he never gave her the shares, and she sued. The trial court gave a directed verdict for International Wood, and Kelsoe appealed.

Issue: Is Hernandez's promise binding?

Excerpts from Justice Houston's Decision: Kelsoe's employer, International Wood, through Rene Hernandez, Sr., one of the corporation's directors and its major stockholder, promised Kelsoe that it would issue 5 percent of the corporation's stock to her. Kelsoe's undisputed trial testimony reflects the nature of that promise:

Q. [by the lawyer for International Wood:] Ms. Kelsoe, you were compensated for your work at International Wood, weren't you?[1]

A. Yes, sir, I received a check.

Q. Were you pleased with your compensation?

A. Yes, sir.

Q. Did you think you were compensated well enough for the work you did?

A. I worked long hours, long hours.

Q. My question was did you think that you were adequately compensated for the work you did?

A. Yes, sir.

Q. Ms. Kelsoe, you never entered an agreement with Mr. Hernandez; "Mr. Hernandez, if I work long and hard and do this" and then he said, "I'll give you five percent of the corporation," did you?

A. No, sir.

Q. You never had that kind of a bargain, did you?

A. No, sir.

Q. And all the time, all the work you did was part of your normal job?

A. Yes, sir.

Q. And then [on] March 8th, you were getting a little reward that you didn't really expect, weren't you?

A. Yes, sir.

Q. You didn't expect to get that five percent, but it was nice, wasn't it?

A. Yes, sir.

Q. And you didn't expect it, though, did you?

A. No, sir.

Q. And you had no reason to expect it?

A. No, sir.

Q. And you just kept right on from March 8th doing your work, didn't you?

A. That's correct.

Q. And you didn't stay on [at] International Wood Products, you didn't commit yourself to Mr. Hernandez, "I'll stay on forever," did you? Or, "I'll stay on for five years in return for this?" You left yourself free to quit at any time, didn't you?

A. Yes, sir, that's correct.

Q. He just up one day and surprised you and said here is five percent of this corporation?

A. Yes, sir.

The trial court directed a verdict for International Wood on the ground that there was no consideration for International Wood's promise to issue the stock to Kelsoe. It is a well-settled general rule ▼

---

[1] International Wood's lawyer is cross-examining Ms. Kelsoe, so he is permitted to ask leading questions.

that consideration is an essential element of a contract. It is generally stated that in order to constitute consideration for a promise, there must have been an act, a forbearance, a detriment, or a return promise, bargained for and given in exchange for the promise. The undisputed evidence here shows that International Wood's promise to issue the stock to Kelsoe was gratuitous in nature and was prompted only by Kelsoe's past favorable job performance. As such, International Wood's promise was without consideration and created no legally enforceable contract right. The directed verdict for International Wood was proper. ■

Ethics

Because Kelsoe had given no consideration, International Wood was legally permitted to escape from its promise. Was that ethical? Use the ethics checklist from Chapter 2. Should a corporation honor all commitments to employees? What policy would create the best workforce? What harm might befall a company that fulfilled all promises? What decision would you have made if you were Hernandez's boss and had the power to award the stock to Kelsoe or deny it? ◆

When trying to enforce a defendant's promise, the plaintiff must show that she did something or promised something in exchange for that promise. What sort of action or promise is good enough? It need not be much. **Consideration can be anything that someone might want to bargain for.** As we explore this idea, we need to use two more legal terms: **promisor,** meaning the person who makes the promise, and **promisee,** the person to whom the promise is made. In consideration cases, a court is typically trying to determine whether the promisee should be able to enforce the promise, and the decision will depend upon whether the promisee gave consideration.

The thing bargained for can be another promise or action. Usually, the thing bargained for is another promise. In the *Kelsoe* case, suppose Hernandez had said, "I will give you 5 percent of our stock if you'll promise not to quit for three years," and Kelsoe had agreed to stay. Her promise would be consideration, making Hernandez's promise enforceable. They would have had a typical bilateral contract. See Exhibit 12.1.

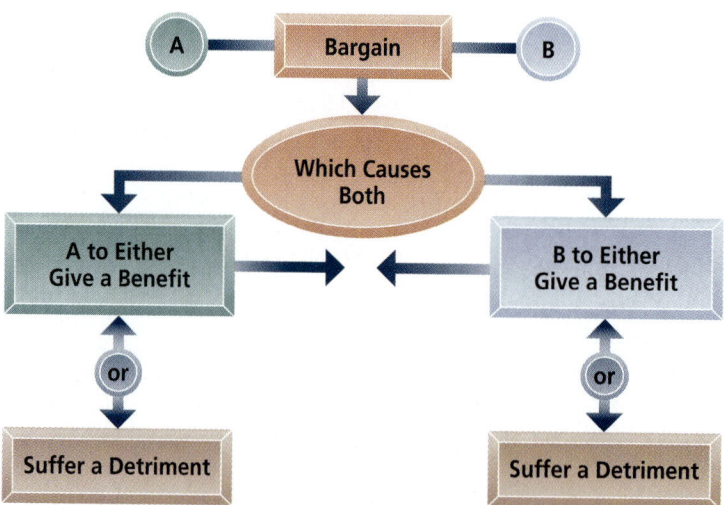

Exhibit 12.1

There is consideration to support a contract when *A* and *B* bargain, and their bargaining causes both *A* and *B* either to give a benefit to the other or to suffer a detriment.

The thing bargained for can be an action, rather than a promise. Suppose Professor Parsley says to Wade, "If you plow my driveway by tonight, I'll pay you $150." Her offer seeks an action, not a promise. If Wade plows the driveway, his work is consideration and the parties have a binding contract.

The thing bargained for can be a benefit to the promisor or a detriment to the promisee. If Hernandez had asked Kelsoe to stay on at International Wood, her promise to do so would have been a benefit to the company. That is consideration.

Suppose Professor Parsley says to the class, "You're all in terrible shape. I offer $25 to anyone who enters next week's marathon and finishes the race." "No way," shouts Joanne. "But I'll do it for $100." Parsley agrees and Joanne completes the entire race. Her running was of no particular benefit to Parsley, but it was clearly a detriment to Joanne, so Parsley owes her $100.

The thing bargained for can be a promise to do something or a promise to refrain from doing something. Megan promises to deliver 1,000 canoes in two months if Casey agrees to pay $300 per canoe. Megan's promise is consideration. Leroy, who runs a beauty parlor, offers Chloe $75,000 not to open a beauty parlor within 30 miles. Chloe's promise *not* to compete is consideration.

The most famous of all consideration lawsuits began in 1869, when a well-meaning uncle made a promise to his nephew. Ever since *Hamer v. Sidway* appeared, generations of American law students have dutifully inhaled the facts and sworn by its wisdom; now you, too, may drink it in.

HAMER V. SIDWAY

124 N.Y. 538, 27 N.E. 256, 1891 N.Y. LEXIS 1396
New York Court of Appeals, 1891

Facts: This is a story with two Stories. William Story wanted his nephew to grow up healthy and prosperous. In 1869, he promised the 15-year-old boy (also William Story) $5,000 if the lad would refrain from drinking liquor, using tobacco, swearing, and playing cards or billiards for money until his twenty-first birthday. (In that wild era—can you believe it?—the nephew had a legal right to do all those things.) The nephew agreed and, what is more, he kept his word. When he reached his twenty-first birthday, the nephew notified his uncle that he had honored the agreement. The uncle congratulated the young man and promised to give him the money, but said he would wait a few more years before handing over the cash, until the nephew was mature enough to handle such a large sum. The uncle died in 1887 without having paid, and his estate refused to honor the promise. Because the nephew had transferred his rights in the money, it was a man named Hamer who eventually sought to collect from the uncle's estate. The estate argued that since the nephew had given no consideration for the uncle's promise, there was no enforceable contract. The trial court found for the plaintiff, and the uncle's estate appealed.

Issue: Did the nephew give consideration for the uncle's promise?

Excerpts from Justice Parker's Decision: The defendant contends that the contract was without consideration to support it, and therefore invalid. He asserts that the promisee, by refraining from the use of liquor and tobacco, was not harmed, but benefited; that that which he did was best for him to do, independently of his uncle's promise,—and insists that it follows that, unless the promisor was benefited, the contract was without consideration,—a contention which, if well founded, would seem to leave open for controversy in many cases whether that which the promisee did or omitted to do was in fact of such benefit to him as to leave no consideration to support the enforcement of the promisor's agreement. Such a rule could not be tolerated, and is without foundation in the law. Courts will not ask whether the thing which forms the consideration does in fact benefit the promisee or a third party, or is of any substantial value to any one. It is enough that something is promised, done, forborne, or suffered by the party to whom the promise is made as consideration for the promise made to him.

▼

Now applying this rule to the facts before us, the promisee used tobacco, occasionally drank liquor, and he had a legal right to do so. That right he abandoned for a period of years upon the strength of the promise of the testator [that is, the uncle] that for such forbearance he would give him $5,000. We need not speculate on the effort which may have been required to give up the use of those stimulants. It is sufficient that he restricted his lawful freedom of action within certain prescribed limits upon the faith of his uncle's agreement, and now, having fully performed the conditions imposed, it is of no moment whether such performance actually proved a benefit to the promisor, and the court will not inquire into it. ■

Adequacy of Consideration

Gold can make people crazy. At the turn of the twentieth century, John Tuppela joined the gold rush to Alaska. He bought a mine and worked it hard, a disciplined man in an unforgiving enterprise. Sadly, his prospecting proved futile and mental problems overwhelmed him. In 1914, a court declared him insane and locked him in an institution in Portland, Oregon. Four years later, Tuppela emerged and learned to his ecstasy that gold had been discovered in his mine, now valued at over half a million dollars. Then the bad news hit: a court-appointed guardian had sold the mine for pennies while Tuppela was institutionalized. Destitute and forlorn, Tuppela turned to his lifelong friend, Embola, saying, "If you will give me $50 so I can go to Alaska and get my property back, I will pay you $10,000 when I win my property." Embola accepted the offer, advancing the $50.

After a long and bitter fight, Tuppela won back his mine, though a guardian would still supervise his assets. Tuppela asked the guardian to pay the full $10,000 to Embola, but the guardian refused. Embola sued, and the issue was whether his $50 was *adequate consideration* to support Tuppela's promise of $10,000. A happy ending: Embola won and recovered his money.

Courts seldom inquire into the adequacy of consideration. Although the difference between Embola's $50 and Tuppela's $10,000 was huge, it was not for a court to decide whether the parties had made an intelligent bargain. Embola undertook a risk and his $50 *was valid consideration*. The question of adequacy is for the parties as they bargain, not for the courts.

MUTUALITY OF OBLIGATIONS

Generally, both sides must be committed to the agreement to make it enforceable. Though courts will not inquire into the adequacy of consideration, they will insist that it be genuine. In some cases a party appears to make a commitment but actually does not. The result: no contract. Here we examine the major issues concerning mutuality.

Illusory Promise

Annabel calls Jim and says, "I'll sell you my bicycle for 325 bucks. Interested?" Jim says, "I'll look at it tonight in the bike rack. If I like what I see, I'll pay you three and a quarter in the morning." At sunrise, Jim shows up with the $325 but Annabel refuses to sell. Can Jim enforce their deal? No. He said he would buy the bicycle *if he liked it*, keeping for himself the power to get out of the agreement for any reason at all. He is not committing himself to do anything, and the law considers his promise illusory, that is, not really a promise at all. **An illusory promise is not consideration.** Because he has given no consideration, there is no contract and *neither party* can enforce the deal. Is the promise in the following case illusory?

you Be The Judge

CULBERTSON V. BRODSKY

788 S.W.2d 156, 1990 Tex. App. LEXIS 1008
Texas Court of Appeals, 1990

Facts: Sam Culbertson had some Texas real estate to sell. He and Frederick Brodsky signed an option contract. Brodsky was to deliver a check for $5,000, representing "earnest money," to a bank. The bank would hold the check in escrow for 60 days. During that period, the bank would not cash it. Brodsky could inspect the property and perform engineering studies to determine whether the real estate could be used for his purposes. If he decided that the land was of no use to him, he could terminate the agreement and demand return of his earnest money. Ultimately, Brodsky decided that he did want to buy the land, but Culbertson refused to sell, claiming that Brodsky gave no consideration to support their contract. The trial court gave judgment for Brodsky, ordering Culbertson to convey the land. Culbertson appealed.

You Be the Judge: Did Brodsky give valid consideration that makes Culbertson's promise enforceable?

Argument for Culbertson: Your honors, Mr. Brodsky made a very sly promise, since it was in fact no promise at all. Brodsky insisted on keeping the right to terminate this phony agreement at any time, for any reason. Mr. Culbertson was expected to leave the property off the market for 60 valuable days while Brodsky took his own sweet time to inspect the land, perform engineering tests, make feasibility calculations, reconsider his position, and ultimately decide whether he had any interest in the property. If he decided for any reason that he no longer wanted the land, Brodsky could simply walk away from the deal. Please note

that he didn't even lose the use of the $5,000. The bank was not permitted to cash the check until Brodsky made up his mind. No money ever left Brodsky's account—indeed, no money even had to be in his account, unless and until he decided to exercise his option.

A true option contract provides something for each party. The landowner is obligated to hold the property open for the buyer, but the buyer pays a fee for this privilege. Here, Brodsky was obligated to pay nothing and do nothing. He made no promise at all, and we urge that no contract resulted.

Argument for Brodsky: Your honors, it is rather disingenuous of Mr. Culbertson to pose as an injured party here. He is, in fact, a sophisticated property owner. He voluntarily entered into a contract with Mr. Brodsky for one reason: it was in his own interest. He concluded that the best way to "land" Mr. Brodsky was first to "hook" him with an option contract. He wanted Mr. Brodsky to show serious interest, and demanded earnest money. He got it. He insisted that Mr. Brodsky's check be held in escrow. He got it. Culbertson hoped that by getting this degree of commitment, Mr. Brodsky would perform the necessary tests on the land and conclude that he wanted to buy it. And that is *precisely what happened.* Mr. Brodsky, in total good faith, performed his tests, decided the land was what he had wanted, and exercised the option that Culbertson had sold him. But Culbertson decided to back out of the deal—presumably to sell elsewhere.

Now Culbertson comes into court and relies on a technical rule of contract law to try to weasel out of a good faith deal. The law of consideration was never intended to permit such chicanery. ∎

Sales Law: Requirements and Output Contracts

You decide to open a "novelty T-shirt" business. You will buy plain white T-shirts from a wholesaler and then arrange for them to be printed with funny pictures and quotes. You will sell them to the public from a small booth you rent in a popular shopping mall. Your single biggest expense will be the wholesale cost of the T-shirts. How many

What are your obligations under a requirements contract?

will you need? You *think* that sales will soar, and you will need hundreds each week. But what if business lags? You do not want to overstock. Your solution may be a requirements contract.

In a requirements contract, the buyer agrees to purchase 100 percent of her goods from one seller. The seller agrees to sell the buyer whatever quantity she reasonably needs. The quantity is not stated in the contract, though it may be estimated, based on previous years or best calculations.

The common law regarded requirements contracts as void because the buyer held all the power. She could purchase a vast quantity or none at all. She was making no commitment, and hence was giving no consideration. Common law courts refused to enforce requirements contracts, as well as their counterpart, output contracts. **In an output contract, the seller guarantees to sell 100 percent of its output to one buyer, and the buyer agrees to accept the entire quantity.** For example, a timber company might agree to sell all of its wood products to a lumber wholesaler. The common law frowned because now it was the seller who was making no real commitment.

The problem with the common law rule was that many merchants valued these contracts. Consider the utility of requirements contracts. From the buyer's viewpoint, a requirements contract provides flexibility. The buyer can adjust purchases based on consumer demands. The agreement also guarantees her a source of goods in a competitive market. For a seller, the requirements agreement will ensure him at least this one outlet and will prevent competitors from selling to this buyer. The contract should enable the seller to spend less on marketing, and may enable him to predict sales more accurately. Output contracts have similar value.

The UCC responded in a forthright fashion: **Section 2-306 expressly allows output and requirements contracts in the sale of goods.**[2] However, the Code places one limitation on how much the buyer may demand (or the seller may offer):

A term which measures the quantity by the output of the seller or the requirements of the buyer means such actual output or requirements as may occur *in good faith,...*

The "good faith" phrase is critical. In requirements contracts, courts have ruled that it is the "good faith" that a buyer brings to the deal that represents her consideration.[3] In other words, by agreeing to act in good faith, she actually is limiting her options. Since she is obligating herself, the deal becomes binding. Beware that this is not just word

---

[2] UCC §2-306(2) permits a related type of contract, the exclusive dealing agreement. Here, either a buyer or a seller of goods agrees to deal exclusively with the other party. The results are similar to an output or requirements agreement. Once again, one party is receiving a guarantee in exchange for a promise that the common law would have considered illusory. Under the Code, such a deal is enforceable.

[3] *Famous Brands, Inc. v. David Sherman Corp.*, 814 F.2d 517, 1987 U.S. App. LEXIS 3634 (8th Cir. 1987).

play. A buyer *must make its requirement demands in good faith*, based on the expectations the parties had when they signed the deal.

Suppose, in your T-shirt business, you and the wholesaler agree on a two-year requirements contract with a fixed price of three dollars per T-shirt and an estimate of 150 T-shirts per week. If business is slow the first two months, you are permitted to purchase only 25 T-shirts per week in the event that is all you are selling. Should sales suddenly boom and you need 200 per week, you may also require that many. Both of those demands are made in good faith. But suppose the price of cotton skyrockets and the wholesale cost of T-shirts everywhere suddenly doubles. You have a two-year guaranteed price of three dollars per T-shirt. Could you demand 2,000 T-shirts per week, knowing that you will be able to resell the shirts to other retailers for a big profit? No. That is not acting in good faith based on the original expectations of the parties. The wholesaler is free to ignore your exorbitant demand. The legal requirement has come full circle: your good faith is valid consideration and makes the deal enforceable—but it is binding on you, too.

Past Consideration

In *Kelsoe v. International Wood Products, Inc.* (discussed earlier in this chapter), International Wood's manager, Hernandez, promised employee Carol Kelsoe some shares of the company stock, but never delivered them. She sued and lost, because there had been no bargaining and no exchange. Yet Hernandez must have had some reason for making the promise. Presumably, it was because of Kelsoe's good work for the company in years past. Could she claim the previous work as consideration? No.

Past consideration is generally no consideration. It all goes back to our basic definition of consideration, which requires bargaining and an exchange of obligations. If one party makes a promise based on what the other party has already done, there is no exchange, and there will usually be no enforceable contract.

DEMENTAS V. ESTATE OF TALLAS

95 Utah Adv. Rep. 28, 764 P.2d 628, 1988 Utah App. LEXIS 174
Utah Court of Appeals, 1988

Facts: Jack Tallas came to the United States from Greece in 1914. He lived in Salt Lake City for nearly 70 years, achieving great success in insurance and real estate. When he died, he left a large estate. During the last 14 years of his life, Tallas was a close friend of Peter Dementas, who helped him with numerous personal and business chores. Two months before his death, Tallas met with Dementas and dictated a memorandum to him, in Greek, stating:

PETER K. DEMENTAS, is my best friend I have in this country and since he came to the United States he treats me like a father and I think of him as my own son. He takes me in his car grocery shopping. He drives me to the doctor and also takes me every week to Bingham to pick up my mail, collect the rents and manage my properties. For all the services Peter has given me all these years, I owe to him the amount of

$50,000 (Fifty Thousand Dollars.) I will shortly change my will to include him as my heir.

Tallas signed the memorandum, but he did not in fact alter his will to include Dementas. The estate refused to pay, and Dementas sued. The trial was entertaining, thanks to Judge Dee, whose remarks included: "It's hearsay, I agree, but its damn good hearsay, and I want to hear it." Urging a lawyer to hurry up, the judge snapped, "Go on to your next question. This witness—who is supposed to be one witness for 15 minutes—is now into the second day, and we've still got the same witness. . . . At the rate we're going, I will have long retired and been happily fishing in Wyoming." Finally hearing something worthwhile from the witness, he interrupted, "Wait a minute. Wait. Wait. Wait. Now, the

▼

factfinder has finally got a fact. He said, 'I did it a lot of times.' I've identified a fact in a day and a half. Let's go to the next witness and see if we can find another one in this case."

Unfortunately for Dementas, when the testimony ground to a halt, Judge Dee ruled that there was no consideration to support Tallas's promise. Dementas appealed.

Issue: Was there consideration to make Tallas's promise enforceable?

Excerpts from Judge Orme's Decision: A generally accepted definition of consideration is that a legal detriment has been bargained for and exchanged for a promise. The mere fact that one man promises something to another creates no legal duty and makes no legal remedy available in case of nonperformance. A performance or a returned promise must be bargained for.

In determining whether consideration to support a personal service contract exists, the focus is not whether the amount promised represents the fair market value for the services rendered. On the contrary, as a general rule it is settled that any detriment no matter how economically inadequate will support a promise. In this regard, the court correctly stated: "If Tallas thought it was worth 50,000 bucks to get one ride to Bingham, that's Tallas' decision. . . . The only thing you can't do is take it with you."

Even though the testimony showed that Dementas rendered at least some services for Tallas, the subsequent promise by Tallas to pay $50,000 for services already performed by Dementas is not a promise supported by legal consideration. Events which occur prior to the making of the promise and not with the purpose of inducing the promise in exchange are viewed as past consideration and are the legal equivalent of no consideration. This is so because the promisor is making his promise because those events occurred, but he is not making his promise in order to get them. There is no "bargaining"; no saying that if you will do this for me I will do that for you.

This rule can surely work unfair results and has accordingly been criticized and the object of legislation. Some courts have sought to enforce promises supported only by past consideration by invoking a "moral obligation" notion to make at least some of these promises enforceable. Although the "moral obligation" exception has not been embraced in Utah, other courts apply the exception in cases where services rendered in the past were rendered with the expectation of payment rather than gratuitously.

Even if the "moral obligation" doctrine applied in Utah, Dementas would not prevail. The trial court found that the services rendered by Dementas to Tallas were not rendered with the expectation of being compensated, but were performed gratuitously. That finding has not been shown to be erroneous.

[Judgment for the estate is *affirmed*.] ■

Exception: Economic Benefit

As the *Dementas* court mentions, there is a modest trend in the law in favor of enforcing promises based on past consideration *if that consideration was an economic benefit that was rendered with the expectation of payment*. The Restatement (Second) of Contracts §86 suggests that promises based on past consideration may be enforceable "to the extent necessary to avoid injustice." But as we can see from the *Kelsoe* and *Dementas* cases, the courts are loathe to carve exceptions into this venerable rule.

Preexisting Duty

A promise to do something the promisor is already obligated to do is not consideration. In the chapter opener, Professor Parsley agrees to show up for the next class if the students pay her $1,000. *They promise to pay.* They are adults, they understood the deal, the cost is only $20 per student, and they strike the bargain. When she arrives to teach, she is entitled to—nothing. Parsley has given no consideration for the $1,000. She was already obligated to teach the class. The students, having paid their tuition, were already entitled to her instruction. Because *her* promise to teach is no consideration, the students are not bound by *their* promise to pay her.

Of course, exceptions are the spice of law, and the preexisting duty rule provides us with a rack full. Courts have created these exceptions because a rigid application of the rule might interfere with legitimate business goals.

Can a builder enforce your promise to pay extra?

© GETTY IMAGES

Exception: Additional Work

When a promisor agrees to do something above and beyond what he is obligated to do, his promise is generally valid consideration. Cecil has promised to build a fabulous swimming pool/cabana for Nathalie for $250,000. When the work is half complete, he offers to build the cabana out of sea shells, rather than pine wood. If Nathalie agrees to a new price of $300,000 for the pool complex, she is obligated to pay, because Cecil's extra work is valid consideration for her promise.

Exception: Modification

If both parties agree that a modification is necessary, the surest way to accomplish that is to rescind the original contract and draft a new one. **To rescind means to cancel.** Thus, if neither party has completed its obligations, the agreement to rescind will terminate each party's rights and obligations under the old contract. This should be done in writing. Then the parties sign the new agreement. Courts will *generally* enforce a rescission and modification provided both parties voluntarily entered into it, in good faith. If one side, determined to earn greater profits, unfairly coerces the other into the changes, the modification is invalid, as we see in the *Zhang* case, later in this section.

Once again the UCC has changed the common law, making it easier for merchants to modify agreements for the sale of goods. UCC §2-209 provides:

- An agreement modifying a contract within this Article needs no consideration to be binding.
- A signed agreement which excludes modification or rescission except by a signed writing cannot be otherwise modified or rescinded.

Here is how these two provisions work together. Mike's Magic Mania agrees to deliver 500 rabbits and 500 top hats to State University, for the school's Sleight of Hand 101 course. The goods, including 100 cages and 1,000 pounds of rabbit food, are to arrive no later than September 1, in time for the new semester, with payment on delivery. By September 20 no rabbits have appeared, in or out of hats. The university buys similar products from another supply house at a 25 percent steeper price, and sues MMM for the difference. Mike claims that in early September the dean had orally agreed to permit delivery in October. The dean is on sabbatical in Tahiti and cannot be reached for comment. Is the alleged modification valid?

Under the common law, the modification would have been void, because MMM gave no consideration for the extended delivery date. However, this is a sale of goods, and under UCC §2-209, an oral modification may be valid even without consideration. Unfortunately for Mike, though, the original agreement included a clause forbidding oral modification. Any changes had to be in writing, signed by both parties. Mike never obtained such a document. Even if the dean did make the oral agreement, the university wins.

The preexisting duty rule often arises when one party agrees to a contract but later believes he could have done better. A realtor will graciously demonstrate for us.

ZHANG V. EIGHTH JUDICIAL DISTRICT COURT OF THE STATE OF NEVADA

103 P.3d 20
Nevada Supreme Court, 2004

Facts: Frank Sorichetti was a Las Vegas realtor. On February 1, he contracted to sell his house to Lanlin Zhang for $532,500, with the closing to occur in one month. On February 3, Sorichetti told Zhang that he was not satisfied with the deal, and was terminating the sale. However, Sorichetti agreed to sell the house if Zhang would pay $578,000. Zhang promised to pay the higher price, but later sued to enforce the first contract.

The trial court dismissed the case, reasoning that the parties had rescinded the original contract, leaving it unenforceable. Their agreement to rescind was consideration for the new deal, said the court. Zhang appealed.

Issue: Was Zhang entitled to enforce the first contract?

Excerpts from the Court's Per Curiam Decision: Contrary to Sorichetti's suggestion, consideration for the February 3 agreement cannot be found in the purported rescission of the February 1 agreement. Overlooking the preexisting duty rule for a simultaneous rescission/modification might permit fraudulent or unfair modifications.

The Iowa Supreme Court addressed these principles in [an earlier case]. The issue was whether a $290,000 agreement for the sale of a farm was enforceable, given that the buyers later agreed to purchase the farm for $300,000. The court concluded that, as the new agreement arose solely from the seller's desire for more money, rather than a wholesale rescission of the earlier sales agreement, the price increase was merely an attempted modification, unsupported by consideration.

[The Iowa decision] is indistinguishable from the instant case. Zhang alleged in her complaint that the February 3 agreement originated from Sorichetti's desire for more money, rather than any desire to end his dealings with Zhang. Consequently, consideration for the February 3 agreement cannot be found in the purported simultaneous rescission of the February 1 agreement. Nor can consideration be found elsewhere, as Zhang alleges in her complaint a lack of "additional consideration" to support the February 3 agreement.

[Reversed and remanded to permit Zhang's lawsuit to go forward.] ■

Public Policy

What does the court mean when it says that overlooking the preexisting duty rule might permit fraudulent or unfair modifications? Is there anything wrong with what Sorichetti did? Doesn't a seller always want to obtain the highest possible price? ◆

Exception: Unforeseen Circumstances

Hugo has a deal to repair major highways. Hugo hires Hal's Hauling to cart soil and debris. Hal's trucks begin work, but after crossing the work site several times they sink to their axles in sinister, sucking slime. Hal demands an additional 35 percent payment from Hugo to complete the job, pointing out that the surface was dry and cracked and that neither Hal nor Hugo was aware of the subsurface water. Hal howls that he must use different trucks with different tires and work more slowly to permit the soil to dry.

Hugo hems and haws and finally agrees. But when the hauling is finished, Hugo refuses to pay the extra money. Is Hugo liable?

Yes. When unforeseen circumstances cause a party to make a promise regarding an unfinished project, that promise is generally valid consideration. Even though Hal is only promising to finish what he was already obligated to do, his promise is valid consideration because neither party knew of the subsoil mud. Hal was facing a situation quite different from what the parties anticipated. It is almost as though he were undertaking a new project. Hal has given consideration and Hugo is bound by his promise to pay extra money.

SETTLEMENT OF DEBTS

You claim that your friend Felicity owes you $90,000, but she refuses to pay. Finally, when you are desperate, Felicity offers you a cashier's check for $60,000—provided you accept it as full settlement. To get your hands on some money, you agree and cash the check. The next day you sue Felicity for $30,000. Who wins? First, an ethical question.

Ethics

Even if you think you have a chance of winning, is it right to accept the money as full settlement and then sue for the balance? From the Chapter 2 ethics checklist: Which values are in conflict? Which of these values are most important? Under what circumstances would you feel ethically correct in suing for the balance? When would you consider it wrong? ◆

As to the legal outcome, it will depend principally upon one major issue: Was Felicity's debt liquidated or unliquidated?

Liquidated Debt

A **liquidated debt** is one in which there is no dispute about the amount owed. A loan is a typical example. If a bank lends you $10,000, and the note obligates you to repay that amount on June 1 of the following year, you clearly owe that sum. The debt is liquidated. **In cases of liquidated debt, if the creditor agrees to take less than the full amount as full payment, her agreement is not binding.** The debtor has given no consideration to support the creditor's promise to accept a reduced payment, and therefore the creditor is not bound by her word. The reasoning is simply that the debtor is already obligated to pay the full amount, so no bargaining could reasonably cause the creditor to accept less. If Felicity's debt to you is liquidated, your agreement to accept $60,000 is not binding, and you will successfully sue for the balance.

Exception: Different Performance

There is one important exception to this rule. If the debtor offers a *different performance* to settle the liquidated debt, and the creditor agrees to take it as full settlement, the agreement is binding. Suppose that Felicity, instead of paying $60,000, offers you five acres in Alaska and you accept. When you accept the deed to the land, you have given up your entire claim, regardless of the land's precise value.

Unliquidated Debt: Accord and Satisfaction

A debt is **unliquidated** for either of two reasons: (1) the parties dispute whether any money is owed, or (2) the parties agree that some money is owed but dispute how much. When a debt is unliquidated, for either reason, the parties may enter into a binding agreement to settle for less than what the creditor demands.

Such a compromise will be enforced if:

- The debt is unliquidated and
- The parties agree that the creditor will accept as full payment a sum less than she has claimed; and
- The debtor pays the amount agreed upon.

This agreement is called an **accord and satisfaction.** The accord is the agreement to settle for less than the creditor claims. The satisfaction is the actual payment of that compromised sum. An accord and satisfaction is valid consideration to support the creditor's agreement to drop all claims. Each party is giving up something: the creditor gives up her full claim, and the debtor gives up his assertion that he owed little or nothing.

Accord and Satisfaction by Check

Most accord and satisfaction agreements involve payment by check. UCC §3-311 governs these agreements, using the same common law rules described above.[7] The Code specifies that when the debtor writes "full settlement" on the check, a creditor who cashes the check generally has entered into an accord and satisfaction. If Felicity's debt is unliquidated, and she gives you a check with "full payment of all debts" written on the face in bold letters, the moment you deposit the check you lose any claim to more money.

What happens, though, if the creditor writes "*not accepted* as full payment" before depositing the check? The following case answers that question, but first it discusses another common issue. The Code requires *good faith* when a debtor offers an accord and satisfaction. That sounds wholesome, but what does it mean in practice?

JONES V. ALLSTATE INSURANCE COMPANY

146 Wash.2d 291, 45 P.3d 1068
Supreme Court of Washington, 2002

Facts: Jeremy France ran a stop sign and broadsided a vehicle driven by Janet Jones. Jones suffered severe facial injuries and damage to her right eye. Her scalp was peeled back and she lost consciousness. She was airlifted to a hospital, underwent several surgeries, and survived.

Allstate Insurance represented France and his parents, who owned the car he was driving when he caused the accident. Christy Klein, an Allstate agent, helped Janet Jones and her husband in various ways, identifying Janet's medical coverage and prodding insurers to pay the medical bills. Klein helped get $30,000 in "underinsured driver" insurance from the Joneses' own company, Farmers. The Joneses con-

sidered Klein more helpful than their own insurance company agent.

Klein then sent Janet Jones a letter, a check for $25,000, and a release form. The check contained this typed notation: "Final settlement of any and all claims arising from bodily injury caused by [the collision with Jeremy France]." The form also released Allstate and the Frances from liability.

The Joneses did not sign the release form. They deposited the check, but nine months later had second thoughts about it, and sent Allstate their own check in the amount of $25,000. Allstate returned the check, saying the claim was settled and closed.

▼

---

[7]   A check is legally an instrument, which is why this section comes from Article 3 of the Code. For a full discussion of instruments, see Chapters 23–25.

The Joneses sued the France family and Allstate. Allstate claimed an accord and satisfaction, but the trial court ruled against the company. The Frances and Allstate appealed, and the case reached the Washington Supreme Court.

Issue: Did the parties enter into an accord and satisfaction?

Excerpts from Justice Bridge's Decision: It does not appear that the [Allstate] check was tendered in good faith as required by [section 3-311 (a)(i)]. "Good faith" is defined in [the Code] as "honesty in fact and the observance of reasonable commercial standards of fair dealing." The Uniform Commercial Code comment on this code section gives as an example of a lack of good faith the routine printing of full satisfaction language on a business's checks.

Another example of lack of good faith is found in the practice of some business debtors in routinely printing full satisfaction language on their check stocks so that all or a large part of the debts of the debtor are paid by checks bearing the full satisfaction language, whether or not there is any dispute with the creditor. Under such a practice the claimant cannot be sure whether a tender in full satisfaction is or is not being made.

Evidence provided by Allstate and Christy Klein indicate that full satisfaction language routinely appeared on Allstate's settlement checks. [The court quotes from Christy Klein's deposition:]

Q. Did you write in—type in the words, "final settlement of any and all claims arising from bodily injury caused by the [collision with Jeremy France]"?
A. I believe that is part of the computer-generated check system. I am not sure at this late date.
Q. Did you read the wording, "Final settlement of any and all claims arising from bodily injury caused by the accident" before you sent the check to the Joneses?
A. I am not sure I read that particular one, but it would have been standard wording that they used in all of their checks.

Allstate's position is that the check was computer generated and that Ms. Klein did not exercise any legal discretion with regard to the preparation of the release or check. It appears therefore that the computer-generated check at issue in this case falls squarely within the example of lack of good faith provided by the Uniform Commercial Code commentary. Under [UCC section 3-311 (a)] the person asserting accord and satisfaction bears the burden of proof. We find that evidence on the record shows that Allstate routinely printed full satisfaction language on its checks. Because the transaction does not meet the good faith requirement, [the defendants] may not assert the affirmative defense of accord and satisfaction.

Affirmed. ∎

Devil's Advocate

Allstate did nothing wrong. The company decided it was willing to send $25,000 to the plaintiff, immediately, without being prompted, but was not prepared voluntarily to offer any more. Allstate believed in good faith that Janet Jones would like the money quickly, and they were right: She promptly cashed the check. If the Joneses had not agreed to the terms of the settlement, they were free to mail the check back. Any bad faith lies with the Joneses, who seized the money but then decided to try for more. ◆

UCC Exceptions

The Code creates two exceptions for accord and satisfaction cases involving checks. The first exception concerns "organizations," which typically are businesses. The general rule of §3-311 is potentially calamitous to them, since a company that receives thousands of checks every day is unlikely to inspect all notations. A consumer who owes $12,000 on a credit card might write "full settlement" on a $200 check, potentially extinguishing the entire debt through accord and satisfaction. Under the exception, if an organization notifies a debtor that any offers to settle for less than the debt claimed must be made to a particular official, and the check is sent to anyone else in the organization, depositing the check generally does *not* create an accord and satisfaction. Thus a clerk who deposits 900 checks daily for payment of MasterCard debts will not have inadvertently entered into dozens of accord and satisfaction agreements.

The second exception allows a way out to most creditors who have inadvertently created an accord and satisfaction. If, within 90 days of cashing a "full payment" check, the creditor offers repayment of the same amount to the debtor, there is no accord and satisfaction. Homer claims that Virgil owes him $7 million, but foolishly cashes Virgil's check for $3 million, without understanding that "paid in full" means just what it says. Homer has created an accord and satisfaction. But if he promptly sends Virgil a check for $3 million, he has undone the agreement and may sue for the full amount.

© DIGITAL VISION/GETTY IMAGES

Chapter Conclusion

This ancient doctrine of consideration is simple to state but subtle to apply. The parties must bargain and enter into an exchange of promises or actions. If they do not, there is no consideration and the courts are unlikely to enforce any promise made.
A variety of exceptions modify the law, but a party wishing to render its future more predictable—the purpose of a contract—will rely on a solid bargain and exchange.

Chapter Review

1. A promise is normally binding only if it is supported by consideration, which requires a bargaining and exchange between the parties.

2. The "thing" bargained for can be another promise or an action—virtually anything that a party might seek. It can create a benefit to the promisor or a detriment to the promisee.

3. The courts will seldom inquire into the adequacy of consideration.

4. An illusory promise is not consideration.

5. Under sales law, requirement and output contracts are valid. Although one side controls the quantity, its agreement to make demands *in good faith* is consideration.

6. Past consideration is generally no consideration.

7. Under the doctrine of preexisting duty, a promise to do something that the promisor is already legally obligated to perform is generally not consideration.

8. A liquidated debt is one in which there is no dispute about the amount owed.

9. For a liquidated debt, a creditor's promise to accept less than the full amount is not binding.

10. For an unliquidated debt, if the parties agree that the creditor will accept less than the full amount claimed and the debtor performs, there is an accord and satisfaction and the creditor may not claim any balance.

11. In most states payment by a check that has a "full payment" notation will create an accord and satisfaction unless the creditor is an organization that has notified the debtor that full payment offers must go to a certain officer.

Practice Test

1. An aunt saw her eight-year-old nephew enter the room, remarked what a nice boy he was, and said, "I would like to take care of him now." She promptly wrote a note, promising to pay the boy $3,000 upon her death. Her estate refused to pay. Is it obligated to do so?

2. **YOU BE THE JUDGE** WRITING PROBLEM Elio Pino took out a health insurance policy with the Union Bankers Insurance Co. Eighteen months later he became ill, suffered medical expenses, and filed a claim for benefits. Union Bankers wrote Pino this letter:

   Dear Mr. Pino:
   While servicing your claim, we learned that the medical facts on the application for this policy were not complete. If we had known the complete health history, we couldn't have issued this insurance. We must place

you and ourselves back where we were when you applied for the policy and consider that the insurance was never in effect. (We are refunding the premiums you've paid us.)

Pino deposited the refund check, which was much less than his claim, and then sued for the full claim. Bankers Insurance argued that Pino had entered into an accord and satisfaction. The trial court gave summary judgment for the insurer, and Pino appealed. Did Pino enter into an accord and satisfaction by cashing the insurance company check? **Argument for Pino:** The insurance company has its contract law wrong. The company attempted to rescind the contract. Then it termed its unilateral act an accord and satisfaction. The company's attempts fail: a rescission requires the agreement of both parties; an accord and satisfaction needs a clear statement that the creditor is accepting the check as full payment. Neither occurred. **Argument for Union Bankers Insurance Co.:** This is classic accord and satisfaction. The company informed Mr. Pino that it regarded his application as false and offered him a partial payment as full settlement. He deposited the check, creating an accord and satisfaction, and has no claim for any more money.

3. **CPA QUESTION** For there to be consideration, there must be:

   a. A bargained-for detriment to the promisor(ee) or a benefit to the promisee(or)

   b. A manifestation of mutual assent

   c. Genuineness of assent

   d. Substantially equal economic benefits to both parties

4. Eagle ran convenience stores. He entered into an agreement with Commercial Movie in which Commercial would provide Eagle with videotape cassettes for rental. Eagle would pay Commercial 50 percent of the rental revenues. If Eagle stopped using Commercial's service, Eagle could not use a competitor's services for 18 months. The agreement also provided: "Commercial shall not be liable for compensation or damages of any kind, whether on account of the loss by Eagle of profits, sales or expenditures, or on account of any other event or cause whatsoever." Eagle complied with the agreement for two years but then began using a competitor's service, and Commercial sued. Eagle claimed that the agreement was unenforceable for lack of consideration. Did Eagle's argument fly?

5. American Bakeries had a fleet of over 3,000 delivery trucks. Because of the increasing cost of gasoline, the company was interested in converting the trucks to propane fuel. It signed a requirements contract with Empire Gas, in which Empire would convert "approximately 3,000" trucks to propane fuel, as American Bakeries requested, and would then sell all required propane fuel to run the trucks. But American Bakeries changed its mind and never requested a single conversion. Empire sued for lost profits. Who won?

6. **CPA QUESTION** Which of the following requires consideration in order to be binding on the parties?

   a. Modification of a contract involving the sale of real estate

   b. Ratification of a contract by a person after reaching the age of majority

   c. A written promise signed by a merchant to keep an offer to sell goods open for 10 days

   d. Modification of a sale of goods contract under the UCC

7. Tindall operated a general contracting business in Montana. He and Konitz entered into negotiations for Konitz to buy the business. The parties realized that Konitz could succeed with the business only if Tindall gave support and assistance for a year or so after the purchase, especially by helping with the process of bidding for jobs and obtaining bonds to guarantee performance. Konitz bought the business and Tindall helped with the bidding and bonding. Two years later, Tindall presented Konitz with a contract for his services up to that point. Konitz did not want to sign but Tindall insisted. Konitz signed the agreement, which said: "Whereas Tindall sold his contracting business to Konitz and thereafter assisted Konitz in bidding and bonding

without which Konitz would have been unable to operate, NOW THEREFORE Konitz agrees to pay Tindall $138,629." Konitz later refused to pay. Comment.

8. CeCe Hylton and Edward Meztista, partners in a small advertising firm, agreed to terminate the business and split assets evenly. Meztista gave Hylton a two-page document showing assets, liabilities, and a bottom line of $35,235.67, with one half due to each partner. Hylton questioned the accounting, and asked to see the books. Meztista did not permit Hylton to see any records, and refused to answer her phone calls. Instead, he gave her a check in the amount of $17,617.83, on which he wrote "Final payment/payment in full." Hylton cashed the check, but wrote on it, "Under protest—cashing this check does not constitute my acceptance of this amount as payment in full." Hylton then filed suit, demanding additional monies. Meztista claimed that the parties had made an accord and satisfaction. What is the best argument for each party? Who should win?

9. **ETHICS** Melnick built a house for Gintzler, but the foundation was defective. Gintzler agreed to accept the foundation if Melnick guaranteed to make future repairs caused by the defects. Melnick agreed but later refused to make any repairs. Melnick argued that his promise to make future repairs was unsupported by consideration. Who will win the suit? Is either party acting unethically? Which one, and why?

10. When White's wife died he filed a claim with Boston Mutual for $10,000 death benefits under her policy. The insurance company rejected the claim, saying that his wife had misrepresented her medical condition in the application form. The company sent White a check for $478.75, which it said represented "a full refund of all applicable premiums paid" for the coverage. Plaintiff deposited the check. Accord and satisfaction?

11. **ROLE REVERSAL** Write a short-answer question that focuses on one of these consideration issues: illusory promise, preexisting duty, or accord and satisfaction.

Internet Research Problem

At http://beatty.westbuslaw.com click on "Article 2." Find your way to §2-209, concerning contract modification. Write a clear one- or two-paragraph explanation of subsections (1) and (2). Explain what these subsections mean (in English) and how they work together.

You can find further practice problems at http://beatty.westbuslaw.com or in the Study Guide that accompanies this text.

Legality

Soheil Sadri, a California resident, did some serious gambling at Caesar's Tahoe casino in Nevada. And lost. To keep gambling, he wrote checks to Caesar's and then signed two memoranda pledging to repay money advanced. After two days, with his losses totaling more than $22,000, he went home. Back in California, Sadri stopped payment on the checks and refused to pay any of the money he owed Caesar's. The casino sued. In defense, Sadri claimed that California law considered his agreements illegal and unenforceable. He was unquestionably correct about one thing: a contract that is illegal is void and unenforceable. ■

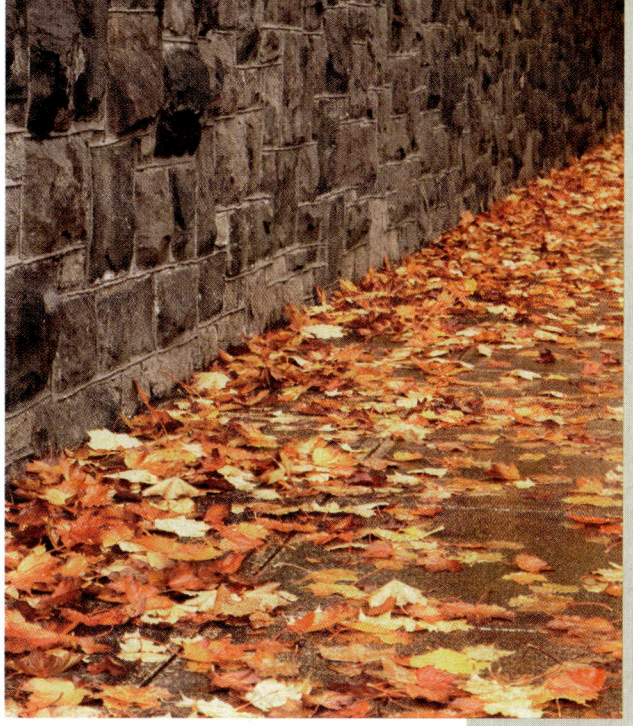

© DAVID PAPAZIAN PHOTOGRAPHY INC/BRAND X PICTURES/GETTY IMAGES

In this chapter we examine a variety of contracts that may be void. Illegal agreements fall into two groups: those that violate a statute, and those that violate public policy.

CONTRACTS THAT VIOLATE A STATUTE

Wagers

Gambling is big business. Almost all states now permit some form of wagering, from casinos to race tracks to lotteries, and they eagerly collect the billions of dollars in revenue generated.

Supporters urge that casinos create jobs and steady income, boost state coffers, and take business away from organized crime. Critics argue that naïve citizens inevitably lose money they can ill afford to forfeit, and that addicted gamblers destroy families and weaken the fabric of communities. With citizens and states divided over the ethics of gambling, it is inevitable that we have conflicts such as the dispute between Sadri and Caesar's. The basic rule, however, is clear: **a gambling contract is illegal unless it is specifically authorized by state statute.**

In California, as in many states, gambling on credit is not allowed. In other words, it is illegal to lend money to help someone wager. But in Nevada, gambling on credit is legal, and debt memoranda such as Sadri's are enforceable contracts. Caesar's sued Sadri in California (where he lived). The result? The court admitted that California's attitude toward gambling had changed, and that bingo, poker clubs, and lotteries were common. Nonetheless, the court denied that the new tolerance extended to wagering on credit:

> There is a special reason for treating gambling on credit differently from gambling itself. Gambling debts are characteristic of pathological gambling, a mental disorder which is recognized by the American Psychiatric Association and whose prevalence is estimated at 2 to 3 percent of the adult population. Characteristic problems include extensive indebtedness and consequent default on debts and other financial responsibilities,. . . and financially motivated illegal activities to pay for gambling. Having lost his or her cash, the pathological gambler will continue to play on credit, if extended, in an attempt to win back the losses. In our view, this is why enforcement of gambling debts has always been against public policy in California and should remain so, regardless of shifting public attitudes about gambling itself. If Californians want to play, so be it. But the law should not invite them to play themselves into debt. The judiciary cannot protect pathological gamblers from themselves, but we can refuse to participate in their financial ruin.[1]

Caesar's lost and Sadri kept his money. The dispute is a useful starting place from which to examine contract legality because it illustrates two important themes. First, morality is a significant part of contract legality. In refusing to enforce an obligation that Sadri undeniably had made, the California court relied on the human and social consequences of gambling and on the ethics of judicial enforcement of gambling debts. Second, "void" really means just that: a court will not intercede to assist either party to an illegal agreement, even if its refusal leaves one party obviously shortchanged.

cyberLaw

Where there is money, there is the Internet. Countless sites now offer online bingo, casino games, and sports betting. Most of these sites operate from offshore locations where they are legal, such as Caribbean countries. Of course, the Internet sites are accessible to anyone in the United States, even though most states outlaw online betting. Technology has once again outpaced the law. The federal government and a few states have tried to block access to these wagering facilities, thus far with limited effect. As this book goes to press, Caribbean nations are appearing before the World Trade Organization, arguing that the United States has no right under international law to restrict casinos in other countries. Early results at the WTO have favored the Caribbean nations, but the final word is not yet in.

In the meantime, we offer for your perusal some of the most popular Internet gambling sites.[2] ◆

---

[1] *Metropolitan Creditors Service of Sacramento v. Sadri,* 15 Cal. App. 4th 1821, 1993 Cal. App. LEXIS 559, 19 Cal. Rptr. 2d 646 (Cal. Ct. App. 1993).

[2] Did you honestly think we would help you squander your money over the Internet? No way.

Insurance

Another market in which "wagering" unexpectedly pops up is that of insurance. You may certainly insure your own life for any sum you choose. But may you insure someone else's life? **Anyone taking out a policy on the life of another must have an insurable interest in that person.** The most common insurable interest is family connection, such as spouses or parents. Other valid interests include creditor-debtor status (the creditor wants payment if the debtor dies), and business association (an executive in the company is so valuable, the firm will need compensation if something happens to him). If there is no insurable interest there is generally no contract. But should that rule *always* be enforced?

you Be The Judge

CHEM V. NEW YORK LIFE INSURANCE COMPANY

168 F.3d 498
Ninth Circuit Court of Appeals, 1999

Facts: Thuan Wu was an insurance agent. An acquaintance named Suulan Chem asked Wu to purchase an insurance policy on the life of her young son, Michael. Wu purchased a short-term policy through Surety Life Insurance. Later, without telling Chem, he renewed the contract, and bought additional policies on Michael's life through New York Life and three other companies. The policies totaled $750,000. On each one, Wu named Suulan Chem as the principal beneficiary and himself as the secondary beneficiary. Wu's plan was grotesque and simple: murder the boy and his mother, collect the money.

Wu gave orders to confederates, who kidnapped and slew the eight-year-old boy. Chem was never killed. Wu was convicted of first-degree murder.

Chem sought to collect the $750,000, but all of the companies refused to pay. She sued. The court dismissed the case, ruling that Wu, who took out the policies without Chem's knowledge, had no insurable interest in Michael's life. Chem appealed.

You Be The Judge: Are the insurance policies void for lack of insurable interest?

Argument for Chem: There is no law that requires a court to ignore basic fairness. When Wu applied for these policies, not one company inquired into his insurable interest in Michael's life. Not one company asked about his relationship with Suulan, or with Michael, or why he named

himself secondary beneficiary. Not one company wondered why it was Wu making the application instead of Suulan. Each insurer was happy to take the money, and issue a policy with Suulan Chem as principal beneficiary. If asked at the time, each company would have said, "These are valid, enforceable contracts." Only when it was time to pay up did the companies become interested in Wu's role.

Obviously, Suulan has a legitimate insurable interest in the life of her son. She is the named beneficiary. It is time to pay her. Yet the companies, oblivious to the murder of a young boy and the grief of a mother, suddenly argue that the contracts for which they happily accepted premiums have been void all along. The law should never endorse such callous hypocrisy.

Argument for New York Life and the other insurers: The companies deeply regret Suulan Chem's appalling loss, but the criminal is Thuan Wu.

Wu was the applicant and he had no insurable interest in Michael's life. As a result, each of these contracts was void from the start. In other words, as a matter of law there never were any contracts. None of the insurers were at any time obligated to Suulan Chem or anyone else. Once a contract is void, that is the end of the matter. No words, actions—or even tragedies—can transform a void contract into a valid one.

Sadly, this case demonstrates exactly why courts demand an insurable interest. The law is designed to assure that someone taking an insurance policy on the life of another *wants the person to live.* Life insurance is supposed to compensate financially for a loss that everyone hopes never occurs. Without the requirement of insurable interest, some would be tempted to take out policies as a crude wager, hoping that the insured would die. Others would plan to murder the insured. Had Wu understood the law, Michael would still be alive. ■

Licensing Statutes

You sue your next-door neighbor in small claims court, charging that he keeps a kangaroo in his backyard and that the beast has disrupted your family barbecues by leaping over the fence, demanding salad, and even punching your cousin in the ear. Your friend Foster, a graduate student from Melbourne, offers to help you prepare the case, and you agree to pay him 10 percent of anything you recover. Foster proves surprisingly adept at organizing documents and arguments. You win $1,200 and Foster demands $120. Must you pay? The answer is determined by the law of licensing.

States require licenses for anyone who practices a profession, such as law or medicine, works as a contractor or plumber, and for many other kinds of work. These licenses are required in order to protect the public. States demand that an electrician be licensed because the work is potentially dangerous to a homeowner: the person doing the work must know an amp from a watt. **When a licensing requirement is designed to protect the public, any contract made by an unlicensed worker is unenforceable.** Your friend Foster is unlicensed to practice law. Even though Foster did a fine job with your small claims case, he cannot enforce his contract for $120.

States use other licenses simply to raise money. For example, most states require a license to open certain kinds of retail stores. This requirement does not protect the public, because the state will not investigate the store owner the way it will examine a prospective lawyer or electrician. The state is simply raising revenue. **When a licensing requirement is designed merely to raise revenue, a contract made by an unlicensed person is generally enforceable.** Thus, if you open a stationery store and forget to pay the state's licensing fee, you can still enforce a contract to buy 10,000 envelopes from a wholesaler at a bargain price.

Should the courts take licensing issues so seriously? Ask the homeowners who hired Lee Poole to exterminate bugs.

NEWS*worthy*

Lee Poole told residents of Houma, Louisiana, that he was a professional pest control expert, but he had never obtained a license to do the work. To eliminate roaches and other bugs common in the humid South, he used methyl parathion. The chemical did the job, all right. But methyl parathion is intended to eradicate boll weevils in cotton fields. In humans, the chemical causes nausea, blurred vision, convulsions, and even death. Farmers who use the product must stay out of their fields for 48 hours. Indoors, the toxic substance may remain for years. The Environmental Protection Agency's Emergency Response Branch evacuated dozens of homes in Houma until the poison could be removed. Poole was sentenced to two years in federal prison and ordered to pay $2.19 million to cover the cost of the cleanup (good luck getting the money). Meanwhile, in suburban Chicago, more than 90 homes were evacuated after another unlicensed worker used the same chemical. Who is the real pest here? ◆

Many cases, such as the following one, involve contractors seeking to recover money for work they did without a license.

you Be The Judge

CEVERN, INC. V. FERBISH

666 A.2d 17, 1995 D.C. App. LEXIS 183
District of Columbia Court of Appeals, 1995

Facts: Cevern, Inc. was a small contractor. The company was bonded and insured, as local law required, but it did not have a license to do home improvement work. Cevern applied for such a license, and this is what then happened:

- August 24: The District of Columbia regulatory agency certified that Cevern met all of the requirements for a license (but it did not yet grant the license).

- August 27: Cevern's agents met with Robert Ferbish and Viola Stanton, and the parties signed a contract for Cevern to do extensive work on the Ferbish-Stanton home (to reFerbish it).

- August 31: The owners made an advance payment of $7,000 for the work. Cevern immediately began work on the project, digging a ditch and perhaps erecting a wall.

- September 5: Cevern paid its licensing fee and received the home improvement license.

Ferbish and Stanton later paid an additional $7,000 for Cevern's work but claimed that it was defective. When the owners refused to make a final payment of $10,295, the company sued. Ferbish counterclaimed for the $14,000 already paid, alleging that he and Stanton had spent an additional $43,000 to repair poor-quality work.

The trial court gave summary judgment for Ferbish and Stanton, ruling that Cevern's contract was void and unenforceable because the company had been unlicensed when the parties made the agreement. The judge ordered restitution (repayment) of the $14,000 the owners had paid. Cevern appealed.

You Be the Judge: Was the contract void because Cevern was unlicensed when the parties reached agreement?

Argument for Cevern: We concede that unlicensed contractors generally may not enforce contracts. That rule makes sense, to discourage unqualified companies from doing work that might endanger the public. This is no such case. The District's regulatory agency had already declared that Cevern met all licensing requirements. Cevern had only to pay the fee and collect its license. The company promptly did this and had the license in hand when it performed the bulk of the work. We are not dealing here with some fly-by-night con artist intent upon cheating innocent homeowners. Instead, we have a fully qualified contractor who had met every substantive requirement the law provides, and was merely a few days late in picking up its license. It is the homeowners who seek to pull a fast one: they wish to take advantage of a technical licensing rule to obtain first-rate work for free. Unfair!

Even if the court refuses to enforce the contract, we urge alternatively that it permit Cevern to collect quasi-contract damages. The owners have benefited and know that Cevern expected payment. Cevern should have a chance at trial to prove the extent of the benefit and to collect quantum meruit damages.

Argument for the Owners: Courts in this jurisdiction and around the country have long held that an unlicensed contractor may never enforce contracts. This old rule is designed to protect the public from shoddy work, and it should be enforced for two reasons. First, a contractor may easily comply. All the company needs to do is demonstrate its competence, fill out certain forms, and pay a fee. A contractor unable to do that is a dubious bet. Second, to permit this builder to recover for unlicensed work would encourage other unqualified contractors to try the same ruse: begin the work with glib assurances of a pending license, then hope for the best. If the license application is rejected, the homeowner might never know it, or might feel obligated to let the company finish, creating exactly the peril the rule is designed to avoid. The court should deny quasi-contract damages for the same reason: a void contract deserves no reward. ■

Usury

Henry Paper and Anthony Pugliese were real estate developers. They bought a $1.7 million property in West Palm Beach, Florida, intending to erect an office building. They needed $1 million to start construction but were able to raise only $800,000. Walter Gross, another developer, agreed to lend them the final $200,000 for 18 months at 15 percent interest. Gross knew the partners were desperate for the money, so at the loan closing, he demanded 15 percent equity (ownership) in the partnership, in addition to the interest. Paper and Pugliese had no choice but to sign the agreement. The two partners never repaid the loan, and when Gross sued, the court ruled they need never pay a cent. It pays to understand usury.

Usury laws prohibit charging excess interest on loans. A lender who charges a usurious rate of interest may forfeit the illegal interest, or all interest, or, in some states, the entire loan. Florida permits interest rates of up to 18 percent on loans such as Gross's. A lender who charges more than 18 percent loses the right to collect any interest. A lender who exceeds 25 percent interest forfeits the entire debt. Where was the usury? Just here: when Gross insisted on a 15 percent share of the partnership, he was simply extracting additional interest and disguising it as partnership equity. The Paper–Pugliese partnership had equity assets of $600,000. A 15 percent equity, plus interest payments of 15 percent over 18 months, was the equivalent of a per annum interest rate of 45 percent. Gross probably thought he had made a deal that was too good to be true. And in the state of Florida, it was. He lost the entire debt.[3]

Ethics

Is it fair for Paper and Pugliese to sign a deal and then walk away from it? Analyze the issue by using these items from the checklist in the ethics chapter: Who are the *stakeholders?* Has the *process been fair?* As you ponder these questions, consider the following news report. ◆

NEWSworthy

The highest loan rates go to those least able to pay, the roughly 35 million people who have no bank account. These workers live from paycheck to (small) paycheck. Frequently, they need cash before the next payday. The solution? A check cashing company. These businesses are legal in most but not all states and are typically unregulated, meaning they are free to charge whatever the market bears. It bears a lot.

Joanne, a fast-food worker, has a $200 check coming in two weeks, but she needs money today. She visits Poundaflesh Check Cashers, Inc. and arranges an "advance" on her pay. The stated interest rate is a tolerable 20 percent. But when her paycheck arrives, Joanne needs all of the money to pay the rent. Instead of repaying the loan, she "rolls it over," that is, extends it for another two weeks. Two weeks later, she repeats the process one last time, then finally pays off the loan. Here is what a six-week "advance" ultimately costs her:

Application fee	$ 15
Interest	40 (20% of $200)
First rollover fee (two additional weeks)	50
Second rollover fee (two additional weeks)	50
Total cost of borrowing $200	**$155**

Joanne paid 77 percent interest for a six-week loan—an annual percentage rate of more than *600 percent!* ◆

---

[3] *Jersey Palm-Gross, Inc. v. Paper*, 639 So. 2d 664, 1994 Fla. App. LEXIS 6597 (Fla. Ct. App. 1994).

CONTRACTS THAT VIOLATE PUBLIC POLICY

In the preceding section, we saw that courts refuse to enforce contracts that violate a statute. In this section we examine cases in which no statute applies but where a *public policy* prohibits certain contracts. In other words, we focus primarily on the common law.

Restraint of Trade

Free trade is the basis of the American economy, and any bargain that restricts it is suspect. Most restraint of free trade is barred by antitrust law. But it is the common law that still regulates one restriction on trade: agreements to refrain from competition. Some of these agreements are legal, some are void.

To be valid, an agreement not to compete must be ancillary to a legitimate bargain. "Ancillary" means that the noncompetition agreement must be part of a larger agreement. Suppose Cliff sells his gasoline station to Mina and the two agree that Cliff will not open a competing gas station within five miles anytime during the next two years. Cliff's agreement not to compete is ancillary to the sale of his service station. His noncompetition promise is enforceable. But suppose that Cliff and Mina already had the only two gas stations within 35 miles. They agree between themselves not to hire each other's workers. Their agreement might be profitable to them, because each could now keep wages artificially low. But their deal is ancillary to no legitimate bargain, and it is therefore void. Mina is free to hire Cliff's mechanic despite her agreement with Cliff.

The two most common settings for legitimate noncompetition agreements are the sale of a business and an employment relationship.

Sale of a Business

Kory has operated a real estate office, Hearth Attack, in a small city for 35 years, building an excellent reputation and many ties with the community. She offers to sell you the business and its goodwill for $300,000. But you need assurance that Kory will not take your money and promptly open a competing office across the street. With her reputation and connections, she would ruin your chances of success. You insist on a noncompete clause in the sale contract. In this clause, Kory promises that for one year she will not open a new real estate office or go to work for a competing company within a 10-mile radius of Hearth Attack. Suppose, six months after selling you the business, Kory goes to work for a competing real estate agency two blocks away. You seek an injunction to prevent her from working. Who wins?

When a noncompete agreement is ancillary to the sale of a business, it is enforceable if reasonable in time, geographic area, and scope of activity. In other words, a court will not enforce a noncompete agreement that lasts an unreasonably long time, covers an unfairly large area, or prohibits the seller of the business from doing a type of work that she never had done before. Measured by this test, Kory is almost certainly bound by her agreement. One year is a reasonable time to allow you to get your new business started. A 10-mile radius is probably about the area that Hearth Attack covers, and realty is obviously a fair business from which to prohibit Kory. A court will probably grant the injunction, barring Kory from her new job.

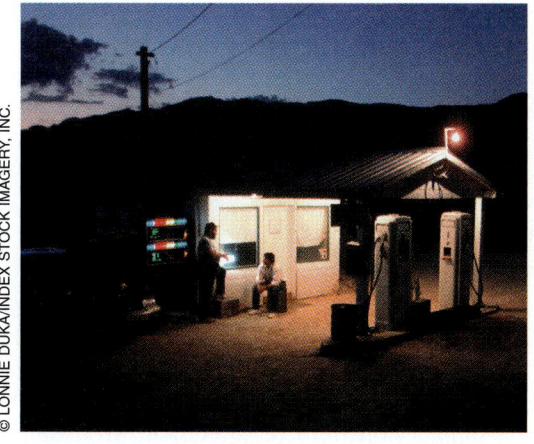

Some agreements to refrain from competition are enforceable and some are not. What is the difference?

If, on the other hand, the noncompetition agreement had prevented Kory from working anywhere within 200 miles of Hearth Attack, and she started working 50 miles away, a court would refuse to enforce the contract. The geographic restriction is unreasonable, since Kory never previously did business 50 miles away, and Hearth Attack is unlikely to be affected if she works there now.

Employment

When you sign an employment contract, the document may well contain a noncompete clause. Employers have legitimate worries that employees might go to a competitor and take with them trade secrets or other proprietary information. Some employers, though, attempt to place harsh restrictions on their employees, perhaps demanding a blanket agreement that the employee will never go to work for a competitor. Once again, courts look at the reasonableness of restrictions placed on an employee's future work. Because the agreement now involves the very livelihood of the worker, a court scrutinizes the agreement more closely.

A noncompete clause in an employment contract is generally enforceable only if it is essential to the employer, fair to the employee, and harmless to the general public. Judges invariably enforce these agreements to protect trade secrets and confidential information. They may protect customer lists that have been expensive to produce. Courts rarely restrain an employee simply because he wants to work for a competitor, and they disfavor agreements that last too long or apply in a very wide area. The following chart summarizes the factors that courts look at in all types of noncompetition agreements.

The Legality of Noncompetition Clauses ("Noncompetes")		
Type of Noncompetition Agreement	**When Enforceable**	
Not ancillary to a sale of business or employment	Never	
Ancillary to a sale of business	If reasonable in time, geography, and scope of activity	
Ancillary to employment	Contract is *more* likely to be enforced when it involves: • Trade secrets or confidential information: these are almost always protected • Customer lists developed over extended period of time and carefully protected • Limited time and geographical scope • Terms essential to protect the employer's business	Contract is *less* likely to be enforced when it involves: • Employee who already had the skills when he arrived, or merely developed general skills on the job • Customer lists that can be derived from public sources • Excessive time or geographical scope • Terms that are unduly harsh on the employee or contrary to public interest

Suppose that Gina, an engineer, goes to work for Fission Chips, a silicon chip manufacturer that specializes in defense work. She signs a noncompete agreement promising never to work for a competitor. Over a period of three years, Gina learns some of Fission's proprietary methods of etching information onto the chips. She acquires a great deal of new expertise about chips generally. And she periodically deals with Fission Chip's customers, all of whom are well-known software and hardware manufacturers. Gina accepts an offer from WriteSmall, a competitor. Fission Chips races into court, seeking an injunction that would prevent Gina from (1) working for WriteSmall; (2) working for any other competitor; (3) revealing any of Fission's trade secrets; (4) using any of the general expertise she acquired at Fission Chips; and (5) contacting any of Fission's customers.

This injunction threatens Gina's career. If she cannot work for a competitor, or use her general engineering skills, what *will* she do? And for exactly that reason, no court will grant such a broad order. The court will allow Gina to work for competitors, including WriteSmall. It will order her not to use or reveal any trade secrets belonging to Fission. She will, however, be permitted to use the general expertise she has acquired, and she may contact former customers since anyone could get their names from the yellow pages.

Was the noncompete in the following case styled fairly, or was the employee clipped?

KING V. HEAD START FAMILY HAIR SALONS, INC.

886 So.2d 769
Supreme Court of Alabama, 2004

Facts: Kathy King was a single mother supporting a college age daughter. For 25 years she had worked as a hair stylist. For the most recent 16 years, she had worked at Head Start, which provided hair cuts, coloring, and styling for men and women. King was primarily a stylist, though she had also managed one of the Head Start facilities.

King quit Head Start and began working as manager of a Sports Clips shop, located in the same mall as the store she just left. Sports Clip offered only hair cuts, and primarily served men and boys. Head Start filed suit, claiming that King was violating the noncompetition agreement that she had signed. The agreement prohibited King from working at a competing business within a two-mile radius of any Head Start facility for 12 months after leaving the company. The trial court issued an injunction enforcing the noncompete. King appealed.

Issue: Was the noncompetition agreement valid?

Excerpts from Justice Lyons's Decision: King's most persuasive argument is that the geographic restriction contained in the noncompetition agreement imposes an undue hardship on her. King has been in the hair-care industry for 25 years, and it is the only industry in which she is skilled and the only industry in which she can find employment. Head Start has 30 locations throughout the Jefferson County and Shelby County area, making it virtually impossible for her to find employment in the hair-care industry at a facility that does not violate the terms of the noncompetition agreement. According to King, the geographic restriction constitutes a blanket prohibition on practicing her trade.

It cannot reasonably be argued that King, at the age of 40 and having spent more than half of her life as a hair stylist, can learn a new job skill that would allow her to be gainfully employed and meet her needs and the needs of her daughter. Under the circumstances presented here, enforcement of the noncompetition agreement works an undue hardship upon King. The noncompetition agreement cannot so burden King that it would result in her impoverishment.

Head Start is nevertheless entitled to some of the protection it sought in the noncompetition agreement. Head Start has a valid concern that King would be able to attract many of her former Head Start customers if she is allowed to provide hair-care services unencumbered by any limitations. To prevent an undue burden on King and to afford some protection to Head Start, the trial court should enforce a more reasonable geographic restriction—such as one prohibiting King from providing hair-care services within a two-mile radius of the location of the Head Start facility at which she was formerly employed or imposing some other limitation that does not unreasonably interfere with King's right to gainful employment while, at the same time, protecting Head Start's interest in preventing King from unreasonably competing with it during the one-year period following her resignation.

Reversed and remanded. ■

Devil's
Advocate

The court decided this case by looking at King's personal circumstances. Enforcement of the agreement (which she signed, fully understanding it) would make it hard for her to support her daughter and herself. Surely that is not how we evaluate a contract. Every defendant in every contract suit finds it inconvenient to fulfill his part of the bargain, which is why the parties are in court. If each defendant is entitled to plead personal difficulties as an excuse for violating the bargain, contracts become useless. Look at it another way. Suppose King had inherited a modest amount of money, and could maintain herself and her daughter while training for a new job. Would the noncompete suddenly be valid? That hardly makes sense. A contract dispute cannot and should not be decided based on the financial difficulties of one party. ◆

Exculpatory Clauses

You decide to capitalize on your expert ability as a skier and open a ski school in Colorado, "Pike's Pique." But you realize that skiing sometimes causes injuries, so you require anyone signing up for lessons to sign this form:

> I agree to hold Pike's Pique and its employees entirely harmless in the event that I am injured in any way or for any reason or cause, including but not limited to any acts, whether negligent or otherwise, of Pike's Pique or any employee or agent thereof.

The day your school opens, Sara Beth, an instructor, deliberately pushes Toby over a cliff because Toby criticized her color combinations. Eddie, a beginning student, "blows out" his knee attempting an advanced racing turn. And Maureen, another student, reaches the bottom of a steep run and slams into a snowmobile that Sara Beth parked there. Maureen, Eddie, and Toby's family all sue Pike's Pique. You defend based on the form you had them sign. Does it save the day?

The form on which you are relying is an **exculpatory clause,** that is, one that attempts to release you from liability in the event of injury to another party. Exculpatory clauses are common. Ski schools use them and so do parking lots, landlords, warehouses, and day-care centers. All manner of businesses hope to avoid large tort judgments by requiring their customers to give up any right to recover. Is such a clause valid? Sometimes. Courts frequently—but not always—ignore exculpatory clauses, finding that one party was forcing the other party to give up legal rights that no one should be forced to surrender.

Exculpatory clauses are important to the operators of ski resorts.

An exculpatory clause is generally unenforceable when it attempts to exclude an intentional tort or gross negligence. When Sara Beth pushes Toby over a cliff, that is the intentional tort of battery. A court will not enforce the exculpatory clause. Sara Beth is clearly liable.[4] As to the snowmobile at the bottom of the run, if a court determines that was gross negligence (carelessness far greater than ordinary negligence), then the exculpatory clause will again be ignored. If, however, it was ordinary negligence, then we must continue the analysis.

An exculpatory clause is generally unenforceable when the affected activity is in the public interest, such as medical care, public transportation, or some essential service. Suppose Eddie

---

4   Note that Pike's Pique is probably not liable, under agency law principles that preclude an employer's liability for an employee's intentional tort.

goes to a doctor for surgery on his damaged knee, and the doctor requires him to sign an exculpatory clause. The doctor negligently performs the surgery, accidentally leaving his cuff links in Eddie's left knee. The exculpatory clause will not protect the doctor. Medical care is an essential service, and the public cannot give up its right to demand reasonable work.

But what about Eddie's suit against Pike's Pique? Eddie claims that he should never have been allowed to attempt an advanced maneuver. His suit is for ordinary negligence, and the exculpatory clause probably *does* bar him from recovery. Skiing is a recreational activity. No one is obligated to do it, and there is no strong public interest in ensuring that we have access to ski slopes.

An exculpatory clause is generally unenforceable when the parties have greatly unequal bargaining power. When Maureen flies to Colorado, suppose that the airline requires her to sign a form contract with an exculpatory clause. Because the airline almost certainly has much greater bargaining power, it can afford to offer a "take it or leave it" contract. The bargaining power is so unequal, though, that the clause is probably unenforceable. Does Pike's Pique have a similar advantage? Probably not. Ski schools are not essential and are much smaller enterprises. A dissatisfied customer might refuse to sign such an agreement and take her business elsewhere. A court probably will not see the parties as grossly unequal.

An exculpatory clause is generally unenforceable unless the clause is clearly written and readily visible. Thus, if Pike's Pique gave all ski students an eight-page contract, and the exculpatory clause was at the bottom of page seven in small print, the average customer would never notice it. The clause would be void.

In the following case, the court focused on the public policy concerns of exculpatory clauses used in a very common setting.

RANSBURG V. RICHARDS

770 N.E.2d 393
Indiana Court of Appeals, 2002

Facts: Barbara Richards leased an apartment at Twin Lakes, a complex owned by Lenna Ransburg. The written lease declared that:

- Twin Lakes would "gratuitously" maintain the common areas.

- Richards' use of the facilities would be "at her own risk."

- Twin Lakes was not responsible for any harm to the tenant or her guests, anywhere on the property (including the parking lot), even if the damage was caused by Twin Lakes' negligence.

It snowed. As Richards walked across the parking lot to her car, she slipped and fell on snow-covered ice. Richards sued Ransburg, who moved for summary judgment based on the exculpatory clause. The trial court denied Ransburg's motion and she appealed.

Issue: Was the exculpatory clause valid?

Excerpts from Judge Barnes's Decision: Resolving the question of whether this lease provision is void as against public policy turns on fairly balancing the parties' freedom to contract against the policy of promoting responsibility for damages caused by one's own negligent acts. We recognize a very strong presumption of enforceability of contracts that represent the freely bargained agreement of the parties. However, in certain circumstances a court may declare an otherwise valid contract unenforceable if it contravenes the public policy of Indiana.

[Some courts have found that the most important principle in these cases is freedom to contract, meaning that the exculpatory clauses are valid. But other courts disagree. One judge declared:]

A tenant must live somewhere. The tenant has no meaningful choices. He can accept this landlord or go to another landlord who charges the same rent and asks the tenant to sign the same standard form lease. But is there any principle which is more familiar or more firmly embedded in the history of Anglo-American law than the basic doctrine that the courts will not permit themselves to be used as instruments of inequity and injustice? The law is not so primitive that it sanctions every injustice except brute force and downright fraud.

A lease is no longer an isolated contract between one landlord and one tenant. The size of the rental industry is so great that construction of an exculpatory clause has an impact on thousands of citizens. Furthermore, the public has an interest in the quality of housing offered for rent to all members of the public.

With these thoughts in mind, we conclude that five factors weigh in favor of not enforcing this type of clause in residential leases. Those factors include: (i) the nature of the subject matter of the contract; (ii) the strength of the public policy underlying the statute; (iii) the likelihood that refusal to enforce the bargain or term will further that policy; (iv) how serious or deserved would be the forfeiture suffered by the party attempting to enforce the bargain; and (v) the parties' relative bargaining power and freedom to contract. Given the vast number of people

clauses like these affect, the inequality of bargaining power caused by the need for housing, the fact that people who are not parties to the contracts could suffer as a result of such clauses, and the desire to promote responsible maintenance by landlords to avoid personal injuries by tenants and third parties, we find that the factors weigh in favor of public policy. We conclude that the exculpatory clause in this residential lease is contrary to public policy insofar as it seeks to immunize Ransburg against damages caused by her negligence, if any, in maintaining common areas.

Affirmed.

Excerpts from Judge Najam's Dissent: The majority opinion nullifies a valid private agreement, rewrites the lease, and reallocates the exchange of costs and benefits between the parties. The majority ignores the plain meaning of the exculpatory clause and violates the well-settled common law right of the parties to make such a provision and to have it enforced according to its terms. In so doing, the majority has unilaterally altered the economic equation in countless residential leases across the state. ■

ECONOMICS & the LAW

Judicial rejection of exculpatory clauses may have a hidden cost, as the dissenting judge in the *Ransburg* case suggests. Presumably, the landlord and tenant each attempted to negotiate the most favorable rent possible, based on the local real estate market. The landlord may have offered a slightly lower rent because of the exculpatory clause. She assumed she could never be found liable for damages. When the court threw the clause out the window, it very effectively notified landlords all across the state that they had better fix up their rental property or obtain more insurance. Landlords probably passed on the increased costs to their tenants, in the form of higher rent. So the court's decision is likely to result in rental units that are safer but more expensive. Some tenants may be pushed down to less desirable apartments, or squeezed out of the market altogether. A judicial ruling that is essentially pro-consumer could leave some families out in the cold. ◆

Bailment Cases

Exculpatory clauses are very common in bailment cases. **Bailment means giving possession and control of personal property to another person.** The person giving up possession is the **bailor,** and the one accepting possession is the **bailee.** When you leave your laptop computer with a dealer to be repaired, you create a bailment. The same is true when you check your coat at a restaurant or lend your Matisse to a museum. Bailees often try to limit their liability for damage to property by using an exculpatory clause.

Judges are slightly more apt to enforce an exculpatory clause in a bailment case, because the harm is to property and not person. But courts will still look at many of the same criteria we have just examined to decide whether a bailment contract is enforceable. In particular, when the bailee is engaged in an important public service, a court is once again likely to ignore the exculpatory clause. The following contrasting cases illustrate this.

In *Weiss v. Freeman*,[5] Weiss stored personal goods in Freeman's self-storage facility. Freeman's contract included an exculpatory clause relieving it of any and all liability. Weiss's goods were damaged by mildew and she sued. The court held the exculpatory clause valid. The court considered self-storage to be a significant business, but not as vital as medical care or housing. It pointed out that a storage facility would not know what each customer stored and therefore could not anticipate the harm that might occur. Freedom of contract should prevail, the clause was enforceable, and Weiss got no money.

In *Gardner v. Downtown Porsche Audi*,[6] Gardner left his Porsche 911 at Downtown for repairs. He signed an exculpatory clause saying that Downtown was "Not Responsible for Loss or Damage to Cars or Articles Left in Cars in Case of Fire, Theft, or Any Other Cause Beyond Our Control." Due to Downtown's negligence, Gardner's Porsche was stolen. The court held the exculpatory clause void. It ruled that contemporary society is utterly dependent upon automobile transportation and Downtown was therefore in a business of great public importance. No repair shop should be able to contract away liability, and Gardner won. (This case also illustrates that using 17 uppercase letters in one sentence does not guarantee legal victory.)

Unconscionable Contracts

Gail Waters was young, naive, and insecure. A serious injury when she was 12 years old left her with an annuity, that is, a guaranteed annual payment for many years. When Gail was 21, she became involved with Thomas Beauchemin, an ex-convict, who introduced her to drugs. Beauchemin suggested that Gail sell her annuity to some friends of his, and she agreed. Beauchemin arranged for a lawyer to draw up a contract, and Gail signed it. She received $50,000 for her annuity, which at that time had a cash value of $189,000 and was worth, over its remaining 25 years, $694,000. Gail later decided this was not a wise bargain. Was the contract enforceable? That depends on the law of unconscionability.

An unconscionable contract is one that a court refuses to enforce because of fundamental unfairness. Historically, a contract was considered unconscionable if it was "such as no man in his senses and not under delusion would make on the one hand, and as no honest and fair man would accept on the other."[7] The two factors that most often led a court to find unconscionability were (1) **oppression,** meaning that one party used its superior power to force a contract on the weaker party, and (2) **surprise,** meaning that the weaker party did not fully understand the consequences of its agreement.

These cases have always been controversial because it is not easy to define oppression and unfair surprise. Further, anytime a court rejects a contract as unconscionable, it diminishes freedom of contract. If one party can escape a deal based on something as hard to define as unconscionability, then no one can rely as confidently on any agreement. This is another of the public policy issues we have seen throughout the law of

---

5   1994 Tenn. App. LEXIS 393 (Tenn. Ct. App. 1993).

6   180 Cal. App. 3d 713, 225 Cal. Rptr. 757, 1986 Cal. App. LEXIS 1542 (Cal. Ct. App. 1986).

7   *Hume v. United States,* 132 U.S. 406, 411, 10 S. Ct. 134, 1889 U.S. LEXIS 1888 (1889), quoting *Earl of Chesterfield v. Janssen,* 38 Eng. Rep. 82, 100 (Ch. 1750).

contracts. As an English jurist said in 1824, "public policy is a very unruly horse, and when once you get astride it you never know where it will carry you."[8] With the creation of the Uniform Commercial Code (UCC), the law of unconscionability got a boost. The Code explicitly adopts unconscionability as a reason to reject a contract.[9] Although officially the Code applies only to the sale of goods, its unconscionability section has proven influential in other cases as well, and courts today are more receptive than they were 100 years ago to a contract defense of fundamental unfairness.

Gail Waters won her case. The Massachusetts high court ruled:

Beauchemin introduced the plaintiff to drugs, exhausted her credit card accounts to the sum of $6,000, unduly influenced her, suggested that the plaintiff sell her annuity contract, initiated the contract negotiations, was the agent of the defendants, and benefited from the contract between the plaintiff and the defendants. The defendants were represented by legal counsel; the plaintiff was not. The cash value of the annuity policy at the time the contract was executed was approximately four times greater than the price to be paid by the defendants. For payment of not more than $50,000 the defendants were to receive an asset that could be immediately exchanged for $189,000, or they could elect to hold it for its guaranteed term and receive $694,000.

The defendants assumed no risk and the plaintiff gained no advantage. We are satisfied that the disparity of interests in this contract is so gross that the court cannot resist the inference that it was improperly obtained and is unconscionable.[10]

Adhesion Contracts

A related issue concerns **adhesion contracts,** which are standard form contracts prepared by one party and given to the other on a "take it or leave it" basis. We have all encountered them many times when purchasing goods or services. When a form contract is vigorously negotiated between equally powerful corporations, the resulting bargain is generally enforced. However, when the contract is simply presented to a consumer, who has no ability to bargain, it is an adhesion contract and subject to an unconscionability challenge.

WORLDWIDE INSURANCE V. KLOPP

603 A.2d 788, 1992 Del. LEXIS 13
Supreme Court of Delaware, 1992

Facts: Ruth Klopp had auto insurance with Worldwide. She was injured in a serious accident that left her with permanent neck and back injuries. The other driver was uninsured, so Klopp filed a claim with Worldwide under her "uninsured motorist" coverage. Her policy required arbitration of such a claim, and the arbitrators awarded Klopp $90,000. But the policy also stated that if the arbitrators awarded more than the statutory minimum amount of insurance ($15,000), either side could appeal the award and request a full trial. Worldwide appealed and demanded a trial.

8 *Richardson v. Mellish,* 2 Bing. 229, 103 Eng. Rep. 294, 303 (1824).
9 UCC §2-302.
10 *Waters v. Min Ltd.,* 412 Mass. 64, 587 N.E.2d 231, 1992 Mass. LEXIS 66 (1992).

In the trial court, Klopp claimed that the appeal provision was unconscionable and void. The trial court agreed and entered judgment for the full $90,000. Worldwide appealed.

Issue: Is the provision that requires arbitration and then permits appeal by either party void as unconscionable?

Excerpts from Justice Walsh's Decision: The parties' views of the arbitration provision are polar opposites. Worldwide contends that the provision is a clear and unambiguous contractual undertaking granting both the insured and the insurer the right to appeal any award in excess of financial responsibility limits. Klopp argues that this provision is unconscionable and void as against public policy because it affords an advantage to one of the parties under a contract of adhesion.

The public policy of this State favors the resolution of disputes through arbitration. An insurance policy which provides for arbitration as its primary mechanism for dispute resolution is thus enforceable against the wishes of either contractual party. [But] our approval of the arbitration concept does not extend to any feature of a contract of adhesion, which, in whole or in part, is unconscionable.

Under the present policy language both parties are bound by a low award which an insurance company is unlikely to appeal. While high awards may be appealed by either party, common experience suggests that it is unlikely that an insured would appeal such an award. It is the insurer who, generally, would be dissatisfied with a high award. The policy provision thus presents an "escape hatch" to the insurer for avoidance of high arbitration awards, whether or not the award was fair and reasonable. However, the insured, who would tend to be dissatisfied with a low award, is barred from appealing such an award, i.e., an award under [$15,000].

In our view, the policy provision at issue here promotes litigation, circumvents the arbitration process and provides an arbitration escape device in favor of an insurance company. So viewed, the provision is contrary to the public policy of this State. Accordingly, we hold that a provision in an insurance policy which allows either party to demand a trial de novo, if the amount of an arbitrators' award exceeds a stated minimum amount but denies review for lesser awards, is void as against public policy and unenforceable. The Chancery Court was correct in striking this unconscionable clause.

The judgment of the Court of Chancery is *affirmed.* ■

Unconscionability and Sales Law

As mentioned above, the drafters of the UCC reinforced the principle of unconscionability by including it in the Code.

Section 2-302 provides:

> If the court as a matter of law finds the contract or any clause of the contract to have been unconscionable at the time it was made the court may refuse to enforce the contract, or it may enforce the remainder of the contract without the unconscionable clause, or it may so limit the application of any unconscionable clause as to avoid any unconscionable result.

In Code cases, the issue of unconscionability often arises when a company attempts to limit the normal contract law remedies. Yet the Code itself allows such limitations, provided they are reasonable.

Section 2-719 provides in part:

> [A contract] may provide for remedies in addition to or in substitution for those provided [by the Code itself] *and may limit or alter the measure of damages recoverable* . . . as by limiting the buyer's remedies to return of the goods and repayment of the price. . . .

In other words the Code includes two potentially competing sections. Section 2-719 permits a seller to insist that the buyer's only remedy for defective goods is return of the purchase price. But §2-302 says that *any unconscionable* provision is unenforceable.

In lawsuits concerning defective goods, the seller often argues that the buyer's only remedies are those stated in the agreement, and the buyer responds that the contract limitation is unconscionable.

Electronic Data Systems (EDS) agreed to create complex software for Chubb Life America at a cost of $21 million. Chubb agreed to make staggered payments over many months, as work proceeded. The contract included a limitation on remedies, stating that if EDS became liable to Chubb, its maximum liability would be equal to two monthly payments.

EDS's work was woefully late and completely unusable, forcing Chubb to obtain its software elsewhere. Chubb sued, claiming $40 million in damages, based on money paid to EDS and funds spent purchasing alternative goods. EDS argued that the contract limited its liability to two monthly payments, a fraction of Chubb's damage. Chubb of course responded that the limitation was unconscionable.

The court noted that both parties were large, sophisticated corporations. As they negotiated the agreement, the companies both used experienced attorneys and independent consultants. This was no contract of adhesion presented to a meek consumer, but an allocation of risk resulting from hard bargaining. The court declared that the clause was valid and EDS owed no more than two monthly payments.[11]

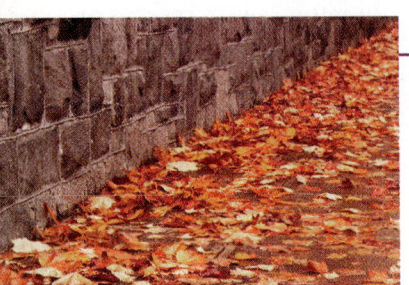

© BRAND X PICTURES/GETTY IMAGES

Chapter Conclusion

It is not enough to bargain effectively and obtain a contract that gives you exactly what you want. You must also be sure that the contract is legal. What appears to be an insurance contract might legally be an invalid wager. Unintentionally forgetting to obtain a state license to perform a certain job could mean you will never be paid for it. Bargaining a contract with a noncompete or exculpatory clause that is too one-sided may lead a court to ignore it. Legality is many faceted, sometimes subtle, and always important.

Chapter Review

Illegal contracts are void and unenforceable. Illegality most often arises in these settings:

1. *Wagering.* A purely speculative contract—whether for gambling or insurance—is likely to be unenforceable.

2. *Licensing.* When the licensing statute is designed to protect the public, a contract by an unlicensed plaintiff is generally unenforceable. When such a statute is designed merely to raise revenue, a contract by an unlicensed plaintiff is generally enforceable.

3. *Usury.* Excessive interest is generally unenforceable and may be fatal to the entire debt.

4. *Noncompete.* A noncompete clause in the sale of a business must be limited to a reasonable time, geographic area, and scope of activity. In an employment contract, such a clause is considered reasonable—and enforceable—only to protect trade secrets, confidential information, and customer lists.

5. *Exculpatory Clauses.* These clauses are generally void if the activity involved is in the public interest, the parties are greatly unequal in bargaining power, or the clause is unclear. In other cases they are generally enforced.

6. *Unconscionability.* Oppression and surprise may create an unconscionable bargain. An adhesion contract is especially suspect when it is imposed

---

[11] *Colonial Life Insurance Co. v. Electronic Data Systems Corp.,* 817 F. Supp. 235, 1993 U.S. Dist. LEXIS 4123 (D.N.H. 1993).

by a corporation on a consumer or small company. Under the UCC, a limitation of liability is less likely to be unconscionable when both parties are sophisticated corporations.

Practice Test

1. At a fraternity party, George mentions that he is going to learn to hang glide during spring break. Vicki, a casual friend, overhears him, and the next day she purchases a $100,000 life insurance policy on George's life. George has a happy week of hang gliding, but on the way home he is bitten by a parrot and dies of a rare tropical illness. Vicki files a claim for $100,000, but the insurance company refuses to pay.

    a. Vicki will win $100,000 but only if she mentioned animal bites to the insurance agent.

    b. Vicki will win $100,000 regardless of whether she mentioned animal bites to the insurance agent.

    c. Vicki will win $50,000.

    d. Vicki will win nothing.

2. For 20 years, Art's Flower Shop relied almost exclusively on advertising in the yellow pages to bring business to its shop in a small West Virginia town. One year the yellow pages printer accidentally omitted to print Art's ad, and Art's suffered an enormous drop in business. Art's sued for negligence and won a judgment of $50,000 from the jury, but the printing company appealed, claiming that under an exculpatory clause in the contract, the company could not be liable to Art's for more than the cost of the ad, about $910. Art's claimed that the exculpatory clause was unconscionable. Please rule.

3. James Wagner agreed to build a house for Nancy Graham. Wagner was not licensed as a contractor and Graham knew it. When the house was finished, Graham refused to pay the final $23,000, and Wagner sued. Who will prevail?

4. Brockwell left his boat to be repaired at Lake Gaston Sales. The boat contained electronic equipment and other personal items. Brockwell signed a form stating that Lake Gaston had no responsibility for any loss to any property in or on the boat. Brockwell's electronic equipment was stolen and other personal items were damaged, and he sued. Is the exculpatory clause enforceable?

5. McElroy owned 104 acres worth about $230,000. He got into financial difficulties and approached Grisham, asking to borrow $100,000. Grisham refused, but ultimately the two reached this agreement: McElroy would sell Grisham his property for $80,000, and the contract would include a clause allowing McElroy to repurchase the land within two years for $120,000. McElroy later claimed the contract was void. Is he right?

6. **ETHICS** Richard and Michelle Kommit traveled to New Jersey to have fun in the casinos. While in Atlantic City, they used their MasterCard to withdraw cash from an ATM conveniently located in the "pit," which is the gambling area of a casino. They ran up debts of $5,500 on the credit card and did not pay. The Connecticut National Bank sued for the money. What argument should the Kommits make? Which party, if any, has the moral high ground here? Should a casino offer ATM services in the gambling pit? If a credit card company allows customers to withdraw cash in a casino, is it encouraging them to lose money? Do the Kommits have any ethical right to use the ATM, attempt to win money by gambling, and then seek to avoid liability?

7. Guyan Machinery, a West Virginia manufacturing corporation, hired Albert Voorhees as a salesman and required him to sign a contract stating that if he left Guyan he would not work for a competing corporation anywhere within 250 miles of West Virginia for a two-year period. Later, Voorhees left Guyan and began working at Polydeck Corp., another West Virginia manufacturer. The only product Polydeck made was urethane screens, which comprised half of 1 percent of Guyan's business. Is Guyan entitled to enforce its noncompete clause?

8. KwikFix, a Fortune 500 company, contracts with Allied Rocket, another huge company, to provide the software for Allied's new Jupiter Probe rocket for $14 million. The software is negligently designed, and when the rocket blasts off from Cape Kennedy, it travels only as far as Fort Lauderdale. Allied Rocket sues for $200 million

and proves that as a result of the disaster it lost a huge government contract, worth at least that much, which KwikFix was aware of. KwikFix responds that its contract with Allied included a clause limiting its liability to the value of the contract. Is the contract clause valid?

a. The clause is unenforceable because it is unconscionable.

b. The clause is unenforceable because it is exculpatory.

c. The clause is enforceable because both parties are sophisticated corporations.

d. The clause is enforceable because $200 million is an unconscionable claim.

9. 810 Associates owned a 42-story skyscraper in midtown Manhattan. The building had a central station fire alarm system, which was monitored by Holmes Protection. A fire broke out and Holmes received the signal. But Holmes's inexperienced dispatcher misunderstood the signal and failed to summon the fire department for about nine minutes, permitting tremendous damage. 810 sued Holmes, which defended based on an exculpatory clause that relieved Holmes of any liability caused in any way. Holmes's dispatcher was negligent. Does it matter *how* negligent he was?

10. *YOU BE THE JUDGE* WRITING PROBLEM Oasis Waterpark, located in Palm Springs, California, sought out Hydrotech Systems, Inc., a New York corporation, to design and construct a surfing pool. Hydrotech replied that it could design the pool and sell all the necessary equipment to Oasis, but could not build the pool because it was not licensed in California. Oasis insisted that Hydrotech do the construction work because Hydrotech had unique expertise in these pools. Oasis promised to arrange for a licensed California contractor to "work with" Hydrotech on the construction; Oasis also assured Hydrotech that it would pay the full contract price of $850,000, regardless of any licensing issues. Hydrotech designed and installed the pool as ordered. But Oasis failed to make the final payment of $110,000. Hydrotech sued. Can Hydrotech sue for either breach of contract or fraud (trickery)? **Argument for Oasis:** The licensing law protects the public from incompetence and dishonesty. The legislature made the section strict: no license, no payment. If the court were to start picking and choosing which unlicensed contractors could win a suit, it would be inviting incompetent workers to endanger the public and then come into court and try their luck. That is precisely the danger the legislature seeks to avoid. **Argument for Hydrotech:** This is not the kind of case the legislature was worried about. Hydrotech has never solicited work in California. Hydrotech went out of its way to avoid doing any contracting work, informing Oasis that it was unlicensed in the state. Oasis insisted on bringing Hydrotech into the state to do work. If Oasis has its way, word will go out that any owner can get free work done by hiring an *unlicensed* builder. Make any promises you want, get the work done to your satisfaction, and then stiff the contractor—you'll never have to pay.

11. The purchaser of a business insisted on putting this clause in the sales contract: The seller would not compete, for five years, "anywhere in the United States, the continent of North America, or anywhere else on earth." What danger does that contract represent *to the purchaser?*

12. *ROLE REVERSAL* Write one multiple-choice question with two noncompete clauses, one of which is valid and the other void.

Internet Research Problem

At http://beatty.westbuslaw.com, choose any state, and then search for that state's law on Internet gambling. Is it legal in that state? Has the state attempted to regulate this subject in any way? Do you believe the state will succeed? Conduct the same search in a second state and compare the results of the two searches.

You can find further practice problems at http://beatty.westbuslaw.com or in the Study Guide that accompanies this text.

Capacity and Consent

For Kevin Green, it was love at first sight. She was sleek, as quick as a cat, and a beautiful deep blue. He paid $4,600 cash for the used Camaro. The car soon blew a gasket, and Kevin demanded his money back. But the Camaro came with no guarantee, and the dealer refused. Kevin repaired the car himself. Next, some unpleasantness on the highway left the car a worthless wreck. Kevin received the full value of the car from his insurance company. Then he sued the dealer, seeking a refund of his purchase price. The dealer pointed out that it was not responsible for the accident, and that the car had no warranty of any kind. Yet the trial court awarded Kevin the full $4,600. How can this be? Should Kevin receive the full purchase price for a demolished car? ■

© AKIRA KAEDE/PHOTODISC/GETTY IMAGES

According to the trial court, the automobile dealer made a basic mistake of law. It ignored *legal capacity*. Kevin Green was only 16 years old when he bought the car, and a minor, said the court, has the right to cancel any agreement he made anytime he wants to, for any reason. We will see how the appellate court resolved the case, as we examine two related issues: capacity and consent.

Capacity concerns the legal ability of a party to enter a contract. Someone may lack capacity because of his young age or mental infirmity. Consent refers to whether a contracting party truly understood what he was getting into and whether he made the agreement voluntarily. Consent issues arise in cases of fraud, mistake, duress, and undue influence.

CAPACITY

Capacity is the legal ability to enter into a contract. An adult of sound mind has the legal capacity to contract. Generally, any deal she enters into will be enforced if all elements we have seen—agreement, consideration, and so forth—are present. But two groups of people usually lack legal capacity: minors and those with a mental impairment.

Minors

A minor is someone under the age of 18. Because a minor lacks legal capacity, she normally can create only a voidable contract. **A voidable contract may be canceled by the party who lacks capacity.** Notice that *only the party lacking capacity* may cancel the agreement. So a minor who enters into a contract generally may choose between enforcing the agreement or negating it. The other party, however, has no such right. Voidable contracts are very different from those that are void, which we examined in Chapter 13, on legality. A *void* contract is illegal from the start and may not be enforced by either party. A *voidable* contract is legal, but permits one party to escape.

Disaffirmance

A minor who wishes to escape from a contract generally may **disaffirm** it; that is, he may notify the other party that he refuses to be bound by the agreement. There are several ways a minor may disaffirm a contract. He may simply tell the other party, orally or in writing, that he will not honor the deal. The minor also has the option of filing a suit to **rescind** the contract, that is, to have a court formally cancel it. Or he may disaffirm a contract simply by refusing to perform his obligations under it.

Kevin Green was 16 when he signed a contract with Star Chevrolet. Since he was a minor, the deal was voidable. When the Camaro blew a gasket and Kevin informed Star Chevrolet that he wanted his money back, he was disaffirming the contract. He happened to do it because the car suddenly seemed a poor buy, but notice that he could have disaffirmed for any reason at all, such as deciding that he no longer liked Camaros. When Kevin disaffirmed, he was entitled to his money back. If Star Chevrolet had understood the law of capacity, it would have towed the Camaro away and returned Kevin's $4,600. At least Star would have had a repairable automobile.

Restitution

A minor who disaffirms a contract must return the consideration he has received, to the extent he is able. Restoring the other party to its original position is called **restitution.** The consideration that Kevin Green received in the contract was, of course, the Camaro. If Star Chevrolet had delivered a check for $4,600, Kevin would have been obligated to return the car.

What happens if the minor is not able to return the consideration because he no longer has it or it has been destroyed? Most states hold that the minor is still entitled to his money back. A minority of states refuse to rescind a contract when the minor cannot return the consideration. Star appealed to the Mississippi Supreme Court, arguing that the state should join those that refuse disaffirmance when a minor cannot make restitution.

STAR CHEVROLET CO. V. GREEN

473 So. 2d 157, 1985 Miss. LEXIS 2141
Supreme Court of Mississippi, 1985

Facts: The facts are summarized in the opening paragraph of this chapter.

Issue: Is Kevin Green entitled to disaffirm the contract with Star Chevrolet even though the Camaro has been destroyed?

Excerpts from Justice Sullivan's Decision: Some general principles warrant restatement. First, the right of a minor to disaffirm his contract is based upon sound public policy to protect the minor from his own improvidence and the overreaching of adults. It is the policy of the law to discourage adults from contracting with minors and the adult cannot complain if, as a consequence of his violation of this rule of conduct, he is injured by the minor's exercise of the right of disaffirmance, since this injury might have been avoided if the adult had declined to enter into the contract.

Second, if upon disaffirmance the minor has in his possession the specific property or any part of it which he received he must return it. Third, the general rule is that upon disaffirmance of a minor's contract, he is required to return the consideration only if it is still in his possession. The minor who disaffirms a contract is not obliged to return the consideration received by him or its equivalent where during his minority he has wasted, squandered, destroyed, used, or otherwise disposed of the consideration.

Turning to the facts of this case, the minor clearly had the consideration, i.e. the vehicle, in his possession when he first notified appellant of the disaffirmance of the contract. Had appellant offered the minor, as the law required, a full refund of his purchase price, the minor clearly would have been required to return the vehicle. Instead, the appellant did not, and while suit was pending the minor repaired the vehicle and began to use it. There is no hint in the record that the accident which destroyed the vehicle was the result of any deliberate design on the minor's part to fraudulently deprive appellant of that which would have placed him in status quo.

[Judgment for Kevin Green, despite the fact that he cannot return the car.][1] ■

Ethics

As the Mississippi court tells us, the rule permitting a minor to disaffirm a contract is designed to discourage adults from making deals with innocent children. The rule is centuries old. But is this rule workable in our consumer society? There are entire industries devoted to (and dependent upon) minors. Think of children's films, and music, and sneakers, and toys. Does this rule imperil retailers? Who are the *stakeholders*? What are the *consequences*? ◆

Timing of Disaffirmance/Ratification

A minor may disaffirm a contract anytime before she reaches age 18. She also may disaffirm within a reasonable time *after* turning 18. Suppose that 17-year-old Betsy signs a contract to buy a $3,000 stereo. The following week she picks up the system and pays for it in full. Four months later she turns 18, and two months after that she disaffirms the contract. Her disaffirmance is effective. In most states, she gets 100 percent of her

---

[1] The court awarded Kevin $3,100, representing the $4,600 purchase price minus $1,500, which was the salvage value of the car when he delivered it to his insurance company. You may wonder why Kevin Green is permitted to keep the insurance money *and* his original purchase price, thus putting him in a better position than he was in before buying the Camaro. The reason is the *collateral source rule,* which states that a defendant (Star Chevrolet) that is found to owe the plaintiff (Green) money may not have its liability reduced because the plaintiff will be compensated by another source (the insurance company). The rule is routinely applied in tort cases. Many courts refuse to use it in contract cases, but the Mississippi court applied it, and as a result, Kevin was in the green.

Does Betsy have the capacity to sign a contract for a stereo?

money back. In some cases minors have been entitled to disaffirm a contract several *years* after turning 18. But the minor's right to disaffirm ends if she later ratifies the contract.

If a minor enters into a contract and then, after turning 18, ratifies the deal, she loses her right to disaffirm and the agreement becomes fully enforceable. **Ratification** is made by any words or action indicating an intention to be bound by the contract. Suppose Betsy, age 17, buys her stereo on credit, promising to pay $150 per month. She has made only four payments by the time she turns 18, but after reaching her majority she continues to pay every month for six more months. Then she attempts to disaffirm. Too late. Her payment of the monthly bill for six months as an adult ratified the contract she entered into as a minor. She is now fully obligated to pay the entire $3,000, on the agreed-upon schedule.

Exception: Necessaries

A necessary is something essential to the minor's life and welfare. **On a contract for necessaries, a minor must pay for the value of the benefit received.** In other words, the minor may still disaffirm the contract and return whatever is unused. But he is liable to pay for whatever benefit he obtained from the goods while he had them. Food, clothing, housing, and medical care are necessaries. Thus a 16-year-old who seeks emergency medical care and signs an agreement to pay for it is probably liable for the full bill. She has received the benefit of the services and must pay. A car, in most states, is *not* considered to be a necessary. Star Chevrolet argued that Kevin's Camaro ought to be considered a necessary, but the Mississippi court followed the general rule and held that it was not.

Exception: Misrepresentation of Age

The rules change somewhat if a minor lies about his age. Sixteen-year-old Dan is delighted to learn from his friend Betsy that a minor can buy a fancy stereo system, use it for a year or so, and then get his money back. Dan drops into SoundBlast and asks to buy a $9,000 surround-sound system. The store clerk says that the store no longer sells expensive systems to punks. Dan produces a fake driver's license indicating that he is 19, and the clerk sells him the system. Two years later, Dan drives up to SoundBlast and unloads the system, now in shambles. He asks for his $9,000 back. Is he still permitted to disaffirm?

States have been troubled by this problem, and there is no clear rule. A few states will still permit Dan to disaffirm the contract entirely. The theory is that a minor must be saved from his own poor judgment, including his foolish lie. Many states, though, will prohibit Dan from disaffirming the contract. They take the reasonable position that the law was intended to protect childhood innocence, not calculated deceit.

Mentally Impaired Persons

You are a trial court judge. Don wants you to rule that his father, Cedric, is mentally incompetent and, on behalf of Cedric, to void a contract he signed. Here is the evidence:

Cedric is a 75-year-old millionaire who keeps $300,000 stuffed in pillow cases in the attic. He lives in a filthy house with a parrot, whom he calls the Bishop, an iguana named Orlando, and a tortoise known as Mrs. Sedgely. All of the pets have small beds in Cedric's grungy bedroom, and each one eats at the food-encrusted dining table with its master. Cedric pays college students $50 an hour to read poetry to the animals, but forbids reading any sonnets, which he regards as "the devil's handiwork." Don has been worried about Cedric's bizarre behavior for several years and has urged his father to enter a nursing home. Last week, when Don stopped in to visit, Cedric became angry at him, accusing his son of "dissing" the Bishop and Mrs. Sedgely, who were, according to Cedric, enjoying a fifteenth-century Castilian poem that Jane, a college student, was reading. Don then blurted out that Cedric was no longer able to take care of himself. Cedric snapped back, "I'll show you how capable I am." On the back of a 40-year-old menu he scratched out a contract, promising to give Jane "$100,000 today and $200,000 one year from today if she agrees to feed, house, and care for the Bishop, Orlando, and Mrs. Sedgely for the rest of their long lives." Jane promptly signed the agreement. Don urges that the court, on Cedric's behalf, declare the contract void. How will you rule? Courts often struggle when deciding cases of mental competence.

A person suffers from a mental impairment if by reason of mental illness or defect he is unable to understand the nature and consequences of the transaction.[2] The mental impairment can be insanity that has been formally declared by a court or mental illness that has never been ruled on but is now evident. The impairment may also be due to some other mental illness, such as schizophrenia, or to mental retardation, brain injury, senility, or any other cause that renders the person unable to understand the nature and consequences of the contract.

A party suffering a mental impairment generally creates only a voidable contract. The impaired person has the right to disaffirm the contract just as a minor does. But again, the contract is voidable, not void. The mentally impaired party generally has the right to full performance if she wishes.[3]

The law presumes that an adult is mentally competent. As always, courts respect the freedom to contract. Anyone seeking to avoid a contract because of mental impairment has the burden of proving the infirmity, since "mental incompetence" could be a very handy way out of a deal gone sour.

How will a court evaluate Cedric's mental status? Of course, if there had already been a judicial determination that he was insane, any contract he signed would be voidable. In fact, in some states his agreements would be void. Since no judge has issued such a ruling about Cedric, the court will listen to doctors or therapists who have evaluated him and to anyone else who can testify about Cedric's recent conduct. Finally, the court may choose to look at the contract itself, to see if it is so lopsided that no competent person would agree to it.

How will Don fare in seeking to preserve Cedric's wealth? Poorly. Unless Don has more evidence than we have heard thus far, he is destined to eat canned tuna while Jane and the Bishop dine on caviar. Cedric is unclean, decidedly eccentric, and possibly unwise. But none of those characteristics proves mental impairment. Neither does leaving a fortune to a poetry reader. If Don could produce evidence from a psychiatrist that Cedric, for example, was generally delusional or could not distinguish a parrot from a religious leader, that would persuade a court of mental impairment. But on the evidence presented thus far, Mrs. Sedgely and friends will be living well.[4]

---

[2] Restatement (Second) of Contracts §15.

[3] As mentioned below, in many states it is the law that if a court has actually judged someone legally insane, a contract he enters into is entirely void, not just voidable.

[4] For a similar case, see *Harwell v. Garrett*, 239 Ark. 551, 393 S.W.2d 256, 1965 Ark. LEXIS 1033 (1965).

Intoxication

Similar rules apply in cases of drug or alcohol intoxication. When one party is so intoxicated that he cannot understand the nature and consequences of the transaction, the contract is voidable. Toby's father gives him a new Jaguar sports car for his birthday, and foolish Toby celebrates by getting drunk. Amy, realizing how intoxicated he is, induces Toby to promise in writing that he will sell his car to her the next day for $1,000. Toby may void the contract and keep his auto.

Restitution

A mentally infirm party who seeks to void a contract must make restitution. If a party succeeds with a claim of mental impairment, the court will normally void the contract but will require the impaired party to give back whatever she got. Suppose Danielle buys a Rolls-Royce and promises in writing to pay $3,000 per month for five years. Three weeks later she seeks to void the contract on the grounds of mental impairment. She must return the Rolls. If the car has depreciated, Danielle normally will have to pay for the decrease in value. What happens if restitution is impossible? Generally, courts require a mentally infirm person to make full restitution if the contract is to be rescinded. If restitution is impossible, the court will not rescind the agreement unless the infirm party can show bad faith by the other. This is because, unlike minority, which is generally easy to establish, mental competence may not be so apparent to the other person negotiating.

REALITY OF CONSENT

Smiley offers to sell you his house for $300,000, and you agree in writing to buy. After you move in, you discover that the house is sinking into the earth at the rate of six inches per week. In 12 months, your only access to the house will be through the chimney. You sue, asking to rescind. You argue that when you signed the contract you did not truly consent because you lacked essential information. In this section we look at four claims that parties make in an effort to rescind a contract based on lack of valid consent: (1) misrepresentation or fraud, (2) mistake, (3) duress, and (4) undue influence.

Misrepresentation and Fraud

Misrepresentation occurs when a party to a contract says something that is factually wrong. "This house has no termites," says a homeowner to a prospective buyer. If the house is swarming with the nasty pests, the statement is a misrepresentation. The misrepresentation might be innocent or fraudulent. If the owner believes the statement to be true and has a good reason for that belief, he has made an **innocent misrepresentation.** If the owner knows that it is false, the statement is **fraudulent misrepresentation.** To explain these concepts, we will assume that two people are discussing a possible deal. One is the "maker," that is, the person who makes the statement that is later disputed. The other is the "injured person," the one who eventually claims to have been injured by the statement. In order to rescind the contract, the injured person must show that the maker's statement was *either* fraudulent *or* a material misrepresentation. She does not have to show both. Innocent misrepresentation and fraud each make a contract voidable and permit the injured party to rescind. **To rescind a contract based on misrepresentation or fraud, a party must show three things: (1) there**

was a false statement of fact; (2) the statement was fraudulent or material; and (3) the injured person justifiably relied on the statement.

Element One: False Statement of Fact

The injured party must show a false statement of fact. Notice that this does not mean the statement was a lie. If a homeowner says that the famous architect Stanford White designed his house, but Bozo Loco actually did the work, it is a false statement. The owner might have a good reason for the error. Perhaps a local history book identifies the house as a Stanford White. Or his words might be an intentional lie. In either case, it is a false statement of fact.

An opinion, though, is not a statement of fact. A realtor says, "I think land values around here will be going up 20 or 30 percent for the foreseeable future." That statement is pretty enticing to a buyer, but it is not a false statement of fact. The maker is clearly stating her own opinion, and the buyer who relies on it does so at his peril. Although there are exceptions, most opinions are no basis to rescind a contract. A close relative of opinion is something called "puffery."

Puffery. Get ready for one of the most astonishing experiences you've ever had! This section on puffery is going to be the finest section of any textbook you have ever read! You're going to find the issue intriguing, the writing dazzling, and the legal summary succinct and literally unforgettable!! "But what happens," you might wonder, "if this section fails to astonish? What if I find the issue dull, the writing mediocre, and the legal summary incomprehensible? Can I sue for misrepresentation?" No. The promises we made were mere puffery. A statement is puffery when a reasonable person would realize that it is a sales pitch, representing the exaggerated opinion of the seller. Puffery is not a statement of fact. Because puffery is not factual, it is never a basis for rescission.

Marie Rodio purchased auto insurance from Allstate and then, after she was involved in a serious accident, received from the company less money than she thought fair. She sued, arguing that the company had committed fraud by advertising that customers would be in "good hands." She lost when the state supreme court ruled that, even if she could prove the company did not treat her well, the ad was mere puffery and not fraud.[5] "The finest automobile you will ever drive" is another example of puffery, as is "The smoothest taste in the world" or "The Sale of the Century." In none of those cases will a disappointed party be allowed to rescind.

That brings us to the end of the section on puffery. The writing was pretty poor, but you still may not sue.

Element Two: Fraud or Materiality

This is the heart of the case. The injured party must demonstrate that the statement was fraudulent *or* material:

- The statement was *fraudulent* if the maker intended to induce the other party to contract, either knowing that her words were false or uncertain that they were true.

- The statement was *material* if the maker expected the other party to rely on her words in reaching an agreement.

Consider the examples in the following chart. In case 1, the homeowner tells a prospective buyer that the heating system works perfectly, when he knows that it barely functions, leaving some rooms suitable only for penguins. The words are fraudulent.

In case 2, the homeowner is not lying when he says his cliff house is built on solid bedrock, but he is making a statement without being certain of its truth. This is also fraud.

---

[5] *Rodio v. Smith*, 123 N.J. 345, 587 A.2d 621, 1991 N. J. LEXIS 21 (1991).

By contrast, in case 3 there is no fraud because the homeowner is acting in good faith. He says that the roof is six years old because half a dozen years ago the previous owner said it was new. In fact, the roof is 25 years old and will soon need replacement. The homeowner's statement is a *material misrepresentation* because it is incorrect and the owner expects the buyer to rely on it.

Finally, in case 4 the homeowner says that the swimming pool is 30 feet long because he measured it himself. But he did the job incorrectly, and the pool is only 29 feet. This is another misrepresentation, but is it *material?* No. An error of a foot or so would not influence a reasonable purchaser, and this buyer has failed to prove her case.

The Difference between Fraud and Misrepresentation

Statement. In each case, the words are false.	Owner's Belief	Legal Result	Explanation
1. "The heating system is perfect."	Owner knows this is false.	Fraud.	Owner knew the statement was false and intended to induce the buyer to enter into a contract.
2. "The house is built on solid bedrock."	Owner has no idea what is under the surface.	Fraud.	Owner was not certain the statement was true and intended to induce the buyer to enter into a contract.
3. "The roof is only six years old."	Owner has a good reason to believe the statement is true.	Material misrepresentation.	Owner acted in good faith, but the statement is material because owner expects the buyer to rely on it.
4. "The pool is 30 feet long."	Owner has a good reason to believe the statement is true.	Not a material misrepresentation.	Although this is a misrepresentation, it is not material, since a reasonable buyer would not make a decision based on a one-foot error in the pool length.

Element Three: Justifiable Reliance

The injured party must also show that she actually did rely on the false statement and that her reliance was reasonable. Suppose the seller of a gas station lies through his teeth about the structural soundness of the building. The buyer believes what he hears but does not much care, because he plans to demolish the building and construct a day-care center. There was fraud but no reliance, and the buyer may not rescind.

The reliance must be justifiable, that is, reasonable. If the seller of wilderness land tells Lewis that the area is untouched by pollution, but a large lake is permanently covered with six inches of thick red scum, Lewis is not justified in relying on the seller's statements. If he goes forward with the purchase, he may not rescind.

No Duty to Investigate. Lewis must act reasonably and keep his eyes open as he walks around the "wilderness" property. But he has no duty to undertake an investigation of what he is told. In other words, if the seller states that the countryside is pure and the lake looks crystal clear, Lewis is not obligated to take water samples and have them tested by a laboratory. A party to a contract has no duty to investigate the other party's factual statements. In the following case, a group of buyers not only alleged fraud, but claimed that the misleading statements were part of a well-orchestrated scam.

HOFFMAN V. STAMPER

2005 WL 263996
Court of Appeals of Maryland, 2005

Facts: Nine plaintiffs in Baltimore sued various defendants, claiming fraud in an elaborate "flipping" scheme. The plaintiffs alleged that Robert Beeman purchased dilapidated houses in poor sections of Baltimore, searched for unsophisticated, low-income buyers, and promised them a renovated home for a mere $500 down payment. Beeman had the buyers sign contracts for greatly inflated prices. Working with a mortgage company officer named Joyce Wood, he obtained 100 percent financing through the Department of Housing and Urban Development, needing only an appraisal to obtain the money. Arthur Hoffman supplied the necessary appraisal at exactly the sales price, and the buyers took possession—only to find that no repairs had been made.

The jury awarded all nine plaintiffs diverse amounts for their economic losses, plus $145,000 each for emotional harm and $200,000 each in punitive damages. Most of the defendants appealed. This part of the appeal focuses on the appraiser, Hoffman.

Issue: Did Hoffman commit fraud?

Excerpts from Justice Wilner's Decision: Beeman purchased the property at 17 N. Kresson Street for $14,500. Less than three weeks later he sold the property to McFadden for $52,000. When the property was sold to McFadden, it was in the same condition as when Beeman bought it. Hoffman, knowing that Beeman had only recently bought the property for $14,500, appraised the property for $52,000. There were a number of deficiencies noted in that report. A glaring, though relatively minor, one was that Hoffman reported that the property was in a residential zone, when, in fact, it was in a manufacturing zone.

Hoffman noted that the property was in "poor condition" when purchased by Beeman but was in "good" condition "now." That could not have been so, for, on an attached Valuation Condition sheet, he listed 14 repairs that still needed to be made, from replacing rotted wood on the porch floor and ceiling, to repairing chipped paint in various parts of the house, to installing a downspout and gutter, to patching, pointing, and painting parts of the house, to replacing windows.

The plaintiffs' expert appraiser described the Kresson Street property as being part of a residential "pocket" surrounded by industrial use properties and fronting on a "heavy truck traffic" road. The three properties used by Hoffman as comparable sales were all in residential areas quite some distance away.

[The court describes similar abuses as to all the properties.]

The evidence—clear and convincing—showed a pattern in all of the appraisals of:

1. actual knowledge by Hoffman in some cases and the ability to know in others, that Beeman had purchased the properties only months earlier for a fraction of what Hoffman appraised them for;

2. an attempt by Hoffman to justify the huge inflation, at least in part, by assuming that major improvements would be made to the properties when, in fact, many of those improvements were not made and, had Hoffman made a reasonable effort to investigate that critical assumption, he would have known that they were not made; and

3. a further attempt by Hoffman to justify the actual appraisal by positing as comparable the sale of distant properties that were not at all comparable.

▼

The end result of this consistent pattern was a seemingly automatic appraisal, in each case, at or just in excess of whatever the contract price happened to be. Hoffman derived 99 percent of his income from appraisals done for [Joyce Wood's mortgage company, and] he knew if the appraisal did not match the contract price, the deal would fall through. He was dependent on Wood for his livelihood, Wood was dependent on people like Beeman for her livelihood, and Hoffman made it all work.

[Affirmed as to Hoffman's liability.] ■

Public Policy

Notice the origin of this scam: a well-intended federal policy, administered by HUD, to help low-income buyers purchase homes they could not obtain in the private market. The assumption is that communities will be stronger when residents have a financial stake in the neighborhood. Where there is federal money, though, there are those who will prey upon it. Government agencies and local prosecutors must be vigilant in guarding public funds. In this case, it was the "unsophisticated" buyers who punished the wrongdoers, using plain old contract law. ◆

Plaintiff's Remedy for Misrepresentation or Fraud

Both innocent and fraudulent misrepresentation permit the injured party to rescind the contract. In other words, the injured party who proves all three elements will get her money back. She will, of course, have to make restitution to the other party. If she bought land and now wants to rescind, she will get her money back but must return the property to the seller.

But the injured party is not forced to rescind the deal if it makes financial sense to go forward with it. After signing a contract to buy a new house, Nancy learns that the building has a terrible heating system. A new one will cost $12,000. If the seller told her the system was "like new," Nancy may rescind the deal. But it may be economically harmful for her to do so. She might have sold her old house, hired a mover, taken a new job, and so forth. She has the option of fully performing the contract and moving into the new house. What are her other remedies? That will depend on whether the misstatement ("the system is like new") was fraudulent or simply a material misrepresentation.

If the maker's statement is fraudulent, the injured party generally has a choice of rescinding the contract or suing for damages. If the seller's mistake was fraudulent, Nancy will generally be allowed to carry out the contract and sue for damages. She could move into the new house and sue for the difference between what she got and what was promised, which is probably about $12,000, the cost of replacing the heating system. But if the seller's mistake was innocent, and Nancy can prove only material misrepresentation, she has no remedy other than rescission. If she chooses to go forward with the contract, she must accept the house the way she finds it.

Finally, in some states a party injured by fraud may both rescind *and* sue for damages. In these states, Nancy could rescind her contract, get her deposit back, and then sue the seller for any damages she has suffered. Her damages might be, for example, a lost opportunity to buy another house or wasted moving expenses.

Sale of Goods

This last option—rescinding and still suing for damages—is available in all states when the contract is for the sale of goods. **UCC §2-721 permits a party to rescind a contract and then sue for damages, whether the misrepresentation was fraudulent or innocent.**

Ted Seaton bought a car (a Chevy Camaro—what else?) from Lawson Chevrolet. It was a demonstrator that had a few thousand miles on it but was supposedly in like-new condition. In fact, a salesman had wrecked the car, which had then been substantially rebuilt. Lawson knew this but did not tell Seaton. After Seaton bought the car for

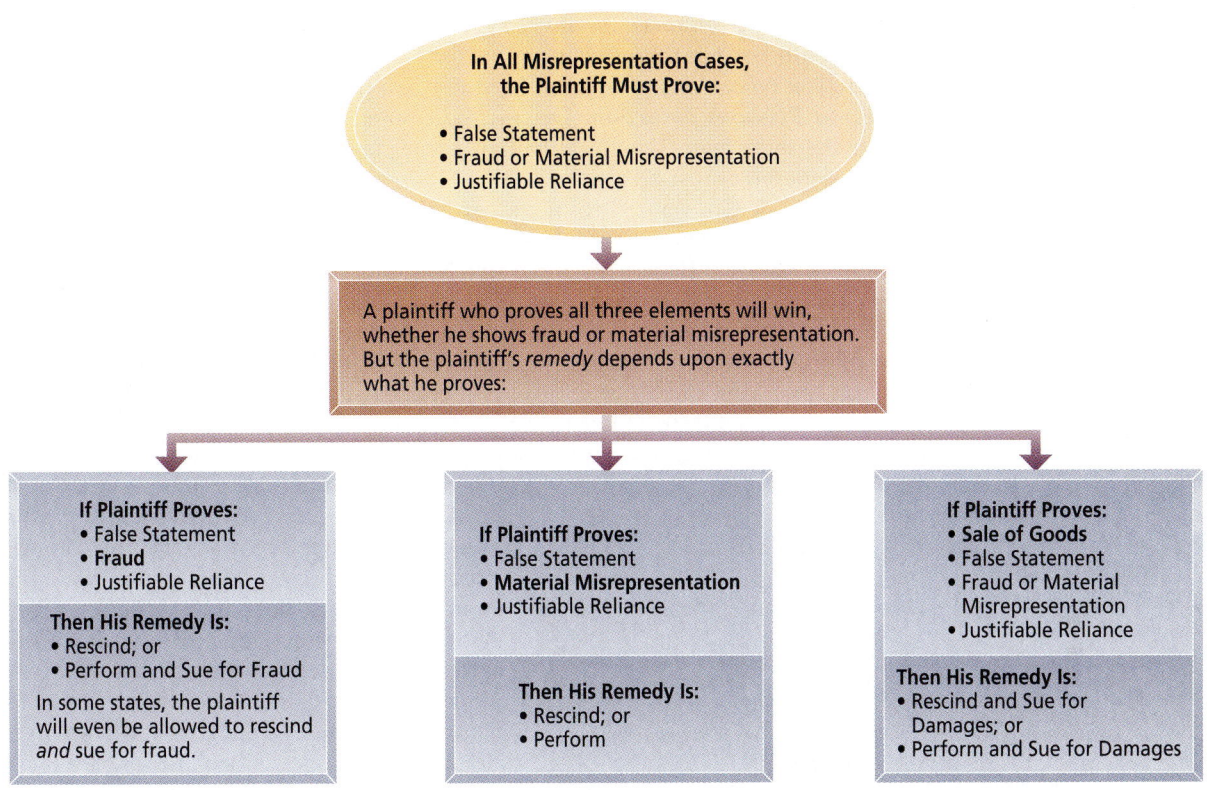

In All Misrepresentation Cases, the Plaintiff Must Prove:

- False Statement
- Fraud or Material Misrepresentation
- Justifiable Reliance

A plaintiff who proves all three elements will win, whether he shows fraud or material misrepresentation. But the plaintiff's *remedy* depends upon exactly what he proves:

If Plaintiff Proves:
- False Statement
- **Fraud**
- Justifiable Reliance

Then His Remedy Is:
- Rescind; or
- Perform and Sue for Fraud

In some states, the plaintiff will even be allowed to rescind *and* sue for fraud.

If Plaintiff Proves:
- False Statement
- **Material Misrepresentation**
- Justifiable Reliance

Then His Remedy Is:
- Rescind; or
- Perform

If Plaintiff Proves:
- **Sale of Goods**
- False Statement
- Fraud or Material Misrepresentation
- Justifiable Reliance

Then His Remedy Is:
- Rescind and Sue for Damages; or
- Perform and Sue for Damages

Exhibit 14.1

$13,000, he discovered the fraud and sued. Seaton won rescission, getting back his $13,000. But this was the sale of goods, so Seaton was entitled to seek money damages as well. The court awarded him $20,000 punitive damages, based upon Lawson's deliberate deceit.[6] See Exhibit 14.1.

Special Problem: Silence

We know that a party negotiating a contract may not misrepresent a material fact. The house seller may not say that "the roof is in great shape" when she sleeps under an umbrella to avoid rain. But what about silence? Suppose the seller knows the roof is in dreadful condition but the buyer never asks. Does the seller have an affirmative obligation to disclose what she knows?

This is perhaps the hottest topic today in the law of misrepresentation. In 1817 the United States Supreme Court laid down the general rule that a party had no duty to disclose, even when he knew that the other person was negotiating under a mistake.[7] In other words, the Court was reinforcing the old rule of *caveat emptor,* "let the buyer beware." But social attitudes about fairness have changed. Today, a seller who knows something that the buyer does not know is often required to divulge it. The Restatement (Second) of Contracts offers guidance:

Nondisclosure of a fact amounts to misrepresentation only in these four cases: (1) where disclosure is necessary to *correct a previous assertion;* (2) where disclosure

---

[6]   *Seaton v. Lawson Chevrolet-Mazda, Inc.,* 821 S.W.2d 137, 1991 Tenn. LEXIS 440 (Tenn. 1991).
[7]   *Laidlaw v. Organ,* 15 U.S. 178, 1817 U.S. LEXIS 396 (1817).

would correct a *basic mistaken assumption* that the other party is relying on; (3) where disclosure would correct the other party's *mistaken understanding about a writing;* or (4) where there is *a relationship of trust* between the two parties.[8]

To Correct a Previous Assertion. During the course of negotiations, one party's perception of the facts may change. When an earlier statement later appears inaccurate, the change generally must be reported.

W. R. Grace & Co. wanted to buy a natural-gas field in Mississippi. An engineer's report indicated large gas reserves. On the basis of the engineering report, the Continental Illinois National Bank committed to a $75 million nonrecourse production loan. A "nonrecourse loan" meant that Continental would be repaid only with revenues from the gas field. After Continental committed but before it had closed on the loan, Grace had an exploratory well drilled and struck it rich—with water. The land would never produce any gas. Without informing Continental of the news, Grace closed the $75 million loan. When Grace failed to repay, Continental sued and won. A party who learns new information indicating that a previous statement is inaccurate must disclose the bad news.[9]

Must a seller disclose problems that lie beneath the surface?

To Correct a Basic Mistaken Assumption. When one party knows that the other is negotiating with a mistaken assumption about an important fact, the party who knows of the error must correct it. Jeffrey Stambovsky agreed to buy Helen Ackley's house in Nyack, New York, for $650,000. Stambovsky signed a contract and made a $32,500 down payment. Before completing the deal, he learned that in several newspaper articles Ackley had publicized the house as being haunted. Ackley had also permitted the house to be featured in a walking tour of the neighborhood as "a riverfront Victorian (*with ghost*)." Stambovsky refused to go through with the deal and sued to rescind. He won. The court ruled that Ackley sold the house knowing Stambovsky was ignorant of the alleged ghosts. She also knew that a reasonable buyer might avoid a haunted house, fearing grisly events—or diminished resale value. Stambovsky could not have discovered the apparitions himself, and Ackley's failure to warn permitted him to rescind the deal.[10]

A seller generally must report any latent defect he knows about that the buyer should not be expected to discover himself. As social awareness of the environment increases, a buyer potentially worries about more and more problems. We now know that underground toxic waste, carelessly dumped in earlier decades, can be dangerous or even lethal. Accordingly, any property seller who realizes that there is toxic waste underground must reveal that fact.

To Correct a Mistaken Understanding about a Writing. Suppose the potential buyer of a vacation property has a town map showing that the land he wants to buy has a legal right of way to a beautiful lake. If the seller of the land knows that the town map is out of date, and that there is no such right of way, she must disclose her information.

---

8   Restatement (Second) of Contracts §161.
9   *FDIC v. W.R. Grace & Co.,* 877 F.2d 614, 1989 U.S. App. LEXIS 8905 (7th Cir. 1989).
10 *Stambovsky v. Ackley,* 169 A.D.2d 254, 572 N.Y.S.2d 672, 1991 N.Y. App. Div. LEXIS 9873 (N.Y. App. Div. 1991).

A Relationship of Trust. Maria is planning to sell her restaurant to her brother Ricardo. Maria has a greater duty to reveal problems in the business because Ricardo assumes she will be honest. **When one party naturally expects openness and honesty, based on a close relationship, the other party must act accordingly.** If the building's owner has told Maria he will not renew her lease, she must pass that information on to Ricardo.

As mentioned above, most courts require a property seller to disclose hidden defects. The judge in the following case states the rule somewhat differently, but the outcome is the same.

FIMBEL V. DECLARK

695 N.E.2d 125
Indiana Court of Appeals, 1998

Facts: Ronald and Patricia Fimbel bought two lakefront lots on Lake Latonka in Indiana, intending to build a summer cottage. However, they discovered that the soil was not suitable for a septic system. They would have to hire an engineer at a substantial expense to determine if it was even possible to construct an alternative system. They decided to sell the land.

The Fimbels met with several interested buyers, including Thomas and Joan DeClark. The Fimbels said nothing about the septic problems. The DeClarks bought the property and, one week later, learned that the property was unbuildable. They sued, and the trial court granted them rescission. The Fimbels appealed.

Issue: Did the Fimbels have a duty to disclose the septic problems?

Excerpts from Judge Staton's Decision: Initially, the Fimbels contend that they cannot be held liable in fraud for failing to disclose the soil condition of the lots since they were under no duty to do so. Ordinarily a seller is not bound to disclose any material facts unless there exists a relationship for which the law imposes a duty of disclosure. Courts have found such a relationship, and therefore a duty to disclose, where the buyer makes inquiries about a condition on, the qualities of, or the characteristics of the property. When a buyer makes such inquiries, it becomes incumbent upon the seller to fully declare any and all problems associated with the subject of the inquiry.

The evidence supports the conclusion that the DeClarks and Fimbels had conversations which imposed a duty upon the Fimbels to disclose the unsuitability of the lots for home construction. Mr. DeClark testified that, while viewing the lots, he asked Mr. Fimbel if he had ever intended to build a home on them. According to Mr. DeClark, Mr. Fim-

bel stated that he was going to build, but he ultimately decided that he preferred some property he owned in Minnesota, noting its peacefulness and that he had a friend that lives there. Mr. DeClark told Mr. Fimbel that he wanted to build a home on the lots. The above inquiry and statement sufficiently introduced the issue of home construction into the parties' transaction such that a duty was imposed on the Fimbels to disclose the information they had regarding the suitability of the lots for residential construction.

The Fimbels also contend that they made no misrepresentation of fact as to whether a home could be constructed on the lots. True, the Fimbels never expressly stated whether or not a home could be constructed on the lots. However, this does not insulate the Fimbels from a judgment in fraud. If a seller undertakes to disclose facts within his knowledge, he must disclose the whole truth without concealing material facts and without doing anything to prevent the other party from making a thorough inspection. For, if in addition to his silence, there is any behavior of the seller which points affirmatively to a suppression of the truth or to a withdrawal or distraction of the other parties' attention to the facts, the concealment becomes fraudulent.

In this case, Mr. Fimbel told Mr. DeClark that the reason he never built on the lots was that he preferred other property. The record is unclear as to whether this was indeed a factor as to the Fimbels' decision not to build on Lake Latonka. Nevertheless, the preference for the other property is, at best, only one reason for not building on Lake Latonka: the other being the inability to place a septic system on the land. One cannot be allowed, under the law, to *partially* disclose the facts as he knows them to be, yet create a false impression in the mind of the hearer by failing to fully reveal the true state of

▼

affairs. At best, Mr. Fimbel's response was only a partial disclosure of the reasons he did not build at Lake Latonka, and, at worst, the response was a misrepresentation of the true reason a home was never erected on the site.

The statement by Mr. DeClark at closing that he intended to build on the lots appears to have been met with silence. Given the circumstances, this silence can also support a judgment for fraud. Silence accompanied by deceptive conduct, results in active concealment, and is actionable.

Affirmed. ■

Ethics

There are various disclosure rules that a state *could* adopt:

- *Caveat emptor*—let the buyer beware.

- Seller has a duty to disclose only if asked.

- Seller has a duty to disclose regardless of whether asked.

- Seller's only duty is to notify buyer of important considerations that *buyer* may wish to investigate (soil condition, building laws, problems with neighboring property, etc.).

Which rule do you prefer, and why? As you answer this question, apply these concepts from the Chapter 2 ethics checklist: What are the alternatives? What outcome does the Golden Rule require? ◆

Mistake

Most contract principles come from appellate courts, but in the area of "legal mistake" a cow wrote much of the law. The cow was Rose 2d of Aberlone, a gentle animal that lived in Michigan in 1886. Rose's owner, Hiram Walker & Sons, had bought her for $850. After a few years, the company concluded that Rose could have no calves. As a barren cow she was worth much less, so Walker contracted to sell her to T. C. Sherwood for $80. But when Sherwood came to collect Rose, the parties realized she was pregnant. Walker refused to part with the happy mother, and Sherwood sued. Walker defended, claiming that both parties had made a mistake and that the contract was voidable.

Mistake can occur in many ways. It may be a basic error about the quality of the thing being sold, as in Rose's case. It could be an erroneous prediction about future prices, such as an expectation that oil prices will rise. It might be a mechanical error, such as a builder offering to build a new home for $300 when he clearly meant to bid $300,000. Some mistakes lead to voidable contracts, others create enforceable deals. The first distinction is between bilateral and unilateral mistakes.

Bilateral Mistake

A **bilateral mistake** occurs when both parties negotiate based on the same factual error. Sherwood and Walker both thought Rose was barren, both negotiated accordingly, and both were wrong. The Michigan Supreme Court gave judgment for Walker, the seller, permitting him to rescind the contract because the parties were both wrong about the essence of what they were bargaining for.

If the parties contract based on an important factual error, the contract is voidable by the injured party. Sherwood and Walker were both wrong about Rose's reproductive ability, and the error was basic enough to cause a tenfold difference in price. Walker, the injured party, was entitled to rescind the contract. Note that the error must be *factual*. Suppose Walker sold Rose thinking that the price of beef was going to drop, when in fact the price rose 60 percent in five months. He made a mistake, but it was simply a business prediction that proved wrong. Walker would have no right to rescind.

Conscious Uncertainty. No rescission is permitted where one of the parties knows he is taking on a risk, that is, he realizes there is uncertainty about the quality of the thing being exchanged. Rufus offers 10 acres of mountainous land to Priscilla. "I can't promise you anything about this land," he says, "but they've found gold on every adjoining parcel." Priscilla, panting with gold lust, buys the land, digs long and hard, and discovers—mud. She may not rescind the contract. She understood the risk she was assuming, and there was no mutual mistake.

Unilateral Mistake

Sometimes only one party enters a contract under a mistaken assumption, a situation called **unilateral mistake.** In these cases it is more difficult for the injured party to rescind a contract. This makes sense, since in a bilateral error neither side really knew what it was getting into, and rescission seems a natural remedy. But with unilateral mistake, one side may simply have made a better bargain than the other. As we have seen throughout this unit on contracts, courts are unwilling to undo an agreement merely because someone made a foolish deal. Nonetheless, if her proof is strong enough, the injured party in a case of unilateral mistakes still may rescind the contract.

To rescind for unilateral mistake, a party must demonstrate that she entered the contract because of a basic factual error and that either (1) enforcing the contract would be unconscionable or (2) the nonmistaken party knew of the error.[11]

Courts are suspicious of unilateral mistake. A contractor who makes a computational error in making a bid may obtain rescission; others seeking this remedy generally fail. Town obtains five bids for construction of a new municipal swimming pool. Four are between $100,000 and $111,000. Fred's bid is for $82,000. His offer includes a figure of $2,000 for excavation work, while the others have allotted about $20,000 for that work. Fred has inadvertently dropped a zero, resulting in a bid that is $18,000 too low. Town officials accept Fred's offer. When he sues to rescind, Fred wins. Town officials knew that the work could not be done that cheaply, and it would be unfair to hold Fred to a mathematical error that the other side perceived.[12]

In contrast, suppose that Rebecca sues Pierce, whose bad driving caused an accident, and Amy, who owned the car that Pierce was operating. While the case is pending, Amy's insurance company, Risknaught, pays Rebecca a $700,000 settlement. Later, the state's supreme court rules that Pierce was an unauthorized driver and an owner's insurer is never liable in such a case. Risknaught seeks to rescind its settlement, claiming unilateral mistake as to its liability. The company loses. Risknaught was aware that an appellate ruling might establish new precedent. The insurer settled based on a decision calculated to minimize its risk.[13]

In the following case an automobile dealer made a mistake—how often does *this* happen?—in the customer's favor.

DONOVAN V. RRL CORPORATION

26 Cal.4th 261, 27 P.3d 702, 109 Ca. Rptr.2d 807
Supreme Court of California, 2001

Facts. Brian Donovan was in the market for a used car. As he scanned the Costa Mesa *Daily Pilot*, he came upon a "Pre-Owned Coup-A-Rama Sale!" at Lexus of Westminster. Of the 16 cars listed in the ad (with vehicle identification numbers), one was a sapphire blue Jaguar XJ6 Vanden Plas, priced at $25,995. ▼

---
11 Restatement (Second) of Contracts §153.
12 See examples provided in Restatement (Second) of Contracts §153.
13 See, e.g., *AID Hawai'i Ins. Co. v. Bateman*, 82 Haw. 453, 923 P.2d 395 (Haw. 1996).

Brian drove to a Jaguar dealership to do some comparison shopping. Jaguars of the same year and mileage cost about $8,000 to $10,000 more than the auto at the Lexus agency. The next day, Brian and his wife hurried over to the Coup-A-Rama event, spotted the Jaguar (which had the correct VIN) and asked a salesperson if they might test drive it. Pleased with the ride, Brian said to the salesman, "O.K. We will take it at your price, $26,000." This figure startled the sales representative, who glanced at the newspaper ad Brian showed him, and responded, "That's a mistake."

As indeed it was. The Lexus agency had paid $35,000 for the Jaguar, and intended to sell it for about $37,000. Brian was adamant. "No, I want to buy it at your advertised price, and I will write you a check right now." The sales manager was called in, and he refused to sell the car for less than $37,000.

It turned out that the *Daily Pilot's* typographical and proofreading errors had caused the mistake, although the Lexus dealership had failed to review the proof sheet, which would have revealed the error before the ad went to press.

Brian sued. The trial court found that unilateral mistake prevented enforcement of the contract. The appellate court reversed, and Donovan appealed to the state's highest court.

The state supreme court first ruled that there *was* in fact a contract between the parties. Generally, a newspaper advertisement is merely a solicitation for an offer, and does not permit the customer to form a contract by accepting. (See Chapter 11, on agreement.) However, a California statute generally holds automobile dealers to the terms of their offers. The court then went on to examine the mistake.

Issue: Did the Lexus dealer's mistake entitle it to rescind the contract?

Excerpts from Justice George's Decision: A significant error in the price term of a contract constitutes a mistake regarding a basic assumption upon which the contract is made, and such a mistake ordinarily has a material effect adverse to the mistaken party. The defendant must show that the resulting imbalance in the agreed exchange is so severe that it would be unfair to require the defendant to perform.

Measured against this standard, defendant's mistake in the contract for the sale of the Jaguar automobile constitutes a material mistake regarding a basic assumption upon which it made the contract. Enforcing the contract with the mistaken price of $25,995 would require defendant to sell the vehicle to plaintiff for $12,000 less than the intended advertised price of $37,995—an error amounting to 32 percent of the price defendant intended. The exchange of performances would be substantially less desirable for defendant and more desirable for plaintiff.

The mere fact that a mistaken party could have avoided the mistake by the exercise of reasonable care does not preclude avoidance on the ground of mistake. Indeed, since a party can often avoid a mistake by the exercise of such care, the availability of relief would be severely circumscribed if he were to be barred by his negligence. Nevertheless, in *extreme cases* the mistaken party's fault is a proper ground for denying him relief for a mistake that he otherwise could have avoided. . . .

If we were to accept plaintiff's position that that the dealer always must be held to the strict terms of a contract arising from an advertisement, we would be holding that the dealer intended to assume the risk of all typographical errors in advertisements, no matter how serious the error and regardless of the circumstances in which the error was made. For example, if an automobile dealer proofread an advertisement but, through carelessness, failed to detect a typographical error listing a $75,000 automobile for sale at $75, the defense of mistake would be unavailable to the dealer.

No evidence presented at trial suggested that defendant knew of the mistake before plaintiff attempted to purchase the automobile, that defendant intended to mislead customers, or that it had adopted a practice of deliberate indifference regarding errors in advertisements. The uncontradicted evidence established that the *Daily Pilot* made the proofreading error resulting in defendant's mistake.

We conclude that the municipal court correctly entered judgment in defendant's favor. ■

Duress

True consent is also lacking when one party agrees to a contract under **duress.** If kindly Uncle Hugo signs over the deed to the ranch because Niece Nelly is holding a Colt .45 to his head, Hugo has not consented in any real sense, and he will have the right to rescind the contract. **If one party makes an improper threat that causes**

the victim to enter into a contract, and the victim had no reasonable alternative, the contract is voidable.[14] The key issues are thus whether there was an improper threat and whether the victim had a reasonable alternative.

On a Sunday morning, Bancroft Hall drove to pick up his daughter Sandra, who had slept at a friend's house. The Halls are black and the neighborhood was white. A suspicious neighbor called the police, who arrived, aggressively prevented the Halls from getting into their own car, and arrested the father. The officers took Hall to the police station for booking but eventually realized there might be some problems with the arrest, since neither of the Halls had violated any law or done anything wrong whatsoever. An officer told Hall that he could leave immediately if he signed a full release (stating that he had no claims of any kind against the police), but that if he refused to sign it he would be detained for a bail hearing. Hall signed the release, but later filed suit for false arrest, false imprisonment, battery, and civil rights violations. The police defended based on the release.

The court held that the release was voidable because Hall had signed it under duress. The threat to detain Hall for a bail hearing was clearly improper because he had committed no crime. He also had no reasonable alternative to signing. The Halls' suit went to trial, where the jury awarded them compensatory and punitive damages, plus attorney's fees, totaling over $525,000.[15]

How do we distinguish hard bargaining from economic duress?

Economic Duress

If improper threats can permit one party to rescind a contract, then why not *economic* intimidation? Many plaintiffs have posed that question over the last half century, and courts have grudgingly yielded. Today, in most but not all states, economic duress can also be used to void a contract. But economic duress sounds perilously close to hard competition, in other words—business. The free market system is expected to produce tough competition. A smart, aggressive executive may bargain fiercely. How do we distinguish economic duress from successful business tactics? Courts have created no single rule to answer the question, but they do focus on certain issues.

In analyzing a claim of economic duress, courts look at these factors:

- Acts that have no legitimate business purpose
- Greatly unequal bargaining power
- An unnaturally large gain for one party
- Financial distress to one party

Is the following case one of duress or hard bargaining?

---

[14] Restatement (Second) of Contracts §175(1).
[15] *Halls v. Ochs*, 817 F.2d 920, U. S. App. LEXIS 5822 (1st Cir. 1987).

you Be The Judge

IN RE RLS LEGAL SOLUTIONS, L.L.C.

2005 WL 171381
Texas Court of Appeals, 2005

Facts: Amy Maida sued her employer, RLS Legal Solutions, for various claims relating to her job. RLS asked that the case be dismissed, because Maida had signed an arbitration agreement. Maida had in fact signed the contract while already working at MLS. However, she responded that the agreement should not be enforced because she had signed it under economic duress. At trial, she was asked whether she had found the agreement acceptable:

> I did not. The arbitration clause was going to allow me not to be able to be in a position that I needed to be in now, and that is, to have someone represent me to help me where I feel like the company did me wrong.
>
> After I refused to agree to this arbitration clause, I was told that my payroll checks would not be direct deposited into my account until I signed the agreement and that I would not be paid until I signed the agreement. I had received my paychecks by direct deposit for three years. [RLS did in fact stop the direct deposit payment of Maida's salary.]
>
> I needed my paycheck to meet my financial responsibilities since I am a single family income household provider. I had no way to pay my mortgage, vehicle note, car and homeowner's insurance as well as any household bills.

Maida testified that after signing and returning the agreement, she received a manual check. Maida said that when she asked why she had not been paid by direct deposit as usual, she was told her paycheck would be held until she signed the agreement.

RLS argued that Maida had eventually received every pay check to which she was entitled, had suffered no losses, and was free to leave RLS at any time if she found her employment terms unacceptable.

The trial court refused to dismiss the case or order arbitration, and RLS appealed.

You Be the Judge: Did Maida sign the arbitration under economic duress?

Argument for RLS: Your honors, it is hard to take seriously a claim of economic duress when the plaintiff has not lost one cent and was never forced to sign anything. RLS runs a business, not a community center. To stay competitive, we constantly revise our commercial practices, and this was one such change. We did not ask for some bizarre or inappropriate change: Arbitration is a widely favored method of settling disputes, quicker and cheaper *for all parties.* Maida signed. Yes, we stopped direct deposit of her check, but we paid her. We were not obligated to pay her in any particular fashion, or even to continue her employment. If she wanted to stay with us, she had to play by our rules.

Argument for Maida: The company could offer an arbitration contract to all workers. But that is distinct from forcing such agreements down employee throats, which is what they did here. RLS knows that its workers depend on prompt payment of payroll checks to avoid falling quickly into debt. The company offered Maida the arbitration agreement, she rejected it, and they responded by stopping direct deposit of her check. Knowing that she was the sole provider for her family, the firm intended to subject her to intolerable economic pressure. It worked. However, the court should have no part of this coercion. The two sides had hugely differing bargaining power, and RLS attempted to use financial distress to obtain what it could not by persuasion. ∎

Undue Influence

She was single and pregnant. A shy young woman in a large city with no family nearby, she needed help and support. She went to the Methodist Mission Home of Texas where she found room and board, support—and a lot of counseling. Her discussions with a minister and a private counselor stressed one point: that she should give up her baby for adoption. She signed the adoption papers, but days later she decided she wanted the baby after all. Was there any ground to rescind? She claimed *undue influence*, in other words, that the Mission Home so dominated her thinking that she never truly consented. Where one party has used undue influence, the contract is voidable at the option of the injured party. There are two elements to the plaintiff's case. **To prove undue influence, the injured party must demonstrate:**

- A relationship between the two parties either of trust or of domination, and
- Improper persuasion by the stronger party.[16]

In other words, a party seeking to rescind based on undue influence must first show that the parties had some close bond, either because one would normally have trusted and relied on the other or because one was able to dominate the other. Second, the party seeking to rescind must show improper persuasion, which is an effort by the stronger party to coerce the weaker one into a decision that she otherwise would not have made.

In the Methodist Mission case, the court held that the plaintiff had been young and extremely vulnerable during the days following the birth of her child. The mission's counselor, to whom she turned for support, had spent day after day forcefully insisting that the young woman had no moral or legal right to keep her child. The harangue amounted to undue influence. The court voided the adoption agreement.[17] In the following case, the age difference is reversed.

SEPULVEDA V. AVILES

762 N.Y.S. 2d 358, 308 A.D.2d 1
New York Supreme Court, Appellate Division, 2003

Facts: Agnes Seals owned and lived in a ten-unit apartment building on East 119th Street in New York City. When she was 80 years old, a fire damaged much of the building's interior, leaving Seals physically and mentally unable to care for the property. Shortly after the fire, she met David Aviles, a 35-year-old neighbor. Aviles convinced Seals to sell him the building, promising to care for her for the rest of her life. She sold him the building for $50,000, taking a down payment of $10,000, with the rest to be paid over time. At the closing, Seals was represented by an attorney, Martin Freedman, whom she had never met before, and who had been referred to her by Aviles's lawyer (with whom he shared office space).

Three years later, Seals died. Her will left her entire estate to Elba and Victor Sepulveda, but the building had been Seals's principal asset. The Sepulvedas sued Aviles, asking the court to set aside the sale of the building, claiming that Aviles had used undue influence to trick Seals into a sale that was not in her interest. The jury found that Aviles had not used undue influence, and the Sepulvedas appealed.

Issue: Did Aviles use undue influence to obtain the apartment building?

Excerpts from Judge Gonzalez's Decision: The jury's verdict here was completely at odds with any fair interpretation of the evidence. The trial testimony established that at the time of the transfer, Seals was an 80-year-old woman in declining health who had recently suffered a traumatic crisis resulting from [the fire], requiring her to vacate the premises for two months. The testimony of social worker Blair established that only 16 months after the conveyance, Seals was totally homebound and dependent on others,

▼

---

16 Restatement (Second) of Contracts §177.

17 *Methodist Mission Home of Texas v. N A B*, 451 S.W.2d 539, 1970 Tex. App. LEXIS 2055 (Tex. Civ. App. 1970).

especially Aviles, to do her banking and shopping and to provide her with transportation to medical appointments. She also was suffering from significant memory impairment by that time. This evidence of Seals's mental condition was corroborated by the medical testimony of Dr. Forster, who provided his expert opinion that Seals was suffering from severe Alzheimer's dementia [at the time of the sale]. In our view, the evidence of Seals's severe mental impairment far outweighed the self-serving, lay opinions of Aviles and Freedman that Seals appeared coherent and lucid at the closing.

Seals's dependence on Aviles was further confirmed by the testimony of two disinterested witnesses, Blair and Sister Lachapelle, who testified that Aviles told Seals shortly before the sale that if she transferred the building to him, he would take care of her for the rest of her life. In addition, that Seals was represented at the closing by an attorney she had never met before and who was referred by the buyer, Mr. Aviles, is a circumstance noted in many prior cases as raising a serious question of improper influence.

Additional clear and convincing evidence adduced by plaintiffs reveal a series of transactions permeated by undue influence. Aviles's unfettered use of Seals's funds and credit cards, which Aviles admitted at trial, provides convincing evidence that he was exploiting Seals's impaired condition for his own financial gain. Finally, his brazen conduct in writing out mortgage checks to Seals, having her endorse them, and then depositing them back into his own account raises the strongest inference that the mortgage agreement was a sham, and his intent was to obtain Seals's building through improper means. In light of the trial evidence, we find that the jury's verdict that Aviles did not obtain Seals's property by undue influence could not have been reached on any fair interpretation of the evidence.

[Reversed and remanded for new trial.] ◼

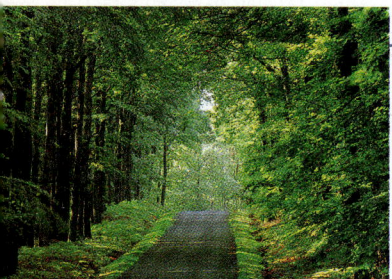

© PHOTODISC/GETTY IMAGES

Chapter Conclusion

An agreement between two parties may not be enough to make a contract enforceable. A minor or a mentally impaired person may generally disaffirm contracts. Even if both parties are adults of sound mind, courts will insist that consent be genuine. Misrepresentation, mistake, duress, and undue influence all indicate that at least one party did not truly consent. As the law evolves, it imposes an increasingly greater burden of *good faith negotiating* on the party in the stronger position. Do not bargain for a contract that is too good to be true.

Chapter Review

1. Capacity and consent are different contract issues that can lead to the same result: a voidable contract. A voidable agreement is one that can be canceled by a party who lacks legal capacity or who did not give true consent.

2. A minor (someone under the age of 18) generally may disaffirm any contract while she is still a minor or within a reasonable time after reaching age 18.

3. A minor who disaffirms must make restitution; that is, she must return to the other party whatever consideration she received, such as goods that she purchased. If she cannot make restitution because the goods are damaged or destroyed, in most (but not all) states the minor is still entitled to disaffirm and receive her money.

4. A mentally impaired person may generally disaffirm a contract. In this case, though, he generally must make restitution.

5. *Fraud and Misrepresentation.* Both fraud and material misrepresentation are grounds for disaffirming a contract. The injured party must prove:

   a. A false statement of fact and

   b. Fraud or materiality; and

   c. Justifiable reliance.

6. Silence amounts to misrepresentation only in four instances:

   a. Where disclosure is necessary to *correct a previous assertion*

b. Where disclosure would correct a *basic mistaken assumption* on which the other party is relying

c. Where disclosure would correct the other party's *mistaken understanding about a writing;* or

d. Where there is a *relationship of trust* between the two parties.

7. *Mistake.* In a case of bilateral mistake, either party may rescind the contract. In a case of unilateral mistake, the injured party may rescind only upon a showing that enforcement would be unconscionable or that the other party knew of her mistake.

Practice Test

1. Raymond Barrows owned a 17-acre parcel of undeveloped land in Seaford, Delaware. For most of his life Mr. Barrows had been an astute and successful businessman, but by the time he was 85 years old, he had been diagnosed as "very senile and confused 90 percent of the time." Glenn Bowen offered to buy the land. Barrows had no idea of its value, so Bowen had it appraised by a friend, who said it was worth $50,000. Bowen drew up a contract, which Barrows signed. In the contract, Barrows agreed to sell the land for $45,000, of which Bowen would pay $100 at the time of closing; the remaining $44,900 was due whenever Bowen developed the land and sold it. There was no time limit on Bowen's right to develop the land nor any interest due on the second payment. Comment.

2. Ron buys from Karen 1,000 "Smudgy Dolls" for his toy store. Karen knows the dolls' heads are not properly attached but says nothing. Ron sells all of the dolls quickly and then has 1,000 unhappy customers with headless dolls. Ron sues to rescind the contract with Karen and also seeks punitive damages. What is the likely outcome?

   a. Ron will be able to rescind, based on fraudulent nondisclosure, but he may not get punitive damages as well.

   b. Ron will be able to rescind, based on fraudulent nondisclosure, and may also obtain punitive damages.

   c. Ron will lose unless he can show that Karen intended to harm Ron's business.

8. *Duress.* If one party makes an improper threat that causes the victim to enter into a contract, and the victim had no reasonable alternative, the contract is voidable.

9. Cases of economic duress are more common but harder to win. Courts will look at the parties' motives, their respective bargaining power, any unnaturally large gains, and resulting financial distress.

10. *Undue Influence.* Once again the injured party may rescind a contract, but only upon a showing of a special relationship and improper persuasion.

   d. Ron will win only if he can show that both parties were mistaken about a basic assumption.

3. Andreini suffered from a nerve problem that was causing him to lose the use of his hands. Dr. Beck operated on Andreini's hands but the problem grew worse. A nurse told Andreini that Beck might have committed a serious error in the operation, causing Andreini's neuropathy to grow worse. Andreini returned to Beck for a second operation, which Beck assured him was certain to correct the problem. But after Andreini had been placed in a surgical gown, shaved, and prepared for surgery, Dr. Beck insisted that he sign a release relieving Beck of any liability for the first operation. Andreini did not want to sign it, but Beck refused to operate until he did. Later, Andreini sued Beck for malpractice. A trial court dismissed Andreini's suit based on the release. You are on the appeals court. Will you affirm the dismissal or reverse?

4. On television and in magazines, Maurine and Mamie Mason saw numerous advertisements for Chrysler Fifth Avenue automobiles. The ads described the car as "luxurious," "quality-engineered," and "reliable." When they went to inspect the car, the salesman told them the warranty was "the best . . . comparable to Cadillacs and Lincolns." After the Masons bought a Fifth Avenue, they began to have many problems with it. Even after numerous repairs, the car was unsatisfactory and required more work. The Masons sued, seeking to rescind the contract based on the ads and the dealer's statement. Will they win?

5. John Marshall and Kirsten Fletcher decided to live together. They leased an apartment, each agreeing to pay one-half of the rent. When he signed the lease, Marshall was 17. Shortly after signing the lease, Marshall turned 18, and two weeks later he moved into the apartment. He paid his half of the rent for two months and then moved out because he and Fletcher were not getting along. Fletcher sued Marshall for one-half of the monthly rent for the remainder of the lease. Who wins?

6. Kerry finds a big green ring in the street. She shows it to Leroy, who says, "Wow. That could be valuable." Neither Kerry nor Leroy knows what the ring is made of or whether it is valuable. Kerry sells the ring to Leroy for $100, saying, "Don't come griping if it turns out to be worth two dollars." Leroy takes the ring to a jeweler who tells him it is an unusually perfect emerald, worth at least $75,000. Kerry sues to rescind.

   a. Kerry will win based on fraud.

   b. Kerry will win based on mutual mistake.

   c. Kerry will win based on unilateral mistake.

   d. Kerry will lose.

7. The McAllisters had several serious problems with their house, including leaks in the ceiling, a buckling wall, and dampness throughout. They repaired the buckling wall by installing I-beams to support it. They never resolved the leaks and the dampness. When they decided to sell the house, they said nothing to prospective buyers about the problems. They stated that the I-beam had been added for reinforcement. The Silvas bought the house for $60,000. Soon afterwards, they began to have problems with leaks, mildew, and dampness. Are the Silvas entitled to any money damages? Why or why not?

8. **ETHICS** Sixteen-year-old Travis Mitchell brought his 19-year-old Pontiac GTO into M&M Precision Body and Paint for body work and a paint job. M&M did the work and charged $1,900, which Travis paid. Travis later complained about the quality of the work and M&M did some touching up, but Travis was still dissatisfied. Travis demanded his $1,900 back, but M&M refused to give it back since all of the work was "in" the car and Travis could not return it to the shop. The state of Nebraska, where this occurred, follows the majority rule on this issue. Does Travis get his money? What is the common law rule? Who *ought* to win? Is the common law rule fair? What is the rationale for the rule?

9. Roy Newburn borrowed money and bought a $49,000 truck from Treadwell Ford. A few months later the truck developed transmission problems. Newburn learned that the truck had 170,000 more miles on it than the odometer indicated. The company admitted the mileage and promised to install a new transmission free. Treadwell did install the new transmission, but when Newburn came to pick up the truck, Treadwell demanded that he sign a general release absolving the dealership of any claims based on the inaccurate mileage. Treadwell refused to turn over the truck until Newburn finally signed. The truck broke down again, and delays cost Newburn so much income that he fell behind on his loan payments and lost the truck. He sued Treadwell, which defended based on the release. Is the release valid?

10. **YOU BE THE JUDGE** WRITING PROBLEM Susan Gould was appointed to a three-year probationary position as a teacher at Sewanhaka High School. Normally, after three years, the school board either grants tenure or dismisses the teacher. The Sewanhaka school board notified Gould she would not be rehired. To keep the termination out of her file, Gould agreed to resign. In fact, because Gould had previously taught at a different New York school, state law required that she be given a tenure decision after only two years. If the board failed to do that, the teacher was automatically tenured. When she learned this, Gould sued to rescind her agreement to resign. Is Gould entitled to rescind the contract (i.e., her agreement to resign)? **Argument for Gould:** Both parties assumed that Gould was on probation and could be dismissed after three years. Neither party understood that after three years, Gould actually *had* tenure under New York State law. Gould would never have resigned had she understood she was entitled to tenure. The misunderstanding goes to the essence of the resignation agreement, and she should be permitted to rescind. **Argument for the School Board:** The school board has done nothing wrong here. It is unfair to penalize the school system for an honest mistake. If Gould is serious about her career, she should understand

the tenure process and should take the trouble to inform the board about unusual rules that pertain to her case. She failed to do that, causing both parties to negotiate under a misperception, and she must bear the loss.

11. Morell bought a security guard business from Conley, including the property on which the business was located. Neither party knew that underground storage tanks were leaking and contaminating the property. After the sale, Morell discovered the tanks and sought to rescind the contract. Should he be allowed to do so?

12. **ROLE REVERSAL** Write a short-essay question that includes one instance each of puffery, misrepresentation, and fraud.

Internet Research Problem

Visit **http://beatty.westbuslaw.com**. Find the link that focuses on marketing to children. Use the ethics checklist from Chapter 2 to analyze the conduct described. Should society limit tobacco marketing? If not, why not? If so, should it be done by legislation, regulation, litigation, or some other means?

> **You can find further practice problems at http://beatty.westbuslaw.com or in the Study Guide that accompanies this text.**

Written Contracts

Oliver and Perry were college roommates, two sophomores with contrasting personalities. They were sitting in the cafeteria with some friends, Oliver chatting away, Perry slumped on a plastic bench. Oliver suggested that they buy a lottery ticket, as the prize for that week's drawing was $13 million. Perry muttered, "Nah. You never win if you buy just one ticket." Oliver bubbled up, "O.K., we'll buy a ticket every week. We'll keep buying them from now until we graduate. Come on, it'll be fun. This month, I'll buy the tickets. Next month, you will, and so on." Other students urged Perry to do it and, finally, grudgingly, he agreed. The two friends carefully reviewed their deal. Each party was providing consideration, namely, the responsibility for purchasing tickets during his month. The amount of each purchase was clearly defined at one dollar. They would start that week and continue until graduation day, two and a half years down the road. Finally, they would share equally any money won. As three witnesses looked on, they shook hands on the bargain. That month, Oliver bought a ticket every week, randomly choosing numbers, and won nothing. The next month, Perry bought a ticket with equally random numbers—and won $52 million. Perry moved out of their dorm room into a suite at the Ritz and refused to give Oliver one red cent. Oliver sued, seeking $26 million, and the return of an Eric Clapton compact disc that he had loaned Perry. If the former friends had understood the statute of frauds,

they would never have slid into this mess.[1] ■

The rule we examine in this chapter is not exactly news. Parliament passed the original statute of frauds in 1677. The purpose was to prevent lying (fraud) in civil law suits. Jury trials of that era invited perjury. Neither the plaintiff nor the defendant was permitted to testify, meaning that the jury never heard from the people who really knew what had happened. Instead, the court heard testimony from people who claimed to have witnessed the contract being created. A plaintiff might concoct a fraudulent claim of contract, knowing that he would never be subjected to aggressive cross-examination, and then bribe witnesses to support his case. A powerful earl, seeking to acquire 300 acres of valuable land owned by a neighboring commoner, might claim that the neighbor had orally promised to sell his land. Although the claim was utterly false, the earl would win if he could bribe enough "reputable" witnesses to persuade the jury.

To provide juries with more reliable evidence that a contract did or did not exist, Parliament passed the statute of frauds. The statute required that in six types of cases, a contract would be enforced only if it were in writing. Almost all states of this country later passed their own statutes making the same requirements. It is important to remember, as we examine the rules and exceptions, that Parliament and the state legislatures all had a commendable, straightforward purpose in passing their respective statutes of fraud: *to provide a court with the best possible evidence of whether the parties intended to make a contract.*

Ironically, the British government has repealed the writing requirement for most contracts. Parliament concluded that the old statute, far from preventing wrongdoing, was *helping* people commit fraud. A wily negotiator could orally agree to terms and then, if the deal turned unprofitable, walk away from the contract, knowing it was unenforceable without written evidence.

Thus far, no state in this country has entirely repealed its statute of frauds. Instead, as we have often seen in the common law, courts have carved exceptions into the original statute to prevent unfairness. Some scholars have urged state legislatures to go further and repeal the law altogether. Other commentators defend the statute of frauds as a valuable tool for justice. They argue that, among other benefits, the requirement of a writing cautions people to be careful before making—or relying on—a promise. For now, the statute of frauds is a vital part of law. Sadly, Oliver will learn this the hard way.

The statute of frauds: A plaintiff may not enforce any of the following agreements, unless the agreement, or some memorandum of it, is in writing and signed by the defendant. The agreements that must be in writing are those:

- For any interest in **land**

- That **cannot be performed within one year**

- To pay the **debt of another**

- Made by an **executor of an estate**

- Made **in consideration of marriage**; and

- For the **sale of goods worth $500 or more**.

---

[1] Based loosely on *Lydon v. Beauregard* (Middlesex Sup. Ct., Mass., Dec. 22, 1989), reported in Paul Langher, "Couple Lose Suit to Share $2.8M Prize," *Boston Globe*, Dec. 23, 1989, p. 21.

Unenforceable

In other words, when two parties make an agreement covered by any one of these six topics, it must be in writing to be enforceable. Oliver and Perry made a definite agreement to purchase lottery tickets during alternate months and share the proceeds of any winning ticket. But their agreement was to last two and one-half years. As the second item on the list indicates, a contract must be in writing if it cannot be performed within one year. The good news is, Oliver gets back his Eric Clapton disc. The bad news is he gets none of the lottery money. Even though three witnesses saw the deal made, it is unlikely to be enforced in any state. Perry the pessimist will probably walk away with all $52 million.[2]

But Not Void

Note that although the Oliver–Perry agreement is unenforceable, it is not void. Suppose that Perry does the right thing, agreeing to share the winnings with Oliver. Over the next 20 years, as he receives the winnings, Perry gives one-half to his friend. But then, having squandered his own fortune, Perry demands the money back from Oliver, claiming that the original contract violated the statute of frauds. Perry loses. **Once a contract is fully executed, it makes no difference that it was unwritten.** The statute of frauds prevents the enforcement of an executory contract, that is, one in which the parties have not fulfilled their obligations. But the contract is not *illegal*. Once both parties have fully performed, neither party may demand rescission.

Ethics

The law permits Perry to keep all of the lottery money. Is that right? Does Perry have a moral right to deny Oliver his half-share, when we know the two friends had agreed? Is the statute of frauds serving a useful purpose here? Remember that Parliament passed the original statute of frauds believing that a written document would be more reliable than the testimony of alleged witnesses. If we permitted Oliver to enforce the oral contract, based on his testimony and that of the witnesses, would we simply be inviting other plaintiffs to conjure up lottery "contracts" that had never been made? ◆

CONTRACTS THAT MUST BE IN WRITING

Agreements for an Interest in Land

A contract for the sale of any interest in land must be in writing to be enforceable. Notice the phrase "interest in land." This means *any legal right* regarding land. A house on a lot is an interest in land. A mortgage, an easement, and a leased apartment are all interests in land. As a general rule, leases must therefore be in writing, although

---

[2]   Perry might also raise *illegality* as a defense, claiming that a contract for gambling is illegal. That defense is likely to fail. Courts appear to distinguish between the simple purchase of a legal lottery ticket, which friends often share, and the more traditional—and socially dangerous—gambling contracts involving horse racing or casino betting. See, e.g., *Pando v. Fernandez*, 118 A.D.2d 474, 499 N.Y.S.2d 950, 1986 N.Y. App. Div. LEXIS 54345 (N.Y. App. Div. 1986), finding no illegality in an agreement to purchase a lottery ticket, even where the purchaser was a minor! Since an illegality defense would probably fail Perry, it is all the more unfortunate that Oliver did not jot down their agreement in writing.

most states have created an exception for short-term leases. A short-term lease is often one for a year or less, although the length varies from state to state.

Kary Presten and Ken Sailer were roommates in a rental apartment in New Jersey, with a view of the Manhattan skyline. The lease was in Sailer's name, but the two split all expenses. Then the building became a "cooperative," meaning that each tenant would have the option of buying the apartment.[3] Sailer learned he could buy his unit for only $55,800 if he promptly paid a $1,000 fee to maintain his rights. He mentioned to Presten that he planned to buy the unit, and Presten asked if he could become half owner. Sailer agreed and borrowed the $1,000 from Presten to pay his initial fee. But as the time for closing on the purchase came nearer, Sailer realized that he could sell the apartment for a substantial profit. He placed an ad in a paper, and promptly received a firm offer for $125,000. Sailer then told Presten that their deal was off, and that he, Sailer, would be buying the unit alone. He did exactly that, and Presten filed suit. Regrettably, the outcome of Presten's suit was only too easy to predict.

A cooperative apartment is an interest in land, said the court. This agreement could be enforced only if put in writing and signed by Sailer. The parties had put nothing in writing, and therefore Presten was out of luck. He was entitled to his $1,000 back, but nothing more. The apartment belonged to Sailer, who could live in it or sell it for a large, quick profit.[4]

at RISK

Suppose that you are interested in buying five expensive acres in a fast-growing rural area. There is no water on the property, and the only way to bring public water to it is through land owned by the neighbor, Joanne, who agrees to sell you an easement through her property. An easement is a legal right that an owner gives to another person to make some use of the owner's land. In other words, Joanne will permit you to dig a 200-foot trench through her land and lay a water pipe there in exchange for $15,000. May you now safely purchase the five acres? Not until Joanne has signed the written easement. You might ignore this "technicality," since Joanne seems friendly and honest. But you could then spend $300,000 buying your property, only to learn that Joanne has changed her mind. She might refuse to go through with the deal unless you pay $150,000 for the easement. Without her permission to lay the pipe, your new land is worthless. Avoid such nightmares: get it in writing. ◆

Exception: Full Performance by the Seller

If the seller completely performs her side of a contract for an interest in land, a court is likely to enforce the agreement even if it was oral. Adam orally agrees to sell his condominium to Maggie for $150,000. Adam delivers the deed to Maggie and expects his money a week later, but Maggie fails to pay. Most courts will allow Adam to enforce the oral contract and collect the full purchase price from Maggie.

Exception: Part Performance by the Buyer

The buyer of land may be able to enforce an oral contract if she paid part of the purchase price *and either* entered upon the land *or* made improvements to it.

---

3 Technically, the residents of a "co-op" do not own their apartments. They own a share of the corporation that owns the building. Along with their ownership shares, residents have a right to lease their unit for a modest fee.

4 *Presten v. Sailer*, 225 N.J. Super. 178, 542 A.2d 7, 1988 N.J. Super. LEXIS 151 (N.J. Super. Ct. App. Div. 1988).

Suppose that Eloise sues Grover to enforce an alleged oral contract to sell a lot in Happydale. She claims they struck a bargain in January. Grover defends based on the statute of frauds, saying that even if the two did reach an oral agreement, it is unenforceable. Eloise proves that she paid 10 percent of the purchase price and that in February she began excavating on the lot, to build a house, and that Grover knew of the work. Eloise has established part performance and will be allowed to enforce her contract.

This exception makes sense if we recall the purpose of the statute of frauds: to provide the best possible evidence of the parties' intentions. The fact that Grover permitted Eloise to enter upon the land and begin building on it is compelling evidence that the two parties had reached an agreement. But be aware that most claims of part performance fail. Merely paying a deposit on a house is not part performance. A plaintiff seeking to rely on part performance must show partial payment *and* either entrance onto the land *or* physical improvements to it.

Did Sullivan rely on the promise of joint ownership?

Exception: Promissory Estoppel

The other exception to the writing requirement is our old friend promissory estoppel. **If a promisor makes an oral promise that should reasonably cause the promisee to rely on it, and the promisee does rely, the promisee may be able to enforce the promise,** despite the statute of frauds, if that is the only way to avoid injustice. This exception potentially applies to any contract that must be written, such as those for land, those that cannot be performed within one year, and so forth.

Maureen Sullivan and James Rooney lived together for seven years, although they never married. They decided to buy a house. The parties agreed that they would be equal owners, but Rooney told Sullivan that in order to obtain Veterans Administration financing he would have to be the sole owner on the deed. They each contributed to the purchase and maintenance of the house, and Rooney repeatedly told Sullivan that he would change the deed to joint ownership. He never did. When the couple split up, Sullivan sued, seeking a 50 percent interest in the house. She won. The agreement was for an interest in land and should have been in writing, said the court. But Rooney had clearly promised Sullivan that she would be a half owner, and she had relied by contributing to the purchase and maintenance. The statute of frauds was passed to *prevent* fraud, not to enable one person to mislead another and benefit at her expense.[5]

In the following case, the defendant seems to have acknowledged *in court* that she agreed to sell her property. Does that satisfy the statute of frauds?

---

[5]   *Sullivan v. Rooney,* 404 Mass. 160, 533 N.E.2d 1372, 1989 Mass. LEXIS 49 (1989).

© AP PHOTO/PAUL SAKUMA

BAKER V. DAVES

83 Ark. App. 145, 119 S.W.3d 53
Court of Appeals of Arkansas, 2003

Facts: Tommy and Eleanor Daves had a daughter, Lisa Baker. The Daves gave Lisa a deed to a two-acre property with a house on it, keeping for themselves a *life interest* in the parcel. In other words, the Daves each had a half interest in the land for the rest of their lives; they could live in the house and use the land any way they wished. When they died, the property returned to their daughter.

Tommy and Eleanor divorced, and settled their affairs amicably. In court, with Lisa watching from the second row, their lawyers informed the court of an agreement that all three parties had allegedly made to sell the two-acre property. Lisa would be reimbursed for taxes and insurance she had paid during the two years she owned the property, and the Daveses would split the rest of the money.

After the agreement was announced, Lisa put the property on the market but then withdrew it, and refused to sell. Tommy Daves sued his daughter. Lisa defended based on the Statute of Frauds, saying she had never agreed in court to the deal, and never signed any contract to sell. The trial court acknowledged that Lisa had signed nothing, but found that the courtroom statements proved the parties had formed a binding contract. The judge ordered Lisa to sell the house, and she appealed.

Issue: Was Lisa obligated to sell the house?

Excerpts from Judge Stroud's Opinion: The record of the divorce proceedings was introduced as an exhibit. The following pertinent portion was abstracted for this appeal:

> [Attorney for Eleanor Daves]: The parties have a joint life estate in 2.2 acres of property and a house on Vimy Ridge Road in Alexander, Arkansas. The parties have agreed to sell the house and 2.2 acres and split the proceeds. They have agreed that Mr. Daves will contact a real estate agency.
>
> [Attorney for Mr. Daves, *appellee*]: They have a life estate. It was placed in her daughter's name and the daughter is the title owner. She is going to cooperate in listing the property for sale. They are actually selling the property not just the life estate.

> [Attorney for Eleanor Daves]: The daughter has agreed to sell her interest in the property as well as the life estate of the two parties.

Appellant contends that she never agreed to sell the property, and that "even if some of the parties thought there was an agreement to sell the land, it cannot be enforced since it was not in writing." Under the facts of this case, we find merit in appellant's argument.

Here, the record does not reveal any writing signed by appellant, or by any other person properly authorized by her, to sell the property in question. Moreover, the fact that appellant was present in the courtroom when the property-settlement agreement was read into the record during the Daveses' divorce proceedings is of no benefit to appellee under these circumstances.

We think that the instant case is an example of the type of situation where a binding agreement was not established with respect to appellant. In short, it is not disputed that the agreement at issue here involves the sale of real property, that appellant was not a party to the original divorce action, that she was not represented by counsel during the divorce proceedings before the trial court, and that she was not asked by the court as part of the record of the divorce proceedings if she heard the agreement and agreed to its terms. Consequently, we hold that the trial court erred in concluding that she was bound by the terms of the agreement.

Reversed and remanded.

Excerpts from Judge Crabtree's Dissent: Appellant admitted that she was present in the hallway with her mother at the time of the divorce hearing when the agreement was being discussed, but she denied taking part in or having any knowledge of the negotiations. She admitted that she was in the courtroom when the agreement was being read into the record, but she denied that she was able to hear what the attorneys were saying. Appellant also admitted that she listed the property for sale pursuant to the agreement. Her conduct unequivocally demonstrates her assent to the agreement. [I would affirm the trial court's decision.] ■

Recall that the Statute of Frauds was created to prevent lying in contract cases. Is Lisa Baker relying on a "legal technicality" to evade a legitimate contract? She was silent during the court session in which two lawyers stated she had agreed to sell. She actually put her house on the market. Judge Crabtree thinks that is clear evidence of an agreement. Is he right, or are there policy reasons to conclude that her behavior is not enough to prove a contract? ◆

Agreements That Cannot Be Performed within One Year

Contracts that cannot be performed within one year are unenforceable unless they are in writing. This one-year period begins on the date the parties make the agreement. The critical phrase here is "*cannot be performed* within one year." If a contract *could* be completed within one year, it need not be in writing. Betty gets a job at Burger Brain, throwing fries in oil. Her boss tells her she can have Fridays off for as long as she works there. That oral contract is enforceable, whether Betty stays one week or fifty-seven years. It *could* have been performed within one year if, say, Betty quit the job after six months. Therefore it does not need to be in writing.[6]

If the agreement will *necessarily* take longer than one year to finish, it must be in writing to be enforceable. If Betty is hired for three years as manager of Burger Brain, the agreement is unenforceable unless put in writing. She cannot perform three years of work in one year.

Type of Agreement	Enforceability
Cannot be performed within one year. *Example:* An offer of employment for three years.	Must be in writing to be enforceable.
Might be performed within one year, although could take many years to perform. *Example:* "As long as you work here at Burger Brain you may have Fridays off."	Enforceable whether it is oral or written, since the employee might quit working a month later.

In the following case, both parties have the same name, which tells us we have a family dispute—and very angry litigants.

you Be The Judge

LOWINGER V. LOWINGER
733 N.Y.S.2d 33, 287 A.D.2d 39
Supreme Court of New York,
Appellate Division, 2001

Facts: Kay, from South Korea, was a flight attendant when she met Louis, whose Orthodox Jewish family owned a major import/export business. The couple married in a civil ceremony in Korea that none of Louis's family attended. After the wedding Kay discovered that although Louis led an extravagant life, with apartments in Tokyo, Paris, and Hong Kong, he was financially dependent on his mother, Edith, who ran the family company. She

▼

---

[6] This is the majority rule. In most states, for example, if a company hires an employee "for life," the contract need not be in writing because the employee could die within one year. "Contracts of uncertain duration are simply excluded [from the statute of frauds]; the provision covers only those contracts whose performance cannot possibly be completed within a year." Restatement (Second) of Contracts §130, Comment a, at 328 (1981). However, a few states disagree. The Illinois Supreme Court ruled that a contract for lifetime employment is enforceable only if written. *McInerney v. Charter Golf, Inc.*, 176 Ill. 2d 482, 680 N.E.2d 1347, 1997 Ill. LEXIS 56 (Ill. 1997).

also learned that her husband was mentally unstable. Louis followed Kay 24 hours a day, even into the bathroom, prevented her from making phone calls, and slept in front of the bedroom door to prevent her escape. Kay attempted suicide once, but the couple eventually had three children.

Kay alleged that Louis and Edith pressured her to convert to Judaism, partly so that the children (ages one to three) could enroll in an orthodox school. Edith orally promised that if Kay joined the religion, she would provide (1) a "wonderful home" for Kay and Louis; (2) a generous lifestyle for the rest of their lives; (3) the best education possible for the children; (4) additional financial support; (5) employment in the family business for the children, if they wished it; and (6) full acceptance of Kay and her children in the family. Kay agreed. The entire family journeyed to Israel, where Edith arranged for a high-ranking Rabbi to convert Kay. The couple married there in a religious ceremony. Edith then provided the family with a 27-room mansion near New York City, increased Kay's monthly allowance from $200 to $12,000, and gave her daughter-in-law a no-limit charge card.

Thirteen years later, when Kay began divorce proceedings, Edith stopped all financial assistance. Kay sued, seeking the home and continued support. Edith denied making the agreement. At trial, the jury found that the parties had in fact made such a bargain. Edith appealed, claiming that even if there had been an oral contract, the statute of frauds barred its enforcement.

You Be the Judge: Does the statute of frauds prevent enforcement of the oral agreement between Kay and Edith?

Argument for Edith: Even if Edith made the promises, none of them can be enforced unless they were put in writing. The promise of a "wonderful home" concerns real estate and it is black letter law that such a contract must be written. No deed or sales agreement indicates that Kay is entitled to the house she has lived in—or any other property. Kay's claim of partial performance also fails. Because partial performance is an exception to the normal rule, it is only enforced when the party's conduct necessarily indicates an underlying agreement. Kay could easily have embraced Judaism to unite the family in one religion, or to please her husband. The conversion does not prove that Edith made any offers.

The other alleged promises fail because none of them can be performed within one year. The children were all under four years of age when the bargain was supposedly struck. They would not begin their education, let alone their working lives, for many years. It would be impossible for Edith to fulfill the promises within a year, and they are unenforceable. Finally, Edith's supposed offers were too vague to create a contract.

Argument for Kay: The purpose of the statute of frauds is to make sure that a court enforces only those agreements that parties really made. Here, we have the best possible evidence that the parties reached a contract—they both performed! Kay was a young woman from South Korea when she met the Lowinger family. She had no plan or reason to convert to another religion. Yet she traveled to Israel and took this enormous personal step because of her mother-in-law's assurances. When the couple returned to the United States, Edith gave them the keys to a mansion and provided exactly the financial support that she had pledged. Both sides kept their part of the bargain for 13 years, which tells us that there was a bargain.

As to the financial support pledges, they could have been completed in one year. If the young family had been wiped out in a terrible accident, all obligations would have been fulfilled within 12 months. While such a gruesome event is unlikely, it is possible, and that is sufficient to avoid the statute of frauds trap. As to vagueness, the terms were clear enough for the parties, and they should be clear enough for the court. ■

Promise to Pay the Debt of Another

When one person agrees to pay the debt of another as a favor to that debtor, it is called a collateral promise, and it must be in writing to be enforceable. D. R. Kemp was a young entrepreneur who wanted to build housing in Tuscaloosa, Alabama. He needed $25,000 to complete a project he was working on, so he went to his old college professor, Jim Hanks, for help. The professor said he would see what he could do about getting Kemp a loan. Professor Hanks spoke with his good friend Travis Chandler, telling him that Kemp was highly responsible and would be certain to repay any money loaned. Chandler trusted Professor Hanks but wanted to be sure of his money. Professor Hanks assured Chandler that if for any reason Kemp did not repay the loan, he, Hanks, would pay Chandler in full. With that assurance, Chandler wrote out a check for $25,000, payable to Kemp, never having met the young man.

Kemp, of course, never repaid the loan. (Thank goodness he did not; this textbook has no use for people who do what they are supposed to.) Kemp exhausted the cash trying to sustain his business, which failed anyway, so he had nothing to give his creditor. Chandler approached Professor Hanks, who refused to pay (what ethics!), and Chandler sued. The outcome was easy to predict. Professor Hanks had agreed to repay Kemp's debt *as a favor to Kemp*, making it a collateral promise. Chandler had nothing in writing, and that is exactly what he got from his lawsuit—nothing.

Exception: The Leading Object Rule

There is one major exception to the collateral promise rule. When the promisor guarantees to pay the debt of another and *the leading object of the promise is some benefit to the promisor himself*, then the contract will be enforceable even if unwritten. In other words, if the promisor makes the guarantee not as a favor to the debtor, but out of self-interest, the statute of frauds does not apply.

Robert Perry was a hog farmer in Ohio. He owed $26,000 to Sunrise Cooperative, a supplier of feed. Because Perry was in debt, Sunrise stopped giving him feed on credit and began selling him feed on a cash-only basis. Perry also owed money to Farm Credit Services, a loan agency. Perry promised Farm Credit he would repay his loans as soon as

When one party promises to pay the debt of another, the enforceability of that promise may depend upon whom the promisor intended to benefit.

his hogs were big enough to sell. But Perry couldn't raise hogs without feed, which he lacked the money to purchase. Farm Credit was determined to bring home the bacon, so it asked Sunrise Cooperative to give Perry the feed on credit. Farm Credit orally promised to pay any debt that Perry did not take care of. When Perry defaulted on his payments to Sunrise, the feed supplier sued Farm Credit based on its oral guarantee. Farm Credit claimed the promise was unenforceable, based on the statute of frauds. But the court found in favor of Sunrise. The *leading object* of Farm Credit's promise to Sunrise was self-interest, and the oral promise was fully enforceable.[7]

Promise Made by an Executor of an Estate

This rule is merely a special application of the previous one, concerning the debt of another person. An executor is the person who is in charge of an estate after someone dies. The executor's job is to pay debts of the deceased, obtain money owed to him, and disburse the assets according to the will. In most cases, the executor will use only the estate's assets to pay those debts. The statute of frauds comes into play only when an executor promises to pay an estate's debts with her *own* funds. **An executor's promise to use her own funds to pay a debt of the deceased must be in writing to be enforceable.** Suppose Esmeralda dies penniless, owing Tina $35,000. Esmeralda's daughter, Sapphire, is the executor of her estate. Tina comes to Sapphire

---

7   Sunrise Cooperative v. Robert Perry, 1992 Ohio App. LEXIS 3913 (Ohio Ct. App., 1992).

and demands her $35,000. Sapphire responds, "There is no money in mamma's estate, but don't worry, I'll make it up to you with my own money." Sapphire's oral promise is unenforceable. Tina should get it in writing while Sapphire is feeling generous.

Promise Made in Consideration of Marriage

Barney is a multimillionaire with the integrity of a gangster and the charm of a tax collector. He proposes to Li-Tsing, who promptly rejects him. Barney then pleads that if Li-Tsing will be his bride, he will give her an island he owns off the coast of California. Li-Tsing begins to see his good qualities and accepts. After they are married, Barney refuses to deliver the deed. Li-Tsing will get nothing from a court either, because **a promise made in consideration of marriage must be in writing to be enforceable.**

WHAT THE WRITING MUST CONTAIN

Each of the five types of contract described above must be in writing in order to be enforceable. What must the writing contain? It may be a carefully typed contract, using precise legal terminology, or an informal memorandum scrawled on the back of a paper napkin at a business lunch. The writing may consist of more than one document, written at different times, with each document making a piece of the puzzle. But there are some general requirements: **the contract or memorandum**

- **Must be signed by the defendant, and**
- **Must state with reasonable certainty the name of each party, the subject matter of the agreement, and all of the essential terms and promises.**[8]

Signature

A statute of frauds typically states that the writing must be "signed by the party to be charged therewith," that is, the party who is resisting enforcement of the contract. Throughout this chapter we refer to that person as the defendant, since when these cases go to court, it is the defendant who is disputing the existence of a contract.

Judges define "signature" very broadly. Using a pen to write one's name, though sufficient, is not required. A secretary who stamps an executive's signature on a letter fulfills this requirement. Any other mark or logo placed on a document to indicate acceptance, even an "X," will likely satisfy the statute of frauds. Electronic commerce creates new methods of signing—and new controversies, discussed in the Cyberlaw feature later in the chapter.

Reasonable Certainty

Suppose Garfield and Hayes are having lunch, discussing the sale of Garfield's vacation condominium. They agree on a price and want to make some notation of the agreement even before their lawyers work out a detailed purchase and sales agreement. A perfectly adequate memorandum might say, "Garfield agrees to sell Hayes his condominium at 234 Baron Boulevard, apartment 18, for $350,000 cash, payable on June 18, 2005, and Hayes promises to pay the sum on that day." They should make two copies

---

[8]   Restatement (Second) of Contracts §131.

of their agreement and sign both. Notice that although Garfield's memo is short, it is *certain* and *complete*. This is critical because problems of vagueness and incompleteness often doom informal memoranda.

Vagueness

Ella Hayden owned valuable commercial property on a highway called Route 9. She wrote a series of letters to her stepson Mark, promising that several of the children, including Mark, would share the property. One letter said: "We four shall fairly divide on the Route 9 property. [sic]" Other letters said: "When the Route 9 Plaza is sold you can take a long vacation," and "The property will be sold. You and Dennis shall receive the same amount." Ella Hayden died, without leaving Mark anything. He sued, but got nothing. The court ruled:

> The above passages written by Ms. Hayden do not recite the essential elements of the alleged contract with reasonable certainty. The writings do not state unequivocally or with sufficient particularity the subject matter to which the writings relate, nor do they provide the terms and conditions of alleged promises made which constitute a contract. The alleged oral contract between Ms. Hayden and Mr. Hayden cannot be identified from the passages from Ms. Hayden's letters quoted above when applied to existing facts. In sum, Mr. Hayden's cause of action seeking an interest in the Route 9 property is foreclosed by the statute of frauds.[9]

Incompleteness

During Ronald McCoy's second interview with Spelman Memorial Hospital, the board of directors orally offered him a three-year job as assistant hospital administrator. McCoy accepted. Spelman's CEO, Gene Meyer, sent a letter confirming the offer, which said:

> To reconfirm the offer, it is as follows: 1. We will pay for your moving expenses. 2. I would like you to pursue your Master's Degree at an area program. We will pay 100% tuition reimbursement. 3. Effective September 26 you will be eligible for all benefits. 4. A starting salary of $48,000 annually with reviews and eligibility for increases at 6 months, 12 months and annually thereafter. 5. We will pay for the expenses of 3 trips, if necessary, in order for you to find housing. 6. Vacation will be for 3 weeks a year after one year, however, we do allow for this to be taken earlier. [Signed] Gene Meyer.

Spelman Hospital fired McCoy less than a year after he started work, and McCoy sued. The hospital's letter seems clear, and it is signed by an authorized official. The problem is, it is incomplete. Can you spot the fatal omission? The court did.

To satisfy the statute of frauds, an employment contract—[or] its memorandum or note—must contain all essential terms, including duration of the employment relationship. Without a statement of duration, an employment at will is created which is terminable at any time by either party with no liability for breach of contract. McCoy's argument that the letter constituted a memorandum of an oral contract fails because the letter does not state an essential element, duration. The letter did not state that Spelman was granting McCoy employment for any term—only that his salary would be reviewed at six months, twelve months and "annually thereafter."[10]

---

9   *Hayden v. Hayden*, Mass. Lawyers Weekly No. 12-299-93 (Middlesex Sup. Ct. 1994).
10   *McCoy v. Spelman Memorial Hospital*, 845 S.W.2d 727, 1993 Mo. App. LEXIS 105 (Mo. Ct. App. 1993).

These two lawsuits demonstrate the continuing force of the statute of frauds. In either case, if the promisor had truly wanted to make a binding commitment, he or she could have written the appropriate contract or memorandum in a matter of minutes. Great formality and expense are unnecessary. But the document *must be clear and complete*, or it will fail.

Because some merchants make dozens or even hundreds of oral contracts every year, the drafters of the UCC wanted to make the writing requirement less onerous for the sale of goods, to which we now turn.

SALE OF GOODS

The UCC requires a writing for the sale of goods worth $500 or more. This is the sixth and final contract that must be in writing, although the Code's requirements are easier to meet than those of the common law. **UCC §2-201,** the statute of frauds section, has three important elements:

1. The basic rule
2. The merchants' exception
3. Special circumstances

UCC §2-201(1)—The Basic Rule

A contract for the sale of goods worth $500 or more is not enforceable unless there is some writing, signed by the defendant, indicating that the parties reached an agreement. The key difference between the common law rule and the UCC rule is that the Code does not require all of the terms of the agreement to be in writing. The Code looks for something simpler: *an indication that the parties reached an agreement.* The two things that *are* essential are the signature of the defendant and the quantity of goods being sold. The quantity of goods is required because this is the one term for which there will be no objective evidence. Suppose a short memorandum between textile dealers indicates that Seller will sell to Buyer "grade AA 100% cotton, white athletic socks." If the writing does not state the price, the parties can testify at court about what the market price was at the time of the deal. If the writing says nothing about the delivery date, the court will assume a reasonable delivery date, say, 60 days. But how many socks were to be delivered? 100 pairs or 100,000? The court will have no objective evidence. The quantity must be written. (A basic sale of goods contract appears at http://www.lectlaw.com/form.html.)

Writing	Result
"Confirming phone conversation today, I will send you 1,000 reams of paper for laser printing, usual quality & price. [Signed,] Seller."	This memorandum satisfies UCC §2-201(1), and the contract may be enforced against the seller. The buyer may testify as to the "usual" quality and price between the two parties, and both sides may rely on normal trade usage.
"Confirming phone conversation today, I will send you best quality paper for laser printing, $3.25 per ream, delivery date next Thursday. [Signed,] Seller."	This memorandum is not enforceable because it states no quantity.

UCC §2-201(2)—The Merchants' Exception

When both parties are "merchants," that is, business people who routinely deal in the goods being sold, the Code will accept an even more informal writing. **Within a reasonable time of making an oral contract, if one merchant sends a written confirmation to the other, and the confirmation is definite enough to bind the *sender herself*, then the merchant who receives the confirmation will *also* be bound by it unless he objects in writing within 10 days.** This exception dramatically changes the rules from the common law. It only applies between two merchants, since the drafters of the Code assumed that experienced merchants are able to take care of themselves in fast-moving negotiations. The critical difference is this: a writing may create a binding contract even when it is not signed by the defendant.

The UCC gives merchants special leeway—and important responsibilities.

© ROLF BRUDERER/CORBIS

Madge manufactures "beanies," that is, silly caps with plastic propellers on top. Rachel, a retailer, telephones her and they discuss the price of the beanies, shipping time, and other details. Madge then faxes Rachel a memo: "This confirms your order for 2,500 beanies at $12.25 per beanie. Colors: blue, green, black, orange, red. Delivery date: 10 days. [Signed] Madge." Rachel receives the fax, reads it while negotiating with another manufacturer, and throws it in the wastebasket. Rachel buys her beanies elsewhere and Madge sues. Rachel defends, claiming there is no written contract because she, Rachel, never signed anything. Madge wins, under UCC §2-201(2). Both parties were merchants, because they routinely dealt in these goods. Madge signed and sent a confirming memo that could have been used to hold her, Madge, to the deal. When Rachel read it, she was not free to disregard it. Obviously, the intelligent business practice would have been to promptly fax a reply saying, "I disagree. We do not have any deal for beanies." Since Rachel failed to respond within 10 days, Madge has an enforceable contract.

The following case arises in a commodities market where speed counts. Did the dealer send the confirming memo within a "reasonable time"?

CONAGRA V. NIERENBERG

301 Mont. 55, 7 P.3d 369
Supreme Court of Montana, 2000

Facts: Dennis Nierenberg and his father, Ralph, operated a wheat farm in Montana. On April 9, Dennis telephoned Marcus Raba, the manager of ConAgra, a grain dealer. According to Raba, the two reached an agreement for the Nierenbergs to sell ConAgra 12,500 bushels of wheat for $5.01 per bushel. Dennis claims that he never agreed to sell, but was merely checking on prices.

ConAgra then prepared a written "confirmation" contract, stating a price of $5.01 for each of 12,500 bushels. A ConAgra executive signed it and held it "for Dennis to come in and sign." According to ConAgra, when Dennis failed to show up, the company mailed the document to him on April 17. Dennis admitted receiving the document on April 19. ▼

Four days later, the Nierenbergs sold all 12,500 bushels to another dealer for $5.85 per bushel. They never notified ConAgra of this sale. ConAgra, believing it owned the wheat, resold it; however, to fulfill that contract, the company was forced to pay the current market price of $6.14 per bushel. ConAgra sued the Nierenbergs.

Dennis had been selling grain to various dealers for ten years, and the trial court concluded that both parties were merchants. ConAgra claimed that under the merchants' exception, a contract was formed when Dennis failed to reject the confirmation notice within ten days. However, the court ruled that ConAgra itself had not sent the confirmation "within a reasonable time of making the oral contract." The court gave judgment for Dennis and ConAgra appealed.

Issue: Had ConAgra complied with the merchant's exception by sending the confirmation within a reasonable time?

Excerpts from Justice Nelson's Decision: The "merchant" exception is one born from the coupling of custom and efficiency in the market place. Wheat, for example, must pass through numerous sales transactions on its journey from field to bakery, a process that simply does not permit the time-consuming enterprise of carefully drafted and executed written agreements stating all material terms. In theory, it is essential to the wheat farmer merchant, as well as to the merchant-buyer, that prices can be contractually fixed orally, by phone, given the constraints of both time and physical proximity. The determination of what constitutes a "reasonable time" under any given specific set of facts depends on the nature, purpose, and circumstances of such action.

Here, ConAgra's "usual" practice was to either hold the confirmation contract until the farmer came in, or mail it to the farmer, depending on the farmer's preference. No definite time period was offered into evidence or otherwise established in this respect. In their brief, the Nierenbergs further suggest that it would be reasonable for the grain elevator to mail confirmation to the farmer "within a day or two of the telephone conversation."

ConAgra's excuse for what amounts to a six, rather than two-day, delay (including a Sunday) in mailing the confirmation is that in the past Dennis had come to the elevator to sign the confirmation, and due to a misunderstanding, acted upon the belief that this same course would be followed. This misunderstanding, in fact, appears in the District Court's contradictory findings which state that Dennis informed Raba "he would visit the elevator offices to sign the contract" and nevertheless found that ConAgra "did not immediately mail such document to Nierenberg." The evidence shows that ConAgra waited for approximately six days for Dennis's arrival, and then mailed the confirmation to his address.

Under these facts, assuming but not deciding that it would be reasonable for ConAgra to mail the confirmation within one or two working days, the slight delay in Dennis's receipt of the confirmation due to an apparent misunderstanding would not be an unreasonable deviation from ConAgra's usual practice under the circumstances. We thus hold that the District Court did not rely on the substantial evidence of this case in determining that Dennis did not receive confirmation of the oral contract within a reasonable time.

[Reversed and remanded] ■

Devil's Advocate

If grain prices change unpredictably and quick action is essential, why did ConAgra dither away ten days? When Dennis failed to show up and sign the agreement, why not hand deliver the document to him? By contrast, ConAgra was very quick to assume it had a binding deal, as it brazenly informed Dennis on April 19. Yet Dennis had just received the document, meaning that no contract could be formed for ten more days. ◆

UCC §2-201(3)—Special Circumstances

An oral contract *may* be enforceable, even without a written memorandum, if:

- **The seller is specially manufacturing the goods for the buyer, *or***
- **The defendant admits in court proceedings that there was a contract, *or***
- **The goods have been delivered or they have been paid for.**

In these three special circumstances, a court may enforce an oral contract even without a memorandum.

Specially Manufactured Goods

If a seller, specially manufacturing goods for the buyer, begins work on them before the buyer cancels, and the goods cannot be sold elsewhere, the oral contract is binding. Bernice manufactures solar heating systems. She phones Jason and orders 75 special electrical converter units designed for her heating system, at $150 per unit. Jason begins manufacturing the units, but then Bernice phones again and says she no longer needs them. Bernice is bound by the contract. The goods are being manufactured for her and cannot be sold elsewhere. Jason had already begun work when she attempted to cancel. If the case goes to court, Jason will win.

Admissions in Court

When the defendant admits in court proceedings that the parties made an oral contract, the agreement is binding. Rex sues Sophie, alleging that she orally agreed to sell him five boa constrictors that have been trained to stand in a line and pass a full wine glass from one snake to the next. Sophie defends the lawsuit, but during a deposition she says, "OK, we agreed verbally, but nothing was ever put in writing, and I knew I didn't have to go through with it. When I went home, the snakes made me feel really guilty, and I decided not to sell." Sophie's admission under oath dooms her defense.

Goods Delivered or Paid For

If the seller has delivered the goods, or the buyer has paid for them, the contract may be enforced even with nothing in writing. Malik orally agrees to sell 500 plastic chairs to University for use in its cafeteria. Malik delivers 300 of the chairs, but then University notifies him that it will not honor the deal. Malik is entitled to payment for the 300 chairs, though not for the other 200. Conversely, if University had sent a check for one-half of the chairs, it would be entitled to 250 chairs.

---

cyberLaw

Electronic Contracts and Signatures. E-commerce has grown at a dazzling rate, and U.S. enterprises buy and sell tens of billions of dollars worth of goods and services over the Internet. What happens to the writing requirement, though, when there is no paper? The present statute of frauds requires some sort of "signing" to ensure that the defendant committed to the deal. Today, an "electronic signature" could mean a name typed (or automatically included) at the bottom of an e-mail message, a retinal or vocal scan, or a name signed by electronic pen on a writing tablet, among others.

Are electronic signatures valid? Yes. State legislatures and Congress are struggling to craft a cohesive law, and the job is incomplete, but here are the rules so far:

- **The Uniform Electronic Transaction Act (UETA).** This law was drafted by the National Conference of Commissioners on Uniform State Laws, who also draft the UCC. As this book goes to press, UETA is the law in 48 states and territories. UETA declares that a contract or signature may not be denied enforceability simply because it is in electronic form. In other words, the normal rules of contract law apply, but one party may not avoid such a deal merely because it originated in cyberspace.

- **The Electronic Signatures in Global and National Commerce Act (E-Sign).** This federal statute, which applies in any state that has not adopted UETA, also declares that contracts will not be denied enforcement simply because they are in electronic form, or signed electronically.

With cyberlaw in its early stages, how can an executive take advantage of the Internet's commercial opportunities while protecting his company against losses unique to the field?

First, acknowledge the risks, which include lost or intercepted communications, fraudulently altered documents, and difficulties authenticating the source of an offer or acceptance. Second, be cautious about "electronic signatures." Assume that any commitments you make electronically can be enforced against you. Paradoxically, if the contract is important, do not assume that the other party's promises, if made electronically, are enforceable unless your lawyer has given you assurance. If in doubt, get a hard copy, signed in ink. ◆

PAROL EVIDENCE

Tyrone agrees to buy Martha's house for $800,000. The contract obligates Tyrone to make a 10 percent down payment immediately and pay the remaining $720,000 in 45 days. As the two parties sign the deal, Tyrone discusses his need for financing. Unfortunately, at the end of 45 days, he has been unable to get a mortgage for the full amount. He claims that the parties orally agreed that he would get his deposit back if he could not obtain financing. But the written agreement says no such thing, and Martha disputes the claim. Who will win? Probably Martha, because of the parol evidence rule. To understand this rule, you need to know two terms. **Parol evidence refers to anything (apart from the written contract itself) that was said, done, or written before the parties signed the agreement or as they signed it.** Martha's conversation with Tyrone about financing the house was parol evidence because it occurred as they were signing the contract. The other important term is **integrated contract,** which means a writing that the parties intend as the final, complete expression of their agreement. Now for the rule.

The parol evidence rule: When two parties make an integrated contract, neither one may use parol evidence to contradict, vary, or add to its terms. Negotiations may last for hours, weeks, or even months. Almost no contract includes everything that the parties said. When parties consider their agreement integrated, any statements they made before or while signing are irrelevant. If a court determines that Martha and Tyrone intended their agreement to be integrated, it will prohibit testimony about Martha's oral promises.

at RISK

One way to avoid parol evidence disputes is to include an *integration clause*. That is a statement clearly proclaiming that this writing is the full and final expression of the parties' agreement, and that anything said before signing or while signing is irrelevant. For example, an art dealer may say to a prospective buyer, "Watteau's paintings have increased in value 10 percent every year for the last decade. They're going to continue to climb, I know it." Perhaps the dealer shows the customer an article on Watteau that claims that his paintings are still undervalued. When it is time to sign the contract, the dealer will not want these statements included, since they were meaningless puffery, and he has no intention of being bound by them. The dealer will include an integration clause, stating that the buyer is not relying on any promises, statements, or documents of any kind made or examined during negotiations, and that the written agreement is the complete expression of their contract. ◆

In the following case, learned people learned about parol evidence the hard way.

MAYO V. NORTH CAROLINA STATE UNIVERSITY

2005 WL 350567
North Carolina Court of Appeals, 2005

Facts: Dr. Robert Mayo was a tenured faculty member of the engineering department at North Carolina State University (NCSU), and director of the school's nuclear engineering program. In July, he informed his department chair, Dr. Paul Turinsky, that he was leaving NCSU effective September 1. Turinsky accepted the resignation.

In October, after Mayo had departed, Phyllis Jennette, the university's payroll coordinator, informed him that he had been overpaid. She explained that for employees who worked 9 months but were paid over 12 months, the salary checks for July and August were in fact prepayments for the period beginning that September. Because Mayo had not worked after September first, the checks for July and August were overpayment. When he refused to refund the money, NCSU sought to claim it in legal proceedings. The first step was a hearing before an administrative agency.

At the hearing, Turinsky and Brian Simet, the university's payroll director, explained that the "prepayment" rule was a basic part of every employee's contract. However, both acknowledged that the prepayment rule was not included in any of the documents that formed Mayo's contract, including his appointment letter, annual salary letter, and policies adopted by the University's trustees. The university officials used other evidence, outside the written documents, to establish the prepayment policy.

Based on the additional evidence, the agency ruled that NCSU was entitled to its money. However, Mayo appealed to court, and the trial judge declared that he owed nothing, ruling that the university was not permitted to rely on parol evidence to establish its policy. NCSU appealed.

Issue: What evidence could NCSU rely upon to establish its prepayment rule?

Excerpts from Judge Bryant's Decision: Here, the language of the employment agreement is clear and unambiguous—petitioner is to be paid in twelve monthly installments for his service as a nine-month, academic year, tenured faculty member.

The terms relied upon by NCSU were not expressly included in the employment agreement. Dr. Turinsky testified that petitioner's written employment agreement is comprised of terms found in petitioner's appointment letter, annual salary letter, and written policies adopted and amended by the UNC Board of Governors and the NCSU Board of Trustees. However, none of these documents forming the employment agreement set forth the compensation policies upon which NCSU bases its claim. Simet, Director of NCSU's Payroll Department, admitted at the agency hearing that the policies were "not stated anywhere specifically." Further, Dr. Turinsky testified he did not know of the existence of the terms until September, after petitioner left his employment with NCSU. NCSU, however, attempts to offer parol evidence to explain that payments made in July and August were prepayments for the following academic year.

The parol evidence rule prohibits the admission of parol evidence to vary, add to, or contradict a written instrument intended to be the final integration of the transaction. The rule is otherwise where it is shown that the writing is not a full integration of the terms of the contract, or when a contract is ambiguous, parol evidence is admissible to show and make certain the intention behind the contract.

Here Dr. Turinsky testified that petitioner's employment agreement consisted only of petitioner's appointment letter, his annual salary letter, and the policies adopted and amended by the UNC Board of Governors and by the NCSU Board of Trustees. It therefore appears the parties intended the above documents to be the final integration of the employment agreement. Additionally, we have already noted the language contained in the documents are unambiguous; thus, parol evidence may not be introduced to explain the terms of the agreement.

We hold petitioner does not owe a debt to NCSU as result of an alleged overpayment of salary.

[Reversed.] ∎

Exception: An Incomplete or Ambiguous Contract

If a court determines that a written contract is incomplete or ambiguous, it will permit parol evidence. Suppose that an employment contract states that the company will provide "full health coverage for Robert Watson and his family." Three years later, Watson divorces and remarries, acquiring three stepchildren, and a year later his second wife has a baby. Watson now has two children by his first marriage, and four by the second. The company refuses to insure Watson's first wife or his stepchildren. A court will probably find that the health care clause is ambiguous. A judge cannot determine exactly what the clause means from the contract itself, so the parties will be permitted to introduce parol evidence to prove whether or not the company must insure Watson's extended family.[11]

Misrepresentation or Duress

A court will permit parol evidence of misrepresentation or duress. To encourage Annette to buy his house, Will assures her that no floodwaters from the nearby river have ever come within two miles of the house. Annette signs a contract, which is silent about flooding and includes an integration clause stating that neither party is relying on any oral statements made during negotiations. When Annette moves in, she discovers that the foundation is collapsing due to earlier flooding, and that Will knew of the flooding and the damage. Despite the integration clause, a court will probably allow Annette to testify about Will's misrepresentations.[12]

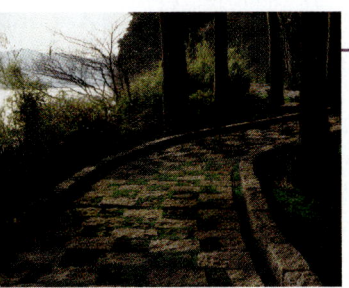

© IMAGE 100/GETTY IMAGES

Chapter Conclusion

Some contracts must be in writing to be enforceable, and the writing must be clear and unambiguous. Drafting the contract need not be arduous. The disputes illustrated in this chapter could all have been prevented with a few carefully crafted sentences. It is worth the time and effort to write them.

Chapter Review

1. Contracts that must be in writing to be enforceable concern:

   - The sale of any interest in land

   - Agreements that cannot be performed within one year

   - Promises to pay the debt of another

   - Promises made by an executor of an estate

   - Promises made in consideration of marriage; and

   - The sale of goods worth $500 or more

2. The writing must be signed by the defendant and must state the name of all parties, the subject matter of the agreement, and all essential terms and promises.

---

[11] See, e.g., *Eure v. Norfolk Shipbuilding & Drydock Corp., Inc.,* 561 S.E.2d 663 (Va. 2002).
[12] *Lindberg v. Roseth,* 137 Idaho 222, 46 P.3d 518 (2002).

3. A contract or memorandum for the sale of goods may be less complete than those required by the common law.

- The basic UCC rule requires only a memorandum signed by the defendant, indicating that the parties reached an agreement and specifying the quantity of goods.

- Between merchants even less is required. If one merchant sends written confirmation of a contract, the merchant who receives the document must object within 10 days or be bound by the writing.

- In the following special circumstances, no writing may be required: the goods are specially manufactured; one party admits in litigation that there was a contract; or one party pays for part of the goods or delivers some of the goods.

4. When an integrated contract exists, neither party may generally use parol evidence to contradict, vary, or add to its terms. Parol evidence refers to anything (apart from the written contract itself) that was said, done, or written before the parties signed the agreement or as they signed it.

Practice Test

1. **CPA QUESTION** Able hired Carr to restore Able's antique car for $800. The terms of their oral agreement provided that Carr was to complete the work within 18 months. Actually, the work could be completed within one year. The agreement is:

   a. Unenforceable because it covers services with a value in excess of $500

   b. Unenforceable because it covers a time period in excess of one year

   c. Enforceable because personal service contracts are exempt from the statute of frauds

   d. Enforceable because the work could be completed within one year

2. Richard Griffin and three other men owned a grain company called Bearhouse, Inc., which needed to borrow money. First National Bank was willing to loan $490,000, but insisted that the four men sign personal guaranties on the loan, committing themselves to repaying up to 25 percent of the loan each if Bearhouse defaulted. Bearhouse went bankrupt. The bank was able to collect some of its money from Bearhouse's assets, but it sued Griffin for the balance. At trial, Griffin wanted to testify that before he signed his guaranty, a bank officer assured him that he would only owe 25 percent of *whatever balance was unpaid*, not 25 percent of the total loan. How will the court decide whether Griffin is entitled to testify about the conversation?

3. Donald Waide had a contracting business. He bought most of his supplies from Paul Bingham's supply center. Waide fell behind on his bills, and Bingham told Waide that he would extend no more credit to him. That same day, Donald's father, Elmer Waide, came to Bingham's store, and said to Bingham that he would "stand good" for any sales to Donald made on credit. Based on Elmer's statement, Bingham again gave Donald credit, and Donald ran up $10,000 in goods before Bingham sued Donald and Elmer. What defense did Elmer make and what was the outcome?

4. James River-Norwalk, Inc., was a paper and textile company that needed a constant supply of wood. James River orally contracted with Gary Futch to procure wood for the company, and Futch did so for several years. Futch actually purchased the wood for his own account and then resold it to James River. Do the parties have an agreement for services or for sale of goods? Why does it matter?

5. When Deana Byers married Steven Byers, she was pregnant with another man's child. Shortly after the marriage Deana gave birth. The marriage lasted only two months, and the couple separated. In divorce proceedings, Deana sought child support. She claimed that Steven had orally promised to support the child if Deana would marry him. Steven claims he never made the promise. Comment on the outcome.

6. **CPA QUESTION** Two individuals signed a contract that was intended to be their entire agreement. The parol evidence rule will prevent the admission of evidence offered to:

a. Explain the meaning of an ambiguity in the written contract

b. Establish that fraud had been committed in the formation of the contract

c. Prove the existence of a contemporaneous oral agreement modifying the contract

d. Prove the existence of a subsequent oral agreement modifying the contract

7. Lonnie Hippen moved to Long Island, Kansas, to work in an insurance company owned by Griffiths. After he moved there, Griffiths offered to sell Hippen a house he owned, and Hippen agreed in writing to buy it. He did buy the house and moved in, but two years later Hippen left the insurance company. He then claimed that at the time of the sale, Griffiths had orally promised to buy back his house at the selling price if Hippen should happen to leave the company. Griffiths defended based on the statute of frauds. Hippen argued that the statute of frauds did not apply because the repurchase of the house was essentially part of his employment with Griffiths. Comment.

8. *ETHICS* Jacob Deutsch owned commercial property. He orally agreed to rent it for six years to Budget Rent-A-Car. Budget took possession, began paying monthly rent, and over a period of several months expended about $6,000 in upgrading the property. Deutsch was aware of the repairs. After a year, Deutsch attempted to evict Budget. Budget claimed it had a six-year oral lease, but Deutsch claimed that such a lease was worthless. Please rule. Is it ethical for Deutsch to use the statute of frauds in attempting to defeat the lease? Assume that, as landlord, you had orally agreed to rent premises to a tenant, but then for business reasons preferred not to carry out the deal. Would you evict a tenant if you thought the statute of frauds would enable you to do so? How should you analyze the problem? What values are most important to you?

9. Landlord owned a clothing store and agreed in writing to lease the store's basement to another retailer. The written lease, which both parties signed, (1) described the premises exactly, (2) identified the parties, and (3) stated the monthly rent clearly. But an appeals court held that the lease did not satisfy the statute of frauds. Why not?

10. *YOU BE THE JUDGE* WRITING PROBLEM Harrison Epperly operated United Brake Sys-

tems in Indianapolis, Indiana, and wanted to open a similar store in Nashville. He offered Kenneth Jarrett a job as manager, promising six months severance pay if the store was not profitable in six months, and 49 percent ownership if he managed the new store for 10 years. Jarrett agreed, but the two men never put the deal in writing. Under Jarrett's management, the Nashville branch grew dramatically. After four years of renting space, the company purchased the land and buildings it used. Epperly periodically acknowledged his promise to make Jarrett 49 percent owner of the Nashville branch, and from time to time he mentioned the arrangement to other workers. But after 10 years, Epperly sold United Brake, which had grown to 23 branches, to another company for $11 million. Jarrett sued Epperly for 49 percent of the Nashville branch. The trial court awarded Jarrett $812,000. Epperly appealed. Is Jarrett's contract with Epperly barred by the statute of frauds? **Argument for Epperly:** This alleged contract is unenforceable for two reasons. First, the agreement includes real estate, namely, the valuable land and buildings the company uses. A contract for the sale of any interest in land is unenforceable unless written. Second, the contract could not have been performed within one year. If there was a deal, then by Jarrett's own words the parties intended it to last 10 years. Ten years' work cannot be performed in one year. **Argument for Jarrett:** The agreement had nothing to do with land. Jarrett and Epperly agreed that Mr. Jarrett would obtain a 49 percent ownership of the *Nashville branch*. At the time they made that agreement, the Nashville branch had no real estate. There is no rule saying that a valid contract becomes invalid because a corporation acquires some land. The "not in one year" argument also misses the point. The primary obligation was to open the branch and manage it for six months. If it was not profitable, Mr. Jarrett would immediately receive six months' severance pay, and the contract would be fully performed by both parties in less than a year. Finally, Epperly made a binding commitment and Mr. Jarrett relied. Promissory estoppel prohibits Mr. Epperly from using deceit to profit.

11. Mast Industries and Bazak International were two textile firms. Mast orally offered to sell certain textiles to Bazak for $103,000. Mast promised to send documents confirming the agreement,

but never did. Finally, Bazak sent a memorandum to Mast confirming the agreement, describing the goods, and specifying their quantity and the price. Bazak's officer signed the memo. Mast received the memo but never agreed to it in writing. When Mast failed to deliver the goods, Bazak sued. Who won?

Internet Research Problem

Examine the lease shown at http://beatty.westbuslaw .com. Is it important for a lease to be in writing? Who probably drafted the lease, a landlord or a tenant? How can you tell? Should any other provisions be included?

12. **ROLE REVERSAL** Write a multiple-choice question that focuses on the merchants' exception to the statute of frauds.

You can find further practice problems at http://beatty.westbuslaw.com or in the **Study Guide that accompanies this text.**

Third Parties

During television's formative days, Howdy Doody was one of the medium's biggest stars. His acting was wooden—as were his head and body—but for 13 years Howdy and an assorted group of puppets starred in one of the most popular children's programs of all time. Rufus Rose maintained and repaired the puppets. When Howdy took his last double-jointed bow (to a chorus of toddler wails), NBC permitted Rose temporarily to keep the various puppets. Six years later, NBC became concerned that Rose was inadequately maintaining them. The network wanted Howdy and friends moved to a safe, public location. Rose claimed the puppets were in good shape and wanted payment for the maintenance he had provided. The two parties agreed in writing that Rose would give Howdy and the other stars of the show (including Dilly Dally and Flub-A-Dub) to a puppet museum at the Detroit Institute of Arts (DIA). NBC agreed to pay the puppeteer for his work. The company permitted Rose to keep some of the minor puppets from the program, provided they were not used for commercial purposes.

© PHOTODISC COLLECTION/GETTY IMAGES

When Rose died, his son Christopher took possession of the famous puppet. At about that time, a copy of Howdy sold at auction for $113,000. Christopher then claimed ownership of Howdy Doody and refused to give him to the museum.

The DIA wanted its famous puppet, but the museum had never been a party to the agreement between NBC and Rose. Did the DIA have any rights to Howdy? The museum filed suit, making a third party claim. ■

The basic pattern in third party law is quite simple. Two parties make a contract, and their rights and obligations are subject to the rules that we have already studied: offer and acceptance, consideration, legality, and so forth. However, sometimes their contract affects a *third party*, one who had no role in forming the agreement itself. The two contracting parties may intend to benefit a third person. Those are cases of *third party beneficiary*. In other cases, one of the contracting parties may actually transfer his rights or responsibilities to a third party, raising issues of *assignment* or *delegation*. We consider the issues one at a time.

THIRD PARTY BENEFICIARY

The two parties who make a contract always intend to benefit themselves. Oftentimes their bargain will also benefit someone else. **A third party beneficiary is someone who was not a party to the contract but stands to benefit from it.** Many contracts create third party beneficiaries. In the chapter's introduction, NBC and Rufus Rose contracted to give Howdy Doody to the Detroit Institute of Arts. The museum stood to benefit from this agreement.

As another example, suppose a city contracts to purchase from Seller 20 acres of an abandoned industrial site in a rundown neighborhood, to be used for a new domed stadium. The owner of a pizza parlor on the edge of Seller's land might benefit enormously. A once marginal operation could become a gold mine of cheese and pepperoni.

When the two contracting parties fulfill their obligations and the third party receives her benefit, there is no dispute to analyze. If Christopher Rose had walked Howdy Doody into the puppet museum, and if the city completed the stadium, there would be no unhappy third parties. Problems arise when one of the parties fails to perform the contract as expected. The issue is this: *May the third party beneficiary enforce the contract?* The museum had no contract with the Rose family. Is the museum entitled to the puppet? The pizza parlor owner was not a party to the contract for the sale of the stadium land. If the city breaks its agreement to buy the property, should the owner recover profits for unsold sausage and green pepper?

The outcome in cases like these depends upon the intentions of the two contracting parties. If they intended to benefit the third party, she will probably be permitted to enforce their contract. If they did not intend to benefit her, she probably has no power to enforce the agreement. The Restatement uses a bit more detail to analyze these cases. We must first recall the terms "promisor" and "promisee." The **promisor** is the one who makes the promise that the third party beneficiary is seeking to enforce. Parts of the contract may not interest her, so the Restatement looks only at the relevant promise, not at the entire contract. The **promisee** is the other party to the contract.

According to the **Restatement (Second) of Contracts §302: A beneficiary of a promise is an intended beneficiary and may enforce a contract if the parties intended her to benefit** *and if either* (a) enforcing the promise will satisfy a duty of the promisee to the beneficiary, or (b) the promisee intended to make a gift to the beneficiary.

Any beneficiary who is not an intended beneficiary is an **incidental beneficiary,** and may not enforce the contract. In other words, a third party beneficiary must show two things in order to enforce a contract that two other people created. First, she must show that the two contracting parties were aware of her situation and knew that she would receive something of value from their deal. Second, she must show that the promisee wanted to benefit her for one of two reasons: either to satisfy some duty owed or to make her a gift.

If the promisee is fulfilling some duty, the third party beneficiary is called a **creditor beneficiary.** Most often, the "duty" that a promisee will be fulfilling is a debt already owed to the beneficiary. If the promisee is making a gift, the third party is a **donee beneficiary.**[1] As long as the third party is either a creditor or a donee beneficiary, she may enforce the contract. If she is only an incidental beneficiary, she may not.

We will apply this rule to the dispute over Howdy Doody. Like most contracts, the deal between NBC and Rufus Rose had two promises: Rose's agreement to give the puppet to the museum, and NBC's promise to pay for the work done on Howdy. The promise that interests us was the one concerning Howdy's destination in Detroit. Rose was the promisor and NBC was the promisee.

Did the two parties intend to benefit the museum? Yes, they did. NBC wanted Howdy to be displayed to the general public, and in a noncommercial venue. Rose, who wanted payment for work already done, was happy to go along with the network's wishes. Did NBC owe a duty to the museum? No. Did the network intend to make a gift to the museum? Yes. The museum wins! The Detroit Institute of Arts was an intended third party beneficiary, and is entitled to Howdy Doody.[2] See Exhibit 16.1.

By contrast, the pizza parlor owner will surely lose. A stadium is a multimillion dollar investment, and it is most unlikely that the city and the seller of the land were even

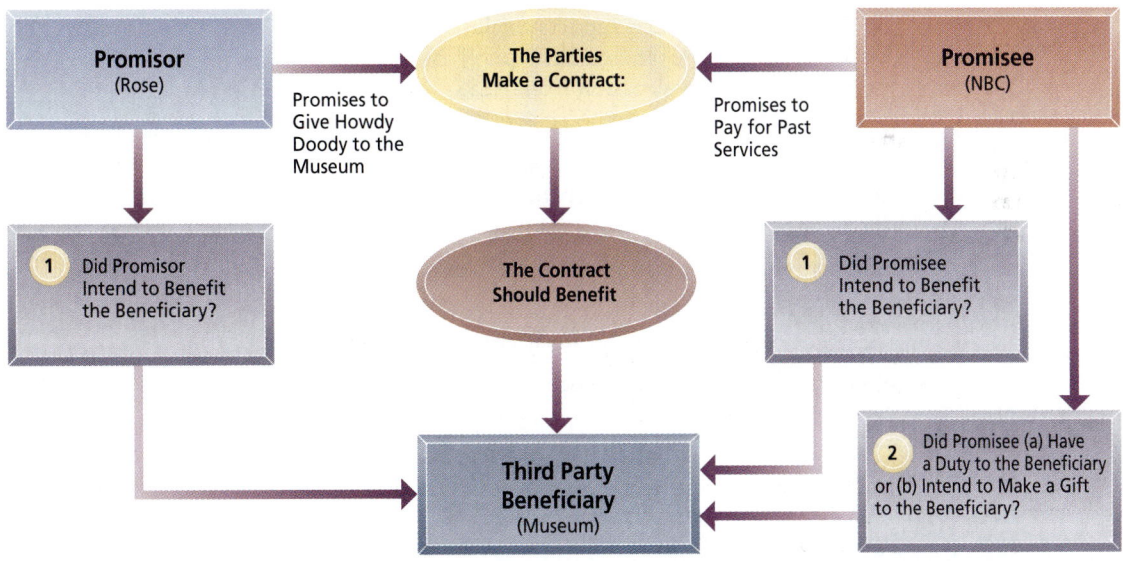

Exhibit 16.1

The issue: **May a third party beneficiary enforce a contract to which it was not a party?**

The answer: **A third party beneficiary may enforce a contract if (1) the parties intended to benefit it and *either* (2)(a) enforcing the promise will satisfy a duty of the promisee to the beneficiary or (2)(b)** the promisee intended to make a gift to the beneficiary.

In this case: **Rose and NBC both intended to benefit the museum. The promisee (NBC) intended to make a *gift* to the museum. The museum is therefore an intended third party beneficiary, entitled to the puppet.**

---

1 "Donee" comes from the word "donate," meaning "to give."
2 *The Detroit Institute of Arts Founders Society v. Rose,* 127 F. Supp. 2d 117 (D. Conn. 2001).

aware of the owner's existence, let alone that they intended to benefit him. He probably cannot prove either the first element or the second element, and certainly not both.

When negotiating an agreement, it is important to anticipate third party claims. Real Estate Support Services (RESS) performed house inspections for potential buyers. RESS contracted with a realtor, Coldwell Banker Relocation Services, Inc., to inspect houses and furnish reports to Coldwell. The agreement stated that the purpose of the reports was:

> To provide the client [Coldwell] with a report of a relocating employee's home, consisting of a series of visual inspection of items contained in pages 1 through 5 of this form, which the client may, at its discretion, disclose to other interested parties.

RESS inspected a house in Greencastle, Indiana, and gave its report to Coldwell, which passed the document on to Paul and Norma Nauman. The Naumans relied on the report and bought the house, but later discovered defects RESS had not mentioned. They sued RESS, claiming to be third party beneficiaries of the company's contract with Coldwell. The court ruled for the Naumans. Coldwell obviously intended to use the reports as a sales tool, and RESS knew it, making buyers such as the Naumans intended beneficiaries.[3]

at RISK

Coldwell presented RESS with a contract that invited claims from third party beneficiaries. That was the time for RESS to decide, "Can we tolerate liability to all buyers who might see the report?" If the company was unwilling to assume such extensive liability, it should have proposed appropriate contract language, such as:

> RESS is preparing these reports exclusively for Coldwell's use. Coldwell will not disclose any report to a house purchaser or any other person without first obtaining written permission from RESS.

If Coldwell had accepted the language, there would have been no lawsuit. Perhaps Coldwell would have insisted on its right to disclose the reports to purchasers. Then RESS would have had two options: sign the contract, acknowledging the company's exposure to third parties, or walk away from the negotiations. To summarize:

- *Anticipate* problems. Examine the deal you are making from the perspective of others—in this case, third party beneficiaries.

- Force yourself to *decide now* what risks you can tolerate.

- *Negotiate* a contract that reflects your decisions. If you are unable to get a deal you can live with, do not sign. ◆

In the following case, a dazzling diamond loses its luster. Who is entitled to sue?

SCHAUER V. MANDARIN GEMS OF CALIFORNIA, INC.

2005 WL 5730
Court of Appeal of California, 2005

Facts: Sarah Schauer and her fiancé, Darin Erstad, went shopping for an engagement ring, first at Tiffany and Cartier, then at Mandarin Gems, where they were captivated by a 3.01 carat diamond with a clarity grading of "S11." Erstad bought the ring the same day for $43,121. Later, Mandarin supplied ▼

---

[3]   *Real Estate Support Services v. Nauman,* 644 N.E.2d 907, 1994 Ind. App. LEXIS 1796 (Ind. Ct. App. 1994).

Erstad with a written appraisal, again rating the ring as an S11, and valuing it at $45,500. Paul Lam, a certified gemologist, signed the appraisal.

Diamonds may last forever but this marriage was short-lived. The divorce decree gave each party the right to keep whatever personal property they currently held, meaning that Schauer could keep the ring. She had the ring appraised by the Gem Trade Laboratory, which gave it a poorer clarity rating, and a value of $20,000.

Schauer sued Mandarin for misrepresentation and breach of contract, but the jeweler defended by saying that it had never contracted with her, and that she was not a third party beneficiary of the company's agreement with Erstad. The trial court dismissed Schauer's suit, and she appealed.

Issue: Does Schauer have any right to sue for breach of contract?

Excerpts from Judge Ikola's Decision: Plaintiff has standing in her own right to sue for breach of contract as a third party beneficiary under the allegation that defendant entered into a written contract with Plaintiff's fiancé to purchase the subject engagement ring for the sole and stated purpose of giving it to Plaintiff.

A contract, made expressly for the benefit of a third person, may be enforced by him or her at any time before the parties thereto rescind it. Because third party beneficiary status is a matter of contract interpretation, a person seeking to enforce a contract as a third party beneficiary must plead a contract which was made expressly for his or her benefit and one in which it clearly appears that he or she was a beneficiary.

An intent to make the obligation inure to the benefit of the third party must have been clearly manifested by the contracting parties. Although this means persons only incidentally or remotely benefited by the contract are not entitled to enforce it, it does not mean both of the contracting parties must intend to benefit the third party: Rather, it means the promisor—in this case, defendant jeweler—must have understood that the promisee (Erstad) had such intent. No specific manifestation by the promisor of an intent to benefit the third person is required.

We conclude the pleading here meets the test of demonstrating plaintiff's standing as a third party beneficiary to enforce the contract between Erstad and defendant. The couple went shopping for an engagement ring. They were together when plaintiff chose the ring she wanted or, as alleged in the complaint, she caused the ring to be purchased for her. Erstad allegedly bought the ring for the sole and *stated* purpose of giving the ring to plaintiff. Under the alleged facts, the jeweler *must* have understood Erstad's intent to enter the sales contract for plaintiff's benefit. Thus, plaintiff has adequately pleaded her status as a third party beneficiary, and she is entitled to proceed with her contract claim against defendant. ■

ASSIGNMENT AND DELEGATION

A contracting party may transfer his rights under the contract, which is called an **assignment of rights.** Or a party may transfer her duties pursuant to the contract, which is a **delegation of duties.** Frequently, a party will make an assignment and delegation simultaneously, transferring both rights and duties to a third party.

Statutory and common law, the Restatement (Second) of Contracts, and the UCC all govern various aspects of assignments. For our purposes, the Restatement serves as a good summary of common law provisions. The UCC rules are generally similar, although we note some differences later on. Our first example is a sale of goods case, governed by the UCC, but the outcome would be the same under the Restatement.

Lydia needs 500 bottles of champagne. Bruno agrees to sell them to her for $10,000, payable 30 days after delivery. He transports the wine to her. Bruno happens to owe Doug $8,000 from a previous deal, so he says to Doug, "I don't have the money, but I'll give you my claim to Lydia's $10,000." Doug agrees. Bruno then *assigns* to Doug *his rights* to Lydia's money, and in exchange Doug gives up his claim for $8,000. Bruno is the **assignor, the one making an assignment,** and Doug is the **assignee, the one receiving an assignment.**

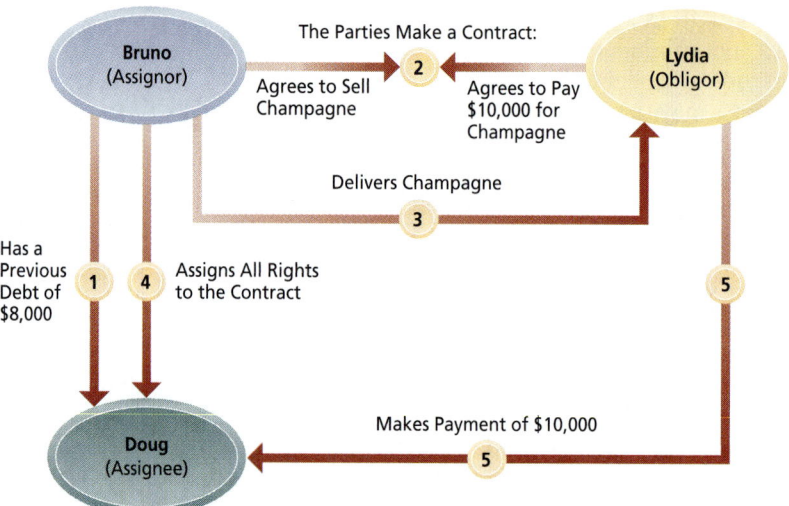

Exhibit 16.2

Why would Bruno offer $10,000 when he owed Doug only $8,000? Because all he has is a *claim* to Lydia's money. Cash in hand is often more valuable. Doug, however, is willing to assume some risk for a potential $2,000 gain.

Bruno notifies Lydia of the assignment. Lydia, who owes the money, is called the **obligor,** that is, the one obligated to do something. At the end of 30 days, Doug arrives at Lydia's doorstep, asks for his money, and gets it, since Lydia is obligated to him. Bruno has no claim to any payment. See Exhibit 16.2.

Lydia bought the champagne because she knew she could sell it at a profit. She promptly agrees to sell and deliver the 500 bottles to Coretta, at a mountaintop wilderness camp. Lydia has no four-wheel drive cars, so she finds Keith, who is willing to deliver the bottles for $1,000. Lydia *delegates her duty* to Keith to deliver the bottles to Coretta. Keith is now obligated to deliver the bottles to Coretta, the **obligee,** that is, the one who has the obligation coming to her. As we see later, Lydia also remains obligated to Coretta, the obligee, to ensure that the bottles are delivered. See Exhibit 16.3.

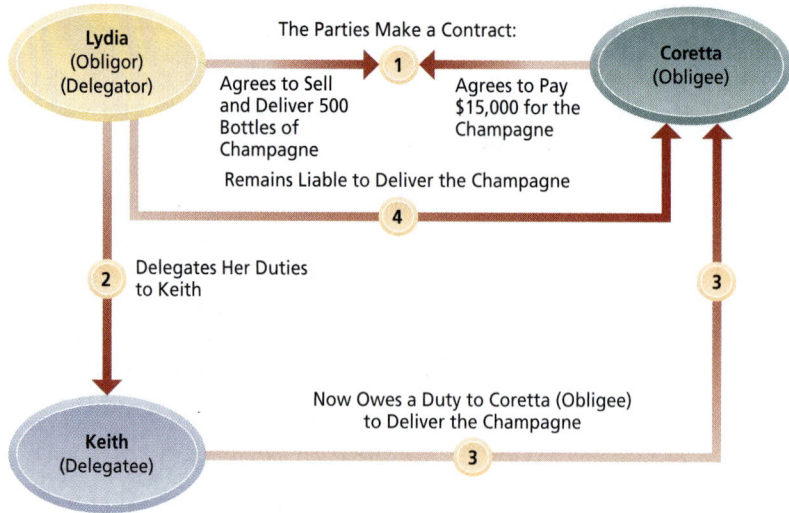

Exhibit 16.3

Assignment and delegation can each create problems. We will examine the most common ones.

Assignment

What Rights Are Assignable?

Most contract rights are assignable, but not all. Disputes sometimes arise between the two contracting parties about whether one of the parties could legally assign her rights to a third party. The Restatement (Second) of Contracts §317(2) sums up the assignability of rights this way:

Any contractual right may be assigned unless assignment

(a) would substantially change the obligor's rights or duties under the contract; or

(b) is forbidden by law or public policy; or

(c) is validly precluded by the contract itself.[4]

Substantial Change. Subsection (a) prohibits an assignment if it would substantially change the obligor's situation. For example, Bruno is permitted to assign to Doug his rights to payment from Lydia because it makes no difference to Lydia whether she writes a check to one or the other. But suppose Erica, who lives on a one-quarter acre lot in Hardscrabble, hires Keith to mow her lawn once per week for the summer, for a total fee of $700. Erica pays up front, before she leaves for the summer. May she assign her right to weekly lawn care to Lloyd, who enjoys a three-acre estate in Halcyon, 60 miles distant? No. The extra travel and far larger yard would dramatically change Keith's obligations, and Erica has no right to make the assignment.

Assignment is also prohibited when the obligor is agreeing to perform **personal services.** The close working relationship in such agreements makes it unfair to expect the obligor to work with a stranger. Warner, a feature film director, hires Mayer to be his assistant on a film to be shot over the next 10 weeks. Warner may not assign his right to Mayer's work to another director.

Public Policy. Some assignments are prohibited by public policy. For example, someone who has suffered a personal injury may not assign her claim to a third person. Vladimir is playing the piano on his roof deck when the instrument rolls over the balustrade and drops 35 stories, striking Wanda and bruising her elbow. Wanda has a valid tort claim against Vladimir, but she may not assign the claim to her father, Arturo. As a matter of public policy, all states have decided that the sale of personal injury claims would create an unseemly and unethical bazaar.

Contract Prohibition. Finally, one of the contracting parties may try to prohibit assignment in the agreement itself. For example, most landlords include in the written lease a clause prohibiting the tenant from assigning the tenancy without the landlord's written permission. Such clauses are generally, but not always, enforced by a court.

Ethics

Suppose a commercial tenant informs its landlord that it wishes to assign its lease. The landlord investigates the assignee, that is, the new tenant, and discovers that it is highly reputable and financially sound. But the landlord also realizes that rental rates have risen. May the landlord deny permission to the tenant to assign its lease, hoping to write a new lease at a higher rent? Most states hold that a landlord may do just that, whether or not it is morally right.

---

[4] Restatement (Second) of Contracts §317(2). And note that UCC §2-210 is, for our purposes, nearly identical.

Two tenants leased the property where they operated a successful deli. The long-term lease prohibited the tenants from assigning the lease without the landlord's permission. The tenants decided to sell their deli, and a buyer offered a good price. But the landlord refused assignment, meaning that the sale could not go through. The tenants sued, claiming that a landlord must permit assignment unless he has a *good faith* reason to deny it. Not so, said the Washington court. A party to a contract must perform an action in good faith *only if the contract requires that action.* This lease imposed no obligation on the landord to consent to assignment, so neither good faith nor bad faith was relevant. The court noted that, when the parties bargain a lease, the tenants could insist on a clause stating that a landlord may not unreasonably withhold permission to assign. These tenants failed to do that.[5]

Exactly the same issue landed before the New Mexico Supreme Court, which reached the opposite conclusion:

The majority of jurisdictions take the position that a landlord may withhold his consent without justification. However, in recent years, the trend is to require the landlord to act reasonably when withholding consent to sublease.

We adopt the latter view. The rationale for requiring a landlord to act reasonably when withholding consent to a subleasing agreement is that a lease, being a contract, should be governed by general contract principles of good faith and commercial reasonableness. Under this view, consent is not to be withheld unless the prospective tenant is unacceptable, using the same standards applied in the acceptance of the original tenant.

New Mexico law has consistently required fairness, justice and right dealing in all commercial practices and transactions. No logical reason exists for not requiring good faith in the rental of commercial premises.[6]

So the court permitted the tenant to assign its rights, even though the lease itself had prohibited assignment without the landlord's permission. Was this ruling a bold step forward for legal ethics? Or was it a fiat by a court imposing its morality on two parties who had, after all, freely entered into a lease? From the Chapter 2 ethics checklist: Has the process been fair? Which values are in conflict? Which of those values are more important? For an example of a residential lease with a no-assignment clause, see **http://www.kinseylaw .com/freestuff/leaseten/ResLease.html**. When you rent an apartment, the lease will probably contain a similar clause. ◆

The following case begins with everyone's dream come true: a winning lottery ticket. The winners want to assign their ticket and receive cash up front, but a statute appears to forbid the plan.

WATSON V. MICHIGAN BUREAU OF STATE LOTTERY

224 Mich. App. 639, 569 N.W.2d 878
Court of Appeals of Michigan, 1997

Facts: The Sweet Sixteen Lotto Club was jackpot winner in the Michigan lotto drawing, with a jackpot of $2,100,000. Each club member's share was $6,562 per year for 20 years. Sweet Sixteen members agreed to sell their installment payments to Prosperity Partners, Inc, in exchange for a present-value lump sum. The Lottery Bureau objected to the assignment, and the club filed suit.

The Bureau opposed assignment for two reasons. First, the Bureau declared that assignments were "awkward and complicated and placed a bur- ▼

---

5   *Johnson v. Yousoofian,* 84 Wash. App. 755, 930 P.2d 921, 1996 Wash. App. LEXIS 788 (Wash. Ct. App. 1996).
6   97 N.M. 239, 638 P.2d 1084 (N.M. 1982).

den on the lottery bureau." Second, a statute barred most assignments:

> The right of any person to a prize drawn is not assignable, except that payment of any prize drawn from the state lottery may be paid to the family members or to the estate of a deceased prizewinner, to a person pursuant to an appropriate judicial order, or to the state [based on tax liability.]

Despite the statute, the trial court permitted the Sweet Sixteen Club to assign its winnings. The Lottery Bureau appealed.

Issue: Should the Club be allowed to assign its winnings, despite the statute?

Excerpts from Judge Hood's Decision: One probable objective of [the statute] is to prohibit voluntary assignments to the extent that there is no procedural safeguard to protect prize winners from their own human frailties. On the other hand, the statute also functions to prevent the state from being unduly burdened. The statute unambiguously places a general prohibition on the assignment of lottery prizes, but specifically provides three exceptions.

The authorized discretionary power of the courts adequately functions to achieve the intent of the statute. We believe that a court can properly exercise its discretion in determining whether a purported assignment is reasonable or in the best interests of the parties involved, including both the state and the prizewinner. Courts have the ability to reject an assignment when this action appears necessary to protect a lottery winner from personal human frailties. Courts also have the power to refuse an assignment if it appears to be unduly burdensome to the state, where, for example, the assignment is for only a temporary period, or where multiple assignments are attempted. While it is true that a winner could petition the courts for an assignment for any reason, however frivolous, that assignment can only be approved by an appropriate court order. It would surely be inappropriate to approve an assignment simply on the whim of a prizewinner.

We therefore conclude that the trial court did not err in issuing an order pursuant to [the statute], allowing petitioners to assign their lottery winnings. The language "appropriate judicial order" does not simply contemplate payments relating to marital property disposition, child support, prior obligations to the state or the equivalent. Courts are capable of properly exercising their discretion in determining whether a purported assignment is reasonable or in the best interests of the parties involved.

Affirmed. ■

Public Policy

The Sweet Sixteen decision demonstrates the strong judicial preference for permitting assignment of contract rights. Critics of the case say that the court went too far, allowing the statutory exception to swallow the rule. They argue that the legislature's primary purpose in passing the law was to prohibit assignment in lottery cases, while allowing narrow exceptions. Yet here, the court shows little respect for the statute, and seems to presume that assignments should be allowed. Is the statute arbitrary and foolish? Is the court's ruling stubborn and presumptuous? How would you rule? ◆

How Rights Are Assigned

Writing. In general, an assignment may be written or oral, and no particular formalities are required. However, when someone wants to assign rights governed by the statute of frauds, she must do it in writing. Suppose City contracts with Seller to buy Seller's land for a domed stadium and then brings in Investor to complete the project. If City wants to assign to Investor its rights to the land, it must do so in writing.

Consideration. An assignment can be valid with or without consideration, but the lack of consideration may have consequences. Two examples should clarify this. Recall Bruno, who sells champagne to Lydia and then assigns to Doug his right to payment. In that case there *is* consideration for the assignment. Bruno assigns his rights only because Doug cancels the old debt, and his agreement to do that is valid consideration. **An assignment for consideration is irrevocable.** Once the two men agree, Bruno may not telephone Doug and say, "I've changed my mind, I want Lydia to pay me after all." Lydia's $10,000 now belongs to Doug.

But suppose that Bruno assigns his contract rights to his sister Brunhilde as a birthday present. This is a **gratuitous assignment,** that is, one made as a gift, for no consideration. **A gratuitous assignment is generally revocable if it is oral and generally irrevocable if it is written.** If Bruno orally assigns his rights to Brunhilde, but then changes his mind, telephones Lydia, and says, "I want you to pay me, after all," that revocation is effective and Brunhilde gets nothing. But if Bruno puts his assignment in writing and Brunhilde receives it, Bruno has given up his right to the money.

If you assign your rights under a contract, inform the obligor immediately—or live with the consequences.

© GETTY IMAGES

Notice to Obligor. The assignment is valid from the moment it is made, regardless of whether the assignor notifies the obligor. But an assignor with common sense will immediately inform the obligor of the assignment. Suppose Maude has a contract with Nelson, who is obligated to deliver 700 live frogs to her shop. If Maude (assignor) assigns her rights to Obie (assignee), Maude should notify Nelson (obligor) the same day. If she fails to inform Nelson, he may deliver the frogs to Maude. Nelson will have no further obligations under the contract, and Maude will owe Obie 700 frogs. For a simple assignment, see http://www.lectlaw.com/forms/f013.htm.

Rights of the Parties after Assignment

Once the assignment is made and the obligor notified, the assignee may enforce her contractual rights against the obligor. If Lydia fails to pay Doug for the champagne she gets from Bruno, Doug may sue to enforce the agreement. The law will treat Doug as though he had entered into the contract with Lydia.

But the reverse is also true. **The obligor may generally raise all defenses against the assignee that she could have raised against the assignor.** Suppose Lydia opens the first bottle of champagne—silently. "Where's the pop?" she wonders. There is no pop because all 500 bottles have gone flat. Bruno has failed to perform his part of the contract, and Lydia may use Bruno's nonperformance as a defense against Doug. If the champagne was indeed worthless, Lydia owes Doug nothing.

Assignor's Warranty. The law implies certain warranties (assurances) on the part of the assignor. Unless the parties expressly agree to exclude them, the assignor warrants that (1) the rights he is assigning actually do exist, and (2) there are no defenses to the rights other than those that would be obvious, like nonperformance. But the assignor *does not* warrant that the obligor is solvent. Bruno is impliedly warranting to Doug that Lydia has no defenses to the contract, but he is not guaranteeing Doug that she has the money to pay, or that she will pay.

Differences under the UCC

As we mentioned, the Code's provisions regarding assignment, found in §2-210, are very similar to the Restatement section quoted above. Assignments are common in sales contracts. The UCC favors them and tends to limit contractual clauses that prohibit assignment. Thus, if a contract states in general terms that assignment is prohibited, the Code will limit that language to mean only that a party may not delegate his duties; assignment of the party's *rights* will still be allowed. If a contracting party wants to prohibit assignment of rights, it must specifically say so.[7]

Article 9 of the UCC governs the assignment of security interests. A **security interest** is a legal right in personal property that assures payment. When an automobile dealer sells you a new car on credit, the dealer will keep a security interest in your car. If you do not make your monthly payments, the dealer retains a right to drive your car away, and that authority is called a security interest. (See Chapter 26 for a full discussion.)

Companies that sell goods often prefer to assign their security interests to some other firm, such as a bank or finance company. The bank is the assignee. Just as we saw with the common law, the assignee of a security interest generally has all of the rights that the assignor had. And the obligor (the buyer) may also raise all of the defenses against the assignee that she could have raised against the assignor.

According to UCC §9-404, in general, the obligor on a sales contract may generally assert any defenses against the assignee that arise from the contract, and any other defenses that arose before notice of assignment. The Code's reference to any defenses that arise from the contract means that if the assignor breached his part of the deal, the obligor may raise that as a defense. Suppose a dealer sells you a new Porsche on credit, retaining a security interest. He assigns the security interest to the bank. The car is great for the first few weeks, but then the roof slides onto the street, both doors fall off, and the engine implodes. You refuse to make any more monthly payments. When the bank sues you, you may raise as a defense the automobile's defects, just as you could have raised them against the dealer itself. Where the Code talks about other defenses that arose before notice of assignment, it refers, for example, to fraud. Suppose the dealer knew that before you bought the Porsche, it had been smashed up and rebuilt. If the dealer told you it was brand new, that was fraud, and you could raise the defense against the bank.

A contract may prohibit an obligor from raising certain defenses against an assignee. Sometimes a seller of goods will require the buyer to sign a contract that permits the seller to assign *and* prohibits the buyer from raising defenses against the assignee that he could have raised against the seller. University wants to buy a computer system on credit from Leland for $85,000. Leland agrees to the deal but insists that the contract permit him to assign his rights to anyone he chooses. He also wants this clause: "University agrees that it will not raise against an assignee any defenses that it may have had against Leland." This clause is sometimes called a *waiver clause*, because the obligor is waiving (giving up) rights. Courts may also refer to it as an *exclusion clause*, since the parties are excluding potential defenses. Leland wants a waiver clause because it makes his contract more valuable. As soon as University signs the agreement, Leland can take his contract to Krushem Collections, a finance company. Krushem might offer Leland $70,000 cash for the contract. Leland can argue, "You have to pay $80,000 for this. You are guaranteed payment by University, since they cannot raise any defenses against you, even if the computer system collapses in the first half-hour." Leland gets cash and need not worry about collecting payments. Krushem receives the full value of the contract, with interest, spread out over several years.

Under UCC §9-403, an agreement by a buyer (or lessee) that he will not assert against an assignee any claim or defense that he may have against the seller (or lessor) is generally enforceable by the assignee if he took the assignment in good faith, for value, without notice of the potential defenses. In other words, Leland's waiver clause with University is enforceable. If Leland assigns the contract to Krushem Collections and the system proves worthless, Krushem is still entitled

---

[7] UCC §2-210(3).

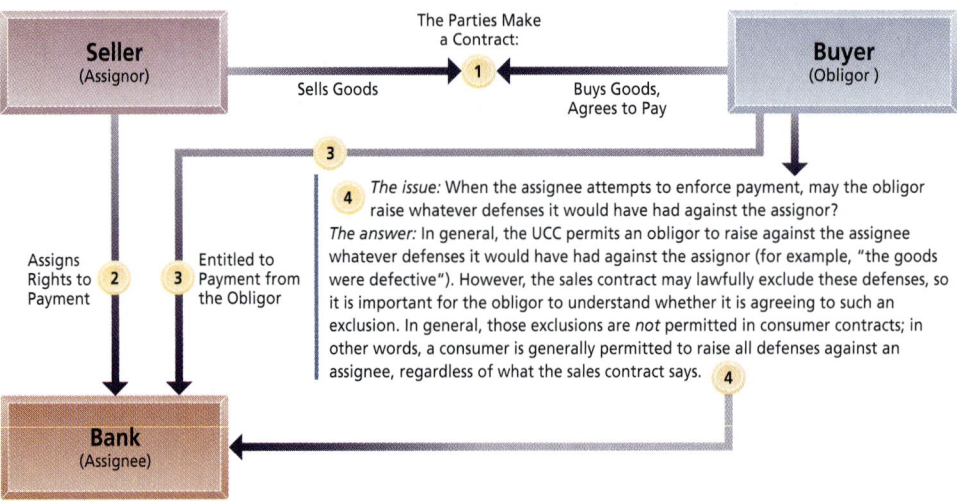

Exhibit 16.4

to its monthly payments from University. The school must seek its damages against Leland—a far more arduous step than simply withholding payment.

These waiver clauses are generally *not* valid in consumer contracts. If Leland sold a computer system to a consumer (an individual purchasing it for her personal use), the waiver would generally be unenforceable. See Exhibit 16.4.

In the following case, one side pushes the waiver rule to its extreme. Can an assignee recover for money advanced . . . when the money was never advanced? You be the judge.

you Be The Judge

WELLS FARGO BANK MINNESOTA V. BROOKSAMERICA MORTGAGE CORPORATION

2004 WL 2072358
United States District Court for the Southern District of New York, 2004

Facts: Michael Brooks desperately needed financing for his company, BrooksAmerica, so he agreed to a sale-leaseback agreement with Terminal Marketing Company. Terminal would pay BrooksAmerica $250,000, and in exchange would obtain title to BrooksAmerica's computers and office equipment. BrooksAmerica would then lease the equipment for three years, for $353,000. The equipment would never leave BrooksAmerica's offices.

The contract included a "hell or high water clause," stating that BrooksAmerica's obligation to pay was "absolute and unconditional." Another clause permitted Terminal to assign its rights without notice to BrooksAmerica, and stated that the assignee took its rights "free from all defenses, setoffs or counterclaims."

Brooks also signed a "Delivery and Acceptance Certificate," stating that BrooksAmerica had received the $250,000 (even though no money had yet changed hands), and reaffirming BrooksAmerica's absolute obligation to pay an assignee, despite any defenses BrooksAmerica might have.

Terminal assigned its rights to Wells Fargo, which had taken about 2,000 other equipment leases from Terminal. Terminal never paid any portion of the promised $250,000. Brooks refused to make the required payments (about $10,000 per month) and Wells Fargo sued. Brooks acknowledged that Wells Fargo paid Terminal for the assignment.

▼

You Be the Judge: **Is Wells Fargo entitled to its monthly lease payments despite the fact that BrooksAmerica never received financing?**

Argument for Wells Fargo: Under UCC 9-403, an assignee such as Wells Fargo may enforce a waiver of defenses clause if the assignment was taken in good faith, for value, and free of knowledge of any claims or defenses. Wells Fargo meets that test. This is our business. We have taken thousands of equipment leases as assignees. In this case, we examined the contract and the Delivery Certificate, and assumed that BrooksAmerica had received its money. If Terminal had not paid, why did Mr. Brooks sign a certificate stating he had received his cash? We are entitled to payment. Any dispute between BrooksAmerica and Terminal is for those parties to resolve.

Argument for BrooksAmerica: We acknowledge the general validity of UCC 9-403. However, in this case Wells Fargo makes an absurd argument. Neither Terminal nor any assignee has a right to enforce a financing contract when Terminal failed to deliver the financing. There is no valid contract to enforce here, because Terminal never paid the $250,000 owed to BrooksAmerica. "Good faith" required Wells Fargo to make sure that Terminal had performed. A simple inquiry would have informed Wells Fargo that Terminal was entitled to no money. This entire transaction is a sham, and section 9-403 was never drafted to encourage financial swindles.

Rebuttal for Wells Fargo: The "simple inquiry" argument has two flaws. First, section 9-403 does not require one. The UCC requires good faith, not an investigation. Second, Wells Fargo *did* investigate, by checking the contract and the Delivery Certificate. We have done more than required.

Rebuttal for BrooksAmerica: BrooksAmerica is being *penalized* for acting in good faith. Mr. Brooks signed the Delivery Certificate assuming that any reasonable company would promptly deliver the money it had promised. Unfortunately Terminal does not operate at the same ethical level—a fact that Wells Fargo should know from its earlier assignments. ■

Delegation of Duties

Garret has always dreamed of racing stock cars. He borrows $250,000 from his sister, Maybelle, in order to buy a car and begin racing. He signs a promissory note in that amount, in other words, a document guaranteeing that he will repay Maybelle the full amount, plus interest, on a monthly basis over 10 years. Regrettably, during his first race, on a Saturday night, Garret discovers that he has a speed phobia. He finishes the race at noon on Sunday and quits the business. Garret transfers the car and all of his equipment to Brady, who agrees in writing to pay all money owed to Maybelle. For a few months Brady sends a check, but he is killed while watching bumper cars at a local carnival. Maybelle sues Garret, who defends based on the transfer to Brady. Will his defense work?

Garret has assigned his rights in the car and business to Brady and that is entirely legal. But more important, he has *delegated his duties* to Brady. Garret was the **delegator** and Brady was the **delegatee**. In other words, the promissory note he signed was a contract, and the agreement imposed certain *duties* on Garret, primarily the obligation to pay Maybelle $250,000 plus interest. Garret had a right to delegate his duties to Brady, but delegating those duties did not relieve Garret of his own obligation to perform them. When Maybelle sues, she will win. Garret, like many debtors, would have preferred to wash his hands of his debt, but the law is not so obliging.

Most duties are delegable. But delegation does not by itself relieve the delegator of his own liability to perform the contract.

Garret
(Obligor)
(Assignor)
(Delegator)

The Parties Make a Contract:

1

Maybelle
(Obligee)

Promises to
Repay the
$250,000 Loan
In Full, with
Interest

Loans
$250,000

5

Assigns
Rights
to the
Business

2 **3**

Delegates
Duty to
Repay
the Loan

Remains Obligated to Repay the Loan

4

Brady
(Assignee)
(Delegatee)

Becomes Obligated to Repay the Loan

4

Exhibit 16.5

One may delegate and one may not.

Garret's delegation to Brady was typical in that it included an assignment at the same time. If he had merely transferred ownership, that would have been only an assignment. If he had convinced Brady to pay off the loan without getting the car, that would have been merely a delegation. He did both at once. See Exhibit 16.5.

What Duties Are Delegable

The rules concerning what duties may be delegated mirror those about the assignment of rights. And once again, the common law, as summarized by the Restatement, agrees with the UCC.

An obligor may delegate his duties unless

(1) delegation would violate public policy, or
(2) the contract prohibits delegation, or
(3) the obligee has a substantial interest in personal performance by the obligor.[8]

Public Policy. Delegation may violate public policy, for example, in a public works contract. If City hires Builder to construct a subway system, state law may prohibit Builder from delegating his duties to Beginner. The theory is that a public agency should not have to work with parties that it never agreed to hire.

---

[8] Restatement (Second) of Contracts §318. And see UCC §2-210, establishing similar limits.

Contract Prohibition. It is very common for a contract to prohibit delegation. We saw in the assignment section that courts may refuse to enforce a clause that limits one party's ability to assign its contract rights. That does not hold true with delegation. The parties may forbid almost any delegation, and the courts will enforce the agreement. Hammer, a contractor, is building a house and hires Spot as his painter, including in his contract a clause prohibiting delegation. Just before the house is ready for painting, Spot gets a better job elsewhere and wants to delegate his duties to Brush. Hammer may refuse the delegation even if Brush is equally qualified.

Substantial Interest in Personal Performance. Suppose Hammer had omitted the "nondelegation" clause from his contract with Spot. Could Hammer still refuse the delegation on the grounds that he has a substantial interest in having Spot do the work? No. Most duties are delegable. There is nothing so special about painting a house that one particular painter is required to do it. But some kinds of work do require personal performance, and obligors may not delegate these tasks. The services of lawyers, doctors, dentists, artists, and performers are considered too personal to be delegated. There is no single test that will perfectly define this group, but generally when the work will test the *character, skill, discretion, and good faith of the obligor,* she *may not* delegate her job.

at RISK

The law can be annoyingly vague, as it is with the test of "personal performance" contracts. But avoiding problems is not difficult. Before entering into a contract, briefly discuss delegation with the other party and decide what duties, if any, may be delegated. Then include an appropriate clause in the contract. As always, if there are differences over delegation, it is better to be aware of them early. ◆

Improper Delegation and Repudiation. Sometimes parties delegate duties they should not. Suppose Spot, having agreed not to delegate his painting job, is so tempted by the higher offer from another contractor that he delegates the work anyway. Hammer informs Spot he will not allow Brush on the job site. If Spot still refuses to work, he has **repudiated** the agreement; in other words, he has formally notified the other side he will not perform his side of the contract. Hammer will probably sue him. On the other hand, if Hammer allows Brush up the ladder and Brush completes the job, Hammer has no claim against anybody.

Novation

As we have seen, a delegator does not get rid of his duties merely by delegating them. But there is one way a delegator can do so. **A novation is a three-way agreement in which the obligor transfers all rights and duties to a third party. The obligee agrees to look only to that third party for performance.**

Recall Garret, the forlorn race car driver. When he wanted to get out of his obligations to Maybelle, he should have proposed a novation. He would assign all rights and delegate all duties to Brady, and Maybelle would agree that *only Brady* was obligated by the promissory note, releasing Garret from his responsibility to repay. Why would Maybelle do this? She might conclude that Brady was a financially better bet than Garret and that this was the best way to get her money. Maybelle would prefer to have both people liable. But Garret might refuse to bring Brady into the deal until Maybelle permits a novation. In the example given, Garret failed to obtain a novation, and hence he and Brady (or Brady's estate) were *both* liable on the promissory note.

Since a novation has the critical effect of releasing the obligor from liability, you will not be surprised to learn that two parties to a contract sometimes fight over whether some event was a simple delegation of duties or a novation. Here is one such contest.

ROSENBERG V. SON, INC.

491 N.W.2d 71, 1992 N.D. LEXIS 202

Supreme Court of North Dakota, 1992

Facts: The Rosenbergs owned a Dairy Queen in Grand Forks, North Dakota. They agreed in writing to sell the Dairy Queen to Mary Pratt. The contract required her to pay $10,000 down and $52,000 over 15 years, at 10 percent interest. Two years later, Pratt assigned her rights and delegated her duties under the sales contract to Son, Inc. The agreement between Pratt and Son contained a "Consent to Assignment" clause that the Rosenbergs signed. Pratt then moved to Arizona and had nothing further to do with the Dairy Queen. The Rosenbergs never received full payment for the Dairy Queen. They sued Mary Pratt.

The trial court gave summary judgment for Pratt, finding that she was no longer obligated on the original contract. The Rosenbergs appealed.

Issue: Did Pratt obtain a novation relieving her of her duties under the original sales contract?

Excerpts from Chief Justice Erickstad's Decision: It is a well-established principle in the law of contracts that a contracting party cannot escape its liability on the contract by merely assigning its duties and rights under the contract to a third party.

It is evident from the express language of the assignment agreement between Pratt and Son, Inc., that only an assignment was intended, not a novation. The agreement made no mention of discharging Pratt from any further liability on the contract.

Furthermore, the agreement was between Pratt and Son, Inc.; they were the parties signing the agreement, not the Rosenbergs. An agreement between Pratt and Son, Inc., cannot unilaterally affect the Rosenbergs' rights under the contract. As mentioned earlier, the Rosenbergs did sign a consent to the assignment at the bottom of the agreement. However, by merely consenting to the assignment, the Rosenbergs did not consent to a discharge of the principal obligor—Pratt. Nothing in the language of the consent clause supports such an allegation. A creditor is free to consent to an assignment without releasing the original obligor.

We *reverse* the summary judgment and *remand* for further proceedings. ■

at RISK

It appears that Mary Pratt, moving to Arizona, honestly thought she was not only out of the ice cream business but relieved of any debt to the Rosenbergs. This lawsuit undoubtedly came as a cold shock. What should she have done to avoid the dispute? ◆

Chapter Conclusion

A moment's caution! That is what enables contracting parties to anticipate and realistically appraise any rights and responsibilities of third parties.

Chapter Review

1. A third party beneficiary is an intended beneficiary and may enforce a contract if the parties intended her to benefit from the agreement and if either (1) enforcing the promise will satisfy a debt of the promisee to the beneficiary, or (2) the promisee intended to make a gift to the beneficiary. The intended beneficiary described in (1) is a *creditor beneficiary*, while (2) describes a *donee beneficiary*. Any beneficiary who meets neither description is an *incidental beneficiary* and has no right to enforce the contract.

2. An assignment transfers the assignor's contract rights to the assignee. A delegation transfers the delegator's duties to the delegatee.

3. A party generally may assign contract rights unless doing so would substantially change the obligor's rights or duties, is forbidden by law, or is validly precluded by the contract.

4. Once the assignment is made and the obligor notified, the assignee may enforce her contractual rights against the obligor. The obligor, in turn, may generally raise all defenses against the assignee that she could have raised against the assignor.

5. Under the UCC, the assignee may generally enforce a waiver that prohibits the obligor from raising defenses. This is not true, however, in most consumer contracts.

6. Duties are delegable unless delegation would violate public policy, the contract prohibits delegation, or the obligee has a substantial interest in personal performance by the obligor.

7. Unless the obligee agrees otherwise, delegation does not discharge the delegator's duty to perform.

8. A *novation* is a three-way agreement in which the obligor delegates all duties to the delegatee and the obligee agrees to hold only the delegatee responsible.

Practice Test

1. Intercontinental Metals Corp. (IMC) contracted with the accounting firm of Cherry, Bekaert & Holland to perform an audit. Cherry issued its opinion about IMC, giving all copies of its report directly to the company. IMC later permitted Dun & Bradstreet to examine the statements, and Raritan River Steel Co. saw a report published by Dun & Bradstreet. Relying on the audit, Raritan sold IMC $2.2 million worth of steel on credit, but IMC promptly went bankrupt. Raritan sued Cherry, claiming that IMC was not as sound as Cherry had reported, and that the accounting firm had breached its contract with IMC. Comment on Raritan's suit.

2. Angelo Zavarella and Yvette Rodrigues were injured in an automobile accident allegedly caused by a vehicle belonging to Truck Equipment of Boston. Travelers Insurance Co. paid insurance benefits to Zavarella and Rodrigues, who then assigned to Travelers their claims against Truck Equipment. Travelers sued Truck Equipment, which moved to dismiss. What is Truck Equipment's claim that the case should be dismissed, and how would you rule?

3. **CPA QUESTION** Yost contracted with Egan for Yost to buy certain real property. If the contract is otherwise silent, Yost's rights under the contract are:

   a. Assignable only with Egan's consent

   b. Nonassignable because they are personal to Yost

   c. Nonassignable as a matter of law

   d. Generally assignable

4. Woodson Walker and Associates leased computer equipment from Park Ryan Leasing. The lease said nothing about assignment. Park Ryan then assigned the lease to TCB as security for a loan. Park Ryan defaulted on its loan, and

Walker failed to make several payments on the lease. TCB sued Walker for the lease payments. Please rule on two issues:

a. Was the assignment valid, given the fact that the original lease made no mention of it?

b. If the assignment was valid, may Walker raise defenses against TCB that it could have raised against Park Ryan?

5. Nationwide Discount Furniture hired Rampart Security to install an alarm in its warehouse. A fire would set off an alarm in Rampart's office, and the security company was then supposed to notify Nationwide immediately. A fire did break out, but Rampart allegedly failed to notify Nationwide, causing the fire to spread next door and damage a building owned by Gasket Materials Corp. Gasket sued Rampart for breach of contract, and Rampart moved for summary judgment. Comment.

6. C. Gaston Whiddon owned Gaston's LP Gas Co., Inc. Curtis Dufour purchased the company. Since Whiddon had personally operated the company for many years, Dufour was worried about competition from him and insisted on a noncompetition clause in the sales contract. The clause stated that Whiddon would not "compete with Gaston's LP Gas Co. anywhere south of Interstate Highway 20 for nine years." Three years later, the Herring Gas Co. offered to buy all of Dufour's gas business, assuming that Whiddon would not be a competitor for six more years. Dufour sold all of the assets to Herring, keeping the actual corporation "Gaston's LP Gas Co." for himself. What mistake in drafting have Dufour and Herring made?

7. **CPA QUESTION** One of the criteria for a valid assignment of a sales contract to a third party is that the assignment must:

a. Not materially increase the other party's risk or duty

b. Not be revocable by the assignor

c. Be supported by adequate consideration from the assignee

d. Be in writing and signed by the assignor

8. **ETHICS** A century and a half ago an English judge stated: "All painters do not paint portraits like Sir Joshua Reynolds, nor landscapes like Claude Lorraine, nor do all writers write dramas like Shakespeare or fiction like Dickens. Rare genius and extraordinary skill are not transferable." What legal doctrine is the judge describing? What is the ethical basis of this rule?

9. Pizza of Gaithersburg, Maryland, owned five pizza shops. Pizza arranged with Virginia Coffee Service to install soft drink machines in each of its stores and maintain them. The contract made no mention of the rights of either party to delegate. Virginia Coffee delegated its duties to the Macke Co., leading to litigation between Pizza and Macke. Pizza claimed that Virginia Coffee was barred from delegating because Pizza had a close working relationship with the president of Virginia Coffee, who personally kept the machines in working order. Was the delegation legal?

10. **YOU BE THE JUDGE** WRITING PROBLEM David Ricupero suspected his wife Polly of having an affair, so he taped her phone conversations and, based on what he heard, sued for divorce. David's lawyer, William Wuliger, had the recorded conversations transcribed for use at trial. The parties settled the divorce out of court and signed an agreement that included this clause:

> Except as herein otherwise provided, each party hereto completely and forever releases the other and his attorneys from any and all rights each has or may have ... to any property, privileges, or benefits accruing to either by virtue of their marriage, or conferred by the Statutory or Common Law of Ohio or the United States of America.

After the divorce was final, Polly sued William Wuliger for invasion of privacy and violation of federal wiretapping law. Wuliger moved to dismiss the case based on the clause quoted. Polly argued that Wuliger was not a party to the divorce settlement and had no right to enforce it. May Wuliger enforce the waiver clause from the Ricuperos' divorce settlement? **Argument for Wuliger:** The contract language demonstrates that the parties intended to release one another and their attorneys from any claims. That makes Wuliger an intended third party beneficiary, and he is entitled to enforce the agreement. If Polly did not want to release Wuliger from such claims, she was free not to sign the agreement. **Argument for Polly Ricupero:** A divorce agreement settles the affairs between the couple. That is all it is ever intended to do, and the parties here never intended to benefit a lawyer. Wuliger is only an incidental beneficiary and cannot use this contract to paper over his violation of federal wiretapping law.

11. Judith and John Brooks hired Wayne Hayes to build a house. The contract required Hayes to "provide all necessary labor and materials and perform all work of every nature whatsoever to be done in the erection of the residence." Hayes hired subcontractors to do all of the work. One of Hayes's employees checked on the work site daily, but neither Hayes nor any of his employees actively supervised the building. The Brookses were aware of this working arrangement and consented to it. The mason negligently installed the fireplace, ultimately leading to a serious fire. The Brookses sued Hayes for breach of contract. Hayes contended that when the Brookses approved of his hiring of subcontractors to do all work, that created a novation, relieving him of any liability. Discuss.

12. *ROLE REVERSAL* Write a short-answer question that highlights the difference between an assignment and a novation.

Internet Research Problem

Go to **http://beatty.westbuslaw.com.** Read clause 5(b) of the lease. What does the clause mean, in English? Do leases commonly include such clauses? Suppose you intend to rent an apartment next year, live there during the school year, and then sublet over the summer. What legal issue will probably arise concerning a sublet?

> **You can find further practice problems at http://beatty.westbuslaw.com or in the Study Guide that accompanies this text.**

Performance and Discharge

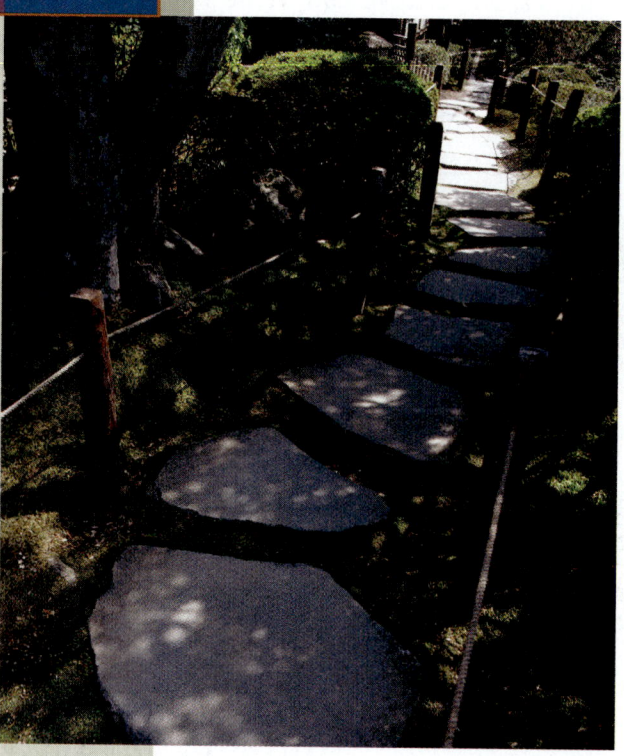

Polly was elated. It was the grand opening of her new restaurant, Polly's Folly, and everything was bubbling. The wait staff hustled and Caesar, the chef, churned out succulent dishes. Polly had signed a contract promising him $1,000 per week for one year, "provided Polly is personally satisfied with his cooking." Polly was determined that her Folly would be a glorious one. Her three-year lease would cost $6,000 per month, and she had signed an advertising deal with Billboard Bonanza for the same period. Polly had also promised Eddie, a publicity agent, a substantial monthly fee, to begin as soon as the restaurant was 80 percent booked for one month. Tonight, with candles flickering at packed tables, Polly beamed.

After a week, Polly's smiles were a bit forced. Some of Caesar's new dishes had been failures, including a grilled swordfish that was hard to pierce and shrimp jambalaya that was too spicy for the owner. The restaurant was only 60 percent full, and the publicity agent yelled at Caesar for costing him money, though the chef pointed out that most of his dishes were very popular. Later that month, Polly disliked a veal dish and gagged on one of Caesar's soups. She fired her chef.

Then troubles gushed forth—literally. A water main burst in front of Polly's restaurant, flooding the street. The city embarked on a two-month repair job that ultimately took four times that long. The street was closed to traffic, and no one could park within blocks of the Folly. For several months Polly bravely served food, but patronage dropped steadily, as hungry customers refused to deal with the bad parking and construction noise. Finally, behind on the rent and in debt to everyone, Polly closed her doors for good. ■

DISCHARGE

Grimly, the court doors swung open, offering a full menu of litigation. Polly's landlord sued for three years' rent, and Billboard Bonanza demanded its money for the same period. Caesar claimed his year's pay. Eddie, the agent, insisted on some money for his hard work.

Polly defended vigorously, seeking to be *discharged* from her various contracts. **A party is discharged when she has no more duties under a contract.** In each lawsuit, Polly asked a court to declare that her obligations were terminated and that she owed no money.

Most contracts are discharged by full performance. In other words, the parties generally do what they promise. Suppose, before the restaurant opened, Walter had promised to deliver 100 sets of cutlery to Polly and she had promised to pay $20 per set. Walter delivered the goods on time, and Polly paid on delivery. The parties got what they expected, and that contract was fully discharged.

Sometimes the parties discharge a contract by agreement. For example, the parties may agree to **rescind** their contract, meaning that they terminate it by mutual agreement.[1] If Polly's landlord believed he could get more rent from a new tenant, he might agree to rescind her lease. But he was dubious about the rental market and refused to rescind.

Defenses That Discharge

At times a court may discharge a party who has not performed. When things have gone amiss, a judge must interpret the contract and issues of public policy to determine who in fairness should suffer the loss. In the lawsuits brought by the landlord and Billboard Bonanza, Polly argued a defense called "commercial impracticability," claiming that she should not be forced to rent space that was useless to her or buy advertising for a restaurant that had closed. From Polly's point of view, the claim was understandable. But we can also respect the arguments made by the landlord and the advertiser, that they did not cause the burst water main. Claims of commercial impracticability are difficult to win, and Polly lost against both of these opponents. Though she was making

---

[1] The parties could also decide that one party's duties will be performed by someone else, a modification called a **novation.** Or they could create an **accord and satisfaction,** in which they agree that one party will substitute a new kind of performance in place of his contract obligations. See Chapter 16, on third parties, and Chapter 12, on consideration.

no money at all from the restaurant, the court found her liable in full for the lease and the advertising contract.[2]

Polly's argument against Caesar raised another issue of discharge. Caesar claimed that his cooking was good professional work and that all chefs have occasional snafus, especially in a new restaurant. But Polly responded that they had a "personal satisfaction" contract. Under such contracts, "good" work may not suffice if it fails to please the promisee. Polly won this argument, and Caesar recovered nothing.

As to Eddie's suit, Polly raised a defense called "condition precedent," meaning that some event had to occur before she was obligated to pay. Polly claimed that she owed Eddie money only if and when the restaurant was 80 percent full, and that had never happened. The court agreed and discharged Polly on Eddie's claim.

We will analyze each of these issues, and begin with a look at conditions.

CONDITIONS

Parties often put conditions in a contract. **A condition is an event that must occur before a party becomes obligated under a contract.** Polly agreed to pay Eddie, the agent, a percentage of her profits, but with an important condition: 80 percent of the tables had to be booked for a month. Unless and until those tables were occupied, Polly owed Eddie nothing. That never happened, or, in contract language, the *condition failed*, and so Polly was discharged.

Conditions can take many forms. Alex would like to buy Kevin's empty lot and build a movie theater on it, but the city's zoning law will not permit such a business in that location. Alex signs a contract to buy Kevin's empty lot in 120 days, *provided that* within 100 days the city re-zones the area to permit a movie theater. If the city fails to re-zone the area by day 100, Alex is discharged and need not complete the deal. As another example, Friendly Insurance issues a policy covering Vivian's house, promising to pay for any loss due to fire, but only if Vivian furnishes proof of her damages within 60 days of the damage. If the house burns down, Friendly becomes liable to pay. But if Vivian arrives with the proof 70 days after the fire, she collects nothing. Friendly, though it briefly had a duty to pay, was discharged when Vivian failed to furnish the necessary information on time.

How Conditions Are Created

Express Conditions

The parties may expressly state a condition. Alex's contract with Kevin expressly discharged all obligations if the city failed to re-zone within the stated period. Notice that **no special language is necessary to create the condition.** Phrases such as "provided that" frequently indicate a condition, but neither those nor any other words are essential. As long as the parties *intended* to create a condition, a court will enforce it.

Because informal language can create a condition, the parties may dispute whether they intended one or not. Sand Creek Country Club, in Indiana, was eager to expand its clubhouse facilities and awarded the design work to CSO Architects. The club wanted the work done quickly but had not secured financing. The architects sent a letter confirming their agreement:

---

[2] Based on *Luminous Neon v. Parscale,* 17 Kan. App. 2d 241, 836 P.2d 1201, 1992 Kan. App. LEXIS 572 (Kan. Ct. App. 1992).

© GETTY IMAGES

The conditions in the contract may be more important than the playing condition of the field.

It was our intent to allow Mr. Dan Moriarty of our office to start work on your project as early as possible in order to allow you to meet the goals that you have set for next fall. Also, it was the intent of CSO to begin work on your project and delay any billings to you until your financing is in place. As I explained to you earlier, we will continue on this course until we reach a point where we can no longer continue without receiving some payment.

The club gave CSO the go-ahead to begin design work, and the architects did their work and billed Sand Creek for $33,000. But the club, unable to obtain financing, refused to pay. Sand Creek claimed that CSO's letter created a *condition* in their agreement, namely, that the club would have to pay only if and when it obtained financing. The court was unpersuaded and ruled that the parties had never intended to create an express condition. The architects were merely delaying their billing as a convenience to the club. It would be absurd, said the court, to assume that CSO intended to perform $33,000 worth of work for free.[3]

at RISK

The Sand Creek case demonstrates the need for clarity in business dealings. The architect's letter should have emphasized that Sand Creek was obligated to pay the full amount, for example by saying: "CSO agrees to delay billing for a reasonable period but the Club remains liable for the full amount of the contract, whether or not it obtains financing." A one-sentence ambiguity meant that the firm could not obtain its money without a lawsuit and an appeal. ◆

Implied Conditions

At other times, the parties say nothing about a condition, but it is clear from their agreement that they have implied one. Charlotte orally rents an apartment to Hakan for one year and promises to fix any problems in the unit. It is an implied condition that Hakan will promptly notify Charlotte of anything needing repair. Although the parties have not said anything about notice, it is only common sense that Hakan must inform his landlord of defects since she will have no other way to learn of them.

NEWS*worthy*

Conditions in the Outfield. Professional sports contracts are often full of conditions. Assume that the San Francisco Giants want to sign Tony Fleet to play center field, a key position. The club considers him a fine defensive player but a dubious offensive performer. The many conditional clauses in his contract reflect hard bargaining over a questionable athlete. The Giants guarantee Fleet $500,000, a modest salary by today's standards. If the speedy outfielder appears in 110 games (out of 162 total), his pay increases to $900,000, and if he plays in 120 games, he earns $1 million. Additional conditional payments relate to a "Gold Glove" award, which coaches and managers throughout the league award annually to the top defensive performers. If Fleet receives even one vote for a Gold Glove, he earns an extra $100,000, and an additional $200,000 if he wins the award. The Giants insist on an option to re-sign Fleet for the following season for $800,000 (he has no say in the matter), but if the center-fielder only plays in 100 games, the team loses that right, leaving Fleet free to negotiate for higher pay with other teams. ◆

---

[3] *Sand Creek Country Club, Ltd. v. CSO Architects, Inc.*, 582 N.E.2d 872, 1991 Ind. App. LEXIS 2151 (Ind. Ct. App. 1991).

Types of Conditions

Courts divide conditional clauses into three categories: (1) condition precedent, (2) condition subsequent, and (3) concurrent conditions.[4] But what they have in common is more important than any of their differences. The key to all conditional clauses is this: **if the condition does not occur, one party will probably be discharged without performing.**

Condition Precedent

In this kind of condition, an event *must occur before* a duty arises. Polly's contract with Eddie concerned a condition precedent. Polly had no obligation to pay Eddie anything *unless and until* the restaurant was 80 percent full for a month. Since that never happened, she was discharged.

Condition Subsequent

The only difference here is that the condition must occur *after* the particular duty arises. If the condition does not occur, the duty is discharged. Vivian's policy with Friendly Insurance contains a condition subsequent. As soon as the fire broke out, Friendly became obligated to pay for the damage. But if Vivian failed to produce her proof of loss on time, Friendly's obligation was discharged.

Condition Precedent and Condition Subsequent Compared

	Condition Created	Does Condition Occur?	Duty Is Determined	Result
Condition Precedent	"Fee to be paid when restaurant is filled to 80% capacity for one month."	Condition DOES occur: restaurant is packed.	Duty arises: Polly owes Eddie his fee.	Polly pays the fee.
		Condition DOES NOT occur: restaurant is empty.	Duty never arises: Polly is discharged.	Polly pays nothing.

	Condition Created	Duty Is Determined	Does Condition Occur?	Result
Condition Subsequent	"Vivian must give proof of loss within 60 days."	Fire damages property, and Friendly Insurance becomes obligated to pay Vivian.	Condition DOES occur: Vivian proves her losses within 60 days.	Friendly pays Vivian for her losses.
			Condition DOES NOT occur: Vivian fails to prove her losses within 60 days.	Friendly is discharged and owes nothing

---

[4] The Restatement (Second) of Contracts has officially abandoned the terms "condition precedent" and "condition subsequent." See Restatement §§224 et seq. But courts routinely use the terms, so it is difficult to avoid the old distinctions.

Precedent/Subsequent Distinction—Who Cares?

The difference between condition precedent and condition subsequent is important for one reason: it tells us *who must prove* whether the condition occurred. If the parties agreed to a condition precedent, the plaintiff has the burden to prove that the condition happened, and hence that the defendant was obligated to perform. But with a condition subsequent, it is normally the defendant who must prove that the condition occurred, relieving him of any obligation. Invariably, the distinction arises in insurance cases. Whether the insured customer or the insurance company must prove the condition often determines who wins the case.

ARKANSAS FARM BUREAU INS. FEDERATION V. RYMAN

309 Ark. 283, 831 S.W.2d 133, 1992 Ark. LEXIS 300
Supreme Court of Arkansas, 1992

Facts: Granville Ryman was killed in an auto accident. His insurance policy with Farm Bureau Mutual stated:

> The Company will pay for accidental death of a person insured under this policy. However, at the time of the accident, the person insured must be wearing a factory installed seat belt or lap and shoulder restraint, verifiable by the investigating officer.

When the investigating police officer arrived at the scene of Ryman's accident, paramedics were already transferring him to an ambulance. The officer could not determine whether Ryman had been wearing a seat belt, and the paramedics did not recall.

Farm Bureau refused to pay, claiming that the seat belt requirement was a condition precedent to its coverage and that Ms. Ryman had the burden of proving her husband *had been wearing a belt* when killed, a burden she failed to meet. Ms. Ryman argued that the clause was a condition subsequent. She claimed that when Granville Ryman died, Farm Bureau became obligated to pay benefits unless *the insurance company* could prove he was *not* wearing a belt.

Issue: Was the seat belt requirement a condition precedent, which Ms. Ryman must prove, or a condition subsequent, which the insurance company must demonstrate?

Excerpts from Justice Holt's Decision: The parties are correct in their respective arguments that the existence of a condition precedent places the burden of proof on the insured, while the insurer has the burden of proving an exclusion [in other words, a condition subsequent]. We agree with Mrs. Ryman, however, that the provision here involved an exclusion [and that the burden is on the company to prove he was *not* wearing a seat belt].

A similarly worded provision was involved in *Life and Casualty Ins. Co. of Tennessee v. Barefield.* There, the insured lost an eye when a stick was thrown toward the insured's car by another passing vehicle. The parties were bound by an insurance policy which covered bodily injuries caused by accidents from motor vehicles "provided that . . . there shall be some external or visible evidence on said vehicle of the collision or accident." This court construed the provision to be in the nature of an exclusion, thereby placing the burden on the insurer to show [no] such external damage to the insured's car. Likewise, the limiting language under the general coverage provision in this case could be construed as an exclusion.

We thus hold the requirement that the insured be wearing a seat belt at the time of the accident, such fact to be verified by the investigating officer, to constitute an exclusion under the policy, rather than a condition precedent, thereby placing the burden on the insurer to prove Mr. Ryman fell within such an exclusion. Since the insurer was unable to do so, we uphold the trial court's granting of summary judgment in Mrs. Ryman's favor.

Affirmed. ■

Concurrent Conditions

Here, both parties have a duty to perform *simultaneously.* Renee agrees to sell her condominium to Tim on July 5. Renee agrees to furnish a valid deed and clear title to the property on that date, and Tim promises to present a cashier's check for $600,000. The parties have agreed to concurrent conditions. Each performance is the condition for the other's performance. If Renee arrives at the Registry of Deeds and can only say, "I'm pretty darn sure I own that property," Tim need not present his check; similarly, if Tim arrives only with an "IOU" scribbled on the back of a candy wrapper, Renee has no duty to hand over a valid deed.

Public Policy

At times a court will refuse to enforce an express condition on the grounds that it is unfair and harmful to the general public. In other words, a court might agree that the parties created a conditional clause but conclude that permitting its enforcement would hurt society. Did the insurance contract in the following case harm society? You be the judge.

you Be The Judge

ANDERSON V. COUNTRY LIFE INS. CO.

180 Ariz. 625, 886 P.2d 1381, 1994 Ariz. App.
LEXIS 240
Arizona Court of Appeals, 1994

Facts: On November 26, a Country Life Insurance agent went to the house of Donald and Anna Mae Anderson. He persuaded the Andersons to buy a life insurance policy and accepted a check for $1,600. He gave the Andersons a "conditional receipt for medical policy," dated that day. The form stated that the Andersons would have a valid life insurance policy with Country Life, effective November 26, but only when all conditions were met. The most important of these conditions was that the Country Life home office accept the Andersons as medical risks. The Andersons were pleased with the new policy and glad that it was effective that same day.

It was not. Donald Anderson died of a heart attack a few weeks later. Country Life declined the Andersons as medical risks and refused to issue a policy. Anna Mae Anderson sued. Country Life pointed out that medical approval was a condition precedent. In other words, the company argued that the policy would be effective as of November 26, but only if it later decided to make the policy effective. Based on this argument, the trial court gave summary judgment for Country Life. Ms.

Anderson appealed, claiming that the conditional clause was a violation of public policy.

You Be the Judge: Did the conditional clause violate public policy?

Argument for Ms. Anderson: Your honors, this policy is a scam. This so called "conditional receipt for medical policy" is designed to trick customers and then steal their money. The company leads people to believe they are covered as of the day they write the check. But they aren't covered until *much later,* when the insurer gets around to deciding the applicant's medical status.

The company gets the customer's money right away and gives nothing in exchange. If the company, after taking its time, decides the applicant is not medically fit, it returns the money, having used it for weeks or even months to earn interest. If, on the other hand, the insurance company decides the applicant is a good bet, it then issues the policy effective for weeks or months *in the past, when coverage is of no use.* No one can die retroactively, your honors. The company is being paid for a period during which it had no risk.

This is a fraud and a disgrace, and the company should pay the benefits it owes.

Argument for Country Life: Your honors, is Country Life supposed to issue life insurance policies without doing a medical check? That is the

▼

road to bankruptcy and would mean that no one could obtain this valuable coverage. Of course we do a medical inquiry, as quickly as possible. It's in our interest to get the policy decided one way or the other.

The policy clearly stated that coverage was effective *only when approved by the home office*, after all inquiries were made. The Andersons knew that as well as the agent. If they were covered immediately, why would the company do a medical check?

Country Life resents suggestions that this policy is a scam, when in reality it is Ms. Anderson who is trying to profit from a tragedy that the company had nothing to do with.

The facts of this case are unusual. Obviously, most insureds do not die between application and acceptance. It would be disastrous for society to rewrite every insurance policy in this state based on one very sad fact pattern. The contract was clear and it should be enforced as written. ■

Ethics	Imagine that you are a young insurance agent, eager to do a good job and advance your career. Your company urges you to sell insurance with "conditional receipts" such as the one used by Country Life. Would you do it? From the Chapter 2 ethics checklist: What values are in conflict? Which of these values are most important? ◆

PERFORMANCE

Caitlin has an architect draw up plans for a monumental new house, and Daniel agrees to build it by September 1. Caitlin promises to pay $900,000 on that date. The house is ready on time but Caitlin has some complaints. The living room was supposed to be 18 feet high but it is only 17 feet; the pool was to be azure yet it is aquamarine; the maid's room was not supposed to be wired for cable television but it is. Caitlin refuses to pay anything for the house. Is she justified? Of course not, it would be absurd to give her a magnificent house for free when it has only tiny defects. And that is how a court would decide the case. But in this easy answer lurks a danger. Technically, Daniel did breach the contract, and yet the law allows him to recover the full contract price, or virtually all of it. Once that principle is established, how far will a court stretch it? Suppose the living room is only 14 feet high, or 12 feet, or 5 feet? What if the foundation has a small crack? A vast and dangerous split? What if Daniel finishes the house a month late? Six months late? Three years late? At some point a court will conclude that Daniel has so thoroughly botched the job that he deserves little or no money. But where is that point? That is a question that businesses—and judges—face everyday.

The more complex a contract, the more certain that at least one party will perform imperfectly. Every house ever built has some defects. A delivery of a thousand bushels of apples is sure to include a few rotten ones. A custom-designed computer system for a huge airline is likely to have some glitches. The cases raise several related doctrines, all concerning how well a party *performed* its contract obligations.

Strict Performance and Substantial Performance

Strict Performance

When Daniel built Caitlin's house with three minor defects, she refused to pay, arguing that he had not *strictly performed* his obligations. She was right, yet she lost anyway. Courts dislike strict performance because it enables one party to benefit without paying, and sends the other one home empty-handed. **A party is generally not required**

to render strict performance unless the contract expressly demands it and such a demand is reasonable. Caitlin's contract never suggested that Daniel would forfeit all payment if there were minor problems. Even if Caitlin had insisted on such a clause, few courts would have enforced it because the requirement would be unreasonable.

There are cases where strict performance does make sense. Marshall agrees to deliver 500 sweaters to Leo's store, and Leo promises to pay $20,000 cash on delivery. If Leo has only $19,000 cash and a promissory note for $1,000, he has failed to perform, and Marshall need not give him the sweaters. Leo's payment represents 95 percent of what he promised, but there is a big difference between cash and a promissory note.

Substantial Performance

Daniel, the house builder, won his case against Caitlin because he fulfilled most of his obligations, even though he did an imperfect job. Courts often rely on the substantial performance doctrine, especially in cases involving services as opposed to those concerning the sale of goods or land. **In a contract for services, a party that substantially performs its obligations will receive the full contract price, minus the value of any defects.** Daniel receives $900,000, the contract price, minus the value of a ceiling that is one foot too low, a pool the wrong color, and so forth. It will be for the trial court to decide how much those defects are worth. If the court decides the low ceiling is a $10,000 damage, the pool color worth $5,000 and the cable television worth $500, then Daniel receives $884,500.

On the other hand, a party that fails to give substantial performance may get nothing. **A party that fails to perform substantially receives nothing on the contract itself and will only recover the value of the work, if any.** If the foundation cracks in Caitlin's house and the walls collapse, Daniel will not receive his $900,000. In such a case he collects only the market value of the work he has done, which is probably zero.

When is performance substantial? There is no perfect test, but courts look at these issues:

- How much benefit has the promisee received?
- If it is a construction contract, can the owner use the thing for its intended purpose?
- Can the promisee be compensated with money damages for any defects?
- Did the promisor act in good faith?

In the following case, did the newspaper substantially perform?

STRATEGIC RESOURCES GROUP V. KNIGHT-RIDDER, INC.

870 So. 2d 846
Court of Appeal of Florida, 2003

Facts: Brighton Homes developed residential housing in the Miami area. The company contracted with Knight-Ridder to run advertisements in the *Miami Herald* newspaper. The contract required Brighton to designate the size of each ad, and stated that Knight-Ridder would print them and "bill for the exact space published." The agreement also permitted Knight-Ridder to "revise, alter or reject any advertisement for any reason but no change in advertising copy will be made without the customer's prior consent."

Brighton assigned to Strategic Resources Group all rights the developer might have for overpayments made to Knight-Ridder. Strategic then sued Knight-Ridder, claiming that for three years the newspaper had routinely printed ads that were 3.83 percent smaller than the copy submitted by Brighton. Strategic sought $83,000 in damages. The trial court found that such reductions were standard in the newspaper industry, that Knight-Ridder had in fact made them, and that the size difference was noticeable only if measured with a ruler. Declaring that Knight-Ridder had substantially performed, the trial court gave summary judgment to the news company, and Strategic appealed.

Issue: Did Knight-Ridder substantially perform its advertising contract?

Excerpts from Judge Ramirez's Decision: Substantial performance is that performance of a contract which, while not full performance, is so nearly equivalent to what was bargained for that it would be unreasonable to deny the promisee the full contract price subject to the promisor's right to recover whatever damages may have been occasioned him by the promisee's failure to render full performance.

For six years, Knight-Ridder ran the advertisements without any complaint from Brighton. Brighton never requested tear sheets or advertising proofs before publication, nor did it measure the advertisements after publication. The size reduction was not easily discernible, even in a side-by-side comparison. Brighton thus received the benefit of its bargain. Even after discovering the reduction, it continued its business relationship with Knight-

Ridder, using the same advertisements under the same terms and conditions.

Strategic makes two arguments as to why the doctrine of substantial performance is not applicable. First, it asserts that the doctrine does not apply to the payment of money. This argument incorrectly places the focus of the parties' transaction upon Brighton's obligation to compensate Knight-Ridder. The focus instead is on Knight-Ridder's responsibility to print a newspaper advertisement that substantially complies with what Brighton bargained for.

Second, Strategic argues that the doctrine is inapplicable where the breach of contract was willful or intentional. In the context of contracts for construction, the doctrine of substantial performance is applicable only where the contractor has not willfully or materially breached the terms of his contract or has not intentionally failed to comply with the specifications. While Knight-Ridder intentionally reduced the size of the advertisements, it did not intentionally breach the contract. It relied on contractual language which authorized it "to revise, alter or reject any advertisement." We agree that, although the better business practice would have been to notify its customers of the size reduction, a reduction to which Brighton obviously would have consented, we conclude that the trial court correctly granted summary judgment.

Affirmed. ■

Devil's Advocate

Knight-Ridder acted in bad faith. If, as the court suggests, it was "obvious" that Brighton would have assented to the ad reduction, then why not ask permission? Was the *Herald* too busy to make one phone call? No. The answer is that the newspaper assumed Brighton would demand an equivalent price reduction. That is why the newspaper deliberately breached the contract, which stated that "no change in advertising copy will be made without the customer's prior consent." At the very least, Strategic should be awarded a price difference of 3.83 percent, along with damages for Knight-Ridder's bad faith. ◆

Personal Satisfaction Contracts

Sujata, president of a public relations firm, hires Ben to design a huge multimedia project for her company, involving computer software, music, and live actors, all designed to sell frozen bologna sandwiches to supermarkets. His contract guarantees him two years' employment, provided all of his work "is acceptable in the sole judgment of Sujata." Ben's immediate supervisor is delighted with his work and his colleagues are impressed—all but Sujata. Three months later she fires him, claiming that his work is "uninspired." Does she have the right to do that?

This is a **personal satisfaction contract, in which the promisee makes a personal, subjective evaluation of the promisor's performance.** Employment contracts may require personal satisfaction of the employer; agreements for the sale of goods may demand that the buyer be personally satisfied with the product; and deals involving a credit analysis of one party may insist that his finances be satisfactory to the other party. In resolving disputes like Ben and Sujata's, judges must decide: When is it fair for the promisee to claim that she is *not* satisfied? May she make that decision for any reason at all, even on a whim?

A court applies a subjective standard only if assessing the work involves personal feelings, taste, or judgment and the contract explicitly demanded personal satisfaction. A "subjective standard" means that the promisee's personal views will greatly influence her judgment, even if her decision is foolish and unfair. Artistic or creative work, or highly specialized tasks designed for a particular employer, may involve subtle issues of quality and personal preference. Ben's work combines several media and revolves around his judgment. Accordingly, the law applies a subjective standard to Sujata's decision. Since she concludes that his work is uninspired, she may legally fire him, even if her decision is irrational.

Note that the promisee, Sujata, has to show two things: that assessing Ben's work involves her personal judgment *and* that their contract explicitly demands personal satisfaction. If the contract were vague on this point, Sujata would lose. Had the agreement merely said, "Ben will at all times make his best efforts," Sujata could not fire him.

In all other cases, a court applies an objective standard to the promisee's decision. In other words, the objective standard will be used if assessing the work does not involve personal judgment *or if* the contract failed to explicitly demand personal satisfaction. An objective standard means that the promisee's judgment of the work must be reasonable. Suppose Sujata hires Leila to install an alarm system for her company, and the contract requires that Sujata be "personally satisfied." Leila's system passes all tests but Sujata claims, "It just doesn't make me feel secure. I know that some day it's going to break down." May Sujata refuse to pay? No. Even though the contract used the phrase "personally satisfied," a mechanical alarm system does not involve personal judgment and taste. Either the system works or it does not. A reasonable person would find that Leila's system is just fine and therefore, under the objective standard, Sujata must pay. The law strongly favors the objective standard because the subjective standard gives unlimited power to the promisee.

Good Faith

The parties to a contract must carry out their obligations in good faith. The Restatement (Second) of Contracts §205 states: **"Every contract imposes upon each party a duty of good faith and fair dealing in its performance and its enforcement."** For its part, the UCC establishes a similar requirement for all contracts governed by the Code.[5] The difficulty, of course, is applying this general rule to the infinite problems that may arise when two people, or companies, do business. How far must one side go to meet its good faith burden? The Restatement emphasizes that the parties must remain faithful to the "agreed common purpose and justified expectations of the other party." Two examples should illustrate.

Marvin Shuster was a physician in Florida. Three patients sued him for alleged malpractice. Shuster denied any wrongdoing and asked his insurer to defend the claims. But

---

[5] UCC §1-203 states: "Every contract or duty within this Act imposes an obligation of good faith in its performance or enforcement." The present Code defines good faith as "honesty in fact." The proposed revision to Article 1 broadens the requirement to "honesty in fact and the observance of reasonable commercial standards of fair dealing," but thus far that is the law in only a few states.

How far must one side go to meet its good faith burden?

the insurance company settled all three claims without defending and with a minimum of investigation. Shuster had to pay nothing, but he sued the insurance company claiming that it acted in bad faith. The doctor argued that the company's failure to defend him caused emotional suffering and meant that it would be impossible for him to obtain new malpractice insurance. The Florida Supreme Court found that the insurer acted in good faith. The contract clearly gave all control of malpractice cases to the company. It could settle or defend as it saw fit. Here, the company considered it more economical to settle quickly, and Shuster should have known, from the contract language, that the insurer might choose to do so.[6]

In the following case, one party to a contract played its cards very close to its chest. Too close?

BRUNSWICK HILLS RACQUET CLUB INC. V. ROUTE 18 SHOPPING CENTER ASSOCIATES

182 N.J. 210, 864 A.2d 387
Supreme Court of New Jersey, 2005

Facts: Brunswick Hills Racquet Club (Brunswick) owned a tennis club on property that it leased from Route 18 Shopping Center Associates (Route 18). The lease ran for 25 years, and Brunswick had spent about $1 million in capital improvements. The lease expired March 30, 2002. Brunswick had the option of either buying the property or purchasing a 99-year lease, both on very favorable terms. To exercise its option, Brunswick had to notify Route 18 no later than September 30, 2001, and had to pay the option price of $150,000. If Brunswick failed to exercise its options, the existing lease automatically renewed as of September 30, for 25 more years, but at more than triple the current rent.

In February, 2000—19 months before the option deadline—Brunswick's lawyer, Gabriel Spector, wrote to Rosen Associates, the company that managed Route 18, stating that Brunswick intended to exercise the option for a 99-year lease. He requested that the lease be sent well in advance so that he could review it. He did not make the required payment of $150,000.

In March, Rosen replied that it had forwarded Spector's letter to its attorney, who would be in touch. In April, Spector again wrote, asking for a reply from Rosen or its lawyer.

Over the next six months, Spector continually asked for a copy of the lease, or information, but neither Route 18's lawyer nor anyone else provided any data. In January 2001, Spector renewed his requests for a copy of the lease. Route 18's lawyer never replied. Sadly, in May 2001, after a long illness, Spector died. In August 2001, Spector's law partner, Arnold Levin, wrote to Rosen, again stating Brunswick's intention to buy the 99-year lease, and requesting a copy of all relevant information. He received no reply, and the September deadline passed.

In February, 2002, Route 18's lawyer dropped the hammer, notifying Levin that Brunswick could not exercise its option to lease, because it had failed to pay the $150,000 by September 30, 2001.

Brunswick sued, claiming that Route 18 had breached its duty of good faith and fair dealing. The trial court found that Route 18 had no duty to notify Brunswick of impending deadlines, and gave summary judgment for Route 18. The appellate court affirmed, and Brunswick appealed to the state supreme court.

▼

---

[6]   *Shuster v. South Broward Hospital Dist. Physicians' Prof. Liability Ins. Trust*, 591 So. 2d 174, 1992 Fla. LEXIS 20 (Fla. 1992).

Issue: Did Route 18 breach its duty of good faith and fair dealing?

Excerpts from Justice Albin's Decision: Courts generally should not tinker with a finely drawn and precise contract entered into by experienced business people that regulates their financial affairs. [However,] every party to a contract is bound by a duty of good faith and fair dealing in both the performance and enforcement of the contract. Good faith is a concept that defies precise definition. Good faith conduct is conduct that does not violate community standards of decency, fairness, or reasonableness. The covenant of good faith and fair dealing calls for parties to a contract to refrain from doing anything which will have the effect of destroying or injuring the right of the other party to receive the benefits of the contract.

Our review of the undisputed facts of this case leads us to the inescapable conclusion that defendant breached the covenant of good faith and fair dealing. Nineteen months in advance of the option deadline, plaintiff notified defendant in writing of its intent to exercise the option to purchase the 99-year lease. Plaintiff mistakenly believed that the purchase price was not due until the time of closing.

During a 19-month period, defendant, through its agents, engaged in a pattern of evasion, sidestepping every request by plaintiff to discuss the option and ignoring plaintiff's repeated written and verbal entreaties to move forward on closing the 99-year lease. After Spector's death, defendant's attorney continued to play possum despite the impending option deadline and obvious potential harm to plaintiff.

Defendant never requested the purchase price of the lease. Indeed, as defendant's attorney candidly admitted at oral argument, defendant did not want the purchase price because the successful exercise of the option was not in defendant's economic interest.

Ordinarily, we are content to let experienced commercial parties fend for themselves and do not seek to introduce intolerable uncertainty into a carefully structured contractual relationship by balancing equities. But there are ethical norms that apply even to the harsh and sometimes cutthroat world of commercial transactions. We do not expect a landlord or even an attorney to act as his brother's keeper in a commercial transaction. We do expect, however, that they will act in good faith and deal fairly with an opposing party. Plaintiff's repeated letters and telephone calls to defendant concerning the exercise of the option and the closing of the 99-year lease obliged defendant to respond, and to respond truthfully.

[Plaintiff is entitled to exercise the 99-year lease.] ■

Public Policy

It is hard to argue against good faith. But how far does this approach go? Suppose Buyer holds a six-month option to purchase land for a shopping mall. With three months remaining, Seller learns through a well-connected friend that the state is likely to construct a new highway interchange one mile from the property. The land will double or triple in value. Is Seller obligated to give Buyer the good news? Or this: Suppose Owner, selling her home, knows that a convicted pedophile has moved into a house on the same block. Must she inform prospective buyers? Is there a difference between the two hypotheticals? ◆

Time of the Essence Clauses

> Go, sir, gallop, and don't forget that the world was made in six days. You can ask me for anything you like, except time.
> Napoleon, to an aide, 1803

Generals are not the only ones who place a premium on time. Ask Gene LaSalle. The Seabreeze Restaurant agreed to sell him all of its assets. The parties signed a contract stating the price and closing date. Seabreeze insisted on a clause saying, "Seabreeze considers that time is of the essence in consummating the proposed transaction." Such clauses are common in real estate transactions and in any other agreement where a delay would cause serious damage to one party. LaSalle was unable to close on the date specified and asked for an extension. Seabreeze refused and sold its assets elsewhere. A Florida court affirmed that Seabreeze acted legally.

A time of the essence clause will generally make contract dates strictly enforceable. Seabreeze regarded a timely sale as important, and LaSalle agreed to the provision. There was nothing unreasonable about the clause, and LaSalle suffered the consequences of his delay.[7]

Suppose the contract had named a closing date but included no time of the essence clause. If LaSalle offered to close three days late, could Seabreeze sell elsewhere? No. **Merely including a date for performance does not make time of the essence.** Courts dislike time of the essence arguments because even a short delay may mean that one party forfeits everything it expected to gain from the bargain. If the parties do not clearly state that prompt performance is essential, then both are entitled to reasonable delays.

BREACH

When one party breaches a contract, the other party is discharged. The discharged party has no obligation to perform and may sue for damages. Edwin promises that on July 1 he will deliver 20 tuxedos, tailored to fit male chimpanzees, to Bubba's circus for $300 per suit. After weeks of delay Edwin concedes he hasn't a cummerbund to his name. Bubba is discharged and obviously owes nothing. In addition, he may sue Edwin for damages. If Bubba is forced to pay $350 elsewhere to obtain similar tuxedos, he will recover the difference in cost. Twenty tuxedos, at $50 extra per suit, means that Bubba will get $1,000 from Edwin.

Material Breach

As we know, parties frequently perform their contract duties imperfectly, which is why courts accept substantial performance rather than strict performance, particularly in contracts involving services. In a more general sense, **courts will only discharge a contract if a party committed a *material* breach.** A material breach is one that substantially harms the innocent party and for which it would be hard to compensate without discharging the contract. Suppose Edwin fails to show up with the tuxedos on June 1, but calls to say they will arrive under the big top the next day. He has breached the agreement. Is his breach material? No. This is a trivial breach, and Bubba is not discharged. When the tuxedos arrive, he must pay.

Anticipatory Breach

Sally will receive her bachelor's degree in May and already has a job lined up for September, a two-year contract as window display designer for Surebet Department Store. The morning of graduation she reads in the paper that Surebet is going out of business that very day. Surebet has told Sally nothing about her status. Sally need not wait until September to learn her fate. Surebet has committed an **anticipatory breach by making it unmistakably clear that it will not honor the contract.** Sometimes a promisor will actually inform the promisee that it will not perform its duties. At other times, as here, the promisor takes some step that makes the breach evident. Sally is discharged and may immediately seek other work. She is also entitled to file suit for breach of contract. The court will treat Surebet's anticipatory breach just as though the store had actually refused to perform on September 1.

---

[7] *Seabreeze Restaurant, Inc. v. Paumgardhen,* 639 So. 2d 69, 1994 Fla. App. LEXIS 4546 (Fla. Dist. Ct. App. 1994).

Statute of Limitations

A party injured by a breach of contract should act promptly. **A statute of limitations begins to run at the time of injury and will limit the time within which the injured party may file suit.** Statutes of limitation vary from state to state and even from issue to issue within a state. In some states, for example, an injured party must sue on oral contracts within three years, on a sale of goods contract within four years, and on some written contracts within five years. Failure to file suit within the time-limits discharges the party who breached the contract. Always consult a lawyer promptly in the case of a legal injury. We have seen the overlap of tort and contract in cases such as fraud, and statutes of limitations for tort are generally shorter than for contract. Further, some related areas of law, such as employment discrimination, have statutes of limitation that are numbered in days, not years. Do not wait, mate.

IMPOSSIBILITY

"Your honor, my client wanted to honor the contract. He just couldn't. *Honest.*" This plea often echoes around courtrooms, as one party seeks discharge without fulfilling his contract obligations. Does the argument work? It depends. If performing a contract was truly impossible, a court will discharge the agreement. But if honoring the deal merely imposed a financial burden, the law will generally enforce the contract.

True Impossibility

These cases are easy—and rare. **True impossibility means that something has happened making it utterly impossible to do what the promisor said he would do.** Francoise owns a vineyard that produces Beaujolais Nouveau wine. She agrees to ship 1,000 cases of her wine to Tyrone, a New York importer, as soon as this year's vintage is ready. Tyrone will pay $50 per case. But a fungus wipes out her entire vineyard. Francoise is discharged. It is theoretically impossible for Francoise to deliver wine from her vineyard, and she owes Tyrone nothing.

Meanwhile, though, Tyrone has a contract with Jackson, a retailer, to sell 1,000 cases of any Beaujolais Nouveau wine at $70 per case. Tyrone has no wine from Francoise, and the only other Beaujolais Nouveau available will cost him $85 per case. Instead of earning $20 per case, Tyrone will lose $15. Does this discharge Tyrone's contract with Jackson? No. It is possible for him to perform, just undesirable. He must fulfill his agreement.

True impossibility is generally limited to these three causes:

- *Destruction of the Subject Matter,* as happened with Francoise's vineyard.

- *Death of the Promisor in a Personal Services Contract.* When the promisor agrees personally to render a service that cannot be transferred to someone else, her death discharges the contract. Producer hires Josephine to write the lyrics for a new Broadway musical, but Josephine dies after writing only two words: "Act One." The contract was personal to Josephine and is now discharged. Neither Josephine's estate nor Producer has any obligation to the other. But notice that most contracts are not for personal services. Suppose that Tyrone, the wine importer, drowns in a bathtub filled with cheap gin. His contract to sell wine to Jackson is not discharged, because anyone can deliver the required wine. Tyrone's estate remains liable on the deal with Jackson.

- ***Illegality.*** Charley, a Silicon Valley entrepreneur, wants to capitalize on his computer expertise. He contracts with Construction Co. to build a factory in Iran that will manufacture computers for sale in that country. Construction Co. fails to build the factory on time and Charley sues. Construction Co. defends by pointing out that the president of the United States has issued an executive order barring trade between the U.S. and Iran. Construction Co. wins; the executive order discharged the contract.

What happens if a contract becomes illegal—but then legal again? The following case sorts out the issues.

WHITE V. J.M. BROWN AMUSEMENT CO, INC.

360 S.C. 366, 601 S.E.2d 342

South Carolina Supreme Court, 2004

Facts: Philip White owned 13 food stores throughout two South Carolina counties, Oconee and Anderson. He contracted with J.M. Brown Amusement to install coin-operated video poker machines in his stores, for a term of 15 years, and the company did so. The machines gave cash payouts to winners.

The next year, because of popular opposition to the gambling machines, the South Carolina legislature passed a statute granting counties the right to hold a referendum on video poker. Oconee and Anderson counties, along with 10 others, voted to ban video poker. Brown removed his poker machines from White's stores and did not replace them with anything else.

Two years later, the South Carolina Supreme Court declared the local referendum law unconstitutional and void. White immediately contracted with Hughes Entertainment, Inc. to place video terminals and other coin operated amusement machines in his stores. White also sued Brown, seeking a court declaration that his contract with Brown was null and void; Brown counterclaimed, arguing that White breached the contract by permitting Hughes to place machines in the food stores.

The trial court found the contract void because of the referendum. However, the court of appeals reversed, declaring that the referendum had had no legal effect because it had been declared void. The case reached the state's highest court.

Issue: Was the White–Brown contract void, or still enforceable?

Excerpts from Justice Toal's Decision: In the present case, both parties were performing as required under the contract until performance of the contract became legally impossible for two reasons. First, the subject matter of the contract—certain video poker machines—became illegal under the local option law and the resulting local referenda. Second, as mandated by the local option law, the Department of Revenue revoked the licenses required to legally possess and use the machines. Consequently, both parties' duty to perform under the contract was discharged, and after that point, White and Brown were free to enter a new contract involving legal machines or seek other contractual relationships.

Moreover, because the subject matter of the contract became illegal, the contract itself was invalidated or rendered dead. Therefore, the next issue we must address is whether the dead contract was revived when this Court deemed the local option law—which permitted counties to hold an individual referendum to determine whether cash payouts for video gaming should remain legal—unconstitutional.

Given the court of appeals' decision, Brown asserts that the invalidation of the local option law somehow revived the dead contract for the remainder of its 15-year term. Brown essentially is asking us to reshape the course of events and impact those events had on the parties' contractual relationship by pretending that the unconstitutional statute and the local referenda never existed.

We reject Brown's argument and hold the contract was not revived by the subsequent invalidation of the local option law. This holding allows parties to conduct business and plan their affairs with some degree of certainty. Life goes on while judicial or legislative processes run their course. In the meantime, parties must arrange and conduct their business ▼

affairs under the law as it presently exists, regardless of a belief or hope the law will later be changed or invalidated.

For the foregoing reasons, we reverse the court of appeals' decision and remand for entry of summary judgment in favor of White on Brown's breach of contract counterclaim. The trial court correctly ruled that the sole subject matter of the contract was the outlawed video poker machines. Neither party breached the contract, and therefore neither party is entitled to damages. ■

Commercial Impracticability and Frustration of Purpose

It is rare for contract performance to be truly impossible, but common for it to become a financial burden to one party. Suppose Bradshaw Steel in Pittsburgh agrees to deliver 1,000 tons of steel beams to Rice Construction in Saudi Arabia at a given price, but a week later the cost of raw ore increases 30 percent. A contract once lucrative to the manufacturer is suddenly a major liability. Does that change discharge Bradshaw? Absolutely not. Rice signed the deal *precisely to protect itself against price increases.* As we have seen, the primary purpose of contracts is to enable the parties to control their future.

Yet there may be times when a change in circumstances is so extreme that it would be unfair to enforce a deal. What if a strike made it impossible for Bradshaw to ship the steel to Saudi Arabia, and the only way to deliver would be by air, at five times the sea cost? Must Bradshaw fulfill its deal? What if war in the Middle East meant that any ships or planes delivering the goods might be fired upon? Other changes could make the contract undesirable for *Rice*. Suppose the builder wanted steel for a major public building in Riyadh, but the Saudi government decided not to go forward with the construction. The steel would then be worthless to Rice. Must the company still accept it?

None of these hypotheticals involves true impossibility. It is physically possible for Bradshaw to deliver the goods and for Rice to receive. But in some cases it may be so dangerous or costly or pointless to enforce a bargain that a court will discharge it instead. Courts use the related doctrines of commercial impracticability and frustration of purpose to decide when a change in circumstances should permit one side to escape its duties.

Commercial impracticability means some event has occurred that neither party anticipated and *fulfilling the contract would now be extraordinarily difficult and unfair to one party*. If a shipping strike forces Bradshaw to ship by air, the company will argue that neither side expected the strike and that Bradshaw should not suffer a fivefold increase in shipping cost. Bradshaw will probably win the argument.

Frustration of purpose means some event has occurred that neither party anticipated and *the contract now has no value for one party*. If Rice's building project is canceled, Rice will argue that the steel now is useless to the company. Frustration cases are hard to predict. Some states would agree with Rice, but others would hold that it was Rice's obligation to protect itself with a government guarantee that the project would be completed. Courts consider the following factors in deciding impracticability and frustration claims:

- *Mere financial difficulties will never suffice to discharge a contract.* Barbara and Michael Luber divorced, and Michael agreed to pay alimony. He stopped making payments and claimed that it was impracticable for him to do so, because he had hit hard times and simply did not have the money. The court dismissed his argument, noting that commercial impracticability requires some objective event that neither party anticipated, not merely the financial deterioration of one party.[8]

---

8   *Luber v. Luber,* 418 Pa. Super. 542, 614 A.2d 771, 1992 Pa. Super. LEXIS 3338 (Pa. Super. Ct. 1992).

- *The event must have been truly unexpected.* Wayne Carpenter bought land from the state of Alaska, intending to farm it and agreeing to make monthly payments. The sales contract stated that Alaska did not guarantee the land for agriculture or any other purpose. Carpenter struggled to farm the land but failed; as soon as the ground thawed, the water table rose too high for crops. Carpenter abandoned the land and stopped making payments. Alaska sued and won. The high court rejected Carpenter's claim of impracticability since the "event"—bad soil—was not unexpected. Alaska had warned that the land might prove unworkable, and Carpenter had no claim for commercial impracticability.[9]

- *If the promisor must use a different means to accomplish her task, at a greatly increased cost, she probably does have a valid claim of impracticability.* If a shipping strike forces Bradshaw to use a different means of delivery—say, air—and this multiplies its costs several times, the company is probably discharged. But a mere increase in the cost of raw materials, such as a 30 percent rise in the price of ore, will almost never discharge the promisor.

- *A* force majeure *clause is significant but not necessarily dispositive.* To protect themselves from unexpected events, companies sometimes include a *force majeure* clause, allowing cancellation of the agreement in case of extraordinary and unexpected events. A typical clause might permit the seller of goods to delay or cancel delivery in the event of "acts of God, fire, labor disputes, accidents or transportation difficulties." A court will always consider a *force majeure* clause, but may not enforce it if one party is trying to escape from routine financial problems.

- *The UCC permits discharge only for major, unforeseen disruptions.* **UCC §2-615** endorses commercial impracticability as a ground for discharge, but emphasizes that mere cost increases will not justify discharge, nor will simple inconvenience or financial loss.

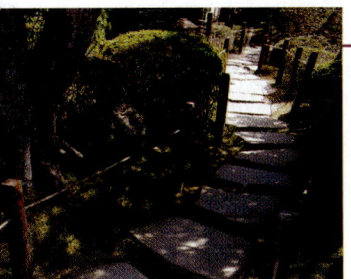

Chapter Conclusion

Negotiate carefully. A casually written letter may imply a condition precedent that the author never intended. The term "personal satisfaction" should be defined so that both parties know whether one party may fire the other on a whim. Never assume that mere inconvenience or financial loss will discharge contractual duties.

Chapter Review

1. A condition is an event that must occur before a party becomes obligated. It may be stated expressly or implied, and no formal language is necessary to create one.

2. Strict performance, which requires one party to fulfill its duties perfectly, is unusual. In construction and service contracts, substantial performance is generally sufficient to entitle the promisor to the contract price, minus the cost of defects in the work.

3. Personal satisfaction contracts are interpreted under an objective standard, requiring reasonable ground for dissatisfaction, unless the work involves personal judgment *and* the parties intended a subjective standard.

---

[9] *State v. Carpenter*, 869 P.2d 1181, 1994 Alaska LEXIS 23 (Alaska 1994).

4. Good faith performance is required in all contracts.

5. Time of the essence clauses result in strict enforcement of contract deadlines.

6. A material breach is the only kind that will discharge a contract; a trivial breach will not.

7. True impossibility means that some event has made it impossible to perform an agreement. It is typically caused by destruction of the subject matter, the death of an essential promisor, or intervening illegality.

8. Commercial impracticability means that some unexpected event has made it extraordinarily difficult and unfair for one party to perform its obligations.

9. Frustration of purpose may occur when an unexpected event renders a contract completely useless to one party.

Practice Test

1. Stephen Krogness was a real estate broker. He signed an agreement to act as an agent for Best Buy Co., which was interested in selling several of its stores. The contract provided that Best Buy would pay Krogness a commission of 2 percent for a sale to "any prospect submitted directly to Best Buy by Krogness." Krogness introduced Corporate Realty Capital (CRC) to Best Buy, and the parties negotiated a possible sale but could not reach agreement. CRC then introduced Best Buy to BB Properties (BB). Best Buy sold several properties to BB for a total of $46 million. CRC acted as the broker on the deal. After the sale, Krogness sought a commission of $528,000. Is he entitled to it?

2. **ETHICS** Commercial Union Insurance Co. (CU) insured Redux, Ltd. The contract made CU liable for fire damage, but stated that the insurer would not pay for harm caused by criminal acts of any Redux employees. Fire destroyed Redux's property. CU claimed that the "criminal acts" clause was a condition precedent, but Redux asserted it was a condition subsequent. What difference does it make, and who is legally right? Does the insurance company's position raise any ethical issues? Who drafted the contract? How clear were its terms?

3. Evans built a house for Sandra Dyer, but the house had some problems. The garage ceiling was too low. Load-bearing beams in the "great room" cracked and appeared to be steadily weakening. The patio did not drain properly. Pipes froze. Evans wanted the money promised for the job, but Dyer refused to pay. Comment.

4. Stephen Muka owned U.S. Robotics. He hired his brother Chris to work in the company. His letter promised Chris $1 million worth of Robotics stock at the end of one year, "provided you work reasonably hard & smart at things in the next year." (We should all have such brothers.) Chris arrived at Robotics and worked the full year, but toward the end of the year Stephen died. His estate refused to give Chris the stock, claiming their agreement was a personal satisfaction contract and only Stephen could decide whether Chris had earned the reward. Comment.

5. Ken Ward was an Illinois farmer who worked land owned by his father-in-law, Frank Ruda. To finance his operation, he frequently borrowed money from Watseka First National Bank, paying back the loans with farming profits. But Ward fell deeper and deeper into debt and Watseka became concerned. When Ward sought additional loans, Watseka insisted that Ruda become a guarantor on all of the outstanding debt, and the father-in-law agreed. The new loans had an acceleration clause, permitting the bank to demand payment of the entire debt if it believed itself "insecure," that is, at risk of a default. Unfortunately, just as Ward's debts reached more than $120,000, Illinois suffered a severe drought, and Ward's crops failed. Watseka asked Ruda to sell some of the land he owned to pay back part of the indebtedness. Ruda reluctantly agreed but never did so. Meanwhile, Ward decreased his payments to the bank because of the terrible crop. Watseka then "accelerated" the loan, demanding that Ruda pay off the entire debt. Ruda defended by claiming that Watseka's acceleration at such a difficult time was bad faith. Who won?

6. In August 1985, Colony Park Associates signed a contract to buy 44 acres of residential land from John Gall. The contract stated that "closing will take place August 20, 1986." The year's delay was to enable Colony Park to obtain building permits to develop condominiums. Colony Park worked diligently to obtain all permits and kept Gall abreast of its efforts. But delays in sewer permits forced Colony Park to notify Gall it could not close on the agreed date. Colony Park suggested a date exactly one month later. Gall refused the new date and declined to convey the property to Colony Park. Colony Park sued. Gall argued that since the parties specified a date, time was of the essence and Colony Park's failure to buy on time discharged Gall. Please rule.

7. Loehmann's clothing stores, a nationwide chain with headquarters in New York, was the anchor tenant in the Lincoln View Plaza Shopping Center in Phoenix, Arizona, with a 20-year lease from the landlord, Foundation Development, beginning in 1978. Loehmann's was obligated to pay rent the first of every month and to pay common area charges four times a year. The lease stated that if Loehmann's failed to pay on time, Foundation could send a notice of default, and that if the store failed to pay all money due within 10 days, Foundation could evict. On February 23, 1987, Foundation sent to Loehmann's the common area charges for the quarter ending January 31, 1987. The balance due was $3,500. Loehmann's believed the bill was in error and sent an inquiry on March 18, 1987. On April 10, 1987, Foundation insisted on payment of the full amount within 10 days. Foundation sent the letter to the Loehmann's store in Phoenix. On April 13, 1987, the Loehmann's store received the bill and, since it was not responsible for payments, forwarded it to the New York office. Because the company had moved offices in New York, a Loehmann's officer did not see the bill until April 20. Loehmann's issued a check for the full amount on April 24 and mailed it the following day. On April 28 Foundation sued to evict; on April 29 the company received Loehmann's check. Please rule.

8. Omega Concrete had a gravel pit and factory. Access was difficult, so Omega contracted with Union Pacific Railroad (UP) for the right to use a private road that crossed UP property and tracks. The contract stated that use of the road was solely for Omega employees and that Omega would be responsible for closing a gate that UP planned to build where the private road joined a public highway. In fact, UP never constructed the gate; Omega had no authority to construct the gate. Mathew Rogers, an Omega employee, was killed by a train while using the private road to reach Omega. Rogers's family sued Omega, claiming, among other things, that Omega failed to keep the gate closed as the contract required. Is Omega liable based on that failure?

9. ***CPA QUESTION*** Nagel and Fields entered into a contract in which Nagel was obligated to deliver certain goods by September 10. On September 3, Nagel told Fields that he had no intention of delivering the goods. Prior to September 10, Fields may successfully sue Nagel under the doctrine of:

   a. Promissory estoppel

   b. Accord and satisfaction

   c. Anticipatory breach

   d. Substantial performance

10. ***YOU BE THE JUDGE*** WRITING PROBLEM Kuhn Farm Machinery, a European company, signed an agreement with Scottsdale Plaza Resort, of Arizona, to use the resort for its North American dealers' convention during March 1991. Kuhn agreed to rent 190 guest rooms and spend several thousand dollars on food and beverages. Kuhn invited its top 200 independent dealers from the United States and Canada and about 25 of its own employees from the United States, Europe, and Australia, although it never mentioned those plans to Scottsdale.

    On August 2, 1990, Iraq invaded Kuwait and on January 16, 1991, the United States and allied forces were at war with Iraq. Saddam Hussein and other Iraqi leaders threatened terrorist acts against the United States and its allies. Kuhn became concerned about the safety of those traveling to Arizona, especially its European employees. By mid-February, 11 of the top 50 dealers with expense-paid trips had either canceled their plans to attend or failed to sign up. Kuhn postponed the convention. The resort sued. The trial court discharged the contract under the doctrines of commercial impracticability and frustration of purpose. The resort appealed. Did commercial impracticability or frustration of purpose discharge the contract? **Argument for Scottsdale Plaza Resort:** The resort had no way of knowing that Kuhn anticipated bringing executives from Europe, and even less reason to expect that if anything interfered with their travel, the entire convention would become pointless. Most of the dealers could have attended the convention, and the resort stood ready to serve them. **Argument for Kuhn:** The parties never anticipated the threat of terrorism. Kuhn wanted this convention so that its European executives, among others, could meet top North American dealers. That is now impossible. No company would risk employee lives for a meeting. As a result, the contract has no value at all to Kuhn, and its obligations should be discharged by law.

Internet Research Problem

Using the Internet, find a contract that contains a "commercial impracticability" clause and/or a "frustration of purpose" clause. They often go together. A good place to look is at http://www.beatty.westbuslaw.com, although many other sites will contain such clauses. What is the subject of the contract generally? What did the drafters of the contract hope to achieve with the clause you have located? In your opinion, will a court enforce the clause? (Refer to the bulleted list of criteria on pages 388 and 389.) Why or why not? If the clause is valid, will it accomplish the purpose you have described?

11. Krug International, an Ohio corporation, had a contract with Iraqi Airways to build aeromedical equipment for training pilots. Krug then contracted for Power Engineering, an Iowa corporation, to build the specialized gearbox to be used in the training equipment, for $150,000. Power did not know that Krug planned to resell the gearbox to Iraqi Airways. When Power had almost completed the gearbox, the Gulf War broke out and the United Nations declared an embargo on all shipments to Iraq. Krug notified Power that it no longer wanted the gearbox. Power sued. Please rule.

12. *ROLE REVERSAL* Write a multiple-choice question focusing on a contractor's claim to substantial performance. The answers should contain dollar amounts that the contractor could possibly recover, from zero to the full value of the contract.

You can find further practice problems at http://beatty.westbuslaw.com or in the Study Guide that accompanies this text.

Remedies

Ben is the general manager of the Starz, a professional football team. Driving home in his rusty, eight-year-old truck, he is in a sour humor. Spencer, the team's best running back, under contract to play for one more year at $2.5 million, has announced he is leaving the team to act in the new sitcom *Cutback*. Ben wonders whether he can stop Spencer from leaving the team. Even if it is possible, would it be worthwhile to make a disgruntled, out-of-condition athlete carry (and fumble) the ball? If Spencer leaves, it will cost at least $5 million to hire a runner with equal speed and power.

The G.M.'s phone rings. Louise, a dealer in rare autos, has bad news in her voice.

"I hate to tell you, Ben, but the Testa deal has fallen through."

"What are you talking about? We both signed! That's a binding contract!." A seller in Florida had agreed in writing to sell Ben a 1955 Ferrari Testarossa for $600,000.

"*I* know it's true, and *you* know it," Louise murmurs soothingly. "But the seller has decided the car is too rare to part with."

Ben slams his cell phone down, turns into his driveway—and notices that the back door is open. Did he leave it that way? No. The burglar did. Ben has lost about

$100,000 worth of jewelry, clothing, and sports memorabilia. Why didn't the alarm sound? When he demands an explanation from Alarmist, the quality assurance representative assures Ben that he will receive the full compensation due under his contract—$600. Later that night, Ben will have a long talk with his lawyer about breached contracts and remedies. ■

BREACHING THE CONTRACT

Someone breaches a contract when he fails to perform a duty without a valid excuse. Spencer is legally committed to play for the Starz for one more year, and is clearly breaching his contract when he informs the team that in the future he will be playing for laughs. But what can the Starz do about the runner's breach? In other words, what is the team's *remedy*? **A remedy is the method a court uses to compensate an injured party.**

Should a court stop Spencer from performing in his new sitcom? Force him to carry the pigskin for the Starz? **An order forcing someone to do something, or refrain from doing something, is an injunction.** Courts frequently grant injunctions to an employer, blocking an employee from *leaving* to work elsewhere. However, courts almost never use an injunction to force an employee to *complete* a contract with his employer, because that would force two antagonistic parties to work together. In other words, Ben can probably stop Spencer from working in television, but no court will order the running back to suit up for the Starz.

Courts also award **expectation damages,** meaning the money required to put one party in the position she would have been in had the other side performed the contract. If the Starz are forced to hire another running back for double the money they expected to pay Spencer, the team will probably recover the difference between the two players' salaries.

The Testarossa seller has breached his deal with Ben. What is his remedy? Ben does not want money damages; he wants that lovely red car. In cases of rare property, courts often award **specific performance,** forcing both parties to complete the deal. Ben should get his car.

Finally, the alarm company is trying to *insist* upon a remedy—a very limited one, which will leave Ben largely uncompensated for the burglary. Alarmist is relying on a **liquidated damages clause,** meaning a provision in the contract that declares in advance what one party will receive if the other side breaches. Courts sometimes—but not always—enforce these clauses. As we see later, Alarmist's liquidated clause may be too harsh, and unenforceable.

How to help an injured party, without unfairly harming the other person, is the focus of remedies. Courts have struggled with remedies for centuries, but we will master the subject in one chapter. The questions and issues created by Ben's Bad Day are typical remedy problems.

Ethics

Though a court may have several alternative remedies available, it is important to note that most have one thing in common: the focus is on compensating the injured party, rather than punishing the party in breach. A court must decide whether to prevent Spencer from leaving the gridiron for the television studio, but it will not consider sending fining or jailing him.

Critics argue that someone who willfully breaches a contract should pay a penalty. The Testarossa seller knows he is obligated to part with his car, but tries to keep it anyway. Spencer blithely ignores his obligations to the team. Should a remedy reflect morality? In this chapter we will see very few instances in which a court punishes unethical conduct. From the Chapter 2 ethics checklist: Does this approach violate important values? ◆

Identifying the "Interest" to Be Protected

The first step that a court takes in choosing a remedy is to decide what interest it is trying to protect. An **interest** is a legal right in something. Someone can have an interest in property, for example, by owning it, or renting it to a tenant, or lending money so someone else may buy it. He can have an interest in a *contract* if the agreement gives him some benefit. There are four principal contract interests that a court may seek to protect:

- *Expectation Interest.* This refers to what the injured party reasonably thought she would get from the contract. The goal is to put her in the position she would have been in if both parties had fully performed their obligations.

- *Reliance Interest.* The injured party may be unable to demonstrate expectation damages, perhaps because it is unclear he would have profited. But he may still prove that he *expended money* in reliance on the agreement and that in fairness he should receive compensation.

- *Restitution Interest.* The injured party may be unable to show an expectation interest or reliance. But perhaps she has conferred a *benefit* on the other party. Here, the objective is to restore to the injured party the benefit she has provided.

- *Equitable Interest.* In some cases, money damages will not suffice to help the injured party. Something more is needed, such as an order to transfer property to the injured party (specific performance) or an order forcing one party to stop doing something (an injunction).

In this chapter, we look at all four interests.

EXPECTATION INTEREST

This is the most common remedy that the law provides for a party injured by a breach of contract. **The expectation interest is designed to put the injured party in the position she would have been in had both sides fully performed their obligations.** A court tries to give the injured party the money she would have made from the contract. If accurately computed, this should take into account all the gains she reasonably expected and all the expenses and losses she would have incurred. The injured party should not end up better off than she would have been under the agreement, nor should she suffer serious loss.

William Colby was a former director of the CIA. He wanted to write a book about his 15 years in Vietnam. He paid James McCarger $5,000 for help in writing an early draft and promised McCarger another $5,000 if the book was published. Then he hired Alexander Burnham to co-write the book. Colby's agent secured a contract with Contemporary Books, which included a $100,000 advance. But Burnham was hopelessly late with the manuscript and Colby missed his publication date. Colby fired Burnham and finished the book without him. Contemporary published *Lost Victory* several years late, and the book flopped, earning no significant revenue. Because the book was so late, Contemporary paid Colby a total of only $17,000. Colby sued Burnham for his lost expectation interest. The court awarded him $23,000, calculated as follows:

	$100,000	advance, the only money Colby was promised
	− 10,000	agent's fee
	= 90,000	Fee for the two authors, combined
divided by 2	= 45,000	Colby's fee
	− 5,000	owed to McCarger under the earlier agreement
	= 40,000	Colby's expectation interest
	− 17,000	Fee Colby received from Contemporary
	= 23,000	Colby's expectation damages, that is, the amount he would have received had Burnham finished on time

The *Colby* case[1] presented an easy calculation of damages. Other contracts are complex. Courts typically divide the expectation damages into three parts: (1) compensatory (or "direct") damages, which represent harm that flowed directly from the contract's breach; (2) consequential (or "special") damages, which represent harm caused by the injured party's unique situation; and (3) incidental damages, which are minor costs such as storing or returning defective goods, advertising for alternative goods, and so forth. The first two, compensatory and consequential, are the important ones.

Compensatory Damages

Compensatory damages are the most common monetary awards for the expectation interest. Courts also refer to these as "direct damages." **Compensatory damages are those that flow directly from the contract.** In other words, these are the damages that inevitably result from the breach. Suppose Ace Productions hires Reina to star in its new movie, *Inside Straight*. Ace promises Reina $3 million, providing she shows up June 1 and works until the film is finished. But in late May, Joker Entertainment offers Reina $6 million to star in its new feature, and on June 1 Reina informs Ace that she will not appear. Reina has breached her contract, and Ace should recover compensatory damages.

What are the damages that flow directly from the contract? Ace obviously has to replace Reina. If Ace hires Kween as its star and pays her a fee of $4 million, Ace is entitled to the difference between what it expected to pay ($3 million) and what the breach forced it to pay ($4 million), or $1 million in compensatory damages. Suppose the rest of the cast and crew are idle for two weeks because of the delay in hiring a substitute, and the lost time costs the producers an extra $2.5 million. Reina is also liable for those expenses. Both the new actress and the delay are inevitable.

Reasonable Certainty

The injured party must prove the breach of contract caused damages that can be quantified with reasonable certainty. What if *Inside Straight*, now starring Kween, bombs at the box office. Ace proves that each of Reina's last three movies grossed over $60 million, but *Inside Straight* grossed only $28 million. Is Reina liable for the lost profits? No. Ace cannot prove that it was Reina's absence that caused the film to fare poorly. The script may have been mediocre, or Kween's co-stars dull, or the publicity efforts inadequate. Ace *hoped* to gross over $60 million, but mere hopes create "speculative damages," worth zero. Because Ace cannot demonstrate a quantifiable box office loss directly attributable to Reina, it will get nothing for the disappointing ticket sales.

---

[1]   *Colby v. Burnham*, 31 Conn. App. 707, 627 A.2d 457, 1993 Conn. App LEXIS 299 (Conn. App. Ct. 1993).

Consequential Damages

In addition to compensatory damages, the injured party may seek consequential damages or, as they are also known, "special damages." **Consequential damages are those resulting from the unique circumstances of *this injured party*.** The rule concerning this remedy comes from a famous 1854 case, *Hadley v. Baxendale*, which all American law students read. Now it is your turn.

HADLEY V. BAXENDALE

9 Ex. 341, 156 Eng. Rep. 145
Court of Exchequer, 1854

Facts: The Hadleys operated a flour mill in Gloucester. The crankshaft broke, causing the mill to grind to a halt. The Hadleys employed Baxendale to cart the damaged part to a foundry in Greenwich, where a new one could be manufactured. Baxendale promised to make the delivery in one day, but he was late transporting the shaft, and as a result the Hadleys' mill was shut for five extra days. They sued, and the jury awarded damages based in part on their lost profits. Baxendale appealed.

Issue: Should the defendant be liable for profits lost because of his delay in delivering the shaft?

Excerpts from Judge Alderson's Decision: Where two parties have made a contract which one of them has broken, the damages which the other party ought to receive in respect of such breach of contract should be such as may fairly and reasonably be considered either arising naturally, i.e. according to the usual course of things, from such breach of contract itself, or such as may reasonably be supposed to have been in the contemplation of both parties, at the time they made the contract, as the probable result of the breach of it. Now, if the special circumstances under which the contract was actually made were communicated by the plaintiffs to the defendants, and thus known to both parties, the damages resulting from the breach of such a contract, which they would reasonably contemplate, would be the amount of injury which would ordinarily follow from a breach of contract under these special circumstances so known and communicated. But, on the other hand, if these special circumstances were wholly unknown to the party breaking the contract, he, at the most, could only be supposed to have had in his contemplation the amount of injury which would arise generally, and in the great multitude of cases not affected by any special circumstances, from such a breach of contract.

Now, in the present case, if we are to apply the principles above laid down, we find that the only circumstances here communicated by the plaintiffs to the defendants at the time the contract was made, were, that the article to be carried was the broken shaft of a mill, and that the plaintiffs were the millers of that mill. But how do these circumstances shew [sic] reasonably that the profits of the mill must be stopped by an unreasonable delay in the delivery of the broken shaft by the carrier to the third person? Suppose the plaintiffs had another shaft in their possession put up or putting up at the time, and that they only wished to send back the broken shaft to the engineer who made it; it is clear that this would be quite consistent with the above circumstances, and yet the unreasonable delay in the delivery would have no effect upon the intermediate profits of the mill. It follows, therefore, that the loss of profits here cannot reasonably be considered such a consequence of the breach of contract as could have been fairly and reasonably contemplated by both the parties when they made this contract.

[The court ordered a new trial, in which the jury would *not* be allowed to consider the plaintiffs' lost profits.] ∎

The rule from *Hadley v. Baxendale* has been unchanged ever since: **the injured party may recover consequential damages only if the breaching party should have foreseen them when the two sides formed the contract.**

Let us return briefly to *Inside Straight*. Suppose that, long before shooting began, Ace had sold the film's soundtrack rights to Spinem Sound for $2 million. Spinem believed it would make a profit only if Reina appeared in the film, so it demanded the right to discharge the agreement if Reina dropped out. When Reina quit, Spinem terminated the contract. Now, when Ace sues Reina, it will also seek $2 million in consequential damages for the lost music revenue. If Reina knew about Ace's contract with Spinem when she signed to do the film, she is liable for $2 million. If she never realized she was an essential part of the music contract, she owes nothing for the lost profits.

Injured plaintiffs often try to recover lost profits, which courts generally award if they can be quantified. The plaintiff need not prove his damages with mathematical precision, but must provide enough information so that the fact finder can reasonably estimate a fair sum for damages. In the following case, lost profits are one of the two issues for you to decide.

you Be The Judge

BERKEL & COMPANY CONTRACTORS, INC. V. PALM & ASSOCIATES, INC.

814 N.E.2d 649 Court of Appeals of Indiana, 2004

Facts: A general contractor was building a large generating plant, and hired Berkel & Co. as a subcontractor. Berkel's job was to install about 800 pilings, as foundation, a process that involves drilling holes as deep as 130 feet and filling them with concrete. Berkel negotiated with Palm & Associates, surveyors, and those two parties agreed that Palm would prepare electronic drawings, grid maps, and other data so that Berkel would know precisely where to drill each piling.

Berkel and Palm agreed that Palm would

- Use two men, full-time
- Prepare all information for approximately 800 auger pilings
- Submit data for specific pilings within 24 hours of Berkel's request
- Be paid $110 per man-hour
- Meet all state, federal and project requirements concerning materials and equipment.

After Palm had done one day's work, Berkel learned that all subcontractors were required to employ union labor. When Berkel told informed Palm of this obligation, Palm replied that it would speak to local unions, and that the price would have to be adjusted based on the new requirement.

Four days later, Palm had not worked out an agreement with the union, and Berkel hired a different surveyor to complete the work.

Palm filed suit for breach of contract. The trial court found that Berkel had breached the agreement, and awarded Palm $41,368 in consequential damages, for lost profits. Berkel appealed, claiming that Palm breached the contract, not Berkel, and further that even if Berkel breached, lost profits were unforeseeable and impossible to calculate.

You Be the Judge: Which party breached the contract? Were lost profits foreseeable? If so, could they be calculated?

Argument for Berkel: The contract required Palm to meet state, federal, and project requirements. One of the project requirements, over which Berkel had no control, was mandatory union labor. Palm was too slow reaching agreement with the unions. Berkel could not wait. To meet its obligations, Berkel hired a surveyor that immediately began work with union labor.

Further, any so-called lost profits were unforeseeable when the parties entered into the agreement, and impossible to calculate. The contract gave no total price or total hours of work. If the parties had been asked what Palm's profits would be, neither side could have answered with certainty. Under the rule of *Hadley v. Baxendale*, consequential damages can only be recovered if at the time of making the contract the parties could have foreseen the harm. This was a very big project and neither side knew exactly what it was dealing with. It is unfair to pretend that the whole job would have gone smoothly and that Palm would have earned a quantifiable profit. Palm did one day's work and then stalled on the job. It should be paid, at most, for one day's labor.

Argument for Palm: The contract did not require Palm to use union labor. The agreement only demanded that materials and equipment meet appropriate standards. Palm had no way of knowing that union labor would be mandatory and should have been allowed a few days to make the major adjustment demanded.

We can in fact calculate Palm's lost profits, with enough precision to satisfy the rule of *Hadley v. Baxendale*. The two sides agreed that there were approximately 800 pilings to be driven. Two men performing this work would take about 520 hours, and the company would be paid $110 per man-hour. Deducting all expenses would have left us with a net profit of about $41,000. These damages were easily foreseeable by both parties at the time they formed the contract. Berkel gave us the contract because they made their own estimate and concluded we were making a reasonable profit. Although we cannot calculate the total time to the exact minute, it is not fair to penalize Palm because of Berkel's behavior. They are the ones who breached, and they should put us in the position we would have been in had they properly performed. ■

Incidental Damages

Incidental damages are the relatively minor costs that the injured party suffers when responding to the breach. When Reina, the actress, breaches the film contract, the producers may have to leave the set and fly back to Los Angeles to hire a new actress. The travel cost is an incidental damage. In another setting, suppose Maud, a manufacturer, has produced 5,000 pairs of running shoes for Foot The Bill, a retail chain, but Foot The Bill breaches the agreement and refuses to accept the goods. Maud will have to store the shoes and advertise for alternate buyers. The storage and advertising costs are incidental expenses, and Maud will recover them.

If the retailer refuses the order, is the manufacturer entitled to incidental damages?

Sale of Goods

Under the Uniform Commercial Code (UCC), remedies for breach of contract in the sale of goods are similar to the general rules discussed throughout this chapter. UCC §§2-703 through 2-715 govern the remedies available to buyers and sellers.[2]

Seller's Remedies

If a buyer breaches a sale of goods contract, the seller generally has at least two remedies. She may resell the goods elsewhere. If she acts in good faith, she will be awarded **the difference between the original contract price and the price she was able to obtain in the open market.** Assume that Maud, the manufacturer, had a contract to sell her shoes to Foot The Bill for $55 per pair and Foot

---

[2]   We discuss these remedies in greater detail in Unit 3, on commercial transactions.

The Bill's breach forces her to sell them on the open market, where she gets only $48 per pair. Maud will win $7 per pair times 5,000 pairs, or $35,000, from Foot The Bill.

Alternatively, the buyer may choose not to resell and settle for the difference between the contract price and the market value of the goods. Maud, in other words, may choose to keep the shoes. If she can prove that their market value is $48 per pair, for example, by showing what other retailers would have paid her for them, she will still get her $7 each, representing the difference between what the contract promised her and what the market would support. In either case, the money represents compensatory damages. Maud is also entitled to incidental damages, such as the storage and advertising expenses described above. But there is one significant difference under the UCC: **Most courts hold that the seller of goods is *not* entitled to consequential damages.** Suppose Maud hired two extra workers to inspect, pack, and ship the shoes for Foot The Bill. Those are consequential damages, but Maud will not recover them because she is the seller and the contract is for the sale of goods.

Buyer's Remedies

The buyer's remedies under the Code are similar to those we have already considered. She typically has two options. First, the buyer can "cover" by purchasing substitute goods. To **cover** means to make a good faith purchase of goods similar to those in the contract. The buyer may then obtain **the difference between the original contract price and her cover price.** Alternatively, if the buyer chooses not to cover, she is entitled to the difference between the original contract price and the market value of the goods.

Suppose Mary has contracted to buy 1,000 six-foot Christmas trees at $25 per tree from Elmo. The market suddenly rises, and in the spirit of the season Elmo breaches his deal and sells the trees elsewhere. If Mary makes a good faith effort to cover but is forced to pay $40 per tree, she may recover the difference from Elmo, meaning $15 per tree times 1,000 trees, or $15,000. Similarly, if she chooses not to cover but can prove that $40 is now the market value of the trees, she is entitled to her $15 per tree.

Under the UCC, **the buyer *is* entitled to consequential damages provided that the seller could reasonably have foreseen them.** If Mary tells Elmo, when they sign their deal, that she has a dozen contracts to resell the trees, for an average price of $50 per tree, she may recover $25 per tree, representing the difference between her contract price with Elmo and the value of the tree *to her*, based on her other contracts.[3] If she failed to inform Elmo of the other contracts, she would not receive any money based on them. The buyer is also entitled to whatever incidental damages may have accrued.

We turn now to cases where the injured party cannot prove expectation damages.

RELIANCE INTEREST

George plans to manufacture and sell silk scarves during the holiday season. In the summer, he contracts with Cecily, the owner of a shopping mall, to rent a high-visibility stall for $100 per day. George then buys hundreds of yards of costly silk and gets to work cutting and sewing. But in September, Cecily refuses to honor the contract. George sues and easily proves Cecily breached a valid contract. But what is his remedy?

George cannot establish an expectation interest in his scarf business. He *hoped* to sell each scarf for a $40 gross profit. He *planned* on making $2,000 per day. But how

---

[3] As we discuss in the section on mitigation, later in the chapter, Mary will get only her consequential damages if she attempts to cover.

much would he actually have earned? Enough to retire on? Enough to buy a salami sandwich for lunch? He has no way of proving his profits, and a court cannot give him his expectation interest. Instead, George will ask for *reliance damages*. **The reliance interest is designed to put the injured party in the position he would have been in had the parties never entered into a contract.** This remedy focuses on the time and money the injured party spent performing his part of the agreement.

George should be able to recover reliance damages from Cecily. Assuming he is unable to sell the scarves to a retail store, which is probable since retailers will have made purchases long ago, George should be able to recover the cost of the silk fabric he bought and perhaps something for the hours of labor he spent cutting and sewing. But reliance damages can be difficult to win because *they are harder to quantify*. Courts prefer to compute damages using the numbers provided in a contract. If a contract states a price of $25 per Christmas tree and one party breaches, the arithmetic is easy. Judges become uncomfortable when asked to base damages on vague calculations. How much was George's time worth in making the scarves? How good was his work? How likely were the scarves to sell? If George has a track record in the industry, he will be able to show a market price for his services. Without such a record, his reliance claim becomes a tough battle.

Reliance Damages and Promissory Estoppel

In several earlier chapters of this unit, we have seen that a plaintiff may sometimes recover damages based on promissory estoppel even when there is no valid contract. The plaintiff must show that the defendant made a promise knowing that the plaintiff would likely rely on it, that the plaintiff did rely, and that the only way to avoid injustice is to enforce the promise. **In promissory estoppel cases, a court will generally award only *reliance damages*.** It would be unfair to give expectation damages for the full benefit of the bargain when, legally, there has been no bargain.

In the following case, the victorious plaintiff demonstrates how unreliable reliance damages are, and how winning can be hard to distinguish from losing.

TOSCANO V. GREENE MUSIC

124 Ca. App. 4th 685, 21 Ca. Rptr. 3d 732
Court of Appeal of California, 2004

Facts: Joseph Toscano was the general manager of Fields Pianos (Fields) in Santa Ana, California. He was unhappy with his job, and decided to seek other employment. Toscano contacted Michael Greene, who owned similar stores. In July, Greene offered Toscano a sales management job, starting September 1. Relying on that offer, Toscano resigned from Fields on August 1. However, in mid-August, Greene withdrew his employment offer. Toscano later found lower-paying jobs in other cities.

Toscano sued Greene for breach of contract and promissory estoppel. Greene argued that Toscano was not entitled to any expectation damages, because his employment with Greene would have been at will, meaning he could lose the job at any time. Greene also urged that because Toscano was an at-will employee at Fields, he could recover at most one month's lost wage.

The trial court ruled that Toscano was entitled to reliance damages for all lost wages at Fields, starting from the day he resigned, going forward until his anticipated retirement in 2017. Toscano's expert accountant calculated his past losses (until the time of trial) at $119,061, and his future lost earnings at $417,772. The trial court awarded Toscano $536,833, and Greene appealed.

▼

Issue: Was Toscano entitled to reliance damages?

Excerpts from Judge O'Rourke's Decision: Given the equitable underpinnings of the promissory estoppel doctrine, we hold that a plaintiff such as Toscano, who relinquished his job in reliance on an unfulfilled promise of employment, may on an appropriate showing recover the lost wages he would have expected to earn from his former employer but for the defendant's promise. Such a damage measure is in keeping with the equitable nature of promissory estoppel. The object of equity is to do right and justice.

Our holding necessarily rejects the notion that the at-will nature of Toscano's former employment with Fields (undisputed by the parties here) is a strict impediment to recovery of future wages that Toscano would have earned at Fields had he not relied on Greene's promise.

[However,] we conclude that even drawing all inferences in Toscano's favor, the evidence was too speculative to lend support to the trial court's award of Toscano's lost future earnings from September 1 to his retirement.

Roberta Spoon, Toscano's damages expert, testified that in calculating Toscano's lost wages for the remainder of his career, "[a]ll I have done is arithmetic. I have simply analyzed the numbers." She testified she was not aware that Toscano's employment with Fields called for any specific tenure. Indeed,

Spoon admitted Toscano could have quit or been fired from that job from the time he resigned to the present. She simply assumed Toscano would have continued employment with Fields or another employer at a comparable salary, observing that he had never in the past changed employers for anything other than a pay increase.

Spoon's testimony does not establish Toscano had a definite expectation of continued employment with Fields for any particular period of time. It is evident her supposition was based only on Toscano's history of remaining with his employers until offered new employment. However, *Toscano's* intentions or practices are not relevant to whether he could expect to remain with Fields until his retirement. Evidence of Toscano's intentions does not establish with any reasonable certainty that Fields, an at-will employer who had the right to terminate Toscano at any time for any reason, had some different understanding of the terms of Toscano's employment, or that it would have continued to employ him until the end of his career. Neither party presented testimony from Jerry Goldman, Toscano's boss at Fields. An expert's opinion must not be based upon speculative or conjectural data.

The award of future earnings calculated from [the day he quit] to the date of Toscano's retirement in 2017 is vacated and the matter remanded for a new trial on the issue of damages only. The judgment is otherwise affirmed. ■

Public Policy

Notice that the court never even mentions that Toscano acted in good faith, relying on Greene's promise, while the latter offered no excuse for suddenly withdrawing his offer. Is it fair to permit Greene to escape all liability? This court, like most, simply will not award significant damages where there is no contract permitting a clear calculation of losses.

The judges, though, have not entirely closed the door on Toscano. What is the purpose of the remand? What might Toscano demonstrate on remand? What practical difficulties will he encounter?   ◆

Law and Equity

Expectation and reliance interests are generally considered **legal remedies.**[4] The other interests we will examine are equitable remedies. The difference is largely historical but still may affect a plaintiff's ability to obtain help from a court. As we saw in the textbook's introductory chapter, the common law developed in England, very gradually, over many centuries. English *law* courts gave money damages to the plaintiff, so money damages became known as "legal remedies."

---

[4]   As the *Toscano* case demonstrates, the terminology is flexible. In a promissory estoppel case, most courts would call reliance damages an equitable remedy.

In some cases, an English law court might refuse to hear a case, claiming that it lacked jurisdiction. Or the injured plaintiff might want more than mere money damages. For example, a plaintiff who had a contract to buy land might want the property itself, not money damages. When a law court would not or could not help, a plaintiff often took his case to the Chancellor in London. There was no jury in a Chancery case, but the Chancellor did have broader, more flexible powers than the law judges. The Chancellor's powers came to be known as **equitable remedies.** In the United States today, trial courts of general jurisdiction have the power to grant legal and equitable remedies. We now turn to an equitable remedy called restitution.

RESTITUTION INTEREST

Lillian and Harold Toews signed a contract to sell 1,500 acres of Idaho farmland to Elmer Funk. He was to take possession immediately, but would not receive the deed until he finished paying for the property, in 10 years. This arrangement enabled him to enroll in a government program that would pay him "set-asides" for *not* farming. Funk kept most aspects of his agreement. He did move onto the land and did receive $76,000 from the government for a year's worth of inactivity. (Nice work if you can get it.) The only part of the bargain Funk did not keep was his promise to pay. The Toewses sued. Funk had clearly breached the deal. But what remedy?

The Toewses still owned the land, so they did not need it reconveyed. Funk had no money to pay for the farm, so the Toewses would never get their expectation interest. And the Toewses had expended almost no money based on the deal, so they had no reliance interest. What they had done, though, was to *confer a benefit* on Funk. They had enabled him to obtain $76,000 in government money. The Toewses wanted a return of the benefit they had conferred on Funk, a remedy called restitution. **The restitution interest is designed to return to the injured party a benefit that he has conferred on the other party, which it would be unjust to leave with that person.** The Toewses argued that they had bestowed a $76,000 benefit on Funk and that it made absolutely no sense for him to keep it. The Idaho Court of Appeals agreed. It ruled that the Toewses had a restitutionary interest in the government set-aside money and ordered Funk to pay the money to the Toewses.[5]

What is the remedy when the buyer fails to pay?

© KEVIN R. MORRIS/CORBIS

Restitution is awarded in two types of cases. First, the law allows restitution when the parties have reached a contract and one of them breaches, as Funk did. In such cases, a court may choose restitution because no other remedy is available or because no other remedy would be as fair. Second, courts may award restitution in cases of

---

[5]   *Toews v. Funk*, 129 Idaho 316, 924 P.2d 217, 1994 Idaho App. LEXIS 75 (Idaho Ct. App. 1994).

quasi-contract, which we examined in earlier chapters. In quasi-contract cases, the parties never made a contract but one side did benefit the other. We consider each kind of restitution interest in turn.

Restitution in Cases of a Valid Contract

Restitution is a common remedy in contracts involving fraud, misrepresentation, mistake, and duress. In these cases, restitution often goes hand-in-hand with **rescission,** which means to "undo" a contract and put the parties where they were before they made the agreement. Courtney sells her favorite sculpture to Adam for $95,000, both parties believing the work to be a valuable original by Barbara Hepworth. Two months later, Adam learns that the sculpture is a mere copy, worth very little. A court will permit Adam to rescind the contract on the ground of mutual mistake. At the same time, Adam is entitled to restitution of the purchase price. Courtney gets the worthless carving and Adam receives his money back.

The following case involved fraud in the sale of a valuable property.

PUTNAM CONSTRUCTION & REALTY CO. V. BYRD

632 So. 2d 961, 1992 Ala. LEXIS 1289
Supreme Court of Alabama, 1992

Facts: Putnam Construction & Realty Co. owned the University Square Business Center (USBC), an office complex with several major tenants, including McDonnell-Douglas, TRW, and the Army Corps of Engineers. William Byrd and some partners (the "buyers") entered into a contract to buy USBC for slightly over $17 million. They financed the purchase with a $16.2 million loan from Northwestern Mutual Life. Northwestern's loan was secured with a mortgage on the USBC, meaning that if the borrowers failed to repay the loan, Northwestern would own the property. Shortly after the sale closed, Byrd learned that several of the major tenants were leaving. The buyers sued Putnam, seeking rescission of the contract and restitution of their money. The trial court found that Putnam (the "sellers") had committed fraud. It rescinded the sales contract, returning the property to the sellers. It ordered the sellers to assume full liability for the mortgage. The trial court did not, however, order restitution of the buyers' expenses, such as the closing costs. The sellers appealed—which proved to be a big mistake.

Issue: Were the buyers entitled to rescission and/or restitution?

Excerpts from Justice Steagall's Decision: As early as December 1988, the sellers were aware that the Corps of Engineers was planning to build its own facility and eventually move into it. In spite of this knowledge, the sellers repeatedly told the buyers that the Corps of Engineers had no intention of leaving USBC and that it would probably agree to lease even more space. In May or June 1989, the sellers learned that McDonnell-Douglas was definitely going to move some of its personnel to new facilities, but did not report this information to the buyers. [The court concluded that the sellers had committed fraud.]

With the departure of its major tenants, the USBC does not have the profit potential the buyers bargained for and is, in fact, a liability to them. While the buyers could receive money damages to approximate the value of the lost leases, such an award would be speculative at best and would not abrogate the fact that the buyers now have a property that operates at an increasing loss. The equitable remedy of rescission, while difficult to execute, would more completely provide the buyers with the compensation they seek. The jury was, therefore, correct in determining that rescission is the proper remedy to be applied in this case.

We agree with the trial court that a reconveyance of USBC to the sellers, subject to the mortgage, "constitutes the most equitable result which can be achieved." Accordingly, we affirm those por-

▼

tions of the court's order relating to the reconveyance of USBC subject to the mortgage. We must also recognize, however, that the buyers incurred other substantial out-of-pocket costs to finance a transaction that was born out of the sellers' fraud. After carefully considering the evidence in this case, we conclude that repayment of the following costs is necessary to more equitably restore the buyers to the position they occupied before the sale: $483,006.75 in closing costs on the purchase of USBC; $121,000 in interest payments they paid to the sellers on the $1.5 million note; and the $500,000 in nonrefundable fees the buyers paid to Northwestern to obtain the loan. We remand this case for the trial court to enter a judgment ordering repayment of these costs. ■

Ethics

Imagine that you are the officer from Putnam in charge of negotiating the sale of USBC to the buyers. You learn that several major tenants are soon to depart and realize that if the buyers learn this they will lower their offer or reject the deal altogether. Your boss insists you tell the buyers that all tenants will be staying. From the Chapter 2 ethics checklist: Who are the stakeholders? Is the conduct that he is urging legal? What are the consequences? What will you do? ◆

Restitution in Cases of a Quasi-Contract

George Anderson owned a valuable 1936 Plymouth. He took it to Ronald Schwegel's repair shop, and the two orally agreed that Schwegel would restore the car for $6,000. Unfortunately, they never agreed on the word "restore." Anderson thought the term meant complete restoration, including body work and engine repairs, whereas Schwegel intended body work but no engine repairs. After doing some of the work, Schwegel told Anderson that the car needed substantial engine work, and asked for Anderson's permission to allow an engine shop to do it. Anderson agreed, believing the cost was included in the original estimate. When the car was finished and running smoothly, Schwegel demanded $9,800. Anderson refused to pay more than the $6,000 agreed price, and Schwegel sued.

The court held that there was no valid contract between the parties. A contract requires a meeting of the minds. Here, said the court, there was no meeting of the minds on what "restore" included, and hence Schwegel could not recover either his expectation or his reliance interest, since both require an enforceable agreement. Schwegel therefore argued "quasi-contract." In other words, he claimed that even if there had been no valid agreement, he had performed a service for Anderson and that it would be unjust for Anderson to keep it without paying. **A court may award restitution, even in the absence of a contract, where one party has conferred a benefit on another and it would be unjust for the other party to retain the benefit.** The court ruled that Schwegel was entitled to the full $3,800 above and beyond the agreed price because that was the fair market value of the additional work. Anderson had asked for the repairs and now had an auto that was substantially improved. It would be unjust, ruled the court, to permit him to keep that benefit for free.[6]

at RISK

Of all the disputes in this unit, the one between Anderson and Schwegel was the easiest to prevent. The parties needed only a few lines on an estimate sheet, listing exactly which repairs would be included for $6,000 and which would not. Indeed, it is remarkable that the parties were able to discuss the matter on several occasions *without* specifying whether Schwegel would repair the engine. Which party is in the better position to ensure a clear agreement? If there was no meeting of the minds, whose fault was it? ◆

---

[6] *Anderson v. Schwegel*, 118 Idaho 362, 796 P.2d 1035, 1990 Idaho App. LEXIS 150 (Idaho Ct. App. 1990).

OTHER EQUITABLE INTERESTS

In addition to restitution, the other three equitable powers that concern us are specific performance, injunction, and reformation.

Specific Performance

Leona Claussen owned Iowa farmland. She sold some of it to her sister-in-law, Evelyn Claussen, and, along with the land, granted Evelyn an option to buy additional property at $800 per acre. Evelyn could exercise her option anytime during Leona's lifetime or within six months of Leona's death. When Leona died, Evelyn informed the estate's executor that she was exercising her option. But other relatives wanted the property and the executor refused to sell. Evelyn sued and asked for *specific performance*. She did not want an award of damages; she wanted the land itself. The remedy of specific performance forces the two parties to perform their contract.

A court will award specific performance, ordering the parties to perform the contract, only in cases involving the sale of land or some other asset that is unique. Courts use this equitable remedy when money damages would be inadequate to compensate the injured party. If the subject is unique and irreplaceable, money damages will not put the injured party in the same position she would have been in had the agreement been kept. So a court will order the seller to convey the rare object and the buyer to pay for it.

Historically, every parcel of land has been regarded as unique, and therefore specific performance is always available in real estate contracts. Evelyn Claussen won specific performance. The Iowa Supreme Court ordered Leona's estate to convey the land to Evelyn, for $800 per acre.[7] Generally speaking, either the seller or the buyer may be granted specific performance. One limitation in land sales is that a buyer may obtain specific performance only if she was ready, willing, and able to purchase the property on time. If Evelyn had lacked the money to buy Leona's property for $800 per acre within the six months' time limit, the court would have declined to order the sale. The following article illustrates a very human mistake that will invoke specific performance.

NEWSworthy

Dear Attorney:

We foolishly listed our home for sale last April. Our realty agent did a fine job and found a buyer by mid-May. The closing was supposed to be June 30. My husband and I bought a Florida condo in February and thought we wanted to move there to live year-round. But in May, after we agreed to sell our home, we went to visit our new condo for a week and encountered terrible heat and humidity. We instantly decided we only want to live in Florida in the winter.

The first week of June we notified our real-estate agent and the buyer that we changed our minds and wanted to cancel the sale. We immediately refunded the buyer's $5,000 deposit. But the buyers refused to take the money. A few weeks later we were served with legal papers for a lawsuit involving something called "specific performance." The buyers really want our house. What can we do to get out of this sale?

Answer: Unless there is a loophole in the sales contract, your home buyers will probably win their specific performance lawsuit to force you to honor the agreement and deliver the deed as you promised to do. Disliking the summer heat and humidity in Florida is not a legal reason for breaching your real estate sales contract.[8] ◆

---

[7] *In re Estate of Claussen*, 482 N.W.2d 381, 1992 Iowa Sup. LEXIS 52 (Iowa 1992).

[8] Robert Bruss, "Compound Mistakes," *Chicago Tribune*, Nov. 5, 1995, p. 7P. © Tribune Media Services, Inc. All Rights Reserved. Reprinted with permission.

Other unique items, for which a court will order specific performance, include such things as rare works of art, secret formulas, patents, and shares in a closely held corporation. Money damages would be inadequate for all these things since the injured party, even if she got the cash, could not go out and buy a substitute item. By contrast, a contract for a new Cadillac Escalade is not enforceable by specific performance. If the seller breaches, the buyer is entitled to the difference between the contract price and the market value of the car. The buyer can take his money elsewhere and purchase a virtually identical auto.

Injunction

You move into your new suburban house on two acres of land, and the fresh air is exhilarating. But the wind shifts to the west, and you find yourself thinking of farm animals, especially pigs. It turns out that your next-door neighbor just started an organic bacon ranch, and the first 15 porkers have checked in. You check out the town's zoning code, discover that it is illegal to raise livestock in the neighborhood, and sue. But money damages will not suffice, because you want the bouquet to disappear. You seek the equitable remedy of injunction. **An injunction is a court order that requires someone to do something or refrain from doing something.**

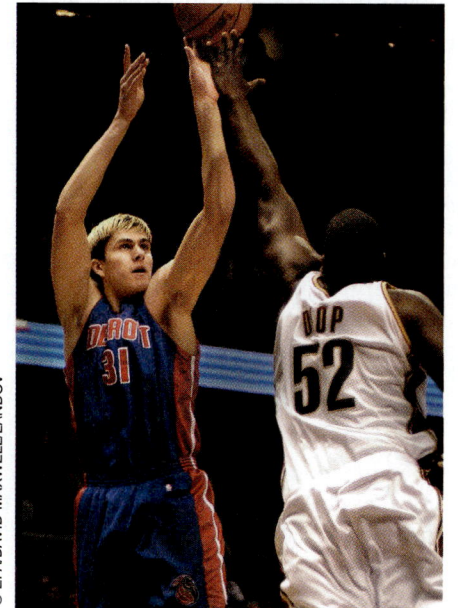

An injunction can halt play as quickly as a referee's whistle.

The court will order your neighbor immediately to cease and desist raising any pigs or other farm animals on his land. "Cease" means to stop, and "desist" means to refrain from doing it in the future. The injunction will not get you any money, but it will move the pigs out of town, and that was your goal.

Injunctions are usually stated in the negative. Look, for example, at noncompetition agreements, where the seller of a business might promise the buyer that he will not open a competing activity in a specified area. If the seller breaches the agreement by opening an identical enterprise across the street, the court will order him *not* to compete within the specified area.

In the increasingly litigious world of professional sports, injunctions are commonplace. In the following basketball case, the trial court issued a **preliminary injunction,** that is, an order issued early in a lawsuit prohibiting a party from doing something *during the course of the lawsuit.* The court attempts to protect the interests of the plaintiff immediately. If, after trial, it appears that the plaintiff has been injured and is entitled to an injunction, the trial court will make its order a **permanent injunction.** If it appears that the preliminary injunction should never have been issued, the court will terminate the order. The Web site **http://www. kinseylaw.com/attyserv/civil/complaints/ injunction.html** provides a sample complaint requesting an injunction.

MILICIC V. BASKETBALL MARKETING COMPANY, INC.

2004 Pa.A Super. 333, 857 A.2d 689
Superior Court of Pennsylvania, 2004

Facts: The Basketball Marketing Company (BMC) markets, distributes, and sells basketball apparel and related products. BMC signed a long-term endorsement contract with a 16-year-old Serbian player,

▼

Darko Milicic, who was virtually unknown in the United States. Two years later, Milicic became the second pick in the National Basketball Association's draft, making him an immensely marketable young man.

Four days after his 18th birthday, Milicic made a buy-out offer to BMC, seeking release from his contract so that he could arrange a more lucrative one elsewhere. BMC refused to release him. A week later, Milicic notified BMC in writing that he was disaffirming the contract, and returned all money and goods he had received from the company. BMC again refused to release Milicic.

Believing that Milicic was negotiating an endorsement deal with either Reebok or Adidas, BMC sent both companies letters informing them it had an enforceable endorsement deal with Milicic that was valid for several more years. Because of BMC's letter, Adidas ceased negotiating with Milicic just short of signing a contract. Milicic sued BMC, seeking a preliminary injunction that would prohibit BMC from sending such letters to competitors. The trial court granted the preliminary injunction and BMC appealed.

Issue: Was Milicic entitled to a preliminary injunction?

Excerpts from Judge McCaffery's Decision:[9]
BMC argues that the trial court erred by concluding that Milicic had proven the four essential prerequisites necessary for injunctive relief. However, Milicic did meet these four requirements.

1. Milicic had a strong likelihood of success on the merits.

Pennsylvania law recognizes, except as to necessities, the contract of a minor is voidable if the minor disaffirms it at any reasonable time after the minor attains majority. Just eleven days after his 18th birthday, Milicic sent BMC a letter withdrawing from the agreement. This letter was sent within a reasonable time after Milicic's reaching the age of majority and stated his unequivocal revocation and voidance of the agreement. There exists more than a reasonable probability that Milicic will succeed in [nullifying the contract with BMC].

2. Injunctive relief was necessary to prevent immediate and irreparable harm that could not be adequately compensated by the awarding of monetary damages.

Top N.B.A. draft picks generally solicit, negotiate, and secure endorsement contracts within a short time after the draft to take advantage of the publicity, excitement, and attendant marketability associated with the promotion. BMC blocked Milicic's efforts to enter into such an endorsement agreement. After being contacted by BMC, advanced negotiations between Milicic and Adidas were suspended. These business opportunity and market advantage losses may aptly be characterized as irreparable injury for purposes of equitable relief.

3. Greater injury would have occurred from denying the injunction than from granting the injunction.

BMC's refusal to acknowledge Milicic's ability to disaffirm the contract is at odds with public policy. Because infants are not competent to contract, the ability to disaffirm protects them from their own immaturity and lack of discretion. It is established practice in Pennsylvania to petition the court to appoint a guardian for the child, to protect the interests of both parties. It confounds the Court that BMC, a corporation of great magnitude, whose business may be said to be based in contract law, failed to have a guardian appointed for Milicic.

Harm to the public is an additional consideration. The public policy consideration underlying the rule which allows a child to disaffirm a contract within a reasonable time after reaching the age of majority is that minors should not be bound by mistakes resulting from their immaturity or the overbearance of unscrupulous adults.

4. The preliminary injunction restored the parties to the status quo that existed prior to the wrongful conduct:

Enjoining BMC from further interfering with Milicic's ability to contract will place the parties where they were prior to BMC's wrongful conduct. As all four of the essential prerequisites have been satisfied in this case, the Court properly granted injunctive relief.

Order affirmed. ∎

---

[9] Because we are unwilling to assume, as the court apparently does, that this decision will be read only by robots, the authors have substituted "BMC" for "appellant," and "Milicic" for "appellee."

Reformation

The final remedy, and perhaps the least common, is **reformation,** a process in which a court will partially "re-write" a contract. Courts seldom do this, because the whole point of a contract is to enable the parties to control their own futures. But a court may reform a contract if it believes a written agreement includes a simple mistake. Suppose that Roger orally agrees to sell 35 acres to Hannah for $600,000. The parties then draw up a written agreement, accidentally describing the land as including 50 additional acres that neither party considered part of the deal. Roger refuses to sell. Hannah sues for specific performance, but asks the court to *reform* the written contract to reflect the true agreement. Most but not all courts would reform the agreement and enforce it.

A court may also reform a contract to save it. If Natasha sells her advertising business to Joseph and agrees not to open a competing agency in the same city anytime in the next 10 years, a court may decide that it is unfair to force her to wait a decade. It could reform the agreement and permit Natasha to compete, say, three years after the sale. But some courts are reluctant to reform contracts and would throw out the entire noncompetition agreement rather than reform it. Parties should never settle for a contract that is sloppy or overbroad, assuming that a court will later reform errors. They may find themselves stuck with a bargain they dislike or with no contract at all.

SPECIAL ISSUES OF DAMAGES

Finally, we consider some special issues of damages, beginning with a party's obligation to minimize its losses.

Mitigation of Damages

A party injured by a breach of contract may not recover for damages that he could have avoided with reasonable efforts. In other words, when one party perceives that the other has breached or will breach the contract, the injured party must try to prevent unnecessary loss. A party is expected to **mitigate** his damages, that is, to keep damages as low as he reasonably can.

Malcolm agrees to rent space in his mall to Zena, for a major department store. As part of the lease, Malcolm agrees to redesign the interior to meet her specifications. After Malcolm has spent $20,000 in architect and design fees, Zena informs Malcolm that she is renting other space and will not occupy his mall. Malcolm nonetheless continues the renovation work, spending an additional $50,000 on materials and labor. Malcolm will recover the lost rental payments and the $20,000 expended in reliance on the deal. He will *not* recover the extra $50,000. He should have stopped work when he learned of Zena's breach.

Mitigation and the Sale of Goods

The UCC emphasizes the importance of mitigation. As mentioned earlier in the chapter, when a seller breaches, a buyer has the option of obtaining cover. If the buyer fails to cover, she will generally be *denied* consequential damages. Mary has a contract to buy 1,000 Christmas trees from Elmo for $25 each. The market value is $40 per tree, but Mary has arranged various contracts to resell the tress at $50 each. If Elmo breaches, Mary should try to cover. If she makes no effort to cover, the court will award her $15 per tree, representing the difference between the contract price and market value, but will not award her the consequential damages based on her own expectation of $50 per tree.

Nominal Damages

Nominal damages are a token sum, such as one dollar, given to a plaintiff who demonstrates that the defendant breached the contract but cannot prove damages. A school board unfairly fires Gemma, a teacher. If she obtains a teaching job at a better school for identical pay the very next day, she probably can show no damages at all. Nonetheless, the school wrongfully terminated her, and a court may award nominal damages.

Liquidated Damages

It can be difficult or even impossible to prove how much damage the injured party has suffered. So lawyers and executives negotiating a deal may include in the contract a **liquidated damages clause, a provision stating in advance how much a party must pay if it breaches.** Assume that Laurie has hired Bruce to build a five-unit apartment building for $800,000. Bruce promises to complete construction by May 15. Laurie insists on a liquidated damages clause providing that if Bruce finishes late, Laurie's final price is reduced by $3,000 for each week of delay. Bruce finishes the apartment building June 30, and Laurie reduces her payment by $18,000. Is that fair? The answer depends on two factors: **A court will generally enforce a liquidated damages clause if (1) at the time of creating the contract it was very difficult to estimate actual damages, and (2) the liquidated amount is reasonable.** In any other case, the liquidated damage will be considered a **penalty** and will prove unenforceable.

We will apply the two factors to Laurie's case. When the parties made their agreement, would it have been difficult to estimate actual damages caused by delay? Yes. Laurie could not prove that all five units would have been occupied or how much rent the tenants would have agreed to pay. Was the $3,000 per week reasonable? Probably. To finance an $800,000 building, Laurie will have to pay at least $6,000 interest per month. She must also pay taxes on the land and may have other expenses. Laurie does not have to prove that every penny of the liquidated damages clause is justified, but only that the figure is reasonable. A court will probably enforce her liquidated damages clause.

On the other hand, suppose Laurie's clause demanded $3,000 per day. There is no basis for such a figure, and a court will declare it a *penalty clause*, and refuse to enforce it. Laurie will be back to square one, forced to prove in court any damages she claims to have suffered from Bruce's delay.

In the chapter's opening scenario, the alarm company tries to invoke a liquidated damage clause that would leave Ben largely uncompensated. Depending on what the parties knew when they made the agreement, a court may well find the clause too harsh, and permit Ben to sue for his actual losses. Similar issues determined the outcome in the case that follows.

LAKE RIDGE ACADEMY V. CARNEY

66 Ohio St. 3d 376, 613 N.E.2d 183, 1993 Ohio LEXIS 1210
Supreme Court of Ohio, 1993

Facts: In March, Mr. Carney reserved a spot in the fourth grade class at Lake Ridge Academy for his son, Michael. He paid a $630 deposit and agreed in writing to pay the balance of the tuition, $5,610, later that year. The contract permitted Carney to cancel the agreement and withdraw his son with no further obligation provided he did so before August

1. If he failed to notify the school before that date, he became liable for the full tuition.

Carney wrote a letter notifying Lake Ridge that Michael would not attend. He dated the letter August 1, mailed it August 7, and the school received it August 14. Lake Ridge demanded its full tuition, Carney refused, and the school sued. One of the disputed issues was whether the liquidated damages clause was a penalty. The trial court found for Carney, but the court of appeals reversed, finding that the clause was valid. Carney appealed to the state's highest court.

Issue: Was the liquidated damages clause enforceable?

Excerpts from Justice Wright's Decision: Contracting parties may provide in advance for damages to be paid in the event of a breach as long as the provision does not disregard the principle of compensation. Determining whether stipulated damages are punitive or liquidated is not always easy. It is necessary to look to the whole instrument, its subject-matter, the ease or difficulty of measuring the breach in damages, and the amount of the stipulated sum, not only as compared with the value of the subject of the contract, but in proportion to the probable consequences of the breach.

We conclude that the damages in this case are liquidated damages [and thus enforceable].

When Carney and Lake Ridge entered into their contract the damages that Lake Ridge might suffer as a result of a breach by Carney were "uncertain as to amount and difficult of proof." Lake Ridge goes through a long budgeting process which begins each year in January and ends in the fall. The tuition money paid by students is pooled and goes towards staff salaries and benefits, department budgets, student materials, maintenance, improvements, and utilities. Trial testimony reveals that the school budget process is often an uncertain science; it is quite clear that Lake Ridge would be unable to calculate and prove the precise damages caused by the loss of one student's tuition.

Nor is the contract as a whole unreasonable. The headmaster testified that August 1 was chosen as the day before which notice of cancellation had to be given simply because the school had to know in order to meet its financial commitments. Carney had almost five months after he signed the contract to decide whether to cancel it. Because Lake Ridge's financial commitments became more firm as the school year approached, it is reasonable to assume that by August 1 the school was relying on Carney's full tuition payment. ■

ECONOMICS & *the* LAW

Some economists think that even *penalty clauses* should be enforced, suggesting that they can be a form of cheap insurance. Vivian has organized a reunion for 35 family members, all of whom will fly on a chartered aircraft from Chicago to San Diego, where they will stay at a luxurious resort. This is a once-in-a-lifetime event for the family, with huge costs and great emotional benefits for parents, grandparents, and others. Vivian wants to be sure the charter flight actually gets everyone to California on time, since she has committed to pay for all rooms, meals, and side trips. She insists on a contract that cancels her charter fee if the plane arrives in San Diego more than four hours late, and forces the company to pay a penalty of $5,000 for every day of delay until the entire family is assembled at the resort. The charter company agrees to the clause but demands a higher than usual fee from Vivian. The parties have agreed to a kind of "emotional insurance," based on the unique significance of the event. Vivian might have purchased such insurance from a third party, but the costs would have been higher because the insurer would have had less confidence in the charter company's ability to perform on time, and would also have insisted on making a profit for its risk.

Notice a second, related reason to enforce such contracts. When the charter company, during contract negotiation, agrees to the high liquidated damages clause, it is saying in the most effective way possible, "We are the best company for this job." By putting its money on the line, the company makes itself more attractive to Vivian, and probably forces its competitors to improve their own performance. The result could be better air service for everyone. ◆

Punitive Damages

We have seen that courts devote little time to morality when granting remedies for breach of contract. In most cases, a party that deliberately breaks its promise is treated the same as one that attempts but fails to honor its bargain. Occasionally, though, a court will take into account the question of what is morally right and order a breaching party to pay extra money damages because its conduct was socially intolerable.

Punitive damages are designed not to compensate the injured party but to punish the breaching party. The courts grant punitive damages in addition to the usual expectation, reliance, or restitution monies. The goal is to prevent the unethical party from repeating its offense and to deter others in society from similar behavior. Bear in mind that these are exceptional cases. In a contract case, courts will consider a punitive damages claim only when the breach of contract involves conduct such as fraud or bad faith.

Although a jury has wide discretion in awarding punitive damages, the Supreme Court has ruled that a verdict must be reasonable. In awarding punitive damages, a court must consider three "guideposts":

- The reprehensibility of the defendant's conduct.
- The ratio between the harm suffered and the award.
- The difference between the punitive award and any civil penalties used in similar cases.

The Court has refused to provide a definitive ratio between compensatory and punitive damages, but has given additional guidance to lower courts:

- A trial court generally should not permit a punitive award more than nine times higher than the compensatory damages.
- The trial court may not use the defendant's wealth as an excuse to award an unreasonably high award.

When an insurance company intentionally deceived a vulnerable married couple, a Utah jury was so outraged it awarded $1 million compensatory and $145 million punitive damages. The Supreme Court reversed, ruling that the pair had suffered only economic harm and that the 145:1 ratio was irrational and intolerable.[10]

A large punitive damages award generally indicates an angry jury, as defense counsel in the following case acknowledged in home-spun fashion.

ORKIN EXTERMINATING COMPANY, INC. V. JETER

2001 W.L. 1391443
832 So.2d 25
Alabama Supreme Court, 2001

Facts: In 1977 Artie Mae Jeter contracted with the Orkin Exterminating Company for a "subterranean-termite-treatment," which included immediate treatment for a minor infestation problem, annual inspections and reports, and a lifetime guarantee against any damage, backed up by a $100,000 bond for any necessary repairs. Beginning in 1984 Orkin inspectors found heavy termite damage to the house,

▼

---

[10] The three guideposts were issued in *BMW of North America, Inc. v. Gore,* 517 U.S. 559, 116 S. Ct. 1589 (1996). The 9:1 ratio comes from *State Farm Mutual Automobile Insurance Co. v. Campbell,* 538 U.S. 408, 123 S. Ct. 1513 (2003).

but continued to report to Jeter that her home was fine. When structural repairs were needed, Orkin told Jeter the damage was caused by water and charged her to install expensive floor supports.

In 1988 Jeter herself discovered swarming termites. Orkin acknowledged some termite damage, but rejected repair estimates because they were too expensive. For another 10 years the company resisted making necessary repairs. A company inspector wrote an internal memo, which included these revelations:

> I used a small hammer and could bury it in every sill plate in the home. . . . To my knowledge, no one has really told [her] the true extent to which her house is infested. . . . We took her money and never really told her the truth about the serious termite problem. . . . Ms. Jeter is 78 years old, black, in poor health, no money, we do not have a graph, her house was improperly treated, we sold her twice with no documentation of existing conditions, home is badly eaten up by termites to the point of breaking apart.

More years went by with no repairs. Finally, in 1999, Jeter sued. At trial, the company's lawyer said during closing arguments:

> I know my county. Y'all ain't going to return no defense verdict. This is going to be a plaintiff verdict. But, again, I speak of atonement versus crucifixion. Now ain't nobody all right; ain't nobody all wrong. Orkin has got some problems. Defense case has got some problems. . . .

He got that last part right. The jury returned a verdict of $800,000 in compensatory damages for Jeter's emotional suffering, and a punitive damages award of $80 million. The trial court remitted the award to $400,000 and $4 million, respectively. Both sides appealed.

Issue: Was a large punitive damages award appropriate?

Excerpts from Justice Lyon's Decision: Mrs. Jeter died before trial. The jury instead heard testimony from her son, Robert Jeter, and her granddaughter. Mrs. Jeter became very upset and angry that she had been betrayed by [the inspector] Orkin because they had not repaired her house as they were required to do under her termite bond. Before learning the truth about how Orkin had treated her, she was happy, but once she discovered the truth, Mrs. Jeter lost her "fighting spirit" and began to worry that she might not live long enough to see justice. Some-

times she would not eat, and she lost interest in people and in going places. Mrs. Jeter chose not to have her family come to her house for what turned out to be her last Thanksgiving because she was concerned that the floor might cave in if she had too many people in her home at one time. In addition, Mrs. Jeter lost sleep and lay awake nights worrying about her house and listening for strange noises.

This Court has recognized that mental anguish and emotional distress are not items for which a precise amount of damages can be assessed; thus, in considering whether a jury verdict awarding, or a trial court's judgment remitting, compensatory damages is excessive, we must view the evidence from the plaintiff's perspective and determine what the evidence supports in terms of the plaintiff's suffering. We conclude that a [high] ratio of punitive damages to compensatory damages is justified. However, in the face of the significant award of compensatory damages, the evidence in this case does not suggest that a ratio higher than 10:1 is warranted.

Orkin's reprehensible conduct in regard to Mrs. Jeter's claim spanned almost 10 years. The evidence is overwhelming that Orkin actively engaged in a plan to deceive Mrs. Jeter about the condition of her home. It is clear that the scheme to deceive Mrs. Jeter spanned from lower level termite inspectors to a branch manager, a district manager, and a regional manager. In addition, there is evidence that Orkin engaged in a pattern of misconduct by failing to inform homeowners of termite damage for which Orkin would be liable to repair.

We now return to a final consideration of the excessiveness of the remitted punitive-damages award in light of *BMW*. Based upon the reprehensibility of the Orkin defendants' conduct, countered by the potential for economic loss by the Orkin defendants for misconduct related to this single transaction, we conclude that a $2,000,000 punitive-damages award is sufficient to punish the Orkin defendants and to deter them from further conduct similar to that evidenced in this case, without compromising their due process rights. The judgment of the trial court is affirmed, on the condition that Mrs. Jeter's estate file with this Court, within 21 days a remittitur of the compensatory-damages award to $300,000 and of the punitive-damages award to $2,000,000; otherwise, the judgment will be reversed and the cause remanded for a new trial.

Affirmed conditionally. ■

Chapter Conclusion

The powers of a court are broad and flexible and may suffice to give an injured party what it deserves. But problems of proof and the uncertainty of remedies demonstrate that the best solution is a carefully drafted contract and socially responsible behavior.

Chapter Review

1. Someone breaches a contract when he fails to perform a duty, without a valid excuse.

2. A remedy is the method a court uses to compensate an injured party.

3. An interest is a legal right in something, such as a contract. The first step that a court takes in choosing a remedy is to decide what interest it is protecting.

4. The expectation interest puts the injured party in the position she would have been in had both sides fully performed. It has three components:

   a. Compensatory damages, which flow directly from the contract.

   b. Consequential damages, which result from the unique circumstances of the particular injured party. The injured party may recover consequential damages only if the breaching party should have foreseen them.

   c. Incidental damages, which are the minor costs an injured party incurs responding to a breach.

5. The reliance interest puts the injured party in the position he would have been in had the parties never entered into a contract. It focuses on the time and money that the injured party spent performing his part of the agreement. If there was no valid contract, a court might still award reliance damages under a theory of promissory estoppel.

6. The restitution interest returns to the injured party a benefit that she has conferred on the other party, which it would be unjust to leave with that person. Restitution can be awarded in the case of a contract created, for example, by fraud, or in a case of quasi-contract, where the parties never created a binding agreement.

7. Specific performance, ordered only in cases of land or a unique asset, requires both parties to perform the contract.

8. An injunction is a court order that requires someone to do something or refrain from doing something.

9. Reformation is the process by which a court will—occasionally—rewrite a contract to ensure that it accurately reflects the parties' agreement and/or to maintain the contract's viability.

10. The duty to mitigate means that a party injured by a breach of contract may not recover for damages that he could have avoided with reasonable efforts.

11. Nominal damages are a token sum, such as one dollar, given to an injured plaintiff who cannot prove damages.

12. A liquidated damages clause will be enforced if and only if, at the time of creating the contract, it was very difficult to estimate actual damages and the liquidated amount is reasonable.

13. Punitive damages are designed not to compensate the injured party but to punish the breaching party.

Practice Test

1. Mr. and Ms. Beard contracted for S/E Joint Venture to build a house on property it owned, and then sell the completed house to the Beards for $785,000. S/E was late with construction and

ultimately never finished the house or conveyed anything to the Beards, who sued. Evidence at trial demonstrated that S/E had clearly breached the contract and that the Beards had spent about $32,000 in rent because of the delay. There was testimony that the market value of the house as promised would have been about $100,000 more than the contract price, but this point was not clearly established because the trial judge considered it irrelevant. The judge awarded only the rental payments. Both sides appealed. Is the market value of the house, as it should have been built, relevant? How much money are the Beards entitled to?

2. Lewis signed a contract for the rights to all timber located on Nine Mile Mine. He agreed to pay $70 per thousand board feet ($70/mbf). As he began work, Nine Mile became convinced that Lewis lacked sufficient equipment to do the job well and forbade him to enter the land. Lewis sued. Nine Mile moved for summary judgment. The mine offered proof that the market value of the timber was exactly $70/mbf, and Lewis had no evidence to contradict Nine Mile. The evidence about market value proved decisive. Why? Please rule on the summary judgment motion.

3. Twin Creeks Entertainment signed a deal with U.S. JVC Corp. in which JVC would buy 60,000 feature film videocassettes from Twin Creeks over a three-year period. JVC intended to distribute the cassettes nationwide. Relying on its deal with JVC, Twin Creeks signed an agreement with Paramount Pictures, agreeing to purchase a minimum of $600,000 worth of Paramount cassettes over a two-year period. JVC breached its deal with Twin Creeks and refused to accept the cassettes it had agreed upon. Twin Creeks sued and claimed, among other damages, the money it owed to Paramount. JVC moved to dismiss the claim based on the Paramount contract, on the ground that Twin Creeks, the seller of goods, was not entitled to such damages. What kind of damages is Twin Creeks seeking? Please rule on the motion to dismiss.

4. Bingo is emerging as a rock star. His last five concerts have all sold out. Lucia signs a deal with Bingo to perform two concerts in one evening in Big City, for a fee of $50,000 for both shows. Lucia then rents the Auditorium for that evening, guaranteeing to pay $50,000. Bingo promptly breaks the deal before any tickets are sold. Lucia sues, pointing out that the Auditorium seats 3,000 and she anticipated selling all tickets for an average of $40 each, for a total gross of $120,000. How much will Lucia recover, if anything?

5. Racicky was in the process of buying 320 acres of ranch land. While that sale was being negotiated, Racicky signed a contract to sell the land to Simon. Simon paid $144,000, the full price of the land. But Racicky then went bankrupt, before he could complete the *purchase* of the land, let alone its sale. Which of these remedies should Simon seek: expectation, restitution, specific performance, or reformation?

6. Ambrose hires Bierce for $25,000 to supervise the production of Ambrose's crop, but then breaks the contract by firing Bierce at the beginning of the season. A nearby grower offers Bierce $23,000 for the same growing season, but Bierce refuses to take such a pay cut. He stays home and sues Ambrose. How much money, if any, will Bierce recover from Ambrose, and why?

7. Parkinson was injured in an auto accident by a driver who had no insurance. Parkinson filed a claim with her insurer, Liberty Mutual, for $2,000 under her "uninsured motorist" coverage. Liberty Mutual told her that if she sought that money, her premiums would go "sky high," so Parkinson dropped the claim. Later, after she had spoken with an attorney, Parkinson sued. What additional claim was her attorney likely to make?

8. **CPA QUESTION** Master Mfg., Inc. contracted with Accur Computer Repair Corp. to maintain Master's computer system. Master's manufacturing process depends on its computer system operating properly at all times. A liquidated damages clause in the contract provided that Accur would pay $1,000 to Master for each day that Accur was late responding to a service request. On January 12, Accur was notified that Master's computer system had failed. Accur did not respond to Master's service request until January 15. If Master sues Accur under the liquidated damage provision of the contract, Master will:

a. Win, unless the liquidated damages provision is determined to be a penalty

b. Win, because under all circumstances liquidated damage provisions are enforceable

c. Lose, because Accur's breach was not material

d. Lose, because liquidated damage provisions violate public policy

9. **CPA QUESTION** Kaye contracted to sell Hodges a building for $310,000. The contract required Hodges to pay the entire amount at closing. Kaye refused to close the sale of the building. Hodges sued Kaye. To what relief is Hodges entitled?

   a. Punitive damages and compensatory damages

   b. Specific performance and compensatory damages

   c. Consequential damages or punitive damages

   d. Compensatory damages or specific performance

10. **YOU BE THE JUDGE** WRITING PROBLEM John and Susan Verba sold a Vermont lakeshore lot to Shane and Deborah Rancourt for $115,000. The Rancourts intended to build a house on the property, but after preparing the land for construction, they learned that a wetland protection law prevented building near the lake. They sued, seeking rescission of the contract. The trial court concluded that the parties had reached their agreement under a "mutual, but innocent, misunderstanding." The trial judge gave the Verbas a choice: they could rescind the contract and refund the purchase price, or they could give the Rancourts $55,000, the difference between the sales price and the actual market value of the land. The Rancourts appealed. Were the Rancourts entitled to rescission of the contract? **Argument for the Rancourts:** When the parties have made a mutual mistake about an important factual issue, either party is entitled to rescind the contract. The land is of no use to us and we want our money back. **Argument for the Verbas:** Both sides were acting in good faith and both sides made an honest mistake. We are willing to acknowledge that the land is worth somewhat less than we all thought, and we are willing to refund $55,000. The buyers shouldn't complain—they are getting the property at about half the original price, and the error was as much their fault as ours.

11. **ETHICS** The National Football League owns the copyright to the broadcasts of its games. It licenses local television stations to telecast certain games and maintains a "blackout rule," which prohibits stations from broadcasting home games that are not sold out 72 hours before the game starts. Certain home games of the Cleveland Browns team were not sold out, and the NFL blocked local broadcast. But several bars in the Cleveland area were able to pick up the game's signal by using special antennas. The NFL wanted the bars to stop showing the games. What did it do? Was it unethical of the bars to broadcast the games that they were able to pick up? Apart from the NFL's legal rights, do you think it had the moral right to stop the bars from broadcasting the games?

12. **ROLE REVERSAL** Write a multiple-choice question involving a contract for the sale of goods. The seller breaches and the buyer definitely has compensatory damages. The test-taker must decide whether there are also consequential damages, and the total amount of damages to which the buyer is entitled.

Internet Research Problem

You represent a group of neighborhood residents in a large city who are protesting construction of a skyscraper that will violate building height limitations. Draft a complaint, requesting an appropriate injunction. You may use the sample injunction complaint found at **http://beatty.westbuslaw.com**.

> **You can find further practice problems at http://beatty.westbuslaw.com or in the Study Guide that accompanies this text.**

Commercial Transactions

Introduction to Sales

HE SUED, SHE SUED. Harold and Maude made a great couple because both were compulsive entrepreneurs. One evening they sat on their penthouse roofdeck, overlooking the twinkling Chicago skyline. Harold sipped a decaf coffee while negotiating, over the phone, with a real estate developer in San Antonio. Maude puffed a cigar as she bargained on a different line with a toy manufacturer in Cleveland. They hung up at the same time. "I did it!" shrieked Maude, "I made an incredible deal for the robots—five bucks each!" "No, I did it!" triumphed Harold, "I sold the 50 acres in Texas for $300,000 more than it's worth." They dashed indoors.

Maude quickly scrawled a handwritten memo, which said, "Confirming our deal—100,000 Psychopath Robots—you deliver Chicago—end of summer." She didn't mention a price, or an exact delivery date, or when payment would be made. She signed her memo and faxed it to the toy manufacturer. Harold took more time. He typed a thorough contract, describing precisely the land he was selling, the $2.3 million price, how and when each payment would be made and the deed conveyed. He signed the contract and faxed it, along with a plot plan showing the surveyed land. Then the happy couple grabbed a bottle of champagne, returned to the deck—and placed a side bet on whose contract would prove more profitable. The loser would have to cook and serve dinner for six months.

Neither Harold nor Maude ever heard again from the other parties. The toy manufacturer sold the Psychopath Robots to another retailer at a higher price. Maude was forced to buy comparable toys elsewhere for $9 each. She sued. And the Texas property buyer changed his mind, deciding to develop a Club Med in Greenland and refusing to pay Harold for his land. He sued. Only one of the two plaintiffs succeeded. Which one? ■

The adventures of Harold and Maude illustrate the Uniform Commercial Code (UCC) in action. The Code is the single most important source of law for people engaged in commerce and controls the vast majority of contracts made every day in every state. The Code is ancient in origin, contemporary in usage, admirable in purpose, and flawed in application. "Yeah, yeah, that's fascinating," snaps Harold, "but who wins the bet?" Relax, Harold, we'll tell you in a minute.

DEVELOPMENT OF COMMERCIAL LAW

During the fifteenth and sixteenth centuries, merchants in England and throughout Europe found the law of their respective nations cumbersome and inadequate for the settlement of commercial disputes. For example, in England, property had historically been the most important asset, and civil law revolved around the rights to land. Decisions in property disputes came slowly, and courts seldom thought in terms of a "contract." Even by the seventeenth century, English judges were only beginning to acknowledge that an exchange of mere promises, with no money or property changing hands, might lead to an enforceable agreement. But merchants dealt in the sale of goods, not real estate. Their livelihood depended upon promises, on the rapid movement of their wares, and on their ability to enforce bargains. Dissatisfied with the few remedies that courts offered, businessmen throughout England and the Continent began to treat their own customs as law and to settle disputes in trade organizations rather than civil courts. The body of rules they relied on became known as the *lex mercatoria*, or **law merchant.** The law merchant was thus a "custom made" law, created by the merchants who used it. The new doctrine focused on promises, the sale and exchange of goods, and payment.

Lord Mansfield (1705–1793), a justly famous English judge, began to use some of these commercial rules in his influential decisions, beginning the slow process of incorporating them into the common law of contract. Over the next two centuries, common law judges employed more and more of the law merchant and at the same time began to develop specialized areas within commercial law. Courts began to distinguish the law for the sale of goods from the law governing, for example, payments by check or other negotiable instruments. Similar changes took place in the United States.

Throughout the first half of the twentieth century, commercial transactions changed dramatically in this country, as advances in transportation and communication revolutionized negotiation and trade. But the law lagged behind, evolving more slowly than commercial practices, hampered by common law differences between the states. The nation needed a modernized business law to give nationwide uniformity and predictability in a new and faster world. In 1942, two groups of scholars, the American Law Institute (ALI) and the National Conference of Commissioners on Uniform State Laws (NCCUSL), began the effort to draft a modern, national law of commerce. Led by Professor Karl N. Llewellyn, the scholars debated and formulated for nearly a decade. Finally, in 1952, Llewellyn and colleagues published their work—the Uniform Commercial Code. The entire Code is available online at http://www.law.cornell.edu/ucc/ucc.table.html.

Article 1: *General Provisions*	The purpose of the code, general guidance in applying it, and definitions.
Article 2: *Sale of Goods*	The sale of *goods*, such as a new car, 20,000 pairs of gloves, or 101 Dalmatians. This is one of the two most important articles in the UCC.
Article 2A: *Leases*	A temporary exchange of goods for money, such as renting a car.
Article 3: *Negotiable Instruments*	The use of checks, promissory notes, and other negotiable instruments.
Article 4: *Bank Deposits and Collections*	The rights and obligations of banks and their customers.
Article 4A: *Funds Transfers*	An instruction, given by a bank customer, to credit a sum of money to another's account.
Article 5: *Letters of Credit*	The use of credit, extended by two or more banks, to facilitate a contract between two parties who do not know each other and require guarantees by banks they trust.
Article 6: *Bulk Transfers*	The sale of a major part of a company's inventory or equipment. This article has been repealed in all but a few states.
Article 7: *Warehouse Receipts, Bills of Lading, and Other Documents of Title*	Documents proving ownership of goods that are being transported or stored. This article is being revised as we go to press.
Article 8: *Investment Securities*	Rights and liabilities concerning shares of stock or other ownership of an enterprise.
Article 9: *Secured Transactions*	A sale of goods in which the seller keeps a financial stake in the goods he has sold, such as a car dealer who may repossess the car if the buyer fails to make payments. This is one of the two most important articles in the Code.

The Code Today

The ALI and the NCCUSL revised the Code in 1957 and once again during the 1970s. Then, beginning in the mid-1980s, the two groups began their most ambitious overhaul, seeking to make substantial changes to almost all of the articles and to add new ones as well. The goals were to acknowledge lessons learned from the Code's first half-century; to accommodate new technology, such as sales made over the Internet; and to serve a business world that had shifted much of its focus from traditional manufacturing to services and information.

The ALI and the NCCUSL have revised the Code several times since then, with important changes coming as recently as 2003. Remember, though, that the UCC is the creation of scholars. No section of the Code has any legal effect until a state legislature adopts it. In fact, all 50 states and the District of Columbia have adopted the UCC, but not all have used identical versions.

This book discusses and applies provisions of the Code that have been widely adopted. Article 9, on secured transactions, is one of the two most important in the Code. The commissioners completely rewrote Article 9 at the turn of the millennium, and this text reflects those changes because every state has adopted them. The commissioners have also revised Article 1, which provides definitions and general guidance, and Article 2, on sales. However, as this book goes to press, very few states have adopted revised Article 1, and none have adopted revised Article 2. We focus on existing law, not the proposed changes to Articles 1 and 2. Finally, Article 6, on bulk transfers, has been repealed in most states, and we will only discuss it briefly, in Chapter 20.

The next four chapters highlight elements of the Code *that have changed the common law rules of contract.*

Harold and Maude, Revisited

Harold and Maude each negotiated what they believed was an enforceable agreement, and both filed suit: Harold for the sale of his land, Maude for the purchase of toy robots. Only one prevailed. The difference in outcome demonstrates one of the changes that the UCC has wrought in the law of commercial contracts and illustrates why everyone in business needs a working knowledge of the Code. As we revisit the happy couple, Harold is clearing the dinner dishes. Maude sits back in her chair, lights a cigar, and compliments her husband on the apple tart. Harold, scowling and spilling coffee, wonders what went wrong.

Harold's contract was for the sale of land and governed by the common law of contracts. The common law statute of frauds requires any agreement for the sale of land to be in writing and *signed by the defendant*, in this case the buyer in Texas. Harold signed it, but the buyer never did, so Harold's meticulously detailed document was worth less than a five-cent cigar.

Maude's quickly scribbled memorandum, concerning psychotic robot toys, was for the sale of goods and was governed by Article 2 of the UCC. The Code requires less detail and formality in a writing. Because Maude and the seller were both merchants, the document she scribbled could be enforced *even against the defendant*, who had never signed anything. The fact that Maude left out the price and other significant terms was not fatal to a contract under the UCC, though under the common law such omissions would have made the bargain unenforceable. We will look in greater detail at these UCC changes. For now it is enough to see that the Code has carved major changes into the common law of contracts, alterations that Harold is beginning to appreciate.

This Unit of the Text

This unit covers three principal subjects, all relating to commercial transactions that the Code governs. The first chapters concern the sale of goods and focus primarily on Article 2. In the present chapter we emphasize how Code provisions work together to change the common law. In the following chapters we examine title to goods (Chapter 20), then warranties and product liability (Chapter 21), and, finally, performance and remedies (Chapter 22).

The next group of three chapters (Chapters 23–25) surveys the law of negotiable instruments. Checks are the most common kind of negotiable instrument, but we will see that there are many other varieties and that each creates different rights and obligations. We conclude the unit with a chapter devoted to secured transactions (Chapter 26), that is, a sale of goods in which the seller keeps a financial stake in the goods he has sold, and a chapter that analyzes bankruptcy law (Chapter 27).

UCC BASICS

Code's Purpose

The Uniform Commercial Code proclaims its purposes clearly:

UCC §1-102(2): Underlying purposes and policies of this Act are
(a) to simplify, clarify and modernize the law governing commercial transactions;
(b) to permit the continued expansion of commercial practices through custom, usage and agreement of the parties;
(c) to make uniform the law among the various jurisdictions.

This is not mere boilerplate. To "modernize," in (a), requires a focus on the needs of contemporary businesspeople, not on rules developed when judges rode horseback. Suppose a court must decide whether a writing is detailed enough to satisfy the Code's statute of frauds. The judge may rely on §1-102 to decide that because modern commerce is so fast, even the skimpiest of writings is good enough to demonstrate that the parties had reached a bargain. In doing so, the judge would deliberately be turning away from legal history to accommodate business practices in an electronic age.

Look at (c), which urges uniformity. Assume that a state supreme court must decide whether a merchant acted in good faith when trying to modify an unprofitable contract. The court may look to the high courts of other states for guidance, not because they are binding (which they are not) or even persuasive (which they may not be) but because uniformity is a valuable goal in itself.

Section 1-102 also states that "[t]his Act shall be liberally construed and applied to promote its underlying purposes," meaning that when in doubt, courts should focus on the goals described. The Code emphasizes *getting the right results*, rather than following rigid rules of contract law.

Scope of Article 2

Because the UCC changes the common law, it is essential to know whether the Code applies in a given case. Negotiations may lead to an enforceable agreement when the UCC applies, even though the same bargaining would create no contract under the common law.

UCC §2-102: Article 2 applies to the sale of goods.[1] **Goods are things that are movable, other than money and investment securities.** Hats are goods, and so are railroad cars, lumber, books, and bottles of wine. Land is not a good, nor is a house. So an agreement for the delivery of 10,000 board feet of white pine is a contract for the sale of goods, and Article 2 governs it. But the article does not apply to a contract for the sale of an office building. A skyscraper is not movable (although an entire city *may* be[2]).

Article 2 regulates **sales,** which means that one party transfers title to the other in exchange for money. If you sell your motorcycle to a friend, that is a sale of goods. If you lend the bike to your friend for the weekend, that is not a sale and Article 2 does not apply. Article 2 also does not apply to the leasing of goods, for example, when you rent a car. A sale involves a permanent change in ownership whereas a lease concerns a temporary change in possession.

Leasing goods is an enormous part of business these days. Virtually every kind of commercial and industrial equipment, from computers to tractors to coffee pots, is leased every day around the country. For example, when you fly home, the aircraft you sit in is quite likely leased to the airline from which you bought your ticket. Over 20 percent of all capital investment in the United States is directly related to equipment leasing. Because leasing is so important, the drafters of the Code added an article to cover the subject.

Article 2A governs the leasing of goods. Most of the states have adopted Article 2A, though unfortunately not all have adopted the same version. The law of leasing is therefore less uniform than that of sales. How does Article 2A compare to Article 2? Overall, it is similar, and many sections are almost identical. But there are some important differences, and anyone engaging in a significant amount of commercial leasing must become familiar with Article 2A. For our purposes, leasing law is a variation on the theme of Article 2, and we will concentrate on the principal melody of sales.

Mixed Contracts

Sophocles University hires ClickOn Computer to design software for the university's computerized grading system, which must be capable of recording and storing all grades, making the grades available to the students by telephone, computing averages, and printing transcripts. ClickOn agrees to design the software, install it, and train the staff in its use. But things go badly from day one. Sophocles gives ClickOn an "F" for effort and refuses to pay a nickel. Did the parties have an enforceable contract? Most of the bargaining was oral, and the only writings were a few short letters. If the common law governs the deal, it will be difficult or impossible to show an offer and acceptance with definite terms. But if the UCC controls, the writings may suffice to show a binding agreement.

To determine whether the UCC governs, we need to know what kind of an agreement the parties made. Was it one for the sale of goods (UCC) or one for services (common law)? In fact the agreement combined both goods and services and was therefore a *mixed contract*. **In a mixed contract involving sales and services, the UCC will govern if the *predominant purpose* is the sale of goods, but the common law will control if the predominant purpose is services.**

---

[1] Officially, Article 2 tells us that it applies to *transactions* in goods, which is a slightly broader category than sale of goods. But most sections of Article 2, and most court decisions, focus exclusively on sales, and so shall we.

[2] "If you are lucky enough to have lived in Paris as a young man, then wherever you go for the rest of your life, it stays with you, for Paris is a moveable feast." Ernest Hemingway, 1950.

If ClickOn sues, the court must determine whether the predominant purpose was the design of the software and the training of staff, which are service work, or the sale of the software, which is a transaction in goods. In this case, the sale of the software predominated. ClickOn did its design work in order to sell an expensive software package to a customer. It was the software that generated the contract, not ClickOn's work in preparing it. So the UCC does govern, and ClickOn may have a valid contract. We return to this issue of mixed contracts later in the chapter, as we see how §2-102 interacts with other Code provisions.

The UCC gives merchants greater freedom to contract—and greater responsibility.

Merchants

The UCC, we know, evolved indirectly from the law merchant, the commercial law developed by business people themselves. And the Code still attempts to meet the unique needs of the business world. But while the UCC offers a contract law that is more flexible than the common law, it also requires a higher level of responsibility from the merchants it serves. Those who make a living by crafting agreements are expected to understand the legal consequences of their words and deeds. Thus many sections of the Code offer two rules: one for "merchants" and one for everybody else.

UCC §2-104: A merchant is someone who routinely deals in the particular goods involved, *or* who appears to have special knowledge or skill in those goods, *or* who uses agents with special knowledge or skill in those goods. A used car dealer is a "merchant" when it comes to selling autos, because he routinely deals in them. He is not a merchant when he goes to a furniture store and purchases a new sofa. The salesman who sells new sofas is a merchant for that purpose.

The UCC frequently holds a merchant to a higher standard of conduct than a non-merchant. For example, a merchant may be held to an oral contract if she received written confirmation of it, even though the merchant herself never signed the confirmation. That same confirmation memo, arriving at the house of a non-merchant, would *not* create a binding deal. We will see many instances of this dual level of responsibility, one for a merchant and the other for a non-merchant. More often than not, it is apparent whether the parties are merchants. If a manufacturer of toy balloons agrees to sell 10,000 boxes of balloons to a toy retailer, both parties obviously are merchants. Other cases are less clear. Is a farmer a merchant? Farmers work long, hard hours in the field, yet today they may also be sophisticated commodities traders. Some courts have concluded they are merchants, but almost as many have decided they are not.

Good Faith and Unconscionability

Good Faith

The UCC imposes a duty of good faith in the performance of all contracts. Here is a $900,000 example.

The Kansas Municipal Gas Agency (KMGA) purchased natural gas for cities and towns in Kansas. KMGA requested proposals for a long-term gas contract from suppliers, stressing its need for a guaranteed supply. Vesta Energy Co. responded, and the two sides agreed on essential terms, including price. Vesta began supplying natural gas while they worked out the last details of a long-term contract.

Suddenly, Vesta asked for a *force majeure* clause, which permits either party to cancel a contract in the event of specified disasters, such as tornadoes or other acts of God. Such clauses are common in the gas industry. But Vesta asked that the clause also permit it to end the arrangement in case of "failure of supply," meaning that Vesta could cancel the deal if it was unable to find affordable supplies. KMGA rejected the proposal, and Vesta stopped supplying gas. KMGA sued, claiming that Vesta had made its *force majeure* proposal in bad faith.

For *non-merchants*, good faith means honesty in fact. For a *merchant*, good faith means honesty in fact *plus* the exercise of reasonable commercial standards of fair dealing.[3] Thus, when parties perform a contract, or in certain cases when they negotiate, neither side may lie or mislead. Further, a party who is a merchant must act as fairly as the business community routinely expects.

The court found that Vesta had acted in bad faith. The parties already had a working agreement, and Vesta had sabotaged it because the price of natural gas had unexpectedly shot up 75 percent. To escape the unprofitable deal, Vesta proposed an outrageous *force majeure* clause, knowing that KMGA would reject it. Based on Vesta's bad faith negotiating, the court awarded KMGA $904,000, the amount the company lost by purchasing gas elsewhere.[4]

Unconscionability

The UCC employs a second principle to encourage fair play and just results: the doctrine of unconscionability. **UCC §2-302: A contract may be unconscionable if it is shockingly one-sided and fundamentally unfair.** If a court concludes that some part of a contract is unconscionable, it will refuse to enforce that provision. Courts seldom find a contract unconscionable if the two parties are businesses, but they are quicker to apply the doctrine when one party is a consumer.

Suppose Bill's Builderia sells building equipment. For every sales contract Bill uses a pre-printed form that says, among other things, that the buyer takes the item "as is" and that Bill is not liable for repairs or for compensatory or consequential damages. If Bill sells a $3,000 power mower to a landscape contractor and the machine falls to pieces, a court will probably enforce the limitation on liability. The law assumes that a professional contractor will have the sophistication to read and understand the contract and can bargain for different terms if he is unhappy. But if the buyer is a consumer, such as a homeowner intent on mowing his own lawn, a court will probably declare the clause *unconscionable*. Bill is in the business of selling the equipment and knows the risks. He has drafted the pre-printed contract. The homeowner is unlikely even to read the entire agreement, let alone understand phrases like "consequential damages." It would be unfair to enforce the clause against the consumer. We will look at this issue in more detail in Chapter 21, on warranties and products liability.

Good Faith and Unconscionability Distinguished. The doctrine of good faith focuses on a party's behavior as it performs an agreement: Was it attempting to carry out its obligations in a reasonable manner and do what both sides expected when they made the deal? Unconscionability looks primarily at the contract itself. Are any terms so grossly unfair that a court should reform or ignore them?

Next we examine how the basic ideas of scope, merchant status, and good faith interact with other UCC provisions in the creation of a contract.

---

[3]   UCC §§1-201(19), 1-203, and 2-103.

[4]   *Kansas Municipal Gas Agency v. Vesta Energy Co.*, 843 F. Supp. 1401, 1994 U.S. Dist. LEXIS 2240 (D. Kan. 1994).

CONTRACT FORMATION

The common law expected the parties to form a contract in a fairly predictable and traditional way: the offeror made a clear offer that included all important terms, and the offeree agreed to all terms. Nothing was left open. The drafters of the UCC recognized that business people frequently do not think or work that way and that the law should reflect business reality.

Formation Basics: Section 2-204

UCC §2-204 provides three important rules that enable parties to make a contract quickly and informally:

1. *Any Manner That Shows Agreement.* The parties may make a contract in any manner sufficient to show that they reached an agreement. They may show the agreement with words, writings, or even their conduct. Lisa negotiates with Ed to buy 300 barbecue grills. The parties agree on a price, but other business prevents them from finishing the deal. Then six months later Lisa writes, "Remember our deal for 300 grills? I still want to do it if you do." Ed doesn't respond, but a week later a truck shows up at Lisa's store with the 300 grills, and Lisa accepts them. The combination of their original discussion, Lisa's subsequent letter, Ed's delivery, and her acceptance all adds up to show that they reached an agreement. The court will enforce their deal, and Lisa must pay the agreed-upon price.

2. *Moment of Making Is Not Critical.* The UCC will enforce a deal even though it is difficult, in common law terms, to say exactly when it was formed. Was Lisa's deal formed when they orally agreed? When he delivered? She accepted? The Code's answer: It does not matter. The contract is enforceable.

3. *One or More Terms May Be Left Open.* The common law insisted that the parties clearly agree on all important terms. If they did not, there was no meeting of minds and no enforceable deal. The Code changes that. **Under the UCC, a court may enforce a bargain even though one or more terms were left open.** Lisa's letter never said when she required delivery of the barbecues or when she would pay. Under the UCC, the omission is not fatal. As long as there is some certain basis for giving damages to the injured party, the court will do just that. Suppose Lisa refused to pay, claiming that the agreement included no date for her payment. A court would rule that the parties assumed she would pay within a commercially reasonable time, such as 30 days.

In the following case, the trial court based its ruling on the common law of contracts. The Georgia Appeals Court used two sections of the Code to reverse the outcome. Since the cases in this chapter all involve more than one Code section, we will outline the relevant provisions at the outset.

Code Provisions Discussed in This Case	
Issue	**Relevant Code Section**
1. What law governs?	UCC §2-102: Article 2 applies to the sale of goods.
2. Did the parties form a contract?	UCC §2-204: The parties may make a contract in any manner sufficient to show agreement.

J. LEE GREGORY, INC. V. SCANDINAVIAN HOUSE, L.P.

209 Ga. App. 285, 433 S.E.2d 687, 1993 Ga. App. LEXIS 857
Georgia Court of Appeals, 1993

Facts: Scandinavian House owned an apartment building that needed new windows. J. Lee Gregory, doing business as Perma Sash, sent a proposal to Scandinavian offering to remove all old windows and install new ones for $453,000. About two-thirds of the price reflected material costs, and one-third labor.

Scandinavian sent back a letter stating: "Please consider this letter an indication of our intent to purchase the windows contained in your proposal. This is your authorization to begin the measuring and the preparation of shop and installation drawings. We reserve the option to negotiate terms and conditions of the proposal which may impact or affect the operation of the building and the installation of the windows."

Perma Sash then spent three weeks measuring windows and preparing shop drawings, which it sent to Scandinavian House. The drawings were fine, but the parties, which had agreed on the price, could not agree on the method of payment. Perma Sash wanted certain guarantees of payment that Scandinavian House refused to make. Scandinavian notified Perma Sash that the deal was off and bought its windows elsewhere.

Perma Sash sued. The trial court gave summary judgment for Scandinavian, finding that the UCC did not govern and that the parties had never finalized an enforceable contract. Perma Sash appealed.

Issues: What law governs the case? Did the parties form a contract?

Excerpts from Judge Murray's Decision: What was the dominant purpose of the transaction in [this] case? Was it the sale of goods or the rendition of services? It can hardly be said that the sale of the windows was "incidental" to the transaction. Rather it would appear that the rendition of services was the incidental factor. After all, approximately two-thirds of the cost of the transaction was allocated to the windows. Besides, the contract did not segregate the total price of the windows from the total price of the services to be rendered. Thus, we think the predominant character of the transaction was the sale of goods, even though a substantial amount of service was involved in installing the goods.

The mere fact that Scandinavian House would not have purchased the windows unless plaintiff installed them is of no consequence. When presented with two elements of a contract, each absolutely necessary if the subject matter is to be of any significant value to the purchaser, it is a futile task to attempt to determine which component is "more necessary." Thus, we must look to the predominant purpose, the thrust of the contract as it would exist in the minds of reasonable parties. There is no surer way to provide for predictable results in the face of a highly artificial classification system. Inasmuch as the predominant purpose of the transaction involved the sale of goods, the UCC applies. The trial court erred in ruling otherwise.

Having determined that the UCC applies to this hybrid transaction, we look to the UCC to determine if plaintiff and Scandinavian House entered into a contract for the sale and installation of the windows.

The UCC expands our conception of contract. It makes contracts easier to form, and it imposes a wider range of obligations than before. Parties may form a contract through conduct rather than merely through the exchange of communications constituting "offer and acceptance."

Assuming arguendo that the letter of intent was equivocal, we would find, nevertheless, that Scandinavian House intended to contract with plaintiff. Why? Because the conduct of the parties demonstrates an intention to contract. Lon Meyers gave a letter of intent to Gregory and informed him that Scandinavian House had awarded the windows contract to plaintiff. The letter of intent authorized plaintiff to take measurements and prepare shop drawings. Pursuant to the letter, plaintiff took measurements in the apartment house. That was no small undertaking and it could not have been done without the cooperation of Scandinavian House. Ultimately, plaintiff completed and delivered the shop drawings to Scandinavian House.

The conduct of the parties is inconsistent with the theory that they only agreed to agree. The mere fact that plaintiff subsequently met with defendants to resolve the guarantee of payment issue does not negate the fact that the parties entered into a contract previously.

Judgment *reversed.* ■

Based on the UCC, J. Lee Gregory won a case that it would have lost under the common law. Next we look at changes the Code has made in the centuries-old requirement of a writing.

Statute of Frauds

UCC §2-201 requires a writing for any sale of goods worth $500 or more. However, under the UCC, the writing need not completely summarize the agreement, and it need not even be entirely accurate. Once again, the Code is modifying the common law rule, permitting parties to enforce deals with less formality. In some cases, the court grants an exception and enforces an agreement with no writing at all. Here are the rules.

Contracts for Goods Worth $500 or More

Section 2-201 demands a writing for any contract of goods over this limit, meaning that virtually every significant sale of goods has some writing requirement. Remember that a contract for goods costing less than $500 is still covered by the UCC, but it may be oral.

Writing Sufficient to Indicate a Contract

The Code only requires a writing *sufficient to indicate* that the parties made a contract. In other words, the writing need not *be* a contract. A simple memo is enough, or a letter or informal note, mentioning that the two sides reached an agreement, is enough. **In general, the writing must be signed by the defendant,** that is, whichever party is claiming there was no deal. Dick signs and sends to Shirley a letter saying, "This is to acknowledge your agreement to buy all 650 books in my rare book collection for $188,000." Shirley signs nothing. A day later, Louis offers Dick $250,000. Is Dick free to sell? No. He signed the memo, it indicates a contract, and Shirley can enforce it against him.

Now reverse the problem. Suppose that after Shirley receives Dick's letter, she decides against rare books in favor of original scripts from the *South Park* television show. Dick sues. Shirley wins because *she* signed nothing.

Incorrect or Omitted Terms

If the writing demonstrates the two sides reached an agreement, it satisfies §2-201 even if it omits important terms or states them incorrectly. Suppose Dick writes "$1888,000," indicating almost $2 million, when he meant to write "$188,000." The letter still shows that the parties made a deal, and the court will enforce it, relying on oral testimony to determine the correct price.

Enforceable Only to Quantity Stated

Since the writing only has to indicate that the parties agreed, it need not state every term of their deal. But one term is essential: quantity. **The Code will enforce the contract only up to the quantity of goods stated in the writing.** This is logical, since a court can surmise other terms, such as price, based on market conditions. Buyer agrees to purchase pencils from Seller. The market value of the pencils is easy to determine, but a court would have no way of knowing whether Buyer meant to purchase 1,000 pencils or 100,000; the quantity must be stated.

Merchant Exception

This is a major change from the common law. **When two merchants make an oral contract, and one sends a confirming memo to the other within a reasonable time, and the memo is sufficiently definite that it could be enforced against the sender herself, then the memo is also valid against the merchant who receives it, unless he objects within 10 days.** Laura, a tire wholesaler, signs and sends a memo to Scott, a retailer, saying, "Confm yr order today—500 tires cat #886—cat price." Scott realizes he can get the tires cheaper elsewhere and ignores the memo. Big mistake. Both parties are merchants, and Laura's memo is sufficient to bind her. So it also satisfies the statute of frauds *against Scott*, unless he objects within 10 days.

The following case illustrates the merchant exception in action.

Code Provisions Discussed in this Case

Issue	Relevant Code Section
1. Was there a writing sufficient to indicate a contract?	UCC §2-201 requires a writing for any sale of goods worth $500 or more.
2. Did the purchase orders satisfy the merchant exception?	UCC §2-201(2), the "merchant exception." When two merchants make an oral contract, and one sends a confirming memo to the other within a reasonable time, and the memo is sufficiently definite that it could be enforced against the sender herself, then the memo is also valid against the merchant who receives it, unless he objects within 10 days.

RAPOCA ENERGY COMPANY, L.P. V. AMCI EXPORT CORPORATION

2001 WL 401424
United States District Court for the Western Division of Virginia, 2001

Facts: Robert Moir, an AMCI executive, met with Rapoca's officer, Gary Chilcot, at O'Charley's Restaurant, and discussed buying a large quantity of coal from Rapoca. According to AMCI, the two agreed that Rapoca would sell 140,000 tons of coal. AMCI confirmed this in two purchase orders (P.O.s), which it sent to Rapoca. Rapoca's version was very different. Chilcot stated that the parties never reached an oral agreement, that the P.O.s were inconsistent as to the quantity of coal, and that the price was too low for a reasonable seller to have agreed. What is clear is that Rapoca did not respond in writing to the P.O.s for several months.

Rapoca filed suit, seeking a declaration from the court that it had no contractual obligation to AMCI. The company argued that there had been no agreement, and that even if the parties had orally agreed, the P.O.s did not satisfy the statute of frauds. AMCI counterclaimed, seeking damages for its costs in buying coal elsewhere. The judge first ruled that the parties had in fact reached an oral agreement. That left one important issue remaining.

Issue: Did the purchase orders satisfy the statute of frauds?

Excerpts from Judge Jones's Decision: The next question that I must resolve is whether the oral contracts are barred by the statute of frauds. It is clear that there is no writing signed by Rapoca in this case sufficient to indicate that the contracts in question were made. However, there is an exception to §2-201. [The court describes the "merchant exception."]

There is no question but that the parties were merchants within the meaning of this exception. Under the circumstances, I find that the two weeks

▼

in which these purchase orders were received by Rapoca was a reasonable time after the oral agreement between Moir and Chilcot. It is unlikely that memories would fade or that Rapoca would be unduly burdened by such a short period of time. The closer question is whether the purchase orders, which were not objected to in writing within ten days, were writings in confirmation of the contracts.

On the one side, the purchase orders here appear to require the recipient to take some affirmative action, by virtue of the printed form language that states, "This order must be acknowledged by the return of the signed second copy" and because the purchase order contains a place for the recipient to sign below the words, "Accepted and Agreed." In addition, the purchase orders contain printed form language that states that delivery of coal after the date of the purchase order constitutes acceptance of the order.

Some courts have held that a purchase order, particularly with language like this, is more akin to an offer for a contract, rather than a confirmation of an existing agreement. Moreover, there is no reference in these purchase orders to any specific antecedent oral agreement, and some courts have found that the absence of such confirming language precludes the use of the writing as a confirmation.

However, I find from the undisputed evidence in this case that the clear trade practice was to use purchase orders such as these to confirm oral agreements. Gary Chilcot's testimony supports this finding:

THE COURT: And why do you think you get a purchase order? What's the ... reason for that?

WITNESS: Well, it's, it's a reconfirmation of what was verbally agreed to.

THE COURT: So that in your experience there normally is an agreement as to the sale which is typically oral?

WITNESS: Typically.

THE COURT: And that ... is followed by the purchaser sending you or your company a purchase order which confirms the terms?

WITNESS: Correct.

In this business, at the time, purchase orders were rarely if ever signed and returned, which is further evidence that they were simply used as confirmations. The practice was not to use them as offers, and they were not offers in this case, but rather confirmations of the prior oral agreement. Thus, the fact that the purchase orders had the acceptance language does not preclude them, under the circumstances of this case, from being writings in confirmation within the meaning of the statute of frauds.

Thus, I find that the contracts in questions are valid and enforceable. ■

Public Policy

The court acknowledges that the purchase orders, by their own terms, require a signature or some other action by the recipient before they become valid. Rapoca never signed the P.O.s or took any other step to indicate an oral agreement. Yet the court has found in favor of AMCI anyway. Why did it do so? Did the court make the right choice? ◆

Special Circumstances

Finally, an oral contract *may* be enforceable, even without a written memorandum, if (1) the seller is specially manufacturing the goods for the buyer, or (2) the defendant admits in court proceedings that there was a contract, or (3) the goods have been delivered or they have been paid for. We discuss these exceptions in detail in Chapter 15, on written contracts.

Added Terms: Section 2-207

Under the common law's mirror image rule, when one party makes an offer, the offeree must accept those exact terms. If the offeree adds or alters any terms, the acceptance is ineffective and the offeree's response becomes a counteroffer. In one of its most significant modifications of contract law, the UCC changes that result. **Under §2-207, an acceptance that adds or alters terms will often create a contract.** The Code has made this change in response to *battles of the form.* Every day, corporations buy and sell millions of dollars of goods using pre-printed forms. The vast majority of all contracts involve such documents. Typically, the buyer places an order using a pre-printed form, and the seller acknowledges with its own pre-printed acceptance form. Because each form contains language favorable to the party sending it, the two documents rarely agree. The Code's drafters concluded that the law must cope with real practices.

We discuss §2-207 in detail in Chapter 11 and summarize it here only to emphasize how it works with other UCC provisions. The section is confusing, and a diagram helps. **For a schematic look at UCC §2-207, see the illustration on page 363.**

Does an additional term eliminate a binding contract?

Intention

The parties must still *intend* to create a contract. Section 2-207 is full of exceptions, but there is no change in this basic requirement of contract law. If the differing forms indicate that the parties never reached agreement, there is no contract.

Additional or Different Terms

An offeree may include a new term in his acceptance and still create a binding deal. Suppose Breeder writes to Pet Shop, offering to sell 100 guinea pigs at $2 each. Pet Shop faxes a memo saying, "We agree to buy 100 g.p. We get credit for any unhealthy pig." Pet Shop has added a new term, concerning unhealthy pigs, but the parties *have* created a binding contract because the writings show they intended an agreement. Now the court must decide what the terms of the contract are, since there is some discrepancy. The first step is to decide whether the new language is an *additional term* or a *different term.*

Additional Terms. Additional terms are those that raise issues not covered in the offer. The "unhealthy pig" issue is an additional term because the offer said nothing about it. **When both parties are *merchants*, additional terms generally become part of the bargain.** Pet Shop's insistence on credit for sick guinea pigs is binding on Breeder. In three circumstances, however, additional terms *do not* bind the parties:

- If the original offer *insisted on its own terms.* If Breeder offered the pets for sale "on these and no other terms," Pet Shop's additional language would not become part of their deal.

- If the additional terms *materially alter* the offer. Pet Shop's new language about credit for unhealthy animals is fairly uncontroversial. But suppose Pet Shop wrote back, "Breeder is liable for any illness of any animal in Pet Shop within 90 days of shipment of guinea pigs." Breeder would potentially have to pay for a $500 iguana with pneumonia or a $6,000 parrot with gout. This is a material alteration of the bargain and is not part of the contract.

- If the offeror *promptly objects* to the new terms. If Breeder received Pet Shop's fax and immediately called up to say, "no credit for unhealthy pigs," then Pet Shop's additional term is not part of their deal.

In all other circumstances, additional terms do become part of an agreement between merchants.

Different Terms. These are terms that contradict those in the offer. Suppose Brilliant Corp. orders 1,500 cellular phones from Makem Co., for use by Brilliant's sales force. Brilliant places the order using a pre-printed form stating that the product is fully warranted for normal use and that seller is liable for compensatory *and consequential* damages. This means, for example, that Makem could be liable for lost profits if a salesman's phone fails during a lucrative sales pitch. Makem responds with its own memo stating that in the event of defective phones, Makem is liable only to repair or replace, and *is not liable for consequential damages, lost profits, or any other damages.*

Makem's acceptance has included a *different* term because its language contradicts the offer. Almost all courts would agree that the parties intended to reach an agreement and therefore the contract is enforceable. The question is, what are its terms? Is the full warranty of the offer included, or the very limited warranty of the acceptance? The majority of states hold that **different terms cancel each other out.** Neither party's language goes into the contract. But what then *are* the terms of the deal?

If the evidence indicates that the parties had orally agreed on the issue disputed in the forms, then the courts will ignore the contradictory writings and enforce the oral contract. **If there is no clear oral agreement, the Code supplies its own terms, called gap-fillers,** which cover prices, delivery dates and places, warranties, and other subjects. In the cellular phone case, the contradicting warranty provisions cancel each other out. The parties had not orally agreed on a warranty, so a court would enforce the Code's gap-filler warranty, which does permit recovery of compensatory and consequential damages. Therefore, Makem *would* be liable for lost profits. We outline most of the gap-filler terms in Chapter 11. Warranty provisions are analyzed in greater detail in Chapter 21.

In the following case, the Rhode Island Supreme Court seeks the fairest method of sorting out conflicting terms.

Code Provisions Discussed in This Case	
Issue	**Relevant Code Section**
1. Which are the terms of this agreement?	UCC §2-207: *Additional* terms generally but not always become part of the bargain. *Different* terms generally cancel each other out.
2. What is the Code's gap-filler provision concerning delivery?	UCC §2-309: The time for shipment or delivery if not agreed upon is a reasonable time.
3. What is a "reasonable" delivery time?	UCC §1-204: A "reasonable" time depends on the nature, purpose, and circumstances of the action.

SUPERIOR BOILER WORKS, INC. V. R. J. SANDERS, INC.

1998 R.I. LEXIS 153
Supreme Court of Rhode Island, 1998

Facts: R. J. Sanders, Inc., had a contract with the federal government to install the heating system at a federal prison camp. The company negotiated with Superior Boiler Works to purchase three large commercial units. On March 27, Superior sent a proposal to Sanders, offering to sell three boilers for a total of $156,000 and estimating time of delivery at four weeks. The parties exchanged further documents and held various discussions. Finally, on July 20, Sanders sent a "purchase order" for three boilers, agreeing to pay $145,827 and stating "Date required: 4 Weeks," that is, August 20. On August 6, Superior sent a "sales order," agreeing to sell the three boilers at that price, but providing a shipping date of October 1. This later delivery date forced Sanders to rent temporary boilers at a cost of $45,315. On October 1, Superior shipped the boilers, which arrived on October 5. Sanders sent a check in the amount of $100,000, claiming that Superior had delivered the boilers late and deducting the cost of its rental equipment. Superior sued for the additional $45,000 and moved for summary judgment, which the trial court granted. Sanders appealed, claiming that the contract had required Superior to deliver the boilers within four weeks.

Issue: **Did Superior's October delivery breach the contract?**

Excerpts from Justice Flanders's Decision: Sanders' amended purchase order of July 20 and Superior's August 6 response agree exactly on the specifications and on the price of the boilers. The fact that these two documents disagree on one important term—the time for delivery—does not prevent the formation of a contract under the UCC because it is apparent from their subsequent conduct that both parties intended to be bound contractually. What becomes of the parties' conflicting positions on the shipment period (Sanders' specified four-week delivery versus Superior's stated October 1 shipping date) is a question that must be considered in light of section 2-207(2).

[The court mentioned that other states had responded in various ways to "different" terms, that is, those that conflict. Judge Flanders declared that Rhode Island would side with the majority and adopt the "knock-out" rule, meaning that conflicting terms knock each other out, leaving a hole in the contract that is filled by one of the Code's gap-filler provisions.] Here, the void relating to delivery time would be filled by Section 2-309, which reads, "The time for shipment or delivery . . . if . . . not agreed upon shall be a reasonable time."

Because of the UCC's gap-filling provisions, we recognize that this approach might result in the enforcement of a contract term that neither party agreed to and, in fact, in regard to which each party expressed an entirely different preference. We note in response to this concern that the offeror and the offeree both have the power to protect any term they deem critical by expressly making acceptance conditional on assent to that term. And as merchants, both parties should have been well aware that their dealings were subject to the UCC and to its various gap-filling provisions. In this case, because the two variant shipping-date terms cancel each other out, the amended purchase order and the August 6 sales order formed a contract that required the three boilers to be delivered within a reasonable period after August 6.

In the usual case the question of what constitutes a reasonable time under the UCC is one for the finder of fact to determine from the nature, the purpose, and the circumstances surrounding the transaction, including the parties' course of dealing, usages of trade in the pertinent industry, or the parties' course of performance. See [UCC §1-204(2). In this case, however, the only available evidence indicated that Superior's performance was reasonable, by industry standards.]

For the foregoing reasons the appeal is denied, and the Superior Court's judgment is affirmed. ∎

at RISK

Section 2-207 is a noble but imperfect attempt to cope with battles of form. The section unfortunately does not resolve all doubt. If a buyer sends your company a purchase order form, with pre-printed terms, and you accept the offer using your own document, what are the terms of the agreement? Are your new terms "additional"? Do they "materially alter" the bargain? Or are your terms "different"? If you understand this section, you can make an educated guess, but you are unlikely to know for sure. How can you avoid a disastrous surprise?

First, *read all terms on both contracts.* Know everybody's terms, and figure out the important differences. This may sound obvious, but many merchants never read the fine print on *either* form. Second, if some of the terms on your contract are essential, *bargain for them.* Do not *assume* that your terms are the final ones; *make* them so by pushing the other party to accept them in writing. Notice, for example, that in the above case, Sanders specified delivery in four weeks, but never insisted on that date. The executives doing the bargaining might have included a phrase such as "these terms and no others." Their failure to do so cost the company $45,000. Third, if the other side refuses to accept terms that you consider essential, *calculate your potential loss.* If your potential liability is more than you consider acceptable, your choices are to terminate the negotiations or to obtain insurance. It takes more time and effort this way, but you stay out of court. ◆

Open Terms: Sections 2-305 and 2-306

Open Prices

Under §2-305, the parties may conclude a contract even though they have not settled the price. Again, this is a change from the common law, which required certainty of such an important contract term. Under the Code, if the parties have not stated one, **the price is a reasonable price at the time of delivery.** A court will use market value and other comparable sales to determine what a reasonable price would have been. If the contract permits the buyer or seller to *determine* the price during contract performance, §2-305 requires that she do so in good faith, as the following case demonstrates.

Code Provisions Discussed in this Case	
Issue	**Relevant Code Sections**
1. May the parties form a binding agreement without specifying the price?	UCC §2-305(1): The parties may conclude a contract even though they have not settled the price.
2. May a contract permit one party to settle the price?	UCC §2-305(2): "A price to be fixed by the seller or by the buyer" requires that it be fixed in good faith.
3. What does *good faith* mean?	UCC §§1-201(19), 1-203 and 2-103: For *non-merchants,* good faith means honesty in fact. For a *merchant,* good faith means honesty in fact *plus* the exercise of reasonable commercial standards of fair dealing.

MATHIS V. EXXON CORPORATION

302 F.3d 448
Fifth Circuit Court of Appeals, 2002

Facts: Exxon marketed gasoline to retailers in three ways. *Franchisees* (who owned local gas stations) were required to purchase a minimum number of gallons per month. Exxon set the price each month, known as the dealer tank wagon price (DTW). *Jobbers* (distributors who could resell to dealers) paid the "rack price," which was generally lower than the DTW. *Company-operated retail stores* (CORS) paid nothing, because Exxon owned them.

A group of 54 Texas franchisees sued, claiming that Exxon set their gasoline prices artificially high. The plaintiffs alleged that Exxon wanted to drive them out of business and replace their franchises with more profitable CORS. The evidence indicated that the franchisees' DTW was consistently higher than the rack price paid by jobbers. Many plaintiffs testified that their franchises had become unprofitable. One study showed that 62 percent of franchisees in Corpus Christi, Texas, were selling gas below the price they paid for it. Plaintiffs' expert testified that 75 percent of their competitors could buy gasoline at a lower price.

The plaintiffs argued that this evidence demonstrated that Exxon set the prices in bad faith. The jury agreed, awarding the plaintiffs $5.7 million, plus $2.3 million in attorney's fees. Exxon appealed.

Issue: Did Exxon set the prices in bad faith?

Excerpts from Judge Smith's Decision: [UCC §2-305(2) rejects the idea that the seller may fix any price he wants.] The price must be fixed in good faith. Good faith includes observance of reasonable commercial standards of fair dealing in the trade if the party is a merchant. In the normal case a "posted price" or a future seller's or buyer's "given price," "price in effect," "market price," or the like satisfies the good faith requirement.

The franchisees here are alleging a breach of good faith grounded not in Exxon's failure to price in accord with an established schedule, but in its failure to set the price in good faith. Suits recognizing such a cause of action are rare, and with good reason: We would be ill-advised to consider a case to be outside the norm based only on an allegation of improper motive by the party setting the price.

Plaintiffs produced enough evidence to escape [the] "normal case" limitation. They showed, for example, that Exxon planned to replace a number of its franchises with CORS, that the DTW price was higher than the sum of the rack price and transportation, that Exxon prevented the franchisees from purchasing gas from jobbers, and that a number of franchisees were unprofitable or noncompetitive.

For example, one Exxon document stated that the company's "Marketing Strategy is to reduce Dealer stores (est. 30%)." Another document set forth Exxon's plans to reduce dealer stations in Houston from 95 to 45, and to increase CORS from 83 to 150. James Carter, the regional director of the Exxon/Mobil Fuels Marketing Company, testified that Exxon made more of a profit from a CORS than from an independent lessee store. These plans and observations were validated by the fact that the number of dealer stations steadily declined.

Further indication of plans to shift from dealer-lessees to CORS is shown by Exxon's dissatisfaction with outlets featuring service bays. Exxon documents showed that service bays—generally associated with lessee-dealer locations—were becoming less profitable, while stations with convenience stores—generally associated with CORS—were the wave of the future.

Exxon's bad faith, in this regard, is shown by the record. Facing the competition of self-service stations that were either selling food and other goods or had bare pumps with no overhead costs incurred in servicing vehicles, Exxon decided years ago that retail marketing through franchise dealers was becoming economically unsound. Although Exxon decided to move to CORS in Houston and jobbers in Corpus Christi, this decision was not communicated to its franchisees. Because of profit from their other sales, CORS could, and did, sell gas for less than the franchise dealers paid to Exxon for their gas. And the jobbers delivered Exxon gas to their dealers for less than Exxon franchisees were required to pay for their delivered gas, but Exxon prohibited its franchisees from buying at this lower price from the jobbers.

Accordingly, the jury's finding that Exxon breached its duty of good faith in setting the DTW price it charged the plaintiffs is not without foundation in the law or the evidence. As we have recounted, plaintiffs offered ample evidence tending to prove their version of price-setting.

[Affirmed.] ∎

Public Policy

Contract law generally focuses on objective standards. For example, whether the parties intended to form a contract is determined not by what they were thinking (which we will never know) but by what their words and actions indicate to a reasonable observer. The court here takes a dramatically different position. How would you describe the court's focus? Do you think the Fifth Circuit decided the case properly?   ◆

Output and Requirements Contracts

Under §2-306, an output contract obligates the seller to sell all of his output to the buyer, who agrees to accept it. Suppose Joel has a small plant in which he manufactures large plants, that is, handcrafted artificial flowers and trees, made of silk and other expensive materials. Joel isn't sure how many he can produce in a year, but wants a guaranteed market. He makes an output contract with Yolanda, in which he promises to sell the entire output of his plant and she agrees to buy it all.

A requirements contract is the reverse, obligating a buyer to purchase all of his needed goods from the seller. Joel might sign a requirements contract with Worm Express, agreeing to buy from Worm all of the silk he needs. Both output and requirements contracts are valid under the Code, although they create certain problems. By definition, the exact quantity of goods is not specified. But then how much may one party demand? Is there any upper or lower limit?

The UCC requires that the parties in an output or requirements contract make their demands in good faith. For example, in a requirements contract, a buyer may not suddenly increase her demand far beyond what the parties expected merely because there has been a market change. Suppose the price of silk skyrockets. Joel's requirements contract obligates Worm Express to sell him all the silk he needs. Could Joel demand 10 times the silk he had anticipated, knowing he could resell it at a big profit to other manufacturers? No. That would be bad faith. Come on, Joel, play by the rules.

May the buyer *reduce* his demand far below what the parties anticipated? Yes, as long as he makes the reduction in good faith.

Modification

Terry, a business consultant, agrees to work for Awkward Co. to create a corporate reorganization plan and oversee its implementation. He promises to finish the job by October 15. By September, Terry is far behind schedule and asks Awkward for an extra three months and for 30 percent extra pay. Terry hints broadly that if the company refuses, he will walk off the job. Awkward agrees in writing to the extra time and money, and Terry finally finishes. Awkward then sues, based on Terry's late completion and overcharge. Who wins? Awkward. This was a services contract. Under the common law, a modification is invalid unless supported by additional consideration, which Terry never gave. Had the contract been one for the sale of goods, however, the outcome would have been different.

UCC §2-209: An agreement modifying a contract needs no consideration to be binding. Suppose Jeanette makes a deal to buy a used Mercedes "in good running order" from her sister, Valerie, for $29,000. Valerie writes to Jeanette confirming the agreement and promising to bring the car the following week. But before Valerie can deliver the car, a major transmission problem makes it inoperable. Valerie pays $1,200 to repair it. She telephones Jeanette and explains the extra cost. Jeanette faxes a note, promising to split the cost of the repair. Is Jeanette's promise enforceable? Valerie was already obligated to deliver a car in good running order. But under the UCC, contract modifications need no additional consideration to be valid. The UCC also permits the parties to modify some contracts orally. Regrettably, the Code is not crystal clear about which changes may be oral and which must be written. The wise executive will insist that all parties sign any proposed modifications. For better or worse, though, §2-209 clearly implies that some alterations may be enforceable even with nothing in writing, so never orally agree to a contract change unless you are prepared to live with it.[5]

Parties make a contract attempting to control their futures. But one party's certainty can be undercut by the ease with which the other party may obtain a modification. Section 2-209 acknowledges this tension by enabling the parties to limit changes. **The parties may agree to prohibit oral modifications and insist that all modifications be in writing and signed. Between merchants, such a clause is valid. But if either party is *not* a merchant, such a clause is valid only if the non-merchant *separately signs* it.**

Once again the Code gives greater protection to non-merchants than to merchants. Two merchants may agree, as part of their bargain, that any future modifications will be valid only if written and signed. But this limitation on modifications is not valid against a non-merchant unless she separately signs the limiting clause itself. Suppose a furniture retailer orders 200 beds from a manufacturer. The retailer's order form requires any modifications to be in writing. The manufacturer initials the retailer's form at the bottom. The parties have a valid agreement and no oral modifications will be enforced. But suppose the retailer sells a bed to a customer. The sales form also bars oral modifications. That prohibition is void unless the customer separately signs it.

The following case looks at an oral modification.

Code Provisions Discussed in this Case

Issue	Relevant Code Sections
1. May the parties prohibit oral modifications of the contract?	UCC §2-209(2): A signed agreement that excludes modification or rescission except by a signed writing cannot be otherwise modified or rescinded.
2. Did Marley's conduct waive the prohibition on modification?	UCC §2-209(4): Although an attempt at modification or rescission does not satisfy the requirements of subsection (2), it can operate as a waiver.

---

[5] The confusion stems from the ambiguous language of §2-209(3), which requires a writing if "the contract as modified" is covered by §2-201, the statute of frauds provision. Some courts have interpreted this to mean that once a contract is covered by §2-201 and needs a writing to be enforceable, any modifications must also be in writing. But others have suggested that a writing is obligatory only if the modification brings the contract within §2-201 *for the first time,* or if the *modification itself* falls within §2-201, or if the modification *changes the quantity* terms of the original contract. There is no definitive answer to this problem, as the court noted in *Flowers Ginning Co. v. Arma, Inc.,* 1997 U.S. App. LEXIS 1054 (4th Cir. 1997). Actually there is: Get it write.

you Be The Judge

THE MARLEY COOLING TOWER COMPANY V. CALDWELL ENERGY & ENVIRONMENTAL, INC.

280 F. Supp. 2d 651
United States District Court for the Western District of Kentucky

Facts: Caldwell manufactured and installed cooling systems for power plants. Caldwell agreed with Duke/Fluor Daniel (D/FD) to install such a system in Aiken, South Carolina. The contract stated that Caldwell would pay liquidated damages of $5,000 per day if the system was late.

Marley agreed to ship to Caldwell all of the material and equipment needed to build the cooling system, and to deliver it no later than April 1. The Marley-Caldwell contract stated that "Neither Marley or the Purchaser shall be responsible or held liable for any special, indirect, consequential, liquidated and/or punitive damages." The agreement also provided that there could be no contract changes without a signed, written modification.

Marley delivered its material almost two months behind schedule, making Caldwell late in fulfilling its obligations to build the cooling system. D/FD assessed Caldwell liquidated damages of $135,000. Caldwell attempted to pass this cost, which it called "backcharges," on to Marley by paying $135,000 less than Marley's invoice demanded.

Marley sent Caldwell a letter, stating "We would like to work with you to resolve this issue. However, before we can agree to these backcharges, we must have [certain specified] documents." Caldwell supplied the documents, and also sent a change order, indicating that Marley accepted the backcharges. The change order stated that it would not be valid until signed by both Caldwell and Marley. A Marley executive agreed on the telephone to accept the backcharges, but Marley never signed or returned the change order. Marley later rejected the charges. When Caldwell refused to pay the full contract price, Marley sued. Both sides moved for summary judgment.

You Be the Judge: Is Marley obligated to pay the backcharges?

Argument for Marley: There are two contracts here, and both are clear. First, Caldwell consented to a large liquidated damage clause with D/FD, and now regrets its contract. Too late. Next time the company agrees to such a clause, it should either obtain insurance or insist on a parallel agreement from *its* suppliers. Caldwell's failure to protect itself entitles the company to sympathy— but no money. Second, Caldwell agreed that Marley would not be liable for any liquidated or consequential damages. The Caldwell-Marley contract also prohibited oral modification. This agreement was made by qualified lawyers representing experienced merchants.

The fact that a Marley executive acknowledged, by phone, the company's ambivalence does not change the contract or the law. UCC section 2-209 was written for cases like this. Companies in the midst of a dispute should discuss the matter freely, without worrying that a spontaneous comment will prove costly. Marley openly considered its options knowing that only a signed modification would create liability. Caldwell asked for such a written modification, but Marley signed nothing. End of case.

Argument for Caldwell: Let us start with what is obvious, undisputed, and most important: Marley caused the problem. Marley delivered its material late, without excuse. In fairness, that should make the outcome clear: A company that causes the harm pays for it.

That of course is why a Marley executive acknowledged the justice of the backcharges. The same executive asked for certain verifying documents. Was that request made in bad faith, or as a joke? No. Marley had agreed in principle to cover the backcharges and wanted assurance that the costs were real. Caldwell promptly supplied the documents, proving that the costs were only too real.

Marley's actions in requesting documents, and then agreeing to pay the backcharges, were a clear waiver of the "no-oral-modification" rule. A signed modification is a silly formality. The Code is designed to cut through legal technicalities and enable experienced merchants to conduct business as usual. Telephone calls, and oral modifications, qualify as routine business. UCC section 2-209(4)

▼

allows a waiver by words-and-action because that is how companies do business. Let Marley pay for the damage it caused *and explicitly acknowledged.* ∎

The following table concludes this chapter with an illustration of the Code's impact on the common law.

Selected Code Provisions That Change the Common Law

Issue	Common Law Rule	UCC Sec.	UCC Rule	Example
Contract formation	Offer must be followed by acceptance that shows meeting of the minds on all important terms.	§2-204 and §2-305	Contract can be made in any manner sufficient to show agreement; moment of making not critical; one or more terms, including the price, may be left open.	Tilly writes Meg, "I need a new van for my delivery company." Meg delivers a van and Tilly starts to use it. Under the common law, there is no contract, because no price was ever mentioned; under the UCC, the writing plus the conduct show an intention to contract (2-204). The price is a *reasonable* one (2-305).
Writing requirement	All essential terms must be in writing.	§2-201	Any writing is sufficient if it indicates a contract; terms may be omitted or misstated; "merchant" exception can create a contract enforceable against a party who receives the writing and does nothing within 10 days.	Douglas, a car dealer, signs and sends to Michael, another dealer, a memo saying, "Confirming our deal for your blue Rolls." Michael reads it but ignores it; 10 days later Douglas has satisfied the statute of frauds under the UCC's merchant exception.
Added terms in acceptance	An acceptance that adds or changes any term is a counteroffer.	§2-207	Additional or different terms are not necessarily counteroffers; their presence does not prevent a contract from being formed, and in some cases the new terms will become a part of the bargain.	Roberts sends a pre-printed form to Julia, offering to buy 25 computers and stating a price; Julia responds with her own pre-printed form, accepting the offer but adding a term that balances unpaid after 30 days incur a finance charge. The additional term is not a counteroffer; there is a valid contract; and the finance charge is part of the bargain.
Modification	A modification is valid only if supported by new consideration.	§2-209	A modification needs no consideration to be binding.	Martin, a computer manufacturer, agrees to sell Steve, a retailer, 500 computers at a specified price, including delivery. The next day Martin learns that his delivery costs have gone up 20%; he calls Steve, who faxes a note agreeing to pay 15% extra. Under the common law, the modification would be void; under the Code, it is enforceable.

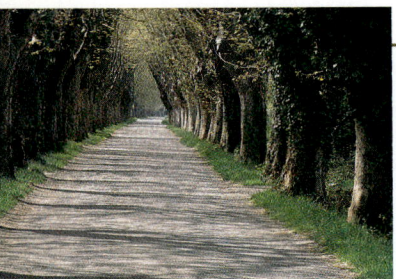

Chapter Conclusion

The Uniform Commercial Code enables parties to create a contract quickly. While this can be helpful in a fast-paced business world, it also places responsibility on executives. Informal conversations may cause at least one party to conclude that it has a binding agreement—and the law may agree.

Chapter Review

1. The Code is designed to modernize commercial law and make it uniform throughout the country.

2. Article 2 applies to the sale of goods, which are movable things other than money and investment securities.

3. Article 2A governs the leasing of goods.

4. In a mixed contract involving goods and services, the UCC applies if the predominant purpose is the sale of goods.

5. A merchant is someone who routinely deals in the particular goods involved, or who appears to have special knowledge or skill in those goods, or who uses agents with special knowledge or skill. The UCC frequently holds a merchant to a higher standard of conduct than a non-merchant.

6. The UCC imposes a duty of good faith in the performance of all contracts.

7. A contract is unconscionable if it is shockingly one-sided and fundamentally unfair. A court is much likelier to use unconscionability to protect a consumer than a corporation.

8. UCC §2-204 permits the parties to form a contract in any manner that shows agreement.

9. For the sale of goods worth $500 or more, UCC §2-201 requires some writing that indicates an agreement. Terms may be omitted or misstated, but the contract will be enforced only to the extent of the quantity stated.

10. When two merchants make an oral contract, and one sends a confirming memo to the other within a reasonable time, and the memo is sufficiently definite that it could be enforced against the sender herself, then the merchant who receives it will also be bound unless he objects within 10 days.

11. UCC §2-207 governs an acceptance that does not "mirror" the offer. *Additional terms* usually, but not always, become part of the contract. *Different terms* contradict a term in the offer. When that happens, most courts reject both parties' proposals and rely on gap-filler terms.

12. Under UCC §2-305 a contract is enforceable even if the price is not stated. In such cases the price must be reasonable.

13. UCC §2-306 requires both parties to perform output and requirements contracts in good faith.

14. UCC §2-209 permits contracts to be modified even if there is no consideration. The parties may prohibit oral modifications, but such a clause is ineffective against a non-merchant unless she signed it.

Practice Test

1. **CPA QUESTION** Cookie Co. offered to sell Distrib Markets 20,000 pounds of cookies at $1.00 per pound, subject to certain specified terms for delivery. Distrib replied in writing as follows: "We accept your offer for 20,000 pounds of cookies at $1.00 per pound, weighing scale to have valid city certificate." Under the UCC:

   a. A contract was formed between the parties

   b. A contract will be formed only if Cookie agrees to the weighing scale requirement

   c. No contract was formed because Distrib included the weighing scale requirement in its reply

d. No contract was formed because Distrib's reply was a counteroffer

2. **CPA QUESTION** With regard to a contract governed by the UCC sales article, which one of the following statements is correct?

 a. Merchants and non-merchants are treated alike.

 b. The contract may involve the sale of any type of personal property.

 c. The obligations of the parties to the contract must be performed in good faith.

 d. The contract must involve the sale of goods for a price $500 or more.

3. Jim Dan, Inc. owned a golf course that had trouble with crab grass. Jim Dan bought 20 bags of Scotts Pro Turf Goosegrass/Crabgrass Control for $835 and applied it to the greens. The Pro Turf harmed the greens, causing over $36,000 in damage. Jim Dan sued Scotts. Scotts defended by claiming that it sold the Pro Turf with a clearly written, easy-to-read disclaimer that stated that in the event of damage, the buyer's only remedy would be a refund of the purchase price. Jim Dan, Inc. argued that the clause was unconscionable. Please rule.

4. **ETHICS** Systems Design designed and installed a software system for the savings accounts of the Kansas City Post Office Employees Credit Union. The software caused many problems and, ultimately, a lawsuit. The court had to decide whether the UCC governed. In similar cases, courts from other states had found that such a contract was *predominantly for the sale of goods*. Based on that, and on the doctrine of *uniformity*, the court ruled that the UCC governed. What does "predominantly for the sale of goods" have to do with the decision? Why is "uniformity" a factor? A word about the ethics of uniformity. From the perspective of two parties in a business dispute, what is potentially *threatening* about the idea of uniformity? Why is the doctrine potentially *attractive* to two business executives attempting to negotiate a contract?

5. Mail Code, Inc. manufactured bar code machines for reading addresses on envelopes. Its offices were in Indiana. John Grauberger, who lived in Kansas, applied to become a dealer for the Mail Code machine in the Kansas area. He signed a dealer application form, agreeing to abide by the terms printed on it. Mail Code informed Grauberger that it accepted him as a dealer and showed him a dealer agreement outlining his duties. The agreement contained a "forum selection" clause, stating that any disputes would be settled in a court in Indiana. Grauberger made no objection. He purchased a bar code machine for $31,000, but it did not work. Grauberger sued in Kansas, but Mail Code attempted to have the case dismissed because it had not been brought in Indiana. Did the parties have a valid agreement? Was the forum selection clause part of the agreement?

6. The Massachusetts Bay Transit Authority (MBTA) awarded the Perini Corp. a large contract to rehabilitate a section of railroad tracks. The work involved undercutting the existing track, removing the ballast and foundation, rebuilding the track, and disposing of the old material. Perini solicited an offer from Atlantic Track & Turnout Co. for Atlantic to buy whatever salvageable material Perini removed. Perini estimated the quantity of salvageable material that would be available. Atlantic offered to purchase "all available" material over the course of Perini's deal with the MBTA, and Perini accepted. But three months into the project, the MBTA ran short of money and told Perini to stop the undercutting part of the project. That was the work that made Perini its profit, so Perini requested that the MBTA terminate the agreement, which the agency did. By that point Perini had delivered to Atlantic only about 15 percent of the salvageable material that it had estimated. Atlantic sued. What kind of contract do the parties have? Who should win and why?

7. Nina owns a used car lot. She signs and sends a fax to Seth, a used car wholesaler who has a huge lot of cars in the same city. The fax says, "Confirming our agrmt—I pick any 15 cars fr yr lot—30% below blue book." Seth reads the fax, laughs, and throws it away. Two weeks later, Nina arrives and demands to purchase 15 of Seth's cars. Is he obligated to sell?

8. The Brugger Corp. owned a farm, operated by Jason Weimer, who acted as the company's business agent. Tri-Circle, Inc. was a farm equipment company. On behalf of Brugger, Weimer offered

to buy from Tri-Circle certain equipment for use on the farm. Tri-Circle accepted the offer, using a pre-printed form. The form included a finance charge for late payment. Weimer's offer had said nothing about finance charges, but he made no objection to the new term. Tri-Circle supplied the farm equipment but later alleged that Brugger had refused to pay for $12,000 worth of the supplies. Tri-Circle sued. In deciding whether Tri-Circle was entitled to finance charges, the court first inquired whether Brugger, Weimer, and Tri-Circle were merchants. Why did it look into that issue? *Were* they merchants?

9. Which one of the following transactions is not governed by Article 2 of the UCC?

   a. Purchasing an automobile for $35,000

   b. Leasing an automobile worth $35,000

   c. Purchasing a radio worth $449

10. To satisfy the UCC statute of frauds regarding the sale of goods, which of the following must generally be in writing?

    a. Designation of the parties as buyer and seller

    b. Delivery terms

    c. Quantity of the goods

    d. Warranties to be made

11. Are you the typical student who just cannot get enough questions and quizzes about the UCC? Type your way to **http://www.fullertonlaw.com/chapt12.htm**. The Web site has a long dis-cussion of the UCC, interspersed with contract hypotheticals and questions.

12. *YOU BE THE JUDGE* WRITING PROBLEM Brewster manufactured plastic bottles. Dial made personal care products at many plants around the country, including one in Salem, Virginia. The companies agreed that Dial would purchase from Brewster all of the plastic bottles it needed for its Salem factory. Dial estimated its requirements for one year at 7,850,000 bottles, but added a clause stating that "quantities are estimated only and do not bind Dial to purchase any minimum quantity." A few months later, Dial concluded that its Salem plant was unprofitable. The company closed the factory and notified Brewster that it would buy no bottles at all. Brewster sued. Did Dial have the right to reduce its orders to zero? **Argument for Brewster:** The parties had a clear contract for a massive number of bottles. Dial knew that this contract was extremely important to Brewster. Although Dial had some right to adjust its orders, it had no right to reduce them to zero. **Argument for Dial:** The issue is whether Dial acted in good faith. It did. The company had a legitimate reason for closing the factory—it was losing money—and with no factory it certainly did not need any bottles.

13. *ROLE REVERSAL* Write a multiple-choice question that contrasts the common law rules of contract formation with those of UCC §2-204.

Internet Research Problem

To find the latest legislation in your state regarding electronic contracts, go to **http://beatty.westbuslaw.com**. Find the "Recent Updates" section and examine pending legislation. What is the goal of the legislation? Can you anticipate any problems that the proposed law might cause?

> **You can find further practice problems at http://beatty.westbuslaw.com or in the Study Guide that accompanies this text.**

Ownership and Risk

He drove his truck fast along the rough country road, hurrying through the shadows of the Cascade Mountains, passing close to the Rogue River. The door panel, freshly painted, read "Ernest Jenkins, Cattle Buyer." Spinning the wheel hard left he drove through an impressive gate, under a wooden sign proclaiming "Double Q Ranch." He knew the ranch by reputation and quickly saw that it was prosperous—a good place for a man like him to do business.

He introduced himself to Kate Vandermeer, the Double Q's business manager, and expressed an interest in buying 300 head of cattle. Vandermeer and the man mounted horses and rode out to inspect the herd. Vandermeer noticed that his boots were brand new and that he rode awkwardly.

He was satisfied with the cattle, so the two bargained, sitting on horseback and looking into the sunset. Vandermeer started at $310,000 and was surprised at how quickly they reached an agreement, at $285,000, a price she considered excellent. They agreed that Vandermeer would deliver the cattle by truck, in one week, in a nearby town. He would pay with a cashier's check and take possession of the cattle and all ownership documents, such as brand inspection certificates and veterinarian's certificates. Back at the ranch, Vandermeer offered him a drink, but he had to hurry to another appointment.

The next week, right on schedule, he arrived on Thursday and presented his cashier's check for the full amount. When they had transferred the livestock, Vandermeer suggested they talk over some future business, but he was again in a rush. They shook hands and parted, the man heading due east, fast.

The Double Q's bank sent the cashier's check for collection, but learned early the following week that it was forged. Vandermeer called the State Police, who traced the man's movements to the state line. Three weeks later and 1,600 miles east, the FBI located the cattle, with the prominent "QQ" brand, in stockyards in Omaha. Ned Munson had purchased the cattle from the man for $225,000, which he considered a bargain. He had paid with a cashier's check. Ernest Jenkins, of course, had disappeared—literally. The truck's freshly painted door now read, "Ted J. Pringle, Grain Merchant," and it was parked a long, long way from Omaha. ■

LEGAL INTEREST

Who owns the cows? The Double Q wanted its cattle back or $285,000. If Munson was dumb enough to pay money to a thief, that wasn't the ranch's problem. But Ned Munson claimed the cows were his. He had paid a fair price to a man who appeared to own them. If Vandermeer was so foolish as to give up the cattle to a con artist, let the ranch suffer the consequences. The Double Q sued. Both parties to this lawsuit are unhappy, but happily they have illustrated the theme for our chapter: When two parties claim a conflicting legal interest in particular goods, *who loses?* Who obtains the law's protection? These are disputes over *conflicting interests in goods.*

An interest is a legal right in something. More than one party can have an interest in particular goods. Suppose you lease a new car from a dealer, agreeing to pay $300 per month for three years. Several parties will have legal interests in the car. The dealer still *owns* the car—interest number one. At the end of three years, the dealer gets it back. For three years, you have the use of the car—interest number two. You may use the car for all normal purposes but are obligated to make monthly payments. Your payments go to a finance agency, which has made an arrangement with the dealer, to obtain the right to your $300 monthly payment. The finance agency has a *security interest* in the car—interest number three. If you fail to pay on time, the finance company has the right to repossess your car. If you take the car to a garage for maintenance, the garage has *temporary possession* of the car—interest number four. The garage has the right to keep the car locked up over night, to work on it, and to test drive it. Sometimes legal interests can clash, and it is those conflicts we look at here.

Often the parties will claim ownership, each arguing that his interest is stronger than the other's. But in this chapter we also consider cases where each party argues that the *other* one owns the goods. Suppose a seller manufactures products for a buyer, but while the goods are being shipped, they are destroyed in a fire. Seller may argue that it no longer owned the goods, but buyer will claim it had not yet acquired them. In other cases, a *third party* will be involved. You pay $30,000 cash to buy a new car and expect to pick it up in three days. But the day before you arrive, the dealer's bank seizes all of the cars on the lot, claiming the dealer has defaulted on loans. Now the fight over legal interest is between you and the bank, with the dealer a relatively passive observer.

In the cattle case, three parties had a legal interest in the goods. The Double Q ranch originally had valid **title** to the cattle, **meaning the normal rights of ownership.** Ernest Jenkins, the scam artist, acquired a lesser interest. His contract with Double Q was fraudulent because Jenkins intended to cheat the ranch. Nonetheless, he did have an agreement. He obtained **voidable title,** meaning limited rights in the goods, inferior to those of the owner.[1] Finally, Ned Munson makes a claim to the cattle based on his payment and his possession of the cows and all documents.

The court will use various sections of the UCC to determine who keeps the cows and who bears the loss. Ned Munson should win the cattle. He was probably acting in good faith and a commercially reasonable manner when he bought the cows from a man who appeared to be a lawful cattle buyer. The Double Q must bear the loss. If, however, the Double Q can convince a court that Munson acted irresponsibly, because he had grounds for suspecting Jenkins, the court might order Munson to pay for the cattle.[2]

Ethics

As we look at this issue and others like it, ask yourself whether the UCC rules and the court decisions accomplish two sensible goals: (1) to be fair to innocent parties and (2) to encourage reasonable business practices nationwide. Both Munson and the Double Q were innocent parties. Jenkins was the bad guy. Why let Munson keep the livestock? Because he probably did all that a reasonable businessperson should do in buying cattle. He paid a fair (though low) price to a man who had all the normal ownership documents. The Code *could* place a greater burden on Munson and require, for example, that he investigate Jenkins's background. The law *could* force Munson to check the history of the cattle and find out how Jenkins acquired them. But such rules would hogtie the cattle industry. Most sales are legitimate; cattle ranchers and buyers must be able to buy and sell quickly, responding to market conditions and opportunities for profit.

Notice that in this case and most others, the Code focuses on basic fairness and sensible business practices. Munson wins because he acted reasonably and in good faith, *not* because he happens to hold certain certificates to the animals. The Code's authors have labored to get away from legal formalities and give results that make sense, as we see in the next section. As you encounter the various commercial problems, bear in mind these issues from the Chapter 2 ethics checklist: Who are the stakeholders? What are the alternatives? Has the process been fair? ◆

IDENTIFICATION, TITLE, AND INSURABLE INTEREST

Historically, courts settled disputes about legal interest by looking at one thing: title. The drafters of the UCC concluded that "title" was too abstract an answer for the assorted practical questions that arose. It could be hard to prove exactly who did have title, and it made no sense to settle a wide variety of business problems with one legal idea. Today, title is only one of several issues that a court will use to resolve conflicting

---

[1] We discuss voidability in detail in Chapter 14, on capacity and consent.

[2] For a cattle case that raises these and other issues, see *Rudiger Charolais Ranches v. Van De Graaf Ranches*, 994 F.2d 670, 1993 U.S. App. LEXIS 12412 (9th Cir. 1993).

interests in goods. *Identification* and *insurable interest* have become more important as title has diminished in significance. We can begin to understand all three doctrines if we examine how title passes from seller to buyer.

Existence and Identification

Title in goods can pass from one person to another only if the goods exist and have been identified to the contract.

Existence

Goods must exist before title can pass.[3] Although most goods do exist when people buy and sell them, some have not yet come into being, such as crops to be grown later. A farmer may contract to sell corn even before it is planted, but title to the corn cannot pass until the corn exists.

Identification

Goods must be identified to the contract before title can pass.[4] This means that the parties must have designated the specific goods being sold. Identification is an important concept that applies in other areas besides the passing of title. Often identification is obvious. If Dealer agrees to sell to Buyer a 60-foot motor yacht with identification number AKX472, the parties have identified the goods. But suppose Paintco agrees to sell Brushworks 1,000 gallons of white base paint at a specified price. Paintco has 25,000 gallons in its warehouse. Title cannot pass until Paintco identifies the specific gallons that will go to Brushworks.

The parties may agree in their contract how and when they will identify the goods.[5] They are free to identify them to the contract any way they want. Paintco and Brushworks might agree, for example, that within one week of signing the sales agreement, Paintco will mark appropriate gallons. If the gallons are stored 50 to a crate, then Paintco will have a worker stick a "Brushworks" label on 20 crates. Once the label is on, the goods are identified to the contract.

If the parties do not specify, identification will occur according to these rules:[6]

- Identification occurs when the parties enter into a contract if the agreement describes specific goods that already exist. If the Dealer agrees to sell a yacht and the parties include the ID number in their contract, the goods are identified (even though the parties never use the term "identify").

- For unborn animals, identification generally takes place when they are conceived; for crops, identification normally happens when they are planted.

- For other goods, identification occurs when the seller marks, ships, or in some other way indicates the exact goods that are going to the buyer.

Passing of Title

Once goods exist and are identified to the contract, title can pass from one person to another. **Title may pass in any manner on which the parties agree (UCC §2-401).** Once again, the Code allows the parties to control their affairs with commonsense

---

[3]   UCC §2-105(2).
[4]   UCC §2-401(1).
[5]   UCC §2-501(1).
[6]   UCC §2-501.

decisions. The parties can agree, for example, that title passes when the goods leave the manufacturer's factory, or when they reach the shipper who will transport them, or at any other time and place. If the parties do not agree on passing title, §2-401 decides. There are two possibilities:

- *When the goods are being moved*, title passes to the buyer when the seller completes whatever transportation it is obligated to do. Suppose the Seller is in Milwaukee and the Buyer is in Honolulu. The contract requires the Seller to deliver the goods to a ship in San Francisco. Title passes when the goods reach the ship.

- *When the goods are not being moved*, title passes when the seller delivers ownership documents to the buyer. Suppose Seller, located in Louisville, has already manufactured 5,000 baseball bats, which are stored in a warehouse in San Diego. Under the terms of their contract, Buyer will take possession of the bats at the warehouse. When Seller gives Buyer ownership documents, title passes. If the contract does not require Seller to give such documents, title passes when the parties form the contract. For example, if the Buyer owns the warehouse where the bats are stored, Buyer needs no documents to take possession; title passes when the parties reach agreement.

The following case raises issues of identification and title.

Code Provisions Discussed in this Case

Issue	Relevant Code Section
1. In which state were goods identified to the contracts?	UCC §2-501(1): The parties may agree in their contract how and when they will identify the goods; otherwise, they are identified as specified in §2-501 (a),(b) or (c).
2. In which state did title pass?	UCC §2-402: Title may pass in any manner on which the parties agree; otherwise, it passes as specified in §2-401.

CIRCUIT CITY STORES, INC. V. COMMISSIONER OF REVENUE

439 Mass. 629, 790 N.E.2d 636
Supreme Judicial Court of Massachusetts, 2003

Facts: Circuit City, which sold electronic goods, permitted customers to pay for goods at one store but pick them up at another. Because Massachusetts imposed a 5 percent sales tax on all goods sold in the state, but neighboring New Hampshire had no sales tax, many Massachusetts customers chose to save the 5 percent by collecting their goods at a New Hampshire store.

For these "alternative location" sales, the customer receipt indicated where the item had been bought and where it would be picked up. The receipt also said, "reserved," meaning simply that in the collection store, one less item was available to other customers. Until the merchandise was picked up, the customer could demand a refund or request to collect the item in the store where she had paid for it.

The Massachusetts Commissioner of Revenue demanded sales tax on the "alternative location" sales, claiming that it was a sale in Massachusetts because that is where title passed. Circuit City claimed that it owed no sales tax, because (1) the goods were not identified to the contract until a customer picked them up in New Hampshire, and (2) title passed in New Hampshire. The case reached the highest court in Massachusetts.

Issue: Where were the goods identified to the contract? Where did title to the goods pass?

Excerpts from Justice Greaney's Decision: We discern no explicit agreement between the parties concerning passage of title. Circuit City claims that testimony at the hearing with respect to its handling ▼

of alternative location sales (i.e., that Circuit City does not book the sale, credit the sale, or consider the sale to have occurred until the product is physically released to the customer) indicates an understanding between the parties that the transaction that takes place in Massachusetts constitutes, not a concluded sale, but only an order for merchandise. We disagree. The events transpiring at the cash register in Massachusetts reflect a significant degree of understanding between Circuit City and its customers that a sale, and not a mere deposit on an order, has occurred. The customer sales receipt, although not a document of title, contains a description of the item or items purchased, as well as the time and date of the sale. The record suggests that, in an ordinary case, any period of warranty relevant to the purchase begins as of this date. The purchase price reflected on the receipt represents full consideration paid for the merchandise. From the vantage point of the customer, the sales receipt represents proof of his or her right to the purchased merchandise. The fact the sale is credited to the Massachusetts store, and the commission accorded the sales associate in Massachusetts, in our view, is indicative of an intent on Circuit City's part that more than an order for merchandise takes place in Massachusetts.

As under the UCC, the inquiry centers, not on physical transfer of the goods, but on whether goods are placed within the actual or constructive possession of another. Here, Circuit City performed its obligations with respect to delivery when the sale was entered as an alternative location sale into Circuit City's system and the purchased merchandise was "reserved" for the customer at the designated location. It was the customer from that point on who assumed responsibility for acquiring physical receipt of the purchased merchandise.

It is clear that, under the UCC, no title can pass under a contract for sale "prior to their identification to the contract." G.L. c. 106, §2-401(1). This was also true in common law. We reject, however, Circuit City's argument that "identification to the contract" cannot be made in alternative location sales prior to the time that the merchandise is physically removed from inventory and the serial number is scanned in the New Hampshire store. The reserve notation marked on the customer sales receipt for the purchased merchandise sufficiently reflects its status of being set aside, or identified, to that particular transaction. The Circuit City district manager described the reserving system as moving merchandise to a "phantom" location to await customer pick up, and, indeed, the situation presented to the customer is just as though the merchandise actually is set aside and waiting for the customer at the pick-up counter. Because customers do not choose items in a store such as Circuit City by a particular serial number, but only by make and model, identification by serial number is unnecessary to the sale.

Affirmed. ∎

Insurable Interest

Closely related to identification and title is the idea of insurable interest. Anyone buying or selling expensive goods should make certain that the goods are insured. There are some limits, though, on who may insure goods, and when. As we saw in Chapter 13, a party may insure something—property, a human life—only when she has a legitimate interest in it. If the person buying the policy lacks a real interest in the thing insured, the law regards the policy as a gambling contract and considers it void.

When does someone have an insurable interest in goods? The Code gives one answer for buyers and one for sellers. **A buyer obtains an insurable interest when the goods are identified to the contract (UCC §2-501).** Suppose, in January, Grain Broker contracts with Farmer to buy his entire wheat crop. Neither party mentions "identification." In January, the crop is not identified, and Broker has no insurable interest. In May, after weeks of breaking the soil, Farmer plants his wheat crop. Once he has planted it, the goods are identified. The Broker, who now has an insurable interest, purchases insurance. In July, a drought destroys the crop, and the Broker never gets one grain of wheat. The Broker need not worry: he is insured.

The seller's insurable interest is different. **The seller retains an insurable interest in goods as long as she has either title to the goods or a security interest in them (UCC §2-501).** "Security interest" refers to cases in which the buyer still owes the seller some money for the goods. Suppose Flyola Manufacturing sells a small aircraft to WingIt, a dealer, for $300,000. WingIt pays $30,000 cash and agrees to pay interest on the balance until it sells the plane. Flyola has an insurable interest even while the aircraft is in WingIt's showroom and may purchase insurance anytime until WingIt pays off the last dime.

What this means is that a seller and buyer can have an insurable interest in the same goods simultaneously. Suppose the heavy metal band Gentle Bunnies hires Inkem Corp., in Minneapolis, to make 25,000 T-shirts with the Gentle Bunnies logo, for sale at rock concerts. The parties agree that the T-shirts are identified as soon as the logo is printed, and that title will pass when Inkem delivers the T-shirts to the office of the Bunnies' manager in Kansas City. Inkem obviously has an insurable interest while the company is making the T-shirts and continues to have an interest until it delivers the T-shirts in Kansas City. But the Gentle Bunnies' insurable interest arises the moment their logo is stamped on

Seller and Buyer may both have an insurable interest in these goods.

each shirt, so the Bunnies could insure the goods while they are still stored in Inkem's factory. Why would the Bunnies spend hard earned cash to insure goods they do not have? They may be uncertain that Inkem has obtained proper insurance.

In the following case, a car accident leads several insurance companies to dispute who owned the damaged auto. Each company wants to claim that the car belonged to—someone *else*.

Code Provisions Discussed in This Case

Issue	Relevant Code Section
1. Which party had title to the car?	UCC §2-401: Title to goods may pass in any manner on which the parties agree.
2. Did the seller have an insurable interest in the car?	UCC §2-501: The seller retains an insurable interest in the goods as long as it holds title to or a security interest in them.

VALLEY FORGE INSURANCE CO. V. GREAT AMERICAN INSURANCE CO.

1995 Ohio App. LEXIS 3939
Ohio Court of Appeals, 1995

Facts: On a Friday afternoon, Karl and Linda Kennedy went to John Nolan Ford to buy a new Ford Mustang. The parties signed all necessary documents, including a New Vehicle Buyer's Order, an Agreement to Provide Insurance, and credit applications. The Kennedys made a down payment, but could not arrange financing before the dealership closed. John Nolan Ford determined that the ▼

Kennedys were creditworthy and allowed them to take the car home for the weekend. That evening, Karl Kennedy permitted his brother-in-law, Cella, to take the car for a drive, along with a passenger named Campbell. Cella wrecked the car, injuring his passenger. Campbell sued, and the question was which insurance company was liable for all of the harm: John Nolan Ford's insurer (Milwaukee Mutual), Cella's insurer (Valley Forge), or Kennedy's insurer (Great American). The trial court ruled that title had never passed to Kennedy and found Milwaukee Mutual liable. The company appealed.

Issue: Had title passed to Kennedy at the time of the accident?

Excerpts from the *Per Curiam* Decision: Milwaukee argues that the risk of loss and insurable interest had passed because the car had been delivered. Further, Milwaukee states that the Kennedys explicitly agreed to provide insurance. Great American counters that the parties had "otherwise explicitly agreed" in the New Vehicle Buyer's Order that any interest in the car would not pass until "either the full purchase price is paid in cash or a satisfactory deferred payment agreement is executed by the parties[.]" No financing had been arranged at the time of the accident.

Two terms of the New Vehicle Buyer's Order apply to the situation at bar. Under the "Agreement" provision, the contract states that "it is expressly agreed that the purchaser acquires no right, title or interest in or to the property which he agrees to purchase hereunder until such property is delivered to him and either the full purchase price is paid in cash or a satisfactory deferred payment agreement is executed by the parties hereto[.]"

Milwaukee also argues that the Kennedys explicitly agreed to provide insurance by signing the "Agreement to Provide Insurance." While the agreement does state that the Kennedys agreed to provide insurance, it is not clear when the Kennedys were to obtain the insurance. In fact, because the agreement refers to an "instalment [sic] contract," it is possible that the Kennedys were to provide insurance once a financing agreement was reached. In light of the fact that the agreement is ambiguous, we construe the contract strictly against the drafter and hold that any agreement to provide insurance was to take effect after financing was obtained.

We hold that because the parties had otherwise agreed that interest in the car, including insurable interest, would not pass until the financing was complete, John Nolan Ford still had the risk of loss and the insurable interest when the accident occurred. [Affirmed.] ∎

WHEN THE SELLER HAS IMPERFECT TITLE

Bona Fide Purchaser

Some people are sleazy, and sales law must accommodate that reality. In the chapter opener we saw a scam artist purchase cattle from a respectable ranch and sell them to an honest dealer. The bad guy skipped town, leaving a dispute between two innocent companies. Either the original owner (the ranch) or the buyer (the cattle dealer) must bear the loss. Who loses?

The Question: Who Must Suffer the Loss?		
Owner ➡	Bad Guy ➡	Buyer
(has valid title)	(obtains goods from Owner and sells)	(buys goods from Bad Guy)

First we need to know what kind of title Bad Guy obtains: Is it void or voidable? If Bad Guy *steals* the goods from Owner, Bad Guy obtains **void title, which is no title at all.** When Bad Guy sells the goods to Buyer, she also gets *no title at all.* Abe steals Marvin's BMW and promptly sells it to Elaine for $35,000 cash. Two weeks later the police locate the car. When Abe stole it, he obtained void title. He had no title to convey to Elaine and that is what she received—none. Elaine must return the car to Marvin and suffer the $35,000 loss for Abe's theft. This policy makes sense because Marvin has done nothing wrong. If the law permitted Elaine to get valid title, it would encourage theft.

If Bad Guy *purchases* the goods from Owner, using fraud or deception, he obtains **voidable title, meaning limited rights in the goods, inferior to those of the owner.** The owner should be able to recover the goods from the Bad Guy, but not from anyone else who ends up with them. Suppose Emily agrees to buy Marvin's *other* car, a Jeep. She gives him a check for $20,000 and he signs the vehicle over to her. Emily knows her check will bounce; she has used fraud to obtain the car. As a result, Emily obtains only voidable title. If Marvin learns of the deception before Emily sells the car to someone else, he will get his Jeep back.

Unfortunately, Emily is slippery, not stupid. She quickly sells the Jeep to Seth for cash. By the time Emily's check bounces, Emily is gone and Seth has the car. Who keeps the Jeep? Seth wins the car if he is a bona fide purchaser. **A person with voidable title has power to transfer valid title for value to a good faith purchaser, generally called a *bona fide purchaser* or *BFP*.**[7]

Seth can prove that he is a bona fide purchaser by showing two things:

- That he gave value for the goods, *and*
- That he acted in good faith.

It is generally easy for purchasers to show that they gave value. The buyer could give cash or a check or could agree to extinguish a debt, that is, to forgive some money that Bad Guy owed. The real issue becomes whether the buyer acted in good faith. If Seth paid a reasonable purchase price and Emily showed him convincing identification and signed over to him all purchase documents, Seth acted in good faith. He keeps the Jeep and Marvin loses.

On the other hand, suppose Seth knows the brand new Jeep is worth more than $28,000. Emily seems in a frantic hurry to sell the car. She cannot produce the car's registration but promises to send it within three days. Emily's conduct together with the $8,000 discount would make a reasonable person suspicious. Seth is not acting in good faith and therefore is not a bona fide purchaser. Marvin receives the car back, and Seth pays dearly for his automotive lust.

The Answer: Who Loses?

Owner →	Bad Guy ⟶	→ Buyer
The Owner has good title.	(1) Bad Guy STEALS the goods, obtaining *void* title (no title) and sells to the Buyer.	Buyer receives no title.
	(2) Bad Guy PURCHASES the goods, obtaining *voidable* title, and sells to the Buyer.	(a) If the Buyer gives value for the goods and acts in good faith, he is a BFP and receives good title. (b) If the Buyer is not a BFP, he receives no title.

In the following case we definitely have a bad guy. Did he obtain voidable title? Could he pass on good title to someone else?

---

[7]   UCC §2-403(1).

PEOPLE V. SIMMONS

2003 WL 21350737
California Court of Appeals, 2003

Facts: Scott Simmons evidently had a sentimental streak, which is why he paid $70,000 for a 15-carat, heart-shaped diamond ring from Archer Estate Jewelers. He had a different streak, as well, which is why he used a fraudulent check to make the purchase.

Simmons took the diamond, and the accompanying gemological certificate, to a jewelry store/pawnshop operated by Glenn Verdult. Verdult bought the ring from Simmons, paying with a $40,000 cashier's check. Simmons was arrested for passing a bad check, and the police seized the rock.

The trial court awarded the ring to Archer and Verdult appealed.

Issue: Who was entitled to the diamond ring?

Excerpts from Judge Gaut's Decision: Generally, a thief cannot convey valid title to property. A thief possesses only void title and, therefore, can transfer only that which he has. Consequently, any subsequent purchaser has no valid interest in the property.

Not so where the thief acquires the property by a transaction of purchase. "Purchase" is defined by the code as a "taking by sale, discount, negotiation, mortgage, pledge, lien, issue or reissue, gift or any other voluntary transaction creating an interest in the property." Thus, only voluntary transactions can constitute transactions of purchase. Based on the code definition of a purchase as a voluntary transaction, case law from other states reasons that a thief who wrongfully takes the goods against the will of the owner is not a purchaser. On the other hand, a swindler who fraudulently induces the victim to deliver the goods voluntarily is a purchaser under the code. Thus, if the original seller voluntarily assents to the transaction and delivers the property, then the thief obtains voidable title. A person with voidable title may transfer good title in an ordinary transaction for value to a good faith purchaser.

Here, Archer voluntarily delivered the diamond to Simmons. The original transfer was a transaction of purchase. Although tainted with obvious fraud or thievery (false pretenses, not larceny), Archer's employee freely exchanged the diamond for a personal check in the amount of $70,000. Only afterward did Archer discover that the bank would not honor Simmons's check. He then stood in the position of an unpaid seller. But he voluntarily relinquished title to Simmons.

Through this transaction, Simmons acquired voidable title. Simmons, therefore, had power to transfer good title to a good faith purchaser for value.

A good faith purchaser is a person who, among other things, takes delivery of the goods pursuant to a preexisting contract for purchase and is honest in fact in the transaction. Whether a person qualifies as a good faith purchaser is determined by applying the reasonable person standard. For instance, if the goods are offered at an unusually low price, a reasonable person would suspect that the goods are stolen and, thus, be put on notice that he may be entering an illegitimate transaction. Usually, whether a person qualifies as a good faith purchaser involves a credibility determination to be made by the trier of fact.

In this case, Verdult stated that Simmons entered his jewelry store and pawnshop with the 15.05-carat, heart-shaped diamond. Simmons also provided Verdult with the gemological certificate for the diamond. Simmons purchased the diamond with a cashier's check in the amount of $40,000. The trial court did not determine, under these circumstances, whether Verdult was a good faith purchaser.

The record indicates that the court awarded the diamond to Archer after rejecting Verdult's argument that Simmons transferred voidable title. The court's ruling, however, was based on the erroneous assumptions that Archer was the rightful owner and, thus, Simmons and Verdult had no interest in the diamond. As discussed above, Simmons had voidable title and Verdult may have had good title. Therefore remand is necessary to give the court an opportunity to decide whether Verdult was a good faith purchaser, as stated above, thereby entitling him to ownership of the diamond.

We reverse and remand this case for the trial court to determine whether Verdult was a good faith purchaser and, based upon this determination, to reinstate the judgment or otherwise enter judgment consistent with the court's factual finding. ∎

Because a thief conveys no title, the law puts pressure on buyers to make sure that their sellers have a valid claim to the goods. As we mentioned, this has the laudable result of discouraging theft. However, it can be difficult to spot a thief. An innocent buyer may suffer an enormous loss when stolen goods are returned to the rightful owner. In economic terms, the law is requiring the buyer to spend whatever time and money is needed to be certain of the seller's title. A buyer who refuses to incur that expense may pay heavily later on, when stolen goods are repossessed.

Other nations allocate the costs differently. In most European countries, a purchaser who has no reason to suspect she is buying stolen goods *generally obtains good title.* An art collector in Milan who makes a bona fide purchase of a Degas painting from a dealer in Zurich can typically keep the work, even if the picture later turns out to have been stolen. Compared to American law, European countries have transferred the financial risk from buyer to owner. In Europe, it is the *owner* of goods who must spend the time and money necessary to make certain that her goods are safe from thieves, because she will not be able to recover stolen articles that are sold to a good faith purchaser.

This difference in cost allocation can have profound emotional impact. During the Holocaust years of 1933–1945, Nazis stole from European Jews more than 200,000 paintings and sculptures, worth billions of dollars. After the war, the German government returned many of the works to the original owners, their survivors, or the country from which they had been looted. Nonetheless, hundreds of people have come forward claiming ownership of paintings that hang in public museums or private homes. Critics claim that European governments made only desultory efforts to locate missing heirs because they wanted to keep valuable works. And the present owners are legally protected, because good faith buyers *do* obtain valid title. Fortunately, most European museums have not used this legal loophole to retain works when presented with valid evidence of theft. However, it is unclear whether private owners of stolen art have been so generous. ◆

*uP*date

Find a current article concerning a dispute over art that has been stolen and sold to a bona fide purchaser. What arguments have the two sides made? In your view, which party has the stronger case, and why? ◆

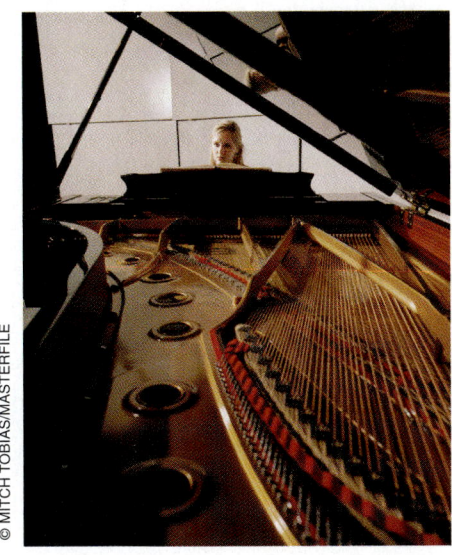

© MITCH TOBIAS/MASTERFILE

Is someone else entitled to buy your beloved piano?

Entrustment

Your old Steinway grand piano needs a complete rebuilding. You hire Fred Showpan, Inc., a company that repairs and sells instruments. Showpan hauls your piano away and promises to return it in perfect shape. Two months later, you are horrified to spot Showpan's showroom boarded up and pasted with bankruptcy notices. Worse still, you learn that Fred sold your beloved instrument to a customer, Frankie List. When you track down List, he gives you nothing but a sonatina, claiming he paid $18,000 for the piano and likes it just fine. Is he entitled to keep it?

Quite likely he is. Section 2-403(1), the BFP provision we just discussed, would not apply because Showpan did not *purchase* the piano from you. But §2-403(2) does apply. This is the "entrustment" section, and it covers cases in which the owner of goods voluntarily leaves them with a merchant, who then sells the goods without permission. According to **UCC §2-403(2), any entrusting to a merchant who deals in goods of that kind gives him power to transfer all rights of the entruster to a buyer in the ordinary course of business.** There are several important ideas in this section:

Entrusting means delivering goods to a merchant or permitting the merchant to retain them.[8] In the piano example, you clearly entrusted goods to a merchant. If you buy a used car from Fast Eddie's Fast Wheels and then leave it there for a week, while you obtain insurance, you have entrusted it to Eddie.

Deals in Goods of That Kind

The purpose of the section is to protect innocent buyers who enter a store, see the goods they expect to find, and purchase something, having no idea that the storekeeper is illegally selling the property of others. Buyers should not have to demand proof of title to everything in the store. Further, if someone has to bear the risk, let it be the person who has entrusted her goods; she is in the best position to investigate the merchant's integrity. But this protection does not extend to a buyer who arrives at a vacuum cleaner store and buys an $80,000 mobile home parked in the lot.

In the Ordinary Course of Business

This means that the buyer must act in good faith, without knowing that the sale violates the owner's rights. If Frank List buys your piano assuming that Showpan owns it, he has acted in good faith. If Frank was your neighbor and recognized your instrument, he is not buying in the ordinary course of business and must hand over the piano.

Of course, a merchant who violates the owner's rights is liable to that owner. If Showpan were still in business when you discovered your loss, you could sue and recover the value of the piano. The problems arise when the merchant is unable to reimburse the owner. The following case explores these concepts. Who gets the fancy car?

you Be The Judge

MADRID V. BLOOMINGTON AUTO COMPANY, INC.

782 N.E.2d 386
Court of Appeals of Indiana, 2003

Facts: Michael and Pamela Madrid went to University Motors, where they had previously bought used cars, and asked its owner, Gary Pratt, to find them a Lincoln Navigator with low miles and all the best options. Pratt located a year-old Navigator at Royal Lincoln/Mercury.

Pratt asked Royal to drive the car to University Motors, so that prospective customers could look at it. The two companies had worked this way in the past. If the customer liked the vehicle, he paid Royal, which gave a finder's fee to University Motors.

Royal delivered the Navigator to University, retaining the certificate of title, a built-in mobile phone, and the owner's manual. The Madrids saw the car later that day, liked it, and bought it, paying *University* $41,500 and taking the car away. Pratt, who said that University owned the Navigator, promised to deliver the title, mobile phone, and other items the next day. He never did so, despite frequent calls from the Madrids.

The Madrids sued to obtain the car's title. Royal joined the case, seeking a judgment that it owned the Navigator. The trial court gave judgment to Royal, for three reasons: first, University was not a merchant who dealt in goods of the same kind as Royal; second, Royal did not entrust the car to University; and third, the Madrids did not buy in the ordinary course of business, because they should have realized University was not an authorized Lincoln dealer. The Madrids appealed.

You Be the Judge: Who owns the Navigator?

▼

---

[8] For a discussion of who is and who is not a merchant, see Chapter 19.

Argument for the Madrids: University sells used cars, Royal new autos. To the average consumer, these are both car dealers, period. They deal in the same kind of goods. The UCC distinction was meant to protect merchants who leave, say a motorcycle with a fine art gallery. The bike buyer would be on notice that the gallery was not a normal motorcycle dealer. Not so, here.

Royal left the Navigator with University for a customer to inspect. Royal hoped that University would conclude a deal to sell the car. There is a good one-word description of what Royal did: entrustment. What Royal is really arguing is that they wish they had not entrusted the car. Too late.

The Madrids had no reason to think there was anything wrong with this sale. The Code's policy is simply stated: Between two innocent victims, the loss falls on the one better equipped to avoid the harm in the first place. Royal should choose its business partners more carefully. The Madrids acted in good faith and should keep the Navigator.

Argument for Royal: This was a pristine Navigator that most consumers would expect to find only in a new car dealership. University does not get its hands on such fine automobiles (for good reasons, it turns out). The Code expects consumers to ask a few reasonable questions when goods are found in an unlikely place. The Madrids were too eager to drive away, and must pay for their disingenuousness.

Royal did not entrust the Navigator. Entrusting means delivering goods to a merchant or permitting the merchant to retain them. Royal was attempting to work with University to arrange a mutually beneficial sale to *a specific customer*. Royal did not simply drop off a $40,000 car and say, "See if you can unload this." Royal assumed that either University would notify it of a deal, instructing Royal to come complete paperwork, or University would return the car the same day. Having worked with University in the past, Royal had no reason to expect the company to sink to this level of fraud.

The Madrids acted in bad faith. When a dealer claims to own the car, but cannot hand over title or a pre-installed mobile phone, something is seriously wrong and any consumer should realize it. You cannot buy a $40,000 car under suspicious circumstances and then complain when the fraud is exposed. ∎

CREDITOR'S RIGHTS

In the entrustment section, we considered the rights of the *owner* of goods and how her interests might conflict with those of a merchant and a buyer. A related issue concerns a *creditor*, that is, someone with a financial stake in the goods that the merchant is selling. Suppose a merchant borrows money from a finance company to buy fish tanks with built-in televisions, to entertain bored guppies. The finance company is now the merchant's creditor. The merchant agrees that when she sells any of the TV Tanks, she will pay a percentage of the proceeds to the finance company. But if she sells tanks to a buyer without giving one cent to her creditor, does the buyer get to keep the fish tanks? To determine an answer, we need to know whether the sale was made in the ordinary course of business.

Ordinary Sales

Article 9 of the Code controls the rights of secured parties. We look closely at it in Chapter 26. Briefly, UCC §9-320 governs the rights of a creditor, a merchant, and a buyer in the ordinary course of business. Suppose the Nickel & Dime Bank loans Yoyo's Yacht Sales $100,000 to purchase two yachts wholesale. The yachts arrive at Yoyo's and remain in the showroom, but Nickel & Dime retains a security interest in both. If Yoyo fails to repay its loan, the bank is entitled to seize the yachts. Further, Yoyo is obligated to notify the bank immediately of a sale and hold the money until the bank gets its share. Unaware of Nickel & Dime's security interest, Liz pays $80,000 for one of the yachts. Yoyo grabs the money and sails into the horizon, leaving the bank in his wake. May Nickel & Dime take Liz's new yacht? No. **UCC §9-320 generally permits a buyer in the ordinary course of business to take the goods free and clear of the security interest.**

Naturally, there are exceptions, and you will *not* want to miss the full story in the secured transactions chapter. But for present purposes, the ordinary customer who purchases goods from a store will keep them regardless of any problems the store has with its creditors. The policy behind the law is obvious: to enable consumers to buy and merchants to sell. If you had to trace the chain of title before you bought a pair of sneakers at Discount City, commerce would grind to a halt and many of us would be barefoot. Section 9-320 keeps things flowing along.

Bulk Sales

Beryl, a rich college student who likes fast cars, strolls into Pearl's High Performance Cars and buys a silver Jaguar. "I think," she says, blithely surveying the showroom and pointing at a yellow Lamborghini, "I'll have that lovely one as well." Before she is done, Beryl buys three Ferraris, an Aston Martin, and four Porsches, along with Pearl's desks, chairs, water cooler, and filing cabinet—everything in the store. Pearl has made a bulk sale. **A bulk sale is one that includes most or all of the inventory in a store.** Historically, these transactions were considered troublesome, because a retailer could purchase his entire inventory on credit, sell it all to one buyer, and flee without paying his creditors. To prevent such fraud, **UCC Article 6 places special obligations on both parties in a bulk transaction,** requiring sellers and buyers to make sure that creditors are notified *before* the sale takes place, so that the creditors can protect their interests.

Today, though, the danger of bulk sale fraud has largely disappeared. Article 9 of the UCC makes it easy and inexpensive for creditors to protect their security interests (see Chapter 26). As a result, **most but not all states have repealed Article 6.** A bulk sale is generally treated like any other.

Returnable Goods

Sometimes the seller will allow the buyer to return goods even when he has no complaints about their quality. This, too, can create a problem for creditors. A bank may extend a loan to a business based on the inventory. The bank is willing to lend money because it can seize the goods if the merchant fails to pay on time. But what if the merchant *does not own* some of the goods, because he intends to return them to the original owner? If the merchant fails to pay his loan, who gets the goods—the creditor (bank) or the owner of the goods? The Code considers two types of contract that permit a buyer to return goods.

Sale on Approval

If a buyer takes goods intending to use them herself, but has the right to return the goods to the seller, it is a "sale on approval." Max manufactures bar code readers, the machines that scan magnetic bar codes on merchandise. He wants to sell half a dozen to Pinky's Superette, but Pinky isn't sure the machines are worth the price. To encourage Pinky, Max allows her to take the machines and try them out. At the end of 60 days she may return them or pay full price. There really is no *sale* until Pinky has formally accepted the goods.

Under UCC §2-326(2), in a sale on approval, the goods *are not* subject to the buyer's creditors until the buyer accepts them. Suppose Pinky has borrowed $200,000 from the bank and has given a security interest "in all goods in the store now or in the future." The bar code machines are "goods in the store," and if Pinky fails to pay her loans, the bank will try to seize the equipment. But this is a sale on approval, and the bank has no right to Max's machines.

at RISK

A finance company will often extend credit based on a merchant's inventory. A creditor considering such a loan must determine what goods, if any, are "sale on approval," since those goods give the creditor no security. ◆

Sale or Return

If a buyer takes goods intending to *resell* them, but has the right to return the goods to the seller, it is a "sale or return." This is generally the same as a *consignment*. The owner is called the *consignor* and the buyer is the *consignee*. Yvonne runs a used car lot. Trent offers to sell Yvonne his used Mustang auto for $937, but it is in such poor shape Yvonne doubts there's a teenager in the county dumb enough to buy it. "My brother's real dumb," Trent suggests hopefully. But Yvonne offers instead to place the car on her lot and try to sell it. She will pay Trent nothing for the car but will keep 20 percent of the price if she can sell it. The name "sale or return" is misleading, since Trent has sold nothing so far and Yvonne will never be a true buyer.

Under UCC §2-326, in a sale or return, the goods are subject to the claims of the buyer's creditors. Suppose Yvonne fails to pay back some loans. Her creditors will instantly round up the Mustang, and Trent will never get a dime for his car.[9]

The issues we have looked at thus far involve someone doing something wrong, often a scoundrel selling goods that he never owned. Now we turn to cases where there may be no wrongdoer.

RISK OF LOSS

Accidents hurt businesses. When goods are damaged, the law may again need to decide whether it is the seller or buyer who must suffer the loss. In the cases we have seen thus far, the parties were arguing, "It's mine!"—"Like heck, it's *mine!*" In risk of loss cases, the parties are generally shouting, "It was yours!"—"No way, chump, it was *yours!*"

Athena, a seafood wholesaler, is gearing up for the Super Bowl, which will bring 110,000 hungry visitors to her city for a week of eating and gabbing. Athena orders 25,000 lobsters from Poseidon's Fishfoods, 500 miles distant, and simultaneously contracts with a dozen local restaurants to resell them. Poseidon loads the lobsters, still kicking, into refrigerated railcars owned by Demeter Trucking. But halfway to the city,

---

[9]   **Article 2 Alert.** Section 2-326 previously permitted a consignor to protect her goods from a creditor by taking any of three specified steps. Those three protective steps *have been deleted* (the changes are not mere proposals), so that this section conforms to Article 9 revisions. Anyone considering consignment should be aware of the risk of losing goods to a creditor, and should take appropriate steps to protect them pursuant to Article 9.

the train collides with a prison van. None of the convicts escape but the lobsters do, hurtling into the swamps from which they are never recaptured. Athena loses all of her profits and sues. As luck would have it, Demeter Trucking had foolishly economized by letting its insurance lapse. Poseidon claims the goods were out of its hands. Who loses?

The common law answered this problem by looking at which party had title to the goods at the time of loss. But the Code again rejects this abstract concept, striving once more for a practical solution. The UCC permits the parties to agree on who bears the risk of loss. **UCC §2-509(4) states that the parties may allocate the risk of loss any way they wish.**

Often the parties will do just that, avoiding arguments and litigation in the event of an accident. As part of her agreement with Poseidon, Athena should have included a one-sentence clause, such as "Seller bears all risk of loss until the lobsters are delivered to Athena's warehouse." As long as the parties make their risk allocation clear, the Code will enforce it.

Shipping Terms

The parties can quickly and easily allocate the risk of loss by using common shipping terms that the Code defines. FOB means free on board; FAS indicates free alongside a ship; and CIF stands for cost, insurance, and freight. By combining these designations with other terms, the parties can specify risk in a few words:

- *FOB place of shipment.* The seller is obligated to put the goods into the possession of the carrier at the place named. The seller bears the expense and risk until they are in the carrier's possession. From that moment onward, the buyer bears the risk.

- *FOB place of destination.* The seller must deliver the goods at the place named and bears the expense *and risk* of shipping.

- *FAS a named vessel.* The seller at his expense *and risk* must deliver the goods alongside the named vessel and obtain proper receipts.

- *CIF.* The price includes in a lump sum the cost of the goods and the insurance and freight to the named destination.

- *C & F.* The price includes in a lump sum the cost of the goods and freight, but *not* insurance.

Thus, if Athena had put a clause in her contract saying, "FOB Athena's warehouse," Poseidon would have born the risk of any loss up to the time the lobsters were unloaded in Athena's possession. Poseidon would then have known that it must insure the lobsters during transit. For an example of all shipping terms, as they actually appear in the statutes of one state (Maine), see **http://janus.state.me.us/legis/statutes**.

When the Parties Fail to Allocate the Risk

If the parties fail to specify when the risk passes from seller to buyer, the Code provides the answer. When neither party breached the contract, §2-509 determines the risk; when a party has breached the contract, §2-510 governs. The full analysis of risk is somewhat intricate, so we first supply you with a short version: **When neither party has breached, the risk of loss generally passes from seller to buyer when the seller has transported the goods as far as he is obligated to. When a party has breached, the risk of loss generally lies with that party.**

And now, for the courageous, the full version of how the Code allocates the risk of loss when the parties failed to specify it.

When Neither Party Breaches

In the example of Athena and Poseidon, both parties did what they were supposed to do, so there was no breach of contract. To settle these cases, we need to know whether the contract obligated the seller to ship the goods or whether the goods were handled in some other way. There are three possibilities: (1) the contract required the seller to ship the goods, or (2) the contract involved a bailment, or (3) other cases.

© AP PHOTO/MAERSK INC.

Most sales contracts are shipment contracts. *What risk does the buyer assume in such a deal?*

If the Seller Must Ship the Goods. Most contracts require the seller to arrange shipment of the goods. In a *shipment contract*, the seller must deliver the goods *to a carrier*, which will then transport the goods to the buyer. The carrier might be a trucking company, railroad, airline, or ship, and is generally located near the seller's place of business. **In a shipment contract, the risk passes to the buyer when the seller delivers the goods to the carrier.** Suppose Old Wood, in North Carolina, agrees to sell $100,000 worth of furniture to Pioneer Company, in Anchorage. The contract requires Old Wood to deliver the goods to Great Northern Railroad lines in Chicago. From North Carolina to Chicago, Old Wood bears the risk of loss. Once the furniture is on board the train in Chicago, the risk of loss passes to Pioneer. If the train derails in Montana and every desk and chair is squashed, Pioneer owes the full $100,000 to Old Wood.

In a *destination contract*, the seller is responsible for delivering the goods *to the buyer*. In a destination contract, risk passes to the buyer when the goods reach the destination. If the contract required Old Wood to deliver the furniture to Pioneer's warehouse in Anchorage, then Old Wood bears the loss for the entire trip. If the train travels 3,000 miles and then plunges off a bridge in Alaska, 45 feet from its destination, Old Wood picks up the tab.

If There Is a Bailment. Freezem Corp. produces 500 room air conditioners and stores them in Every-Ware's Warehouse. This is a **bailment, meaning that one person or company is legally holding goods for the benefit of another.** Freezem is the **bailor,** the one who owns the goods, and Every-Ware is the **bailee,** the one with temporary possession. (For a sample bailment contract, see **http://agebb.missouri.edu/mgt/agcontract/hosoy.htm.**) Suppose Freezem agrees to sell 300 of its air conditioners to Keep-Kool Appliances. KeepKool does not need the machines in its store for six months, so it plans to keep them at Every-Ware's until then. But two weeks after Freezem and KeepKool make their deal, Every-Ware burns to the ground. Who bears the loss of the 300 air conditioners? **If the contract requires a bailee to hold the goods for the buyer, the risk passes when the buyer obtains documents entitling her to possession, or when the bailee acknowledges her right to the goods.** If fire broke out in Every-Ware's before KeepKool received any documents enabling it to take the air conditioners away, then the loss would fall on Freezem.

Other Cases. The great majority of contracts involve either shipment by the seller or a bailment. In the remaining cases, if the seller is a *merchant*, risk passes to the buyer on receipt. This means that a merchant is only off the hook if the buyer actually accepts the goods. If the seller is *not a merchant*, risk passes when the seller tenders the goods,

Exhibit 20.1

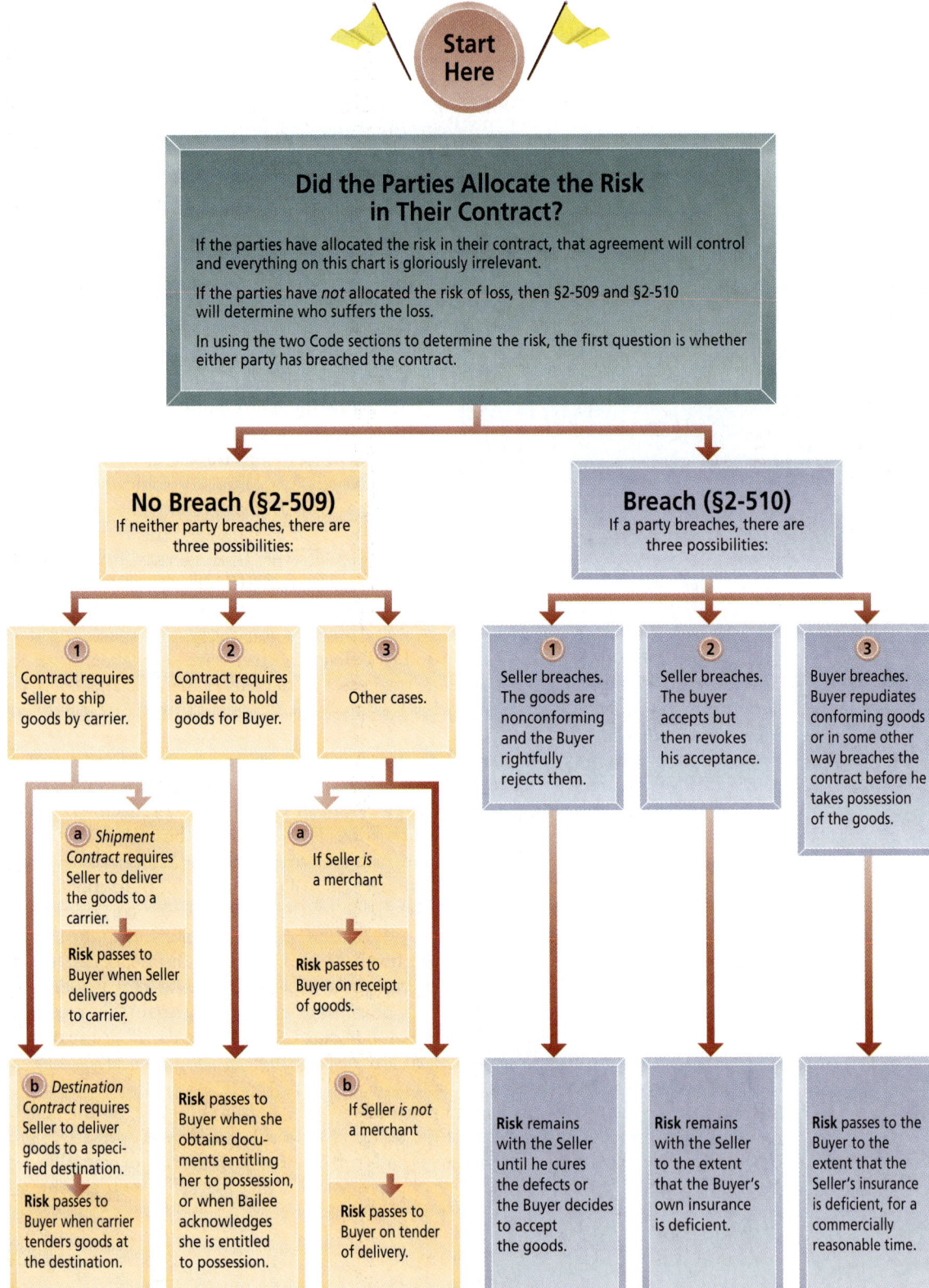

Start Here

Did the Parties Allocate the Risk in Their Contract?

If the parties have allocated the risk in their contract, that agreement will control and everything on this chart is gloriously irrelevant.

If the parties have *not* allocated the risk of loss, then §2-509 and §2-510 will determine who suffers the loss.

In using the two Code sections to determine the risk, the first question is whether either party has breached the contract.

No Breach (§2-509)
If neither party breaches, there are three possibilities:

Breach (§2-510)
If a party breaches, there are three possibilities:

1 Contract requires Seller to ship goods by carrier.

2 Contract requires a bailee to hold goods for Buyer.

3 Other cases.

1 Seller breaches. The goods are nonconforming and the Buyer rightfully rejects them.

2 Seller breaches. The buyer accepts but then revokes his acceptance.

3 Buyer breaches. Buyer repudiates conforming goods or in some other way breaches the contract before he takes possession of the goods.

a *Shipment Contract* requires Seller to deliver the goods to a carrier.

Risk passes to Buyer when Seller delivers goods to carrier.

a If Seller *is* a merchant

Risk passes to Buyer on receipt of goods.

b *Destination Contract* requires Seller to deliver goods to a specified destination.

Risk passes to Buyer when carrier tenders goods at the destination.

Risk passes to Buyer when she obtains documents entitling her to possession, or when Bailee acknowledges she is entitled to possession.

b If Seller *is not* a merchant

Risk passes to Buyer on tender of delivery.

Risk remains with the Seller until he cures the defects or the Buyer decides to accept the goods.

Risk remains with the Seller to the extent that the Buyer's own insurance is deficient.

Risk passes to the Buyer to the extent that the Seller's insurance is deficient, for a commercially reasonable time.

meaning that she makes them available to the buyer. The Code is giving more protection to buyers when they deal with a merchant. But if the buyer is purchasing from a non-merchant, the Code assumes they are on equal footing, and the seller is relieved of liability when she merely tenders the goods.

When One Party Breaches

Still there? Excellent. We now look at how the Code allocates risk when one of the parties does breach. Again there are three possibilities: (1) seller breaches and buyer rejects; (2) seller breaches, buyer accepts, but then revokes; or (3) buyer breaches.

Seller Breaches and Buyer Rejects. PlayStore, a sporting goods store, orders 75 canoes from Floataway. PlayStore specifies that the canoes must be 12 feet long, lightweight metal, dark green. Floataway delivers 75 canoes to Truckit, a trucking company. When Truckit's trucks arrive, PlayStore finds that the canoes are the right material and color, but 18 feet long. PlayStore rejects the craft, and Truckit heads back to Floataway. But one of the trucks is hijacked and the 25 canoes it carries are never recovered. Floataway demands its money for the 25 lost canoes. Who loses?

Floataway had delivered **nonconforming goods,** that is, merchandise that is different from what the contract specified. A buyer has a right to reject nonconforming goods. **When the buyer rejects nonconforming goods, the risk of loss remains with the seller until he cures the defect or the buyer decides to accept the goods.** In our example, Floataway must suffer the loss for the stolen canoes. If PlayStore had decided to accept the canoes, even though they were the wrong size, then the risk would have passed to the sports store.

Seller Breaches, Buyer Accepts, but Then Revokes. PlayStore orders 200 tennis rackets from High Strung. When the rackets arrive, they seem fine, so the store accepts them. But then a salesperson notices that the grips are loose. Every racket has the same problem. PlayStore returns the rackets to High Strung, but they are destroyed when a blimp crashes into the delivery truck. **When a buyer accepts goods but then rightfully revokes acceptance, the risk remains with the seller to the extent the buyer's insurance will not cover the loss.** If PlayStore's insurance covers the damaged rackets, there is no problem. If PlayStore's insurance does not cover the loss of goods in transit, High Strung must pay.

Buyer Breaches. One last time. PlayStore orders 60 tents from ExploreMore. About the time the tents leave the factory, PlayStore decides to drop its line of camping goods and specialize in team sports. PlayStore notifies ExploreMore it wants to explore less, and will not pay. The tents are destroyed in a collision involving a prison van and a train carrying lobsters. This time, PlayStore is liable. **When a buyer breaches the contract before taking possession, it assumes the risk of loss to the extent the seller's insurance is deficient.**

Exhibit 20.1 on page 460 should clarify.

In the following case, neither party breached, so §2-509 governs.

Code Provisions Discussed in This Case	
Issue	**Relevant Code Section**
1. Did the parties create a bailment?	In a bailment, one person legally holds goods for the benefit of another.
2. Which party bore the risk of the horse's death?	UCC §2-509(2): If the contract requires a bailee to hold the goods for the buyer, the risk passes when the buyer obtains documents entitling her to possession, or when the bailee acknowledges her right to the goods.

HARMON V. DUNN

1997 Tenn. App. LEXIS 217
Tennessee Court of Appeals, 1997

Facts: Bess Harmon owned a two-year-old Tennessee Walking Horse named Phantom Recall. Harmon, who lived in Tennessee, boarded her horse with Steve Dunn, at his stables in Florence, Alabama. Dunn cared for Phantom Recall and showed him at equestrian events. Harmon instructed Dunn to sell the horse for $25,000, and Dunn arranged for his friend Scarbrough to buy the colt. On June 30, Dunn delivered Scarbrough's $25,000 check to Harmon, who handed over the horse's certificate of registration and a "transfer of ownership" document. That night at a horse show Dunn told Scarbrough that he had delivered the check and had the ownership papers in his car. Dunn did not actually give the documents to his friend. Scarbrough knew that Phantom Recall was at Dunn's stable, where Scarbrough had boarded other horses. Sadly, the colt developed colitis and died suddenly, on July 4. Scarbrough stopped payment on his check, and Harmon sued for her money. The trial court found for Harmon and Scarbrough appealed.

Issue: Which party bore the risk of Phantom Recall's death?

Excerpts from Judge Farmer's Decision: [UCC §2-509 states:] Risk of loss in the absence of breach. . . .

   (2) Where the goods are held by a bailee to be delivered without being moved, the risk of loss passes to the buyer:
   (a) on his receipt of a negotiable document of title covering the goods, or
   (b) on acknowledgment by the bailee of the buyer's right to possession of the goods, or
   (c) after his receipt of a non-negotiable document of title or other written direction to deliver. . .

We conclude that the facts before us clearly establish a bailor-bailee relationship between Harmon and Dunn. It is not disputed that the latter was the agent of the former. Here, it was agreed that Dunn would train and care for Phantom Recall at the Dunn Stables in Florence, Alabama. He was also responsible for transporting the horse to various shows. The record establishes that prior to the horse's death, he had been entered and shown by Dunn himself in three separate events.

Having established Dunn a bailee for purposes of [§2-509(2)] and in the absence of any prior arrangement with Dunn or Harmon that the horse be delivered elsewhere upon purchase from the latter, we find that the risk of loss passed to Scarbrough if and when the applicable provisions under subsection (2) occurred. Subsection (2)(a) and (b) provide that the risk of loss passes to the buyer "on his receipt of a negotiable document of title covering the goods; or on acknowledgment by the bailee of the buyer's right to possession of the goods."

We find that Scarbrough received the ability to control possession of the horse no later than July 1 irrespective of the fact that he did not actually receive physical possession of the ownership documents at that time. The documents which were necessary for transfer of ownership and taking possession of the horse were already in the hands of the bailee. We find an actual physical back and forth exchange between the two unnecessary under these facts where the bailee and the seller's agent are one and the same. Certainly Scarbrough had the ability to control possession of the horse no later than July 1 when he was made aware that Dunn had the transfer papers.

[Affirmed.] ∎

Chapter Conclusion

The Code enables the parties in most commercial transactions to control their own destiny. It reduces the importance of abstract terms like "title," and allows buyer and seller to specify when goods are identified and when risk shifts. Owners and creditors can anticipate problems and protect themselves. But the provisions only work if business people understand the rules and apply them.

Chapter Review

1. An *interest* is a legal right in something. *Title* means the normal rights of ownership.

2. Goods must *exist* and be *identified* to the contract before title can pass. The parties may agree in their contract how and when they will identify goods; if they do not specify, the Code stipulates when it happens. The parties may also state when title passes, and once again, if they do not, the Code provides rules.

3. A buyer obtains an *insurable interest* when the goods are identified to the contract. A seller retains an insurable interest in goods as long as she has either title or a security interest in them.

4. *Void title* is no title at all. *Voidable title* means limited rights in the goods, inferior to those of the owner. A person with voidable title has power to transfer good title to a *bona fide purchaser (BFP)*, that is, someone who purchases in good faith, for value.

5. Any *entrusting* of goods to a merchant who deals in goods of that kind gives him the power to transfer all rights of the entruster to a buyer in the ordinary course of business.

6. A buyer in the ordinary course of business generally takes goods free and clear of any security interest.

7. In a sale on approval, the goods *are not* subject to the buyer's creditors until the buyer accepts them; in a sale or return, the goods *are* subject to the buyer's creditors.

8. In their contract, the parties may allocate the *risk of loss* any way they wish. If they fail to do so, the Code provides several steps to determine who pays for any damage. When neither party has breached, the risk of loss generally passes from seller to buyer when the seller has transported the goods as far as he is obligated to. When a party has breached, the risk of loss generally lies with the party that has breached.

Practice Test

1. **CPA QUESTION** On Monday, Wolfe paid Aston Co., a furniture retailer, $500 for a table. On Thursday, Aston notified Wolfe that the table was ready to be picked up. On Saturday, while Aston was still in possession of the table, it was destroyed in a fire. Who bears the loss of the table?

   a. Wolfe, because Wolfe had title to the table at the time of loss

   b. Aston, unless Wolfe is a merchant

   c. Wolfe, unless Aston breached the contract

   d. Aston, because Wolfe had not yet taken possession of the table

2. **CPA QUESTION** Under UCC Article 9 on secured transactions, which of the following statements is correct concerning the disposition of goods by a secured creditor after a debtor defaults on a loan?

   a. A good faith purchaser of the goods for value and without knowledge of any defects in the sale takes free of any security interest.

   b. The debtor may not redeem the goods after the default.

   c. Secured creditors retain the right to redeem the goods after they are sold to a third party.

   d. The goods may be disposed of only at a public sale.

3. Franklin Miller operated Miller Seed Co. in Pea Ridge, Arkansas. He bought, processed, and sold fescue seed, which is used for growing pasture and fodder grass. Farmers brought seed to Miller who would normally clean, bag, and store it. In some cases the farmers authorized Miller to sell the seed, in some cases not. Miller mixed together the seed that was for sale with the seed in storage so that a customer could not see any difference between them. Miller defaulted on a $380,000 loan from the First State Bank of Purdy. First State attempted to seize all of the seed in the store. Tony Havelka, a farmer, protested that his 490,000 pounds of seed was merely in storage and not subject to First State's claim. Who is entitled to the seed?

4. **ETHICS** Myrna and James Brown ordered a $35,000 motor home from R.V. Kingdom, Inc. The manufacturer delivered the vehicle to R.V. Kingdom, with title in the dealer's name. The

Browns agreed to accept the motor home, but soon regretted spending the money and asked R.V. Kingdom to resell it. The motor home stayed on R.V. Kingdom's lot for quite a few months, but when the Browns decided to come get it, they learned that R.V. Kingdom had illegally used the vehicle as collateral for a loan and that a bank had repossessed it. The Browns filed a claim with their insurance company, State Farm. The insurer agreed that the vehicle had been stolen and agreed that the Browns' policy covered newly acquired vehicles. But the company refused to pay, claiming that the Browns had not taken title or possession to the goods and therefore had no insurable interest. The Browns sued. Please rule on their case. Let us also look at the ethics of the case by creating a contrasting hypothetical. Suppose that among the insurance company's thousands of customers was Arvee, a recreational vehicle dealership similar to the one in the real case. Imagine that Arvee had taken in an automobile for resale from a customer named Parker, and kept the vehicle on its lot. If Parker's auto were stolen, what argument would the insurance company be making? How would the company define insurable interest in *that* case?

5. John C. Clark, using an alias, rented a Lexus from Alamo Rent-A-Car in San Diego, California. Clark never returned the car to Alamo and obtained a California "quick title" using forged signatures. He then advertised in the *Las Vegas Review Journal* newspaper and sold the car to Terry and Vyonne Mendenhall for $34,000 in cash. The Mendenhalls made improvements to the car, had it insured, smog and safety tested, registered, licensed, and titled in the state of Utah. When Alamo reported the car stolen, the Nevada Department of Motor Vehicles seized the auto and returned it to Alamo. The Mendenhalls sued Alamo. The trial court concluded that the Mendenhalls had purchased the car for value and without notice that it was stolen, and were bona fide purchasers entitled to the Lexus. Alamo appealed. Please rule.

6. Fay Witcher owned a Ford Bronco. Steve Risher operated a used car lot. (We know where this one's heading.) Witcher delivered his automobile to Risher, asking him to resell it if he could. Witcher specified that he wanted all cash for his car, not part cash plus a trade-in. Risher sold the car to Richard Parker for $12,800, but took a trade-in as part payment. Risher promised to deliver the Bronco's certificate of title to Parker within a few days, but never did. He was also obligated to deliver most of the proceeds of the sale to Witcher, the owner, but also failed to do that. Parker claimed that the car was rightfully his. Witcher argued that Parker owned nothing because he never got the title and because Witcher never got his money. Who loses?

7. Universal Consolidated Cos. contracted with China Metallurgical Import and Export Corp. (CMIEC) to provide CMIEC with new and used equipment for a cold rolling steel mill. Universal then contracted with Pittsburgh Industrial Furnace Co. (Pifcom) to engineer and build much of the equipment. The contract required Pifcom to deliver the finished equipment to a trucking company, which would then transport it to Universal. Pifcom delivered the goods to the trucking company as scheduled. But before all of the goods reached Universal, CMIEC notified Universal it was canceling the deal. Universal, in turn, notified Pifcom to stop work, but all goods had been delivered to the shipper and ultimately reached Universal. Pifcom claimed that it retained title to the goods, but Universal claimed that title had passed to it. Who is right?

8. Bradkeyne International, Ltd., an English company, bought a large quantity of batteries from Duracell, Inc. The contract specified delivery "FOB Jacksonville, Florida." Duracell supervised the loading of the batteries onto a ship in Jacksonville in early July, and they arrived in England in August. When loaded onto the ship, the batteries were conforming goods that could be used for normal purposes. But on board the ship, excessive heat damaged them. By the time they reached England, they were worth only a fraction of the original price. Bradkeyne sued Duracell. Who loses?

9. **CPA QUESTION** On September 10, Bell Corp. entered into a contract to purchase 50 lamps from Glow Manufacturing. Bell prepaid 40 percent of the purchase price. Glow became insolvent on September 19 before segregating, in its inventory, the lamps to be delivered to Bell. Bell will not be able to recover the lamps because:

a. Bell is regarded as a merchant

b. The lamps were not identified to the contract

c. Glow became insolvent fewer than 10 days after receipt of Bell's prepayment

d. Bell did not pay the full price at the time of purchase

10. ***YOU BE THE JUDGE*** WRITING PROBLEM Construction Helicopters paid Heli-Dyne Systems $315,000 for three helicopters that were in Argentina. Two were ready to fly and one was disassembled for routine maintenance. The contract said nothing about risk of loss (the parties could have saved a lot of money by reading this chapter). Heli-Dyne arranged for an Argentine company to oversee their loading on board the freight ship *Lynx*. The two helicopters and 25 crates containing the disassembled craft were properly loaded, but when the ship arrived in Miami, only 7 of the crates appeared. Heli-Dyne refused to supply more parts and Construction sued. Who bears the loss? **Argument for Construction:** Construction had no control over the goods until they reached Miami. Although we do not know exactly what happened to the crates, we know the one party that had *nothing* to do with the loss: Construction. The company should not pay for damage it never caused. **Argument for Heli-Dyne:** Because the contract

failed to specify risk of loss, it is a shipment contract. In such an agreement, risk of loss passes to the buyer when the seller delivers the goods to a carrier. Heli-Dyne delivered the goods and has no further responsibility.

11. ***CPA QUESTION*** Quick Corp. agreed to purchase 200 typewriters from Union Suppliers, Inc. Union is a wholesaler of appliances and Quick is an appliance retailer. The contract required Union to ship the typewriters to Quick by common carrier, "FOB Union Suppliers, Inc. Loading Dock." Which of the parties bears the risk of loss during shipment?

a. Union, because the risk of loss passes only when Quick receives the typewriters

b. Union, because both parties are merchants

c. Quick, because title to the typewriters passed to Quick at the time of shipment

d. Quick, because the risk of loss passes when the typewriters are delivered to the carrier

12. ***ROLE REVERSAL*** Write a multiple-choice question concerning either insurable interest, bona fide purchaser, or entrustment.

Internet Research Problem

You own two powerful Clydesdale draft horses. A friend asks to borrow the horses for three months to give hayrides. You agree, provided your friend takes proper care of these valuable animals, providing good feed, adequate rest, and veterinary treatment. Examine the bailment contract at **http://beatty.westbuslaw .com.**

You can find further practice problems at
http://beatty.westbuslaw.com or in the
Study Guide that accompanies this text.

Warranties and Product Liability

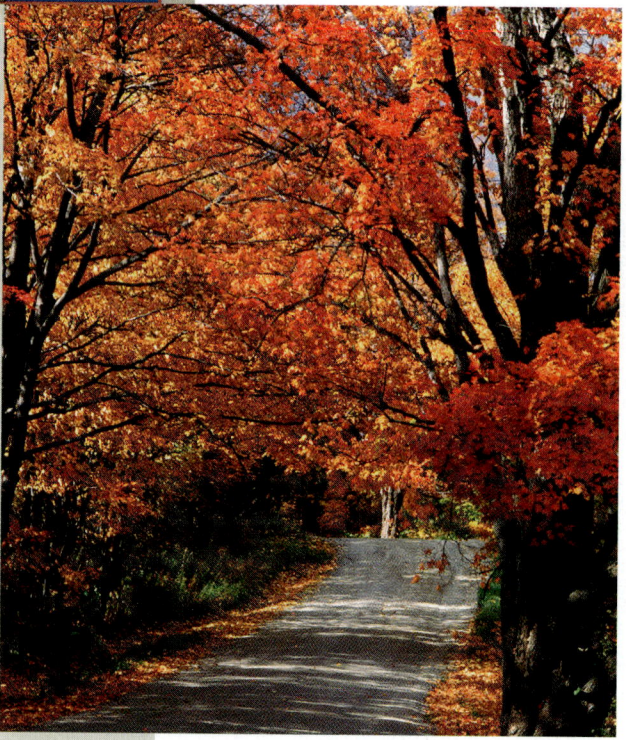

Y ou are sitting in a fast-food restaurant in Washington, D.C. Your friend Harley, who works for a congressman, is eating with one hand and gesturing with the other. "We want product liability reform and we want it now," he proclaims, stabbing the air with his free hand. "It's absurd, these multimillion dollar verdicts, just because something has a *slight defect*." He waves angrily at the absurdity, takes a ferocious bite from his burger—and with a loud CRACK breaks a tooth. Harley howls in pain and throws down the bun, revealing a large piece of bone in the meat. As he tips back in misery, his defective chair collapses, and Harley slams into the tile, knocking himself unconscious. Hours later, when he revives in the hospital, he refuses to speak to you until he puts in a call to his lawyer. ■

© PHOTO 24/BRAND X PICTURES/ GETTY IMAGES

PRODUCT LIABILITY

Harley and his lawyer will be chatting about **product liability,** which refers to goods that have caused an injury. The harm may be physical, as it was in Harley's case. Or it can be purely economic, as when a corporation buys a computer so defective it must be replaced, costing the buyer lost time and profits. The injured party may have a choice of possible remedies, including:

- *Warranty,* which is an assurance provided in a sales contract
- *Negligence,* which refers to unreasonable conduct by the defendant, and
- *Strict liability,* which prohibits defective products whether the defendant acted reasonably or not.

We discuss each of these remedies in this chapter. What all product liability cases have in common is that a person or business has been hurt by goods. We focus primarily on cases where the *sale* of goods leads to the injury, but we also examine product liability issues where there has been no sale. We begin with warranties.

A warranty is a contractual assurance that goods will meet certain standards. It is normally a manufacturer or a seller who gives a warranty, and a buyer who relies on it. A warranty might be explicit and written: "The manufacturer warrants that the light bulbs in this package will provide 100 watts of power for 2,000 hours." Or a warranty could be oral: "Don't worry, this machine can harvest any size of wheat crop ever planted in the state." The manufacturer may offer a warranty as a means of attracting buyers: "We provide the finest, bumper-to-bumper warranty in the automobile industry." Or *the law itself* may impose a warranty on goods, requiring the manufacturer to meet certain standards whether it intends to or not. Here we consider two broad categories: express warranties and implied warranties.

EXPRESS WARRANTIES

An express warranty is one that the seller creates with his words or actions.[1] Whenever a seller *clearly indicates* to a buyer that the goods being sold will meet certain standards, she has created an express warranty. For example, if the sales clerk for a paint store tells a professional house painter that "this exterior paint will not fade for three years, even in direct sunlight," that is an express warranty and the store is bound by it. Or, if the clerk gives the painter a brochure that makes the same promise, the store is again bound by its express warranty. On the other hand, if the sales person merely says, "I know you're going to be happy with this product," there is no warranty, because the promise is too vague. The UCC establishes that the seller may create an express warranty in three ways: (1) with an affirmation of fact or a promise; (2) with a description of the goods; or (3) with a sample or model. In addition, the buyer must demonstrate that what the seller said or did was the *basis of the bargain.*

Affirmation of Fact or Promise

Any affirmation of fact—or any promise—can create an express warranty.[2] An affirmation of fact is simply a statement about the nature or quality of the goods, such as "This scaffolding is made from the highest grade of steel available at any price," or "This car will accelerate from 0 to 60 in 8.3 seconds." A promise includes phrases such as "We guarantee you that this air conditioning system will cool your building to 72 degrees, regardless of the outdoor temperature."

---

[1] UCC §2-313.
[2] UCC §2-313(1)(a).

A common problem in cases of express warranty is to separate true affirmations of fact from mere sales puffery or seller's opinion, which creates no express warranty. "You meet the nicest people on a Honda" is mere puffery. If you purchase a Honda and meet only deadbeats, the manufacturer owes you nothing.

A statement is more likely to be an affirmation of fact if:

- *It is specific and can be proven true or false.* Suppose the brochures of a home builder promise to meet "the strictest building codes." Since there is a code on file, the builder's work can be compared to it, and his promise is binding.

- *It is written.* An oral promise *can* create an express warranty. But promises in brochures are more likely to be taken seriously. Statements in a *written contract* are the likeliest of all to create a binding warranty.

- *Defects are not obvious.* If a used car salesman tells you that a car is rust free, when the driver's door is pockmarked with rust, you should not take the statement seriously—since a court will not, either.

- *Seller has greater expertise.* If the seller knows more than the buyer, his statements will be more influential with buyer and court alike. If your architect assures you that the new porch will be warm in winter, the law recognizes that you will naturally rely on her expertise.

Description of Goods

Any description of the goods can create an express warranty.[3] The phrase could be oral or written. A description might be a label on a bag of seed, referring to the seed as a particular variety of tomato; it could be a tag on airplane parts, assuring the buyer that the goods have met safety tests. Wherever the words appear, if they describe the goods as having particular characteristics or qualities, the seller has probably created an express warranty.

Sample or Model

Any sample or model can create an express warranty.[4] A sample can be a very effective way of demonstrating the quality of goods to a customer. However, a seller who uses a sample is generally warranting that the merchandise sold will be just as good.

Basis of Bargain

The seller's conduct must have been part of the basis of the bargain. To prove an express warranty, a buyer must demonstrate that the two parties *included the statements or acts in their bargain.* Some courts have interpreted this to mean that the buyer must have *relied* on the seller's statements. There is logic to this position. For example, suppose a sales brochure makes certain assurances about the quality of goods, but the buyer never sees the brochure until she files suit. Should the seller be held to an express warranty? Some courts would rule that the seller is not liable for breach of warranty.

Other courts, however, have ruled that a seller's statement can be part of the basis of the bargain even when the buyer has not clearly relied on it. These courts are declaring that a seller who chooses to make statements about his goods will be held to

---

[3] UCC §2-313(1)(b).
[4] UCC §2-313(1)(c).

them, *unless the seller can convince a court that he should not be liable*. This is a policy decision, taken by many courts, to give the buyer the benefit of the doubt, since the seller is in the best position to control what he says.

In the following case, a ventilation company wrote a letter hoping to clear the air (and sell the product). Was the letter an express warranty?

KELLER V. INLAND METALS ALL WEATHER CONDITIONING, INC.

139 Idaho 233, 76 P.3d 977
Supreme Court of Idaho, 2003

Facts: When Brian and Clarice Keller installed an indoor swimming pool in the athletic club they owned, customers began to complain that the air near the pool was hot, humid, and foul smelling. The Kellers sought help from two contractors. Inland Metal submitted a bid to install a 7 1/2-ton dehumidifier for about $30,000, and another company offered to install a 10-ton machine for about $40,000.

The Kellers were worried that the 7 1/2-ton dehumidifier might be too small, so Inland's president visited the club, accompanied by a representative of the machine's manufacturer. The men assured the Kellers that the 7 1/2-ton dehumidifier would work. Inland's president followed up with a letter to the Kellers, which said:

> As in any indoor pool, the air needs to be treated with outdoor fresh air, dehumidified, air conditioned in the summer, and heated in the winter. This ducted system will rid you of the sweating walls and eliminate those offensive odors, and overall "bad air". This is not an uncommon problem, and all commercial pool owners face the same thing until they install one of these systems.
>
> Once you complete this installation your air problems should be over, and your customers should be satisfied and happy.

The Kellers bought the system from Inland, but the dehumidifier did not improve the problem. The Kellers sued, and the trial court found that Inland had breached an express warranty. Inland appealed.

Issues: Did Inland make an express warranty? If so, did the company breach it?

Excerpts from Justice Trout's Decision: An express warranty by the seller can be created by any affirmation of fact or promise made by the seller to the buyer that relates to the goods and becomes part of the basis of the bargain. In order to create an express warranty, the seller need not use formal words such as "warrant" or "guarantee," nor need the seller have a specific intention to make a warranty.

The issue Mr. Keller wanted addressed at the meeting did not concern the value of the 7 1/2-ton dehumidifier, or its quality, or whether it was better than those from other manufacturers, or whether that particular brand was, in general, a good dehumidifier. The issue Mr. Keller wanted addressed was whether a 7 1/2-ton dehumidifier was large enough to remedy the odor and humidity problems in the athletic club. Inland Metals' president and Mr. Ash both orally assured Mr. Keller that, based upon calculations made, the 7 1/2-ton dehumidifier was large enough to remedy the problems. In the letter sent after the meeting, Inland Metals' president stated, "This ducted system will rid you of the sweating walls and eliminate those offensive odors, and overall 'bad air.'" There was substantial, competent evidence supporting the district court's finding that Inland Metals made an express warranty that the 7 1/2-ton dehumidifier was fit for the particular purpose of eliminating the odor and humidity problems at the athletic club.

Inland Metals also argues that the district court erred in finding that the Kellers relied upon the representations made by its president when deciding to accept Inland Metals' bid. It argues that the evidence shows that the Kellers relied upon statements by Mr. Ash and purchased the least expensive of the dehumidifiers offered. The buyer of goods need not *rely* on an affirmation of fact or promise or description for the same to become part of the basis of the bargain and hence an express warranty.

Finally, Inland Metals contends that the district court erred in finding that it breached the express warranty. It argues that any failure of the dehumidifier

▼

resulted from the Kellers' failure to maintain the air temperature in the pool area two to four degrees higher than the water temperature, as anticipated by the manufacturer of the dehumidifier.

The primary issue in the trial was whether the dehumidification system failed to properly maintain humidity because it was too small or because the Kellers failed to maintain the air and water temperatures within the appropriate range. The trial court found, based upon the evidence presented, that the 7 1/2-ton dehumidifier was inadequate to maintain

relative humidity in the pool area according to the industry standard and that the persons upon whom Inland Metals had relied when sizing the dehumidifier had made numerous incorrect assumptions when making their calculations. It is the province of the trial court to weigh conflicting evidence and to judge the credibility of witnesses. The district court's finding that Inland Metals breached the express warranty is supported by substantial, competent evidence.

Affirmed. ■

IMPLIED WARRANTIES

Can Emily get away with her snow job about a warranty?

© GETTY IMAGES

Sean decides to plow driveways during the winter. Emily sells him a snowplow and installs it on his truck, but makes no promises about its performance. When winter arrives, Sean has plenty of business, but finds that the plow cannot be raised or lowered whenever the temperature falls below 40 degrees. He demands a refund from Emily, but she declines, saying, "I never said that thing would work in the winter. No express warranties, no luck." Scandalous! Is she off the hook? No. It is true she made no express warranties. But many sales are covered by implied warranties.

Implied warranties are those created by the Code itself, not by any act or statement of the seller. The Code's drafters concluded that goods should generally meet certain standards of quality, regardless of what the seller did or did not say. So the Code creates an implied warranty of merchantability and an implied warranty of fitness.

Implied Warranty of Merchantability

This is the most important warranty in the Code. Buyers, whether individual consumers or billion dollar corporations, are likelier to rely on this than any other section, and sellers must understand it thoroughly when they market goods. **Unless excluded or modified, a warranty that the goods shall be merchantable is implied in a contract for their sale, if the seller is a merchant with respect to goods of that kind.** *Merchantable* means that the goods are fit for the ordinary purposes for which they are used.[5] This rule contains several important principles:

- *Unless excluded or modified* means that the seller does have a chance to escape this warranty. We later discuss what steps a seller may take if she wants to sell goods that are *not* merchantable.

- *Merchantability* requires that goods be fit for their normal purposes. A ladder, to be merchantable, must be able to rest securely against a building and support someone who is climbing it. The ladder need not be serviceable as a boat ramp.

- *Implied* means that the law itself imposes this liability on the seller.

- *A merchant with respect to goods of that kind* means that the seller is someone who routinely deals in these goods or holds himself out as having special knowledge about these goods.

Dacor Corp. manufactured and sold scuba diving equipment. Dacor ordered air hoses from Sierra Precision, specifying the exact size and couplings so that the hose would fit tightly and safely into Dacor's oxygen units. Within about one year, customers returned a dozen Dacor units, complaining that the hose connections had cracked or sheared and were unusable. Dacor recalled 16,000 units and refit them with safe hoses, at a cost of more than $136,000. Dacor sued Sierra, claiming a breach of the implied warranty of merchantability. The Illinois court first ruled that Sierra was a merchant with respect to scuba hoses, because it routinely manufactured and sold them. The court then ruled:

> There is no evidence suggesting that these hose assemblies were subjected to anything other than normal use. Since the kind of failure experienced in connection with the returned hose assemblies would be life-threatening if it occurred under water, the hose assemblies were not fit for the purpose for which they were used within the meaning of section 2-314.

The court ordered Sierra to pay $136,721.[6]

The scuba equipment was not merchantable, because a properly made scuba hose should never crack under normal use. But what if the product being sold is food, and the food contains something that is harmful—yet quite normal?

GOODMAN V. WENCO FOODS, INC.

333 N.C. 1, 423 S.E.2d 444, 1992 N.C. LEXIS 671
Supreme Court of North Carolina, 1992

Facts: Fred Goodman and a friend stopped for lunch at a Wendy's restaurant in Hillsborough, North Carolina. Goodman had eaten about half of his double hamburger when he bit down and felt immediate pain in his lower jaw. He took from his mouth a triangular piece of cow bone, about one-sixteenth to one-quarter inch thick and one-half inch long, along with several pieces of his teeth. Goodman's pain was intense and his dental repairs took months.

The restaurant purchased all of its meat from Greensboro Meat Supply Company (GMSC).

---

[5] UCC §2-314(1).
[6] *Dacor Corp. v. Sierra Precision,* 1993 U.S. Dist. LEXIS 8009 (N.D. Ill. 1993).

Wendy's required its meat to be chopped and "free from bone or cartilage in excess of 1/8 inch in any dimension." GMSC beef was inspected continuously by state regulators and was certified by the United States Department of Agriculture (USDA). The USDA considered any bone fragment less than three-quarters of an inch long to be "insignificant."

Goodman sued, claiming a breach of the implied warranty of merchantability. The trial court dismissed the claim, ruling that the bone was natural to the food and that the hamburger was therefore fit for its ordinary purpose. The appeals court reversed this, holding that a hamburger could be unfit even if the bone occurred naturally. Wendy's appealed to the state's highest court.

Issue: Was the hamburger unfit for its ordinary purpose because it contained a harmful but natural bone?

Excerpts from Justice Exum's Decision: We hold that when a substance in food causes injury to a consumer of the food, it is not a bar to recovery against the seller that the substance was "natural" to the food, provided the substance is of such a size, quality or quantity, or the food has been so processed, or both, that the substance's presence should not reasonably have been anticipated by the consumer.

A triangular, one-half-inch, inflexible bone shaving is indubitably "inherent" in or "natural" to a cut of beef, but whether it is so "natural" to hamburger as to put a consumer on his guard—whether it "is to be reasonably expected by the consumer"—is, in most cases, a question for the jury. We are not requiring that the respondent's hamburgers be perfect, only that they be fit for their intended purpose. It is difficult to conceive of how a consumer might guard against the type of injury present here, short of removing the hamburger from its bun, breaking it apart and inspecting its small components.

Wendy's argues that the evidence supported its contention that its hamburger complied with [federal and state] standards. Wendy's reasons that [state and federal regulators permit] some bone fragments in meat and that its hamburgers are therefore merchantable as a matter of law. The court of appeals rejected this argument, noting that compliance "with all state and federal regulations is only some evidence which the jury may consider in determining whether the product was merchantable." We agree.

We thus conclude, as did the court of appeals majority, that a jury could reasonably determine the meat to be of such a nature, i.e., hamburger, and the bone in the meat of such a size that a consumer of the meat should not reasonably have anticipated the bone's presence. The court of appeals therefore properly reversed the directed verdict for Wendy's on plaintiff's implied warranty of merchantability claim. ■

at **RISK**

Notice some important implications of the *Goodman* ruling. The court says that a hamburger need not be perfect, but it must be fit for its ordinary purpose, that is, being eaten by someone who has not brought an X-ray machine with him to the restaurant. Whether this hamburger, or any other, *is* fit for its ordinary purpose will be a question for the jury. How will a jury tend to vote in a defective food case? To rephrase the question, did you wince just a bit reading about broken teeth? Will a jury? If that is so, how should a restaurant protect itself?

Wendy's had relied in part on the certification of the state and federal inspectors, but the court found that a consumer's expectations were more important. What other options does Wendy's have? ◆

Implied Warranty of Fitness for a Particular Purpose

The other warranty that the law imposes on sellers is the implied warranty of fitness for a particular purpose. This cumbersome name is often shortened to the *warranty of fitness.* **Where the seller at the time of contracting knows about a particular purpose for which the buyer wants the goods, and knows that the buyer is relying on the seller's skill or judgment, there is (unless excluded or modified) an implied warranty that the goods shall be fit for the purpose.**[7] Here are the key points:

---

[7] UCC §2-315.

- *Particular Purpose.* The seller must know about some special use that the buyer plans for the goods. For example, if a lumber salesman knows that a builder is purchasing lumber to construct houses in swampland, the Code implies a warranty that the lumber will withstand water.

- *Seller's Skill.* The buyer must be depending upon the seller's skill or judgment in selecting the product, and the seller must know it. Suppose the builder says to the lumber salesman, "I need four-by-eights that I will be using to build a house in the swamp. What do you have that will do the job?" The builder's reliance is obvious and the warranty is established. By contrast, suppose that an experienced Alaskan sled-driver offers to buy your three huskies, telling you she plans to use them to pull sleds. She has the experience and you do not, and if the dogs refuse to pull more than a one-pound can of dog food, you have probably breached no implied warranty.

- *Exclusion or Modification.* Once again, the seller is allowed to modify or exclude any warranty of fitness, as we see below.

Warranties Compared

Express Warranty	Implied Warranty of Merchantability	Implied Warranty of Fitness for a Particular Purpose
The Rule: Seller can create an express warranty with any affirmation or promise, with any description of the goods, or with any sample or model, provided the words or sample are part of the basis of the bargain.	*The Rule:* With certain exceptions, the Code implies a warranty that the goods will be fit for their ordinary purpose.	*The Rule:* With some exceptions, the Code implies a warranty that the goods are fit for the buyer's special purpose, provided that the seller knows of that purpose when the contract is made and knows of the buyer's reliance.
Example: Manufacturer sends Retailer a brochure describing its brand of children's bicycle. The brochure states that "these bikes will last for a minimum of eight years of normal use." If the handlebars snap off after six months, Manufacturer has breached its express warranty.	*Example:* Manufacturer sells Retailer 300 "children's bicycles." There is no brochure and no promise made by Manufacturer about the bikes' quality. The UCC implies a warranty that the bikes will be fit for ordinary riding by children. But the cycles might not be strong enough to withstand mountain racing, and there is no warranty to that effect.	*Example:* Retailer orders from Manufacturer "300 mountain bikes, for racing," and Manufacturer agrees. The UCC implies a warranty that the bikes will withstand the added stress of mountain racing.

Two Last Warranties: Title and Infringement

Strapped for cash, Maggie steals her boyfriend's rusty Chevy and sells it to Paul for $2,500. As we saw in Chapter 20, Maggie gets no valid title by her theft, and therefore Paul receives no title either. When the boyfriend finds his car parked at a nightclub, he notifies the police and gets his wheels back. Poor Paul is out of pocket $2,500 and has no car to show for it. That clearly is unjust, and the UCC provides Paul with a remedy: **the seller of goods warrants that her title is valid and that the goods are free of any security interest that the buyer knows nothing about, unless the seller has clearly excluded or modified this warranty.**[8] Once again, the Code is imposing a warranty on any seller except those who explicitly exclude or modify it. When Maggie sells the car to Paul, she warrants her valid title to the car and

---

[8] UCC §2-312(1).

simultaneously breaches that warranty, since she obviously has no title. Paul will win a lawsuit against Maggie for $2,500.

The same Code section imposes a warranty against claims of infringement by third parties. **Unless otherwise agreed, a seller who is a merchant warrants that the goods are free of any rightful claim of copyright, patent, or trademark infringement.**[9] Wesley sells to Komputer Corp. a device that automatically blasts purple smoke out of a computer screen anytime a student's paper is really dreadful. Unless Komputer Corp. agrees otherwise, Wesley is automatically giving the buyer a warranty that no one else invented the device or has any copyright, patent, or trademark in it.

DISCLAIMERS AND DEFENSES

There are several limitations on warranties. A seller may disclaim *warranties*, meaning that he eliminates express or implied warranties covering the goods. Or the seller may limit the buyer's *remedy*, which means that even if there is a breach of warranty, the buyer still may have only a very limited chance to recover against the seller.

Disclaimers

A disclaimer is a statement that a particular warranty *does not* apply. The Code permits the seller to disclaim most warranties.

Oral Express Warranties

Would you fly in a helicopter protected by an oral express warranty?

Under the Code, a seller may disclaim an oral express warranty. Suppose Traffic Co. wants to buy a helicopter from HeliCorp for use in reporting commuter traffic. HeliCorp's salesman tells Traffic Co., "Don't worry, you can fly this bird day and night for six months with nothing more than a fuel stop." HeliCorp's contract may disclaim the oral warranty. The contract could say, "HeliCorp's entire warranty is printed below. Any statements made by any agent or salesperson are disclaimed and form no part of this contract." That disclaimer is valid. If the helicopter requires routine servicing between flights, HeliCorp has not breached an oral warranty.

Written Express Warranties

This is the one type of warranty that is difficult or impossible to disclaim. If a seller includes an express warranty in the *sales contract*, any disclaimer is invalid. Suppose HeliCorp sells an industrial helicopter for use in hauling building equipment. The sales contract describes the aircraft as "operable to 14,000 feet." Later, in the contract, a limited warranty disclaims "any other warranties or statements that appear in this document or in any other document." That disclaimer is invalid. The Code will not permit a seller to take contradictory positions in one document. The goal is simply to be fair, and the

---

[9] UCC §2-313(3).

Code assumes that it is confusing and unjust for the seller to say one thing to help close a deal and the opposite to limit its losses.[10]

What if the express written statement is in a different document, such as a sales brochure? The disclaimer is void if it would *unfairly surprise* the buyer. Assume, again, that HeliCorp promises a helicopter that requires no routine maintenance for six months, but this time the promise appears in a sales brochure that Traffic Co. reads and relies on. If HeliCorp attempts to disclaim the written warranty, it will probably fail. Most people take written information seriously.

Implied Warranties

A seller may disclaim the implied warranty of merchantability provided he *actually mentions the word "merchantability"* and makes the disclaimer conspicuous. Courts demand to see the word "merchantability" in the disclaimer to be sure the buyer realized she was giving up this fundamental protection. If the word is there and the disclaimer is conspicuous enough that the buyer should have seen it, she has forfeited the warranty. A seller may disclaim the implied warranty of fitness with any language that is clear and conspicuous.

General Disclaimers

To make life easier, the Code permits a seller to disclaim all implied warranties by conspicuously stating that the goods are sold "as is" or "with all faults." Notice the tension between this provision and the discussion about disclaiming a warranty of merchantability. A seller who wants to disclaim *only* the warranty of merchantability must explicitly mention that term; but a seller wishing to exclude *all* implied warranties may do so with a short expression, such as "sold as is."

Consumer Sales

As we have seen many times in the Code, protection is often stronger for consumers than for businesses. *Many states prohibit a seller from disclaiming implied warranties in the sale of consumer goods.* In these states, if a home furnishings store sells a bunk bed to a consumer, and the top bunk tips out the window on the first night, the seller is liable. If the sales contract clearly stated "no warranties of merchantability or fitness," the court would reject the clause and find that the seller breached the implied warranty of merchantability.

---

at RISK

Some courts dislike disclaimers. Other courts respect the right of a seller to disclaim but insist on strict compliance with disclaimer rules, such as mentioning the word "merchantability." An astute seller will take no chances. Disclaimers must be conspicuous, so the seller should print them in boldface with large capital letters that are, ideally, a different color from the rest of the contract. ◆

Remedy Limitations

Simon Aerials, Inc., manufactured boomlifts, the huge cranes used to construct multi-storied buildings. Simon agreed to design and build eight unusually large machines for Logan Equipment Corp. Simon delivered the boomlifts late, and they functioned poorly. Logan requested dozens of repairs and modifications, which Simon attempted to accomplish over many months, but the equipment never worked well. Logan gave

---

[10] UCC §2-316(1).

up and sued for $7.5 million, representing the profits it expected to make from renting the machines and the damage to its reputation. Logan clearly had suffered major losses, and it recovered—nothing. How could that be?

Simon had negotiated a **limitation of remedy** clause, by which **the parties may limit or exclude the normal remedies permitted under the Code.**[11] These important rights are entirely distinct from disclaimers. A disclaimer limits the seller's warranties and thus affects whether the seller has breached her contract. A remedy limitation, by contrast, states that if a party does breach its warranty, the injured party will not get all of the damages the Code normally allows.

In its contract, Simon had agreed to repair or replace any defective boomlifts, but that was all. The agreement said that if a boomlift was defective, and Logan lost business, profits, and reputation, Simon was not liable. The court upheld the remedy limitation. Since Simon had repeatedly attempted to repair and redesign the defective machines, it had done everything it promised to do. Logan got nothing.[12]

We compare disclaimers and remedy limitations in the table below.

Comparison of Disclaimers and Remedy Limitations

Code Section	Purpose	Setting	Contract Language	Result
Disclaimers: UCC §2-316	Limits warranties, whether express or implied. This section will determine *whether there has been a breach.*	Seller sells Buyer a used "tire shredding machine." UCC §2-314 implies a warranty of merchantability, meaning that the machine will be good for its ordinary purpose, which is shredding tires in a commercial recycling business.	Seller includes in the contract a clause stating that the tire shredder is sold "as is." Under §2-316, this phrase excludes all implied warranties, meaning that the implied warranty of merchantability will NOT apply here.	One tire goes through the machine, the tire emerges completely intact, and the machine falls to pieces. *Result:* Seller has NOT breached the contract, and Buyer gets no damages.
Remedy limitations: UCC §2-719	Limits the remedies available *when one party has breached* the contract.	Seller sells Buyer 10,000 computer circuit boards at $200 each, which Buyer uses in its laptops.	Seller requires a clause limiting Buyer's remedies to "replace or repair." If the boards fail, Seller will replace or repair them for free. But Buyer is permitted NO OTHER REMEDY. Buyer may not seek consequential damages, which would include lost profits and injured reputation.	All of the boards malfunction, and Buyer's customers are angry *at Buyer.* Buyer must take the computers back, losing all of its expected profits and also suffering a serious loss of reputation in the high-tech world. Seller IS in breach of the contract and must repair or replace all circuit boards at its expense. But Seller owes NOTHING for Buyer's lost profits or injured reputation.

---

[11] UCC §2-719. A few states prohibit remedy limitations, but most permit them.

[12] *Logan Equipment Corp. v. Simon Aerials, Inc.,* 736 F. Supp. 1188, 1990 U.S. Dist. LEXIS 5720 (D. Mass. 1990).

Consequential Damages

Simon's contract clause was a typical one. Sellers frequently use a remedy limitation to avoid liability for consequential damages, which can be vast. Recall that a party injured by breach of contract normally gets *compensatory* damages.[13] In the sale of goods that means the difference between the value of the goods promised and those actually delivered. A seller can anticipate and probably tolerate such damages, since the seller understands exactly how much it costs to repair or replace the goods it has sold. **Consequential damages,** however, are different. They are losses stemming from the particular requirements of the buyer. The buyer might have entered into dozens of contracts in reliance on the goods it expects from the seller. The seller will have no way of knowing how great the consequential damages could be. Logan Equipment claimed that it would have earned profits in the millions, and it was just such a claim that Simon had determined to avoid.

Notice that there is one major limitation on these clauses: **an exclusion of consequential damages is void if it is unconscionable.** "Unconscionable" means that a remedy restriction is shockingly one-sided and fundamentally unfair.[14] If the buyer is a consumer, a court will be likelier to consider such an exclusion unfair, since the typical consumer will not understand the terms and may never even notice them. If the buyer is a consumer who suffers a *personal injury*, a court is nearly certain to reject the exclusion. It is unfair for a corporation to market defective goods and escape liability because an unsuspecting consumer failed to understand contract language. Suppose Byron buys a hot-air popper that comes with a label excluding consequential damages. Byron is seriously burned when the popper ignites. Virtually all courts will ignore the consequential damages exclusion and apply a warranty of merchantability to the popper, permitting Byron to recover his full damages. His compensatory damages are insignificant: the cost of a new popper. His consequential damages are enormous: medical expenses, pain and suffering, and lost income.

However, when the buyer is a corporation, courts assume it had adequate legal advice and an opportunity to reject unacceptable terms. When two companies agree to a remedy limitation, they are allocating the risk of loss as one part of their bargain. A court will seldom substitute its judgment for that of the contracting companies. In the *Logan Equipment* case, both parties were corporations, and sophisticated executives negotiated the boomlift sale. The court found nothing unconscionable in the bargain and enforced the limitation that the parties had agreed to.[15]

Privity

When two parties contract, they are *in privity*. If Lance buys a chain saw from the local hardware store, he is in privity with the store. But Lance has no privity with Kwiksaw, the manufacturer of the chain saw. Under traditional contract law, a plaintiff injured by a breach of contract could only sue a defendant with whom he had privity. So, a hundred years ago, if Lance's chain saw had been seriously defective, he could have sued only the store. Kwiksaw would have defended successfully, claiming "lack of privity." This hurt consumers because the local retailer might have lacked assets to compensate for serious injuries. Today, privity is gradually disappearing as a defense. The various states are approaching the issue in different ways, so there is no one rule. We can, however, highlight the trends.

---

[13] Compensatory, consequential, and incidental damages are discussed in Chapter 18, on remedies.
[14] UCC §2-719. We discuss unconscionability under the Code in Chapter 19.
[15] *Logan Equipment,* 736 F. Supp. at 1195.

Personal Injury

Where a product causes a personal injury, most states permit a warranty suit even without privity. If the chain on Lance's power saw flies off and slashes his arm, he has suffered a personal injury. Of course, he may sue the store, with which he has privity. But he wants to sue the manufacturer, which has more money. In the majority of states, he will be able to sue the manufacturer for breach of warranty even though he had no privity with it.[16] (Note that Lance is sure to make other claims against the manufacturer, including *negligence* and *strict liability*, both discussed below.)

Economic Loss

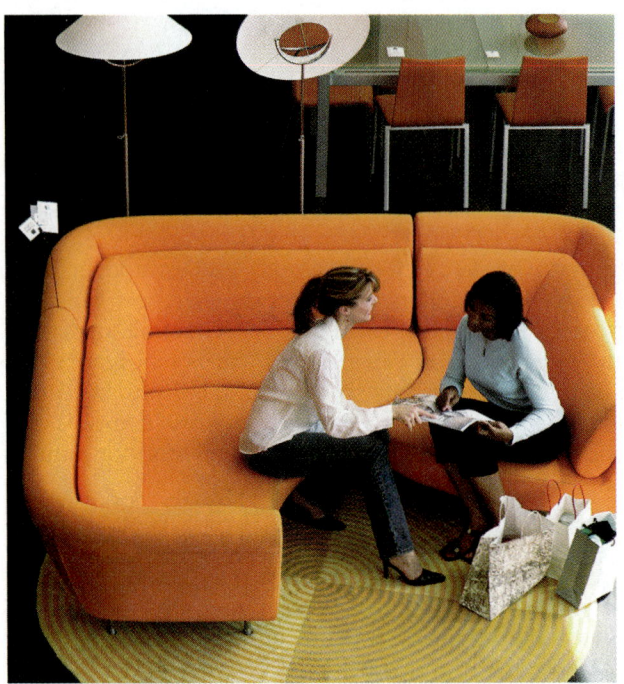

The sofa manufacturer is in privity with the fabric wholesaler, but not the fabric manufacturer.

If the buyer suffers only economic loss, privity *may* still be required to bring a suit for breach of warranty. If the buyer is a business, the majority of states require privity. Fab-Rik makes fabric for furniture and drapes, which it sells to various wholesalers. Siddown makes sofas. Siddown buys Fab-Rik fabric from a wholesaler and, after installing it on 200 sofas, finds the material defective. Siddown may sue the wholesaler but, in most states, will be unable to sue Fab-Rik for breach of any warranties. There was no privity.

By contrast, when the buyer is a consumer, more states will permit a suit against the manufacturer, even without privity. Lance, the consumer, buys his power saw to landscape his property. This time the saw malfunctions without injuring him, but Lance must buy a replacement saw for considerably more money. Many states—but not all—will permit him to recover his losses from Kwiksaw, the manufacturer, on the theory that Kwiksaw intends its product to reach consumers and is in the best position to control losses.

In the following case, a jailhouse tragedy prompts a product liability suit.

---

[16] The Code offers three alternative version of its rule concerning privity: UCC §2-318, Alternatives A, B, and C, with each state free to adopt whichever version the legislature prefers. Alternative A, the most restrictive, extends a warranty in the cases of personal injury to the buyer and members of his household. But the comments of this section indicate that this extension to household members does not *preclude* claims brought by non-household members. The drafters have left it up to the states to decide whether additional injured parties could sue. Several states that have adopted this version of the privity rule have permitted warranty claims by injured parties who were not household members. Dahlia buys a weed cutter manufactured by Thorn and sold by Hardware, and loans it to Rose, who is cut when it malfunctions. Many, but not all, states that have adopted Alternative A would allow Rose to sue Thorn.

Alternative B is more expansive, explicitly permitting a warranty suit by any injured natural person, (non-corporation) who could reasonably be affected by the product. In states that have adopted this section, Rose would certainly be permitted to sue Thorn. Alternative C, the most expansive, permits recovery by natural persons and corporations and allows suits for economic loss as well as personal injury. What does all this mean? The privity requirement is disappearing in personal injury cases and diminishing in cases of economic loss.

REED V. CITY OF CHICAGO

263 F.Supp.2d 1123
United States District Court for the Northern District of Illinois, 2003

Facts: J.C. Reed was arrested and brought to Chicago's Fifth District Police Station. Police were allegedly aware that he was suicidal, having seen him slash his wrists earlier. They removed his clothing and dressed him in a paper isolation gown. Sadly, Reed used the gown to hang himself.

Reed's mother, on his behalf, sued the police (for failing to monitor a suicidal inmate) and also Cypress Medical Products, the manufacturer of the isolation gown. The claim was that the gown should have been made of material that would tear if someone attempted to hang himself with it. Cypress moved to dismiss the suit, claiming that Reed had no privity with the company.

Issue: Could Reed maintain a lawsuit against Cypress despite lack of privity?

Excerpts from Judge Moran's Decision: The single issue we must decide is whether plaintiff, as a non-purchaser, can recover from the manufacturer and designer of the gown for breach of warranty. Historically, Illinois law has required plaintiffs suing for breach of warranty to establish both horizontal and vertical privity. Lack of vertical privity occurs when a consumer seeks to sue a remote manufacturer who was not involved in the sale to the consumer. Lack of horizontal privity occurs when a user of the product, beside the consumer, is injured. Section 2-318 of the Uniform Commercial Code (UCC), as adopted by the Illinois legislature, contains mandatory exceptions to the general requirement of privity:

> A seller's warranty whether express or implied extends to any natural person who is in the family or household of his buyer or who is a guest in his home if it is reasonable to expect that such person may use, consume or be affected by the goods and who is injured in person by breach of the warranty.

The Illinois Supreme Court has determined that the privity is no longer an absolute requirement for breach of warranty actions. While section 2-318 lists specific exceptions to the privity requirement, Illinois courts have noted that this list is not necessarily exhaustive.

The vast majority of cases examining the limits of section 2-318 in Illinois have dealt with the employment context, expanding the class of potential breach of warranty plaintiffs to employees of the ultimate purchaser. In [a case called *Whitaker*,] plaintiff was injured while using a bandsaw that had been purchased by his employer. The court determined that the employee was essentially a third party beneficiary to the sale in that the employee's safety while using the bandsaw was "either explicitly or implicitly part of the basis of the bargain when the employer purchased the goods."

In cases examining the limits of section 2-318 in other contexts, courts have been reluctant to find additional exceptions to the privity requirement. In [a case called *Hemphill*,] the court refused to allow a breach of warranty claim by a university football player against the manufacturer of his helmet.

While no Illinois courts have expanded the plaintiff class for breach of warranty actions beyond employees, we believe that the law requires us to do so here. The beneficiary of any warranty made by the manufacturer and designer of the gown is necessarily a potentially suicidal detainee like Reed. If protection is not provided to plaintiffs like Reed, any warranty as to the safety of the gown would have little, if any, effect. In designing and manufacturing the gown, defendants contemplated that the users of the gown would be detainees. Moreover, the safety of these detainees was necessarily a part of the bargain, whether explicitly or implicitly, between the seller and buyer. For these reasons, a detainee of the City like Reed must be able to enforce the protections of any warranties made by the manufacturer and designer of the gown.

For the foregoing reasons, defendants' motion to dismiss is denied. ■

Public Policy | These isolation gowns are used only by potentially suicidal detainees. Does that argue for expanding liability or contracting it? What position does the court take? What is the opposing argument? Which view do you find more persuasive? ◆

Buyer's Misconduct

Misuse by the buyer will generally preclude a warranty claim[17]. Common sense tells us that the seller only warrants its goods if they are properly used. Lord & Taylor warranted that its false eyelashes would function well and cause no harm. But when Ms. Caldwell applied them, they severely irritated one eye. She sued but the store prevailed. Why? Caldwell applied the eyelashes improperly, getting the glue into one eye. On her other eye she used the product correctly and suffered no harm. Her misuse proved painful to her eye—and fatal to her lawsuit.[18]

Statute of Limitations and Notice of Breach

It is right that a seller be responsible for the goods it places in the market. On the other hand, a seller should not face potential liability *forever*. A company cannot be a perpetual insurer for goods that it sold decades earlier. And so the UCC imposes two important time limits on a buyer's claim of breach.

The Code prescribes a four-year statute of limitations. This means that the buyer must bring any lawsuit for breach of a warranty no later than four years after the goods were delivered. When the parties contract, they may shorten that period to no less than one year, but they may not extend it. Suppose PlaneJane, an airline, buys 10 new aircraft from Flyem, a manufacturer, taking delivery on June 1, 2004. In the fall of 2007, PlaneJane begins to discover structural weaknesses in the wings, which Flyem repeatedly repairs over the next few months. PlaneJane must decide whether to file a lawsuit. If the airline believes all problems are corrected, fine. But if it has any doubts about the aircraft fitness, PlaneJane must sue promptly. On June 2, 2008, any lawsuit for breach of warranty is barred by the statute of limitations.

The Code puts an additional burden on a buyer asserting a breach of warranty. **The UCC requires that a buyer notify the seller of defects within a reasonable time.**[19] The purpose here is to enable the seller to cure, by repairing or replacing, any problems with the goods. Ideally, a seller that receives notice of a potential breach will fix the problem and there will *be* no lawsuit.

The circumstances will determine what is a "reasonable" amount of time. An inexperienced consumer could reasonably take many months to figure out that a new laptop computer had a serious operating defect. Further, a delay of six or eight months would not harm a large computer manufacturer. On the other hand, a corporate buyer of perishable food products must act very fast if it claims the goods are defective.

NEGLIGENCE

A buyer of goods may have remedies other than warranty claims. One is negligence, which we discuss in detail in Chapter 7. Here we focus on how this law applies to the sale of goods. Negligence, as you will recall, is notably different from contract law. In a contract case, the two parties have reached an agreement, and the terms of their bargain will usually determine how to settle any dispute. If the parties agreed that the

---

[17] Some courts characterize the misuse as "comparative negligence" or "contibutory negligence" or "failure of proximate cause." These tort terms are discussed in Chapter 7, dealing with negligence and strict liability. For our purposes here, it is enough to understand that misuse generally precludes a warranty claim.

[18] *Caldwell v. Lord & Taylor, Inc.,* 142 Ga. App. 137, 235 S.E.2d 546 (Ga. Ct. App. 1977).

[19] UCC §2-607.

seller disclaimed all warranties, then the buyer may be out of luck. But in a negligence case, there has been no bargaining between the parties, who may never have met. A consumer injured by an exploding cola bottle is unlikely to have bargained for her beverage with the CEO of the cola company. Instead, the law *imposes* a standard of conduct on everyone in society, corporation and individual alike. The two key elements of this standard, for present purposes, are *duty* and *breach*. A plaintiff injured by goods she bought must show that the defendant, usually a manufacturer or seller of a product, had a duty to her and breached that duty.[20] A defendant has a duty of due care to anyone who could foreseeably be injured by its misconduct. Generally, it is the duty to act as *a reasonable person* would in like circumstances; a defendant who acts unreasonably has breached its duty.

In negligence cases concerning the sale of goods, plaintiffs most often raise one or more of these claims:

- *Negligent Design.* The buyer claims that the product injured her because the manufacturer designed it poorly. Negligence law requires a manufacturer to design a product free of *unreasonable* risks. The product does not have to be absolutely safe. An automobile that guaranteed a driver's safety could be made but would be prohibitively expensive. Reasonable safety features must be built in, if they can be included at a tolerable cost.

- *Negligent Manufacture.* The buyer claims that the design was adequate but that failure to inspect or some other sloppy conduct caused a dangerous product to leave the plant.

- *Failure to Warn.* A manufacturer is liable for failing to warn the purchaser or users about the dangers of normal use and also foreseeable misuse. However, there is no duty to warn about obvious dangers, a point evidently lost on some manufacturers. A Batman costume came with this statement: "For play only: Mask and chest plate are not protective; cape does not enable user to fly."

In the following case, the plaintiffs raise issues of negligent design and failure to warn, concerning a disposable lighter. You decide.

you Be The Judge

BOUMELHEM V. BIC CORP.

211 Mich. App. 175, 535 N.W.2d 574, 1995 Mich. App.
LEXIS 228
Michigan Court of Appeals, 1995

Facts: Ibrahim Boumelhem, aged four, began playing with a Bic disposable lighter that his parents had bought. He started a fire that burned his legs and severely burned his six-month-old brother over 85 percent of his body. Ibrahim's father sued Bic, claiming that the lighter was negligently designed because it could have been child-proof.

He also claimed failure to warn, because the lighter did not clearly warn of the danger to children.

The *Boumelhem* court considered evidence and analyses from several other cases against Bic. The court noted that consumers use over 500 million disposable lighters annually in the United States. Each lighter provides 1,000 to 2,000 lights. During one three-year period, children playing with disposable lighters started 8,100 fires annually, causing an average of 180 people to die every year, of whom 140 were children under

▼

---

[20] A plaintiff in a negligence case must also prove three other elements: factual causation, foreseeable type of harm, and injury. For a discussion of those elements, see Chapter 7. We focus in this chapter on duty and breach because those two elements take on special importance in product liability cases.

five. Another 990 people were injured. The average annual cost of deaths, injuries, and property damage from child-play fires was estimated at $310 to $375 million, or 60 to 75 cents per lighter sold. Bic had acknowledged in earlier litigation that it was foreseeable lighters would get into children's hands and injure them. Bic had also agreed that it was feasible to make a more child-resistant lighter.

The trial court relied on a Michigan case. In Adams v. Perry Furniture Co.,[21] four minor children had died in a fire started when one of them was playing with a Bic lighter. The Adams court had found no negligent design and no failure to warn, and dismissed all claims. The trial court in the present case followed Adams and dismissed Boumelhem's claims. He appealed.

You Be the Judge: Did Bic negligently design its disposable lighter? Did Bic negligently fail to warn of the lighter's dangers?

Argument for Boumelhem: Your honors, the *Adams* court decided the issues wrongly. There is a reason that new plaintiffs are back in this court, the year after *Adams*, raising related issues against Bic: the company is killing hundreds of children every year. In its efforts to maximize corporate profits, it is literally burning these children to death and injuring hundreds more. That's wrong.

Bic has acknowledged that its disposable lighters can and will get into the hands of children. Bic knows full well that its product will injure or kill a certain percentage of these children—very young children. Bic has admitted that it could design a child-proof lighter, and it knows perfectly well how to include effective warnings on its lighters. But rather than improve product design and give effective warnings, Bic prefers to do business as usual and litigate liability for injured and murdered children.

We ask this court to rule that Bic breached its duty to design and manufacture a lighter that will keep our kids safe, and breached its duty to warn.

Argument for Bic: Your honors, the Bic Corp. is as horrified as anyone over the injuries to these children and the deaths of other kids. But Bic is not responsible. The children's parents are responsible. We sympathize with their grief but not with their attempt to pass parental responsibility onto the shoulders of a corporation. There are several reasons Bic is not liable in this case.

First, the *Adams* court decided the matter, and that precedent is binding.

Second, Bic has no duty to design a different lighter. The test in design defect cases is whether the risks are unreasonable in light of the foreseeable injuries. Young children can hurt themselves in countless ways, from falls to poisonings to automobile injuries. There is one answer to these dangers, and it is called good parenting. The parents who bought this lighter purchased it because it could start a fire. The moment they purchased it, they assumed the obligation to keep it away from their children. These are useful products, which is why Bic sells hundreds of millions per year. Other consumers should not be forced to pay an outrageously high price for a simple tool, just because some parents fail to do their job.

The failure to warn argument is even weaker. The law imposes no failure to warn when the danger is obvious. Every adult knows that lighters are *potentially* dangerous, if misused, or if passed on to children. Does the court really think anyone would be helped by a warning that said, "This lighter starts fires. Don't give it to children." ∎

*up*date The tragic deaths in cases like *Boumelhem* prompted a federal agency, the Consumer Product Safety Commission, to take action. What did the CPSC do, and with what results? You can search for news articles online, or go directly to the agency's Web site at http://www.cpsc.gov. ◆

---

[21] 198 Mich. App. 1, 497 N.W.2d 514, 1993 Mich. App. LEXIS 33 (Mich. Ct. App. 1993).

STRICT LIABILITY

The other tort claim that an injured person can bring against the manufacturer or seller of a product is strict liability. Like negligence, strict liability is a burden created by the law rather than by the parties. And, as with all torts, strict liability concerns claims of physical harm. But there is a key distinction between negligence and strict liability: in a negligence case, the injured buyer must demonstrate that the seller's conduct was unreasonable. Not so in strict liability.

In strict liability, the injured person need not prove that the defendant's conduct was unreasonable. The injured person must show only that the defendant manufactured or sold a product that was defective and that the defect caused harm. Almost all states permit such lawsuits, and most of them have adopted the summary of strict liability provided by the Restatement (Second) of Torts **§402A.** Because §402A is the most frequently cited section in all of tort law, we quote it in full:

(1) One who sells any product in a defective condition unreasonably dangerous to the user or consumer or to his property is subject to liability for physical harm thereby caused to the ultimate user or consumer, or to his property, if
  (a) the seller is engaged in the business of selling such a product, and
  (b) it is expected to and does reach the user or consumer without substantial change in the condition in which it is sold.

(2) The rule stated in Subsection (1) applies although
  (a) the seller has exercised all possible care in the preparation and sale of his product, and
  (b) the user or consumer has not bought the product from or entered into any contractual relation with the seller.

These are the key terms in subsection (1):

- ***Defective condition unreasonably dangerous to the user.*** The defendant is liable only if the product is defective when it leaves his hands. There must be something wrong with the goods. If they are reasonably safe and the buyer's mishandling of the goods causes the harm, there is no strict liability. If you attempt to open a soda bottle by knocking the cap against a counter, and the glass shatters and cuts you, the manufacturer owes nothing.
  A carving knife can produce a lethal wound, but everyone knows that, and a sharp knife is not unreasonably dangerous. On the other hand, prescription drugs may harm in ways that neither a layperson nor a doctor would anticipate. The manufacturer *must provide adequate warnings* of any dangers that are not apparent.

- ***In the business of selling.*** The seller is liable only if she normally sells this kind of product. Suppose your roommate makes you a peanut butter sandwich and, while eating it, you cut your mouth on a sliver of glass that was in the jar. The peanut butter manufacturer faces strict liability as does the grocery store where your roommate bought the goods. But your roommate is not strictly liable because he does not serve sandwiches as a business.

- ***Reaches the user without substantial change.*** Obviously, if your roommate put the glass in the peanut butter thinking it was funny, neither the manufacturer nor the store is liable.

And here are the important phrases in subsection (2).

- *Has exercised all possible care.* This is the heart of strict liability, which makes it a potent claim for consumers. *It is no defense that the seller used reasonable care.* If the product is dangerously defective and injures the user, the seller is liable even if it took every precaution to design and manufacture the product safely. Suppose the peanut butter jar did in fact contain a glass sliver when it left the factory. The manufacturer proves that it uses extraordinary care in keeping foreign particles out of the jars and thoroughly inspects each container before it is shipped. The evidence is irrelevant. The manufacturer has shown that it was not *negligent* in packaging the food, but reasonable care is irrelevant in strict liability.

- *No contractual relation.* Remember "privity," from the warranty discussion? Privity only exists between the user and the person from whom she actually bought the goods. This sentence in §402A means that *privity is not required*. Suppose the manufacturer that made the peanut butter sold it to a distributor, which sold it to a wholesaler, which sold it to a grocery store, which sold it to your roommate. You may sue the manufacturer, distributor, wholesaler, and store, even though you had no privity with any of them.

Restatement (Third) and Contemporary Trends

We saw that under traditional negligence law, a company could be found liable based on design, manufacture, or failure to warn. The same three activities can give rise to a claim of strict liability. It will normally be easier for a plaintiff to win a claim of strict liability, because she does not need to demonstrate that the manufacturer's conduct was unreasonable.

If the steering wheel on a brand new car falls off, and the driver is injured, that is a clear case of defective manufacturing, and the company will be strictly liable. Those are the easy cases. As courts have applied §402A, defective design cases have been more contentious. Suppose a vaccine that prevents serious childhood illnesses inevitably causes brain damage in a very small number of children, because of the nature of the drug. Is the manufacturer liable? What if a racing sailboat, designed only for speed, is dangerously unstable in the hands of a less experienced sailor? Is the boat's maker responsible for fatalities? Suppose an automobile made of lightweight metal uses less fuel but exposes its occupants to more serious injuries in an accident. How is a court to decide whether the design was defective? Often, these design cases also involve issues of warnings: Did drug designer diligently detail dangers to doctors? Should sailboat seller sell speedy sailboat solely to seasoned sailors?

Over the years, most courts have adopted one of two tests for design and warning cases. The first is *consumer expectation*. Here, a court finds the manufacturer liable for defective design if the product is less safe than a reasonable consumer would expect. If a smoke detector has a 3 percent failure rate, and the average consumer has no way of anticipating that danger, effective cautions must be included, though the design may be defective anyway. Many states have moved away from that test, and now use a *risk-utility test*. Here, a court must weigh the benefits for society against the dangers that the product poses. Principal factors in the risk-utility test include:

- The *value* of the product,
- The *gravity* of the danger (how bad will the harm be),
- The *likelihood* that such danger will occur (the odds),
- The mechanical feasibility of a *safer alternative* design, and
- The *adverse consequences* of an alternative design (greater cost, different risks created).

Because of the conflicting court decisions, the American Law Institute drafted the Restatement (Third) of Torts: Product Liability, in an attempt to harmonize judicial opinions about product liability generally and design defects in particular. The new Restatement treats manufacturing cases differently from those involving design defects and failure to warn.

- In manufacturing cases, a product is defective whenever it departs from its intended design, regardless of how much care was taken. This is the traditional standard.

- In design and warnings cases, a product is defective only when the *foreseeable risks* of harm could have been reduced by using a reasonable alternative design or warning. So-called "strict" liability in these cases is beginning to resemble plain old negligence. If courts adopt this new approach, it will become more difficult for plaintiffs to win a design or warning case, because they will need to prove that the manufacturer should have foreseen the danger and could have done something about it.

There is no strong trend in how judges examine these cases: courts tend to pick and choose the analytic tools they use. Most still regard §402A as the basic law for all strict liability lawsuits. In design cases, many courts use the risk-utility test, quite a few still examine consumer expectation, and some permit both analyses. Most states consider the availability of alternative designs to be important, and some consider it essential. And finally, as the following case indicates, some courts employ elements of the Restatement Third—with plenty of disagreement.

UNIROYAL GOODRICH TIRE COMPANY V. MARTINEZ

977 S.W.2d 328
Texas Supreme Court, 1998

Facts: When Roberto Martinez, a mechanic, attempted to mount a 16-inch tire on a 16.5-inch rim (wheel), the tire exploded, causing him serious, permanent injuries. He sued Goodrich, the tire manufacturer; the Budd Company, which made the rim; and Ford Motor Company, which designed it. Budd and Ford settled out of court, and the case proceeded against Goodrich.

The tire had a conspicuous label, advising users never to mount a 16-inch tire on a 16.5-inch rim, warning of the danger of severe injury or death, and including a picture of a worker thrown into the air by an explosion. The label also urged the user never to lean or reach over the assembly while working. Martinez ignored the warnings.

Martinez admitted that the warnings were adequate, but claimed that Goodrich was strictly liable for failing to use a safer "bead" design. The bead, a rubber-encased steel wire, encircles the tire and holds it to the rim. Martinez's expert testified that an alternate design, used by other tire manufacturers, would have prevented his injury. The trial court gave judgment for Martinez in the amount of $10,308,792.45, the Court of Appeals affirmed, and Goodrich appealed to the state's highest court.

Issue: When warnings are adequate, is a manufacturer still obligated to use a safer alternative design?

Excerpts from Chief Justice Phillips' Decision: This Court has adopted the products liability standard set forth in section 402A of the Restatement (Second) of Torts. A product may be unreasonably dangerous because of a defect in manufacturing, design, or marketing. To prove a design defect, a claimant must establish, among other things, that the defendant could have provided a safer alternative design. [If] there are no safer alternatives, a product is not unreasonably dangerous as a matter of law.

The newly released Restatement (Third) of Torts: Product Liability carries forward this focus on reasonable alternative design:

> A broad range of factors may be considered in determining whether an alternative design is reasonable and whether its omission renders a product not reasonably safe. The factors include, among others, the magnitude and probability of the foreseeable risks of harm, the instructions and warnings accompanying the product, and the nature and strength of consumer expectations regarding the product, including expectations arising from product portrayal and marketing. . . . Thus, the likely effects of the alternative design on production costs; the effects of the alternative design on product longevity, maintenance, repair, and esthetics; and the range of consumer choice among products are factors that may be taken into account. . . .

Goodrich urges this Court to depart from this standard by following certain language from

▼

Comment j of the Restatement (Second) of Torts. Comment j provides in part: "Where warning is given, the seller may reasonably assume that it will be read and heeded; and a product bearing such a warning, which is safe for use if it is followed, is not in defective condition, nor is it unreasonably dangerous." The new Restatement, however, expressly rejects the Comment j approach [and we refuse to adopt it].

The dissenting justices argue that Goodrich's warning was clear and that it could have been followed, and consequently Martinez was injured only by "[i]gnoring . . . his own good sense." Even if this were true, it is precisely because it is not at all unusual for a person to fail to follow basic warnings and instructions, that we have rejected the superseded Comment j. The dissent also notes that there have been few reported mismatch accidents involving tires with this particular warning label. While this is certainly relevant, and perhaps would persuade many juries, we cannot say that it conclusively establishes that the tire is reasonably safe when weighed against the other evidence. The jury heard firsthand how an accident can occur despite the warning label, and how a redesigned tire would have prevented that accident. The jury also heard evidence that Goodrich's competitors had incorporated the single strand programmed bead by the early 1980s, and that Goodrich itself adopted this design in 1991, a year after manufacturing the tire that injured Martinez.

The Martinezes offered some evidence that their alternative design would have prevented the injury to Martinez. It is undisputed that the single strand programmed bead is more resistant to breaking in mismatch situations. Goodrich expert Tom Conner testified that in a mismatch situation the tape bead may break at 60 psi, while a single strand bead will not break until at least 130 psi. Conner also testified that he has never heard of a single strand bead breaking during the inflating of a mismatched tire. Goodrich representative Stanley Lew testified that the single strand bead is more resistant in a mismatch situation. Lew also testified that if the tire inflated by Martinez had a single strand bead it would not have exploded. Both Conner and Lew testified that they would prefer a tire inflated by their loved one to have a single strand bead.

For the foregoing reasons, we affirm the judgment of the court of appeals. [Affirmed]

Excerpts from the Dissenting Opinion of Justice Hecht: Although a 16.5″ wheel can be designed so that a 16″ tire cannot be mounted on it, a 16″ tire cannot be designed so that it cannot be mounted on a 16.5″ wheel. A tire manufacturer's only options to reduce the risk of injury from attempting to mount a 16″ tire on a 16.5″ wheel are to place a warning on the tire or to design the bead wire so that it will withstand higher inflation pressure before exploding. The Uniroyal Goodrich Tire Company, which made the tire Martinez was using, chose to put a prominent, pictographic label on it, which, as I have said, Martinez actually saw but did not heed. Had he done so, he would not have been injured. In fact, according to the record, only one other person has ever claimed to have been injured attempting to mount a 16″ tire with a warning label like Goodrich's on a 16.5″ wheel, although thousands of labeled tires and more than thirty million 16.5″ wheels have been manufactured in the past two decades.

[The] Court holds that a product can be found to be defective whenever it could be more safely designed without substantially impairing its utility. This is not, and should not be, the law. As the Restatement (Third) of Torts: Product Liability advises, a "broad range of factors" besides the utility of a reasonable alternate design should be considered in determining whether its use is necessary to keep the product reasonably safe, including "the magnitude and probability of the foreseeable risks of harm [and] the instructions and warnings accompanying the product". When the undisputed evidence is that the magnitude and probability of a risk are low, an alternative design could reduce but not eliminate that risk, and the instructions and warnings given do eliminate the risk, the product should be determined not to be defective as a matter of law. ∎

ECONOMICS & the LAW

Smoking is expensive. In fact, virtually all state governments concluded that tobacco use causes lung cancer, emphysema, heart disease, and other illnesses, and that these ailments are very expensive to treat. The states filed suit against the tobacco industry, which settled most of the cases for a total of about $206 *billion,* to be paid gradually between the years 2000 and 2025. That is a lot of money, even for a profitable industry.

Ironically, one economist claims that the settlements make little money sense, because cigarettes are self-financing. This expert concedes that tobacco use causes expensive ill-

nesses, yet argues that the increased costs are offset by savings due to earlier mortality! Because smokers die younger than others, states pay less money for nursing homes and pensions. These savings more than offset the increased medical costs of smoking.

If that is correct, then why would the tobacco industry agree to the pricey settlements? This economist suggests that a tobacco industry defense based on earlier mortality would be very risky to make in court. Jurors might find the argument so offensive that they would impose even higher punitive damages.[22] ◆

Tort Reform

Some people believe that jury awards are excessive and need statutory reform. About one-half of the states have passed limits on tort awards. The laws vary, but many work this way. A jury is permitted to award whatever it considers fair for *economic* damages, meaning lost wages and medical expenses. However, *non-economic* damages (pain and suffering), together with any punitive award, may not exceed a prescribed limit, such as three times the economic damages, or sometimes a flat cap, such as $250,000 total. These restrictions can drastically lower the total verdict.

Other states have created special rules for particular kinds of product liability. *Unavoidably unsafe* prescription drugs are an example. Suppose that a plaintiff proves that a prescription medicine caused her grievous, permanent harm, and that one percent of all users will suffer similar damage. If the pharmaceutical company can demonstrate that it is impossible to manufacture the drug to eliminate all danger, many states will deny the plaintiff any damages. These states have essentially decided that the benefits of that prescription medicine outweigh its risks. If the medicine is unavoidably unsafe, that is, it cannot be made safer, the company should not be held liable; large verdicts might drive pharmaceutical firms out of a business that has great social value.

Opponents consider tort reform misleading and dangerous to society. They state that the real goal of the so-called "reform" is to free irresponsible corporations from any potential liability, enabling them to save money while injuring innocent people. Opponents argue that there is no evidence linking product liability cases to higher insurance costs. Jury verdicts nationwide have been declining. They insist that giving 12 average members of society a say in product safety benefits everyone.

Time Limits: Tort versus Contract

Statutes of Limitations in Tort

We have seen that for *warranty* cases, the UCC imposes a four-year statute of limitation. By contrast, most states have a different statute of limitations for tort claims. Many states set a three-year limit, though some are shorter and others longer. But the key element is this: in a tort case, the statute of limitations runs *from the time the defect was discovered*. Even though the three-year period is shorter, the time for filing a suit may be much longer because a defect may not appear for many years.

Many product liability cases involve both warranty and tort claims. Should a court apply the statute of limitations from the Code or from tort law? The analysis begins with the **economic loss doctrine: when an injury is purely economic, and arises from a contract made by two businesses, the injured party may only sue under the UCC.** This rule is primarily for contracts between two businesses; if the buyer is a consumer, most courts will not apply it. The economic loss doctrine has two important consequences for corporate buyers.

---

[22] W. Kip Viscusi, "The Governmental Composition of the Insurance Costs of Smoking," *Journal of Law and Economics*, 1999, vol. 42, p. 575.

First, **the four-year statute of limitations will apply in all cases of economic loss.** Suppose a corporation discovers that a product it purchased six years ago is defective and has caused major losses. The company probably has no remedy. Neibarger purchased an automated milking system for his dairy from Universal Cooperatives. Over the next few years, many of his cows became sick with mastitis; some died, and others had to be sold for beef. Seven years after he bought the equipment, Neibarger learned that Universal had improperly designed and installed the vacuum system that is an essential part of the machine. He sued, claiming massive damage to his farming operation, but the Michigan Supreme Court applied the economic loss doctrine. Neibarger's loss was commercial, resulting from a contract that two corporations had negotiated. His only possible remedy was under the UCC, but the Code's statute of limitations had expired. In the end he had no remedy.[23]

Second, **where the sales contract includes proper disclaimers or remedy limitations, a buyer barred from a negligence case may have no remedy at all.** The economic loss doctrine prohibits a corporation from suing in negligence when its loss is purely commercial. That leaves a lawsuit under the UCC. But if the seller has disclaimed all warranties and/or prohibited certain remedies (such as consequential damages), the buyer may be left with no basis for a lawsuit.

A Final Issue: Statutes of Repose

In tort cases, the passage of time provides a seller with two possible defenses. We have seen that the statute of limitations requires that a lawsuit be brought within a specified period, such as three years, beginning when the defect is discovered or should have been discovered. **A statute of repose places an absolute limit on when a lawsuit may be filed, regardless of when the defect is discovered.** Jeffrey Oats was riding in the back seat of a Nissan sports car when it was involved in an accident. Tragically, Oats suffered spinal cord injuries that left him a quadriplegic. Oats sued Nissan, based on defective design, claiming that the rear seat lacked adequate head and leg room and that the car's body panels lacked sufficient strength. He argued that these defects only became apparent in an accident. But the Idaho Supreme Court dismissed his claims because the car was 11 years old at the time of the accident. The Idaho statute of repose prohibits most product liability suits filed more than 10 years after the goods were sold, regardless of when the defects were discoverable.[24]

OTHER LEGISLATION

Congress and state legislatures frequently pass statutes affecting product liability. A summary of all the legislation would create an overwhelming and uninformative list, so we mention only a few statutes to indicate that sellers must consider other laws when designing and marketing goods, and that buyers who believe they have been injured may have remedies beyond those discussed in the chapter.

Lemon Laws

It is intensely frustrating—and expensive—for consumers when a new car is defective and spends more time in the repair shop than on the road. So, many states have passed lemon laws, which entitle the buyer to receive a refund if the car has defects that substantially impair its value and safety. This right may prove more valuable than a limited warranty, which might only entitle the buyer to repeated attempts at servicing.

---

[23] *Neibarger v. Universal Cooperatives, Inc.*, 439 Mich. 512, 486 N.W.2d 612, 1992 Mich. LEXIS 1502 (1992).
[24] *Oats v. Nissan Motor Corp.*, 126 Idaho 162, 879 P.2d 1095, 1994 Ida. LEXIS 116 (1994).

Check out the lemon law in your state. Drive to http://autopedia.com and find your way to the material on lemon laws. What obligations does the law impose on buyers and sellers? In your view does the law strike a fair balance, or does it favor one side?   ◆

The public has clamored for more laws to protect it against unscrupulous sellers. Some states have added lemon laws for used cars. California, among others, has responded with a *puppy* lemon law, enabling buyers to obtain refunds for cats and dogs that were sick when purchased. You may view the law—but please do not feed it—at http://www.dog-play.com/lemonlaw.html.

Consumer Protection Laws

Virtually all states also have consumer protection laws, which focus on a merchant's bad faith or deceit. Consumers can use these statutes, which are discussed in Chapter 40, to recover for defective goods or inadequate service.

Magnuson-Moss Warranty Act

This statute protects consumers who purchase household goods by ensuring basic fairness in the seller's warranty. The statute does not *require* any warranties at all, but covers cases in which a seller chooses to give one. Most sellers of consumer goods do provide some form of express warranty to attract buyers. Magnuson-Moss requires the seller to indicate whether a warranty is full or limited, and to describe clearly what is and is not warranted. The Act also sets certain minimum standards for an express warranty, requiring, for example, that at the very least a seller agree to repair or replace a defective item. Finally, the Act generally forbids a seller who has chosen to give an express warranty to disclaim implied warranties such as the Code's warranties of merchantability and fitness. For a detailed look at Magnuson-Moss, visit http://www.ftc.gov.

Suppose Flybynite Corp. wants to unload 10,000 snowmobiles that it knows do not work in the snow. To attract customers, it prominently features "EXPRESS WARRANTY" in its ads. But the warranty only promises that "the snowmobile is guaranteed to start within 10 seconds, every time, for 60 days." The warranty then goes on to say, "Seller disclaims all other warranties, express or implied, whether of merchantability, fitness, or any other kind." Buyers discover that their snowmobiles start up quickly but cannot be operated in the snow because the treads are defective. Under Magnuson-Moss, Flybynite cannot disclaim the warranties of merchantability and fitness. Since the snowmobiles are not merchantable, any consumer will get his money back. The company has also violated the consumer protection laws of most states, and an angry buyer might even get treble damages and attorney's fees.

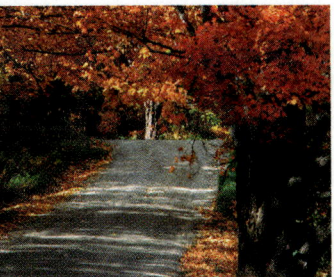

Chapter Conclusion

Both sellers and buyers of goods must understand the basic principles of product liability law. A seller must understand warranty, negligence, and strict liability law and consider all of those principles when designing, manufacturing, and marketing goods. A buyer, on the other hand, should be aware that each theory provides a possible basis for compensation and that consumers receive particularly strong protection.

Chapter Review

Products can injure. The harm may be economic or physical. The plaintiff might have a remedy in *warranty*, which is found in the UCC, or one in *tort*, either for negligence or strict liability. The economic loss doctrine states that, when the injured party is a corporation and the harm is purely economic, the only remedies available are the warranty provisions of the Code. If a corporation suffers physical injury, it will probably be able to sue in tort. A consumer who suffers a physical injury can definitely sue in both tort and warranty, and a consumer who suffers an economic injury can generally, but not always, sue in both.

The Code prescribes a four-year statute of limitations for breaches of warranty. In tort cases, the statute of limitations runs from whenever the plaintiff should have discovered the defect. For ease of review, the following chart summarizes the different warranty and tort remedies.

	Contract or Tort	Source of Law	Summary of the Rule	Example	Potential Issue
Express Warranty	Contract	UCC §2-313	May be created by an affirmation of fact, a promise, a description of goods, or a sample, but it must have been the basis of the bargain.	Salesman says, "This helicopter will operate perfectly at 16,000 feet."	Written contract may disclaim any and all *oral* warranties.
Implied Warranty of Merchantability	Contract	UCC §2-314	The Code implies that the goods are fit for their ordinary use.	Buyer purchases a deep freezer. The Code implies a warranty that it will keep food frozen.	Seller may disclaim this warranty only if a conspicuous disclaimer includes the word "merchantability."
Implied Warranty of Fitness	Contract	UCC §2-315	The Code implies that the goods are fit for buyer's special purpose that seller knows about.	Where seller knows (1) buyer wants pine trees to plant in sandy soil, and (2) buyer is relying on seller's judgment, the trees carry an implied warranty that they will grow in that soil.	Seller may disclaim this warranty with conspicuous writing, but note that some states will disregard a disclaimer of *any* implied warranty in a consumer sale.
Implied Warranty of Title	Contract	UCC §2-312	The Code implies that seller has good title, free of any security interests and claims of patent, copyright, or trademark.	Seller sells a stolen car to buyer, who must later return it to the rightful owner. Seller has breached his warranty of good title and owes buyer her full damages.	Buyer is not protected against any security interests that she knows about.

	Contract or Tort	Source of Law	Summary of the Rule	Example	Potential Issue
Negligence	Tort	Common law	Seller is liable if she fails to show level of conduct that a *reasonable person* would use.	Manufacturer sells bathing suit made of miracle fabric; buyer swims in ocean where saltwater makes garment transparent; seller's failure to test the suit in saltwater was unreasonable and leaves seller liable. If seller had thoroughly tested and this was a freak occurrence, there would probably be no negligence.	No duty to warn if the danger is obvious. (In the bathing suit example, the danger is *not* obvious and there was a duty to warn.)
Strict Liability	Tort	Reinstatement §402A (subject to new revisions) and common law	Seller liable if the product leaves in a dangerously a defective condition.	Can of barbecue lighter fluid explodes in the users hand because the can's metal was defective; manufacturer took every reasonable precaution to test and inspect every can leaving factory; that reasonable care is *irrelevant* and seller is liable.	Injured buyer need not prove negligence but must prove that the product was defective.

Practice Test

1. **CPA QUESTION** Vick bought a used boat from Ocean Marina that disclaimed "any and all warranties." Ocean was unaware the boat had been stolen from Kidd. Vick surrendered it to Kidd when confronted with proof of the theft. Vick sued Ocean. Who prevails?

   a. Vick, because the implied warranty of title has been breached

   b. Vick, because a merchant cannot disclaim implied warranties

   c. Ocean, because of the disclaimer of warranties

   d. Ocean, because Vick surrendered the boat to Kidd

2. **CPA QUESTION** To establish a cause of action based on strict liability in tort for personal injuries resulting from using a defective product, one of the elements the plaintiff must prove is that the seller (defendant):

   a. Failed to exercise due care

   b. Was in privity of contract with the plaintiff

   c. Defectively designed the product

   d. Was engaged in the business of selling the product

3. Leighton Industries needed steel pipe to build furnaces for a customer. Leighton sent Callier

Steel an order for a certain quantity of "A 106 Grade B" steel. Callier confirmed the order and created a contract by sending an invoice to Leighton, stating that it would send "A 106 Grade B" steel, as ordered. Callier delivered the steel and Leighton built the furnaces, but they leaked badly and required rebuilding. Tests demonstrated that the steel was not, in fact, "A 106 Grade B," but an inferior steel. Leighton sued. Who wins?

4. ***YOU BE THE JUDGE*** WRITING PROBLEM United Technologies advertised a used Beechcraft Baron airplane for sale in an aviation journal. Attorney Thompson Comerford was interested and spoke with a United agent who described the plane as "excellently maintained" and said it had been operated "under §135 flight regulations," meaning the plane had been subject to airworthiness inspections every 100 hours. Comerford arrived at a Dallas airport to pick up the plane, where he paid $80,000 for it. He signed a sales agreement stating that the plane was sold "as is" and that there were "no representations or warranties, express or implied, including the condition of the aircraft, its merchantability or its fitness for any particular purpose." Comerford attempted to fly the plane home, but immediately experienced problems with its brakes, steering, ability to climb, and performance while cruising. (Otherwise it was fine.) He sued, claiming breach of express and implied warranties. Did United Technologies breach express or implied warranties? **Argument for Comerford:** United described the airplane as "excellently maintained," knowing that Mr. Comerford would rely on that information. United bragged about §135 servicing, when that was obviously a lie. The company should not be allowed to say one thing and put the opposite in writing. **Argument for United Technologies:** Comerford is a lawyer, and we assume he can read. The contract could not have been clearer. The plane was sold as is. There were no warranties. If Comerford disliked the terms, he should have bargained for a different contract—or walked away. He knew he was buying a risky plane, and it is his to keep.

5. Round Tire Co. sells 1,000 tires to Green Rent-a-Car for use on Green's fleet. The same day it sells one new tire to Betty Blue for use on her car. For both sales, Round uses a sales agreement that includes: "LIMITATION OF REMEDIES. Round agrees to repair or replace any tire which Round determines was defective, within 12 months or 25,000, whichever comes first. Buyer agrees that this is Buyer's SOLE REMEDY; Buyer is not entitled to consequential or incidental damages or any other remedy of any kind." All of Round's tires prove defective. Green is so disgusted it immediately purchases substitute tires from another manufacturer. Green loses $12,000 in extra tire costs and $75,000 in lost rental payments because many of its cars must be off the road waiting for tires. Betty Blue's new tire blows out as she is driving to church, and Betty suffers broken bones. Green and Blue both sue. Predict the outcomes.

6. **ETHICS** Texaco, Inc., and other oil companies sold mineral spirits in bulk to distributors, which then resold to retailers. Mineral spirits are used for cleaning. Texaco allegedly knew that the retailers, such as hardware stores, frequently packaged the mineral spirits (illegally) in used half-gallon milk containers and sold them to consumers, often with no warnings on the packages. Mineral spirits are harmful or fatal if swallowed. David Hunnings, aged 21 months, found a milk container in his home, swallowed the mineral spirits, and died. The Hunnings sued Texaco in negligence. The trial court dismissed the complaint and the Hunnings appealed. What is the legal standard in a negligence case? Have the plaintiffs made out a valid case of negligence? Remember that at this stage a court is not deciding who wins, but what standard a plaintiff must meet in order to take its case to a jury. Assume that Texaco knew about the repackaging and the grave risk, but continued to sell in bulk because doing so was profitable. (If the plaintiffs cannot prove those facts, they will lose even if they *do* get to a jury.) Would that make you angry? Does that mean such a case should go to a jury? Or would you conclude that the fault still lies with the retailer and/or the parents? In that case, the court should dismiss the suit against Texaco.

7. Boboli Co. wanted to promote its "California style" pizza, which it sold in supermarkets. The company contracted with Highland Group, Inc., to produce two million recipe brochures, which would be inserted in the carton when the freshly baked pizza was still very hot. Highland contracted

with Comark Merchandising to print the brochures. But when Comark asked for details concerning the pizza, the carton, and so forth, Highland refused to supply the information. Comark printed the first lot of 72,000 brochures, which Highland delivered to Boboli. Unfortunately, the hot bread caused the ink to run, and customers opening the carton often found red or blue splotches on their pizzas. Highland refused to accept additional brochures, and Comark sued for breach of contract. Highland defended by claiming that Comark had breached its warranty of merchantability. Please comment.

8. **CPA QUESTION** Which of the following conditions must be met for an implied warranty of fitness for a particular purpose to arise?: I. The warranty must be in writing. II. The seller must know that the buyer was relying on the seller in selecting the goods.
   a. I only
   b. II only
   c. Both I and II
   d. Neither I nor II

9. **CPA QUESTION** Under the UCC sales article, an action for breach of the implied warranty of merchantability by a party who sustains personal injuries may be successful against the seller of the product only when:

   a. The seller is a merchant of the product involved
   b. An action based on negligence can also be successfully maintained
   c. The injured party is in privity of contract with the seller
   d. An action based on strict liability in tort can also be successfully maintained

10. **CPA QUESTION** Which of the following factors is least important in determining whether a manufacturer is strictly liable in tort for a defective product?
    a. The negligence of the manufacturer
    b. The contributory negligence of the plaintiff
    c. Modifications to the product by the wholesaler
    d. Whether the product caused injuries

11. **ROLE REVERSAL** Write an essay question concerning a household product that injures a buyer. The buyer sues under theories of warranty and strict liability. The buyer should have a strong claim based on one theory but no reasonable claim based on the other.

Internet Research Problem

Go to **http://beatty.westbuslaw.com** and find the crash test results. Which cars are safer than average? Less safe? How important is auto safety to you? Are you willing to pay more for a safe car? Who should be the final judge of auto safety: auto companies, insurance companies, juries, government regulators, or consumers?

> **You can find further practice problems at http://beatty.westbuslaw.com or in the Study Guide that accompanies this text.**

Performance and Remedies

Was it a 1930s roadster? A drag racing car from the 1950s? Both. Neither. *Untouchable.* When the Plymouth Prowler first hit the road, with its motorcycle-styled front fenders and low-slung hot rod body, it was nearly impossible to get your hands on one. Dealers were swamped with orders, but did not know if they would receive a single car from the manufacturer. Donald Hessler was one of those who wanted a Prowler—and he was a determined man.

Hessler went to Crystal Lake Chrysler-Plymouth, met with its owner, Gary Rosenberg, and signed an agreement to buy a Prowler anytime during the next year for $5,000 over the manufacturer's list price. Three months later Rosenberg revealed that the list price would be $39,000. However, the car dealer also entered into a contract to sell a Prowler to another customer for $50,000.

The next time they spoke, Rosenberg told Hessler that Crystal Lake would not be allotted any Prowlers. The eager buyer, though, responded that a Chrysler representative had told him Crystal Lake would receive at least one car. Rosenberg was furious with a customer who had "gone behind his back" to contact Chrylser, and said he would not sell Hessler a car, even if he did receive one.

Hessler telephoned 38 Chrysler dealers, but none would promise him a car. One month later, at a promotional event for the car, he saw a new Prowler—with Crystal Lake's name on it! He located Rosenberg, offered to buy the car on the spot—and was again rebuffed. Frustrated and angry, but still determined, Hessler somehow found a Prowler later the same day from another dealer, and bought it—for $77,706.

Ecstatic with his new car, Hessler drove straight to court, where he sued Crystal Lake.

Was Rosenberg within his rights, refusing to sell a car to Hessler? Was the customer entitled to any compensation for spending so much more on the coveted auto? These are typical issues of *contract performance* under the Code, which we look at in this chapter, along with principles of *remedy*. Technically, when Hessler bought a car elsewhere, he was *covering*. Did he act reasonably in spending $30,000 above the price set by Crystal Lake, and almost $40,000 above list price? You will have to wait a few pages to find out, but we promise to give you the answer before anyone else gets it.

Surely it is a good idea to begin this final chapter on sale of goods issues in good faith. ■

GOOD FAITH

The R. G. Ray Corp. needed T-bolts to use in certain automobile parts it was manufacturing for the Garrett Co. Ray contracted for Maynard Manufacturing to deliver 57,000 T-bolts and provided Maynard with detailed specifications. The contract stated that Ray would be the "final judge" of whether the T-bolts conformed to its specifications and that Ray had the right to return any or all non-conforming bolts. **Conforming goods satisfy the contract terms. Non-conforming goods do not.**[1] Unfortunately, Ray rejected the 57,000 bolts and sued, demanding every penny it had paid as well as additional damages for its lost business with Garrett. Ray moved for summary judgment, pointing out that the contract explicitly allowed it to judge the bolts, to reject any it found unsatisfactory, and to cancel the contract. The court acknowledged that the contract did give Ray these one-sided powers, yet it denied summary judgment. There was still an issue of *good faith*.

The Code requires *good faith* in the performance and enforcement of every contract. Good faith means honesty in fact. Between merchants, it also means the use of reasonable commercial standards of fair dealing.[2] So Ray's right to reject the T-bolts was not absolute. There was some evidence that Ray had lost its contract with Garrett for reasons having nothing to do with Maynard's T-bolts. If that was true, and Ray had rejected the T-bolts simply because it no longer needed them, then

---

[1]   UCC §2-106(2).
[2]   UCC §§1-203, 2-103(1)(b).

Ray acted in bad faith and would be fully liable on the contract. The court ruled that Maynard should have its day in court to prove bad faith.[3]

With this good faith requirement in mind, we look first at the seller's obligations, and then at those of the buyer.

SELLER'S OBLIGATIONS (AND A FEW RIGHTS)

The seller's primary obligation is to deliver conforming goods to the buyer.[4] But because a buyer might not be willing or able to accept delivery, the UCC demands only that the seller make a reasonable *attempt* at delivery. **The seller must *tender* the goods, which means to make conforming goods available to the buyer.**[5] Normally, the contract will state where and when the seller is obligated to tender delivery. For example, the parties may agree that Manufacturer is to tender 1,000 computer printers at a certain warehouse on July 3. If Manufacturer makes the printers available on that date, Buyer is obligated to pick them up then and there, and is in breach if it fails to do so.

Although a seller must always tender delivery, that does not mean a seller always transports the goods. Sometimes the contract will require the buyer to collect the goods. Regardless of where delivery is being made, however, the seller must (1) make the goods available at a reasonable time, (2) keep the goods available for a reasonable period, and (3) deliver to the buyer any documents that it needs to take possession. And as we have said, the seller is expected to deliver *conforming* goods, which brings us to the next rule.

Perfect Tender Rule

Under the perfect tender rule, the buyer may reject the goods if they fail *in any respect* to conform to the contract.[6] Under the common law, before the Code was drafted, the perfect tender rule required that the seller deliver goods that conformed absolutely to the contract specifications. The buyer had the right to reject goods with even minor deviations. Although commentators had criticized the rule for decades and courts had carved many exceptions into the rule, the drafters of the UCC retained it.

Stanley and Joan Jakowski agreed to buy a new Camaro automobile from Carole Chevrolet. The contract stated that Carole would apply a polymer undercoating. The Jakowskis paid in full for the car but the next day informed Carole that the car lacked the undercoating. Carole acknowledged the defect and promised to apply the undercoating, but before it could do so, a thief stole the car. The Jakowskis demanded their money back, but Carole refused, saying that the risk of loss had passed to the Jakowskis when Carole tendered delivery. The Jakowskis sued, claiming that they had rejected the Camaro as non-conforming. Carole responded that this was absurd: the car was perfect in every respect except for the very minor undercoating, which Carole had promised to fix promptly. Carole Chevrolet was correct in its description of the car, but lost the case because of the perfect tender rule.

The New Jersey court found that the defect was minor, but said that, "despite seller's assertion to the contrary, the degree of their nonconformity is irrelevant in assessing the buyer's concomitant right to reject them. . . . [N]o particular quantum of nonconformity is required." The Jakowskis had lawfully rejected non-conforming goods, and Carole Chevrolet was forced to pay them the full value of the missing car.[7]

---

[3] *R. G. Ray Corp. v. Maynard Manufacturing Co.*, 1993 U.S. Dist. LEXIS 15754 (N.D. Ill. 1993).

[4] UCC §2-301.

[5] UCC §2-503.

[6] UCC §2-601.

[7] *Jakowski v. Carole Chevrolet, Inc.*, 180 N.J. Super. 122, 433 A.2d 841, 1981 N.J. Super. LEXIS 635 (N.J. Super. Ct. 1981).

Restrictions on the Perfect Tender Rule

The Code includes sections that limit the perfect tender rule's effect. Indeed, courts often apply the limitations more enthusiastically than the rule itself, and so while perfect tender is the law, it must be understood in the context of other provisions. We will look at the most common ways that the law—or the parties themselves—undercut the perfect tender rule. In doing so, we will see the typically flexible approach that the Code takes to a business transaction, in contrast to the inflexible and potentially harsh results of the perfect tender rule.

Usage of Trade, Course of Dealing, and Course of Performance

The Code takes the commonsense view that a contract for the sale of goods does not exist in a vacuum. **"Usage of trade" means any practice that members of an industry *expect* to be part of their dealings.**[8] The Code requires that courts consider trade usage when they interpret contracts, which means that the perfect tender rule may not permit a buyer to reject goods with minor flaws. For example, the textile industry interprets the phrase "first quality fabric" to permit a limited number of flaws in most materials. If a seller delivers 1,000 bolts of fabric and 5 of them have minor defects, the seller *has not* violated the perfect tender rule; in the textile industry, such a minor nonconformity *is* perfect tender.

The course of dealing between the two parties may also limit the rule. **"Course of dealing" refers to previous commercial transactions between the same parties.**[9] The Code requires that the current contract be interpreted in the light of any past dealings that have created reasonable expectations. Suppose a buyer orders 20,000 board feet of "highest grade pine" from a lumber company, just as it has in each of the three previous years. In the earlier deliveries, the buyer accepted the lumber even though 1 or 2 percent was not the highest grade. That course of dealing will probably control the present contract, and the buyer will not be permitted suddenly to reject an entire shipment because 1 percent is a lower grade of pine.

The course of performance has the same effect on contract interpretation. **"Course of performance" refers to the history of dealings between the parties *in this one contract*, and thus assumes that it is the kind of contract demanding an ongoing relationship.**[10] Suppose a newspaper company signs a deal to purchase five tons of newsprint from a paper company every week for a year, and the contract also specifies the grade of paper to be delivered. If, during the first three months, the newspaper company routinely accepts paper containing a small number of flaws, that course of performance will control the contract. During the final month, the newspaper may not suddenly reject the type of paper it had earlier accepted.

Parties' Agreement

The parties may limit the effect of the perfect tender rule by drafting a contract that permits imperfection in the goods. In some industries this is routine practice. For example, contracts requiring the seller to design or engineer goods specially for the buyer will generally state a level of performance that the equipment must meet. If the goods meet the level described, the buyer has no right to reject, even if the product has some flaws.

at RISK

Computer software plays an ever growing role in all business, and corporations routinely purchase software designed especially for them. But software almost always has at least

---

[8] UCC §1-205(2).
[9] UCC §1-205(1).
[10] UCC §2-208(1).

minor flaws, and a software manufacturer might fail the perfect tender rule on every sale. A wise software seller will insist that the contract establish tolerances for expected levels of failure and permit adequate opportunities to correct any defects. ◆

Cure

A basic goal of the UCC is a fully performed contract that leaves both parties satisfied. The seller's right to *cure* helps achieve this goal. **When the buyer rejects non-conforming goods, the seller has the right to cure, by delivering conforming goods before the contract deadline.**[11] LightCo is obligated to deliver 10,000 specially manufactured bulbs to Burnout Corp. by September 15. LightCo delivers the bulbs on August 20, and on August 25 Burnout notifies the seller that the bulbs do not meet contract specifications. If LightCo promptly notifies Burnout that it intends to cure and then delivers conforming light bulbs on September 15, it has fulfilled its contract obligations, and Burnout must accept the goods. A contract should not fail when a seller shows every willingness to cure the problem.

A seller who delivers non-conforming goods is generally entitled to a reasonable opportunity to cure.

The seller may even cure *after the contract deadline* if the seller (1) reasonably believed the original goods were acceptable and (2) promptly notified the buyer of his intent to cure within a reasonable time. This gives the seller a second chance to replace defective goods. Suppose Chip Co. delivers 25,000 computer chips to Assembler one day before the contract deadline, and two days later Assembler notifies Chip that the goods are defective. If Chip had thoroughly tested the chips before they left its factory and reasonably believed they met contract specifications, then Chip may cure by promptly notifying Assembler that it will supply conforming goods within a reasonable period. Thus, even if the conforming chips arrive two weeks after the contract deadline, Chip will have cured unless Assembler can show that the delay caused it serious harm.

In the case that follows, the choir can sing much better than the appellate judges—but how do their *robes* compare?

ZION TEMPLE FIRST PENTECOSTAL CHURCH OF CINCINNATI, OHIO, INC. V. BRIGHTER DAY BOOKSTORE & GIFTS

2004 WL 23150323
Court of Appeals of Ohio, 2004

Facts: Zion Temple First Pentecostal Church needed new choir robes. Brighter Day Bookstore was a retailer that sold robes manufactured by Murphy Cap & Gown. Rosalind Bush of Brighter Day showed Glenda Evans of Zion a robe and a sample board of Murphy products. The board showed various fabrics in diverse colors. A disclaimer on the board said, "all shades subject to dye lot variations." Evans ordered choir robes and overlays in colors and fabrics that she selected.

---

[11] UCC §2-508.

Murphy then sent sample swatches to Brighter Day, stating they were cut from the actual cloth that would be used for the Zion Temple robes. Bush called Evans to see if she wished to see the swatches, but Evans declined, saying she trusted Bush's judgment. Bush told Murphy to proceed with the order.

When Brighter Day delivered the robes to the Zion Temple, Evans and other church members found many faults. They did not like the color or material, which they considered very different from the board sample. The sleeves had been attached facing the wrong way. And on the overlays, the Velcro and tags were visible.

Zion complained to Murphy. The manufacturer offered to repair the sleeves, but Zion declined the offer because of the other problems. Zion returned the robes, and when it failed to get its money back, filed suit.

Zion claimed Murphy breached its warranty by delivering goods that differed from the sample board, and had the sleeve and overlay problems. The trial court gave summary judgment for the defendants, and Zion Temple appealed.

Issues: Did Murphy breach its warranty? Did Zion Temple afford Murphy a chance to cure?

Excerpts from Judge Doan's Decision: The record shows that Evans and the choir members actually inspected the robes when Brighter Day delivered them and Zion found what it deemed to be nonconformities. This inspection was reasonable and was made within a reasonable time. Thus, Zion never accepted the robes, but instead rejected them as not conforming to the contract. Since Zion rejected the goods, Murphy had a right to cure.

Further, the swatches themselves created an express warranty as to the appearance of the material

that became a part of the contract. Zion did not have the right to reject the robes based solely upon the color and feel of the material, because the material conformed to the requirements of the contract.

As to the sleeves, Murphy offered to cure any problem with the sleeves. Where the buyer rejects a nonconforming tender which the seller had reasonable ground to believe would be acceptable with or without money allowance, the seller may, if he seasonably notifies the buyer, have a further reasonable time to substitute a conforming tender. Murphy manufactured the sleeves on the robes according to its design specifications. Because of an error in the catalog that Zion had consulted before placing its order, the sleeves as properly manufactured appeared different from the sleeves as depicted in the catalog. Murphy clearly had the right to cure this nonconformity and indicated its intention to do so within a reasonable time.

Zion had other reasons for contending that the robes did not conform to the contract. It claimed that Velcro was visible on the reversible overlays and that the tags on the overlays could be seen when the overlays were reversed. Murphy never indicated its intention to cure these alleged nonconformities.

In addition to the sample board, Murphy also provided to Zion a sample robe. That sample robe also created an express warranty that became part of the contract. Material issues of fact exist as to whether the alleged defects related to the tags and Velcro violated the express warranty created by the sample robe and whether they rendered the robes nonconforming tender subject to rejection. Consequently, the trial court erred in granting Murphy's motion for summary judgment.

We reverse the entry of summary judgment for Murphy and remand this case for trial or further proceedings consistent with this court's opinion. ■

Devil's Advocate

The Zion Temple complained about five problems with the robes—three of which the church caused! If church leaders had checked out the swatches, there would have been no problem with color or fabric. If they had permitted Murphy to remake the sleeves, that issue would have been eliminated. The Zion Temple has behaved unreasonably from start to finish—yet we have to go *back* to the trial court about Velcro and tags? The trial court had it right—summary judgment for defendants. ◆

Substantial Impairment

In two cases the Code permits a buyer to refuse goods only if their non-conformity *substantially impairs their value*. This is a higher standard for the buyer to meet. **A buyer who claims goods are non-conforming must show that the defects *substantially impair* their value (1) if the buyer is revoking acceptance of goods or (2) if the**

buyer is rejecting an installment. So a buyer who accepts a dozen cement mixers, but later discovers problems with their engines, may revoke his acceptance only by showing that the defects have caused him serious problems. Similarly, if a contract requires a buyer to accept one shipment of diesel fuel each month for two years, the buyer may reject one monthly installment only if the problem with the fuel substantially lowers its value. We consider this issue from the buyer's perspective later in the chapter.

Destruction of the Goods

A farmer contracts to sell 250,000 pounds of sunflowers to a broker. The contract describes the 250 acres that the farmer will plant to grow the flowers. He plants his crop on time but a drought destroys most of the plants, and he is able to deliver only 75,000 pounds. Is the farmer liable for the flowers he could not deliver? No. Is the broker required to accept the smaller crop? No. **If identified goods are totally destroyed before risk passes to the buyer, the contract is void. If identified goods are partially destroyed, the buyer may choose whether to accept the goods at a reduced price or void the contract.**[12]

The crop of sunflowers was identified to the contract when the farmer planted it. When a drought destroyed most of the crop, the contract became voidable. The buyer had the right to accept the smaller crop, at a reduced price, or to reject the crop entirely. The farmer is not liable for the shortfall, because the destruction was not his fault.[13]

Commercial Impracticability

Commercial impracticability means that a supervening event excuses performance of a contract, if the event was not within the parties' contemplation when they made the agreement.[14] An event is "supervening" if it interrupts the normal course of business and dominates performance of the contract. But a supervening event will excuse performance only if neither party had thought there was any serious chance it would happen.

Harris RF Systems was an American company that manufactured radio equipment. Svenska, a Swedish corporation, bought Harris radio systems and sold them in many countries, including Iran. One contract required Harris to ship a large quantity of spare radio parts, which Svenska would pay $600,000 for and then resell in Iran. Harris attempted to ship the parts to Svenska but U.S. Customs seized the goods, and the U.S. Department of Defense then notified Harris that it feared the parts would be of military value to Iran. Harris executives met several times with Defense Department officials and officers of Svenska, attempting to work out a compromise.

The Defense Department acknowledged that technically Harris was licensed to ship the goods but made two things clear: first, that it would litigate rather than permit the goods to reach Iran, and second, that if Harris attempted to complete the sale in Iran, the department would place all of Harris's future radio shipments on a Munitions List, making it difficult to ship them anywhere in the world. Svenska, on the other hand, pointed out that it had binding contracts to deliver the radio parts to various customers in Iran. If the parts were not forthcoming, Svenska would hold Harris liable for all of its losses. Harris attempted to reach a satisfactory compromise with all parties but failed and eventually agreed not to ship the parts overseas.

Svenska sued. Harris defended, relying on commercial impracticability. Harris persuaded the court that neither party had foreseen the government's intervention and

---

[12] UCC §2-613. Identification of goods is discussed in Chapter 20, on ownership and risk.
[13] Based on *Red River Commodities, Inc. v. Eidsness,* 459 N.W.2d 805, 1990 N.D. LEXIS 159 (N.D. 1990).
[14] UCC §2-615.

that both parties realized it would be virtually impossible to export goods the Defense Department was determined to block. The court dismissed Svenska's suit.[15]

Sellers offer many excuses to avoid contracts. A merchant may plead that her own supply of goods failed. Courts generally assume that the parties did contemplate failure of supply, and therefore reject the excuse, holding the seller liable. On the other hand, natural disasters, such as hurricanes or tornadoes, may relieve a party from performing.

In the following case, you decide whether the seller's unexpected problem created true impossibility.

you Be The Judge

SPECIALTY TIRES OF AMERICA, INC. V. THE CIT GROUP/EQUIPMENT FINANCING, INC.

82 F. Supp. 2d 434
United States District Court for the Western District of Pennsylvania, 2000

Facts: CIT Group, a major equipment leasing company, leased 11 tire press machines to Condere Corporation, in Natchez, Mississippi, maintaining the right to repossess the goods if Condere defaulted on its payments. After making some payments, Condere (did you guess?) stopped making payments and filed for bankruptcy in the Southern District of Mississippi. Specialty Tires wanted to expand production in that area and was interested in purchasing the machines. CIT and Specialty executives toured the Condere factory to examine the tire presses and discuss the logistics of their removal. Condere officials cooperated fully, acknowledging that CIT had the right to immediate possession and assisting in the transportation plans. CIT then agreed to sell the goods to Specialty for $250,000.

When CIT attempted to ship the presses to Specialty, Condere surprised everyone by refusing access to the equipment. Instead, Condere (without the necessary permission of the bankruptcy court) offered CIT a check to cover its lease payments. CIT refused the payment and filed a complaint in the bankruptcy case, asking the court in Mississippi to award it the goods. Meanwhile, Specialty filed suit against CIT, in Pennsylvania, for breach of contract. In the Pennsylvania court, CIT moved for summary judgment, claiming commercial impracticability.

You Be the Judge: Should CIT be discharged based on commercial impracticability?

Argument for CIT: Your honor, CIT cannot deliver goods that it cannot even get its hands on. Specialty bargained for these 11 tire presses, not for just any machines. The parties toured Condere's factory, identified all the equipment, and negotiated terms based on delivery of these goods. Condere assured everyone that the presses would be ready for delivery. CIT could not have foreseen Condere's bizarre turn-about or made provisions to protect itself. This is not a case where a seller, unable to deliver 1,000 bushels of apples, can supply identical goods from another source. There was nothing CIT could do to remedy the situation but direct Specialty to the bankruptcy court, and Specialty has refused to enter into those proceedings. While we are sympathetic to Specialty's frustration, the fault lies entirely with Condere. It is impossible to move these goods without an order from the bankruptcy court, and neither CIT nor any other company should suffer a large loss for failing to do something that it cannot physically, theoretically, or legally accomplish.

Argument for Specialty: Your honor, companies enter into contracts to control future events and protect against risks. When CIT agreed to this contract, the company was promising either to deliver the goods or suffer the consequences. We realize it is Condere's irresponsible behavior that has induced this logjam. The question, though, is not who caused the snafu, but who must suffer the consequences. Specialty planned a major expansion

[15] *Harriscom Svenska AB v. Harris Corp.,* 1990 U.S. Dist. LEXIS 20006 (W.D.N.Y. 1990).

in the area using these tire presses, and now is losing money based on factory space rented, other overhead incurred, and lost profits. Specialty has done nothing wrong at all, and should not endure those losses. CIT chose to lease the goods to Condere, and chose to promise our client that the presses would be delivered on time. Perhaps CIT should select its business partners more scrupulously, or buy additional insurance. Those are risk/benefit decisions for CIT to make in the future. Right now it is time for CIT to pay up. ■

The accompanying chart outlines the seller's obligations.

Basic Obligation: The seller's basic obligation is to deliver conforming goods. **The perfect tender rule permits the buyer to reject the goods if they are in any way non-conforming.** But many Code provisions limit the harshness of the perfect tender rule.

Limitation on Seller's Obligation	Code Provision	Effect on Seller's Obligations
Good faith	§1-201(19) and §2-103(1)(b)	Prohibits the buyer from using the perfect tender rule as a way out of a contract that has become unprofitable.
Course of dealing, usage of trade, and course of performance	§1-205(1), §1-205(2), and §2-208	If applicable, will limit the buyer's right to reject for relatively routine defects.
The parties' agreement	§2-106	May describe tolerances for imperfections in the goods.
Cure	§2-508	Allows the seller to replace defective goods with conforming goods, if time permits.
Revocation of acceptance	§2-608	A buyer who has accepted goods may later revoke them only if she can show that the defects *substantially impair* its value.
Installment contracts	§2-612	A buyer may reject an installment only if the defects *substantially impair* its value.
Destruction of goods	§2-613	If goods identified to the contract are destroyed, the contract is void.
Commercial impracticability	§2-615	A supervening event excuses performance of a contract, if the event was not within the parties' contemplation when they made the agreement.

BUYER'S OBLIGATIONS (AND A FEW RIGHTS)

The buyer's primary obligation is to accept conforming goods and pay for them.[16] The buyer must also **provide adequate facilities to receive the goods.**[17] For example, if the contract requires the seller to deliver to the buyer's warehouse, and the parties anticipate that delivery will be by rail, then the buyer must have facilities for unloading railcars at its warehouse.

---

[16] UCC §2-301.
[17] UCC §2-503(1)(b).

Inspection and Acceptance

The buyer generally has the right to inspect the goods before paying or accepting.[18] If the contract is silent on this issue, the buyer may inspect. Typically, a buyer will insist on this right. An exception is contracts in which the parties agree there is *no* right to inspect—for example, a contract allowing shipment *C.O.D.*, which means "cash on delivery." In that case, the buyer must pay upon receipt and do her inspecting later.

Along with the right of inspection comes the obligation to do it within a reasonable time and to notify the seller promptly if the buyer intends to reject the goods. **The buyer accepts goods** if (1) after a reasonable opportunity to inspect, she indicates to the seller that the goods are conforming or that she will accept them in spite of non-conformity; or (2) she has had a reasonable opportunity to inspect the goods and has *not rejected them;* or (3) she performs some act indicating that she now owns the goods, such as altering or reselling them.[19]

Partial Acceptance

A buyer has the right to accept some goods while rejecting others if the goods can be divided into *commercial units.* Such a unit is any grouping of goods that the industry normally treats as a whole. For example, one truckload of gravel would be a commercial unit. If the contract called for 100 truckloads of gravel, a buyer could accept the 10 that conformed to contract specifications while rejecting the 90 that did not.

Revocation

As we mentioned earlier, a buyer has a limited right to revoke acceptance of goods. **A buyer may revoke acceptance but only if the non-conformity *substantially impairs the value of the goods and only if she had a legitimate reason for the initial acceptance.***[20] This means the perfect tender rule does *not* apply: a buyer in this situation may not revoke because of minor defects. Further, the buyer must show that she had a good reason for accepting the goods originally. Acceptable reasons would include defects that were not visible on inspection or defects that the seller promised but failed to cure.

In the following case, was the revocation effective?

H.A.S. OF FORT SMITH, LLC V. J.V. MANUFACTURING, INC.

2004 WL 2102009
Arkansas Court of Appeals, 2004

Facts: J.V. Manufacturing manufactured industrial equipment. H.A.S. of Fort Smith sold press brake systems, which are complex machines used in industrial manufacturing. H.A.S. sold J.V. a linear press brake system for $52,653, agreeing to install it over a two-day period. J.V. paid $32,767 as down payment.

H.A.S. did install the brake system but it did not work. An essential hydraulic tank leaked, and other parts malfunctioned. Over the next three weeks, H.A.S. made numerous unsuccessful attempts at repair. J.V. was unable to perform its normal work, meaning that its inventory of finished work steadily dropped. With the seller's permission, J.V. used its own employees and third party workers to try to make the brake system operable. After three futile

---

[18] UCC §2-513.
[19] UCC §2-606.
[20] UCC §§2-607, 608.

weeks, J.V. dismissed H.A.S. from the project and reinstalled its old press brake system.

J.V. sued H.A.S., and recovered $49,500 from the trial court. H.A.S. appealed, claiming that J.V. did not properly revoke acceptance of the system.

Issue: Did J.V. properly revoke acceptance?

Excerpts from Judge Roaf's Decision:[21] What constitutes a non-conforming delivery depends upon the facts of the case. Here, it is undisputed that the press brake system never worked and that H.A.S. could not make it work. Therefore, there is no question that the system's value to J.V. was substantially impaired and that J.V. was entitled to revoke its acceptance. Although the UCC does not expressly give the seller a right to attempt to cure when a buyer attempts to revoke acceptance, a seller in Arkansas is afforded a chance to cure a non-conforming delivery before an effective revocation of acceptance may occur. [The court quotes a treatise on this subject:]

> Where the seller can and does readily repair there is no substantial impairment. But a seller usually cannot bar revocation where its "repairing" constitutes substituting a major new integral part in the whole—such as an engine in a *new* car. Moreover, where a whole series of defects arises seriatim, the seller cannot bar revocation indefinitely simply by repairing, and standing by to repair every defect that has or will emerge. As one court puts it, there comes a time when "enough is enough."

The testimony overwhelmingly supports J.V.'s position that, after three weeks of futile attempts by H.A.S. to make the system work, "enough was enough." [J.V.'s plant engineer] Mr. Leblanc testified at length about the many problems the parties encountered over those three weeks while production hours were lost and J.V.'s inventory decreased: the power unit was not painted; H.A.S.'s employees lacked the proper tools; the new tank leaked; H.A.S. did not supply a full crew, and J.V. was required to devote its employees' time to the installation; third parties were consulted at an additional cost in an attempt to determine why the system would not work.

The damages awarded to J.V. were proper for a revocation-of-acceptance claim. A buyer who properly revokes his acceptance has the same rights and duties with regard to the goods as if he had rejected them. Where the buyer rightfully rejects or justifiably revokes acceptance, with respect to the whole if the breach goes to the whole contract, the buyer may cancel and recover so much of the price as has been paid. Clearly, H.A.S.'s breach went to the whole contract.

H.A.S. further argues that J.V. unreasonably delayed giving H.A.S. notice of its revocation of acceptance and thereby rendered the revocation ineffective. Revocation of acceptance must occur within a reasonable time after the buyer discovers the grounds for revocation. What is a reasonable time depends upon the nature, purposes, and circumstances of the action or inaction. Where the delay is attributable to efforts to repair the goods, the revocation may even come long after sale and still be timely.

We hold that, under these circumstances, J.V. did not unreasonably delay giving H.A.S. notice of revocation. The testimony overwhelmingly shows that J.V. gave H.A.S. three weeks to make the system conform before it removed H.A.S. from the premises.

[Affirmed.] ■

Public Policy

The court ruled that a buyer can take *weeks* before revoking acceptance, attempting to make the product work. Why so generous? Why not require a buyer to make up its mind within a day or two? ◆

Rejection

The buyer may reject non-conforming goods by notifying the seller within a reasonable time.[22] Huntsville Hospital purchased electrocardiogram equipment from Mortara Instrument for $155,000. The equipment failed to work properly and caused continual problems for the hospital, which notified Mortara within a reasonable time that it was rejecting. The hospital asked Mortara to pick up the equipment and refund

---

[21] Once again the authors of this text have substituted the parties' names for the court's "appellant" and "appellee."

[22] UCC §§2-601, 602.

the full purchase price, but Mortara did neither. When the hospital sued, Mortara claimed that the hospital should have returned the equipment to Mortara and that its failure left it liable for the full cost. The court of appeals was unpersuaded and gave judgment for the hospital, declaring that the hospital's only obligation was to notify the seller of a rejection and hold the goods for the seller to collect.[23]

Installment Contracts

An **installment contract** is one that requires goods to be delivered in separate lots. If Bus Co. contracts for Oil Co. to deliver 5,000 gallons of gasoline every week for one year, that is an installment contract. **A buyer may reject a non-conforming installment but only if it *substantially impairs* the value of that installment and cannot be cured.**[24] The perfect tender rule does not apply. Bus Co. has no right to reject an installment containing 4,900 gallons of gasoline, because the minor shortfall does not impair the shipment's substantial value. On the other hand, if Oil Co. delivered gasoline with lead in it, Bus Co. could reject it, since Bus Co. is legally prohibited from using the gas. (Remember, though, that Oil Co., like all sellers, has the right to cure.)

REMEDIES: ASSURANCE AND REPUDIATION

We have looked at the rights and obligations of the two parties. Now we turn our attention to the remedies they may employ. The first, assurance and repudiation, is available to both buyer and seller.

Assurance

One party to a contract may begin to fear that the other is not going to perform its obligations. **When there are reasonable grounds for insecurity, a party may demand written assurance of performance from the other party, and until he receives it, generally may suspend his own performance.**[25] Suppose Auto Co. plans to give away 50,000 videos as a promotion for its new car, to be introduced October 1. VidKids has promised to copy, package, and deliver the tapes no later than September 20. On September 1, Auto learns that VidKids has not yet begun to package the video. Auto may demand written assurance that VidKids will meet the deadline. VidKids is obligated to respond promptly and assure Auto that it will perform.

Repudiation

A party repudiates a contract by indicating that it will not perform. A party may repudiate by notifying the other party that it will not perform, by making it clear from its conduct, or by failing to answer a demand for assurance. Suppose VidKids' president calls Auto and admits, "We're having a lot of staff problems. The earliest we're going to get you that video is mid- or late October." VidKids has repudiated the contract. Similarly, if VidKids fails to respond to Auto's demand for assurance, Auto may consider that a repudiation.

When one party repudiates the contract, the other party may (1) for a reasonable time await performance or (2) resort to any remedy for breach of

---

[23] *Huntsville Hospital v. Mortara Instrument*, 57 F.3d 1043, 1995 U.S. App. LEXIS 16925 (11th Cir. 1995).

[24] UCC §2-612.

[25] UCC §2-609.

contract. **In *either* case it may suspend its own performance.**[26] In the VidKids case, it would be unreasonable for Auto to wait, because time is of the essence. So once Vid-Kids has repudiated, Auto should protect itself by pursuing a remedy for breach, such as arranging for another company to produce the goods. (We discuss the buyer's remedies for breach later in this chapter.)

We turn now to remedies intended exclusively for the seller.

SELLER'S REMEDIES

When a buyer breaches a contract, the Code provides the seller with a variety of potential remedies. Exactly which ones are available depends upon who has the goods (buyer or seller) and what steps the seller took after the buyer breached. The seller can always **cancel the contract.** She may also be able to:

- Stop delivery of the goods
- Identify goods to the contract
- Resell and recover damages
- Obtain damages for non-acceptance, or
- Obtain the contract price.

Stop Delivery

Sometimes a buyer breaches before the seller has delivered the goods, for example, by failing to make a payment due under the contract or perhaps by repudiating the contract. If that happens, **the seller may refuse to deliver the goods.**[27] If, when the buyer breaches, the seller has already placed the goods in the hands of a carrier, the seller may instruct the carrier not to deliver the goods provided the shipment is at least a carload or larger.

Identify Goods to the Contract

If the seller has not yet identified goods to the contract when the buyer breaches, he may do so as soon as he learns of the breach.[28] Suppose an electronics manufacturer, with 5,000 compact disc players in its warehouse, learns that a retailer refuses to pay for the 800 units it contracted to buy. The manufacturer may now attach a label to 800 units in its warehouse, identifying them to the contract. This will help it recover damages when it resells the identified goods or uses one of the other remedies described below.

Resale

A seller may resell goods that the buyer has refused to accept, provided she does it reasonably. **If the resale is commercially reasonable, the seller may recover the dif-**

---

[26] UCC §2-610.
[27] UCC §2-705.
[28] UCC §2-704.

ference between the resale price and contract price, plus incidental damages, minus expenses saved.[29] Incidental damages are expenses the seller incurs in holding the goods and reselling them, costs such as storage, shipping, and advertising for resale. The seller must deduct expenses saved by the breach. For example, if the contract required the seller to ship heavy machinery from Detroit to San Diego, and the buyer's breach enables the seller to sell its goods in Detroit, the seller must deduct from its claimed losses the transportation costs that it saved.

A seller who acts in a commercially reasonable manner is entitled to the following damages:

> Contract price (the price Seller expected from the original contract)
> − the resale price (the money Seller got at resale)
> + incidental damages (storage, advertising, etc.)
> − <u>expenses saved</u>
> = Seller's damages

A seller is also permitted to resell goods privately, that is, by simply negotiating a deal with another party. But if the seller does so, she must first give the buyer reasonable notice of the private resale.

Damages for Non-Acceptance

A seller who does not resell, or who resells unreasonably, may recover the difference between the original contract price and the market value of the goods at the time of delivery.[30] Oilko agrees to sell Retailer 100,000 barrels of a certain grade of gasoline for $60 per barrel, to be delivered in Long Beach, California, on November 1. Oilko tenders the gasoline on November 1, but Retailer refuses to accept it. On February 20, Oilko resells the gasoline to another purchaser for $52 per barrel and sues Retailer for $800,000 (the difference between its contract price and what it finally obtained), plus the cost of storage. Will Oilko win? No. Oilko's resale was unreasonable. Because there is a ready market for gasoline, Oilko should have resold immediately. Because Oilko acted unreasonably, it will not obtain damages under the Code's resale provision. Oilko will be forced to base its damages on market value.

Often this remedy will be less valuable to the seller than resale damages. Suppose that on November 1 the market value of Oilko's gasoline was $59 per barrel. Oilko's contract with Retailer was actually worth only one dollar per barrel to Oilko, the amount by which its contract price exceeded the market value. That is all that Oilko will get in court.[31] A seller with a chance to resell should be certain to do it reasonably. If Oilko had resold promptly and for some reason obtained only $52 per barrel, it probably would have recovered its entire $800,000 loss. The following chart compares resale and non-acceptance damages:

Resale Damages §2-706		Non-Acceptance Damages §2-708	
Contract price	$6,000,000	Contract price	$6,000,000
Resale price	−5,200,000	Market value of goods	−5,900,000
	$ 800,000		$ 100,000

---

[29] UCC §2-706.

[30] UCC §2-708.

[31] Based on *Baii Banking Corp. v. Atlantic Richfield Co.*, 1993 U.S. Dist. LEXIS 14107 (S.D.N.Y. 1993).

Action for the Price

The seller may recover the contract price if (1) the buyer has accepted the goods *or* (2) the seller's goods are conforming and the seller is unable to resell after a reasonable effort.[32] Royal Jones was a company that constructed rendering plants, that is, factories that use sophisticated equipment to extract valuable minerals from otherwise useless material. Royal Jones contracted for First Thermal to construct three rendering tanks, at a cost of $64,350. First Thermal built the tanks to Royal Jones's specifications but Royal Jones never accepted or paid for them, and First Thermal sued. Royal Jones argued that First Thermal deserved no money because it had not attempted to resell the goods, but the court awarded the full contract price, stating:

> First Thermal proved that any effort at resale would have been unavailing because these were the only rendering tanks First Thermal ever made, the tanks were manufactured according to Royal Jones's specifications, First Thermal had no other customers to which it could resell the tanks, and it was unaware how the tanks could have been marketed for resale.[33]

Resale is normally the safest route for an injured seller to recover the maximum amount, but when it is unrealistic, as in the *First Thermal* case, a lawsuit for the full price is appropriate. All of the seller's remedies are summarized in the chapter review at the end of the chapter. We now move on to the buyer's remedies.

BUYER'S REMEDIES

The buyer, too, has a variety of potential remedies. If a seller fails to deliver goods or if the buyer rightfully rejects the goods, the buyer is entitled to **cancel the contract.** She may also **recover money paid** to the seller, assuming she has not received the goods. In addition, she may be able to:

- Cover
- Obtain damages for non-delivery
- Obtain incidental *and consequential* damages
- Recover the goods themselves by an order for specific performance, or
- Recover liquidated damages.

Cover

If the seller breaches, the buyer may "cover" by reasonably obtaining substitute goods; it may then obtain the difference between the contract price and its cover price, plus incidental and consequential damages, minus expenses saved.[34] Casein, a protein derived from milk, is used to make cheese and to process many other foods. Erie Casein Co. contracted with Anric Corp. to supply several hundred thousand pounds of casein for about $1 per pound. Half was to be delivered in March of the first year and the other half in March of the second year. By May of the first year, Anric had not finished its first delivery because it was having difficulty obtaining the casein, but

---

[32] UCC §2-709.
[33] *Royal Jones & Associates, Inc. v. First Thermal Systems, Inc.,* 566 So. 2d 853, 1990 Fla. App. LEXIS 6596 (Fla. Ct. App. 1990).
[34] UCC §2-712.

Erie told Anric to keep trying. Anric delivered some of the casein later the same year, but by March of the second year was forced to admit it could not meet the second delivery. Anric suggested that it might be able to obtain more casein in the autumn of that second year.

Erie waited until August of the second year, but finally obtained its casein elsewhere at a price of $1.45 per pound. Erie sued Anric for the extra money it had paid, about $66,000. Anric argued that Erie had no right to the difference, because Erie had waited until the price of casein was sky-high before obtaining substitute goods.

The court found for Erie. Even though the company might have covered a year earlier, when the price was much lower, it was reasonable for the buyer to wait because Anric indicated it might be able to supply the goods later. Erie had acted in good faith, and when it ultimately covered, it did so at the best price it could find. An injured buyer does not have to do a perfect job of covering, only a reasonable job, and Erie got its full $66,000.[35]

Note that an injured buyer may also be awarded consequential damages, which we discuss below. Finally, if covering saves expense, the savings are deducted from any damages.

We hope that you recall Donald Hessler, whom we met in the chapter opener. We last saw him circling the courthouse in his Plymouth Prowler, anxiously awaiting the outcome of his suit against the dealership that promised him the same car for a lot less money. It has been a long wait; you and Donald deserve an answer.

HESSLER V. CRYSTAL LAKE CHRYSLER-PLYMOUTH, INC.

338 Ill.App.3d 1010, 788 N.E.2d 405, 273 Ill.Dec. 96
Appellate Court of Illinois, 2003

Facts: The facts are provided in the chapter opening. The trial court awarded Hessler $29,853, representing the difference between his contract with Crystal Lake and the sum he ultimately spent purchasing a new Prowler. Crystal Lake appealed, arguing that Hessler covered unreasonably.

Issue: **Did Hessler cover reasonably?**

Excerpts from Judge Callum's Decision: We conclude that the trial court did not err in finding that defendant's foregoing actions reasonably indicated to plaintiff that defendant would not deliver to him a Prowler under the Agreement. As we determined above, defendant contracted to deliver a Prowler to plaintiff as soon as possible. It was not against the manifest weight of the evidence for the trial court to find that defendant [breached] the Agreement when it repeatedly informed plaintiff that it would not deliver to him the first Prowler it received. Such actions made it sufficiently clear to plaintiff that defendant would not perform under the Agreement.

Defendant's final argument is that the trial court erred in calculating the damages award because plaintiff effected an inappropriate cover. Defendant contends that plaintiff did not recontact the 38 dealers he had called in September to inquire if they would sell him a Prowler. Instead, on the same day that Rosenberg refused to sell him a car, plaintiff visited another dealership and purchased a Prowler for about $40,000 over the list price.

Comment 2 to section 2-712 of the UCC provides, in relevant part:

> The test of proper cover is whether at the time and place the buyer acted in good faith and in a reasonable manner, and it is immaterial that hindsight may later prove that the method of cover used was not the cheapest and most effective.

Plaintiff testified that he called Rosenberg on September 22 to inform him that defendant was on a

▼

---

35 *Erie Casein Co. v. Anric Corp.*, 217 Ill. App. 3d 602, 577 N.E.2d 892, 1991 Ill. App. LEXIS 1429 (Ill. App. Ct. 1991).

tentative list to receive a Prowler and that Rosenberg responded that he would not sell to plaintiff a car and that plaintiff was not the first person with whom he had contracted. Rosenberg testified that he informed plaintiff on this date that the Prowler was "already committed." The trial court also heard plaintiff's testimony that, following his September 22 conversation with Rosenberg, he had "serious doubts" that defendant would sell to him a Prowler and he contacted about 38 dealerships to inquire about purchasing a vehicle, but was unable to obtain a car.

Following Rosenberg's refusal to sell a car to plaintiff on October 25, plaintiff visited another dealership on that day and purchased a Prowler for about $30,000 over what he would have paid defendant for the same car. The trial court concluded that the price plaintiff ultimately paid for a Prowler was the "best price" he could receive after defendant refused to sell a car to him. We agree. The trial court heard testimony from both parties about the Prowler's limited supply. It also heard plaintiff's testimony about his efforts to obtain a car one month before his purchase date. We conclude that the court's determination that plaintiff effected a proper cover was not against the manifest weight of the evidence.

For the foregoing reasons, the judgment of the circuit court is affirmed. ■

Devil's Advocate

It is fine for a buyer to cover, but Hessler's conduct is absurd. He bought a car for nearly *double* the contract price. A buyer's behavior must be reasonable, and no court should reward conduct that is clearly obsessive. This purchase was not required by business or financial pressures. We have here a man who believes he is entitled to whatever he wants. If Hessler decides he must have a Prowler *at any price* then in fairness he should be the one to *pay* that price. ◆

Non-Delivery

In some cases the buyer does not cover, or fails to cover *reasonably*, leaving it with damages for non-delivery. **The measure of damages for non-delivery is the difference between the market price at the time the buyer learns of the breach and the contract price, plus incidental and consequential damages, minus expenses saved.**[36] Suppose that, in the case described above, Erie had not covered but simply filed suit against Anric. Instead of its $66,000, Erie would have obtained the difference between its contract price with Anric and the market value on the date of breach. That market price was probably only a few pennies higher than the contract price, and Erie would have obtained less than $10,000.

Acceptance of Non-Conforming Goods

A buyer will sometimes accept non-conforming goods from the seller, either because no alternative is available or because the buyer expects to obtain some compensation for the defects. **Where the buyer has accepted goods but notified the seller that they are non-conforming, he may recover damages for the difference between the goods as promised and as delivered, plus incidental and consequential damages.**[37]

Incidental and Consequential Damages

An injured buyer is generally entitled to incidental and consequential damages. Incidental damages cover such costs as advertising for replacements, sending buyers to obtain new goods, and shipping the replacement goods. Consequential damages can be

---

[36] UCC §2-713.
[37] UCC §2-714.

much more extensive and may include lost profits. A buyer expecting to resell goods may obtain the loss of profit caused by the seller's failure to deliver.

A buyer, however, only gets consequential damages for harm that was unavoidable. Suppose Wholesaler has a contract to sell 10,000 rosebushes at $10 per bush to Flora-Mora. Wholesaler contracts to buy 10,000 rosebushes from Growem at $6 per bush, but Growem fails to deliver. Wholesaler in fact could obtain comparable roses at $8 per bush, but fails to do so and loses the chance to sell to FloraMora. Wholesaler sues Growem, seeking the $4 per bush profit it would have made on the FloraMora deal. The company will receive only $2 per bush, representing the difference between its contract price and the market value of the plants. Wholesaler will be denied the additional $2 per bush because it failed to cover.

In the following case, the court decides whether *future* profits may be too speculative to award as consequential damages.

SMITH V. PENBRIDGE ASSOCIATES, INC.

440 Pa. Super. 410, 655 A.2d 1015, 1995 Pa. Super. LEXIS 574
Superior Court of Pennsylvania, 1995

Facts: Donna and Alan Smith wanted to raise emus, which are flightless Australian birds that look like ostriches. The creatures produce rapidly in almost any terrain and are sold for their meat, which is high in protein and low in fat, and for their oil, leather, and feathers. The Smiths paid Tomie Clark, the manager of Penbridge Farms, $4,000 as a down payment for "Andrew" and "Rachel," which the farm called a "proven breeder pair." Since it is impossible to discern an emu's gender by looking, the Smiths asked Clark several times if the two birds were male and female, and he assured them that the pair had successfully produced chicks the previous breeding season.

The Smiths placed the prospective lovebirds in the same pen, but the breeding season passed without a hint of romance. Donna Smith noticed that both birds were grunting, something that only male emus do. She phoned Penbridge Farms, which advised her to "vent sex" the animals, a manual procedure used to determine gender. Donna performed this agreeable task and learned that Andrew and Rachel were both gentlemen. The would-be breeders asked for their money back but Penbridge refused, so the Smiths flew into court. The trial judge awarded the couple $105,215, representing lost profits from their anticipated chicks. Penbridge appealed, arguing that a buyer cannot count her chicks before they have hatched.

Issue: **Did the trial court err by awarding lost profits?**

Excerpts from Judge Popovich's Decision: [Penbridge claimed that the] evidence was speculative and insufficient to support an award of consequential damages, including damages for lost profits. [Penbridge argued that, since] the breeding of emus is a relatively new business, and there is no reliable data to project the ultimate success in breeding emus, the [Smiths'] claims for loss of chick production are entirely speculative and do not meet the "reasonable certainty" requirement of the law of damages.

The birds cannot fly. Will the claims?

The Uniform Commercial Code provides the following circumstances for the recovery of consequential damages resulting from the breach of the seller: any loss resulting from general or particular requirements and needs of which the seller at the time of contracting had reason to know and which could not reasonably be prevented by "cover" or otherwise. [UCC §2-715(2).]

The "proven breeder pair" had produced sixteen (16) chicks in the previous breeding season. [The Smiths] presented testimony revealing that it was reasonable to expect a doubling of chick production from a proven breeder pair in the following year.

The determination of damages lies with the fact finder, who weighs the evidence and assesses the credibility of the witnesses. Although the court recognized that emu breeding was a relatively new commercial business, it determined that the award of consequential damages could be calculated with a reasonable degree of certainty from the evidence adduced at trial. The court below initially found that the value of a three-month old chick produced from the [previous] season was $5,000.00. The lower court then concluded that [the Smiths] suffered incidental and consequential damages in the amount of $90,000.00. In arriving at that figure, the court below was conservative in its finding of the expected chick production from the [previous] breeding season absent appellant's breach. From our thorough evaluation of the record, we conclude that the evidence was sufficient for the lower court to measure [the Smith's] lost profits with a reasonable degree of certainty. The basis for this rule is that the breaching party should not be allowed to shift the loss to the injured party when damages, even if uncertain in amount, were certainly the responsibility of the party in breach.

Order affirmed. ■

Specific Performance

If the contract goods are unique, or the buyer is unable to obtain cover, the buyer may be allowed *specific performance,* which means a court order requiring the seller to deliver those particular goods.[38] This remedy is most common when the goods are one-of-a-kind. Suppose Gallery agreed to sell to Trisha an original Corot painting for $120,000, but then refused to perform (because another buyer offered more money). Trisha can obtain specific performance because the painting cannot be replaced: the court will order Gallery to deliver the work. By contrast, a car rental company stymied by a dealer's refusal to sell 500 new Ford Mustangs will not obtain specific performance, since the rental company can simply buy the same cars from another dealer (cover) and sue for the difference.

Liquidated Damages

Liquidated damages are those that the parties agree, at the time of contracting, will compensate the injured party. **They are enforceable, but only in an amount that is reasonable in light of the harm, the difficulties of proving actual loss, and the absence of other remedies.**[39] A clause that establishes unreasonably large or unreasonably small liquidated damages is void. Courts only enforce a liquidated damages clause if it would have been difficult to estimate actual damages when the parties reached the agreement.

Cessna Aircraft agreed to build a "Citation V" business jet and sell it to Aero Consulting for $3,995,000. Cessna's contract required Aero to pay an initial deposit of $125,000, a second deposit of $300,000 six months prior to delivery, and the balance upon delivery. The contract also stated that if Aero failed to pay the balance due, Cessna would keep all deposited monies by way of liquidated damages.

---

[38] UCC §2-716.
[39] UCC §2-718.

Aero made both deposits and Cessna built the plane and tendered it to Aero, but Aero refused to pay the full balance due. Cessna notified Aero that it would keep the $425,000 deposited. When Aero sued, seeking a return of the deposits, the issue was whether this liquidated damage was fair. The court concluded that it was. At the time Cessna entered into the deal, it was difficult to estimate actual damages in the event of Aero's breach. The long period required to build a jet aircraft and the uncertainties about supply and demand in the marketplace meant that neither party could say for sure how much Cessna would lose should Aero breach. Further, the liquidated damage here was about 10 percent of the total cost, not an unreasonably high figure. Cessna kept the money (and the plane).[40]

at RISK

Liquidated damages can be a powerful tool to ensure fair play in the international market. Consider the problem of gray-market goods. These are products that a manufacturer intends for sale in foreign countries but which wind up in the hands of an unauthorized local retailer. You own a vineyard that has strong domestic sales, and you wish to expand into Europe. To penetrate the Italian market, you offer your product at steep discounts to an Italian importer; your intent is that the company will sell your wine cheap to retailers, and the low prices will entice consumers to try it. The importer, however, sells every available bottle to a local Italian merchant, who ships all the wine back to the United States and undersells your own product, taking advantage of your advertising and infuriating established dealers. Indeed, such a resale could occur before your wine ever left the country. What to do? Include a liquidated damages clause in the sales contract with the Italian importer, requiring a substantial penalty if any of your exported wine finds its way back home. ◆

Damage Limitations and Exclusions

The Code allows parties to draft a contract that limits or excludes the normal remedies discussed in this chapter. For example, parties can agree that if the seller delivers non-conforming goods, the buyer's only remedy is to demand repair or replacement. We discussed these limits in the preceding chapter and will not repeat the information here. By way of a quick summary, we can say that while the parties may exclude most remedies, there are two important restrictions:

- **A court generally will not enforce a limitation that leaves the injured party with no remedy at all.** Suppose a remedy limitation states that a buyer of software is only entitled to repair, but the software is so badly designed that no amount of repairing solves the problem. A court will ignore the limitation, and the buyer will be entitled to the full range of remedies we have discussed.

- **A court will not enforce an unconscionable exclusion of consequential damages.** If the buyer is a consumer, a court is likely to ignore any exclusion of consequential damages. So, if a consumer purchases a used car from a dealer who excludes such damages, and the consumer is injured when the radiator explodes, the contract limitation will do the seller no good.

---

[40] *Aero Consulting Corp. v. Cessna Aircraft Co.*, 867 F. Supp. 1480, 1994 U.S. Dist. LEXIS 16668 (D. Kan. 1994).

Chapter Conclusion

The drafters of the code intended the law to reflect contemporary commercial practices, but also to require a satisfactory level of sensible, ethical behavior. For example, the Code allows numerous exceptions to the perfect tender rule so that a buyer may not pounce on minor defects in goods to avoid a contract that has become financially burdensome. Similarly, a seller forced to resell his goods must do so in a commercially reasonable manner. Good faith and common sense are the hallmarks of contract performance and remedies.

Chapter Review

1. Conforming goods are those that satisfy the contract terms; non-conforming goods fail to do so.

2. The Code requires good faith in the performance and enforcement of every contract.

3. The seller must tender the goods, which means make conforming goods available to the buyer. The perfect tender rule permits a buyer to reject goods that are non-conforming in any respect, although there are numerous exceptions.

4. Usage of trade, course of dealing, and course of performance may enable a seller to satisfy the perfect tender rule even though there are some defects in the goods.

5. When the buyer rejects non-conforming goods, the seller has the right to cure by delivering conforming goods before the contract deadline.

6. If identified goods are destroyed before risk passes to the buyer, the contract is void.

7. Under commercial impracticability, a supervening event excuses performance if it was not within the parties' contemplation when they made the contract.

8. The buyer generally has the right to inspect goods before paying or accepting. If the buyer does not reject goods within a reasonable time after inspecting them, she may be deemed to have accepted them.

9. A buyer may revoke his acceptance of non-conforming goods, but only if the defects substantially impair the value of the goods.

10. A buyer may reject non-conforming goods by notifying the seller within a reasonable time.

The following chart summarizes the contrasting remedies available to the two parties.

Seller's Remedies	Issue	Buyer's Remedies
§2-705: The seller generally may stop delivery, whether it was to be done by the seller herself or a carrier.	DELIVERY	§2-716: Specific performance: buyer may obtain specific performance only if the goods are unique.
§2-706: Resale: If the resale is made in good faith and a commercially reasonable manner, the seller may recover the difference between the resale price and the contract price, plus incidental costs, minus savings.	WHEN THE INJURED PARTY MAKES AN ALTERNATE CONTRACT	§2-712: Cover: The buyer may purchase alternate goods and obtain the difference in price, plus incidental and consequential damages, minus expenses saved.
§2-708: Non-acceptance: The measure of damages for non-acceptance is the difference between the market price at the time and place of tender and and the contract price (plus incidental damages minus expenses saved).	WHEN THE GOODS HAVE NOT CHANGED HANDS	§2-713: Non-delivery: If the seller fails to deliver, the buyer's damages are the difference between the market price at the time he learned of the breach and the contract price (plus incidental and consequential damages, minus expenses saved).

§2-709: The seller may sue for the price.	WHEN THE BUYER HAS ACCEPTED THE GOODS	§2-714: A buyer who has accepted non-conforming goods and notified the seller may recover damages for resulting losses.
§§2-706, 2-708, 2-709, 2-710: The seller is entitled to incidental damages but not consequential damages.	INCIDENTAL AND CONSEQUENTIAL DAMAGES	§2-715: The buyer is entitled to incidental and consequential damages.

LIQUIDATED DAMAGES

§2-718: Either party may obtain liquidated damages but only in an amount that is reasonable at the time of the contract.

REMEDY LIMITATION

§2-719: The parties may add or exclude remedies, but no remedy limitation will be allowed if it results in the injured party obtaining no relief at all; consequential damages may not be limited in cases where doing so would be unconscionable.

Practice Test

1. **CPA QUESTION** Smith contracted in writing to sell Peters a used personal computer for $600. The contract did not specifically address the time for payment, place of delivery, or Peters's right to inspect the computer. Which of the following statements is correct?

   a. Smith is obligated to deliver the computer to Peters's home.

   b. Peters is entitled to inspect the computer before paying for it.

   c. Peters may not pay for the computer using a personal check unless Smith agrees.

   d. Smith is not entitled to payment until 30 days after Peters receives the computer.

2. **CPA QUESTION** Cara Fabricating Co. and Taso Corp. agreed orally that Taso would custom manufacture a compressor for Cara at a price of $120,000. After Taso completed the work at a cost of $90,000, Cara notified Taso that the compressor was no longer needed. Taso is holding the compressor and has requested payment from Cara. Taso has been unable to resell the compressor for any price. Taso incurred storage fees of $2,000. If Cara refuses to pay Taso and Taso sues Cara, the most Taso will be entitled to recover is:

   a. $92,000

   b. $105,000

   c. $120,000

   d. $122,000

3. Jewell-Rung was a Canadian corporation that imported and sold men's clothing at wholesale. Haddad was a New York corporation that manufactured and sold men's clothing under the "Lakeland" label. The companies agreed that Haddad would sell 2,325 Lakeland garments to Jewell-Rung, for $250,000. Jewell-Rung began to take orders for the garments from its Canadian customers. Jewell-Rung had orders for about 372 garments when it learned that Haddad planned to allow another company, Olympic, the exclusive Canadian right to manufacture and sell Lakeland garments. Jewell-Rung sued Haddad for its lost profits. Haddad moved for summary judgment, claiming that Jewell-Rung could not recover lost profits because it had not "covered." Is Haddad right? Why might Jewell-Rung not have covered?

4. **ETHICS** Laura and Bruce Trethewey hired Basement Waterproofing Nationwide, Inc., to waterproof the walls in their basement for a fee of $2,500. BWNI's contract stated: "BWNI will service any seepage in the areas waterproofed at no additional cost to the customer. All labor and materials will be at the company's expense. Liability for any damage shall be limited to the total price paid for this contract." The material that BWNI used to waterproof the Tretheweys' walls swelled and caused large cracks to open in the walls. Water poured into the basement, and the Tretheweys ultimately spent $38,000 to repair

the damage. They sued, claiming negligence and breach of warranty, but BWNI claimed its liability was limited to $2,500. Please rule. Apart from the legal ruling, comment on ethics. BWNI wanted to protect itself against unlimited damage claims. Is this a legitimate way to do it? Is this how BWNI would wish to be treated itself? If you think BWNI *did* behave ethically, what advice would you have for consumers who hire home improvement companies? If you believe the company did *not* behave ethically, imagine that you are a BWNI executive, charged with drafting a standard contract for customers. How would you protect your company's interests while still acting in a way you consider moral?

5. Cargill, Inc., sold cottonseed, which is used in feed for dairy cattle. Bill Storms, a dairy farmer, agreed to buy 17 truckloads of cottonseed from Cargill for $176 per ton, to be delivered at Storms's farm. Storms had the option of accepting the seed at any time during the next nine months. Over the first two months, Storms ordered three truckloads of seed and paid Cargill, but Storms then informed Cargill that he would accept no more cottonseed. What rights does Cargill have?

6. Mastercraft Boat manufactured boats and often used instrument panels and electrical systems assembled and/or manufactured by Ace Industries. Typically, Ace would order electrical instruments and other parts and assemble them to specifications that Mastercraft provided. Mastercraft decided to work with a different assembler, M & G Electronics, so it terminated its relationship with Ace. Mastercraft then requested that Ace deliver all of the remaining instruments and other parts that it had purchased for use in Mastercraft boats. Ace delivered the inventory to Mastercraft, which inspected it and kept some of the items, but returned others to Ace, stating that the shipment had been unauthorized. Later, Mastercraft requested that Ace deliver the remaining parts (which Mastercraft had sent back to Ace) to M & G, which Ace did. Mastercraft then refused to pay for these parts, claiming that they were non-conforming. Is Ace entitled to its money for the parts?

7. Allied Semi-Conductors International agreed to buy 50,000 computer chips from Pulsar, for a total price of $365,750. Pulsar delivered the chips, which Allied then sold to Apple Computer. But at least 35,000 of the chips proved defective so Apple returned them to Allied, which sent them back to Pulsar. Pulsar agreed to replace any defective chips, but only after Allied, at its expense, tested each chip and established the defect. Allied rejected this procedure and sued. Who wins?

8. Lewis River Golf, Inc., grew and sold sod. It bought seed from defendant, O. M. Scott & Sons, under an express warranty. But the sod grown from the Scott seeds developed weeds, a breach of Scott's warranty. Several of Lewis River's customers sued, unhappy with the weeds in their grass. Lewis River lost most of its customers, cut back its production from 275 acres to 45 acres, and destroyed all remaining sod grown from Scott's seeds. Eventually, Lewis River sold its business at a large loss. A jury awarded Lewis River $1,026,800, largely for lost profits and loss of goodwill. Scott appealed, claiming that a plaintiff may not recover for lost profits and goodwill. Comment.

9. **CPA QUESTION** On February 15, Mazur Corp. contracted to sell 1,000 bushels of wheat to Good Bread, Inc., at $6 per bushel with delivery to be made on June 23. On June 1, Good advised Mazur that it would not accept or pay for the wheat. On June 2, Mazur sold the wheat to another customer at the market price of $5 per bushel. Mazur had advised Good that it intended to resell the wheat. Which of the following statements is correct?

    a. Mazur can successfully sue Good for the difference between the resale price and the contract price.

    b. Mazur can resell the wheat only after June 23.

    c. Good can retract its anticipatory breach at any time before June 23.

    d. Good can successfully sue Mazur for specific performance.

10. *CPA QUESTION* Under a contract governed by the UCC sales article, which of the following statements is correct?

    a. Unless both the seller and the buyer are merchants, neither party is obligated to perform the contract in good faith.

    b. The contract will not be enforceable if it fails to expressly specify a time and a place for delivery of the goods.

    c. The seller may be excused from performance if the goods are accidentally destroyed before the risk of loss passes to the buyer.

    d. If the price of the goods is less than $500, the goods need not be identified to the contract for title to pass to the buyer.

11. The AM/PM Franchise association was a group of 150 owners of ARCO Mini-Market franchises in Pennsylvania and New York. Each owner had an agreement to operate a gas station and mini-market, obtaining all gasoline, food, and other products, from ARCO. The Association sued, claiming that ARCO had experimented with its formula for unleaded gasoline, using oxinol, and that the poor-quality gas had caused serious engine problems and a steep drop in customers. The Association demanded (1) lost profits for gasoline sales, (2) lost profits for food and other items, and (3) loss of goodwill. The trial court dismissed the case, ruling that the plaintiff's claims were too speculative, and the Association appealed. Please rule.

12. *YOU BE THE JUDGE* WRITING PROBLEM Clark Oil agreed to sell Amerada Hess several hundred thousand barrels of oil at $24 each by January 31, with the sulfur content not to exceed 1 percent. On January 26, Clark tendered oil from various ships. Most of the oil met specifications, but a small amount contained excess sulfur. Hess rejected all of the oil. Clark recirculated the oil, meaning that it blended the high-sulfur oil with the rest, and notified Amerada that it could deliver 100 percent of the oil, as specified, by January 31. Hess did not respond. On January 30, Clark offered to replace the oil with an entirely new shipment, due to arrive February 1. Hess rejected the offer. On February 6, Clark retendered the original oil, all of which met contract terms, and Hess rejected it. Clark sold the oil elsewhere for $17.75 per barrel and filed suit. Is Clark entitled to damages? **Argument for Clark:** A seller is entitled to cure any defects. Clark did so in good faith and offered all of the oil by the contract deadline. Clark went even further, offering an entirely new shipment of oil. Hess acted in bad faith, seeking to obtain cheaper oil. Clark is entitled to the difference between the contract price and its resale price. **Argument for Hess:** Hess was entitled to conforming goods, and Clark failed to deliver. Under the perfect tender rule, that is the end of the discussion. Hess had the right to reject nonconforming goods, and it promptly did so. Hess chose not to deal further with Clark because it had lost confidence in Clark's ability to perform.

13. *ROLE REVERSAL* Write a multiple-choice question that involves a buyer's rejection of goods, the perfect tender rule, and one of the following: usage of trade, course of dealing, or course of performance.

Internet Research Problem

Go to **http://beatty.westbuslaw.com**, click on "Article 2," and find your way to §2-615. You represent a buyer of goods who insists that the goods be delivered on time, regardless of any natural disasters. Read the opening sentence, as well as the subsection (a). Draft a provision that requires the seller to deliver on time, period.

> **You can find further practice problems at http://beatty.westbuslaw.com or in the Study Guide that accompanies this text.**

Creating a Negotiable Instrument

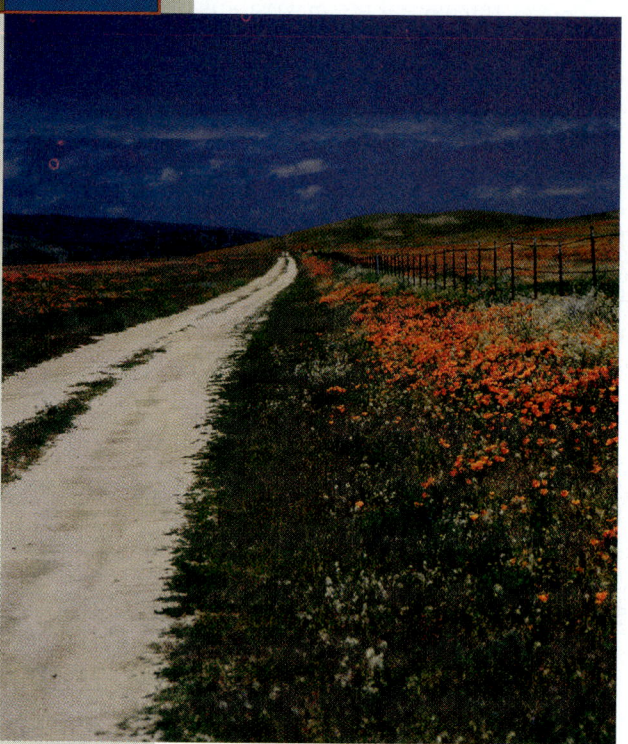

The figure lay on the couch by the fireplace. No signs of violence were visible, and a casual observer would have thought the man was napping. But Detective Waterston's trained eye immediately recognized the unnatural stiffness and pallor of a corpse. Walking behind the body, she saw matted blood against black hair and a heavy brass fireplace iron on the floor. She also noticed the crumpled document clutched in the victim's hand.

As the coroner was removing the body, Waterston slipped the crumpled paper out of the corpse's grasp. Sergeant Malloy asked whether she was ready to interview witnesses. "No," she said thoughtfully, looking at the document, "I believe I have everything I need right here." An hour later, the police arrested Tony Jenkins, the dead man's business partner. Jenkins immediately confessed.

"How did you know?" Malloy demanded.

"Simple," Waterston responded, "The answer is right here on this promissory note." She spread the crumpled page on the table. "On the front, it's a straightforward note for $1 million, payable by Tony Jenkins, the accused, to Letitia Lamour on August 1. You remember—she was recently arrested for selling fraudulent securities. Jenkins must have invested in one of her enterprises.

© PHOTO 24/BRAND X PICTURES/GETTY IMAGES

"It gets even more interesting on the back, though," she said, turning the paper over. "Lamour held on to the note for some time. But you see, on August 15th, she wrote on the back 'Pay to the order of Sebastian Haverstock.'"

"The dead man," Malloy whistled through his teeth.

"Precisely. Haverstock and Jenkins were planning to take their computer software company public in a month or two. The sale would have made them both wealthy men. But Haverstock called Jenkins to demand payment on the note. Jenkins did not have a million dollars; he had lost everything in a series of unfortunate investments. Haverstock demanded that Jenkins turn over his shares in the company as payment for the note. In his rage and frustration, Jenkins picked up the first thing that came to hand and struck Haverstock with the brass iron. An antique instrument and very heavy.

"It's a shame, really," Detective Waterston continued. "If Jenkins had understood Article 3 of the Uniform Commercial Code, he would not have been tempted to murder. In fact, he owed Haverstock nothing. You see, the note was overdue—it should have been paid on August 1st, but today is the 31st. You can't be a holder in due course on an overdue note. Since Haverstock was not a holder in due course, Jenkins could have used the fraud claim he had against Lamour as a defense to Haverstock's demand for payment. In any event, Haverstock was well aware that Lamour had committed fraud—he was the one who set her up in business in the first place. Jenkins could have used Haverstock's knowledge of the fraud as another weapon against any demands for payment. That legal weapon would have been a better choice than a fireplace iron," Waterston concluded wryly. ∎

COMMERCIAL PAPER

Commercial paper plays an important role in your life if you write checks or borrow money. Historically speaking, however, commercial paper is a relatively new development. In early human history, people lived on whatever they could hunt, grow, or make for themselves. Imagine what your life would be like if you had to subsist only on what you could make yourself. Over time, people improved their standard of living by bartering for goods and services they could not make themselves. But traders needed a method for keeping account of who owed how much to whom. That was the role of currency. Many items have been used for currency over the years, including silver, gold, copper, and cowrie shells. Even cigarettes were used briefly in Greece at the end of World War II after Hitler's troops left. These currencies have two disadvantages—they are easy to steal and cumbersome to carry.

Sweden had traditionally used copper as currency. These ingots were very large and heavy (heavier even than gold) so it is not surprising that, in 1661, Sweden became the first country in Europe to try paper currency. This effort was not a success because too much paper money was printed, and so the president of the bank went to prison.

Ultimately paper currency did catch on but it created new problems—it was even easier to steal than gold. As a result, money had to be kept in a safe place, and banks developed to meet that need. However, money in a vault is not very useful unless it can be readily spent. Society needed a system for transferring paper funds easily. Commercial paper is that system. Electronic alternatives may ultimately dominate the marketplace, but for now paper is still king. (For more on the history of money, see http://www.ex.ac.uk/~RDavies/arian/llyfr.html.)

Commercial paper is a contract to pay money. It is used as:

- *A Substitute for Money.* When Darla stops at Drive-In-Convenience to buy food for dinner, she has only 32¢ in her wallet. Not a problem, she can pay by check. Darla's check is a promise that she has money in the bank. It is also an order to the bank to transfer funds to Drive-In-Convenience. Darla is going to eat immediately (in the car on the way home), and the store would also like to be paid expeditiously. For commercial paper to be a substitute for money, it must be payable on demand.

- *A Loan of Money.* This type of commercial paper is a contract to pay what is owed sometime in the future. Darla buys a beautiful concert grand piano that costs more than her parents paid for their first house. She does not have enough money in the bank to write a check for the full amount, so she signs a **promissory note,** that is, an assurance that she will pay for the piano in five years. The manager at the Angel House of Music does not expect to take the note to Darla's bank and be paid right away; he understands that he will have to wait.

The four previous chapters covered the Uniform Commercial Code (UCC) and the sale of goods. This chapter and the following two focus on Articles 3 and 4 of the UCC as they regulate commercial paper.[1] The purpose of the UCC articles on negotiable instruments is to facilitate commerce. When the United States Treasury issues money, it is consistent—all dollar bills look alike. But when practically the entire population of the United States issues commercial paper, creativity takes over and consistency disappears. The purpose of Articles 3 and 4 is to transform these pieces of paper into something almost as easily transferable and reliable as currency.

The fundamental "rule" of commercial paper can be stated this way:

The possessor of a piece of commercial paper has an unconditional right to be paid, as long as (1) the paper is *negotiable;* (2) it has been *negotiated* to the possessor; (3) the possessor is a *holder in due course;* and (4) the issuer cannot claim any of a limited number of "real" *defenses*.

This rule is the backbone of the chapter, and in the following sections we define and explain its terms: "negotiable," "negotiated," "holder in due course," and "defenses." You will want to keep this rule in mind throughout the chapter.

TYPES OF NEGOTIABLE INSTRUMENTS

There are two kinds of commercial paper: negotiable and non-negotiable instruments. Article 3 of the Code covers only negotiable instruments; non-negotiable instruments

---

[1]   In 2002, the Uniform Law Commissioners approved a revision of Articles 3 and 4 that deals with changing technology for checks and other paper instruments. So far, Minnesota is the only state to have passed this new version. Therefore, this chapter is based on the older version.

are governed by ordinary contract law. There are also two categories of negotiable instruments: notes and drafts. The essential difference between the two is that a note is a promise to do something while a draft is an *order* to someone else to do it. This is an overview; now for the details.

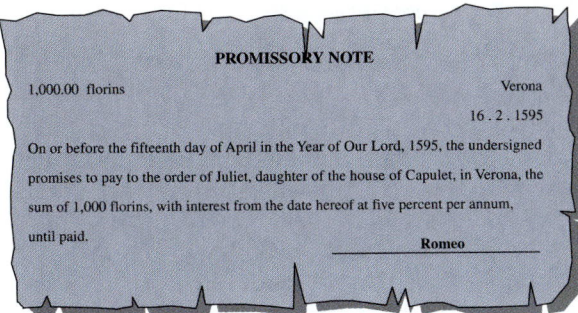

In this note, Romeo is the maker and Juliet is the payee.

A **note** (also called a **promissory note**) is your promise that you will pay money. A promissory note is used in virtually every loan transaction, whether the borrower is buying a multimillion dollar company, a house, or a TV set. For example, the National Basketball Association permits players to borrow money from their team. If LeBron James borrows $5 million from the Cleveland Cavaliers, he must sign a note promising to repay the money. James is the **maker** because he is the one who has made the promise. His team is called the **payee** because it expects to be paid. Remember that only *two* parties are involved in a note: the maker and the payee. Some notes are due at a definite date in the future. Others are **payable on demand,** which means that the maker must pay whenever he is asked. Thus, James's note could be payable, say, in three years when his contract expires, or it could be payable on demand (which means that, if his team is ever annoyed at him, it could insist on immediate payment). The Web site **http://www. legaldocs.com/** provides a sample promissory note with fill-in blanks.

If the note is made by a bank, it is called a **certificate of deposit** (also known as a CD). When investors loan money to a bank, the bank gives them a note promising to repay the loan at a specific date in the future. The bank is the maker and the investor is the payee. The bank pays a higher rate of interest on CDs than it does on regular savings accounts because the investor cannot demand payment on the CD until its due date. In return for the lower rate on a savings account, the depositor can withdraw that money anytime. To compare CD and savings account rates, see **http://www.bankrate.com/brm/default.asp?web=brm**.

A **draft** is an order directing someone else to pay money for you. A **check** is the most common form of a draft—it is an order telling a bank to pay money. In a draft three people are involved: the **drawer** orders the **drawee** to pay money to the **payee.** Now before you slam the book shut in despair, let us sort out the players. Suppose that Se Ri Pak wins a tournament. The Jamie Farr Kroger Classic writes her a check for $150,000. This check is an order by the Jamie Farr Kroger Classic (the drawer) to its bank (the drawee) to pay money to Se Ri Pak (the payee). The terms make sense if you remember that, when you take money out of your account, you *draw* it out. Therefore, when you write a check, you are the draw*er* and the bank is the draw*ee*. The person to whom you make out the check is being paid, so he is called the pay*ee.*

The following table illustrates the difference between notes and drafts. Even courts sometimes confuse the terms *drawer* (the person who signs a check) and *maker* (someone who signs a promissory note). But the UCC is a very precise set of rules, so it is important to get the details right. **Issuer** is an all-purpose term that means both maker and drawer.

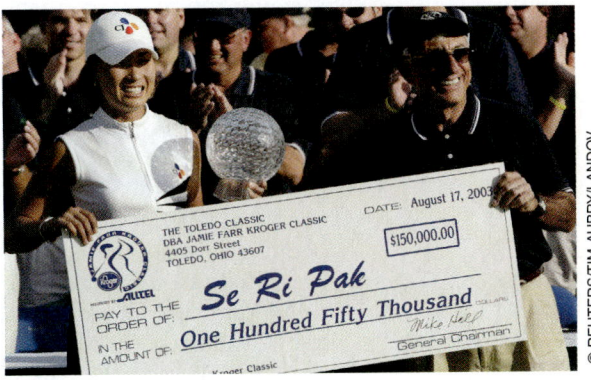

In this check, the Jamie Farr Kroger Classic is the drawer and Se Ri Pak is the payee.

	Who Pays	Who Plays
Note	You make a promise that you will pay.	Two people are involved: maker and payee.
Draft	You order someone else to pay.	Three people are involved: drawer, drawee, and payee.

Se Ri Pak presumably feels confident that the Jamie Farr Kroger Classic has enough money in its account to cover the check. When Stewart Student goes to the MegaLoud store to buy a $3,000 sound system, MegaLoud has no way of knowing if his check is good. Even if MegaLoud calls the bank to confirm Stewart's balance, he could withdraw it all by the time the check is deposited that evening. To protect itself, MegaLoud insists upon a cashier's check. A **cashier's check** is drawn by a bank on itself. When Stewart asks for a cashier's check, the bank takes the money out of his account on the spot and then issues a check itself, payable out of its own funds. When MegaLoud gets the cashier's check from Stewart, it knows that the check is good as long as the bank itself is solvent.

All checks are drafts, but not all drafts are checks. A draft is a check only if it is drawn on a bank. Sometimes drafts are drawn on individuals or companies. Suppose that in September, Sasha's Saddlery sells 16 saddles to the Circle S Stable. The stable expects that, in December, it will receive its first deposits from tourists making reservations for the following summer. The stable promises to pay Sasha $8,000 in January. Sasha is happy to make the sale, but she needs the funds now. So she prepares a draft ordering Circle S to pay $8,000 to Citizen's Bank in January. After Circle S signs (**accepts**) the draft, Sasha takes it to Citizen's, which investigates Circle S's credit reputation. Satisfied, it agrees to buy the draft for $7,000. (It pays less than the full amount because it has to wait for the money and because there is always a chance Circle S will not pay.) Sasha is the drawer, Circle S the drawee, and Citizen's Bank the payee. So Sasha's Saddlery receives $7,000 from Citizen's in September. In January, Circle S pays Citizen's the full $8,000.

The draft on Circle S is a **trade acceptance,** which is a draft drawn by a seller of goods on the buyer and payable to the seller or some third party. In our case, Sasha is the seller, Circle S the buyer, and Citizen's the third party that will be paid. To be valid, the draft must be accepted (that is, signed) by the buyer. A **sight draft** is payable on demand; a **time draft** is payable in the future. Circle S's draft is a time draft because it is not payable until January.

Sasha books a trip to England to find a new supplier of saddles. Concerned about carrying too much cash, she decides to buy $1,000 of **traveler's checks.** To purchase the checks, Sasha goes to a bank (such as Citizen's) or a company (such as American Express) and pays $1,000 plus a handling fee of about 1 percent. Before she leaves the building, she signs the front of the checks. When she needs to make a purchase in England, she signs the front of the check again. The payee then compares the two signatures to make sure they are the same, indicating that the checks are valid. Once the payee has accepted the checks, only Citizen's is liable. The payee's bank presents the checks to Citizen's for payment. Note that Citizen's is both the drawer and the drawee because it issues the checks in its own name (as drawer) and it pays the checks when presented (as drawee). If the checks are drawn on American Express, they are technically drafts, not checks, because American Express is not a bank. Traveler's checks have two advantages: (1) the English merchant accepts a check from Sasha, whom he does not know, because he trusts Citizen's (or American Express); and (2) if Sasha loses the checks, Citizen's (or American Express) will replace them for free.

NEGOTIABILITY

To work as a substitute for money, commercial paper must be freely transferable in the marketplace. In other words, it must be *negotiable*. Suppose that Krystal buys a used car from the Trustie Car Lot for her business, Krystal Rocks. She cannot afford to pay the full $15,000 right now, but she is willing to sign a note promising to pay later. As long as Trustie keeps the note, Krystal's obligation to pay is contingent upon the validity of the underlying contract. If, for instance, the car is defective, then Krystal might not be liable to Trustie for the full amount of the note. Trustie, however, does not want to keep the note. He needs the cash *now* so that he can buy more cars to sell to other customers. Reggie's Finance Co. is happy to buy Krystal's promissory note from Trustie, but the price Reggie is willing to pay depends upon whether her note is negotiable.

The possessor of *non*-negotiable commercial paper has the same rights—no more, no less—as the person who made the original contract. With non-negotiable commercial paper the transferee's rights are *conditional* because they depend upon the rights of the original party to the contract. If, for some reason, the original party loses his right to be paid, so does the transferee. The value of non-negotiable commercial paper is greatly reduced because the transferee cannot be absolutely sure what his rights are or whether he will be paid at all.

If Krystal's promissory note is non-negotiable, Reggie gets exactly the same rights that Trustie had. As the saying goes, he steps into Trustie's shoes. Other people's shoes may not be a good fit. Suppose that Trustie tampered with the odometer and, as a result, Krystal's car is worth only $12,000 instead of the $15,000 she paid for it. If, under contract law, she owes Trustie only $12,000, then that is all she has to pay Reggie, even though the note *says* $15,000.

The possessor of *negotiable* commercial paper has *more* rights than the person who made the original contract. With negotiable commercial paper, the transferee's rights are *unconditional* and generally do not depend upon the rights of the original party to the contract. As long as the transferee is a *holder in due course* (discussed later in this chapter), he is entitled to be paid the full amount of the note, regardless of the relationship between the original parties (with a few limited exceptions). If Krystal's promissory note is a negotiable instrument, she must pay the full amount to whoever has possession of it, no matter what complaints she might have against Trustie. Even if the car explodes within the month, Krystal must still pay Reggie the full $15,000. If, however, Trustie keeps the note, Krystal can subtract from what she owes *him* any claims she has against him for breach of contract because, as the original party to the note, Trustie cannot be a holder in due course. Therefore, Reggie (and any subsequent holder in due course) is in a better position than Trustie.

Exhibit 23.1 illustrates the difference between negotiable and non-negotiable commercial paper.

Requirements for Negotiability

Because negotiable instruments are more valuable than non-negotiable ones, it is important for buyers and sellers to be able to tell, easily and accurately, if an instrument is indeed negotiable. An instrument is negotiable if it meets the six standards set out in UCC §3-104(a).[2]

---

[2]   Section 3-104(a) sets out all the requirements of negotiability. Sections 3-105 to 3-119 then describe the requirements in more detail.

Exhibit 23.1

1. ***The Instrument Must Be in* Writing.** Trustie cannot negotiate Krystal's *oral* promise to pay $15,000. However, the writing need not be on any official form or even on paper. To protest a speeding ticket, Barry Lee Brown of Missoula, Montana, wrote a check for the $35 fine on a pair of old (but clean!) underpants. The bank cashed it.

2. ***The Instrument Must Be* Signed *by the Maker or Drawer.*** Any signature counts—initials, an "X," a stamp—as long as the issuer intends to indicate her signature. If Krystal normally signs her documents with an interlocking heart logo, that symbol counts as a signature. Since Krystal is buying the car for her business, Krystal Rocks, she can simply sign the document using this trade name, and that is a valid signature.

3. ***The Instrument Must Contain an* Unconditional Promise *or* Order *to Pay.*** The whole point of a negotiable instrument is that the holder can sleep soundly at night confident that he will be paid *without conditions*. If Krystal's promissory note says, "I will pay $15,000 as long as the car is still in working order," it is not negotiable. If, however, the note says, "I will pay $15,000 for the yellow car," it is negotiable because this statement is not a *condition*, it is simply describing the transaction.

   The instrument must also contain a promise or order to pay. It is not enough simply to say, "Krystal owes Trustie $15,000." She has to indicate that she owes the money and also that she intends to pay it. "Krystal promises to pay Trustie $15,000," would work.

4. ***The Instrument Must State a* Definite Amount *of Money.*** It is not easy to sell an instrument if the buyer cannot tell how much it is worth; to be negotiable, therefore, the document must clearly state how much money is owed. If the document is a note, with interest due, matters become more complicated. The holder may not be able to tell how much interest is owing simply by looking at the note. If Krystal's note says, "$15,000 with annual interest of 10 percent," Reggie can easily calculate the interest. If, on the other hand, the note says, "with interest at 1 percent above prime rate," Reggie cannot tell the total amount owed unless he checks the prime rate in his newspaper. No matter: under §3-112, an instrument with a variable interest rate is considered to be negotiable, even though the holder must look elsewhere to calculate the amount owing. Suppose that Krystal's note says, "I promise to pay $15,000 worth of diamonds." This note is not negotiable because it does not state a definite amount of *money*.

5. ***The Instrument Must Be Payable on* Demand *or at a* Definite Time.** To determine what an instrument is worth, the holder must know when he will be paid. Ten thousand dollars today is worth more than $10,000 the day the earth stands still.

A demand instrument must be paid whenever the holder requests payment. If an instrument is undated, it is treated as a demand instrument and is negotiable. There is one exception to this rule. If an undated promissory note says, "payable in 90 days," the instrument is not payable on demand and is non-negotiable. The maker of the note clearly did not intend to pay it on demand, but there is no way of knowing when she did intend to pay it.

An instrument can be negotiable even if it will not be paid until some time in the future, provided that the payment date can be determined *when the document is made*. A graduate of a well-known prep school wrote a generous check to his alma mater, but for payment date he put, "The day the headmaster is fired." This check is not negotiable because it is neither payable on demand nor at a definite time. When the check was written, no one knew when (or whether) the headmaster would be fired. If the headmaster is finally fired, the check does not suddenly become negotiable.

Suppose that Krystal simply signs her note without specifying the due date. Reggie can demand payment anytime. By contrast, if the due date on the note is Easter 2008, Reggie may have to check his calendar to figure out when that is (since the date of Easter changes every year), but the note is nonetheless negotiable. If, however, the due date on the note is "three months after Krystal receives her MBA degree," the note is non-negotiable because the date of Krystal's graduation is uncertain.

6. ***The Instrument Must Be Payable to* Order *or to* Bearer.** To be negotiable, an instrument must be either order paper or bearer paper. **Order paper** must include the words "Pay to the order of" Trustie (or an equivalent, such as "Pay to Trustie, or order"). If the note simply says "Pay to Trustie," it is not negotiable. By including the word "order," the maker is indicating that the instrument is not limited to only one person. "Pay to the order of Trustie Car Lot" means that the money will be paid to Trustie *or to anyone Trustie designates.*

If the note is made out "To bearer," it is **bearer paper** and can be redeemed by any holder in due course. The good news is that bearer paper is easily and freely transferable, but the bad news is that it may be too easily redeemed. Suppose that Krystal's note is payable to bearer and Reggie mails it to his sweetheart Sue as a birthday present. If dastardly Dan steals the note from Sue's mailbox and sells it to unknowing Neal, Krystal will have to pay Neal when he presents the note.

A note is bearer paper if it is made out to "bearer" or it is *not* made out to any specific person. If Krystal's note says, "Pay to the order of cash," or "Pay to the order of a Happy Birthday," it is bearer paper. If Krystal signs a note but leaves blank the space after "Pay to the order of," that note is bearer paper, and any holder in due course can redeem it.

The rules for checks are different from other negotiable instruments. All checks are, by definition, negotiable. Most checks are pre-printed with the words, "Pay to the order of," but sometimes people inadvertently cross out "order of." Even so, the check is still negotiable. Checks are frequently received by consumers who, sadly, have not completed a course on business law. The drafters of the UCC did not think it fair to penalize them when the drawer of the check was the one who made the mistake. If a check is made out to "Reggie *and* Sue," both payees must sign it before it can be transferred. If the check is made out to "Reggie *or* Sue," the signature of either is sufficient.

cyberLaw

An instrument must be *signed* by the maker or drawer. This sounds straightforward, but what does it mean to sign a note or draft? Many people, for example, pay bills online. How do they sign an online check? How does their bank know the signature is valid? Many states now grant digital signatures the same legal status under the UCC as a traditional paper signature (which is called a "wet" signature).[3] A computer signature does not look like handwriting; instead, it is a unique series of letters and numbers in code. A digital signature can actually be safer than the traditional wet signature. If the digital document is dishonestly altered, the sender and recipient can tell. ◆

In the following case, the *intent* of the parties is clear. But is the note enforceable? You be the judge.

you Be The Judge

YYY CORPORATION V. GAZDA

145 N.H. 53; 761 A.2d 395; 2000 N.H. LEXIS 17
Supreme Court of New Hampshire, 2000

Facts: Craig Krisel and William Volante borrowed $1,360,000 from United Federal Bank to buy two apartment buildings in Rochester, New York. They gave the bank a promissory note in this amount. Krisel and Volante then sold the apartment buildings to Richard and Everette Gazda. The Gazdas agreed to assume liability on the note. The Gazdas executed the following agreement with the bank:

> Witness that: [That is the way lawyers sometimes write agreements.]
> WHEREAS, the Bank loaned to Krisel and Volante the sum of $1,360,000.00; and
> WHEREAS, by mutual agreement the Gazdas and Bank wish to revise the terms of payment of the note signed by Krisel and Volante,
> NOW IT IS HEREBY AGREED THAT;
> (1) the rate of interest on the unpaid balance shall be 10.00 percent per annum.
> (2) The Gazdas agree to make and the Bank agrees to accept principal and interest payments in the amount of $12,217.91. The Gazdas agree that on March 1, 2012, the entire balance due under the note shall be due and payable at the option of the Bank.

This agreement shall not otherwise waive any of the terms of the original note signed by Krisel and Volante.

United Federal sold the note to another bank. Ultimately, the note ended up in the hands of the YYY Corporation. When the Gazdas failed to pay the sums due under the note, YYY sued to enforce it. The Gazdas argued that YYY could not enforce this note because the note was not a negotiable instrument under the UCC.

You be the Judge: Was the note that the Gazdas signed a negotiable instrument?

Argument for the Gazdas: To be a negotiable instrument, a note must

- contain an unconditional promise or order to pay; and
- be payable to order or bearer.

This note is not a negotiable instrument because it does not contain an unconditional promise to pay. The words "we promise to pay" are never stated. Nor is the note payable to order or bearer.

Argument for YYY: The note provides that the "Gazdas agree to make and the Bank agrees to accept principal and interest payments in the amount of $12,217.91. The Gazdas agree that on March 1, 2012 the entire balance due under the note shall be due and payable. . . ." That is an unconditional promise to pay. What else could those words mean?

The agreement also provided that it did not "waive any of the terms of the original note." That note was payable to order or bearer and, therefore, so is this note.

The Gazdas borrowed this money and now they do not want to repay it. A finding for the Gazdas would be a serious miscarriage of justice. ■

Public Policy

If the system of negotiable instruments is to work, buyers and sellers must be able to tell, easily and accurately, whether an instrument is indeed negotiable. It is also essential—and fair—that lenders be repaid what they are owed. Both of these interests are important to commerce. In this case, which interest is most crucial? ◆

---

[3] The federal Electronic Signatures in Global and National Commerce Act expanded the definition of electronic signature to include "biometric" identifications such as fingerprints, retina scans, and voiceprints. However, the federal statute does not apply to UCC Articles 3 and 4.

Interpretation of Ambiguities

Perhaps you have noticed that people sometimes make mistakes. Although the UCC establishes simple and precise rules for creating negotiable instruments, people do not always follow these rules to the letter. It might be tempting simply to invalidate defective documents (after all, money is at stake here). But instead, the UCC favors negotiability and has rules to resolve uncertainty and supply missing terms.

Notice anything odd about the check pictured here? Is it for $1,500 or $15,000? When the terms in a negotiable instrument contradict each other, three rules apply:

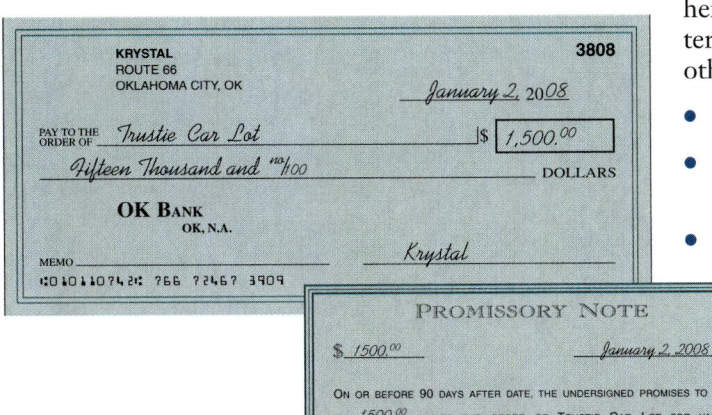

- Words take precedence over numbers.

- Handwritten terms prevail over typed and printed terms.

- Typed terms win over printed terms.

According to these rules, Krystal's check is for $15,000 because, in a conflict between words and numbers, words win.

What is wrong with the promissory note shown here? The interest rate is left blank. When this happens, UCC §3-112 directs that the judgment rate applies. The **judgment rate** is simply the rate that courts use on court-ordered judgments.

NEGOTIATION

Remember the fundamental rule that underlies this chapter: the possessor of a piece of commercial paper has an unconditional right to be paid, as long as (1) the paper is negotiable, (2) it has been negotiated to the possessor, (3) the possessor is a holder in due course, and (4) the issuer cannot claim any of a limited number of "real" defenses. **Negotiation means that an instrument has been transferred to the holder by someone *other than the issuer*.** If the issuer has transferred the instrument to the holder, then it has not been negotiated and the issuer can refuse to pay the holder if there was some flaw in the underlying contract. Thus, if Jake gives Madison a promissory note for $2,000 in payment for a new computer, but the computer crashes and burns the first week, Jake has the right to refuse to pay the note. Jake was the issuer and the note was not negotiated. But if, before the computer self-destructs, Madison indorses and transfers the note to Kayla, then Jake is liable to Kayla for the full amount of the note, regardless of his claims against Madison.

To be negotiable, an instrument must be order paper (payable to the order of someone) or bearer paper (payable to anyone in possession). These two types of instrument have different rules for negotiation: **to be negotiated, order paper must first be** *indorsed* and then *delivered* to the transferee. **Bearer paper must simply be *delivered* to the transferee; no indorsement is required.**[4]

In its simplest form, **an indorsement is the signature of the payee.** Tess writes a rent check for $475 to her landlord, Larnell. He would like to use this money to pay Patty for painting the building. If Larnell signs the back of the check and delivers it to Patty, he has met the two requirements for negotiating order paper: indorsement and delivery. If Larnell delivers the check to Patty but forgets to sign it, the check has not been indorsed and therefore cannot be negotiated—it has no value to Patty. Similarly, the check is no use to Patty if Larnell signs it but never gives it to her. If someone forges Larnell's name, the indorsement is invalid and no subsequent transfer counts as a negotiation.

There are three different types of indorsements:

- *Blank Indorsement.* A blank indorsement occurs when Larnell simply signs the check on the back without designating any particular payee. A blank indorsement turns the check into bearer paper. Larnell can give the check to Patty the painter or Ellen the electrician. In either case, he has properly negotiated the check.

- *Special Indorsement.* A special indorsement limits an instrument to one particular person. If Larnell writes on the back of the check, "Pay Ellen Wilson" or "Pay to the order of Ellen Wilson," then only Ellen can cash the check.

- *Restrictive Indorsement.* A restrictive indorsement limits the check to one particular use. When Ellen receives the check from Larnell, she writes on the back, "For deposit only," and then signs her name. The check can only be deposited in Ellen's account. If Conrad finds the check, he cannot cash it or deposit it in his own account. This type of indorsement is the safest.

Note that indorsements can be used to change an instrument from order paper to bearer paper or vice versa. If Tess makes a check out to cash, it is bearer paper. When Larnell writes on the back, "Pay to the order of Patty," it becomes order paper. If Patty simply signs her name, the check becomes bearer paper again. And so on it could go forever.[5]

HOLDER IN DUE COURSE

A holder in due course has an automatic right to receive payment for a negotiable instrument (unless the issuer can claim a limited number of "real" defenses). If the possessor of an instrument is not a holder in due course, then his right to payment depends upon the relationship between the issuer and payee. He inherits whatever claims and defenses arise out of that contract. Clearly, then, holder in due course status dramatically increases the value of an instrument because it enhances the probability of being paid.

Requirements for Being a Holder in Due Course

Under §3-302 of the UCC, a holder in due course is a *holder* who has given *value* for the instrument, in *good faith*, *without notice* of outstanding claims or other defects.

---

[4] §3-201. The UCC spells the word "indorsed." Outside the UCC, the word is more commonly spelled "endorsed."

[5] Even when all the space on the back of the check is filled, the holder can attach a separate paper for indorsements, called an **allonge**.

Holder

A holder in due course must, first of all, be a holder. For order paper, a **holder** is anyone in possession of the instrument if it is payable to or indorsed to her. For bearer paper, a **holder** is anyone in possession. When Felix borrows money from his mother, she insists that he sign a promissory note for the loan. He promptly writes, "I hereby promise to pay to the order of Imogene $5,000." He signs his name and gives the note to her. She is a holder because she has possession of the instrument and it is payable to her. She would like to give the note to her lawyer, Lance, to pay the legal bill she incurred when Felix smashed up a nightclub. If she simply hands the note to Lance, he is not a holder because the note is not payable to him. If she writes on the back of the note, "Pay to the order of Lance," but does not give it to him, he is not a holder either.

Value

A holder in due course must give value for an instrument. **Value** means that the holder has *already* done something in exchange for the instrument. Lance has already represented Felix, so he has given value. Once Imogene indorses and delivers the note to Lance, he is a holder in due course.

Although a promise to do something in the future is *consideration* under contract law, such a promise does not count as *value* under Article 3. If the holder receives an instrument in return for a promise, he does not deserve to be paid unless he performs the promise. But if he were a holder in due course, he would be entitled to payment whether he performed or not. For example, suppose that Imogene gave Lance the promissory note in exchange for his promise to represent Felix in an upcoming arson trial. Lance would not be a holder in due course because he has not yet performed the service. It would be unfair for him to be a holder in due course, with an unconditional right to be paid, if he, in fact, does not represent Felix.

Someone who receives a negotiable instrument as a gift is not a holder in due course because he has not given value. If Imogene gives Felix's note to her daughter, Joy, as a birthday present, Joy is not a holder in due course.

Good Faith

Should Hope have faith in Felix's fabulous beauty cream?

There are two tests to determine if a holder acquired an instrument in good faith. The holder must meet both of these tests:

- **Subjective Test.** Did the holder *believe* the transaction was honest in fact?

- **Objective Test.** Did the transaction *appear* to be commercially reasonable?

Felix persuades his elderly neighbor, Hope, that he has invented a fabulous beauty cream guaranteed to remove wrinkles. She gives him a $10,000 promissory note, payable in 90 days, in return for exclusive sales rights in Pittsburgh. Felix sells the note to his old friend Dick for $2,000. Felix never delivers the sales samples to Hope. When Dick presents the note to Hope, she refuses to pay on the grounds that Dick is not a holder in due course. She contends that he did not buy the note in good faith.

Dick fails both tests. Any friend of Felix knows he is not trustworthy, especially when presenting a promissory note signed by an elderly neighbor. Dick did not believe the transaction was honest in fact. Also, $10,000 notes are not usually discounted to $2,000; $9,000 would be more normal. This transaction is not commercially reasonable, and Dick should have realized immediately that Felix was up to no good.

In the following case, the plaintiff also failed two tests: he neither gave value nor acted in good faith.

ROSENBAUM V. BULOW

1997 Bankr. LEXIS 555
United States Bankruptcy Court for the Eastern District of North Carolina, 1997

Facts: Maude Knox Rosenbaum was convicted of "obtaining property by false pretenses" (more commonly referred to as "fraud"). Pending the outcome of her appeal, she was sent to Women's Prison in Raleigh, North Carolina. Prison was not to her liking, but she could not raise bail of $50,000. Nor could she find a bondsman willing to post bail for her.[6]

Rosenbaum turned to her sister, Louise Knox, for help. Knox asked for money from a number of friends and acquaintances, who evidently felt Rosenbaum was just fine where she was. Finally, Harvey Bowen, a local used-car dealer, agreed to post the $7,500 bond in exchange for a $7,500 promissory note secured by Rosenbaum's house. In other words, Bowen asked to be paid $7,500 even though he was entitled to a refund of his entire bond if Rosenbaum returned to prison as required. There was only one problem with this arrangement: Bowen was not a licensed bondsman. Thus, under state law, Rosenbaum had no obligation to pay him for posting bail. Shortly after obtaining the note from Rosenbaum, Bowen attempted to solve this problem by asking her to sign a second note that was identical to the first, except this time W. F. Bulow was the payee. (Bulow was married to Bowen's niece, but he was not a licensed bondsman either.) When Bulow tried to collect on the note, Rosenbaum argued that he was not entitled to be paid because he neither gave value nor acted in good faith.

Issues: Did Bulow give value for the promissory note? Did he act in good faith?

Excerpts from Judge Leonard's Decision: Bulow gave no value to Rosenbaum in exchange for her execution of the note. It is true that Bowen gave something of value to Rosenbaum, and that Bowen then arranged for Bulow to be named the beneficiary of these instruments. However, there is no credible evidence that Bulow gave value to Bowen in exchange for this benefit. To the contrary, the evidence establishes that Bowen simply used Bulow's name to mask his own illegal activity. At most, these facts support the inference that Bulow was the gratuitous beneficiary of Bowen's illegally obtained profit. This inference does not satisfy the "for value" requirement of §3-302.

Nor can Bulow show that he took these instruments in good faith as required by §3-302. Bulow has presented no credible explanation for his acquisition of Rosenbaum's note. He concedes that he gave nothing of value to Rosenbaum in exchange for these documents, and in particular, that he did not give the $7,500 consideration recited in the note. It is also clear that he and Rosenbaum had no acquaintance prior to her execution of these documents. On these facts, it strains credulity to think that Bulow was unaware of the true arrangement between Bowen and Rosenbaum. However, even if Bulow knew nothing of Bowen's unsavory activity, his failure to acquaint himself with the circumstances of this transaction would amount to bad faith. When a perfect stranger makes an unsolicited promise to pay $7,500 and secures this promise with a lien on her house, good faith and common sense impose a minimal duty of inquiry on the recipient. Bulow's acceptance of these documents without some investigation into their origin precludes a finding that he took them in good faith.

Based on the foregoing, the court holds that the promissory note granted by Maude Lee Knox Rosenbaum to W. F. Bulow [is] void and unenforceable. ∎

---

[6] Typically, a prisoner will be released if a licensed bail bondsman is willing to post a cash bond equal to 15 percent of bail (in this case $7,500). The prisoner pays the bondsman a fee equal to 10 percent of the bond (here it would be $750). If the prisoner fails to return to prison when ordered by the court, the bondsman must pay the balance owing (that is, $42,500). Naturally, a licensed bondsman will post bail only if he is quite sure the defendant will return as promised. When the defendant does return, the bondsman gets back the bond of $7,500 and keeps the $750 fee as well.

Ethics

In Chapter 2 on ethics, we talked about Right v. Right. This case is, in some sense, about Wrong v. Wrong. Harvey Bowen serves as a bondsman, although he is not licensed. Maude Rosenbaum refuses to pay $7,500, although she has signed a promissory note. Why did the court view her act as less wrong than his? ◆

Notice of Outstanding Claims or Other Defects

In certain circumstances, a holder is on notice that an instrument has an outstanding claim or other defect.

1. **The Instrument Is Overdue.** An instrument is overdue the day after its due date. At that point, the recipient is on notice that it may have a defect. He ought to wonder why no one has bothered to collect the money owed. However, an instrument is not overdue simply because the interest is unpaid. If, on July 25, Dick buys Harriet's note that was due on July 24, Dick is not a holder in due course because the note is overdue. But if he buys the note on July 23, knowing that Harriet has not paid all the interest owing, he can still be a holder in due course.

   A check is overdue 90 days after its date. Any other *demand* instrument is overdue (1) the day after a request for payment is made or (2) a reasonable time after the instrument was issued. Suppose that Felix tries to sell Tom a demand note from Hope. If Felix happens to mention, "I asked the old lady for the money yesterday, but so far, no luck," then Tom is not a holder in due course because he knows the note is overdue.

```
              PROMISSORY NOTE


$500.00                        September 5, 1950

On or before 60 days after date, I promise to pay $500 to

the order of Soames for value received.

                          Irene
           _____
```

The holder of this note should realize that there may be a problem.

2. **The Instrument Is Dishonored.** To dishonor an instrument is to refuse to pay it. If Tom knows that Hope has refused to pay her note, then Tom cannot be a holder in due course. Likewise, once a check has been stamped, "Insufficient Funds" by the bank, it has been dishonored, and no one who obtains it afterward can be a holder in due course.

3. **The Instrument Is Altered, Forged, or Incomplete.** Anyone who knows that an instrument has been altered or forged cannot be a holder in due course. Suppose Joe wrote a check to Tony for $200. While showing the check to Liza, Tony cackles to himself and says, "Can you believe what that goof did? Look, he left the line blank after the words 'two hundred.'" Taking his pen out with a flourish, Tony changes the zeroes to nines and adds the words, "ninety-nine." He then indorses the check over to Liza, who is definitely not a holder in due course. However, if, instead of giving the check to Liza, Tony sells it to Kate, she is a holder in due course because she had no idea the check had been altered.

   Likewise, if Joe filled out the check, but failed to sign it, Liza cannot be a holder in due course after she watches Tony fill in Joe's signature. And even if Liza did not see the forgery, she might be on notice if Tony has misspelled Joe's name as "Jo."

   Sometimes people (foolishly) sign blank promissory notes or checks. These issuers are liable for any amount subsequently filled in. However, anyone who is aware that a material term was added later is not a holder in due course. Suppose that Joe gives Tony a signed, blank check. If Tony fills in the amount in front of Liza, then naturally she is not a holder in due course. But if Tony fills in the check *before* he gives it to Liza, she is a holder in due course.

4. ***The Holder Has Notice of Certain Claims or Disputes.*** No one can qualify as a holder in due course if she is on notice that (1) someone else has a claim to the instrument or (2) there is a dispute between the original parties to the instrument. Matt hires Sheila to put aluminum siding on his house. In payment, he gives her a $15,000 promissory note with the due date left blank. They agree that the note will not be due until 60 days after completion of the work. Despite the agreement, Sheila fills in the date immediately and sells the note to Rupert at American Finance Corp., who has bought many similar notes from Sheila. Rupert knows that the note is not supposed to be due until after the work is finished. Usually, before he buys a note from her, he demands a signed document from the homeowner certifying that the work is complete. Also, he lives near Matt and can see that Matt's house is only half finished. Rupert is not a holder in due course because he has reason to suspect there is a dispute between Sheila and Matt.

Holder in due course status is determined *when the holder receives the instrument.* If, at the very moment when he takes possession, the holder has no notice of outstanding claims or other defects, then he is a holder in due course, no matter what else happens afterward. If Rupert knows nothing of Sheila's sneaky ways when he buys Matt's note, then he is a holder in due course even if Matt calls him 10 minutes later to report that Sheila has violated their contract.

In the following case, Avon thought that American Express should have realized something fishy was going on.

HARTFORD ACCIDENT & INDEMNITY CO. V. AMERICAN EXPRESS, CO.

74 N.Y.2d 153, 542 N.E.2d 1090, 1989 N.Y. LEXIS 881
New York Court of Appeals, 1989

Facts: As manager of the import/export department at Avon Products, Stratford Skalkos had authority to requisition checks up to $25,000 on his signature alone. For nearly three years, Skalkos used that authority to steal $162,538.65 from Avon. Skalkos followed a simple pattern: he altered the names of the payees so that, although they still sounded like company suppliers, the checks could be cashed by businesses to which he owed money personally. He used these checks to pay for personal expenses such as credit card charges, an opera subscription, car maintenance bills, and apartment furnishings. For example, he sent American Express 15 Avon checks that were payable to "Amerex Corp." Similarly, he sent three Avon checks to the Metropolitan Opera Association, Inc., payable to "Metropolitan Opng. Co.," "Metropolitan Opptg. Inc." and "Metropolitan Oprtg. Co." By the movement of one letter, E.J. Audi, Inc. (a furniture store) became "E. Jaudi, Inc."

Avon sued the recipients of the checks, demanding that the funds be returned. The trial court ruled against Avon and granted defendants' motion for summary judgment, concluding that defendants were holders in due course and thus took the checks free of any claims or defenses. The appellate division affirmed. Avon appealed.

Issue: Were the defendants holders in due course?

Excerpts from Judge Kaye's Decision: To be a holder in due course a party must take the instrument "without notice that it is overdue or has been dishonored or of any defense against or claim to it on the part of any person." Plaintiff contends that defendants took the checks from Skalkos with notice of Avon's claim—in particular, that they took with notice that Avon had not authorized defendants to apply its funds to Skalkos' personal indebtedness.

▼

[It] will be rare that an instrument will be so irregular as to call into question its validity, terms or ownership. By any measure, the misnomers—correctly portrayed by [the trial court] as minor errors or misspellings—were not irregularities of such magnitude as to put a holder on notice that something was wrong.

As [the trial court] observed, the use of corporate checks to pay employees' debts "is an every day occurrence in the business world. Employers often help an employee to maintain a residence as an inducement to continued employment in an area where living expenses are high. Employers often pay for the entertainment of customers by an employee. Employers often pay for travel and transportation expenses of an employee." Defendants themselves in their summary judgment submissions have indicated that they regularly receive payment through corporate accounts for goods or services furnished to individuals.

Parties who take commercial paper for value [are] not bound at [their] peril to be upon the alert for circumstances which might possibly excite the suspicions of wary vigilance. Thus we conclude as a matter of law that defendants did not have notice of Avon's claim under UCC §3-304.

Finally, the result we reach promotes the policy favoring ready negotiability of commercial paper, assuring that good faith purchasers need not stand as insurers of the honesty of a drawer corporation's employees. And it assigns losses by the relative responsibility of the parties, allocating liability to the party best able to prevent them. As among the eight parties to this dispute Avon—whose misplaced trust or inattention enabled its employee to misappropriate funds, undetected, for several years—was plainly the party best able to prevent the losses and to protect itself by insurance. The losses were therefore properly allocated to Avon, not defendants.

Accordingly, the order of the appellate division dismissing the complaint should be *affirmed*, with costs. ■

Shelter Rule

Under the shelter rule, the transferor of an instrument passes on all of his rights. When a holder in due course transfers an instrument, the recipient acquires all the same rights *even if she is not a holder in due course herself.*[7]

Cigna Insurance Company sent James Mills a check for $484.12 in payment for his insurance claim. Dishonest fellow that he was, Mills told Cigna that he had never received the check because it had been sent to the wrong address. Cigna stopped payment and issued a new check. Mills took the old check to Sun's Market and used it to buy goods there. When Sun deposited the check at its bank, the bank refused to pay and stamped the check "Stop Payment." At this point, Sun was a holder in due course and was entitled to payment from Cigna. Instead of presenting the check itself, Sun sold it to Robert Triffin, who was in the business of buying dishonored instruments. Triffin then sued Cigna for payment. Triffin acknowledged that he was not a holder in due course because he knew the check had been dishonored. However, under the shelter rule, he acquired Sun's rights as a holder in due course and he was entitled to payment.[8]

The point of the shelter rule is not to benefit Mills or Triffin, it is to protect Sun. It would not do Sun much good to be a holder in due course if it were unable to sell the instrument to anyone.

There is one small exception to the shelter rule. If a holder in due course transfers the instrument back to a prior holder who was a party to fraud involving the instrument, that prior holder does not acquire the rights of a holder in due course. Thus, if

---

[7] §3-203(b).
[8] *Triffin v. Cigna,* 297 N.J. Super. 199; 687 A.2d 1045; 1997 N.J. Super. LEXIS 50 (Sup. Ct. N.J., App. Div., 1997).

Triffin transferred the check back to Mills, then Mills would not be entitled to payment from Cigna (even if he had the nerve to ask).

Defenses against a Holder in Due Course

Negotiable instruments are meant to be a close substitute for money, and, as a general rule, holders expect to be paid. However, an issuer may legitimately refuse to pay an instrument under certain circumstances. Section 3-305 of the UCC lists so-called *real* defenses that an issuer may legitimately use even against a holder in due course. If the holder is not in due course but is simply a plain ordinary holder, the issuer may use both real defenses and *personal* defenses. **Real and personal defenses are valid against an ordinary holder; only real defenses can be used against a holder in due course.**

Real Defenses

The following real defenses are valid against both a holder and a holder in due course:

Forgery. If Sharon forges Jared's name to a promissory note and sells it to Jennifer, Jared does not have to pay Jennifer, even if she is a holder in due course.

Bankruptcy. If Jared's debts are discharged in a bankruptcy proceeding after he has signed a promissory note, he does not have to pay the note, even to a holder in due course.

Minority. If a minor has the right to void a contract under state law, then he also has the right not to pay a negotiable instrument, even to a holder in due course.

Alteration. If the amount of an instrument is wrongfully changed, the holder in due course can collect only the original (correct) amount. If the instrument was incomplete, the holder in due course can collect the full face amount, even if the instrument was incorrectly filled in. Suppose that Jared gives a $2,000 promissory note to Rose. As soon as he leaves, she whips out her pen and adds a zero to the note. She then takes it to the auto showroom to pay for her new car. If the showroom is a holder in due course, it is entitled to be paid the original amount of the note ($2,000), not the altered amount ($20,000). But, if Jared had accidentally forgotten to fill out the amount of the note, and Rose wrote in $20,000, the showroom could recover the full $20,000. Although the two notes *look* the same, they have a different result. In the case where Rose changed the amount, Jared was not to blame; but he *was* at fault for signing a blank note.

Duress, Mental Incapacity, or Illegality. These are customary contract defenses that you remember well from your study of contracts. They are a defense against a holder in due course if they are severe enough to make the underlying transaction void (not simply voidable) under state law. An instrument is not valid even in the hands of a holder in due course if, for example, Rose holds a gun to Jared's head to force him to sign it; or Jared has been declared mentally incompetent at the time he signs it; or Jared is using the instrument to pay for something illegal (cocaine, say).

Fraud in the Execution. In cases of fraud in the execution, the issuer has been tricked into signing without knowing what the instrument is and without any reasonable way to find out. In such instances, even a holder in due course cannot recover. Jared cannot read English. Helen, his boss, tells him that he must sign a document required by the company's health insurance plan. In fact, the document is a promissory note, payable to Helen. Jared does not have to pay the note, even to a holder in due course, because of fraud in the execution.

Personal Defenses

Personal defenses are valid against a holder, but *not* against a holder in due course. Typically, personal defenses have some connection to the initial transaction in which the instrument was issued.

Breach of Contract. Ross signs a contract to sell a new airplane to Paige in return for a $1 million promissory note. If Paige discovers that the plane is defective and that Ross has breached the contract, she can refuse to pay him because he is a mere holder. If, however, Ross sells the note to Helga, a holder in due course, Paige must pay her.

Lack of Consideration. Ross gives his mother, Gertrude, a $1,000 check for her birthday. Then they have a disagreement over where to spend Thanksgiving, so Ross stops payment on Gertrude's check. Gertrude has no right to the $1,000 because she is a mere holder who did not give value for the check. But if Gertrude has already cashed the check at her bank, Ross must pay the bank because it is a holder in due course. Even though the check was a gift, and therefore lacking in value, the bank is a holder in due course because it has given value for the check, even if Gertrude has not.

Prior Payment. Two years before, Gertrude had loaned Ross money to start his airplane business. When he paid off the note to Gertrude, he forgot to retrieve the original from her. Angry at him over the check, she sells the note to Carla. Of course, Ross would not have to pay Gertrude *again*, but he cannot refuse to pay Carla, who is a holder in due course. The moral is: when you pay off a note, be sure to retrieve it or mark it canceled.

Unauthorized Completion. Ross writes a check to Carla to pay the note. He forgets to fill in the amount of the check, but Carla very helpfully does, for $5,000 more than he actually owes. If she uses that check to pay her debt at the bank, the bank is a holder in due course, and Ross must honor the check. Remember, however, that if the bank knew Carla had filled in the amount, it would not be a holder in due course and could not recover on the check.

Fraud in the Inducement. Suppose that Carla gives Sean a promissory note to buy stock in his company. It turns out that the company is a fraud. Carla would not have to pay Sean (a holder), but, if Sean transfers the note to Peter, a holder in due course, Carla must pay Peter even though the underlying contract was fraudulent. Note that *fraud in the execution* (real defense) has a different result from *fraud in the inducement* (personal defense).

Non-Delivery. The note that Carla issued to Sean was bearer paper. When Oliver steals it and sells it to a holder in due course, Carla must pay the note even though neither she nor Sean had ever delivered it to the holder. Carla would not have to pay Oliver because he is a mere holder and she did not deliver it to him.

The following table lists, for quick reference, real and personal defenses.

Real Defenses	Personal Defenses
Forgery	Breach of contract
Bankruptcy	Lack of consideration
Minority	Prior payment
Alteration	Unauthorized completion
Duress	Fraud in the inducement
Mental incapacity	Non-delivery
Illegality	
Fraud in the execution	

Claims in Recoupment

A **claim in recoupment** is not the same as a defense, but it has a similar impact. It means that the issuer subtracts (i.e., "sets off") any other claims he has against the initial payee from the amount he owes on the instrument. The distinction is subtle, but a *claim in recoupment* means, "I'm not going to pay the full amount of the instrument because she owes me money for something else" whereas a *defense* means, "I'm not going to pay the full amount of the instrument because there is some problem with the instrument itself or the underlying deal on which the instrument is based."

A claim in recoupment is valid against a holder but not against a holder in due course. Carla gives Sean a promissory note to pay for stock that turns out to be fraudulent. Therefore, Carla has a defense against Sean when he requests that she pay her note. Suppose, however, that the stock is perfectly legitimate, but Sean has never paid Carla $18,000 for the used car he bought from her. When Sean presents the note on the stock deal for payment, Carla makes a claim for recoupment and subtracts $18,000 from the amount owing on the note. If, however, Sean had already sold the note to Olaf, a holder in due course, Carla would have to pay the full amount of the note and then sue Sean for the $18,000.

Consumer Exception

In the eighteenth and nineteenth centuries, negotiable instruments often circulated through several hands. The business community treated them as money. The concept of holder in due course was essential because the instruments had little use if they could not be transferred for value. In the modern banking system, however, instruments are much less likely to circulate. Currently, the most common use for negotiable instruments is in consumer transactions. A consumer pays for a refrigerator by giving the store a promissory note. The store promptly sells the note to a finance company. Even if the refrigerator is defective, under Article 3 the consumer must pay full value on the note because the finance company is a holder in due course.

Some commentators have argued that the concept of holder in due course no longer serves a useful purpose and that it should be eliminated once and for all (and with it Article 3 of the UCC). No state has yet taken such a dramatic step. Instead, some states require promissory notes given by a consumer to carry the words "consumer paper." Notes with this legend are non-negotiable.

Meanwhile, the Federal Trade Commission (FTC) has special rules for consumer credit contracts. A **consumer credit contract** is one in which a consumer borrows money from a lender to purchase goods and services from a seller who is affiliated with the lender. If Sears loans money to Gerald to buy a big-screen TV at Sears, that is a consumer credit contract. It is not a consumer credit contract if Gerald borrows money from his cousin Vinnie to buy the TV from Sears. The FTC requires all promissory notes in consumer credit contracts to contain the following language:

NOTICE
ANY HOLDER OF THIS CONSUMER CREDIT CONTRACT IS SUB-
JECT TO ALL CLAIMS AND DEFENSES WHICH THE DEBTOR
COULD ASSERT AGAINST THE SELLER OF GOODS OR SERVICES
OBTAINED WITH THE PROCEEDS HEREOF.

Under §3-106(d) of the UCC, no one can be a holder in due course of an instrument with this language. If the language is omitted from a consumer note, it is possible to be a holder in due course, but the seller can be punished by a fine of up to $10,000.

In the following case, the plaintiff borrowed money from Sterling to pay Mayflower. The FTC rule applied because the two companies were "affiliated."

SCOTT V. MAYFLOWER HOME IMPROVEMENT CORP.

363 N.J. Super. 145; 831 A.2d 564; 2001 N.J. Super. LEXIS 524
Superior Court of New Jersey, 2001

Facts: Mary Johnson signed a contract with Mayflower Home Improvement Corporation for repair work on her home. The contract specified a fee of $25,900. Later, Mayflower arranged for Johnson to pay for this work by borrowing money from Sterling Resources. In the note she signed with Sterling, the price was unconscionably high—$50,108.60—and so was the interest rate—17.98 percent.

Johnson alleges that Mayflower was running a scam. It hired unlicensed salespeople who targeted minority neighborhoods. The contracts prepared by the salespersons specified the work in general terms but omitted the name, make, quality, and model of the products and materials to be used. The contracts did not specify the interest rate or the total cost. The contractor's work was done in a shoddy or incomplete manner often using poor quality materials.

Sterling routinely loaned money to Mayflower customers. The interest rates on these loans were between 15 percent and 19 percent. Sterling then sold the loans to banks and other financial institutions (the Lender). BankAtlantic purchased from Sterling over $60 million of consumer loans in a three year period.

When Johnson failed to make the payments due on the note, the Lender sued her. It moved for summary judgment against Johnson on the grounds that, as a holder in due course, it was entitled to enforce the note regardless of her claims against Mayflower or Sterling. She responded that, under the FTC consumer exception rule, the Lender was not a holder in due course. Therefore, the Lender was subject to whatever defenses she had against Sterling or Mayflower.

Issue: Was the Lender a holder in due course?

Excerpts from Judge Humphrey's Decision: The assignees argue that they are holders in due course of negotiable instruments, and therefore immune from the claims of the [defendant]. In recent years a large body of law has developed restricting the use of the holder in due course doctrine in consumer transactions. The FTC spearheaded that new body of law some 25 years ago by adopting the FTC Holder Rule. The reasons for the FTC Holder Rule have been described as follows:

[T]he FTC concluded that unethical merchants and their financiers were using the venerable Holder in Due Course doctrine from the law of negotiable instruments to victimize thousands of innocent consumers. Inner-city stores were selling shoddy furniture, fly-by-night contractors were promising to install aluminum siding that never appeared, the proverbial used-car dealers were hawking lemons, and countless other shady characters were operating in similar fashion in scores of different fields. In each of these cases, the defrauded consumer was saddled with the bill when a holder in due course demanded payment. The note [that Sterling assigned had] the FTC Holder notice conspicuously printed thereon. Consequently, the assignees were on notice that the FTC Holder Rule was applicable to the notes that they were purchasing from Sterling. The FTC Holder Rule, is therefore, applicable to the consumer obligations here. The Holder in Due Course doctrine will not immunize the financial institutions from the claims of the [plaintiff].

The FTC Holder Rule is designed to require the assignee of a consumer contract to step into the shoes of the seller with respect to the claims and defenses of the consumer. If the seller's shoes are too tight a fit, then the assignee need not purchase the consumer contract. The creditor faced with the loss of the holder in due course defense against the victimized consumer has a variety of acceptable options, e.g., buy the commercial paper with some type of recourse, or protect against losses by raising the interest rate or purchase insurance.

[Summary judgment is denied for the plaintiff, but granted for the defendant.] ∎

Public Policy | Someone—either the plaintiff or the defendant—will lose money in this case. Although one could argue that the buyer should beware, that Mary Johnson should not have signed such an unfair contract, the court decided that the Lender was in a better position to protect itself than she was. What does the court suggest that the Lender should have done? Is it reasonable to expect the Lender to take such steps? Why is it important to protect Mary Johnson? ◆

Chapter Conclusion

Whenever someone acquires commercial paper, the first question he ought to ask is "How certain is it that I will be paid the face value of this document?" Article 3 of the UCC contains the answer to this question: if a negotiable instrument is negotiated to a holder in due course, then that holder knows he has an unconditional right (subject only to a few real defenses) to be paid the value of the note. In some ways, Article 3 is like a marine drill instructor: rigid, but predictable if you follow the rules.

Chapter Review

1. Commercial paper is a contract to pay money. It can be used either as a substitute for money or as a loan of money.

2. The possessor of a piece of commercial paper has an unconditional right to be paid, as long as:
   - The paper is negotiable
   - It has been negotiated to the possessor
   - The possessor is a holder in due course, and
   - The issuer cannot claim any of the few "real" defenses.

3. The possessor of non-negotiable commercial paper has the same rights—no more, no less—as the person who made the original contract. The possessor of negotiable commercial paper has more rights than the person who made the original contract.

4. To be negotiable, an instrument must:
   - Be in writing
   - Be signed by the maker or drawer
   - Contain an unconditional promise or order to pay
   - State a definite amount of money
   - Be payable on demand or at a definite time, and
   - Be payable to order or to bearer.

5. When the terms in a negotiable instrument contradict each other, three rules apply:
   - Words take precedence over numbers.
   - Handwritten terms prevail over typed and printed terms.
   - Typed terms win over printed terms.

6. To be negotiated, order paper must first be indorsed and then delivered to the transferee. Bearer paper must simply be delivered to the transferee; no indorsement is required.

7. A holder in due course is a holder who has given value for the instrument, in good faith, without notice of outstanding claims or other defects.

8. These real defenses are valid against both a holder and a holder in due course:
   - Forgery
   - Bankruptcy
   - Minority
   - Alteration
   - Duress, mental incapacity, or illegality
   - Fraud in the execution

9. These personal defenses are valid against any holder except a holder in due course:
   - Breach of contract
   - Lack of consideration

- Prior payment
- Unauthorized completion
- Fraud in the inducement
- Non-delivery

Practice Test

1. Gary Culver, a farmer in Missouri, was having financial problems. He agreed to let Nasib Ed Kalliel assume control of the farm's finances. After a few months, Culver urgently asked Kalliel for money. One week later, $30,000 was wire-transferred to Culver from the Rexford State Bank. Culver thought that Kalliel would be responsible for repaying this sum. A man who worked for Kalliel stopped Culver on the street and asked him to sign a receipt for the $30,000. Culver signed without intending to commit himself to repaying the money. In fact, the document Culver signed was a blank promissory note, payable to Rexford. Someone later filled in the blanks, putting in $50,000 instead of $30,000. Kalliel had received $50,000 before transferring $30,000 to Culver. When Rexford sued Culver to enforce the note, Culver asserted the defense of fraud. Is Culver liable on the note?

2. CPA QUESTION In order to negotiate bearer paper, one must:

  a. Indorse the paper

  b. Indorse and deliver the paper with consideration

  c. Deliver the paper

  d. Deliver and indorse the paper

3. CPA QUESTION Bond fraudulently induced Teal to make a note payable to Wilk, to whom Bond was indebted. Bond delivered the note to Wilk. Wilk negotiated the instrument to Monk, who purchased it with knowledge of the fraud and after it was overdue. If Wilk qualifies as a holder in due course, which of the following statements is correct?

  a. Monk has the standing of a holder in due course through Wilk.

  b. Teal can successfully assert the defense of fraud in the inducement against Monk.

10. A claim in recoupment cannot be used against a holder in due course.

11. The Federal Trade Commission requires all promissory notes in consumer credit contracts to contain language preventing any subsequent holder from being a holder in due course.

  c. Monk personally qualifies as a holder in due course.

  d. Teal can successfully assert the defense of fraud in the inducement against Wilk.

4. Shelby wrote the following check to Dana. When is it payable and for how much?

5. After Irene Nusor fell behind on her mortgage payments, she answered an advertisement from Best Financial Consultants offering attractive refinancing opportunities. During a meeting at a McDonald's restaurant, a Best representative told her that the company would arrange for a complete refinancing of her home, pay off two of her creditors, and give her an additional $5,000 in spending money. Nusor would only have to pay Best $4,000. Nusor signed a blank promissory note that was filled in later by Best representatives for $14,986.61 payable in 60 days at an annual interest rate of 18 percent. Within two weeks, Best sold the note to Parkhill for just under $14,000. Best paid $5,997.25 to one of Nusor's creditors but never fulfilled its other promises. Nusor refused to pay the note, alleging that Parkhill was not a holder in due course. Is Nusor liable to Parkhill?

6. On June 30, John N. Willis signed a demand promissory note for $1,620 to the Camelot Country Club in Carrollton, Texas. The note stated that it was being given in payment for a membership in the country club, but, in fact, the club was insolvent, its memberships had no value, and Willis was already a member. He was also the club's golf pro. Willis signed the note at the request of the club's manager to enable the club to borrow money from the Commonwealth National Bank to meet its payroll. The Bank of Dallas purchased the note on July 14 and immediately made demand. Willis alleged the note was overdue and therefore the bank could not be a holder in due course. Do you agree?

7. Sam Kay signed a promissory note for $220,000 that was payable to Investments, S.A., Inc., a company of which he was the principal stockholder. The company then indorsed the note over to its lawyers, Arthur B. Cunningham and Philip T. Weinstein, to pay past and future legal fees. Kay claimed the company owed $3,557.53 in fees; the lawyers testified they had performed "more than $20,000" worth of work on the date they received the note. Were the lawyers holders in due course?

8. *YOU BE THE JUDGE* WRITING PROBLEM A columnist for the *Arizona Republic/Phoenix Gazette* received the following problem from a reader. How would you answer it?

A check cashing company was suing a local businessman. The check cashing company said they accepted a check this businessman had given an ex-employee and later found out he had stopped payment. "We cannot locate the ex-employee so we opted to sue the issuing company," they said. The businessman said that he found out after he had given this ex-employee a check that he had made a mistake. He had the bank issue a stop payment. "I have a right to tell our bank not to pay a check. The check is null and void," the businessman said. "It is a worthless piece of paper. Go after the person who gave you the check." The check company argued that a check is a negotiable instrument. Placed in interstate commerce, the check is a promise to pay the holder in due course. The stop payment only stopped the bank from paying the check. The company that issued the check placed it in inter-

state commerce and is legally bound to pay the face amount of the check, the check company argued. "We are the holder and have a right to be paid." Who is right?[9]

9. How would you advise this troubled newspaper reader?

Q: I have paid off a loan and have a receipt from the lender for payment, but the lender will not give me the original promissory note. Do I need the original promissory note?

10. Gina and Douglas Felde purchased a Dodge Daytona with a 70,000-mile warranty. They signed a loan contract with the dealer to pay for the car in 48 monthly installments of $250. The dealer sold the contract to the Chrysler Credit Corp. Soon, the Feldes complained that the car had developed a tendency to accelerate abruptly and without warning. Neither of two Dodge dealers was able to correct the problem. The Feldes filed suit against Chrysler Credit Corp., but the company refused to rescind the loan contract. The company argued that, as a holder in due course on the note, it was entitled to be paid regardless of any defects in the car. How would you decide this case if you were the judge?

11. *ETHICS* S. J. Littlegreen owned the Lookout Mountain Hotel. In financial trouble, he put the hotel on the market at a price of $850,000. C. Abbott Gardner was his real estate agent. To obtain more time to sell, Littlegreen decided to refinance his debt. Mr. Rupe agreed to lend Littlegreen $300,000. When this loan was ready for closing, Gardner informed Littlegreen that he expected a commission of 5 percent of the amount of the loan, or $15,000. Gardner threatened to block the loan if his demands were not met. Littlegreen needed the proceeds of the loan badly, so he agreed to give Gardner $4,000 in cash and a promissory note for $11,000. On what grounds might Littlegreen claim that the note is invalid? Would this be a valid defense? Even if Gardner was in the right legally, was he in the right ethically? Would he like everyone in town to know that he had squeezed Littlegreen in this way? How would he have felt if he had been in Littlegreen's position? Does might make right?

---

9 Quentin V. Tolby, "Stopping Payment Not Always Enough," Arizona Republic/Phoenix Gazette, July 4, July 4, 1995, p. 3. Reprinted with permission of the author.

12. Catherine Wagner suffered serious physical injuries in an automobile accident and became acutely depressed as a result. One morning, she received a check for $17,400 in settlement of her claims arising out of the accident. She indorsed the check and placed it on the kitchen table. She then called Robert Scherer, her long-time roommate, to tell him the check had arrived. That afternoon, she jumped from the roof of her apartment building, killing herself. The police found the check and a note from her, stating that she was giving it to Scherer. Had Wagner negotiated the check to Scherer?

13. *ROLE REVERSAL* Write a multiple-choice question that concerns a holder in due course.

Internet Research Problem

Go to http://beatty.westbuslaw.com and fill in the blanks of a promissory note. Who is the maker, and who is the payee of your note? Did you create a demand note?

> **You can find further practice problems at http://beatty.westbuslaw.com or in the Study Guide that accompanies this text.**

Liability for Negotiable Instruments

Willie groaned under his breath. How had he ever gotten into this mess? Producing a rock video for the Hot Tamales had seemed a golden opportunity. He loved the music, and he didn't even mind living in a trailer on location, but the business end was driving him to despair. That morning, he had glanced out his trailer window and seen Vidalia slinking across the set. How could he have been so stupid as to let her finance the video? "Willie, darling," she had purred, as a circle of smoke from her cigarette caught in his throat, "I know that your promissory note for $50,000 isn't due 'til next month, but I simply do *not* like the music in this video, and I *cannot* support what I do not like. It would be so bad for my karma. But, take your time, dearest one, my driver will be back this afternoon to collect what you owe me."

Sitting in his trailer holding his head in his hands, Willie heard a timid knock. Opening the door, he saw a teenage girl smiling at him. "Hi, Mister Willie," she beamed. "I'm Vera Brown. My mom sent me over to collect the rent check for the trailer. And could I please, please have your autograph? Your work is so awesome."

Willie smiled. "Sure, kiddo, here's my autograph and here's the rent check."

Seeing a helpful, enthusiastic kid like Vera helped brighten an otherwise dark day. But his spirits took a blow later that afternoon when the landlady came by for her check and Willie discovered she had no daughter. He immediately called his bank to stop payment on the check, only to discover that his balance was zero dollars and zero cents. Vera had used her computer to create a second check drawn on Willie's account. She had then forged his signature and cashed both checks before skipping town. ■

To understand the full impact of the day's catastrophes, Willie needs a crash course on liability for negotiable instruments:

- **The Promissory Note to Vidalia.** When Willie gave a promissory note in payment for the debt, the debt was *suspended* until the note comes due. *Verdict:* Vidalia cannot collect her money until next month when the note is due.
- **The Rent Check to the Landlady.** Vera was not Mrs. Brown's lovely daughter; she was an impostor. Banks are not liable on checks that the issuer voluntarily gives to an impostor.[1] *Verdict:* The bank will not reimburse Willie for the rent check. Of course, Willie must still pay the landlady.
- **The Check That Vera Forged.** A bank is liable if it pays a check on which the issuer's name is forged. *Verdict:* The bank must reimburse Willie for the second check.

INTRODUCTION

In Chapter 23, you learned that the issuer of a negotiable instrument is liable to a holder in due course, unless the issuer can assert one of a limited number of real defenses. Against a mere holder, an issuer can assert both personal and real defenses. The life of a negotiable instrument, however, is more complicated than these simple statements indicate. Not everyone who signs a negotiable instrument is an issuer, and not everyone who presents an instrument for payment is a holder in due course or even a holder. This chapter focuses on the liability of these extra players: non-issuers who sign an instrument and non-holders who receive payment. The liability of someone who has signed an instrument is called **signature liability.** The liability of someone who receives payment is called **warranty liability.**

WARNING: The material in this chapter is complex. Please do not proceed further until you understand the prior paragraph.

The Contract versus the Instrument

People generally do not hand out promissory notes or checks to random strangers. Negotiable instruments are issued to fulfill a contract. The instruments create a *second*

---

[1] You remember from Chapter 23 that *issuer* means the *drawer* of a check or the *maker* of a note.

contract to pay the debt created by the *first* agreement. When Beverly agrees to buy a house from John, that is Contract No. 1. When she gives him a promissory note in payment, that is Contract No. 2. When Jodie buys lunch with a Visa card, her promise to repay Visa by check at the end of the month is Contract No. 1. The check she mails to Visa is Contract No. 2.

Once an instrument has been accepted in payment for a debt, the debt is *suspended* until the instrument is paid or dishonored. When Beverly buys a house from John, she pays with a promissory note that is not due for five years. Until she defaults on the note, he cannot sue her for payment even if, after a year, he decides he wants all the money right away. When Visa receives Jodie's check, her debt is suspended until the company tries to cash the check. If the check is returned for insufficient funds, the obligation is revived and Visa can pursue Jodie until she pays it for real.

Enforcing an Instrument

The signature liability rules determine who is liable on an instrument. But *to whom* are they liable? Who has the right to demand payment? Uniform Commercial Code (UCC) §3-301 provides this list:

- A holder of the instrument
- Anyone to whom the **shelter rule** applies (that is, any non-holder with the rights of a holder; review the shelter rule discussion in Chapter 23 if this explanation makes no sense to you)
- A holder who has lost the instrument[2]

Recall that a holder is someone in possession of an instrument that has been validly negotiated.[3] Keep in mind, however, that the real and personal defenses discussed in Chapter 23 can be used against a holder. Therefore, in practice, the answer to the question "Who has the right to demand payment on an instrument?" is "A holder against whom no defenses can be used." Exhibit 24.1 illustrates this concept.

Exhibit 24.1

Primary versus Secondary Liability

A number of different people may be liable on the same negotiable instrument, but some are *primarily* liable, others are only *secondarily* liable. Someone with **primary liability** is unconditionally liable—he must pay unless he has a valid defense. Those with

---

[2]   Although technically some non-holders (such as a holder who has lost the instrument) can demand payment, in this chapter we use "holder" as shorthand to include anyone entitled to enforce an instrument.

[3]   Negotiation is discussed in Chapter 23.

secondary liability only pay if the person with primary liability does not. The holder of an instrument must first ask for payment from those who are primarily liable before making demand against anyone who is only secondarily liable.

The Payment Process

The payment process comprises as many as three steps:

- *Presentment.* Presentment means that the holder of the instrument demands payment from someone who is obligated to pay it (such as the maker or drawee).[4] To present, the holder must (1) exhibit the instrument, (2) show identification, and (3) surrender the instrument (if paid in full) or give a receipt (if only partially paid).

- *Dishonor.* The instrument is due, but the maker (of a note) or the drawee (of a draft) refuses to pay.[5]

- *Notice of Dishonor.* The holder of the instrument notifies those who are secondarily liable that the instrument has been dishonored.[6] This notice can be given by any reasonable means, including oral, written, or electronic communication. It must, however, be given within 30 days of the dishonor (except in the case of banks, which must give notice by midnight of the next banking day). The notice must simply identify the instrument and indicate that it has been dishonored. Anyone who has ever bounced a check has received a notice of dishonor—a check stamped "Insufficient Funds."

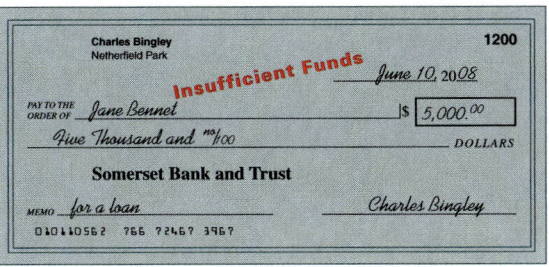

This check has been dishonored.

In the following case, the holder of a check presented it for payment to a bank. But then the holder gave a thumbs-down to the bank's request for identification. Was the bank's requirement a reasonable effort to prevent check fraud or an illegitimate encroachment on privacy? You be the judge.

you Be The Judge

MESSING V. BANK OF AMERICA

373 Md. 672, 2003 Md. LEXIS 155
Court of Appeals of Maryland, 2003

Facts: Jeff Messing attempted to cash a check for $976 at a Bank of America branch office in Baltimore. The check was made out to Messing and drawn on the Bank of America. A teller confirmed the availability of the funds on deposit, and then gave the check back to Messing to endorse. In response to the teller's request for identification, Messing presented his driver's license and a major credit card. The teller wrote the identification information on the back of the check.

Bank of America policy required a thumbprint signature from anyone wishing to cash a check who did not have an account at the bank. A thumbprint signature is created by applying one's right thumb to an inkless fingerprinting device that leaves no ink stain or residue. The thumbprint is then placed on the face of the check between the memo and signature line. This process is neither messy nor time consuming.

Because Messing was not an accountholder at the Bank of American, the teller asked him to give his thumbprint. When Messing declined, the teller refused to cash the check.

---

[4] UCC §3-501.

[5] UCC §3-502.

[6] UCC §3-503.

You Be the Judge: Was the bank's thumbprint policy permissible under the UCC? Had Messing provided reasonable identification?

Argument for Messing: The UCC provides that anyone wishing to cash a check must provide "reasonable identification." Messing provided a driver's license and credit card—which are standard methods of identification, acceptable virtually everywhere. He had, in short, provided reasonable identification. The bank is trying to expand the scope of the UCC.

To require a thumbprint is an invasion of privacy that smacks of Big Brother. Messing would not be able to prevent the bank from using this print for some other purpose. The bank could, for example, turn the thumbprint over to the police without Messing's permission. Moreover, it is difficult to see how a thumbprint would prevent check fraud since the teller did not have Messing's prints on file. Therefore, she could not tell if he was really Jeff Messing or not.

Argument for the Bank: The official comment to the UCC provides that "Authentication may be printed, stamped or written; it may be by initials or by thumbprint." So the UCC certainly contemplates that thumbprints can be used for identification. Moreover, the process of giving a thumbprint signature is not inconvenient—it requires only one finger and no ink.

The bank's objective is not to invade Messing's privacy, but to prevent check fraud. These losses have been growing at an average rate of 17.5 percent per year. The American Bankers Association and more than 30 state bankers associations have endorsed thumbprint programs.

Although Messing is correct that a thumbprint cannot be used, in most instances, to confirm the identity of the person cashing the check, it does assist in the identification of the checkholder should the check later prove to be bad. It therefore serves as a powerful deterrent to those who might otherwise attempt to pass a bad check. ■

SIGNATURE LIABILITY

Virtually everyone who signs an instrument is potentially liable for it, but the liability depends upon the capacity in which it was signed. The maker of a note, for example, has different liability from an indorser. Capacity can sometimes be difficult to determine if the signature is not labeled—"maker," "indorser," "guarantor," "acceptor," etc. (All of these terms will be defined below.) In the absence of a label, courts generally look at the location of the signature. Someone who signs a check or a note in the lower right-hand corner is presumed to be an issuer. If a drawee bank signs on the face of a check, it is an acceptor. Someone who signs on the back of an instrument is considered to be an indorser.

Maker

As you remember from Chapter 23, the issuer of a note is called the **maker. The maker is *primarily* liable.**[7] He has promised to pay, and pay he must, unless he has a valid defense.[8] If two makers sign a note, they are both **jointly and severally** liable. The holder can demand full payment from either or partial payment from both. Suppose that Shane offers to buy Marilyn's bookstore in return for a $20,000 promissory note. Because Shane has no assets, Marilyn insists that his supplier, Alexis, also sign the note as co-maker. Once Alexis signs the note, Marilyn has the right to demand full

---

[7]   UCC §3-412.

[8]   For example, if the maker goes bankrupt, he does not have to pay the note because bankruptcy is a defense even against a holder in due course.

payment from either her or Shane. Of course, if Alexis pays the note, she can demand that Shane reimburse her. If Shane refuses, it is Alexis's problem, not Marilyn's.

Drawer

A check is the most common form of a draft—it is an order telling a bank to pay money. Throughout this chapter, we will use checks as an example because they are the most familiar form of draft, but these same rules apply to all drafts. The drawer is the person who writes the check.

The drawer of a check has *secondary* liability. He is not liable until he has received notice that the bank has dishonored the check.[9] Although the bank pays the check with the drawer's funds, the drawer is secondarily liable in the sense that he does not have to write a new check or give cash to the holder unless the bank dishonors the original check. Suppose that Shane writes a $10,000 check to pay Casey for new inventory. Casey is nervous and, before he can get to the bank to deposit the check, he calls Shane seven times to ask whether the check is good. He even asks Shane for payment in cash instead of by check. Shane finally snarls at Casey, "Just go cash the check and get off my back, will you?" At this point, Casey has no recourse against Shane because Shane is only secondarily liable.

Sadly, however, Casey's fears are realized. When he presents the check to the bank teller, she informs him that Shane's account is overdrawn. Casey snatches the check off the counter and hurries over to Shane's shop. It makes no difference that Casey forgot to let the teller stamp "Insufficient Funds" on the check—notice of dishonor can be made orally. Once the bank has refused to pay, the check has been dishonored. Casey has informed Shane, who must now pay the $10,000.

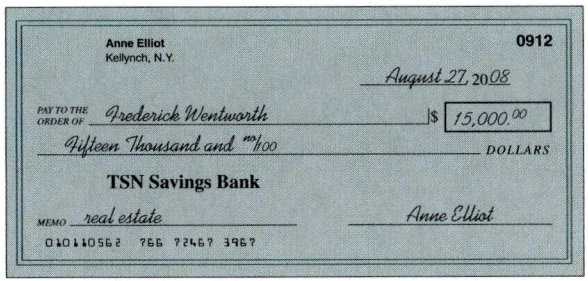

Anne Elliot is only secondarily liable, but no one is primarily liable until the bank accepts the check.

Drawee

The **drawee** is the bank on which a check is drawn. Since the draw*er* of a check is only secondarily liable, logically you might expect the drawee bank to be primarily liable. That is not the case, however. When a drawer signs a check, the instrument enters a kind of limbo. **The bank is not liable to the holder and owes no damages to the holder for refusing to pay the check.**[10] The bank may be liable to the *drawer* for violating their checking account agreement, but this contract does not extend to the holder of the check.

When a holder presents a check, the bank can do one of the following:

- Pay the check. In this case, the holder has no complaints.

- Dishonor the check. In this case, the holder must pursue remedies against the drawer.

What if Casey is afraid to take a check from Shane? After all, even if Shane has enough money in his account at the moment, it may be gone by the time Casey deposits the check and his bank presents it for payment. To protect himself, Casey can insist that Shane give him a certified check. A **certified** or **accepted** check is one that the drawee bank has signed.[11] This signature is a promise that the bank will pay the

---

[9] UCC §3-414.
[10] UCC §3-408.
[11] UCC §3-409.

check out of its own funds. The bank then becomes *primarily* liable, and Casey is sure to be paid as long as the bank stays solvent. To protect itself once it certifies the check, Shane's bank will immediately remove that money from his account.

In the following case, the real estate lawyer relied on written and oral promises, but not on a certified check. As the court pointed out, he was "bamboozled."

HARRINGTON V. MACNAB

163 F. Supp. 2d 583; 2001 U.S. Dist. LEXIS 15314
United States District Court for the District of Maryland

Facts: The MacNabs purchased a piece of property from Richard Harrington's client. Although Harrington was an experienced attorney, he made a grievous error. The MacNabs came to the closing with a personal check drawn on their Merrill Lynch cash management account for $150,128.70. The check had not been certified. Harrington should have refused to close, but instead called the Merrill Lynch office in Delaware where the MacNabs had their account. Ms. Ruark, an employee of Merrill Lynch, told him that there were sufficient funds in the MacNabs' account to cover the check and that she would put a hold on the account in the amount of the check. When asked to confirm this in writing, Ruark sent the following fax to Harrington: "This letter is to verify that the funds are available in the Merrill Lynch account. There is a pend on the funds for the check that was given you."

In fact, the MacNabs' account did not contain sufficient cleared funds to cover the check, which bounced. The MacNabs repeatedly promised to make the check good, but never did. Harrington paid his clients the amount owing and then sued the MacNabs. Although he eventually obtained a judgment against them, they did not pay him the full amount. He also sought recovery from Merrill Lynch.

Issue: Is Merrill Lynch liable to Harrington as the drawee of the check?

Excerpts from Judge Smalkin's Decision: [T]he Court of Appeals of Maryland has been careful, in cases of negligent misrepresentation resulting in

economic loss, to confine the tort claim to situations where the giver and the recipient of the negligently made misrepresentation or promise have an "intimate nexus," such as contractual privity or its equivalent. Here, there is simply no contractual privity or its equivalent between Mr. Harrington and Merrill Lynch, which was in a position equivalent to that of the drawee on the MacNabs' check.

That is, to hold that an "intimate nexus" relationship existed in this case would lead to the result that any payee on a check who makes inquiry is in the equivalent of contractual privity with the drawee, a proposition that would place substantial and potentially unlimited liability on drawees for uncertified checks, in contravention of the basic policies underlying the checking system in the United States as codified in the Uniform Commercial Code. U.C.C. § 3-408 specifically provides that a drawee is not liable as an assignee of the drawer on a check.

Even more to the point, a drawee has no contract liability on a check to a payee unless and until it has accepted the check, *viz.*, certified it. Acceptance requires, as it has since Lord Mansfield's day, the formality of the drawee's signature on the check. To recognize a cause of action under the circumstances of this case essentially would create a tort remedy allowing suit to be brought for oral certification of checks, in clear violation of the policies of the Commercial Code and hundreds of years of commercial law.

Accordingly, an Order will be entered granting Merrill Lynch's motion for summary judgment, and closing this case. ■

Public Policy | Money is important and should be treated with respect. The UCC establishes very precise rules that must be complied with precisely. Although one could argue in this case (and, indeed, Harrington did argue) that Merrill Lynch was negligent and he relied on their misrepresentation, none of that mattered because Merrill Lynch had not certified the check. Close only works in hand grenades and horseshoes, not in the UCC. ◆

Indorser

An **indorser** is anyone, other than an issuer or acceptor, who signs an instrument. Shane gives Hannah a check to pay her for installing new shelves in his bookstore. On the back of Shane's check, Hannah writes, "Pay to Christian," signs her name, and then gives the check to Christian in payment for back rent. Underneath Hannah's name, Christian signs his own name and gives the check to Trustie Car Lot as a deposit on his new Volkswagen bug. Hannah and Christian are both indorsers. This is the chain of ownership:

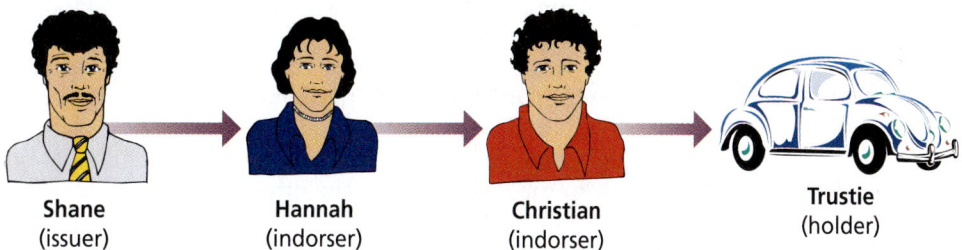

Shane	Hannah	Christian	Trustie
(issuer)	(indorser)	(indorser)	(holder)

Indorsers are *secondarily* liable; they must pay if the issuer or drawee does not. But indorsers are only liable to those who come *after* them in the chain of ownership, not to those who held the instrument beforehand.[12] If Shane refuses to pay Trustie, the auto dealership can demand payment from Christian or Hannah. If Christian pays Trustie, Christian can then demand payment from Hannah. If, however, Hannah pays Trustie, she has no right to go after Christian because he is not liable to a previous indorser.

There are some exceptions to this rule. **Indorsers are not liable if:**

1. they write the words "without recourse" next to their signature on the instrument,

2. a bank certifies the check,

3. the check is presented for payment more than 30 days after the indorsement, or

4. the check is dishonored and the indorser is not notified within 30 days.[13]

Christian has doubts about the creditworthiness of Hannah and Shane, so he writes the words "without recourse" when he indorses the check to Trustie. This sounds like a good idea and perhaps every indorser should try it. However, if the manager of Trustie Car Lot is familiar with the UCC, he will not accept an instrument that has been indorsed without recourse because he wants to make sure that Christian is also liable, not just Shane and Hannah. After all, Christian is the person he knows.

Accommodation Party

An **accommodation party** is someone—other than an issuer, acceptor, or indorser—who adds her signature to an instrument for the purpose of being liable on it.[14] The accommodation party typically receives no direct benefit from the instrument but is acting for the benefit of the **accommodated party.** Shane wants to buy a truck from the Trustie Car Lot. Trustie, however, will not accept a promissory note from Shane unless his father, Walter, also signs it. Shane has no assets, but Walter is wealthy. When Walter signs, he becomes an accommodation party to Shane, who is the accommodated party. The accommodation party can sign for an issuer, acceptor, or indorser. Anyone

---

[12] UCC §3-415.
[13] UCC §3-415.
[14] UCC §3-419.

who signs an instrument is deemed to be an accommodation party unless it is clear that he is an issuer, acceptor, or indorser.

An accommodation party has the same liability to the holder as the person for whom he signed. The holder can make a claim directly against the accommodation party without first demanding payment from the accommodated party. Walter is liable to Trustie, whether or not Trustie first demands payment from Shane. If forced to pay Trustie, Walter can try to recover from Shane.

An accommodation party sounds like what non-lawyers would call a "guarantor," but under the UCC these terms sometimes have a different meaning. Someone who writes "I guarantee this *instrument*" is an accommodation party. But someone who writes "I guarantee *collection*" is not liable until the accommodated party fails to pay. If Walter had written "to guarantee collection" before signing his name, Trustie could not have collected from him until Shane refused to pay the note.

In an earlier example, Shane's supplier, Alexis, had signed a note as co-maker. What is the difference between a co-maker and an accommodation party? The co-maker is liable both to the holder and to the other co-maker. The accommodation party is liable only to the holder, not to the other maker. If Shane pays the note on which Alexis is co-maker, then Alexis is liable to him for half the payment. But if Shane pays the note on which Walter is the accommodation party, Walter has no liability to Shane.

at RISK

People sign for the debts of their friends and relatives with such abandon that one can only assume they do not fully understand the situation. As the saying goes, nothing is more dangerous than a fool with a pen. Certainly, Yeung Sau-lin caused some serious damage with her pen. The 53-year-old mother of four was jailed for two years when her decision to guarantee a friend's $300,000 loan went horribly wrong. The friend defaulted and disappeared, leaving Yeung to face loan sharks who pressured her into taking part in a bad check scheme. Yeung pleaded guilty to charges that she had written $4.1 million in bad checks.[15] ◆

In the following case, an accommodation party argued that she was not liable because she did not receive the proceeds from the loan. Was she correct in her interpretation of the UCC?

In Re COUCHOT

169 B.R. 40, 1994 Bankr. LEXIS 899
United States Bankruptcy Court, Southern District of Ohio, 1994

Facts: Kathy J. Couchot and her mother-in-law, Jean Couchot, borrowed $6,317.48 from Star Bank to pay the funeral expenses of Kathy's husband. Jean executed a note to the bank, and Kathy signed as an accommodation party. To disburse the proceeds of the loan, Star Bank issued a check payable to "Kathy *and* Jean Couchot." Somehow this check was altered to read "Kathy *or* Jean Couchot." Jean cashed the check and used the loan proceeds to pay her son's funeral expenses and some of Kathy's back taxes and insurance premiums. Jean did not repay the loan to the bank; Kathy made six payments before defaulting.

Issues: Is an accommodation party liable for the full amount of a note when she received only a small portion of the proceeds? Is an accommodation party liable even though the check was altered?

Excerpts from Judge Clark's Decision: [Kathy Couchot]'s contention that she is only liable to Star Bank for the consideration she directly received from the loan is incorrect and misconstrues the nature of an accommodation party. It is basic hornbook law that consideration does not have to be received by an accommodation party to support her obligation. Time and again sureties respond to a holder's suit by arguing, "I am a surety and I did not

▼

---

[15] "Loan Decision Leads to Prison," *South China Morning Post*, Aug. 6, 1994, p. 5.

receive consideration for my contract." This is a losing argument. Regardless whether the surety signs gratuitously or receives compensation, his obligation is supported by the consideration which moves from the creditor to the principal debtor.

Also unavailing is [Kathy Couchot]'s argument that the check issued by Star Bank relieves her from the terms of the [note]. [Kathy Couchot] relies on U.C.C. 3-407 which provides that: "(A) Any alteration of an instrument is material which changes the contract of any party thereto in any respect...."

While it is clear that the check was materially altered, there is absolutely no evidence that the check was fraudulently altered. [Kathy Couchot]'s own testimony established that the loan proceeds were used precisely as envisioned by the parties. In any event, finding no fraud in this case, it is unnecessary to further examine the effects of the altered check. The court finds that [Kathy Couchot] cosigned the promissory note to Star Bank and that the loan proceeds were used as anticipated by [her].

[Kathy Couchot was ordered to pay the note.] ∎

Agent

Many business transactions are conducted by agents acting on behalf of a principal. A corporation, for example, cannot sign an instrument itself; all of its transactions must be conducted by company employees. When signing for a principal, the agent must be careful to ensure that only the principal is liable.

To avoid personal liability when signing an instrument, an agent must (1) indicate that she is signing as an agent and (2) give the name of the principal.[16] An agent who fails to follow these two simple steps will be *personally* liable on the instrument to any holder in due course who did not know that the agent was acting for someone else. The agent will not be liable to holders who are not in due course if she can prove that the original parties did not intend for her to be liable. An agent who signs her name, "Harley Calhoun, as agent for Slippery Corp." is safe; she is not liable on the instrument. But if Harley simply signs the note, "Harley Calhoun, Agent," then she will be personally liable to Ralph, a holder in due course, unless she can prove that Ralph knew she was acting for someone else when he acquired the note. (That is a great deal of trouble easily avoided by simply including the name of the principal.) Even if Ralph is not a holder in due course, Harley will be liable unless she can prove that the original parties never intended her to be.

The principal is liable if the agent signs correctly, the agent signs just her own name, or the agent signs only the name of the principal. Thus, if Harley signs the note, "Harley Calhoun" or "Slippery Corp.," the corporation is liable to Ralph (and so is Harley). He can sue either. If Ralph recovers from Harley, she can try to recover from Slippery; but if the company goes out of business, Harley will find herself in a sticky situation. Exhibit 24.2 illustrates the liability of agents and principals.

at **R!SK**	This rule establishing an agent's liability on negotiable instruments is, in some ways, the perfect kind of law: it is a simple, straightforward guideline that guarantees protection to those who follow it. Never sign an instrument (or any contract for that matter) as an agent without giving the name of the principal and indicating that you are an agent. ◆

Checks are an exception to this general rule on agent liability. If an agent is authorized to sign a check on the principal's bank account, the agent is not personally liable even if she forgets to indicate that she is simply an agent. Because the check is probably printed with the principal's name anyway, no one is likely to think that the check is coming out of the agent's personal funds.

---

[16] UCC §3-402.

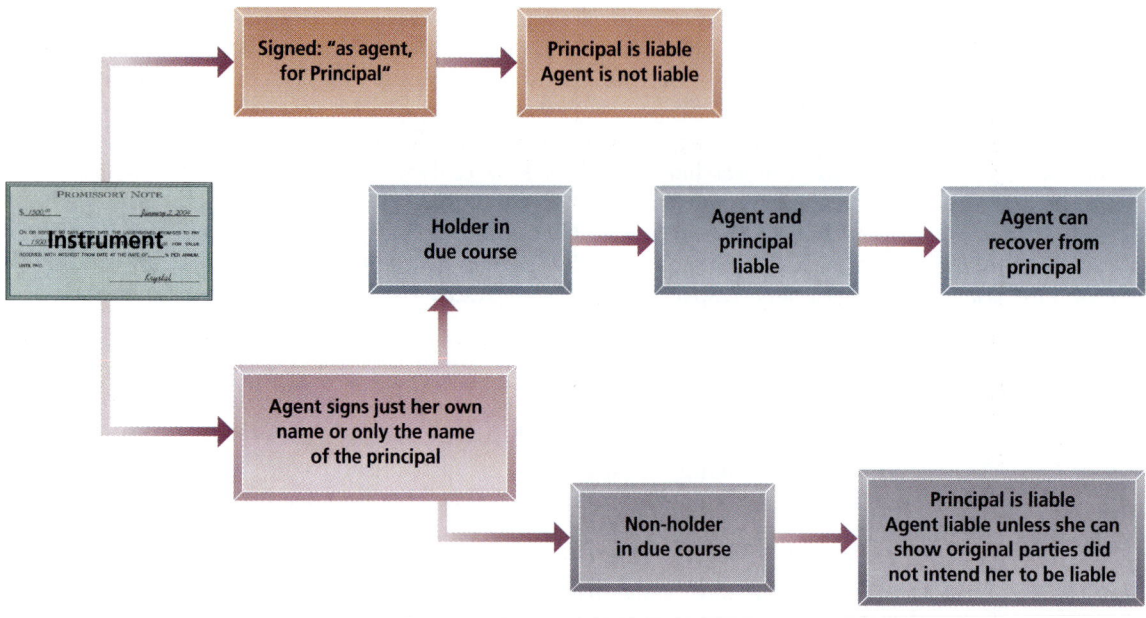

Exhibit 24.2

WARRANTY LIABILITY

Warranty liability rules apply when someone receives payment on an instrument that is invalid because it has been forged, altered, or stolen.

Basic Rules of Warranty Liability

1. **The culprit is always liable.** If a forger signs someone else's name to an instrument, that signature counts as the forger's, not as that of the person whose name she signed. The forger is liable for the value of the instrument plus any other expenses or lost interest that subsequent parties may experience because of the forgery. If Hope signs David's name on one of his checks, Hope is liable, but not David. Although this is a sensible rule, the problem is that forgers are difficult to catch and, even when found, often do not have the money to pay what they owe. (For everything you ever wanted to know about forgery, sneak over to http://www.bham.ac.uk/english/bibliography/handwriting/hwbiblio/hwbiblio.htm.)

2. **The drawee bank is liable if it pays a check on which the *drawer's* name is forged. The bank can recover from the payee only if the payee had reason to suspect the forgery.**[17] If a bank cashes David's forged check, it must reimburse him whether or not it ever recovers from Hope. Suppose that Hope forged the check to pay for a new tattoo. If Gus, the owner of the tattoo parlor, deposits the check and the bank pays it, the bank cannot recover from Gus unless he had reason to suspect the forgery. Perhaps Gus did suspect because the mystery customer asked to have

---

[17] UCC §3-418.

"Hope" tattooed on her biceps, not "David." She did not look much like a "David" either.

Why hold the bank liable for something that is not its fault? In theory, the bank has David's signature on file and can determine that Hope's version does not match. As the saying goes, the drawee must know the drawer's signature as a mother knows her own child. Such a rule may have been appropriate in an era when people went to their neighborhood bank to cash checks and a teller would indeed recognize dear Miss Plotkin's signature. In this day and age, most checks—especially those for small amounts—are handled by machine, so perhaps this rule makes less sense. Nonetheless, the rule stands, for good reason or bad. Banks have two choices: (1) examine the signature on each presented check or (2) purchase forgery insurance.

3. **In any other case of wrongdoing, a person who first acquires an instrument from a culprit is ultimately liable to anyone else who pays value for it.** This rule is based on the provisions in Article 3 of the UCC that establish transfer and presentment warranties.

Transfer Warranties

When someone transfers an instrument, she warrants that:

- She is a holder of the instrument
- All signatures are authentic and authorized
- The instrument has not been altered
- No defense can be asserted against her, and
- As far as she knows the issuer is solvent.[18]

When someone transfers an instrument, she promises that it is valid. The culprit—the person who created the defective instrument in the first place—is always liable, but if he does not pay what he owes, the person who took it from him is liable in his place. She may not be that much at fault, but she is more at fault than any of the other innocent people who paid good value for the instrument.

Suppose that Annie writes a check for $100 to pay for a fancy dinner at Barbara's Bistro. Cecelia steals the check from Barbara's cash register, indorses Barbara's name, and uses the check to buy a leather jacket from Deirdre. In her turn, Deirdre takes the check home and indorses it over to her condominium association to pay her monthly service fee. Barbara notices the check is gone and asks Annie to stop payment on it. Once payment is stopped, the condominium association cannot cash the check. Who is liable to whom? The chain of ownership looks like this:

Annie   Barbara   Cecelia (the culprit)   Deirdre   Condominium Association

---

[18] UCC §3-416.

Cecelia is the culprit and, of course, she is liable. Unfortunately, she is currently studying at the University of the Azores and refuses to return to the United States. The condominium association makes a claim against Deirdre. When she transferred the check, she warranted that all the signatures were authentic and authorized, but that was not true because Barbara's signature was forged. (Deirdre should have asked Cecelia for identification.) Deirdre cannot make a claim against Annie or Barbara because neither of them violated their transfer warranties—all the signatures at that point were authentic and authorized.

There are a few additional wrinkles to the transfer warranty rules:

- When someone violates the transfer warranties, she is liable for the value of the instrument, plus expenses and interest. If the condominium association is charged a fee by the bank for the returned check, Deirdre must pay it.

- Transfer warranties flow to all subsequent holders in good faith who have indorsed the instrument. If the condominium association indorses the check over to its maintenance company, Deirdre is liable to the condo association when the maintenance company makes a claim against it.

- If the instrument is *bearer* paper, the transfer warranties extend only to the first transferee. If Annie had made her check out to cash, it would have been bearer paper, and her transfer warranties would have extended only to Barbara. If Barbara transfers the check to Hannah, Barbara's transfer warranties extend to Hannah; Annie's do not.

- If a warranty claim is not made within 30 days of discovering the breach, damages are reduced by the amount of harm that the delay caused. Suppose that the condominium association waits two months to tell Deirdre the check is invalid. Cecelia has been into Deirdre's store several times to try on matching leather pants. By the time Deirdre finds out the check is bad, Cecelia has again left town. Deirdre may not be liable on the check at all because the delay has prevented her from making a claim against Cecelia.

- Transfer warranties apply only if the instrument has been transferred for consideration. Suppose Deirdre gives the check to an employee, Emily, as a birthday present. When the check turns out to be worthless, Emily has no claim against Deirdre.

Comparison of Signature Liability and Transfer Warranties

Transfer warranties fill in holes left by the signature liability rules:

- A forged signature is invalid and therefore creates no signature liability on the part of the person whose name was signed. However, someone who receives a forged instrument may recover under transfer warranty rules, which provide that anyone who transfers a forged instrument is liable for it.

- The signature liability rules do not apply to the transfer of bearer paper. Bearer paper can be negotiated simply by delivery; no indorsement is required. No signature means no signature liability (for anyone other than the issuer—who is the only person actually signing the instrument). Transfer warranties apply to each transfer of bearer paper (although the transferor of bearer paper is liable only to the person to whom he gives the instrument, not to any transferees further down the line).

- Under the signature liability rules, the holder of an instrument cannot make a claim until the indorser or drawer has been notified that the instrument was presented and dishonored.[19] Under the transfer warranty rules, the holder need not wait for presentment or dishonor before making a claim against the transferor.

---

[19] UCC §3-503(a).

Presentment Warranties

Transfer warranties impose liability on anyone who sells a negotiable instrument, such as Deirdre. **Presentment warranties** apply to someone who demands payment for an instrument from the maker, drawee, or anyone else liable on it. Thus, if the condominium association cashes Annie's check, it is subject to presentment warranties because it is demanding payment from her bank, the drawee. In a sense, transfer warranties apply to all transfers *away* from the issuer; presentment warranties apply when the instrument *returns* to the maker or drawee for payment. As a general rule, payment on an instrument is final, and the payer has no right to a refund, unless the presentment warranties are violated.

Anyone who presents a *check* for payment warrants that:

- She is a holder
- The check has not been altered, and
- She has no reason to believe the drawer's signature is forged.[20]

If any of these promises is untrue, the bank has a right to demand a refund from the presenter. Suppose that Adam writes a $500 check to pay Bruce for repairing his motorcycle. Bruce changes the amount of the check to $1,500 and indorses it over to Chip as payment for an oil bill. When Chip deposits the check, the bank credits his account for $1,500 and deducts the same amount from Adam's account. When Adam discovers the alteration, the bank is forced (for reasons discussed in Chapter 25) to credit his account for $1,000. Chip violated his *presentment* warranties when he deposited an altered check (even though he did not *know* it was altered). Although Chip was not at fault, he must still reimburse the bank for $1,000. But Chip is not without recourse—Bruce violated his *transfer* warranties to Chip (by transferring an altered check). Bruce must repay the $1,000. Chip loses out only if he cannot make Bruce pay. In the following case, a bank is accused of violating its presentment warranty.

HSBC BANK USA V. F&M BANK–NORTHERN VIRGINIA

246 F.3d 335; 2001 U.S. App. LEXIS 5588
United States Court of Appeals for the Fourth Circuit, 2001

Facts: Donald Lynch purchased a check in the amount of US $250.00 from Allied Irish Bank (AIB) in Ireland. The check was drawn on HSBC Bank USA (HSBC) and was payable to Advance Marketing and Investment Inc. (AMI). The amount of the check was handwritten as "Two Hundred + Fifty" on the center line, and "US $250.00" on the upper right-hand side (in the numerical portion of the check). The drawer (AIB) left slightly less than one-half inch of open space in the numerical portion and one inch of open space on the center line of the check.

Sometime before AMI deposited the check into its account at F&M Bank–Northern Virginia (F&M), the amount on the check was altered from $250.00 to $250,000.00. In the numerical portion of the check, the period was changed to a comma and three zeros were added. The letters "Thoud" were added to the center line. F&M presented the check for payment to HSBC. It paid $250,000.00 to F&M, and debited AIB's account for that amount. The following diagram traces the route of the check:

▼

---

[20] UCC §3-417.

AIB   Donald Lynch   AMI   F&M   HSBC

AIB later notified HSBC that the check had been altered. HSBC recredited AIB's account for the amount of the unauthorized alteration and filed suit against F&M for breach of presentment warranty. F&M claimed that it was not liable because AIB had failed to exercise due care in filling out the check. The district court found for HSBC and F&M appealed.

Issues: Did AIB fail to exercise due care in filling out the check? Did F&M violate its presentment warranty to HSBC?

Excerpts from Judge Hamilton's Decision: AIB is precluded from asserting the unauthorized alteration of the Check against HSBC under [the UCC], if AIB failed to exercise ordinary care in preparing the check and such failure substantially contributed to the unauthorized alteration of the Check. The district court found that AIB had exercised ordinary care in preparing the Check. In this last regard, the district court stated:

> I have examined this check. And, of course, there does have [sic] to be sufficient writing on a check that there is not an open space so someone can fill it in for additional amounts and alter the check. But regardless of what you do about writing in zero, zero over 100 and

then put a line in, which is, I guess, the standard way to do it—I don't know that if I looked at all the checks in this country that I would know the standard. It is the way I have always done it. There is still some kind of an open space regardless of what you do. And so, the test has got to be is that line sufficiently filled so that someone cannot come along and add into that writing in a way that just alters the check so that it will go through unnoticed.

That certainly wasn't done on this check. This check was substantially written across the line. As a matter of fact, it was written far enough along the line that you could not write the word "thousand" in. It had to be scrawled up in the manner in which it was. And I just, looking at this check, and the way it is made out, I can't find that the preparer was negligent or participated in the alteration of it. There was sufficient writing there that any alteration that was made was obvious. And I can't find negligence in that regard.

After reviewing a copy of the Check, we see sound logic in the district court's rationale that if the written portion of the Check contained enough writing such that the Check's alteration could only be accomplished with the "scrawled up," abbreviated form of the word "thousand," i.e., "Thoud," ordinary care was exercised in making out the Check. [W]e affirm the judgment in favor of HSBC.

The presentment warranty rules for a promissory note are different from those for a check. **Anyone who presents a *promissory note* for payment makes only one warranty—that he is a holder of the instrument.** Someone presenting a note does not need to warrant that the note is unaltered or the maker's signature is authentic because a note is presented for payment to the issuer himself. The issuer presumably remembers the amount of the note and whether he signed it. Suppose Adam gives a promissory note to Bruce to pay for a new motorcycle. If Bruce increases the note from $5,000 to $10,000 before he presents it for payment in six months' time, Adam will almost certainly realize the note has been changed and refuse to pay it.

The presenter of a note warrants that he is a holder. A forged signature prevents subsequent owners from being a holder, so anyone who presents a note with a forged signature is violating the presentment warranties. Suppose that Bruce is totally honest and does not alter the note, but Chip steals it and forges Bruce's indorsement before passing the note on to Donald, who presents it to Adam for payment. Donald has violated his *presentment* warranties because he is not a holder. Adam can refuse to pay him. For his part, Donald can claim repayment from Chip who violated his *transfer* warranties by passing on a note with a forged signature.

at **RISK**

The person who first takes a forged or altered instrument from the culprit is liable to everyone thereafter who gives value for the instrument. Therefore, before accepting an instrument, it is absolutely essential to obtain foolproof identification and to examine the instrument carefully for any signs of alteration. For advice on how to avoid check fraud, see **http://www.bizcashflow.com/faqs/checkfraud.htm** and also **http://www.treas .gov/usss/faq.html#check_fraud**. ◆

OTHER LIABILITY RULES

This section contains other UCC rules that establish liability for wrongdoing on instruments.

Conversion Liability

Conversion means that (1) someone has stolen an instrument or (2) a bank has paid a check that has a forged indorsement.[21] The rightful owner of the instrument can recover from either the thief or the bank.

For example, Glenn Altman was a lawyer representing Barbara Kirchoff. He settled her case for $12,000, but when he received the check, he forged her indorsement and deposited the check in his own account without telling her. He gave her the money four months later, but by then she had discovered his dishonesty. What claims do the various parties have?

Kirchoff has a claim against the bank because it paid a check with a forged indorsement. If the bank pays Kirchoff, then it can recover from Altman because he violated his presentment warranties. Note, however, that Kirchoff could not sue Altman for violating presentment warranties because he had not presented the check to her for payment. Nor could she sue him for violating transfer warranties because he had not transferred the check *to* her. To the contrary, he had transferred the check *away* from her.

Kirchoff also has a claim against Altman for conversion because he stole the check from her.[22] What about the issuer of the check—can it also sue Altman for conversion? No, an action for conversion cannot be brought by an issuer because the check technically belongs to the payee (Kirchoff). The issuer can bring a claim only against the bank that pays the forged check.

Impostor Rule

If someone issues an instrument to an impostor, then any indorsement in the name of the payee is valid as long as the person (a bank, say) who pays the instrument does not know of the fraud.[23] A teenager knocks on your door one afternoon. He tells you he is selling magazine subscriptions to pay for a school trip to Washington, D.C. After signing up for *Career* and *Popular Accounting*, you make out a check to "Family Magazine Subscriptions." Unfortunately, the boy does not represent Family Magazine at all. He does cash the check, however, by forging an indorsement for the magazine company. Is the bank liable for cashing the fraudulent check?

---

[21] UCC §3-420.

[22] A payee (i.e., Kirchoff) cannot bring a claim for conversion unless she actually *receives* the check. In this case, Altman was Kirchoff's agent and he received the check for her so she could bring a conversion action against him.

[23] UCC §3-404(a).

No. The teenager was an impostor—he said he represented the magazine company, but he did not. If anyone indorses the check in the name of the payee (Family Magazine Subscriptions), you must pay the check and the bank is not liable. Does this rule seem harsh? Maybe, but you were in the best position to determine if the teenager really worked for the magazine company. You were more at fault than the bank, and you must pay. Of course, the teenager would be liable to you, if you could ever find him.

Fictitious Payee Rule

If someone issues an instrument to a person who does not exist, then any indorsement in the name of the payee is valid as long as the person (a bank, say) who pays the instrument does not know of the fraud.[24] The *impostor* rule applies if you give a check with a real name to the wrong person. The *fictitious payee* rule applies if you write a check to someone who does not exist. The following article illustrates that this type of fraud can be very difficult to prevent. Even a law firm was victimized.

Until yesterday, Dennis Masellis hardly seemed to need a lawyer. For 12 years he was surrounded by them, as a manager in the accounting department of one of the world's largest law firms. But yesterday, his own lawyer stood by his side as he pleaded guilty to stealing $7 million from his former employer, Baker & McKenzie, which has 2,700 lawyers in 61 offices around the world. Now, Mr. Masellis faces up to 15 years in prison.

As manager of the payroll unit in the firm's New York office, Mr. Masellis had the right to issue money to employees and process records. He created fictitious employees and then deposited their salaries in his personal bank account.

At the firm's Chicago office, a partner, William J. Linklater, said, "The firm is, of course, dismayed and disappointed to learn of this breach of trust from a trusted employee." The loss was limited to Baker & McKenzie itself, rather than clients, Mr. Linklater said, concluding, "We are hopeful that there may be some restitution."[25] ◆

Employee Indorsement Rule

If an employee with responsibility for issuing instruments forges a check or other instrument, then any indorsement in the name of the payee, or a similar name, is valid as long as the person (a bank, say) who pays the instrument does not know of the fraud.[26] A dishonest employee, especially one with the authority to issue checks, has the opportunity to steal a great deal of money. The employer cannot shift blame (and liability) onto the bank that unknowingly cashes the forged checks because the employer was more to blame—it not only hired the thief, it failed to supervise him carefully.

Dennis M. Hartotunian had a major gambling problem—he owed nearly $10 million. Unfortunately, he was also the controller and accountant for the Aesar Group, a precious metals company. Over the course of three years, he wrote himself 154 checks worth $9.24 million. Any check for more than $500 required the signature of Aesar's general manager, but Hartotunian forged it. After an internal audit revealed that millions were missing, company officers asked to talk with Hartotunian. When he heard they were coming, he walked out and never came back.

It is always a bad sign when the company controller disappears. If an employee is generally authorized to prepare or sign checks, then the bank is not liable on checks

---

24 UCC §3-404(b).

25 Katherine E. Finkelstein, "Direct Deposit Used to Embezzle $7 Million," *New York Times,* June 9, 2000, §B, p. 3. Copyright © 2000 The New York Times Co. Reprinted by permission.

26 UCC §3-405.

that the employee forges. Hartotunian was clearly covered by this rule because he was the company controller. If he had been a mailroom employee without authority to sign checks, the bank would have been liable. The employee indorsement rule applies to both single and double forgeries. In a ***single forgery,*** the employee writes a check to himself, signs his employer's name, and cashes the check. In a ***double forgery,*** the employee writes a check to someone else, forges his employer's name, and also forges the name of the payee.

Who will lose this bet, the employer or the bank?

Negligence

Regardless of the impostor rule, the fictitious payee rule, and the employee indorsement rule (the "three rules"), **anyone who behaves negligently in creating or paying an unauthorized instrument is liable to an innocent third party.** If two people are negligent, they share the loss according to their negligence. Here are two examples:

- Anyone who is careless in paying an unauthorized instrument is liable, despite the three rules.[27] Suppose that the boy selling bogus magazine subscriptions goes into the bank and indorses the check: "Family Magazine Subscriptions, by Butch McGraw." The teller peers over her counter and sees a 13-year-old boy standing there with torn jeans and a baseball cap on backwards. She may be negligent if she cashes the check without asking for further identification. Or suppose that a local bank teller knew that no one by the name of Elizabeth W. Nehring worked at Columbia Association. Then the bank could be liable for having paid the checks that were deposited into this fictitious person's account.

- **Anyone who is careless in allowing a forged or altered instrument to be created is also liable, whether or not he has violated one of the three rules.** The classic case establishing this rule was *Young v. Grote,* an 1827 English case. A businessman who was going abroad signed five checks and gave them to his wife with instructions that they were to be used for business expenses. A clerk in the company helpfully showed the missus how to fill out the checks, carefully instructing her to leave a blank space in front of the number. The clerk used this space to add a "3" in front of a "50" and then cashed the £350 check. The court held that the drawee bank was not liable because, "If Young, instead of leaving the check with a female, had left it with a man of business, he would have guarded against fraud in the mode of filling it up."[28] Today, we hiss at the sexist sentiment, but it illustrates the point. Anyone who carelessly creates a situation that facilitates the forgery or alteration of an instrument cannot recover against a party who pays the instrument in good faith. Contrast this decision with the HSBC Bank case earlier in the chapter. There, the court held that the issuer of the check (AIB) was not negligent even though it had left enough space on the face of the check for someone to alter it dramatically. Why the different result in these two cases?

In the following case, the Professional Golf Association had a bad lie. Who must take penalty strokes—the PGA or its bank?

---

[27] UCC §§3-404(d), 3-405(b).

[28] *Young v. Grote,* 4 Bing. 253 (Common Pleas), quoted in Douglas J. Whaley, *Problems and Materials on Payment Law* (Boston: Little, Brown & Co., 1995), at 253.

you Be The Judge

GULF STATES SECTION, PGA, INC. V. WHITNEY NATIONAL BANK OF NEW ORLEANS

689 So. 2d 638, 1997 La. App. LEXIS 167
Court of Appeal of Louisiana, Fourth Circuit, 1997

Facts: Robert Brown was the executive director of the Gulf States Section of the Professional Golf Association (PGA). He was responsible for paying bills and handling the bank account. Brown used Quicken, a computer program, to write checks. These checks were kept in a box beneath the printer stand in his office.

Adrenetti Collins was a secretary who worked in the PGA office with Brown. During a four-month period, she forged 18 PGA checks totaling $22,699.81. To avoid detection, she intercepted two of the bank statements sent by Whitney National Bank and replaced them with forged statements that left out the numbers of the checks she had stolen. The usual Whitney statement was printed on vanilla-colored paper measuring a nonstandard $6\frac{3}{4} \times 11$ inches. The forged statements were on standard $8\frac{1}{2} \times 11$ inch white paper. They were not dated but they did contain the Whitney logo. Brown received two forged statements and then no statements at all for two months. Shortly thereafter, Collins asked for a leave of absence.

Whitney's policy was to verify signatures on checks equal to or greater than $5,000. One of the forged checks was in the amount of $5,000, but Whitney did not verify Brown's signature before paying it. Brown's signature was a semilegible letter or two and a long loop. The forged signature on the check looked very similar to the real one.

You Be the Judge: Is Whitney liable to the PGA for the forged checks it paid?

Argument for the PGA: The general rule is that a person is not liable on an instrument unless his signature appears on it. Brown's signature did not appear on these checks, so only the bank is liable on them.

As for the PGA's alleged negligence, Brown traveled extensively and was not available to supervise the office staff carefully. If this is negligence, then half the companies in America are negligent, too. Don't forget that Brown stored the checks in his private office. Whitney admits that it did not verify the signatures on any of the checks, even the one for $5,000. This is in direct violation of its own policies. If Whitney had simply followed its policies, the forgeries would have been detected months earlier.

Argument for Whitney: Generally, a bank is liable for forged checks unless it can show that (1) the customer was negligent; (2) the negligence substantially contributed to the forgery; and (3) the bank paid the forged instruments in accordance with reasonable commercial banking industry standards.

The PGA was clearly negligent in this case. The checks should have been locked up, not sitting under the printer in an open box. Brown should have realized that checks were missing, and he should have noticed that the bank statements were forged. Without his negligence, Collins could never have committed the forgeries. In any event, she would have been caught much earlier—when the first bank statement was received, not four months later.

As for the bank's failure to verify Brown's signature, the forgery was close enough to his sloppy writing that no one could have realized the signature was a fake. ∎

Crimes

It is beyond the scope of this chapter to catalogue all of the crimes that can be committed with negotiable instruments, but students should be aware of these.

Bouncing a Check

It is illegal to write a check on an account that has insufficient funds. Generally, no serious penalties are imposed if sufficient funds are immediately deposited. (This is a good thing, considering that more than 400 *million* checks bounce each year.) However, both banks and merchants impose substantial fees for their trouble. People who make a career of bouncing checks may find they have plenty of time to bone up on UCC Article 3 in the prison library.

Check Kiting

It is illegal to kite checks. E. F. Hutton was a thriving brokerage firm until ambitious branch managers began boosting profits with a check-kiting scheme. A Hutton manager would overdraw an account in Bank A and deposit that check in Bank B. Bank B would begin paying interest on the funds before the check had cleared. The manager would then write a check on Bank B to cover the deficit in Bank A, in the process overdrawing Bank B. One Hutton account in a Virginia bank was overdrawn by an average of $9 million a day. Interest earned on these overdrafts accounted for as much as 70 percent of the Washington office's gross income. In 20 months, Hutton made at least $8 million, but the resulting scandal drove the firm out of business.

Forgery

It is illegal to forge an instrument or to pass on (**utter**) an instrument that one knows to be forged. In the United States each year, more than 500 million checks are forged, with a total value of more than $20 billion.

at RISK

How can you safeguard against forgery?

- ***Do not leave checks lying around where others can find them.*** In the PGA case, the checks were left in a box under the printer stand. In another case, a woman left blank checks in the apartment that she sublet. The tenant promptly forged six checks.

- ***Tear up any unused checks before throwing them away.*** Crooks have been known to hunt through trash barrels for just such prey.

- ***Review your bank statements to see if there are any checks you do not recognize.*** Cautious folk even check their bank balances several times each month to make sure that their balance is about where they expect it to be. You can check your bank balance easily each time you withdraw funds from an ATM. ◆

DISCHARGE

Discharge of the Obligor

Discharge means that liability on an instrument terminates. Article 3 establishes five different ways to discharge an instrument[29]:

- ***By Payment.*** Payment discharges an instrument, as long as the payment is *from* someone obliged to pay and goes *to* the holder. If you mail a check to the wrong bank when paying off a promissory note, you obviously have not discharged the note. Or if you

---

[29] UCC Article 3, Part 6.

ask an employee to take money to the bank to pay off the note, but she goes to Hawaii instead, no discharge has occurred. Similarly, payment does not discharge an instrument if the payor knows that the instrument is stolen. Suppose you have given a promissory note to Lou. He complains to you that his employee Stephanie stole it. If you pay Stephanie when she presents the note, you have not discharged it.

- *By Agreement.* The parties to the instrument can agree to a discharge, even if the instrument is not paid. The discharge, however, must be in writing; it cannot be oral. You give a promissory note to your company to pay for company stock. The company president tells you that the company will forgive the loan and discharge the note as a reward for your fabulous performance. A few months later the president is ousted. Your agreement was not in writing and you are liable on the note. (You may have a contract claim against the company, but the note itself is still valid.)

One way to cancel an instrument.

- *By Cancellation* Cancellation means the intentional, voluntary surrender, destruction, or disfigurement of an instrument. If Ted accidentally forgets to take a check out of his pocket before throwing his shirt in the wash, he has not canceled the check (even though it was destroyed) because the destruction was unintentional. If, while arguing with his business partner, he takes her promissory note and tears it into a thousand pieces while screaming, "This is what I think of you and your business skills," he has canceled the note. He could achieve the same result less dramatically by simply writing "canceled" on it or by giving it back to her.

- *By Certification.* When a bank certifies or accepts a check, the drawer and all indorsers of the check are discharged, and only the bank is liable.

- *By Alteration.* An instrument is discharged if its terms are intentionally changed. Laura gives Todd a promissory note. Thinking he is being very clever, Todd changes the amount of her note from $200 to $2,000. He has actually done Laura a favor because he has discharged the note.

Keep in mind, however, that no discharge is effective against a holder in due course who acquires the instrument without knowledge of the discharge. If Todd sells Laura's note to Max, who does not know of the discharge, Max can enforce the instrument against Laura, but only for the original amount of $200.

Discharge of an Indorser or Accommodation Party

Article 3 provides that virtually any change in an instrument that harms an indorser or accommodation party also discharges them unless they consent to the change. These fatal changes include an extension of the due date on the instrument, a material modification of the instrument, or any impairment of the collateral that secures the instrument. When Chelsea borrows money from Jordan, she signs a promissory note due on December 24. Helena guarantees the note. Chelsea cannot pay, but Jordan does not have the stomach for declaring Chelsea in default on Christmas Eve. He generously extends the due date for another week. Helena is no longer liable, even secondarily, because Jordan has granted an extension of the due date.

Chapter Conclusion

It is never wise to play an important game without understanding the rules. Virtually everyone uses negotiable instruments regularly to pay bills or borrow money. Although the rules sometimes seem complex, it is important to know them well.

Chapter Review

1. Someone who is primarily liable on a negotiable instrument must pay unless he has a valid defense. Those with secondary liability only pay if the person with primary liability does not.

2. The payment process for a negotiable instrument comprises as many as three steps:

   - *Presentment.* The holder makes a demand for payment to the issuer.

   - *Dishonor.* The instrument is due, but the issuer does not pay.

   - *Notice of Dishonor.* The holder of the instrument notifies those who are secondarily liable that the instrument has been dishonored.

3. The maker of a note is primarily liable.

4. The drawer of a check has secondary liability: he is not liable until he has received notice that the bank has dishonored the check.

5. Indorsers are secondarily liable; they must pay if the issuer does not. But an indorser is only liable to those who come after him in the chain of ownership, not to those who held the instrument before he did.

6. The accommodation party signs an instrument to benefit the accommodated party. By signing the instrument, an accommodation party agrees to be liable on it, whether or not she directly benefits from it.

7. To avoid personal liability when signing an instrument, an agent must indicate that he is signing as an agent and must give the name of the principal.

8. The basic rules of warranty liability are as follows:

   - The culprit is always liable.

   - The drawee bank is responsible if it pays a check on which the drawer's name is forged.

   - In any other case of wrongdoing, a person who initially acquires an instrument from a culprit is ultimately liable to anyone else who pays value for it.

9. When someone transfers an instrument, she warrants that:

   - She is a holder of the instrument

   - All signatures are authentic and authorized

   - The instrument has not been altered

   - No defense can be asserted against her, and

   - As far as she knows the issuer is solvent.

10. Anyone who presents a check for payment warrants that:

    - She is a holder

    - The check has not been altered, and

    - She has no reason to believe the drawer's signature is forged.

11. The presenter of a note only warrants that he is a holder.

12. Conversion means that (1) someone has stolen an instrument or (2) a bank has paid a check that has a forged indorsement.

13. *Impostor Rule.* If someone issues an instrument to an impostor, then any indorsement in the

name of the payee is valid as long as the person who pays the instrument is ignorant of the fraud.

14. *Fictitious Payee Rule.* If someone issues an instrument to a person who does not exist, then any indorsement in the name of the payee is valid as long as the person who pays the instrument does not know of the fraud.

15. *Employee Indorsement Rule.* If an employee with responsibility for issuing instruments forges a check or other instrument, then any indorsement in the name of the payee is valid as long as

the person who pays the instrument is ignorant of the fraud.

16. Anyone who behaves negligently in creating or paying an unauthorized instrument is liable to an innocent third party.

17. Discharge means that liability on an instrument terminates. An instrument may be discharged by payment, agreement, cancellation, certification, or alteration.

Practice Test

1. Marie Kless hired an attorney, James R. Gunderman, to collect money owed her on a mortgage. Gunderman was successful in his attempt to recover the money, but when he received the check payable to Kless for $26,676.16, he forged her indorsement and deposited the check in his own account at Manufacturers Hanover Trust Co. He later withdrew the entire amount. Is the bank liable to Kless?

2. **CPA QUESTION** Vex Corp. executed a negotiable promissory note payable to Tamp, Inc. The note was collaterized by some of Vex's business assets. Tamp negotiated the note to Miller for value. Miller indorsed the note in blank and negotiated it to Bilco for value. Before the note became due, Bilco agreed to release Vex's collateral. Vex refused to pay Bilco when the note became due. Bilco promptly notified Miller and Tamp of Vex's default. Which of the following statements is correct?

   a. Bilco will be unable to collect from Miller because Miller's indorsement was in blank.

   b. Bilco will be able to collect from either Tamp or Miller because Bilco was a holder in due course.

   c. Bilco will be unable to collect from either Tamp or Miller because of Bilco's release of the collateral.

   d. Bilco will be able to collect from Tamp because Tamp was the original payee.

3. **CPA QUESTION** A check has the following indorsements on the back:

Paul Frank
without recourse
George Hopkins
payment guaranteed
Ann Quarry
Collection guaranteed
Rachel Ott

Which of the following conditions occurring subsequent to the indorsements would discharge all of the indorsers?

   a. Lack of notice of dishonor

   b. Late presentment

   c. Insolvency of maker

   d. Certification of check

4. **CPA QUESTION** Which of the following actions does not discharge a prior party to a commercial instrument?

   a. Good faith payment or satisfaction of the instrument

   b. Cancellation of that prior party's indorsement

   c. The holder's oral renunciation of that prior party's liability

   d. The holder's intentional destruction of the instrument

5. Phariss operated a business known as Railroad Salvage Co. He filed a claim in bankruptcy court against the Chicago, Rock Island and Pacific Railroad. Phariss then left Iowa and closed his bank account with the Security State Bank in

Independence. Somehow, Carl Eddy obtained possession of the check that the railroad issued in payment of Phariss's claim. Eddy indorsed the check "Railroad Salvage Co. Carl Eddy" and deposited it in his own account at Security State Bank. After Eddy filed for bankruptcy, Phariss sued the bank, alleging that it was liable to him for having paid the check over an unauthorized indorsement. Is Security State Bank liable to Phariss? On what theory?

6. **YOU BE THE JUDGE** WRITING PROBLEM Melco, Inc., issued a promissory note for $12,000, payable to the order of Marjorie Irene Floor. On the back of the note, Charles Melvin had signed the following statement: "For and in consideration of funds advanced herein to Melco, Inc., we irrevocably guarantee Marjorie Irene Floor against loss by reason of non-payment of this note." Floor sued Melvin to enforce the note before demanding payment from the issuer. Is Melvin liable on the note before demand is made on the issuer? **Argument for Floor:** Melvin was an accommodation party and, as such, was liable on the instrument even if no demand had been made on the issuer. **Argument for Melvin:** If the accommodation party writes, "I guarantee collection," he is not liable until the issuer fails to pay. In this case, the words Melvin wrote are the equivalent of "I guarantee collection." **Floor's response:** To avoid liability in this case, Melvin had to comply with the exact requirements of the statute. How was she to know that he thought he was writing the equivalent of "I guarantee collection"?

7. Sidney Knopf entered into a contract for $35,000 with MacDonald Roofing Co., Inc., to reroof Knopf's building. Knopf made his initial payment by writing a check for $17,500 payable to "MacDonald Roofing Company, Inc., and D-FW Supply Company." MacDonald took the check to D-FW and requested an indorsement. MacDonald Roofing was a customer of D-FW, so D-FW indorsed the check. When MacDonald failed to complete the roofing work, Knopf filed suit for damages against D-FW. Knopf argues that D-FW was liable as an indorser. Do you agree?

8. **ETHICS** Steven was killed in an automobile accident. His wife, Debra, was the beneficiary of a life insurance policy for $60,000. She decided to move from Bunkie to Sulphur, Louisiana. Before she could leave, however, arrangements had to be made to settle outstanding debts. Debra executed a document authorizing her mother-in-law, Helen, to sign checks on Debra's account at the bank. Debra also signed several blank checks and gave them to Helen with instructions to use them to pay off the remaining debt on Debra's trailer. When Helen received the life insurance checks, she deposited them in Debra's account. So far so good. But then she immediately withdrew $50,000 from the account by using one of the blank checks Debra had left her. She did not use these funds to pay off the trailer debt. When Debra discovered the theft, she sued the bank for having paid an unauthorized check. How would you rule in this case? Debra has suffered a grievous loss—her husband died tragically in an automobile accident. She trusted her mother-in-law and counted on her help. Should the bank show compassion? If the bank made good on the forged checks, how great would be the injury to the bank's shareholders compared with the harm to Debra if she loses this entire sum?

9. James A. Arnold and Marvin D. Smith signed two promissory notes for a total of $25,000 payable to the Bostwick Banking Co. The defendants argued that they were not liable on the notes because they had signed as agents for Sunshine Sales Corp. The notes made no reference to Sunshine, but the defendants alleged that an officer at Bostwick had promised to type "Sunshine Sales Corporation" above their signatures on the notes. Are the defendants liable on the notes?

10. Merlyn Yagow borrowed money from P.C.A. to finance his farming expenses. Fearing that Yagow would not be able to pay his debt, P.C.A. required him to accept payment for his crops with checks that named him and P.C.A. as co-payees. This way, Yagow could not cash the checks without P.C.A.'s indorsement. Yagow sold corn to Farmer's Co-op Elevator, which paid $5,698.71 by check made out to "Merlyn Yagow, Alvin Yagow, P.C.A." When Yagow deposited this check, the comma between Alvin Yagow and P.C.A. appeared as "or." The check was indorsed by Merlin Yagow alone, not by P.C.A. When P.C.A. sued the bank for having paid this check, the bank in turn, filed suit against Yagow demanding indemnification for the P.C.A. claims. What claim did the bank make against Yagow?

11. Using the company's check-signing machine, Doris Britton forged $148,171.30 of checks on the account of her employer, Winkie, Inc. One of Britton's jobs at the company was to prepare checks for the company president, W. J. Winkie, Jr., to sign. He did not (1) look at the sequence of check numbers; (2) examine the monthly account statements; or (3) reconcile company records with bank statements. Winkie's bank, as a matter of policy, did not check indorsements on checks with a face value of less than $1,000. By accident, it paid a forged check that had not even been indorsed. Is the bank liable to Winkie, Inc., for the forged checks?

12. **ROLE REVERSAL** Write a short-answer question that tests the reader's knowledge of at least one of the transfer warranties.

Internet Research Problem

At **http://beatty.westbuslaw.com**, the United States Secret Service offers advice on how to avoid check fraud. Click on "FAQs" and then "How can I protect myself against check fraud?" Have you ever violated this advice and left yourself vulnerable to fraud?

> You can find further practice problems at **http://beatty.westbuslaw.com** or in the **Study Guide that accompanies this text.**

Liability for Negotiable Instruments: Banks and Their Customers

Arriving in New York from his native Bangladesh, Abdul Matin worked as a waiter in a restaurant in lower Manhattan. Through grueling effort and remarkable thrift, he managed to save $70,000, which he deposited in an account at the Chase Manhattan Bank. Then word came from home that his father was ill. Matin left in a hurry, expecting to return promptly. In the end, though, it was two years before he arrived back in New York. Imagine his horror and panic when he discovered upon his return that his bank account had no money left. Someone had used forged checks to empty the account. Matin told bank employees what had happened and begged for his money back. But Chase refused to make good on the missing funds because Matin had not reported the forgeries within one year, as the Uniform Commercial Code requires.

Is Matin simply out of luck? Does he have to start all over again, working and saving, saving and working? To find out, read on. ■

INTRODUCTION

Americans write over 40 billion checks each year. They also execute 11 billion transactions at the more than 371,000 automatic teller machines (ATMs) found every place, including in banks, grocery stores, airports, the Grand Canyon, Antarctica, and Buckingham Palace. This chapter is about the laws that govern the relationship between banks and their customers, both for traditional activities such as check writing and newer activities like electronic fund transfers at ATMs. Parts of this chapter will seem familiar to you from reading Chapter 24. Because checks are a form of draft, they are covered by Article 3 of the Uniform Commercial Code (UCC). Article 4 governs bank deposits and collections. Some of the provisions in Article 4 are very similar to those in Article 3. When the two conflict, Article 4 controls.

Who's Who

UCC §4-105 defines the different roles of banks:

- **Depositary Bank.** The first bank to *take* a check is called the depositary bank. (A bank that *cashes* a check is not a depositary bank.) Suppose that the New York Yankees, Inc., writes a check on its account at Citibank to pay star player Derek Jeter. If he deposits the check in his account at Bank of America, then Bank of America is the depositary bank.

- **Payor Bank.** A bank that is called a *drawee* bank in Article 3 is termed a *payor* bank in Article 4 because it pays the issuer's check. The New York Yankees, Inc., is the issuer of the check, and Citibank is the payor bank.

- **Intermediary Bank.** An intermediary bank is any bank that handles a check during the collection process, *except* the depositary or payor bank. Instead of presenting the check directly to Citibank for payment, Bank of America may send it to the Federal Reserve bank, which serves as a central clearinghouse for checks. The Federal Reserve then sends the check to Citibank for payment. The Federal Reserve is an intermediary bank.

- **Collecting Bank.** A collecting bank is any bank that handles a check during the collection process, except the payor bank. Both Bank of America and the Federal Reserve are collecting banks.

- **Presenting Bank.** A presenting bank is a bank that submits a check to the payor bank. The Federal Reserve is the presenting bank.

As you can see, the same bank may carry several different labels. Exhibit 25.1 sets out the roles that the various banks play in the transaction between the Yankees and Derek Jeter.

Check deposited in **Bank of America**

Depositary bank
Collecting bank

Check sent to **Federal Reserve** for collection

Intermediary bank
Collecting bank
Presenting bank

Check presented to **Citibank**, which pays the check

Payor bank

Exhibit 25.1

CHECKING ACCOUNTS

When a customer deposits money in a checking account, the bank becomes a debtor to the customer—the bank owes the customer money. At the same time, the bank serves as an agent for the customer. The legal relationship between the customer and the bank is based on both the checking account agreement and Article 4. The checking account agreement is simply a contract between the bank and the customer. Article 4 is, in essence, a default option; it applies unless the bank and customer agree to different terms. No matter what the agreement says, however, a bank cannot avoid liability for careless or bad faith actions. To pursue a complaint against a bank, see http://www.federalreserve.gov/pubs/complaints/.

The Bank's Duty to Provide Information

The UCC does not require banks to provide customers with a monthly statement that lists transactions. Virtually every bank does so, however, because customers expect it. If a bank provides a statement, it must either include canceled checks or a list of check numbers, amounts, and dates of payment.[1] Returning canceled checks is an expensive habit that many banks would like to break.[2] Nonetheless, most banks still do return canceled checks because customers like to have them. People find that a photocopy of a canceled check is the best proof that a bill has been paid. If a bank does not return canceled checks, it must keep legible copies on hand for seven years and provide copies to customers within a reasonable time.

The Truth in Savings Act[3] requires banks that send statements to include:

- The interest rate paid on the account
- The amount of interest the account has earned
- Any fees imposed by the bank
- The number of days covered by the statement

Before customers open an account (and in advertisements), a bank must disclose:

- The interest rate paid on the account
- How long this interest rate will be in effect
- Any requirements (such as minimum account balance or initial deposit) that the customer must meet to earn the advertised rate
- Any fees or penalties imposed by the bank

The Bank's Duty to Pay

A bank must pay a check if the check is authorized by the customer and complies with the terms of the checking account agreement.[4] A bank may, however, choose the order in which it pays authorized checks. Suppose that Elizabeth writes a check to each of her four sisters: Jane ($100), Mary ($50), Lydia ($40), and Kitty ($10). When the sisters appear at the bank the next morning to cash the checks, they discover

---

[1] UCC §4-406.
[2] Originally, banks returned checks because they did not want the expense of storing all that paper. With advances in technology and increases in postal rates, it is now cheaper simply to store microcopies.
[3] 12 U.S.C. §§4301-4313.
[4] UCC §§4-401(a), 4-402(a).

Elizabeth has only $100 in her account. The bank is free to choose which sisters it pays. It is not forced to pay the sister who appears first nor must it pay Mary, Lydia, and Kitty together, instead of Jane by herself.

A bank does not have to bounce checks; it can, if it chooses, pay a check even if that causes an overdraft. Once an account has an overdraft, the bank may either repay itself out of the customer's next deposit or try to collect the amount directly from the customer. For example, a bookie demanded that a gambler repay his debts *immediately*. The gambler did not want to pay, but he also did not want his legs broken. It was midnight and no banks were open. He wrote a check, knowing that his account was virtually on empty. It is not clear what he thought the bookie would do when the check bounced, but at that particular midnight, he was more concerned with the present than the future. His plan was upset, however, when the bank honored his check, despite the overdraft, and then demanded payment from him. Though highly indignant, he nonetheless had to pay. There is a moral to this story about both overdrafts and gambling.

Wrongful Dishonor

If a bank violates its duty and wrongfully dishonors an authorized check, it is liable to the customer for all *actual* and *consequential* damages. Bouncing a check is not only embarrassing, it can cost real money—a retailer may charge for a returned check, the customer's credit rating may suffer, or the customer may even be arrested. When it has wrongfully dishonored a check, the bank is liable for these damages. What should the bank's liability be in the following case?

CITY NATIONAL BANK OF FORT SMITH V. GOODWIN

301 Ark. 182, 783 S.W.2d 335, 1990 Ark. LEXIS 49
Supreme Court of Arkansas, 1990

Facts: City National Bank of Fort Smith (CNB) had two customers with similar names: Larry J. Goodwin and Larry K. Goodwin. Larry K. defaulted on two loans from CNB. Jim Geels, a collection officer at the bank, sought to take money from Larry K.'s checking account and credit it to the loan (which he had the right to do). On November 26, he pulled Larry K.'s loan file to check his Social Security number, but the file had Larry J.'s number instead. Geels took $3,229.07 from the checking account of Larry J. and his wife, Sandra.

On November 30, Sandra Goodwin received written notice from CNB that four checks she had written between November 21 and 26 had not been paid because of insufficient funds and that the Goodwins' joint checking account had a zero balance. Ms. Goodwin knew the bank was in error and requested that CNB both call and send certified letters of apology to the merchants involved. On December 2, she called three of the businesses to which she had written the checks. None of them had received a call or letter. Later in the day, Geels

promised Ms. Goodwin that letters would be sent to the merchants stating that the bank was at fault. On the next day, December 3, he did mail the letters.

Subsequently, CNB learned in a letter from the Goodwins' attorney that other checks written to merchants on November 12 and 21 had also bounced. CNB wrote a letter to one merchant and called the other, stating that it was the bank's fault that the checks were returned. On February 6, the Goodwins filed suit against CNB alleging that CNB wrongfully dishonored seven checks. The jury found for the Goodwins and awarded compensatory damages of $10,000 and punitive damages of $30,000. The bank appealed.

Issue: Is a bank liable for punitive damages when it wrongfully dishonors a customer's check?

Excerpts from Judge Holt's Decision: This court has indicated that punitive damages may be recoverable where a payor bank wrongfully dishonors a check written by its customer. However, only actual damages are recoverable where the dishonor occurs through a mistake. The word "mistake" is to be construed as limited to wrongful dishonor made in good faith.

There was simply no evidence presented that CNB acted in bad faith or that it deliberately or willfully dishonored the Goodwins' checks. It simply confused the identities of Larry K. and Larry J. Goodwin and, as a result, setoff the checking account of Larry J. Goodwin and Sandra Goodwin instead of the accounts of Larry K. Goodwin. In sum, the dishonor of the Goodwins' checks occurred through a mistake. Accordingly, punitive damages were not recoverable.

In law cases, the issues of punitive and compensatory damages may be so interwoven that an error with respect to one requires a retrial of the whole case. This court has held that where the issue of punitive damages is erroneously submitted to the jury, together with the defendant's financial condition, an award of compensatory damages cannot stand. Accordingly, we *reverse* and *remand* the entire case for further proceedings consistent with this opinion. ■

Banks are in a difficult position. If they refuse to pay an *authorized* check, they are liable for damages. On the other hand, if they pay an *unauthorized* check, they must bear the liability and recredit the customer's account. Following are the most common problems banks face in determining which checks to pay and which to dishonor.

The Death of a Customer

If a customer dies, the bank may continue to pay checks *for 10 days* after it learns of the death, unless it receives a stop payment order from someone claiming an interest in the account.[5] After all, the customer was alive when he wrote the checks. Refusing to pay may cause hardship for innocent merchants who accepted checks in return for goods. A refusal to pay may also complicate matters for his family when they sort out his financial affairs. Certainly, the last thing his widow wants is for all his checks to bounce.

In reality, however, banks typically do freeze an account after the holder dies. First, a bank must stop payment on checks if someone else makes a claim to the funds in the account, no matter how weak that claim is. If Mildred, a seventh cousin twice removed, makes a claim, the bank must stop payment. Second, although Article 4 permits banks to pay checks even after the customer has died, most states require banks to freeze enough money to cover the decedent's taxes. Since the bank does not know what the decedent will ultimately owe, it typically freezes the entire account.

Incompetent Customers

Once a bank is notified that a court has found a customer to be incompetent, it is liable if it pays the customer's checks. The bank is under no obligation to determine competence itself. It may continue to pay checks until it has received notice that a court has determined the customer is incompetent.

Forgery

If a bank pays a check on which the issuer's name is forged, it must recredit the issuer's account. When a bank pays a forged check, either the bank or the customer will lose money, except in the unlikely event that the forger repays what he has stolen. As a matter of policy, the drafters of the UCC decided that the payor bank should bear the risk of forgery, rather than the customer. Most banks take two steps to guard against losses: they examine the signatures on all checks above a certain dollar amount, and they carry forgery insurance.

---

[5] UCC §4-405.

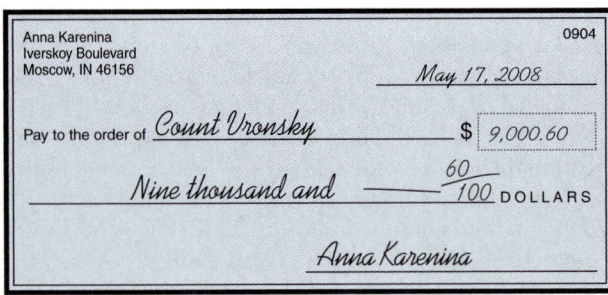

Exhibit 25.2

If the bank pays this check, it is liable for the full amount because the check has obviously been altered.

Anna Karenina originally wrote this check for $9.60. Because the check looks unaltered, she is liable for $9.60, and the bank is liable for the balance.

Alteration

If a bank pays a check that has been altered, the customer is liable only for the original terms of the check, and the bank is liable for the balance.[6] There is one exception to this rule: if the alteration is obvious, the bank is liable for the full amount of the check because it should have known better than to pay it in the first place. Exhibit 25.2 illustrates this rule.

Completion

If an incomplete check is later filled in by someone other than the original issuer, the bank is not liable unless it was on notice that the completion was improper.[7] Joey and Lisa want to buy, renovate, and resell a two-family house. They think they have located the perfect choice, but negotiations are still incomplete when Joey leaves town on business for a few days. He signs a blank check and leaves it with Lisa to pay his half of the deposit, if their offer is accepted. Lisa absentmindedly uses the check as a bookmark and forgets to remove it before she returns the book to the library. Marian the librarian finds the check and, glorying in the thought of hundreds of new books, fills in the library's name and the amount of $10,000. If Lisa realizes the check is missing and notifies the bank, then the bank is liable to Joey if it later pays the check. Otherwise, the bank owes Joey nothing.

Comparative Negligence and Bank Statements

Customers must use reasonable care in examining their bank statements to look for forged or altered checks. If a customer is careless, the bank is not liable for the faulty checks. Moreover, if a customer fails to notify the bank of a forgery or alteration within 30 days of receiving a statement, then the bank is not liable for any subsequent bad checks by the same wrongdoer. However, if both the customer and the bank are careless, a comparative negligence standard is used, and the bank's liability is reduced by the amount of the customer's negligence.[8] In any case, a customer cannot recover for a forgery or alteration if it is reported more than one year after receiving the statement that first revealed the problem.

In the following case, Abdul Matin failed to report forgeries on his account within the one-year period. Is the bank liable? You be the judge.

---

[6]   UCC §4-401(d).
[7]   UCC §4-401(d).
[8]   UCC §4-406.

you Be The Judge

MATIN V. CHASE MANHATTAN BANK

**10 A.D.3d 447; 781 N.Y.S.2d 158; 2004 N.Y. App. Div.
LEXIS 10387
Supreme Court of New York, 2004**

Facts: Abdul Matin returned home from a lengthy trip abroad only to discover that some unknown person had used forged checks to empty his account at the Chase Manhattan Bank. The culprit also forged a change of address card so that the bank sent the monthly statements to a different address. When Matin asked for a refund, the bank refused on the grounds that Matin had not reported the forgeries within one year as required by the UCC. After Matin filed suit, the court granted Chase's motion for summary judgment.

You Be the Judge: Is the bank liable for forged checks that were not reported within one year?

Argument for Matin: Under the UCC, a bank is liable for any forged checks that it pays as long as the customer reports the forgeries within one year after the bank makes the statement *available to him*. In this case, Matin never received the bank statements because they were sent to the wrong address. He did report the loss within minutes after he realized what had happened. He complied with the UCC and the bank is liable to him.

Argument for Chase Manhattan: Matin was away for two years. Even if the bank had mailed the statements to his correct address in America, he would never have received them and would never have noticed the forgeries. If he had a friend or family member checking his mail then that person should have notified the bank when no statements arrived. In that case, the bank could have prevented further forgeries.

Under the UCC one-year rule, bank customers need to check periodically to make sure that nothing is wrong with their accounts. Matin failed to do this. ∎

Stale Checks

A bank is not *required* to pay checks that are presented more than six months after their date, but it is not liable if it does pay.[9] In 1962, John Glenn became the first person to orbit the earth. Many people were so eager to have his autograph that they did not cash checks he gave them. In 1974, Glenn was elected senator from Ohio. Suppose that one of his admirers became so disgusted with his political views that she no longer treasured his autograph and tried, in 1974, to cash a check from 1962. Would she be successful? Although Glenn's bank, as a matter of policy, would probably reject the 12-year-old check, it would not be liable to Glenn if it paid.

Post-Dated Checks

A post-dated check is one that is presented for payment before its date. **A bank is not liable for paying a post-dated check unless the customer has notified the bank in advance that a post-dated check is coming.**[10] Under the old version of Article 4, banks were not supposed to cash checks until their due date. So, for example, customers could mail off a set of post-dated checks to pay all their bills while on vacation, knowing that the bank would not pay the checks until their due dates. When Article 4 was revised, however, banks argued that this rule was impractical at a time when most banks use machines to process checks. The extra expense of manually reviewing each check is not worth the limited benefit to a few customers.

---

[9]   UCC §4-404.
[10]   UCC §4-401(c).

Stop Payment Orders

Even if a check is authorized when issued, the customer has the right to stop payment later. **As a general rule, if a bank pays a check over a stop payment order, it is liable to the customer for any loss he suffers.**[11] However, a bank customer must be aware of these additional rules:

- Any account holder has the right to stop payment, even someone who did not sign the check.

- A stop payment order is valid only if it describes the check with reasonable certainty and the bank receives the order before paying, or certifying, the check.

- An oral stop payment order is valid for only 14 days; a written order expires in six months. This is an important point. Many people think that, once they have stopped payment on a check, they can relax and forget about it. Not true. One woman, for example, wrote a $1,000 check to a contractor. When he told her he had lost the check, she stopped payment and gave him a new one, which he promptly cashed. Ten months later, he cashed the old check, too. The customer could have continued to renew the stop payment order every six months, but that would have been a hassle. The only surefire method for stopping a check permanently is to close the old account and open a new one.

Typically, a customer issues a stop payment order because she is having a disagreement over a contract. The customer may or may not be in the right. If a bank accidentally pays a check in violation of a stop payment order, it retains the right to recover from whichever party to the contract was wrong. The "bank is **subrogated to**" the rights of the parties, which means that the bank can substitute for, or take the place of, either party. Section 4-407 provides: **If a bank pays a check despite a valid stop payment order, it inherits the rights of the customer against the payee and of the payee against the customer.** In the following case, the plaintiff gambled and lost—twice: once in a casino and once in court.

SEIGEL V. MERRILL LYNCH, PIERCE, FENNER & SMITH, INC.

745 A.2d 301; 2000 D.C. App. LEXIS 21
District of Columbia Court of Appeals, 2000

Facts: During a two-month period, Walter Seigel gambled—a lot—at casinos in Atlantic City, New Jersey. To buy gambling chips, he wrote checks to the various casinos. These checks were drawn on his cash management account at Merrill Lynch.[12] Once the spree was over, and Seigel had lost all of his chips (if not his marbles), he called his broker to ask if there was any way he could avoid paying his gambling debts. At the broker's suggestion, Seigel placed a stop payment order on the checks. Merrill Lynch did dishonor many of the checks but accidentally paid checks totaling $143,000. (This number provides some evidence of the extent of Seigel's problem.)

Seigel sued Merrill Lynch, demanding a return of the $143,000 plus interest. The trial court granted Merrill Lynch's motion for summary judgment.

Issue: Did Seigel suffer a loss when Merrill Lynch paid a check over his stop payment order?

Excerpts from Judge Steadman's Decision: [L]iability on the bank for payment over a stop payment order is far from automatic. On the contrary,

▼

---

[11] UCC §4-403.

[12] Article 4 of the UCC technically only applies to banks. However, the parties to this case agreed that the negotiable instruments drawn by Seigel were checks. Furthermore, the official comment to UCC §4-403 notes that "by analogy the rule extends to drawers other than banks" Therefore, the court treated Merill Lynch as a bank.

section 4-403(c) provides: "The burden of establishing the fact and amount of loss resulting from the payment of an item contrary to a stop-payment order is on the customer."

In assessing whether any such loss was actually incurred, Merrill Lynch must be treated as the subrogee of any rights of the casino payees against Seigel. As the payee of a dishonored check, the casino would have a prima facie right to recover its amount from Seigel as drawer, and the burden would be on Seigel to establish any defense he might assert on the instrument.

Seigel asserts two such defenses: duress and illegality. Seigel first argues that the casinos would have no right to enforce the checks even under New Jersey law because enforcement of checks by a casino against a compulsive gambler would run counter to New Jersey's Casino Control Act. However, there is nothing in the record to suggest that these checks were accepted contrary to a specific order of the Casino Control Commission, and therefore there is no genuine issue of fact on this point.

[I]t appears to be true that intoxication, duress, and unconscionability may, in certain circumstances, be valid defenses to the enforcement of gambling contracts in New Jersey. However, compulsive gambling, in and of itself, is not a defense to a contract action in New Jersey. [Siegel] fails to produce any evidence in the record, specific or otherwise, regarding his problem and its relation to any unconscionable duress in the transactions at issue. We therefore conclude that Seigel's assertion that the checks would be unenforceable in New Jersey fails.

[E]ven if payment had been stopped, the casinos could have enforced the checks in New Jersey, where the transaction was entered into. Merrill Lynch therefore, under the Code scheme, conceptually has the same right. We conclude that Seigel failed to establish that he ultimately suffered any actual loss as a result of the payment of the checks by Merrill Lynch. Accordingly, the judgment of the trial court must be

Affirmed. ■

Devil's Advocate

If Merrill Lynch had dishonored all the checks, it is possible that Seigel might not have had to pay in the end—the casinos might not have bothered to sue him. He lived in Maryland, not New Jersey, and the expense and effort of filing suit in another jurisdiction might not have been worth the effort. Also, he was a good customer at the casinos and had already paid them substantial sums. They might not have wanted to alienate him. In any event, a lawsuit would have taken some years and delayed the day on which Seigel actually had to pay. He would have been better off if Merrill Lynch had done as it promised and dishonored the checks. ◆

---

at RISK

Consumer advocates suggest that bank customers should follow these safeguards:

- *Read bank statements.* Many financial advisers now say that it is not crucial to balance a checkbook, but it is important to look at bank statements (and canceled checks, if there are any) to detect anything out of the ordinary.

- *Keep bank statements and canceled checks.* Without this documentation, it is difficult to prove the bank has made an error.

- *Keep receipts from ATMs.* Don't walk away without a record of the transaction, and make sure it is correct.

- *Write immediately to the bank if there is an error in a statement or ATM receipt.* Mail the information to a specific person who handles consumer complaints; then keep a record of when you contacted the bank, the names of any people you spoke to, and what they said. Be persistent. If you do not hear from the bank, or the answer is unsatisfactory, take your complaint to a higher level in the bank.

- *If you cannot resolve your dispute directly with the bank, write to the agency that regulates it.* Ask someone at your bank for the name of its primary regulator, or call your state banking department and ask for help.[13] ◆

---

[13] Christine Dugas, "Fighting the Bank," *Newsday*, Nov. 13, 1994, p. 3. Copyright 1994 Newsday, Inc.

Substitute Checks

Suppose that you own a cottage on the coast in Florida which you rent to Ella from Seattle. As soon as her rent check arrives, you deposit it into your account. The next day, you want to write a check against those funds to pay your credit card bill. No chance the bank will let you do that. Ella's check has a long route to travel before your bank can tell if it is good or not. Your Miami bank will send the check to the Federal Reserve Bank in Atlanta, which will send the check to the Federal Reserve Bank in San Francisco, which will present the check for payment at Ella's bank in Seattle. Like a game of hot potato, each bank in the collection process must pass a check along before midnight of the next banking day after it receives the check (the so-called **midnight deadline**).

The rent check is not money in the bank until the check clears.

© PHOTODISC/PICTUREQUEST

If the check is good, the Seattle bank simply lets the midnight deadline expire in silence. If the Seattle bank dishonors the check, it can either return the item along the same route that the check originally traveled, or the bank can return the check directly to Miami.

Checks are physically transported by airplane or ground transportation—so that even with the midnight deadline, the process is slow and expensive. This problem was compounded after September 11, 2001, when air traffic was shut down for days. Checks piled up at banks across the country.

In an effort to bring the banking system into the twenty-first century, Congress recently passed the Check 21 Act. This statute creates a new negotiable instrument called a **substitute check.** Any bank that receives a paper check has the right to encode both the front and back electronically and then destroy the original. It can then send that check electronically to the other banks in the check-clearing process. However, if a bank prefers not to accept an electronic check, it has the right to receive a substitute check instead. This substitute is simply a paper printout of the electronic version. **The substitute check is legally the same as the original check.** (Exhibit 25.3 is a picture of a substitute check.) Note that Check 21 does not require a bank to create substitute checks or to accept electronic checks; it simply requires banks to accept paper substitute checks. The hope is that, as banks gradually switch to electronic transmissions, checks will travel faster and depositors will have access to their funds sooner. Imagine how much faster Ella's check could travel electronically than on planes, trains, and airplanes.

In the previous chapter, we learned about warranty liability. Under Check 21, **a bank that transfers or presents an electronic or a substitute check gives a *warranty of legal equivalency*.** The bank is warranting to the drawer, the payee, the depositor, any indorser, and any bank that receives the check that:

- The substitute check is an accurate image of the original check

- No bank, issuer, or indorser will be asked to pay a check that he has already paid.

If someone does end up paying a check twice, then the bank that created the substitute check in the first place is liable.

What does Check 21 mean to you? Funds may clear faster, which means that you need to be sure you have enough money in your account to cover checks that you

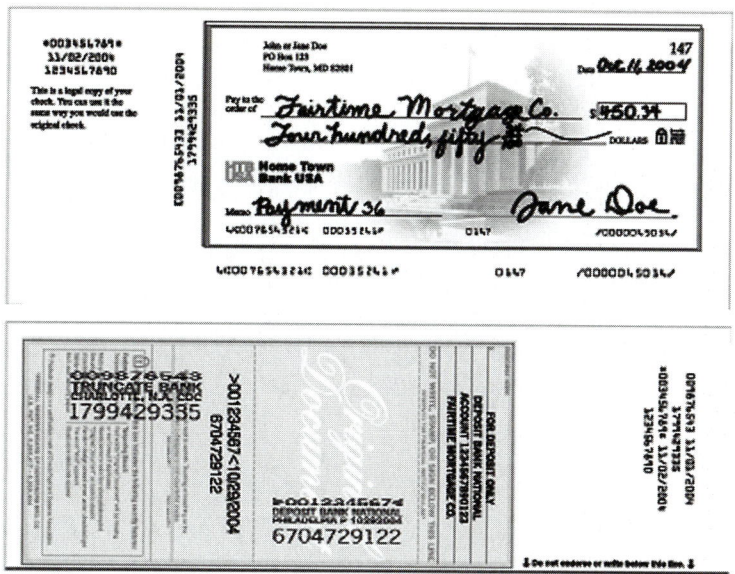

Exhibit 25.3
A substitute check.

write. It also means that you may receive some substitute checks with your bank statement each month. If you request a copy of a check from your bank, it may give you the original check, a substitute check, or a copy of the original check. For more about this statute, including the refund process if your bank makes an error, check out **http://federalreserve.gov**.

Expedited Funds Availability Act

Although, in theory, Check 21 will permit banks to process checks more quickly and put money in a customer's bank account faster, this statute does not regulate how soon funds must be available for withdrawal. That is left to the Expedited Funds Availability Act (EFAA),[14] which specifies the maximum time a bank may hold funds before allowing a customer to withdraw them. (A bank can always pay earlier if it wants.) Exhibit 25.4 lists rules that establish how quickly you can write a check against funds in your account.

Customers must, however, wait longer to withdraw cash than they do to write a check.[15] Banks are at greater risk when customers withdraw cash than when they write a check: the bank still has a number of days before a check must be paid; the cash is gone immediately. Thus, under the EFAA, a customer can only withdraw the first $100 in cash on the next business day after depositing a check. He can withdraw $400 more in cash by 5:00 P.M. on the same day that the funds are available for check writing. The rest of the deposit can be withdrawn the day after funds are available for check writing. Exhibit 25.5 illustrates these rules on funds availability.

---

[14] 12 U.S.C. §§4001-4010.

[15] These hold periods do not apply to new accounts, accounts with repeated overdrafts, and any other situation in which a bank has reasonable cause to believe the check is uncollectible.

Item Deposited	When Funds May be Withdrawn by Check
Cash Cashiers Check Certified Check Government Check Check Drawn on same bank Wire Transfer	• Next business day, if deposited with a teller • Second business day, if deposited in an ATM
Local Check (both the depositary bank and the payor bank are in the same region)	• Next business day, for the first $100 • Second business day, for the balance up to $5,000 • Ninth business day, for the balance over $5,000
Nonlocal Check	• Next business day, for the first $100 • Fifth business day, for the balance up to $5,000 • Ninth business day, for the balance over $5,000

Exhibit 25.4

Exhibit 25.5[16]
When Cash May Be Withdrawn.

---

[16] Adapted from a chart prepared by the Federal Reserve Board. *Reprinted in* Douglas J. Whaley, *Problems and Materials on Payment Law* (Boston: Little, Brown & Co., 1995), p. 218.

ELECTRONIC BANKING

Back to the Future

In 1968, a bank in Philadelphia installed the first automated teller machine (ATM) in the United States. Until that time, anyone who needed money for the weekend had two choices: cash a check at the bank before it closed (at 3:00 P.M. on Friday, 1:00 P.M. on Saturday) or find a local merchant who would cash a small check after hours. The same person had two options for paying a bill: cash or check. Today, thanks to advances in electronic fund transfers, we have options that were barely imagined a generation ago, such as debit cards and online payment of bills. In 2003, for the first time, consumers used debit and credit cards in stores more often than checks or cash.

Now consumers can obtain cash day or night and pay their bills with a few clicks of the mouse. And banks save money—electronic transmission is less expensive than shipping billions of checks around the globe. But the advances in technology are so new that this area of the law is changing rapidly and will undoubtedly continue to do so for some time.

Electronic Fund Transfer Act

In the beginning, electronic fund transfers were governed by contract between a bank and its customers, not by state or national statutes. Some banks treated their customers better than others. For example, roughly one-third of banks refused to recredit a customer for unauthorized transfers. Thus, if Biff stole Marty's ATM card and emptied his account, Marty was simply out of luck. Gradually, states began to regulate electronic transfers. This was better than nothing, but it did not solve the problem of interstate transfers. In 1978, Congress passed the Electronic Fund Transfer Act (EFTA)[17] to protect **consumers.** The statute defines a consumer as "any natural person," that is, not a corporation or business. Following are the major provisions of the EFTA.

Required Electronic Fund Transfers

An employer may require its employees to receive paychecks via an electronic fund transfer but it cannot specify the particular bank. Suppose the CEO of MegaCorp. has decided that the company must cut costs to stay competitive in its industry. Her chief financial officer tells her the company can save thousands of dollars in administrative expenses if it pays employees via electronic fund transfers instead of by check. In addition, the Dawes Bank will agree to give MegaCorp. favorable financing on a major loan if the company pays all employees by electronic fund transfer to Dawes. Under the EFTA, MegaCorp. can require all employees to receive their pay via an electronic fund transfer, but the company cannot require employees to be paid at Dawes.

Cards

If a bank sends an electronic fund transfer card (for example, an ATM card) to a consumer who has not requested it, the card must be invalid until the consumer requests validation. Otherwise, if banks sent valid ATM cards to consumers who were not expecting them, the cards could be stolen and used without the consumer ever knowing. To validate a card, the bank typically assigns the consumer a PIN. The card does not work unless the PIN is entered with each transaction.

Documentation

A bank must provide consumers with (1) a transaction statement each time an electronic fund transfer is made at an ATM and (2) a monthly (or, in the case of infrequent transactions, quarterly) statement reporting all electronic fund transfers for the period.

---

[17] 15 U.S.C. §1693.

Preauthorized Transfers

Consumers sometimes ask banks to wire funds on a regular basis—to pay the monthly mortgage, say. A bank may not make preauthorized transfers without written instructions from the consumer. The consumer can stop payment of the transfer by oral or written notice up to three business days before the scheduled date. In the following case, a customer sued her bank for making a preauthorized transfer that she thought she had stopped.

BROXTON-KING V. LASALLE BANK, N.A.

2001 U.S. Dist. LEXIS 14653
United States District Court for the Northern District of Illinois, 2001

Facts: Eunice Broxton-King paid $28 a month to belong to the YMCA. On the first day of each month, this sum was transferred automatically from her account at the LaSalle Bank to the YMCA. On August 31, Broxton-King went to the bank, paid an overdraft on her account, and then closed it. However, on September 1, the bank transferred $28 to the YMCA. Because there was no money in her account, the bank charged an overdraft fee of $22 and a service charge of $3. The overdraft totaled $53. On September 7, the bank sent Broxton-King a notice of this overdraft. She told the bank that her account had been closed on August 31, that the debit to the YMCA should be stopped, and the fees refunded. But on October 1, the bank again debited plaintiff's checking account for the $28 YMCA fee and added an additional $27 in overdraft and service fees.

Alleging that the bank had violated the EFTA, Broxton-King filed a *pro se*[18] lawsuit. The bank filed a motion to dismiss.

Issue: Did the bank violate the EFTA?

Excerpts from Judge Gottschall's Decision: Section 1693e of the EFTA provides that "[a] consumer may stop payment of a preauthorized electronic fund transfer by notifying the financial institution orally or in writing at any time up to three business days preceding the scheduled date of such transfer." Defendant moves to dismiss plaintiff's EFTA claim, arguing that the EFTA cannot help the plaintiff. Defendant argues that plaintiff failed to properly prevent the transfer of funds to the YMCA. Defendant contends that if plaintiff had wished to prevent

the first transfer of funds in question (the one that occurred on September 1), plaintiff should have, pursuant to the EFTA, requested a stop to the funds transfer three days prior to the transfer date. Instead, defendant notes, plaintiff alleges that she closed her account and ended all transactions with her account on August 31: the day before the transfer date.

As for the October 1 transfer of funds, defendant argues, it had properly allowed the funds transfer because plaintiff had failed to pay off the overdraft resulting from the first transfer of funds. Therefore, the account remained open during the time of the funds transfer.

Defendant's motion to dismiss is granted as to plaintiff's EFTA claim regarding the September 1 transfer. Because the request happened less than three days prior to September 1, defendant is correct in principle that plaintiff cannot sue under §1693e of the EFTA for the transfer that occurred on September 1.

It appears, however, that under §1693e of the EFTA, the fact that plaintiff's account was open is immaterial to whether plaintiff could stop a funds transfer from her account. Nowhere in the language of §1693e does the Act require that plaintiff have made the request to stop a funds transfer at a time when the account was closed, as defendant appears to argue. Defendant's motion to dismiss is denied as to plaintiff's EFTA claim regarding the October 1 transfer.

Defendant's motion to dismiss is granted in part and denied in part. ∎

---

[18] Instead of hiring a lawyer, she represented herself.

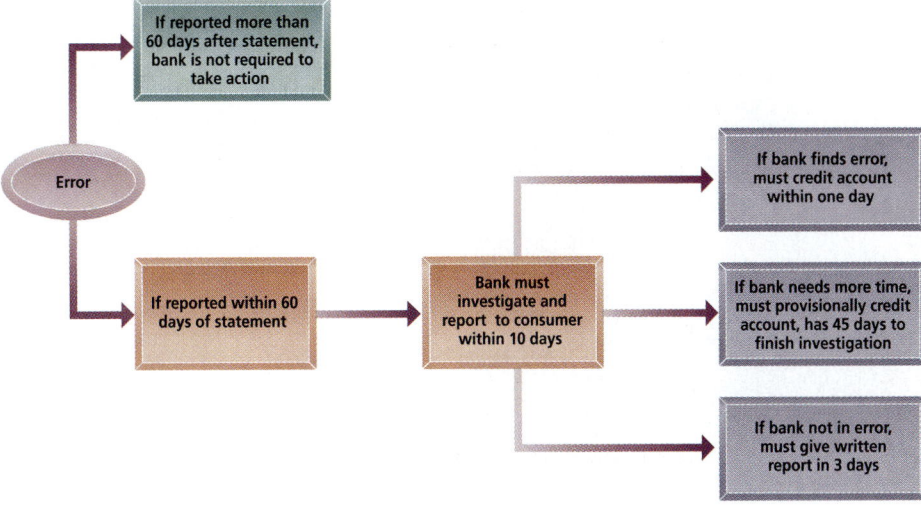

Exhibit 25.6

Errors

If, within 60 days of receiving a bank statement, a consumer tells the bank (either orally or in writing) that the account is in error, the bank must investigate and report the result of its investigation to the consumer within 10 business days. If the bank discovers an error, it must recredit the consumer's account (including interest) within one business day. If the bank cannot complete its investigation within 10 business days, it must provisionally recredit the consumer's account (including interest) pending the termination of its investigation, which must be completed within 45 calendar days. If the bank finds there was no error, it must give the consumer a full explanation in writing within three business days of so finding. When a bank violates this provision, it must pay the consumer treble damages (three times the amount in dispute). Exhibit 25.6 illustrates these rules.

The EFTA addresses the following kinds of errors:

- *Unauthorized Transfer.* Someone withdraws money from an account without permission.

- *Disbursement Error.* The consumer receives $80 from the ATM, but $100 is deducted from her account.

- *Omitted Transfer.* A transfer is never applied to an account. (For some reason, omitted deposits are reported more often than omitted withdrawals.)

- *Computational Error.* The bank makes a mathematical miscalculation.

Consumer Liability for Unauthorized Transactions

When a thief steals an ATM or debit card, it is important for the consumer to report the theft to the bank as quickly as possible.[19] If she reports the loss within two days of discovering it, she is liable only for the first $50 stolen. If she reports the loss after two

---

[19] The Web page **http://www.ftc.gov/bcp/conline/edcams/credit/coninfo_loans.htm** tells you what to do if you lose a credit card.

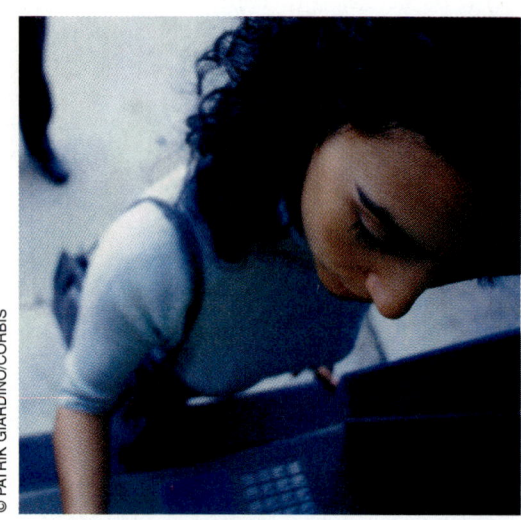

When a consumer is robbed at an ATM, the bank is liable for any losses over $50 if reported to the bank within two days.

days, but within 60 days of receiving her bank statement that shows the unauthorized withdrawal, she is liable for a maximum of $500. After 60 days, she is liable for the full amount.

If an unauthorized transfer takes place without the use of a stolen card, then the consumer is not liable at all as long as she reports the loss within 60 days of receiving a bank statement that shows the loss. After 60 days, however, she is liable for the full amount. If the bank fails to give a consumer either a PIN or some other device to make unauthorized withdrawals difficult, the consumer is not liable for any amount. You remember that, if a customer's negligence contributes to a check forgery, the bank may not be liable. That is not true for electronic funds: the bank is liable even if the customer was negligent. Suppose Marty writes his PIN on his ATM card and then accidentally leaves the card at the ATM. When Biff uses the card to withdraw funds, the bank is still liable for any withdrawal in excess of $50 (which is why many banks limit daily withdrawals to, say, $500).

Crimes at ATMs have become increasingly common. For instance, when a man robbed a convenience store in Orlando, Florida, he locked the clerk in the bathroom and took her purse. Forty minutes later, he used her ATM card to withdraw money from a bank. Who is liable for the money removed from the clerk's account? Robbery is an "unauthorized electronic fund transfer," so the clerk is liable only for $50, provided she notifies the bank within two days of the theft. As the following news story indicates, thieves no longer need a card to steal money.

NEWS*worthy*

He fenced stolen jewels, committed bank and credit-card fraud, and had been accused of having links to an Albanian-Yugoslavian criminal gang. Cloaking himself in nine aliases and Armani jackets, he was a smooth, multilingual master of the con, investigators and people who knew him say. His name is Iljmija Frljuckic, and by all accounts, he had no business being around anybody else's money.

Yet after being deported in the late 1990s, he slipped back into the United States and set up shop as a banker, not in a marble lobby under the watchful eyes of auditors and regulators, but in the virtually unregulated world of privately owned automated teller machines. To tap into this electronic network, Mr. Frljuckic (pronounced Furl-YOU-kich) did not have to produce so much as a valid driver's license. After buying these machines—the kind commonly found in convenience stores, delicatessens and other retail outlets—he and his associates installed devices that captured, or "skimmed," personal bank account information from at least 21,000 people, prosecutors say. They used that information to make fake ATM cards, then stole at least $3.5 million, mostly from ATMs in New York City.

Before Mr. Frljuckic came along, small-time crooks had made crude forays into ATM fraud. But in its size and technical sophistication, investigators say, the Frljuckic case is a con of an entirely different order—a new turn on identity theft, a jolting warning of the vulnerability of an ATM system that has exploded in size in the last few years.[20] ◆

Bank's Liability

As we have seen, the bank's liability for *unauthorized* transfers depends upon how soon the consumer reports the loss. In addition, a bank is liable to a consumer for any damages caused by the bank's failure to make an *authorized* electronic fund transfer. Bert

---

[20] Walt Bogdanich, "Stealing the Code: Con Men and Cash Machines; Criminals Focus on A.T.M.'s, Weak Link in Banking System," *The New York Times*, August 3, 2003, p. 1.

asks the Tomes Bank to transfer funds every month to pay his mortgage. He goes off hiking in Alaska for the summer, secure in the knowledge that his mortgage will be paid while he is gone. When he returns to find his house in foreclosure proceedings because the bank did not make the payments, he can recover damages from the bank.

System Malfunction

If a system malfunction prevents an electronic fund transfer, the consumer's obligation to make the payment is suspended until the malfunction is repaired or until the intended recipient has, in writing, requested nonelectronic payment. If Bert's mortgage payment is not made because of a system malfunction, the mortgage company cannot charge him a penalty or foreclose on his house during the time the system is down. In fact, he has no obligation to make the payment until the system is working again or until the mortgage company, in writing, requests payment by check.

Disclosure

All of these rules must be disclosed to the consumer (in readily understandable language!) before she opens an account that has electronic fund transfer capability. In addition, banks are required to notify customers of all ATM fees. This notice must appear on or near the machine and also on the screen at a point during the transaction where the customer still has an opportunity to back out without paying a fee.[21]

The goal of the EFTA is to protect consumers. As the following case illustrates, however, that protection goes only so far. It is important for consumers to pay careful attention to the EFTA time limits.

KRUSER V. BANK OF AMERICA

230 Cal. App. 3d 741, 1991 Cal. App. LEXIS 523, 281 Cal. Rptr. 463
Court of Appeal of California, 1991

Facts: Mr. and Mrs. Kruser each had an ATM card for their joint account at the Bank of America (Bank). The Bank referred to this as a "Versatel" card. Mr. Kruser believed his card was destroyed in September 1986. It turned out, however, that someone used it to make an unauthorized withdrawal of $20 from the account in December 1986. That same month, Mrs. Kruser underwent surgery and was hospitalized for 11 days. She then spent six or seven months recuperating at home. Her recovery underwent a nasty setback, however, when she discovered in September 1987 that someone had illegally withdrawn $9,020 from the account during July and August 1987. The Bank refused to refund the money. The Krusers sued, but the trial court granted the Bank's motion for summary judgment. The Krusers appealed.

Issue: Did the Krusers' failure to report the unauthorized withdrawal in December prevent them from recovering the much larger amount stolen in July and August?

Excerpts from Judge Stone's Decision: Appellants [that is, Mr. and Mrs. Kruser] contend the December withdrawal of $20 was so isolated in time and minimal in amount that it cannot be considered in connection with the July and August withdrawals. They assert the [lower] court's interpretation would have absurd results which would be inconsistent with the primary objective of the EFTA—to protect the consumer. They argue that if a consumer receives a bank statement which reflects an unauthorized minimal electronic transfer and fails to report the transaction to the bank within 60 days of transmission of the bank statement, unauthorized transfers many years later, perhaps totaling thousands of dollars, would remain the responsibility of the consumer.

The result appellants fear is avoided by the requirement that the bank establish the subsequent

▼

---

21   ATM Fee Reform Act of 1999, 15 U.S.C. 1693b(d).

unauthorized transfers could have been prevented had the consumer notified the bank of the first unauthorized transfer. Here, although the unauthorized transfer of $20 occurred approximately seven months before the unauthorized transfers totaling $9,020, it is undisputed that all transfers were made by someone using Mr. Kruser's card which the Krusers believed had been destroyed prior to December 1986. According to the declaration of Yvonne Maloon, the Bank's Versatel risk manager, the Bank could have and would have canceled Mr. Kruser's card had it been timely notified of the December unauthorized transfer. In that event Mr. Kruser's card could not have been used to accomplish the unauthorized transactions in July and August.

Appellants contend the facts establish that Mrs. Kruser, who was solely responsible for reconciling the bank statements, was severely ill when the December withdrawal occurred. Therefore, they claim they were entitled to an extension of time within which to notify the Bank. The evidence appellants rely upon indicates Mrs. Kruser left her house infrequently during the first six or seven months of 1987 while she was recuperating. Mrs. Kruser admits, however, she received and reviewed bank statements during her recuperation. Therefore, we need not consider whether Mrs. Kruser's illness created circumstances which might have excused her failure to notice the unauthorized withdrawal pursuant to the applicable sections. She in fact did review the statements in question.

Moreover, nothing in the record reflects any extenuating circumstances which would have prevented Mr. Kruser from reviewing the bank statements. The understanding he had with Mrs. Kruser that she would review the bank statements did not excuse him from his obligation to notify the bank of any unauthorized electronic transfers.

We affirm the judgment and award costs on appeal to respondent. ■

Ethics

Someone uses Mr. Kruser's ATM card to withdraw $20. Mrs. Kruser undergoes major surgery and fails to notice the unauthorized withdrawal. (How many healthy people would notice one unauthorized $20 withdrawal?) Six months later, someone steals more than $9,000 from the Krusers' account and the Bank refuses to pay. It litigates the case to the appeals court, undoubtedly incurring well more than $9,000 in legal fees. Why did the Bank do this? Was it the right thing to do? What are the consequences of the Bank's decision?

Wire Transfers

Electronic fund transfers are important to consumers, but the amount of money they transfer pales in comparison with wholesale wire transfers among banks and their commercial customers. Within the United States, the Federal Reserve system maintains a wire transfer system called "Fedwire." More than $380 trillion is sent each year via Fedwire; the average amount per transaction is $3.5 million. International wire transfers are handled by Clearinghouse Interbank Payments System (CHIPS), based in New York. About $287 trillion is sent through CHIPS each day; the average wire is over $5 million.

UCC Article 4A regulates *nonconsumer* wire transfers, which are a type of **payment order.** Article 3 deals with checks.[22] The difference between a check and a payment order has sometimes been described as push-pull. A check permits the payee to *pull* money out of the issuer's account while a payment order *pushes* money out of the issuer's account into the payee's.

Suppose that Cooper, Inc., plans to buy Maxine, Inc.'s, water ride park in Columbia, South Carolina. Cooper could write a check for $1 million to Maxine on Cooper's CoopBank. When Maxine presents that check for payment, CoopBank will pull $1 million out of Cooper's account. If, however, Cooper sends a wire to Maxine for the same amount, CoopBank takes the money out of the account and then uses a wire to push that money to the local Federal Reserve bank. The Federal Reserve bank debits CoopBank's account there and pushes the funds to Maxine's bank, MaxBank. The Federal Reserve notifies MaxBank that it has received $1 million for Maxine. MaxBank

---

[22] You remember that the Electronic Fund Transfer Act regulates wire transfers involving consumers.

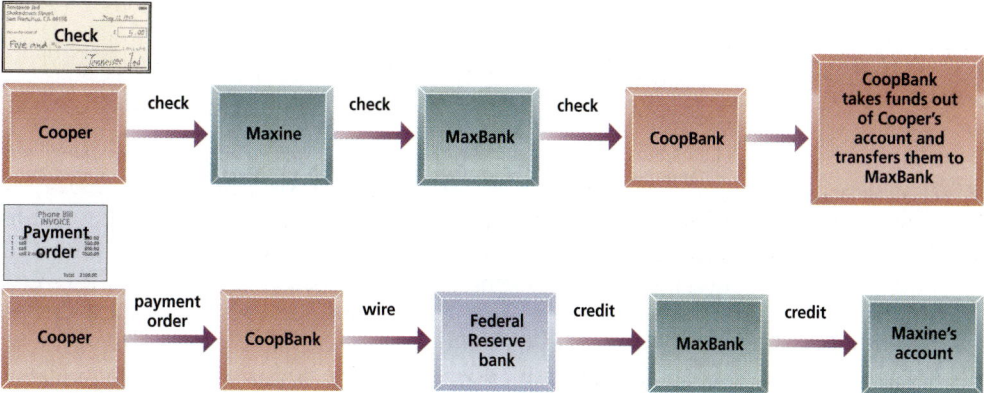

Exhibit 25.7

pushes the money into Maxine's account. Exhibit 25.7 illustrates the difference between checks and payment orders.

Article 4A uses the following terminology to describe the various participants in a wire transfer:

- *Originator.* The person who sends the first payment order in a transaction (Cooper)
- *Originator's Bank.* The bank that issues the originator's payment order (CoopBank)
- *Sender.* Anyone who gives instructions to a receiving bank (Cooper, CoopBank, and Federal Reserve bank)
- *Beneficiary.* The person who receives the payment order (Maxine)
- *Receiving Bank.* Any bank to which the sender's instructions are sent (CoopBank, Federal Reserve bank, and MaxBank)
- *Intermediary Bank.* Any receiving bank other than the originator's bank or the beneficiary's bank (Federal Reserve bank)
- *Beneficiary's Bank.* The bank identified in the payment order, which has an account in the beneficiary's name (MaxBank)

Exhibit 25.8 illustrates the terminology used to describe the participants in Cooper's wire transfer to Maxine.

Wire transfers often involve very large sums of money. What happens when mistakes occur, as mistakes inevitably will?

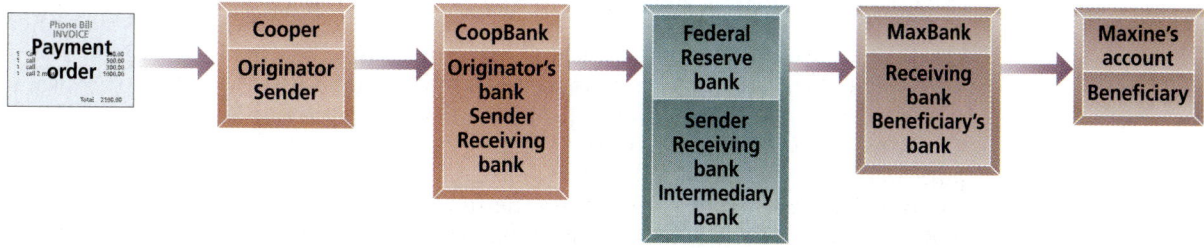

Exhibit 25.8

Bank Sends the Wrong Amount of Money

If a bank sends more money than the payment order specified, it is liable for the extra amount. Its recourse is to recover the excess from the beneficiary. If the bank sends too little money, the originator must pay only the amount sent, not the amount of the order.[23]

Bank Sends Money to the Wrong Person

If any bank issues a payment order to the wrong person, the bank is liable for the full amount of the payment. It can try to recover from the unintended recipient. The originator and any prior bank are not liable.[24]

Sometimes, a beneficiary's bank receives a payment order with an account name and number that do not match. If the bank notices the mismatch, it should not pay any account. If the bank does not notice and pays the account specified by the number, it is not liable even if that turns out to be the wrong account. The originator is liable. If the beneficiary's bank relies on the name instead of the number, it is liable and must reimburse the originator. As you can imagine, banks have a tendency to look only at the account number, not at the name. There is, however, one major exception to this rule. If a nonbank originator gives the wrong number and the right name, he is not liable when the payment is made to the wrong person unless his bank warned him that the beneficiary's bank would make payment based on the number, not the name.[25]

PRIVACY

Think about how much information your bank knows about you. Add to that what your insurance company, stock brokerage, and credit card companies know. Imagine that they can sell that information to anyone they wish, without telling you. Are you nervous yet?

This is the problem that the Gramm-Leach-Bliley Act of 1999 (GLB) sought to solve.[26] **Under this statute, banks and other financial institutions must disclose to consumers any non-public information they wish to reveal to third parties. A financial institution cannot disclose this private information if the consumer opts out (that is, denies permission).** Note that GLB permits financial institutions to provide information to third parties unless the consumer affirmatively requests privacy.

After this statute passed, consumers were inundated with a blizzard of notification forms. Thinking that these notices were junk mail, many customers never even bothered to open them. Consumer advocates complained that in many cases opting out was made deliberately difficult—the instructions were unclear and opting out generally had to be done by snail mail instead of online. Also, many companies failed to send out the required notices.

A small number of states have established rules that go further than the GLB. These states require an "opt-in" standard, which means that a financial institution cannot divulge private data unless the consumer affirmatively grants permission. The distinction between opt in and opt out is important—typically 30 percent of consumers opt out, while only 1 percent of consumers are expected to opt in.

---

[23] UCC §4A-303(a), (b).
[24] UCC §4A-303(c).
[25] UCC §4A-207.
[26] 15 U.S.C. §6801.

Chapter Conclusion

This area of law merits careful study for two reasons. First, it is important to everyone who has ever written a check or used an ATM, which is to say, virtually everyone. Second, the law is changing rapidly. A generation ago, no one would have asked "How much do I owe if my ATM card is stolen?" because ATMs did not exist. In some cases, the questions are still the same—"When can a bank pay a post-dated check?"—but now the answer is different.

Chapter Review

1. If a bank wrongfully dishonors an authorized check, it is liable to the customer for all actual and consequential damages.

2. A bank is not liable for paying the checks of an incompetent customer until it knows that the customer has been adjudicated incompetent. If a customer dies, the bank may continue to pay checks for 10 days after it learns of the death, unless it receives a stop payment order from someone claiming an interest in the account.

3. If a bank pays a check on which the issuer's name is forged, it must recredit the issuer's account.

4. If a bank pays a check that has been altered, the customer is liable only for the original terms of the check, and the bank is liable for the balance.

5. If a bank pays an incomplete check that was filled in by someone other than the original issuer, the bank is not liable unless it was on notice that the completion was improper.

6. A bank is not required to pay checks that are presented more than six months after their date, but it is not liable if it does pay.

7. A bank has no liability for paying a check before its date unless the customer notifies the bank in advance that the check is coming.

8. If a bank pays a check over a stop payment order, it is liable to the customer for any loss he suffers as a result. The bank is subrogated to the rights of both the customer and the payee.

9. A substitute check is legally the same as an original check. A bank that transfers or presents an electronic or a substitute check gives a *warranty of legal equivalency.* The bank is warranting to the drawer, the payee, the depositor, any indorser and to any bank that receives the check that the substitute check is an accurate image of the original check.

10. If a bank sends an electronic fund transfer card (for example, an ATM card) to a consumer who has not requested it, the card must be invalid until the consumer requests validation.

11. If, within 60 days of receiving a bank statement, a consumer tells the bank (either orally or in writing) that the account is in error, the bank must investigate and report the result of its investigation to the consumer within 10 business days.

12. When a thief uses a stolen ATM or debit card to withdraw money from a bank, the consumer is not liable for more than $50, provided she notifies the bank within two business days that the card has been stolen.

13. If a bank issues a payment order to the wrong person, the bank is liable for the full amount of the payment.

14. Banks and other financial institutions must disclose to consumers any non-public information they wish to reveal to third parties. A financial institution cannot disclose this private information if the consumer *opts out* (that is, denies permission).

Practice Test

1. On May 1, Lucile Fischer indorsed a $2,000 check. That same day, Nevada State Bank cashed the check and initiated collection through Valley Bank. Ninety days later, on July 28, Valley Bank notified State Bank that the check had been dishonored, stating "original lost in transit—account closed." On July 29, State Bank debited Fischer's account for $2,000. Fischer sued State Bank for a refund, alleging that the notice of dishonor had not been made in a timely fashion. State Bank initiated collection within one day of Fischer's indorsement and gave notice of dishonor within one day of receiving such notice. Must State Bank refund the $2,000?

2. Hassan Qassemzadeh had an account at the IBM Poughkeepsie Employees Federal Credit Union.

On December 1, he wrote a check for $9.60, which was altered and subsequently cashed for $9,000.60. In January, the Credit Union mailed his statement to his niece, as he had directed. This statement indicated that the check had been paid on January 6 for $9,000.60. Qassemzadeh notified the Credit Union of the alteration the following January. Is the Credit Union liable to Qassemzadeh for the amount of the altered check?

3. Begg & Daigle, Inc., wrote a check for $31,989.80 to Newwall Interior Partitions, Inc. Begg then asked Chemical Bank to stop payment on the check. In November, the bank accidentally paid the check. This payment was reflected in Begg's November statement, but Begg did not discover the mistaken payment until the following February. In the meantime, Begg sent a second check to Newwall in payment of the full amount. Begg demanded that the bank recredit its account for the amount of the stopped check. Is the bank liable for paying this check over the stop payment order?

4. This question appeared in the (Minneapolis) *Star Tribune* in 1993. How would you answer it?

    Q.—I have a payroll check issued to me that was misplaced and recently found. The check is from 1974 but nothing on the check says it must be cashed within a certain amount of time. Will a bank accept this check?

5. Woodhaven Knitting Mills wrote a check to Ava Industries for $19,500, drawn on Manufacturers Hanover Trust Co. Woodhaven asked Manufacturers Hanover to stop payment on the check, but the bank paid the check accidentally. The bank was subrogated to Woodhaven's interest against Ava, and Ava paid the bank $5,000. As a result, the bank's loss was reduced from $19,500 to $14,500. The bank filed suit against Woodhaven for $14,500, alleging that Woodhaven owed that sum to Ava. Does the bank have a valid claim against Woodhaven?

6. The following article appeared in the *Los Angeles Times*. Is there anything Elowsky could have done to reduce Prudential Bache's losses?

    A former Prudential Bache Finance vice president testified Friday that she accepted a $2-million postdated check from ZZZZ Best carpet cleaning kingpin Barry Minkow after he flew her to Los Angeles, showered her with flowers and took her out for an intimate seaside dinner in Malibu. After a "lark" of a weekend, Sheri Elowsky called Minkow to tell him she had approved a $225,000 extension on the young entrepreneur's $5 million credit line with Prudential Bache. Two days later, ZZZZ Best's stock dropped by nearly 25 percent. Minkow failed to return [Elowsky's] frantic phone calls. A day later, she reached two members of ZZZZ Best's board of directors, who told her that Minkow had resigned "for health reasons" and that the $2 million postdated check "would not be honored."[27]

7. Rev. Janet Hooper Ritchie knew that the shoe store at Buckland Hills mall in Manchester, Connecticut, would not accept a Discover credit card, so she stopped at an ATM for a $100 cash advance. Ritchie, a Congregational minister, inserted her card only to have it returned with a slip that said her withdrawal had been rejected. Ritchie thought that it was odd the slip did not bear the name of a bank. A few days later, she learned she was one of more than 100 customers bilked of confidential code information through the phony ATM. The crooks made off with a total of $100,000 after using the code information obtained by the ATM to make counterfeit bank cards. They used these fake cards to hit ATMs up and down the East Coast and pillage customer accounts. Who is liable for these losses—the banks or the customers whose accounts were looted?

8. **CPA QUESTION** In general, which of the following statements is correct concerning the priority among checks drawn on a particular account and presented to the drawee bank on a particular day?

    a. The checks may be charged to the account in any order convenient to the bank.
    b. The checks may be charged to the account in any order provided no charge creates an overdraft.
    c. The checks must be charged to the account in the order in which the checks were dated.
    d. The checks must be charged to the account in the order of lowest amount to highest amount to minimize the number of dishonored checks.

9. Harriet goes to the teller window and deposits a $1,000 tax refund check from the United States Treasury into her checking account. Two business days later, she sees the apartment of her dreams and wants to withdraw the entire $1,000 in cash to put down a security deposit and first month's rent on the apartment before anyone else sees it. She:

---

[27] Kim Murphy, "Minkow Wooed and Swindled Her, Loan Officer Says," *Los Angeles Times*, Oct. 22, 1988, Part 2, p. 1. Copyright 1988, Los Angeles Times.

a. Can withdraw only $100
b. Can withdraw only $400
c. Can withdraw the whole amount
d. Cannot withdraw anything

10. **ETHICS** Sandra Bisbey authorized her bank to make monthly electronic fund transfers to her life insurance company. In September, Bisbey's account did not have enough funds to cover this payment so no transfer was made. In October, Bisbey's account still lacked sufficient funds, but the bank made payments for both months anyway and sent two overdraft notices to her (but did not charge an overdraft fee). Bisbey, having forgotten her nonpayment in September, believed that the bank had erroneously made two payments in October. She called the bank to report this alleged error. Ten days later, an official of the bank telephoned her and explained that both payments had been proper. Bisbey filed suit under the EFTA, alleging that the bank unlawfully failed to inform her of the result of its investigation. Did the bank violate the EFTA? Is it liable even if its violation caused no harm to the plaintiff? The bank's actions actually benefited Bisbey: she received insurance coverage without paying an overdraft fee. Was it right for her to file suit under these circumstances? What guidance can you obtain from the ethics checklist in Chapter 2?

11. Shawmut Bank in Massachusetts transferred $10,000 from the account of American Optical Corp. via Fedwire to the account of Fernando Degan at the First American Bank in West Palm Beach, Florida. Although the money was intended for Degan and the payment order had his name alone, Shawmut listed an account number at First American that was jointly held by Degan and Joseph Merle, rather than the account that was held solely by Degan. Once the money was transferred into the joint account, Merle withdrew it. Shawmut sued First American, alleging that First American was liable for the mistaken transfer because it had placed the funds in a joint account, not in Degan's sole account as the payment order had indicated. Is First American liable to Shawmut?

Internet Research Problem

Visit the Federal Reserve Board's Web page at **http://beatty.westbuslaw.com** to find out where the Federal Reserve bank for your region is located. Where did you send the last check you mailed? Was it in the same region? What difference does it make if you sent a check out of the region?

12. **YOU BE THE JUDGE** WRITING PROBLEM Roger Duchow (owner of Duchow's Marine, Inc.) borrowed money from General Electric Capital Corp. (GECC) to buy boats for his business. He agreed that when he sold a boat, he would deposit the funds in a blocked account at Central Bank. Funds could be withdrawn from this blocked account only with GECC's signature. Duchow also had a separate, unrestricted account at Central. Duchow sold a yacht and, in an effort to defraud GECC, told the buyer to wire the $215,000 purchase price to the unrestricted account. The buyer's bank sent the wire transfer to an intermediary bank, Banker's Bank. But Banker's instructions to Central included only Duchow's name, omitting his account number. As luck would have it, the money was put in the blocked account. Duchow immediately ordered Central to transfer the funds to his unrestricted account, which Central did. Duchow quickly spent the money and had no other assets. Is Central liable to GECC? **Argument for Central:** The Bank simply followed instructions that Banker's had originally issued and that had been accidentally left off the payment order. Central was not to blame for Duchow's fraud. **Argument for GECC:** Central had an obligation to follow the wire instructions. But once the funds landed in the blocked account, Central had to make a non-clerical decision—to move or not to move. No law required it to transfer the funds, especially since the account clearly had GECC's name on it.

13. When Heidi submits a claim to her health insurance company, it refuses to reimburse her unless she also provides a copy of the check that she used to pay the doctor. The company wants proof that she has indeed paid. When she requests the cancelled check from her bank, it sends her a substitute check. Her health insurance company refuses to accept this check—it demands a copy of the original. How can Heidi provide proof to the insurance company?

14. **ROLE REVERSAL** Write a multiple-choice question that involves consumer liability for unauthorized transactions.

You can find further practice problems at http://beatty.westbuslaw.com or in the Study Guide that accompanies this text.

Secured Transactions

Dear Help-For-All:

Look, somebody out there is crazy. When I got out of school, I paid $18,000 for a used Jeep. I made every payment—*every one*—for over two years. I shelled out over 9,000 bucks for that car. Then I got laid off through no fault of my own which even my boss admits. I missed a few payments and the bank repossessed the car. OK, fair enough, I can see that. They auction off the Jeep. Now the bank's lawyer phones and says I'm still liable for over $5,000. What is this, a joke? I owe money for a car I can't even drive anymore? Come on, admit something is out of whack here.

Signed,

Still Sane, I Hope

Dear Still Sane,

I am sympathetic with your story but unfortunately the bank is entitled to its money. Here is how the law sees your plight. When you bought the car, you signed two documents: a note, in which you promised to pay the full balance owed, and a security agreement, which said that if you stopped making payments, the bank could repossess the vehicle and sell it.

There are two problems. First, even after two years of writing checks you might still have owed about $10,000 (because of interest). Second, cars depreciate quickly. Your $18,000 vehicle probably had a market value of about $8,000 thirty months later. The security agreement allowed the bank to sell the Jeep at auction, where prices are still lower. Your car evidently fetched about $5,000. That leaves a deficiency of $5,000—for which you are legally responsible, regardless of who is driving the car.

Hoping the busses are on time,

Help-for-Almost-All ■

REVISED ARTICLE 9: TERMS AND SCOPE[1]

We can sympathize with "Still Sane," but the bank is entitled to its money. The buyer and the bank had entered into a secured transaction, meaning that one party gave credit to another, demanding in return an assurance of repayment. Whether a used car lot sells a car on credit for $18,000, or a bank takes collateral for a $600 million corporate loan, the parties have created a secured transaction.

Article 9 of the Uniform Commercial Code (UCC) governs secured transactions in personal property. It is essential to understand the basics of this law because we live and work in a world economy based solidly—or shakily—on credit. Gravity may cause the earth to spin, but secured transactions keep the commercial world going 'round. The quantity of disputes tells us how important this law is: about *one-half of all UCC lawsuits* involve Article 9. This part of the Code employs terms not used elsewhere, so we must lead off with some definitions:

- **Fixtures** are goods that have become attached to real estate. For example, heating ducts are *goods* when a company manufactures them and also when it sells them to a retailer. But when a contractor installs the ducts in a new house, they become *fixtures*.

- **Security interest** means an interest in personal property or fixtures that secures the performance of some *obligation*. If an automobile dealer sells you a new car on credit and retains a security interest in the car, it means she is keeping legal rights *in your car*, including the right to drive it away if you fall behind in your payments. Usually, the obligation is to pay money, such as the money due on the new car. Occasionally, the obligation is to perform some other action, but in this chapter, we concentrate on the payment of money because that is what security interests are generally designed to ensure.

- **Secured party** is the person or company that holds the security interest. The automobile dealer who sells you a car on credit is the secured party.

---

[1]   In this chapter we use more footnotes than usual, for two reasons. First, Article 9 is a challenging series of interlocking provisions, and many readers will want to peruse the actual Code (in the appendix) to reinforce the myriad concepts. Second, the revised Article 9 is substantially rewritten and entirely renumbered; experienced practitioners may appreciate guidelines as they encounter new rules and discover familiar concepts in unexpected places.

- **Collateral** is the property subject to a security interest. When a dealer sells you a new car and keeps a security interest, the vehicle is the collateral.

- **Debtor and Obligor.** For our purposes, **debtor** refers to a person who has some original ownership interest in the collateral. (Having a security interest in the collateral does not make one a debtor.) If Alice borrows money from a bank and uses her Mercedes as collateral, she is the debtor because she owns the car. **Obligor** means a person who must repay money, or perform some other task.

   Throughout this chapter, the obligor and debtor will generally be the same person, but not always. When Alice borrows money from a bank and uses her Mercedes as collateral, she is the obligor, because she must repay the loan; as we know, Alice is also the debtor. However, suppose that Toby borrows money from a bank and provides no collateral; Jake co-signs the loan as a favor to Toby, using his Steinway piano as collateral. *Jake* is the only debtor, because he owns the piano. *Both parties* are obligors, because both have agreed to repay the loan.

- **Security agreement** is the contract in which the debtor gives a security interest to the secured party. This agreement protects the secured party's rights in the collateral.

- **Default** occurs when the debtor fails to pay money that is due, for example, on a loan or for a purchase made on credit. Default also includes other failures by the debtor, such as failing to keep the collateral insured.

- **Repossession** occurs when the secured party takes back collateral because the debtor has defaulted. Typically, the secured party will demand that the debtor deliver the collateral; if the debtor fails to do so, the secured party may find the collateral and take it.

- **Perfection** is a series of steps the secured party must take to protect its rights in the collateral against people other than the debtor. This is important because if the debtor cannot pay his debts, several creditors may attempt to seize the collateral, but only one may obtain it. To perfect its rights in the collateral, the secured party will typically file certain papers with a state agency.

- **Financing statement** is a document that the secured party files to give the general public notice that it has a secured interest in the collateral.

- **Record** refers to information written on paper *or* stored in an electronic or other medium.

- **Authenticate** means to sign a document *or* to use any symbol or encryption method that identifies the person and clearly indicates she is adopting the record as her own. You authenticate a security agreement when you sign the papers at an auto dealership. A corporation electronically authenticates a loan agreement by using the Internet to transmit an encrypted signature.

   Here is an example using the terms just discussed. A medical equipment company manufactures a CAT scan machine and sells it to a clinic for $2 million, taking $500,000 cash and the clinic's promise to pay the rest over five years. The clinic simultaneously authenticates a security agreement, giving the manufacturer a security interest in the CAT scan. If the clinic fails to make its payments, the manufacturer can repossess the machine. The manufacturer then electronically files a financing statement in an appropriate state agency. This *perfects* the manufacturer's rights, meaning that its security interest in the CAT scanner is now valid against all the world. Exhibit 26.1 illustrates this transaction.

   If the clinic goes bankrupt and many creditors try to seize its assets, the manufacturer has first claim to the CAT scan machine. The clinic's bankruptcy is of great

Exhibit 26.1

A simple security agreement:

(1) The manufacturer sells a CAT scan machine to a clinic, taking $500,000 and the clinic's promise to pay the balance over five years.

(2) The clinic simultaneously authenticates a security agreement.

(3) The manufacturer perfects by electronically filing a financing statement.

importance. When a debtor has money to pay all of its debts, there are no concerns about security interests. A creditor insists on a security interest to protect itself in the event the debtor *cannot* pay all of its debts. The secured party intends (1) to give itself a legal interest in specific property of the debtor and (2) to establish a priority claim in that property, ahead of other creditors. In this chapter, we look at a variety of issues that arise in secured transactions.

Article 9 Revisions

Throughout the 1990s, the American Law Institute and the National Conference of Commissioners on Uniform State Laws worked on significant revisions of Article 9. The drafters made their final recommendations in 2000, and the proposed revisions are now the law in all states. The revisions have expanded the number of transactions that Article 9 covers, and clarified the rules for creating, perfecting, and enforcing security interests. In a bow to e-commerce, Article 9 is now **medium-neutral,** meaning that it permits security interests to be created and filed electronically or in any other form (as well as on paper). The revisions also strengthen some provisions concerning consumer transactions.

All citations in this chapter are to the 2000 Revision of Article 9. The Uniform Commercial Code is available online at http://www.law.cornell.edu/ucc/ucc .table.html.[2] For the actual statutory versions of Article 9 that have been adopted state-by-state, go to http://www.law.cornell.edu/uniform/ucc.html.

Scope of Revised Article 9

Article 9 applies to any transaction intended to create a security interest in personal property or fixtures. The personal property used as collateral may be goods, such as cars or hats, but it may also be a variety of other things:

- **Instruments.** Drafts, checks, certificates of deposit, and notes may all be used as collateral, as may stocks, bonds, and other securities.

- **Investment Property,** which refers primarily to securities and related rights.

- **Documents of Title.** These are papers used by an owner of goods who ships or stores them. The documents are the owner's proof that he owns goods no longer in his possession. For example, an owner sending goods by truck will obtain a *bill of lading*, a receipt indicating where the goods will be shipped and who gets them when they arrive. Similarly, a *warehouse receipt* is the owner's receipt for goods stored at a warehouse. The owner may use these and other similar documents of title as collateral.

- **Account** means a right to receive payment for goods sold or leased. This includes, for example, accounts receivable, indicating various buyers owe a merchant money for goods they have already received. The category now includes health-care-insurance receivables.

- **Deposit Accounts.** Article 9 now covers security interests in deposit accounts (money placed in banks).

- **Commercial Tort Claims.** An organization that has filed a tort suit may use its claim as collateral. Personal injuries to individuals are not covered by this article.

- **General Intangibles.** This is a residual category, designed to include many kinds of collateral that do not appear elsewhere on the list, such as copyrights, patents, trademarks, goodwill, and the right to payment of some loans.

- **Chattel Paper.** This is a record that indicates two things: (1) an obligor owes money and (2) a secured party has a security interest in specific goods. Chattel paper most commonly occurs in a consumer sale on credit. If a dealer sells an air conditioner to a customer, who agrees in writing to make monthly payments and also agrees that the dealer has a security interest in the air conditioner, that agreement is chattel paper. The confusing point is that the same chattel paper may be collateral for a second security interest. The dealer who sells the air conditioner could use the chattel paper to obtain a loan. If the dealer gives the chattel paper to a bank as collateral for the loan, the bank has a security interest *in the chattel paper*, while the dealer continues to have a security interest *in the air conditioner*. **Electronic chattel paper** is the same thing except that it is an electronic record rather than a written one.

- **Goods** means movable things, including fixtures, crops, and manufactured homes. For purposes of secured transactions, the Code divides goods into additional categories. In some cases, the rights of the parties will depend upon what category the goods fall into. These are the key categories:
  - *Consumer goods* are those used primarily for personal, family, or household purposes.

---

[2] When researching any article of the Code online, be certain that you are reading the most recent revision.

- *Farm products* are crops, livestock, or supplies used directly in farming operations (as opposed to the business aspects of farming).

- *Inventory* consists of goods held by someone for sale or lease, such as all of the beds and chairs in a furniture store.

- *Equipment* refers to things used in running a business, such as the desks, telephones, and computers needed to operate a retail store.

cyberLaw

Software. Article 9 takes into account the increasingly important role that computer software plays in all business. The Code distinguishes *software* from *goods,* and this becomes important when competing creditors are fighting over both a computer system and the software inside it. A program embedded in a computer is goods *if* it is customarily considered part of those goods *or if* by purchasing the goods the owner acquires the right to use the program. A program that does *not* meet those criteria is termed *software,* and will be treated differently for some purposes. ◆

In sum, Article 9 applies anytime the parties intended to create a security interest in any of the items listed above.

ATTACHMENT OF A SECURITY INTEREST

Attachment is a vital step in a secured transaction. This means that the secured party has taken three steps to create an enforceable security interest:

- The two parties made a security agreement, *and either* the debtor has *authenticated a security agreement* describing the collateral *or* the secured party has obtained *possession* or *control;*

- The secured party has given value to obtain the security agreement; and

- The debtor has rights in the collateral.[3]

© AP PHOTO/WILFREDO LEE

Many "big ticket" consumer sales are secured transactions.

Agreement

Without an agreement, there can be no security interest. Generally, the agreement will be in writing and signed by the debtor, or electronically recorded and authenticated by the debtor. The agreement must reasonably identify the collateral. A description of collateral by *type* is often acceptable. For example, a security agreement may properly describe the collateral as "all equipment in the store at 123 Periwinkle Street."[4] In a security agreement for consumer goods, however, a description by type is *not* sufficient, and more specificity is required.

---

[3]   UCC §9-203.

[4]   A security agreement may not use a **super-generic term** such as "all of Smith's personal property." We will see later that, by contrast, such a super-generic description is legally adequate in a *financing statement.*

A security agreement at a minimum might:

- State that Happy Homes, Inc., and Martha agree that Martha is buying an Arctic Co. refrigerator and identify the exact unit by its serial number;

- Give the price, the down payment, the monthly payments, and interest rate;

- State that because Happy Homes is selling Martha the refrigerator on credit, it has a security interest in the refrigerator; and

- Provide that if Martha defaults on her payments, Happy Homes is entitled to repossess the refrigerator.

An actual security agreement will add many details, such as Martha's obligation to keep the refrigerator in good condition and to deliver it to the store if she defaults; a precise definition of "default"; and how Happy Homes may go about repossessing the goods if Martha defaults.

Control and Possession

In many cases, the security agreement need not be in writing if the parties have an oral agreement and the secured party has either **control** or **possession.** For many kinds of collateral it is safer for the secured party actually to take the item than to rely upon a security agreement. The rules follow.

Control

For deposit accounts, electronic chattel paper and certain other collateral, the security interest attaches if the secured party has *control*. The Code specifies exactly what the secured party must do to obtain control for each type of collateral. In a general sense, *control means that the secured party has certain exclusive rights to dispose of the collateral.*

- Deposit account (in a bank). The secured party has control if it is itself the bank holding the deposit or if the debtor has authorized the bank to dispose of funds according to the secured party's instructions.

- Electronic chattel paper. A secured party has control of electronic chattel paper when it possesses the only authoritative copy of it, and the record(s) designate the secured party as the assignee. This means that the parties have agreed on an electronic method to verify the uniqueness of the record, so that any copies of the electronic original are clearly recognizable as reproductions.

- Investment property and letter-of-credit rights. The Code specifies analogous methods of controlling investment properties and letter-of-credit rights.[5]

Possession

For most other forms of collateral, including goods, securities, and most other items, a security interest attaches if the secured party has *possession*. For example, if you loan your neighbor $175,000 and he gives you a Winslow Homer watercolor as collateral, you have an attached security interest in the painting once it is in your possession. It would still be wise to put the agreement in writing, to be certain both parties understand all terms and can prove them if necessary, but the writing is not legally required.

The following case is typical of Article 9 disputes in that it was fought out in bankruptcy court. A debtor claimed to have a security interest in property owned by a bankrupt company. Had the parties made a security agreement? The court decided the case based on former Article 9, but the outcome would be the same under the revised Code.

---

[5] *Control* is described in the following sections: 9-104 (deposit accounts), 9-105 (electronic chattel paper), 9-106 (investment property), and 9-107 (letter-of-credit rights).

In Re CFLC, INC.

209 B.R. 508, 1997 Bankr. LEXIS 821
United States Bankruptcy Appellate Panel of the Ninth Circuit, 1997

Facts: Expeditors was a freight company that supervised importing and exporting for Everex Systems, Inc. Expeditors negotiated rates and services for its client and frequently had possession of Everex's goods. During a 17-month period, Expeditors sent over 300 invoices to Everex. Each invoice stated that the customer either had to accept all of the invoice's terms or to pay cash, receiving no work on credit. One of those terms gave Expeditors a general lien on all of the customer's property in its possession. In other words, if the customer failed to pay a bill, Expeditors claimed the right to retain the goods, auction them, and keep enough of the proceeds to pay its overdue bills.

Everex filed for bankruptcy. Expeditors expedited its way into the court proceedings, claiming the right to sell Everex's goods, worth about $81,000. The trial judge rejected the claim, ruling that Expeditors lacked a valid security interest. Expeditors appealed.

Issue: Did Expeditors have a security interest in Everex's goods?

Excerpts from Judge Ollason's Decision: Under the common law, silence in the face of an offer is not an acceptance, unless there is a relationship between the parties or a previous course of dealing pursuant to which silence would be understood as acceptance.

In this case, Expeditors and Everex had been doing business for about one and one-half years. They had never discussed the terms of the invoice nor negotiated for a security interest. Everex had never expressly acknowledged the invoice terms by accepting or objecting to them, nor did it take actions which acknowledged Expeditors' alleged general lien on the goods. Its only pertinent acts were its payment of the invoices and silence as to the added terms.

The evidence consisting of Everex's receipt and payment of invoices containing terms for a general lien in the goods in favor of Expeditors did not amount to an agreement for such a security interest, pursuant to [revised section 9-102]. As a matter of law, the repetitive sending by Expeditors to Everex of terms which Expeditors wished to be made part of the oral contract was not evidence of course of dealing because an agreement did not exist as to the security interest which could be supplemented by such evidence.

Affirmed. ∎

Value

For the security interest to attach, the secured party must give value. Usually, the value will be apparent. If a bank loans $400 million to an airline, that money is the value, and the bank, therefore, may obtain a security interest in the planes that the airline is buying. If a store sells a living room set to a customer for a small down payment and two years of monthly payments, the value given is the furniture.

Future Value

The parties may also agree that some of the value will be given in the future. For example, a finance company might extend a $5 million line of credit to a retail store, even though the store initially takes only $1 million of the money. The remaining credit is available whenever the store needs it to purchase inventory. The Code considers the entire $5 million line of credit to be value.[6]

---

[6]   UCC §9-204(c).

Debtor Rights in the Collateral

The debtor can only grant a security interest in goods if he has some legal right to those goods himself. Typically, the debtor owns the goods. But a debtor may also give a security interest if he is leasing the goods or even if he is a bailee, meaning that he is lawfully holding them for someone else. Suppose Importer receives a shipment of scallops on behalf of Seafood Wholesaler. Wholesaler asks Importer to hold the scallops for three days as a favor, and to keep a customer happy, Importer agrees. Importer then arranges a $150,000 loan from a bank, using the scallops as collateral. Although Importer has acted unethically, it does have *some right* in the collateral—the right to hold them for three days. That is enough to satisfy this rule.

By contrast, suppose Railroad is transporting 10 carloads of cattle on behalf of Walter, the owner. A devious Meat Dealer uses forged documents to trick Railroad into believing that Meat Dealer is entitled to the animals. Meat Dealer trucks the cattle away and uses them to obtain a bank loan, giving the bank a security interest in the animals. That "security interest" has never attached and is invalid, because Dealer had *no* legal interest in the cattle. When Walter, the rightful owner, locates his cattle, he may take them back. The bank can only hope to find the deceitful Dealer, who in fact has probably disappeared.

Result

Once the security interest has attached to the collateral, the secured party is protected against the debtor. If the debtor fails to pay, the secured party may repossess the collateral.

Attachment to Future Property

The security agreement may specify that the security interest attaches to personal property that the debtor does not yet possess but might obtain in the future.

After-Acquired Property

After-acquired property refers to items that the debtor obtains after the parties have made their security agreement. **The parties may agree that the security interest attaches to after-acquired property.**[7] Basil is starting a catering business, but owns only a beat-up car. He borrows $55,000 from the Pesto Bank, which takes a security interest in the car. But Pesto also insists on an after-acquired clause. When Basil purchases a commercial stove, cooking equipment, and freezer, Pesto's security interest attaches to each item as Basil acquires it.

Proceeds

Proceeds are whatever is obtained by a debtor who sells the collateral or otherwise disposes of it. **The secured party automatically obtains a security interest in the proceeds of the collateral, unless the security agreement states otherwise.**[8] Suppose the Pesto Bank obtains a security interest in Basil's $4,000 freezer. Basil then decides he needs a larger model and sells the original freezer to his neighbor for $3,000. The $3,000 cash is proceeds, in which Pesto automatically obtains a security interest. If for some reason the parties do not want the security interest to extend to proceeds (which would be very unusual), they must make that clear in the security agreement.

---

[7] UCC §9-204(a).
[8] UCC §9-203(f).

PERFECTION

Nothing Less than Perfection

Once the security interest has attached to the collateral, the secured party is protected *against the debtor*. Pesto Bank loaned money to Basil and has a security interest in all of his property. If Basil defaults on his loan, Pesto may insist he deliver the goods to the bank. If he fails to do that, the bank can seize the collateral. But Pesto's security interest is valid only against Basil; if a third person claims some interest in the goods, the bank may never get them. For example, Basil might have taken out *another* loan, from his friend Olive, and used the same property as collateral. Olive knew nothing about the bank's original loan. To protect itself against Olive, and all other parties, the bank must *perfect* its interest.

There are several kinds of perfection:

- Perfection by filing
- Perfection by possession
- Perfection of consumer goods
- Perfection of movable collateral and fixtures

In some cases, the secured party will have a choice of which method to use; in other cases, only one method works.

Perfection by Filing

The most common way to perfect is by filing a financing statement with one or more state agencies. A **financing statement** gives the names of all parties, describes the collateral, and outlines the security interest, enabling any interested person to learn about it. Suppose the Pesto Bank obtains a security interest in Basil's catering equipment and then perfects by filing with the Secretary of State in the state capital. When Basil asks his friend Olive for a loan, she will check the records to see if anyone has a security interest in the catering equipment. Olive's search uncovers Basil's previous security agreement, and she realizes it would be unwise to make the loan. If Basil were to default, the collateral would go straight to Pesto Bank, leaving Olive empty-handed. See Exhibit 26.2.

Article 9 prescribes one form, to be used nationwide for financing statements.[9] The financing form is available online at **http://www.dos.state.ny.us/corp/pdfs/ucc1.pdf**. Remember that the filing may be done on paper or electronically.

If the collateral is either *accounts* or *general intangibles*, filing is the only way to perfect. Suppose Nester uses his copyright in a screenplay as collateral for a loan. The bank that gives him the loan may perfect *only* by filing.

The most common problems that arise in filing cases are (1) whether the financing statement contained enough information to put other people on notice of the security interest and (2) whether the secured party filed the papers in the right place.

Contents of the Financial Statement

A financing statement is sufficient if it provides the name of the debtor, the name of the secured party and an indication of the collateral.[10]

---

[9]   UCC §9-521.
[10]   UCC §9-502(a).

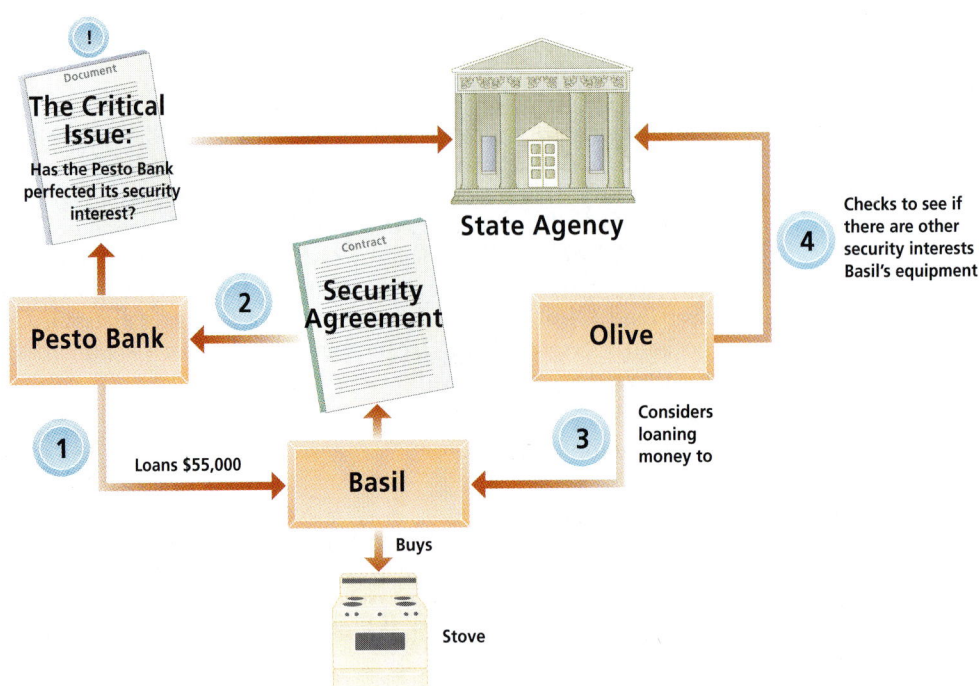

Exhibit 26.2
The Pesto Bank:
(1) Loans money to Basil and
(2) Takes a security interest in his equipment.
Later, when Olive:
(3) Considers loaning Basil money, she will
(4) Check to see if any other creditors already have a security interest in his goods.

The name of the debtor is critical because that is what an interested person will use to search among the millions of other financing statements on file. Faulty descriptions of the debtor's name have led to thousands of disputes and untold years of litigation, as subsequent creditors have failed to locate any record of an earlier claim on the debtor's property. In response, the Code is now very precise about what name must be used. If the debtor is a "registered organization," such as a corporation, limited partnership, or limited liability company, the official, registered name of the company is the only one acceptable. If the debtor is a person, or an unregistered organization (such as a club), then the *correct* name is required. Trade names are not sufficient. Because misnamed debtors have created so much conflict, the Code now offers a straightforward test: if a computer search under the debtor's *correct name* would reveal the financing statement, then the record is valid.[11]

The collateral must be described reasonably so that another party contemplating a loan to the debtor will understand which property is already secured. A financing statement could properly state that it applies to "all inventory in the debtor's Houston warehouse." If the debtor has given a security interest in everything he owns, then it is sufficient to state simply that the financing statement covers "all assets" or "all personal property."

---

[11] UCC §9-506(c).

Even though revised Article 9 has provided considerable detail about how to indicate the debtor's name, there are still some holes that need filling in, as the following case indicates.

ERWIN V. BUCKLIN NATIONAL BANK

2003 WL 21513158
United States Bankruptcy Court, District of Kansas, 2003

Facts: The Bucklin National Bank ("Bank") had a security interest in Michael Erwin's machinery and equipment. The Bank filed a financing statement describing the collateral and giving the debtor's name as "Mike Erwin," which it had used in all loan papers.

Three years later, Erwin filed for bankruptcy. On court papers, his name was given as "Michael A. Erwin." The court appointed a trustee, whose job was to gather Erwin's assets and divide them among creditors with legitimate claims. The trustee did an electronic search for secured parties, using the name "Michael A. Erwin," which did not reveal the Bank's security interest. Later, when the Bank claimed Erwin's machinery and equipment, the trustee argued that the security interest was never perfected.

In court, the parties agreed that a search for "Michael A. Erwin" would not have led to the Bank's security interest in Erwin's property, while a search for "Erwin," "M. Erwin," or "Mike Erwin" would have revealed the Bank's financing statement.

Issue: Did the Bank perfect its security interest?

Excerpts from Judge Nugent's Decision: Some new concepts and rules have been injected by revised Article Nine, particularly § 9-503(a) and § 9-506, that give further guidance concerning the debtor name requirement and the seriously misleading standard. § 9-503(a) gives specific rules for determining the sufficiency of a debtor's name, but only for certain types of debtor organizations and entities: corporations, estates, and trusts. In the case of debtor corporations or registered organizations, the name of the debtor is the name on file in the state of organization. However, § 9-503(a) does not give any specific criteria for the sufficiency of an individual's name. Accordingly, the Court concludes that the full legal name of an individual debtor is not necessarily required on a financing statement in order to be sufficient under § 9-503(a).

Now, § 9-506 deems a financing statement seriously misleading if the debtor's name does not comply with § 9-503(a), *unless* a search under the debtor's correct name, using the filing office's "standard search logic," would reveal the financing statement.

This is the crux of the instant case. The trustee contends that debtor's "correct name" is his full legal name and since the search logic under the debtor's full legal name did not reveal the Bank's financing statement, it is seriously misleading. The Bank, of course, argues that Mike Erwin is debtor's "correct name," and a search under this name, using the Secretary of State Office's search logic, would have revealed the Bank's financing statement. The Court must determine the meaning of "correct name."

Under the revised UCC, the Secretary of State's Office is required to adopt "filing-office" rules to implement revised Article Nine. These new regulations contain the search logic standards employed by the Secretary of State's office. The search standards do not require a search by the debtor's "legal name," "full name," or "correct name." Moreover, with knowledge of the search logic standards, the person requesting a search can formulate a narrow or broad search of the debtor's name and fairly predict the search results. The regulations permit a party to search the UCC records by nothing more than an individual debtor's last name, the broadest of search requests. Therefore, the Court concludes that as to individuals, drafters of search requests should exercise some reasonable diligence in formulating those requests.

The Bank used "Mike Erwin" as the debtor's name on the financing statement. Was the name of debtor sufficient under § 9-503(a)? The Court concludes that it was. Since § 9-503(a) does not *require* the use of an individual debtor's full legal name, nor expressly prohibit nicknames or common derivations for an individual debtor's first name, the use of Mike Erwin was a sufficient debtor name.

The Court concludes that a reasonably diligent searcher would have requested searches not only for "Michael A. Erwin," but also for "Erwin" or "Erwin, M." As the record shows, these latter two requests would have yielded the Bank's financing statement.

The Bank is entitled to judgment as a matter of law. ■

Public Policy

The bank concludes that a reasonably prudent searcher would look under different names. Why not put that burden on creditors? After all, they initiate the whole process by drafting the financial statement. We could if we chose demand that Bucklin Bank, intent upon protecting its security interest against all the world, take the painless steps of filing under "Michael Erwin," "Michael A. Erwin," and "Mike Erwin." Which approach is better?   ◆

Debtor's Signature. Notice one important item that is not required on a financing statement: the debtor's signature. The drafters have greatly facilitated electronic filing by eliminating the old requirement that a debtor sign. Does this allow a secured party to create any financing statement it wishes? No. The debtor must have entered into a valid security agreement before the secured party is entitled to file any financing statement. Of course, there is the possibility of a fraudulent filing, but the drafters reasoned that the efficiency achieved far outweighs the dangers.

Place of Filing

This is a big country, and potential creditors do not want to stagger from one end of it to the other to learn whether particular collateral is already secured elsewhere. Article 9 specifies *where* a secured party must file. These provisions may vary from state to state, so it is essential to check local law, because a misfiled record accomplishes nothing. The general rules are as follows.

A secured party must file **in the state of the debtor's location.** An *individual* is located at his principal residence. If Luigi, the debtor, lives in Baltimore, works in Virginia, and has a vacation home in Key West, a secured party must file in Maryland. An organization that has only one place of business is located in that state. If the organization has more than one place of business, it is located at its chief executive office.[12]

Article 9 prescribes central filing within the state for most types of collateral. For *goods*, the central location will typically be the Secretary of State's office, although a state may designate some other office if it wishes. For *fixtures*, the secured party generally has a choice between filing in the same central office that is used for goods, or filing in the local county office that would be used to file real estate mortgages.[13]

Duration of Filing

Once a financing statement has been filed, it is effective for five years (except for a manufactured home, where it lasts 30 years). After five years the statement will expire and leave the secured party unprotected, unless she files a continuation statement within six months prior to expiration. The continuation statement is valid for an additional five years and a secured party may file one periodically, forever.[14] You may see a standard amendment form, which can be used for a continuation statement, at http://www.dos.state.ny.us/corp/pdfs/ucc3.pdf.

Perfection by Possession or Control

For most types of collateral, in addition to filing, a secured party generally may perfect by possession or control. So if the collateral is a diamond brooch or 1,000 shares of stock, a bank may perfect its security interest by holding the items until the loan is paid off. When the debtor gives collateral to the secured party, it is often called a **pledge:** the debtor pledges her goods to secure her performance, and the secured

---

[12] UCC §9-307.
[13] UCC §9-501.
[14] UCC §9-515.

A bank may wish to perfect its security interest by holding this brooch in its vault.

party (sometimes called the **pledgee**) takes the goods to perfect its interest.

Possession

When may a party use possession? Whenever the collateral is **goods, negotiable documents, instruments, money, chattel paper that is tangible (as opposed to electronic), or most securities.**[15]

Perfection by possession has some advantages. First, notice to other parties is very effective. No reasonable finance company assumes that it can obtain a security interest in a Super Bowl championship ring when *another creditor* already holds the ring. Second, possession enables the creditor to ensure that the collateral will not be damaged during the life of the security interest. A bank that loans money based on a rare painting may worry about the painting's condition, but it knows the painting is safe if it is locked up in the bank's vault. Third, if the debtor defaults, a secured party obviously has no difficulties repossessing goods that it already holds.

Of course, for some collateral, possession is impractical. If a consumer buys a new yacht on credit, the seller can hardly expect to perfect its security interest by possession. The buyer would become edgy sailing the boat around the dealer's parking lot. In such a case, the secured party must perfect by filing.

Mandatory Possession

A party *must* perfect a security interest in money by taking possession.[16] Money is easy to transfer and impossible to distinguish from other cash. So a party with a security interest in money must take possession to perfect. Suppose Ed's Real Estate claims that Jennifer, a former employee, has opened her own realty business in violation of their noncompetition agreement. Jennifer promises to move her business to another city within 90 days, and Ed agrees not to sue. To secure Jennifer's promise to move, Ed takes a security interest in $50,000 cash. If she fails to move on time, he is entitled to the money. To perfect that interest, Ed must take possession of the money and hold it until Jennifer is out of town.

Control

A security interest in investment property, deposit accounts, letter-of-credit rights, and electronic chattel paper may be perfected by control.[17] We have described control above, in the section on attachment. In general, *control means that the secured party has certain exclusive rights to dispose of the collateral.* Recall, for example, that a secured party which is a bank has control of any deposit account located in that bank. **Mandatory Control. Security interests in deposit accounts and letter-of-credit rights may be perfected *only* by control.**[18] Once again, filing would be ineffectual

---

[15] UCC §9-313.

[16] UCC §9-312(b)(3). Note that this section is an important change from the former article, which required possession for money *and* instruments. The revised article permits perfection of instruments by filing, which will be useful when a debtor has a continuous stream of notes arriving from the makers of the notes (borrowers).

[17] UCC §9-314(a).

[18] UCC §9-312(b)(1).

with forms of collateral so easily moved, and the Code will grant perfection only to a secured party that has control.

Care of the Collateral

Possession and control give several advantages to the secured party, but also one important duty: **a secured party must use reasonable care in the custody and preservation of collateral in her possession or control.**[19] If the collateral is something tangible, such as a painting, the secured party must take reasonable steps to ensure that it is safe from harm. What does "reasonable care" mean when the collateral is something as volatile as shares of stock? The following case is an early response under the revised article.

LAYNE V. BANK ONE

395 F.3d 271
United States Court of Appeals for the Sixth Circuit, 2005

Facts: Charles E. Johnson was the founder and CEO of PurchasePro.com, Inc., and Geoff Layne was its marketing director. When their Internet stock went public, both officers suddenly owned shares worth millions of dollars. To increase his liquidity, Johnson took out a loan for $2.8 million from Bank One, and Layne borrowed $3.25 million. Each secured the loan with shares of PurchasePro stock.

The loan agreement required a loan-to-value (LTV) ratio of 50 percent, meaning that the value of the shares had to be at least double the outstanding loan balance. If the value of the shares sank below the required level, the two men could either pay off some of the loan or offer additional security. If the two borrowers failed to remedy the problem, the Bank was entitled (but not obligated) to sell the shares. Johnson secured his loan with $6.9 million worth of PurchasePro stock.

In February, Internet stocks suddenly plummeted, and both loans immediately exceeded their LTV ratio. Johnson and Layne spoke with the Bank several times, stating that they would offer additional collateral. During March and April, more calls went back and forth, with the debtors occasionally suggesting that the collateral be sold, while at other times agreeing to provide more security. Finally, in July, over a four-day period, the Bank sold Johnson's PurchasePro shares for $524,757, less than 10 percent of its original worth.

Johnson and Layne both filed suit against the Bank, claiming that it failed to exercise reasonable care of the collateral. The trial court gave judgment for the Bank, and the plaintiffs appealed.

Issue: Did the Bank exercise reasonable care of the shares?

Excerpts from Judge Moore's Decision: We first consider Johnson's argument that Bank One violated a duty under Kentucky law to preserve the value of the collateral held in its possession. With respect to the regulation of secured transactions, Kentucky has adopted the Uniform Commercial Code ("U.C.C."), which states that "a secured party shall use reasonable care in the custody and preservation of collateral in the secured party's possession. In the case of chattel paper or an instrument, reasonable care includes taking necessary steps to preserve rights against prior parties unless otherwise agreed."

The comment to § 9-207 states that the provision "imposes a duty of care, similar to that imposed on a pledgee at common law, on a secured party in possession of collateral," and cites to [a different treatise, called the Restatement of Security. The explanatory comment in that Restatement says,] "The pledgee is not liable *for a decline in the value* of pledged instruments, even if timely action could have prevented such decline." In the context of pledged stock, courts have used this language from the Restatement to hold that "a bank has no duty to its borrower to sell collateral stock of declining value."

▼

---

[19] UCC §9-207.

As [another court] stated, "It is the borrower who makes the investment decision to purchase stock. A lender in these situations merely accepts the stock as collateral, and does not thereby itself invest in the issuing firm. Given the volatility of the stock market, a requirement that a secured party sell shares held as collateral, at a particular time, would be to shift the investment risk from the borrower to the lender."

We conclude that under Kentucky law a lender has no obligation to sell pledged stock held as collateral merely because of a market decline. If the borrower is concerned with the decline in the share value, it is his responsibility, rather than that of the lender, to take appropriate remedial steps, such as paying off the loan in return for the collateral, substituting the pledged stock with other equally valued assets, or selling the pledged stock himself and paying off the loan. ■

Devil's Advocate

Although a bank cannot be expected to do a perfect job anticipating stock price changes, it must perform reasonably, as we would expect from an experienced financial institution. Bank One failed. The bank should either have sold the stock quickly, or decided to wait and give the shares a chance to rebound. Instead, it foolishly split the difference, dithering while PurchasePro lost more than 90 percent of its value, and *then* selling, when the shares were nearly worthless. We would get a more prudent hold/sell strategy from a chimpanzee flipping coins. Bank One is liable. ◆

Perfection of Consumer Goods

The Code gives special treatment to security interests in most consumer goods. Merchants sell a vast amount of consumer goods on credit. They cannot file a financing statement for every bed, television, and stereo for which a consumer owes money. Yet perfecting by possession is also impossible, since the consumer will take the goods home. To understand the UCC's treatment of these transactions, we need to know two terms. The first is *consumer goods*, which as we saw earlier means goods used primarily for personal, family, or household purposes. The second term is *purchase money security interest*.

A purchase money security interest (PMSI) is one taken by the person who sells the collateral or by the person who advances money so the debtor can buy the collateral.[20] Assume the Gobroke Home Center sells Marion a $5,000 stereo system. The sales document requires a payment of $500 down and $50 per month for the next 300 years, and gives Gobroke a security interest in the system. Because the security interest was "taken by the seller," the document is a PMSI. It would also be a PMSI if a bank had loaned Marion the money to buy the system and the document gave the bank a security interest.

But aren't all security interests PMSIs? No, many are not. Suppose a bank loans a retail company $800,000 and takes a security interest in the store's present inventory. That is not a PMSI since the store did not use the money to purchase the collateral.

---

[20] UCC §9-103. This is a complete rewrite of the former PMSI section. The most important substantive changes concern *non-consumer* PMSIs, and are only of passing interest to us. One noteworthy point is that in non-consumer cases, the section explicitly permits collateral to have *dual status,* meaning that goods can be subject simultaneously to a PMSI and an ordinary security interest. Suppose a bank loans $100,000 to a restaurant to purchase furniture, taking a PMSI in the goods. Two years later, the restaurant refinances, agreeing to borrow an additional $25,000, and using the furniture as collateral for the entire $125,000. The bank has a PMSI *only* for $100,000; as to the remaining $25,000, the bank has an ordinary security interest. The difference may be crucial if competing creditors seek to repossess the same tables and chairs. The bank should obtain priority for its PMSI, but may not fare as well for the remaining security interest.

What must Gobroke Home Center do to perfect its security interest? Nothing. **A PMSI in consumer goods perfects automatically, without filing.**[21] Marion's new stereo is clearly consumer goods, because she will use it only in her home. Gobroke's security interest is a PMSI, so the interest has perfected automatically. (See Exhibit 26.3.)

Exhibit 26.3
A purchase money security interest can arise in either of two ways. In the first example, a store sells a stereo to a consumer on credit; the consumer in turn signs a PMSI, giving the store a security interest in the stereo. In the second example, the consumer buys the stereo with money loaned from a bank; the consumer signs a PMSI giving the *bank* a security interest in the stereo.

cyberLaw

A PMSI may be created only in goods, fixtures, or software.[22] No other types of collateral are allowed. Recall that for Article 9 purposes, *software* is defined to mean a computer program that is not embedded in hardware. A seller may obtain a PMSI in software if the debtor is buying the program to run hardware purchased in the same transaction and if the secured party also has a PMSI in that hardware. Merry Bank advances $250,000 to Ben's Books to enable Ben to purchase a new computer system and some separate software to run the computer. Merry may acquire a PMSI in the software, provided it is obtaining a PMSI in the computer as well. ◆

Perfection of Movable Collateral and Fixtures

The rules for perfection are slightly different for security interests in movable goods, such as cars and boats, and in fixtures. We look briefly at each.

---

[21] UCC §9-309(1).
[22] UCC §9-103(b)(c).

Movable Goods Generally

Goods that are easily moved create problems for creditors. Suppose a bank in Colorado loans Dorothy money, takes a security interest in her Degas sculpture, and perfects its interest in the proper state offices in Colorado. But then Dorothy moves to Ohio and uses the same collateral for another loan. A lender in Ohio will never discover the security interest perfected in Colorado. If Dorothy defaults, who gets the sculpture?

For most collateral, when the *debtor moves* to a new state, a security interest from the old state remains perfected for four months; when the *collateral is transferred* to a new state, the security interest remains perfected for one year.[23] If the secured party re-perfects in the new state within the time limits mentioned, the security interest remains valid until it would normally expire. If the secured party fails to re-perfect in the new state, the security interest lapses. Suppose Dorothy takes her Degas into Ohio on February 10 and on March 5 uses it as collateral for a new loan. The original Colorado bank still has a valid security interest in the sculpture and may seize the art if Dorothy defaults. But if Dorothy applies for her new loan on October 10, and the Colorado bank has failed to re-perfect, the Colorado bank has lost its protection.

Motor Vehicles and the Like

The Code provisions about perfecting generally do not apply to motor vehicles, trailers, mobile homes, boats, or farm tractors.[24] Because all of these are so numerous and so mobile, filing may be ineffective and possession is impossible. As a result, almost all states have created special laws to deal with this problem. Anyone offering or taking a security interest in any of these goods must consult local law.

State title laws generally require that a security interest in an automobile be noted directly on the vehicle's certificate of title. A driver needs a certificate of title to obtain registration plates, so the law presumes that the certificate will stay with the car. By requiring that the security interest be noted on the certificate, the law gives the best possible notice to anyone thinking of buying the car or accepting it as collateral. Generally, if a buyer or lender examines the certificate and finds no security interest, he may accept the vehicle for sale, or as collateral, and take it free of any interest. In most states, the same requirement applies to boats.

Fixtures

Fixtures, you recall, are goods that have become attached to real estate. A security interest may be created in goods that *are* fixtures and may continue in goods that *become* fixtures; however, the Code does not permit a security interest in ordinary building materials, such as lumber and concrete, once they become part of a construction project.

The primary disputes in these cases are between a creditor holding a security interest in a fixture, such as a furnace, and another creditor with rights in the real estate, such as a bank holding a mortgage on the house. The issues are complex, involving local real property law, and we cannot undertake here a thorough explanation of them. However, we can highlight the issues that arise so that you can anticipate the potential problems. Common disputes concern:

- The status of the personal property when the security interest was created (was it still goods or already a fixture?);
- The status of the real estate (does the debtor *also* have a legal interest in the *real property?*);

---

[23] UCC §9-316(a).
[24] UCC §9-311(a)(2).

- The type of perfection (which was recorded first, the security interest in the fixture or the real estate? does the secured party hold a PMSI?); and
- The physical status of the fixture (can it be removed without harming the real estate?).[25]

Any creditor who considers accepting collateral that might become a fixture must anticipate these problems and clarify with the debtor exactly what she plans to do with the goods. Armed with that information, the creditor should consult local law on fixtures and make an appropriate security agreement (or refuse to accept the fixture as collateral).

PROTECTION OF BUYERS

Generally, once a security interest is perfected, it remains effective regardless of whether the collateral is sold, exchanged, or transferred in some other way. Bubba's Bus Co. needs money to meet its payroll, so it borrows $150,000 from Francine's Finance Co., which takes a security interest in Bubba's 180 buses and perfects its interest. Bubba, still short of cash, sells 30 of his buses to Antelope Transit. But even that money is not enough to keep Bubba solvent: he defaults on his loan to Francine and goes into bankruptcy. Francine pounces on Bubba's buses. May she repossess the 30 that Antelope now operates? Yes. The security interest continued in the buses even after Antelope purchased them, and Francine can whisk them away. (Antelope has a valid claim against Bubba for the value of the buses, but the claim may prove fruitless, since Bubba is bankrupt.)

There are some exceptions to this rule. The Code gives a few buyers special protection.

Buyers in Ordinary Course of Business

A buyer in ordinary course of business (BIOC) is someone who buys goods in good faith from a seller who routinely deals in such goods.[26] For example, Plato's Garden Supply purchases 500 hemlocks from Socrates' Farm, a grower. Plato is a BIOC: he is buying in good faith, and Socrates routinely deals in hemlocks. This is an important status, because a BIOC is generally not affected by security interests in the goods. However, if Plato realized that the sale violated another party's rights in the goods, there would be no good faith. If Plato knew that Socrates was bankrupt and had agreed with a creditor not to sell any of his inventory, Plato would not achieve BIOC status.

A buyer in ordinary course of business takes the goods free of a security interest created by his seller even though the security interest is perfected.[27] Suppose that, a month before Plato made his purchase, Socrates borrowed $200,000 from the Athenian Bank. Athenian took a security interest in all of Socrates' trees and perfected by filing. Then Plato purchased his 500 hemlocks. If Socrates defaults on the

---

[25] UCC §9-334.

[26] UCC §1-201(9).

[27] UCC §9-320(a). In fact, the buyer takes free of the security interest *even if the buyer knew of it.* Yet a BIOC, by definition, must be acting in good faith. Is this a contradiction? No. Plato might know that a third party has a security interest in Socrates' crops, yet not realize that his purchase violates the third party's rights. Generally, for example, a security interest will permit a retailer to sell consumer goods, the presumption being that part of the proceeds will go to the secured party. A BIOC cannot be expected to determine what a retailer plans to do with the money he is paid.

loan, Athenian will have *no right* to repossess the 500 trees that are now at the Garden Supply. Plato took them free and clear. (Of course, Athenian can still attempt to repossess other trees from Socrates.)

The BIOC exception is designed to encourage ordinary commerce. A buyer making routine purchases should not be forced to perform a financing check before buying. But the rule creates its own problems. A creditor may extend a large sum of money to a merchant based on collateral, such as inventory, only to discover that by the time the merchant defaults the collateral has been sold. Because the BIOC exception undercuts the basic protection given to a secured party, the courts interpret it narrowly. BIOC status is available only if the *seller created the security interest*. Oftentimes, a buyer will purchase goods that have a security interest created by someone other than the seller. If that happens, the buyer is not a BIOC. However, should that rule be strictly enforced even when the results are harsh? You make the call.

you Be The Judge

CONSECO FINANCE SERVICING CORP. V. LEE

2004 WL 1243417
Court of Appeals of Texas, 2004

Facts: Lila Williams purchased a new Roadtrek 200 motor home from New World R.V. Inc. She paid about $14,000 down and financed $63,000, giving a security interest to New World. The RV company assigned its security interest to Conseco Finance, which perfected. Two years later, Williams returned the vehicle to New World (the record does not indicate why), and New World sold the RV to Robert and Ann Lee, for $42,800. A year later, Williams defaulted on her payments to Conseco.

The Lees sued Conseco, claiming to be BIOCs and asking for a court declaration that they had sole title to the Roadtrek. Conseco counterclaimed, seeking title based on its perfected security interest. The trial court ruled that the Lees were BIOCs, with full rights to the vehicle. Conseco appealed.

You Be the Judge: Were the Lees BIOCs?

Conseco's Argument: Under UCC section 9-319, a buyer in ordinary course takes free of a security interest *created by the buyer's seller*. The buyers were the Lees. The seller was New World. New World did not create the security interest—Lila Williams did. There is no security interest created by New World. The security interest held by Conseco was created by someone else (Williams) and is not affected by the Lees' status as BIOC. The law is clear and Conseco is entitled to the Roadtrek.

The Lees' Argument: Conseco weaves a clever argument, but let's remove the mumbo-jumbo and look at what they are saying. Two honest buyers, acting in perfect good faith, can walk into an RV dealership, spend $42,000 for a used vehicle, and end up with—nothing. Conseco claims it is entitled to an RV that the Lees paid for because someone that the Lees have never dealt with, never even heard of, gave *to this RV seller* a security interest which the seller, years earlier, passed on to a finance company. Conseco's argument defies common sense and the goals of Article 9.

Conseco's Rebuttal: The best part of the Lees' argument is the emotional appeal, the worst part is the law. Yes, $42,000 is a lot of money. That is why a reasonable buyer is careful to do business with conscientious, ethical sellers. New World, which knew that Williams financed the RV and knew who held the security interest, never bothered to check on the status of the payments. If the Lees have suffered wrongdoing, it is at the hands of an irresponsible seller—the company they chose to work with, the company from whom they must seek relief.

The Lees' Rebuttal: The purpose of the Code is to make dealing fair and commerce work; one of its methods is to get away from obscure, technical arguments. Conseco's suggestion would demolish the used-car industry. What buyers will ever pay serious money—*any* money—for a used vehicle, knowing that thousands of dollars later the car might be towed out of their driveway by a finance company they never heard of? ■

Buyers of Consumer Goods

Another exception exists to protect buyers of consumer goods who do not realize that the item they are buying has a security interest in it. This exception tends to apply to relatively casual purchases, such as those between friends. Typically the pattern is that one purchaser buys consumer goods on credit and then resells. The original purchaser is considered a debtor-seller, since she still owes money but is now selling to a second buyer. **In the case of consumer goods purchased from a debtor-seller, a buyer takes free of a security interest if he is not aware of the security interest, he pays value for the goods, he is buying for his own family or household use, and the second party has not yet filed a financing statement.**[28]

Here is how this exception works. Charles Lau used a Sears credit card to buy a 45-inch TV, a sleeper sofa, love seat, entertainment center, diamond ring, gold chain, and microwave. He had the items delivered to the house of his girlfriend, Teresa Rierman, because he did not want his father to know he had been using the credit card (can't imagine why). Lau later sold the items to Rierman's family and then (need we say it?) defaulted on his payments to Sears and declared bankruptcy. Sears attempted to repossess its merchandise, but the Riermans claimed they were innocent buyers. The court ruled that if the Riermans could show that they knew nothing about Sears's security interest in the goods, they could keep the goods.[29]

This rule may be confusing because earlier we discussed the automatic perfection of a security interest in consumer goods. When Sears sold the merchandise to Lau, it took a purchase money security interest in consumer goods. That interest perfected automatically (without filing) and was valid against *almost* everyone. Suppose Lau had used the furniture as collateral to obtain a bank loan. Sears would have retained its perfected security interest in the goods, and when Lau defaulted, Sears could have repossessed everything, leaving the bank with no collateral and no money.

The one person that Sears's perfect security interest could not defeat, however, was a buyer purchasing for *personal use without knowledge of the security interest*, in other words, the Riermans. Assuming the Riermans knew nothing of the security interest, they win. If Sears considers this type of loss important, it must, in the future, protect itself by filing a financing statement. Taking this extra step will leave Sears protected against everyone. Then, if a buyer defaults, Sears can pull the sofa out from under any purchaser.

Buyers of Chattel Paper, Instruments, and Documents

We have seen that debtors often use chattel paper, instruments, or documents as collateral. Because each of these is so easily transferred, the Code gives buyers special protection. **A buyer who purchases chattel paper or an instrument in the ordinary course of her business, and then takes possession, generally takes free of any security interest.**[30]

Suppose Tele-Maker sells 500 televisions to Retailer on credit, keeping a security interest in the televisions and the proceeds. The proceeds are any money or paper that Retailer earns from selling the sets. Retailer sells 300 of the sets to customers, most of whom pay on credit. The customers sign chattel paper, promising to pay for the sets

---

[28] UCC §9-320.
[29] *In re Lau,* 140 B.R. 172, 1992 Bankr. LEXIS 671 (N.D. Ohio 1992). The case was decided under the former Article 9 but the outcome would be the same under the revised version.
[30] UCC §9-330(a)(b)(d).

Exhibit 26.4
The buyer of chattel paper takes it free of a perfected security interest. In this case, Tele-Maker (1) sells 500 units to Retailer on credit, keeping (2) a security interest in the televisions and the proceeds. Retailer (3) sells the sets to customers who (4) sign chattel paper. Retailer (5) sells the chattel paper to Financer and then defaults on its obligations to Tele-Maker.

over time (and giving Retailer a security interest in the sets). All of this chattel paper is proceeds, so Tele-Maker has a perfected security interest in it. The chattel paper is worth about $150,000 if all of the customers pay in full. But Retailer wants money now, so Retailer sells its chattel paper to Financer, who pays $120,000 cash for it. Next, Retailer defaults on its obligation to pay Tele-Maker for the sets. Tele-Maker cannot repossess the televisions, because each customer was a BIOC (buyer in ordinary course of business) and took the goods free of any security interest. So Tele-Maker attempts to repossess the *chattel paper*. Will it succeed? No. The buyer of chattel paper takes it free of a perfected security interest. See Exhibit 26.4.

What could Tele-Maker have done to prevent this disaster?

Other Paper

Similar rules apply for holders in due course of instruments (discussed in Chapters 23 and 24, on negotiable instruments) and for purchasers of securities and documents of title. Those parties obtain special rights, described in Articles 3, 7, and 8 of the Code. The details of those rules are beyond the scope of this chapter, but once again, the lesson for any lender is simple: a security interest is safest when the collateral is in your vault. If you do not take possession of the paper, you may lose it to an innocent buyer.[31]

---

[31] UCC §9-331.

Liens

Law student Paul King got a costly lesson when his $28.09 check for an oil change bounced and the repo man snatched his prized Corvette. The bill for the car's return: $644. King was a third-year law student, working part-time in a private firm in Houston. He had just walked in from lunch when co-workers told him his car was being towed.

"I thought they were joking," King said. They weren't. King saw a tow truck backing up to his car and hurried out to speak with the workers. They advised him that Texas law authorized them to pick up his car to satisfy a lien, for work done to the car. King hurried inside to telephone the company that had performed the oil change. Unable to make a deal on the phone, he ran back outside and found—no car.

King phoned Harris County Repossession to see about getting his car back. That's easy, they told him. But you owe some fees: $28.09 for the oil change, $20 for the returned check, $25 for the legal notice in the newspapers, $21.24 per day for storage—plus, of course, the $550 repossession fee.[32] ◆

Is that legal? Probably. The service station had a lien on the car. **A lien is a security interest created by law (rather than by agreement).** State and federal law both allow parties to assert a lien against a debtor under prescribed conditions. For example, a state may claim a lien based on unpaid taxes; the state is giving notice to the world that it may seize the debtor's property and sell it. A company may claim a lien based on work performed by the debtor.

To understand the difference between a lien and a security interest, assume that when Paul King bought his Corvette, he made a down payment and signed a security agreement to ensure future payments. *His agreement* gave the dealer a security interest in the sports car. Later, when he paid for an oil change, his check bounced. *State law* gave the service station a lien on the auto, meaning the right to hold the car if it is in the garage and to seize the auto if it is elsewhere. Because automobile repossessions provide such a graphic view of secured transactions, we will return to the subject later in the chapter. In the meantime, the commercial Web site **http://www.pimall.com/ nais/n.repo.html** offers a blunt, grimly intriguing look at car repossession from the perspective of those who earn a living at it.

In this case, the oil company had an **artisan's lien, meaning a security interest in personal property** created when a worker makes some improvement to the property. A car mechanic, a computer repairman, and a furniture restorer all create artisan's liens. **A mechanic's lien is similar, created when a worker improves real property.** A carpenter who puts an addition on a kitchen and a painter who paints the kitchen's interior both have a mechanic's lien on the house. The owner of an apartment may obtain a **landlord's lien** in a tenant's personal property if the tenant fails to pay the rent. These security interests vary from state to state, so an affected person must consult local law. For an example of a mechanic's lien, go to **http://www.nvlaw.com/** and click on "mechanic's lien."

Because liens are the creation of statutes, rather than agreements, Article 9 generally does not apply. The one aspect of liens that Article 9 does govern is priority between lienholders and other secured parties, which we examine in the following section. In Paul King's case, the repair shop certainly had a valid lien on his car, even though the amount in question was small. The company's method of *collecting* on its

---

[32] Rad Sallee and James T. Campbell, "Repo Men Hitch Up Big Fee to Car," *Houston Chronicle*, Oct. 15, 1991, §A, p. 21. Copyright 1991 Houston Chronicle Publishing Company. Reprinted with permission. All rights reserved.

lien is more debatable. King admitted that the company had telephoned him and given him a chance to pay for the bounced check. Some courts would hold that the repair shop had done all it was required to do, but others might rule that it should have shown more patience and avoided running up the bill.

PRIORITIES AMONG CREDITORS

What happens when two creditors have a security interest in the same collateral? The party who has **priority** in the collateral gets it. Typically, the debtor lacks assets to pay everyone, so all creditors struggle to be the first in line. After the first creditor has repossessed the collateral, sold it, and taken enough of the proceeds to pay off his debt, there may be nothing left for anyone else. (There may not even be enough to pay the first creditor all that he is due, in which case that creditor will sue for the deficiency.) Who gets priority? There are three principal rules.

The first rule is easy: **a party with a perfected security interest takes priority over a party with an unperfected interest.**[33] This, of course, is the whole point of perfecting: to ensure that your security interest gets priority over everyone else's. On August 15, Meredith's Market, an antique store, borrows $100,000 from the Happy Bank, which takes a security interest in all of Meredith's inventory. Happy Bank does not perfect. On September 15, Meredith uses the same collateral to borrow $50,000 from the Suspicion Bank, which files a financing statement the same day. On October 15, as if on cue, Meredith files for bankruptcy and stops paying both creditors. Suspicion wins because it holds a perfected interest, whereas the Happy Bank holds merely an unperfected interest.

The second rule: **if neither secured party has perfected, the first interest to attach gets priority.**[34] Suppose that Suspicion Bank and Happy Bank had both failed to perfect. In that case, Happy Bank would have the first claim to Meredith's inventory, since Happy's interest *attached* first.

And the third rule follows logically: **between perfected security interests, the first to file or perfect wins.**[35] Diminishing Perspective, a railroad, borrows $75 million from the First Bank, which takes a security interest in Diminishing's rolling stock (railroad cars) and immediately perfects by filing. Two months later, Diminishing borrows $100 million from Second Bank, which takes a security interest in the same collateral and also files. When Diminishing arrives, on schedule, in bankruptcy court, both banks will race to seize the rolling stock. First Bank gets the railcars because it perfected first.

March 1:	April 2:	May 3:	The Winner:
First Bank loans money and perfects its security interest by filing a financing statement.	Second Bank loans money and perfects its security interest by filing a financing statement.	Diminishing goes bankrupt, and both banks attempt to take the rolling stock.	First Bank, because it perfected first.

---

[33] UCC §9-322(a)(2).
[34] UCC §9-322(a)(3).
[35] UCC §9-322(a)(1).

The general rules of priority are quite straightforward; however, you will not be surprised to learn that there are some exceptions.

Filing versus Control or Possession

Recall that a secured party *may* use either filing or control to perfect its security interest in deposit accounts, investment property, and letter-of-credit rights. Which method *should* the secured party use? Control. **For these three types of collateral, a secured party who has control wins over a party who merely filed.**[36] Early Bank obtains a security interest in Lionel's investment property, and perfects by filing. Nine months later, Late Bank obtains a security interest in the same property, and perfects by taking control. Late Bank wins.

Similarly, a secured party may perfect its interest in an *instrument* either by filing or possession. Once again, possession is the better idea: **between competing secured parties, the one who possesses wins, even over one who filed earlier.**[37]

Priority Involving a Purchase Money Security Interest

You may recall that a purchase money security interest (PMSI) is a security interest taken by the seller of the collateral or by a lender whose loan enables the debtor to buy the collateral. A PMSI can be created only in goods, fixtures and software. On November 1, Manufacturer sells a specially built lathe to Tool Shop for $80,000 and takes a security interest in the lathe. The parties have created a PMSI. Parties holding a PMSI often take priority over other perfected security interests in the same goods, even if the other security interest was perfected first. How can the conflict arise? Suppose that on February 1, Tool Shop had borrowed $100,000 from the Gargoyle Bank, giving Gargoyle a security interest in after-acquired property. When the lathe arrives at the Tool Shop on November 1, Gargoyle's security interest attaches to it. But Manufacturer has a PMSI in the lathe, and hence the conflict.

We need to examine PMSIs involving inventory and those involving noninventory. **Inventory means goods that the seller is holding for sale or lease in the ordinary course of its business.** The furniture in a furniture store is inventory; the store's computer, telephones, and filing cabinets are not.

PMSI in Inventory

A PMSI in inventory takes priority over a conflicting perfected security interest (even one perfected earlier), if two conditions are met:

- Before filing its PMSI, the secured party must check for earlier security interests and, if there are any, must notify the holder of that interest concerning the new PMSI; and

- The secured party must then perfect its PMSI (normally by filing) *before* the debtor receives the inventory.[38]

If the holder of the PMSI has met both of these conditions, its PMSI takes priority over any security interests filed earlier, as illustrated in the following chart.

---

[36] UCC §§9-327, 9-328, 9-329. If more than one creditor has control of the same collateral, the security interests rank according to the time of obtaining control.

[37] UCC §9-330(d).

[38] UCC §9-324(b)(c).

A PMSI in Inventory May Obtain Priority

1. February 1:	2. March 2:	3. March 3:	4. March 4:
Coltrane Bank loans Monk's Jazz Store $90,000, taking a security interest in all after-acquired property, including inventory.	Monk offers to buy 10 saxophones from Webster's Supply for $3,000 each.	Webster checks the financing records and learns that Coltrane Bank has a security interest in all of Monk's after-acquired property.	Webster notifies Coltrane Bank that he is selling 10 saxophones to Monk for $30,000 and is taking a PMSI in the instruments, which Webster carefully describes.
5. March 4:	**6. March 5:**	**7. September:**	**8. The Winner:**
Webster files a financing statement indicating a PMSI in the 10 saxophones.	Webster sells the 10 saxophones to Monk.	Monk goes bankrupt.	Webster. His PMSI in inventory takes priority over Coltrane's earlier interest.

PMSI in Noninventory Collateral

PMSIs are often given for noninventory goods. When Tool Shop bought the lathe, in the example above, the company gave a PMSI to the seller. The bank simultaneously obtained a security interest in the same lathe, based on its after-acquired property interest. Who wins?

A PMSI in collateral other than inventory takes priority over a conflicting security interest if the PMSI is perfected at the time the debtor receives the collateral or within 20 days after he receives it.[39] As long as Computer Co. perfects (by filing) within 20 days of delivering the computer, its PMSI takes priority over the bank's earlier security interest. Manufacturer may repossess the machine, and the bank may never get a dime back.

Again, we must note that the PMSI exception undercuts the ability of a creditor to rely on its perfected security interest. As a result, courts insist that a party asserting the PMSI exception demonstrate that it has complied with every requirement.

The following case, a conflict between a purchase money security interest and an earlier perfected interest, was decided under the former Article 9, but the outcome would be the same under the revised law.

CITIZENS BANK OF AMERICUS V. FEDERAL FINANCIAL SERVICES, INC.

509 S.E.2d 339
Georgia Court of Appeals, 1998

Facts: The court intertwines its explanation of the facts with its decision, so we will allow Judge Beasley to do the talking.

Issue: Does the PMSI holder obtain priority?

Excerpts from Judge Beasley's Decision: Federal Financial Services, Inc., sought a judgment declaring that it has a purchase money security interest with priority over the earlier perfected security interest of Citizens Bank of Americus in the same logging

▼

---

[39] UCC §9-324(a).

skidder. The court entered judgment in Federal Financial's favor. The bank appeals.

Where conflicting security interests are perfected by the filing of financing statements, the general rule is that they rank according to priority in time of filing. But under [section 9-324], a purchase money security interest in collateral other than inventory has priority over a previously perfected security interest in the same collateral, if the purchase money security interest is perfected "at the time the debtor receives possession of the collateral or within [20] days thereafter." The issue is, which comes first, Citizens or Federal? The answer lies in the determination of the triggering event, quoted above, which establishes the time period during which the purchase money security interest holder must file a financing statement.

The stipulated facts are as follows. Charles H. Logging, Inc., began negotiations to purchase a logging skidder from Pioneer Machinery, Inc., sometime prior to December 5. On December 5, the logging company borrowed $22,520 from Citizens Bank of Americus and signed a promissory note in favor of the bank and a UCC financing statement listing the skidder as collateral. The bank filed the financing statement the next day. The logging company used the loan proceeds to satisfy debts. It did not possess or own the skidder.

About two weeks later, on December 18, Pioneer delivered the skidder to the company for demonstration purposes only. Toward the end of December, the company decided to purchase the skidder from Pioneer. On December 30, the company indicated its intention by executing a contract of sale and invoice which were subject to the company's obtaining adequate physical damage insurance showing Pioneer and Federal Financial Services, the intended purchase money lender, as loss payees. The contract was also expressly subject to signature by Pioneer, the seller.

A little more than a month thereafter, on February 6, the company acquired ownership of the skidder after obtaining the required insurance. The same day, it executed a note to Federal Financial, signed a UCC financing statement listing the skidder as collateral, and Federal Financial remitted the loan proceeds to Pioneer in payment of the purchase price. Federal Financial filed the financing statement on February 10.

It is uncontested that Citizens Bank's perfected security interest in the skidder does not qualify as a purchase money security interest because the funds it lent were not in fact used by the logging company to purchase the skidder. Whether Federal Financial's purchase money security interest achieved priority over the bank's previously perfected security interest depends on the date of the event statutorily described as "the time the debtor receive[d] possession of the collateral."

The eventual purchaser received possession of the collateral on December 18 for a specific purpose and thereby became its bailee. The skidder was still owned by the seller and, insofar as the bailee's creditor bank was concerned, the skidder was property which was to become acquired.

The bailee became a purchaser on February 6, thereby acquiring ownership of the property, and its status as bailee ceased. It paid for the skidder by way of its loan that day from the purchase money lender, which paid the seller directly. At that time the purchaser became debtor to the purchase money lender. The purchaser already had possession of the collateral on that day, so it is then that the two factors (indebtedness for purchase price and possession) first coincided. The lender had [20] days from that date to file the financing statement, which it did.

It is undisputed that Federal Financial is the only creditor holding a purchase money security interest, and that it perfected this interest by filing its financing statement within [20] days after the logging company acquired ownership of the skidder and executed the note evidencing its obligation to pay the purchase price. Under these circumstances, it has priority.

Judgment affirmed. ∎

Rights of Third Parties

Article 9 now explicitly provides the rights and duties of *third parties*, meaning those who may be affected by a secured transaction even though they are neither debtor nor secured party. Significant issues raised include the rights and duties of assignees. (This textbook discusses assignment and assignees in Chapter 16, on third parties.) These issues go beyond the scope of this chapter; interested readers should consult Part Four of Article 9, Sections 9-401 through 9-408.

DEFAULT AND TERMINATION

We have reached the end of the line. Either the debtor has defaulted, or it has performed its obligations and may terminate the security agreement.

Default

The parties define "default" in their security agreement. **Generally, a debtor defaults when he fails to make payments due or enters bankruptcy proceedings.** The parties can agree that other acts will constitute default, such as the debtor's failure to maintain insurance on the collateral. When a debtor defaults, the secured party has two principal options: (1) it may take possession of the collateral, or (2) it may file suit against the debtor for the money owed. The secured party does not have to choose between these two remedies; it may try one remedy, such as repossession, and if that fails, attempt the other.[40]

Taking Possession of the Collateral

When the debtor defaults, the secured party may take possession of the collateral.[41] How does the secured party accomplish this? In either of two ways. The secured party may act on its own, without any court order, and simply take the collateral, provided this can be done *without a breach of the peace*. Otherwise, the secured party must file suit against the debtor and request that the court *order* the debtor to deliver the collateral.

© JEFF GREENBERG/PHOTO EDIT, INC.

If you do not make your loan payments, can the secured party repossess your car?

Suppose a consumer bought a refrigerator on credit and defaulted. The security agreement may require the consumer to make the collateral available in a reasonable time and manner, such as by emptying the refrigerator of all food and having it ready for a carrier to take away. When the refrigerator is ready, the retailer can haul it away. What if the consumer refuses to cooperate? May the retailer break into the consumer's house to take the collateral? No. Breaking into a house is a clear breach of the peace and violates Article 9.

Secured parties often repossess automobiles without the debtor's cooperation. Typically, the security agreement will state that, in the event of default, the secured party has a right to take possession of the car and drive it away. As we saw earlier, the secured party could be the seller, or it could be a mechanic with an artisan's lien on the car.

---

[40] UCC §9-601(a)(b)(c).
[41] UCC §9-609.

corners with stark naked people who are wielding machetes. No experience necessary but driver's license and good night vision essential.

We are, in short, seeking a "repo person," someone who will help us recover cars from purchasers who have failed to make monthly payments. Automobile dealers hire us to repossess a vehicle, and we assign the jobs to our agents. If hired, you will be expected to do your job as quietly as possible, stealing unseen onto the debtor's property, often at night, attempting to drive away unnoticed. You should repossess 100 to 125 cars a year. That allows for a day or so to locate particularly troublesome owners, and additional time to gain safe access.

You should be aware that modest problems may occur when an owner does spot one of our agents. Unpleasantness in the past included:

- Angry owners who have howled at, bitten, and attacked repo agents.

- An enraged debtor who leapt out of bed and ran screaming down the street, naked, in pursuit of his former car.

- Various deadbeats who forced their children to lie in the street, blocking the vehicle's departure.

- A doctor who leaned out of the window of a distinguished teaching hospital and fired four shots at our agent, who was attempting to repossess the doctor's BMW.

Every year, one or two repo agents are killed somewhere in the United States. This is a lively job, with good pay and benefits, including life insurance. ◆

Disposition of the Collateral

Once the secured party has obtained possession of the collateral, it has two choices. The secured party may (1) dispose of the collateral or (2) retain the collateral as full satisfaction of the debt.

Disposal of the Collateral. A secured party may sell, lease, or otherwise dispose of the collateral in any commercially reasonable manner.[42] Typically, the secured party will sell the collateral in either a private or a public sale. First, however, the debtor must receive *reasonable notice* of the time and place of the sale so that she may bid on the collateral. The higher the price that the secured party gets for the collateral, the lower the balance still owed by the debtor. Giving the debtor notice of the sale, and a chance to bid, ensures that the collateral will not be sold for an unreasonably low price.

Suppose Bank loans $65,000 to Farmer to purchase a tractor. While still owing $40,000, Farmer defaults. Bank takes possession of the tractor and then notifies Farmer that it intends to sell the tractor at an auction. Farmer has the right to attend and bid on the tractor.

When the secured party has sold the collateral, it applies the proceeds of the sale: first, to its expenses in repossessing and selling the collateral, and second, to the debt.[43] Assume Bank sold the tractor for $35,000 and that the process of repossessing and selling the tractor cost $5,000. Bank applies the remaining $30,000 to the debt.

Deficiency or Surplus. The sale of the tractor yielded $30,000 to be applied to the debt, which was $40,000. The disposition has left a **deficiency**, that is, insufficient funds to pay off the debt. **The debtor is liable for any deficiency.** So the bank will sue the farmer for the remaining $10,000. On the other hand, sometimes the sale of the collateral yields a **surplus**, that is, a sum greater than the debt. In that case, the secured party must pay the surplus to the debtor.[44]

---

[42] UCC §9-610.
[43] UCC §9-615(a).
[44] UCC §9-615(d).

When a secured party disposes of collateral in a *commercially unreasonable* manner, then a deficiency or surplus claim may be adjusted based on the sum that *should* have been obtained.[45] Suppose that Seller, who is owed $300,000, repossesses 500 bedroom sets from a hotel and, without giving proper notice, quickly sells them for a net amount of $200,000. Seller sues for the $100,000 deficiency. If a court determines that a properly announced sale would have netted $250,000, Seller is only entitled to a deficiency judgment of $50,000. Similarly, if the collateral is sold *to the secured party* or someone related, and the price obtained is significantly below what would be expected, then any deficiency or surplus must be calculated on what the sale would normally have brought. This protects the debtor from a sale in which the secured party has followed all formalities but ended up owning the goods for a suspiciously low price.[46]

Acceptance of Collateral. In many cases, the secured party has the option to satisfy the debt simply by keeping the collateral. **Acceptance refers to a secured party's retention of the collateral as full or partial satisfaction of the debt.** *Partial satisfaction* means that the debtor will still owe some deficiency to the secured party. This is how the system works.[47]

A secured party who wishes to accept the collateral must notify the debtor. If the debtor agrees in an authenticated record, then the secured party may keep the collateral as full *or* partial satisfaction of the debt. If the debtor does not respond within 20 days, the secured party may still accept the collateral as *full* satisfaction but *not* as partial satisfaction. In other words, the debtor's silence does not give the secured party the right to keep the goods and still sue for more money.

Suppose the buyer of a $13 million yacht, *Icarus*, has defaulted, and the retailer has repossessed the boat. The firm may decide the boat is worth more than the debt, so it notifies the buyer that it plans to keep *Icarus*. If the buyer does not object, the retailer automatically owns the boat after 20 days.

If the buyer promptly objects to acceptance, the retailer must then dispose of *Icarus* as described above, typically by sale. Why would a debtor object? Because she believes the boat is worth more than the debt. The debtor anticipates that a sale will create a surplus.

Consumers receive additional protection. A secured party may not accept collateral that is consumer goods if the debtor has possession of the goods *or* if the debtor has paid 60 percent of the purchase price. If Maud has defaulted on an oven that is in her kitchen, the Gobroke retail store may be entitled to repossess the oven, but the company must then dispose of the goods (sell the oven) and apply the proceeds to Maud's debt. Similarly, if Ernest is paying for his $10,000 television set in a "layaway" plan, with Gobroke warehousing the goods until the full price is paid, the store may not accept the television once Ernest has paid $6,000. Finally, a secured party is never permitted to accept consumer goods in partial satisfaction.[48]

Right of Redemption. Up to the time the secured party disposes of the collateral, the debtor has the right to **redeem** it, that is, to pay the full value of the debt. If the debtor redeems, she obtains the collateral back. Sylvia borrows $25,000 from the bank and pledges a ruby necklace as collateral. She defaults, still owing $9,000, and the bank notifies her that it will sell the necklace. If Sylvia pays the full $9,000 before the sale occurs, plus any expenses the bank has incurred in arranging the sale, she receives her necklace back.[49]

---

[45] UCC §9-626(a)(3).

[46] UCC §§9-615(f), 9-626(a)(5).

[47] UCC §9-620.

[48] UCC §9-620(a)(3), (e), (g).

[49] UCC §9-623.

Proceeding to Judgment

Occasionally, the secured party will prefer to ignore its rights in the collateral and simply sue the debtor. **A secured party may sue the debtor for the full debt.**[50] Why would a creditor, having gone to so much effort to perfect its security interest, ignore that interest and simply file a lawsuit? The collateral may have decreased in value and be insufficient to cover the debt. Suppose a bank loaned $300,000 to a debtor to buy a rare baseball cap. The debtor defaults, owing $190,000. The bank discovers that the cap is now worth only $110,000. It is true that the bank could sell the cap and sue for the deficiency. But the sale will take time, and the outcome is uncertain. Suppose the bank knows that the debtor has recently paid cash for a $2 million house. The bank may promptly file suit for the full $190,000. The bank will ask the court to freeze the debtor's bank account and legally hold the house until the suit is resolved. The bank expects to prove the debt quickly—the loan documents are clear, and the amount of debt is easily calculated. It will obtain its $190,000 without ever donning the cap. Of course, the bank has the option of doing both things simultaneously: It may slap on the cap and a lawsuit all at once.

Termination

Finally, we need to look at what happens when a debtor *does not* default, but pays the full debt. (You are forgiven if you lost track of the fact that things sometimes work out smoothly.) Once that happens, the secured party must complete a **termination statement,** a document indicating that it no longer claims a security interest in the collateral.[51]

For a consumer debt, the secured party must file the termination statement in every place that it filed a financing statement. The secured party must do this within one month from the date the debt is fully paid, or within 20 days of a demand from the consumer, whichever comes first. For other transactions, the secured party must within 20 days either file the termination statement or send it to the secured party so that he may file it himself. In both cases, the goal is the same: to notify all interested parties that the debt is extinguished.

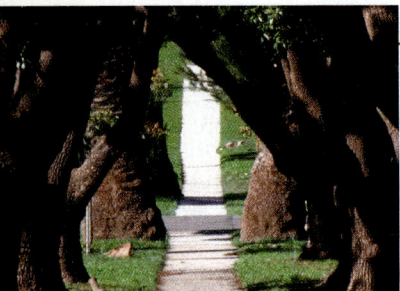

Chapter Conclusion

Secured transactions are essential to modern commerce. Billions of dollars' worth of goods are sold on credit annually, and creditors normally demand an assurance of payment. A secured party that understands Article 9 and follows its provisions to the letter should be well protected. A company that operates in ignorance of Article 9 invites disaster, because others may obtain superior rights in the goods, leaving the "secured" party with no money, no security— and no sympathy from the courts.

---

[50] UCC §9-601(a).
[51] UCC §9-513.

Chapter Review

1. Article 9 applies to any transaction intended to create a security interest in personal property or fixtures.

2. Attachment means that (1) the two parties made a security agreement, *and* either the debtor has *authenticated a security agreement* describing the collateral *or* the secured party has obtained *possession* or *control*; and (2) the secured party gave value in order to get the security agreement; and (3) the debtor has rights in the collateral.

3. A security interest may attach to after-acquired property.

4. Attachment protects against the debtor. Perfection of a security interest protects the secured party against parties other than the debtor.

5. Filing is the most common way to perfect. For many forms of collateral, the secured party may also perfect by obtaining either possession or control.

6. A purchase money security interest (PMSI) is one taken by the person who sells the collateral or advances money so the debtor can buy the collateral.

7. A PMSI in consumer goods perfects automatically, without filing.

8. A buyer in ordinary course of business (BIOC) takes the goods free of a security interest created by his seller even though the security interest is perfected.

9. A buyer who purchases chattel paper or an instrument in good faith in the ordinary course of his business, and then obtains possession or control, generally takes free of any security interest.

10. Priority among secured parties is generally as follows:

    a. A party with a perfected security interest takes priority over a party with an unperfected interest.

    b. If neither secured party has perfected, the first interest to attach gets priority.

    c. Between perfected security interests, the first to file or perfect wins.

11. A PMSI may take priority over a conflicting perfected security interest (even one perfected earlier) if the holder of the PMSI meets certain conditions.

12. For deposit accounts, investment property, letter-of-credit rights, and instruments, a secured party who obtains control or possession takes priority over one who merely filed.

13. When the debtor defaults, the secured party may take possession of the collateral on its own, without a court order, if it can do so without a breach of the peace.

14. A secured party may sell, lease, or otherwise dispose of the collateral in any commercially reasonable way; in many cases it may accept the collateral in full or partial satisfaction of the debt. The secured party may also ignore the collateral and sue the debtor for the full debt.

15. When the debtor pays the full debt, the secured party must complete a termination statement, notifying the public that it no longer claims a security interest in the collateral.

Practice Test

Note to the student: The following cases and problems were decided under the former Article 9. In each instance the outcome would be the same under the revised code, although the relevant sections of Article 9 have been renumbered and probably rewritten.

1. **CPA QUESTION** Under the UCC Secured Transactions Article, which of the following actions will best perfect a security interest in a negotiable instrument against any other party?

   a. Filing a security agreement

   b. Taking possession of the instrument

c. Perfecting by attachment

d. Obtaining a duly executed financing statement

2. **CPA QUESTION** Under the UCC Secured Transactions Article, perfection of a security interest by a creditor provides added protection against other parties in the event the debtor does not pay its debts. Which of the following parties is not affected by perfection of a security interest?

a. Other prospective creditors of the debtor

b. The trustee in a bankruptcy case

c. A buyer in ordinary course of business

d. A subsequent personal injury judgment creditor

3. Eugene Ables ran an excavation company. He borrowed $500,000 from the Highland Park State Bank. Ables signed a note promising to repay the money and an agreement giving Highland a security interest in all of his equipment, including after-acquired equipment. Several years later, Ables agreed with Patricia Myers to purchase a Bantam Backhoe from her for $16,000, which he would repay at the rate of $100 per month, while he used the machine. Ables later defaulted on his note to Highland, and the bank attempted to take the backhoe. Myers and Ables contended that the bank had no right to take the backhoe. Was the backhoe covered by Highland's security interest? Did Ables have sufficient rights in the backhoe for the bank's security interest to attach?

4. Jerry Payne owed the First State Bank of Pflugerville $342,000. The loan was secured by a 9.25-carat diamond ring. The bank claimed a default on the loan and, without notifying Payne, sold the ring. But the proceeds did not pay off the full debt, and the bank sued Payne for the deficiency. Is Payne liable for the deficiency?

5. John and Clara Lockovich bought a 22-foot Chaparrel Villian II boat from Greene County Yacht Club for $32,500. They paid $6,000 cash and borrowed the rest of the purchase money from Gallatin National Bank, which took a security interest in the boat. Gallatin filed a financing statement in Greene County, Pennsylvania, where the bank was located. But Pennsylvania law requires financing statements to be filed in the county of the debtor's residence, and the Lockoviches lived in Allegheny County. The

Lockoviches soon washed up in Bankruptcy Court. Other creditors demanded that the boat be sold, claiming that Gallatin's security interest had been filed in the wrong place. Who wins? (Please be advised: this is a trick question.)

6. The Copper King Inn, Inc., had money problems. It borrowed $62,500 from two of its officers, Noonan and Patterson, but that did not suffice to keep the inn going. So Noonan, on behalf of Copper King, arranged for the inn to borrow $100,000 from Northwest Capital, an investment company that worked closely with Noonan in other ventures. Copper King signed an agreement giving Patterson, Noonan, and Northwest a security interest in the inn's furniture and equipment. But the financing statement that the parties filed made no mention of Northwest. Copper King went bankrupt. Northwest attempted to seize assets, but other creditors objected. Is Northwest entitled to Copper King's furniture and equipment?

7. McMann Golf Ball Co. manufactured, as you might suppose, golf balls. Barwell, Inc., sold McMann a "preformer," a machine that makes golf balls, for $55,000. Barwell delivered the machine on February 20. McMann paid $3,000 down, the remainder to be paid over several years, and signed an agreement giving Barwell a security interest in the preformer. Barwell did not perfect its interest. On March 1, McMann borrowed $350,000 from First of America Bank, giving the bank a security interest in McMann's present and after-acquired property. First of America perfected by filing on March 2. McMann, of course, became insolvent, and both Barwell and the bank attempted to repossess the preformer. Who gets it?

8. Sears sold a lawn tractor to Cosmo Fiscante for $1,481. Fiscante paid with his personal credit card. Sears kept a valid security interest in the lawnmower but did not perfect. Fiscante had the machine delivered to his business, Trackers Raceway Park, the only place he ever used the machine. When Fiscante was unable to meet his obligations, various creditors attempted to seize the lawnmower. Sears argued that because it had a purchase money security interest (PMSI) in the lawnmower, its interest had perfected automatically. Is Sears correct?

9. The state of Kentucky filed a tax lien against Panbowl Energy, claiming unpaid taxes. Six months later, Panbowl bought a powerful drill from Whayne Supply, making a down payment of $11,500 and signing a security agreement for the remaining debt of $220,000. Whayne perfected the next day. Panbowl defaulted. Whayne sold the drill for $58,000, leaving a deficiency of just over $100,000. The state filed suit, seeking the $58,000 proceeds. The trial court gave summary judgment to the state and Whayne appealed. Who gets the $58,000?

10. CPA QUESTION Mars, Inc., manufactures and sells VCRs on credit directly to wholesalers, retailers, and consumers. Mars can perfect its security interest in the VCRs it sells without having to file a financing statement or take possession of the VCRs if the sale is made to which of the following:

a. Retailers

b. Wholesalers that sell to distributors for resale

c. Consumers

d. Wholesalers that sell to buyers in ordinary course of business

11. ETHICS The Dannemans bought a Kodak copier worth over $40,000. Kodak arranged financing by GECC and assigned its rights to that company. Although the Dannemans thought they had purchased the copier on credit, the papers described the deal as a lease. The Dannemans had constant problems with the machine and stopped making payments. GECC repossessed the machine and, without notifying the Dannemans, sold it back to Kodak for $12,500, leaving a deficiency of $39,927. GECC sued the Dannemans for that amount. The Dannemans argued that the deal was not a lease but a sale on credit. Why does it matter whether the parties had a sale or a lease? Is GECC entitled to its money? Finally, comment on the ethics. Why did the Dannemans not understand the papers they had signed? Who is responsible for that? Are you satisfied with the ethical conduct of the Dannemans? Kodak? GECC?

12. YOU BE THE JUDGE WRITING PROBLEM Dupont Feed bought and sold agricultural products. Dupont borrowed $300,000 from Wells Fargo Bank and gave Wells Fargo a security interest in all inventory, including after-acquired inventory. Wells Fargo perfected its interest by filing on June 17, 1982. Later, Dupont borrowed $150,000 from the Rushville National Bank and used the money to buy fertilizer. Dupont gave a PMSI to Rushville in the amount of $150,000. Rushville filed its financing statement in February 1984 at the County Recorder's office—the wrong place to file a financing statement for inventory. Then Dupont took possession of the fertilizer, and finally, in December 1984, Rushville filed correctly, with the Indiana Secretary of State. Dupont defaulted on both loans. Rushville seized the fertilizer, and Wells Fargo sued, claiming that it had perfected first. Rushville asserted that it had a PMSI, which took priority over an earlier-filed security interest. Does Rushville's PMSI take priority over Wells Fargo? (Go slowly, the rules are very technical.) **Argument for Rushville:** It is black letter law that PMSIs take priority over virtually everything, including interests perfected earlier. We are not fools at Rushville: we would not loan $150,000 to buy inventory if our security interest in that inventory was instantly inferior to someone else's. **Argument for Wells Fargo:** A PMSI in inventory gets priority only if the secured party perfects before the debtor receives the collateral. When Dupont obtained the fertilizer, Rushville had not perfected, because it had filed in the wrong office. It only perfected long after Dupont bought the inventory; thus, Rushville's PMSI does not get priority.

13. ROLE REVERSAL Write a multiple-choice question with a conflict between a secured party and a buyer in ordinary course of business.

Internet Research Problem

Draft a security agreement in which your friend gives you a security interest in her $20,000 home entertainment system, in exchange for a loan of $12,000. Because the collateral is something that she uses daily, what special concerns do you have? How will you protect yourself? Next, find the UCC1 financing form at http://beatty.westbuslaw.com.

Print the form, then complete it. In what office of your state should you file in order to perfect?

You can find further practice problems at http://beatty.westbuslaw.com or in the Study Guide that accompanies this text.

Bankruptcy

George Bryan Brummell, known as Beau Brummell, was a celebrity in nineteenth-century England. Known for his impeccable sense of style, he was the leading arbiter of taste and fashion for more than 20 years. This role was demanding—he routinely spent five hours a day simply getting dressed. After bathing in eau de cologne and water, he would spend an hour with his hairdresser and another two hours tying his cravat. Although he had inherited modest wealth, his extravagant lifestyle brought him to ruin. He fled to France to escape his creditors, taking his lavish tastes with him. After 14 years in France, he was thrown in debtors' prison.

For actor Kim Basinger, a modern celebrity, bankruptcy had a different outcome. A Los Angeles jury ordered her to pay $8.1 million to Main Line Pictures, Inc., because she broke her promise to appear in *Boxing Helena,* a film about a doctor who cuts off his lover's arms and legs. Five days after the verdict, she filed for bankruptcy protection, claiming $5 million in assets and $11 million in liabilities.

Despite filing for bankruptcy, Basinger spent $43,000 per month, including $6,100 for clothes; $4,000 for recreation, clubs, and entertainment; $7,000 for pet care and other personal expenses; as well as $9,000 in alimony to her ex-husband.

© JAMES GRITZ/PHOTODISC/GETTY IMAGES

She also reported owning $592,000 in furniture and clothing and $192,000 in jewelry.

In the meantime, she made no payments to creditors—those who had arranged her

travel, repaired her home, or cut her grass.[1] ∎

Traditionally, the goal of English bankruptcy law was to protect creditors and punish debtors. Creditors had the right to seize a bankrupt's assets and have him incarcerated in a squalid debtors' prison. Once in jail, the debtor had no way to earn money to pay his debts. His only hope was the kindness of family and friends. Many of America's first settlers fled England to escape debtors' prison. As if to compensate for England's harsh regime, American bankruptcy laws were traditionally more lenient toward debtors.

Public Policy

In response to intense lobbying by the credit card industry, Congress passed the **Bankruptcy Abuse Prevention and Consumer Protection Act of 2005 (the BAPCPA),** which makes the bankruptcy process more difficult for debtors. Before filing, individual debtors must now submit to credit counseling—an expensive process that does not necessarily reduce bankruptcy filings. Moreover, if debtors earn more than their state's median income, the new amendment requires them to pay back some of their debt. Those in favor of this amendment argued that all consumers would benefit from lower prices if fewer people were allowed to avoid their debts by going bankrupt. In the prior decade the number of bankruptcies had doubled—perhaps in part because people no longer felt ashamed of bankruptcy. Critics of the statute countered that credit card companies were to blame for the high rate of bankruptcy. These companies issued credit cards willy-nilly without adequate credit checks and then charged high (and sometimes misleading) late fees. Most bankrupts are in the middle class but have suffered a misfortune shortly before filing—unemployment, illness, or divorce. As you read this chapter, formulate your own view on this debate. ◆

OVERVIEW OF THE BANKRUPTCY CODE

The federal Bankruptcy Code (Code) is divided into eight chapters. All chapters except one have odd numbers. Chapters 1, 3, and 5 are administrative rules that generally apply to all types of bankruptcy proceedings. These chapters, for example, define terms and establish the rules of the bankruptcy court. Chapters 7, 9, 11, 12, and 13 are substantive rules for different types of bankruptcies. All of these substantive chapters have one of two objectives—rehabilitation or liquidation.

Rehabilitation

The objective of Chapters 11 and 13 is to rehabilitate the debtor. Many debtors can return to financial health provided they have the time and breathing space to work out their problems. These chapters hold creditors at bay while the debtor develops a payment plan. In return for retaining some of their assets, debtors typically promise to pay creditors a portion of their future earnings.

---

[1] Carol Marie Cropper, "The Basinger Bankruptcy Bomb," *New York Times,* Jan. 1, 1995, §3, p. 1. Copyright © 1995 by The New York Times Co. A California appeals court overturned the judgment against Basinger in the Main Line suit and ordered a new trial. On the eve of retrial, Basinger settled for $3.8 million.

Liquidation

When debtors are unable to develop a feasible plan for rehabilitation under Chapter 11 or 13, Chapter 7 provides for liquidation (also known as a **straight bankruptcy**). Most of the debtor's assets are distributed to creditors, but the debtor has no obligation to share future earnings.

Chapter Description

The following options are available under the Bankruptcy Code:

Number	Topic	Description
Chapter 7	Liquidation	The bankrupt's assets are sold to pay creditors. If the debtor owns a business, it terminates. The creditors have no right to the debtor's future earnings.
Chapter 9	Municipal bankruptcies	This chapter is not covered in this book.
Chapter 11	Reorganization	This chapter is designed for businesses and wealthy individuals. Businesses continue in operation, and creditors receive a portion of both current assets and future earnings.
Chapter 12	Family farmers	This chapter is not covered in this book.
Chapter 13	Consumer reorganizations	Chapter 13 offers reorganizations for the typical consumer. Creditors usually receive a portion of the individual's current assets and future earnings.

Debtors are sometimes eligible to file under more than one chapter. No choice is irrevocable because both debtors and creditors have the right to ask the court to convert a case from one chapter to another at any time during the proceedings. For example, if creditors have asked for liquidation under Chapter 7, a consumer debtor may request rehabilitation under Chapter 13. Kim Basinger originally filed under Chapter 11 but, unable to reach agreement with her creditors, converted to liquidation under Chapter 7.

Goals

The Bankruptcy Code has three primary goals:

- *To preserve as much of the debtor's property as possible.* In keeping with this goal, the Code requires debtors to disclose all of their assets and prohibits them from transferring assets immediately before a bankruptcy filing.

- *To divide the debtor's assets fairly between the debtor and creditors.* On the one hand, creditors are entitled to payment. On the other hand, debtors are often so deeply in debt that full payment is virtually impossible in any reasonable period of time. The Code tries to balance the creditors' desire to be paid with the debtors' right to get on with their lives unburdened by prior debts.

- *To divide the debtor's assets fairly among creditors.* Creditors rarely receive all they are owed, but at least they are treated fairly, according to established rules. Creditors do not benefit from simply being the first to file or from any other gamesmanship.

CHAPTER 7 LIQUIDATION

All bankruptcy cases proceed in a roughly similar pattern, regardless of chapter. We use Chapter 7 as a template to illustrate common features of all bankruptcy cases. Later on, the discussions of the other chapters will indicate how they differ from Chapter 7. The latest news on bankruptcy is available at **http://www.abiworld.org**.

Filing a Petition

Any individual, partnership, corporation, or other business organization that lives, conducts business, or owns property in the United States can file under the Code. (Chapter 13, however, is available only to individuals.) The traditional term for someone who could not pay his debts was "**bankrupt**," but the Code uses the term "**debtor**" instead. We use both terms interchangeably.

A case begins with the filing of a bankruptcy petition in federal district court. The district court typically refers bankruptcy cases to a specialized bankruptcy judge. Either party can appeal the decision of the bankruptcy judge back to the district court and, from there, to the federal appeals court.

Debtors may go willingly into the bankruptcy process by filing a **voluntary petition** or they may be dragged into court by creditors who file an **involuntary petition**. Originally, when the goal of bankruptcy laws was to protect creditors, voluntary petitions did not exist; all petitions were involuntary. Because the bankruptcy process is now viewed as being favorable to debtors, the vast majority of bankruptcy filings in this country are voluntary petitions.

Voluntary Petition

Any debtor may file for bankruptcy. It is not necessary that the debtor's liabilities exceed assets. Debtors sometimes file a bankruptcy petition because cash flow is so tight they cannot pay their debts, even though they are not technically insolvent. Under the BAPCPA, however, there are two new criteria for a bankruptcy filing:

- Within 180 days before filing, a debtor must undergo credit counseling with an approved agency.

- Debtors may file under Chapter 7 if they earn less than the median income in their state *or* they cannot afford to pay back at least $6,000 over five years.[2] Generally, all other debtors must file under Chapters 11 or 13. (These Chapters require the bankrupt to repay some debt.) To determine the median income in your state, click on **http://www.census.gov/hhes/income/4person.html**.

The voluntary petition must include the following documents:

Document	Description
Petition	Begins the case. Easy to fill out, it requires checking a few boxes and typing in little more than name, address, and Social Security number.
List of Creditors	The names and addresses of all creditors.

---

[2]   In some circumstances, debtors with income higher than $6,000 may still be eligible to file under Chapter 7, but the formula is highly complex and more than most readers want to know. The formula is available at 11 USC §707(b)(2)(A).

Document	Description
Schedule of Assets and Liabilities	A list of the debtor's assets and debts.
Claim of Exemptions	A list of all assets that the debtor is entitled to keep.
Schedule of Income and Expenditures	The debtor's job, income, and expenses.
Statement of Financial Affairs	A summary of the debtor's financial history and current financial condition. In particular, the debtor must list any recent payments to creditors and any other property held by someone else for the debtor.

Involuntary Petition

Creditors may force a debtor into bankruptcy by filing an involuntary petition. The creditors' goal is to preserve as much of the debtor's assets as possible and to ensure that all creditors receive a fair share. Naturally, the Code sets strict limits—debtors cannot be forced into bankruptcy every time they miss a credit card payment. **An involuntary petition must meet all of the following requirements:**

- The debtor must owe at least $12,300 in unsecured claims to the creditors who file.[3]

- If the debtor has at least 12 creditors, 3 or more must sign the petition. If the debtor has fewer than 12 creditors, any one of them can file a petition.

- The creditors must allege either that a custodian for the debtor's property has been appointed in the prior 120 days or that the debtor has generally not been paying debts that are due.

What does "a custodian for the debtor's property" mean? *State* laws sometimes permit the appointment of a custodian to protect a debtor's assets. The Code allows creditors to pull a case out from under state law and into federal bankruptcy court by filing an involuntary petition. Creditors also have the right to file an involuntary petition if they can show that the debtor is not paying debts. In the event that a debtor objects to an involuntary petition, the bankruptcy court must hold a trial to determine whether the creditors have met the Code's requirements.

Once a voluntary petition is filed or an involuntary petition approved, the bankruptcy court issues an **order for relief.** This order is an official acknowledgment that the debtor is under the jurisdiction of the court, and it is, in a sense, the start of the whole bankruptcy process. An involuntary debtor must now make all the filings that accompany a voluntary petition. Official bankruptcy forms are available at **http://www .uscourts.gov/bkforms/index.html**.

---

[3] In Chapter 26, on secured transactions, we discuss the difference between secured and unsecured claims at some length. A secured claim is one in which the creditor has the right to foreclose on a specific piece of the debtor's property (known as **collateral**) if the debtor fails to pay the debt when due. For example, if Lee borrows money from GMAC Finance to buy a car, the company has the right to repossess the car if Lee fails to repay the loan. GMAC's loan is **secured**. An **unsecured** loan has no collateral. If the debtor fails to repay, the creditor can make a general claim against the debtor but has no right to foreclose on a particular item of the debtor's property.

Trustee

The trustee is responsible for gathering the bankrupt's assets and dividing them among creditors. This is a critical role in a bankruptcy case. Trustees are typically lawyers or CPAs, but any generally competent person can serve. Creditors have the right to elect the trustee, but often they do not bother. If the creditors do not elect a trustee, then the **U.S. Trustee** appoints one. Each region of the country has a U.S. Trustee selected by the U.S. attorney general. Besides appointing trustees as necessary, this U.S. Trustee oversees the administration of bankruptcy law in the region. More information about the U.S. Trustee program is available at **http://www.usdoj.gov/ust/ about_ustp.htm**.

Creditors

After the court issues an order for relief, the U.S. Trustee calls a meeting of creditors. At the meeting, the bankrupt must answer (under oath) any question the creditors pose about his financial situation. If the creditors want to elect a trustee, they do so at this meeting.

After the meeting of creditors, unsecured creditors must submit a *proof of claim*. This document is a simple form stating the name of the creditor and the amount of the claim. The trustee and the debtor also have the right to file on behalf of a creditor. But if a claim is not filed, the creditor loses any right to be paid. The trustee, debtor, or any creditor can object to a claim on the grounds that the debtor does not really owe that money. The court then holds a hearing to determine the validity of the claim.

Secured creditors do not file proofs of claim unless the claim exceeds the value of their collateral. In this case, they are unsecured creditors for the excess amount and must file a proof of claim for it. Suppose that Deborah borrows $750,000 from Morton in return for a mortgage on her house. If she does not repay the debt, he can foreclose. Unfortunately, property values plummet, and by the time Deborah files a voluntary petition in bankruptcy, the house is worth only $500,000. Morton is a secured creditor for $500,000 and need file no proof of claim for that amount. But he is an unsecured creditor for $250,000 and will lose his right to this excess amount unless he files a proof of claim for it.

Automatic Stay

A fox chased by hounds has no time to make rational long-term decisions. What that fox needs is a safe burrow. Similarly, it is difficult for debtors to make sound financial decisions when hounded night and day by creditors shouting, "Pay me! Pay me!" The Code is designed to give debtors enough breathing space to sort out their affairs sensibly. An automatic stay is a safe burrow for the bankrupt. It goes into effect as soon as the petition is filed. **An automatic stay prohibits creditors from collecting debts that the bankrupt incurred before the petition was filed.** Creditors may not sue a bankrupt to obtain payment nor may they take other steps, outside of court, to pressure the debtor for payment. The following case illustrates how persistent creditors can be.

At least debtors are entitled to an automatic stay.

JACKSON V. HOLIDAY FURNITURE

309 B.R. 33, 2004 Bankr. LEXIS 548
United States Bankruptcy Court for the Western District of Missouri, 2004

Facts: Chris Wilcoxon and her mother, Alice Bokonich, owned Dan Holiday Furniture. Wilcoxon's sister, Judith Bokonich, was an employee. In April, Cora and Frank Jackson purchased a recliner chair on credit from the store. They made payments until November. That month, they filed for protection under the Bankruptcy Code. Dan Holiday received a notice of the bankruptcy. This notice stated that the store must stop all efforts to collect on the Jacksons' debt.

Despite this notice, a Dan Holiday collector telephoned the Jacksons' house ten times between November 15 and December 1 and left a card in their door threatening repossession of the chair. On Dec 1, Frank—without Cora's knowledge—went to Dan Holiday to pay the $230.00 owed for November and December. He told Wilcoxon about the bankruptcy filing, but allegedly added that he and his wife wanted to continue making payments directly to Dan Holiday.

In early January, employees at Dan Holiday learned that Frank had died the month before. Nevertheless, after Cora failed to make the payment for the month of January, a collector telephoned her house 26 times between January 14 and February 19. One of the taped messages from her answering machine stated:

> Hello. This is Judy over at Dan Holiday Furniture. And this is the last time I am going to call you. If you do not call me I will be at your house. And I expect you to call me today. If there is a problem I need to speak to you about it. You need to call me. We need to get this thing going. You are a January and February payment behind. And if you think you are going to get away with it, you've got another thing coming.

Judith Bokonich admitted that she had made this call.

When Cora returned home on February 18, she found seven bright yellow slips of paper in her door jamb stating that a Dan Holiday truck had stopped by to repossess her furniture. The cards read:

> "OUR TRUCK was here to **REPOSSESS** Your furniture (sic). 241-6933 Dan Holiday Furn. & Appl. Co."

The threat to send a truck was merely a ruse designed to frighten Cora into paying. Wilcoxon testified that Dan Holiday does not typically send a truck and that they do not want the furniture back. What they want is to talk directly to the customer about making payments.

Also on February 18, Dan Holiday sent Cora a letter stating that she had 24 hours to bring her account current or else **"Repossession Will Be Made and Legal Action Will Be Taken."** That same day, Cora's bankruptcy attorney contacted Dan Holiday. Thereafter all collection activity ceased.

Issues: Did Dan Holiday violate the automatic stay provisions of the Bankruptcy Code? What is the penalty for a violation?

Excerpts from Judge Venters's Decision:[4] The automatic stay prohibits the commencement or continuation of any action against the debtor that arose before the commencement of the bankruptcy case and forbids any act by a pre-petition creditor to obtain possession of property of the bankruptcy estate. An individual injured by a creditor's violation of the automatic stay shall recover actual damages, including costs and attorneys' fees, and in appropriate circumstances, may recover punitive damages.

In this case, there is no question that Dan Holiday repeatedly violated the automatic stay. [T]he Court finds that the Jacksons suffered financial damages in the amount of $230.00, which represents the coerced payments that Dan Holiday received from Frank Jackson on December 1.

The Court finds that punitive damages are warranted in this case based on Dan Holiday's egregious, intentional violations of the automatic stay. Dan Holiday's conduct was remarkably bad in that, after it had actual knowledge of the Jacksons' bankruptcy, and after coercing payments from the Jacksons covering the months of November and December, it made no less than twenty-six telephone calls to the Jacksons' household in January and February. Dan Holiday's continued collection efforts were in

▼

---

[4] For readability's sake, we refer to the plaintiffs as "the Jacksons," not "debtors" as the court did.

flagrant violation of the protections Congress afforded to debtors under the automatic stay.

In this matter the Court is somewhat hampered in assessing punitive damages by the lack of evidence concerning the ability of Dan Holiday to pay. Wilcoxon testified that Dan Holiday was a family-owned business that has been in existence for 52 years, and the Court assumes that it is a relatively small business. Under the circumstances of this case, the Court believes that an appropriate penalty would be $100.00 for each illegal contact with the Jacksons after December 1, when it is crystal clear that Dan Holiday had actual knowledge of the Jacksons' bankruptcy filing, for a total of $2,800.00. The Court believes that this penalty will be sufficient to sting the pocketbook of Dan Holiday and impress upon Dan Holiday and its owners and employees the importance of debtor protections under the Bankruptcy Code, as well as to deter further transgressions.

The Court also will award the Jacksons their attorneys' fees and costs in the amount of $1,142.42, an amount the Court considers eminently fair and reasonable under the circumstances of this case. ■

Bankruptcy Estate

The filing of the bankruptcy petition creates a new legal entity separate from the debtor—the **bankruptcy estate.** All of the bankrupt's assets pass to the estate, except exempt property and new property that the debtor acquires after the petition is filed.

Exempt Property

Unpaid creditors may be angry, but generally they do not want the debtor to starve to death. **The Code permits *individual* debtors (but not organizations) to keep some property for themselves.** This exempt property saves the debtor from destitution during the bankruptcy process and provides the foundation for a new life once the process is over.

In this one area of bankruptcy law, the Code defers to state law. Although the Code lists various types of exempt property, it permits states to opt out of the federal system and define a different set of exemptions. A majority of states have indeed opted out of the Code, and for their residents the Code exemptions are irrelevant. Alternatively, some states allow the debtor to choose between state or federal exemptions.

Under the *federal* Code, a debtor is allowed to exempt only $18,450 of the value of her home. If the house is worth more than that, the trustee sells it and returns $18,450 of the proceeds to the debtor. Most *states* exempt items such as the debtor's home, household goods, cars, work tools, disability and pension benefits, alimony, and health aids. Indeed, some states set no limit on the value of exempt property. Both Florida and Texas, for example, permit debtors to keep homes of unlimited value and a certain amount of land. (Texas also allows debtors to hang on to two firearms; athletic and sporting equipment; two horses, mules, or donkeys and a saddle, blanket, and bridle for each.) Not surprisingly, these generous exemptions sometimes lead to abuses. Therefore, under the BAPCPA, debtors can take advantage of state exemptions only if they have lived in that state for two years prior to the bankruptcy. And they can exempt only $125,000 of any house that was acquired during the 40 months before the bankruptcy.

Voidable Preferences

A major goal of the bankruptcy system is to divide the debtor's assets fairly among creditors. It would not be fair, or in keeping with this goal, if debtors were permitted to pay off some of their creditors immediately before filing a bankruptcy petition. These transfers are called **preferences** because they give unfair preferential treatment to some creditors. The trustee has the right to void such preferences.

Preferences can take two forms: payments and liens. A payment simply means that the debtor gives a creditor cash that would otherwise end up in the bankruptcy estate.

The debtor who hides assets from the approaching storm of bankruptcy is making a fraudulent transfer.

A lien means a security interest in the debtor's property. In bankruptcy proceedings, secured creditors are more likely to be paid than unsecured creditors. If the debtor grants a security interest in specific property, he vaults that creditor out of the great unwashed mass of unsecured creditors and into the elite company of secured creditors. If it happens immediately before the petition is filed, it is unfair to other unsecured creditors.

The trustee can void any transfer (whether payment or lien) that meets all of the following requirements:

- The transfer was to a creditor of the bankrupt.
- It was to pay an existing debt.
- The creditor received more from the transfer than she would have received during the bankruptcy process.
- The debtor's liabilities exceeded assets at the time of the transfer.
- The transfer took place in the 90-day period before the filing of the petition.

In addition, the trustee can void a transfer to an insider that occurs in the *year* preceding the filing of the petition. **Insiders** are family members of an individual, officers and directors of a corporation, or partners of a partnership.

Fraudulent Transfers

Suppose that a debtor sees bankruptcy inexorably approaching across the horizon like a tornado. He knows that, once the storm hits and he files a petition, everything he owns except a few items of exempt property will become part of the bankruptcy estate. Before that happens, he may be tempted to give some of his property to friends or family to shelter it from the tornado. If he succumbs to temptation, however, he is committing a fraudulent transfer.

A transfer is fraudulent if it is made within the year before a petition is filed and its purpose is to hinder, delay, or defraud creditors. The trustee can void any fraudulent transfer. Fraudulent transfers sound similar to voidable preferences, but there is an important distinction: voidable preferences pay legitimate debts, while fraudulent transfers protect the debtor's assets from legitimate creditors. For example, Lawrence Williams and his wife, Diana, enjoyed a luxurious lifestyle while his investment bank flourished. But when the bank failed, Lawrence was faced with debts of $6 million. On the eve of the bankruptcy filing, Diana suddenly announced that she wanted a divorce. In what had to be the most amicable breakup ever, Lawrence willingly transferred all of his assets to her. The unhappy couple went on to obtain their divorce in only two months, a speed that the bankruptcy court referred to as "astonishing." The court indignantly found that the transfer had been fraudulent.[5]

Not all payments by a debtor prior to filing are considered voidable preferences or fraudulent transfers. **A trustee cannot void pre-petition payments made *in the ordinary course.*** In a business context, that means a trustee cannot void payments from, say, a grocery store to its regular cookie supplier. For consumers, the trustee cannot

---

[5] *In re Williams,* 159 B.R. 648, 1993 Bankr. LEXIS 1482 (Bankr. D.R.I. 1993); remanded, 190 B.R. 728, 1996 U.S. Dist. LEXIS 539.

void payments below $600 or other routine payments, say, to the electric or water company. In these situations, the bankrupt is clearly not trying to cheat creditors. Even the insolvent are allowed to shower with the light on.

Payment of Claims

Imagine a crowded delicatessen on Saturday evening. People are pushing and shoving because they know there is not enough food for everyone; some customers will go home hungry. The delicatessen could simply serve whoever pushes to the front of the line, or it could establish a number system to ensure that the most deserving customers are served first—long-time patrons or those who called ahead. The Code has, in essence, adopted a number system to prevent a free-for-all fight over the bankrupt's assets. Indeed, one of the Code's primary goals is to ensure that creditors are paid in the proper order, not according to who pushes to the front of the line.

All claims are placed in one of three classes: (1) secured claims, (2) priority claims, and (3) unsecured claims. The second class—priority claims—has seven subcategories; the third class—unsecured claims—has three. **The trustee pays the bankruptcy estate to the various classes of claims in order of rank.** A higher class is paid in full before the next class receives any payment at all. In the case of *priority* claims, each *subcategory* is paid in order, with the higher subcategory receiving full payment before the next subcategory receives anything. If there are not enough funds to pay an entire subcategory, all claimants in that group receive a pro rata share. The rule is different for unsecured claims. All categories of *unsecured* claims are treated the same, and if there are not enough funds to pay the *entire* class, everyone in the class shares pro rata. If, for example, there is only enough money to pay 10 percent of the claims owing to unsecured creditors, then each creditor receives 10 percent of her claim. In bankruptcy parlance, this is referred to as "getting 10 cents on the dollar." The debtor is entitled to any funds remaining after all claims have been paid. The payment order is shown in Exhibit 27.1.

Secured Claims

Creditors whose loans are secured by specific collateral are paid first. Secured claims are fundamentally different from all other claims because they are paid by selling a specific asset, not out of the general funds of the estate. Sometimes, however, collateral is not valuable enough to pay off the entire secured debt. In this case, the creditor must wait in line with the unsecured creditors for the balance. Deborah (whom we met earlier in the section entitled "Creditors") borrowed $750,000 from Morton, secured by a mortgage on her house. By the time she files a voluntary petition, the house is worth only $500,000. Morton is a secured creditor for $500,000 and is paid that amount as soon as the trustee sells the house. But Morton is an unsecured creditor for $250,000

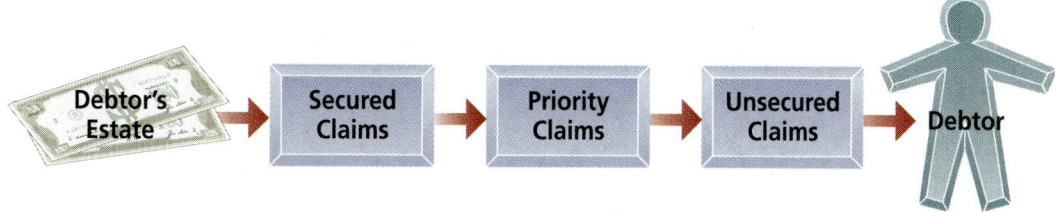

Exhibit 27.1

and will only receive this amount if the estate has enough funds to pay the unsecured creditors.

Priority Claims

There are seven subcategories of priority claims. Each category is paid in order, with the first group receiving full payment before the next group receives anything.

- *Alimony and Child Support.* The trustee must first pay any claims for alimony and child support. However, if the trustee is administering assets that could pay these support claims, then the trustee's fees are paid first.

- *Administrative Expenses.* These include fees to the trustee, lawyers, and accountants.

- *Gap Expenses.* If creditors file an involuntary petition, the debtor will continue to operate her business until the order for relief. Any expenses she incurs in the ordinary course of her business during this so-called **gap period** are paid now.

- *Payments to Employees.* The trustee now pays back wages to the debtor's employees for work performed during the 180 days prior to the date of the petition. The trustee, however, can pay no more than $10,000 to each employee. Any other wages become unsecured claims.

- *Employee Benefit Plans.* The trustee pays what the debtor owes to employee pension, health, or life insurance plans for work performed during the 180 days prior to the date of the petition. The total payment for wages and benefits under this and the prior paragraph cannot exceed $10,000 times the number of employees.

- *Consumer Deposits.* Any individual who has put down a deposit with the bankrupt for consumer goods is entitled to a refund of up to $2,225. If Stewart puts down a $3,000 deposit on a Miata sports car, he is entitled to a refund of $2,225 when the Trustie Car Lot goes bankrupt.

- *Taxes.* The trustee pays the debtor's income taxes for the three years prior to filing and property taxes for one prior year.

- *Drunken Injuries.* The trustee next pays the claims of anyone injured by a bankrupt who was driving a vehicle while drunk or on drugs.

Unsecured Claims

Last, and frequently very much least, the trustee pays unsecured claims. All three of these unsecured subcategories have an equal claim and must be paid together.

- *Secured Claims That Exceed the Value of the Available Collateral.* If funds permit, the trustee pays Morton the $250,000 that his collateral did not cover.

- *Priority Claims That Exceed the Priority Limits.* The trustee now pays employees, Stewart, and the tax authorities who were not paid in full the first time around because their claims exceeded the priority limits.

- *All Other Unsecured Claims.* Unsecured creditors have now reached the delicatessen counter. They can only hope that some food remains.

Discharge

Filing a bankruptcy petition is embarrassing, time-consuming, and disruptive. It can affect the debtor's credit rating for years, making the simplest car loan a challenge. To encourage debtors to file for bankruptcy despite the pain involved, the Code offers a powerful incentive: the **fresh start.** Once a bankruptcy estate has been distributed to creditors, they cannot make a claim against the debtor for money owed before the filing, *whether or not they actually received any payment.* These pre-petition debts are **discharged.** All is forgiven, if not forgotten.

Discharge is an essential part of bankruptcy law. Without it, debtors would have little incentive to take part. To avoid abuses, however, the Code limits both the type of debts that can be discharged and the circumstances under which discharge can take place. In addition, a debtor must complete an approved course on financial management before receiving a discharge.

As the following case illustrates, however, discharge is sometimes easier said than done.

In Re VISIAN

In Re VIVIAN

150 B.R. 832, 1992 Bankr. LEXIS 2102
United States Bankruptcy Court for the Southern District of Florida, 1992

Facts: NationsBank continued to send bills to John and Margaret Vivian for a debt that a bankruptcy court had discharged. Mr. Vivian wrote to the bankruptcy judge angrily demanding that NationsBank be ordered to stop.

Issue: Was NationsBank in contempt of court?

Excerpts from Judge Cristol's Decision: Following the entry of discharge in bankruptcy to John Coffey Vivian and Margaret Vivian, NationsBank sent them a dunning letter on a debt which had been discharged. NationsBank went to the expense of flying a high executive from North Carolina to Miami to appear and testify that the letter was sent in error and the court was satisfied that no intentional violation of the injunction had occurred. The NationsBank computer had generated the notice and NationsBank wrote a letter of apology to the Vivians and proceeded to appropriately chastise their computer and directed it not to send any more notices to the Vivians.

Only a month went by and the Vivians received a computer generated document from the bank which contained the words, "Please make checks payable to NationsBank and remit with top part of this statement to". Never mind that the document also showed no balance due and no payment due date, the Vivians were annoyed. It appearing to the court that this was not an intentional act of any human at NationsBank but rather the rampage of a rogue computer, the court entered an order suggesting that counsel for the bank communicate with the bank and the Vivians and try and make clear that this was not an intentional violation and it would not happen again.

Lo and behold, another month rolled around and that rogue computer did it again. The account statement showing no balance due and no date to make payment was mailed on NationsBank's red, white and blue stationery to Mr. and Mrs. Vivian. It is this final document that has truly established, beyond any reasonable doubt, that Mr. and Mrs. Vivian have no sense of humor and no gratitude whatsoever for the court's prior efforts on their behalf. They have, in their letter queried "May I ask a question? Why can't you or your Court get these continuing and very annoying letters STOPPED." (The question mark was omitted by the Vivians, not by the court but the court understood what they meant.) The Vivians were so annoyed that they went on to threaten that perhaps they should write to their family friend, a very well known, renowned and respected federal judge, about this serious matter. They then went on to say "May I hear from you or your secretary by return mail?". It is apparent that the Vivians are mad as you know what and they are not going to take it anymore. Likewise, this court is mad as you know what and is not going to take it anymore. Accordingly, and pursuant to Federal Rule of Bankruptcy Procedure 9020, the court determines the NationsBank computer to be in civil contempt of this court. Upon consideration, it is

ORDERED that the NationsBank computer, having been determined in civil contempt, is fined 50 megabytes of hard drive memory and 10 megabytes random access memory. The computer may purge itself of this contempt by ceasing the production and mailing of documents to Mr. and Mrs. Vivian. ■

Debts That Cannot Be Discharged

The following debts are *never* discharged, and the debtor remains liable in full until they are paid:

- Income taxes for the three years prior to filing and property taxes for the prior year.

- Money obtained fraudulently. Kenneth Smith ran a home repair business that fleeced senior citizens by making unnecessary repairs. Three months after he was found liable for fraud, he filed a voluntary petition in bankruptcy. The court held that his liability on the fraud claim could not be discharged.[6]

- Any loan of more than $500 that a consumer uses to purchase luxury goods within 90 days before the order for relief is granted.

- Cash advances on a credit card totaling more than $750 that an individual debtor takes out within 70 days before the order of relief.

- Debts omitted from the Schedule of Assets and Liabilities that the debtor filed with the petition, if the creditor did not know about the bankruptcy and therefore did not file a proof of claim.

- Money that the debtor stole or obtained through a violation of fiduciary duty.

- Money owed for alimony or child support.

- Debts stemming from intentional and malicious injury.

- Fines and penalties owed to the government.

- Liability for injuries caused by the debtor while operating a vehicle under the influence of drugs or alcohol. Yet another reason why friends don't let friends drive drunk.

- Liability for breach of duty to a bank. During the 1980s, a record number of savings and loans failed because their officers had made too many risky loans (in some cases to friends and family). This provision, added to the Code in 1990, was designed to prevent these officers from declaring bankruptcy to avoid their liability to bank shareholders.

- Debts stemming from a violation of securities laws. (This provision, added in 2002, was a response to Enron and similar cases, discussed in Chapter 36 on shareholders.)

- Student loans made or guaranteed by the government. These loans can only be discharged if repayment would cause undue hardship. As the following case illustrates, proving undue hardship is difficult.

In Re STERN

288 B.R. 36; 2002 Bankr. LEXIS 1609
United States Bankruptcy Court for the Northern District of New York, 2002

Facts: After graduating from Bates College in Lewiston, Maine, James Stern went to Syracuse College of Law. After law school, he had difficulty finding a job so he opened his own law practice specializing in civil rights work. He also handled criminal defense work for the Teamsters union. During the six years that he practiced, Stern's annual income ranged from $11,000 to $34,000, with an average of $17,000. In this same period, his wife's earnings were between $5,000 and $33,000, with an average of $18,000.

▼

---

[6] *In re Smith*, 848 F.2d 813, 1988 U.S. App. LEXIS 8037 (7th Cir. 1988).

Stern was sued for malpractice. Although he was ultimately found not liable, his malpractice premiums increased so much that he could no longer afford to practice on his own. He did not seek other legal jobs, believing that his debt and his default on student loans made him unemployable as a lawyer. He closed his practice and moved with his wife to her native country, France. She wanted to be with her father, who had suffered a stroke. Stern did not speak French and was, as he put it, not even qualified to be a street sweeper. At the time of trial, he was taking French language classes.

Stern had borrowed money to attend both college and law school. Having paid back $27,000, he still owed $147,000, which included $56,000 in principal and $91,000 in interest. Many of his living expenses were higher in France than in the United States, including gas, food, housing, and the cost of travel to visit his family. His monthly expenses averaged about $2,100. His income was $2,000, which represented residual income from his law practice. That income was not expected to continue for long. Stern's wife had almost completed a masters degree in France. She was freelancing as an English teacher but had not been able to obtain full-time employment. Her total income during the six months prior to trial had been $2,200.

Stern calculated that paying his debt would cost $1,167 per month over 30 years. He asked the court to discharge these student loans on grounds of undue hardship. As he put it, "I'm never going to be able to get a house, I'm never going to be able to have a car, and I won't—you know, I want to have kids. I want to be responsible, and I can't—I can't possibly pay this amount and have a life, not with what I expect I'll be able to earn."

Issue: Is Stern entitled to a discharge of his student loans on grounds of undue hardship?

Excerpts from Judge Gerling's Decision:[7] Congress, in enacting the [student loan provision of the Bankruptcy] statute, was cognizant of the fact that educational loans are different from most loans. They are made without business considerations, without security, without cosigners, and rely for repayment solely on the debtor's future increased income resulting from the education. In this sense, the loan is viewed as a mortgage on the debtor's future.

[To obtain a discharge] Stern must prove more than his present inability to pay his student loan obligations. He must also establish that his current financial hardship is likely to be long-term. In this case, Stern possesses both a bachelor's degree and a Juris Doctorate. Stern apparently has decided that he no longer wishes to pursue a legal career. He is certainly well within his rights to make such a choice. Nevertheless, [b]orrowers under the various guaranteed student loan programs are obligated to repay their loans even if they are unable to obtain employment in their chosen field of study.

The Court finds disturbing Stern's failure to maximize his income and minimize his expenses. He and his wife have elected to relocate to France where Stern admitted that the cost of living is higher. Nor is there any evidence that he ever made any effort to obtain employment in the United States in order to enhance his earnings, whether it be in business, government, or in a private law firm in Syracuse or elsewhere. Instead, he opted to move to a country where he acknowledges he cannot even get a job as a street sweeper because of his inability to speak the language.

Obviously, Stern would prefer to be in a position that would allow him to allocate those monies [he owes] to a mortgage on a home or to the raising of children. Those are certainly commendable goals; however, but the fact that they may not be attainable at this time because of the student loans and Stern's, as well as his wife's, current employment situation, does not meet the fundamental standard from which "undue hardship" is measured and does not provide a basis for granting Stern [even] a partial discharge at this time.

While Stern and his wife have experienced some "bumps in the road," the direction they take in the future appears very much in their control based on their age, health, and education. Indeed, it is the very education that he obtained as a result of the student loans at both the undergraduate and graduate levels, which, arguably, should ultimately allow him to pursue employment opportunities not available to others who were unable to pursue higher education for whatever reason. While Stern testified that he no longer wishes to continue in the legal profession, certainly, there are other career opportunities available to him by virtue on his education, training, and experience. ■

---

[7] Although the court refers to Stern as "Debtor," we use his surname.

Circumstances That Prevent Debts from Being Discharged

Apart from identifying the *kinds* of debts that cannot be discharged, the Code also prohibits the discharge of debts under the following *circumstances:*

- *Business Organizations.* Under Chapter 7 (but *not* the other chapters), only the debts of individuals can be discharged, not those of business organizations. Once its assets have been distributed, the organization must cease operation. If it continues in business, it is responsible for all pre-petition debts. Shortly after E. G. Sprinkler Corp. entered into an agreement with its union employees, it filed for bankruptcy under Chapter 7. Its debts were discharged, and the company began operation again. A court ordered it to pay its obligations to the employees because, once the company resumed business, it was responsible for all of its pre-filing debts.[8]

- *Repeated Filings for Bankruptcy.* Congress feared that some debtors, attracted by the lure of a fresh start, would make a habit of bankruptcy. Therefore, a debtor who has received a discharge under Chapter 7 or 11 cannot receive another discharge under Chapter 7 for at least eight years after the prior filing.

- *Revocation.* A court can revoke a discharge within one year if it discovers the debtor engaged in fraud or concealment.

- *Dishonesty or Bad Faith Behavior.* The court may deny discharge altogether if the debtor has, for example, made fraudulent transfers, hidden assets, falsified records, disobeyed court orders, refused to testify, or otherwise acted in bad faith. For instance, a court denied discharge under Chapter 7 to a couple who failed to list 15 pounds of marijuana on their Schedule of Assets and Liabilities. The court was unsympathetic to their arguments that a listing of this asset might have caused larger problems than merely being in debt.[9]

Reaffirmation

Sometimes debtors are willing to **reaffirm** a debt, meaning they promise to pay even after discharge. They may want to reaffirm a secured debt to avoid losing the collateral. For example, a debtor who has taken out a loan secured by a car may reaffirm that debt so that the finance company will agree not to repossess it. Sometimes debtors reaffirm because they feel guilty, or they want to maintain a good relationship with the creditor. They may have borrowed from a family member or an important supplier. Because discharge is a fundamental pillar of the bankruptcy process, courts look closely at each reaffirmation to ensure that the creditor has not unfairly pressured the bankrupt. To be valid, the reaffirmation must meet the following requirements:

- It must not violate common law standards for fraud, duress, or unconscionability. If creditors force a bankrupt into reaffirming a debt, the reaffirmation is invalid.

- It must have been filed in court before the discharge is granted.

- It must include the detailed disclosure statement required by the statute (§524).

- It must clearly disclose that the debtor has the right to rescind at any time up to the date of the discharge or 60 days after the agreement is filed in court, whichever is later.

- Either the court must determine that the agreement is in the debtor's best interest and does not impose undue hardship, or the attorney representing the debtor must

---

[8] *In re Goodman,* 873 F.2d 598, 1989 U.S. App. LEXIS 5472 (2d Cir. 1989).
[9] *In re Tripp,* 224 B.R. 95, 1998 Bankr. LEXIS 1108 (1998).

file an affidavit in court stating that the debtor's consent was informed and voluntary and the agreement does not create a hardship.

- In the case of an individual debtor, the court must explain both the terms of the agreement and the fact that it is not required by law.

In the following case, a lawyer agreed to repay a discharged debt. Did she know what she was doing? Is she liable on this debt? You be the judge.

you Be The Judge

RENWICK V. BENNETT

298 F.3d 1059; 2002 U.S. App. LEXIS 15547
United States Court of Appeals for the Ninth Circuit, 2002

Facts: Roberta Bennett and Diane Abbitt were law partners. To finance their partnership, they borrowed $150,000 from Abbitt's parents, the Renwicks. The day after the loan was due, Bennett and Abbitt each filed a separate petition for bankruptcy. The debt to the Renwicks was listed on each of their schedules. The bankruptcy court later discharged this debt.

Two years later, Bennett and Abbitt dissolved their partnership. During this process, they signed a settlement agreement. Paragraph 11 of the agreement provided:

11. *No Effect on Joint Personal Debts to the Renwicks* Abbitt and Bennett expressly agree that, notwithstanding anything to the contrary contained herein, they shall each remain liable for one half of the debt that Abbitt and Bennett currently owe to Martin and Annette Renwick. Abbitt and Bennett will remain liable to those creditors in the same manner as before this Settlement Agreement was executed.

Bennett allegedly agreed to reaffirm this debt in exchange for Abbitt's release of her claims against Bennett.

Following the settlement agreement, Bennett made interest-only payments to the Renwicks. Then the Renwicks demanded payment in full. Bennett refused and the Renwicks filed suit.

You Be the Judge: Is Bennett liable to the Renwicks for the money she borrowed from them?

Argument for the Renwicks: After the bankruptcy court discharged Bennett's debt, she entered into a new agreement to pay it. In return, Abbitt released the claims she had against Bennett. Thus, there was consideration for the new agreement.

Furthermore, Bennett is a lawyer who clearly understood the implications of what she was doing when she signed the new agreement. There were no threats or other duress; she entered into the new agreement voluntarily. Perhaps she was feeling guilty. But whatever the reason, she signed the new agreement and it is enforceable.

Argument for Bennett: The new agreement states: "Abbitt and Bennett will remain liable to those creditors in the same manner as before this Settlement Agreement was executed." When the new agreement was signed, Bennett was not liable to the Renwicks because the bankruptcy court had discharged that debt. Indeed, the whole point of discharge in bankruptcy is for the debtor *not* to remain liable on pre-filing debts. This may have been a new agreement, but it was an attempt to revive liability for the old debt.

Even if what the Renwicks said was true and Bennett signed the new agreement in exchange for Abbitt's release of her claims against Bennett, the agreement is still not enforceable. The fact that Abbitt offered Bennett new consideration for repayment of the discharged debt is irrelevant. This agreement did not meet the requirements for reaffirmation. ■

CHAPTER 11 REORGANIZATION

For a business, the goal of a Chapter 7 bankruptcy is euthanasia—putting it out of its misery by shutting it down and distributing its assets to creditors. Chapter 11 has a much more complicated and ambitious goal—resuscitating a business so that it can ultimately emerge as a viable economic concern. Keeping a business in operation benefits virtually all company stakeholders: employees, customers, creditors, shareholders, and the community.

Both individuals and businesses can use Chapter 11. Businesses usually prefer Chapter 11 over Chapter 7 because Chapter 11 does not require them to dissolve at the end as Chapter 7 does. The threat of death creates a powerful incentive to try rehabilitation under Chapter 11. Individuals, however, tend to prefer Chapter 13 because it is specifically designed for them.

A Chapter 11 proceeding follows many of the same steps as Chapter 7: a petition (either voluntary or involuntary), order for relief, meeting of creditors, proofs of claim, and an automatic stay. There are, however, some significant differences.

Debtor in Possession

Chapter 11 does not require a trustee. The bankrupt is called the **debtor in possession** and, in essence, serves as trustee. The debtor in possession has two jobs: to operate the business and to develop a plan of reorganization. A trustee is chosen only if the debtor is incompetent or uncooperative. In that case, the creditors can elect the trustee, but if they do not choose to do so, the U.S. Trustee appoints one.

Creditors' Committee

In a Chapter 11 case, the creditors' committee plays a particularly important role because typically there is no neutral trustee to watch over their interests. The committee has the right to help develop the plan of reorganization and to participate in any other way necessary to protect the interests of its constituency. Moreover, the BAPCPA requires the committee to communicate diligently with all creditors. The U.S. Trustee typically appoints the seven largest *un*secured creditors to the committee. However, under the BAPCPA, the court may require the U.S. Trustee to appoint some small business creditors to the committee. Secured creditors do not serve because their interests require less protection. If the debtor is a corporation, the U.S. Trustee may also appoint a committee of shareholders. The Code refers to the **claims** of creditors and the **interests** of shareholders.

Plan of Reorganization

Once the bankruptcy petition is filed, an automatic stay goes into effect to provide the debtor with temporary relief from creditors. The next stage is to develop a plan of reorganization that provides for the payment of debts and the continuation of the business. For the first 120 days after the order for relief, the debtor has the exclusive right to propose a plan. If the plan is accepted by the shareholders and creditors within 180 days of the order for relief, then the bankruptcy case terminates and the debtor implements the plan. Generally, the creditors and shareholders will accept a plan only if they expect to be better off with a reorganization than they would be with a liquidation. If they reject the debtor's plan, the creditors or shareholders may file alternative plans. The debtor has a strong incentive to develop a fair plan the first time because the creditors' proposals are likely to be less favorable.

Confirmation of the Plan

Anyone who proposes a plan of reorganization must also prepare a **disclosure statement** to be mailed out with the plan. The purpose of this statement is to provide creditors and shareholders with enough information to make an informed judgment. The statement describes the company's business, explains the plan, calculates the company's liquidation value, and assesses the likelihood that the debtor can be rehabilitated. The court must approve a disclosure statement before it is sent to creditors and shareholders.

All the creditors and shareholders have the right to vote on the plan of reorganization. In preparation for the vote, each creditor and shareholder is assigned to a class. Everyone in a class has similar claims or interests. Chapter 11 classifies claims in the same way as Chapter 7: (1) secured claims, (2) priority claims, and (3) unsecured claims. Each secured claim is usually in its own class because each one is secured by different collateral. Shareholders are also divided into classes, depending upon their interests. For example, holders of preferred stock are in a different class from common shareholders.

Creditors and shareholders receive a ballot with their disclosure statement to vote for or against the plan of reorganization. After the vote, the bankruptcy court holds a **confirmation hearing** to determine whether it should accept the plan. **The court will approve a plan if a majority *of each class* votes in favor of it.** Even if some classes vote against the plan, the court can still confirm it under what is called a **cramdown** (as in "the plan is crammed down the creditors' throats"). The court will not impose a cramdown unless, in its view, the plan is feasible and fair. If the court rejects the plan of reorganization, the creditors must develop a new one. In the following case, the court did impose a cramdown.

In Re FOX

2000 Bankr. LEXIS 1713
United States Bankruptcy Court, District of Kansas, 2000

Facts: Donald Fox founded Midland Fumigant, Inc., a company in the business of fumigating stored wheat, corn, and other grain. In a prior case, a competitor United Phosphorus, Ltd., obtained a verdict of $2 million against Midland and Fox for fraud.

Unable to pay the judgment, Fox filed a voluntary petition under Chapter 11 of the Bankruptcy Code. His plan of reorganization envisioned that he would use revenues from Midland to pay off his creditors in full over five years, with interest. To ensure that the plan of reorganization was feasible, Fox hired CPA Kirk W. Wiesner to analyze Midland's financial statements and prepare projections of its income and expenses. Wiesner also reviewed Midland's operations, business, products, and the industry. He concluded that the plan's projections were conservative and could easily be met.

Midland had six classes of creditors. All of the classes accepted the plan, except the two classes in which United was a member. The bankruptcy judge noted that United had an incentive to oppose Midland's reorganization because this business was highly competitive and, if Midland were to cease operations, United would be able to raise its prices substantially.

Issues: Was Fox's plan of reorganization feasible and fair? Should the court impose a cramdown?

Excerpts from Judge Robinson's Decision: Debtor has proposed a plan which pays all creditors in full, with interest. United, the only objecting creditor, will be paid in full [within 16 months]. Debtor has provided a reasonable and orderly repayment of his debts. Debtor's desire and intent to provide a mechanism for him to retain his business interests and assets is consistent with the purposes of the Bankruptcy Code. The plan may satisfy [the Code] even though the plan may not be one which the creditors would themselves design.

▼

United contends that the Plan is not feasible because the projections of Midland's income and expenses are unreliable. The purpose [of the Bankruptcy Code] is to prevent confirmation of visionary schemes that promise creditors and equity security holders more than the debtor can possibly attain after confirmation.

Will the reorganized debtor emerge from bankruptcy solvent and with a reasonable prospect of success? Debtor's expert, Kirk Wiesner, analyzed Midland's financial statements, and determined that Midland would have sufficient income and cash flow during the life of Debtor's Plan, to make the anticipated distributions and loans that will fund Debtor's Plan. Based on Wiesner's Projections, which proved conservative in [the past], when Midland's actual income doubled the projected income, the Court concludes that Midland will have a continuing ability to distribute and loan funds to the Debtor as contemplated.

The Plan has a reasonable assurance of success and is not likely to be followed by liquidation, or the need for further financial reorganization. As such, the Debtor's Plan meets the feasibility requirement. The Court further notes that the United States Trustee has filed a statement in support of confirmation of the Plan.

[T]he Court finds that the Debtor's Plan is fair and equitable and, as a result, the fact that [two] Classes did not accept the Plan does not preclude confirmation.

The Debtor's Plan is confirmed over the objection of United and over the dissenting votes of [two] Classes for the reasons stated. ∎

Discharge

A confirmed plan of reorganization is binding on the debtor, creditors, and shareholders. **The debtor now owns the assets in the bankrupt estate, free of all obligations except those listed in the plan.** Under a typical plan of reorganization, the debtor gives some current assets to creditors and also promises to pay them a portion of future earnings. In contrast, the Chapter 7 debtor typically relinquishes all assets (except exempt property) to creditors but then has no obligation to turn over future income. Exhibit 27.2 illustrates the steps in a Chapter 11 bankruptcy.

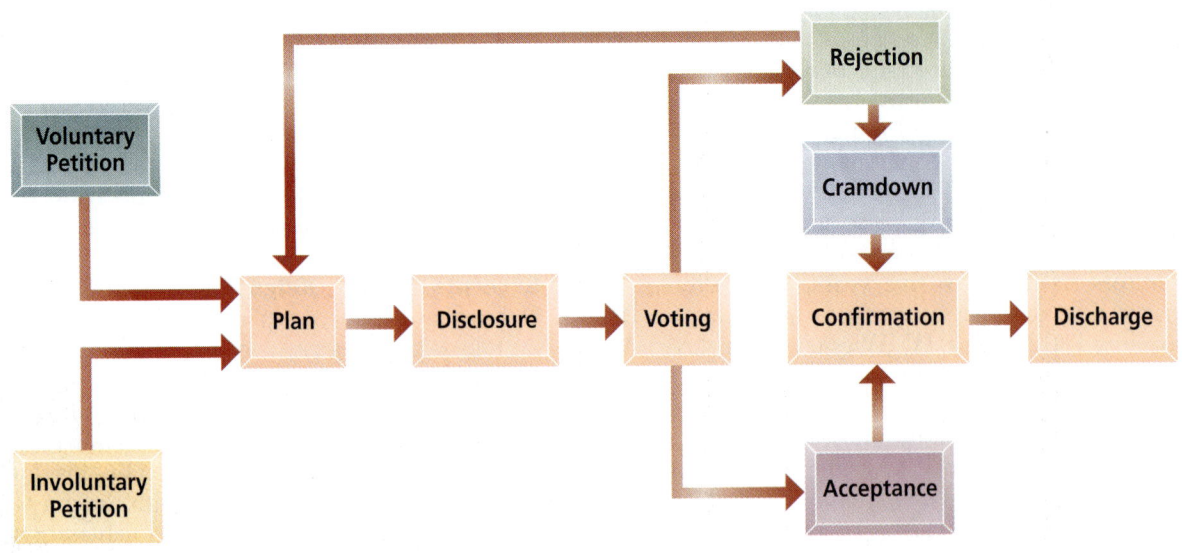

Exhibit 27.2

Small Business Bankruptcy

Out of concern that the lengthy procedure in Chapter 11 was harming the creditors of small businesses, Congress included provisions in the BAPCPA designed to speed up the process for businesses with less than $2 million in debt. After the order of relief, the bankrupt has the exclusive right to file a plan for 180 days. Both a plan and a disclosure statement must be filed within 300 days. The court must confirm or reject the plan within 45 days after its filing. If these deadlines are not met, the case can be converted to Chapter 7 or dismissed. This amendment may well cause more small companies to go out of business.

CHAPTER 13 CONSUMER REORGANIZATIONS

The purpose of Chapter 13 is to rehabilitate an individual debtor. It is not available at all to businesses or to individuals with more than $307,675 in unsecured debts or $922,975 in secured debts. Under Chapter 13, the bankrupt consumer typically keeps most of her assets in exchange for a promise to repay some of her debts using future income. Therefore, to be eligible, the debtor must have a regular source of income. Individuals usually choose this chapter because it is easier and cheaper than Chapters 7 and 11. Consequently, more money is retained for both creditors and debtor.

A bankruptcy under Chapter 13 generally follows the same course as Chapter 11: the debtor files a petition, creditors submit proofs of claim, the court imposes an automatic stay, the debtor files a plan and the court confirms the plan. But there are some differences.

Beginning a Chapter 13 Case

To initiate a Chapter 13 case, the debtor must file a voluntary petition. **Creditors cannot use an involuntary petition to force a debtor into Chapter 13.** In all Chapter 13 cases, the U.S. Trustee appoints a trustee to supervise the debtor, although the debtor remains in possession of the bankruptcy estate. The trustee also serves as a central clearinghouse for the debtor's payments to creditors. The debtor pays the trustee who, in turn, transmits these funds to creditors. For this service, the trustee is allowed to keep 10 percent of the payments.

Plan of Payment

The debtor must file a plan of payment within 15 days after filing the voluntary petition. Only the debtor can file a plan; the creditors have no right to file their own version. Under the plan, the debtor must (1) commit some future earnings to pay off debts, (2) promise to pay all secured and priority claims in full, and (3) treat all remaining classes equally. If the plan does not provide for the debtor to pay off creditors in full, then all of the debtor's disposable income for the next five years must go to creditors.

Within 30 days after filing the plan of payment, the debtor must begin making payments to the trustee under the plan. The trustee holds these payments until the plan is confirmed and then transmits them to creditors. The debtor continues to make payments to the trustee until the plan has been fully implemented. If the plan is rejected, the trustee returns the payments to the debtor.

Only the bankruptcy court has the authority to confirm or reject a plan of payment. Creditors have no right to vote on it. However, to confirm a plan, the court must ensure that:

- The creditors have the opportunity to voice their objections at a hearing;
- All of the unsecured creditors receive at least as much as they would have under Chapter 7;
- The plan is feasible and the bankrupt will be able to make the promised payments;
- The plan does not extend beyond three years without good reason and in no event lasts longer than five years; and
- The debtor is acting in good faith, making a reasonable effort to pay obligations.

In the following case, a creditor argued that the debtor's plan was not made in good faith.

In Re LEMAIRE

898 F.2d 1346, 1990 U.S. App. LEXIS 4374
United States Court of Appeals for the Eighth Circuit, 1990

Facts: As Paul Handeen got out of his car one Sunday morning, Gregory LeMaire shot at him nine times with a bolt action rifle. Bullets struck Handeen in the mouth, neck, spine, arm, knee, and ankle. LeMaire pleaded guilty to a charge of aggravated assault and served 27 months in prison. After his release, he earned a doctorate from the University of Minnesota.

Handeen received a judgment of $50,000 against LeMaire. To avoid paying this judgment, LeMaire filed a bankruptcy petition under Chapter 13. He proposed a plan under which he would pay his creditors 42 percent of their claims. The bankruptcy court confirmed the plan over Handeen's objection. Handeen appealed to the district court, arguing that LeMaire had not filed his plan in good faith. The district court affirmed and, upon appeal, the appeals court also affirmed. Handeen then asked for a rehearing. This time, the appeals court granted a rehearing *en banc*. (Usually, only three judges hear an appeal. *En banc* means that all the judges on the court hear it.)

Issues: Is a judgment awarded to the victim of an intentional shooting dischargeable under Chapter 13? Did LeMaire file his plan in good faith?

Excerpts from Judge Gibson's Decision: In evaluating LeMaire's motivation and sincerity, the bankruptcy court balanced Handeen's desire to be compensated for his injuries against LeMaire's desire to have a fresh start and found the latter to outweigh the former in importance. The court noted that, while LeMaire had been unable to pay his debt to his victim, he had paid his debt to society by serving a prison sentence and had attempted to reorder his life and make a fresh start. The court found that forcing LeMaire to be burdened the rest of his life with a judgment which would continue to accrue interest, result in endless garnishments, and prevent him from accumulating property would be inimical to such a fresh start. The court concluded that LeMaire had made a wholehearted attempt to pay Handeen as much as possible, and that LeMaire's motivation was proper and his sincerity real.

We do not believe that LeMaire has fulfilled the good faith requirement of Chapter 13. The record here very clearly indicates that LeMaire intended to kill Handeen, and he nearly succeeded in his intention. While pre-filing conduct is not determinative of the good faith issue, it is nevertheless relevant. When we consider the pre-filing conduct here, including the maliciousness of the injury which LeMaire inflicted upon Handeen, in light of the lack of other factors sufficient to establish good faith, we are persuaded that the bankruptcy court clearly erred in finding that LeMaire proposed his plan in good faith.

We remand this case to the district court with instructions to remand, in turn, to the bankruptcy court for further proceedings consistent with this opinion. ∎

Discharge

Once confirmed, a plan is binding on all creditors, whether they like it or not. **The debtor is washed clean of all pre-petition debts except those provided for in the plan, but, unlike Chapter 7, the debts are not** *permanently* **discharged.** If the debtor violates the plan, all of the debts are revived, and the creditors have a right to recover them under Chapter 7. The debts become permanently discharged only when the bankrupt fully complies with the plan.

If the debtor's circumstances change, the debtor, the trustee, or unsecured creditors can ask the court to modify the plan. Most such requests come from debtors whose income has declined. However, if the debtor's income rises, the creditors or the trustee can ask that payments increase, too.

NEWSworthy

The BAPCPA has been criticized for making bankruptcy more difficult for individuals. At the same time, some argue that bankruptcy is too easy for companies. Take the airline industry, for instance. United Airlines was in bankruptcy for three years. In this process, it dramatically cut the pay and benefits of rank-and-file workers, terminated employee pensions plans, and renegotiated leases on its airplanes. At least its employees still had jobs. Meanwhile, its CEO was the highest paid executive at any domestic airline, with compensation over $1 million. For United, bankruptcy was an effective competitive strategy.

Was it fair for United to remain in business, competing against its rivals with the aid of the bankruptcy court? The airline industry had substantial excess capacity and only one airline among the largest seven was profitable. If some of these companies closed down, perhaps more of the survivors would make money. ◆

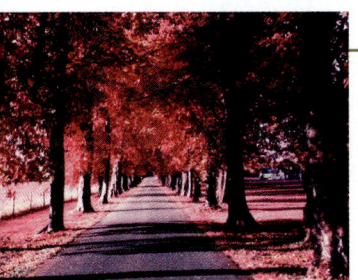

© PHOTODISC/GETTY IMAGES

Chapter Conclusion

Whenever an individual or organization incurs more debts than it can pay in a timely fashion, everyone loses. The debtor loses control of his assets and the creditors lose money. Bankruptcy laws cannot create assets where there are none (or not enough), but they can ensure that the debtor's assets, however limited, are fairly divided between the debtor and creditors. Any bankruptcy system that accomplishes this goal must be deemed a success. Is the U.S. Bankruptcy Code fair?

Chapter Review

This chart sets out the important elements of each bankruptcy chapter.

	Chapter 7	**Chapter 11**	**Chapter 13**
Objective	Liquidation	Reorganization	Consumer reorganization
Who May Use It	Individual or organization	Individual or organization	Individual
Type of Petition	Voluntary or involuntary	Voluntary or involuntary	Only voluntary

	Chapter 7	**Chapter 11**	**Chapter 13**
Administration of Bankruptcy Estate	Trustee	Debtor in possession (trustee selected only if debtor is unable to serve).	Trustee
Selection of Trustee	Creditors have right to elect trustee; otherwise, U.S. Trustee makes appointment.	Usually no trustee.	Appointed by U.S. Trustee.
Participation in Formulation of Plan	No plan is filed.	Both creditors and debtor can propose plans.	Only debtor can propose a plan.
Creditor Approval of Plan	Creditors do not vote.	Creditors vote on plan, but court may approve plan without the creditors' support.	Creditors do not vote on plan.
Impact on Debtor's Post-petition Income	Not affected; debtor keeps all future earnings.	Must contribute toward payment of pre-petition debts.	Must contribute toward payment of pre-petition debts.

Practice Test

1. Mark Milbank built custom furniture in Port Chester, New York. His business was unsuccessful, and he repeatedly borrowed money from his wife and her father. He promised that the loans would enable him to spend more time with his family. Instead, he spent more time in bed with his next-door neighbor. After the divorce, his ex-wife and her father demanded repayment of the loans. When Milbank filed under Chapter 13, his ex-wife and her father asked the court not to discharge Milbank's debts on the grounds that he had acted in bad faith toward them. Should the bankruptcy court discharge Milbank's loans?

2. **CPA QUESTION** Decal Corp. incurred substantial operating losses for the past three years. Unable to meet its current obligations, Decal filed a petition of reorganization under Chapter 11 of the federal Bankruptcy Code. Which of the following statements is correct?

   a. A creditors' committee, if appointed, will consist of unsecured creditors.

   b. The court must appoint a trustee to manage Decal's affairs.

   c. Decal may continue in business only with the approval of a trustee.

   d. The creditors' committee must select a trustee to manage Decal's affairs.

3. James Hartley, the owner of an auto parts store, told an employee, Rickey D. Jones, to clean and paint some tires in the basement. Highly flammable gasoline fumes accumulated in the poorly ventilated space. Hartley threw a firecracker into the basement, as a joke, intending only to startle Jones. Sparks from the firecracker caused an explosion and fire that severely burned Jones. He filed a personal injury suit against Hartley for $1 million. Is this debt dischargeable under Chapter 7?

4. **CPA QUESTION** A voluntary petition filed under the liquidation provisions of Chapter 7 of the federal Bankruptcy Code:

   a. Is not available to a corporation unless it has previously filed a petition under the reorganization provisions of Chapter 11 of the Code

   b. Automatically stays collection actions against the debtor **except** by secured creditors

c. Will be dismissed unless the debtor has 12 or more unsecured creditors whose claims total at least $5,000

d. Does **not** require the debtor to show that the debtor's liabilities exceed the fair market value of assets

5. After filing for bankruptcy, Yvonne Brown sought permission of the court to reaffirm a $6,000 debt to her credit union. The debt was unsecured and she was under no obligation to pay it. The credit union had published the following notice in its newsletter:

> If you are thinking about filing bankruptcy THINK about the long-term implications. This action, filing bankruptcy, closes the door on TOMORROW. Having no credit means no ability to purchase cars, houses, credit cards. Look into the future—no loans for the education of your children.

Should the court approve Brown's reaffirmation?

6. **ETHICS** On November 5, The Fred Hawes Organization, Inc., a small subcontractor, opened an account with Basic Distribution Corp., a supplier of construction materials. Hawes promised to pay its bills within 30 days of purchase. Although Hawes purchased a substantial quantity of goods on credit from Basic, it made few payments on the accounts until the following March when it paid Basic over $21,000. On May 14, Hawes filed a voluntary petition under Chapter 7. Does the bankruptcy trustee have a right to recover this payment? Is it fair to Hawes's other creditors if Basic is allowed to keep the $21,000 payment?

7. Robert Britton was an office manager at the Academy of Cosmetic Surgery Medical Group. Mary Price made an appointment for a consultation about a lipectomy (removal of abdominal fat). Britton wore a name tag that identified him as a doctor, and was addressed as "doctor" by the nurse. Britton and the nurse then examined Price. Britton touched the area of her stomach where there was excess fat and showed her where the incision would be made. A doctor who worked for the Academy actually performed the surgical procedure on Price at the Academy's offices, with Britton present. After the procedure, Price went to a hospital suffering from

severe pain. The hospital staff found that a tube had been left in her body at the site of the incision. The area of the incision became infected, and Price ultimately required corrective surgery. The jury awarded her $275,000 in damages in a fraud suit against Britton. He subsequently filed a Chapter 7 bankruptcy petition. Is this judgment dischargeable in bankruptcy court?

8. Why did Kim Basinger (see the chapter introduction) file under Chapter 11 rather than Chapter 13?

9. **CPA QUESTION** Unger owes a total of $50,000 to eight unsecured creditors and one fully secured creditor. Quincy is one of the unsecured creditors and is owed $6,000. Quincy has filed a petition against Unger under the liquidation provisions of Chapter 7 of the federal Bankruptcy Code. Unger has been unable to pay debts as they become due. Unger's liabilities exceed Unger's assets. Unger has filed papers opposing the bankruptcy petition. Which of the following statements regarding Quincy's petition is correct?

a. It will be dismissed because the secured creditor failed to join in the filing of the petition.

b. It will be dismissed because three unsecured creditors must join in the filing of the petition.

c. It will be granted because Unger's liabilities exceed Unger's assets.

d. It will be granted because Unger is unable to pay Unger's debts as they become due.

10. **YOU BE THE JUDGE** WRITING PROBLEM Lydia D'Ettore received a degree in computer programming at DeVry Institute of Technology, with a grade-point average of 2.51. To finance her education, she borrowed $20,516.52 from a federal student loan program. After graduation, she could not find a job in her field, so she went to work as a clerk at a salary of $12,500. D'Ettore and her daughter lived with her parents free of charge. After setting aside $50 a month in savings and paying bills that included $233 for a new car (a Suzuki Samurai) and $50 for jewelry from Zales, her disposable income was $125 per month. D'Ettore asked the bankruptcy court to discharge the debts she owed for her DeVry education. Did the debts to DeVry Institute impose an undue hardship on D'Ettore? **Argument for D'Ettore:** Lydia D'Ettore lives at home with her parents. Even so, her disposable income is a

meager $125 a month. She would have to spend every single penny of her disposable income for nearly 15 years to pay back her $20,000 debt to DeVry. That would be an undue hardship. **Argument for the Creditors:** The U.S. government guaranteed D'Ettore's loan. Therefore, if the court discharges it, the American taxpayer will have to pay the bill. Why should taxpayers subsidize an irresponsible student? D'Ettore must also stop buying new cars and jewelry. And why should the government pay her debts while she saves money every month?

11. Dr. Ibrahim Khan caused an automobile accident in which a fellow physician, Dolly Yusufji, became a quadriplegic. Dr. Khan signed a contract for the lifetime support of Dr. Yusufji. When he refused to make payments under the contract, she sued him and obtained a judgment for $1,205,400. Dr. Khan filed a Chapter 11 petition. At the time of the bankruptcy hearing, five years after the accident, Dr. Khan had not paid Dr. Yusufji anything. She was dependent on a motorized wheelchair; he drove a Rolls-Royce. Is Dr. Khan's debt dischargeable under Chapter 11?

12. *ROLE REVERSAL* Write a multiple-choice question that highlights the difference between Chapters 7 and 11.

Internet Research Problem

What are your state's exemption rules? (You can find them at http://beatty.westbuslaw.com or elsewhere on the Web.) Compared with other states and the federal government, is your state generous or stingy with exemptions? In considering a new bankruptcy statute, Congress struggled mightily over this issue. What do you think is a fair exemption?

You can find further practice problems at http://beatty.westbuslaw.com **or in the Study Guide that accompanies this text.**

Agency and Employment Law

Agency: The Inside Relationship

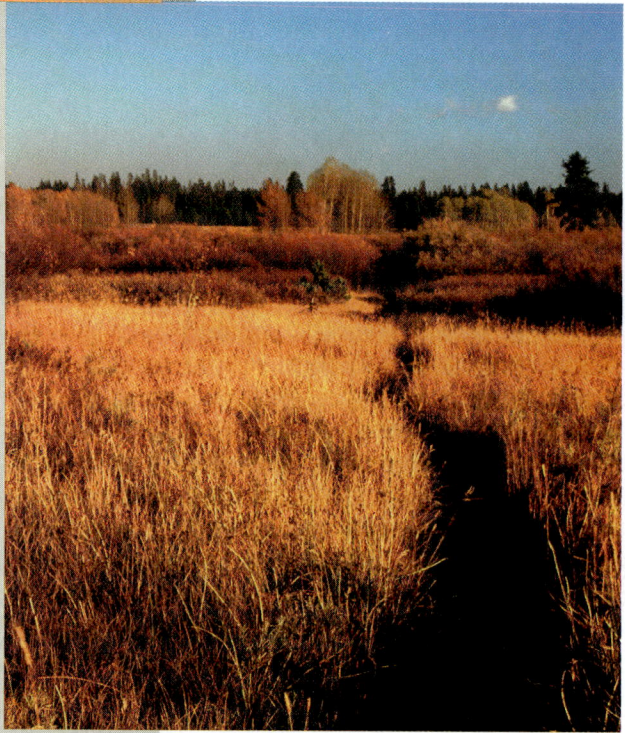

As Leo Tolstoy observed, "Happy families are all alike; every unhappy family is unhappy in its own way."[1] The Gagnon family of Massachusetts found its own way to be unhappy. Eighty-five-year-old Francis Gagnon and his wife lived on a 184-acre farm in Shelburne. They also owned a smaller parcel of land in Hillsborough, New Hampshire. Their daughter Joan Coombs resided 20 miles from Shelburne while their son, Frank, lived in a trailer on a far corner of the farm.

Because of their advancing age, Jean suggested that her parents sign powers of attorney appointing her as their agent. In this way, if they became ill she would have the legal authority to take care of them and their property. In theory, this was a sensible step that estate lawyers often recommend. But in this family sensible took a backseat to jealousy and resentment. No one told Frank about the power of attorney.

The next year, Mrs. Gagnon went into a nursing home. In the process of admitting her, Frank learned of Joan's power of attorney. He was not exactly pleased. After moving from his trailer into the main house, Frank prevailed upon his father to revoke the power of attorney. Naturally, neither Frank nor Francis told Joan this inter-

---

1   Leo Tolstoy, *Anna Karenina*, Barnes & Noble Books, p.1.

esting fact. (At trial the siblings each accused the other of undue influence on their father, but the judge concluded that Francis was mentally competent during this entire episode.)

Two months later, Mrs. Gagnon died and Francis decided to sell the Shelburne farm. Shortly thereafter, he signed a purchase and sale agreement on the property at a price of $750,000. He then gave the property in New Hampshire to Frank.

When Francis told Joan about the sale of the land and his intention to move to New Hampshire to live with Frank, she crafted her own plan. Not realizing that her power of attorney had been revoked, she used it to transfer the Shelburne property to a trust that she had created and that she controlled. When Joan wrote Frank to tell him about these developments, he was furious. This unhappy family was now reduced to communicating through their attorneys. Francis's lawyer wrote to Joan demanding that she return the Shelburne property to him. She refused, setting the family on the path to court.

Although this case undoubtedly raises issues that could keep a family therapist employed for some time, it is the questions of agency law that concern us. Was Joan an agent for her father? As an agent, did she have the right to convey his property to her trust? Later in this chapter, the case of *Gagnon v. Coombs* lays out the arguments for both sides. ■

Thus far, this book has primarily dealt with issues of individual responsibility: What happens if *you* knock someone down or *you* sign an agreement? Agency law, on the other hand, is concerned with your responsibility for the actions of others. What happens if your agent assaults someone or enters into an agreement? Agency law presents a significant trade-off: if you do everything yourself, you have control over the result. But the size and scope of your business (and your life) will be severely limited. Once you hire other people, you can accomplish a great deal more, but your risk of legal liability increases immensely. Though it might be safer to do everything yourself, that is not a practical decision for most business owners (or most people). The alternative is to hire carefully and to limit the risks as much as possible by understanding the law of agency.

CREATING AN AGENCY RELATIONSHIP

Principals have substantial liability for the actions of their agents.[2] Therefore, disputes about whether an agency relationship exists are not mere legal quibbles but important issues with potentially profound financial consequences. According to the Restatement of Agency:

---

[2] The word "principal" is always used when referring to a person. It is not to be confused with the word "principle," which refers to a fundamental idea.

Agency is the fiduciary relation which results from the manifestation of consent by one person to another that the other shall act on his behalf and subject to his control, and consent by the other so to act.[3]

In other words, in an agency relationship, someone (the agent) agrees to perform a task for, and under the control of, someone else (the principal). To create an agency relationship, there must be:

- A **principal** and
- An **agent**
- Who mutually **consent** that the agent will act on behalf of the principal and
- Be subject to the principal's **control**
- Thereby creating a **fiduciary** relationship.

Consent

To establish consent, the principal must ask the agent to do something and the agent must agree. In the most straightforward example, Francis Gagnon asked his daughter to act as his agent and she agreed. Matters were more complicated, however, when Steven James met some friends one evening at a restaurant. During the two hours he was there, he drank four to six beers. (It is probably a bad sign that he cannot remember how many.) From then on, one misfortune piled upon another. After leaving the restaurant at about 7:00 P.M., James sped down a highway and crashed into a car that had stalled on the roadway, thereby killing the driver. James told the police at the scene that he had not seen the parked car (another bad sign). Evidently, James's lawyer was not as perceptive as the police in recognizing drunkenness. In a misguided attempt to help his client, James's lawyer took him to the local hospital for a blood test. Unfortunately, the test confirmed that James had indeed been drunk at the time of the accident.

The attorney knew that if this evidence was admitted at trial, his client would soon be receiving free room and board from the Massachusetts Department of Corrections. So at trial, the lawyer argued that the blood test was protected by the client–attorney privilege because the hospital had been his agent and therefore a member of the defense team. After a review of agency law, however, the court concluded that:

> no such agency relationship [was] shown between the defendant and the hospital personnel. Nothing in the record indicates that the hospital's employees manifested the requisite consent to act in that capacity.[4]

The court upheld James's conviction of murder in the first degree by reason of extreme atrocity or cruelty.

Control

Principals are liable for the acts of their agents because they exercise control over the agents. If principals direct their agents to commit an act, it seems fair to hold the principal liable when that act causes harm. In the following example, did Northwest Airlines exercise control over Kuwait Air?

NEWS*worthy*

The horse-drawn caisson wound slowly through Arlington National Cemetery and stopped in front of lot number 59, the section reserved for victims of terrorist acts. The flag-draped casket of William L. Stanford, one of the two Agency for International Development audi-

---

[3] Section 1 of the Restatement (Second) of Agency (1958), prepared by the American Law Institute.
[4] *Commonwealth v. James*, 427 Mass. 312, 693 N.E.2d 148, 1998 Mass. LEXIS 175.

tors killed by plane hijackers in Iran, was carried to the gravesite amid full military honors. Three volleys of rifle fire pierced the unusually warm December air as scores of family, friends and colleagues lowered their heads and wept. Stanford, 52, was killed as he was traveling to join his wife and 13-year-old daughter in Karachi, Pakistan, where he intended to spend the holidays.[5] ◆

The hijacked plane—with William Stanford aboard—was a Kuwait Airways (KA) flight from Kuwait to Pakistan. Stanford had originally purchased a ticket on Northwest Airlines but had traded in his Northwest ticket for a seat on the KA flight. Stanford's widow sued Northwest on the theory that KA was Northwest's agent. The airlines had an agreement permitting passengers to exchange tickets from one to another. In this case, however, the court found that no agency relationship existed because Northwest had no *control* over KA.[6] Northwest did not tell KA how to fly planes or handle terrorists; therefore it should not be liable when KA made fatal errors. An agent and principal must not only *consent* to an agency relationship, but the principal must also have *control* over the agent.

Fiduciary Relationship

A fiduciary relationship is a special relationship, with high standards. The beneficiary places special confidence in the fiduciary who, in turn, is obligated to act in good faith and candor, putting his own needs second. The purpose of a fiduciary relationship is for one person to benefit another. **Agents have a fiduciary duty to their principals.**

All three elements—consent, control, and a fiduciary duty—are necessary to create an agency relationship. In some relationships, for example, there might be a *fiduciary duty* but no *control*. A trustee of a trust must act for the benefit of the beneficiaries, but the beneficiaries have no right to control the trustee. Therefore, a trustee is not an agent of the beneficiaries. *Consent* is present in every contractual relationship, but that does not necessarily mean that the two parties are agent and principal. If Horace sells his car to Lily, they both expect to benefit under the contract, but neither has a *fiduciary duty* to the other and neither *controls* the other, so there is no agency relationship.

In the following case, a customer was injured while waiting at a Southwest ticket counter. Were the workers behind the counter agents for Southwest?

ELSON V. KOEHR

856 S.W.2d 57, 1993 Mo. LEXIS 77
Supreme Court of Missouri, 1993

Facts: Rose Elson was injured in a fall at the Southwest Airlines ticket counter at Lambert–St. Louis International Airport during a layover on a flight from Houston to Indianapolis. She filed suit against Southwest for negligence. Elson was a resident of Texas and Southwest is a Texas corporation, but she filed the case in St. Louis. Southwest's only connection with St. Louis was that passenger reservations and ticket sales for Southwest flights were made through independent travel agents located in the city.

Under Missouri state law, suit could be filed against a corporation in "any county where the corporations shall have or usually keep an office or agent. . . ." The trial court dismissed Elson's case on the grounds that the ticket sellers were not true agents under agency law. ▼

---

[5] Mary Jordan, "Terrorists' Victim Is Buried," *Washington Post*, Dec. 18, 1984, p. A14. © 1984, The Washington Post.
[6] *Stanford v. Kuwait Airways Corp.*, 648 F. Supp. 1158, 1986 U.S. Dist. LEXIS 18880 (S.D.N.Y. 1986).

Issues: **Could Elson file suit against Southwest in St. Louis? Were the workers behind the Southwest counter agents of Southwest?**

Excerpts from Judge Limbaugh's Decision: In this case, Southwest and the independent travel agencies agreed in writing to establish an agency relationship in which the agents are given the express authority to sell and promote air travel on the airline. The existence of the agency is confirmed by matching the three essential agency characteristics to the provisions of the agency agreement.

It is uncontested that Southwest is bound to provide air travel to customers who buy airline tickets from the travel agencies. Nor is there any dispute that the travel agencies operate as fiduciaries of Southwest within the scope of the agency agreement. That fiduciary relationship is evidenced, in part, by the fact that the travel agency makes reservations and sells tickets on behalf of the airline, and the moneys collected from those sales are forwarded to the airline, all to the airline's direct benefit.

Finally, it is obvious that Southwest exercises control over the efforts of the travel agencies to sell and promote air travel. [T]he agreement between Southwest and the travel agencies is replete with conditions and restrictions on the authority of the agencies to act on behalf of the airline.

Under these circumstances, we hold that St. Louis travel agencies are agents of Southwest. ■

Elements Not Required for an Agency Relationship

Consent, control, and a fiduciary relationship are necessary to establish an agency relationship. The following elements are **not** required:

- *A Written Agreement.* In most cases, an agency agreement does not have to be in writing. An oral understanding is valid, except in one circumstance—the **equal dignities rule.** According to this rule, if an agent is empowered to enter into a contract that must be in writing, then the appointment of the agent must also be written. For example, under the statute of frauds a contract for the sale of land is unenforceable unless in writing, so the agency agreement to sell land must also be in writing. Suppose that Albert hires Hannah to find a buyer for his house. If Albert wants Hannah to sign the sales contract for him, he must grant her that authority *in writing*.

- *A Formal Agreement.* The principal and agent need not agree formally that they have an agency relationship. They do not even have to think the word "agent." As long as they act like an agent and principal, the law will treat them as such.

- *Consideration.* An agency relationship need not meet all the standards of contract law. For example, a contract is not valid without consideration, but an agency agreement is valid *even if the agent is not paid.* If Hannah is Albert's friend and agrees to find a buyer for his house without charging a commission, she is nonetheless his agent.

DUTIES OF AGENTS TO PRINCIPALS

Agents owe a fiduciary duty to their principals. In the following example, employees of Steinberg, Moorad & Dunn (SMD) were agents of the firm—they had agreed to act on behalf of SMD and be subject to its control. Did they violate their fiduciary duty?

NEWS*worthy*

Sports agent Leigh Steinberg, whose story inspired the Tom Cruise film *Jerry Maguire,* is caught up in a legal battle with his former partner that echoes moments from the movie. Steinberg's firm, SMD, has sued David Dunn, claiming Dunn was planning to form his own stable of sports stars while working for SMD. Dunn and agents at his new firm, Athletes

First, have said that as many as 80 percent of SMD's clients plan to switch management firms or already have.

SMD plans to ask Los Angeles Superior Court Judge Marilyn Hoffman to order Dunn to stop representing athletes he knew through SMD. "Earlier this year, Dunn orchestrated a despicable raid on [SMD] and its clientele," SMD says in court papers for its suit. Dunn counters that SMD "neglected and lost clients it now accuses Athletes First of stealing."

Overall, about one-third of SMD's former 30-person staff in Newport Beach, California, has since joined Dunn at Athletes First. Steinberg claims that Dunn and his recruits downloaded lists of clients and their specific contract terms and needs, as well as information on prospective clients, while still at SMD.[7] ◆

UPdate Search on the Web for further information about the dispute between Leigh Steinberg and David Dunn. If Dunn won, what were the important factors in the court's decision? If Steinberg was victorious, what penalties were imposed on Dunn? ◆

Duty of Loyalty

The agent must act solely for the benefit of the principal in all matters connected with the agency.[8] The agent has an obligation to put the principal first, to strive to accomplish the principal's goals. If Dunn and his colleagues stole client information from SMD in preparation for their departure to Athletes First, they were violating their duty of loyalty to their principal because they were acting in their own interest, not that of their principal. The various components of the duty of loyalty follow.

Hope could keep this Maybach only with BEAT's permission.

© REBECCA COOK/REUTERS/LANDOV

Outside Benefits

An agent may not receive profits unless the principal knows and approves. Suppose that Hope is an employee of the agency Big Egos and Talents, Inc. (BEAT). She has been representing Will Smith in his latest movie negotiations.[9] Smith often drives her to meetings in his new Maybach. He is so thrilled that she has arranged for him to star in the movie *Little Men* that he buys her a Maybach. Can Hope keep this generous gift? Only with BEAT's permission. She must tell BEAT about the Maybach; the company may then take the vehicle itself or allow her to keep it.

Confidential Information

The ability to keep secrets is important in any relationship, but especially a fiduciary relationship. **Agents can neither disclose nor use for their own benefit any confidential information they acquire during their agency.** As the following case shows, this duty continues even after the agency relationship ends.

---

[7] Joyzelle Davis, "Real-Life Breakup of 'Jerry Maguire' Agency Mirrors Movie," *Houston Chronicle,* Aug. 12, 2001, Sports, p. 2.

[8] Restatement (Second) of Agency §387.

[9] Do not be confused by the fact that Hope works as an agent for movie stars. As an employee of BEAT, her duty is to the company. She is an agent of BEAT, and BEAT works for the celebrities.

ABKCO MUSIC, INC. V. HARRISONGS MUSIC, LTD.

722 F.2d 988, 1983 U.S. App. LEXIS 15562
United States Court of Appeals for the Second Circuit, 1983

Facts: Bright Tunes Music Corp. (Bright Tunes) owned the copyright to the song "He's So Fine." The company sued George Harrison, a Beatle, alleging that the Harrison composition "My Sweet Lord" copied "He's So Fine." At the time the suit was filed, Allen B. Klein handled the business affairs of the Beatles.

Klein (representing Harrison) met with the president of Bright Tunes to discuss possible settlement of the copyright lawsuit. Klein suggested that Harrison might be interested in purchasing the copyright to "He's So Fine." Shortly thereafter, Klein's management contract with the Beatles expired. Without telling Harrison, Klein began negotiating with Bright Tunes to purchase the copyright to "He's So Fine" for himself. To advance these negotiations, Klein gave Bright Tunes information about royalty income for "My Sweet Lord"—information that he had gained as Harrison's agent.

The trial judge in the copyright case ultimately found that Harrison had infringed the copyright on "He's So Fine" and assessed damages of $1,599,987. After the trial, Klein purchased the "He's So Fine" copyright from Bright Tunes and with it, the right to recover from Harrison for the breach of copyright.

Issue: Did Klein violate his fiduciary duty to Harrison by using confidential information after the agency relationship terminated?

Excerpts from Judge Pierce's Decision: There is no doubt that the relationship between Harrison and [Klein] prior to the termination of the management agreement was that of principal and agent, and that the relationship was fiduciary in nature. [A]n agent has a duty not to use confidential knowledge acquired in his employment in competition with his principal. This duty exists as well after the employment is terminated as during its continuance. On the other hand, use of information based on general business knowledge or gleaned from general business experience is not covered by the rule, and the former agent is permitted to compete with his former principal in reliance on such general publicly available information. The evidence presented herein is not at all convincing that the information imparted to Bright Tunes by Klein was publicly available.

While the initial attempt to purchase [the copyright to "He's So Fine"] was several years removed from the eventual purchase on [Klein]'s own account, we are not of the view that such a fact rendered [Klein] unfettered in the later negotiations. Taking all of these circumstances together, we agree that [Klein's] conduct did not meet the standard required of him as a former fiduciary. ■

To listen to the two songs involved in this case, tune in to **http://www.copyrightwebsite.com/audio/harrison/harrison.asp**.

Ethics

Klein was angry that the Beatles had failed to renew his management contract. Was it reasonable for him to think that he owed no duty to the principal who had fired him? Should his sense of ethics have told him that his behavior was wrong? Would the ethics checklist in Chapter 2 have helped Klein to make a better decision? Why would George Harrison prefer to owe money to Bright Tunes than to Klein? ◆

Competition with the Principal

Agents are not allowed to compete with their principal in any matter within the scope of the agency business. If Allen Klein had purchased the "He's So Fine" copyright while he was George Harrison's agent, he would have committed an additional sin against the agency relationship. Owning song rights was clearly part of the agency business, so Klein could not make such purchases without Harrison's consent. Once the agency relationship ends, however, so does the rule against competition. Klein was entitled to buy the "He's So Fine" copyright after the agency relationship ended (as long as he did not use confidential information).

Conflict of Interest between Two Principals

Unless otherwise agreed, an agent may not act for two principals whose interests conflict. Suppose Travis represents both director Steven Spielberg and actress Julia Roberts. Spielberg is casting the title role in his new movie, *Nancy Drew: Girl Detective*, a role that Roberts covets. Travis cannot represent these two clients when they are negotiating with each other, unless they both know about the conflict and agree to ignore it. Similarly, a real estate agent cannot represent both the buyer and the seller of a piece of land. The following article illustrates the dangers of acting for two principals at once.

Faced with growing health care and retirement costs, the Sisters of Charity decided to sell a 207-acre property that they owned in New Jersey. The order of nuns soon found, however, that the world is not always a charitable place. They agreed to sell the land to Linpro for nearly $10 million. But before the deal closed, Linpro signed a contract to resell the property to Sammis for $34 million. So, you say, the sisters made a bad deal. There is no law against that. But it turned out that the nuns' lawyer, Peter Berkley, also represented Sammis. He knew about the deal between Sammis and Linpro, but never told the sisters. Was that the charitable—or legal—thing to do? For ideas on how Berkley should have handled this delicate situation, look at the discussion on dual agency at **http://www.thbuyers .com/Business/newsbusiness/archivesbusiness.htm.** ◆

Secretly Dealing with the Principal

If a principal hires an agent to arrange a transaction, the agent may not become a party to the transaction without the principal's permission. Matt Damon became an overnight sensation after starring in the movie *Good Will Hunting*. Suppose that he hired Trang to read scripts for him. Unbeknownst to Damon, Trang had written her own script, which she thought would be ideal for him. She may not sell it to him without revealing that she wrote it herself. Damon may be perfectly happy to buy Trang's script, but he has the right, as her principal, to know that she is the person selling it.

Appropriate Behavior

An agent may not engage in inappropriate behavior that reflects badly on the principal. This rule applies even to *off-duty* conduct. For example, two of the flight attendants featured in the following article were fired for inappropriate off-duty behavior; the third was given a warning letter.

The guests at a hotel bar in London were stunned when British Airways flight attendant Shirlie Johns raised her shirt so that colleague Stefania Lanza could caress her breasts while kissing her on the mouth. Johns then lowered her trousers, revealing her underwear. Meanwhile, crew member Matthew Swadling took off his shirt and poured wine down his trousers. All three rubbed up against each other provocatively while downing beer, vodka, and wine. It was, bystanders agreed, a huge embarrassment for British Airways. ◆

One of the most common, and difficult, issues facing employees is their duty to their principal after they have decided to seek employment elsewhere. How do they comply with their *duty of loyalty* when they know they are going to quit their job? The following case offers guidance.

READING RADIO, INC. V. FINK

2003 PA Super 353, 833 A.2d 199, 2003 Pa. Super. LEXIS 3181
Superior Court of Pennsylvania, 2003

Facts: David L. Kline was the station manager/sales manager of Reading Radio, Inc., which broadcast as WAGO Radio. As station manager, Kline was in charge of supervising the station's sales representatives, including Molly Fink and Isaac Ulrich. Fink and Ulrich were two of WAGO's top salespeople. They had both signed a non-compete agreement with WAGO that prohibited them from taking a job for six months after leaving WAGO with any radio or television broadcasting station located within a 50-mile radius of Reading, Pennsylvania. Kline did not have a covenant not to compete.

Reading Eagle Company approached WAGO about possibly buying the station. In the end, the sale fell through but Eagle offered Kline a job as manager of its station, WEEU. Kline accepted the position and resigned from his job at WAGO. To ensure a smooth transition, he agreed to stay at WAGO for 30 days. Kline assured his superiors at WAGO that he would continue to work as diligently for WAGO as he had in the past and that the station would be in better shape after he left it than it had been prior to his accepting the new job.

It did not exactly turn out that way. He began the "smooth transition" by canceling his bluegrass music program on WAGO without telling anyone. He transferred a significant advertising account from a car dealership to Eagle and with it his right to use a car that the dealership provided him. Although Kline was aware that Fink and Ulrich had non-compete agreements, he asked them to violate those contracts by coming to work for him at WEEU.

Fink and Ulrich gave their resignations to the WAGO station manager, who just happened also to be their new boss—Kline. He did not attempt to enforce the agreements on WAGO's behalf. After Fink and Ulrich left, sales revenue at WAGO fell by $1.6 million dollars.

WAGO sued both Kline and Eagle. The jury returned a verdict for WAGO in the amount of $1,105,000. The defendants appealed.

Issue: Did Kline violate his duty of loyalty to his employer, WAGO?

Excerpts from Judge Popovich's Decision: To prevail on a claim of breach of fiduciary duty of loyalty, a plaintiff must demonstrate that his agent acted for a person or entity whose interests conflicted with the plaintiff. Restatement (Second) of Agency § 394 (1958). The jury found that Kline breached his fiduciary duty of loyalty to his principal, WAGO. We agree.

The facts demonstrate that, while still employed by WAGO, Kline actively engaged in diverting Fink and Ulrich from WAGO to WEEU, and he refused to enforce the covenants-not-to-compete to which they were bound. Kline's failure to protect the integrity of the covenants-not-to-compete and the sales staff at WAGO were clear violations of his duty of loyalty, for which he was liable in damages. Therefore, we are satisfied that the trial court did not err when it refused to enter judgment in [Kline's] favor with respect to this claim. ■

Public Policy

Agency law does not prevent employees from changing jobs. The law would be absurd—and unenforceable—if it did. But the law does require employees to be loyal to whoever is signing the paycheck. When people switch jobs, they often find themselves facing great temptation to curry favor with the new employer no matter the harm to the old one. Kline meant to start his new job on a high note. Instead, Eagle found itself in a messy trial, forced to pay substantial damages. ◆

An agent is bound by the duty of loyalty, *whether or not the agent and principal have consciously agreed to it.* It is irrelevant that George Harrison never expressly prohibited his agent from revealing the royalty income on "My Sweet Lord." The agent should have known his obligations. However, a principal and agent can change the rules by agreement. If the agent had gone to Harrison and asked permission to reveal confidential information, it would have been up to Harrison to grant permission or not, as he chose. If he had agreed, the agent would not have been liable. **The duty of loyalty applies unless the principal and agent expressly agree to change it.**

Other Duties of an Agent

Before Taylor left for a five-week trip to England, he hired Angie to rent his vacation house. Angie never got around to listing his house on the regional rental list used by all the area brokers, but when the Fords contacted her looking for rental housing, she did show them Taylor's place. They offered to rent it for $750 per month.

Angie called Taylor in England to tell him. He responded that he would not accept less than $850 a month, which Angie thought the Fords would be willing to pay. He told Angie to call back if there was any problem. The Fords decided that they would go no higher than $800 a month. Instead of calling Taylor in England, Angie left a message on his home answering machine. When the Fords pressed her for an answer, she said she could not get in touch with Taylor. Not until Taylor returned home did he learn that the Fords had rented another house. Did Angie violate any of the duties that agents owe to their principals?

Duty to Obey Instructions

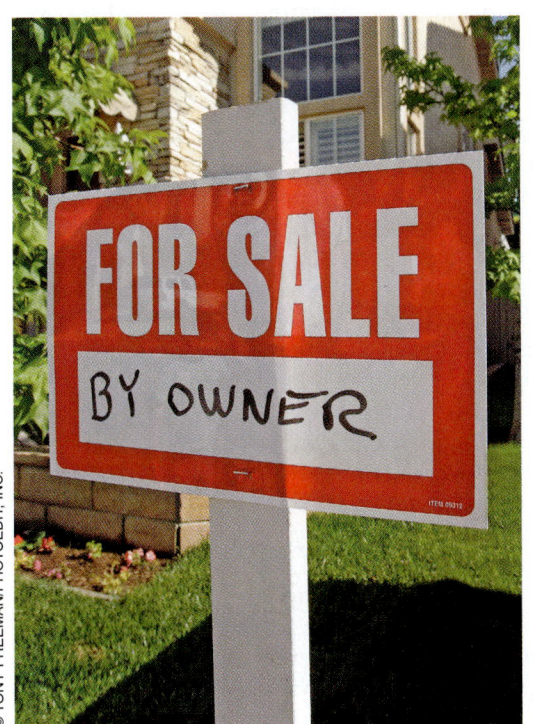

An agent must obey her principal's instructions, unless the principal directs her to behave illegally or unethically. Taylor instructed Angie to call him if the Fords rejected the offer. When Angie failed to do so, she violated her duty to obey instructions. If, however, Taylor had asked her to say that the house's basement was dry, when in fact it looked like a rice paddy every spring, Angie would be under no obligation to follow those illegal instructions.

Duty of Care

An agent has a duty to act with reasonable care. In other words, an agent must act as a reasonable person would, under the circumstances. A reasonable person would not have left a message on Taylor's home answering machine when she knew he was in Europe.

Under some circumstances, an agent is held to a higher—or lower—standard than usual. **An agent with special skills is held to a higher standard because she is expected to use those skills.** A trained real estate agent should know enough to use the regional rental list.

But suppose Taylor had asked his neighbor, Clementine, to help him sell the house. Clementine is not a trained real estate agent, and she is not being paid, which makes her a *gratuitous agent*. A gratuitous agent is held to a lower standard because she is doing her principal a favor and, as the old saying goes,

Neither Clementine nor her sign is professional.

© TONY FREEMAN/PHOTOEDIT, INC.

you get what you pay for—up to a point. **Gratuitous agents are liable if they commit *gross* negligence, but not *ordinary* negligence.** If Clementine, as a gratuitous agent, left an important message on Taylor's answering machine because she forgot about the trip to England, she would not be liable to Taylor for that ordinary negligence. But if the answering machine had a message that *warned* her Taylor was away and would not be picking up messages, she would be liable for gross negligence and a violation of her duty.

Duty to Provide Information

An agent has a duty to provide the principal with all information in her possession that she has reason to believe the principal wants to know. She also has a duty to provide accurate information. In the following case, the agent violated both its duty of care and its duty to provide information.

GRIGSBY V. O.K. TRAVEL

118 Ohio App. 3d 671, 693 N.E.2d 1142, 1997 Ohio App. LEXIS 875
Court of Appeals of Ohio, 1997

Facts: In the window of O.K. Travel, Oma Grigsby saw an advertisement for a tour of Israel that was organized by Trinity Tours. Grigsby signed up for the tour and paid O.K. About a week before Grigsby was to leave for the tour, O.K. discovered that Trinity was out of business. O.K. contacted the American Society of Travel Agents, which notified O.K. that Trinity did not carry the financial bond required by the state of Ohio. Grigsby filed suit against O.K., alleging that it had violated its duty of care and its duty to provide information.

Issue: Did O.K. violate the duties it owed Grigsby?

Excerpts from Judge Painter's Decision: Customers come to travel agents because these agents hold themselves out as having knowledge about how to travel to places "foreign" to the traveler. For this reason, travel agents are the special agents of the traveler for securing a trip. A travel agent is more than a ticket supplier. Travel agents have become a professional segment of today's complex travel world.

When assisting in planning a vacation, a travel agent has a duty to act with the care, skill, and diligence that a fiduciary rendering that kind of service would reasonably be expected to use. The agent must make reasonable inquiries into the current financial stability of the person or entity with whom she recommended her principal do business. The duty, then, is to discover and disclose material information that is reasonably obtainable. If a tour operator or promoter defaults due to discoverable circumstances, the travel agent earning a commission from selling the tours should bear the loss if the agent fails to disclose the relevant risks.

Trinity, as a tour promoter, was required to register with the Secretary of State before commencing business in this state. A tour promoter must also provide a bond ($50,000 for interstate or international travel) in favor of the state before commencing operations. Upon registration, a tour promoter shall use the statement "registered Ohio tour promoter" and its registration number in any and all advertisements in Ohio. The advertisement for the Israel tour from Trinity was devoid of this statement and Trinity's registration number. Trinity could not have even provided a registration number because it was not registered in Ohio and never provided a bond, as statutorily required.

▼

O.K. breached its duty to Grigsby by failing to disclose to Grigsby that Trinity was not registered in Ohio and had no bond posted which could have provided security in case it defaulted. This information was reasonably obtainable, and in fact should have been clear to O.K. (at least O.K. was put on notice), because Trinity's advertisement did not have the statutorily required language and registration number. ■

Principal's Remedies When the Agent Breaches a Duty

A principal has three potential remedies when an agent breaches her duty:

- The principal can recover from the agent any **damages** the breach has caused. Thus, if Taylor can only rent his house for $600 a month instead of the $800 the Fords offered, Angie would be liable for $2,400—$200 a month for one year.

- If an agent breaches the duty of loyalty, he must turn over to the principal any **profits** he has earned as a result of his wrongdoing. Thus, after Klein violated his duty of loyalty to Harrison, he forfeited profits he would have earned from the copyright of "He's So Fine."

- If the agent has violated her duty of loyalty, the principal may **rescind** the transaction. When Trang sold a script to her principal, Matt Damon, without telling him that she was the author, she violated her duty of loyalty. Damon could rescind the contract to buy the script.[10]

DUTIES OF PRINCIPALS TO AGENTS

In a typical agency relationship, the agent agrees to perform tasks for the principal, and the principal agrees to pay the agent. The range of tasks undertaken by an agent is limited only by the imagination of the principal. Because the agent's job can be so varied, the law has needed to define an agent's duties carefully. The role of the principal, on the other hand, is typically less complicated—often little more than writing a check to pay the agent. Thus the law enumerates fewer duties for the principal. Primarily, the principal must reimburse the agent for reasonable expenses and cooperate with the agent in performing agency tasks. The respective duties of agents and principals can be summarized as follows:

Duties of Agents to Principals	Duty of Principals to Agents
Duty of loyalty	Duty to reimburse
Duty to obey instructions	Duty to cooperate
Duty of care	
Duty to provide information	

---

[10] A principal can rescind his contract with an agent who has violated her duty, but, as we shall see in the next chapter, the principal might not be able to rescind a contract with a third party when the agent misbehaves.

Duty to Reimburse the Agent

As a general rule, the principal must **indemnify** (that is, reimburse) the agent for any expenses she has reasonably incurred. These reimbursable expenses fall into three categories.

Payments Made by the Agent While Carrying out His Duties

Peace Baptist Church of Birmingham, Alabama, asked its pastor, W. L. Lauderdale, to borrow money and buy land for a new church. Lauderdale repaid some of the borrowed money out of his own pocket. After his death, his heirs sued the church, asking for repayment. In finding in favor of the heirs, the court held that **a principal must indemnify an agent for any expenses or damages reasonably incurred in carrying out his agency responsibilities.**[11]

In this case, the church had specifically authorized Reverend Lauderdale to borrow the money and purchase the land. **A principal must also indemnify an agent for an *unauthorized* purchase if the agent *reasonably* believed he was authorized and the principal received a *benefit*.** Even if Reverend Lauderdale was not authorized, if he believed he was and the church obtained the land it needed at a favorable price, it would have to reimburse him for his expenses.

Torts Committed by the Agent

A principal must indemnify an agent for tort claims brought by a third party if the principal authorized the agent's behavior and the agent did not realize he was committing a tort. Marisa owns all the apartment buildings on Elm Street, except one. She hires Rajiv to manage the units and tells him that, under the terms of the leases, she has the right to ask guests to leave if a party becomes too rowdy. But she forgets to tell Rajiv that she does not own one of the buildings, which happens to house a college sorority. One night, when the sorority is having a rambunctious party, Rajiv hustles over and starts ejecting the noisy guests. The sorority is furious and sues Rajiv for trespass. If the sorority wins its suit against Rajiv, Marisa would have to pay the judgment, plus Rajiv's attorney's fees, because she had told him to quell noisy parties, and he did not realize he was trespassing.

Contracts Entered into by the Agent

The principal must indemnify the agent for any liability she incurs from third parties as a result of entering into a contract on the principal's behalf, including attorney's fees and reasonable settlements. An agent signed a contract to buy cucumbers for Vlasic Food Products Co. to use in making pickles. When the first shipment of cucumbers arrived, Vlasic inspectors found them unsuitable and directed the agent to refuse the shipment. The agent found himself in a pickle when the cucumber farmer sued. The agent notified Vlasic, but the company refused to defend him. He settled the claim himself and, in turn, sued Vlasic. The court ordered Vlasic to reimburse the agent because he had notified them of the suit and had acted reasonably and in good faith.[12]

---

[11] *Lauderdale v. Peace Baptist Church of Birmingham*, 246 Ala. 178, 19 So. 2d 538, 1944 Ala. LEXIS 508 (1944).

[12] *Long v. Vlasic Food Products Co.*, 439 F.2d 229, 1971 U.S. App. LEXIS 11455 (4th Cir. 1971).

Duty to Cooperate

Principals have a duty to cooperate with their agent; they cannot impede the agent's efforts.

The principal must furnish the agent with the opportunity to work. If Lewis agrees to serve as Ida's real estate agent, Ida must allow Lewis access to the house. It is unlikely that Lewis will be able to sell the house without taking anyone inside.

The principal cannot unreasonably interfere with the agent's ability to accomplish his task. Suppose that Ida allows Lewis to show the house, but she refuses to clean it and then makes disparaging comments to prospective purchasers. "I really get tired of living in such a dank, dreary house," she says. "And the neighborhood children are vicious juvenile delinquents." This behavior would constitute unreasonable interference with an agent.

Note, however, that **unless the agency contract provides otherwise, the principal is allowed to compete with her agent.** Unless Ida has promised Lewis the exclusive right to sell the house, Ida can hire other real estate agents or even sell the house herself.

The principal must perform her part of the contract. Once the agent has successfully completed the task, the principal must pay him, even if the principal has changed her mind and no longer wants the agent to perform. Ida is a 78-year-old widow who has lived alone for many years in a house that she loves. Her asking price is outrageously high but, lo and behold, Lewis finds a couple who are happy to pay this price. There is only one problem. Ida does not really want to sell. She put her house on the market because she enjoys showing it to all the folks who move to town. She rejects the offer. Now there is a second problem. The contract provided that Lewis would find a willing buyer at the asking price. Since he has done so, Ida must pay his real estate commission, even if she does not want to sell her house.

TERMINATING AN AGENCY RELATIONSHIP

Either the agent or the principal can terminate the agency relationship at any time. In addition, the relationship terminates automatically if the principal or agent can no longer perform their required duties or a change in circumstances renders the agency relationship pointless.

Termination by Agent or Principal

The two parties—principal and agent—have five choices available for terminating their relationship:

- *Term Agreement.* The principal and agent can agree in advance how long their relationship will last. Alexandra hires Boris to help her purchase exquisite enameled Easter eggs made for the Russian czars by Fabergé. If they agree that the relationship will last five years, they have a term agreement.

- *Achieving a Purpose.* The principal and agent can agree that the agency relationship will terminate when the principal's goals have been achieved. Alexandra and Boris might agree that their relationship will end when Alexandra has purchased 10 eggs.

- *Mutual Agreement.* No matter what the principal and agent agree at the start, they can always change their minds later on, as long as the change is mutual. If Boris and

This is one of the Fabergé eggs that Alexandra is seeking.

Alexandra originally agree to a five-year term, but after only three years Boris decides he wants to go back to business school and Alexandra runs out of money, they can decide together to terminate the agency.

- *Agency at Will.* If they make no agreement in advance about the term of the agreement, either principal or agent can terminate at any time.

- *Wrongful Termination.* An agency relationship is a *personal* relationship. Hiring an agent is not like buying a book. You might not care which copy of the book you buy, but you do care which agent you hire. If an agency relationship is not working out, the courts will not force the agent and principal to stay together. **Either party always has the *power* to walk out. They may not, however, have the *right*.** If one party's departure from the agency relationship violates the agreement and causes harm to the other party, the wrongful party must pay damages. He will nonetheless be permitted to leave. If Boris has agreed to work for Alexandra for five years but he wants to leave after three, he can leave, provided he pays Alexandra the cost of hiring and training a replacement.

If the agent is a *gratuitous* agent (i.e., is not being paid), he has both the power and the right to quit any time he wants, regardless of the agency agreement. If Boris is doing this job for Alexandra as a favor, he will not owe her damages when he stops work.

Principal or Agent Can No Longer Perform Required Duties

If the principal or the agent is unable to perform the duties required under the agency agreement, the agreement terminates.

Loss of Qualification

The agent or the principal may need a license to perform duties under the agency agreement. If either one of them is unable to obtain—or keep—the necessary license, the agency agreement ends. Caleb hires Allegra to represent him in a lawsuit. If she is disbarred, their agency agreement terminates because the agent is no longer allowed in court. Alternatively, suppose that Emil hires Bess to work in his gun shop. If he loses his license to sell firearms, their agency relationship terminates.

Bankruptcy

The bankruptcy of the agent or the principal terminates an agency relationship only if it affects their ability to perform. Bankruptcy rarely interferes with an agent's responsibilities. After all, there is generally no reason why an agent cannot continue to act for the principal whether the agent is rich or poor. Suppose that Lewis, the real estate agent, gets in over his head buying real estate for his own account. During a downturn in the market, he is unable to meet his mortgage payments, so he seeks the protection of the bankruptcy courts. He can continue to represent Ida or anyone else who wants to sell a house.

If the agent's bankruptcy does interfere with his ability to perform, then the agency relationship terminates. Chung works for Blue Chip Investments as a financial adviser, helping individuals organize their finances. If he were to go bankrupt, he would not exactly be a good advertisement for his employer, and his agency relationship would terminate.

The bankruptcy of a principal is different, however, because after filing for bankruptcy, the principal loses control of his assets. A bankrupt principal may be unable to pay the agent or honor contracts that the agent enters into on his behalf. Therefore, the bankruptcy of a principal is more likely to terminate an agency relationship.

Death or Incapacity of the Principal or Agent

An agency relationship terminates upon the death or incapacity of either the principal or the agent. Agency is a personal relationship, and when the principal dies, the agent cannot act on behalf of a nonexistent person.[13] Of course, a nonexistent person cannot act either, so the relationship also terminates when the agent dies. Incapacity has the same legal effect because either the principal or the agent is, at least temporarily, unable to act. Incapacity includes physical or mental disability.

Disloyalty of Agent

If the agent violates her duty of loyalty, the agency agreement automatically terminates. Agents are appointed to represent the principal's interest; if they fail to do so, there is no point to the relationship. Sam is negotiating a military procurement contract on behalf of his employer, Missiles R Us, Inc. In the midst of these negotiations, he becomes very friendly with Louisa, the government negotiator. One night over drinks, he tells Louisa what Missiles' real costs are on the project and the lowest bid it could possibly make. By passing on this confidential information, Sam has violated his duty of loyalty, and his agency relationship terminates.

Change in Circumstances

After the agency agreement is negotiated, circumstances may change. If these changes are significant enough to undermine the purpose of the agreement, then the relationship ends automatically. Andrew hires Melissa to sell his country farm for $100,000. Shortly thereafter, the largest oil reserve in North America is discovered nearby. The farm is now worth 10 times Andrew's asking price. Melissa's authority terminates automatically.

Change of Law

If the agent's responsibilities become illegal, the agency agreement terminates. Oscar has hired Marta to ship him succulent avocados from California's Imperial Valley. Before she sends the shipment, Mediterranean fruit flies are discovered in the area and all fruits and vegetables in California are quarantined. The agency agreement terminates because it is now illegal to ship the California avocados.

---

[13] Restatement (Second) of Agency §120, Comment a.

Loss or Destruction of Subject Matter

Andrew is fortunate that his farm is now worth so much, because his financial affairs are in grave disorder. Earlier in the year, he hired Damian to sell his Palm Beach condominium, but before Damian could even measure the living room, Andrew's creditors attached the condo. Damian is no longer authorized to sell the real estate because Andrew does not have the right to sell it. He has "lost" the subject matter of his agency agreement with Damian.

The following case not only deals with the issue of loss or destruction of subject matter, it provides a useful review of many of the agency issues in this chapter.

you Be The Judge

GAGNON V. COOMBS

39 Mass. App. Ct. 144, 654 N.E.2d 54, 1995
Mass. App. LEXIS 545
Appeals Court of Massachusetts, 1995

Facts: The facts of this case are set out in the scenario at the beginning of the chapter. The trial court found that Joan had the authority under the power of attorney to convey the Shelburne property to the trust. Francis appealed.

You Be the Judge: Did Joan have the right to convey the Shelburne farm to a trust that she had established? Does the property belong to the trust or to Francis?

Argument for Joan: Francis had the right to terminate the agency agreement with Joan, but he had to *tell* her that he had done so. Joan cannot read minds. When she transferred the property to the trust she was, as far as she knew, an authorized agent. Now the land has been transferred; it is a done deal. The land belongs to the trust.

Francis did indeed sign a purchase & sale agreement (P&S) to sell the Shelburne farm. That document indicated his *intent* to sell the property. But even after he signed the P&S, he still owned the land. He had not yet "lost" it, for the purposes of agency law and would not until he actually sold it.

Everything Joan did was designed to protect Francis. He was eighty-five years old and clearly not as strong as he had once been. For years, he

and Frank had barely spoken but now suddenly he was doing whatever Frank told him to do. Without the protection of the trust, he might end up with no assets at all.

Argument for Francis: Admittedly, Francis never told Joan that he had terminated her agency, but she should have been able to figure it out when she discovered that he was planning to sell the property. She must have known then that he no longer wanted her to act for him. Her job as an agent was to further his desires, not thwart them. Likewise, when Francis's lawyer wrote demanding that she return the land, her duty as an agent was to comply with his request.

Joan's authority ended when Francis signed the P&S for the farm. At that point, he had "lost" the property. He no longer had the right to dispose of it because he had legally promised it to someone else. If it was no longer his, she could not act for him in transferring it to the trust.

As an agent, Joan had an obligation to inform Francis of any material facts. Certainly her transfer of the property to the trust was material. By failing to tell him, she violated her duty of loyalty. Once an agent violates her duty of loyalty, the agency agreement automatically terminates.

Joan also violated her duty of loyalty by self-dealing. She was the person who primarily benefited from her transfer of the land to the trust, not Francis. ■

Effect of Termination

Once an agency relationship ends, the agent no longer has the authority to act for the principal. If she continues to act, she is liable to the principal for any damages he incurs as a result. The Mediterranean fruit fly quarantine ended Marta's agency. If she sends Oscar the avocados anyway and he is fined for possession of a fruit fly, Marta must pay the fine.

The agent loses her authority to act, but some of the duties of both the principal and agent continue even after the relationship ends.

Principal's Duty to Indemnify Agent

Oscar must reimburse Marta for expenses she incurred before the agency ended. If Marta accumulated mileage on her car during her search for the perfect avocado, Oscar must pay her for gasoline and depreciation. But he owes her nothing for her expenses after the agency relationship ends.

Confidential Information

Remember the "He's So Fine" case earlier in the chapter. George Harrison's agent used confidential information to negotiate, on his own behalf, the purchase of the "He's So Fine" copyright. An agent is not entitled to use confidential information, even after the agency relationship terminates.

Irrevocable Agency Relationship

Michele borrows money from Gustav. As collateral, she grants him a mortgage on her land. If she does not pay her debt to Gustav, he has the right to sell her land and recover what she owes him. In theory, when Gustav sells Michele's land, he looks a lot like her agent. However, their relationship is different from a true agency. You remember that a typical agency relationship is established to benefit the principal. But here, Gustav has the right to sell Michele's land to benefit himself. He has what is called a **power coupled with an interest**. In other words, he has the right to sell Michele's land because she owes him something. He has benefited her by loaning her the money; now she must benefit him by allowing him to sell the land if she does not pay the debt.

In the case of a power coupled with an interest, only the agent can terminate the relationship. The principal has neither the *power* nor the *right* to terminate. Michele would like to terminate if she could, because then her land would not be at risk, but it would be unfair to Gustav if she did. This special kind of agency relationship (a power coupled with an interest) does not terminate upon the death or incapacity of either the principal or agent. If Gustav were to die, Michele would owe the money to his heirs, and they would have the right to sell her land if she did not pay her debt. If Michele died, her estate would be obligated to pay the debt to Gustav before it could distribute any assets to her heirs.

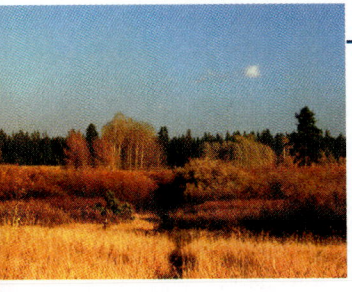

Chapter Conclusion

When students enroll in a business law course, they fully expect to learn about torts and contracts, corporations and partnerships. They probably do not think much about agency law; many of them have not even heard the term before. Yet it is an area of the law that affects us all because each of us has been and will be both an agent and a principal many times in our lives.

Chapter Review

1. In an agency relationship, a principal and an agent mutually consent that the agent will act on behalf of the principal and be subject to the principal's control, thereby creating a fiduciary relationship.

2. An agency relationship can exist without either a written agreement, a formal agreement, or consideration.

3. An agent owes these duties to the principal: duty of loyalty, duty to obey instructions, duty of care, and duty to provide information.

4. The principal has three potential remedies when the agent breaches her duty: recovery of damages the breach has caused, recovery of any profits earned by the agent from the breach, and rescission of any transaction with the agent.

5. The principal has two duties to the agent: to reimburse legitimate expenses, and to cooperate with the agent.

6. Both the agent and the principal have the power to terminate an agency relationship, but they may not have the right. If the termination violates the agency agreement and causes harm to the other party, the wrongful party must pay damages.

7. An agency relationship automatically terminates if the principal or agent can no longer perform the required duties or if a change in circumstances renders the agency relationship pointless.

8. Once an agency relationship ends, the agent no longer has the authority to act for the principal. If she continues to act, she is liable to the principal for any damages he incurs as a result.

9. In the case of a power coupled with an interest, only the agent has the right to terminate the relationship.

Practice Test

1. This is a tale of marital woe. At the urging of her husband, Phyllis Thropp placed $40,000 in a brokerage account with her husband's friend Richard Gregory, a broker at Bache Halsey. Mrs. Thropp opened the account in her name alone and did not authorize Gregory to discuss the account with Mr. Thropp, nor did she authorize Mr. Thropp to act for her. Undeterred by this technicality, Mr. Thropp forged his wife's name to a power of attorney that authorized him to make decisions for her. He gave this document to Gregory. In the course of the next year, Mr. Thropp ordered Gregory to sell his wife's securities and issue checks to her. After forging her name to the checks, he cashed them and used the money to pay his gambling debts. Gregory did not process the power of attorney form according to standard Bache procedures. When the Thropps saw Gregory socially, Mrs. Thropp frequently asked him how her account was doing. Gregory somehow neglected to mention that it was not doing very well at all. He never told her about the numerous sales. Can this marriage be saved? No, the Thropps were divorced. Did Richard Gregory violate his fiduciary duty to Mrs. Thropp?

2. Herbert Chew worked for Bethlehem Steel Co. The company required all employees who missed work to produce a written explanation within 15 days. A medical excuse required a note from a doctor. Dr. Paul Meyer operated on Chew. The day after the surgery, Chew asked Meyer to sign a form for the company. He told the doctor that failure to send in the form could "cost me my job." Meyer refused to sign the form at that moment, but promised to have his secretary send it within the week. Chew asked the doctor several times in the next week whether the form had been sent. Meyer did finally send the form—one day late. Chew was fired. A rational question is: Who would want to work for this employer anyway? But the legal issue is: As a gratuitous agent, did Dr. Meyer have any obligation to Mr. Chew? Meyer was a gratuitous agent because he had been hired to operate on Chew, not to fill out forms. Once he agreed to notify the company, he became a gratuitous agent for that purpose.

3. The German-American Vocational League was formed in New York during World War II to serve as a propaganda agency for the German Reich. Under U.S. law, all foreign agents were required to register. Neither the Vocational League nor its officers registered. When they were charged with violating U.S. law, they argued that they were not agents of the German government because they had no formal agency agreement. Their one written agreement with the German Reich said nothing about being a propaganda agency. Is a formal contract necessary to establish an agency relationship?

4. **CPA QUESTION** Pell is the principal and Astor is the agent in an agency coupled with an interest. Who has the right to terminate the agency before the interest has expired?

Pell	Astor
a. Yes	Yes
b. No	Yes
c. No	No
d. Yes	No

5. **CPA QUESTION** A principal and agent relationship requires a:

   a. Written agreement

   b. Power of attorney

   c. Meeting of the minds and consent to act

   d. Specified consideration

6. **YOU BE THE JUDGE** WRITING PROBLEM Frank Secan sought to buy land in Arizona that was owned by David Egelston. Secan gave a written offer on the land to a real estate agent, Becky Gogle, and asked her to transmit it to Egelston. Gogle told Secan that she was working with two other men who were interested in buying the land, but she would transmit the offer. She duly did so. She failed, however, to tell Secan that Egelston made a counteroffer to the two other men, who then bought the property. Did Gogle violate her duty to Secan? **Argument for Secan:** As Secan's agent, Gogle had a duty to provide information. Her failure to tell him about the counteroffer caused him harm. **Argument for Gogle:** Gogle had only one duty—to transmit the offer. Once she did that, her agency relationship with Secan ended, and she had no further obligation.

7. **ETHICS** Radio TV Reports (RTV) was in the business of recording, transcribing, and monitoring radio and video programming for its clients. The Department of Defense (DOD) in Washington was one of RTV's major clients. Paul Ingersoll worked for RTV until August 31. In July, the DOD solicited bids for a new contract for the following year. During this same month, Ingersoll formed his own media monitoring business, Transmedia. RTV and Transmedia were the only two bidders on the DOD contract, which was awarded to Transmedia. Did Ingersoll violate his fiduciary duty to RTV? Aside from his legal obligations, did Ingersoll behave ethically? How does his behavior look in the light of day? Was it right?

8. Barbara Gelfand and her husband asked Action Travel Center, Inc., to book a cruise for them. They told the agency that they had to travel on a new cruise ship because of Mrs. Gelfand's medical condition. Older ships had chemicals that made her ill. The Travel Center sent Mrs. Gelfand a brochure for the *Costa Riviera*, described as a new ship making its maiden voyage. During the course of the cruise, Mrs. Gelfand became very ill and was forced to fly to Fort Lauderdale for hospitalization. It turned out that the *Costa Riviera* was an old ship that had merely been refurbished. Has the Travel Center violated its duty of care?

9. The Fellowship is a not-for-profit corporation whose primary purpose is promoting fellowship among Baptists. Its annual meeting was held at the Indianapolis Baptist Temple. Dr. Greg Dixon, the head of the Temple, invited various missions and vendors to attend the meeting and set up display booths. Rodger Keener wanted to buy a bus for his church. One of the Temple employees suggested he talk with Robert Crist, who had a booth at the annual meeting. Crist and Keener flew to Crist's business in Perryville, Indiana. The plane crashed and Keener was killed. Was Crist an agent of the Fellowship?

10. David and Fiona Rookard purchased tickets for a trip through Mexico from a Mexicoach office in San Diego. Mexicoach told them that the trip would be safe. It did not tell them, however, that their tickets had disclaimers written in Spanish

warning that, under Mexican law, a bus company is not liable for any harm that befalls its passengers. The Rookards did not read Spanish. They were injured in a bus accident caused by gross negligence on the part of the driver. Did Mexicoach violate its duty to the Rookards?

11. Penny Wilson went to Arlington Chrysler-Plymouth-Dodge to buy an automobile. Penny told Arlington that, as a minor, she could not buy the car unless she obtained credit life insurance that would pay the balance of any loan owing if her mother died. She also disclosed that her mother had cancer. Arlington was an agent for Western Pioneer Life Insurance Co. Western Pioneer reported that a credit insurance policy would be invalid if Mrs. Wilson died within six months. In fact, the policy was invalid if Mrs. Wilson died of cancer within *one year*. Seven months later, Mrs. Wilson died and Western Pioneer refused to pay. Penny Wilson sued Western Pioneer and Arlington. The trial court found Western Pioneer liable, but not Arlington. Was Western Pioneer liable for Arlington's legal expenses?

12. **ROLE REVERSAL** Write a multiple-choice question that focuses on an agent's duty of loyalty.

Internet Research Problem

The Code of Ethics for the National Association of Realtors is at http://beatty.westbuslaw.com. Do these rules require realtors to treat clients better—or worse—than agency law demands? In what ways?

You can find further practice problems at http://beatty.westbuslaw.com or in the Study Guide that accompanies this text.

Agency: The Outside Relationship

One night on the way home in the family car, 15-year-old Naeun Yoon had an argument with her brother. It proved to be a fatal dispute. To calm the children down, their mother pulled the van over to the side of the road. Still furious, the two teenagers leapt out of the van in the dark and started walking along the road in opposite directions. At that moment, Jane Wagner, a 29-year-old lawyer at a large firm, was driving her Mercedes, talking on her cell phone. She never saw the teenage girl before she hit her, knocking her over the guardrail. Nor did she stop her car. She said afterwards that she thought she had hit a deer.

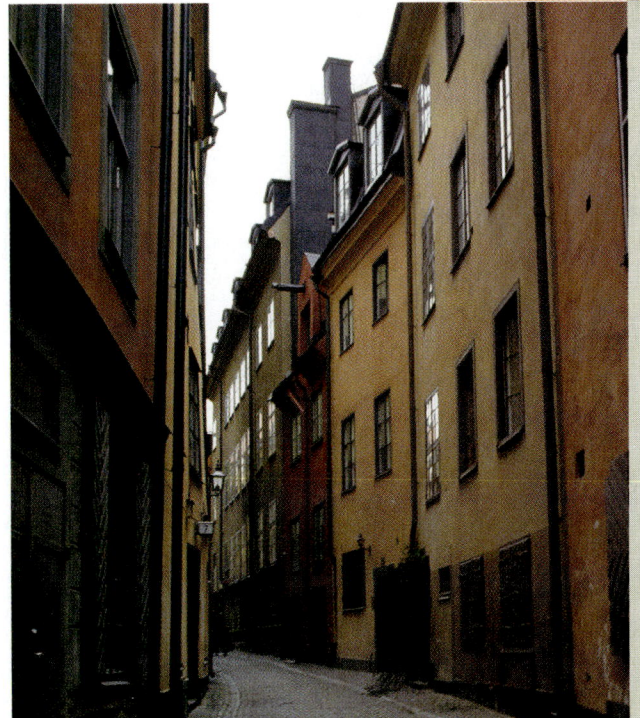

© PHOTO 24/BRAND X PICTURES/GETTY IMAGES

Whose fault was the accident? Wagner pleaded guilty to a felony, served in a one-year work release program, and lost her license to practice law. But Yoon's family also sued Wagner's law firm, Cooley, Godward. They claimed that Wagner was talking on the phone as part of her job and for the benefit of the firm. The law firm ultimately settled the $30 million case.

Cell phone lawsuits are becoming increasingly common. After a broker for Smith, Barney killed a motorcyclist while talking on his cell phone, the investment bank paid the bereaved family $500,000. The state of Hawaii paid $1.5 million to a man who was killed by a teacher talking on her phone. But in a different case, a

Minnesota hospital was found not liable for a nurse who was in a car accident while talking with her daughter on a cell phone.

Why the different results? Under agency law, a principal is liable for the negligent torts of an employee that occur within the scope of employment. Although the nurse was using a cell phone that the hospital had provided, she was talking with her daughter—and therefore, was not within the scope of employment. The other employees arguably were acting within the scope of their employment and for the benefit of their employers. ■

It is virtually impossible to run a modern business without agents. However, hiring an agent dramatically increases the risk of legal liability. A principal may be liable in contract for agreements that the agent signs and also liable in tort for any harm the agent causes. Indeed, once a principal hires an agent, he may be liable to third parties for her acts, even if she *disobeys* instructions. Thus even businesses with policies that prohibit employees from talking on a cell phone while driving a car could still be liable for someone who violates that policy. This risk of liability means that it is important to understand agency law.

PRINCIPAL'S LIABILITY FOR CONTRACTS

Many agents are hired for the primary purpose of entering into contracts on behalf of their principals. Salespeople, for example, may do little other than sign on the dotted line. Most of the time, the principal is delighted to be bound by these contracts. But that is not always the case, because sometimes the agent disobeys orders. As a general rule, however, the principal has no right to rescind a contract entered into by his agent. After all, if someone is going to be penalized, it should be the principal who hired the disobedient agent, not the innocent third party.

The principal is bound by the acts of an agent if (1) the agent has *authority*, or (2) the principal, for reasons of fairness, is *estopped* from denying that the agent had authority, or (3) the principal *ratifies* the acts of the agent.

To say that the principal is "bound by the acts" of the agent means that the principal is as liable as if he had performed the acts himself. It also means that the principal is liable for statements the agent makes to a third party. Thus, when a lawyer lied on an application for malpractice insurance, the insurance company was allowed to void the policy for the entire law firm. It was as if the firm had lied. In addition, the principal is deemed to know any information that the agent knows or should know.

Authority

A principal is bound by the acts of an agent if the agent has authority. **There are three types of authority: express, implied, and apparent.** Express and implied authority are categories of **actual** authority because the agent *is* truly authorized to act for the principal. In apparent authority, the principal is liable for the agent's actions even though the agent was *not* authorized.

Express Authority

The principal grants **express authority** by words or conduct that, reasonably interpreted, cause the agent to believe the principal desires her to act on the principal's account.[1] In other words, the principal asks the agent to do something and the agent does it. Craig calls his stockbroker, Alice, and asks her to buy 100 shares of Banshee Corp. for his account. She has *express authority* to carry out this transaction.

Sometimes reasonable people might disagree about what the principal actually asked the agent to do. **In cases of ambiguity about the principal's intent, the courts look at the principal's *objective* manifestation, not his *subjective* intent.** Craig stops by the brokerage house and leaves a signed note on Betsy's desk that says, "Please buy 100 shares of Banshee Corp. stock." Craig thought he was leaving the note on Alice's desk. Betsy has the right to purchase the stock (and Alice loses out on the commission) because Craig's actions count, not his thoughts.

Likewise, it does not matter how the principal's wishes are communicated. As long as the agent receives them, she is authorized to act. If, instead of leaving a note to Alice, Craig had told Betsy what he wanted Alice to do and Betsy had, in turn, passed the word to Alice, then Alice would be authorized to act.

Implied Authority

Unless otherwise agreed, authority to conduct a transaction includes authority to do acts that are reasonably necessary to accomplish it.[2] David has recently inherited a house from his grandmother in Wichita Falls, Kansas. He hires Nell, one of his grandmother's neighbors, to auction off the house and its contents. As David well knows, only a licensed auctioneer is permitted to conduct an auction. Nell hires an auctioneer, advertises the event, rents a tent, and generally does everything necessary to conduct a successful auction. She withholds the amounts she has spent and sends the tidy balance to David, along with receipts for her expenses. Totally outraged, he calls her on the phone, "How dare you hire an auctioneer and rent a tent? I never gave you permission! Who said you could run advertisements? I absolutely refuse to pay these expenses!"

David is wrong. A principal almost never gives an agent absolutely complete instructions. Unless some authority were implied, David would have had to say, "Open the car door, get in, put the key in the ignition, drive to the store, buy stickers, mark an auction number on each sticker" . . . and so forth. To solve this problem, the law assumes that the agent has authority to do anything that is *reasonably* necessary to accomplish her task.

Apparent Authority

A principal can be liable for the acts of an agent who is not, in fact, acting with authority if the principal's conduct causes a third party reasonably to believe that the agent is authorized. In the case of *express* and *implied* authority, the principal has authorized the agent to act. Apparent authority is different: the principal has not authorized the agent, but has done something to make an innocent third party believe the agent is authorized. As a result, the principal is every bit as liable to the third party as if the agent did have authority. Mary works for Dinners Delite, a company that sells tasty, low-fat frozen foods door-to-door. She enjoys calling on people, but often ends up spending the dinner hour with only one customer, talking away and eating samples.

---

[1] Restatement (Second) of Agency §26.
[2] Restatement (Second) of Agency §35.

Finally, her boss fires her. When he asks her to return her samples and order forms, she lies and tells him that everything was stolen. She then calls on all her customers, takes many large orders, and keeps the payments herself. The orders go in the trash. When last sighted, Mary was sunning herself at a Cuban resort.

Someone is going to be out a good deal of money. Although it should be Mary, the customers will not be able to reach her in Cuba. Either her customers will go hungry, or the company will have to reimburse them. What is the fair result? The law takes the view that the principal is liable, not the third party, because the principal, by word or deed, allowed the third party to believe that the agent was acting on the principal's behalf. The principal could have prevented the third party from losing money. When Mary stole the customers' money, she was *not* an agent for Dinners Delite, *but the customers believed she was* because the company had never told them that she had been dismissed. Nor did the company retrieve her samples and order forms. Dinners Delite must reimburse the customers for the money Mary took. Thus, in apparent authority, the agent *appears* to have authority, even though she does not. Of course, Dinners Delite has the right to recover from Mary, if it can track her down.

Remember that the issue in apparent authority is always what the *principal* has done to make the *third party* believe that the *agent* actually has authority. Suppose that Mary had never worked for Dinners Delite but, on her own, printed order forms and prepared phony samples. The company would not be liable for the orders she took, because it had never done or said anything that would *reasonably* make a third party believe Mary was its agent.

In the following case, neighbors had no reason to know the wife owned the house and that the husband was not authorized to make decisions about landscaping.

DICKINSON V. CHARTER OAKS

2003 Ohio 2055, 2003 Ohio App. LEXIS 1940
Court of Appeals of Ohio, 2003

Facts: Marlee Snowdon and her husband, Richard Snowdon, bought a house next door to Hal and Carol Dickinson. Carol had owned the house for 30 years; Hal Dickinson had moved in 10 to 15 years later when he and Carol married. Under the terms of a prenuptial agreement, Hal had no ownership interest in the property.

The Snowdons decided to clean out an area of overgrowth in their back yard and along the side of their property next to the Dickinson land. Richard spoke with Hal, who said it was fine for the Snowdons to have this work done. Marlee hired Charter Oaks for the project. Shortly thereafter, Hal cornered Richard and accused him of not doing the work that he had promised he would do. Richard told Hal that Charter was coming soon.

As Charter was working the first day, Hal came out into the yard to look at what was going on and then went back into the house. The next day, Carol returned from an out-of-town trip and was upset to see what Charter had done. She ordered the company to stop work. She then filed a lawsuit seeking damages for the harm to her property.

Charter admitted that Carol had not personally given permission for the landscaping work, but claimed it they had relied on Hal's apparent authority. The jury returned a verdict for Charter and Carol appealed.

Issue: **Did Hal Dickinson have apparent authority to make decisions about Carol's property?**

Excerpts from Judge Bryant's Decision: [P]laintiff contends an essential element of apparent agency is evidence the alleged principal *by the principal's own words or conduct* represented to the public that a person is the principal's agent with authority to act on behalf of the principal. No presumption of agency between a husband and wife arises based merely upon their marital relationship.

▼

[T]he record contains competent evidence to support a reasonable conclusion that Hal Dickinson had apparent authority to grant permission to defendants to enter upon plaintiff's property and to remove vegetation. Specifically the evidence shows that not only did Hal Dickinson work frequently in the Dickinson yard, both alone and with Carol Dickinson, but he trimmed and removed vegetation from the Dickinson property, including the area along the joint property line with the Snowdons. Notably, other evidence revealed Hal Dickinson dealt with contractors, including a tree service Carol Dickinson hired that performed work on the Dickinson property.

No evidence suggested the Snowdons were advised Hal Dickinson had limited or no authority to make decisions regarding landscaping matters on the Dickinson property. [A] reasonable inference could be made that Carol Dickinson knowingly permitted Hal Dickinson to act as having apparent authority over landscaping matters on the Dickinson property.

Judgment affirmed. ■

Devil's Advocate

The Snowdons assumed that Hal was authorized to make decisions about the property because he was married to Carol. But husbands are not automatically authorized to make decisions for their wives. If the Snowdons had seen Carol's son working in the yard, would they have assumed he was authorized? What about a handyman who regularly worked around the house? The court says that Carol had never told them about Hal's lack of authority, but that is not what the law requires. What had *she* ever done to make the Snowdons believe *he* was authorized? ◆

Estoppel

No one may claim that a person was *not* his agent, if he knew that others thought the person *was* acting on his behalf, and he failed to correct their belief. He is *estopped* from denying an agency relationship. Paul Murphy approached the Sperry Rand Corp. with a promising idea for marketing Remington shavers. He showed the company a report from Dr. William Hill, Jr., indicating that Remington shavers were better for the skin than ordinary razors or other electric shavers. Sperry Rand publicized this report in full-page advertisements in newspapers and magazines. There was only one problem—Hill had not written the report and had not agreed to allow his name to be used in the ad campaign. Murphy had *said* he was Hill's agent and had negotiated on Hill's behalf, but he was not, in fact, Hill's agent. Murphy did *not* have *apparent authority*, because Hill had done nothing to lead Sperry Rand to believe Murphy was his agent.

The court, however, found Sperry Rand not liable on a theory of estoppel. Hill discovered the ad campaign in March but did not complain to Sperry Rand until November. By the simple act of making a prompt phone call, the doctor could have prevented most of the harm the advertisements caused him.[3]

© SUSAN VAN ETTEN

Does Dr. Hill really think this shaver is better?

Ratification

If a person accepts the benefit of an unauthorized transaction or fails to repudiate it, then he is as bound by the act as if he had originally authorized it. He has *ratified*

---

3 *Sperry Rand Corp. v. Hill*, 356 F.2d 181, 1966 U.S. App. LEXIS 7491 (1st Cir. 1966).

the act.[4] Many of the cases in agency law involve instances in which one person acts *without* authority for another. To avoid liability, the alleged principal shows that he had not authorized the task at issue. But sometimes, after the fact, the principal decides that he approves of what the agent has done even though it was not authorized at the time. The law would be perverse if it did not permit the principal, under those circumstances, to agree to the deal the agent has made. The law is not perverse, but it is careful. Even if an agent acts without authority, the principal can decide later to be bound by her actions as long as these requirements are met:

- The "agent" indicates to the third party that she is acting for a principal.
- The "principal" knows all the material facts of the transaction.
- The "principal" accepts the benefit of the whole transaction, not just part.
- The third party does not withdraw from the contract before ratification.

A night clerk at the St. Regis Hotel in Detroit, Michigan, was brutally murdered in the course of a robbery. A few days later, the *Detroit News* reported that the St. Regis management had offered a $1,000 reward for any information leading to the arrest and conviction of the killer. Two days after the article appeared, Robert Jackson turned in the man who was subsequently convicted of the crime. But then it was Jackson's turn to be robbed—the hotel refused to pay the reward on the grounds that the manager who had made the offer had no authority. Jackson still had one weapon left: he convinced the court that the hotel had ratified the offer. One of the hotel's owners admitted he read the *Detroit News*. The court concluded that if someone reads a newspaper, he is sure to read any articles about a business he owns; therefore, the owner must have been aware of the offer. He accepted the benefit of the reward by failing to revoke it publicly. This failure to revoke constituted a ratification and the hotel was liable.[5]

Estoppel and ratification are easy to confuse. *Ratification* applies when the principal accepts the benefit of the contract. The hotel owner benefited from the reward because he wanted the murderer to be caught. *Estoppel* applies when the alleged principal does *not* want the benefit of the contract, but delays in telling the innocent third party of the mistake. The doctor did not want his name tied to a nonexistent research report in a national ad campaign. If the doctor had accepted the benefit of the contract, by receiving payment, for instance, then he would have *ratified* the contract. As it was, he accepted no benefit, but he waited so long to contact Sperry Rand that he was *estopped* from recovering damages.

Subagents

Many of the examples offered thus far in this chapter involve a single agent acting for a principal. Real life is often more complex. Daniel, the owner of a restaurant, hires Michaela to manage it. She in turn hires chefs, waiters, and dishwashers. Daniel has never even met the restaurant help, yet they are also his agents, albeit a special category called **subagent**. Michaela is called an **intermediary agent**—someone who hires subagents for the principal.

As a general rule, an agent has no authority to delegate her tasks to another unless the principal authorizes her to. But when an agent is authorized to hire a subagent, the principal is as liable for the acts of the subagent as he is for the acts of a regular agent. Daniel authorizes Michaela to hire a restaurant staff. She hires Lydia to serve as produce buyer. When Lydia buys food for the restaurant, Daniel must pay the bill.

---

[4] Restatement (Second) of Agency §82.

[5] *Jackson v. Goodman*, 69 Mich. App. 225, 244 N.W.2d 423, 1976 Mich. App. LEXIS 741 (Mich. Ct. App. 1976).

The intermediary agent is not liable to the principal for the misdeeds of the subagent, unless she was negligent in hiring. Lydia is supposed to buy premium lettuces like arugula and radicchio. But iceberg is much cheaper so she orders a carload of these plebeian greens. Daniel is furious because he must pay for all the lettuce, even though the restaurant cannot possibly serve it. He blames Michaela for hiring Lydia in the first place. But Michaela is not liable unless she had some reason to know that Lydia was trouble.

AGENT'S LIABILITY FOR CONTRACTS

The agent's liability on a contract depends upon how much the third party knows about the principal. Disclosure is the agent's best protection against liability.

Fully Disclosed Principal

An agent is not liable for any contracts she makes on behalf of a *fully* disclosed principal. A principal is fully disclosed if the third party knows of his *existence* and his *identity*. Augusta acts as agent for Parker when he buys Tracey's prize-winning show horse. Augusta and Tracey both grew up in posh Grosse Pointe, Michigan, where they attended the same elite schools. Tracey does not know Parker, but she figures any friend of Augusta's must be okay. She figures wrong—Parker is a charming deadbeat. He injures Tracey's horse, fails to pay the full contract price, and promptly disappears. Tracey angrily demands that Augusta make good on Parker's debt. Unfortunately for Tracey, Parker was a fully disclosed principal—Tracey knew of his *existence* and his *identity*. Although Tracey partly relied on Augusta's good character when contracting with Parker, Augusta is not liable because Tracey knew who the principal was and could have (should have) investigated him. Augusta did not promise anything herself, and Tracey's only recourse is against the principal, Parker (wherever he may be).

at **R!SK**
To avoid liability when signing a contract on behalf of a principal, an agent must clearly state that she is an agent and must also identify the principal. Augusta should sign a contract on behalf of her principal, Parker, as follows: "Augusta, as agent for Parker" or "Parker, by Augusta, Agent." ◆

Partially Disclosed Principal

In the case of a *partially* disclosed principal, the third party can recover from either the agent or the principal. A principal is partially disclosed if the third party knew of his *existence* but not his *identity*. Suppose that, when approaching Tracey about the horse, Augusta simply says, "I have a friend who is interested in buying your champion." Any friend of Augusta's is a friend of Tracey's—or so Tracey thinks. Parker is a partially disclosed principal because Tracey knows only that he exists, not who he is. She cannot investigate his creditworthiness because she does not know his name. Tracey relies solely on what she is able to learn from the agent, Augusta. Both Augusta and Parker are liable to Tracey. (They are jointly and severally liable, which means that Tracey can recover from either or both of them. She cannot, however, recover more than the total that she is owed: if her damages are $100,000, she can recover that amount from either Augusta or Parker, or partial amounts from both, but in no event more than $100,000.)

Undisclosed Principal

In the case of an *undisclosed* principal, the third party can recover from either the agent or the principal. A principal is undisclosed if the third party did not know of his existence. Suppose that Augusta simply asks to buy the horse herself, without mentioning that she is purchasing it for Parker. In this case, Parker is an undisclosed principal because Tracey does not know that Augusta is acting for someone else. Both Parker and Augusta are jointly and severally liable. As Exhibit 29.1 illustrates, the principal is *always* liable, but the agent is not unless the principal's identity is a mystery.

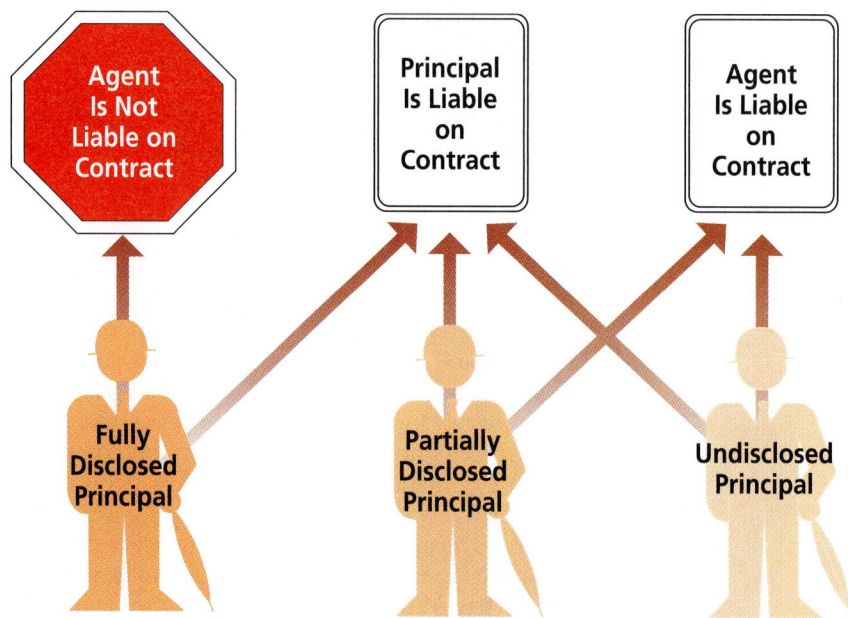

Exhibit 29.1

In some ways, the concept of an undisclosed principal violates principles of contract law. If Tracey does not even know that Parker exists, how can they have an agreement or a meeting of the minds? Is such an arrangement fair to Tracey? As Supreme Court Justice Oliver Wendell Holmes put it, "common sense is opposed to allowing a stranger to my overt acts and to my intentions, a man of whom I have never heard, to set up a contract against me which I had supposed I was making with my personal friend."[6] Nonetheless, a contract with an undisclosed principal is binding. The following incident illustrates why.

William Zeckendorf was a man with a plan. For years he had been eyeing a six-block tract of land along New York's East River. It was a wasteland of slums and slaughterhouses, but he could see its potential. The meat packers had refused to sell to him, however, because they knew they would never be permitted to build slaughterhouses in Manhattan again. Finally, in 1946, he got the phone call he had been waiting for. The companies were willing to sell—at $17 a square foot, when surrounding land cost less than $5. Undeterred, Zeckendorf immediately put down a $1 million deposit. But to make his investment worthwhile, he needed to buy the neighboring property— once the slaughterhouses were gone, this other land would be much more valuable. Zeckendorf was well-known as a wealthy developer; he had begun his business career

---

6 O. W. Holmes, "The History of Agency," in *Association of American Law Schools, Select Essays in Anglo-American Legal History* (Boston: Little, Brown & Co., 1909), vol. 3, p. 368.

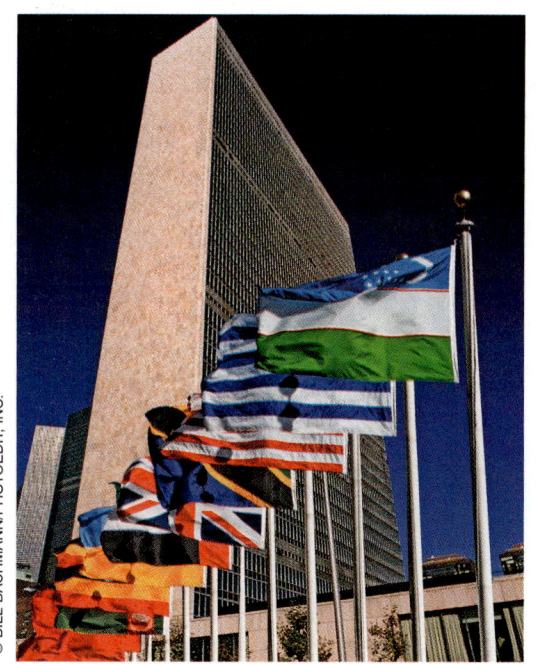

© BILL BACHMANN/PHOTOEDIT, INC.

If it were not for William Zeckendorf and his agents, UN headquarters might be in Boston.

managing the Astor family's real estate holdings. If he personally tried to negotiate the purchase of the surrounding land, word would soon get out that he was trying to put together a large parcel. Prices would skyrocket and the project would become too costly. So he hired agents to purchase the land for him. To further conceal his involvement, he went to South America for a month. When he returned, his agents had completed 75 different purchases, and he owned 18 acres of land.

Shortly afterwards, the United Nations began seeking a site for its headquarters. President Truman favored Boston, Philadelphia, or a location in the Midwest. The UN committee suggested Greenwich or Stamford, Connecticut. But John D. Rockefeller settled the question once and for all. He purchased Zeckendorf's land for $8.5 million and donated it to the UN (netting Zeckendorf a profit of $2 million). Without the cooperation of agency law, the UN headquarters would not be in New York today.

The law permits the concept of an undisclosed principal out of commercial necessity. There are times when the right of the third party to know the identity of the principal is outweighed by the law's interest in ensuring the smooth operation of commerce. The following article suggests that Harvard behaved unethically when it purchased land secretly. Do you agree?

NEWSworthy

Harvard University has bought 52 acres during the past nine years in a secret buying spree that increases the school's land in Allston (across the river from its Cambridge headquarters) by more than a third. Working through the Beal Cos., a prominent real estate development company, Harvard spent $88 million to buy 14 separate parcels. Harvard officials said the university made the purchases without revealing its identity to the sellers, residents, local politicians, or city officials because property owners would have drastically inflated the prices if they knew Harvard was the buyer. "We were really driven by the need to get these properties at fair market value" and avoid "overly inflated acquisition costs," said James H. Rowe, vice-president for public affairs at Harvard. But those who were left in the dark—including Mayor Thomas M. Menino—weren't buying it. "That's absurd," Menino scoffed. "Without informing anyone or telling anybody? That's total arrogance." Menino was so incensed that he adopted a mocking singsong tone to express his view of Harvard's attitude, saying: "We're from Harvard, and we're going to do what we want."

"As far as I'm concerned, they practiced a deception," said Ray Mellone, chairman of a neighborhood task force. "There are a lot of people who are going to say we can't trust them. We have to make the process work, and that means making the neighborhood involved, not having deals made in a back room and then coming to us and saying: 'Take it or leave it.'"[7] ◆

Because of concerns about fair play, there are some exceptions to the rule on undisclosed principals. **A third party is not bound to the contract with an undisclosed principal if (1) the contract specifically provides that the third party is not bound to anyone other than the agent, or (2) the agent lies about the principal because**

[7] Tina Cassidy and Dan Aucoin, "Harvard Reveals Secret Purchases of 52 Acres Worth $88M in Allston," *Boston Globe*, June 10, 1997, p. A1. Republished with permission of *The Boston Globe*; permission conveyed through the Copyright Clearance Center, Inc.

she knows the third party would refuse to contract with him. A cagey property owner, when approached by one of Harvard's agents, could have asked for a clause in the contract providing that the agent was not representing someone else. If the agent told the truth, the owner could have demanded a higher price. If the agent lied, then the owner could have rescinded the contract when the truth emerged. Suppose that a property owner said to one of the agents, "I don't mind selling this land to you, but I certainly wouldn't want Harvard to get it." The agent responded, "You can be sure this land will never end up in Harvard's hands." When the irate owner later discovers the agent lied, he can rescind the contract.

In the following case, a Degas painting raced around Alabama and New York. In the end, no one wanted it. But someone had to lose the race.

WEIL V. MURRAY

161 F. Supp. 2d 250, 2001 U.S. Dist. LEXIS 4117
United States District Court for the Southern District of New York, 2001

Facts: Mark Murray, an art dealer in New York, heard that Jean and Robert Weil were interested in selling some of their pictures. He was particularly keen on their painting by Edgar Degas entitled "Aux Courses" ("The Races").[8] Murray discussed this painting with Ian Peck, a fellow art dealer, who expressed an interest in buying it and asked Murray

© CORBIS/FRANCIS MAYER

Edgar Degas was off to the races in this painting.

to arrange to have it brought to New York from the Weils' home in Alabama.

Murray alleges that, after Peck saw the painting, Peck agreed to buy it for $1 million. Indeed, Peck's attorney wrote the first draft of the purchase agree-

ment. Murray retyped that draft, changing the name of the buyer from Peck to Murray. Weil then prepared an alternative version. Murray contends that Peck approved the Weil version of the agreement. Peck, on the other hand, claims that there was no discussion of the Weil version, and that Murray merely brought it to him so he would know how much to pay.

Murray and Weil both signed the agreement. It stated that the "Buyer" was Mark Murray and further that:

> It is understood that the eventual Buyer is an Undisclosed Principal client of Mark Murray, and that said undisclosed principal shall also be bound by this agreement. Should Sellers not receive full payment by December 8th, Buyer agrees to divulge to the Sellers the exact identity of the Undisclosed Principal, and the Undisclosed Principal must hereby guarantee this purchase and stand in the shoes of the Buyer, should there be cause for non-performance in any particular by said Ultimate Buyer.

When the Weils did not receive the $1 million, they filed suit against Murray and Peck. The Weils and Peck also filed motions for summary judgment.

Issue: Are Murray and Peck liable to the Weils for the purchase price of the Degas?

Excerpts from Judge Mukasey's Decision: The contract clearly defines Murray as the "Buyer." Mur-

▼

---

[8] A series of Degas racetrack paintings is on view at **http://www.nga.gov/cgi-bin/psearch?Request=A&Person=7850**.

ray advocates a reading of the contract that would make him neither the buyer, nor an agent for the partially disclosed principal, but rather an intermediary whose only contractual obligation was to reveal the identity of the undisclosed principal.

The contract's reference to an undisclosed principal who "shall also be bound by [the] agreement" does not extinguish Murray's obligation as the buyer. Even assuming that Murray was merely signing the contract as an agent for the so-called "undisclosed principal," an agent who enters into an agreement on behalf of a partially disclosed principal is obligated to perform the contract.

Peck argues that he is entitled to summary judgment because the written agreement is explicitly a bilateral agreement between Murray and plaintiffs,

and therefore, Peck cannot be bound by it. If the jury were to determine that Murray was acting as Peck's agent, with authority to sign the contract, then Peck could be bound. Furthermore, although Murray signed the contract in his name, not as the agent for Peck or the undisclosed principal, a partially disclosed principal is subject to liability upon an authorized contract in writing although it purports to be the contract of the agent. An agent who enters into an agreement on behalf of an undisclosed or partially disclosed principal is jointly and severally liable with the principal.

For the reasons stated above, plaintiffs' motion for summary judgment against Murray is granted. Peck's motion for summary judgment against plaintiffs is denied. ■

Unauthorized Agent

Thus far in this section, we have been discussing an agent's liability to a third party for a transaction that was authorized by the principal. Sometimes, however, agents act without the authority of a principal. **If the agent has no authority (express, implied, or apparent), the principal is not liable to the third party and the agent is.** Suppose that Augusta agrees to sell Parker's horse to Tracey. Unfortunately, Parker has never met Augusta and has certainly not authorized this transaction. Augusta is hoping that she can persuade him to sell, but Parker refuses. Augusta, but not Parker, is liable to Tracey for breach of contract.

PRINCIPAL'S LIABILITY FOR TORTS

A master is liable for physical harm caused by the negligent conduct of servants within the scope of employment.[9] This principle of liability is called *respondeat superior,* which is a Latin phrase that means "let the master answer." Under the theory of *respondeat superior,* the master (that is, the principal) is liable for the agent's misbehavior whether or not the principal was at fault. Indeed, the principal is liable even if he forbade or tried to prevent the agent from misbehaving. Thus a company could be liable for the damage an employee causes while using her cell phone, even if she is violating company policy at the time. This sounds like a harsh rule. The logic is that, since the principal controls the agent, he should be able to *prevent* misbehavior. If he cannot prevent it, at least he can *insure* against the risks. Furthermore, the principal may have deeper pockets than the agent or the injured third party and thus be better able to *afford* the cost of the agent's misbehavior.

To apply the principle of *respondeat superior,* it is important to understand each of the following terms: *master and servant, scope of employment, negligent and intentional torts,* and *physical harm.*

[9] Restatement (Second) of Agency §243.

Master and Servant

There are two kinds of agents: (1) *servants* and (2) *independent contractors.* **A principal *may be* liable for the torts of a servant but generally is *not* liable for the torts of an independent contractor.** Because of this rule, the distinction between a servant and an independent contractor is important.

Servant or Independent Contractor?

The more control the principal has over an agent, the more likely that the agent will be considered a servant. Therefore, when determining if agents are servants or independent contractors, courts consider whether:

- The principal controls details of the work.
- The principal supplies the tools and place of work.
- The agents work full-time for the principal.
- The agents are paid by time, not by the job.
- The work is part of the regular business of the principal.
- The principal and agents believe they have an employer-employee relationship.
- The principal is in business.[10]

Do not be misled by the term *servant.* A servant does not mean Jeeves, the butler, or Maisie, the maid. In fact, if Mrs. Dillworth hires Jeeves and Maisie for the evening from a catering firm, they are *not* her servants; they are independent contractors. On the other hand, the president of General Motors is a servant of that corporation.

cyberLaw

With computers, e-mail, and cell phones at their fingertips, more employees than ever work outside the office—at home, in the car, by the pool. This freedom to roam may increase productivity and enhance job satisfaction, but it also scrambles the legal picture. Traditionally, courts determined if an agent was a servant or an independent contractor by looking at the principal's control. If the employee was working on an assembly line under the eagle eye of a supervisor, the control was obvious. But what about an employee who is telecommuting from home? Suppose that he calls a repair person for his computer. When she informs him that his hard drive may be dead and gone, his hands tremble so badly that he accidentally drop his coffee cup, spilling hot liquid all over her. Who is liable for her injuries? ◆

In the following case, a Boston University basketball player injured an opposing player. Was BU liable?

KAVANAGH V. TRUSTEES OF BOSTON UNIVERSITY

440 Mass. 195, 795 N.E.2d 1170; 2003 Mass. LEXIS 643
Supreme Judicial Court of Massachusetts, 2003

Facts: The Boston University men's basketball team played a game against Manhattan College. Following a contested rebound, the referee blew his whistle to signal a foul. Some of the players began to push and elbow each other. Kenneth Kavanagh, a Manhattan College player, intervened to break up a developing scuffle. LeVar Folk, a Boston University player, punched him in the nose. Folk was immediately ejected from the game. Kavanagh was treated ▼

---

[10] Restatement (Second) of Agency §220(2).

for what turned out to be a broken nose and returned to play later in the same game.

Folk was at the university on a full athletic scholarship. Kavanagh contends that Folk's status as a scholarship athlete made him an agent of the university and that the university is therefore liable for any torts committed by Folk while playing for the basketball team.

The trial court granted summary judgment to the university. Kavanagh appealed.

Issue: Is a basketball player on scholarship an agent of the university team for which he plays?

Excerpts from Justice Sosman's Decision: Broadly speaking, *respondeat superior* is the proposition that an employer, or master, should be held vicariously liable for the torts of its employee, or servant, committed within the scope of employment.

In determining whether an employer-employee relationship exists, various factors are to be considered, including the method of payment (e.g., whether the employee receives a W-2 form from the employer), and whether the parties themselves believe they have created an employer-employee relationship. A student's status as student does not, by itself, make the student an "employee" or "servant" of the school the student attends. Neither party understands the student's relationship with the school to be one of employment. Students attend school to serve their own interests, not the interests of the school. The student is a buyer of education rather than an agent. A student retains the benefit of that education for himself rather than for the university.

While schools may benefit in various ways from the presence of a particular student, or may benefit in the future from a former student's later success, the student does not attend school to do the school's bidding.

While scholarships may introduce some element of "payment" into the relationship, scholarships are not wages. Nor does a scholarship student "work for" the school in exchange for that scholarship. The benefits that may accrue to a school from the attendance of particularly talented athletes is conceptually no different from the benefits that schools obtain from the attendance of other forms of talented and successful students—both as undergraduates and later as alumni, such students enhance the school's reputation, draw favorable attention to the school, and may increase the school's ability to raise funds.

It is undeniable that a successful athletic program, particularly in popular sports like basketball, can garner substantial revenues for colleges and universities, both directly from the sporting activities themselves (e.g., gate receipts, sale of broadcasting rights) and indirectly from the attention those activities attract (e.g., increased alumni giving). In recent years, the enormity of the revenues at stake in collegiate sports has prompted some to recommend that colleges and universities be allowed to compensate student athletes for their "services" and thereby transform them into employees. It is recognized, however, that the current relationship of a player to a school remains that of scholarship student, not employee.

Kavanagh argues that scholarship athletes should nevertheless be treated as "agents" of their schools because it is said that they "represent" their schools. When one speaks of an athlete, or any other student, as a "representative" of his or her school, the term is not being used in its legal sense. Rather, it connotes only that a student's performance will reflect on the school and will be seen as indicative of the school's quality. Students do not "represent" their schools in the sense of being able to bind their schools to agreements, or to act on behalf of their schools.

Judgment affirmed. ∎

Negligent Hiring

Principals prefer agents to be considered independent contractors not servants because, as a general rule, principals are not liable for the torts of an independent contractor. There is, however, one exception to this rule: **The principal is liable for the physical torts of an independent contractor *only if* the principal has been negligent in hiring or supervising her.** Remember that, under *respondeat superior*, the principal is liable *without fault* for the physical torts of servants. The case of independent contractors is different: the principal is liable only if he was *at fault* by being careless in his hiring or supervising. Was the supermarket at fault in the following case?

DURAN V. FURR'S SUPERMARKETS, INC.

921 S.W.2d 778, 1996 Tex. App. LEXIS 1345
Court of Appeals of Texas, 1996

Facts: Steve Romero was an off-duty police officer working as a security guard for Furr's Supermarkets. He approached a car parked in the supermarket's fire lane and began yelling at a passenger to move it. The passenger, Graciela Duran, asked Romero for his name. He opened the car door and tried to pull her out, all the while threatening to arrest her. Duran ultimately required surgery to repair the injury that his tugs and twists caused to her left arm.

Duran filed suit against Furr's. The supermarket filed a motion for summary judgment on the grounds that it was not responsible for Romero's conduct because he was an independent contractor. Duran argued that Furr's had been negligent in hiring Romero. The trial court granted the motion for summary judgment.

Issues: Did the trial court properly grant Furr's motion for summary judgment? Is Duran entitled to a trial?

Excerpts from Judge McClure's Decision: The basis of responsibility under the doctrine of negligent hiring is the master's own negligence in hiring or retaining in his employ an incompetent servant whom the master knows or by the exercise of reasonable care should have known was incompetent or unfit and thereby creating an unreasonable risk of harm to others. The evidence showed that Furr's did not require Romero to complete a job application and otherwise made no inquiry into his background as a police officer. Furr's never interviewed Romero or spoke with him before he began working at the store. If Furr's had conducted an investigation of Romero's performance as a police officer, it would have learned that Romero had a prior complaint for using vulgar and abusive language towards a member of the public while on duty as a police officer.

Duran argues that this complaint demonstrates Romero's propensity for aggressive behavior so that Furr's could have reasonably anticipated that Romero might verbally and physically abuse a patron of the store. On the other hand, Furr's argues that even if it had discovered the prior complaint, the information would not have caused Furr's to reasonably anticipate his physical assault upon Duran. In attempting to distinguish between the prior verbal abuse complaint and the physical assault upon Duran, Furr's ignores the evidence showing that Romero first verbally abused Duran during this incident. According to Duran, the verbal abuse escalated into the physical assault. We find that a fact question is raised whether knowledge of this abusive language complaint would put a reasonable person on notice that Romero might verbally abuse a store patron, and that such conduct might escalate into a physical assault. Because of the existence of this fact issue, summary judgment on this ground is improper. ■

Exhibit 29.2 illustrates the difference in liability between a servant and an independent contractor.

Scope of Employment

Principals are only liable for torts that a servant commits within the *scope of employment*. If an employee leaves a pool of water on the floor of a store and a customer slips and falls, the employer is liable. But if the same employee leaves water on his own kitchen floor and a friend falls, the employer is not liable because the employee is not acting within the scope of employment. A servant is acting within the scope of employment if the act:

- Is one that servants are generally responsible for
- Takes place during hours that the servant is generally employed

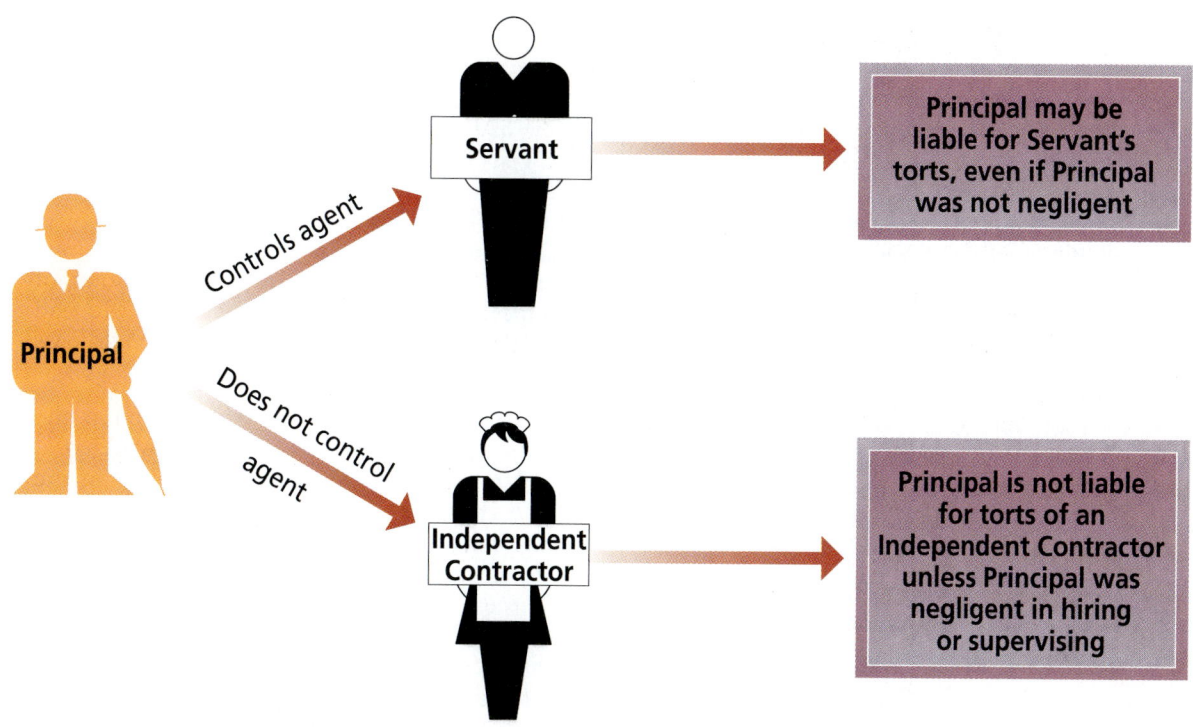

Exhibit 29.2

- Is part of the principal's business
- Is similar to the one the principal authorized
- Is one for which the principal supplied the tools; and
- Is not seriously criminal.

Scope of employment cases raise two major issues: *authorization* and *abandonment*.

Authorization

In authorization cases, the agent is clearly working for the principal but commits an act that the principal has not authorized. Although Jane has often told the driver of her delivery van not to speed, Hank ignores her instructions and plows into Bernadette. At the time of the accident, he is working for Jane, delivering flowers for her shop, but his act is not authorized. **An act is within the scope of employment, even if expressly forbidden, if it is of the same general nature as that authorized or if it is incidental to the conduct authorized.**[11] Hank was authorized to drive the van, but not to speed. However, his speeding was of the same general nature as the authorized act, so Jane is liable to Bernadette.

　　Was the employee in the following case acting within the scope of his employment? You be the judge.

---

[11] Restatement (Second) of Agency §229(1).

you Be The Judge

KASHIN V. KENT

333 F. Supp. 2d 926, 2004 U.S. Dist. LEXIS 17381
United States District Court for the Southern District of California, 2004

Facts: Douglas Kent was the Consul General of the United States in Vladivostok, Russia. One evening, he drove from his office to a gym and then home. On the way home, he was involved in an accident that left Aleksandr Kashin severely injured.

Kashin sued the United States government, claiming that Kent was within the scope of his employment at the time of the accident.

You Be the Judge: Was Kent within the scope of his employment while driving home from the gym?

Argument for Kashin: Kent was expected to, and did, work on behalf of the United States around the clock, seven days a week. He sometimes worked from home. Kent also sometimes conducted government business from his apartment or had to leave it in the middle of the night on official business. The Department of State leased and furnished Kent's apartment, which was provided to him without cost.

Kent was required to pass regular and thorough medical examinations or face revocation of his medical clearance to work overseas. He had gone to the gym to work out so that he could pass this medical exam.

Argument for the United States: On the day of the accident, Kent had not been working at home. Nor was he engaged in any diplomatic activity at the time of the accident. The visit to the gym was his personal business. He had not visited the gym for purposes of taking the medical exam, nor did the State Department require him to work out at the gym.

The Department of State provided Kent with a driver and a car for any purpose; however, he elected to use his own car after he was advised that the overtime costs accrued to his driver had become high. At the time of the accident, Kent was driving his own car. ■

Abandonment

The second major issue in a *scope of employment* case involves abandonment. **The master is liable for the actions of the servant that occur while the servant is at work, but not for actions that occur after the servant has abandoned the master's business.** Although the rule sounds straightforward, the difficulty lies in determining whether the employee has in fact abandoned the master's business. The employer is liable if the employee is simply on a *detour* from company business, but the employer is not liable if the employee is off on a *frolic of his own.* Suppose that Hank, the delivery van driver, speeds during his afternoon commute home. A servant is generally not acting within the scope of his employment when he commutes to and from work, so his master, Jane, is not liable. Or suppose that, while on the way to a delivery, he stops to view his favorite movie classic, *Dead on Arrival.* Unable to see in the darkened theater, he knocks Anna down, causing grave harm. Jane is not liable because Hank's visit to the movies is outside the scope of his employment. On the other hand, if Hank stops at the Burger King drive-in window en route to making a delivery, Jane is liable when he crashes into Anna on the way out of the parking lot, because this time he is simply making a detour. The distinction between a *frolic* and a *detour* can sometimes seem obscure. The following case clarifies the distinction.

O'CONNOR V. MCDONALD'S RESTAURANTS OF CALIFORNIA, INC.

220 Cal. App. 3d 25, 1990 Cal. App. LEXIS 448
California Court of Appeals, 1990

Facts: One August evening from about 8 P.M. until 2 A.M. Evans and several co-workers scoured the children's playground at McDonald's San Ysidro restaurant. This special cleaning prepared the restaurant for inspection as part of McDonald's "spring-blitz" competition. Evans—who aspired to a managerial position—worked without pay in the cleanup party. His voluntary contribution of work and time was the type of extra effort necessary for advancement in the McDonald's organization.

After completing the cleanup, Evans and four fellow employees went to the house of Joe Duffer, who had also participated in the evening's work. Evans and the others talked shop and socialized for several hours. On his way home at 6:30 A.M., Evans collided with a motorcycle driven by Martin O'Connor. The motorcyclist was seriously injured, and his left leg had to be amputated below the knee.

O'Connor filed a lawsuit for negligence against Evans and McDonald's. The trial court found that Evans was acting outside the scope of his employment at the time of the accident, and granted summary judgment for McDonald's. O'Connor appealed.

Issue: Was Evans acting within the scope of his employment at the time of the accident?

Excerpts from Judge Kremer's Decision: The record contains evidence McDonald's encourages its employees and aspiring managers to show greater dedication than simply working a shift and going home. O'Connor presented McDonald's operations and training manual and employee handbook to demonstrate how McDonald's fosters employee initiative and involvement in problem solving. Such evidence could reasonably support a finding of a direct and specific connection between McDonald's business and the gathering at Duffer's because the gathering was consistent with the "family" spirit and teamwork emphasized by McDonald's in its communications with employees. Such evidence could also reasonably support a finding McDonald's emphasis on teamwork made a group discussion of McDonald's business at Duffer's house a foreseeable continuation of Evans's special errand. Much of the conversation during the gathering centered on McDonald's business or concerned employee-manager relations. The group discussed the cleaning activities of the spring blitz to determine whether they might return to the restaurant to correct any deficiencies.

McDonald's contends the asserted managerial discussions at Duffer's house went beyond the scope of work Evans was hired to do. Evans's direct supervisor Cardenas asserted Evans "was under no instruction from me, or any other authorized employee of McDonald's, with respect to his activities after he left the restaurant. I had no knowledge that other co-employees would go to Joe Duffer's house after the final clean-up." McDonald's also presented evidence it required official employee conferences be attended by a salaried manager and no such salaried manager attended the Duffer gathering. However, these facts do not compel a finding as a matter of law contrary to O'Connor's claim McDonald's implicitly encouraged Evans to continue his special errand by conferring with co-employees on what they might do to win the spring blitz competition.

Such evidence raises a triable factual issue about the combination of personal entertainment and company business at Duffer's house. Where the employee may be deemed to be pursuing a business errand and a personal objective simultaneously, he will still be acting within the scope of his employment.

The summary judgment is *reversed*. ■

Negligent and Intentional Torts

The master is liable if the servant commits a *negligent* tort that causes physical harm to a person or property. When Evans crashed into O'Connor, he committed a negligent tort, and McDonald's is liable if all the other requirements for *respondeat superior* are met.

A master is *not* liable for the *intentional* torts of the servant unless the servant was motivated, at least in part, by a desire to serve the master, or the conduct

was reasonably foreseeable. During an NBA basketball game, Kobe pushes Shaq into some chairs under the basket to prevent him from scoring a breakaway layup. Kobe's team is liable for his actions because he was motivated, at least in part, by a desire to help his team. But if Kobe hits Shaq in the parking lot after the playoffs are over, Kobe's team is *not* liable because he is no longer motivated by a desire to help the team. His motivation now is personal revenge or frustration.

The courts (of law, not basketball) are generally expansive in their definition of behavior that is intended to serve the master. In one case, a police trainee shot a fellow officer while practicing his quick draw technique. In another, a drunken sailor knocked a shipmate out of bed with the admonition, "Get up, you big son of a bitch, and turn to," after which the two men fought. The courts ruled that both the police trainee and the sailor were motivated by a desire to serve their master and, therefore, the master was liable for their intentional torts.[12]

Even if the servant was not motivated by a desire to serve his master, the master is liable if the conduct was reasonably foreseeable. Barbara Marston went to see a psychiatrist, Dr. E. Philip Nuernberger, for biofeedback therapy to cure her chronic headaches and back pain. After two sessions Dr. Nuernberger began kissing and fondling her. Marston became increasingly depressed. Under a theory of *respondeat superior,* she sued the clinic where Dr. Nuernberger worked. At trial, experts testified that any sexual contact with a patient is totally unethical, has no therapeutic purpose, is purely personal, and could not be motivated by any desire to serve the clinic. But the court held for the patient on the grounds that "[s]exual relations between a psychologist and a patient is a well-known hazard and thus, to a degree, foreseeable and a risk of employment."[13]

Physical Harm

In the case of *physical* torts, a master is liable for the negligent conduct of a servant that occurs within the scope of employment. The rule for *nonphysical* torts (that is, torts that harm only reputation, feelings, or wallet) is different. **Nonphysical torts are treated more like a contract claim, and the principal is liable only if the servant acted with actual, implied, or apparent authority.** For example, the Small Business Administration (SBA) granted Midwest Knitting Mills, Inc., more than $2 million in loans, but the SBA employee in charge of the case never told Midwest. (He was allegedly a drug addict.) The company sued the SBA for the negligence of its employee. Although the conduct had occurred within the scope of employment, it was a nonphysical tort. Since the employee had not acted with actual, implied, or apparent authority, the SBA was not liable.[14]

Misrepresentation and defamation are, however, treated differently from other nonphysical torts.

Misrepresentation

A principal is liable if:

- The agent makes a misrepresentation
- The agent has express, implied, or apparent authority
- The third party relies on the misrepresentation; and
- The third party suffers harm.

---

[12] *Nelson v. American-West African Line, Inc.,* 86 F.2d 730, 1936 U.S. App. LEXIS 3841 (2d Cir. 1936), and *Thompson v. United States,* 504 F. Supp. 1087, 1980 U.S. Dist. LEXIS 15834 (D.S.D. 1980).

[13] *Marston v. Minneapolis Clinic of Psychiatry & Neurology, Ltd.,* 329 N.W.2d 306, 1982 Minn. LEXIS 1891 (Minn. 1982).

[14] *Midwest Knitting Mills, Inc. v. United States,* 741 F. Supp. 1345, 1990 U.S. Dist. LEXIS 8663 (E.D. Wis. 1990).

This rule applies to any agent, not just a servant. If the agent is authorized to make a *truthful* statement, the principal is liable for any related *false* statement.

Althea hires Morris, a real estate agent, to sell a piece of land. Morris knows that part of the land floods every spring, but when Helen inquires about flooding, Morris lies. He is not authorized to make the *false* statement, but he is authorized to make statements about the land. Althea is liable to Helen for any harm caused by Morris's misrepresentation, even though Morris is an independent contractor.

Defamation

A principal is liable if:

- The agent makes a defamatory statement
- The agent has express, implied, or apparent authority; and
- The third party is harmed by the statement.

Again, this rule applies to all agents, not simply to servants. If the agent is authorized to make a *truthful* statement, the principal is liable for any related *defamatory* statements.

A newspaper reporter writes an untrue story alleging that the mayor has been taking kickbacks from contractors who work for the city. The reporter has defamed the mayor, and the newspaper is liable because the reporter is an agent authorized to write the article, even though he is not authorized to write false statements.

cyberLaw

Electronic communication has created new risks for employers. They fear that their employees may commit libel by sending flaming e-mails or violate intellectual property laws by downloading copyrighted software from the Internet. Is the company liable in these circumstances? What if an employee posts defamatory information on an Internet bulletin board? Even if the employee is not authorized, she may have *apparent* authority—especially if the posting appears with a company e-mail address. For this reason, companies increasingly monitor their employees' e-mail content and Internet usage. Some companies also require employees, when posting on a bulletin board, to include a disclaimer that they do not speak for their company. ◆

AGENT'S LIABILITY FOR TORTS

The focus of this chapter has been on the *principal's* liability for the agent's torts. But it is important to remember that **agents are always liable for their own torts.** Agents who commit torts are personally responsible, whether or not their principal is also liable. In the *McDonald's* case, the plaintiff filed suit against *both* Evans (the agent) and McDonald's (the principal). Even if the tort was committed to benefit the principal, the agent is still liable. So the sailor who got into a fistfight while rousting a shipmate from bed is liable even though he thought he was acting for the benefit of his principal.

This rule makes obvious sense. If the agent were not liable, he would have little incentive to be careful. Imagine Hank driving his delivery van for Jane. If he were not personally liable for his own torts, he might think, "If I drive fast enough, I can make it through that light even though it just turned red. And if I don't, what the heck, it'll be Jane's problem, not mine." Agents, as a rule, may have fewer assets than their principal, but it is important that their personal assets be at risk in the event of their negligent behavior.

If the agent and principal are *both* liable, which does the injured third party sue? The principal and the agent are *jointly and severally* liable, which means, as we have seen, that the injured third party can sue either one or both, as she chooses. If she recovers from the principal, he can sue the agent.

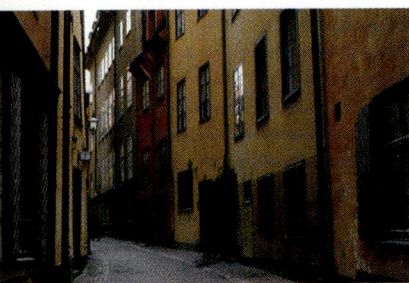
© BRAND X PICTURES/GETTY IMAGES

Chapter Conclusion

Most people will, at some point in their lives, serve as a principal and as an agent. This is particularly true for those in business—few businesses operate without agents. Though essential, the agent-principal relationship is nonetheless a potential minefield of liability. In some sense, this entire chapter is a lesson in preventive law. By understanding agency law, principals and agents can both avoid liability.

Chapter Review

1. A principal is bound by the contracts of the agent if the agent has express, implied, or apparent authority. The principal is also bound by the contracts of the agent if the principal is estopped from denying the agent had authority, or if the principal ratifies the acts of the agent.

2. The principal grants express authority by words or conduct that, reasonably interpreted, cause the agent to believe that the principal desires her to act on the principal's account.

3. Implied authority includes authority to do acts that are incidental to a transaction, usually accompany it, or are reasonably necessary to accomplish it.

4. Apparent authority means that a principal is liable for the acts of an agent who is not, in fact, acting with authority if the principal's conduct causes a third party reasonably to believe that the agent is authorized.

5. Under the theory of estoppel, no one may claim that a person was *not* his agent if he knew that others thought the person *was* acting on his behalf and he failed to correct their belief.

6. Ratification means that someone agrees to an act that he had not originally authorized. A ratified transaction is treated as if it had been authorized from the beginning.

7. An agent is not liable for any contract she makes on behalf of a fully disclosed principal. The principal is liable. In the case of a partially disclosed or undisclosed principal, both the agent and the principal are liable on the contract.

8. Under *respondeat superior*, a master is liable when a servant acting within the scope of employment commits a negligent tort that causes physical harm to a person or property. Under some limited circumstances, a master is also liable for a servant's intentional torts.

9. The principal is only liable for the physical torts of an independent contractor if the principal has been negligent in hiring or supervising him.

10. A principal is liable for nonphysical torts only if the servant acts with actual, implied, or apparent authority.

11. Agents are always liable for their own torts.

Practice Test

1. It was Christmas time in the city, and Mrs. Pommert decided to surprise her husband by buying holiday decorations for his hardware store. Singing along with the carols on the car radio, Mrs. Pommert ran a stop sign and crashed into Mr. Bryan's car. Called to the scene by the police, Mr. Pommert took the decorations out of his wife's car and placed them in his own. Mr. Bryan alleged that Mr. Pommert was liable as Mrs. Pommert's principal because he had ratified her purchase of the Christmas decorations when he placed them in his car. Do you agree?

2. **CPA QUESTION** Cox engaged Datz as her agent. It was mutually agreed that Datz would not disclose that he was acting as Cox's agent. Instead he was to deal with prospective customers as if he were a principal acting on his own behalf. This he did and made several contracts for Cox. Assuming Cox, Datz, or the customer seeks to avoid liability on one of the contracts involved, which of the following statements is correct?
   a. Cox must ratify the Datz contracts in order to be held liable.

b. Datz has **no** liability once he discloses that Cox was the real principal.

c. The third party can avoid liability because he believed he was dealing with Datz as a principal.

d. The third party may choose to hold either Datz or Cox liable.

3. This article appeared in *Newsday:*

As the first legal claim was filed in the wake of yesterday's deadly subway crash at Union Square, personal injury attorneys said the city Transit Authority was certain to be held responsible for the loss of life and injuries in the wreck. Even if the motorman were found to have been under the influence of drugs or alcohol, the Transit Authority bears responsibility for the negligence of its employees.[15]

Is this story accurate? Under what legal theory would the Transit Authority be liable?

4. **ETHICS** Dr. James Leonard wrote Dr. Edward Jacobson offering him the position of Chief of Audiology at Jefferson Medical College in Philadelphia. In the letter, Leonard stated that this appointment would have to be approved by the promotion and appointment committee. Jacobson believed that the appointment committee acted only as a "rubber stamp" affirming whatever recommendation Leonard made. Jacobson accepted Leonard's offer and proceeded to sell his house and quit his job in Colorado. You can guess what happened next. Two weeks later, Leonard sent Jacobson another letter, rescinding his offer because of opposition from the appointment committee. Jacobson conceded that Leonard did not have express or implied authority to enter into binding employment contracts on behalf of the medical college. On what grounds could Jacobson bring a lawsuit? Would he prevail? Regardless of the medical school's legal obligation, does the appointment committee have an ethical obligation to Dr. Jacobson? Would any of the questions on the ethical checklist in Chapter 2 make the committee members think twice about what they have done?

5. One Friday afternoon, a custodian at the Lazear Elementary School in Oakland, California, raped an 11-year-old student in his office on the school premises. The student sued the school district on a theory of *respondeat superior.* Is the school district liable for this intentional tort by its employee?

6. Jack and Rita Powers purchased 312 head of cattle at an auction conducted by Coffeyville Livestock Sales Co. They did not know who owned the cattle they bought. The Powers, in turn, sold 159 of this lot to Leonard Hoefling. He sued the Powers, alleging the cattle were diseased and dying in large numbers, and recovered $38,360. Are the Powers entitled to reimbursement from Coffeyville?

7. This article appeared in the *New York Times:*

A week after criminal charges were announced in the death of tennis star Vitas Gerulaitis, his mother filed suit yesterday against eight defendants, including the owner of the Long Island estate where Mr. Gerulaitis died of carbon monoxide poisoning last fall. Prosecutors have charged that a new swimming pool heater, installed at a cost of $8,000, was improperly vented and sent deadly fumes into a pool house where Mr. Gerulaitis was taking a nap. The lawsuit accuses the companies that manufactured, installed and maintained the pool heater, and the mechanic who installed it, with negligence and reckless disregard for human life. It makes similar charges against the owners of the oceanfront estate, Beatrice Raynes and her son Martin, a real-estate executive.[16]

Why would the owners of the estate be liable?

8. **CPA QUESTION** A principal will **not** be liable to a third party for a tort committed by an agent:

a. Unless the principal instructed the agent to commit the tort

b. Unless the tort was committed within the scope of the agency relationship

c. If the agency agreement limits the principal's liability for the agent's tort

---

[15] Anthony M. DeStefano, "Wreck's 1st Legal Claim Seeks $10M for Injuries," *Newsday,* Aug. 29, 1991, p. 10. Copyright 1991 Newsday, Inc.

[16] Vivian S. Toy, "Gerulaitis's Mother Files Suit in Son's Carbon Monoxide Death," *New York Times,* June 1, 1995, p. B5. Copyright © 1995 by The New York Times Co.

d. If the tort is also regarded as a criminal act

9. As a child, Clive Thomas became a permanent resident of the United States. Three decades later, still not a citizen, he pleaded guilty to conspiracy to possess cocaine for sale and was sentenced to seven years' imprisonment. He was released from prison after two years because of his cooperation in a major narcotics investigation. Thomas and an Assistant United States Attorney signed a formal "letter of agreement" in which Thomas promised to work as a cooperating witness for two years. In return, the United States government agreed not to deport him. Shortly thereafter, the United States Immigration and Naturalization Service (INS) ordered him deported. Thomas argued that the Assistant United States Attorney had implied authority to bind the United States government and therefore the INS could not deport him. Do you agree?

10. A. B. Rains worked as a broker for the Joseph Denunzio Fruit Co. Raymond Crane offered to sell Rains nine carloads of Emperor grapes. Rains accepted the offer on behalf of Denunzio. Later, Rains and Denunzio discovered that Crane was an agent for John Kazanjian. Who is liable on this contract?

11. Roy Watson bought vacuum cleaners from T & F Distributing Co. and then resold them door-to-door. He was an independent contractor. Before hiring Watson, the president of T & F checked with two former employers but could not remember if he called Watson's two references. Watson had an extensive criminal record, primarily under the alias Leroy Turner, but he was listed in FBI records under both Leroy Turner and Roy Watson. T & F granted Watson sales territory that included Neptune City, New Jersey. This city required that all "peddlers" such as Watson be licensed. Applicants for this license were routinely fingerprinted. T & F never insisted that Watson apply for such a license. Watson attacked Miriam Bennett after selling a vacuum cleaner to her at her home in Neptune City. Is T & F liable to Bennett?

12. **YOU BE THE JUDGE** WRITING PROBLEM Sara Kearns went to an auction at Christie's to bid on a tapestry for her employer, Nardin Fine Arts Gallery. The good news is that she purchased a Dufy tapestry for $77,000. The bad news is that it was not the one her employer had told her to buy. In the excitement of the auction, she forgot her instructions. Nardin refused to pay and Christie's filed suit. Is Nardin liable for the unauthorized act of its agent? **Argument for Christie's:** Kearns executed a bidder form as agent for Nardin. This is a common practice for many purchasers. Christie's cannot possibly ascertain in each case the exact nature of the bidder's authority. Whether or not Kearns had actual authority, she certainly had apparent authority and Nardin is liable. **Argument for Nardin:** Kearns was not authorized to purchase the Dufy tapestry, and therefore Christie's must recover from her, not Nardin.

13. **ROLE REVERSAL** Draft a multiple-choice question that deals with the liability of principals for the acts of their servants.

Internet Research Problem

Acting as an undisclosed principal, William Zeckendorf employed agents to purchase the land in New York on which the United Nations headquarters was ultimately built. Can you find any other examples on the Internet of business dealings in which agents made purchases for an undisclosed principal? Were these business arrangements ethical? What risks did the agents face?

> **You can find further practice problems at** http://beatty.westbuslaw.com **or in the Study Guide that accompanies this text.**

Employment Law

"**O**n the killing beds you were apt to be covered with blood, and it would freeze solid; if you leaned against a pillar, you would freeze to that, and if you put your hand upon the blade of your knife, you would run a chance of leaving your skin on it. The men would tie up their feet in newspapers and old sacks, and these would be soaked in blood and frozen, and then soaked again, and so on, until by nighttime a man would be walking on great lumps the size of the feet of an ele-phant. Now and then, when the bosses were not looking, you would see them plunging their feet and ankles into the steaming hot carcass of the steer. . . . The cruelest thing of

all was that nearly all of them—all of those who used knives—were unable to wear gloves, and their arms would be white with frost and their hands would grow numb, and then of course there would be accidents."[1] ▪

---

[1]   From Upton Sinclair, *The Jungle* (New York: Bantam Books, 1981), p. 80, a 1906 novel about the meat-packing industry.

INTRODUCTION

For most of history, the concept of career planning was unknown. By and large, people were born into their jobs. Whatever their parents had been—landowner, soldier, farmer, servant, merchant, or beggar—they became, too. People not only knew their place, they also understood the rights and obligations inherent in each position. The landowner had the right to receive labor from his tenants, but he also cared for them if they fell ill. Certainly, there were abuses, but at a time when people held religious convictions about their position in life and workers had few expectations that their lives would be better than their parents', the role of law was limited. The primary English law of employment simply established that, in the absence of a contract, an employee was hired for a year at a time. This rule was designed to prevent injustice in an agrarian society. If an employee worked through harvest time, the landowner could not fire him in the unproductive winter. Conversely, a worker could not stay the winter and then leave for greener pastures in the spring.

In the eighteenth and nineteenth centuries, the Industrial Revolution profoundly altered the employment relationship. Many workers left the farms and villages for large factories in the city. Bosses no longer knew their workers personally, so they felt little responsibility toward them. The old laws that had suited an agrarian economy with stable relationships did not fit the new employment conditions. Instead of duties and responsibilities, courts emphasized the freedom to contract. Since employees could quit their factory jobs whenever they wanted, it was only fair for employers to have the same freedom to fire a worker. That was indeed the rule adopted by the courts: unless workers had an explicit employment contract, they were employees at will. **An *employee at will* could be fired for a good reason, a bad reason, or no reason at all.** For nearly a century, this was the basic common law rule of employment. A court explained the rule this way:

> Precisely as may the employee cease labor at his whim or pleasure, and, whatever be his reason, good, bad, or indifferent, leave no one a legal right to complain; so, upon the other hand, may the employer discharge, and, whatever be his reason, good, bad, or indifferent, no one has suffered a legal wrong.[2]

However evenhanded this common law rule of employment may have sounded in theory, in practice it could lead to harsh results. The lives of factory workers were grim.[3] It was not as if they could simply pack up and leave; conditions were no better elsewhere. For the worker, freedom to contract often meant little more than freedom to starve. Courts and legislatures gradually began to recognize that individual workers were generally unable to negotiate fair contracts with powerful employers. Since the beginning of the twentieth century, employment law has changed dramatically. Now, the employment relationship is more strictly regulated by statutes and by the common law. No longer can a boss discharge an employee for any reason whatsoever.

Note that many of the statutes discussed in this chapter were passed by Congress and therefore apply nationally. The common law, however, comes from state courts and only applies locally. We will look at a sampling of cases that illustrates national trends, even though the law may not be the same in every state.

This chapter covers four topics in employment law: (1) employment security, (2) safety and privacy in the workplace, (3) financial protection, and (4) employment discrimination.

---

[2] *Union Labor Hospital Assn. v. Vance Redwood Lumber Co.*, 112 P.886, 888, 1910 Cal. LEXIS 417 (Cal. 1910).

[3] For examples of some truly grim modern jobs, work your way over to **http://www.worstjob.com**.

EMPLOYMENT SECURITY

National Labor Relations Act

Without unions to represent employee interests, employers could simply fire any troublemaking workers who complained about conditions in factories or mines. By joining together, workers could bargain with their employers on more equal terms. Naturally, the owners fought against the unions, firing organizers and even hiring goons to beat them up. Distressed by anti-union violence, Congress passed the **National Labor Relations Act** in 1935. Known as the **NLRA** or the **Wagner Act,** this statute:

- Created the National Labor Relations Board to enforce labor laws
- Prohibits employers from penalizing workers who engage in union activity (for example, joining a preexisting union or forming a new one); and
- Requires employers to "bargain in good faith" with unions.

Labor law is covered at greater length in Chapter 31.

Family and Medical Leave Act

In 1993, Congress passed the Family and Medical Leave Act (FMLA), which guarantees both men and women up to 12 weeks of *unpaid* leave each year for childbirth, adoption, or medical emergencies for themselves or a family member. An employee who takes a leave must be allowed to return to the same or an equivalent job with the same pay and benefits. The FMLA applies only to companies with at least 50 workers and to employees who have been with the company full-time for at least a year—this is about 60 percent of all employees. The Labor Department answers questions about the FMLA at http://www.dol.gov/dol/esa/fmla.htm.

When Randy Seale's wife went into premature labor with triplets, he stayed home from his job as a truck driver with Associated Milk Producers, Inc., in Roswell, New Mexico. However, the milk of human kindness did not flow in this company's veins: it promptly fired the expectant father. Since Seale was an employee at will, the company's action would have been perfectly legal without the FMLA. But after the U.S. Department of Labor filed suit, the company agreed to pay Seale $10,000.

COBRA

Many companies provide health insurance for their employees. The problem with this system used to be that losing your job meant losing your health insurance on the spot. Then Congress passed the Consolidated Omnibus Budget Reconciliation Act (COBRA). This statute provides that former employees must be allowed to continue their health insurance for 18 months after leaving their job. The catch is that employees must pay for it themselves, up to 102 percent of the cost. (The extra 2 percent covers administrative expenses.)

COBRA applies to any company with 20 or more workers. Both employees and their families are covered. So, for example, if the child of a worker graduates from college and is no longer eligible under her parent's health insurance plan, she can elect to continue her coverage by paying for it herself.

Wrongful Discharge

Olga Monge was a schoolteacher in her native Costa Rica. After moving to New Hampshire, she attended college in the evenings to earn U.S. teaching credentials. At night, she worked at the Beebe Rubber Co. During the day, she cared for her husband and three children. When she applied for a better job at her plant, the foreman offered to promote her if she would be "nice" and go out on a date with him. When she refused, he assigned her to a lower wage job, took away her overtime, made her clean the washrooms, and generally ridiculed her. Finally, she collapsed at work and he fired her.[4]

Imagine that you are one of the judges who decided this case. Olga Monge has been treated abominably, but she was an employee at will and, as you well know, could be fired for any reason. But how can you let the foreman get away with this despicable behavior? The New Hampshire Supreme Court decided that even an employee at will has rights:

> We hold that a termination by the employer of a contract of employment at will which is motivated by bad faith or malice or based on retaliation is not in the best interest of the economic system or the public good and constitutes a breach of the employment contract.[5]

The employment at will doctrine was created by the courts. Because that rule has sometimes led to absurdly unfair results, the courts have now created a major exception to the rule—**wrongful discharge.** The *Monge* case illustrates this concept. ***Wrongful discharge* prohibits an employer from firing a worker for a *bad reason*.** There are three categories of wrongful discharge claims: public policy, contract law, and tort law.

Public Policy

The *Monge* case is an example of the **public policy rule.** Unfortunately, naming the rule is easier than defining it, because its definition and application vary from state to state. **In essence, the public policy rule prohibits an employer from firing a worker for a reason that violates basic social rights, duties, or responsibilities.** Almost every employee who has ever been fired feels that a horrible injustice has been done. The difficulty, from the courts' perspective, is to distinguish those cases of dismissal that are offensive enough to affront the community at large from those that outrage only the employee. The courts have primarily applied the public policy rule when an employee refuses to violate the law or insists upon exercising a legal right or performing a legal duty.

Refusing to Violate the Law. Larry Downs went to Duke Hospital for surgery on his cleft palate. When he came out of the operating room, the doctor instructed a nurse, Marie Sides, to give Downs enough anesthetic to immobilize him. Sides refused because she thought the anesthetic was wrong for this patient. The doctor angrily administered the anesthetic himself. Shortly thereafter, Downs stopped breathing. Before the doctors could resuscitate him, he suffered permanent brain damage. When Downs's family sued the hospital, Sides was called to testify. A number of Duke doctors told her that she would be "in trouble" if she testified. She did testify and, after three months of harassment, was fired. When she sued Duke University, the court held:

> It would be obnoxious to the interests of the state and contrary to public policy and sound morality to allow an employer to discharge any employee, whether

---

[4] *Monge v. Beebe*, 114 N.H. 130, 316 A.2d 549, 1974 N.H. LEXIS 223 (1974).

[5] *Id.* at 133.

the employment be for a designated or unspecified duration, on the ground that the employee declined to commit perjury, an act specifically enjoined by statute. To hold otherwise would be without reason and contrary to the spirit of the law.[6]

As a general rule, employees may not be discharged for refusing to break the law. For example, courts have protected employees who refused to participate in an illegal price-fixing scheme, falsify pollution control records required by state law, pollute navigable waters in violation of federal law, or assist a supervisor in stealing from customers.[7]

Exercising a Legal Right. **As a general rule, an employer may not discharge a worker for exercising a legal right if that right supports public policy.** Dorothy Frampton injured her arm while working at the Central Indiana Gas Co. Her employer (and its insurance company) paid her medical expenses and her salary during the four months she was unable to work. When she discovered that she also qualified for benefits under the state's workers' compensation plan, she filed a claim and received payment. One month later, the company fired her without giving a reason. In her suit against the gas company, the court held:

> The [Workers' Compensation] Act creates a duty in the employer to compensate employees for work-related injuries and a right in the employee to receive such compensation. If employers are permitted to penalize employees for filing workmen's compensation claims, a most important public policy will be undermined. Employees will not file claims for justly deserved compensation—opting, instead, to continue their employment without incident. The end result, of course, is that the employer is effectively relieved of his obligation.[8]

Performing a Legal Duty. **Courts have consistently held that an employee may not be fired for serving on a jury.** Employers sometimes have difficulty replacing employees who are called up for jury duty and, therefore, prefer that their workers find some excuse for not serving. But jury duty is an important civic obligation that employers are not permitted to undermine.

What about an employee who performs a good deed that is not legally required? Kevin Gardner had just parked his armored truck in front of a bank in Spokane, Washington, when he saw a man with a knife chase the manager out of the bank. While running past the truck, the manager looked directly at Gardner and yelled, "Help me, help me." Gardner got out of his truck and locked the door. By then, the suspect had grabbed another woman, put his knife to her throat, and dragged her into the bank. Gardner followed them in, tackled the suspect, and disarmed him. The rescued woman hailed Gardner as a hero, but his employer fired him for violating a "fundamental" company rule that prohibited drivers from leaving their armored trucks unattended. However, the court held for Gardner on the grounds that, although there is no affirmative legal duty to intervene in such a situation, society values and encourages voluntary rescuers when a life is in danger.[9]

In the following case, the court adopts an expansive view of the public policy rule.

---

[6] *Sides v. Duke University*, 74 N.C. App. 331, 328 S.E.2d 818, 1985 N.C. App. LEXIS 3501 (N.C. Ct. App. 1985).

[7] *Tameny v. Atlantic Richfield Co.*, 27 Cal. 3d 167, 610 P.2d 1330, 1980 Cal. LEXIS 171 (1980); *Trombetta v. Detroit, T. & I. R.*, 81 Mich. App. 489, 265 N.W.2d 385, 1978 Mich. App. LEXIS 2153 (Mich. Ct. App. 1978); *Sabine Pilot Service, Inc. v. Hauck*, 28 Tex. Sup. J. 339, 687 S.W.2d 733, 1985 Tex. LEXIS 755 (1985); *Vermillion v. AAA Pro Moving & Storage*, 146 Ariz. 215, 704 P.2d 1360, 1985 Ariz. App. LEXIS 592 (Ariz. Ct. App. 1985).

[8] *Frampton v. Central Indiana Gas Co.*, 260 Ind. 249, 297 N.E.2d 425, 1973 Ind. LEXIS 522 (1973).

[9] *Gardner v. Loomis Armored, Inc.*, 913 P.2d 377, 1996 Wash. LEXIS 109 (1996).

WELLS V. ORMET CORP.

1999 Ohio App. LEXIS 1087
Court of Appeals of Ohio, 1999

Facts: Mark Wells had worked for the Ormet Corporation for 19 years and was foreman of one of its plants. One evening, he had to cancel an overtime shift when five workers failed to show up. Wells and Lee Smith, one of the company's labor relations specialists, then met with union officials to determine if the employees had legitimate excuses for not working or if they had collaborated to shut the plant down.

After the meeting, Wells and Smith concluded that the employees had had good excuses for their absences and that they had not been part of an organized effort to cause trouble. However, Dunlap, the general manager of the plant, disagreed and suspended the five employees. The union requested a formal hearing. At the hearing, a union official asked Wells if he believed that the absences were part of a concerted plan. After Smith gave Wells permission to answer, Wells responded that he did not believe the employees had collaborated.

Three days later, Dunlap had Wells fired. Wells sued the company, alleging wrongful discharge under the public policy exception to the employment-at-will doctrine. Ormet filed a motion to dismiss, which the trial court granted.

Issue: Does the public policy doctrine protect an employee from being fired for disagreeing with his boss at a hearing?

Excerpts from Judge Vukovich's Decision: [T]he issue before this court is whether there exists a sufficiently clear public policy against the corporate firing of a member of management for answering a question in a way that favors the laborers' position at a grievance hearing. Due to the fact that appellant was a nineteen-year veteran worker at the corporation and the fact that he was only answering the question in a manner that he believed was being directed by the corporation's labor relations specialist, we hold that, as limited to the facts alleged in the complaint, a sufficiently clear public policy was violated by appellant's discharge.

The public policy in the case consists of various established interests of society as a whole. These broad societal interests include a fair workplace, truthful grievance proceedings, job stability for long-term employees, and economic productivity. There is a clear public policy supporting the aforementioned interests, the violation of which is of similar import to the violation of a statute. The adoption of such a policy exception to employment-at-will adequately inures to the benefit of the general public. ■

Whistleblowing. No one likes to be accused of wrongdoing even if (or, perhaps, especially if) the accusations are true. **This is exactly what whistleblowers do: they are employees who disclose illegal behavior on the part of their employer.** Not surprisingly, many companies, when faced with such an accusation by an employee, prefer to shoot the messenger. Here is the story of Henry Boisvert.

NEWS*worthy*

FMC Corp. sold 9,000 Bradley Fighting Vehicles to the U.S. Army for as much as $1.5 million each. But the Bradley was controversial from the moment it began rolling off FMC's manufacturing lines. Designed to carry soldiers around battlefields in Eastern Europe, its ability to "swim" across rivers and lakes was an important part of its job description. But Henry Boisvert, a testing supervisor for FMC, charged that the Bradley swam like a rock. Boisvert said he first encountered problems with the Bradley in the early days of the Army procurement process. He had one driven into a test pond and watched it quickly fill with water. FMC welders who worked on Bradleys claimed they weren't given enough time to do their work properly and so would simply fill gaps with putty. FMC quashed Boisvert's report on the Bradley and fired him when he refused to sign a falsified version. FMC disputes his account, but a jury ultimately agreed with him.[10] ◆

_____
[10] *Lee Gomes, "A Whistle-Blower Finds Jackpot at the End of His Quest," The Wall Street Journal, April 27, 1998, p. B1.*

The law on whistleblowers varies across the country. As a general rule, however, whistleblowers are protected in the following situations:

- *The False Claims Act.* Henry Boisvert refused to sign his name to a report he thought was inaccurate. As a result, he earned the right to sign a check from FMC for about $20 million. Boisvert recovered under the federal False Claims Act, a statute that permits anyone to bring suit against a "person" (including a company) who defrauds the government. The Act also prohibits employers from firing workers who file suit under the statute. A successful whistleblower receives between 15 and 30 percent of any damages awarded to the government.

- *Constitutional Protection for Government Employees.* Employees of federal, state, and local governments have a right to free speech under the United States Constitution. Therefore, the government cannot retaliate against public employees who blow the whistle, as long as the employee is speaking out on a matter of public concern. For example, a New York City child welfare agency received numerous reports that six-year-old Elisa Izquierdo was being abused. After Elisa was beaten to death by her mother, ABC News broadcast an interview with a social worker from the agency. She stated on air that "The workers who are considered the best workers are the ones who seem to be able to move cases out quickly. . . . There are lots of fatalities the press doesn't know anything about." By giving this interview, the social worker violated New York City rules prohibiting employees from disclosing information about families supervised by city agencies. The city suspended the social worker from her job, and she sued. The court acknowledged that the government has the right to prohibit some employee speech. However, if the employee speaks on matters of public concern, the government bears the burden of justifying any retaliation. In this case, the court held for the social worker. The city reinstated her and gave her back pay.[11]

- *Statutory Protection for Federal Employees.* Congress passed the Civil Service Reform Act in 1978 and the Whistleblower Protection Act in 1989. These two statutes prevent retaliation against federal employees who report wrongdoing. They also permit the award of back pay and attorney's fees to the whistleblower. This statute was used to prevent the National Park Service from disciplining two managers who wrote a report expressing concern over development in Yellowstone National Park.

- *Employees of Publicly Traded Companies.* In response to a series of corporate financial scandals, Congress passed the Sarbanes-Oxley Act of 2002. Among other provisions, this Act protects employees of publicly traded companies who provide evidence of fraud to investigators (whether in or outside the company). A successful plaintiff is entitled to reinstatement, back pay, and attorney's fees. The Web page **http://www .oalj.dol.gov/Public/WBLOWER/REFRNC/sox.htm** provides a summary of some recent whistleblower complaints filed under Sarbanes-Oxley.

- *State Statutes.* The good news is that all 50 states have statutes that protect whistleblowers from retaliation by their employers. The bad news is that the scope of this protection varies greatly from state to state. For example, in some states, protection only extends to public employees, while in other states, all employees are covered.

- *Common Law.* Most courts will prohibit the discharge of employees who report illegal activity that relates to their own jobs. For example, a Connecticut court held a company liable when it fired a quality control director for reporting to his boss that some products had failed the quality tests.[12] Sometimes, however, courts have held that employees do not have a right to report wrongdoing if it does not relate to their own job functions. For example, Donald Smith's boss told him to ignore the fact that 73,000 pounds of caustic soda had spilled into the river next to a company

---

[11] *Harman v. City of New York,* 140 F.3d 111, 1998 U.S. App. LEXIS 5567 (2d Cir. 1998).
[12] *Sheets v. Teddy's Frosted Foods, Inc.,* 179 Conn. 471, 427 A.2d 385, 1980 Conn. LEXIS 690 (1980).

warehouse. When Smith instead reported the spill to corporate headquarters, he was fired. The court held that, since Smith had no responsibility for reporting spills, the public's interest "in harmony and productivity in the workplace must prevail over the public's interest in encouraging an employee in Smith's position to express his 'informed view.'"[13]

PublicPolicy

Which public interest is greater—harmony in the workplace or protection of the environment? Why should it matter that Donald Smith was not responsible for reporting spills? If you were living downstream from 73,000 pounds of caustic soda, would you want Smith to report that spill? ◆

Contract Law

Traditionally, many employers (and employees) thought that only a formal, signed document qualified as an employment contract. Increasingly, however, courts have been willing to enforce an employer's more casual promises, whether written or oral. Sometimes courts have also been willing to *imply* contract terms in the absence of an *express* agreement.

Truth in Hiring. **Oral promises made during the hiring process can be enforceable, even if not approved by the company's top executives.** When the Tanana Valley Medical-Surgical Group, Inc. hired James Eales as a physician's assistant, it promised him that as long as he did his job, he could stay there until retirement age. Six years later the company fired him without cause. The Alaska Supreme Court held that the clinic's promise was enforceable.[14]

In the following case, an insurance company was tackled for a big loss when it failed to disclose information during the hiring process.

NEWSworthy

While a player with the New York Giants football team, Phil McConkey was used to rough treatment. He expected life in the insurance business to be more civilized. But shortly after Alexander & Alexander hired him, it was acquired by Aon Corp. and the new company sacked him immediately. McConkey filed suit, alleging that Alexander & Alexander should have told him during the hiring process that it was engaged in merger talks (even though those discussions were, at that point, secret). A jury agreed, awarding the downed player $10 million. ◆

Employee Handbooks. The employee handbook at Blue Cross & Blue Shield stated that employees could be fired only for just cause and then only after warnings, notice, a hearing, and other procedures. Charles Toussaint was fired summarily five years after he joined the company. Although this decision was ultimately reviewed by the personnel department, company president, and chairman of the board of trustees, Toussaint was not given the benefit of all of the procedures in the handbook. The court held that **an employee handbook creates a contract.**[15]

at R**I**SK

Employers are now taking steps to protect themselves from liability for implied contracts. Some employers require new hires to sign a document acknowledging that (1) they are employees at will, (2) they can be terminated at any time for any reason, and (3) no one at the company has made any oral representations concerning the terms of employment. These employers caution interviewers not to make promises. Their employee handbooks now feature stern legal warnings, rather than friendly welcomes. And some companies have dispensed with handbooks altogether. ◆

---

[13] *Smith v. Calgon Carbon Corp.*, 917 F.2d 1338, 1990 U.S. App. LEXIS 19193 (3rd Cir. 1990).

[14] *Eales v. Tanana Valley Medical-Surgical Group, Inc.*, 663 P.2d 958, 1983 Alas. LEXIS 430 (Alaska 1983).

[15] *Toussaint v. Blue Cross & Blue Shield*, 408 Mich. 579, 292 N.W.2d 880, 1980 Mich. LEXIS 227 (1980).

Covenant of Good Faith and Fair Dealing. A covenant of good faith and fair dealing prohibits one party to a contract from interfering with the other's right to benefit under the contract. All parties are expected to behave in a fair, decent, and reasonable manner. **In some cases, courts will imply a covenant of good faith and fair dealing in an at-will employment relationship.**

When Forrest Fleming went to work for Parametric Technology Corp., the company promised him valuable stock options if he met his sales goals. He would not be able to *exercise* the options (that is, purchase the stock), however, until several years after they were granted and then only if he was still employed by the company. During his four years with Parametric, Fleming received options to purchase about 18,000 shares for a price as low as 25 cents each. The shares ultimately traded in the market for as much as $50. Although Fleming exercised some options, the company fired him three months before he became eligible to purchase an additional 1,000 shares. The jury awarded him $1.6 million in damages. Although Parametric had not violated the explicit terms of the option agreement, the jury believed it had violated the covenant of good faith and fair dealing by firing Fleming to prevent him from exercising his remaining options.[16]

Tort Law

Workers have successfully sued their employers under the following tort theories.

Defamation. **Employers may be liable for defamation when they give false and unfavorable references about a former employee.** John R. Glennon, Jr., was the branch manager of Dean Witter's Nashville office. Dean Witter fired him and filed a termination notice with the National Association of Securities Dealers saying that Glennon "was under internal review for violating investment-related statutes." This statement was untrue, and Witter had to pay $1.5 million in damages for defamation.

More than half of the states, however, recognize a qualified privilege for employers who give references about former employees. A qualified privilege means that employers are liable only for false statements that they know to be false or that are primarily motivated by ill will. After Becky Chambers left her job at American Trans Air, Inc., she discovered that her former boss was telling anyone who called for a reference that Chambers "does not work good with other people," is a "troublemaker," and "would not be a good person to rehire." Chambers was unable, however, to present compelling evidence that her boss had been primarily motivated by ill will. Neither Trans Air nor the boss was held liable for these statements because they were protected by the qualified privilege.[17]

Even if the employer wins, a trial is an expensive and time-consuming undertaking. Not surprisingly, companies are leery about offering any references for former employees. The company gains little benefit from giving an honest evaluation and may suffer substantial liability. As a matter of policy, many companies instruct their managers to reveal only a person's salary and dates of employment and not to offer an opinion on job performance. According to one survey, only 55 percent of former employers are totally honest when they give references.

NEWS*worthy*

Human resources managers have been drilled for years by their lawyers to provide only the most limited job references on former employees. Now they have even more reason to be cautious. Growing numbers of job applicants are hiring companies to find out what their former employers are saying about them. Job seekers can use information from these

---

[16] *Fleming v. Parametric Tech. Corp.*, 1999 U.S. App. LEXIS 14864
[17] *Chambers v. American Trans Air, Inc.*, 577 N.E.2d 612, 1991 Ind. App. LEXIS 1413 (Ind. Ct. App. 1991).

companies to confront former employers or even to bolster legal action they may take after being let go. Companies like References-etc., Documented Reference Check, and Allison & Taylor Inc. will provide a reference-check report for a fee between $50 and $90.

The reference-checking companies are adding to the difficulty that employers have long had in providing references on former employees. A company that gives a glowing reference on an employee fired with cause could soon be defending a wrongful termination case. A company that fails to mention negative information about a former employee with known dangerous tendencies could be sued by a future employer for failing to disclose the damaging information.[18] ◆

Employers are afraid of liability if they give a negative reference, but this article suggests that they are liable if they tell less than the whole truth. **Generally, courts have held that employers do not have a legal obligation to disclose information about former employees.** For example, while Jeffrey St. Clair worked at the St. Joseph Nursing Home, he was disciplined 24 times for actions ranging from extreme violence to drug and alcohol use. When he applied for a job with Maintenance Management Corp. (MMC), St. Joseph refused to give any information other than St. Clair's dates of employment. After he savagely murdered a security guard at his new job, the guard's family sued, but the court dismissed the case.[19]

In some recent cases, however, courts have held that, when a former worker is potentially dangerous, employers do have an obligation to disclose this information. For example, officials from two junior high schools gave Robert Gadams glowing letters of recommendation without mentioning that he had been fired for inappropriate sexual conduct with students. While an assistant principal at a new school, he molested a 13-year-old. Her parents sued the former employers. The court held that the writer of a letter of recommendation owes to third parties (in this case, the student) "a duty not to misrepresent the facts in describing the qualifications and character of a former employee, if making these misrepresentations would present a substantial, foreseeable risk of physical injury to the third persons."[20] As a result of cases such as this, it makes sense to disclose past violent behavior.

To assist employers who are asked for references, Lehigh economist Robert Thornton has written "The Lexicon of Intentional Ambiguous Recommendations" (LIAR). For a candidate with interpersonal problems, he suggests saying, "I am pleased to say that this person is a former colleague of mine." For the lazy worker, "In my opinion, you will be very fortunate to get this person to work for you." For the criminal, he suggests, "He's a man of many convictions" and "I'm sorry we let her get away." For the untrustworthy candidate, "Her true ability is deceiving."[21]

Ethics

All joking aside, what if someone calls you to check references on a former employee who had a drinking problem? The job is driving a van for junior high school sports teams. What is the manager's ethical obligation in this situation? Many managers say that, in the case of a serious problem such as alcoholism, sexual harassment, or drug use, they will find a way to communicate that an employee is unsuitable. What if the ex-employee says she is reformed? Aren't people entitled to a second chance? Is it right to risk a defamation suit

---

[18] Marci Alboher Nusbaum, "When a Reference Is Not What It Seems," *The New York Times*, October 19, 2003. Section 3, p. 12.

[19] *Moore v. St. Joseph Nursing Home, Inc.,* 184 Mich. App. 766, 459 N.W.2d 100, 1990 Mich. App. LEXIS 285 (Mich. Ct. App. 1990).

[20] *Randi W. v. Muroc Joint Unified School District,* 14 Cal. 4th 1066, 929 P.2d 582, 1997 Cal. LEXIS 10 (1997), modified, 14 Cal. 4th 1282c, 97 Cal. Daily Op. Service 1439.

[21] *Wall Street Journal,* Mar. 22, 1994, p. 1.

against your company to protect others from harm? What solutions does the Ethics Checklist in Chapter 2 suggest? Would it be just to reveal private information about a former employee? Is the process fair if you provide information that the job applicant has no opportunity to rebut because it is kept secret? ◆

Intentional Infliction of Emotional Distress. **Employers who condone cruel treatment of their workers face liability under the tort of intentional infliction of emotional distress.** For example:

- When a 57-year-old social-work manager at Yale–New Haven Hospital was fired, she was forced to place her personal belongings in a plastic bag and was escorted out the door by security guards in full view of gaping co-workers. A supervisor told her that she would be arrested for trespassing if she returned. A jury awarded her $105,000.

- An employee swore at a co-worker and threatened her with a knife because she rejected his sexual advances. Her superiors fired her for complaining about the incident. A court held that the employer had inflicted emotional distress.[22]

- On the other hand, another court held that an employee who was fired for dating a co-worker did not have a valid claim for infliction of emotional distress.[23]

SAFETY AND PRIVACY IN THE WORKPLACE

Workplace Safety

In 1970, Congress passed the Occupational Safety and Health Act (OSHA) to ensure safe working conditions. Under OSHA:

- Employers must comply with specific health and safety standards. For example, health care personnel who work with blood are not permitted to eat or drink in areas where the blood is kept and must not put their mouths on any instruments used to store blood. Protective clothing—gloves, gowns, and laboratory coats—must be impermeable to blood.

- Employers are under a general obligation to keep their workplace "free from recognized hazards that are causing or are likely to cause death or serious physical harm" to employees.

- Employers must keep records of all workplace injuries and accidents.

- The Occupational Safety and Health Administration (also known as OSHA) may inspect workplaces to ensure that they are safe. OSHA may assess fines for violations and order employers to correct unsafe conditions.

OSHA has done a lot to make the American workplace safer. In 1900, roughly 35,000 workers died and 350,000 were injured at work. One hundred years later, the workforce had grown five times larger but the number of annual deaths had fallen to 5,100. You can report hazards at your worksite to OSHA online at **http://www.osha-slc .gov/as/opa/worker/complain.html**.

---

[22] *Hogan v. Forsyth Country Club Co.,* 79 N.C. App. 483, 340 S.E.2d 116, 1986 N.C. App. LEXIS 2098 (N.C. Ct. App. 1986).

[23] *Patton v. J. C. Penney Co.,* 301 Or. 117, 719 P.2d 854, 1986 Ore. LEXIS 1144 (1986).

Employee Privacy

Upon opening the country's first moving assembly line in the early 1900s, Henry Ford issued a booklet, "Helpful Hints and Advice to Employees," that warned against drinking, gambling, borrowing money, taking in boarders, and practicing poor hygiene. Ford also created a department of 100 investigators for door-to-door checks on his employees' drinking habits, sexual practices, and housekeeping skills. It sounds outrageous, but in modern times employees have been fired or disciplined for such extracurricular activities as playing dangerous sports, dating co-workers, or even having high cholesterol.

The right to hire, fire, and make an honest profit is enshrined in American tradition. But so is the right to privacy. Justice Louis D. Brandeis called it the "right to be let alone—the most comprehensive of rights and the right most valued by civilized men." What protection do workers have against intrusive employers?

Off-Duty Conduct

In an era of rapidly expanding health care costs, employers are concerned about the health of their workers. Some companies have banned off-duty smoking and have even fired employees who show traces of nicotine in their blood. In response, more than half the states have passed laws that protect the right of employees to smoke cigarettes while off-duty. Some of these statutes permit *any* lawful activity when off-duty, including drinking socially, having high cholesterol, being overweight, or engaging in dangerous hobbies—bungee jumping or roller blading, for instance.

Alcohol and Drug Testing

Government employees can be tested for drug and alcohol use only if they show signs of use or if they are in a job where this type of abuse endangers the public. Most states permit private employers to administer alcohol and drug tests. According to one survey, more than 80 percent of large firms test employees for drugs.

Lie Detector Tests

Under the Employee Polygraph Protection Act of 1988, employers may not require, or even *suggest*, that an employee or job candidate submit to a lie detector test, except as part of an "on-going investigation" into crimes that have occurred.

Electronic Monitoring of the Workplace

Technological advances in communications have raised a host of new privacy issues.

cyberLaw

Many companies monitor employee use of electronic equipment in the workplace: telephone calls, voice mail, e-mail, and Internet usage. **The Electronic Communications Privacy Act of 1986 (ECPA) permits employers to monitor workers' telephone calls and e-mail messages if (1) the employee consents, (2) the monitoring occurs in the ordinary course of business, or (3) in the case of e-mail, the employer provides the e-mail system.** However, bosses may not disclose any private information revealed by the monitoring.

Although workers may feel that their e-mail should be private, employers argue that this monitoring improves employee productivity and protects the company from lawsuits. For example, a West Coast company fired a woman "because of a tough economy." When she sued, her attorneys demanded access to the company's e-mail system as part of the discovery process. They found a message from the woman's supervisor saying, "Get that bitch out of here as fast as you can. I don't care what it takes. Just do it." The supervisor had long since erased the message from his computer, but it had remained buried in the system. A few hours after the message was revealed in court, the company settled for $250,000.

When companies monitor employee use of the Internet, they are concerned not only about lawsuits but also that workers may be wasting time. During one month, employees at IBM, Apple Computer, and AT&T logged on to *Penthouse* magazine's Web site 12,823 times, using the equivalent of more than 347 workdays. One company discovered that some of its employees were using their company computers to buy and sell child pornography. Employers fear that even legal logging on to sexually explicit sites may give rise to sexual harassment claims. ◆

FINANCIAL PROTECTION

Congress and the states have enacted laws that provide employees with a measure of financial security. All of the laws in this section were created by statute, not by the courts.

Fair Labor Standards Act

Passed in 1938, the Fair Labor Standards Act (FLSA) regulates wages and limits child labor. The wage provisions do not apply to managerial, administrative, or professional staff, which means that accounting, consulting, and law firms (among others) are free to require as many hours a week as their employees can humanly perform without having to pay overtime or the minimum wage.

Minimum Wage

The current federal minimum wage is $5.15 per hour, although some states have set a higher minimum. To find the minimum wage in your state, check in at http://www.dol.gov/esa/minwage/america.htm. Employers can pay students and apprentices under age 20 a training wage of $4.25 per hour. The Department of Labor Web site lists any changes in the minimum wage and also answers related questions: http://www.dol.gov/dol/topic/wages/index.htm.

Overtime Pay

The FLSA does not limit the number of hours a week that an employee can work, but it does specify that workers must be paid time and a half for any hours over 40 in one week.

Child Labor

The FLSA prohibits "oppressive child labor," which means that children under 14 may work only in agriculture and entertainment. Fourteen- and 15-year-olds are permitted to work *limited* hours after school in nonhazardous jobs. Sixteen- and 17-year-olds may work *unlimited* hours in nonhazardous jobs.

Workers' Compensation

Workers' compensation statutes ensure that employees receive payment for injuries incurred at work. Before workers' comp, injured employees could recover damages only if they sued their employer. It is the brave (or carefree) worker who is willing to risk a suit against his own boss. Lawsuits poison the atmosphere at work. Moreover, employers frequently won these suits by claiming that (1) the injured worker was contributorily negligent, (2) a fellow employee had caused the accident, or (3) the injured worker had assumed the risk of injury. As a result, seriously injured workers (or their families) often had no recourse against the employer.

Workers' comp statutes provide a fixed, certain recovery to the injured employee, no matter who was at fault for the accident. In return, employees are not permitted to sue their employers for negligence. The amounts allowed (for medical expenses and lost wages) under workers' comp statutes are often less than a worker might recover in court, but the injured employee trades the certainty of some recovery for the higher risk of rolling the dice at trial. Payments are approved by an administrative board that conducts an informal hearing into each claim. These payments are funded either through the purchase of private insurance or by a tax on employers—a tax that is based on how many injuries their employees have suffered. Thus employers have an incentive to maintain a safe working environment.

Social Security

The federal Social Security system began in 1935, during the depths of the Great Depression, to provide a basic safety net for the elderly, ill, and unemployed. **Currently, the Social Security system pays benefits to workers who are retired, disabled, or temporarily unemployed and to the spouses and children of disabled or deceased workers.** It also provides medical insurance to the retired and disabled. The Social Security program is financed through a tax on wages that is paid by employers, employees, and the self-employed.

Before Social Security, breadlines were often the only safety net available to the unemployed.

Although the Social Security system has done much to reduce poverty among the elderly, many worry that it cannot survive in its current form. When workers pay taxes, the proceeds do not go into a savings account for their retirement, but instead are used to pay benefits to current retirees. In 1940, there were 40 workers for each retiree; currently, there are 3.3. By 2030, when the last baby boomers retire, there will be only 2 workers to support each retiree—a prohibitive burden. No wonder baby boomers are often cautioned not to count on Social Security when making their retirement plans.

The Federal Unemployment Tax Act (FUTA) is the part of the Social Security system that provides support to the unemployed. FUTA establishes some national standards, but states are free to set their own benefit levels and payment schedules. These payments are funded by a tax on employers. A worker who quits voluntarily or is fired for just cause is ineligible for benefits. While receiving payments, she must make a good faith effort to look for other employment.

Pension Benefits

In 1974, Congress passed the Employee Retirement Income Security Act (ERISA) to protect workers covered by private pension plans. Under ERISA, employers are not required to establish pension plans, but if they do, they must follow these federal rules. The law was aimed, in particular, at protecting benefits of retired workers if their companies subsequently go bankrupt. The statute also prohibits risky investments by pension plans. In addition, the statute sets rules on the vesting of benefits. (An employer cannot cancel *vested* benefits; *nonvested* benefits are forfeited when the employee leaves.) Before ERISA, retirement benefits at some companies did not vest until the employee retired—if he quit or was fired before retirement, even after years of service, he lost his pension. Under current law, employee benefits vest after five years of employment.

EMPLOYMENT DISCRIMINATION

In the last five decades, Congress has enacted important legislation to prevent discrimination in the workplace.

Equal Pay Act of 1963

Under the Equal Pay Act, an employee may not be paid at a lesser rate than employees of the opposite sex for equal work. "Equal work" means tasks that require equal skill, effort, and responsibility under similar working conditions. If the employee proves that she is not being paid equally, the employer will be found liable unless the pay difference is based on merit, productivity, seniority, or some factor other than sex. A "factor other than sex" includes prior wages, training, profitability, performance in an interview, and value to the company. For example, female agents sued Allstate Insurance Co. because its salary for new agents was based, in part, on prior salary. The women argued that this system was unfair because it perpetuated the historic wage differences between men and women. The court, however, held for Allstate.[24]

To find out how much less women earn than men, in spite of the Equal Pay Act, click on **http://www.aflcio.org/issuespolitics/women/equalpay/**.

Title VII

Title VII of the Civil Rights Act of 1964 prohibits employers from discriminating on the basis of race, color, religion, sex, or national origin. More specifically, it prohibits (1) discrimination in the workplace, (2) sexual harassment, and (3) discrimination because of pregnancy. It also permits employers to develop affirmative action plans. The following article reveals what life was like before Title VII.

NEWSworthy

Fresh out of college in 1963, I got my first job at *Newsweek* magazine. In those days, women were hired as researchers and men were hired as writers . . . and that was that. It was, as we used to say, a good job for a woman. If we groused about working for the men we studied with in college, we did it privately. It was the way things were.

I don't share my garden-variety piece of personal history as a lament or gripe. Woe isn't me. Nor am I one to regale the younger generation with memories of the bad old days

---

[24] *Kouba v. Allstate Insurance Co.*, 691 F.2d 873, 1982 U.S. App. LEXIS 24479 (9th Cir. 1982).

when I walked 4 miles in the snow to school. They already know that women were treated as second-class citizens. But what they don't know, I have found, is that this was legal.

It was legal to have segregated ads that read "male wanted" and "female wanted." It was legal to fire a flight attendant if she got married. It was legal to get rid of a teacher when she became pregnant. If a boss paid a woman less because she was a woman, he was unapologetic. If he didn't want to hire a woman for a "man's job," he just didn't.

When President Johnson signed the Civil Rights Act of 1964, it became illegal for the first time to discriminate in employment on the grounds of sex. What had seemed to many like a "natural" way of treating men and women differently because of their roles in the family and society became what the courts now call "invidious."

In the first Title VII case, the Supreme Court ruled that it was illegal to refuse to hire a woman because she had small children. Under pressure, newspapers stopped segregating their employment pages. Women tiptoed into some "male jobs" and took hold in others.[25] ◆

Proof of Discrimination

Discrimination under Title VII means firing, refusing to hire, failing to promote, or otherwise reducing a person's employment opportunities because of race, color, religion, sex, or national origin. This protection applies to every stage of the employment process from job ads to postemployment references and includes placement, wages, benefits, and working conditions.

Plaintiffs in Title VII cases can prove discrimination two different ways: disparate treatment and disparate impact.

Disparate Treatment. To prove a disparate treatment case, the plaintiff must show that she was *treated* differently because of her sex, race, color, religion, or national origin. The required steps in a disparate treatment case are:

> **Step 1.** The plaintiff presents evidence that the defendant has discriminated against her because of a protected trait. This is called a ***prima facie*** **case.** The plaintiff is not required to prove discrimination; she need only create a *presumption* that discrimination occurred.
>
> Suppose that Louisa applies for a job coaching a boys' high school ice hockey team. She was an All-American hockey star in college. Although Louisa is obviously qualified for the job, Harry, the school principal, rejects her and continues to interview other people. This is not proof of discrimination, because Harry may have a perfectly good, nondiscriminatory explanation. However, his behavior *could have been* motivated by discrimination.
>
> **Step 2.** The defendant must present evidence that its decision was based on *legitimate, nondiscriminatory* reasons. Harry might say, for example, that he wanted someone with prior coaching experience. Although Louisa is clearly a great player, she has never coached before.
>
> **Step 3.** To win, the plaintiff must now prove that the employer discriminated. She may do so by showing that the reasons offered were simply a *pretext.* Louisa might show that Harry had recently hired a male tennis coach who had no prior coaching experience. Or Harry's assistant might testify that Harry said, "No way I'm going to put a woman on the ice with those guys." If she can present evidence such as this, Louisa wins.

In the following case, was the bartender treated differently because of her sex? You be the judge.

---

[25] Ellen Goodman, "The Next Step for Women," *The Boston Globe,* June 27, 2004, p. D11.

you Be The Judge

JESPERSEN V. HARRAH'S

392 F.3d 1076, 2004 U.S. App. LEXIS 26892
United States Court of Appeals for the Ninth Circuit, 2004

Facts: Darlene Jespersen was a bartender at the sports bar in Harrah's Casino in Reno, Nevada. She was an outstanding employee. Her supervisors commented that she was "highly effective," her attitude was "very positive," and she made a "positive impression" on Harrah's guests. Harrah's customers repeatedly praised Jespersen on employee feedback forms, writing that Jespersen's excellent service and good attitude enhanced their experience at the sports bar and encouraged them to come back.

When Jespersen first went to work for Harrah's, the casino encouraged, but did not require, its female beverage servers to wear makeup. Jespersen tried for a short period of time, but found that it made her feel sick, degraded, exposed, and violated. Moreover, wearing makeup interfered with her ability to deal with unruly, intoxicated guests because it "took away [her] credibility as an individual and as a person."

After Jespersen had been at Harrah's for almost 20 years, the casino implemented a program whose goal was to create a "brand standard of excellence." The program required beverage servers to be "well groomed, appealing to the eye, be firm and body toned, and be comfortable with maintaining this look while wearing the specified uniform." More explicitly, the rules for men were:

- Hair must not extend below top of shirt collar. Ponytails are prohibited.
- Hands and fingernails must be clean and nails neatly trimmed at all times.
- No colored polish is permitted.
- Eye and facial makeup is not permitted.
- Shoes will be solid black leather or leather type with rubber (non skid) soles.

The rules for women were:

- Hair must be teased, curled, or styled every day you work. Hair must be worn down at all times, no exceptions.
- Stockings are to be of nude or natural color consistent with employee's skin tone. No runs.

- Nail polish can be clear, white, pink, or red color only. No exotic nail art or length.
- Shoes will be solid black leather or leather type with rubber (non skid) soles.
- Makeup (foundation/concealer and/or face powder, as well as blush and mascara) must be worn and applied neatly in complimentary colors, and lip color must be worn at all times.

An expert was brought in to show the employees how to dress. The workers (both male and female) were then photographed and told that they must look like the photographs every day at work.

Jespersen refused to wear makeup. She was told either to comply or to apply for a position that did not require makeup. When she did neither, Harrah's fired her. Jespersen sued under Title VII. The district court granted Harrah's motion for summary judgment. Jespersen appealed.

You Be The Judge: Did Harrah's requirement that women wear makeup violate Title VII?

Argument for Jespersen: Jespersen refused to wear makeup to work because the cost—in time, money, and personal dignity—was too high. Despite the fact that she did not wear makeup, numerous customers and supervisors consistently gave her glowing recommendations. Nonetheless, Harrah's fired her.

Employers are free to adopt different appearance standards for each sex, but these standards may not impose a greater burden on one sex than the other. Men were not required to wear makeup, women were. That difference meant a savings for men of hundreds of dollars and hours of time. Harrah's did not have the right to fire Jespersen for violating a rule that applies only to women, with no equivalent for men.

Argument for Harrah's: Employers are permitted to impose different appearance rules on men than on women as long as the overall burden on employees is the same. For example, it is not discriminatory to require men to wear their hair short. When looking at all of Harrah's rules, on balance the burden on men was no heavier than on women. ■

Disparate Impact. Disparate impact becomes an issue if the employer has a rule that, *on its face*, is not discriminatory, but *in practice* excludes too many people in a protected group. The steps in a disparate impact case are:

Step 1. The plaintiff must present a *prima facie* case. The plaintiff is not required to prove discrimination; he need only show a disparate impact—that the employment practice in question excludes a disproportionate number of people in a protected group (women and minorities, for instance).

Suppose that Harry will only hire teachers who are at least 5 feet 10 inches tall and weigh 170 pounds. He says he is afraid that students will literally push around anyone smaller. When Chou Ping, an Asian male, applies for a job, he cannot meet Harry's physical requirements. Chou Ping must show that Harry's rule, *in fact*, eliminates more women or minorities than white males. He might offer evidence that 50 percent of all white males can meet Harry's standard, but only 20 percent of white women and Asian males qualify.

Step 2. The defendant must offer some evidence that the employment practice was a *job-related business necessity*. Harry might produce evidence that teachers are regularly expected to wrestle students into their classroom seats. Further, he might cite studies showing his standards are essential for this task.

Step 3. To win, the plaintiff must now prove either that the employer's reason is a *pretext* or that other, *less discriminatory* rules would achieve the same results. Chou Ping might suggest that all teachers could take a self-defense course or engage in martial arts training.

Note that the mere existence of a disparate impact does not *necessarily* mean that an employment practice violates the law. When the Illinois Law Enforcement Officers Training Board created an exam to test aspiring police officers, a higher percentage of minority applicants than white candidates failed the test. Some of the unsuccessful aspirants filed suit, alleging that the exam was illegal because it had a disparate impact. In response, the board presented evidence that the exam had been very carefully prepared by a consulting company that specialized in creating such exams. The court held that the exam was legal because it was "demonstrably a reasonable measure of job performance."[26]

Color

Title VII prohibits discrimination based on both race and color. Many people assume that these are essentially the same issue. Not so, as the following article demonstrates:

NEWS*worthy*

Dwight Burch says the insults began soon after he started working as a waiter at an Applebee's restaurant in Jonesboro, GA. His boss called him a "black monkey" and "tar baby" and suggested he bleach his skin, he says, and then co-workers began taunting him, too. "You name it, any dark-skinned, monstrous name you can think of, they called me it—porch monkey, jig-a-boo, blackie," Mr. Burch recalls. "I was the brunt of every joke. . .from the moment I got there until I left."

A case of racial discrimination? No, the alleged abuse came from fellow African-Americans. But Mr. Burch sued anyway, becoming one of an increasing number or workers publicly complaining about "color discrimination" at the hands of fellow minority-group members. Mr. Burch has very dark skin, and his alleged tormentors were lighter-skinned.[27] ◆

---

[26] *Bew v. Chicago,* 252 F.3d 891, 2001 U.S. App. LEXIS 9247 (7th Cir. 2001).

[27] Marjorie Valbrun, "EEOC Sees Rise in Intrarace Complaints of Color Bias," *Wall Street Journal,* August 7, 2003, p. B1.

Title VII prohibits the type of treatment that Dwight Burch allegedly suffered. While denying any wrong-doing, Applebee's settled the case by paying Burch $40,000 and agreeing to conduct antidiscrimination training.

Religion

Employers must make *reasonable accommodation* for a worker's religious beliefs unless the request would cause *undue hardship* for the business. Scott Hamby told his manager at Wal-Mart that he could never work on Sunday because that was his Sabbath. It also happened to be one of the store's busiest days. When the manager forced Hamby to quit, he promptly sued on the grounds of religious discrimination. Lawsuits such as his are on the rise as more businesses remain open on Sundays. Wal-Mart denied wrongdoing but settled the case with a cash payment of undisclosed amount. It also established a company-wide training program on religious accommodation.

Defenses to Charges of Discrimination

Under Title VII, the defendant has three possible defenses.

Merit. A defendant is not liable if he shows that the person he favored was the most qualified. Test results, education, or productivity can all be used to demonstrate merit, provided they relate to the job in question. Harry can show that he hired Bruce instead of Louisa because Bruce has a master's degree in physical education and seven years of coaching experience. On the other hand, the fact that Bruce scored higher on the National Latin Exam in the eighth grade is not a good reason to hire him over Louisa.

ECONOMICS & *the* LAW

It is easy to say that the most qualified person should be hired or promoted. But how do you measure merit? Take the case of Santa Clara, California, for example. No woman had ever held the job of radio dispatcher there. Although Paul Johnson scored higher on the dispatcher exam than Diane Joyce, the county hired Joyce.[28] This case ultimately reached the U.S. Supreme Court on the issue of whether a less qualified woman could be promoted over a more qualified man. (The court ruled that she could.)

So do we feel sorry for Paul Johnson? Of course, we feel sorry for anyone who does not get the job of his dreams. It turns out, however, that his score on the dispatcher exam had been 75 out of 100; hers was 73. This two-point difference is simply not persuasive evidence that Johnson would be a better radio dispatcher than Joyce. Indeed, employment tests are typically not very good predictors of on-the-job performance. They are at best blunt instruments. Moreover, a 2-point differential on a 100-point test is meaningless. As an affirmative action case, *Johnson* was unusual only in that the court actually reported the test scores. Typically, in such cases the actual difference in scores is rarely reported or discussed.

The moral of the story? Before concluding that a less qualified applicant has been promoted over a more qualified competitor, it is wise to ask about the validity of the test and the significance of the difference in scores.[29] ◆

Seniority. A legitimate seniority system is legal, even if it perpetuates past discrimination. Suppose that Harry has always chosen the most senior assistant coach to take over as head coach when a vacancy occurs. Since the majority of the senior assistant coaches are male, most of the head coaches are, too. Such a system does not violate Title VII.

---

[28] *Johnson v. Transportation Agency,* 489 U.S. 616, 1987 U.S. LEXIS 1387 (1987).

[29] Michael Selmi, "Testing for Equality: Merit, Efficiency, and the Affirmative Action Debate," *UCLA Law Review,* June 1995, vol. 42, p. 1251.

Bona Fide Occupational Qualification. An employer is permitted to establish discriminatory job requirements if they are *essential* to the position in question. Such a requirement is called a **bona fide occupational qualification (BFOQ).** Catholic schools may, if they choose, refuse to hire non-Catholic teachers; mail order companies may refuse to hire men to model women's clothing. Generally, however, courts are not sympathetic to claims of BFOQ. They have, for example, almost always rejected BFOQ claims that are based on customer preference. Thus airlines could not refuse to hire male flight attendants even though travelers prefer female attendants.[30] The major exception to this customer preference rule is sexual privacy: an employer may refuse to hire women to work in a men's bathroom and vice versa.

Affirmative Action

Affirmative action has become a hot political issue: white males protest that such programs are reverse discrimination against them; political candidates campaign on anti-affirmative action platforms.

Affirmative action is not required by Title VII, nor is it prohibited. Affirmative action programs have three different sources:

- *Litigation.* Courts have the power under Title VII to order affirmative action to remedy the effects of past discrimination.

- *Voluntary Action.* Employers can voluntarily introduce an affirmative action plan to remedy the effects of past practices or to achieve equitable representation of minorities and women.

- *Government Contracts.* In 1965, President Johnson signed Executive Order 11246, which prohibits discrimination by federal contractors. This order had a profound impact on the American workplace because one-third of all workers are employed by companies that do business with the federal government. If an employer found that women or minorities were underrepresented in its workplace, it was required to establish goals and timetables to correct the deficiency.

In 1995, however, the Supreme Court dramatically limited the extent to which the government can require contractors to establish affirmative action programs. The Court ruled that these programs are permissible only if they serve a "compelling national interest" and are "narrowly tailored" so that they minimize the harm to white males. The government must be able to show that (1) the programs are needed to overcome specific past discrimination, (2) they have time limits, and (3) nondiscriminatory alternatives are not available.[31] This case led to a sharp decrease in the number of federal contracts awarded to companies owned by women and minorities.

Sexual Harassment

When Professor Anita Hill accused Supreme Court nominee Clarence Thomas of sexually harassing her, people across the country were glued to their televisions, watching the Senate hearings on her charges. Thomas was ultimately confirmed to the Supreme Court, but "sexual harassment" became a household phrase. The number of cases—and the size of the damage awards—sky-rocketed.

Everyone has heard of sexual harassment, but few people know exactly what it is. Men fear that a casual comment or glance will be met with career-ruining charges; women claim that men "just don't get it." So what is sexual harassment anyway? **Sexual harassment involves unwelcome sexual advances, requests for sexual favors, and**

---

[30] *Diaz v. Pan American World Airways, Inc.,* 442 F.2d 385, 1971 U.S. App. LEXIS 10920 (5th Cir. 1971).

[31] *Adarand Constructors, Inc. v. Pena,* 515 U.S. 200, 115 S. Ct. 2097, 1995 U.S. LEXIS 4037 (1995).

other verbal or physical conduct of a sexual nature. There are two major categories of sexual harassment: (1) *quid pro quo* and (2) hostile work environment.

Quid Pro Quo. From a Latin phrase that means "this for that," *quid pro quo* harassment occurs if any aspect of a job is made contingent upon sexual activity. In other words, when a banker says to a secretary, "You can be promoted to teller if you sleep with me," that is *quid pro quo* sexual harassment.

Hostile Work Environment. This is a more subtle claim and the one that managers worry about most. An employee has a valid claim of sexual harassment if sexual talk and innuendo are so pervasive that they interfere with her (or his) ability to work. Courts have found that offensive jokes, comments about clothes or body parts, and public displays of pornographic pictures create a hostile environment. In the following case, the company president repeatedly insulted and demeaned his female employees.

TERESA HARRIS V. FORKLIFT SYSTEMS, INC.

510 U.S. 17, 114 S. Ct. 367, 1993 U.S. LEXIS 7155
United States Supreme Court, 1993

Facts: Teresa Harris was a manager at Forklift Systems; Charles Hardy was its president. Hardy frequently made inappropriate sexual comments to Harris and other women at the company. For example, he said to Harris, in the presence of others, "You're a woman, what do you know?" and "We need a man as the rental manager." He called her "a dumb ass woman" and suggested that the two of them "go to the Holiday Inn to negotiate her raise." He also asked Harris and other female employees to get coins from his front pants pocket. He insisted that Harris and other women pick up objects he had thrown on the ground. When Harris complained to Hardy, he apologized and claimed he was only joking. A month later, while Harris was arranging a deal with one of Forklift's customers, he asked her, in front of other employees, "What did you do, promise the guy some sex Saturday night?"

Harris sued Forklift, claiming that Hardy had created an abusive work environment. The federal trial court ruled against Harris on the grounds that Hardy's comments might offend a reasonable woman, but they were not severe enough to have a serious impact on Harris's psychological well-being. The appeals court confirmed, and the Supreme Court granted *certiorari*.

Issue: To be a violation of Title VII, must sexual harassment seriously affect the employee's psychological well-being?

Excerpts from Justice O'Connor's Decision: Title VII of the Civil Rights Act of 1964 makes it "an unlawful employment practice for an employer to discriminate against any individual with respect to his compensation, terms, conditions, or privileges of employment, because of such individual's race, color, religion, sex, or national origin." [T]his language is not limited to economic or tangible discrimination. The phrase "terms, conditions, or privileges of employment" evinces a congressional intent to strike at the entire spectrum of disparate treatment of men and women in employment, which includes requiring people to work in a discriminatorily hostile or abusive environment. When the workplace is permeated with discriminatory intimidation, ridicule, and insult, that is sufficiently severe or pervasive to alter the conditions of the victim's employment and create an abusive working environment, Title VII is violated.

This standard takes a middle path between making actionable any conduct that is merely offensive and requiring the conduct to cause a tangible psychological injury. [M]ere utterance of an epithet which engenders offensive feelings in an employee does not sufficiently affect the conditions of employment to implicate Title VII. Conduct that is not severe or pervasive enough to create an objectively hostile or abusive work environment—an environment that a reasonable person would find hostile or abusive—is beyond Title VII's purview. Likewise, if the victim does not subjectively perceive the environment to be abusive, the conduct has not actually altered the conditions of the victim's employment, and there is no Title VII violation.

▼

But Title VII comes into play before the harassing conduct leads to a nervous breakdown. A discriminatorily abusive work environment, even one that does not seriously affect employees' psychological well-being, can and often will detract from employees' job performance, discourage employees from remaining on the job, or keep them from advancing in their careers. Moreover, even without regard to these tangible effects, the very fact that the discriminatory conduct was so severe or pervasive that it created a work environment abusive to employees because of their race, gender, religion, or national origin offends Title VII's broad rule of workplace equality.

We therefore believe the [trial court] erred in relying on whether the conduct "seriously affected plaintiff's psychological well-being" or led her to "suffer injury." So long as the environment would reasonably be perceived, and is perceived, as hostile or abusive there is no need for it also to be psychologically injurious. ∎

Employees who commit sexual harassment are liable for their own misdeeds. But is their company also liable? The Supreme Court has held that:

- If the victimized employee has suffered a "tangible employment action" such as firing, demotion, or reassignment, the company is liable to her for sexual harassment by a supervisor.

- If the victimized employee has not suffered a tangible employment action, the company is not liable if it can prove that (1) it used reasonable care to prevent and correct sexually harassing behavior, and (2) the employee unreasonably failed to take advantage of the complaint procedure or other preventive opportunities provided by the company.[32]

---

at **RISK**

Corning Consumer Products Co. asks its employees to apply four tests in determining whether their behavior constitutes sexual harassment:

- Would you say or do this in front of your spouse or parents?

- What about in front of a colleague of the opposite sex?

- Would you like your behavior reported in your local newspaper?

- Does it need to be said or done at all? ◆

Procedures and Remedies

Before a plaintiff in a Title VII case brings suit, she must first file a complaint with a federal agency, the Equal Employment Opportunity Commission (EEOC). The EEOC then has the right to sue on behalf of the plaintiff. This arrangement is favorable for the plaintiff because the government pays the legal bill. If the EEOC decides *not* to bring the case, or does not make a decision within six months, it issues a **right to sue letter**, and the plaintiff may proceed on her own in court. Many states also have their own version of the EEOC, but these state commissions are often understaffed.

Remedies available to the successful plaintiff include hiring, reinstatement, retroactive seniority, back pay, reasonable attorney's fees, and damages of up to $300,000. Two recent trends, however, have reduced employees' chances of taking home substantial damages. Concerned about a rise in discrimination lawsuits, employers now often require new hires to agree in advance to arbitrate, not litigate, any future employment claims. The Supreme Court has upheld the employers' right to do so.[33] Typically,

---

[32] *Burlington Industries, Inc. v. Ellerth*, 524 U.S. 742, 118 S. Ct. 2257, 1998 U.S. LEXIS 4217 (1998); *Faragher v. Boca Raton*, 524 U.S. 775, 118 S. Ct. 2275, 1998 U.S. LEXIS 4216 (1998).

[33] *Circuit City Stores, Inc. v. Adams*, 532 U.S. 105, 2001 U.S. LEXIS 2459 (2001).

employees receive worse results in the arbitrator's office than in the courtroom, largely because arbitrators tend to favor repeat customers (such as management) over one-time users (such as employees). But even if a case does go to trial, plaintiffs in job discrimination cases have a much worse track record than other types of plaintiffs. About 43 percent of all plaintiffs in federal district court win their cases; for discrimination plaintiffs, the win rate is only about 30 percent. Even if discrimination plaintiffs win at trial, they have a 44 percent probability of losing on appeal. Victorious plaintiffs in other types of cases are overturned only 33 percent of the time.

Pregnancy

Under the Pregnancy Discrimination Act of 1978, an employer may not fire, refuse to hire, or fail to promote a woman because she is pregnant. An employer must also treat pregnancy as any other temporary disability. If, for example, employees are allowed time off from work for other medical disabilities, women must also be allowed a maternity leave. The United States and Australia are the only industrialized nations that do not require employers to provide paid maternity leave.

Age Discrimination

The Age Discrimination in Employment Act (ADEA) of 1967 prohibits age discrimination against employees or job applicants who are at least 40 years old. An employer may not fire, refuse to hire, fail to promote, or otherwise reduce a person's employment opportunities because he is 40 or older. Under this statute, an employer may not require a worker to retire at any age. These retirement rules do not apply to police and top-level corporate executives, who may indeed be forced to retire at a certain age.

The procedure for an age-bias claim is similar to that under Title VII—plaintiffs must first file a charge with the EEOC. If the EEOC does not take action, they can file suit themselves.

During tight economic times, companies often feel great pressure to lower costs. They are sometimes tempted to replace older, higher paid workers with younger, less expensive employees. Courts traditionally held that replacing expensive, older workers with cheaper, younger ones was illegal discrimination under the ADEA. In some recent cases, however, courts have held that an employer is entitled to prefer *lower paid* workers even if that preference results in the company also choosing *younger* workers. As the court put it in one case, "An action based on price differentials represents the very quintessence of a legitimate business decision."[34]

As we have seen, Title VII permits employees to prove discrimination two way: *disparate treatment* and *disparate impact*. Although the courts had always agreed that disparate treatment was a violation of the ADEA, they were divided on the illegality of disparate impact. In the following case, the plaintiffs convinced the Supreme Court that disparate impact is a violation of the law, but they still lost their case. Recall

Oliver Wendell Holmes, Jr., one of the greatest Supreme Court Justices of the twentieth century, was 61 when appointed to the high court. He served with distinction for over 30 years.

© BETTMAN/CORBIS

---

[34]   *Marks v. Loral Corp.,* 57 Cal. App. 4th 30, 1997 Cal. App. LEXIS 611 (Cal. Ct. App. 1997).

when reading this case that the opinion was written by the court's oldest member, 84-year-old Justice Stevens.

SMITH V. CITY OF JACKSON

2005 U.S. LEXIS 2931
Supreme Court of the United States, 2005

Facts: The city of Jackson, Mississippi (the City), granted pay raises to everyone on its police force. One of the City's goals in granting these increases was to attract new recruits. Under this plan, officers with less than five years of service received proportionately greater raises than their more senior colleagues. Senior officers tended to be older. Some of these older officers filed suit under the ADEA claiming a disparate impact: that they were adversely affected by the plan because of their age. The District Court granted summary judgment to the City. The Court of Appeals affirmed.

Issues: Is disparate impact a violation of the ADEA? Were these police officers adversely affected because of their age?

Excerpts from Justice Steven's Decision:[35]
Except for substitution of the word "age" for the words "race, color, religion, sex, or national origin," the language of that provision in the ADEA is identical to that found in Title VII. Unlike Title VII, however, the ADEA contains language that significantly narrows its coverage by permitting any "otherwise prohibited" action "where the differentiation is based on reasonable factors other than age" (RFOA provision).

In determining whether the ADEA authorizes disparate-impact claims, we begin with the premise that when Congress uses the same language in two statutes having similar purposes, particularly when one is enacted shortly after the other, it is appropriate to presume that Congress intended that text to have the same meaning in both statutes. We [have already] held that Title VII did not require a showing of discriminatory intent. Finally, we note that both the Department of Labor, which initially drafted the legislation, and the EEOC, which is the agency charged by Congress with responsibility for implementing the statute, have consistently interpreted the ADEA to authorize relief on a disparate-impact theory.

[But] the scope of disparate-impact liability under ADEA is narrower than under Title VII. Congress' decision to limit the coverage of the ADEA by including the RFOA provision is consistent with the fact that age, unlike race or other classifications protected by Title VII, not uncommonly has relevance to an individual's capacity to engage in certain types of employment. Thus, it is not surprising that certain employment criteria that are routinely used may be reasonable despite their adverse impact on older workers as a group. Moreover, intentional discrimination on the basis of age has not occurred at the same levels as discrimination against those protected by Title VII. While the ADEA reflects Congress' intent to give older workers employment opportunities whenever possible, the RFOA provision reflects this historical difference.

Turning to the case before us, we initially note that plaintiffs have done little more than point out that the pay plan at issue is relatively less generous to older workers than to younger workers. They have not identified any specific test, requirement, or practice within the pay plan that has an adverse impact on older workers. [I]t is not enough to simply allege that there is a disparate impact on workers, or point to a generalized policy that leads to such an impact. Rather, the employee is responsible for isolating and identifying the *specific* employment practices that are allegedly responsible for any observed statistical disparities. Plaintiffs have failed to do so. Their failure to identify the specific practice being challenged is the sort of omission that could result in employers being potentially liable for the myriad of innocent causes that may lead to statistical imbalances. In this case not only did plaintiffs thus err by failing to identify the relevant practice, but it is also clear from the record that the City's plan was based on reasonable factors other than age.

▼

---

[35] For clarity, we have substituted the word "plaintiffs" for "petitioners."

Plaintiffs' evidence established two principal facts: First, almost two-thirds (66.2 percent) of the officers under 40 received raises of more than 10 percent while less than half (45.3 percent) of those over 40 did. Second, the average percentage increase for the entire class of officers with less than five years of tenure was somewhat higher than the percentage for those with more seniority. The basic explanation for the differential was the City's perceived need to raise the salaries of junior officers to make them competitive with comparable positions in the market. Reliance on seniority and rank is unquestionably reasonable given the City's goal of raising employees' salaries to match those in surrounding communities.

While there may have been other reasonable ways for the City to achieve its goals, the one selected was not unreasonable. Accordingly, while we do not agree with the Court of Appeals' holding that that the disparate-impact theory of recovery is never available under the ADEA, we affirm its judgment.

It is so ordered. ■

Devil's Advocate

The court says that the plaintiffs needed to show a "specific test, requirement, or practice within the pay plan that has an adverse impact on older workers." Otherwise, an employer might be liable for the "myriad of innocent causes that may lead to statistical imbalances." The City gave larger raises to junior officers than their more senior colleagues. The senior officers were older. What could be more specific than that? This plan was hardly an "innocent cause" that led to a "statistical imbalance." ◆

Americans with Disabilities Act

Passed in 1990, the Americans with Disabilities Act (ADA) prohibits employers from discriminating on the basis of disability. (The Justice Department's ADA home page is http://www.usdoj.gov/crt/ada.) As with Title VII, a plaintiff under the ADA must first file a charge with the EEOC. If the EEOC decides not to file suit, the individual may do so himself.

A disabled person is someone with a physical or mental impairment that substantially limits a major life activity, or someone who is regarded as having such an impairment. This definition includes people with mental illness, visual impairment, epilepsy, dyslexia, and AIDS, or who are *recovered* drug addicts and alcoholics. It does not cover people with sexual disorders, pyromania, exhibitionism, or compulsive gambling.

An employer may not disqualify an employee or job applicant because of disability as long as she can, with *reasonable accommodation*, perform the *essential functions* of the job. An accommodation is not reasonable if it would create *undue hardship* for the employer. In one case, a court held that a welder who could perform 88 percent of a job was doing the essential functions. Reasonable accommodation includes buying necessary equipment, providing readers or interpreters, or permitting a part-time schedule. In determining undue hardship, *relative* cost, not *absolute* cost, is the issue. Even an expensive accommodation—such as hiring a full-time reader—is not considered an undue hardship unless it imposes a significant burden on the overall finances of the company.

An employer may not ask about disabilities before making a job offer. The interviewer may ask only whether an applicant can perform the work. Nor can an employer require applicants to take a medical exam unless the exam is (1) job-related and (2) required of all applicants for similar jobs. However, drug testing is permitted.

After a job offer has been made, an employer may require a medical test, but it must be related to the *essential functions* of the job. For example, an employer could not test the cholesterol of someone applying for an accounting job because high cholesterol is no impediment to good accounting.

An employer may not discriminate against someone because of his *relationship* with a disabled person. For example, an employer cannot refuse to hire an applicant because he has a child with Down's syndrome or a spouse with cancer.

In 1997, the EEOC issued rules on the treatment of mental disabilities. These rules were based on an assumption of parity—that physical and mental disabilities should be treated the same. The difficulty is that physical ailments such as diabetes and deafness may be easy to diagnose, but what does a supervisor do when an employee is chronically late, rude, or impulsive? Does this mean the worker is mentally disabled or just a lazy, irresponsible jerk? Among other accommodations, the EEOC rules indicated that employers should be willing to put up barriers to isolate people who have difficulty concentrating, provide detailed day-to-day feedback to those who need greater structure in performing their jobs, or allow workers on antidepressants to come to work later if they are groggy in the morning.

It appears that courts may not be as accommodating of mental illness as the EEOC. In one case, for example, an engineer had been criticized for his "negative attitude." Later his supervisor warned him that he might be terminated if his behavior did not improve. He then told the company that the warning had caused him to be depressed, which, in turn, affected his ability to interact with other people. He asked, as a special accommodation, to be assigned to clerical work that did not require him to run meetings. The company fired him. Although EEOC guidelines state that interacting with others is a major life activity, the court held that it is not. Therefore the engineer was not disabled for purposes of the ADA.[36]

While lauding the ADA's objectives, many managers have been apprehensive about its impact on the workplace. Most acknowledge, however, that society is clearly better off if every member has the opportunity to work. And as advocates for the disabled point out, we are all, at best, only temporarily able-bodied. Even with the ADA, only 29 percent of the disabled population who are of working age are actually employed, while 79 percent of able-bodied persons have jobs.

When cases go to litigation, employers win more than 93 percent of the time. Workers are caught in something of a legal Catch-22: they must prove that they can perform the essential functions of the job, but they must also show that their disability limits a major life activity. In the following case, the Supreme Court takes a close look at the definition of "major life activity."

TOYOTA V. WILLIAMS

534 U.S. 184, 122 S. Ct. 681, 2002 U.S. LEXIS 400
United States Supreme Court, 2002

Facts: Ella Williams worked in a Toyota manufacturing plant in Georgetown, Kentucky. Her job required her to use pneumatic tools. When her arms and hands began to hurt, she went to see a doctor who diagnosed her with carpal tunnel syndrome. He advised her to avoid using pneumatic tools or lifting more than 20 pounds. Toyota transferred Williams to a position in Quality Control Inspection Operations (QCIO). Employees in this department typically performed four different jobs, but Williams was initially assigned only two tasks. Toyota then changed its policy and required QCIO employees to rotate through all four jobs.

Williams began to perform the "shell body audit." After applying oil to the outside of cars, she visually inspected each car for flaws. To perform this task, she had to hold her hands and arms up around shoulder height for several hours at a time.

A short while after beginning this job, she began to experience pain in her neck and shoulders. She asked permission to perform only the two tasks that she could do without difficulty. Williams claimed

▼

---

[36] *Soileau v. Guildford of Maine,* 105 F.3d 12, 1997 U.S. App. LEXIS 1171 (1st Cir. 1997).

that Toyota refused this request. Toyota said that Williams simply began missing work regularly. Ultimately, Williams's doctor told her she should not do any work of any kind. Toyota fired her.

When Williams sued Toyota, alleging that the company had violated the Americans with Disabilities Act, the district court granted summary judgment to Toyota on the grounds that Williams's impairments did not substantially limit any of her major life activities. The Court of Appeals for the Sixth Circuit reversed, finding that the impairments substantially limited Williams in the major life activity of performing manual tasks. The Supreme Court granted *certiorari*.

Issues: Was Williams disabled, within the terms of the Americans with Disabilities Act? Did Toyota violate the ADA?

Excerpts from Justice O'Connor's Decision, Writing for a Unanimous Court: When it enacted the ADA in 1990, Congress found that some 43,000,000 Americans have one or more physical or mental disabilities. If Congress intended everyone with a physical impairment that precluded the performance of some isolated, unimportant, or particularly difficult manual task to qualify as disabled, the number of disabled Americans would surely have been much higher. We therefore hold that to be substantially limited in performing manual tasks, an individual must have an impairment that prevents or severely restricts the individual from doing activities that are of central importance to most people's daily lives. The impairment's impact must also be permanent or long-term.

When addressing the major life activity of performing manual tasks, the central inquiry must be whether the claimant is unable to perform the variety of tasks central to most people's daily lives, not whether the claimant is unable to perform the tasks associated with her specific job. In this case, "repetitive work with hands and arms extended at or above shoulder levels for extended periods of time" is not an important part of most people's daily lives. The court, therefore, should not have considered respondent's inability to do such manual work in her specialized assembly line job as sufficient proof that she was substantially limited in performing manual tasks.

[T]he Court of Appeals treated as irrelevant the fact that respondent can tend to her personal hygiene and carry out personal or household chores. Yet household chores, bathing, and brushing one's teeth are among the types of manual tasks of central importance to people's daily lives, and should have been part of the assessment of whether respondent was substantially limited in performing manual tasks.

The District Court noted that at the time respondent sought an accommodation from petitioner, she admitted that she was able to do the manual tasks required by her original two jobs in QCIO. In addition, even after her condition worsened, she could still brush her teeth, wash her face, bathe, tend her flower garden, fix breakfast, do laundry, and pick up around the house. The record also indicates that her medical conditions caused her to avoid sweeping, to quit dancing, to occasionally seek help dressing, and to reduce how often she plays with her children, gardens, and drives long distances. But these changes in her life did not amount to such severe restrictions in the activities that are of central importance to most people's daily lives that they establish a manual-task disability as a matter of law.

Accordingly, we reverse the Court of Appeals' judgment granting summary judgment to respondent and remand the case for further proceedings consistent with this opinion.

So ordered. ■

---

at RISK | Every applicant feels slightly apprehensive before a job interview, but now the interviewer may be even more nervous—fearing that every question is a potential land mine of liability. Most interviewers (and students who have read this chapter) would know better than Delta Airlines interviewers who allegedly asked applicants about their sexual preference, birth control methods, and abortion history. The following list provides guidelines for interviewers. ◆

Don't Even Consider Asking	Go Ahead and Ask
Can you perform this function with or without reasonable accommodation?	Would you need reasonable accommodation in this job?
How many days were you sick last year?	How many days were you absent from work last year?
What medications are you currently taking?	Are you currently using drugs illegally?
Where were you born? Are you a United States citizen?	Are you authorized to work in the United States?
How old are you?	What work experience have you had?
How tall are you? How much do you weigh?	Could you carry a 100-pound weight, as required by this job?
When did you graduate from college?	Where did you go to college?
How did you learn this language?	What languages do you speak and write fluently?
Have you ever been arrested?	Have you ever been convicted of a crime that would affect the performance of this job?
Do you plan to have children? How old are your children? What method of birth control do you use?	Can you work weekends? Travel extensively? Would you be willing to relocate?
What is your corrected vision?	Do you have 20/20 corrected vision?
Are you a man or a woman? Are you single or married? What does your spouse do? What will happen if your spouse is transferred? What clubs, societies, or lodges do you belong to?	Leave well enough alone!

The most common gaffe on the part of interviewers? Asking women about their child-care arrangements. That question assumes the woman is responsible for child-care.

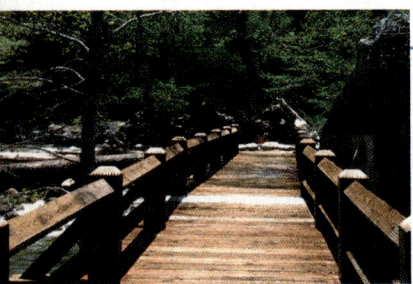

© BRAND X PICTURES/GETTY IMAGES

Chapter Conclusion

Although managers sometimes feel overwhelmed by the long list of laws that protect workers, the United States guarantees its workers fewer rights than virtually any other industrialized nation. For instance, Japan, Great Britain, France, Germany, and Canada all require employers to show just cause before terminating workers. Although American employers are no longer insulated from minimum standards of fairness, reasonable behavior, and compliance with important policies, they still have great freedom to manage their employees.

Chapter Review

1. The traditional common law rule of employment provided that an employee at will could be fired for a good reason, a bad reason, or no reason at all.

2. The National Labor Relations Act prohibits employers from penalizing workers for union activity.

3. The Family and Medical Leave Act guarantees workers up to 12 weeks of unpaid leave each year for childbirth, adoption, or medical emergencies for themselves or a family member.

4. An employer who fires a worker for a bad reason is liable under a theory of wrongful discharge.

5. Generally, an employee may not be fired for refusing to break the law, exercising a legal right, or performing a legal duty.

6. Whistleblowers receive some protection under both federal and state laws.

7. Oral promises made during the hiring process may be enforceable, even if not approved by the company's top executives. An employee handbook may create a contract.

8. Employers may be liable for defamation if they give false and unfavorable references.

9. The goal of the Occupational Safety and Health Act is to ensure safe conditions in the workplace.

10. Employees have a limited right to privacy in the workplace.

11. The Fair Labor Standards Act regulates minimum and overtime wages. It also limits child labor.

12. Workers' compensation statutes ensure that employees receive payment for injuries incurred at work.

13. The Social Security system pays benefits to workers who are retired, disabled, or temporarily unemployed and to the spouses and children of disabled or deceased workers.

14. The Employee Retirement Income Security Act regulates private pension plans.

15. Under the Equal Pay Act, an employee may not be paid at a lesser rate than employees of the opposite sex for equal work.

16. Title VII of the Civil Rights Act of 1964 prohibits employers from discriminating on the basis of race, color, religion, sex, or national origin.

17. The Age Discrimination in Employment Act prohibits age discrimination against employees or job applicants who are age 40 or older.

18. The Americans with Disabilities Act prohibits employers from discriminating on the basis of disability.

Practice Test

1. When Theodore Staats went to his company's "Council of Honor Convention," he was accompanied by a woman who was not his wife although he told everyone she was. The company fired him. Staats alleged that his termination violated public policy because it infringed upon his freedom of association. He also alleged that he had been fired because he was too successful—his commissions were so high, he out-earned even the highest paid officer of the company. Has Staat's employer violated public policy?

2. This article appeared in *The Wall Street Journal*:

When Michelle Lawrence discovered she was pregnant, she avoided telling Ron Rogers, the owner of the Los Angeles public relations agency where she worked as manager of media relations. "I had heard he wasn't crazy about pregnant women," she says. Instead, she asked her immediate supervisor to pass along the news. Mr. Rogers didn't speak to her for a week. His first comment was, "Congratulations on your pregnancy. My sister vomited for months." A few weeks later, Ms. Lawrence was fired. Mr. Rogers told her the business was shifting away from her area of expertise.[37]

---

[37] Sue Shellenbarger, "As More Pregnant Women Work, Bias Complaints Rise," *Wall Street Journal*, Dec. 6, 1993, p. B1.

Does Lawrence have a valid claim against Rogers? Under what law?

3. Reginald Delaney managed a Taco Time restaurant in Portland, Oregon. Some of his customers told Mr. Ledbetter, the district manager, that they would not be eating there so often because there were too many black employees. Ledbetter told Delaney to fire Ms. White, who was black. Delaney did as he was told. Ledbetter's report on the incident said: "My notes show that Delaney told me that White asked him to sleep with her and that when he would not that she started causing dissension within the crew. She asked him to come over to her house and that he declined." Delaney refused to sign the report because it was untrue, so Ledbetter fired him. What claim might Delaney make against his former employer?

4. When Walton Weiner interviewed for a job with McGraw-Hill, Inc., he was assured that the company would not terminate an employee without "just cause." Weiner also signed a contract specifying that his employment would be subject to the provisions of McGraw-Hill's handbook. The handbook said, "[The] company will resort to dismissal for just and sufficient cause only, and only after all practical steps toward rehabilitation or salvage of the employee have been taken and failed. However, if the welfare of the company indicates that dismissal is necessary, then that decision is arrived at and is carried out forthrightly." After eight years, Weiner was fired suddenly for "lack of application." Does Weiner have a valid claim against McGraw-Hill?

5. **ETHICS** John Mundorf hired three women to work for Gus Construction Co. as traffic controllers at road construction sites in Iowa. Male members of the construction crew incessantly referred to the women as "f—king flag girls." They repeatedly asked the women if they "wanted to f—k" or engage in oral sex. One crew member held a woman up to the cab window so other men could touch her. Another male employee exposed himself to the women. Male employees also urinated in a woman's water bottle and the gas tank of her car. Mundorf, the supervisor, was present during some of these incidents. He talked to crew members about their conduct, but the abuse continued until the women quit. What claim might the women make

against their co-workers? Is Gus Construction Co. liable for the acts of its employees? What procedure must the women follow to pursue their claim? Why do you think these men behaved this way? Why did they want to humiliate their co-workers? What should the supervisor have done when he observed these incidents? What would you have done if you were the supervisor? A fellow employee?

6. **CPA QUESTION** An unemployed CPA generally would receive unemployment compensation benefits if the CPA:

   a. Was fired as a result of the employer's business reversals

   b. Refused to accept a job as an accountant while receiving extended benefits

   c. Was fired for embezzling from a client

   d. Left work voluntarily without good cause

7. Debra Agis worked in a Ground Round restaurant. The manager, Roger Dionne, informed the waitresses that "there was some stealing going on." Until he found out who was doing it, he intended to fire all the waitresses in alphabetical order, starting with the letter "A." Dionne then fired Agis. Does she have a valid claim against her employer?

8. The Duke Power Co. refused to transfer any employees at its generating plant to better jobs unless they had a high school diploma or could pass an intelligence test. The company was willing to pay two-thirds of the tuition for an employee's high school training. Neither a high school education nor the intelligence test was significantly related to successful job performance. Both requirements disqualified African Americans at a substantially higher rate than white applicants. Is the company in violation of Title VII?

9. The Lillie Rubin boutique in Phoenix would not permit Dick Kovacic to apply for a job as a salesperson. It only hired women to work in sales because fittings and alterations took place in the dressing room or immediately outside. The customers were buying expensive clothes and demanded a male-free dressing area. Has the Lillie Rubin store violated Title VII? What would its defense be?

10. ***YOU BE THE JUDGE*** WRITING PROBLEM Nationwide Insurance Co. circulated a memorandum asking all employees to lobby in favor of a bill that had been introduced in the Pennsylvania House of Representatives. By limiting the damages that an injured motorist could recover from a person who caused an accident, this bill would have saved Nationwide significant money. Not only did John Novosel refuse to lobby, but he privately criticized the bill for harming consumers. Nationwide was definitely not on his side—it fired him. Novosel filed suit, alleging that his discharge had violated public policy by infringing his right to free speech. Did Nationwide violate public policy by firing Novosel? **Argument for Novosel:** The United States Constitution and the Pennsylvania Constitution both guarantee the right to free speech. Nationwide has violated an important public policy by firing Novosel for expressing his opinions. **Argument for Nationwide:** For all the high-flown talk about the Constitution, what we have here is an employee who refused to carry out company policy. If the employee prevails in this case, where will it all end? What if an employee for a tobacco company refuses to market cigarettes because he does not approve of smoking? How can businesses operate without loyalty from their employees?

11. When Thomas Lussier filled out a Postal Service employment application, he did not admit that he had twice pleaded guilty to charges of disorderly conduct. Lussier suffered from Post Traumatic Stress Disorder (PTSD) acquired during military service in Vietnam. Because of this disorder, he sometimes had panic attacks that required him to leave meetings. He was also a recovered alcoholic and drug user. During his stint with the Postal Service, he had some personality conflicts with other employees. Once another employee hit him. He also had one episode of "erratic emotional behavior and verbal outburst." In the meantime, a postal employee in Ridgewood, New Jersey, killed four colleagues. The Postmaster General encouraged all supervisors to identify workers who had dangerous propensities. Lussier's boss discovered that he had lied on his employment application about the disorderly conduct charges and fired him. Is the Postal Service in violation of the law?

12. The following question appeared in *The Wall Street Journal.* How would you answer it?

Q: Imagine an employer and a male job candidate discussing employment. The candidate discloses that his wife is pregnant, and the employer is turned off, thinking the candidate will need time off during a busy time. The employer may even ask the candidate if he's planning to take family leave after the birth. If the candidate says yes, the employer might not hire him because of that. Would this be discriminatory?[38]

13. ***ROLE REVERSAL*** Prepare a short-answer question in which an employee alleges that his discharge violated public policy, but you think a court would not agree.

Internet Research Problem

Go to http://beatty.westbuslaw.com. The EEOC offers advice on how to comply with some aspects of the Americans with Disabilities Act. Employers sometimes complain that the EEOC unfairly favors workers. What do you think of these EEOC guidelines? Are they fair and even-handed? As an employee, would you like your company to follow these guidelines? If you were in a supervisory role, would your view of these guidelines be different?

> **You can find further practice problems at** http://beatty.westbuslaw.com **or in the Study Guide that accompanies this text.**

---

[38] Sue Shellenbarger, "Work and Family Mailbox," *The Wall Street Journal,* March 10, 2005, p. D4.

Labor Law

A strike! For five weeks the union workers have been walking picket lines at JMJ, a manufacturer of small electrical engines. An entire town of 70,000 citizens, most of them blue-collar workers, is sharply divided, right down to the McNally kitchen table. Buddy, age 48, has worked on the assembly lines at JMJ for more than 25 years. Now he's sipping coffee in the house where he grew up. His sister Kristina, age 46, is a vice-president for personnel at JMJ. The two have always been close. In high school, Kristina idolized her older brother, the football and track star. Buddy was immensely proud of his kid sister's academic triumphs, boasting to the world that she would "be the first lady president." Today, though, conversation is halting.

"It's time to get back together, Buddy," Kristina murmurs. "The strike is hurting the whole company—and the town."

Not the *whole* town, Kristina," he tries to quip lightly. "Your management pals still have fat incomes and nice houses."

"Oh yeah?" she attempts to joke, "you haven't seen our porch lately."

Go talk to Tony Falcione," Buddy replies. "He can't pay his rent."

"Talk to the Ericksons," Kristina snaps back, "they don't even work for JMJ. Their sandwich shop is going under because none of you guys stop in for lunch. Come back to work."

"Not with that clause on the table."

That clause is management's proposal for the new union contract—one that Kristina helped draft. The company officers want the right to subcontract work, that is, to send it out for other companies to perform.

"Buddy, we need the flexibility. K-Ball is underselling us by 35 percent. If we can't compete, there won't be *any* jobs or *any* contract!"

"The way to save money is not by sending our jobs overseas, where a bunch of foreigners will work for 50 bucks a month."

"O.K., fine. Tell me how we *should* save money."

"Kristina, I really do not know how you can sit at this table and say these things—in this household. You never would have got a fancy college degree if Dad hadn't made union wages."

"If we can't sell motors to Latin America, we're out of business. *Then* what's your union going to do for you? All we're asking is the right to subcontract some of the smallest components. Everything else gets built here."

"This is just the start. Next it'll be the wiring, then the batteries, then you'll assemble the whole thing over there—and that'll be it for me. You take that clause off the table, we'll be back in 15 minutes."

"Never."

Buddy stands up. They stare silently, sadly, at each other, and then Kristina says, in a barely audible voice, "I have to tell you this. My boss is starting to talk about hiring replacement workers." Buddy walks out. ■

Some Americans revere unions, believing that organized labor has pulled the working class up from poverty and shielded it from exploitative management. Others loathe organized labor, convinced that unions foment mindless conflicts, decrease productivity, increase costs, and harm corporations and the economy generally. Why do unions exist?

UNIONS DEVELOP . . . AND THE LAW RESPONDS

During the nineteenth century, as industrialization spread across America, workers found employment conditions increasingly unbearable and wages inadequate. Here is a contemporary account of mining in the American West:

> View their work! Descending from the surface in the shaft-cages, they enter narrow galleries where the air is scarce respirable. By the dim light of their lanterns a dingy rock surface, braced by rotting props, is visible. The stenches of

decaying vegetable matter, hot foul water, and human excretions intensify the effects of the heat. The men throw off their clothes at once. Only a light breech-cloth covers their hips, and thick-soled shoes protect their feet from the scorching rocks and steaming rills of water that trickle over the floor. Except for these coverings they toil naked, with heavy drops of sweat starting from every pore.[1]

Temperatures in the mines were well over 100 degrees. Miners drank more than three gallons of water every day. Some suddenly collapsed, with swollen veins, purple faces, and glazed eyes. Within minutes they were dead, but even before they died, their places in the mine were taken by other workers desperate for pay.

Conditions were equally oppressive in the new factories back east. Workers, often women and sometimes children, worked 60 to 70 hours per week and sometimes more, standing at assembly lines in suffocating, dimly lit factories, performing monotonous yet dangerous work with heavy machinery. A visitor to a factory in Lowell, Massachusetts, in 1855 was shocked by the degrading conditions and the exhausting hours required of all workers.

> I inquired of the agent of a principal factory whether it was the custom of the manufacturers to do anything for the physical, intellectual, and moral welfare of their work-people. "We never do," he said. "As for myself, I regard my work-people just as I regard my machinery. So long as they can do my work for what I choose to pay them, I keep them, getting out of them all I can. What they do or how they fare outside my walls I don't know, nor do I consider it my business to know. When my machines get old and useless, I reject them and get new, and these people are part of my machinery."[2]

Because of the intolerable conditions and impoverishing wages, workers began to band together into unions. But early in the nineteenth century, American courts regarded any coordinated effort by workers as a criminal conspiracy. Courts convicted workers merely for the *act of joining together*, even if no strike took place. In 1842 the Massachusetts high court became the first to reject this use of the criminal law. The court ruled that workers could join together for legitimate economic goals; their efforts would become criminal only if the workers used illegal means to achieve them.[3] Other courts came to agree, and so management resorted to the civil law to curtail unions.

In 1890 Congress passed the Sherman Act to outlaw monopolies.[4] For the next 40 years, courts relied on this statute to issue anti-strike injunctions, declaring that strikes illegally restrained trade. A company could usually obtain an immediate injunction merely by alleging that a strike *might* cause harm. Courts were so quick to issue injunctions that most companies became immune to union efforts. But with the economic collapse of 1929 and the vast suffering of the Great Depression, public sympathy shifted to the workers. Congress responded with the first of several landmark statutes.

In 1932 Congress passed the **Norris-LaGuardia Act,** which prohibited federal court injunctions in nonviolent labor disputes. No longer could management obtain an injunction merely by mentioning the word "strike." By taking away the injunction rem-

---

[1] Eliot Lord, *Comstock Mining and Miners* (Washington: G.P.O., 1883), p. 386, *quoted in* Richard E. Lingenfelter, *The Hardrock Miners* (Berkeley: University of California Press, 1974), p. 13.

[2] Massachusetts Senate Dock. no. 21, 1868, p. 23, *quoted in* Norman Ware, *The Industrial Worker* (Chicago: Quadrangle Books, 1964), p. 77.

[3] *Commonwealth v. Hunt*, 45 Mass. 111, 4 Met. 111 (1842).

[4] See Chapter 39, on antitrust law.

edy, Congress was declaring that workers should be permitted to organize unions and to use their collective power to achieve legitimate economic ends. The statute led to explosive growth in union membership.

In 1935 Congress passed the Wagner Act, generally known as the **National Labor Relations Act (NLRA).** This is the most important of all labor laws. A fundamental aim of the NLRA is the establishment and maintenance of industrial peace, to preserve the flow of commerce. The NLRA ensures the right of workers to form unions and encourages management and unions to bargain collectively and productively. For our purposes, §§7 and 8 of the NLRA are the most important.

Section 7 guarantees employees the right to organize and join unions, bargain collectively through representatives of their own choosing, and engage in other concerted activities. This is the cornerstone of union power. With the enactment of the NLRA, Congress put an end to any notion that unions were criminal or inherently illegal by explicitly recognizing that workers could join together and bargain as a group, using their collective power to seek better conditions. Section 8 reinforces these rights by outlawing *unfair labor practices.*

Section 8(a) makes it an unfair labor practice (ULP) for an employer:

- To interfere with union organizing efforts
- To dominate or interfere with any union
- To discriminate against a union member, or
- To refuse to bargain collectively with a union.

The NLRA also established the **National Labor Relations Board (NLRB)** to administer and interpret the statute and to adjudicate labor cases. For example, when a union charges that an employer has committed an unfair labor practice—say, by refusing to bargain—the ULP charge goes first to the NLRB.

The NLRB has two primary tasks:

- *Representation.* The Board decides whether a particular union is entitled to represent a group of employees.

- *Unfair Labor Practices.* The Board adjudicates claims by either the employer or workers that the other side has committed a ULP.

To accomplish these tasks, the NLRB has several divisions. Although the agency is headquartered in Washington, it performs the greatest volume of its work in local offices. **Regional offices,** each headed by a regional director, are located throughout the country. These local offices handle most ULP claims. The General Counsel, a staff of lawyers, investigates such claims. If the General Counsel's office believes that a party has committed a ULP, it prosecutes the case before an administrative law judge (ALJ).

The **Board** itself, which sits in Washington, has five members, all appointed by the president. The Board makes final agency decisions about representation and ULP cases. But note that the Board has no

As industry changes, labor changes with it. Do these changes spell the end of unionization, or are the unions merely undergoing a transition as labor catches up with the modern economy?

power to *enforce* its orders. If it is evident that the losing party will not comply, the Board must petition a federal appeals court to enforce the order. Typically, the steps resulting in an appeal follow this pattern: the Board issues a decision, for example, finding that a company has unfairly refused to bargain with a union. The Board orders the company to bargain. The Board then appeals to the United States Court of Appeals to enforce its order, and the company *cross-appeals*, requesting the court *not* to enforce the Board's order. (The NLRB describes its mission and methods at http://www.nlrb.gov/.)

Throughout the 1930s and 1940s, unions grew in size and power. As strikes became more common, employers complained loudly of union abuse. Unions coerced unwilling workers to join and engaged in *secondary boycotts*, picketing an innocent company to stop it from doing business with an employer the union was fighting. In 1947 Congress responded with the Taft-Hartley Act, also known as the **Labor-Management Relations Act,** designed to curb union abuses. The statute amended §8 of the NLRA to outlaw certain unfair labor practices *by unions.*

Section 8(b) makes it an unfair labor practice for a union:

- To interfere with employees who are exercising their labor rights under §7
- To encourage an employer to discriminate against a particular employee because of a union dispute
- To refuse to bargain collectively, or
- To engage in an illegal strike or boycott, particularly secondary boycotts.

Finally, in the 1950s the public became aware that certain labor leaders were corrupt. Some officers stole money from large union treasuries, rigged union elections, and stifled opposition within the organization. In response, in 1959 Congress passed the Landrum-Griffin Act, generally called the **Labor-Management Reporting and Disclosure Act (LMRDA).** The LMRDA requires union leadership to make certain financial disclosures and guarantees free speech and fair elections within a union.

These landmark federal labor laws are outlined below:

Four Key Labor Statutes	
Norris-LaGuardia Act (1932)	Prohibits federal court injunctions in peaceful strikes.
National Labor Relations Act (1935)	Guarantees workers' right to organize unions and bargain collectively. Prohibits an employer from interfering with union organizing or discriminating against union members. Requires an employer to bargain collectively.
Labor-Management Relations Act (1947)	Prohibits union abuses such as coercing employees to join. Outlaws secondary boycotts.
Labor-Management Reporting and Disclosure Act (1959)	Requires financial disclosures by union leadership. Guarantees union members free speech and fair elections.

NEWS*worthy*

Today, labor abuses are less visible—but as ugly as ever. From New York City to Los Angeles, desperately poor, frightened immigrants cut and sew about half of all the garments this country produces, often working in appalling sweatshops where conditions are little better than in nineteenth-century factories. Frequently, the employees are undocumented immigrants who speak no English, know nothing of their rights, and fear that any complaints they make will lead to deportation. Exploitative owners force the workers to toil 50 to 60 hours a week with few breaks in cramped rooms with weak lighting, no ventilation, and inadequate sanitation. Pay is below the minimum wage—and vicious bosses often steal the small amounts they promised. For a report on sweatshops in the United States, see http://www.uniteunion.org/sweatshops/sweatshop.html. ◆

State Labor Law

All states have labor statutes. Some are comprehensive, while others focus on narrow issues. For example, certain states prohibit particular kinds of picketing, while many states outlaw strikes by public employees. A court enforces a state statute when no federal law applies. In general, when a federal law such as the NLRA does apply, it controls the outcome. This is the doctrine of *preemption*, discussed in Chapter 5, on constitutional law. **Preemption: states have no jurisdiction to regulate any labor issue that is governed by federal law.**

In this chapter, we look principally at federal law because it is uniform and because it controls the most fundamental issues of labor policy.

Labor Unions Today

Organized labor is shrinking in the United States. In the 1950s about 25 percent of the workforce belonged to a union. Today, only about 13.5 percent of all workers are union members. Employers point to this figure with satisfaction and claim that it shows that unions have failed their memberships. In an increasingly high-tech, service-oriented economy, employers argue, there is no place for organized labor. Union supporters respond that although the country has shed many old factories, workers have not benefited. Throughout the last 20 years, they assert, compensation for executives has soared into the stratosphere, with many CEOs earning several *million* dollars per year, while wages for the average worker, in real dollars, have fallen for two decades.

Whether organized labor is disappearing from the United States or is only retreating temporarily, labor law still affects many. About 16 million workers are union members. The largest unions are national in scope, with hundreds of affiliated **locals** throughout the country. A local is the regional union, which represents workers at a particular company. For example, over 2.2 million teachers belong to the National Education Association, with thousands of locals spread throughout the nation. Here are some current labor numbers:[5]

Who Are Union Workers?
- Government employees—36.4 percent are in unions
- Private sector—7.9 percent are in unions

Which Occupational Groups Have Higher Membership?
- Education—37.6 percent unionized
- Police and fire—37.3 percent unionized

Which Private Industries Have the Highest Percentages of Union Workers?
- Transportation and utilities—24.9 percent
- Construction—14.7 percent
- Information industries—14.2 percent
- Manufacturing—12.9 percent

---

[5] All statistics from the Bureau of Labor Statistics Web site, at http://bls.gov/.

Where Do Union Workers Live?
- Union membership is highest in the Northeast, North Central, and Pacific states.
- Half of all union workers live in just six states: California, New York, Illinois, Michigan, Ohio, and Pennsylvania.
- Union membership is lowest in the South.
- In four states, union membership is below five percent: North Carolina, South Carolina, Arkansas, and Mississippi.

How Does Union/Non-Union Pay Compare? (Wage and Salary Workers)
- Union members average $781 per week
- Non-union members average $612 per week

ORGANIZING A UNION

Exclusivity

It is difficult to organize a union. When a worker starts to talk about collective action, or when an organizer appears from a national union, many employees are suspicious or fearful; some may be hostile. Management will generally be opposed—sometimes fiercely opposed—to any union organizing effort. The fight can become ugly, and all because of one principle: *exclusivity*.

Under §9 of the NLRA, a validly recognized union is the *exclusive* representative of the employees. This means that the union will represent all of the designated employees, regardless of whether a particular worker *wants* to be represented. The company may not bargain directly with any employee in the group, nor with any other organization representing the designated employees.

A collective bargaining unit is the precisely defined group of employees who will be represented by a particular union. Suppose a hotel workers' union attempts to organize the Excelsior Hotel. The union will seek to represent some of Excelsior's employees, but not all. The union may represent, for example, all maids, busboys, and bellhops. Those employees are in the collective bargaining unit. Many other people who work for the hotel will *not* be in the collective bargaining unit. Managers who run the hotel, reservation agents who work in other cities, launderers who work in separate facilities for a different employer—all of these people are *outside* the collective bargaining unit and will be unaffected by the union's bargaining.

It is the union's *exclusive* right to bargain for the unit that gives the organization its power. But some employees may be unhappy with the way a union exercises this power. In the following case, workers believed the union was failing to represent them on a vital issue. Should they be allowed to bargain on their own behalf? You be the judge.

you Be The Judge

EMPORIUM CAPWELL CO. V. WESTERN ADDITIONAL COMMUNITY ORGANIZATION

420 U.S. 50, 95 S. Ct. 977, 1975 U.S. LEXIS 134
United States Supreme Court, 1975

Facts: Emporium Capwell operated a department store in San Francisco. The Department Store Employees Union represented all stock workers. Several black union members complained to the union about racial discrimination in promotions, asserting that highly qualified black workers were routinely passed over in favor of less qualified whites. The union promised to pursue the issue ▼

with management, but the black employees were not satisfied with the union's effort. The unhappy workers demanded to speak with top management of the store and then, without the union's permission, picketed the store and handed out leaflets accusing the company of discrimination. Emporium Capwell fired the picketing employees. The resulting case went all the way to the Supreme Court.

In most labor cases, the union is on one side and management is on the other. In this case, the black employees were on one side, with the union on the other. The union argued that exclusivity prohibited any group of workers from demanding to meet separately with management. It claimed that the disgruntled workers violated the NLRA by insisting on separate bargaining, and that it was proper for the company to fire the workers. In other words, the union placed a higher value on exclusivity than on maintaining the jobs of those employees. The black workers, on the other hand, argued that eliminating discrimination was more important than union exclusivity. They insisted that management had no right to fire them and that they were entitled to get their jobs back and to bargain independently.

You Be the Judge: **Did the picketing employees violate the NLRA by demanding to bargain directly with management?**

Argument for the Union: Your honors, exclusivity is the core of a union's strength. If management is free to talk with employees individually—or if it can be *compelled* to talk with them—the union has no leverage. An astute manager will quickly use worker conflicts as a tool to divide the union and destroy it. By cutting deals with favored employees, management could demonstrate to all workers that affiliation with the union is a losing tactic, and that the smart worker bargains for himself—and then does what management tells him to do.

Racial discrimination is a terrible evil. It must be eradicated from the workplace. This union is committed to fighting prejudice. But the union must do it *collectively*. If an exception to the principle of exclusivity can be carved out for one important issue, such as race discrimination, then an exception can be carved out for other important issues, such as gender bias, age discrimination, language differences, retirement pay, health benefits . . . and on and on. To allow this group of picketers to pursue a worthy goal with separate bargaining would be to destroy the union—and ensure that *no* valuable goals are obtained.

Argument for the Picketing Workers: Congress granted employees the right to organize *for their mutual benefit*, not to advance the cause of unions. A labor organization is a means to an end, not an end in itself. When a union fails to support its members on a vital issue, employees must be free to fend for themselves. Race discrimination is not a simple bargaining issue like retirement benefits; it is a vital matter of human dignity. This union failed to act promptly and vigorously to protect its black members and end discrimination. Why should those employees now be shackled to an organization that has failed them?

It makes no difference *why* the union failed to protect its members. Weak-kneed, docile union leadership can be just as devastating to the cause of racial equality as bad faith. We are not asking that union members be free to pursue every petty complaint directly with management. To equate racial justice with retirement benefits is to ignore the singular evil of discrimination. We merely ask that, when a union fails to protect its members concerning a profound issue such as this, the injured employees be allowed to speak for themselves. ■

Organizing

A union organizing effort generally involves the following pattern.

Campaign

Union organizers talk with employees—or attempt to talk—and interest them in forming a union. The organizers may be employees of the company, who simply chat with fellow workers about unsatisfactory conditions. Or a union may send nonemployees of the company to hand out union leaflets to workers as they arrive and depart from the factory.

Authorization Cards

Union organizers ask workers to sign authorization cards, which state that the particular worker requests the specified union to act as her sole bargaining representative.

Recognition

If a union obtains authorization cards from a sizable percentage of workers, it seeks **recognition** as the exclusive representative for the bargaining unit. The union may ask the employer to recognize it as the bargaining representative, but most of the time employers refuse to recognize the union voluntarily. The NLRA permits an employer to refuse recognition.

Petition

Assuming that the employer does not voluntarily recognize a union, the union generally petitions the NLRB for an election. It must submit to the NLRB regional office authorization cards signed by at least 30 percent of the workers. The regional office verifies whether there are enough valid cards to warrant an election and looks closely at the proposed bargaining unit to make sure that it is appropriate. If the regional director determines that the union has identified an appropriate bargaining unit and has enough valid cards, it orders an election.

Election

The NLRB closely supervises the election to ensure fairness. All members of the proposed bargaining unit vote on whether they want the union to represent them. If more than 50 percent of the workers vote for the union, the NLRB designates that union as the exclusive representative of all members of the bargaining unit. When unions hold representation elections in private corporations, they win about half the time. Labor organizations claim that management typically uses paid company time to campaign against the union. Employers respond that labor loses elections because workers fear that a union will hurt them, not help. Among public employers, unions generally do much better, winning about 85 percent of representation campaigns. Public employers often do not campaign against the union.

These are some of the issues that most commonly arise during an organizing effort: (1) What may a union do during its organizing campaign? (2) What may the employer do to defeat the campaign? (3) What is an appropriate bargaining unit?

What Workers May Do

The NLRA guarantees employees the right to talk among themselves about forming a union, to hand out literature, and ultimately to join a union.[6] Workers may urge other employees to sign authorization cards and may vigorously push their cause. When employees hand out leaflets, the employer generally may not limit the content. In one case a union distributed leaflets urging workers to vote against political candidates who opposed minimum wage laws. The employer objected to the union using company property to distribute the information, but the Supreme Court upheld

---

[6] NLRA §7.

the union's right. Even though the content of the writing was not directly related to the union, the connection was close enough that the NLRA protected the union's activity.[7]

There are, of course, limits to what union organizers may do. The statute permits an employer to restrict organizing discussions if they interfere with discipline or production. A worker on a moving assembly line has no right to walk away from his task to talk with other employees about organizing a union; the employer may insist that the worker stay at his job and leave discussions until lunch or some other break.[8]

What Employers May Do

As mentioned above, an employer may prohibit employees from organizing if the efforts interfere with the company's work. In a retail store, for example, management may prohibit union discussions in the presence of customers, because the discussions could harm business.

May the employer speak out against a union organizing drive? Yes. Management is entitled to communicate to the employees why it believes a union will be harmful to the company. But the employer's efforts must be limited to explanation and advocacy. **The employer may vigorously present anti-union views to its employees, but may not use either threats or promises of benefits to defeat a union drive.**[9] Notice that the employer is prohibited not only from threatening reprisals, such as firing a worker who favors the union, but also from offering benefits designed to defeat the union. A company that has vigorously rejected employee demands for higher wages may not suddenly grant a 10 percent pay increase in the midst of a union campaign.

It is an unfair labor practice for an employer to interfere with a union organizing effort. Normally, a union claiming such interference will file a ULP charge. If the Board upholds the union's claim, it will order the employer to stop its interference and permit a fair election. In some cases, though, management's interference is so pervasive and intrusive that the Board may conclude an election would be pointless. **When an employer outrageously interferes with a union organizing campaign, the NLRB may forgo the normal election, certify the union as the exclusive representative, and order the company to bargain.** This *bargaining order* is an extreme measure, and the Board uses it only when an employer has shown extreme anti-union animus. In the following case, the union contended that the employer had done just that.

GARVEY MARINE, INC. V. NATIONAL LABOR RELATIONS BOARD

245 F.3d 819
United States District Court of Appeals for the District of Columbia Circuit, 2001

Facts: Garvey Marine operated a fleet of tugboats. Each boat had two or more pilots and various deckhands, assigned by a company dispatcher. The International Longshoremen's Association, Local 2038, AFL-CIO, sought to represent the deckhands. When the Union lost the representation vote, it filed a complaint with the NLRB, stating that Garvey had intimidated the deckhands. The ALJ found numerous ULPs. He declared that Garvey made its pilots promise deckhands pay increases if the union were defeated but wage reductions and a strike if it won. He found that Garvey instituted a stricter ▼

---

[7] *Eastex, Inc. v. NLRB*, 434 U.S. 1045, 98 S. Ct. 888, 1978 U.S. LEXIS 547 (1978).
[8] *NLRB v. Babcock & Wilcox Co.*, 351 U.S. 105, 76 S. Ct. 679, 1956 U.S. LEXIS 1721 (1956).
[9] *NLRB v. Gissel Packing Co.*, 395 U.S. 575, 89 S. Ct. 1918, 1969 U.S. LEXIS 3172 (1969).

disciplinary policy and used it to fire deckhand Steven Bradley. The NLRB affirmed the findings and ordered Garvey to bargain with the union, without another election. Garvey appealed.

Issues: Had Garvey committed ULPs? Did the NLRB properly issue an order to bargain?

Excerpts from Judge Ginsburg's Decision: According to Garvey, the deckhands could not reasonably have believed that the pilots who made promises and threats to union adherents were acting on the Company's behalf. Garvey points out that its vice president, Hudson, made repeated written and oral statements disclaiming any promises or threats and assuring deckhands there would be no reprisals taken for their union activity. The Board took the opposite position. Garvey required its pilots to sign a policy that they would support the Company in the Union campaign—and the deckhands knew it. A reasonable deckhand, therefore, would not necessarily have assumed that a pilot's statement in contravention of Garvey's official policies was unauthorized; he would as likely have concluded that Garvey's public statements were primarily for show while the pilot's private warnings reflected management's actual position.

The Board was justified in concluding that Bradley's dismissal was motivated in part by his union advocacy: Garvey's dispatcher told him so. The Board also relied upon Garvey's elaborate choreography of Bradley's initial suspension, which preceded his formal dismissal by a few days: Garvey sent Bradley's boat back to the dock midshift, where Bradley—observed by the crews of three boats that had been held at the dock, presumably so they could witness the event—was met by a sheriff's officer who escorted him off the premises. This procedure suggests that Garvey at the least wanted to make an example of Bradley; it had staged no such spectacle when, on an earlier occasion, it delayed until shift's end the dismissal of a deckhand who had threatened a pilot with a knife.

Garvey objects to several features of the Board's analysis. First, the Company points out that the threats cited by the Board in support of its order were made during one-on-one encounters between pilots and a relatively small number of deckhands. Moreover, those most seriously threatened—[Bradley and others]—were undeterred in their union advocacy and, according to Garvey, there was no evidence that the many deckhands who were not personally threatened ever learned of the threats. Garvey also marshals the ALJ's point that the threats were less serious because they came only from pilots and were at odds with the official statements made by Vice President Hudson.

These arguments do not show that the Board acted unreasonably. The Board acknowledged that relatively few deckhands were threatened in person, but it balanced that fact against the small size of the unit, which had only 22 voters; the frequency of the threats, of which there were more than 30 during the two-month union campaign; and the nature of those threats, several of which menaced union adherents with physical harm. The Board believed that Bradley's suspension alone, having been "carried out in a manner that would ensure a dramatic and lasting impression on other employees . . . obviates any argument that other employees would not have been aware of the unlawful conduct and its import."

The Board was also reasonable in hypothesizing that a "rough and ready" threat made by an immediate supervisor "may be far more credible and influential so far as the ordinary worker is concerned than a necessarily more formal, structured, and purposeful statement of a high-ranking executive."

We grant the Board's application for enforcement. ■

Public Policy   Is the court being overly protective of the workers? These are deckhands on tugboats. Are they so easily intimidated? The order to bargain means that the union "wins" without an election. Is that right? ◆

Unlike the company in the *Garvey* case, the employer in the following dispute admitted a glaring violation of labor law, yet claimed it should pay no damages because the injured worker was in the country illegally.

HOFFMAN PLASTIC COMPOUNDS, INC. V. NATIONAL LABOR RELATIONS BOARD

122 S. Ct. 1275, 152 L. Ed. 2d 271
United States Supreme Court, 2002

Facts: The United Rubber, Cork, Linoleum and Plastic Workers of America began an organizing campaign at Hoffman Plastic Compounds, Inc. (Hoffman). Jose Castro and others supported this effort and, in retaliation, Hoffman fired them. Several years later (labor cases move very slowly), during hearings concerning his termination, Castro revealed for the first time that he was illegally in the United States. He had used false documents to obtain the job at Hoffman. Despite his illegal status, the NLRB found that Hoffman's retaliatory firing violated the NLRA and ordered the company to pay Castro $66,951, representing backpay from the date of firing until the employer learned that he was ineligible to work. The company appealed and the issue reached the United States Supreme Court.

Issue: May an employer who has fired a worker for union organizing be ordered to pay back wages when the employee was illegally in the country?

Excerpts from Chief Justice Rehnquist's Decision: Under the [Immigration Reform and Control Act (IRCA), which regulates immigration into the United States], it is impossible for an undocumented alien to obtain employment in the United States without some party directly contravening explicit congressional policies. Either the undocumented alien tenders fraudulent identification, which subverts the cornerstone of IRCA's enforcement mechanism, or the employer knowingly hires the undocumented alien in direct contradiction of its IRCA obligations. The Board asks that we overlook this fact and allow it to award backpay to an illegal alien for years of work not performed, for wages that could not lawfully have been earned, and for a job obtained in the first instance by a criminal fraud. We find, however, that awarding backpay to illegal aliens runs counter to policies underlying IRCA, policies the Board has no authority to enforce or administer. Therefore, as we have consistently held in like circumstances, the award lies beyond the bounds of the Board's remedial discretion.

The Board contends that awarding limited backpay to Castro "reasonably accommodates" IRCA, because, in the Board's view, such an award is not "inconsistent" with IRCA. The Board argues that because the backpay period was closed as of the date Hoffman learned of Castro's illegal status, Hoffman could have employed Castro during the backpay period without violating IRCA. The Board further argues that while IRCA criminalized the misuse of documents, "it did not make violators ineligible for backpay awards or other compensation flowing from employment secured by the misuse of such documents." This latter statement, of course, proves little. What matters here, and what sinks both of the Board's claims, is that Congress has expressly made it criminally punishable for an alien to obtain employment with false documents. There is no reason to think that Congress nonetheless intended to permit backpay where but for an employer's unfair labor practices, an alien-employee would have remained in the United States illegally, and continued to work illegally, all the while successfully evading apprehension by immigration authorities. Far from "accommodating" IRCA, the Board's position, recognizing employer misconduct but discounting the misconduct of illegal alien employees, subverts it.

[The NLRB's ruling is reversed.]

Excerpts from Justice Breyer's Dissent: The Court does not deny that the employer in this case dismissed an employee for trying to organize a union—a crude and obvious violation of the labor laws. And it cannot deny that the Board has especially broad discretion in choosing an appropriate remedy for addressing such violations. Nor can it deny that in such circumstances backpay awards serve critically important remedial purposes. Those purposes involve more than victim compensation; they also include deterrence, *i.e.*, discouraging employers from violating the Nation's labor laws.

[Denying backpay] lowers the cost to the employer of an initial labor law violation (provided, of course, that the only victims are illegal aliens). It thereby increases the employer's incentive to find and to hire illegal-alien employees. Were the Board forbidden to assess backpay against a *knowing* employer—a circumstance not before us today—this

▼

perverse economic incentive, which runs directly contrary to the immigration statute's basic objective, would be obvious and serious. But even if limited to cases where the employer did not know of the employee's status, the incentive may prove significant—for, as the Board has told us, the Court's rule offers employers immunity in borderline cases, thereby encouraging them to take risks, *i.e.*, to hire with a wink and a nod those potentially unlawful aliens whose unlawful employment (given the Court's views) ultimately will lower the costs of labor law violations. ■

Appropriate Bargaining Unit

When a union petitions the NLRB for an election, the Board determines whether the proposed bargaining unit is appropriate. **The Board generally certifies a proposed bargaining unit if and only if the employees share a community of interest.** Employers frequently assert that the bargaining unit is inappropriate. If the Board agrees with the employer and rejects the proposed bargaining unit, it dismisses the union's request for an election. The Board pays particular attention to two kinds of employees: managerial and confidential.

Managerial employees must be excluded from the bargaining unit.[10] An employee is managerial if she is so closely aligned with management that her membership in the bargaining unit would create a conflict of interest between her union membership and her actual work. Courts generally find such a conflict only if *the employee is substantially involved in the employer's labor policy.*

For example, a factory worker who spends one-third of his time performing assembly work but two-thirds of his time supervising a dozen other workers is so closely aligned with management that he could not fairly be part of the bargaining unit. There would be constant tension between his supervisory work and his advocacy on behalf of the union. By contrast, an engineer who analyzes production methods and merely reports her findings to management may not be closely aligned with the employer. Unless the engineer has actual control over personnel decisions, she can probably be included in a bargaining unit of other engineers.[11]

Confidential employees are generally excluded from the bargaining unit.[12] A confidential employee is one who works so closely with executives or other management employees that there would be a conflict of interest if the employee were in the bargaining unit. An executive secretary may be so intimately acquainted with her boss's ideas, plans, and other confidential information that it would be unfair to allow her to join a bargaining unit of other secretaries.

Once the Board has excluded managerial and confidential employees, it looks at various criteria to decide whether the remaining employees should logically be grouped in one bargaining unit, that is, whether they share a **community of interest.** The Board looks for:

- Rough equality of pay and benefits, and methods of computing both
- Similar total hours per week and type of work
- Similar skills and training, and
- Previous bargaining history and the number of authorization cards from any different groups within the unit.

---

[10] *NLRB v. Bell Aerospace Co., Div. of Textron, Inc.*, 416 U.S. 267, 94 S. Ct. 1757, 1974 U.S. LEXIS 35 (1974).
[11] See, e.g., *NLRB v. Case Corp.*, 995 F.2d 700, 1993 U.S. App. LEXIS 13246 (7th Cir. 1993).
[12] Ibid.

Having applied these criteria to all members of the proposed unit, the Board either certifies the bargaining unit or rejects the unit and dismisses the union's petition. Suppose the employees in a public high school decide to organize. The Board will probably find that an appropriate bargaining unit includes all academic teachers and physical education teachers because they do roughly similar work and are paid similarly. The principal and vice-principal will not be included in the unit because their work is supervisory and administrative and they are paid on a separate scale.

COLLECTIVE BARGAINING

The goal of bargaining is a contract, which is called a **collective bargaining agreement (CBA).** As mentioned, Congress passed the NLRA to foster industrial peace, and a CBA is designed to do that. But problems arise as union and employer advocate their respective positions. Three of the most common conflicts are (1) whether an issue is a mandatory subject of bargaining, (2) whether the parties are bargaining in good faith, and (3) how to enforce the agreement. For a Web page devoted to articles and reports on collective bargaining, see **http://www.ilr.cornell.edu/depts/ICB/briefing/**.

Subjects of Bargaining

The NLRA *permits* the parties to bargain almost any subject they wish, but *requires* them to bargain certain issues. **Mandatory subjects include wages, hours, and other terms and conditions of employment.** Either side may propose to bargain *other* subjects, but neither side may insist upon bargaining them.

Management and unions often disagree as to whether a particular topic is mandatory or not. Typically, unions attempt to expand the number of mandatory subjects, seeking more input into a greater number of issues, while the company argues that subjects are not mandatory and are none of the union's business. In general, a court is likely to find a given issue mandatory when it *directly relates* to individual workers; when a subject only indirectly affects employees, it is likely to be found not mandatory. In passing the NLRA, Congress never intended a union negotiator to become an equal partner in running the business.

Can American labor compete with lower paid foreign workers? Should management have the unfettered right to transfer jobs overseas?

Courts generally find these subjects to be mandatory: pay, benefits, order of layoffs and recalls, production quotas, work rules (such as safety practices), retirement benefits, and in-plant food service and prices (e.g., cafeteria food). Courts usually consider these subjects to be nonmandatory: product type and design, advertising, sales, financing, corporate organization, and location of plants.

Today, some of the angriest disputes between management and labor arise from a company's desire to subcontract work and/or to move plants to areas with cheaper costs. **Subcontracting** means that a manufacturer, rather than producing all parts of a product and then assembling them, contracts for other companies, frequently overseas, to make some of the parts. Is a business free to subcontract work? That depends on management's motive. **A company that subcontracts** in order to maintain its economic viability is probably *not* required to bargain first; however, bargaining *is* mandatory if the subcontracting is designed to replace union workers with cheaper labor.

Dorsey Trailers manufactured dump trucks. During a period of heavy sales, Dorsey subcontracted some of its production work to Bankhead Enterprises, which agreed to manufacture two trucks per week and split the profits. The union filed a ULP charge, claiming that subcontracting was a mandatory subject of bargaining, and that Dorsey had no right to make the deal before negotiating with the union.

The court noted that Dorsey was losing business because it could not fill orders fast enough. The dump truck industry was cyclical, and in a period of strong demand, the company had to be able to manufacture its goods quickly. Dorsey had been unable to hire enough welders and other skilled workers to keep up with demand. The court stated that Dorsey could not survive without the subcontracting. Further, the company had not reduced union jobs; it had simply failed to add more union workers—through no fault of its own. Dorsey was free to subcontract without bargaining the issue.[13]

Plant closings, which can result in hundreds or thousands of lost jobs, are also a volatile issue. Although the job losses are potentially greater than those that result from subcontracting, management is not obligated to bargain such a decision. **An employer is not required to bargain over the closing of a plant, only the *effects* of the closing.**[14]

The reasoning behind this rule is basic: the company that opened a plant ought to be able to close it. The competing interest of the employees—the need for work—is obviously strong but not strong enough to mandate bargaining. Further, having concluded that the employer has the right to shut down a facility, courts also allow the employer to do so fairly quickly. Management may need speed and flexibility in effecting such major business changes. In contrast, the union will want to slow down or prevent the closing. The two sides will have few things to discuss, and mandated bargaining will gain little for employees while potentially costing the company time and money. When a plant closing will cost jobs, management must bargain such things as the order of layoffs, but it need not bargain the closing itself.

Employer and Union Security

Both the employer and the union will seek clauses making their positions more secure. Management, above all, wants to be sure that there will be no strikes during the course of the agreement. For its part, the union tries to ensure that its members cannot be turned away from work during the CBA's term, and that all newly hired workers will affiliate with the union. We look at several union security issues.

No Strike/No Lockout. Most agreements include some form of no-strike clause, meaning that the union promises not to strike during the term of the contract. In turn, unions insist on a no-lockout clause, meaning that in the event of a labor dispute, management will not prevent union members from working. **No-strike and no-lockout clauses are both legal.**

Closed Shop. A closed shop means the employer must hire only union members. Though obviously very attractive to a union, effectively giving it veto power over new hires, a closed shop is not possible. **A closed shop is illegal.** Indeed, for a union to bargain for a closed shop violates the NLRA.

Union and Agency Shops. In a union shop, membership in the union becomes compulsory *after* the employee has been hired. Thus management retains an unfettered right to hire whom it pleases, but all new employees who fit into the bargaining unit

---

[13] *Dorsey Trailers, Inc. Northumberland PA Plant v. NLRB,* 134 F.3d 125, 1998 U.S. App. LEXIS 764 (3rd. Cir. 1998).

[14] *First National Maintenance Corp. v. NLRB,* 452 U.S. 666, 101 S. Ct. 2573, 1981 U.S. LEXIS 117 (1981).

must affiliate with the union. **A union shop is generally legal.** There are two limitations, however. First, new members need not join the union for 30 days. Second, the new members, after joining the union, can only be required to pay initiation fees and union dues. If the new hire decides he does not want to participate in the union, the union may not compel him to do so, and management may not terminate him (pursuant to a CBA) for his refusal. This is a compromise, designed to protect workers from having to play an active role in a union, while ensuring that the union receives normal dues from all employees, whether they participate in union affairs or not. If employees could avoid dues, they would be "free riders," benefiting from the union's bargaining without paying for it.

An **agency shop** is similar to a union shop. Here, the new hire must pay union fees but need not actually join the organization. In both a union shop and an agency shop, the worker may insist on paying only the percentage of dues that is devoted to collective bargaining, contract administration, and grievances. An employee may refuse to pay, for example, the percentage of union dues devoted to organizing other companies.[15]

Some states have passed so-called **right to work** laws, which restrict or even outlaw union shop and agency shop agreements. These statutes typically prohibit a labor organization from demanding that all employees join the union or pay dues. Right to work laws prompt an intense response from both supporters and opponents of organized labor, and the Internet offers plenty of evidence. At **http://www.nrtw.org/**, the National Right to Work Legal Defense Foundation explains these statutes and counsels employees about their rights to reject union membership and avoid paying dues. The organization also discusses what it considers to be union abuses. Meanwhile the AFL-CIO, the nation's largest labor organization, offers statistics demonstrating that union workers earn higher pay than their nonunion counterparts in virtually all jobs and professions, and that wages are lower in right to work states than elsewhere in the country. See its Web site at **http://www.aflcio.org/**.

Hot Cargo Clause. A hot cargo clause would prohibit an employer from doing business with a specified company. A union might like such a clause to put pressure on the *other* company, where the union already has a dispute. But the effort must fail: **hot cargo clauses are illegal.**

Duty to Bargain

Both the union and the employer must bargain in good faith with an open mind. However, they are *not* obligated to reach an agreement. This means that the two sides must meet and make a reasonable effort to reach a contract. The goal is good faith bargaining, with the hope that it will lead to a contract and labor peace. Each side must listen to the other's proposals and consider possible compromises. But the NLRA does not require agreement. Suppose a union proposes a 15 percent pay increase, and management offers a 1 percent raise. Each side is required to attend bargaining sessions, listen to the other side's proposal, and consider its supporting argument. But neither side has to agree. Management need not raise its offer to 2 percent, nor must the union drop its demand. However, **if an employer states that it is financially unable to meet the union's demands, the union is entitled to see records that support the claim.** It is an unfair labor practice for an employer to say, "We can't afford a pay raise now," and then refuse to supply its financial data. An employer could easily destroy good faith bargaining if it were allowed to claim financial impossibility without demonstrating it. Similarly, if an employer argues that it must subcontract work to save money, it must furnish the documents it is relying on in making its proposal.

---

[15] *Communications Workers of America v. Beck,* 487 U.S. 735, 108 S. Ct. 2641, 1988 U.S. LEXIS 3030 (1988).

Sometimes an employer will attempt to make changes without bargaining the issues at all. However, **management may not unilaterally change wages, hours, or terms and conditions of employment without bargaining the issues to impasse.** "Bargaining to impasse" means that both parties must continue to meet and bargain in good faith until it is clear that they cannot reach an agreement. The goal in requiring collective bargaining is to bring the parties together, to reach an agreement that brings labor peace. In one case, the union won an election, but before bargaining could begin, management changed the schedule from five 8-hour days to four 10-hour days a week. The company also changed its layoff policy from one of strict seniority to one based on ability and began laying off employees based on alleged poor performance. The court held that each of these acts violated the company's duty to bargain. The employer ultimately might be allowed to make every one of these changes, but first it had to bargain the issues to impasse.[16]

For the same reasons, though the employer may implement new policies after impasse, it may *implement only what it has proposed at the table.* Again, it would defeat the purpose of the NLRA if a company were free to implement a business decision that it had never proposed; the two sides *could not* have discussed plans that were never offered at the table. Exhibit 31.1 outlines the respective bargaining rights and responsibilities between employers and unions.

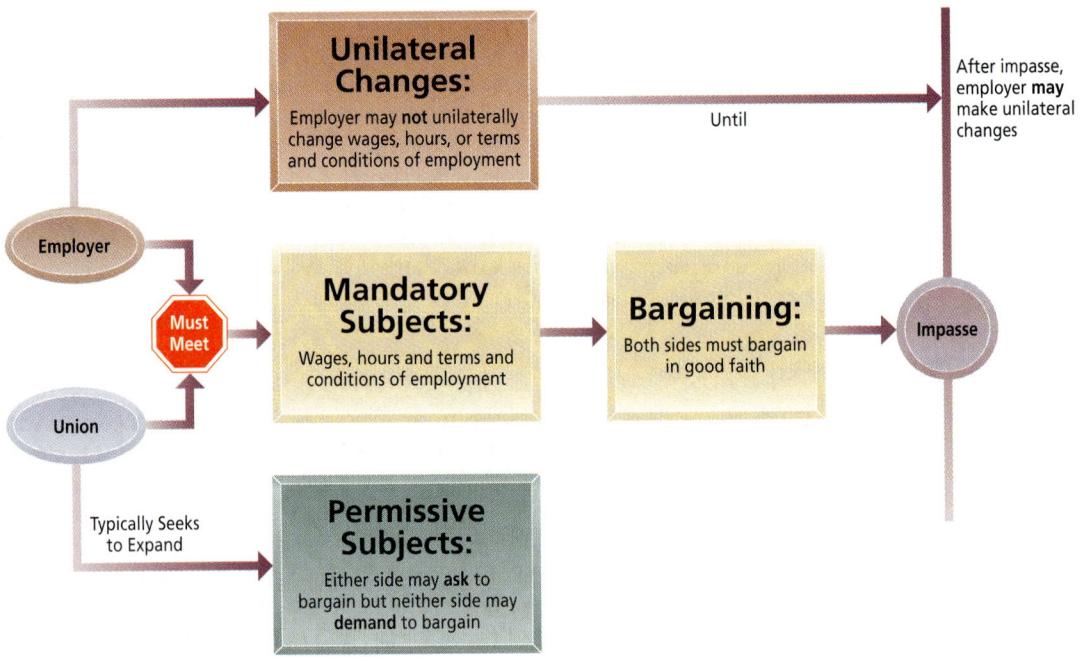

Exhibit 31.1
The NLRA requires that the employer and the union meet. They *must* bargain mandatory subjects and *may* bargain permissive subjects. The employer may not make any unilateral change concerning a mandatory subject until bargaining has reached an impasse.

---

[16] *Adair Standish Corp. v. NLRB*, 912 F.2d 854, 1990 U.S. App. LEXIS 14670 (6th Cir. 1990).

Illegal implementation put major league baseball players back on the field after the longest strike in sports history. The CBA had expired, and the players' union bargained with team owners throughout the spring and summer. The two sides could not agree, primarily because the owners demanded a salary cap, which would give all teams equal payrolls. In August the players struck, ending the season without a World Series for the first time in more than 100 years. The two sides continued talking until December, when the owners announced they were implementing their salary cap proposal and changing various aspects of "free agency," the policy that allows a player to seek the highest salary from any team. A federal district court judge ruled that the owners had violated the NLRA by unilaterally imposing new rules concerning a mandatory subject (free agency) that they had never bargained. The judge ordered the owners back to the table, and the parties finally agreed to a new CBA.

Enforcement

Virtually all collective bargaining agreements provide for their own enforcement, typically through **grievance-arbitration.** Suppose a company transfers an employee from the day shift to the night shift, and the worker believes the contract prohibits such a transfer for any employee with her seniority. The employee complains to the union, which files a **grievance,** that is, a formal complaint with the company, notifying management that the union claims a contract violation. Generally, the CBA establishes some kind of informal hearing, usually conducted by a member of management, at which the employee, represented by the union, may state her case and respond to the company's assertions. The manager has a limited time period—say, seven days—to decide the grievance.

If, after the manager's decision, the employee is still dissatisfied, the union normally has the right to appeal to some kind of formal hearing, perhaps before a top company executive or committee. This appeal hearing is slightly more formal. If this hearing still fails to satisfy the employee, the union typically may file for **arbitration,** that is, a formal hearing before a neutral arbitrator. In the arbitration hearing, each side is represented by its lawyer. The arbitrator is required to decide the case based on the CBA. An arbitrator finds either for the employee, and orders the company to take certain corrective action, or for the employer, and dismisses the grievance. (The American Arbitration Association offers its rules, procedures, and forms at http://www.adr.org/.)

A CBA also permits the company to file a grievance. Its complaint normally goes directly to arbitration. In the vast majority of grievances, the arbitrator's decision is final. In a limited number of cases, however, the losing party attempts to convince a federal court that the arbitration award is unjust. Usually, such an appeal is futile. **Courts generally do not examine the merits of an arbitrator's decision.** The idea of all contracts, including CBAs, is to give the parties a chance to control their own destiny. When a CBA states that grievances should be settled by arbitration, courts seldom undercut the contract by reviewing the arbitrator's award. Of course, a rule would hardly be a rule without an exception. **A court may refuse to enforce an arbitrator's award that is contrary to public policy.** So if an arbitrator's decision encourages either party to violate the law or engage in clearly immoral conduct, a court will probably nullify the award. The following cases demonstrates how reluctant courts are to interfere with an arbitrator's decision.

BRENTWOOD MEDICAL ASSOCIATES V. UNITED MINE WORKERS OF AMERICA

396 F.3d 237
United States Court of Appeals for the Third Circuit, 2005

Facts: Brentwood Medical Associates operated a hospital. The United Mine Workers of America represented one unit of employees, which included Denise Cope, a phlebotomist (someone who draws blood). Exercising her seniority rights, Cope changed jobs to Charge Entry Associate. A year and a half later, BMA announced it was terminating the position. Cope asked to return to her old job. This would have required "bumping" the least senior phlebotomist out of a job. BMA refused, claiming that bumping was not allowed under the collective bargaining agreement (CBA). Cope filed a grievance, which an arbitrator heard.

The arbitrator ruled in Cope's favor. In his decision, he asked rhetorically why, if the CBA disallowed bumping, did it include the following language:

> ...employees who exercise seniority rights and bump must have the skill to perform all of the work [in the new job].

The problem with the quoted language was that it did not in fact exist anywhere in the CBA. BMA filed suit, asking a federal court to overturn the arbitration decision. The trial court upheld the award and BMA appealed.

Issue: Should the arbitration award be affirmed even though the arbitrator relied on language that cannot be found in the CBA?

Excerpts from Judge Van Antwerpen's Decision: The narrow issue before us is whether the arbitrator's conclusion is supported, in any way, by a rational interpretation of the collective bargaining agreement. We ask merely whether the parties to the collective bargaining agreement got what they bargained for, namely an arbitrator who would first provide an interpretation of the contract that was rationally based on the language of the agreement, and second would produce a rational award. BMA contends that the arbitrator's reference to the language not found in the collective bargaining agreement fatally taints the award, because this reference is essential to the arbitrator's ultimate conclusion and is inseparable from the remainder of the award. As such, our focus must be on whether the arbitrator's discussion can still support the award if we excise the anomalous language.

In additional support for his conclusion, the arbitrator cited several provisions of the agreement. For example, Section 1 defines seniority as "bargaining unit-wide" and not within classification. Section 2 provides that the principle of seniority is a factor in layoffs, recalls, and certain types of promotional opportunities provided the employee is fully qualified. Section 5 specifies that in filling vacancies when the qualifications of two or more applicants are relatively equal, preference will be based on seniority.

After reviewing the totality of the arbitrator's decision, we are confident that his award does not rest solely upon the aberrant language added by the arbitrator. Faced with what he perceived as an incongruity between BMA's position and the bargaining unit-wide seniority rights of employees, the arbitrator attempted to construe together, and then give effect to, all provisions of the agreement. While BMA may take issue with his contractual interpretation, this is not sufficient to justify [overturning] the award.

Full-blown judicial review of the arbitrator's decision would annul the bargain between BMA and UMWA for an arbitrator's construction of their agreement and replace it with a judicial interpretation that was not bargained for. Only where there is manifest disregard for the agreement can we override an arbitrator. Because the remainder of the justification for the award offered by the arbitrator was capable of separation from the aberrant language, his decision reflects an interpretation of the contract that is at least minimally rooted in the collective bargaining agreement, and not his own brand of industrial justice.

For the foregoing reasons, we affirm the decision of the District Court. ■

Devil's
Advocate

It is one thing to respect an arbitrator's award and presume it final; it is quite another to rubber-stamp a decision. This arbitrator based his opinion in large part on alleged "CBA language" that in fact came out of thin air. The court blithely suggests that the imaginary language was not of overriding importance—but the *arbitrator* thought so! This is the rare, even bizarre case in which a court should say, "Not good enough. We are taking over." ◆

CONCERTED ACTION

Concerted action refers to any tactics union members take in unison to gain some bargaining advantage. It is this power that gives a union strength. **The NLRA guarantees the right of employees to engage in concerted action for mutual aid or protection.**[17] The most common forms of concerted action are strikes and picketing.

Strikes

The NLRA guarantees employees the right to strike, but with some limitations.[18] A union has a guaranteed right to call a strike if the parties are unable to reach a collective bargaining agreement. A union may call a strike to exert economic pressure on management, to protest an unfair labor practice, or to preserve work that the employer is considering sending elsewhere. Note that the right to strike can be waived. Management will generally insist that the CBA include a **no-strike clause,** which prohibits the union from striking while the CBA is in force. A strike is illegal in several other situations as well; here we mention the most important.

Cooling Off Period

Once the union agrees to a CBA, it may not strike to terminate the agreement, or modify it, without giving management 60 days' notice. Suppose a union contract expires July 1. The two sides attempt to bargain a new contract, but progress is slow. The union may strike as an economic weapon, but must notify management of its intention to do so *and then must wait 60 days*. This cooling off period is designed to give both sides a chance to reassess negotiations and to decide whether some additional compromise would be wiser than enduring a strike.

Statutory Prohibition

Many states have outlawed strikes by public employees. In some states, the prohibition applies to selected employees, such as firefighters or teachers. In other states, all public employees are barred from striking, whether or not they have a contract. The purpose of these statutes is to ensure that unions do not use the public health or welfare as a weapon to secure an unfair bargaining advantage. However, even employees subject to such a rule may find other tactics to press their cause.

Ethics

Jen has worked hard throughout high school, achieving a 3.8 GPA and high test scores, and now she is ready to apply to some of the best colleges in the country. All of her teachers think she is an extraordinary student—yet no one will write her a letter of recommendation.

The teacher's union has been bargaining a new contract for a year and a half. The teachers seek a 4 percent raise; the school board has offered 1 percent. The struggle has grown increasingly bitter. There will be no strike—state law prohibits that—but the teachers have decided they will "work to rule," meaning that they will do only what their (expired) contract requires: teach classes, issue grades, and so forth. No teacher will write a letter of recommendation, coach a team, supervise detention, or offer extra help to a student.

"This stinks," wails Jen. "I've never asked for extra assistance. I've tried to be helpful in class, and a lot of times, I've tutored other kids. This is the one time in my life I really need my teachers to be there for me, and they're turning their backs."

---

[17] NLRA §7.
[18] NLRA §13.

"My heart goes out to Jen," responds her American history teacher, "but our problem is simple: as long as we quietly ask for decent pay, no one listens. Students and parents notice us only when they suffer inconvenience."

"This is a moral outrage!" shouts Jen's father. "These so-called teachers have no right to hurt my child over their pay disputes. If they were serious about their profession, they would do everything they could to help the children who are entrusted to them. Our high school normally sends 95 percent of its students to good colleges, and now the teachers are sabotaging everything."

"If the parents were serious about education," the history teacher retorts, "or truly concerned about their children's welfare, they would demand that the town pay respectable salaries. They prefer lower taxes so they can spend more on fancy cars."

Who is right? From the Chapter 2 Ethics Checklist: What are the alternatives? What are the consequences of each? ◆

Violent Strikes

The NLRA prohibits violent strikes. Violence does sometimes occur on the picket line, when union members attempt to prevent other workers from entering the job site. Or a union may stage a **sit-down strike,** in which members stop working but remain at their job posts, physically blocking replacement workers from taking their places. Any such violence is illegal.

Partial Strikes

A partial strike occurs when employees stop working temporarily, then resume, then stop again, and so forth. This tactic is particularly disruptive because management cannot bring in replacement workers. A union may either walk off the job or stay on it, but it may not alternate.

Replacement Workers

When employees go on strike, management generally wants to replace them to keep the company operating. When replacement workers begin to cross a union picket line, tempers are certain to explode, and entire communities may feel the repercussions. Are replacement workers legal? Yes. **Management has the right to hire replacement workers during a strike.** May the employer offer the replacement workers *permanent* jobs, or must the company give union members their jobs back when the strike is over? It depends on the type of strike.

After an *economic strike,* **an employer may not discriminate against a striker, but the employer is *not* obligated to lay off a replacement worker to give a striker his job back.** An economic strike is one intended to gain wages or benefits. When a union bargains for a pay raise but fails to get it and walks off the job, that is an economic strike. During such a strike, an employer may hire permanent replacement workers. When the strike is over, the company has no obligation to lay off the replacement workers to make room for the strikers. However, if the company does hire more workers, it may not discriminate against the strikers.

After a *ULP strike,* **a union member is entitled to her job back, even if that means the employer must lay off a replacement worker.** Suppose management refuses to bargain in good faith, by claiming poverty without producing records to substantiate its claim. The union strikes. Management's refusal to bargain was an unfair labor practice, and the strike is a ULP strike. When it ends, the striking workers must get their jobs back. The following case raises the pivotal distinction concerning a strike: Was this one sparked by a ULP—or by money?

CITIZENS PUBLISHING AND PRINTING COMPANY V. NATIONAL LABOR RELATIONS BOARD

263 F.3d 224
United States Court of Appeals for the Third Circuit, 2001

Facts: Citizens Publishing was a family-owned corporation that published the *Ellwood City Ledger* and another local newspaper. Bud Dimeo had been the company's sole photographer for over 35 years. When the needs for daytime photography declined, Citizens began requiring Dimeo to work at night and on weekends as well. Citizens also occasionally employed stringers, meaning freelance photographers who were paid per photo.

Teamsters Local No. 261 was certified as the representative for certain Citizens' employees, including photographers but excluding stringers. While the company and union were negotiating a contract, Dimeo retired, and Citizens assigned most of the night/weekend photography to stringers. The union filed a ULP charge with the NLRB, claiming that Citizens had unilaterally changed the terms and conditions of employment without bargaining, by giving to stringers work previously done by Dimeo, a bargaining unit member.

On July 23, fully 18 months after contract negotiations had started, the union met with employees and informed them that the NLRB intended to issue a complaint based on Citizens' use of stringers. The members voted to strike, and walked out on July 24. The paper continued to publish, using family members, supervisors, and non-striking employees. The following February, six months into the strike, Citizens reassured the union that that none of the replacement workers were considered permanent; the strikers could return if they wished.

The parties met to bargain on March 14. The union representative indicated the union was prepared to return to work. Company representatives took a break to caucus; when they returned, they informed the union that all replacements were permanent. In other words, the strikers had lost their jobs. The next day, Citizens informed the replacement workers they were permanent. The NLRB found that the union's job action was a ULP strike and ordered Citizens to offer the union members their jobs back. Citizens appealed.

Issue: Was the job action a ULP strike?

Excerpts from Judge Fuentes's Decision: An employer violates § 8(a)(5) if, without bargaining to impasse, it effects a unilateral change of an existing term or condition of employment. By unilaterally changing the employees' terms and conditions of employment, an employer minimizes the influence of organized bargaining and emphasizes to the employees that there is no necessity for a collective bargaining agent.

Here, substantial evidence supports the Board's finding that Citizens Publishing's night/weekend work became an integral part of the regular full-time photographer's work, and thus, became bargaining unit work. When Citizens Publishing assigned the night/weekend work to Dimeo, that work became a necessary and integral part of the full-time photographer's position. Additionally, Dimeo did not receive any additional remuneration for his night/weekend work. Thus, at the time of the Union's certification, the status quo included a full-time photographer's position with night/weekend work. Accordingly, substantial evidence supports the determination that Citizens Publishing violated the Act when it unilaterally subcontracted the bargaining unit work during the negotiations over the initial collective-bargaining agreement.

We next address whether the strike was an "unfair labor practice strike," as opposed to a mere economic strike. Unfair labor practice strikers are entitled to immediate reinstatement upon their unconditional offers to return to work; any replacements hired during the strike must be dismissed, if necessary, to effect reinstatement of the strikers.

Here, substantial evidence supports the Board's finding that the strike was an unfair labor practice strike. The Union convened a meeting of bargaining unit members on the day before the strike began. After learning of Citizens Publishing's action, numerous employees indicated their desire to go on strike, and the membership held a strike vote. These facts support the Board's finding that its decision to issue a complaint galvanized the bargaining unit members' belief that an unfair labor practice had been committed and served as the flashpoint for discussion about calling a strike.

Moreover, even if Citizens Publishing's subcontracting of night/weekend work did not constitute an unfair labor practice, its discharge of the striking

▼

employees on March 14 converted the strike into an unfair labor practice strike because it prolonged the strike. Citizens Publishing's false declaration that it had permanently replaced the strikers prolonged the strike by thwarting the Union's attempt to make an unconditional offer to return to work that day. Indeed, the Union informed Citizens Publishing at the March 14 bargaining session of its intent to make an unconditional offer to return to work. Before the Union could make its offer, however, Citizens Publishing preemptively notified the Union that it had permanently replaced the strikers, thereby effectively informing the Union that any unconditional offer to return to work would be futile.

We will enforce the Board's order in its entirety. ■

Find a thorough description of a current strike. What issues caused the union to walk out? Is this an economic or a ULP strike? In your opinion, which side is making the stronger case, and why? ◆

Picketing

Picketing the employer's workplace in support of a strike is generally lawful. Striking workers are permitted to establish picket lines at the employer's job site and to urge all others—employees, replacement workers, and customers—not to cross the line. But the picketers are not permitted to use physical force to *prevent* anyone from crossing the line. The NLRA does not authorize or protect violence on the picket line. The company may terminate violent picketers and permanently replace them, regardless of the nature of the strike.

Secondary boycotts are generally illegal. A secondary boycott is a picket line established not at the employer's premises but at the workplace of a *different* company that does business with the union's employer. Such a boycott is designed to put pressure on the union's employer by forcing other companies to stop doing business with it. Suppose Union is on strike against Truck Co. Union is free to picket Truck Co.'s office or terminal. If Truck Co. hires replacement workers, the trucks will be back on the road, making deliveries. Now Union wants to put additional pressure on Truck Co., so it sets up picket lines at a *supermarket* where Truck Co. delivers. Union attempts to persuade customers not to shop at the store and other workers, including delivery drivers, not to enter the premises. If allowed, the picketing might result in the supermarket demanding that Truck Co. compromise with Union. But this is a secondary boycott, so it is illegal. Truck Co. and the supermarket will obtain an injunction, prohibiting the secondary boycott. See Exhibit 31.2.

Lockouts

The workers have bargained with management for weeks, and discussions have turned belligerent. It is 6:00 AM, the start of another day at the factory. But as 150 employees arrive for work, they are amazed to find the company's gate locked and armed guards standing on the other side. What is this? A lockout.

The power of a union comes ultimately from its potential to strike. But management, too, has weapons. In a lockout, management prohibits workers from entering the premises, denying the employees work and a chance to earn a paycheck. Most, but not all, lockouts are legal.

A defensive lockout is almost always legal. It is one way management can respond to union pressure such as a sit-down strike or a **whipsaw strike,** which may occur when a union is simultaneously bargaining with various employers. Suppose a machinists' union is simultaneously bargaining a contract with three engine manufacturers, attempting to obtain an identical contract from all of the companies. To pressure

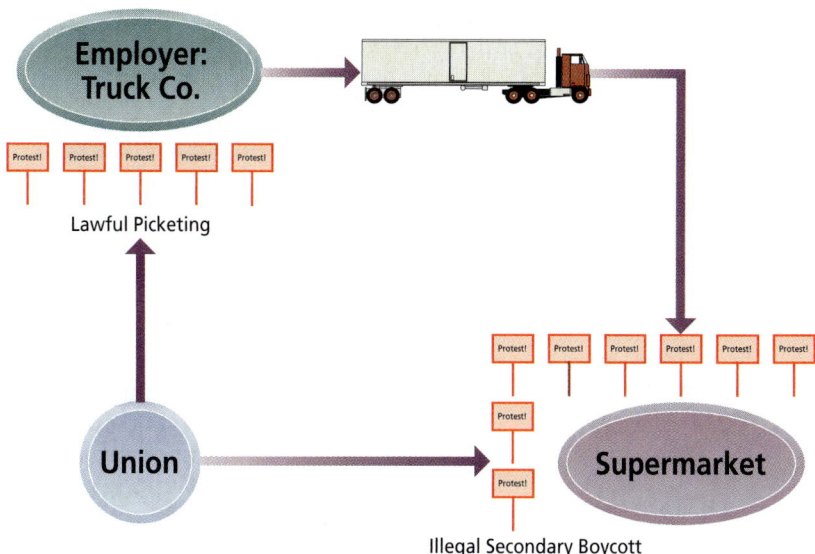

Lawful Picketing

Illegal Secondary Boycott

Exhibit 31.2
A union striking against Truck Co. may lawfully picket the employer, using peaceful means to urge all others to stay away. But if the union attempts to put indirect pressure on Truck Co. by picketing one of the company's customers, it is engaging in an illegal secondary boycott.

the companies, the union might choose to strike against only *one* of the manufacturers. This is a whipsaw strike, and it can be very effective because the struck company, losing money while the others profit, will push strongly for a compromise. But management of all three companies may respond by locking out the workers from *all* factories, even those where no strike is under way. That is a defensive lockout, and it is legal.

An offensive lockout is legal if the parties have reached a bargaining impasse. Management, bargaining a new CBA with a union, may wish to use a lockout to advance its position. It is allowed to do so *provided the parties have reached an impasse.* If there is no impasse, a lockout will *probably* be illegal. Most courts consider that a lockout before impasse indicates hostility to the union. That kind of general antagonism to a union is illegal because the NLRA guarantees employees the right to organize. In addition, management usually *must notify the union before locking it out.* Again, the purpose of the NLRA is to bring the parties together through bargaining. A lockout is a legitimate method to pressure a union into compromise, but it can have that effect only if the union is warned and given a chance to bargain.

REGULATING UNION AFFAIRS

Along with a union's exclusive bargaining power goes a duty of fairness to all of its members. The union's *duty of fair representation* was created by the NLRA and the Labor-Management Reporting and Disclosure Act. **The duty of fair representation requires that a union represent all members fairly, impartially, and in good faith.** A union is not entitled to favor some members over others. No union may discriminate against a member based on impermissible characteristics such as race or sex. A union is allowed to discipline a member for certain acts, such as engaging in an illegal strike or working for wages below union scale. But the union may *not* discipline a member for criticizing union leadership or attempting to replace the leadership through a proper election.

Unions must make reasonable decisions about whether to pursue an employee's grievance. A member may sue his union, claiming that the organization violated its duty of fair representation by deciding not to pursue a grievance on his behalf. But courts generally allow unions a *wide range of latitude* in deciding whether to pursue a grievance. **A union's decision not to file a grievance is illegal only if it was arbitrary, discriminatory, or in bad faith.**

Most employees fail when claiming that a union violated its duty of fair representation. Ramon Hayes worked at the Peoples Gas, Light and Coke Co. Peoples Gas fired him for theft, and the union filed a grievance. Before the grievance could be arbitrated, Hayes was convicted on drug charges. The union, mistakenly believing Hayes had been convicted on the *theft* accusation, withdrew its grievance. Later, the union learned of its error, but refused to pursue the grievance because Peoples Gas had added the drug charge as a reason for the dismissal. A court ruled that the union had probably been inept and negligent in dismissing the original grievance, but had shown no *bad faith* in its belief that the grievance was futile. The union had not violated its duty of fair representation.[19]

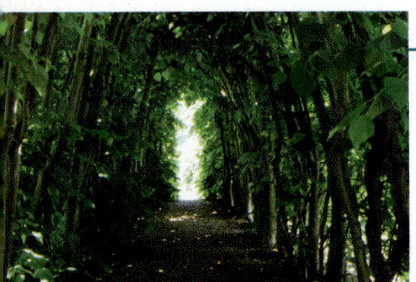

Chapter Conclusion

Workers first attempted to organize unions in this country about 200 years ago in response to appalling working conditions. These conditions are *generally* better today, and contemporary clashes between union and management are less likely to stem from sweltering temperatures in a mine than from a management decision to subcontract work or from a teacher's refusal to write college recommendations. But although the flash points have changed, labor law is still dominated by issues of organizing, collective bargaining, and concerted action.

Chapter Review

1. Section 7 of the National Labor Relations Act (NLRA) guarantees employees the right to organize and join unions, bargain collectively, and engage in other concerted activities.

2. Section 8(a) of the NLRA makes it an unfair labor practice for an employer to interfere with union organizing, discriminate against a union member, or refuse to bargain collectively.

3. Section 8(b) of the NLRA makes it an unfair labor practice for a union to interfere with employees who are exercising their rights under §7, to encourage an employer to discriminate against an employee because of a labor dispute, to refuse to bargain collectively, or to engage in an illegal strike or boycott.

4. Section 9 of the NLRA makes a validly recognized union the *exclusive* representative of the employees.

5. During a union organizing campaign, an employer may vigorously present anti-union views to its employees, but it may not use threats or promises of benefits to defeat the union effort.

6. The National Labor Relations Board (NLRB) will certify a proposed bargaining unit only if the employees share a community of interest.

7. The employer and the union *must* bargain over wages, hours, and other terms and conditions of employment. They *may* bargain other subjects, but neither side may insist on doing so.

---

[19] *Hayes v. People's Gas, Light and Coke Co.*, 1992 U.S. App. LEXIS 30592 (7th Cir. 1992).

8. The union and the employer must bargain in good faith, but they are not obligated to reach an agreement. Management may not unilaterally change wages, hours, or terms and conditions of employment without bargaining to impasse.

9. The NLRA guarantees employees the right to strike, with some limitations.

10. After an *economic* strike, an employer is not obligated to lay off replacement workers to give a striker her job back, but it may not discriminate against a striker. After a *ULP* strike, the striking worker must get her job back.

11. Picketing the employer's workplace in support of a strike is generally lawful; a secondary boycott is generally illegal.

12. An employer may lock out workers, but only after giving them notice.

13. Multi-employer bargaining and implementation do not violate antitrust laws.

14. The duty of fair representation requires that a union represent all members fairly, impartially, and in good faith.

Practice Test

1. Power, Inc., operated a surface coal mine in central Pennsylvania. Financial losses led it to lay off a number of employees. After that, several employees contacted the United Mine Workers of America (UMWA), which began an organizing drive at the company. Power's general manager and foreman both warned the miners that if the company was unionized, it would be shut down. An office manager told one of the miners that the company would get rid of union supporters. Shortly before the election was to take place, Power laid off 13 employees, all of whom had signed union cards. One employee, who had not signed a union card, had low seniority but was not laid off. Later, one of Power's lawyers told several miners that anyone caught helping the 13 laid-off workers by contributing to a union hardship fund would "be out there looking for help from somebody else." Comment.

2. Triec, Inc., is a small electrical contracting company in Springfield, Ohio, owned by its executives Yeazell, Jones, and Heaton. Employees contacted the International Brotherhood of Electrical Workers, which began an organizing drive. Six of the 11 employees in the bargaining unit signed authorization cards. The company declined to recognize the union, which petitioned the NLRB to schedule an election. The company then granted several new benefits for all workers, including higher wages, paid vacations, and other measures. When the election was held, only 2 of the 11 bargaining unit members voted for the union. Did the company violate the NLRA?

3. Q-1 Motor Express was an interstate trucking company. When a union attempted to organize Q-1's drivers, it met heavy resistance. A supervisor told one driver that if he knew what was good for him, he would stay away from the union organizer. The company president told another employee that he had the right to fire everybody, close the company, and then rehire new drivers after 72 hours. He made numerous other threats to workers and their families. Based on the extreme nature of the company's opposition, what exceptional remedy did the union seek before the NLRB?

4. Douglas Kuroda worked for the Hertz Corp. He and his supervisor had a heated argument in which Kuroda told his boss, "You may have a master's degree but you don't know shit." The supervisor instructed Kuroda to punch out for the day, but Kuroda refused to leave until security officers escorted him off the premises. Hertz fired him, and Kuroda filed a grievance. The union represented Kuroda at an arbitration hearing. During the hearing, the union made no objection to certain evidence that the company offered to demonstrate why it fired Kuroda. The arbitrator ruled in favor of the company. Kuroda sued his union (and also Hertz). What kind of claim is he making against the union? Is he likely to win his claim?

5. Gibson Greetings, Inc., had a plant in Berea, Kentucky, where the workers belonged to the International Brotherhood of Firemen & Oilers. The old CBA expired, and the parties negotiated a

new one, but were unable to reach an agreement on economic issues. The union struck. At the next bargaining session, the company claimed that the strike violated the *old* CBA, which had a no-strike clause and which stated that the terms of the old CBA would continue in force as long as the parties were bargaining a *new* CBA. The company refused to bargain until the union at least agreed that by bargaining, the company was not giving up its claim of an illegal strike. The two sides returned to bargaining, but meanwhile the company hired replacement workers. Eventually, the striking workers offered to return to work, but Gibson refused to rehire many of them. In court, the union claimed that the company had committed a ULP by (1) insisting the strike was illegal and (2) refusing to bargain until the union acknowledged the company's position. Why is it very important to the union to establish the company's act as a ULP? *Was* it a ULP?

6. **YOU BE THE JUDGE** WRITING PROBLEM Plainville Ready Mix Concrete Co. was bargaining a CBA with the drivers' union. Negotiations went forward, on and off, over many months, with wages the major source of disagreement. Plainville made its final offer of $9.50 per hour, with step increases of $.25 per hour in a year and another $.25 per hour the following year. The plan also included certain incentive pay. The union refused to accept the offer, and the two sides reached an impasse. Plainville then announced it was implementing its plans. It established a wage rate of $9.50 per hour but eliminated the step increases and incentive pay. Was the company's implementation of the wage increase legal? **Argument for Plainville:** The NLRA only requires the company to bargain in good faith, which we did. The law does not obligate us to agree to anything. Once the parties reached an impasse, Plainville could implement any plan it wanted. **Argument for the Union:** When the parties reach an impasse, the employer is permitted to implement whatever it proposed at the bargaining table. It would defeat the purpose of collective bargaining if a company could implement plans it had never proposed.

7. Eads Transfer, Inc., was a moving and storage company with a small workforce represented by the General Teamsters, Chauffeurs and Helpers Union. When the CBA expired, the parties failed to reach agreement on a new one, and the union

struck. As negotiations continued, Eads hired temporary replacement workers. After 10 months of the strike, some union workers offered to return to work, but Eads made no response to the offer. Two months later, more workers offered to return to work, but Eads would not accept any of the offers. Eventually, Eads notified all workers that they would not be allowed back to work until a new CBA had been signed. The union filed ULP claims against the company. Please rule.

8. Olivetti Office U.S.A., Inc., was located in Newington, Connecticut, and its workers were represented by the United Automobile, Aerospace and Agriculture Implement Workers of America. The company's president reported to the union that Olivetti was losing money. He insisted that unless the union renegotiated certain wage increases in the current CBA, Olivetti would subcontract work to cheaper parts of the country to save money. The union requested to bargain over the proposed subcontracting, and Olivetti agreed. But when the sides met, the company would not permit the union to see the financial data that supported its arguments. After several meetings, the company declared an impasse, implemented its subcontracting proposal, and laid off workers in Connecticut. The union claimed this was a ULP. Was it?

9. Fred Schipul taught English at the Thomaston (Connecticut) High School for 18 years. When the position of English Department chairperson became vacant, Schipul applied, but the Board of Education appointed a less senior teacher. Schipul filed a grievance, based on a CBA provision that required the Board to promote the most senior teacher where two or more applicants were equal in qualification. Before the arbitrator ruled on the grievance, the Board eliminated all department chairpersons. The arbitrator ruled in Schipul's favor. The Board then reinstated all department chairs—all but the English Department. Comment.

10. Labor Day is a national holiday originally intended to celebrate the contributions of working men and women. But for most people today it simply means a day off from work—or the day before school begins. What are some reasons that unions have declined in membership and power? Are there are any reasons to think that

organized labor may rebound and increase its strength?

11. *ETHICS* The chapter refers in several places to the contentious issue of subcontracting. Make an argument for management in favor of a company's ethical right to subcontract, and one for unions in opposition.

Internet Research Problem

Find a web site that is campaigning against sweat-shops. What are sweatshops? Do they exist in the United States? Describe a current campaign about this issue. Do you agree or disagree with what is being done? Why?

12. *ROLE REVERSAL* Write an essay question involving a union organizing campaign and a management response that includes both permissible advocacy and illegal conduct.

You can find further practice problems at http://beatty.westbuslaw.com or in the Study Guide that accompanies this text.

Business Organizations

Starting a Business

James Parker founded Factory Connections, Inc. (FCI) to sell franchises of automotive parts. First, a distributor would purchase a territory (which cost $30,000 to $250,000, depending on the size). Then an FCI sales team would set up accounts at garages in that area, stocking each garage with various FCI car parts. The distributor paid for this initial supply, but was reimbursed by the garage after the parts were used. To resupply the garages, the distributors would purchase parts from FCI.

Unfortunately for all involved, nothing went according to plan. Parker promised in the sales brochures that FCI products were of the highest quality. That was not the case: Among other problems, the brakes squealed and then quickly disintegrated. When distributors complained to Parker, he told them that the products had worked fine for everyone else but the mechanics must have ruined them during installation. These accusations soured relationships between the distributors and their garages. Parker also promised that the FCI sales staff would set up accounts at high quality garages. Instead, the customers were oftentimes not garages at all, but were dump sites for the salesperson's inventory, such as bait shops and junkyards. To entice garage owners to accept an FCI account, sales people would tell the owners that they need not use the products but could keep them on hand for emergencies.

FCI promotional materials included wildly optimistic profitability estimates. Although Parker knew that profitability was declining, he predicted a 10 percent annual increase in sales and profits. He told potential investors that FCI distributorships were 100 percent successful, but that was not true. FCI advertised that, according to an independent survey, it was "Number 1." No survey had ever been conducted. ■

Every business, no matter how large, was at some point little more than a gleam in an entrepreneur's eye. The goal of the law is to balance the rights, obligations, and liabilities of entrepreneurs, managers, investors, and customers. Time and again in these next chapters we will see that legal issues can have as profound an impact on the success of a company as any business decision. The law affects virtually every aspect of business. Wise (and successful) entrepreneurs know how to use the law to their advantage. Because James Parker was not wise, he soon found himself on the wrong end of the law. Parker violated the FTC rules on franchises and, as a result, was sentenced to prison for fraud.[1]

To begin, entrepreneurs must select a form of organization. The correct choice can reduce taxes, liability, and conflict while facilitating outside investment. If entrepreneurs do not make a choice for themselves, the law will automatically select a (potentially undesirable) default option. Numerous alternatives are available: sole proprietorship, general partnership, limited partnership, corporation, limited liability company, limited liability partnership, joint venture, business trust, or cooperative. At http://www.onlinewbc.gov/docs/starting/test.html, the U.S. Small Business Administration offers advice about starting a business, and includes an entrepreneurial test to help you assess your potential as an entrepreneur.

Sole Proprietorships

A sole proprietorship is an unincorporated business owned by a single person. It is the most common form of business organization. For example, Linda runs ExSciTe (which stands for Excellence in Science Teaching), a company that helps teachers prepare hands-on science experiments in the classroom using such basic items as vinegar, lemon juice, and red cabbage.

Sole proprietorships are easy and inexpensive to create and operate. There is no need to hire a lawyer or register with the government. The company is not even required to file a separate tax return—all profits and losses are reported on the owner's personal return. A very few states and some cities and towns require sole proprietors to obtain a business license. And states generally require sole proprietors to register their business name if it is different from their own. Linda, for example, would file a "d/b/a" or "doing business as" certificate for "ExSciTe."

Sole proprietorships also have some serious disadvantages. First, the owner of the business is responsible for all of the business's debts. If ExSciTe cannot pay its suppliers or if a student is injured by an exploding cabbage, Linda is *personally* liable. She may have to sell her house and car to pay the debt. Second, the owner of a sole proprietorship has limited options for financing her business. Debt is generally her only source of working capital because she has no stock or memberships to sell. If someone else brings in capital and helps with the management of the business, then it is a partnership, not a

---

[1] *United States of America v. Parker*, 364 F.3d 934; 2004 U.S. App. LEXIS 7549 (2004).

sole proprietorship. For this reason, sole proprietorships work best for small businesses without large capital needs.

No form of organization is right—or wrong—for everyone. Consider these very different experiences of two small-business owners.

Judith Gross felt that the fees and taxes imposed on her young corporation were a major factor in its failure:

> It seemed like a dream come true. I always thought I had the right instincts to publish a newsletter. When 500 people packed a seminar on a controversial new technology sweeping my industry, dollar signs danced in my head. I was on my way. Now, two and a half years later, I realize that what I was on my way to was becoming one of those small-business owners who list failure on their resumes.
>
> Incorporating my business was a major mistake because the expenses were more than I could afford. I did not find out until later that 76 percent of all small businesses operate as sole proprietorships. Although being a corporation protected me in case of a lawsuit, I got a shock when my accountant pointed out the disadvantages of incorporation in the heavily taxed, heavily regulated nation's capital. Now I realize that incorporating is good for a company when raising capital is an essential part of the ongoing business. Real estate and construction are two examples that come to mind. But a service business, which relies mostly on money put up by the people involved, would be better operated as a sole proprietorship or partnership.[2] ◆

For Beth and Drexel Wright, however, a sole proprietorship was disastrous. Mr. Wright was the founder and sole proprietor of Quaker Siding Co., a construction and remodeling business in Millville, Pennsylvania. Within a year of their marriage, the Wrights went into bankruptcy proceedings. Because the company was a sole proprietorship, the court liquidated many of their personal assets—farm equipment, cattle, vehicles, rental properties—to pay creditors. For a time, they were afraid they might even lose their home. Four years later, the Wrights reached an agreement with their creditors and were allowed out of bankruptcy. They immediately incorporated their business as Quaker Construction Services, Inc.

GENERAL PARTNERSHIPS

A partnership is an unincorporated association of two or more co-owners who carry on a business for profit.[3] Each co-owner is called a *general partner.*

Liability

Each partner is personally liable for the debts of the enterprise whether or not she caused them. Thus a partner is liable for any injury that another partner or an employee causes while on partnership business as well as for any contract signed on behalf of the partnership. This form of organization can be particularly risky if the group of owners is large and the partners do not know each other.

---

[2] Judith Gross, "Autopsy of a Business," *Home Office Computing,* Oct. 1993, vol. 11, no. 10, p. 52. Reprinted with permission.

[3] Uniform Partnership Act §6(1).

Daniel Matter knows firsthand about the risks of a partnership. A former partner in the accounting firm Pannell Kerr Foster, he thought he had heard the last of the firm when he resigned his partnership. He was wrong. *Seven* years later, he and 260 other former partners of the California firm were served with a 78-page lawsuit seeking $24 million in damages. The lawsuit alleged that Pannell Kerr had been negligent in preparing financial reports for a bankrupt Tennessee savings and loan. Although Daniel Matter had never worked for that particular client, he was potentially liable because he had been a partner when the audit was done. At age 53, Matter feared losing everything he owned.

Management

As many law, accounting, and consulting firms have grown larger, they have discovered another disadvantage to partnerships: management can be difficult. In theory, all partners in a firm are equal and have an equal right to share in management. When two sisters-in-law form a small accounting firm, they can easily discuss business issues—from hiring a new associate to choosing a brand of telephone. But when the partnership has 1,000 accountants speaking four different languages on three continents, consultation becomes difficult. Although most large firms authorize a management committee to make day-to-day decisions, other partners may still expect to be consulted. One partner in a law firm complained bitterly when all 163 partners were assembled to vote on the style of ceiling tile for the conference room. Yet, to be fair, the managing partner had called for the vote because everyone had complained when he changed the typeface on the firm's stationery without consulting them.

Transfer of Ownership

Financing a partnership may be difficult because the firm cannot sell shares as a corporation does. The capital needs of the partnership must be provided by contributions from partners or by borrowing. Likewise, a partner only has the right to transfer the *value* of her partnership interest, not the interest itself. She cannot, for example, transfer the right to participate in firm management. Take the case of Evan and his mother. She is a partner in the immensely profitable McBain Consulting firm. She dies, leaving him an orphan with no siblings. He overcomes his grief as best he can and goes to her office on the next Monday to take over her job and her partnership. Imagine his surprise when her partners tell him that, as her sole heir, he can inherit the *value* of her partnership, but not the partnership itself. He is out on the sidewalk within the hour. The partners have promised him a check in the mail.

---

at RISK

If a partner decides to leave a partnership, he is typically entitled to his share of the value of the partnership. But how does the partnership determine that value? Often with great difficulty. The departing person is in the odd position of arguing that, although he no longer cares to be a partner, the business is nonetheless immensely valuable. Naturally, the partnership asserts the opposite. It is wise, therefore, for partners to agree in advance how a partnership interest will be valued when a partner leaves (or dies). A typical agreement might specify a formula for calculating the value as well as a mechanism for resolving disputes. ◆

Dissociation

When a partner quits, that event is called a *dissociation*. A dissociation is a fork in the road: the partnership can either buy out the departing partner(s) and continue in business or wind up the business and terminate the partnership. Most large firms provide in their partnership agreement that, upon dissociation, the business continues.

Formation

Given the disadvantages, why does anyone do business as a partnership? Like sole proprietorships, partnerships are easy to form. Although a partnership should have a written agreement, it is perfectly legal without one (a sample agreement is available at http://biz.findlaw.com/bookshelf/sblg/sblgchp3_h1.html). In fact, nothing is required in the way of forms or filings or agreements. The partnership simply needs at least two people who share in the management and profits. Forming a partnership is so easy that sometimes people do so without knowing it, but that is a story for the next chapter.

A partnership has an important advantage over a sole proprietorship—partners. Sole proprietors are on their own; partners have colleagues to help them and, equally important, to supply capital for the business. Sole proprietorships often turn into partnerships for exactly this reason.

Taxes

A partnership is not a taxable entity, which means it does not pay taxes itself. All income and losses are passed through to the partners and reported on their personal income tax returns. Corporations, by contrast, are taxable entities and pay income tax on their profits. Shareholders must then pay tax on dividends from the corporation. Thus a dollar is taxed only once before it ends up in a partner's bank account, but twice before it is deposited by a shareholder.

Exhibit 32.1 compares the single taxation of partnerships with the double taxation of corporations. Suppose, as shown in the exhibit, that a corporation and a partnership each receive $10,000 in additional income. The corporation pays tax at a top rate of 35 percent.[4] Thus the corporation pays $3,500 of the $10,000 in tax. The corporation pays out the remaining $6,500 as a dividend of $2,167 to each of its three shareholders.

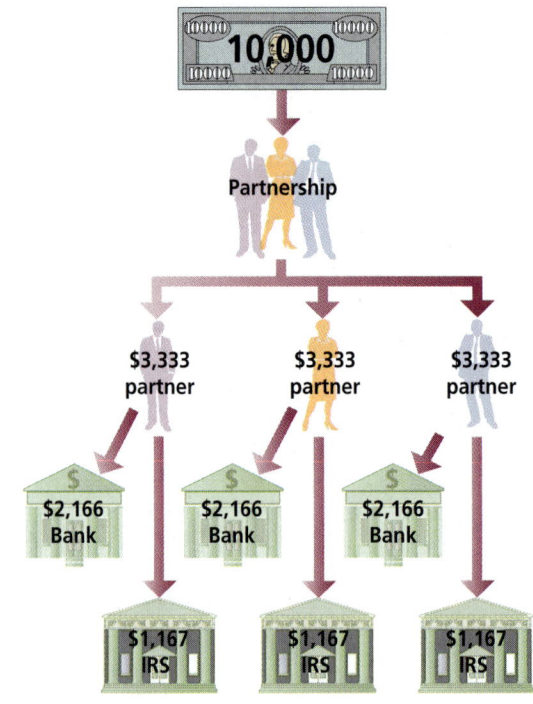

Exhibit 32.1

---

[4] This is the federal tax rate; most states also levy a corporate tax.

Then the shareholders are taxed at the special dividend rate of 15 percent, which means they each pay a tax of $325. They are each left with $1,842. Of the initial $10,000, almost 45 percent ($4,475) has gone to the Internal Revenue Service (IRS).

Compare the corporation to a partnership. The partnership itself pays no taxes, so it can pass on $3,333 to each of its partners. At a 35 percent individual rate, they will each pay an income tax of $1,167. As partners, they pocket $2,166, which is $324 more than they could keep as shareholders. Of the partnership's initial $10,000, 35 percent ($3,501) has gone to the IRS—compared with the corporation's 45 percent.

LIMITED LIABILITY PARTNERSHIPS

A limited liability partnership (LLP) is a type of general partnership that most states now permit. There is a very important distinction, however, between these two forms of organization: **in an LLP, the partners are not liable for the debts of the partnership.**[5] To form an LLP, the partners must file a statement of qualification with state officials. LLPs must also file annual reports. The other attributes of a partnership remain the same. Thus, an LLP is not a taxable entity and it has the right to choose its duration (that is, it can, but does not have to, survive the dissociation of a member).

Although an LLP can be much more advantageous for partners than a general partnership, the following case provides an important warning: it is essential to comply with all the technicalities of the LLP statute.

APCAR V. GAUS

2005 Tex. App. LEXIS 379
Court of Appeals of Texas, 2005

Facts: Smith & West, LLP had two partners: Michael L. Gaus and John C. West. The partnership registered in Texas as a limited liability partnership. The Texas statute requires LLPs to renew their registrations each year, but Smith & West never did so. Four years after its initial registration, the partnership entered into a lease with MF Partners, which subsequently assigned the lease to Apcar. Three years into the lease, Smith & West stopped paying rent and abandoned the premises. Apcar filed suit against the two partners individually and against the partnership. Gaus, West, and Apcar each filed a motion for summary judgment. The trial court granted Gaus and West's motions while denying Apcar's.

Issue: Were Gaus and West personally liable for payments due under Smith & West's lease?

Excerpts from Judge McCall's Decision: [The Texas Limited Liability Partnership statute] provides:

An initial application filed under this subsection and registered by the secretary of state expires one year after the date of registration or later effective date unless earlier withdrawn or revoked or unless renewed.

Smith & West did not file a renewal application before the expiration date. Therefore, its status as a registered limited liability partnership expired [one year after the initial filing]. Smith & West entered into the lease three years after its status as a registered limited liability partnership expired.

Smith & West was not a registered limited liability partnership when it incurred the lease obligations. Thus, the clear language [of the statute] supports Apcar's position that Gaus and West are not protected from individual liability for the lease obligations.

Gaus and West argue that a limited liability partnership is not required to strictly comply with the registration requirements for its partners to be protected from individual liability. [But the statute] does not contain a "substantial compliance" section, nor does it contain a grace period for filing a renewal ▼

---

[5] UPA §306(c).

application. We hold that a partnership must be in compliance with the registration requirements for its partners to receive protection from individual liability. Smith & West was not a registered limited liability partnership when it incurred the lease obligations; therefore, Gaus and West are not protected from individual liability for the lease obligations.

The judgment of the trial court is reversed, and this cause is remanded for further proceedings consistent with this opinion. ■

PROFESSIONAL CORPORATIONS

Most states now allow professionals to incorporate, but in a special way. These organizations are called "professional corporations" or "PCs." **In many states, PCs provide more liability protection than a general partnership.** If a member of a PC commits malpractice, the corporation's assets are at risk, but not the personal assets of the innocent members. If Drs. Sharp, Payne, and Graves form a *partnership*, all the partners will be personally liable when Dr. Payne accidentally leaves her scalpel inside a patient. If the three doctors have formed a *PC* instead, Dr. Payne's Aspen condo and the assets of the PC will be at risk, but not the personal assets of the two other doctors.

Generally, the shareholders of a PC are not personally liable for the contract debts of the organization, such as leases or bank loans. Thus, if Sharp, Payne & Graves, P.C. is unable to pay its rent, the landlord cannot recover from the personal assets of any of the doctors. As partners, the doctors would be personally liable.

PCs have some limitations. First, all shareholders of the corporation must be members of the same profession. For Sharp, Payne & Graves, P.C., that means all shareholders must be licensed physicians. Other valued employees cannot own stock. Second, like other corporations, the required legal technicalities for forming and maintaining a PC are expensive and time-consuming. Third, tax issues can be complicated. A PC is a separate taxable entity, like any other corporation. It must pay tax on its profits, and then its shareholders pay tax on any dividends they receive. *Salaries*, however, are deductible from firm profits. Thus the PC can avoid taxes on its profits by paying out all profits as salary. But any profits remaining in firm coffers *at the end of the year* are taxable. To avoid tax, PCs must be careful to calculate their profits accurately and pay them out before year's end. This chore can be time-consuming, and any error may cause unnecessary tax liability.

LIMITED PARTNERSHIPS AND LIMITED LIABILITY LIMITED PARTNERSHIPS

The owners of the Montreal Expos asked investment banker Jacques Menard to find a buyer for the baseball team. Instead, he found 11 other people to help him buy the team. They formed a limited partnership, and each purchaser invested between $1 million and $7 million. During their first year of ownership, the Expos lost nearly $5 million and their final 14 home games, finishing in the cellar of their division. Given this dismal showing, management had no choice but to fire the popular team manager. Then a concrete beam in the team's stadium collapsed.

Fortunately, the owners had formed a *limited* partnership. Limited partnerships and general partnerships have similar names but, like many siblings, they operate very differently. Here are the major differences between these two types of organizations.

Structure

General partnerships have only *general* partners. Limited partnerships have two types of partners—*limited* partners and *general* partners. A limited partnership must have at least one of each.

Liability

All the partners in a general partnership are *personally* liable for the debts of the partnership. **In a limited partnership, however, the limited partners are not *personally* liable.** The limited partners are like corporate shareholders—they risk only their investment in the partnership (which is called their "capital contribution"). No matter how much money the Expos lost, creditors could not take the personal property of the limited partners.

The Montreal Expos are owned by a limited partnership.

General partners are personally liable for the debts of a limited partnership. To avoid this liability, most general partners are, in fact, corporations. Thus Claude Brochu, the Expos' general manager, could form a corporation—Brochu, Inc.—to serve as general partner. Then, only the assets of the corporation, not Brochu's personal assets, would be at risk.

The revised version of the Uniform Limited Partnership Act, however, permits a limited partnership, in its certificate of formation, simply to declare itself a *limited liability* limited partnership.[6] **In a limited liability limited partnership, the general partner is not personally liable for the debts of the partnership.** This provision effectively removes the major disadvantage of limited partnerships. Although, at this writing, fewer than 10 states have actually passed the revised version of the Uniform Limited Partnership Act, this revision would seem to indicate the trend for the future.

Taxes

Limited partnerships, like general partnerships, are not taxable entities. Income is taxed only once before landing in a partner's pocket.

Formation

General partnerships can be formed very casually, sometimes without the partners even being aware of it. Not so for limited partnerships: the general partners must file a **certificate of limited partnership** with their Secretary of State. Although most limited partnerships do have a partnership agreement, it is not required. (A sample limited partnership agreement is available at **http://www.worldlawdirect.com/builddoc.php**.)

Management

General partners have the right to manage a limited partnership. Limited partners are essentially passive investors with few management rights beyond the right to be

---

[6] ULPA §102(9).

informed about the partnership business. Limited partnership agreements can, however, expand the rights of limited partners. These agreements, for example, often permit a substantial majority (i.e., two-thirds) of the limited partners to remove a general partner. In any event, when *general* partnerships grow large, management becomes difficult. But because *limited* partners are not allowed to manage, a limited partnership can handle a very large number of partners.

Transfer of Ownership

As is the case with a general partnership, limited partners always have the right to transfer the *value* of their partnership interest, but they can only sell or give away the interest itself if the partnership agreement permits. Thus, if Sadie is a limited partner in the Expos, but decides to invest in basketball instead, she does not have the automatic right to sell her limited partnership interest to Pedro. Although she could sell Pedro the right to receive profit distributions from the Expos, he would not *be* a limited partner, with the right to vote in meetings.

Duration

Unless the partnership agreement provides otherwise, limited partnerships enjoy perpetual existence—they continue even as partners come and go.

Although a limited partnership structure protected the Expos' owners from liability, it did not solve the team's problems on the ball field or at the bank. Perhaps the team's move to Washington, D.C. (and its transformation into the Washington Nationals) will bring athletic and financial success.

CORPORATIONS

Although the concept of a corporation is very old—it began with the Greeks and spread from them through the Romans into English law—corporations were traditionally viewed with deep suspicion. What were shareholders doing that they needed limited liability? Why did they have to cower behind a corporate shield? For this reason, shareholders originally had to obtain special permission to form a corporation. In England, corporations could be created only by special charter from the king or, later, from Parliament. But with the advent of the Industrial Revolution, large-scale manufacturing enterprises needed huge amounts of capital from investors who were not involved in management and did not want to be personally liable for the debts of an organization that they were not managing. In 1811, New York became the first jurisdiction in the United States to permit routine incorporation.[7]

State laws regulate corporations, but federal statutes determine their tax status. Many states treat small corporations differently and even give them a different name: close corporations. The federal tax code also provides more favorable tax treatment to some small corporations and calls them S corporations. But the two sets of statutes are completely independent. Thus a close corporation or a regular (nonclose) corporation may or may not be an S corporation. Exhibit 32.2 illustrates the difference between state and IRS regulation of corporations.

---

[7] An Act Relative to Incorporation for Manufacturing Purpose, 1811 N.Y. Laws, ch. 67, §111.

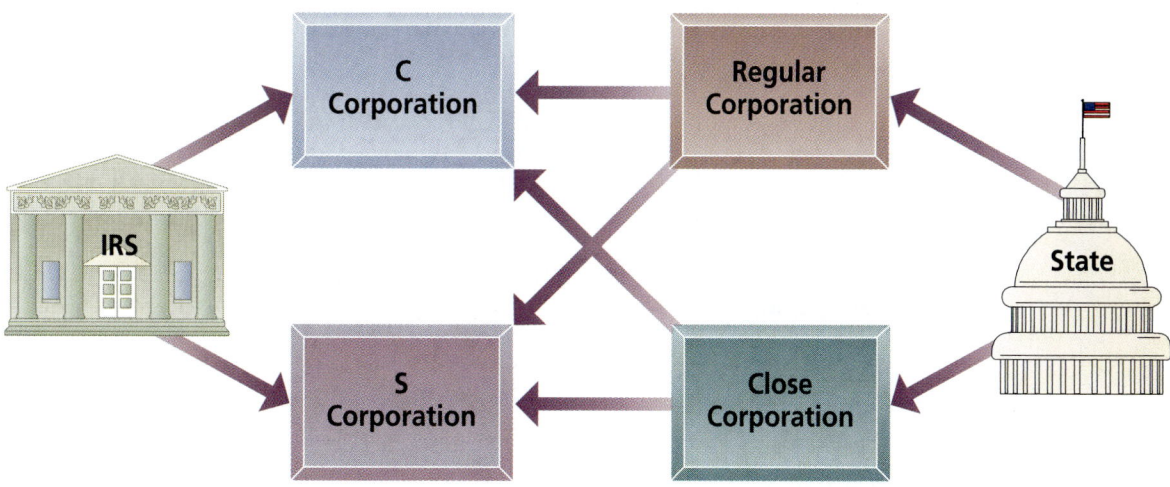

Exhibit 32.2
Both a regular and a close corporation can be either a C or an S corporation.

Corporations in General

When Judy George was a young child, her parents started a plating business using a process her father had invented. Like many entrepreneurs, her parents devoted so much time and energy to this new project that they were rarely at home. Feeling abandoned by her parents, George became obsessed with her surroundings. If she could make her room just the way she wanted it, she would feel safe. As she put it, "Design was a way of fulfilling my own personal fantasy." She also vowed that one day she would start her own business to make money and create beautiful designs. George realized her dream when she started Domain, an upscale, European-style chain of furniture stores.

George's lawyer suggested that she incorporate Domain. He explained that a corporation would offer the protection of limited liability. If Domain flopped, and could not pay its bills, George and her backers would lose their investment in the company, but not their other assets.

He also explained that limited liability does not protect against all debts. Individuals are always responsible for their *own* acts. If a Domain employee was in an accident while driving a company van, Domain would be liable for any harm to the other driver, but its shareholders would not be personally liable. If George herself crashed the van, Domain would be liable, and *so would George*. If Domain did not pay the judgment, George would have to, from her personal assets if necessary. A corporation protects managers and investors from personal liability for the debts of the corporation and the actions of others, but not against personal negligence (or other torts and crimes).

Corporations have other advantages besides limited liability. They provide flexibility for enterprises small (with one owner) and large (thousands of shareholders). For example, partnership interests are not transferable without the permission of the other partners, whereas corporate stock can be easily bought and sold. Further, when a sole proprietor dies, legally so does the business. But corporations have perpetual existence: they can continue without their founders.

There are two major disadvantages of a corporation: logistics and taxes. Corporations require substantial expense and effort to create and operate. Because corporations are taxable entities, they must pay taxes and file returns. The cost of establishing a corporation may exceed $1,000 in legal and filing fees, not to mention the cost of the annual filings that states require. Corporations must also hold annual meetings for both shareholders and directors. Minutes of these meetings must be kept indefinitely in the company minute book.

Judy George knew that she needed at least $3 million to get Domain up and running. She could not borrow that much money, so she needed to sell stock. She chose the corporate form of organization because, at the time she formed Domain, limited liability companies (LLCs) were not as well known or as well understood by potential investors as they are now. (LLCs are discussed later in this chapter.)

Close Corporations

Although most entrepreneurs would now choose to form an LLC rather than a close corporation, it is important to understand the legal contours of close corporations simply because so many still exist. Originally, the terms **"close corporation"** and **"closely held corporation"** referred simply to a company whose stock was not publicly traded on a stock exchange (in other words, a "privately held" company). Most close corporations are small, although some privately held corporations, such as Hallmark Cards, Inc., and Mars, Inc. (maker of Mars candy bars), are huge. Beginning in New York in 1948, some states amended their corporation statutes to make special provisions for entrepreneurs. In some cases, a corporation must affirmatively elect to be treated as a close corporation; in others, any corporation can take advantage of these special provisions. Now when lawyers refer to close corporations, they usually mean not merely a privately held company, but one that has taken advantage of the close corporation provisions of its state code.

Although the provisions of close corporation statutes vary from state to state, they tend to have certain common themes:

- **Protection of Minority Shareholders.** As there is no public market for the stock of a close corporation, a minority shareholder who is being mistreated by the majority cannot simply sell his shares and depart. Therefore, close corporation statutes often provide some protection for minority shareholders. For example, the charter of a close corporation could require a unanimous vote of all shareholders to choose officers, set salaries, or pay dividends. It could grant each shareholder veto power over all important corporate decisions.

- **Transfer Restrictions.** The shareholders of a close corporation often need to work closely together in the management of the company. Therefore, statutes typically permit the corporation to require that a shareholder first offer shares to the other owners before selling them to an outsider. In that way, the remaining shareholders have some control over who their new co-owners will be.

- **Flexibility.** Close corporations can typically operate without a board of directors, a formal set of bylaws, or annual shareholder meetings.

- **Dispute Resolution.** The shareholders are allowed to agree in advance that any one of them can dissolve the corporation if some particular event occurs or, if they choose, for any reason at all. If the shareholders are in a stalemate, the problem can be solved by dissolving the corporation. Even without such an agreement, a shareholder can ask a court to dissolve a close corporation if the other owners behave "oppressively" or "unfairly."

S Corporations

Although entrepreneurs are often optimistic about the likely success of their new enterprise, in truth, the majority of new businesses lose money in their early years. Congress created S corporations (aka "S corps") to encourage entrepreneurship by offering tax breaks. The name "S corporation" comes from the provision of the Internal Revenue Code that created this form of organization.[8] **Shareholders of S corps have both the limited liability of a corporation and the tax status of a partnership.** Like a partnership, an S corp is not a taxable entity—all of the company's profits and losses pass through to the shareholders, who pay tax at their individual rates. It avoids the double taxation of a regular corporation (called a "C corporation"). If, as is often the case, the start-up loses money, investors can deduct these losses against their other income.

S corps do face some major restrictions:

- There can be only one class of stock (although voting rights can vary within the class).

- There can be only 75 shareholders.

- Shareholders must be individuals, estates, charities, pension funds, or trusts, not partnerships or corporations.

- Shareholders must be citizens or residents of the United States, not non-resident aliens.

- All shareholders must agree that the company should be an S corporation.

Although *most* states follow the federal lead on S corporations, a small number treat an S corp like a regular C corporation. In these states, the companies must pay state corporate tax.

These rules governing S corps can be burdensome. Therefore, most companies do not remain S corps forever, and most entrepreneurs would choose an LLC over an S corp. However, S corps do have some advantages. The rules governing LLCs are not as established as those for S corps. Thus the process of organizing an LLC is less standardized and more expensive. Also, LLC statutes have changed rapidly and can vary dramatically from state to state. It is perhaps for these reasons that S corps are the single most popular choice of corporate entity. There are 3.2 million of them, with total assets that exceed $2 trillion. In contrast, there are only about 1 million LLCs.

LIMITED LIABILITY COMPANIES

Limited liability companies (LLCs) are a relatively new form of organization. Wyoming passed the first LLC statute in 1977 but most states did not follow suit until after 1991. **An LLC offers the limited liability of a corporation and the tax status of a partnership.**

An LLC is an extremely useful form of organization increasingly favored by entrepreneurs. It is not, however, as simple as it perhaps should be. Owing to a complex history that involves painful interaction between IRS regulations and state laws (the details of which we will spare you), the specific provisions of state laws vary greatly. An effort to remedy this confusion—the Uniform Limited Liability Company Act—has not at this point been widely accepted and, in fact, has been heavily criticized. Thus, we can only discuss general trends in state laws. Before forming an LLC, you should carefully review the laws in your particular state.

---

[8] 26 U.S.C. §1361.

Formation

To organize an LLC, you generally need two documents: a charter and an operating agreement. The charter is short, containing basic information such as name and address. It must be filed with the Secretary of State in the jurisdiction. An operating agreement sets out the rights and obligations of the owners, called members. If an LLC does not adopt its own operating agreement, most LLC statutes provide a default option. However, these standardized provisions are usually not what members would choose if they thought about it. Therefore, it is often better for an LLC to prepare its own personalized operating agreement. A sample agreement is shown at http://www.tannedfeet.com/simple_operating_Agreement_for_llc.doc.

Limited Liability

As in a corporation, members are not personally liable for debts of the company. They risk only their investment, just as they would if they were shareholders of a corporation. Are the members of an LLC liable in the following case? You be the judge.

you Be The Judge

RIDGAWAY V. SILK

2004 Conn. Super. LEXIS 548
Superior Court of Connecticut, 2004

Facts: Norman Costello and Joseph Ruggiero were members of Silk, LLC, the owner of Silk Stockings and Cafe Del Mar, which was a bar and adult entertainment nightclub in Groton, Connecticut. Anthony Sulls went drinking there one night—and drinking heavily. Although he was obviously drunk, employees at Silk Stockings continued to serve him. Giordano and Costello were working there that night. They both greeted customers (who numbered in the hundreds), supervised employees, and performed "other PR work." When Sulls left the nightclub at 1:45 A.M. with two friends, he drove off the highway at high speed, killing himself and one of his passengers, William Ridgaway, Jr.

Ridgaway's estate sued Costello and Giordano personally. The defendants filed a motion for summary judgment seeking dismissal of the complaint.

You Be the Judge: Are Costello and Giordano personally liable to Ridgaway's estate?

Argument for Costello and Giordano: The defendants did not own Silk Stockings, they were simply members of an LLC that owned the nightclub. The whole point of an LLC is to protect members against personal liability. The assets of Silk, LLC, are at risk, but not the personal assets of Costello and Giordano.

Argument for Ridgaway's Estate: The defendants are not liable for being *members* of Silk, LLC, they are liable for their own misdeeds as *employees* of the LLC. They were both present at Silk Stockings on the night in question, meeting and greeting customers and supervising employees. It is possible that they might actually have served drinks to Sulls, but in any event they did not adequately supervise and train their employees so as to prevent them from serving alcohol to someone who was clearly drunk. The world would be an intolerable place to live if employees were free to be as careless as they wished, knowing that they were not liable because they were members of an LLC. ■

Tax Status

As in a partnership, income flows through the company to the individual members, avoiding the double taxation of a corporation.

Flexibility

Unlike S corporations, LLCs can have members that are corporations, partnerships, or nonresident aliens. LLCs can also have different classes of stock. Unlike corporations, LLCs are not required to hold annual meetings or maintain a minute book.

Standard Forms

Corporations are so familiar that the standard documents (such as a charter, by-laws, and shareholder agreement) are well established and widely available. Lawyers can form a corporation easily and the Internet offers a host of free forms. This is not the case with LLCs. As yet, there are no standard forms to make the formation of an LLC both easy and inexpensive. With state laws varying so widely, standard forms may even be dangerous.

Transferability of Interests

In corporations, shareholders can generally sell or give their shares to whomever they want. In partnerships, partners generally must obtain the unanimous approval of the other partners before transferring their partnership interest. In keeping with the flexible approach of LLCs, members have a choice. If they want, the operating agreement can give them the right to transfer their interests freely to anyone. However, if the operating agreement is silent on this issue, then typically the members of the LLC must obtain the unanimous permission of the remaining members before transferring their ownership rights.

Duration

It used to be that LLCs automatically dissolved upon the withdrawal of a member (owing to, for example, death, resignation, or bankruptcy). The current trend in state laws, however, is to permit an LLC to continue in operation even after a member withdraws. Unless the operating agreement provides otherwise, the LLC must usually pay the departing member the value of her interest.

Going Public

Once an LLC goes public, it loses its favorable tax status and is taxed as a corporation, not a partnership.[9] Thus, there is no real advantage to using the LLC form of organization for a publicly traded company. And there are some disadvantages: unlike corporations, LLCs do not enjoy a well-established set of statutory and case law that is relatively consistent across the many states. For this reason, it may well turn out that most privately held companies begin as LLCs but change to corporations when they go public.

Changing Forms

Some companies that are now corporations might prefer to be LLCs. However, the IRS would consider this change to be a sale of the corporate assets, and would levy a tax on the value of these assets. For this reason, few corporations have made the change. However, switching from a partnership to an LLC or from an LLC to a corporation is not considered a sale and does not have the same adverse tax impact.

---

[9] 26 U.S.C. §7704.

JOINT VENTURES

NEWSworthy

Ckrush Entertainment, Inc. announced today that it has entered into a joint venture with Identity Films, LLC. Ckrush and Identity formed "Identity Films & Company, LLC" for the purpose of, among other things, developing, financing, and producing feature films. Ckrush is obligated to contribute overhead financing to the joint venture and it is anticipated that Identity will contribute approximately twelve film properties in various stages of development. Lisa Fielding and Anthony Mastromauro, of Identity Films, will be responsible for the day-to-day management of the joint venture. Jeremy Dallow and Jim DiLorenzo of Ckrush Entertainment will serve as officers of the joint venture along with Fielding and Mastromauro.

"We believe that the joint venture and the formation of Identity Films & Company is a real milestone for Ckrush Entertainment, Inc. We feel that this joint venture gives Ckrush Entertainment the opportunity to participate in a number of quality film projects alongside Lisa Fielding and Anthony Mastromauro. It is our position that the slate of properties currently in development and production are outstanding. We further feel that the joint venture is positioned to execute on these properties and can result in the growth of Identity Films & Company in the film business," said Jim DiLorenzo, President of Ckrush Entertainment.

"We are thrilled beyond our expectations to be in business with Ckrush. We have the opportunity to not only work with people we respect but to truly grow our company into a presence in the film business. We're coming into this joint venture knowing that producing award-winning films will be the first item on our agenda. Fortune has smiled on Identity Films," said Lisa Fielding of Identity Films, LLC.[10] ◆

© WENN/LANDOV

Identity Films is not liable on a contract between Ckrush Entertainment and Chris Rock because the contract is not related to the limited purpose of their joint venture.

This newspaper article refers to a joint venture between Identity Films and Ckrush Entertainment. **A joint venture is a partnership for a limited purpose.** Ckrush and Identity are not merging; they are simply working together on some movies. Each organization retains its own identity (so to speak). If they had joined in a full-scale partnership, both parties would be bound by contracts that any one of them signed. In a joint venture, only contracts relating to the limited purpose are binding on both. If Ckrush Entertainment signed a contract with Chris Rock to make a boxing movie, Identity Films would not be liable on that contract. But if the joint venture enters into a contract with Jennifer Aniston to star in a movie, both Ckrush and Identity would be liable. Nonprofit enterprises do not qualify as joint ventures—the purpose, however limited, must include making a profit.

OTHER FORMS OF ORGANIZATION

When starting a business, most entrepreneurs choose one of the forms of organization that we have discussed. There are, however, an assortment of other, less common forms that we must briefly cover—not so much because you are likely to use one of them yourself, but so that you will know what they are if you come across them in your business life or in reading the newspaper.

---

[10] "Ckrush Entertainment, Inc. Closes on Joint Venture with Identity Films," Business Wire, July 5, 2005.

Business Trusts

A business trust is an unincorporated association run by trustees for the benefit of investors (who are called "beneficiaries"). This arrangement sounds like an unfavorable one for investors. They buy certificates in the trust, just as shareholders buy stock in a corporation, but they have fewer rights than shareholders. They do not elect the trustees; if a trustee resigns or dies, the other trustees choose a replacement. The trustees can take almost any action without approval of the investors and can issue an unlimited number of shares. The beneficiaries are not liable for the debts of the trust. Theoretically, the trustees are liable, but the trust agreement usually protects them from liability.

Ordinary businesses usually do not consider this form of organization, but it does make sense for mutual funds and other investment management companies. Investors buy shares or certificates in the trust. The trustees, who are investment experts, invest the funds, paying out any returns to the investors, minus management fees. If investors are unhappy with a fund's performance, they do not have the right to vote out the trustees, but they can sell their shares and take their money elsewhere. It would be difficult to run an investment company if the beneficiaries were always changing trustees and investment style. A mutual fund is the one type of investment where it makes sense that investors *cannot* replace trustees.

Cooperatives

Cooperatives are groups of individuals or businesses that join together to gain the advantages of volume purchases or sales. Profits are distributed to members using whatever formula they choose. Unincorporated cooperatives are generally subject to partnership law; incorporated cooperatives are governed by corporation law.

NEWS*worthy*

For example, the Harvard Cooperative Society is the oldest retail cooperative in the country. Founded in 1882 by Harvard students aiming to undercut price-gouging local merchants, the Coop (rhymes with "hoop") originally sold just textbooks and firewood. It has long since outgrown its first location—a five-foot shelf in a local tobacco store. Now the Coop is a landmark in Harvard Square, selling textbooks, clothing, and dorm supplies. Owned by its members, who are primarily students and alumni of Harvard and MIT, its sales exceed $40 million a year. ◆

FRANCHISES

This chapter has presented an overview of the various forms of organization. Franchises are not, strictly speaking, a separate form of organization. They are included here because they represent an important option for entrepreneurs. In the United States, 1 in 12 small businesses is a franchise. Franchises generate sales of close to $1 trillion each year and provide jobs for more than eight million people. Well-known franchises include Dunkin' Donuts, McDonald's, and Mail Boxes Etc. Most franchisors and franchisees are corporations, although they could legally choose to be any of the forms discussed in this chapter.

Buying a franchise is a compromise between starting one's own business as an entrepreneur and working for someone else as an employee. Franchisees are free to choose which franchise to buy, where to locate it, and how to staff it. But they are not completely on their own. They are buying an established business with all the kinks worked out. In case the owner has never boiled water before, the McDonald's operations manual explains everything from how to set the temperature controls on the stove, to the number of seconds that fries must cook, to the length of time they can be held in the rack before being discarded. And a well-known name like McDonald's or Mrs. Fields ought, by itself, to bring customers through the door.

There is, however, a fine line between being helpful and being oppressive. Franchisees sometimes complain that franchisor control is too tight—tips on cooking fries might be appreciated, but rules on how often to sweep the floor are not. Sometimes franchisors, in their zeal to maintain standards, prohibit innovation that appeals to regional tastes. Just because spicy biscuits are not popular in New England does not mean they should be banned in the South.

Franchises can be very costly to acquire, anywhere from several thousand dollars to several million. That fee is usually payable up front, whether or not a cookie or burger is ever sold. On top of the up-front fee, franchisees also pay an annual fee that is a percentage of *gross sales revenues,* not *profit.* Sometimes the fee seems to eat up all the profits. Franchisees also complain when they are forced to buy supplies from headquarters. In theory, the franchisors can purchase hamburger meat and paper plates more cheaply in bulk. On the other hand, the franchisees are a captive audience, and they sometimes allege that headquarters has little incentive to keep prices low. Franchisees also grumble when they are forced to contribute to expensive "co-op advertising" that benefits all the outlets in the region. The following article illustrates the good news—and bad—about buying a franchise.

NEWS*worthy*

Bellingham, Mass.—Stephen Gurwitz is proud that his Hilltop Farms convenience store has long been a fixture here in this small town on the Rhode Island border. His grandfather, Milton Gurwitz, opened the little roadside building in 1955 as a place to sell milk and eggs from his farm. His father, Gary Gurwitz, added a deli counter. Four years ago, Stephen converted half the store to a Subway fast-food franchise.

Mr. Gurwitz, 32, said he felt no shame at trading in the old deli counter for a nationally promoted name and formulaic sandwiches that taste the same as their Subway counterparts around the world. For Mr. Gurwitz, joining Subway was a welcome respite from the myriad decisions he has to make in running the convenience store. "They give you the operations manual, which is as thick as the New York City telephone book, and it tells you within a millimeter how thick to slice the onions," said Mr. Gurwitz.

Indeed, Mr. Gurwitz discovered that many issues were no longer his sole responsibility. "Someone stubs his toe in the store, you call the Subway legal department," he said. "How many convenience stores have a legal department?" Research and development, pricing and menus—all are handled for him. The Subway brand also brings name recognition. Mr. Gurwitz credits it with increasing the traffic in his store by about 1,000 customers a week— roughly a 10 percent gain—more than making up for the 11.5 percent of revenues from the sandwich operation he pays to headquarters.

It seems enticing, but Susan P. Kezios learned to be wary of such a deal. She put all her money into a franchise operation of VR Business Brokers in Chicago Heights, Ill. While she managed to keep the doors open, she struggled with what she calls "the flaws in the system." They began with the contract, which usually imposes an iron-clad form with no exceptions for a franchisee's particular needs.

"These franchise contracts are often legal works of art with franchisor attorneys determining every possible scenario during the entire length of time you'll own the franchise, to the franchisor's benefit—not yours," she said. When the contract comes up for renewal, the terms often change. "If they were taking a 5 percent royalty, they might change it to 8 percent," she said. Some franchisors force their licensees to purchase from certain vendors at inflated prices. They can open franchise units close by, intensifying competition. Franchisees often find it difficult to sell their businesses if they want out, or to open another business in the same industry because of "noncompete" agreements.

Although Subway allowed Mr. Gurwitz to stray from the standard menu by offering Willow Tree Farms chicken salad, a popular local brand, he has few other opportunities to personalize the business. Still, he said, that is all the sovereignty he needs. "If you're a free-spirited person and want to do it your own way," he advised, "you don't buy a franchise."[11] ◆

Although franchises were once relatively unregulated, the states and the federal government have dramatically increased their supervision and regulation of these businesses. The Federal Trade Commission (FTC) requires that, at least 10 business days prior to the sale, franchisors must give prospective franchisees an **offering circular.** This circular must comply either with FTC rules or with the provisions of the Uniform Franchise Offering Circular (UFOC) Guidelines of the North American Securities Administrators' Association (available at http://www.nasaa.org). Most franchisors choose to comply with the UFOC guidelines, because they are accepted by more states than the FTC rules. The circular must include the following information:

- Any litigation against the company
- Whether it has gone through bankruptcy proceedings in the prior 10 years
- All fees

- Estimates of the required initial investment
- What goods must be purchased from the franchisor
- The number of franchisees in operation
- How many franchisees have gone out of business in the prior three years

The offering circular must also contain audited financial statements and a sample set of the contracts that a franchisee is expected to sign.

The purpose of the offering circular is to ensure that the franchisor discloses all relevant facts. It is not a guarantee of quality. Under UFOC Guidelines, the following statement must appear on the cover page of the offering circular:

> Registration of this franchise by a state does not mean that the state recommends it or has verified the information in this offering circular. If you learn that anything in the offering circular is untrue, contact the Federal Trade Commission and (State or Provincial authority).

Because the franchise offering circular is not a guarantee of quality, you may end up needing more psychiatric care than the cats.

Suppose you obtain an offering circular for "Shrinking Cats," a franchise that offers psychiatric services for neurotic felines. The company has lost money on all the outlets it operates itself; it has sold only three franchises, two of which have gone out of business; and all the required contracts are ridiculously favorable to the franchisor. Nevertheless, the FTC will still permit sales as long as the franchisor discloses all the information required in the offering circular. Nor will the FTC investigate to make sure that the information is accurate. After the fact, if the FTC discovers the

---

[11] Julie Flaherty, "By the Book: Individuality vs. Franchising; Trading Spark of Creativity for the Safety of Numbers," New York Times, Feb. 17, 2001, §C, p. 1. Copyright © 2001 by The New York Times Co. Reprinted by permission.

franchisor has violated the rules, it may sue on your behalf. (You do not have the right to bring suit personally against someone who violates the FTC franchise rules.)

As we have seen, some states also regulate the sale of franchises. They often require franchisors to register and to provide offering circulars, but the franchisor can use the UFOC guidelines to meet the requirements of both the state and the FTC. The states that do regulate franchisors are often stricter than the FTC. Some states, for instance, require franchisors to file all advertisements ahead of time and meet minimum capital requirements. State laws may also prohibit unfair terms in the franchising contract. Unlike FTC rules, some states permit franchisees themselves to sue for damages or rescission anyone who violates franchise laws.

In the following case, a franchisee filed suit under the Illinois Franchise Disclosure Act.

BIXBY'S FOOD SYSTEMS, INC. V. MCKAY

193 F. Supp. 2d 1053, 2002 U.S. Dist. LEXIS 5243
United States District Court for the Northern District of Illinois, 2002

Fact: Phillip McKay was a dentist and his wife, Jan, worked for Ameritech. They were looking for a business to buy when a friend told them about Bixby's, a franchisor of bagel restaurants. This same friend introduced them to Ken Miyamoto, Bixby's president.

Miyamoto gave the McKays a franchise offering circular (FOC), which stated that the initial investment for a franchise, including the initial franchise fee, would be between $143,000 and $198,000. It also stated that, with a store space of between 1,400 and 2,200 square feet, each franchise would have annual sales of $625,000 and would earn an annual profit of $139,450. Miyamoto told the McKays that the FOC figures were conservative, that "existing bagel stores were doing annual sales in excess of $1 million," and that "Bixby's franchises would exceed these revenue figures."

The McKays purchased the right to own a Bixby's franchise. They found a 2,000-square-foot space for lease but Miyamoto urged them repeatedly to lease an additional space next door, for a total of more than 3,000 square feet. Miyamoto assured them that the site would bring in annual revenues in excess of $1 million. No other Bixby's restaurant nationwide was as large as 3,000 square feet.

At a reception that the McKays attended for existing and prospective Bixby's franchisees, Miyamoto told the guests that the company had 340 franchise agreements. In fact, the company had no more than 15 such agreements. Miyamoto was also quoted in a company newsletter as stating that Bixby's had 340

signed and paid-for agreements, which represented "a $68 million vote of confidence."

The McKays executed a lease for the 3,000-square-foot space and proceeded to renovate the property. Their initial investment was more than $400,000, significantly higher than the estimated investment of between $143,000 and $198,000 in the FOC. Miyamoto assured them that the FOC was accurate, their costs were normal, and that their sales would cover their costs. Miyamoto knew that these statements were false.

After the McKays opened their store, monthly sales ranged from $25,000 to $30,000, far less than Miyamoto had predicted. Because the McKays fell behind on their payments, Bixby's terminated their franchise agreement after only eight months.

Bixby's sued the McKays for violating the franchise agreement. The McKays counter-claimed against Bixby's, alleging that the company had violated the Illinois Franchise Disclosure Act (IFDA). They then filed a motion for summary judgment.

Issue: Did Bixby's violate the Illinois Franchise Disclosure Act?

Excerpts from Judge Nolan's Decision: The McKays claim that Miyamoto violated the IFDA by providing false information with respect to the franchise sale. The McKays relied on these representations when they executed their franchise agreement.

To be actionable under the IFDA, the misrepresentation must be an untrue statement of a material fact. A material fact is one in which a buyer would have acted differently knowing the information. In other words, the fact must be essential to the transaction between the parties.

A statement expressing an opinion or that relates to future or contingent events rather than to present facts, however, ordinarily does not constitute an actionable misrepresentation under Illinois law. For example, predictions of future sales or profitability are not considered representations of preexisting material facts.

The McKays have not shown that, contrary to the general rule, Miyamoto's statements about future events, costs, and profitability are actionable misrepresentations under the IFDA, so summary judgment cannot be granted based upon those statements.

The McKays have, however, conclusively shown that Miyamoto falsely claimed that Bixby's had 340 signed and paid-for agreements when no more than fifteen agreements had in fact been executed. Miyamoto's untrue statement was material to the McKays' decision to execute the Bixby's franchise agreement a week later. [T]herefore summary judgment should be granted as to the McKays' claim under the IFDA. ■

Chapter Conclusion

The process of starting a business is immensely time-consuming. Eighteen-hour days are the norm. Not surprisingly, entrepreneurs are sometimes reluctant to spend their valuable time on legal issues that, after all, do not contribute directly to the bottom line. No customer buys more biscuits because the franchise is a limited liability company instead of a corporation. Wise entrepreneurs know, however, that careful attention to legal issues is an essential component of success. The form of organization affects everything from taxes to liability to management control. The idea for the business may come first, but legal considerations occupy a close second place.

Chapter Review

	Separate Taxable Entity	Personal Liability for Owners	Ease of Formation	Transferable Interests (Easily Bought and Sold)	Perpetual Existence	Other Features
Sole Proprietorship	No	Yes	Very easy	No, can only sell entire business	No	
General Partnership	No	Yes	Easy	No	Depends on the partnership agreement	Management can be difficult.
Limited Liability Partnership	No	No	Difficult	No	Depends on the partnership agreement	
Professional Corporation	Yes	No	Difficult	Shareholders must all be members of same profession	Yes, as long as it has shareholders	Complex tax issues.

	Separate Taxable Entity	Personal Liability for Owners	Ease of Formation	Transferable Interests (Easily Bought and Sold)	Perpetual Existence	Other Features
Limited Partnership	No	Yes, for general partner No, for limited partners	Difficult	Yes (for limited partners), if partnership agreement permits	Yes	
Limited Liability Limited Partnership	No	No	Difficult	Yes (for limited partners), if partnership agreement permits	Yes	
Corporation	Yes	No	Difficult	Yes	Yes	
Close Corporation	Yes, for C corporation No, for S corporation	No	Difficult	Transfer restrictions	Yes	Protection of minority shareholders. No board of directors required.
S Corporation	No	No	Difficult	Transfer restrictions	Yes	Only 75 shareholders. Only one class of stock. Shareholders must be individuals, estates, trusts, charities, or pension funds and be citizens or residents of the United States. All shareholders must agree to S status.
Limited Liability Company	No	No	Difficult	Yes, if the operating agreement permits	Varies by state, but generally, yes	No limit on the number shareholders, the number of classes of stock, or the type of shareholder.
Joint Venture	No	Yes	Easy	No	No	Partnership for a limited purpose.
Business Trust	Yes	No	Difficult	Yes	Yes	Most commonly used by mutual funds and other investment companies.

	Separate Taxable Entity	Personal Liability for Owners	Ease of Formation	Transferable Interests (Easily Bought and Sold)	Perpetual Existence	Other Features
Cooperative	All these issues depend on the form of organization chosen by participants.					Groups of individuals or businesses that join together to gain the advantages of volume purchases or sales.
Franchise	All these issues depend on the form of organization chosen by participants.					Established business. Name recognition. Management assistance. Loss of control. Fees may be high.

Practice Test

1. **ETHICS** Lee McNeely told Hardee's officials that he was interested in purchasing multiple restaurants in Arkansas. A Hardee's officer assured him that any of the company-owned stores in Arkansas would be available for purchase. However, the company urged him to open a new store in Maumelle and sent him a letter estimating first-year sales at around $800,000. McNeely built the Maumelle restaurant, but gross sales the first year were only $508,000. When McNeely asked to buy an existing restaurant, a Hardee's officer refused, informing him that Hardee's rarely sold company-owned restaurants. The offering circular contained no misstatements, but McNeely brought suit alleging fraud in the sale of the Maumelle franchise. Does McNeely have a valid claim against Hardee's? Apart from the legal issues, did Hardee's officers behave ethically? Would they want their behavior to be publicized? Would they like to be treated this way themselves? Is all fair in love, war, and franchising?

2. **CPA QUESTION** Assuming all other requirements are met, a corporation may elect to be treated as an S corporation under the Internal Revenue Code if it has:

   a. Both common and preferred stockholders

   b. A partnership as a stockholder

   c. Seventy-five or fewer stockholders

   d. The consent of a majority of the stockholders

3. Under Delaware law, a corporation cannot appear in court without a lawyer, but a partnership can. Fox Hollow Ventures, Ltd., was a limited liability company. One of its employees, who was not a lawyer, appeared in court to represent the company. Does an LLC more closely resemble a partnership, which may represent itself in court, or a corporation, which requires representation by a lawyer?

4. Glenleigh Falls Development Co. was a limited liability company that hired architects John and Marion Zaugg to design a residential golf course. The Zauggs were to receive partial payment for their services plus part ownership in the LLC. Although the articles of organization had been filed with the Secretary of State in Ohio, the operating agreement had not yet been signed by the members. The Zauggs signed the agreement, but two of the original four members did not. The agreement provided that no member could voluntarily withdraw. When the LLC refused to pay the Zauggs' bill for architectural services, they withdrew from the LLC and filed suit, seeking payment of their bill. The LLC counterclaimed, alleging that the Zauggs had wrongfully withdrawn. Did the Zauggs have the right to withdraw?

5. Alan Dershowitz, a law professor famous for his wealthy clients (O. J. Simpson, Claus von Bulow, Leona Helmsley), joined with other lawyers to

open a kosher delicatessen, Maven's Court. Dershowitz met with greater success at the bar than in the kitchen—the deli failed after barely a year in business. One supplier sued for overdue bills. What form of organization would have been the best choice for Maven's Court?

6. *CPA QUESTION* A joint venture is a(an):

   a. Association limited to no more than two persons in business for profit

   b. Enterprise of numerous co-owners in a non-profit undertaking

   c. Corporate enterprise for a single undertaking of limited duration

   d. Association of persons engaged as co-owners in a single undertaking for profit

7. Mrs. Meadows opened a biscuit shop called The Biscuit Bakery. The business was not incorporated. Whenever she ordered supplies, she was careful to sign the contract in the name of the business, not personally: The Biscuit Bakery by Daisy Meadows. Unfortunately, she had no money to pay her flour bill. When the vendor threatened to sue her, Mrs. Meadows told him that he could only sue the business, because all the contracts were in the business's name. Will Mrs. Meadows lose her dough?

8. *YOU BE THE JUDGE* WRITING PROBLEM Cellwave was a limited partnership that applied to the Federal Communications Commission (FCC) for a license to operate cellular telephone systems. After the FCC awarded the license it discovered that, although all the limited partners had signed the limited partnership agreement, Cellwave had never filed its limited partnership certificate with the Secretary of State in Delaware. The FCC dismissed Cellwave's application on the grounds that the partnership did not exist when the application was filed. Did the FCC have the right to dismiss Cellwave's application? **Argument for Cellwave:** The limited partnership was effectively in existence as soon as the limited partners signed the agreement. The Secretary of State could not refuse to accept the certificate for filing; that was a mere formality. **Argument for the FCC:** When Cellwave applied for a license, it did not exist legally. Formalities matter.

9. Arnold and Judith Germain bought two franchises from My Pie International, Inc. They did not receive the franchise disclosure statement from My Pie until two years after the purchase. Did My Pie violate franchise law?

10. Leonard C. Blum, an attorney, was negligent in his representation of Louis Anthony, Sr. In settlement of Anthony's claim against him, Blum signed a promissory note for $10,400 on behalf of his law firm, an LLC. When the law firm did not pay, Anthony filed suit against Blum personally for payment of the note. Is a member personally liable for the debt of an LLC that was caused by his own negligence?

11. *ROLE REVERSAL* Draft a multiple-choice question that focuses on the difference between an LLC and an S corporation.

Internet Research Problem

At http://beatty.westbuslaw.com, the Federal Trade Commission provides information on enforcement cases it has brought against franchisors who violate FTC rules. Do you see a pattern? Are some violations more common than others? How can you avoid falling prey to an unsuitable franchise offering?

You can find further practice problems at http://beatty.westbuslaw.com or in the Study Guide that accompanies this text.

Partterships

C hase stood at the edge of a meadow near the top of the Porcupine Mountains in the Upper Peninsula of Michigan. The sun glistened off apple blossoms, birds called to each other, and the Lake of the Clouds stretched out to the horizon below. Chase had never been happier. As an architect, he believed in designing houses that blended with nature. Sharing his vision, Danielle had hired him to create a house for this perfect location. The large budget would allow Chase to realize many of his architectural beliefs. But he needed help—a landscape designer and a decorator who could work with the spectacular setting and his splendid design.

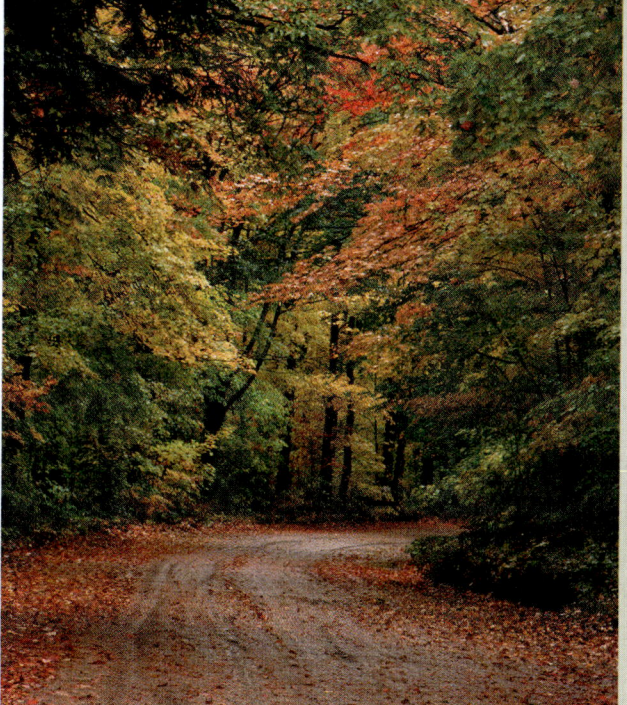

© PHOTO 24/ BRAND X PICUTRES/GETTY IMAGES

Bailey was Chase's choice for the interior design; she could create the sleek, warm look he sought. With Zack's landscape plan, the house would appear to be a natural part of the site. At their first meeting, all three designers committed to the project and rapidly agreed to a deal: Chase would receive 50 percent of the profits, Bailey and Zack 25 percent each. All three would have veto rights over the work of the other two. As the meeting ended, Chase poured glasses of sparkling water. "Here's to our new partnership. We'll build the most beautiful house in America," he said, rising to his feet. The three raised a toast to their success.

The honeymoon lasted only a few weeks. Chase and Bailey immediately fell out over the width of the hallways. Chase designed them unusually narrow to create a dramatic entrance into each room. But none of Bailey's antique Persian carpets would fit. When Bailey suggested consulting the owner, Chase blew up. "What do owners know?" he demanded. Zack sided with Bailey on that issue. But then both Chase and Bailey disagreed with Zack, who wanted to relocate the house to save some specimen trees. "Lose the view to save a few ratty old trees?" Bailey asked incredulously. Outvoted, Zack quit in disgust. Bailey and Chase began to suspect they were in trouble.

Their apprehension proved all too well founded. Outraged that her house was not finished on time, Danielle sued the three designers. When Chase protested that it was not *his* fault Zack quit, Danielle snarled into the phone, "I don't know and I don't care whose fault it is. All I know is that my house isn't ready. I'll see you and your partners in court!" Meanwhile, Zack was last spotted recuperating on Bora Bora, far from the reach of the U.S. legal system.

The plight of this threesome illustrates common partnership problems. Although Chase, Bailey, and Zack never signed an agreement or filed a form, they nonetheless had formed a partnership. Not only did they refer to themselves as partners, but they intended to share profits and co-manage the business. The partnership is liable to Danielle for any damages the delay caused. If the partnership does not have enough assets to pay, each of the partners is personally liable—even if the delay was totally Zack's fault. When Zack left before finishing the project, he wrongfully dissociated from the partnership. Chase and Bailey must pay him the value of his share of the partnership, but they can subtract from that total any damages he caused. If the damages are more than the value of his partnership share, he owes them money. But his former partners must pay Danielle, whether or not they can actually recover from Zack in Bora Bora.

INTRODUCTION

Partnerships have two important advantages: they do not pay taxes and they are easy to form.[1] Many professionals, such as accountants and lawyers, have traditionally favored this form of organization. Some of the rules can be complex, however, and, like any relationship, a partnership requires careful tending.

Traditionally, partnerships were regulated by common law, but a lack of consistency among the states became troublesome as interstate commerce grew. To solve this problem, the National Conference of Commissioners on Uniform State Laws proposed the Uniform Partnership Act (UPA) in 1914. Since then there have been several revisions,

---

[1] These issues are discussed at greater length in Chapter 32, on starting a business. Although the partnership itself does not pay taxes, each partner must pay taxes on his share of the partnership's profits.

the most recent in 1997. A majority of states have now passed the latest revisions, so we include them in our discussion of partnership law.

Although the UPA has made life easier, common law still plays an important role in regulating partnerships. To some degree, that is always true with statutes. No matter how well written they are, the courts are called upon to interpret some provisions. In addition, the UPA directs courts to apply common law to resolve any issue that they do not cover. Finally, many of the rules in the UPA are so-called **default rules,** meaning that they apply unless the partners reach a different agreement. When partners write their own rules, they must sometimes ask the courts to interpret ambiguous provisions.

CREATING A PARTNERSHIP

Some legal relationships are carefully delineated. By and large, people know whether or not they are married. Similarly, people usually know if they have formed a corporation. Partnerships are trickier, more like living together than getting married. It can be difficult to tell if a live-in relationship—or a partnership—really exists. The UPA does not require partnerships to prepare a written agreement or make a formal filing. (For examples of a partnership agreement, go to **http://www.lectlaw.com/formb.htm**. However, the UPA does permit a partnership to file a statement with the local Secretary of State that contains basic information about the partnership.[2]

How can you tell if you have a partnership? According to the UPA:

> **The association of two or more persons to carry on as co-owners a business for profit forms a partnership, whether or not the persons intend to form a partnership.**[3]

Note that a partnership is an association of two or more people. If only one person is involved in the business, it is a sole proprietorship, not a partnership.

Association

An "association" means a voluntary relationship. The law does not, however, require a formal agreement, either written or oral. Nor is a formal agreement enough on its own to create a partnership. In a partnership, actions speak louder than words. If the people act like partners, then the law will treat them as such. If they do not act like partners, then nothing they say or write will make them a partnership.

For example, Kevin and Brenda formed an electrical contracting business. The business did so well that Kevin's first wife, Cynthia, asked the court to increase his child support payments. Kevin argued that, because he and Brenda were partners, he was entitled to only half of the business's profits. Therefore, his child support should not be increased.

Cynthia claimed that Kevin and Brenda were *not* partners because Kevin had reported all the income from the business on his personal tax return while Brenda had reported none. Kevin had even put "sole proprietorship" in bold letters on the top of his return. No written partnership agreement existed. Kevin and Brenda never informed their accountant that they were a partnership. When Kevin answered interrogatories for Cynthia's lawsuit, he stated that he was sole owner and that Brenda

---

[2] UPA §105.
[3] UPA §202(a).

worked for him. Nonetheless, the court held that Brenda and Kevin were partners because Brenda helped manage the business and shared in its profits.[4]

In contrast, when Nancy Green borrowed money from Joseph DiFebo to make a down payment on four houses, they agreed that they were partners. Although Green bought the properties in her name alone, the two signed this document:

> Nancy R. Green and Joseph A. DiFebo are equal partners in the following Wilmington, Delaware, properties: 807 Pine Street, 427 East 3rd St., 611 East 7th Street, 613 East 7th Street.
>
> On the death of Nancy R. Green, her half interest is left to her daughters, Kelly R. Green and Stacy R. Green. On the death of Joseph A. DiFebo, his half interest is left to his daughters, Amy DiFebo and Beth Durham.
>
> If Nancy R. Green survives Joseph A. DiFebo she makes all decisions on the above properties.
>
> DiFebo did some repair work on the buildings, but never asked Green for a share of the rentals. When the city condemned one of the properties, Green refused to give DiFebo half the proceeds. DiFebo testified that, in his mind, the money he transferred to Green established a partnership between them. Green testified that at no time did she consider their arrangement to be a partnership.

The court was less concerned about what the agreement *said* than how the parties acted. Although they had called themselves "equal partners," they did not share profits. DiFebo said he had not taken his share of the profits because he did not want his wife to find out about his arrangements (financial and otherwise) with Green. Finding that their contract was a will, not a partnership agreement, the court denied DiFebo's claim.[5]

Co-Owners of a Business for Profit

As these cases demonstrate, a written agreement is neither necessary nor sufficient for creating a partnership. The following factors are crucial in determining whether a partnership exists:

- **To be a partnership, the participants must share profits.** Nancy Green and Joseph DiFebo may have signed a document declaring themselves to be partners, but because they did not share profits, they were not partners.

- **Partners share in the management of the business.** If participants are not involved in management, the courts will generally not consider them to be partners.

- **An agreement to share in losses is strong evidence of a partnership.** Although landlords, employees, and even creditors may share in business profits, usually no one other than a partner is willing to sign on for a share of the losses.

- **Referring to yourselves as partners is not enough to create a partnership, but in a close case, it may help sway a court.** In the *Green* case, the two litigants said in writing that they were partners, but that was not enough to persuade the court because other more important factors, such as profit sharing, were missing.

- **Charitable businesses are not partnerships.** When Aaron and Elijah agree to run the annual jamboree at their children's school, they expect to clear a profit of $35,000 after expenses, but they are not partners because their fund-raising has a charitable purpose.

In the following case, father and son could have avoided the entire drama if only they had decided earlier whether or not they were a partnership.

---

[4] *In re Marriage of Cynthia Hassiepen*, 269 Ill. App. 3d 559, 646 N.E.2d 1348, 1995 Ill. App. LEXIS 101.
[5] *Green v. Schagrin*, 1989 Del. Super. LEXIS 295.

you Be The Judge

RIGSBY V. RIGSBY

346 Ark. 337, 57 S.W.3d 206, 2001 Ark. LEXIS 580
Supreme Court of Arkansas, 2001

Facts: Harold Rigsby bought a piece of land on which he then lived in a mobile home with his son Brett. The two men had a falling out. Brett filed a complaint in court alleging that he and his father owned the land as partners. He also alleged that he and his father had been partners in a cattle business operated on the land. Brett asked for half the proceeds from the sale of the cattle. Harold filed a

Partnership property?

counterclaim asking that Brett be evicted from the property.

Both men testified that, at Brett's suggestion, the two of them had taken out a bank loan to build a house on the land. The loan was secured by a mortgage on the property. Brett agreed to make the monthly loan payments, while Harold offered to pay all other bills, including taxes, insurance, maintenance, utilities, and groceries. Brett first testified that he had made all the loan payments, but then admitted that his father had made a one-time principal payment of $4,000. Harold countered that he had also paid three and one-half of the monthly loan payments. He also claimed to have spent $6,230 for improvements to the house.

Brett testified:

Q. You put money into it with Harold's knowledge?
A. Correct.

Q. And what was your relationship with him? I think you said earlier that you thought you were partners on the cattle; how about in regards to the real estate?
A. It was my understanding—he told me to do what I wanted to do with it—some day it was all going to be mine anyway.

Brett further testified that he and his father ran the cattle operation together and that he (Brett) had spent a significant amount of money on it. On cross-examination, Brett did admit, however, that he worked daily at the Whirlpool Corporation from 7:00 A.M. until 3:42 P.M. Harold testified that he alone ran the cattle operation, but admitted that his son helped occasionally, such as taking care of the cattle while Harold was hospitalized.

Brett further testified that he had made substantial improvements to the land to take care of the cattle, including clearing parts of it, fertilizing it, erecting fences, and building a barn. On cross-examination, Brett admitted that he and his father sometimes disagreed about the necessity of those improvements, such as the building of a new barn. He said that his father tried to dissuade him from tearing down the old barn, and even offered to pay him not to build a new barn. Harold testified that he had no control over his son when it came to his desire to make improvements. According to Harold, Brett had undertaken many of the improvements, such as clearing the land and dredging a pond, to attract dove, deer, turkeys, and other wild game for hunting. Although Harold admitted that he had received some benefit from these improvements; he claimed he was not allowed to use the cleared land for his cattle until after hunting season was over.

The trial court found that the two men had formed a partnership for the house, but not for the cattle business. Both men appealed.

You Be the Judge: Were Harold and Brett Rigsby partners? For the land? For the cattle business?

Argument for Brett: Harold and Brett took out a joint loan to improve the property. They shared the expenses—both payments on the mortgage and

▼

improvements to the land. Harold told Brett the land would all be his.

Both men cared for the cattle. Brett cleared land, dredged a pond, and built a barn for the benefit of the cattle operation. Why would he have done this if he were not a partner?

Argument for Harold: Brett made some contributions to the cost of the land and the new house, but those payments were in lieu of rent, not an indication of a partnership. The land was not a business, there were no profits, and Brett was not a partner.

As for Brett's contributions to the cattle business, many of these were made against Harold's wishes. He offered to pay Brett *not* to build a new barn. Brett cleared the land and dredged the pond to attract game that he could hunt. Harold may have been an indulgent father, but he was not a partner. ■

Partnership by Estoppel

Brett wanted to be considered a partner in the cattle business so that he could share in the profits of the enterprise. *Partnership by estoppel* is concerned with the opposite situation—a person does not want to be considered a partner because he wishes to avoid the *liability* of the partnership. The twist is that partnership by estoppel applies in situations where the participants are *not*, in fact, partners but are held to be liable as if they were.

Partnership by estoppel applies if:

- **Participants tell other people that they are partners (even though they are not), or they allow other people to say, without contradiction, that they are partners**
- **A third party relies on this assertion; and**
- **The third party suffers harm.**

Dr. William Martin was held liable under a theory of partnership by estoppel because he told a patient that he and Dr. John Maceluch were partners (although they were not); the patient relied on this statement and made appointments to see Dr. Maceluch; and she was harmed by Dr. Maceluch's malpractice. He refused to come to the hospital when she was in labor and, as a result, her child was born with brain damage. Although Dr. Martin was out of the country at the time, he was also liable.[6]

at RISK

Dr. Martin could have avoided this problem by being very careful not to refer to Dr. Maceluch as his partner. Presumably, he used the word "partner" to reassure Mrs. Haught. Instead of "partner," he could have said "colleague," "associate," or "assistant." Dr. Martin should also have been careful to correct anyone who referred to Dr. Maceluch as his partner. ◆

RELATIONSHIP BETWEEN PARTNERS AND OUTSIDERS

Under the UPA, **the rules governing the liability of partners to outsiders are** *mandatory*. Partners may not change them. **In contrast, most of the rules governing the relationship** *among* **partners are** *default* **provisions,** meaning that the partners can change these rules if they desire.[7]

---

[6] *Haught v. Maceluch*, 681 F.2d 290, 1982 U.S. App. LEXIS 17123 (5th Cir. 1982).

[7] The exceptions are listed in UPA §103.

In the relationship between partners and outsiders, two questions arise: When is the partnership liable to outsiders? If the partnership is liable, who must pay the debt?

Liability of the Partnership to Outsiders

Under the UPA, **every partner is an agent of the partnership for the purpose of its business.**[8]

Authority

Partnership liability is based on the rules of agency law, discussed in Chapters 28 and 29. As an agent, a partner has three types of authority:

- **Actual Authority.** A partnership is liable for any act of a partner that it authorized. Suppose Tamika and Daniel have a partnership that buys and sells used books. They decide that they would be willing to pay up to $100 for any first edition *Harry Potter* books. When Daniel agrees to pay $75 to a customer who brings in such a book, the partnership is liable.

- **Implied Authority.** A partnership is liable for any act of a partner that is reasonably necessary to carry out an authorized transaction. Daniel does not have enough cash on hand to buy the *Harry Potter*, so he withdraws funds from the partnership's bank account. Again, the partnership is liable.

- **Apparent Authority.** A partnership is liable for an unauthorized act of a partner if the partner appears to be carrying on the business of the partnership or even business of the same type. Without Daniel's knowledge, Tamika promises to pay a large sum for Jane's record collection. Jane is a regular customer of the TD partnership and simply assumes that Tamika has authority to act. The TD partnership is liable because buying used records is the same kind of business as buying used books. Daniel was in the dark, but now he is in the red.

The UPA permits a partnership to limit the authority of a partner to transfer real estate by filing a statement in the relevant registry of deeds.[9] Thus, if the TD partnership files a notice that neither Tamika nor Daniel is authorized to sell the partnership's real estate, then Tamika's sale of their storefront to Kayla would not be valid, even if Kayla does not actually know about the notice. A general limitation on authority can also be filed with state officials, but in this case, it is only valid if Kayla actually knows about it. Thus, if TD files a notice saying that only Daniel is authorized to buy inventory for the partnership, but Kayla does not know about this filing, then the partnership is still liable on any contract for the sale of records that Kayla enters into with Tamika.

Ratification

As with every agency relationship, partners can ratify unauthorized acts. **If the partnership accepts the benefit of the unauthorized transaction or fails to repudiate it, the partnership has ratified it.** Once ratified, these actions are as valid as if they had been authorized from the beginning. Thus, Daniel exceeds his authority when he offers Matthew $1,000 for any Stephen King first edition. Tamika is outraged, but she never tells Matthew that the deal is no good. After scouring the city, Matthew finds a first edition of *Misery*. The partnership must pay for the book, no matter how miserable it makes Tamika.

---

[8]   UPA §301(1).
[9]   UPA §303.

Information

As agent, a partner has a duty to pass on all relevant information to the partnership. Whether or not a partner actually fulfills this obligation, the partnership is treated as if it had been notified. Under the UPA, **whatever one partner knows, the partnership is deemed to know.** Under the terms of TD's storefront lease, the landlord must give 90 days notice if he does not want to renew. He gives notice to Tamika who forgets to tell Daniel. The notice is nonetheless valid, and the landlord has every right to evict the partnership. If someone is going to suffer harm because of Tamika's mistake, in all fairness it should be the partnership, which had the bad judgment to take on an unreliable partner.

Tort Liability

A partnership is responsible for the *intentional* and *negligent* torts of a partner that occur *in the ordinary course* of the partnership's business or with the *actual* authority of the partners. When Daniel tells a customer that a book is a valuable first edition Tom Clancy, when really it is a worthless Book of the Month Club edition, the partnership is liable for this intentional misrepresentation because it occurred in the ordinary course of the partnership's business.

Paying the Debts of the Partnership

The basic rule of partnership liability is simply stated: **all partners are personally liable for all debts of the partnership.** All of a partner's assets are at risk. This rule applies whether or not the individual partner was in any way responsible for the debts. Thus, for example, when the accounting firm Laventhol & Horwath went bankrupt, the partners were personally liable and some had to sell their houses to pay the partnership's debts.

Joint and Several Liability

Partners have *joint* and *several* liability for partnership obligations. Joint and several liability means that a creditor can sue the partnership and the partners together or in separate lawsuits or in any combination. The partnership and the partners are all individually liable for the full amount of the debt, but, obviously, the creditor cannot keep collecting after he has already received the total amount owed. **Also note that, even if creditors have a judgment against an individual partner, they cannot go after that partner's assets until all the partnership's assets are exhausted.**[10]

Letitia, one of the world's wealthiest people, enters into a partnership with penniless Harry to drill for oil on her estate. While driving on partnership business, Harry crashes into Gus, seriously injuring him. Gus can sue any combination of the partnership, Letitia, and Harry for the full amount, even though Letitia was 2,000 miles away on her Caribbean island when the accident occurred and she had many times cautioned Harry to drive carefully. Even if Gus obtains a judgment against Letitia, however, he cannot recover against her while the partnership still has assets. So, for all practical purposes, he must try to collect first against the partnership. If the partnership is bankrupt and he manages to collect the full amount from Letitia, he cannot then try to

---

[10] UPA §307.

recover against Harry. (As we will see in a minute, Letitia may be able to recover from Harry some portion of what she paid Gus.)

Letitia is not wild about Harry's behavior, so she insists that he agree in writing to share all liabilities of the partnership 50/50. Unfortunately for Letitia, the liability rule is *mandatory*, not a default provision, so her agreement with Harry has absolutely no impact on the rights of Gus or any other creditor. He can still recover from Letitia for all debts of the partnership. She can always try to recover from Harry, but he is penniless, so good luck.

Liability of Incoming Partners

A partner is personally liable only for obligations the partnership incurred while he was a partner. His liability for debts incurred before he became partner is limited to his investment in the partnership.[11] Does this rule make sense? Why should an incoming partner be liable in any way for debts the partnership incurred before he became a partner? Consider these questions in light of the following article about Englishman Robert Maxwell. Long known as an international wheeler-dealer, Maxwell stole money from his companies' pension plans to pay for the purchase of newspapers and publishing houses around the world. He drowned after falling—or jumping—over the side of his yacht late one evening. After his death, investigators discovered that more than $1 billion was missing from his various enterprises.

NEWS*worthy*

Though British publisher Robert Maxwell drowned at sea several years ago, his ghost still haunts his investment bank, Goldman Sachs. A tussle is brewing among Goldman partners over how they should divide $250 million in costs from a settlement that the securities firm reached with pension funds looted by the late publisher. Goldman allegedly sold pension assets without returning the proceeds to the pension funds.

Now Goldman management is grappling with the nettlesome issue of which partners will pay the settlement. Senior partners have proposed allocating the cost to those who were Goldman partners when the Maxwell transactions occurred. But some ex-partners are balking because they would end up paying nearly half of the settlement—as much as $4 million apiece. These alumni argue that all of Goldman's current partners will benefit from the settlement and so the partnership should pay a share of the costs, too. The ex-partners also complain that they had no say over the amount of the settlement, so why should they be asked to write a check for it?[12] ◆

In a sense, the UPA supports both of these positions. Goldman's ex-partners are personally liable for debts incurred while they were members of the firm. However, current partners are also liable, up to the amount of their investment in the partnership, for debts incurred even before they joined. Of course, Goldman's current assets are substantial, so it is up to the management committee to decide how much should be paid personally by the former partners and how much by the current partnership. In any event, former partners generally are not liable for debts of the partnership incurred after they have left.

---

[11] UPA §306.

[12] Anita Raghavan, "Goldman's Partners Contend with Maxwell Legacy," *Wall Street Journal*, Apr. 12, 1995, p. C1. Republished with permission of The Wall Street Journal; permission conveyed through the Copyright Clearance Center, Inc.

RELATIONSHIP AMONG PARTNERS

The rules governing the relationship between partners and outsiders are mandatory; the partners cannot change them. In contrast, the rules regulating the relationship among partners are more flexible—the partners can alter many of them by agreement. If these rules can be changed, why are they in the UPA at all? Partnerships are often formed casually. Sometimes the partners themselves do not even realize they have a partnership. In situations such as these, the default rules apply. Also, some partnerships may not want to undertake the effort and expense of preparing their own agreement. For them, the off-the-rack rules work well enough, and they do not need a custom-tailored version.

Financial Rights

Sharing Profits

Partners share profits equally, unless they agree otherwise. This basic rule applies no matter how much money, time, or effort an individual partner contributes to the partnership. After graduation, Dawn convinces her friends, Niels and Sonya, to return with her to Jackson, Mississippi, to open a coffee bar. Niels and Sonya each contribute the $15,000 they won as prizes during their last year in business school. Since their school awarded no prizes for giving the best parties, Dawn has nothing to contribute financially. But she does know Jackson. When Dawn's Coffee Bar opens for business, she attracts sell-out crowds. Meanwhile, Niels and Sonya are working 20-hour days, first renovating the building and then serving customers. Dawn rarely sees the dawn, or even noon. Niels and Sonya have contributed more time and money and may have done more for the bar's success, but they must share profits equally with Dawn, unless the three agreed otherwise.

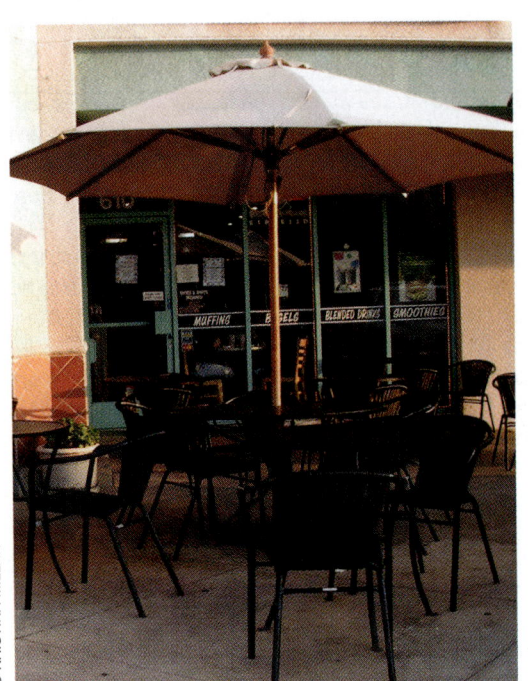

What is Dawn's share of the profits?

© KRISTINA MILLAR

Sharing Losses

Partners share losses according to their share of profits, unless they agree otherwise. If Dawn's Coffee Bar fizzles after the first few months of success, then Dawn is responsible for one-third of the losses because she received one-third of the profits. Too late for her to argue that it was not her fault the business failed.

Payment for Work Done

Partners are not entitled to any payment beyond their share of profits, unless they agree otherwise. Niels and Sonya have no right to a greater share of the profits in return for their extra work. It is simply too difficult for the courts to evaluate each partner's contributions. ("Sonya didn't get to work until 9:15." "That's not true, I was there at 8:45 but you didn't see me because I was out back washing your dirty dishes. . . .") This rule may seem arbitrary, but at least it is easy to enforce. The only exception, which we will see later, is that partners are entitled to remuneration for services performed in winding up the partnership.

In the following case, did one of the Hooper brothers deserve payment for the extra work he performed for the partnership? Did the court make the right decision legally? Ethically?

HOOPER V. HOOPER

2002 Cal. App. unpub. LEXIS 835
Court of Appeal of California, 2002

Facts: Charles Hooper owned Lako, a scrap metal business. He offered his brother, William, a partnership in the business. The two brothers never discussed salary or compensation. Instead, they agreed they would each be entitled to 50 percent of the profits of the partnership, but they would take out only what was necessary to live, and the remainder would stay in the business.

Lako began purchasing real estate. The two brothers also agreed that Lako would hold and manage real estate and stocks they had inherited from their grandfather. These inherited holdings generated most of the partnership's income.

Ten years after forming the partnership, Charles and William were both injured in a car accident. William's injuries were more serious and required two major surgeries. He could no longer drive a car and had to depend upon Charles for information about the partnership. Charles took over management responsibility. Although William never returned to the office, he did do some partnership work at home, such as reviewing leases and researching the metal market.

A Lako building was destroyed. William was willing to accept the settlement offer from the insurer, but Charles wanted to hold out for more. Charles became so angry that he refused to speak with William and, thenceforth, all communication between them went through Charles's girlfriend. Charles refused to give William any information about the partnership.

William filed suit, asking the court to order an accounting and to dissolve the partnership. Charles alleged that he was entitled to payment for the services he performed for the partnership after William's accident. The lower court found for William and Charles appealed.

Issue: Is a partner entitled to compensation for the services he provides the partnership?

Excerpts from Judge Woods's Decision: Appellants [that is, Charles] contend the court erred in its allocation of partnership assets by not taking into account the enhanced value of partnership income and partnership assets by reason of Charles's unilateral services and time. Appellants posit that Charles is entitled in kind to the property his services enhanced and to the additional income generated by his services. Alternatively, appellants argue the court should have valued the property improved by Charles at what it would have been worth without his unilateral additional services and enhancement.

The general rule is that, in the absence of an express or implied agreement, a partner is not entitled to any compensation for his services to the partnership other than his share of the profits. This is predicated on the theory that during the lifetime of the partners each of them is required to donate his time and talents to the affairs of the partnership, the service and labor of the one offsetting that of the others. The fact that one partner contributes greater skill and takes over the management of the business does not give rise to a right to extra compensation without an agreement therefor.

Appellants argue the court should have found an implied agreement based on William's testimony it was agreed both partners would work full time and contribute equally and the partnership would not exist if one partner was not around. Appellants argue that testimony constituted an agreement to proportionate pay based upon their work. William's testimony shows an agreement for an equal partnership and not an agreement to pay compensation to a partner for services rendered to the partnership. William testified there were to be equal responsibilities and equal commitment for an equal share, i.e., an equal share in profits and losses. William did not mention pay, salary or compensation.

Although it can be implied the partners agreed they would work equally, they did not anticipate the situation which arose here where one partner was unable to continue to fully participate in the partnership. Even after William was unable to return to work, Charles was not paid a salary for his services. Moreover, even though appellants argue there was an implied agreement, they do not suggest what Charles should have been paid or how his compensation was to be determined.

The judgment is affirmed. ∎

Partnership Property

All partnership property belongs to the partnership as a whole, not to the individual partners. A partner has no right to use or sell property, except for the benefit of the partnership. Suppose that the partnership owns the building that houses their coffee bar. Upstairs, above the bar, are three apartments. "Wow! This is great," says Niels, "I get the front unit." Does Niels have the right to live in one of the three apartments? After all, Dawn and Sonya can have the other two. Although the arrangement sounds fair, in fact, Niels has no right to live there, unless the other partners agree.

Right to Transfer a Partnership Interest

A partnership is a personal relationship built on trust. Therefore, a partner can no more sell his partnership share to a stranger than a spouse can come home one night and announce, "I'm leaving the marriage but, don't worry, I've found a substitute." **Without the approval of the other partners, a partner cannot sell her share; she can only transfer her right to receive profits and losses. A new partner can only be admitted to a partnership by unanimous consent of the other partners.**[13] It would be unfair to force partners to work with, or face unlimited liability for, someone they do not consider trustworthy. Sonya gets in serious debt to a fellow gambler, Nathan Detroit. Fearful that Nathan will ruin her manicure if she does not pay her debt, she agrees to give him her share of the partnership, which is her only asset. He knows a lot about coffee, and she is sure he will do fine as a partner. Although Niels and Dawn feel sorry for Sonya's predicament, they refuse to admit Nathan as a partner. Without their permission, Sonya has no right to transfer ownership rights or management authority to Nathan. Niels and Dawn cannot be forced to work with someone they do not want to touch with a 10-foot pole. However, Sonya can transfer to Nathan the right to receive her share of the partnership's profits.

What if Sonya refuses to assign to Nathan her right to receive profits from the partnership? **Creditors can attach partnership profits through a charging order. A charging order** is simply a court order granting a third party the right to receive a share of partnership profits.

Similar rules apply when a partner dies. A partner's heirs have no right to specific partnership property; they do not become partners themselves, nor do they have any say in partnership management. They do have a right to receive the value of a partnership share. In large, sophisticated partnerships, the partnership agreement will usually short-circuit arguments by establishing in advance how to calculate the value of a share.

Management Rights

Right to Manage

Each and every partner has equal rights in the management and conduct of the business, unless the partners agree otherwise. In a large partnership, with hundreds of partners, too many cooks can definitely spoil the firm's profitability. That is why large partnerships are almost always run by one or a few partners who are designated as managing partners or members of the executive committee. Some firms are run almost dictatorially by the partner who brings in the most business (called a "rainmaker"). Nonetheless, even in relatively autocratic firms, the atmosphere tends to be less hierarchical than in a corporation, where employees are accustomed to the concept of having

---

[13] UPA §401(i).

a boss. Whatever the reality, partners by and large like to think of themselves as being the equal of every other partner.

Right to Bind the Partnership

As we have discussed, partners are agents of the partnership and have the power to bind the partnership through actual, implied, or apparent authority. The partnership is liable to third parties for a partner's actions. **If these actions are not authorized by the partnership, the partner still has the *power* to bind the partnership, but not the *right*.** In this case, the partnership is liable to the third party, and the partner is liable to the partnership. If the partner has both the *power* and the *right*, he is not personally liable to the partnership no matter how harmful his actions.

A partner is authorized to bind the partnership for any transaction within the ordinary course of its business, unless the partner knows that the other partners would disapprove. Dawn decides she would rather buy coffee from Hadley than from the regular supplier in New York. She has the authority to switch suppliers, unless she knows that Sonya and Niels think Hadley's coffee tastes too much like the Mississippi River. If Dawn signs a contract with Hadley, knowing that her partners disapprove, the partnership is liable to Hadley, but she is liable to the partnership.

Right to Vote

Unless the partners agree otherwise, all partners have an equal vote, regardless of their contributions to the partnership. For ordinary partnership affairs, the majority has the right to make a decision. To amend the partnership agreement or to make decisions outside the ordinary course of business, the vote must be unanimous. What happens when Dawn wants to introduce herbal teas, over Niels's dead body? The partners vote. Since this is an ordinary partnership matter, the majority rules. If Dawn can get Sonya on her side, she will win approval for the healthy teas. It makes no difference that Dawn never contributed any cash to the partnership; she has the right to vote.

This is the default rule, but many partnerships change it by agreement. Accounting or law firms, for instance, often award partners a certain number of points each year, based on how much business they bring in or how hard they work. The more points, the higher their compensation and the more their votes count. Some firms, run by a particularly powerful partner, may effectively have only one vote—his. The managing partner of a large law firm once said, "This partnership has a one man, one vote rule, and I'm the one man."

Right to Know

It is difficult to manage an enterprise without adequate information. **Therefore, the UPA grants each partner the right to inspect and copy the partnership's books and records.** This right is unconditional and does not depend upon the partner's purpose or motive. However, books and records are not enough, by themselves, to keep a partner fully informed. Therefore, the UPA requires all partners and the partnership to volunteer any information that might reasonably be necessary for other partners to exercise their rights. All partners and the partnership also have a duty to supply any other information that a partner reasonably requests. These rules are mandatory; the partners may not change them by agreement among themselves.

Management Duties

Partners have the right to manage the partnership. In addition, they also have duties to the partnership and the other partners. These duties are mandatory; the partners may not waive them.

Duties of Care

Partners are liable to the partnership for gross negligence, reckless conduct, intentional misconduct, or a knowing violation of the law. Partners are not liable for ordinary negligence.[14] As you remember from earlier in this chapter, a partnership is liable for the intentional and negligent torts of a partner that occur in the ordinary course of business. But, as you have just learned, the partner is not liable to the partnership for ordinary negligence. These two rules intersect in the following case.

MOREN V. JAX RESTAURANT

679 N.W.2d 165, 2004 Minn. App. LEXIS 459
Court of Appeals of Minnesota, 2004

Facts: Jax is a pizza restaurant in Foley, Minnesota, owned by two sisters: Nicole Moren and Amy Benedetti. They operated it as a partnership. One afternoon, Moren ended her regular shift at 4:00 P.M. and left to pick up her two-year-old son, Remington, from day care. When her sister called her to say that one of the cooks had not come to work, Moren returned to the restaurant with Remington. Moren's husband said he would pick the child up in about 20 minutes.

Because Moren did not want Remington running around the restaurant, she brought him into the kitchen with her, set him on top of the counter, and began rolling out pizza dough using the dough-pressing machine. As she was making pizzas, Remington reached his hand into the dough press. His hand was crushed, causing permanent injuries. His father brought suit on Remington's behalf against the partnership for negligence. The partnership, in its turn, sued Moren, arguing that she had to reimburse the partnership for any payments to Remington. The district court granted summary judgment to Moren. The restaurant appealed.

Issue: Is Moren liable to the partnership for her own negligence?

Excerpts from Judge Crippen's Decision: The partnership [argues] that its obligation to compensate Remington is diminished in proportion to the predominating negligence of Moren as a mother, although it is responsible for her conduct as a business owner. Under Minnesota's Uniform Partnership Act of 1994 (UPA), a partnership is liable for loss or injury caused to a person as a result of a wrongful act or omission, or other actionable conduct, of a partner acting in the ordinary course of business of the partnership or with authority of the partnership. [Moreover], a partnership [must] indemnify a partner for liabilities incurred by the partner in the ordinary course of the business of the partnership. Thus, under the plain language of the UPA, a partner has a right to indemnity from the partnership, but the partnership's claim of indemnity from a partner is not authorized or required.

The district court correctly concluded that Nicole Moren's conduct was in the ordinary course of business of the partnership and, as a result, indemnity by the partner to the partnership was inappropriate. It is undisputed that one of the cooks scheduled to work that evening did not come in, and that Moren's partner asked her to help in the kitchen. It also is undisputed that Moren was making pizzas for the partnership when her son was injured. Because her conduct at the time of the injury was in the ordinary course of business of the partnership, under the UPA, her conduct bound the partnership and it owes indemnity to her for her negligence.

[The restaurant] also claims that because Nicole Moren's action of bringing Remington into the kitchen was partly motivated by personal reasons, her conduct was outside the ordinary course of business. Even if the predominant motive of the partner was to benefit himself or third persons, such does not prevent the concurrent business purpose from being within the scope of the partnership. [W]e conclude that the conduct of Nicole Moren was no less in the ordinary course of business because it also served personal purposes. It is undisputed that Moren was acting for the benefit of the partnership by making pizzas when her son was injured, and even though she was simultaneously acting in her role as a mother, her conduct remained in the ordinary course of the partnership business.

Affirmed. ■

---

[14] UPA §404.

Public Policy

What is the logic behind this case? A mother is careless, her son is injured, and the partnership must pay. Why shouldn't she be liable for her own negligence? ◆

Duty of Loyalty

Partners have a limited fiduciary duty to their partnership.

Competing with the Partnership. Each partner must turn over to the partnership all earnings from any activity that is related to the partnership's business. Cara, Max, and Brooke are partners in a Beverly Hills law firm. While Cara is vacationing near Santa Fe, a guest in the next-door hacienda is arrested in the middle of the night for drunk driving. Cara goes down to the police station and persuades the police officer to release the guest. Her new client gratefully insists on paying her $5,000 for her efforts. Cara figures the fee will go a long way toward paying the cost of her vacation. Cara figures wrong. She must turn the fee over to the partnership because she earned it doing the kind of work that the partnership does. It is irrelevant that she was on vacation.

Taking a Business Opportunity. A partner may not take an opportunity away from the partnership unless the other partners consent. The partnership wants to buy new conference room furniture. Max notices an advertisement in the paper for a lovely antique table and chairs that would be perfect for the conference room. If he buys them himself for his dining room at home without telling his partners, he is violating his duty by taking an opportunity away from the partnership. The partnership is entitled either to the furniture or to the value of the opportunity Max took.

Using Partnership Property. A partner must turn over to the partnership any profit he earns from use of partnership property without the consent of the partners. The partnership's office is in an old, beautifully restored historic building. Max runs a party-planning service on the side—MAXimum Fun. He occasionally holds parties on the weekends in the partnership's elegant foyer without telling Brooke and Cara. When they find out, they are maximum angry, and for good reason—Max has violated his duty to the partnership.

Conflict of Interest. A partner has a conflict of interest whenever the partnership does business with him, a member of his family, or a business partly or fully owned by him. Suppose that Max hires MAXimum Fun to put on the firm's tenth anniversary celebration. Unless the other partners consent in advance, Max must turn over to the partnership any profits he earns from the party. In the following case, one partner bought partnership property at a public auction. Is that a conflict of interest?

MARSH V. GENTRY

642 S.W.2d 574, 1982 Ky. LEXIS 315

Supreme Court of Kentucky, 1982

Facts: Tom Gentry and John Marsh were partners in a business that bought and sold racehorses. The partnership paid $155,000 for Champagne Woman, who subsequently had a foal named Excitable Lady. The partners decided to sell Champagne Woman at the annual Keeneland auction, the world's premier thoroughbred horse auction. On the day of the auction, Gentry decided to bid on the horse personally, without telling Marsh. Gentry bought Champagne Woman for $135,000. Later, he told Marsh that someone from California had approached him about buying Excitable Lady. Marsh agreed to the sale. Although he repeatedly asked Gentry the name of the purchaser, Gentry refused to tell him. Not until 11 months later, when Excitable Lady won a race at Churchill Downs, did Marsh learn that Gentry had been the purchaser. Marsh became the Excitable Man.

▼

Issue: Did Gentry violate his fiduciary duty when he bought partnership property without telling his partner?

Excerpts from Justice O'Hara's Decision: Admittedly, at an auction sale, the specific identity of a purchaser cannot be ascertained before the sale, but [Kentucky partnership law] required a full disclosure by Gentry to Marsh that he would be a prospective purchaser.

As to the private sale of Excitable Lady, Marsh consented to a sale from the partnership, at a specified price, to the prospective purchaser in California. Even though Marsh obtained the stipulated purchase price, a partner has an absolute right to know when his partner is the purchaser. Partners scrutinize buy-outs by their partners in an entirely different light than an ordinary third party sale. This distinction is vividly made without contradiction when Marsh later indicated that he would not have con-

sented to either sale had he known that Gentry was the purchaser. Under these facts, it is obvious that Gentry failed to disclose all that he knew concerning the sales, including his desire to purchase partnership property.

[P]artners, in their relations with other partners, [must] maintain a higher degree of good faith due to the partnership agreement. The requirement of full disclosure among partners as to partnership business cannot be escaped.

Finally, Gentry maintains that it is an accepted practice at auction sales of thoroughbreds for one partner to secretly bid on partnership stock to accomplish a buy-out. We would emphatically state, however, for the benefit of those engaged in such practices, that where an "accepted business practice" conflicts with existing law, the law whether statutory or court ordered, is controlling. To hold otherwise would be chaotic. ■

Good Faith and Fair Dealing

Partners have an obligation of good faith and fair dealing to each other and to the partnership. They must deal with each other *fairly* and *without coercion*. Behavior that would be acceptable in an arm's-length transaction may be unacceptable between partners. Hartz Mountain Industries, Inc., was the managing partner of a real estate business in northern New Jersey. Eugene Heller was Hartz's partner. According to the partnership agreement, when Heller left the partnership, Hartz would have the properties appraised and buy Heller's share. Hartz had the right to choose the appraiser. Over Heller's objection, Hartz chose Robert DiFalco. Hartz's own internal appraisals valued the properties at more than $214 million, but DiFalco produced an appraisal of $133 million—a slight discrepancy of more than $80 million.

The court found that, while Hartz had technically complied with the partnership agreement, it had breached its obligation of good faith and fair dealing. Courts generally pay a great deal of respect to appraisals, especially when both parties have agreed in advance to the appraisal process. But the court did not accept the appraisal in this case because Hartz had violated its duty to Heller by choosing such an unreliable appraiser.[15]

TERMINATING A PARTNERSHIP

The rules on termination depend, in part, on the type of partnership. If the partners have not agreed how long their partnership will last, they have a **partnership at will,** and any of them can leave at any time, for any reason. Taylor, Jay, and Gabriela are partners in the Donut Partnership, which owns a racehorse by the name of Speedy Donut. They see their business as a lark, to last as long as they are having fun, so they

---

[15] *Heller v. Hartz Mountain Industries, Inc.,* 270 N.J. Super. 143, 636 A.2d 599, 1993 N.J. Super. LEXIS 903 (N.J. Super. Ct. Law Div. 1993).

make no decision about its duration. When Taylor decamps after only two months, leaving Jay and Gabriela holding the feedbag, they have no legal right to complain.

With a **term partnership,** the partners have agreed in advance how long it will last. At the end of the specified term, the partnership automatically ends. If Taylor, Jay, and Gabriela agree to sell Speedy Donut and end their business relationship in five years, or if they agree the partnership will end when Speedy runs in the Kentucky Derby, they have a term partnership.

Dissociation

A partnership begins with an association of two or more people. Appropriately, the end of a partnership begins with a *dissociation*. **A dissociation occurs when a partner quits.** However, a dissociation does not inevitably lead to the termination of the partnership business. A dissociation is a fork in the road: **when one or more partners dissociate, the partnership can either buy out the departing partner(s) and continue in business or wind up the business and terminate the partnership.** Exhibit 33.1 illustrates the dissociation process under the UPA.

Exhibit 33.1

Rightful versus Wrongful Dissociation

A partnership is a personal relationship built on trust. As we have seen, all partners are agents for the partnership, and each partner is personally liable for its debts. The actions of one partner can profoundly affect the financial health of every other partner. Under these circumstances, courts will not force someone to remain in a partnership, no matter what the partnership agreement says, any more than they will force a couple to stay married because of their vows at the altar. Partners can always dissociate, but like any divorcing spouse, they may have to pay damages for the harm that their departure causes. As courts are wont to say: **a partner always has the power to leave a partnership but may not have the right.**

Rightful Dissociation. A rightful dissociation occurs if:

- *A partner in a partnership at will serves notice that he intends to withdraw.*
- *The partners agree in advance on an event that causes dissociation.* Jay plans to attend business school in three years, so the partnership agreement provides that he will be automatically dissociated from the partnership at that point.
- *A partner dies or becomes incompetent.*
- *A partner is expelled by the other partners.* Partnership agreements can establish a process for expelling a partner. Often, under such agreements, the partnership does not even have to give a reason for expulsion. If a certain percentage of the partners (say, 75 percent) vote against someone, she is out. However, in the absence of such a provision in the partnership agreement, the UPA permits the expulsion of a partner only if (1) it is illegal to carry on the business with her or (2) she has transferred her partnership interest.

The following article illustrates that even law firms sometimes forget the law.

NEWS*worthy*

A state-court jury here awarded $3 million to a former partner of Cadwalader, Wickersham & Taft, saying the prestigious New York law firm had no right to expel him. In the case, Steven A. Ruskin, a former tax partner in the New York office, was awarded $1.4 million for the loss of past earnings and $1.6 million for the loss of future earnings. Next month, the judge will decide whether Mr. Ruskin is entitled to a share of the firms' assets.

The Ruskin case hinged on the fact that Cadwalader's partnership agreement contained no provisions for expelling a partner. Unlike employees of a corporation, law firm partners can't be fired unless their partnership agreement specifically allows for it.[16] ◆

Wrongful Dissociation. A wrongful dissociation occurs if:

- *A partner violates the partnership agreement.* The Donut Partnership agreement prohibits racetrack betting. When Taylor wins the Pick Six, he is automatically dissociated.
- *A partner in a term partnership withdraws before the end of the term.* The Donut Partnership is supposed to last five years, but Jay withdraws after five months.
- *A court expels a partner in a term partnership because her behavior is harmful.* A court has the right to expel a partner who engages in wrongful conduct that harms the partnership or violates the partnership agreement in a serious way. Gabriela drugs the favored Speedy Donut so that she can win a bet on a long shot in the race. A court could expel her and that would constitute a wrongful dissociation.
- *A partner in a term partnership becomes bankrupt.*

Once a partner is dissociated, the remaining partners must decide how to proceed; they can either continue the partnership as an ongoing business or terminate it.

Continuation of the Partnership Business

If a partner is dissociated from the partnership, the other partners can, by unanimous vote, continue the business, but they must buy out the ex-partner.[17] Most large firms simply provide in their partnership agreement that, upon dissociation, the business continues.

---

[16] Dean Starkman, "Former Partner at Cadwalader Wins Lawsuit," *Wall Street Journal*, Dec. 23, 1997, p. B5.

[17] If the ex-partner's dissociation was rightful, she can vote in this decision. If her dissociation was wrongful, she has no right to vote.

Financial Settlement

If the partnership decides to continue, it must pay the ex-partner the value of her share of the business. This value is equal to her share of the proceeds if (1) the partnership were sold as an ongoing business or (2) the partnership's assets were liquidated, whichever calculation is greater. For example, if Gabriela is adjudged incompetent by a court, she is automatically dissociated from the Donut Partnership. At that point, Speedy is worth $500,000 and the partnership has debts of $50,000, for a total value of $450,000. Gabriela is entitled to at least a one-third share—$150,000. If, however, the partnership is worth $600,000 as an ongoing business, Gabriela is entitled to $200,000.

Now the plot thickens. If Gabriela's dissociation was *wrongful*, the partnership can subtract any damages she caused from the amount it owes her. A court expels Gabriela from the partnership because she drugged Speedy. His recovery is slow and he is unable to race for months, costing the partnership $50,000. Taylor and Jay could subtract that $50,000 from the $200,000 they owe her, so she ultimately receives a check for only $150,000. If her bad acts caused more than $200,000 in damage, she owes them money.

Liability of the Dissociated Partner to Outsiders for Debts Incurred **before** Dissociation

A dissociated partner is liable to outsiders for debts incurred during her term as a partner, but the partnership must indemnify her for these debts. After Gabriela departs, a bank sues the partnership for failure to repay its loan. Although Gabriela is no longer a partner, she was one when the partnership borrowed the money. As we have seen, the bank may be able to recover from her. If it does, however, the partnership must indemnify her; that is, the partnership must reimburse her for any amounts she pays the bank. This outcome is only fair because, when the partnership purchased her share, it reduced the payment to reflect liabilities such as this.

Liability of the Dissociated Partner to Outsiders for Debts Incurred **after** Dissociation

A dissociated partner is liable to outsiders for the debts of the partnership incurred within two years after she leaves, but only if the creditor reasonably believes she is still a partner. The partnership must indemnify her for these debts. If Taylor and Jay buy an expensive saddle on credit from their regular supplier, Gabriela is also liable unless the saddler knows she is dissociated. The partnership would have to reimburse her (if it has enough funds). To protect herself, however, Gabriela can file a statement of dissociation with the Secretary of State. Although the saddler rarely spends his free afternoons perusing the public records, he is deemed to have notice of this filing 90 days after Gabriela makes it.

Liability of the Dissociated Partner to the Partnership

If the ex-partner harms the partnership after she leaves, she is liable for the damage she causes. If Gabriela lets a feed supplier believe that she is still a partner and then buys feed on credit, the partnership may be liable for her charges. If so, she must reimburse the partnership.

Termination of the Partnership Business

When a partner is dissociated, the partnership may choose to terminate the business rather than continue it. **Ending a partnership business involves three steps: dissolution, winding up, and termination.**

Dissolution

The UPA lists circumstances under which a partnership automatically dissolves. This provision is a default rule, meaning that the partners can agree otherwise if they want. **Partners can always decide (by unanimous vote) to continue a partnership.** Indeed, even after the winding up process begins, the partners can change their minds and continue the business.

Unless the partners agree otherwise, a partnership dissolves under the following circumstances:

- *In a partnership at will, when a partner notifies the partnership that he intends to withdraw.*
- *In a term partnership when:*
  - *A partner is dissociated and half of the remaining partners vote to wind up the partnership business.* When Jay dies, he is dissociated from the partnership. If Gabriela votes to wind up the business, the partnership is dissolved.
  - *All the partners agree to dissolve.* Although the Donut Partnership is supposed to last five years, Taylor, Jay, and Gabriela can agree among themselves to wind up the business whenever they want. If Speedy Donut is a cream puff on the racetrack, they can decide to dissolve their partnership and sell the pastry.
  - *The term expires or the partnership achieves its goal.* If Speedy Donut runs in the Derby, the Donut Partnership automatically dissolves.
- *In any partnership when:*
  - *An event occurs which the partners had agreed would cause dissolution.* The Donut Partnership agreement provided that the partnership would dissolve if Speedy failed to win a race in any 12-month period. When Speedy goes winless, the partnership dissolves.
  - *The partnership business becomes illegal.* If horse racing is banned, the Donut Partnership automatically dissolves.
  - *A court determines that the partnership is unlikely to succeed.* If the partners simply cannot get along or they cannot make a profit, any partner has the right to ask a court to dissolve the partnership. If Taylor and Jay quarrel over everything and are unable to reach agreement on anything, a court is likely to agree to dissolve the partnership.

Winding Up

During the winding up process, all debts of the partnership are paid, and the remaining proceeds are distributed to the partners.
Who Does It? Unless the partnership agreement provides otherwise, any partner who has not wrongfully dissociated has the right to oversee the winding up.
Are They Paid? Partners are entitled to reasonable compensation for their work in winding up the partnership.
What Do They Do? The winding up process can be complex and take as long as several years to complete. The partners in charge can either sell the entire business as a whole, sell the individual assets of the business, distribute specific assets to the partners, or some combination of these options. They have the right to complete unfinished transactions and do whatever is necessary to wind up the business, but they do not have the right to take on new business.

If Taylor is winding up the Donut Partnership, he can sell Speedy Donut outright, buy feed for him until the sale, sue to recover any winnings that have not been paid, and settle partnership debts. But can he enter the horse in additional races? In a similar case, a court permitted the partner in charge of winding up a racing business to pay entrance fees for races, even though the horses would, in all likelihood, be sold before the races. The court assumed that buyers would pay more for horses that were eligible to race in upcoming events.[18]

The partnership is bound by the acts of the partners in charge of winding up. As the following case illustrates, this rule can sometimes lead to unhappy results.

JEFFERSON INSURANCE CO. V. CURLE

771 S.W.2d 424, 1989 Tenn. App. LEXIS 30
Tennessee Court of Appeals, 1989

Facts: Michael Curle and Steven Shelley were partners doing business under the name C & S Roofing. When the partnership dissolved, Curle agreed to complete one unfinished project (the Bishop house) and left Shelley to wind up the other partnership business. Shelley canceled the partnership's general liability insurance policy without telling Curle. While painting the Bishop house, Dennis Whitsett fell through a hole in the roof that the partnership had left covered only with tar paper. When Whitsett sought to recover from the partnership for his serious injuries, Curle and Shelley asked the insurance company to pay the claim.

The trial court found the policy canceled as to Steven Shelley, individually, but in full force and effect as to the partnership and Michael Curle, individually. The insurance company appealed.

Issue: Was the partnership bound by Shelley's decision during the winding up process to cancel the policy, even though he had not told Curle?

Excerpts from Judge McLemore's Decision: [The Tennessee Partnership Act] clearly states: "After dissolution a partner can bind the partnership . . . by any act appropriate for winding up partnership affairs or completing transactions unfinished at dissolution." The liquidating partner owes a continuing fiduciary duty to the other partners and has an obligation to act equitably toward them. However, these obligations run between partners and do not absolve any partner from being bound by the liquidating partner's actions in winding up partnership affairs. In the present case, we hold Shelley's cancellation of the partnership insurance policy and collection of unused premiums to be within his authority in winding up the partnership's affairs.

For the foregoing reasons, the judgment of the trial court holding the policy canceled as to Steven Shelley, individually, is affirmed, but that portion of the judgment holding that the policy is in full force and effect as to C & S Roofing, a partnership, and Michael Curle, individually, is reversed; and we hold that the policy is canceled as to all insureds and, thus, provides no coverage to any of the defendants for the accident alleged by Dennis Whitsett. ∎

Public Policy

What is the public policy behind this rule? Either the insurance company or the partnership must pay for Dennis Whitsett's injuries. Michael Curle made the mistake of entering into a partnership with Steven Shelley, so he is more at fault than the insurance company, which did nothing more than follow orders. ◆

Who Is Liable If a Partner Takes on New Business? During the winding up process, the partners continue to be liable for the debts of the partnership that were incurred

---

[18] *Central Trust & S. Deposit Co. v. Respass*, 112 Ky. 606, 66 S.W. 421 (1902).

before dissolution. But what if a partner oversteps her bounds during the winding up process and takes on new business? All of the other partners are liable unless they have filed a statement of dissolution with the Secretary of State. This statement is effective 90 days after it is filed. A sample notice of dissolution is available at http://www.4hb.com/letters/ltrnotdispa.html.

How Are Partnership Proceeds Distributed? During the winding up process, the assets of the partnership are paid out in the following order:

- First, to creditors of the partnership, including creditors who are partners. Suppose that the Donut Partnership has assets of $30,000. It owes $20,000 each to the feed supplier, the stabler, and Jay, for a total of $60,000. It will pay $10,000 to each of the three creditors—Jay is treated exactly like the outsiders.

- Second, any leftover funds (or obligations) are distributed to the partners. Unless the partnership agreement provides otherwise, partners share equally in profits—and losses. In this example, the Donut Partnership had only enough assets to pay half its $60,000 debt. Each partner would then contribute $10,000 to pay the amount still owing. Jay's payment would be a wash—he owes $10,000, but he is also entitled to be paid $10,000.

Termination

After the sometimes lengthy and complex winding up, the actual termination of a partnership is anticlimactic. Termination happens automatically once the winding up is finished. The partnership is not required to do anything official; it can go out of the world even more quietly and simply than it came in.

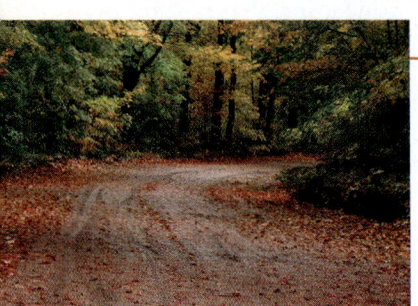

Chapter Conclusion

In some ways, a partnership is an old-fashioned form of organization. From the late 1770s until the mid-nineteenth century, virtually all businesses were partnerships. Then corporations gained in popularity, and now new forms have arisen such as limited liability companies and limited liability partnerships (both discussed in Chapter 32). These new forms of organization have many of the advantages of a partnership without the unlimited liability.

It is no surprise that to protect their partners from personal liability, many accounting firms, law firms, brokerage houses, advertising agencies, and investment banks that were originally partnerships have changed their form of organization to one of the newer options. On the other hand, many organizations continue to act like partnerships even though they have changed their official form of organization. And, before the partnership baby gets thrown out with the liability bath water, it is worth noting that many organizations—law, accounting, and investment banking firms to name a few—have been highly successful as partnerships. The lack of hierarchy in partnerships encourages collaboration and teamwork while the lure of ownership motivates and inspires employees.

Partnership law is important for another reason. As we have seen in this chapter, partnerships are often formed inadvertently by people who do not realize they are in such a relationship until a dispute arises. It is useful to know in advance the kind of behavior that will create a partnership, and the consequences.

Chapter Review

1. In determining whether a partnership exists, a court will consider whether the parties:
   - Share the profits of the business
   - Share management of the business
   - Share the losses of the business
   - Refer to themselves as partners

2. If someone is not a member of a partnership, she will nonetheless be considered a partner by estoppel if (1) she tells other people she is a partner or allows other people to say, without contradiction, that she is a partner; (2) a third party relies on this assertion; and (3) the third party suffers harm.

3. Every partner is an agent of the partnership for the purpose of its business. A partnership is responsible for the intentional and negligent torts of a partner that occur in the ordinary course of the partnership's business or with the actual authority of the other partners.

4. All partners are personally liable for all debts of the partnership. Partners have joint and several liability for partnership obligations.

5. A partner is personally liable only for obligations the partnership incurred while she was a partner. Her liability for debts incurred before she became a partner is limited to her investment in the partnership.

6. Unless they agree otherwise, partners:
   - Share profits equally
   - Share losses according to their share of profits
   - Are not entitled to any payment beyond their share of profits
   - Have no right to use or sell specific partnership property, except for the benefit of the partnership
   - Each have an equal vote, regardless of their contributions to the partnership, and
   - Each have an equal right in the management of the business.

7. Without the approval of the other partners, a partner cannot sell her share. She can only transfer the right to receive profits and losses. A new partner can be admitted to a partnership only by unanimous consent of the other partners.

8. Creditors can attach partnership profits through a charging order.

9. Partners are liable to the partnership for any damages resulting from their gross negligence, reckless conduct, intentional misconduct, or a knowing violation of the law. Partners are not liable to the partnership for ordinary negligence.

10. Each partner must turn over to the partnership all earnings from any activity that is related to the partnership's business.

11. A partner may not take an opportunity away from the partnership unless the other partners consent.

12. A partner has a conflict of interest whenever the partnership does business with him, a member of his family, or a business partly or fully owned by him.

13. Partners have an obligation of good faith and fair dealing to each other and to the partnership.

14. A dissociation occurs when a partner leaves the partnership.

15. When one or more partners dissociate, the partnership can either buy out the departing partner(s) and continue in business or wind up the business and terminate the partnership.

16. A partner always has the power to leave a partnership but may not have the right.

17. If partners do not have an agreement about the duration of their partnership, it is called a partnership at will, and any of them can leave at any time for any reason.

18. With a term partnership, the partners have agreed in advance how long the partnership will last.

19. A dissociated partner is liable to outsiders for debts incurred during her term as a partner, but the partnership must indemnify her for these debts.

20. A dissociated partner is liable for the debts of the partnership incurred within two years after she leaves, but only if the creditor reasonably believes she is still a partner. The partnership must indemnify her for these debts.

21. If the partners decide to end the partnership business, they must take three steps: dissolution, winding up, and termination.

22. During the winding up process, the partners have the right to complete unfinished transactions and do whatever is necessary to terminate

the business. They do not have the right to take on new business.

23. During the winding up process, the assets of the partnership are paid out:

- First, to creditors of the partnership, including creditors who are partners.
- Second, to partners.

Practice Test

1. Mrs. Perry parked her new Chevrolet in the parking lot at the airport in Springfield, Ohio. Bryan Little was giving flying lessons to Edward Selders. Little told Selders to taxi a plane off the runway. Selders, standing on the ground next to the plane, cranked up the engine. The throttle was set too far open, so the plane began to move. Selders chased the plane on foot, grabbed its left wing, and swung the airplane in a semicircle, crashing it into Perry's car. Little operated his flying business under the name "Little-Greiner Air Service." Bryan Little and Carl Greiner were not partners, but Perry sued them both on a theory of partnership by estoppel. She argued that they had used a name for their business that sounded like a partnership. She had never heard of their business until the collision. Is Greiner liable to Perry as a partner by estoppel?

2. Suppose that in the chapter's opening vignette, Chase, Bailey, and Zack signed a document stating, "The undersigned expressly agree that they are not partners." If they continued to work together on the house, sharing the profits and the management, would they have been partners?

3. **CPA QUESTION** Which of the following is not necessary to create a partnership?

   a. Execution of a written partnership agreement

   b. Agreement to share ownership of the partnership

   c. Intention of conducting a business for profit

   d. Intention of creating a relationship recognized as a partnership

4. **ETHICS** Arthur Engelbrecht, John McCullough, and George Gilling formed a partnership to drill and maintain cesspools for two years. After less than two months, McCullough and Gilling sent a letter to Engelbrecht informing him that they were dissolving the partnership. Engelbrecht sued McCullough and Gilling, asking the court to declare that the partnership still existed and he had the right to continue in the business. Do McCullough and Gilling have the power to dissolve a term partnership before the end of the term? Aside from the legal issue, is it fair to Engelbrecht to allow his two partners to walk away from their partnership? He had counted on a two-year commitment; they gave only two months.

5. If a partner dissociates, he is entitled to:

   a. Force the termination of the partnership

   b. Receive indemnification from liability for present partnership debt

   c. Receive indemnification from damages he caused the partnership

   d. Receive only his share of the value of the partnership assets when it ultimately liquidates

6. While Warren Lyon was representing Betty Cook in divorce proceedings, she inherited $60,000. Lyon suggested Cook invest her money in a corporation of which he was president. Although he promised her a substantial return, the company went bankrupt shortly thereafter. Lyon was a partner in the law firm Brundidge, Fountain, Elliott & Churchill. The firm was not in the business of giving investment advice, it did not know that Lyon was giving such advice, nor did it receive any fee from Cook for the "investment service." Is the law firm liable for Cook's loss?

7. **CPA QUESTION** Cobb, Inc., a partner in TLC Partnership, assigns its partnership interest to Bean, who is not made a partner. After the assignment, Bean asserts the right to (1) participate in the management of TLC and (2) Cobb's share of TLC's partnership profits. Bean is correct as to which of these rights?

   a. 1 only

   b. 2 only

   c. 1 and 2

   d. Neither 1 nor 2

8. **YOU BE THE JUDGE** WRITING PROBLEM Hubert Shuptrine, an artist, entered into an agreement with R. L. Brown for the reproduction and distribution of his paintings. Shuptrine

was to receive 50 percent of the gross sales revenues. Brown was responsible for all losses and for management of the business. Before leaving on a trip to Israel, where he feared he might be in some danger, Brown signed a partnership agreement with Shuptrine stating that they jointly owned the business. Shortly after Brown returned from the trip, the two men terminated their business relationship, and Shuptrine revoked his authorization for the sale of prints. When Brown continued selling the prints, Shuptrine filed suit. Brown argued that the two had formed a partnership and that he was authorized to sell assets of the partnership. Were Shuptrine and Brown partners? **Argument for Shuptrine:** A partnership agreement does not create a partnership. Brown alone managed the business. Shuptrine shared only revenues, not profits. **Argument for Brown:** Shuptrine and Brown both provided services to the business: Brown paid for the printing, and Shuptrine did the artwork. These two men signed a partnership agreement, and they obviously intended to be partners.

9. Seventy-Three Land, Inc., sued Maxlar Partners for the balance due on a note made by the partnership. Max Odlen, a partner, asked the court to dismiss the claim against him personally because the plaintiff had not first tried to collect against the partnership. Must a creditor attempt to collect against the partnership first, before it sues an individual partner?

10. Dutch, Bill, and Heidi were equal partners in a lawn care business. Bill and Heidi wanted to borrow money from the bank to buy more trucks and expand the business. Dutch was dead set against the idea. When the matter came to a vote, Bill and Heidi voted in favor, Dutch against. Dutch was so annoyed that he told the bank not to lend the money and, further, that he

would not be responsible for repaying the loan. The bank loaned the money, the business failed, and the bank sued all three partners. Is Dutch liable on the loan?

11. **CPA QUESTION** Ted Fein, a partner in the ABC Partnership, wishes to withdraw from the partnership and sell his interest to Gold. All of the other partners in ABC have agreed to admit Gold as a partner and to hold Fein harmless for the past, present, and future liabilities of ABC. A provision in the original partnership agreement states that the partnership will continue upon the death or withdrawal of one or more of the partners. As a result of Fein's withdrawal and Gold's admission to the partnership, Gold:

   a. Is personally liable for partnership liabilities arising before and after his admission as a partner
   b. Has the right to participate in the management of ABC
   c. Acquired only the right to receive Fein's share of the profits of ABC
   d. Must contribute cash or property to ABC in order to be admitted with the same rights as the other partners

12. Brothers Sydney and Ashley Altman were partners in a real estate partnership in southeastern Pennsylvania. They received identical salaries. Sydney moved to Florida to establish residency so that he could obtain a divorce there. His lawyer told him not to return to Pennsylvania until he had resolved his marital problems. After Sydney had been gone almost a year, Ashley decided to increase his own salary to compensate for the additional work he was doing. Does Ashley have the right to pay himself more if he is doing more work?

13. **ROLE REVERSAL** Write an essay question that illustrates the dissociation process.

Internet Research Problem

The Web site http://beatty.westbuslaw.com has posted a sample partnership agreement. Meet with one or two of your classmates and form a hypothetical partnership. Can you foresee any problems that might arise under this agreement? Would this sample form protect your interests? How would you want to change it? Can you negotiate a more sensible or more favorable agreement?

You can find further practice problems at http://beatty.westbuslaw.com or in the Study Guide that accompanies this text.

Life and Death of a Corporation

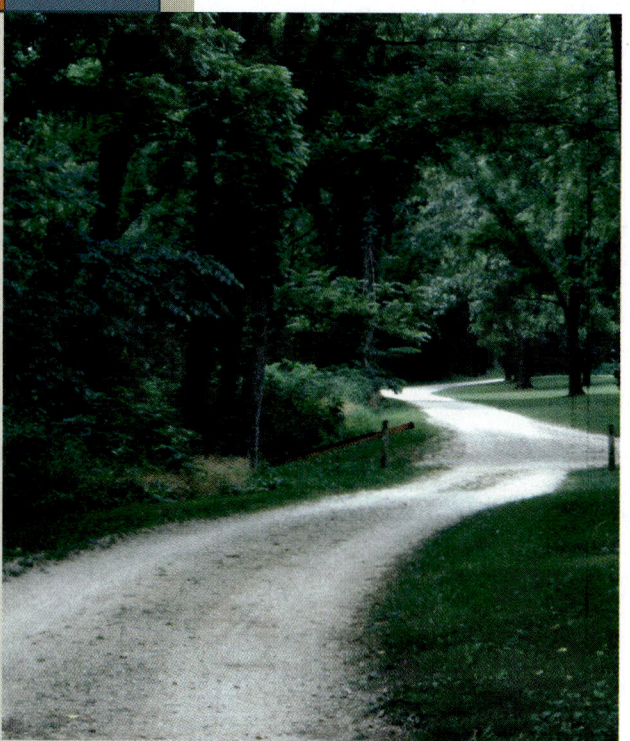

Becker Interiors, Inc., was overseeing a major renovation of a house in McLean, Virginia. The company hired Stephen Brooks as a subcontractor on the project. When the corporation refused to pay him, Brooks sued it.

Ronald Becker was the sole shareholder, officer, and director of Becker Interiors. Becker and his companion, Robert LaPointe, used approximately $300,000 of Becker Interiors' funds to renovate their residence, pay their personal credit card bills, and invest in another company of which Becker was president. Becker sold a corporate car for $73,700 and deposited those funds into his personal account, along with the corporation's income tax refund check of $12,850.

Brooks won his lawsuit against Becker Interiors and the court ordered the company to pay him $54,597.09. But when Brooks tried to collect the judgment he discovered that Becker Interiors had no assets.

Can Brooks recover what Becker Interiors owes him? Is Ronald Becker *personally* liable for the corporation's debts? Are shareholders ever liable for the debts of their corporation? Later in this chapter, the case of *Brooks v. Becker* will reveal the answer. ■

© PHOTO 24/BRAND X PICTURES/GETTY IMAGES

In this chapter you will learn how to form a corporation and also how to avoid traps that await the unwary entrepreneur, before and after a business is formed. Finally, you will learn how to dissolve a corporation.

BEFORE THE CORPORATION IS FORMED

Judy George was bound and determined to open Domain—a chain of furniture stores selling upscale European-style furnishings and accessories. (To understand her concept, rest your weary mouse on **http://www.domain-home.com**) At the beginning, George had more to do than seemed humanly possible. She had to find store locations, buy inventory, hire employees—it all seemed overwhelming. Her lawyer cautioned her not to do *too* much, *too* quickly. The corporation had not been formed, and she needed to be careful to avoid liability as a promoter.

Promoter's Liability

The promoter is the person who creates the corporation. It is her idea; she raises the capital, hires the lawyers, calls the shots. Judy George was Domain's promoter. Sometimes, promoters are so eager to get their business going that they sign contracts on behalf of the corporation before it is legally formed. Suppose that George finds the perfect location for her flagship store. She is desperate to sign the lease before someone else snatches the opportunity away, but Domain does not yet legally exist—it is not incorporated. What would happen if she signed the lease anyway? The rules are straightforward:

- **The promoter is personally liable on any contract signed before the corporation is formed.** If George signs the lease before Domain, Inc. legally exists, she is personally liable for the rent due.

- **The corporation is not liable on any contracts signed *before* incorporation unless it *adopts* the contract *after* incorporation.** What does **adoption** mean? Either the board of directors takes a formal vote saying, "We hereby adopt this contract," or they act as if they had adopted it. If Domain uses the space George rented, it has adopted the contract. But George is still on the hook.

- **Even if the corporation adopts the contract, the promoter is still liable until the third party (in this case, the landlord) agrees to a *novation*.** A novation creates a *new* contract with different parties. Even if Domain adopts the contract, George is still personally liable to the landlord until the landlord signs a new contract with George and Domain explicitly stating that only the corporation is liable, not George.

Like most sets of rules, this one has an exception:

- **If the contract clearly indicates that the other party is relying *only* on the corporation, although he knows the corporation does not yet exist, the promoter is released from liability once the corporation adopts the contract.** To protect herself, George would want the lease to state that Domain is not yet formed but will be liable when it is formed, and that George is not personally liable for rental payments once Domain adopts the contract.

In the following case, the entrepreneur did not understand the rules of promoter liability.

HARDY V. SOUTHWESTERN BELL YELLOW PAGES, INC.

2001 Tex. App. LEXIS 587
Court of Appeals of Texas, 2001

Facts: Bruce Hardy signed a contract on behalf of A-Z Business Products, Inc., agreeing to pay Southwestern Bell $23,240.00 for an advertisement in its yellow pages. The contract was in the name of A-Z Business Products, Inc. Next to Hardy's signature on the contract was a line marked "Title:" where Hardy wrote "Pres."

At the time, A-Z Business Products, Inc., had not yet been formed. After Hardy failed to make any payments on the contract, Southwestern Bell sued him individually, d/b/a A-Z Business Products. Hardy argued that only A-Z Business Products, Inc., was liable. The trial court found for Southwestern and Hardy appealed.

Issue: Is Hardy personally liable on the contract with Southwestern Bell?

Excerpts from Justice Kinkeade's Decision: Hardy contends that the contract was between Southwestern Bell and A-Z Business Products, Inc., and that he signed the document in his capacity as president of A-Z. Southwestern Bell argues, and we agree, that even assuming he signed the contract as the president of A-Z, he is still personally liable because A-Z was not yet formed as a corporation at the time of the contract.

Although Hardy asserts that he acted as an agent for the corporation, he admitted at trial that the corporation was not in existence at the time he signed the contract. Further, the corporate charter showing the date of incorporation, several months after the contract was signed, was admitted into evidence. Hardy could not have acted as an agent for a nonexistent corporation, because a nonexistent corporation can have no agent. He could only have acted as a promoter in contemplation of the formation of a corporation.

A promoter who enters a contract on behalf of an unformed corporation is personally liable on the contract unless (1) there is an agreement with the contracting party that the promoter is not liable, (2) the contract is made in the name and on the credit of the proposed corporation and the contracting party knows that the corporation does not yet exist, or (3) the corporation adopts the agreement after its incorporation.

The only evidence Hardy offered was his own testimony that when he signed the contract, he advised Southwestern Bell that he had applied for, but not yet received, the corporate charter number. Absent proof that A-Z adopted the agreement after its incorporation or that the agreement was in A-Z's name and that Southwestern Bell agreed at the time of contracting that it would look only to A-Z's credit, Hardy is bound individually.

We hold the evidence is legally and factually sufficient to support the trial court's verdict that Hardy is personally liable on the contract. ■

Defective Incorporation

A promoter is liable on contracts signed before the corporation exists. But what if the promoter signs a contract *thinking* the corporation has been formed only to discover later that the incorporation is somehow defective? In these situations, the law is reasonably tolerant. Consider the following examples.

De Jure *Corporation*

"De jure" is Latin for "by law." **A *de jure* corporation means that the promoter has substantially complied with the requirements for incorporation, but has made some minor error.** She has perhaps misspelled the name of the corporation's registered agent (more about the registered agent later). In this case, no one, not even the state, can challenge the validity of the corporation.

De Facto *Corporation*

"De facto" is Latin for "in fact." **A *de facto* corporation means that the promoter has made a good faith effort to incorporate and has actually used the corporation to conduct business.** In this case, the state can challenge the validity of the corporation, but a third party cannot. Suppose that Judy George fills out the incorporation form and files it, but the Secretary of State does not stamp it for weeks. In the meantime, George signs a lease for Domain. In many states, no stamp means no corporation. Nonetheless, George has a *de facto* corporation because she made a reasonable effort to incorporate and has used the corporation to conduct business. The landlord cannot challenge the validity of the corporation and claim that George is personally liable on the lease. Only the corporation is liable.

Corporation by Estoppel

A corporation by estoppel means that, if a party enters into a contract *believing* in good faith that the corporation exists, he cannot later take advantage of the fact that it does not. Suppose that George's attorney tells her that Domain, Inc., has been formed but, in fact, he never even attempted to incorporate it. In the meantime, George orders truckloads of furniture in Domain's name. Under the theory of corporation by estoppel, George is *not* personally liable even though the corporation does not exist. Both she and the furniture dealer thought she was buying on behalf of the corporation. Why should the dealer receive a windfall, and why should George be penalized, simply because her lawyer made a mistake? This rule works both ways: if a bank loans money to Domain, Inc., George cannot refuse to pay it back simply because Domain does not yet exist. At the time George received the loan, she believed the corporation had been formed.

Ethics	Whenever courts use the term "estoppel," it means that they are basing a decision on fairness rather than strict legal rules. Is corporation by estoppel a fair concept? What about *de facto* corporation? What is fair in the following case? ◆

you **Be The Judge**

VALLEY VICTORY CHURCH V. SANDON

2005 MT 72, 109 P.3d 273, 2005 Mont. LEXIS 72
Supreme Court of Montana 2005

Facts: Valley Victory Church incorporated in Montana. The next year, its lawyer filed the annual report required of all corporations. The lawyer then left Montana without telling the church that it needed to continue filing annual reports to retain its status as a corporation. Because the church did not file any more reports, the Secretary of State suspended its corporate status and involuntarily dissolved the corporation. The Secretary of State sent notice of the suspension to the church's lawyer, but his office was then vacant. The church continued operating in good faith (so to speak) as a corporation.

Darvin and Bonnie Struck gave a plot of land to Valley Victory for a new building. Before starting work on the building, the church needed to raise the level of the land. It placed a sign on the land inviting anyone and everyone to dump fill dirt on the property. Many people took advantage of this opportunity. Unfortunately, much of what they dumped contained asphalt and garbage. The Department of Environmental Quality ordered the church to remove all of this improper fill. Valley

▼

Victory filed a tort suit against those who had done the dumping. One of these defendants then filed suit against the Strucks.

At some point during the litigation, the parties discovered that Valley Victory's corporate status had been dissolved some three years earlier. The Strucks could not obtain a tax deduction for their gift unless the church was a legal corporation. However, the Strucks had never sought a deduction, even when they thought the church was legally incorporated.

The Strucks tried to revoke their gift. If they regained ownership of the land, the church would not be able to pursue its lawsuit. At the same time, the Secretary of State reinstated the church's corporate status.

Defendants moved for summary judgment, arguing that because Valley Victory was not in existence at the time of the gift, it could not legally accept the land from the Strucks. The church argued that the gift was valid under the theory of corporation by estoppel.

You Be the Judge: Was the gift of land to Valley Victory Church valid even though the church was not legally a corporation at the time?

Argument for the Strucks and other defendants: The Strucks wanted to give this land to Valley Victory but the church did not exist at the time of the gift. Therefore, the gift is invalid. The Strucks also intended to take a tax deduction for the land that they gave the church. For the Strucks to qualify for this deduction, Valley Victory had to be a corporation. Before the church was reinstated as a corporation, the Strucks withdrew their gift. Therefore, they now own the land.

Argument for the Valley Victory: At the time the gift was made, both sides believed that Valley Victory Church was a corporation. The doctrine of corporation by estoppel prevents one party to a contract from denying the other party's corporate status if it turns out that the corporation did not exist because of some mere technicality.

The Strucks talk about their tax deduction, but they never applied for one, even when they thought Valley Victory was a corporation. The reality is that now they want to avoid any potential liability in the tort lawsuit. It would be not be fair to allow them to escape this liability just because the church, acting in good faith, was involuntarily dissolved at the time the liability arose. ■

INCORPORATION PROCESS

The mechanics of incorporation are easy: simply fill out the form online or mail or fax it to the Secretary of State for your state. But do not let this easy process fool you; the incorporation document needs to be completed with some care. The corporate charter defines the corporation, including everything from the company's name to the number of shares it will issue and the liability of its directors. States use different terms to refer to a charter; some call it the "articles of incorporation," others use "articles of organization," and still others say "certificate" instead of "articles." All of these terms mean the same thing. Similarly, some states use the term "shareholders," and others use "stockholders"; they are both the same.

There is no federal corporation code, which means that a company can incorporate only under state law, not federal law. No matter where a company actually does business, it may incorporate in any state. This decision is important because the organization must live by the laws of whichever state it chooses for incorporation. To encourage similarity among state corporation statutes, the American Bar Association drafted the Model Business Corporation Act as a guide. Many states do use the Act as a model, although Delaware does not. In discussing corporate law in this and the following chapters, we will give examples from both the Model Act and specific states, especially Delaware. Why Delaware? Despite its small size, it has a disproportionate influence on

More than half of all public corporations are incorporated in Delaware, which has a huge influence on corporate law.

corporate law. Although only one third of one percent of the American population lives in Delaware, more than half of all public companies are incorporated there, including 58 percent of Fortune 500 companies.

Where to Incorporate?

Traditionally, companies incorporated either in their home state or in Delaware. They typically must pay filing fees and franchise taxes in their state of incorporation as well as in any state in which they do business. To avoid this double set of fees, a business that will be operating primarily in one state would probably select that state for incorporation rather than Delaware. But if a company is going to do business in several states, it might consider choosing Delaware (or, perhaps, Ohio, Pennsylvania, or Nevada). More information about Delaware corporate law is available at **http://www.state.de.us/corp**. Or browse **http://www.findlaw.com/11stategov/indexcorp .html** for links to all state corporation Web sites.

Delaware has not always been a popular choice for corporations. In the early 1900s, New Jersey held the position that Delaware does today. When Woodrow Wilson became governor (on his way to the White House), he toughened New Jersey's laws. Looking for a state with a more hospitable environment, companies found one across the Delaware River. What is good for business is good for Delaware, too. Each year it collects substantial filing fees and taxes from companies that, for the most part, conduct little business in the state.

Delaware offers corporations several advantages:

- *Laws That Favor Management.* Delaware laws offer flexibility. For example, if the shareholders want to take a vote in writing instead of holding a meeting, many other states require the vote to be unanimous; Delaware requires only a majority to agree. The Delaware legislature also tries to keep up-to-date by changing its code to reflect new developments in corporate law. For example, it was one of the first states to eliminate a rigid format for corporate charters.

- *An Efficient Court System.* Delaware has a special court (called "Chancery Court") that hears nothing but business cases and has judges who are experts in corporate law. In other states, judges who practiced in fields such as criminal law or divorce also hear corporate cases.[1] In an emergency involving, say, a hostile takeover, Delaware judges will hear cases and reach decisions on short notice. This preferential treatment is typically not available in other states.

- *An Established Body of Precedent.* Because so many businesses incorporate in the state, its courts hear a vast number of corporate cases, creating a large body of precedent. Thus lawyers feel they can more easily predict the outcome of a case in Delaware than in a state where few corporate disputes are tried each year.

---

[1] When Pennzoil sued Texaco in Texas over a breach of contract, the judge who tried the case was experienced in hearing divorce cases. Many lawyers felt that his ignorance of corporate matters contributed to the jury's Texas-sized verdict—$11 *billion*.

The financial bonanza that Delaware realizes from its incorporation business has not gone unnoticed by other states. New York, Ohio, Pennsylvania, and, ironically, New Jersey have all modified their corporate laws to attract incorporation business. Large companies in the western part of the country often choose Nevada as their home state because of its attractive laws. Of course, management—not shareholders—chooses the state of incorporation and pays the state fees. Some commentators argue that states are so eager to attract corporate revenue that their laws unfairly favor management over shareholders. They refer to this competition as the "race to the bottom."[2] However, some recent studies indicate that, when a company reincorporates in Delaware, its stock price does not go down. Evidently, financial markets do not perceive shareholders to be at a disadvantage in Delaware.

Ethics

Is it ethical for promoters deliberately to choose a state of incorporation that offers less protection to shareholders than, say, the state in which they do most of their business? What rules do you think a promoter should follow in selecting a state of incorporation? From the Chapter 2 Ethics Checklist: Who are the stakeholders? Does a promoter violate important values by incorporating in a state with lax laws? ◆

Once a company has decided *where* to incorporate, the next step is to prepare and file the charter. The charter must always be filed with the Secretary of State; some jurisdictions also require that it be filed in a county office. Some states supply a form to be completed. Delaware and the Model Act require that certain information be included, but the incorporators can list it any way they want. The incorporators may also include some optional provisions. Sample articles of incorporation for Delaware are available at http://www.state.de.us/corp.

Charter's Required Provisions

Name

The Model Act imposes two requirements in selecting a name. First, all corporations must use one of the following words in their name: "corporation," "incorporated," "company," or "limited." Delaware also accepts some additional terms, such as "association" or "institute." Both the Model Act and Delaware permit abbreviations (such as "inc." or "corp.") or equivalent terms in another language (such as "S.A.," which is French for corporation—it literally means "Société Anonyme").

Second, under both the Model Act and Delaware law, a new corporate name must be different from that of any corporation that already exists in that state. If your name is Freddy du Pont, you cannot name your corporation "Freddy du Pont, Inc.," because Delaware already has a company named E. I. du Pont de Nemours and Company. It does not matter that Freddy du Pont is your real name or that the existing company is a large chemical business while you want to open a video arcade. The names are too similar.

What if you wake from a deep sleep late one night with the perfect corporate name in your head, but the charter is not quite ready for filing? You can reserve a name online in Delaware at http://www.state.de.us/corp for a fee of $10. That takes care of Delaware, but you know your corporation will soon be going national. How can you protect your name in other states? The Model Act also permits the advance registration of a corpo-

---

[2] When Delaware passed its corporation law in 1899, the *American Law Review* attacked its pro-management bias as an effort by a "little community of truck-farmers and clam diggers . . . determined to get her little, tiny, sweet, round, baby hand into the grab bag." Quoted in the *Economist* 10/25/03, p. 55.

rate name. Alternatively, you can form a "nameholder" organization: a corporation that incurs minimum annual fees because it is inactive but does reserve its name.

All this bother and expense discourage most start-ups from reserving their names nationwide. If they later expand into another state where someone else is already using their name, they either buy the name back or use a different name in that jurisdiction. The problem multiplies if they want to register their name overseas as well. When Steven Spielberg, Jeffrey Katzenberg, and David Geffen launched their Hollywood studio, DreamWorks SKG, they spent nearly $500,000 to clear rights to the name in 108 countries around the world. (Of course, that was a small drop in the $2 billion bucket they raised from investors.) The following article illustrates the perils of choosing a name first and checking later.

Citigroup, Inc., the colossus that Travelers Group and Citicorp propose creating, may have hit a bump in the race to the financial future: Renata McGriff. Ms. McGriff started a computer business that distributes gift certificates over the Internet. It just happens to bear the name Citigroup, Inc. Ms. McGriff turned on her TV set and saw Travelers Chairman Sanford I. Weill and Citicorp Chairman John S. Reed announcing their merger. "A reporter asks Sandy, 'What is the name of your new company?' and he says, 'Citigroup,'" she recalled. "And my whole stomach fell out. I said, 'Oh my God, how can this be?'"

Neither Citicorp nor Travelers executives returned her calls in the first days after the merger. She did get through to an acquaintance at Citicorp and explained the problem, she said. Soon afterward, a man came to the lobby of the apartment building where she lives and quizzed the concierge about the existence of a "Citigroup" in the building. When the concierge demanded a name, the man left a name and a phone number that later turned out to be a nonworking exchange, she said.

Richard Howe, a Citicorp spokesman, said that the company sent a "representative" to investigate Ms. McGriff. "It's a standard procedure to determine whether the company is legitimate." "What we want is them to come to us with respect and with courtesy even though I'm small," Ms. McGriff responded. "What we want is not to be investigated. Who are we to them? I think this is despicable."

Mr. Howe confirmed that a Citicorp attorney did finally phone Ms. McGriff. "We have been in touch with her and we're sure we can resolve this in a positive way," he said. Mr. Howe also said that Messrs. Weill and Reed hadn't researched names when they picked one for their $70 billion merger. The transaction "came together very late," he said.[3] ◆

As this article indicates, choosing the right corporate name can be difficult. When Judy George started her company, she considered other names such as Intimacy and Sanctuary before settling on Ciao Italia, Inc. Afterwards, her advertising agency suggested a change to Domain. "It was probably the most emotional part of the process of putting this deal together," George explained. "When I heard 'Domain' I couldn't even talk. I couldn't work. All the heartfelt stuff about the concept just exploded. I just *knew*."

Address and Registered Agent

A company must have an official address in the state in which it is incorporated so that the Secretary of State knows where to contact it—and so that anyone who wants to sue the corporation can serve the complaint in state. Since most companies incorporated in

---

[3] Matt Murray, "Citigroup Inc. Merger May Break New Ground, But Name Doesn't," *Wall Street Journal*, Apr. 13, 1998, p. C1. Republished with permission of The Wall Street Journal; permission conveyed through the Copyright Clearance Center, Inc.

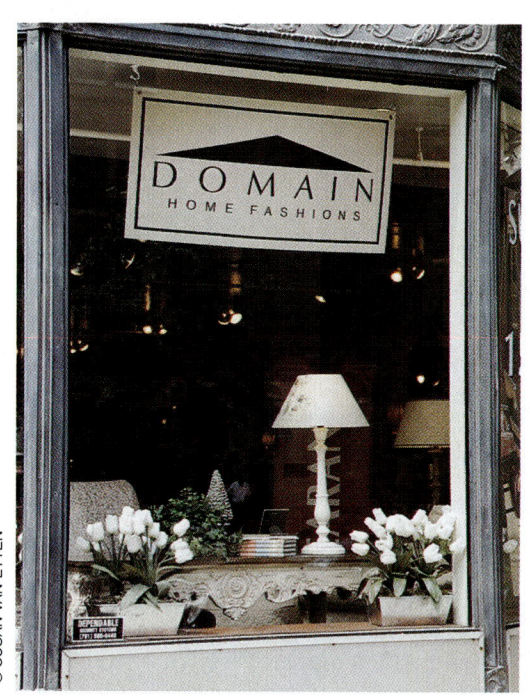

Judy George felt that Domain was the perfect name for her chain of stores.

Delaware do not actually have an office there, they hire a registered agent to serve as their official presence in the state. Agents typically charge about $100 annually for this service.

Incorporators

The incorporator signs the charter and delivers it to the Secretary of State for filing. The incorporator is not required to buy stock nor does he necessarily have any future relationship with the company. Domain's incorporator was William B. Simmons, Jr., the young lawyer who prepared the charter. If no lawyer is involved, the promoter typically serves as incorporator. The incorporator can incur liability only if he knows that something in the charter is not true when he signs it.

Purpose

The corporation is required to give its purpose for existence. In the nineteenth century, when corporations were a new concept, states thought it important to keep tight control over them. Under the ***ultra vires* doctrine,** a corporation cannot undertake any transaction unless its charter specifically permits it. For example, if the purpose clause in Domain's charter said "To operate a retail home furnishings business," then the company might not be allowed to sell clothing or open restaurants.

Corporate officers understandably chafed at this restriction. To avoid problems of *ultra vires*, most companies now use a very broad purpose clause such as Domain's:

> The nature of the business or purposes to be conducted or promoted is to engage in any lawful act or activity for which corporations may be organized under the General Corporation Law of Delaware.

Essentially, the only way to violate this purpose clause is to commit an illegal act.

Stock

The charter must provide three items of information about the company's stock.

Par Value. The concept of par value was designed to protect investors. Originally, par value was supposed to be close to market price. A company could not issue stock at a price less than par, which meant that it could not sell to insiders at a sweetheart price well below market value. (Once the stock was *issued*, it could be *traded* at any price.) In modern times, par value does not relate to market value; it is usually some nominal figure such as 1¢ or $1 per share. Companies can dispense with the concept altogether and issue stock that has no par value. When making this decision, the company should check the state's filing fees because they may be based on the par value of the company's stock. Domain stock has a par value of 1¢ per share.

Number of Shares. Before stock can be sold, it must first be authorized in the charter. The corporation can authorize as many shares as the incorporators choose, but the more shares, the higher the filing fee. In Delaware, the basic filing fee for a certificate of incorporation is $89. That fee includes 1,500 shares at no par value. The filing fee is higher if the corporation wants more shares or shares with par value. After incorporation, a company can add authorized shares by simply amending its charter and paying the additional fee. The Domain charter initially authorized 10,000 shares, but soon increased this number to over 10 million.

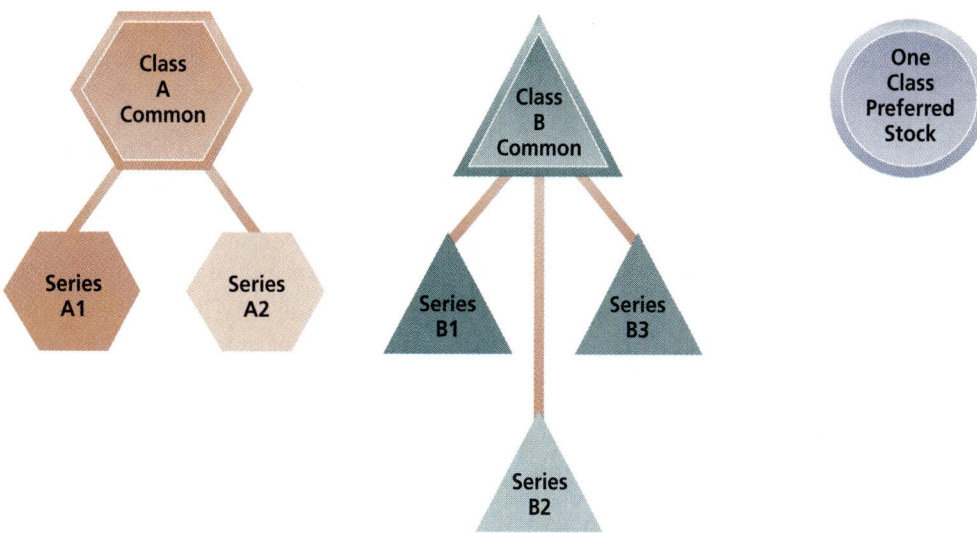

Exhibit 34.1

Stock that has been authorized but not yet sold is called **authorized and unissued.** Stock that has been sold is termed **authorized and issued** or **outstanding.** Stock that the company has sold but later bought back is **treasury stock.**

Classes and Series. Different shareholders often make different contributions to a company. Some may be involved in management, while others may simply contribute financially. Early investors may feel that they are entitled to more control than those who come along later (and who perhaps take less risk). Corporate structure can be infinitely flexible in defining the rights of these various shareholders. Stock can be divided into categories called **classes,** and these classes can be further divided into subcategories called **series.** All stock in a series has the same rights, and all series in a class are fundamentally the same, except for minor distinctions. For example, in a class of preferred stock, all shareholders may be entitled to a dividend, but the amount of the dividend may vary by series. Different classes of stock, however, may have very different rights—a class of preferred stock is different from a class of common stock. Exhibit 34.1 illustrates the concept of class and series. Defining the rights of a class or series of stock is like baking a cake—the stock can contain virtually any combination of the following ingredients (although the result may not be to everyone's taste):

- *Dividend Rights.* The charter establishes whether the shareholder is entitled to dividends and, if so, in what amount. No matter what the charter says, the corporation may not pay dividends unless it is solvent, that is, unless it has enough assets to pay its debts.

- *Voting Rights.* Shareholders are usually entitled to elect directors and vote on charter amendments, among other issues, but these rights can vary among different series and classes of stock. When Ford Motor Co. went public in 1956, it issued Class B common stock to members of the Ford family. This class of stock holds about 40 percent of the voting power and, thereby, effectively controls the company. Not surprisingly, the chairman of the company is often named "Ford."

- *Liquidation Rights.* The charter specifies the order in which classes of stockholders will be paid upon dissolution of the company. This provision is important if there are not enough assets to pay everyone.

- *Preemptive Rights.* If a corporation later issues additional shares of its stock, the original shareholders will own a smaller percentage of the company. For example, if a company has 10 shareholders, each owning one share, and it later issues another 10 shares to others, each of the old shareholders will then own 5 percent of the company instead of 10 percent. To prevent this **dilution,** some companies grant preemptive rights: the old shareholders have the right to acquire enough new stock to prevent their share of the company from being diminished. In our example, each old shareholder would be entitled to buy enough new shares to keep their ownership at 10 percent. Of course, they are not required to buy this stock.

- *Conversion Rights.* Some classes of stock may have the right to convert into shares of a different class. For example, if a company does not meet its financial projections, nonvoting stock may have the right to convert into voting stock.

- *Redemption Rights.* Similarly, the shareholders of some classes of stock may have the right to force a company to buy their stock back if, for example, the company does not meet its financial goals.

These are the ingredients for any class or series of stock. Some stock comes prepackaged like a cake mix. "Preferred" and "common" stock are two classic types.

Owners of *preferred stock* have preference on dividends and also, typically, in liquidation. If a class of preferred stock is entitled to dividends, then it must receive its dividends before common stockholders are paid theirs. If holders of **cumulative preferred** stock miss their dividend one year, common shareholders cannot receive a dividend until the cumulative preferred shareholders have been paid, no matter how long that takes. Alternatively, holders of **non-cumulative preferred** stock lose an annual dividend for good if the company cannot afford it in the year it is due. When a company dissolves, preferred stockholders typically have the right to receive their share of corporate assets before common shareholders. Exhibit 34.2 illustrates the order of payment for dividends.

Preferred stock can have any combination of other ingredients, such as preemptive rights or conversion rights. Sometimes preferred shareholders have voting rights, but usually they do not. Venture capitalists (professional investors who are in the business of financing companies) often choose preferred stock because it enables them to share the increased equity value if the company does well and also to be ahead of the other stockholders (such as the founders) when it comes to dividends and liquidation.

Common stock is last in line for any corporate payouts, including dividends and liquidation payments. If the company is liquidated, creditors of the company and preferred shareholders are typically paid before common shareholders. But being a common shareholder is not all bad news—common shareholders often have most of

Exhibit 34.2

the voting rights. They also have greater profit potential; preferred stock typically has a limit on the size of dividends, common does not. If the business does well, common stock will often increase in value faster than preferred stock.

The Domain charter demonstrates how flexible stock classes and series can be. The company began with common stock only. Then it added a class of cumulative preferred, which is divided into 11 series, one for each group of investors. Both classes have one vote for each share of stock, and the preferred shareholders may convert their stock into common shares, but the conversion rate is different for each series.

This ends our discussion of Domain. Like many businesses, the company has seen some lean times, but it has survived and flourished.

Charter's Optional Provisions

Many corporations add optional provisions to their charters. Bear in mind, however, that once a provision is in the charter, it can be changed only by a vote of the shareholders and the filing of an amendment with the Secretary of State. This process can be cumbersome and expensive. Therefore, when in doubt, it is usually a good idea not to include extra provisions in the charter. Nonetheless, some provisions are so important that they belong there, despite the effort and expense.

Indemnification of Directors

Although incorporation protects shareholders against personal liability for the debts of the company, anyone involved in the management of the business can be personally liable for his own wrongdoing. For example, shareholders may sue directors for making an unprofitable decision. The potential liability in such a lawsuit is enormous. Even if the director is found not liable, the legal fees can be devastating. Consider the following example.

NEWS*worthy*

Leonard Shoen not only founded U-Haul, the truck rental company, he also raised 12 children. His family may have been big, but it was not happy. Son Joe forced Leonard into retirement and took over management. Joe then assaulted brother Sam at one board meeting and brother Mike at another. Two years later, Leonard joined forces with six of his children to regain his place on the board. Their goal was to sell the company.

When Joe resisted, Leonard and his allies filed suit, charging that the board of directors had violated its duty to shareholders. A jury agreed—it ordered Joe and the other directors to pay the plaintiffs $1.47 *billion*. The judge ultimately reduced the verdict to $461 million. Because U-Haul had promised to indemnify its directors "to the full extent of the law," the company was forced to authorize new shares of stock to raise the money owed. ◆

Under most state statutes, a corporation may include in its charter a provision indemnifying directors unless they have engaged in egregious misbehavior involving, for example, bad faith or intentional misconduct.[4] Not surprisingly, many people refuse to serve as a director unless the company **indemnifies** them, that is, pays any liability (including legal fees) they incur from doing their job.

Cumulative Voting

For sheer drama, few corporate battles have exceeded the fight between the elephant, Gulf Oil, and the flea, Mesa Petroleum. When T. Boone Pickens, the CEO of Mesa, announced that Gulf Oil was badly managed, he was picking on the sixth largest oil

---

[4] See, for example, 8 Del. C. §102(7).

company in America. Pickens nominated himself to be Gulf's savior. His plan was to buy enough of the company's shares so that he could elect himself to the board of directors. Pickens's goal was possible only because Gulf was incorporated in Pennsylvania, a state that then had cumulative voting.

At the time, Gulf Oil had 15 directors, all elected annually. Under a *regular* voting system, the 15 people who receive the most votes are awarded the seats. If Pickens owned one share, he could vote for as many as 15 *different* candidates, but he could not pool his votes; that is, he could not cast multiple votes for any one candidate. Thus he could only vote for himself once. To be sure of getting elected to the board, he would have to buy half of Gulf's shares, plus one. Gulf had 165 million shares outstanding, so Pickens would have to buy 82,500,001 shares. Once he had bought that many shares, he could elect *all* the directors, because he would own a majority of the company's stock. As Gulf's stock was trading at around $40 per share, Pickens would have had to invest more than $3 billion ($3,300,000,040) to achieve his goal.

Under a cumulative voting system, however, Pickens is allowed to pool his shares and vote them all for the same person (in this case, himself). How many shares would Pickens have to own to elect himself to the board? This is the formula:

$$\frac{\text{Number of shares}}{\text{needed to elect one director}} = \frac{\text{Number of shares outstanding}}{\text{Number of directors being elected} + 1} + 1$$

This is how the formula worked in Pickens's case, where x stands for the number of shares he needed to elect one director:

$$x = \frac{165,000,000}{15 + 1} + 1$$

$$x = 10,312,501$$

This 10 million shares is a lot less than the 82 million he needed under a regular voting system. At a price per share of $40, Pickens would have to invest roughly $400 million ($412,500,040) under a cumulative voting system, compared with $3 billion under a regular system.

In a desperate effort to prevent Pickens from being elected to its board of directors, Gulf called a special meeting of shareholders to change its state of incorporation from Pennsylvania to Delaware and eliminate cumulative voting. For months, both sides ran full-page advertisements in newspapers across the country to persuade shareholders. Gulf spent $9 million and Mesa $8 million on the fight alone, not counting money spent buying Gulf shares. In the end, Gulf won the battle but lost the war. It won the shareholder vote by a small margin, but the company was so weakened by this fight that it sold out to Chevron Oil shortly thereafter. The fight so frightened other companies that many changed their state of organization to Delaware to avoid cumulative voting. Pennsylvania changed its statute to agree with the Model Act: any company can choose to have cumulative voting; none is required to.

AFTER INCORPORATION

Once the charter has been filed (and the filing fee paid), the corporation legally exists, but work is not done yet. The shareholders must still complete a few additional tasks.

Directors and Officers

Once the corporation is organized, the incorporators elect the first set of directors. Thereafter, shareholders elect directors. Under the Model Act, a corporation is required to have at least one director, unless (1) *all* the shareholders sign an agreement that eliminates the board, or (2) the corporation has 50 or fewer shareholders. To elect directors, the shareholders may hold a meeting, or, in the more typical case for a small company, they elect directors by **written consent.** (In most states and under the Model Act, all the shareholders must sign, but in Delaware a majority is sufficient.) A typical written consent looks like this:

Classic American Novels, Inc.
Written Consent

The undersigned shareholders of Classic American Novels, Inc., a corporation organized and existing under the General Corporation Law of the State of Wherever, hereby agree that the following action shall be taken with full force and effect as if voted at a validly called and held meeting of the shareholders of the corporation:

    Agreed: That the following people are elected to serve as directors for one year, or until their successors have been duly elected and qualified:

        Herman Melville

        Louisa May Alcott

        Mark Twain

Dated: _____ Signed: _____
                                    Willa Cather

Dated: _____ Signed: _____
                                 Nathaniel Hawthorne

Dated: _____ Signed: _____
                                Harriet Beecher Stowe

Once the incorporators or shareholders have chosen the directors, the directors must elect the officers of the corporation. They can use a consent form, if they wish. The Model Act is flexible. It simply requires a corporation to have whatever officers are described in the bylaws. The same person can hold more than one office.

The written consents and any records of actual meetings are kept in a **minute book,** which is the official record of the corporation. Entrepreneurs sometimes feel they are too busy to bother with all these details, but, if a corporation is ever sold, the lawyers for the buyers will *insist* on a well-organized and complete minute book. In one case, a company that was seeking a $100,000 bank loan could not find all of its minutes. Many of its early shareholders and directors were not available to reauthorize prior deeds. In the end, the company had to merge itself into a newly created corporation so it could start fresh with a new set of corporate records. The company spent $10,000 on this task, a large chunk out of the $100,000 loan.

Bylaws

The **bylaws** list all the "housekeeping" details for the corporation. For example, bylaws set the date of the annual shareholders' meeting, define what a quorum is (i.e., what percentage of stock must be represented for a meeting to count), indicate how many directors there will be, give titles to officers, fix the procedure for calling a special meeting of the shareholders or directors, and establish the fiscal (i.e., tax) year of the corporation. When there is a choice, it is usually better to place provisions in the bylaws rather than the charter, because the bylaws are easier to change. Under the Model Act, directors can amend the bylaws without calling a meeting of the shareholders or paying a filing fee. The shareholders can always override the directors if they want, but they rarely do. A sample set of bylaws is available at http://www.lectlaw.com/forms/f151.htm and http://www.tannedfeet.com/by-laws_for_a_business_corporation.doc. In the following case, the directors' ignorance of company bylaws led to disaster.

In Re BIGMAR

2002 Del. Ch. LEXIS 45
Court of Chancery, Delaware, 2002

Facts: Bigmar was a Delaware corporation that manufactured and marketed pharmaceuticals in Europe. While trying to raise additional capital, the company's founder, John Tramontana, met Cynthia May. She lied to him about her education, wealth, and connections in the investment community. Unfortunately, he believed her. The upshot was that May became Bigmar's president and a director of the company. She soon took control of the company's financial records and refused to give Tramontana any information (always a bad sign).[5] When Bigmar ran out of money, Tramontana sent May an e-mail asking for her resignation. She did not respond. (Also a bad sign.)

The company was in desperate financial shape, but Tramontana managed to find a bank willing to buy $1 million of Bigmar stock. He called a special meeting of the board of directors to approve the sale of shares and to fire May. The meeting was to take place by telephone. To establish a quorum necessary for the meeting to be valid, at least five of the nine directors had to take part. May and her three allies on the board refused to participate.

Tramontana testified that, at the appointed time, he met with two directors in his office. They used a speaker feature on a cell phone that Tramontana borrowed from Danilo Graticola to call two other directors, one of whom was in Heathrow airport in London. The five directors unanimously resolved to issue the stock to the bank. The meeting then adjourned so that they could consult counsel. It was reconvened the next day, at which time they voted to fire May.

The following day, the bank transferred $1 million to Bigmar. Tramontana instructed the company's transfer agent to send stock certificates to the bank, but May contradicted his order. Tramontana and May went to court to determine if the director's meeting was valid and the bank entitled to the shares.

Issue: Was the meeting of the Bigmar board of directors valid?

Excerpts from Judge Jacobs's Decision: Ms. May attacks the validity of the meeting(s) [claiming that] no meeting at which a quorum of directors was present, ever took place.

There is evidence that the meeting(s) did occur. Minutes of the meetings were prepared, and all but one of the Tramontana directors gave sworn testimony that the meeting(s) took place exactly as the minutes recite. Ordinarily that would be sufficient, but this is not an ordinary case, for several reasons.

First, the minutes were prepared by counsel, who was not present at the meetings, and who simply reduced to writing what Mr. Tramontana told him had occurred. Second, there is no independent documentation or testimony of any third party witness that corroborates the directors' testimony. Moreover, any notes taken at the meeting(s) were destroyed.

▼

---

[5]   She did, however, send him this e-mail: I wish for GOd's sake that you would GROW [UP] just a little . . . you've F the banking up here in Sweden so I can't get the money that I made [arrangements] for . . . damn idiot . . . take a shower and clean your ears out . . . you can't follow a straight line without having your ego and little hissy fits . . . Get off the play ground . . . before the big boys beat you up. . .

Further, many of the telephone records whose production was requested were not produced, and the records that were produced either fail to corroborate the Tramontana directors' testimony,[6] or those documents are inconsistent with that testimony.[7]

Third, for the directors' testimony to be accepted, the Court would have to "buy into" a scenario that (to put it charitably) is most improbable. Although Mr. Tramontana had a speaker phone in his office, he testified that he decided to conduct the board meeting on Mr. Graticola's borrowed cell phone. His explanation for that unusual decision was that Mr. Graticola had described his new cell phone's technology in glowing terms and Mr. Tramontana elected to use the telephone to ingratiate his company with Graticola. [T]he story does have some plausibility, however slight. But even that minimal plausibility vanishes when one is told that the same identical scenario occurred a second time, at the adjourned meeting. I find this scenario too implausible for even a gullible fact finder to swallow. Accordingly, the Court is unable to determine that those directors' meetings were validly convened and conducted.

Although the analysis could stop here, that would leave the Court (and perhaps a reader of this Opinion) with a sense of dissatisfaction, because Mr. Tramontana's testimony leaves unanswered questions. In purely human terms, this issue was most difficult and perplexing for the Court.

It is plausible, and the available evidence does indicate, that Mr. Tramontana attempted to assemble all of his colleagues for a telephonic meeting.

[But one director] was unavailable, as he was en route from London to Ireland at that time. Because a quorum required the attendance of five directors, [this director's] unavailability meant that the telephonic meeting failed for lack of a quorum. Mr. Tramontana believed, nonetheless, that the problem could be solved by obtaining from himself and his colleagues' individual written consent resolutions taking the actions recited in the minutes. Unfortunately (and unbeknownst to Mr. Tramontana), Bigmar's by-laws required that any director action by written consent must be unanimous. [When] Mr. Tramontana learned of that unanimity requirement, [he] decided to [say] that a quorum of five directors was present, and that a board meeting was held.

I am persuaded that [Mr. Tramontana and his colleagues acted] in the good-faith belief that unless the issuance of the shares to the Bank was upheld, the Company would fall into the hands of Ms. May, who was incapable of saving the Company. I think it plausible that they believed that at worst, they failed to observe a highly technical legal requirement that, on balance, was too insignificant to justify the ruination of the Company.

The principles of corporate governance, such as those violated here, exist precisely because those procedures enable courts and parties to distinguish between acts that lawfully bind the corporation and its constituents, from those that do not. The directors may have believed in good faith that they had no alternative but to testify as they did, but good faith is not sufficient to validate a procedurally invalid proceeding. ■

Shareholder Agreements

Sometimes shareholders want to agree in advance how they will vote their stock. For example, Craig O. McCaw was willing to sell a majority interest in Cellular One to Affiliated Publications, but he was not willing to give up control of the company. After all, he had single-handedly built it into the largest cell phone company in the United States. His solution? McCaw and Affiliated entered into a shareholder agreement requiring Affiliated to vote its stock in Cellular One as McCaw directed. Affiliated trusted McCaw's business acumen enough to want him to continue running the company although he was only a minority shareholder.

---

6 [The] cell phone bills for the [director who is supposed to have received a call in the London airport] do not show any incoming calls to him at Heathrow Airport at 3:00 P.M., London time, which is when the meeting is said to have started. Since [his] cell phone provider was located in Ireland where he lived, [this director] would have incurred a roaming charge for any calls received outside of Ireland, and the roaming charge would have been reflected on his cell phone bill.

7 For example, Mr. Tramontana's telephone records show that he made an 11-minute telephone call to Mr. Graticola's cell phone number at 7:12 P.M.—a time that Mr. Tramontana claimed to have had Mr. Graticola's cell phone in his possession.

Sometimes, shareholders use a voting trust instead of a shareholder agreement to accomplish the same goal. The shareholders transfer their stock to a trust, granting the trustee power to vote it. While a shareholder agreement may be limited to votes on specific issues (such as electing directors), the trustee has control over the trust shares for every vote. For a sample shareholder agreement, browse **http://www.alllaw.com/ forms/BUSINESS/Corporation/shareholder_agreemen**.

at RISK

The shareholders of a start-up company often work together intensively. If a shareholder sells her stock to someone who does not share the same vision, conflict is inevitable. To avoid this situation, shareholders of start-ups typically sign a shareholder agreement, granting a right of first refusal on the company's stock. In a typical agreement, if a shareholder wants to sell, she must first offer the stock to the company at the same price that the outsider has offered. If, after 30 days, the company has not agreed to buy the stock, she must then offer it to the other shareholders. Only if they also refuse to buy it within 30 days, can she then sell it to an outsider at the same price that she offered to the company and shareholders. Similarly, if a shareholder dies, his estate may be required to offer the stock to the company or other shareholders. In the case of death, it is more difficult to determine the market value of the stock, so the shareholder agreement often provides a formula for making this determination. ◆

Issuing Debt

Most start-up companies begin with some combination of equity and debt. Equity (i.e., stock) is described in the charter; debt is not. Authorizing debt is often one of the first steps a new company takes. There are several types of debt:

- **Bonds** are long-term debt secured by some of the company's assets. If the company is unable to pay the debt, creditors have a right to specific assets, such as accounts receivable or inventory.

- **Debentures** are long-term *unsecured* debt. If the company cannot meet its obligations, the debenture holders are paid after bondholders, but before stockholders.

- **Notes** are short-term debt, typically payable within five years. They may be either secured or unsecured.

Foreign Corporations

A company is called a *domestic* corporation in the state where it incorporates and a *foreign* corporation everywhere else. States have only limited control over foreign corporations.

Ned has sworn that he will never again suffer through a bitter Chicago winter. No, he is not relocating; he has invented a new fabric that looks like fur. It is better than the original, though, because it breathes, repels water, and is washable. He knows that his business will soon be a national success.

Ned, like many entrepreneurs before him, incorporates Fabulous Fake Furs, Inc. (FFF), in Delaware. He is still, however, living in Chicago (where he now *adores* the winter). Company headquarters are down the street from his condominium. The main manufacturing facility is in Texas, with warehouses in Minnesota and New York. A sales staff calls on all the major department stores, catalog companies, and online merchants across the country.

Ned has obligations to the state of Delaware because he incorporated there—he must pay taxes and annual fees. But what about the other states where he is doing business? Someone had to pay to build the roads and educate the workforce in these states.

Must he contribute, too? The states certainly think so. They require a foreign corporation that is doing business within their borders to register with them and obtain a "certificate of authority." This registration process is called **qualifying to do business.**

What constitutes "doing business"? **Opening an office or establishing any other ongoing presence counts as doing business.** Clearly, FFF must register in Illinois, Texas, Minnesota, and New York because it has a permanent presence in these states. Typically, the following activities do *not* count as doing business: holding meetings, opening a bank account, soliciting sales orders, or any isolated transaction. If FFF's directors hold a meeting in Alaska, Ned attends a trade show in Wisconsin, or a sales rep takes an order at a store in California, these activities do not constitute doing business, and FFF does not have to register in these states.

To qualify, a company must file corporate documents with the state, list a registered agent, and pay annual fees and taxes on income generated in that jurisdiction. As a general rule, of course, companies would prefer not to register. Some states fine any companies they catch doing business without registering. Under the Model Act, a company that is doing business without qualifying cannot bring a lawsuit in that state until it registers (and pays back fees, taxes, and penalties). But note that, if the company is not actually doing business, then it may file suit without qualifying first. And whether or not it has qualified, a company can always *defend* against a lawsuit.

DEATH OF THE CORPORATION

Sometimes, business ideas are not successful and the corporation fails. This death can be voluntary (the shareholders elect to terminate the corporation) or forced (by court order). Sometimes, a court takes a step that is much more damaging to shareholders than simply dissolving the corporation—it removes the shareholders' limited liability.

Piercing the Corporate Veil

One of the major purposes of a corporation is to protect its owners—the shareholders—from personal liability for the debts of the organization. Sometimes, however, a court will **pierce the corporate veil;** that is, the court will hold shareholders personally liable for the debts of the corporation. Courts generally pierce a corporate veil in four circumstances:

- *Failure to Observe Formalities.* If an organization does not act like a corporation, it will not be treated like one. It must, for example, hold required shareholders' and directors' meetings (or sign consents), keep a minute book as a record of these meetings, and make all the required state filings. Even a corporation with only one shareholder must comply with these formalities. Sole shareholders usually just sign a written consent in lieu of a meeting. In addition, officers must be careful to sign all corporate documents with a corporate title, not as an individual. Otherwise, creditors may well be in doubt about whether they were dealing with an individual or a corporation. An officer should sign like this:

Classic American Novels, Inc.

By: *Stephen Crane*

Stephen Crane, President

If he signs simply, "Stephen Crane," creditors may successfully claim that he is personally liable.

- *Commingling of Assets.* Nothing makes a court more willing to pierce a corporate veil than evidence that shareholders have mixed their assets with those of the corporation. Sometimes, for example, shareholders use corporate assets to pay their personal debts or even mix corporate and personal funds in one bank account. If shareholders commingle assets, it is genuinely difficult for creditors to determine which assets belong to whom. This confusion is generally resolved in favor of the creditors—*all* assets are deemed to belong to the corporation.

Fireworks cause injuries. If a corporation that sells fireworks fails to purchase adequate insurance, its shareholders may be personally liable.

- *Inadequate Capitalization.* If the founders of a corporation do not raise enough capital (either through debt or equity) to give the business a fighting chance of paying its debts, courts may require shareholders to pay corporate obligations. Therefore, if the corporation does not have sufficient capital, it needs to buy insurance, particularly to protect against tort liability. Judges are likelier to hold shareholders liable if the alternative is to send an injured tort victim away empty-handed. For example, Oriental Fireworks Co. had hundreds of thousands of dollars in annual sales, but only $13,000 in assets. The company did not bother to obtain any liability insurance, keep a minute book, or defend lawsuits. There was no need because the company had no money. But then a court pierced the corporate veil and found the owner of the company personally liable.[8]

- *Fraud.* Corporations cannot be used to shelter fraud. Imagine that a con artist forms a corporation entitled Brooklyn Bridge, Inc. He then sells shares in the organization by convincing "investors," aka "pigeons," that the company really does own the famous New York landmark. If he is caught, the pigeons can go after his personal assets, even though the fraud was committed in the name of a corporation.

The following case is a good example of when a court should pierce the corporate veil.

BROOKS V. BECKER

2005 Va. Cir. LEXIS 13
Circuit Court of Fairfax County, Virginia, 2005

Facts: The facts are set out in the opening scenario. Brooks sued Becker in an attempt to pierce the corporate veil and hold Becker personally liable for the debts of the corporation.

Issues: Can Brooks pierce the corporate veil? Is Becker personally liable for the debts of the corporation?

Excerpts from Judge Roush's Decision: The decision to ignore the separate existence of a corporate entity and impose personal liability upon shareholders for debts of the corporation is an extraordinary act to be taken only when necessary to promote justice. Disregarding the corporate entity is usually warranted only under the extraordinary circumstances where: the shareholder sought to be held personally liable has controlled or used the corpora-

---

8   *Rice v. Oriental Fireworks Co.*, 75 Or. App. 627, 707 P.2d 1250, 1985 Ore. App. LEXIS 3928.

tion to evade a personal obligation, to perpetrate fraud or a crime, to commit an injustice, or to gain an unfair advantage. Piercing the corporate veil is justified when the unity of interest and ownership is such that the separate personalities of the corporation and the individual no longer exist and to adhere to that separateness would work an injustice.

In this case, the evidence convinces the court that the extraordinary remedy of piercing the corporate veil should be granted. Becker knowingly violated his duties as an officer, director and shareholder of Becker Interiors and treated the corporation's funds as his personal piggy bank. His testimony that the corporate expenditures on his personal residence were a legitimate business expense because he wanted to use the residence as a showcase of his work was simply not credible. Nor did the court believe Becker's testimony that he commingled his personal funds with the corporation's funds on the advice of his accountant. The court found more credible Becker's later testimony that his accountant was "mystified" by his comingling of funds between his personal and corporate accounts.

Accordingly, the court will enter judgment against Becker in the amount of $54,597.09. ■

Termination

Terminating a corporation is a three-step process:

- *Vote.* The directors recommend to the shareholders that the corporation be dissolved, and a majority of the shareholders agree.
- *Filing.* The corporation files "Articles of Dissolution" with the Secretary of State.
- *Winding Up.* The officers of the corporation pay its debts and distribute the remaining property to shareholders. When the winding up is completed, the corporation ceases to exist.

The Secretary of State may dissolve a corporation that violates state law by, for example, failing to pay the required annual fees (as happened in the *Valley Victory Church* case earlier in this chapter). Indeed, many corporations, particularly small ones, do not bother with the formal dissolution process. They simply cease paying their required annual fees and let the Secretary of State act. A court may dissolve a corporation if it is insolvent or if its directors and shareholders cannot resolve conflict over how the corporation should be managed. The court will then appoint a receiver to oversee the winding up.

© BRAND X PICTURES/GETTY IMAGES

Chapter Conclusion

Most of the country's largest businesses, and many of its small ones, are corporations. Although corporations are an exceedingly useful form of organization, they are also exceedingly formal. State corporation codes contain precise rules that must be followed to the letter. To do otherwise is to court disaster.

Chapter Review

1. Promoters are personally liable for contracts they sign before the corporation is formed unless the corporation and the third party agree to a novation.

2. Companies generally incorporate in the state in which they will be doing business. However, if they intend to operate in several states, they may choose to incorporate in a jurisdiction known for its favorable corporate laws, such as Delaware or Nevada.

3. A corporate charter must generally include the company's name, address, registered agent, purpose, and a description of its stock. The charter must be signed by at least one incorporator.

4. A company's charter may include a number of optional provisions such as cumulative voting and indemnification for officers and directors.

5. A corporation must register in every state in which it is doing business.

6. A court may, under certain circumstances, pierce the corporate veil and hold shareholders personally liable for the debts of the corporation.

7. Termination of a corporation is a three-step process requiring a shareholder vote, the filing of "Articles of Dissolution," and the winding up of the enterprise's business.

Practice Test

1. Michael Ferns incorporated Erin Homes, Inc., to manufacture mobile homes. He issued himself a stock certificate for 100 shares for which he made no payment. He and his wife served as officers and directors of the organization, but, during the eight years of its existence, the corporation held only one meeting. Erin always had its own checking account, and all proceeds from the sales of mobile homes were deposited there. It filed federal income tax returns each year, using its own federal identification number. John and Thelma Laya paid $17,500 to purchase a mobile home from Erin, but the company never delivered it to them. The Layas sued Erin Homes and Michael Ferns, individually. Should the court "pierce the corporate veil" and hold Ferns personally liable?

2. **YOU BE THE JUDGE** WRITING PROBLEM Davis Ajouelo signed an employment contract with William Wilkerson. The contract stated: "Whatever company, partnership, or corporation that Wilkerson may form for the purpose of manufacturing shall succeed Wilkerson and exercise the rights and assume all of Wilkerson's obligations as fixed by this contract." Two months later, Wilkerson formed Auto-Soler Co. Ajouelo entered into a new contract with Auto-Soler providing that the company was liable for Wilkerson's obligations under the old contract. Neither Wilkerson nor the company ever paid Ajouelo. He sued Wilkerson personally. Does Wilkerson have any obligations to Ajouelo? **Argument for Ajouelo:** The first contract with Wilkerson provided that a subsequent company would "assume all of Wilkerson's obligations." It did not say that Wilkerson was no longer liable, simply that the new corporation was *also* on the hook. Ajouelo did the work and deserves to be paid. **Argument for Wilkerson:** The new contract was a novation and, therefore, Wilkerson is not liable.

3. **CPA QUESTION** Destiny Manufacturing, Inc., is incorporated under the laws of Nevada. Its principal place of business is in California, and it has permanent sales offices in several other states. Under the circumstances, which of the following is correct?

a. California may validly demand that Destiny incorporate under the laws of the state of California.

b. Destiny must obtain a certificate of authority to transact business in California and the other states in which it does business.

c. Destiny is a foreign corporation in California, but **not** in the other states.

d. California may prevent Destiny from operating as a corporation if the laws of California differ regarding organization and conduct of the corporation's internal affairs.

4. **CPA QUESTION** Generally, a corporation's articles of incorporation must include all of the following **except** the:

a. Name of the corporation's registered agent

b. Name of each incorporator

c. Number of authorized shares

d. Quorum requirements

5. **ETHICS** This case arises out of an unpaid hotel bill. An organization called the 21st Century Commission on African American Males made arrangements for a conference at the Omni Shoreham Hotel in Washington. J. D. Andrews signed the contract on behalf of the commission. Although the commission made some payments, $88,044.07 was still outstanding on the bill. The commission was not incorporated at the time of the conference, but it did subsequently incorporate. The Carnegie Corp., Xerox Corp., former

Virginia Governor L. Douglas Wilder, and former United States Senator Terry Sanford were active participants in and organizers of the commission. Their employees served on a planning committee for the commission. This planning committee entered into the agreement with the Shoreham Hotel. Were Carnegie, Xerox, Wilder, and Sanford liable for the hotel bill as promoters of the commission? Whether or not the defendants were *legally* responsible for the debt, did they have an *ethical* obligation to pay? Did their wealth and fame lure the hotel into a contract with the commission? What would the Ethics Checklist in Chapter 2 suggest as a possible answer?

6. **CPA QUESTION** A corporate stockholder is entitled to which of the following rights?

   a. Elect officers

   b. Receive annual dividends

   c. Approve dissolution

   d. Prevent corporate borrowing

7. The Resolution Trust Corp. (RTC) sued the directors of the Commonwealth Savings Association seeking to recover from them personally $200 million that the bank lost in bad real estate loans. The directors approved the loans after state and federal regulatory agencies had issued reports criticizing the bank's loan practices. The directors failed to implement policies and procedures to prevent problems with the loan portfolio and failed to monitor loan officers adequately. There was no evidence that the directors knowingly committed illegal acts or acts outside their authority. Under Texas law, the RTC could recover for the directors' negligence only if their acts were *ultra vires*. Were these acts *ultra vires*?

8. Waste Management, Inc., the country's largest waste hauler, changed its name to WMX Technologies, Inc. Similarly, U.S. Steel changed its moniker to USX Corp. and American Airlines became AMR Corp. What legal steps would be necessary for WMX to protect its new corporate name?

9. Angelica is planning to start a home security business in McGehee, Arkansas. She plans to start modestly but hopes to expand her business within 5 years to neighboring towns and, perhaps, within 10 years to neighboring states. Her inclination is to incorporate her business in Delaware? Is her inclination correct?

10. **ROLE REVERSAL** A number of the cases in this chapter focus on companies that suffered harmful consequences because they failed to comply with corporate technicalities. Write a short-answer question in which students are asked to identify several examples of such laxity.

Internet Research Problem

Think of an idea for a new company and prepare a corporate charter for your business. You can find examples of Delaware charters at **http://beatty.west-buslaw.com**. For extra credit, find a sample charter for your own state.

> **You can find further practice problems at http://beatty.westbuslaw.com or in the Study Guide that accompanies this text.**

Corporate Management

Suppose that you were a shareholder of Wallace Computer Services, Inc. The company's stock was trading between $35 and $40 when, out of the blue, Moore Corp. offered to buy all the stock for $56 a share. A few days later, Moore raised its offer to $60. Wow! You quickly tendered your stock to Moore and sat back to wait for the check, while visions of luxury danced in your head. You were in good company: the owners of nearly three-quarters of Wallace stock also tendered. But the check never came because Wallace's board of directors turned down the offer. How is that? The board said that the company was worth more. How much more? Well, a year after the board rejected Moore's $60 offer, Wallace stock was trading at $56. During the same period, the stock market had risen 20 percent. If you had sold your Wallace stock and invested the proceeds in the market, your $60 would have been worth $72. Wallace shareholders lost out on $74 million in that year alone. But the worst was not over. During the next few years, while the stock market continued to rise, Wallace stock hit a low of $15.44.

You had hoped that your profits from Wallace would enable you to quit your day job at Chase Manhattan Bank and start a business of your own. Bitter that your dream had been deferred, you often complained to your co-workers about this grave injustice, "How totally unfair, how outrageous for a board to ignore the best interests of its own shareholders!" Then one day over lunch the conversation turned to Michael Price, a prominent mutual fund manager, who had purchased 6.1 percent of Chase's stock. He reportedly was pushing the bank's board to start an auction for its stock and then sell out to the highest bidder. Your co-workers were nervous because they knew the new owner would try to increase profits by firing as many workers as possible. Rumors were flying that, to preempt Price, the board would soon start to fire employees itself. You and your fellow workers feared pink slips in the next paycheck. How could the board turn its back on loyal, long-term employees? And how would you survive with no savings and no job?[1] ■

Before the Industrial Revolution in the eighteenth and nineteenth centuries, a business owner typically supplied both capital and management. However, the capital needs of the great manufacturing enterprises spawned by the Industrial Revolution were larger than any small group of individuals could supply. To find capital, firms sought outside investors, who often had neither the knowledge nor the desire to manage the enterprise. Investors without management skills complemented managers without capital. (Throughout this chapter, "manager" includes both directors and officers.)

Modern businesses still have the same vast need for capital and the same division between managers and investors. Because shareholders are too numerous and too uninformed to manage the enterprises they own, they elect directors to manage for them. The directors set policy and then appoint officers to implement corporate goals. The Model Business Corporation Act describes the directors' role thus: "All corporate powers shall be exercised by or under the authority of, and the business and affairs of the corporation managed by or under the direction of, its board of directors. . . ."

Directors have the authority to manage the corporate business, but they also have important responsibilities to shareholders and perhaps also to other **stakeholders**—employees, customers, creditors, suppliers, and neighbors—who are affected by corporate decisions. As the opening vignette illustrates, the interests of these various stakeholders often conflict. This chapter is about the rights—and the responsibilities—of directors and officers to manage these conflicts.

MANAGERS VERSUS SHAREHOLDERS: THE INHERENT CONFLICT

NEWSworthy

The mood here in reaction to the sale of *The Los Angeles Times* to the Tribune Company may have been best summed up by Mark H. Willes, the company's chairman, when he left the board meeting that approved the transaction late Sunday evening. Mr. Willes burst into tears and wept openly, according to several people who saw him. The sale of the paper and

---

[1] If you are interested in following the stock price of a particular company, click on **http://finance.yahoo.com**. If you want to pretend to play the market for Hollywood movies, try **http://www.hsx.com**.

its parent, the Times Mirror Company, would make Mr. Willes an immensely wealthy man. And it would earn tens of thousands of dollars, in some instances more, for each of the reporters, editors and many other employees of the Times Mirror Company who hold stock and stock options.

But for many people in this city, both in *The Los Angeles Times* newsroom and outside, the deal felt humiliating, they said, as if something precious had been stolen away. "There is a feeling that yesterday, a part of this city's soul was *The Los Angeles Times*," said Geoffrey Cowan, dean of the Annenberg School of Communications at the University of Southern California. "I'm not sure how much that is true tomorrow." He added, "There is a loss of identity."

Within the newsroom, many people expressed anger that the Chandler family, which has controlled the company for decades, had sold the company to an outsider, in spite of assurances in recent years that it never would. "The Chandler family long ago lost interest in running a newspaper and they're just interested in the profits," said Ken Reich, a columnist who has worked at *The Los Angeles Times* for 35 years.[2] ◆

This episode illustrates the ongoing debate over corporate governance in America. Managers serve at least three masters: themselves, shareholders, and other stakeholders. These masters have conflicting goals:

- **Managers** want, first, to keep their jobs and, second, to build an institution that will survive them. Mark Willes, chairman of *The Los Angeles Times*, wept when his company was sold, despite the immense wealth he received from the sale. To him, the job was what mattered.

- **Shareholders** want a high stock price, *right now*, not five years from now. As owners, the members of the Chandler family cared more about their own profits than they did about the newspaper and its important role in the life of the city.

- **Stakeholders,** those who work for the *LA Times*, read it, sell it ink, or own the food-shop across the street from its plant, want the newspaper to stay in business. The speaker of the California State Assembly lamented the sale because the paper had been a booster for the whole city of Los Angeles. (Generally, managers are not included in the stakeholder category because their interests may be different from those of lower level employees.)

Did the Chandler family have a legal or ethical obligation to consider the impact of this sale on the community and other stakeholders? Or should the stakeholders simply accept that shareholders—and their profits—come first? These are the difficult questions facing managers around the world. Only one thing is clear: managers cannot please all the stakeholders all the time.

The courts have generally held that **managers have a fiduciary duty to act in the best interests of the corporation's shareholders.** Since shareholders are primarily concerned about their return on investment, managers must *maximize shareholder value*, which means providing shareholders with the highest possible financial return from dividends and stock price. However, reality is more complicated than this simple rule indicates. It is often difficult to determine which strategy will best maximize shareholder value. And what about *stake*holders? Must managers totally ignore their interests? In the following case, the court explicitly permits the board to consider the interests of stakeholders over those of some shareholders.

---

[2]   James Sterngold, "In Los Angeles, Tears and a Feeling of Loss," *New York Times*, Mar. 14, 2000, p. C16. Copyright © 2000 by The New York Times Co. Reprinted by permission.

UNOCAL CORP. V. MESA PETROLEUM CO.

493 A.2d 946, 1985 Del. LEXIS 482
Supreme Court of Delaware, 1985

Facts: Mesa Petroleum Co. offered to purchase 64 million shares of Unocal's stock at a cash price of $54 per share. Upon merger of the two companies, Mesa planned to exchange the remaining Unocal shares for "junk bonds" that Mesa (but no one else, including the court) valued at $54 per share. Unocal's investment bankers advised the board of directors that the Mesa proposal was wholly inadequate and that an offer of over $60 per share would have been reasonable. The board rejected the Mesa offer and then made its own competing offer of $72 per share to all shareholders except Mesa. (This type of offer is called a "selective exchange offer.") The board's offer effectively preempted Mesa, because no shareholder would accept the $54 Mesa offer when the $72 Unocal offer was also available. The Delaware court issued a preliminary injunction against Unocal's offer unless it included Mesa.

Issues: Could Unocal make an offer to buy stock from all shareholders except Mesa? In making this offer, did Unocal have the right to consider the interests of other stakeholders?

Excerpts from Justice Moore's Decision: In the board's exercise of corporate power to forestall a takeover bid our analysis begins with the basic principle that corporate directors have a fiduciary duty to act in the best interests of the corporation's stockholders. The restriction placed upon a selective stock repurchase is that the directors may not have acted solely or primarily out of a desire to perpetuate themselves in office. This entails an analysis by the directors of the nature of the takeover bid and its effect on the corporate enterprise. Examples of such concerns may include: inadequacy of the price offered, nature and timing of the offer, questions of illegality, the impact on "constituencies" other than shareholders (i.e., creditors, customers, employees, and perhaps even the community generally), the risk of nonconsummation, and the quality of securities being offered in the exchange. While not a controlling factor, it also seems to us that a board may reasonably consider the basic stockholder interests at stake, including those of short term speculators, whose actions may have fueled the coercive aspect of the offer at the expense of the long-term investor.

In adopting the selective exchange offer, the board stated that its objective was either to defeat the inadequate Mesa offer or, should the offer still succeed, provide its stockholders with $72 a share. We find that both purposes are valid. However, such efforts would have been thwarted by Mesa's participation in the exchange offer. First, if Mesa could tender its shares, Unocal would effectively be subsidizing the former's continuing effort to buy Unocal stock at $54 per share. Second, Mesa could not, by definition, fit within the class of shareholders being protected from its own coercive and inadequate tender offer. Thus, we are satisfied that the selective exchange offer is reasonably related to the threats posed.

The decision of the Court of Chancery is therefore *reversed*, and the preliminary injunction is *vacated*. ■

Devil's Advocate

In this case, the court says that the board cannot act with the primary goal of keeping itself in office. One could argue, however, that that is precisely what the board did. It *said* that it was concerned about stakeholders but, conveniently, stakeholder interests coincided precisely with its own. When forced to choose between shareholders, who in fact *own the company,* and stakeholders, why should the board be allowed to choose stakeholders? This choice seems particularly tainted given the board's conflict of interest. ◆

A number of states have adopted statutes that codify the *Unocal* decision. These statutes permit directors, when making a decision, to consider, for example, "both the short term and long term best interests of the corporation, taking into account, and weighing as the directors deem appropriate, the effects thereof on the corporation's shareholders and the other corporate constituent groups. . . ."[3] The next section looks more closely at directors' responsibilities to their various constituencies.

RESOLVING THE CONFLICT: THE BUSINESS JUDGMENT RULE

Officers and directors have a fiduciary duty to act in the best interests of their stockholders, but under the **business judgment rule** the courts allow managers great leeway in carrying out this responsibility. The business judgment rule is a common law concept that virtually every court in the country recognizes. In addition, some states have enacted statutes that codify the business judgment rule. To be protected by the business judgment rule, managers must act in good faith:

Duty of Loyalty	1. Without a conflict of interest
Duty of Care	2. With the care that an ordinarily prudent person would take in a similar situation, and
	3. In a manner they reasonably believe to be in the best interests of the corporation.

The business judgment rule is two shields in one: it protects both the manager and her decision. If a manager has complied with the rule, a court will not hold her personally liable for any harm her decision has caused the company, nor will the court rescind her decision. If the manager violates the business judgment rule, then she has the burden of proving that her decision was fair to the shareholders. If it was not fair, she may be held personally liable, and the decision can be rescinded.

The business judgment rule accomplishes three goals:

- *It permits directors to do their job.* Business is risky. No one can guarantee perfect decision making all the time. If directors were afraid they would be liable for every decision that led to a loss, they would never make a decision, or at least not a risky one.

- *It keeps judges out of corporate management.* Shareholders would generally prefer that their investments be overseen by experienced corporate managers, not judges. Without the business judgment rule, judges would be tempted, if not required, to second-guess managers' decisions.

- *It encourages directors to serve.* No one in his right mind would serve as a director if he knew that every decision was open to attack in the courtroom. Even if the company pays the legal bills, who wants to spend years in litigation?

Analysis of the business judgment rule is typically divided into two parts. The obligation of a manager to act without a conflict of interest is called the **duty of loyalty.** The requirements that a manager act with care and in the best interests of the corporation are referred to as the **duty of care.**

Duty of Loyalty

The duty of loyalty prohibits managers from making a decision that benefits them at the expense of the corporation.

---

[3] Indiana Code §23-1-35-1.

Self-Dealing

Self-dealing means that a manager makes a decision benefiting either himself or another company with which he has a relationship. While working at the Blue Moon restaurant, Zeke signs a contract on behalf of the restaurant to purchase bread from Rising Sun Bakery. Unbeknownst to anyone at Blue Moon, he is a part owner of Rising Sun. Zeke has engaged in self-dealing, which is a violation of the duty of loyalty.

Once a manager engages in self-dealing, the business judgment rule no longer applies. This does not mean the manager is automatically liable to the corporation or that his decision is automatically void. All it means is that the court will no longer presume that the transaction was acceptable. Instead, the court will scrutinize the deal more carefully. A self-dealing transaction is valid in any one of the following situations:

- **The disinterested members of the board of directors approve the transaction.** Disinterested directors are those who do not themselves benefit from the transaction.

- **The disinterested shareholders approve it.** The transaction is valid if the shareholders who do not benefit from it are willing to approve it.

- **The transaction was entirely fair to the corporation.** In determining fairness, the courts will consider whether the price was reasonable and the impact of the transaction on the corporation.

Exhibit 35.1 illustrates the rules on self-dealing.

Exhibit 35.1

In the following case, the CEO negotiated a highly favorable deal—for himself. Even board approval was not enough to protect this decision.

STRASSBURGER V. EARLEY

752 A.2d 557, 2000 Del. Ch. LEXIS 21
Court of Chancery of Delaware, 2000

Facts: Ridgewood was a small, publicly held real estate company that purchased partially empty mobile home parks, marketed the vacant spaces, and then, once the parks were full, sold them to someone else to operate. The company also owned a few hotels, apartment buildings, and some vacant land. Russell Walden was Ridgewood's president and a member of its board of directors. Ridgewood's three largest stockholders were Triton (with a 74.4 percent stake), Hesperus[4] (which owned 9 percent), and Walden (who owned 6.9 percent). The remaining 9.7 percent of Ridgewood's shares were owned by members of the public.

At the time our story opens, Ridgewood was nearly destitute. Because of a recession in the mobile home market, the company did not have enough revenue to pay its expenses, so was forced to sell off its inventory of vacant land and borrow money from Triton. As Walden reported to the board, "If we don't get the apartment sale closed in early March, we may be in deep dog droppings."

Walden had reason to be concerned. His Ridgewood stock represented 65 percent of his net worth and all of his income. The company gave him $200,000 a year in salary plus cash bonuses, a generous severance package and retirement pay. It also provided insurance and a country club membership.

Walden was even more concerned when his company's largest shareholder, Triton, filed for bankruptcy protection and began the process of liquidating its assets. Walden was afraid that Triton might pressure Ridgewood to liquidate, too. Walden developed an alternative: he got Ridgewood to buy out both Triton and Hesperus, giving him a controlling interest in the company. This was an expensive undertaking: To raise the cash, Ridgewood had to sell off most of its assets. In the end, it sold its five remaining mobile home parks, leaving it with only two hotels plus several parcels of vacant land that it had been trying unsuccessfully to sell for many years.

In short, Triton and Hesperus sold their stock for a good price and Walden personally acquired a controlling interest in Ridgewood. His position as president was safe, as was his lucrative employment contract. Everyone benefited from this deal except Ridgewood's minority stockholders, who remained holders of an illiquid minority interest. At Walden's urging, Ridgewood's board of directors approved the deal.

Minority shareholders brought suit alleging that Walden had engaged in self-dealing and that the deal was not entirely fair.

Issues: Did Walden violate his duty of loyalty? Did he engage in self-dealing? Was the transaction entirely fair to the other shareholders?

Excerpts from Judge Jacobs's Decision: The plaintiff claims that the defendants breached their fiduciary duty of loyalty to Ridgewood and its minority shareholders [by] effectuating a self-dealing transaction that was unfair to the minority. [T]he overwhelming weight of the evidence shows that the repurchase of the Ridgewood shares held by Triton and Hesperus constituted an expenditure of corporate funds for the primary purpose of conferring and perpetuating control upon Walden.

[T]he defendants have not carried their burden of proving that the repurchase transactions were entirely fair. Ridgewood was so desperately in need of cash that it had to sell assets just to pay expenses. In those straitened circumstances, for Ridgewood's board to sell off the mobile home parks—Ridgewood's then-crown jewel—and then use a significant part of the proceeds to repurchase the control block, would strike any prudent businessman striving to serve the interests of all shareholders as an extravagance. That would be not unlike an unemployed person whose savings account is depleted, deciding to sell his family's only valuable asset (the house) and use the proceeds to buy a luxury car.[5] In these circumstances,

▼

---

[4]　As it turns out, this company was aptly named. See Henry Wadsworth Longfellow's poem "The Wreck of the Hesperus."

[5]　Had Ridgewood used the mobile home proceeds to buy a fleet of luxury vehicles, it might have been better off since that might at least position the company to go into the limousine transportation business.

only a crisis that threatened the ongoing viability of the Company, and that was so grave as to outweigh these negative business concerns, might arguably justify a repurchase of control.

The board, at Walden's initiation and urging, approved a transaction structure that would benefit only Walden and the two largest shareholders whose holdings were to be repurchased. Missing from the negotiating process and the board decision making process, however, was any independent representa-

tion of the interests of Ridgewood's minority public stockholders. In those circumstances, there was no fair dealing, because there was no advocate committed to protect the minority's interests, and because the players were either indifferent, or had objectives adverse, to those interests.

I therefore conclude that the repurchases are invalid for the reason that the defendants have not demonstrated that those transactions were entirely fair to Ridgewood or its minority stockholders. ■

Corporate Opportunity

The self-dealing rules prevent managers from *forcing* their companies into unfair deals. The corporate opportunity doctrine is the reverse—it prohibits managers from *excluding* their company from favorable deals. **Managers are in violation of the corporate opportunity doctrine if they compete against the corporation without its consent.**

Charles Guth was president of Loft, Inc., which operated a chain of candy stores. These stores sold Coca-Cola. Guth purchased the Pepsi-Cola Co. personally, without offering the opportunity to Loft. The Delaware court found that Guth had violated the corporate opportunity doctrine and ordered him to transfer all his shares in Pepsi to Loft.[6] That was in 1939 and Pepsi-Cola was bankrupt; today, PepsiCo, Inc., is worth $96 billion.

If a manager first offers an opportunity to disinterested directors or shareholders, and they turn it down, the manager then has the right to take advantage of the opportunity himself. (Remember that "disinterested directors or shareholders" are those who do not personally benefit from the transaction.) Sometimes, however, either through oversight or ignorance, managers do not seek permission in advance. To avoid violating the corporate opportunity doctrine, the manager must show after the fact that the company would have been unable to benefit from the opportunity. For example, Cellular Information Systems, Inc., had just emerged from bankruptcy proceedings when one of its directors learned that a cell-phone license covering part of Michigan was for sale. The director purchased the license himself, and the company sued. The court found the director not liable because the company could not have afforded to purchase the license itself.[7]

A manager will often find it difficult to prove that the company could not have used an opportunity itself. However, these disputes are easy to avoid—the manager must simply ask permission first. If the company finds out after the fact that a manager has taken a corporate opportunity, it may not choose to litigate the issue, but the manager's career at that company will effectively be over. Certainly, if a manager suspects that company officers would be displeased to learn about his new sideline, that is an indication that he is skating on thin ice.

In the following case, the manager felt that he had a good reason for taking a corporate opportunity. Unfortunately, the court disagreed.

---

[6]   *Guth v. Loft,* 5 A.2d 503, 23 Del. Ch. 255, 1939 Del. LEXIS 13 (Del. 1939).
[7]   *Broz v. Cellular Information Systems, Inc.,* 673 A.2d 148, 1996 Del. LEXIS 105.

ANDERSON V. BELLINO

265 Neb. 577, 658 N.W.2d 645, 2003 Neb. LEXIS 49
Supreme Court of Nebraska, 2003

Facts: The city of LaVista, Nevada, was looking for someone to operate a restaurant and lounge that included a keno game.[8] Richard Bellino, who was an electrician, wanted to bid on this opportunity but he needed to find someone to share the financial risk. He joined forces with Robert Anderson and the two men formed LaVista Lottery, Inc. Anderson and Bellino each owned 50 percent of the stock of Lottery, and both were officers and directors. The division of labor was left vague—each agreed to participate as much as he could.

Lottery's bid was successful and the company signed a contract with the city of LaVista. During the next nine years, Lottery grossed more than $100 million. Bellino and Anderson each received over $4 million in salary and dividends. Although Bellino and Anderson both continued to be involved in Lottery, Bellino spent more time, in part because of his personal relationship with Lottery's lounge manager. During this period, Bellino did not complain to Anderson about his lack of involvement in Lottery and Anderson never refused to do anything that Bellino asked him to do.

Increasingly resentful of Anderson's work ethic, Bellino set up a meeting with LaVista's city administrator. Until that meeting, the city had been satisfied with Lottery's performance. But after the meeting, the administrator recommended to the city council that the keno contract be put up for competitive bid. Bellino incorporated LaVista Keno, Inc., to bid on the contract. He was Keno's sole shareholder.

Bellino wrote to Anderson complaining that he (Bellino) was doing too much work for Lottery at too little pay. (Evidently, $4 million is not as much as it used to be.) Therefore, Bellino intended to resign from Lottery and bid on the city contract himself. Anderson offered to do more work or whatever Bellino wanted, but Bellino refused any effort at reconciliation. He then submitted a bid on behalf of Keno. At the time he submitted the bid, he was still an officer of Lottery, as well as a director and a 50 percent shareholder. Anderson also bid on the contract on behalf of Lottery. The city awarded the new contract to Keno.

Anderson and Lottery filed suit against Bellino and Keno, alleging that they had usurped a corporate opportunity. The lower court found for Anderson and Lottery. It ordered Bellino to pay $644,992.63 but provided that Bellino could receive a credit of $172,514.63 against the judgment, if Bellino transferred the stock of Keno to Lottery and persuaded the city to relicense the keno contract from Keno to Lottery.

Issues: Did Bellino usurp a corporate opportunity? Is he liable to Lottery?

Excerpts from Justice Miller-Lerman's Decision: Bellino and Keno claim that if a corporate opportunity existed, it was limited to the opportunity to bid for the keno contract, that Bellino did nothing to impede Lottery from bidding for the keno contract by merely submitting a competing bid, and that, therefore, Bellino did not usurp a corporate opportunity.

Contrary to the arguments asserted by Bellino and Keno, the corporate opportunity was not the right to bid; the bidding process was merely the "preliminary step" by which Lottery sought to acquire the opportunity embodied in the award of the keno contract. The facts thus establish that the keno contract was a corporate opportunity for Lottery.

When discussing a corporate officer or director's fiduciary duty to the corporation, we have stated:

> Although an officer or a director of a corporation is not necessarily precluded from entering into a separate business because it is in competition with the corporation, his fiduciary relationship to the corporation and its stockholders is such that if he does so he must prove that he did so in good faith and did not act in such a manner as to cause or contribute to the injury or damage of the corporation, or deprive it of business; if he fails in this proof, there has been a breach of that fiduciary trust or relationship.

The evidence is uncontroverted that Bellino's successful bid for the LaVista keno contract deprived Lottery of its only source of business. Thus, under the law governing the fiduciary duty of corporate directors and given the facts of this case, Bellino, through Keno, should not have competed with Lottery for the LaVista keno contract.

We affirm the district court's order. ∎

---

[8] Keno is a game of chance similar to bingo except that in keno the players choose the numbers on their ticket.

Duty of Care

In addition to the *duty of loyalty*, managers also owe a *duty of care*. **The duty of care requires officers and directors to act in the best interests of the corporation and to use the same care that an ordinarily prudent person would in the management of her own assets.** In managing her own property, an ordinarily prudent person would have a rational business purpose, avoid illegal behavior, and make informed decisions. Officers and directors of corporations must do no less.

Rational Business Purpose

Courts generally agree in principle that directors and officers are liable to shareholders for decisions that have no rational business purpose. In practice, however, these same courts have been extremely supportive of managerial decisions, looking hard to find some justification. For decades, the Chicago Cubs baseball team refused to install lights in Wrigley Field. Cubs' fans could only take themselves out to the ball game during the day. A shareholder sued on the grounds that the Cubs' revenues were peanuts and crackerjack compared with those generated by other teams that played at night. The Cubs defended their decision on the grounds that a large night crowd would cause the neighborhood to deteriorate, depressing the value of Wrigley Field (which was not owned by the Cubs). The court rooted for the home team and found that the Cubs' excuse was a "rational purpose" and a legitimate exercise of the business judgment rule.[9]

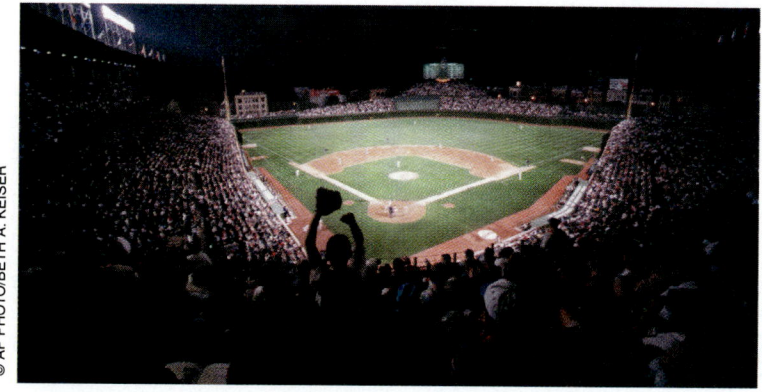

The Chicago Cubs ultimately decided to light Wrigley Field, but it was management's decision, not the shareholders'.

If a decision does not have a rational business purpose, the managers are liable and the decision can be rescinded. If a court decides that there is a rational business purpose, both the manager and the decision are protected.

Legality

Courts are generally unsympathetic to managers who engage in illegal behavior, even if their goal is to help the company. For example, the managing director of an amusement park in New York used corporate funds to purchase the silence of people who threatened to complain that the park was illegally operating on Sunday. The court ordered the director to repay the money he had spent on bribes, even though the company had earned large profits on Sundays.[10]

Informed Decision

Generally, courts will protect managers who make an *informed* decision, even if the decision ultimately harms the company. Making an informed decision means carefully investigating the facts. However, even if the decision is uninformed, the directors will not be held liable if the decision was entirely fair to the shareholders. The board of Technicolor, Inc., agreed to sell the film processing company, knowing little about the

---

[9] *Shlensky v. Wrigley,* 95 Ill. App. 2d 173, 237 N.E.2d 776, 1968 Ill. App. LEXIS 1107 (Ill. App. Ct. 1968).
[10] *Roth v. Robertson,* 64 Misc. 343, 118 N.Y.S. 351, 1909 N.Y. Misc. LEXIS 279 (N.Y. 1909).

Exhibit 35.2

terms of the deal and without seeking other bidders. The directors simply knew that the sales price was higher than the appraised value of the company. Five years later, the buyer sold the company for a $750 million profit. The former shareholders sued, alleging that the directors had made an uninformed decision. The state supreme court held that, because the directors had been so careless, they had to prove that the price, and the process by which it had been determined, were both fair.[11]

Exhibit 35.2 provides an overview of the duty of care.

In the following case, shareholders sued the board of directors for accepting a purchase price that they felt was too low. Did the directors violate their duty of care? You be the judge. It is a long and complex case but an important one.

you Be The Judge

SMITH V. VAN GORKOM

488 A.2d 858, 1985 Del. LEXIS 421
Supreme Court of Delaware, 1985

Facts: Trans Union was a publicly traded company in the railcar leasing business. Jerome Van Gorkom had been its chief executive officer for more than 17 years. He was nearing the mandatory retirement age of 65 and was concerned about maximizing the value of his 75,000 shares of Trans Union stock. In the preceding five years, Trans Union's stock had traded at a high of $39.50 and a low of $24.25 per share. The price was now about $37.

Although Trans Union had hundreds of millions of dollars in annual cash flow, it did not have enough income to take advantage of large investment tax credits (ITCs). Van Gorkom fretted that competitors who could efficiently use their ITCs would be able to cut their lease prices and take business away from Trans Union. He believed that

▼

---

[11] The state supreme court sent the case back to the lower court to determine whether the deal had been fair to the shareholders. *Cede & Co., Inc. v. Technicolor, Inc.,* 634 A.2d 345, 1993 Del. LEXIS 398 (Del. 1993). The lower court ultimately decided that the transaction had indeed been fair. *Cinerama, Inc. v. Technicolor, Inc.,* 663 A.2d 1134, 1994 Del. Ch. LEXIS 178 (Del. Ch. 1994). The state supreme court, however, disagreeing with the valuation method used by the trial court, reversed that decision and remanded it once again to the trial court for further proceedings. *Cede & Co. v. Technicolor,* 684

Trans Union would be more profitable if it was bought by a company that could use the credits.

On September 13, Van Gorkom met with Jay Pritzker, a well-known corporate takeover specialist, to discuss the potential market for Trans Union. Van Gorkom suggested to Pritzker that a leveraged buyout (LBO) could be done at $55 per share. (In an LBO the acquiring company buys the target company's stock using a loan secured by the target's assets.) On Thursday, September 18, Pritzker offered to buy all of Trans Union's stock for $55 per share. The offer expired three days later, on Sunday evening.

On Saturday, Van Gorkom met separately with senior managers and later with the board of directors. Salomon Brothers, the company's investment banker, was not invited to attend. At both meetings, Van Gorkom disclosed the offer and described its terms, but furnished no copies of the proposed agreement. At the first meeting with senior management, the managers' reaction to the Pritzker proposal was completely negative—they feared losing their jobs, they did not like Pritzker, and they thought the price was too low. Nevertheless, Van Gorkom proceeded to the board meeting.

The board was composed of five inside and five outside directors. Of the outside directors, four were corporate CEOs and one was the former Dean of the University of Chicago Business School. None was an investment banker or trained financial analyst. All members of the board were familiar with the company's financial condition and the ITC problem. They had all recently reviewed the company's five-year forecast as well as a comprehensive 18-month study by a well-known consulting firm.

Van Gorkom explained that the issue was not whether $55 per share was the highest price the company could obtain, but whether it was a fair price that the stockholders should be given the opportunity to accept or reject. He also explained that the company had the right to accept a higher offer, if one was made. Van Gorkom did not disclose to the board that he had proposed the $55 price in his negotiations with Pritzker. The company's attorney advised the directors that they might be sued if they failed to accept the offer. The company's chief financial officer said that $55 was "in the range of a fair price" for an LBO, but "at the beginning of the range." The board approved the sale.

Van Gorkom executed the agreement at a formal social event that he hosted for the opening of the Chicago Lyric Opera. Neither he nor any other director read the agreement before signing it. The company issued a press release announcing that Trans Union had entered into a "definitive" agreement with Pritzker. At the same time, it hired Salomon Brothers to solicit other offers. No one else made a firm offer, perhaps because other bidders believed the company was already committed to Pritzker. On February 10, 69 percent of the stockholders of Trans Union voted in favor of the Pritzker proposal.

The plaintiff, Alden Smith, objected to the sale because he did not want to pay tax on the huge profits he realized.

You Be the Judge: **Did the directors of Trans Union violate their duty of care to the corporation by making an uninformed decision? Did the shareholders consent to the board's decision?**

Argument for the Shareholders: The whole procedure for this sale was shockingly casual. Van Gorkom signed the final agreement at a social function. When the directors voted to sell the company, they had not (1) tried to negotiate a higher price with Pritzker, (2) read the agreement, (3) consulted their investment bankers, or (4) determined the intrinsic value of the company. The stock price simply represents the value of a minority stake (one share); a controlling share is worth more, but the board did not know how much more.

▼

A.2d 289, 1996 Del. LEXIS 386 (Del. 1996). Yet again, in 2000, the Delaware Supreme Court (somewhat apologetically) overruled the trial court and returned the case for another trial. *Cede & Co. v. Technicolor, Inc.,* 758 A.2d 485, 2000 Del. LEXIS 283 (Del. 2000). The results from this trial were again appealed. Finally, in 2005, the Supreme Court of Delaware upheld most of the trial court rulings and remanded with simple instructions to change the interest rate it used to calculate damages. *Cede & Co. v. Technicolor, Inc.,* 2005 Del. LEXIS 177 (Del. 2000). The original sale of stock took place in 1983. This has been the longest case in the 200-year history of the Delaware Court of Chancery.

The board did not know this important information and neither did the shareholders when they approved the sale. For that reason, the shareholder consent is invalid.

Argument for the Board of Directors:
Pritzker paid a fair price for the Trans Union stock. It represented a premium of (1) 62 percent over the average of the high and low price in the prior year, (2) 48 percent over the last closing price, and (3) 39 percent over the highest price at which the stock had ever traded. The plaintiffs suggest that the "intrinsic value" of the company was higher. The board hired Salomon Brothers to look for better offers and agreed to pay them millions of dollars in fees if they were successful, but they could not find a buyer willing to pay more than Pritzker.

Jerome Van Gorkom served the company for 24 years, and he knew $55 was a favorable price.

He also had an enormous incentive to obtain the highest possible price because he personally owned 75,000 shares. The five inside directors had collectively worked for the company for 116 years. The outside directors knew the company well, and they were experienced business people; four of them were CEOs of their own large companies. The board was forced to make a decision quickly because Pritzker's offer expired in three days. What could an expert have discovered in three days that the board did not already know? The Trans Union lawyer warned the directors that if they refused the offer, they would be sued.

Alden Smith's tax problems are not a legitimate reason to hold the board liable. The business judgment rule is meant to protect a board that makes a good faith decision. This board did what it thought best for all of the company's shareholders, not for Alden Smith alone. ■

Remember that managers are only liable if they make an uninformed decision *and* the transaction is unfair to the shareholders. If the appeals court in the *Trans Union* case determined that the directors had violated their duty of care, it would remand the case to the lower court to determine if $55 was a fair price.

Some states have modified their business judgment rule to increase protection for directors. These states either limit liability by statute or permit corporations to include charter provisions that shield directors from personal liability.[12]

Public Policy

At the beginning of the next chapter, you will read about Enron—a high-flying company destroyed by the fraudulent activities of its managers. Enron directors agreed to pay $13 million out of their own pockets to settle claims brought by enraged shareholders. Is it a good idea for directors to be *personally* liable?

Yes: If directors are liable, then presumably they will pay more careful attention to what goes on in the boardroom. Moreover, when a company pays a settlement itself, that money ultimately comes out of the pockets of shareholders. Even if an insurance company pays directly, the shareholders are still penalized indirectly because the cost of insurance will rise. The directors are more at fault than shareholders, so the money should come from them.

No: Settlements like Enron will simply discourage good people from serving on boards of directors. No board can prevent all wrong-doing on the part of determined employees. Enron paid these directors an average of $79,107 a year; is it fair for them to be on the hook for $13 million? ◆

---

[12] For instance, the Delaware code permits a corporation to include in its charter a provision limiting a director's personal liability except in certain cases such as intentional misconduct. 8 Del. C. §102(b)(7).

MORE CONFLICT: TAKEOVERS

The business judgment rule is an important guideline for officers and directors in the routine management of corporations. The business judgment rule also plays a crucial role in corporate takeover battles. But the business judgment rule is not, by itself, sufficient for resolving all the issues that arise in these battles. Therefore, both Congress and many state legislatures have passed statutes that define the roles of the various combatants in hostile takeovers. Thus the law of takeovers is rooted in both common and statutory law.

There are three ways to acquire control of a company:

- **Buy the company's assets.** Such a sale must be approved by both the shareholders and the board of directors of the acquired company.

- **Merge with the company.** In a merger, one company absorbs another. The acquired company ceases to exist. A merger must also be approved by the shareholders and the board of directors of the target. Even if the current directors object, an acquiring company could buy enough stock to replace the board, but these battles are difficult and often end in defeat for the acquirer (for reasons discussed in Chapter 36, on shareholders).

- **Buy stock from the shareholders.** This method is called a **tender offer** because the acquirer asks shareholders to "tender," or offer their stock for sale. Unlike the other methods of obtaining control, approval from the board of directors of the target company is not strictly necessary. As long as shareholders tender enough stock, the acquirer gains control. Typically, the bidder makes an offer (at a price above market value). This offer is usually contingent—that is, if a certain percentage of the shareholders do not tender, the offer terminates automatically. A tender offer is called a **hostile takeover** if the board of the target resists.

Two scenarios are common in hostile takeovers:

- The target has assets that the bidder genuinely wants.

- A speculator plans to acquire control and then resell all or part of the company at a profit. Speculators, sometimes called **corporate raiders,** often say that they are acquiring stock in a company because it is undervalued; their ostensible goal is to improve management and raise stock prices. In practice, however, they rarely manage the companies they acquire. Either another bidder comes along who buys their stock at a higher price; the raiders dismember the company and sell its parts; or the company buys its own stock back at a higher-than-market price. (Management is willing to pay a premium price to keep the company intact and their jobs safe.)

In the beginning, state and federal governments barely regulated tender offers at all. Over time, targets began to ask Congress and their state legislatures to umpire these increasingly rancorous battles. Both states and the federal government have stepped into the ring as referees, generally more on the side of the target than of the bidder. As a shareholder, would you prefer for the law to favor the target or the bidder? Economic research suggests an answer.

ECONOMICS *& the* LAW

Suppose you are thinking about buying stock in two companies. The directors and officers of Bright Future, Inc., own 30 percent of the company while the managers of Dim Bulb Co. own virtually none. You might think that it would be better to invest in a company in which the managers own substantial amounts of stock. In such a case, managers have the same incentives as shareholders—you both benefit from higher stock prices. Moreover, you assume that managers who own lots of stock must have reason to believe that their company's future is promising. Because managers are likely to know more about the inner workings of a company than an ordinary shareholder would, you might legitimately conclude that Bright Future has, well, the brighter future.

It turns out that reality is more complex. If managers own so much stock that they can defeat takeovers, then they tend to become complacent and care less about shareholder value. This phenomenon is called the "entrenchment effect." According to some estimates, the entrenchment effect is most pronounced in companies in which managers own between 5 and 25 percent of the stock.[13] Investors might be wise to investigate such companies carefully. Dim Bulb could be a better choice than Bright Future. ◆

Federal Regulation of Tender Offers: The Williams Act

The Williams Act applies only if the target company's stock is publicly traded. Under the Williams Act:

- Any individual or group who together acquire more than 5 percent of a company's stock must file a public disclosure document (called a "Schedule 13D") with the Securities and Exchange Commission (SEC)

- On the day a tender offer begins, a bidder must file a disclosure statement with the SEC

- A bidder must keep a tender offer open for at least 20 business days initially and for at least 10 business days after any substantial change in the terms of the offer

- Any shareholder may withdraw acceptance of the tender offer at any time while the offer is still open

- If the bidder raises the price offered, all selling shareholders must be paid the higher price, regardless of when they tendered; and

- If the stockholders tender more shares than the bidder wants to buy, it must purchase shares pro rata (in other words, it must buy the same proportion from everyone, *not* first come, first served).

Companies have been creative in fighting off sharks.

Observe that the Williams Act regulates only the behavior of the *bidder*, not that of the *target* company. After Congress passed the Act, the number of tender offers declined and the average premium over market price increased. But target companies did not rely merely on the Williams Act to protect against the threat of takeovers. They were busy formulating other defenses.

State Regulation of Takeovers

A company's response to a takeover attempt is largely governed by state law, both common and statutory.

---

[13] R. Morck, A. Schleifer, and R.W. Vishny, "Management Ownership and Market Valuation: An Empirical Analysis," Working Paper No. 23, Institute for Financial Research, Faculty of Business, University of Alberta, quoted in P.-O. Bjuggren, "Ownership and Efficiency in Companies Listed on Stockholm Stock Exchange 1985," in M. Faure and R. Van den Bergh, *Essays in Law and Economics* (MAKLU, Antwerp, 1985).

Common Law of Takeovers

To protect themselves from hostile takeovers, companies adopt defensive measures known as **antitakeover devices** or **shark repellents.** (The acquiring shareholder in a hostile takeover is sometimes referred to as a "shark.") Common shark repellents include the following:

- **Asset Lockup.** Suppose that Ingrid is the CEO of Casablanca, Inc., a successful film production company that owns a vast and valuable library of old films. Turner has indicated that he may want to acquire Casablanca because he covets its library. Ingrid tries to pass the bait to someone else either by selling the film library or by giving someone else the option to buy it.

- **Greenmail.** Ingrid suspects that Turner is not really interested in owning Casablanca stock; he simply wants to turn a quick profit. Ingrid offers to buy back Turner's stock at a price 30 percent higher than he paid for it.

- **Shareholder Rights Plan (aka Poison Pill).** Now Ingrid becomes truly creative. She gets Casablanca to issue a special share of preferred stock to each shareholder.[14] If a shark purchases more than 20 percent of Casablanca's stock and subsequently merges with Casablanca, this preferred stock can be converted into 10 shares of the acquiring company. Thus, for each share of Casablanca that Turner buys, he also has to give away 10 of his own shares, making the takeover much more expensive for him. No wonder these, and other similar tactics, are called "poison pills"; they could certainly prove fatal to a shark.

- **Chewable Poison Pills.** In the face of complaints by institutional shareholders that poison pills are nothing more than protection for incompetent managers, some companies have adopted chewable poison pills instead. These pills are exactly like a poison pill except that they expire automatically if a cash tender offer is made for 100 percent of the company's stock, at a price at least, say, 25 percent above market value. This provision gives Ingrid plenty of clout when negotiating with outsiders, but limits her ability to turn down an offer that is clearly in the shareholders' best interest.

- **Dead-Hand Poison Pills.** Turner might try to elect some of his supporters to the board of Casablanca so that they could eliminate the poison pill. But a dead-hand poison pill can be removed only by vote of the directors who installed the pill, or by their handpicked successors. In this way, the decision is in the "dead hands" of the prior board. Dead-hand poison pills are invalid in some states, but if Casablanca is incorporated in a state that does permit this defense, Turner's supporters would not be able to remove Casablanca's poison pill.

- **Staggered Board of Directors.** Although in many companies directors must run for reelection each year, Casablanca has a staggered board. Each director serves a three-year term, and only 4 of the 12 directors are elected each year. If Turner takes over the company, he will not gain control of the board for two years, and it will be three before he can replace all the directors. Although staggered boards have been shown to reduce shareholder value, 60 percent of S&P 500 firms have them.

- **Supermajority Voting.** Ordinarily, shareholders can approve charter amendments by a majority vote. If Ingrid wants to make a takeover more difficult, she can ask shareholders to amend Casablanca's charter to require a *supermajority* vote of, say, 80 percent to approve a merger. Thus Turner will not be able to merge his company with Casablanca unless he buys 80 percent of Casablanca.

---

[14] Although in theory the shareholders must approve the issuance of a new class of stock, many companies have so-called *blank check preferred stock* in their charters. When this stock is authorized, its rights and other characteristics are left blank, to be filled in by the board of directors upon issuance. It is like an unloaded gun that can be armed by the board whenever a shark threatens.

- **White Knight.** Because Turner has publicly criticized Ingrid's management of Casablanca, she despises him and would prefer to sell to *anyone* else. She locates another buyer who she hopes will retain her management team.

Management typically cannot use staggered boards of directors, supermajority voting, and white knights without shareholder approval. However, traditionally shareholders have voted in favor of management proposals without asking many questions. Shareholder approval is not required to implement the other shark repellents.

Conventional wisdom views antitakeover devices as a mixed blessing—beneficial if used to ensure that shareholders receive the highest possible price for their stock in the event of a sale, but harmful to shareholders if used only to protect management from being fired. However, recent research indicates that the stock prices of companies with few shark repellents significantly outperform those of companies that provide more protection to their managers.[15]

The legal rules on antitakeover devices are complex and sometimes seem to depend on the idiosyncrasies of a particular case. But these are the general guidelines:

- **When establishing takeover defenses, shareholder welfare must be the board's primary concern.** The directors may institute shark repellents, but they must do so to ensure that bids are high, not to protect their own jobs. A poison pill is acceptable if it gives management enough bargaining power to negotiate a high price for shareholders, but not if it makes a takeover impossible.

- **If it is clear that the company will ultimately be sold, the board must auction the company to the highest bidder; it cannot give preferential treatment to a lower bidder.** The board cannot sell the company to a white knight at a lower price than someone else has offered, no matter how much management might personally dislike the shark.

In the chapter's opening vignette, Wallace Computer Services fought off a takeover attempt. Read on to find out how.

MOORE CORP. LTD. V. WALLACE COMPUTER SERVICES, INC.

907 F. Supp. 1545, 1995 U.S. Dist. LEXIS 18882
United States District Court for the District of Delaware, 1995

Facts: Under the terms of a poison pill adopted by Wallace Computer Services, Inc., each existing shareholder had the right to purchase Wallace stock at half price, in the event that 20 percent of Wallace's stock was acquired in a hostile takeover. Five years later, Moore Corp. offered to buy all Wallace's stock for $56 a share, which was 27 percent over the existing market price. However, the offer was contingent upon the Wallace board eliminating the poison pill.

Wallace consulted with Goldman, Sachs, its investment banker, which advised the company that the offer was inadequate, but did not indicate what the shares were really worth. Moore then raised its offer price to $60 per share, and again the bankers opined that the offer was inadequate. Both the board and Goldman believed that Wallace's recently adopted corporate strategy would lead to an increased stock price. Indeed, the company's recent financial results had been better than expected.

Despite these improved results, more than 73 percent of Wallace shareholders offered their shares to Moore. When Wallace refused to remove the poison pill, Moore filed suit.

Issue: Was the board's refusal to remove the poison pill a violation of the business judgment rule?

Excerpts from Judge Schwartz's Decision: When a board is confronted with a hostile tender offer, it

▼

---

[15] P.A. Gompers, J. Ishii, A. Metrick, "Corporate Governance and Equity Prices," *Quarterly Journal of Economics*, 118(1), Feb. 2003.

has the obligation to determine whether the offer is in the best interests of the corporation and its shareholders. Collectively, the Board considered Wallace's current business plans and strategies, its financial projections, its current financial results and future projections, and the opinion of Goldman in arriving at its decision that the $56 offer was inadequate. Further, several individual members of the Board took the position that, based on their knowledge and experience, the offer seemed to be a "low ball" offer. The same investigative procedure was followed when Moore raised its offer price to $60. The Wallace Board's decision reflected the belief that the fourth quarter of [the fiscal year] promised to be a good one. That belief became a reality: sales had increased 32 percent to 33 percent over the prior year, and profits had increased 32 percent. These data suggested to the Board that Wallace could achieve returns greater than Moore's offer, while allowing the shareholders to retain their ownership interest. Accordingly, the Court cannot conclude that the Wallace Board lacked good faith or acted unreasonably in its investigation of the Moore offer.

Moore's tender offer poses a threat that shareholders might tender their shares without appreciating the fact that after substantial capital investment, Wallace is actually witnessing the beginning of the pay-off of its business strategy. The Court therefore finds that Moore's tender offer poses a threat to Wallace that shareholders, because they are uninformed, will cash out before realizing the fruits of the substantial technological innovations achieved by Wallace.

[F]ailing to redeem a poison pill can be justified by considerations other than maximizing current share value. In [a prior case], the Supreme Court of Delaware noted, "[A] board of directors, while always required to act in an informed manner, is not under any per se duty to maximize shareholder value in the short term, even in the context of a takeover."

In light of the foregoing, the Court concludes the Wallace Board has demonstrated that its retention of the poison pill falls within the range of reasonableness. ■

Devil's Advocate

The shareholders own the company. They should have the right to determine when, and at what price, they are willing to sell. The board of directors had the opportunity to *persuade* shareholders that the company strategy was about to pay off. Why should it be able to *impose* its view on the shareholders? They are not, after all, children; in many cases they are sophisticated adults. And, in the end, the shareholders were right. Eight years after the first takeover attempt, the Wallace board agreed to merge with Moore—at a price that was $5 less per share than Moore had originally offered. ◆

State Antitakeover Statutes

In fighting takeover battles, companies have also found support in state governments because legislators fear the impact on the local economy if a major employer leaves. When the Belzberg family threatened a hostile takeover of auto parts manufacturer Arvin Industries, the Indiana legislature quickly passed a tough antitakeover bill that had been drafted by Arvin's own lawyers. Shortly thereafter, Arvin and the Belzbergs settled. Arvin was not only the second largest employer in Columbus, Indiana, it was an all-purpose fairy godmother. Among its charitable activities, it built two new schools, subsidized the salary of the school superintendent, and opened a summer camp. Columbus residents were delighted that Arvin survived the takeover attempt, but company shareholders might have preferred a bidding war for their stock. After all, shareholders do not necessarily care if the children of Columbus spend their summers at leafy Camp Grenada or sleazy Mall City. Once again, the interests of these two corporate constituencies clash.

Most states have now passed laws to deter hostile takeovers. Among the common varieties are the following:

- **Statutes That Automatically Impede Hostile Takeovers.** These statutes, for instance, might ban hostile mergers for five years after the acquirer buys 10 percent of a company. Or investors who acquire as much as 20 percent of a company lose their voting rights unless the other shareholders move to reinstate them (not likely!). These provisions do not apply to bids that have been approved by the board of directors of the target company. In many states, such as Delaware, the board can opt out of the statute altogether and refuse to accept its protection.

- **Statutes That Authorize Companies to Fight Off Hostile Takeovers.** These statutes typically permit management, when responding to a hostile takeover, to consider the welfare of company stakeholders, such as the community, customers, suppliers, and employees. Some even go so far as to allow management to consider the regional or national economy. Since takeovers are almost always harmful to these other constituencies, company management has a ready excuse for fighting the takeover.

Most of these statutes do not totally eliminate hostile takeovers. A determined, well-financed bidder can still be successful. But these state statutes do tip the playing field in favor of management. In the process, they prevent some takeovers that shareholders might want, but they also ensure that shareholders receive a high price in those takeovers that are successful.

Ethics

Supporters of these state statutes argue that large, publicly traded corporations owe a duty to all of their constituencies. The loss of a large corporate presence can be immensely disruptive to a community. Perhaps a state should have the right to prevent economic upheaval within its borders.

Opponents contend that shareholders own the company and their interests ought to be paramount. Antitakeover legislation entrenches management and prevents shareholders from obtaining the premium that accompanies a takeover. Opponents also argue that, if other *stake*holders are so concerned with the well-being of the company, let them put their money where their mouths are and buy stock. And if current managers cannot offer shareholders as high a stock price as an outside raider, they ought to be replaced.

Delaware companies can choose not to accept the protection of the antitakeover statute. Is that the ethical choice for directors? What guidance does the Chapter 2 Ethics Checklist offer? Who are the stakeholders? What values are important to a company director? If a director owned stock in another company, how would she wish the directors of that company to respond to a takeover? ◆

© BRAND X PICTURES/GETTY IMAGES

Chapter Conclusion

Managers of corporations have a fiduciary duty to shareholders and are charged with running the organization for their benefit. The law, whether federal or state, common or statutory, grants managers great freedom in deciding how to promote the shareholders' interest. Particularly in the takeover arena, lawmakers have given managers considerable leeway in defending their organizations from outside attack.

Chapter Review

1. Officers and directors have a fiduciary duty to act in the best interests of the shareholders of the corporation.

2. The business judgment rule protects managers from liability for their decisions as long as the managers observe the duty of care and the duty of loyalty.

3. Managers may not enter into an agreement on behalf of their corporation that benefits them personally, unless the disinterested directors or shareholders have first approved it. If the manager does not seek the necessary approval, the business judgment rule no longer applies, and the manager will be liable unless the transaction was fair to the corporation.

4. Under the duty of loyalty, managers may not take advantage of an opportunity that rightfully belongs to the corporation.

5. Under the duty of care, managers must make honest, informed decisions that have a rational business purpose.

6. The Williams Act regulates the activities of a bidder in a tender offer for stock in a publicly traded corporation.

7. Under common law, shareholder welfare must be the board's primary concern when establishing takeover defenses. If it is clear that the company will ultimately be sold, the board must auction the company to the highest bidder; it cannot give preferential treatment to a lower bidder.

8. Many states have passed antitakeover statutes that render hostile takeovers more difficult for the bidder.

Practice Test

1. Vern Hayes owned 32 percent of Coast Oyster Co. and served as president and director. The company owned several large oyster beds, including two located in Washington State. Coast was struggling to pay its debts, so Hayes suggested that the company sell the Washington beds to Keypoint Co. After the sale, other officers at Coast discovered that Hayes owned 50 percent of Keypoint. They demanded that he give the Keypoint stock to Coast. Did Hayes violate his duty to Coast?

2. ***YOU BE THE JUDGE*** WRITING PROBLEM Asher Hyman and Stephen Stahl formed a corporation named "Ampersand" to produce plays. Both men were employed by the corporation. After producing one play, Stahl decided to write *Philly's Beat*, focusing on the history of rock and roll in Philadelphia. As the play went into production, however, the two men quarreled over Hyman's repeated absences from work and the company's serious financial difficulties. Stahl resigned from Ampersand and formed another corporation to produce the play. Did the opportunity to produce *Philly's Beat* belong to Ampersand? **Argument for Stahl:** Ampersand was formed for the purpose of producing plays, not writing them. When Stahl wrote *Philly's Beat*, he was not competing against Ampersand. Furthermore, Ampersand could not afford to produce the play even if it had had the opportunity. **Argument for Hyman:** Ampersand was in the business of producing plays, and it wanted *Philly's Beat*. Ampersand was perfectly able to afford the cost of production—until Stahl resigned.

3. Some companies adopt a staggered board of directors as an antitakeover defense. How does a staggered board affect cumulative voting?

4. ***ETHICS*** Ronald O. Perelman, chairman of the board and CEO of Pantry Pride, met with his counterpart at Revlon, Michel C. Bergerac, to discuss a friendly acquisition of Revlon by Pantry Pride. Revlon rebuffed Pantry Pride's overtures, perhaps in part because Bergerac did not like Perelman. The Revlon board of directors agreed to sell the company to Forstmann Little & Co. at a price of $56 per share. Pantry Pride announced that it would engage in fractional bidding to top any Forstmann offer by a slightly higher one. To discourage Pantry Pride, the Revlon board granted Forstmann the right to purchase Revlon's Vision Care and National Health Laboratories divisions at a price some $100–$175 million below their value. Was the board within its rights in selling off these two divisions? Do the shareholders of Revlon have the right to prevent a sale of the company to Forstmann at a price lower than Pantry Pride offered? Is it ethical for a board to base a takeover decision on personal animosity? What are a board's ethical obligations to shareholders?

5. An appraiser valued a subsidiary of Signal Co. at between $230 million and $260 million. Six months later, Burmah Oil offered to buy the subsidiary at $480 million, giving Signal only three

days to respond. The board of directors accepted the offer, without obtaining an updated evaluation of the subsidiary or determining if other companies would offer a higher price. Members of the board were sophisticated, with a great deal of experience in the oil industry. A Signal Co. shareholder sued to prevent the sale. Is the Signal board protected by the business judgment rule?

6. Employees of Exxon Corp. paid some $59 million in corporate funds as bribes to Italian political parties to secure special favors and other illegal commitments. Several Exxon directors were aware of these illegal payments. The board of directors decided not to sue the employees and directors who had committed the illegal acts. Was this decision protected by the business judgment rule?

7. Four employees of Allis-Chalmers Manufacturing Co. were indicted for violations of U.S. antitrust laws. The directors had no knowledge of the violations until the indictments were announced. Plaintiffs alleged that the directors had violated their duty of care by not establishing an antitrust prevention program at the company. Are these directors protected by the business judgment rule?

8. The board of Harmony, Inc., is concerned that the company may be the target of a hostile takeover. It has decided to adopt antitakeover devices. Which one of the following statements is **not** true?

   a. Harmony may divest one of its divisions, as long as it does so at fair market value.

   b. Harmony may adopt a poison pill, as long as the purpose is to give management enough bargaining power to negotiate a high price for shareholders.

   c. If it becomes clear that Harmony is going to be sold, the directors have an obligation to auction the company off to the highest bidder, no matter how loathsome the directors find the bidder to be.

   d. If Harmony offers to buy back any of its stock, it must treat its shareholders equally.

9. Klinicki and Lundgren started an air taxi service in Berlin, Germany, under the name Berlinair, Inc. Lundgren was approached by a group of travel agents who were interested in hiring an air charter business to take German tourists on vacation to warmer climes. Lundgren formed Air Berlin Charter Co. (ABC) and was its sole owner. On behalf of ABC, he entered into an air charter contract with the Berlin travel agents. Lundgren concealed his negotiations from Klinicki, even though he used Berlinair working time, staff, money, and facilities. Lundgren defended his behavior on the grounds that Berlinair could not afford to enter into a contract with the travel agents. Has Lundgren violated the corporate opportunity doctrine?

10. Both Viacom and Paramount owned a diverse group of entertainment businesses. QVC was a televised shopping channel. The Paramount board of directors accepted a merger offer from Viacom at a price of $69 per share. QVC and Viacom then entered a bidding war for Paramount. QVC ultimately made the highest offer at $90 per share. The Paramount board rejected QVC's bid on the grounds that a Viacom merger would be more in keeping with Paramount's business strategy. Does a board of directors have the right to reject a high bidder on the belief that the low bidder would be better for the company?

11. **ROLE REVERSAL** Write a short-answer question that deals with the duty of care under the business judgment rule.

Internet Research Problem

Using the Internet, find a newspaper article that discusses a failed takeover attempt. Track the stock price of the two companies involved in the dispute. Would the shareholders of the target company have been better or worse off if the company had been acquired?

You can find further practice problems at http://beatty.westbuslaw.com **or in the Study Guide that accompanies this text.**

Shareholders

In little more than a decade, Enron Corp. transformed itself from a modest pipeline company into a $65 billion global energy business. Enron's officers earned fabulous wealth and became major celebrities. But no sooner had the ink dried on newspaper and magazine articles lauding the Enron business model when suddenly, shockingly, the company collapsed into bankruptcy court. What happened to Enron?

Enron had become, in essence, an energy trading enterprise that required a lot of cash. To obtain the cash, it created subsidiaries that held substantial sums in safe investments. Enron borrowed money that was secured by these subsidiaries, but—and here is the catch—it excluded this debt from its financial statements. The income from energy sales appeared as revenue for Enron, but the debt to support this income was off the books. None of these "special" arrangements was disclosed clearly to shareholders.

Moreover, compensation for top executives was tied directly to the company's stock price. So managers had a powerful incentive to raise the stock price in any way possible, legal or not. Stock manipulation and questionable accounting practices became standard operating procedure at the firm. The company would, for

© AUTHUR S. AUBRY/PHOTODISC/GETTY IMAGES

example, book as current revenues its (optimistic) assessment of what future revenues might be for new deals.

After a few stock analysts began to ask tough questions, Enron restated its earnings by nearly $600 million. In turn, this restatement caused investors to lose confidence. Enron stock entered a death spiral into bankruptcy, destroying the net worth (and the dreams) of many employees and shareholders. It turned out, however, that not all employees suffered dramatic financial losses—the top executives had sold hundreds of millions of dollars in stock before the collapse, even as they were exhorting other employees and shareholders to continue buying.

Outrage and uproar ensued. Inquiring minds wanted to know: Why did the law fail to protect Enron shareholders? Why did the impressive board of directors miss—or ignore—obvious signs of trouble? At the same time, other prominent companies confessed to shady accounting practices: Xerox Corp., Merrill Lynch, and Lucent, among others. The CEO of investment bank Goldman Sachs said, "I cannot think of a time when business over all has been held in less repute."

So what is the solution to this raft of corporate wrongdoing? Some commentators claim that there are simply a few bad apples in the executive orchard. More pessimistic commentators argue that wholesale changes are needed in the regulation of public companies. After reading this chapter, you decide. ■

INTRODUCTION

Shareholders technically own the companies in which they invest, but their power over these enterprises is very limited. As Chapter 35 revealed, **directors, not shareholders, have the right to manage the corporate business.** However, not all directors are created equal. **Inside directors,** who are also officers in the corporation, have typically controlled their company's board. **Outside directors** (also called **independent directors**) do not work for the company and have traditionally played a lesser role.[1] They have been described derisively as "ornaments on a corporate Christmas tree" or "parsley on the fish." Nominated by their friend, the chief executive (CEO), and elected by shareholders without question, these directors could collect handsome paychecks while simply rubber-

---

[1] Although the terms *outside* and *independent* are often used interchangeably, an outside director does not always act independently. In the eBay case later in the chapter, for example, shareholders alleged that outside directors were not, in fact, independent because they were under the influence of the company's CEO and its founders.

stamping the CEO's decisions. Without a watchdog board, CEOs and other officers have great latitude in running their companies. As the Enron episode illustrates, they sometimes abuse this power. The results are predictable: studies show that a weak board means higher pay for the boss and lower stock prices for the shareholders.

At one time, corporate stock was primarily owned by individuals, but now institutional investors—pension plans, mutual funds, insurance companies, banks, foundations, and university endowments—own more than 50 percent of all shares publicly traded in the United States.[2] Institutional investors, with enormous sums to invest, have little choice but to buy the stock of large companies. If they are unhappy with management, it is difficult for them to do the "Wall Street walk"—that is, sell their shares—because a sale of their stock holdings would depress the market price. And where would they invest the proceeds? Institutional investors cannot all profit simply by trading shares among themselves. For better or worse, the fate of fund managers hangs on the success of these large companies. So what can shareholders, large and small, do to protect their investment? This chapter discusses the ways in which existing laws do (and do not) safeguard their interests.

Ethics

Enron was a "win at all cost" culture. Nothing, but nothing, was more important than keeping the stock price high. The company's focus was on short-term results, not long-term value. Its top executives worried about their income this year, not the impact on lower level employees, shareholders, and society. Would the Ethics Checklist from Chapter 2 have been helpful to Enron executives? Should they have considered the consequences of their actions? What would happen to the economy if all executives behaved in a similar fashion? The New York Stock Exchange (NYSE) requires each of its listed companies to publish a code of ethics. Would such a code have prevented abuses at Enron? ◆

What control do shareholders have over executives who run the companies that the shareholders own? The first section of this chapter explores the rights of shareholders. The second section looks at how shareholders enforce these rights. The Corporate Governance Web site (**http://www.corpgov.net**) provides more information about these issues.

RIGHTS OF SHAREHOLDERS

If you own a car, you expect to be able to drive it whenever you want. If you own it with four of your friends, you may not be able to use it every Saturday night, but you will get to drive it *sometimes*, even if only on Sunday mornings. Of course, you will also be responsible for changing the oil sometimes, too. Owning stock in a corporation is different. As an owner, you have no right to use any *specific* asset of the corporation. If you own stock in Starbucks Corp., your share of stock plus $3.68 entitles you to a cup of Mocha Valencia, the same as everyone else. By the same token, if the pipes freeze and the local Starbucks store floods, the manager has no right to call you, as a shareholder, to help clean up the mess. **As a shareholder you have neither the *right* nor**

---

[2] Shareholders play a very different role in privately held companies than in publicly traded corporations. Not only do privately held corporations have fewer shareholders, but these owners take a more active role in management, often serving as a director, officer, or employee. A public corporation is one that (1) has completed a public offering under the Securities Act of 1933, or (2) has securities traded on a national exchange, or (3) has at least 500 shareholders and total assets that exceed $10 million. For a discussion of public corporations, see Chapter 37, on securities law.

the *obligation* to manage the day-to-day business of the enterprise. What rights do you have?

Right to Information

A company's obligation to provide shareholders with financial information depends on whether it is publicly or privately held. States, which regulate private corporations, generally do not require automatic disclosure of financial information to shareholders. Although the Model Business Corporation Act (Model Act) does require some disclosure, most states do not follow its recommendation. In contrast, the Securities and Exchange Commission (SEC) carefully regulates publicly held corporations and requires them to provide shareholders with extensive financial data.

Even if a corporation is not required to volunteer information, shareholders have the right to obtain certain data upon request. **Under the Model Act, shareholders acting in good faith and with a proper purpose have the right to inspect and copy the corporation's minute book, accounting records, and shareholder lists.** A **proper purpose** is one that aids the shareholder in managing and protecting her investment. If Celeste receives an offer to sell her shares in a bakery, Devil Desserts, Inc., she may want to look carefully at the company's accounting records to determine the value of her stock. Or, if she is convinced the directors are mismanaging the company, she might demand a list of shareholders so that she can ask them to join her in a lawsuit. This purpose is proper—though the company may not like it—and the company is required to give her the list. If, however, Celeste wants to use the shareholder list as a potential source for her new mail-order catalog featuring exercise equipment, the company could legitimately turn her down. Did the shareholders in the following case have a proper purpose?

you Be The Judge

MARATHON PARTNERS L.P. V. M&F WORLDWIDE CORPORATION

2004 Del. Ch. LEXIS 101
Court of Chancery of Delaware, 2004

Facts: M&F Worldwide (M&F) was a publicly traded company that made flavorings for use in cigarettes. Marathon Partners was a shareholder of M&F—an unhappy shareholder, as it turns out. Marathon wanted M&F to sell itself to Schweitzer-Mauduit International (SMI), but M&F refused. Marathon thought about suing M&F to force a sale. But before Marathon could make this decision, it needed more information and it wanted to talk with other shareholders. So it sent a letter to M&F demanding access to the company's shareholder list. Marathon also sought

(1) all records of any discussions with SMI; (2) any internal valuations of M&F; and (3) financial forecasts for M&F. Marathon's stated purpose for requesting these documents was to (1) assess the value of its shares in M&F; and (2) communicate with other stockholders about management and a possible sale.

Why was Marathon intent upon a sale of M&F? Ronald O. Perelman was a director of M&F and owned 36.2 percent of its stock. He sought to buy more shares of M&F so that he could increase his ownership to 41.3 percent. Marathon preferred for M&F to be sold outright rather than for Perelman to increase his ownership.

To thwart Perelman, M&F had approached SMI to inquire whether it might be interested in purchasing the company. SMI investigated the possibility for two months before reporting back that if it did make an offer, the price would be

▼

between $9 and $9.50 per share. M&F rejected this price as too low.

Two years later, M&F contacted SMI again to discuss the possibility of a sale. Then Marathon got into the act when its principal, Mario Cibelli, tried to encourage SMI to buy M&F. During his presentation to SMI, Cibelli revealed that in prior litigation, M&F had stated that its stock was worth $4 per share. Cibelli also said that if the sale went through, he would expect a finder's fee of $300,000 plus a percentage of the total price SMI paid. Cibelli later admitted that he should not have mentioned the $4 figure to SMI.

In the end, M&F told SMI that the company was not for sale at any price. Cibelli continued to prod SMI to buy M&F, but SMI was interested only in a friendly takeover. At this point, Marathon sent its request for documents. M&F refused to comply and Marathon filed suit.

You Be the Judge: Did Marathon have a proper purpose in requesting these documents of M&F?

Argument for Marathon: As a shareholder of M&F, Marathon wanted to find out why M&F refused to sell the company to SMI. By law, a shareholder is entitled to see records that would aid the shareholder in managing and protecting its investment. That is exactly what Marathon wanted to do in this case. Besides, what is the harm in allowing Marathon to see these records?

Marathon asked for internal valuations of the company and financial forecasts. Both of these would be useful in determining the value of its shares, which is certainly a proper purpose.

As a shareholder, Marathon had the right to talk with other owners of the company about a sale of the company. Perhaps other shareholders also believed that the board was not acting in the best interests of the company's owners.

Argument for M&F: Marathon wanted to investigate possible mismanagement by the M&F board. But Marathon failed to present any evidence either that the M&F board had a conflict of interest or that it failed to properly consider the sale. Rather, the evidence showed that M&F initiated communications with SMI but that the proffered price was too low. Such a decision was squarely within the realm of M&F's business judgment.

Moreover, Marathon was part of the problem, not part of the solution. Cibelli's revelation about the $4 valuation plus his demand for a finders fee and a commission undermined the negotiation process.

M&F is a publicly traded company. There is enough public information available for Marathon to value its shares without asking for internal company documents.

Marathon is intent on doing mischief. If it is allowed to see the list of M&F shareholders, there is no telling what harm it will cause. It would be better for the company to keep that information private. ■

Public Policy

Marathon was a shareholder of M&F; in other words, it was a part owner of the company. Should there be any constraints on the rights of an owner to see the records of the company? Does the law adequately balance the rights of the owners with those of managers? ◆

Right to Vote

A corporation must have at least one class of stock with voting rights. Typically, common shareholders have the right to vote and preferred shareholders do not, but there are many exceptions to this rule.

Proxies

Under common law, shareholders could cast a vote only by attending the shareholders' meeting. Such a rule in a publicly traded corporation would effectively disfranchise many shareholders who have neither the time nor the interest to travel around the country attending meetings. Modern statutory law permits shareholders to appoint someone else to vote for them. Confusingly, both this person and the document the shareholder signs to appoint the substitute voter are called a **proxy.**

Under the Model Act, a proxy is valid for only 11 months, unless the form provides for a longer period. For public corporations, however, SEC rules specify that a proxy is valid only for the next meeting. After that, it automatically expires. Under both state and federal law, the shareholder can generally revoke a proxy at any time.

Under SEC rules, companies are not required to solicit proxies. However, a meeting is invalid unless a certain percentage of shareholders attend, either in person or by proxy. This attendance requirement is referred to as a **quorum.** As a practical matter, if a public company with thousands of investors does not solicit proxies, it will not obtain a quorum. Therefore, virtually all public companies do solicit proxies. Along with the proxy, the company must also give shareholders a **proxy statement** and an **annual report.** The proxy statement provides information on everything from management compensation to a list of directors who miss too many meetings. The annual report contains detailed financial data.

Even if a company decides not to solicit proxies for a shareholder meeting, it cannot avoid its obligation to communicate with its shareholders. The SEC requires public companies, whether or not they solicit proxies, to give shareholders all the information required in a proxy statement and an annual report.

cyberLaw

Under SEC rules, companies can offer (but not require) electronic delivery of proxy statements and annual reports. Intel Corp. was one of the first companies to make its proxy statements and annual reports available on its Web site. See **http://www.intel.com/intel/finance/savethetrees.htm.** You can also read about Intel's policies on corporate governance at **http://www.intel.com/intel/finance/corp_gov.htm.** ◆

Typically, only the company itself solicits proxies for a shareholder meeting. But sometimes shareholders who disapprove of company policies try to convince other shareholders to appoint them as proxy instead of management. These dissident shareholders must also prepare a proxy statement that discloses, among other information, who they are, how they are financing their opposition, and how many other proxy contests they have participated in. If enough shareholders give their proxies to the dissidents, then the dissidents can elect themselves or their representatives to replace the board of directors.

The first proxy contest was held in 1915, when the shareholders of General Motors removed the founder from office (although they later voted him back in). It was not until 1998, however, that an institutional investor actually dismissed an entire board from office. TIAA-CREF, one of the nation's largest pension and insurance funds, led a proxy contest to replace the directors of Furr's/Bishop's, Inc. TIAA-CREF was spurred to action when the price of the cafeteria company plummeted from $33.75 to $1.25. Circumstances were particularly favorable for a shareholder revolt—not only had Furr's stock price fallen precipitously, but eight investors owned 84 percent of the stock. TIAA-CREF could stage the coup with a few phone calls and without the expense or effort of having to persuade thousands of shareholders. Nonetheless, this victory has been referred to, dramatically if not originally, as "the shot heard round the world."

Shareholder Proposals

Some shareholders who oppose a company policy may not aspire to a board seat or perhaps cannot afford to send material individually to other investors. Such shareholders may use an alternative method, provided by the SEC, for communicating with fellow shareholders. **Under SEC rules, any shareholder who has continuously owned for one year at least 1 percent of the company or $2,000 of stock can require that one proposal be placed in the company's proxy statement to be voted on at the shareholder meeting.** In practice, many of these resolutions have a political agenda: save the environment, withdraw from Myanmar, ban genetically modified ingredients. Others relate to corporate-governance issues: reduce executive compensation, permit secret ballots, adopt cumulative voting. Over the last three years, public companies voted on 370 shareholder proposals. Prior to 1985, only *two* proposals had been approved—ever. Currently, about a quarter of all shareholder proposals receive a majority vote, a definite improvement (or deterioration, depending on your perspective).

Despite the long history of shareholder proposals, an essential question remains unanswered: are shareholder proposals binding on the company? The SEC recommends that proposals be couched in the form of a request or recommendation because state laws sometimes prohibit binding resolutions. Although shareholders traditionally followed this advice, many activists have been angered by companies that refuse to implement proposals that receive a majority vote from shareholders. In response, an increasing number of shareholders have begun to propose binding resolutions. The Supreme Court of Oklahoma provided ammunition when it ruled that a shareholder vote on takeover defenses could be binding.[3]

Ironically, companies sometimes implement shareholder proposals that have not received support from a majority of the shareholders. The pressure of shareholder proposals is credited with inducing many American companies to withdraw from South Africa in protest against its apartheid regime. Other companies implement shareholder proposals without even putting them up for a vote. Indeed, nearly half of all shareholder proposals are now withdrawn before a vote because the company capitulates. Many companies feel they have little choice but to negotiate, particularly with institutional investors over issues of corporate governance. For instance, Colgate-Palmolive Co. agreed to a proposal by institutional investors to permit secret ballots at shareholder meetings. The following article illustrates the influence of even "unsuccessful" proposals.

Colgate-Palmolive Co. implemented secret ballots at shareholder meetings in response to a shareholder proposal that was never voted on.

NEWS*worthy*

Decades ago, during the Vietnam war, many churches were at the forefront of antiwar efforts. A band of Catholic nuns has remained true to the cause of peace—though today's activism takes them to corporate boardrooms and shareholders' meetings. At the moment, nuns from dozens of orders are completing a series of resolutions to be introduced at shareholder meetings this spring. The shareholder proposals to be offered by the nuns are making military executives squirm. At the top of their agenda is limiting military sales in countries where the arms can fall into the hands of child soldiers or perpetuate long-running wars. The nuns are also promoting a code of conduct that holds arms makers accountable for the effect of their business on the environment, and on the political and social stability of countries where they operate.

---

[3]   *International Bhd. of Teamsters Gen. Fund v. Fleming Cos.,* 1999 OK 3, 975 P.2d 907, 1999 Okla. LEXIS 3 (OK, 1999).

Last year, shareholder proposals from religious orders gained 11 percent of the vote at Textron, nearly 9 percent at Raytheon, and 5 percent at General Dynamics. Religious groups say this compares with 2 percent to 3 percent of the vote in years past.

Nicholas D. Chabraja, the chief executive of General Dynamics, said he had given serious thought to some of the issues raised by the nuns, especially in the area of foreign military sales. While he said he was comfortable with selling arms to foreign countries at the request of the United States government, in the smaller number of cases where the United States government was not party to the transaction, the words of the nuns gave him pause.

Judging the success of the nuns' activism by the shareholder ballot box may be short-sighted, according to Nell Minnow, editor at the Corporate Library, an online organization that promotes corporate governance. Ms. Minnow said that while the nuns' campaign might be seen as "quixotic," such efforts "often turn out to be the leading edge of a cultural phenomenon." Ms. Minnow pointed to early antitobacco shareholders and environmental activists who raised issues at corporate annual meetings long before they caught on with the public at large.[4] ◆

If a company refuses to include a shareholder proposal in its proxy material, shareholders can appeal to the SEC. These are the major SEC regulations on shareholder resolutions:

- *If dissident shareholders are running for director, they must prepare their own proxy statement; they cannot piggyback on the company's.* If shareholders could run for director simply by placing their name in the proxy statement, the result might be hundreds of candidates and thousands of confused shareholders.

- *The proposal cannot relate to the ordinary business operations of the corporation.* Shareholders of Excalibur Technologies, Inc. proposed that the company post its SEC filings on the company Web site. You might think that a "Technologies" company would willingly agree. You might also think that the SEC would favor the widest possible disclosure. You would be wrong. The SEC ruled the proposal out of bounds because it related to ordinary business operations.

- *The proposal must relate to operations accounting for at least 5 percent of total assets, gross sales, or net earnings.* AT&T refused to include in its proxy statement an anti-Israel proposal from a white supremacy group on the grounds that the company's business with Israel accounted for less than 1 percent of sales.

- *The proposal cannot interfere with the company's proxy solicitation.* Management can exclude more than one proposal on the same topic and proposals that were voted down decisively in the past.

- *The proposal cannot require the company to violate a federal or state law.* Bell & Howell excluded a shareholder proposal that called for the company to hire qualified women because the proposal might require the company to violate federal and state antidiscrimination laws.

- *The shareholder cannot use a proposal to seek satisfaction of a personal grievance against the company.* Lee Data Corp. excluded a proposal requested by an employee/shareholder who had been fired for sexual harassment. The goal of his proposal was to embarrass the company and provide fodder for his lawsuit.

The Corporate Library Web site provides information about recent shareholder proposals at **http://www.thecorporatelibrary.com/Research/shareholder-proposals/default.asp**.

---

4   Leslie Wayne, "Shareholders Who Answer to a Higher C.E.O.," *New York Times*, 2/19/2005, p. 1.

Shareholder Meetings

Annual shareholder meetings are the norm for publicly traded companies. (Although technically not all states require public companies to hold an annual meeting of shareholders, the NYSE requires companies listed with it to do so.) Companies whose stock is not publicly traded can either hold an annual meeting or use written consents from their shareholders. (Written consents are discussed in Chapter 34.) Under the Model Act, the board of directors and shareholders owning at least 10 percent of the company's stock each have the right to call a special meeting to vote on an emergency issue that cannot wait until the next annual meeting—for example, to conclude a merger or sell off substantial assets.

Everyone who owns stock on the **record date** must be sent notice of a meeting, whether it is an annual or special meeting. The record date can be any day that is no more than 70 days before the meeting. The votes taken at a shareholder meeting are not valid unless a quorum is present, meaning that shareholders representing a certain percentage of the shares entitled to vote either attend or send in their proxy cards.

cyberLaw

Delaware law has entered cyberspace. It now permits companies to send official notices to their shareholders electronically and allows shareholders to vote electronically both before and during a meeting. Shareholder meetings can be held in cyberspace as long as shareholders have a reasonable opportunity to participate in and vote at the meeting. Many corporations now provide a live Webcast of their annual meetings in real time, and permit shareholders to send in e-mail questions. So far, though, very few companies have held an annual meeting that is exclusively online. ◆

Election and Removal of Directors

The process of electing directors of a publicly traded company is different from what most people think. The nominating committee of the board of directors produces a slate of directors, with one name per opening. This slate is then sent to shareholders whose only choice is to vote in favor of a nominee or to withhold their vote (i.e., not vote at all). If a large number of shareholders withhold their votes, the nominee may be embarrassed a little but the reality is that as long as he receives at least one vote (which can be his own), he is elected. If shareholders want to have a choice, they have to nominate their own slate, prepare and distribute a proxy statement to shareholders, and then communicate to shareholders why their slate is superior. This process is complex and expensive. Not surprisingly, each year only about one or two shareholder groups in the country undertake this effort.

This process would be fairer if the nominating committee of the board was independent. Although the NYSE does not permit the CEO of a listed company to serve on the board's nominating committee, these committees rarely, if ever, nominate someone to whom the CEO is opposed.

What are unhappy shareholders to do? In the waning years of Michael Eisner's rule at Disney Enterprises Inc., shareholders withheld 43 percent of their votes from him. But that vote of no-confidence did not cause the board to fire him, nor did he resign, at least not immediately. To oust Eisner, the shareholders would have had to nominate their own slate, pay for the preparation and distribution of their own proxy statement, and then compete against the company's almost unlimited budget to persuade other shareholders to vote for the rebel slate. Although shareholders theoretically elect directors who then choose the officers, the reality is that officers (particularly the CEO) really choose the directors.

The board of directors at Enron was rife with conflicts of interest. Two directors received substantial consulting fees. Two others worked at educational or medical institutions that received charitable contributions from Enron. For example, John Mendelson, a member of the board's audit committee, was president of the M. D. Anderson Cancer Center at the University of Texas, which received a pledge of $1.5 million from the Enron Foundation and $600,000 from Kenneth Lay, Enron's CEO. However, under recent NYSE rules, only independent directors can serve on a listed company's audit, compensation, and nominating committees.[5] Moreover, independent directors must comprise a majority of the total board. They must also meet regularly on their own without inside directors. Neither the Enron directors who received consulting fees nor the ones who (indirectly) received charitable donations would be considered independent.

Compensation for Officers and Directors

Given the control that the CEO has over the selection process for the board of directors, it is not surprising that when the board sets the CEO's compensation, the results can sometimes appear to unfairly favor the CEO over the shareholders whose money is being used to compensate her.

For many children, *Pat the Bunny* is their first book. It contains few words but much interaction. "Readers" can pat the bunny, sniff the flowers, and play peekaboo with the blanket. After *Pat the Bunny,* many children graduate to *The Poky Little Puppy* and *Richard Scarry's Busy, Busy Town,* all published by Golden Books Family Entertainment, Inc.

Despite its portfolio of classics, Golden Books was having financial difficulties. The company hired Richard Snyder, an experienced publishing executive, to solve its distribution and sales problems. Such experience does not come cheap. At Golden Books, he was the third highest paid executive in the publishing industry. But an executive does not live by pay alone. Snyder relocated the company to posh new quarters, hired a private chef, and used the corporate jet for his vacations. He also hired other executives (including his wife) at salaries two to three times the industry average. In return, investors expected the stock price to zoom. They just did not expect it to zoom *down.* Not only did the stock price plummet 80 percent, but the company was put up for sale. In the midst of this turmoil, the board doubled Snyder's salary and paid him a $500,000 signing bonus for extending his contract two years. The company's stock price promptly plummeted again. Golden Books ended up filing for bankruptcy protection, not once, but twice, under Snyder's leadership. Ultimately, it was bought out and Snyder received close to $8 million in severance pay for a job well done. This sum was about 11 percent of the total purchase price for the company. ◆

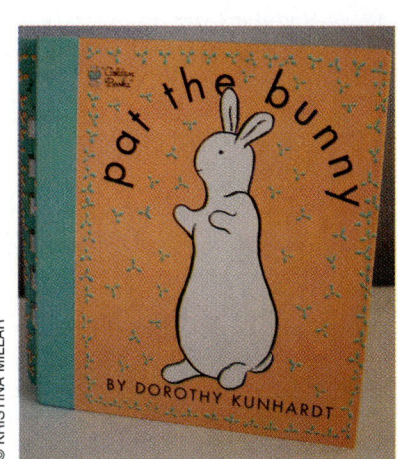

While readers patted the bunny, Golden Books padded its executive payroll.

© KRISTINA MILLAR

To many investors, sky-high executive salaries have become the symbol of all that is wrong with corporate governance. It is difficult to justify CEO compensation that runs as high as $872 million in one year. In many companies, salaries are the least of the compensation. Executives also receive stock options, retirement plans, and lavish perks. Executives have long received perks such as country club memberships and cars, but the roster of options has expanded to include private school tuition for children and million dollar birthday parties for spouses. One company spent $8 million to buy the personal papers of Franklin Roosevelt for an executive who was writing a biography of the former president.

---

5   Under NYSE rules, "independent" means a director who does not earn any compensation from the company outside of the usual director's fees (that is, a director who is not an employee and who has no consulting contracts).

As we saw with Golden Books, even failure is well rewarded. When AT&T fired John Walter after less than one year, the board of directors offered him $26 million in severance pay. Indeed, many CEO employment contracts provide that the employee is entitled to severance pay unless fired for committing a particular type of felony. Incompetence does not disqualify the CEO from receiving a massive reward at the end. The chief of J.C. Penney would lose his severance pay only for "theft or moral turpitude" (and signing this contract does not count).

How much more does a CEO earn than an average worker? In 1975, the answer for the top 100 CEOs was 39 times as much. By 2005, that ratio had risen to over 1,000. No wonder that executive compensation has become a hot topic for shareholder proposals. And no surprise that, so far, these shareholder efforts have had little impact. More information about CEO compensation is available at **http://www .thecorporatelibrary.com**.

Why has executive pay become so lavish?

- *Directors, not shareholders, set executive compensation.* Unless directors are major shareholders of the company (which is seldom the case), generous executive compensation has little impact on directors' income. It is easy to be generous with other people's money. And, as we will see in the eBay case later in this chapter, even nominally independent directors are often beholden to the CEO.

- *Executives have a great deal of influence over their own pay.* In principle, directors set executive compensation after arm's-length negotiations. However, in practice, these negotiations are not so neutral after all, almost always working to the advantage of the executive. For example:

  - Compensation is rarely linked closely to individual performance, but instead to overall industry or stock market performance, which is defined in a way to favor executives. Two-thirds of the largest 1,000 U.S. companies report that they performed better than their peers.[6]

  - The full extent of compensation packages is often camouflaged so that shareholders cannot tell exactly how much executives are earning.[7]

  - Fired executives receive substantial severance packages, even if their contracts do not require them.

  - Retirement pay and perks are also exceedingly generous; executives are well-paid long after their contribution to the company has ended.

- *The busier the directors, the higher the executive pay.* Generally, executives are more likely to be overpaid if directors serve on many boards. These directors may be too busy to pay attention to such details. Such trophy directors may also be afraid that if they offend a chief executive at one company, word will get around, jeopardizing their position on other boards.

- *Most executives are above average.* Of course, not everyone can be above average, but most directors believe that their executives are. No one wants to admit to hiring

---

6 Kevin J. Murphy, "Politics, Economics and Executive Compensation," reported in Lucian Bebchuk and Jesse Fried, *Pay without Performance,* Harvard University Press, 2004, p. 71.

7 Take the annual report of any public company and see if it discloses clearly and accessibly how much the executives earn in base pay, bonus, deferred compensation, stock options, and perquisites. For example, when Terrence Murray retired from FleetBoston Financial Corporation, the company increased his retirement pay at an annual cost to shareholders of $3.1 million. This figure is available only because a newspaper hired an actuary to make the calculation.

incompetents. Suppose that you are on a company's compensation committee and have data about industry averages. If your executives are above average in performance, you should pay them above-average salaries. If they are not above average, you should fire them, which few boards want to do, except in the face of disaster. If *you* raise salaries, the industry average also rises. The next company that sets compensation has an even higher bar to jump. For example, Colgate-Palmolive awarded two million stock options to its CEO on the understanding that he would receive no further grants for five years. Three years later, however, when consultants found that the CEO's compensation had fallen below the median, the company immediately awarded him an additional 2.6 million options.

- *Stock options.* Concerned about escalating executive salaries, shareholder activists began advocating "pay-for-performance" plans. The theory was that if executives received stock options instead of cash salaries, their incentives would be more closely aligned with those of shareholders. It was a good theory, but in practice, it did not work out as intended.

  Stock options became a "heads, I win; tails, you lose" game. When stock prices soared in a bull market, options became unexpectedly valuable. In some cases, managers were richly rewarded even when their company had underperformed the (rising) market. However, when stock prices fell, boards lowered the price of the options. For example, during one three-month period, the stock price of (the inaccurately named) Ascend Communications fell from $86 to $36. Many stock options were then underwater; that is, the exercise price (at which employees could buy stock) was higher than the market price. No problem: the board simply repriced the options so that the exercise price was lower than market value. When the Ascend stock continued its descent to $23, the board again lowered the option price. These actions transferred $1 billion from shareholders to employees.

  The other problem with options is that they create a dangerous incentive for an executive to do whatever it takes (whether illegal or just exceedingly risky) to ensure a high stock price. As it turns out, then, managers do not have the same incentives as shareholders—because shareholders bear the risk if the stock price goes down, while managers do not.

Public Policy

Corporate executives are not the only people to earn fabulous salaries. Some athletes earn more even than CEOs. What is the difference between athletes and executives (besides a hook shot)? Athletes' salaries are indeed negotiated at arm's length. This negotiation process means that (1) their pay is not camouflaged; (2) they do not receive enormous severance packages on their way out the door; and (3) their retirement pay ranges from modest to nonexistent.[8] Also, an athlete's performance is transparent and easy to measure. ◆

To make matters even worse for shareholders, lavish compensation does not appear to improve the business's success. A study of the 58 companies that were most generous to their CEOs found that, on average, these companies significantly underperformed both the market generally and their industry in particular.[9]

---

[8] Some of the material in this section on executive compensation is drawn from Lucian Bebchuk and Jesse Fried, *Pay without Performance,* Harvard University Press, 2004.

[9] Reed Abelson, "Who Profits If the Boss Is Overfed?" *New York Times,* June 20, 1999, Business Section, p. 9.

For more information about executive compensation, pay attention to **http://www
.paywatch.org**. Run by the AFL-CIO labor union, this Web site has an understandably
skeptical view of lavish paychecks.

As the following case demonstrates, shareholders' efforts to challenge executive
compensation have met with little success. An officer's salary is presumed to be reasonable unless she voted for it as a director of the company. (Officers should excuse themselves from all such votes.) To be successful in challenging an executive's compensation,
shareholders must prove that the board was *grossly uninformed* or that the amount was
so high that it had *no relation* to the value of the services performed and was really a
gift. As the following case indicates, courts tend to be unsympathetic to this line of
argument.

In Re THE WALT DISNEY COMPANY DERIVATIVE LITIGATION

2005 Del. Ch. LEXIS 113
COURT OF CHANCERY OF DELAWARE, 2005

Facts: Michael Ovitz was an important talent broker
in Hollywood. He was also a long-time friend of
Disney Chairman and CEO Michael Eisner.
Although Ovitz lacked experience managing a diver-
sified public company, Disney hired him to be its
president. Eisner negotiated Ovitz's employment
agreement and the board approved it.

After 14 months, all parties agreed that the
experiment had failed, so Ovitz left Disney—but not
empty-handed. Under his contract, he was entitled
to $140 million in severance pay.[10] When the board
originally approved this agreement, it had known
how the severance payment would be calculated but
it had not realized how high the total cost could be.
Graef Crystal, the compensation expert who had
advised the directors, later said that he wished he
had done this calculation for them.

Shareholders of Disney sued the board, alleging
that its members had violated the business judgment
rule.[11]

**Issues: Did the Disney directors have the right
to pay $140 million to an employee who had
worked at the company unsuccessfully and for
only 14 months? Had they violated the business
judgment rule?**

Excerpts from Chancellor Chandler's Decision:
It is easy, of course, to fault a decision that ends in a
failure, once hindsight makes the result of that deci-

sion plain to see. But the essence of business is
risk—the application of informed belief to contin-
gencies whose outcomes can sometimes be predicted, but never known. The decision-makers
entrusted by shareholders must act out of loyalty to
those shareholders. They must in good faith act to
make informed decisions on behalf of the shareholders, untainted by self-interest. Where they fail to do
so, this Court stands ready to remedy breaches of
fiduciary duty.

Even where decision-makers act as faithful servants, however, their ability and the wisdom of their
judgments will vary. The redress for failures that
arise from faithful management must come from the
markets, through the action of shareholders and the
free flow of capital, and not from this Court. Should
the Court apportion liability based on the ultimate
outcome of decisions taken in good faith by faithful
directors or officers, those decision-makers would
necessarily take decisions that minimize risk, not
maximize value. The entire advantage of the risk-
taking, innovative, wealth-creating engine that is the
Delaware corporation would cease to exist, with disastrous results for shareholders and society alike.
That is why, under our corporate law, corporate
decision-makers are held strictly to their fiduciary
duties, but within the boundaries of those duties are
free to act as their judgment and abilities dictate,
free of penalties from a reviewing court using perfect hindsight.

▼

---

[10] As Ira Gershwin put it, "Nice work if you can get it, and if you get it—won't you tell me how?"
[11] Chapter 35 contains an in-depth discussion of the business judgment rule.

For the future, many lessons of what not to do can be learned from defendants' conduct here. Nevertheless, I conclude that the only reasonable application of the law to the facts as I have found them, is that the defendants did not act in bad faith, and were at most ordinarily negligent. In accordance with the business judgment rule (because, as it turns out, business judgment *was* exercised), ordinary negligence is insufficient to constitute a violation of the fiduciary duty of care.

By virtue of his Machiavellian (and imperial) nature as CEO, Eisner to a large extent is responsible for the failings in process that infected and handicapped the board's decisionmaking abilities. Despite all of the legitimate criticisms that may be leveled at Eisner, especially at having enthroned himself as the omnipotent and infallible monarch of his personal Magic Kingdom, I nonetheless conclude, after care-fully considering and weighing all the evidence, that Eisner's actions were taken in good faith. That is, Eisner's actions were taken with the subjective belief that those actions were in the best interests of the Company—he believed that his taking charge and acting swiftly and decisively to hire Ovitz would serve the best interests of the Company notwithstanding the high cost of Ovitz's hiring. Those actions do not represent a knowing violation of law or evidence a conscious and intentional disregard of duty. In conclusion, Eisner acted in good faith and did not breach his fiduciary duty of care because he was not grossly negligent.

For all the foregoing reasons, I conclude that none of the defendants breached their fiduciary duties or acted in anything other than good faith in connection with Ovitz's hiring. ■

As we have seen, directors set the salaries of company officers. **Typically, directors also set their own compensation (unless the charter or bylaws provide otherwise).** Directors of Fortune 200 companies are paid on average $152,000 annually, while directors of Fortune 1000 companies earn on average $116,000.

Fundamental Corporate Changes

A corporation must seek shareholder approval before undergoing any of the following fundamental changes:

- **Mergers.** As a general rule, one corporation cannot merge with another unless a majority of both sets of shareholders approve. This rule is always true for shareholders of the *acquired* company, because they are always affected by the merger. But when an elephant acquires a peanut, it makes little sense for the elephant to vote. So shareholders of the *acquiring* company vote only if the merger will have a major impact on their company.

- **Sale of Assets.** Generally, shareholders are not asked to approve the sale of corporate assets. After all, one could hardly ask shareholders of Philip Morris to approve the sale of every pack of cigarettes at every convenience store in the country. But shareholders must approve any sale that involves "all or substantially all" of the company's assets.

- **Dissolution.** A corporation cannot *voluntarily* dissolve without shareholder approval. However, as discussed in Chapter 34, on the life and death of a corporation, the state or a court can *involuntarily* dissolve a corporation regardless of shareholder views.

- **Amendments to the Charter.** Directors propose amendments to the charter, but these amendments are not valid unless approved by shareholders.

- **Amendments to the Bylaws.** Both directors and shareholders have the right to amend the bylaws. Shareholder activists have begun using bylaw amendments in creative ways because, unlike the typical shareholder proposal, an amendment is *binding* on the company. For example, CalPERS proposed a bylaw amendment at Advanced Micro Devices, Inc., to separate the jobs of chairman and CEO.

Right to Dissent

If a private corporation (i.e., one whose stock is not publicly traded) decides to undertake a fundamental change, the Model Act and many state laws require the company to buy back the stock of any shareholders who object to this decision. This process is referred to as **dissenters' rights,** and the company must pay "fair value" for the stock. Fundamental changes include a merger or a sale of most of the company's assets. Devil Desserts, Inc., manufactures sinfully rich chocolate delights. The board of directors is now considering a merger with Angel Treats Ltd., a company that sells low-fat, low-calorie (and in shareholder Celeste's opinion, low-taste) desserts. Celeste fully expects the value of the company to plummet after the merger, but her fellow shareholders support the board's decision. In a public company, Celeste could simply sell her stock, but Devil is a private corporation and there is no market for its stock. She has the right to dissent because a merger is a fundamental change.

Right to Protection from Other Shareholders

Anyone who owns enough stock to control a corporation has a fiduciary duty to minority shareholders (those with less than a controlling interest). The courts have long recognized that minority shareholders are entitled to extra protection because it is easy (perhaps even natural) for controlling shareholders to take advantage of them. In the following case, a husband owed a greater obligation to his wife in her role as a shareholder of a corporation than he owed her as his wife.

MICHAEL L. RETZER V. NANCY B. RETZER

578 So. 2d 580, 1990 Miss. LEXIS 858
Supreme Court of Mississippi, 1990

Facts: Shortly after Mr. and Mrs. Retzer were married, they moved to Greenville, Mississippi, and opened a McDonald's restaurant. Mr. Retzer managed the restaurant, working 18 hours a day. Mrs. Retzer made little contribution to the business. Mr. Retzer subsequently purchased four additional McDonald's restaurants, transferring ownership of them to Retzer and Retzer, Inc., a close corporation.[12] Mr. and Mrs. Retzer each owned 1,600 shares of the corporation.

Mr. Retzer discovered that his wife was having an affair with their attorney. As a condition for salvaging their marriage, Mrs. Retzer agreed to end the affair. She also permitted the corporation to issue 10 additional shares to Mr. Retzer to give him corporate control.

Mrs. Retzer was a profligate spender, often paying more than $3,000 for a dress. When she overdrew her checking account, an officer at the bank would notify Mr. Retzer so that he could replenish her account. Once, when he let her checks bounce, Mrs. Retzer came to his office and began throwing pieces of valuable porcelain. Mr. Retzer called their pastor to calm her down.

Despite the agreement with her husband, Mrs. Retzer continued her affair. The Retzers subsequently divorced on the grounds of Mrs. Retzer's adultery. Their joint net worth was $4 million.

Issue: What are Mr. Retzer's obligations to Mrs. Retzer as a minority shareholder in Retzer and Retzer, Inc.?

▼

---

[12] As you remember from Chapter 32, a close corporation is one whose stock is not publicly traded.

Excerpts from Justice Hawkins's Decision: Where divorce has been granted to the husband on the ground of the wife's adultery, this court has consistently denied any alimony, period. Mr. Retzer does have substantial financial obligations to Mrs. Retzer, however, arising from her ownership of almost half of the shares of Retzer and Retzer, Inc.

Courts look quite differently upon the respective duties existing between majority and minority shareholders in publicly held and close corporations. Retzer and Retzer, Inc., is a very close corporation, which has existed solely for the financial benefit of two people, the Retzers. For almost two decades, and through Mr. Retzer's management, the corporation has indeed furnished them both with large incomes. Now, through ownership of ten more shares than she, Mr. Retzer has control of the management of Retzer and Retzer. As such, under well-settled principles he has a fiduciary obligation to Mrs. Retzer in the management of her property. He has a trustee's duty to preserve, protect, and produce income from her corporate shares.

He must manage the corporation prudently, and after paying necessary and reasonable expenses, and setting aside whatever is reasonably necessary for corporate reserves and equipment and facilities, pay her 49.8 percent of the net remaining. He will not be acting at arm's length, but as trustee over her shares. He must keep her currently, fully, and accurately informed and abreast of his management, and under regular periodic accounting. While their interest as husband and wife was essentially identical, now they are adverse to each other. This will make his conduct as trustee that much more subject to close scrutiny by a court. ∎

Ordinary Business Transactions

Minority shareholders have the right to overturn an ordinary business transaction between the corporation and a controlling shareholder, unless the corporation can show that the transaction is fair to the minority shareholders. The Sinclair Oil Co. owned 97 percent of Sinclair Venezuelan Oil Co. (Sinven). Sinven's minority shareholders complained that Sinclair

- Forced Sinven to pay dividends so large that the subsidiary faced bankruptcy

- Hired other, wholly owned, subsidiaries but not Sinven, and

- Refused to force its other subsidiaries to abide by their contracts with Sinven; for instance, a Sinclair subsidiary signed a contract with Sinven to buy crude oil but failed to purchase the required amount.[13]

Were these transactions fair to Sinven's minority shareholders?

Excluding Minority Shareholders

Controlling shareholders must include minority shareholders in any favorable arrangements that they make for their own stock. A successful savings and loan (S&L) had stock that, in theory, was worth $2,400 a share but, in reality, it rarely traded because of the high price. The controlling shareholder could have split the stock so that shareholders received 100 shares worth $24 each. Instead, he concocted a shrewd plan whereby he and his friends (who together owned 85 percent of the stock) exchanged their S&L stock for shares in a new corporation. Stock of the new company sold well, but there was still virtually no market for the remaining S&L shares. The court held that the controlling shareholders could not exclude the minority without a compelling business purpose, which did not exist in this case.[14]

---

[13] *Sinclair Oil Corp. v. Levien*, 280 A.2d 717, 1971 Del. LEXIS 225 (Del. 1971).
[14] *Jones v. H. F. Ahmanson & Co.*, 1 Cal. 3d 93, 460 P.2d 464, 1969 Cal. LEXIS 195 (1969).

Expelling Shareholders

There is an old saying that you can choose your friends but not your family. Can you choose your fellow shareholders? Sometimes, relations between shareholders become so bitter that the majority attempts to expel a minority owner. **Many states prohibit a company from expelling shareholders unless the firm pays a fair price for the minority stock and the expulsion has a legitimate business purpose.** Delaware has an even higher standard—the transaction must be "entirely fair." This standard requires that both the price and the process of approval be fair. Theodore Lerner owned 70 shares in the family real estate company, Lawrence Lerner only 25. When Lawrence sued Theodore for mismanagement, Theodore amended the charter to reclassify each share of stock into 1/35th of a share and to buy out any fractional shares. Lawrence ended up with 5/7ths of a share, which the company purchased. The court, however, halted the squeeze-out because it had no legitimate business purpose.[15]

Right to Monitor

As owners of an enterprise, shareholders play a relatively passive role. Primarily, they have the right to *monitor*, meaning the right to receive information and the right to vote on proposals put to them by the board. Shareholders do not, by and large, have the right to *initiate* corporate changes.

What could Enron shareholders have done to stop the abuses committed by the officers? At the time, not much. They could neither have fired the officers nor prevented the board from awarding lavish compensation. Nor could the shareholders have vetoed the array of complex deals that ultimately brought the company down. However, under new NYSE rules, shareholders of listed companies have the opportunity to vote on stock option plans that are often an important component of executive compensation.

Corporate Governance in Publicly Traded Companies: Sarbanes-Oxley and Stock Exchange Rules

In response to Enron and other corporate scandals, Congress passed the Sarbanes-Oxley Act (SOX) in 2002. This statute applies to all publicly traded corporations in the United States as well as to all foreign companies listed on a U.S. stock exchange. Under SOX:

- Rule 404 requires each company to adopt effective financial controls.

- CEOs and CFOs must personally certify their company's financial statements. These officers are subject to criminal penalties for violations.

- All members of a board's audit committee must be independent.

- A company cannot make personal loans to its directors or officers.

- If a company has to restate its earnings, its CEO and CFO must reimburse the company for any bonus or profits they have received from selling company stock within a year of the release of the flawed financials.

- Each company must disclose if it has an ethics code and, if it does not, why not.

- It is a felony to interfere with a federal investigation into fraud.

- Whistleblowing employees are protected.

---

[15] *Lerner v. Lerner*, 306 Md. 771, 511 A.2d 501 (Md. App. 1986).

- A new Public Accounting Oversight Board has been established to oversee the auditing of public companies.

The text of the statute is available at http://sarbanes-oxley.com.

The NYSE and Nasdaq responded to the Enron-era scandals by establishing a new role for independent directors at listed companies:

- Independent directors must comprise a majority of the board.
- They must meet regularly on their own without inside directors.
- Only independent directors can serve on audit, compensation, or nominating committees.
- Audit committees must have at least three directors who are financially literate.

Public Policy

The goal of these reforms was to prevent corporate abuses and restore investor confidence. Have the goals been achieved? Were they worth the cost? For large companies (those with annual revenues that exceeded $5 billion), the cost of compliance with Rule 404 averaged $4.6 million in the first year of the act. These firms also required on average 70,000 hours of their employees' time to comply. Some smaller companies have spent a substantial portion of their total revenue on SOX. Indeed, 20 percent of public companies have considered going private simply to avoid this heavy compliance expense. Some foreign companies decided not to be listed in the United States because of this statute.

It is difficult to quantify the benefit that investors gain from a reduction in accounting fraud and an increase in confidence in the stock market. Only time will reveal whether SOX has given the boot to corporate scandals. ◆

ENFORCING SHAREHOLDER RIGHTS

Shareholders in serious conflict with management have three different mechanisms for enforcing their rights: a derivative lawsuit, a direct lawsuit, or a class action.

Derivative Lawsuits

A derivative lawsuit is brought by *shareholders* to remedy a wrong to the *corporation*. The suit is brought in the name of the corporation, and all proceeds of the litigation go to the corporation. Thus, the Enron shareholders could not sue either the directors or Kenneth Lay directly because, technically, the shareholders were not injured—the corporation was. Of course, the shareholders might have felt they were harmed when their stock became worthless. Nonetheless, the corporation, *not the shareholders*, has the right to sue. And who would authorize a suit against the directors on behalf of the corporation? The directors, of course. Because the directors are unlikely to sue themselves, the law permits derivative actions by which shareholders can sue managers who have violated their duty to the corporation. Because damages go *to the corporation*, the individual shareholders benefit only to the extent that the settlement causes their stock to rise in value.

The same rule applies if an outsider harms the corporation. If Enron decided not to sue a customer that refused to pay its bill, the shareholders could do so, but only in a derivative action, that is, only in the name of the corporation. Once again, any recovery goes to the corporation.

Litigation is tremendously expensive. How can shareholders afford to sue if they are not entitled to damages? A corporation that loses a derivative suit must pay the legal fees of the victorious shareholders. Most derivative lawsuits are litigated by lawyers eager to earn these fees. (Losing shareholders are not required to pay the corporation's legal fees.[16]) It is likely for instance, that any cases against Enron would be initiated by lawyers who sought out shareholders and persuaded them to sue. Without this incentive, few shareholders would bring derivative suits, and much corporate wrongdoing would go unpunished. As we have seen, shareholders have limited power; derivative lawsuits are a means of protecting their rights.

There is some concern, however, that lawyers who bring derivative suits have an incentive to settle quickly to ensure that they receive *some* compensation. Even if the shareholders' claim is strong, their lawyers might prefer a small, but guaranteed, payment rather than an uncertain chance at a larger amount after trial. If the case goes to trial and their clients lose, the lawyers receive nothing. In some cases, these settlement payments are little more than bribes to ignore wrongdoing.

On the other hand, lawyers sometimes bring so-called **strike suits**—claims without merit that corporations settle simply to avoid the nuisance of litigation. Many states and the federal government have established rules that are meant to curb abuses while fairly balancing the rights of the various parties. Most derivative suits are brought in Delaware, so this discussion is based on Delaware law. In most cases federal law and other state statutes are similar to those of Delaware.

Approval of Settlements

To ensure that lawyers consider the welfare of their clients when settling a derivative action, all settlements must be approved by the court.

Making Demand

Before bringing suit, shareholders must first "make demand" on the board of directors. In other words, they must notify the board that the corporation has been wronged and ask the board to bring suit in the name of the corporation directly. There is one crucial exception to this rule: shareholders are not required to make demand if it would *clearly be futile* because a majority of the directors either have a conflict of interest or were careless when making the decision. In the following case, the court ruled that making demand on eBay would be futile.

In Re EBAY, INC. SHAREHOLDERS LITIGATION

2004 Del. Ch. LEXIS 4
Court of Chancery of Delaware, 2004

Facts: In 1995, Pierre M. Omidyar and Jeffrey Skoll founded eBay, a company that hosts an online auction site. Robert C. Kagle joined the eBay board in 1997. Margaret C. Whitman became president, CEO, and a director of the company in 1998. She also became a director of the investment bank Goldman Sachs Group, Inc. in 2001. Goldman Sachs served as lead underwriter when eBay went public in 1998, and

again in 1999 when the company sold more shares to the public. Goldman also served as eBay's financial advisor when it acquired PayPal, Inc. in 2001.

During this period in which Goldman engaged in three major transactions with eBay, the market for stock in high-tech companies was very active. Goldman served as underwriter for a substantial number of technology companies that went public. Many

▼

---

[16] Under the Private Securities Litigation Reform Act, class action plaintiffs in suits brought under the securities laws must pay the corporation's legal expenses if the court determines that the suit was frivolous or abusive. 104 Pub. L. No. 67, 109 Stat. 737.

investors wanted to buy stock in these initial public offerings (IPOs) because an immediate and large profit was virtually guaranteed. Often stock prices doubled or tripled on the day of the offering. Goldman allowed Omidyar, Skoll, Kagle, and Whitman, all directors of eBay, to buy shares in hundreds of its IPOs, effectively giving them millions of dollars in profits. The following chart reveals the percentage of eBay shares that each director owned and the number of Goldman IPOs in which he or she was allowed to invest:

Director	Percentage of eBay shares owned	Number of IPOs in which director took part
Omidyar	> 23%	40
Skoll	13%	75
Whitman	3.3%	> 100
Kagle	Not disclosed in case	25

In each case, the eBay directors sold the stock immediately for millions of dollars in total profit.

eBay shareholders sued, alleging that Goldman had effectively bribed the defendants to continue giving business to the bank. The lawsuit was brought as a derivative action in the name of eBay. The plaintiffs alleged that demand was futile because the directors had a conflict of interest.

eBay's board of directors had seven members: Omidyar, Kagle, Whitman, Philippe Bourguignon, Scott D. Cook, Dawn G. Lepore, and Howard D. Schultz. (At the time of the lawsuit, Skoll was no longer a director.) The court determined that the three defendants had a conflict of interest because they were the targets of the lawsuit. It was obvious they would not vote for eBay to pursue the litigation. If one of the remaining four directors also had a conflict, then that would constitute a majority and demand would be excused. The shareholders could then bring the lawsuit themselves.

Issues: Did a majority of the board of directors have a conflict of interest? Was demand on the board futile?

Excerpts from Chancellor Chandler's Decision: Plaintiffs allege that Cook, Lepore, Schultz, and Bourguignon have received huge financial benefits as a result of their positions as eBay directors and, furthermore, that they owe their positions on the board to Omidyar, Whitman, Kagle, and Skoll.

eBay pays no cash compensation to its directors, but it does award substantial stock options. For example, in 1998, when Cook joined eBay's board, it awarded him 900,000 options. One fourth of these options (225,000) vested immediately, and an additional 2 percent vests each subsequent month so long as Cook remains a director. ["Vested" means that the owner is allowed to keep the options, even if he leaves the company.] In 1998, eBay adopted a director's stock option plan pursuant to which each non-employee director was to be awarded 30,000 options each year. [T]he stock options, which are not yet fully vested, and will never vest unless Cook retains his position as a director, are worth potentially millions of dollars.

I need not address each of the four outside directors, as I agree with plaintiffs that the allegations of the complaint are sufficient to raise a reasonable doubt as to Cook's independence from the eBay insider directors who accepted Goldman Sachs' IPO allocations.

First, Whitman, Omidyar, Kagle, and Skoll (and their affiliates) own about one-half of eBay's outstanding common stock. As a result, these eBay officers and directors effectively have the ability to control eBay and to direct its affairs and business, including the election of directors and the approval of significant corporate transactions.

Second, although many of the options awarded to Cook and the other outside directors have in fact vested, a significant number of options have not yet vested and will never vest unless the outside directors remain directors of eBay. Given that the value of the options for Cook (and allegedly for the other outside directors) potentially run into the millions of dollars, one cannot conclude realistically that Cook would be able to objectively and impartially consider a demand to bring litigation against those to whom he is beholden for his current position and future position on eBay's board. With the specific allegations of the complaint in mind, I conclude that plaintiffs have adequately demonstrated that demand on eBay's board should be excused as futile. ∎

Ethics	The activities described in this case were standard operating procedure at the time. Yet, these defendants were *billionaires*. Why would they engage in behavior that was potentially damaging to their reputation and to their company? Is behavior right just because other people are doing it? What guidance might the directors have gained from the ethics checklist? Would they have bought the IPO stock if they had known that their behavior would see the light of day? ◆

If Demand Is Required

If shareholders are required to make demand, the board has three choices:

1. It can agree with the shareholders and file suit on behalf of the corporation. In this case, the shareholders cannot bring their own derivative action. Although, technically, the board is required to put the interests of the corporation first, boards almost never decide to file suit themselves.

2. The board can reject the demand (or fail to respond). To proceed with their suit in this case, the plaintiffs must convince the court that the board has violated the business judgment rule because it had a conflict of interest or was careless in rejecting the demand.

3. The board can appoint a Special Litigation Committee (SLC). The SLC is typically comprised of at least two independent directors (usually those elected after the disputed activity occurred). If the SLC determines that the lawsuit is without merit, then the court must generally dismiss the case unless the shareholders can show the rejection was uninformed or not in good faith. There does not appear to be a single case in which an SLC recommended that litigation continue or a court overturned the decision of an SLC.

Exhibit 36.1 illustrates the course of derivative litigation. The most important issue is whether a court will require demand. Shareholders know that, if they make demand, the directors will appoint an SLC, which will then kill the suit. Therefore, shareholders typically file suit without making demand and wait for the company to go to court to ask that the suit be dismissed unless demand is made. If the court indeed requires demand, the shareholders know they have lost and typically withdraw the case. If, however, the shareholders can convince the court that demand is not required, the shareholders have won and the parties settle.

More Fortune 500 companies are incorporated in Delaware than in any other state, making its corporate law the most influential in the nation. The Model Act has, however, deviated from Delaware law by proposing that demand be required in *all* derivative cases. This approach essentially ignores the possibility that demand might be futile. Recently, the Supreme Court of Pennsylvania adopted the same approach.[17] Although Pennsylvania law is not as important as Delaware's, it is nonetheless growing in influence and could well represent the future of derivative actions.

Direct Lawsuits

Shareholders are permitted to sue the corporation directly only if their own rights have been harmed. If, for example, the corporation denies shareholders the right to inspect its books and records or to hold a shareholder meeting, they may sue in their own name and keep any damages awarded. The corporation is not required to

---

[17] *Cuker v. Mikalauskas,* 547 Pa. 600, 692 A.2d 1042, 1997 Pa. LEXIS 789 (Pa. 1997).

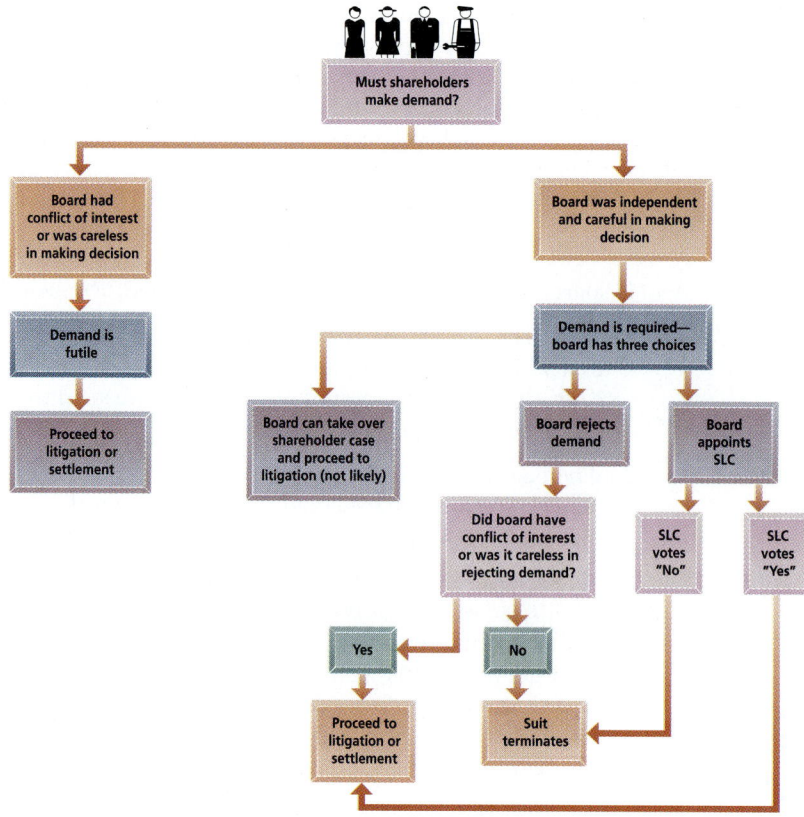

Exhibit 36.1

pay the shareholders' legal fees; winning shareholders can use part of any damage award for this purpose. With a direct action, shareholders are more likely to get their day in court because they are not required to make demand first.

Class Action Lawsuits

If a group of shareholders all have the same claim, they can join together and file suit as a class action, rather than suing separately. By joining forces, they can share the expense and effort of litigation. It is also far more efficient for the judicial system for one court to try one case than for tens or hundreds of courts all over the country to try the same issue. For obvious reasons, companies tend to resist class actions. In such suits, management is assailed by many small shareholders who otherwise could not afford to (or would not bother to) sue individually.

Most jurisdictions have strict requirements governing class actions, such as the following:

- The case cannot proceed unless a judge **certifies** the class. To be certified, all the members of the class must have a similar case without any conflicts of interest.

- A judge will not certify a class unless it is so large that individual suits are impractical. A class comprised of all Enron shareholders would be large enough.

- Any settlement must be approved by a judge. This requirement is meant to ensure fairness to all class members and to protect the class from their lawyers who may prefer to settle early on terms favorable to themselves (that is, with a large award of attorney's fees) rather than going to trial or insisting on a settlement that is best for shareholders.

Note that a class action can be either a derivative suit or a direct action. If a group of Enron shareholders sued the board for breaching its fiduciary duty to the company, that would be a derivative action in the name of the corporation. If the company refused to pay a dividend that it owed, the shareholders could sue the corporation directly, in a class action representing all shareholders.

The following table displays some of the important distinguishing features of derivative suits, direct actions, and class actions:

Features	Derivative Action	Direct Action	Class Action
Enforces the Rights of:	The corporation	The shareholder(s)	Either the shareholder(s) or the corporation depending on whether the suit is a derivative or direct action
Damages Are Paid to:	The corporation	The shareholder(s)	Either the corporation or the shareholder(s) depending on whether the suit is a derivative or direct action
Number of Plaintiffs	One or more	One or more	Many
Procedural Requirements	• Plaintiffs make demand on the board unless clearly futile. • If demand is futile, plaintiffs proceed with the case. • If demand is made, either the board or the SLC can terminate the case. • Settlement must be approved by the court.	The same as regular litigation	Class must be certified by the court. Settlement must be approved by the court.

Chapter Conclusion

At the beginning of this chapter, we asked the question: What happened to Enron (and Merrill Lynch and Xerox and all those other companies)? Commentators point to the following causes for trouble at Enron and other companies:

1. *A focus on stock prices.* Because corporate officers could earn vast wealth by exercising stock options, their incentive to raise stock prices was, for many, irresistible. They were willing to use complex (and even illegal) accounting methods. For instance, Yahoo! Inc. calculated its earnings one quarter by omitting depreciation, amortization, some payroll taxes, investment gains and losses, and acquisition-related and restructuring costs. In short, earnings were whatever Yahoo said they were.

2. *Ineffectual board of directors.* The Enron board was ignorant—either they did not know about or they ignored many of the company's abuses. They also approved exorbitant compensation packages.

3. *Lax supervision by lawyers and accountants.* Financial reporting standards were not sufficiently rigorous, as the Yahoo example illustrates. Even worse, Arthur Andersen, Enron's accounting firm, turned a blind eye to many questionable activities. Enron's lawyers did question a number of the company's activities but were not aggressive about reporting their concerns to the board.

What can be done to improve corporate governance in America, to prevent other Enrons?

In addition to SOX, commentators have suggested:

1. Require greater transparency in the disclosure of executive compensation. Every shareholder should be able to determine easily the total amount that top executives earn, now and in the future.

2. Instead of stock options, base compensation on the company's growth in earnings compared with those of its competitors. (Presumably executives should not be rewarded when their company's earnings grow at a slower pace than those of their competitors.)

3. Shareholders holding a substantial number of shares should be able to nominate candidates for the board of directors, and these nominees should be included in the company's proxy material. In this way, shareholders would be saved the expense of preparing and distributing their own proxy statements.

4. Make shareholder resolutions binding.

5. Permit shareholders, not just the board of directors, to make changes in the company's charter and state of incorporation. Currently, state corporation laws tend to favor managers because they decide the state of incorporation. If shareholders had a say, these laws might become more balanced.

Ethics

In analyzing Enron and its aftermath, a *Wall Street Journal* article concluded: "[N]ot one of the instances of egregious abuse of shareholder interest could have occurred if the CEO had simply said, 'No!' It takes a person of character to know what lines you don't cross. That part of the equation of corporate management hasn't had the emphasis it should have had in the last decade or two."[18] Would you have the strength of character to resist the temptations faced by many CEOs? ◆

Chapter Review

1. The Securities and Exchange Commission (SEC) regulates the relationship between publicly held corporations and their shareholders. The SEC plays a less active role in privately held corporations.

2. Shareholders have the right to:

- Receive annual financial statements
- Inspect and copy the corporation's records (for a proper purpose)
- Elect and remove directors; and
- Approve fundamental corporate changes, such as a merger or a major sale of assets.

---

18 David Wessel, "Why the Bad Guys of the Boardroom Emerged en Masse," *Wall Street Journal*, June 20, 2002, p. A1.

3. Virtually all publicly held companies solicit proxies from their shareholders. A proxy authorizes someone else to vote in place of the shareholder.

4. Under certain circumstances, public companies must include shareholder proposals in the proxy statement.

5. A shareholder who objects to a fundamental change in the corporation can insist that her shares be bought out at fair value. This protection is referred to as "dissenters' rights."

6. Controlling shareholders:

   • May not enter into unfair business transactions with the corporation

   • Have a fiduciary duty to minority shareholders

   • May not exclude minority shareholders from beneficial arrangements involving stock; and

   • Are prohibited from expelling minority shareholders, unless the expulsion is done for a legitimate business purpose

7. Congress, the NYSE, and Nasdaq have all taken steps to prevent management abuses. These new regulations require that companies adopt effective financial controls. They also require more independent directors on the board as a whole and on important subcommittees.

8. A derivative lawsuit is brought by shareholders to remedy a wrong to the corporation. The suit is brought in the name of the corporation, and all proceeds of the litigation go to the corporation.

9. If a group of shareholders all have the same claim against the corporation, they can join together and file a class action, rather than suing separately.

Practice Test

1. The New York State Common Retirement Fund wanted A&P (the grocery store chain) to permit large shareholders to place comments about the company's financial performance in its proxy statement. Which would be a better strategy for achieving this goal: a shareholder proposal or an amendment to the company's bylaws?

2. Shareholders lost their gamble when they bought stock of Jackpot Enterprises, Inc. Fed up with management, a shareholder asked the company to include a proposal in the proxy statement that would require the board of directors to sell or merge the company. Must Jackpot include this proposal in its proxy statement?

3. William H. Sullivan, Jr., purchased all the voting shares of the New England Patriots Football Club, Inc. (the Old Patriots). He organized a new corporation called the New Patriots Football Club, Inc. The boards of directors of the two companies agreed to merge. After the merger, the nonvoting stock in the Old Patriots was to be exchanged for cash. Do minority shareholders of the Old Patriots have the right to prevent the merger? If so, under what theory?

4. Daniel Cowin was a minority shareholder of Bresler & Reiner, Inc., a public company that developed real estate in Washington, D.C. He alleged numerous instances of corporate mismanagement, fraud, self-dealing, and breach of fiduciary duty by the board of directors. He sought damages for the diminished value of his stock. Could Cowin bring this suit as a direct action, or must it be a derivative suit?

5. The board of directors of Finalco Group, Inc., decided to sell most of the company's assets to Western Savings and Loan Association. Shortly after the proposed sale was announced, Finalco's largest shareholder said he opposed the transaction. Does Finalco need his approval for the sale?

6. **ETHICS** Edgar Bronfman, Jr., dropped out of high school to go to Hollywood and write songs and produce movies. Eventually, he left Hollywood to work in the family business—the Bronfmans owned 36 percent of Seagram Co., a liquor and beverage conglomerate. Promoted to president of the company at the age of 32, Bronfman seized a second chance to live his dream. Seagram received 70 percent of its earnings from its 24 percent ownership of DuPont Co. Bronfman sold this stock *at less than market value* to purchase (at an inflated price) 80 percent of MCA, a movie and music company that had been a financial disaster for its prior owners. Some observers thought Bronfman had gone Hollywood, others

that he had gone crazy. After the deal was announced, the price of Seagram shares fell 18 percent. Was there anything Seagram shareholders could do to prevent what to them was not a dream but a nightmare? Apart from legal issues, was Bronfman's decision ethical? What ethical obligations does he owe Seagram's shareholders?

7. When Classic Corp. went public at $12 a share, its waterbed business was floating along nicely—the company had annual sales of $23 million and turned a hefty profit. The company then sprang a leak and suffered through many years of losses. Isaac Fogel, who owned 64 percent of the stock, decided to take the company private again (by buying shareholders' stock) at a price of 20 *cents* a share. Classic hired two financial advisers who opined that the buyout price was fair. The board of directors voted in favor of the sale and then scheduled a special shareholder meeting to vote on the buyout. Do the minority shareholders have any rights?

8. The president of R. Hoe & Co., Inc., refused to call a special meeting of the shareholders although 55 percent of the shareholders requested it. One purpose of the meeting was to demand that the former president be reinstated. Are these two requests within the power of the shareholders?

9. Prior to the DuPont Co.'s annual shareholder meeting, Friends of the Earth Oceanic Society submitted a proposal requiring the company to (1) accelerate its phaseout of the production of chlorofluorocarbons and halons, (2) present to shareholders a report detailing research and development efforts to find environmentally sound substitutes, and (3) report to shareholders on marketing plans to sell those substitutes. Must DuPont include this proposal in its proxy material for the annual meeting?

10. *YOU BE THE JUDGE* WRITING PROBLEM Two shareholders of Bruce Co., Harry and Yolan Gilbert, were fighting management for control of the company. They asked for permission to inspect Bruce's stockholder list so that they could either solicit support for their slate of directors at the upcoming stockholder meeting, or attempt to buy additional stock from other stockholders, or both. Bruce's board refused to allow the Gilberts to see the shareholder list on the grounds that the Gilberts owned another corporation that competed with Bruce. Do the Gilberts have the right to see Bruce's shareholder list? **Argument for the Gilberts:** If shareholders of a company have a proper purpose, they are entitled to inspect shareholder lists. Soliciting votes and buying stock are both proper purposes. **Argument for Bruce:** The Gilberts are simply offering a pretext. They could use this information to compete against the company. No shareholder has the right to cause harm.

11. *ROLE REVERSAL* Write a short-answer question that focuses on whether a shareholder would be able to bring a derivative suit without first making demand.

Internet Research Problem

Using the Internet, find information on a company's shareholder proposals in the last year. (You can, for example, type into Google: "shareholder proposals 2006") What were these proposals about? What was the outcome of the shareholder vote? Can you find a proposal that shareholders supported?

You can find further practice problems at http://beatty.westbuslaw.com or in the Study Guide that accompanies this text.

Securities Regulation

In 1926, America was gripped by a fever of stock market speculation. "Playing the market" became a national mania. The most engrossing news on any day's front page was the market. Up and up it soared. The cause of this psychological virus is uncertain, but the focus of the infection was the New York Stock Exchange. Between 1926 and 1929, annual volume leaped from 451 million to over 1.1 billion shares. In one year alone, the price of AT&T went from $179.50 to $335.62.

© ARTHUR S. AUBRY/PHOTODISC/GETTY IMAGES

Much of this feverish trading was done on margin. Customers put down only 10 or 20 percent of a stock's purchase price and then borrowed the rest from their broker. This easy-payment plan excited the gambling instinct of unwary amateurs and professional speculators alike. By September 1929, the volume of these margin loans was equal to about half the entire public debt of the United States.

On September 4, 1929, stock prices began to soften, and for the next month they slid gently. Over the weekend of October 19, brokers sent out thousands of margin calls, asking customers to pay down loans that now exceeded the value of their stock. If customers failed to pay, brokers dumped their stock on the market, causing prices to fall further and brokers to make more margin calls. Soon there was a mad scramble of selling as prices plunged in wild disorder. Tens of thousands of investors

The effect of the 1929 stock market crash was immediate and devastating.

across the country were wiped out. On Tuesday, October 29, 1929, the speculative boom completely collapsed. That day, 4 million shares were traded, a record that stood for 30 years. From the peak of the bull market in September to the debacle of October 29, over $32 billion of equity value simply vanished from the earth.

The stock market crash spawned the Great Depression—the most pervasive, persistent, and destructive economic crisis the nation has ever faced. Retail trade fell by one-half, automobile production by two-thirds, steel by three-quarters. In 1933, more businesses failed than in any other year in history. Surviving businesses responded to the crisis by cutting dividends, reducing inventories, laying off workers, slashing wages, and canceling capital investments.

Unemployment statistics were the most poignant of all. In 1932, one in every five people in the labor force was out of a job. Million of others were underemployed, working only two or three days a week for wages that could not support a family. Distress cut indiscriminately across all economic and social classes. Bankers, insurance agents, architects, and lawyers joined the throng of unemployed. Articles such as the following were common in newspapers across the land:

New York, Jan. 6, 1933 (AP)—After vainly trying to get a stay of dispossession until Jan. 15 from his apartment in Brooklyn, yesterday, Peter J. Cornell, 48 years old, a former roofing contractor out of work and penniless, fell dead in the arms of his wife. A doctor gave the cause of his death as heart disease, and the police said it had at least partly been caused by the bitter disappointment of a long day's fruitless attempt to prevent himself and his family being put out on the streets.[1] ■

---

[1]   The material in this section is adapted from Cabell Phillips, *From the Crash to the Blitz* (Toronto: Macmillan, 1969).

INTRODUCTION

At the time of the great stock market crash, there was no federal securities law, only state law. Congress recognized that the country needed a national securities system if it was to avoid another such catastrophe. In 1933, Congress passed the Securities Act of 1933 (1933 Act) to regulate the issuance of new securities. The next year, it passed the Securities Exchange Act of 1934 (1934 Act) to regulate companies with publicly traded securities. The 1934 Act also established the Securities and Exchange Commission (SEC), the regulatory agency that oversees the securities industry.

The Securities and Exchange Commission

The SEC creates law in three different ways:

- **Rules.** The securities statutes are often little more than general guides. Through its rules, the SEC fills in the crucial details.

- **Releases.** These are informal pronouncements from the SEC on current issues. Releases often operate as two-way communication. When the SEC issues a release to announce a proposed change in the rules, it also asks for comments on the proposal.

- **No-Action Letters.** Anyone who is in doubt about whether a particular transaction complies with the securities laws can ask the SEC directly. The response is called a no-action letter because it states that "the staff will recommend that the Commission take no action" if the transaction is done in a specified manner.

In addition to creating laws, the SEC has the power to enforce them. It can bring **cease and desist orders** against those who violate the securities laws, and it can also levy fines or confiscate profits from illegal transactions. Those accused of wrongdoing can appeal these sanctions to the courts. The SEC does not have the authority to bring a criminal action; it refers criminal cases to the Justice Department.

What Is a Security?

Both the 1933 and the 1934 Acts regulate securities. The official definition of a security includes a note, stock, treasury stock, bond, debenture, evidence of indebtedness, certificate of interest or participation in any profit-sharing agreement, and 17 other equivalents. Courts have interpreted this definition to mean that **a security is any transaction in which the buyer (1) invests money in a common enterprise and (2) expects to earn a profit predominantly from the efforts of others.**

This definition covers investments that are not necessarily called *securities*. For example, they may be called orange trees. W. J. Howey Co. owned large citrus groves in Florida. It sold these trees to investors, most of whom were from out of state and knew nothing about farming. Purchasers were expected to hire someone to take care of their trees. Someone like Howey-in-the-Hills, Inc., a related company that just happened to be in the service business. Customers were free to hire any service company, but 85 percent of the acreage was covered by service contracts with Howey-in-the-Hills. The court held that Howey was selling a security (no matter how orange or tart), because the purchaser was investing in a common enterprise (the orange grove) expecting to earn a profit from Howey's farmwork.

Other courts have interpreted the term "security" to include animal breeding arrangements (chinchillas, silver foxes, or beavers, take your pick); condominium purchases in which the developer promises the owner a certain level of income from rentals; and even investments in whiskey.

SECURITIES ACT OF 1933

The 1933 Act requires that, before offering or selling securities, the issuer must register the securities with the SEC, unless the securities qualify for an exemption. An **issuer** is the company that issues the stock. Registering securities with the SEC in a public offering is a major undertaking, but the 1933 Act exempts some securities and also some particular types of securities transactions from the full-blown registration requirements of a public offering.

It is also important to remember that **when an issuer registers securities, the SEC does not investigate the quality of the offering.** Permission from the SEC to sell securities does not mean that the company has a good product or will be successful. SEC approval simply means that, on the surface, the company has answered all relevant questions about itself and its major products. The guiding principle of the federal securities laws is that investors can make a reasoned decision on whether to buy or sell securities if they have full and accurate information about a company and the security it is selling. For example, the Green Bay Packers football team sold an offering of stock to finance stadium improvements. The prospectus admitted:

> IT IS VIRTUALLY IMPOSSIBLE that any investor will ever make a profit on the stock purchase. The company will pay no dividends, and the shares cannot be sold.

This does not sound like a stock you want in your retirement fund; on the other hand, the SEC will not prevent Green Bay from selling it, or you from buying it, as long as you understand what the risks are.

One last point: **the 1933 Act prohibits fraud in *any* securities transaction.** Anyone who issues fraudulent securities is in violation of the 1933 Act, whether or not the securities are registered. Both the SEC and any purchasers of the stock can sue the issuer.

cyberLaw

Companies must deliver certain documents to investors and also file them with the SEC. Almost all filings with the SEC must be made electronically, using the EDGAR (Electronic Data Gathering, Analysis, and Retrieval) system. Once filed with the SEC, this information is available online (at **http://www.sec.gov**).

Companies file online with the SEC, but delivering documents to investors electronically is more difficult because computer literacy and availability among investors vary widely. The SEC does *permit* (but not require) issuers to communicate electronically with investors, provided that the following standards are met:

- *Consent.* Although many investors have computers, an issuer cannot assume that all do, or that all want to receive data this way. Therefore, an electronic document is valid only if the investor agrees to receive information in this form.

- *Notice.* A company cannot simply post information on its Internet Web site, because investors will not necessarily know it is there. The issuer must notify investors, via e-mail or snail mail, that information is available.

- *Access.* The recipients must have access to the information for a reasonable period of time and be able to download or print it. The investor can always request the paper version of a document, even after consenting to electronic delivery. ◆

General Exemption

Before offering securities for sale, the issuer must determine whether they are exempt from registration under the 1933 Act. Typically, exemptions are based on two factors: the type of security and the type of transaction. However, the National Securities Markets Improvement Act of 1996 gave the SEC new authority under both the 1933 and the 1934 Acts to grant exemptions that are "in the public interest" and "consistent with the protection of investors."

Exempt Securities

The 1933 Act exempts some types of securities from registration because they (1) are inherently low risk, (2) are regulated by other statutes, or (3) are not really investments. The following securities are exempt from registration:

- **Government securities,** which include any security issued or guaranteed by federal or state government

- **Bank securities,** which include any security issued or guaranteed by a bank

- **Short-term notes,** which are high-quality negotiable notes or drafts that are due within nine months of issuance and are not sold to the general public

- **Nonprofit issues,** which include any security issued by a nonprofit religious, educational, or charitable organization

- **Insurance policies and annuity contracts,** which are governed by insurance regulations

Exempt Transactions

Section 4(2) of the 1933 Act exempts from registration "transactions by an issuer not involving any public offering." These are simple words to define a complex problem. In effect, the 1933 Act says that an issuer is not required to register securities that are sold in a private offering, that is, an offering with only a few investors or a relatively small amount of money involved. In private offerings, the full-blown disclosure of a public offering is neither necessary nor appropriate. For instance, a group of sophisticated investors who know an industry well do not need full disclosure. Or, if the amount at stake is relatively small, it would not make economic sense for the issuer to incur the heavy expense of a public offering.

There is an important distinction between exempt *securities* and exempt *transactions.* Exempt *securities* are always exempt, throughout their lives, no matter how many times they are sold. Stock sold in an exempt *transaction* is exempt only that one time, not necessarily in any subsequent sale. Suppose that Country Bank sells stock to the public. Under the 1933 Act, the bank is never required to register these securities, no matter how many times they are sold. On the other hand, suppose that Tumbleweed, Inc., a quilt maker, sells $5 million worth of stock in a private offering that is exempt from registration. Shamika buys 100 shares of this stock. Seven years later, the company decides to sell stock in a public offering that must be registered. As part of this public offering, Shamika sells her 100 shares. This time, the shares must be registered because they are being sold in a *public offering.*

Most small companies use private, not public, offerings to raise capital. There are three different types of private offerings—intrastate, Regulation D, and Regulation A—each with its own set of rules.

Intrastate Offering Exemption

Under SEC Rule 147, an issuer is not required to register securities that are *offered* and *sold* only to residents of the state in which the issuer is incorporated and does business. This exemption was designed to provide local financing for local businesses. To qualify under Rule 147, 80 percent of the issuer's revenues and assets must be in-state, and it must also intend to spend 80 percent of the offering's proceeds in-state. Neither the issuer nor any purchaser can sell the securities outside the state for nine months after the offering.

Rule 147 is a **safe harbor**—if an issuer totally complies with it, the offering definitely qualifies as intrastate. But even if the issuer does not comply absolutely with the rule, the SEC or the courts may still consider the offering to be intrastate; however, the issuer cannot be sure in advance how the decision will come out. Sonic was a Utah corporation that sold stock to Utah residents. *Seven* months later, the company sold stock to an Illinois company. Although Sonic violated Rule 147 by making the second sale too early, the court held that the company had nonetheless qualified for an intrastate offering because it had not intended, at the time of the original offering, to sell stock outside Utah.[2] Although Sonic had not totally complied with Rule 147, it had come close enough to avoid liability. A safe harbor is less dangerous, but a voyage outside its boundaries does not necessarily end in disaster.

Regulation D

Three different types of private offerings can be made under Regulation D (often referred to as Reg D) under Rules 504, 505, and 506.

Rule 504. Under this rule (know as the "seed capital" rule), a company:

- May sell up to $1 million in securities during each 12-month period.
- May advertise the stock and solicit an unlimited number of investors if:
  - The transaction is registered under a state law with disclosure requirements, or
  - Sales are limited to accredited investors. **Accredited investors** are institutions (such as banks and insurance companies) or wealthy individuals (with a net worth of more than $1 million or an annual income of more than $200,000).

If the securities are neither registered under state law nor sold exclusively to accredited investors, they are **restricted** stock, which means they must be purchased for investment purposes. As a general rule, the buyer cannot resell restricted securities, either publicly or privately, for one year.

Rule 505. This rule permits a company to sell up to $5 million of stock during each 12-month period, subject to the following restrictions:

- The company may not advertise the stock publicly.
- The issuer can sell to as many accredited investors as it wants, but is limited to only 35 unaccredited investors.
- The company need not provide information to accredited investors but must make some disclosure to unaccredited investors. This requirement provides issuers with a serious incentive to avoid unaccredited investors because the disclosure requirements, although less demanding than for a public offering, are nonetheless burdensome.
- Stock purchased under this rule is restricted.

Rule 506. This rule is similar to Rule 505. The differences are that:

- There is no limit on the amount of stock a company can sell.
- If an unaccredited purchaser is unsophisticated, he must have a **purchaser representative** to help him evaluate the investment. Is an *unsophisticated* investor someone who does not care for opera? No, it is someone who is unable to assess the risks of the offering himself.

The following table sets out the menu of choices under Reg D:

---

[2] *Busch v. Carpenter*, 827 F.2d 653, 1987 U.S. App. LEXIS 11034 (10th Cir. 1987).

	Maximum Value of Securities Sold in a 12-Month Period	Maximum Number of Investors		Is Disclosure Required?	Is Public Advertising Permitted?	Are Securities Restricted?
Rule 504 Option 1:	$1 million	No limit on accredited investors	or	Disclosure under state law	Yes	No
Option 2:	$1 million	No limit	and	No	No	Yes
Rule 505	$5 million	No limit on accredited investors; no more than 35 unaccredited investors		Only for unaccredited investors	No	Yes
Rule 506	No limit	No limit on accredited investors; no more than 35 unaccredited investors, who must either be sophisticated or have a purchaser representative		Only for unaccredited investors	No	Yes

Regulation A

Although an offering under Regulation A is *called* a private offering, it really is a small public offering. **Reg A permits an issuer to sell $5 million of securities *publicly* in any 12-month period.** The issuer must give each purchaser an offering circular that provides the same disclosure required for unaccredited investors under Reg D. The following table compares a public offering, Reg A, and Reg D:

	Initial Public Offering	Regulation A	Regulation D
Maximum Value of Securities Sold	No limit	$5 million	$1 million, $5 million, or no limit, depending on the rule
Public Solicitation of Purchasers	Permitted	Permitted	Permitted only under Rule 504
Suitability Requirements for Purchasers	No requirements	No requirements	Must determine if investors are accredited or sophisticated
Disclosure Requirements	Elaborate registration statement, audited financials	Offering circular that is less detailed than a registration statement	Rule 504: may require disclosure under state law Rules 505 and 506: none for accredited investors, the same requirements as Reg A for unaccredited investors

	Initial Public Offering	Regulation A	Regulation D
Resale of Securities	Permitted	Permitted	Sometimes permitted under Rule 504, otherwise not permitted for one year
Number of Offerings in 2004	630	25	15,795

Direct Public Offerings

Traditionally, a small company either sold stock to people it knew well or hired an investment banker to place the securities with a wider public. But now, instead of going through Wall Street, many companies trying to raise capital for the first time sell stock to the public themselves through a direct public offering (DPO). In a DPO, the issuer typically sells shares to its stakeholders: customers, employees, suppliers, or the community. The issuer makes a DPO offering under Regulation A or Rule 504, because both permit public offerings without full-blown registration and disclosure requirements.

The advantages of a DPO are

- It is much cheaper than a regular public offering done through an underwriter.

- It can be an effective marketing tool—shareholders tend to become even more loyal customers.

The downside:

- Each investor must receive written information about the company. The cost of this disclosure can be prohibitive when dealing with many small investors. Mailing a $10 disclosure document to hundreds of investors who only want to buy $50 worth of stock each may not be an efficient means of raising money.

- Although shareholders are warned that they should view their purchases as long-term investments, some will inevitably want to sell their shares. Setting up a system to permit these trades can be tricky and time consuming.

Although the companies featured in the following article found their DPOs worthwhile, the process consumed significant management time.

NEWS*worthy*

In 1995, Spring Street Brewery, a New York microbrewery, became the first company to conduct an offering on the Internet. It established a home page that allowed potential investors to examine and download its offering documents. In the end, it raised $1.6 million.

Thanksgiving Coffee Co. of Fort Bragg, California, used both cybertechnology and the old-fashioned face-to-face approach. It had originally planned simply to sell to its loyal customer base. "You think that everybody who knows about you will line up around the block to buy stock, but you have to put the offering in front of potential investors' faces seven times to get them to take action," says Thanksgiving general manager Rick Moon. He did just that. He put offering notices on coffee-bean bags; he hung announcements on bean dispensers. Vendors got the advertisements, as did mail-order customers. Information about the stock sale appeared on the company's Web site, in its catalog, and in advertisements in targeted magazines. Anyone who called about the stock got regular updates on the offering. In the end, the huge effort paid off. By the time the offering closed, Thanksgiving Coffee had sold 20 percent of its stock for $1.25 million.[3] ◆

---

[3] Stephanie Gruner, "When Mom & Pop Go Public," *INC.*, Dec. 1996, p. 66. Republished with permission of INC. Magazine; permission conveyed through the Copyright Clearance Center, Inc.

The "screen test" at http://www.dfdpo.com can help you gauge whether you and your company are ready for a DPO.

Public Offerings

When a company wishes to raise significant amounts of capital from a large number of people, it is time for a public offering. A company's first public sale of securities is called an **initial public offering** or an **IPO.** Here is one company's experience with an IPO.

Shortly after graduating from the Massachusetts Institute of Technology, Daniel Schwinn and Frank Slaughter founded Shiva Corp. (pronounced SHE-va) in Burlington, Massachusetts. The company made hardware and software that allowed personal computers to tie directly into a corporate network from outside the office. Although within a decade sales had reached $42 million and net income was $2.7 million, the company was constantly strapped for cash to fund expansion. Its two founders began thinking about a public offering.

Underwriting

As we have seen, companies can sell stock directly to the public themselves, but they primarily do so if the amounts involved are small. Shiva sought to raise more than $20 million, so it decided to hire an investment bank to serve as underwriter. In a **firm commitment** underwriting, the underwriter buys the stock from the issuer and resells it to the public. The underwriter bears the risk that the stock may sell at a lower price than expected. In a **best efforts** underwriting, the underwriter does not buy the stock but instead acts as the company's agent in selling it. If the stock sells at a low price, the company, not the underwriter, is the loser.

In underwriting, as in life, timing is everything. As it happened, just when Shiva hoped to complete its offering, Wall Street's interest in the high-tech sector suddenly cooled. Investment bankers offered the company only $6 a share for its stock. Shiva decided to wait. Within three months, the market in high-tech stocks picked up again. The company's president, Frank Ingari, and its chief financial officer, Cynthia Deysher, went to New York to sign on with the investment bank Goldman Sachs. Shiva agreed to sell Goldman 2.4 million shares at a tentative price of $12 per share.

Registration Statement

The **registration statement** has two purposes: to notify the SEC that a sale of securities is pending and to disclose information to prospective purchasers. The registration statement must include detailed information about the issuer and its business, a description of the stock, the proposed use of the proceeds from the offering, and audited balance sheets and income statements. Preparing a registration statement is neither quick—it typically takes two to three months—nor inexpensive. Shiva spent $900,000 on audits and other expenses.

Within a month of hiring an investment bank, Shiva filed its *preliminary* draft of the registration statement with the SEC. This preliminary draft is called a **red herring** because it contains a notice in red ink warning that the securities cannot yet be sold.[4] The SEC typically spends between 30 and 100 days reviewing this preliminary draft of the registration statement. Remember that the Commission does not assess the value of the stock or the merit of the investment. Its role is to ensure that the company has disclosed enough to enable investors to make an informed decision.

---

[4]   The term "red herring" is a bit of a joke because, outside securities offerings, it means a false clue.

Prospectus

Typically, buyers never see the registration statement; they are given the **prospectus** instead. (The prospectus is also included in the registration statement that is sent to the SEC.) The prospectus includes all of the important disclosures about the company, while the registration statement includes additional information that is of interest to the SEC but not to the typical investor, such as the names and addresses of the lawyers for the issuer and underwriter. All investors must receive a copy of the prospectus before purchasing the stock.

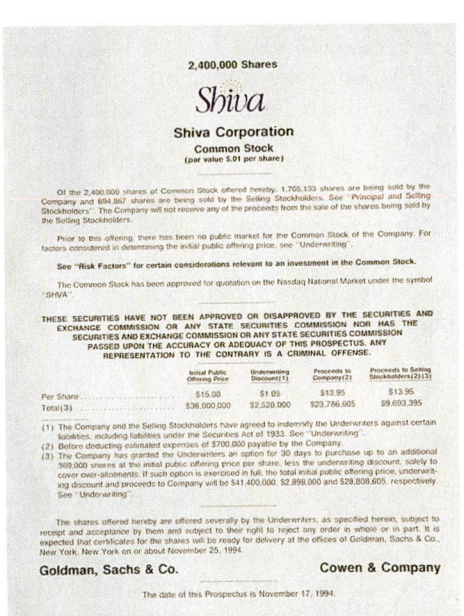

Each investor who purchased stock in Shiva Corp.'s initial public offering received this prospectus. Shiva also filed it with the SEC as part of the company's registration statement. The inside cover illustrates the dual nature of a prospectus—both disclosure document and sales pitch.

Sales Effort

The SEC closely regulates an issuer's sales effort.

Quiet Period. The quiet period begins when a company hires an underwriter and ends 25 days after the stock is first sold to the public. During this period, company officers must guard their words carefully to avoid any appearance of hyping the stock. For example, the SEC delayed an offering of stock by Saleforce.com after *The New York Times* published a profile of its CEO during the company's quiet period. A few months later, *Playboy* magazine printed an interview with the founders of Google and the SEC delayed its public offering. Although the SEC recently relaxed the rules for the quiet period, it seems unlikely that even under the new standards the SEC will ignore interviews with *Playboy.*

Waiting Period. This is the time after the registration statement has been filed but before the SEC has approved it. The underwriter can publish a **tombstone ad,** that is, a simple, unadorned announcement of the offering that includes the amount and type of security, the name of the underwriter, and the price of stock. You can see many of these ads in *The Wall Street Journal* and also on company Web sites. During the waiting period, the underwriter may distribute the preliminary prospectus. It can also solicit offers, but cannot make sales. The underwriter uses this period to estimate market demand for the stock. It **makes book,** meaning that it talks with traders to determine how many shares it can sell and at what price. It also takes **indications of interest** from traders but makes no sales.

Road Show. During the waiting period, Goldman and Shiva began the **road show—** the cross-country road trip to convince traders that Shiva was a stock their clients should buy. Ingari and Schwinn spent a grueling two weeks visiting 16 cities. At each stop, they made the same impassioned pitch to influential traders. Sometimes road shows are broadcast on the Web so that they can be viewed by a larger group that includes wealthy individuals. "We felt like door-to-door salesmen," Ingari said. So strong was the response to Shiva that in the second week of the road show, Goldman suggested raising the price to $15 a share, from $12, and selling an additional 360,000 shares. When the road show ended, orders for the stock exceeded the number of shares by a factor of 30. That the IPO would be hot was certain. But how hot?

Going Effective

Once its review of the preliminary registration statement is complete, the SEC sends the issuer a **comment letter,** listing changes that must be made to the registration statement. An issuer almost always amends the registration statement at least once, and sometimes more than once. After the SEC has approved a final registration statement (which includes, of course, the final prospectus), the issuer then decides on a date to **go effective,** that is, to begin selling the stock. One last step remained: Goldman and Shiva had to agree on an opening price. They decided to raise the price from $12 to $15 per share. Shiva would sell to Goldman at $13.95 per share, and Goldman, in turn, would sell it on the market at $15.

The night before the sale, Shiva executives and the underwriters met for dinner and made bets about the next day's closing price and trading volume. No one guessed nearly high enough. As soon as Goldman sold at $15, the price zoomed to $30.50. The stock closed that day at $31.50 per share. At Goldman, there were hugs, tears of joy, and champagne toasts. But founders Schwinn and Slaughter, with their stock suddenly worth $30 million each, suffered chest pains. And Ingari, the president and chief executive, felt even worse. As the value of his stake in Shiva soared past $14 million, he fled to the men's room. "I was ready to throw up, I was sweating badly, and I could barely stand up. When I looked in the mirror, I had blood coming out of my nose."

In the end, Shiva raised $28 million that day, and its founders and other insiders, who sold about 700,000 shares, took home another $10 million. Goldman earned almost $3 million, or 7 percent of the proceeds. Did Goldman price the offering too low? Pricing an IPO is more art than science. Everyone would like the price to rise gently. At all cost, however, the underwriter wishes to avoid a disaster in which the stock price collapses, leaving it with a large loss. Of course, the underwriter looks bad if the company sells stock for a lot less than it is worth. Shares that Goldman sold in the morning for $15 were trading for twice that amount later in the day. Half of the initial worth of Shiva's stock, or about $43 million, went into the pockets of early buyers who "flipped" the stock, selling it immediately to other investors. In hindsight, Goldman should have priced the stock higher, but it is not clear that it or anyone else could reasonably have predicted the market's reaction.

Frank Slaughter went home after the IPO and spent a day "scrubbing toilets—to retain some humility." He had come through one of the most unnerving, and quintessential, rites of passage of the American capitalist system. The company obtained money to develop new products and build factories. The public got a chance to buy in. And the company's founders, and other key insiders, found a way to cash out.[5]

So what happened to Shiva? Its stock continued an upward climb for two years, reaching a peak of $87 per share. But when the company failed to develop new products, both its business and its stock price faltered. Five years after the public offering, Intel Corp. acquired Shiva at a price of $6 per share.

In the following case, eToys sued its underwriter, Goldman Sachs (also Shiva's underwriter), for underpricing its stock offering. Should Goldman be liable? You be the judge.

---

[5]   The information about Shiva Corp. is from Glenn Rifkin, "Anatomy of a Highflying IPO, Nosebleeds and All," *New York Times,* Feb. 19, 1995, p. F7. Copyright © 1995 by The New York Times Co. Reprinted by permission.

you Be The Judge

EBC I, INC. V. GOLDMAN SACHS & CO.

2005 N.Y. LEXIS 1178
Court of Appeals of New York, 2005

Facts: Goldman Sachs was the lead underwriter for eToys' initial public offering. eToys agreed to sell 8,320,000 shares of its stock to Goldman at a price of $18.65 per share, for resale to the public at $20. (Goldman had the option to buy an additional 1,248,000 shares at the same price.) The bank's potential profit was $1.35 per share, for a maximum of $12,916,800.

On the first day of the offering, the price of eToys' stock rose as high as $85 and closed at $76.56. Within a year, however, the price had fallen below $20. eToys ultimately filed for bankruptcy protection.

eToys alleged that Goldman made side deals with other clients allowing them to purchase shares in eToys' offering in exchange for kickbacks to Goldman of a portion of their profits on the stock. This arrangement would have created an incentive for Goldman to underprice the stock. eToys also alleged that Goldman had a fiduciary duty to eToys that it violated by not disclosing this conflict of interest.

Goldman filed a motion to dismiss denying that it had a fiduciary relationship to eToys.

You Be the Judge: Did Goldman have a fiduciary duty to eToys? Did it violate this duty?

Argument for eToys: A fiduciary relationship exists between two parties if one of them is under a duty to act for or to give advice for the benefit of the other. eToys hired Goldman for its expertise and paid handsomely for its advice about many aspects of going public. The company would never have relied on this advice had it known about the side deals with other clients—deals that could harm eToys.

eToys trusted Goldman, the bank betrayed that trust, and eToys suffered an enormous financial penalty as a result.

Argument for Goldman Sachs: This is a simple case: eToys sold stock, Goldman bought it. Goldman negotiated the best price it could. If eToys was unhappy with this deal, it had no one to blame but itself.

If eToys expected Goldman to act as a fiduciary, the agreement should have stated so explicitly. The company always knew that its interests were different from Goldman's. eToys sought the highest price; Goldman had to ensure that it could resell the shares at a profit. The lower the price to eToys, the lower the risk to Goldman. Goldman took a substantial risk buying this stock, and in this case the risk paid off. It does not always do so.

eToys was a sophisticated company with sophisticated advisors. Its stockholders included well-known venture-capital firms. Its largest single stockholder, Idealab, was an incubator for successful technology companies (see http://www.idealab .com). eToys' law firm—the Venture Law Group, P.C.—specialized in representing high-tech companies. During one year, this law firm was fourth on the list of firms that handled the most initial public offerings for technology companies.

In short, the offering price was not "set" by Goldman, it was negotiated by two sophisticated parties. ■

Sales of Restricted Securities

After the public offering, Shiva insiders still owned a substantial block of stock. Between them, Schwinn, Slaughter, and Ingari held stock or options for 2.8 million shares. With the stock trading as high as $87 per share, on paper they were worth $245 million, but they could not actually sell their stock, at least not right away. **Rule 144 limits the resale of two types of securities:** *control securities* and *restricted securities.*

A **control security** is stock held by any shareholder who owns more than 10 percent of a class of stock or by any officer or director. In any three-month period, such an insider can sell only an amount of stock equal to the average weekly trading volume for the prior four weeks or 1 percent of the number of shares outstanding, whichever is greater. Shiva had 9,589,000 shares outstanding and an (unusually high) average weekly trading volume of roughly 938,000. A Shiva insider could sell at most 938,000 shares during each three-month period. In a company with a more typical trading volume, the number might be a tenth of that. The purpose of this rule is to protect other investors from precipitous declines in stock price. If company insiders sold all of their stock in one day, the price would plunge, causing losses to the other shareholders.

For owners of restricted securities, the rules are more complex. A **restricted security** is any stock purchased from the issuer in a private offering (such as Regulation D). These securities may not be sold within one year of the offering. After the first year, restricted securities can be sold as long as the sale does not exceed the limitations that apply to control stock: the greater of the average weekly trading volume for the prior four weeks or 1 percent of the number of shares outstanding. After two years, restricted securities can be sold freely, unless they are also control securities, in which case those restrictions still apply. Exhibit 37.1 illustrates the sale of restricted securities under Rule 144.

Exhibit 37.1

The sale of restricted securities under Rule 144

Liability

Liability for Unregistered Securities

Section 12(a)(1) of the 1933 Act imposes liability on anyone who sells a security that is not registered and not exempt. The purchaser of the security can demand rescission—a return of his money in exchange for the stock—or, if he no longer owns the stock, he can ask for damages.

Fraud

Under §12(a)(2) of the 1933 Act, the seller of a security is liable for making any material misstatement or omission, either oral or written, in connection with the offer or sale of a security. This provision applies to both *public* and *private* offerings if there is some use of interstate commerce, such as the mails, telephone (even for an *intra*state call), or check (which clears). It is difficult to imagine a securities transaction that does not involve interstate commerce. The SEC provides information on how to invest wisely and avoid securities fraud at http://www.sec.gov/investor.shtml. The North American Securities Administrators Association also offers advice on "how to spot a con artist" and popular securities scams (http://www.nasaa.org). You can obtain disciplinary reports on securities firms or individual brokers at http://www.nasdr.com. To report fraud, contact the SEC at its Complaint Center (http://www.sec.gov/complaint.shtml).

Criminal Liability

Under §24 of the 1933 Act, the Justice Department can prosecute anyone who willfully violates the Act.

Liability for the Registration Statement

Section 11 of the 1933 Act establishes the penalties for any errors in a registration statement. **If a final registration statement contains a material misstatement or omission, the purchaser of the security can recover from everyone who signed the registration statement.** This list of signatories includes the issuer, its directors, and chief officers; experts (such as auditors, engineers, or lawyers); and the underwriters. Everyone who signed the registration statement is jointly and severally liable for any error, except the experts, who are liable only for misstatements in the part of the registration statement for which they were responsible.[6] Thus an auditor is liable for misstatements in the financials but not, say, for omissions about the CEO's criminal past.

Damages. To prevail under §11, the plaintiff need only prove that there was a material misstatement or omission and that she lost money. **Material** means important enough to affect an investor's decision. The plaintiff does not have to prove that she relied on (or even *read*) the registration statement, that she bought the stock from the issuer, or that the defendant was negligent. The plaintiff can recover the difference between what she paid for the stock and its value on the date of the lawsuit. Suppose that Pet Detective, Inc., does an IPO. A week later, Ace Investora buys 1,000 shares at $10 a share. He knows nothing about the company, but he likes the name. This stock turns out to be a dog—Pet Detective has only two agencies, not the 200 stated in the registration statement. When the stock falls to 10 cents, Investora can sue under §11 for $9,900.

Due Diligence. All is not hopeless, however, for those who have signed the registration statement. If the statement contains a material misstatement or omission, the company is liable and has no defense. But everyone else who signed the registration statement can avoid liability by showing that he investigated the registration statement as thoroughly as a "prudent person in the management of his own property." This investigation is called **due diligence.** Its importance cannot be overstated. The SEC does not conduct its own investigation to ensure that the registration statement is accurate. It can only ensure that, on the surface, the issuer has supplied all relevant information. If an issuer chooses to lie, the SEC has no way of knowing. It is the job of the underwriters to check the accuracy of the filing. Thus underwriters typically spend two or three weeks visiting the company, reading all its corporate documents (including minutes back to the beginning), and calling its bankers, customers, suppliers, and competitors to ensure that the registration statement is accurate and no skeletons have been overlooked.

When §11 was first passed, investment bankers were outraged. Some predicted that this liability provision would cause capital in America to dry up, that grass would grow on Wall Street. In fact, the first case under §11 arose 35 years and 27,000 registration statements later. In this case—*Escott v. Barchris Construction Corp.*—the registration statement was seriously flawed.[7] The underwriter failed to read the minutes of the executive committee meetings that revealed the company to be in serious financial condition. Much of the company's alleged backlog of orders was from nonexistent corporations. Proceeds of the offering were earmarked to pay off debt, not to buy new plant and equipment, as the registration statement had indicated. The company's directors, underwriters, and underwriters' counsel were held liable.

Although *Barchris* still strikes fear in the hearts of underwriters, some commentators now argue that underwriters do not take their due diligence obligations seriously enough. Was there adequate disclosure in the following case?

---

[6] Joint and several liability is discussed in Chapter 33.
[7] 283 F. Supp. 643, 1968 U.S. Dist. LEXIS 3853 (S.D.N.Y. 1968).

ROMBACH V. CHANG

355 F.3d 164, 2004 U.S. App. LEXIS 778
United States Court of Appeals for the Second Circuit, 2004

Facts: Family Golf Centers, Inc. was a public company that owned and operated 119 golf courses nationwide. To raise funds for the purchase of additional courses, it sold shares in a second public offering. During the year following that second offering, Family Golf had lower than expected earnings and its stock price plummeted by more than 43 percent. Within two years of the offering, the company filed for bankruptcy protection.

The plaintiffs purchased stock from the company in the second public offering. They filed suit against the company's officers and underwriters, alleged that the registration statement contained misrepresentations about Family Golf's financial performance and projected income. The district court granted defendants' motion to dismiss and the plaintiffs appealed.

Issue: Did the defendants violate §11 by issuing a false or misleading registration statement?

Excerpts from Judge Jacobs's Decision: Plaintiffs do not identify any materially false statements in the registration statement that were false or misleading when made. Plaintiffs, rather, simply allege generally that the registration statement "failed to disclose that the Offering was necessitated by pressure from the Company's lenders and its deteriorating cash position, and it failed to disclose that the integration of recently acquired sites was proceeding poorly and that the Company was experiencing operation problems associated with these acquired properties."

Such allegations, however, are undercut by the fact that the offering documents contained cautionary language and information about the financial risks, including:

- that the company experienced a net loss of $3.6 million for [the prior] fiscal year
- that some Family Golf facilities had experienced losses
- that no assurance could be given that additional facilities would be readily integrated into the Company's operating structure
- that the company had lower cash reserves [than it had the year before]
- that there existed a need to raise substantial additional capital for continued long-term expansion, and the caution that there was no assurance Family Golf would be able to raise enough
- that the company had a $180 million debt, coupled with the admonition that there was no assurance the company would be able to generate sufficient cash to service that debt; and
- that the company's past performance was "not necessarily indicative of future results."

While some of these cautionary statements were formulaic, we conclude that as a whole they provided a sobering picture of Family Golf's financial condition and future plans.

For the foregoing reasons, we affirm the decision of the district court. ■

SECURITIES EXCHANGE ACT OF 1934

Most buyers do not purchase new securities from the issuer in an initial public offering. Rather they buy stock that is publicly traded in the open market. This stock is, in a sense, *secondhand* because others, perhaps many others, have already owned it. The purpose of the 1934 Act is to maintain the integrity of this secondary market.

General Provisions of the 1934 Act

Registration Requirements

As we have seen, the 1933 Act requires an issuer to register securities before selling them. That is a onetime effort for the company. The 1933 Act does not require the issuer to provide shareholders with any additional information in later years. Suppose that an automobile company registered and sold securities for the first time in 1946. Purchasers of those securities knew a lot about the firm—in 1946. But how can current investors assess the company? The 1934 Act plugs this hole. It requires issuers with publicly traded stock to continue to make information available to the public so that current—and potential—shareholders can evaluate the company. It is often said that the 1933 Act registers securities, and the 1934 Act registers companies.

Under the 1934 Act, an issuer must register with the SEC if (1) it completes a public offering under the 1933 Act, or (2) its securities are traded on a national exchange (such as the New York Stock Exchange), or (3) it has at least 500 shareholders and total assets that exceed $10 million. A company can *de*register if its number of shareholders falls below 300 or if it has fewer than 500 shareholders and assets of less than $10 million.

Disclosure Requirements—Section 13

Like the 1933 Act, the 1934 Act focuses on disclosure. The difference is that the 1933 Act requires onetime disclosure when a company sells stock to the public. The 1934 Act requires *ongoing*, regular disclosure for any company with a class of stock that is publicly traded. Companies that are required to register under the 1934 Act are called **reporting companies.**

Section 13 requires reporting companies to file the following documents:

- An initial, detailed information statement when the company first registers (similar to the filing required under the 1933 Act)

- Annual reports on Form 10-K, containing audited financial statements, a detailed analysis of the company's performance, and information about officers and directors

- Quarterly reports on Form 10-Q, which are less detailed than 10-Ks and contain unaudited financials

- Form 8-Ks to report any significant developments, such as bankruptcy, a change in control, a purchase or sale of significant assets, the resignation of a director as a result of a policy dispute, or a change in auditing firms

In response to corporate scandals involving Enron Corp. and other companies (discussed in Chapter 36), Congress passed the Sarbanes-Oxley Act of 2002. It requires each company's CEO and CFO to certify that:

- The information in the quarterly and annual reports is true,

- The company has effective internal controls, and

- The officers have informed the company's audit committee and its auditors of any concerns that they have about the internal control system.

A reporting company must send its annual report to shareholders. All annual reports and other 1934 Act filings are available on the SEC Web site (**http://www .sec.gov**). For particularly lively examples of this form of literature, check out the filings for Jack in the Box Inc. The Web site at **http://www.sidcato.com** provides an (often humorous) analysis of annual reports.

Proxy Requirements—Section 14

As discussed in Chapter 36, most shareholders of public corporations do not attend annual shareholder meetings. Instead, the company solicits their proxies, permitting them to vote by mail rather than in person. If a company solicits proxies, it is required to supply shareholders with a proxy statement that is intended to give them enough information to make informed decisions about the company. The proxy statement contains detailed information about officers and directors, including their experience, relationship with the company, and compensation. (The annual report provides financial information.) Proxy statements must also be filed with the SEC. Proxy contests and shareholder proposals are discussed in Chapter 36.

Under SEC rules, a company is not *required* to solicit proxies from shareholders, but if it does not, it is unlikely to obtain the quorum needed for the meeting to be held. In any event, a company cannot avoid its responsibility to inform shareholders. Whether or not it solicits proxies, it is still required to furnish shareholders with an information statement that contains essentially the same material as a proxy statement.

Short-Swing Trading—Section 16

During congressional hearings after the 1929 stock market crash, witnesses testified that insiders had manipulated the stock market. For example, insiders would buy a large block of stock, announce a substantial dividend, and then divest before the dividend was reduced. Section 16 was designed to prevent corporate insiders—officers, directors, and shareholders who own more than 10 percent of the company—from taking unfair advantage of privileged information to manipulate the market.

Section 16 takes a two-pronged approach:

- First, insiders must **report** their trades within two business days. This report must also reveal their total stock holdings in the company. The filings must be made to the SEC electronically, and both the SEC and the company are required to post them on their respective Web sites within one business day after they are made.

- Second, insiders must **turn over to the corporation** any profits they make from the purchase and sale or sale and purchase of company securities in a six-month period. Section 16 is a strict liability provision. It applies even if the insider did not actually take advantage of secret information or try to manipulate the market; if she bought and sold or sold and bought stock in a six-month period, she is liable.

Suppose that Manuela buys 20,000 shares of her company's stock in June at $10 a share. In September, her (uninsured) summer house in Florida is destroyed by a hurricane. To raise money for rebuilding, she sells the stock at $12 per share, making a profit of $40,000. Her house will have to remain in ruins because she has violated §16 and must turn over the profit to her company.

Liability

Section 18

Under §18, anyone who makes a false or misleading statement in a filing under the 1934 Act is liable to buyers or sellers who (1) acted in reliance on the statement and (2) can prove that the price at which they bought or sold was affected by the false filing. Section 18 applies to all filings under the 1934 Act, including proxy statements and annual reports.

Section 10(b)

Section 18 applies only to *filings* under the 1934 Act. What happens if a company executive makes a false public *statement* about the company? Or writes an untrue statement somewhere other than in a filing? In one case, a corporate officer bought up shares of his company's stock even as he made pessimistic public statements about the company. That is the type of behavior that §10(b) is designed to prevent. **Section 10(b) prohibits**

fraud in connection with the purchase and sale of any security, whether or not the security is registered under the 1934 Act.

The SEC adopted Rule 10b-5 to clarify §10(b), but the rule is still a relatively vague, catch-all provision designed to fill any holes left by other sections of the securities laws.[8] Interpretation has largely been left to the courts, which generally have interpreted Rule 10b-5 to require:

- **A Misstatement or Omission of a Material Fact.** Anyone who fails to disclose material information, or makes incomplete or inaccurate disclosure, is liable. **Material** has the same meaning as under the 1933 Act: important enough to affect an investor's decision. For example, a company repeatedly and falsely denied that it was involved in merger negotiations. It was liable even though the negotiations had only been in a preliminary stage.[9]

- **Scienter.** This is a legal term meaning *willfully, knowingly, or recklessly.* To be liable under Rule 10b-5, the defendant must have (1) known (or been reckless in not knowing) that the statement was inaccurate and (2) intended for the plaintiff to rely on the statement. Negligence is not enough. A group of shareholders sued the accounting firm Ernst & Ernst because it had failed to discover, during the course of an audit, that a company's chief executive was stealing funds. According to the shareholders, the auditors should have discovered that the executive refused to allow anyone else to open his mail and, therefore, should have been suspicious of wrongdoing. The court found Ernst & Ernst not liable. Although it may have been negligent, it had not *intentionally* or even *recklessly* facilitated fraud.[10]

- **Purchase or Sale.** Rule 10b-5 covers both buyers and sellers. It does not include, however, someone who failed to purchase stock because of a material misstatement. In the case of the company executive who spread negative rumors about his company while he bought stock, those who sold because of his false rumors could sue under Rule 10b-5, but not those who simply failed to buy.

- **Reliance.** To bring suit, a plaintiff must show that she relied on the misstatement or omission. In the case of open-market trades, reliance is difficult to prove, so the courts are willing to assume it.

- **Economic Loss.** The plaintiffs must suffer a loss in the value of their investment. For example, a couple sold their pharmaceutical business to another company in exchange for stock of the purchaser. Some time later, they discovered that the purchaser had lied about its financial condition. However, the court held that the couple could not recover because, by the time they sold their stock in the purchaser, it was worth substantially more than when they acquired it. Thus, they had not suffered an economic loss.

- **Loss Causation.** The economic loss must have been caused by the misstatement of a material fact.

---

[8] Rule 10b-5 prohibits any person, in connection with a purchase or sale of any security, from (1) employing any device, scheme, or artifice to defraud; (2) making any untrue statement of a material fact or omitting to state a material fact necessary in order to make the statements made, in light of the circumstances under which they were made, not misleading; or (3) engaging in any act, practice, or course of business that operates or would operate as a fraud or deceit upon any person.

[9] *Basic Inc. v. Levinson*, 485 U.S. 224, 108 S. Ct. 978, 1988 U.S. LEXIS 1197 (1988).

[10] *Ernst & Ernst v. Hochfelder*, 425 U.S. 185, 96 S. Ct. 1375, 1976 U.S. LEXIS 2 (1976).

In the following case, the Supreme Court decided that the misrepresentation did not cause a loss.

DURA PHARMACEUTICALS, INC. V. BROUDO

125 S. Ct. 1627, 2005 U.S. LEXIS 3478
Supreme Court of the United States, 2005

Facts: Over the course of a year, plaintiffs bought stock in Dura Pharmaceuticals, Inc., a publicly traded company. They alleged that during this time Dura executives falsely stated that (1) company drug sales would be profitable and (2) the Food and Drug Administration (FDA) would approve its new asthma spray device.

The plaintiffs halted their purchases of Dura stock on the day the company announced that, owing to slow drug sales, its earnings would be lower than expected. After this announcement, Dura shares lost almost half their value. About eight months later, Dura announced that the FDA would not approve the new asthma spray device. The next day Dura's share price temporarily fell but almost fully recovered within one week.

The district court dismissed the plaintiff's complaint on the grounds they had not shown that the false statements caused the fall in stock price. The Court of Appeals for the Ninth Circuit reversed, holding that the defendants' false statements had indeed caused the plaintiffs' loss. The Ninth Circuit reasoned that if it had not been for the misrepresentations, the stock price would have been lower when the plaintiffs purchased it and then would not have fallen as far (or at all) when the truth came out. Dura appealed and the Supreme Court granted *certiorari*.

Issue: Did the defendants' false statements cause the plaintiffs' loss?

Excerpts from Justice Breyer's Decision: [T]he logical link between the inflated share purchase price and any later economic loss is not invariably strong. Shares are normally purchased with an eye toward a later sale. But if, say, the purchaser sells the shares quickly before the relevant truth begins to leak out, the misrepresentation will not have led to any loss. If the purchaser sells later after the truth makes its way into the market place, an initially inflated purchase price *might* mean a later loss. But that is far from inevitably so.

When the purchaser subsequently resells such shares, even at a lower price, that lower price may reflect, not the earlier misrepresentation, but changed economic circumstances, changed investor expectations, new industry-specific or firm-specific facts, conditions, or other events, which taken separately or together account for some or all of that lower price. Other things being equal, the longer the time between purchase and sale, the more likely that this is so, i.e., the more likely that other factors caused the loss.

Given the tangle of factors affecting price, the most logic alone permits us to say is that the higher purchase price will *sometimes* play a role in bringing about a future loss. It may prove to be a necessary condition of any such loss, and in that sense one might say that the inflated purchase price suggests that the misrepresentation (using language the Ninth Circuit used) "touches upon" a later economic loss. But, even if that is so, it is insufficient. To "touch upon" a loss is not to *cause* a loss, and it is the latter that the law requires. [A] plaintiff in such a case [must] show not only that had he known the truth he would not have acted but also that he suffered actual economic loss.

Finally, the Ninth Circuit's approach overlooks an important securities law objective. The securities statutes seek to maintain public confidence in the marketplace. They do so by deterring fraud, in part, through the availability of private securities fraud actions. But the statutes make these latter actions available, not to provide investors with broad insurance against market losses, but to protect them against those economic losses that misrepresentations actually cause. Allowing recovery in the face of affirmative evidence of nonreliance would effectively convert Rule 10b-5 into a scheme of investor's insurance. There is no support in the Securities Exchange Act for such a result.

For these reasons, we find the plaintiffs' complaint legally insufficient. We reverse the judgment of the Ninth Circuit. ■

If the Dura stock price is inflated because of false claims made by company executives, it seems virtually inevitable that, once the truth comes out, shareholders will lose money. It may be difficult to estimate exactly what the stock was worth on the day the plaintiffs bought it, but courts are often called upon to make difficult decisions. Would it be better for the stock market if these defendants were held liable?   ◆

The Private Securities Litigation Reform Act of 1995

The Private Securities Litigation Reform Act is an amendment to the 1934 Act intended to discourage fraud suits by shareholders. Under this amendment, companies are liable to shareholders for so-called forward-looking statements (that is, financial projections or statements about future plans) *only if* (1) the company fails to include a warning that the predictions may not come to pass, *and* (2) the shareholders can show that company executives knew the predictions were false. Suppose a pharmaceutical company predicts that a new drug will generate billions in sales, but two years later the drug is a total failure. Before 1995, shareholders would have had a strong case, but now the company would not be liable as long as it had disclosed, at the time of making the prediction, reasons why the drug might not be a success. Even if the company failed to mention these reasons, it would be liable only if executives knew the prediction to be false when they made it.

Despite this statute, the number of securities fraud lawsuits and the cost of settling them has continued to increase each year. (Shareholders even sued Shiva, the company discussed earlier in the chapter, when its stock price fell.) For more information about these lawsuits, browse at http://securities.stanford.edu.

Insider Trading

Insider trading is immensely tempting. Anyone with reliable secret information can earn millions of dollars overnight. Costandi Nasser bought shares of Santa Fe International, Inc., after learning that Kuwait Petroleum Co. was set to acquire the company. His profit? $4.6 million in three weeks. The downside? Insider trading is a crime punishable by fines and imprisonment. The guilty party may also be forced to turn over to the SEC three times the profit made. Ivan Boesky paid $100 million and spent two years in prison. Dennis Levine suffered an $11.6 million penalty and three years in prison.

Why is insider trading a crime? Who is harmed? After all, if you buy or sell stock in a company, presumably you are reasonably content with the price or you would not have traded. Insider trading is illegal because:

- It offends our fundamental sense of fairness. No one wants to be in a poker game with marked cards.

- Investors will lose confidence in the market if they feel that insiders have an unfair advantage.

- Investment banks typically "make a market" in stocks, meaning that they hold extra shares so that orders can be filled smoothly. If an insider buys stock because she knows the company is about to sign an important contract, she earns the profit on that information at the expense of the marketmaker who sold her the stock. These marketmakers expect to earn a certain profit. If they do not earn it from normal stock appreciation, they simply raise the commission they charge for being a marketmaker. As a result, everyone who buys and sells stock pays a slightly higher price because insider trading skims off some of the profits.

In the following feature, economists argue that there is another reason insider trading is illegal.

Although economists generally laud free markets, at times markets create inefficient results. The market for information is particularly subject to inefficiencies. Stock markets, for example, tend to create too much information. (And, as we will see in Chapter 43, intellectual property markets have the opposite problem.)

Generally, economists think that society benefits when financial information spreads widely and quickly. Investors are thereby able to make more informed decisions. However, insider trading is an exception to this rule. When someone trades on inside information, she can quickly earn vast profits—but she has effectively stolen these profits from uninformed shareholders. The benefit that society gains from having this hidden information indirectly revealed to the market (via her purchase or sale of stock) is less than the harm to the shareholders who trade in ignorance. True, everyone now knows that the stock is more or less valuable than the market thought, but they have learned this information at a high price. Thus, the government prohibits insider trading to prevent society from "paying too much" for this private information.

Recent research supports the view that insider trading harms securities markets. In comparing returns in all 103 stock markets in the world, two economists found that markets in those countries that enforced insider trading laws earned 5 percent higher returns than did markets in countries with no laws or with lax enforcement. Five percent of the world's stock market capitalization amounts to $1.75 trillion.[11] ◆

As noted, Rule 10b-5 is a vaguely worded rule that generally prohibits fraud. The language of the rule never explicitly mentions insider trading, but courts have interpreted it to prohibit this activity. Although the courts are nominally *interpreting* the rule, in fact, they are more or less fashioning this crime out of whole cloth. Insider trading has been described as "the judicial oak that has grown from little more than a legislative acorn." The current rules on insider trading are as follows:

- **Strangers.** The SEC has argued many times that anyone in possession of nonpublic material information must disclose it or refrain from trading. The courts, however, have definitively rejected this approach. The Supreme Court has held that **someone who trades on inside information is liable only if he has a fiduciary duty to the company whose stock he has traded.** Suppose that, while looking in a dumpster, Harry finds correspondence indicating that MediSearch, Inc., will shortly announce a major breakthrough in the treatment of AIDS. Harry buys the stock, which promptly quadruples in value. Harry will be dining at the Ritz, not in the dumpster nor in federal prison, because he has no fiduciary duty to MediSearch.

- **Fiduciaries.** Anyone who works for a company is a fiduciary. **A fiduciary violates Rule 10b-5 if she trades stock of her company while in possession of nonpublic material information.** If the director of research for MediSearch learns of the promising new treatment for AIDS and buys stock in the company before the information is public, she has violated Rule 10b-5. This rule applies not only to employees who work for the company, but also to **constructive insiders**—others who have an indirect employment relationship, such as employees of the company's auditors or law firm. Thus, if a lawyer who works at the firm that is patenting MediSearch's new discovery buys stock before the information is public, she has violated Rule 10b-5.

- ***Possession* versus *use* of information.** Suppose that an insider sells stock just after learning that her company is about to report lower earnings but before this information is public. When challenged by the SEC, she argues that she sold her stock for other reasons—say, to buy a new house, or set her son up in business. The appeals

---

[11] Hazem Daouk and Utpal Bhattacharya, "The World Price of Insider Trading," *Journal of Finance,* 2002, vol. 57, pp. 75–108. Discussed in *The Economist,* Jan. 22, 2000, p. 75.

courts were divided on whether the SEC actually had to prove that the insider had traded because of the secret information and not for some other (legitimate) reason. To clarify this murky issue, the SEC issued Rule 10b5-1. **This rule provides that an insider violates Rule 10b-5 if she trades while in possession of material, non-public information, unless she has committed in advance to a plan to sell those securities.** Thus, if an insider knows that she will want to sell stock to pay college tuition, she can establish such a sales plan in advance. (And, then, despite any change in circumstances, she must sell according to the plan.) She will then not be liable for the sales, no matter what inside information she ultimately learns.

- **Tippers.** Now things become really complicated. **Insiders who pass on nonpublic, material information are liable under Rule 10b-5, even if they do not trade themselves, as long as (1) they know the information is confidential and (2) they expect some personal gain.** Personal gain is loosely defined. Essentially, any gift to a friend counts as personal gain. W. Paul Thayer was a corporate director, deputy secretary of defense, and former fighter pilot ace who gave stock tips to his girlfriend in lieu of paying her rent. That counted as personal gain and he spent a year and a half in prison.

- **Tippees.** Those who receive tips—tippees—are liable for trading on inside information, even if they do not have a fiduciary relationship to the company, as long as (1) they know the information is confidential, (2) they know it came from an insider who was violating his fiduciary duty, and (3) the insider expected some personal gain.** Barry Switzer, then head football coach at the University of Oklahoma, went to a track meet to see his son compete. While sunbathing on the bleachers, he overheard someone talking about a company that was going to be acquired. Switzer bought the stock but was acquitted of insider trading charges, because the insider had not breached his fiduciary duty. He had not tipped anyone on purpose—he had simply been careless. Also, Switzer did not know that the insider was breaching a fiduciary duty, and the insider expected no personal gain.[12]

Illegal insider trading or just good luck?

- **Takeovers.** Frustrated by its lack of success under Rule 10b-5, the SEC adopted Rule 14e-3. **This rule prohibits trading on inside information during a tender offer if the trader knows the information was obtained from either the bidder or the target company.** The trader or tipper need not have violated a fiduciary duty. (Tender offers are discussed in detail in Chapter 35, on corporate management.)

- **Misappropriation.** In an effort to tighten the insider trading noose further, the SEC developed a new theory—misappropriation. Under this theory, **a person is liable if he trades in securities (1) for personal profit, (2) using confidential information, and (3) in breach of a fiduciary duty to the source of the information.** This theory applies even if that source was not the company whose stock was traded.

---

[12] *SEC v. Switzer,* 590 F. Supp. 756, 1984 U.S. Dist. LEXIS 15303 (W.D. Okla. 1984). After this case, some wags joked, "When Barry Switzer listens, people talk."

Foster Winans wrote a column for *The Wall Street Journal* entitled "Heard on the Street" in which he reported rumors he had heard about companies. Frequently, the stock of these companies would rise or fall in response to his story. He began leaking information about his columns in advance to Peter Brant, a stockbroker at Kidder, Peabody & Co. Brant would trade the stock and split the profits with Winans. After the first episode, the SEC noticed the abnormally large trade. When it called the company to find out who was buying, the officers said they could think of no explanation except that the company had been the subject of a "Heard on the Street" column. It was all over for Winans, though the SEC let him pass on information a few more times, to make sure.

But had Winans and Brant violated Rule 10b-5? Not according to traditional insider trading rules. Neither of them had a fiduciary relationship to the company whose stock was traded. When the case went to the Supreme Court, it split 4–4 on the issue of misappropriation (there were only eight justices because one had resigned and his successor had not yet been appointed). However, the Court did find 8–0 that Winans was guilty of mail and wire fraud for having violated *The Wall Street Journal's* rules about confidentiality.[13] Ten years later, the Supreme Court finally resolved the misappropriation issue.

UNITED STATES V. O'HAGAN

521 U.S. 642, 117 S. Ct. 2199, 1997 U.S. LEXIS 4033
United States Supreme Court, 1997

Facts: Grand Metropolitan PLC (Grand Met) hired the law firm of Dorsey & Whitney to represent it in a takeover of Pillsbury Co. James O'Hagan, a partner in Dorsey & Whitney, did not work for Grand Met, but he found out about the deal and purchased significant amounts of Pillsbury stock. After Grand Met publicly announced its takeover attempt, the price of Pillsbury stock rose dramatically. O'Hagan sold his stock at a profit of more than $4.3 million. A jury convicted O'Hagan of misappropriation in violation of §10(b), and he was sentenced to prison.[14] The appeals court reversed, ruling that misappropriation is not a violation of §10(b). The Supreme Court granted *certiorari*.

Issue: Is misappropriation a violation of §10(b)?

Excerpts from Justice Ginsburg's Decision: Under the "traditional" or "classical theory" of insider trading liability, §10(b) and Rule 10b-5 are violated when a corporate insider trades in the securities of his corporation on the basis of material,

nonpublic information. The classical theory applies not only to officers, directors, and other permanent insiders of a corporation, but also to attorneys, accountants, consultants, and others who temporarily become fiduciaries of a corporation.

The "misappropriation theory" holds that a person commits fraud "in connection with" a securities transaction, and thereby violates §10(b) and Rule 10b-5, when he misappropriates confidential information for securities trading purposes, in breach of a duty owed to the source of the information. Under this theory, a fiduciary's undisclosed, self-serving use of a principal's information to purchase or sell securities, in breach of a duty of loyalty and confidentiality, defrauds the principal of the exclusive use of that information.

The two theories are complementary, each addressing efforts to capitalize on nonpublic information through the purchase or sale of securities. The classical theory targets a corporate insider's breach of duty to shareholders with whom the insider transacts; the misappropriation theory outlaws trading on the

▼

---

[13] *Carpenter v. United States*, 484 U.S. 19, 108 S. Ct. 316, 1987 U.S. LEXIS 4815 (1987).

[14] O'Hagan used the profits he gained through this trading to conceal his previous embezzlement of client funds. There is a moral here.

basis of nonpublic information by a corporate "outsider" in breach of a duty owed not to a trading party, but to the source of the information. The misappropriation theory is thus designed to protect the integrity of the securities markets against abuses by "outsiders" to a corporation who have access to confidential information that will affect the corporation's security price when revealed, but who owe no fiduciary or other duty to that corporation's shareholders.

A company's confidential information qualifies as property to which the company has a right of exclusive use. The undisclosed misappropriation of such information, in violation of a fiduciary duty constitutes fraud akin to embezzlement.

The theory is also well-tuned to an animating purpose of the Exchange Act: to insure honest securities markets and thereby promote investor confi-dence. Although informational disparity is inevitable in the securities markets, investors likely would hesitate to venture their capital in a market where trading based on misappropriated nonpublic information is unchecked by law. An investor's informational disadvantage vis-à-vis a misappropriator with material, nonpublic information stems from contrivance, not luck; it is a disadvantage that cannot be overcome with research or skill.

It makes scant sense to hold a lawyer like O'Hagan a §10(b) violator if he works for a law firm representing the target of a tender offer, but not if he works for a law firm representing the bidder. The text of the statute requires no such result. The misappropriation at issue here was properly made the subject of a §10(b) charge because it meets the statutory requirement that there be "deceptive" conduct "in connection with" securities transactions. ■

After the *O'Hagan* case established the principle of misappropriation, it was still not clear how this rule applied to family members. If a wife told her husband that her company was about to be taken over and he then sold company stock as a result, was he in violation of 10b-5? Did he have a fiduciary duty to her? Rule 10b-5-2 establishes that anyone who receives non-public, material information from a spouse, parent, child or sibling, has a fiduciary duty unless the trader can prove that he did not have a duty of trust or confidence to the family member in question.

at RISK | If you learn confidential information about a company, what can you do? Of course, it is always safe *not* to trade. If you want to trade anyway, you should wait 24 to 48 hours after the information is disseminated through wire services or in the financial press. ◆

Foreign Corrupt Practices Act

In the 1970s, more than 450 major U.S. corporations paid millions of dollars in foreign bribes. The Japanese premier and the Italian president both resigned after it was revealed that Lockheed had paid them off. In the Netherlands, members of the royal family were implicated in the scandal. Many of these payments had been labeled "commissions" or other legitimate business expenses and then illegally deducted from the company's income tax. In response, Congress passed the Foreign Corrupt Practices Act as an amendment to the 1934 Act.

Under the Foreign Corrupt Practices Act, it is a crime for *any American company* (whether reporting under the 1934 Act or not) to make or promise to make payments or gifts to foreign officials, political candidates, or parties in order to influence a governmental decision, even if the payment is legal under local law. There is one exception: it is legal for a company to make payments to a foreign official to expedite a "routine governmental action." Anyone who violates the law is subject to fines and imprisonment. The Department of Justice reveals its enforcement guidelines at http://www.usdoj.gov/criminal/fraud/fcpa/dojdocb.htm.

Congress believed that the ready availability of corporate "slush funds" had facilitated the payment of bribes. Therefore, it also tightened accounting standards for companies that report under the 1934 Act. It requires *reporting companies* to (1) keep books that accurately and fairly reflect the transactions of the issuer, and (2) maintain a system of internal controls that ensures transactions are executed only "in accordance with management's authorization."

For years, American companies complained that they were handicapped when competing against rivals who could bribe their way to success overseas. The U.S. government estimated that American companies lost contracts worth more than $15 billion a year to competitors who paid bribes. But in 1997, 34 developed countries signed a treaty in Paris outlawing bribery of foreign officials.

Ethics

What's wrong with bribery anyway? Many businesspeople think it is relatively harmless, just a cost of doing business, like New York City's high taxes or Germany's high labor costs. Corruption is not a victimless crime. Poor people in poor countries are the losers when officials are on the take: corruption means that good projects are squeezed out by bad ones. And corruption can reduce a country's entire administration to a state of decay. Honest officials give up. Bribes grow ever bigger and more ubiquitous. The trough becomes less well stocked; the snouts plunge deeper.[15] Worldwide about $400 billion is lost each year to corruption in government procurement. The anticorruption czar in Mexico estimated that bribes reduce Mexico's GDP annually by 9.5 percent. This sum is twice the country's education budget. From the Chapter 2 Ethics Checklist: Who are the stakeholders? What are the consequences of corruption? ◆

Which countries are most corrupt? As rules of thumb:

- Poor countries are more corrupt than rich ones, although corruption can be found everywhere.

- Autocratic countries are more corrupt than democratic ones. Democratic institutions—an independent judiciary, a free press, and strong opposition parties—reduce corruption.

- Economies based on natural resources are more corrupt than those based on trade. Thus, for example, countries that produce oil tend to be more corrupt than traditional trading powers, such as Hong Kong, Singapore, and Chile.[16]

According to Transparency International, an international non-profit agency, Cote d'Ivoire, Georgia, Indonesia, Tajikistan, Turkmenistan, Azerbaijan, Paraguay, Chad, Myanmar, Nigeria, Bangladesh, and Haiti lead the list of shame. The most honest? Finland, New Zealand, Denmark, Iceland, Singapore, Sweden, Switzerland, Norway, Australia, and the Netherlands. (The United States was 17th on the honest list.) A complete list is available at http://www.transparency.org.

BLUE SKY LAWS

At the end of the nineteenth century, years before the great stock market crash, states had already begun to regulate the sale of securities. These statutes are called **blue sky laws** (because crooks were willing to sell naive investors a "piece of the great blue sky"). Currently, all states and the District of Columbia have blue sky laws.

---

[15] "Who Will Listen to Mr. Clean?" *The Economist*, Aug. 2, 1997, p. 52.

[16] Tina Rosenberg, "The Taint of the Greased Palm," *New York Times*, August 10, 2003.

Exemption from State Regulation

To make life easier for issuers of stock, Congress passed the **National Securities Markets Improvement Act** (NSMIA) **of 1996.** Essentially, states may no longer regulate offerings of securities that are:

- Traded on a national exchange
- Exempt under Rule 506, or
- Sold to "qualified purchasers."

State Regulation

Any securities offerings not covered by the NSMIA must comply with state securities laws. Easier said than done. The 50 states have exhibited great creativity in crafting their securities laws and, as a result, have caused many headaches for issuers of securities. To begin, the 1933 Act is primarily concerned with disclosure, but many state statutes focus on the quality of the investment and require a so-called *merit review.* For example, in 1981, the Massachusetts securities commissioner refused to allow Apple Computer Co. to sell its initial public offering in Massachusetts because he believed the stock, selling at 92 times earnings, was too risky. He "protected" Massachusetts residents from this investment.

Typically, states take one of the following approaches to securities offerings:

- *Registration by notification.* Some states permit issuers with an established track record simply to file a notice before offering their securities.

- *Registration by coordination.* Some states permit issuers that have registered with the SEC simply to file copies of the federal registration statement (and perhaps some additional documents) with the state.

- *Registration by qualification.* Some states require issuers to undergo a full-blown registration, complete with a merit review.

Facilitating State Regulation

All is not bleak, however. There are three options that ease the process of complying with state securities requirements.

Coordinated Equity Review (CER)

For offerings over $5 million that are registered with the SEC, the issuer might be able to take advantage of the **Coordinated Equity Review** (CER) program. Under this program, the issuer deals with only one state, which takes responsibility for coordinating the comments from all other states. The process is simpler, but state officials still have the right to conduct a merit review.

Small Company Offering Registration (SCOR)

Most states permit a so-called **SCOR (small company offering registration)** for use in offerings of up to $1 million over any 12-month period. The issuer has the right to advertise publicly (even on the Internet) and can sell any amount of securities to any number of investors (as long as the total offering does not exceed $1 million). The relatively simple form (U-7) is in a question-and-answer format. It is designed to be filled out by company executives without the assistance of lawyers or accountants who are securities experts. Any company using a SCOR form can request a coordinated review from the states in which it has filed. Under this system, a designated lead state takes responsibility for coordinating the process with all other states. The result is a faster, simpler process. States do have the right to conduct a merit review, although it tends to be less burdensome than the usual merit examination. SCOR registration is designed to be used with

- Rule 147
- Rule 504
- Regulation A

Uniform Limited Offering Exemption

Under the **Uniform Limited Offering Exemption,** most states largely exempt from registration any offerings under Rule 505.

The moral of the story? Securities offerings are exceedingly complex and require professional supervision. Do not attempt this at home!

Chapter Conclusion

The 1929 stock market crash and the Great Depression that followed were an economic catastrophe for the United States. The Securities Act of 1933 and the Securities Exchange Act of 1934 were designed to prevent such disasters from ever occurring again. This country has enjoyed years of prosperity that is based, at least in part, on a reliable and honest securities market. The securities laws deserve some of the credit for that stability.

Chapter Review

1. A security is any transaction in which the buyer invests money in a common enterprise and expects to earn a profit predominantly from the efforts of others.

2. Before any offer or sale, an issuer must register securities with the SEC, unless the securities qualify for an exemption.

3. These securities are exempt from the registration requirement: government securities, bank securities, short-term notes, nonprofit issues, insurance policies, and annuity contracts.

4. The following table compares the different types of securities offerings:

	Public Offering	Intrastate Offering	Regulation A	Regulation D: Rule 504	Regulation D: Rule 505	Regulation D: Rule 506
Maximum Value of Securities Sold	Unlimited	Unlimited	$5 million	$1 million	$5 million	Unlimited
Public Solicitation of Purchasers	Permitted	Permitted	Permitted	Sometimes permitted	Not permitted	Not permitted
Suitability Requirements for Purchasers	No requirements	Must reside in issuer's state	No requirements	May be limited to accredited investors	No limit on accredited investors; no more than 35 unaccredited investors	No limit on accredited investors; no more than 35 unaccredited investors who, if unsophisticated, must have a purchaser representative
Disclosure Requirements	Elaborate registration statement; audited financials	None	Offering circular that is less detailed than a registration statement	May be required under state law	Same requirements as Reg A for unaccredited investors; no disclosure to accredited investors	Same requirements as Reg A for unaccredited investors; no disclosure to accredited investors
Resale of Securities	Permitted	Permitted, but may not be made out of state for nine months	Permitted	Sometimes permitted	Not permitted for one year	Not permitted for one year

5. If a final registration statement contains a material misstatement or omission, the purchaser of a security offered under that statement can recover from everyone who signed it.

6. The 1934 Act requires public companies to make regular filings with the SEC.

7. Under §16, insiders who buy and sell or sell and buy company stock within a six-month period must turn over to the corporation any profits from the trades. They must also disclose any trades they make in company stock.

8. Section 10(b) prohibits fraud in connection with the purchase and sale of any security, whether or not the issuer is registered under the 1934 Act.

9. Section 10(b) also prohibits insider trading.

10. Under the Foreign Corrupt Practices Act, it is a crime for any U.S. company to make payments to foreign officials to influence a government decision. This statute also requires reporting companies to keep accurate records.

11. The NSMIA prohibits states from regulating securities offerings that are:

    • Traded on a national exchange

    • Exempt under Rule 506, or

    • Sold to "qualified purchasers."

12. Any securities offerings not covered by the NSMIA must comply with state securities laws, which are varied and complex.

Practice Test

1. Christopher Stenger bought 12 Impressionist paintings from R. H. Love Galleries for $1.5 million. Love told Stenger that art investment would produce a safe profit. The two men agreed that Stenger could exchange any painting within five years for any one or two other paintings with the same or greater value. When Stenger's paintings did not increase in value, he sued Love, arguing that the right to trade paintings made them securities. Is Stenger correct?

2. **CPA QUESTION** When a common stock offering requires registration under the Securities Act of 1933:

   a. The registration statement is automatically effective when filed with the SEC

   b. The issuer would act unlawfully if it were to sell the common stock without providing the investor with a prospectus

   c. The SEC will determine the investment value of the common stock before approving the offering

   d. The issuer may make sales 10 days after filing the registration statement

3. Fluor, an engineering and construction company, was awarded a $1 billion project to build a coal gasification plant in South Africa. Fluor signed an agreement with a South African client that prohibited them both from announcing the agreement until March 10. Accordingly, Fluor denied all rumors that a major transaction was pending. Between March 3 and March 6, the State Teachers Retirement Board pension fund sold 288,257 shares of Fluor stock. After the contract was announced, the stock price went up. Did Fluor violate Rule 10b-5?

4. **CPA QUESTION** Hamilton Corp. makes a $4.5 million securities offering under Rule 505 of Regulation D of the Securities Act of 1933. Under this regulation, Hamilton is:

   a. Required to provide full financial information to accredited investors only

   b. Allowed to make the offering through a general solicitation

   c. Limited to selling to no more than 35 nonaccredited investors

   d. Allowed to sell to an unlimited number of investors both accredited and nonaccredited

5. Does this excerpt from the *Boston Globe* reveal any potential securities law problems?

   Berkshire Ice Cream's down-home investment strategy is paying off for more than 100 people who last year put up $800 to $1,000 to "own" a company cow. Last month, the company sent out about $32,000 to investors who bought a total of 110 cows a year ago, with the expectation of a 20 percent annual return on their money. [I]nitially, there were 63 investors who agreed to finance the purchase of a cow—which the company then cares for—in return for a piece of the company's profits.[17]

6. **ETHICS** ETS Payphones, Inc., sold pay phones to the public. The company then leased back the pay phones from the purchaser, promising a fixed 14 percent annual return on their investment. Although ETS's marketing materials trumpeted the "incomparable pay phone" as "an exciting business opportunity," the pay phones did not generate enough revenue for ETS to make the required payments, so the company depended on funds from new investors to meet its obligations to its existing customers. After ETS filed for bankruptcy protection, the SEC sued, alleging that ETS had been selling unregistered securities. Were the pay phone contracts securities under the 1933 Act? ETS advertised this investment as low risk (offering a "guaranteed" fixed return). These sorts of advertisements are particularly attractive to individuals more vulnerable to investment fraud, including older and less sophisticated investors. Whether or not the pay phone contracts were securities, was it ethical to pitch what was, in fact, a high risk investment to vulnerable investors who were

---

[17] Ellen Labr, "Investors Milk Profits of Ice Cream Firm," *Boston Globe*, July 30, 1995, p. 38. Republished with permission of The Boston Globe; permission conveyed through the Copyright Clearance Center, Inc.

unable to accurately assess the risks? Were these actions right? How would the CEO of ETS have felt if someone had sold such an investment to his poor, elderly mother?

7. **CPA QUESTION** Pace Corp. previously issued 300,000 shares of its common stock. The shares are now actively traded on a national securities exchange. The original offering was exempt from registration under the Securities Act of 1933. Pace has $2.5 million in assets and 425 shareholders. With regard to the Securities Exchange Act of 1934, Pace is:

   a. Required to file a registration statement because its assets exceed $2 million in value

   b. Required to file a registration statement even though it has fewer than 500 shareholders

   c. Not required to file a registration statement because the original offering of its stock was exempt from registration

   d. Not required to file a registration statement unless insiders own at least 5 percent of its outstanding shares of stock

8. **YOU BE THE JUDGE** WRITING PROBLEM World-Wide Coin Investments Ltd. sold rare coins, precious metals, camera equipment, and Coca-Cola collector items. Its stock was registered with the SEC under the 1934 Act. Joseph Hale was the controlling shareholder, chairman of the board, CEO, and president. World-Wide's independent auditor warned Hale that the company's faulty system of accounting procedures was causing problems with inventory control. Furthermore, the auditor could not document transactions, and it had found that the books and records of the company were inaccurate. Is World-Wide in violation of the Foreign Corrupt Practices Act? **Argument for the SEC:** Without exception, all reporting companies are required to maintain accurate books and records. **Argument for World-Wide:** This is a small company, and the cost of such an elaborate internal control system would bankrupt it.

9. Consider this scenario from the periodical *Investor's Business Daily, Inc.*:

   > You're in line at the grocery store when you overhear a stranger say: "That new widget is going to make XYZ Co. a fortune. I can't wait until the product launches tomorrow."

   > What do you do? (a) Nothing? (b) Call your broker and buy as much XYZ Co. stock as you possibly can?

10. Malaga Arabian Limited Partnership sold investments in the Spanish Arabian horse industry under Rule 506. James E. Mark, who purchased one of the partnership interests, alleged that the partnership violated Rule 506 because it never gave him any disclosure about the risks of the investment. He was not an accredited investor. At trial, the partnership said that it had surveyed investors to ensure that they were either accredited or sophisticated but had not actually read the surveys and did not have them available for the trial court. Is this offering exempt from registration under the 1933 Act?

11. CoolCom, Inc., sends notice to all of its shareholders that its annual report and proxy soliciting materials are on its Internet Web site. It provides investors with the Internet location and a telephone number that they may call to request a paper copy. Is CoolCom in compliance with SEC rules?

12. **ROLE REVERSAL** Prepare a multiple-choice question that focuses on an issue involving Rule 504, restricted securities, or insider trading.

Internet Research Problem

Choose a company, go to the EDGAR database at the SEC (http://beatty.westbuslaw.com/), and look at all filings this company has made during the last year. What filings has it made and why? Extra credit: search EDGAR for a prospectus for an initial public offering.

You can find further practice problems at http://beatty.westbuslaw.com or in the Study Guide that accompanies this text.

Accountants' Liability

© PHILIP & KAREN SMITH/PHOTODISC/GETTY IMAGES

The accounting firm Arthur Andersen prided itself on its ethics. Old-timers would tell new recruits the legend of the firm's founder: how in 1914 the young Arthur Andersen had refused a client's request to certify a dubious earnings report. Although Andersen knew his firm would be fired, and he might not be able to meet payroll, he nonetheless stood on principle. He was vindicated a few months later when the client went bankrupt. This emphasis on ethics continued—the firm later established a program to train business school faculty to teach ethics. The firm paid all expenses to bring in faculty from around the country for training at its country club campus outside Chicago. This was a company that walked the talk. Or so everyone thought.

The firm that began its life as the exemplar of ethical behavior, the firm whose audits were considered the gold standard in the industry, died ignominiously—convicted of obstructing a government investigation into the infamous Enron case (discussed at the beginning of Chapter 36).[1] How did this once noble firm go so wrong? And what lessons does this sad fable teach about the accounting profession?

---

[1] Although, as we will see later in the chapter, this conviction was overturned, the damage was already done. It was too late to resurrect the firm.

For its first 35 years, Andersen was primarily in the business of auditing public companies. Although its partners did not become rich, they made a good living. In the 1960s, a typical Andersen partner made the equivalent of $160,000 a year in today's dollars. Then, one of the partners had a breakthrough, which at the time seemed marvelous but ultimately started the firm down a dangerous and slippery slope. This fellow figured out how to take one of those new-fangled devices—a computer—out of the science lab and into the bookkeeping department. Soon, Andersen was earning huge profits advising companies on how to automate their bookkeeping.

The technology consultants in the firm began generating much greater profits—and earning much higher salaries—than the auditors. Competition in the auditing field was driving income down anyway. Audits were fast becoming loss leaders to attract consulting business. Lower costs led to lower quality as Andersen (and other auditors) felt they could not afford to invest as many hours in their audits. And the audits were becoming less effective because partners were increasingly afraid to deliver bad news, for fear of losing both audit and consulting fees.

Across the industry, major accounting firms earned only about one-quarter of their revenues from auditing; the rest came from consulting. Like its competitors, Andersen drove its auditors to bring in revenues from other sources such as tax advising or technology consulting. The firm began offering internal bookkeeping services to its audit clients—thereby creating a situation in which it was auditing itself. Audit partners who could not bring in enough revenue from other sources faced termination. The Andersen Web site described its mission as "Convergence: We help you navigate the forces of change." There was no mention of "We carefully audit your books."

To save money, the firm began to force partners to retire at 56. These actions drove average salaries up to $600,000, but reduced the general level of experience and expertise. At the same time, accounting was becoming more complicated. Rules for manufacturing plants were less useful when it came to, say, valuing intangible assets such as intellectual property and goodwill.

Predictably, mistakes happened, lawsuits were filed, settlements were made. Andersen's pristine name was soiled by its role in financial disasters at Boston Market,

Sunbeam, Waste Management, Global Crossing, and WorldCom. And then there was Enron. Andersen opened an office in Enron's headquarters staffed with more than 150 Andersen employees, who dressed like, acted like, and partied with Enron employees. In some cases, Enron failed to fix problems in its accounts, but Andersen certified them anyway. The company paid Andersen $23 million a year for auditing services and $29 million for its consulting advice.

When the federal government began investigating Enron's bankruptcy, panicked Andersen employees shredded documents, leading the government to file a criminal charge of obstructing justice. And so, the firm that began as a model of ethics in the accounting profession collapsed in disgrace, the first major accounting firm ever to be convicted of a crime.[2]

Worse was to come. As more accounting irregularities came to light involving other companies and other auditors, and as scores of major companies restated (i.e., lowered reports of) their earnings, investors doubted they could rely on public financial statements. The stock market went into a tailspin, losing 20 percent of its value in the month following the Andersen verdict. ■

INTRODUCTION

To begin our study of the accounting industry, it is important to understand what accountants do. Many of the cases in this chapter involve audits that went awry, so we start there.

Audits

Traditionally, auditors were primarily a watchdog for management, charged with detecting and anticipating financial problems. As the public ownership of stocks increased, however, investors began to need reliable financial information for evaluating their investments. Whereas the accountant had traditionally been a watchdog *for* management, investors needed a watchdog to keep an eye *on* management. Now, one of the accountant's most important roles is to serve as an independent evaluator of the financial statements issued by management to investors and creditors. The audit report of a CPA firm, particularly one of the Big Four,[3] is practically required as an admission ticket to the capital markets—investors will not put up their money without it. In a

---

[2] Based in part on information in Ken Brown and Ianthe Jeanne Dugan, "Andersen's Fall from Grace Is a Tale of Greed and Miscues," *Wall Street Journal,* June 7, 2002, p.1.

[3] The Big Four are Deloitte & Touche, Ernst & Young, KPMG, and PricewaterhouseCoopers.

very real sense, accountants serve two masters—company management and the investing public. It is sometimes difficult for auditing firms to forget, however, that of the two masters, management pays the fees.

When conducting an audit, accountants verify information provided by management. Since it is impossible to check each and every transaction, they verify a sample of various types of transactions. If these are accurate, they assume all are. To verify transactions, accountants use two mirror image processes—vouching and tracing. In **vouching,** they choose a transaction listed in the company's books and check backwards to make sure that there are original data to support it. They might, for example, find in accounts payable a bill for the purchase of 1,000 reams of photocopy paper. They would check to ensure that all the paper had actually arrived and that the receiving department had properly signed and dated the invoice. The auditors would also check the original purchase order to ensure the acquisition was properly authorized in the first place. In **tracing,** the accountant begins with an item of original data and traces it forward to ensure that it has been properly recorded throughout the bookkeeping process. For example, the sales ledger might report that 1,000 copies of a software program were sold to a distributor. The accountant checks the information in the sales ledger against the original invoice to ensure that the date, price, quantity, and customer's name all match. The auditor then verifies each step along the paper trail until the software leaves the warehouse.

Since accountants do not check every transaction, the process of selecting those items to verify requires skill and experience. Auditors must continually modify their original plan to reflect discoveries they make during the audit. If they find that one aspect of the company's accounting system seems weak, they need to check those results more carefully.

In performing their duties, accountants must follow two sets of rules: (1) generally accepted accounting principles (GAAP) and (2) generally accepted auditing standards (GAAS). **GAAP** are the rules for preparing financial statements, and **GAAS** are the rules for conducting audits. These two sets of standards include broadly phrased general principles as well as specific guidelines and illustrations. The application and interpretation of these rules require acute professional skill.

Opinions

After an audit is complete, the accountant issues an opinion that indicates how accurately the financial statements reflect the company's true financial condition. The auditor has four choices:

- **Unqualified Opinion.** Also known as a **clean** opinion, this is the most favorable report an auditor can give. It indicates that the company's financial statements fairly present its financial condition in accordance with GAAP. A less than clean opinion is a warning to potential investors and creditors that something may be wrong.

- **Qualified Opinion.** This opinion indicates that although the financial statements are generally accurate, there is nonetheless an outstanding, unresolved issue. This may be a violation of GAAP or perhaps some important issue whose ultimate impact is uncertain. For example, the company may face potential liability from environmental law violations, but the liability cannot yet be accurately estimated. Depending upon the reason for the qualification, this type of opinion does not necessarily prevent a company from borrowing money or selling stock.

- **Adverse Opinion.** This opinion is definitely bad news. In the auditor's view, the company's financial statements do not accurately reflect its financial position. In other words, the company is lying about its finances (or to put it more politely, is "materially misstating certain items on its financial statements"). A company with an adverse opinion is generally unable to sell stock or borrow money.

- **Disclaimer of Opinion.** Although not as damning as an adverse opinion, a disclaimer is still not good news. It is issued when the auditor does not have enough information to form an opinion. If the auditor knows that the statements are inaccurate, she cannot hide behind a disclaimer of opinion; she must issue an adverse opinion.

The following article suggests that an accountant's role can be more complex than the public appreciates.

NEWS*worthy*

Not all GAAP is created equal.

Every accountant knows that there is good GAAP and not-so-good GAAP. For many transactions, companies have a choice of accounting methods that can affect the numbers that are reported. So, too, can decisions on estimates that affect profit numbers.

Auditors are supposed to discuss with a company's directors the decisions the company made and let them know whether the company is being quite aggressive or very cautious in its accounting. But that is where that information stops. Nobody tells the public. The only thing investors hear directly from the auditor is the boilerplate letter in every annual report. "One of the things that bothers me is that there is so little flexibility in what you can say about your work after you have done an audit," said James E. Copeland, Jr., the chief executive of Deloitte & Touche.

As it is, with auditors giving the same grade to every company that barely meets accounting standards, we have a sort of Gresham's Law in operation, in which bad GAAP drives out good. If investors assume every company is pushing the accounting envelope, then those that use more conservative accounting derive no benefit from acting responsibly.

The fact that some of Enron's most ridiculous accounting had at least a veneer of complying with accounting rules shows how difficult auditors' decisions can be. Had Arthur Andersen been able and willing to point out how aggressive the accounting was, perhaps the Enron story might have been very different.[4] ◆

Congress Responds to Enron: Sarbanes-Oxley

As the stock market tumbled after the Andersen verdict, Congress acted to restore investor confidence by passing the Sarbanes-Oxley Act of 2002 (SOX). The major provisions of this act as it relates to auditors are as follows.

The Public Company Accounting Oversight Board

Congress established the **Public Company Accounting Oversight Board** (PCAOB) to ensure that investors receive accurate and complete financial information. The board has the authority to regulate public accounting firms, establishing everything from audit rules to ethics guidelines. All accounting firms that audit public companies must register with the board and the board must inspect them regularly. The PCAOB has the authority to revoke an accounting firm's registration or prohibit it from auditing public companies.

In an effort to keep the foxes out of the henhouse, the statute provides that no more than two of the five PCAOB board members may be certified public accountants. This board has the authority and, it is hoped, will have the political will to revise lax accounting

---

4   Floyd Norris, "Let the Auditors Tell Us What They Know," *New York Times*, Feb. 1, 2002, p. C1.
    Copyright © 2002 by The New York Times Co. Reprinted with permission.

rules that contributed to the Enron financial earthquake. The PCAOB's first inspection of the Big Four accounting firms found audit and accounting problems at all of them but the board still expressed confidence in the general quality of their work.

Reports to Audit Committee

Traditionally, auditors reported to the senior management of a client. This reporting relationship created obvious conflicts of interest—the auditors were reporting concerns to the very people who could be causing, or at least benefiting from, these problems. Under SOX, auditors must report to the audit committee of the client's board of directors, not to senior management. The accountants must inform the audit committee of any: (1) significant flaws they find in the company's internal controls; (2) alternative options that the firm considered in preparing the financial statements; and (3) accounting disagreements with management.

Consulting Services

As we saw in the chapter opening, Enron paid Arthur Andersen more for its consulting services than for its auditing efforts. For years, the SEC tried to restrict consulting by accounting firms, but the firms found powerful allies in Congress to protect them. SOX prohibits accounting firms that audit public companies from providing consulting services to those clients on topics such as bookkeeping, financial information systems, human resources, and legal issues (unrelated to the audit). Any consulting agreements must be approved by a client's audit committee. Auditing firms cannot base their employees' compensation on sales of consulting services to clients.

Some large companies are finding compliance with this provision difficult. Sun Microsystems, for instance, uses all the Big Four firms: KPMG (internal controls); Deloitte & Touche (tax); PricewaterhouseCoopers (internal audit), and Ernst & Young (external audit).[5]

Conflicts of Interest

An accounting firm cannot audit a company if one of the client's top officers has worked for that accounting firm within the prior year and was involved in the company's audit. In short, a client cannot hire one of its auditors to ensure a friendly attitude.

Term Limits on Audit Partners

After five years with a client, the lead audit partner must rotate off the account for at least five years. Other partners must rotate off an account every seven years for at least two years.

Consolidation in the Accounting Profession

Congress noted that since 1989, the Big Eight accounting firms had become the Big Four (sometimes called the Final Four). It ordered the GAO (Government Accountability Office) to prepare a study on the factors that have caused this consolidation, the potential impact, and possible methods for increasing competition within the industry.

---

[5]   "The future of auditing," *Economist*, 11/20/2004, p. 71.

In its study, the GAO found that the accounting industry is so concentrated that the largest firms do, in theory, have substantial market power. The Big Four audit 97 percent of all public companies in the United States that have sales over $250 million. However, the GAO did not find any evidence of collusion among the top firms. Nor was there conclusive evidence that consolidation had led to an increase in audit fees or a decline in quality or independence. However, smaller audit firms face substantial barriers to entry, so that it seems unlikely that the Big Four will increase in number.

The GAO concluded with a warning that further consolidation would be harmful and additional study was warranted. Ten months after this report was released, Ernst & Young was banned for six months from accepting any new audit clients in the United States. The firm was being punished for violating rules on auditor independence by entering into business with a client to sell both consulting and tax services.

Although it is early days yet to assess fully the impact of the Sarbanes-Oxley Act, no one doubts that Congress and the public believe that transparent and accurate financial statements are an essential foundation for capital markets throughout the world.

Lawyers think that laws are the solution to most problems; economists believe in markets. How effective do you think the following economic solution would be?

ECONOMICS & *the* LAW

The basic problem, at least for economists, can be reduced to the question of incentives. Even under the Sarbanes-Oxley Act, auditors have an overwhelming incentive to please the client, thereby retaining the stream of income from auditing fees.

One nifty solution has been advanced by Joshua Ronen, accounting professor at New York University. This new approach is embodied in what Mr. Ronen calls financial statement insurance. Corporations would buy insurance from carriers, but auditors would be selected by, and work for, the insurance companies. Accountants would perform the same set of auditing services as before, but from an entirely different perspective—as outsiders.

Insurance companies, armed with their own auditors' assessment of the risk that a company was not forthcoming—either by misrepresenting financial data, omitting data, or otherwise engaging in dubious practices—would then determine how much coverage to offer and at what premium. Risky companies would pay higher premiums than less risky ones. The insurance company bearing the risk of a bad audit would have an incentive to hire tough (not to mention competent) auditors. At the same time, auditors would know that if they fail to minimize the insurer's risk (e.g., they incorrectly assess the firm's financial condition), they will not only lose the business of that insurance carrier for that company, but for all other companies the carrier has assigned them to audit.

Both the amount of coverage and the size of the premiums would be publicly disclosed. Investors would then be alerted to companies that have a small amount of coverage with a high premium. Riskier firms would be punished by lower stock prices. All without one drop more of government regulation.[6] ◆

LIABILITY TO CLIENTS

When clients sue their accountants, these suits are based on contract, negligence, fraud, or breach of trust.

---

[6]   Susan Lee, "A Market Remedy for Our Nasty Accounting Virus," *Wall Street Journal,* July 7, 2002, p. A4. Republished with permission of The Wall Street Journal; permission conveyed through the Copyright Clearance Center, Inc.

Contract

Contracts between accountants and their clients are either written or oral. A written contract is often called an **engagement letter.** The contract has both express and implied terms. The accountant *expressly* promises to perform a particular project by a given date. The accountant also *implies* that she will work as carefully as an ordinarily prudent accountant would under the circumstances. When an accountant enters into a contract to prepare, say, tax returns, she is making two promises—to complete the returns on time and to prepare them accurately. If she fails to do either, she has breached her contract and may be liable for any damages that result.

Negligence

An accountant is liable for negligence to a client who can prove both of the following elements:

- **The accountant breached his duty to his client by failing to exercise the degree of skill and competence that an ordinarily prudent accountant would under the circumstances.** For example, if the accountant fails to follow GAAP or GAAS, he has almost certainly breached his duty. But the reverse is not true—compliance with GAAP and GAAS does not necessarily protect an accountant from liability.

- **The accountant's violation of duty caused harm to the client.** To recover damages, the client must be able to show that the accountant's misdeeds injured her.

In the following case, the accounting firm was clearly negligent. But had its wrongdoing actually caused harm to the client?

OREGON STEEL MILLS, INC. V. COOPERS & LYBRAND, LLP

336 Ore. 329, 83 P.3d 322, 2004 Ore. LEXIS 55
Supreme Court of Oregon, 2004

Facts: Oregon Steel Mills, Inc., was a publicly traded company whose financial statements were audited by Coopers & Lybrand, LLP, for many years. When Oregon sold the stock in one of its subsidiaries, Coopers advised Oregon that the transaction should be reported as a $12.3 million gain. This advice was wrong and Coopers was negligent in giving it.

Two years later, Oregon began a public offering of additional shares of stock. It intended to sell these shares to the public around May 2. Shortly before Oregon filed the stock offering with the SEC, it found out from Coopers that the sale of its subsidiary had been misreported and that it would have to revise its financial statements. As a result, the offering was delayed from May 2 to June 13. During this period of delay, the price of the stock fell from $16 to $13.50.

Oregon filed suit against Coopers, seeking as damages the difference between what Oregon actually received for its stock and what it would have received if the offering had occurred on May 2, an amount equal to approximately $35 million.

The trial court granted Coopers motion for summary judgment but the court of appeals reversed. Coopers appealed.

Issue: Did Coopers' negligence cause the loss to Oregon?

Excerpts from Justice Balmer's Decision:[7] [T]he critical issue is whether Oregon's market losses were a reasonably foreseeable result of Coopers' wrongful conduct. [N]o one could foresee, at the time of Coopers' accounting errors, the risk that Oregon would suffer a loss because its securities would be

▼

---

[7] For readability, we have changed "defendant" and "plaintiff" to "Coopers" and "Oregon."

sold at market-determined prices on June 13, rather than on May 2.

Oregon argues that it is foreseeable that stock prices will fluctuate, and that is certainly true. It also is foreseeable that negligent conduct by an accounting firm may harm a client by impairing its ability to raise capital. Coopers' conduct caused the delay in the offering that led to an unintended adverse result. However, the intervening action of market forces on the price of Oregon's stock was the harm-producing force, and Coopers' actions did not cause the decline in the stock price so as to support liability for that decline. As a matter of law, the risk of a decline in Oregon's stock price in June was not a reasonably foreseeable consequence of Coopers' negligent acts.

Oregon argues that the losses in this case were foreseeable because Coopers knew that Oregon intended to enter the market and sell its securities at a specific and favorable time. However, the record does not support Oregon's assertion. First, Oregon's complaint does not allege that the securities offering was scheduled to occur at a specific, advantageous time. Although Coopers knew that Oregon contemplated a public offering at some point, the timing of that offering was known only in the most general sense at the time of Coopers' wrongful conduct. Nor does the record contain any other suggestion by Oregon that it expected that market conditions would be favorable at the time the offering was originally planned, why those conditions were favorable, or why conditions would be any less favorable six weeks later. On the contrary, the uncontroverted evidence in the record shows that the increase and then decrease in steel company stock prices, including Oregon's, between April and June was due to market forces unrelated to Oregon's financial condition or to Coopers' conduct.

For the reasons discussed above, we conclude that, although Coopers breached its duty to Oregon by failing to provide competent accounting services, Coopers had no duty to protect Oregon against market fluctuations in Oregon's stock price. The trial court correctly granted Coopers' motion for summary judgment. ■

Fraud

An accountant is liable for fraud if (1) she makes a false statement of fact, (2) she either knows it is not true or recklessly disregards the truth, and (3) the client justifiably relies on the statement.[8] For example, William deliberately inflated numbers in the financial statements he prepared for Tess so that she would not discover that he had made some disastrous investments for her. Because of these distortions, Tess did not realize her true financial position for some years. William committed fraud.

A fraud claim is an important weapon because it permits the client to ask for punitive damages. In negligence or contract cases, a client is typically entitled only to compensatory damages.[9] For example, the singer Billy Joel sued his business manager (and ex-wife's brother) for financial mismanagement. He claimed a mere $30 million on the negligence and breach of contract claims but asked for $60 million in punitive damages on a fraud claim.

Breach of Trust

Accountants occupy a position of enormous trust because financial information is often sensitive and confidential. Clients may put as much trust in their accountants as they do in their lawyers,

Billy Joel may have liked uptown girls, but he had a downtown accountant.

---

8 Fraud is discussed in greater length in Chapter 14, on capacity and consent.
9 Compensatory and punitive damages are discussed in Chapter 6, on intentional torts, and Chapter 18, on remedies.

clergy, or psychiatrists. **Accountants have a legal obligation to (1) keep all client information confidential, and (2) use client information only for the benefit of the client.** For example, Alexander Grant & Co. did accounting work for Consolidata Services, Inc. (CDS), a company that provided payroll services. The two firms had a number of clients in common. When Alexander Grant discovered discrepancies in CDS's client funds accounts, it notified those companies that were clients of both firms. Not surprisingly, these mutual clients fired CDS, which then went out of business. The court held that Alexander Grant had violated its duty of trust to CDS.[10]

LIABILITY TO THIRD PARTIES

Suppose that a professional basketball team signs a star college player to a three-year contract. A leading cardiologist examines the player and pronounces him "in perfect health." You purchase stock in the team in reliance on this assertion. Unfortunately, the cardiologist is wrong, and the player collapses in his first pro game. His career is over and the team's future is bleak. The value of your stock plummets. Although you feel the doctor has singlehandedly wiped out your investment, you cannot recover from him because he owes you no duty.

Suppose, on the other hand, that you had purchased stock in the team because you were impressed with its financial prospects as revealed in its audited financial statements. Unfortunately, the auditors had failed to detect that the company had overstated its income. The value of the stock dives when the mistake comes to light. You may be able to recover from the auditors. Why are accountants different from doctors or other professionals?

No issue in the accounting field is more controversial than liability to third parties. Plaintiffs argue that auditors owe a duty to a trusting public that doctors (and other professionals) do not. The job of the auditor, they say, is to provide an independent, professional source of assurance that a company's audited financial statements are accurate. If the auditors do their job properly, they have nothing to fear.

The accounting profession rebuts, however, that if everyone who has ever been harmed even remotely by a faulty audit can recover damages, there will soon be no auditors left. In return for a limited fee on the upside, auditors face potentially unlimited liability when things go wrong. Big Four firms spend between 10 and 20 percent of their revenues on litigation (including settlements and insurance).

One observation before beginning: accountants are generally not liable to third parties in *contract* because there is no *privity of contract* between the parties.[11] Most third parties are incidental beneficiaries who are not entitled to enforce a contract. (We discuss third party beneficiaries in Chapter 16.)

Negligence

Accountants' liability for negligence to third parties is determined by state law. Most states follow one of the following rules: the *Ultramares* doctrine, the foreseeable doctrine, or the Restatement doctrine.

---

[10] *Wagenheim v. Alexander Grant & Co.,* 19 Ohio App. 3d 7, 482 N.E.2d 955, 1983 Ohio App. LEXIS 11194 (App. Ct. Ohio 1983).

[11] Two parties are in "privity of contract" if they have entered into a contract with each other. If two parties enter into a contract that affects a third party, that third party is not in privity.

Ultramares *Doctrine*

In 1931, while serving on the New York Court of Appeals, Judge Benjamin Cardozo decided the case of *Ultramares Corp. v. Touche*,[12] an influential decision that is still the law in a number of states. Fred Stern & Co. imported rubber. Stern asked the Ultramares Corp. for a loan to finance these purchases. As a condition of any loans, Ultramares insisted upon an audited balance sheet. The auditors, Touche, Niven & Co., were never told exactly who would see the financial statements, but knew a number of potential creditors might. On the basis of a balance sheet listing a net worth of $1 million, Ultramares loaned money to Stern. In reality, however, management had falsified the books and the company was insolvent. The auditors failed to follow paper trails leading to "off-the-books" transactions that, if properly analyzed, would have revealed the company's insolvency. When Stern failed to repay the loans, Ultramares sued Touche for negligence. The jury awarded Ultramares $187,576.32. (The case was decided in 1931, at the height of the Great Depression. That was real money.)

Cardozo overturned the jury's verdict. If third parties were able to recover for negligence against an accounting firm, then "[a] thoughtless slip or blunder, the failure to detect a theft or forgery beneath the cover of deceptive entries, may expose accountants to a liability in an indeterminate amount for an indeterminate time to an indeterminate class." Cardozo thought this hazard too extreme. **Under the *Ultramares* doctrine, accountants who fail to exercise due care are liable to a third party only if they know that the third party (1) will see their work product and (2) will rely on the work product for a particular, known purpose.** To be liable, the accountants must know the identity of the third party.

Consider an example of a later case in which a court found an accountant liable under the *Ultramares* doctrine: a limited partner sued an accountant who failed to disclose in an audit report that the general partners were withdrawing funds in violation of the partnership agreement. The limited partnership agreement contained an express provision requiring an annual audit by a CPA, and the auditor had also prepared the partnership's tax returns on which the limited partners relied in preparing their personal returns. The accountant knew that his work product would be shown to the limited partners, and he knew their identity.[13]

Cardozo decided *Ultramares* in 1931, and since then, some of the country's notions about liability have changed. Although some states still follow the *Ultramares* doctrine, other jurisdictions have adopted different rules.

Foreseeable *Doctrine*

The courts in a limited number of states have held that an accountant is liable to any *foreseeable* users who suffer harm as a result of her carelessness. For example, Harry and Barry (we are not making this up) Rosenblum sold their business to Giant Stores Corp. in return for Giant common stock. In assessing the value of this stock, the two men relied on an audit by Touche Ross & Co. (which had the bad luck to be the accounting firm in the landmark cases that established both the *Ultramares* doctrine and the foreseeable doctrine). You will not be surprised to learn that Giant's financial statements turned out to be fraudulent and the stock worthless. Giant had manipulated its books by falsely recording assets that it did not own and omitting substantial amounts of accounts payable. **The court held that an accountant who fails to exercise due**

---

[12] 255 N.Y. 170, 174 N.E. 441, 1931 N.Y. LEXIS 660 (1931).
[13] *White v. Guarente*, 43 N.Y.2d 356, 372 N.E.2d 315, 1977 N.Y. LEXIS 2470 (1977).

care is liable to a third party if (1) it was foreseeable that the third party would receive financial statements from the accountant's client, and (2) the third party relied on these statements.[14] This standard creates greater liability for accountants than the *Ultramares* doctrine.

Restatement Doctrine

The majority of state courts have rejected the *Ultramares* doctrine as too narrow and the foreseeable doctrine as too broad. They prefer, instead, a middle ground that was adopted by the Restatement (Second) of Torts. **According to the Restatement, accountants who fail to exercise due care are liable to (1) anyone they knew would rely on the information and (2) anyone else in the same class.**

Suppose, for example, that Adrienne knows she is preparing financial statements for the BeachBall Corp. to use in obtaining a bank loan from the First National Bank of Tucson. If Adrienne is careless in preparing the statements and BeachBall bursts, she will be liable to First Bank *under all three tests:* the *Ultramares* doctrine, the foreseeable doctrine, and the Restatement doctrine.

Suppose, however, that the company takes its financial statements to the Last National Bank of Tucson instead. Under the *Ultramares* doctrine, Adrienne would not be liable because she did not prepare the documents for the Last Bank. She would be liable under the foreseeable doctrine because it was foreseeable that the Last Bank would receive the financial statements from the client and rely on them. She would also be liable under the Restatement doctrine because the Last Bank is in the *same class* as the First Bank. Once Adrienne knows that a bank will rely on the statements she has prepared, the identity of the particular bank should not make any difference to her when doing her work.

Suppose that BeachBall uses the financial statements to persuade a landlord to rent it a manufacturing facility. In this case, Adrienne would be liable under the foreseeable doctrine because this was a foreseeable use of the financial statements. She would not be liable under the Restatement doctrine, however, because the landlord is not in the same class as the First Bank, for whom Adrienne knew she was preparing the documents. Finally, if a major shareholder of BeachBall uses the financial statements to convince her boyfriend to marry her, Adrienne is not liable under any doctrine. The following table summarizes the three doctrines:

Under this doctrine:	Accountants who fail to exercise due care are liable to a third party if:
Ultramares Doctrine	They know the identity of the third party who: • Will see their work product, and • Will rely on the work product for a particular, known purpose
Foreseeable Doctrine	• It is foreseeable that the third party will receive financial statements from the accountant's client, and • The third party relies on these statements
Restatement Doctrine	• The accountants knew the third party would rely on the information, or • The third party was in the same class as someone who the accountant knew would rely on the information

---

[14] *H. Rosenblum, Inc. v. Adler,* 93 N.J. 324, 461 A.2d 138, 1983 N.J. LEXIS 2717 (N.J. 1983).

In the following case, investors relied on audited financial statements that proved to be faulty. Was Deloitte & Touche (not again!) liable?

TARA CAPITAL PARTNERS I, L.P. V. DELOITTE & TOUCHE, L.L.P.

2004 Tex. App. LEXIS 4577
Court of Appeals of Texas, 2004

Facts: Over a four-month period, Tara Capital Partners bought stock in Just For Feet, Inc., an athletic footwear company. In making these purchases, Tara Partners relied in part on financial statements prepared by Deloitte & Touche. Six weeks after Tara's last purchase of stock, Just For Feet filed for bankruptcy. Tara brought suit against Deloitte, alleging that the accounting firm had been negligent in its preparation of Just For Feet's financial documents. The trial court granted Deloitte's motion for summary judgment and Tara appealed.

Issue: Is Deloitte liable to purchasers of stock in Just For Feet?

Excerpts from Judge Francis's Decision:[15] [The Restatement] narrows the scope of liability to situations where the information supplier is aware of the third party and intends that the third party rely on the information. While the Restatement's approach is less restrictive than others requiring strict or near privity between the accountant and the plaintiff, it does not permit recovery for every foreseeable user of its audited financial statements.

Tara Partners do not dispute that Deloitte had no knowledge of their specific identity or their contemplated purchases of Just For Feet stock. The evidence conclusively establishes that Deloitte issued its last audit report for Just for Feet over a month before Tara Partners made their first Just For Feet stock purchase. The critical inquiry for purposes of our analysis is whether the evidence conclusively established that Tara Partners were not members of an identifiable limited group of which Deloitte was aware and intended to influence.

Tara Partners initially attempt to characterize themselves as a limited group of potential shareholders who utilized a value investment strategy. At the time Deloitte's last audit report was issued Tara Partners were indistinguishable from any other potential open market buyers. There is absolutely nothing in the record suggesting Deloitte intended or knew Just for Feet intended to utilize its work for the purpose of attracting investors like Tara Partners. At best the record reflects Deloitte's general awareness that such value investors exist. To conclude that Tara Partners raised a fact issue on whether value investors comprise a limited group to which Deloitte owed a duty based on the facts before us would implicitly endorse a foreseeability approach to accountant liability for negligent misrepresentation that was specifically rejected by the Restatement.

Next, Tara Partners assert their agent was one of several investment analysts who participated in conference calls with Just For Feet management where financial information was discussed. The fact that Tara Partners' *agent* was one among several analysts who participated in conference calls with Just for Feet executives where financial information was discussed is also insufficient to qualify *Tara Partners* as members of a limited group. Again, aside from Deloitte's general knowledge that the company held such conference calls, there is nothing in the record to indicate that Deloitte intended to or had knowledge that Just for Feet intended to supply its work to Tara Partners through such analysts.

Finally, Tara Partners contend that after their first purchase of Just For Feet stock, they became part of the limited group of existing shareholders to whom Deloitte owed a duty. For purposes of an accountant's liability for negligent misrepresentation, the pivotal inquiry is the accountant's intent toward this limited group at the time the representation is made. In this case, Deloitte's last audit report was issued before Tara Partners ever made their first stock purchase. Because Tara Partners were not existing shareholders at the time the audit report was issued, they could not be part of the limited group of existing shareholders to which the audit was addressed.

We affirm the trial court's judgment. ■

---

[15] For readability, we refer to Tara Partners by name and not as "appellant."

Fraud

Under common law, courts consider fraud to be much worse than negligence because it is intentional. Therefore, the penalty is heavier. **An accountant who commits fraud is liable to any *foreseeable* user of the work product who justifiably relied on it.** This rule applies in all jurisdictions, even those that have adopted the *Ultramares* doctrine. For example, consider TechDisk, a manufacturer of disk drives. Customers were buying disk drives faster than the company could make them. Afraid that the stock price would plummet if investors found out about the shortage, company officers helped their sales numbers by shipping out bricks wrapped up to look like disk drives. Company accountants altered the financial statements to pretend that the bricks were indeed computer parts. These accountants would be liable to any foreseeable users—including investors, creditors and customers.

Liability for Qualified Opinions

Auditors can, under some circumstances, protect themselves from liability by issuing a less than clean opinion, that is, a qualified, adverse, or disclaimer of opinion. To avoid liability, the less than clean opinion must be issued for the right reasons. For example, if the auditor indicates that it has issued a qualified opinion because of uncertainty about environmental litigation, then it is not liable when that lawsuit bankrupts the company. But if the company runs into financial trouble because of some other problem that the auditors should have discovered, they are liable, despite their qualified opinion. For example, if the company survives its environmental lawsuit unscathed but runs into trouble because of inventory thefts that the auditors should have caught, the auditors would be liable.

Securities Act of 1933

Third parties who have been injured by an accountant's error often file suit under the securities laws. Chapter 37, on securities regulation, provides a general overview of the liability provisions for both the Securities Act of 1933 (1933 Act) and the Securities Exchange Act of 1934 (1934 Act). This chapter offers a summary of these liability provisions as they affect accountants.

The 1933 Act requires an issuer to register securities before offering them for sale to the public. To do this, the issuer files a registration statement with the Securities and Exchange Commission (SEC). This registration statement must include audited financial statements. **Under §11 of the 1933 Act, auditors are liable for any material misstatement or omission in the financial statements that they prepare for a registration statement.**

To prevail under §11, the plaintiff must prove only that (1) the registration statement contained a material misstatement or omission and (2) she lost money. Ernst & Young served as the auditor for FP Investments, Inc., a company that sold interests in tax shelter partnerships. These partnerships were formed to cultivate tropical plants in Hawaii. The prospectus for this investment neglected to mention that the partnerships did not have enough cash on hand to grow the plants. A jury found

Without the cash to grow these plants, the offering was a flop.

© KRISTINA MILLAR

that Ernst & Young violated §11 and awarded damages of $18.9 million to the investors.[16]

However, auditors can avoid liability under §11 by showing that they made a reasonable investigation of the financial statements and had reasonable grounds to believe the statements contained no material omissions or misstatements. This investigation is called **due diligence.** Typically, auditors will not be liable if they can show that they complied with GAAP and GAAS.

In the following case, the registration statement revealed some, but not all, of an investment's risks. The fund declined in value—for a reason that *was* disclosed. Should the accountant be liable for the *undisclosed* risks?

you Be The Judge

RODNEY V. KPMG PEAT MARWICK

143 F.3d 1140, 1998 U.S. App. LEXIS 9454
United States Court of Appeals for the Eighth Circuit, 1998

Facts: The plaintiffs invested in the Piper Funds Institutional Government Income Portfolio (the Fund). The Fund invested heavily in a type of security, called a "derivative," that is very sensitive to fluctuations in interest rates. If rates go up, the value of derivatives goes down, and vice versa. The Fund had disclosed this interesting fact in its registration statement. When the Federal Reserve Board tightened monetary policy, interest rates rose, and the price of Fund shares fell sharply. The investors filed suit against KPMG under §11 of the 1933 Act, alleging that its audit should have disclosed the following discrepancies:

- The Fund invested in a type of derivative that was not disclosed in the registration statement. This new type of investment was also sensitive to interest rate changes.

- The Fund's portfolio had a longer life expectancy than disclosed. For this type of investment, the longer the life expectancy, the higher the risk.

- The Fund's registration statement promised that it would not invest in illiquid securities (that is, securities that are not readily marketable). As much as 52 percent of the Fund's portfolio was illiquid.

You Be the Judge: Was KPMG's failure to disclose this information a material omission? Should the accounting firm be liable to investors?

Argument for KPMG: After reading the registration statement, no reasonable person could fail to understand that the Fund intended to purchase highly risky investments. In particular, investors were on full notice that, if interest rates went up, the value of their investment would go down. That is exactly what happened. The Fund's investments may not have complied *exactly* with the guidelines in the registration statement, but the risk was the same. When the information in a registration statement clearly discloses the precise risks that ultimately cause a decline in the stock's value, investors can hardly claim that they were misled.

Argument for the Investors: Under §11, plaintiffs need prove only that the registration statement contained a material misstatement and they lost money. The registration statement in this case was inaccurate. Although investors were warned about the danger of rising interest rates, they were not told about the other risks. If the truth about the Fund's investments had been disclosed, the plaintiffs might have avoided the Fund or at least bought it at a cheaper price. Investors had the right to know not only that their purchase was risky, but how risky and why. ■

---

[16] *Hayes v. Haushalter,* 1994 U.S. App. LEXIS 23608 (9th Cir. 1994).

Securities Exchange Act of 1934

A company that is subject to the 1934 Act must file with the SEC an annual report containing audited financial statements and quarterly reports with unaudited financials.

Liability for Inaccurate Disclosure in a Required Filing

Under §18 of the 1934 Act, an auditor who makes a false or misleading statement in a required filing is liable to any buyer or seller of the stock who has acted in reliance on the statement. The auditors can avoid liability by showing that they acted in *good faith* and did not know the information was misleading.

Fraud

Primary Liability. Most securities litigation against accountants is brought under §10(b) and Rule 10b-5 of the 1934 Act. **Under §10(b), an auditor is liable for making (1) a misstatement or omission of a material fact (2) knowingly or recklessly (3) that the plaintiff relies on in purchasing or selling a security.** This is called primary liability because the accountants are liable for statements that they make themselves. Accountants are liable under §10(b) only if they are reckless. For example, when Price Waterhouse audited Altris Software, it failed to notice some obvious red flags: on the last day of the year, Altris recorded revenue from two customers that was more than 50 times greater than it had ever received from this type of transaction. The court held, however, that although Price Waterhouse may have been grossly negligent, it had not had actual knowledge of the falsehoods, nor had it been deliberately reckless.[17]

Aiding and Abetting. For a *primary* violation of §10(b), the defendant must have made a knowing or reckless omission or misstatement himself. That can be difficult to prove. Some plaintiffs successfully argued that even an accountant who had not made knowing or reckless misstatements himself could be liable for **aiding and abetting** others who made untrue statements. These cases created enormous potential liability for accountants. In 1994, however, the Supreme Court overruled this whole line of cases, holding that private plaintiffs cannot recover damages on claims of aiding and abetting.[18] What the Supreme Court giveth, Congress (at least partly) taketh away. Congress amended the 1934 Act to permit the SEC to prosecute those who aid and abet others in making untrue statements in connection with the purchase or sale of a security.[19]

Whistleblowing

Under §10A of the 1934 Act, auditors who suspect that a client has committed an illegal act must ensure that the client's board of directors is notified. If the board fails to take appropriate corrective action, the auditors must issue an official report to the board. If the board receives such a report from its auditors, it must notify the SEC within one business day (and send a copy of this notice to its accountant). If the auditors do not receive this copy, they must notify the SEC themselves.

The scope of §10A is broad, covering insider trading, price-fixing, and any other violations of state and federal law. While doing an audit of the Cronos Group, Arthur Andersen questioned a $1.5 million "disbursement." When the shipping company refused either to provide an explanation or to investigate this mysterious payment, the accounting firm filed an official report with the board of directors and resigned as

---

[17] *DSAM Global Value Fund v. Altris Software, Inc.*, 288 F.3d 385, 2002 U.S. App. LEXIS 7213 (9th Cir. 2002).

[18] *Central Bank v. First Interstate Bank*, 511 U.S. 164, 114 S. Ct. 1439, 1994 U.S. LEXIS 3120 (1994).

[19] Private Securities Litigation Reform Act, Pub. L. No. 104-67, 109 Stat. 737 (1995).

Cronos's auditor. Cronos then filed the Andersen report with the SEC, which investigated the incident. Not surprisingly, many auditors are unenthusiastic about this statute. It is not a pretty choice—the wrath of the SEC if they fail to cooperate or the anger of their clients if they do comply.

Joint and Several Liability

Traditionally, liability under the 1934 Act was **joint and several.** When several different participants were potentially liable, a plaintiff could sue any one defendant or any group of defendants for the full amount of the damages. If a company committed fraud and then went bankrupt, its accounting firm might well be the only defendant with assets. Even if the accountants had caused only, say, 5 percent of the damages, they could be liable for the full amount.

Congress has amended the 1934 Act to provide that accountants are liable jointly and severally only if they knowingly violate the law. Otherwise, the defendants are proportionately liable, meaning that they are liable only for the share of the damages that they themselves caused.

CRIMINAL LIABILITY

Thus far the discussion has focused on civil liability. The penalty for a civil offense is the payment of monetary damages. However, some offenses are criminal acts for which the punishment is a fine and imprisonment:

- The Justice Department has the right to prosecute willful violations under either the 1933 Act or the 1934 Act.

- The Internal Revenue Code imposes various criminal penalties on accountants for wrongdoing in the preparation of tax returns.

- Many states prosecute violations of their securities laws.

As we saw in the opening scenario, Arthur Andersen was convicted of a crime for its handling of the Enron investigation. The following case reveals the outcome of that conviction.

ARTHUR ANDERSEN LLP V. UNITED STATES

125 S. Ct. 2129, 2005 U.S. LEXIS 4348
Supreme Court of the United States, 2005

Facts: Arthur Andersen audited Enron Corporation's financial statements. Enron had been highly profitable and rapidly growing, but its financial performance was faltering. At the beginning of August, a senior accountant at Enron told two Andersen partners that Enron could face severe accounting scandals. These two partners were David Duncan, head of the Enron engagement team, and his supervisor, Michael Odom.

On August 28, an article in *The Wall Street Journal* suggested there were improprieties at Enron. The SEC opened an informal investigation. By early September, Andersen had formed an Enron "crisis response" team, which included Nancy Temple, an in-house lawyer. Early in October, Temple realized that an SEC investigation was highly probable. A few days later, at a general training meeting attended by 89 employees, including 10 from the Enron engagement team, Odom urged everyone to comply with the firm's document retention policy.[20] He added: "If it's destroyed in the course of the normal policy and litigation is filed the next day, that's great.... We've followed our own policy, and whatever there was that might have been of interest to somebody is gone and irretrievable." Three times that month, Temple reminded Andersen employees to follow the document retention policy. Andersen employees did indeed destroy a substantial number of paper and electronic documents. At a meeting on October 31, Duncan picked up a document with the words "smoking gun" written on it and began to destroy it, adding "we don't need this."

On October 30, the SEC opened a formal investigation and sent Enron a letter that requested accounting documents. In November, the SEC served Enron and Andersen with subpoenas for records. Duncan's assistant then sent an e-mail that stated: "Per Dave—No more shredding.... We have been officially served for our documents."

Andersen was indicted on the grounds that it "did knowingly, intentionally and corruptly persuade other persons, to wit: its employees, with intent to cause them to withhold documents from, and alter documents for use in, official proceedings." A jury returned a guilty verdict. The Court of Appeals for the Fifth Circuit affirmed and the Supreme Court granted *certiorari*.

Issue: Did Andersen employees commit a crime when they destroyed Enron documents?

Excerpts from Chief Justice Rehnquist's Decision for a Unanimous Court:[21] Document retention policies, which are created in part to keep certain information from getting into the hands of others, including the Government, are common in business. It is, of course, not wrongful for a manager to instruct his employees to comply with a valid document retention policy under ordinary circumstances.

[The statute] punishes not just "corruptly persuading" another, but "knowingly ... corruptly persuading" another. Only persons conscious of wrongdoing can be said to "knowingly ... corruptly persuade." The jury instructions at issue simply failed to convey the requisite consciousness of wrongdoing. Indeed, it is striking how little culpability the instructions required. For example, the jury was told that, "even if [Andersen] honestly and sincerely believed that its conduct was lawful, you may find [Andersen] guilty."

The jury was told to convict if it found Andersen intended to "subvert, undermine, or impede" governmental factfinding by suggesting to its employees that they enforce the document retention policy. No longer was any type of "dishonesty" necessary to a finding of guilt, and it was enough for Andersen to have simply "impeded" the Government's factfinding ability. As the Government conceded at oral argument, "impede" has broader connotations than "subvert" or even "undermine," and [does] not incorporate any "corruptness" at all.

The instructions also were infirm for another reason. They led the jury to believe that it did not have to find any nexus between the "persuasion" to destroy documents and any particular proceeding. A "knowingly ... corrupt persuader" cannot be someone who persuades others to shred documents under a document retention policy when he does not have in contemplation any particular official proceeding in which those documents might be material. If the defendant lacks knowledge that his actions are likely to affect the judicial proceeding, he lacks the requisite intent to obstruct.

For these reasons, the jury instructions here were flawed in important respects. The judgment of the Court of Appeals is reversed, and the case is remanded for further proceedings consistent with this opinion.

It is so ordered. ■

Although the reversal of this conviction may have been gratifying for Andersen employees, it did not undo the harm that had been done to the firm. Andersen was dead and this opinion did not resurrect it.

---

[20] The firm's policy called for a single central engagement file, which "should contain only that information which is relevant to supporting our work." The policy stated that, "in cases of threatened litigation, ... no related information will be destroyed."

[21] For ease of reading, we refer to Andersen by name and not as "Petitioner" as the court did.

Auditors play an important role in assuring investors that financials have been honestly prepared. Melissa Harmon, the judge who tried the Arthur Andersen case, commented that Andersen had shown a "callous, reckless disregard for its duty to investors and the public trust for decades." If this is true, one would expect investors to distrust the financials of all Andersen clients and, accordingly, downgrade their stock prices. Apparently, however, it was not until Andersen collapsed that the markets penalized its clients. This penalty probably reflected the costs of switching auditors and defending against lawsuits more than anything else.

The markets may have given Andersen clients a pass because that firm was no worse than its competitors. According to a study by two law professors, all of the (then) Big Five auditing firms had about the same error rate when they audited large companies (with more than $1 billion in sales).[22] Indeed, Andersen was better than average when it came to restatements because of problems with revenue recognition, the kind of error that has the greatest impact on stock price. Only 2.8 percent of Andersen's clients had this problem, compared with, say, 5.6 percent at Deloitte & Touche. For most auditors, the larger the client, the more likely a restatement; but this was not true for Andersen. If all auditors have about the same mistake rate, it is perhaps not surprising that companies tend to select their auditors based on price. And maybe they are getting what they pay for. ◆

OTHER ACCOUNTANT-CLIENT ISSUES

The Accountant-Client Relationship

The SEC has long been concerned about the relationship between accountants and the companies they audit. Its rules require accountants to maintain independence from their clients. The accountant must be "capable of exercising objective and impartial judgment on all issues. . . ."[23] To this general guideline, the SEC also adds specific rules. An auditor or her family must not, for example, maintain a financial or business relationship with the client.

SEC rules on independence specifically prohibit accountants or their families from owning stock in a company that their firm audits. To take one woeful example, during an investigation the SEC discovered that most of PricewaterhouseCoopers' partners were in violation, including half of the partners who were charged with enforcing the rule. All told, firm employees had committed more than *8,000* violations. Although the firm had been caught violating the same rule only a few years before, it nonetheless had a trifecta in place: many partners pleaded ignorance of the rule, the firm made little effort to enforce it, and, as a result, violations were widespread. In response to this second infraction, the firm fired 10 employees, including 5 partners. The SEC notified 52 of the firm's clients that there were potential concerns about the integrity of their financial statements and even requested that some of the companies, such as Compaq Computer Corp., select a new auditor.

SEC rules of practice specify that an accountant who engages in "unethical or improper professional conduct" may be banned from practice before the SEC.[24] Auditors who are banned or suspended cannot perform the audits that are required by the 1933 and 1934 Acts—quite a professional blow.

---

[22] Theodore Eisenberg and Jonathan Macey, "Was Arthur Andersen Different?," *Journal of Empirical Legal Studies,* July 2004, vol. 1, issue 2, pp. 263–300(38); discussed in "How Bad was Andersen," *Economist,* Dec. 6, 2003, p. 68. This discussion is based on that article.

[23] 17 CFR §210.2-01(b).

[24] 17 CFR §201.102(e)(1)(iv).

Accountant-Client Privilege

Traditionally, an accountant-client privilege did not exist under federal law. Accountants were under no obligation to keep confidential any information they received from their clients. In one notorious case, the IRS suspected that the owner of a chain of pizza parlors was underreporting his income. The agency persuaded the owner's CPA, James Checksfield, to spy on him for eight years. (The IRS agreed to drop charges against Checksfield, who had not paid his own taxes for three years.) Thanks to the information that Checksfield passed to the IRS, his client was indicted on criminal charges of evading taxes by failing to report over $300,000 in income.

Congress passed the Internal Revenue Service Restructuring and Reform Act to reduce IRS abuse of taxpayers. This statute provides limited protection for confidential communications between accountants and clients. That is the good news. The bad news is the word "limited." This new privilege applies only in civil cases involving the IRS or the U.S. government. It does not apply to criminal cases, civil cases not involving the U.S. government, or cases with other federal agencies such as the SEC. Nor does it apply to the preparation of tax returns. Thus, for example, this new accountant-client privilege would not have protected Checksfield's client because he was charged with a criminal offense.

Some states do recognize an accountant-client privilege, but a state privilege applies only to issues of state law and provides no protection against federal charges. The Checksfield case took place in Missouri, which does have an accountant-client privilege. However, because the IRS filed suit, federal law applied and Checksfield's information could be used in court. In the end, however, the IRS dropped the tax evasion charges out of concern that a jury would not believe Checksfield's testimony. Ironically, Checksfield suffered worse punishment than his client—the Missouri state board of accountancy revoked his CPA license for violating state law.

Working Papers

When working for a client, accountants use the client's own documents and also prepare working papers of their own—notes, memoranda, research. In theory, each party owns whatever it has prepared itself. Thus accountants own the working papers they have created. In practice, however, the client controls even the accountant's working papers. The accountant (1) cannot show the working papers to anyone without the client's permission (or a valid court order) and (2) must allow the client access to the working papers. Under the Sarbanes-Oxley Act, accountants for public companies must keep all audit work papers for at least seven years.

© PHOTODISC/GETTY IMAGES

Chapter Conclusion

Accountants serve many masters and, therefore, face numerous potential conflicts. Clients, third parties, and the government all rely on their work. Privy to clients' most intimate financial secrets, accountants must decide which of these secrets to reveal and which to keep confidential. The wrong decision may destroy the client, impoverish its shareholders, and subject its auditors to substantial penalties. Because America was dismayed by revelations of widespread inaccuracies in the financial statements of public companies, Congress took action to increase regulation of the industry. It is a time of change for the accounting profession.

Chapter Review

1. The Sarbanes-Oxley Act:

   a. Establishes the Public Company Accounting Oversight Board.

   b. Requires an accounting firm to make regular and complete reports to the audit committees of its clients.

   c. Prohibits accounting firms that audit public companies from providing consulting services to those companies on certain topics, such as bookkeeping, financial information systems, human resources, and legal issues (unrelated to the audit).

   d. Prohibits an accounting firm from auditing a company if one of the company's top officers has worked for the firm within the last year and was involved in the company's audit.

   e. Provides that a lead audit partner cannot work for a client in any auditing role for more than five years.

2. Accountants are liable to their clients for negligence if:

   • They breach their duty to their clients by failing to exercise the degree of skill and competence that an ordinarily prudent accountant would under the circumstances, and

   • The violation of this duty causes harm to the client.

3. Accountants are liable for fraud if:

   • They make a false statement of fact

   • They know it is not true or recklessly disregard the truth, and

   • The client justifiably relies on the statement.

4. Accountants have a legal obligation to:

   • Keep all client information confidential, and

   • Use client information only for the benefit of the client.

5. State law determines an accountant's liability for negligence to third parties. Most states follow one of the following three rules:

   a. *Ultramares* Doctrine. Accountants who fail to exercise due care are only liable to a third party if they know the identity of the third party who:

   • Will see their work product, and

   • Will rely on the work product for a particular, known purpose.

   b. Foreseeable Doctrine. Accountants who fail to exercise due care are liable to a third party if:

   • It is foreseeable that the third party will receive financial statements from the client, and

   • The third party relies on these statements.

   c. Restatement Doctrine. Accountants who fail to exercise due care are liable to:

   • Anyone they knew would rely on the information, and

   • Anyone else in the same class.

6. An accountant who commits fraud is liable to any foreseeable user of the work product who justifiably relies on it.

7. Under §11 of the 1933 Act, auditors are liable for any material misstatement or omission in the financial statements that they provide for a registration statement.

8. Under §10(b) of the 1934 Act, an auditor is liable for making (1) any misstatement or omission of a material fact in financial statements (2) knowingly or recklessly (3) that the plaintiff relies on in purchasing or selling a security.

9. The SEC can prosecute those who aid and abet others in making untrue statements in connection with the purchase or sale of a security.

10. Under §10A of the 1934 Act, auditors who suspect that a client has committed an illegal act must ensure that the client's board of directors is notified.

11. Under the 1934 Act, accountants are liable jointly and severally only if they knowingly violate the law. Otherwise, they are proportionately liable.

12. The SEC prohibits auditors or their families from owning stock in companies that their firm audits.

13. A limited accountant-client privilege exists under federal law. Some states also recognize this privilege and apply it in matters involving state law.

Practice Test

1. Krouse, Kern & Co., Inc., made errors in its audit of Summit Power. Toro Co. relied on Krouse's faulty financial statements when making loans to Summit. Krouse did not know that Toro would rely on these reports. Indiana adheres to the *Ultramares* doctrine. Is Krouse liable to Toro?

2. **ETHICS** Wayne and Arlene Selden invested in Competition Aircraft, a company that had once sold airplanes. Sometime later, however, it became a fraud and simply pretended to sell airplanes. After the company went bankrupt, the Seldens sought to recover from accountant William Burnett. He had recommended the investment to several of his clients, who communicated his recommendation to the Seldens. The Seldens were not Burnett's clients. The court adopted the Restatement doctrine. Is Burnett liable? Whether or not Burnett faces legal liability, was it a good idea for him to recommend investments to his clients? Does it create any potential conflicts of interest?

3. Color-Dyne printed patterns on carpets. After reviewing the company's audited financial statements, the plaintiffs provided materials to Color-Dyne on credit. These financial statements showed that Color-Dyne owned $2 million in inventory. The audit failed to reveal, however, that various banks held secured interests in this inventory. The accountant did not know that the company intended to give the financial statements to plaintiffs or any other creditors. Color-Dyne went bankrupt. Is the accountant liable to plaintiffs under the Restatement doctrine?

4. **CPA QUESTION** To be successful in a civil action under §11 of the Securities Act of 1933 concerning liability for a misleading registration statement, the plaintiff must prove:

	Defendant's Intent to Deceive	Plaintiff's Reliance on the Registration Statement
a.	No	Yes
b.	No	No
c.	Yes	No
d.	Yes	Yes

5. James and Penelope Monroe purchased securities offered by Hughes Homes, Inc., a retailer of manufactured housing in Tacoma, Washington. During its audit, Deloitte & Touche found that Hughes Homes' internal controls had flaws. As a result, the accounting firm adjusted the scope of its audit to perform independent testing to verify the accuracy of the company's financial records. Satisfied that the internal controls were functional, Deloitte issued a clean opinion. After Hughes Homes became insolvent, the Monroes sued Deloitte for violating §11 of the 1933 Act. They alleged that Deloitte's failure to disclose that it had found flaws in Hughes's internal control system was a material omission. GAAS did not require disclosure. Is Deloitte liable?

6. **CPA QUESTION** One of the elements necessary to hold a CPA liable to a client for conducting an audit negligently is that the CPA:

   a. Acted with *scienter* or guilty knowledge

   b. Was a fiduciary of the client

   c. Failed to exercise due care

   d. Executed an engagement letter

7. When Jeff Hall told one of the general partners of the Edge Energies limited partnerships that he did not wish to invest in these ventures, the general partner suggested he call Ronald W. Jackson, the partnerships' accountant. Jackson told Hall that Edge Energies partnerships were a "good deal," that they were "good moneymakers," and "they were expecting something like a two-year payoff." In fact, Jackson knew that the operators were mismanaging these ventures, and that the partnerships were bad investments. Hall relied on Jackson's recommendation and invested in Edge Energies. He subsequently lost his entire investment. Is Jackson liable to Hall? Does it matter which negligence doctrine applies?

8. **CPA QUESTION** A CPA's duty of due care to a client most likely will be breached when a CPA:

a. Gives a client an oral instead of a written report

b. Gives a client incorrect advice based on an honest error judgment

c. Fails to give tax advice that saves the client money

d. Fails to follow generally accepted auditing standards

9. The British Broadcasting Corp. (BBC) broadcast a TV program alleging that Terry Venables, a former professional soccer coach, had fraudulently obtained a £1 million loan by misrepresenting the value of his company. Venables had been a sportscaster for the BBC but had switched to a competing network. The source of the BBC's story was "confidential working papers" from Venables's accountant. According to the accountant, the papers had been stolen. Who owns these working papers? Does the accountant have the right to disclose the content of working papers?

10. **YOU BE THE JUDGE** WRITING PROBLEM Medtrans, an ambulance company, was unable to pay its bills. In need of cash, it signed an engagement letter with Deloitte & Touche to perform an audit that could be used to attract investors. Unfortunately, the audit had the opposite effect. The unaudited statements showed earnings of $1.9 million, but the accountants calculated that the company had actually lost about $500,000. While in the process of negotiating adjustments to the financials, Deloitte resigned. Some time passed before Medtrans found another auditor, and, in that interim, a potential investor withdrew its $10 million offer. Is Deloitte liable for breach of contract? **Argument for Medtrans:** Once an accountant has undertaken to serve a client, he cannot resign in a manner that causes harm to the client. Deloitte should have been more persistent in resolving the dispute and should not have resigned until the company could find another auditor. **Argument for Deloitte:** An auditor's duty is not only to the client but also to the public trust. Thus an auditor is required to place the integrity of the financial reporting process above the client. Deloitte had no choice but to resign, and quickly, when the client was uncooperative.

11. A partnership of doctors in Billings, Montana, sought to build a larger office building. They decided to finance this project using industrial revenue bonds under a complex provision of the Internal Revenue Code. They hired Peat Marwick to do the required financial work. The deal was all set to close when it was discovered that the accountants had made an error in structuring the deal. As a result, the partnership was forced to pay a significantly higher rate of interest. When the partnership sued Peat for breach of contract, the accounting firm asked the court to dismiss the claim on the grounds that the client could only sue in tort. Peat argued that it had performed its duties under the contract. The statute of limitations had expired for a tort case but not for a contract case. Should the doctors' case be dismissed?

12. **ROLE REVERSAL** Prepare a multiple-choice question like those found on the CPA exam. The earlier questions in the practice test provide some examples.

Internet Research Problem

Go to http://beatty.westbuslaw.com and find five examples of actions that the SEC has brought against accountants. (You might try typing the term "accounting violations" in the search box.) What does the SEC allege that the accountants have done? What provisions of the securities laws has the SEC accused them of violating?

> **You can find further practice problems at http://beatty.westbuslaw.com or in the Study Guide that accompanies this text.**

UNIT 6

Government Regulation

Antitrust

Mike Elliott was not looking for trouble when he brought an order form for Girl Scout cookies to work. Mr. Elliott, an employee at DaimlerChrysler's factory in Dearborn, Michigan, started asking co-workers to buy a few boxes on behalf of his girlfriend's eight-year-old daughter. "I worked for four or five hours, and suddenly this lady came up to me and said that a guy who worked 50 feet down the line from me was selling them cheaper," Mr. Elliott says. "The first thing that everyone thinks is, 'You're trying to rip me off.'"

In an increasingly competitive market-place, price wars are breaking out over Thin Mints and Peanut Butter Patties. The 36,500-member Michigan Metro Council, citing rising costs and the need to subsidize inner city troops, reluctantly raised its price to $3 a box this year. The neighboring—but much smaller—Macomb County Girl Scout Council stayed at $2.50 a box, setting the stage for a marketing battle. However, most of the troops in this skirmish are not Scouts: they are grown-ups who peddle the cookies at work. Such scenarios have been repeated in other parts of the country, as many of the nation's 330 Girl

Scout councils go through their annual pricing debate. Why don't the councils simply agree on one national price? Because antitrust laws prohibit price-fixing.[1] ■

Competition is an essential element of the American economic system. Antitrust laws are the rules that govern that competition. As this chapter opening illustrates, these laws affect many aspects of our lives—both as consumers and as businesspeople.

IN THE BEGINNING

Throughout much of the nineteenth century, competition in America was largely a local affair. The country was so big and transportation so poor that companies primarily competed in small local markets. It was too costly to transport goods great distances. State laws rather than national statutes regulated competition.

By the second half of the nineteenth century, four railroad lines crossed the continent from coast to coast. For the first time, national markets were a real possibility. John D. Rockefeller saw the potential. In 1859, Edwin L. Drake, a retired railroad conductor, drilled the first commercially successful oil well in the United States. Three years later, when the 23-year-old Rockefeller entered the scene, the oil industry was full of producers too small to benefit from economies of scale. Production was inefficient, and prices varied dramatically in different parts of the country.

Rockefeller set out to reorganize the industry. He began by buying refineries, first in Cleveland and then in other cities. He and his partners spread into all segments of the oil industry—buying oil fields, building pipelines, and establishing an efficient marketing system. To unify the management of these companies, they transferred their stock to the Standard Oil Trust. By 1870, Rockefeller had achieved his goal—the Standard Oil Trust controlled virtually all the oil in the country, from producer to consumer. Rockefeller was the wealthiest person in the world.

Some of Rockefeller's tactics were controversial. When a competitor tried to build an oil pipeline, Rockefeller used every weapon short of violence to stop it. He planted stories in the press suggesting the pipes would leak and ruin nearby fields. He flooded local builders with orders for tank cars so no workers would be available to build the pipeline. When the pipeline was finished, he refused to allow his oil to flow through it. These tactics were frightening, especially in an industry as important as oil. What if Rockefeller decided to raise prices unfairly? Or cut off oil altogether? Newspapers began to attack him ferociously.

Sherman Act

With the coming of the railroads, it became clear that large companies might be able to control other industries as well. To prevent extreme concentrations of economic power, Congress passed the **Sherman Act** in 1890. It was one of the first national laws

---

[1] Rebecca Blumenstein, "Cookie Price War Sends Adult Troops into Marketing Battle," *Wall Street Journal,* Mar. 8, 1996, p. A1. Republished with permission of The Wall Street Journal; permission conveyed through the Copyright Clearance Center, Inc.

designed to regulate competition. Because this statute was aimed at the Standard Oil Trust and other similar organizations, it was termed **antitrust** legislation. In 1892, the Ohio Supreme Court dissolved the Standard Oil Trust, which was replaced by the Standard Oil Co. But the government was not satisfied until a spring day in 1911, when Supreme Court Chief Justice Edward White quietly read aloud his dramatic 20,000-word opinion ordering the breakup of Standard Oil.[2] The 33 companies that made up Standard Oil were forced to compete as separate businesses. Today, descendants of Standard Oil include Amoco, Atlantic Richfield, Chevron, ExxonMobil, and Pennzoil. Imagine what kind of giant they would be if still united.

For the first 70 or so years after the passage of the Sherman Act, most scholars and judges took the view that large concentrations of economic power were suspect, even if they had no obvious impact on competition itself. Big was bad. Big meant too much economic and political power. As Senator John Sherman, sponsor of the Sherman Act, put it, a nation that "would not submit to an emperor should not submit to an autocrat of trade." Fragmented, competitive markets were desirable in and of themselves. Standard Oil should not control the oil markets, even if the company was very efficient and had gained control by completely acceptable methods.

Chicago School

Beginning in the 1960s and 1970s, however, a group of influential economists and lawyers at the University of Chicago began to argue that the goal of antitrust enforcement should be *efficiency*. Let a company grow as large as it likes provided that this growth is based on a superior product or lower costs, not ruthless tactics. Insist on a clean fight, but do not handicap large successful companies to help weaker competitors. Some companies will thrive, others will die, but in either case, the consumer will come out ahead. Adherents of the **Chicago School** argued further that the market should decide the most efficient size for each industry. In some cases, such as automobiles or aircrafts, the most efficient size might be very large indeed. Under traditional antitrust analysis, courts often asked, "Has a competitor been harmed?" The Chicago School suggests that courts should ask instead, "Has *competition* been harmed?"

At the turn of the twentieth century, President Theodore Roosevelt personally plotted the breakup of Standard Oil. (As one of Rockefeller's compatriots said of Roosevelt, "We bought the son of a bitch, and then he didn't stay bought.") At the turn of the twenty-first century, two descendants of Standard Oil—Exxon and Mobil—announced their intention to merge. This time, not one politician so much as grabbed a microphone to object to the recombination. Where once size alone was cause for concern, now regulators believe that a certain bulk may be necessary if American companies are to compete in the intense global economy.

Antitrust policy, however, continues to evolve. Adherents of the so-called **Post Chicago School** are beginning to recognize that competition alone may not be enough to protect consumers. For example, an industry with a large number of competitors may foster collusion, not competition. Or, activities that appear consumer-friendly, such as giving a product away for free, may in the long run harm consumers. (Take, for example, Microsoft's decision to give away its Internet browser. Although consumers benefited in the short run, the Justice Department alleged that this giveaway harmed consumers by driving competitors out of business.) Now, when deciding

---

2   *Standard Oil Company of New Jersey v. United States*, 221 U.S. 1, 31 S. Ct. 502, 1911 U.S. LEXIS 1725 (1911).

whether to take action, federal trustbusters are beginning to focus directly on consumers, asking two questions: Will this action cause consumers to pay higher prices? Are the higher prices sustainable in the face of existing competition? As you read the cases in this chapter, think about which factors the court considered important: size, competition, or the impact on consumers.

It is worth noting that throughout the twentieth century, the United States had stricter antitrust laws than most other countries. Indeed, our markets are more competitive than most. No matter what standard of law the government has applied, it has managed to prevent the worst competitive abuses.

OVERVIEW OF ANTITRUST LAWS

The major provisions of the antitrust laws are:

- Section 1 of the Sherman Act prohibits all agreements "in restraint of trade."
- Section 2 of the Sherman Act bans "monopolization"—the wrongful acquisition of a monopoly.
- The Clayton Act prohibits anticompetitive mergers, tying arrangements, and exclusive dealing agreements.
- The Robinson-Patman Act bans price discrimination that reduces competition.

The full text of the antitrust statutes is available at **http://www.antitrustinstitute.org/links/codes.cfm**.

In 1914, Congress passed the **Clayton Act** in part because the courts were not enforcing the Sherman Act as strictly as it had intended. The purpose of the Clayton Act was to clarify the earlier statute. As a result, the two laws overlap significantly. The **Robinson-Patman Act** (passed in 1936) is an amendment to the Clayton Act. Rather than systematically reviewing the terms of each statute in order, this chapter focuses instead on the *kinds of behavior* that the antitrust laws regulate.

Violations of the antitrust laws are divided into two categories: *per se* and **rule of reason.** As the name implies, *per se* violations are automatic. Defendants charged with this type of violation cannot defend themselves by saying, "But the impact wasn't so bad" or "No one was hurt." The court will not listen to excuses, and the defendants are subject to both *criminal* and *civil* penalties. Typically, the Justice Department has sought criminal sanctions only against *per se* violators.

Rule of reason violations, on the other hand, are illegal only if they have an anticompetitive impact. To determine if an activity is an unreasonable restraint of trade, the courts consider its circumstances, intent, and impact. For example, if competitors join together and agree that they will not deal with a particular supplier, their action is illegal only if it harms competition. Although rule of reason violators may be subject to civil penalties or private lawsuits, traditionally the Justice Department has not sought criminal penalties against them.

Both the Justice Department and the Federal Trade Commission (FTC) have authority to enforce the antitrust laws. However, only the Justice Department can bring criminal proceedings; the FTC is limited to civil injunctions and other administrative remedies. In addition to the government, anyone injured by an antitrust violation has the right to sue for damages. The United States is unusual in this regard—in most other countries, only the government is able to sue antitrust violators. A successful plaintiff can recover treble (that is, triple) damages from the defendant.

In developing a competitive strategy, managers typically consider two different approaches:

- Cooperative strategies that allow companies to work together to their mutual advantage
- Aggressive strategies, designed to create an advantage over competitors

COOPERATIVE STRATEGIES

Three types of cooperative strategies are potentially illegal:

- **Horizontal agreements** among competitors. An agreement between Levi Strauss and Wrangler—both manufacturers of denim jeans—would be a horizontal agreement.

- **Vertical agreements** among participants at different stages of the production process. An agreement between Levi Strauss and Macy's—one company makes jeans, the other sells them—would be a vertical agreement.

- **Mergers and joint ventures** among competitors. Here, companies go beyond simple agreements to combine forces more permanently.

The following table lists the cooperative strategies that will be discussed in this chapter:

Horizontal Strategies	Vertical Strategies	Mergers
Market division	Reciprocal dealing	Horizontal mergers
Price-fixing	Price discrimination	Vertical mergers
Bid-rigging		Joint ventures
Refusal to deal		

Horizontal Cooperative Strategies

Although the term "cooperative strategies" *sounds* benign, these tactics are often harmful to competition. Many horizontal cooperative strategies are *per se* violations of the law and can lead to prison terms, heavy fines, and expensive lawsuits with customers and competitors.

Market Division

Any effort by a group of competitors to divide its market is a *per se* violation of §1 of the Sherman Act. Illegal arrangements include agreements to allocate customers, territory, or products. For example, these business schools would be in violation if:

- Georgetown agreed to accept only men and, in return, George Washington would take only women[3]

---

[3]   This, of course, does not mean that all single-sex schools are violating the antitrust laws. They are in violation only if their admissions policy results from an agreement with competitors.

- Stanford agreed to accept only students from west of the Mississippi, leaving the east to Yale, or

- Northwestern agreed not to provide courses in entrepreneurship, while the University of Chicago eliminated its international offerings.

Price-Fixing and Bid-Rigging

When competitors agree on the prices at which they will buy or sell products or services, their price-fixing is a *per se* violation of §1 of the Sherman Act. Bid-rigging is also a *per se* violation. In bid-rigging, competitors eliminate price competition by agreeing on who will submit the lowest bid. In an early case, the defendants argued that price-fixing was only wrong if the prices were *unfair.* The Supreme Court disagreed. In its view, prices should be set by markets, not by competitors—or judges. Moreover, "The reasonable price fixed today may through economic and business changes become the unreasonable price of tomorrow."[4]

For the better part of a century, price-fixing and bid-rigging have been illegal, yet they never seem to go away. Here are some examples:

- *Dairy Industry.* Using a computer to analyze the bids that schools received on their milk contracts, the Florida Attorney General uncovered a pervasive price-fixing scheme. By some estimates, price-fixing raised milk prices in Florida by 14 percent. Forty-three companies were convicted or pleaded guilty; two dozen individuals went to prison. Companies paid fines in excess of $90 million.

- *College Athletics.* Colleges were concerned about the cost of their athletic programs. In particular, the cost of the coaching staffs seemed out of control. Some assistant coaches were being paid as much as $70,000 a year. In response, NCAA schools (that is, members of the National Collegiate Athletic Association) agreed to cap the salaries of assistant coaches at (a very stingy) $12,000. But a court blew the whistle, finding that the NCAA had engaged in illegal price-fixing. A jury awarded the coaches $66 million.

The following article discusses the Justice Department's successful strategy for ensnaring price-fixers.

NEWS*worthy*

Meeting clandestinely at an airport hotel outside London, top executives from the leading makers of a crucial raw material for forging steel reached an agreement to fix global prices. The executives were from France, Germany, Japan, and the United States. But the cartel began to unravel after a steel maker complained to federal investigators about the lack of competition. The U.S. government filed suit and ultimately obtained corporate fines in the case of $437 million. Two executives pleaded guilty, paid large fines, and received prison sentences.

The antitrust division, once a small and sleepy backwater of the Justice Department, has become a power center against white-collar crime. All told, the antitrust division has won fines—corporate and individual—of more than $1.7 billion in the last four years. No one doubts that the global price-fixing collusions it has exposed affected every American consumer. These collusions have raised prices for gasoline, vitamins, soft drinks, and other food products.

The recent takeoff in investigations and prosecutions is a result of a new Justice Department policy that made amnesty automatic if the company came in before an investigation began and permitted broad amnesty afterward to the first company to offer assistance. It also covered all executives from that company who cooperated, a significant inducement

---

[4] *United States v. Trenton Potteries Co.,* 273 U.S. 392, 397, 1927 U.S. LEXIS 975 (1927).

because violations of the Sherman Act carry a potential prison sentence of three years for every count, in addition to virtually limitless fines. Almost immediately, the change could be seen in the quantity and quality of tips coming to prosecutors. Before the new rule, the division reported an average of one amnesty request a year. Since the change, it is one a month.[5] ◆

As this Newsworthy feature indicates, the Justice Department sometimes finds a smoking gun. But what if there is no obvious weapon, only circumstantial evidence? Suppose competitors just happen to charge the same prices. Is that practice illegal? The following case discusses the legality of so-called *conscious parallelism*.

FEARS V. WILHELMINA MODEL AGENCY, INC.

2004 U.S. Dist. LEXIS 4502
United States District Court for the Southern District of New York, 2004

Facts: A group of models sued some of the top agencies in New York, alleging that these firms had violated §1 of the Sherman Act by conspiring to fix the commissions that they charged the models for placing them. The agencies were all members of the International Model Managers Association, Inc. (IMMA).

Under New York law, *employment* agencies could not charge a commission of more than 10 percent, but *management* agencies could. All agencies that were members of IMMA changed their state registration from employment agency to management agency and then raised their standard commission to 20 percent. Several of the agencies used identical language in their contracts, specifying that they were personal managers, not employment agencies. At IMMA meetings, executives at various agencies announced that they were raising their commissions to 20 percent. One executive stated, "We are all committing suicide, if we do not stick together. . ."

During depositions, executives at the agencies admitted that they knew instantly every time an agency raised prices. One executive stated, "the more uniformity in the prices, the more I think it was—it was something that you could then compete on the quality of your models on the service, and not just on—on rates, you know. So we were always favorable to letting everyone know as much as possible about—about our pricing policies."

The models also presented memoranda from the agencies, stating:

- "IMMA should send out a letter stating that we plan on pursuing a 1½ percent finance charge on clients who pay after 30 days in lieu of increasing our service charge."

- The commission would increase from 15 to 20 percent, and "all other agencies will go along with this increase. Please inform your clients accordingly so that there is no misunderstanding."

- "Pauline's agreed with me but as usual, Bill Weinberg cautioned me about price fixing. . .Ha! Ha! Ha! . . . the usual bulls–t! I warned him that by not sticking together, we would have to make 40 percent more volume in order to make the same figures as last year, but

Michele Weweje's agency violated the rules—but were the rules legal?

---

[5] Stephen Labaton, "The World Gets Tough on Fixing Prices," *New York Times*, June 3, 2001, §3, p. 1. Copyright © 2001 by The New York Times Co. Reprinted by permission.

you know Bill, he always thinks he can get more if he acts that way."

IMMA minutes reported that members had adopted uniform schedules for the Christmas holiday. In addition, the agencies agreed to operate "ethically," by which they meant that they would not try to hire models from other agencies. A letter to all members of IMMA reported that one agency had broken this rule by hiring model Michele Weweje.

The agencies admitted that they had engaged in parallel behavior but they argued that these activities were not sufficient to support a charge of illegal price-fixing. The agencies moved for summary judgment.

Issues: Did the modeling agencies engage in illegal price-fixing? Is parallel behavior illegal?

Excerpts from Judge Baer's Decision: To be sure, business behavior is admissible circumstantial evidence from which the fact finder may infer agreement. But this Court has never held that proof of parallel business behavior conclusively establishes agreement or, phrased differently, that such behavior itself constitutes a Sherman Act offense. Because parallel activity may be equally suggestive of independent conduct, plaintiffs offering parallel conduct as evidence of an antitrust conspiracy must demonstrate additional circumstances, often referred to as "plus factors," which provide a supplemental basis to infer a conspiracy. Among recognized plus factors, two in particular have received significant exposure in case law, both of which have a strong presence in this case—a motive to conspire and a high level of inter-firm communication.

With regard to the first plus factor, there is no question that defendants possessed a common rational motive to conspire—the ability to raise models' commissions without suffering loss of business. While I agree with defendants that the majority of this evidence more directly demonstrates agreement on elements other than models' commissions, I do not agree that, as a result, such evidence is irrelevant. Rather, I find that the extensive evidence of agreements between IMMA members, on various components of their businesses, such as client service fees, holiday closing schedules, cancellation policies, and penalties borne by management companies who attract models from competitors, may reasonably be inferred to demonstrate an industry inundated with collusion.

Plaintiffs have established that all defendants who were members of IMMA, and therefore participated in or were privy to the conversations and agreements discussed above, had a unity of purpose or a common design and understanding, or a meeting of minds in an unlawful arrangement. [Therefore, the court denies the agencies' motion for summary judgment.] ■

Refusals to Deal

Every company generally has the right to decide with whom it will or will not do business. **However, a refusal to deal is a rule of reason violation of the Sherman Act, illegal if it harms competition.** In a **refusal to deal,** a group of competitors boycotts a buyer, supplier, or even another competitor. For example, a group of clothing manufacturers agreed that they would not sell apparel to retailers who also bought from style pirates—companies that copied the manufacturers' designs. The Supreme Court held that this was an illegal refusal to deal because it was harming competition.[6]

Vertical Cooperative Strategies

Vertical cooperative strategies are agreements among participants at different stages of the production process.

---

6 *Fashion Originators' Guild of America, Inc. v. Federal Trade Commission,* 312 U.S. 457, 61 S. Ct. 703, 1941 U.S. LEXIS 1318 (1941).

Reciprocal Dealing Agreements

Under a reciprocal dealing agreement, a buyer refuses to purchase goods from a supplier unless the supplier also purchases items from the buyer. Imagine that you are in the business of processing beets into sugar. During this process, it is easy to separate the seeds, which can then be used to grow more beets. Why not suggest to your beet suppliers that they buy their seeds from you? Why not further suggest that if *they* are not willing, you will find other suppliers who are?[7]

You are proposing a reciprocal dealing agreement. In the past, such arrangements were common. Many major corporations even kept computer records of purchases, sales, and "balance of trade" with other companies. Although these arrangements might have made *business* sense, the government took the view that they were also *rule of reason* violations of the Sherman Act; that is, they were illegal if they had an anticompetitive effect. The government brought suit against several companies, including a beet processor. It also halted a number of mergers that might have resulted in internal reciprocal arrangements. In recent years, however, the government has brought few of these cases. Reciprocal dealing agreements are likely to be a problem now only if they foreclose a *significant share* of the market and if the participants *agree* not to buy from others.

Price Discrimination

Under the Robinson-Patman Act, it is illegal to charge different prices to different purchasers if:

- The items are the same, and
- The price discrimination lessens competition.

However, it is legal to charge a lower price to a particular buyer if:

- The costs of serving this buyer are lower, or
- The seller is simply meeting competition.

Congress passed the Robinson-Patman Act (RPA) in 1936 to prevent large chains from driving small, local stores out of business. Owners of these "Ma and Pa stores" complained that the large chains could sell goods cheaper because suppliers charged them lower prices. As a result of the RPA, managers who would otherwise like to develop different pricing strategies for specific customers or regions may hesitate to do so for fear of violating this statute. In reality, however, they have little to fear.

Under the RPA, a plaintiff must prove that price discrimination occurred and that it lessened competition. It is now perfectly permissible, for example, for a supplier to sell at a different price to its Texas and California distributors, or to its health care and educational distributors, as long as the distributors are not in competition with each other.

The RPA also expressly permits price variations that are based on differences in cost. Thus Kosmo's Kitchen would be perfectly within its legal rights to sell its frozen cheese enchiladas to Giant at a lower price than to Corner Grocery if Kosmo's costs are lower to do so. Giant often buys shipments the size of railroad containers that cost less to deliver than smaller boxes.

During the last decade, the federal government has dramatically reduced its enforcement of the RPA. Some federal officials have even urged that the RPA be repealed to prevent it from interfering with the smooth operation of the market. This fade-out of government action has left enforcement in the hands of individual plaintiffs, but these cases are receiving little encouragement from the courts.

---

[7]   See *Betaseed, Inc. v. U & I, Inc.*, 681 F.2d 1203, 1982 U.S. App. LEXIS 17190 (9th Cir. 1982).

The Supreme Court has, for instance, made it much more difficult for plaintiffs to win damages in price discrimination cases. Chrysler Motors charged the J. Truett Payne dealership more than other car dealers in Birmingham, Alabama. Unable to compete, Payne went out of business. The accepted formula for determining damages in a Robinson-Patman Act case *had been* the difference between the two prices multiplied by the number of units purchased. These numbers were easy to calculate. However, in *Payne*, the Supreme Court held that it is not enough to prove that competitors are able to buy at a lower cost. The plaintiff must also show that these competitors passed their savings on to customers and, as a result, plaintiff lost profits.[8] These are difficult facts to prove. As a result of cases such as this, antitrust lawyers sometimes advise their clients not to worry too much about price discrimination suits because dissatisfied customers will usually not seek damages in court but will instead try to negotiate a better price.

Mergers and Joint Ventures

The Clayton Act prohibits mergers that are anticompetitive. Companies with substantial assets must notify the FTC *before* consummating a merger.[9] This notification gives the government an opportunity to prevent a merger ahead of time, rather than trying to untangle one after the fact.

Horizontal Mergers

A horizontal merger involves companies that compete in the same market. Traditionally, the government has aggressively sought to prevent horizontal mergers that could lead to a monopoly or even a highly concentrated industry. In the *Von's Grocery* case, decided in 1966, the Supreme Court upheld the Justice Department in its suit to prevent the merger of two grocery chains that represented only 7.5 percent of the grocery market in Los Angeles.[10] Compare that decision with the following case, decided almost 20 years later.

UNITED STATES V. WASTE MANAGEMENT, INC.

743 F.2d 976, 1984 U.S. App. LEXIS 18843
United States Court of Appeals for the Second Circuit, 1984

Facts: Waste Management, Inc. (WMI), acquired Texas Industrial Disposal, Inc. (TIDI). Both companies were in the trash collection business. In Dallas, their combined market share was 48.8 percent. The trial court held that the merger was illegal and ordered WMI to divest itself of TIDI.

Issue: Did WMI violate the Clayton Act by acquiring TIDI?

Excerpts from Judge Winter's Decision: A post-merger market share of 48.8 percent is sufficient to establish *prima facie* illegality under *United States v. Philadelphia National Bank* and its progeny. That decision held that large market shares are a convenient

▼

---

[8] *J. Truett Payne Co., Inc. v. Chrysler Motors Corp.,* 451 U.S. 557, 101 S. Ct. 1923, 1981 U.S. LEXIS 49 (1981).

[9] If, for example, the acquiring company is purchasing stock or assets of the acquired company that is worth more than $212 million (adjusted annually for inflation).

[10] *United States v. Von's Grocery Co.,* 384 U.S. 270, 86 S. Ct. 1478, 1966 U.S. LEXIS 2823 (1966).

proxy for appraising the danger of monopoly power resulting from a horizontal merger. Under its rationale, a merger resulting in a large market share is presumptively illegal, rebuttable only by a demonstration that the merger will not have anticompetitive effects.

[In the present case, the *Philadelphia National Bank*] presumption is rebutted by the fact that competitors can enter the Dallas waste hauling market with such ease. WMI argues that it is unable to raise prices over the competitive level because new firms would quickly enter the market and undercut them. A person wanting to start in the trash collection business can acquire a truck, a few containers, drive the truck himself, and operate out of his home. A

great deal depends on the individual's personal initiative, and whether he has the desire and energy to perform a high quality of service. If he measures up well by these standards, he can compete successfully with any other company for a portion of the trade, even though a small portion. Over the last 10 years or so a number of companies have started in the commercial trash collection business.

We conclude that the 48.8 percent market share attributed to WMI does not accurately reflect future market power. Since that power is in fact insubstantial, the merger does not, therefore, substantially lessen competition in the relevant market and does not violate the [Clayton Act]. ■

Traditionally, market share was the most important factor in evaluating mergers. As *Waste Management* indicates, however, market share is no longer the sole issue in merger cases. The government and the courts now also consider how the merger will affect competition and consumers. Thus the government cleared a merger between aircraft giants Boeing and McDonnell Douglas, which together had a virtual monopoly on the American aircraft business. But the aircraft market is global, and American companies faced severe competition from Europe's Airbus consortium. Therefore, the government believed that the merger would not harm competition.

Conversely, the FTC blocked the merger of office supply giants, Staples, Inc., and Office Depot. Nationally, these two retailers controlled only 4 percent of the market for office supplies. Was the FTC harking back to the days of *Von's Grocery*? Not exactly. The office superstores' *national* market share was relatively low because they had no stores at all in many areas of the country. Rather than national market share, the FTC focused instead on their ability to control prices locally. The agency found that, when both stores operated in the same market, prices were significantly lower than when only one store was present. Thus a box of file folders cost $1.72 in Orlando, Florida (where both stores competed), and $4.17 in nearby Leesburg (where Office Depot had a monopoly). In the FTC's view, if the two stores combined, they would have had enough power in local markets to raise prices and harm consumers.

FTC merger guidelines are available at **http://www.ftc.gov/bc/docs/horizmer.htm**. As the following article illustrates, antitrust enforcement is a worldwide issue.

NEWS*worthy*

The United States has always felt perfectly comfortable enforcing its antitrust laws overseas, as long as the activity had some impact within its borders. (Remember the article earlier about the price-fixing charges against foreign companies.) Now the gavel is in the other hand: the European Union scuttled a proposed merger between General Electric and Honeywell International—a marriage between two American companies that had already been approved in Washington. More trouble may be ahead because Europe and the United States each applies a different standard when evaluating mergers. The European Commission considers whether a merger would create or strengthen a *dominant position*. The commission reasoned that since GE makes jet engines and Honeywell manufactures avionics equipment, this portfolio of products together might make them more dominant. To U.S. authorities, the important issue was whether the merger would reduce competition or harm consumers. ◆

Vertical Mergers

A vertical merger involves companies at different stages of the production process—for example, when a producer of a final good acquires a supplier or vice versa. Vertical mergers can also be anticompetitive, especially if they reduce entry into a market by locking up an important supplier or a top distributor. Consider the following example.

NEWSworthy

International Management Group (IMG) is a management conglomerate that dominates the tennis world. IMG operates tournaments, sets up exhibitions, holds broadcast rights, and manages the careers of more than 100 pros. IMG even acquired the Nick Bolletieri Tennis Academy, training ground for many of the sport's present and future stars. IMG's competitors questioned whether this acquisition violated the antitrust laws. Says the head coach of another tennis academy, "You name it, IMG owns it, owns tournaments, owns the players, owns the academy. It's impossible to compete at that level, so we don't even bother to try.[11] ◆

IMG's acquisition of the Nick Bolletieri Tennis Academy was a vertical merger—IMG acquired a source of supply for its management group. The Justice Department has not been overly concerned about vertical mergers. The department's guidelines provide that it will challenge vertical mergers only if they are likely to increase entry barriers in a concentrated market.

Joint Ventures

A joint venture is a partnership for a limited purpose—the companies do not combine permanently, they simply work together on a specific project. The government will usually permit a joint venture, even between competitors with significant market power. The FTC approved, over strenuous objections from competitors, a joint venture between General Motors and Toyota to produce cars.

AGGRESSIVE STRATEGIES

The goal of an aggressive strategy is to gain an unfair advantage over competitors.

Monopolization

Aggressive competition is beneficial for consumers—up until the moment a company develops enough power to control a market. One purpose of the Sherman Act is to prevent this type of control. **Under §2 of the act, it is illegal to monopolize or attempt to monopolize a market.** To monopolize means to acquire a monopoly in the wrong way. *Having* a monopoly is legal unless it is *gained* or *maintained* by using wrongful tactics.

ECONOMICS
& the LAW

What is so bad about a monopoly? Imagine, for example, that you owned the only movie theater in town. Although the price of movie tickets in other towns is $10, you are able to charge $20 or maybe even $30 (for *Star Wars*, Part XVII). Although fewer customers might buy tickets at this expensive price, your profits are still higher because you earn so much

---

[11]   Robin Finn, "Mixed Doubles: Players as Business," *New York Times*, Mar. 16, 1994, p. B17.

on each ticket. There are two things wrong with this picture: fewer people are able to afford the movies and, when they do attend, they have less choice about what to see. The owner of the only theater in town might not be in tune with the tastes of his audiences. Economists believe that it is harmful for the movie theater to have many buyers while the customers have only one seller. ◆

To determine if a defendant has illegally monopolized, we must ask three questions:

- **What is the market?** Without knowing the market, it is impossible to determine if someone is controlling it.
- **Does the company control the market?** Without control, there is no monopoly.
- **How did the company acquire or maintain its control?** Monopolization is illegal only if gained or kept in the wrong way.

What Is the Market?

This question is not as easy to answer as it sounds. Some people refer to the antitrust laws as the "Economists' Full-Employment Acts" because antitrust litigation requires detailed testimony from economic experts.

Imagine that your company sells soft drinks with unusual food flavors—steak and cheese, among others. For some reason, you are the only company that sells food-flavored soft drinks so, by definition, you control 100 percent of the market. But is that the *relevant* market? Perhaps the relevant market is flavored drinks or soft drinks or all beverages. The question economists ask is: **How high can your prices rise before your buyers will switch to a different product?** If a price rise from $1.00 to $1.05 a bottle causes many of your customers to desert to Snapple or Coke, it is clear you are part of a larger market. Moreover, if changes in the prices of other drinks affect *your* sales, your products and theirs are probably close competitors. However, if you could raise your price to $5.00 per bottle and still hold on to many of your customers, then you might well be in your own market.

The following case illustrates the importance of market definition in an antitrust case. What is the relevant market in this case?

CUPP V. ALBERTO-CULVER USA, INC.

310 F. Supp. 2d 963, 2004 U.S. Dist. LEXIS 5244
United States District Court for the Western District of Tennessee, 2004

Facts: Billy Cupp and his wife, Cathy R. Craig, owned and operated the Looks hair salon in Cordova, Tennessee, a suburb of Memphis. The salon used hair care products that were sold only to salons, not to consumers. It bought Paul Mitchell products from Heil Beauty Systems (Heil) and Redken products from Arnold's, Inc. (Arnold's).

Beauty Systems Group, Inc. (BSG) purchased both Heil and Arnold's. Without warning, it stopped all product deliveries to Cupp and Craig unless they would agree to sign a distribution agreement. The agreement included restrictions on where the products could be used and how they could be resold. It also prohibited purchasers from changing product tracking codes. Cupp and Craig refused to sign the agreement, so BSG stopped supplying them. The salon lost customers as a result.

Cupp and Craig filed sued against BSG, alleging that it had monopolized the market in violation of §2 of the Sherman Act. The defendant filed a motion to dismiss.

Issue: Did BSG engage in illegal monopolization?

Excerpts from Judge Donald's Decision: A plaintiff must first define the relevant market in order to state a claim under the antitrust statutes. Determining the relevant market enables the court to assess whether the defendant has monopoly power in that market, what the area of competition is, and whether the allegedly unlawful acts have anticompetitive effects in that market. The relevant market analysis includes both a product market and a geographic market.

The essential test for ascertaining the relevant product market involves the identification of those products or services that are either (1) identical to or (2) available substitutes for the defendant's product or service. Reasonable interchangeability may be gauged by (1) the product uses, i.e., whether the substitute products or services can perform the same function, and/or (2) consumer response (cross-elasticity); that is, consumer sensitivity to price levels at which they elect substitutes for the defendant's product or service. Unless a product is completely unique or exceptional market conditions exist, one brand in a market of competing brands may not constitute the relevant market.

The court determines the geographic market by assessing the market area in which the seller operates and to which the buyer can practically turn for supplies. Plaintiff neglects entirely to define a geographic market. In the complaint, Plaintiff simultaneously mentions, without elaboration, both Defendants' international reach and its own inability to obtain Redken and Paul Mitchell products in the Memphis, Tennessee, area. Similarly, Plaintiff states both that SBC [BSG's parent corporation] is the "largest marketer of professional beauty care products in the world" and that BSG sells beauty products in "exclusive geographic territories," which Plaintiff leaves unspecified. The disconnect between a strictly local or exclusive geographic area and Defendants' global reach leaves the Court without any ability to formulate a relevant geographic market.

Furthermore, Plaintiff's attempted definition of the relevant product market is insufficient and fatally vague. In the complaint, Plaintiff refers to the relevant product market as "exclusive salon hair care products . . . those sold exclusively through salons under the advice of professional hair stylists." First, Plaintiff offered no allegation of which hair care product brands are interchangeable with Defendants' products. From the face of the complaint, it is clear that many brands and suppliers of hair care products exist. Defendants themselves manufacture or distribute several product lines other than those purchased by Plaintiff or distributed by BSG. Plaintiff even names one other distributor of hair care products in the Memphis area, which carried Redken products. The Court would be skeptical of any claim that such other hair care products are not reasonably interchangeable with Defendants' products, given the conformity of uses among hair care products, or that other, unnamed distributors could not supply those other hair care products in suitable amounts for Plaintiff's use.

Without a more specific definition and accounting of the brands and suppliers to be included in the relevant market, the Court cannot determine the boundaries of the market. It is thus unable to assess Defendants' market power, which is one of the purposes of defining a relevant market.

Second, the Court is unsure why the product market should be limited only to those hair care products sold in salons. The interchangeability among retail and salon products of this type seems high, particularly given that the price of hair care products retailed directly to consumers is generally lower than those retailed through salons, thus providing readily available substitutes.

Third, the description "hair care products" is itself so vague that it leaves the Court at a loss as to what sorts of products to include. [T]hose products could include shampoos, cosmetics, hair rinses, styling aids, or something more. Each category considered could expand the relevant market further, and Plaintiff's allegations do not indicate how broad the category is.

The Court therefore *grants* Defendants' motion to dismiss. ∎

Does the Company Control the Market?

You have 100 percent of the food-flavored soft drink market (although only 1 percent of the overall soft drink market and an infinitesimal percentage of the total beverage market). Traditionally, courts considered a share anywhere between 70 and 90 percent to constitute a monopoly. However, under modern antitrust law, market share is not important if other competitors can enter the market anytime they want (or anytime you raise your prices or lower your quality). **No matter what your market share, you do not have a monopoly unless you can exclude competitors or control prices.** For example, the Justice Department sued a movie theatre chain that possessed a 93 percent share of the box office in Las Vegas. But the court ruled against the Justice Department because the chain's market share decreased to 75 percent within three years. This decline indicated that the company did not control the market and that barriers to entry were low.[12]

How Did the Company Acquire or Maintain Its Control?

Possessing a monopoly is not necessarily illegal; using *"bad acts"* to acquire or maintain one is. If the law prohibited the mere possession of a monopoly, it might discourage companies from producing excellent products or offering low prices. Anyone who can produce a better product cheaper is entitled to a monopoly. In your case, you have very cleverly developed a secret method for adding flavors to carbonated water. You also have an efficient factory and highly trained workers, so you can sell your drinks for 5¢ a bottle less than your competitors. If, in fact, you do have a monopoly, it is for all the right reasons. You have demonstrated exactly the kind of innovative, efficient behavior that benefits consumers. If you were sued for a violation of the antitrust laws, you would win.

Some companies use ruthless tactics to acquire or maintain a monopoly. It is these "bad acts" that render a monopoly illegal. In the past, the definition of bad acts was broad, and any company with a monopoly could be in violation unless it showed that, despite its best efforts to duck, a monopoly had been *thrust upon* it. In 1945, a famous judge, with the appropriate name of Learned Hand, found that Alcoa's monopoly in the aluminum industry was illegal because the company had repeatedly expanded capacity to anticipate demand.[13] In his view, the company should have waited to expand until demand actually existed. Alcoa was in violation because it could have easily *avoided* a monopoly—the monopoly had not been thrust upon it.

Everyone makes mistakes. Although Learned Hand is generally considered one of the greatest judges of his era, most commentators now believe that Alcoa was wrongly decided. *Berkey Photo* is a more typical modern case.[14] Berkey accused Eastman Kodak Co. of repeatedly and unnecessarily changing the size of its cameras to confound competitors who manufactured film to fit them. Although Learned Hand most likely would have found such actions to be illegal, the *Berkey* court rejected the view that monopolies are acceptable only if *thrust upon* the defendant and instead held that aggressive competitive strategies are legal even if they have the effect of hindering competitors. In finding Kodak not liable, the court reasoned that the company would not have repeatedly changed camera and film specifications if consumers had objected. The success or failure of Kodak's strategy ought to be determined in the market and not by the courts.

---

[12] *United States v. Syufy Enterprises*, 903 F.2d 659, 1990 U.S. App. LEXIS 7396 (9th Cir. 1990).

[13] *United States v. Aluminum Co. of America*, 148 F.2d 416, 1945 U.S. App. LEXIS 4091 (2d Cir. 1945). Judge Hand's parents did not necessarily foresee his illustrious career when naming him. "Learned" was his mother's maiden name, and it was the tradition in his family to give the mother's name to one of the children.

[14] *Berkey Photo, Inc. v. Eastman Kodak Co.*, 603 F.2d 263, 1979 U.S. App. LEXIS 13692 (2d Cir. 1979), cert. denied, 444 U.S. 1093, 1980 U.S. LEXIS 923 (1980).

Predatory Pricing

Predatory pricing occurs when a company lowers its prices below cost to drive competitors out of business. Once the predator has the market to itself, it raises prices to make up lost profits—and more besides.

Recall that, under §2 of the Sherman Act, it is illegal "to monopolize" and also to "attempt to monopolize." Typically, the goal of a predatory pricing scheme is either to win control of a market or to maintain it. A ban on these schemes prevents monopolization and attempts to monopolize. To win a predatory pricing case, the plaintiff must prove three elements:

- The defendant is selling its products *below cost.*

- The defendant *intends* that the plaintiff go out of business.

- If the plaintiff does go out of business, the defendant will be able to earn sufficient profits to *recoup* its prior losses.

The classic example of predatory pricing is a large grocery store that comes into a small town offering exceptionally low prices subsidized by profits from its other branches. Once all the "Ma and Pa" corner groceries go out of business, MegaGrocery raises its prices to much higher levels.

Predatory pricing offers a good example of how attitudes toward antitrust laws have changed. Formerly, courts took predatory pricing very seriously. The term certainly *sounds* bad. But despite its name, courts generally are not as concerned about predatory pricing now as they used to be. For one thing, consumers benefit from price wars, at least in the short run. For another, the cases are hard to prove. Here is why:

- **The defendant is selling its products below cost.** This rule sounds sensible, but what does "cost" mean? As you know from your economics courses, there are many different kinds of costs—total, average variable, marginal, to name a few. Under current law, any price below *average variable cost* is generally presumed to be predatory.[15] The rule may be easy to state, but, in real life, average variable cost is difficult to calculate. First, plaintiffs must obtain most of the data from the defendant. Even if a defendant has a good idea of what its average variable costs are, it will not willingly tell all in court. Moreover, many of the economic decisions about what items fit into which cost category are subjective. It is difficult for the plaintiff to prove that its subjective view is closer to the truth than the defendant's.

- **The defendant intends that the plaintiff go out of business.** Even if Ma and Pa can calculate MegaGrocery's average variable cost to the satisfaction of a court, they will not necessarily win their case. They must prove that MegaGrocery intended to put them out of business. That is a pretty tall order, short of finding some smoking gun like a strategic plan that explicitly says MegaGrocery wants Ma and Pa gone.

- **If the plaintiff does go out of business, the defendant will be able to earn sufficient profits to recoup its prior losses.** Until Ma and Pa go out of business, Mega-Grocery will lose money—after all, it is selling food below cost. To win their case, Ma and Pa must show that MegaGrocery will be able to make up all its lost profits once the corner grocery is out of the way. They need to prove, for example, that no other grocery chain will come to town. It is difficult to prove a negative proposition like that, especially in the grocery business where barriers to entry are low.

Recently, plaintiffs have not had much success with predatory pricing suits. For example, Liggett began selling generic cigarettes 30 percent below the price of branded

---

[15] To calculate average variable cost, add all the firm's costs except its fixed costs and then divide by the total quantity of output.

cigarettes. Brown & Williamson retaliated by introducing its own generics at an even lower price. Liggett sued, claiming that Brown's prices were below cost. The Supreme Court agreed that Brown was not only selling below cost but also intended to harm Liggett. Brown still won the case, however, because there was no evidence that it would be able to recover its losses from the below-cost pricing. If Brown raised its prices, other competitors would come back into the market.[16]

Tying Arrangements

A tying arrangement is an agreement to sell a product on the condition that the buyer also purchases a different (or tied) product. A tying arrangement is illegal under §3 of the Clayton Act and §1 of the Sherman Act if:

- The two products are clearly separate
- The seller requires the buyer to purchase the two products together
- The seller has significant power in the market for the tying product, and
- The seller is shutting out a significant part of the market for the tied product.

Should a movie distributor have to buy Tugboat Annie to get Ingrid Bergman?

© SUSAN VAN ETTEN

Six movie distributors refused to sell individual films to television stations. Instead, they insisted that a station buy an entire package of movies. To obtain classics such as *Treasure of the Sierra Madre* and *Casablanca* (the **tying product**), the station also had to purchase such forgettable films as *Nancy Drew Troubleshooter, Gorilla Man*, and *Tugboat Annie Sails Again* (the **tied product**).[17] The distributors engaged in an illegal tying arrangement. These are the questions that the court asked:

- **Are the two products clearly separate?** A left and right shoe are not separate products, and a seller can legally require that they be purchased together. *Gorilla Man*, on the other hand, is a separate product from *Casablanca*.

- **Is the seller requiring the buyer to purchase the two products together?** Yes, that is the whole point of these "package deals."

- **Does the seller have significant power in the market for the tying product?** In this case, the tying products are the classic movies. Since they are copyrighted, no one else can show them without the distributor's permission. The six distributors controlled a great many classic movies. So, yes, they do have significant market power.

- **Is the seller shutting out a significant part of the market for the tied product?** In this case, the tied products are the undesirable films like *Tugboat Annie Sails Again*. Television stations forced to take the unwanted films did not buy "B" movies from other distributors. These other distributors were effectively foreclosed from a substantial part of the market.

16   *Brooke Group Ltd. v. Brown & Williamson Tobacco Corp.*, 509 U.S. 209, 113 S. Ct. 2578, 1993 U.S. LEXIS 4245 (1993).

17   *United States v. Loew's Inc.*, 371 U.S. 38, 83 S. Ct. 97, 1962 U.S. LEXIS 2332 (1962).

Controlling Distributors and Retailers

The goal of an aggressive strategy is to force competitors out of a market—by undercutting their prices or tying products together, for example. Controlling distributors and retailers is another method for excluding competitors. It is difficult to compete in a market if you are foreclosed from the best distribution channels.

Allocating Customers and Territory

As we saw earlier in this chapter, a *horizontal* agreement by *competitors* to allocate customers and territories is a *per se* violation of §1 of the Sherman Act. **However, a vertical allocation of customers or territory is illegal only if it adversely affects competition in the market as a whole.** It is a rule of reason, not a *per se*, violation.

Suppose that Hot Sound, Inc., produces expensive, high-quality speakers. It grants its distributors the exclusive right to sell in a particular territory or the exclusive right over a particular type of customer (consumers, corporate, automobiles). In return for these exclusive rights, Hot Sound requires the distributors to stock a wide range of inventory, hire highly trained (expensive) sales help, and advertise widely. Such requirements not only increase sales but also enhance distributor loyalty. The distributors have such a large investment in Hot Sound's products that they are reluctant to switch to another manufacturer. A change would mean unloading a large inventory, developing new advertisements, and retraining or laying off some of the sales force.

Hot Sound clearly has good business reasons for adopting such a plan. It is reducing intrabrand competition (among its dealers) but enhancing interbrand competition (between brands). With its committed dealer network, Hot Sound can compete more fiercely against other brands. Vertical allocation is a rule of reason violation, which means that the law will intervene only if Hot Sound's activities have an anticompetitive impact on the market as a whole. But since Hot Sound's plan increases interbrand competition, it is unlikely to have an anticompetitive impact.

Exclusive Dealing Agreements

An **exclusive dealing contract** is one in which a distributor or retailer agrees with a supplier not to carry the products of any other supplier. **Under §1 of the Sherman Act and §3 of the Clayton Act, exclusive dealing contracts are subject to a rule of reason and are illegal only if they have an anticompetitive effect.**

Consider the case of Ben & Jerry's. With more than $100 million in sales, it was a major player in the ice cream market. And some of its competitors alleged that it was playing hardball. Just ask Amy Miller. She started Amy's Ice Creams in a small storefront in Austin, Texas. Her ice cream was so popular that she decided to begin producing pints for sale in grocery stores. But when she tried to enter the Houston market, Sunbelt, the dominant distributor in the area, refused to carry her desserts. She thinks Sunbelt turned her down because Ben & Jerry's had forbidden it to carry other premium brands.

Ironically, the ice cream was once in the other bowl, so to speak. When Ben and Jerry were the new boys on the block, they discovered that Pillsbury (owner of Häagen-Dazs) included provisions in its contracts that prohibited distributors from carrying Ben & Jerry's brand. When Ben & Jerry's produced written contracts containing these exclusory clauses, Pillsbury backed down immediately. Thereafter, no one in the industry used written distribution contracts.

Amy Miller threatened to sue Ben & Jerry's for violating the antitrust laws with exclusive dealing contracts. In determining if these agreements had an anticompetitive impact on the market, a court would consider the following factors:

- **The number of other distributors available.** Amy said that no one but Sunbelt would do because only the best distributors were able to preserve her ice cream's quality.

- **The portion of the market foreclosed by the exclusive dealing agreements.** Without Sunbelt, Amy's Ice Creams could not penetrate the Houston market, so it had to shut down its pint production line.

- **The ease with which new distributors could enter the market.** Sunbelt had few, if any, competitors. Presumably, the market was a difficult one to enter.

- **The possibility that Amy could distribute the products herself.** Not likely. Amy's talents lay in *making* a good ice cream, not distributing it.

- **The legitimate business reasons that might have led the distributor to accept an exclusive contract.** Here is what Sunbelt's vice-president had to say: "We already had our table full with super premium pints. We felt Amy's was an underfinanced product and we would have had to replace a high-volume product to give it a shot. And we personally did not think the product was very good."[18]

Would an exclusive dealing agreement between Ben & Jerry's and Sunbelt be anti-competitive? If so, would their business reasons justify the contract?

Resale Price Maintenance

Peter Polites (pronounced po-LEE-tus), owner of a Nine West store in New Jersey, slashed the price of a popular, smart-looking women's shoe last winter, knowing he would attract many more customers—and still earn a smooth 60 percent on each pair. But Mr. Polites's sale irritated some managers at large department stores down the hall in the Mall at Short Hills. One Nordstrom manager, he said, walked into Mr. Polites's small store, picked some shoes off the shelf, looked at the prices, slammed them down, and left without a word.

Mr. Polites said the Nordstrom manager later explained that the flats Mr. Polites had reduced to $49.99 from $60 were included on a confidential list of styles—known as the "off-limits list"—whose prices Nine West Group, Inc., rarely, if ever, lets stores mark down. Mr. Polites's low prices also maddened executives at Nine West, the footwear giant that says it sells one out of every five pairs of shoes sold to women in the United States. Vincent Camuto, chief executive of Nine West, called Mr. Polites and demanded that he end his sale. When Mr. Polites refused, Mr. Camuto told him that in that case, "We can't ship you those shoes."[19] ◆

Is it legal for Nine West to cut off a retailer who refuses to raise his prices? This question is at the heart of an important antitrust conundrum—the validity of **resale price maintenance (RPM)**. RPM means the manufacturer sets *minimum* prices that retailers may charge. In other words, it prevents retailers from discounting. Why does the manufacturer care? After all, once the retailer purchases the shoes, the manufacturer has made its profit. The only way the manufacturer makes more money is to raise its *wholesale* price, not the *retail* price. RPM guarantees a profit margin for the *retailer*.

Manufacturers argue that they ought to have the right to decide how and at what price their products are sold. They may, for instance, want to promote an upscale

---

[18] Rickie Windle, "Ben & Jerry's Creams Amy's," *Austin Business Journal,* Oct. 4, 1993, vol. 13, no. 33, §1, p. 1.

[19] Melody Petersen, "Treading a Contentious Line," *New York Times,* Jan. 13, 1999, p. C1. Copyright © 1999 by The New York Times Co. Reprinted by permission.

Who should determine how much consumers will pay for these shoes?

brand image, one that could be destroyed by discount prices. Or the manufacturer may expect its dealers to provide a higher level of service than discounters can afford. Consumer advocates contend, however, that manufacturers such as Nine West are simply protecting dealers from competition. Discounting may or may not harm products, but, they insist, RPM certainly hurts consumers.

To settle this controversy, the Supreme Court has spoken. Spray-Rite was an herbicide dealer selling products manufactured by Monsanto. Spray-Rite claimed that Monsanto terminated the dealership contract because other dealers had complained about Spray-Rite's discount prices. Monsanto countered that Spray-Rite had not spent enough money training its salespeople or promoting the products. The jury, however, found for Spray-Rite and awarded $3.5 million in damages, which were trebled to $10.5 million. Monsanto appealed to the Supreme Court.[20]

Many commentators expected the Supreme Court to decide that RPM was a rule of reason, not a *per se*, violation. The Court ruled unanimously, however, that **RPM is a *per se* violation of §1 of the Sherman Act. A manufacturer may not enter into an agreement with distributors to fix prices.** The Court did create a potential loophole by saying that an agreement cannot be inferred simply because a manufacturer cuts off one distributor after receiving complaints from another. Unilateral action by a manufacturer to set prices is legal; an agreement with distributors about prices is not.[21]

And what happened to Nine West? It agreed to end RPM and to pay a settlement of $34 million to be used for women's health, educational, and safety programs.

In the following case, a clothing manufacturer terminated its sales to a store. Was this illegal RPM or simply a change in business strategy?

you Be The Judge

EUROMODAS, INC. V. ZANELLA, LTD.

253 F. Supp. 2d 201, 2003 U.S. Dist. LEXIS 5431
United States District Court for the District of Puerto Rico, 2003

Facts: Zanella, Ltd., was a manufacturer of men's clothing that distributed its products in Puerto Rico through the Clubman and Euromodas stores. Euromodas sold Zanella trousers at a much lower price than Clubman did. A Zanella executive told Euromodas that Clubman was unhappy about this price competition. Nonetheless, Zanella continued to sell to Euromodas. Clubman cancelled its Zanella order because Euromodas's discount pricing was undermining Clubman's image as an upscale clothing boutique.

▼

---

[20] *Monsanto Co. v. Spray-Rite Corp.*, 465 U.S. 752, 104 S. Ct. 1464, 1984 U.S. LEXIS 39 (1984).
[21] The court decided that Monsanto had engaged in RPM because it had terminated Spray-Rite as part of an agreement with other distributors.

The following year, Clubman proposed that it create "Zanella corners" in its stores to display and promote Zanella trousers. Shortly thereafter, Zanella cut Euromodas off as a distributor, without giving any reason.

Euromodas filed suit alleging that Zanella had violated §1 of the Sherman Act by committing resale price maintenance. Zanella filed a motion for summary judgment.

You Be the Judge: Did Zanella engage in resale price maintenance?

Argument for Euromodas: Section 1 of the Sherman Act prohibits a manufacturer from entering into an agreement with distributors to fix prices. Clubman complained to Zanella that Euromodas was discounting, then Zanella terminated Euromodas. Clearly, there was some sort of agreement, whether implicit or explicit. Clubman did not want to compete against a discounter. As a reward for terminating Euromodas, Zanella was given a special corner in the Clubman stores.

The law on resale price maintenance is designed to protect consumers. Now consumers in Puerto Rico no longer have a low-cost option for buying Zanella trousers—they will be forced to pay Clubman's high prices.

Argument for Zanella: Clubman offered Zanella an exclusive deal to set up special displays of Zanella trousers. The decision to terminate Euromodas had nothing to do with pricing; the company simply wanted to sell more trousers and Clubman provided that opportunity. This choice was a perfectly legal business decision.

Yes, it is illegal for a manufacturer to agree with its distributors to fix prices. However, the simple decision to terminate a discounter—even in response to complaints from other distributors—does not in and of itself prove an illegal conspiracy. There must be some further evidence of an agreement. No such evidence is present in this case. ∎

Vertical Maximum Price-Fixing

In *Spray-Rite*, the Supreme Court held that resale price maintenance is a *per se* violation of the Sherman Act. In that case, the manufacturer set the *minimum* prices its distributors could charge. **Vertical *maximum* price-fixing (when a manufacturer sets *maximum* prices), however, is a rule of *reason violation* of the Sherman Act.** The defendant is liable only if the price-fixing harms competition. (You remember, from earlier in this chapter, that all *horizontal* price-fixing is a *per se* violation.)

When State Oil Co. leased a gas station to Barkat Khan, it set a maximum price that Khan could charge for gas. Khan sued State Oil, but the Supreme Court ruled in favor of the oil company, on the grounds that cutting prices to increase business is the very essence of competition and, furthermore, low prices benefit consumers.[22]

---

[22] *State Oil Co. v. Khan*, 522 U.S. 3, 118 S. Ct. 275, 1997 U.S. LEXIS 6705 (1997).

© PHOTODISC/GETTY IMAGES

Chapter Conclusion

The purpose of the antitrust laws in the United States is to keep businesses on a narrow road. On the one hand, they may not swerve to one side and work too closely with competitors. Nor may they swerve to the other side and attack competitors too aggressively. Although managers sometimes resent the constraints imposed on them by antitrust laws, it is these laws that ensure the fair and open competition necessary for a healthy economy. In the end, the antitrust laws benefit us all.

Chapter Review

1. There are two categories of antitrust violations: *per se* and rule of reason. *Per se* violations are automatic; courts do not consider mitigating circumstances. Rule of reason violations, on the other hand, are illegal only if they have an anticompetitive impact.

2. Any effort by a group of competitors to divide their market is a *per se* violation of the Sherman Act. Illegal arrangements include agreements to allocate customers, territory, or products.

3. Price-fixing and bid-rigging are *per se* violations of the Sherman Act.

4. Every company generally has the right to decide with whom it will do business. However, the Sherman Act prohibits competitors from joining together in an agreement to exclude a particular supplier, buyer, or even another competitor, if the agreement would hurt competition.

5. Under a reciprocal dealing agreement, a buyer refuses to purchase goods from a supplier unless the supplier also purchases items from the buyer. Reciprocal dealing agreements violate the Sherman Act if they foreclose competitors from a significant part of the market.

6. The Robinson-Patman Act prohibits companies from selling the same item at different prices if the sale lessens competition. However, a seller may charge different prices if these prices reflect different costs.

7. Under the Clayton Act, the federal government has the authority to prohibit anticompetitive mergers and joint ventures.

8. Possessing a monopoly need not be illegal; acquiring or maintaining it through "bad acts" is.

9. To determine if a company is guilty of monopolization, ask three questions:
   - What is the market?
   - Does the company control the market?
   - How did the company acquire its control?

10. To win a predatory pricing case, a plaintiff must prove three elements:
   - The defendant is selling its products below cost.
   - The defendant intends that the plaintiff go out of business.
   - If the plaintiff does go out of business, the defendant will be able to earn sufficient profit to recoup its prior losses.

11. A tying arrangement is illegal if:
   - The two products are clearly separate
   - The seller requires that the buyer purchase the two products together
   - The seller has significant power in the market for the tying product, and
   - The seller is shutting out a significant part of the market for the tied product.

12. Efforts by a manufacturer to allocate customers or territory among its distributors are subject to a rule of reason. These allocations are illegal only if they adversely affect competition in the market.

13. An exclusive dealing contract is one in which a distributor or retailer agrees with a supplier not to carry the products of any other supplier. Exclusive dealing contracts are subject to a rule

of reason and are prohibited only if they have an anticompetitive effect.

14. When a manufacturer enters into an agreement with distributors or retailers to fix minimum prices, this arrangement is called resale price maintenance. RPM is a *per se* violation of the law.

15. Vertical maximum price-fixing is a rule of reason violation of the Sherman Act. It is illegal only if it has an adverse impact on competition.

Practice Test

1. Harcourt Brace Jovanovich (HBJ) granted BRG an exclusive license to market HBJ's bar review materials in Georgia and to use HBJ's trade name. HBJ agreed not to compete with BRG in Georgia, and BRG agreed not to compete with HBJ outside the state. HBJ was entitled to receive $100 per student enrolled by BRG and 40 percent of revenues over $350 per student. Did this agreement violate the antitrust laws?

2. Fifty bakeries in New York formed an association. They developed a system of distribution under which stores were only allowed to buy from a single baker. A store that wanted to shift to another baker had to consult the association and pay cash to the former baker. The association also decided to raise the retail price of bread from 75 to 85 cents. All the association's members printed the new price on their bread sleeves. Are the bakeries in violation of the antitrust laws?

3. Fifty restaurants in Boston threatened to stop accepting the American Express card if the company refused to reduce the commission it charged on each purchase. Visa International, one of American Express's rivals, offered to pay the group's legal expenses. American Express then lowered its commission. For restaurants that processed more than $10 million in annual volume, American Express reduced charges from 3.25 percent to 2.75 percent. Rates for restaurants processing less than $10 million but more than $1 million a year fell to 3 percent. The company did not lower rates for restaurants with volume lower than $1 million a year. Have either the restaurants, Visa, or American Express potentially violated the antitrust laws?

4. Reserve Supply Corp., a cooperative of 379 lumber dealers, charged that Owens-Corning Fiberglass Corp. violated the Robinson-Patman Act by selling at lower prices to Reserve's competitors. Owens-Corning had granted lower prices to a number of Reserve's competitors to meet, but not beat, the prices of other insulation manufacturers. Is Owens-Corning in violation of the Robinson-Patman Act?

5. BAR/BRI is a company that prepares law students for bar exams. With branches in 45 states, it has the largest share of the bar review market in the country. Barpassers is a much smaller company located only in Arizona and California. BAR/BRI distributed pamphlets on campuses falsely suggesting Barpassers was near bankruptcy. Enrollments in Barpassers' courses dropped, and the company was forced to postpone plans for expansion. Does Barpassers have an antitrust claim against BAR/BRI?

6. **YOU BE THE JUDGE** WRITING PROBLEM American Academic Suppliers (AAS) and Beckley-Cardy (B-C) both sold educational supplies to schools. B-C's sales began to plummet, and it was rapidly losing market share. The company responded by reducing its catalog prices 5 to 12 percent. It also offered a discount of 25 to 40 percent in states in which AAS was making substantial gains. What claim might AAS make against B-C? Is it likely to prevail in court? **Argument for AAS:** B-C has committed predatory pricing. The company is selling below cost for the purpose of driving us out of business. **Argument for B-C:** Even if we were to drive AAS out of business, we do not have enough market power to recoup our losses.

7. Two medical supply companies in the San Francisco area provide oxygen to homes of patients. The companies are owned by the doctors who prescribe the oxygen. These doctors make up 60 percent of the lung specialists in the area. Does this arrangement create an antitrust problem?

8. After acquiring the Schick brand name and electric shaver assets, North American Phillips controlled 55 percent of the electric shaver industry in the United States. Remington, a competitor, claimed that the acquisition of such a large mar-

ket share was a violation of the law because the increased competition from Phillips would decrease Remington's profits. Does Remington have a valid claim?

9. Videos of *Jurassic Park* and *Snow White and the Seven Dwarfs* were due in stores the same month. The stores ought to have been delighted at the prospect of having two blockbusters to sell, but instead they were worried—how to price the videos? Both Disney (*Snow White*) and MCA/Universal (*Jurassic Park*) were longtime proponents of MAP—minimum advertised pricing. In other words, if retailers sold the videos at prices below $14.95, the studios would not subsidize their advertising budgets. Many retailers would have *liked* to sell the videos at $14.95, but they were afraid competitors would undercut them. To make matters even more complicated, they had all heard rumors that Disney planned to take other steps against retailers who ignored MAP, such as delaying shipment of the next

hit—*The Lion King*. Is MAP legal? What if the studios take "other steps"?

10. **ETHICS** An 18-year-old woman with a mental disability and her mother (the Nelsons) brought a malpractice suit against one of the doctors at the Monroe Regional Medical Center. As a result, the Monroe Clinic notified the Nelsons that it would no longer treat them on a non-emergency basis. The patients then went to another local clinic, which was later acquired by Monroe. The merged clinic refused to treat the Nelsons on a nonemergency basis, so the Nelsons were obliged to seek medical treatment in another town 40 miles away. Has Monroe violated the antitrust laws? Whether or not the Monroe clinic has violated the law, is it ethical to deny treatment to a patient?

11. **ROLE REVERSAL** Prepare a short-answer question based on an article you have found in the newspaper that involves an antitrust issue.

Internet Research Problem

Choose one of the cases featured at http://beatty.westbuslaw.com. Read the Information (that is, the complaint) in the case. Then see if you can find out how the case was ultimately resolved. You could try looking on WestLaw or LEXIS, in newspaper reports, at the company Web site, or you could even call the Justice Department.

You can find further practice problems at http://beatty.westbuslaw.com or in the Study Guide that accompanies this text.

Consumer Law

The women signed up for a lesson at the Arthur Murray dance studio in Washington, D.C. Expecting a session of decorous fun, they instead found themselves in a nightmare of humiliation and coercion:

- "First of all, I did not want the [additional] lesson, and I think it was unpleasant because I had three, maybe four, people, as I say, pressuring me to buy something by a certain time, and I do recall asking that I be let to think, let me think it over, and I was told that the contest would end at 6 o'clock or something to that effect and if I did not sign by a certain time it would be too late. I think we got under the deadline by maybe a minute or two. If I had been given time to think, I would not have signed that contract."

- "I tried to say no and get out of it and I got very, very upset because I got frightened at paying out all that money and having nothing to fall back on. I remember I started crying and couldn't stop crying. All I thought of was getting out of there. So finally after—I don't know how much time, Mr. Mara said, well, I could sign up for 250 hours, which was half the 500 Club, which would amount to $4,300. So I finally signed it. After that, I tried to raise the money from the bank and found I couldn't get a loan for that amount and I didn't have any savings and I had to get a bank loan to pay for it. That was when I went back and asked him to cancel that contract. But Mr. Mara said that he couldn't cancel it."

- I did not join the carnival. I did not wish to join the carnival, and while it was only an additional $55, I had no desire to join. [My instructor] asked everyone in the room to sit down in a circle around me and he stood me up in that circle, in the middle of the circle, and said, 'Everybody, I want you to look at this woman here who is too cheap to join the carnival. I just want you to look at a woman like that. Isn't it awful?'"

Because of abuses such as these, the Federal Trade Commission (FTC) ordered the Arthur Murray dance studio to halt its high-pressure sales techniques, limit each contract to no more than $1,500 in dance lessons, and permit all contracts to be canceled within seven days.[1]

INTRODUCTION

Years ago consumers typically dealt with merchants they knew well. A dance instructor in a small town would not stay in business long if he tormented his elderly, vulnerable clients. As the population of this country grew and cities expanded, however, merchants became less and less subject to community pressure. The law has supplemented, if not replaced, these informal policing mechanisms. Both Congress and the states have passed statutes that protect consumers from the unscrupulous. But the legal system in America is generally too slow and expensive to handle small cases. The women who fell into the web of Arthur Murray had neither the wealth nor the energy to sue the studio themselves. To aid consumers such as these, Congress empowered federal agencies to enforce consumer laws. The FTC is the most important of these agencies.

Federal Trade Commission

Congress created the FTC in 1915 to regulate business. Although its original focus was on antitrust law, it now regulates a wide range of business activities that affect consumers, everything from advertising to consumer loans to warranties to debt collection practices.[2] It is, if you will, the consumer's best friend in Washington. The FTC has several options for enforcing the law:

- *Voluntary Compliance.* When the FTC determines that a business has violated the law, it first asks the offender to sign a voluntary compliance affidavit promising to stop the prohibited activity.

---

[1] *In re Arthur Murray Studio of Washington, Inc.*, 78 F.T.C. 401, 1971 FTC LEXIS 75 (1971).
[2] Chapter 39 discusses the FTC's role in antitrust enforcement.

- *Administrative Hearings and Appeals.* If the company refuses to stop voluntarily, the FTC takes the case to an administrative law judge (ALJ) within the agency. The violator may settle the case at this point by signing a **consent order.** If the case proceeds to a hearing, the ALJ has the right to issue a **cease and desist order,** commanding the violator to stop the offending activity. The FTC issued a cease and desist order against the Arthur Murray dance studio. A defendant can appeal such an order to the five Commissioners of the FTC, from there to a federal appeals court, and ultimately to the United States Supreme Court. Both the Commissioners and the Fifth Circuit Court of Appeals confirmed the cease and desist order against Arthur Murray. The case never reached the Supreme Court.

- *Penalties.* The FTC can impose a fine for each violation of:

  - a voluntary compliance affidavit

  - a consent order

  - a cease and desist order

  - an FTC rule or

  - a cease and desist order issued against *someone else.*

  For example, the Arthur Murray studio could be liable for violating an FTC cease and desist order prohibiting high-pressure sales by the Fred Astaire studio. In addition, the FTC can file suit in federal court asking for damages on behalf of an injured consumer if (1) the defendant has violated FTC rules and (2) a reasonable person would have known under the circumstances that the conduct was dishonest or fraudulent.

SALES

Section 5 of the Federal Trade Commission Act (FTC Act) prohibits "unfair and deceptive acts or practices." You can report an unfair or deceptive practice to the FTC at its Web site (http://www.ftc.gov).

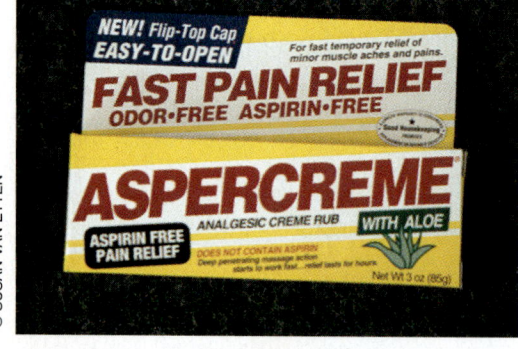

To avoid confusing consumers, the FTC required Aspercreme to disclose that it offers "Aspirin-Free Pain Relief."

Deceptive Acts or Practices

Many deceptive acts or practices involve advertisements. **Under the FTC Act, an advertisement is deceptive if it contains an important misrepresentation or omission that is likely to mislead a reasonable consumer.** A company advertised that a pain-relief ointment called "Aspercreme" provided "the strong relief of aspirin right where you hurt." From this ad and the name of the product, do you assume that the ointment contains aspirin? Are you a reasonable consumer? Consumers surveyed in a shopping mall believed the product contained aspirin. In fact, it does not. The FTC required the company to disclose that there is no aspirin in Aspercreme.[3]

---

[3] *In re Thompson Medical Co., Inc.,* 104 F.T.C. 648, 1984 FTC LEXIS 6 (1984).

Is there anything wrong with the following ads?

Do not believe a word of them, warns the FTC. It takes more than three minutes a day to get six-pack abs, no matter what equipment you use. As for the #1 Doctor Recommended Ensure, the doctors in the survey were asked which liquid meal they would choose, if they were going to recommend one to a patient. In fact, most doctors would not recommend Ensure to the healthy adults pictured in the advertisements. The half-price cars were for lease, not sale. By the end of the lease, owners would have paid only half the value of the cars, but they would also have to return the cars to the dealer. Was the company in the following case deceptive about its business opportunity?

you Be The Judge

FEDERAL TRADE COMMISSION V. TASHMAN

318 F.3d 1273, 2003 U.S. App. LEXIS 1123
United States Court of Appeals for the Eleventh Circuit, 2003

Facts: Stephen Tashman owned Telecard Dispensing Corp. (TDC), which sold dispensing machines for phone cards (and the cards to go in them). To get the attention of passersby, these machines would call out, "Hi there! Get your long distance phone card and call anywhere, anytime, from any touchtone phone without a penny in your pocket and save up to 50 percent. Buy it here, buy it now."

TDC ran the following radio advertisement:

"Do you really want to make more money—an additional 25 to 35 thousand dollars a year or more, possibly a lot more, and only work three to five hours per week? Stop the excuses. You can do it. You can change your life."

Anyone who answered this ad was connected with a telemarketer, known as a "fronter," who claimed: (1) TDC's locators would put machines in public places with traffic flow of at least 500 peo-

ple per day; (2) according to TDC's experience, 2 percent of passersby were likely to purchase phone cards from the machines; and (3) entrepreneurs could be expected to pay off their machines in about six months. Disclosure statements sent to prospective customers claimed that TDC had received 287 positive letters and only 20 negative ones from purchasers. TDC also encouraged prospective customers to speak to references who would give first-hand testimony about the profitability of this business. Some of these references had never owned phone card vending machines, and all of them were paid for their praise.

Most of TDC's claims were false. Locators put machines anyplace that was available, no matter what the foot traffic. The 2 percent figure was completely made up. In one TDC experiment, the machines made no sales whatsoever. Undaunted, TDC began reporting the usage rate from an unrelated business—vending machines in which people attempted to catch stuffed animals with a mechanical crane. Most of the customers who bought machines did not recoup their original ▼

investment. TDC received 20 to 30 calls per day complaining about sluggish phone card sales. The FTC presented 14 witnesses who claimed to have lost substantial sums as TDC customers. TDC presented only one witness who claimed to have made a profit, but half of his machines were purchased from other sources and they had four times the capacity of the TDC machines. There was some evidence, however, that migrant workers purchased phone cards from dispensing machines.

The FTC filed suit against TDC. The trial court found for the company and the FTC appealed.

You Be the Judge: Did TDC violate §5 of the FTC Act?

Argument for the FTC: Many of TDC's claims were false. How could it claim that each machine had daily foot traffic of 500 and that 2 percent of the passersby would purchase phone cards? The company's only data were based upon an entirely different product.

Argument for TDC: The phone card business is new and unproven. That does not mean it is fraudulent. This business is potentially an important and viable one but it is also a high-risk entrepreneurial activity. Prospective customers bear the responsibility of weighing the risks and profit potential, and of following up their investment with the hard work and business savvy necessary to make the venture successful. Not every business venture will work for every person. Moreover, reasonable customers would have understood that they could not make tens of thousands of dollars while working only three to five hours per week. They cannot expect protection from sheer gullibility.

The FTC's Rebuttal: The FTC Act does not provide immunity for new businesses. Indeed, it is precisely in the context of a new venture that investors are most likely to need accurate data because they are unlikely to have any of their own. *Caveat emptor* is simply not the law. ∎

Unfair Practices

The FTC Act also prohibits unfair acts or practices. **The Commission considers a practice to be *unfair* if it meets all of the following three tests:**

- *It causes a substantial consumer injury.* This can mean physical or financial injury. A furnace repair company that dismantled home furnaces for "inspection" and then refused to reassemble them until the consumers agreed to buy services or replacement parts had caused a substantial consumer injury.

- *The harm of the injury outweighs any countervailing benefit.* A pharmaceutical company sold a sunburn remedy without conducting adequate tests to ensure that it worked. The expense of these tests would have forced the company to raise the product's price. The company had demonstrated that the product was safe, and there was evidence in the medical literature that the ingredients when used in other products were effective. The FTC determined that, although the company was technically in violation of its rules, the benefit to consumers of a cheaper product more than outweighed the risk of injury to them.

- *The consumer could not reasonably avoid the injury.* The FTC is particularly vigilant in protecting susceptible consumers—such as the elderly or the ill—who are less able to avoid injury. For instance, the Commission looks especially carefully at those who offer a cure for cancer.

In addition, the FTC may decide that a practice is unfair simply because it violates public policy even if it does not meet these three tests. The Commission refused to allow a mail-order company to file collection suits in states far from where the defendants lived because the practice was unfair, whether or not it met the three tests.

What is the difference between *deceptive* and *unfair?* Consider this case: Audio Communications, Inc. (ACI), ran a telephone service for children. By dialing a 900 number, children could listen to recorded stories or games featuring characters such as Santa Claus and the Easter Bunny. ACI ran advertisements on children's TV shows and in children's magazines. The FTC held that the ads were *deceptive* because they did not reveal that the phone calls cost money. Moreover, the ads promised a free gift in return for one phone call. In reality, callers (who were, after all, young children) could not obtain a gift without following several complicated steps that were explained very rapidly. Often, more than one call was necessary to obtain the gift. This practice was also *unfair* because children often made the calls without parental permission. Parents (who paid the bill) had little control over children (who made the call). In its consent order, the FTC required ACI to include in all of its advertisements the following statement: "Kids, you must ask your mom or dad and get their permission before you call. This call costs money."[4]

Other Sales Practices

Bait and Switch

FTC rules prohibit bait and switch advertisements: a merchant may not advertise a product and then disparage it to consumers in an effort to sell a different item. In addition, merchants must have enough stock on hand to meet reasonable demand for any advertised product. Sears ran many advertisements like the one on the left.

Portable Zig-Zag Sewing Machine

from SEARS $58

Sews on buttons, sews buttonholes
Does zig-zag or straight stitching
monograms, appliqués, other fancy work
for household linens, gifts
Sews forward and reverse for her convenience

When eager customers went to buy this fabulous item, they were told that the machines were noisy, did not come with Sears's standard sewing machine guarantee, and could neither stitch in reverse nor do buttonholes. Also, the store was out of stock and would not be receiving any new machines for a long time.[5]

This is bait and switch advertising and it violates FTC rules. The **bait** is an alluring offer that sounds almost too good to be true. Of course, it is. The advertiser does not wish to sell the advertised merchandise; it wants to **switch** consumers to another, higher priced product. The real purpose of the advertisement is simply to find customers who are interested in buying.

Mail or Telephone Order Merchandise

Many Americans rely on catalogs to buy everything from clothing to medicine to furnishings, so it is important that these merchants deliver as promised. The FTC has established the following guidelines on mail or telephone order merchandise:

- Mail-order companies must ship an item within the time stated or, if no time is given, within 30 days after receipt of the order.

---

[4] F.T.C., 56 C.F.R. 22432 (May 15, 1991).
[5] *In re Sears, Roebuck and Co.*, 89 F.T.C. 229, 1977 FTC LEXIS 225 (1977).

- If a company cannot ship the product when promised, it must send the customer a notice with the new shipping date and an opportunity to cancel. If the new shipping date is within 30 days of the original one, and the customer does not cancel, the order is still on.

- If the company cannot ship within 30 days of the original date, it must send the customer another notice. This time, however, the company must cancel the order unless the customer returns the notice, indicating that he still wants the item.

For example, Dell Computer Corp. advertised that its Dimension computer came with the "Dell Software Suite." In fact, for several months the suite was not available. Instead of the software, Dell sent customers a coupon for the suite "when available." The FTC charged Dell with violations of the mail or telephone order rules because the company:

- Knew it could not ship the software within 30 days

- Failed to offer buyers the opportunity to cancel their orders, and

- Did not cancel the orders automatically as it should have under the rules.[6]

Telemarketing

The telephone rings: "Could I speak with Alexander Johannson? This is Denise from Master Chimney Sweeps." It is 7:30 P.M.; you have just straggled in from work and are looking forward to a peaceful dinner of takeout cuisine. You are known as Sandy, your last name is pronounced Yohannson and you live in a modern apartment without a chimney. A telemarketer has struck again! What can you do to protect your peace and quiet?

The FTC prohibits telemarketers from calling any telephone number listed on its do-not-call registry. You can register your telephone numbers with the FTC online at http://www.donotcall.gov or by telephone at (888) 382-1222. FTC rules also prohibit telemarketers from blocking their names and telephone numbers on Caller ID systems.

Unordered Merchandise

Under §5 of the FTC Act, anyone who receives unordered merchandise in the mail can treat it as a gift. She can use it, throw it away, or do whatever else she wants with it.

There you are, watching an infomercial for Anushka products, guaranteed to fight that scourge of modern life—cellulite! Rushing to your phone, you place an order. The Anushka cosmetics arrive, but for some odd reason, the cellulite remains. A month later another bottle arrives, like magic, in the mail. The magic spell is broken, however, when you get your credit card bill and see that, without your authorization, the company has charged you for the new supply of Anushka. Is this a hot new marketing technique? Not exactly. The FTC ordered the company to cease and desist this unfair and deceptive practice. The company improperly billed its customers, said the FTC, and should have notified them that they were free to treat the unauthorized products as a gift, to use or throw out as they wished.[7]

Door-to-Door Sales

Consumers at home need special protection from unscrupulous salespeople. In a store, customers can simply walk out, but at home they may feel trapped. Also, it is difficult at home to compare products or prices offered by competitors. Under the FTC door-to-door rules, **a salesperson is required to notify the buyer that she has the right to cancel the transaction prior to midnight of the third business day thereafter.**

---

6   *United States v. Dell Computer Corp.,* 1998 FTC LEXIS 30 (1998).
7   *In the Matter of Synchronal Corp.,* 116 F.T.C. 1189, 1993 FTC LEXIS 280 (1993).

This notice must be given both orally and in writing; the actual cancellation must be in writing. The seller must return the buyer's money within 10 days. The following news report illustrates an illegal method of selling magazine subscriptions.

NEWS*worthy*

A federal judge assessed a $50,000 civil penalty against a door-to-door magazine sales company. Customers who purchased magazine subscriptions from Tork & Associates were given (partial) receipts that misrepresented their right to cancel. The receipt indicated that a customer wishing to cancel was required to submit a copy of the complete receipt, the canceled check, the salesperson's name, the magazine name, the date of the transaction, and the total cost. Because the salesperson never gave the customer the complete receipt, it was difficult to comply. In two years, Tork generated $2 million in revenues.[8] ◆

Ethics

A vice-president of Grolier, the encyclopedia company, made the following statement:

> The proposition that a buyer should have the right to whimsically change his mind with respect to a transaction which has been formalized by an agreement containing all of the elements of a legally binding contract, is indeed, a revolutionary legal concept. This proposal represents an attack on the basic contractual concepts which are the foundation of the American economic system.[9]

Do you agree with this statement? From the Chapter 2 Ethics Checklist: What answer would the Golden Rule provide? If you were head of Grolier, would you support or resist the FTC door-to-door rule? ◆

CONSUMER CREDIT

Historically, the practice of charging interest on loans was banned by most countries and by three of the most prominent religions—Christianity, Islam, and Judaism. As the European economy developed, however, money lending became essential. To compromise, governments began to permit interest charges but limited the maximum rate to 6 percent. European settlers carried this concept to the United States, which soon adopted the 6 percent rule, too.

Even in modern times, most states limit the maximum interest rate a lender may charge. The penalty for violating usury statutes varies among the states. Depending upon the jurisdiction, the borrower may be allowed to keep (1) the interest above the usury limit, (2) all of the interest, or (3) all of the loan and the interest.

Before Congress passed the Truth in Lending Act (TILA), lenders found many creative methods to disguise the real interest rate and circumvent the law. For example, they would use a so-called add-on rate. That is, they would charge the permissible interest rate but would insist that the borrower begin to repay the loan in installments immediately. The borrower only had effective use of the money for half the term of the loan. Suppose that a car dealer loaned a customer $3,600 for three years, at 8 percent. The total interest would be $0.08 \times \$3,600 \times 3 = \$864$. If the borrower was required to repay $100 of the principal each month, she would be repaying half the loan within 18 months, but would still pay the full $864 in interest. This customer's real interest rate was 16 percent, not 8 percent.

---

[8] Nancy Stancill, "Door-to-Door Firm Hit with $50,000 Penalty," *Houston Chronicle*, Jan. 28, 1993, p. A17.

[9] Quoted in Douglas Whaley, *Problems and Materials on Consumer Law* (Boston: Little, Brown & Co., 1991), at p. 135.

Truth in Lending Act

The problem with add-ons and other such devices designed to hide the real rate of interest from the authorities is that they also hide it from the borrower. Before TILA, many consumers had no idea what interest rate they were really paying. Congress passed the statute to ensure that consumers were adequately informed about credit terms before entering into a loan and could compare the cost of credit. TILA does not regulate interest rates or the terms of a loan; these are still set by state law. It simply requires lenders to *disclose* the terms of a loan in an understandable and complete manner. **TILA applies to a transaction only if all of the following tests are met:**

- *It is a consumer loan.* That means a loan to an individual for personal, family, or household purposes but not a loan to a business. For example, TILA does not apply to a loan on a truck used to sell produce.

- *The loan has a finance charge or will be repaid in more than four installments.* Sometimes finance charges masquerade as installment plans. Boris can pay for his big-screen TV in six monthly installments of $200 each, or he can pay $900 cash up front. If he chooses the installment plan, he is effectively paying a finance charge of $300. That is why TILA applies to loans with more than four installments.

- *The loan is for less than $25,000 or secured by a mortgage on real estate.* If Boris borrows money to buy a $1 million house, TILA applies, but not if he buys a $50,000 yacht.

- *The loan is made by someone in the business of offering credit.* If Boris borrows $5,000 from his friend Ludmilla to buy a riding mower, TILA does not apply. If he borrows the money from Friendly Neighborhood Loan Depot, Inc., TILA does apply.

Required Disclosure

In all loans regulated by TILA:

- *The disclosure must be clear and in meaningful sequence.* A finance company violated TILA when it loaned money to Dorothy Allen. The company made all the required disclosures but scattered them throughout the loan document and intermixed them with confusing terms that were not required by TILA.[10] A TILA disclosure statement should not be a game of *Where's Waldo.*

- *The lender must disclose the finance charge.* The finance charge is the amount, in dollars, the consumer will pay in interest and fees over the life of the loan. It is important for consumers to know this amount because otherwise they may not understand the real cost of the loan. Of course, the longer the loan, the higher the finance charge. Someone who borrows $5 for 10 years at 10 percent annual interest will pay $.50 each year for 10 years, for a total finance charge of $5—equal to the principal borrowed. In 25-year mortgages, the finance charge will almost always exceed the amount of the principal.

- *The creditor must also disclose the annual percentage rate (APR).* This number is the actual rate of interest the consumer pays on an annual basis. Without this disclosure, it would be easy in a short-term loan to disguise a very high APR because the finance charge is low. Boris borrows $5 for lunch from his employer's credit union. Under the terms of the loan, he must repay $6 the following week. His finance charge is only $1, but his APR is astronomical—20 percent per week – which is over 1000 percent for a year.

---

[10] *Allen v. Beneficial Fin. Co. of Gary,* 531 F.2d 797, 1976 U.S. App. LEXIS 12935 (7th Cir. 1976).

All TILA loans must meet these three requirements. TILA requires additional disclosure for two types of loans: open-end credit and closed-end credit.

Open-End Credit. This is a credit transaction in which the lender makes a *series* of loans that the consumer can repay at once or in installments. The typical VISA or MasterCard account is open-end credit—the cardholder has a choice of paying his balance in full each month or making only the required minimum payment.[11] In any advertisement or solicitation, the lender must disclose credit terms. If the lender is offering a *teaser rate* it must clearly disclose that the rate is introductory, when it expires, and the permanent rate that will replace it. In addition, before beginning an open-end credit account, the lender must disclose to the consumer when a finance charge will be imposed and how the finance charge will be calculated (for example, whether it will be based on the account balance at the beginning of the billing cycle, the end, or somewhere in between). **In each statement, the lender must disclose the following:** the amount owed at the beginning of the billing cycle (the previous balance); amounts and dates of all purchases, credits and payments; finance charges and late fees; the date by which a bill must be paid to avoid these charges; and either the consequences of making the monthly minimum payment or a toll free number at which to obtain such information. The Federal Reserve Board offers advice on choosing a credit card at **http://www.federalreserve.gov/pubs/shop**.

Closed-End Credit. In a closed-end transaction, there is only one loan, and the borrower knows the amount and the payment schedule in advance. Boris enters into a closed-end transaction when he buys a $30,000 car and agrees to make specified monthly payments over five years. Before a consumer enters into a closed-end transaction, the lender must disclose the cash price; the total down payment; the amount financed; an itemized list of all other charges; the number, amount, and due dates of payments; the total amount of payments; late payment charges; penalties for prepaying the loan; and the lender's security interest in the item purchased.[12]

Other TILA Provisions

Home Equity Loans. Scam artists sometimes prey upon the elderly who are vulnerable to pressure and upon the poor who may not have access to conventional financing. These swindlers offer home equity loans, secured by a second mortgage, to finance fraudulent repairs. (There are, of course, many legitimate lenders in the home equity business.) The following news report shows scam artists at work.

NEWS*worthy*

Mack and Jacqueline Moon of East Baltimore hired a home improvement contractor to install a dropped ceiling, paneling, and cabinets in the unfinished basement of their rowhouse. The couple were determined not to put a second mortgage on their house, anticipating they would need backup money to pay medical expenses for their 10-year-old daughter, who had lupus. They signed the contract a few days later after a second salesman assured them, "We were able to work it out, and you don't have to worry about a mortgage." The Moons were never given copies of the loan documents nor told of the 17 percent interest rate. A year later, when they tried to use their home's equity to pay medical bills for their daughter, who had since died, they discovered they had given a second mortgage to the lender without knowing it.[13] ◆

---

[11] Open-end credit rules apply to all consumer credit cards, even those that require the balance to be paid each month.

[12] See Chapter 26, on secured transactions, for a discussion of security interests.

[13] Lorraine Mirabella, "With Hopes of Improving Their Homes, Many Owners Fall Prey to Loan Scams," Baltimore Sun, Sep. 4, 1994, p. 1K.

In response to such scams, TILA was amended to provide additional consumer safeguards for home equity installment loans. If a home equity installment loan:

- Has an APR (interest rate) that is more than 10 percentage points higher than Treasury securities, or
- The consumer must pay fees and points at closing that are higher than 8 percent of the total loan amount,

  then,

- At least three business days before the loan closing the lender must notify the consumer that (1) he does not have to go through with the loan (even if he has signed the loan agreement) and (2) he could lose his house if he fails to make payments, and
- Loans that are for less than five years may not contain balloon payments (that is, a payment at the end that is more than twice the regular monthly payment).

Rescission. This change in the law came too late to help the Moons, but they found relief in a different TILA provision. Under TILA, consumers have the right to rescind a mortgage for up to three business days after the signing (including Saturdays). If the lender does not comply with the disclosure provisions of TILA, the consumer can rescind for up to three years from the date of the mortgage.

The Moons were able to rescind the loan because the lender had not made adequate disclosure. This right of rescission does *not* apply to a *first* mortgage used to finance a house purchase or to any refinancing with the consumer's existing lender. (Note that some states have passed, and others are considering, predatory lending laws that more strictly regulate loans with high fees or interest rates.)

The table below summarizes the major provisions of TILA.

TILA applies to a transaction only if:	• It is a consumer loan • The loan has a finance charge or will be repaid in more than four installments • The loan is for less than $25,000 or to secure a mortgage on real estate, and • The loan is made by someone in the business of offering credit.
In all loans regulated by TILA:	• The disclosure must be clear and in meaningful sequence, and • The lender must disclose the finance charge and the annual percentage rate (APR).
Consumers have the right to rescind a mortgage:	• For up to three business days after the signing, or • For up to three years from the date of the mortgage if the lender does not comply with TILA disclosure provisions. • This provision does not apply if the mortgage is a first mortgage used to finance a house purchase or a refinancing with the consumer's existing lender.

Advertising. TILA is meant to enable consumers to shop around and compare available financing alternatives. With this goal in mind, the statute requires lenders to advertise their rates accurately. A lender cannot **bait and switch;** that is, it cannot advertise rates unless they are generally available to anyone who applies. Moreover, if the lender advertises any credit terms, it must tell the whole story. For example, if it advertises "Nothing down, 12 months to pay," it must also disclose the APR and other terms of repayment.

Enforcement. The FTC generally has the right to enforce TILA. In addition, consumers who have been injured by any violation (except for the advertising provisions) have the right to file suit.

What is the economic impact of TILA? This statute requires lenders to provide a service against their will: detailed information about loans. Although this information is important to consumers, it is relatively expensive for them to produce while being relatively easy for lenders. Without TILA, consumers could compile credit information only by spending hours on the phone, asking questions of each lender. With TILA, all of this information to consumers is available more or less for free. (Although lenders do pass their costs on to consumers, this cost is low compared with the value of the information or the cost to consumers if they had to find out the information on their own.)

Economists believe in efficiency, which means, among other things, that a product should be produced as cheaply as possible. TILA is consistent with this goal: it insures that loan information is produced cheaply (by lenders) rather than at great cost (by consumers).

Access to detailed loan information permits borrowers to compare competing offers. The ability to comparison shop enhances consumers' market power. Greater customer power leads to lower prices. In short, TILA not only protects consumers from entering into loans that are more expensive than they realized, it also lowers the cost of borrowing money. ◆

Special Credit Card Rules. Your wallet is missing, and with it your cash, your driver's license, a photo of your dog, a coupon for a free DVD rental and—oh! no!—all your credit cards! It is a disaster, to be sure. But it could have been worse. There was a time when you would have been responsible for every charge the thief rang up. **Now, under TILA, you are liable only for the first $50 in charges the thief makes before you notify the credit card company.** If you call the company before any charges are made, you have no liability at all. But if, by the time you contact the company, the speedy robber has completely furnished her apartment on your card, you are still liable only for $50. Of course, if you carry a wallet full of cards, $50 for each one can add up to a sizable total. If the thief steals just your credit card number, but not the card itself, you are not liable for any unauthorized charges.

These two pieces of plastic look the same, but offer different legal protections.

Suppose that a credit card company mails a card to you that you did not order and someone steals it out of your mailbox. You know nothing about the card until the bills arrive. If you did not request the card, and it is not a renewal or substitute for a card you already have, you are not liable, even for the $50.

You use your credit card to buy a new computer at Shady-Computers. When you arrive home and start to load software, you discover the hard disk is only 1 gigabyte, not the 80 that was advertised. The computer crashes six times the first day. In short, you have a major, $1,500 problem. But all is not lost. **In the event of a dispute between a customer and a merchant, the credit card company cannot bill the customer if** (1) she makes a good faith effort to resolve the dispute, (2) the dispute is for more than $50, and (3) the merchant is in the same state where she lives or is within 100 miles of her house.

What happens if the merchant and the consumer cannot resolve their dispute? Or if the merchant is not in the same state as the consumer? Clearly, credit card companies do not want to be caught in the middle between consumer and merchant. In practice, they now require all merchants to sign a contract specifying that, in the event of a dispute between the merchant and a customer, the credit card company has the right to charge back the merchant's account. If a customer seems to have a reasonable claim against a merchant, the credit card company will typically transfer the credit it has given the merchant back to the customer's account. Of course, the merchant can try to sue the customer for any money owed.

Debit Cards. So your wallet is missing, and with it your debit card. No problem, right, it is just like a credit card? Wrong. Debit cards look and feel like credit cards, but legally they are a different plastic altogether. Debit cards work like checks (which is why they are also called **check cards**). When you use your debit card, the bank deducts money directly from your account, which means there is no bill to pay at the end of the month (and no interest charges on unpaid bills). That is the good news. The bad news is that your liability for a stolen debit card is much greater. If you report the loss before anyone uses your card, you are not liable for any unauthorized withdrawals. If you report the theft within two days of discovering it, the bank will make good on all losses above $50. If you wait until after two days, your bank will only replace stolen funds above $500. After 60 days of receipt of your bank statement, all losses are yours: the bank will not repay any stolen funds. If an unauthorized transfer takes place using just your number, not your card, then you are not liable at all as long as you report the loss within 60 days of receiving the bank statement showing the loss. After 60 days, however, you are liable for the full amount.

Fair Credit Billing Act

The Fair Credit Billing Act (FCBA) provides additional protection for credit card holders. Is there anyone in America who has not sometime or other discovered an error in a credit card bill? Before Congress passed the FCBA in 1975, a dispute with a credit card company often deteriorated into an avalanche of threatening form letters that ignored any response from the hapless cardholder. **Under the FCBA:**

- If, within 60 days of receipt of a bill, a consumer writes to a credit card company to complain about the bill, the company must acknowledge receipt of the complaint within 30 days.

- Within two billing cycles (but no more than 90 days) the credit card company must investigate the complaint and respond:

  - In the case of an error, by correcting the mistake and notifying the consumer

  - If there is no error, by writing to the consumer with an explanation

- Whether or not there was a mistake, if the consumer requests it, the credit card company must supply documentary evidence to support its position—for example, copies of the bill signed by the consumer or evidence that the package actually arrived.

- The credit card company cannot try to collect the disputed debt or close or suspend the account until it has responded to the consumer complaint.

- The credit card company cannot report to credit agencies that the consumer has an unpaid bill until 10 days after the response. If the consumer still disputes the charge, the credit card company may report the amount to a credit agency but must disclose that it is disputed.

At **http://www.ftc.gov/bcp/conline/pubs/credit/fcb.htm** the FTC provides a sample form letter to send to a credit card company if you want to dispute a bill.

In the following case, American Express made a big mistake picking on a law professor. The court's opinion was written by Abner J. Mikva, a highly regarded judge on the federal appeals court. He was clearly exasperated by American Express's arguments and used strong language to reprimand the company—and the lower court. Since Judge Mikva had served in Congress, he could speak with some authority about Congress's approach to consumer legislation.

GRAY V. AMERICAN EXPRESS CO.

743 F.2d 10, 240 U.S. App. D.C. 10, 1984 U.S. App. LEXIS 19033
United States Court of Appeals for the District of Columbia Circuit, 1984

Facts: In December, Oscar Gray used his American Express credit card to buy airline tickets costing $9,312. American Express agreed that Gray could pay for the tickets in 12 monthly installments. In January, Gray paid $3,500 and then in February an additional $1,156. In March, American Express billed Gray by mistake for the entire remaining balance, which he did not pay. In April, Gray and his wife went out for dinner to celebrate their wedding anniversary. When he tried to pay with his American Express card, the restaurant told him that the credit card company had not only refused to accept the charges for the meal, but had instructed the restaurant to confiscate and destroy the card. While still at the restaurant, Gray spoke to an American Express employee on the telephone who informed him, "Your account is canceled as of now."

Gray wrote to American Express, pointing out the error. For more than a year, the company failed to respond to Gray or to investigate his claim. It then turned the bill over to a collection agency. Gray sued American Express for violating the Fair Credit Billing Act. The trial court granted summary judgment to American Express and dismissed the complaint on the grounds that Gray had waived his rights under the act.

Issue: Is American Express liable to Gray for violating the Fair Credit Billing Act?

Excerpts from Judge Mikva's Decision: The contract between Gray and American Express provides: "We can revoke your right to use [the card] at any time. We can do this with or without cause and without giving you notice." American Express concludes from this language that the cancellation was not of the kind prohibited by the Act, even though the Act regulates other aspects of the relationship between the cardholder and the card issuer.

[T]he Act states that, during the pendency of a disputed billing, the card issuer shall not cause the cardholder's account to be restricted or closed because of the failure of the obligor to pay the amount in dispute. American Express seems to argue that, despite that provision, it can exercise its right to cancellation for cause unrelated to the disputed amount, or for no cause, thus bringing itself out from under the statute. At the very least, the argument is audacious. American Express would restrict the efficacy of the statute to those situations where the parties had not agreed to a "without cause, without notice" cancellation clause, or to those cases where the cardholder can prove that the sole reason for cancellation was the amount in dispute. We doubt that Congress painted with such a faint brush.

The effect of American Express's argument is to allow the equivalent of a "waiver" of coverage of the Act simply by allowing the parties to contract it away. Congress usually is not so tepid in its approach to consumer problems. The rationale of consumer protection legislation is to even out the inequalities that consumers normally bring to the bargain. To allow such protection to be waived by boiler plate language of the contract puts the legislative process to a foolish and unproductive task. A court ought not impute such nonsense to a Congress intent on correcting abuses in the market place.

The district court's order of summary judgment and dismissal is hereby *vacated*. ■

Fair Credit Reporting Act

Gossip and rumor can cause great harm. Bad enough when whispered behind one's back, worse yet when placed in files and distributed to potential creditors. Most adults rely on credit—to acquire a house, credit cards, or overdraft privileges at the bank. A sullied credit report makes life immensely more difficult. The goal of the Fair Credit Reporting Act (FCRA) is to ensure that consumer credit reports are accurate.

The FCRA regulates **consumer reporting agencies.** These are businesses that supply consumer reports to third parties. If an insurance agency or bank conducts its own investigation to determine whether a consumer is creditworthy, the FCRA does not apply. A **consumer report** is any communication about a consumer's creditworthiness, character, general reputation, or lifestyle that is considered as a factor in establishing credit, obtaining insurance, securing a job, acquiring a government license, or for any other legitimate business need.

Under the FCRA:

- A consumer report can be used only for a legitimate business need, and a consumer reporting agency must be careful not to supply reports that will be used for any other purpose. A nosy neighbor does not have the right to order a report.

- A consumer reporting agency cannot report obsolete information. Ordinary credit information is obsolete after seven years, bankruptcies after 10 years. (But if a consumer is applying for more than $150,000 of credit or life insurance, or for a job that pays more than $75,000 a year, then there is no time limit.) **Investigative reports** that discuss character, reputation, or lifestyle become obsolete in three *months*. Some commentators argue that the type of information contained in investigative reports is not relevant and should not be used at all. Although the FCRA does not limit the kinds of information that can be collected and reported, it does specify that an investigative report cannot be ordered without first informing the consumer.

- A consumer reporting agency cannot report medical information without the consumer's permission.

- An employer cannot request a consumer report on any current or potential employee without the employee's permission. An employer cannot take action because of information in the consumer report without first giving the current or potential employee a copy of the report and a description of the employee's rights under this statute.

- Anyone who makes an adverse decision against a consumer because of a credit report must reveal the name and address of the reporting agency that supplied the information. An "adverse decision" includes denying credit or charging higher rates.

- Upon request from a consumer, a reporting agency must disclose all information in his file, the source of the information (except for investigative reports), the name of anyone to whom a report has been sent in the prior year (two years for employment purposes), and the name of anyone who has requested a report in the prior year.

- If a consumer tells an agency that some of the information in his file is incorrect, the agency must both investigate and forward the data to the information provider. The information provider must investigate and report the results to the agency. If the data are inaccurate, the information provider must so notify all national credit agencies. The consumer also has the right to give the agency a short report telling his side of the story. The agency must then include the consumer's statement with any credit reports it supplies and also, at the consumer's request, send the statement to anyone who has received a report within six months (or two years for employment purposes).
The following article illustrates the usefulness of the FCRA.

NEWS*worthy*

Kimberly Dorcik wanted a new job. An assistant manager at a Lechters housewares store, she applied for the manager's position at Ups 'N Downs, a women's clothing store a dozen doors away in Solano Mall, in Fairfield, California. But her hopes for the job, which paid a few thousand dollars more than she was earning, vanished, she said, when the staff member taking her application whispered: "We're not supposed to tell anybody, but we pull credit reports on people. Is that going to be a problem?"

Ms. Dorcik remembers mumbling a noncommittal response, but she knew that it was going to be a problem. Three years earlier, when she was 19, she had had emergency surgery resulting from complications from pregnancy. Because of what she calls a clerical error, $30,000 in medical bills were still unpaid and in dispute, tainting her credit history. Ms. Dorcik did not get the job, and she said she was almost certain that the deciding factor was her credit history. The FCRA now requires employers to tell applicants like Ms. Dorcik if credit histories are being used as part of hiring. Employers will also have to obtain written permission from applicants before even requesting a credit history. If someone is turned down for a job and a credit report was used in the decision, the applicant can presumably weed out wrong information in the report and reapply.[14] ◆

Fair and Accurate Credit Transactions Act

In identity theft, a fraudster steals his victim's personal information, such as social security number, credit card information, or mother's maiden name, and uses it to obtain credit or goods in the victim's name. In short, to wreak havoc in the victim's life. The goal of the Fair and Accurate Credit Transactions Act (FACTA) is to reduce identity theft.

FACTA provides that consumers are entitled by law to one free credit report every year from each of the three major reporting agencies: Equifax, Experian, and Trans-Union. You can order these reports at https://www.annualcreditreport.com. Consumer advocates recommend that you do check your credit reports every year to make sure they are accurate and also that no one else has been obtaining credit in your name. If you find any errors, notify the agency in writing and warn it that failing to make corrections is a violation of the law. At http://www.ftc.gov/bcp/conline/pubs/credit/crdtdis.htm, the FTC offers advice on how to dispute credit report errors.

FACTA also created the National Fraud Alert System, which permits consumer who fear they may be the victim of identity theft to place an alert in their credit files, warning financial institutions to investigate carefully before issuing any new credit. It also requires credit bureaus to share information about identity theft.

Also, under the Gramm-Leach-Bliley Privacy Act of 1999, banks, other financial institutions, and consumer reporting agencies must notify a consumer (1) before disclosing any personal information to a third party or (2) if there has been unauthorized access to the consumer's sensitive personal information.[15] The company cannot disclose private information if the consumer *opts out* (that is, denies permission).

Fair Debt Collection Practices Act

The introduction to the Fair Debt Collection Practices Act (FDCPA) states that "Abusive debt collection practices contribute to the number of personal bankruptcies, to marital instability, to the loss of jobs, and to invasions of individual privacy."[16] Debt collection practices can also disrupt Super Bowl Sunday. Debt collectors seek to catch their prey off guard, and what better time than when the entire nation is at home, glued to the television? If the phone rings, sports fans assume it is a friend calling to gab about the game.

Is that legal? It depends. **The FDCPA provides** that a collector must, within five days of contacting a debtor, send the debtor a written notice containing the amount of the debt, the name of the creditor to whom the debt is owed, and a statement that if

---

[14] Anthony Ramirez, "Name, Resume, References. And How's Your Credit," *New York Times*, Aug. 31, 1997, p. F8. Copyright © 1997 by The New York Times Co. Reprinted by permission.

[15] 15 U.S.C. §6801.

[16] 15 U.S.C. §1692(a).

the debtor disputes the debt (in writing), the collector will cease all collection efforts until it has sent evidence of the debt. **Also under the FDCPA, collectors may not:**

- Call or write a debtor who has notified the collector in writing that he wishes no further contact
- Call or write a debtor who is represented by an attorney
- Call a debtor before 8:00 A.M. or after 9:00 P.M.
- Threaten a debtor or use obscene or abusive language
- Call or visit the debtor at work if the consumer's employer prohibits such contact
- Imply that they are attorneys or government representatives when they are not, or use a false name
- Threaten to arrest consumers who do not pay their debts
- Make other false or deceptive threats, that is, threats that would be illegal if carried out or which the collector has no intention of doing—such as suing the debtor or seizing property
- Contact acquaintances of the debtor for any reason other than to locate the debtor (and then only once), or
- Tell acquaintances that the consumer is in debt.

Of course, these rules do not prevent the collector from filing suit against the debtor. In the event of a violation of the FDCPA, the debtor is entitled to damages, court costs, and attorney's fees. The FTC also has authority to enforce the Act.

The following case illustrates the types of abuses that the FDCPA was designed to prevent.

GRADISHER V. CHECK ENFORCEMENT UNIT, INC.

2002 U.S. Dist. LEXIS 6003
United States District Court for the Western District of Michigan, 2002

Facts: Check Enforcement Unit, Inc. (CEU), was in the business of helping merchants collect on bad checks. When a merchant received a dishonored check, it would forward the check directly to CEU, which would then send out a series of notices to the check writer, using the letterhead of the local Sheriff's Department. CEU had permission to use this letterhead, but the Sheriff's Department was not otherwise involved in the collection effort. Only after the three notices had been sent, and no payment received, would CEU notify the Sheriff's Department about a bad check. Even then, the check did not become a criminal matter until the Sheriff's Department assigned a complaint number.

After Sherri Gradisher bounced a check for $81.30 at Doug Born's Smokehouse, she received three notices from CEU. Gradisher filed suit alleging that CEU had violated the FDCPA.

Issue: Did CEU violate the FDCPA?

Excerpts from Judge Quist's Decision: CEU admits that the Notice did not contain the exact language required by the statute but contends that it did contain much of the information required, such as the amount of the debt, the name of the creditor, and a telephone number and address which Gradisher could use to contact CEU if she wished to dispute the debt. [But] the Notice does not state [as required by law] that the debtor may dispute the validity of the debt by notifying the debt collector in writing within thirty days after receipt of the Notice.

▼

Gradisher contends that CEU violated [the statute] because CEU's use of the letterhead of the Office of the Sheriff gave the false and misleading impression that the notices were from the Sheriff's Department when they were actually from CEU. In addition, Gradisher contends that CEU violated the FDCPA by failing to disclose its true name.

[The Notices] all conveyed the impression that they were authorized, created, and sent by the Sheriff's Department without any indication that CEU, an independent contractor of the County, was actually the entity that generated the notices. The fact that CEU had an "affiliation" with the Sheriff's Department is irrelevant because CEU's notices created the false impression that the notices were generated by the Sheriff's Department. Moreover, CEU's notices violated [the statute] because CEU used a name other than its own name.

Gradisher's next claim is that CEU violated the FDCPA by implying that Gradisher would be arrested or imprisoned if she failed to pay the debt. The back side of the Notice stated:

> WARNING
> Failure To Make Payment Can Result In A Warrant For Your Arrest

[Any] debtor would conclude after reading CEU's notices that the Sheriff's Department had determined that the debtor committed a crime and arrest or criminal prosecution was certain to occur if the debt was not paid. In fact, the Sheriff's Department had no involvement with the notices sent by CEU and never made any determination regarding violation of the law or arrest. Gradisher has shown that criminal prosecution occurs infrequently on files CEU sends to the Sheriff's Department. Thus, in any given case there is only a slight possibility of criminal prosecution. Under these circumstances, CEU's notices violated [the statute]. ■

---

at RISK

If a debt collector calls you, what can you do? First of all, be sure to write down his name and the name of the agency for which he works. Tell the caller that you are recording the conversation and then do so. Send a letter to the agency, requesting that it not contact you. Report any violations to the FTC at http://www.ftc.gov/bcp/conline/pubs/credit/fdc.htm. ◆

Equal Credit Opportunity Act

The Equal Credit Opportunity Act (ECOA) prohibits any creditor from discriminating against a borrower because of race, color, religion, national origin, sex, marital status, age (as long as the borrower is old enough to enter into a legal contract), or because the borrower is receiving welfare. A lender must respond to a credit application within 30 days. If a lender rejects an application, it must either tell the applicant why or notify him that he has the right to a written explanation of the reasons for this *adverse action*. The following news report illustrates the types of abuses that the ECOA is designed to prevent.

NEWS*worthy*

Florence and Joe made an offer to buy a new home at the Meadowood housing development near Tampa. The developer accepted their offer, contingent upon their obtaining a mortgage. When the couple filed an application with Rancho Mortgage and Investment Corp., they were surprised by the hostility of Rancho's loan processor. She requested information they had already supplied and repeatedly questioned them about whether they intended to occupy the house, which was about 80 miles from their jobs. Florence and Joe insisted they wanted to live near their son and daughter-in-law and escape city crime. Rancho turned down their mortgage, refusing to give either an oral or a written explanation. The house was sold to another buyer.

Joe and Florence didn't get mad, they got even. They sued under the ECOA. Rancho was ordered to pay the African American couple $35,000.[17] ◆

---

[17] Robert J. Bruss, "Home Buyers Sue Mortgage Lender for Racial Discrimination," *Tampa Tribune*, Nov. 5, 1994, p. 3.

As the following case illustrates, the ECOA protects against a broad range of wrongdoing.

TREADWAY V. GATEWAY CHEVROLET OLDSMOBILE INC.

362 F.3d 971, 2004 U.S. App. LEXIS 6325
United States Court of Appeals for the Seventh Circuit, 2004

Facts: Gateway Chevrolet Oldsmobile (GCO), a car dealership, sent an unsolicited letter to Tonja Treadway notifying her that she was "pre-approved" for the financing to purchase a car. GCO did not provide financing itself; instead, it arranged loans through banks or finance companies.

Treadway called the dealer to say that she was interested in purchasing a used car. She divulged her social security number so that GCO could obtain her credit report. Based on this report, the dealer determined that Treadway was not eligible for financing. This was not surprising, given that GCO had purchased Treadway's name for the direct-mail solicitation from a list of people who had recently filed for bankruptcy.

Instead of applying for a loan on behalf of Treadway, GCO called her and invited her to come to the dealership. At the dealership, Gateway told her that it had found a bank that would finance her transaction, but only if she purchased a new car and provided a cosigner. Treadway agreed to purchase a new car and came up with Pearlie Smith, her godmother, to serve as a cosigner.

Concerned as it was with customer convenience, GCO had an agent deliver papers directly to Smith's house to be signed immediately. If Smith had read the papers before she signed them, she might have realized that she had committed herself to be the sole purchaser and owner of the car. But she had no idea that she was the owner until she began receiving bills on the car loan. After Treadway made the first payment on behalf of Smith, both women refused to pay more—Smith because she did not want a new car; Treadway because the car was not hers. The car was repossessed but the financing company continued to demand payment.

On closer inspection, it appears that GCO was running a scam. It would lure desperate prospects off the bankruptcy rolls and into the showroom with promises of financing for a used car, and then sell a new car to their "co-signer" (who was, in fact, the sole signer). Instead of selling a used car to Tonja Treadway, GCO sold a new car to Pearlie Smith.

Treadway filed suit against GCO, alleging that it had violated the ECOA by not notifying her that it had taken an adverse action against her. The district court granted GCO's motion for summary judgment on the grounds that GCO had not committed an adverse action under the ECOA. This appeal followed.

Issue: Did Gateway violate the ECOA?

Excerpts from Judge Cudahy's Decision: The term "adverse action" is defined in relevant part by the ECOA as "a denial or revocation of credit." By unilaterally deciding not to send Treadway's application to *any* lender, Gateway effectively denied credit to Treadway. Whether it is the lender or the dealership that makes the decision, both the action and the outcome are the same. In both cases, the decision maker (1) reviews the applicant's credit report to determine whether she is creditworthy, (2) makes a determination adverse to the applicant (i.e., that she is not creditworthy), (3) decides not to proceed any further in arranging credit and (4) as a result the applicant is not granted credit. There is no logical reason why these same steps would be considered an "adverse action" when taken by a lender but not when taken by a dealership, given that the result is the same in either case.

If an automobile dealership that decides against referring a particular applicant to any lender need not provide notice of this decision to the applicant, then it becomes significantly easier for it to discriminate. [I]f an applicant never receives notice, it will be difficult for her to ever determine that she was the victim of discrimination. This is particularly true because, as was the case here, without proper notice, the applicant may assume that her application *was* sent to lenders, and it was the lenders who did the rejecting. Car dealers could throw the credit report of every minority applicant in the "circular file" and none would be the wiser.

Therefore, based on the foregoing analysis, we find that Gateway's action constitutes an "adverse action" for purposes of the ECOA. ■

Consumer Leasing Act

If you, like many other consumers, lease a car rather than buy it, you are protected under the Consumer Leasing Act (CLA). The CLA does not apply to the rental of real property—that is, to house or apartment leases. **Before a lease is signed, a lessor must disclose the following in writing:**

- All required payments, including deposits, down payments, taxes, and license fees
- The number and amount of each monthly payment and how payments are calculated
- Balloon payments (that is, payments due at the end of the lease)
- Required insurance payments
- The total amount the consumer will have paid by the end of the lease
- Available warranties
- Maintenance requirements and a description of the lessor's wear and use standards
- Penalties for late payments
- The consumer's right to purchase the leased property and at what price
- The consumer's right to terminate a lease early
- Any penalties for early termination

The government brochure "Keys to Vehicle Leasing" is available at **http://www .federalreserve.gov/pubs/leasing/**. It lays out the lessor's rights and compares the advantages and disadvantages of leasing versus purchasing a car.

MAGNUSON-MOSS WARRANTY ACT

When Senator Frank E. Moss sponsored the Magnuson-Moss Warranty Act, this is how he explained the need for such a statute:

> [W]arranties have for many years confused, misled, and frequently angered American consumers. . . . Consumer anger is expected when purchasers of consumer products discover that their warranty may cover a 25-cent part but not the $100 labor charge or that there is full coverage on a piano so long as it is shipped at the purchaser's expense to the factory. . . . There is a growing need to generate consumer understanding by clearly and conspicuously disclosing the terms and conditions of the warranty and by telling the consumer what to do if his guaranteed product becomes defective or malfunctions.[18]

The Magnuson-Moss Warranty Act does not require manufacturers or sellers to provide a warranty on their products. **The Act does require any supplier that offers a written warranty on a consumer product that costs more than $15 to disclose the terms of the warranty in simple, understandable language** *before the sale*. This statute covers sales by catalog or on the Internet. Required disclosure includes the following:

- The name and address of the person the consumer should contact to obtain warranty service
- The parts that are covered and those that are not
- What services the warrantor will provide, at whose expense, and for what period of time
- A statement of what the consumer must do and what expenses he must pay

---

[18] *Quoted in* David G. Epstein and Steve H. Nickles, *Consumer Law* (Eagan, Minn.: West, 1981).

Although suppliers are not required to offer a warranty, if they do offer one they must indicate whether it is *full* or *limited*. Under a **full warranty,** the warrantor must promise to fix a defective product for a reasonable time without charge. If, after a reasonable number of efforts to fix the defective product, it still does not work, the consumer must have the right to a refund or a replacement without charge; but the warrantor is not required to cover damage caused by the consumer's unreasonable use.

CONSUMER PRODUCT SAFETY

In 1969, the federal government estimated that consumer products caused 30,000 deaths, 110,000 disabling injuries, and 20 million trips to the doctor. Toys were among the worst offenders, injuring 700,000 children a year. Children were cut by Etch-a-Sketch glass panels, choked by Zulu gun darts, and burned by Little Lady toy ovens. Although injured consumers had the right to seek damages under tort law, the goal of the Consumer Product Safety Act of 1972 (CPSA) was to prevent injuries in the first place. This act created the Consumer Product Safety Commission to evaluate consumer products and develop safety standards. The Commission can impose civil and criminal penalties on those who violate its standards. Individuals have the right to sue under the CPSA for damages, including attorney's fees, from anyone who knowingly violates a consumer product safety rule. You can find out about product recalls or file a report on an unsafe product at the Commission's Web site (**http://www.cpsc.gov**).

Chapter Conclusion

Virtually no one will go through life without reading an advertisement, ordering from a catalog, borrowing money, needing a credit report, or using a consumer product. It is important to know your rights.

Chapter Review

1. The Federal Trade Commission (FTC) prohibits "unfair and deceptive acts or practices." A practice is unfair if it meets the following three tests:

   - It causes a substantial consumer injury.
   - The harm of the injury outweighs any countervailing benefit.
   - The consumer could not reasonably avoid the injury.

2. The FTC considers an advertisement to be deceptive if it contains an important misrepresentation or omission that is likely to mislead a reasonable consumer.

3. FTC rules prohibit bait and switch advertisements. A merchant may not advertise a product and then disparage it to consumers in an effort to sell a different item.

4. The FTC prohibits telemarketers from calling telephone numbers listed on its do-not-call registry.

5. Consumers may keep as a gift any unordered merchandise that they receive in the mail.

6. Under the FTC door-to-door rules, a salesperson is required to notify the buyer that she has the right to cancel the transaction prior to midnight of the third business day thereafter.

7. In all loans regulated by the Truth in Lending Act (TILA), the disclosure must be clear and in meaningful sequence. The lender must disclose the finance charge and the annual percentage rate.

8. In the case of a high-rate home equity loan, the lender must notify the consumer at least three business days before the closing that (1) he does not have to go through with the loan (even if he has signed the loan agreement) and (2) he could lose his house if he fails to make payments. If the duration of a high-rate home equity loan is less than five years, it may not contain balloon payments.

9. Under TILA, consumers have the right to rescind a mortgage (other than a first mortgage) for three business days after the signing. If the lender does not comply with the disclosure provisions of TILA, the consumer may rescind for up to three years from the date of the mortgage.

10. Under TILA, a *credit* card holder is liable only for the first $50 in unauthorized charges made before the credit card company is notified that the card was stolen. If, however, you wait more than two days to report the loss of a *debit* card, your bank will only reimburse you for losses in excess of $500. If you fail to report the lost debit card within 60 days of receipt of your bank statement, the bank is not liable at all.

11. In the event of a dispute between a customer and a merchant, the credit card company cannot bill the customer if:

    • She makes a good faith effort to resolve the dispute

    • The dispute is for more than $50, and

    • The merchant is in the same state where she lives or is within 100 miles of her house.

12. Under the Fair Credit Billing Act, a credit card company must promptly investigate and respond to any consumer complaints about a credit card bill.

13. Under the Fair Credit Reporting Act:

    • A consumer report can be used only for a legitimate business need

    • A consumer reporting agency cannot report obsolete information

    • An employer cannot request a consumer report on any current or potential employee without the employee's permission, and

    • Anyone who makes an adverse decision against a consumer because of a credit report must reveal the name and address of the reporting agency that supplied the negative information.

14. The Fair and Accurate Credit Transactions Act permits consumers to obtain one free credit report every year from each of the three major reporting agencies.

15. Under the Fair Debt Collection Practices Act, a debt collector may not harass or abuse debtors.

16. The Equal Credit Opportunity Act prohibits any creditor from discriminating against a borrower on the basis of race, color, religion, national origin, sex, marital status, age, or because the borrower is receiving welfare.

17. The Magnuson-Moss Warranty Act requires any supplier that offers a written warranty on a consumer product costing more than $15 to disclose the terms of the warranty in simple and readily understandable language before the sale.

18. The Consumer Product Safety Commission evaluates consumer products and develops safety standards.

Practice Test

1. In August, Dorothy Jenkins went to First American Mortgage and Loan Association of Virginia (the Bank) to sign a second mortgage on her home. Her first mortgage was with a different bank. She left the closing without a copy of the required Truth in Lending Act disclosure forms. Jenkins defaulted on her loan payments, and, the following May, the Bank began foreclosure proceedings on her house. In June, she notified the Bank that she wished to rescind the loan. Does Jenkins have a right to rescind the loan 10 months after it was made?

2. **YOU BE THE JUDGE** WRITING PROBLEM
Process cheese food slices must contain at least 51 percent natural cheese. Imitation cheese slices, by contrast, contain little or no natural cheese and consist primarily of water, vegetable oil, flavoring, and fortifying agents. Kraft, Inc., makes Kraft Singles, which are individually wrapped process cheese food slices. When Kraft began losing market share to imitation slices that were advertised as both less expensive and equally nutritious as Singles, Kraft responded with a

series of advertisements informing consumers that Kraft Singles cost more than imitation slices because they are made from five ounces of milk. Kraft does use five ounces of milk in making each Kraft Single, but 30 percent of the calcium contained in the milk is lost during processing. Imitation slices contain the same amount of calcium as Kraft Singles. Are the Kraft advertisements deceptive? **Argument for Kraft:** This statement is completely true—Kraft does use five ounces of milk in each Kraft Single. The FTC is assuming that the only value of milk is the calcium. In fact, people might prefer having milk rather than vegetable oil, regardless of the calcium. **Argument for the FTC:** It is deceptive to advertise more milk if the calcium is the same after all the processing.

3. Joel Curtis was two and his brother, Joshua, was three years old when their father left both children asleep in the rear seat of his automobile while visiting a friend. His cigarette lighter was on the dashboard of the car. After awaking, Joshua began playing with the lighter and set fire to Joel's diaper. Do the parents have a claim against the manufacturer of the lighter under the Consumer Product Safety Act?

4. Josephine Rutyna was a 60-year-old widow who suffered from high blood pressure and epilepsy. A bill collector from Collections Accounts Terminal, Inc., called her and demanded that she pay $56 she owed to Cabrini Hospital Medical Group. She told him that Medicare was supposed to pay the bill. Shortly thereafter, Rutyna received a letter from Collections that stated:

> You have shown that you are unwilling to work out a friendly settlement with us to clear the above debt. Our field investigator has now been instructed to make an investigation in your neighborhood and to personally call on your employer. The immediate payment of the full amount, or a personal visit to this office, will spare you this embarrassment.

Has Collections violated the law?

5. Thomas Pinner worked at a Sherwin-Williams paint store that was managed by James Schmidt. Pinner and Schmidt had a falling out when, according to Pinner, "a relationship began to bloom between Pinner and one of the young female employees, the one Schmidt was obsessed with." Pinner quit. Schmidt claimed that Pinner owed the company $121.71 for paint he had taken but not paid for. Sherwin-Williams reported this information to Chilton, who ran a credit reporting agency. Pinner's attorney sent a letter to Chilton notifying him that Pinner disputed the accuracy of the Sherwin-Williams charges. Chilton contacted Schmidt who confirmed that Pinner's account remained delinquent. Chilton failed to note in Pinner's file that a dispute was pending. Thereafter, Pinner was denied credit cards at two stores. Have Schmidt and Chilton violated the Fair Credit Reporting Act?

6. Kathleen Carroll, a single woman, applied for an Exxon credit card. Exxon rejected her application without giving any specific reason and without providing the name of the credit bureau it had used. When Carroll asked for a reason for the rejection, she was told that the credit bureau did not have enough information about her to establish creditworthiness. In fact, Exxon had denied her credit application because she did not have a major credit card or a savings account, she had been employed for only one year, and she had no dependents. Did Exxon violate the law?

7. In October, Renie Guimond discovered that her credit report at TransUnion Credit Information Co. incorrectly stated that she was married, used the name "Ruth Guimond," and had a credit card from Saks Fifth Avenue. After she reported the errors, TransUnion wrote her in November to say that it had removed this information. However, in March, TransUnion again published the erroneous information. The following October, TransUnion finally removed the incorrect information from her file. Guimond was never denied credit because of these mistakes. Is Trans-Union liable for violating the Fair Credit Reporting Act?

8. The National Coalition for Consumer Education and MasterCard International created the following quiz to help consumers find out how smart they are about buying on credit:

   a. What's the best way to correct a mistake on your credit card bill?

      i. Call your credit card issuer immediately and explain the mistake.

      ii. Circle the mistake in red and return the bill to your card issuer.

      iii. Immediately write a letter to your credit card issuer and clearly describe the problem.

b. How should you handle an unauthorized charge (a purchase that you didn't make) if you see one on your credit card statement?

    i. Write a letter to the company that accepted your card for payment to absolve yourself of any liability.

    ii. Call your credit issuer immediately to alert them.

    iii. Note the error on your credit card bill and refuse to pay it.[19]

9. Thomas Waldock purchased a 1983 BMW 320i from Universal Motors, Inc. It was warranted "to be free of defects in materials or workmanship for a period of three years or 36,000 miles, whichever occurs first." Within the warranty period, the car's engine failed and upon examination was found to be extensively damaged. Universal denied warranty coverage because it concluded that Waldock damaged the engine by over-revving it. Waldock vehemently disputed BMW's contention. He claimed that, while being driven at a low speed, the engine emitted a gear-crunching noise, ceased operation, and would not restart. Is Universal in violation of the law?

10.

> GET ENOUGH BROADLOOM TO CARPET ANY AREA OF YOUR HOME OR APARTMENT UP TO 150 SQUARE FEET CUT, MEASURED, AND READY FOR INSTALLATION FOR ONLY $77.
> GET 100% DUPONT CONTINUOUS FILAMENT NYLON PILE BROADLOOM.
> CALL COLLECT

When customers called the number provided, New Rapids Carpet Center, Inc., sent salespeople to visit them at home to sell them carpet that was not as advertised—it was not continuous filament nylon pile broadloom, and the price was not $77. Has New Rapids violated a consumer law?

11. *ETHICS* After TNT Motor Express hired Joseph Bruce Drury as a truck driver, it ordered a background check from Robert Arden & Associates. TNT provided Drury's Social Security number and date of birth, but not his middle name. Arden discovered that a Joseph *Thomas* Drury, who coincidentally had the same birth date as Joseph *Bruce* Drury, had served a prison sentence for drunk driving. Not knowing that it had the wrong Drury, Arden reported this information to TNT, which promptly fired Drury. When he asked why, the TNT executive merely stated, "We do not discuss these matters." Did TNT violate the law? Whether or not TNT was in violation, did its executives behave ethically? Who would have been harmed or helped if TNT managers had informed Drury of the Arden report?

12. Advertisements for Listerine mouthwash claimed that it was as effective as flossing in preventing tooth plaque and gum disease. This statement was true, but only if the flossing was done incorrectly. In fact, many consumers do floss incorrectly. However, if flossing is done right, it is more effective against plaque and gum disease than Listerine. Is this advertisement deceptive? Does it violate §5 of the FTC Act?

13. *ROLE REVERSAL* Prepare a short-answer question that focuses on deceptive advertisements. Include a sample ad in the question (either a real ad or one that you have made up.)

Internet Research Problem

The Consumer Product Safety Commission (**http://beatty.westbuslaw.com**) lists products that have been recalled and provides consumers with a telephone number for contacting the manufacturer. Choose a recalled product and telephone the manufacturer to find out how it is handling the problem. Also see if you can find the manufacturer's Web site to learn if it has disclosed the recall there. What do you think of the manner in which the manufacturer has handled the recall? Is the manufacturer providing adequate protection to consumers?

> **You can find further practice problems at http://beatty.westbuslaw.com or in the Study Guide that accompanies this text.**

---

[19] "Give Yourself Some Credit If You Pass This Quiz", *Times-Picayune*, Apr. 7, 1994, p. E5. Permission granted by the Times-Picayune Publishing Corporation. All rights reserved. Reprinted with permission.

Environmental Law

"**W**hen my mother was left a widow almost 50 years ago, she taught school to support her family. A few years after my father's death, she took her savings and bought a small commercial building on a downtown lot in our little town in Oregon. The building, she said, would offer what my father couldn't—a source of support in her old age. In one half of the building was a children's clothing store, in the other a dry cleaners. The two stores served Main Street shoppers for years."

"Now the building that once represented security has produced a menace with the potential to bankrupt my mother. The discovery of contamination in city park well water triggered groundwater tests in the area. Waste products discarded by dry cleaners were identified as a likely source of contamination. Although a dry cleaner hasn't operated for 20 years on my mother's property, chemicals remain in the soil. Mother knew nothing of this hazard until a letter came from the Oregon Department of Environmental Quality. It said she should decide if she would oversee further testing and cleanup herself or if she would let the government handle it. In either case, my mother would pay the costs."

"The building is worth just under $70,000. Cleanup costs will be at least $200,000. At 84, my mother has enough savings to preserve her independence. She does not have enough money to bear the enormous costs of new community standards. The dry cleaner that operated in my mother's building disposed of chemicals the same way other dry cleaners did. None of these businesses was operated in a negligent fashion. They followed standards accepted by the community at the time. Now we are learning that we must live more carefully if we are to survive in a world that is safe and clean. My question is: Who will pay? Who will be responsible for cleaning up environmental messes made before we knew better?"[1] ◾

INTRODUCTION

The environmental movement in the United States began in 1962 with the publication of Rachel Carson's book *Silent Spring*. She was the first to expose the deadly—and lingering—impact of DDT and other pesticides. These chemicals spread a wide web, poisoning not only the targeted insects, but the entire food chain—fish, birds, and even humans. Since Carson first sounded the alarm, environmental issues have appeared regularly in the news—everything from acute disasters such as the *Exxon Valdez* tanker oil spill in Alaska to chronic concerns over pesticide residues in food. For more about Rachel Carson (and links to other environmental Web sites), visit http://www.rachelcarson.org. To find out about environmental quality in your area, look at http://epa.gov/enviro/wme.

The environmental movement began with the fervor of a moral crusade. How could anyone be against a clean environment? It has become clear, however, that the issue is more complex. It is not enough simply to say, "We are against pollution." As the opening vignette reveals, the question is: Who will pay? Who will pay for past damage inflicted before anyone understood the harm that pollutants cause? Who will pay for current changes necessary to prevent damage now and in the future? Are car owners willing to spend $100 or $1,000 more per car to prevent air pollution? Are easterners ready to ban oil drilling in the Arctic National Wildlife Refuge in Alaska if that means higher prices for heating oil? Will loggers in the West give up their jobs to protect endangered species? Are all consumers willing to pay more to insulate their homes? The first President George Bush, a Republican, said, "Beyond all the studies, the figures, and the debates, the environment is a moral issue." But Newt Gingrich, a Republican Speaker of the House of Representatives, called the Environmental Protection Agency "the biggest job-killing agency in inner-city America."[2]

The cost-benefit trade-off is particularly complex in environmental issues because those who pay the cost often do not receive the benefit. If a company dumps toxic wastes into a stream, its shareholders benefit by avoiding the expense of safe disposal. Those who fish or drink the waters pay the real costs without receiving any of the

---

[1] Carolyn Scott Kortge, "Taken to the Cleaners," *Newsweek*, Oct. 23, 1995, p. 16. Reprinted with permission of the author.

[2] Both men are quoted in Robert V. Percival, Alan S. Miller, Christopher H. Schroeder, and James P. Leape, *Environmental Regulation* (Boston: Little, Brown & Co., 1992), p. 1, and 1995 supp. p. 2.

benefit. Economists use the term *externality* to describe the situation in which people do not bear the full cost of their decisions. Externalities prevent the market system from achieving a clean environment on its own. Only government involvement can realign costs and benefits.

Environmental Protection Agency

Thirty-five years ago, environmental abuses were (ineffectively) governed by tort law and a smattering of local ordinances. Now, environmental law is a mammoth structure of federal and state regulation. In 1970, Congress created the Environmental Protection Agency (EPA) to consolidate environmental regulation under one roof. When Congress passes a new environmental law, the EPA issues regulations to implement it. The agency can bring administrative enforcement action against those who violate its regulations. An administrative law judge within the agency hears these actions. Either party can appeal this decision to a United States Court of Appeals and, from there, to the Supreme Court. Those who violate environmental laws are liable for civil damages. In addition, some statutes, such as the Clean Water Act, the Resource Conservation and Recovery Act, and the Endangered Species Act, provide for *criminal* penalties, including imprisonment. The EPA is not shy about seeking criminal prosecutions of those who knowingly violate these statutes, and of those corporate officers who fail to prevent criminal negligence by their employees.

AIR POLLUTION

On October 26, 1948, almost half of the 10,000 people in Donora, Pennsylvania, fell ill from air pollution. A weather inversion trapped industrial pollutants in the air, creating a lethal smog. Twenty residents ultimately died. Although air pollution rarely causes this type of acute illness, it can cause or increase the severity of diseases that are annoying, chronic, or even fatal—such as pneumonia, bronchitis, emphysema, and cancer. A rise in ozone levels is associated with an increase in deaths from heart and lung disease. Even apart from the health risks, air pollution can be irritating: it blocks visibility, damages car exteriors, and grimes windowsills. To find out the air quality today where you live, view http://www.epa.gov/airnow.

There are three major sources of air pollution: coal-burning utility plants, factories, and motor vehicles. Residential furnaces, farm operations, forest fires, and dust from mines and construction sites also contribute. Local regulation is ineffective in controlling air pollution. For instance, when cities limited pollution from factory smokestacks, plants simply built taller stacks that sent the pollution hundreds, or even thousands, of miles away. Local governments had little incentive to prevent this long-distance migration. Recognizing the national nature of the problem, Congress enacted three air pollution laws during the 1950s and 1960s. With little enforcement bite and no EPA to ensure implementation, these statutes had minimal impact.

Clean Air Act

Dissatisfied by this lack of progress, Congress passed the Clean Air Act of 1970. **The Clean Air Act has four major provisions:**

- **Primary Standards.** Congress directed the EPA to establish **national ambient air quality standards** (known as NAAQSs) for primary pollution, that is, pollution that harms the public health. The EPA's mandate was to set standards that protected public health and provided an adequate margin of safety *without regard to cost.* Pollution may not exceed these limits anyplace in the country. The EPA must regularly update the rules to reflect the latest scientific evidence.

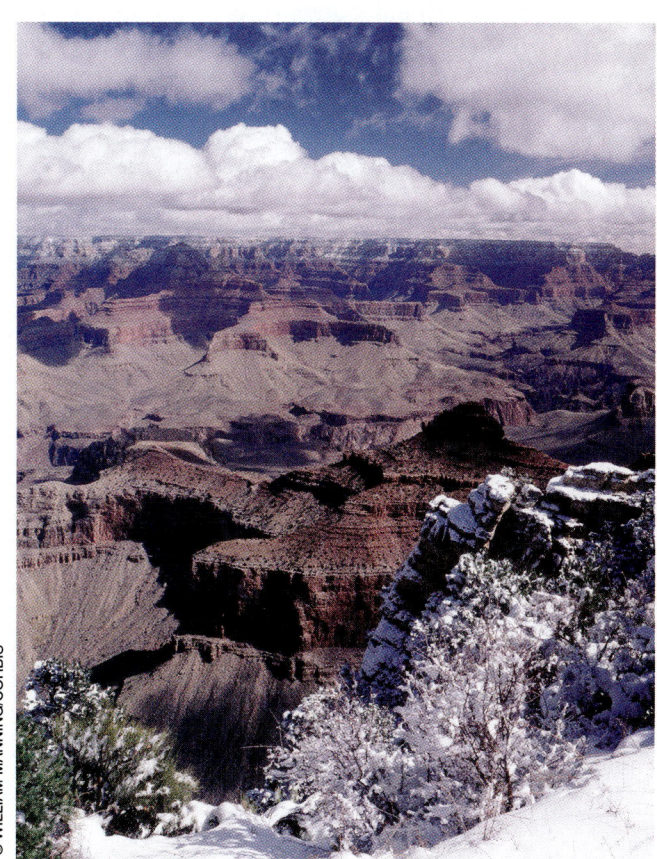

© WILLIAM MANNING/CORBIS

Is it worth half a billion dollars to improve winter visibility at the Grand Canyon by 7 percent?

- **Secondary Standards.** Congress also directed the EPA to establish NAAQSs for pollution that may not be a threat to health but has other unpleasant effects, such as obstructing visibility and harming plants or other materials.

- **State Implementation Plans (SIPs).** The Clean Air Act envisioned a partnership between the EPA and the states. After the EPA set primary and secondary standards, states would produce SIPs to meet the primary standards within three years and the secondary standards within a reasonable time. If a SIP was not acceptable, the EPA would produce its own plan for that state. In formulating their SIPs, states were required to identify the major sources of pollution. Each polluter would then be given a pollution limit to bring the area into compliance with national standards. The worse the pollution in a particular area, the tougher the regulations.

- **Citizen Suits.** The Clean Air Act (and many other environmental statutes) permits anyone to file suit against a polluter or against the EPA for failing to enforce the statute. Citizens have often been more assertive than the EPA in enforcing environmental statutes. For instance, the Arizona Center for Law in the Public Interest has sued the EPA more than a dozen times for failing to impose sufficiently strict air quality standards on Phoenix and Tucson.

Although air quality throughout the country improved dramatically, a 1990 EPA study revealed that, 20 years after passage of the Clean Air Act, virtually every American was still breathing unsafe levels of some pollutants. In 1990, Congress amended the Act, setting more realistic goals but also higher penalties for failure. For instance, the deadline for Los Angeles was extended, but the penalty for noncompliance was increased—a cutoff of federal highway funds (a serious blow indeed in Los Angeles) and the threat of even stricter controls. Already, everything in California from lawn mowers to bakeries to barbecue grills is subject to increasingly strict standards.

To find out about the general air quality in your community, feel your way over to http://www.scorecard.org.

In the following case, a power plant argued that the EPA had imposed a solution whose cost far outweighed its benefit. There is only one Grand Canyon. Should visibility there be preserved at any cost?

you Be The Judge

CENTRAL ARIZONA WATER CONSERVATION DISTRICT V. EPA

990 F.2d 1531, 1993 U.S. App. LEXIS 5881
United States Court of Appeals for the Ninth
Circuit, 1993

Facts: In the Clean Air Act, Congress directed the EPA to issue regulations that would protect visibility at national landmarks. The Navaho Generating Station (NGS) is a power plant 12 miles from the Grand Canyon. In response to a citizen suit filed by the Environmental Defense Fund under the Clean Air Act, the EPA ordered NGS to reduce its sulfur dioxide emissions by 90 percent. To do so would cost NGS $430 million initially in capital expenditures and then $89.6 million annually. Average winter visibility in the Grand Canyon would be improved by at most 7 percent, but perhaps less. NGS sued to prevent implementation of the EPA's order. A court may nullify an EPA order if it determines that the agency action was arbitrary and capricious.

You Be the Judge: Did the EPA act arbitrarily and capriciously in requiring NGS to spend half a billion dollars to improve winter visibility at the Grand Canyon by at most 7 percent?

Argument for NGS: This case is a perfect example of environmentalism run amok. Half a billion dollars for the *chance* of increasing winter visibility at the Grand Canyon by 7 percent? No rational person would choose to spend his own money that way, but the EPA is happy to spend NGS's. Winter visitors to the Grand Canyon would undoubtedly prefer that NGS provide them with a free lunch rather than a 7 percent improvement in visibility. The EPA order is simply a waste of money.

Argument for the EPA: Under the Clean Air Act, Congress instructed the EPA to protect visibility at national landmarks such as the Grand Canyon. How can NGS, or anyone else, measure the benefit of protecting a national treasure like the Grand Canyon? Even people who never have and never will visit it during the winter sleep better at night knowing that the Canyon is protected. NGS has been causing harm to the Grand Canyon, and now it should remedy the damage.

Courts generally defer to federal agencies, whose experts deal with similar problems all the time. The EPA has greater expertise in these matters than either NGS or this court. ■

**ECONOMICS
& the LAW**

The Office of Management and Budget, the White House's research branch, calculated that over the past decade the benefit from environmental regulations has been five to seven times their cost. The benefits, which include fewer deaths, illnesses, and lost workdays, have been between $120 billion and $193 billion while the costs have been from $23 billion to $26 billion. Of course, these types of calculations are by their very nature speculative. In any event, the Clean Air Act directs the EPA to set air quality standards without regard to cost. Should cost-benefit analysis matter? ◆

New Sources of Pollution

Some states had air so clean that they could have allowed air quality to decline and still have met EPA standards. However, the Clean Air Act declared that one of its purposes was to "protect and enhance" air quality. Using this phrase, the Sierra Club sued the EPA to prevent it from approving any SIPs that met EPA standards but nonetheless permitted a decline in air quality. As a result of this suit, the EPA developed a **prevention of significant deterioration (PSD)** program. **No one may undertake a build-**

ing project that will cause a major increase in pollution without first obtaining a permit from the EPA. The agency will grant permits only if an applicant can demonstrate that (1) its emissions will not cause an overall decline in air quality and (2) it has installed the **best available control technology** for every pollutant.

The PSD program prohibits any deterioration in current air quality, *regardless of health impact*. In essence, national policy values a clean environment for its own sake, apart from any health benefits.

Acid Rain

In some places, rain is now 10 times more acidic than it would naturally be. The results of acid rain are visible in the eastern United States and Canada—damaged forests, crops, and lakes. Acid is primarily created by sulfur emissions from large coal-burning

utility plants in the Midwest. Many of these plants were built before the Clean Air Act, when the easiest way to meet state and local standards (while keeping electricity prices low) was to build tall stacks that would send the sulfur dioxide far away. Terrific for Ohio, not so wonderful for Maine.

The Clean Air Act banned the tall-stack solution, leaving coal plants, in theory, with two choices: install (expensive) scrubbers or buy (cheaper) low-sulfur western coal. Under pressure from members who represented states with high-sulfur coal, Congress compromised and required all power plants to install scrubbers regardless of the coal they burned. In this way, western coal would have no advantage.

In 1990, Congress amended the Clean Air Act to require power plants to cut their sulfur dioxide emissions by half. This time, however,

The acid rain that caused this damage probably came from a power plant hundreds, if not thousands, of miles away.

Congress did not specify how the goal should be achieved and instead offered new methods for minimizing costs and maximizing economic efficiency. **Power plants have four options for meeting emissions standards: (1) installing scrubbers, (2) using low-sulfur coal, (3) switching to alternative fuels (such as natural gas), or (4) trading emissions allowances.** This last alternative requires some explanation. Each year, every utility receives an emissions allowance, meaning that it is allowed to emit a certain number of tons of pollutants. If a company does not need its entire allowance, because it uses cleaner fuels or has installed pollution control devices, it can sell the leftover allowance to other companies or stockpile the allowance for future use. Plants with high levels of pollution either buy more allowances or reduce their own emissions, depending on which alternative is cheaper. In effect, the government establishes the maximum amount of pollution, and then the market sets the price for meeting the national standard.

The market for sulfur dioxide emissions has become remarkably efficient and effective. Power plants now have a financial incentive to reduce pollution through innovation. In some years, pollution from sulfur dioxide has declined by as much as 25 percent, at a cost one-tenth the original estimate. For more information on the emissions trading program, click on **http://www.epa.gov/airmarkets/trading/index.html**. This Web site reveals who has bought allowances and at what cost. Note that sometimes the highest bidders are organizations such as the Birney Elementary School, which buys emissions allowances simply to keep polluters from using them.

There is, however, one catch to the emissions trading system: **new source review.** Originally, Congress had exempted the oldest power plants and factories from the Clean Air Act on the theory that they would be very expensive to upgrade and would be replaced soon enough anyway. As it turned out, many companies discovered it was easier to patch up the old plants than it was to replace them with new, clean operations. Congress amended the Act to impose the new source review system: companies are required to upgrade pollution devices anytime they renovate a plant (but not when they undertake routine maintenance). In the end, though, few plants have complied with the new source review requirements, at least in part because the EPA issued weak regulations to implement the law. For instance, the EPA defines routine maintenance as any activity that costs less than 20 percent of the value of the generating unit—which means a company could spend hundreds of millions of dollars on so-called routine maintenance and not be required to upgrade pollution facilities. The American Lung Association termed these rules "the most harmful and unlawful air-pollution initiative ever undertaken by the federal government."[3]

Automobile Pollution

The Clean Air Act of 1970 directed the EPA to reduce automobile pollution levels by 90 percent within six years. Although the technology to achieve this goal did not then exist, Congress believed that the auto industry could, if forced, be able to develop the necessary innovations. This approach has been referred to as **technology forcing,** in the sense that industry is forced to develop the technology. Indeed, by 1975, General Motors developed a catalytic converter that not only reduced harmful emissions but improved fuel economy.

Although new cars are 97 percent cleaner than 1970 models, motor vehicles are still a major source of air pollution, releasing more than 50 percent of the hazardous pollutants in the air. Each car may be cleaner, but Americans are driving more—and bigger—cars more miles on more trips. During 1970, Americans traveled one trillion miles, but by 2000 the annual total had increased to four trillion miles. To counteract this increase, Congress has required oil companies to produce cleaner gasoline and automakers to build **low-emission vehicles,** such as cars powered by electricity or natural gas. The most polluted cities must also reduce auto use by encouraging car pools. However, in 2002, the auto industry fought off congressional efforts to increase automobile fuel efficiency requirements.

Plagued as it is by smog, California has been more aggressive than Congress in limiting automobile pollution. The state recently passed tough emission rules that, beginning with the 2016 model year, would require about a 30 percent decrease in emissions from cars and trucks sold in California. These regulations are now in limbo because automakers have challenged them in court. (To show support for these new rules, Governor Arnold Schwarzenegger traded in his fuel-guzzling Hummer for a specially designed version that runs on hydrogen.) Ten other states, including New York, Connecticut, Washington, and Oregon have also adopted California's tougher car emission standards. Inhabitants of these states buy 29 percent of the cars purchased in America. This market power will presumably pressure the auto industry to produce more fuel-efficient cars.

---

[3] Bruce Barcott, "Changing all the Rules," *New York Times*, Apr. 4, 2004, §6, p. 38.

Soot Particles

Produced primarily by power plants and diesel fuel, microscopic soot particles substantially increase the risk of premature death from lung cancer and other breathing and heart disorders. Because of these particles, residing in a city has the same impact on one's lungs as living with a smoker. The life expectancy of residents in cities with the cleanest air is on average two years longer than those in the dirtiest cities. In 1997, the EPA issued regulations limiting soot. However, a lawsuit by power plant operators and automobile manufacturers delayed the rules until 2001, when the Supreme Court ruled that the EPA had the right to impose these new regulations without conducting a cost-benefit analysis.[4]

Air Toxics

Some pollutants are so potent that even tiny amounts cause harm. For instance, the EPA has never been able to identify a safe level of exposure to asbestos. Each year, 2.7 billion pounds of toxics spew into the air in the United States, causing an estimated annual increase of 3,000 cancer deaths. Two-thirds of Americans face an increased cancer risk from exposure to toxic chemicals in the air. Because the Clean Air Act directed the EPA to set safety standards that provided an adequate margin of safety without regard to cost, the agency in theory has no choice except an outright ban on some pollutants. Since such a ban would shut down the steel, chemical, and petroleum industries, among others, the EPA does not consider such a strategy to be politically viable.

The Environmental Defense Fund sued the EPA to force compliance with the law. Nevertheless, by 1990, the agency had proposed standards for only seven substances. Although these standards do not eliminate health risks, they are set at the lowest feasible level given existing technology, and the courts have upheld them.

In 1990 amendments to the Clean Air Act, Congress directed the EPA to set standards for each of 189 specific pollutants and any other toxics the EPA wanted to include. The EPA was permitted to base these standards initially on the **maximum achievable control technology (MACT).** Within eight years of developing MACT rules, the EPA was instructed to tighten the standards to a level at which the risk of cancer from these substances was no more than one in one million over a lifetime. This two-step process was meant to create an incentive for polluters to continue to develop better technology.

Global Warming

During the last 100 years, the average temperature worldwide has increased between 0.5° and 1.1°F. If current trends continue, the world's average temperature during the next 100 years will rise another 2° to 6°F, producing the warmest climate in the history of humankind. (By comparison, the planet is only 5° to 9°F warmer than during the last ice age.) The impact of this climate change is potentially catastrophic: a rise in sea level that would engulf coastal areas, a devastating decline in fishing stocks, the death of major forests, and a loss of farmland worldwide. It has been estimated that these changes could cost between 1 and 2.5 percent of global GDP. For a long time, the scientific evidence underlying the theory of global warming was subject to doubt and debate. But today, most reasonable scientists accept that the burning of fossil fuels produces gases—carbon dioxide, methane, and nitrous oxide—that do indeed create a greenhouse effect by trapping heat in the earth's atmosphere.

---

[4] *Whitman v. American Trucking Associations,* 531 U.S. 457; 2001 U.S. LEXIS 1952.

Identifying the problem, however, does not illuminate the solution. Global warming is the most complex environmental problem of the new millennium because any solution requires international political cooperation coupled with major lifestyle changes. The Energy Department has estimated that, to fight global warming effectively, U.S. gasoline prices would have to rise by nearly $2 a gallon and electricity prices might have to increase by 86 percent.

The United States plays a particularly important role in finding a solution because with 5 percent of the world's population, it consumes 25 percent of the world's energy. Thus far, however, this country has largely elected to be part of the problem, not part of the solution. It is the only leading industrialized nation that refused to ratify the Kyoto Protocol. This treaty requires emissions to be reduced by the year 2012 to a level 5.2 percent below 1990 amounts.

In 2002, the American government sent the U.S. Climate Action Report to the United Nations. In this document, the United States acknowledged that the use of fossil fuels causes global warming. The report also conceded that global warming was likely to have a damaging impact on this country—causing severe heat waves, coastal flooding, and water shortages. However, the report also pointed out some potential benefits, such as a longer growing season, at least in the short run. Its proposed solution was not prevention but adaptation. It suggested, for example, that increased use of air conditioning could mitigate the impact of heat waves. The report stated that "In the real world, no one will forego meeting basic family needs to protect the global commons."

Although the United States has not ratified the Kyoto Protocol, there have been some grassroots efforts to comply voluntarily with some parts of it. As we have seen, California has become an important player in the global warming debate by tightening its fuel emission standards. Some business leaders have agreed to voluntary limits on the greenhouse gases that their companies produce. For example, the heads of seven electric-power companies volunteered to reduce their greenhouse gas emissions by 3 percent to 5 percent and General Motors has reduced its plant emissions in North America by 10 percent. It seems as if, by hook or by crook, bit by bit, we will all be affected by efforts to limit greenhouse gases.

WATER POLLUTION

One day, thousands of Milwaukeeans began to suffer nausea, cramps, and diarrhea. The suspected culprit? *Cryptosporidium*, a tiny protozoan that usually resides in the intestines of cattle and other animals. Ironically, the parasite may have entered Milwaukee's water supply at a purification plant on Lake Michigan. Officials suspect that infected runoff from dairy farms spilled into Lake Michigan near the plant's intake pipe. Doctors advised those with a damaged immune system (such as AIDS patients) to avoid drinking municipal water. Most Milwaukeeans were taking no chances—more than 800,000 switched to boiled or bottled water.

Polluted water can cause a number of loathsome diseases, such as typhus and dysentery. But by 1930, most American cities had dramatically reduced outbreaks of waterborne diseases by chlorinating their water. (The parasite that caused the Milwaukee outbreak is relatively immune to chlorine.) However, industrial discharges into the water supply have increased rapidly, with a significant impact on water quality. These industrial wastes may not induce acute illnesses like typhus, but they can cause serious diseases such as cancer. There is more at stake than health alone; clean water is valued for esthetics, recreation, and fishing.

Clean Water Act

In 1972, Congress passed a statute, now called the Clean Water Act (CWA), with two ambitious goals: (1) to make all navigable water suitable for swimming and fishing by 1983, and (2) to eliminate the discharge of pollutants into navigable water by 1985. Like the Clean Air Act, the CWA sets goals without regard to cost; leaves enforcement primarily to the states, with oversight by the EPA; and permits citizen suits. Also, like the Clean Air Act, the CWA's goals have not been met.

Industrial Discharges

The CWA prohibits any single producer from discharging pollution into water without a permit from the EPA. Before granting a permit, the EPA must set limits, by industry, on the amount of each type of pollution any single producer (called a **point source**) can discharge. These limits must be based on the **best available technology.** The EPA faces a gargantuan task in determining the best available technology that *each* industry can use to reduce pollution. Furthermore, standards become obsolete quickly as technology changes.

The CWA also requires the EPA to measure water quality broadly to determine if the permit system is working. Until clean water standards are met, every point source is held to the same standard, whether it is discharging into a clean ocean that can handle more pollution or a stagnant lake that cannot. Since determining the impact of a particular discharge may not be possible, especially when it is mingled with others, it is easier for the EPA to set the same standards for everyone. Easier and fairer—Congress did not want states to lure industry with promises of laxer pollution rules.

In the following case, the Supreme Court discusses the definition of "point source."

SOUTH FLORIDA WATER MANAGEMENT DISTRICT V. MICCOSUKEE TRIBE OF INDIANS

541 U.S. 95, 124 S. Ct. 1537, 2004 U.S. LEXIS 2376
Supreme Court of the United States, 2004

Facts: The land between south Florida's coastal hills and the Everglades was once part of the Everglades, and its surface and groundwater flowed south in a uniform and unchanneled sheet. Starting in the early 1900s, however, Florida began building canals to drain the Everglades and make parts of them suitable for cultivation. These canals proved to be trouble: they caused flooding and they lowered the water table, allowing salt water into coastal wells.

In 1948, Congress instructed the United States Army Corps of Engineers to solve these problems. In response, the Corps constructed the Central and South Florida Flood Control Project (Project): a vast array of levees, canals, pumps, and water storage areas. The Project fundamentally altered the hydrology of the Everglades, changing the natural sheet flow of the water. The South Florida Water Management District (District) operates the Project.

C-11 is a canal that collects groundwater and rainwater from a 104-square-mile area of Broward County that has a population of 136,000 people. When the water in C-11 rises too high, it is pumped into a wetland area (called WCA-3) that is a remnant of the original Everglades. Before entering C-11, the rainwater absorbs contaminants produced by human activities, including phosphorus from fertilizer used by farmers. When this phosphorus is pumped into WCA-3 (by a pump called S-9), it alters the balance of the WCA-3 ecosystem and stimulates the growth of algae and plants foreign to the Everglades.

A number of initiatives were underway to reduce these impacts and thereby restore the ecological

▼

integrity of the Everglades. The Miccosukee Tribe of Indians (the Tribe), impatient with the pace of this progress, brought suit under the Clean Water Act (the Act) to halt the pumping of water from C-11 into WCA-3. The Tribe alleged that C-11 was a point source and, therefore, could not discharge pollutants into WC-3 without a permit. The District argued that the canal was not a point source because it did not create the pollutants; it simply transported them. The Tribe filed a motion for summary judgment, which the trial court granted and the appellate court affirmed. The Supreme Court granted *certiorari*.

Issue: Is a canal a point source when it transmits pollutants that it did not create?

Excerpts from Justice O'Connor's Decision: Congress enacted the Act in 1972. Its stated objective was "to restore and maintain the chemical, physical, and biological integrity of the Nation's waters." To serve those ends, the Act prohibits the discharge of any pollutant by any person unless done in compliance with some provision of the Act. The provision relevant to this case requires dischargers to obtain permits that place limits on the type and quantity of pollutants that can be released into the Nation's waters. The Act defines the phrase "discharge of a pollutant" to mean "any addition of any pollutant to navigable waters from any point source." A "point source," in turn, is defined as "any discernible, confined and discrete conveyance," such as "a pipe, ditch, channel, or tunnel from which pollutants are or may be discharged."

The question is whether the operation of the S-9 pump constitutes the discharge of a pollutant within the meaning of the Act. The District argued that the [permit requirement] covers a point source only when a pollutant originates from the point source, and not when pollutants originating elsewhere merely pass through the point source.

A point source is, by definition, a "discernible, confined, and discrete *conveyance*." (emphasis added). That definition makes plain that a point source need not be the original source of the pollutant; it need only convey the pollutant to navigable waters, which are, in turn, defined as "the waters of the United States." Tellingly, the examples of "point sources" listed by the Act include pipes, ditches, tunnels, and conduits, objects that do not themselves generate pollutants but merely transport them. In addition, one of the Act's primary goals was to impose permitting requirements on municipal wastewater treatment plants. But under the District's interpretation of the Act, the [permit] program would not cover such plants, because they treat and discharge pollutants added to water by others. We therefore reject the District's proposed reading of the definition of "discharge of a pollutant." That definition includes within its reach point sources that do not themselves generate pollutants. ∎

Water Quality Standards

The CWA requires states to set EPA-approved water quality standards and develop plans to achieve them. The first step in developing a plan is to determine how each body of water is used. Standards may vary depending upon the designated use—higher for recreational lakes than for a river used to irrigate farmland. No matter what the water's designated use, standards may not be set at a level lower than its current condition. Congress is not in the business of permitting *more* pollution.

States are supposed to pay special attention to so-called **non-point sources,** that is, pollutants with no single source, such as water runoff from agricultural land or city streets. This runoff may contain gasoline, pesticides, or bacteria. Congress left non-point source pollution to the states because it is so difficult to regulate. This regulation also involves complex issues such as land use planning that are, in theory, better handled at the local level than by national fiat. However optimistic Congress may have been, to date the states have not successfully implemented this section of the CWA. They appear to lack both the political will and the technological know-how, for which they are not totally to blame. Determining the impact of individual pollutants on the overall quality of a body of water used for many different purposes is a complex problem. Land use planning requires a delicate and volatile mix of consensus and control.

As the ambitious goals set by the CWA have not been met, Congress has granted numerous extensions. At the same time, environmental advocates have filed citizen suits to force the EPA to toughen its enforcement.

Wetlands

Wetlands are the transition areas between land and open water. They may look like swamps, they may even be swamps, but their unattractive appearance should not disguise their vital role in the aquatic world. They are natural habitats for many fish and wildlife. They also serve as a filter for neighboring bodies of water, trapping chemicals and sediments. Moreover, they are an important aid in flood control because they can absorb a high level of water and then release it slowly after the emergency is past.

Although wetlands may not look attractive, they fill an important ecological role.

The CWA prohibits any discharge of dredge and fill material into wetlands without a permit. Although filling in wetlands requires a permit, many other activities that harm wetlands, such as draining them, originally did not. (However, many states require permits for draining wetlands.) After some particularly egregious abuses, the EPA issued regulations to limit the destruction of wetlands. These new regulations were, however, successfully challenged in the courts.[5] The EPA then rewrote the regulations to accomplish the same goal within the parameters set out by the courts. These new regulations will certainly be challenged, too.

Although, in theory, the government's official policy is no net loss of wetlands, the reality has been different. Since the country was settled, about half of the original 230 million acres of wetlands in the continental United States have been destroyed. In 2002, the Bush administration amended the "no net loss" rule so that it could issue waivers in some cases. The Web site **http://www.nwi.fws.gov** shows an inventory of wetlands in the United States.

Sewage

Plumbing drains must be attached to either a septic system or a sewer line. A septic system is, in effect, a freestanding waste treatment plant. A sewer line, on the other hand, feeds into a publicly owned wastewater treatment plant, also known as a municipal sewage plant. **Under the CWA, a municipality must obtain a permit for any discharge from a wastewater treatment plant.** To obtain a permit, the municipality must first treat the waste to reduce its toxicity. However, taxpayers have stubbornly resisted the large increases in taxes or fees necessary to fund required treatments. Since the fines imposed by the EPA are almost always less than the cost of treatment, some cities have been slow to comply. The following news report illustrates the complex trade-offs between costs and benefits.

---

[5]   *National Mining Ass'n v. U.S. Army Corps of Engineers,* 145 F.3d 1399 (D.C. Cir. 1998).

In the two years since Tom Cox took over as general manager of Constitution Marina, located in one of the sludgiest pockets of Boston's infamously sludgy Inner Harbor, he has seen an entire ecosystem reborn before his eyes. At the mouth of a now-sealed effluent pipe that once poured sewer waste directly into his anchorage, baby herring and krill shrimp feed. "This spring, for the first time in a decade, we even had porpoises in the Inner Harbor, and seals flopping onto my docks. Boston Harbor," Cox says, "is definitely back."[6]

Back? The Boston Harbor? The harbor that was gruesomely swamped with human waste during the disastrous crash of the old Deer Island treatment plant? The harbor that only a few years ago still reeked of 350 years of ill use?

The harbor has passed a vital milestone on its voyage from toilet bowl for 43 cities and towns to tourist attraction and recharging jobs engine. The new $183 million Deer Island sewage-treatment plant received a formal commission, and its predecessor, an obsolete and overburdened albatross that once channeled raw sewage directly in the bay, was bulldozed into dust.

This transformation has not come cheap. Sewer user charges for residents of the greater Boston area have risen more than 560 percent in the past decade, becoming among the highest in the country. These charges are expected to rise an additional 50 to 75 percent in the next few years. In protest, angry ratepayers dumped tea boxes full of sewer bills into the harbor. ◆

Other Water Pollution Statutes

The Safe Drinking Water Act of 1974:

- Requires the EPA to set national standards for contaminants potentially harmful to human health that are found in drinking water

- Assigns enforcement responsibility to the states but permits the EPA to take enforcement action against states that do not adhere to the standards

- Prohibits the use of lead in any pipes through which drinking water flows, and

- Requires community water systems to send every customer an annual *consumer confidence report* disclosing the level of contaminants in the drinking water. (One can only hope that consumers will remain confident after receiving the report.) To find out more about your drinking water, turn on http://www.epa.gov/ogwdw/dwinfo.htm.

The **Ocean Dumping Act of 1972** prohibits the dumping of wastes in ocean water without a permit from the EPA.

Congress passed the **Oil Pollution Act of 1990** in response to the mammoth 1989 *Exxon Valdez* tanker oil spill in Prince William Sound, Alaska. To prevent defective boats from leaking oil, this statute sets design standards for ships operating in U.S. waters. It also requires shipowners to pay for damage caused by oil discharged from their ships.

Although few would argue with the concept that those who spill ought to pay, there has been great controversy over how to measure damages. The U.S. government proposed that damages should be based on the subjective value that people assign to an injured area. Suppose that an oil spill prevents 1,000 people from using a beach. The government proposal would base the fine on the value that these people report (in a survey) that they place on a day of swimming or walking on the beach. If sea fowl are injured by the spill, nearby residents would be asked what they would be willing to pay to save a bird from death. Oil companies prefer to pay only the cost of fixing the dam-

---

6 Tom Mashberg, "Harbor Cleans Up Its Act," *Boston Herald,* July 30, 1995, p. 1.

age. If 1,000 seagulls are killed by a spill, oil companies contend that the proper fine should equal the cost of cleaning up the area and increasing the number of seagulls. That might mean importing seagulls or augmenting their food supply.

WASTE DISPOSAL

The time is 1978. The place is 96th Street in Niagara Falls, New York. Six women are afflicted with breast cancer, one man has bladder cancer, another suffers from throat cancer. A seven-year-old boy suddenly goes into convulsions and dies of kidney failure. Other residents have chromosomal abnormalities, epilepsy, respiratory problems, and skin diseases. This street is three blocks away from Love Canal.

In 1945, Hooker Chemical Co. disposed of 21,800 tons of 82 different chemicals by dumping them into Love Canal or burying them nearby. An internal memorandum warned that this decision would lead to "potential future hazard" and be a "potential source of lawsuits." A year later, the company's lawyer wrote that "children in the neighborhood use portions of the water for swimming and, as a matter of fact, just before we left the site we saw several young children walking down the path with what appeared to be bathing costumes in hand." He suggested that Hooker build a fence around the canal, but the company never did. Instead, it sold the land to the local school board to build an elementary school. When the company's executive vice-president recommended against the sale, the company inserted a clause in the deed to eliminate the company's liability.

Schoolchildren tripped over drums of chemicals that worked their way up to the surface. Some children were burned playing with hot balls of chemical residue—what they called "fire stones"—that popped up through the ground. Homeowners noticed foul odors in their basements after heavy rains. Finally, a national health emergency was declared at Love Canal, and a joint federal-state program relocated 800 families. In 1994, Occidental Chemical Corp. (which had since bought Hooker) agreed to pay the state of New York $98 million to settle a lawsuit over Love Canal.[7] Two years later, the EPA settled its lawsuit with Occidental for $129 million. In the end, the cleanup cost almost $400 million and took 21 years to complete.

In its time, what Hooker did was not unusual. Companies historically dumped waste in waterways, landfills, or open dumps. Out of sight was out of mind. Waste disposal continues to be a major problem in the United States. It has been estimated that the cost of cleaning up existing waste products will exceed $1 *trillion*. At the same time, the country continues to produce more than six billion tons of agricultural, commercial, industrial, and domestic waste each year. Ironically, air and water pollution control devices have added to the problem because the pollutants they remove from the air and water become waste that must be discarded somewhere.

Two major statutes regulate wastes. The Resource Conservation and Recovery Act (RCRA) focuses on *preventing* future Love Canals by regulating the production and disposal of solid wastes, both toxic and otherwise. The Comprehensive Environmental Response, Compensation, and Liability Act (CERCLA), also referred to as **Superfund,** focuses on *cleaning up* existing hazardous waste sites.

---

[7]   William Glaberson, "Love Canal: Suit Focuses on Records from 1940s," *New York Times*, Oct. 22, 1990, p. B1. Copyright © 1990 by The New York Times Co. Reprinted by permission.

Resource Conservation and Recovery Act

The RCRA establishes rules for treating both hazardous wastes and other forms of solid waste (such as ordinary garbage).

Solid Waste

Before 1895, the city of New York did not collect garbage. Residents simply piled it up in the streets, causing the streets to rise five feet in height over the century. At present, each American generates 4.5 pounds of solid waste a *day*, an increase of 60 percent since 1960 and more waste per capita than any other country.

But most Americans never gave much thought to their waste until the infamous case of the garbage barge. The trouble arose in 1983 when the New York legislature banned new landfills (garbage dumps) on Long Island. Three years later, the landfill began to fill up in Islip, a bedroom community outside New York City. Lowell Herrelson, an Alabama businessman, offered to put the Islip garbage on a barge and ship it to another state. But once he filled the barge, no other state would take the garbage. Loaded with 3,186 tons of waste, the barge traveled over 6,000 miles in five months and was turned away by six states and three countries before returning to New York and anchoring near the Statue of Liberty. Its movements were reported daily in the newspapers and even became the subject of the *Tonight Show* monologue: "The only town to send its garbage on a 6,000 mile cruise." The garbage was ultimately burned in a Brooklyn incinerator, but not before Herrelson had lost $500,000 in the venture. Islip introduced recycling and built a $38 million garbage incinerator.

The disposal of nonhazardous solid waste has generally been left to the states, but they must follow guidelines set by the RCRA. **The RCRA:**

- Bans new open dumps
- Requires that garbage be sent to sanitary landfills
- Sets minimum standards for landfills
- Requires landfills to monitor nearby groundwater
- Requires states to develop a permit program for landfills; and
- Provides some financial assistance to aid states in waste management.

ECONOMICS & the LAW

The federal Office of Management and Budget (OMB) objected to the solid waste regulations that the EPA intended to issue under the RCRA because, according to the OMB's calculations, complying with the proposed regulations would have cost more than $19 billion for every life saved. Not worth it, said the OMB. As a result, the EPA's revised regulations are more flexible than the original version.

This dispute typifies the ongoing conflict in environmental law. On the one hand, the EPA argues that scientific data are uncertain and the health risks of pollutants may be much worse than we realize. The EPA's goal is to stop pollution virtually without regard to cost. The OMB, on the other hand, prefers to base decisions on a numerical cost-benefit analysis. The OMB believes that a clean-air-and-water-for-its-own-sake approach makes little economic sense. Is a human life worth $19 billion? Is your life? ◆

Ethics

Computers and other consumer electronic devices have created the most rapidly growing waste problem in the world. Containing chemicals such as lead and mercury, these products produce not only large volume, but also dangerous toxicity. Industrialized nations have found a simple solution—between 50 and 80 percent of the "e-waste" collected for recycling is sent to countries such as China, India, and Pakistan.

Once the e-waste is in Asia, adults and children, working without any protective clothing or equipment, burn the plastic casings in the open air, dismantle toner cartridges by hand, and melt circuit boards. The ground, air, and water are polluted with the residue of these toxic components. Because this disposal method is so easy and cheap (for the industrialized nations), manufacturers have not attempted to reduce toxic components in electronic products, and governments have not forced them to take responsibility for safe disposal at the end of the product's life.[8]

What is the ethical obligation of developed nations to dispose of toxic e-waste? From the Chapter 2 Ethics Checklist: What would the Golden Rule suggest? What values are at stake?

What will you do with your old computer when you buy a new one? Hewlett Packard will safely recycle e-waste, whether or not HP made it, for a fee of $13 to $34 per item (see http://www.hp.com/go/recycle). Would you be willing to pay that sum?   ◆

Underground Storage Tanks

Concerned that underground gasoline storage tanks were leaking into water supplies, Congress required the EPA to issue regulations for detecting and correcting leaks in existing tanks and establishing specifications for new receptacles. Anyone who owns property with an underground storage tank must notify the EPA and comply with regulations that require installation of leak detectors, periodic testing, and, in some cases, removal of old tanks.

Identifying Hazardous Wastes

The EPA must establish criteria for determining what is, and is not, hazardous waste. It must then prepare a list of wastes that qualify as hazardous.

Tracking Hazardous Wastes

Anyone who creates, transports, stores, treats, or disposes of more than a certain quantity of hazardous wastes must apply for an EPA permit. All hazardous wastes must be tracked from creation to final disposal. They must be disposed of at a certified facility. Any company that generates more than 100 kilograms of hazardous waste in any month (roughly 200,000 firms nationwide) must obtain an identification number for its wastes. When it ships this waste to a disposal facility, it must send along a multicopy manifest that identifies the waste, the transporter, and the destination. The company must notify the EPA if it does not receive a receipt from the disposal site indicating that the waste has been received.

Superfund

In the vignette that opened this chapter, an elderly woman faced financial ruin from the cost of cleaning up pollutants that her dry cleaner tenants had left. The RCRA was designed to ensure safe disposal of current hazardous wastes. In contrast, the goal of Superfund (also known as CERCLA) is to clean up hazardous wastes improperly dumped in the past.

---

[8]   The Basel Action Networks, "Exporting Harm: The Techno-Trashing of Asia," Feb. 25, 2002, available at http://www.ban.org.

The philosophy of Superfund is "the polluter pays." **Therefore, anyone who has ever owned or operated a site on which hazardous wastes are found, or who has transported wastes to the site, or who has arranged for the disposal of wastes that were released at the site, is liable for (1) the cost of cleaning up the site, (2) any damage done to natural resources, and (3) any required health assessments.**

In a "shovels first, lawyers later" approach, Congress established a $15.2 billion revolving trust fund for the EPA to use in cleaning up sites even before obtaining reimbursement from those responsible for the damage. Any reimbursements go into the trust fund to be used to repair other sites. The trust fund was initially financed by a tax on the oil and chemical industries, which produce the bulk of hazardous waste. In 1995, however, the taxes expired, and Congress refused to renew them, thereby threatening the viability of the statute. The EPA has identified 428 sites that need immediate cleanup, but the agency spends 52 percent of its annual $450 million Superfund budget on just nine of these sites. According to the EPA, there could be as many as 355,000 hazardous waste sites that would require up to $250 billion to restore.

Meanwhile, one in four Americans, including 10 million children below the age of 12, lives within four miles of a Superfund site. To find out about hazardous waste sites in your community, click on http://www.epa.gov/oerrpage/superfund/sites.

Property owners have complained, and litigated, bitterly because:

- Current and former owners are liable, even though they did nothing illegal at the time, and indeed even if they did nothing more than own property where someone else dumped hazardous wastes. In addition, officers or controlling shareholders in closely held corporations can be personally liable for operations of the company.

- Polluters have joint and several liability—each polluter is responsible for the entire cost of cleaning up a site, even if it contributed only a portion of the pollution. A polluter can reduce its liability only by proving that it caused a smaller percentage of the damage, but that proof is often impossible.

- The expense of a Superfund cleanup can be devastating—higher than $100 million on some sites. Property owners have often viewed litigation as a better investment. More than 50 percent of total Superfund spending has gone to administrative and legal expenses.

- Congress requires that land be returned to pristine condition. Owners point to scientific evidence indicating that this goal is often impossible to achieve, given existing knowledge. Once again, cost-benefit analysis enters the picture as property owners argue that the cost of perfection is higher than the benefit. To encourage redevelopment of contaminated land, the EPA has implemented a "Brownfields" program that bases the cleanup levels for some property on potential risk to human health. However, Superfund proponents counter that, to be safe, all hazardous wastes should be removed. They offer as Exhibit A the Forrest Glen real estate development in upstate New York. The developers knew they could buy the land cheap because it had been used as a hazardous waste dump. Instead of cleaning it up, they slapped on a bucolic name. Now chemicals ooze up on lawns.

---

at RISK   Virtually any commercial real estate is at risk for Superfund liability. Before purchasing land, it is important to investigate whether it has ever been used to dispose of hazardous wastes. Consider testing the soil and groundwater. It might also be a good idea to ask the seller for indemnification against Superfund liability or to purchase Superfund insurance. ◆

Unfortunately, as the following case illustrates, incentives under Superfund can sometimes be perverse.

COOPER INDUSTRIES, INC. V. AVIALL SERVICES, INC.

125 S. Ct. 577, 2004 U.S. LEXIS 8271
Supreme Court of the United States, 2004

Facts: Cooper Industries, Inc. owned and operated four aircraft engine maintenance sites in Texas. In 1981, it sold them to Aviall Services, Inc. During the time that Cooper owned the property and later when Aviall owned it, petroleum and other hazardous substances leaked into the ground and ground water from underground storage tanks. No one knew this, however, until Aviall owned the property. As soon as it discovered the contamination, Aviall notified the Texas Natural Resource Conservation Commission (Commission). The Commission directed Aviall to clean up the site, and threatened suit if it did not. Aviall cleaned up the property so neither the Commission nor the EPA needed to file suit. Aviall spent about $5 million in cleanup costs but was not yet finished.

Aviall filed a lawsuit against Cooper alleging that, as a former owner, it was also liable under CERCLA for the cleanup costs. Both parties moved for summary judgment. The trial court granted Cooper's motion on the grounds that Cooper did not have to contribute to the cleanup because Aviall had never been sued under CERCLA. A panel of the Court of Appeals for the Fifth Circuit affirmed, but on a rehearing *en banc* the Fifth Circuit reversed by a divided vote, holding for Aviall.[9] The Supreme Court granted *certiorari*.

Issue: **If the owner of a contaminated site has not been sued under CERCLA but has paid cleanup costs, can it seek contribution from prior owners of the property?**

Excerpts from Justice Thomas's Decision: The first sentence, the enabling clause that establishes the right of contribution, provides: "Any person *may* seek contribution ... *during or following* any civil action under [CERCLA]." Aviall answers that "may" should be read permissively, such that "during or following" a civil action is one, but not the exclusive, instance in which a person may seek contribution. We disagree.

[If CERCLA] were read to authorize contribution actions at any time, regardless of the existence of a civil action, then Congress need not have included the explicit "during or following" condition. In other words, Aviall's reading would render part of the statute entirely superfluous, something we are loath to do. There is no reason why Congress would bother to specify conditions under which a person may bring a contribution claim, and at the same time allow contribution actions absent those conditions.

[CERCLA] authorizes contribution claims only "during or following" a civil action and it is undisputed that Aviall has never been subject to such an action. Aviall therefore has no claim. ■

Public Policy

Aviall cooperated with the authorities in Texas and voluntarily cleaned up its contaminated site. If it had refused to clean up the site and forced Texas to sue, Aviall would have been entitled to some contribution from Cooper. As it is, Aviall got nothing and had to pay all the expenses itself. Does this result make sense? Is it in keeping with the goal of CERCLA: "shovels first, lawyers later"? Should Congress amend the statute? ◆

ECONOMICS *& the* **LAW**

In a perfect world, the EPA would make rational decisions based on sound science, using its limited resources to solve the most severe problems. Reality can be a bit different.

If you were head of the EPA, for instance, how would you decide which Superfund sites the EPA should address first? You might think that the environmental agency should focus on the most harmful sites. That may sound sensible, but it is not how the system works. A recent study reveals that the EPA's priorities are largely determined by two factors: the

---

9   Typically, a panel of three judges hears the appeal to a U.S. circuit court of appeals. However, sometimes the entire court will hear a case, and that is called sitting "en banc."

polluters and the local communities. An aggressive defendant can stave off EPA action or an eager community can persuade the EPA to clean up their town first, even as a neighboring community with a more pressing problem finds itself moved down the waiting list.[10] Likewise, one would expect that decisions about which species to add to the endangered list (discussed later in the chapter) should perhaps be based solely on the rarity and importance of the species in question. In fact, public opinion (whether in favor or against) can dramatically affect the listing decision.[11]

Can you think of any way to render the decision-making process more effective? ◆

CHEMICALS

More than 70,000 chemicals are used in food, drugs, cosmetics, pesticides, and other products. Some of these chemicals are known to accumulate in human tissue and cause, among other harm, cancer, birth defects, and neurological damage. However, only 2 percent of these 70,000 chemicals have been adequately tested to determine their total health impact. Almost 70 percent have not been tested at all. Scientists know virtually nothing about their impact on the health of wildlife.

Several federal agencies share responsibility for regulating chemicals. The Food and Drug Administration (FDA) has control over foods, drugs, and cosmetics. The Occupational Safety and Health Administration (OSHA) is responsible for protecting workers from exposure to toxic chemicals. The Nuclear Regulatory Commission (NRC) regulates radioactive substances. The EPA regulates pesticides and other toxic chemicals.

Federal Insecticide, Fungicide, and Rodenticide Act

The Federal Insecticide, Fungicide, and Rodenticide Act (FIFRA) requires manufacturers to register all pesticides with the EPA. Before registering a pesticide, the EPA must ensure that its benefits exceed its (then-known) risks. However, many of the 50,000 pesticides currently registered with the EPA were approved at a time when little was known about their risks. In 1972, Congress directed the EPA to reevaluate all registered pesticides and cancel those whose risks exceed their benefits. This process has been very slow. Before the EPA cancels a registration, the manufacturer is entitled to a formal hearing, which may take several years. In the event of an emergency, the EPA may order an immediate suspension; otherwise the chemical stays on the market until the hearing. If a pesticide is banned, the EPA must reimburse end users of the chemicals for their useless inventory.

Federal Food, Drug, and Cosmetic Act

The Federal Food, Drug, and Cosmetic Act requires the EPA to set maximum levels for pesticide residue in raw or processed food. The Food and Drug Administration can confiscate food with pesticide levels that exceed the EPA standards.

---

[10] Hilary Sigman, "The Pace of Progress at Superfund Sites: Policy Goals and Interest Group Influence," *Journal of Law and Economics,* April 2001, vol. 44, p. 315.

[11] Amy Whritenour Ando, "Waiting to Be Protected Under the Endangered Species Act: The Political Economy of Regulatory Delay," *Journal of Law and Economics,* April 1999, vol. 42, p.29.

Food Quality Protection Act of 1996

The Food Quality Protection Act requires the EPA to set pesticide standards at levels that are safe for children. If the data for children are unclear, the EPA must reduce levels to one-tenth the amount now permitted in food. The EPA must also consider all sources of exposure. Thus, for example, in setting limits for pesticides on grapes, the EPA must factor in other sources of pesticides, such as drinking water.

This statute is highly controversial. The pesticide industry argues that the EPA could effectively ban many valuable chemicals for years while careful research into their impact on children is conducted. Environmental advocates, on the other hand, are dismayed that the EPA has not demanded more thorough research before setting standards for some pesticides.

Toxic Substances Control Act

The Toxic Substances Control Act (TSCA) regulates chemicals other than pesticides, foods, drugs, and cosmetics. For example, it regulates lead in gasoline and paints. **Before selling a new chemical (or an old chemical being used for a new purpose), the manufacturer must register it with the EPA.** As part of the registration process, the manufacturer must present evidence of the chemical's impact on health and the environment. The EPA may prohibit the manufacture, sale, or a particular use of any chemical that poses an unreasonable risk.

NATURAL RESOURCES

Thus far, this chapter has focused on the regulation of pollution. Congress has also passed statutes whose purpose is to preserve the country's natural resources.

National Environmental Policy Act

The National Environmental Policy Act of 1969 (NEPA) requires all *federal agencies* to prepare an *environmental impact statement* (EIS) for every major federal action significantly affecting the quality of the human environment. An EIS is a major undertaking—often hundreds, if not thousands, of pages long. It must discuss (1) environmental consequences of the proposed action, (2) available alternatives, (3) direct and indirect effects, (4) energy requirements, (5) impact on urban quality, historic, and cultural resources, and (6) means to mitigate adverse environmental impacts. Once a draft report is ready, the federal agency must hold a hearing to allow for outside comments.

The EIS requirement applies not only to actions *undertaken* by the federal government, but also to activities *regulated* or *approved* by the government. For instance, the following projects required an EIS:

- Expanding the Snowmass ski area in Aspen, Colorado—because approval was required by the Forest Service

- Killing a herd of wild goats that was causing damage at the Olympic National Park (outside Seattle)

- Closing a road to create a beachside pavilion in Redondo Beach, California

- Creating a golf course outside Los Angeles—because the project required a government permit to build in wetlands.

The EIS process is controversial. If a project is likely to have an important impact, environmentalists almost always litigate the adequacy of the EIS. Industry advocates argue that environmentalists are simply using the EIS process to delay—or halt—any projects they oppose. In 1976, seven years after NEPA was passed, a dam on the Teton River in Idaho burst, killing 17 people and causing $1 billion in property damage. The Department of the Interior had built the dam in the face of allegations that its EIS was incomplete; it did not, for example, confirm that a large earth-filled dam resting on a riverbed was safe. To environmentalists, this tragedy graphically illustrated the need for a thorough EIS.

Researchers have found that the EIS process generally has a beneficial impact on the environment. The mere prospect of preparing an EIS tends to eliminate the worst projects. Litigation over the EIS eliminates the next weakest group. If an agency does a good faith EIS, honestly looking at the available alternatives, projects tend to be kinder to the environment, at little extra cost.

Endangered Species Act

The Endangered Species Act (ESA):

- Requires the Secretary of Commerce or the Secretary of the Interior to prepare a list of species that are in danger of becoming extinct

- Requires the government to develop plans to revive these species

- Requires all federal agencies to ensure that their actions will not jeopardize an endangered species

- Prohibits any sale or transport of these species

- Makes any taking of an endangered animal species unlawful—taking is defined as harassing, harming, killing, or capturing any endangered species or modifying its habitat in such a way that its population is likely to decline—and

- Prohibits the taking of any endangered plant species on federal property.

No environmental statute has been more controversial than the ESA. In theory, everyone is in favor of saving endangered species. There are currently 991 endangered species (392 animals and 599 plants) on the U.S. list, and species are becoming extinct at 100 to 1,000 times the rate one would expect to occur naturally. To quote the House of Representatives Report on the ESA:

> As we homogenize the habitats in which these plants and animals evolved . . . we threaten their—and our own—genetic heritage. . . . Who knows, or can say, what potential cures for cancer or other scourges, present or future, may lie locked up in the structures of plants which may yet be undiscovered, much less analyzed?

In practice, however, the cost of saving a species can be astronomical. One of the earliest ESA battles involved the snail darter—a three-inch fish that lived in the Little Tennessee River. The Supreme Court upheld a decision under the ESA to halt work on a dam that would have blocked the river, flooding 16,500 acres of farmland and destroying the snail darter's habitat. To the dam's supporters, this decision was ludicrous: stopping a dam (on which $100 million in taxpayer money had already been spent) to save a little fish that no one had ever even thought of before the dam (or damn) controversy. The real agenda, they argued, was simply to halt development. Environmental advocates argued, however, that the wanton destruction of whole species will ultimately and inevitably lead to disaster for humankind. In the end, Congress overruled the Supreme Court and authorized completion of the dam. It turned out that the snail darter has survived in other rivers.

The snail darter was the first in a long line of ESA controversies that have included the bighorn sheep, the spotted owl, the gnatcatcher, the island fox, and the pygmy rabbit, among others. Opponents argue that too much time and money have been spent on litigation to save too few species of too little importance. The following case, however, discusses the advantages of the ESA.

GIBBS V. BABBITT

214 F.3d 483, 2000 U.S. App. LEXIS 12280
United States Court of Appeals for the Fourth Circuit, 2000

Facts: The red wolf used to roam throughout the southeastern United States. Owing to wetlands drainage, dam construction, and hunting, this wolf is now on the endangered species list. The Fish and Wildlife Service (FWS) trapped the remaining red wolves, placed them in a captive breeding program, and then reintroduced them into the wild. Ultimately, the FWS reintroduced 75 wolves into the 120,000-acre Alligator River National Wildlife Refuge in eastern North Carolina and the Pocosin Lakes National Wildlife Refuge in Tennessee.

After reintroduction, about 41 red wolves wandered from federal refuges onto private property. Plaintiff Richard Lee Mann shot a red wolf that he feared might threaten his cattle. Mann pled guilty to violating a provision of the ESA that prohibits the taking of any endangered species without a permit.

Two individuals and two counties in North Carolina filed suit against the U.S. government, alleging that the anti-taking regulation as applied to the red wolves on private land exceeded Congress's power under the interstate Commerce Clause of the U.S. Constitution.

Issue: Is the anti-taking provision of the ESA constitutional?

Excerpts from Justice Wilkinson's Decision: Congress' commerce authority includes the power to regulate those activities having a substantial relation to interstate commerce. Although the connection to economic or commercial activity plays a central role in whether a regulation will be upheld under the Commerce Clause, economic activity must be understood in broad terms.

The red wolves are part of a $29.2 billion national wildlife-related recreational industry that involves tourism and interstate travel. Many tourists travel to North Carolina from throughout the country for "howling events"—evenings of listening to wolf howls accompanied by educational programs. According to a study conducted by Dr. William E. Rosen of Cornell University, the recovery of the red wolf and increased visitor activities could result in a significant regional economic impact. Rosen estimates that northeastern North Carolina could see an increase of between $39.61 and $183.65 million per year in tourism-related activities, and that the Great Smoky Mountains National Park could see an increase of between $132.09 and $354.50 million per year. This is hardly a trivial impact on interstate commerce.

Appellants argue that the tourism rationale relates only to howling events on national park land or wildlife refuges because people do not travel to private land. Yet this argument misses the mark. Indeed, wolves are known to be "great wanderers." Because so many members of this threatened species wander on private land, the regulation of takings on private land is essential to the entire program of reintroduction and eventual restoration of the species. Such regulation is necessary to conserve enough red wolves to sustain tourism.

The regulation of red wolf takings is also closely connected to a second interstate market—scientific research. Scientific research generates jobs. It also deepens our knowledge of the world in which we live. The red wolf reintroduction program has already generated numerous scientific studies. Scientists have studied how the red wolf affects small mammal populations and how the wolves interact with the ecosystem as a whole. Scientific research can also reveal other uses for animals—for instance, approximately 50 percent of all modern medicines are derived from wild plants or animals.

The anti-taking regulation is also connected to a third market—the possibility of a renewed trade in fur pelts. Wolves have historically been hunted for

▼

their pelts. Congress had the renewal of trade in mind when it enacted the ESA. In such a case businessmen may profit from the trading and marketing of that species for an indefinite number of years, where otherwise it would have been completely eliminated from commercial channels. The American alligator is a case in point. In 1975, the American alligator was nearing extinction and listed as endangered, but by 1987 conservation efforts restored the species. Now there is a vigorous trade in alligator hides.

Finally, the taking of red wolves is connected to interstate markets for agricultural products and livestock. For instance, appellant landowners find red wolves a menace because they threaten livestock and other animals of economic and commercial value. This effect on commerce, however, still qualifies as a legitimate subject for regulation. It is well-settled under Commerce Clause cases that a regulation can involve the promotion or the restriction of commercial enterprises and development.

It is anything but clear that red wolves harm farming enterprises. They may in fact help them, and in so doing confer additional benefits on commerce. For instance, red wolves prey on animals like raccoons, deer, and rabbits—helping farmers by killing the animals that destroy their crops.

[I]t is reasonable for Congress to decide that conservation of species will one day produce a substantial commercial benefit to this country and that failure to preserve a species will result in permanent, though unascertainable, commercial loss. If a species becomes extinct, we are left to speculate forever on what we might have learned or what we may have realized. If we conserve the species, it will be available for the study and benefit of future generations. We therefore hold that the anti-taking provision at issue here involves regulable economic and commercial activity as understood by current Commerce Clause jurisprudence. ∎

The government has introduced the Habitat Conservation Plan (HCP) as a blueprint for compromise over the ESA. In an HCP, developers agree to conserve some land in return for developing other property as they want. These deals contain a "no surprises" clause, meaning that the government has no right to retrieve land once it has been approved for development, even if scientists later determine that a particular species needs that habitat for survival. Unfortunately, the natural world is full of surprises, and environmentalists worry about the ultimate impact of these HCPs. In the short run, however, the success has been striking. For example, to save the gnatcatcher, a songbird found near San Diego, federal and local governments agreed to set aside 82,000 acres that they owned. They bought an additional 27,000 acres, at a cost of $300 million, and developers donated 63,000 acres more. In return, the developers earned the right to build on their remaining land without limitation. More than 16 million acres, including 10 percent of timberland in the Pacific Northwest, are now designated HCPs.

In the long run, the real issue is not how much land developers will give up, but how each of us will change our lifestyle. The government recently announced that nine wild salmon species in the Pacific Northwest are threatened. The Columbia River was once home to 16 million salmon, but dozens of dams now block the river, interfering with the fish's annual migration. Fewer than a million salmon remain. The following article discusses some of the remedies that may be necessary to save the salmon.

NEWS*worthy*

With the salmon crisis, you step out the door and the rain that's running off your front lawn, awash in fertilizer, is a problem. You drive to work (alone) and you are adding to the oil and other chemicals that all eventually drain into the streams. You work for a company that wants to expand its offices into what is a salmon habitat, which describes just about every wetland within a day's drive of Seattle. At home, you turn on a light that is fed cheaply by the very dams that make it nearly impossible for salmon to swim upstream. For us to change this chain of events requires changing our lifestyles, which is something most Northwesterners have always seemed loath to do. We don't want anyone to tell us what to do with our lot size or with that instrument that is most integral to life here: the sport utility vehicle. All of a sudden being for the salmon means being against building a new home wherever you'd like, being for increased taxes, being prepared to change suburban life.

As this new debate begins, the phrase "putting salmon before people" will be heard over and over. Somehow the people need to line up behind the fish, knowing that the fish are like the canary in the coal mine. Now, the salmon are making us look not just at what we can do with the rivers but at what we can do with the way we commute and choose our homes and shop and live. The question is, Will it be too much of a hassle for us to look at ourselves?[12] ◆

Chapter Conclusion

Environmental laws have a pervasive impact on our lives. The cost has been great—whether it is the higher price for cars with pollution control devices or the time spent filling out environmental impact statements. Some argue that cost is irrelevant, that a clean environment has incalculable value for its own sake. Others insist on a more pragmatic approach and want to know if the benefits outweigh the costs.

What benefits has the country gained from environmental regulation? Since 1970, when Congress created the EPA, the record on common air pollutants, such as lead, has been extraordinarily successful. Total emissions of lead nationwide have declined by 96 percent. Before 1970, emissions of sulfur dioxide had been increasing rapidly. Since then, in spite of strong economic growth and an increase in population, these emissions have dropped. Despite this progress, however, many Americans live in areas that still do not meet EPA quality standards.

As for water, wetland acreage continues to decline at a rapid rate. However, the number of Americans whose sewage goes to wastewater treatment facilities has more than doubled. Two-thirds of the nation's waters are safe for fishing and swimming, up from only one-third when the Clean Water Act was passed.

Despite this progress, as a nation we still face many intractable problems. We have not developed a political consensus on global warming. The health effects of pesticides in our food supply are uncertain. Superfund and the Endangered Species Act are mired in a thornbush of litigation.

In short, despite significant progress, much work remains to be done. In a study of worldwide environmental sustainability, which ranked countries on issues such as air quality, water quality, and biodiversity, the United States ranked 45th out of 146 countries, behind Japan and all of Western Europe. Although many people, and many politicians, readily acknowledge the importance of the environment to both present and future generations, when the time comes to allocate resources, change lifestyles, make tough choices, the consensus too often breaks down, with the result that resources are spent on litigation, instead of the environment.

---

[12] Robert Sullivan, "And Now, the Salmon War," *New York Times,* Mar. 20, 1999, p. A15. Copyright © 1999 by The New York Times Co. Reprinted by permission.

Chapter Review

1. The following table provides a list of environmental statutes:

Air Pollution	Water Pollution	Waste Disposal	Chemicals	Natural Resources
Clean Air Act	Clean Water Act Safe Drinking Water Act	Resource Conservation and Recovery Act	Federal Insecticide, Fungicide, and Rodenticide Act	National Environmental Policy Act
	Ocean Dumping Act Oil Pollution Act	Comprehensive Environmental Response, Compensation, and Liability Act (Superfund or CERCLA)	Federal Food, Drug, Cosmetic Act Food Quality Protection Act Toxic Substances Control Act	Endangered Species Act

2. Under the Clean Air Act of 1970, the Environmental Protection Agency must establish national ambient air quality standards for both primary and secondary pollution. States must produce implementation plans to meet the EPA standards.

3. Under the Clean Air Act, power plants may trade emission allowances.

4. The Clean Water Act prohibits the discharge of pollution into water without a permit from the EPA. States must set EPA-approved water quality standards and develop plans to achieve them. The Clean Water Act also prohibits any discharge of dredge and fill material into a wetland without a permit.

5. The Safe Drinking Water Act requires the EPA to set national standards for every contaminant potentially harmful to human health that is found in drinking water.

6. The Ocean Dumping Act prohibits the dumping of wastes in ocean water without a permit from the EPA.

7. The Oil Pollution Act of 1990 sets design standards for ships operating in U.S. waters and requires shipowners to pay for damage caused by oil discharged from their ships.

8. The Resource Conservation and Recovery Act establishes rules for treating hazardous wastes and other forms of solid waste.

9. Under Superfund (CERCLA), anyone who has ever owned or operated a site on which hazardous wastes are found, or who has transported wastes to the site, or who has arranged for the disposal of wastes that were released at the site, is liable for (1) the cost of cleaning up the site, (2) any damage done to natural resources, and (3) any required health assessments.

10. The Federal Insecticide, Fungicide, and Rodenticide Act requires manufacturers to register all pesticides with the EPA.

11. The Federal Food, Drug, and Cosmetic Act requires the EPA to set maximum levels for pesticide residue in raw or processed food. The Food Quality Protection Act requires the EPA to set pesticide standards at levels that are safe for children.

12. Under the Toxic Substances Control Act, manufacturers must register new chemicals with the EPA.

13. The National Environmental Policy Act requires all federal agencies to prepare an environmental impact statement for every major federal action significantly affecting the quality of the environment.

14. The Endangered Species Act prohibits activities that cause harm to endangered species.

Practice Test

1. Astro Circuit Corp. in Lowell, Massachusetts, manufactured printed circuit boards. David Boldt was in charge of the production line. In theory, the company pretreated its industrial waste to remove toxic metals, but, in practice, the factory was producing twice as much wastewater as the treatment facility could handle. The company often bypassed the treatment facility and dumped wastewater directly into the city sewer. Once, when caught by the city, Boldt wrote a letter implying that the violation was a temporary aberration. Boldt felt that he was caught "between the devil and the deep blue sea." It was his job to keep the production line moving, but he had no place to put the waste product. Has Boldt violated the law? What penalties might he face?

2. The U.S. Forest Service planned to build a road in the Nez Perce National Forest in Idaho to provide access to loggers. Is the Forest Service governed by any environmental statutes? Must it seek permission before building the road?

3. In 1963, FMC Corp. purchased a manufacturing plant in Virginia from American Viscose Corp., the owner of the plant since 1937. During World War II, the government's War Production Board had commissioned American Viscose to make rayon for airplanes and truck tires. In 1982, inspections revealed carbon disulfide, a chemical used to manufacture this rayon, in groundwater near the plant. American Viscose was out of business. Who is responsible for cleaning up the carbon disulfide? Under what statute?

4. Tariq Ahmad owned Shankman Laboratories. He decided to dispose of some of the lab's hazardous chemicals by shipping them to his home in Pakistan. He sent the chemicals to Castelazo & Associates (in the United States) to prepare the materials for shipment. Ahmad did not tell the driver who picked up the chemicals that they were hazardous. Nor did he give the driver any written documentation. Ahmad had packed the chemicals hurriedly in flimsy containers that were unsafe for transporting hazardous materials. He also grossly misrepresented to Castelazo the amount and type of hazardous material that he was shipping to Pakistan. Has Ahmad violated U.S. law? What penalties might he face?

5. Suppose that you are the manager of the General Motors Hummer plant in Mishawaka, Indiana. Hummers are the successor to the U.S. Army jeep and have become popular recreational vehicles among the rich and famous. Arnold Schwarzenegger has several. The Hummer requires special protective paint that, as it turns out, reacts with other chemicals during the application process to create ozone, a pollutant. You want to increase production of Hummers. Are there any legal requirements you must observe?

6. Alcan Aluminum Corp. manufactures aluminum sheet in Oswego, New York. It hired the Mahler Cos. to dispose of an emulsion used during the manufacturing process. This emulsion contained a variety of hazardous substances. Without Alcan's knowledge, Mahler dumped the emulsion into a borehole that connected to deep underground mines along the Susquehanna River in Pennsylvania. You can guess what happened next. Approximately 100,000 gallons of water contaminated with hazardous substances spilled from the borehole into the river. The EPA paid to clean up the river and then sued Alcan along with others who had hired Mahler for hazardous waste disposal. All other defendants settled. The court entered judgment against Alcan in the amount of $473,790.18, which was the difference between the full response costs the government had incurred in cleaning the river and the amount the government had recovered from the settling defendants. Is Alcan required to pay this amount?

7. In 1991, Illinois passed a statute requiring its four largest generating plants to install scrubbers so that they could continue using high-sulfur Illinois coal. What federal law was this Illinois statute designed to overcome? *Extra credit question:* On what grounds did a federal appeals court strike down the Illinois statute?

8. The marbled murrelet is a rare seabird that lives only in old-growth forests on the West Coast. Logging has destroyed so much of its habitat that its numbers in California have declined from 60,000 to between 2,000 and 5,000. Pacific Lumber Co. wanted to harvest trees from 137 acres of land it owned in the Owl Creek forest in California. It originally received approval to log, on

the condition that it would cooperate with regulators to protect the murrelet. But the company sneaked in one weekend and cut down trees before it met the condition. Caught in the act, it promised no more logging until it had a plan to protect the birds. This time it waited until the long weekend over Thanksgiving to take down some more trees. Finally, a federal court ordered a permanent halt to any further logging. There was no evidence that the company had harmed the murrelet. Had it violated the law?

9. **ETHICS** Geronimo Villegas owned a blood-testing lab in Brooklyn, New York. He threw vials of human blood from the lab into the Hudson River. A group of eighth graders on a field trip to Staten Island discovered 70 of these glass vials along the shore. Ten vials contained blood infected with the highly contagious hepatitis-B virus. Did Villegas violate the Clean Water Act? Why had Villegas disposed of the vials in this way? Whether or not he was in violation of the statute, was his behavior ethical? Did he violate any of the ethical tests from Chapter 2?

10. ***YOU BE THE JUDGE*** WRITING PROBLEM The Lordship Point Gun Club operated a trap and skeet shooting club in Stratford, Connecticut, for 70 years. During this time, customers deposited close to 5 million tons of lead shot and 11 million pounds of clay target fragments on land around the club and in Long Island Sound. Forty-five percent of sediment samples taken from the Sound exceeded the established limits for lead. Was the Gun Club in violation of the RCRA? **Argument for the Gun Club:** The Gun Club does not *dispose* of hazardous wastes, within the meaning of the RCRA. Congress meant the statute to apply only to companies in the business of manufacturing articles that produce hazardous waste. If the Gun Club happens to produce wastes, that is only *incidental* to the normal use of a product. **Argument for the plaintiff:** Under the RCRA, lead shot is hazardous waste. The law applies to anyone who produces hazardous waste, no matter how.

11. **ROLE REVERSAL** Write a short-answer question that poses an ethics or economics question under the environmental laws.

Internet Research Problem

Using the information provided at **http://beatty .westbuslaw.com**, write an essay summarizing your views on global warming. What should our own government, and other governments, do? What should you do personally?

> **You can find further practice problems at http://beatty.westbuslaw.com or in the Study Guide that accompanies this text.**

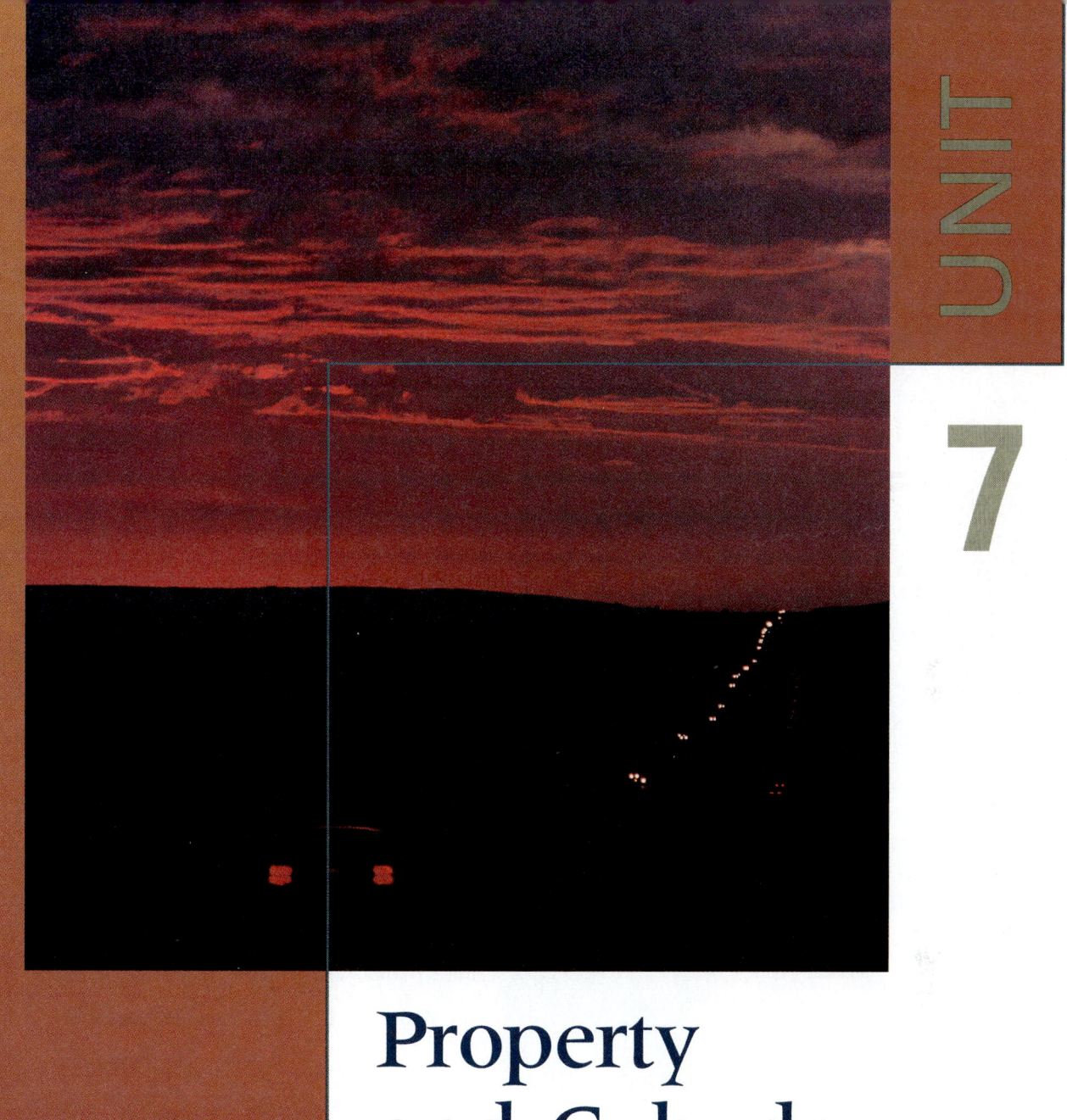

Property
and Cyberlaw

Cyberlaw

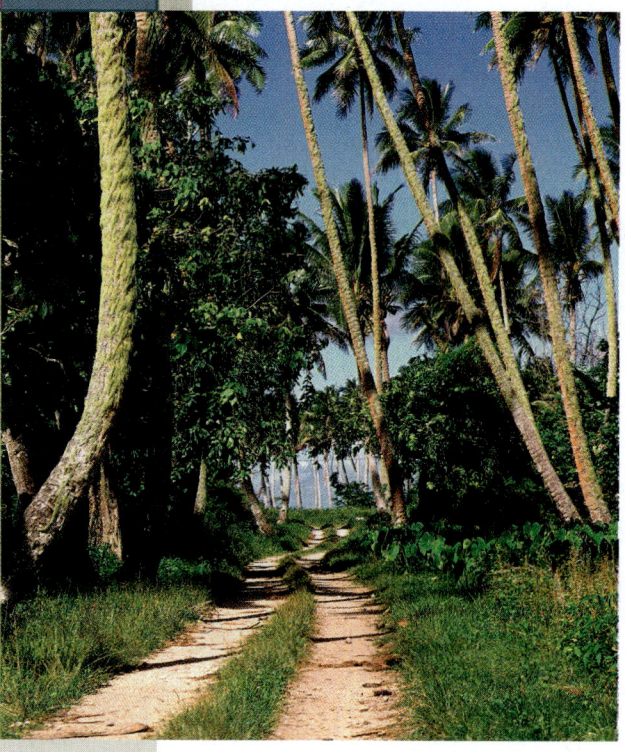

Garrett always said that his computer was his best friend. He was online all the time, sending instant messages to his friends, listening to music, doing research for his courses, and, okay, maybe playing a few games now and again. Occasionally, the computer could be annoying. It would crash once in a while, trashing part of a paper he had forgotten to save. And there was the time that a copy of an e-mail he sent Lizzie complaining about Caroline somehow ended up in Caroline's mailbox. He was pretty irritated when the White Sox tickets he bought in an online auction turned out to be for a Little League team. And he was tired of all the spam advertising pornographic Web sites. But these things happen and, despite the petty annoyances, his computer was an important part of his life.

Then one day, Garrett received a panicked instant message from a teammate on the college wrestling squad telling him to click on a certain Web site pronto to see someone they knew. Garrett eagerly clicked on the Web site and discovered, to his horror, that *he* was featured—in the nude. The Web site was selling videos showing him and other members of the wrestling team in the locker room in various states of undress. Other videos, from other locker and shower rooms, were for sale, too, showing football players and wrestlers from dozens of universities. The videos had titles like "Straight Off the Mat" and "Voyeur Time." No longer trusting technology,

Garrett pulled on his running shoes and dashed over to the office of his business law

professor. ■

Computers and the Internet—cyberspace—together comprise one of the great technological developments of the twentieth century.[1] Inevitably, new technologies create the need for new law. In the thirteenth century, England was one of the first countries to develop passable roads. Like the Internet, these roadways greatly enhanced communication, creating social and business opportunities, but also enabled new crimes. Good roads meant that bad guys could sneak out of town without paying their bills. Parliament responded with laws to facilitate the collection of out-of-town debts. Similarly, while the Internet has opened up enormous opportunities in both our business and personal lives, it has also created the need for new laws, both to pave the way for these opportunities and to limit their dangers.

The process of lawmaking never stops. Judges sit and legislatures meet—all in an effort to create better rules and a better society. However, in an established area of law, such as contracts, the basic structure changes little. Cyberlaw is different because it is still very much in its infancy. Not only are new laws being created almost daily but whole areas of regulation are, as yet, unpaved roads. Although the process of rule making has progressed well, much debate still surrounds cyberspace law and much work remains to be done. This chapter focuses on the existing rules and also discusses the areas of regulation that are still incomplete and in debate.

Cyberlaw affects many areas of our lives. You will have noticed that this book contains numerous Cyberlaw features throughout. Chapter 15, for instance, discusses the validity of electronic contracts and signatures, Chapter 37 deals with cyber issues in securities law, and Chapter 43 contains a lengthy discussion of cyberlaw and intellectual property. This chapter, however, deals with issues that are unique to the cyber world, such as online privacy, hacking, and spam. If some of the words confuse you, consult the glossary of Internet terms at **http://www.matisse.net/files/glossary.html**.

Before beginning the chapter in earnest, let's return briefly to Garrett, the wrestler. What recourse does Garrett have for his Internet injuries? The nude video incident happened at Illinois State University and seven other colleges. Approximately 30 athletes filed suit against GTE and PSINet for selling the videos online, but the two Web hosts were found not liable under the Communications Decency Act because they had not produced the videos themselves, they had simply permitted the sale of someone else's content. What about Garrett's other computer injuries? Lizzie was not being a good friend, but it was perfectly legal for her to forward Garrett's e-mail to Caroline. The seller of the White Sox tickets violated both federal and state fraud statutes. The federal Can-Spam Act prohibits spam—unsolicited commercial e-mail—but a lawsuit is a slow and awkward tool for killing such a flourishing weed. Thus far, the available legal tools have been relatively ineffectual (as you can tell from your e-mail inbox).

---

[1]   The term "Internet" means "the international computer network of both Federal and non-Federal interoperable packet switched data networks." 47 U.S. §230 (f)(1). It began in the 1960s as a project to link military contractors and universities. Now, it is a giant network that connects smaller groups of linked computer networks. The World Wide Web was created in 1991 by Tim Berners-Lee as a subnetwork of the Internet. It is a decentralized collection of documents containing text, pictures, and sound. Users can move from document to document using links that form a "web" of information.

PRIVACY

The Internet has vastly increased our ability to communicate quickly and widely. There was a time when intraoffice memos were typed, photocopied, and then hand-delivered by messengers. Catalog orders were sent via regular mail, a comparatively slow, inefficient, and costly method.

As wonderful as computerized communication can be, though, it is not without its dangers. Consumers enter the most personal data—credit card numbers, bank accounts, lists of friends, medical information, product preferences—on the Internet. Who will have access to this data? Who can see it, use it, sell it? Many people fear that the Internet is a very large window through which the government, employers, business, and criminals can find out more than they should about you and your money, habits, beliefs and health. Even e-mail has its dangers: Who has not been embarrassed by an e-mail that ended up in the wrong mailbox?

Many commentators argue that, without significant changes in the law, our privacy will be obliterated. At the moment, however, privacy on the Internet is very much like the weather—everyone talks about it, but (so far) no one has done much about it.

Of Cookies and Caches

If you order a book from Amazon.com, you may notice that the next time you log on, you will be greeted with the message, "Hello, [Your Name]. We have recommendations for you." Click on the link and you may find that, because you previously bought a GMAT study guide, Amazon will entice you with other guides for standardized tests. However did Amazon know? Many Web sites automatically place a cookie on the hard drive of your computer when you visit them. **A cookie is a small file that includes an identification number and may also include personal data such as your address, phone and credit card numbers, and searches you have made or advertisements you have clicked on.**[2]

Some cookies are designed to follow a user from site to site, along the entire Internet trail. Indeed, a whole industry of Internet marketing firms knows how to target Web banners to individual surfers. Thus, if you visit Web sites for hotels in Togo you might, without your knowledge, be invisibly linked to an Internet marketing company that will automatically record this site visit in a cookie on your hard drive. Then, when you visit a travel site, in less time than it takes you to say "click," the marketing company can automatically retrieve your cookie, realize you are interested in Togo, and show you banner ads for travel there. You, meanwhile, are blissfully unaware that you have a dossier in cyberspace.

Other cookies can be used to authenticate who you are, storing such information as your name, address, and credit card number. Amazon.com has patented its so-called "One-Click" system that permits a shopper to buy an item by clicking once on the button. What could be easier than that? One-click buying would not be possible without cookies. No doubt, cookies are convenient. And not just for one-click shopping. Consumers benefit from targeted advertisements—for instance, long-distance runners see

---

[2]   Legend has it that the term "cookie" refers to the Hansel and Gretel fairy tale. An evil stepmother forced her husband to take his two young children out into the woods and lose them. Anticipating such a plan, the children left a trail of bread crumbs to follow home. Legend does not reveal why these files are called cookies rather than crumbs.

ads for running shoes, not cigarettes. Industry representatives also argue that, without the revenue from cookie-based ads, many Internet sites would not be free to consumers.

But there is no such thing as a free lunch, or even a free snack. Cookies raise privacy issues. When you traipse around the Internet, cookies create a dossier that could come back to haunt you. Although much of the information gathered is anonymous (that is, the consumer is identified only by a computer identification number), this anonymous information can be linked to **personally identifiable information (PII)**, such as name and address. One company now markets a databank with the names of 150 million registered voters. Anyone can buy a list of voters that is sliced and diced however they want, say, Republicans between the ages of 45 and 60 with Hispanic surnames and incomes greater than $50,000. This company can also transmit specially tailored banner ads to voters surfing the Web.[3]

If marketers can put together a databank of Hispanic Republican voters, they can also find out that you have visited a Web site for recovering alcoholics or unrecovered gamblers or Nazi sympathizers. Do you want information about every Web site you visit to be public?

Even without cookies, your computer creates a dossier about you. When you surf the Web, your computer stores a copy of the Web pages you visit in a cache file on your hard drive. Thus, anyone with access to your hard drive could get a good idea of your regular stopping places. Would you be concerned if your boss knew that you were visiting sites that specialized in job searches, cancer, or, for that matter, *any* non-job-related site? (For advice on how to protect your privacy, slip over to **http://www .consumerprivacyguide.org/topthings**.)

Self Regulation of Online Privacy

Congress and the Federal Trade Commission (FTC) have been reluctant to establish laws that would regulate and protect consumer privacy on the Internet. They have instead favored self-regulation. In 2000, the commissioners of the FTC voted 3-2 to recommend that Congress enact Internet privacy legislation, but the next year a new FTC chair revoked that recommendation. Although the FTC promotes its Fair Information Practices (available at **http://www.ftc.gov/reports/privacy3/fairinfo.htm**), which are voluntary standards, few businesses have elected to follow them. Privacy protection on the Internet is now an uncertain, piecemeal affair. There is not, for instance, any law requiring Web sites to have or disclose a privacy policy, although if they do have one they are expected to abide by it. Consumers are largely unable to detect or prevent the collection and sharing of their personal information. Surfer beware!

Government Regulation of Online Privacy

Members of Congress have filed many bills to regulate online privacy. So intense, however, is the debate between industry and consumer advocates that no consensus—and little law—has emerged. There has, however, been some government regulation.

---

[3] For example, during the 2000 Republican presidential primaries, time was running short for John McCain to obtain enough voter signatures to get his name on the Virginia ballot. For $5,000, his campaign hired a company to send Internet advertisements to registered Republican voters in Virginia. When people in this database went online, they would see a McCain banner asking them to sign his petition.

The FTC

As we saw in Chapter 40 on consumer law, **Section 5 of the FTC Act prohibits unfair and deceptive acts or practices.** The FTC applies this statute to online privacy policies: It does not require Web sites to have a privacy policy, but if they do have one, they must follow it. For example, Gateway Learning Corporation sold *Hooked on Phonics* products online. The privacy policy on its Web site sounded good: it promised that the company would not give PII to third parties without the customer's consent and would not change its privacy policy without first notifying customers. Wrong on both counts—the company changed its policy, gave PII to third parties, and never told its customers. Gateway admitted that it was in violation of the FTC Act and agreed to discontinue its illegal practices.

Electronic Communications Privacy Act of 1986

The Electronic Communications Privacy Act of 1986 (ECPA) is a federal statute that prohibits unauthorized interception or disclosure of wire and electronic communications or unauthorized access to stored communications. The definition of electronic communication includes e-mail and transmissions from pagers and cellular phones. Violators are subject to both criminal and civil penalties. An action does not violate the ECPA if it is <u>unintentional</u> or if either party consents. Also, the USA Patriot Act, passed after the September 11th attacks, has broadened the *government's* right to monitor electronic communications.

Under the ECPA:

1. **Any intended recipient of an electronic communication has the right to disclose it.** Thus, if you sound off in an e-mail to a friend about your boss, the (erstwhile) friend may legally forward that e-mail to the boss or anyone else.

2. **Internet service providers (ISPs) are generally prohibited from disclosing electronic messages to anyone other than the addressee,** unless this disclosure is necessary for the performance of their service or for the protection of their own rights or property.

3. **An employer has the right to monitor workers' electronic communications if (1) the employee consents, (2) the monitoring occurs in the ordinary course of business, or (3) the employer provides the computer system (in the case of e-mail).** Note that an employer has the right to monitor electronic communication even if it does not relate to work activities.

4. **The government has the right to access electronic communication if it first obtains a search warrant or court order.**

One lesson from the ECPA: e-mail is not private and it is dangerous. Sixty percent of employers monitor their employees' e-mail. In the event of litigation, the other party can access e-mail, even messages that have in theory been deleted. The following article illustrates some of the many dangers.

NEWS*worthy*

Let's be clear. Harry Stonecipher wasn't fired simply because he had an extramarital affair with an employee. Plenty of chief executives have done that in the past, and plenty more will do it in the future. It's a bad, idea, it often violates company policies, but for the most part, it isn't a firing offense—yet.

No, the Boeing CEO was fired because, among other things, he had the bad judgment to detail his actions and desires in a series of very explicit e-mails to the woman in question. To borrow from one of my favorite country-music songs: We know what you were feeling, Harry. But what were you thinking?

E-mail, unlike love, is forever. You may think you've destroyed every last vestige of it, but it lives on, in some forgotten corner of some far-off server, waiting like Sleeping Beauty to be brought back to life by a zealous prosecutor or an overcompensated trial lawyer.

Has Mr. Stonecipher ever heard of Eliot Spitzer? The New York attorney general has built an awe-inspiring career on indiscreet e-mail, and now believes they are his e-ticket to the governor's mansion. Among his most prized discoveries were Henry Blodget's e-mail using the acronym POS (hint: the first two words are "piece" and "of") to refer to a tech stock that he was touting to the public on behalf of Merrill Lynch. Then there was Jack Grubman's e-mail boasting that Citigroup Chairman Sandy Weill had helped his children get into an exclusive Manhattan nursery school after he boosted his rating of AT&T stock.

The lesson of all this couldn't be clearer. Don't ever put anything in an e-mail that you wouldn't want to read on the jumbotron at Times Square.[4] ◆

What about information that consumers provide online—is that private? In the following case, consumers discovered that their PII was being collected by pharmaceutical company Web sites.

you Be The Judge

In Re PHARMATRAK, INC. PRIVACY LITIGATION

329 F.3d 9, 2003 U.S. App. LEXIS 8758
United States Court of Appeals for the First Circuit, 2003

Facts: Pharmatrak provided software that enabled pharmaceutical companies to compare traffic on different parts of their Web sites with the same information from competitors' sites. This software, called NETcompare, recorded the time a viewer spent on each Web page, her IP address, and the Web page she viewed immediately before arriving at the client's site. NETcompare was not designed to collect personal information about individual visitors, and Pharmatrak promised potential clients that the software could not and did not collect PII. Some of the pharmaceutical clients explicitly conditioned their purchase of NETcompare on Pharmatrak's guarantees of visitor confidentiality.

Pharmatrak sent monthly reports to its clients covering topics such as the most important links to a site and its most heavily visited pages. The monthly reports did not contain any PII. It turned out, though, that by an accident of programming, NETcompare did collect some personal information on a small number of users. Some of these mistakes occurred because of an interaction between NETcompare and the computer code used by clients on their Web pages. Pharmatrak could have warned its clients not to use this particular type of code, but it did not. Other data were mistakenly collected because of a bug in a popular e-mail program. Pharmatrak never collated or used this information.

Plaintiffs were a group of Internet users whose personal data were collected by NETcompare. Although the company monitored approximately 18.7 million Web site visitors, the computer expert hired by the plaintiffs was able to develop individual profiles for just 232 users. This information included name, address, telephone number, e-mail address, date of birth, gender, insurance status, education level, occupation, medical conditions, medications taken, and reasons for visiting the particular Web site. Occasionally, NETcompare also recorded the subject, sender, and date of the Web-based e-mail message a user was reading immediately prior to visiting a Web site.

Plaintiffs filed a class action complaint against Pharmatrak, alleging that the company had violated the Electronic Communications Privacy Act

▼

[4] Alan Murray, "Indiscreet E-Mail Claims a Fresh Casualty," *Wall Street Journal*, Mar. 9, 2005, p. A2

(ECPA). Both parties moved for summary judgment. The district court held for the defendants on the grounds that the pharmaceutical companies had consented to the placement of NETcompare on their Web sites. Plaintiffs appealed.

You Be the Judge: **Is Pharmatrak liable under the ECPA for having gathered PII about Web site visitors? Did Pharmatrak act intentionally? Was there consent?**

Argument for the Web Site Visitors: Pharmatrak promised that it would not collect PII, yet it did. The Web site visitors did not consent. The pharmaceutical companies consented to the installation of NETcompare, but not to the collection of the personal data. Pharmatrak had an obligation to live up to its promises. At a minimum, it should have warned its clients about the possible interaction between their software and NETcompare.

Argument for Pharmatrak: The ECPA only applies if there is intent and lack of consent. Pharmatrak did not design NETcompare so that it would gather PII and it never used the information. This information could be gleaned only by a computer expert. Any violation by Pharmatrak was at worst inadvertent, not intentional. Also, the pharmaceutical companies had consented to the installation of this software. ∎

Children's Online Privacy Protection Act of 1998

The Children's Online Privacy Protection Act of 1998 (COPPA) prohibits Internet operators from collecting information from children under 13 without parental permission. It also requires sites to disclose how they will use any information they acquire. The standard for obtaining parental consent is on a sliding scale—a higher standard applies if the information will be disclosed publicly. Enforcement is in the hands of the FTC. (An explanation of the statute is available at http://www.ftc.gov/bcp/conline/pubs/buspubs/coppa.htm.)

The Web site for Mrs. Fields cookies offered birthday coupons for free cookies to children under 13. Although the company did not share information with outsiders, it did collect PII without parental consent from 84,000 children. This information included name, home address, and birthdate. Mrs. Fields paid a penalty of $100,000 and agreed not to violate the law again.

But first you have to give me some personal information.

Gramm-Leach-Bliley Privacy Act of 1999

The Gramm-Leach-Bliley Privacy Act of 1999 (GLB) requires banks and other financial institutions to disclose to consumers any non-public information they wish to reveal to third parties.[5] A financial institution cannot disclose this private information if the consumer opts out (that is, denies permission). Advice on how to opt out is available at http://www.privacyrights.org/fs/fs24a-optout.htm.

GLB also prohibits *pretexting*, a process by which so-called *information brokers* use deception to find out private financial information. Thus, an FTC investigator contacted a Web site that was offering to sell private financial information. She offered to pay for information about her "fiancé's" bank balances. Someone working for the Web site successfully obtained this information by calling the bank and pretending

---

[5]   15 U.S.C. §6801.

to be the fiancé. The Web site settled with the FTC and agreed not to violate the GLB in future.

State Regulation

A few states have passed their own online privacy statutes. For instance, the California Online Privacy Act of 2003 requires any Web site that collects PII from California residents to post a privacy policy conspicuously and then abide by its terms.

The European Directive

The European Union (EU) has established strict privacy rules for the collection of personal data. This directive could have far-reaching impact outside of Europe because it prohibits the transfer of personal data to any countries that do not provide adequate privacy protection. Canada, South America, Australia, New Zealand, and parts of Asia have passed legislation to comply with the directive. Because the United States has not done so, the Department of Commerce reached agreement with the EU on so-called *safe harbor principles*. Any company that complies with the safe harbor rules will be permitted to receive data from European companies.

To be in compliance with the safe harbor principles, a company must:

1. Tell consumers how it intends to use their data and how they can limit its use.

2. Provide consumers with the opportunity to prevent disclosure of their personal data (in other words, to opt out). If the data are particularly sensitive (involving, for example, health or sex), then the data cannot be used unless the consumer opts in.

3. Provide adequate security for the data.

4. Provide customers with reasonable access to their data.

5. Establish a procedure for resolving disputes with customers.

To date, fewer than 500 U.S. companies are in compliance with the safe harbor principles. Most American companies have not complied because:

- The rules are cumbersome and require major changes in how companies manage customer data.

- European countries are not aggressively enforcing the rules, even against their own companies.

- If a U.S. company announces that it will comply with the safe harbor principles and then does not, the FTC has the authority to sanction the company. Therefore, companies may be better off complying with a weak policy rather than violating a strict one.

Spyware

Is your computer running sluggishly? Does it crash frequently? Has the home page on your Web browser suddenly changed without your consent? Is there a program in your systems tray that you do not recognize? You might have **spyware** on your computer. Spyware is a computer program that slips onto your computer without your permission—through e-mails, Internet downloads, or software installations. These programs monitor your activities, log your keystrokes and can report e-mail addresses, passwords and credit card numbers to outsiders. For more about spyware (and how to get rid of it), sneak over to **http://getnetwise.org/**.

Congress has considered legislation to control spyware, but has not taken final action. California has enacted the Consumer Protection Against Computer Spyware Act, which makes spyware illegal.

at RISK

What can you do to protect your privacy online? Here are some options:

- Use a fake name or provide false personal information when browsing Web sites (without committing fraud, of course!).
- Use secondary e-mail addresses to disguise your identity.
- Remember, before you click, to look for a Web site's privacy policy. If you cannot find one, or do not like what you find, you have the right to go elsewhere.
- Use privacy tools, such as those offered by The Electronic Privacy Information Center at **http://www.epic.org/privacy/tools.html**. ◆

Your Hard Drive as Witness (Against You)

Many people confide their deepest secrets to their computers. Would you want everything you have ever typed into your computer to be revealed publicly? Monica Lewinsky certainly did not. Investigators in the President Clinton impeachment case discovered damaging evidence on the hard drive of Lewinsky's computer—evidence she clearly thought was private, including copies of deleted e-mails and drafts of letters she had never sent. What protection do you have for information stored on your computer?

Criminal Law

The Fourth Amendment to the Constitution prohibits unreasonable searches and seizures by the government. In enforcing this provision of the Constitution, the courts ask: Did the person being searched have a legitimate expectation of privacy in the place searched or the item seized? If yes, then the government must obtain a warrant from a court before conducting the search. (For more on this topic, investigate Chapter 8, on crime.) The Fourth Amendment applies to computers.

The architecture professor in the following case would have benefited from a course in business law and perhaps in computer science, too.

UNITED STATES OF AMERICA V. ANGEVINE

281 F.3d 1130, 2002 U.S. App. LEXIS 2746
United States Court of Appeals for the Tenth Circuit, 2002

Facts: Professor Eric Angevine taught architecture at Oklahoma State University. The university provided him with a computer that was linked to the university network, and through it to the Internet. Professor Angevine used this computer to download more than 3,000 pornographic images of young boys. After viewing the images and printing some of them, he deleted the files. Tipped off by Professor Angevine's wife, police officers seized the computer and turned it over to a police computer expert who retrieved the pornographic files that the professor had deleted.

The Oklahoma State University computer policy states that:

- The contents of all storage media owned or stored on university computing facilities are the property of the university.
- Employees cannot use university computers to access obscene material.
- The university reserves the right to view or scan any file or software stored on a computer or passing through the network, and will do so periodically to audit the use of university resources. The university cannot guarantee confidentiality of stored data.
- System administrators keep logs of file names that may indicate why a particular data file is

▼

being erased, when it was erased, and what user identification has erased it.

The trial court held that federal agents did not need a warrant to search Professor Angevine's office computer because he had no expectation of privacy. He was sentenced to 51 months in prison for "knowing possession of child pornography." The professor appealed.

Issue: Did Professor Angevine have a reasonable expectation of privacy in his office computer?

Excerpts from Judge Brorby's Decision: Oklahoma State University policies and procedures prevent its employees from reasonably expecting privacy in data downloaded from the Internet onto University computers. The University computer-use policy reserved the right to randomly audit Internet use and to monitor specific individuals suspected of misusing University computers. The policy explicitly cautions computer users that information flowing through the University network is not confidential either in transit or in storage on a University computer. These office practices and procedures should have warned reasonable employees not to access child pornography with University computers.

We are reluctant to find a reasonable expectation of privacy where the circumstances reveal a careless effort to maintain a privacy interest. Professor Angevine downloaded child pornography through a monitored University computer network. The policy explained network administrators actively audit network transmissions for such misuse. While Professor Angevine did attempt to erase the child pornography, the University computer policy warned system administrators kept file logs recording when and by whom files were deleted. Moreover, given his transmission of the pornographic data through a monitored University network, deleting the files alone was not sufficient to establish a reasonable expectation of privacy.

We hold Professor Angevine could not have an objectively reasonable expectation of privacy. ■

Civil Litigation

Increasingly, computers are fair game in civil litigation. Suppose that you sue your company for wrongful termination. The company counterclaims, alleging that you cheated on your expense account. During litigation, it might subpoena your computer to find support for its allegations. Or suppose that, during the midst of a bitter divorce, your spouse alleges that you have shown pornography to your children. Your computer—with its Web trail—could end up in court. The following article illustrates how fragile privacy is when hard drives become pawns in litigation.

NEWS*worthy*

Each day, Ted Reeve pours his life into his home computer. He spends hours reading news online, and dutifully records monthly payments for his Visa card and Toyota Camry, along with ATM withdrawals. He regularly types up notes from talks with his doctor. It never occurred to him that such personal data could be extracted and shared among strangers. But that's what happened when his computer's hard drive was copied by two investigators retained for his employer, Northwest Airlines. Working right in his living room with a program called EnCase, they excavated every last bit and byte from his desktop hard drive.

Northwest suspected that its flight-attendant union had used the Internet to run an illegal call-in-sick campaign to disrupt the airline. So the airline won a court order to search 20 or so hard drives at flight attendants' homes and union offices. As people commit an ever-growing pile of information to computers, their hard drives are becoming a digital mother lode for lawyers. More federal courts are approving searches of home PCs for evidence in civil cases.[6] ◆

---

6 Michael J. McCarthy, "In Airline's Suit, PC Becomes Legal Pawn, Raising Privacy Issues," *Wall Street Journal*, May 24, 2000, p. 1.

SPAM

Spam is officially known as unsolicited commercial e-mail (UCE) or unsolicited bulk e-mail (UBE). Whatever it is called, it can be annoying as millions of these messages clog ISP computers and consumer mailboxes. As much as 80 percent of all e-mail is spam. It is estimated that roughly half of all spam is fraudulent—either in content (promoting a scam) or in packaging (the headers or return address are false). At a minimum, bulk e-mail adds to the cost of connecting to the Internet. ISPs must, for example, increase server capacity to handle the millions of spam e-mails. Moreover, both consumers and ISPs must endure the cost of outages caused by an overload of bulk e-mail. ISPs also argue that their reputations as service providers are harmed when consumers blame them for unsolicited advertisements. ISPs typically use filters to block this unwanted mail, but these programs are not foolproof and much spam sneaks through. The average worker spends ten business days a year dealing with spam. This lost productivity costs business $50 billion worldwide.

The Controlling the Assault of Non-Solicited Pornography and Marketing Act (Can-Spam) is a federal statute regulating spam. This statute applies to virtually all promotional e-mails, whether or not the sender has a pre-existing relationship with the recipient. E-mails covered by Can-Spam must:

- Provide an opt-out system that permits the recipient to unsubscribe
- Clearly indicate that the e-mail is an advertisement
- Provide a valid physical return address (not a post office box)
- Clearly indicate the nature of pornographic messages

A company can avoid these requirements by obtaining advance permission from the recipients.

Although one can only applaud the effort, the Can-Spam Act has not in truth noticeably decreased the amount of spam. Spammers operate in the netherworld of cyberspace where they are difficult to identify and locate. It may be, too, that the opt-out provision is having a perverse effect—instead of inspiring a spammer to remove e-mail addresses from his list, an opt-out request simply confirms to him that a live person is receiving his e-mails. But the statute does provide a new tool for fighting spam and ISPs have filed hundreds of lawsuits against spammers. For the optimistic, Spam-Cop (http://spamcop.net) offers a service to which you can report spammers.

In the following case, Intel tried to prevent unsolicited bulk e-mail from a former employee. The company used a common law principle: trespass to chattels. Did the company have the right to prevent this ex-employee from getting inside Intel with e-mail?

INTEL CORPORATION V. HAMIDI

30 Cal. 4th 1342, 71 P.3d 296, 2003 Cal. LEXIS 4205
Supreme Court of California, 2003

Facts: Kourosh Kenneth Hamidi, a former Intel engineer, founded an organization named Former and Current Employees of Intel (FACE-Intel) to disseminate information critical of Intel's employment practices. In addition to maintaining a Web site with critical information about Intel, FACE- ▼

Intel sent six mass e-mails to Intel employees. Each message was sent to as many as 35,000 addresses. These messages criticized Intel's employment practices, warned employees of the dangers those practices posed to their careers, suggested that employees consider moving to other companies, solicited employees' participation in FACE-Intel, and urged employees to inform themselves further by visiting FACE-Intel's Web site.

If any recipient asked to be removed from FACE-Intel's mailing list, Hamidi complied. He did not breach any computer security barriers. Nor did his e-mails cause physical damage or functional disruption to the company's computers. Intel was not deprived of the use of its computers. Many employees did ask the company to stop the messages, and staff members spent time attempting to block further messages. Employees also spent time discussing the content of the messages.

Intel sought an injunction against Hamidi to prevent him from sending any more e-mails on the grounds that he was committing the tort of trespass to chattels. The trial court granted Intel's motion for summary judgment and enjoined Hamidi from any further mailings. The Court of Appeal affirmed. The Supreme Court of California agreed to hear the case.

Issue: Did Intel have the right to prevent Hamidi from sending e-mails to its employees?

Excerpts from Justice Werdegar's Decision: [T]he tort of trespass to chattels allows recovery for interferences with possession of personal property. [T]he defendant's interference must, to be actionable, have caused some injury to the chattel or to the plaintiff's rights in it. The dispositive issue in this case, therefore, is whether the facts demonstrate Hamidi's actions caused or threatened to cause damage to Intel's computer system, or injury to its rights in that personal property.

[A] series of federal district court decisions held that sending UCE [spam] through an ISP's equipment may constitute trespass to the ISP's computer system. In each of these spamming cases, the plaintiff showed, or was prepared to show, some interference with the efficient functioning of its computer system. Intel has demonstrated neither any appreciable effect on the operation of its computer system from Hamidi's messages, nor any likelihood that Hamidi's actions will be replicated by others if found not to constitute a trespass. The functional burden on Intel's computers, or the cost in time to individual recipients, of receiving Hamidi's occasional advocacy messages cannot be compared to the burdens and costs caused ISPs and their customers by the ever-rising deluge of commercial e-mail.

Intel's workers were allegedly distracted from their work not because of the frequency or quantity of Hamidi's messages, but because of assertions and opinions the messages conveyed. Intel's complaint is thus about *the contents of the messages* rather than the functioning of the company's e-mail system. Intel's theory would expand the tort of trespass to chattels to cover virtually any unconsented-to communication that, solely because of its content, is unwelcome to the recipient or intermediate transmitter. Indeed, if a chattel's receipt of an electronic communication constitutes a trespass to that chattel, then unwelcome radio waves and television signals also constitute a trespass to chattel every time the viewer inadvertently sees or hears the unwanted program.

Nor, finally, can the fact Intel staff spent time attempting to block Hamidi's messages be bootstrapped into an injury to Intel's possessory interest in its computers. [I]t is circular to premise the damage element of a tort solely upon the steps taken to prevent the damage. Injury can only be established by the completed tort's consequences, not by the cost of the steps taken to avoid the injury and prevent the tort; otherwise, we can create injury for every supposed tort.

We conclude, therefore, that Intel has not presented undisputed facts demonstrating an injury to its personal property, or to its legal interest in that property, that support, under California tort law, an action for trespass to chattels. ■

Devil's Advocate

Hamidi's goal was to undermine Intel. Why should the company be forced to allow him access to its e-mail system when his goal is to cause harm? ◆

INTERNET SERVICE PROVIDERS AND WEB HOSTS: COMMUNICATIONS DECENCY ACT OF 1996

ISPs are companies, such as AOL, that provide connection to the Internet. Web hosts post Web pages on the Internet. Both play important roles in the Internet. As the legal structure that supports the Internet develops, so have legal issues involving these players.

The Internet is an enormously powerful tool for disseminating information. But what if some of this information happens to be false or in violation of our privacy rights? Is an ISP liable for transmitting it to the world? In 1995, a trial judge in New York held that an ISP, Prodigy Services Company, was potentially liable for defamatory statements that an unidentified person posted on one of its bulletin boards.[7] The message alleged that the president of an investment bank had committed "criminal and fraudulent acts." It was not only a false statement, it was posted on the most widely read financial computer bulletin board in the country. Although one can only feel sympathy for the target of this slur, the decision nonetheless alarmed many observers who argued that there was no way ISPs could review every piece of information that hurtles through their portals. The next year, Congress overruled the Prodigy case by passing the Communications Decency Act of 1996 (CDA).[8] **Under the CDA, ISPs and Web hosts are not liable for information that is provided by someone else. Only content providers are liable.** The following case lays out the arguments in favor of the CDA, but also illustrates some of the costs of the statute (and of the Internet).

CARAFANO V. METROSPLASH.COM, INC.

339 F.3d 1119, 2003 U.S. App. LEXIS 16548
United States Court of Appeals for the Ninth Circuit, 2003

Facts: Matchmaker.com is an Internet dating service that permits members to post profiles of themselves and to view the profiles of other members. Matchmaker reviews photos for impropriety before posting them but does not examine the profiles themselves.

Christianne Carafano pursues a career as an actor under the stage name Chase Masterson. She has appeared in numerous films and television shows, such as *Star Trek: Deep Space Nine* and *General Hospital*. Without her knowledge or consent, someone in Berlin posted a profile of her in the Los Angeles section of Matchmaker. In answer to the question "Main source of current events?," the person posting the profile put "*Playboy Playgirl*" and for "Why did you call?" responded "Looking for a one-night stand." In addition, the essays indicated that she was looking for a "hard and dominant" man with "a strong sexual appetite" and that she "liked sort of

being controlled by a man, in and out of bed." Pictures of the actor taken off the Internet were included with the profile. The profile also provided her home address and an e-mail address, which, when contacted, produced an automatic e-mail reply stating, "You think you are the right one? Proof it !!" [sic], and providing Carafano's home address and telephone number.

Unaware of the improper posting, Carafano began receiving sexually explicit messages on her home voice mail as well as a sexually explicit fax that threatened her and her son. She received numerous phone calls, letters, and e-mail from male fans, expressing concern that she had given out her address and phone number (but simultaneously indicating an interest in meeting her). Feeling unsafe, Carafano and her son stayed in hotels or away from Los Angeles for several months.   ▼

---

[7]   *Stratton Oakmont, Inc. v. Prodigy Services Company*, 1995 N.Y. Misc. LEXIS 229.
[8]   47 U.S.C. 230.

One Saturday a week or two after the profile was first posted, Carafano's assistant, Siouxzan Perry, learned of the false profile through a message from "Jeff." Acting on Carafano's instructions, Perry contacted Matchmaker, demanding that the profile be removed immediately. The Matchmaker employee did not remove it then because Perry herself had not posted it, but on Monday morning the company blocked the profile from public view and then deleted it the following day.

Carafano filed suit against Matchmaker alleging invasion of privacy, misappropriation of the right of publicity, defamation, and negligence. The district court rejected Matchmaker's argument for immunity under the CDA on the grounds that the company provided part of the profile content.

Issue: Does the CDA protect Matchmaker from liability?

Excerpts from Judge Thomas's Decision:
Through [the CDA], Congress granted most Internet services immunity from liability for publishing false or defamatory material so long as the information was provided by another party. As a result, Internet publishers are treated differently from corresponding publishers in print, television, and radio. Congress enacted this provision for two basic policy reasons: to promote the free exchange of information and ideas over the Internet and to encourage voluntary monitoring for offensive or obscene material.

Interactive computer services have millions of users. It would be impossible for service providers to screen each of their millions of postings for possible problems. Faced with potential liability for each message republished by their services, interactive computer service providers might choose to severely restrict the number and type of messages posted. Congress considered the weight of the speech interests implicated and chose to immunize service providers to avoid any such restrictive effect. Under [the CDA], therefore, so long as a third party willingly provides the essential published content, the interactive service provider receives full immunity regardless of the specific editing or selection process.

The fact that some of the content [in Carafano's fake profile] was formulated in response to Matchmaker's questionnaire does not [make Matchmaker liable]. Doubtless, the questionnaire facilitated the expression of information by individual users. However, the selection of the content was left exclusively to the user. Matchmaker cannot be considered an "information content provider" under the statute because no profile has any content until a user actively creates it.

Further, even assuming Matchmaker could be considered an information content provider, the statute would still bar Carafano's claims unless Matchmaker created or developed the particular information at issue. In this case, critical information about Carafano's home address and the e-mail address that revealed her phone number were transmitted unaltered to profile viewers. Thus Matchmaker did not play a significant role in creating, developing, or "transforming" the relevant information.

Thus, despite the serious and utterly deplorable consequences that occurred in this case, we conclude that Congress intended that service providers such as Matchmaker be afforded immunity from suit. ■

Public Policy

As we saw in the case of the college athletes whose nude pictures were sold online, a great deal of harm can be done very quickly over the Internet. But Congress made a policy decision to protect open and free expression on the Internet without regard to the harm caused. The Carafano case discussed the reasons behind this policy. Do you agree with Congress' approach? If you were a legislator, what approach would you advocate? ◆

CRIME ON THE INTERNET

Despite its great benefits, the Internet has also opened new frontiers in crime for the dishonest and unscrupulous. For examples of recent cybercrimes, investigate **http://computerworld.com/securitytopics/security/cybercrime/news**.

Hacking

Gaining unauthorized access to a computer system is called *hacking*. The Pentagon reports that hackers make more than 250,000 attempts annually on its computers. The goal of hackers is varied; some do it for little more than the thrill of the challenge. The objective for other hackers may be industrial espionage, extortion, or theft of credit card information. Whatever the motive, hacking is a major crime. A survey of U.S. corporations, government agencies, and colleges revealed that 70 percent had experienced computer security breaches within the year. No surprise then that American companies spend more than $6 billion annually on computer security systems. The Federal Bureau of Investigation ranks cybercrime as its third highest priority, right behind terrorism and spying.

Hacking is illegal under the federal Computer Fraud and Abuse Act of 1986 (CFAA).[9] This statute applies to any computer attached to the Internet. **The CFAA prohibits:**

- Computer espionage
- Theft of financial information
- Theft of information from the U.S. government
- Theft from a computer
- Computer trespass
- Computer fraud
- Intentional, reckless, and negligent damage to a computer
- Trafficking in computer passwords
- Computer extortion

Some states have also adopted statutes prohibiting computer crime. A list of these statutes is available at http://www.cybercrimes.net/State/state_index.html. For advice on how to report a computer crime, visit http://cybercrimes.net/Reporting/reporting.html.

There are two problems with the CFAA. First, while the statute prohibits the use of a virus to harm a computer, it does not ban the creation of viruses that someone else could use for hacking. Thus, it is legal for Web sites such as American Eagle Publications (http://www.ameaglepubs.com) to sell source code for viruses—codes that even beginners can use destructively.

Second, the CFAA applies only to U.S. criminals. Because the Internet is truly international, cybercriminals do not always fall within the jurisdiction of American laws. For example, a computer virus called ILOVEYOU caused an estimated $7 billion worth of damage worldwide. Although the perpetrator would have been subject to prosecution under the CFAA in the United States, he lived in the Philippines, which did not have laws prohibiting cybercrime. Nor could the suspect be extradited automatically to the United States because the extradition treaty only applied if both nations had the same law. The Philippines ultimately dropped all charges against the suspect.

Fraud

Fraud is a growth business on the Internet. The Internet's anonymity and speed facilitate fraud, and computers help criminals identify and contact victims. Common scams include the sale of merchandise that is either defective or nonexistent, the so-called

---

[9]   18 U.S.C. §1030.

Nigerian letter scam,[10] billing for services that are touted as "free," fraudulent stock offers, fake scholarship search services, business opportunity scams (for a small investment, you will get rich), and credit card scams (for a fee, you can get a credit card, even with a poor credit rating). To learn more about Internet fraud, steal over to http://fraud.org.

Fraud is the deception of another person for the purpose of obtaining money or property from him. It can be prosecuted under state law or the Computer Fraud and Abuse Act. In addition, federal mail and wire fraud statutes prohibit the use of mail or wire communication in furtherance of a fraudulent scheme.[11] The FTC can bring civil cases under §5 of the FTC act. (Chapter 8, on crime, discusses fraud, while Chapter 40, on consumer law, contains a detailed discussion of the FTC act.)

Auctions

Internet auctions are the number one source of consumer complaints about online fraud. Wrongdoers either sell goods they do not own, provide defective goods, or offer fakes. Fewer than 1 percent of online auctions involve fraud, but with upwards of $9 billion worth of goods being auctioned on the Internet each year, even 1 percent begins to add up.

Shilling is an increasingly popular online auction fraud. **Shilling means that a seller either bids on his own goods or agrees to cross-bid with a group of other sellers.** Shilling is prohibited because the owner drives up the price of his own item by bidding on it. Thus, for example, Kenneth Walton, a San Francisco lawyer, put up for auction on eBay an abstract painting purportedly by famous artist Richard Diebenkorn. A bidder offered $135,805 before eBay withdrew the item in response to charges that Walton had placed a bid on the painting himself and had also engaged in cross-bidding with a group of other eBay users. Although Walton claimed that he had placed the bids for friends, he ultimately pleaded guilty to charges of federal wire and mail fraud. He was sentenced to almost four years in prison and paid almost $100,000 in restitution to those who overpaid for the items he bid on.

To date, eBay has generally responded to shillers by suspending them for 30 days on the first offense and indefinitely on the second. Shillers are also subject to suit under general anti-fraud statutes. In addition, some states explicitly prohibit shilling.[12]

What is a fair price for this Diebenkorn painting?

© RICHARD DIEBENKORN, OCEAN PARK #54; 1972 OIL ON CANVAS; 100 IN. X 81 IN. (254CM X 205.74CM); SAN FRANCISCO MUSEUM OF MODERN ART, GIFT OF FRIENDS OF GERALD NORLAND, © ESTATE OF RICHARD DIEBENKORN

---

[10] Victims receive an e-mail from someone alleging to be a Nigerian government official who has stolen money from the government. He needs some place safe to park the money for a short time. The official promises that, if the victim will permit her account to be used for this purpose, she will be allowed to keep a percentage of the stolen money. Instead, of course, once the "official" has the victim's bank information, he cleans out the account. The highest average dollar losses are reported in this Internet scam—$5,575 per victim.

[11] U.S.C. §§1341–1346.

[12] For example, New Mexico law provides that "It shall be unlawful to employ shills or puffers at any such auction sale or to offer or to make or to procure to be offered or made any false bid or offer any false bid to buy or pretend to buy any article sold or offered for sale." N.M. Stat. §61-16-14.

The FTC has initiated Project Safebid, under which it educates law enforcement officials and then maintains a national database of Internet auction fraud complaints so that it can refer cases to the appropriate law enforcement agencies. To file a fraud complaint, click on **http://www.ifccfbi.gov**.

Identity Theft

Identity theft is one of the scariest crimes against property. Although it existed before computers, the Internet has made it much easier. For example, consumer activists were able to purchase the social security numbers of the director of the CIA, the Attorney General of the United States, and other top administration officials. The cost? $26 each. No surprise then that 10 million Americans are victims of this crime each year, at an estimated cost of $55 billion. The following article describes what it is like to be a victim of identity fraud.

NEWS*worthy*

I was working at Home Depot, where I'm a manager, when the Discover Card fraud unit called to find out why I'd requested an additional credit card. The Discover agent asked when I had moved to 1919 Madison Avenue, Norfolk, Va. My stomach turned inside out; I live on Long Island. I'd never even been to Virginia. The agent told me to notify the credit bureaus immediately.

A woman at one bureau told me someone had applied for eight cards in my name within the last month. My heart raced as I called each company to confirm my worst fear—they were all carrying large balances in my name. Even though I was able to cancel each card, I was freaking out. Two weeks later, I received more credit reports. He had opened 21 accounts overall. After two computers were delivered to his Norfolk address, I called the Norfolk police. They refused to arrest him. My wife had to stop me from going to sit in front of his house myself. In less than a month, this guy spent more than $40,000, a large chunk on stuff I'd never buy for myself, like Tommy Hilfiger and Nautica clothes and designer shoes.

I finally contacted the FBI, which discovered that the address he was using was fake and that the guy had a driver's license in my name. In the end, the FBI nabbed him in a stolen car. Turns out he conned 50 or 60 people out of more than $500,000. He plea-bargained and got six and a half years, but will probably get out earlier. This guy wrecked my credit history. What's worse is that he still knows my Social Security number. What would stop him from doing it again?[13] ◆

Although the owner of a credit card must generally pay only the first $50 that is stolen (as discussed in Chapter 40 on consumer law), the time and effort required to undo the damage can be substantial. And credit cards may be the least of it. Armed with data such as a Social Security number and mother's maiden name, thieves can obtain loans, acquire a passport and driver's license, or even commit (additional) crimes under their new identities. Meanwhile, the victim may find himself unable to obtain a credit card, loan, or job. One victim spent several nights in jail after he was arrested for a crime that his alter ego had committed.

---

[13] Adam Ray, as told to Liz Welch, "Taken to the Bank," *New York Times,* June 2, 2002, Sec. 6, p. 106. Copyright © 2002 by The New York Times Co. Reprinted by permission.

Responding to these concerns, Congress passed the Identity Theft and Assumption Deterrence Act of 1998.[14] **This statute prohibits the use of false identification to commit fraud or other crime and it also permits the victim to seek restitution in court.**

A number of states have also passed identity theft statutes. California, for example, prohibits the use of Social Security numbers on ID cards or on bank statements or other documents sent by mail. Also, consumers can place a security freeze on their credit reports. When a freeze is in place, thieves cannot obtain a credit card or loan in the consumer's name. California is the only state with a law requiring companies to notify consumers when their personal information has been stolen. Congress is considering similar legislation.

update

Has Congress passed legislation requiring companies to notify customers if their PII is stolen? ◆

at RISK

What can you do to prevent the theft of your identity?

1. Check your credit reports at least once a year. (Consumers are entitled by law to one free credit report every year from each of the three major reporting agencies. You can order these reports at https://www.annualcreditreport.com.)

2. Subscribe to a credit monitoring service that will notify you each week if there are any major changes to your credit reports.

3. If you suspect that your identity has been stolen, contact the FTC at 877-IDTHEFT, 877-438-4338, or http://www.consumer.gov/idtheft. Also, file a police report immediately and keep a copy to show creditors. Notify the three credit agencies.

For additional tips, visit http://www.ftc.gov/bcp/conline/pubs/credit/idtheft.htm. ◆

Phishing

Have you ever received an e-mail like this:

> We regret to inform you that your eBay account could be suspended if you don't re-update your account information. To resolve this problems [sic] please use the link below and re-enter your account information. If your problems could not be resolved your account will be suspended for a period of 24 hours, after this period your account will be terminated.

This e-mail is not from eBay, but rather from a fraudster hoping to lure the recipient into revealing her eBay account information, including credit card numbers and passwords. It is part of one of the most rapidly growing areas of Internet fraud: **phishing. In this crime, a fraudster sends an e-mail directing the recipient to enter personal information on a Web site that is an illegal imitation of a legitimate site.** Prosecutors can bring criminal charges against phishers for fraud. The targeted companies have sued these criminals for fraud, trademark infringement, false advertising and cybersquatting (discussed in Chapter 43, on intellectual property). No reputable company will ask customers to respond to an e-mail with personal information. When in doubt, close down the suspicious e-mail, re-launch your Web browser and then go to the company's main Web site. If the legitimate company needs information from you, it will so indicate on the site.

---

[14] 18 U.S. §1028.

Chapter Conclusion

The Internet has changed our lives in ways that were inconceivable a generation ago, and the law is rushing to catch up. Old laws will be applied in new ways, other laws will need to change completely and, as legislators and courts learn from experience, new laws will be enacted.

Inevitably, the law of cyberspace will become increasingly international. What does Europe accomplish by regulating Internet privacy if its citizens spend a good portion of their time on American Web sites? What will the FTC do if scam artists, or spammers, operate offshore? Leaders of e-commerce companies around the world have formed the Global Business Dialogue on Electronic Commerce to develop policies and advise governments on cyberspace issues. (To learn more about this organization, travel to http://www.gbd.org.) Effective regulation of cyberspace will require cooperation among nations and between government and industry.

Chapter Review

1. Section 5 of the FTC Act prohibits unfair and deceptive practices.

2. The Electronic Communications Privacy Act of 1986 is a federal statute that prohibits unauthorized interception or disclosure of wire and electronic communications or unauthorized access to stored communications.

3. The Children's Online Privacy Protection Act of 1998 prohibits Internet operators from collecting information from children under 13 without parental permission. It also requires sites to disclose how they will use any information they acquire.

4. The Gramm-Leach-Bliley Privacy Act of 1999 requires banks and other financial institutions to disclose to consumers any non-public information they wish to reveal to third parties.

5. The U.S. Department of Commerce and the European Union have established safe harbor principles for the collection of personal data. Any company that complies with the safe harbor rules will be permitted to receive data from European companies.

6. Spyware is a computer program that slips onto your computer without your permission—through e-mails, Internet downloads, or software installations. Congress has considered legislation to control spyware, but has not taken final action. California has enacted the Consumer Protection Against Computer Spyware Act, which makes spyware illegal.

7. The Fourth Amendment to the Constitution prohibits unreasonable searches and seizures by government agents. This provision applies to computers.

8. Controlling the Assault of Non-Solicited Pornography and Marketing Act (Can-Spam) is a federal statute regulating spam. This statute applies to virtually all promotional e-mails, whether or not the sender has a pre-existing relationship with the recipient. E-mails covered by Can-Spam must:

    • Provide an opt-out system that permits the recipient to unsubscribe

    • Clearly indicate that the e-mail is an advertisement

    • Provide a valid physical return address (not a post office box)

    • Clearly indicate the nature of pornographic messages

9. Under the Communications Decency Act of 1996, ISPs and Web hosts are not liable for information that is provided by someone else.

10. Hacking is illegal under the federal Computer Fraud and Abuse Act of 1986. The CFAA prohibits:

    • Computer espionage

    • Theft of financial information

    • Theft of information from the U.S. government

    • Theft from a computer

    • Computer trespass

    • Computer fraud

- Intentional, reckless, and negligent damage to a computer
- Trafficking in computer passwords
- Computer extortion

11. Fraud is the deception of another person for the purpose of obtaining money or property from him.

12. The Identity Theft and Assumption Deterrence Act of 1998 prohibits the use of false identification to commit fraud or other crime.

Practice Test

1. Three travel agents used fictitious accounts to steal 61 million frequent flyer miles from American Airlines. They traded this mileage in for 546 free tickets, with a value of $1.3 million. As evidence in the criminal trial, prosecutors used electronic communications from the agents on SABRE, American's computerized travel reservations system. The agents alleged that this search was illegal under the Fourth Amendment to the Constitution. Do you agree?

2. **ETHICS** Matt Drudge published a report on his Web site (http://www.drudgereport.com) that White House aide Sidney Blumenthal "has a spousal abuse past that has been effectively covered up.... There are court records of Blumenthal's violence against his wife." The Drudge Report is an electronic publication focusing on Hollywood and Washington gossip. AOL paid Drudge $3,000 a month to make the Drudge Report available to AOL subscribers. Drudge e-mailed his reports to AOL, which then posted them. Before posting, however, AOL had the right to edit content. Drudge ultimately retracted his allegations against Blumenthal, who sued AOL. He alleged that under the Communications Decency Act of 1996, AOL was a "content provider" because it paid Drudge and edited what he wrote. Do you agree? Putting liability aside, what moral obligation did AOL have to its members? To Blumenthal? Should AOL be liable for content it bought and provided to its members?

3. To demonstrate the inadequacies of existing computer security systems, Cornell student Robert Morris created a computer virus. His plan, however, went awry, as plans sometimes do. He thought his virus would be relatively harmless but it ran amok, crashing scores of computers at universities, military sites, and medical research sites. Under what statute might Morris be charged? Has he committed a crime, or is he liable only for civil penalties? Does it matter that he did not intend to cause damage?

4. **YOU BE THE JUDGE** WRITING PROBLEM Jerome Schneider wrote several books on how to avoid taxes. These books were sold on Amazon.com. Amazon permits visitors to post comments about items for sale. Amazon's policy suggests that these comments should be civil (e.g., no profanity or spiteful remarks). The comments about Schneider's books were not so kind. One person alleged Schneider was a felon. When Schneider complained, an Amazon representative agreed that some of the postings violated its guidelines and promised that they would be removed within one to two business days. Two days later, the posting had not been removed. Schneider filed suit. **Argument for Schneider:** Amazon has editorial discretion over the posted comments: It both establishes guidelines and then monitors the comments to ensure that they comply with the guidelines. These activities make Amazon an information content provider, not protected by the Communications Decency Act. **Argument for Amazon:** The right to edit material is not the same thing as creating the material in the first place.

5. During the course of 10 months, Joseph Melle sent more than 60 million unsolicited e-mail advertisements to AOL members. What charges could be brought against him?

6. Anthony Davis operated a computer bulletin board system that permitted users to send and receive e-mail, access the Internet, and download software. Davis's system had one attribute that distinguished it from, say, AOL. It specialized in pornography. Alerted by an anonymous tip, the Oklahoma City Police Department obtained a warrant to search his premises for "equipment, order materials, papers, membership lists and other paraphernalia pertaining to the distribution or display of pornographic material." During their raid, the officers seized computer equipment that contained 150,000 e-mails in electronic storage, some of which had not been

retrieved by the recipients. Alleging that the e-mails had not been included in the warrant, Davis filed suit against the police officers for violations of the Electronic Communications Privacy Act. Does Davis have a valid claim?

7. Ton Cremers was the director of security at Amsterdam's famous Rijksmuseum and the operator of the Museum Security Network ("the Network") Web site. Robert Smith, a handyman working for Ellen Batzel in North Carolina, sent an e-mail to the Network alleging that Batzel was the granddaughter of Heinrich Himmler (one of Hitler's henchman) and that she had art that Himmler had stolen. These allegations were completely untrue. Cremers posted Smith's e-mail on the Network's Web site and sent it to the Network's subscribers. Cremers exercised some editorial discretion in choosing which e-mails to send to subscribers, generally omitting any that were unrelated to stolen art. Is Cremers liable to Batzel for the harm that this inaccurate information caused?

8. What can you do to protect your privacy online? Draw up a concrete list of steps that you might reasonably consider. Are there some actions that you would not be willing to take, either because they are not worth the effort or because they are too sneaky?

9. Craig Hare offered computers and related equipment for sale on various Internet auction Web sites. He accepted payment but not responsibility—he never shipped the goods. Both the FTC and the U.S. attorney general in Florida (that is, the prosecutor for the federal government) brought charges against him. What charges did they bring? Why would these two separate agencies of the federal government both bring suit?

10. **ROLE REVERSAL** Write a short-answer question that deals with an issue involving crime in cyberspace.

Internet Research Problem

1. The FTC offers advice to Web site operators about how to comply with the Children's Online Privacy Protection Act at **http://beatty.westbuslaw .com**. Find a Web site that does comply and one that does not.

2. The FTC provides an online brochure titled Site Seeing on the Internet (at **http://beatty.westbuslaw .com**) that offers suggestions for safe travel on the Internet. Have you ever violated the FTC's advice on how to protect yourself in cyberspace?

You can find further practice problems at http://beatty.westbuslaw.com or in the Study Guide that accompanies this text.

Intellectual Property

J ason, a senior at the University of Maryland, ran one of the most popular Web sites on campus out of his shoebox dorm room here. The site let his 8,500 fellow dorm residents search for music files, among other things, stored on one another's computers and copy them in seconds.

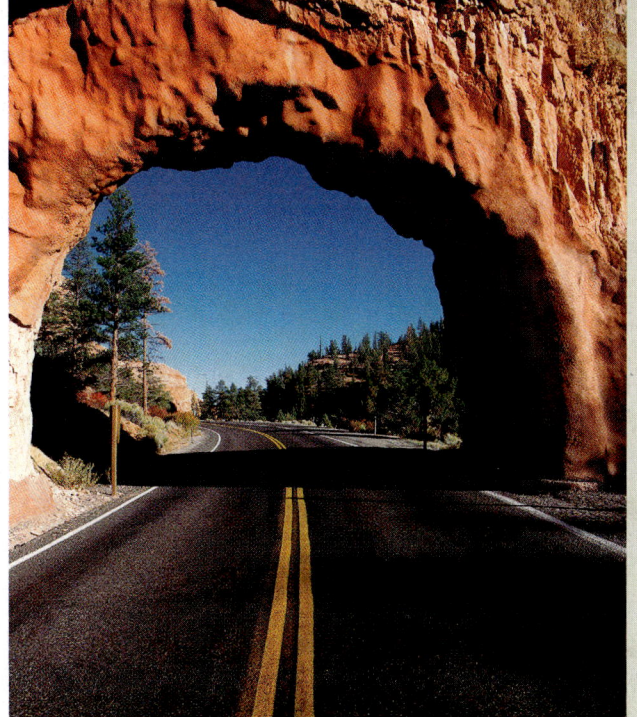

Then came the news that the record industry had filed lawsuits against four students running similar sites at other universities, accusing them of enabling large-scale copyright infringement and asking for billions of dollars in damages. Within an hour, Jason, who insisted on anonymity for fear of being sued himself, had dismantled his site. "I don't think I was doing anything wrong," said Jason, a computer science major. "But who wants to face a $98 billion debt for the rest of their lives? I was scared."

These lawsuits are the most aggressive legal action the record industry has ever directed against college students, who in recent years have exercised an enduring predisposition to consume large quantities of music by copying it over the Internet without ever paying for it. College campuses, the record industry says, have become far and away the prime locus for online piracy.

Wary of alienating young customers who continue to generate a large chunk of their revenue, record companies until recently focused on prodding university administrators to discipline their students. But freshman orientation sessions on respect for intellectual property have had little effect. With CD sales in a tailspin that record executives attribute at least partly to the downloading frenzy in academia's hallowed halls, they said they needed to try another approach.

"We have decided to bring to the attention of universities just how much music piracy is going on college campuses and universities," said Cary Sherman, president of the Recording Industry Association of America, which brought the suits, "and we think that message has been received."

"It's been very difficult because students have grown up viewing the Internet as a place where you go to get lots of free access to things," said Graham Spanier, president of Pennsylvania State University. "As we have tried to educate our students, half of them understand it's like going into a store and putting a CD in your pocket and the other half just can't see it that way."[1] ■

INTRODUCTION

For much of history, land was the most valuable form of property. It was the primary source of wealth and social status. Today, intellectual property is a major source of wealth. New ideas—for manufacturing processes, computer programs, medicines, books—bring both affluence and influence.

**ECONOMICS
& the LAW**

Land and intellectual property, though both valuable assets, are fundamentally different. The value of land lies in the owner's right to exclude, to prevent others from entering or using it. Intellectual property, however, has little economic value unless it is used by many.

The crux of the economic problem is this: Intellectual property is typically expensive to *produce* but cheap to *reproduce and transmit*. Movies or computer software, for example, cost millions to make but can be copied or reproduced for virtually nothing. (How much does it cost to download software?) But if too much intellectual property is transmitted too freely, then those who create ideas will not be paid the full value of their efforts. Those who simply transmit ideas will tend to be overpaid. The resulting imbalance creates too many transmitters and not enough producers. So the next time you are tempted to copy a friend's CD or download music free from the Internet, remember that lost royalty payments to musicians may ultimately mean less music for you.

Because producers of intellectual property are likely to be underpaid in the free market, the government provides three remedies: It *protects* the property rights of producers (with patents and copyrights), *produces* information itself (such as weather reports), and *subsidizes* production by others (via government research grants).

---

[1]   Amy Harmon, "Recording Industry Goes After Students Over Music Sharing," *New York Times*, Apr. 23, 2003, Sec. A, p. 1.

> Some commentators suggest that the United States has been a technological leader partly because its laws have provided strong protection for intellectual property since early in the country's history. Indeed, the Constitution provides for patent protection. In contrast, one of the oldest civilizations in the world, China, has been much slower in developing new technology. It did not institute a patent system until 1985 and its protection of patents is weak. ◆

The conflict between those who have intellectual property and those who want to use it has taken on a global dimension. Developing countries argue that American intellectual property laws increase the price of medicines, such as AIDS drugs and vaccines, that could save lives if only they were cheaper and, therefore, more readily available. "Patents kill" is their slogan. The United States responds that, without patent protection, there would be no innovation, no miracle drugs. In India, for example, biotech entrepreneurs hesitate to sell their new products at home where intellectual property laws offer little protection. Their inventions go overseas.

But even U.S. drug companies admit that patents can sometimes stifle innovation. The pharmaceutical company Bristol-Meyers Squibb says that it cannot conduct research on many cancer-fighting drugs because of patents held by its competitors. Information technology firms make a similar complaint. In a study of the American semiconductor business, researchers found that more patents did not necessarily mean there was more innovation. Instead, some companies were simply more aggressive about patenting every possible aspect of their research. Nor was there any evidence that innovation increased as patent rights were enhanced. And, in a study of developing companies, researchers could find no evidence that patent protection promoted innovation.

The role of intellectual property law is to balance the rights of those who create intellectual property and those who would enjoy it. And as this chapter reveals, such a balancing act is no easy feat.

What about the four students in the opening scenario? They agreed to pay between $12,000 and $17,000 to settle the suits. The record industry expanded its legal action beyond students and ultimately sued thousands of people across the country who had illegally downloaded music from the Internet.

PATENTS

A patent is a grant by the government permitting the inventor exclusive use of an invention for 20 years (or 14 years in the case of design patents). During this period, no one may make, use, or sell the invention without permission. In return, the inventor publicly discloses information about the invention that anyone can use upon expiration of the patent.

Types of Patents

There are three types of patents: utility patents, design patents, and plant patents.

Utility Patent

Whenever people use the word "patent" by itself, they are referring to a utility patent. This type of patent is available to those who invent (or significantly improve) any of the following:

Type of Invention	Example
Mechanical invention	A hydraulic jack used to lift heavy aircraft
Electrical invention	A prewired, portable wall panel for use in large, open-plan offices
Chemical invention	The chemical 2-chloroethylphosphonic acid used as a plant growth regulator
Process	A method for applying a chemical compound to an established plant such as rice in order to inhibit the growth of weeds selectively; the application can be patented separately from the actual chemical
Machine	A device that enables a helicopter pilot to control all flight functions (pitch, roll, and heave) with one hand
Composition of matter	A sludge used as an explosive at construction sites; the patent specifies the water content, the density, and the types of solids contained in the mixture

A patent is not available solely for an idea, but only for its tangible application. Thus patents are not available for laws of nature, scientific principles, mathematical algorithms, or formulas such as $a^2 + b^2 = c^2$. In recent years, the status of computer software has been controversial: Is it an (unpatentable) mathematical formula or a (patentable) process or machine? The following case answers this question.

STATE STREET BANK & TRUST CO. V. SIGNATURE FINANCIAL GROUP, INC.

149 F.3d 1368, 1998 U.S. App. LEXIS 16869
United States Court of Appeals for the Federal Circuit,[2] 1998

Facts: Signature Financial Group, Inc., owns a patent on a computer software program that aids in the administration of mutual funds. The so-called Hub and Spoke System allows several mutual funds, or "Spokes," to pool their investment funds into a single portfolio, or "Hub." In this way, the funds can share administrative costs. Each Spoke sells shares to the public, and the cost of these shares depends upon the value of the assets pooled in the Hub. Therefore, each day within hours of the close of the stock market, each fund's administrator must know the value to the nearest penny of its pooled shares. The Signature software makes this calculation.

State Street Bank and Trust Co. negotiated with Signature for a license to use its software. When negotiations broke down, State Street brought suit alleging that the patent was invalid. The trial court granted State Street's motion for summary judgment.

Issue: Is data processing software patentable?

Excerpts from Judge Rich's Decision: [The Supreme] Court has held that mathematical algorithms are not patentable subject matter to the extent that they are merely abstract ideas. From a practical standpoint, this means that to be patentable an algorithm must be applied in a "useful" way.

Today, we hold that the transformation of data, representing discrete dollar amounts, by a machine through a series of mathematical calculations into a final share price, constitutes a practical application of a mathematical algorithm, formula, or calculation, because it produces "a useful, concrete and tangible result"—a final share price momentarily fixed for recording and reporting purposes.

The question of whether a claim encompasses statutory subject matter should focus on the essential characteristics of the subject matter, in particular, its practical utility. For purpose of our analysis, [this] claim is directed to a machine programmed with the Hub and Spoke software and admittedly produces a "useful, concrete, and tangible result." This renders it statutory subject matter, even if the useful result is expressed in numbers, such as price, profit, percentage, cost, or loss.

Reversed and remanded. ∎

---

2   Recall from Chapter 3 that the Court of Appeals for the Federal Circuit is the thirteenth United States Court of Appeals. It hears appeals from specialized trial courts.

Public Policy

The State Street case could have a profound impact on e-commerce as companies rush to patent techniques for doing business over the Internet. For example, Amazon.com received a patent for its One-Click method of instant ordering. The company then obtained an injunction to prevent barnesandnoble.com from using its Express Lane service that was similar to One-Click. The judge directed barnesandnoble.com to add an additional step to its ordering process.

Proponents of these patents argue that they permit innovators on the Internet to protect their ideas. Otherwise, it is easy for copycats to open a rival Web site overnight. Critics counter that these patents could stifle e-commerce by limiting the use of new ideas. Companies have been forced to increase their patent applications simply to remain competitive—they fear that if they do not patent an idea, their rivals will. Apple developed a scroll wheel for the iPod, but Microsoft patented the idea first. The result is a dramatic increase in the number of patent applications. The Patent and Trademark Office (PTO) now receives about 350,000 applications a year and has a backlog of half a million. The process for accepting a patent is much simpler than for rejecting it, which gives patent examiners an incentive to accept even dubious applications. As many as 30 percent of patents make duplicate claims—an indication that too many are being accepted. ◆

Design Patent

© DAVID YOUNG-WOLFF/PHOTOEDIT, INC.

Braun patented the design, not the function, of this blender.

A design patent protects the appearance, not the function, of an item. It is granted to anyone who invents a new, original, and ornamental design for an article. For example, Braun, Inc., patented the look of its handheld electric blenders. Design patents last only 14 years, not 20.

Plant Patent

Anyone who creates a new type of plant can patent it, *provided that* the inventor is able to reproduce it asexually—through grafting, for instance, not by planting its seeds. For example, one company patented its unique heather plant.

Requirements for a Patent

To obtain a patent, the inventor must show that her invention meets all of the following tests:

- **Novel.** An invention is not patentable if it (1) is known or has already been used in this country, or (2) has been described in a publication here or overseas. For example, an inventor discovered a new use for existing chemical compounds but was not permitted to patent it because the compounds had already been described in prior publications, though the new uses had not.[3]

- **Nonobvious.** An invention is not patentable if it is obvious to a person with ordinary skill in that particular area. An inventor was not allowed to patent a waterflush system designed to remove cow manure from the floor of a barn because it was obvious.[4]

- **Useful.** To be patented, an invention must be useful. It need not necessarily be commercially valuable, but it must have some current use. Being merely of scientific

---

[3] *In re Schoenwald*, 964 F.2d 1122, 1992 U.S. App. LEXIS 10181 (Fed. Cir. 1992).
[4] *Sakraida v. Ag Pro, Inc.*, 425 U.S. 273, 96 S. Ct. 1532, 1976 U.S. LEXIS 146 (1976).

interest is not enough. Thus a company was denied a patent for a novel process for making steroids because they had no therapeutic value.[5]

A searchable database of all patents issued since 1976 is available at the Patent and Trademark Office's Web site: **http://www.uspto.gov/patft/index.html**. To find out just how creative inventors can be, check out the Wacky Patent of the Month at **http://www.colitz.com/site/wacky.htm**.

Patent Application and Issuance

To obtain a patent, the inventor must file a complex application with the PTO Office in Washington, D.C. If a patent examiner determines that the application meets all legal requirements, the PTO will issue the patent. If the examiner denies the patent application, the inventor can appeal that decision to the PTO Board of Appeals and from there to the Court of Appeals for the Federal Circuit in Washington. Alternatively, upon denial of the application, the inventor can file suit against the PTO in the federal district court in Washington.

Priority between Two Inventors

When two people invent the same product, who is entitled to a patent—the first to invent or the first to file an application? Generally, the person who invents and *puts the invention into practice* has priority over the first filer. Having the idea is not enough— the inventor must actually use the product.

Prior Sale

However, an inventor must apply for a patent within one year of selling the product commercially. The purpose of this rule is to encourage prompt disclosure of inventions. It prevents someone from inventing a product, selling it for years, and then obtaining a 20-year monopoly with a patent.

Provisional Patent Application

Investors who are unable to assess the market value of their ideas sometimes hesitate to file a patent application because the process is expensive and cumbersome. To solve this problem, the PTO now permits inventors to file a **provisional patent application (PPA).** The PPA is a simpler, shorter, cheaper application that gives inventors the opportunity to show their ideas to potential investors without incurring the full expense of a patent application. PPA protection lasts only one year. To maintain protection after that time, the inventor must file a regular patent application.

Duration of a Patent

Patents are valid for 20 years from the date of *filing* the application (except design patents, which are valid for 14 years from date of *issuance*). Currently, approval of a patent takes about 27 months from the date of filing, which means that patent holders effectively receive a little less than 18 years of protection (although in the case of exceptional delays, it is possible to request an extension).

Eighteen months after patents are filed, the PTO publishes them. This means that patent applications are often published before they have been approved. Although there is some concern that patent ideas are therefore easier to steal, publication also

---

[5]   *Brenner v. Manson*, 383 U.S. 519, 86 S. Ct. 1033, 1966 U.S. LEXIS 2907 (1966).

gives anyone with knowledge in the field an opportunity to provide the PTO with additional information about why the patent should or (more likely) should not be granted.

How long should patents last? Holders enjoy a monopoly that protects them from competition and permits them to charge higher prices. But these monopoly profits are not all bad—they also provide inventors with the incentive to spend large sums hoping to develop new products. In theory, the duration of a patent should be individually tailored to each product. The goal is to ensure that a patent creates the right incentive for each product. Take, for example, a complex, life-saving drug that costs $400 million to develop. No drug company would undertake such a project without assurance that it could recoup its costs. But if the company can make $300 million in the first year of sale, it needs only a short patent life to recoup its costs. On the other hand, if the company could only make $25 million a year, it should have at least a 16-year patent. Likewise, if a product has little value to society, its patent should be of short duration.

Of course, the PTO would be in chaos if examiners had to decide how much protection each individual patent deserved, but Germany has gone some distance along this path. It awards a standard patent for important inventions. Less important products receive a so-called *petty patent* that lasts only three years. Moreover, all patent owners pay an annual maintenance fee. At the beginning, this fee is low, but it increases so much each year that only 5 percent of German patents are maintained for a full term. Most owners abandon ship in less than eight years.[6] ◆

WIPO headquarters in Geneva

Infringement

A patent holder has the exclusive right to use the invention during the term of the patent. A holder can prohibit others from using any product that is substantially the same, license the product to others for a fee, and recover damages from anyone who uses the product without permission.

International Patent Treaties

Suppose you have a great idea that you want to protect around the world. It used to be that filing an application in other countries was a logistical nightmare because almost every country had its own unique filing procedures and standards. Several treaties now facilitate this process, although it is still not the one-stop (or one-click) effort that inventors desire. These treaties were drafted by the World Intellectual Property Organization (WIPO) of the United Nations and are available on its Web site at http://www.wipo.int.

The Paris Convention for the Protection of Industrial Property (Paris Convention) requires each member country to grant to citizens of other member countries the same rights under patent law as its own citizens enjoy. Thus, the patent office in each member country must accept and recognize all patent and trademark applications filed with it by anyone who lives in any member country. For

6 R. Cooter and T. Ulen, *Law and Economics,* 2nd ed. (Reading, Mass.: Addison-Wesley, 1997).

example, the French patent office cannot refuse to accept an application from an American, as long as the American has complied with French law.

The Patent Law Treaty requires that countries use the same standards for the form and content of patent applications (whether submitted on paper or electronically). This treaty reduces the procedural conflicts over issues such as translations and fees. In short, it takes an important first step in standardizing the application *process*. Still to be worked out, however, is an international standard for the *substance* of patent laws. For instance, the U.S. "first to invent" rule conflicts with the "first to file" rule used in most other countries. Also countries often have very different definitions of what constitutes "novelty" under patent law.

In addition to these treaties, any country that joins the World Trade Organization must agree to TRIPS (trade-related aspects of intellectual property rights). This agreement does not create an international patent system but it does require all participants to meet minimum standards for the protection of intellectual property. How individual countries achieve that goal is left to them.

COPYRIGHTS

The holder of a copyright owns the *particular tangible expression* of an idea, but not the underlying idea or method of operation. Abner Doubleday could copyright a book setting out his particular version of the rules of baseball, but he could not copyright the rules themselves nor could he require players to pay him a royalty. Similarly, the inventor of double-entry bookkeeping could copyright a pamphlet explaining his system but not the system itself.

Unlike patents, the ideas underlying copyrighted material need not be novel. Two movies that came out at the same time—*The Incredibles* and *Sky High*—were each about a family of superheroes. Neither violated the other's copyright because their *expressions* of the basic idea were different—indeed, one was a cartoon and the other a live action film.

The Copyright Act protects literature, music, drama, choreography, pictures, sculpture, movies, recordings, architectural works, and "computer data bases, and computer programs to the extent that they incorporate authorship in the programmer's expression of original ideas, as distinguished from the ideas themselves."

A copyright is valid until 70 years after the death of the work's only or last living author. In the case of works owned by a corporation—Mickey Mouse, for instance—the copyright lasts 95 years from publication or 120 years from creation. Once the copyright expires, anyone may use the material. Mark Twain died in 1910, so anyone may now publish *Tom Sawyer* without permission and without paying a copyright fee.

A work is automatically copyrighted once it is in tangible form. For example, once a songwriter puts notes on paper, the work is copyrighted without further ado. But if she whistles a happy tune without writing it down, the song is not copyrighted, and anyone else can use it without permission. Registration with the Copyright Office of the Library of Congress is necessary only if the holder wishes to bring suit to enforce the copyright. Although authors still routinely place the copyright symbol (©) on their works, such a precaution is not necessary in the United States. However, some lawyers still recommend using the copyright symbol because other countries recognize it. Also, the penalties for intentional copyright infringement are heavier than for unintentional violations, and the presence of a copyright notice is evidence that the infringer's actions were intentional.

Infringement

Anyone who uses copyrighted material without permission is violating the Copyright Act. **To prove a violation, the plaintiff must present evidence that the work was original** and that either:

- The infringer actually copied the work, or
- The infringer had access to the original and the two works are substantially similar.

A court may (1) prohibit the infringer from committing further violations, (2) order destruction of the infringing material, and (3) require the infringer to pay damages, profits earned, and attorney's fees.

Fair Use

The purpose of copyright laws is to encourage creative work. A writer who can control, and profit from, artistic work will be inclined to produce more. If enforced oppressively, however, the copyright laws could stifle creativity by denying access to copyrighted work. **The doctrine of *fair use* permits limited use of copyrighted material without permission of the author for purposes such as criticism, comment, news reporting, scholarship, or research.** Courts generally do not permit a use that will decrease revenues from the original work by, say, competing with it. A reviewer is permitted, for example, to quote from a book without the author's permission, but, as we see below, online music companies cannot download entire versions of copyrighted songs.

Also under the fair use doctrine, faculty members are permitted to photocopy and distribute copyrighted materials to students, as long as the materials are brief and the teacher's action is spontaneous. If, over his breakfast coffee one morning, Professor Learned spots a terrific article in *Mad Magazine* that perfectly illustrates a point he intends to make in class that day, the fair use doctrine permits him to photocopy the page and distribute it to his class. However, under a misinterpretation of the fair use doctrine, some faculty had been in the habit of routinely preparing lengthy course packets of copyrighted material without permission of the authors. In *Basic Books, Inc. v. Kinko's Graphic Corp.*[7] a federal court held that this practice violated the copyright laws because the material was more than one short passage and because it was sold to students. Now, when professors put together course packets, they (or the copy shop) must obtain permission and pay a royalty for the use of copyrighted material. Likewise, it is illegal for students to make photocopies of a classmate's course packet or textbook.

Parody

Parody has a long history in the United States—some of our most cherished songs have been the basis of parodies. Before Francis Scott Key wrote the words to the Star-Spangled Banner, other lyrics that mocked colonial governors had been set to the same music. (The tune was well known as a drinking song.) During the Civil War, this parody of "Battle Hymn of the Republic" expressed anti-war sentiment:

Tell Abe Lincoln of Antietam's bloody dell
Tell Abe Lincoln where a thousand heroes fell
Tell Abe Lincoln and his gang to go to hell
And we'll go marching home.

---

[7] 758 F. Supp. 1522, 1991 U.S. Dist. LEXIS 3804 (S.D.N.Y. 1991). A federal appeals court reached the same result in *Princeton University Press v. Michigan Document Services, Inc.*, 99 F.3d 1381, 1996 U.S. App. LEXIS 29132 (6th Cir. 1996).

The Capitol Steps, a singing group in Washington, wrote this version of Lee Greenwood's song "God Bless the USA," renamed "God Bless My SUV":

But my Daddy wasn't fighting on Normandy that day
For the right to drive a Hyundai, I refuse to live that way.
And I'm proud to be an American, who gets just 5 mpg
Though I live alone the car I own can seat one hundred three.

(For more parodies by the Capitol Steps, dance over to their Web site at **http:// www.capsteps.com.**) Have the Capitol Steps violated Greenwood's copyright? After all, they did use his music. What if the words or opinions expressed in a parody are ones with which the original creators (or whoever now owns the rights) do not agree? The Capitol Steps appear to be on safe ground. The United States has a long history of protecting the expression of unpopular ideas.

The Supreme Court faced this issue in a case involving the rap group 2 Live Crew. The group wanted to record a parody of the song "Oh, Pretty Woman," but the copyright holder refused permission. Undaunted, 2 Live Crew went ahead anyway, and the group was sued, all the way to the Supreme Court. The following lyrics are excerpted from the Court's decision in this case:

Original:	Parody:
Pretty Woman, walking down the street,	Big hairy woman you need to shave that stuff
Pretty Woman, the kind I like to meet,	Big hairy woman you know I bet it's tough
Pretty Woman, I don't believe you, you're not the truth,	Big hairy woman all that hair it ain't legit
No one could look as good as you Mercy	'Cause you look like "Cousin It" Big hairy woman

The Court decided in favor of 2 Live Crew, holding that **parody is a fair use of copyrighted material as long as the use of the original is not excessive.** The parody may copy enough to remind the audience of the original work but not so much that the parody harms the market for the original. The Supreme Court remanded the case to the trial court to determine if the 2 Live Crew version had copied too much or harmed the market for a nonparody rap version of "Oh, Pretty Woman."[8] The two sides ultimately settled with 2 Live Crew agreeing to pay royalties.

Linking

A *link* is a connection between two files on the Web or between two parts of the same file. The ability to link is fundamental to the World Wide Web but used improperly, linking violates copyright law.

Leslie Kelly was a photographer specializing in images of the American West. He posted some of his pictures on his Web site. Arriba Soft Corp. operated an Internet search engine (at **http://www.ditto.com**) that searches for graphic images. It displays its results in the form of small pictures called *thumbnails*. By double-clicking on one of these thumbnails, a large version of that same picture is automatically copied from the

---

8 *Campbell v. Acuff-Rose Music, Inc.,* 510 U.S. 569, 114 S. Ct. 1164, 1994 U.S. LEXIS 2052 (1994).

originating Web page onto Arriba's site, complete with Arriba advertising. The user might think that the image was, in fact, on Arriba's Web site. Kelly alleged that Arriba was violating his copyright. Arriba claimed that its activities were protected by the fair use doctrine. The court ruled that, while the thumbnails were a fair use, the display of the larger image was a copyright violation. The thumbnails did not compete with Kelly's use of the works, but the full-size display did.[9]

The impact of this case is uncertain. Critics argue that it threatens the use of linking, not just for pictures, but for text as well. If search engines are required to obtain the permission of every copyright holder before setting up a link, they will soon be out of business. Other commentators argue, however, that neither Arriba nor anyone else needs permission to create a link to Kelly's site, they are simply forbidden from competing with Kelly by offering his images in the same size and quality.

Digital Music and Movies

Copyright protection is as old as the country itself, having been included in the Constitution. But intellectual property has changed dramatically in the last 250 years, and legal protections suitable for the eighteenth century do not work as well today. Now Congress and the courts are playing catch-up, trying to mend and patch the laws to cover the digital world.

One of the major challenges for legal institutions in regulating copyrights is simply that modern intellectual property is so easy to copy. Many consumers have been in the habit of violating the law by downloading copyrighted material—both music and movies—for free. The entertainment world used to turn a blind eye, but recording companies and movie studios have come to believe that illegal downloading is hurting profitability. For the first time, CD sales actually declined nationally. One study found that the decline was particularly sharp in areas around college campuses. Perhaps even more insidious, a whole generation has grown up believing that music and even movies were, and should be, free. While an older sibling might have purchased a thousand CDs during her teens and twenties, her younger brother would buy none at all. Although at least one study seemed to indicate that downloading does not harm CD sales, the entertainment industry remained convinced that it does.[10] As the chapter opener illustrates, the Recording Industry Association of America (RIAA) has begun aggressively suing those who downloaded illegally. Then a coalition of entertainment businesses sued two companies that distributed the software used by many consumers to violate copyright law. So important was this issue that the Supreme Court waded into these murky waters.

METRO-GOLDWYN-MAYER STUDIOS INC. V. GROKSTER, LTD.

125 S. Ct. 2764, 2005 U.S. LEXIS 5212
Supreme Court of the United States, 2005

Facts: Grokster, Ltd., and StreamCast Networks, Inc., distributed free software that allowed computer users to share electronic files through peer-to-peer networks, so called because users' computers

▼

---

[9] *Kelly v. Arriba Soft Corporation*, 280 F.3d 934, 2002 U.S. App. LEXIS 1786, United States Court of Appeals (9th Cir. 2002).

[10] Felix Oberholzer-Gee and Koleman Strumpf, "The Effect of File Sharing on Record Sales." 2004, available at http://www.unc.edu/~cigar/papers/FileSharing_March2004.pdf.

communicated directly with each other, not through central servers. The Grokster and StreamCast software could be used for legal purposes. Indeed, peer-to-peer networks were utilized by universities, government agencies, corporations, libraries, and individuals, among others. Even the briefs in this very case could be downloaded legally with the StreamCast software.

Nonetheless, nearly 90 percent of the files available for download through Grokster or StreamCast were copyrighted. Billions of files were shared each month—the probable scope of copyright infringement was staggering. The two companies encouraged the illegal uses of their software. For example, the chief technology officer of StreamCast said that "the goal is to get in trouble with the law and get sued. It's the best way to get in the news."

A group of copyright holders (MGM and others) sued Grokster and StreamCast alleging that they were violating the copyright law by knowingly and intentionally distributing their software to users who would reproduce and distribute copyrighted works illegally. Both parties moved for summary judgment. The trial court held for Grokster and StreamCast; the appeals court affirmed. The Supreme Court granted *certiorari*.

Issue: Were Grokster and StreamCast violating copyright law?

Excerpts from Justice Souter's Decision: The more artistic protection is favored, the more technological innovation may be discouraged; the administration of copyright law is an exercise in managing the trade-off. [T]he indications are that the ease of copying songs or movies using software like Grokster's is fostering disdain for copyright protection. When a widely shared service or product is used to commit infringement, it may be impossible to enforce rights in the protected work effectively against all direct infringers, the only practical alternative being to go against the distributor of the copying device. We hold that one who distributes a

device with the object of promoting its use to infringe copyright, as shown by clear expression or other affirmative steps taken to foster infringement, is liable for the resulting acts of infringement by third parties.

We are, of course, mindful of the need to keep from trenching on regular commerce or discouraging the development of technologies with lawful and unlawful potential. Accordingly, mere knowledge of infringing potential or of actual infringing uses would not be enough here to subject a distributor to liability. The inducement rule, instead, premises liability on purposeful, culpable expression and conduct, and thus does nothing to compromise legitimate commerce or discourage innovation having a lawful promise.

Grokster distributed an electronic newsletter containing links to articles promoting its software's ability to access popular copyrighted music. And both companies communicated a clear message by responding affirmatively to requests for help in locating and playing copyrighted materials. [N]either company attempted to develop filtering tools or other mechanisms to diminish the infringing activity using their software. It is useful to recall that StreamCast and Grokster make money by selling advertising space, by directing ads to the screens of computers employing their software. As the record shows, the more the software is used, the more ads are sent out and the greater the advertising revenue becomes. Since the extent of the software's use determines the gain to the distributors, the commercial sense of their enterprise turns on high-volume use, which the record shows is infringing. The unlawful objective is unmistakable.

In addition to intent to bring about infringement and distribution of a device suitable for infringing use, [MGM must show] evidence of actual infringement by recipients of the software. As the account of the facts indicates, there is evidence of infringement on a gigantic scale.

On remand, reconsideration of MGM's motion for summary judgment will be in order. ∎

PublicPolicy

The media industry argued that free downloads were killing profitability. Technology businesses countered that restrictions on downloading would hamper technology and that the media business model was simply out-of-date. Upstart (and illegal) companies like Grokster and its predecessor, Napster, created a whole industry around downloading music. It took years for legitimate businesses such as iTunes to follow this lead legally. But now iTunes is an enormous success. Without Napster, would iTunes even exist?

And perhaps the entertainment industry is unfairly aggressive over the copyright laws. The theory of copyright was that publishers and creative talent needed a brief period of monopoly to ensure that they could earn a fair return. Originally, copyright protection lasted only 28 years, now it can be as long as 95 years. The period of protection has tripled even as publication and distribution have become much cheaper and faster. In theory, publishers should need a shorter, not longer, monopoly. ◆

The No Electronic Theft Act

Enacted in 1997, the **No Electronic Theft Act** is intended to deter the downloading of copyrighted material. It provides for criminal penalties for the reproduction or distribution of copyrighted material that has a retail value greater than $1,000, even if the offender has no profit motive. Thus, for instance, if a student photocopied for ten of her friends a text book that is worth $150, she could be subject to criminal penalties, including a prison term of one year. Originally, the Justice Department did not enforce this statute, but it has now begun to do so, particularly against those who set up networks to trade games, movies and music.

The Family Entertainment and Copyright Act

Under the **Family Entertainment and Copyright Act** it is a criminal offense to use a camcorder to film a movie in the theater. This statute also establishes criminal penalties for willful copyright infringement that involves distributing software, music, or film on a computer network.

The Digital Millennium Copyright Act

The good news is that Mary Schmich wrote an influential article in the *Chicago Tribune*. The bad news is that people deleted her name, attributed the article to Kurt Vonnegut, and sent it around the world via e-mail. Tom Tomorrow's cartoon was syndicated to 100 newspapers, but, by the time the last papers received it, the cartoon had already gone zapping around cyberspace. Because his name had been deleted, some editors thought he had plagiarized it.

In response to such incidents, Congress passed the **Digital Millennium Copyright Act** (DMCA), which provides that:

- **It is illegal to delete copyright information, such as the name of the author or the title of the article.** It is also illegal to distribute false copyright information. Thus, anyone who e-mailed Schmich's article without her name on it, or who claimed it was his own work, would be violating the law.

- **It is illegal to circumvent encryption or scrambling devices that protect copyrighted works.** For example, some software programs are designed so that they can only be copied once. Anyone who overrides this protective device to make another copy is violating the law. (The statute does permit purchasers of copyrighted software to make one backup copy.) If you buy a Disney DVD that prevents you from fastforwarding through commercials, you are violating the DMCA if you figure out how to do it anyway.

- **It is illegal to distribute tools and technologies used to circumvent encryption devices.** If you tell others how to fastforward through the Disney commercials, you have violated the statute.

The DMCA has been controversial. Its goal was laudable: to protect legitimate businesses from copyright pirates. However, opponents allege that:

- The DMCA interferes with legal activities. For instance, copy-protected CDs prevent consumers from making copies for their own use. These copies are legal under the fair use doctrine.

- The DMCA interferes with legitimate scientific research. An organization called the Secure Digital Music Initiative (SDMI) developed a technology to encrypt digital music. It issued a public challenge to see if anyone could override the encryption. Edward Felten, a Princeton professor, did manage to circumvent the technology, but when he tried to present his results at an academic conference, the SDMI threatened him with suit for violating the DMCA. He ultimately was able to publish part of his research, but only after filing suit against SDMI.

International Copyright Treaties

The Berne Convention requires member countries to provide automatic copyright protection to any works created in another member country. The protection does not expire until 50 years after the death of the author.[11] The WIPO Copyright Treaty and the WIPO Performances and Phonograms Treaty add computer programs, movies, and music to the list of copyrightable materials.

In 2004, Congress enacted a law that permits the president to appoint a copyright law enforcement officer charged with the responsibility of stopping copyright infringement overseas. Also, for the first time, Congress funded the National Intellectual Property Law Enforcement Coordination Council, which was established to protect American intellectual property internationally.

TRADEMARKS

A trademark is any combination of words and symbols that a business uses to identify its products or services and distinguish them from others. Trademarks are important to both consumers and businesses. Consumers use trademarks to distinguish between competing products. People who feel that Nike shoes fit their feet best can rely on the Nike trademark to know they are buying the shoe they want. A business with a high-quality product can use a trademark to develop a loyal base of customers who are able to distinguish its product from another.

Types of Marks

There are four different types of marks:

- **Trademarks** are affixed to *goods* in interstate commerce.

- **Service marks** are used to identify services, not products. Fitness First, Burger King, and Weight Watchers are service marks. In this chapter, the terms "trademark" and "mark" are used to refer to both trademarks and service marks.

- **Certification marks** are words or symbols used by a person or organization to attest that products and services produced by others meet certain standards. The Good

---

[11] Under U.S. law, copyrights last 70 years. The United States must grant works created in other signatory countries a copyright that lasts either 50 years or the length of time granted in that country, whichever is longer, but in no case longer than 70 years.

Housekeeping Seal of Approval means that the Good Housekeeping organization has determined that a product meets its standards.

- **Collective marks** are used to identify members of an organization. The Lions Club, the Girls Scouts of America, and the Masons are examples of collective marks.

Ownership and Registration

Under common law, the first person to use a mark in trade owns it. Registration with the federal government is not necessary. However, under the federal Lanham Act, the owner of a mark may register it on the Lanham Act Principal Register. A trademark owner may use the symbol ™ at any time, even before registering it, but not until the mark is registered can the symbol ® be placed next to it. Registration has several advantages:

- Even if a mark has been used in only one or two states, registration makes it valid nationally.

- Registration notifies the public that a mark is in use because anyone who applies for registration first searches the Public Register to ensure that no one else has rights to the mark.

- Five years after registration, a mark becomes virtually incontestable because most challenges are barred.

- The damages available under the Lanham Act are higher than under common law.

- The holder of a registered trademark generally has the right to use it as an Internet domain name.

Under the Lanham Act, the owner files an application with the PTO. The PTO will accept an application only if the owner has already used the mark attached to a product in interstate commerce or promises to use the mark within six months after the filing. In addition, the applicant must be the *first* to use the mark in interstate commerce. Initially, the trademark is valid for 10 years, but the owner can renew it for an unlimited number of 10-year terms as long as the mark is still in use. Trademark searches are free on PTO's Web site: **http://www.uspto.gov/main/trademarks.htm**.

Valid Trademarks

Words (Reebok), symbols (Microsoft's flying window logo), phrases ("Just do it"), shapes (a Coca-Cola bottle), sounds (NBC's three chimes), colors (Owens Corning's pink insulation), and even scents (plumeria blossoms on sewing thread) can be trademarked. **To be valid, a trademark must be distinctive**—that is, the mark must clearly distinguish one product from another. There are five basic categories of distinctive marks:

- **Fanciful marks** are made-up words such as Converse or Saucony.

- **Arbitrary marks** use existing words that do *not* describe the product—Prince tennis racquets, for example. No one really thinks that these racquets are designed by or for royalty.

- **Suggestive marks** *indirectly* describe the product's function. Greyhound implies that the bus line is swift, and Coppertone suggests what customers will look like after applying the product.

- Marks with **secondary meaning** cannot, by themselves, be trademarked, unless they have been used so long that they are now associated with the product in the public's mind. When a film company released a movie called *Ape*, it used as an illustration a picture that looked like a scene from *King Kong*—a gigantic gorilla astride the World Trade Center in New York City. The court held that the movie posters of *King Kong* had acquired a secondary meaning in the mind of the public, so the *Ape* producers were forced to change their poster.[12]

- **Trade dress** is the image and overall appearance of a business or product. It may include size, shape, color, or texture. The Supreme Court held that a Mexican restaurant was entitled to protection under the Lanham Act for the shape and general appearance of the exterior of its building as well as the decor, menu, servers' uniforms, and other features reflecting the total image of the restaurant.[13]

The following categories are not distinctive and *cannot* be trademarked:

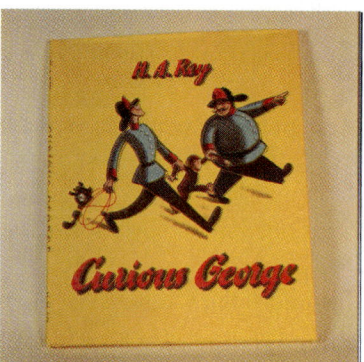

Is Furious George too similar to Curious George?

- **Similar to an Existing Mark.** To avoid confusion, the PTO will not grant a trademark that is similar to one already in existence on a similar product. Once the PTO had granted a trademark for "Pledge" furniture polish, it refused to trademark "Promise" for the same product. "Chat noir" and "black cat" were also too similar because one is simply a translation of the other. Houghton-Mifflin Co. sued to prevent a punk rock band from calling itself Furious George because the name is too similar to Curious George, the star of a series of children's books.

- **Generic Trademarks.** No one is permitted to trademark an item's ordinary name— "shoe" or "book," for example. Sometimes, however, a word begins as a trademark and later becomes a generic name. Zipper, escalator, aspirin, linoleum, thermos, yo-yo, band-aid, ping-pong, and nylon all started out as trademarks, but became generic. Once a name is generic, the owner loses the trademark because the name can no longer be used to distinguish one product from another—all products are called the same thing. That is why, in advertisements for Sanka, people ask for "a cup of Sanka-brand decaffeinated coffee." And why Xerox Corp. encourages people to say, "I'll photocopy this document," rather than "I'll xerox it." Jeep, Rollerblade, and TiVo are trademarks that seem destined for generic status.

- **Descriptive Marks.** Words cannot be trademarked if they simply describe the product—such as "low-fat," "green," or "crunchy." Descriptive words can, however, be trademarked if they do *not* describe that particular product because they then become distinctive rather than descriptive. "Blue Diamond" is an acceptable trademark for nuts as long as the nuts are neither blue nor diamond shaped.

- **Names.** The PTO generally will not grant a trademark in a surname because other people are already using it and have the right to continue. No one could register "Jefferson" as a trademark. However, a surname can be used as part of a longer title—"Jefferson Home Tours," for instance. Similarly, no one can register a geographical name such as "Boston" unless it is also associated with another word, such as "Boston Ale."

---

[12] *Paramount Pictures Corp. v. Worldwide Entertainment Corp.*, 2 Media L. Rep. 1311, 195 U.S.P.Q. (BNA) 539, 1977 U.S. Dist. LEXIS 17931 (S.D.N.Y. 1977).

[13] *Two Pesos, Inc. v. Taco Cabana, Inc.*, 505 U.S. 763, 112 S. Ct. 2753, 1992 U.S. LEXIS 4533 (1992).

- **Deceptive Marks.** The PTO will not register a mark that is deceptive. It refused to register a trademark with the words "National Collection and Credit Control" and an eagle superimposed on a map of the United States because this trademark gave the false impression that the organization was an official government agency.

- **Scandalous or Immoral Trademarks.** The PTO refused to register a mark that featured a nude man and woman embracing. In upholding the PTO's decision, the court was unsympathetic to arguments that this was the perfect trademark for a newsletter on sex.[14]

Infringement

To win an infringement suit, the trademark owner must show that the defendant's trademark is likely to deceive customers about who has made the goods or provided the services. The rightful owner is entitled to (1) an injunction prohibiting further violations, (2) destruction of the infringing material, (3) up to three times actual damages, (4) any profits the infringer earned on the product, and (5) attorney's fees.

What about a perfume for dogs? Would a reasonable consumer confuse Pucci with Gucci, Bono Sports with Ralph Lauren Polo Sports, or Miss Claybone for Liz Claiborne? None of these companies challenged the parody use of their names for a dog perfume. But Tommy Hilfiger Licensing, Inc. did not see the humor in the name Timmy Holedigger. The court, however, advised Hilfiger "to chill," pointing out that there was no evidence of actual confusion.[15]

cyberLaw

Many Web sites give away free information and (try to) make money selling advertisements. To be successful, the sites must attract hordes of visitors. What can they do to lure cybersurfers? Some site operators embed words like "sex" and "nudity" in invisible coding, even if the sites have nothing to do with sex. Although visitors cannot see the words, search engines will still call up the site. Not content with these generic lures, Calvin Designer Label (no relation to Calvin Klein, the clothing designer) embedded the words "Playboy" and "Playmate" in machine-readable code on its Web site. A federal court entered a restraining order preventing Calvin Designer from infringing on Playboy's trademarks.[16] ◆

Federal Trademark Dilution Act of 1995

Before Congress passed the Federal Trademark Dilution Act of 1995 (FTDA), a trademark owner could win an infringement lawsuit only by proving that consumers would be deceived about who had really made the product. **The new statute prevents others from using a trademark in a way that dilutes its value,** even though consumers are not confused about the origin of the product. For example, this statute would prohibit the use of Dupont shoes, Buick aspirin or Kodak pianos.

In the following case, Victoria's Secret thought of itself as an upscale women's lingerie chain and Victor's Little Secret was, well, vulgar with its offerings of handcuffs and adult videos. Did Victor's Little Secret dilute the value of the Victoria's Secret trademark?

---

[14] *In re McGinley,* 660 F.2d 481, 211 U.S.P.Q. (BNA) 668, 1981 CCPA LEXIS 177 (C.C.P.A. 1981).

[15] *Tommy Hilfiger Licensing, Inc. v. Nature Labs, LLC,* 221 F. Supp. 2d 410; 2002 U.S. Dist. LEXIS 14841 (2002).

[16] *Playboy Enterprises, Inc. v. Calvin Designer Label,* 985 F. Supp. 1220, 1997 U.S. Dist. LEXIS 14345 (N.D. Cal. 1997).

you Be The Judge

VICTOR MOSELEY V. V SECRET CATALOGUE, INC.

537 U.S. 418; 123 S. Ct. 1115
United States Supreme Court, 2002

Facts: Victoria's Secret was a chain that sold women's lingerie, nightwear, caftans, kimonos, slippers, sachets, lingerie bags, candles, soaps, cosmetic brushes, bath products, and fragrances. The company operated over 750 stores and distributed 400 million copies of its catalog each year. Sales exceeded $1.5 billion annually. The name "Victoria's Secret" was trademarked.

Victor Moseley owned a store near the military base in Fort Knox, Kentucky, called "Victor's Little Secret." He sold clocks, patches, temporary tattoos, stuffed animals, coffee mugs, leather biker wallets, Zippo lighters, diet formula, jigsaw puzzles, handcuffs, hosiery, bubble machines, greeting cards, calendars, incense burners, car air fresheners, sunglasses, jewelry, candles, lava lamps, blacklights, rock and roll prints, lingerie, pagers, candy, adult video tapes, and adult novelties. Women's lingerie represented only about 5 percent of his sales. Moseley placed an advertisement for his store in the military base's weekly newspaper.

An army colonel on the base was offended by what he considered to be an attempt to use a reputable company's trademark to promote the sale of unwholesome, tawdry merchandise. The colonel sent a copy of the ad to Victoria's Secret. The company filed suit under the FTDA alleging that Moseley's use of such a similar name was likely to blur the distinctiveness and tarnish the reputation of the Victoria's Secret trademark.

You Be the Judge: Does the name Victor's Little Secret dilute the trademark of Victoria's Secret?

Argument for Victoria's Secret: This case is a classic instance of dilution by tarnishing (associating the Victoria's Secret name with sex toys and lewd coffee mugs) and by blurring (linking the chain with a single, unauthorized store). While no consumer is likely to go to Moseley's store expecting to find Victoria's Secret's famed Miracle Bra, consumers who hear the name 'Victor's Little Secret' will automatically think of the more famous store and link it to Moseley's tawdrier shop. There is great potential for damage.

To prove that Victor's Little Secret had actually tarnished the name of Victoria's Secret would be difficult and expensive. This expense is unnecessary because it is obvious that a sleazy store using a very similar name will by its mere existence devalue the more upscale store.

Argument for Victor's Little Secret: The FTDA prohibits the use of a name that causes dilution of the famous mark. In other words, the law requires that there actually *be* dilution, not just that there be the *chance* of dilution. That does not mean that Victoria's Secret must prove an actual loss of sales or profits, but it must prove more than the mere fact that consumers mentally associate Victor's Little Secret with the more famous mark. The army officer who saw the advertisement in the base newspaper did associate Moseley's store with Victoria's Secret, but the ad did not change his perception of Victoria's Secret. It simply made him angry at Moseley.

It may be expensive to prove that dilution has taken place but that is not a reason to dispense with some reasonable standard of proof. It may also be expensive to show that someone has committed a murder, but we do not convict without it. ■

Domain Names

Roughly 50 million Internet addresses, known as domain names, have been registered, so it is often difficult to find a distinctive name for a new business. Domain names can be immensely valuable as they are an important component of doing business. Suppose you want to buy a new pair of jeans. Without thinking twice, you type in http://www.jcrew.com and there you are, ready to order. What if that address took you to a different site altogether, say, the personal site of one Jackie Crew? The store might lose out on a sale. Companies not only want to own their own domain name, they want to prevent complaint sites such as http://www.untied.com (about United Airlines), http://www.ihatestarbucks.com, or the always popular variation on the "sucks" theme, such as http://www.aolsucks.org. Generic domain names can be valuable, too. Shopping.com paid $750,000 to acquire its domain name from the previous (lucky) owner.

Who has the right to a domain name? In the beginning, the National Science Foundation, which maintained the Internet, granted Network Solutions, Inc. (NSI), a private company, the right to allocate domain names. NSI charged no fee for domain names and the rule was "first come, first served." Then so-called "cybersquatters" began to register domain names, not to use, but to sell to others. Someone, for example, tried to sell the name "Bill Gates" for $1 million.

In response to complaints, NSI began suspending any domain name that was challenged by the holder of a registered trademark. For instance, NSI would not allow Princeton Review to keep kaplan.com, which Princeton had acquired simply to inconvenience its arch-rival in the test preparation business. Congress then passed the **Anticybersquatting Consumer Protection Act, which permits both trademark owners and famous people to sue anyone who registers their name as a domain name in "bad faith."** The rightful owner of a trademark is entitled to damages of up to $100,000.

Although the goal of this statute was laudable, in practice it sometimes looked like a heavy club in the hands of corporations who used it to threaten innocent holders of domain names. The maker of Pokey toys threatened a boy who had registered his nickname, Pokey, and Archie Comics went after a girl named Veronica. The Chilling Effects Clearinghouse at http://www.chillingeffects.org provides a database of so-called "cease and desist" letters sent to holders of domain names.

As both the value and the number of domain names soared, the U.S. government transferred management of the Internet, including the allocation of names, to a private, nonprofit, international organization, the Internet Corporation for Assigned Names and Numbers (ICANN). Disputes over domain names can be decided by arbitration under ICANN's Uniform Domain Name Dispute Resolution Policy (UDRP) rather than by litigation under the Anticybersquatting Consumer Protection Act.

If a domain name is confusingly similar to a trademark, the owner has the right to bring a UDRP proceeding. To bring a case under the ICANN policy, the complainant (i.e., the plaintiff) must allege that:

- The domain name creates confusion because it is similar to a registered trademark.

- The respondent (i.e., the defendant) has no legitimate reason to use the domain name.

- The respondent registered the domain name in bad faith. If the respondent is a competitor of the complainant and has acquired the domain name to disrupt the complainant's business (à la Princeton Review), that is evidence of bad faith. So is an attempt by the respondent to sell the name to the complainant.

If the complainant wins, it is entitled either to take over the domain name or to cancel it.

For example, in a dispute over wal-martsucks.com, the WIPO arbitrator ordered that the name be transferred to Wal-Mart. The respondent had demonstrated his bad faith by attempting to sell the name for $530,000. In a similar case, however, the WIPO arbitrator found for a respondent who had registered Wallmartcanadasucks.com. In this case, the respondent had not tried to sell the name and was using the Web site to criticize Wal-Mart. As the arbitrator stated in his opinion: "Posting defamatory material on a Web site would not justify revocation of a domain name. The Policy should not be used to shut down robust debate and criticism." (These cases, and others, are available at **http://arbiter.wipo.int/ domains/search/index.html**.)

Critics have complained that WIPO arbitrators unfairly favor trademark holders, who win roughly 81 percent of the cases they bring. Either party has the option before or after an ICANN arbitration to litigate the issue in court. Of course, litigation is slower and more expensive.

Our discussion thus far has been about registering a trademark as a domain name. Sometimes businesses want to do the opposite—trademark a domain name. The PTO will issue such a trademark only for services offered via the Internet. Thus it trademarked "eBay" for "on-line trading services in which seller posts items to be auctioned and bidding is done electronically." The PTO will not trademark a domain name that is merely an address and does not identify the service provided.

International Trademark Treaties

Under the **Paris Convention**, if someone registers a trademark in one country, then he has a grace period of six months during which he can file in any other country using the same original filing date. Under the **Madrid Agreement**, any trademark registered with the international registry is valid in all signatory countries. (The United States is a signatory.) The **Trademark Law Treaty** simplifies and harmonizes the process of applying for trademarks around the world.

TRADE SECRETS

As the following news report indicates, trade secrets can be a company's most valuable asset.

NEWS*worthy*

At Slick 50, Inc., sneakiness is company policy. The handful of employees privy to the secret formula for the fancy engine treatment, which has nearly $80 million in annual sales, must swear a notarized oath of silence. Only those few who need to know are in possession of the combination to the fireproof vault with eight-inch-thick walls in which the sole printed copy of the Slick 50 recipe is housed. They alone are entrusted with the multiple passwords to the specially encoded database where the computer version is filed. When the company ships ingredients to hired blenders around the country, it dispatches them in odd allotments of containers identified only by numbered codes and mixing instructions. Masking chemicals are included in every batch so that chemical analysis to determine exactly what it takes to concoct the stuff is virtually impossible.

Despite the company's precautions, an employee at a Slick processing plant in the Cayman Islands was able to figure out the formula. He threatened to disclose it unless the company paid him $2.5 million. Fortunately for the company, when the extortionist faxed his demands, he included a cover page listing his mailbox address. The police arrested him immediately. As criminals go, he was not very slick.[17] ◆

---

[17] Anne Reifenberg, "How Secret Formula for Coveted Slick 50 Fell into Bad Hands," *Wall Street Journal*, Oct. 25, 1995, p. A1. Republished with permission of The Wall Street Journal; permission conveyed through the Copyright Clearance Center, Inc.

Although a company can patent some types of trade secrets, it may be reluctant to do so because patent registration requires that the formula be disclosed publicly. In addition, patent protection expires after 20 years. Some types of trade secrets cannot be patented—customer lists, business plans, manufacturing processes, and marketing strategies.

It has been estimated that the theft of trade secrets costs U.S. businesses $100 billion a year. In response, the National Conference of Commissioners on Uniform State Laws drafted the Uniform Trade Secrets Act (UTSA), which most states have now adopted. **A trade secret is a formula, device, process, method, or compilation of information that, when used in business, gives the owner an advantage over competitors who do not know it.** In determining if information is a trade secret, courts consider:

- How difficult (and expensive) was the information to obtain? Was it readily available from other sources?
- Does the information create an important competitive advantage?
- Did the company make a reasonable effort to protect it?

Anyone who misappropriates a trade secret is liable to the owner for (1) actual damages, (2) unjust enrichment, or (3) a reasonable royalty. If the misappropriation was willful or malicious, the court may award attorney's fees and double damages. A jury recently awarded Avery Dennison Corp. $40 million in damages from a competitor that had misappropriated secret information about the adhesives used in self-stick stamps.

The following case deals with a typical issue: How much information can employees take with them when they start their own, competing business?

POLLACK V. SKINSMART DERMATOLOGY AND AESTHETIC CENTER P.C.

2004 Pa. D. & C. LEXIS 99 2004
Common Pleas Court of Philadelphia County, Pennsylvania, 2004

Facts: Dr. Andrew Pollack owned the Philadelphia Institute of Dermatology (PID), a dermatology practice. Drs. Toby Shawe and Samy Badawy worked for PID as independent contractors, receiving a certain percentage of the revenues from each patient they treated. Natalie Wilson was Dr. Pollack's medical assistant.

Pollack tentatively agreed to sell the practice to Shawe and Badawy. But instead of buying his practice, the two doctors decided to start their own, which they called Skinsmart. They executed a lease for the Skinsmart office space, offered Wilson a job, and instructed PID staff members to make copies of their appointment books and printouts of the patient list. Then they abruptly resigned from PID. Wilson called PID patients to reschedule procedures at Skinsmart. The two doctors also called patients and

sent out a mailing to patients and referring physicians to tell them about Skinsmart.

Pollack filed suit, alleging that the two doctors had misappropriated trade secrets.

Issue: Did Shawe and Badawy misappropriate trade secrets from PID?

Excerpts from Judge Cohen's Decision: The right of a business person to be protected against unfair competition stemming from the usurpation of his or her trade secrets must be balanced against the right of an individual to the unhampered pursuit of the occupations and livelihoods for which he or she is best suited. For this reason, to qualify for protection, the information must be the particular secrets of the complaining employer, not general secrets of the trade in which he is engaged.

▼

Against this backdrop, it is clear the patient list is a trade secret, worthy of protection. As conceded by defendants, the confidentiality of patient information ensures that it remain unknown to those outside the practice and makes the patient list valuable. Through the substantial efforts of plaintiff, the patient list was compiled over numerous years, and contained 20,000 names with related information. PID spent money for computers, software, and employees to keep and maintain the patient list. Within the offices of PID, the information was not universally known or accessible. Not every staff member, including the practicing physicians, could pull the records. Wilson did not have access to them and the doctors relied on other PID employees to access the patient list. These same factors demonstrate that plaintiff sought to protect the secrecy of the information.

The plaintiff must demonstrate that the trade secret has value and importance to him and his business. As noted above, defendants acknowledge the value of the patient list to PID's practice. In addition, plaintiff relied upon the patient list as the core component of his practice.

To have the rights to the use of the trade secret, the plaintiff needs to show he either discovered or owned the trade secret. Plaintiff compiled the patient list over numerous years. The patient list was maintained on PID's computers by PID's employees. Plaintiff's tax returns show that PID was owned solely by plaintiff. These facts establish plaintiff's ownership of the patient list.

Summary judgment is granted on the issue of liability against defendants Shawe, Badawy, and Wilson. ■

Only civil penalties are available under the Uniform Trade Secrets Act. To safeguard national security and maintain the nation's industrial and economic edge, Congress passed the **Economic Espionage Act of 1996, which makes it a *criminal* offense to steal (or attempt to steal) trade secrets for the benefit of someone other than the owner, including for the benefit of any foreign government.** Kai-Lo Hsu was charged under this statute for his alleged attempt to steal the formula for manufacturing Taxol, an anticancer drug produced by Bristol-Myers. His employer, Yuen Foong Paper Co. in Taiwan, had directed him to steal this information because it sought to diversify into biotechnology and obtain technology from other countries.[18]

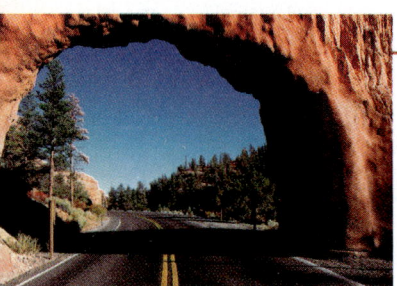

Chapter Conclusion

Intellectual property takes many different forms. It can be an Internet domain name, a software program, a cartoon character, a formula for motor oil, or a process for making anticancer drugs. Because of its great variety, intellectual property is difficult to protect. Yet, for many individuals and companies, intellectual property is the most valuable asset they will ever own. As its economic value increases, so does the need to understand the rules of intellectual property law.

---

[18] *United States v. Kai-Lo Hsu,* 155 F.3d 189, 1998 U.S. App. LEXIS 20810 (3rd Cir. 1998).

Chapter Review

	Patent	Copyright	Trademark	Trade Secrets
Protects:	Mechanical, electrical, chemical inventions; processes; machines; composition of matter; designs; plants	The tangible expression of an idea, but not the idea itself	Words and symbols that a business uses to identify its products or services	A formula, device, process, method, or compilation of information that, when used in business, gives the owner an advantage over competitors who do not know it
Requirements for Legal Protection:	Application approved by PTO	An item is automatically copyrighted once it is in tangible form	Use is the only requirement; registration is not necessary but does offer some benefits	Must be kept confidential
Duration:	20 years after the application is filed (14 years from date of issuance for a design patent)	70 years after the death of the work's only or last living author or, for a corporation, 95 years from publication	Valid for 10 years but the owner can renew for an unlimited number of terms as long as the mark is still being used	As long as it is kept confidential

Practice Test

1. For many years, the jacket design for Webster's Ninth New Collegiate Dictionary featured a bright red background. The front was dominated by a "bull's-eye" logo. The center of the bull's-eye was white with the title of the book in blue. Merriam-Webster registered this logo as a trademark. Random House published a dictionary with a red dust jacket, the title in large black and white letters, and Random House's "house" logo—an angular drawing of a house—in white. What claim might Merriam-Webster make against Random House? Would it be successful?

2. "Hey, Paula," a pop hit that spent months on the music charts, was back on the radio 30 years later, but in a form the song's author never intended. Talk-show host Rush Limbaugh played a version with the same music as the original but with lyrics that poked fun at President Bill Clin-ton's alleged sexual misconduct with Paula Jones. Has Limbaugh violated the author's copyright?

3. From the following description of Jean-Pierre Foissey's activities one evening, can you guess what he is doing and why?

   Mr. Foissey waits until sundown. Then it is time to move. A friend whom he employs drops him off by car near the plum orchard, turning off the headlights as they approach. Mr. Foissey and another operative move quickly through adjacent cornfields and enter the orchard, careful not to leave footprints. Armed with a flashlight, his associate crawls through the orchard reading aloud the numbers on labels attached to the trees by the grower. Mr. Foissey picks leaves off the trees and marks the tree numbers on them. He takes those leaves back to an expert who will examine their size, shape, color, and texture, and also test their DNA.[19]

4. Rebecca Reyher wrote (and copyrighted) a children's book entitled *My Mother Is the Most Beautiful Woman in the World*. The story was based on a Russian folktale told to her by her own mother. Years later, the children's TV show *Sesame Street* televised a skit entitled "The Most Beautiful Woman in the World." The *Sesame Street* version took place in a different locale and had fewer frills, but the sequence of events in both stories was identical. The author of the *Sesame Street* script denied he had ever seen Reyher's book but said his skit was based on a story told to his sister some 20 years before. Has *Sesame Street* infringed Reyher's copyright?

5. Roger Schlafly applied for a patent for two prime numbers. (A prime number cannot be evenly divided by any number other than itself and 1— 2, 3, 5, 7, 11, 13, for example.) Schlafly's numbers are a bit longer—one is 150 digits, the other is 300. His numbers, when used together, can help perform the type of mathematical operation necessary for exchanging coded messages by computer. Should the PTO issue this patent?

6. DatagraphiX manufactured and sold computer graphics equipment that allowed users to transfer large volumes of information directly from computers to microfilm. Customers were required to keep maintenance documentation on-site for the DatagraphiX service personnel. The service manual carried this legend: "No other use, direct or indirect, of this document or of any information derived therefrom is authorized. No copies of any part of this document shall be made without written approval by DatagraphiX." Additionally, on every page of the maintenance manual the company placed warnings that the information was proprietary and not to be duplicated. Frederick J. Lennen left DatagraphiX to start his own company that serviced DatagraphiX equipment. Can DatagraphiX prevent Lennen from using its manuals?

7. A man asked a question of the advice columnist at his local newspaper. His wife had thought of a clever name for an automobile. He wanted to know if there was any way they could own or register the name so that no one else could use it. If you were the columnist, how would you respond?

8. Babe Ruth was one of the greatest baseball players of all time. After Ruth's death, his daughters registered the words "Babe Ruth" as a trademark. MacMillan, Inc., published a baseball calendar that contained three Babe Ruth photos. Ruth's daughters did not own the specific photographs, but they objected to the use of Ruth's likeness. As holders of the Babe Ruth trademark, do his daughters have the right to prevent others from publishing pictures of Ruth without their permission?

9. Harper & Row signed a contract with former President Gerald Ford to publish his memoirs. As part of the deal, the two agreed that *Time* magazine could print an excerpt from the memoirs shortly before the book was published. *Time* was to pay $25,000 for this right. Before *Time* published its version, *Nation* magazine published an unauthorized excerpt. *Time* canceled its article and refused to pay the $25,000. Harper sued *Nation* for copyright infringement. What was *Nation*'s defense? Was it successful?

10. Frank B. McMahon wrote one of the first psychology textbooks to feature a light and easily readable style. He also included many colloquialisms and examples that appealed to a youthful student market. Charles G. Morris wrote a psychology textbook that copied McMahon's style. Has Morris infringed McMahon's copyright?

11. **ETHICS** After Edward Miller left his job as a salesperson at the New England Insurance Agency, Inc., he took some of his New England customers to his new employer. At New England, the customer lists had been kept in file cabinets. Although the company did not restrict access to these files, it claimed there was a "you do not peruse my files and I do not peruse yours" understanding. The lists were not marked "confidential" or "not to be disclosed." Did Miller steal New England's trade secrets? Whether or not he violated the law, was it ethical for him to use this information at his new job?

---

[19] Thomas Kamm, "Patented Plums Give French Fruit Sleuth His Raison D'être," *Wall Street Journal*, Sep. 18, 1995, p. A1.

12. *YOU BE THE JUDGE* WRITING PROBLEM Three inventors developed a software program that generated a particularly clear screen display on a computer. The PTO refused to issue a patent for this software. Do the inventors have a right to a patent? **Argument for the PTO:** This software is merely a series of mathematical for- mulas that cannot be patented. **Argument for the inventors:** The program is not merely a mathematical concept or an abstract idea, but rather a specific machine to produce a useful, concrete, and tangible result.

13. *ROLE REVERSAL* Draft a multiple-choice ques- tion that focuses on an issue of copyright law.

Internet Research Problem

Think of a name for an interesting new pro- duct. Click on Search Trademarks at http://beatty. westbuslaw.com to see if this name is available as a trademark. Also look at http://beatty.westbuslaw.com, which provides a list of domain name registrars. See if your name is available as an Internet domain name.

> **You can find further practice problems at** http://beatty.westbuslaw.com **or in the Study Guide that accompanies this text.**

Real Property

S ome men have staked claims to land for its oil, others for its gold. But Paul Termarco and Gene Murdoch are staking their claim to an island using . . . hot dogs. Their quest to market frankfurters in the New Jersey wilderness has made their children blush with embarrassment, their wives shrug in bewilderment, and strangers burst into laughter. But for three years, the two friends from West Milford have sold chili dogs, cheese dogs, and the ever traditional, hold-everything-but-the-mustard hot dogs from a tiny island in Greenwood Lake. Now it seems as though everyone knows about "Hot Dog Island."

"People love it," said Termarco. "They say, 'Thank you for being here.' I always say, 'No. Thank *you.*'" The personalized service and the inexpensive prices (hot dogs cost $1.75; chili dogs, cheese dogs, and sauerkraut, $2.00) have cultivated a base of regulars. "I think it's great. It's better than going to a restaurant for two hours and spending a lot of money," said Joan Vaillant, who frequently jet skis to the island for hot dogs slathered in mustard.

At two-eighths of an acre, the island's pile of craggy rocks, scrubby bushes, and a few ash trees are difficult to spot. Termarco doesn't mind. "Not everyone can say they own an island," he boasted. Termarco and Murdoch decided to claim the

© AKIRA KAEDE/PHOTODISC/GETTY IMAGES

slip of land after chatting with a local restaurateur a few years ago. Termarco had just finished suggesting that the man expand his lake-side business to the island when Murdoch kicked his friend under the table.

"We left thinking, 'We can do this ourselves,'" said Murdoch, who rushed to the township offices the following day to see who owned the island.

Property records showed that the state owned the lake and lake floor, but nobody owned the island. An attorney told them about the law of adverse possession written in the 1820's. If Murdoch and Termarco could show that they used the island for five years, it would be theirs. As crazy as the scheme sounded, Murdoch figured it was worth trying.[1] ■

Can two friends acquire an island simply by *pretending* they own it? Yes. As we will see, the law of adverse possession permits people to obtain title to land by using it, if they meet certain stringent criteria. We examine the rules later in the chapter and decide how likely Murdoch and Termarco are to succeed. For now, the lesson is that real property law can provide surprises—and profit.

NATURE OF REAL PROPERTY

We need to define a few terms. A **grantor** is an owner who conveys his property, or some interest in it, to someone else, called the **grantee.** If you sell your house to Veronica, you are the grantor and she is the grantee. Real property may be any of the following:

- **Land.** Land is the most common and important form of real property. In England, land was historically the greatest source of wealth and social status, far more important than industrial or commercial enterprises. As a result, the law of real property has been of paramount importance for nearly 1,000 years, developing very gradually to reflect changing conditions. Some real property terms sound medieval for the simple reason that they *are* medieval. By contrast, the common law of torts and contracts is comparatively new. (For a fascinating look at the Roman roots of our property law, dig down to **http://www.libertystory.net** and find the link to ancient Roman law.)

- **Buildings.** Buildings are real property. Houses, office buildings, and factories all fall (or stand) in this category.

- **Subsurface Rights.** In most states, the owner of the land also owns anything under the surface, down to the center of the earth. In some cases the subsurface rights may be worth far more than the surface land, for example if there is oil or gold underfoot.

---

[1] Leslie Haggin, "Pair Stake Their Claim to Hot Dog Island," *Record* (Bergen, N.J.), Sep. 5, 1994, p. A12. Excerpted with permission of The Record, Hackensack, NJ.

Although the landowner generally owns these rights, she may sell them, while retaining ownership of the surface land. Suppose Terry buys land in the country to get away from the materialistic rat race and then discovers natural gas under the surface. She may choose to sell the natural gas rights to an energy company. Terry keeps the rights to use the surface for whatever she wishes, but the energy company owns the subsurface rights. It will have the right to enter Terry's land, drill for the gas, and conduct it away by pipe. The company could also sell the subsurface rights, if it wished.

- **Air Rights.** The owner of land owns the air space above the land. You own an urban parking lot. The owner of an adjacent office building wishes to build a walkway across your parking lot to join her building with a neighboring skyscraper. The office owner needs your permission to build across the air space and will expect to pay you a handsome fee for the privilege. Because cities are by definition crowded, air space is often very valuable. Some companies, such as railroads, own a great deal of air space and earn considerable coin selling thin air.

- **Plant Life.** Plant life growing on land is real property, whether the plants are naturally occurring, such as trees, or cultivated crops. When a landowner sells his property, plant life is automatically included in the sale, unless the parties agree otherwise. A landowner may also sell the plant life separately, if he wishes. A sale of the plant life alone, without the land, is a sale of goods. (Goods, as you may recall, are movable things.) If Douglas agrees to sell all of the fir trees on his property, this sale of goods will be governed by the Uniform Commercial Code (UCC), regardless of whether Douglas or the buyer is obligated to cut the trees.[2]

- **Fixtures.** Fixtures are goods that have become attached to real property. A house (which is real property) contains many fixtures. The furnace and heating ducts were goods when they were manufactured and when they were sold to the builder, because they were movable. But when the builder attached them to the house, the items became fixtures. By contrast, neither the refrigerator nor the grand piano is a fixture.

When an owner sells real property, the buyer normally obtains the fixtures, unless the parties specify otherwise. Sometimes it is difficult to determine whether something is a fixture. The general rule is this: **an object is a fixture if a reasonable person would consider the item to be a permanent part of the property,** taking into account attachment, adaptation, and other objective manifestations of permanence:

- *Attachment.* If an object is attached to property in such a way that removing it would damage the property, it is probably a fixture. Heating ducts could be removed from a house, but only by ripping open walls and floors, so they are fixtures.

- *Adaptation.* Something that is made or adapted especially for attachment to the particular property is probably a fixture, such as custom-made bookshelves fitted in a library.

- *Other Manifestations of Permanence.* If the owner of the property clearly intends the item to remain permanently, it is probably a fixture. Suppose a homeowner constructs a large concrete platform in his backyard, then buys a heavy metal shed and bolts it to the platform. His preparatory work indicates that he expects the shed to remain permanently, and a court would likely declare it a fixture.

In the following case, there was no doubt about one thing: the object was *big*. Did that make it a fixture?

---

2   UCC §2-107(2).

ALL CITY COMMUNICATION COMPANY, INC. V. STATE DEPARTMENT OF REVENUE

263 Wis.2d 394, 661 N.W.2d 845, 2003 WI App 77
Court of Appeals of Wisconsin, 2003

Facts: Waukesha Tower leased rural land from All City Communication. The ten-year lease gave Waukesha the right to construct a 500-foot communication tower and, at lease end, to take away the tower. The rest of the land could be used for farming. Waukesha built a 480-foot tower on a concrete foundation, with 30 guy wires. The company rented space on it to radio stations and other firms. Several years after Waukesha began operating the tower, the state department of revenue (DOR) informed the company that it was liable for sales tax on all past and future revenue.

In Wisconsin, sales tax was due for the sale, lease, or rental of *personal* property. No such tax was due for the use of real property or fixtures (also called improvements) to real estate. The trial court agreed with the DOR that the tower was personal property, and that the company owed sales tax for its rentals. Waukesha appealed, arguing that the tower was a fixture.

Issue: Was the communications tower a fixture?

Excerpts from Judge Lundsten's Decision: The annexation factor asks whether the property has been actually physically [attached] to the real estate. There is no dispute in this case that the tower is annexed to the real property, and so we turn our attention to the second factor.

The second factor in the test considers the degree of application or adaptation to the use or purpose to which the realty is devoted. [Some courts determine] the degree to which the realty is well suited to the use or purpose of the property in question. [Other courts examine] the degree to which the property in question has been adapted to the realty in such a way that it loses its marketability and demonstrates an intent to make the property permanent. [We conclude] that the land is well suited for farming and, at the same time, is equally well

suited for use as a base for a broadcasting tower. Apart from the required engineering necessary to erect all broadcasting towers, the Companies do not allege that this tower has been adapted in some way unique to this particular plot of land. Because neither side presents a stronger argument on this factor, factor three (intent) will overshadow any determination regarding factor two.

The third factor considers whether there is an intent to make a permanent accession to the freehold. The intent factor is regarded as the most important of the three factors. [Waukesha argues] that, viewed objectively, the erection of a 480-foot-tall tower evinces an intent to permanently annex the property to the land. In addition, [Waukesha argues] that the tower is permanently annexed to the land due to the substantial concrete foundations required to attach it to the land. DOR responds that the commission found that the tower is movable. Thus, according to DOR, the fact that the tower was erected on leased land is more important than the degree to which the tower is annexed to the land.

There is no dispute that the substantial foundations associated with a 480-foot tower mean moving the properties could not be done with ease. However, the commission determined that a market existed for the sale and purchase of used towers, and that the tower could be disassembled and reassembled at another site. Waukesha Tower had the right to remove the tower from the land, and the landowner had the right to terminate the lease at the end of the lease term. Despite the tower's large size, nothing in [case law] suggests that size alone can manifest intent to create a permanent accession to the land. In view of the undisputed facts, we conclude that a reasonable person would not have intended the tower to be a permanent accession to the land.

Order affirmed. ■

Devil's Advocate

A 480-foot tower? On a massive concrete foundation? With 30 guy wires? Yes, it is theoretically possible to disassemble and haul away a tower. For that matter, you can move a house. But this tower is the height of a 40- or 50-story building. If intent is the key, then this is a fixture. Waukesha surely intended to leave the tower where it stood. Who wouldn't? ◆

ESTATES IN REAL PROPERTY

Use and ownership of real estate can take many different legal forms. A person may own property outright, having the unrestricted use of the land and an unlimited right to sell it. However, someone may also own a lesser interest in real property. For example, you could inherit the *use* of a parcel of land during your lifetime, but have no power to leave the land to your heirs. Or you could retain ownership and possession of some land yet allow a corporation to explore for oil and drill wells. The different rights that someone can hold in real property are known as **estates** or **interests**. Both terms simply indicate specified rights in property.

Freehold Estates

The owner of a freehold estate has the present right to possess the property and to use it in any lawful way she wants. The three most important freehold estates are (1) fee simple absolute, (2) fee simple defeasible, and (3) life estate.

Cecily's fee simple absolute enables her to decide what use to make of this vineyard.

Fee Simple Absolute

A fee simple absolute provides the owner with the greatest possible control of the property. When we think of buying a house or owning land outright, we are usually referring to fee simple absolute, the most common form of land ownership. Suppose Cecily inherits a fee simple interest in a 30-acre vineyard. Cecily may use the land for any purpose that the law allows. She may continue to raise grapes, or, if she hates wine, she may rip up the vines and plant apple trees, build a condominium complex, or allow the land to go to waste. Although zoning laws may regulate her use, nothing in Cecily's estate itself limits her use of the land.

Cecily may pass on to her heirs her entire estate, that is, her full fee simple absolute. This makes a fee simple absolute potentially infinite in duration, with each generation leaving the same full ownership privileges to the next.

Fee Simple Defeasible

Other estates contain more limited rights than the fee simple absolute. Suppose that during his life, Wily establishes the Wily Church of Perfection. Upon his death, Wily leaves a 100-acre estate to the church for as long as it keeps the name "Wily Church of Perfection." Wily has included a significant limitation in the church's ownership. The church has a fee simple defeasible.

A fee simple defeasible may terminate upon the occurrence of some limiting event. If the congregation decides to rename itself the Happy Valley Church of Perfection, the church automatically loses its estate in the 100 acres. Ownership of the land then **reverts** to Wily's heirs, meaning title goes back to them. Because the heirs might someday inherit the land, they are said to have a *future interest* in the 100 acres. We look at future interests later.

A landowner who creates a fee simple defeasible generally does so to ensure that property is used in a particular way, perhaps as a school or church or playground. In some cases a landowner will create such a fee to guarantee that a particular activity, such as gambling or residential subdivision, does *not* take place. In the following case, a California city was surprised to learn that this ancient doctrine still has plenty of life.

WALTON V. CITY OF RED BLUFF

2 Cal. App. 4th 117, 3 Cal. Rptr. 2d 275, 1991 Cal. App. LEXIS 1474

California Court of Appeal, 1991

Facts: In 1908 and 1916, Mrs. Elizabeth Kraft and her son, Edward Kraft, granted to the city of Red Bluff two adjoining properties, with buildings, for use as a public library. The grants from the Krafts required continuous use as a public library and stated that the property would return to the Kraft family if the city ever used it for other purposes.

In 1986, Red Bluff decided that the buildings were too small for its needs and moved all of the books to a new building nearby. The city used the Kraft property for other civic purposes such as town meetings, social gatherings, and school tutoring. Herbert Kraft Walton, a descendant and heir, filed suit seeking to have the property reconveyed to him. The trial court found for Red Bluff, and Walton appealed.

Issue: **Did Red Bluff violate the terms of the grants, so the property must now revert to Walton?**

Excerpts from Judge Carr's Decision: The grants provide in part: "If the property herein conveyed shall at any time be abandoned by the said Town of Red Bluff,. . . or if the said property shall cease to be used, for library purposes, by said Town,. . . or shall be put to [any] use other [than] the uses and purposes herein specifically referred to,. . . then the grant and conveyance herein made shall cease and terminate, and the title to the said property and all the improvements thereon shall at once revert to [the Kraft family].

Red Bluff admits all the books were removed from the library as of September 1986. The trial court framed the issue as one of abandonment. But the grantors specified that "if the said property shall cease to be used, for library purposes" the grants terminate.

Whether Red Bluff intended to "abandon" the use purpose of the property or not, it removed the books and stopped using the premises for library purposes. The grants defined library purposes broadly to include various educational endeavors, but there is no evidence any of these other activities took place. It stopped using the grant for library purposes and the property must go back to the Kraft heir.

At oral argument Red Bluff focused on the "changed conditions" doctrine. The power of termination expires when it becomes "obsolete." In a leading case involving a covenant restricting the use of lots to residential purposes it was said that "where there has been a change in the uses to which the property in the neighborhood is being put, so that such property is no longer residence property, it would be unjust, oppressive, and inequitable to give effect to the restrictions, if such change has resulted from causes other than their breach." In this case the alleged change in circumstance is that Red Bluff needs a bigger, modern library building, not that the present building cannot be used for the purposes of the grant or that the use of surrounding property makes operation of a library impracticable. In these circumstances there is nothing inequitable about enforcing the restriction in the grant.

The judgment is *reversed* with directions to the trial court to enter a judgment [granting title to] Walton. ∎

Life Estate

A life estate is exactly what you would think: **an estate for the life of some named person.** For example, Aretha owns Respect Farm, and in her will she leaves it to Max, for his lifetime. Max is the **life tenant.** He is entitled to live on the property and work it as a normal farm during his lifetime. He may grow and harvest crops and retain all the profits. But the moment Max dies, the farm reverts to Aretha or her heirs.

The life tenant must keep the property in reasonable repair during his lifetime and may not damage the property. As we saw earlier, Cecily, the owner of a fee simple absolute in a vineyard, was entitled to mow down the vines and turn the property into a miniature-golf park if she wanted; Max, a life tenant, has no such rights. Aretha's heirs, who will obtain the property on Max's death, are entitled to enter upon the farm to ensure that he is not damaging the property and to take any other sensible steps to ensure that their future property is protected. For example, if a stream through the farm threatens to flood a valuable field, Aretha's heirs have the right to charge onto the property yelling "Dam it!" and then, if Max failed to do so, to dam it.

Non-Freehold Estates

A non-freehold is entirely different from the freehold estates we have seen. It involves a **lease** in which the owner, the landlord, agrees to permit a tenant to use and possess the property. When you lease an apartment from a landlord you have a leasehold, or a non-freehold estate. We discuss these estates in detail in Chapter 45, on landlord-tenant law.

Concurrent Estates

When two or more people own real property at the same time, they have **concurrent estates.** The most common forms of concurrent estates are tenancy in common, joint tenancy, marital property, and condominiums and cooperatives.

Tenancy in Common

The most common form of concurrent estate is **tenancy in common.** Suppose Patricia owns a house or, in legal terms, owns a fee simple absolute estate in the house. Patricia agrees to sell her house to Quincy and Rebecca. When she **conveys** the deed, that is, transfers the deed, "to Quincy and Rebecca," those two now have a tenancy in common. This kind of estate can also be created in a will. If Patricia had died still owning the house, and left it in her will to "Sam and Tracy," then Sam and Tracy would have a tenancy in common.

A tenancy in common might have 2 owners or 22. Each owner is called a **tenant in common** or **co-tenant.** The tenants in common do not own a particular section of the property; they own an equal interest in the entire property. Quincy and Rebecca each own a 50 percent interest in the entire house.

Any co-tenant may convey her interest in the property to another person. Thus, if Rebecca moves 1,000 miles away, she may sell her 50 percent interest in the house to Sidney. Further, when a co-tenant dies, her interest in the property passes to her heirs, along with all of her other assets.

Partition. Since any tenant in common has the power to convey her interest, some people may find themselves sharing ownership with others they do not know or, worse, dislike. What to do? **Partition,** or division of the property among the co-tenants. Any co-tenant is entitled to demand partition of the property. If the various co-tenants cannot agree on a fair division, a co-tenant may request a court to do it. **All co-tenants have an absolute right to partition.**

A court will normally attempt a **partition by kind,** meaning that it actually divides the land equally among the co-tenants. If three co-tenants own a 300-acre farm, and the court can divide the land so that the three sections are of roughly equal value, it will perform a partition in kind, even if one or two of the co-tenants oppose partition.

If partition by kind is impossible because there is no fair way to divide the property, the court will order the real estate sold and the proceeds divided equally.

Joint Tenancy

Joint tenancy is similar to tenancy in common but is used less frequently. The parties, called joint tenants, again own a percentage of the entire property and also have the absolute right of partition. The primary difference is that a **joint tenancy includes the right of survivorship.** This means that when one joint tenant dies, his interest in the property passes to *the surviving joint tenants*. Recall that a tenant in common, by contrast, has the power to leave his interest in the real estate to his heirs. Because a joint tenant cannot leave the property to his heirs, courts do not favor this form of ownership. The law presumes that a concurrent estate is a tenancy in common; a court will interpret an estate as a joint tenancy only if the parties creating it clearly intended that result.

Joint tenancy has one other curious feature. Although joint tenants may not convey their interest by will, they may do so during their lifetime. If Frank and George own vacation property as joint tenants, Frank has the power to sell his interest to Harry. But as soon as he does so, the joint tenancy is **severed,** that is, broken. Harry and George are now tenants in common, and the right of survivorship is destroyed. Exhibit 44.1 illustrates tenancy in common and joint tenancy.

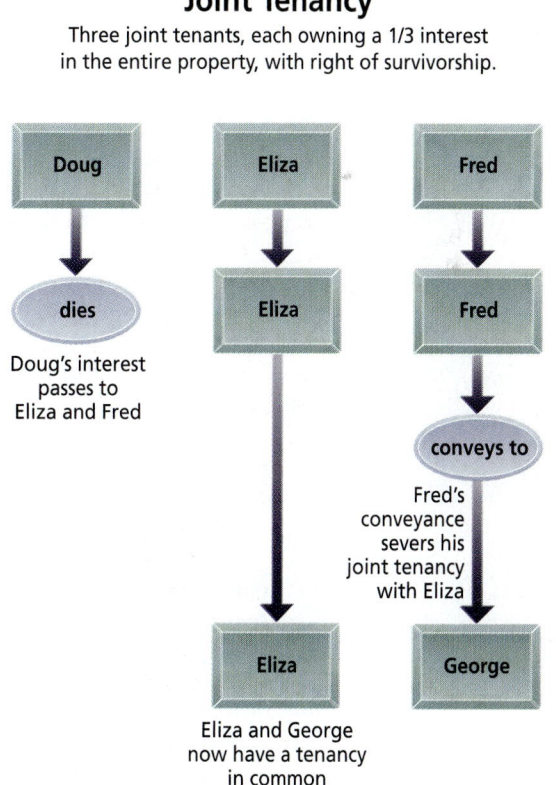

Tenancy in Common

Three tenants in common, each owning a 1/3 interest in the entire property.

Alice → dies → Kate

Kate inherits and becomes a tenant in common with Ben and Clem

Ben → Ben → sells → Larry

Clem → Clem → Clem

Larry buys and becomes a tenant in common with Kate and Clem

Joint Tenancy

Three joint tenants, each owning a 1/3 interest in the entire property, with right of survivorship.

Doug → dies

Doug's interest passes to Eliza and Fred

Eliza → Eliza → Eliza

Fred → Fred → conveys to → George

Fred's conveyance severs his joint tenancy with Eliza

Eliza and George now have a tenancy in common

Exhibit 44.1

Marital Property

Two forms of concurrent ownership are available only to married couples: tenancy by the entirety and community property.

Tenancy by the Entirety. This form of ownership exists in slightly over half of the states. **The husband and wife each own the entire property, and they both have a right of survivorship.** So when the husband dies, his one-half interest in the property automatically passes to his wife. Neither party has a right to convey his or her interest. If the parties wish to sell their interests, they must do so together. An advantage of this is that no creditor may seize the property based on a debt incurred by only one spouse. If a husband goes bankrupt, creditors may not take his house if he and his wife own it as tenants by the entirety. Divorce terminates a tenancy by the entirety and leaves the two parties as tenants in common.

Community Property. French and Spanish settlers brought **community property** law to the South and West, and nine states still use this form of ownership for a married couple.[3] This system allows the husband and wife to maintain separate ownership of assets they bring to the marriage or inherit. Those assets are called **separate property.** They remain the private property of each spouse during the marriage. Either spouse may convey separate property to another person during the marriage and may leave the separate property to anyone he or she wishes. But income or assets that either party *earns* during the marriage are considered **community property, which must be equally shared** during the marriage, regardless of who earns it. Neither party may convey community property without the consent of the other. When a spouse dies, one-half of the community property goes to the surviving spouse, and the other half goes to the heirs of the deceased.

Suppose Margarita marries Jean Claude in Texas, a community property state. At the time of the marriage, Jean Claude owns a ranch but Margarita owns nothing. Jean Claude's ranch is separate property. He is free to convey it to someone else during his lifetime, and at his death he may leave it to anyone he wishes. During the marriage, Margarita inherits a Renoir painting worth $3 million; it is separate property, which she may freely dispose of. While married, Jean Claude earns $6,000 per year, translating children's poetry. Margarita earns $900,000 producing gory television shows. The income is community property, and each spouse is entitled to $453,000 per year.

Condominiums and Cooperatives

Condominiums and cooperatives are forms of concurrent ownership that have enjoyed increasing popularity as the cost of home ownership has skyrocketed. Both forms of ownership are most common in apartment buildings with multiple units, though they can be used in other settings, such as a cluster of houses on a single parcel of land. Here we look at the typical setting, a multi-unit apartment building.

In a condominium, the owner of the apartment typically has a fee simple absolute in his particular unit. He is normally entitled to sell or lease the unit, must pay taxes on it, and may

There is a major difference between a condominium and a cooperative. How does that difference affect life inside the building?

---

3   Arizona, California, Idaho, Louisiana, Nevada, New Mexico, Texas, and Washington all have a community property law, while Wisconsin's system is a variation of the same principle.

receive the normal tax deduction if he is carrying a mortgage. The apartment owner is also a tenant in common as to all common areas, such as hallways, parking areas, roofdeck, exterior grounds, and so forth. All unit owners belong to a condominium association, which manages the common areas. The association arranges exterior maintenance, such as snow plowing, lawn care, and painting. Each unit owner pays a set monthly fee for routine maintenance. The association may impose additional **assessments,** that is, special fees for unusual work, such as major roof repair.

In a cooperative, the residents generally do not own their particular unit. Instead, they are shareholders in a corporation that owns the building and leases specified units to the shareholders. Suppose Mandy buys unit 5F in an apartment building in New York City, where cooperatives are the norm. What Mandy is actually buying is a block of shares in the corporation that owns her building; she has no freehold estate in unit 5F. However, her shares entitle her to a perpetual lease on unit 5F.

The corporation not only owns the cooperative building, it *runs* the building, too. This means the corporation's board of directors have near dictatorial power over who buys shares in the cooperative and how owners live.

NEWSworthy

New York City has more cooperative apartments than anyplace else in the country and offers copious evidence of the unrestricted authority of co-op boards. Before permitting the sale of a unit, boards scrutinize prospective buyers, demanding exhaustive evidence of long-term financial stability. A board might reject an investment banker who earns $300,000 per year because she is a recent graduate, or because it disapproves of her social life—or without even giving a reason. Once in a co-op, a new owner may find the board even more intrusive. In some buildings, no dogs are allowed. Some boards require dogs to ride in freight elevators, while another went further, also restricting poorly dressed *guests* to service elevators. (Would the dogs resent this?) Various buildings ban pianos; some prohibit cooking in woks, because other residents complain about the smell; and at least one co-op board outlawed sitting in the lobby while wearing flippers. The managers of a 29-story, 452-unit building became the first in the nation to prohibit new owners from smoking *in their apartments,* asserting that residents had complained for years that smoke entered their units through vents, and claiming that this ban was the only way to solve the problem. (Current owners may continue to smoke in their apartments.) ◆

The case that follows looks at the ultimate issue: May a co-op board *evict* an owner?

LONDON TERRACE TOWERS, INC. V. DAVIS

6 Misc.3d 600, 2004 N.Y. Slip Op. 24497, 2004 WL 2827658
Civil Court, City of New York, 2004

Facts: Michael Davis owned shares in a New York cooperative and leased the corresponding apartment, number 2F. London Terrace Towers owned and operated the building. From the beginning, Davis created problems, and over a period of several years, the co-op board charged Davis with playing loud music at night, allowing his dog to roam freely in the halls, inviting loud guests who sometimes got into fights with him, spray-painting furniture in the common areas, and leaving his personal belongings in the hallways.

The board held a hearing to consider terminating his lease. Davis admitted most of the alleged behavior and begged for a second chance, promising to obey the rules. The board granted him another opportunity, but a year later, finding that nothing had changed, it held a second meeting. Davis brought a lawyer and had a full opportunity to

▼

defend himself. The board voted unanimously to end his lease. Davis refused to leave, and the board filed suit to enforce the lease termination.

Issue: Does a co-op board have the power to terminate the lease of a shareholder?

Excerpts from Judge Lebovits's Decision:[4] The board let Davis try to refute the board's claims and explain his conduct. Davis chose to refute only some of the allegations. He admitted that [although] he once had left his apartment wearing only a shirt and one sock, he did so unintentionally because he was sleep-walking.

In response to the board's allegations that he let his dog roam the public hallways without a leash, he stated that his dog is well behaved. Davis then argued that it was a mischaracterization to state that his dog roamed around, because the dog never left his floor.

Davis spent a significant amount of time responding to the board's accusation that he engaged in sexual relations [with a guest] in the health club's shower. Davis admitted that they were naked in the same shower at the same time, but he explained that he was merely trying to free an ingrown hair from his guest's back. When a board member asked Davis why he did not shower with the homeless man in his apartment, he replied that his apartment was a mess and he did not want to bring a stranger near his dog.

[The court next discussed how much deference it should give to the board's decision.]

The business-judgment rule is a standard of reviewing business decisions that courts use to prevent judicial interference and second guessing of corporate decisions made in good faith and in furtherance of the corporate purpose. Courts have given business-judgment deference to a wide range of cooperative board actions and decisions, although not yet to a vote to evict.

The issue in this case is whether a board vote terminating a shareholder-tenant's proprietary lease is entitled to business-judgment deference. Some commentators support extending business-judgment deference to board votes to terminate tenancies for objectionable conduct. Those who oppose granting business-judgment deference to board votes are ultimately concerned with eroding tenant protection. Allowing boards to terminate cooperative tenancies might affect the value of cooperatives. But cases cannot be decided on market forces. Market forces have no force of law. [The court ruled that a court should respect a board's decision to terminate a lease.]

A properly elected board acted within its authority and according to the proprietary lease to terminate Davis's tenancy. The board gave Davis proper notice of its proposed action. After Davis acknowledged his behavior in writing and agreed to change, the board gave Davis one more last chance to conform his conduct to the cooperative community's standards. When he failed to comply with the agreement, the board gave him another notice of objectionable conduct and asked him to appear for a special meeting. Davis appeared and defended himself against the board's allegations. The board listened but found him unconvincing. After unanimously voting to terminate his tenancy, the board passed a corporate resolution and sent Davis a notice to terminate his tenancy. The cooperative unfailingly followed the procedures contained in the proprietary lease to terminate Davis's tenancy The board is entitled to judgment on the papers. ∎

Public Policy

Davis was clearly a headache for his cooperative neighbors. However, this is a man who has paid a substantial sum to *own* permanent residency rights. Should the board have the power to throw him out? As a society in which more and more people live jammed together in ever smaller spaces, should we require some kind of mediation, or a formal court trial, before allowing a cooperative to take away basic property rights from wayward residents? ◆

Future Interests

A property owner may convey less than all of his rights to another person. For example, if Andrew has a fee simple absolute in Serenity Farm, he may convey a life estate to Claire, meaning that Claire gets the property only for her life. The remaining rights in the land are called future interests.

---

[4]   Once again, the authors have substituted the parties' names for "petitioner" and "respondent."

Future interests are presently existing nonpossessory rights that may or may not develop later. The rights are *presently existing* because they can be bought and sold immediately. They are *nonpossessory* because they do not permit the holder to take immediate possession of the land. Some future interests definitely create the right to possession later on, while other future interests create only the possibility of possession. We look at three future interests: a reversion, a remainder, and a possibility of reverter.

Reversion

If Andrew conveys Serenity Farm "to Claire for her life," Claire has a life estate in the property. Andrew has a **reversion,** meaning that upon Claire's death the property automatically returns to him or to his heirs. The significance of a future interest is this: even though Claire may live for 50 more years, Andrew may convey his reversion at any time. The right to own Serenity Farm upon Claire's death is a valuable right, and Andrew may sell the reversion to Xerxes for $1 million. Xerxes has to bide his time until Claire's death, but when she dies, the land is his.

Remainder

Suppose Andrew conveys Tranquility Farm "to Douglas for life, and then to Ernie." Douglas has a life estate and Ernie has a **remainder.** A remainder has exactly the same value as a reversion. The difference is that when the life tenant dies, the property goes to a named third person, not to the original owner.

Possibility of Reverter

This future interest applies when a property owner has granted a fee simple defeasible. Suppose Andrew conveys Utopia Farm "to Fredericka for as long as she continues to raise winter wheat." Fredericka has a fee simple defeasible and will keep the farm, and may leave it to her heirs, as long as the winter wheat grows. Andrew has the possibility of reverter because the farm will revert to him (or his heirs) if Fredericka (or her heirs) fails to grow winter wheat.

Example: Andrew owns a fee simple absolute in property and . . .	What was conveyed?	What future interest remains?
Conveys the property "to Betty."	Sale of the entire estate	None
Conveys the property "to Claire for her life."	Life estate	Andrew has a reversion. The property reverts to him or his heirs upon Claire's death.
Conveys the property "to Douglas for his life and then to Ernie."	Life estate	Ernie has a remainder and Andrew has nothing.
Conveys "to Fredericka as long as she grows winter wheat."	Fee simple defeasible	Andrew has a possibility of reverter. The property reverts to him or his heirs if Fredericka or any of her heirs cease to grow winter wheat.

Nonpossessory Interests

All of the estates and interests that we have examined thus far focused on one thing: possession of the land. Now we look at interests that *never* involve possession. These interests may be very valuable, even though the holder never lives on the land.

Easements

The Alabama Power Co. drove a flatbed truck over land owned by Thomas Burgess, damaging the property. The power company did this to reach its power lines and wooden transmission poles. Burgess had never given Alabama Power permission to enter his land, and he sued for the damage that the heavy trucks caused. He recovered—nothing. Alabama Power had an *easement* to use Burgess's land.

An easement gives one person the right to enter land belonging to another and make a limited use of it, without taking anything away. Burgess had bought his land from a man named Denton, who years earlier had sold an easement to Alabama Power. The easement gave the power company the right to construct several transmission poles on one section of Denton's land and to use reasonable means to reach the poles. Alabama Power owned that easement forever, and when Burgess bought the land, he took it subject to the easement. Alabama Power drove its trucks across a section of land where the power company had never gone before, and the easement did not explicitly give the company this right. But the court found that the company had no other way to reach its poles, and therefore the easement allowed this use. Burgess is stuck with his uninvited guest as long as he owns the land.[5]

There are two kinds of easements. The first, an **easement appurtenant,** benefits its owner in the use of *another parcel of land*. Suppose Madeline buys vacation land that is near a lake but without waterfront access. Wade owns lakefront land, and he sells Madeline an easement, allowing her to cross his property, on foot or in a car, to reach the water. This is an easement appurtenant, since it benefits its owner (Madeline) in the use of her land. Madeline's land is the **dominant tenement,** that is, the property that benefits from the easement. Wade's parcel is the **servient tenement,** the land that is burdened by the easement. Typically, the dominant tenement is adjacent to the servient, but it need not be.

An easement appurtenant *runs with the land*, meaning that if the owner of the dominant tenement sells her land, the buyer acquires the easement as well. However, the owner may *not* sell an easement by itself to someone else. If Madeline sells her property to Jason, he acquires the right to waltz across Wade's land. But Madeline has no right to sell only the easement to Jason, while retaining her property.

The second kind of easement, an **easement in gross,** benefits its owner but *not in the use of other land*. The Alabama Power Co. had an easement in gross in Burgess's land. The company had the right to install power lines across the property and use reasonable means to reach them. However, this right did not benefit any other property owned by the company, so it was an easement in gross. Most easements in gross *may* be sold. If Alabama Power no longer needed its power lines on Burgess's land, it could sell its easement to another company, for example, a cable television company.[6]

---

[5] *Burgess v. Alabama Power Co.*, 658 So. 2d 435, 1995 Ala. LEXIS 119 (Ala. 1995).

[6] A related nonpossessory estate—and one that can benefit society and posterity—is a **conservation easement,** in which a property owner agrees to forbid certain development on her property, forever. For an interesting discussion of how the Canadian province of Ontario uses these easements to preserve historic architecture and virgin wilderness, take a look at **http://www.heritagefdn.on.ca** and click on the "Conservation Easements" link under "Programs."

Creation of Easements

Grant or Reservation. Property owners normally create easements in one of two ways. A **grant** occurs when a landowner expressly intends to convey an easement to someone else. This is how Alabama Power acquired its easement. The company offered to buy the right to use the land, and Denton agreed to sell. The parties signed an agreement and *recorded* the easement, meaning they placed it on file in the land registry, so that interested parties were on notice. When Burgess bought the land from Denton, he knew (or should have known) about the easement.

A **reservation** occurs when an owner sells land but keeps some right to enter the property. A farmer might sell 40 acres to a developer but reserve an easement giving him the right to drive his equipment across a specified strip of the land.

Implication or Necessity. Easements are less frequently created in these two ways. An **easement by implication** arises when an owner subdivides land in a way that *clearly implies* the creation of an easement in favor of the new parcels. Suppose Jason owns lakefront property with a boat ramp. He subdivides his land and sells several parcels that do not reach the lake, promising all purchasers use of the boat ramp. This subdivision clearly implies the right to cross Jason's land to use the boat ramp, since there is no other access. The new owners have an easement by implication.

An **easement by necessity** arises when the dominant tenement *absolutely must* make use of other property. Yolanda leases a ninth floor apartment to Darrin. Darrin has an easement by necessity to use the stairs and elevators, since he has no other method of reaching his apartment, short of skydiving.

Prescription. Joseph Leto bought undeveloped land in 1946 and used it on weekends for family gatherings, picnicking, and nature walks. He reached his property by using a jeep trail that crossed land he did not own, land eventually purchased by Digital Equipment Corp. (DEC). Leto continued to use the trail for nearly 30 years, until DEC sued to keep him off its property. Neither DEC nor the previous owner had ever given Leto permission to use the land. Did Leto have an easement? Yes, he had an **easement by prescription.**[7] An easement by prescription may arise when someone makes use of property belonging to another, if his use is:

- Open and notorious
- Adverse to the owner, and
- Continuous and uninterrupted for the number of years required by local statute.

The theory of easement by prescription is that landowners must take some initiative to protect their property rights. If they fail to do so, they may lose certain rights in their land (or, as we will see in the section on adverse possession, they may lose the land altogether). But someone seeking an easement by prescription must satisfy each element. His use of the property must be open and notorious, so that a reasonable landowner would be aware of what is happening and have a chance to stop it. The use must be adverse to the owner, meaning without the owner's permission. A landowner who *permits* another to cross his land nullifies any possibility of easement by implication. Finally, the use must continue without interruption for as long as required by the state statute, which is often 7 years but may be more or less in a particular state. Joseph Leto continued his use of the trail for nearly 30 years, much longer than the local statute

---

[7] *Digital Equipment Corp. v. Leto,* Mass. Lawyers Weekly No. 14-008-94 (Mass. Land Court 1994).

required. Once he acquired the easement by prescription, it was potentially his forever, and when DEC acquired the land, it did so subject to Leto's easement.

NEWS*worthy*

During the nineteenth century, many railroads obtained easements to lay down rails, and, by 1900, trains ran on over 300,000 miles of track throughout the country. Today, railroads use less than half that much track. What happens to the thousands of miles of unused land? Some state laws, and some contracts, require property to revert to the owner when an easement is abandoned. Yet federal, state, and local governments have turned many miles of unused track into trails for hiking and biking. Environmentalists strongly support this "rails to trails" conversion. Some property owners believe that their reversionary rights are being violated and demand compensation. Local governments point out that they continue to shore up and maintain the original rail bank, for possible future train use, and that the easements are therefore not abandoned. ◆

Easements, whether created by grant or otherwise, come in all sizes. Is the easement in the following case *too* big?

you Be The Judge

CARVIN V. ARKANSAS POWER AND LIGHT

14 F.3d 399, 1993 U.S. App. LEXIS 33986
United States Court of Appeals for the Eighth Circuit, 1993

Facts: Between 1923 and 1947, Arkansas Power & Light (AP&L) constructed several dams on two Arkansas lakes, Hamilton and Catherine. The company then obtained "flood easements" on property adjoining the lakes. AP&L obtained some of the easements by grant and others by reservation, selling lakeside property and keeping the easement. These flood easements permitted AP&L to "clear of trees, brush and other obstructions and to submerge by water" certain acreage, which was described exactly. AP&L properly recorded the easements, and when the current landowners bought lakeside property, they were aware of the documents.

During one 12-hour period in May 1990, extraordinarily heavy rains fell in the Ouachita River Basin, including both lakes. In some areas, over 10 inches of rain fell, causing the water to reach the highest levels ever recorded, even washing away the equipment designed to measure rainfall. To avoid flooding Lake Hamilton, AP&L opened the gates of a dam called Carpenter. This caused Lake Catherine to flood, with water in some places rising 25 feet. This flood caused massive damage to the plaintiffs' houses, with water in some cases rising to the roof level.

Several dozen landowners sued, claiming that AP&L was negligent in opening one dam without simultaneously opening another and also in failing to warn homeowners of the intended action. The federal district court granted summary judgment for AP&L, based on the flood easements, and the landowners appealed.

You Be the Judge: Did the easements relieve AP&L from liability for flooding?

Argument for the Landowners: Your honors, no sane homeowner would give a power company the right to do what this company has done. AP&L has destroyed land, demolished houses, and ruined lives. AP&L opened a dam knowing that this would flood the shores of Lake Catherine and inundate dozens of properties. Does the power   ▼

company think the homeowners are simply crazy? That is the only reason someone would voluntarily permit such conduct.

These flood easements were many years old, created long before many of the present owners bought their property. None of them ever dreamed something like this could happen. Even if the easements were once valid, they should not be enforced any longer.

Further, even if the easements were still valid, and we maintain they were not, no easement authorizes negligence. At most the easements would permit some minimal flooding by a carefully controlled process, after adequate notice to everyone concerned. Here there was no notice, no care, no decency at all. AP&L should not be allowed to rely on ancient pieces of paper to wash away land and ruin lives.

Argument for AP&L: Your honors, the flooding was caused by an act of God—unprecedented rain—not by anything AP&L did. It is true that the company opened the dam without notice, for the simple reason that there was no time to give notice. AP&L not only had the right to act quickly, it had the *duty* to act quickly, to protect residents of a much wider area.

Your honors, a flood easement exists for one reason: to allow a company, when necessary, to flood land. The company knew it had the legal right to do this, based on the easements, and that there was no alternative.

The landowners argue that no sane person would grant such an easement, but in every instance here, that is just what has happened. It is true that many of these owners did not grant the easements, but their predecessors did. The value of the property would naturally decline somewhat with a flood easement attached, and as a result these owners paid less for their property. They were on notice of the easements, every one of which was recorded, and they had plenty of opportunity to decide whether to take on the risk. All of the owners made calculated decisions to accept the risk, and they must now live with their choices. ■

Profit

A *profit* gives one person the right to enter land belonging to another and take something away. You own 100 acres of vacation property, and suddenly a mining company informs you that the land contains valuable nickel deposits. You may choose to sell a profit to the mining company, allowing it to enter your land and take away the nickel. You receive cash up front, and the company earns money from the sale of the mineral. The rules about creating and transferring easements apply to profits, as well.

License

A license gives the holder temporary permission to enter upon another's property. Unlike an easement or profit, a license is a *temporary* right. When you attend a basketball game by buying a ticket, the basketball club that sells you the ticket is the licensor and you are the licensee. You are entitled to enter the licensor's premises, namely the basketball arena, and to remain during the game, though the club can revoke the license if you behave unacceptably.

Mortgage

Generally, in order to buy a house, a prospective owner must borrow money. The bank or other lender will require security before it hands over its money, and the most common form of security for a real estate loan is a mortgage. **A mortgage is a security interest in real property.** The homeowner who borrows money is the **mortgagor,** because she is *giving* the mortgage to the lender. The lender, in turn, is the **mortgagee,** the party acquiring a security interest. The mortgagee in most cases obtains a **lien** on the house, meaning the right to foreclose on the property if the mortgagor fails to pay back the money borrowed. A mortgagee forecloses by taking legal possession of the property, auctioning it to the highest bidder, and using the proceeds to pay off the loan.

SALE OF REAL PROPERTY

For most people, buying or selling a house is the biggest, most important financial transaction they will make. Here we consider several of the key issues that may arise.

Seller's Obligations Concerning the Property

Historically, the common law recognized the rule of *caveat emptor* in the sale of real property—that is, let the buyer beware. If a buyer walked into his new living room and fell through the floor into a lake of toxic waste, it was his tough luck. But the common law changes with the times, and today courts place an increasing burden of fairness on the sellers of real estate. Two of the most significant obligations are the implied warranty of habitability and the duty to disclose defects.

Implied Warranty of Habitability

Most states now impose an implied warranty of habitability on a builder who sells a new home. This means that, whether he wants to or not, the builder is guaranteeing that the new house contains **adequate materials and good workmanship.** The law implies this warranty because of the inherently unequal position of builder and buyer. Some defects might be obvious to a lay observer, such as a room with no roof or a front porch that sways whenever the neighbors sneeze. But only the builder will know if he made the frame with proper wood, if the heating system was second rate, the electrical work shabby, and so forth. Note that the law implies this warranty only to protect buyers of residential property. There is *no* such implied warranty for the sale of new *commercial* buildings, although over the next decade or two some courts could begin to impose one.

Duty to Disclose Defects

The seller of a home must disclose facts that a buyer does not know and cannot readily observe, if they materially affect the property's value. Roy and Charlyne Terrell owned a house in the Florida Keys, where zoning codes required all living areas to be 15 feet above sea level. They knew that their house violated the code because a bedroom and bathroom were on the ground floor. They offered to sell the house to Robert Revitz, assuring him that the property complied with all codes and that flood insurance would cost about $350 per year. Revitz bought the house, moved in, and later learned that because of the code violations, flood insurance would be slightly more expensive—costing just over *$36,000 per year.* He sued and won. The court declared that the Terrells had a duty to disclose the code violations; it ordered a rescission of the contract, meaning that Revitz got his money back. The court mentioned that the duty to disclose was wide ranging and included leaking roofs, insect infestation, cracks in walls and foundations, and any other problems that a buyer might be unable to discern.[8] We discuss this rapidly evolving area of the law more fully in Chapter 14, on capacity and consent.

Sales Contract and Title Examination

The statute of frauds requires that an agreement to sell real property must be in writing to be enforceable. A contract for the sale of a house is often several pages of dense legal reading, in which the lawyers for the buyer and seller attempt to allocate risks for every problem that might go wrong. However, the contract *need* not be so thorough. A written contract for the sale of land is generally valid if it includes the names of all parties, a precise description of the property being sold, the price, and signatures.

Once the parties have agreed to the terms and signed a contract, the buyer's lawyer performs a **title examination,** which means that she, or someone she hires, searches through the local land registry for all documents that relate to the property. The purpose is to ensure that the seller actually has valid title to this land, since it is dispiriting to give someone half a million dollars for property and then discover that he never owned it and neither do you. Even if the seller owns the land, his title may be subject to other claims, such as an easement or profit. In some cases the buyer's lawyer will issue a certificate of title, describing precisely what title the seller has (such as fee simple absolute) and whether there are any limitations to it (such as a profit to remove all trees). Or the lawyer may hire a title company to perform the search and issue a report. A buyer may also choose to buy title insurance, a policy in which the insurance company, after making its own title examination, guarantees to pay the buyer for any losses if she later discovers the seller lacked good title.

Closing and Deeds

While the buyer is checking the seller's title, she also probably needs to arrange financing, as described above in the section on mortgages. When the title work is complete and the buyer has arranged financing, the parties arrange a **closing,** a meeting at which the property is actually sold. The seller brings to the closing a **deed,** which is the document proving ownership of the land. The seller signs the deed over to the buyer in exchange for the purchase price. The buyer pays the price either with a certified check and/or by having her lender pay. If a lender pays part or all of the price, the buyer executes a mortgage to the lender as part of the closing.

Different types of deeds provide different assurances about what the seller is conveying to the buyer. **A general warranty deed normally contains the following five covenants (promises):**

- *Covenant of Seisin.* (Did we mention that some terms might sound medieval?) Here, the grantor warrants that he owns whatever estate he is conveying. If the deed describes a fee simple absolute, this covenant guarantees that is what the grantor is delivering.

- *Covenant of Right to Convey.* The grantor promises that he has the power to make this conveyance.

- *Covenant against Encumbrances.* Here the grantor is assuring that the land is free of any easement, profit, mortgage, and the like.

- *Covenant of Quiet Enjoyment.* The grantor assures that no other person can lawfully claim the land.

---

[8] *Revitz v. Terrell,* 572 So. 2d 996, 1990 Fla. App. LEXIS 9655 (Fla. Dist. Ct. App. 1990).

- *Covenant of Warranty.* The grantor promises to defend the grantee if any third party claims to own the land.

The general warranty deed normally makes all of these covenants against problems arising *before* the grantor took the land or *while* he owned it. That makes this the best deed from the buyer's point of view.

A **special warranty deed** is more limited. It typically includes the same five covenants listed above, but the covenants apply only against problems arising *while* the grantor owned the land, *not* those that might have arisen earlier.

A **quitclaim deed** warrants nothing. The grantor simply transfers whatever right, title, or interest he has, if any. Most buyers of property will refuse to accept a quitclaim deed. The real value of this deed lies in clearing up property disputes. Suppose there is a possible claim that Becky has an easement by prescription to drive across Nick's land, even though Becky never uses that route. To have clear title to his land, Nick may ask Becky to execute a quitclaim deed. If she does so, the parties never need to determine whether Becky had a valid claim, since she is conveying any rights she may have had to Nick. For a sample quitclaim deed, pack up and move to **http://www.legaldocs.com/htsgif .d/xquitdee.mv.**

Recording

Recording the deed means filing it with the official state registry. The registry clerk places a photocopy of the deed in the agency's bound volumes and indexes the deed by the name of the grantor and the grantee. (The states are moving cautiously toward electronic recording, but the process is slow because the stakes are so high.) Recording is a critical step in the sale of land, because it puts all the world on notice that the grantor has sold the land. It has little effect between grantor and grantee: once the deed and money are exchanged, the sale is generally final between those two. But recording is vital to protect the general public.

Suppose Roger sells his farm to Alicia for $600,000. Alicia records her deed within minutes of the purchase. The public is now on notice that Alicia owns the property. A month later Roger offers to sell the land to Dana for $500,000. Dana must check the registry, where she will quickly learn that Roger does not own the land. Suppose that, without checking the registry of deeds, Dana pays the full amount and Roger gives her a fraudulent deed. Alicia's property is safe, and Dana gets nothing: she was obligated to search the registry before buying. Dana has a valid claim against Roger, but if he has skipped town, the claim may be useless.

By contrast, suppose that Alicia sells the land to Pete, who *fails* to record his deed. A week later, Alicia offers the same property to Reggie, who checks the registry and sees no mention of the sale to Pete. If Reggie pays for the land, he will probably get valid title to it because he is a **bona fide purchaser,** that is, someone who gives value (money) in good faith for property. Reggie believed in good faith that Alicia owned the farm, since his search of the registry indicated no defects in his title. He gave value by paying $500,000. A bona fide purchaser generally takes the land over a buyer (Pete) who failed to record.

Dana thought that she bought this farm from Roger, but Alicia recorded her deed a month earlier. Alicia gets to keep the property and Dana has to press a claim against Roger.

ADVERSE POSSESSION

You may recall Paul Termarco and Gene Murdoch, who opened this chapter by trying to sell you—and all the world—a hot dog from an island in the middle of a New Jersey lake. As we mentioned then, Termarco and Murdoch had their sights set on more than mustard and relish: they hoped that by using the island *as if* they owned it, they *would* own it. They were relying on the doctrine of adverse possession. This old rule of law is analogous to easement by prescription, which we analyzed earlier. Under certain conditions, easement by prescription permits a person who makes use of land continuously to establish an easement for that use. Adverse possession goes even farther and allows someone to take title to land if she meets certain tests.

To gain ownership of land by adverse possession, the user must prove:

- Entry and exclusive possession
- Open and notorious possession
- A claim adverse to the owner, and
- Continuous possession for a statutory period.

Entry and Exclusive Possession

The user must take physical possession of the land and must be the only one to do so. If the owner is still occupying the land, or if other members of the public share its use, there can be no adverse possession.

Open and Notorious Possession

The user's presence must be visible and generally known in the area, so that the owner is on notice that his title is contested. This ensures that the owner can protect his property by ejecting the user. Someone making secret use of the land gives the owner no opportunity to do this, and hence acquires no rights in the land.

A Claim Adverse to the Owner

The user must clearly assert that the land is his. He does not need to register a deed or take other legal steps, but he must act as though he is the sole owner. If the user occupies the land with the owner's permission, there is no adverse claim and the user acquires no rights in the property. To succeed, the user must protect his possession of the land against all others the way any normal landowner would. This may mean erecting a home if the area is residential, or fencing property that is used to graze cattle, or posting "no trespassing" signs in a wilderness area.

Must the user *believe* he has a title or only act as though he does? The states are divided on this question. Many states focus only on the adverse *acts* of the user: it is sufficient if his conduct indicates he is the sole owner, regardless of what he thinks. This is the modern trend. But other states require a mistaken *belief* that the user has title to the land. For example, some states require that the user demonstrate "color of title," meaning that he has some document that *he believed* gave him good title to the land, though in reality it never did.

Continuous Possession for the Statutory Period

State statutes on adverse possession prescribe a period of years for continuous use of the land. Originally, most states required about 20 years to gain adverse possession, but the trend has been to shorten this period. Many states now demand 10 years, but a few require only 5 years' use. The reason for shortening the period is to reward those who *make use* of land. Even within a single state, statutes may prescribe various periods for different types of land. For example, adverse possession in a wilderness area may require more than 20 years' possession.

Regardless of the length required, the use must be continuous. In a residential area, the user would have to occupy the land year round for the prescribed period. In a wilderness area generally used only in the summer, a user could gain ownership by seasonal use.

A user may be able to meet the statutory period by **tacking,** which permits her to add onto her years of occupancy any years certain predecessors were in possession. The predecessors must have been in *privity* with the current user, meaning there was some legal relationship. Suppose that for 12 years, Martha adversely possesses land owned by Jake. Martha then moves, selling her interest in the land to Nancy, who occupies the land for 9 years. The total of 21 years is sufficient for adverse possession in any state, and Nancy now owns the land.

Sailing back to Hot Dog Island, how did Murdoch and Termarco fare? They certainly entered on the land and established themselves as the exclusive occupants. Their use has been open and notorious, allowing anyone who claimed ownership to take steps to eject them from the property. Their actions have been adverse to anyone else's claim. If the two hot dog entrepreneurs have grilled those dogs for the full statutory period, they should take title to the island.[9]

In the following case, the couple claiming adverse possession must do without friendly hot dog sellers because they have taken up residence in a ghost town.

RAY V. BEACON HUDSON MOUNTAIN CORP.

88 N.Y.2d 154, 666 N.E.2d 532, 1996 N.Y. LEXIS 676
Court of Appeals of New York, 1996

Facts: In 1931, Rose Ray purchased a cottage in a mountain-top resort town in the Adirondacks, at the same time agreeing to rent the land on which the structure stood. The long-term lease required her to pay the real estate taxes and provided that when the tenancy ended, the landlord would buy back the cottage at fair market value. In 1960, the landlord terminated the lease of everyone in the town, so Ray and all other residents packed up and left. She died in 1962, without ever getting a penny for the cottage. The next year, Mt. Beacon Incline Lands, Inc., bought all rights to the abandoned 156-acre resort.

Robert and Margaret Ray, the son and daughter-in-law of Rose Ray, reentered the cottage and began to use it one month per year, every summer from 1963 to 1988. They paid taxes, insured the property, installed utilities, and posted "no trespassing" signs.

In 1978, Beacon Hudson bought the resort in a tax foreclosure sale. Finally, in 1988, the Rays filed suit, claiming title to the cottage by adverse possession. Beacon Hudson counter-claimed, seeking to eject the Rays. The trial court ruled for the couple. The appellate court reversed, stating that the Rays had been absent too frequently to achieve adverse possession. The Rays appealed to New York's highest court.

Issue: Did the Rays acquire title by adverse possession?

Excerpts from Judge Titone's Decision: The element of continuity will be defeated where the adverse possessor interrupts the period of possession by abandoning the premises. However, the hostile claimant's actual possession of the property need not

---

9   Unfortunately, there are no press accounts to inform us of the island's current status.

be constant to satisfy the "continuity" element of the claim. Rather, the requirement of continuous possession is satisfied when the adverse claimant's acts of possessing the property are consistent with acts of possession that ordinary owners of like properties would undertake.

Here, defendant claims that plaintiffs' possession of the property was not continuous because they were physically present there for only one month out of the summer season. However, this argument fails to take into consideration plaintiffs' other acts of dominion and control over the premises that are indicative of their actual possession of an estate in land. Here, plaintiffs' installation of utilities and over-all preservation of the cottage, a permanent and substantial structure, in a veritable ghost town, for the duration of the statutory period demonstrates continuous, actual occupation of land by improvement. Thus, plaintiffs' actual summertime use for a full month each season, coupled with their repeated acts of repelling trespassers, improving, posting, padlocking and securing of the property in their absences throughout the statutory period, demonstrated their continuous dominion and control over, and thus possession of, the property.

Such seasonal presence, coupled with plaintiffs' preservation of the premises for the statutory period of 10 years—which was made more obvious by the fact that all neighboring structures had collapsed due to vandalism and abandonment—was sufficient to place the record owner on notice of their hostile and exclusive claim of ownership.

[The appellate court is reversed and the Rays obtain title by adverse possession.] ∎

LAND USE REGULATION

Nuisance Law

A nuisance is an unprivileged interference with a person's use and enjoyment of her property. Offensive noise, odors, or smoke often give rise to nuisance claims. Courts typically balance the utility of the act that is causing the problem against the harm done to neighboring property owners. If a suburban homeowner begins to raise pigs in her backyard, the neighbors may find the bouquet offensive; a court will probably issue an **abatement,** that is, an order requiring the homeowner to eliminate the nuisance. For some practical advice on how to quiet noisy neighbors, go to **http://findlaw.com** and enter a search for "nuisance."

NEWSworthy

Community members can use the old doctrine of nuisance for more serious problems than pigs. An apartment building in Berkeley, California, became widely known as a drug house, and the neighbors suffered. Here is how two of the neighbors described their lives:

> I have been confronted by the drug dealers, drug customers, and prostitutes that frequent and work around and from 1615–1617 Russell Street. Weekly I have lost many hours of sleep from the cars that burn rubber after each drug buy in the middle of the night.
>
> Because of this illegal activity my child is unable to use our front yard and I even have to check the back yard since it has been intruded upon from time to time by people running from the police. He is learning to count by how many gunshots he hears and can't understand why he can't even enjoy our rose garden.

These were but two of the affidavits written by neighbors of a 36-unit building owned by Albert Lew. Month after month neighbors complained to Lew that his tenants were destroying the neighborhood. But Lew refused to evict the drug dealers or take any serious steps to limit the crime. So the neighbors used the law of nuisance to restore their community.

Sixty-six neighbors of the drug house each filed a small claims case against Lew, claiming that he was permitting a nuisance to exist on his property. The neighbors won their small claims cases, but Lew appealed, as he had a right to, for a new trial in Superior Court. A sergeant testified that he had been to the building over 250 times during two years. Residents testified about how frightening life had become. The Superior Court awarded damages of $218,325 to the neighbors and the court of appeals affirmed the award, holding that neighbors injured by a nuisance may seek an abatement and damages. As Lew discovered, the law of nuisance can be a powerful weapon for a better neighborhood.[10] ◆

Zoning

Zoning statutes are state laws that permit local communities to regulate building and land use. The local communities, whether cities, towns, or counties, then pass zoning ordinances that control many aspects of land development. For example, a town's zoning ordinance may divide the community into an industrial zone where factories may be built, a commercial zone in which stores of a certain size are allowed, and several residential zones in which only houses may be constructed. Within the residential zones there may be further divisions, for example, permitting two-family houses in certain areas and requiring larger lots in others.

An owner prohibited by an ordinance from erecting a certain kind of building, or adding on to his present building, may seek a **variance** from the zoning board, meaning an exception granted for special reasons unique to the property. Whether a board will grant a variance generally depends upon the type of the proposed building, the nature of the community, the reason the owner claims he is harmed by the ordinance, and the reaction of neighbors.

Ethics

Many people abhor "adult" businesses, such as strip clubs and pornography shops. Urban experts agree that a large number of these concerns in a neighborhood often causes crime to increase and property values to drop. Nonetheless, many people patronize such businesses, which can earn a good profit. Should a city have the right to restrict adult businesses? New York City officials determined that the number of sex shops had grown steadily for two decades and that their presence harmed various neighborhoods. With the support of community groups, the city passed a zoning ordinance that prohibited adult businesses from all residential neighborhoods, from some commercial districts, *and* from being within 500 feet of schools, houses of worship, day-care centers, or other sex shops (to avoid clustering). Owners and patrons of these shops protested, claiming that the city was unfairly denying the public access to a form of entertainment that it obviously desired. From the Chapter 2 Ethics Checklist: Who are the stakeholders? Has the process been fair? Are there any superior alternatives? ◆

Eminent Domain

Eminent domain is the power of the government to take private property for public use. A government may need land to construct a highway, airport, university, or public housing. All levels of government—federal, state, and local—have this power. But the Fifth Amendment of the United States Constitution states: "...nor shall private property be taken for public use, without just compensation." The Supreme Court has held that this clause, the Takings Clause, applies not only to the federal government but also to state and local governments. So, although all levels of government have the power to take property, they must pay the owner a fair price.

A "fair price" generally means the reasonable market value of the land. Generally, if the property owner refuses the government's offer, the government will file suit seeking **condemnation** of the land, that is, a court order specifying what compensation is just and awarding title to the government.

---

[10] *Lew v. Superior Court*, 20 Cal. App. 4th 866, 1993 Cal. App. LEXIS 1198 (Cal. Ct. App. 1993).

A related issue concerns local governments requiring property owners to *dedicate* some of their land to public use, in exchange for zoning permission to build or expand on their own property. For example, if a store owner wishes to expand his store, a town might grant zoning permission only if the owner dedicates a different part of his property for use as a public bike path. The Supreme Court has recently diminished the power of local governments to require such dedication.[11]

Chapter Conclusion

Real property law is ancient but forceful, as waterfront property owners discovered when a power company flooded their land and an old-fashioned *easement* deprived them of compensation. Had the owners truly understood nonpossessory interests when they bought their property, they would have realized the risk the investment represented. Similarly, a knowledge of the various freehold estates will enable a property owner to avoid the kind of error that cost the city of Red Bluff its library building. Although real property today is not the dominant source of wealth that it was in medieval England, it is still the greatest asset that most people will ever possess—and is worth understanding.

Chapter Review

1. Real property includes land, buildings, air and subsurface rights, plant life, and fixtures. A fixture is any good that has become attached to other real property, such as land.

2. A fee simple absolute provides the owner with the greatest possible control of the property, including the right to make any lawful use of it and to sell it.

3. A fee simple defeasible may terminate upon the occurrence of some limiting event.

4. A life estate permits the owner to possess the property during her life, but not to sell it or leave it to heirs.

5. When two or more people own real property at the same time, they have a concurrent estate. In both a tenancy in common and a joint tenancy, all owners have a share in the entire property. The primary difference is that joint tenants have the right of survivorship, meaning that when a joint tenant dies, his interest passes to the other joint tenants. A tenant in common has the power to leave her estate to her heirs.

6. Tenancy by the entirety and community property are both concurrent estates available only to married couples.

7. In a condominium, the owner of an apartment generally has a fee simple absolute in the particular unit, whereas in a cooperative, a resident owns shares in a corporation and then leases his unit from the corporation.

8. Future interests are presently existing nonpossessory rights that may or may not develop later.

9. An easement gives a person the right to enter land belonging to another and make a limited use of it, without taking anything away.

10. A profit gives one person the right to enter land belonging to another and take something away, such as timber or minerals.

11. The implied warranty of habitability means that a builder selling a new home guarantees the adequacy of materials and workmanship.

12. The seller of a home must disclose facts that a buyer does not know and cannot readily observe, if they materially affect the property's value.

---

[11] The Supreme Court's ruling came in *Dolan v. City of Tigard,* 512 U.S. 374, 114 S. Ct. 2309, 1994 U.S. LEXIS 4836 (1994), which we discuss in more detail in Chapter 5, on constitutional law.

13. A general warranty deed offers the greatest protection to a buyer, a special warranty deed less protection, and a quitclaim deed very little.

14. Adverse possession permits the user of land to gain title if he can prove entry and exclusive possession, open and notorious possession, a claim adverse to the owner, and continuous possession for the required statutory period.

15. Nuisance law, zoning ordinances, and eminent domain all permit a government to regulate property and in some cases to take it for public use.

Practice Test

1. Thayer owned a farm in Illinois. For over half a century, various farmers had cut across his land to reach a second farm that had no other access to the road. Thayer never granted permission to these other farmers, but neither had he ever stopped them. In 1989, Page bought the second farm, of about 120 acres. He, too, cut across Thayer's property to reach the town road. Shortly after buying his farm, Page began to improve his access across Thayer's property. Page brought in large road-building equipment to level and solidify the road and make it safe for his heavy farm equipment. Thayer attempted to stop this work by constructing a barricade across the entrance to the disputed area. Page sued. Was he entitled to use and improve the "road" across Thayer's property?

2. Paul and Shelly Higgins had two wood stoves in their home. Each rested on, but was not attached to, a built-in brick platform. The downstairs wood stove was connected to the chimney flue and was used as part of the main heating system for the house. The upstairs stove, in the master bedroom, was purely decorative. It had no stovepipe connecting it to the chimney. The Higginses sold their house to Jack Everitt, and neither party said anything about the two stoves. Is Everitt entitled to either stove? Both stoves?

3. In 1944, W. E. Collins conveyed land to the Church of God of Prophecy. The deed said: "This deed is made with the full understanding that should the property fail to be used for the Church of God, it is to be null and void and property to revert to W. E. Collins or heirs." In the late 1980s, the church wished to move to another property and sought a judicial ruling that it had the right to sell the land. The trial court ruled that the church owned a fee simple absolute and had the right to sell the property. Comment.

4. Howard Geib, Walker McKinney, and John D. McKinney owned two vacation properties as joint tenants with right of survivorship. The parties were not getting along well, and Geib petitioned the court to partition the properties. The trial court ruled that the fairest way to do this was to sell both properties and divide the proceeds. The two McKinneys appealed, claiming that a partition by sale was improper because it would destroy their right of survivorship. Comment.

5. Summey Building Systems built a condominium project in Myrtle Beach, South Carolina. The project included an adjacent parking deck. Shortly after Summey relinquished control to the condominium association, the deck began to experience problems. Water and caustic materials leaked through the upper deck and dripped onto cars parked underneath. Cracks appeared, and an expert concluded that the bond between the top deck and the structural supports was insufficient. Repairs would cost about $205,000. Summey had never warranted that the deck would be free of all problems. Is the company liable for the repairs?

6. Mark Wasser negotiated to purchase a 67-year-old apartment building from Michael and Anna Sasoni. The Sasonis told Wasser that the building was "a very good building" and "an excellent deal." The contract stated that the Wassers took the building "as is" and that there were no express or implied warranties or representations. After Wasser took over the building, he discovered that it needed major structural repairs. He sued the Sasonis, claiming that they had failed to disclose defects. Who wins? (Slow down before answering.)

7. Nome 2000, a partnership, owned a large tract of wilderness land in Alaska. The Fagerstrom family had used the property for camping and holidays since about 1944. In 1966, Charles and

Peggy Fagerstrom marked off an area for a cabin and brought material to build the cabin, but never did so. In about 1970, they built a picnic area on the land, and in about 1974, they placed a camper trailer on the land, where it remained until the lawsuit. In 1987, Nome 2000 sued to eject the Fagerstroms from the land. The Fagerstroms had used the land only during the summer months. No one lived in the area during the winter months, when it was virtually uninhabitable. Who wins Nome's suit?

8. *YOU BE THE JUDGE* WRITING PROBLEM Frank Deluca and his son David owned the Sportsman's Pub on Fountain Street in Providence, Rhode Island. The Delucas applied to the city for a license to employ topless dancers in the pub. Did the city have the power to deny the Delucas' request? **Argument for the Delucas:** Our pub is perfectly legal. Further, no law in Rhode Island prohibits topless dancing. We are morally and legally entitled to present this entertainment. The city should not use some phony moralizing to deny customers what they want. **Argument for Providence:** This section of Providence is zoned to prohibit topless dancing, just as it is zoned to bar manufacturing. There are other parts of town where the Delucas can open one of their sleazy clubs if they want to, but we are entitled to deny a permit in this area.

9. *CPA QUESTION* On July 1, 1992, Quick, Onyx, and Nash were deeded a piece of land as tenants in common. The deed provided that Quick owned one-half the property and Onyx and Nash owned one-quarter each. If Nash dies, the property will be owned as follows:

   a. Quick ½, Onyx ½.

   b. Quick ⅝, Onyx ⅜.

   c. Quick ⅓, Onyx ⅓, Nash's heirs ⅓.

   d. Quick ½, Onyx ¼, Nash's heirs ¼.

10. *ETHICS* In 1966, Arketex Ceramic Corp. sold land in rural Indiana to Malcolm Aukerman. The deed described the southern boundary as the section line between sections 11 and 14 of the land. Further south than this section line stood a dilapidated fence running east to west. Aukerman and Arketex both believed that this fence was the actual southern boundary of his new land, though in fact it lay on Arketex's property.

    Aukerman installed a new electrified fence, cleared the land on "his" side of the new fence, and began to graze cattle there. In 1974, Harold Clark bought the land that bordered Aukerman's fence, assuming that the fence was the correct boundary. In 1989, Clark had his land surveyed and discovered that the true property line lay north of the electric fence. Aukerman filed suit, seeking a court order that he had acquired the disputed land by adverse possession. The statutory period in Indiana is 20 years. Who wins? Who *ought* to win? Does adverse possession make sense as a social policy? Why or why not?

11. *CPA QUESTION* Which of the following deeds will give a real property purchaser the greatest protection?

    a. Quitclaim

    b. Bargain and sale

    c. Special warranty

    d. General warranty

12. *ROLE REVERSAL* Write a short-answer question focusing on one of these issues: a fixture, an easement, or adverse possession.

Internet Research Problem

Your sister Samantha owns a Montana ranch. For years, she and a neighbor have disputed ownership of 200 valuable acres. Samantha, exhausted, refuses to litigate, but you are willing to fight it out with her neighbor because the land is so valuable. How might a quitclaim deed be useful? Examine such a document at http://beatty.westbuslaw.com. Then draft an agreement between you and Samantha concerning the land.

You can find further practice problems at http://beatty.westbuslaw.com or in the Study Guide that accompanies this text.

Landlord-Tenant

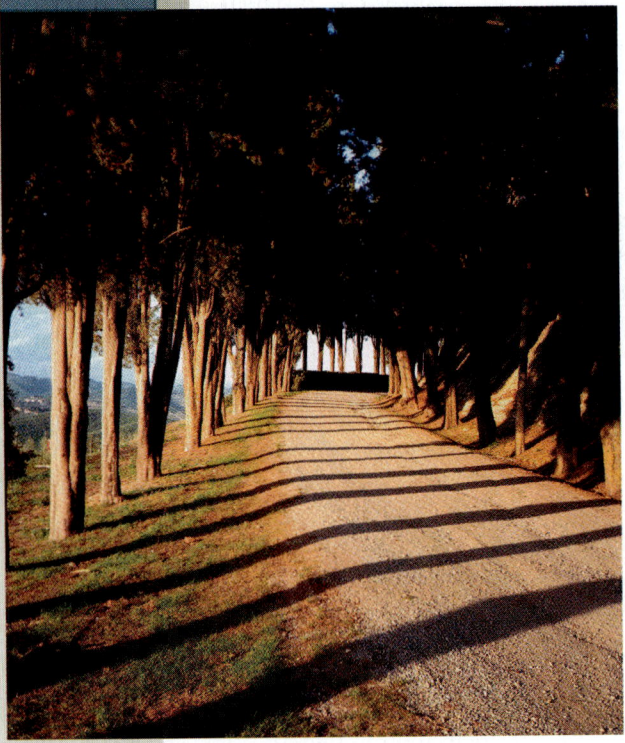

O n a January morning in Studio City, California, Alpha Donchin took her small Shih Tzu dog for a walk. Suddenly, less than a block from her house, two large rottweilers attacked Donchin and her pet. The heavy animals mauled the 14-pound Shih Tzu, and when Donchin picked her dog up, the rottweilers knocked her down, breaking her hip and causing other serious injuries.

Ubaldo Guerrero, who lived in a rented house nearby, owned the two rottweilers, and Donchin sued him. But she also sued Guerrero's landlord, David Swift, who lived four blocks away from the rental property. Donchin claimed that the landlord was liable for her injuries, because he knew of the dogs' vicious nature and permitted them to escape from the property he rented to Guerrero. Should the landlord be liable for injuries caused by his tenant's dogs?

As is typical of many landlord-tenant issues, the law in this area is in flux. Under the common law, a landlord had no liability for injuries caused by animals belonging to a tenant, and many states adhere to that rule. But some states are expanding the landlord's liability for injuries caused on or near his property. The California court ruled that Donchin *could* maintain her suit against Swift.

If Donchin could prove that Swift knew the dogs were dangerous and allowed them to escape through a defective fence, the landlord would be liable for her injuries.[1] ■

One reason for the erratic evolution of landlord-tenant law is that it is really a combination of three venerable areas of law: property, contract, and negligence. The confluence of these legal theories produces results that are unpredictable but interesting and important. (To survey a variety of articles and laws in this rapidly evolving area, visit **http://www.law.cornell.edu/topics/landlord_tenant.html**.) We begin our examination of landlord-tenant law with an analysis of the different types of tenancy.

A freehold estate is the right to possess real property and use it in any lawful manner. What we think of as "owning" land is in fact a freehold estate. **When an owner of a freehold estate allows another person temporary, exclusive possession of the property, the parties have created a landlord-tenant relationship.** The freehold owner is the **landlord,** and the person allowed to possess the property is the **tenant.** The landlord has conveyed a **leasehold** interest to the tenant, meaning the right to temporary possession. Courts also use the word **"tenancy"** to describe the tenant's right to possession.

A leasehold may be commercial or residential. In a commercial tenancy, the owner of a building may rent retail space to a merchant, offices to a business, or industrial space to a manufacturer. When someone rents an apartment or house, he has a residential leasehold.

Three Legal Areas Combined

Property law influences landlord-tenant cases because the landlord is conveying rights in real property to the tenant. She is also keeping a **reversionary interest** in the property, meaning the right to possess the property when the lease ends. Contract law plays a role because the basic agreement between the landlord and tenant is a contract. **A lease is a contract that creates a landlord-tenant relationship.** And negligence law increasingly determines the liability of landlord and tenant when there is an injury to a person or property. Many states have combined these three legal issues into landlord-tenant statutes; you can see a typical statute by going to **http://www.law.cornell.edu/topics/landlord_tenant.html** and, under "State Material," finding the link to the uniform residential landlord-tenant act.

Notice the difference between a leasehold and a **license,** which is discussed in Chapter 44, on real property. A licensor, such as the owner of a football stadium, licenses patrons to enter the premises (the stadium) for a limited period, such as for one football game. But the licensor retains possession and control of the property, and the licensee (the patron) shares his right with thousands of others. A landlord, by contrast, gives up possession of the premises to the tenant and may regain possession only when the lease has terminated. The tenant has exclusive possession during the tenancy.

Lease

The statute of frauds generally requires that a lease be in writing. Some states will enforce an oral lease if it is for a short term, such as one year or less, but even when an oral lease is permitted, it is wiser for the parties to put their agreement in

---

[1]   *Donchin v. Guerrero,* 34 Cal. App. 4th 1832, 1995 Cal. App. LEXIS 462 (Cal. Ct. App. 1995).

writing, because a written lease avoids many misunderstandings. At a minimum, a lease must state the names of the parties, the premises being leased, the duration of the agreement, and the rent. But a well-drafted lease generally includes many provisions, called covenants. A **covenant** is simply a promise by either the landlord or the tenant to do something or refrain from doing something. For example, most leases include a covenant concerning the tenant's payment of a security deposit and the landlord's return of the deposit, a covenant describing how the tenant may use the premises, and several covenants about who must maintain and repair the property, who is liable for damage, and so forth. The parties should also agree about how the lease may be terminated and whether the parties have the right to renew it.

In a residential lease, the landlord generally presents the tenant with a form lease, and the tenant has little opportunity or power to negotiate the terms. This does not mean that the tenant is powerless. If the terms of a lease are too one-sided, a court may refuse to enforce them. We will look later, for example, at exculpatory clauses in leases and see that they are often void. In a commercial lease, both parties generally have the opportunity to negotiate terms that provide adequate protection.

TYPES OF TENANCY

There are four types of tenancy: a tenancy for years, a periodic tenancy, a tenancy at will, and a tenancy at sufferance. The most important feature distinguishing one from the other is how each tenancy terminates. In some cases, a tenancy terminates automatically, while in others, one party must take certain steps to end the agreement.

Tenancy for Years

Any lease for a stated, fixed period is a tenancy for years. If a landlord rents a summer apartment for the months of June, July, and August of next year, that is a tenancy for years. A company that rents retail space in a mall beginning January 1, 2006, and ending December 31, 2009, also has a tenancy for years. A tenancy for years terminates automatically when the agreed period ends.

Periodic Tenancy

A periodic tenancy is created for a fixed period and then automatically continues for additional periods until either party notifies the other of termination. This is probably the most common variety of tenancy, and the parties may create one in either of two ways. Suppose a landlord agrees to rent you an apartment "from month to month, rent payable on the first." That is a periodic tenancy. The tenancy automatically renews itself every month, unless either party gives adequate notice to the other that she wishes to terminate. A periodic tenancy could also be for one-year periods—in which case it automatically renews for an additional year if neither party terminates— or for any other period.

The parties also create a periodic tenancy if, when a *tenancy for years* expires, the tenant continues to pay rent and the landlord accepts it. Ariadne agrees to rent property called Naxos for three years, with rent payable once per month. When the three years are up, the tenancy for years expires automatically. Ariadne continues to pay the monthly rent, however, and the landlord accepts her checks. The parties have created a periodic tenancy.

What is the period? If the tenant is renting *commercial property*, the new periodic tenancy is for the same period as the old tenancy for years, up to a maximum of one year. In other words, if Naxos is an office building, Ariadne's new periodic tenancy is for one year (since her original lease was for more than a year). Once the landlord accepts a single monthly rental check, both he and Ariadne are bound for the full year. In many states, if the property is *residential*, the new periodic tenancy is month-to-month. If Naxos is a vacation house, either party can end the lease with 30 days' notice. A landlord's notice terminating a tenancy is often called a **notice to quit.**

Tenancy at Will

A tenancy at will has no fixed duration and may be terminated by either party at any time. Tenancies at will are unusual tenancies.[2] Typically, the agreement is vague, with no specified rental period and with payment, perhaps, to be made in kind. The parties might agree, for example, that a tenant farmer could use a portion of his crop as rent. Since either party can end the agreement at any time, it provides no security for either landlord or tenant.

Tenancy at Sufferance

A tenancy at sufferance occurs when a tenant remains on the premises, against the wishes of the landlord, after the expiration of a true tenancy. Thus a tenancy at sufferance is not a true tenancy because the tenant is staying without the landlord's agreement. The landlord has the option of seeking to evict the tenant or of forcing the tenant to pay rent for a new rental period. The following case illustrates the difference between two types of tenancy, and the importance of that distinction to an owner attempting to gain control of its property.

CITY OF NEW YORK V. UTSEY

185 Misc. 2d 715, 714 N.Y.S.2d 410
Supreme Court of New York, Appellate Term, 2000

Facts: The city of New York (City) took legal title to an abandoned house in Brooklyn, but the building became a haven for drug dealers. Thelma Utsey then took charge. She and her three adult children and one grandchild cleaned the house and installed pipes, plumbing, wiring, new flooring, and a new roof at the cost of thousands of dollars and countless hours of hard work. Two years later, claiming that the Utseys were squatters who had no legal right to occupy the house, the City began eviction proceedings. The City planned to develop the area as part of an urban renewal project. However, when funding collapsed the government abandoned its effort to evict the Utseys. Believing that they had the City's permission to remain, the family installed aluminum siding, new windows, and a stairway and made other major improvements.

About six years later, planning another large redevelopment effort, the City again began squatter proceedings against the Utseys by serving a 10-day notice to quit. The trial court granted summary judgment for the City. The Utseys appealed, claiming that they were tenants at will entitled to a *30-day* notice to quit before eviction proceedings could begin.

▼

---

[2] The courts of some states, annoyingly, use the term "tenancy at will" for what are, in reality, periodic tenancies. They do this to bewilder law students and even lawyers, a goal at which they are quite successful. This text uses tenancy at will in its more widely known sense, meaning a tenancy terminable at any time.

Issue: **Were the occupants tenants at will, entitled to a 30-day notice to quit before eviction?**

Excerpts from the Court's Memorandum Decision: Occupants indicated that they remain committed to purchasing the home from the City. Citing [an earlier case called *Walls v. Giuliani*], occupants claimed that by virtue of the City's inaction for seven years they became tenants at sufferance or at will.

The Housing Court granted the City's motion for summary judgment, reasoning that contrary to the holding in *Walls*, a tenancy at sufferance arises only when one holds over after the termination of a lawful tenancy. An estate at sufferance is an interest in land which exists when a person who had a possessory interest in land by virtue of an effective conveyance wrongfully continues in possession of the land after the termination of said interest. It is essential to the creation of this interest that the party previously have had a possessory interest. As the Housing Court correctly held, the occupancy by a trespasser who never had such a possessory interest cannot ripen into a tenancy at sufferance.

However, an occupancy by a squatter or trespasser can ripen into a tenancy at will as, for instance, where there is an express agreement of the parties or an acceptance of rent. A tenancy at will may also arise by implication, and an obligation to pay rent is not a necessary incident of such a tenancy. The Court of Appeals has stated that an owner's acquiescence in a continued occupancy (where the occupancy is subordinate to the title of the owner) may, where the facts so warrant, justify an inference that a tenancy at will has been created.

In *Walls*, the squatters' occupancy was adverse to the City's title, and the squatters were claiming title by adverse possession. In contrast, the occupancy here was at all relevant times subordinate to the interest of the City since the occupants had acknowledged the City's title.

The record shows, contrary to the findings of the Housing Court, that the City, after bringing the unsuccessful squatter proceeding, made a conscious decision to allow occupants to remain in the premises for an indefinite term because the funding to proceed with the urban renewal project was not available. At the time the City made this decision, it was already clear from the preceding litigations and from occupants' submission to the City of the receipts and of the engineering report, that occupants were not claiming title and that they were interested in working with the City to purchase the property from it. The City was also aware of the substantial improvements that occupants had made and were continuing to make to the premises and of their stabilizing influence upon the neighborhood. Under these circumstances, we hold that they remained in occupancy as tenants at will. Based upon the City's failure to serve a 30-day notice the petition must be dismissed. ∎

LANDLORD'S DUTIES

Duty to Deliver Possession

The landlord's first important duty is to deliver possession of the premises at the beginning of the tenancy, that is, to make the rented space available to the tenant. In most cases this presents no problems and the new tenant moves in. But what happens if the previous tenant has refused to leave when the new tenancy begins?

The **"English rule"** obligates the landlord to remove the previous tenant in time for the new tenant to take possession. The majority of American states enforce this rule. If the old tenant is still in possession when the new tenant arrives, the landlord has breached the lease. The new tenant has two alternative remedies. She may terminate the lease and sue the landlord for costs she incurs obtaining other accommodations. Or she may affirm the lease, refuse to pay rent for the period in which she cannot take possession, sue for the cost of other accommodations, and then take possession when the old tenant is finally evicted.

The **"American rule"** is more favorable to the landlord. (Although called the American rule, this is in fact the minority rule in this country—anything to keep you off balance.) This rule holds that the landlord has no duty to deliver actual possession of the premises. If the previous tenant remains in possession, the landlord has not breached the lease. Under this rule, the new tenant generally has the power to act as a landlord toward the old tenant. The new tenant may evict the old tenant and recover damages caused by her delay in leaving. Alternatively, the new tenant may treat the holdover as a tenant at will for a new rental period and may charge the normal rent for that period.

Quiet Enjoyment

All tenants are entitled to quiet enjoyment of the premises, meaning the right to use the property without the interference of the landlord. Most leases expressly state this covenant of quiet enjoyment. And if a lease includes no such covenant, the law implies the right of quiet enjoyment anyway, so all tenants are protected. If a landlord interferes with the tenant's quiet enjoyment, he has breached the lease, entitling the tenant to damages.

The most common interference with quiet enjoyment is an **eviction,** meaning some act that forces the tenant to abandon the premises. Of course, some evictions are legal, as when a tenant fails to pay the rent. But some evictions are illegal. There are two types of eviction: actual and constructive.

Actual Eviction

If a landlord prevents the tenant from possessing the premises, he has actually evicted her. Suppose a landlord decides that a group of students are "troublemakers." Without going through lawful eviction procedures in court, the landlord simply waits until the students are out of the apartment and changes all the locks. By denying the students access to the premises, the landlord has actually evicted them and has breached their right of quiet enjoyment. He is liable for all expenses they suffer, such as retrieving their possessions, the cost of alternate housing, and moving expenses. In some states he may be liable for punitive damages for failing to go through proper eviction procedures.

Even a partial eviction is an interference with quiet enjoyment. Suppose Louise rents an apartment with a storage room. If the landlord places his own goods in the storage room, he has partially evicted Louise because a tenant is entitled to the *exclusive* possession of the premises. In all states Louise would be allowed to deduct from her rent the value of the storage space, and in many states she would not be obligated to pay any rent for the apartment as long as the landlord continued the partial eviction.

Constructive Eviction

If a landlord substantially interferes with the tenant's use and enjoyment of the premises, he has constructively evicted her. Courts construe certain behavior as the equivalent of an eviction. In these cases, the landlord has not actually prevented the tenant from *possessing* the premises, but has instead interfered so greatly with her *use and enjoyment* that the law regards the landlord's actions as equivalent to an eviction. Suppose the

If conditions are intolerable, the landlord has constructively evicted the tenant.

heating system in an apartment house in Juneau, Alaska, fails during January. The landlord, an avid sled dog racer, tells the tenants he is too busy to fix the problem. If the tenants move out, the landlord has constructively evicted them and is liable for all expenses they suffer.

To claim a constructive eviction, the tenant must vacate the premises. The tenant must also prove that the interference was sufficiently serious and lasted long enough that she was forced to move out. A lack of hot water for two days is not fatal, but lack of any water for two weeks creates a constructive eviction.

Other Interference

A landlord's conduct may interfere with quiet enjoyment even when it is not so harmful as to force a constructive eviction. Suppose a landlord, living in the ground floor unit, gives trumpet lessons in his apartment six nights a week until 1:00 A.M., producing such a cacophony that a group of students, living upstairs, can neither study nor sleep. If the students continue to live in the apartment, because they cannot afford a better place, there has been no constructive eviction. But the landlord's conduct interferes with the tenants' quiet enjoyment, and the students are entitled to damages.

Duty to Maintain Premises

Historically, the common law placed no burden on the landlord to repair and maintain the premises. This made sense because rental property had traditionally been farmland. Buildings, such as a house or barn, were far less important than the land itself, and no one expected the landlord to fix a leaking roof. Today, the vast majority of rental property is used for housing or business purposes. Space in a building is frequently all that a tenant is renting, and the condition of the building is of paramount importance. Most states have changed the common law rule and placed various obligations on the landlord to maintain the property.

In most states, a landlord has a duty to deliver the premises in a habitable condition and a continuing duty to maintain the habitable condition. This duty overlaps with the quiet enjoyment obligation, but it is not identical. The tenant's right to quiet enjoyment focuses primarily on the tenant's *ability to use* the rented property. The landlord's duty to maintain the property focuses on whether the property *meets a particular legal standard.* The required standard may be stated in the lease, created by a state statute, or implied by law.

Lease

The lease itself generally obligates the landlord to maintain the exterior of any buildings and the common areas. If a lease does not do so, state law may imply the obligation.

Building Codes

Many state and local governments have passed building codes, which mandate minimum standards for commercial and/or residential property. The codes are likely to be stricter for residential property and may demand such things as minimum room size, sufficient hot water, secure locks, proper working kitchens and bathrooms, absence of insects and rodents, and other basics of decent housing. Generally,

© GETTY IMAGES

A landlord's duty to maintain the premises may be stated in the lease, created by statute, or implied by law.

all rental property must comply with the building code, whether the lease mentions the code or not.

Implied Warranty of Habitability

Students Maria Ivanow, Thomas Tecza, and Kenneth Gearin rented a house from Les and Martha Vanlandingham. The monthly rent was $900. But the roommates failed to pay any rent for the final five months of the tenancy. After they moved out, the Vanlandinghams sued. How much did the landlords recover? Nothing. The landlords had breached the implied warranty of habitability.

The implied warranty of habitability requires that a landlord meet all standards set by the local building code, or that the premises be fit for human habitation. Most states, though not all, *imply* this warranty of habitability, meaning that the landlord must meet this standard whether the lease includes it or not. In some states, the implied warranty means that the premises must at least satisfy the local building code. Other states require property that is "fit for human habitation," which means that a landlord might comply with the building code yet still fail the implied warranty of habitability, if the rental property is unfit to live in.

The Vanlandinghams breached the implied warranty. The students had complained repeatedly about a variety of problems. The washer and dryer, which were included in the lease, frequently failed. A severe roof leak caused water damage in one of the bedrooms. Defective pipes flooded the bathroom. The refrigerator frequently malfunctioned, and the roommates repaired it several times. The basement often flooded, and when it was dry, rats and opossums lived in it. The heat sometimes failed.

In warranty of habitability cases, a court normally considers the severity of the problems and their duration. If the defective conditions seriously interfere with the tenancy, the court declares the implied warranty breached and orders a **rent abatement,** that is, a reduction in the rent owed. The longer the defects continued and the greater their severity, the more the rent is abated. In the case of Maria Ivanow and friends, the court abated the rent 50 percent. The students had already paid more than the abated rent to the landlord, so they owed nothing for the last five months.[3]

Tenant Remedies for Defective Conditions

The students in the above case demonstrated one remedy often available to a tenant whose landlord has breached the warranty of habitability. Not all states permit rent abatement, but the majority do. Other states allow alternative, or additional, remedies for defective conditions. A tenant must check the law of his state before using any of the remedies discussed. For tenant rights in your state, go to **www.worldtenant.com** and click on your state. For a useful series of form letters concerning defective conditions, problems with neighbors, interference with quiet enjoyment, and other common tenant concerns, go to **www.tenantsunion.org**.

Rent Withholding. Many states allow a tenant to withhold rent, representing the decreased value of the premises. The tenant must first notify the landlord of the problems and allow her a reasonable period to make repairs. If she fails to remedy the problem, the tenant may then withhold a portion of the rent, while continuing to live in the premises. The tenant should withhold a portion of the rent that approximates the seriousness of the defective conditions. A wise tenant saves the withheld rent, in case a

---

[3] *Vanlandingham v. Ivanow,* 246 Ill. App. 3d 348, 615 N.E.2d 1361, 1993 Ill. App. LEXIS 985 (Ill. Ct. App. 1993).

court later orders part or all of it paid to the landlord. In a *rent strike*, a group of tenants in the same building refuses to pay their landlord because of uniformly deplorable conditions. By acting collectively, the tenants may wield greater power against an abusive landlord than they could individually.

Repair and Deduct. In some states, if a tenant notifies the landlord of a serious defect and the landlord fails to remedy the problem, the tenant may deduct a reasonable amount of money from the rental payment and have the repair made himself. States that allow this remedy place a maximum figure on the amount of money a tenant may deduct, such as one or two months' rent.

Suit for Damages. A landlord who refuses to repair significant defects is breaching the lease and/or state law, and the tenant may simply sue for damages. Often, though, rent withholding is a more effective way to force repairs, since the landlord may respond more quickly when the money stops flowing.

Duty to Return Security Deposit

Most landlords require tenants to pay a security deposit, in case the tenant damages the premises. In many states, a landlord must either return the security deposit soon after the tenant has moved out or notify the tenant of the damage and the cost of the repairs. In addition, landlords are often obligated to credit tenants with interest earned on the deposit. In many states a landlord who fails to return the deposit in a timely fashion can be forced to pay double or even triple damages to the tenant, a question raised in the following dispute.

MISHKIN V. YOUNG

____ P.3d ____, 2005 WL 452168
Supreme Court of Colorado

Facts: A Colorado statute required a landlord either to return a security deposit or provide an accounting of why money was being withheld. The landlord had to do this within one month of the tenant's surrender of the property, or up to 60 days if the lease permitted. If the landlord failed to refund the money, the tenant, after giving seven days' notice, could sue for treble damages. The landlord could avoid the treble damages by refunding the deposit within those seven days.

Marc Mishkin leased an apartment from Dean Young, paying a security deposit of $1,625. The lease stated that the deposit would be returned no later than 45 days after the tenant moved out. After Mishkin left, Young did not return the money. Forty-eight days after leaving, Mishkin sent a demand for the deposit, notifying Young that in seven days he would sue for treble damages. Six days later, Young gave Mishkin a statement detailing $1,574.60 worth of property damage, along with a check for $50.40.

Mishkin sued. The trial court ruled that Young was entitled to withhold the money because of the damages. Mishkin appealed. The appellate court ruled that the Colorado statute required the landlord to return the full security deposit within the seven day period. Young appealed.

Issue: May a landlord avoid the treble damages by accounting for the security deposit within seven days of the tenant's notice to sue?

Excerpts from Justice Kourlis's Decision: [Earlier] cases implicitly indicate that a landlord's failure to account for a security deposit as required by subsection (1) [of the statute] constitutes a forfeiture of all rights to withhold any portion of the deposit and subjects the landlord to treble damages. A landlord may avoid treble damages only by returning the entire security deposit during the seven days following a tenant's demand notice. An accounting during this seven-day period does not protect a landlord

▼

from treble damages because this period is beyond the statutory deadline of subsection (1) and the landlord has already forfeited all rights to retain the deposit. The purpose of the seven-day notice provision is to give landlords one last week to avoid treble damages by returning the security deposit. It does not give landlords a second chance to account for the deposit. The money actually belongs to the tenant; it was only security for the landlord, who has by unilateral action forfeited all right to retain any of it. Therefore, we now make explicit what has been implicit in our prior rulings: We hold that a landlord may not avoid treble damages by accounting for a security deposit during the seven-day period following a tenant's demand notice.

Contrary to the landlord's contention, our interpretation does not render the remaining provisions of the Act meaningless. Subsection (2) [which states that the landlord forfeits the entire deposit if he fails to return the money or account for it within the statutory period] performs a critical function by encouraging most landlords to expeditiously account for their tenants' security deposits. Yet the case may arise where a landlord finds forfeiture an insufficient inducement to account for the withholding of a tenant's security deposit. In such situations, the prospect of treble damages provided for by subsection (3) proves instrumental. Not only do treble damages act as a formidable deterrent to landlords who might otherwise wrongfully withhold a tenant's security deposit, but they also give tenants an enticing legal remedy where the alternative is to forgo a relatively small but often vital sum of money.

[Affirmed.] ■

Public Policy

The typical remedy in a contract dispute is to restore the injured plaintiff to the position he would have been in had both sides performed, but not to make the plaintiff better off than he would have been had the defendant kept her side of the bargain. Yet in *Mishkin,* the court permits a tenant to profit from the landlord's breach of contract. Why? Is that the right result? ◆

Final Word on Security Deposits

The discussion and case both concerned residential leases, where security deposits are almost inevitable. Note that, in a commercial lease, the tenant may have less statutory protection but more bargaining power. A financially sound company might negotiate a lease with no security deposit or perhaps offer a letter of credit for security, instead of cash. The interest saved over several years could be substantial.

Your authors are always grateful when a litigant volunteers to illustrate half a dozen legal issues in one lawsuit. The landlord in the following case demonstrates problems of quiet enjoyment, constructive eviction, implied warranty, and . . . well, see how many you can count.

HARRIS V. SOLEY

2000 Me. 150, 756 A.2d 499
Supreme Judicial Court of Maine, 2000

Facts: Here is an apartment adventure that begins as a horror story but ends happily. The court will tell you what happened.

Issue: Are the tenants entitled to such large damages?

Excerpts from Justice Saufley's Decision: Near Labor Day, Andrea Harris, Kimberly Nightingale, Karen Simard, and Michelle Dussault moved into a large apartment that was located in the Old Port area of Portland and owned by Joseph Soley. Soley had promised the tenants that the apartment, which had previously been condemned by the City of

▼

Portland, would be repaired by the time they moved in. When they arrived, the condemnation notice was still on the door. Upon entering the apartment, they found it in an uninhabitable condition. They spoke to Soley's property manager who indicated that if the tenants were willing to clean the apartment themselves, she would credit them with $750 of their $1000 monthly rent for the month of September. They rented a steam cleaner, bought various cleaning supplies, and cleaned the apartment themselves. Soley's property manager also suggested that they buy a new refrigerator and deduct it from the rent because the one in the apartment did not work.

Despite their efforts to clean the apartment, the tenants continued to have problems with infestations of mice and cockroaches, as well as a persistent odor of cat urine. A dead cat was eventually found beneath the floorboards. The apartment had no heat during the month of October. One tenant slept with blankets over her head, not only because of the cold, but also to keep bugs away from her. These problems persisted into November, and the tenants submitted to Soley a list of complaints including a broken skylight, a broken toilet, a broken garbage disposal, a leaking roof, and cockroach infestation. As winter arrived, snow would fall into the living room through the broken skylight. When Soley did not make the needed repairs, the tenants stopped paying rent. Soley telephoned them on several occasions regarding the rent and spoke to the tenants in a rude and abrasive manner. In February, the property manager told the tenants that Soley had begun eviction proceedings against them.

The tenants eventually found another place to live and had begun moving [when] Soley's agents broke into the apartment and took many of the tenants' remaining belongings. Upon confrontation with the returning tenants and police officers who had been called to the scene, Soley's agents indicated that Soley had directed their actions. Eventually, the officers and one of the tenants went to an apartment nearby and recovered some, but not all, of the missing property.

The tenants then sought out Soley to request that he return their remaining possessions. They located him at his restaurant, the Seamen's Club. According to one of the tenants, he replied that he would return their property only after they paid him $3000. He then ordered them to leave and threatened to call the police and have them forcibly removed. Soley told the tenants that he knew where they were moving and where their families lived, a statement that the tenants took as a threat.

The tenants brought suit against the defendants in a complaint that included claims for conversion [the wrongful taking of property], intentional infliction of emotional distress, punitive damages, breach of contract, wrongful eviction, and wrongful retention of a security deposit. [For months, Soley refused to respond to discovery requests and finally the trial court gave a default judgment for the plaintiffs. The judge instructed the jury that all of the plaintiffs' allegations were deemed true, and that their job was simply to award damages.]

The jury awarded each of the tenants $15,000 as damages for emotional distress. The defendants argue that the evidence does not support an award to each of the tenants in identical amounts. In addition, Soley relies on the fact that the awards are identical to support a claim that the awards are the result of passion and prejudice.

Contrary to Soley's argument, the jury was not required to find that each of the tenants suffered identical emotional distress in order to award the same amount of damages to each; rather, the jury need only have found that the emotional distress suffered by each, regardless of the nature of that distress, warranted comparable monetary compensation. The evidence introduced at trial, including evidence of Soley's conduct and the tenants' testimony regarding their emotional responses, could support a determination that the tenants suffered comparable emotional distress.

Finally, Soley challenges the award of $1 million in punitive damages as excessive. Again, we begin with the facts of the complaint as conclusively established by the default judgment. Among other things, those facts included the following:

Plaintiffs were shaken up, infuriated, violated, intimidated and in fear for their physical safety. . . . The conduct of Defendants, and each of them, was so extreme and outrageous as to exceed all possible bounds of decency. . . . Defendants acted intentionally, knowingly, willfully, wantonly and with malice.

There can be no question that the jury was justified in deciding that an award of punitive damages was warranted. The tenants had to endure the presence of insect and rodent infestations, dead animals, snow falling into the apartment, and a total lack of response from their landlord after repeated complaints. Soley's continued refusal to repair conditions that rendered the apartment unfit for human occu-

▼

pation, the violent removal of tenants' property before eviction proceedings had proceeded, the retention of property belonging to the tenants, the destruction of their property, and his threatening behavior combined to create a pattern of conduct that must be considered intolerable.

Judgment affirmed. ■

TENANT'S DUTIES

Duty to Pay Rent

My landlord said he's gonna raise the rent. "Good," I said, " 'cause I can't raise it."

Slappy White, comedian, 1921–1995

Rent is the compensation the tenant pays the landlord for use of the premises, and paying the rent, despite Mr. White's wistful hope, is the tenant's foremost obligation. The lease normally specifies the amount of rent and when it must be paid. Typically, the landlord requires that rent be paid at the beginning of each rental period, whether that is monthly, annually, or otherwise.

Both parties must be certain they understand whether the rent includes utilities such as heat and hot water. Some states mandate that the landlord pay certain utilities, such as water. Many leases include an **escalator clause,** permitting the landlord to raise the rent during the course of the lease if his expenses increase for specified reasons. For example, a tax escalator clause allows the landlord to raise the rent if his real estate taxes go up. Any escalator clause should state the percentage of the increase that the landlord may pass on to the tenant.

Landlord's Remedies for Nonpayment of Rent

If the tenant fails to pay rent on time, the landlord has several remedies. She is entitled to apply the security deposit to the unpaid rent. She may also sue the tenant for nonpayment of rent, demanding the unpaid sums, cost of collection, and interest. Finally, the landlord may evict a tenant who has failed to pay rent.

State statutes prescribe the steps a landlord must take to evict a tenant for nonpayment. Typically, the landlord must serve a termination notice on the tenant and wait for a court hearing. At the hearing the landlord must prove that the tenant has failed to pay rent on time. If the tenant has no excuse for the nonpayment, the court grants an order evicting him. The order authorizes a sheriff to remove the tenant's goods and place them in storage, at the tenant's expense. However, if the tenant was withholding rent because of unlivable conditions, the court may refuse to evict.

Duty to Mitigate

Pickwick & Perkins, Ltd., was a store in the Burlington Square Mall in Burlington, Vermont. Pickwick had a five-year lease, but abandoned the space almost two years early and ceased paying rent. The landlord waited approximately eight months before renting the space to a new tenant and then sued, seeking the unpaid rent. Pickwick defended on the grounds that Burlington had failed to **mitigate damages,** that is, to keep its losses to a minimum by promptly seeking another tenant. Burlington argued that it had no legal obligation to mitigate. Burlington's position accurately reflected the common law rule, which permitted the landlord to let the property lie vacant and allow the damages to add up. But the common law evolves over time, and this time the Vermont Supreme Court changed the rule. The judges pointed out that, historically, a lease was a conveyance of an estate, and property law had never required mitigation. However, the court asserted, a lease is now regarded as both a contract and a conveyance. Under contract law, the nonbreaching party must make a reasonable effort to minimize losses, and that same rule applies, said the court, to a landlord. Burlington lost. The Vermont ruling is typical of current decisions, although some courts still do not require mitigation.[4]

Duty to Use Premises for Proper Purpose

A lease normally lists what a tenant may do in the premises and prohibits other activities. For example, a residential lease allows the tenant to use the property for normal living purposes, but not for any retail, commercial, or industrial purpose. A commercial lease might allow a tenant to operate a retail clothing store, but not a restaurant. A landlord may evict a tenant who violates the lease by using the premises for prohibited purposes.

A tenant may not use the premises for any illegal activity, such as gambling or selling drugs. The law itself implies this condition in every lease, so a tenant who engages in illegal acts on the leased property is subject to eviction, regardless of whether the lease mentions such conduct.

Duty Not to Damage Premises

A tenant is liable to the landlord for any significant damage he causes to the property. The tenant is not liable for normal wear and tear. If, however, he knocks a hole in a wall or damages the plumbing, the landlord may collect the cost of repairs, either by using the security deposit or by suing, if necessary. A landlord may also seek to evict a tenant for serious damage to the property.

A tenant is permitted to make reasonable changes in the leased property so that he can use it as intended. Someone leasing an apartment is permitted to hang pictures on the wall. But a tenant leasing commercial space should make certain that the lease specifies the alterations he can make and whether he is obligated to return the premises to their original condition at the end of the lease.

Recall from Chapter 44 that a **fixture** is an item of personal property that is permanently attached to real estate. A furnace is a fixture, as are custom cabinets installed in a kitchen. The common law rule held that all fixtures belonged to the landlord. The contemporary trend, though, is the opposite. In commercial leases, it is common for tenants to install expensive equipment as part of their business, for example, commercial ovens in a restaurant. These are called **trade fixtures.** Most states permit commercial tenants to remove trade fixtures, provided the tenant restores the property to its original condition. In residential leases, some states still prohibit the tenant from removing a fixture, but courts today are likelier to permit removal, provided the tenant does not harm the premises in the process.

Duty Not to Disturb Other Tenants

Most leases, commercial and residential, include a covenant that the tenant will not disturb other tenants in the building. A landlord may evict a tenant who unreasonably disturbs others. The test is *reasonableness.* A landlord does not have the right to evict a

---

[4]   *O'Brien v. Black,* 162 Vt. 448, 648 A.2d 1374, 1994 Vt. LEXIS 89 (1994).

residential tenant for giving one loud party but may evict a tenant who repeatedly plays loud music late at night and disturbs the quiet enjoyment of other tenants.

at RISK | Landlords not only have the *right* to evict tenants who seriously disturb others, they may have the *duty* as well. Carmen Burgos lived in an apartment in the Queens borough of New York City, with her elderly mother and two teenage children. Ms. Burgos had no problems for over 10 years, until the landlord rented a neighboring unit to tenants who began to deal drugs from their apartment. Ms. Burgos repeatedly complained to the landlord, but he did nothing. The drug dealer began to terrorize Ms. Burgos and her family, smashing her car windows, throwing things at her door, and cursing at her family at all hours of the night. Still the landlord took no steps. Finally, Ms. Burgos abandoned her unit, leaving several months' rent unpaid. The landlord sued her for unpaid rent, but the court found he had failed to protect Ms. Burgos from other tenants and was entitled to no rent. This landlord lost rental income and watched his building deteriorate, all because he failed to enforce the terms of the tenancy against the troublemaker.[5] ◆

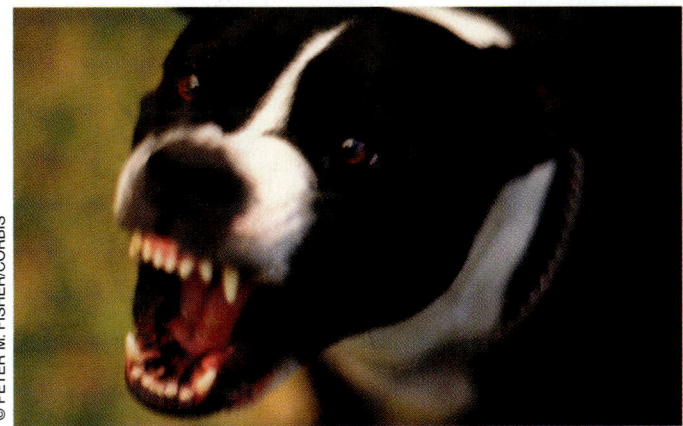

Is the tenant or the landlord liable when the tenant's dog attacks?

© PETER M. FISHER/CORBIS

Animal Attacks

Dogs bite, cats scratch, wolves maul. In most states, the owner of an animal is responsible for any harm it causes. A tenant is liable if her dog intimidates or attacks other tenants. The landlord has the right to evict a tenant whose animal abuses other tenants. In some states, a landlord may have a *duty* to evict, following the logic of the *Burgos* decision, above.

States do not agree, however, on whether the landlord is liable for harm caused by a tenant's animals. The common law rule holds a landlord free of any responsibility for harm caused by a tenant's animal. California and some other states disagree and declare a landlord potentially liable. We revisit this issue later in the chapter. Of course, if either the landlord *or* the tenant were to show common sense and respond quickly to a dangerous animal, there would be no injury and no need for a court to rule on liability.

CHANGE IN THE PARTIES

Sometimes the parties to a lease change. This can happen when the landlord sells the property or when a tenant wants to turn the leased property over to another tenant.

Sale of the Property

Generally, the sale of leased property does not affect the lease but merely substitutes one landlord, the purchaser, for another, the seller. The lease remains valid, and the tenant enjoys all rights and obligations until the end of the term. The new

---

[5] *Auburn Leasing Corp. v. Burgos*, 609 N.Y.S.2d 549, 1994 N.Y. Misc. LEXIS 68 (N.Y. Civ. Ct. 1994).

landlord may not raise the rent during the period of the existing lease or make any other changes in the tenant's rights.

There is one exception. If the tenant is not in possession when the property is sold *and* the tenant's lease was never recorded with the registry of deeds, then the buyer need not honor the lease. If the buyer has no way of knowing there *is* a tenant, she should not be required to respect the lease.

Assignment and Sublease

A tenant who wishes to turn the property over to another tenant will attempt to assign the lease or to sublet it. In an **assignment,** the tenant transfers all of his legal interest to the other party. The original tenant is the **assignor** and the new tenant is the **assignee.**[6] If a tenant validly assigns a lease, the assignee obtains all rights and liabilities under the lease. The assignee is permitted to use and enjoy the property and must pay the rent. The assignor remains liable to the landlord unless the landlord explicitly releases him, which the landlord is unlikely to do. This means that if the new tenant fails to pay the rent on time, the landlord can sue both parties, old and new, seeking to evict both and to recover the unpaid rent from both.

A landlord generally insists on a covenant in the lease prohibiting the tenant from assigning without the landlord's written permission. The landlord chose to do business with one person and should not be forced to accept a stranger as tenant. How much discretion does a landlord have in deciding whether to permit assignment? It depends on state law and the language of the lease.

Many leases include a covenant that the landlord will not "unreasonably withhold" permission to assign. That covenant is enforceable, and a landlord who arbitrarily refuses permission to assign is liable for all damage she has caused. If the lease contains no limit on the landlord's ability to refuse assignment, may she refuse for no valid reason? It depends on the state. **A dwindling majority of states allows a landlord to reject assignment for any reason or no reason.** An increasing number of courts require the landlord to make her decision *reasonably*. She may consider the assignee's financial stability and intended use of the premises, but may not reject an assignment simply because it is inconvenient.

In a **sublease,** the tenant remains a tenant of the landlord and turns over *some* of his rights to a new tenant. The original tenant is the **sublessor** and the new tenant is the **sublessee.** The sublessor remains fully liable to the landlord for all provisions of the lease, including payment of rent and proper care of the premises. The sublessee has no legal relationship with the landlord, but has a normal tenant's obligations to the sublessor. The sublessee must pay rent to the sublessor and must return the property in good condition at the end of the sublease.

Why would a tenant sublet property rather than assign it? Often because rental rates have risen during the course of the original tenancy, and the tenant believes he can make a profit by subletting the premises at a higher rent than he is paying the landlord.

Must a landlord agree to a sublease? The rules are essentially the same as for an assignment. The lease probably requires the tenant to obtain the landlord's permission before subletting. In a growing minority of states, the landlord may not unreasonably withhold that permission.

D. L. Development, Inc., was a tenant on five acres of commercial property owned by Bessie Nance. The lease was for 99 years, with 68 years remaining. Property values

---

[6] We discuss assignment of contracts in Chapter 16, on third parties.

had increased dramatically, and the lease was no longer profitable to Nance. D. L. Development wished to sublease some of its space to McCaw Cellular Communications for installation of a cellular telephone antenna, and McCaw signed a sublease for 10 years. D. L. Development then asked Nance to approve the sublease, but she refused, stating that she would agree to it only if D. L. Development renegotiated the terms of the original lease. The court held that Nance was holding the sublease hostage in an effort to squeeze more rent out of D. L. Development, and that this was unreasonable. The court ordered Nance to pay her tenant all profits lost from the failed sublease.[7]

INJURIES

You invite a friend to dinner in your rented home, but after the meal she slips and falls, seriously injuring her back. Are you liable? Is the landlord?

Tenant's Liability

A tenant is generally liable for injuries occurring within the premises she is leasing, whether that is an apartment, a store, or otherwise. If a tenant permits grease to accumulate on a kitchen floor and a guest slips and falls, the tenant is liable. If a merchant negligently installs display shelving that tips onto a customer, the merchant pays for the harm. Generally, a tenant is not liable for injuries occurring in common areas over which she has no control, such as exterior walkways. If a tenant's dinner guest falls because the building's common stairway has loose steps, the landlord is probably liable.

Landlord's Liability

Common Law Rules

Historically, the common law held a landlord responsible for injuries on the premises only in a limited number of circumstances, which we will describe. In reading these common law rules, be aware that many states have changed them, dramatically increasing the landlord's liability.

Latent Defects. If the landlord knows of a dangerous condition on the property and realizes the tenant will not notice it, the landlord is liable for any injuries. For example, if a landlord knows that a porch railing is weak and fails to inform the tenant, the landlord is responsible if the tenant plunges off the porch. But notice that, under the common law, if the landlord notifies the tenant of the latent defect, he is no longer liable.

Common Areas. The landlord is usually responsible for maintaining the common areas, and along with this obligation may go liability for torts. As we saw above, if your guest falls down stairs in a common hallway because the stairs were defective, the landlord is probably liable.

Negligent Repairs. Even in areas where the landlord has no duty to make repairs, if he volunteers to do so and does the work badly, he is responsible for resulting harm.

---

[7] *D. L. Development, Inc. v. Nance*, 894 S.W.2d 258, 1995 Mo. App. LEXIS 431 (Mo. Ct. App. 1995).

Public Use. If the premises are to be used for a public purpose, such as a store or office, the landlord is generally obligated to repair any dangerous defects, although the tenant is probably liable as well. The purpose of this stricter rule is to ensure that the general public can safely visit commercial establishments. If a landlord realizes that the plate glass in a store's door is loose, he must promptly repair it or suffer liability for any injuries.

Modern Trend

Increasingly, state legislatures and courts are discarding the common law classifications described above and holding landlords liable under the normal rules of negligence law. **In many states, a landlord must use reasonable care to maintain safe premises and is liable for foreseeable harm.** For example, the common law rule merely required a landlord to notify a tenant of a latent defect, such as a defective porch railing. Most states now have building codes that require a landlord to maintain structural elements such as railings in safe condition. States further imply a warranty of habitability, which mandates reasonably safe living conditions. So, in many states, a landlord is no longer saved from negligence suits merely by giving notice of defects—he has to fix them. Suppose that a bathroom faucet is loose, causing hot water to leak continuously, and the landlord has failed to repair it in spite of frequent requests by the tenant. If the faucet suddenly breaks open and hot water scalds the tenant's guest, the landlord is liable in many states. The landlord's responsibility, however, depends upon his receiving notice of the defect from the tenant.

As always, the common law advances in a disorderly fashion, and state courts disagree about what "reasonable care" requires. The following pair of cases illustrate the diversity of issues—and conflicting arguments—that a landlord must consider before renting units. You make the calls.

you Be The Judge

MCGUIRE V. K & G MANAGEMENT CO.

1998 Ohio App. LEXIS 4742
Ohio Court of Appeals, 1998

Facts: The McGuire family rented a second-story apartment from K & G Management, which managed a residential complex on behalf of Avant Co. Robin McGuire notified K & G that a window screen in her son's bedroom was loose and had fallen out once. Neighbors had also complained about loose-fitting screens. Five days after Robin reported the loose screen, her son, 26-month-old Devin, was playing in his bedroom with his eight-year-old cousin. Somehow, Devin fell or leaned into the window screen, which gave way. Devin fell to the ground and was seriously hurt.

The McGuires filed suit against K & G and Avant, claiming negligence. In Ohio (and most

states), a landlord has a statutory duty to "make all repairs and do whatever is reasonably necessary to put and keep the premises in a fit and habitable condition." The trial court granted summary judgment for both defendants, ruling that the defendants had no duty to install screens strong enough to restrain a child. The McGuires appealed.

You Be the Judge: **Are the McGuires entitled to a trial on their claim of negligence?**

Argument for the McGuires: Both defendants have a statutory duty to keep the apartment fit and habitable, and both failed to do that. The screen was loose and they knew it, but failed to fix it. The danger of a child falling was entirely foreseeable, and the defendants are responsible. No parent can watch a child 24 hours a day. Young children climb and play anywhere they can reach. A landlord who makes a profit renting apartments

▼

to families should use reasonable care to protect all family members, young and old.

Argument for K & G and Avant: A window screen is not a child restraint. A screen is designed to keep insects and birds out, not to hold children in. A normal window screen, no matter how tightly installed, would not restrain a child. If all landlords throughout the state are suddenly obligated to install child-proof screens, let the legislature announce the new rule and provide time to comply. We do not think that the voters want to pay the additional rent required to cover such a huge expense. ■

you Be The Judge

MATTHEWS V. AMBERWOOD ASSOCIATES LIMITED PARTNERSHIP, INC.
351 Md. 544, 719 A.2d 199, 1998 Md. LEXIS 807
Maryland Court of Appeals, 1998

Facts: Shelly Morton leased an apartment owned by Amberwood and operated by Monocle Management. The lease permitted the landlord to evict any tenant who broke the "House Rules," one of which prohibited pets. Morton kept her boyfriend's pit bull, named Rampage (!), in her apartment. At times she kept Rampage chained outside the apartment house. When Morton was near the dog, he was not violent, but when she was absent, Rampage would attempt to attack anyone who came near him. Numerous maintenance workers had been unable to perform service work because Rampage barked and lunged at them. The workers reported each of these incidents to Monocle.

Shanita Matthews and her 16-month-old son, Tevin, visited Morton and her child, something they had done many times. As the adults worked on a puzzle in the dining room, the children played in the living room. Morton briefly left the apartment, and suddenly Rampage attacked Tevin. The dog grabbed the boy by the neck and shook him. Matthews was unable to free her son. She yelled for help and called 911. Morton reentered the apartment, could not free the boy, grabbed a knife, and repeatedly stabbed the animal, which finally released Tevin. An ambulance arrived, but an hour after reaching the hospital, Tevin died from his injuries.

Matthews sued Amberwood and Monocle. The jury awarded her $5,018,750 for the wrongful death of her son. The defendants appealed.

You Be the Judge: Does a landlord owe a duty to a social guest of a tenant for an attack within the tenant's apartment?

Argument for Matthews: The House Rules prohibited pets. Monocle knew that Morton was breaking the rule and keeping an especially dangerous animal. Monocle should have acted to protect the other residents and all guests to the complex. The companies' failure to enforce their own rules led directly to the death of a child.

Argument for the Defendants: Neither the owner nor the management company has control over the apartment or what goes on inside it. The companies could not have foreseen this attack, nor could they have done anything to stop it. Matthews knew the dog's nature. She had no business leaving her son alone with such a vicious beast. ■

Pit bulls and other so-called attack dogs have become such a menace in some French neighborhoods that the French Assembly voted unanimously to ban them from French soil. Owners of various breeds deemed dangerous must sterilize their pets immediately. The law prohibits breeding, importing, buying, or selling any of the animals. The French agricultural minister predicts that the affected breeds will disappear within the first decade of the new century.

Exculpatory Clauses

You have found an apartment you can afford, in the right neighborhood, and the landlord presents you with a lease to sign. You notice an **exculpatory clause,** which states that the landlord is *not* liable for any injuries that occur on the rented premises, whether to you or your guests, regardless of the cause. You feel uncomfortable about the clause because it seems to suggest that the landlord can ignore serious defects and still escape liability. Should you sign the lease?

Today, **exculpatory clauses are generally void in residential leases.** Courts dislike such clauses because the parties typically have unequal bargaining power, and the goal of the law is to encourage safe housing managed by responsible landlords. So courts in many states simply ignore exculpatory clauses and apply normal rules of negligence to determine whether or not a landlord is liable for an injury. However, this is not universally the case; in some states, a court may still enforce an exculpatory clause in a residential lease. A concerned tenant should learn the local law before signing such a lease.

Exculpatory clauses are much more likely to be enforced in commercial leases. A court assumes that a merchant is capable of effective bargaining. A business tenant might agree to an exculpatory clause because the landlord accommodated him in some way, such as with a lower rent.

Crime

Landlords may be liable in negligence to tenants or their guests for criminal attacks that occur on the premises. Courts have struggled with this issue and have reached opposing results in similar cases. The very prevalence of crime sharpens the debate. What must a landlord do to protect a tenant? Courts typically answer the question by looking at four factors.

- *Nature of the Crime.* How did the crime occur? Could the landlord have prevented it?

- *Reasonable Person Standard.* What would a reasonable landlord have done to prevent this type of crime? What did the landlord actually do?

- *Foreseeability.* Was it reasonably foreseeable that such a crime might occur? Were there earlier incidents or warnings?

- *Prevalence of Crime in the Area.* If the general area, or the particular premises, has a high crime rate, courts are more likely to hold that the crime was foreseeable and the landlord responsible.

The following case highlights some of the issues facing courts as they apply changing mores to a tragic loss.

DICKINSON ARMS-REO, L.P. V. CAMPBELL

4 S.W.3d 333
Texas Court of Appeals, 1999

Facts: About midnight, Joe Campbell and his girlfriend, Jenny Cady, left a club in separate cars, agreeing to meet at her apartment. Campbell parked his pickup truck in a space at the Dickinson Arms Apartments, where Cady lived.

Meanwhile, two 16-year-olds, Jeremy Gartrell and Donald Nichols, members of the Assassins, were

▼

visiting a fellow gang member who lived at the apartments. Gartrell approached Campbell, demanded the truck, and shot Campbell with a .22 caliber pistol, killing him. Gartrell was convicted of murder and sentenced to 50 years.

Campbell's parents sued the Dickinson Arms, claiming that the landlord's neglect of security had permitted the killing. Testimony indicated that over a three-year period, there had been 184 reported criminal offenses at the apartments. The property manager testified that no one told her gang members lived in the complex; that company policy required her to check with police for possible preventive safety programs, but she had never done so; and that she had never performed a security survey of the complex. The plaintiffs' expert witness testified that because of the high crime rates, the Dickinson Arms should have been protected with a perimeter fence, gates, and a security guard.

The jury found that the landlord failed to provide adequate security, and gave a judgment of $341,000 for the plaintiffs. The Dickinson Arms appealed.

Issue: Was the landlord liable for the murder?

Excerpts from Justice Mirabal's Decision: For a landowner to foresee criminal conduct on property, there must be evidence that other crimes have occurred on the property or in its immediate vicinity. Foreseeability also depends on how recently and how often criminal conduct has occurred in the past. The previous crimes must be sufficiently similar to the crime in question as to place the landowner on notice of the specific danger. However, the prior crimes need not be identical. The following evidence is relevant to similarity of other crimes: Out of the 184 crimes described in exhibit no. 38, there are included:

20 burglaries
13 auto thefts
11 assaults
8 thefts

These types of crimes could make the risk of other violent crimes, such as murder, foreseeable if there would be a confrontation.

Defendants argue that the shooter, Jeremy Gartrell, was an unstoppable and undeterrable individual whose conduct had no relation to defendant's alleged negligence. Defendants assert that the carjacking and shooting would have taken place even if defendants had used all reasonable care.

Defendants rely heavily on the testimony of their expert witness who testified that a security guard, perimeter fencing, and limited access gates would not have stopped an offender like Gartrell, who was an impulsive, explosive type individual—a time bomb just waiting to happen. Defendants also rely on the testimony of the former high school principal and Gartrell's peers regarding his violent nature, lack of respect for authority, and undeterrability.

Plaintiffs counter that the evidence shows Gartrell had wanted to do a car-jacking throughout much of the day and had ample opportunities to do so, but he was deterred by the surroundings. For example, before going to the Dickinson Arms Apartments, Gartrell and Nichols were at the nearby Taco Bell and Gartrell told Nichols he was going to carjack a green Mustang that had pulled up. There were people present and Taco Bell was well lit; Nichols said something like "Don't be stupid." Gartrell did not car-jack the green Mustang. Then Gartrell and Nichols walked to the next-door parking lot of Kroger's on the way to the apartments; the parking lot presented the opportunity to car-jack someone, but it was well-lit and Gartrell did not do so. Though he had spoken of car-jacking someone most of the day, it was not until Gartrell came to the Dickinson Arms Apartments—a place Nichols testified was dark and where they knew there was no security guard or access control gates—that he actually did a car-jacking. The evidence was conflicting regarding lighting in the parking lot the night of Campbell's murder: Charlotte Davis testified the lighting in the parking lot was good enough for her to see Campbell's body and truck from her apartment window; Nichols specifically testified it was dark in the parking lot that night and that there were no lights working in that area.

Plaintiffs' expert witness testified that if defendants had access control gates, a night security guard, and perimeter fencing, this offense, in all probability, would not have happened. Mindful that it is the role of the jury to resolve conflicts in the evidence, we conclude the evidence is legally and factually sufficient to support the jury's cause in fact determination.

We affirm the judgment. ■

Devil's Advocate

Gartrell was a lawful visitor to the apartments, as he would have been had there been more security. If there had been a guard, was he supposed to search all guests? All residents? Only suspected gang members? The court does not explain how the improved security would have prevented this crime. The decision imposes an unfair punishment on a low-rent apartment complex. The result will be greater expense to the owner, higher rents for tenants—and no guarantee of more security for anyone.   ◆

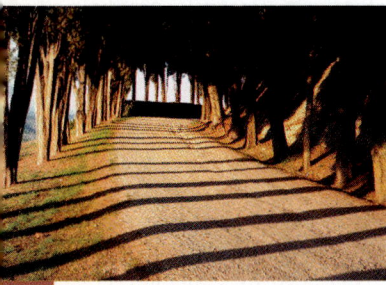

Chapter Conclusion

A century ago no plaintiff would even have argued that a landlord was responsible for bites inflicted by a tenant's dog, for children falling from windows, or for a tenant's death by murder. But living patterns alter, social mores reflect the change, and the law—in theory—responds to both. The current trend is clearly for expanded landlord liability, but how far that will continue is impossible to divine.

Chapter Review

1. When an owner of a freehold estate allows another person temporary, exclusive possession of the property, the parties have created a landlord-tenant relationship.

2. Any lease for a stated, fixed period is a tenancy for years. A periodic tenancy is created for a fixed period and then automatically continues for additional periods until either party notifies the other of termination. A tenancy at will has no fixed duration and may be terminated by either party at any time. A tenancy at sufferance occurs when a tenant remains, against the wishes of the landlord, after the expiration of a true tenancy.

3. All tenants are entitled to the quiet enjoyment of the premises, without the interference of the landlord.

4. A landlord may be liable for constructive eviction if he substantially interferes with the tenant's use and enjoyment of the premises.

5. The implied warranty of habitability requires that a landlord meet all standards set by the local building code and/or that the premises be fit for human habitation.

6. The tenant is obligated to pay the rent, and the landlord may evict for nonpayment. The modern trend is to require a landlord to mitigate damages caused by a tenant who abandons the premises before the lease expires.

7. A tenant is liable to the landlord for any significant damage he causes to the property.

8. A tenant must not disturb other tenants.

9. A tenant typically may assign a lease or sublet the premises only with the landlord's permission, but the current trend is to prohibit a landlord from unreasonably withholding permission.

10. At common law, a landlord had very limited liability for injuries on the premises, but today many courts require a landlord to use reasonable care and hold her liable for foreseeable harm.

11. Landlords may be liable in negligence to tenants or their guests for criminal attacks on the premises. Courts determine liability by looking at factors such as the nature of the crime, what a reasonable landlord would have done to prevent it, and the foreseeability of the attack.

Practice Test

1. **CPA QUESTION** Which of the following forms of tenancy will be created if a tenant stays in possession of the leased premises without the landlord's consent, after the tenant's one-year written lease expires?

a. Tenancy at will

b. Tenancy for years

c. Tenancy from period to period

d. Tenancy at sufferance

2. **CPA QUESTION** A tenant's personal property will become a fixture and belong to the landlord if its removal would:

   a. Increase the value of the personal property

   b. Cause a material change to the personal property

   c. Result in substantial harm to the landlord's property

   d. Change the use of the landlord's property back to its prior use

3. Loren Andreo leased retail space in his shopping plaza to Tropical Isle Pet Shop for five years, at a monthly rent of $2,100. Tropical Isle vacated the premises 18 months early, turned in the key to Andreo, and acknowledged liability for the unpaid rent. Andreo placed a "for rent" sign in the store window and spoke to a commercial real estate broker about the space. But he did not enter into a formal listing agreement with the broker, or take any other steps to rent the space, for about nine months. With approximately nine months remaining on the unused part of Tropical's lease, Andreo hired a commercial broker to rent the space. He also sued Tropical for 18 months' rent. Comment.

4. Philip Schwachman owned a commercial building and leased space to Davis Radio Corp. for use as a retail store. In the same building, Schwachman leased other retail space to Pampered Pet, a dog grooming shop. Davis Radio complained repeatedly to Schwachman that foul odors from Pampered Pet entered its store and drove away customers and workers. Davis abandoned the premises, leaving many months' rent unpaid. Schwachman sued for unpaid rent and moved for summary judgment. What ruling would you make on the summary judgment motion?

5. William Bryant was walking along the street in Conway, Arkansas, when a rottweiler (sound familiar?) and two pit bulls attacked and seriously injured him. Mona Jones owned the dogs, who had escaped from the house she rented from Karen and Ted Putnam. Bryant sued the Putnams for negligence, and they moved for summary judgment. Arkansas applies the traditional common law rule to this case. Who wins on the summary judgment motion?

6. **YOU BE THE JUDGE** WRITING PROBLEM Jane Doe (not her real name) worked as a secretary in a large commercial building in Washington, D.C. Dominion Bank, which owned the building, decided to sell it. It stopped giving new leases for office space, in anticipation of the sale, and gradually 5 of the building's 13 floors became vacant. The bank did not close off the vacant floors, and as the vacancies increased, tenants in the building began to complain to the landlord about vagrants, "street persons," "strange people," and others entering the building and engaging in drug deals or prostitution in the uncontrolled spaces. Jane Doe left her office one morning about 9:20 A.M. to go to a nearby shop. She entered the elevator on the eleventh floor and rode down, but the elevator stopped at an abandoned floor, and a large male boarded. He grabbed Doe in a choke hold and dragged her down the hallway through unlocked doors to a vacant office, where he raped and robbed her. Doe sued the Dominion Bank in United States District Court. A security expert testified that all vacant offices and floors should have been sealed off. Is the bank liable for Doe's injuries? **Argument for Jane Doe:** The bank created a dangerous situation by gradually abandoning a commercial building. Tenants repeatedly told the bank about the vagrants, and it was entirely foreseeable that a violent crime would result. The bank should be held to a "reasonable person" standard, one that it clearly failed to meet. **Argument for Dominion Bank:** A landlord is not and should not be liable for violent crime. The bank is not a police force. The bank's obligation was to keep the rented premises, meaning Doe's office, in good working order, which it did. Do not try to hold a bank liable just because there has been a personal tragedy.

7. Doris Rowley rented space from the city of Mobile, Alabama, to run the Back Porch Restaurant. Her lease prohibited assignment or subletting without the landlord's permission. Rowley's business became unprofitable, and she asked the

city's real estate officer for permission to assign her lease. She told the officer that she had "someone who would accept if the lease was assigned." Rowley provided no other information about the assignee. The city refused permission. Rowley repeated her requests several times without success, and finally she sued. Rowley alleged that the city had unreasonably withheld permission to assign and had caused her serious financial losses as a result. Comment.

8. Kenmart Realty sued to evict Mr. and Ms. Alghalabio for nonpayment of rent and sought the unpaid monies, totaling several thousand dollars. In defense, the Alghalabios claimed that their apartment was infested with rats. They testified that there were numerous rat holes in the walls of the living room, bedroom, and kitchen, that there were rat droppings all over the apartment, and that on one occasion they saw their toddler holding a live rat. They testified that the landlord had refused numerous requests to exterminate. Please rule on the landlord's suit.

9. **CPA QUESTION** To be enforceable, a residential real estate lease must:

   a. Require the tenant to obtain liability insurance

   b. Entitle the tenant to exclusive possession of the leased property

   c. Specify a due date for rent

   d. Be in writing

10. **CPA QUESTION** A tenant renting an apartment under a three-year written lease that does not contain any specific restrictions may be evicted for:

    a. Counterfeiting money in the apartment

    b. Keeping a dog in the apartment

    c. Failing to maintain a liability insurance policy on the apartment

    d. Making structural repairs to the apartment

11. **ETHICS** Lisa Preece rented an apartment from Turman Realty, paying a $300 security deposit. Georgia law states: "Any landlord who fails to return any part of a security deposit which is required to be returned to a tenant pursuant to this article shall be liable to the tenant in the amount of three times the sum improperly withheld plus reasonable attorney's fees." When Preece moved out, Turman did not return her security deposit, and she sued for triple damages plus attorney's fees, totaling $1,800. Turman offered evidence that its failure to return the deposit was inadvertent and that it had procedures reasonably designed to avoid such errors. Is Preece entitled to triple damages? Attorney's fees? What is the rationale behind a statute that requires triple damages? Is it ethical to force a landlord to pay $1,800 for a $300 debt?

12. **ROLE REVERSAL** Write a multiple-choice question concerning one of these issues: tenancy for years, security deposit, or sublease.

Internet Research Problem

Go to http://beatty.westbuslaw.com, and search for the law of your state concerning a landlord's obligation to provide a habitable apartment. Now assume that you are living in a rental unit with serious defects. Draft a letter to the landlord asking for prompt repairs. For sample letters, go to http://beatty .westbuslaw.com and click on the appropriate links.

> **You can find further practice problems at** http://beatty.westbuslaw.com **or in the Study Guide that accompanies this text.**

Personal Property
and Bailment

"**M**y only child is a no-good thief," Riley murmurs sadly to his visitors. "He has always treated me contemptuously. Now he's been sentenced to five years for stealing from a children's charity. He is my only heir, but why should I leave him everything?" Riley continues talking to his three guests: a bishop, a rabbi, and Earnest, a Boy Scout leader. "I have $500,000 in stocks and bonds in my bank deposit box. Tomorrow morning I'm going down to the bank, take out all the papers, and hand them over to the Boy Scouts so that other kids won't turn out so bad." Everyone applauds his generosity, and they photograph Riley and Earnest shaking hands.

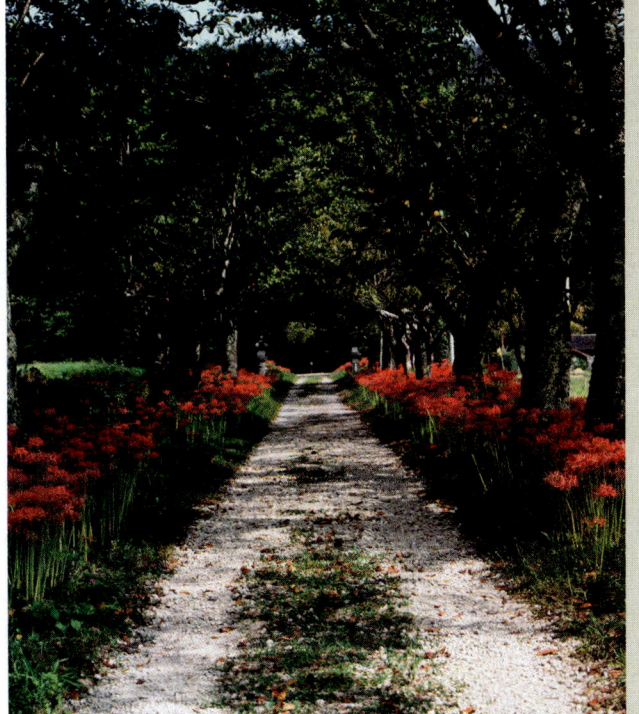

© AKIRA KAEDE/PHOTODISC/GETTY IMAGES

But the following morning, on his way to the bank, Riley is struck by an ambulance and killed. A dispute arises over the money. The three witnesses assure the court that Riley was on his way to give the money to the Boy Scouts. From prison, the ne'er-do-well son demands the money as Riley's sole heir. Who wins? This is a typical issue of personal property law. ■

Personal property means all property other than real property. In Chapter 44 we saw that real property means land and things firmly attached to it, such as buildings, crops, and minerals. All other property is personal property—a bus, a toothbrush, a share of stock. Most personal property is goods, meaning something that can be moved. We have already examined the purchase and sale of goods, which are governed by the Uniform Commercial Code. In this chapter we look at several other ways in which personal property can be acquired, including gifts and found property. In the section on gifts we learn that Riley's no-good son gets the money. Riley intended to give the stocks and bonds to the Boy Scouts the following day, but he never completed a valid gift because he failed to *deliver* the papers. Then we turn to disputes over found property. And finally we examine bailments, which occur when the owner of personal property permits another to possess it.

GIFTS

A gift is a voluntary transfer of property from one person to another without any consideration. It is the lack of consideration that distinguishes a gift from a contract. Contracts usually consist of mutual promises to do something in the future. Each promise is consideration for the other one, and the mutual consideration makes each promise enforceable. But a gift is a one-way transaction, without consideration. The person who gives property away is the **donor** and the one who receives it is the **donee**.
   A gift involves three elements:

- The donor intends to transfer ownership of the property to the donee immediately.
- The donor delivers the property to the donee.
- The donee accepts the property.

Intention to Transfer Ownership

The donor must intend to transfer ownership to the property right away, immediately giving up all control of the item. Notice the two important parts of this element. First, the donor's intention must be to *transfer ownership*, that is, to give title to the donee. Merely proving that the owner handed you property does not guarantee that you have received a gift; if the owner only intended that you use the item, there is no gift and she can demand it back.

   Second, the donor must also intend the property to transfer *immediately*. A promise to make a gift in the future is unenforceable. Promises about future behavior are governed by contract law, and a contract is unenforceable without consideration. If Sarah hands Lenny the keys to a $600,000 yacht and says, "Lenny, it's yours," then it *is* his, since Sarah intends to transfer ownership right away. But if Sarah says to Max, "Next week I'm going to give you my used bicycle," Max has not received a gift of the bike because Sarah did not intend an immediate transfer. Nor does Max have an enforceable contract, since there is no consideration for Sarah's promise.

   A *revocable gift* is a contradiction in terms, because it violates the rule just discussed. It is not a gift and the donee keeps nothing.[1] Suppose Harold tells his daughter Faith, "The mule is yours from now on, but if you start acting stupid again, I'm taking her

---

[1] The only exception to this rule is a gift *causa mortis,* discussed later in the chapter.

back." Harold has retained some control over the animal, which means he has not intended to transfer ownership. There is no gift, and Harold still owns the mule.

When Dominic Tenaglia's automobile broke down, his brother Nick generously offered to give him a replacement car. Nick delivered a Chevrolet to Dominic, and both brothers understood that the car was a gift. Nick wrote "gift" on the car's certificate of title, but did not immediately give the certificate to Dominic. A week later, while Dominic was driving the Chevrolet, he was involved in an accident. Both brothers had insurance, through different insurers, for cars they owned. The two companies disputed which one was responsible for Dominic's accident. The court determined that Nick's company was still liable for any damage caused by the Chevrolet. Nick had presented the car to Dominic but had not relinquished all control over it. Ownership of a car requires possession of the certificate of title. Because Nick still had the certificate at the time of the accident, he had the power to take back the Chevrolet whenever he wanted, and he had not made a valid gift of the automobile. Dominic's insurer won the case.[2]

Delivery

Physical Delivery

The donor must deliver the property to the donee. Generally, this involves physical delivery. If Anna hands Eddie a Rembrandt drawing, saying "I want you to have this forever," she has satisfied the delivery requirement. In the chapter opening, Riley promised to give half a million dollars to the Boy Scouts the following day. But he never delivered the stocks and bonds, so there was no gift. The Boy Scouts received nothing, and all of the money became part of Riley's estate, to be inherited by his unworthy son.

Constructive Delivery

Physical delivery is the most common and the surest way to make a gift, but it is not always necessary. **A donor makes constructive delivery by transferring ownership without a physical delivery.** Most courts permit constructive delivery only when physical delivery is impossible or extremely inconvenient. Suppose Anna wants to give her niece Jen a blimp, which is parked in a hangar at the airport. The blimp will not fit through the doorway of Jen's dorm. Instead of flying the aircraft to the university, Anna may simply deliver to Jen the certificate of title and the keys to the blimp. When she has done that, Jen owns the aircraft.

Delivery to an Agent

A donor might deliver the property to an agent, either someone working for him or for the donee. If the donor delivers the property to his own agent, there is no gift. By definition the agent works for the donor, and thus the donor still has control and ownership of the property. But if the donor delivers the property to the donee's agent, the gift is made.

Property Already in Donee's Possession

Sometimes a donor decides to give property to a donee who already has possession of it. In that case, no delivery is required, and the donee need only demonstrate that the

2 *Motorists Mutual Insurance Co. v. State Farm Mutual Automobile Insurance Co.*, 1990 Ohio App. LEXIS 3027 (Ohio Ct. App. 1990).

donor intended to transfer present *ownership*. Larry lends a grand piano to Leslie for the summer. At the end of the summer, Larry announces that she can keep the instrument. As long as Larry clearly intends that Leslie gets ownership of the piano, the gift is completed.

Inter Vivos Gifts and Gifts *Causa Mortis*

A gift can be either *inter vivos* or *causa mortis*. An **inter vivos gift** means a gift made "during life," that is, when the donor is not under any fear of impending death. The vast majority of gifts are *inter vivos*, involving a healthy donor and donee. Shirley, age 30 and in good health, gives her husband Terry an eraser for his birthday. This is an *inter vivos* gift, which is absolute. The gift becomes final upon delivery, and the donor *may not* revoke it. If Shirley and Terry have a fight the next day, Shirley has no power to erase her eraser gift.

A **gift *causa mortis*** is one made in contemplation of approaching death. The gift is valid if the donor dies as expected, but is revoked if he recovers. Suppose Lance's doctors have told him he will probably die of a liver ailment within a month. Lance calls Jane to his bedside and hands her a fistful of emeralds, saying, "I'm dying, these are yours." Jane sheds a tear, then sprints to the bank. If Lance dies of the liver ailment within a few weeks, Jane gets to keep the emeralds. The law permits the gift *causa mortis* to act as a substitute for a will, since the donor's delivery of the property clearly indicates his intentions. But note that this kind of gift is revocable. Since a gift *causa mortis* is conditional (upon the donor's death), the donor has the right to revoke it at any time before he dies. If Lance telephones Jane the next day and says that he has changed his mind, he gets the jewels back. Further, if the donor recovers and does not die as expected, the gift is automatically revoked.

Acceptance

The donee must accept the gift. This rarely leads to disputes, but if a donee should refuse a gift and then change her mind, she is out of luck. Her repudiation of the donor's offer means there is no gift, and she has no rights in the property.

The following case offers a combination of love and anger, alcohol and diamonds—always a volatile mix.

you Be The Judge

ALBINGER V. HARRIS

2002 Mont. 118, 2002 WL 1226858
Montana Supreme Court, 2002

Facts: Michelle Harris and Michael Albinger lived together, on and off, for three years. Their roller-coaster relationship was marred by alcohol abuse and violence. When they announced their engagement, Albinger gave Harris a $29,000 diamond ring, but the couple broke off their wedding plans because of emotional and physical turmoil.

Harris returned the ring. Later, they reconciled and resumed their marriage plans, and Albinger gave his fiancee the ring again. This cycle repeated several times over the three years. Each time they broke off their relationship, Harris returned the ring to Albinger, and each time they made up, he gave it back to her.

On one occasion, Albinger held a knife over Harris as she lay in bed, threatening to chop off her finger if she didn't remove the ring. He beat her and forcibly removed the ring. Criminal

▼

charges were brought but then dropped when, inevitably, the couple reconciled. Another time, Albinger told her to "take the car, the horse, the dog and the ring and get the hell out." Finally, mercifully, they ended their stormy affair, and Harris moved to Kentucky—keeping the ring.

Albinger sued for the value of the ring. The trial court found that the ring was a conditional gift, made in contemplation of marriage, and ordered Harris to pay its full value. She appealed. The Montana Supreme Court had to decide, in a case of first impression, whether an engagement ring was given in contemplation of marriage. (In Montana, and many states, neither party to a broken engagement may sue for breach of contract, because it is impossible to determine who is responsible for ending the relationship.)

You Be the Judge: Who owns the ring?

Argument for Harris: The main problem with calling the ring a "conditional gift" is that there is no such thing. The elements of a gift are intent, delivery, and acceptance, and Harris has proven all three. A gift is not a contract, nor is it a loan. Once a gift has been accepted, the donor has no more rights in the property and may not demand its return. Hundreds of years of litigation have resulted in only one exception to this rule—a gift *causa mortis*—and despite some cynical claims to the contrary, marriage is not death. If this court carves a new exception to the long-standing rule, other unhappy donors will dream up more "conditions" that supposedly entitle them to their property. What is more, to create a special rule for engagement rings would be blatant gender bias, because the exception would only benefit men. This court should stick to settled law, and permit the recipient of a gift to keep it.

Argument for Albinger: The symbolism of an engagement ring is not exactly news. For decades, Americans have given rings—frequently diamond—in contemplation of marriage. All parties understand why the gift is made and what is expected if the engagement is called off: the ring must be returned. Albinger's *intent*, to focus on one element, was conditional—and Michelle Harris understood that. Each time the couple separated, she gave the ring back. She knew that she could wear this beautiful ring in anticipation of their marriage, but that custom and decency required its return if the wedding was off. She knew it, that is, until greed got the better of her and she fled to Kentucky, attempting to profit at the expense of Albinger's generosity. We are not asking for new law, but for confirmation of what everyone has known for generations: there is no wedding ring when there is no wedding. ■

The following table distinguishes between a contract and a gift:

A Contract and a Gift Distinguished

A Contract:

Lou: I will pay you $2,000 to paint the house, if you promise to finish by July 3.

Abby: I agree to paint the house by July 3, for $2,000.

Lou and Abby have a contract. Each promise is consideration in support of the other promise. Lou and Abby can each enforce the other's promise.

A Gift:

Lou hands Phil two opera tickets, while saying: I want you to have these two tickets to *Rigoletto*.

Phil: Hey, thanks.

This is a valid *inter vivos* gift. Lou intended to transfer ownership immediately and delivered the property to Phil, who now owns the tickets.

Neither Contract nor Gift:

Lou: You're a great guy. Next week, I'm going to give you two tickets to *Rigoletto*.

Jason: Hey, thanks.

There is no gift because Lou did not intend to transfer ownership immediately, and he did not deliver the tickets. There is no contract because Jason has given no consideration to support Lou's promise.

FOUND PROPERTY

Dejected and ashamed, you walk to the university with your head hung low, knowing that your failure to study means you will fare poorly on today's quiz concerning *found property*. Suddenly, there is a gleam of light, not in your mind (which is vacant), but right there on the sidewalk. You stoop to pick it up—a ring! You stop in at the local jewelry shop, where you learn this ruby marvel is worth just over $700,000. Dazzled and delighted, you walk into the classroom and take the test. Question 1 reads: "A student discovers a ruby ring while walking to class. May the student keep the ring?" You have no idea what the answer is and you cannot concentrate anyway. So you write the two safest words in the law: "It depends." That is a fine start, but to learn the full answer, read on.

The law of found property has bewitched the courts of this country for nearly two centuries. Judges have made valiant attempts to base their rulings on principles of sound public policy, but the results have been confusing and contradictory. **The primary goal of the common law has been to get found property back to its proper owner, if possible.** The finder must make a good faith effort to locate the owner of the property and return the goods to him. In some states, the finder is obligated to notify the police of what she has found and entrust the property to them until the owner can be located or until a stated period has passed. **A second policy has been to reward the finder if no owner can be located.** But courts are loath to encourage trespassing, so finders who discover personal property on someone else's land generally cannot keep it. Those basic policies yield various outcomes, depending on the nature of the property. There are four kinds of found property:

- **Abandoned property** is something that the owner has knowingly discarded because she no longer wants it. A vase thrown into a garbage can is abandoned. Generally, the finder is permitted to keep abandoned property. But because the owner loses all rights in abandoned property, a court never *presumes* abandonment. The finder must prove that the owner intended to relinquish all rights.

- **Lost property** is something accidentally given up. A ring that falls off a finger into the street is lost property. Usually, the finder of lost property has rights superior to all the world except the true owner. If the true owner comes forward, he gets his property back; otherwise, the finder may keep it. However, if the finder has discovered the item on land belonging to another, the landowner is probably entitled to keep it.

- **Mislaid property** is something the owner has intentionally placed somewhere and then forgotten. A book deliberately placed on a bus seat by an owner who forgets to take it with her is mislaid property. Generally, the finder gets no rights in property that has simply been mislaid. If the true owner cannot be located, the mislaid item belongs to the owner of the premises where the item was found.

- **Treasure trove** is coins or currency concealed by an owner so long ago that it is likely the owner has died. A sackful of 1850 gold coins, found under the roots of a 150-year-old tree, is treasure trove. The finder can generally keep treasure trove.

Many states have enacted laws, called **finding statutes** or **estray statutes,** governing found property. In some cases, the legislation incorporates the common law principles outlined above, but in other states the new law modifies the old rules. A New York statute, for example, has removed the distinction between lost and mislaid property and now generally permits the finder to keep what he has discovered, regardless of where he found it. The finder is, however, required to turn over the property either to the police or the owner of the premises where the item was found. If the true owner is not located during a stated period, the finder is then entitled to whatever he found.

In the following case, the facts are clear and undisputed. But what do they tell us about the property owner's intention?

FRANKS V. PRITCHETT

2004 WL 2453930
Court of Appeals of Arkansas, 2004

Facts: Alex Franks spent two nights at a Comfort Inn in Searcy, Arkansas. As he prepared to leave, clearing out the left drawer of the dresser, he discovered two bundles of cash, each wrapped with masking tape. He notified the hotel manager, who gave the money to the police. The bundles contained 46 one-hundred-dollar bills and 480 twenty-dollar bills, for a total value of $14,200. The city of Searcy held the money until a court could determine its owner.

The trial court acknowledged that the hotel was often used by narcotics traffickers. However, the judge rejected Franks' assertion that the currency was abandoned drug money, ruling instead that it was mislaid property. He awarded the money to the hotel's owners, Perri and Seddika Kazi, to be held in trust until the rightful owner claimed it. Franks appealed.

Issue: Was the money mislaid, lost, or abandoned property?

Excerpts from Judge Griffen's Decision:[3] Franks argues that the circuit court erred in reasoning that, simply because the money was placed in a drawer, it was mislaid. He asserts that this reasoning also supports a finding that the property was lost, abandoned, or treasure trove property. Franks argues that there is no reason to believe that the true owner left the money in the drawer of a public motel room for security purposes with the expectation of returning to claim it. The Kazis argue that the circuit court properly inferred that the money was placed into the drawer intentionally. They point to the fact that the money was intentionally and meticulously wrapped. They also argue that common sense and logic defy that the owner intended to part with such a large amount of money.

From the bench and in its written order, the court noted that if the money had been found on the floor instead of in a drawer, it could have been said to have been lost. The court also stated:

> It appears to me that the only way I can see this is that somebody put the money in the drawer. Again, it did not fall in the drawer. If they put the money in the drawer, they knew they put the money in the drawer. There is insufficient evidence to find that it's abandoned property. The only conclusion then that I can reach is that it was mislaid property and the court is going to find that it is mislaid property.

Thus, the trial court concluded that, because the money was intentionally placed in the drawer, it had not been abandoned (voluntarily forsaken by the owner) or lost (through neglect, carelessness, or inadvertence).

The trial court's reasoning is consistent with the principle that the place where money or property is found is an important factor in determining whether it was lost or mislaid. To reason by analogy, if one leaves a wallet in a drawer, there is no greater reason to believe it was lost rather than intentionally placed there and forgotten. Similarly, here, as the trial court found, the fact that the money was placed in the drawer supports a finding that the property was not abandoned or lost, but was mislaid.

Affirmed.

Excerpts from Judge Baker's Dissenting Opinion: Following the majority's reasoning, someone meticulously wrapped forty-six one-hundred dollar bills all facing the same direction into one bundle, and meticulously wrapped 480 twenty dollar bills all facing the same direction into another bundle, then wrapped the two bundles into a block the size of a brick using masking tape, intentionally placed the $14,200 block of money into a drawer in a public

▼

---

[3] Once again the authors substitute the parties' names for the court's "appellant" and "appellees."

motel room, planning to later reclaim it, and then somehow forgot where he put it.

I cannot agree with the majority that leaving a wallet in a drawer is in any way analogous to leaving a $14,200 block of cash in the same drawer. Unless those in the majority customarily travel with significantly larger amounts of cash in their wallets than I, there is no validity in the comparison. The nature of the property is itself sufficient to refute the notion that it was intentionally placed in the drawer and then forgotten.

When all of the facts and circumstances in this case are considered, they lead logically to only one conclusion; that regardless of whether the money was placed in the motel room drawer intentionally, the true owner has abandoned his interest in it. ■

Public Policy

What is the primary policy of found-property law? How should that policy affect this dispute? ◆

ACCESSION

Accession occurs when one person uses labor and/or materials to add value to personal property belonging to another. This generally occurs by agreement. Suppose Leasing Corp. agrees to lease a truck to Delivery Co., for use in its business. The contract may permit Delivery to modify the truck's storage space to meet its special needs. If so, the agreement should also state whether Delivery has to return the truck to its original condition at the end of the lease, and whether Delivery is entitled to any payment for improvements made.

Sometimes one party makes accessions without agreement. If the improvements can be "undone" without damage to the property, then the improver must do that. For example, if Delivery Co. simply bolts a few shelves into the truck, it should remove them before returning the truck. Problems arise when the improvements cannot be removed without damaging the property. Assuming the property has become more valuable, must the owner pay the improver for the work done? It normally depends upon whether the improver acted wrongfully or mistakenly.

Wrongful Accessions

If the improver knows he is making accessions without authority, the owner may generally take the improved property without compensating for the work done. Suppose the lease between Leasing Corp. and Delivery Co. states that Delivery may not modify the truck without written permission. Delivery goes ahead anyway and reconfigures the truck to meet its needs. Even if the work substantially increases the truck's value, Leasing Corp. probably owes nothing for the accessions.

Mistaken Accessions

If the improver mistakenly believes he is entitled to add accessions, the owner probably has to pay for the increased value. Suppose that, based on its previous leases with Leasing Corp., Delivery Co. believes it has the right to modify its new truck, though in fact it has no such permission. If the modifications increase the value of the vehicle, Leasing probably has to pay for the accessions.

BAILMENT

A bailment is the rightful possession of goods by one who is not the owner. The one who delivers the goods is the **bailor** and the one in possession is the **bailee.** Bailments are common. Suppose you are going out of town for the weekend and loan your motorcycle to Stan. You are the bailor and your friend is the bailee. When you check your suitcase with the airline, you are again the bailor and the airline is the bailee. If you rent a car at your destination, you become the bailee while the rental agency is the bailor. In each case, someone other than the true owner has rightful, temporary possession of personal property.

When you lend your motorcycle to Stan, you are the bailor and Stan is the bailee.

The parties generally—but not always—create a bailment by agreement. In each of the examples, the parties agreed to the bailment. In two cases, the agreement included payment, which is common but not essential. When you buy your airline ticket, you pay for your ticket, and the price includes the airline's agreement, as bailee, to transport your suitcase. When you rent a car, you pay the bailor for the privilege of using it. By loaning your motorcycle, you engage in a bailment without either party paying compensation.

A bailment without any agreement is called a constructive, or involuntary, bailment. Suppose you find a wristwatch in your house that you know belongs to a friend. As we saw in the section above, you are obligated to return the watch to the true owner, and until you do so, you are the bailee, liable for harm to the property. This is called a constructive bailment because, with no agreement between the parties, the law is *construing* a bailment.

Control

To create a bailment, the bailee must assume physical control with intent to possess. A bailee may be liable for loss or damage to the property. But it is not fair to hold him liable unless he has taken physical control of the goods, intending to possess them.

Disputes about whether someone has taken control often arise in parking lot cases. When a car is damaged or stolen, the lot's owner may try to avoid liability by claiming it lacked control of the parked auto and therefore was not a bailee. If the lot is a "park and lock" facility, where the car's owner retains the key and the lot owner exercises *no control at all*, then there may be no bailment, and no liability for damage.

Jack Sonneveldt was a guest at the O'Hare Marriott Hotel outside Chicago. Sonneveldt arrived at the hotel in a 40-foot customized coach. He attempted to park in the hotel's valet parking area, but employees asked him to leave the vehicle in the hotel's general parking lot across the street. During the night, the $265,000 coach was stolen. If the hotel was a bailee, it would be liable. Sonneveldt's insurance company, Michigan Mutual, sued the hotel—and lost. The court ruled:

The complaint indicates that the Sonneveldt driver drove the Prevost coach into the lot and parked the vehicle himself. Nowhere does it suggest that Marriott was left with a set of keys to the coach, or that the hotel otherwise accepted or obtained actual control over the vehicle. Without the keys, Marriott had neither partial nor complete control over the Prevost coach.[4]

By contrast, when a driver leaves her keys with a parking attendant, the lot clearly is exercising control of the auto, and the parties have created a bailment. The lot is probably liable for loss or damage.

The parties may use a contract to specify whether they have created a bailment, hoping to protect their rights. But even then things do not always go smoothly, as the following case demonstrates.

MITCHELL V. BANK OF AMERICA NATIONAL ASSOCIATION

2002 WL 31139375
Court of Appeals of Texas, 2002

Facts: Donna and Timothy Mitchell rented a safe deposit box from a Dallas branch of Bank of America. The lease agreement stated that the bank "had no possession or custody of, nor control over, the contents of the Box, and the Lessee [the couple] assumes all risks in connection with the depositing of such content." The lease also permitted the bank to remove the box's contents if the rental fee went unpaid.

Bank officers, believing the Mitchells were behind in their rental fees, drilled into the box and removed the contents, which they inventoried and sent to a central vault elsewhere. When the Mitchells learned of this, they were very upset, and "loudly discussed the value of the contents" in the lobby of the Dallas branch.

A week later, the bank informed the Mitchells the contents were back at the Dallas branch. The couple placed the contents into a bag, which they put under the front seat of their car. Shortly after leaving the bank, the Mitchells had a flat tire. A stranger offered assistance. While they were all changing the tire, the bag disappeared.

The Mitchells sued the bank, claiming that its negligence enabled bank employees to learn of the box's contents. In a well-prepared scam, an employee or his accomplice let the air out of the couple's tire, offered roadside assistance, and stole the bag.

The trial court gave summary judgment for the bank, finding that the contract language quoted above meant that there was no bailment, and no possible negligence. The Mitchells appealed.

Issue: Was there a bailment?

Excerpts from Judge Farris's Decision: The Bank moved for summary judgment on the Mitchells' breach of bailment claim on the grounds the lease superseded any common law bailment claim. Generally, bailment relationships are governed by common law principles of negligence. However, the parties to the bailment can abrogate the law of bailment through an express written agreement that clearly varies the liability imposed by the law. To the extent the lease agreement clearly addressed the duties and liabilities of the Bank for the Mitchells' property, the lease agreement controls.

To establish a bailment, there must be a delivery of personal property from one person to another for a specific purpose. The lease clearly provides that so long as the contents of the box remained in the box, there was no delivery of the property to the Bank. Accordingly, no bailment occurred due to the deposit of the Mitchells' property into the box.

However, the lease authorized the Bank to remove the contents of the box for the non-payment of rent. The lease thus contemplated a delivery of the property to the Bank under certain circumstances and did not change the duties imposed by law once the Bank exercised its right to take control of the property. The trial court thus erred in granting summary judgment for the Bank on the grounds the Mitchells' common law cause of action for breach of bailment was superseded by the written contract. ■

---

[4]   *Michigan Mutual Insurance Co. v. Marriott Corp.*, 1992 U.S. Dist. LEXIS 5696 (N.D. Ill. 1992).

Rights of the Bailee

The bailee's primary right is possession of the property. **Anyone who interferes with the bailee's rightful possession is liable to her.** Suppose that, after you loan your motorcycle to Stan, Mel sees Stan park the bike, realizes Stan isn't the owner, rides the motorcycle away, and locks it up until you return. Mel is liable to Stan for any damages Stan suffered while deprived of transportation.

Even a bailor is liable if he wrongfully takes back property from a bailee. If a car agency rents Francine a car for a three-day weekend but then repossesses it for use elsewhere, it is liable to her for any damages, even though it owns the car. The bailor must abide by the agreement.

The bailee is typically, though not always, permitted to use the property. Obviously, a customer is permitted to drive a car rented from an agency. When a farmer loans his tractor to a neighbor, the bailee is entitled to use the machine for normal farm purposes. But some bailees have no authority to use the goods. If you store your furniture in a warehouse, the storage company is your bailee, but it has no right to curl up in your bed.

The bailee may be entitled to compensation. This depends upon the agreement. If Owner leaves a power boat at the boatyard for repairs, the boatyard, a bailee, is entitled to payment for the work it does. As with any contract, the exact compensation should be clearly agreed upon before any work begins. If there is no agreement, the boatyard will probably receive the reasonable value of its services.

Duties of the Bailee

The bailee is strictly liable to redeliver the goods on time to the bailor or to whomever the bailor designates. Strict liability means there are virtually no exceptions. Rudy stores his $6,000 drum set with Melissa's Warehouse while he is on vacation. Blake arrives at the warehouse and shows a forged letter, supposedly from Rudy, granting Blake permission to remove the drums. If Melissa permits Blake to take the drums, she will owe Rudy $6,000, even if the forgery was a high-quality job.

Due Care

The bailee is obligated to exercise due care. **The level of care required depends upon who receives the benefit of the bailment.** There are three possibilities.

- *Sole Benefit of Bailee.* If the bailment is for the sole benefit of the bailee, the bailee is required to use **extraordinary care** with the property. Generally, in these cases, the bailor loans something for free to the bailee. Since the bailee is paying nothing for the use of the goods, most courts (though not all) consider her the only one to benefit from the bailment. If your neighbor loans you a power lawn mower, the bailment is probably for your sole benefit. You are liable if you are even slightly inattentive in handling the lawn mower and can expect to pay for virtually any harm done.

- *Mutual Benefit.* When the bailment is for the mutual benefit of bailor and bailee, the bailee must use **ordinary care** with the property. Ordinary care is what a reasonably prudent person would use under the circumstances. When you rent a car, you benefit from the use of the car, and the agency profits from the fee you pay. When the airline hauls your suitcase to your destination, both parties benefit. Most bailments benefit both parties, and courts decide the majority of bailment disputes under this standard.

- *Sole Benefit of Bailor.* When the bailment benefits only the bailor, the bailee must use **only slight care.** This kind of bailment is called a **gratuitous bailment,** and the bailee is liable only for **gross negligence.** Sheila enters a greased-pig contest and asks you to hold her $140,000 diamond engagement ring while she competes. You put the ring in your pocket. Sheila wins the $20 first prize but the ring has disappeared. This was a gratuitous bailment, and you are not liable to Sheila unless she can prove gross negligence on your part. If the ring dropped from your pocket or was stolen, you are not liable. If you used the ring to play catch with friends, you are liable.

Burden of Proof

In an ordinary negligence case, the plaintiff has the burden of proof to demonstrate that the defendant was negligent and caused the harm alleged. In bailment cases, the burden of proof is reversed. **Once the bailor has proven the existence of a bailment and loss or harm to the goods, a presumption of negligence arises, and the burden shifts to the bailee to prove adequate care.** This is a major change from ordinary negligence cases. Georgina's car is struck by another auto. If Georgina sues for negligence, it is her burden to prove that the defendant was driving unreasonably and caused the harm. By comparison, assume that Georgina rents Charley her sailboat for a month. At the end of the month, Charley announces that the boat is at the bottom of Lake Michigan. If Georgina sues Charley, she only needs to demonstrate that the parties had a bailment and that Charley failed to return the boat. The burden then shifts to Charley to prove that the boat was lost through no fault of his own. If Charley cannot meet that burden, Georgina recovers the full value of the boat.

Exculpatory Clauses

Bailees often use exculpatory clauses in an effort to limit their liability. **An exculpatory clause is any part of a contract that attempts to relieve one of the parties of future liability.** Exculpatory clauses are commonly employed in parking garages, coat check locations (restaurants or museums), warehouses, suitcase lockers, and so forth. For example, an exculpatory clause at a coat check might state that the restaurant is not responsible for any loss or damage to the customer's coat. Are such clauses valid? Occasionally.

If the bailor is a corporation and it has bargaining power roughly equal to the bailee's, a court will probably enforce a bailment exculpatory clause. If Manufacturer agrees to park five of its aircraft in a hangar owned by Hannah Corp., and Hannah's storage contract states that it is not responsible for any losses caused by fire, flood, or hurricane, then Hannah is probably protected when fire destroys Manufacturer's planes. Both parties are corporations, and the law assumes they should live with whatever agreement they bargained. However, even if the parties have equal bargaining power, an exculpatory clause is generally unenforceable if it attempts to exclude an intentional tort or gross negligence.

When the bailor is a consumer, the exculpatory clause stands on shaky ground, because judges generally presume the parties have unequal bargaining power. Courts look to see whether the clause was clearly written and easily visible.

The following case arises in a familiar setting, and indicates the wide reach of bailment principles.

TANNENBAUM V. NEW YORK DRY CLEANING, INC.

2001 N.Y. Slip Op. 40076 (U), 2001 WL 913272
Civil Court of the City of New York, 2001

Facts: When Rob Tannenbaum picked up his $160 shirt at the dry cleaners, he found it too badly torn to wear. He sued, claiming negligence. New York Cleaners denied causing the tear. In addition, the cleaners claimed that even if the company damaged the shirt, an exculpatory clause on the back of the ticket limited its liability to $20.

Issues: Were the cleaners negligent? If so, did the exculpatory clause limit the company's liability?

Excerpts from Judge Samuels' Decision: To the customer, it doesn't seem reasonable that he should be able to recover only $20.00 for the destruction of the $160 shirt he took to the dry cleaner to be laundered. To the dry cleaner, it doesn't seem reasonable that he should risk liability of $160.00—an extraordinary price for a shirt—in exchange for the lousy $2.00 laundering fee he charges.

The Limitation Clause, titled, in bold, italic 14-point type, "CONDITIONS," first states, in italic 12-point type, "WE ARE NOT RESPONSIBLE FOR ARTICLES NOT CLAIMED WITHIN 30 DAYS." The remainder of the Limitation Clause, in plain 8-point type (the minimum size legally admissible for a consumer transaction), reads as follows:

> We exercise utmost care in processing articles entrusted to us. Nevertheless, we cannot assume responsibility for inherent weaknesses of or defects in materials that are not readily apparent prior to processing.
>
> In laundering, we cannot guarantee against color loss, and shrinkage; or against damage to weak and tender fabrics. The company's liability with respect to any lost article shall not exceed 10 times our charge for processing it.

The foregoing is printed in gray type, against a light yellow background, and is significantly more difficult for a person with good eyesight to read than the text on the front of the claim ticket.

On its face, the Limitation Clause does not apply to the damage alleged in this case. Defendant does not allege that the Shirt was damaged because of "inherent weaknesses of or defects in" the material [or] complain of "color loss" or "shrinkage." Defendant has not alleged that the Shirt was made of "weak [or] tender fabrics."

This case is clearly one of bailment for hire. When a bailee is unable to return the bailed item, or (as here) returns it in damaged condition, a rebuttable presumption arises that the loss of, or damage to, the item is attributable to the bailee's negligence.

At trial, Defendant denied that the Shirt had been damaged while in its care, but did not offer, in the alternative, any explanation negating the presumption of negligence that follows from the Court's finding that the Shirt was damaged while in Defendant's care. Accordingly, Defendant is liable for negligence, unless its disclaimer is effective.

New York law, however, has long disfavored exculpatory clauses that relieve a party to a contract from liability for the consequences of its own negligence. The law's disfavor has been expressed not in a prohibition of such clauses, but in strict requirements that the disclaimer of liability for negligence be made explicit and be communicated in such a way as to ensure that the party who is to be bound by the disclaimer has knowingly accepted such disclaimer as part of the contract between the parties.

It appears that Defendant sought to enjoy the protections of a disclaimer without alarming its customers by causing them actually to contemplate the parade of horribles addressed in the Limitation Clause. There is no language on the front of the Claim Ticket referring the customer to the terms on the reverse side, let alone the caption "Contract" in red ink.

As Claimant testified credibly that he had not read the text on the back of the Claim Ticket and was not aware of the Limitation Clause when he entrusted the Shirt to Defendant, and Defendant offered no evidence that it had taken any steps to call Claimant's attention to its terms beyond giving him the Claim Ticket, the Court finds that Claimant was not aware of, and did not assent to be bound by, the Limitation Clause. Accordingly, even if the language of the Limitation Clause did make it applicable to the damage suffered by the Shirt, Claimant would not be bound by its terms and would be entitled to recover the full reasonable value of the Shirt.

Claimant is awarded judgment in the amount of $160.00, plus interest and costs. ■

Devil's
A*dvocate*
The exculpatory clause clearly capped the cleaner's liability, but the court finds the company failed to inform the customer of the limits imposed. How is a company supposed to do that, without driving business out the door? If a clerk asks everyone to read the back of the ticket, won't that alienate potential customers? Realistically, the court is imposing absolute liability on a dry cleaning company—a heavy burden on a small business with a thin profit margin. ◆

Rights and Duties of the Bailor

The bailor's rights and duties are the reverse of the bailee's. The bailor is entitled to the return of his property on the agreed-upon date. He is also entitled to receive the property in good condition and to recover damages for harm to the property, if the bailee failed to use adequate care.

Liability for Defects

Depending upon the type of bailment, the bailor is potentially liable for known or even unknown defects in the property. **If the bailment is for the sole benefit of the bailee, the bailor must notify the bailee of any known defects.** Suppose Megan lends her stepladder to Dave. The top rung is loose and Megan knows it, but forgets to tell Dave. The top rung crumbles and Dave falls onto his girlfriend's iguana. Megan is liable to Dave and the girlfriend unless the defect in the ladder was obvious. Notice that Megan's liability is not only to the bailee, but also to any others injured by the defects. Megan would not be liable if she had notified Dave of the defective rung.

In a mutual-benefit bailment, the bailor is liable not only for known defects but also for unknown defects that the bailor could have discovered with reasonable diligence. Suppose RentaLot rents a power sander to Dan. RentaLot does not realize that the sander has faulty wiring, but a reasonable inspection would have revealed the problem. When Dan suffers a serious shock from the defect, RentaLot is liable to him, even though it was unaware of the problem.

If the bailor is in the business of renting property, the bailment is probably subject to implied warranties. As we saw in Chapter 21, on product liability, the Uniform Commercial Code creates various implied warranties for goods sold (Article 2) or leased (Article 2A) by a merchant. A merchant is someone in the business of selling or leasing that type of goods. A car rental company is a merchant with respect to its cars, so it rents the autos subject to implied warranties that they are fit for their normal purposes. Because these warranties are implied by law, they normally exist whether the parties say anything about them or not. Bailors may attempt to limit these implied warranties by provisions in the bailment agreement, but courts disfavor such limitations, especially when the bailee is a consumer. For a full discussion of implied warranties, see Chapter 21, on product liability.

Common Carriers and Contract Carriers

A carrier is a company that transports goods for others. It is a bailee of every shipment entrusted to it. There are two kinds of carriers: common carriers and contract carriers. The distinction is important because each type of company has a different level of liability.

A **common carrier** makes its services available on a regular basis to the general public. For example, a trucking company located in St. Louis that is willing to haul freight for anyone, to any destination in the country, is a common carrier. **Generally, a common carrier is strictly liable for harm to the bailor's goods.** Common carriers are governed by a statute known as the Carmack Amendment.[5] Under this law, a bailor needs only to establish that it delivered property to the carrier in good condition and that the cargo arrived damaged. The carrier is then liable unless it can show that it was not negligent *and* that the loss was caused by an act of God (such as a hurricane), an act of a public enemy (a nation at war with the United States), an act of the bailor itself (for example, by packaging the goods improperly), an act of a public authority (for example, a state inspector forcing a delay), or the inherent nature of the goods (such as fruit that spoiled naturally). These are hard defenses to prove, and in most cases a common carrier is liable for harm to the property.

When checking into a hotel, it is best to make no assumptions about the safety of your valuables or the innkeeper's liability for their loss.

A common carrier is, however, allowed to limit its liability by contract. For example, a common carrier might offer the bailor the choice of two shipping rates: a low rate, with a maximum liability, say, of $10,000, or a higher shipping rate, with full liability for any harm to the goods. In that case, if the bailor chooses the lower rate, the limitation on liability is enforceable. Even if the bailor proves a loss of $300,000, the carrier owes merely $10,000.

A **contract carrier** does not make its services available to the general public, but engages in continuing agreements with particular customers. Assume that Steel Curtain Shipping is a trucking company in Pittsburgh that hauls cargo to California for two or three steel producers and carries manufactured goods from California to Pennsylvania and New York for a few West Coast companies. Steel Curtain is a contract carrier. **A contract carrier does not incur strict liability.** The normal bailment rules apply, and a contract carrier can escape liability by demonstrating that it exercised due care of the property.

Innkeepers

Hotels, motels, and inns frequently act as bailees of their guests' property. Most states have special innkeeper statutes that regulate liability.

| at **R!SK** | Hotel patrons often assume that anything they bring to a hotel is safe. But some state innkeeper statutes impose an absolute limit on a hotel's liability. Other statutes require guests to leave valuables in the inn's safe deposit box. And even that may not be enough to protect them fully. For example, a state statute might require the guest to register the nature and value of the goods with the hotel. Savvy travelers make no assumptions about safety—nor do their hosts, as the Four Seasons Hotel will cheerfully help us demonstrate. ◆ |

---

5   49 U.S.C. §11707.

PARASKEVAIDES V. FOUR SEASONS WASHINGTON

292 F.3d 886, 2002 WL 1300031
United States District Court for the District of Columbia, 2002

Facts: Thelma and Christina Paraskevaides arrived in Washington, D.C., for a few days of fancy socializing (see below). They checked into the Four Seasons hotel bringing with them close to $1.2 million worth of jewelry (they had to look *decent*). Their hotel suite had two bedrooms and a living room. Each room had a "convenience safe" located in the back of a closet, accessible via keys provided by the hotel.

The guests placed the jewels and other valuables in the bedroom safes rather than in the safety deposit boxes provided by the hotel near the reception area. When they returned from a night out, they found (can you guess?) that the room had been entered without force and the safes emptied. The jewels were never found. The hotel manager stated that safes could be opened either by the key supplied or by one of two master keys. One of the master keys had been missing for six months.

The Paraskevaides sued the hotel. The district court gave summary judgment for the Four Seasons, ruling that a local innkeeper statute protected the hotel. The statute, D.C. Code §30-101, provides that under specified circumstances, a hotel is not liable for loss of personal property. The trial court also ruled that the two guests had committed contributory negligence by failing to use the hotel's safety deposit boxes. In the District of Columbia, any contributory negligence by a plaintiff bars a defendant's liability. The Paraskevaides appealed.

Issues: Was the hotel entitled to innkeeper immunity? Did the Paraskevaides commit contributory negligence?

Excerpts from Judge Sentelle's Decision: In limiting a hotel's liability, section 30-101 deviates from the general common law [which holds innkeepers strictly liable for lost personal items] and must therefore be strictly construed. The plain language of the statute states quite clearly that a hotel must "display conspicuously in the guest *and public rooms* of [the hotel] a printed copy" of the limiting statute (or summary thereof). It is undisputed that the Four Seasons only posted a copy of the limiting statute in the guest rooms of the hotel, thereby failing to post

notices in any of the hotel's "public rooms." The Four Seasons nonetheless contends that its posting of the "summary of the statute and the accompanying disclaimer notice were sufficient to place the Paraskevaides on notice of the liability limitations provided by the Innkeeper Statute." The district court agreed, ruling that by posting a printed copy of section 30-101 next to the in-room convenience safe, the Four Seasons "place[d] the plaintiffs on notice and satisf[ied] [its] obligation under the statute to do such." Perhaps the Paraskevaides had notice; perhaps not. But whether they did is irrelevant to our disposition of this case. What is clear is that the Four Seasons did not display, conspicuously or otherwise, a copy or summary of the statute in its public rooms. Therefore, when we strictly construe this statute, as we must, we conclude that the Four Seasons failed to comply fully with the statute's requirements for limiting its liability to the Paraskevaides.

Once we conclude that the Innkeeper Statute does not apply to the Four Seasons, we are left with the question: What law, in fact, does apply? The district court noted, as do we, that under the common law doctrine of *infra hospitium* an innkeeper is strictly liable for loss or damage to a guest's property. However, the district court reached no conclusion as to whether this particular common law doctrine applies in the District of Columbia. We conclude that in the interests of justice, the appropriate action is to remand this issue to the district court for further proceedings.

Contributory Negligence

[Because the District Court ruled as a matter of law that the Paraskevaides committed contributory negligence, no jury would be allowed to decide that issue.] Whether a plaintiff is contributorily negligent is usually a question for the jury. The district court's decision reflects its conclusion that this is the rare and exceptional case—that the Paraskevaides demonstrated such a "lack of prudence in choosing to place $1.2 million dollars worth of jewelry in a hotel room safe" that a fair-minded jury could reach this and only this conclusion. Based on the facts before us, we conclude otherwise.

▼

The Paraskevaides provided evidence that even though they normally do not travel with $1.2 million worth of jewelry, they did so on this particular trip because they were scheduled to attend such functions as lunch on Capitol Hill, a reception hosted by the First Lady, dinner with the Secretary of State, and breakfast at the Vice President's residence. They also provided evidence that they were uncomfortable placing their jewelry in the safety deposit boxes provided by the Four Seasons because the location of the boxes was "not in a . . . private place in the hotel," but was instead in a room with a door that faced the lobby. According to the Paraskevaides, "when you go in to get some things or put things in [the safety deposit boxes], then you walk [among] people [in the lobby]." Given the location of the safety deposit boxes, the Paraskevaides "felt it was safer" to place their valuables in the locked in-room convenience safes.

We cannot conclude that by traveling with valuable jewelry to attend high-level political functions in Washington, D.C., and by placing those valuables in a locked room safe because it was more remote and appeared safer than a safety deposit box, the Paraskevaides were negligent as a matter of law. We conclude instead that these facts present a genuine issue of material fact that is more appropriately resolved by a jury.

[Reversed and remanded.] ■

Ethics

In the Paraskevaides case, which party do you think was ethically right? From the Chapter 2 Ethics Checklist: What are the critical issues? The guests raised concerns about using safety deposit boxes that are visible from the lobby. Is their claim legitimate? How should the hotel respond to that concern? Is it fair to place lock boxes in hotel rooms but then deny liability when they are broken into? ◆

Chapter Conclusion

One deduction from this chapter is that carrying a suitcase filled with jewelry is as risky as . . . one would think. A more general conclusion is that personal property law plays an almost daily role in all of our lives. The manager of a dry cleaning company, the finder of lost property, and a bank officer who rents safe deposit boxes must all realize that they could incur substantial liability for personal property, whether they intend to accept that obligation or not. Understanding personal property law can be worth a lot of money—but never carry all of it with you.

Chapter Review

1. A gift is a voluntary transfer of property from one person to another without consideration. The elements of a gift are intention to transfer ownership immediately, delivery, and acceptance.

2. The finder of property must attempt to locate the true owner, unless the property was abandoned. State estray statutes have made some changes in the common law, but the following principles generally govern:

   • Abandoned property—the finder may keep it.

   • Lost property—the finder generally has rights superior to everyone but the true owner, except that if she found it on land belonging to another, the property owner generally is entitled to it.

   • Mislaid property—generally, the finder has no rights in the property.

   • Treasure trove—generally, the finder may keep it.

3. Accession occurs when one person uses labor and/or materials to add value to personal property belonging to another. If the improver knows he is making accessions without authority, the owner may generally take the improved property without compensating for the work done. If the improver mistakenly believes he is entitled to

add accessions, the owner probably has to pay for the increased value.

4. A bailment is the rightful possession of goods by one who is not the owner. The one who delivers the goods is the bailor and the one in possession is the bailee. To create a bailment, the bailee must assume physical control with intent to possess.

5. The bailee is always entitled to possess the property, is frequently allowed to use it, and may be entitled to compensation.

6. The bailee is strictly liable to redeliver the goods to the bailor.

7. The bailee is obligated to exercise due care. The level of care required depends upon who receives the benefit of the bailment: if the bailee is the sole beneficiary, she must use extraordinary care; if the parties mutually benefit, the bailee must use ordinary care; and if the bailor is the sole beneficiary of the bailment, the bailee must use only slight care.

8. Once the bailor has proven the existence of a bailment and loss, a presumption of negligence arises, and the burden shifts to the bailee to prove adequate care.

9. Exculpatory clauses, seeking to relieve a bailee of liability for damage to the goods, may be enforced between two corporations of equal bargaining power but are seldom enforced against a consumer.

10. The bailor must keep the property in suitable repair, free of any hidden defects. If the bailor is in the business of renting property, the bailment is probably subject to implied warranties.

11. Generally, a common carrier is strictly liable for harm to the bailor's goods. A contract carrier incurs only normal bailment liability.

12. The liability of an innkeeper is regulated by state statute. A guest intending to store valuables with an innkeeper must follow the statute to the letter.

Practice Test

1. While in her second year at the Juilliard School of Music in New York City, Ann Rylands had a chance to borrow for one month a rare Guadagnini violin, made in 1768. She returned the violin to the owner in Philadelphia, but telephoned her father to ask if he would buy it for her. He borrowed money from his pension fund and paid the owner. Ann traveled to Philadelphia to pick up the violin. She had exclusive possession of the violin for the next 20 years, using it in her professional career. Unfortunately, she became an alcoholic, and during one period when she was in a treatment center, she entrusted the violin to her mother for safekeeping. At about that time, her father died. When Ann was released from the center, she requested return of the violin, but her mother refused. Who owns the violin?

2. **ETHICS** Jane says to Cody, "If you will agree to work as my yard man, I'll pay you $1,000 per week for a normal workweek. You can start on Monday, and I'll guarantee you eight months' work." Cody is elated at his good fortune and agrees to start work on Monday. Later that day, Cody, still rejoicing, says to Beth, his girlfriend, "You know those sapphire earrings in the jewelry store that you're wild about? At the end of next week I'm going to buy them for you." On Monday, Jane realizes what a foolish thing she said, and refuses to hire Cody. Cody, in turn, refuses to buy the earrings for Beth. Cody sues Jane and wins; Beth sues Cody and loses. Why the opposite outcomes? What basic ideas of fairness underlie the two results?

3. Ronald Armstead worked for First American Bank as a courier. His duties included making deliveries between the bank's branches in Washington, D.C. Armstead parked the bank's station wagon near the entrance of one branch in violation of a sign saying: "No Parking Rush Hour Zone." In the rear luggage section of the station wagon were four locked bank dispatch bags, containing checks and other valuable documents. Armstead had received tickets for illegal parking at this spot on five occasions. Shortly after Armstead entered the bank, a tow truck arrived and its operator prepared to tow the station wagon. Transportation Management, Inc., operated the towing service on behalf of the District of Columbia. Armstead ran out to the vehicle and told the tow truck operator that he was prepared to drive the vehicle away immediately. But the

operator drove away with the station wagon in tow. One and one-half hours later, a bank employee paid for the car's release, but one dispatch bag, containing documents worth $107,000, was missing. First American sued Transportation Management and the District of Columbia. The defendants sought summary judgment, claiming they *could not* be liable. Were they correct?

4. During the Great Depression of the 1930s, the federal government's Works Progress Administration hired artists to create public works of art. The goal was to provide employment and beautify the nation. The artist James Daugherty painted six murals on the walls of the public high school in Stamford, Connecticut. During the 1970s, the city began to restore its high school. The architect and school officials agreed that the Daugherty murals should be preserved. They arranged for the construction workers to remove the murals to prevent harm. By accident, the workers rolled them up and placed them near the trash dumpsters for disposal. A student found the murals and took them home, and later notified the federal government's General Services Administration (GSA) of his find. The GSA arranged to transport the murals to an art restorer, named Hiram Hoelzer, for storage and eventual restoration, when funds could be arranged. Over *19 years* went by before anyone notified the Stamford School system where the murals were. In the meantime, neither the GSA nor anyone else paid Hoelzer for the storage or restoration. By 1989 the murals were valued at $1.25 million by Sotheby's, an art auction house. Hoelzer filed suit, seeking a declaration that the murals had been abandoned. Were they abandoned? What difference does it make?

5. **CPA QUESTION** Which of the following requirements must be met to create a bailment?

   I. Delivery of personal property to the intended bailee

   II. Possession by the intended bailee

   III. An absolute duty on the intended bailee to return or dispose of the property according to the bailor's directions

   a. I and II only

   b. I and III only

   c. II and III only

   d. I, II, and III

6. Shannon borrows Marty's car, but when she returns the auto, she hands the keys to Scott, who claims he is Marty's brother. Scott offers a driver's license and passport to reassure Shannon. Scott is actually a con artist. Marty sues Shannon. Outcome?

   a. Marty will win.

   b. Marty will win only if a *reasonable person* would have spotted the fraud.

   c. Marty will win only if he in fact has no brother named Scott.

   d. Marty will lose, because Scott offered reasonable identification.

7. Marjan International Corp. sells handmade oriental rugs. V. K. Putman, Inc., is a Montana trucking company. Marjan delivered valuable rugs to Putman for shipment from New York City to Tacoma, Washington. Unfortunately, there were several delays in transit. The truck driver encountered snow storms and closed roads. His truck also overheated and required repairs in a garage. Before the driver resumed the trip, he stopped to pick up and load other goods. When the truck finally arrived in Tacoma, two bales of rugs were missing. Marjan sued, on the grounds that Putman was a common carrier, but Putman claimed it was a contract carrier. What difference does it make whether Putman was a common carrier or a contract carrier, and how is that determined?

8. Lonny Joe owned two rare 1955 Ford Thunderbird automobiles, one red and one green, both in mint condition. He stored the cars in his garage. His friend Stephanie wanted to use the red car in a music video, so Lonny Joe rented it to her for two days, for $300 per day. When she returned the red car, Lonny Joe discovered a long scratch along one side. That same day, he noticed a long scratch along the side of the green car. He sued Stephanie for harm to the red car. Lonny Joe sued an electrician for damage to the green car, claiming that the scratch occurred while the electrician was fixing a heater in the garage. Explain the different burdens of proof in the two cases.

9. The government accused Carlo Francia and another of stealing a purse belonging to Frances Bainlardi. A policeman saw Francia sorting through the contents of the purse, which included a photo identification of Bainlardi. Francia kept some items, such as cash, while discarding others. At trial, Francia claimed that he had thought the purse was lost or abandoned. Besides the fact that Francia's accomplice was holding burglary tools, what is the weakness in Francia's defense?

10. *YOU BE THE JUDGE* WRITING PROBLEM Eileen Murphy often cared for her elderly neighbor, Thomas Kenney. He paid her $25 per day for her help and once gave her a bank certificate of deposit worth $25,000. She spent the money. Murphy alleged that shortly before his death, Kenney gave her a large block of shares in three corporations. He called his broker, intending to instruct him to transfer the shares to Murphy's name, but the broker was ill and unavailable. So Kenney told Murphy to write her name on the shares and keep them, which she did. Two weeks later Kenney died. When Murphy presented the shares to Kenney's broker to transfer ownership to her, the broker refused because Kenney had never endorsed the shares as the law requires, that is, signed them over to Murphy. Was Murphy entitled to the $25,000? To the shares? **Argument for Murphy:** The purpose of the law is to do what a donor intended, and it is obvious that Kenney intended Murphy to have the $25,000 and the shares. Why else would he have given them to her? A greedy estate should not be allowed to interfere with the deceased's intention. **Argument for the Estate:** Murphy is not entitled to the $25,000 because we have no way of knowing what Kenney's intentions were when he gave her the money. She is not entitled to the shares of stock because Kenney's failure to endorse them over to her meant he never *delivered* them, and that is an essential element of a gift.

11. You decide to open a rental store, renting everything from lawn mowers to power saws to complete dinner service for 150. What principles of bailment law should you be aware of?

12. *ROLE REVERSAL* Write a multiple-choice question focusing on one of these topics: a gift *causa mortis*, lost property, or a bailment.

Internet Research Problem

You own a helicopter worth $250,000. A business associate wishes to use it for one week to show prospective clients around various islands in the Caribbean. You are willing to let him use it, for a fee of $15,000. Draft a bailment agreement. Find a sample bailment form online to use as a model.

> **You can find further practice problems at** http://beatty.westbuslaw.com **or in the Study Guide that accompanies this text.**

Planning for the Future: Estates and Insurance

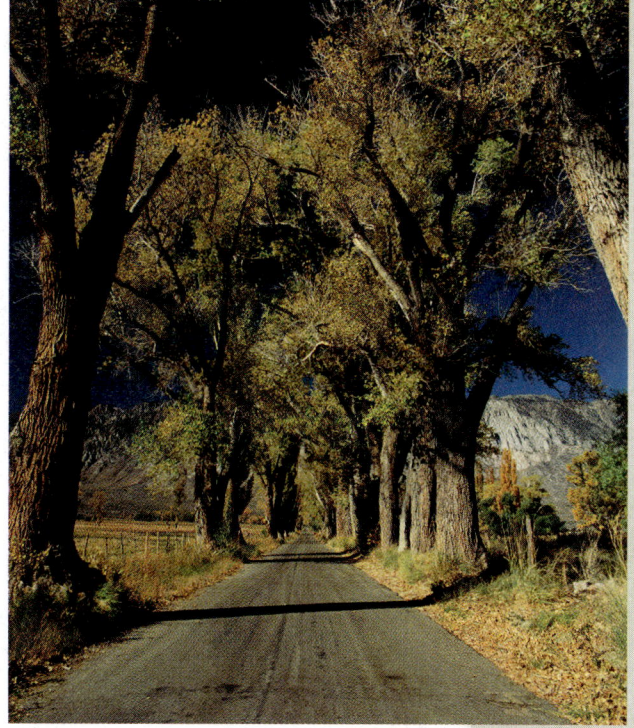

Emily and Nick had been friends since childhood. In high school they were teammates on the cross-country squad; in college they often commiserated over tough courses and difficult romances. After college, Emily went to business school and from there to a venture capital firm. Nick followed his life-long dream of becoming a high school teacher. But they still kept in touch and were members of the same running club. They even bought houses near each other. When an old estate went on the market, Emily bought the manor house, Nick the gatekeeper's cottage.

By age 45, Nick was married with two children. Although his salary was modest, he saved carefully, purchased enough life insurance to replace his income if he died prematurely, and signed a will that would divide his assets in an orderly way. To pay the premiums on his life insurance, his family gave up resort vacations and went to visit their families instead.

"Boring!" thought Emily. "I can't believe you spend so much on life insurance," she scolded Nick, "you can't afford it." For her part, Emily was making a fortune each and every year. She had been divorced once, was currently separated from her second husband, had one child by each marriage and was involved in a passionate affair with a clerk at her office. Her husband was living in the house with their child, while Emily resided with her boyfriend in a fancy condo she owned downtown. She took lavish vacations, bought expensive jewelry and artwork, and kept intending to write a will. She earned so much money, she did not need life insurance.

One bright fall day, Emily and Nick were driving in Emily's new Viper sports car to a road race. She was so busy showing Nick all the gadgets that she did not notice when the truck in front of them stopped suddenly. Her car plowed into the truck, killing them both instantly.

Nick's widow was devastated. But because of Nick's careful planning, she was able to keep her house and maintain her family's lifestyle. Emily's extended family did not fare so well. The ex-spouse, estranged spouse, children, and boyfriend spent years and hundreds of thousands of dollars squabbling and ultimately litigating the rights to her money, the house, the downtown condo, and the rest of her estate. Her venture capital firm went out of business and was unable to pay her pension or even her salary for the last year. Because her ex-spouse and her husband were no longer receiving support from her, they had to sell their houses and move the children to new school districts. For children who were already suffering from the loss of their mother, this was an added emotional blow. ■

Bad things happen to good people (and good businesses). This chapter is about mitigating the risks of these bad things by planning for the future. Virtually everyone should have a will and absolutely everyone should make careful, considered decisions on how much and what kinds of insurance coverage they need.

INTRODUCTION TO ESTATE PLANNING

There is one immutable law of the universe: "You can't take it with you." As the Egyptian pharaohs discovered, regardless of your fame or wealth, eventually you and your material goods will part. But you can control where your assets go after your death. Or you can decide not to bother with an estate plan and leave all in chaos behind you.

Definitions

Like many areas of the law, estate planning uses its own terminology:

- **Estate Planning.** The process of giving away property after (or in anticipation of) death.

- **Estate.** The legal entity that holds title to assets after the owner dies and before the property is distributed.
- **Decedent.** The person who has died.
- **Testator** or **Testatrix.** Someone who has signed a valid will. **Testatrix** is the female version (from the Latin).
- **Intestate.** To die without a will.
- **Heir.** Technically, the term "heir" refers to someone who inherits from a decedent who died intestate. **Devisee** means someone who inherits under a will. However, common parlance and many courts use "heir" to refer to anyone who inherits property, and we follow that usage in this chapter.
- **Probate.** The process of carrying out the terms of a will.
- **Executor** or **Executrix.** A personal representative chosen by the decedent to carry out the terms of the will. An **executrix** is a female executor.
- **Administrator** or **Administratrix.** A personal representative appointed by the probate court to oversee the probate process for someone who has died intestate. As you can guess, an **administratrix** is a female administrator.
- **Grantor or Settlor.** Someone who creates a trust.
- **Donor.** Someone who makes a gift or creates a trust.

Throughout this chapter, we use the masculine and feminine versions of testator, executor, and administrator interchangeably. These are dated terms that reflect a sexist era when men and women had different legal rights. It would be more progressive to bury these words in the same graveyard as "authoress" and "poetess," but courts and lawyers still use them and so must we.

Purpose

Estate planning has two primary goals: to ensure that property is distributed as the owner desires and to minimize estate taxes. Although tax issues are beyond the scope of this chapter, they are an important element of estate planning, often affecting not only how people transfer their property but, in some cases, to whom. For instance, wealthy people may give money to charity, at least in part, to minimize the taxes on the rest of their estate.

As this chapter goes to press, Congress is considering legislation to reduce or eliminate the estate tax. Has it done so? ◆

Probate Law

The federal government and many states currently levy estate taxes, although the tax rate imposed by states is typically much lower. Only the states, and not the federal government, have probate codes to regulate the creation and implementation of wills and trusts. These codes vary from state to state. This chapter, therefore, speaks only of general trends among the states. Certainly, anyone who is preparing a will must consult the laws of the relevant state. To make probate law more consistent, the National Conference of Commissioners on Uniform State Laws issued a Uniform Probate Code (UPC). However, fewer than half of the states have adopted it.

WILLS

A will is a legal document that disposes of the testator's property after death. It can, in most instances, be revoked or altered at any time until death. (To find out how much longer you will live, check out http://www.northwesternmutual.com/games/longevity.) Virtually every adult, even those with only modest assets, should have a will:

- To ensure that their assets (modest though they may be) are distributed in accordance with their wishes.

- To select a personal representative to oversee the estate. If the decedent does not name an executor in a will, the court will appoint an administrator. Generally, people prefer to have a friend, rather than a court, in charge of their property.

- To avoid unnecessary expenses. Those who die intestate often leave behind issues for lawyers to resolve. A properly drafted will can also reduce the estate tax bill.

- To provide guardians for minor children. If parents do not appoint a guardian before they die, a court will. Presumably, the parents are best able to make this choice.

Wondering how to talk with your family about wills and inheritance? Find advice on the family dynamics of estate planning at http://www.yellowpieplate.umn.edu. The AARP also offers advice about writing wills at http://www.aarp.org/estate_planning.

The following article suggests another purpose for a will: to take revenge on your enemies.[1]

NEWS*worthy*

I give to the Lieutenant-General Cromwell one of my words . . . which he must want, seeing that he hath never kept any of his own.

—Philip, fifth Earl of Pembroke, seventeenth century

Seeing that I had the misfortune to be married to the aforesaid Elizabeth, who, ever since our union, has tormented me in every possible way; that not content with making game of all my remonstrances, she has done all she could to render my life miserable; that Heaven seems to have sent her into the world solely to drive me out of it; that the strength of Samson, the genius of Homer, the prudence of Augustus, the skill of Pyrrhus, the patience of Job, the philosophy of Socrates, the subtlety of Hannibal, the vigilance of Hermogenes, would not suffice to subdue the perversity of her character . . . weighing seriously all these considerations . . . I bequeath, to my said wife Elizabeth, the sum of one shilling.

—John George, 1791

I leave Parson Chavasse (Maggy's husband) the snuff box I got from the Sarnia Militia, as a small token of gratitude for the service he has done my family in taking a sister that no man of taste would have taken.

—William Dunlop, Canada, 1842

Before anything else is to be done 50 cents is to be paid to my son-in-law to enable him to buy for himself a good stout rope with which to hang himself, and thus rid mankind of one of the most infamous scoundrels that ever roamed this broad land or dwelt outside of a penitentiary.

—Garvey B. White, 1908 ◆

Legal Technicalities

A testator must comply with the legal requirements for executing a will: it must be in writing, and the testator must sign it or direct someone else to sign it for him, if he is

---

[1] Jeff Stryker, "They Couldn't Resist: Oh, One Last Thing . . . ," *New York Times*, May 21, 2000, §4, p. 7.

too weak. Generally, two witnesses must also sign the will. No one named in a will should also serve a witness because, in many states, a witness may not inherit under a will. The importance of abiding by the legal technicalities cannot be overstated. No matter what the testator's intent, courts generally do not enforce a will unless each requirement of the law has been fully met.

Holographic Will

Some states recognize a *holographic will*: a will that is handwritten and signed by the testatrix, but not witnessed. Suppose Rowena is on a plane that suffers engine trouble. For 15 minutes, the pilot struggles to control the plane. Despite his efforts, it crashes, killing everyone aboard. During those 15 minutes, Rowena writes on a Post-it note, "This is my last will and testament. I leave all my assets to the National Gallery of Art in Washington, D.C." She signs her name, but her fellow passengers are too frantic to witness it. This note is found in the wreckage of the plane. Her previous will, signed and witnessed in a lawyer's office, left everything to her beau, Ivan. If Rowena resides in one of the majority of states that accepts a holographic will, then Ivan is out of luck and the National Gallery will inherit all. One court has, indeed, accepted as a will a handwritten Post-it note that had not been witnessed.

Nuncupative Will

Some states will also accept a **nuncupative will.** This is the formal term for an oral will. For a nuncupative will to be valid, the testatrix must know she is dying, there must be three witnesses, and these witnesses must know that they are listening to her will. Suppose that Rowena survives the airplane crash for a few hours. Instead of writing a will on the plane, she whispers to a nurse in the hospital, "I'd like all my property to go to the Angell Memorial Cat Hospital." This oral will is valid if there are two other witnesses and Rowena also says, "I'm dying. Please witness my oral will." The cat hospital, however, is only entitled to her personal property. Nuncupative wills cannot be used to dispose of real estate. Ivan would inherit her farm.

Spouse's Share

A spouse is entitled to a **forced share** of the decedent's estate (unless she waives that right by written contract). In community property states, a spouse can override the will and claim one-half of all marital property acquired during the marriage, except property that the testator inherited or received as a gift.[2] Although this rule sounds easy and fair, implementation can be troublesome. If a couple has been married for many years and has substantial assets, it can be very difficult to sort out what is and is not community property. Suppose that the testatrix inherited a million dollars 20 years before her death. She and her husband both earned sizable incomes during their careers. How can a court tell what money bought which asset? Anyone in a situation such as this should keep detailed records.

In most non-community property states, a spouse can override the will and claim some percentage (usually one-third to one-half) of the decedent's probate estate (again, unless she has waived that right by written contract). Under the Uniform Probate Code (UPC), a surviving spouse is entitled to whichever is greater: $50,000, or a percentage of the decedent's assets. The percentage depends upon how long the couple was married. At 5 years, a spouse is entitled to 15 percent; at 10 years, 30 percent; and

---

2 Arizona, California, Idaho, Louisiana, Nevada, New Mexico, Texas, and Washington all have community property law; Wisconsin's system is a variation of the same principle.

at 15 years, 50 percent.[3] Suppose that, when Drew and Sandy marry, Drew has assets of $500,000 while Sandy has virtually nothing. If Drew dies anytime during the first five years of their marriage, Sandy is entitled to $50,000. At five years, the share automatically goes up to $75,000. After 15 years, it reaches the maximum of $250,000.

Children's Share

Parents are not required to leave assets to their children. They may disinherit their children for any reason.[4] In most states, this is true even if the children are minors whom the testator was obligated to support while alive.

However, the law presumes that a **pretermitted child** (that is, a child left nothing in the parent's will) was omitted by accident, unless the parent clearly indicates in the will that he has omitted the child on purpose. To do so, he must either leave her some nominal amount, such as $1, or specifically write in the will that the omission was intentional: "I am making no bequest to my daughter because she has chosen a religion of which I disapprove."

If a pretermitted child is left out by accident, she is generally entitled to the same share she would have received if her parent had died intestate. How likely is it that a parent would *forget* a child? Do you think the father in the following case simply forgot?

In Re ESTATE OF JOSIAH JAMES TRELOAR, JR.

151 N.H. 460; 859 A.2d 1162; 2004 N.H. LEXIS 177
Supreme Court of New Hampshire, 2004

Facts: Josiah James Treloar, Jr.'s first will left his estate to his wife unless she died before he did, in which case one piece of land was to go to his daughter Evelyn, another to his son, Rodney, and the rest of his estate was to be divided equally among Evelyn, Rodney, and another daughter, Beverly.

After his daughter Evelyn died, Josiah executed a new will. To help his lawyer in preparing this document, Josiah gave him a copy of the old will with handwritten changes, including Evelyn's name crossed out. The new will left the land to Rodney and the remainder of the estate to Rodney and Beverly equally. Evelyn's husband and children got nothing, although Evelyn's husband, Leon, was named as executor. The will stated: "I hereby nominate and so far as I legally may appoint as Executor of this will, my son-in-law, Leon Merrill of Concord, New Hampshire."

Under New Hampshire law, all issue (including children and grandchildren) can qualify as pretermitted heirs. The law assumes that if the testator does not leave anything to his issue or does not refer to them in his will, it is because he has forgotten them. They are therefore entitled to a share of his estate. If Josiah had mentioned Evelyn, then the assumption would be that he had not forgotten her or her children. Evelyn's children argued that they were entitled to a share of Josiah's estate because he had not left her or them out on purpose. Josiah's attorney was serving as executor (not Leon). When he refused to pay the children, they sued.

Issue: Are Evelyn's children entitled to a share of Josiah's estate?

Excerpts from Justice Galway's Decision:[5] The purpose of the statute [on pretermitted heirs] is to

▼

---

[3]   UPC §2-201.

[4]   The only exception to this rule is Louisiana, whose laws are based on the French model.

[5]   For readability, we use the term "Evelyn's children" instead of "respondents" and "executor" instead of "petitioner."

prevent a mistake or unintended failure by the testator to remember the natural object of his or her bounty. This rule of law is conclusive unless there is evidence in the will itself that the omission was intentional. To be a pretermitted heir, the child must not be named in the will, referred to in the will, or be a devisee or legatee under the will.

The executor asserts that, although the will names neither Evelyn nor her children, there are sufficient indirect references to Evelyn to satisfy the statute. The executor first argues that the reference in the will to revoking "all prior wills and testamentary instruments" coupled with evidence of the prior will, which specifically named Evelyn, and the testator's handwritten changes to it, demonstrate that he had Evelyn in mind when he prepared the will.

The court's task is not to investigate the circumstances to divine the intent of the testator; rather, it is to review the language contained within the four corners of the will for a determination of whether the testator named or referred to Evelyn's children.

We disagree with the executor that we must read the wills together. [The new] will stands on its own.

The executor next argues that the reference to Leon as the testator's "son-in-law" showed that he had Evelyn in mind when he drafted the [new] will. [T]he testator did not use his daughter's name. Nor did he use the phrase "son-in-law" in a bequest. Rather, he used the phrase "son-in-law" to identify the individual he wished to appoint as his executor.

Even if the will indirectly referred to Evelyn, these indirect references would not satisfy the statute for the purposes of disinheriting Evelyn's children. [T]he naming of one person, however closely related to another, without more, is no reference to that other. It is well established that there must be a reference in the will to the child himself. It is not sufficient to infer that the child was not forgotten because a sibling or other relative was remembered in the will.

For all of the above reasons, we conclude that Evelyn's children are pretermitted heirs. ■

PublicPolicy

Could Josiah possibly have *forgotten* his grandchildren? It seems more likely that he deliberately left them out. He crossed his daughter's name out of the earlier will and specifically appointed his son-in-law to be executor. But Josiah's intent is irrelevant; the will must comply with the technicalities of the statute, period. Does this rule make sense? Should the courts look to the testator's intent rather than to the technicalities? The law generally takes the view that wills are too important to permit guessing as to what the testator meant; the technicalities must be met exactly. As the old saying goes, close only counts in hand grenades and horseshoes. ◆

In drafting a will, lawyers almost always use the term **issue** instead of children. Issue means all descendants such as children, grandchildren, great-grandchildren, and so on. If the will leaves property to "my children" and one child dies before the testator, the child's children would not inherit their parent's share.

The will must also indicate whether issue are to inherit per stirpes or per capita. **Per stirpes** means that each *branch* of the family receives an equal share. Each child of the deceased receives the same amount, and, if a child has already died, her heirs inherit her share. **Per capita** means that each *heir* receives the same amount. If the children have died, then each grandchild inherits the same amount. Suppose that Gwendolyn has two children, Lance and Arthur. Lance has one child, Arthur has four. Both sons predecease their mother. If Gwendolyn's will says "per stirpes," Lance's child will inherit her father's entire share, which is half of Gwendolyn's estate. Arthur's four children will share their father's portion, so each will receive one-eighth ($1/4 \times 1/2$). If Gwendolyn's will says, "per capita," each of her grandchildren will inherit one-fifth of her estate. Although it might sound fairer to give all grandchildren the same inheritance, most people choose a per stirpes distribution, on the theory that they are treating their *children* equally. The following chart illustrates the difference between per stirpes and per capita.

Should decedents be allowed to leave their money to whomever they wish? Many societies have traditionally regulated inheritances. In England, for example, until 1925 **primogeniture** was the order of the day. Under this system, a father was required in most cases to leave all his property to his eldest son. Over time, however, countries have tended to allow testators a wider choice in devising their property. As we have seen, in the United States a testator can generally leave his property to whomever he wishes, except that his spouse is entitled to some portion of his estate.

Spending money to get around the law is an inefficient waste of societal resources. If the law forces people to leave their money to someone against their wishes, they will find ways to circumvent the law, and those ways will be inefficient. Suppose, for example, that a father, Osbert, must by law leave his property to his ne'er do well son, Cuthbert. Osbert would probably strive to find a way around this (in his view) unfair law. He might, for example, give all his property to his daughter, Alberta, and then lease it back from her for $1 a year. Making this plan work, however, would entail some expensive trips to the lawyer. Economists take the view that the cost of his efforts to avoid the law is a net waste of societal resources. According to this view, there are better ways to spend money than by paying unnecessary lawyer's fees.

Osbert might also decide that, rather than leaving his money to Cuthbert, he would prefer to spend it all himself. Economists do not approve of this attitude either. They would prefer that Osbert spend his money buying productive assets rather than frittering it away in a gambling den. These are two economic reasons why testators now have great latitude in preparing their wills. Under the law testators generally are required to leave some portion of their estate to their spouses for the simple reason that if a spouse is disinherited, the government may have to support her. ◆

Amending a Will

A testator can generally revoke or alter a will at any time prior to death. In most states, he can revoke a will by destroying it, putting an X through it, writing "revoked" (or some synonym) on it, or signing a new will. He can also execute an amendment—called a **codicil**—to change specific terms of the will, while keeping the rest of it intact. A codicil must meet all the requirements of a will, such as two witnesses. Suppose that Uncle Herman, who has a long and elaborate will, now wants his sterling silver Swiss Army knife to go to Cousin Larry rather than Niece Shannon. Instead of redoing his whole will, he can ask his lawyer to draw up a codicil changing only that one provision.

A change in family situation may also revoke part or all of a will automatically. Under the UPC, divorce or annulment cancels the ex-spouse's inheritance under a will. In some states, marriage, divorce, or the birth of a child revokes a will unless the instrument was clearly executed with that event in mind. A testatrix can state in the will, for instance, that she is making it in anticipation of her marriage.

Intestacy

When singer John Denver died unexpectedly in a plane accident, he had had several marriages, children, and platinum albums. His estate was worth $20 million. What he did not have was a will. He was in good company—almost three-quarters of Americans die intestate, that is, without a will. In this event, the law steps in and determines how to distribute the decedent's property. Although, in theory, intestacy laws are supposed to be based on what most people would prefer, in practice, they are not. The vast majority of married people, for instance, leave all their assets to their surviving spouse. Most intestacy laws do not. In some states, if a married person dies intestate, some portion of her property (one-half or two-thirds) goes to her spouse, and the remainder to her issue (including grandchildren). Few people would actually want grandchildren to take a share of their estate in preference to their spouse. In other states, the decedent's estate is shared among her issue, her spouse, and her parents. If she has no issue, her spouse shares the estate with her parents. The moral of the story? As the late great law professor A. James Casner used to say, "Only a fool would die without a will."

at RISK

If intestacy is a bad idea, what about drafting your own will? Warren Burger did. Of course, he was the retired Chief Justice of the United States Supreme Court. Except for misspelling the word "executor," and omitting language that would have permitted his executor to sell real estate, he did fine. These errors were relatively harmless, and his property ended up going to his children, as he had planned. He was not an estate planner, but he was a lawyer and, presumably, a fairly competent one. Someone less competent runs the risk of making an error on some picky detail. For example, an heir might find that his inheritance has been voided because he witnessed the will. Advice on drafting a will is available on the Internet (for example, at **http://www.mtpalermo.com**). Computer software or form books in the library can also be helpful. Nonetheless, it is usually safer to hire an estate lawyer, especially if you have enough property to incur estate taxes. Still, a do-it-yourself will is often better than none. ◆

Power of Attorney

A **durable power of attorney** is a document that permits the **attorney-in-fact** to act for the principal. (An attorney-in-fact need not be a lawyer.) The power of attorney is effective until the principal dies or revokes it. An **immediate power** becomes effective when signed; a **springing power** is effective at some time in the future, typically when the principal becomes incompetent and is no longer able to manage his affairs.

Lawyers generally recommend that their clients execute a durable power of attorney, particularly if they are elderly or in poor health. The power of attorney permits the client not only to choose an attorney-in-fact, but also to give advance instructions, such as "loan money to my son, Billy, if ever he needs it." If a client becomes incompetent and has no power of attorney, a court will appoint a guardian.

Probate

The testatrix cannot implement the terms of the will from beyond the grave, so she appoints an executor for this task. Typically, the executor is a family member, lawyer, or close friend. If the decedent does not select an executor, the probate court appoints an administrator to fulfill the same functions. The executor (or the administrator) has important responsibilities and, in a large estate, may spend a significant amount of time carrying out his functions. He has a fiduciary duty to the estate and is potentially liable to the heirs for any mistakes—from bad investment choices to errors in property valuation. Both the executor and the administrator are entitled to reasonable compensation—typically between 1 and 5 percent of the estate's value, although family members and friends often waive the fee.

Property Not Transferred by Will

A will does not control the distribution of joint property, retirement benefits, or life insurance. As explained in Chapter 44, property that is held in a joint tenancy automatically passes to the surviving owner, regardless of provisions in the decedent's will. This form of ownership is often used by family members—spouses or parents and children—as a simple method of transferring ownership without a will. Pension plans, other retirement benefits, and life insurance are also excluded from the decedent's estate and pass to whomever she has named as beneficiary.

Anatomical Gifts

As immunosuppressant drugs improve, doctors are increasingly successful at transplanting human organs. The demand for these organs—hearts, corneas, kidneys, livers, pituitary glands, skin—is much greater than the supply. **The Uniform Anatomical Gift Act (UAGA) allows an individual to indicate her desire to be a donor either by putting a provision in her will or by signing an organ donation card in the presence of two witnesses.** A sample organ donation card is available at http://www.delafe.com/form/frmdonor.htm. If the donor makes the gift by will, this provision takes effect before probate. (After a lengthy probate process, the organs would be less useful.) The UAGA also provides that, unless a decedent has affirmatively indicated her desire not to be a donor, family members have the right to make a gift of her organs after death.

Living Wills

NEWS*worthy*

Three times a day, a nurse snapped the flip tops on two small cans and poured the protein into a bag suspended from an IV-stand. A pump clicked on and the whitish liquid flowed through a pencil-thin plastic tube directly into the stomach of Nancy Cruzan, 32. An automobile accident had deprived her of oxygen for 14 minutes, destroying the part of her brain that controlled her thoughts, emotions, and actions. She spent seven years in a deep coma at the Missouri Rehabilitation Center, apparently perceiving neither herself nor her surroundings.

Cruzan's knees and arms were permanently curved into a fetal position. Her hands were twisted so tightly that the fingernails cut her wrists. She had primitive, involuntary functions, such as sleep and wake cycles. When her eyes opened, they moved randomly around the room. She responded to pain, and one nurse swore that Cruzan cried when a Valentine's Day card was read to her. Medical history has no record of anyone in her condition ever recovering. But experts said that if she continued to be fed, she could live for another 25 years.

Cruzan's parents found the thought of such a prolonged existence unbearable for their once-attractive, vibrant, and fun-loving daughter. Nancy would not have chosen to continue living that way, they said. They wanted to let her die. The Cruzans' decision to stop feeding their daughter turned into a two-year legal battle that stretched from the small probate courtroom in Joplin, Missouri, to the marble chamber of the United States Supreme Court.[6]

---

6   Rita Ciolli, "Is There a Right to Die?" *Newsday,* Dec. 3, 1989, p. 12.

Gary Rickman and Yvette Williams were among a group that petitioned two Missouri courts to resume the feeding of Cruzan. Rickman stated, "As for myself, I can't think of any case where euthanasia is OK. I want to live." Williams added, "They said Nancy wouldn't want to live like this. Well, nobody would like to live like that. But everybody goes through hard times in their lives. I'm not happy all the time either. Nancy was a very healthy disabled person. She didn't even have bedsores. Like, what is a good quality of life?"[7] ◆

Nancy Cruzan's tragedy led to a national debate over the right to die. **The Supreme Court ruled that family members can choose to discontinue treatment for an incompetent person if there is evidence the patient would have made that choice herself.**[8] After the Supreme Court decision, the probate court in Missouri heard new witnesses testify that Cruzan had said she would not want to live "like a vegetable." The lower court considered this clear and convincing evidence about Cruzan's wishes and granted the family permission to withhold feeding.

Spurred by the *Cruzan* case, many people executed so-called **living wills** or **advance directives.** Living wills permit adults to refuse extreme medical treatment that would prolong their lives, such as artificial feeding, cardiac resuscitation, or mechanical respiration. In addition, a living will can be used to appoint a **health care proxy** to make decisions for a person who has become incompetent.

Living wills become particularly important if family members disagree about appropriate treatment. Terri Schiavo was only 26 years old when her heart stopped beating one evening, causing brain damage that put her in a persistent vegetative state. Her husband said she would not have wanted to live that way and asked to have her feeding tube removed; her parents disagreed and fought him through the courts. Even Congress intervened to try to keep the tube in place. Her husband ultimately prevailed and the tube was removed, but only after 15 years of litigation and public uproar. If Schiavo had had a living will, her family would have had more privacy, fewer legal bills, and, perhaps, greater peace. Information about living wills and samples are available at http://www. partnershipforcaring.org, http://abalawinfo.org, and http://www.health.harvard.edu/LW.

Doctors are permitted to shorten a patient's life by withholding medical treatment. Can they go the next step and prescribe medication to end the life of a terminal patient who is suffering intolerably? In the following case, the court considered the legality of a statute in the state of Washington that makes **assisted suicide** a felony. Other states have similar statutes. Should a state have the right to punish someone for assisting the suicide of a terminally ill person? You be the judge.

you Be The Judge

WASHINGTON V. GLUCKSBERG
521 U.S. 702, 117 S. Ct. 2258, 1997 U.S. LEXIS 4039
United States Supreme Court, 1997

Facts: The plaintiffs are five physicians who treat terminally ill patients, three patients in the terminal stage of excruciatingly painful illnesses, and Compassion in Dying (an organization that provides support to mentally competent, fatally ill adults considering suicide). The defendant is the state of Washington, which passed a statute making assisted suicide a felony punishable by up to five years in prison and a $10,000 fine. Plaintiffs argued that this statute was unconstitutional. The trial court found for the plaintiffs, but the court of appeals reversed. The Supreme Court of the United States granted *certiorari*.

▼

---

7 Pamela Warrick, "Protesters Plotted 'Rescue'—And Then It Was Too Late," *Los Angeles Times,* Jan. 10, 1991, p. E1.

8 *Cruzan v. Director, Missouri Department of Health,* 497 U.S. 261, 110 S. Ct. 2841, 1990 U.S. LEXIS 3301 (1990).

You Be the Judge: Does a state have the right to punish those who assist the terminally ill to commit suicide?

Argument for the Plaintiffs: The Fourteenth Amendment of the United States Constitution declares that the state may not "deprive any person of life, liberty, or property, without due process of law." The Supreme Court has, in the past, interpreted this provision to prevent the government from interfering in personal decisions relating to marriage, procreation, contraception, family relationships, child rearing, and education. For example, in *Roe v. Wade*, the Supreme Court held that a woman has the right to an abortion. If she has the right to terminate her pregnancy, surely she must have the right to terminate her own life. The choice to end one's life, to avoid unbearable pain, is among the most intimate and personal choices a person may make, a choice central to personal dignity and autonomy, central to the liberty protected by the Fourteenth Amendment.

In the *Cruzan* case, the Supreme Court suggested that an individual has the right to refuse life-saving treatment. No constitutional distinction can be drawn between the withdrawal of medical treatment that results in death and the hastening of death by taking prescribed drugs. The plaintiffs in this case suffered horribly from incurable diseases. Would any of us want to be in their place? If we were, wouldn't we want the right to control when and how we die?

Argument for the State of Washington: The plaintiffs argue that, since *Cruzan* permits doctors to withhold life support, it also permits them to aid in a suicide. There is an enormous difference between *withholding* aid and actively *killing* someone. This difference has long been recognized in tort law. You may not be liable for allowing someone to drown, but you will certainly be liable for pushing him into the pond.

The American Medical Association's Code of Medical Ethics declares, "Physician-assisted suicide is fundamentally incompatible with the physician's role as healer." The AMA also argues that the physician's constant search for weapons to combat disease would be impeded if killing were as acceptable an option for the physician as curing.

Without this anti-suicide statute, the elderly and the infirm will be pressured to consent to their own deaths. Minorities and the poor would also be susceptible to manipulation in a regime of assisted suicide. Pain is a significant factor in creating a desire for assisted suicide, and doctors are notoriously less aggressive in providing pain relief to the underprivileged.

For over 700 years, Anglo-American common law has punished those who help suicides. Most states that have considered this issue have decided that assisted suicide should be illegal. Given this history, it is difficult to argue that the Constitution somehow protects, as a fundamental liberty, the right to assisted suicide. ∎

Oregon is the only state that specifically allows doctors to prescribe a fatal dose of drugs to a dying patient. About 20 terminally ill Oregonians take advantage of this law each year.

*up*date   Attorney General John Ashcroft issued a directive instructing the federal Drug Enforcement Administration to revoke the license of any physician who prescribes drugs to assist in a suicide. The Ninth Circuit Court of Appeals struck down this directive and the Supreme Court granted *certiorari*. Has the Supreme Court ruled yet? If so, what was the outcome of the case? ◆

TRUSTS

Trusts are an increasingly popular method for managing assets, both during life and after death. Over a trillion dollars are held by personal trusts. **A trust is an entity that**

separates legal and beneficial ownership. It involves three people: the grantor (also called the settlor or donor), who creates and funds it; the trustee, who manages the assets; and the beneficiary, who receives the financial proceeds. The trustee technically owns the property, but she must use it for the good of the beneficiary. In other words, the trustee holds **legal** title, while the beneficiary holds **equitable** title. A grantor can create a trust during her lifetime or after her death through her will. **There are four requirements for establishing a trust:**

- **Legal Capacity.** As with any contract, the grantor must be of legal age and sound mind.

- **Trustee.** The grantor must appoint at least one trustee (who may be the grantor himself). The trust does not end if the appointed trustee dies or resigns. Either the trust instrument provides for successor trustees, or a court can appoint one.

- **Beneficiary.** A trust must have specific beneficiaries although it need not list them by name. It can instead list a class, such as "living children of the grantors."

- **Trust Property.** The grantor must transfer specific assets to the trust, although these assets can be nominal. A grantor might, for instance, establish a trust with $10 and then add other assets later.

The National Conference of Commissioners on Uniform State Laws has drafted a Uniform Trust Code (UTC) to establish consistent laws on the creation and administration of trusts. Nearly half the states have passed some version of this code.

Advantages and Disadvantages

Why do people use trusts? These are among the advantages:

- **Control.** The grantor can control her assets after her death. In the trust document, she can direct the trustees to follow a specific investment strategy, and she can determine how much income the beneficiaries receive. As an example, suppose the grantor has a husband and children. She wants to provide her husband with adequate income after her death, but she does not want him to spend so lavishly that nothing is left for the children. Nor does she want him to spend all her money on his second wife. The grantor could create a trust in her will that allows her husband to spend the income and, upon his death, gives the principal to their children.

- **Caring for Children.** Minor children cannot legally manage property on their own, so parents or grandparents often establish trusts to take care of these assets until the children grow up.

- **Tax Savings.** Although tax issues are beyond the scope of this chapter, it is worth noting that many married couples use a so-called **marital trust** to minimize their estate taxes.

- **Privacy.** A will is filed in probate court and becomes a matter of public record. Anyone can obtain a copy of it. Some companies are even in the business of providing copies to celebrity hounds. Jacqueline Kennedy Onassis's will is particularly popular. Trusts, however, are private documents and are not available to the public. To see summaries of celebrity wills, dig into **http://www.megadox.com/documents.php/1206**.

- **Probate.** Because a will must go through the often lengthy probate process, the heirs may not receive assets for some time. Assets that are put into a trust *before the grantor dies* do not go through probate; the beneficiaries have immediate access to them.

The major *disadvantage* of a trust is expense. Although it is always possible for the grantor to establish a trust himself with the aid of software or form books, trusts are complex instruments with many potential pitfalls. Do-it-yourself trusts are a recipe for disaster. In addition to the legal fees required to establish a trust, the trustees may have to be paid. Professional trustees typically charge an annual fee of about 1 percent of the trust's assets. Family members usually do not expect payment. Trusts can also save some money, however, because the grantor will have fewer assets to probate and therefore the executor's fees will be lower.

Types of Trusts

Depending upon the goal in establishing a trust, a grantor has two choices.

Living Trust

Also known as an *inter vivos trust*, a living trust is established while the grantor is still alive. In the typical living trust, the grantor serves as trustee during his lifetime. He maintains total control over the assets and avoids a trustee's fee. If the grantor becomes disabled or dies, the successor trustee, who is named in the trust instrument, takes over automatically. All of the assets stay in the trust and avoid probate. Most living trusts are **revocable,** meaning that the grantor can undo the trust or change it at any time.

Testamentary Trust

A testamentary trust is created by a will. It goes into effect when the grantor dies. Naturally, it is **irrevocable** because the grantor is dead. The grantor's property must first go through probate, on its way to the trust. Living trusts are particularly popular with older people because they want to ensure that their assets will be properly managed if they become disabled. Younger people typically opt for a testamentary trust because the probability they will become disabled any time soon is remote. Also they want to avoid the effort of transferring their assets to the trust.

Trust Administration

The primary obligation of trustees is to carry out the terms of the trust. They may exercise any powers expressly granted to them in the trust instrument and any implied powers reasonably necessary to implement the terms of the trust, unless that power has been specifically prohibited. **In carrying out the terms of the trust, the trustees have a fiduciary duty to the beneficiary.** This fiduciary duty includes:

- **A Duty of Loyalty.** In managing the trust, the trustees must put the interests of the beneficiaries first. They must disclose any relevant information to the beneficiaries. They may not commingle their own assets with those of the trust, do business with the trust (unless expressly permitted by the terms of the trust), or favor one beneficiary over another.

- **A Duty of Care.** The trustee must act as a reasonable person would when managing the assets of *another*. (This is a higher standard than requiring a trustee to act as a reasonable person would when managing his *own* affairs.) The trustee must make careful investments, keep accurate records, and collect debts owed the trust.

A trustee is liable to the beneficiaries of the trust if she breaches her duty. W. Averell Harriman was the scion of a wealthy New York family. When he died, he left half of his $65 million estate outright to his wife, Pamela Harriman, and half in trust for his two daughters from an earlier marriage (who were in their 70s). Pamela was a trustee and had the right to appoint the other trustees. She had been married twice

Ambassador to France and fundraiser extraordinaire for the Democratic Party, Pamela Harriman had many skills. Managing trust funds does not appear to have been one of them.

© TIME LIFE PICTURES/GETTY IMAGES

before, to Winston Churchill's son and to Hollywood producer Leland Hayward. After Averell's death, she became ambassador to France, partly because of her generous contributions to the Democratic Party.

Under Pamela's care, the trust assets were invested in a series of risky real estate deals, including a seedy conference center in New Jersey that had once been a Playboy Club. The beneficiaries filed suit against her when they discovered that trust assets had declined in value from $30 million to $3 million. She and the children ultimately settled their litigation for an undisclosed sum, and then both sides filed suit against the two other trustees. This litigation also was settled.

Termination

A trust ends upon the occurrence of any of these events:

- On the date indicated by the grantor.

- If the trust is revocable, when revoked by the grantor. Even if the trust is irrevocable, the grantor and all the beneficiaries can agree to revoke it.

- When the purpose of the trust has been fulfilled. If the grantor established the trust to pay college tuition for his grandchildren, the trust ends when the last grandchild graduates.

Even if one of these events does not occur, the **Rule Against Perpetuities** provides that a trust must end within 21 years of the death of some named person who is alive when the trust is created. Thus, for instance, a grantor could legitimately establish a trust that ends 21 years after the death of whichever of his children was living when he made the trust. He could not, however, create a trust that ends upon the death of all of his grandchildren, because that might well be more than 21 years after the death of any person he could name who was living when he made the trust.

For centuries, the Rule Against Perpetuities has been the law in England and the United States. However, nearly half the states now permit **dynasty trusts,** that is, trusts that last forever. These trusts avoid estate taxes, protect assets from ex-spouses and creditors, and generally allow donors to control their money forever. Whether or not eternal control is a good idea is best left to psychology texts.

INTRODUCTION TO INSURANCE

No matter how careful our behavior, we are all subject to risk—from automobile accidents, injury, illness, fires, early death, and other catastrophes. No wonder that, from earliest times, people have sought insurance against these unpredictable and unpreventable dangers. For general advice from the insurance industry on everything from what to do after a car accident to avoiding catastrophes at work, click on http://www.iii.org. You can learn more about your insurance companies or file a complaint against them at http://www.naic.org.

It is important to begin by defining these key terms:

- **Person.** An individual, corporation, partnership, or any other legal entity.
- **Insurance.** A contract in which one person, in return for a fee, agrees to guarantee another against loss caused by a specific type of danger.
- **Insurer.** The person who issues the insurance policy and serves as guarantor.
- **Insured.** The person whose loss is the subject of the insurance policy.
- **Owner.** The person who enters into the insurance contract and pays the premiums.
- **Premium.** The consideration that the owner pays under the policy.
- **Beneficiary.** The person who receives the proceeds from the insurance policy.

The beneficiary, the insured, and the owner can be, but are not necessarily, the same person. If a homeowner buys fire insurance for her house, she is the insured, the owner, and the beneficiary because she bought the policy and receives the proceeds if her house burns down. If a mother buys a life insurance policy on her son that is payable to his children in the event of his death, then the mother is the owner, the son is the insured, and the grandchildren are the beneficiaries.

ECONOMICS & the LAW

Before beginning a study of insurance law, it is important to understand the economics of the insurance industry. Suppose that you have recently purchased a $500,000 house. The probability your house will burn down in the next year is 1 in 1,000. That is a low risk, but the consequences would be devastating, especially since you could not afford to rebuild. Instead of bearing that risk yourself, you take out a fire insurance policy. You pay an insurance company $1,200 in return for a promise that, if your house burns down in the next 12 months, the company will pay you $500,000. The insurance company sells the same policy to 1,000 similar homeowners, expecting that on average one of these houses will burn down. If all 1,000 policyholders pay $1,200, the insurance company takes in $1.2 million each year, but expects to pay out only $500,000. It will put some money aside in case two houses burn down, or even worse, a major forest fire guts a whole tract of houses. It must also pay overhead expenses such as marketing and administration. And, of course, shareholders expect profits. ◆

INSURANCE CONTRACT

An insurance policy must meet all the common law requirements for a contract. There must be an offer, acceptance, and consideration. The owner must have legal capacity; that is, he must be an adult of sound mind. Fraud, duress, or undue influence invalidates a policy. In theory, insurance contracts need not be in writing because the statute of frauds does not apply to any contract that can be performed within one year and it is possible that the house may burn down or the car may crash within a year. Some states, however, specifically require insurance contracts to be in writing.[9]

Offer and Acceptance

The purchaser of a policy makes an offer by delivering an application and a premium to the insurer. The insurance company then has the option of either accepting or rejecting the offer. **It can accept by oral notice, by written notice, or by delivery**

---

[9] See Unit 2 for a general discussion of contracts. Chapter 15, on written contracts, covers the statute of frauds.

of the policy. It also has a fourth option—a written binder. A binder is a short document acknowledging receipt of the application and premium. It indicates that a policy is *temporarily* in effect but does not constitute *final* acceptance. The insurer still has the right to reject the offer once it has examined the application carefully. Kyle buys a house on April 1 and wants insurance right away. The insurance company issues a binder to him the same day. If Kyle's house burns down on May 1, the insurer must pay, even though it has not yet issued the final policy. If, however, there is no fire, but on May 1 the company decides Kyle is a bad risk, it has the right to reject his application at that time.

Limiting Claims by the Insured

Insurance policies can sometimes look like a quick way to make easy money. More than one person suffering from overwhelming financial pressure has insured a building to the hilt and then burned it down for the insurance money. Unbelievably, more than one parent has killed a child to collect the proceeds of a life insurance policy. Therefore, the law has created a number of rules to protect insurance companies from fraud and bad faith on the part of insureds.

Insurable Interest

An insurance contract is not valid unless the owner has an *insurable interest* in the subject matter of the policy. To understand why an insurable interest is important, read this tragic story. Twenty-year-old Deana Wild was thrilled when James Coates pro-

© MILES ERTMAN/MASTERFILE

posed to her. To celebrate their engagement, they took a sight-seeing trip along the California coast with Coates's mother, Virginia Rearden. They seemed to be just one big happy family. Only one problem: Wild slipped while walking along the edge of a cliff at Big Sur and fell to her death. That would have been the end of the story except that, the day before, Wild had taken out a $35,000 life insurance policy, naming Coates and Rearden as beneficiaries. When the insurance company investigated, it learned that Coates was married to someone else. Therefore, he could not be Wild's fiancé, and neither he nor Rearden had an insurable interest in Wild. It also turned out that Rearden had taken out the policy without Wild's knowledge. Rearden was convicted of first degree murder and sentenced to life in prison without parole.

Virginia Rearden pushed Deana Wild to her death from a Big Sur cliff. If the insurance company had known that Rearden did not have an insurable interest in Wild, the company would have refused to issue the policy, and Wild might not have died.

These are the rules on insurable interest:

- **Definition.** A person has an **insurable interest** if she would be harmed by the danger that she has insured against. If Jessica takes out a fire insurance policy on her own barn, she will presumably be reluctant to burn it down. However, if she buys a policy on Nathan's barn, she will not mind, she may even be delighted, when fire sweeps through the building. It is a small step to saying that she might even burn the barn down herself.

- **Amount of Loss.** The insurable interest can be no greater than the actual amount of loss suffered. If the barn is worth $50,000, but Jessica insures it (and pays premiums) for $100,000, she will recover only $50,000 when it burns down. The goal is to make sure that Jessica does not profit from the policy.

- **Life Insurance.** A person always has an insurable interest in his own life and the life of his spouse or fiancée. Parents and minor children also have an insurable interest in each other.

- **Work Relationships.** Business partners, employers, and employees have an insurable interest in each other if they would suffer some financial harm from the death of the insured. For example, a start-up company will often buy **key person life insurance** on its officers to compensate the company if an important person dies.

Misrepresentation

Insurers have the right to void a policy if, during the application process, the insured makes a material misstatement or conceals a material fact. The policy is voidable whether the misstatement was oral or in writing, intentional or unintentional. **Material** means that the misstatement or omission affected the insurer's willingness to issue the policy. As the following case illustrates, two large dogs are definitely material.

DANBURY INSURANCE COMPANY V. GINNETTI

2004 U.S. Dist. LEXIS 17857
United States District Court for the District of Connecticut, 2004

Facts: Jason Ginnetti applied for a homeowner's policy through CPM Insurance Services, Inc. An employee of CPM filled out the application form using information provided by Ginnetti's housemate, Tricia Farace. The two-page form asked: "Does applicant or any tenant have any animals or exotic pets?" The CPM employee checked an adjacent box stating that the answer was "No." At the time, Ginnetti owned two dogs, a German shepherd/Doberman mix and a German shepherd. Although Ginnetti had not read this part of the form, he nonetheless signed the application attesting that he had read it and that the answers were true. CPM issued the homeowner's policy.

Ginnetti was sued by someone who claimed to have been bitten by one of his dogs. But when Ginnetti filed a claim with CPM, the company rescinded his policy for material misrepresentation. Ginnetti then sued CPM. The trial court granted CPM's motion for summary judgment. Ginnetti appealed.

Issues: Does CPM have the right to rescind Ginnetti's policy? Did his application contain a material misrepresentation?

Excerpts from Judge Chatigny's Decision:[10] Ginnetti's "No" answer to the question concerning "animals or exotic pets" constitutes a misrepresentation. Ginnetti contends that a jury could find otherwise on the ground that the question is vague and a reasonable reader of it could conclude that a 'non-exotic pet' such as a dog was not the subject of the question. I agree that the question would be more plainly all-encompassing if it asked only about "animals" or, alternatively, only about "pets." But it does not follow that a reasonable applicant could think that the question in its present form does not apply to dogs.

Ginnetti contends that a jury could credit his testimony that he did not review the application for accuracy and thus find that the misrepresentation was not knowingly made. This argument is also unavailing. Under Connecticut law a person may not claim that a misrepresentation is innocent solely

▼

---

[10] We have substituted proper names for "defendant" and "plaintiff."

because the person failed to read the application before signing it. The law requires that the insured shall not only, in good faith, answer all the interrogatories correctly, but shall use reasonable diligence to see that the answers are correctly written. Ginnetti offers no justification for his failure to read the application before signing it. He admits that he had an opportunity to read the two-page form in full, had no physical or mental conditions or disabilities, read part of the form, had no difficulty understanding it, added information to the form, and signed it. There is no allegation that he was induced to sign the application without reading it.

Ginnetti contends that CPM is not entitled to rescind the policy because CPM's employee was told about the two dogs before the application was completed. Connecticut law does not relieve an insured of responsibility for a misrepresentation inserted in an application by an agent in the absence of circumstances justifying the insured's failure to read the application before signing it. No such circumstances are presented here.

Ginnetti does not deny that the representation was material. Accordingly, CPM is entitled to rescission of the policy as a matter of law. For the foregoing reasons, CPM's motion for summary judgment is hereby granted. The policy is rescinded. CPM will return Ginnetti's premium. ■

Bad Faith by the Insurer

Insurance policies often contain a *covenant of good faith and fair dealing*. Even if the policy itself does not *explicitly* include such a provision, an increasing number of courts (but not all) *imply* this covenant. An insurance company can violate the covenant of good faith and fair dealing by (1) fraudulently inducing someone to buy a policy, (2) refusing to pay a valid claim, or (3) refusing to accept a reasonable settlement offer that has been made to an insured. When an insurance company violates the covenant of good faith and fair dealing, it becomes liable for both compensatory and punitive damages.[11]

Fraud

In recent years, a number of insurance companies have paid serious damages to settle fraud charges involving the sale of life insurance. The companies trained their salespeople to tell elderly customers that a new policy was better when, in fact, it was much worse. State Farm Insurance agreed to pay its customers $200 million to settle such a suit. As the following article indicates, State Farm was not alone in this scam.

NEWS*worthy*

After a two-year investigation of the Prudential Insurance Company of America, the nation's largest insurer, officials in Florida concluded that the company deliberately set out to cheat its customers for more than a decade. Prudential has agreed to pay restitution that could run to as much as $2 billion.

The tactic used repeatedly by Prudential agents was to persuade customers to use the cash that had built up in their life insurance policies to buy new policies with greater coverage, with the promise that their premiums would not increase. The agents earned new commissions and the company's market share grew. But when the cash value of the original policies was depleted by the demands for premiums for the second policies, customers began receiving much higher bills. Many people could not make the payments and lost all their coverage. In those cases, the company had received years of premiums and now no longer faced the prospect of ever having to pay a death benefit.

In some of its training seminars, Prudential taught agents either to commit fraud or to use misleading techniques. Agents were also trained to target the elderly. One complaint received by the Florida Department of Insurance was from a 60-year-old woman who had

---

[11] Compensatory and punitive damages are covered in Chapter 18, on remedies.

told an agent that she could not afford more insurance. "The next thing I know," she said, "a nurse comes to my door to give me a physical" as required for a new policy. "It wasn't until then," the woman told investigators, "that I realized I had another policy that would drain my old policy."[12] ◆

Refusing to Pay a Valid Claim

Perhaps because juries feel sympathy for those who must deal with an immovable bureaucracy, damage awards are often sizeable when an insurance company has refused to pay a legitimate claim. For example, a jury in Ohio entered a $13 million verdict against Buckeye Union Insurance Co. for its bad faith refusal to pay a claim. An Ohio sheriff stopped the automobile of 19-year-old Eugene Leber. As the sheriff approached Leber's car, he slipped on ice and his gun discharged. By incredible bad luck, the bullet struck Leber, permanently paralyzing him from the rib cage down. The insurance company recognized that it was liable under the policy, but it nonetheless fought the case for *16* years.

Consumers complain that insurance companies often "low-ball"—that is, they make an unreasonably low offer to settle a claim. Some insurance companies even set claims quotas that limit how much their adjusters can pay out each year, regardless of the merits of each individual claim. If juries continue to award multimillion dollar verdicts, insurance companies may decide simply to pay the claims.

In the following case, the insurance company ultimately paid the claim but not fast enough to satisfy the jury.

GOODSON V. AMERICAN STANDARD INSURANCE COMPANY OF WISCONSIN

89 P.3d 409, 2004 Colo. LEXIS 388
Supreme Court of Colorado, 2004

Facts: Dawn Goodson and her two children were in an automobile accident while driving a car owned by Chet Weber. He was insured by American Standard Insurance Company of Wisconsin.

To treat injuries that she and her children suffered in the accident, Goodson sought care from a chiropractor. She submitted these bills, totaling about $8,000, to American Standard. The insurance company offered a number of erroneous reasons why it should not pay the claims: that the chiropractor was not a member of American Standard's preferred provider organization; that Weber's policy was not in effect at the time of the accident; that Goodson and her children needed to undergo an independent medical evaluation to determine whether their injuries were related to the accident and whether their medical treatment was reasonable and necessary. In the end, American Standard did pay Goodson's bills, but it took 18 months to do so.

Goodson filed suit against American Standard, alleging that it had engaged in a bad faith breach of the insurance contract. Although the company's delay in payment had not caused Goodson any economic damage, it had caused her substantial emotional distress. The jury awarded Goodson and her children $75,000 in actual damages and an additional $75,000 in punitive damages. The appeals court overturned the verdict. Goodson appealed to the state Supreme Court.

▼

---

[12] Joseph B. Treaster and Melody Petersen, "Florida Study Claims That Prudential Cheated Customers," *New York Times*, Dec. 22, 1997, p. A20. Copyright © 1997 by The New York Times Co. Reprinted by permission.

Issue: Can Goodson recover damages for emotional distress without showing any economic loss caused by American Standard's delay in paying her claim?

Excerpts from Justice Hobbs's Decision: To establish that the insurer breached its duties of good faith and fair dealing, the insured must show that a reasonable insurer under the circumstances would have paid or otherwise settled the claim. Compensatory damages for economic and non-economic losses are available to make the insured whole and, where appropriate, punitive damages are available to punish the insurer and deter wrongful conduct by other insurers. Non-economic losses recognized under the rubric of compensatory damages include emotional distress; pain and suffering; inconvenience; fear and anxiety; and impairment of the quality of life. To recover punitive damages, the insured must establish that the insurer's breach was accom-panied by circumstances of fraud, malice, or willful and wanton conduct. A punitive damages award cannot exceed the amount of actual damages and, in certain situations, may be increased or decreased by the court.

Goodson proved to the jury that she suffered emotional distress as a result of this delay. The anxiety, fear, stress, and uncertainty she experienced occurred as a result of her worry about whether she would be financially responsible for her medical bills, which American Standard refused to pay. An insured purchases insurance in the first place so as not to suffer such anxiety, fear, stress, and uncertainty. The fact that an insurer finally pays in full does not erase the distress caused by the bad faith conduct.

Accordingly, we reverse the court of appeals and remand the case to that court with instructions to reinstate the trial court's judgment entered on the jury verdict. ■

Refusing to Accept a Settlement Offer

An insurer also violates the covenant of good faith and fair dealing when it wrongfully refuses to settle a claim. Suppose that Dmitri has a $100,000 automobile insurance policy. After he injures Tanya in a car accident, she sues him for $5 million. As provided in the policy, Dmitri's insurance company defends him against Tanya's claim. She offers to settle for $100,000, but the insurance company refuses because it only has $100,000 at risk anyway. It may get lucky with the jury. Instead, a jury comes in with a $2 million verdict. The insurance company is only liable for $100,000, but Dmitri must pay $1.9 million. A court might well find that the insurance company had violated its covenant of good faith and fair dealing.

TYPES OF INSURANCE

Insurance is available for virtually any risk. Bruce Springsteen, Michael Jackson, Billy Joel, and the Rolling Stones have insured their voices. When Kerry Wallace shaved her head in the Star Trek films, she bought insurance in case her hair failed to grow back. Food critic Egon Ronay insured his taste buds. Forty members of a Whiskers Club insured their beards against fire and theft. And an amateur dramatics group took out insurance to protect against the risk that a member of the audience might die laughing. Most people, however, get by with six different types of insurance: property, life, health, disability, liability, and automobile.

Property Insurance

Property insurance (also known as **casualty insurance**) covers physical damage to real estate, personal property (boats, furnishings), or inventory from causes such as fire, smoke, lightning, wind, riot, vandalism, or theft.

Life Insurance

Life insurance is really death insurance—it provides for payments to a beneficiary upon the death of the insured. The purpose is to replace at least some of the insured's income so that her family will not be financially devastated.

Term Insurance

Term insurance is the simplest, cheapest life insurance option. It is purchased for a specific period, such as 1, 5, or 20 years. If the insured dies during the period of the policy, the insurance company pays the policy amount to the beneficiary. If the owner stops paying premiums, the policy terminates and the beneficiary receives nothing. As the probability of death rises with age, so do the premiums. A $200,000 10-year-term policy on a 25-year-old nonsmoker in good health costs as little as $100 annually; at age 60 the same policy costs $560. Term insurance is the best choice for a person who simply wants to protect his family by replacing his income if he dies young.

Whole Life Insurance

Whole life or **straight life** insurance is designed to cover the insured for his entire life. A portion of the premiums pays for insurance, and the remainder goes into savings. This savings portion is called the **cash value** of the policy. The company pays dividends on this cash value and typically, after some years, the dividends are large enough to cover the premium so that the owner does not have to pay any more. The cash value accrues without being taxed until the policy is cashed in. The owner can borrow against the cash value, in many cases at a below-market rate. In addition, if the owner cancels the policy, the insurance company will pay her the policy's cash value. When the owner purchases the policy, the company typically sets a premium that stays constant over the life of the policy. A 25-year-old nonsmoker pays annual premiums of roughly $2,000 per year on a $200,000 policy.

The advantage of a whole life policy is that it forces people to save. It also has some significant disadvantages:

- The investment returns from the savings portion of whole life insurance have traditionally been mediocre. Mutual funds may offer better investment opportunities.

- A significant portion of the premium for the first year goes to pay overhead and commissions. Agents have a great incentive to sell whole life policies, rather than term, because their commissions are much higher.

- Unless the customer holds a policy for about 20 years, it will typically generate little cash value. Half of all whole life policyholders drop their policies in the first seven or eight years. At that point, the policy has generated little more than commissions for the agent.

- Whole life insurance provides the same amount of insurance throughout the insured's life. In contrast, most people need more insurance when they have young children and less as they approach retirement age.

Universal Life

Universal life insurance is a flexible combination of whole life and term. The owner can adjust the premiums over the life of the policy and also adjust the allocation of the premiums between insurance and savings. The options are complex and often difficult for the customer to understand.

Annuities

As life expectancy has increased, people have begun to worry as much about supporting themselves in their old age as they do about dying young. Sales of life insurance have stagnated while the number of annuities sold each year is growing rapidly. **Annuities are the reverse of life insurance—they make payments *until* death whereas life insurance pays *after* death.** In the basic annuity contract, the owner makes a lump-sum payment to an insurance company in return for a fixed annual income for the rest of her life, no matter how long she lives. If she dies tomorrow, the insurance company makes a huge profit. If she lives to be 95, the company loses money. But whatever happens, she knows she will have an income until the day she dies.

In a **deferred annuity contract,** the owner makes a lump-sum payment but receives no income until some later date, say, in 10 or 20 years when he retires. From that date forward, he will receive payments for the rest of his life.

Health Insurance

Traditional health insurance plans are **pay for service.** The insurer pays for virtually any treatment that any doctor orders. The good news under this system is that policyholders have the largest possible choice of doctor and treatment. The bad news is that doctors and patients have an incentive to overspend on health care because the insurance company picks up the tab. It has been estimated that as many as one-third of the medical procedures performed in pay for service plans have little medical justification, which in the end is not good for the patient.

Instead of, or in addition to, pay for service plans, many insurers offer **managed care plans.** There are many variations on this theme, but they all work to limit treatment choices. In some plans, the patient has a primary care physician who must approve all visits to specialists. In **health maintenance organizations,** known as **HMOs,** the patient can be treated only by doctors in the organization, unless there is some extraordinary need for an outside specialist.

Neither type of plan is perfect. In pay for service plans, doctors have an incentive to overtreat. In managed care plans, they may have an incentive to undertreat. For example, a recent study revealed that managed care plans tend to treat mental illness primarily with drugs. A combination of drugs and therapy is more successful but also more expensive. Many managed care plans provide excellent care, but whatever their strengths and weaknesses, they seem destined to become the norm in American health care.

Disability Insurance

Disability insurance replaces the insured's income if he becomes unable to work because of illness or injury. "Ah!" you think, "that will never happen to me." In fact, the average person is seven times more likely to be disabled for at least 90 days than she is to die before age 65. Half of all mortgage foreclosures are caused by an owner's disability. Everyone should have disability insurance to replace between 60 and 75 percent of their income. (There is no need for 100 percent replacement because expenses while unemployed are lower.) Many employers provide disability protection.

Liability Insurance

Most insurance—property, life, health, disability—is designed to reimburse the insured (or her family) for any harm she suffers. Liability insurance is different. **Its purpose is**

to reimburse the insured for any liability she incurs by (accidentally) harming someone else. This type of insurance covers tort claims by:

- Those injured on property owned by the insured—the mail carrier who slips and falls on the front sidewalk or the child who drowns in the pool
- Those injured by the insured away from home or business—the jogger crushed by an insured who loses control of his rollerblades, and
- Those whose property is damaged by the insured—the owner whose stone wall is pulverized by the insured's swerving car.

These are the types of claims covered in a *personal* liability policy. *Business* liability policies may also protect against other sorts of claims:

- Professional malpractice on the part of an accountant, architect, doctor, engineer, or lawyer.
- Product liability for any injuries caused by the company's products.
- Employment practices liability insurance to protect employers against claims of sexual harassment, discrimination, and wrongful termination. About 30 percent of American firms carry this type of insurance.

Automobile Insurance

An automobile insurance policy is a combination of several different types of coverage that, depending on state law, are either mandatory or optional. These are the basic types of coverage:

- **Collision** covers the cost of repairing or replacing a car that is damaged in an accident.
- **Comprehensive** covers fire, theft, and vandalism—but not collision.
- **Liability** covers harm the owner causes to other people or their property—their body, car, or stone wall. Most states require drivers to carry liability insurance.
- **Uninsured Motorist** covers the owner and anyone else in the car who is injured by an uninsured motorist.

at **R!SK**

Most Americans spend a considerable percentage of their disposable income on insurance. What can you do to reduce this expense?

- **Do not insure against every risk.** If you can afford the loss yourself, it is better not to purchase insurance. About half of every dollar that consumers spend on insurance is paid back in claims; the other half goes to the company's profits and overhead. For example, salespeople often try very hard to sell extended warranties on consumer electronic devices and appliances such as televisions, and refrigerators. These warranties are simply insurance plans that require the store to fix the item if something goes wrong. Stores often make a larger profit from the warranty than from the product itself. If you self-insure, odds are you will come out ahead in the long run.
- **Do not buy "special occasion" insurance.** After a major plane crash, sales of flight accident insurance jump. If you need life insurance, you should have it, no matter how you die. Your family does not need more money because you die in a plane crash rather than a car accident. The same rule holds true for other special occasion policies such as cancer insurance. You need health insurance regardless of your illness. Indeed, to protect the elderly who buy most of these policies, some states have outlawed cancer insurance.

- **Select as high a deductible as you can afford.** The higher the deductible, the lower the premium. Over the lifetime of your house or car, you can save thousands of dollars by self-insuring the small losses and buying insurance to protect only against major catastrophes.

- **Shop for the best price.** The lowest cost company may charge as little as two-thirds as much as its highest price competitor. The Internet offers a great opportunity to compare prices for different types of insurance. Try **http://www.answercenter.com**, **http://www.quicken.com/insurance**, **http://www.insweb.com**, **http://quickquote.com**, or **http://www.quotesmith.com**.

- **Shop for quality.** An insurance company can fail as easily as any other business. What a disaster to pay premiums, only to discover later that you are not in safe hands after all. ◆

© BRAND X PICTURES/GETTY IMAGES

Chapter Conclusion

Life is a risky business. Cars crash, people die, houses burn. So what can we do? Sign a will, buy insurance, and get on with our lives, knowing that we have prepared as best we can.

Chapter Review

1. A holographic will is handwritten by the testator but not witnessed.

2. A spouse is entitled to a certain share of the decedent's estate, but children have no automatic right to share in a parent's estate.

3. In a will, a per stirpes distribution means that each *branch* of the family receives an equal share. Per capita means that each *heir* receives the same amount.

4. A testator may generally revoke or alter a will at any time prior to death.

5. Almost three-quarters of Americans die intestate—that is, without a will. In this event, the law determines how the decedent's property will be distributed.

6. A will does not control the distribution of joint property, life insurance, or retirement benefits.

7. A living will permits an adult to refuse medical treatment that would prolong life.

8. A trust is an entity that separates legal and beneficial ownership.

9. In carrying out the terms of a trust, the trustees have a fiduciary duty to the beneficiary.

10. An insurance policy must meet all the common law requirements for a contract—offer, acceptance, and consideration.

11. A person has an insurable interest if she would be harmed by the danger that she has insured against.

12. Insurers have the right to void a policy if the insured makes a material misstatement, or conceals a material fact.

13. Many courts have held that insurance policies contain a covenant of good faith and fair dealing and have found insurance companies liable for compensatory and punitive damages if they refuse to pay legitimate claims in a timely manner.

14. Property insurance covers physical damage to real estate, personal property (boats, furnishings), or inventory from causes such as fire, smoke, lightning, wind, riot, vandalism, or theft.

15. Annuities are the reverse of life insurance policies; they make payments *until* death.

16. Health insurance is available in pay for service plans, managed care plans, or HMOs.

17. Disability insurance replaces the insured's income if he becomes unable to work because of illness or injury.

18. Liability insurance reimburses the insured for any liability she incurs by accidentally harming someone else.

Practice Test

1. When Frank Gilbert died, he left behind an eight-page typed will, prepared by an attorney, and handwritten notes dated two years later. The notes were found folded together in a sealed envelope. On the back of a business card, Frank had written: "Jim and Margaret I have appro $50,000.00 in Safe. See Buzz if anything happens [signed] Frank Gilbert." On the back of a pay stub, Frank had written: "Jim & Margaret $20,000.00 the Rest divided Equally the other Living Survivors Bro. & Sisters [signed] Frank Gilbert." He had written on the envelope: "I gave to Jim and Margaret this card which I Stated what to do." Jim was one of Frank's brothers; Margaret was Jim's wife. The typed will granted Jim a share of Frank's other assets besides the $50,000 in the safe. Jim's siblings argued that the handwritten notes were a new will that revoked the typed document and that, therefore, Jim and Margaret were entitled to $20,000 and nothing more. Jim argued that the handwritten notes were a codicil, giving him $20,000 in addition to his share under the will. Who is correct?

2. **CPA QUESTION** A decedent's will provided that the estate was to be divided among the decedent's issue, per capita and not per stirpes. If there are two surviving children and three grandchildren who are children of a predeceased child at the time the will is probated, how will the estate be divided?

   a. 1/2 to each surviving child

   b. 1/3 to each surviving child and 1/9 to each grandchild

   c. 1/4 to each surviving child and 1/6 to each grandchild

   d. 1/5 to each surviving child and grandchild

3. **CPA QUESTION** A personal representative of an estate would breach her fiduciary duties if she:

   a. Combined personal funds with funds of the estate so that both could purchase treasury bills

   b. Represented the estate in a lawsuit brought against it by a disgruntled relative of the decedent

   c. Distributed property in satisfaction of the decedent's debts

   d. Engaged a non-CPA to prepare the records for the estate's final accounting

4. Josh was a crotchety fellow, often at outs with his family. In his will, he left his son an autographed copy of his book, *A Guide to Federal Prisons*. He completely omitted his wife of 35 years and his daughter, instead leaving the rest of his substantial estate to the Society for the Assistance of Convicted Felons. Under the UPC, which member of his family fared best?

5. This question appeared in the *Minneapolis Star Tribune*'s annual Consumer Quiz: What does intestate mean?

   a. A highway that crosses from one state to another

   b. A highway that remains within a state

   c. A male hormonal imbalance

   d. None of the above

6. **YOU BE THE JUDGE** WRITING PROBLEM Linda Richmond and Eddie Durham had two children before they were divorced. Under the terms of their divorce decree, Durham obtained title to their house. When he died suddenly of a heart attack, the children inherited the house. Richmond moved into the house with the children and began paying the mortgage that was in Durham's name. She also took out fire insurance. Ten months later, fire totally destroyed the house. The insurance company refused to pay a

benefit under the policy because Richmond did not have an insurable interest in the property. Do you agree? **Argument for the insurance company:** Linda Richmond did not own the house; therefore, she had no insurable interest. **Argument for Richmond:** She was harmed when the house burned down because she and her children had no place to live. She was paying the mortgage, so she also had a financial interest.

7. Mark Zulcosky applied for life insurance with Farm Bureau Life Insurance Co. On the application he indicated that he had not received any traffic tickets in the preceding five years. In fact, he had received several such citations for driving while intoxicated. Two years later, Mark was shot to death. When Farm Bureau discovered the traffic tickets, it denied coverage to his beneficiary. Was Farm Bureau in the right?

8. Dannie Harvey sued her employer, O. R. Whitaker, for sexual harassment, discrimination, and defamation. Whitaker counter-claimed for libel and slander, requesting $1 million in punitive damages. Both Whitaker and Harvey were insured by Allstate, under identical homeowner's policies. This policy explicitly promised to defend Harvey against the exact claim Whitaker had made against her. Harvey's Allstate agent, however, told her that she was not covered. Because the agent kept all copies of Harvey's insurance policies in his office, she took him at his word. She had no choice but to defend against the claim on her own. Whitaker mounted an exceedingly hostile litigation attack, taking 80 depositions. After a year, Allstate agreed to defend Harvey. However, instead of hiring the lawyer who had been representing her, it chose another lawyer who had no expertise in this type of case and was a close friend of Whitaker's attorney. Harvey's new lawyer refused to meet her or to attend any depositions. Harvey and Whitaker finally settled. Whitaker had spent $1 million in legal fees, Harvey $169,000, and Allstate $2,513. Does Harvey have a claim against Allstate?

Internet Research Problem

Fill out your own organ donor card (available at http://beatty.westbuslaw.com) or advance directive (see http://beatty.westbuslaw.com).

9. Clyde Anderson received a letter from his automobile insurance company notifying him that it would not renew his policy that was set to expire on February 28. Anderson did not obtain another policy, and, on March 1, at 2:30 A.M., he struck another vehicle, killing two men. Later that day, Anderson applied for insurance coverage. As part of this application, he indicated that he had not been involved in any accident in the last three years. The new policy was effective as of 12:01 A.M. on March 1. Will the estates of the two dead men be able to recover under this policy?

10. **ETHICS** Donna and Carl Nichols each bought term life insurance from Prudential Insurance Company of America. These policies contained a rider providing that, if the insured became disabled, the premiums did not have to be paid and the policy would still stay in effect. This term is called a "waiver of premium." Carl became totally disabled and his premiums were waived. Some years later, two Prudential sales managers convinced the Nicholses to convert their term life insurance policies into whole life insurance policies. They promised that, once Carl made the conversion, he would only have to pay premiums on the new policy for a six-month waiting period. They even wrote "WP to be included in this policy" on the application form. "WP" stood for waiver of premium benefit. Only after the new policy was issued did the Nicholses learn that Prudential would not waive the premium. The Nicholses had exchanged a policy on which they owed nothing further for a policy on which they now had to pay premiums that they could not afford. Do the Nicholses have a claim against Prudential? Regardless of the legal outcome, did Prudential have an ethical obligation to the Nicholses?

11. **ROLE REVERSAL** Write a short-answer question dealing with either misrepresentation on the part of an applicant for insurance or bad faith by an insurer.

You can find further practice problems at http://beatty.westbuslaw.com **or in the Study Guide that accompanies this text.**

Appendix A

The Constitution of the United States

Preamble   We the People of the United States, in Order to form a more perfect Union, establish Justice, insure domestic Tranquility, provide for the common defense, promote the general Welfare, and secure the Blessings of Liberty to ourselves and our Posterity, do ordain and establish this Constitution for the United States of America.

ARTICLE I

Section 1.

All legislative Powers herein granted shall be vested in a Congress of the United States, which shall consist of a Senate and House of Representatives.

Section 2.

The House of Representatives shall be composed of Members chosen every second Year by the People of the several States, and the Electors in each State shall have the Qualifications requisite for Electors of the most numerous Branch of the State Legislature.

No Person shall be a Representative who shall not have attained to the Age of twenty five Years, and been seven Years a Citizen of the United States, and who shall not, when elected, be an Inhabitant of that State in which he shall be chosen.

Representatives and direct Taxes shall be apportioned among the several States which may be included within this Union, according to their respective Numbers, which shall be determined by adding to the whole Number of free Persons, including those bound to Service for a Term of Years, and excluding Indians not taxed, three fifths of all other Persons. The actual Enumeration shall be made within three Years after the first Meeting of the Congress of the United States, and within every subsequent Term of ten Years, in such Manner as they shall by Law direct. The number of Representatives shall not exceed one for every thirty Thousand, but each State shall have at Least one Representative; and until such enumeration shall be made, the State of New Hampshire shall be entitled to chuse three, Massachusetts eight, Rhode Island and Providence Plantations one, Connecticut five, New-York six, New Jersey four, Pennsylvania eight, Delaware one, Maryland six, Virginia ten, North Carolina five, South Carolina five, and Georgia three.

When vacancies happen in the Representation from any State, the Executive Authority thereof shall issue Writs of Election to fill such vacancies.

The House of Representatives shall chuse their Speaker and other Officers; and shall have the sole Power of Impeachment.

Section 3.

The Senate of the United States shall be composed of two Senators from each State, chosen by the Legislature thereof, for six Years; and each Senator shall have one Vote.

Immediately after they shall be assembled in Consequence of the first Election, they shall be divided as equally as may be into three Classes. The Seats of the Senators of the first Class shall be vacated at the Expiration of the second Year, of the second Class at the Expiration of the fourth Year, and of the third Class at the Expiration of the sixth Year, so that one third may be chosen every second Year; and if Vacancies happen by Resignation or otherwise, during the Recess of the Legislature of any State, the Executive thereof may make temporary Appointments until the next Meeting of the Legislature, which shall then fill such Vacancies.

No Person shall be a Senator who shall not have attained to the Age of thirty Years, and been nine Years a Citizen of the United States, and who shall not, when elected, be an Inhabitant of that State for which he shall be chosen.

The Vice President of the United States shall be President of the Senate, but shall have no Vote, unless they be equally divided.

The Senate shall chuse their other Officers, and also a President pro tempore, in the Absence of the Vice President, or when he shall exercise the Office of President of the United States.

The Senate shall have the sole power to try all Impeachments. When sitting for that Purpose, they shall be an Oath or Affirmation. When the President of the United States is tried, the Chief Justice shall preside: And no Person shall be convicted without the Concurrence of two thirds of the Members present.

Judgment in Cases of Impeachment shall not extend further than to removal from Office, and disqualification to hold and enjoy any Office of honor, Trust or Profit under the United States: but the Party convicted shall nevertheless be liable and subject to Indictment, Trial, Judgment and Punishment, according to Law.

Section 4.

The Times, Places and Manner of holding Elections for Senators and Representatives, shall be prescribed in each State by the Legislature thereof: but the Congress may at any time by Law make or alter such Regulations, except as to the Places of chusing Senators.

The Congress shall assemble at least once in every Year, and such Meeting shall be on the first Monday in December, unless they shall by Law appoint a different Day.

Section 5.

Each House shall be the Judge of the Elections, Returns and Qualifications of its own Members, and a Majority of each shall constitute a Quorum to do Business; but a smaller Number may adjourn from day to day, and may be authorized to compel the Attendance of absent Members, in such Manner, and under such Penalties as each House may provide.

Each House may determine the Rules of its Proceedings, punish its Members for disorderly Behaviour, and, with the Concurrence of two thirds, expel a Member.

Each House shall keep a Journal of its Proceedings, and from time to time publish the same, excepting such Parts as may in their Judgment require Secrecy; and the Yeas and Nays of the Members of either House on any question shall, at the Desire of one fifth of those Present, be entered on the Journal.

Neither House, during the Session of Congress, shall, without the Consent of the other, adjourn for more than three days, nor to any other Place than that in which the two Houses shall be sitting.

Section 6.

The Senators and Representatives shall receive a Compensation for their Services, to be ascertained by Law, and paid out of the Treasury of the United States. They shall in all Cases, except Treason, Felony and Breach of the Peace, be privileged from Arrest during their Attendance at the Session of their respective Houses, and in going to and returning from the same; and for any Speech or Debate in either House, they shall not be questioned in any other Place.

No Senator or Representative shall, during the Time for which he was elected, be appointed to any civil Office under the Authority of the United States, which shall have been created, or the Emoluments whereof shall have been encreased during such time; and no Person holding any Office under the United States, shall be a Member of either House during his Continuance in Office.

Section 7.

All Bills for raising Revenue shall originate in the House of Representatives; but the Senate may propose or concur with Amendments as on other Bills.

Every Bill which shall have passed the House of Representatives and the Senate, shall, before it become a Law, be presented to the President of the United States; If he approve he shall sign it, but if not he shall return it, with his Objections to that House in which it shall have originated, who shall enter the Objections at large on their Journal, and proceed to reconsider it. If after such Reconsideration two thirds of that House shall agree to pass the Bill, it shall be sent, together with the Objections, to the other House, by which it shall likewise be reconsidered, and if approved by two thirds of that House, it shall become a Law. But in all such Cases the Votes of both Houses shall be determined by Yeas and Nays, and the Names of the Persons voting for and against the Bill shall be entered on the Journal of each House respectively. If any Bill shall not be returned by the President within ten Days (Sundays excepted) after it shall have been presented to him, the Same shall be a Law, in like Manner as if he had signed it, unless the Congress by their Adjournment prevent its Return, in which Case it shall not be a Law.

Every Order, Resolution, or Vote to which the Concurrence of the Senate and House of Representatives may be necessary (except on a question of Adjournment) shall be presented to the President of the United States; and before the Same shall take Effect, shall be approved by him, or being disapproved by him, shall be repassed by two thirds of the Senate and House of Representatives, according to the Rules and Limitations prescribed in the Case of a Bill.

Section 8.

The Congress shall have Power to lay and collect Taxes, Duties, Imposts and Excises, to pay the Debts and provide for the common Defence and general Welfare of the United States; but all Duties, Imposts and Excises shall be uniform throughout the United States;

To borrow Money on the credit of the United States;

To regulate Commerce with foreign Nations, and among the several States, and with the Indian Tribes;

To establish an uniform Rule of Naturalization, and uniform Laws on the subject of Bankruptcies throughout the United States;

To coin Money, regulate the Value thereof, and of foreign Coin, and fix the Standard of Weights and Measures;

To provide for the Punishment of counterfeiting the Securities and current Coin of the United States;

To establish Post Offices and post Roads;

To promote the Progress of Science and useful Arts, by securing for limited Times to Authors and Inventors the exclusive Right to their respective Writings and Discoveries;

To constitute Tribunals inferior to the supreme Court;

To define and punish Piracies and Felonies committed on the high Seas, and Offenses against the Law of Nations;

To declare War, grant Letters of Marque and Reprisal, and make Rules concerning Captures on Land and Water;

To raise and support Armies, but no Appropriation of Money to that Use shall be for a longer Term than two Years;

To provide and maintain a Navy;

To make Rules for the Government and Regulation of the land and naval Forces;

To provide for calling forth the Militia to execute the Laws of the Union, suppress Insurrections and repel Invasions;

To provide for organizing, arming, and disciplining, the Militia, and for governing such Part of them as may be employed in the Service of the United States, reserving to the States respectively, the Appointment of the Officers, and the Authority of training the Militia according to the discipline described by Congress;

To exercise exclusive Legislation in all Cases whatsoever, over such District (not exceeding ten Miles square) as may, by Cession of particular States, and the Acceptance of Congress, become the Seat of the Government of the United States, and to exercise like Authority over all Places purchased by the Consent of the Legislature of the State in which the Same shall be, for the Erection of Forts, Magazines, Arsenals, dock-Yards, and other needful Buildings;—And

To make all Laws which shall be necessary and proper for carrying into Execution the foregoing Powers, and all other Powers vested by this Constitution in the Government of the United States, or in any Department or Officer thereof.

Section 9.

The Migration or Importation of such Persons as any of the States now existing shall think proper to admit, shall not be prohibited by the Congress prior to the Year one thousand eight hundred and eight, but a Tax or Duty may be imposed on such Importation, not exceeding ten dollars for each Person.

The Privilege of the Writ of Habeas Corpus shall not be suspended, unless when in Cases of Rebellion or Invasion the public Safety may require it.

No Bill of Attainder or ex post facto Law shall be passed.

No Capitation, or other direct, Tax shall be laid, unless in Proportion to the Census or Enumeration herein before directed to be taken.

No Tax or Duty shall be laid on Articles exported from any State.

No Preference shall be given by any Regulation of Commerce or Revenue to the Ports of one State over those of another; nor shall Vessels bound to, or from, one State, be obliged to enter, clear, or pay Duties in another.

No Money shall be drawn from the Treasury, but in Consequence of Appropriations made by Laws; and a regular Statement and Account of the Receipts and Expenditures of all public Money shall be published from time to time.

No Title of Nobility shall be granted by the United States: And no Person holding any Office of Profit or Trust under them, shall, without the Consent of the Congress, accept of any present, Emolument, Office, or Title, of any kind whatever, from any King, Prince, or foreign State.

Section 10.

No State shall enter into any Treaty, Alliance, or Confederation; grant Letters of Marque and Reprisal; coin Money; emit Bills of Credit; make any Thing but gold and silver Coin a Tender in Payment of Debts; pass any Bill of Attainder, ex post facto Law, or Law impairing the Obligation of Contracts, or grant any Title of Nobility.

No State shall, without the Consent of the Congress, lay any Imposts or Duties on Imports or Exports, except what may be absolutely necessary for executing its inspection Laws: and the net Produce of all Duties and Imposts, laid by any State on Imports or Exports, shall be for the Use of the Treasury of the United States; and all such Laws shall be subject to the Revision and Controul of the Congress.

No State shall, without the Consent of Congress, lay any Duty of Tonnage, keep Troops, or Ships of War in time of Peace, enter into any Agreement or Compact with another State, or with a foreign Power, or engage in War, unless actually invaded, or in such imminent Danger as will not admit of delay.

ARTICLE II

Section 1.

The executive Power shall be vested in a President of the United States of America. He shall hold his Office during the Term of four Years, and, together with the Vice President, chosen for the same Term, be elected, as follows:

Each State shall appoint, in such Manner as the Legislature thereof may direct, a Number of Electors, equal to the whole Number of Senators and Representatives to which the State may be entitled in the Congress: but no Senator or Representative, or Person holding an Office of Trust or Profit under the United States, shall be appointed an Elector.

The Electors shall meet in their respective States, and vote by Ballot for two Persons, of whom one at least shall not be an Inhabitant of the same State with themselves. And they shall make a list of all the Persons voted for, and of the Number of Votes for each; which List they shall sign and certify, and transmit sealed to the Seat of the Government of the United States, directed to the President of the Senate. The President of the Senate shall, in the presence of the Senate and House of Representatives, open all the Certificates, and the Votes shall be counted. The Person having the greatest Number of Votes shall be the President, if such Number be a Majority of the whole Number of Electors appointed; and if there be more than one who have such Majority, and have an equal Number of Votes, then the House of Representatives shall immediately chuse by Ballot one of them for President; and if no Person have a Majority, then from the five highest on the List the said House shall in like Manner chuse the President. But in chusing the President, the Votes shall be taken by States, the Representation from each State having one Vote; A quorum for this Purpose shall consist of a Member or Members from two thirds of the States, and a Majority of all the States shall be necessary to a Choice. In every Case, after the Choice of the President, the Person having the greatest Number of Votes of the Electors shall be the Vice President. But if there should remain two or more who have equal Votes, the Senate shall chuse from them by Ballot the Vice President.

The Congress may determine the Time of Chusing the Electors, and the Day on which they shall give their Votes; which Day shall be the same throughout the United States.

No Person except a natural born Citizen, or a Citizen of the United States, at the time of the Adoption of this Constitution, shall be eligible to the Office of President; neither shall any Person be eligible to that Office who shall not have attained to the Age of thirty five Years, and been fourteen Years a Resident within the United States.

In Case of the Removal of the President from Office, or of his Death, Resignation, or Inability to discharge the Powers and Duties of the said Office, the Same shall devolve on the Vice President, and the Congress may by Law provide for the Case of Removal, Death, Resignation or Inability, both of the President and Vice President, declaring what Officer shall then act as President, and such Officer shall act accordingly, until the Disability be removed, or a President shall be elected.

The President shall, at stated Times, receive for his Services, a Compensation, which shall neither be encreased nor diminished during the Period for which he shall have been elected, and he shall not receive within that Period any other Emolument from the United States, or any of them.

Before he enter on the Execution of his Office, he shall take the following Oath or Affirmation:—"I do solemnly swear (or affirm) that I will faithfully execute the Office of President of the United States, and will to the best of my Ability, preserve, protect and defend the Constitution of the United States."

Section 2.

The President shall be Commander in Chief of the Army and Navy of the United States, and of the Militia of the several States, when called into the actual Service of the United States; he may require the Opinion, in writing, of the principal Officer in each of the executive Departments, upon any Subject relating to the Duties of their respective Offices, and he shall have Power to grant Reprieves and Pardons for Offenses against the United States, except in Cases of Impeachment.

He shall have Power, by and with the Advice and Consent of the Senate, to make Treaties, providing two thirds of the Senators present concur; and he shall nominate, and by and with the Advice and Consent of the Senate, shall appoint Ambassadors, other public Ministers and Consuls, Judges of the supreme Court, and all other Officers of the United States, whose Appointments are not herein otherwise provided for, and which shall be established by Law: but the Congress may by Law vest the Appointment of such inferior Officers, as they think proper, in the President alone, in the Courts of Law, or in the Heads of Departments.

The President shall have Power to fill up all Vacancies that may happen during the Recess of the Senate, by granting Commissions which shall expire at the End of their next Session.

Section 3.

He shall from time to time give to the Congress Information of the State of the Union, and recommend to their Consideration such Measures as he shall judge necessary and expedient; he may, on extraordinary Occasions, convene both Houses, or either of them, and in Case of Disagreement between them, with Respect to the Time of Adjournment, he may adjourn them to such Time as he shall think proper, he shall receive Ambassadors and other public Ministers; he shall take Care that the Laws be faithfully executed, and shall Commission all the Offices of the United States.

Section 4.

The President, Vice President and all civil Officers of the United States, shall be removed from Office on Impeachment for, and Conviction of, Treason, Bribery, or other high Crimes and Misdemeanors.

ARTICLE III

Section 1.

The judicial Power of the United States, shall be vested in one supreme Court, and in such inferior Courts as the Congress may from time to time ordain and establish. The Judges, both of the supreme and inferior Courts, shall hold their Offices during good Behaviour, and shall, at Times, receive for their Services, a Compensation, which shall not be diminished during their Continuance in Office.

Section 2.

The judicial Power shall extend to all Cases, in Law and Equity, arising under this Constitution, the Laws of the United States, and Treaties made, or which shall be made, under their Authority;—to all Cases affecting Ambassadors, other public Ministers and Consuls;—to all Cases of admiralty and maritime Jurisdiction;—to Controversies to which the United States shall be a Party;—to controversies between two or more States;—between a State and Citizens of another State;—between Citizens of different States;—between Citizens of the same State claiming Lands under Grants of different States; and between a State, or the Citizens thereof, and foreign States, Citizens or Subjects.

In all Cases affecting Ambassadors, other public Ministers and Consuls, and those in which a State shall be Party, the supreme Court shall have original Jurisdiction. In all the other Cases before mentioned, the supreme Court shall have appellate Jurisdiction, both as to Law and Fact, with such Exceptions, and under such Regulations as the Congress shall make.

The Trial of all Crimes, except in Cases of Impeachment, shall be by Jury; and such Trial shall be held in the State where the said Crimes shall have been committed; but when not committed within any State, the Trial shall be at such Place or Places as the Congress may by Law have directed.

Section 3.

Treason against the United States, shall consist only in levying War against them, or in adhering to their Enemies, giving them Aid and Comfort. No Person shall be convicted of Treason unless on the Testimony of two Witnesses to the same overt Act, or on Confession in open Court.

The Congress shall have Power to declare the Punishment of Treason, but no Attainder of Treason shall work Corruption of Blood, or Forfeiture except during the Life of the Person attainted.

ARTICLE IV

Section 1.

Full Faith and Credit shall be given in each State to the public Acts, Records, and judicial Proceedings of every other State. And the Congress may by general Laws prescribe the Manner in which such Acts, Records and Proceedings shall be proved, and the Effect thereof.

Section 2.

The Citizens of each State shall be entitled to all Privileges and Immunities of Citizens in the several States.

A Person charged in any State with Treason, Felony, or other Crime, who shall flee from Justice, and be found in another State, shall on Demand of the executive Authority of the State from which he fled, be delivered up, to be removed to the State having Jurisdiction of the Crime.

No Person held to Service or Labour in one State, under the Laws thereof, escaping into another, shall, in Consequence of any Law or Regulation therein, be discharged from such Service or Labour, but shall be delivered up on Claim of the Party to whom such Service or Labour may be due.

Section 3.

New States may be admitted by the Congress into this Union; but no new State shall be formed or erected within the Jurisdiction of any other State; nor any State be formed by the Junction of two or more States, or Parts of States, without the Consent of the Legislatures of the States concerned as well as the Congress.

The Congress shall have Power to dispose of and make all needful Rules and Regulations respecting the Territory or other Property belonging to the United States; and nothing in this Constitution shall be so construed as to Prejudice any Claims of the United States, or of any particular State.

Section 4.

The United States shall guarantee to every State in this Union a Republican Form of Government, and shall protect each of them against Invasion; and on Application of the Legislature, or of the Executive (when the Legislature cannot be convened) against domestic Violence.

ARTICLE V

The Congress, whenever two thirds of both Houses shall deem it necessary, shall propose Amendments to this Constitution, or, on the Application of the Legislatures of two thirds of the several States, shall call a Convention for proposing Amendments, which, in either Case, shall be valid to all Intents and Purposes, as Part of this Constitution, when ratified by the Legislatures of three fourths of the several States, or by Conventions in three fourths thereof, as the one or the other Mode of Ratification may be proposed by the Congress; Provided that no Amendment which may be made prior to the Year One thousand eight hundred and eight shall in any Manner affect the first and fourth Clauses in the Ninth Section of the first Article; and that no State, without its Consent, shall be deprived of its equal Suffrage in the Senate.

ARTICLE VI

All Debts contracted and Engagements entered into, before the Adoption of this Constitution, shall be as valid against the United States under this Constitution, as under the Confederation.

This Constitution, and the Laws of the United States which shall be made in Pursuance thereof; and all Treaties made, or which shall be made, under the Authority of the United States, shall be the supreme Law of the Land; and the Judges in every State shall be bound thereby, any Thing in the Constitution or Laws of any State to the Contrary notwithstanding.

The Senators and Representatives before mentioned, and the Members of the several State Legislatures, and all executive and judicial Officers, both of the United States and of the Several States, shall be bound by Oath or Affirmation, to support this Constitution; but no religious Test shall ever be required as a Qualification to any Office or public Trust under the United States.

ARTICLE VII

The Ratification of the Conventions of nine States, shall be sufficient for the Establishment of this Constitution between the States so ratifying the Same.

Amendment I [1791].

Congress shall make no law respecting an establishment of religion, or prohibiting the free exercise thereof; or abridging the freedom of speech, or the press; or the right of the people peaceably to assemble, and to petition the Government for a redress of grievances.

Amendment II [1791].

A well regulated Militia, being necessary to the security for a free State, the right of the people to keep and bear Arms, shall not be infringed.

Amendment III [1791].

No Soldier shall, in time of peace be quartered in any house, without the consent of the Owner, nor in time of war, but in a manner to be prescribed by law.

Amendment IV [1791].

The right of the people to be secure in their persons, houses, papers, and effects, against unreasonable searches and seizures, shall not be violated, and no Warrants shall issue, but upon probable cause, supported by Oath or Affirmation, and particularly describing the place to be searched, and the persons or things to be seized.

Amendment V [1791].

No person shall be held to answer for a capital, or otherwise infamous crime, unless on a presentment or indictment of a Grand Jury, except in cases arising in the land or naval forces, or in the Militia, when in actual service in time of

War or public danger; nor shall any person be subject for the same offense to be twice put in jeopardy of life or limb; nor shall be compelled in any criminal case to be a witness against himself, nor be deprived of life, liberty, or property, without due process of law; nor shall private property be taken for public use, without just compensation.

Amendment VI [1791].

In all criminal prosecutions, the accused shall enjoy the right to a speedy and public trial, by an impartial jury of the State and district wherein the crime shall have been committed, which district shall have been previously ascertained by law, and to be informed of the nature and cause of the accusation; to be confronted with the Witnesses against him; to have compulsory process for obtaining witnesses in his favor, and to have the Assistance of counsel for his defence.

Amendment VII [1791].

In suits at common law, where the value in controversy shall exceed twenty dollars, the right of trial by jury shall be preserved, and no fact tried by a jury, shall be otherwise re-examined in any Court of the United States, than according to the rules of the common law.

Amendment VIII [1791].

Excessive bail shall not be required, no excessive fines imposed, nor cruel and unusual punishments inflicted.

Amendment IX [1791].

The enumeration in the Constitution, of certain rights, shall not be construed to deny or disparage others retained by the people.

Amendment X [1791].

The powers not delegated to the United States by the Constitution, nor prohibited by it to the States, are reserved to the States respectively, or to the people.

Amendment XI [1798].

The judicial power of the United States shall not be construed to extend to any suit in law or equity, commenced or prosecuted against one of the United States by Citizens of another State, or by Citizens or Subjects of any Foreign State.

Amendment XII [1804].

The Electors shall meet in their respective states and vote by ballot for President and Vice-President, one of whom, at least, shall not be an inhabitant of the same state with themselves; they shall name in their ballots the person voted for as President, and in distinct ballots the person voted for as Vice-President, and they shall make distinct lists of all persons voted for as President, and of all persons voted for as Vice-President, and of the number of votes for each, which lists they shall sign and certify, and transmit sealed to the seat of the government of the United States, directed to the President of the Senate;—The President of the Senate shall, in the presence of the Senate and House of Representatives, open all the certificates and the votes shall then be counted;—The person having the greatest number of votes for President, shall be the President, if such number be a majority of the whole number of Electors appointed; and if no person have such majority, then from the persons having the highest numbers not exceeding three on the list of those voted for as President, the House of Representatives shall choose immediately, by ballot, the President. But in choosing the President, the votes shall be taken by states, the representation from each state having one vote; a quorum for this purpose shall consist of a member or members from two-thirds of the states, and a majority of all the states shall be necessary to a choice. And if the House of Representatives shall not choose a President whenever the right of choice shall devolve upon them, before the fourth day of March next following, then the Vice-President shall act as President, as in the case of the death or other constitutional disability of the President. The person having the greatest number of votes as Vice-President, shall be the Vice-President, if such number be a majority of the whole number of Electors appointed, and if no person have a majority, then from the two highest numbers on the list, the Senate shall choose the Vice-President; a quorum for the purpose shall consist of two-thirds of the whole number of Senators, and a majority of the whole number shall be necessary to a choice. But no person constitutionally ineligible to the office of President shall be eligible to that of the Vice-President of the United States.

Amendment XIII [1865].

Section 1. Neither slavery nor involuntary servitude, except as a punishment for crime whereof the party shall have been duly convicted, shall exist within the United States, or any place subject to their jurisdiction.

Section 2. Congress shall have power to enforce this article by appropriate legislation.

Amendment XIV [1868].

Section 1. All persons born or naturalized in the United States, and subject to the jurisdiction thereof, are citizens of the United States and of the State wherein they reside. No State shall make or enforce any law which shall abridge the privileges or immunities of citizens of the United States; nor shall any State deprive any person of life, liberty, or property, without due process of law; nor deny to any person within its jurisdiction the equal protection of the laws.

Section 2. Representatives shall be appointed among the several States according to their respective numbers, counting the whole number of persons in each State, excluding Indians not taxed. But when the right to vote at any election for the choice of electors for President and Vice President of the United States, Representatives in Congress, the Executive and Judicial officers of a State, or the members of the Legislature thereof, is denied to any of the male inhabitants of such State, being twenty-one years of age, and citizens of the United States, or in any way abridged, except for participation in rebellion, or other crime, the basis of representation therein shall be reduced in the proportion which the number of such male citizens shall bear the whole number of male citizens twenty-one years of age in such State.

Section 3. No person shall be a Senator or Representative in Congress, or elector of President and Vice President, or hold any office, civil or military, under the United States, or under any State, who, having previously taken an oath, as a member of Congress, or as an officer of the United States, or as a member of any State legislature, or as an executive or judicial officer of any State, to support the Constitution of the United States, shall have engaged in insurrection or rebellion against the same, or given aid or comfort to the enemies thereof. But Congress may by a vote of two-thirds of each House, remove such disability.

Section 4. The validity of the public debt of the United States, authorized by law, including debts incurred for payment of pensions and bounties for services in suppressing insurrection or rebellion, shall not be questioned. But neither the United States nor any State shall assume or pay any debt or obligation incurred in aid of insurrection of rebellion against the United States, or any claim for the loss or emancipation of any slave; but all such debts, obligations and claims shall be held illegal and void.

Section 5. The Congress shall have power to enforce, by appropriate legislation, the provisions of this article.

Amendment XV [1870].

Section 1. The right of citizens of the United States to vote shall not be denied or abridged by the United States or by any State on account of race, color, or previous condition of servitude.

Section 2. The Congress shall have power to enforce this article by appropriate legislation.

Amendment XVI [1913].

The Congress shall have power to lay and collect taxes on incomes, from whatever source derived, without apportionment among the several States, and without regard to any census or enumeration.

Amendment XVII [1913].

The Senate of the United States shall be composed of two Senators from each State, elected by the people thereof, for six years; and each Senator shall have one vote. The electors in each State shall have the qualifications requisite for electors of the most numerous branch of the State legislatures.

When vacancies happen in the representation of any State in the Senate, the executive authority of each State shall issue writs of election to fill such vacancies; *Provided,* That the legislature of any State may empower the executive thereof to make temporary appointments until the people fill the vacancies by election as the legislature may direct.

This amendment shall not be construed as to affect the election or term of any Senator chosen before it becomes valid as part of the Constitution.

Amendment XVIII [1919].

Section 1. After one year from the ratification of this article the manufacture, sale, or transportation of intoxicating liquors within, the importation thereof into, or the exportation thereof from the United States and all territory subject to the jurisdiction thereof for beverage purposes is hereby prohibited.

Section 2. The Congress and the several States shall have concurrent power to enforce this article by appropriate legislation.

Section 3. This article shall be inoperative unless it shall have been ratified as an amendment to the Constitution by the legislatures of the several States, as provided in the Constitution, within seven years from the date of the submission hereof to the States by the Congress.

Amendment XIX [1920].

The right of citizens of the United States to vote shall not be denied or abridged by the United States or by any State on account of sex.

Congress shall have power to enforce this article by appropriate legislation.

Amendment XX [1933].

Section 1. The terms of the President and Vice President shall end at noon on the 20th day of January, and the terms of Senators and Representatives at noon on the 3d day of January, of the years in which such terms would have ended if this article had not been ratified; and the terms of their successors shall then begin.

Section 2. The Congress shall assemble at least once in every year, and such meeting shall begin at noon on the 3d day of January, unless they shall by law appoint a different day.

Section 3. If, at the time fixed for the beginning of the term of the President, the President elect shall have died, the Vice President elect shall become President. If a President shall not have been chosen before the time fixed for the beginning of his term, or if the President elect shall have failed to qualify, then the Vice President elect shall act as President until a President shall have qualified; and the Congress may by law provide for the case wherein neither a President elect nor a Vice President elect shall have qualified, declaring who shall then act as President, or the manner in which one who is to act shall be selected, and such person shall act accordingly until a President or Vice President shall have qualified.

Section 4. The Congress may by law provide for the case of the death of any of the persons from whom the House of Representatives may choose a President whenever the right of choice shall have devolved upon them, and for the case of the death of any of the persons from whom the Senate may choose a Vice President whenever the right of choice shall have devolved upon them.

Section 5. Sections 1 and 2 shall take effect on the 15th day of October following the ratification of this article.

Section 6. This article shall be inoperative unless it shall have been ratified as an amendment to the Constitution by the legislatures of three-fourths of the several States within seven years from the date of its submission.

Amendment XXI [1933].

Section 1. The eighteenth article of amendment to the Constitution of the United States is hereby repealed.

Section 2. The transportation or importation into any State, Territory, or possession of the United States for delivery or use therein of intoxicating liquors, in violation of the laws thereof, is hereby prohibited.

Section 3. This article shall be inoperative unless it shall have been ratified as an amendment to the Constitution by conventions in the several States, as provided in the Constitution, within seven years from the date of the submission hereof to the States by the Congress.

Amendment XXII [1951].

Section 1. No person shall be elected to the office of the President more than twice, and no person who has held the office of President, or acted as President, for more than two years of a term to which some other person was elected President shall be elected to the office of the President more than once. But this Article shall not apply to any person holding the office of President when this Article was proposed by the Congress, and shall not prevent any person who may be holding the office of President, or acting as President, during the term within which this Article becomes operative from holding the office of President, or acting as President during the remainder of such term.

Section 2. This article shall be inoperative unless it shall have been ratified as an amendment to the Constitution by the legislatures of three-fourths of the several States within seven years from the date of its submission to the States by the Congress.

Amendment XXIII [1961].

Section 1. The District constituting the seat of Government of the United States shall appoint in such manner as the Congress may direct:

A number of electors of President and Vice President equal to the whole number of Senators and Representatives in Congress to which the District would be entitled if it were a State, but in no event more than the least populous State; they shall be in addition to those appointed by the States, but they shall be considered, for the purposes of the election of President and Vice President, to be electors appointed by a State; and they shall meet in the District and perform such duties as provided by the twelfth article of amendment.

Section 2. The Congress shall have power to enforce this article by appropriate legislation.

Amendment XXIV [1964].

Section 1. The right of citizens of the United States to vote in any primary or other election for President or Vice President, for electors for President or Vice President, or for Senator or Representative in Congress, shall not be denied or abridged by the United States or any State by reason of failure to pay any poll tax or other tax.

Section 2. The Congress shall have power to enforce this article by appropriate legislation.

Amendment XXV [1967].

Section 1. In case of the removal of the President from office or of his death or resignation, the Vice President shall become President.

Section 2. Whenever there is a vacancy in the office of the Vice President, the President shall nominate a Vice President who shall take office upon confirmation by a majority vote of both Houses of Congress.

Section 3. Whenever the President transmits to the President pro tempore of the Senate and the Speaker of the House of Representatives his written declaration that he is unable to discharge the powers and duties of his office, and until he transmits to them a written declaration to the contrary, such powers and duties shall be discharged by the Vice President as Acting President.

Section 4. Whenever the Vice President and a majority of either the principal officers of the executive departments or of such other body as Congress may by law provide, transmit to the President pro tempore of the Senate and the Speaker of the House of Representatives their written declaration that the President is unable to discharge the powers and duties of his office, the Vice President shall immediately assume the powers and duties of the office as Acting President.

Thereafter, when the President transmits to the President pro tempore of the Senate and the Speaker of the House of Representatives his written declaration that no inability exists, he shall resume the powers and duties of his office unless the Vice President and a majority of either the principal officers of the executive department or of such other body as Congress may by law provide, transmit within four days to the President pro tempore of the Senate and the Speaker of the House of Representatives their written declaration that the President is unable to discharge the powers and duties of his office. Thereupon Congress shall decide the issue, assembling within forty-eight hours for that purpose if not in session. If the Congress, within twenty-one days after receipt of the latter written declaration, or, if Congress is not in session, within twenty-one days after Congress is required to assemble, determines by two-thirds vote of both Houses that the President is unable to discharge the powers and duties of his office, the Vice President shall continue to discharge the same as Acting President; otherwise, the President shall resume the powers and duties of his office.

Amendment XXVI [1971]. **Section 1.** The right of citizens of the United States, who are eighteen years of age or older, to vote shall not be denied or abridged by the United States or by any State on account of age.

Section 2. The Congress shall have power to enforce this article by appropriate legislation.

Amendment XXVII [1992]. No law, varying the compensation for the services of the Senators and Representatives, shall take effect, until an election of Representatives shall have intervened.

Appendix B

Uniform Commercial Code (Selected Provisions)

The Code consists of the following articles:

Art.

1. General Provisions
2. Sales
2A. Leases
3. Negotiable Instruments
4. Bank Deposits and Collections
4A. Fund Transfers
5. Letters of Credit
6. Repealer of Article 6—Bulk Transfers and [Revised] Article 6—Bulk Sales
7. Warehouse Receipts, Bills of Lading and Other Documents of Title
8. Investment Securities
9. Secured Transactions
10. Effective Date and Repealer
11. Effective Date and Transmission Provisions

ARTICLE 1

GENERAL PROVISIONS

PART 1   Short Title, Construction, Application and Subject Matter of the Act

§ 1–101.   Short Title.

This Act shall be known and may be cited as Uniform Commercial Code.

§ 1–102.   Purposes; Rules of Construction; Variation by Agreement.

(1) This Act shall be liberally construed and applied to promote its underlying purposes and policies.

(2) Underlying purposes and policies of this Act are

   (a) to simplify, clarify and modernize the law governing commercial transactions;

   (b) to permit the continued expansion of commercial practices through custom, usage and agreement of the parties;

   (c) to make uniform the law among the various jurisdictions.

(3) The effect of provisions of this Act may be varied by agreement, except as otherwise provided in this Act and except that the obligations of good faith, diligence, reasonableness and care prescribed by this Act may not be disclaimed by agreement but the parties may by agreement determine the standards by which the performance of such obligations is to be measured if such standards are not manifestly unreasonable.

(4) The presence in certain provisions of this Act of the words "unless otherwise agreed" or words of similar import does not imply that the effect of other provisions may not be varied by agreement under subsection (3).

(5) In this Act unless the context otherwise requires

   (a) words in the singular number include the plural, and in the plural include the singular;

   (b) words of the masculine gender include the feminine and the neuter, and when the sense so indicates words of the neuter gender may refer to any gender.

§ 1–103.   Supplementary General Principles of Law Applicable.

Unless displaced by the particular provisions of this Act, the principles of law and equity, including the law merchant and the law relative to capacity to contract, principal and agent, estoppel, fraud, misrepresentation, duress, coercion, mistake, bankruptcy, or other validating or invalidating cause shall supplement its provisions.

§ 1-104.   Construction Against Implicit Repeal.

This Act being a general act intended as a unified coverage of its subject matter, no part of it shall be deemed to be impliedly repealed by subsequent legislation if such construction can reasonably be avoided.

§ 1-105.   Territorial Application of the Act; Parties' Power to Choose Applicable Law.

(1) Except as provided hereafter in this section, when a transaction bears a reasonable relation to this state and also to another state or nation the parties may agree that the law either of this state or of such other state or nation shall govern their rights and duties. Failing such agreement this Act applies to transactions bearing an appropriate relation to this state.

(2) Where one of the following provisions of this Act specifies the applicable law, that provision governs and a contrary agreement is effective only to the extent permitted by the law (including the conflict of laws rules) so specified:

Rights of creditors against sold goods. Section 2–402.

Applicability of the Article on Leases. Sections 2A–105 and 2A–106.

Applicability of the Article on Bank Deposits and Collections. Section 4–102.

Governing law in the Article on Funds Transfers. Section 4A–507.

Letters of Credit, Section 5–116.
Bulk sales subject to the Article on Bulk Sales. Section 6–103.

Applicability of the Article on Investment Securities. Section 8–106.

Law governing perfection, the effect of perfection or nonperfection, and the priority of security interests and agricultural liens. Sections 9–301 through 9–307.

As amended in 1972, 1987, 1988, 1989, 1994, 1995, and 1999.

§ 1-106.   Remedies to Be Liberally Administered.

(1) The remedies provided by this Act shall be liberally administered to the end that the aggrieved party may be put in as good a position as if the other party had fully performed but neither consequential or special nor penal damages may be had except as specifically provided in this Act or by other rule of law.

(2) Any right or obligation declared by this Act is enforceable by action unless the provision declaring it specifies a different and limited effect.

§ 1-107.   Waiver or Renunciation of Claim or Right After Breach.

Any claim or right arising out of an alleged breach can be discharged in whole or in part without consideration by a written waiver or renunciation signed and delivered by the aggrieved party.

§ 1-108.   Severability.

If any provision or clause of this Act or application thereof to any person or circumstances is held invalid, such invalidity shall not affect other provisions or applications of the Act which can be given effect without the invalid provision or application, and to this end the provisions of this Act are declared to be severable.

§ 1-109.   Section Captions.

Section captions are parts of this Act.

PART 2   General Definitions and Principles of Interpretation

§ 1-201.   General Definitions.

Subject to additional definitions contained in the subsequent Articles of this Act which are applicable to specific Articles or Parts thereof, and unless the context otherwise requires, in this Act:

(1) "Action" in the sense of a judicial proceeding includes recoupment, counterclaim, set-off, suit in equity and any other proceedings in which rights are determined.

(2) "Aggrieved party" means a party entitled to resort to a remedy.

(3) "Agreement" means the bargain of the parties in fact as found in their language or by implication from other circumstances including course of dealing or usage of trade or course of performance as provided in this Act (Sections 1–205 and 2–208). Whether an agreement has legal consequences is determined by the provisions of this Act, if applicable; otherwise by the law of contracts (Section 1–103). (Compare "Contract".)

(4) "Bank" means any person engaged in the business of banking.

(5) "Bearer" means the person in possession of an instrument, document of title, or certificated security payable to bearer or indorsed in blank.

(6) "Bill of lading" means a document evidencing the receipt of goods for shipment issued by a person engaged in the business of transporting or forwarding goods, and includes an airbill. "Airbill" means a document serving for air transportation as a

bill of lading does for marine or rail transportation, and includes an air consignment note or air waybill.

(7) "Branch" includes a separately incorporated foreign branch of a bank.

(8) "Burden of establishing" a fact means the burden of persuading the triers of fact that the existence of the fact is more probable than its non-existence.

(9) "Buyer in ordinary course of business" means a person that buys goods in good faith, without knowledge that the sale violates the rights of another person in the goods, and in the ordinary course from a person, other than a pawnbroker, in the business of selling goods of that kind. A person buys goods in the ordinary course if the sale to the person comports with the usual or customary practices in the kind of business in which the seller is engaged or with the seller's own usual or customary practices. A person that sells oil, gas, or other minerals at the wellhead or minehead is a person in the business of selling goods of that kind. A buyer in ordinary course of business may buy for cash, by exchange of other property, or on secured or unsecured credit, and may acquire goods or documents of title under a pre-existing contract for sale. Only a buyer that takes possession of the goods or has a right to recover the goods from the seller under Article 2 may be a buyer in ordinary course of business. A person that acquires goods in a transfer in bulk or as security for or in total or partial satisfaction of a money debt is not a buyer in ordinary course of business.

(10) "Conspicuous": A term or clause is conspicuous when it is so written that a reasonable person against whom it is to operate ought to have noticed it. A printed heading in capitals (as: NON-NEGOTIABLE BILL OF LADING) is conspicuous. Language in the body of a form is "conspicuous" if it is in larger or other contrasting type or color. But in a telegram any stated term is "conspicuous". Whether a term or clause is "conspicuous" or not is for decision by the court.

(11) "Contract" means the total legal obligation which results from the parties' agreement as affected by this Act and any other applicable rules of law. (Compare "Agreement".)

(12) "Creditor" includes a general creditor, a secured creditor, a lien creditor and any representative of creditors, including an assignee for the benefit of creditors, a trustee in bankruptcy, a receiver in equity and an executor or administrator of an insolvent debtor's or assignor's estate.

(13) "Defendant" includes a person in the position of defendant in a cross-action or counterclaim.

(14) "Delivery" with respect to instruments, documents of title, chattel paper, or certificated securities means voluntary transfer of possession.

(15) "Document of title" includes bill of lading, dock warrant, dock receipt, warehouse receipt or order for the delivery of goods, and also any other document which in the regular course of business or financing is treated as adequately evidencing that the person in possession of it is entitled to receive, hold and dispose of the document and the goods it covers. To be a document of title a document must purport to be issued by or addressed to a bailee and purport to cover goods in the bailee's possession which are either identified or are fungible portions of an identified mass.

(16) "Fault" means wrongful act, omission or breach.

(17) "Fungible" with respect to goods or securities means goods or securities of which any unit is, by nature or usage of trade, the equivalent of any other like unit. Goods which are not fungible shall be deemed fungible for the purposes of this Act to the extent that under a particular agreement or document unlike units are treated as equivalents.

(18) "Genuine" means free of forgery or counterfeiting.

(19) "Good faith" means honesty in fact in the conduct or transaction concerned.

(20) "Holder" with respect to a negotiable instrument, means the person in possession if the instrument is payable to bearer or, in the cases of an instrument payable to an identified person, if the identified person is in possession. "Holder" with respect to a document of title means the person in possession if the goods are deliverable to bearer or to the order of the person in possession.

(21) To "honor" is to pay or to accept and pay, or where a credit so engages to purchase or discount a draft complying with the terms of the credit.

(22) "Insolvency proceedings" includes any assignment for the benefit of creditors or other proceedings intended to liquidate or rehabilitate the estate of the person involved.

(23) A person is "insolvent" who either has ceased to pay his debts in the ordinary course of business or cannot pay his debts as they become due or is insolvent within the meaning of the federal bankruptcy law.

(24) "Money" means a medium of exchange authorized or adopted by a domestic or foreign government and includes a monetary unit of account established by an intergovernmental organization or by agreement between two or more nations.

(25) A person has "notice" of a fact when

(a) he has actual knowledge of it; or

(b) he has received a notice or notification of it; or

(c) from all the facts and circumstances known to him at the time in question he has reason to know that it exists.

A person "knows" or has "knowledge" of a fact when he has actual knowledge of it. "Discover" or "learn" or a word or phrase of similar import refers to knowledge rather than to reason to know. The time and circumstances under which a notice or notification may cease to be effective are not determined by this Act.

(26) A person "notifies" or "gives" a notice or notification to another by taking such steps as may be reasonably required to inform the other in ordinary course whether or not such other

actually comes to know of it. A person "receives" a notice or notification when

(a) it comes to his attention; or

(b) it is duly delivered at the place of business through which the contract was made or at any other place held out by him as the place for receipt of such communications.

(27) Notice, knowledge or a notice or notification received by an organization is effective for a particular transaction from the time when it is brought to the attention of the individual conducting that transaction, and in any event from the time when it would have been brought to his attention if the organization had exercised due diligence. An organization exercises due diligence if it maintains reasonable routines for communicating significant information to the person conducting the transaction and there is reasonable compliance with the routines. Due diligence does not require an individual acting for the organization to communicate information unless such communication is part of his regular duties or unless he has reason to know of the transaction and that the transaction would be materially affected by the information.

(28) "Organization" includes a corporation, government or governmental subdivision or agency, business trust, estate, trust, partnership or association, two or more persons having a joint or common interest, or any other legal or commercial entity.

(29) "Party", as distinct from "third party", means a person who has engaged in a transaction or made an agreement within this Act.

(30) "Person" includes an individual or an organization (See Section 1–102).

(31) "Presumption" or "presumed" means that the trier of fact must find the existence of the fact presumed unless and until evidence is introduced which would support a finding of its non-existence.

(32) "Purchase" includes taking by sale, discount, negotiation, mortgage, pledge, lien, issue or re-issue, gift or any other voluntary transaction creating an interest in property.

(33) "Purchaser" means a person who takes by purchase.

(34) "Remedy" means any remedial right to which an aggrieved party is entitled with or without resort to a tribunal.

(35) "Representative" includes an agent, an officer of a corporation or association, and a trustee, executor or administrator of an estate, or any other person empowered to act for another.

(36) "Rights" includes remedies.

(37) "Security interest" means an interest in personal property or fixtures which secures payment or performance of an obligation. The term also includes any interest of a consignor and a buyer of accounts, chattel paper, a payment intangible, or a promissory note in a transaction that is subject to Article 9. The special property interest of a buyer of goods on identification of those goods to a contract for sale under Section 2–401 is not a "security interest", but a buyer may also acquire a

"security interest" by complying with Article 9. Except as otherwise provided in Section 2–505, the right of a seller or lessor of goods under Article 2 or 2A to retain or acquire possession of the goods is not a "security interest", but a seller or lessor may also acquire a "security interest" by complying with Article 9. The retention or reservation of title by a seller of goods notwithstanding shipment or delivery to the buyer (Section 2–401) is limited in effect to a reservation of a "security interest".

Whether a transaction creates a lease or security interest is determined by the facts of each case; however, a transaction creates a security interest if the consideration the lessee is to pay the lessor for the right to possession and use of the goods is an obligation for the term of the lease not subject to termination by the lessee, and

(a) the original term of the lease is equal to or greater than the remaining economic life of the goods,

(b) the lessee is bound to renew the lease for the remaining economic life of the goods or is bound to become the owner of the goods,

(c) the lessee has an option to renew the lease for the remaining economic life of the goods for no additional consideration or nominal additional consideration upon compliance with the lease agreement, or

(d) the lessee has an option to become the owner of the goods for no additional consideration or nominal additional consideration upon compliance with the lease agreement.

A transaction does not create a security interest merely because it provides that

(a) the present value of the consideration the lessee is obligated to pay the lessor for the right to possession and use of the goods is substantially equal to or is greater than the fair market value of the goods at the time the lease is entered into,

(b) the lessee assumes risk of loss of the goods, or agrees to pay taxes, insurance, filing, recording, or registration fees, or service or maintenance costs with respect to the goods,

(c) the lessee has an option to renew the lease or to become the owner of the goods,

(d) the lessee has an option to renew the lease for a fixed rent that is equal to or greater than the reasonably predictable fair market rent for the use of the goods for the term of the renewal at the time the option is to be performed, or

(e) the lessee has an option to become the owner of the goods for a fixed price that is equal to or greater than the reasonably predictable fair market value of the goods at the time the option is to be performed.

For purposes of this subsection (37):

(x) Additional consideration is not nominal if (i) when the option to renew the lease is granted to the lessee the rent is stated to be the fair market rent for the use of the goods for the term of the renewal determined at the time the option is to be performed, or (ii) when the option to become the owner of the goods is granted to the lessee the price is stated to be the fair market value of the goods determined at the time the option is to be performed. Additional consideration is nominal if it is less than the lessee's reasonably predictable cost of performing under the lease agreement if the option is not exercised;

(y) "Reasonably predictable" and "remaining economic life of the goods" are to be determined with reference to the facts and circumstances at the time the transaction is entered into; and

(z) "Present value" means the amount as of a date certain of one or more sums payable in the future, discounted to the date certain. The discount is determined by the interest rate specified by the parties if the rate is not manifestly unreasonable at the time the transaction is entered into; otherwise, the discount is determined by a commercially reasonable rate that takes into account the facts and circumstances of each case at the time the transaction was entered into.

(38) "Send" in connection with any writing or notice means to deposit in the mail or deliver for transmission by any other usual means of communication with postage or cost of transmission provided for and properly addressed and in the case of an instrument to an address specified thereon or otherwise agreed, or if there be none to any address reasonable under the circumstances. The receipt of any writing or notice within the time at which it would have arrived if properly sent has the effect of a proper sending.

(39) "Signed" includes any symbol executed or adopted by a party with present intention to authenticate a writing.

(40) "Surety" includes guarantor.

(41) "Telegram" includes a message transmitted by radio, teletype, cable, any mechanical method of transmission, or the like.

(42) "Term" means that portion of an agreement which relates to a particular matter.

(43) "Unauthorized" signature means one made without actual, implied or apparent authority and includes a forgery.

(44) "Value". Except as otherwise provided with respect to negotiable instruments and bank collections (Sections 3–303, 4–210 and 4–211) a person gives "value" for rights if he acquires them

(a) in return for a binding commitment to extend credit or for the extension of immediately available credit whether or not drawn upon and whether or not a chargeback is provided for in the event of difficulties in collection; or

(b) as security for or in total or partial satisfaction of a preexisting claim; or

(c) by accepting delivery pursuant to a preexisting contract for purchase; or

(d) generally, in return for any consideration sufficient to support a simple contract.

(45) "Warehouse receipt" means a receipt issued by a person engaged in the business of storing goods for hire.

(46) "Written" or "writing" includes printing, typewriting or any other intentional reduction to tangible form.

§1–202.   Prima Facie Evidence by Third Party Documents.

A document in due form purporting to be a bill of lading, policy or certificate of insurance, official weigher's or inspector's certificate, consular invoice, or any other document authorized or required by the contract to be issued by a third party shall be prima facie evidence of its own authenticity and genuineness and of the facts stated in the document by the third party.

§ 1–203.   Obligation of Good Faith.

Every contract or duty within this Act imposes an obligation of good faith in its performance or enforcement.

§ 1–204.   Time; Reasonable Time; "Seasonably".

(1) Whenever this Act requires any action to be taken within a reasonable time, any time which is not manifestly unreasonable may be fixed by agreement.

(2) What is a reasonable time for taking any action depends on the nature, purpose and circumstances of such action.

(3) An action is taken "seasonably" when it is taken at or within the time agreed or if no time is agreed at or within a reasonable time.

§ 1–205.   Course of Dealing and Usage of Trade.

(1) A course of dealing is a sequence of previous conduct between the parties to a particular transaction which is fairly to be regarded as establishing a common basis of understanding for interpreting their expressions and other conduct.

(2) A usage of trade is any practice or method of dealing having such regularity of observance in a place, vocation or trade as to justify an expectation that it will be observed with respect to the transaction in question. The existence and scope of such a usage are to be proved as facts. If it is established that such a usage is embodied in a written trade code or similar writing the interpretation of the writing is for the court.

(3) A course of dealing between parties and any usage of trade in the vocation or trade in which they are engaged or of which they are or should be aware give particular meaning to and supplement or qualify terms of an agreement.

(4) The express terms of an agreement and an applicable course of dealing or usage of trade shall be construed wherever reasonable as consistent with each other; but when such construction is unreasonable express terms control both course of dealing and usage of trade and course of dealing controls usage trade.

(5) An applicable usage of trade in the place where any part of performance is to occur shall be used in interpreting the agreement as to that part of the performance.

(6) Evidence of a relevant usage of trade offered by one party is not admissible unless and until he has given the other party such notice as the court finds sufficient to prevent unfair surprise to the latter.

§ 1–206.   Statute of Frauds for Kinds of Personal Property Not Otherwise Covered.

(1) Except in the cases described in subsection (2) of this section a contract for the sale of personal property is not enforceable by way of action or defense beyond five thousand dollars in amount or value of remedy unless there is some writing which indicates that a contract for sale has been made between the parties at a defined or stated price, reasonably identifies the subject matter, and is signed by the party against whom enforcement is sought or by his authorized agent.

(2) Subsection (1) of this section does not apply to contracts for the sale of goods (Section 2–201) nor of securities (Section 8–113) nor to security agreements (Section 9–203).

As amended in 1994.

§ 1–207.   Performance or Acceptance Under Reservation of Rights.

(1) A party who with explicit reservation of rights performs or promises performance or assents to performance in a manner demanded or offered by the other party does not thereby prejudice the rights reserved. Such words as "without prejudice", "under protest" or the like are sufficient.

(2) Subsection (1) does not apply to an accord and satisfaction.

As amended in 1990.

§ 1–208.   Option to Accelerate at Will.

A term providing that one party or his successor in interest may accelerate payment or performance or require collateral or additional collateral "at will" or "when he deems himself insecure" or in words of similar import shall be construed to mean that he shall have power to do so only if he in good faith believes that the prospect of payment or performance is impaired. The burden of establishing lack of good faith is on the party against whom the power has been exercised.

§ 1–209.   Subordinated Obligations.

An obligation may be issued as subordinated to payment of another obligation of the person obligated, or a creditor may subordinate his right to payment of an obligation by agreement with either the person obligated or another creditor of the person obligated. Such a subordination does not create a security interest as against either the common debtor or a subordinated creditor. This section shall be construed as declaring the law as it existed prior to the enactment of this section and not as modifying it. Added 1966.

Note: *This new section is proposed as an optional provision to make it clear that a subordination agreement does not create a security interest unless so intended.*

ARTICLE 2

SALES

PART I   Short Title, General Construction and Subject Matter

§ 2–101.   Short Title.

This Article shall be known and may be cited as Uniform Commercial Code—Sales.

§ 2–102.   Scope; Certain Security and Other Transactions Excluded From This Article.

Unless the context otherwise requires, this Article applies to transactions in goods; it does not apply to any transaction which although in the form of an unconditional contract to sell or present sale is intended to operate only as a security transaction nor does this Article impair or repeal any statute regulating sales to consumers, farmers or other specified classes of buyers.

§ 2–103.   Definitions and Index of Definitions.

(1) In this Article unless the context otherwise requires

 (a) "Buyer" means a person who buys or contracts to buy goods.

 (b) "Good faith" in the case of a merchant means honesty in fact and the observance of reasonable commercial standards of fair dealing in the trade.

 (c) "Receipt" of goods means taking physical possession of them.

 (d) "Seller" means a person who sells or contracts to sell goods.

 (2) Other definitions applying to this Article or to specified Parts thereof, and the sections in which they appear are:

  "Acceptance". Section 2–606.

  "Banker's credit". Section 2–325.

  "Between merchants". Section 2–104.

  "Cancellation". Section 2–106(4).

  "Commercial unit". Section 2–105.

  "Confirmed credit". Section 2–325.

  "Conforming to contract". Section 2–106.

  "Contract for sale". Section 2–106.

  "Cover". Section 2–712.

  "Entrusting". Section 2–403.

"Financing agency". Section 2–104.

"Future goods". Section 2–105.

"Goods". Section 2–105.

"Identification". Section 2–501.

"Installment contract". Section 2–612.

"Letter of Credit". Section 2–325.

"Lot". Section 2–105

"Merchant". Section 2–104.

"Overseas". Section 2–323.

"Person in position of seller". Section 2–707.

"Present sale". Section 2–106.

"Sale". Section 2–106.

"Sale on approval". Section 2–326.

"Sale or return". Section 2–326.

"Termination". Section 2–106.

(3) The following definitions in other Articles apply to this Article:

"Check". Section 3–104.

"Consignee". Section 7–102.

"Consignor". Section 7–102.

"Consumer goods". Section 9–109.

"Dishonor". Section 3–507.

"Draft". Section 3–104.

(4) In addition Article 1 contains general definitions and principles of construction and interpretation applicable throughout this Article.

As amended in 1994 and 1999.

§ 2–104. Definitions: "Merchant"; "Between Merchants"; "Financing Agency".

(1) "Merchant" means a person who deals in goods of the kind or otherwise by his occupation holds himself out as having knowledge or skill peculiar to the practices or goods involved in the transaction or to whom such knowledge or skill may be attributed by his employment of an agent or broker or other intermediary who by his occupation holds himself out as having such knowledge or skill.

(2) "Financing agency" means a bank, finance company or other person who in the ordinary course of business makes advances against goods or documents of title or who by arrangement with either the seller or the buyer intervenes in ordinary course to make or collect payment due or claimed under the contract for sale, as by purchasing or paying the seller's draft or making advances against it or by merely taking it for collection whether or not documents of title accompany the draft. "Financing agency" includes also a bank or other person who similarly intervenes between persons who are in the position of seller and buyer in respect to the goods (Section 2–707).

(3) "Between merchants" means in any transaction with respect to which both parties are chargeable with the knowledge or skill of merchants.

§ 2–105. Definitions: Transferability; "Goods"; "Future" Goods; "Lot"; "Commercial Unit".

(1) "Goods" means all things (including specially manufactured goods) which are movable at the time of identification to the contract for sale other than the money in which the price is to be paid, investment securities (Article 8) and things in action. "Goods" also includes the unborn young of animals and growing crops and other identified things attached to realty as described in the section on goods to be severed from realty (Section 2–107).

(2) Goods must be both existing and identified before any interest in them can pass. Goods which are not both existing and identified are "future" goods. A purported present sale of future goods or of any interest therein operates as a contract to sell.

(3) There may be a sale of a part interest in existing identified goods.

(4) An undivided share in an identified bulk of fungible goods is sufficiently identified to be sold although the quantity of the bulk is not determined. Any agreed proportion of such a bulk or any quantity thereof agreed upon by number, weight or other measure may to the extent of the seller's interest in the bulk be sold to the buyer who then becomes an owner in common.

(5) "Lot" means a parcel or a single article which is the subject matter of a separate sale or delivery, whether or not it is sufficient to perform the contract.

(6) "Commercial unit" means such a unit of goods as by commercial usage is a single whole for purposes of sale and division of which materially impairs its character or value on the market or in use. A commercial unit may be a single article (as a machine) or a set of articles (as a suite of furniture or an assortment of sizes) or a quantity (as a bale, gross, or carload) or any other unit treated in use or in the relevant market as a single whole.

§ 2–106. Definitions: "Contract"; "Agreement"; "Contract for Sale"; "Sale"; "Present Sale"; "Conforming" to Contract; "Termination"; "Cancellation".

(1) In this Article unless the context otherwise requires "contract" and "agreement" are limited to those relating to the present or future sale of goods. "Contract for sale" includes both a present sale of goods and a contract to sell goods at a future time. A "sale" consists in the passing of title from the seller to the buyer for a price (Section 2–401). A "present sale" means a sale which is accomplished by the making of the contract.

(2) Goods or conduct including any part of a performance are "conforming" or conform to the contract when they are in accordance with the obligations under the contract.

(3) "Termination" occurs when either party pursuant to a power created by agreement or law puts an end to the contract

otherwise than for its breach. On "termination" all obligations which are still executory on both sides are discharged but any right based on prior breach or performance survives.

(4) "Cancellation" occurs when either party puts an end to the contract for breach by the other and its effect is the same as that of "termination" except that the cancelling party also retains any remedy for breach of the whole contract or any unperformed balance.

§ 2–107. Goods to Be Severed From Realty: Recording.

(1) A contract for the sale of minerals or the like (including oil and gas) or a structure or its materials to be removed from realty is a contract for the sale of goods within this Article if they are to be severed by the seller but until severance a purported present sale thereof which is not effective as a transfer of an interest in land is effective only as a contract to sell.

(2) A contract for the sale apart from the land of growing crops or other things attached to realty and capable of severance without material harm thereto but not described in subsection (1) or of timber to be cut is a contract for the sale of goods within this Article whether the subject matter is to be severed by the buyer or by the seller even though it forms part of the realty at the time of contracting, and the parties can by identification effect a present sale before severance.

(3) The provisions of this section are subject to any third party rights provided by the law relating to realty records, and the contract for sale may be executed and recorded as a document transferring an interest in land and shall then constitute notice to third parties of the buyer's rights under the contract for sale.

As amended in 1972.

PART 2 Form, Formation and Readjustment of Contract

§ 2–201. Formal Requirements; Statute of Frauds.

(1) Except as otherwise provided in this section a contract for the sale of goods for the price of $500 or more is not enforceable by way of action or defense unless there is some writing sufficient to indicate that a contract for sale has been made between the parties and signed by the party against whom enforcement is sought or by his authorized agent or broker. A writing is not insufficient because it omits or incorrectly states a term agreed upon but the contract is not enforceable under this paragraph beyond the quantity of goods shown in such writing.

(2) Between merchants if within a reasonable time a writing in confirmation of the contract and sufficient against the sender is received and the party receiving it has reason to know its con-

tents, its satisfies the requirements of subsection (1) against such party unless written notice of objection to its contents is given within ten days after it is received.

(3) A contract which does not satisfy the requirements of subsection (1) but which is valid in other respects is enforceable

(a) if the goods are to be specially manufactured for the buyer and are not suitable for sale to others in the ordinary course of the seller's business and the seller, before notice of repudiation is received and under circumstances which reasonably indicate that the goods are for the buyer, has made either a substantial beginning of their manufacture or commitments for their procurement; or

(b) if the party against whom enforcement is sought admits in his pleading, testimony or otherwise in court that a contract for sale was made, but the contract is not enforceable under this provision beyond the quantity of goods admitted; or

(c) with respect to goods for which payment has been made and accepted or which have been received and accepted (Sec. 2–606).

§ 2–202. Final Written Expression: Parol or Extrinsic Evidence.

Terms with respect to which the confirmatory memoranda of the parties agree or which are otherwise set forth in a writing intended by the parties as a final expression of their agreement with respect to such terms as are included therein may not be contradicted by evidence of any prior agreement or of a contemporaneous oral agreement but may be explained or supplemented

(a) by course of dealing or usage of trade (Section 1–205) or by course of performance (Section 2–208); and

(b) by evidence of consistent additional terms unless the court finds the writing to have been intended also as a complete and exclusive statement of the terms of the agreement.

§ 2–203. Seals Inoperative.

The affixing of a seal to a writing evidencing a contract for sale or an offer to buy or sell goods does not constitute the writing a sealed instrument and the law with respect to sealed instruments does not apply to such a contract or offer.

§ 2–204. Formation in General.

(1) A contract for sale of goods may be made in any manner sufficient to show agreement, including conduct by both parties which recognizes the existence of such a contract.

(2) An agreement sufficient to constitute a contract for sale may be found even though the moment of its making is undetermined.

(3) Even though one or more terms are left open a contract for sale does not fail for indefiniteness if the parties have intended to make a contract and there is a reasonably certain basis for giving an appropriate remedy.

§ 2–205.   Firm Offers.

An offer by a merchant to buy or sell goods in a signed writing which by its terms gives assurance that it will be held open is not revocable, for lack of consideration, during the time stated or if no time is stated for a reasonable time, but in no event may such period of irrevocability exceed three months; but any such term of assurance on a form supplied by the offeree must be separately signed by the offeror.

§ 2–206.   Offer and Acceptance in Formation of Contract.

(1) Unless other unambiguously indicated by the language or circumstances

(a) an offer to make a contract shall be construed as inviting acceptance in any manner and by any medium reasonable in the circumstances;

(b) an order or other offer to buy goods for prompt or current shipment shall be construed as inviting acceptance either by a prompt promise to ship or by the prompt or current shipment of conforming or nonconforming goods, but such a shipment of non-conforming goods does not constitute an acceptance if the seller seasonably notifies the buyer that the shipment is offered only as an accommodation to the buyer.

(2) Where the beginning of a requested performance is a reasonable mode of acceptance an offeror who is not notified of acceptance within a reasonable time may treat the offer as having lapsed before acceptance.

§ 2–207.   Additional Terms in Acceptance or Confirmation.

(1) A definite and seasonable expression of acceptance or a written confirmation which is sent within a reasonable time operates as an acceptance even though it states terms additional to or different from those offered or agreed upon, unless acceptance is expressly made conditional on assent to the additional or different terms.

(2) The additional terms are to be construed as proposals for addition to the contract. Between merchants such terms become part of the contract unless:

(a) the offer expressly limits acceptance to the terms of the offer;

(b) they materially alter it; or

(c) notification of objection to them has already been given or is given within a reasonable time after notice of them is received.

(3) Conduct by both parties which recognizes the existence of a contract is sufficient to establish a contract for sale although the writings of the parties do not otherwise establish a contract. In such case the terms of the particular contract consist of those terms on which the writings of the parties agree, together with any supplementary terms incorporated under any other provisions of this Act.

§ 2–208.   Course of Performance or Practical Construction.

(1) Where the contract for sale involves repeated occasions for performance by either party with knowledge of the nature of the performance and opportunity for objection to it by the other, any course of performance accepted or acquiesced in without objection shall be relevant to determine the meaning of the agreement.

(2) The express terms of the agreement and any such course of performance, as well as any course of dealing and usage of trade, shall be construed whenever reasonable as consistent with each other; but when such construction is unreasonable, express terms shall control course of performance and course of performance shall control both course of dealing and usage of trade (Section 1–205).

(3) Subject to the provisions of the next section on modification and waiver, such course of performance shall be relevant to show a waiver or modification of any term inconsistent with such course of performance.

§ 2–209.   Modification, Rescission and Waiver.

(1) An agreement modifying a contract within this Article needs no consideration to be binding.

(2) A signed agreement which excludes modification or rescission except by a signed writing cannot be otherwise modified or rescinded, but except as between merchants such a requirement on a form supplied by the merchant must be separately signed by the other party.

(3) The requirements of the statute of frauds section of this Article (Section 2–201) must be satisfied if the contract as modified is within its provisions.

(4) Although an attempt at modification or rescission does not satisfy the requirements of subsection (2) or (3) it can operate as a waiver.

(5) A party who has made a waiver affecting an executory portion of the contract may retract the waiver by reasonable notification received by the other party that strict performance will be required of any term waived, unless the retraction would be unjust in view of a material change of position in reliance on the waiver.

§ 2–210.   Delegation of Performance; Assignment of Rights.

(1) A party may perform his duty through a delegate unless otherwise agreed or unless the other party has a substantial interest in having his original promisor perform or control the acts required by the contract. No delegation of performance relieves the party delegating of any duty to perform or any liability for breach.

(2) Except as otherwise provided in Section 9–406, unless otherwise agreed, all rights of either seller or buyer can be assigned except where the assignment would materially change the duty of the other party, or increase materially the burden or risk imposed on him by his contract, or impair materially his chance of obtaining return performance. A right to damages for breach of the whole contract or a right arising out of the assignor's due performance of his entire obligation can be assigned despite agreement otherwise.

(3) The creation, attachment, perfection, or enforcement of a security interest in the seller's interest under a contract is not a transfer that materially changes the duty of or increases materially the burden or risk imposed on the buyer or impairs materially the buyer's chance of obtaining return performance within the purview of subsection (2) unless, and then only to the extent that, enforcement actually results in a delegation of material performance of the seller. Even in that event, the creation, attachment, perfection, and enforcement of the security interest remain effective, but (i) the seller is liable to the buyer for damages caused by the delegation to the extent that the damages could not reasonably by prevented by the buyer, and (ii) a court having jurisdiction may grant other appropriate relief, including cancellation of the contract for sale or an injunction against enforcement of the security interest or consummation of the enforcement.

(4) Unless the circumstances indicate the contrary a prohibition of assignment of "the contract" is to be construed as barring only the delegation to the assignee of the assignor's performance.

(5) An assignment of "the contract" or of "all my rights under the contract" or an assignment in similar general terms is an assignment of rights and unless the language or the circumstances (as in an assignment for security) indicate the contrary, it is a delegation of performance of the duties of the assignor and its acceptance by the assignee constitutes a promise by him to perform those duties. This promise is enforceable by either the assignor or the other party to the original contract.

(6) The other party may treat any assignment which delegates performance as creating reasonable grounds for insecurity and may without prejudice to his rights against the assignor demand assurances from the assignee (Section 2–609).

As amended in 1999.

PART 3   General Obligation and Construction of Contract

§ 2–301.   General Obligations of Parties.

The obligation of the seller is to transfer and deliver and that of the buyer is to accept and pay in accordance with the contract.

§ 2–302.   Unconscionable Contract or Clause.

(1) If the court as a matter of law finds the contract or any clause of the contract to have been unconscionable at the time it was made the court may refuse to enforce the contract, or it may enforce the remainder of the contract without the unconscionable clause, or it may so limit the application of any unconscionable clause as to avoid any unconscionable result.

(2) When it is claimed or appears to the court that the contract or any clause thereof may be unconscionable the parties shall be afforded a reasonable opportunity to present evidence as to its commercial setting, purpose and effect to aid the court in making the determination.

§ 2–303.   Allocations or Division of Risks.

Where this Article allocates a risk or a burden as between the parties "unless otherwise agreed", the agreement may not only shift the allocation but may also divide the risk or burden.

§ 2–304.   Price Payable in Money, Goods, Realty, or Otherwise.

(1) The price can be made payable in money or otherwise. If it is payable in whole or in part in goods each party is a seller of the goods which he is to transfer.

(2) Even though all or part of the price is payable in an interest in realty the transfer of the goods and the seller's obligations with reference to them are subject to this Article, but not the transfer of the interest in realty or the transferor's obligations in connection therewith.

§ 2–305.   Open Price Term.

(1) The parties if they so intend can conclude a contract for sale even though the price is not settled. In such a case the price is a reasonable price at the time for delivery if

(a) nothing is said as to price; or

(b) the price is left to be agreed by the parties and they fail to agree; or

(c) the price is to be fixed in terms of some agreed market or other standard as set or recorded by a third person or agency and it is not so set or recorded.

(2) A price to be fixed by the seller or by the buyer means a price for him to fix in good faith.

(3) When a price left to be fixed otherwise than by agreement of the parties fails to be fixed through fault of one party the other may at his option treat the contract as cancelled or himself fix a reasonable price.

(4) Where, however, the parties intend not to be bound unless the price be fixed or agreed and it is not fixed or agreed there is no contract. In such a case the buyer must return any goods already received or if unable so to do must pay their reasonable value at the time of delivery and the seller must return any portion of the price paid on account.

§ 2–306.   Output, Requirements and Exclusive Dealings.

(1) A term which measures the quantity by the output of the seller or the requirements of the buyer means such actual output or requirements as may occur in good faith, except that no quantity unreasonably disproportionate to any stated estimate or in the absence of a stated estimate to any normal or otherwise comparable prior output or requirements may be tendered or demanded.

(2) A lawful agreement by either the seller or the buyer for exclusive dealing in the kind of goods concerned imposes unless otherwise agreed an obligation by the seller to use best efforts to supply the goods and by the buyer to use best efforts to promote their sale.

§ 2–307.   Delivery in Single Lot or Several Lots.

Unless otherwise agreed all goods called for by a contract for sale must be tendered in a single delivery and payment is due only on such tender but where the circumstances give either party the right to make or demand delivery in lots the price if it can be apportioned may be demanded for each lot.

§ 2–308.   Absence of Specified Place for Delivery.

Unless otherwise agreed

(a) the place for delivery of goods is the seller's place of business or if he has none his residence; but

(b) in a contract for sale of identified goods which to the knowledge of the parties at the time of contracting are in some other place, that place is the place for their delivery; and

(c) documents of title may be delivered through customary banking channels.

§ 2–309.   Absence of Specific Time Provisions; Notice of Termination.

(1) The time for shipment or delivery or any other action under a contract if not provided in this Article or agreed upon shall be a reasonable time.

(2) Where the contract provides for successive performances but is indefinite in duration it is valid for a reasonable time but unless otherwise agreed may be terminated at any time by either party.

(3) Termination of a contract by one party except on the happening of an agreed event requires that reasonable notification be received by the other party and an agreement dispensing with notification is invalid if its operation would be unconscionable.

§ 2–310.   Open Time for Payment or Running of Credit; Authority to Ship Under Reservation.

Unless otherwise agreed

(a) payment is due at the time and place at which the buyer is to receive the goods even though the place of shipment is the place of delivery; and

(b) if the seller is authorized to send the goods he may ship them under reservation, and may tender the documents of title, but the buyer may inspect the goods after their arrival before payment is due unless such inspection is inconsistent with the terms of the contract (Section 2–513); and

(c) if delivery is authorized and made by way of documents of title otherwise than by subsection (b) then payment is due at the time and place at which the buyer is to receive the documents regardless of where the goods are to be received; and

(d) where the seller is required or authorized to ship the goods on credit the credit period runs from the time of shipment but post-dating the invoice or delaying its dispatch will correspondingly delay the starting of the credit period.

§ 2–311.   Options and Cooperation Respecting Performance.

(1) An agreement for sale which is otherwise sufficiently definite (subsection (3) of Section 2–204) to be a contract is not made invalid by the fact that it leaves particulars of performance to be specified by one of the parties. Any such specification must be made in good faith and within limits set by commercial reasonableness.

(2) Unless otherwise agreed specifications relating to assortment of the goods are at the buyer's option and except as otherwise provided in subsections (1)(c) and (3) of Section 2–319 specifications or arrangements relating to shipment are at the seller's option.

(3) Where such specification would materially affect the other party's performance but is not seasonably made or where one party's cooperation is necessary to the agreed performance of the other but is not seasonably forthcoming, the other party in addition to all other remedies

(a) is excused for any resulting delay in his own performance; and

(b) may also either proceed to perform in any reasonable manner or after the time for a material part of his own performance treat the failure to specify or to cooperate as a breach by failure to deliver or accept the goods.

§ 2–312.   Warranty of Title and Against Infringement; Buyer's Obligation Against Infringement.

(1) Subject to subsection (2) there is in a contract for sale a warranty by the seller that

(a) the title conveyed shall be good, and its transfer rightful; and

b) the goods shall be delivered free from any security interest or other lien or encumbrance of which the buyer at the time of contracting has no knowledge.

(2) A warranty under subsection (1) will be excluded or modified only by specific language or by circumstances which give the buyer reason to know that the person selling does not claim title in himself or that he is purporting to sell only such right or title as he or a third person may have.

(3) Unless otherwise agreed a seller who is a merchant regularly dealing in goods of the kind warrants that the goods shall be delivered free of the rightful claim of any third person by way of infringement or the like but a buyer who furnishes specifications to the seller must hold the seller harmless against any such claim which arises out of compliance with the specifications.

§ 2–313.   Express Warranties by Affirmation, Promise, Description, Sample.

(1) Express warranties by the seller are created as follows:

(a) Any affirmation of fact or promise made by the seller to the buyer which relates to the goods and becomes part of the basis of the bargain creates an express warranty that the goods shall conform to the affirmation or promise.

(b) Any description of the goods which is made part of the basis of the bargain creates an express warranty that the goods shall conform to the description.

(c) Any sample or model which is made part of the basis of the bargain creates an express warranty that the whole of the goods shall conform to the sample or model.

(2) It is not necessary to the creation of an express warranty that the seller use formal words such as "warrant" or "guarantee" or that he have a specific intention to make a warranty, but an affirmation merely of the value of the goods or a statement purporting to be merely the seller's opinion or commendation of the goods does not create a warranty.

§ 2–314.   Implied Warranty: Merchantability; Usage of Trade.

(1) Unless excluded or modified (Section 2–316), a warranty that the goods shall be merchantable is implied in a contract for their sale if the seller is a merchant with respect to goods of that kind. Under this section the serving for value of food or drink to be consumed either on the premises or elsewhere is a sale.

(2) Goods to be merchantable must be at least such as

(a) pass without objection in the trade under the contract description; and

(b) in the case of fungible goods, are of fair average quality within the description; and

(c) are fit for the ordinary purposes for which such goods are used; and

(d) run, within the variations permitted by the agreement, of even kind, quality and quantity within each unit and among all units involved; and

(e) are adequately contained, packaged, and labeled as the agreement may require; and

(f) conform to the promises or affirmations of fact made on the container or label if any.

(3) Unless excluded or modified (Section 2–316) other implied warranties may arise from course of dealing or usage of trade.

§ 2–315.   Implied Warranty: Fitness for Particular Purpose.

Where the seller at the time of contracting has reason to know any particular purpose for which the goods are required and that the buyer is relying on the seller's skill or judgment to select or furnish suitable goods, there is unless excluded or modified under the next section an implied warranty that the goods shall be fit for such purpose.

§ 2–316.   Exclusion or Modification of Warranties.

(1) Words or conduct relevant to the creation of an express warranty and words or conduct tending to negate or limit warranty shall be construed wherever reasonable as consistent with each other; but subject to the provisions of this Article on parol or extrinsic evidence (Section 2–202) negation or limitation is inoperative to the extent that such construction is unreasonable.

(2) Subject to subsection (3), to exclude or modify the implied warranty of merchantability or any part of it the language must mention merchantability and in case of a writing must be conspicuous, and to exclude or modify any implied warranty of fitness the exclusion must be by a writing and conspicuous. Language to exclude all implied warranties of fitness is sufficient if it states, for example, that "There are no warranties which extend beyond the description on the face hereof."

(3) Notwithstanding subsection (2)

(a) unless the circumstances indicate otherwise, all implied warranties are excluded by expressions like "as is", "with all faults" or other language which in common understanding calls the buyer's attention to the exclusion of warranties and makes plain that there is no implied warranty; and

(b) when the buyer before entering into the contract has examined the goods or the sample or model as fully as he desired or has refused to examine the goods there is no implied warranty with regard to defects which an examination ought in the circumstances to have revealed to him; and

(c) an implied warranty can also be excluded or modified by course of dealing or course of performance or usage of trade.

(4) Remedies for breach of warranty can be limited in accordance with the provisions of this Article on liquidation or limitation of damages and on contractual modification of remedy (Sections 2–718 and 2–719).

§ 2–317.   Cumulation and Conflict of Warranties Express or Implied.

Warranties whether express or implied shall be construed as consistent with each other and as cumulative, but if such construction is unreasonable the intention of the parties shall determine which warranty is dominant. In ascertaining that intention the following rules apply:

(a) Exact or technical specifications displace an inconsistent sample or model or general language of description.

(b) A sample from an existing bulk displaces inconsistent general language of description.

(c) Express warranties displace inconsistent implied warranties other than an implied warranty of fitness for a particular purpose.

§ 2–318.   Third Party Beneficiaries of Warranties Express or Implied.

Note: If this Act is introduced in the Congress of the United States this section should be omitted. (States to select one alternative.)

Alternative A   A seller's warranty whether express or implied extends to any natural person who is in the family or household of his buyer or who is a guest in his home if it is reasonable to expect that such person may use, consume or be affected by the goods and who is injured in person by breach of the warranty. A seller may not exclude or limit the operation of this section.

Alternative B   A seller's warranty whether express or implied extends to any natural person who may reasonably be expected to use, consume or be affected by the goods and who is injured in person by breach of the warranty. A seller may not exclude or limit the operation of this section.

Alternative C   A seller's warranty whether express or implied extends to any person who may reasonably be expected to use, consume or be affected by the goods and who is injured by breach of the warranty. A seller may not exclude or limit the operation of this section with respect to injury to the person of an individual to whom the warranty extends.

As amended 1966.

§ 2–319.   F.O.B. and F.A.S. Terms.

(1) Unless otherwise agreed the term F.O.B. (which means "free on board") at a named place, even though used only in connection with the stated price, is a delivery term under which

(a) when the term is F.O.B. the place of shipment, the seller must at that place ship the goods in the manner provided in this Article (Section 2–504) and bear the expense and risk of putting them into the possession of the carrier; or

(b) when the term is F.O.B. the place of destination, the seller must at his own expense and risk transport the goods to that place and there tender delivery of them in the manner provided in this Article (Section 2–503);

(c) when under either (a) or (b) the term is also F.O.B. vessel, car or other vehicle, the seller must in addition at his own expense and risk load the goods on board. If the term is F.O.B. vessel the buyer must name the vessel and in an appropriate case the seller must comply with the provisions of this Article on the form of bill of lading (Section 2–323).

(2) Unless otherwise agreed the term F.A.S. vessel (which means "free alongside") at a named port, even though used only in connection with the stated price, is a delivery term under which the seller must

(a) at his own expense and risk deliver the goods alongside the vessel in the manner usual in that port or on a dock designated and provided by the buyer; and

(b) obtain and tender a receipt for the goods in exchange for which the carrier is under a duty to issue a bill of lading.

(3) Unless otherwise agreed in any case falling within subsection (1)(a) or (c) or subsection (2) the buyer must seasonably give any needed instructions for making delivery, including when the term is F.A.S. or F.O.B. the loading berth of the vessel and in an appropriate case its name and sailing date. The seller may treat the failure of needed instructions as a failure of cooperation under this Article (Section 2–311). He may also at his option move the goods in any reasonable manner preparatory to delivery or shipment.

(4) Under the term F.O.B. vessel or F.A.S. unless otherwise agreed the buyer must make payment against tender of the required documents and the seller may not tender nor the buyer demand delivery of the goods in substitution for the documents.

§ 2–320.   C.I.F. and C. & F. Terms.

(1) The term C.I.F. means that the price includes in a lump sum the cost of the goods and the insurance and freight to the named destination. The term C. & F. or C.F. means that the price so includes cost and freight to the named destination.

(2) Unless otherwise agreed and even though used only in connection with the stated price and destination, the term C.I.F. destination or its equivalent requires the seller at his own expense and risk to

(a) put the goods into the possession of a carrier at the port for shipment and obtain a negotiable bill or bills of lading covering the entire transportation to the named destination; and

(b) load the goods and obtain a receipt from the carrier (which may be contained in the bill of lading) showing that the freight has been paid or provided for; and

(c) obtain a policy or certificate of insurance, including any war risk insurance, of a kind and on terms then current at the port of shipment in the usual amount, in the currency of the contract, shown to cover the same goods covered by the bill of lading and providing for payment of loss to the order of the buyer or for the account of whom it may concern; but the seller may add to the price the amount of the premium for any such war risk insurance; and

(d) prepare an invoice of the goods and procure any other documents required to effect shipment or to comply with the contract; and

(e) forward and tender with commercial promptness all the documents in due form and with any indorsement necessary to perfect the buyer's rights.

(3) Unless otherwise agreed the term C. & F. or its equivalent has the same effect and imposes upon the seller the same obligations and risks as a C.I.F. term except the obligation as to insurance.

(4) Under the term C.I.F. or C. & F. unless otherwise agreed the buyer must make payment against tender of the required documents and the seller may not tender nor the buyer demand delivery of the goods in substitution for the documents.

§ 2–321.   C.I.F. or C. & F.: "Net Landed Weights"; "Payment on Arrival"; Warranty of Condition on Arrival.

Under a contract containing a term C.I.F. or C. & F.

(1) Where the price is based on or is to be adjusted according to "net landed weights", "delivered weights", "out turn" quantity or quality or the like, unless otherwise agreed the seller must reasonably estimate the price. The payment due on tender of the documents called for by the contract is the amount so estimated, but after final adjustment of the price a settlement must be made with commercial promptness.

(2) An agreement described in subsection (1) or any warranty of quality or condition of the goods on arrival places upon the seller the risk of ordinary deterioration, shrinkage and the like in transportation but has no effect on the place or time of identification to the contract for sale or delivery or on the passing of the risk of loss.

(3) Unless otherwise agreed where the contract provides for payment on or after arrival of the goods the seller must before payment allow such preliminary inspection as is feasible; but if the goods are lost delivery of the documents and payment are due when the goods should have arrived.

§ 2–322.   Delivery "Ex-Ship".

(1) Unless otherwise agreed a term for delivery of goods "ex-ship" (which means from the carrying vessel) or in equivalent language is not restricted to a particular ship and requires delivery from a ship which has reached a place at the named port of destination where goods of the kind are usually discharged.

(2) Under such a term unless otherwise agreed

(a) the seller must discharge all liens arising out of the carriage and furnish the buyer with a direction which puts the carrier under a duty to deliver the goods; and

(b) the risk of loss does not pass to the buyer until the goods leave the ship's tackle or are otherwise properly unloaded.

§ 2–323.   Form of Bill of Lading Required in Overseas Shipment; "Overseas".

(1) Where the contract contemplates overseas shipment and contains a term C.I.F. or C. & F. or F.O.B. vessel, the seller unless otherwise agreed must obtain a negotiable bill of lading stating that the goods have been loaded on board or, in the case of a term C.I.F. or C. & F., received for shipment.

(2) Where in a case within subsection (1) a bill of lading has been issued in a set of parts, unless otherwise agreed if the documents are not to be sent from abroad the buyer may demand tender of the full set; otherwise only one part of the bill of lading need be tendered. Even if the agreement expressly requires a full set

(a) due tender of a single part is acceptable within the provisions of this Article on cure of improper delivery (subsection (1) of Section 2–508); and

(b) even though the full set is demanded, if the documents are sent from abroad the person tendering an incomplete set may nevertheless require payment upon furnishing an indemnity which the buyer in good faith deems adequate.

(3) A shipment by water or by air or a contract contemplating such shipment is "overseas" insofar as by usage of trade or agreement it is subject to the commercial, financing or shipping practices characteristic of international deep water commerce.

§ 2–324.   "No Arrival, No Sale" Term.

Under a term "no arrival, no sale" or terms of like meaning, unless otherwise agreed,

(a) the seller must properly ship conforming goods and if they arrive by any means he must tender them on arrival but he assumes no obligation that the goods will arrive unless he has caused the non-arrival; and

(b) where without fault of the seller the goods are in part lost or have so deteriorated as no longer to conform to the contract or arrive after the contract time, the buyer may proceed as if there had been casualty to identified goods (Section 2–613).

§ 2–325.   "Letter of Credit" Term; "Confirmed Credit".

(1) Failure of the buyer seasonably to furnish an agreed letter of credit is a breach of the contract for sale.

(2) The delivery to seller of a proper letter of credit suspends the buyer's obligation to pay. If the letter of credit is dishonored, the seller may on seasonable notification to the buyer require payment directly from him.

(3) Unless otherwise agreed the term "letter of credit" or "banker's credit" in a contract for sale means an irrevocable credit issued by a financing agency of good repute and, where the shipment is overseas, of good international repute. The

term "confirmed credit" means that the credit must also carry the direct obligation of such an agency which does business in the seller's financial market.

§ 2–326.   Sale on Approval and Sale or Return; Rights of Creditors.

(1) Unless otherwise agreed, if delivered goods may be returned by the buyer even though they conform to the contract, the transaction is

(a) a "sale on approval" if the goods are delivered primarily for use, and

(b) a "sale or return" if the goods are delivered primarily for resale.

(2) Goods held on approval are not subject to the claims of the buyer's creditors until acceptance; goods held on sale or return are subject to such claims while in the buyer's possession.

(3) Any "or return" term of a contract for sale is to be treated as a separate contract for sale within the statute of frauds section of this Article (Section 2–201) and as contradicting the sale aspect of the contract within the provisions of this Article or on parol or extrinsic evidence (Section 2–202).

As amended in 1999.

§ 2–327.   Special Incidents of Sale on Approval and Sale or Return.

(1) Under a sale on approval unless otherwise agreed

(a) although the goods are identified to the contract the risk of loss and the title do not pass to the buyer until acceptance; and

(b) use of the goods consistent with the purpose of trial is not acceptance but failure seasonably to notify the seller of election to return the goods is acceptance, and if the goods conform to the contract acceptance of any part is acceptance of the whole; and

(c) after due notification of election to return, the return is at the seller's risk and expense but a merchant buyer must follow any reasonable instructions.

(2) Under a sale or return unless otherwise agreed

(a) the option to return extends to the whole or any commercial unit of the goods while in substantially their original condition, but must be exercised seasonably; and

(b) the return is at the buyer's risk and expense.

§ 2–328.   Sale by Auction.

(1) In a sale by auction if goods are put up in lots each lot is the subject of a separate sale.

(2) A sale by auction is complete when the auctioneer so announces by the fall of the hammer or in other customary manner. Where a bid is made while the hammer is falling in acceptance of a prior bid the auctioneer may in his discretion reopen the bidding or declare the goods sold under the bid on which the hammer was falling.

(3) Such a sale is with reserve unless the goods are in explicit terms put up without reserve. In an auction with reserve the auctioneer may withdraw the goods at any time until he announces completion of the sale. In an auction without reserve, after the auctioneer calls for bids on an article or lot, that article or lot cannot be withdrawn unless no bid is made within a reasonable time. In either case a bidder may retract his bid until the auctioneer's announcement of completion of the sale, but a bidder's retraction does not revive any previous bid.

(4) If the auctioneer knowingly receives a bid on the seller's behalf or the seller makes or procures such as bid, and notice has not been given that liberty for such bidding is reserved, the buyer may at his option avoid the sale or take the goods at the price of the last good faith bid prior to the completion of the sale. This subsection shall not apply to any bid at a forced sale.

PART 4   Title, Creditors and Good Faith Purchasers

§ 2–401.   Passing of Title; Reservation for Security; Limited Application of This Section.

Each provision of this Article with regard to the rights, obligations and remedies of the seller, the buyer, purchasers or other third parties applies irrespective of title to the goods except where the provision refers to such title. Insofar as situations are not covered by the other provisions of this Article and matters concerning title became material the following rules apply:

(1) Title to goods cannot pass under a contract for sale prior to their identification to the contract (Section 2–501), and unless otherwise explicitly agreed the buyer acquires by their identification a special property as limited by this Act. Any retention or reservation by the seller of the title (property) in goods shipped or delivered to the buyer is limited in effect to a reservation of a security interest. Subject to these provisions and to the provisions of the Article on Secured Transactions (Article 9), title to goods passes from the seller to the buyer in any manner and on any conditions explicitly agreed on by the parties.

(2) Unless otherwise explicitly agreed title passes to the buyer at the time and place at which the seller completes his performance with reference to the physical delivery of the goods, despite any reservation of a security interest and even though a document of title is to be delivered at a different time or place; and in particular and despite any reservation of a security interest by the bill of lading

(a) if the contract requires or authorizes the seller to send the goods to the buyer but does not require him to deliver them at destination, title passes to the buyer at the time and place of shipment; but

(b) if the contract requires delivery at destination, title passes on tender there.

(3) Unless otherwise explicitly agreed where delivery is to be made without moving the goods,

(a) if the seller is to deliver a document of title, title passes at the time when and the place where he delivers such documents; or

(b) if the goods are at the time of contracting already identified and no documents are to be delivered, title passes at the time and place of contracting.

(4) A rejection or other refusal by the buyer to receive or retain the goods, whether or not justified, or a justified revocation of acceptance revests title to the goods in the seller. Such revesting occurs by operation of law and is not a "sale".

§ 2–402.   Rights of Seller's Creditors Against Sold Goods.

(1) Except as provided in subsections (2) and (3), rights of unsecured creditors of the seller with respect to goods which have been identified to a contract for sale are subject to the buyer's rights to recover the goods under this Article (Sections 2–502 and 2–716).

(2) A creditor of the seller may treat a sale or an identification of goods to a contract for sale as void if as against him a retention of possession by the seller is fraudulent under any rule of law of the state where the goods are situated, except that retention of possession in good faith and current course of trade by a merchant-seller for a commercially reasonable time after a sale or identification is not fraudulent.

(3) Nothing in this Article shall be deemed to impair the rights of creditors of the seller

(a) under the provisions of the Article on Secured Transactions (Article 9); or

(b) where identification to the contract or delivery is made not in current course of trade but in satisfaction of or as security for a pre-existing claim for money, security or the like and is made under circumstances which under any rule of law of the state where the goods are situated would apart from this Article constitute the transaction a fraudulent transfer or voidable preference.

§ 2–403.   Power to Transfer; Good Faith Purchase of Goods; "Entrusting".

(1) A purchaser of goods acquires all title which his transferor had or had power to transfer except that a purchaser of a limited interest acquires rights only to the extent of the interest purchased. A person with voidable title has power to transfer a good title to a good faith purchaser for value. When goods have been delivered under a transaction of purchase the purchaser has such power even though

(a) the transferor was deceived as to the identity of the purchaser, or

(b) the delivery was in exchange for a check which is later dishonored, or

(c) it was agreed that the transaction was to be a "cash sale", or

(d) the delivery was procured through fraud punishable as larcenous under the criminal law.

(2) Any entrusting of possession of goods to a merchant who deals in goods of that kind gives him power to transfer all rights of the entruster to a buyer in ordinary course of business.

(3) "Entrusting" includes any delivery and any acquiescence in retention of possession regardless of any condition expressed between the parties to the delivery or acquiescence and regardless of whether the procurement of the entrusting or the possessor's disposition of the goods have been such as to be larcenous under the criminal law.

(4) The rights of other purchasers of goods and of lien creditors are governed by the Articles on Secured Transactions (Article 9), Bulk Transfers (Article 6) and Documents of Title (Article 7).

As amended in 1988.

PART 5   Performance

§ 2–501.   Insurable Interest in Goods; Manner of Identification of Goods.

(1) The buyer obtains a special property and an insurable interest in goods by identification of existing goods as goods to which the contract refers even though the goods so identified are non-conforming and he has an option to return or reject them. Such identification can be made at any time and in any manner explicitly agreed to by the parties. In the absence of explicit agreement identification occurs

(a) when the contract is made if it is for the sale of goods already existing and identified;

(b) if the contract is for the sale of future goods other than those described in paragraph (c), when goods are shipped, marked or otherwise designated by the seller as goods to which the contract refers;

(c) when the crops are planted or otherwise become growing crops or the young are conceived if the contract is for the sale of unborn young to be born within twelve months after contracting or for the sale of crops to be harvested within twelve months or the next normal harvest season after contracting whichever is longer.

(2) The seller retains an insurable interest in goods so long as title to or any security interest in the goods remains in him and where the identification is by the seller alone he may until default or insolvency or notification to the buyer that the identification is final substitute other goods for those identified.

(3) Nothing in this section impairs any insurable interest recognized under any other statute or rule of law.

§ 2–502.   Buyer's Right to Goods on Seller's Insolvency.

(1) Subject to subsections (2) and (3) and even though the goods have not been shipped a buyer who has paid a part or all of the price of goods in which he has a special property under the provisions of the immediately preceding section may on making and keeping good a tender of any unpaid portion of their price recover them from the seller if:

(a) in the case of goods bought for personal, family, or household purposes, the seller repudiates or fails to deliver as required by the contract; or

(b) in all cases, the seller becomes insolvent within ten days after receipt of the first installment on their price.

(2) The buyer's right to recover the goods under subsection (1)(a) vests upon acquisition of a special property, even if the seller had not then repudiated or failed to deliver.

(3) If the identification creating his special property has been made by the buyer he acquires the right to recover the goods only if they conform to the contract for sale.

As amended in 1999.

§ 2–503.   Manner of Seller's Tender of Delivery.

(1) Tender of delivery requires that the seller put and hold conforming goods at the buyer's disposition and give the buyer any notification reasonably necessary to enable him to take delivery. The manner, time and place for tender are determined by the agreement and this Article, and in particular

(a) tender must be at a reasonable hour, and if it is of goods they must be kept available for the period reasonably necessary to enable the buyer to take possession; but

(b) unless otherwise agreed the buyer must furnish facilities reasonably suited to the receipt of the goods.

(2) Where the case is within the next section respecting shipment tender requires that the seller comply with its provisions.

(3) Where the seller is required to deliver at a particular destination tender requires that he comply with subsection (1) and also in any appropriate case tender documents as described in subsections (4) and (5) of this section.

(4) Where goods are in the possession of a bailee and are to be delivered without being moved

(a) tender requires that the seller either tender a negotiable document of title covering such goods or procure acknowledgment by the bailee of the buyer's right to possession of the goods; but

(b) tender to the buyer of a non-negotiable document of title or of a written direction to the bailee to deliver is sufficient tender unless the buyer seasonably objects, and receipt by the bailee of notification of the buyer's rights fixes those rights as against the bailee and all third persons; but risk of loss of the goods and of any failure by the bailee to honor the non-

negotiable document of title or to obey the direction remains on the seller until the buyer has had a reasonable time to present the document or direction, and a refusal by the bailee to honor the document or to obey the direction defeats the tender.

(5) Where the contract requires the seller to deliver documents

(a) he must tender all such documents in correct form, except as provided in this Article with respect to bills of lading in a set (subsection (2) of Section 2–323); and

(b) tender through customary banking channels is sufficient and dishonor of a draft accompanying the documents constitutes non-acceptance or rejection.

§ 2–504.   Shipment by Seller.

Where the seller is required or authorized to send the goods to the buyer and the contract does not require him to deliver them at a particular destination, then unless otherwise agreed he must

(a) put the goods in the possession of such a carrier and make such a contract for their transportation as may be reasonable having regard to the nature of the goods and other circumstances of the case; and

(b) obtain and promptly deliver or tender in due form any document necessary to enable the buyer to obtain possession of the goods or otherwise required by the agreement or by usage of trade; and

(c) promptly notify the buyer of the shipment.

Failure to notify the buyer under paragraph (c) or to make a proper contract under paragraph (a) is a ground for rejection only if material delay or loss ensues.

§ 2–505.   Seller's Shipment under Reservation.

(1) Where the seller has identified goods to the contract by or before shipment:

(a) his procurement of a negotiable bill of lading to his own order or otherwise reserves in him a security interest in the goods. His procurement of the bill to the order of a financing agency or of the buyer indicates in addition only the seller's expectation of transferring that interest to the person named.

(b) a non-negotiable bill of lading to himself or his nominee reserves possession of the goods as security but except in a case of conditional delivery (subsection (2) of Section 2–507) a non-negotiable bill of lading naming the buyer as consignee reserves no security interest even though the seller retains possession of the bill of lading.

(2) When shipment by the seller with reservation of a security interest is in violation of the contract for sale it constitutes an improper contract for transportation within the preceding section but impairs neither the rights given to the buyer by shipment and identification of the goods to the contract nor the seller's powers as a holder of a negotiable document.

§ 2–506.   Rights of Financing Agency.

(1) A financing agency by paying or purchasing for value a draft which relates to a shipment of goods acquires to the extent of the payment or purchase and in addition to its own rights under the draft and any document of title securing it any rights of the shipper in the goods including the right to stop delivery and the shipper's right to have the draft honored by the buyer. (2) The right to reimbursement of a financing agency which has in good faith honored or purchased the draft under commitment to or authority from the buyer is not impaired by subsequent discovery of defects with reference to any relevant document which was apparently regular on its face.

§ 2–507.   Effect of Seller's Tender; Delivery on Condition.

(1) Tender of delivery is a condition to the buyer's duty to accept the goods and, unless otherwise agreed, to his duty to pay for them. Tender entitles the seller to acceptance of the goods and to payment according to the contract.

(2) Where payment is due and demanded on the delivery to the buyer of goods or documents of title, his right as against the seller to retain or dispose of them is conditional upon his making the payment due.

§ 2–508.   Cure by Seller of Improper Tender or Delivery; Replacement.

(1) Where any tender or delivery by the seller is rejected because non-conforming and the time for performance has not yet expired, the seller may seasonably notify the buyer of his intention to cure and may then within the contract time make a conforming delivery.

(2) Where the buyer rejects a non-conforming tender which the seller had reasonable grounds to believe would be acceptable with or without money allowance the seller may if he seasonably notifies the buyer have a further reasonable time to substitute a conforming tender.

§ 2–509.   Risk of Loss in the Absence of Breach.

(1) Where the contract requires or authorizes the seller to ship the goods by carrier

(a) if it does not require him to deliver them at a particular destination, the risk of loss passes to the buyer when the goods are duly delivered to the carrier even though the shipment is under reservation (Section 2–505); but

(b) if it does require him to deliver them at a particular destination and the goods are there duly tendered while in the possession of the carrier, the risk of loss passes to the buyer when the goods are there duly so tendered as to enable the buyer to take delivery.

(2) Where the goods are held by a bailee to be delivered without being moved, the risk of loss passes to the buyer

(a) on his receipt of a negotiable document of title covering the goods; or

(b) on acknowledgment by the bailee of the buyer's right to possession of the goods; or

(c) after his receipt of a non-negotiable document of title or other written direction to deliver, as provided in subsection (4)(b) of Section 2–503.

(3) In any case not within subsection (1) or (2), the risk of loss passes to the buyer on his receipt of the goods if the seller is a merchant; otherwise the risk passes to the buyer on tender of delivery.

(4) The provisions of this section are subject to contrary agreement of the parties and to the provisions of this Article on sale on approval (Section 2–327) and on effect of breach on risk of loss (Section 2–510).

§ 2–510.   Effect of Breach on Risk of Loss.

(1) Where a tender or delivery of goods so fails to conform to the contract as to give a right of rejection the risk of their loss remains on the seller until cure or acceptance.

(2) Where the buyer rightfully revokes acceptance he may to the extent of any deficiency in his effective insurance coverage treat the risk of loss as having rested on the seller from the beginning.

(3) Where the buyer as to conforming goods already identified to the contract for sale repudiates or is otherwise in breach before risk of their loss has passed to him, the seller may to the extent of any deficiency in his effective insurance coverage treat the risk of loss as resting on the buyer for a commercially reasonable time.

§ 2–511.   Tender of Payment by Buyer; Payment by Check.

(1) Unless otherwise agreed tender of payment is a condition to the seller's duty to tender and complete any delivery.

(2) Tender of payment is sufficient when made by any means or in any manner current in the ordinary course of business unless the seller demands payment in legal tender and gives any extension of time reasonably necessary to procure it.

(3) Subject to the provisions of this Act on the effect of an instrument on an obligation (Section 3–310), payment by check is conditional and is defeated as between the parties by dishonor of the check on due presentment.

As amended in 1994.

§ 2–512.   Payment by Buyer Before Inspection.

(1) Where the contract requires payment before inspection non-conformity of the goods does not excuse the buyer from so making payment unless

(a) the non-conformity appears without inspection; or

(b) despite tender of the required documents the circumstances would justify injunction against honor under this Act (Section 5–109(b)).

(2) Payment pursuant to subsection (1) does not constitute an acceptance of goods or impair the buyer's right to inspect or any of his remedies.

As amended in 1995.

§ 2–513.   Buyer's Right to Inspection of Goods.

(1) Unless otherwise agreed and subject to subsection (3), where goods are tendered or delivered or identified to the contract for sale, the buyer has a right before payment or acceptance to inspect them at any reasonable place and time and in any reasonable manner. When the seller is required or authorized to send the goods to the buyer, the inspection may be after their arrival.

(2) Expenses of inspection must be borne by the buyer but may be recovered from the seller if the goods do not conform and are rejected.

(3) Unless otherwise agreed and subject to the provisions of this Article on C.I.F. contracts (subsection (3) of Section 2–321), the buyer is not entitled to inspect the goods before payment of the price when the contract provides

(a) for delivery "C.O.D." or on other like terms; or

(b) for payment against documents of title, except where such payment is due only after the goods are to become available for inspection.

(4) A place or method of inspection fixed by the parties is presumed to be exclusive but unless otherwise expressly agreed it does not postpone identification or shift the place for delivery or for passing the risk of loss. If compliance becomes impossible, inspection shall be as provided in this section unless the place or method fixed was clearly intended as an indispensable condition failure of which avoids the contract.

§ 2–514.   When Documents Deliverable on Acceptance; When on Payment.

Unless otherwise agreed documents against which a draft is drawn are to be delivered to the drawee on acceptance of the draft if it is payable more than three days after presentment; otherwise, only on payment.

§ 2–515.   Preserving Evidence of Goods in Dispute.

In furtherance of the adjustment of any claim or dispute

(a) either party on reasonable notification to the other and for the purpose of ascertaining the facts and preserving evidence has the right to inspect, test and sample the goods including such of them as may be in the possession or control of the other; and

(b) the parties may agree to a third party inspection or survey to determine the conformity or condition of the goods and may agree that the findings shall be binding upon them in any subsequent litigation or adjustment.

PART 6   Breach, Repudiation and Excuse

§ 2–601.   Buyer's Rights on Improper Delivery.

Subject to the provisions of this Article on breach in installment contracts (Section 2–612) and unless otherwise agreed under the sections on contractual limitations of remedy (Sections 2–718 and 2–719), if the goods or the tender of delivery fail in any respect to conform to the contract, the buyer may

(a) reject the whole; or

(b) accept the whole; or

(c) accept any commercial unit or units and reject the rest.

§ 2–602.   Manner and Effect of Rightful Rejection.

(1) Rejection of goods must be within a reasonable time after their delivery or tender. It is ineffective unless the buyer seasonably notifies the seller.

(2) Subject to the provisions of the two following sections on rejected goods (Sections 2–603 and 2–604),

(a) after rejection any exercise of ownership by the buyer with respect to any commercial unit is wrongful as against the seller; and

(b) if the buyer has before rejection taken physical possession of goods in which he does not have a security interest under the provisions of this Article (subsection (3) of Section 2–711), he is under a duty after rejection to hold them with reasonable care at the seller's disposition for a time sufficient to permit the seller to remove them; but

(c) the buyer has no further obligations with regard to goods rightfully rejected.

(3) The seller's rights with respect to goods wrongfully rejected are governed by the provisions of this Article on Seller's remedies in general (Section 2–703).

§ 2–603.   Merchant Buyer's Duties as to Rightfully Rejected Goods.

(1) Subject to any security interest in the buyer (subsection (3) of Section 2–711), when the seller has no agent or place of business at the market of rejection a merchant buyer is under a duty after rejection of goods in his possession or control to follow any reasonable instructions received from the seller with respect to the goods and in the absence of such instructions to make reasonable efforts to sell them for the seller's account if they are perishable or threaten to decline in value speedily.

Instructions are not reasonable if on demand indemnity for expenses is not forthcoming.

(2) When the buyer sells goods under subsection (1), he is entitled to reimbursement from the seller or out of the proceeds for reasonable expenses of caring for and selling them, and if the expenses include no selling commission then to such commission as is usual in the trade or if there is none to a reasonable sum not exceeding ten per cent on the gross proceeds.

(3) In complying with this section the buyer is held only to good faith and good faith conduct hereunder is neither acceptance nor conversion nor the basis of an action for damages.

§ 2–604.   Buyer's Options as to Salvage of Rightfully Rejected Goods.

Subject to the provisions of the immediately preceding section on perishables if the seller gives no instructions within a reasonable time after notification of rejection the buyer may store the rejected goods for the seller's account or reship them to him or resell them for the seller's account with reimbursement as provided in the preceding section. Such action is not acceptance or conversion.

§ 2–605.   Waiver of Buyer's Objections by Failure to Particularize.

(1) The buyer's failure to state in connection with rejection a particular defect which is ascertainable by reasonable inspection precludes him from relying on the unstated defect to justify rejection or to establish breach

(a) where the seller could have cured it if stated seasonably; or

(b) between merchants when the seller has after rejection made a request in writing for a full and final written statement of all defects on which the buyer proposes to rely.

(2) Payment against documents made without reservation of rights precludes recovery of the payment for defects apparent on the face of the documents.

§ 2–606.   What Constitutes Acceptance of Goods.

(1) Acceptance of goods occurs when the buyer

(a) after a reasonable opportunity to inspect the goods signifies to the seller that the goods are conforming or that he will take or retain them in spite of their nonconformity; or

(b) fails to make an effective rejection (subsection (1) of Section 2–602), but such acceptance does not occur until the buyer has had a reasonable opportunity to inspect them; or

(c) does any act inconsistent with the seller's ownership; but if such act is wrongful as against the seller it is an acceptance only if ratified by him.

(2) Acceptance of a part of any commercial unit is acceptance of that entire unit.

§ 2–607.   Effect of Acceptance; Notice of Breach; Burden of Establishing Breach After Acceptance; Notice of Claim or Litigation to Person Answerable Over.

(1) The buyer must pay at the contract rate for any goods accepted.

(2) Acceptance of goods by the buyer precludes rejection of the goods accepted and if made with knowledge of a non-conformity cannot be revoked because of it unless the acceptance was on the reasonable assumption that the non-conformity would be seasonably cured but acceptance does not of itself impair any other remedy provided by this Article for non-conformity.

(3) Where a tender has been accepted

(a) the buyer must within a reasonable time after he discovers or should have discovered any breach notify the seller of breach or be barred from any remedy; and

(b) if the claim is one for infringement or the like (subsection (3) of Section 2–312) and the buyer is sued as a result of such a breach he must so notify the seller within a reasonable time after he receives notice of the litigation or be barred from any remedy over for liability established by the litigation.

(4) The burden is on the buyer to establish any breach with respect to the goods accepted.

(5) Where the buyer is sued for breach of a warranty or other obligation for which his seller is answerable over

(a) he may give his seller written notice of the litigation. If the notice states that the seller may come in and defend and that if the seller does not do so he will be bound in any action against him by his buyer by any determination of fact common to the two litigations, then unless the seller after seasonable receipt of the notice does come in and defend he is so bound.

(b) if the claim is one for infringement or the like (subsection (3) of Section 2–312) the original seller may demand in writing that his buyer turn over to him control of the litigation including settlement or else be barred from any remedy over and if he also agrees to bear all expense and to satisfy any adverse judgment, then unless the buyer after seasonable receipt of the demand does turn over control the buyer is so barred.

(6) The provisions of subsections (3), (4) and (5) apply to any obligation of a buyer to hold the seller harmless against infringement or the like (subsection (3) of Section 2–312).

§ 2–608.   Revocation of Acceptance in Whole or in Part.

(1) The buyer may revoke his acceptance of a lot or commercial unit whose non-conformity substantially impairs its value to him if he has accepted it

(a) on the reasonable assumption that its nonconformity would be cured and it has not been seasonably cured; or

(b) without discovery of such non-conformity if his acceptance was reasonably induced either by the difficulty of discovery before acceptance or by the seller's assurances.

(2) Revocation of acceptance must occur within a reasonable time after the buyer discovers or should have discovered the ground for it and before any substantial change in condition of the goods which is not caused by their own defects. It is not effective until the buyer notifies the seller of it.

(3) A buyer who so revokes has the same rights and duties with regard to the goods involved as if he had rejected them.

§ 2–609.   Right to Adequate Assurance of Performance.

(1) A contract for sale imposes an obligation on each party that the other's expectation of receiving due performance will not be impaired. When reasonable grounds for insecurity arise with respect to the performance of either party the other may in writing demand adequate assurance of due performance and until he receives such assurance may if commercially reasonable suspend any performance for which he has not already received the agreed return.

(2) Between merchants the reasonableness of grounds for insecurity and the adequacy of any assurance offered shall be determined according to commercial standards.

(3) Acceptance of any improper delivery or payment does not prejudice the party's right to demand adequate assurance of future performance.

(4) After receipt of a justified demand failure to provide within a reasonable time not exceeding thirty days such assurance of due performance as is adequate under the circumstances of the particular case is a repudiation of the contract.

§ 2–610.   Anticipatory Repudiation.

When either party repudiates the contract with respect to a performance not yet due the loss of which will substantially impair the value of the contract to the other, the aggrieved party may

    (a) for a commercially reasonable time await performance by the repudiating party; or

    (b) resort to any remedy for breach (Section 2–703 or Section 2–711), even though he has notified the repudiating party that he would await the latter's performance and has urged retraction; and

    (c) in either case suspend his own performance or proceed in accordance with the provisions of this Article on the seller's right to identify goods to the contract notwithstanding breach or to salvage unfinished goods (Section 2–704).

§ 2–611.   Retraction of Anticipatory Repudiation.

(1) Until the repudiating party's next performance is due he can retract his repudiation unless the aggrieved party has since the repudiation cancelled or materially changed his position or otherwise indicated that he considers the repudiation final.

(2) Retraction may be by any method which clearly indicates to the aggrieved party that the repudiating party intends to perform, but must include any assurance justifiably demanded under the provisions of this Article (Section 2–609).

(3) Retraction reinstates the repudiating party's rights under the contract with due excuse and allowance to the aggrieved party for any delay occasioned by the repudiation.

§ 2–612.   "Installment Contract"; Breach.

(1) An "installment contract" is one which requires or authorizes the delivery of goods in separate lots to be separately accepted, even though the contract contains a clause "each delivery is a separate contract" or its equivalent.

(2) The buyer may reject any installment which is nonconforming if the non-conformity substantially impairs the value of that installment and cannot be cured or if the non-conformity is a defect in the required documents; but if the non-conformity does not fall within subsection (3) and the seller gives adequate assurance of its cure the buyer must accept that installment.

(3) Whenever non-conformity or default with respect to one or more installments substantially impairs the value of the whole contract there is a breach of the whole. But the aggrieved party reinstates the contract if he accepts a non-conforming installment without seasonably notifying of cancellation or if he brings an action with respect only to past installments or demands performance as to future installments.

§ 2–613.   Casualty to Identified Goods.

Where the contract requires for its performance goods identified when the contract is made, and the goods suffer casualty without fault of either party before the risk of loss passes to the buyer, or in a proper case under a "no arrival, no sale" term (Section 2–324) then

    (a) if the loss is total the contract is avoided; and

    (b) if the loss is partial or the goods have so deteriorated as no longer to conform to the contract the buyer may nevertheless demand inspection and at his option either treat the contract as voided or accept the goods with due allowance from the contract price for the deterioration or the deficiency in quantity but without further right against the seller.

§ 2–614.   Substituted Performance.

(1) Where without fault of either party the agreed berthing, loading, or unloading facilities fail or an agreed type of carrier becomes unavailable or the agreed manner of delivery otherwise becomes commercially impracticable but a commercially reasonable substitute is available, such substitute performance must be tendered and accepted.

(2) If the agreed means or manner of payment fails because of domestic or foreign governmental regulation, the seller may

withhold or stop delivery unless the buyer provides a means or manner of payment which is commercially a substantial equivalent. If delivery has already been taken, payment by the means or in the manner provided by the regulation discharges the buyer's obligation unless the regulation is discriminatory, oppressive or predatory.

§ 2–615. Excuse by Failure of Presupposed Conditions.

Except so far as a seller may have assumed a greater obligation and subject to the preceding section on substituted performance:

(a) Delay in delivery or non-delivery in whole or in part by a seller who complies with paragraphs (b) and (c) is not a breach of his duty under a contract for sale if performance as agreed has been made impracticable by the occurrence of a contingency the nonoccurrence of which was a basic assumption on which the contract was made or by compliance in good faith with any applicable foreign or domestic governmental regulation or order whether or not it later proves to be invalid.

(b) Where the causes mentioned in paragraph (a) affect only a part of the seller's capacity to perform, he must allocate production and deliveries among his customers but may at his option include regular customers not then under contract as well as his own requirements for further manufacture. He may so allocate in any manner which is fair and reasonable.

(c) The seller must notify the buyer seasonably that there will be delay or non-delivery and, when allocation is required under paragraph (b), of the estimated quota thus made available for the buyer.

§ 2–616. Procedure on Notice Claiming Excuse.

(1) Where the buyer receives notification of a material or indefinite delay or an allocation justified under the preceding section he may by written notification to the seller as to any delivery concerned, and where the prospective deficiency substantially impairs the value of the whole contract under the provisions of this Article relating to breach of installment contracts (Section 2–612), then also as to the whole,

(a) terminate and thereby discharge any unexecuted portion of the contract; or

(b) modify the contract by agreeing to take his available quota in substitution.

(2) If after receipt of such notification from the seller the buyer fails so to modify the contract within a reasonable time not exceeding thirty days the contract lapses with respect to any deliveries affected.

(3) The provisions of this section may not be negated by agreement except in so far as the seller has assumed a greater obligation under the preceding section.

PART 7 Remedies

§ 2–701. Remedies for Breach of Collateral Contracts Not Impaired.

Remedies for breach of any obligation or promise collateral or ancillary to a contract for sale are not impaired by the provisions of this Article.

§ 2–702. Seller's Remedies on Discovery of Buyer's Insolvency.

(1) Where the seller discovers the buyer to be insolvent he may refuse delivery except for cash including payment for all goods theretofore delivered under the contract, and stop delivery under this Article (Section 2–705).

(2) Where the seller discovers that the buyer has received goods on credit while insolvent he may reclaim the goods upon demand made within ten days after the receipt, but if misrepresentation of solvency has been made to the particular seller in writing within three months before delivery the ten day limitation does not apply. Except as provided in this subsection the seller may not base a right to reclaim goods on the buyer's fraudulent or innocent misrepresentation of solvency or of intent to pay.

(3) The seller's right to reclaim under subsection (2) is subject to the rights of a buyer in ordinary course or other good faith purchaser under this Article (Section 2–403). Successful reclamation of goods excludes all other remedies with respect to them.

§ 2–703. Seller's Remedies in General.

Where the buyer wrongfully rejects or revokes acceptance of goods or fails to make a payment due on or before delivery or repudiates with respect to a part or the whole, then with respect to any goods directly affected and, if the breach is of the whole contract (Section 2–612), then also with respect to the whole undelivered balance, the aggrieved seller may

(a) withhold delivery of such goods;

(b) stop delivery by any bailee as hereafter provided (Section 2–705);

(c) proceed under the next section respecting goods still unidentified to the contract;

(d) resell and recover damages as hereafter provided (Section 2–706);

(e) recover damages for non-acceptance (Section 2–708) or in a proper case the price (Section 2–709);

(f) cancel.

§ 2–704. Seller's Right to Identify Goods to the Contract Notwithstanding Breach or to Salvage Unfinished Goods.

(1) An aggrieved seller under the preceding section may

(a) identify to the contract conforming goods not already identified if at the time he learned of the breach they are in his possession or control;

(b) treat as the subject of resale goods which have demonstrably been intended for the particular contract even though those goods are unfinished.

(2) Where the goods are unfinished an aggrieved seller may in the exercise of reasonable commercial judgment for the purposes of avoiding loss and of effective realization either complete the manufacture and wholly identify the goods to the contract or cease manufacture and resell for scrap or salvage value or proceed in any other reasonable manner.

§ 2–705.   Seller's Stoppage of Delivery in Transit or Otherwise.

(1) The seller may stop delivery of goods in the possession of a carrier or other bailee when he discovers the buyer to be insolvent (Section 2–702) and may stop delivery of carload, truckload, planeload or larger shipments of express or freight when the buyer repudiates or fails to make a payment due before delivery or if for any other reason the seller has a right to withhold or reclaim the goods.

(2) As against such buyer the seller may stop delivery until

(a) receipt of the goods by the buyer; or

(b) acknowledgment to the buyer by any bailee of the goods except a carrier that the bailee holds the goods for the buyer; or

(c) such acknowledgment to the buyer by a carrier by reshipment or as warehouseman; or

(d) negotiation to the buyer of any negotiable document of title covering the goods.

(3) (a) To stop delivery the seller must so notify as to enable the bailee by reasonable diligence to prevent delivery of the goods.

(b) After such notification the bailee must hold and deliver the goods according to the directions of the seller but the seller is liable to the bailee for any ensuing charges or damages.

(c) If a negotiable document of title has been issued for goods the bailee is not obliged to obey a notification to stop until surrender of the document.

(d) A carrier who has issued a non-negotiable bill of lading is not obliged to obey a notification to stop received from a person other than the consignor.

§ 2–706.   Seller's Resale Including Contract for Resale.

(1) Under the conditions stated in Section 2–703 on seller's remedies, the seller may resell the goods concerned or the undelivered balance thereof. Where the resale is made in good faith and in a commercially reasonable manner the seller may recover the difference between the resale price and the contract price together with any incidental damages allowed under the provisions of this Article (Section 2–710), but less expenses saved in consequence of the buyer's breach.

(2) Except as otherwise provided in subsection (3) or unless otherwise agreed resale may be at public or private sale including sale by way of one or more contracts to sell or of identification to an existing contract of the seller. Sale may be as a unit or in parcels and at any time and place and on any terms but every aspect of the sale including the method, manner, time, place and terms must be commercially reasonable. The resale must be reasonably identified as referring to the broken contract, but it is not necessary that the goods be in existence or that any or all of them have been identified to the contract before the breach.

(3) Where the resale is at private sale the seller must give the buyer reasonable notification of his intention to resell.

(4) Where the resale is at public sale

(a) only identified goods can be sold except where there is a recognized market for a public sale of futures in goods of the kind; and

(b) it must be made at a usual place or market for public sale if one is reasonably available and except in the case of goods which are perishable or threaten to decline in value speedily the seller must give the buyer reasonable notice of the time and place of the resale; and

(c) if the goods are not to be within the view of those attending the sale the notification of sale must state the place where the goods are located and provide for their reasonable inspection by prospective bidders; and

(d) the seller may buy.

(5) A purchaser who buys in good faith at a resale takes the goods free of any rights of the original buyer even though the seller fails to comply with one or more of the requirements of this section.

(6) The seller is not accountable to the buyer for any profit made on any resale. A person in the position of a seller (Section 2–707) or a buyer who has rightfully rejected or justifiably revoked acceptance must account for any excess over the amount of his security interest, as hereinafter defined (subsection (3) of Section 2–711).

§ 2–707.   "Person in the Position of a Seller".

(1) A "person in the position of a seller" includes as against a principal an agent who has paid or become responsible for the price of goods on behalf of his principal or anyone who otherwise holds a security interest or other right in goods similar to that of a seller.

(2) A person in the position of a seller may as provided in this Article withhold or stop delivery (Section 2–705) and resell (Section 2–706) and recover incidental damages (Section 2–710).

§ 2–708. Seller's Damages for Non-Acceptance or Repudiation.

(1) Subject to subsection (2) and to the provisions of this Article with respect to proof of market price (Section 2–723), the measure of damages for non-acceptance or repudiation by the buyer is the difference between the market price at the time and place for tender and the unpaid contract price together with any incidental damages provided in this Article (Section 2–710), but less expenses saved in consequence of the buyer's breach.

(2) If the measure of damages provided in subsection (1) is inadequate to put the seller in as good a position as performance would have done then the measure of damages is the profit (including reasonable overhead) which the seller would have made from full performance by the buyer, together with any incidental damages provided in this Article (Section 2–710), due allowance for costs reasonably incurred and due credit for payments or proceeds of resale.

§ 2–709. Action for the Price.

(1) When the buyer fails to pay the price as it becomes due the seller may recover, together with any incidental damages under the next section, the price

(a) of goods accepted or of conforming goods lost or damaged within a commercially reasonable time after risk of their loss has passed to the buyer; and

(b) of goods identified to the contract if the seller is unable after reasonable effort to resell them at a reasonable price or the circumstances reasonably indicate that such effort will be unavailing.

(2) Where the seller sues for the price he must hold for the buyer any goods which have been identified to the contract and are still in his control except that if resale becomes possible he may resell them at any time prior to the collection of the judgment. The net proceeds of any such resale must be credited to the buyer and payment of the judgment entitles him to any goods not resold.

(3) After the buyer has wrongfully rejected or revoked acceptance of the goods or has failed to make a payment due or has repudiated (Section 2–610), a seller who is held not entitled to the price under this section shall nevertheless be awarded damages for non-acceptance under the preceding section.

§ 2–710. Seller's Incidental Damages.

Incidental damages to an aggrieved seller include any commercially reasonable charges, expenses or commissions incurred in stopping delivery, in the transportation, care and custody of goods after the buyer's breach, in connection with return or resale of the goods or otherwise resulting from the breach.

§ 2–711. Buyer's Remedies in General; Buyer's Security Interest in Rejected Goods.

(1) Where the seller fails to make delivery or repudiates or the buyer rightfully rejects or justifiably revokes acceptance then with respect to any goods involved, and with respect to the whole if the breach goes to the whole contract (Section 2–612), the buyer may cancel and whether or not he has done so may in addition to recovering so much of the price as has been paid

(a) "cover" and have damages under the next section as to all the goods affected whether or not they have been identified to the contract; or

(b) recover damages for non-delivery as provided in this Article (Section 2–713).

(2) Where the seller fails to deliver or repudiates the buyer may also

(a) if the goods have been identified recover them as provided in this Article (Section 2–502); or

(b) in a proper case obtain specific performance or replevy the goods as provided in this Article (Section 2–716).

(3) On rightful rejection or justifiable revocation of acceptance a buyer has a security interest in goods in his possession or control for any payments made on their price and any expenses reasonably incurred in their inspection, receipt, transportation, care and custody and may hold such goods and resell them in like manner as an aggrieved seller (Section 2–706).

§ 2–712. "Cover"; Buyer's Procurement of Substitute Goods.

(1) After a breach within the preceding section the buyer may "cover" by making in good faith and without unreasonable delay any reasonable purchase of or contract to purchase goods in substitution for those due from the seller.

(2) The buyer may recover from the seller as damages the difference between the cost of cover and the contract price together with any incidental or consequential damages as hereinafter defined (Section 2–715), but less expenses saved in consequence of the seller's breach.

(3) Failure of the buyer to effect cover within this section does not bar him from any other remedy.

§ 2–713. Buyer's Damages for Non-Delivery or Repudiation.

(1) Subject to the provisions of this Article with respect to proof of market price (Section 2–723), the measure of damages for non-delivery or repudiation by the seller is the difference between the market price at the time when the buyer learned of the breach and the contract price together with any incidental and consequential damages provided in this Article (Section 2–715), but less expenses saved in consequence of the seller's breach.

(2) Market price is to be determined as of the place for tender or, in cases of rejection after arrival or revocation of acceptance, as of the place of arrival.

§ 2–714. Buyer's Damages for Breach in Regard to Accepted Goods.

(1) Where the buyer has accepted goods and given notification (subsection (3) of Section 2–607) he may recover as damages for any non-conformity of tender the loss resulting in the ordi-

nary course of events from the seller's breach as determined in any manner which is reasonable.

(2) The measure of damages for breach of warranty is the difference at the time and place of acceptance between the value of the goods accepted and the value they would have had if they had been as warranted, unless special circumstances show proximate damages of a different amount.

(3) In a proper case any incidental and consequential damages under the next section may also be recovered.

§ 2–715.   Buyer's Incidental and Consequential Damages.

(1) Incidental damages resulting from the seller's breach include expenses reasonably incurred in inspection, receipt, transportation and care and custody of goods rightfully rejected, any commercially reasonable charges, expenses or commissions in connection with effecting cover and any other reasonable expense incident to the delay or other breach.

(2) Consequential damages resulting from the seller's breach include

(a) any loss resulting from general or particular requirements and needs of which the seller at the time of contracting had reason to know and which could not reasonably be prevented by cover or otherwise; and

(b) injury to person or property proximately resulting from any breach of warranty.

§ 2–716.   Buyer's Right to Specific Performance or Replevin.

(1) Specific performance may be decreed where the goods are unique or in other proper circumstances.

(2) The decree for specific performance may include such terms and conditions as to payment of the price, damages, or other relief as the court may deem just.

(3) The buyer has a right of replevin for goods identified to the contract if after reasonable effort he is unable to effect cover for such goods or the circumstances reasonably indicate that such effort will be unavailing or if the goods have been shipped under reservation and satisfaction of the security interest in them has been made or tendered. In the case of goods bought for personal, family, or household purposes, the buyer's right of replevin vests upon acquisition of a special property, even if the seller had not then repudiated or failed to deliver.

As amended in 1999.

§ 2–717.   Deduction of Damages From the Price.

The buyer on notifying the seller of his intention to do so may deduct all or any part of the damages resulting from any breach of the contract from any part of the price still due under the same contract.

§ 2–718.   Liquidation or Limitation of Damages; Deposits.

(1) Damages for breach by either party may be liquidated in the agreement but only at an amount which is reasonable in the light of the anticipated or actual harm caused by the breach, the difficulties of proof of loss, and the inconvenience or nonfeasibility of otherwise obtaining an adequate remedy. A term fixing unreasonably large liquidated damages is void as a penalty.

(2) Where the seller justifiably withholds delivery of goods because of the buyer's breach, the buyer is entitled to restitution of any amount by which the sum of his payments exceeds

(a) the amount to which the seller is entitled by virtue of terms liquidating the seller's damages in accordance with subsection (1), or

(b) in the absence of such terms, twenty per cent of the value of the total performance for which the buyer is obligated under the contract or $500, whichever is smaller.

(3) The buyer's right to restitution under subsection (2) is subject to offset to the extent that the seller establishes

(a) a right to recover damages under the provisions of this Article other than subsection (1), and

(b) the amount or value of any benefits received by the buyer directly or indirectly by reason of the contract.

(4) Where a seller has received payment in goods their reasonable value or the proceeds of their resale shall be treated as payments for the purposes of subsection (2); but if the seller has notice of the buyer's breach before reselling goods received in part performance, his resale is subject to the conditions laid down in this Article on resale by an aggrieved seller (Section 2–706).

§ 2–719.   Contractual Modification or Limitation of Remedy.

(1) Subject to the provisions of subsections (2) and (3) of this section and of the preceding section on liquidation and limitation of damages,

(a) the agreement may provide for remedies in addition to or in substitution for those provided in this Article and may limit or alter the measure of damages recoverable under this Article, as by limiting the buyer's remedies to return of the goods and repayment of the price or to repair and replacement of nonconforming goods or parts; and

(b) resort to a remedy as provided is optional unless the remedy is expressly agreed to be exclusive, in which case it is the sole remedy.

(2) Where circumstances cause an exclusive or limited remedy to fail of its essential purpose, remedy may be had as provided in this Act.

(3) Consequential damages may be limited or excluded unless the limitation or exclusion is unconscionable. Limitation of consequential damages for injury to the person in the case of consumer goods is prima facie unconscionable

but limitation of damages where the loss is commercial is not.

§ 2–720.   Effect of "Cancellation" or "Rescission" on Claims for Antecedent Breach.

Unless the contrary intention clearly appears, expressions of "cancellation" or "rescission" of the contract or the like shall not be construed as a renunciation or discharge of any claim in damages for an antecedent breach.

§ 2–721.   Remedies for Fraud.

Remedies for material misrepresentation or fraud include all remedies available under this Article for non-fraudulent breach. Neither rescission or a claim for rescission of the contract for sale nor rejection or return of the goods shall bar or be deemed inconsistent with a claim for damages or other remedy.

§ 2–722.   Who Can Sue Third Parties for Injury to Goods.

Where a third party so deals with goods which have been identified to a contract for sale as to cause actionable injury to a party to that contract

(a) a right of action against the third party is in either party to the contract for sale who has title to or a security interest or a special property or an insurable interest in the goods; and if the goods have been destroyed or converted a right of action is also in the party who either bore the risk of loss under the contract for sale or has since the injury assumed that risk as against the other;

(b) if at the time of the injury the party plaintiff did not bear the risk of loss as against the other party to the contract for sale and there is no arrangement between them for disposition of the recovery, his suit or settlement is, subject to his own interest, as a fiduciary for the other party to the contract;

(c) either party may with the consent of the other sue for the benefit of whom it may concern.

§ 2–723.   Proof of Market Price: Time and Place.

(1) If an action based on anticipatory repudiation comes to trial before the time for performance with respect to some or all of the goods, any damages based on market price (Section 2–708 or Section 2–713) shall be determined according to the price of such goods prevailing at the time when the aggrieved party learned of the repudiation.

(2) If evidence of a price prevailing at the times or places described in this Article is not readily available the price prevailing within any reasonable time before or after the time described or at any other place which in commercial judgment or under usage of trade would serve as a reasonable substitute for the one described may be used, making any proper allowance for the cost of transporting the goods to or from such other place.

(3) Evidence of a relevant price prevailing at a time or place other than the one described in this Article offered by one party is not admissible unless and until he has given the other party such notice as the court finds sufficient to prevent unfair surprise.

§ 2–724.   Admissibility of Market Quotations.

Whenever the prevailing price or value of any goods regularly bought and sold in any established commodity market is in issue, reports in official publications or trade journals or in newspapers or periodicals of general circulation published as the reports of such market shall be admissible in evidence. The circumstances of the preparation of such a report may be shown to affect its weight but not its admissibility.

§ 2–725.   Statute of Limitations in Contracts for Sale.

(1) An action for breach of any contract for sale must be commenced within four years after the cause of action has accrued. By the original agreement the parties may reduce the period of limitation to not less than one year but may not extend it.

(2) A cause of action accrues when the breach occurs, regardless of the aggrieved party's lack of knowledge of the breach. A breach of warranty occurs when tender of delivery is made, except that where a warranty explicitly extends to future performance of the goods and discovery of the breach must await the time of such performance the cause of action accrues when the breach is or should have been discovered.

(3) Where an action commenced within the time limited by subsection (1) is so terminated as to leave available a remedy by another action for the same breach such other action may be commenced after the expiration of the time limited and within six months after the termination of the first action unless the termination resulted from voluntary discontinuance or from dismissal for failure or neglect to prosecute.

(4) This section does not alter the law on tolling of the statute of limitations nor does it apply to causes of action which have accrued before this Act becomes effective.

ARTICLE 2 AMENDMENTS (EXCERPTS)[1]

PART 1   Short Title, General Construction and Subject Matter

§ 2–103.   Definitions and Index of Definitions.

* * * *

(1) In this article unless the context otherwise requires

* * * *

(b) "Conspicuous", with reference to a term, means so written, displayed, or presented that a reasonable person against which it is to operate ought to have noticed it. A term in an electronic record intended to evoke a response by an electronic agent is conspicuous if it is presented in a form that would enable a reasonably configured electronic agent to take it into account or react to it without review of the record by an individual. Whether a term is "conspicuous" or not is a decision for the court. Conspicuous terms include the following:

(i) for a person:

(A) a heading in capitals equal to or greater in size than the surrounding text, or in contrasting type, font, or color to the surrounding text of the same or lesser size;

(B) language in the body of a record or display in larger type than the surrounding text, or in contrasting type, font, or color to the surrounding text of the same size, or set off from surrounding text of the same size by symbols or other marks that call attention to the language; and

(ii) for a person or an electronic agent, a term that is so placed in a record or display that the person or electronic agent cannot proceed without taking action with respect to the particular term.

(c) "Consumer" means an individual who buys or contracts to buy goods that, at the time of contracting, are intended by the individual to be used primarily for personal, family, or household purposes.

(d) "Consumer contract" means a contract between a merchant seller and a consumer.

* * * *

(j) "Good faith" means honesty in fact and the observance of reasonable commercial standards of fair dealing.

(k) "Goods" means all things that are movable at the time of identification to a contract for sale. The term includes future goods, specially manufactured goods, the unborn young of animals, growing crops, and other identified things attached to realty as described in Section 2–107. The term does not include information, the money in which the price is to be paid, investment securities under Article 8, the subject matter of foreign exchange transactions, and choses in action.

* * * *

(m) "Record" means information that is inscribed on a tangible medium or that is stored in an electronic or other medium and is retrievable in perceivable form.

(n) "Remedial promise" means a promise by the seller to repair or replace the goods or to refund all or part of the price upon the happening of a specified event.

* * * *

(p) "Sign" means, with present intent to authenticate or adopt a record,

(i) to execute or adopt a tangible symbol; or

(ii) to attach to or logically associate with the record an electronic sound, symbol, or process.

* * * *

PART 2   Form, Formation, Terms and Readjustment of Contract; Electronic Contracting

§ 2–201.   Formal Requirements; Statute of Frauds.

(1) A contract for the sale of goods for the price of $5,000 or more is not enforceable by way of action or defense unless there is some record sufficient to indicate that a contract for sale has been made between the parties and signed by the party against whom which enforcement is sought or by the party's authorized agent or broker. A record is not insufficient because it omits or incorrectly states a term agreed upon but the contract is not enforceable under this subsection beyond the quantity of goods shown in the record.

(2) Between merchants if within a reasonable time a record in confirmation of the contract and sufficient against the sender is received and the party receiving it has reason to know its contents, it satisfies the requirements of subsection (1) against such party the recipient unless notice of objection to its contents is given in a record within 10 days after it is received.

(3) A contract which does not satisfy the requirements of subsection (1) but which is valid in other respects is enforceable

(a) if the goods are to be specially manufactured for the buyer and are not suitable for sale to others in the ordinary course of the seller's business and the seller, before notice of repudiation is received and under circumstances which reasonably indicate that the goods are for the buyer, has made either a substantial beginning of their manufacture or commitments for their procurement; or

(b) if the party against whom which enforcement is sought admits in the party's pleading, or in the party's testimony or otherwise under oath that a contract for sale was made, but the contract is not enforceable under this paragraph beyond the quantity of goods admitted; or

(c) with respect to goods for which payment has been made and accepted or which have been received and accepted (Sec. 2–606).

(4) A contract that is enforceable under this section is not rendered unenforceable merely because it is not capable of being

performed within one year or any other applicable period after its making.

* * * *

§ 2–207. Terms of Contract; Effect of Confirmation.

If (i) conduct by both parties recognizes the existence of a contract although their records do not otherwise establish a contract, (ii) a contract is formed by an offer and acceptance, or (iii) a contract formed in any manner is confirmed by a record that contains terms additional to or different from those in the contract being confirmed, the terms of the contract, subject to Section 2–202, are:

(a) terms that appear in the records of both parties;

(b) terms, whether in a record or not, to which both parties agree; and

(c) terms supplied or incorporated under any provision of this Act.

* * * *

PART 3 General Obligation and Construction of Contract

* * * *

§ 2–312. Warranty of Title and Against Infringement; Buyer's Obligation Against Infringement.

(1) Subject to subsection (2) there is in a contract for sale a warranty by the seller that

(a) the title conveyed shall be good, good and its transfer rightful and shall not, because of any colorable claim to or interest in the goods, unreasonably expose the buyer to litigation; and

(b) the goods shall be delivered free from any security interest or other lien or encumbrance of which the buyer at the time of contracting has no knowledge.

(2) Unless otherwise agreed a seller that is a merchant regularly dealing in goods of the kind warrants that the goods shall be delivered free of the rightful claim of any third person by way of infringement or the like but a buyer that furnishes specifications to the seller must hold the seller harmless against any such claim that arises out of compliance with the specifications.

(3) A warranty under this section may be disclaimed or modified only by specific language or by circumstances that give the buyer reason to know that the seller does not claim title, that the seller is purporting to sell only the right or title as the seller or a third person may have, or that the seller is selling subject to any claims of infringement or the like.

§ 2–313. Express Warranties by Affirmation, Promise, Description, Sample; Remedial Promise.

(1) In this section, "immediate buyer" means a buyer that enters into a contract with the seller.

* * * *

(4) Any remedial promise made by the seller to the immediate buyer creates an obligation that the promise will be performed upon the happening of the specified event.

§ 2–313A. Obligation to Remote Purchaser Created by Record Packaged with or Accompanying Goods.

(1) This section applies only to new goods and goods sold or leased as new goods in a transaction of purchase in the normal chain of distribution. In this section:

(a) "Immediate buyer" means a buyer that enters into a contract with the seller.

(b) "Remote purchaser" means a person that buys or leases goods from an immediate buyer or other person in the normal chain of distribution.

(2) If a seller in a record packaged with or accompanying the goods makes an affirmation of fact or promise that relates to the goods, provides a description that relates to the goods, or makes a remedial promise, and the seller reasonably expects the record to be, and the record is, furnished to the remote purchaser, the seller has an obligation to the remote purchaser that:

(a) the goods will conform to the affirmation of fact, promise or description unless a reasonable person in the position of the remote purchaser would not believe that the affirmation of fact, promise or description created an obligation; and

(b) the seller will perform the remedial promise.

(3) It is not necessary to the creation of an obligation under this section that the seller use formal words such as "warrant" or "guarantee" or that the seller have a specific intention to undertake an obligation, but an affirmation merely of the value of the goods or a statement purporting to be merely the seller's opinion or commendation of the goods does not create an obligation.

(4) The following rules apply to the remedies for breach of an obligation created under this section:

(a) The seller may modify or limit the remedies available to the remote purchaser if the modification or limitation is furnished to the remote purchaser no later than the time of purchase or if the modification or limitation is contained in the record that contains the affirmation of fact, promise or description.

(b) Subject to a modification or limitation of remedy, a seller in breach is liable for incidental or consequential damages under Section 2–715, but the seller is not liable for lost profits.

(c) The remote purchaser may recover as damages for breach of a seller's obligation arising under subsection (2) the loss resulting in the ordinary course of events as determined in any manner that is reasonable.

(5) An obligation that is not a remedial promise is breached if the goods did not conform to the affirmation of fact, promise or description creating the obligation when the goods left the seller's control.

§ 2-313B. Obligation to Remote Purchaser Created by Communication to the Public.

(1) This section applies only to new goods and goods sold or leased as new goods in a transaction of purchase in the normal chain of distribution. In this section:

(a) "Immediate buyer" means a buyer that enters into a contract with the seller.

(b) "Remote purchaser" means a person that buys or leases goods from an immediate buyer or other person in the normal chain of distribution.

(2) If a seller in advertising or a similar communication to the public makes an affirmation of fact or promise that relates to the goods, provides a description that relates to the goods, or makes a remedial promise, and the remote purchaser enters into a transaction of purchase with knowledge of and with the expectation that the goods will conform to the affirmation of fact, promise, or description, or that the seller will perform the remedial promise, the seller has an obligation to the remote purchaser that:

(a) the goods will conform to the affirmation of fact, promise or description unless a reasonable person in the position of the remote purchaser would not believe that the affirmation of fact, promise or description created an obligation; and

(b) the seller will perform the remedial promise.

(3) It is not necessary to the creation of an obligation under this section that the seller use formal words such as "warrant" or "guarantee" or that the seller have a specific intention to undertake an obligation, but an affirmation merely of the value of the goods or a statement purporting to be merely the seller's opinion or commendation of the goods does not create an obligation.

(4) The following rules apply to the remedies for breach of an obligation created under this section:

(a) The seller may modify or limit the remedies available to the remote purchaser if the modification or limitation is furnished to the remote purchaser no later than the time of purchase. The modification or limitation may be furnished as part of the communication that contains the affirmation of fact, promise or description.

(b) Subject to a modification or limitation of remedy, a seller in breach is liable for incidental or consequential damages under Section 2–715, but the seller is not liable for lost profits.

(c) The remote purchaser may recover as damages for breach of a seller's obligation arising under subsection (2) the loss resulting in the ordinary course of events as determined in any manner that is reasonable.

(5) An obligation that is not a remedial promise is breached if the goods did not conform to the affirmation of fact, promise or description creating the obligation when the goods left the seller's control.

* * * *

§ 2-316.   Exclusion or Modification of Warranties.

* * * *

(2) Subject to subsection (3), to exclude or modify the implied warranty of merchantability or any part of it in a consumer contract the language must be in a record, be conspicuous and state "The seller undertakes no responsibility for the quality of the goods except as otherwise provided in this contract," and in any other contract the language must mention merchantability and in case of a record must be conspicuous. Subject to subsection (3), to exclude or modify the implied warranty of fitness the exclusion must be in a record and be conspicuous. Language to exclude all implied warranties of fitness in a consumer contract must state "The seller assumes no responsibility that the goods will be fit for any particular purpose for which you may be buying these goods, except as otherwise provided in the contract," and in any other contract the language is sufficient if it states, for example, that "There are no warranties which extend beyond the description on the face hereof." Language that satisfies the requirements of this subsection for the exclusion and modification of a warranty in a consumer contract also satisfies the requirements for any other contract.

(3) Notwithstanding subsection (2):

(a) unless the circumstances indicate otherwise, all implied warranties are excluded by expressions like "as is", "with all faults" or other language which in common understanding calls the buyer's attention to the exclusion of warranties, makes plain that there is no implied warranty, and in a consumer contract evidenced by a record is set forth conspicuously in the record; and

(b) when the buyer before entering into the contract has examined the goods or the sample or model as fully as desired or has refused to examine the goods after a demand by the seller there is no implied warranty with regard to defects which an examination ought in the circumstances to have revealed to the buyer; and

(c) an implied warranty can also be excluded or modified by course of dealing or course of performance or usage of trade.

* * * *

§ 2-318.   Third Party Beneficiaries of Warranties Express or Implied.

(1) In this section:

(a) "Immediate buyer" means a buyer that enters into a contract with the seller.

(b) "Remote purchaser" means a person that buys or leases goods from an immediate buyer or other person in the normal chain of distribution.

Alternative A to subsection (2)   (2) A seller's warranty whether express or implied to an immediate buyer, a seller's remedial promise to an immediate buyer, or a seller's obligation to a remote purchaser under Section 2-313A or 2-313B extends to any natural person who is in the family or household of the immediate buyer or the remote purchaser or who is a guest in the home of either if it is reasonable to expect that the person may use, consume or be affected by the goods and who is injured in person by breach of the warranty, remedial promise or obligation. A seller may not exclude or limit the operation of this section.

Alternative B to subsection (2)   (2) A seller's warranty whether express or implied to an immediate buyer, a seller's remedial promise to an immediate buyer, or a seller's obligation to a remote purchaser under Section 2-313A or 2-313B extends to any natural person who may reasonably be expected to use, consume or be affected by the goods and who is injured in person by breach of the warranty, remedial promise or obligation. A seller may not exclude or limit the operation of this section.

Alternative C to subsection (2)   (2) A seller's warranty whether express or implied to an immediate buyer, a seller's remedial promise to an immediate buyer, or a seller's obligation to a remote purchaser under Section 2-313A or 2-313B extends to any person that may reasonably be expected to use, consume or be affected by the goods and that is injured by breach of the warranty, remedial promise or obligation. A seller may not exclude or limit the operation of this section with respect to injury to the person of an individual to whom the warranty, remedial promise or obligation extends.

* * * *

PART 5   Performance

* * * *

§ 2-502.   Buyer's Right to Goods on Seller's Insolvency.

(1) Subject to subsections (2) and (3) and even though the goods have not been shipped a buyer who that has paid a part or all of the price of goods in which the buyer has a special property under the provisions of the immediately preceding section may on making and keeping good a tender of any unpaid portion of their price recover them from the seller if:

(a) in the case of goods bought by a consumer, the seller repudiates or fails to deliver as required by the contract; or

(b) in all cases, the seller becomes insolvent within ten days after receipt of the first installment on their price.

(2) The buyer's right to recover the goods under subsection (1) vests upon acquisition of a special property, even if the seller had not then repudiated or failed to deliver.

(3) If the identification creating the special property has been made by the buyer, the buyer acquires the right to recover the goods only if they conform to the contract for sale.

* * * *

§ 2-508.   Cure by Seller of Improper Tender or Delivery; Replacement.

(1) Where the buyer rejects goods or a tender of delivery under Section 2-601 or 2-612 or except in a consumer contract justifiably revokes acceptance under Section 2-608(1)(b) and the agreed time for performance has not expired, a seller that has performed in good faith, upon seasonable notice to the buyer and at the seller's own expense, may cure the breach of contract by making a conforming tender of delivery within the agreed time. The seller shall compensate the buyer for all of the buyer's reasonable expenses caused by the seller's breach of contract and subsequent cure.

(2) Where the buyer rejects goods or a tender of delivery under Section 2-601 or 2-612 or except in a consumer contract justifiably revokes acceptance under Section 2-608(1)(b) and the agreed time for performance has expired, a seller that has performed in good faith, upon seasonable notice to the buyer and at the seller's own expense, may cure the breach of contract, if the cure is appropriate and timely under the circumstances, by making a tender of conforming goods. The seller shall compensate the buyer for all of the buyer's reasonable expenses caused by the seller's breach of contract and subsequent cure.

§ 2-509.   Risk of Loss in the Absence of Breach.

(1) Where the contract requires or authorizes the seller to ship the goods by carrier

(a) if it does not require the seller to deliver them at a particular destination, the risk of loss passes to the buyer when the goods are delivered to the carrier even though the shipment is under reservation (Section 2-505); but

(b) if it does require the seller to deliver them at a particular destination and the goods are there tendered while in the possession of the carrier, the risk of loss passes to the buyer when the goods are there so tendered as to enable the buyer to take delivery.

(2) Where the goods are held by a bailee to be delivered without being moved, the risk of loss passes to the buyer

(a) on the buyer's receipt of a negotiable document of title covering the goods; or

(b) on acknowledgment by the bailee to the buyer of the buyer's right to possession of the goods; or

(c) after the buyer's receipt of a non-negotiable document of title or other direction to deliver in a record, as provided in subsection (4)(b) of Section 2–503.

(3) In any case not within subsection (1) or (2), the risk of loss passes to the buyer on the buyer's receipt of the goods.

* * * *

§ 2–513.   Buyer's Right to Inspection of Goods.

* * * *

(3) Unless otherwise agreed, the buyer is not entitled to inspect the goods before payment of the price when the contract provides

(a) for delivery on terms that under applicable course of performance, course of dealing, or usage of trade are interpreted to preclude inspection before payment; or

(b) for payment against documents of title, except where such payment is due only after the goods are to become available for inspection.

* * * *

PART 6   Breach, Repudiation and Excuse

* * * *

§ 2–605.   Waiver of Buyer's Objections by Failure to Particularize.

(1) The buyer's failure to state in connection with rejection a particular defect or in connection with revocation of acceptance a defect that justifies revocation precludes the buyer from relying on the unstated defect to justify rejection or revocation of acceptance if the defect is ascertainable by reasonable inspection

(a) where the seller had a right to cure the defect and could have cured it if stated seasonably; or

(b) between merchants when the seller has after rejection made a request in a record for a full and final statement in record form of all defects on which the buyer proposes to rely.

(2) A buyer's payment against documents tendered to the buyer made without reservation of rights precludes recovery of the payment for defects apparent on the face of the documents.

* * * *

§ 2–607.   Effect of Acceptance; Notice of Breach; Burden of Establishing Breach After Acceptance; Notice of Claim or Litigation to Person Answerable Over.

(3) Where a tender has been accepted

(a) the buyer must within a reasonable time after the buyer discovers or should have discovered any breach notify the seller; however, failure to give timely notice bars the buyer from a remedy only to the extent that the seller is prejudiced by the failure and

(b) if the claim is one for infringement or the like (subsection (3) of Section 2–312) and the buyer is sued as a result of such a breach the buyer must so notify the seller within a reasonable time after the buyer receives notice of the litigation or be barred from any remedy over for liability established by the litigation.

* * * *

§ 2–608.   Revocation of Acceptance in Whole or in Part.

* * * *

(4) If a buyer uses the goods after a rightful rejection or justifiable revocation of acceptance, the following rules apply:

(a) Any use by the buyer that is unreasonable under the circumstances is wrongful as against the seller and is an acceptance only if ratified by the seller.

(b) Any use of the goods that is reasonable under the circumstances is not wrongful as against the seller and is not an acceptance, but in an appropriate case the buyer shall be obligated to the seller for the value of the use to the buyer.

* * * *

§ 2–612.   "Installment Contract"; Breach.

* * * *

(2) The buyer may reject any installment which is non-conforming if the non-conformity substantially impairs the value of that installment to the buyer or if the non-conformity is a defect in the required documents; but if the non-conformity does not fall within subsection (3) and the seller gives adequate assurance of its cure the buyer must accept that installment.

(3) Whenever non-conformity or default with respect to one or more installments substantially impairs the value of the whole contract there is a breach of the whole. But the aggrieved party reinstates the contract if the party accepts a non-conforming installment without seasonably notifying of cancellation or if the party brings an action with respect only to past installments or demands performance as to future installments.

* * * *

PART 7   Remedies

§ 2–702.   Seller's Remedies on Discovery of Buyer's Insolvency.

* * * *

(2) Where the seller discovers that the buyer has received goods on credit while insolvent the seller may reclaim the goods upon demand made within a reasonable time after the buyer's receipt of the goods. Except as provided in this subsection the seller may not base a right to reclaim goods on the buyer's fraudulent or innocent misrepresentation of solvency or of intent to pay.

* * * *

§ 2–705.   Seller's Stoppage of Delivery in Transit or Otherwise.

(1) The seller may stop delivery of goods in the possession of a carrier or other bailee when the seller discovers the buyer to be insolvent (Section 2–702) or when the buyer repudiates or fails to make a payment due before delivery or if for any other reason the seller has a right to withhold or reclaim the goods.

* * * *

§ 2–706.   Seller's Resale Including Contract for Resale.

(1) In an appropriate case involving breach by the buyer, the seller may resell the goods concerned or the undelivered balance thereof. Where the resale is made in good faith and in a commercially reasonable manner the seller may recover the difference between the contract price and the resale price together with any incidental or consequential damages allowed under the provisions of this Article (Section 2–710), but less expenses saved in consequence of the buyer's breach.

* * * *

§ 2–708.   Seller's Damages for Non-Acceptance or Repudiation.

(1) Subject to subsection (2) and to the provisions of this Article with respect to proof of market price (Section 2–723)

(a) the measure of damages for non-acceptance by the buyer is the difference between the contract price and the market price at the time and place for tender together with any incidental or consequential damages provided in this Article (Section 2–710), but less expenses saved in consequence of the buyer's breach; and

(b) the measure of damages for repudiation by the buyer is the difference between the contract price and the market price at the place for tender at the expiration of a commercially reasonable time after the seller learned of the repudiation, but no later than the time stated in paragraph (a), together with any incidental or consequential damages provided in this Article (Section 2–710), but less expenses saved in consequence of the buyer's breach.

(2) If the measure of damages provided in subsection (1) or in Section 2–706 is inadequate to put the seller in as good a position as performance would have done then the measure of damages is the profit (including reasonable overhead) which the seller would have made from full performance by the buyer, together with any incidental or consequential damages provided in this Article (Section 2–710).

§ 2–709.   Action for the Price.

(1) When the buyer fails to pay the price as it becomes due the seller may recover, together with any incidental or consequential damages under the next section, the price

(a) of goods accepted or of conforming goods lost or damaged within a commercially reasonable time after risk of their loss has passed to the buyer; and

(b) of goods identified to the contract if the seller is unable after reasonable effort to resell them at a reasonable price or the circumstances reasonably indicate that such effort will be unavailing.

* * * *

* * * *

* * * *

§ 2–710.   Seller's Incidental and Consequential Damages.

(1) Incidental damages to an aggrieved seller include any commercially reasonable charges, expenses or commissions incurred in stopping delivery, in the transportation, care and custody of goods after the buyer's breach, in connection with return or resale of the goods or otherwise resulting from the breach.

(2) Consequential damages resulting from the buyer's breach include any loss resulting from general or particular requirements and needs of which the buyer at the time of contracting had reason to know and which could not reasonably be prevented by resale or otherwise.

(3) In a consumer contract, a seller may not recover consequential damages from a consumer.

* * * *

§ 2–713.   Buyer's Damages for Non-Delivery or Repudiation.

(1) Subject to the provisions of this Article with respect to proof of market price (Section 2–723), if the seller wrongfully fails to deliver or repudiates or the buyer rightfully rejects or justifiably revokes acceptance

(a) the measure of damages in the case of wrongful failure to deliver by the seller or rightful rejection or justifiable revocation of acceptance by the buyer is the difference between the market price at the time for tender under the contract and the contract price together with any incidental or consequential damages provided in this Article (Section 2–715), but less expenses saved in consequence of the seller's breach; and

(b) the measure of damages for repudiation by the seller is the difference between the market price at the expiration of a commercially reasonable time after the buyer learned of the repudiation, but no later than the time stated in paragraph (a), and the contract price together with any incidental or consequential damages provided in this Article (Section 2–715), but less expenses saved in consequence of the seller's breach.

* * * *

§ 2–725.   Statute of Limitations in Contracts for Sale.

(1) Except as otherwise provided in this section, an action for breach of any contract for sale must be commenced within the later of four years after the right of action has accrued under subsection (2) or (3) or one year after the breach was or should have been discovered, but no longer than five years after the right of action accrued. By the original agreement the parties may reduce the period of limitation to not less than one year but may not extend it; however, in a consumer contract, the period of limitation may not be reduced.

(2) Except as otherwise provided in subsection (3), the following rules apply:

(a) Except as otherwise provided in this subsection, a right of action for breach of a contract accrues when the breach occurs, even if the aggrieved party did not have knowledge of the breach.

(b) For breach of a contract by repudiation, a right of action accrues at the earlier of when the aggrieved party elects to treat the repudiation as a breach or when a commercially reasonable time for awaiting performance has expired.

(c) For breach of a remedial promise, a right of action accrues when the remedial promise is not performed when due.

(d) In an action by a buyer against a person that is answerable over to the buyer for a claim asserted against the buyer, the buyer's right of action against the person answerable over accrues at the time the claim was originally asserted against the buyer.

(3) If a breach of a warranty arising under Section 2–312, 2–313(2), 2–314, or 2–315, or a breach of an obligation other than a remedial promise arising under Section 2–313A or 2–313B, is claimed the following rules apply:

(a) Except as otherwise provided in paragraph (c), a right of action for breach of a warranty arising under Section 2–313(2), 2–314 or 2–315 accrues when the seller has tendered delivery to the immediate buyer, as defined in Section 2–313, and has completed performance of any agreed installation or assembly of the goods.

(b) Except as otherwise provided in paragraph (c), a right of action for breach of an obligation other than a remedial promise arising under Section 2–313A or 2–313B accrues when the remote purchaser, as defined in sections 2–313A and 2–313B, receives the goods.

(c) Where a warranty arising under Section 2–313(2) or an obligation other than a remedial promise arising under 2–313A or 2–313B explicitly extends to future performance of the goods and discovery of the breach must await the time for performance the right of action accrues when the immediate buyer as defined in Section 2–313 or the remote purchaser as defined in Sections 2–313A and 2–313B discovers or should have discovered the breach.

(d) A right of action for breach of warranty arising under Section 2–312 accrues when the aggrieved party discovers or should have discovered the breach. However, an action for breach of the warranty of non-infringement may not be commenced more than six years after tender of delivery of the goods to the aggrieved party.

* * * *

ARTICLE 2A

LEASES

PART I   General Provisions

§ 2A–101. Short Title.

This Article shall be known and may be cited as the Uniform Commercial Code—Leases.

§ 2A–102. Scope.

This Article applies to any transaction, regardless of form, that creates a lease.

§ 2A–103. Definitions and Index of Definitions.

(1) In this Article unless the context otherwise requires:

(a) "Buyer in ordinary course of business" means a person who in good faith and without knowledge that the sale to him [or her] is in violation of the ownership rights or security interest or leasehold interest of a third party in the goods buys in ordinary course from a person in the business of selling goods of that kind but does not include a pawnbroker. "Buying" may be for cash or by exchange of other property or on secured or unsecured credit and includes receiving goods or documents of title under a pre-existing contract for sale but does not include a transfer in bulk or as security for or in total or partial satisfaction of a money debt.

(b) "Cancellation" occurs when either party puts an end to the lease contract for default by the other party.

(c) "Commercial unit" means such a unit of goods as by commercial usage is a single whole for purposes of lease and division of which materially impairs its character or value on the market or in use. A commercial unit may be a single article, as a machine, or a set of articles, as a suite of furniture or a line of machinery, or a quantity, as a gross or carload, or any other unit treated in use or in the relevant market as a single whole.

(d) "Conforming" goods or performance under a lease contract means goods or performance that are in accordance with the obligations under the lease contract.

(e) "Consumer lease" means a lease that a lessor regularly engaged in the business of leasing or selling makes to a lessee who is an individual and who takes under the lease primarily for a personal, family, or household purpose [, if the total payments to be made under the lease contract, excluding payments for options to renew or buy, do not exceed $_____].

(f) "Fault" means wrongful act, omission, breach, or default.

(g) "Finance lease" means a lease with respect to which:

(i) the lessor does not select, manufacture or supply the goods;

(ii) the lessor acquires the goods or the right to possession and use of the goods in connection with the lease; and

(iii) one of the following occurs:

(A) the lessee receives a copy of the contract by which the lessor acquired the goods or the right to possession and use of the goods before signing the lease contract;

(B) the lessee's approval of the contract by which the lessor acquired the goods or the right to possession and use of the goods is a condition to effectiveness of the lease contract;

(C) the lessee, before signing the lease contract, receives an accurate and complete statement designating the promises and warranties, and any disclaimers of warranties, limitations or modifications of remedies, or liquidated damages, including those of a third party, such as the manufacturer of the goods, provided to the lessor by the person supplying the goods in connection with or as part of the contract by which the lessor acquired the goods or the right to possession and use of the goods; or

(D) if the lease is not a consumer lease, the lessor, before the lessee signs the lease contract, informs the lessee in writing (a) of the identity of the person supplying the goods to the lessor, unless the lessee has selected that person and directed the lessor to acquire the goods or the right to possession and use of the goods from that person, (b) that the lessee is entitled under this Article to any promises and warranties, including those of any third party, provided to the lessor by the person supplying the goods in connection with or as part of the contract by which the lessor acquired the goods or the right to possession and use of the goods, and (c) that the lessee may communicate with the person supplying the goods to the lessor and receive an accurate and complete statement of those promises and warranties, including any disclaimers and limitations of them or of remedies.

(h) "Goods" means all things that are movable at the time of identification to the lease contract, or are fixtures (Section 2A–309), but the term does not include money, documents, instruments, accounts, chattel paper, general intangibles, or minerals or the like, including oil and gas, before extraction. The term also includes the unborn young of animals.

(i) "Installment lease contract" means a lease contract that authorizes or requires the delivery of goods in separate lots to be separately accepted, even though the lease contract contains a clause "each delivery is a separate lease" or its equivalent.

(j) "Lease" means a transfer of the right to possession and use of goods for a term in return for consideration, but a sale, including a sale on approval or a sale or return, or retention or creation of a security interest is not a lease. Unless the context clearly indicates otherwise, the term includes a sublease.

(k) "Lease agreement" means the bargain, with respect to the lease, of the lessor and the lessee in fact as found in their language or by implication from other circumstances including course of dealing or usage of trade or course of performance as provided in this Article. Unless the context clearly indicates otherwise, the term includes a sublease agreement.

(l) "Lease contract" means the total legal obligation that results from the lease agreement as affected by this Article and any other applicable rules of law. Unless the context clearly indicates otherwise, the term includes a sublease contract.

(m) "Leasehold interest" means the interest of the lessor or the lessee under a lease contract.

(n) "Lessee" means a person who acquires the right to possession and use of goods under a lease. Unless the context clearly indicates otherwise, the term includes a sublessee.

(o) "Lessee in ordinary course of business" means a person who in good faith and without knowledge that the lease to him [or her] is in violation of the ownership rights or security interest or leasehold interest of a third party in the goods, leases in ordinary course from a person in the business of selling or leasing goods of that kind but does not include a pawnbroker. "Leasing" may be for cash or by exchange of other property or on secured or unsecured credit and includes receiving goods or documents of title under a pre-existing lease contract but does not include a transfer in bulk or as security for or in total or partial satisfaction of a money debt.

(p) "Lessor" means a person who transfers the right to possession and use of goods under a lease. Unless the context clearly indicates otherwise, the term includes a sublessor.

(q) "Lessor's residual interest" means the lessor's interest in the goods after expiration, termination, or cancellation of the lease contract.

(r) "Lien" means a charge against or interest in goods to secure payment of a debt or performance of an obligation, but the term does not include a security interest.

(s) "Lot" means a parcel or a single article that is the subject matter of a separate lease or delivery, whether or not it is sufficient to perform the lease contract.

(t) "Merchant lessee" means a lessee that is a merchant with respect to goods of the kind subject to the lease.

(u) "Present value" means the amount as of a date certain of one or more sums payable in the future, discounted to the date certain. The discount is determined by the interest rate specified by the parties if the rate was not manifestly unreasonable at the time the transaction was entered into; otherwise, the discount is determined by a commercially reasonable rate that takes into account the facts and circumstances of each case at the time the transaction was entered into.

(v) "Purchase" includes taking by sale, lease, mortgage, security interest, pledge, gift, or any other voluntary transaction creating an interest in goods.

(w) "Sublease" means a lease of goods the right to possession and use of which was acquired by the lessor as a lessee under an existing lease.

(x) "Supplier" means a person from whom a lessor buys or leases goods to be leased under a finance lease.

(y) "Supply contract" means a contract under which a lessor buys or leases goods to be leased.

(z) "Termination" occurs when either party pursuant to a power created by agreement or law puts an end to the lease contract otherwise than for default.

(2) Other definitions applying to this Article and the sections in which they appear are:

"Accessions". Section 2A–310(1).
"Construction mortgage". Section 2A–309(1)(d).
"Encumbrance". Section 2A–309(1)(e).
"Fixtures". Section 2A–309(1)(a).
"Fixture filing". Section 2A–309(1)(b).
"Purchase money lease". Section 2A–309(1)(c).

(3) The following definitions in other Articles apply to this Article:

"Accounts". Section 9–106.
"Between merchants". Section 2–104(3).
"Buyer". Section 2–103(1)(a).
"Chattel paper". Section 9–105(1)(b).
"Consumer goods". Section 9–109(1).

"Document". Section 9–105(1)(f).
"Entrusting". Section 2–403(3).
"General intangibles". Section 9–106.
"Good faith". Section 2–103(1)(b).
"Instrument". Section 9–105(1)(i).
"Merchant". Section 2–104(1).
"Mortgage". Section 9–105(1)(j).
"Pursuant to commitment". Section 9–105(1)(k).
"Receipt". Section 2–103(1)(c).
"Sale". Section 2–106(1).
"Sale on approval". Section 2–326.
"Sale or return". Section 2–326.
"Seller". Section 2–103(1)(d).

(4) In addition Article 1 contains general definitions and principles of construction and interpretation applicable throughout this Article.

As amended in 1990 and 1999.

§ 2A-104. Leases Subject to Other Law.

(1) A lease, although subject to this Article, is also subject to any applicable:

(a) certificate of title statute of this State: (list any certificate of title statutes covering automobiles, trailers, mobile homes, boats, farm tractors, and the like);

(b) certificate of title statute of another jurisdiction (Section 2A–105); or

(c) consumer protection statute of this State, or final consumer protection decision of a court of this State existing on the effective date of this Article.

(2) In case of conflict between this Article, other than Sections 2A–105, 2A–304(3), and 2A–305(3), and a statute or decision referred to in subsection (1), the statute or decision controls.

(3) Failure to comply with an applicable law has only the effect specified therein.

As amended in 1990.

§ 2A-105. Territorial Application of Article to Goods Covered by Certificate of Title.

Subject to the provisions of Sections 2A–304(3) and 2A–305(3), with respect to goods covered by a certificate of title issued under a statute of this State or of another jurisdiction, compliance and the effect of compliance or noncompliance with a certificate of title statute are governed by the law (including the conflict of laws rules) of the jurisdiction issuing the certificate until the earlier of (a) surrender of the certificate, or (b) four months after the goods are removed from that jurisdiction and thereafter until a new certificate of title is issued by another jurisdiction.

§ 2A-106. Limitation on Power of Parties to Consumer Lease to Choose Applicable Law and Judicial Forum.

(1) If the law chosen by the parties to a consumer lease is that of a jurisdiction other than a jurisdiction in which the lessee resides at the time the lease agreement becomes enforceable or within 30 days thereafter or in which the goods are to be used, the choice is not enforceable.

(2) If the judicial forum chosen by the parties to a consumer lease is a forum that would not otherwise have jurisdiction over the lessee, the choice is not enforceable.

§ 2A-107. Waiver or Renunciation of Claim or Right After Default.

Any claim or right arising out of an alleged default or breach of warranty may be discharged in whole or in part without consideration by a written waiver or renunciation signed and delivered by the aggrieved party.

§ 2A-108. Unconscionability.

(1) If the court as a matter of law finds a lease contract or any clause of a lease contract to have been unconscionable at the time it was made the court may refuse to enforce the lease contract, or it may enforce the remainder of the lease contract without the unconscionable clause, or it may so limit the application of any unconscionable clause as to avoid any unconscionable result.

(2) With respect to a consumer lease, if the court as a matter of law finds that a lease contract or any clause of a lease contract has been induced by unconscionable conduct or that unconscionable conduct has occurred in the collection of a claim arising from a lease contract, the court may grant appropriate relief.

(3) Before making a finding of unconscionability under subsection (1) or (2), the court, on its own motion or that of a party, shall afford the parties a reasonable opportunity to present evidence as to the setting, purpose, and effect of the lease contract or clause thereof, or of the conduct.

(4) In an action in which the lessee claims unconscionability with respect to a consumer lease:

(a) If the court finds unconscionability under subsection (1) or (2), the court shall award reasonable attorney's fees to the lessee.

(b) If the court does not find unconscionability and the lessee claiming unconscionability has brought or maintained an action he [or she] knew to be groundless, the court shall award reasonable attorney's fees to the party against whom the claim is made.

(c) In determining attorney's fees, the amount of the recovery on behalf of the claimant under subsections (1) and (2) is not controlling.

§ 2A-109. Option to Accelerate at Will.

(1) A term providing that one party or his [or her] successor in interest may accelerate payment or performance or require collateral or additional collateral "at will" or "when he [or she] deems himself [or herself] insecure" or in words of similar import must be construed to mean that he [or she] has power to do so only if he [or she] in good faith believes that the prospect of payment or performance is impaired.

(2) With respect to a consumer lease, the burden of establishing good faith under subsection (1) is on the party who exercised the power; otherwise the burden of establishing lack of good faith is on the party against whom the power has been exercised.

PART 2 Formation and Construction of Lease Contract

§ 2A-201. Statute of Frauds.

(1) A lease contract is not enforceable by way of action or defense unless:

(a) the total payments to be made under the lease contract, excluding payments for options to renew or buy, are less than $1,000; or

(b) there is a writing, signed by the party against whom enforcement is sought or by that party's authorized agent, sufficient to indicate that a lease contract has been made between the parties and to describe the goods leased and the lease term.

(2) Any description of leased goods or of the lease term is sufficient and satisfies subsection (1)(b), whether or not it is specific, if it reasonably identifies what is described.

(3) A writing is not insufficient because it omits or incorrectly states a term agreed upon, but the lease contract is not enforceable under subsection (1)(b) beyond the lease term and the quantity of goods shown in the writing.

(4) A lease contract that does not satisfy the requirements of subsection (1), but which is valid in other respects, is enforceable:

(a) if the goods are to be specially manufactured or obtained for the lessee and are not suitable for lease or sale to others in the ordinary course of the lessor's business, and the lessor, before notice of repudiation is received and under circumstances that reasonably indicate that the goods are for the lessee, has made either a substantial beginning of their manufacture or commitments for their procurement;

(b) if the party against whom enforcement is sought admits in that party's pleading, testimony or otherwise in court that a lease contract was made, but the lease contract is not enforceable under this provision beyond the quantity of goods admitted; or

(c) with respect to goods that have been received and accepted by the lessee.

(5) The lease term under a lease contract referred to in subsection (4) is:

(a) if there is a writing signed by the party against whom enforcement is sought or by that party's authorized agent specifying the lease term, the term so specified;

(b) if the party against whom enforcement is sought admits in that party's pleading, testimony, or otherwise in court a lease term, the term so admitted; or

(c) a reasonable lease term.

§ 2A–202. Final Written Expression: Parol or Extrinsic Evidence.

Terms with respect to which the confirmatory memoranda of the parties agree or which are otherwise set forth in a writing intended by the parties as a final expression of their agreement with respect to such terms as are included therein may not be contradicted by evidence of any prior agreement or of a contemporaneous oral agreement but may be explained or supplemented:

(a) by course of dealing or usage of trade or by course of performance; and

(b) by evidence of consistent additional terms unless the court finds the writing to have been intended also as a complete and exclusive statement of the terms of the agreement.

§ 2A–203. Seals Inoperative.

The affixing of a seal to a writing evidencing a lease contract or an offer to enter into a lease contract does not render the writing a sealed instrument and the law with respect to sealed instruments does not apply to the lease contract or offer.

§ 2A–204. Formation in General.

(1) A lease contract may be made in any manner sufficient to show agreement, including conduct by both parties which recognizes the existence of a lease contract.

(2) An agreement sufficient to constitute a lease contract may be found although the moment of its making is undetermined.

(3) Although one or more terms are left open, a lease contract does not fail for indefiniteness if the parties have intended to make a lease contract and there is a reasonably certain basis for giving an appropriate remedy.

§ 2A–205. Firm Offers.

An offer by a merchant to lease goods to or from another person in a signed writing that by its terms gives assurance it will be held open is not revocable, for lack of consideration, during the time stated or, if no time is stated, for a reasonable time, but in no event may the period of irrevocability exceed 3 months. Any such term of assurance on a form supplied by the offeree must be separately signed by the offeror.

§ 2A–206. Offer and Acceptance in Formation of Lease Contract.

(1) Unless otherwise unambiguously indicated by the language or circumstances, an offer to make a lease contract must be construed as inviting acceptance in any manner and by any medium reasonable in the circumstances.

(2) If the beginning of a requested performance is a reasonable mode of acceptance, an offeror who is not notified of acceptance within a reasonable time may treat the offer as having lapsed before acceptance.

§ 2A–207. Course of Performance or Practical Construction.

(1) If a lease contract involves repeated occasions for performance by either party with knowledge of the nature of the performance and opportunity for objection to it by the other, any course of performance accepted or acquiesced in without objection is relevant to determine the meaning of the lease agreement.

(2) The express terms of a lease agreement and any course of performance, as well as any course of dealing and usage of trade, must be construed whenever reasonable as consistent with each other; but if that construction is unreasonable, express terms control course of performance, course of performance controls both course of dealing and usage of trade, and course of dealing controls usage of trade.

(3) Subject to the provisions of Section 2A–208 on modification and waiver, course of performance is relevant to show a waiver or modification of any term inconsistent with the course of performance.

§ 2A–208. Modification, Rescission and Waiver.

(1) An agreement modifying a lease contract needs no consideration to be binding.

(2) A signed lease agreement that excludes modification or rescission except by a signed writing may not be otherwise modified or rescinded, but, except as between merchants, such a requirement on a form supplied by a merchant must be separately signed by the other party.

(3) Although an attempt at modification or rescission does not satisfy the requirements of subsection (2), it may operate as a waiver.

(4) A party who has made a waiver affecting an executory portion of a lease contract may retract the waiver by reasonable notification received by the other party that strict performance will be required of any term waived, unless the retraction would be unjust in view of a material change of position in reliance on the waiver.

§ 2A–209. Lessee under Finance Lease as Beneficiary of Supply Contract.

(1) The benefit of the supplier's promises to the lessor under the supply contract and of all warranties, whether express or implied, including those of any third party provided in connection with or as part of the supply contract, extends to the lessee to the extent of the lessee's leasehold interest under a finance lease related to the supply contract, but is subject to the terms warranty and of the supply contract and all defenses or claims arising therefrom.

(2) The extension of the benefit of supplier's promises and of warranties to the lessee (Section 2A–209(1)) does not: (i) modify the rights and obligations of the parties to the supply contract, whether arising therefrom or otherwise, or (ii) impose any duty or liability under the supply contract on the lessee.

(3) Any modification or rescission of the supply contract by the supplier and the lessor is effective between the supplier and the lessee unless, before the modification or rescission, the supplier has received notice that the lessee has entered into a finance lease related to the supply contract. If the modification or rescission is effective between the supplier and the lessee, the lessor is deemed to have assumed, in addition to the obligations of the lessor to the lessee under the lease contract, promises of the supplier to the lessor and warranties that were so modified or rescinded as they existed and were available to the lessee before modification or rescission.

(4) In addition to the extension of the benefit of the supplier's promises and of warranties to the lessee under subsection (1), the lessee retains all rights that the lessee may have against the supplier which arise from an agreement between the lessee and the supplier or under other law.

As amended in 1990.

§ 2A–210. Express Warranties.

(1) Express warranties by the lessor are created as follows:

(a) Any affirmation of fact or promise made by the lessor to the lessee which relates to the goods and becomes part of the basis of the bargain creates an express warranty that the goods will conform to the affirmation or promise.

(b) Any description of the goods which is made part of the basis of the bargain creates an express warranty that the goods will conform to the description.

(c) Any sample or model that is made part of the basis of the bargain creates an express warranty that the whole of the goods will conform to the sample or model.

(2) It is not necessary to the creation of an express warranty that the lessor use formal words, such as "warrant" or "guarantee," or that the lessor have a specific intention to make a warranty, but an affirmation merely of the value of the goods or a statement purporting to be merely the lessor's opinion or commendation of the goods does not create a warranty.

§ 2A–211. Warranties Against Interference and Against Infringement; Lessee's Obligation Against Infringement.

(1) There is in a lease contract a warranty that for the lease term no person holds a claim to or interest in the goods that arose from an act or omission of the lessor, other than a claim by way of infringement or the like, which will interfere with the lessee's enjoyment of its leasehold interest.

(2) Except in a finance lease there is in a lease contract by a lessor who is a merchant regularly dealing in goods of the kind a warranty that the goods are delivered free of the rightful claim of any person by way of infringement or the like.

(3) A lessee who furnishes specifications to a lessor or a supplier shall hold the lessor and the supplier harmless against any claim by way of infringement or the like that arises out of compliance with the specifications.

§ 2A–212. Implied Warranty of Merchantability.

(1) Except in a finance lease, a warranty that the goods will be merchantable is implied in a lease contract if the lessor is a merchant with respect to goods of that kind.

(2) Goods to be merchantable must be at least such as

(a) pass without objection in the trade under the description in the lease agreement;

(b) in the case of fungible goods, are of fair average quality within the description;

(c) are fit for the ordinary purposes for which goods of that type are used;

(d) run, within the variation permitted by the lease agreement, of even kind, quality, and quantity within each unit and among all units involved;

(e) are adequately contained, packaged, and labeled as the lease agreement may require; and

(f) conform to any promises or affirmations of fact made on the container or label.

(3) Other implied warranties may arise from course of dealing or usage of trade.

§ 2A–213. Implied Warranty of Fitness for Particular Purpose.

Except in a finance of lease, if the lessor at the time the lease contract is made has reason to know of any particular purpose for which the goods are required and that the lessee is relying on the lessor's skill or judgment to select or furnish suitable goods, there is in the lease contract an implied warranty that the goods will be fit for that purpose.

§ 2A–214. Exclusion or Modification of Warranties.

(1) Words or conduct relevant to the creation of an express warranty and words or conduct tending to negate or limit a warranty must be construed wherever reasonable as consistent

with each other; but, subject to the provisions of Section 2A–202 on parol or extrinsic evidence, negation or limitation is inoperative to the extent that the construction is unreasonable.

(2) Subject to subsection (3), to exclude or modify the implied warranty of merchantability or any part of it the language must mention "merchantability", be by a writing, and be conspicuous. Subject to subsection (3), to exclude or modify any implied warranty of fitness the exclusion must be by a writing and be conspicuous. Language to exclude all implied warranties of fitness is sufficient if it is in writing, is conspicuous and states, for example, "There is no warranty that the goods will be fit for a particular purpose".

(3) Notwithstanding subsection (2), but subject to subsection (4),

(a) unless the circumstances indicate otherwise, all implied warranties are excluded by expressions like "as is" or "with all faults" or by other language that in common understanding calls the lessee's attention to the exclusion of warranties and makes plain that there is no implied warranty, if in writing and conspicuous;

(b) if the lessee before entering into the lease contract has examined the goods or the sample or model as fully as desired or has refused to examine the goods, there is no implied warranty with regard to defects that an examination ought in the circumstances to have revealed; and

(c) an implied warranty may also be excluded or modified by course of dealing, course of performance, or usage of trade.

(4) To exclude or modify a warranty against interference or against infringement (Section 2A–211) or any part of it, the language must be specific, be by a writing, and be conspicuous, unless the circumstances, including course of performance, course of dealing, or usage of trade, give the lessee reason to know that the goods are being leased subject to a claim or interest of any person.

§ 2A–215. Cumulation and Conflict of Warranties Express or Implied.

Warranties, whether express or implied, must be construed as consistent with each other and as cumulative, but if that construction is unreasonable, the intention of the parties determines which warranty is dominant. In ascertaining that intention the following rules apply:

(a) Exact or technical specifications displace an inconsistent sample or model or general language of description.

(b) A sample from an existing bulk displaces inconsistent general language of description.

(c) Express warranties displace inconsistent implied warranties other than an implied warranty of fitness for a particular purpose.

§ 2A–216. Third-Party Beneficiaries of Express and Implied arranties.

Alternative A   A warranty to or for the benefit of a lessee under this Article, whether express or implied, extends to any natural person who is in the family or household of the lessee or who is a guest in the lessee's home if it is reasonable to expect that such person may use, consume, or be affected by the goods and who is injured in person by breach of the warranty. This section does not displace principles of law and equity that extend a warranty to or for the benefit of a lessee to other persons. The operation of this section may not be excluded, modified, or limited, but an exclusion, modification, or limitation of the warranty, including any with respect to rights and remedies, effective against the lessee is also effective against any beneficiary designated under this section.

Alternative B   A warranty to or for the benefit of a lessee under this Article, whether express or implied, extends to any natural person who may reasonably be expected to use, consume, or be affected by the goods and who is injured in person by breach of the warranty. This section does not displace principles of law and equity that extend a warranty to or for the benefit of a lessee to other persons. The operation of this section may not be excluded, modified, or limited, but an exclusion, modification, or limitation of the warranty, including any with respect to rights and remedies, effective against the lessee is also effective against the beneficiary designated under this section.

Alternative C   A warranty to or for the benefit of a lessee under this Article, whether express or implied, extends to any person who may reasonably be expected to use, consume, or be affected by the goods and who is injured by breach of the warranty. The operation of this section may not be excluded, modified, or limited with respect to injury to the person of an individual to whom the warranty extends, but an exclusion, modification, or limitation of the warranty, including any with respect to rights and remedies, effective against the lessee is also effective against the beneficiary designated under this section.

§ 2A–217. Identification.

Identification of goods as goods to which a lease contract refers may be made at any time and in any manner explicitly agreed to by the parties. In the absence of explicit agreement, identification occurs:

(a) when the lease contract is made if the lease contract is for a lease of goods that are existing and identified;

(b) when the goods are shipped, marked, or otherwise designated by the lessor as goods to which the lease contract refers, if the lease contract is for a lease of goods that are not existing and identified; or

(c) when the young are conceived, if the lease contract is for a lease of unborn young of animals.

§ 2A–218. Insurance and Proceeds.

(1) A lessee obtains an insurable interest when existing goods are identified to the lease contract even though the goods identified are nonconforming and the lessee has an option to reject them.

(2) If a lessee has an insurable interest only by reason of the lessor's identification of the goods, the lessor, until default or insolvency or notification to the lessee that identification is final, may substitute other goods for those identified.

(3) Notwithstanding a lessee's insurable interest under subsections (1) and (2), the lessor retains an insurable interest until an option to buy has been exercised by the lessee and risk of loss has passed to the lessee.

(4) Nothing in this section impairs any insurable interest recognized under any other statute or rule of law.

(5) The parties by agreement may determine that one or more parties have an obligation to obtain and pay for insurance covering the goods and by agreement may determine the beneficiary of the proceeds of the insurance.

§ 2A–219. Risk of Loss.

(1) Except in the case of a finance lease, risk of loss is retained by the lessor and does not pass to the lessee. In the case of a finance lease, risk of loss passes to the lessee.

(2) Subject to the provisions of this Article on the effect of default on risk of loss (Section 2A–220), if risk of loss is to pass to the lessee and the time of passage is not stated, the following rules apply:

(a) If the lease contract requires or authorizes the goods to be shipped by carrier

(i) and it does not require delivery at a particular destination, the risk of loss passes to the lessee when the goods are duly delivered to the carrier; but

(ii) if it does require delivery at a particular destination and the goods are there duly tendered while in the possession of the carrier, the risk of loss passes to the lessee when the goods are there duly so tendered as to enable the lessee to take delivery.

(b) If the goods are held by a bailee to be delivered without being moved, the risk of loss passes to the lessee on acknowledgment by the bailee of the lessee's right to possession of the goods.

(c) In any case not within subsection (a) or (b), the risk of loss passes to the lessee on the lessee's receipt of the goods if the lessor, or, in the case of a finance lease, the supplier, is a merchant; otherwise the risk passes to the lessee on tender of delivery.

§ 2A–220. Effect of Default on Risk of Loss.

(1) Where risk of loss is to pass to the lessee and the time of passage is not stated:

(a) If a tender or delivery of goods so fails to conform to the lease contract as to give a right of rejection, the risk of their loss remains with the lessor, or, in the case of a finance lease, the supplier, until cure or acceptance.

(b) If the lessee rightfully revokes acceptance, he [or she], to the extent of any deficiency in his [or her] effective insurance coverage, may treat the risk of loss as having remained with the lessor from the beginning.

(2) Whether or not risk of loss is to pass to the lessee, if the lessee as to conforming goods already identified to a lease contract repudiates or is otherwise in default under the lease contract, the lessor, or, in the case of a finance lease, the supplier, to the extent of any deficiency in his [or her] effective insurance coverage may treat the risk of loss as resting on the lessee for a commercially reasonable time.

§ 2A–221. Casualty to Identified Goods.

If a lease contract requires goods identified when the lease contract is made, and the goods suffer casualty without fault of the lessee, the lessor or the supplier before delivery, or the goods suffer casualty before risk of loss passes to the lessee pursuant to the lease agreement or Section 2A–219, then:

(a) if the loss is total, the lease contract is avoided; and

(b) if the loss is partial or the goods have so deteriorated as to no longer conform to the lease contract, the lessee may nevertheless demand inspection and at his [or her] option either treat the lease contract as avoided or, except in a finance lease that is not a consumer lease, accept the goods with due allowance from the rent payable for the balance of the lease term for the deterioration or the deficiency in quantity but without further right against the lessor.

PART 3   Effect of Lease Contract

§ 2A–301. Enforceability of Lease Contract.

Except as otherwise provided in this Article, a lease contract is effective and enforceable according to its terms between the parties, against purchasers of the goods and against creditors of the parties.

§ 2A–302. Title to and Possession of Goods.

Except as otherwise provided in this Article, each provision of this Article applies whether the lessor or a third party has title to the goods, and whether the lessor, the lessee, or a third party has possession of the goods, notwithstanding any statute or rule of law that possession or the absence of possession is fraudulent.

§ 2A–303. Alienability of Party's Interest Under Lease Contract or of Lessor's Residual Interest in Goods; Delegation of Performance; Transfer of Rights.

(1) As used in this section, "creation of a security interest" includes the sale of a lease contract that is subject to Article 9, Secured Transactions, by reason of Section 9–109(a)(3).

(2) Except as provided in subsections (3) and Section 9–407, a provision in a lease agreement which (i) prohibits the voluntary or involuntary transfer, including a transfer by sale, sublease, creation or enforcement of a security interest, or attachment,

levy, or other judicial process, of an interest of a party under the lease contract or of the lessor's residual interest in the goods, or (ii) makes such a transfer an event of default, gives rise to the rights and remedies provided in subsection (4), but a transfer that is prohibited or is an event of default under the lease agreement is otherwise effective.

(3) A provision in a lease agreement which (i) prohibits a transfer of a right to damages for default with respect to the whole lease contract or of a right to payment arising out of the transferor's due performance of the transferor's entire obligation, or (ii) makes such a transfer an event of default, is not enforceable, and such a transfer is not a transfer that materially impairs the propsect of obtaining return performance by, materially changes the duty of, or materially increases the burden or risk imposed on, the other party to the lease contract within the purview of subsection (4).

(4) Subject to subsection (3) and Section 9–407:

(a) if a transfer is made which is made an event of default under a lease agreement, the party to the lease contract not making the transfer, unless that party waives the default or otherwise agrees, has the rights and remedies described in Section 2A–501(2);

(b) if paragraph (a) is not applicable and if a transfer is made that (i) is prohibited under a lease agreement or (ii) materially impairs the prospect of obtaining return performance by, materially changes the duty of, or materially increases the burden or risk imposed on, the other party to the lease contract, unless the party not making the transfer agrees at any time to the transfer in the lease contract or otherwise, then, except as limited by contract, (i) the transferor is liable to the party not making the transfer for damages caused by the transfer to the extent that the damages could not reasonably be prevented by the party not making the transfer and (ii) a court having jurisdiction may grant other appropriate relief, including cancellation of the lease contract or an injunction against the transfer.

(5) A transfer of "the lease" or of "all my rights under the lease", or a transfer in similar general terms, is a transfer of rights and, unless the language or the circumstances, as in a transfer for security, indicate the contrary, the transfer is a delegation of duties by the transferor to the transferee. Acceptance by the transferee constitutes a promise by the transferee to perform those duties. The promise is enforceable by either the transferor or the other party to the lease contract.

(6) Unless otherwise agreed by the lessor and the lessee, a delegation of performance does not relieve the transferor as against the other party of any duty to perform or of any liability for default.

(7) In a consumer lease, to prohibit the transfer of an interest of a party under the lease contract or to make a transfer an event of default, the language must be specific, by a writing, and conspicuous.

As amended in 1990 and 1999.

§ 2A–304. Subsequent Lease of Goods by Lessor.

(1) Subject to Section 2A–303, a subsequent lessee from a lessor of goods under an existing lease contract obtains, to the extent of the leasehold interest transferred, the leasehold interest in the goods that the lessor had or had power to transfer, and except as provided in subsection (2) and Section 2A–527(4), takes subject to the existing lease contract. A lessor with voidable title has power to transfer a good leasehold interest to a good faith subsequent lessee for value, but only to the extent set forth in the preceding sentence. If goods have been delivered under a transaction of purchase the lessor has that power even though:

(a) the lessor's transferor was deceived as to the identity of the lessor;

(b) the delivery was in exchange for a check which is later dishonored;

(c) it was agreed that the transaction was to be a "cash sale"; or

(d) the delivery was procured through fraud punishable as larcenous under the criminal law.

(2) A subsequent lessee in the ordinary course of business from a lessor who is a merchant dealing in goods of that kind to whom the goods were entrusted by the existing lessee of that lessor before the interest of the subsequent lessee became enforceable against that lessor obtains, to the extent of the leasehold interest transferred, all of that lessor's and the existing lessee's rights to the goods, and takes free of the existing lease contract.

(3) A subsequent lessee from the lessor of goods that are subject to an existing lease contract and are covered by a certificate of title issued under a statute of this State or of another jurisdiction takes no greater rights than those provided both by this section and by the certificate of title statute.

As amended in 1990.

§ 2A–305. Sale or Sublease of Goods by Lessee.

(1) Subject to the provisions of Section 2A–303, a buyer or sublessee from the lessee of goods under an existing lease contract obtains, to the extent of the interest transferred, the leasehold interest in the goods that the lessee had or had power to transfer, and except as provided in subsection (2) and Section 2A–511(4), takes subject to the existing lease contract. A lessee with a voidable leasehold interest has power to transfer a good leasehold interest to a good faith buyer for value or a good faith sublessee for value, but only to the extent set forth in the preceding sentence. When goods have been delivered under a transaction of lease the lessee has that power even though:

(a) the lessor was deceived as to the identity of the lessee;

(b) the delivery was in exchange for a check which is later dishonored; or

(c) the delivery was procured through fraud punishable as larcenous under the criminal law.

(2) A buyer in the ordinary course of business or a sublessee in the ordinary course of business from a lessee who is a merchant dealing in goods of that kind to whom the goods were entrusted by the lessor obtains, to the extent of the interest transferred, all of the lessor's and lessee's rights to the goods, and takes free of the existing lease contract.

(3) A buyer or sublessee from the lessee of goods that are subject to an existing lease contract and are covered by a certificate of title issued under a statute of this State or of another jurisdiction takes no greater rights than those provided both by this section and by the certificate of title statute.

§ 2A–306. Priority of Certain Liens Arising by Operation of Law.

If a person in the ordinary course of his [or her] business furnishes services or materials with respect to goods subject to a lease contract, a lien upon those goods in the possession of that person given by statute or rule of law for those materials or services takes priority over any interest of the lessor or lessee under the lease contract or this Article unless the lien is created by statute and the statute provides otherwise or unless the lien is created by rule of law and the rule of law provides otherwise.

§ 2A–307. Priority of Liens Arising by Attachment or Levy on, Security Interests in, and Other Claims to Goods.

(1) Except as otherwise provided in Section 2A–306, a creditor of a lessee takes subject to the lease contract.

(2) Except as otherwise provided in subsection (3) and in Sections 2A–306 and 2A–308, a creditor of a lessor takes subject to the lease contract unless the creditor holds a lien that attached to the goods before the lease contract became enforceable.

(3) Except as otherwise provided in Sections 9–317, 9–321, and 9–323, a lessee takes a leasehold interest subject to a security interest held by a creditor of the lessor.

As amended in 1990 and 1999.

§ 2A–308. Special Rights of Creditors.

(1) A creditor of a lessor in possession of goods subject to a lease contract may treat the lease contract as void if as against the creditor retention of possession by the lessor is fraudulent under any statute or rule of law, but retention of possession in good faith and current course of trade by the lessor for a commercially reasonable time after the lease contract becomes enforceable is not fraudulent.

(2) Nothing in this Article impairs the rights of creditors of a lessor if the lease contract (a) becomes enforceable, not in current course of trade but in satisfaction of or as security for a pre-existing claim for money, security, or the like, and (b) is made under circumstances which under any statute or rule of law apart from this Article would constitute the transaction a fraudulent transfer or voidable preference.

(3) A creditor of a seller may treat a sale or an identification of goods to a contract for sale as void if as against the creditor retention of possession by the seller is fraudulent under any statute or rule of law, but retention of possession of the goods pursuant to a lease contract entered into by the seller as lessee and the buyer as lessor in connection with the sale or identification of the goods is not fraudulent if the buyer bought for value and in good faith.

§ 2A–309. Lessor's and Lessee's Rights When Goods Become Fixtures.

(1) In this section:

(a) goods are "fixtures" when they become so related to particular real estate that an interest in them arises under real estate law;

(b) a "fixture filing" is the filing, in the office where a mortgage on the real estate would be filed or recorded, of a financing statement covering goods that are or are to become fixtures and conforming to the requirements of Section 9–502(a) and (b);

(c) a lease is a "purchase money lease" unless the lessee has possession or use of the goods or the right to possession or use of the goods before the lease agreement is enforceable;

(d) a mortgage is a "construction mortgage" to the extent it secures an obligation incurred for the construction of an improvement on land including the acquisition cost of the land, if the recorded writing so indicates; and

(e) "encumbrance" includes real estate mortgages and other liens on real estate and all other rights in real estate that are not ownership interests.

(2) Under this Article a lease may be of goods that are fixtures or may continue in goods that become fixtures, but no lease exists under this Article of ordinary building materials incorporated into an improvement on land.

(3) This Article does not prevent creation of a lease of fixtures pursuant to real estate law.

(4) The perfected interest of a lessor of fixtures has priority over a conflicting interest of an encumbrancer or owner of the real estate if:

(a) the lease is a purchase money lease, the conflicting interest of the encumbrancer or owner arises before the goods become fixtures, the interest of the lessor is perfected by a fixture filing before the goods become fixtures or within ten days thereafter, and the lessee has an interest of record in the real estate or is in possession of the real estate; or

(b) the interest of the lessor is perfected by a fixture filing before the interest of the encumbrancer or owner is of record, the lessor's interest has priority over any conflicting interest of a predecessor in title of the encumbrancer or owner, and the lessee has an interest of record in the real estate or is in possession of the real estate.

(5) The interest of a lessor of fixtures, whether or not perfected, has priority over the conflicting interest of an encumbrancer or owner of the real estate if:

(a) the fixtures are readily removable factory or office machines, readily removable equipment that is not primarily used or leased for use in the operation of the real estate, or readily removable replacements of domestic appliances that are goods subject to a consumer lease, and before the goods become fixtures the lease contract is enforceable; or

(b) the conflicting interest is a lien on the real estate obtained by legal or equitable proceedings after the lease contract is enforceable; or

(c) the encumbrancer or owner has consented in writing to the lease or has disclaimed an interest in the goods as fixtures; or

(d) the lessee has a right to remove the goods as against the encumbrancer or owner. If the lessee's right to remove terminates, the priority of the interest of the lessor continues for a reasonable time.

(6) Notwithstanding paragraph (4)(a) but otherwise subject to subsections (4) and (5), the interest of a lessor of fixtures, including the lessor's residual interest, is subordinate to the conflicting interest of an encumbrancer of the real estate under a construction mortgage recorded before the goods become fixtures if the goods become fixtures before the completion of the construction. To the extent given to refinance a construction mortgage, the conflicting interest of an encumbrancer of the real estate under a mortgage has this priority to the same extent as the encumbrancer of the real estate under the construction mortgage.

(7) In cases not within the preceding subsections, priority between the interest of a lessor of fixtures, including the lessor's residual interest, and the conflicting interest of an encumbrancer or owner of the real estate who is not the lessee is determined by the priority rules governing conflicting interests in real estate.

(8) If the interest of a lessor of fixtures, including the lessor's residual interest, has priority over all conflicting interests of all owners and encumbrancers of the real estate, the lessor or the lessee may (i) on default, expiration, termination, or cancellation of the lease agreement but subject to the agreement and this Article, or (ii) if necessary to enforce other rights and remedies of the lessor or lessee under this Article, remove the goods from the real estate, free and clear of all conflicting interests of all owners and encumbrancers of the real estate, but the lessor or lessee must reimburse any encumbrancer or owner of the real estate who is not the lessee and who has not otherwise agreed for the cost of repair of any physical injury, but not for any diminution in value of the real estate caused by the absence of the goods removed or by any necessity of replacing them. A person entitled to reimbursement may refuse permission to remove until the party seeking removal gives adequate security for the performance of this obligation.

(9) Even though the lease agreement does not create a security interest, the interest of a lessor of fixtures, including the lessor's residual interest, is perfected by filing a financing statement as a fixture filing for leased goods that are or are to become fixtures in accordance with the relevant provisions of the Article on Secured Transactions (Article 9).

As amended in 1990 and 1999.

§ 2A–310. Lessor's and Lessee's Rights When Goods Become Accessions.

(1) Goods are "accessions" when they are installed in or affixed to other goods.

(2) The interest of a lessor or a lessee under a lease contract entered into before the goods became accessions is superior to all interests in the whole except as stated in subsection (4).

(3) The interest of a lessor or a lessee under a lease contract entered into at the time or after the goods became accessions is superior to all subsequently acquired interests in the whole except as stated in subsection (4) but is subordinate to interests in the whole existing at the time the lease contract was made unless the holders of such interests in the whole have in writing consented to the lease or disclaimed an interest in the goods as part of the whole.

(4) The interest of a lessor or a lessee under a lease contract described in subsection (2) or (3) is subordinate to the interest of

(a) a buyer in the ordinary course of business or a lessee in the ordinary course of business of any interest in the whole acquired after the goods became accessions; or

(b) a creditor with a security interest in the whole perfected before the lease contract was made to the extent that the creditor makes subsequent advances without knowledge of the lease contract.

(5) When under subsections (2) or (3) and (4) a lessor or a lessee of accessions holds an interest that is superior to all interests in the whole, the lessor or the lessee may (a) on default, expiration, termination, or cancellation of the lease contract by the other party but subject to the provisions of the lease contract and this Article, or (b) if necessary to enforce his [or her] other rights and remedies under this Article, remove the goods from the whole, free and clear of all interests in the whole, but he [or she] must reimburse any holder of an interest in the whole who is not the lessee and who has not otherwise agreed for the cost of repair of any physical injury but not for any diminution in value of the whole caused by the absence of the goods removed or by any necessity for replacing them. A

person entitled to reimbursement may refuse permission to remove until the party seeking removal gives adequate security for the performance of this obligation.

§ 2A–311. Priority Subject to Subordination.

Nothing in this Article prevents subordination by agreement by any person entitled to priority.

As added in 1990.

PART 4 Performance of Lease Contract: Repudiated, Substituted and Excused

§ 2A–401. Insecurity: Adequate Assurance of Performance.

(1) A lease contract imposes an obligation on each party that the other's expectation of receiving due performance will not be impaired.

(2) If reasonable grounds for insecurity arise with respect to the performance of either party, the insecure party may demand in writing adequate assurance of due performance. Until the insecure party receives that assurance, if commercially reasonable the insecure party may suspend any performance for which he [or she] has not already received the agreed return.

(3) A repudiation of the lease contract occurs if assurance of due performance adequate under the circumstances of the particular case is not provided to the insecure party within a reasonable time, not to exceed 30 days after receipt of a demand by the other party.

(4) Between merchants, the reasonableness of grounds for insecurity and the adequacy of any assurance offered must be determined according to commercial standards.

(5) Acceptance of any nonconforming delivery or payment does not prejudice the aggrieved party's right to demand adequate assurance of future performance.

§ 2A–402. Anticipatory Repudiation.

If either party repudiates a lease contract with respect to a performance not yet due under the lease contract, the loss of which performance will substantially impair the value of the lease contract to the other, the aggrieved party may:

(a) for a commercially reasonable time, await retraction of repudiation and performance by the repudiating party;

(b) make demand pursuant to Section 2A–401 and await assurance of future performance adequate under the circumstances of the particular case; or

(c) resort to any right or remedy upon default under the lease contract or this Article, even though the aggrieved party has notified the repudiating party that the aggrieved party would await the repudiating party's performance and assurance and has urged retraction. In addition, whether or not the aggrieved party is pur-

suing one of the foregoing remedies, the aggrieved party may suspend performance or, if the aggrieved party is the lessor, proceed in accordance with the provisions of this Article on the lessor's right to identify goods to the lease contract notwithstanding default or to salvage unfinished goods (Section 2A–524).

§ 2A–403. Retraction of Anticipatory Repudiation.

(1) Until the repudiating party's next performance is due, the repudiating party can retract the repudiation unless, since the repudiation, the aggrieved party has cancelled the lease contract or materially changed the aggrieved party's position or otherwise indicated that the aggrieved party considers the repudiation final.

(2) Retraction may be by any method that clearly indicates to the aggrieved party that the repudiating party intends to perform under the lease contract and includes any assurance demanded under Section 2A–401.

(3) Retraction reinstates a repudiating party's rights under a lease contract with due excuse and allowance to the aggrieved party for any delay occasioned by the repudiation.

§ 2A–404. Substituted Performance.

(1) If without fault of the lessee, the lessor and the supplier, the agreed berthing, loading, or unloading facilities fail or the agreed type of carrier becomes unavailable or the agreed manner of delivery otherwise becomes commercially impracticable, but a commercially reasonable substitute is available, the substitute performance must be tendered and accepted.

(2) If the agreed means or manner of payment fails because of domestic or foreign governmental regulation:

(a) the lessor may withhold or stop delivery or cause the supplier to withhold or stop delivery unless the lessee provides a means or manner of payment that is commercially a substantial equivalent; and

(b) if delivery has already been taken, payment by the means or in the manner provided by the regulation discharges the lessee's obligation unless the regulation is discriminatory, oppressive, or predatory.

§ 2A–405. Excused Performance.

Subject to Section 2A–404 on substituted performance, the following rules apply:

(a) Delay in delivery or nondelivery in whole or in part by a lessor or a supplier who complies with paragraphs (b) and (c) is not a default under the lease contract if performance as agreed has been made impracticable by the occurrence of a contingency the nonoccurrence of which was a basic assumption on which the lease contract was made or by compliance in good faith with any applicable foreign or domestic governmental regulation or order, whether or not the regulation or order later proves to be invalid.

(b) If the causes mentioned in paragraph (a) affect only part of the lessor's or the supplier's capacity to perform, he [or she] shall allocate production and deliveries among his [or her] customers but at his [or her] option may include regular customers not then under contract for sale or lease as well as his [or her] own requirements for further manufacture. He [or she] may so allocate in any manner that is fair and reasonable.

(c) The lessor seasonably shall notify the lessee and in the case of a finance lease the supplier seasonably shall notify the lessor and the lessee, if known, that there will be delay or nondelivery and, if allocation is required under paragraph (b), of the estimated quota thus made available for the lessee.

§ 2A–406. Procedure on Excused Performance.

(1) If the lessee receives notification of a material or indefinite delay or an allocation justified under Section 2A–405, the lessee may by written notification to the lessor as to any goods involved, and with respect to all of the goods if under an installment lease contract the value of the whole lease contract is substantially impaired (Section 2A–510):

(a) terminate the lease contract (Section 2A–505(2)); or

(b) except in a finance lease that is not a consumer lease, modify the lease contract by accepting the available quota in substitution, with due allowance from the rent payable for the balance of the lease term for the deficiency but without further right against the lessor.

(2) If, after receipt of a notification from the lessor under Section 2A–405, the lessee fails so to modify the lease agreement within a reasonable time not exceeding 30 days, the lease contract lapses with respect to any deliveries affected.

§ 2A–407. Irrevocable Promises: Finance Leases.

(1) In the case of a finance lease that is not a consumer lease the lessee's promises under the lease contract become irrevocable and independent upon the lessee's acceptance of the goods.

(2) A promise that has become irrevocable and independent under subsection (1):

(a) is effective and enforceable between the parties, and by or against third parties including assignees of the parties, and

(b) is not subject to cancellation, termination, modification, repudiation, excuse, or substitution without the consent of the party to whom the promise runs.

(3) This section does not affect the validity under any other law of a covenant in any lease contract making the lessee's promises irrevocable and independent upon the lessee's acceptance of the goods.

As amended in 1990.

PART 5 Default

A. In General
§ 2A–501. Default: Procedure.

(1) Whether the lessor or the lessee is in default under a lease contract is determined by the lease agreement and this Article.

(2) If the lessor or the lessee is in default under the lease contract, the party seeking enforcement has rights and remedies as provided in this Article and, except as limited by this Article, as provided in the lease agreement.

(3) If the lessor or the lessee is in default under the lease contract, the party seeking enforcement may reduce the party's claim to judgment, or otherwise enforce the lease contract by self-help or any available judicial procedure or nonjudicial procedure, including administrative proceeding, arbitration, or the like, in accordance with this Article.

(4) Except as otherwise provided in Section 1–106(1) or this Article or the lease agreement, the rights and remedies referred to in subsections (2) and (3) are cumulative.

(5) If the lease agreement covers both real property and goods, the party seeking enforcement may proceed under this Part as to the goods, or under other applicable law as to both the real property and the goods in accordance with that party's rights and remedies in respect of the real property, in which case this Part does not apply.

As amended in 1990.

§ 2A–502. Notice After Default.

Except as otherwise provided in this Article or the lease agreement, the lessor or lessee in default under the lease contract is not entitled to notice of default or notice of enforcement from the other party to the lease agreement.

§ 2A–503. Modification or Impairment of Rights and Remedies.

(1) Except as otherwise provided in this Article, the lease agreement may include rights and remedies for default in addition to or in substitution for those provided in this Article and may limit or alter the measure of damages recoverable under this Article.

(2) Resort to a remedy provided under this Article or in the lease agreement is optional unless the remedy is expressly agreed to be exclusive. If circumstances cause an exclusive or limited remedy to fail of its essential purpose, or provision for an exclusive remedy is unconscionable, remedy may be had as provided in this Article.

(3) Consequential damages may be liquidated under Section 2A–504, or may otherwise be limited, altered, or excluded unless the limitation, alteration, or exclusion is unconscionable. Limitation, alteration, or exclusion of consequential damages for injury to the person in the case of consumer goods is prima facie unconscionable but limitation, alteration, or exclusion

of damages where the loss is commercial is not prima facie unconscionable.

(4) Rights and remedies on default by the lessor or the lessee with respect to any obligation or promise collateral or ancillary to the lease contract are not impaired by this Article.

As amended in 1990.

§ 2A–504. Liquidation of Damages.

(1) Damages payable by either party for default, or any other act or omission, including indemnity for loss or diminution of anticipated tax benefits or loss or damage to lessor's residual interest, may be liquidated in the lease agreement but only at an amount or by a formula that is reasonable in light of the then anticipated harm caused by the default or other act or omission.

(2) If the lease agreement provides for liquidation of damages, and such provision does not comply with subsection (1), or such provision is an exclusive or limited remedy that circumstances cause to fail of its essential purpose, remedy may be had as provided in this Article.

(3) If the lessor justifiably withholds or stops delivery of goods because of the lessee's default or insolvency (Section 2A–525 or 2A–526), the lessee is entitled to restitution of any amount by which the sum of his [or her] payments exceeds:

(a) the amount to which the lessor is entitled by virtue of terms liquidating the lessor's damages in accordance with subsection (1); or

(b) in the absence of those terms, 20 percent of the then present value of the total rent the lessee was obligated to pay for the balance of the lease term, or, in the case of a consumer lease, the lesser of such amount or $500.

(4) A lessee's right to restitution under subsection (3) is subject to offset to the extent the lessor establishes:

(a) a right to recover damages under the provisions of this Article other than subsection (1); and

(b) the amount or value of any benefits received by the lessee directly or indirectly by reason of the lease contract.

§ 2A–505. Cancellation and Termination and Effect of Cancellation, Termination, Rescission, or Fraud on Rights and Remedies.

(1) On cancellation of the lease contract, all obligations that are still executory on both sides are discharged, but any right based on prior default or performance survives, and the cancelling party also retains any remedy for default of the whole lease contract or any unperformed balance.

(2) On termination of the lease contract, all obligations that are still executory on both sides are discharged but any right based on prior default or performance survives.

(3) Unless the contrary intention clearly appears, expressions of "cancellation," "rescission," or the like of the lease contract may not be construed as a renunciation or discharge of any claim in damages for an antecedent default.

(4) Rights and remedies for material misrepresentation or fraud include all rights and remedies available under this Article for default.

(5) Neither rescission nor a claim for rescission of the lease contract nor rejection or return of the goods may bar or be deemed inconsistent with a claim for damages or other right or remedy.

§ 2A–506. Statute of Limitations.

(1) An action for default under a lease contract, including breach of warranty or indemnity, must be commenced within 4 years after the cause of action accrued. By the original lease contract the parties may reduce the period of limitation to not less than one year.

(2) A cause of action for default accrues when the act or omission on which the default or breach of warranty is based is or should have been discovered by the aggrieved party, or when the default occurs, whichever is later. A cause of action for indemnity accrues when the act or omission on which the claim for indemnity is based is or should have been discovered by the indemnified party, whichever is later.

(3) If an action commenced within the time limited by subsection (1) is so terminated as to leave available a remedy by another action for the same default or breach of warranty or indemnity, the other action may be commenced after the expiration of the time limited and within 6 months after the termination of the first action unless the termination resulted from voluntary discontinuance or from dismissal for failure or neglect to prosecute.

(4) This section does not alter the law on tolling of the statute of limitations nor does it apply to causes of action that have accrued before this Article becomes effective.

§ 2A–507. Proof of Market Rent: Time and Place.

(1) Damages based on market rent (Section 2A–519 or 2A–528) are determined according to the rent for the use of the goods concerned for a lease term identical to the remaining lease term of the original lease agreement and prevailing at the times specified in Sections 2A–519 and 2A–528.

(2) If evidence of rent for the use of the goods concerned for a lease term identical to the remaining lease term of the original lease agreement and prevailing at the times or places described in this Article is not readily available, the rent prevailing within any reasonable time before or after the time described or at any other place or for a different lease term which in commercial judgment or under usage of trade would serve as a reasonable substitute for the one described may be

used, making any proper allowance for the difference, including the cost of transporting the goods to or from the other place.

(3) Evidence of a relevant rent prevailing at a time or place or for a lease term other than the one described in this Article offered by one party is not admissible unless and until he [or she] has given the other party notice the court finds sufficient to prevent unfair surprise.

(4) If the prevailing rent or value of any goods regularly leased in any established market is in issue, reports in official publications or trade journals or in newspapers or periodicals of general circulation published as the reports of that market are admissible in evidence. The circumstances of the preparation of the report may be shown to affect its weight but not its admissibility.

As amended in 1990.

B. Default by Lessor

§ 2A–508. Lessee's Remedies.

(1) If a lessor fails to deliver the goods in conformity to the lease contract (Section 2A–509) or repudiates the lease contract (Section 2A–402), or a lessee rightfully rejects the goods (Section 2A–509) or justifiably revokes acceptance of the goods (Section 2A–517), then with respect to any goods involved, and with respect to all of the goods if under an installment lease contract the value of the whole lease contract is substantially impaired (Section 2A–510), the lessor is in default under the lease contract and the lessee may:

(a) cancel the lease contract (Section 2A–505(1));

(b) recover so much of the rent and security as has been paid and is just under the circumstances;

(c) cover and recover damages as to all goods affected whether or not they have been identified to the lease contract (Sections 2A–518 and 2A–520), or recover damages for nondelivery (Sections 2A–519 and 2A–520);

(d) exercise any other rights or pursue any other remedies provided in the lease contract.

(2) If a lessor fails to deliver the goods in conformity to the lease contract or repudiates the lease contract, the lessee may also:

(a) if the goods have been identified, recover them (Section 2A–522); or

(b) in a proper case, obtain specific performance or replevy the goods (Section 2A–521).

(3) If a lessor is otherwise in default under a lease contract, the lessee may exercise the rights and pursue the remedies provided in the lease contract, which may include a right to cancel the lease, and in Section 2A–519(3).

(4) If a lessor has breached a warranty, whether express or implied, the lessee may recover damages (Section 2A–519(4)).

(5) On rightful rejection or justifiable revocation of acceptance, a lessee has a security interest in goods in the lessee's possession or control for any rent and security that has been paid and any expenses reasonably incurred in their inspection, receipt, transportation, and care and custody and may hold those goods and dispose of them in good faith and in a commercially reasonable manner, subject to Section 2A–527(5).

(6) Subject to the provisions of Section 2A–407, a lessee, on notifying the lessor of the lessee's intention to do so, may deduct all or any part of the damages resulting from any default under the lease contract from any part of the rent still due under the same lease contract.

As amended in 1990.

§ 2A–509. Lessee's Rights on Improper Delivery; Rightful Rejection.

(1) Subject to the provisions of Section 2A–510 on default in installment lease contracts, if the goods or the tender or delivery fail in any respect to conform to the lease contract, the lessee may reject or accept the goods or accept any commercial unit or units and reject the rest of the goods.

(2) Rejection of goods is ineffective unless it is within a reasonable time after tender or delivery of the goods and the lessee seasonably notifies the lessor.

§ 2A–510. Installment Lease Contracts: Rejection and Default.

(1) Under an installment lease contract a lessee may reject any delivery that is nonconforming if the nonconformity substantially impairs the value of that delivery and cannot be cured or the nonconformity is a defect in the required documents; but if the nonconformity does not fall within subsection (2) and the lessor or the supplier gives adequate assurance of its cure, the lessee must accept that delivery.

(2) Whenever nonconformity or default with respect to one or more deliveries substantially impairs the value of the installment lease contract as a whole there is a default with respect to the whole. But, the aggrieved party reinstates the installment lease contract as a whole if the aggrieved party accepts a nonconforming delivery without seasonably notifying of cancellation or brings an action with respect only to past deliveries or demands performance as to future deliveries.

§ 2A–511. Merchant Lessee's Duties as to Rightfully Rejected Goods.

(1) Subject to any security interest of a lessee (Section 2A–508(5)), if a lessor or a supplier has no agent or place of business at the market of rejection, a merchant lessee, after rejection of goods in his [or her] possession or control, shall follow any reasonable instructions received from the lessor or the supplier with respect to the goods. In the absence of those instructions, a merchant lessee shall make reasonable efforts to sell, lease, or otherwise dispose of the goods for the lessor's account if they threaten to decline in value speedily.

Instructions are not reasonable if on demand indemnity for expenses is not forthcoming.

(2) If a merchant lessee (subsection (1)) or any other lessee (Section 2A–512) disposes of goods, he [or she] is entitled to reimbursement either from the lessor or the supplier or out of the proceeds for reasonable expenses of caring for and disposing of the goods and, if the expenses include no disposition commission, to such commission as is usual in the trade, or if there is none, to a reasonable sum not exceeding 10 percent of the gross proceeds.

(3) In complying with this section or Section 2A–512, the lessee is held only to good faith. Good faith conduct hereunder is neither acceptance or conversion nor the basis of an action for damages.

(4) A purchaser who purchases in good faith from a lessee pursuant to this section or Section 2A–512 takes the goods free of any rights of the lessor and the supplier even though the lessee fails to comply with one or more of the requirements of this Article.

§ 2A–512. Lessee's Duties as to Rightfully Rejected Goods.

(1) Except as otherwise provided with respect to goods that threaten to decline in value speedily (Section 2A–511) and subject to any security interest of a lessee (Section 2A–508(5)):

(a) the lessee, after rejection of goods in the lessee's possession, shall hold them with reasonable care at the lessor's or the supplier's disposition for a reasonable time after the lessee's seasonable notification of rejection;

(b) if the lessor or the supplier gives no instructions within a reasonable time after notification of rejection, the lessee may store the rejected goods for the lessor's or the supplier's account or ship them to the lessor or the supplier or dispose of them for the lessor's or the supplier's account with reimbursement in the manner provided in Section 2A–511; but

(c) the lessee has no further obligations with regard to goods rightfully rejected.

(2) Action by the lessee pursuant to subsection (1) is not acceptance or conversion.

§ 2A–513. Cure by Lessor of Improper Tender or Delivery; Replacement.

(1) If any tender or delivery by the lessor or the supplier is rejected because nonconforming and the time for performance has not yet expired, the lessor or the supplier may seasonably notify the lessee of the lessor's or the supplier's intention to cure and may then make a conforming delivery within the time provided in the lease contract.

(2) If the lessee rejects a nonconforming tender that the lessor or the supplier had reasonable grounds to believe would be acceptable with or without money allowance, the lessor or the supplier may have a further reasonable time to substitute a conforming tender if he [or she] seasonably notifies the lessee.

§ 2A–514. Waiver of Lessee's Objections.

(1) In rejecting goods, a lessee's failure to state a particular defect that is ascertainable by reasonable inspection precludes the lessee from relying on the defect to justify rejection or to establish default:

(a) if, stated seasonably, the lessor or the supplier could have cured it (Section 2A–513); or

(b) between merchants if the lessor or the supplier after rejection has made a request in writing for a full and final written statement of all defects on which the lessee proposes to rely.

(2) A lessee's failure to reserve rights when paying rent or other consideration against documents precludes recovery of the payment for defects apparent on the face of the documents.

§ 2A–515. Acceptance of Goods.

(1) Acceptance of goods occurs after the lessee has had a reasonable opportunity to inspect the goods and

(a) the lessee signifies or acts with respect to the goods in a manner that signifies to the lessor or the supplier that the goods are conforming or that the lessee will take or retain them in spite of their nonconformity; or

(b) the lessee fails to make an effective rejection of the goods (Section 2A–509(2)).

(2) Acceptance of a part of any commercial unit is acceptance of that entire unit.

§ 2A–516. Effect of Acceptance of Goods; Notice of Default; Burden of Establishing Default after Acceptance; Notice of Claim or Litigation to Person Answerable Over.

(1) A lessee must pay rent for any goods accepted in accordance with the lease contract, with due allowance for goods rightfully rejected or not delivered.

(2) A lessee's acceptance of goods precludes rejection of the goods accepted. In the case of a finance lease, if made with knowledge of a nonconformity, acceptance cannot be revoked because of it. In any other case, if made with knowledge of a nonconformity, acceptance cannot be revoked because of it unless the acceptance was on the reasonable assumption that the nonconformity would be seasonably cured. Acceptance does not of itself impair any other remedy provided by this Article or the lease agreement for nonconformity.

(3) If a tender has been accepted:

(a) within a reasonable time after the lessee discovers or should have discovered any default, the lessee shall notify the lessor and the supplier, if any, or be barred from any remedy against the party notified;

(b) except in the case of a consumer lease, within a reasonable time after the lessee receives notice of litigation for infringement or the like (Section 2A–211) the lessee shall notify the lessor or be barred from any remedy over for liability established by the litigation; and

(c) the burden is on the lessee to establish any default.

(4) If a lessee is sued for breach of a warranty or other obligation for which a lessor or a supplier is answerable over the following apply:

(a) The lessee may give the lessor or the supplier, or both, written notice of the litigation. If the notice states that the person notified may come in and defend and that if the person notified does not do so that person will be bound in any action against that person by the lessee by any determination of fact common to the two litigations, then unless the person notified after seasonable receipt of the notice does come in and defend that person is so bound.

(b) The lessor or the supplier may demand in writing that the lessee turn over control of the litigation including settlement if the claim is one for infringement or the like (Section 2A–211) or else be barred from any remedy over. If the demand states that the lessor or the supplier agrees to bear all expense and to satisfy any adverse judgment, then unless the lessee after seasonable receipt of the demand does turn over control the lessee is so barred.

(5) Subsections (3) and (4) apply to any obligation of a lessee to hold the lessor or the supplier harmless against infringement or the like (Section 2A–211).

As amended in 1990.

§ 2A–517. Revocation of Acceptance of Goods.

(1) A lessee may revoke acceptance of a lot or commercial unit whose nonconformity substantially impairs its value to the lessee if the lessee has accepted it:

(a) except in the case of a finance lease, on the reasonable assumption that its nonconformity would be cured and it has not been seasonably cured; or

(b) without discovery of the nonconformity if the lessee's acceptance was reasonably induced either by the lessor's assurances or, except in the case of a finance lease, by the difficulty of discovery before acceptance.

(2) Except in the case of a finance lease that is not a consumer lease, a lessee may revoke acceptance of a lot or commercial unit if the lessor defaults under the lease contract and the default substantially impairs the value of that lot or commercial unit to the lessee.

(3) If the lease agreement so provides, the lessee may revoke acceptance of a lot or commercial unit because of other defaults by the lessor.

(4) Revocation of acceptance must occur within a reasonable time after the lessee discovers or should have discovered the ground for it and before any substantial change in condition of the goods which is not caused by the nonconformity. Revocation is not effective until the lessee notifies the lessor.

(5) A lessee who so revokes has the same rights and duties with regard to the goods involved as if the lessee had rejected them.

As amended in 1990.

§ 2A–518. Cover; Substitute Goods.

(1) After a default by a lessor under the lease contract of the type described in Section 2A–508(1), or, if agreed, after other default by the lessor, the lessee may cover by making any purchase or lease of or contract to purchase or lease goods in substitution for those due from the lessor.

(2) Except as otherwise provided with respect to damages liquidated in the lease agreement (Section 2A–504) or otherwise determined pursuant to agreement of the parties (Sections 1–102(3) and 2A–503), if a lessee's cover is by lease agreement substantially similar to the original lease agreement and the new lease agreement is made in good faith and in a commercially reasonable manner, the lessee may recover from the lessor as damages (i) the present value, as of the date of the commencement of the term of the new lease agreement, of the rent under the new lease agreement applicable to that period of the new lease term which is comparable to the then remaining term of the original lease agreement minus the present value as of the same date of the total rent for the then remaining lease term of the original lease agreement, and (ii) any incidental or consequential damages, less expenses saved in consequence of the lessor's default.

(3) If a lessee's cover is by lease agreement that for any reason does not qualify for treatment under subsection (2), or is by purchase or otherwise, the lessee may recover from the lessor as if the lessee had elected not to cover and Section 2A–519 governs.

As amended in 1990.

§ 2A–519. Lessee's Damages for Non-Delivery, Repudiation, Default, and Breach of Warranty in Regard to Accepted Goods.

(1) Except as otherwise provided with respect to damages liquidated in the lease agreement (Section 2A–504) or otherwise determined pursuant to agreement of the parties (Sections 1–102(3) and 2A–503), if a lessee elects not to cover or a lessee elects to cover and the cover is by lease agreement that for any reason does not qualify for treatment under Section 2A–518(2), or is by purchase or otherwise, the measure of damages for non-delivery or repudiation by the lessor or for rejection or revocation of acceptance by the lessee is the present value, as of

the date of the default, of the then market rent minus the present value as of the same date of the original rent, computed for the remaining lease term of the original lease agreement, together with incidental and consequential damages, less expenses saved in consequence of the lessor's default.

(2) Market rent is to be determined as of the place for tender or, in cases of rejection after arrival or revocation of acceptance, as of the place of arrival.

(3) Except as otherwise agreed, if the lessee has accepted goods and given notification (Section 2A–516(3)), the measure of damages for non-conforming tender or delivery or other default by a lessor is the loss resulting in the ordinary course of events from the lessor's default as determined in any manner that is reasonable together with incidental and consequential damages, less expenses saved in consequence of the lessor's default.

(4) Except as otherwise agreed, the measure of damages for breach of warranty is the present value at the time and place of acceptance of the difference between the value of the use of the goods accepted and the value if they had been as warranted for the lease term, unless special circumstances show proximate damages of a different amount, together with incidental and consequential damages, less expenses saved in consequence of the lessor's default or breach of warranty.

As amended in 1990.

§ 2A-520. Lessee's Incidental and Consequential Damages.

(1) Incidental damages resulting from a lessor's default include expenses reasonably incurred in inspection, receipt, transportation, and care and custody of goods rightfully rejected or goods the acceptance of which is justifiably revoked, any commercially reasonable charges, expenses or commissions in connection with effecting cover, and any other reasonable expense incident to the default.

(2) Consequential damages resulting from a lessor's default include:

   (a) any loss resulting from general or particular requirements and needs of which the lessor at the time of contracting had reason to know and which could not reasonably be prevented by cover or otherwise; and

   (b) injury to person or property proximately resulting from any breach of warranty.

§ 2A-521. Lessee's Right to Specific Performance or Replevin.

(1) Specific performance may be decreed if the goods are unique or in other proper circumstances.

(2) A decree for specific performance may include any terms and conditions as to payment of the rent, damages, or other relief that the court deems just.

(3) A lessee has a right of replevin, detinue, sequestration, claim and delivery, or the like for goods identified to the lease contract if after reasonable effort the lessee is unable to effect cover for those goods or the circumstances reasonably indicate that the effort will be unavailing.

§ 2A-522. Lessee's Right to Goods on Lessor's Insolvency.

(1) Subject to subsection (2) and even though the goods have not been shipped, a lessee who has paid a part or all of the rent and security for goods identified to a lease contract (Section 2A–217) on making and keeping good a tender of any unpaid portion of the rent and security due under the lease contract may recover the goods identified from the lessor if the lessor becomes insolvent within 10 days after receipt of the first installment of rent and security.

(2) A lessee acquires the right to recover goods identified to a lease contract only if they conform to the lease contract.

C. Default by Lessee

§ 2A-523. Lessor's Remedies.

(1) If a lessee wrongfully rejects or revokes acceptance of goods or fails to make a payment when due or repudiates with respect to a part or the whole, then, with respect to any goods involved, and with respect to all of the goods if under an installment lease contract the value of the whole lease contract is substantially impaired (Section 2A–510), the lessee is in default under the lease contract and the lessor may:

   (a) cancel the lease contract (Section 2A–505(1));

   (b) proceed respecting goods not identified to the lease contract (Section 2A–524);

   (c) withhold delivery of the goods and take possession of goods previously delivered (Section 2A–525);

   (d) stop delivery of the goods by any bailee (Section 2A–526);

   (e) dispose of the goods and recover damages (Section 2A–527), or retain the goods and recover damages (Section 2A–528), or in a proper case recover rent (Section 2A–529)

   (f) exercise any other rights or pursue any other remedies provided in the lease contract.

(2) If a lessor does not fully exercise a right or obtain a remedy to which the lessor is entitled under subsection (1), the lessor may recover the loss resulting in the ordinary course of events from the lessee's default as determined in any reasonable manner, together with incidental damages, less expenses saved in consequence of the lessee's default.

(3) If a lessee is otherwise in default under a lease contract, the lessor may exercise the rights and pursue the remedies provided in the lease contract, which may include a right to cancel the lease. In addition, unless otherwise provided in the lease contract:

   (a) if the default substantially impairs the value of the lease contract to the lessor, the lessor may exercise the rights and pursue the remedies provided in subsections (1) or (2); or

(b) if the default does not substantially impair the value of the lease contract to the lessor, the lessor may recover as provided in subsection (2).

As amended in 1990.

§ 2A–524. Lessor's Right to Identify Goods to Lease Contract.

(1) After default by the lessee under the lease contract of the type described in Section 2A–523(1) or 2A–523(3)(a) or, if agreed, after other default by the lessee, the lessor may:

(a) identify to the lease contract conforming goods not already identified if at the time the lessor learned of the default they were in the lessor's or the supplier's possession or control; and

(b) dispose of goods (Section 2A–527(1)) that demonstrably have been intended for the particular lease contract even though those goods are unfinished.

(2) If the goods are unfinished, in the exercise of reasonable commercial judgment for the purposes of avoiding loss and of effective realization, an aggrieved lessor or the supplier may either complete manufacture and wholly identify the goods to the lease contract or cease manufacture and lease, sell, or otherwise dispose of the goods for scrap or salvage value or proceed in any other reasonable manner.

As amended in 1990.

§ 2A–525. Lessor's Right to Possession of Goods.

(1) If a lessor discovers the lessee to be insolvent, the lessor may refuse to deliver the goods.

(2) After a default by the lessee under the lease contract of the type described in Section 2A–523(1) or 2A–523(3)(a) or, if agreed, after other default by the lessee, the lessor has the right to take possession of the goods. If the lease contract so provides, the lessor may require the lessee to assemble the goods and make them available to the lessor at a place to be designated by the lessor which is reasonably convenient to both parties. Without removal, the lessor may render unusable any goods employed in trade or business, and may dispose of goods on the lessee's premises (Section 2A–527).

(3) The lessor may proceed under subsection (2) without judicial process if that can be done without breach of the peace or the lessor may proceed by action.

As amended in 1990.

§ 2A–526. Lessor's Stoppage of Delivery in Transit or Otherwise.

(1) A lessor may stop delivery of goods in the possession of a carrier or other bailee if the lessor discovers the lessee to be insolvent and may stop delivery of carload, truckload, plane-

load, or larger shipments of express or freight if the lessee repudiates or fails to make a payment due before delivery, whether for rent, security or otherwise under the lease contract, or for any other reason the lessor has a right to withhold or take possession of the goods.

(2) In pursuing its remedies under subsection (1), the lessor may stop delivery until

(a) receipt of the goods by the lessee;

(b) acknowledgment to the lessee by any bailee of the goods, except a carrier, that the bailee holds the goods for the lessee; or

(c) such an acknowledgment to the lessee by a carrier via reshipment or as warehouseman.

(3) (a) To stop delivery, a lessor shall so notify as to enable the bailee by reasonable diligence to prevent delivery of the goods.

(b) After notification, the bailee shall hold and deliver the goods according to the directions of the lessor, but the lessor is liable to the bailee for any ensuing charges or damages.

(c) A carrier who has issued a nonnegotiable bill of lading is not obliged to obey a notification to stop received from a person other than the consignor.

§ 2A–527. Lessor's Rights to Dispose of Goods.

(1) After a default by a lessee under the lease contract of the type described in Section 2A–523(1) or 2A–523(3)(a) or after the lessor refuses to deliver or takes possession of goods (Section 2A–525 or 2A–526), or, if agreed, after other default by a lessee, the lessor may dispose of the goods concerned or the undelivered balance thereof by lease, sale, or otherwise.

(2) Except as otherwise provided with respect to damages liquidated in the lease agreement (Section 2A–504) or otherwise determined pursuant to agreement of the parties (Sections 1–102(3) and 2A–503), if the disposition is by lease agreement substantially similar to the original lease agreement and the new lease agreement is made in good faith and in a commercially reasonable manner, the lessor may recover from the lessee as damages (i) accrued and unpaid rent as of the date of the commencement of the term of the new lease agreement, (ii) the present value, as of the same date, of the total rent for the then remaining lease term of the original lease agreement minus the present value, as of the same date, of the rent under the new lease agreement applicable to that period of the new lease term which is comparable to the then remaining term of the original lease agreement, and (iii) any incidental damages allowed under Section 2A–530, less expenses saved in consequence of the lessee's default.

(3) If the lessor's disposition is by lease agreement that for any reason does not qualify for treatment under subsection (2), or is by sale or otherwise, the lessor may recover from the lessee as if the lessor had elected not to dispose of the goods and Section 2A–528 governs.

(4) A subsequent buyer or lessee who buys or leases from the lessor in good faith for value as a result of a disposition under this section takes the goods free of the original lease contract and any rights of the original lessee even though the lessor fails to comply with one or more of the requirements of this Article. (5) The lessor is not accountable to the lessee for any profit made on any disposition. A lessee who has rightfully rejected or justifiably revoked acceptance shall account to the lessor for any excess over the amount of the lessee's security interest (Section 2A–508(5)).

As amended in 1990.

§ 2A–528. Lessor's Damages for Non-acceptance, Failure to Pay, Repudiation, or Other Default.

(1) Except as otherwise provided with respect to damages liquidated in the lease agreement (Section 2A–504) or otherwise determined pursuant to agreement of the parties (Section 1–102(3) and 2A–503), if a lessor elects to retain the goods or a lessor elects to dispose of the goods and the disposition is by lease agreement that for any reason does not qualify for treatment under Section 2A–527(2), or is by sale or otherwise, the lessor may recover from the lessee as damages for a default of the type described in Section 2A–523(1) or 2A–523(3)(a), or if agreed, for other default of the lessee, (i) accrued and unpaid rent as of the date of the default if the lessee has never taken possession of the goods, or, if the lessee has taken possession of the goods, as of the date the lessor repossesses the goods or an earlier date on which the lessee makes a tender of the goods to the lessor, (ii) the present value as of the date determined under clause (i) of the total rent for the then remaining lease term of the original lease agreement minus the present value as of the same date of the market rent as the place where the goods are located computed for the same lease term, and (iii) any incidental damages allowed under Section 2A–530, less expenses saved in consequence of the lessee's default.

(2) If the measure of damages provided in subsection (1) is inadequate to put a lessor in as good a position as performance would have, the measure of damages is the present value of the profit, including reasonable overhead, the lessor would have made from full performance by the lessee, together with any incidental damages allowed under Section 2A–530, due allowance for costs reasonably incurred and due credit for payments or proceeds of disposition.

As amended in 1990.

§ 2A–529. Lessor's Action for the Rent.

(1) After default by the lessee under the lease contract of the type described in Section 2A–523(1) or 2A–523(3)(a) or, if agreed, after other default by the lessee, if the lessor complies with subsection (2), the lessor may recover from the lessee as damages:

(a) for goods accepted by the lessee and not repossessed by or tendered to the lessor, and for conforming goods lost or damaged within a commercially reasonable time after risk of loss passes to the lessee (Section 2A–219), (i) accrued and unpaid rent as of the date of entry of judgment in favor of the lessor (ii) the present value as of the same date of the rent for the then remaining lease term of the lease agreement, and (iii) any incidental damages allowed under Section 2A–530, less expenses saved in consequence of the lessee's default; and

(b) for goods identified to the lease contract if the lessor is unable after reasonable effort to dispose of them at a reasonable price or the circumstances reasonably indicate that effort will be unavailing, (i) accrued and unpaid rent as of the date of entry of judgment in favor of the lessor, (ii) the present value as of the same date of the rent for the then remaining lease term of the lease agreement, and (iii) any incidental damages allowed under Section 2A–530, less expenses saved in consequence of the lessee's default.

(2) Except as provided in subsection (3), the lessor shall hold for the lessee for the remaining lease term of the lease agreement any goods that have been identified to the lease contract and are in the lessor's control.

(3) The lessor may dispose of the goods at any time before collection of the judgment for damages obtained pursuant to subsection (1). If the disposition is before the end of the remaining lease term of the lease agreement, the lessor's recovery against the lessee for damages is governed by Section 2A–527 or Section 2A–528, and the lessor will cause an appropriate credit to be provided against a judgment for damages to the extent that the amount of the judgment exceeds the recovery available pursuant to Section 2A–527 or 2A–528.

(4) Payment of the judgment for damages obtained pursuant to subsection (1) entitles the lessee to the use and possession of the goods not then disposed of for the remaining lease term of and in accordance with the lease agreement.

(5) After default by the lessee under the lease contract of the type described in Section 2A–523(1) or Section 2A–523(3)(a) or, if agreed, after other default by the lessee, a lessor who is held not entitled to rent under this section must nevertheless be awarded damages for non-acceptance under Sections 2A–527 and 2A–528.

As amended in 1990.

§ 2A–530. Lessor's Incidental Damages.

Incidental damages to an aggrieved lessor include any commercially reasonable charges, expenses, or commissions incurred in stopping delivery, in the transportation, care and custody of goods after the lessee's default, in connection with return or disposition of the goods, or otherwise resulting from the default.

§ 2A-531. Standing to Sue Third Parties for Injury to Goods.

(1) If a third party so deals with goods that have been identified to a lease contract as to cause actionable injury to a party to the lease contract (a) the lessor has a right of action against the third party, and (b) the lessee also has a right of action against the third party if the lessee:

(i) has a security interest in the goods;

(ii) has an insurable interest in the goods; or

(iii) bears the risk of loss under the lease contract or has since the injury assumed that risk as against the lessor and the goods have been converted or destroyed.

(2) If at the time of the injury the party plaintiff did not bear the risk of loss as against the other party to the lease contract and there is no arrangement between them for disposition of the recovery, his [or her] suit or settlement, subject to his [or her] own interest, is as a fiduciary for the other party to the lease contract.

(3) Either party with the consent of the other may sue for the benefit of whom it may concern.

§ 2A-532. Lessor's Rights to Residual Interest.

In addition to any other recovery permitted by this Article or other law, the lessor may recover from the lessee an amount that will fully compensate the lessor for any loss of or damage to the lessor's residual interest in the goods caused by the default of the lessee.

As added in 1990.

REVISED ARTICLE 3

NEGOTIABLE INSTRUMENTS

PART 1   General Provisions and Definitions

§ 3-101.   Short Title.

This Article may be cited as Uniform Commercial Code–Negotiable Instruments.

§ 3-102.   Subject Matter.

(a) This Article applies to negotiable instruments. It does not apply to money, to payment orders governed by Article 4A, or to securities governed by Article 8.

(b) If there is conflict between this Article and Article 4 or 9, Articles 4 and 9 govern.

(c) Regulations of the Board of Governors of the Federal Reserve System and operating circulars of the Federal Reserve

Banks supersede any inconsistent provision of this Article to the extent of the inconsistency.

§ 3-103.   Definitions.

(a) In this Article:

(1) "Acceptor" means a drawee who has accepted a draft.

(2) "Drawee" means a person ordered in a draft to make payment.

(3) "Drawer" means a person who signs or is identified in a draft as a person ordering payment.

(4) "Good faith" means honesty in fact and the observance of reasonable commercial standards of fair dealing.

(5) "Maker" means a person who signs or is identified in a note as a person undertaking to pay.

(6) "Order" means a written instruction to pay money signed by the person giving the instruction. The instruction may be addressed to any person, including the person giving the instruction, or to one or more persons jointly or in the alternative but not in succession. An authorization to pay is not an order unless the person authorized to pay is also instructed to pay.

(7) "Ordinary care" in the case of a person engaged in business means observance of reasonable commercial standards, prevailing in the area in which the person is located, with respect to the business in which the person is engaged. In the case of a bank that takes an instrument for processing for collection or payment by automated means, reasonable commercial standards do not require the bank to examine the instrument if the failure to examine does not violate the bank's prescribed procedures and the bank's procedures do not vary unreasonably from general banking usage not disapproved by this Article or Article 4.

(8) "Party" means a party to an instrument.

(9) "Promise" means a written undertaking to pay money signed by the person undertaking to pay. An acknowledgment of an obligation by the obligor is not a promise unless the obligor also undertakes to pay the obligation.

(10) "Prove" with respect to a fact means to meet the burden of establishing the fact (Section 1–201(8)).

(11) "Remitter" means a person who purchases an instrument from its issuer if the instrument is payable to an identified person other than the purchaser.

(b) [Other definitions' section references deleted.]

(c) [Other definitions' section references deleted.]

(d) In addition, Article 1 contains general definitions and principles of construction and interpretation applicable throughout this Article.

§ 3-104.   Negotiable Instrument.

(a) Except as provided in subsections (c) and (d), "negotiable instrument" means an unconditional promise or order to pay a fixed amount of money, with or without interest or other charges described in the promise or order, if it:

(1) is payable to bearer or to order at the time it is issued or first comes into possession of a holder;

(2) is payable on demand or at a definite time; and

(3) does not state any other undertaking or instruction by the person promising or ordering payment to do any act in addition to the payment of money, but the promise or order may contain (i) an undertaking or power to give, maintain, or protect collateral to secure payment, (ii) an authorization or power to the holder to confess judgment or realize on or dispose of collateral, or (iii) a waiver of the benefit of any law intended for the advantage or protection of an obligor.

(b) "Instrument" means a negotiable instrument.

(c) An order that meets all of the requirements of subsection (a), except paragraph (1), and otherwise falls within the definition of "check" in subsection (f) is a negotiable instrument and a check.

(d) A promise or order other than a check is not an instrument if, at the time it is issued or first comes into possession of a holder, it contains a conspicuous statement, however expressed, to the effect that the promise or order is not negotiable or is not an instrument governed by this Article.

(e) An instrument is a "note" if it is a promise and is a "draft" if it is an order. If an instrument falls within the definition of both "note" and "draft," a person entitled to enforce the instrument may treat it as either.

(f) "Check" means (i) a draft, other than a documentary draft, payable on demand and drawn on a bank or (ii) a cashier's check or teller's check. An instrument may be a check even though it is described on its face by another term, such as "money order."

(g) "Cashier's check" means a draft with respect to which the drawer and drawee are the same bank or branches of the same bank.

(h) "Teller's check" means a draft drawn by a bank (i) on another bank, or (ii) payable at or through a bank.

(i) "Traveler's check" means an instrument that (i) is payable on demand, (ii) is drawn on or payable at or through a bank, (iii) is designated by the term "traveler's check" or by a substantially similar term, and (iv) requires, as a condition to payment, a countersignature by a person whose specimen signature appears on the instrument.

(j) "Certificate of deposit" means an instrument containing an acknowledgment by a bank that a sum of money has been received by the bank and a promise by the bank to repay the sum of money. A certificate of deposit is a note of the bank.

§ 3–105.   Issue of Instrument.

(a) "Issue" means the first delivery of an instrument by the maker or drawer, whether to a holder or nonholder, for the purpose of giving rights on the instrument to any person.

(b) An unissued instrument, or an unissued incomplete instrument that is completed, is binding on the maker or drawer, but

nonissuance is a defense. An instrument that is conditionally issued or is issued for a special purpose is binding on the maker or drawer, but failure of the condition or special purpose to be fulfilled is a defense.

(c) "Issuer" applies to issued and unissued instruments and means a maker or drawer of an instrument.

§ 3–106.   Unconditional Promise or Order.

(a) Except as provided in this section, for the purposes of Section 3–104(a), a promise or order is unconditional unless it states (i) an express condition to payment, (ii) that the promise or order is subject to or governed by another writing, or (iii) that rights or obligations with respect to the promise or order are stated in another writing. A reference to another writing does not of itself make the promise or order conditional.

(b) A promise or order is not made conditional (i) by a reference to another writing for a statement of rights with respect to collateral, prepayment, or acceleration, or (ii) because payment is limited to resort to a particular fund or source.

(c) If a promise or order requires, as a condition to payment, a countersignature by a person whose specimen signature appears on the promise or order, the condition does not make the promise or order conditional for the purposes of Section 3–104(a). If the person whose specimen signature appears on an instrument fails to countersign the instrument, the failure to countersign is a defense to the obligation of the issuer, but the failure does not prevent a transferee of the instrument from becoming a holder of the instrument.

(d) If a promise or order at the time it is issued or first comes into possession of a holder contains a statement, required by applicable statutory or administrative law, to the effect that the rights of a holder or transferee are subject to claims or defenses that the issuer could assert against the original payee, the promise or order is not thereby made conditional for the purposes of Section 3–104(a); but if the promise or order is an instrument, there cannot be a holder in due course of the instrument.

§ 3–107.   Instrument Payable in Foreign Money.

Unless the instrument otherwise provides, an instrument that states the amount payable in foreign money may be paid in the foreign money or in an equivalent amount in dollars calculated by using the current bank-offered spot rate at the place of payment for the purchase of dollars on the day on which the instrument is paid.

§ 3–108.   Payable on Demand or at Definite Time.

(a) A promise or order is "payable on demand" if it (i) states that it is payable on demand or at sight, or otherwise indicates that it is payable at the will of the holder, or (ii) does not state any time of payment.

(b) A promise or order is "payable at a definite time" if it is payable on elapse of a definite period of time after sight or acceptance or at a fixed date or dates or at a time or times readily ascertainable at the time the promise or order is issued, subject to rights of (i) prepayment, (ii) acceleration, (iii) extension at the option of the holder, or (iv) extension to a further definite time at the option of the maker or acceptor or automatically upon or after a specified act or event.

(c) If an instrument, payable at a fixed date, is also payable upon demand made before the fixed date, the instrument is payable on demand until the fixed date and, if demand for payment is not made before that date, becomes payable at a definite time on the fixed date.

§ 3–109.   Payable to Bearer or to Order.

(a) A promise or order is payable to bearer if it:

(1) states that it is payable to bearer or to the order of bearer or otherwise indicates that the person in possession of the promise or order is entitled to payment;

(2) does not state a payee; or

(3) states that it is payable to or to the order of cash or otherwise indicates that it is not payable to an identified person.

(b) A promise or order that is not payable to bearer is payable to order if it is payable (i) to the order of an identified person or (ii) to an identified person or order. A promise or order that is payable to order is payable to the identified person.

(c) An instrument payable to bearer may become payable to an identified person if it is specially indorsed pursuant to Section 3–205(a). An instrument payable to an identified person may become payable to bearer if it is indorsed in blank pursuant to Section 3–205(b).

§ 3–110.   Identification of Person to Whom Instrument Is Payable.

(a) The person to whom an instrument is initially payable is determined by the intent of the person, whether or not authorized, signing as, or in the name or behalf of, the issuer of the instrument. The instrument is payable to the person intended by the signer even if that person is identified in the instrument by a name or other identification that is not that of the intended person. If more than one person signs in the name or behalf of the issuer of an instrument and all the signers do not intend the same person as payee, the instrument is payable to any person intended by one or more of the signers.

(b) If the signature of the issuer of an instrument is made by automated means, such as a check-writing machine, the payee of the instrument is determined by the intent of the person who supplied the name or identification of the payee, whether or not authorized to do so.

(c) A person to whom an instrument is payable may be identified in any way, including by name, identifying number, office, or account number. For the purpose of determining the holder of an instrument, the following rules apply:

(1) If an instrument is payable to an account and the account is identified only by number, the instrument is payable to the person to whom the account is payable. If an instrument is payable to an account identified by number and by the name of a person, the instrument is payable to the named person, whether or not that person is the owner of the account identified by number.

(2) If an instrument is payable to:

(i) a trust, an estate, or a person described as trustee or representative of a trust or estate, the instrument is payable to the trustee, the representative, or a successor of either, whether or not the beneficiary or estate is also named;

(ii) a person described as agent or similar representative of a named or identified person, the instrument is payable to the represented person, the representative, or a successor of the representative;

(iii) a fund or organization that is not a legal entity, the instrument is payable to a representative of the members of the fund or organization; or

(iv) an office or to a person described as holding an office, the instrument is payable to the named person, the incumbent of the office, or a successor to the incumbent.

(d) If an instrument is payable to two or more persons alternatively, it is payable to any of them and may be negotiated, discharged, or enforced by any or all of them in possession of the instrument. If an instrument is payable to two or more persons not alternatively, it is payable to all of them and may be negotiated, discharged, or enforced only by all of them. If an instrument payable to two or more persons is ambiguous as to whether it is payable to the persons alternatively, the instrument is payable to the persons alternatively.

§ 3–111.   Place of Payment.

Except as otherwise provided for items in Article 4, an instrument is payable at the place of payment stated in the instrument. If no place of payment is stated, an instrument is payable at the address of the drawee or maker stated in the instrument. If no address is stated, the place of payment is the place of business of the drawee or maker. If a drawee or maker has more than one place of business, the place of payment is any place of business of the drawee or maker chosen by the person entitled to enforce the instrument. If the drawee or maker has no place of business, the place of payment is the residence of the drawee or maker.

§ 3–112.   Interest.

(a) Unless otherwise provided in the instrument, (i) an instrument is not payable with interest, and (ii) interest on an interest-bearing instrument is payable from the date of the instrument.

(b) Interest may be stated in an instrument as a fixed or variable amount of money or it may be expressed as a fixed or variable rate or rates. The amount or rate of interest may be stated or described in the instrument in any manner and may require reference to information not contained in the instrument. If an instrument provides for interest, but the amount of interest payable cannot be ascertained from the description, interest is payable at the judgment rate in effect at the place of payment of the instrument and at the time interest first accrues.

§ 3–113.   Date of Instrument.

(a) An instrument may be antedated or postdated. The date stated determines the time of payment if the instrument is payable at a fixed period after date. Except as provided in Section 4–401(c), an instrument payable on demand is not payable before the date of the instrument.

(b) If an instrument is undated, its date is the date of its issue or, in the case of an unissued instrument, the date it first comes into possession of a holder.

§ 3–114.   Contradictory Terms of Instrument.

If an instrument contains contradictory terms, typewritten terms prevail over printed terms, handwritten terms prevail over both, and words prevail over numbers.

§ 3–115.   Incomplete Instrument.

(a) "Incomplete instrument" means a signed writing, whether or not issued by the signer, the contents of which show at the time of signing that it is incomplete but that the signer intended it to be completed by the addition of words or numbers.

(b) Subject to subsection (c), if an incomplete instrument is an instrument under Section 3–104, it may be enforced according to its terms if it is not completed, or according to its terms as augmented by completion. If an incomplete instrument is not an instrument under Section 3–104, but, after completion, the requirements of Section 3–104 are met, the instrument may be enforced according to its terms as augmented by completion.

(c) If words or numbers are added to an incomplete instrument without authority of the signer, there is an alteration of the incomplete instrument under Section 3–407.

(d) The burden of establishing that words or numbers were added to an incomplete instrument without authority of the signer is on the person asserting the lack of authority.

§ 3–116.   Joint and Several Liability; Contribution.

(a) Except as otherwise provided in the instrument, two or more persons who have the same liability on an instrument as makers, drawers, acceptors, indorsers who indorse as joint payees, or anomalous indorsers are jointly and severally liable in the capacity in which they sign.

(b) Except as provided in Section 3–419(e) or by agreement of the affected parties, a party having joint and several liability who pays the instrument is entitled to receive from any party having the same joint and several liability contribution in accordance with applicable law.

(c) Discharge of one party having joint and several liability by a person entitled to enforce the instrument does not affect the right under subsection (b) of a party having the same joint and several liability to receive contribution from the party discharged.

§ 3–117.   Other Agreements Affecting Instrument.

Subject to applicable law regarding exclusion of proof of contemporaneous or previous agreements, the obligation of a party to an instrument to pay the instrument may be modified, supplemented, or nullified by a separate agreement of the obligor and a person entitled to enforce the instrument, if the instrument is issued or the obligation is incurred in reliance on the agreement or as part of the same transaction giving rise to the agreement. To the extent an obligation is modified, supplemented, or nullified by an agreement under this section, the agreement is a defense to the obligation.

§ 3–118.   Statute of Limitations.

(a) Except as provided in subsection (e), an action to enforce the obligation of a party to pay a note payable at a definite time must be commenced within six years after the due date or dates stated in the note or, if a due date is accelerated, within six years after the accelerated due date.

(b) Except as provided in subsection (d) or (e), if demand for payment is made to the maker of a note payable on demand, an action to enforce the obligation of a party to pay the note must be commenced within six years after the demand. If no demand for payment is made to the maker, an action to enforce the note is barred if neither principal nor interest on the note has been paid for a continuous period of 10 years.

(c) Except as provided in subsection (d), an action to enforce the obligation of a party to an unaccepted draft to pay the draft must be commenced within three years after dishonor of the draft or 10 years after the date of the draft, whichever period expires first.

(d) An action to enforce the obligation of the acceptor of a certified check or the issuer of a teller's check, cashier's check, or traveler's check must be commenced within three years after demand for payment is made to the acceptor or issuer, as the case may be.

(e) An action to enforce the obligation of a party to a certificate of deposit to pay the instrument must be commenced within six years after demand for payment is made to the maker, but if the instrument states a due date and the maker is not required to pay before that date, the six-year period begins when a demand for payment is in effect and the due date has passed.

(f) An action to enforce the obligation of a party to pay an accepted draft, other than a certified check, must be commenced (i) within six years after the due date or dates stated in the draft or acceptance if the obligation of the acceptor is payable at a definite time, or (ii) within six years after the date of the acceptance if the obligation of the acceptor is payable on demand.

(g) Unless governed by other law regarding claims for indemnity or contribution, an action (i) for conversion of an instrument, for money had and received, or like action based on conversion, (ii) for breach of warranty, or (iii) to enforce an obligation, duty, or right arising under this Article and not governed by this section must be commenced within three years after the [cause of action] accrues.

§ 3–119.   Notice of Right to Defend Action.

In an action for breach of an obligation for which a third person is answerable over pursuant to this Article or Article 4, the defendant may give the third person written notice of the litigation, and the person notified may then give similar notice to any other person who is answerable over. If the notice states (i) that the person notified may come in and defend and (ii) that failure to do so will bind the person notified in an action later brought by the person giving the notice as to any determination of fact common to the two litigations, the person notified is so bound unless after seasonable receipt of the notice the person notified does come in and defend.

PART 2   Negotiation, Transfer, and Indorsement

§ 3–201.   Negotiation.

(a) "Negotiation" means a transfer of possession, whether voluntary or involuntary, of an instrument by a person other than the issuer to a person who thereby becomes its holder.

(b) Except for negotiation by a remitter, if an instrument is payable to an identified person, negotiation requires transfer of possession of the instrument and its indorsement by the holder. If an instrument is payable to bearer, it may be negotiated by transfer of possession alone.

§ 3–202.   Negotiation Subject to Rescission.

(a) Negotiation is effective even if obtained (i) from an infant, a corporation exceeding its powers, or a person without capacity, (ii) by fraud, duress, or mistake, or (iii) in breach of duty or as part of an illegal transaction.

(b) To the extent permitted by other law, negotiation may be rescinded or may be subject to other remedies, but those reme-

dies may not be asserted against a subsequent holder in due course or a person paying the instrument in good faith and without knowledge of facts that are a basis for rescission or other remedy.

§ 3–203.   Transfer of Instrument; Rights Acquired by Transfer.

(a) An instrument is transferred when it is delivered by a person other than its issuer for the purpose of giving to the person receiving delivery the right to enforce the instrument.

(b) Transfer of an instrument, whether or not the transfer is a negotiation, vests in the transferee any right of the transferor to enforce the instrument, including any right as a holder in due course, but the transferee cannot acquire rights of a holder in due course by a transfer, directly or indirectly, from a holder in due course if the transferee engaged in fraud or illegality affecting the instrument.

(c) Unless otherwise agreed, if an instrument is transferred for value and the transferee does not become a holder because of lack of indorsement by the transferor, the transferee has a specifically enforceable right to the unqualified indorsement of the transferor, but negotiation of the instrument does not occur until the indorsement is made.

(d) If a transferor purports to transfer less than the entire instrument, negotiation of the instrument does not occur. The transferee obtains no rights under this Article and has only the rights of a partial assignee.

§ 3–204.   Indorsement.

(a) "Indorsement" means a signature, other than that of a signer as maker, drawer, or acceptor, that alone or accompanied by other words is made on an instrument for the purpose of (i) negotiating the instrument, (ii) restricting payment of the instrument, or (iii) incurring indorser's liability on the instrument, but regardless of the intent of the signer, a signature and its accompanying words is an indorsement unless the accompanying words, terms of the instrument, place of the signature, or other circumstances unambiguously indicate that the signature was made for a purpose other than indorsement. For the purpose of determining whether a signature is made on an instrument, a paper affixed to the instrument is a part of the instrument.

(b) "Indorser" means a person who makes an indorsement.

(c) For the purpose of determining whether the transferee of an instrument is a holder, an indorsement that transfers a security interest in the instrument is effective as an unqualified indorsement of the instrument.

(d) If an instrument is payable to a holder under a name that is not the name of the holder, indorsement may be made by the holder in the name stated in the instrument or in the holder's name or both, but signature in both names may be required by a person paying or taking the instrument for value or collection.

§ 3–205. Special Indorsement; Blank Indorsement; Anomalous Indorsement.

(a) If an indorsement is made by the holder of an instrument, whether payable to an identified person or payable to bearer, and the indorsement identifies a person to whom it makes the instrument payable, it is a "special indorsement." When specially indorsed, an instrument becomes payable to the identified person and may be negotiated only by the indorsement of that person. The principles stated in Section 3–110 apply to special indorsements.

(b) If an indorsement is made by the holder of an instrument and it is not a special indorsement, it is a "blank indorsement." When indorsed in blank, an instrument becomes payable to bearer and may be negotiated by transfer of possession alone until specially indorsed.

(c) The holder may convert a blank indorsement that consists only of a signature into a special indorsement by writing, above the signature of the indorser, words identifying the person to whom the instrument is made payable.

(d) "Anomalous indorsement" means an indorsement made by a person who is not the holder of the instrument. An anomalous indorsement does not affect the manner in which the instrument may be negotiated.

§ 3–206. Restrictive Indorsement.

(a) An indorsement limiting payment to a particular person or otherwise prohibiting further transfer or negotiation of the instrument is not effective to prevent further transfer or negotiation of the instrument.

(b) An indorsement stating a condition to the right of the indorsee to receive payment does not affect the right of the indorsee to enforce the instrument. A person paying the instrument or taking it for value or collection may disregard the condition, and the rights and liabilities of that person are not affected by whether the condition has been fulfilled.

(c) If an instrument bears an indorsement (i) described in Section 4–201(b), or (ii) in blank or to a particular bank using the words "for deposit," "for collection," or other words indicating a purpose of having the instrument collected by a bank for the indorser or for a particular account, the following rules apply:

(1) A person, other than a bank, who purchases the instrument when so indorsed converts the instrument unless the amount paid for the instrument is received by the indorser or applied consistently with the indorsement.

(2) A depositary bank that purchases the instrument or takes it for collection when so indorsed converts the instrument unless the amount paid by the bank with respect to the instrument is received by the indorser or applied consistently with the indorsement.

(3) A payor bank that is also the depositary bank or that takes the instrument for immediate payment over the counter from a person other than a collecting bank converts the instrument unless the proceeds of the instrument are received by the indorser or applied consistently with the indorsement.

(4) Except as otherwise provided in paragraph (3), a payor bank or intermediary bank may disregard the indorsement and is not liable if the proceeds of the instrument are not received by the indorser or applied consistently with the indorsement.

(d) Except for an indorsement covered by subsection (c), if an instrument bears an indorsement using words to the effect that payment is to be made to the indorsee as agent, trustee, or other fiduciary for the benefit of the indorser or another person, the following rules apply:

(1) Unless there is notice of breach of fiduciary duty as provided in Section 3–307, a person who purchases the instrument from the indorsee or takes the instrument from the indorsee for collection or payment may pay the proceeds of payment or the value given for the instrument to the indorsee without regard to whether the indorsee violates a fiduciary duty to the indorser.

(2) A subsequent transferee of the instrument or person who pays the instrument is neither given notice nor otherwise affected by the restriction in the indorsement unless the transferee or payor knows that the fiduciary dealt with the instrument or its proceeds in breach of fiduciary duty.

(e) The presence on an instrument of an indorsement to which this section applies does not prevent a purchaser of the instrument from becoming a holder in due course of the instrument unless the purchaser is a converter under subsection (c) or has notice or knowledge of breach of fiduciary duty as stated in subsection (d).

(f) In an action to enforce the obligation of a party to pay the instrument, the obligor has a defense if payment would violate an indorsement to which this section applies and the payment is not permitted by this section.

§ 3–207. Reacquisition.

Reacquisition of an instrument occurs if it is transferred to a former holder, by negotiation or otherwise. A former holder who reacquires the instrument may cancel indorsements made after the reacquirer first became a holder of the instrument. If the cancellation causes the instrument to be payable to the reacquirer or to bearer, the reacquirer may negotiate the instrument. An indorser whose indorsement is canceled is discharged, and the discharge is effective against any subsequent holder.

PART 3   Enforcement of Instruments

§ 3–301. Person Entitled to Enforce Instrument.

"Person entitled to enforce" an instrument means (i) the holder of the instrument, (ii) a nonholder in possession of the instrument who has the rights of a holder, or (iii) a person not in possession of the instrument who is entitled to enforce the instrument pursuant to Section 3–309 or 3–418(d). A person may be a person entitled to enforce the instrument even though the person is not the owner of the instrument or is in wrongful possession of the instrument.

§ 3–302.   Holder in Due Course.

(a) Subject to subsection (c) and Section 3–106(d), "holder in due course" means the holder of an instrument if:

(1) the instrument when issued or negotiated to the holder does not bear such apparent evidence of forgery or alteration or is not otherwise so irregular or incomplete as to call into question its authenticity; and

(2) the holder took the instrument (i) for value, (ii) in good faith, (iii) without notice that the instrument is overdue or has been dishonored or that there is an uncured default with respect to payment of another instrument issued as part of the same series, (iv) without notice that the instrument contains an unauthorized signature or has been altered, (v) without notice of any claim to the instrument described in Section 3–306, and (vi) without notice that any party has a defense or claim in recoupment described in Section 3–305(a).

(b) Notice of discharge of a party, other than discharge in an insolvency proceeding, is not notice of a defense under subsection (a), but discharge is effective against a person who became a holder in due course with notice of the discharge. Public filing or recording of a document does not of itself constitute notice of a defense, claim in recoupment, or claim to the instrument.

(c) Except to the extent a transferor or predecessor in interest has rights as a holder in due course, a person does not acquire rights of a holder in due course of an instrument taken (i) by legal process or by purchase in an execution, bankruptcy, or creditor's sale or similar proceeding, (ii) by purchase as part of a bulk transaction not in ordinary course of business of the transferor, or (iii) as the successor in interest to an estate or other organization.

(d) If, under Section 3–303(a)(1), the promise of performance that is the consideration for an instrument has been partially performed, the holder may assert rights as a holder in due course of the instrument only to the fraction of the amount payable under the instrument equal to the value of the partial performance divided by the value of the promised performance.

(e) If (i) the person entitled to enforce an instrument has only a security interest in the instrument and (ii) the person obliged to pay the instrument has a defense, claim in recoupment, or claim to the instrument that may be asserted against the person who granted the security interest, the person entitled to enforce the instrument may assert rights as a holder in due course only to an amount payable under the instrument which, at the time of enforcement of the instrument, does not exceed the amount of the unpaid obligation secured.

(f) To be effective, notice must be received at a time and in a manner that gives a reasonable opportunity to act on it.

(g) This section is subject to any law limiting status as a holder in due course in particular classes of transactions.

§ 3–303.   Value and Consideration.

(a) An instrument is issued or transferred for value if:

(1) the instrument is issued or transferred for a promise of performance, to the extent the promise has been performed;

(2) the transferee acquires a security interest or other lien in the instrument other than a lien obtained by judicial proceeding;

(3) the instrument is issued or transferred as payment of, or as security for, an antecedent claim against any person, whether or not the claim is due;

(4) the instrument is issued or transferred in exchange for a negotiable instrument; or

(5) the instrument is issued or transferred in exchange for the incurring of an irrevocable obligation to a third party by the person taking the instrument.

(b) "Consideration" means any consideration sufficient to support a simple contract. The drawer or maker of an instrument has a defense if the instrument is issued without consideration. If an instrument is issued for a promise of performance, the issuer has a defense to the extent performance of the promise is due and the promise has not been performed. If an instrument is issued for value as stated in subsection (a), the instrument is also issued for consideration.

§ 3–304.   Overdue Instrument.

(a) An instrument payable on demand becomes overdue at the earliest of the following times:

(1) on the day after the day demand for payment is duly made;

(2) if the instrument is a check, 90 days after its date; or

(3) if the instrument is not a check, when the instrument has been outstanding for a period of time after its date which is unreasonably long under the circumstances of the particular case in light of the nature of the instrument and usage of the trade.

(b) With respect to an instrument payable at a definite time the following rules apply:

(1) If the principal is payable in installments and a due date has not been accelerated, the instrument becomes overdue upon default under the instrument for nonpayment of an installment, and the instrument remains overdue until the default is cured.

(2) If the principal is not payable in installments and the due date has not been accelerated, the instrument becomes overdue on the day after the due date.

(3) If a due date with respect to principal has been accelerated, the instrument becomes overdue on the day after the accelerated due date.

(c) Unless the due date of principal has been accelerated, an instrument does not become overdue if there is default in payment of interest but no default in payment of principal.

§ 3–305.   Defenses and Claims in Recoupment.

(a) Except as stated in subsection (b), the right to enforce the obligation of a party to pay an instrument is subject to the following:

(1) a defense of the obligor based on (i) infancy of the obligor to the extent it is a defense to a simple contract, (ii) duress, lack of legal capacity, or illegality of the transaction which, under other law, nullifies the obligation of the obligor, (iii) fraud that induced the obligor to sign the instrument with neither knowledge nor reasonable opportunity to learn of its character or its essential terms, or (iv) discharge of the obligor in insolvency proceedings;

(2) a defense of the obligor stated in another section of this Article or a defense of the obligor that would be available if the person entitled to enforce the instrument were enforcing a right to payment under a simple contract; and

(3) a claim in recoupment of the obligor against the original payee of the instrument if the claim arose from the transaction that gave rise to the instrument; but the claim of the obligor may be asserted against a transferee of the instrument only to reduce the amount owing on the instrument at the time the action is brought.

(b) The right of a holder in due course to enforce the obligation of a party to pay the instrument is subject to defenses of the obligor stated in subsection (a)(1), but is not subject to defenses of the obligor stated in subsection (a)(2) or claims in recoupment stated in subsection (a)(3) against a person other than the holder.

(c) Except as stated in subsection (d), in an action to enforce the obligation of a party to pay the instrument, the obligor may not assert against the person entitled to enforce the instrument a defense, claim in recoupment, or claim to the instrument (Section 3–306) of another person, but the other person's claim to the instrument may be asserted by the obligor if the other person is joined in the action and personally asserts the claim against the person entitled to enforce the instrument. An obligor is not obliged to pay the instrument if the person seeking enforcement of the instrument does not have rights of a holder in due course and the obligor proves that the instrument is a lost or stolen instrument.

(d) In an action to enforce the obligation of an accommodation party to pay an instrument, the accommodation party may assert against the person entitled to enforce the instrument any defense or claim in recoupment under subsection (a) that the accommodated party could assert against the person entitled to enforce the instrument, except the defenses of discharge in insolvency proceedings, infancy, and lack of legal capacity.

§ 3–306.   Claims to an Instrument.

A person taking an instrument, other than a person having rights of a holder in due course, is subject to a claim of a property or possessory right in the instrument or its proceeds, including a claim to rescind a negotiation and to recover the instrument or its proceeds. A person having rights of a holder in due course takes free of the claim to the instrument.

§ 3–307.   Notice of Breach of Fiduciary Duty.

(a) In this section:

(1) "Fiduciary" means an agent, trustee, partner, corporate officer or director, or other representative owing a fiduciary duty with respect to an instrument.

(2) "Represented person" means the principal, beneficiary, partnership, corporation, or other person to whom the duty stated in paragraph (1) is owed.

(b) If (i) an instrument is taken from a fiduciary for payment or collection or for value, (ii) the taker has knowledge of the fiduciary status of the fiduciary, and (iii) the represented person makes a claim to the instrument or its proceeds on the basis that the transaction of the fiduciary is a breach of fiduciary duty, the following rules apply:

(1) Notice of breach of fiduciary duty by the fiduciary is notice of the claim of the represented person.

(2) In the case of an instrument payable to the represented person or the fiduciary as such, the taker has notice of the breach of fiduciary duty if the instrument is (i) taken in payment of or as security for a debt known by the taker to be the personal debt of the fiduciary, (ii) taken in a transaction known by the taker to be for the personal benefit of the fiduciary, or (iii) deposited to an account other than an account of the fiduciary, as such, or an account of the represented person.

(3) If an instrument is issued by the represented person or the fiduciary as such, and made payable to the fiduciary personally, the taker does not have notice of the breach of fiduciary duty unless the taker knows of the breach of fiduciary duty.

(4) If an instrument is issued by the represented person or the fiduciary as such, to the taker as payee, the taker has notice of the breach of fiduciary duty if the instrument is (i) taken in payment of or as security for a debt known by the taker to be the personal debt of the fiduciary, (ii) taken in a transaction known by the taker to be for the personal benefit of the fiduciary, or (iii) deposited to an account other than an account of the fiduciary, as such, or an account of the represented person.

§ 3–308.   Proof of Signatures and Status as Holder in Due Course.

(a) In an action with respect to an instrument, the authenticity of, and authority to make, each signature on the instrument is admitted unless specifically denied in the pleadings. If the validity of a signature is denied in the pleadings, the burden of establishing validity is on the person claiming validity, but the signature is presumed to be authentic and authorized unless the action is to enforce the liability of the purported signer and the signer is dead or incompetent at the time of trial of the issue of validity of the signature. If an action to enforce the instrument is brought against a person as the undisclosed principal of a person who signed the instrument as a party to the instrument, the plaintiff has the burden of establishing that the defendant is liable on the instrument as a represented person under Section 3–402(a).

(b) If the validity of signatures is admitted or proved and there is compliance with subsection (a), a plaintiff producing the instrument is entitled to payment if the plaintiff proves entitlement to enforce the instrument under Section 3–301, unless the defendant proves a defense or claim in recoupment. If a defense or claim in recoupment is proved, the right to payment of the plaintiff is subject to the defense or claim, except to the extent the plaintiff proves that the plaintiff has rights of a holder in due course which are not subject to the defense or claim.

§ 3–309.   Enforcement of Lost, Destroyed, or Stolen Instrument.

(a) A person not in possession of an instrument is entitled to enforce the instrument if (i) the person was in possession of the instrument and entitled to enforce it when loss of possession occurred, (ii) the loss of possession was not the result of a transfer by the person or a lawful seizure, and (iii) the person cannot reasonably obtain possession of the instrument because the instrument was destroyed, its whereabouts cannot be determined, or it is in the wrongful possession of an unknown person or a person that cannot be found or is not amenable to service of process.

(b) A person seeking enforcement of an instrument under subsection (a) must prove the terms of the instrument and the person's right to enforce the instrument. If that proof is made, Section 3–308 applies to the case as if the person seeking enforcement had produced the instrument. The court may not enter judgment in favor of the person seeking enforcement unless it finds that the person required to pay the instrument is adequately protected against loss that might occur by reason of a claim by another person to enforce the instrument. Adequate protection may be provided by any reasonable means.

§ 3–310.   Effect of Instrument on Obligation for Which Taken.

(a) Unless otherwise agreed, if a certified check, cashier's check, or teller's check is taken for an obligation, the obligation is discharged to the same extent discharge would result if an amount of money equal to the amount of the instrument were taken in payment of the obligation. Discharge of the obligation does not affect any liability that the obligor may have as an indorser of the instrument.

(b) Unless otherwise agreed and except as provided in subsection (a), if a note or an uncertified check is taken for an obligation, the obligation is suspended to the same extent the obligation would be discharged if an amount of money equal to the amount of the instrument were taken, and the following rules apply:

(1) In the case of an uncertified check, suspension of the obligation continues until dishonor of the check or until it is paid or certified. Payment or certification of the check results in discharge of the obligation to the extent of the amount of the check.

(2) In the case of a note, suspension of the obligation continues until dishonor of the note or until it is paid. Payment of the note results in discharge of the obligation to the extent of the payment.

(3) Except as provided in paragraph (4), if the check or note is dishonored and the obligee of the obligation for which the instrument was taken is the person entitled to enforce the instrument, the obligee may enforce either the instrument or the obligation. In the case of an instrument of a third person which is negotiated to the obligee by the obligor, discharge of the obligor on the instrument also discharges the obligation.

(4) If the person entitled to enforce the instrument taken for an obligation is a person other than the obligee, the obligee may not enforce the obligation to the extent the obligation is suspended. If the obligee is the person entitled to enforce the instrument but no longer has possession of it because it was lost, stolen, or destroyed, the obligation may not be enforced to the extent of the amount payable on the instrument, and to that extent the obligee's rights against the obligor are limited to enforcement of the instrument.

(c) If an instrument other than one described in subsection (a) or (b) is taken for an obligation, the effect is (i) that stated in subsection (a) if the instrument is one on which a bank is liable as maker or acceptor, or (ii) that stated in subsection (b) in any other case.

§ 3–311.   Accord and Satisfaction by Use of Instrument.

(a) If a person against whom a claim is asserted proves that (i) that person in good faith tendered an instrument to the claimant as full satisfaction of the claim, (ii) the amount of the claim was unliquidated or subject to a bona fide dispute, and (iii) the claimant obtained payment of the instrument, the following subsections apply.

(b) Unless subsection (c) applies, the claim is discharged if the person against whom the claim is asserted proves that the instrument or an accompanying written communication contained a conspicuous statement to the effect that the instrument was tendered as full satisfaction of the claim.

(c) Subject to subsection (d), a claim is not discharged under subsection (b) if either of the following applies:

(1) The claimant, if an organization, proves that (i) within a reasonable time before the tender, the claimant sent a conspicuous statement to the person against whom the claim is asserted that communications concerning disputed debts, including an instrument tendered as full satisfaction of a debt, are to be sent to a designated person, office, or place, and (ii) the instrument or accompanying communication was not received by that designated person, office, or place.

(2) The claimant, whether or not an organization, proves that within 90 days after payment of the instrument, the claimant tendered repayment of the amount of the instrument to the person against whom the claim is asserted. This paragraph does not apply if the claimant is an organization that sent a statement complying with paragraph (1)(i).

(d) A claim is discharged if the person against whom the claim is asserted proves that within a reasonable time before collection of the instrument was initiated, the claimant, or an agent of the claimant having direct responsibility with respect to the disputed obligation, knew that the instrument was tendered in full satisfaction of the claim.

§ 3–312.   Lost, Destroyed, or Stolen Cashier's Check, Teller's Check, or Certified Check.*

(a) In this section:

(1) "Check" means a cashier's check, teller's check, or certified check.

(2) "Claimant" means a person who claims the right to receive the amount of a cashier's check, teller's check, or certified check that was lost, destroyed, or stolen.

(3) "Declaration of loss" means a written statement, made under penalty of perjury, to the effect that (i) the declarer lost possession of a check, (ii) the declarer is the drawer or payee of the check, in the case of a certified check, or the remitter or payee of the check, in the case of a cashier's check or teller's check, (iii) the loss of possession was not the result of a transfer by the declarer or a lawful seizure, and (iv) the declarer cannot reasonably obtain possession of the check because the check was destroyed, its whereabouts cannot be determined, or it is in the wrongful possession of an unknown person or a person that cannot be found or is not amenable to service of process.

(4) "Obligated bank" means the issuer of a cashier's check or teller's check or the acceptor of a certified check.

(b) A claimant may assert a claim to the amount of a check by a communication to the obligated bank describing the check with reasonable certainty and requesting payment of the amount of the check, if (i) the claimant is the drawer or payee of a certified check or the remitter or payee of a cashier's check or teller's check, (ii) the communication contains or is accompanied by a declaration of loss of the claimant with respect to the check, (iii) the communication is received at a time and in a manner affording the bank a reasonable time to act on it

before the check is paid, and (iv) the claimant provides reasonable identification if requested by the obligated bank. Delivery of a declaration of loss is a warranty of the truth of the statements made in the declaration. If a claim is asserted in compliance with this subsection, the following rules apply:

(1) The claim becomes enforceable at the later of (i) the time the claim is asserted, or (ii) the 90th day following the date of the check, in the case of a cashier's check or teller's check, or the 90th day following the date of the acceptance, in the case of a certified check.

(2) Until the claim becomes enforceable, it has no legal effect and the obligated bank may pay the check or, in the case of a teller's check, may permit the drawee to pay the check. Payment to a person entitled to enforce the check discharges all liability of the obligated bank with respect to the check.

(3) If the claim becomes enforceable before the check is presented for payment, the obligated bank is not obliged to pay the check.

(4) When the claim becomes enforceable, the obligated bank becomes obliged to pay the amount of the check to the claimant if payment of the check has not been made to a person entitled to enforce the check. Subject to Section 4–302(a)(1), payment to the claimant discharges all liability of the obligated bank with respect to the check.

(c) If the obligated bank pays the amount of a check to a claimant under subsection (b)(4) and the check is presented for payment by a person having rights of a holder in due course, the claimant is obliged to (i) refund the payment to the obligated bank if the check is paid, or (ii) pay the amount of the check to the person having rights of a holder in due course if the check is dishonored.

(d) If a claimant has the right to assert a claim under subsection (b) and is also a person entitled to enforce a cashier's check, teller's check, or certified check which is lost, destroyed, or stolen, the claimant may assert rights with respect to the check either under this section or Section 3–309.

Added in 1991.

PART 4   Liability of Parties

§ 3–401.   Signature.

(a) A person is not liable on an instrument unless (i) the person signed the instrument, or (ii) the person is represented by an agent or representative who signed the instrument and the signature is binding on the represented person under Section 3–402.

(b) A signature may be made (i) manually or by means of a device or machine, and (ii) by the use of any name, including a trade or assumed name, or by a word, mark, or symbol executed or adopted by a person with present intention to authenticate a writing.

§ 3–402.   Signature by Representative.

(a) If a person acting, or purporting to act, as a representative signs an instrument by signing either the name of the represented person or the name of the signer, the represented person is bound by the signature to the same extent the represented person would be bound if the signature were on a simple contract. If the represented person is bound, the signature of the representative is the "authorized signature of the represented person" and the represented person is liable on the instrument, whether or not identified in the instrument.

(b) If a representative signs the name of the representative to an instrument and the signature is an authorized signature of the represented person, the following rules apply:

(1) If the form of the signature shows unambiguously that the signature is made on behalf of the represented person who is identified in the instrument, the representative is not liable on the instrument.

(2) Subject to subsection (c), if (i) the form of the signature does not show unambiguously that the signature is made in a representative capacity or (ii) the represented person is not identified in the instrument, the representative is liable on the instrument to a holder in due course that took the instrument without notice that the representative was not intended to be liable on the instrument. With respect to any other person, the representative is liable on the instrument unless the representative proves that the original parties did not intend the representative to be liable on the instrument.

(c) If a representative signs the name of the representative as drawer of a check without indication of the representative status and the check is payable from an account of the represented person who is identified on the check, the signer is not liable on the check if the signature is an authorized signature of the represented person.

§ 3–403.   Unauthorized Signature.

(a) Unless otherwise provided in this Article or Article 4, an unauthorized signature is ineffective except as the signature of the unauthorized signer in favor of a person who in good faith pays the instrument or takes it for value. An unauthorized signature may be ratified for all purposes of this Article.

(b) If the signature of more than one person is required to constitute the authorized signature of an organization, the signature of the organization is unauthorized if one of the required signatures is lacking.

(c) The civil or criminal liability of a person who makes an unauthorized signature is not affected by any provision of this Article which makes the unauthorized signature effective for the purposes of this Article.

§ 3–404.   Impostors; Fictitious Payees.

(a) If an impostor, by use of the mails or otherwise, induces the issuer of an instrument to issue the instrument to the impostor, or to a person acting in concert with the impostor, by impersonating the payee of the instrument or a person authorized to act for the payee, an indorsement of the instrument by any person in the name of the payee is effective as the indorsement of the payee in favor of a person who, in good faith, pays the instrument or takes it for value or for collection.

(b) If (i) a person whose intent determines to whom an instrument is payable (Section 3–110(a) or (b)) does not intend the person identified as payee to have any interest in the instrument, or (ii) the person identified as payee of an instrument is a fictitious person, the following rules apply until the instrument is negotiated by special indorsement:

(1) Any person in possession of the instrument is its holder.

(2) An indorsement by any person in the name of the payee stated in the instrument is effective as the indorsement of the payee in favor of a person who, in good faith, pays the instrument or takes it for value or for collection.

(c) Under subsection (a) or (b), an indorsement is made in the name of a payee if (i) it is made in a name substantially similar to that of the payee or (ii) the instrument, whether or not indorsed, is deposited in a depositary bank to an account in a name substantially similar to that of the payee.

(d) With respect to an instrument to which subsection (a) or (b) applies, if a person paying the instrument or taking it for value or for collection fails to exercise ordinary care in paying or taking the instrument and that failure substantially contributes to loss resulting from payment of the instrument, the person bearing the loss may recover from the person failing to exercise ordinary care to the extent the failure to exercise ordinary care contributed to the loss.

§ 3–405.   Employer's Responsibility for Fraudulent Indorsement by Employee.

(a) In this section:

(1) "Employee" includes an independent contractor and employee of an independent contractor retained by the employer.

(2) "Fraudulent indorsement" means (i) in the case of an instrument payable to the employer, a forged indorsement purporting to be that of the employer, or (ii) in the case of an instrument with respect to which the employer is the issuer, a forged indorsement purporting to be that of the person identified as payee.

(3) "Responsibility" with respect to instruments means authority (i) to sign or indorse instruments on behalf of the employer, (ii) to process instruments received by the employer for bookkeeping purposes, for deposit to an account, or for other disposition, (iii) to prepare or process instruments for issue in the name of the employer, (iv) to supply information determining the names or addresses of payees of instruments to be issued in the name of the employer, (v) to control the disposition of

instruments to be issued in the name of the employer, or (vi) to act otherwise with respect to instruments in a responsible capacity. "Responsibility" does not include authority that merely allows an employee to have access to instruments or blank or incomplete instrument forms that are being stored or transported or are part of incoming or outgoing mail, or similar access.

(b) For the purpose of determining the rights and liabilities of a person who, in good faith, pays an instrument or takes it for value or for collection, if an employer entrusted an employee with responsibility with respect to the instrument and the employee or a person acting in concert with the employee makes a fraudulent indorsement of the instrument, the indorsement is effective as the indorsement of the person to whom the instrument is payable if it is made in the name of that person. If the person paying the instrument or taking it for value or for collection fails to exercise ordinary care in paying or taking the instrument and that failure substantially contributes to loss resulting from the fraud, the person bearing the loss may recover from the person failing to exercise ordinary care to the extent the failure to exercise ordinary care contributed to the loss.

(c) Under subsection (b), an indorsement is made in the name of the person to whom an instrument is payable if (i) it is made in a name substantially similar to the name of that person or (ii) the instrument, whether or not indorsed, is deposited in a depositary bank to an account in a name substantially similar to the name of that person.

§ 3–406.   Negligence Contributing to Forged Signature or Alteration of Instrument.

(a) A person whose failure to exercise ordinary care substantially contributes to an alteration of an instrument or to the making of a forged signature on an instrument is precluded from asserting the alteration or the forgery against a person who, in good faith, pays the instrument or takes it for value or for collection.

(b) Under subsection (a), if the person asserting the preclusion fails to exercise ordinary care in paying or taking the instrument and that failure substantially contributes to loss, the loss is allocated between the person precluded and the person asserting the preclusion according to the extent to which the failure of each to exercise ordinary care contributed to the loss.

(c) Under subsection (a), the burden of proving failure to exercise ordinary care is on the person asserting the preclusion. Under subsection (b), the burden of proving failure to exercise ordinary care is on the person precluded.

§ 3–407.   Alteration.

(a) "Alteration" means (i) an unauthorized change in an instrument that purports to modify in any respect the obligation of a party, or (ii) an unauthorized addition of words or numbers or other change to an incomplete instrument relating to the obligation of a party.

(b) Except as provided in subsection (c), an alteration fraudulently made discharges a party whose obligation is affected by the alteration unless that party assents or is precluded from asserting the alteration. No other alteration discharges a party, and the instrument may be enforced according to its original terms.

(c) A payor bank or drawee paying a fraudulently altered instrument or a person taking it for value, in good faith and without notice of the alteration, may enforce rights with respect to the instrument (i) according to its original terms, or (ii) in the case of an incomplete instrument altered by unauthorized completion, according to its terms as completed.

§ 3–408.   Drawee Not Liable on Unaccepted Draft.

A check or other draft does not of itself operate as an assignment of funds in the hands of the drawee available for its payment, and the drawee is not liable on the instrument until the drawee accepts it.

§ 3–409.   Acceptance of Draft; Certified Check.

(a) "Acceptance" means the drawee's signed agreement to pay a draft as presented. It must be written on the draft and may consist of the drawee's signature alone. Acceptance may be made at any time and becomes effective when notification pursuant to instructions is given or the accepted draft is delivered for the purpose of giving rights on the acceptance to any person.

(b) A draft may be accepted although it has not been signed by the drawer, is otherwise incomplete, is overdue, or has been dishonored.

(c) If a draft is payable at a fixed period after sight and the acceptor fails to date the acceptance, the holder may complete the acceptance by supplying a date in good faith.

(d) "Certified check" means a check accepted by the bank on which it is drawn. Acceptance may be made as stated in subsection (a) or by a writing on the check which indicates that the check is certified. The drawee of a check has no obligation to certify the check, and refusal to certify is not dishonor of the check.

§ 3–410.   Acceptance Varying Draft.

(a) If the terms of a drawee's acceptance vary from the terms of the draft as presented, the holder may refuse the acceptance and treat the draft as dishonored. In that case, the drawee may cancel the acceptance.

(b) The terms of a draft are not varied by an acceptance to pay at a particular bank or place in the United States, unless the acceptance states that the draft is to be paid only at that bank or place.

(c) If the holder assents to an acceptance varying the terms of a draft, the obligation of each drawer and indorser that does not expressly assent to the acceptance is discharged.

§ 3–411.   Refusal to Pay Cashier's Checks, Teller's Checks, and Certified Checks.

(a) In this section, "obligated bank" means the acceptor of a certified check or the issuer of a cashier's check or teller's check bought from the issuer.

(b) If the obligated bank wrongfully (i) refuses to pay a cashier's check or certified check, (ii) stops payment of a teller's check, or (iii) refuses to pay a dishonored teller's check, the person asserting the right to enforce the check is entitled to compensation for expenses and loss of interest resulting from the nonpayment and may recover consequential damages if the obligated bank refuses to pay after receiving notice of particular circumstances giving rise to the damages.

(c) Expenses or consequential damages under subsection (b) are not recoverable if the refusal of the obligated bank to pay occurs because (i) the bank suspends payments, (ii) the obligated bank asserts a claim or defense of the bank that it has reasonable grounds to believe is available against the person entitled to enforce the instrument, (iii) the obligated bank has a reasonable doubt whether the person demanding payment is the person entitled to enforce the instrument, or (iv) payment is prohibited by law.

§ 3–412.   Obligation of Issuer of Note or Cashier's Check.

The issuer of a note or cashier's check or other draft drawn on the drawer is obliged to pay the instrument (i) according to its terms at the time it was issued or, if not issued, at the time it first came into possession of a holder, or (ii) if the issuer signed an incomplete instrument, according to its terms when completed, to the extent stated in Sections 3–115 and 3–407. The obligation is owed to a person entitled to enforce the instrument or to an indorser who paid the instrument under Section 3–415.

§ 3–413.   Obligation of Acceptor.

(a) The acceptor of a draft is obliged to pay the draft (i) according to its terms at the time it was accepted, even though the acceptance states that the draft is payable "as originally drawn" or equivalent terms, (ii) if the acceptance varies the terms of the draft, according to the terms of the draft as varied, or (iii) if the acceptance is of a draft that is an incomplete instrument, according to its terms when completed, to the extent stated in Sections 3–115 and 3–407. The obligation is owed to a person entitled to enforce the draft or to the drawer or an indorser who paid the draft under Section 3–414 or 3–415.

(b) If the certification of a check or other acceptance of a draft states the amount certified or accepted, the obligation of the acceptor is that amount. If (i) the certification or acceptance does not state an amount, (ii) the amount of the instrument is subsequently raised, and (iii) the instrument is then negotiated to a holder in due course, the obligation of the acceptor is the amount of the instrument at the time it was taken by the holder in due course.

§ 3–414.   Obligation of Drawer.

(a) This section does not apply to cashier's checks or other drafts drawn on the drawer.

(b) If an unaccepted draft is dishonored, the drawer is obliged to pay the draft (i) according to its terms at the time it was issued or, if not issued, at the time it first came into possession of a holder, or (ii) if the drawer signed an incomplete instrument, according to its terms when completed, to the extent stated in Sections 3–115 and 3–407. The obligation is owed to a person entitled to enforce the draft or to an indorser who paid the draft under Section 3–415.

(c) If a draft is accepted by a bank, the drawer is discharged, regardless of when or by whom acceptance was obtained.

(d) If a draft is accepted and the acceptor is not a bank, the obligation of the drawer to pay the draft if the draft is dishonored by the acceptor is the same as the obligation of an indorser under Section 3–415(a) and (c).

(e) If a draft states that it is drawn "without recourse" or otherwise disclaims liability of the drawer to pay the draft, the drawer is not liable under subsection (b) to pay the draft if the draft is not a check. A disclaimer of the liability stated in subsection (b) is not effective if the draft is a check.

(f) If (i) a check is not presented for payment or given to a depositary bank for collection within 30 days after its date, (ii) the drawee suspends payments after expiration of the 30-day period without paying the check, and (iii) because of the suspension of payments, the drawer is deprived of funds maintained with the drawee to cover payment of the check, the drawer to the extent deprived of funds may discharge its obligation to pay the check by assigning to the person entitled to enforce the check the rights of the drawer against the drawee with respect to the funds.

§ 3–415.   Obligation of Indorser.

(a) Subject to subsections (b), (c), and (d) and to Section 3–419(d), if an instrument is dishonored, an indorser is obliged to pay the amount due on the instrument (i) according to the terms of the instrument at the time it was indorsed, or (ii) if the indorser indorsed an incomplete instrument, according to its terms when completed, to the extent stated in Sections 3–115 and 3–407. The obligation of the indorser is owed to a person entitled to enforce the instrument or to a subsequent indorser who paid the instrument under this section.

(b) If an indorsement states that it is made "without recourse" or otherwise disclaims liability of the indorser, the indorser is not liable under subsection (a) to pay the instrument.

(c) If notice of dishonor of an instrument is required by Section 3–503 and notice of dishonor complying with that section is not given to an indorser, the liability of the indorser under subsection (a) is discharged.

(d) If a draft is accepted by a bank after an indorsement is made, the liability of the indorser under subsection (a) is discharged.

(e) If an indorser of a check is liable under subsection (a) and the check is not presented for payment, or given to a depositary bank for collection, within 30 days after the day the indorsement was made, the liability of the indorser under subsection (a) is discharged.

As amended in 1993.

§ 3–416.   Transfer Warranties.

(a) A person who transfers an instrument for consideration warrants to the transferee and, if the transfer is by indorsement, to any subsequent transferee that:

(1) the warrantor is a person entitled to enforce the instrument;

(2) all signatures on the instrument are authentic and authorized;

(3) the instrument has not been altered;

(4) the instrument is not subject to a defense or claim in recoupment of any party which can be asserted against the warrantor; and

(5) the warrantor has no knowledge of any insolvency proceeding commenced with respect to the maker or acceptor or, in the case of an unaccepted draft, the drawer.

(b) A person to whom the warranties under subsection (a) are made and who took the instrument in good faith may recover from the warrantor as damages for breach of warranty an amount equal to the loss suffered as a result of the breach, but not more than the amount of the instrument plus expenses and loss of interest incurred as a result of the breach.

(c) The warranties stated in subsection (a) cannot be disclaimed with respect to checks. Unless notice of a claim for breach of warranty is given to the warrantor within 30 days after the claimant has reason to know of the breach and the identity of the warrantor, the liability of the warrantor under subsection (b) is discharged to the extent of any loss caused by the delay in giving notice of the claim.

(d) A [cause of action] for breach of warranty under this section accrues when the claimant has reason to know of the breach.

§ 3–417.   Presentment Warranties.

(a) If an unaccepted draft is presented to the drawee for payment or acceptance and the drawee pays or accepts the draft, (i) the person obtaining payment or acceptance, at the time of presentment, and (ii) a previous transferor of the draft, at the time of transfer, warrant to the drawee making payment or accepting the draft in good faith that:

(1) the warrantor is, or was, at the time the warrantor transferred the draft, a person entitled to enforce the draft or

authorized to obtain payment or acceptance of the draft on behalf of a person entitled to enforce the draft;

(2) the draft has not been altered; and

(3) the warrantor has no knowledge that the signature of the drawer of the draft is unauthorized.

(b) A drawee making payment may recover from any warrantor damages for breach of warranty equal to the amount paid by the drawee less the amount the drawee received or is entitled to receive from the drawer because of the payment. In addition, the drawee is entitled to compensation for expenses and loss of interest resulting from the breach. The right of the drawee to recover damages under this subsection is not affected by any failure of the drawee to exercise ordinary care in making payment. If the drawee accepts the draft, breach of warranty is a defense to the obligation of the acceptor. If the acceptor makes payment with respect to the draft, the acceptor is entitled to recover from any warrantor for breach of warranty the amounts stated in this subsection.

(c) If a drawee asserts a claim for breach of warranty under subsection (a) based on an unauthorized indorsement of the draft or an alteration of the draft, the warrantor may defend by proving that the indorsement is effective under Section 3–404 or 3–405 or the drawer is precluded under Section 3–406 or 4–406 from asserting against the drawee the unauthorized indorsement or alteration.

(d) If (i) a dishonored draft is presented for payment to the drawer or an indorser or (ii) any other instrument is presented for payment to a party obliged to pay the instrument, and (iii) payment is received, the following rules apply:

(1) The person obtaining payment and a prior transferor of the instrument warrant to the person making payment in good faith that the warrantor is, or was, at the time the warrantor transferred the instrument, a person entitled to enforce the instrument or authorized to obtain payment on behalf of a person entitled to enforce the instrument.

(2) The person making payment may recover from any warrantor for breach of warranty an amount equal to the amount paid plus expenses and loss of interest resulting from the breach.

(e) The warranties stated in subsections (a) and (d) cannot be disclaimed with respect to checks. Unless notice of a claim for breach of warranty is given to the warrantor within 30 days after the claimant has reason to know of the breach and the identity of the warrantor, the liability of the warrantor under subsection (b) or (d) is discharged to the extent of any loss caused by the delay in giving notice of the claim.

(f) A [cause of action] for breach of warranty under this section accrues when the claimant has reason to know of the breach.

§ 3–418.   Payment or Acceptance
by Mistake.

(a) Except as provided in subsection (c), if the drawee of a draft pays or accepts the draft and the drawee acted on the mistaken belief that (i) payment of the draft had not been stopped pursuant to Section 4–403 or (ii) the signature of the drawer of the draft was authorized, the drawee may recover the amount of the draft from the person to whom or for whose benefit payment was made or, in the case of acceptance, may revoke the acceptance. Rights of the drawee under this subsection are not affected by failure of the drawee to exercise ordinary care in paying or accepting the draft.

(b) Except as provided in subsection (c), if an instrument has been paid or accepted by mistake and the case is not covered by subsection (a), the person paying or accepting may, to the extent permitted by the law governing mistake and restitution, (i) recover the payment from the person to whom or for whose benefit payment was made or (ii) in the case of acceptance, may revoke the acceptance.

(c) The remedies provided by subsection (a) or (b) may not be asserted against a person who took the instrument in good faith and for value or who in good faith changed position in reliance on the payment or acceptance. This subsection does not limit remedies provided by Section 3–417 or 4–407.

(d) Notwithstanding Section 4–215, if an instrument is paid or accepted by mistake and the payor or acceptor recovers payment or revokes acceptance under subsection (a) or (b), the instrument is deemed not to have been paid or accepted and is treated as dishonored, and the person from whom payment is recovered has rights as a person entitled to enforce the dishonored instrument.

§ 3–419.   Instruments Signed for Accommodation.

(a) If an instrument is issued for value given for the benefit of a party to the instrument ("accommodated party") and another party to the instrument ("accommodation party") signs the instrument for the purpose of incurring liability on the instrument without being a direct beneficiary of the value given for the instrument, the instrument is signed by the accommodation party "for accommodation."

(b) An accommodation party may sign the instrument as maker, drawer, acceptor, or indorser and, subject to subsection (d), is obliged to pay the instrument in the capacity in which the accommodation party signs. The obligation of an accommodation party may be enforced notwithstanding any statute of frauds and whether or not the accommodation party receives consideration for the accommodation.

(c) A person signing an instrument is presumed to be an accommodation party and there is notice that the instrument is signed for accommodation if the signature is an anomalous indorsement or is accompanied by words indicating that the signer is acting as surety or guarantor with respect to the obligation of another party to the instrument. Except as provided in Section 3–605, the obligation of an accommodation party to pay the instrument is not affected by the fact that the person enforcing the obligation had notice when the instrument was taken by that person that the accommodation party signed the instrument for accommodation.

(d) If the signature of a party to an instrument is accompanied by words indicating unambiguously that the party is guaranteeing collection rather than payment of the obligation of another party to the instrument, the signer is obliged to pay the amount due on the instrument to a person entitled to enforce the instrument only if (i) execution of judgment against the other party has been returned unsatisfied, (ii) the other party is insolvent or in an insolvency proceeding, (iii) the other party cannot be served with process, or (iv) it is otherwise apparent that payment cannot be obtained from the other party.

(e) An accommodation party who pays the instrument is entitled to reimbursement from the accommodated party and is entitled to enforce the instrument against the accommodated party. An accommodated party who pays the instrument has no right of recourse against, and is not entitled to contribution from, an accommodation party.

§ 3–420.   Conversion of Instrument.

(a) The law applicable to conversion of personal property applies to instruments. An instrument is also converted if it is taken by transfer, other than a negotiation, from a person not entitled to enforce the instrument or a bank makes or obtains payment with respect to the instrument for a person not entitled to enforce the instrument or receive payment. An action for conversion of an instrument may not be brought by (i) the issuer or acceptor of the instrument or (ii) a payee or indorsee who did not receive delivery of the instrument either directly or through delivery to an agent or a co-payee.

(b) In an action under subsection (a), the measure of liability is presumed to be the amount payable on the instrument, but recovery may not exceed the amount of the plaintiff's interest in the instrument.

(c) A representative, other than a depositary bank, who has in good faith dealt with an instrument or its proceeds on behalf of one who was not the person entitled to enforce the instrument is not liable in conversion to that person beyond the amount of any proceeds that it has not paid out.

PART 5   Dishonor

§ 3–501.   Presentment.

(a) "Presentment" means a demand made by or on behalf of a person entitled to enforce an instrument (i) to pay the instrument made to the drawee or a party obliged to pay the instrument or, in the case of a note or accepted draft payable at a bank, to the bank, or (ii) to accept a draft made to the drawee.

(b) The following rules are subject to Article 4, agreement of the parties, and clearing-house rules and the like:

(1) Presentment may be made at the place of payment of the instrument and must be made at the place of payment if the instrument is payable at a bank in the United States; may be made by any commercially reasonable means, including an oral, written, or electronic communication; is effective when the demand for payment or acceptance is received by the person to whom presentment is made; and is effective if made to any one of two or more makers, acceptors, drawees, or other payors.

(2) Upon demand of the person to whom presentment is made, the person making presentment must (i) exhibit the instrument, (ii) give reasonable identification and, if presentment is made on behalf of another person, reasonable evidence of authority to do so, and (. . .) sign a receipt on the instrument for any payment made or surrender the instrument if full payment is made.

(3) Without dishonoring the instrument, the party to whom presentment is made may (i) return the instrument for lack of a necessary indorsement, or (ii) refuse payment or acceptance for failure of the presentment to comply with the terms of the instrument, an agreement of the parties, or other applicable law or rule.

(4) The party to whom presentment is made may treat presentment as occurring on the next business day after the day of presentment if the party to whom presentment is made has established a cut-off hour not earlier than 2 P.M. for the receipt and processing of instruments presented for payment or acceptance and presentment is made after the cut-off hour.

§ 3–502. Dishonor.

(a) Dishonor of a note is governed by the following rules:

(1) If the note is payable on demand, the note is dishonored if presentment is duly made to the maker and the note is not paid on the day of presentment.

(2) If the note is not payable on demand and is payable at or through a bank or the terms of the note require presentment, the note is dishonored if presentment is duly made and the note is not paid on the day it becomes payable or the day of presentment, whichever is later.

(3) If the note is not payable on demand and paragraph (2) does not apply, the note is dishonored if it is not paid on the day it becomes payable.

(b) Dishonor of an unaccepted draft other than a documentary draft is governed by the following rules:

(1) If a check is duly presented for payment to the payor bank otherwise than for immediate payment over the counter, the check is dishonored if the payor bank makes timely return of the check or sends timely notice of dishonor or nonpayment under Section 4–301 or 4–302, or becomes accountable for the amount of the check under Section 4–302.

(2) If a draft is payable on demand and paragraph (1) does not apply, the draft is dishonored if presentment for payment is duly made to the drawee and the draft is not paid on the day of presentment.

(3) If a draft is payable on a date stated in the draft, the draft is dishonored if (i) presentment for payment is duly made to the drawee and payment is not made on the day the draft becomes payable or the day of presentment, whichever is later, or (ii) presentment for acceptance is duly made before the day the draft becomes payable and the draft is not accepted on the day of presentment.

(4) If a draft is payable on elapse of a period of time after sight or acceptance, the draft is dishonored if presentment for acceptance is duly made and the draft is not accepted on the day of presentment.

(c) Dishonor of an unaccepted documentary draft occurs according to the rules stated in subsection (b)(2), (3), and (4), except that payment or acceptance may be delayed without dishonor until no later than the close of the third business day of the drawee following the day on which payment or acceptance is required by those paragraphs.

(d) Dishonor of an accepted draft is governed by the following rules:

(1) If the draft is payable on demand, the draft is dishonored if presentment for payment is duly made to the acceptor and the draft is not paid on the day of presentment.

(2) If the draft is not payable on demand, the draft is dishonored if presentment for payment is duly made to the acceptor and payment is not made on the day it becomes payable or the day of presentment, whichever is later.

(e) In any case in which presentment is otherwise required for dishonor under this section and presentment is excused under Section 3–504, dishonor occurs without presentment if the instrument is not duly accepted or paid.

(f) If a draft is dishonored because timely acceptance of the draft was not made and the person entitled to demand acceptance consents to a late acceptance, from the time of acceptance the draft is treated as never having been dishonored.

§ 3–503. Notice of Dishonor.

(a) The obligation of an indorser stated in Section 3–415(a) and the obligation of a drawer stated in Section 3–414(d) may not be enforced unless (i) the indorser or drawer is given notice of dishonor of the instrument complying with this section or (ii) notice of dishonor is excused under Section 3–504(b).

(b) Notice of dishonor may be given by any person; may be given by any commercially reasonable means, including an oral, written, or electronic communication; and is sufficient if it reasonably identifies the instrument and indicates that the instrument has been dishonored or has not been paid or accepted. Return of an instrument given to a bank for collection is sufficient notice of dishonor.

(c) Subject to Section 3–504(c), with respect to an instrument taken for collection by a collecting bank, notice of dishonor must be given (i) by the bank before midnight of the next banking day following the banking day on which the bank receives notice of dishonor of the instrument, or (ii) by any other person within 30 days following the day on which the person receives notice of dishonor. With respect to any other instrument, notice of dishonor must be given within 30 days following the day on which dishonor occurs.

§ 3–504.   Excused Presentment and Notice of Dishonor.

(a) Presentment for payment or acceptance of an instrument is excused if (i) the person entitled to present the instrument cannot with reasonable diligence make presentment, (ii) the maker or acceptor has repudiated an obligation to pay the instrument or is dead or in insolvency proceedings, (iii) by the terms of the instrument presentment is not necessary to enforce the obligation of indorsers or the drawer, (iv) the drawer or indorser whose obligation is being enforced has waived presentment or otherwise has no reason to expect or right to require that the instrument be paid or accepted, or (v) the drawer instructed the drawee not to pay or accept the draft or the drawee was not obligated to the drawer to pay the draft.

(b) Notice of dishonor is excused if (i) by the terms of the instrument notice of dishonor is not necessary to enforce the obligation of a party to pay the instrument, or (ii) the party whose obligation is being enforced waived notice of dishonor. A waiver of presentment is also a waiver of notice of dishonor.

(c) Delay in giving notice of dishonor is excused if the delay was caused by circumstances beyond the control of the person giving the notice and the person giving the notice exercised reasonable diligence after the cause of the delay ceased to operate.

§ 3–505.   Evidence of Dishonor.

(a) The following are admissible as evidence and create a presumption of dishonor and of any notice of dishonor stated:

(1) a document regular in form as provided in subsection (b) which purports to be a protest;

(2) a purported stamp or writing of the drawee, payor bank, or presenting bank on or accompanying the instrument stating that acceptance or payment has been refused unless reasons for the refusal are stated and the reasons are not consistent with dishonor;

(3) a book or record of the drawee, payor bank, or collecting bank, kept in the usual course of business which shows dishonor, even if there is no evidence of who made the entry.

(b) A protest is a certificate of dishonor made by a United States consul or vice consul, or a notary public or other person authorized to administer oaths by the law of the place where dishonor occurs. It may be made upon information satisfactory to that person. The protest must identify the instrument and certify either that presentment has been made or, if not made, the reason why it was not made, and that the instrument has been dishonored by nonacceptance or nonpayment. The protest may also certify that notice of dishonor has been given to some or all parties.

PART 6   Discharge and Payment

§ 3–601.   Discharge and Effect of Discharge.

(a) The obligation of a party to pay the instrument is discharged as stated in this Article or by an act or agreement with the party which would discharge an obligation to pay money under a simple contract.

(b) Discharge of the obligation of a party is not effective against a person acquiring rights of a holder in due course of the instrument without notice of the discharge.

§ 3–602.   Payment.

(a) Subject to subsection (b), an instrument is paid to the extent payment is made (i) by or on behalf of a party obliged to pay the instrument, and (ii) to a person entitled to enforce the instrument. To the extent of the payment, the obligation of the party obliged to pay the instrument is discharged even though payment is made with knowledge of a claim to the instrument under Section 3–306 by another person.

(b) The obligation of a party to pay the instrument is not discharged under subsection (a) if:

(1) a claim to the instrument under Section 3–306 is enforceable against the party receiving payment and (i) payment is made with knowledge by the payor that payment is prohibited by injunction or similar process of a court of competent jurisdiction, or (ii) in the case of an instrument other than a cashier's check, teller's check, or certified check, the party making payment accepted, from the person having a claim to the instrument, indemnity against loss resulting from refusal to pay the person entitled to enforce the instrument; or

(2) the person making payment knows that the instrument is a stolen instrument and pays a person it knows is in wrongful possession of the instrument.

§ 3–603.   Tender of Payment.

(a) If tender of payment of an obligation to pay an instrument is made to a person entitled to enforce the instrument, the effect of tender is governed by principles of law applicable to tender of payment under a simple contract.

(b) If tender of payment of an obligation to pay an instrument is made to a person entitled to enforce the instrument and the tender is refused, there is discharge, to the extent of the amount of the tender, of the obligation of an indorser or accommodation party having a right of recourse with respect to the obligation to which the tender relates.

(c) If tender of payment of an amount due on an instrument is made to a person entitled to enforce the instrument, the obligation of the obligor to pay interest after the due date on the amount tendered is discharged. If presentment is required with respect to an instrument and the obligor is able and ready to pay on the due date at every place of payment stated in the instrument, the obligor is deemed to have made tender of payment on the due date to the person entitled to enforce the instrument.

§ 3–604.   Discharge by Cancellation or Renunciation.

(a) A person entitled to enforce an instrument, with or without consideration, may discharge the obligation of a party to pay the instrument (i) by an intentional voluntary act, such as surrender of the instrument to the party, destruction, mutilation, or cancellation of the instrument, cancellation or striking out of the party's signature, or the addition of words to the instrument indicating discharge, or (ii) by agreeing not to sue or otherwise renouncing rights against the party by a signed writing.

(b) Cancellation or striking out of an indorsement pursuant to subsection (a) does not affect the status and rights of a party derived from the indorsement.

§ 3–605.   Discharge of Indorsers and Accommodation Parties.

(a) In this section, the term "indorser" includes a drawer having the obligation described in Section 3–414(d).

(b) Discharge, under Section 3–604, of the obligation of a party to pay an instrument does not discharge the obligation of an indorser or accommodation party having a right of recourse against the discharged party.

(c) If a person entitled to enforce an instrument agrees, with or without consideration, to an extension of the due date of the obligation of a party to pay the instrument, the extension discharges an indorser or accommodation party having a right of recourse against the party whose obligation is extended to the extent the indorser or accommodation party proves that the extension caused loss to the indorser or accommodation party with respect to the right of recourse.

(d) If a person entitled to enforce an instrument agrees, with or without consideration, to a material modification of the obligation of a party other than an extension of the due date, the modification discharges the obligation of an indorser or accommodation party having a right of recourse against the person whose obligation is modified to the extent the modification causes loss to the indorser or accommodation party with respect to the right of recourse. The loss suffered by the indorser or accommodation party as a result of the modifica-

tion is equal to the amount of the right of recourse unless the person enforcing the instrument proves that no loss was caused by the modification or that the loss caused by the modification was an amount less than the amount of the right of recourse.

(e) If the obligation of a party to pay an instrument is secured by an interest in collateral and a person entitled to enforce the instrument impairs the value of the interest in collateral, the obligation of an indorser or accommodation party having a right of recourse against the obligor is discharged to the extent of the impairment. The value of an interest in collateral is impaired to the extent (i) the value of the interest is reduced to an amount less than the amount of the right of recourse of the party asserting discharge, or (ii) the reduction in value of the interest causes an increase in the amount by which the amount of the right of recourse exceeds the value of the interest. The burden of proving impairment is on the party asserting discharge.

(f) If the obligation of a party is secured by an interest in collateral not provided by an accommodation party and a person entitled to enforce the instrument impairs the value of the interest in collateral, the obligation of any party who is jointly and severally liable with respect to the secured obligation is discharged to the extent the impairment causes the party asserting discharge to pay more than that party would have been obliged to pay, taking into account rights of contribution, if impairment had not occurred. If the party asserting discharge is an accommodation party not entitled to discharge under subsection (e), the party is deemed to have a right to contribution based on joint and several liability rather than a right to reimbursement. The burden of proving impairment is on the party asserting discharge.

(g) Under subsection (e) or (f), impairing value of an interest in collateral includes (i) failure to obtain or maintain perfection or recordation of the interest in collateral, (ii) release of collateral without substitution of collateral of equal value, (iii) failure to perform a duty to preserve the value of collateral owed, under Article 9 or other law, to a debtor or surety or other person secondarily liable, or (iv) failure to comply with applicable law in disposing of collateral.

(h) An accommodation party is not discharged under subsection (c), (d), or (e) unless the person entitled to enforce the instrument knows of the accommodation or has notice under Section 3–419(c) that the instrument was signed for accommodation.

(i) A party is not discharged under this section if (i) the party asserting discharge consents to the event or conduct that is the basis of the discharge, or (ii) the instrument or a separate agreement of the party provides for waiver of discharge under this section either specifically or by general language indicating that parties waive defenses based on suretyship or impairment of collateral.

ADDENDUM TO REVISED ARTICLE 3

Notes to Legislative Counsel

1. If revised Article 3 is adopted in your state, the reference in Section 2–511 to Section 3–802 should be changed to Section 3–310.

2. If revised Article 3 is adopted in your state and the Uniform Fiduciaries Act is also in effect in your state, you may want to consider amending Uniform Fiduciaries Act § 9 to conform to Section 3–307(b)(2)(iii) and (4)(iii). See Official Comment 3 to Section 3–307.

REVISED ARTICLE 4

BANK DEPOSITS AND COLLECTIONS

PART I   General Provisions and Definitions

§ 4–101.   Short Title.

This Article may be cited as Uniform Commercial Code—Bank Deposits and Collections.

As amended in 1990.

§ 4–102.   Applicability.

(a) To the extent that items within this Article are also within Articles 3 and 8, they are subject to those Articles. If there is conflict, this Article governs Article 3, but Article 8 governs this Article.

(b) The liability of a bank for action or non-action with respect to an item handled by it for purposes of presentment, payment, or collection is governed by the law of the place where the bank is located. In the case of action or non-action by or at a branch or separate office of a bank, its liability is governed by the law of the place where the branch or separate office is located.

§ 4–103.   Variation by Agreement; Measure of Damages; Action Constituting Ordinary Care.

(a) The effect of the provisions of this Article may be varied by agreement, but the parties to the agreement cannot disclaim a bank's responsibility for its lack of good faith or failure to exercise ordinary care or limit the measure of damages for the lack or failure. However, the parties may determine by agreement the standards by which the bank's responsibility is to be measured if those standards are not manifestly unreasonable.

(b) Federal Reserve regulations and operating circulars, clearing-house rules, and the like have the effect of agreements under subsection (a), whether or not specifically assented to by all parties interested in items handled.

(c) Action or non-action approved by this Article or pursuant to Federal Reserve regulations or operating circulars is the exercise of ordinary care and, in the absence of special instructions, action or non-action consistent with clearing-house rules and the like or with a general banking usage not disapproved by this Article, is prima facie the exercise of ordinary care.

(d) The specification or approval of certain procedures by this Article is not disapproval of other procedures that may be reasonable under the circumstances.

(e) The measure of damages for failure to exercise ordinary care in handling an item is the amount of the item reduced by an amount that could not have been realized by the exercise of ordinary care. If there is also bad faith it includes any other damages the party suffered as a proximate consequence.

As amended in 1990.

§ 4–104.   Definitions and Index of Definitions.

(a) In this Article, unless the context otherwise requires:

(1) "Account" means any deposit or credit account with a bank, including a demand, time, savings, passbook, share draft, or like account, other than an account evidenced by a certificate of deposit;

(2) "Afternoon" means the period of a day between noon and midnight;

(3) "Banking day" means the part of a day on which a bank is open to the public for carrying on substantially all of its banking functions;

(4) "Clearing house" means an association of banks or other payors regularly clearing items;

(5) "Customer" means a person having an account with a bank or for whom a bank has agreed to collect items, including a bank that maintains an account at another bank;

(6) "Documentary draft" means a draft to be presented for acceptance or payment if specified documents, certificated securities (Section 8–102) or instructions for uncertificated securities (Section 8–102), or other certificates, statements, or the like are to be received by the drawee or other payor before acceptance or payment of the draft;

(7) "Draft" means a draft as defined in Section 3–104 or an item, other than an instrument, that is an order;

(8) "Drawee" means a person ordered in a draft to make payment;

(9) "Item" means an instrument or a promise or order to pay money handled by a bank for collection or payment. The term does not include a payment order governed by Article 4A or a credit or debit card slip;

(10) "Midnight deadline" with respect to a bank is midnight on its next banking day following the banking day on which it receives the relevant item or notice or from which the time for taking action commences to run, whichever is later;

(11) "Settle" means to pay in cash, by clearing-house settlement, in a charge or credit or by remittance, or otherwise as agreed. A settlement may be either provisional or final;

(12) "Suspends payments" with respect to a bank means that it has been closed by order of the supervisory authorities, that a public officer has been appointed to take it over, or that it ceases or refuses to make payments in the ordinary course of business.

(b) [Other definitions' section references deleted.]

(c) [Other definitions' section references deleted.]

(d) In addition, Article 1 contains general definitions and principles of construction and interpretation applicable throughout this Article.

§ 4–105. "Bank"; "Depositary Bank"; "Payor Bank"; "Intermediary Bank"; "Collecting Bank"; "Presenting Bank".

In this Article:

(1) "Bank" means a person engaged in the business of banking, including a savings bank, savings and loan association, credit union, or trust company;

(2) "Depositary bank" means the first bank to take an item even though it is also the payor bank, unless the item is presented for immediate payment over the counter;

(3) "Payor bank" means a bank that is the drawee of a draft;

(4) "Intermediary bank" means a bank to which an item is transferred in course of collection except the depositary or payor bank;

(5) "Collecting bank" means a bank handling an item for collection except the payor bank;

(6) "Presenting bank" means a bank presenting an item except a payor bank.

§ 4–106. Payable Through or Payable at Bank: Collecting Bank.

(a) If an item states that it is "payable through" a bank identified in the item, (i) the item designates the bank as a collecting bank and does not by itself authorize the bank to pay the item, and (ii) the item may be presented for payment only by or through the bank.

Alternative A (b) If an item states that it is "payable at" a bank identified in the item, the item is equivalent to a draft drawn on the bank.

Alternative B (b) If an item states that it is "payable at" a bank identified in the item, (i) the item designates the bank as a collecting bank and does not by itself authorize the bank to pay the item, and (ii) the item may be presented for payment only by or through the bank.

(c) If a draft names a nonbank drawee and it is unclear whether a bank named in the draft is a co-drawee or a collecting bank, the bank is a collecting bank.

As added in 1990.

§ 4–107. Separate Office of Bank.

A branch or separate office of a bank is a separate bank for the purpose of computing the time within which and determining the place at or to which action may be taken or notices or orders shall be given under this Article and under Article 3.

As amended in 1962 and 1990.

§ 4–108. Time of Receipt of Items.

(a) For the purpose of allowing time to process items, prove balances, and make the necessary entries on its books to determine its position for the day, a bank may fix an afternoon hour of 2 P.M. or later as a cutoff hour for the handling of money and items and the making of entries on its books.

(b) An item or deposit of money received on any day after a cutoff hour so fixed or after the close of the banking day may be treated as being received at the opening of the next banking day.

As amended in 1990.

§ 4–109. Delays.

(a) Unless otherwise instructed, a collecting bank in a good faith effort to secure payment of a specific item drawn on a payor other than a bank, and with or without the approval of any person involved, may waive, modify, or extend time limits imposed or permitted by this [act] for a period not exceeding two additional banking days without discharge of drawers or indorsers or liability to its transferor or a prior party.

(b) Delay by a collecting bank or payor bank beyond time limits prescribed or permitted by this [act] or by instructions is excused if (i) the delay is caused by interruption of communication or computer facilities, suspension of payments by another bank, war, emergency conditions, failure of equipment, or other circumstances beyond the control of the bank, and (ii) the bank exercises such diligence as the circumstances require.

§ 4–110. Electronic Presentment.

(a) "Agreement for electronic presentment" means an agreement, clearing-house rule, or Federal Reserve regulation or operating circular, providing that presentment of an item may be made by transmission of an image of an item or information describing the item ("presentment notice") rather than delivery of the item itself. The agreement may provide for procedures governing retention, presentment, payment, dishonor, and other matters concerning items subject to the agreement.

(b) Presentment of an item pursuant to an agreement for presentment is made when the presentment notice is received.

(c) If presentment is made by presentment notice, a reference to "item" or "check" in this Article means the presentment notice unless the context otherwise indicates.

As added in 1990.

§ 4–111.   Statute of Limitations.

An action to enforce an obligation, duty, or right arising under this Article must be commenced within three years after the [cause of action] accrues.

As added in 1990.

PART 2   Collection of Items: Depositary and Collecting Banks

§ 4–201.   Status of Collecting Bank as Agent and Provisional Status of Credits; Applicability of Article; Item Indorsed "Pay Any Bank".

(a) Unless a contrary intent clearly appears and before the time that a settlement given by a collecting bank for an item is or becomes final, the bank, with respect to an item, is an agent or sub-agent of the owner of the item and any settlement given for the item is provisional. This provision applies regardless of the form of indorsement or lack of indorsement and even though credit given for the item is subject to immediate withdrawal as of right or is in fact withdrawn; but the continuance of ownership of an item by its owner and any rights of the owner to proceeds of the item are subject to rights of a collecting bank, such as those resulting from outstanding advances on the item and rights of recoupment or setoff. If an item is handled by banks for purposes of presentment, payment, collection, or return, the relevant provisions of this Article apply even though action of the parties clearly establishes that a particular bank has purchased the item and is the owner of it.

(b) After an item has been indorsed with the words "pay any bank" or the like, only a bank may acquire the rights of a holder until the item has been:

(1) returned to the customer initiating collection; or

(2) specially indorsed by a bank to a person who is not a bank.

As amended in 1990.

§ 4–202.   Responsibility for Collection or Return; When Action Timely.

(a) A collecting bank must exercise ordinary care in:

(1) presenting an item or sending it for presentment;

(2) sending notice of dishonor or nonpayment or returning an item other than a documentary draft to the bank's transferor after learning that the item has not been paid or accepted, as the case may be;

(3) settling for an item when the bank receives final settlement; and

(4) notifying its transferor of any loss or delay in transit within a reasonable time after discovery thereof.

(b) A collecting bank exercises ordinary care under subsection (a) by taking proper action before its midnight deadline following receipt of an item, notice, or settlement. Taking proper action within a reasonably longer time may constitute the exercise of ordinary care, but the bank has the burden of establishing timeliness.

(c) Subject to subsection (a)(1), a bank is not liable for the insolvency, neglect, misconduct, mistake, or default of another bank or person or for loss or destruction of an item in the possession of others or in transit.

As amended in 1990.

§ 4–203.   Effect of Instructions.

Subject to Article 3 concerning conversion of instruments (Section 3–420) and restrictive indorsements (Section 3–206), only a collecting bank's transferor can give instructions that affect the bank or constitute notice to it, and a collecting bank is not liable to prior parties for any action taken pursuant to the instructions or in accordance with any agreement with its transferor.

§ 4–204.   Methods of Sending and Presenting; Sending Directly to Payor Bank.

(a) A collecting bank shall send items by a reasonably prompt method, taking into consideration relevant instructions, the nature of the item, the number of those items on hand, the cost of collection involved, and the method generally used by it or others to present those items.

(b) A collecting bank may send:

(1) an item directly to the payor bank;

(2) an item to a nonbank payor if authorized by its transferor; and

(3) an item other than documentary drafts to a nonbank payor, if authorized by Federal Reserve regulation or operating circular, clearing-house rule, or the like.

(c) Presentment may be made by a presenting bank at a place where the payor bank or other payor has requested that presentment be made.

As amended in 1990.

§ 4–205.   Depositary Bank Holder of Unindorsed Item.

If a customer delivers an item to a depositary bank for collection:
(1) the depositary bank becomes a holder of the item at the time it receives the item for collection if the customer at the time of delivery was a holder of the item, whether or not the customer indorses the item, and, if the bank satisfies the other requirements of Section 3–302, it is a holder in due course; and
(2) the depositary bank warrants to collecting banks, the payor bank or other payor, and the drawer that the amount of the item was paid to the customer or deposited to the customer's account.

As amended in 1990.

§ 4–206.   Transfer Between Banks.

Any agreed method that identifies the transferor bank is sufficient for the item's further transfer to another bank.

As amended in 1990.

§ 4–207.   Transfer Warranties.

(a) A customer or collecting bank that transfers an item and receives a settlement or other consideration warrants to the transferee and to any subsequent collecting bank that:

(1) the warrantor is a person entitled to enforce the item;

(2) all signatures on the item are authentic and authorized;

(3) the item has not been altered;

(4) the item is not subject to a defense or claim in recoupment (Section 3–305(a)) of any party that can be asserted against the warrantor; and

(5) the warrantor has no knowledge of any insolvency proceeding commenced with respect to the maker or acceptor or, in the case of an unaccepted draft, the drawer.

(b) If an item is dishonored, a customer or collecting bank transferring the item and receiving settlement or other consideration is obliged to pay the amount due on the item (i) according to the terms of the item at the time it was transferred, or (ii) if the transfer was of an incomplete item, according to its terms when completed as stated in Sections 3–115 and 3–407. The obligation of a transferor is owed to the transferee and to any subsequent collecting bank that takes the item in good faith. A transferor cannot disclaim its obligation under this subsection by an indorsement stating that it is made "without recourse" or otherwise disclaiming liability.

(c) A person to whom the warranties under subsection (a) are made and who took the item in good faith may recover from the warrantor as damages for breach of warranty an amount equal to the loss suffered as a result of the breach, but not more than the amount of the item plus expenses and loss of interest incurred as a result of the breach.

(d) The warranties stated in subsection (a) cannot be disclaimed with respect to checks. Unless notice of a claim for breach of warranty is given to the warrantor within 30 days after the claimant has reason to know of the breach and the identity of the warrantor, the warrantor is discharged to the extent of any loss caused by the delay in giving notice of the claim.

(e) A cause of action for breach of warranty under this section accrues when the claimant has reason to know of the breach.

As amended in 1990.

§ 4–208.   Presentment Warranties.

(a) If an unaccepted draft is presented to the drawee for payment or acceptance and the drawee pays or accepts the draft, (i) the person obtaining payment or acceptance, at the time of presentment, and (ii) a previous transferor of the draft, at the time of transfer, warrant to the drawee that pays or accepts the draft in good faith that:

(1) the warrantor is, or was, at the time the warrantor transferred the draft, a person entitled to enforce the draft or authorized to obtain payment or acceptance of the draft on behalf of a person entitled to enforce the draft;

(2) the draft has not been altered; and

(3) the warrantor has no knowledge that the signature of the purported drawer of the draft is unauthorized.

(b) A drawee making payment may recover from a warrantor damages for breach of warranty equal to the amount paid by the drawee less the amount the drawee received or is entitled to receive from the drawer because of the payment. In addition, the drawee is entitled to compensation for expenses and loss of interest resulting from the breach. The right of the drawee to recover damages under this subsection is not affected by any failure of the drawee to exercise ordinary care in making payment. If the drawee accepts the draft (i) breach of warranty is a defense to the obligation of the acceptor, and (ii) if the acceptor makes payment with respect to the draft, the acceptor is entitled to recover from a warrantor for breach of warranty the amounts stated in this subsection.

(c) If a drawee asserts a claim for breach of warranty under subsection (a) based on an unauthorized indorsement of the draft or an alteration of the draft, the warrantor may defend by proving that the indorsement is effective under Section 3–404 or 3–405 or the drawer is precluded under Section 3–406 or 4–406 from asserting against the drawee the unauthorized indorsement or alteration.

(d) If (i) a dishonored draft is presented for payment to the drawer or an indorser or (ii) any other item is presented for payment to a party obliged to pay the item, and the item is paid, the person obtaining payment and a prior transferor of the item warrant to the person making payment in good faith that the warrantor is, or was, at the time the warrantor transferred the item, a person entitled to enforce the item or authorized to obtain payment on behalf of a person entitled to enforce the item. The person making payment may recover from any warrantor for breach of warranty an amount equal to the amount paid plus expenses and loss of interest resulting from the breach.

(e) The warranties stated in subsections (a) and (d) cannot be disclaimed with respect to checks. Unless notice of a claim for breach of warranty is given to the warrantor within 30 days after the claimant has reason to know of the breach and the identity of the warrantor, the warrantor is discharged to the extent of any loss caused by the delay in giving notice of the claim.

(f) A cause of action for breach of warranty under this section accrues when the claimant has reason to know of the breach.

As amended in 1990.

§ 4–209.   Encoding and Retention Warranties.

(a) A person who encodes information on or with respect to an item after issue warrants to any subsequent collecting bank and to the payor bank or other payor that the information is correctly encoded. If the customer of a depositary bank encodes, that bank also makes the warranty.

(b) A person who undertakes to retain an item pursuant to an agreement for electronic presentment warrants to any subsequent collecting bank and to the payor bank or other payor that retention and presentment of the item comply with the agreement. If a customer of a depositary bank undertakes to retain an item, that bank also makes this warranty.

(c) A person to whom warranties are made under this section and who took the item in good faith may recover from the warrantor as damages for breach of warranty an amount equal to the loss suffered as a result of the breach, plus expenses and loss of interest incurred as a result of the breach.

As added in 1990.

§ 4–210.   Security Interest of Collecting Bank in Items, Accompanying Documents and Proceeds.

(a) A collecting bank has a security interest in an item and any accompanying documents or the proceeds of either:

(1) in case of an item deposited in an account, to the extent to which credit given for the item has been withdrawn or applied;

(2) in case of an item for which it has given credit available for withdrawal as of right, to the extent of the credit given, whether or not the credit is drawn upon or there is a right of charge-back; or

(3) if it makes an advance on or against the item.

(b) If credit given for several items received at one time or pursuant to a single agreement is withdrawn or applied in part, the security interest remains upon all the items, any accompanying documents or the proceeds of either. For the purpose of this section, credits first given are first withdrawn.

(c) Receipt by a collecting bank of a final settlement for an item is a realization on its security interest in the item, accompanying documents, and proceeds. So long as the bank does not receive final settlement for the item or give up possession of the item or accompanying documents for purposes other than collection, the security interest continues to that extent and is subject to Article 9, but:

(1) no security agreement is necessary to make the security interest enforceable (Section 9–203(1)(a));

(2) no filing is required to perfect the security interest; and

(3) the security interest has priority over conflicting perfected security interests in the item, accompanying documents, or proceeds.

As amended in 1990 and 1999.

§ 4–211.   When Bank Gives Value for Purposes of Holder in Due Course.

For purposes of determining its status as a holder in due course, a bank has given value to the extent it has a security interest in an item, if the bank otherwise complies with the requirements of Section 3–302 on what constitutes a holder in due course.

As amended in 1990.

§ 4–212.   Presentment by Notice of Item Not Payable by, Through, or at Bank; Liability of Drawer or Indorser.

(a) Unless otherwise instructed, a collecting bank may present an item not payable by, through, or at a bank by sending to the party to accept or pay a written notice that the bank holds the item for acceptance or payment. The notice must be sent in time to be received on or before the day when presentment is due and the bank must meet any requirement of the party to accept or pay under Section 3–501 by the close of the bank's next banking day after it knows of the requirement.

(b) If presentment is made by notice and payment, acceptance, or request for compliance with a requirement under Section 3–501 is not received by the close of business on the day after maturity or, in the case of demand items, by the close of business on the third banking day after notice was sent, the presenting bank may treat the item as dishonored and charge any drawer or indorser by sending it notice of the facts.

As amended in 1990.

§ 4–213.   Medium and Time of Settlement by Bank.

(a) With respect to settlement by a bank, the medium and time of settlement may be prescribed by Federal Reserve regulations or circulars, clearing-house rules, and the like, or agreement. In the absence of such prescription:

(1) the medium of settlement is cash or credit to an account in a Federal Reserve bank of or specified by the person to receive settlement; and

(2) the time of settlement is:

(i) with respect to tender of settlement by cash, a cashier's check, or teller's check, when the cash or check is sent or delivered;

(ii) with respect to tender of settlement by credit in an account in a Federal Reserve Bank, when the credit is made;

(iii) with respect to tender of settlement by a credit or debit to an account in a bank, when the credit or debit is made or, in the case of tender of settlement by authority to charge an account, when the authority is sent or delivered; or

(iv) with respect to tender of settlement by a funds transfer, when payment is made pursuant to Section 4A–406(a) to the person receiving settlement.

(b) If the tender of settlement is not by a medium authorized by subsection (a) or the time of settlement is not fixed by subsection (a), no settlement occurs until the tender of settlement is accepted by the person receiving settlement.

(c) If settlement for an item is made by cashier's check or teller's check and the person receiving settlement, before its midnight deadline:

(1) presents or forwards the check for collection, settlement is final when the check is finally paid; or

(2) fails to present or forward the check for collection, settlement is final at the midnight deadline of the person receiving settlement.

(d) If settlement for an item is made by giving authority to charge the account of the bank giving settlement in the bank receiving settlement, settlement is final when the charge is made by the bank receiving settlement if there are funds available in the account for the amount of the item.

As amended in 1990.

§ 4–214. Right of Charge-Back or Refund; Liability of Collecting Bank: Return of Item.

(a) If a collecting bank has made provisional settlement with its customer for an item and fails by reason of dishonor, suspension of payments by a bank, or otherwise to receive settlement for the item which is or becomes final, the bank may revoke the settlement given by it, charge back the amount of any credit given for the item to its customer's account, or obtain refund from its customer, whether or not it is able to return the item, if by its midnight deadline or within a longer reasonable time after it learns the facts it returns the item or sends notification of the facts. If the return or notice is delayed beyond the bank's midnight deadline or a longer reasonable time after it learns the facts, the bank may revoke the settlement, charge back the credit, or obtain refund from its customer, but it is liable for any loss resulting from the delay. These rights to revoke, charge back, and obtain refund terminate if and when a settlement for the item received by the bank is or becomes final.

(b) A collecting bank returns an item when it is sent or delivered to the bank's customer or transferor or pursuant to its instructions.

(c) A depositary bank that is also the payor may charge back the amount of an item to its customer's account or obtain refund in accordance with the section governing return of an item received by a payor bank for credit on its books (Section 4–301).

(d) The right to charge back is not affected by:

(1) previous use of a credit given for the item; or

(2) failure by any bank to exercise ordinary care with respect to the item, but a bank so failing remains liable.

(e) A failure to charge back or claim refund does not affect other rights of the bank against the customer or any other party.

(f) If credit is given in dollars as the equivalent of the value of an item payable in foreign money, the dollar amount of any charge-back or refund must be calculated on the basis of the bank-offered spot rate for the foreign money prevailing on the day when the person entitled to the charge-back or refund learns that it will not receive payment in ordinary course.

As amended in 1990.

§ 4–215. Final Payment of Item by Payor Bank; When Provisional Debits and Credits Become Final; When Certain Credits Become Available for Withdrawal.

(a) An item is finally paid by a payor bank when the bank has first done any of the following:

(1) paid the item in cash;

(2) settled for the item without having a right to revoke the settlement under statute, clearing-house rule, or agreement; or

(3) made a provisional settlement for the item and failed to revoke the settlement in the time and manner permitted by statute, clearing-house rule, or agreement.

(b) If provisional settlement for an item does not become final, the item is not finally paid.

(c) If provisional settlement for an item between the presenting and payor banks is made through a clearing house or by debits or credits in an account between them, then to the extent that provisional debits or credits for the item are entered in accounts between the presenting and payor banks or between the presenting and successive prior collecting banks seriatim, they become final upon final payment of the item by the payor bank.

(d) If a collecting bank receives a settlement for an item which is or becomes final, the bank is accountable to its customer for the amount of the item and any provisional credit given for the item in an account with its customer becomes final.

(e) Subject to (i) applicable law stating a time for availability of funds and (ii) any right of the bank to apply the credit to an obligation of the customer, credit given by a bank for an item in a customer's account becomes available for withdrawal as of right:

(1) if the bank has received a provisional settlement for the item, when the settlement becomes final and the bank has had a reasonable time to receive return of the item and the item has not been received within that time;

(2) if the bank is both the depositary bank and the payor bank, and the item is finally paid, at the opening of the bank's second banking day following receipt of the item.

(f) Subject to applicable law stating a time for availability of funds and any right of a bank to apply a deposit to an obligation of the depositor, a deposit of money becomes available for withdrawal as of right at the opening of the bank's next banking day after receipt of the deposit.

As amended in 1990.

§ 4–216.   Insolvency and Preference.

(a) If an item is in or comes into the possession of a payor or collecting bank that suspends payment and the item has not been finally paid, the item must be returned by the receiver, trustee, or agent in charge of the closed bank to the presenting bank or the closed bank's customer.

(b) If a payor bank finally pays an item and suspends payments without making a settlement for the item with its customer or the presenting bank which settlement is or becomes final, the owner of the item has a preferred claim against the payor bank.

(c) If a payor bank gives or a collecting bank gives or receives a provisional settlement for an item and thereafter suspends payments, the suspension does not prevent or interfere with the settlement's becoming final if the finality occurs automatically upon the lapse of certain time or the happening of certain events.

(d) If a collecting bank receives from subsequent parties settlement for an item, which settlement is or becomes final and the bank suspends payments without making a settlement for the item with its customer which settlement is or becomes final, the owner of the item has a preferred claim against the collecting bank.

As amended in 1990.

PART 3   Collection of Items: Payor Banks

§ 4–301.   Deferred Posting; Recovery of Payment by Return of Items; Time of Dishonor; Return of Items by Payor Bank.

(a) If a payor bank settles for a demand item other than a documentary draft presented otherwise than for immediate payment over the counter before midnight of the banking day of receipt, the payor bank may revoke the settlement and recover the settlement if, before it has made final payment and before its midnight deadline, it

(1) returns the item; or

(2) sends written notice of dishonor or nonpayment if the item is unavailable for return.

(b) If a demand item is received by a payor bank for credit on its books, it may return the item or send notice of dishonor and may revoke any credit given or recover the amount thereof withdrawn by its customer, if it acts within the time limit and in the manner specified in subsection (a).

(c) Unless previous notice of dishonor has been sent, an item is dishonored at the time when for purposes of dishonor it is returned or notice sent in accordance with this section.

(d) An item is returned:

(1) as to an item presented through a clearing house, when it is delivered to the presenting or last collecting bank or to the clearing house or is sent or delivered in accordance with clearing-house rules; or

(2) in all other cases, when it is sent or delivered to the bank's customer or transferor or pursuant to instructions.

As amended in 1990.

§ 4–302.   Payor Bank's Responsibility for Late Return of Item.

(a) If an item is presented to and received by a payor bank, the bank is accountable for the amount of:

(1) a demand item, other than a documentary draft, whether properly payable or not, if the bank, in any case in which it is not also the depositary bank, retains the item beyond midnight of the banking day of receipt without settling for it or, whether or not it is also the depositary bank, does not pay or return the item or send notice of dishonor until after its midnight deadline; or

(2) any other properly payable item unless, within the time allowed for acceptance or payment of that item, the bank either accepts or pays the item or returns it and accompanying documents.

(b) The liability of a payor bank to pay an item pursuant to subsection (a) is subject to defenses based on breach of a presentment warranty (Section 4–208) or proof that the person seeking enforcement of the liability presented or transferred the item for the purpose of defrauding the payor bank.

As amended in 1990.

§ 4–303.   When Items Subject to Notice, Stop-Payment Order, Legal Process, or Setoff; Order in Which Items May Be Charged or Certified.

(a) Any knowledge, notice, or stop-payment order received by, legal process served upon, or setoff exercised by a payor bank comes too late to terminate, suspend, or modify the bank's right or duty to pay an item or to charge its customer's account for the item if the knowledge, notice, stop-payment order, or legal process is received or served and a reasonable time for the bank to act thereon expires or the setoff is exercised after the earliest of the following:

(1) the bank accepts or certifies the item;

(2) the bank pays the item in cash;

(3) the bank settles for the item without having a right to revoke the settlement under statute, clearing-house rule, or agreement;

(4) the bank becomes accountable for the amount of the item under Section 4–302 dealing with the payor bank's responsibility for late return of items; or

(5) with respect to checks, a cutoff hour no earlier than one hour after the opening of the next banking day after the bank-

ing day on which the bank received the check and no later than the close of that next banking day or, if no cutoff hour is fixed, the close of the next banking day after the banking day on which the bank received the check.

(b) Subject to subsection (a), items may be accepted, paid, certified, or charged to the indicated account of its customer in any order.

As amended in 1990.

PART 4   Relationship Between Payor Bank and Its Customer

§ 4–401.   When Bank May Charge Customer's Account.

(a) A bank may charge against the account of a customer an item that is properly payable from the account even though the charge creates an overdraft. An item is properly payable if it is authorized by the customer and is in accordance with any agreement between the customer and bank.

(b) A customer is not liable for the amount of an overdraft if the customer neither signed the item nor benefited from the proceeds of the item.

(c) A bank may charge against the account of a customer a check that is otherwise properly payable from the account, even though payment was made before the date of the check, unless the customer has given notice to the bank of the postdating describing the check with reasonable certainty. The notice is effective for the period stated in Section 4–403(b) for stop-payment orders, and must be received at such time and in such manner as to afford the bank a reasonable opportunity to act on it before the bank takes any action with respect to the check described in Section 4–303. If a bank charges against the account of a customer a check before the date stated in the notice of postdating, the bank is liable for damages for the loss resulting from its act. The loss may include damages for dishonor of subsequent items under Section 4–402.

(d) A bank that in good faith makes payment to a holder may charge the indicated account of its customer according to:

(1) the original terms of the altered item; or

(2) the terms of the completed item, even though the bank knows the item has been completed unless the bank has notice that the completion was improper.

As amended in 1990.

§ 4–402.   Bank's Liability to Customer for Wrongful Dishonor; Time of Determining Insufficiency of Account.

(a) Except as otherwise provided in this Article, a payor bank wrongfully dishonors an item if it dishonors an item that is properly payable, but a bank may dishonor an item that would create an overdraft unless it has agreed to pay the overdraft.

(b) A payor bank is liable to its customer for damages proximately caused by the wrongful dishonor of an item. Liability is limited to actual damages proved and may include damages for an arrest or prosecution of the customer or other consequential damages. Whether any consequential damages are proximately caused by the wrongful dishonor is a question of fact to be determined in each case.

(c) A payor bank's determination of the customer's account balance on which a decision to dishonor for insufficiency of available funds is based may be made at any time between the time the item is received by the payor bank and the time that the payor bank returns the item or gives notice in lieu of return, and no more than one determination need be made. If, at the election of the payor bank, a subsequent balance determination is made for the purpose of reevaluating the bank's decision to dishonor the item, the account balance at that time is determinative of whether a dishonor for insufficiency of available funds is wrongful.

As amended in 1990.

§ 4–403.   Customer's Right to Stop Payment; Burden of Proof of Loss.

(a) A customer or any person authorized to draw on the account if there is more than one person may stop payment of any item drawn on the customer's account or close the account by an order to the bank describing the item or account with reasonable certainty received at a time and in a manner that affords the bank a reasonable opportunity to act on it before any action by the bank with respect to the item described in Section 4–303. If the signature of more than one person is required to draw on an account, any of these persons may stop payment or close the account.

(b) A stop-payment order is effective for six months, but it lapses after 14 calendar days if the original order was oral and was not confirmed in writing within that period. A stop-payment order may be renewed for additional six-month periods by a writing given to the bank within a period during which the stop-payment order is effective.

(c) The burden of establishing the fact and amount of loss resulting from the payment of an item contrary to a stop-payment order or order to close an account is on the customer. The loss from payment of an item contrary to a stop-payment order may include damages for dishonor of subsequent items under Section 4–402.

As amended in 1990.

§ 4–404.   Bank Not Obliged to Pay Check More Than Six Months Old.

A bank is under no obligation to a customer having a checking account to pay a check, other than a certified check, which is presented more than six months after its date, but it may charge its customer's account for a payment made thereafter in good faith.

§ 4–405.   Death or Incompetence of Customer.

(a) A payor or collecting bank's authority to accept, pay, or collect an item or to account for proceeds of its collection, if otherwise effective, is not rendered ineffective by incompetence of a customer of either bank existing at the time the item is issued or its collection is undertaken if the bank does not know of an adjudication of incompetence. Neither death nor incompetence of a customer revokes the authority to accept, pay, collect, or account until the bank knows of the fact of death or of an adjudication of incompetence and has reasonable opportunity to act on it.

(b) Even with knowledge, a bank may for 10 days after the date of death pay or certify checks drawn on or before the date unless ordered to stop payment by a person claiming an interest in the account.

As amended in 1990.

§ 4–406.   Customer's Duty to Discover and Report Unauthorized Signature or Alteration.

(a) A bank that sends or makes available to a customer a statement of account showing payment of items for the account shall either return or make available to the customer the items paid or provide information in the statement of account sufficient to allow the customer reasonably to identify the items paid. The statement of account provides sufficient information if the item is described by item number, amount, and date of payment.

(b) If the items are not returned to the customer, the person retaining the items shall either retain the items or, if the items are destroyed, maintain the capacity to furnish legible copies of the items until the expiration of seven years after receipt of the items. A customer may request an item from the bank that paid the item, and that bank must provide in a reasonable time either the item or, if the item has been destroyed or is not otherwise obtainable, a legible copy of the item.

(c) If a bank sends or makes available a statement of account or items pursuant to subsection (a), the customer must exercise reasonable promptness in examining the statement or the items to determine whether any payment was not authorized because of an alteration of an item or because a purported signature by or on behalf of the customer was not authorized. If, based on the statement or items provided, the customer should reasonably have discovered the unauthorized payment, the customer must promptly notify the bank of the relevant facts.

(d) If the bank proves that the customer failed, with respect to an item, to comply with the duties imposed on the customer by subsection (c), the customer is precluded from asserting against the bank:

(1) the customer's unauthorized signature or any alteration on the item, if the bank also proves that it suffered a loss by reason of the failure; and

(2) the customer's unauthorized signature or alteration by the same wrongdoer on any other item paid in good faith by the bank if the payment was made before the bank received notice from the customer of the unauthorized signature or alteration and after the customer had been afforded a reasonable period of time, not exceeding 30 days, in which to examine the item or statement of account and notify the bank.

(e) If subsection (d) applies and the customer proves that the bank failed to exercise ordinary care in paying the item and that the failure substantially contributed to loss, the loss is allocated between the customer precluded and the bank asserting the preclusion according to the extent to which the failure of the customer to comply with subsection (c) and the failure of the bank to exercise ordinary care contributed to the loss. If the customer proves that the bank did not pay the item in good faith, the preclusion under subsection (d) does not apply.

(f) Without regard to care or lack of care of either the customer or the bank, a customer who does not within one year after the statement or items are made available to the customer (subsection (a)) discover and report the customer's unauthorized signature on or any alteration on the item is precluded from asserting against the bank the unauthorized signature or alteration. If there is a preclusion under this subsection, the payor bank may not recover for breach or warranty under Section 4–208 with respect to the unauthorized signature or alteration to which the preclusion applies.

As amended in 1990.

§ 4–407.   Payor Bank's Right to Subrogation on Improper Payment.

If a payor has paid an item over the order of the drawer or maker to stop payment, or after an account has been closed, or otherwise under circumstances giving a basis for objection by the drawer or maker, to prevent unjust enrichment and only to the extent necessary to prevent loss to the bank by reason of its payment of the item, the payor bank is subrogated to the rights

(1) of any holder in due course on the item against the drawer or maker;

(2) of the payee or any other holder of the item against the drawer or maker either on the item or under the transaction out of which the item arose; and

(3) of the drawer or maker against the payee or any other holder of the item with respect to the transaction out of which the item arose.

As amended in 1990.

PART 5   Collection of Documentary Drafts

§ 4–501.   Handling of Documentary Drafts; Duty to Send for Presentment and to Notify Customer of Dishonor.

A bank that takes a documentary draft for collection shall present or send the draft and accompanying documents for presentment and, upon learning that the draft has not been paid or accepted in due course, shall seasonably notify its customer of the fact even though it may have discounted or bought the draft or extended credit available for withdrawal as of right.

As amended in 1990.

§ 4–502.   Presentment of "On Arrival" Drafts.

If a draft or the relevant instructions require presentment "on arrival", "when goods arrive" or the like, the collecting bank need not present until in its judgment a reasonable time for arrival of the goods has expired. Refusal to pay or accept because the goods have not arrived is not dishonor; the bank must notify its transferor of the refusal but need not present the draft again until it is instructed to do so or learns of the arrival of the goods.

§ 4–503.   Responsibility of Presenting Bank for Documents and Goods; Report of Reasons for Dishonor; Referee in Case of Need.

Unless otherwise instructed and except as provided in Article 5, a bank presenting a documentary draft:

(1) must deliver the documents to the drawee on acceptance of the draft if it is payable more than three days after presentment, otherwise, only on payment; and

(2) upon dishonor, either in the case of presentment for acceptance or presentment for payment, may seek and follow instructions from any referee in case of need designated in the draft or, if the presenting bank does not choose to utilize the referee's services, it must use diligence and good faith to ascertain the reason for dishonor, must notify its transferor of the dishonor and of the results of its effort to ascertain the reasons therefor, and must request instructions.

However, the presenting bank is under no obligation with respect to goods represented by the documents except to follow any reasonable instructions seasonably received; it has a right to reimbursement for any expense incurred in following instructions and to prepayment of or indemnity for those expenses.

As amended in 1990.

§ 4–504.   Privilege of Presenting Bank to Deal With Goods; Security Interest for Expenses.

(a) A presenting bank that, following the dishonor of a documentary draft, has seasonably requested instructions but does not receive them within a reasonable time may store, sell, or otherwise deal with the goods in any reasonable manner.

(b) For its reasonable expenses incurred by action under subsection (a) the presenting bank has a lien upon the goods or their proceeds, which may be foreclosed in the same manner as an unpaid seller's lien.

As amended in 1990.

ARTICLE 4A

FUNDS TRANSFERS

PART 1   Subject Matter and Definitions

§ 4A–101. Short Title.

This Article may be cited as Uniform Commercial Code—Funds Transfers.

§ 4A–102. Subject Matter.

Except as otherwise provided in Section 4A–108, this Article applies to funds transfers defined in Section 4A–104.

§ 4A–103. Payment Order-Definitions.

(a) In this Article:

(1) "Payment order" means an instruction of a sender to a receiving bank, transmitted orally, electronically, or in writing, to pay, or to cause another bank to pay, a fixed or determinable amount of money to a beneficiary if:

(i) the instruction does not state a condition to payment to the beneficiary other than time of payment,

(ii) the receiving bank is to be reimbursed by debiting an account of, or otherwise receiving payment from, the sender, and

(iii) the instruction is transmitted by the sender directly to the receiving bank or to an agent, funds-transfer system, or communication system for transmittal to the receiving bank.

(2) "Beneficiary" means the person to be paid by the beneficiary's bank.

(3) "Beneficiary's bank" means the bank identified in a payment order in which an account of the beneficiary is to be credited pursuant to the order or which otherwise is to make payment to the beneficiary if the order does not provide for payment to an account.

(4) "Receiving bank" means the bank to which the sender's instruction is addressed.

(5) "Sender" means the person giving the instruction to the receiving bank.

(b) If an instruction complying with subsection (a)(1) is to make more than one payment to a beneficiary, the instruction is a separate payment order with respect to each payment.

(c) A payment order is issued when it is sent to the receiving bank.

§ 4A-104. Funds Transfer–Definitions.

In this Article:

(a) "Funds transfer" means the series of transactions, beginning with the originator's payment order, made for the purpose of making payment to the beneficiary of the order. The term includes any payment order issued by the originator's bank or an intermediary bank intended to carry out the originator's payment order. A funds transfer is completed by acceptance by the beneficiary's bank of a payment order for the benefit of the beneficiary of the originator's payment order.

(b) "Intermediary bank" means a receiving bank other than the originator's bank or the beneficiary's bank.

(c) "Originator" means the sender of the first payment order in a funds transfer.

(d) "Originator's bank" means (i) the receiving bank to which the payment order of the originator is issued if the originator is not a bank, or (ii) the originator if the originator is a bank.

§ 4A-105. Other Definitions.

(a) In this Article:

(1) "Authorized account" means a deposit account of a customer in a bank designated by the customer as a source of payment of payment orders issued by the customer to the bank. If a customer does not so designate an account, any account of the customer is an authorized account if payment of a payment order from that account is not inconsistent with a restriction on the use of that account.

(2) "Bank" means a person engaged in the business of banking and includes a savings bank, savings and loan association, credit union, and trust company. A branch or separate office of a bank is a separate bank for purposes of this Article.

(3) "Customer" means a person, including a bank, having an account with a bank or from whom a bank has agreed to receive payment orders.

(4) "Funds-transfer business day" of a receiving bank means the part of a day during which the receiving bank is open for the receipt, processing, and transmittal of payment orders and cancellations and amendments of payment orders.

(5) "Funds-transfer system" means a wire transfer network, automated clearing house, or other communication system of a clearing house or other association of banks through which a payment order by a bank may be transmitted to the bank to which the order is addressed.

(6) "Good faith" means honesty in fact and the observance of reasonable commercial standards of fair dealing.

(7) "Prove" with respect to a fact means to meet the burden of establishing the fact (Section 1–201(8)).

(b) Other definitions applying to this Article and the sections in which they appear are:

"Acceptance" Section 4A–209
"Beneficiary" Section 4A–103
"Beneficiary's bank" Section 4A–103
"Executed" Section 4A–301
"Execution date" Section 4A–301
"Funds transfer" Section 4A–104
"Funds-transfer system rule" Section 4A–501
"Intermediary bank" Section 4A–104
"Originator" Section 4A–104
"Originator's bank" Section 4A–104
"Payment by beneficiary's bank to beneficiary" Section 4A–405
"Payment by originator to beneficiary" Section 4A–406
"Payment by sender to receiving bank" Section 4A–403
"Payment date" Section 4A–401
"Payment order" Section 4A–103
"Receiving bank" Section 4A–103
"Security procedure" Section 4A–201
"Sender" Section 4A–103

(c) The following definitions in Article 4 apply to this Article:
"Clearing house" Section 4–104
"Item" Section 4–104
"Suspends payments" Section 4–104

(d) In addition, Article 1 contains general definitions and principles of construction and interpretation applicable throughout this Article.

§ 4A-106. Time Payment Order Is Received.

(a) The time of receipt of a payment order or communication cancelling or amending a payment order is determined by the rules applicable to receipt of a notice stated in Section 1–201(27). A receiving bank may fix a cut-off time or times on a funds-transfer business day for the receipt and processing of payment orders and communications cancelling or amending payment orders. Different cut-off times may apply to payment orders, cancellations, or amendments, or to different categories of payment orders, cancellations, or amendments. A cut-off time may apply to senders generally or different cut-off times may apply to different senders or categories of payment orders. If a payment order or communication cancelling or amending a payment order is received after the close of a funds-transfer business day or after the appropriate cut-off time on a funds-transfer business day, the receiving bank may treat the payment order or communication as received at the opening of the next funds-transfer business day.

(b) If this Article refers to an execution date or payment date or states a day on which a receiving bank is required to take action, and the date or day does not fall on a funds-transfer business day, the next day that is a funds-transfer business day is treated as the date or day stated, unless the contrary is stated in this Article.

§ 4A–107. Federal Reserve Regulations and Operating Circulars.

Regulations of the Board of Governors of the Federal Reserve System and operating circulars of the Federal Reserve Banks supersede any inconsistent provision of this Article to the extent of the inconsistency.

§ 4A–108. Exclusion of Consumer Transactions Governed by Federal Law.

This Article does not apply to a funds transfer any part of which is governed by the Electronic Fund Transfer Act of 1978 (Title XX, Public Law 95–630, 92 Stat. 3728, 15 U.S.C. § 1693 et seq.) as amended from time to time.

PART 2   Issue and Acceptance of Payment Order

§ 4A–201. Security Procedure.

"Security procedure" means a procedure established by agreement of a customer and a receiving bank for the purpose of (i) verifying that a payment order or communication amending or cancelling a payment order is that of the customer, or (ii) detecting error in the transmission or the content of the payment order or communication. A security procedure may require the use of algorithms or other codes, identifying words or numbers, encryption, callback procedures, or similar security devices. Comparison of a signature on a payment order or communication with an authorized specimen signature of the customer is not by itself a security procedure.

§ 4A–202. Authorized and Verified Payment Orders.

(a) A payment order received by the receiving bank is the authorized order of the person identified as sender if that person authorized the order or is otherwise bound by it under the law of agency.

(b) If a bank and its customer have agreed that the authenticity of payment orders issued to the bank in the name of the customer as sender will be verified pursuant to a security procedure, a payment order received by the receiving bank is effective as the order of the customer, whether or not authorized, if (i) the security procedure is a commercially reasonable method of providing security against unauthorized payment orders, and (ii) the bank proves that it accepted the payment order in good faith and in compliance with the security procedure and any written agreement or instruction of the customer restricting acceptance of payment orders issued in the name of the customer. The bank is not required to follow an instruction that violates a written agreement with the customer or notice of which is not received at a time and in a manner affording the bank a reasonable opportunity to act on it before the payment order is accepted.

(c) Commercial reasonableness of a security procedure is a question of law to be determined by considering the wishes of the customer expressed to the bank, the circumstances of the customer known to the bank, including the size, type, and frequency of payment orders normally issued by the customer to the bank, alternative security procedures offered to the customer, and security procedures in general use by customers and receiving banks similarly situated. A security procedure is deemed to be commercially reasonable if (i) the security procedure was chosen by the customer after the bank offered, and the customer refused, a security procedure that was commercially reasonable for that customer, and (ii) the customer expressly agreed in writing to be bound by any payment order, whether or not authorized, issued in its name and accepted by the bank in compliance with the security procedure chosen by the customer.

(d) The term "sender" in this Article includes the customer in whose name a payment order is issued if the order is the authorized order of the customer under subsection (a), or it is effective as the order of the customer under subsection (b).

(e) This section applies to amendments and cancellations of payment orders to the same extent it applies to payment orders.

(f) Except as provided in this section and in Section 4A–203(a)(1), rights and obligations arising under this section or Section 4A–203 may not be varied by agreement.

§ 4A–203. Unenforceability of Certain Verified Payment Orders.

(a) If an accepted payment order is not, under Section 4A–202(a), an authorized order of a customer identified as sender, but is effective as an order of the customer pursuant to Section 4A–202(b), the following rules apply:

(1) By express written agreement, the receiving bank may limit the extent to which it is entitled to enforce or retain payment of the payment order.

(2) The receiving bank is not entitled to enforce or retain payment of the payment order if the customer proves that the order was not caused, directly or indirectly, by a person (i) entrusted at any time with duties to act for the customer with respect to payment orders or the security procedure, or (ii) who obtained access to transmitting facilities of the customer or who obtained, from a source controlled by the customer and without authority of the receiving bank, information facilitating breach of the security procedure, regardless of how the information was obtained or whether the customer was at fault. Information includes any access device, computer software, or the like.

(b) This section applies to amendments of payment orders to the same extent it applies to payment orders.

§ 4A–204. Refund of Payment and Duty of Customer to Report with Respect to Unauthorized Payment Order.

(a) If a receiving bank accepts a payment order issued in the name of its customer as sender which is (i) not authorized and not effective as the order of the customer under Section 4A–202, or (ii) not enforceable, in whole or in part, against the customer under Section 4A–203, the bank shall refund any payment of the payment order received from the customer to the extent the bank is not entitled to enforce payment and shall pay interest on the refundable amount calculated from the date the bank received payment to the date of the refund. However, the customer is not entitled to interest from the bank on the amount to be refunded if the customer fails to exercise ordinary care to determine that the order was not authorized by the customer and to notify the bank of the relevant facts within a reasonable time not exceeding 90 days after the date the customer received notification from the bank that the order was accepted or that the customer's account was debited with respect to the order. The bank is not entitled to any recovery from the customer on account of a failure by the customer to give notification as stated in this section.

(b) Reasonable time under subsection (a) may be fixed by agreement as stated in Section 1–204(1), but the obligation of a receiving bank to refund payment as stated in subsection (a) may not otherwise be varied by agreement.

§ 4A–205. Erroneous Payment Orders.

(a) If an accepted payment order was transmitted pursuant to a security procedure for the detection of error and the payment order (i) erroneously instructed payment to a beneficiary not intended by the sender, (ii) erroneously instructed payment in an amount greater than the amount intended by the sender, or (iii) was an erroneously transmitted duplicate of a payment order previously sent by the sender, the following rules apply:

(1) If the sender proves that the sender or a person acting on behalf of the sender pursuant to Section 4A–206 complied with the security procedure and that the error would have been detected if the receiving bank had also complied, the sender is not obliged to pay the order to the extent stated in paragraphs (2) and (3).

(2) If the funds transfer is completed on the basis of an erroneous payment order described in clause (i) or (iii) of subsection (a), the sender is not obliged to pay the order and the receiving bank is entitled to recover from the beneficiary any amount paid to the beneficiary to the extent allowed by the law governing mistake and restitution.

(3) If the funds transfer is completed on the basis of a payment order described in clause (ii) of subsection (a), the sender is not obliged to pay the order to the extent the amount received by the beneficiary is greater than the amount intended by the sender. In that case, the receiving bank is entitled to recover from the beneficiary the excess amount received to the extent allowed by the law governing mistake and restitution.

(b) If (i) the sender of an erroneous payment order described in subsection (a) is not obliged to pay all or part of the order, and (ii) the sender receives notification from the receiving bank that the order was accepted by the bank or that the sender's account was debited with respect to the order, the sender has a duty to exercise ordinary care, on the basis of information available to the sender, to discover the error with respect to the order and to advise the bank of the relevant facts within a reasonable time, not exceeding 90 days, after the bank's notification was received by the sender. If the bank proves that the sender failed to perform that duty, the sender is liable to the bank for the loss the bank proves it incurred as a result of the failure, but the liability of the sender may not exceed the amount of the sender's order.

(c) This section applies to amendments to payment orders to the same extent it applies to payment orders.

§ 4A–206. Transmission of Payment Order through Funds-Transfer or Other Communication System.

(a) If a payment order addressed to a receiving bank is transmitted to a funds-transfer system or other third party communication system for transmittal to the bank, the system is deemed to be an agent of the sender for the purpose of transmitting the payment order to the bank. If there is a discrepancy between the terms of the payment order transmitted to the system and the terms of the payment order transmitted by the system to the bank, the terms of the payment order of the sender are those transmitted by the system. This section does not apply to a funds-transfer system of the Federal Reserve Banks.

(b) This section applies to cancellations and amendments to payment orders to the same extent it applies to payment orders.

§ 4A–207. Misdescrizption of Beneficiary.

(a) Subject to subsection (b), if, in a payment order received by the beneficiary's bank, the name, bank account number, or other identification of the beneficiary refers to a nonexistent or unidentifiable person or account, no person has rights as a beneficiary of the order and acceptance of the order cannot occur.

(b) If a payment order received by the beneficiary's bank identifies the beneficiary both by name and by an identifying or bank account number and the name and number identify different persons, the following rules apply:

(1) Except as otherwise provided in subsection (c), if the beneficiary's bank does not know that the name and number refer to different persons, it may rely on the number as the proper identification of the beneficiary of the order. The beneficiary's bank need not determine whether the name and number refer to the same person.

(2) If the beneficiary's bank pays the person identified by name or knows that the name and number identify different persons, no person has rights as beneficiary except the person paid by the beneficiary's bank if that person was entitled to receive payment from the originator of the funds transfer. If no person has rights as beneficiary, acceptance of the order cannot occur.

(c) If (i) a payment order described in subsection (b) is accepted, (ii) the originator's payment order described the beneficiary inconsistently by name and number, and (iii) the beneficiary's bank pays the person identified by number as permitted by subsection (b)(1), the following rules apply:

(1) If the originator is a bank, the originator is obliged to pay its order.

(2) If the originator is not a bank and proves that the person identified by number was not entitled to receive payment from the originator, the originator is not obliged to pay its order unless the originator's bank proves that the originator, before acceptance of the originator's order, had notice that payment of a payment order issued by the originator might be made by the beneficiary's bank on the basis of an identifying or bank account number even if it identifies a person different from the named beneficiary. Proof of notice may be made by any admissible evidence. The originator's bank satisfies the burden of proof if it proves that the originator, before the payment order was accepted, signed a writing stating the information to which the notice relates.

(d) In a case governed by subsection (b)(1), if the beneficiary's bank rightfully pays the person identified by number and that person was not entitled to receive payment from the originator, the amount paid may be recovered from that person to the extent allowed by the law governing mistake and restitution as follows:

(1) If the originator is obliged to pay its payment order as stated in subsection (c), the originator has the right to recover.

(2) If the originator is not a bank and is not obliged to pay its payment order, the originator's bank has the right to recover.

§ 4A–208. Misdescription of Intermediary Bank or Beneficiary's Bank.

(a) This subsection applies to a payment order identifying an intermediary bank or the beneficiary's bank only by an identifying number.

(1) The receiving bank may rely on the number as the proper identification of the intermediary or beneficiary's bank and need not determine whether the number identifies a bank.

(2) The sender is obliged to compensate the receiving bank for any loss and expenses incurred by the receiving bank as a result of its reliance on the number in executing or attempting to execute the order.

(b) This subsection applies to a payment order identifying an intermediary bank or the beneficiary's bank both by name and an identifying number if the name and number identify different persons.

(1) If the sender is a bank, the receiving bank may rely on the number as the proper identification of the intermediary or beneficiary's bank if the receiving bank, when it executes the sender's order, does not know that the name and number identify different persons. The receiving bank need not determine whether the name and number refer to the same person or whether the number refers to a bank. The sender is obliged to compensate the receiving bank for any loss and expenses incurred by the receiving bank as a result of its reliance on the number in executing or attempting to execute the order.

(2) If the sender is not a bank and the receiving bank proves that the sender, before the payment order was accepted, had notice that the receiving bank might rely on the number as the proper identification of the intermediary or beneficiary's bank even if it identifies a person different from the bank identified by name, the rights and obligations of the sender and the receiving bank are governed by subsection (b)(1), as though the sender were a bank. Proof of notice may be made by any admissible evidence. The receiving bank satisfies the burden of proof if it proves that the sender, before the payment order was accepted, signed a writing stating the information to which the notice relates.

(3) Regardless of whether the sender is a bank, the receiving bank may rely on the name as the proper identification of the intermediary or beneficiary's bank if the receiving bank, at the time it executes the sender's order, does not know that the name and number identify different persons. The receiving bank need not determine whether the name and number refer to the same person.

(4) If the receiving bank knows that the name and number identify different persons, reliance on either the name or the number in executing the sender's payment order is a breach of the obligation stated in Section 4A–302(a)(1).

§ 4A–209. Acceptance of Payment Order.

(a) Subject to subsection (d), a receiving bank other than the beneficiary's bank accepts a payment order when it executes the order.

(b) Subject to subsections (c) and (d), a beneficiary's bank accepts a payment order at the earliest of the following times:

(1) When the bank (i) pays the beneficiary as stated in Section 4A–405(a) or 4A–405(b), or (ii) notifies the beneficiary of receipt of the order or that the account of the beneficiary has been credited with respect to the order unless the notice indicates that the bank is rejecting the order or that funds with respect to the order may not be withdrawn or used until receipt of payment from the sender of the order;

(2) When the bank receives payment of the entire amount of the sender's order pursuant to Section 4A–403(a)(1) or 4A–403(a)(2); or

(3) The opening of the next funds-transfer business day of the bank following the payment date of the order if, at that time, the amount of the sender's order is fully covered by a

withdrawable credit balance in an authorized account of the sender or the bank has otherwise received full payment from the sender, unless the order was rejected before that time or is rejected within (i) one hour after that time, or (ii) one hour after the opening of the next business day of the sender following the payment date if that time is later. If notice of rejection is received by the sender after the payment date and the authorized account of the sender does not bear interest, the bank is obliged to pay interest to the sender on the amount of the order for the number of days elapsing after the payment date to the day the sender receives notice or learns that the order was not accepted, counting that day as an elapsed day. If the withdrawable credit balance during that period falls below the amount of the order, the amount of interest payable is reduced accordingly.

(c) Acceptance of a payment order cannot occur before the order is received by the receiving bank. Acceptance does not occur under subsection (b)(2) or (b)(3) if the beneficiary of the payment order does not have an account with the receiving bank, the account has been closed, or the receiving bank is not permitted by law to receive credits for the beneficiary's account.

(d) A payment order issued to the originator's bank cannot be accepted until the payment date if the bank is the beneficiary's bank, or the execution date if the bank is not the beneficiary's bank. If the originator's bank executes the originator's payment order before the execution date or pays the beneficiary of the originator's payment order before the payment date and the payment order is subsequently cancelled pursuant to Section 4A–211(b), the bank may recover from the beneficiary any payment received to the extent allowed by the law governing mistake and restitution.

§ 4A–210. Rejection of Payment Order.

(a) A payment order is rejected by the receiving bank by a notice of rejection transmitted to the sender orally, electronically, or in writing. A notice of rejection need not use any particular words and is sufficient if it indicates that the receiving bank is rejecting the order or will not execute or pay the order. Rejection is effective when the notice is given if transmission is by a means that is reasonable in the circumstances. If notice of rejection is given by a means that is not reasonable, rejection is effective when the notice is received. If an agreement of the sender and receiving bank establishes the means to be used to reject a payment order, (i) any means complying with the agreement is reasonable and (ii) any means not complying is not reasonable unless no significant delay in receipt of the notice resulted from the use of the noncomplying means.

(b) This subsection applies if a receiving bank other than the beneficiary's bank fails to execute a payment order despite the existence on the execution date of a withdrawable credit balance in an authorized account of the sender sufficient to cover the order. If the sender does not receive notice of rejection of the order on the execution date and the authorized account of

the sender does not bear interest, the bank is obliged to pay interest to the sender on the amount of the order for the number of days elapsing after the execution date to the earlier of the day the order is cancelled pursuant to Section 4A–211(d) or the day the sender receives notice or learns that the order was not executed, counting the final day of the period as an elapsed day. If the withdrawable credit balance during that period falls below the amount of the order, the amount of interest is reduced accordingly.

(c) If a receiving bank suspends payments, all unaccepted payment orders issued to it are are deemed rejected at the time the bank suspends payments.

(d) Acceptance of a payment order precludes a later rejection of the order. Rejection of a payment order precludes a later acceptance of the order.

§ 4A–211. Cancellation and Amendment of Payment Order.

(a) A communication of the sender of a payment order cancelling or amending the order may be transmitted to the receiving bank orally, electronically, or in writing. If a security procedure is in effect between the sender and the receiving bank, the communication is not effective to cancel or amend the order unless the communication is verified pursuant to the security procedure or the bank agrees to the cancellation or amendment.

(b) Subject to subsection (a), a communication by the sender cancelling or amending a payment order is effective to cancel or amend the order if notice of the communication is received at a time and in a manner affording the receiving bank a reasonable opportunity to act on the communication before the bank accepts the payment order.

(c) After a payment order has been accepted, cancellation or amendment of the order is not effective unless the receiving bank agrees or a funds-transfer system rule allows cancellation or amendment without agreement of the bank.

(1) With respect to a payment order accepted by a receiving bank other than the beneficiary's bank, cancellation or amendment is not effective unless a conforming cancellation or amendment of the payment order issued by the receiving bank is also made.

(2) With respect to a payment order accepted by the beneficiary's bank, cancellation or amendment is not effective unless the order was issued in execution of an unauthorized payment order, or because of a mistake by a sender in the funds transfer which resulted in the issuance of a payment order (i) that is a duplicate of a payment order previously issued by the sender, (ii) that orders payment to a beneficiary not entitled to receive payment from the originator, or (iii) that orders payment in an amount greater than the amount the beneficiary was entitled to receive from the originator. If the payment order is cancelled or amended, the beneficiary's bank is entitled to recover from the beneficiary any amount paid to the beneficiary to the extent allowed by the law governing mistake and restitution.

(d) An unaccepted payment order is cancelled by operation of law at the close of the fifth funds-transfer business day of the receiving bank after the execution date or payment date of the order.

(e) A cancelled payment order cannot be accepted. If an accepted payment order is cancelled, the acceptance is nullified and no person has any right or obligation based on the acceptance. Amendment of a payment order is deemed to be cancellation of the original order at the time of amendment and issue of a new payment order in the amended form at the same time.

(f) Unless otherwise provided in an agreement of the parties or in a funds-transfer system rule, if the receiving bank, after accepting a payment order, agrees to cancellation or amendment of the order by the sender or is bound by a funds-transfer system rule allowing cancellation or amendment without the bank's agreement, the sender, whether or not cancellation or amendment is effective, is liable to the bank for any loss and expenses, including reasonable attorney's fees, incurred by the bank as a result of the cancellation or amendment or attempted cancellation or amendment.

(g) A payment order is not revoked by the death or legal incapacity of the sender unless the receiving bank knows of the death or of an adjudication of incapacity by a court of competent jurisdiction and has reasonable opportunity to act before acceptance of the order.

(h) A funds-transfer system rule is not effective to the extent it conflicts with subsection (c)(2).

§ 4A–212. Liability and Duty of Receiving Bank Regarding Unaccepted Payment Order.

If a receiving bank fails to accept a payment order that it is obliged by express agreement to accept, the bank is liable for breach of the agreement to the extent provided in the agreement or in this Article, but does not otherwise have any duty to accept a payment order or, before acceptance, to take any action, or refrain from taking action, with respect to the order except as provided in this Article or by express agreement. Liability based on acceptance arises only when acceptance occurs as stated in Section 4A–209, and liability is limited to that provided in this Article. A receiving bank is not the agent of the sender or beneficiary of the payment order it accepts, or of any other party to the funds transfer, and the bank owes no duty to any party to the funds transfer except as provided in this Article or by express agreement.

PART 3 Execution of Sender's Payment Order by Receiving Bank

§ 4A–301. Execution and Execution Date.

(a) A payment order is "executed" by the receiving bank when it issues a payment order intended to carry out the payment order received by the bank. A payment order received by the beneficiary's bank can be accepted but cannot be executed.

(b) "Execution date" of a payment order means the day on which the receiving bank may properly issue a payment order in execution of the sender's order. The execution date may be determined by instruction of the sender but cannot be earlier than the day the order is received and, unless otherwise determined, is the day the order is received. If the sender's instruction states a payment date, the execution date is the payment date or an earlier date on which execution is reasonably necessary to allow payment to the beneficiary on the payment date.

§ 4A–302. Obligations of Receiving Bank in Execution of Payment Order.

(a) Except as provided in subsections (b) through (d), if the receiving bank accepts a payment order pursuant to Section 4A–209(a), the bank has the following obligations in executing the order:

(1) The receiving bank is obliged to issue, on the execution date, a payment order complying with the sender's order and to follow the sender's instructions concerning (i) any intermediary bank or funds-transfer system to be used in carrying out the funds transfer, or (ii) the means by which payment orders are to be transmitted in the funds transfer. If the originator's bank issues a payment order to an intermediary bank, the originator's bank is obliged to instruct the intermediary bank according to the instruction of the originator. An intermediary bank in the funds transfer is similarly bound by an instruction given to it by the sender of the payment order it accepts.

(2) If the sender's instruction states that the funds transfer is to be carried out telephonically or by wire transfer or otherwise indicates that the funds transfer is to be carried out by the most expeditious means, the receiving bank is obliged to transmit its payment order by the most expeditious available means, and to instruct any intermediary bank accordingly. If a sender's instruction states a payment date, the receiving bank is obliged to transmit its payment order at a time and by means reasonably necessary to allow payment to the beneficiary on the payment date or as soon thereafter as is feasible.

(b) Unless otherwise instructed, a receiving bank executing a payment order may (i) use any funds-transfer system if use of that system is reasonable in the circumstances, and (ii) issue a payment order to the beneficiary's bank or to an intermediary bank through which a payment order conforming to the sender's order can expeditiously be issued to the beneficiary's bank if the receiving bank exercises ordinary care in the selection of the intermediary bank. A receiving bank is not required to follow an instruction of the sender designating a funds-transfer system to be used in carrying out the funds transfer if the receiving bank, in good faith, determines that it is not feasible to follow the instruction or that following the instruction would unduly delay completion of the funds transfer.

(c) Unless subsection (a)(2) applies or the receiving bank is otherwise instructed, the bank may execute a payment order by transmitting its payment order by first class mail or by any means reasonable in the circumstances. If the receiving bank is instructed to execute the sender's order by transmitting its payment order by a particular means, the receiving bank may issue its payment order by the means stated or by any means as expeditious as the means stated.

(d) Unless instructed by the sender, (i) the receiving bank may not obtain payment of its charges for services and expenses in connection with the execution of the sender's order by issuing a payment order in an amount equal to the amount of the sender's order less the amount of the charges, and (ii) may not instruct a subsequent receiving bank to obtain payment of its charges in the same manner.

§ 4A–303. Erroneous Execution of Payment Order.

(a) A receiving bank that (i) executes the payment order of the sender by issuing a payment order in an amount greater than the amount of the sender's order, or (ii) issues a payment order in execution of the sender's order and then issues a duplicate order, is entitled to payment of the amount of the sender's order under Section 4A–402(c) if that subsection is otherwise satisfied. The bank is entitled to recover from the beneficiary of the erroneous order the excess payment received to the extent allowed by the law governing mistake and restitution.

(b) A receiving bank that executes the payment order of the sender by issuing a payment order in an amount less than the amount of the sender's order is entitled to payment of the amount of the sender's order under Section 4A–402(c) if (i) that subsection is otherwise satisfied and (ii) the bank corrects its mistake by issuing an additional payment order for the benefit of the beneficiary of the sender's order. If the error is not corrected, the issuer of the erroneous order is entitled to receive or retain payment from the sender of the order it accepted only to the extent of the amount of the erroneous order. This subsection does not apply if the receiving bank executes the sender's payment order by issuing a payment order in an amount less than the amount of the sender's order for the purpose of obtaining payment of its charges for services and expenses pursuant to instruction of the sender.

(c) If a receiving bank executes the payment order of the sender by issuing a payment order to a beneficiary different from the beneficiary of the sender's order and the funds transfer is completed on the basis of that error, the sender of the payment order that was erroneously executed and all previous senders in the funds transfer are not obliged to pay the payment orders they issued. The issuer of the erroneous order is entitled to recover from the beneficiary of the order the payment received to the extent allowed by the law governing mistake and restitution.

§ 4A–304. Duty of Sender to Report Erroneously Executed Payment Order.

If the sender of a payment order that is erroneously executed as stated in Section 4A–303 receives notification from the receiving bank that the order was executed or that the sender's account was debited with respect to the order, the sender has a duty to exercise ordinary care to determine, on the basis of information available to the sender, that the order was erroneously executed and to notify the bank of the relevant facts within a reasonable time not exceeding 90 days after the notification from the bank was received by the sender. If the sender fails to perform that duty, the bank is not obliged to pay interest on any amount refundable to the sender under Section 4A–402(d) for the period before the bank learns of the execution error. The bank is not entitled to any recovery from the sender on account of a failure by the sender to perform the duty stated in this section.

§ 4A–305. Liability for Late or Improper Execution or Failure to Execute Payment Order.

(a) If a funds transfer is completed but execution of a payment order by the receiving bank in breach of Section 4A–302 results in delay in payment to the beneficiary, the bank is obliged to pay interest to either the originator or the beneficiary of the funds transfer for the period of delay caused by the improper execution. Except as provided in subsection (c), additional damages are not recoverable.

(b) If execution of a payment order by a receiving bank in breach of Section 4A–302 results in (i) noncompletion of the funds transfer, (ii) failure to use an intermediary bank designated by the originator, or (iii) issuance of a payment order that does not comply with the terms of the payment order of the originator, the bank is liable to the originator for its expenses in the funds transfer and for incidental expenses and interest losses, to the extent not covered by subsection (a), resulting from the improper execution. Except as provided in subsection (c), additional damages are not recoverable.

(c) In addition to the amounts payable under subsections (a) and (b), damages, including consequential damages, are recoverable to the extent provided in an express written agreement of the receiving bank.

(d) If a receiving bank fails to execute a payment order it was obliged by express agreement to execute, the receiving bank is liable to the sender for its expenses in the transaction and for incidental expenses and interest losses resulting from the failure to execute. Additional damages, including consequential damages, are recoverable to the extent provided in an express written agreement of the receiving bank, but are not otherwise recoverable.

(e) Reasonable attorney's fees are recoverable if demand for compensation under subsection (a) or (b) is made and refused before an action is brought on the claim. If a claim is made for breach of an agreement under subsection (d) and the agreement does not provide for damages, reasonable attorney's fees are recoverable if demand for compensation under subsection (d) is made and refused before an action is brought on the claim.

(f) Except as stated in this section, the liability of a receiving bank under subsections (a) and (b) may not be varied by agreement.

PART 4   Payment

§ 4A–401. Payment Date.

"Payment date" of a payment order means the day on which the amount of the order is payable to the beneficiary by the beneficiary's bank. The payment date may be determined by instruction of the sender but cannot be earlier than the day the order is received by the beneficiary's bank and, unless otherwise determined, is the day the order is received by the beneficiary's bank.

§ 4A–402. Obligation of Sender to Pay Receiving Bank.

(a) This section is subject to Sections 4A–205 and 4A–207.

(b) With respect to a payment order issued to the beneficiary's bank, acceptance of the order by the bank obliges the sender to pay the bank the amount of the order, but payment is not due until the payment date of the order.

(c) This subsection is subject to subsection (e) and to Section 4A–303. With respect to a payment order issued to a receiving bank other than the beneficiary's bank, acceptance of the order by the receiving bank obliges the sender to pay the bank the amount of the sender's order. Payment by the sender is not due until the execution date of the sender's order. The obligation of that sender to pay its payment order is excused if the funds transfer is not completed by acceptance by the beneficiary's bank of a payment order instructing payment to the beneficiary of that sender's payment order.

(d) If the sender of a payment order pays the order and was not obliged to pay all or part of the amount paid, the bank receiving payment is obliged to refund payment to the extent the sender was not obliged to pay. Except as provided in Sections 4A–204 and 4A–304, interest is payable on the refundable amount from the date of payment.

(e) If a funds transfer is not completed as stated in subsection (c) and an intermediary bank is obliged to refund payment as stated in subsection (d) but is unable to do so because not permitted by applicable law or because the bank suspends payments, a sender in the funds transfer that executed a payment order in compliance with an instruction, as stated in Section 4A–302(a)(1), to route the funds transfer through that interme-diary bank is entitled to receive or retain payment from the sender of the payment order that it accepted. The first sender in the funds transfer that issued an instruction requiring routing through that intermediary bank is subrogated to the right of the bank that paid the intermediary bank to refund as stated in subsection (d).

(f) The right of the sender of a payment order to be excused from the obligation to pay the order as stated in subsection (c) or to receive refund under subsection (d) may not be varied by agreement.

§ 4A–403. Payment by Sender to Receiving Bank.

(a) Payment of the sender's obligation under Section 4A–402 to pay the receiving bank occurs as follows:

(1) If the sender is a bank, payment occurs when the receiving bank receives final settlement of the obligation through a Federal Reserve Bank or through a funds-transfer system.

(2) If the sender is a bank and the sender (i) credited an account of the receiving bank with the sender, or (ii) caused an account of the receiving bank in another bank to be credited, payment occurs when the credit is withdrawn or, if not withdrawn, at midnight of the day on which the credit is withdrawable and the receiving bank learns of that fact.

(3) If the receiving bank debits an account of the sender with the receiving bank, payment occurs when the debit is made to the extent the debit is covered by a withdrawable credit balance in the account.

(b) If the sender and receiving bank are members of a funds-transfer system that nets obligations multilaterally among participants, the receiving bank receives final settlement when settlement is complete in accordance with the rules of the system. The obligation of the sender to pay the amount of a payment order transmitted through the funds-transfer system may be satisfied, to the extent permitted by the rules of the system, by setting off and applying against the sender's obligation the right of the sender to receive payment from the receiving bank of the amount of any other payment order transmitted to the sender by the receiving bank through the funds-transfer system. The aggregate balance of obligations owed by each sender to each receiving bank in the funds-transfer system may be satisfied, to the extent permitted by the rules of the system, by setting off and applying against that balance the aggregate balance of obligations owed to the sender by other members of the system. The aggregate balance is determined after the right of setoff stated in the second sentence of this subsection has been exercised.

(c) If two banks transmit payment orders to each other under an agreement that settlement of the obligations of each bank to the other under Section 4A–402 will be made at the end of the day or other period, the total amount owed with respect to all orders transmitted by one bank shall be set off against the total amount owed with respect to all orders transmitted by the other bank. To the extent of the setoff, each bank has made payment to the other.

(d) In a case not covered by subsection (a), the time when payment of the sender's obligation under Section 4A–402(b) or 4A–402(c) occurs is governed by applicable principles of law that determine when an obligation is satisfied.

§ 4A–404. Obligation of Beneficiary's Bank to Pay and Give Notice to Beneficiary.

(a) Subject to Sections 4A–211(e), 4A–405(d), and 4A–405(e), if a beneficiary's bank accepts a payment order, the bank is obliged to pay the amount of the order to the beneficiary of the order. Payment is due on the payment date of the order, but if acceptance occurs on the payment date after the close of the funds-transfer business day of the bank, payment is due on the next funds-transfer business day. If the bank refuses to pay after demand by the beneficiary and receipt of notice of particular circumstances that will give rise to consequential damages as a result of nonpayment, the beneficiary may recover damages resulting from the refusal to pay to the extent the bank had notice of the damages, unless the bank proves that it did not pay because of a reasonable doubt concerning the right of the beneficiary to payment.

(b) If a payment order accepted by the beneficiary's bank instructs payment to an account of the beneficiary, the bank is obliged to notify the beneficiary of receipt of the order before midnight of the next funds-transfer business day following the payment date. If the payment order does not instruct payment to an account of the beneficiary, the bank is required to notify the beneficiary only if notice is required by the order. Notice may be given by first class mail or any other means reasonable in the circumstances. If the bank fails to give the required notice, the bank is obliged to pay interest to the beneficiary on the amount of the payment order from the day notice should have been given until the day the beneficiary learned of receipt of the payment order by the bank. No other damages are recoverable. Reasonable attorney's fees are also recoverable if demand for interest is made and refused before an action is brought on the claim.

(c) The right of a beneficiary to receive payment and damages as stated in subsection (a) may not be varied by agreement or a funds-transfer system rule. The right of a beneficiary to be notified as stated in subsection (b) may be varied by agreement of the beneficiary or by a funds-transfer system rule if the beneficiary is notified of the rule before initiation of the funds transfer.

§ 4A–405. Payment by Beneficiary's Bank to Beneficiary.

(a) If the beneficiary's bank credits an account of the beneficiary of a payment order, payment of the bank's obligation under Section 4A–404(a) occurs when and to the extent (i) the beneficiary is notified of the right to withdraw the credit, (ii) the bank lawfully applies the credit to a debt of the beneficiary, or

(iii) funds with respect to the order are otherwise made available to the beneficiary by the bank.

(b) If the beneficiary's bank does not credit an account of the beneficiary of a payment order, the time when payment of the bank's obligation under Section 4A–404(a) occurs is governed by principles of law that determine when an obligation is satisfied.

(c) Except as stated in subsections (d) and (e), if the beneficiary's bank pays the beneficiary of a payment order under a condition to payment or agreement of the beneficiary giving the bank the right to recover payment from the beneficiary if the bank does not receive payment of the order, the condition to payment or agreement is not enforceable.

(d) A funds-transfer system rule may provide that payments made to beneficiaries of funds transfers made through the system are provisional until receipt of payment by the beneficiary's bank of the payment order it accepted. A beneficiary's bank that makes a payment that is provisional under the rule is entitled to refund from the beneficiary if (i) the rule requires that both the beneficiary and the originator be given notice of the provisional nature of the payment before the funds transfer is initiated, (ii) the beneficiary, the beneficiary's bank, and the originator's bank agreed to be bound by the rule, and (iii) the beneficiary's bank did not receive payment of the payment order that it accepted. If the beneficiary is obliged to refund payment to the beneficiary's bank, acceptance of the payment order by the beneficiary's bank is nullified and no payment by the originator of the funds transfer to the beneficiary occurs under Section 4A–406.

(e) This subsection applies to a funds transfer that includes a payment order transmitted over a funds-transfer system that (i) nets obligations multilaterally among participants, and (ii) has in effect a loss-sharing agreement among participants for the purpose of providing funds necessary to complete settlement of the obligations of one or more participants that do not meet their settlement obligations. If the beneficiary's bank in the funds transfer accepts a payment order and the system fails to complete settlement pursuant to its rules with respect to any payment order in the funds transfer, (i) the acceptance by the beneficiary's bank is nullified and no person has any right or obligation based on the acceptance, (ii) the beneficiary's bank is entitled to recover payment from the beneficiary, (iii) no payment by the originator to the beneficiary occurs under Section 4A–406, and (iv) subject to Section 4A–402(e), each sender in the funds transfer is excused from its obligation to pay its payment order under Section 4A–402(c) because the funds transfer has not been completed.

§ 4A–406. Payment by Originator to Beneficiary; Discharge of Underlying Obligation.

(a) Subject to Sections 4A–211(e), 4A–405(d), and 4A–405(e), the originator of a funds transfer pays the beneficiary of the originator's payment order (i) at the time a payment order for the benefit of the beneficiary is accepted by the beneficiary's bank in the funds transfer and (ii) in an amount equal to the amount of the order accepted by the beneficiary's bank, but not more than the amount of the originator's order.

(b) If payment under subsection (a) is made to satisfy an obligation, the obligation is discharged to the same extent discharge would result from payment to the beneficiary of the same amount in money, unless (i) the payment under subsection (a) was made by a means prohibited by the contract of the beneficiary with respect to the obligation, (ii) the beneficiary, within a reasonable time after receiving notice of receipt of the order by the beneficiary's bank, notified the originator of the beneficiary's refusal of the payment, (iii) funds with respect to the order were not withdrawn by the beneficiary or applied to a debt of the beneficiary, and (iv) the beneficiary would suffer a loss that could reasonably have been avoided if payment had been made by a means complying with the contract. If payment by the originator does not result in discharge under this section, the originator is subrogated to the rights of the beneficiary to receive payment from the beneficiary's bank under Section 4A–404(a).

(c) For the purpose of determining whether discharge of an obligation occurs under subsection (b), if the beneficiary's bank accepts a payment order in an amount equal to the amount of the originator's payment order less charges of one or more receiving banks in the funds transfer, payment to the beneficiary is deemed to be in the amount of the originator's order unless upon demand by the beneficiary the originator does not pay the beneficiary the amount of the deducted charges.

(d) Rights of the originator or of the beneficiary of a funds transfer under this section may be varied only by agreement of the originator and the beneficiary.

PART 5   Miscellaneous Provisions

§ 4A–501. `Variation by Agreement and Effect of Funds-Transfer System Rule.

(a) Except as otherwise provided in this Article, the rights and obligations of a party to a funds transfer may be varied by agreement of the affected party.

(b) "Funds-transfer system rule" means a rule of an association of banks (i) governing transmission of payment orders by means of a funds-transfer system of the association or rights and obligations with respect to those orders, or (ii) to the extent the rule governs rights and obligations between banks that are parties to a funds transfer in which a Federal Reserve Bank, acting as an intermediary bank, sends a payment order to the beneficiary's bank. Except as otherwise provided in this Article, a funds-transfer system rule governing rights and obli-

gations between participating banks using the system may be effective even if the rule conflicts with this Article and indirectly affects another party to the funds transfer who does not consent to the rule. A funds-transfer system rule may also govern rights and obligations of parties other than participating banks using the system to the extent stated in Sections 4A–404(c), 4A–405(d), and 4A–507(c).

§ 4A–502. Creditor Process Served on Receiving Bank; Setoff by Beneficiary's Bank.

(a) As used in this section, "creditor process" means levy, attachment, garnishment, notice of lien, sequestration, or similar process issued by or on behalf of a creditor or other claimant with respect to an account.

(b) This subsection applies to creditor process with respect to an authorized account of the sender of a payment order if the creditor process is served on the receiving bank. For the purpose of determining rights with respect to the creditor process, if the receiving bank accepts the payment order the balance in the authorized account is deemed to be reduced by the amount of the payment order to the extent the bank did not otherwise receive payment of the order, unless the creditor process is served at a time and in a manner affording the bank a reasonable opportunity to act on it before the bank accepts the payment order.

(c) If a beneficiary's bank has received a payment order for payment to the beneficiary's account in the bank, the following rules apply:

(1) The bank may credit the beneficiary's account. The amount credited may be set off against an obligation owed by the beneficiary to the bank or may be applied to satisfy creditor process served on the bank with respect to the account.

(2) The bank may credit the beneficiary's account and allow withdrawal of the amount credited unless creditor process with respect to the account is served at a time and in a manner affording the bank a reasonable opportunity to act to prevent withdrawal.

(3) If creditor process with respect to the beneficiary's account has been served and the bank has had a reasonable opportunity to act on it, the bank may not reject the payment order except for a reason unrelated to the service of process.

(d) Creditor process with respect to a payment by the originator to the beneficiary pursuant to a funds transfer may be served only on the beneficiary's bank with respect to the debt owed by that bank to the beneficiary. Any other bank served with the creditor process is not obliged to act with respect to the process.

§ 4A–503. Injunction or Restraining Order with Respect to Funds Transfer.

For proper cause and in compliance with applicable law, a court may restrain (i) a person from issuing a payment order to initiate a funds transfer, (ii) an originator's bank from executing the payment order of the originator, or (iii) the beneficiary's bank from releasing funds to the beneficiary or the beneficiary from withdrawing the funds. A court may not otherwise restrain a person from issuing a payment order, paying or receiving payment of a payment order, or otherwise acting with respect to a funds transfer.

§ 4A–504. Order in Which Items and Payment Orders May Be Charged to Account; Order of Withdrawals from Account.

(a) If a receiving bank has received more than one payment order of the sender or one or more payment orders and other items that are payable from the sender's account, the bank may charge the sender's account with respect to the various orders and items in any sequence.

(b) In determining whether a credit to an account has been withdrawn by the holder of the account or applied to a debt of the holder of the account, credits first made to the account are first withdrawn or applied.

§ 4A–505. Preclusion of Objection to Debit of Customer's Account.

If a receiving bank has received payment from its customer with respect to a payment order issued in the name of the customer as sender and accepted by the bank, and the customer received notification reasonably identifying the order, the customer is precluded from asserting that the bank is not entitled to retain the payment unless the customer notifies the bank of the customer's objection to the payment within one year after the notification was received by the customer.

§ 4A–506. Rate of Interest.

(a) If, under this Article, a receiving bank is obliged to pay interest with respect to a payment order issued to the bank, the amount payable may be determined (i) by agreement of the sender and receiving bank, or (ii) by a funds-transfer system rule if the payment order is transmitted through a funds-transfer system.

(b) If the amount of interest is not determined by an agreement or rule as stated in subsection (a), the amount is calculated by multiplying the applicable Federal Funds rate by the amount on which interest is payable, and then multiplying the product by the number of days for which interest is payable. The applicable Federal Funds rate is the average of the Federal Funds rates published by the Federal Reserve Bank of New York for each of the days for which interest is payable divided by 360. The Federal Funds rate for any day on which a published rate is not available is the same as the published rate for the next preceding day for which there is a published rate. If a receiving bank that accepted

a payment order is required to refund payment to the sender of the order because the funds transfer was not completed, but the failure to complete was not due to any fault by the bank, the interest payable is reduced by a percentage equal to the reserve requirement on deposits of the receiving bank.

§ 4A–507. Choice of Law.

(a) The following rules apply unless the affected parties otherwise agree or subsection (c) applies:

(1) The rights and obligations between the sender of a payment order and the receiving bank are governed by the law of the jurisdiction in which the receiving bank is located.

(2) The rights and obligations between the beneficiary's bank and the beneficiary are governed by the law of the jurisdiction in which the beneficiary's bank is located.

(3) The issue of when payment is made pursuant to a funds transfer by the originator to the beneficiary is governed by the law of the jurisdiction in which the beneficiary's bank is located.

(b) If the parties described in each paragraph of subsection (a) have made an agreement selecting the law of a particular jurisdiction to govern rights and obligations between each other, the law of that jurisdiction governs those rights and obligations, whether or not the payment order or the funds transfer bears a reasonable relation to that jurisdiction.

(c) A funds-transfer system rule may select the law of a particular jurisdiction to govern (i) rights and obligations between participating banks with respect to payment orders transmitted or processed through the system, or (ii) the rights and obligations of some or all parties to a funds transfer any part of which is carried out by means of the system. A choice of law made pursuant to clause (i) is binding on participating banks. A choice of law made pursuant to clause (ii) is binding on the originator, other sender, or a receiving bank having notice that the funds-transfer system might be used in the funds transfer and of the choice of law by the system when the originator, other sender, or receiving bank issued or accepted a payment order. The beneficiary of a funds transfer is bound by the choice of law if, when the funds transfer is initiated, the beneficiary has notice that the funds-transfer system might be used in the funds transfer and of the choice of law by the system. The law of a jurisdiction selected pursuant to this subsection may govern, whether or not that law bears a reasonable relation to the matter in issue.

(d) In the event of inconsistency between an agreement under subsection (b) and a choice-of-law rule under subsection (c), the agreement under subsection (b) prevails.

(e) If a funds transfer is made by use of more than one funds-transfer system and there is inconsistency between choice-of-law rules of the systems, the matter in issue is governed by the law of the selected jurisdiction that has the most significant relationship to the matter in issue.

REVISED ARTICLE 9

SECURED TRANSACTIONS

PART I   General Provisions

[Subpart 1. Short Title, Definitions, and General Concepts]

§ 9–101.   Short Title.

This article may be cited as Uniform Commercial Code—Secured Transactions.

§ 9–102.   Definitions and Index of Definitions.

(a) In this article:

(1) "Accession" means goods that are physically united with other goods in such a manner that the identity of the original goods is not lost.

(2) "Account", except as used in "account for", means a right to payment of a monetary obligation, whether or not earned by performance, (i) for property that has been or is to be sold, leased, licensed, assigned, or otherwise disposed of, (ii) for services rendered or to be rendered, (iii) for a policy of insurance issued or to be issued, (iv) for a secondary obligation incurred or to be incurred, (v) for energy provided or to be provided, (vi) for the use or hire of a vessel under a charter or other contract, (vii) arising out of the use of a credit or charge card or information contained on or for use with the card, or (viii) as winnings in a lottery or other game of chance operated or sponsored by a State, governmental unit of a State, or person licensed or authorized to operate the game by a State or governmental unit of a State. The term includes health-care insurance receivables. The term does not include (i) rights to payment evidenced by chattel paper or an instrument, (ii) commercial tort claims, (iii) deposit accounts, (iv) investment property, (v) letter-of-credit rights or letters of credit, or (vi) rights to payment for money or funds advanced or sold, other than rights arising out of the use of a credit or charge card or information contained on or for use with the card.

(3) "Account debtor" means a person obligated on an account, chattel paper, or general intangible. The term does not include persons obligated to pay a negotiable instrument, even if the instrument constitutes part of chattel paper.

(4) "Accounting", except as used in "accounting for", means a record:

(A) authenticated by a secured party;

(B) indicating the aggregate unpaid secured obligations as of a date not more than 35 days earlier or 35 days later than the date of the record; and

(C) identifying the components of the obligations in reasonable detail.

(5) "Agricultural lien" means an interest, other than a security interest, in farm products:

(A) which secures payment or performance of an obligation for:

(i) goods or services furnished in connection with a debtor's farming operation; or

(ii) rent on real property leased by a debtor in connection with its farming operation;

(B) which is created by statute in favor of a person that:

(i) in the ordinary course of its business furnished goods or services to a debtor in connection with a debtor's farming operation; or

(ii) leased real property to a debtor in connection with the debtor's farming operation; and

(C) whose effectiveness does not depend on the person's possession of the personal property.

(6) "As-extracted collateral" means:

(A) oil, gas, or other minerals that are subject to a security interest that:

(i) is created by a debtor having an interest in the minerals before extraction; and

(ii) attaches to the minerals as extracted; or

(B) accounts arising out of the sale at the wellhead or minehead of oil, gas, or other minerals in which the debtor had an interest before extraction.

(7) "Authenticate" means:

(A) to sign; or

(B) to execute or otherwise adopt a symbol, or encrypt or similarly process a record in whole or in part, with the present intent of the authenticating person to identify the person and adopt or accept a record.

(8) "Bank" means an organization that is engaged in the business of banking. The term includes savings banks, savings and loan associations, credit unions, and trust companies.

(9) "Cash proceeds" means proceeds that are money, checks, deposit accounts, or the like.

(10) "Certificate of title" means a certificate of title with respect to which a statute provides for the security interest in question to be indicated on the certificate as a condition or result of the security interest's obtaining priority over the rights of a lien creditor with respect to the collateral.

(11) "Chattel paper" means a record or records that evidence both a monetary obligation and a security interest in specific goods, a security interest in specific goods and software used in the goods, a security interest in specific goods and license of software used in the goods, a lease of specific goods, or a lease of specific goods and license of software used in the goods. In this paragraph, "monetary obligation" means a monetary obligation secured by the goods or owed under a lease of the goods and includes a monetary obligation with respect to

software used in the goods. The term does not include (i) charters or other contracts involving the use or hire of a vessel or (ii) records that evidence a right to payment arising out of the use of a credit or charge card or information contained on or for use with the card. If a transaction is evidenced by records that include an instrument or series of instruments, the group of records taken together constitutes chattel paper.

(12) "Collateral" means the property subject to a security interest or agricultural lien. The term includes:

(A) proceeds to which a security interest attaches;

(B) accounts, chattel paper, payment intangibles, and promissory notes that have been sold; and

(C) goods that are the subject of a consignment.

(13) "Commercial tort claim" means a claim arising in tort with respect to which:

(A) the claimant is an organization; or

(B) the claimant is an individual and the claim:

(i) arose in the course of the claimant's business or profession; and

(ii) does not include damages arising out of personal injury to or the death of an individual.

(14) "Commodity account" means an account maintained by a commodity intermediary in which a commodity contract is carried for a commodity customer.

(15) "Commodity contract" means a commodity futures contract, an option on a commodity futures contract, a commodity option, or another contract if the contract or option is:

(A) traded on or subject to the rules of a board of trade that has been designated as a contract market for such a contract pursuant to federal commodities laws; or

(B) traded on a foreign commodity board of trade, exchange, or market, and is carried on the books of a commodity intermediary for a commodity customer.

(16) "Commodity customer" means a person for which a commodity intermediary carries a commodity contract on its books.

(17) "Commodity intermediary" means a person that:

(A) is registered as a futures commission merchant under federal commodities law; or

(B) in the ordinary course of its business provides clearance or settlement services for a board of trade that has been designated as a contract market pursuant to federal commodities law.

(18) "Communicate" means:

(A) to send a written or other tangible record;

(B) to transmit a record by any means agreed upon by the persons sending and receiving the record; or

(C) in the case of transmission of a record to or by a filing office, to transmit a record by any means prescribed by filing-office rule.

(19) "Consignee" means a merchant to which goods are delivered in a consignment.

(20) "Consignment" means a transaction, regardless of its form, in which a person delivers goods to a merchant for the purpose of sale and:

(A) the merchant:

(i) deals in goods of that kind under a name other than the name of the person making delivery;

(ii) is not an auctioneer; and

(iii) is not generally known by its creditors to be substantially engaged in selling the goods of others;

(B) with respect to each delivery, the aggregate value of the goods is $1,000 or more at the time of delivery;

(C) the goods are not consumer goods immediately before delivery; and

(D) the transaction does not create a security interest that secures an obligation.

(21) "Consignor" means a person that delivers goods to a consignee in a consignment.

(22) "Consumer debtor" means a debtor in a consumer transaction.

(23) "Consumer goods" means goods that are used or bought for use primarily for personal, family, or household purposes.

(24) "Consumer goods transaction" means a consumer transaction in which:

(A) an individual incurs an obligation primarily for personal, family, or household purposes; and

(B) a security interest in consumer goods secures the obligation.

(25) "Consumer obligor" means an obligor who is an individual and who incurred the obligation as part of a transaction entered into primarily for personal, family, or household purposes.

(26) "Consumer transaction" means a transaction in which (i) an individual incurs an obligation primarily for personal, family, or household purposes, (ii) a security interest secures the obligation, and (iii) the collateral is held or acquired primarily for personal, family, or household purposes. The term includes consumer-goods transactions.

(27) "Continuation statement" means an amendment of a financing statement which:

(A) identifies, by its file number, the initial financing statement to which it relates; and

(B) indicates that it is a continuation statement for, or that it is filed to continue the effectiveness of, the identified financing statement.

(28) "Debtor" means:

(A) a person having an interest, other than a security interest or other lien, in the collateral, whether or not the person is an obligor;

(B) a seller of accounts, chattel paper, payment intangibles, or promissory notes; or

(C) a consignee.

(29) "Deposit account" means a demand, time, savings, passbook, or similar account maintained with a bank. The term does not include investment property or accounts evidenced by an instrument.

(30) "Document" means a document of title or a receipt of the type described in Section 7–201(2).

(31) "Electronic chattel paper" means chattel paper evidenced by a record or records consisting of information stored in an electronic medium.

(32) "Encumbrance" means a right, other than an ownership interest, in real property. The term includes mortgages and other liens on real property.

(33) "Equipment" means goods other than inventory, farm products, or consumer goods.

(34) "Farm products" means goods, other than standing timber, with respect to which the debtor is engaged in a farming operation and which are:

(A) crops grown, growing, or to be grown, including:

(i) crops produced on trees, vines, and bushes; and

(ii) aquatic goods produced in aquacultural operations;

(B) livestock, born or unborn, including aquatic goods produced in aquacultural operations;

(C) supplies used or produced in a farming operation; or

(D) products of crops or livestock in their unmanufactured states.

(35) "Farming operation" means raising, cultivating, propagating, fattening, grazing, or any other farming, livestock, or aquacultural operation.

(36) "File number" means the number assigned to an initial financing statement pursuant to Section 9–519(a).

(37) "Filing office" means an office designated in Section 9–501 as the place to file a financing statement.

(38) "Filing-office rule" means a rule adopted pursuant to Section 9–526.

(39) "Financing statement" means a record or records composed of an initial financing statement and any filed record relating to the initial financing statement.

(40) "Fixture filing" means the filing of a financing statement covering goods that are or are to become fixtures and satisfying Section 9–502(a) and (b). The term includes the filing of a financing statement covering goods of a transmitting utility which are or are to become fixtures.

(41) "Fixtures" means goods that have become so related to particular real property that an interest in them arises under real property law.

(42) "General intangible" means any personal property, including things in action, other than accounts, chattel paper, commercial tort claims, deposit accounts, documents, goods, instruments, investment property, letter-of-credit rights, letters of credit, money, and oil, gas, or other minerals before extraction. The term includes payment intangibles and software.

(43) "Good faith" means honesty in fact and the observance of reasonable commercial standards of fair dealing.

(44) "Goods" means all things that are movable when a security interest attaches. The term includes (i) fixtures, (ii) standing timber that is to be cut and removed under a conveyance or contract for sale, (iii) the unborn young of animals, (iv) crops grown, growing, or to be grown, even if the crops are produced on trees, vines, or bushes, and (v) manufactured homes. The term also includes a computer program embedded in goods and any supporting information provided in connection with a transaction relating to the program if (i) the program is associated with the goods in such a manner that it customarily is considered part of the goods, or (ii) by becoming the owner of the goods, a person acquires a right to use the program in connection with the goods. The term does not include a computer program embedded in goods that consist solely of the medium in which the program is embedded. The term also does not include accounts, chattel paper, commercial tort claims, deposit accounts, documents, general intangibles, instruments, investment property, letter-of-credit rights, letters of credit, money, or oil, gas, or other minerals before extraction.

(45) "Governmental unit" means a subdivision, agency, department, county, parish, municipality, or other unit of the government of the United States, a State, or a foreign country. The term includes an organization having a separate corporate existence if the organization is eligible to issue debt on which interest is exempt from income taxation under the laws of the United States.

(46) "Health-care-insurance receivable" means an interest in or claim under a policy of insurance which is a right to payment of a monetary obligation for health-care goods or servies provided.

(47) "Instrument" means a negotiable instrument or any other writing that evidences a right to the payment of a monetary obligation, is not itself a security agreement or lease, and is of a type that in ordinary course of business is transferred by delivery with any necessary indorsement or assignment. The term does not include (i) investment property, (ii) letters of credit, or (iii) writings that evidence a right to payment arising out of the use of a credit or charge card or information contained on or for use with the card.

(48) "Inventory" means goods, other than farm products, which:

(A) are leased by a person as lessor;

(B) are held by a person for sale or lease or to be furnished under a contract of service;

(C) are furnished by a person under a contract of service; or

(D) consist of raw materials, work in process, or materials used or consumed in a business.

(49) "Investment property" means a security, whether certificated or uncertificated, security entitlement, securities account, commodity contract, or commodity account.

(50) "Jurisdiction of organization", with respect to a registered organization, means the jurisdiction under whose law the organization is organized.

(51) "Letter-of-credit right" means a right to payment or performance under a letter of credit, whether or not the beneficiary has demanded or is at the time entitled to demand payment or performance. The term does not include the right of a beneficiary to demand payment or performance under a letter of credit.

(52) "Lien creditor" means:

(A) a creditor that has acquired a lien on the property involved by attachment, levy, or the like;

(B) an assignee for benefit of creditors from the time of assignment;

(C) a trustee in bankruptcy from the date of the filing of the petition; or

(D) a receiver in equity from the time of appointment.

(53) "Manufactured home" means a structure, transportable in one or more sections, which, in the traveling mode, is eight body feet or more in width or 40 body feet or more in length, or, when erected on site, is 320 or more square feet, and which is built on a permanent chassis and designed to be used as a dwelling with or without a permanent foundation when connected to the required utilities, and includes the plumbing, heating, air-conditioning, and electrical systems contained therein. The term includes any structure that meets all of the requirements of this paragraph except the size requirements and with respect to which the manufacturer voluntarily files a certification required by the United States Secretary of Housing and Urban Development and complies with the standards established under Title 42 of the United States Code.

(54) "Manufactured-home transaction" means a secured transaction:

(A) that creates a purchase-money security interest in a manufactured home, other than a manufactured home held as inventory; or

(B) in which a manufactured home, other than a manufactured home held as inventory, is the primary collateral.

(55) "Mortgage" means a consensual interest in real property, including fixtures, which secures payment or performance of an obligation.

(56) "New debtor" means a person that becomes bound as debtor under Section 9–203(d) by a security agreement previously entered into by another person.

(57) "New value" means (i) money, (ii) money's worth in property, services, or new credit, or (iii) release by a transferee of an interest in property previously transferred to the transferee. The term does not include an obligation substituted for another obligation.

(58) "Noncash proceeds" means proceeds other than cash proceeds.

(59) "Obligor" means a person that, with respect to an obligation secured by a security interest in or an agricultural lien on the collateral, (i) owes payment or other performance of the obligation, (ii) has provided property other than the collateral to secure payment or other performance of the obligation, or (iii) is otherwise accountable in whole or in part for payment or

other performance of the obligation. The term does not include issuers or nominated persons under a letter of credit.

(60) "Original debtor", except as used in Section 9–310(c), means a person that, as debtor, entered into a security agreement to which a new debtor has become bound under Section 9–203(d).

(61) "Payment intangible" means a general intangible under which the account debtor's principal obligation is a monetary obligation.

(62) "Person related to", with respect to an individual, means:

(A) the spouse of the individual;

(B) a brother, brother-in-law, sister, or sister-in-law of the individual;

(C) an ancestor or lineal descendant of the individual or the individual's spouse; or

(D) any other relative, by blood or marriage, of the individual or the individual's spouse who shares the same home with the individual.

(63) "Person related to", with respect to an organization, means:

(A) a person directly or indirectly controlling, controlled by, or under common control with the organization;

(B) an officer or director of, or a person performing similar functions with respect to, the organization;

(C) an officer or director of, or a person performing similar functions with respect to, a person described in subparagraph (A);

(D) the spouse of an individual described in subparagraph (A), (B), or (C); or

(E) an individual who is related by blood or marriage to an individual described in subparagraph (A), (B), (C), or (D) and shares the same home with the individual.

(64) "Proceeds", except as used in Section 9–609(b), means the following property:

(A) whatever is acquired upon the sale, lease, license, exchange, or other disposition of collateral;

(B) whatever is collected on, or distributed on account of, collateral;

(C) rights arising out of collateral;

(D) to the extent of the value of collateral, claims arising out of the loss, nonconformity, or interference with the use of, defects or infringement of rights in, or damage to, the collateral; or (E) to the extent of the value of collateral and to the extent payable to the debtor or the secured party, insurance payable by reason of the loss or nonconformity of, defects or infringement of rights in, or damage to, the collateral.

(65) "Promissory note" means an instrument that evidences a promise to pay a monetary obligation, does not evidence an order to pay, and does not contain an acknowledgment by a bank that the bank has received for deposit a sum of money or funds.

(66) "Proposal" means a record authenticated by a secured party which includes the terms on which the secured party is

willing to accept collateral in full or partial satisfaction of the obligation it secures pursuant to Sections 9–620, 9–621, and 9–622.

(67) "Public-finance transaction" means a secured transaction in connection with which:

(A) debt securities are issued;

(B) all or a portion of the securities issued have an initial stated maturity of at least 20 years; and

(C) the debtor, obligor, secured party, account debtor or other person obligated on collateral, assignor or assignee of a secured obligation, or assignor or assignee of a security interest is a State or a governmental unit of a State.

(68) "Pursuant to commitment", with respect to an advance made or other value given by a secured party, means pursuant to the secured party's obligation, whether or not a subsequent event of default or other event not within the secured party's control has relieved or may relieve the secured party from its obligation.

(69) "Record", except as used in "for record", "of record", "record or legal title", and "record owner", means information that is inscribed on a tangible medium or which is stored in an electronic or other medium and is retrievable in perceivable form.

(70) "Registered organization" means an organization organized solely under the law of a single State or the United States and as to which the State or the United States must maintain a public record showing the organization to have been organized.

(71) "Secondary obligor" means an obligor to the extent that:

(A) the obligor's obligation is secondary; or

(B) the obligor has a right of recourse with respect to an obligation secured by collateral against the debtor, another obligor, or property of either.

(72) "Secured party" means:

(A) a person in whose favor a security interest is created or provided for under a security agreement, whether or not any obligation to be secured is outstanding;

(B) a person that holds an agricultural lien;

(C) a consignor;

(D) a person to which accounts, chattel paper, payment intangibles, or promissory notes have been sold;

(E) a trustee, indenture trustee, agent, collateral agent, or other representative in whose favor a security interest or agricultural lien is created or provided for; or

(F) a person that holds a security interest arising under Section 2–401, 2–505, 2–711(3), 2A–508(5), 4–210, or 5–118.

(73) "Security agreement" means an agreement that creates or provides for a security interest.

(74) "Send", in connection with a record or notification, means:

(A) to deposit in the mail, deliver for transmission, or transmit by any other usual means of communication, with postage or cost of transmission provided for, addressed to any address reasonable under the circumstances; or

(B) to cause the record or notification to be received within the timce that it would have been received if properly sent under subparagraph (A).

(75) "Software" means a computer program and any supporting information provided in connection with a transaction relating to the program. The term does not include a computer program that is included in the definition of goods.

(76) "State" means a State of the United States, the District of Columbia, Puerto Rico, the United States Virgin Islands, or any territory or insular possession subject to the jurisdiction of the United States.

(77) "Supporting obligation" means a letter-of-credit right or secondary obligation that supports the payment or performance of an account, chattel paper, a document, a general intangible, an instrument, or investment property.

(78) "Tangible chattel paper" means chattel paper evidenced by a record or records consisting of information that is inscribed on a tangible medium.

(79) "Termination statement" means an amendment of a financing statement which:

(A) identifies, by its file number, the initial financing statement to which it relates; and

(B) indicates either that it is a termination statement or that the identified financing statement is no longer effective.

(80) "Transmitting utility" means a person primarily engaged in the business of:

(A) operating a railroad, subway, street railway, or trolley bus;

(B) transmitting communications electrically, electromagnetically, or by light;

(C) transmitting goods by pipeline or sewer; or

(D) transmitting or producing and transmitting electricity, steam, gas, or water.

(b) The following definitions in other articles apply to this article:

"Applicant." Section 5–102

"Beneficiary." Section 5–102

"Broker." Section 8–102

"Certificated security." Section 8–102

"Check." Section 3–104

"Clearing corporation." Section 8–102

"Contract for sale." Section 2–106

"Customer." Section 4–104

"Entitlement holder." Section 8–102

"Financial asset." Section 8–102

"Holder in due course." Section 3–302

"Issuer" (with respect to a letter of credit or letter-of-credit right). Section 5–102

"Issuer" (with respect to a security). Section 8–201

"Lease." Section 2A–103

"Lease agreement." Section 2A–103

"Lease contract." Section 2A–103

"Leasehold interest." Section 2A–103

"Lessee." Section 2A–103

"Lessee in ordinary course of business." Section 2A–103

"Lessor." Section 2A–103

"Lessor's residual interest." Section 2A–103

"Letter of credit." Section 5–102

"Merchant." Section 2–104

"Negotiable instrument." Section 3–104

"Nominated person." Section 5–102

"Note." Section 3–104

"Proceeds of a letter of credit." Section 5–114

"Prove." Section 3–103

"Sale." Section 2–106

"Securities account." Section 8–501

"Securities intermediary." Section 8–102

"Security." Section 8–102

"Security certificate." Section 8–102

"Security entitlement." Section 8–102

"Uncertificated security." Section 8–102

(c) Article 1 contains general definitions and principles of construction and interpretation applicable throughout this article.

Amended in 1999 and 2000.

§ 9–103.   Purchase-Money Security Interest; Application of Payments; Burden of Establishing.

(a) In this section:

(1) "purchase-money collateral" means goods or software that secures a purchase-money obligation incurred with respect to that collateral; and

(2) "purchase-money obligation" means an obligation of an obligor incurred as all or part of the price of the collateral or for value given to enable the debtor to acquire rights in or the use of the collateral if the value is in fact so used.

(b) A security interest in goods is a purchase-money security interest:

(1) to the extent that the goods are purchase-money collateral with respect to that security interest;

(2) if the security interest is in inventory that is or was purchase-money collateral, also to the extent that the security interest secures a purchase-money obligation incurred with respect to other inventory in which the secured party holds or held a purchase-money security interest; and

(3) also to the extent that the security interest secures a purchase-money obligation incurred with respect to software in which the secured party holds or held a purchase-money security interest.

(c) A security interest in software is a purchase-money security interest to the extent that the security interest also secures a purchase-money obligation incurred with respect to goods in which the secured party holds or held a purchase-money security interest if:

(1) the debtor acquired its interest in the software in an integrated transaction in which it acquired an interest in the goods; and

(2) the debtor acquired its interest in the software for the principal purpose of using the software in the goods.

(d) The security interest of a consignor in goods that are the subject of a consignment is a purchase-money security interest in inventory.

(e) In a transaction other than a consumer-goods transaction, if the extent to which a security interest is a purchase-money security interest depends on the application of a payment to a particular obligation, the payment must be applied:

(1) in accordance with any reasonable method of application to which the parties agree;

(2) in the absence of the parties' agreement to a reasonable method, in accordance with any intention of the obligor manifested at or before the time of payment; or

(3) in the absence of an agreement to a reasonable method and a timely manifestation of the obligor's intention, in the following order:

(A) to obligations that are not secured; and

(B) if more than one obligation is secured, to obligations secured by purchase-money security interests in the order in which those obligations were incurred.

(f) In a transaction other than a consumer-goods transaction, a purchase-money security interest does not lose its status as such, even if:

(1) the purchase-money collateral also secures an obligation that is not a purchase-money obligation;

(2) collateral that is not purchase-money collateral also secures the purchase-money obligation; or

(3) the purchase-money obligation has been renewed, refinanced, consolidated, or restructured.

(g) In a transaction other than a consumer-goods transaction, a secured party claiming a purchase-money security interest has the burden of establishing the extent to which the security interest is a purchase-money security interest.

(h) The limitation of the rules in subsections (e), (f), and (g) to transactions other than consumer-goods transactions is intended to leave to the court the determination of the proper rules in consumer-goods transactions. The court may not infer from that limitation the nature of the proper rule in consumer-goods transactions and may continue to apply established approaches.

§ 9–104.   Control of Deposit Account.

(a) A secured party has control of a deposit account if:

(1) the secured party is the bank with which the deposit account is maintained;

(2) the debtor, secured party, and bank have agreed in an authenticated record that the bank will comply with instructions originated by the secured party directing disposition of

the funds in the deposit account without further consent by the debtor; or

(3) the secured party becomes the bank's customer with respect to the deposit account.

(b) A secured party that has satisfied subsection (a) has control, even if the debtor retains the right to direct the disposition of funds from the deposit account.

§ 9–105.   Control of Electronic Chattel Paper.

A secured party has control of electronic chattel paper if the record or records comprising the chattel paper are created, stored, and assigned in such a manner that:

(1) a single authoritative copy of the record or records exists which is unique, identifiable and, except as otherwise provided in paragraphs (4), (5), and (6), unalterable;

(2) the authoritative copy identifies the secured party as the assignee of the record or records;

(3) the authoritative copy is communicated to and maintained by the secured party or its designated custodian;

(4) copies or revisions that add or change an identified assignee of the authoritative copy can be made only with the participation of the secured party;

(5) each copy of the authoritative copy and any copy of a copy is readily identifiable as a copy that is not the authoritative copy; and

(6) any revision of the authoritative copy is readily identifiable as an authorized or unauthorized revision.

§ 9–106.   Control of Investment Property.

(a) A person has control of a certificated security, uncertificated security, or security entitlement as provided in Section 8–106.

(b) A secured party has control of a commodity contract if:

(1) the secured party is the commodity intermediary with which the commodity contract is carried; or

(2) the commodity customer, secured party, and commodity intermediary have agreed that the commodity intermediary will apply any value distributed on account of the commodity contract as directed by the secured party without further consent by the commodity customer.

(c) A secured party having control of all security entitlements or commodity contracts carried in a securities account or commodity account has control over the securities account or commodity account.

§ 9–107.   Control of Letter-of-Credit Right.

A secured party has control of a letter-of-credit right to the extent of any right to payment or performance by the issuer or any nominated person if the issuer or nominated person has consented to an assignment of proceeds of the letter of credit under Section 5–114(c) or otherwise applicable law or practice.

§ 9–108.   Sufficiency of Description.

(a) Except as otherwise provided in subsections (c), (d), and (e), a description of personal or real property is sufficient, whether or not it is specific, if it reasonably identifies what is described.

(b) Except as otherwise provided in subsection (d), a description of collateral reasonably identifies the collateral if it identifies the collateral by:

(1) specific listing;

(2) category;

(3) except as otherwise provided in subsection (e), a type of collateral defined in [the Uniform Commercial Code];

(4) quantity;

(5) computational or allocational formula or procedure; or

(6) except as otherwise provided in subsection (c), any other method, if the identity of the collateral is objectively determinable.

(c) A description of collateral as "all the debtor's assets" or "all the debtor's personal property" or using words of similar import does not reasonably identify the collateral.

(d) Except as otherwise provided in subsection (e), a description of a security entitlement, securities account, or commodity account is sufficient if it describes:

(1) the collateral by those terms or as investment property; or

(2) the underlying financial asset or commodity contract.

(e) A description only by type of collateral defined in [the Uniform Commercial Code] is an insufficient description of:

(1) a commercial tort claim; or

(2) in a consumer transaction, consumer goods, a security entitlement, a securities account, or a commodity account.

[Subpart 2. Applicability of Article]

§ 9–109.   Scope.

(a) Except as otherwise provided in subsections (c) and (d), this article applies to:

(1) a transaction, regardless of its form, that creates a security interest in personal property or fixtures by contract;

(2) an agricultural lien;

(3) a sale of accounts, chattel paper, payment intangibles, or promissory notes;

(4) a consignment;

(5) a security interest arising under Section 2–401, 2–505, 2–711(3), or 2A–508(5), as provided in Section 9–110; and

(6) a security interest arising under Section 4–210 or 5–118.

(b) The application of this article to a security interest in a secured obligation is not affected by the fact that the obligation is itself secured by a transaction or interest to which this article does not apply.

(c) This article does not apply to the extent that:

(1) a statute, regulation, or treaty of the United States preempts this article;

(2) another statute of this State expressly governs the creation, perfection, priority, or enforcement of a security interest created by this State or a governmental unit of this State;

(3) a statute of another State, a foreign country, or a governmental unit of another State or a foreign country, other than a statute generally applicable to security interests, expressly governs creation, perfection, priority, or enforcement of a security interest created by the State, country, or governmental unit; or

(4) the rights of a transferee beneficiary or nominated person under a letter of credit are independent and superior under Section 5–114.

(d) This article does not apply to:

(1) a landlord's lien, other than an agricultural lien;

(2) a lien, other than an agricultural lien, given by statute or other rule of law for services or materials, but Section 9–333 applies with respect to priority of the lien;

(3) an assignment of a claim for wages, salary, or other compensation of an employee;

(4) a sale of accounts, chattel paper, payment intangibles, or promissory notes as part of a sale of the business out of which they arose;

(5) an assignment of accounts, chattel paper, payment intangibles, or promissory notes which is for the purpose of collection only;

(6) an assignment of a right to payment under a contract to an assignee that is also obligated to perform under the contract;

(7) an assignment of a single account, payment intangible, or promissory note to an assignee in full or partial satisfaction of a preexisting indebtedness;

(8) a transfer of an interest in or an assignment of a claim under a policy of insurance, other than an assignment by or to a health-care provider of a health-care-insurance receivable and any subsequent assignment of the right to payment, but Sections 9–315 and 9–322 apply with respect to proceeds and priorities in proceeds;

(9) an assignment of a right represented by a judgment, other than a judgment taken on a right to payment that was collateral;

(10) a right of recoupment or set-off, but:

(A) Section 9–340 applies with respect to the effectiveness of rights of recoupment or set-off against deposit accounts; and

(B) Section 9–404 applies with respect to defenses or claims of an account debtor;

(11) the creation or transfer of an interest in or lien on real property, including a lease or rents thereunder, except to the extent that provision is made for:

(A) liens on real property in Sections 9–203 and 9–308;

(B) fixtures in Section 9–334;

(C) fixture filings in Sections 9–501, 9–502, 9–512, 9–516, and 9–519; and

(D) security agreements covering personal and real property in Section 9–604;

(12) an assignment of a claim arising in tort, other than a commercial tort claim, but Sections 9–315 and 9–322 apply with respect to proceeds and priorities in proceeds; or

(13) an assignment of a deposit account in a consumer transaction, but Sections 9–315 and 9–322 apply with respect to proceeds and priorities in proceeds.

§ 9–110. Security Interests Arising under Article 2 or 2A.

A security interest arising under Section 2–401, 2–505, 2–711(3), or 2A–508(5) is subject to this article. However, until the debtor obtains possession of the goods:

(1) the security interest is enforceable, even if Section 9–203(b)(3) has not been satisfied;

(2) filing is not required to perfect the security interest;

(3) the rights of the secured party after default by the debtor are governed by Article 2 or 2A; and

(4) the security interest has priority over a conflicting security interest created by the debtor.

PART 2 Effectiveness of Security Agreement; Attachment of Security Interest; Rights of Parties to Security Agreement

[Subpart 1. Effectiveness and Attachment]

§ 9–201. General Effectiveness of Security Agreement.

(a) Except as otherwise provided in [the Uniform Commercial Code], a security agreement is effective according to its terms between the parties, against purchasers of the collateral, and against creditors.

(b) A transaction subject to this article is subject to any applicable rule of law which establishes a different rule for consumers and [insert reference to (i) any other statute or regulation that regulates the rates, charges, agreements, and practices for loans, credit sales, or other extensions of credit and (ii) any consumer-protection statute or regulation].

(c) In case of conflict between this article and a rule of law, statute, or regulation described in subsection (b), the rule of law, statute, or regulation controls. Failure to comply with a statute or regulation described in subsection (b) has only the effect the statute or regulation specifies.

(d) This article does not:

(1) validate any rate, charge, agreement, or practice that violates a rule of law, statute, or regulation described in subsection (b); or

(2) extend the application of the rule of law, statute, or regulation to a transaction not otherwise subject to it.

§ 9–202. Title to Collateral Immaterial.

Except as otherwise provided with respect to consignments or sales of accounts, chattel paper, payment intangibles, or promissory notes, the provisions of this article with regard to rights and obligations apply whether title to collateral is in the secured party or the debtor.

§ 9–203. Attachment and Enforceability of Security Interest; Proceeds; Supporting Obligations; Formal Requisites.

(a) A security interest attaches to collateral when it becomes enforceable against the debtor with respect to the collateral, unless an agreement expressly postpones the time of attachment.

(b) Except as otherwise provided in subsections (c) through (i), a security interest is enforceable against the debtor and third parties with respect to the collateral only if:

(1) value has been given;

(2) the debtor has rights in the collateral or the power to transfer rights in the collateral to a secured party; and

(3) one of the following conditions is met:

(A) the debtor has authenticated a security agreement that provides a description of the collateral and, if the security interest covers timber to be cut, a description of the land concerned;

(B) the collateral is not a certificated security and is in the possession of the secured party under Section 9–313 pursuant to the debtor's security agreement;

(C) the collateral is a certificated security in registered form and the security certificate has been delivered to the secured party under Section 8–301 pursuant to the debtor's security agreement; or

(D) the collateral is deposit accounts, electronic chattel paper, investment property, or letter-of-credit rights, and the secured party has control under Section 9–104, 9–105, 9–106, or 9–107 pursuant to the debtor's security agreement.

(c) Subsection (b) is subject to Section 4–210 on the security interest of a collecting bank, Section 5–118 on the security interest of a letter-of-credit issuer or nominated person, Section 9–110 on a security interest arising under Article 2 or 2A, and Section 9–206 on security interests in investment property.

(d) A person becomes bound as debtor by a security agreement entered into by another person if, by operation of law other than this article or by contract:

(1) the security agreement becomes effective to create a security interest in the person's property; or

(2) the person becomes generally obligated for the obligations of the other person, including the obligation secured under the security agreement, and acquires or succeeds to all or substantially all of the assets of the other person.

(e) If a new debtor becomes bound as debtor by a security agreement entered into by another person:

(1) the agreement satisfies subsection (b)(3) with respect to existing or after-acquired property of the new debtor to the extent the property is described in the agreement; and

(2) another agreement is not necessary to make a security interest in the property enforceable.

(f) The attachment of a security interest in collateral gives the secured party the rights to proceeds provided by Section 9–315 and is also attachment of a security interest in a supporting obligation for the collateral.

(g) The attachment of a security interest in a right to payment or performance secured by a security interest or other lien on personal or real property is also attachment of a security interest in the security interest, mortgage, or other lien.

(h) The attachment of a security interest in a securities account is also attachment of a security interest in the security entitlements carried in the securities account.

(i) The attachment of a security interest in a commodity account is also attachment of a security interest in the commodity contracts carried in the commodity account.

§ 9–204. After-Acquired Property; Future Advances.

(a) Except as otherwise provided in subsection (b), a security agreement may create or provide for a security interest in after-acquired collateral.

(b) A security interest does not attach under a term constituting an after-acquired property clause to:

(1) consumer goods, other than an accession when given as additional security, unless the debtor acquires rights in them within 10 days after the secured party gives value; or

(2) a commercial tort claim.

(c) A security agreement may provide that collateral secures, or that accounts, chattel paper, payment intangibles, or promissory notes are sold in connection with, future advances or other value, whether or not the advances or value are given pursuant to commitment.

§ 9–205. Use or Disposition of Collateral Permissible.

(a) A security interest is not invalid or fraudulent against creditors solely because:

(1) the debtor has the right or ability to:

(A) use, commingle, or dispose of all or part of the collateral, including returned or repossessed goods;

(B) collect, compromise, enforce, or otherwise deal with collateral;

(C) accept the return of collateral or make repossessions; or

(D) use, commingle, or dispose of proceeds; or

(2) the secured party fails to require the debtor to account for proceeds or replace collateral.

(b) This section does not relax the requirements of possession if attachment, perfection, or enforcement of a security interest depends upon possession of the collateral by the secured party.

§ 9–206.   Security Interest Arising in Purchase or Delivery of Financial Asset.

(a) A security interest in favor of a securities intermediary attaches to a person's security entitlement if:

(1) the person buys a financial asset through the securities intermediary in a transaction in which the person is obligated to pay the purchase price to the securities intermediary at the time of the purchase; and

(2) the securities intermediary credits the financial asset to the buyer's securities account before the buyer pays the securities intermediary.

(b) The security interest described in subsection (a) secures the person's obligation to pay for the financial asset.

(c) A security interest in favor of a person that delivers a certificated security or other financial asset represented by a writing attaches to the security or other financial asset if:

(1) the security or other financial asset:

(A) in the ordinary course of business is transferred by delivery with any necessary indorsement or assignment; and

(B) is delivered under an agreement between persons in the business of dealing with such securities or financial assets; and

(2) the agreement calls for delivery against payment.

(d) The security interest described in subsection (c) secures the obligation to make payment for the delivery.

[Subpart 2. Rights and Duties]

§ 9–207.   Rights and Duties of Secured Party Having Possession or Control of Collateral.

(a) Except as otherwise provided in subsection (d), a secured party shall use reasonable care in the custody and preservation of collateral in the secured party's possession. In the case of chattel paper or an instrument, reasonable care includes taking necessary steps to preserve rights against prior parties unless otherwise agreed.

(b) Except as otherwise provided in subsection (d), if a secured party has possession of collateral:

(1) reasonable expenses, including the cost of insurance and payment of taxes or other charges, incurred in the custody, preservation, use, or operation of the collateral are chargeable to the debtor and are secured by the collateral;

(2) the risk of accidental loss or damage is on the debtor to the extent of a deficiency in any effective insurance coverage;

(3) the secured party shall keep the collateral identifiable, but fungible collateral may be commingled; and

(4) the secured party may use or operate the collateral:

(A) for the purpose of preserving the collateral or its value;

(B) as permitted by an order of a court having competent jurisdiction; or

(C) except in the case of consumer goods, in the manner and to the extent agreed by the debtor.

(c) Except as otherwise provided in subsection (d), a secured party having possession of collateral or control of collateral under Section 9–104, 9–105, 9–106, or 9–107:

(1) may hold as additional security any proceeds, except money or funds, received from the collateral;

(2) shall apply money or funds received from the collateral to reduce the secured obligation, unless remitted to the debtor; and

(3) may create a security interest in the collateral.

(d) If the secured party is a buyer of accounts, chattel paper, payment intangibles, or promissory notes or a consignor:

(1) subsection (a) does not apply unless the secured party is entitled under an agreement:

(A) to charge back uncollected collateral; or

(B) otherwise to full or limited recourse against the debtor or a secondary obligor based on the nonpayment or other default of an account debtor or other obligor on the collateral; and

(2) subsections (b) and (c) do not apply.

§ 9–208.   Additional Duties of Secured Party Having Control of Collateral.

(a) This section applies to cases in which there is no outstanding secured obligation and the secured party is not committed to make advances, incur obligations, or otherwise give value.

(b) Within 10 days after receiving an authenticated demand by the debtor:

(1) a secured party having control of a deposit account under Section 9–104(a)(2) shall send to the bank with which the deposit account is maintained an authenticated statement that releases the bank from any further obligation to comply with instructions originated by the secured party;

(2) a secured party having control of a deposit account under Section 9–104(a)(3) shall:

(A) pay the debtor the balance on deposit in the deposit account; or

(B) transfer the balance on deposit into a deposit account in the debtor's name;

(3) a secured party, other than a buyer, having control of electronic chattel paper under Section 9–105 shall:

(A) communicate the authoritative copy of the electronic chattel paper to the debtor or its designated custodian;

(B) if the debtor designates a custodian that is the designated custodian with which the authoritative copy of the electronic chattel paper is maintained for the secured party, communicate to the custodian an authenticated record releasing the designated custodian from any further obligation to comply with instructions originated by the secured party and instructing the custodian to comply with instructions originated by the debtor; and

(C) take appropriate action to enable the debtor or its designated custodian to make copies of or revisions to the authoritative copy which add or change an identified assignee of the authoritative copy without the consent of the secured party;

(4) a secured party having control of investment property under Section 8–106(d)(2) or 9–106(b) shall send to the securities intermediary or commodity intermediary with which the security entitlement or commodity contract is maintained an authenticated record that releases the securities intermediary or commodity intermediary from any further obligation to comply with entitlement orders or directions originated by the secured party; and

(5) a secured party having control of a letter-of-credit right under Section 9–107 shall send to each person having an unfulfilled obligation to pay or deliver proceeds of the letter of credit to the secured party an authenticated release from any further obligation to pay or deliver proceeds of the letter of credit to the secured party.

§ 9–209. Duties of Secured Party If Account Debtor Has Been Notified of Assignment.

(a) Except as otherwise provided in subsection (c), this section applies if:

(1) there is no outstanding secured obligation; and

(2) the secured party is not committed to make advances, incur obligations, or otherwise give value.

(b) Within 10 days after receiving an authenticated demand by the debtor, a secured party shall send to an account debtor that has received notification of an assignment to the secured party as assignee under Section 9–406(a) an authenticated record that releases the account debtor from any further obligation to the secured party.

(c) This section does not apply to an assignment constituting the sale of an account, chattel paper, or payment intangible.

§ 9–210. Request for Accounting; Request Regarding List of Collateral or Statement of Account.

(a) In this section:

(1) "Request" means a record of a type described in paragraph (2), (3), or (4).

(2) "Request for an accounting" means a record authenticated by a debtor requesting that the recipient provide an accounting of the unpaid obligations secured by collateral and reasonably identifying the transaction or relationship that is the subject of the request.

(3) "Request regarding a list of collateral" means a record authenticated by a debtor requesting that the recipient approve or correct a list of what the debtor believes to be the collateral securing an obligation and reasonably identifying the transaction or relationship that is the subject of the request.

(4) "Request regarding a statement of account" means a record authenticated by a debtor requesting that the recipient approve or correct a statement indicating what the debtor believes to be the aggregate amount of unpaid obligations secured by collateral as of a specified date and reasonably identifying the transaction or relationship that is the subject of the request.

(b) Subject to subsections (c), (d), (e), and (f), a secured party, other than a buyer of accounts, chattel paper, payment intangibles, or promissory notes or a consignor, shall comply with a request within 14 days after receipt:

(1) in the case of a request for an accounting, by authenticating and sending to the debtor an accounting; and

(2) in the case of a request regarding a list of collateral or a request regarding a statement of account, by authenticating and sending to the debtor an approval or correction.

(c) A secured party that claims a security interest in all of a particular type of collateral owned by the debtor may comply with a request regarding a list of collateral by sending to the debtor an authenticated record including a statement to that effect within 14 days after receipt.

(d) A person that receives a request regarding a list of collateral, claims no interest in the collateral when it receives the request, and claimed an interest in the collateral at an earlier time shall comply with the request within 14 days after receipt by sending to the debtor an authenticated record:

(1) disclaiming any interest in the collateral; and

(2) if known to the recipient, providing the name and mailing address of any assignee of or successor to the recipient's interest in the collateral.

(e) A person that receives a request for an accounting or a request regarding a statement of account, claims no interest in the obligations when it receives the request, and claimed an interest in the obligations at an earlier time shall comply with the request within 14 days after receipt by sending to the debtor an authenticated record:

(1) disclaiming any interest in the obligations; and

(2) if known to the recipient, providing the name and mailing address of any assignee of or successor to the recipient's interest in the obligations.

(f) A debtor is entitled without charge to one response to a request under this section during any six-month period. The secured party may require payment of a charge not exceeding $25 for each additional response.

As amended in 1999.

PART 3   Perfection and Priority

[Subpart 1. Law Governing Perfection and Priority]

§ 9–301.   Law Governing Perfection and Priority of Security Interests.

Except as otherwise provided in Sections 9–303 through 9–306, the following rules determine the law governing perfection, the effect of perfection or nonperfection, and the priority of a security interest in collateral:

(1) Except as otherwise provided in this section, while a debtor is located in a jurisdiction, the local law of that jurisdiction governs perfection, the effect of perfection or nonperfection, and the priority of a security interest in collateral.

(2) While collateral is located in a jurisdiction, the local law of that jurisdiction governs perfection, the effect of perfection or nonperfection, and the priority of a possessory security interest in that collateral.

(3) Except as otherwise provided in paragraph (4), while negotiable documents, goods, instruments, money, or tangible chattel paper is located in a jurisdiction, the local law of that jurisdiction governs:

(A) perfection of a security interest in the goods by filing a fixture filing;

(B) perfection of a security interest in timber to be cut; and

(C) the effect of perfection or nonperfection and the priority of a nonpossessory security interest in the collateral.

(4) The local law of the jurisdiction in which the wellhead or minehead is located governs perfection, the effect of perfection or nonperfection, and the priority of a security interest in as-extracted collateral.

§ 9–302.   Law Governing Perfection and Priority of Agricultural Liens.

While farm products are located in a jurisdiction, the local law of that jurisdiction governs perfection, the effect of perfection or nonperfection, and the priority of an agricultural lien on the farm products.

§ 9–303.   Law Governing Perfection and Priority of Security Interests in Goods Covered by a Certificate of Title.

(a) This section applies to goods covered by a certificate of title, even if there is no other relationship between the jurisdiction under whose certificate of title the goods are covered and the goods or the debtor.

(b) Goods become covered by a certificate of title when a valid application for the certificate of title and the applicable fee are delivered to the appropriate authority. Goods cease to be cov-ered by a certificate of title at the earlier of the time the certificate of title ceases to be effective under the law of the issuing jurisdiction or the time the goods become covered subsequently by a certificate of title issued by another jurisdiction.

(c) The local law of the jurisdiction under whose certificate of title the goods are covered governs perfection, the effect of perfection or nonperfection, and the priority of a security interest in goods covered by a certificate of title from the time the goods become covered by the certificate of title until the goods cease to be covered by the certificate of title.

§ 9–304.   Law Governing Perfection and Priority of Security Interests in Deposit Accounts.

(a) The local law of a bank's jurisdiction governs perfection, the effect of perfection or nonperfection, and the priority of a security interest in a deposit account maintained with that bank.

(b) The following rules determine a bank's jurisdiction for purposes of this part:

(1) If an agreement between the bank and the debtor governing the deposit account expressly provides that a particular jurisdiction is the bank's jurisdiction for purposes of this part, this article, or [the Uniform Commercial Code], that jurisdiction is the bank's jurisdiction.

(2) If paragraph (1) does not apply and an agreement between the bank and its customer governing the deposit account expressly provides that the agreement is governed by the law of a particular jurisdiction, that jurisdiction is the bank's jurisdiction.

(3) If neither paragraph (1) nor paragraph (2) applies and an agreement between the bank and its customer governing the deposit account expressly provides that the deposit account is maintained at an office in a particular jurisdiction, that jurisdiction is the bank's jurisdiction.

(4) If none of the preceding paragraphs applies, the bank's jurisdiction is the jurisdiction in which the office identified in an account statement as the office serving the customer's account is located.

(5) If none of the preceding paragraphs applies, the bank's jurisdiction is the jurisdiction in which the chief executive office of the bank is located.

§ 9–305.   Law Governing Perfection and Priority of Security Interests in Investment Property.

(a) Except as otherwise provided in subsection (c), the following rules apply:

(1) While a security certificate is located in a jurisdiction, the local law of that jurisdiction governs perfection, the effect of perfection or nonperfection, and the priority of a security interest in the certificated security represented thereby.

(2) The local law of the issuer's jurisdiction as specified in Section 8–110(d) governs perfection, the effect of perfection or

nonperfection, and the priority of a security interest in an uncertificated security.

(3) The local law of the securities intermediary's jurisdiction as specified in Section 8–110(e) governs perfection, the effect of perfection or nonperfection, and the priority of a security interest in a security entitlement or securities account.

(4) The local law of the commodity intermediary's jurisdiction governs perfection, the effect of perfection or nonperfection, and the priority of a security interest in a commodity contract or commodity account.

(b) The following rules determine a commodity intermediary's jurisdiction for purposes of this part:

(1) If an agreement between the commodity intermediary and commodity customer governing the commodity account expressly provides that a particular jurisdiction is the commodity intermediary's jurisdiction for purposes of this part, this article, or [the Uniform Commercial Code], that jurisdiction is the commodity intermediary's jurisdiction.

(2) If paragraph (1) does not apply and an agreement between the commodity intermediary and commodity customer governing the commodity account expressly provides that the agreement is governed by the law of a particular jurisdiction, that jurisdiction is the commodity intermediary's jurisdiction.

(3) If neither paragraph (1) nor paragraph (2) applies and an agreement between the commodity intermediary and commodity customer governing the commodity account expressly provides that the commodity account is maintained at an office in a particular jurisdiction, that jurisdiction is the commodity intermediary's jurisdiction.

(4) If none of the preceding paragraphs applies, the commodity intermediary's jurisdiction is the jurisdiction in which the office identified in an account statement as the office serving the commodity customer's account is located.

(5) If none of the preceding paragraphs applies, the commodity intermediary's jurisdiction is the jurisdiction in which the chief executive office of the commodity intermediary is located.

(c) The local law of the jurisdiction in which the debtor is located governs:

(1) perfection of a security interest in investment property by filing;

(2) automatic perfection of a security interest in investment property created by a broker or securities intermediary; and

(3) automatic perfection of a security interest in a commodity contract or commodity account created by a commodity intermediary.

§ 9–306.   **Law Governing Perfection and Priority of Security Interests in Letter-of-Credit Rights.**

(a) Subject to subsection (c), the local law of the issuer's jurisdiction or a nominated person's jurisdiction governs perfection,

the effect of perfection or nonperfection, and the priority of a security interest in a letter-of-credit right if the issuer's jurisdiction or nominated person's jurisdiction is a State.

(b) For purposes of this part, an issuer's jurisdiction or nominated person's jurisdiction is the jurisdiction whose law governs the liability of the issuer or nominated person with respect to the letter-of-credit right as provided in Section 5–116.

(c) This section does not apply to a security interest that is perfected only under Section 9–308(d).

§ 9–307.   **Location of Debtor.**

(a) In this section, "place of business" means a place where a debtor conducts its affairs.

(b) Except as otherwise provided in this section, the following rules determine a debtor's location:

(1) A debtor who is an individual is located at the individual's principal residence.

(2) A debtor that is an organization and has only one place of business is located at its place of business.

(3) A debtor that is an organization and has more than one place of business is located at its chief executive office.

(c) Subsection (b) applies only if a debtor's residence, place of business, or chief executive office, as applicable, is located in a jurisdiction whose law generally requires information concerning the existence of a nonpossessory security interest to be made generally available in a filing, recording, or registration system as a condition or result of the security interest's obtaining priority over the rights of a lien creditor with respect to the collateral. If subsection (b) does not apply, the debtor is located in the District of Columbia.

(d) A person that ceases to exist, have a residence, or have a place of business continues to be located in the jurisdiction specified by subsections (b) and (c).

(e) A registered organization that is organized under the law of a State is located in that State.

(f) Except as otherwise provided in subsection (i), a registered organization that is organized under the law of the United States and a branch or agency of a bank that is not organized under the law of the United States or a State are located:

(1) in the State that the law of the United States designates, if the law designates a State of location;

(2) in the State that the registered organization, branch, or agency designates, if the law of the United States authorizes the registered organization, branch, or agency to designate its State of location; or

(3) in the District of Columbia, if neither paragraph (1) nor paragraph (2) applies.

(g) A registered organization continues to be located in the jurisdiction specified by subsection (e) or (f) notwithstanding:

(1) the suspension, revocation, forfeiture, or lapse of the registered organization's status as such in its jurisdiction of organization; or

(2) the dissolution, winding up, or cancellation of the existence of the registered organization.

(h) The United States is located in the District of Columbia.

(i) A branch or agency of a bank that is not organized under the law of the United States or a State is located in the State in which the branch or agency is licensed, if all branches and agencies of the bank are licensed in only one State.

(j) A foreign air carrier under the Federal Aviation Act of 1958, as amended, is located at the designated office of the agent upon which service of process may be made on behalf of the carrier.

(k) This section applies only for purposes of this part.

[Subpart 2. Perfection]

§ 9–308.   When Security Interest or Agricultural Lien Is Perfected; Continuity of Perfection.

(a) Except as otherwise provided in this section and Section 9–309, a security interest is perfected if it has attached and all of the applicable requirements for perfection in Sections 9–310 through 9–316 have been satisfied. A security interest is perfected when it attaches if the applicable requirements are satisfied before the security interest attaches.

(b) An agricultural lien is perfected if it has become effective and all of the applicable requirements for perfection in Section 9–310 have been satisfied. An agricultural lien is perfected when it becomes effective if the applicable requirements are satisfied before the agricultural lien becomes effective.

(c) A security interest or agricultural lien is perfected continuously if it is originally perfected by one method under this article and is later perfected by another method under this article, without an intermediate period when it was unperfected.

(d) Perfection of a security interest in collateral also perfects a security interest in a supporting obligation for the collateral.

(e) Perfection of a security interest in a right to payment or performance also perfects a security interest in a security interest, mortgage, or other lien on personal or real property securing the right.

(f) Perfection of a security interest in a securities account also perfects a security interest in the security entitlements carried in the securities account.

(g) Perfection of a security interest in a commodity account also perfects a security interest in the commodity contracts carried in the commodity account.

Legislative Note: Any statute conflicting with subsection (e) must be made expressly subject to that subsection.

§ 9–309.   Security Interest Perfected upon Attachment.

The following security interests are perfected when they attach:

(1) a purchase-money security interest in consumer goods, except as otherwise provided in Section 9–311(b) with respect to consumer goods that are subject to a statute or treaty described in Section 9–311(a);

(2) an assignment of accounts or payment intangibles which does not by itself or in conjunction with other assignments to the same assignee transfer a significant part of the assignor's outstanding accounts or payment intangibles;

(3) a sale of a payment intangible;

(4) a sale of a promissory note;

(5) a security interest created by the assignment of a health-care-insurance receivable to the provider of the health-care goods or services;

(6) a security interest arising under Section 2–401, 2–505, 2–711(3), or 2A–508(5), until the debtor obtains possession of the collateral;

(7) a security interest of a collecting bank arising under Section 4–210;

(8) a security interest of an issuer or nominated person arising under Section 5–118;

(9) a security interest arising in the delivery of a financial asset under Section 9–206(c);

(10) a security interest in investment property created by a broker or securities intermediary;

(11) a security interest in a commodity contract or a commodity account created by a commodity intermediary;

(12) an assignment for the benefit of all creditors of the transferor and subsequent transfers by the assignee thereunder; and

(13) a security interest created by an assignment of a beneficial interest in a decedent's estate; and

(14) a sale by an individual of an account that is a right to payment of winnings in a lottery or other game of chance.

§ 9–310.   When Filing Required to Perfect Security Interest or Agricultural Lien; Security Interests and Agricultural Liens to Which Filing Provisions Do Not Apply.

(a) Except as otherwise provided in subsection (b) and Section 9–312(b), a financing statement must be filed to perfect all security interests and agricultural liens.

(b) The filing of a financing statement is not necessary to perfect a security interest:

(1) that is perfected under Section 9–308(d), (e), (f), or (g);

(2) that is perfected under Section 9–309 when it attaches;

(3) in property subject to a statute, regulation, or treaty described in Section 9–311(a);

(4) in goods in possession of a bailee which is perfected under Section 9–312(d)(1) or (2);

(5) in certificated securities, documents, goods, or instruments which is perfected without filing or possession under Section 9–312(e), (f), or (g);

(6) in collateral in the secured party's possession under Section 9–313;

(7) in a certificated security which is perfected by delivery of the security certificate to the secured party under Section 9–313;

(8) in deposit accounts, electronic chattel paper, investment property, or letter-of-credit rights which is perfected by control under Section 9–314;

(9) in proceeds which is perfected under Section 9–315; or

(10) that is perfected under Section 9–316.

(c) If a secured party assigns a perfected security interest or agricultural lien, a filing under this article is not required to continue the perfected status of the security interest against creditors of and transferees from the original debtor.

§ 9–311. Perfection of Security Interests in Property Subject to Certain Statutes, Regulations, and Treaties.

(a) Except as otherwise provided in subsection (d), the filing of a financing statement is not necessary or effective to perfect a security interest in property subject to:

(1) a statute, regulation, or treaty of the United States whose requirements for a security interest's obtaining priority over the rights of a lien creditor with respect to the property preempt Section 9–310(a);

(2) [list any certificate-of-title statute covering automobiles, trailers, mobile homes, boats, farm tractors, or the like, which provides for a security interest to be indicated on the certificate as a condition or result of perfection, and any non-Uniform Commercial Code central filing statute]; or

(3) a certificate-of-title statute of another jurisdiction which provides for a security interest to be indicated on the certificate as a condition or result of the security interest's obtaining priority over the rights of a lien creditor with respect to the property.

(b) Compliance with the requirements of a statute, regulation, or treaty described in subsection (a) for obtaining priority over the rights of a lien creditor is equivalent to the filing of a financing statement under this article. Except as otherwise provided in subsection (d) and Sections 9–313 and 9–316(d) and (e) for goods covered by a certificate of title, a security interest in property subject to a statute, regulation, or treaty described in subsection (a) may be perfected only by compliance with those requirements, and a security interest so perfected remains perfected notwithstanding a change in the use or transfer of possession of the collateral.

(c) Except as otherwise provided in subsection (d) and Section 9–316(d) and (e), duration and renewal of perfection of a security interest perfected by compliance with the requirements prescribed by a statute, regulation, or treaty described in subsection (a) are governed by the statute, regulation, or treaty. In other respects, the security interest is subject to this article.

(d) During any period in which collateral subject to a statute specified in subsection (a)(2) is inventory held for sale or lease by a person or leased by that person as lessor and that person is in the business of selling goods of that kind, this section does not apply to a security interest in that collateral created by that person.

Legislative Note: This Article contemplates that perfection of a security interest in goods covered by a certificate of title occurs upon receipt by appropriate State officials of a properly tendered application for a certificate of title on which the security interest is to be indicated, without a relation back to an earlier time. States whose certificate-of-title statutes provide for perfection at a different time or contain a relation-back provision should amend the statutes accordingly.

§ 9–312. Perfection of Security Interests in Chattel Paper, Deposit Accounts, Documents, Goods Covered by Documents, Instruments, Investment Property, Letter-of-Credit Rights, and Money; Perfection by Permissive Filing; Temporary Perfection without Filing or Transfer of Possession.

(a) A security interest in chattel paper, negotiable documents, instruments, or investment property may be perfected by filing.

(b) Except as otherwise provided in Section 9–315(c) and (d) for proceeds:

(1) a security interest in a deposit account may be perfected only by control under Section 9–314;

(2) and except as otherwise provided in Section 9–308(d), a security interest in a letter-of-credit right may be perfected only by control under Section 9–314; and

(3) a security interest in money may be perfected only by the secured party's taking possession under Section 9–313.

(c) While goods are in the possession of a bailee that has issued a negotiable document covering the goods:

(1) a security interest in the goods may be perfected by perfecting a security interest in the document; and

(2) a security interest perfected in the document has priority over any security interest that becomes perfected in the goods by another method during that time.

(d) While goods are in the possession of a bailee that has issued a nonnegotiable document covering the goods, a security interest in the goods may be perfected by:

(1) issuance of a document in the name of the secured party;

(2) the bailee's receipt of notification of the secured party's interest; or

(3) filing as to the goods.

(e) A security interest in certificated securities, negotiable documents, or instruments is perfected without filing or the taking of possession for a period of 20 days from the time it attaches to the extent that it arises for new value given under an authenticated security agreement.

(f) A perfected security interest in a negotiable document or goods in possession of a bailee, other than one that has issued a negotiable document for the goods, remains perfected for 20 days without filing if the secured party makes available to the debtor the goods or documents representing the goods for the purpose of:

(1) ultimate sale or exchange; or

(2) loading, unloading, storing, shipping, transshipping, manufacturing, processing, or otherwise dealing with them in a manner preliminary to their sale or exchange.

(g) A perfected security interest in a certificated security or instrument remains perfected for 20 days without filing if the secured party delivers the security certificate or instrument to the debtor for the purpose of:

(1) ultimate sale or exchange; or

(2) presentation, collection, enforcement, renewal, or registration of transfer.

(h) After the 20-day period specified in subsection (e), (f), or (g) expires, perfection depends upon compliance with this article.

§ 9–313. When Possession by or Delivery to Secured Party Perfects Security Interest without Filing.

(a) Except as otherwise provided in subsection (b), a secured party may perfect a security interest in negotiable documents, goods, instruments, money, or tangible chattel paper by taking possession of the collateral. A secured party may perfect a security interest in certificated securities by taking delivery of the certificated securities under Section 8–301.

(b) With respect to goods covered by a certificate of title issued by this State, a secured party may perfect a security interest in the goods by taking possession of the goods only in the circumstances described in Section 9–316(d).

(c) With respect to collateral other than certificated securities and goods covered by a document, a secured party takes possession of collateral in the possession of a person other than the debtor, the secured party, or a lessee of the collateral from the debtor in the ordinary course of the debtor's business, when:

(1) the person in possession authenticates a record acknowledging that it holds possession of the collateral for the secured party's benefit; or

(2) the person takes possession of the collateral after having authenticated a record acknowledging that it will hold possession of collateral for the secured party's benefit.

(d) If perfection of a security interest depends upon possession of the collateral by a secured party, perfection occurs no earlier than the time the secured party takes possession and continues only while the secured party retains possession.

(e) A security interest in a certificated security in registered form is perfected by delivery when delivery of the certificated security occurs under Section 8–301 and remains perfected by delivery until the debtor obtains possession of the security certificate.

(f) A person in possession of collateral is not required to acknowledge that it holds possession for a secured party's benefit.

(g) If a person acknowledges that it holds possession for the secured party's benefit:

(1) the acknowledgment is effective under subsection (c) or Section 8–301(a), even if the acknowledgment violates the rights of a debtor; and

(2) unless the person otherwise agrees or law other than this article otherwise provides, the person does not owe any duty to the secured party and is not required to confirm the acknowledgment to another person.

(h) A secured party having possession of collateral does not relinquish possession by delivering the collateral to a person other than the debtor or a lessee of the collateral from the debtor in the ordinary course of the debtor's business if the person was instructed before the delivery or is instructed contemporaneously with the delivery:

(1) to hold possession of the collateral for the secured party's benefit; or

(2) to redeliver the collateral to the secured party.

(i) A secured party does not relinquish possession, even if a delivery under subsection (h) violates the rights of a debtor. A person to which collateral is delivered under subsection (h) does not owe any duty to the secured party and is not required to confirm the delivery to another person unless the person otherwise agrees or law other than this article otherwise provides.

§ 9–314. Perfection by Control.

(a) A security interest in investment property, deposit accounts, letter-of-credit rights, or electronic chattel paper may be perfected by control of the collateral under Section 9–104, 9–105, 9–106, or 9–107.

(b) A security interest in deposit accounts, electronic chattel paper, or letter-of-credit rights is perfected by control under Section 9–104, 9–105, or 9–107 when the secured party obtains control and remains perfected by control only while the secured party retains control.

(c) A security interest in investment property is perfected by control under Section 9–106 from the time the secured party obtains control and remains perfected by control until:

(1) the secured party does not have control; and

(2) one of the following occurs:

(A) if the collateral is a certificated security, the debtor has or acquires possession of the security certificate;

(B) if the collateral is an uncertificated security, the issuer has registered or registers the debtor as the registered owner; or

(C) if the collateral is a security entitlement, the debtor is or becomes the entitlement holder.

§ 9–315. Secured Party's Rights on Disposition of Collateral and in Proceeds.

(a) Except as otherwise provided in this article and in Section 2–403(2):

(1) a security interest or agricultural lien continues in collateral notwithstanding sale, lease, license, exchange, or other disposition thereof unless the secured party authorized the disposition free of the security interest or agricultural lien; and

(2) a security interest attaches to any identifiable proceeds of collateral.

(b) Proceeds that are commingled with other property are identifiable proceeds:

(1) if the proceeds are goods, to the extent provided by Section 9–336; and

(2) if the proceeds are not goods, to the extent that the secured party identifies the proceeds by a method of tracing, including application of equitable principles, that is permitted under law other than this article with respect to commingled property of the type involved.

(c) A security interest in proceeds is a perfected security interest if the security interest in the original collateral was perfected.

(d) A perfected security interest in proceeds becomes unperfected on the 21st day after the security interest attaches to the proceeds unless:

(1) the following conditions are satisfied:

(A) a filed financing statement covers the original collateral;

(B) the proceeds are collateral in which a security interest may be perfected by filing in the office in which the financing statement has been filed; and

(C) the proceeds are not acquired with cash proceeds;

(2) the proceeds are identifiable cash proceeds; or

(3) the security interest in the proceeds is perfected other than under subsection (c) when the security interest attaches to the proceeds or within 20 days thereafter.

(e) If a filed financing statement covers the original collateral, a security interest in proceeds which remains perfected under subsection (d)(1) becomes unperfected at the later of:

(1) when the effectiveness of the filed financing statement lapses under Section 9–515 or is terminated under Section 9–513; or

(2) the 21st day after the security interest attaches to the proceeds.

§ 9–316. Continued Perfection of Security Interest Following Change in Governing Law.

(a) A security interest perfected pursuant to the law of the jurisdiction designated in Section 9–301(1) or 9–305(c) remains perfected until the earliest of:

(1) the time perfection would have ceased under the law of that jurisdiction;

(2) the expiration of four months after a change of the debtor's location to another jurisdiction; or

(3) the expiration of one year after a transfer of collateral to a person that thereby becomes a debtor and is located in another jurisdiction.

(b) If a security interest described in subsection (a) becomes perfected under the law of the other jurisdiction before the earliest time or event described in that subsection, it remains perfected thereafter. If the security interest does not become perfected under the law of the other jurisdiction before the earliest time or event, it becomes unperfected and is deemed never to have been perfected as against a purchaser of the collateral for value.

(c) A possessory security interest in collateral, other than goods covered by a certificate of title and as-extracted collateral consisting of goods, remains continuously perfected if:

(1) the collateral is located in one jurisdiction and subject to a security interest perfected under the law of that jurisdiction;

(2) thereafter the collateral is brought into another jurisdiction; and

(3) upon entry into the other jurisdiction, the security interest is perfected under the law of the other jurisdiction.

(d) Except as otherwise provided in subsection (e), a security interest in goods covered by a certificate of title which is perfected by any method under the law of another jurisdiction when the goods become covered by a certificate of title from this State remains perfected until the security interest would have become unperfected under the law of the other jurisdiction had the goods not become so covered.

(e) A security interest described in subsection (d) becomes unperfected as against a purchaser of the goods for value and is deemed never to have been perfected as against a purchaser of the goods for value if the applicable requirements for perfection under Section 9–311(b) or 9–313 are not satisfied before the earlier of:

(1) the time the security interest would have become unperfected under the law of the other jurisdiction had the goods not become covered by a certificate of title from this State; or

(2) the expiration of four months after the goods had become so covered.

(f) A security interest in deposit accounts, letter-of-credit rights, or investment property which is perfected under the law of the bank's jurisdiction, the issuer's jurisdiction, a nominated person's jurisdiction, the securities intermediary's jurisdiction, or the commodity intermediary's jurisdiction, as applicable, remains perfected until the earlier of:

(1) the time the security interest would have become unperfected under the law of that jurisdiction; or

(2) the expiration of four months after a change of the applicable jurisdiction to another jurisdiction.

(g) If a security interest described in subsection (f) becomes perfected under the law of the other jurisdiction before the earlier of the time or the end of the period described in that subsection, it remains perfected thereafter. If the security interest does not become perfected under the law of the other jurisdiction before the earlier of that time or the end of that period, it becomes unperfected and is deemed never to have been perfected as against a purchaser of the collateral for value.

[Subpart 3. Priority]

§ 9–317.   Interests That Take Priority over or Take Free of Security Interest or Agricultural Lien.

(a) A security interest or agricultural lien is subordinate to the rights of:

   (1) a person entitled to priority under Section 9–322; and

   (2) except as otherwise provided in subsection (e), a person that becomes a lien creditor before the earlier of the time:

       (A) the security interest or agricultural lien is perfected; or

       (B) one of the conditions specified in Section 9–203(b)(3) is met and a financing statement covering the collateral is filed.

(b) Except as otherwise provided in subsection (e), a buyer, other than a secured party, of tangible chattel paper, documents, goods, instruments, or a security certificate takes free of a security interest or agricultural lien if the buyer gives value and receives delivery of the collateral without knowledge of the security interest or agricultural lien and before it is perfected.

(c) Except as otherwise provided in subsection (e), a lessee of goods takes free of a security interest or agricultural lien if the lessee gives value and receives delivery of the collateral without knowledge of the security interest or agricultural lien and before it is perfected.

(d) A licensee of a general intangible or a buyer, other than a secured party, of accounts, electronic chattel paper, general intangibles, or investment property other than a certificated security takes free of a security interest if the licensee or buyer gives value without knowledge of the security interest and before it is perfected.

(e) Except as otherwise provided in Sections 9–320 and 9–321, if a person files a financing statement with respect to a purchase-money security interest before or within 20 days after the debtor receives delivery of the collateral, the security interest takes priority over the rights of a buyer, lessee, or lien creditor which arise between the time the security interest attaches and the time of filing.

As amended in 2000.

§ 9–318.   No Interest Retained in Right to Payment That Is Sold; Rights and Title of Seller of Account or Chattel Paper with Respect to Creditors and Purchasers.

(a) A debtor that has sold an account, chattel paper, payment intangible, or promissory note does not retain a legal or equitable interest in the collateral sold.

(b) For purposes of determining the rights of creditors of, and purchasers for value of an account or chattel paper from, a debtor that has sold an account or chattel paper, while the buyer's security interest is unperfected, the debtor is deemed to have rights and title to the account or chattel paper identical to those the debtor sold.

§ 9–319.   Rights and Title of Consignee with Respect to Creditors and Purchasers.

(a) Except as otherwise provided in subsection (b), for purposes of determining the rights of creditors of, and purchasers for value of goods from, a consignee, while the goods are in the possession of the consignee, the consignee is deemed to have rights and title to the goods identical to those the consignor had or had power to transfer.

(b) For purposes of determining the rights of a creditor of a consignee, law other than this article determines the rights and title of a consignee while goods are in the consignee's possession if, under this part, a perfected security interest held by the consignor would have priority over the rights of the creditor.

§ 9–320.   Buyer of Goods.

(a) Except as otherwise provided in subsection (e), a buyer in ordinary course of business, other than a person buying farm products from a person engaged in farming operations, takes free of a security interest created by the buyer's seller, even if the security interest is perfected and the buyer knows of its existence.

(b) Except as otherwise provided in subsection (e), a buyer of goods from a person who used or bought the goods for use primarily for personal, family, or household purposes takes free of a security interest, even if perfected, if the buyer buys:

   (1) without knowledge of the security interest;

   (2) for value;

   (3) primarily for the buyer's personal, family, or household purposes; and

   (4) before the filing of a financing statement covering the goods.

(c) To the extent that it affects the priority of a security interest over a buyer of goods under subsection (b), the period of effectiveness of a filing made in the jurisdiction in which the seller is located is governed by Section 9–316(a) and (b).

(d) A buyer in ordinary course of business buying oil, gas, or other minerals at the wellhead or minehead or after extraction takes free of an interest arising out of an encumbrance.

(e) Subsections (a) and (b) do not affect a security interest in goods in the possession of the secured party under Section 9–313.

§ 9–321.   Licensee of General Intangible and Lessee of Goods in Ordinary Course of Business.

(a) In this section, "licensee in ordinary course of business" means a person that becomes a licensee of a general intangible in good faith, without knowledge that the license violates the rights of another person in the general intangible, and in the ordinary course from a person in the business of licensing general intangibles of that kind. A person becomes a licensee in the ordinary course if the license to the person comports with the usual or customary practices in the kind of business in which the licensor is engaged or with the licensor's own usual or customary practices.

(b) A licensee in ordinary course of business takes its rights under a nonexclusive license free of a security interest in the general intangible created by the licensor, even if the security interest is perfected and the licensee knows of its existence.

(c) A lessee in ordinary course of business takes its leasehold interest free of a security interest in the goods created by the lessor, even if the security interest is perfected and the lessee knows of its existence.

§ 9–322.   Priorities among Conflicting Security Interests in and Agricultural Liens on Same Collateral.

(a) Except as otherwise provided in this section, priority among conflicting security interests and agricultural liens in the same collateral is determined according to the following rules:

(1) Conflicting perfected security interests and agricultural liens rank according to priority in time of filing or perfection. Priority dates from the earlier of the time a filing covering the collateral is first made or the security interest or agricultural lien is first perfected, if there is no period thereafter when there is neither filing nor perfection.

(2) A perfected security interest or agricultural lien has priority over a conflicting unperfected security interest or agricultural lien.

(3) The first security interest or agricultural lien to attach or become effective has priority if conflicting security interests and agricultural liens are unperfected.

(b) For the purposes of subsection (a)(1):

(1) the time of filing or perfection as to a security interest in collateral is also the time of filing or perfection as to a security interest in proceeds; and

(2) the time of filing or perfection as to a security interest in collateral supported by a supporting obligation is also the time of filing or perfection as to a security interest in the supporting obligation.

(c) Except as otherwise provided in subsection (f), a security interest in collateral which qualifies for priority over a conflicting security interest under Section 9–327, 9–328, 9–329, 9–330, or 9–331 also has priority over a conflicting security interest in:

(1) any supporting obligation for the collateral; and

(2) proceeds of the collateral if:

(A) the security interest in proceeds is perfected;

(B) the proceeds are cash proceeds or of the same type as the collateral; and

(C) in the case of proceeds that are proceeds of proceeds, all intervening proceeds are cash proceeds, proceeds of the same type as the collateral, or an account relating to the collateral.

(d) Subject to subsection (e) and except as otherwise provided in subsection (f), if a security interest in chattel paper, deposit accounts, negotiable documents, instruments, investment property, or letter-of-credit rights is perfected by a method other than filing, conflicting perfected security interests in proceeds of the collateral rank according to priority in time of filing.

(e) Subsection (d) applies only if the proceeds of the collateral are not cash proceeds, chattel paper, negotiable documents, instruments, investment property, or letter-of-credit rights.

(f) Subsections (a) through (e) are subject to:

(1) subsection (g) and the other provisions of this part;

(2) Section 4–210 with respect to a security interest of a collecting bank;

(3) Section 5–118 with respect to a security interest of an issuer or nominated person; and

(4) Section 9–110 with respect to a security interest arising under Article 2 or 2A.

(g) A perfected agricultural lien on collateral has priority over a conflicting security interest in or agricultural lien on the same collateral if the statute creating the agricultural lien so provides.

§ 9–323.   Future Advances.

(a) Except as otherwise provided in subsection (c), for purposes of determining the priority of a perfected security interest under Section 9–322(a)(1), perfection of the security interest dates from the time an advance is made to the extent that the security interest secures an advance that:

(1) is made while the security interest is perfected only:

(A) under Section 9–309 when it attaches; or

(B) temporarily under Section 9–312(e), (f), or (g); and

(2) is not made pursuant to a commitment entered into before or while the security interest is perfected by a method other than under Section 9–309 or 9–312(e), (f), or (g).

(b) Except as otherwise provided in subsection (c), a security interest is subordinate to the rights of a person that becomes a lien creditor to the extent that the security interest secures an advance made more than 45 days after the person becomes a lien creditor unless the advance is made:

(1) without knowledge of the lien; or

(2) pursuant to a commitment entered into without knowledge of the lien.

(c) Subsections (a) and (b) do not apply to a security interest held by a secured party that is a buyer of accounts, chattel paper, payment intangibles, or promissory notes or a consignor.

(d) Except as otherwise provided in subsection (e), a buyer of goods other than a buyer in ordinary course of business takes free of a security interest to the extent that it secures advances made after the earlier of:

(1) the time the secured party acquires knowledge of the buyer's purchase; or

(2) 45 days after the purchase.

(e) Subsection (d) does not apply if the advance is made pursuant to a commitment entered into without knowledge of the buyer's purchase and before the expiration of the 45-day period.

(f) Except as otherwise provided in subsection (g), a lessee of goods, other than a lessee in ordinary course of business, takes the leasehold interest free of a security interest to the extent that it secures advances made after the earlier of:

(1) the time the secured party acquires knowledge of the lease; or

(2) 45 days after the lease contract becomes enforceable.

(g) Subsection (f) does not apply if the advance is made pursuant to a commitment entered into without knowledge of the lease and before the expiration of the 45-day period.

As amended in 1999.

§ 9–324.   Priority of Purchase-Money Security Interests.

(a) Except as otherwise provided in subsection (g), a perfected purchase-money security interest in goods other than inventory or livestock has priority over a conflicting security interest in the same goods, and, except as otherwise provided in Section 9–327, a perfected security interest in its identifiable proceeds also has priority, if the purchase-money security interest is perfected when the debtor receives possession of the collateral or within 20 days thereafter.

(b) Subject to subsection (c) and except as otherwise provided in subsection (g), a perfected purchase-money security interest in inventory has priority over a conflicting security interest in the same inventory, has priority over a conflicting security interest in chattel paper or an instrument constituting proceeds of the inventory and in proceeds of the chattel paper, if so provided in Section 9–330, and, except as otherwise provided in Section 9–327, also has priority in identifiable cash proceeds of the inventory to the extent the identifiable cash proceeds are received on or before the delivery of the inventory to a buyer, if:

(1) the purchase-money security interest is perfected when the debtor receives possession of the inventory;

(2) the purchase-money secured party sends an authenticated notification to the holder of the conflicting security interest;

(3) the holder of the conflicting security interest receives the notification within five years before the debtor receives possession of the inventory; and

(4) the notification states that the person sending the notification has or expects to acquire a purchase-money security interest in inventory of the debtor and describes the inventory.

(c) Subsections (b)(2) through (4) apply only if the holder of the conflicting security interest had filed a financing statement covering the same types of inventory:

(1) if the purchase-money security interest is perfected by filing, before the date of the filing; or

(2) if the purchase-money security interest is temporarily perfected without filing or possession under Section 9–312(f), before the beginning of the 20-day period thereunder.

(d) Subject to subsection (e) and except as otherwise provided in subsection (g), a perfected purchase-money security interest in livestock that are farm products has priority over a conflicting security interest in the same livestock, and, except as otherwise provided in Section 9–327, a perfected security interest in their identifiable proceeds and identifiable products in their unmanufactured states also has priority, if:

(1) the purchase-money security interest is perfected when the debtor receives possession of the livestock;

(2) the purchase-money secured party sends an authenticated notification to the holder of the conflicting security interest;

(3) the holder of the conflicting security interest receives the notification within six months before the debtor receives possession of the livestock; and

(4) the notification states that the person sending the notification has or expects to acquire a purchase-money security interest in livestock of the debtor and describes the livestock.

(e) Subsections (d)(2) through (4) apply only if the holder of the conflicting security interest had filed a financing statement covering the same types of livestock:

(1) if the purchase-money security interest is perfected by filing, before the date of the filing; or

(2) if the purchase-money security interest is temporarily perfected without filing or possession under Section 9–312(f), before the beginning of the 20-day period thereunder.

(f) Except as otherwise provided in subsection (g), a perfected purchase-money security interest in software has priority over a conflicting security interest in the same collateral, and, except as otherwise provided in Section 9–327, a perfected security interest in its identifiable proceeds also has priority, to the extent that the purchase-money security interest in the goods in which the software was acquired for use has priority in the goods and proceeds of the goods under this section.

(g) If more than one security interest qualifies for priority in the same collateral under subsection (a), (b), (d), or (f):

(1) a security interest securing an obligation incurred as all or part of the price of the collateral has priority over a security interest securing an obligation incurred for value given

to enable the debtor to acquire rights in or the use of collateral; and

(2) in all other cases, Section 9–322(a) applies to the qualifying security interests.

§ 9–325. Priority of Security Interests in Transferred Collateral.

(a) Except as otherwise provided in subsection (b), a security interest created by a debtor is subordinate to a security interest in the same collateral created by another person if:

(1) the debtor acquired the collateral subject to the security interest created by the other person;

(2) the security interest created by the other person was perfected when the debtor acquired the collateral; and

(3) there is no period thereafter when the security interest is unperfected.

(b) Subsection (a) subordinates a security interest only if the security interest:

(1) otherwise would have priority solely under Section 9–322(a) or 9–324; or

(2) arose solely under Section 2–711(3) or 2A–508(5).

§ 9–326. Priority of Security Interests Created by New Debtor.

(a) Subject to subsection (b), a security interest created by a new debtor which is perfected by a filed financing statement that is effective solely under Section 9–508 in collateral in which a new debtor has or acquires rights is subordinate to a security interest in the same collateral which is perfected other than by a filed financing statement that is effective solely under Section 9–508.

(b) The other provisions of this part determine the priority among conflicting security interests in the same collateral perfected by filed financing statements that are effective solely under Section 9–508. However, if the security agreements to which a new debtor became bound as debtor were not entered into by the same original debtor, the conflicting security interests rank according to priority in time of the new debtor's having become bound.

§ 9–327. Priority of Security Interests in Deposit Account.

The following rules govern priority among conflicting security interests in the same deposit account:

(1) A security interest held by a secured party having control of the deposit account under Section 9–104 has priority over a conflicting security interest held by a secured party that does not have control.

(2) Except as otherwise provided in paragraphs (3) and (4), security interests perfected by control under Section 9–314 rank according to priority in time of obtaining control.

(3) Except as otherwise provided in paragraph (4), a security interest held by the bank with which the deposit account is maintained has priority over a conflicting security interest held by another secured party.

(4) A security interest perfected by control under Section 9–104(a)(3) has priority over a security interest held by the bank with which the deposit account is maintained.

§ 9–328. Priority of Security Interests in Investment Property.

The following rules govern priority among conflicting security interests in the same investment property:

(1) A security interest held by a secured party having control of investment property under Section 9–106 has priority over a security interest held by a secured party that does not have control of the investment property.

(2) Except as otherwise provided in paragraphs (3) and (4), conflicting security interests held by secured parties each of which has control under Section 9–106 rank according to priority in time of:

(A) if the collateral is a security, obtaining control;

(B) if the collateral is a security entitlement carried in a securities account and:

(i) if the secured party obtained control under Section 8–106(d)(1), the secured party's becoming the person for which the securities account is maintained;

(ii) if the secured party obtained control under Section 8–106(d)(2), the securities intermediary's agreement to comply with the secured party's entitlement orders with respect to security entitlements carried or to be carried in the securities account; or

(iii) if the secured party obtained control through another person under Section 8–106(d)(3), the time on which priority would be based under this paragraph if the other person were the secured party; or

(C) if the collateral is a commodity contract carried with a commodity intermediary, the satisfaction of the requirement for control specified in Section 9–106(b)(2) with respect to commodity contracts carried or to be carried with the commodity intermediary.

(3) A security interest held by a securities intermediary in a security entitlement or a securities account maintained with the securities intermediary has priority over a conflicting security interest held by another secured party.

(4) A security interest held by a commodity intermediary in a commodity contract or a commodity account maintained with the commodity intermediary has priority over a conflicting security interest held by another secured party.

(5) A security interest in a certificated security in registered form which is perfected by taking delivery under Section 9–313(a) and not by control under Section 9–314 has priority over a conflicting security interest perfected by a method other than control.

(6) Conflicting security interests created by a broker, securities intermediary, or commodity intermediary which are perfected without control under Section 9–106 rank equally.

(7) In all other cases, priority among conflicting security interests in investment property is governed by Sections 9–322 and 9–323.

§ 9–329.   Priority of Security Interests in Letter-of-Credit Right.

The following rules govern priority among conflicting security interests in the same letter-of-credit right:

(1) A security interest held by a secured party having control of the letter-of-credit right under Section 9–107 has priority to the extent of its control over a conflicting security interest held by a secured party that does not have control.

(2) Security interests perfected by control under Section 9–314 rank according to priority in time of obtaining control.

§ 9–330.   Priority of Purchaser of Chattel Paper or Instrument.

(a) A purchaser of chattel paper has priority over a security interest in the chattel paper which is claimed merely as proceeds of inventory subject to a security interest if:

(1) in good faith and in the ordinary course of the purchaser's business, the purchaser gives new value and takes possession of the chattel paper or obtains control of the chattel paper under Section 9–105; and

(2) the chattel paper does not indicate that it has been assigned to an identified assignee other than the purchaser.

(b) A purchaser of chattel paper has priority over a security interest in the chattel paper which is claimed other than merely as proceeds of inventory subject to a security interest if the purchaser gives new value and takes possession of the chattel paper or obtains control of the chattel paper under Section 9–105 in good faith, in the ordinary course of the purchaser's business, and without knowledge that the purchase violates the rights of the secured party.

(c) Except as otherwise provided in Section 9–327, a purchaser having priority in chattel paper under subsection (a) or (b) also has priority in proceeds of the chattel paper to the extent that:

(1) Section 9–322 provides for priority in the proceeds; or

(2) the proceeds consist of the specific goods covered by the chattel paper or cash proceeds of the specific goods, even if the purchaser's security interest in the proceeds is unperfected.

(d) Except as otherwise provided in Section 9–331(a), a purchaser of an instrument has priority over a security interest in the instrument perfected by a method other than possession if the purchaser gives value and takes possession of the instrument in good faith and without knowledge that the purchase violates the rights of the secured party.

(e) For purposes of subsections (a) and (b), the holder of a purchase-money security interest in inventory gives new value for chattel paper constituting proceeds of the inventory.

(f) For purposes of subsections (b) and (d), if chattel paper or an instrument indicates that it has been assigned to an identified secured party other than the purchaser, a purchaser of the chattel paper or instrument has knowledge that the purchase violates the rights of the secured party.

§ 9–331.   Priority of Rights of Purchasers of Instruments, Documents, and Securities under Other Articles; Priority of Interests in Financial Assets and Security Entitlements under Article 8.

(a) This article does not limit the rights of a holder in due course of a negotiable instrument, a holder to which a negotiable document of title has been duly negotiated, or a protected purchaser of a security. These holders or purchasers take priority over an earlier security interest, even if perfected, to the extent provided in Articles 3, 7, and 8.

(b) This article does not limit the rights of or impose liability on a person to the extent that the person is protected against the assertion of a claim under Article 8.

(c) Filing under this article does not constitute notice of a claim or defense to the holders, or purchasers, or persons described in subsections (a) and (b).

§ 9–332.   Transfer of Money; Transfer of Funds from Deposit Account.

(a) A transferee of money takes the money free of a security interest unless the transferee acts in collusion with the debtor in violating the rights of the secured party.

(b) A transferee of funds from a deposit account takes the funds free of a security interest in the deposit account unless the transferee acts in collusion with the debtor in violating the rights of the secured party.

§ 9–333.   Priority of Certain Liens Arising by Operation of Law.

(a) In this section, "possessory lien" means an interest, other than a security interest or an agricultural lien:

(1) which secures payment or performance of an obligation for services or materials furnished with respect to goods by a person in the ordinary course of the person's business;

(2) which is created by statute or rule of law in favor of the person; and

(3) whose effectiveness depends on the person's possession of the goods.

(b) A possessory lien on goods has priority over a security interest in the goods unless the lien is created by a statute that expressly provides otherwise.

§ 9–334.   Priority of Security Interests in Fixtures and Crops.

(a) A security interest under this article may be created in goods that are fixtures or may continue in goods that become fixtures.

A security interest does not exist under this article in ordinary building materials incorporated into an improvement on land.

(b) This article does not prevent creation of an encumbrance upon fixtures under real property law.

(c) In cases not governed by subsections (d) through (h), a security interest in fixtures is subordinate to a conflicting interest of an encumbrancer or owner of the related real property other than the debtor.

(d) Except as otherwise provided in subsection (h), a perfected security interest in fixtures has priority over a conflicting interest of an encumbrancer or owner of the real property if the debtor has an interest of record in or is in possession of the real property and:

(1) the security interest is a purchase-money security interest;

(2) the interest of the encumbrancer or owner arises before the goods become fixtures; and

(3) the security interest is perfected by a fixture filing before the goods become fixtures or within 20 days thereafter.

(e) A perfected security interest in fixtures has priority over a conflicting interest of an encumbrancer or owner of the real property if:

(1) the debtor has an interest of record in the real property or is in possession of the real property and the security interest:

(A) is perfected by a fixture filing before the interest of the encumbrancer or owner is of record; and

(B) has priority over any conflicting interest of a predecessor in title of the encumbrancer or owner;

(2) before the goods become fixtures, the security interest is perfected by any method permitted by this article and the fixtures are readily removable:

(A) factory or office machines;

(B) equipment that is not primarily used or leased for use in the operation of the real property; or

(C) replacements of domestic appliances that are consumer goods;

(3) the conflicting interest is a lien on the real property obtained by legal or equitable proceedings after the security interest was perfected by any method permitted by this article; or

(4) the security interest is:

(A) created in a manufactured home in a manufactured-home transaction; and

(B) perfected pursuant to a statute described in Section 9–311(a)(2).

(f) A security interest in fixtures, whether or not perfected, has priority over a conflicting interest of an encumbrancer or owner of the real property if:

(1) the encumbrancer or owner has, in an authenticated record, consented to the security interest or disclaimed an interest in the goods as fixtures; or

(2) the debtor has a right to remove the goods as against the encumbrancer or owner.

(g) The priority of the security interest under paragraph (f)(2) continues for a reasonable time if the debtor's right to remove the goods as against the encumbrancer or owner terminates.

(h) A mortgage is a construction mortgage to the extent that it secures an obligation incurred for the construction of an improvement on land, including the acquisition cost of the land, if a recorded record of the mortgage so indicates. Except as otherwise provided in subsections (e) and (f), a security interest in fixtures is subordinate to a construction mortgage if a record of the mortgage is recorded before the goods become fixtures and the goods become fixtures before the completion of the construction. A mortgage has this priority to the same extent as a construction mortgage to the extent that it is given to refinance a construction mortgage.

(i) A perfected security interest in crops growing on real property has priority over a conflicting interest of an encumbrancer or owner of the real property if the debtor has an interest of record in or is in possession of the real property.

(j) Subsection (i) prevails over any inconsistent provisions of the following statutes:

[List here any statutes containing provisions inconsistent with subsection (i).]

Legislative Note: States that amend statutes to remove provisions inconsistent with subsection (i) need not enact subsection (j).

§ 9–335. Accessions.

(a) A security interest may be created in an accession and continues in collateral that becomes an accession.

(b) If a security interest is perfected when the collateral becomes an accession, the security interest remains perfected in the collateral.

(c) Except as otherwise provided in subsection (d), the other provisions of this part determine the priority of a security interest in an accession.

(d) A security interest in an accession is subordinate to a security interest in the whole which is perfected by compliance with the requirements of a certificate-of-title statute under Section 9–311(b).

(e) After default, subject to Part 6, a secured party may remove an accession from other goods if the security interest in the accession has priority over the claims of every person having an interest in the whole.

(f) A secured party that removes an accession from other goods under subsection (e) shall promptly reimburse any holder of a security interest or other lien on, or owner of, the whole or of the other goods, other than the debtor, for the cost of repair of any physical injury to the whole or the other goods. The secured party need not reimburse the holder or owner for any diminution in value of the whole or the other goods caused by the absence of the accession removed or by any necessity for replacing it. A person entitled to reimbursement may refuse permission to remove until the secured party gives adequate assurance for the performance of the obligation to reimburse.

§ 9–336.   Commingled Goods.

(a) In this section, "commingled goods" means goods that are physically united with other goods in such a manner that their identity is lost in a product or mass.

(b) A security interest does not exist in commingled goods as such. However, a security interest may attach to a product or mass that results when goods become commingled goods.

(c) If collateral becomes commingled goods, a security interest attaches to the product or mass.

(d) If a security interest in collateral is perfected before the collateral becomes commingled goods, the security interest that attaches to the product or mass under subsection (c) is perfected.

(e) Except as otherwise provided in subsection (f), the other provisions of this part determine the priority of a security interest that attaches to the product or mass under subsection (c).

(f) If more than one security interest attaches to the product or mass under subsection (c), the following rules determine priority:

(1) A security interest that is perfected under subsection (d) has priority over a security interest that is unperfected at the time the collateral becomes commingled goods.

(2) If more than one security interest is perfected under subsection (d), the security interests rank equally in proportion to the value of the collateral at the time it became commingled goods.

§ 9–337.   Priority of Security Interests in Goods Covered by Certificate of Title.

If, while a security interest in goods is perfected by any method under the law of another jurisdiction, this State issues a certificate of title that does not show that the goods are subject to the security interest or contain a statement that they may be subject to security interests not shown on the certificate:

(1) a buyer of the goods, other than a person in the business of selling goods of that kind, takes free of the security interest if the buyer gives value and receives delivery of the goods after issuance of the certificate and without knowledge of the security interest; and

(2) the security interest is subordinate to a conflicting security interest in the goods that attaches, and is perfected under Section 9–311(b), after issuance of the certificate and without the conflicting secured party's knowledge of the security interest.

§ 9–338.   Priority of Security Interest or Agricultural Lien Perfected by Filed Financing Statement Providing Certain Incorrect Information.

If a security interest or agricultural lien is perfected by a filed financing statement providing information described in Section 9–516(b)(5) which is incorrect at the time the financing statement is filed:

(1) the security interest or agricultural lien is subordinate to a conflicting perfected security interest in the collateral to the extent that the holder of the conflicting security interest gives value in reasonable reliance upon the incorrect information; and

(2) a purchaser, other than a secured party, of the collateral takes free of the security interest or agricultural lien to the extent that, in reasonable reliance upon the incorrect information, the purchaser gives value and, in the case of chattel paper, documents, goods, instruments, or a security certificate, receives delivery of the collateral.

§ 9–339.   Priority Subject to Subordination.

This article does not preclude subordination by agreement by a person entitled to priority.

[Subpart 4. Rights of Bank]

§ 9–340.   Effectiveness of Right of Recoupment or Set-Off against Deposit Account.

(a) Except as otherwise provided in subsection (c), a bank with which a deposit account is maintained may exercise any right of recoupment or set-off against a secured party that holds a security interest in the deposit account.

(b) Except as otherwise provided in subsection (c), the application of this article to a security interest in a deposit account does not affect a right of recoupment or set-off of the secured party as to a deposit account maintained with the secured party.

(c) The exercise by a bank of a set-off against a deposit account is ineffective against a secured party that holds a security interest in the deposit account which is perfected by control under Section 9–104(a)(3), if the set-off is based on a claim against the debtor.

§ 9–341.   Bank's Rights and Duties with Respect to Deposit Account.

Except as otherwise provided in Section 9–340(c), and unless the bank otherwise agrees in an authenticated record, a bank's rights and duties with respect to a deposit account maintained with the bank are not terminated, suspended, or modified by:

(1) the creation, attachment, or perfection of a security interest in the deposit account;

(2) the bank's knowledge of the security interest; or

(3) the bank's receipt of instructions from the secured party.

§ 9–342.   Bank's Right to Refuse to Enter into or Disclose Existence of Control Agreement.

This article does not require a bank to enter into an agreement of the kind described in Section 9–104(a)(2), even if its customer so requests or directs. A bank that has entered into such an agreement is not required to confirm the existence of the agreement to another person unless requested to do so by its customer.

PART 4   Rights of Third Parties

§ 9–401.   Alienability of Debtor's Rights.

(a) Except as otherwise provided in subsection (b) and Sections 9–406, 9–407, 9–408, and 9–409, whether a debtor's rights in collateral may be voluntarily or involuntarily transferred is governed by law other than this article.

(b) An agreement between the debtor and secured party which prohibits a transfer of the debtor's rights in collateral or makes the transfer a default does not prevent the transfer from taking effect.

§ 9–402.   Secured Party Not Obligated on Contract of Debtor or in Tort.

The existence of a security interest, agricultural lien, or authority given to a debtor to dispose of or use collateral, without more, does not subject a secured party to liability in contract or tort for the debtor's acts or omissions.

§ 9–403.   Agreement Not to Assert Defenses against Assignee.

(a) In this section, "value" has the meaning provided in Section 3–303(a).

(b) Except as otherwise provided in this section, an agreement between an account debtor and an assignor not to assert against an assignee any claim or defense that the account debtor may have against the assignor is enforceable by an assignee that takes an assignment:

  (1) for value;

  (2) in good faith;

  (3) without notice of a claim of a property or possessory right to the property assigned; and

  (4) without notice of a defense or claim in recoupment of the type that may be asserted against a person entitled to enforce a negotiable instrument under Section 3–305(a).

(c) Subsection (b) does not apply to defenses of a type that may be asserted against a holder in due course of a negotiable instrument under Section 3–305(b).

(d) In a consumer transaction, if a record evidences the account debtor's obligation, law other than this article requires that the record include a statement to the effect that the rights of an assignee are subject to claims or defenses that the account debtor could assert against the original obligee, and the record does not include such a statement:

  (1) the record has the same effect as if the record included such a statement; and

  (2) the account debtor may assert against an assignee those claims and defenses that would have been available if the record included such a statement.

(e) This section is subject to law other than this article which establishes a different rule for an account debtor who is an individual and who incurred the obligation primarily for personal, family, or household purposes.

(f) Except as otherwise provided in subsection (d), this section does not displace law other than this article which gives effect to an agreement by an account debtor not to assert a claim or defense against an assignee.

§ 9–404.   Rights Acquired by Assignee; Claims and Defenses against Assignee.

(a) Unless an account debtor has made an enforceable agreement not to assert defenses or claims, and subject to subsections (b) through (e), the rights of an assignee are subject to:

  (1) all terms of the agreement between the account debtor and assignor and any defense or claim in recoupment arising from the transaction that gave rise to the contract; and

  (2) any other defense or claim of the account debtor against the assignor which accrues before the account debtor receives a notification of the assignment authenticated by the assignor or the assignee.

(b) Subject to subsection (c) and except as otherwise provided in subsection (d), the claim of an account debtor against an assignor may be asserted against an assignee under subsection (a) only to reduce the amount the account debtor owes.

(c) This section is subject to law other than this article which establishes a different rule for an account debtor who is an individual and who incurred the obligation primarily for personal, family, or household purposes.

(d) In a consumer transaction, if a record evidences the account debtor's obligation, law other than this article requires that the record include a statement to the effect that the account debtor's recovery against an assignee with respect to claims and defenses against the assignor may not exceed amounts paid by the account debtor under the record, and the record does not include such a statement, the extent to which a claim of an account debtor against the assignor may be asserted against an assignee is determined as if the record included such a statement.

(e) This section does not apply to an assignment of a health-care-insurance receivable.

§ 9–405.   Modification of Assigned Contract.

(a) A modification of or substitution for an assigned contract is effective against an assignee if made in good faith. The assignee acquires corresponding rights under the modified or substituted contract. The assignment may provide that the modification or substitution is a breach of contract by the assignor. This subsection is subject to subsections (b) through (d).

(b) Subsection (a) applies to the extent that:

  (1) the right to payment or a part thereof under an assigned contract has not been fully earned by performance; or

  (2) the right to payment or a part thereof has been fully earned by performance and the account debtor has not received notification of the assignment under Section 9–406(a).

(c) This section is subject to law other than this article which establishes a different rule for an account debtor who is an individual and who incurred the obligation primarily for personal, family, or household purposes.

(d) This section does not apply to an assignment of a health-care-insurance receivable.

§ 9–406.   Discharge of Account Debtor; Notification of Assignment; Identification and Proof of Assignment; Restrictions on Assignment of Accounts, Chattel Paper, Payment Intangibles, and Promissory Notes Ineffective.

(a) Subject to subsections (b) through (i), an account debtor on an account, chattel paper, or a payment intangible may discharge its obligation by paying the assignor until, but not after, the account debtor receives a notification, authenticated by the assignor or the assignee, that the amount due or to become due has been assigned and that payment is to be made to the assignee. After receipt of the notification, the account debtor may discharge its obligation by paying the assignee and may not discharge the obligation by paying the assignor.

(b) Subject to subsection (h), notification is ineffective under subsection (a):

(1) if it does not reasonably identify the rights assigned;

(2) to the extent that an agreement between an account debtor and a seller of a payment intangible limits the account debtor's duty to pay a person other than the seller and the limitation is effective under law other than this article; or

(3) at the option of an account debtor, if the notification notifies the account debtor to make less than the full amount of any installment or other periodic payment to the assignee, even if:

(A) only a portion of the account, chattel paper, or payment intangible has been assigned to that assignee;

(B) a portion has been assigned to another assignee; or

(C) the account debtor knows that the assignment to that assignee is limited.

(c) Subject to subsection (h), if requested by the account debtor, an assignee shall seasonably furnish reasonable proof that the assignment has been made. Unless the assignee complies, the account debtor may discharge its obligation by paying the assignor, even if the account debtor has received a notification under subsection (a).

(d) Except as otherwise provided in subsection (e) and Sections 2A–303 and 9–407, and subject to subsection (h), a term in an agreement between an account debtor and an assignor or in a promissory note is ineffective to the extent that it:

(1) prohibits, restricts, or requires the consent of the account debtor or person obligated on the promissory note to the assignment or transfer of, or the creation, attachment, perfection, or enforcement of a security interest in, the account, chattel paper, payment intangible, or promissory note; or

(2) provides that the assignment or transfer or the creation, attachment, perfection, or enforcement of the security interest

may give rise to a default, breach, right of recoupment, claim, defense, termination, right of termination, or remedy under the account, chattel paper, payment intangible, or promissory note.

(e) Subsection (d) does not apply to the sale of a payment intangible or promissory note.

(f) Except as otherwise provided in Sections 2A–303 and 9–407 and subject to subsections (h) and (i), a rule of law, statute, or regulation that prohibits, restricts, or requires the consent of a government, governmental body or official, or account debtor to the assignment or transfer of, or creation of a security interest in, an account or chattel paper is ineffective to the extent that the rule of law, statute, or regulation:

(1) prohibits, restricts, or requires the consent of the government, governmental body or official, or account debtor to the assignment or transfer of, or the creation, attachment, perfection, or enforcement of a security interest in the account or chattel paper; or

(2) provides that the assignment or transfer or the creation, attachment, perfection, or enforcement of the security interest may give rise to a default, breach, right of recoupment, claim, defense, termination, right of termination, or remedy under the account or chattel paper.

(g) Subject to subsection (h), an account debtor may not waive or vary its option under subsection (b)(3).

(h) This section is subject to law other than this article which establishes a different rule for an account debtor who is an individual and who incurred the obligation primarily for personal, family, or household purposes.

(i) This section does not apply to an assignment of a health-care-insurance receivable.

(j) This section prevails over any inconsistent provisions of the following statutes, rules, and regulations:

[List here any statutes, rules, and regulations containing provisions inconsistent with this section.]

Legislative Note: States that amend statutes, rules, and regulations to remove provisions inconsistent with this section need not enact subsection (j).

As amended in 1999 and 2000.

§ 9–407.   Restrictions on Creation or Enforcement of Security Interest in Leasehold Interest or in Lessor's Residual Interest.

(a) Except as otherwise provided in subsection (b), a term in a lease agreement is ineffective to the extent that it:

(1) prohibits, restricts, or requires the consent of a party to the lease to the assignment or transfer of, or the creation, attachment, perfection, or enforcement of a security interest in an interest of a party under the lease contract or in the lessor's residual interest in the goods; or

(2) provides that the assignment or transfer or the creation, attachment, perfection, or enforcement of the security interest

may give rise to a default, breach, right of recoupment, claim, defense, termination, right of termination, or remedy under the lease.

(b) Except as otherwise provided in Section 2A–303(7), a term described in subsection (a)(2) is effective to the extent that there is:

(1) a transfer by the lessee of the lessee's right of possession or use of the goods in violation of the term; or

(2) a delegation of a material performance of either party to the lease contract in violation of the term.

(c) The creation, attachment, perfection, or enforcement of a security interest in the lessor's interest under the lease contract or the lessor's residual interest in the goods is not a transfer that materially impairs the lessee's prospect of obtaining return performance or materially changes the duty of or materially increases the burden or risk imposed on the lessee within the purview of Section 2A–303(4) unless, and then only to the extent that, enforcement actually results in a delegation of material performance of the lessor.

As amended in 1999.

§ 9–408.   Restrictions on Assignment of Promissory Notes, Health-Care-Insurance Receivables, and Certain General Intangibles Ineffective.

(a) Except as otherwise provided in subsection (b), a term in a promissory note or in an agreement between an account debtor and a debtor which relates to a health-care-insurance receivable or a general intangible, including a contract, permit, license, or franchise, and which term prohibits, restricts, or requires the consent of the person obligated on the promissory note or the account debtor to, the assignment or transfer of, or creation, attachment, or perfection of a security interest in, the promissory note, health-care-insurance receivable, or general intangible, is ineffective to the extent that the term:

(1) would impair the creation, attachment, or perfection of a security interest; or

(2) provides that the assignment or transfer or the creation, attachment, or perfection of the security interest may give rise to a default, breach, right of recoupment, claim, defense, termination, right of termination, or remedy under the promissory note, health-care-insurance receivable, or general intangible.

(b) Subsection (a) applies to a security interest in a payment intangible or promissory note only if the security interest arises out of a sale of the payment intangible or promissory note.

(c) A rule of law, statute, or regulation that prohibits, restricts, or requires the consent of a government, governmental body or official, person obligated on a promissory note, or account debtor to the assignment or transfer of, or creation of a security interest in, a promissory note, health-care-insurance receivable, or general intangible, including a contract, permit, license, or franchise between an account debtor and a debtor, is ineffective to the extent that the rule of law, statute, or regulation:

(1) would impair the creation, attachment, or perfection of a security interest; or

(2) provides that the assignment or transfer or the creation, attachment, or perfection of the security interest may give rise to a default, breach, right of recoupment, claim, defense, termination, right of termination, or remedy under the promissory note, health-care-insurance receivable, or general intangible.

(d) To the extent that a term in a promissory note or in an agreement between an account debtor and a debtor which relates to a health-care-insurance receivable or general intangible or a rule of law, statute, or regulation described in subsection (c) would be effective under law other than this article but is ineffective under subsection (a) or (c), the creation, attachment, or perfection of a security interest in the promissory note, health-care-insurance receivable, or general intangible:

(1) is not enforceable against the person obligated on the promissory note or the account debtor;

(2) does not impose a duty or obligation on the person obligated on the promissory note or the account debtor;

(3) does not require the person obligated on the promissory note or the account debtor to recognize the security interest, pay or render performance to the secured party, or accept payment or performance from the secured party;

(4) does not entitle the secured party to use or assign the debtor's rights under the promissory note, health-care-insurance receivable, or general intangible, including any related information or materials furnished to the debtor in the transaction giving rise to the promissory note, health-care-insurance receivable, or general intangible;

(5) does not entitle the secured party to use, assign, possess, or have access to any trade secrets or confidential information of the person obligated on the promissory note or the account debtor; and

(6) does not entitle the secured party to enforce the security interest in the promissory note, health-care-insurance receivable, or general intangible.

(e) This section prevails over any inconsistent provisions of the following statutes, rules, and regulations:

[List here any statutes, rules, and regulations containing provisions inconsistent with this section.]

Legislative Note: States that amend statutes, rules, and regulations to remove provisions inconsistent with this section need not enact subsection (e).

As amended in 1999.

§ 9–409.   Restrictions on Assignment of Letter-of-Credit Rights Ineffective.

(a) A term in a letter of credit or a rule of law, statute, regulation, custom, or practice applicable to the letter of credit which prohibits, restricts, or requires the consent of an applicant, issuer, or nominated person to a beneficiary's assignment of or creation of a security interest in a letter-of-credit right is ineffective to the extent that the term or rule of law, statute, regulation, custom, or practice:

(1) would impair the creation, attachment, or perfection of a security interest in the letter-of-credit right; or

(2) provides that the assignment or the creation, attachment, or perfection of the security interest may give rise to a default, breach, right of recoupment, claim, defense, termination, right of termination, or remedy under the letter-of-credit right.

(b) To the extent that a term in a letter of credit is ineffective under subsection (a) but would be effective under law other than this article or a custom or practice applicable to the letter of credit, to the transfer of a right to draw or otherwise demand performance under the letter of credit, or to the assignment of a right to proceeds of the letter of credit, the creation, attachment, or perfection of a security interest in the letter-of-credit right:

(1) is not enforceable against the applicant, issuer, nominated person, or transferee beneficiary;

(2) imposes no duties or obligations on the applicant, issuer, nominated person, or transferee beneficiary; and

(3) does not require the applicant, issuer, nominated person, or transferee beneficiary to recognize the security interest, pay or render performance to the secured party, or accept payment or other performance from the secured party.

As amended in 1999.

PART 5   Filing

[Subpart 1. Filing Office; Contents and Effectiveness of Financing Statement]

§ 9–501.   Filing Office.

(a) Except as otherwise provided in subsection (b), if the local law of this State governs perfection of a security interest or agricultural lien, the office in which to file a financing statement to perfect the security interest or agricultural lien is:

(1) the office designated for the filing or recording of a record of a mortgage on the related real property, if:

(A) the collateral is as-extracted collateral or timber to be cut; or

(B) the financing statement is filed as a fixture filing and the collateral is goods that are or are to become fixtures; or

(2) the office of [ ] [or any office duly authorized by [ ]], in all other cases, including a case in which the collateral is goods that are or are to become fixtures and the financing statement is not filed as a fixture filing.

(b) The office in which to file a financing statement to perfect a security interest in collateral, including fixtures, of a transmit-

ting utility is the office of [ ]. The financing statement also constitutes a fixture filing as to the collateral indicated in the financing statement which is or is to become fixtures.

Legislative Note: The State should designate the filing office where the brackets appear. The filing office may be that of a governmental official (e.g., the Secretary of State) or a private party that maintains the State's filing system.

§ 9–502.   Contents of Financing Statement; Record of Mortgage as Financing Statement; Time of Filing Financing Statement.

(a) Subject to subsection (b), a financing statement is sufficient only if it:

(1) provides the name of the debtor;

(2) provides the name of the secured party or a representative of the secured party; and

(3) indicates the collateral covered by the financing statement.

(b) Except as otherwise provided in Section 9–501(b), to be sufficient, a financing statement that covers as-extracted collateral or timber to be cut, or which is filed as a fixture filing and covers goods that are or are to become fixtures, must satisfy subsection (a) and also:

(1) indicate tha1t it covers this type of collateral;

(2) indicate that it is to be filed [for record] in the real property records;

(3) provide a description of the real property to which the collateral is related [sufficient to give constructive notice of a mortgage under the law of this State if the description were contained in a record of the mortgage of the real property]; and

(4) if the debtor does not have an interest of record in the real property, provide the name of a record owner.

(c) A record of a mortgage is effective, from the date of recording, as a financing statement filed as a fixture filing or as a financing statement covering as-extracted collateral or timber to be cut only if:

(1) the record indicates the goods or accounts that it covers;

(2) the goods are or are to become fixtures related to the real property described in the record or the collateral is related to the real property described in the record and is as-extracted collateral or timber to be cut;

(3) the record satisfies the requirements for a financing statement in this section other than an indication that it is to be filed in the real property records; and

(4) the record is [duly] recorded.

(d) A financing statement may be filed before a security agreement is made or a security interest otherwise attaches.

Legislative Note: Language in brackets is optional. Where the State has any special recording system for real property other than the usual grantor-grantee index (as, for instance, a tract system or a title registration or Torrens system) local adaptations of subsection (b) and Section 9–519(d) and (e) may be necessary. See, e.g., Mass. Gen. Laws Chapter 106, Section 9–410.

§ 9–503.   Name of Debtor and Secured Party.

(a) A financing statement sufficiently provides the name of the debtor:

(1) if the debtor is a registered organization, only if the financing statement provides the name of the debtor indicated on the public record of the debtor's jurisdiction of organization which shows the debtor to have been organized;

(2) if the debtor is a decedent's estate, only if the financing statement provides the name of the decedent and indicates that the debtor is an estate;

(3) if the debtor is a trust or a trustee acting with respect to property held in trust, only if the financing statement:

(A) provides the name specified for the trust in its organic documents or, if no name is specified, provides the name of the settlor and additional information sufficient to distinguish the debtor from other trusts having one or more of the same settlors; and

(B) indicates, in the debtor's name or otherwise, that the debtor is a trust or is a trustee acting with respect to property held in trust; and

(4) in other cases:

(A) if the debtor has a name, only if it provides the individual or organizational name of the debtor; and

(B) if the debtor does not have a name, only if it provides the names of the partners, members, associates, or other persons comprising the debtor.

(b) A financing statement that provides the name of the debtor in accordance with subsection (a) is not rendered ineffective by the absence of:

(1) a trade name or other name of the debtor; or

(2) unless required under subsection (a)(4)(B), names of partners, members, associates, or other persons comprising the debtor.

(c) A financing statement that provides only the debtor's trade name does not sufficiently provide the name of the debtor.

(d) Failure to indicate the representative capacity of a secured party or representative of a secured party does not affect the sufficiency of a financing statement.

(e) A financing statement may provide the name of more than one debtor and the name of more than one secured party.

§ 9–504.   Indication of Collateral.

A financing statement sufficiently indicates the collateral that it covers if the financing statement provides:

(1) a description of the collateral pursuant to Section 9–108; or

(2) an indication that the financing statement covers all assets or all personal property.

As amended in 1999.

§ 9–505.   Filing and Compliance with Other Statutes and Treaties for Consignments, Leases, Other Bailments, and Other Transactions.

(a) A consignor, lessor, or other bailor of goods, a licensor, or a buyer of a payment intangible or promissory note may file a financing statement, or may comply with a statute or treaty described in Section 9–311(a), using the terms "consignor", "consignee", "lessor", "lessee", "bailor", "bailee", "licensor", "licensee", "owner", "registered owner", "buyer", "seller", or words of similar import, instead of the terms "secured party" and "debtor".

(b) This part applies to the filing of a financing statement under subsection (a) and, as appropriate, to compliance that is equivalent to filing a financing statement under Section 9–311(b), but the filing or compliance is not of itself a factor in determining whether the collateral secures an obligation. If it is determined for another reason that the collateral secures an obligation, a security interest held by the consignor, lessor, bailor, licensor, owner, or buyer which attaches to the collateral is perfected by the filing or compliance.

§ 9–506.   Effect of Errors or Omissions.

(a) A financing statement substantially satisfying the requirements of this part is effective, even if it has minor errors or omissions, unless the errors or omissions make the financing statement seriously misleading.

(b) Except as otherwise provided in subsection (c), a financing statement that fails sufficiently to provide the name of the debtor in accordance with Section 9–503(a) is seriously misleading.

(c) If a search of the records of the filing office under the debtor's correct name, using the filing office's standard search logic, if any, would disclose a financing statement that fails sufficiently to provide the name of the debtor in accordance with Section 9–503(a), the name provided does not make the financing statement seriously misleading.

(d) For purposes of Section 9–508(b), the "debtor's correct name" in subsection (c) means the correct name of the new debtor.

§ 9–507.   Effect of Certain Events on Effectiveness of Financing Statement.

(a) A filed financing statement remains effective with respect to collateral that is sold, exchanged, leased, licensed, or otherwise disposed of and in which a security interest or agricultural lien continues, even if the secured party knows of or consents to the disposition.

(b) Except as otherwise provided in subsection (c) and Section 9–508, a financing statement is not rendered ineffective if, after the financing statement is filed, the information provided in the financing statement becomes seriously misleading under Section 9–506.

(c) If a debtor so changes its name that a filed financing statement becomes seriously misleading under Section 9–506:

(1) the financing statement is effective to perfect a security interest in collateral acquired by the debtor before, or within four months after, the change; and

(2) the financing statement is not effective to perfect a security interest in collateral acquired by the debtor more than four months after the change, unless an amendment to the financing statement which renders the financing statement not seriously misleading is filed within four months after the change.

§ 9–508.   Effectiveness of Financing Statement If New Debtor Becomes Bound by Security Agreement.

(a) Except as otherwise provided in this section, a filed financing statement naming an original debtor is effective to perfect a security interest in collateral in which a new debtor has or acquires rights to the extent that the financing statement would have been effective had the original debtor acquired rights in the collateral.

(b) If the difference between the name of the original debtor and that of the new debtor causes a filed financing statement that is effective under subsection (a) to be seriously misleading under Section 9–506:

(1) the financing statement is effective to perfect a security interest in collateral acquired by the new debtor before, and within four months after, the new debtor becomes bound under Section 9B–203(d); and

(2) the financing statement is not effective to perfect a security interest in collateral acquired by the new debtor more than four months after the new debtor becomes bound under Section 9–203(d) unless an initial financing statement providing the name of the new debtor is filed before the expiration of that time.

(c) This section does not apply to collateral as to which a filed financing statement remains effective against the new debtor under Section 9–507(a).

§ 9–509.   Persons Entitled to File a Record.

(a) A person may file an initial financing statement, amendment that adds collateral covered by a financing statement, or amendment that adds a debtor to a financing statement only if:

(1) the debtor authorizes the filing in an authenticated record or pursuant to subsection (b) or (c); or

(2) the person holds an agricultural lien that has become effective at the time of filing and the financing statement covers only collateral in which the person holds an agricultural lien.

(b) By authenticating or becoming bound as debtor by a security agreement, a debtor or new debtor authorizes the filing of an initial financing statement, and an amendment, covering:

(1) the collateral described in the security agreement; and

(2) property that becomes collateral under Section 9–315(a)(2), whether or not the security agreement expressly covers proceeds.

(c) By acquiring collateral in which a security interest or agricultural lien continues under Section 9–315(a)(1), a debtor authorizes the filing of an initial financing statement, and an amendment, covering the collateral and property that becomes collateral under Section 9–315(a)(2).

(d) A person may file an amendment other than an amendment that adds collateral covered by a financing statement or an amendment that adds a debtor to a financing statement only if:

(1) the secured party of record authorizes the filing; or

(2) the amendment is a termination statement for a financing statement as to which the secured party of record has failed to file or send a termination statement as required by Section 9–513(a) or (c), the debtor authorizes the filing, and the termination statement indicates that the debtor authorized it to be filed.

(e) If there is more than one secured party of record for a financing statement, each secured party of record may authorize the filing of an amendment under subsection (d).

As amended in 2000.

§ 9–510.   Effectiveness of Filed Record.

(a) A filed record is effective only to the extent that it was filed by a person that may file it under Section 9–509.

(b) A record authorized by one secured party of record does not affect the financing statement with respect to another secured party of record.

(c) A continuation statement that is not filed within the six-month period prescribed by Section 9–515(d) is ineffective.

§ 9–511.   Secured Party of Record.

(a) A secured party of record with respect to a financing statement is a person whose name is provided as the name of the secured party or a representative of the secured party in an initial financing statement that has been filed. If an initial financing statement is filed under Section 9–514(a), the assignee named in the initial financing statement is the secured party of record with respect to the financing statement.

(b) If an amendment of a financing statement which provides the name of a person as a secured party or a representative of a secured party is filed, the person named in the amendment is a secured party of record. If an amendment is filed under Section 9–514(b), the assignee named in the amendment is a secured party of record.

(c) A person remains a secured party of record until the filing of an amendment of the financing statement which deletes the person.

§ 9–512.   Amendment of Financing Statement.

[Alternative A]

(a) Subject to Section 9–509, a person may add or delete collateral covered by, continue or terminate the effectiveness of, or, subject to subsection (e), otherwise amend the information provided in, a financing statement by filing an amendment that:

(1) identifies, by its file number, the initial financing statement to which the amendment relates; and

(2) if the amendment relates to an initial financing statement filed [or recorded] in a filing office described in Section 9–501(a)(1), provides the information specified in Section 9–502(b).

[Alternative B]

(a) Subject to Section 9–509, a person may add or delete collateral covered by, continue or terminate the effectiveness of, or, subject to subsection (e), otherwise amend the information provided in, a financing statement by filing an amendment that:

(1) identifies, by its file number, the initial financing statement to which the amendment relates; and

(2) if the amendment relates to an initial financing statement filed [or recorded] in a filing office described in Section 9–501(a)(1), provides the date [and time] that the initial financing statement was filed [or recorded] and the information specified in Section 9–502(b).

[End of Alternatives]

(b) Except as otherwise provided in Section 9–515, the filing of an amendment does not extend the period of effectiveness of the financing statement.

(c) A financing statement that is amended by an amendment that adds collateral is effective as to the added collateral only from the date of the filing of the amendment.

(d) A financing statement that is amended by an amendment that adds a debtor is effective as to the added debtor only from the date of the filing of the amendment.

(e) An amendment is ineffective to the extent it:

(1) purports to delete all debtors and fails to provide the name of a debtor to be covered by the financing statement; or

(2) purports to delete all secured parties of record and fails to provide the name of a new secured party of record.

Legislative Note: States whose real-estate filing offices require additional information in amendments and cannot search their records by both the name of the debtor and the file number should enact Alternative B to Sections 9–512(a), 9–518(b), 9–519(f), and 9–522(a).

§ 9–513. Termination Statement.

(a) A secured party shall cause the secured party of record for a financing statement to file a termination statement for the financing statement if the financing statement covers consumer goods and:

(1) there is no obligation secured by the collateral covered by the financing statement and no commitment to make an advance, incur an obligation, or otherwise give value; or

(2) the debtor did not authorize the filing of the initial financing statement.

(b) To comply with subsection (a), a secured party shall cause the secured party of record to file the termination statement:

(1) within one month after there is no obligation secured by the collateral covered by the financing statement and no commitment to make an advance, incur an obligation, or otherwise give value; or

(2) if earlier, within 20 days after the secured party receives an authenticated demand from a debtor.

(c) In cases not governed by subsection (a), within 20 days after a secured party receives an authenticated demand from a debtor, the secured party shall cause the secured party of record for a financing statement to send to the debtor a termination statement for the financing statement or file the termination statement in the filing office if:

(1) except in the case of a financing statement covering accounts or chattel paper that has been sold or goods that are the subject of a consignment, there is no obligation secured by the collateral covered by the financing statement and no commitment to make an advance, incur an obligation, or otherwise give value;

(2) the financing statement covers accounts or chattel paper that has been sold but as to which the account debtor or other person obligated has discharged its obligation;

(3) the financing statement covers goods that were the subject of a consignment to the debtor but are not in the debtor's possession; or

(4) the debtor did not authorize the filing of the initial financing statement.

(d) Except as otherwise provided in Section 9–510, upon the filing of a termination statement with the filing office, the financing statement to which the termination statement relates ceases to be effective. Except as otherwise provided in Section 9–510, for purposes of Sections 9–519(g), 9–522(a), and 9–523(c), the filing with the filing office of a termination statement relating to a financing statement that indicates that the debtor is a transmitting utility also causes the effectiveness of the financing statement to lapse.

As amended in 2000.

§ 9–514. Assignment of Powers of Secured Party of Record.

(a) Except as otherwise provided in subsection (c), an initial financing statement may reflect an assignment of all of the secured party's power to authorize an amendment to the financing statement by providing the name and mailing address of the assignee as the name and address of the secured party.

(b) Except as otherwise provided in subsection (c), a secured party of record may assign of record all or part of its power to authorize an amendment to a financing statement by filing in the filing office an amendment of the financing statement which:

(1) identifies, by its file number, the initial financing statement to which it relates;

(2) provides the name of the assignor; and

(3) provides the name and mailing address of the assignee.

(c) An assignment of record of a security interest in a fixture covered by a record of a mortgage which is effective as a financing statement filed as a fixture filing under Section 9–502(c) may be made only by an assignment of record of the mortgage in the manner provided by law of this State other than [the Uniform Commercial Code].

§ 9–515.   Duration and Effectiveness of Financing Statement; Effect of Lapsed Financing Statement.

(a) Except as otherwise provided in subsections (b), (e), (f), and (g), a filed financing statement is effective for a period of five years after the date of filing.

(b) Except as otherwise provided in subsections (e), (f), and (g), an initial financing statement filed in connection with a public-finance transaction or manufactured-home transaction is effective for a period of 30 years after the date of filing if it indicates that it is filed in connection with a public-finance transaction or manufactured-home transaction.

(c) The effectiveness of a filed financing statement lapses on the expiration of the period of its effectiveness unless before the lapse a continuation statement is filed pursuant to subsection (d). Upon lapse, a financing statement ceases to be effective and any security interest or agricultural lien that was perfected by the financing statement becomes unperfected, unless the security interest is perfected otherwise. If the security interest or agricultural lien becomes unperfected upon lapse, it is deemed never to have been perfected as against a purchaser of the collateral for value.

(d) A continuation statement may be filed only within six months before the expiration of the five-year period specified in subsection (a) or the 30-year period specified in subsection (b), whichever is applicable.

(e) Except as otherwise provided in Section 9–510, upon timely filing of a continuation statement, the effectiveness of the initial financing statement continues for a period of five years commencing on the day on which the financing statement would have become ineffective in the absence of the filing. Upon the expiration of the five-year period, the financing statement lapses in the same manner as provided in subsection (c), unless, before the lapse, another continuation statement is filed pursuant to subsection (d). Succeeding continuation statements may be filed in the same manner to continue the effectiveness of the initial financing statement.

(f) If a debtor is a transmitting utility and a filed financing statement so indicates, the financing statement is effective until a termination statement is filed.

(g) A record of a mortgage that is effective as a financing statement filed as a fixture filing under Section 9–502(c) remains effective as a financing statement filed as a fixture filing until the mortgage is released or satisfied of record or its effectiveness otherwise terminates as to the real property.

§ 9–516.   What Constitutes Filing; Effectiveness of Filing.

(a) Except as otherwise provided in subsection (b), communication of a record to a filing office and tender of the filing fee or acceptance of the record by the filing office constitutes filing.

(b) Filing does not occur with respect to a record that a filing office refuses to accept because:

(1) the record is not communicated by a method or medium of communication authorized by the filing office;

(2) an amount equal to or greater than the applicable filing fee is not tendered;

(3) the filing office is unable to index the record because:

(A) in the case of an initial financing statement, the record does not provide a name for the debtor;

(B) in the case of an amendment or correction statement, the record:

(i) does not identify the initial financing statement as required by Section 9–512 or 9–518, as applicable; or

(ii) identifies an initial financing statement whose effectiveness has lapsed under Section 9–515;

(C) in the case of an initial financing statement that provides the name of a debtor identified as an individual or an amendment that provides a name of a debtor identified as an individual which was not previously provided in the financing statement to which the record relates, the record does not identify the debtor's last name; or

(D) in the case of a record filed [or recorded] in the filing office described in Section 9–501(a)(1), the record does not provide a sufficient description of the real property to which it relates;

(4) in the case of an initial financing statement or an amendment that adds a secured party of record, the record does not provide a name and mailing address for the secured party of record;

(5) in the case of an initial financing statement or an amendment that provides a name of a debtor which was not previously provided in the financing statement to which the amendment relates, the record does not:

(A) provide a mailing address for the debtor;

(B) indicate whether the debtor is an individual or an organization; or

(C) if the financing statement indicates that the debtor is an organization, provide:

(i) a type of organization for the debtor;

(ii) a jurisdiction of organization for the debtor; or

(iii) an organizational identification number for the debtor or indicate that the debtor has none;

(6) in the case of an assignment reflected in an initial financing statement under Section 9–514(a) or an amendment filed under Section 9–514(b), the record does not provide a name and mailing address for the assignee; or

(7) in the case of a continuation statement, the record is not filed within the six-month period prescribed by Section 9–515(d).

(c) For purposes of subsection (b):

(1) a record does not provide information if the filing office is unable to read or decipher the information; and

(2) a record that does not indicate that it is an amendment or identify an initial financing statement to which it relates, as required by Section 9–512, 9–514, or 9–518, is an initial financing statement.

(d) A record that is communicated to the filing office with tender of the filing fee, but which the filing office refuses to accept for a reason other than one set forth in subsection (b), is effective as a filed record except as against a purchaser of the collateral which gives value in reasonable reliance upon the absence of the record from the files.

§ 9–517.   Effect of Indexing Errors.

The failure of the filing office to index a record correctly does not affect the effectiveness of the filed record.

§ 9–518.   Claim Concerning Inaccurate or Wrongfully Filed Record.

(a) A person may file in the filing office a correction statement with respect to a record indexed there under the person's name if the person believes that the record is inaccurate or was wrongfully filed.

[Alternative A]

(b) A correction statement must:

(1) identify the record to which it relates by the file number assigned to the initial financing statement to which the record relates;

(2) indicate that it is a correction statement; and

(3) provide the basis for the person's belief that the record is inaccurate and indicate the manner in which the person believes the record should be amended to cure any inaccuracy or provide the basis for the person's belief that the record was wrongfully filed.

[Alternative B]

(b) A correction statement must:

(1) identify the record to which it relates by:

(A) the file number assigned to the initial financing statement to which the record relates; and

(B) if the correction statement relates to a record filed [or recorded] in a filing office described in Section 9–501(a)(1), the date [and time] that the initial financing statement was filed [or recorded] and the information specified in Section 9–502(b);

(2) indicate that it is a correction statement; and

(3) provide the basis for the person's belief that the record is inaccurate and indicate the manner in which the person believes the record should be amended to cure any inaccuracy or provide the basis for the person's belief that the record was wrongfully filed.

[End of Alternatives]

(c) The filing of a correction statement does not affect the effectiveness of an initial financing statement or other filed record.

Legislative Note: States whose real-estate filing offices require additional information in amendments and cannot search their records by both the name of the debtor and the file number should enact Alternative B to Sections 9–512(a), 9–518(b), 9–519(f), and 9–522(a).

[Subpart 2. Duties and Operation of Filing Office]

§ 9–519.   Numbering, Maintaining, and Indexing Records; Communicating Information Provided in Records.

(a) For each record filed in a filing office, the filing office shall:

(1) assign a unique number to the filed record;

(2) create a record that bears the number assigned to the filed record and the date and time of filing;

(3) maintain the filed record for public inspection; and

(4) index the filed record in accordance with subsections (c), (d), and (e).

(b) A file number [assigned after January 1, 2002,] must include a digit that:

(1) is mathematically derived from or related to the other digits of the file number; and

(2) aids the filing office in determining whether a number communicated as the file number includes a single-digit or transpositional error.

(c) Except as otherwise provided in subsections (d) and (e), the filing office shall:

(1) index an initial financing statement according to the name of the debtor and index all filed records relating to the initial financing statement in a manner that associates with one another an initial financing statement and all filed records relating to the initial financing statement; and

(2) index a record that provides a name of a debtor which was not previously provided in the financing statement to which the record relates also according to the name that was not previously provided.

(d) If a financing statement is filed as a fixture filing or covers as-extracted collateral or timber to be cut, [it must be filed for record and] the filing office shall index it:

(1) under the names of the debtor and of each owner of record shown on the financing statement as if they were the mortgagors under a mortgage of the real property described; and

(2) to the extent that the law of this State provides for indexing of records of mortgages under the name of the mortgagee, under the name of the secured party as if the secured party were the mortgagee thereunder, or, if indexing is by description, as if the financing statement were a record of a mortgage of the real property described.

(e) If a financing statement is filed as a fixture filing or covers as-extracted collateral or timber to be cut, the filing office shall index an assignment filed under Section 9–514(a) or an amendment filed under Section 9–514(b):

(1) under the name of the assignor as grantor; and

(2) to the extent that the law of this State provides for indexing a record of the assignment of a mortgage under the name of the assignee, under the name of the assignee.

[Alternative A]

(f) The filing office shall maintain a capability:

(1) to retrieve a record by the name of the debtor and by the file number assigned to the initial financing statement to which the record relates; and

(2) to associate and retrieve with one another an initial financing statement and each filed record relating to the initial financing statement.

[Alternative B]

(f) The filing office shall maintain a capability:

(1) to retrieve a record by the name of the debtor and:

(A) if the filing office is described in Section 9–501(a)(1), by the file number assigned to the initial financing statement to which the record relates and the date [and time] that the record was filed [or recorded]; or

(B) if the filing office is described in Section 9–501(a)(2), by the file number assigned to the initial financing statement to which the record relates; and

(2) to associate and retrieve with one another an initial financing statement and each filed record relating to the initial financing statement.

[End of Alternatives]

(g) The filing office may not remove a debtor's name from the index until one year after the effectiveness of a financing statement naming the debtor lapses under Section 9–515 with respect to all secured parties of record.

(h) The filing office shall perform the acts required by subsections (a) through (e) at the time and in the manner prescribed by filing-office rule, but not later than two business days after the filing office receives the record in question.

[(i) Subsection[s] [(b)] [and] [(h)] do[es] not apply to a filing office described in Section 9–501(a)(1).]

Legislative Notes:

1. States whose filing offices currently assign file numbers that include a verification number, commonly known as a "check digit," or can implement this requirement before the effective date of this Article should omit the bracketed language in subsection (b).

2. In States in which writings will not appear in the real property records and indices unless actually recorded the bracketed language in subsection (d) should be used.

3. States whose real-estate filing offices require additional information in amendments and cannot search their records by both the name of the debtor and the file number should enact Alternative B to Sections 9–512(a), 9–518(b), 9–519(f), and 9–522(a).

4. A State that elects not to require real-estate filing offices to comply with either or both of subsections (b) and (h) may adopt an applicable variation of subsection (i) and add "Except as otherwise provided in subsection (i)," to the appropriate subsection or subsections.

§ 9–520.   **Acceptance and Refusal to Accept Record.**

(a) A filing office shall refuse to accept a record for filing for a reason set forth in Section 9–516(b) and may refuse to accept a record for filing only for a reason set forth in Section 9–516(b).

(b) If a filing office refuses to accept a record for filing, it shall communicate to the person that presented the record the fact of and reason for the refusal and the date and time the record would have been filed had the filing office accepted it. The communication must be made at the time and in the manner prescribed by filing-office rule but [, in the case of a filing office described in Section 9–501(a)(2),] in no event more than two business days after the filing office receives the record.

(c) A filed financing statement satisfying Section 9–502(a) and (b) is effective, even if the filing office is required to refuse to accept it for filing under subsection (a). However, Section 9–338 applies to a filed financing statement providing information described in Section 9–516(b)(5) which is incorrect at the time the financing statement is filed.

(d) If a record communicated to a filing office provides information that relates to more than one debtor, this part applies as to each debtor separately.

Legislative Note: A State that elects not to require real-property filing offices to comply with subsection (b) should include the bracketed language.

§ 9–521.   **Uniform Form of Written Financing Statement and Amendment.**

(a) A filing office that accepts written records may not refuse to accept a written initial financing statement in the following form and format except for a reason set forth in Section 9–516(b):

[NATIONAL UCC FINANCING STATEMENT (FORM UCC1)(REV. 7/29/98)]

[NATIONAL UCC FINANCING STATEMENT ADDENDUM (FORM UCC1Ad)(REV. 07/29/98)]

(b) A filing office that accepts written records may not refuse to accept a written record in the following form and format except for a reason set forth in Section 9–516(b):

[NATIONAL UCC FINANCING STATEMENT AMEND-
MENT (FORM UCC3)(REV. 07/29/98)]
[NATIONAL UCC FINANCING STATEMENT AMEND-
MENT ADDENDUM (FORM UCC3Ad)(REV. 07/29/98)]

§ 9–522. Maintenance and Destruction of Records.

[Alternative A]

(a) The filing office shall maintain a record of the information provided in a filed financing statement for at least one year after the effectiveness of the financing statement has lapsed under Section 9–515 with respect to all secured parties of record. The record must be retrievable by using the name of the debtor and by using the file number assigned to the initial financing statement to which the record relates.

[Alternative B]

(a) The filing office shall maintain a record of the information provided in a filed financing statement for at least one year after the effectiveness of the financing statement has lapsed under Section 9–515 with respect to all secured parties of record. The record must be retrievable by using the name of the debtor and:

(1) if the record was filed [or recorded] in the filing office described in Section 9–501(a)(1), by using the file number assigned to the initial financing statement to which the record relates and the date [and time] that the record was filed [or recorded]; or

(2) if the record was filed in the filing office described in Section 9–501(a)(2), by using the file number assigned to the initial financing statement to which the record relates.

[End of Alternatives]

(b) Except to the extent that a statute governing disposition of public records provides otherwise, the filing office immediately may destroy any written record evidencing a financing statement. However, if the filing office destroys a written record, it shall maintain another record of the financing statement which complies with subsection (a).

Legislative Note: States whose real-estate filing offices require additional information in amendments and cannot search their records by both the name of the debtor and the file number should enact Alternative B to Sections 9–512(a), 9–518(b), 9–519(f), and 9–522(a).

§ 9–523. Information from Filing Office; Sale or License of Records.

(a) If a person that files a written record requests an acknowledgment of the filing, the filing office shall send to the person an image of the record showing the number assigned to the record pursuant to Section 9–519(a)(1) and the date and time of the filing of the record. However, if the person furnishes a copy of the record to the filing office, the filing office may instead:

(1) note upon the copy the number assigned to the record pursuant to Section 9–519(a)(1) and the date and time of the filing of the record; and

(2) send the copy to the person.

(b) If a person files a record other than a written record, the filing office shall communicate to the person an acknowledgment that provides:

(1) the information in the record;

(2) the number assigned to the record pursuant to Section 9–519(a)(1); and

(3) the date and time of the filing of the record.

(c) The filing office shall communicate or otherwise make available in a record the following information to any person that requests it:

(1) whether there is on file on a date and time specified by the filing office, but not a date earlier than three business days before the filing office receives the request, any financing statement that:

(A) designates a particular debtor [or, if the request so states, designates a particular debtor at the address specified in the request];

(B) has not lapsed under Section 9–515 with respect to all secured parties of record; and

(C) if the request so states, has lapsed under Section 9–515 and a record of which is maintained by the filing office under Section 9–522(a);

(2) the date and time of filing of each financing statement; and

(3) the information provided in each financing statement.

(d) In complying with its duty under subsection (c), the filing office may communicate information in any medium. However, if requested, the filing office shall communicate information by issuing [its written certificate] [a record that can be admitted into evidence in the courts of this State without extrinsic evidence of its authenticity].

(e) The filing office shall perform the acts required by subsections (a) through (d) at the time and in the manner prescribed by filing-office rule, but not later than two business days after the filing office receives the request.

(f) At least weekly, the [insert appropriate official or governmental agency] [filing office] shall offer to sell or license to the public on a nonexclusive basis, in bulk, copies of all records filed in it under this part, in every medium from time to time available to the filing office.

Legislative Notes:

1. States whose filing office does not offer the additional service of responding to search requests limited to a particular address should omit the bracketed language in subsection (c)(1)(A).

2. A State that elects not to require real-estate filing offices to comply with either or both of subsections (e) and (f) should specify in the appropriate subsection(s) only the filing office described in Section 9–501(a)(2).

§ 9–524.   Delay by Filing Office.

Delay by the filing office beyond a time limit prescribed by this part is excused if:

(1) the delay is caused by interruption of communication or computer facilities, war, emergency conditions, failure of equipment, or other circumstances beyond control of the filing office; and

(2) the filing office exercises reasonable diligence under the circumstances.

§ 9–525.   Fees.

(a) Except as otherwise provided in subsection (e), the fee for filing and indexing a record under this part, other than an initial financing statement of the kind described in subsection (b), is [the amount specified in subsection (c), if applicable, plus]:

(1) $[X] if the record is communicated in writing and consists of one or two pages;

(2) $[2X] if the record is communicated in writing and consists of more than two pages; and

(3) $[1/2X] if the record is communicated by another medium authorized by filing-office rule.

(b) Except as otherwise provided in subsection (e), the fee for filing and indexing an initial financing statement of the following kind is [the amount specified in subsection (c), if applicable, plus]:

(1) $——— if the financing statement indicates that it is filed in connection with a public-finance transaction;

(2) $——— if the financing statement indicates that it is filed in connection with a manufactured-home transaction.

[Alternative A]

(c) The number of names required to be indexed does not affect the amount of the fee in subsections (a) and (b).

[Alternative B]

(c) Except as otherwise provided in subsection (e), if a record is communicated in writing, the fee for each name more than two required to be indexed is $———.

[End of Alternatives]

(d) The fee for responding to a request for information from the filing office, including for [issuing a certificate showing] [communicating] whether there is on file any financing statement naming a particular debtor, is:

(1) $——— if the request is communicated in writing; and

(2) $——— if the request is communicated by another medium authorized by filing-office rule.

(e) This section does not require a fee with respect to a record of a mortgage which is effective as a financing statement filed as a fixture filing or as a financing statement covering as-extracted collateral or timber to be cut under Section 9–502(c). However, the recording and satisfaction fees that otherwise would be applicable to the record of the mortgage apply.

Legislative Notes:

1. To preserve uniformity, a State that places the provisions of this section together with statutes setting fees for other services should do so without modification.

2. A State should enact subsection (c), Alternative A, and omit the bracketed language in subsections (a) and (b) unless its indexing system entails a substantial additional cost when indexing additional names.

As amended in 2000.

§ 9–526.   Filing-Office Rules.

(a) The [insert appropriate governmental official or agency] shall adopt and publish rules to implement this article. The filing-office rules must be[:

(1) consistent with this article[; and

(2) adopted and published in accordance with the [insert any applicable state administrative procedure act]].

(b) To keep the filing-office rules and practices of the filing office in harmony with the rules and practices of filing offices in other jurisdictions that enact substantially this part, and to keep the technology used by the filing office compatible with the technology used by filing offices in other jurisdictions that enact substantially this part, the [insert appropriate governmental official or agency], so far as is consistent with the purposes, policies, and provisions of this article, in adopting, amending, and repealing filing-office rules, shall:

(1) consult with filing offices in other jurisdictions that enact substantially this part; and

(2) consult the most recent version of the Model Rules promulgated by the International Association of Corporate Administrators or any successor organization; and

(3) take into consideration the rules and practices of, and the technology used by, filing offices in other jurisdictions that enact substantially this part.

§ 9–527.   Duty to Report.

The [insert appropriate governmental official or agency] shall report [annually on or before ———] to the [Governor and Legislature] on the operation of the filing office. The report must contain a statement of the extent to which:

(1) the filing-office rules are not in harmony with the rules of filing offices in other jurisdictions that enact substantially this part and the reasons for these variations; and

(2) the filing-office rules are not in harmony with the most recent version of the Model Rules promulgated by the International Association of Corporate Administrators, or any successor organization, and the reasons for these variations.

PART 6   Default

[Subpart 1. Default and Enforcement of Security Interest]

§ 9–601.   Rights after Default; Judicial Enforcement; Consignor or Buyer of Accounts, Chattel Paper, Payment Intangibles, or Promissory Notes.

(a) After default, a secured party has the rights provided in this part and, except as otherwise provided in Section 9–602, those provided by agreement of the parties. A secured party:

(1) may reduce a claim to judgment, foreclose, or otherwise enforce the claim, security interest, or agricultural lien by any available judicial procedure; and

(2) if the collateral is documents, may proceed either as to the documents or as to the goods they cover.

(b) A secured party in possession of collateral or control of collateral under Section 9–104, 9–105, 9–106, or 9–107 has the rights and duties provided in Section 9–207.

(c) The rights under subsections (a) and (b) are cumulative and may be exercised simultaneously.

(d) Except as otherwise provided in subsection (g) and Section 9–605, after default, a debtor and an obligor have the rights provided in this part and by agreement of the parties.

(e) If a secured party has reduced its claim to judgment, the lien of any levy that may be made upon the collateral by virtue of an execution based upon the judgment relates back to the earliest of:

(1) the date of perfection of the security interest or agricultural lien in the collateral;

(2) the date of filing a financing statement covering the collateral; or

(3) any date specified in a statute under which the agricultural lien was created.

(f) A sale pursuant to an execution is a foreclosure of the security interest or agricultural lien by judicial procedure within the meaning of this section. A secured party may purchase at the sale and thereafter hold the collateral free of any other requirements of this article.

(g) Except as otherwise provided in Section 9–607(c), this part imposes no duties upon a secured party that is a consignor or is a buyer of accounts, chattel paper, payment intangibles, or promissory notes.

§ 9–602.   Waiver and Variance of Rights and Duties.

Except as otherwise provided in Section 9–624, to the extent that they give rights to a debtor or obligor and impose duties on a secured party, the debtor or obligor may not waive or vary the rules stated in the following listed sections:

(1) Section 9–207(b)(4)(C), which deals with use and operation of the collateral by the secured party;

(2) Section 9–210, which deals with requests for an accounting and requests concerning a list of collateral and statement of account;

(3) Section 9–607(c), which deals with collection and enforcement of collateral;

(4) Sections 9–608(a) and 9–615(c) to the extent that they deal with application or payment of noncash proceeds of collection, enforcement, or disposition;

(5) Sections 9–608(a) and 9–615(d) to the extent that they require accounting for or payment of surplus proceeds of collateral;

(6) Section 9–609 to the extent that it imposes upon a secured party that takes possession of collateral without judicial process the duty to do so without breach of the peace;

(7) Sections 9–610(b), 9–611, 9–613, and 9–614, which deal with disposition of collateral;

(8) Section 9–615(f), which deals with calculation of a deficiency or surplus when a disposition is made to the secured party, a person related to the secured party, or a secondary obligor;

(9) Section 9–616, which deals with explanation of the calculation of a surplus or deficiency;

(10) Sections 9–620, 9–621, and 9–622, which deal with acceptance of collateral in satisfaction of obligation;

(11) Section 9–623, which deals with redemption of collateral;

(12) Section 9–624, which deals with permissible waivers; and

(13) Sections 9–625 and 9–626, which deal with the secured party's liability for failure to comply with this article.

§ 9–603.   Agreement on Standards Concerning Rights and Duties.

(a) The parties may determine by agreement the standards measuring the fulfillment of the rights of a debtor or obligor and the duties of a secured party under a rule stated in Section 9–602 if the standards are not manifestly unreasonable.

(b) Subsection (a) does not apply to the duty under Section 9–609 to refrain from breaching the peace.

§ 9–604.   Procedure If Security Agreement Covers Real Property or Fixtures.

(a) If a security agreement covers both personal and real property, a secured party may proceed:

(1) under this part as to the personal property without prejudicing any rights with respect to the real property; or

(2) as to both the personal property and the real property in accordance with the rights with respect to the real property, in which case the other provisions of this part do not apply.

(b) Subject to subsection (c), if a security agreement covers goods that are or become fixtures, a secured party may proceed:

(1) under this part; or

(2) in accordance with the rights with respect to real property, in which case the other provisions of this part do not apply.

(c) Subject to the other provisions of this part, if a secured party holding a security interest in fixtures has priority over all owners and encumbrancers of the real property, the secured party, after default, may remove the collateral from the real property. (d) A secured party that removes collateral shall promptly reimburse any encumbrancer or owner of the real property, other than the debtor, for the cost of repair of any physical injury caused by the removal. The secured party need not reimburse the encumbrancer or owner for any diminution in value of the real property caused by the absence of the goods removed or by any necessity of replacing them. A person entitled to reimbursement may refuse permission to remove until the secured party gives adequate assurance for the performance of the obligation to reimburse.

§ 9–605. Unknown Debtor or Secondary Obligor.

A secured party does not owe a duty based on its status as secured party:

(1) to a person that is a debtor or obligor, unless the secured party knows:

(A) that the person is a debtor or obligor;

(B) the identity of the person; and

(C) how to communicate with the person; or

(2) to a secured party or lienholder that has filed a financing statement against a person, unless the secured party knows:

(A) that the person is a debtor; and

(B) the identity of the person.

§ 9–606. Time of Default for Agricultural Lien.

For purposes of this part, a default occurs in connection with an agricultural lien at the time the secured party becomes entitled to enforce the lien in accordance with the statute under which it was created.

§ 9–607. Collection and Enforcement by Secured Party.

(a) If so agreed, and in any event after default, a secured party:

(1) may notify an account debtor or other person obligated on collateral to make payment or otherwise render performance to or for the benefit of the secured party;

(2) may take any proceeds to which the secured party is entitled under Section 9–315;

(3) may enforce the obligations of an account debtor or other person obligated on collateral and exercise the rights of the debtor with respect to the obligation of the account debtor or other person obligated on collateral to make payment or otherwise render performance to the debtor, and with respect to any property that secures the obligations of the account debtor or other person obligated on the collateral;

(4) if it holds a security interest in a deposit account perfected by control under Section 9–104(a)(1), may apply the balance of the deposit account to the obligation secured by the deposit account; and

(5) if it holds a security interest in a deposit account perfected by control under Section 9–104(a)(2) or (3), may instruct the bank to pay the balance of the deposit account to or for the benefit of the secured party.

(b) If necessary to enable a secured party to exercise under subsection (a)(3) the right of a debtor to enforce a mortgage nonjudicially, the secured party may record in the office in which a record of the mortgage is recorded:

(1) a copy of the security agreement that creates or provides for a security interest in the obligation secured by the mortgage; and

(2) the secured party's sworn affidavit in recordable form stating that:

(A) a default has occurred; and

(B) the secured party is entitled to enforce the mortgage nonjudicially.

(c) A secured party shall proceed in a commercially reasonable manner if the secured party:

(1) undertakes to collect from or enforce an obligation of an account debtor or other person obligated on collateral; and

(2) is entitled to charge back uncollected collateral or otherwise to full or limited recourse against the debtor or a secondary obligor.

(d) A secured party may deduct from the collections made pursuant to subsection (c) reasonable expenses of collection and enforcement, including reasonable attorney's fees and legal expenses incurred by the secured party.

(e) This section does not determine whether an account debtor, bank, or other person obligated on collateral owes a duty to a secured party.

As amended in 2000.

§ 9–608. Application of Proceeds of Collection or Enforcement; Liability for Deficiency and Right to Surplus.

(a) If a security interest or agricultural lien secures payment or performance of an obligation, the following rules apply:

(1) A secured party shall apply or pay over for application the cash proceeds of collection or enforcement under Section 9–607 in the following order to:

(A) the reasonable expenses of collection and enforcement and, to the extent provided for by agreement and not prohibited by law, reasonable attorney's fees and legal expenses incurred by the secured party;

(B) the satisfaction of obligations secured by the security interest or agricultural lien under which the collection or enforcement is made; and

(C) the satisfaction of obligations secured by any subordinate security interest in or other lien on the collateral subject to the security interest or agricultural lien under which the collection or enforcement is made if the secured party receives an authenticated demand for proceeds before distribution of the proceeds is completed.

(2) If requested by a secured party, a holder of a subordinate security interest or other lien shall furnish reasonable proof of the interest or lien within a reasonable time. Unless the holder complies, the secured party need not comply with the holder's demand under paragraph (1)(C).

(3) A secured party need not apply or pay over for application noncash proceeds of collection and enforcement under Section 9–607 unless the failure to do so would be commercially unreasonable. A secured party that applies or pays over for application noncash proceeds shall do so in a commercially reasonable manner.

(4) A secured party shall account to and pay a debtor for any surplus, and the obligor is liable for any deficiency.

(b) If the underlying transaction is a sale of accounts, chattel paper, payment intangibles, or promissory notes, the debtor is not entitled to any surplus, and the obligor is not liable for any deficiency.

As amended in 2000.

§ 9–609. Secured Party's Right to Take Possession after Default.

(a) After default, a secured party:

(1) may take possession of the collateral; and

(2) without removal, may render equipment unusable and dispose of collateral on a debtor's premises under Section 9–610.

(b) A secured party may proceed under subsection (a):

(1) pursuant to judicial process; or

(2) without judicial process, if it proceeds without breach of the peace.

(c) If so agreed, and in any event after default, a secured party may require the debtor to assemble the collateral and make it available to the secured party at a place to be designated by the secured party which is reasonably convenient to both parties.

§ 9–610. Disposition of Collateral after Default.

(a) After default, a secured party may sell, lease, license, or otherwise dispose of any or all of the collateral in its present condition or following any commercially reasonable preparation or processing.

(b) Every aspect of a disposition of collateral, including the method, manner, time, place, and other terms, must be commercially reasonable. If commercially reasonable, a secured party may dispose of collateral by public or private proceedings, by one or more contracts, as a unit or in parcels, and at any time and place and on any terms.

(c) A secured party may purchase collateral:

(1) at a public disposition; or

(2) at a private disposition only if the collateral is of a kind that is customarily sold on a recognized market or the subject of widely distributed standard price quotations.

(d) A contract for sale, lease, license, or other disposition includes the warranties relating to title, possession, quiet enjoyment, and the like which by operation of law accompany a voluntary disposition of property of the kind subject to the contract.

(e) A secured party may disclaim or modify warranties under subsection (d):

(1) in a manner that would be effective to disclaim or modify the warranties in a voluntary disposition of property of the kind subject to the contract of disposition; or

(2) by communicating to the purchaser a record evidencing the contract for disposition and including an express disclaimer or modification of the warranties.

(f) A record is sufficient to disclaim warranties under subsection (e) if it indicates "There is no warranty relating to title, possession, quiet enjoyment, or the like in this disposition" or uses words of similar import.

§ 9–611. Notification before Disposition of Collateral.

(a) In this section, "notification date" means the earlier of the date on which:

(1) a secured party sends to the debtor and any secondary obligor an authenticated notification of disposition; or

(2) the debtor and any secondary obligor waive the right to notification.

(b) Except as otherwise provided in subsection (d), a secured party that disposes of collateral under Section 9–610 shall send to the persons specified in subsection (c) a reasonable authenticated notification of disposition.

(c) To comply with subsection (b), the secured party shall send an authenticated notification of disposition to:

(1) the debtor;

(2) any secondary obligor; and

(3) if the collateral is other than consumer goods:

(A) any other person from which the secured party has received, before the notification date, an authenticated notification of a claim of an interest in the collateral;

(B) any other secured party or lienholder that, 10 days before the notification date, held a security interest in or other lien on the collateral perfected by the filing of a financing statement that:

(i) identified the collateral;

(ii) was indexed under the debtor's name as of that date; and

(iii) was filed in the office in which to file a financing statement against the debtor covering the collateral as of that date; and

(C) any other secured party that, 10 days before the notification date, held a security interest in the collateral perfected by compliance with a statute, regulation, or treaty described in Section 9–311(a).

(d) Subsection (b) does not apply if the collateral is perishable or threatens to decline speedily in value or is of a type customarily sold on a recognized market.

(e) A secured party complies with the requirement for notification prescribed by subsection (c)(3)(B) if:

(1) not later than 20 days or earlier than 30 days before the notification date, the secured party requests, in a commercially reasonable manner, information concerning financing statements indexed under the debtor's name in the office indicated in subsection (c)(3)(B); and

(2) before the notification date, the secured party:

(A) did not receive a response to the request for information; or

(B) received a response to the request for information and sent an authenticated notification of disposition to each secured party or other lienholder named in that response whose financing statement covered the collateral.

§ 9–612.   Timeliness of Notification before Disposition of Collateral.

(a) Except as otherwise provided in subsection (b), whether a notification is sent within a reasonable time is a question of fact.

(b) In a transaction other than a consumer transaction, a notification of disposition sent after default and 10 days or more before the earliest time of disposition set forth in the notification is sent within a reasonable time before the disposition.

§ 9–613.   Contents and Form of Notification before Disposition of Collateral: General.

Except in a consumer-goods transaction, the following rules apply:

(1) The contents of a notification of disposition are sufficient if the notification:

(A) describes the debtor and the secured party;

(B) describes the collateral that is the subject of the intended disposition;

(C) states the method of intended disposition;

(D) states that the debtor is entitled to an accounting of the unpaid indebtedness and states the charge, if any, for an accounting; and

(E) states the time and place of a public disposition or the time after which any other disposition is to be made.

(2) Whether the contents of a notification that lacks any of the information specified in paragraph (1) are nevertheless sufficient is a question of fact.

(3) The contents of a notification providing substantially the information specified in paragraph (1) are sufficient, even if the notification includes:

(A) information not specified by that paragraph; or

(b) minor errors that are not seriously misleading.

(4) A particular phrasing of the notification is not required.

(5) The following form of notification and the form appearing in Section 9–614(3), when completed, each provides sufficient information:

NOTIFICATION OF DISPOSITION OF COLLATERAL

To: [*Name of debtor, obligor, or other person to which the notification is sent*]

From: [*Name, address, and telephone number of secured party*]

Name of Debtor(s): [*Include only if debtor(s) are not an addressee*]

[*For a public disposition:*]

We will sell [or lease or license, *as applicable*] the [*describe collateral*] [to the highest qualified bidder] in public as follows:

Day and Date: _____

Time: _____

Place: _____

[*For a private disposition:*]

We will sell [or lease or license, *as applicable*] the [*describe collateral*] privately sometime after [*day and date*].

You are entitled to an accounting of the unpaid indebtedness secured by the property that we intend to sell [or lease or license *as applicable*] [for a charge of $———]. You may request an accounting by calling us at [*telephone number*].

[End of Form]

As amended in 2000.

§ 9–614.   Contents and Form of Notification before Disposition of Collateral: Consumer-Goods Transaction.

In a consumer-goods transaction, the following rules apply:

(1) A notification of disposition must provide the following information:

(A) the information specified in Section 9–613(1);

(B) a description of any liability for a deficiency of the person to which the notification is sent;

(C) a telephone number from which the amount that must be paid to the secured party to redeem the collateral under Section 9–623 is available; and

(D) a telephone number or mailing address from which additional information concerning the disposition and the obligation secured is available.

(2) A particular phrasing of the notification is not required.

(3) The following form of notification, when completed, provides sufficient information:

[*Name and address of secured party*]

[*Date*]

NOTICE OF OUR PLAN TO SELL PROPERTY

[*Name and address of any obligor who is also a debtor*]

Subject: [*Identification of Transaction*]

We have your [*describe collateral*], because you broke promises in our agreement.

[*For a public disposition:*]

We will sell [*describe collateral*] at public sale. A sale could include a lease or license. The sale will be held as follows:

Date:_____

Time: _____

Place: _____

You may attend the sale and bring bidders if you want.

[*For a private disposition:*]

We will sell [*describe collateral*] at private sale sometime after [*date*]. A sale could include a lease or license.

The money that we get from the sale (after paying our costs) will reduce the amount you owe. If we get less money than you owe, you [*will or will not, as applicable*] still owe us the difference. If we get more money than you owe, you will get the extra money, unless we must pay it to someone else.

You can get the property back at any time before we sell it by paying us the full amount you owe (not just the past due payments), including our expenses. To learn the exact amount you must pay, call us at [*telephone number*].

If you want us to explain to you in writing how we have figured the amount that you owe us, you may call us at [*telephone number*] [or write us at [*secured party's address*]] and request a written explanation. [We will charge you $_____ for the explanation if we sent you another written explanation of the amount you owe us within the last six months.]

If you need more information about the sale call us at [*telephone number*] [or write us at [*secured party's address*]].

We are sending this notice to the following other people who have an interest in [*describe collateral*] or who owe money under your agreement:

[*Names of all other debtors and obligors, if any*]

[End of Form]

(4) A notification in the form of paragraph (3) is sufficient, even if additional information appears at the end of the form.

(5) A notification in the form of paragraph (3) is sufficient, even if it includes errors in information not required by paragraph (1), unless the error is misleading with respect to rights arising under this article.

(6) If a notification under this section is not in the form of paragraph (3), law other than this article determines the effect of including information not required by paragraph (1).

§ 9–615. Application of Proceeds of Disposition; Liability for Deficiency and Right to Surplus.

(a) A secured party shall apply or pay over for application the cash proceeds of disposition under Section 9–610 in the following order to:

(1) the reasonable expenses of retaking, holding, preparing for disposition, processing, and disposing, and, to the extent provided for by agreement and not prohibited by law, reasonable attorney's fees and legal expenses incurred by the secured party;

(2) the satisfaction of obligations secured by the security interest or agricultural lien under which the disposition is made;

(3) the satisfaction of obligations secured by any subordinate security interest in or other subordinate lien on the collateral if:

(A) the secured party receives from the holder of the subordinate security interest or other lien an authenticated demand for proceeds before distribution of the proceeds is completed; and

(B) in a case in which a consignor has an interest in the collateral, the subordinate security interest or other lien is senior to the interest of the consignor; and

(4) a secured party that is a consignor of the collateral if the secured party receives from the consignor an authenticated demand for proceeds before distribution of the proceeds is completed.

(b) If requested by a secured party, a holder of a subordinate security interest or other lien shall furnish reasonable proof of the interest or lien within a reasonable time. Unless the holder does so, the secured party need not comply with the holder's demand under subsection (a)(3).

(c) A secured party need not apply or pay over for application noncash proceeds of disposition under Section 9–610 unless the failure to do so would be commercially unreasonable. A secured party that applies or pays over for application noncash proceeds shall do so in a commercially reasonable manner.

(d) If the security interest under which a disposition is made secures payment or performance of an obligation, after making the payments and applications required by subsection (a) and permitted by subsection (c):

(1) unless subsection (a)(4) requires the secured party to apply or pay over cash proceeds to a consignor, the secured party shall account to and pay a debtor for any surplus; and

(2) the obligor is liable for any deficiency.

(e) If the underlying transaction is a sale of accounts, chattel paper, payment intangibles, or promissory notes:

(1) the debtor is not entitled to any surplus; and

(2) the obligor is not liable for any deficiency.

(f) The surplus or deficiency following a disposition is calculated based on the amount of proceeds that would have been realized in a disposition complying with this part to a transferee other than the secured party, a person related to the secured party, or a secondary obligor if:

(1) the transferee in the disposition is the secured party, a person related to the secured party, or a secondary obligor; and

(2) the amount of proceeds of the disposition is significantly below the range of proceeds that a complying disposition to a person other than the secured party, a person related to the secured party, or a secondary obligor would have brought.

(g) A secured party that receives cash proceeds of a disposition in good faith and without knowledge that the receipt violates the rights of the holder of a security interest or other lien that is not subordinate to the security interest or agricultural lien under which the disposition is made:

(1) takes the cash proceeds free of the security interest or other lien;

(2) is not obligated to apply the proceeds of the disposition to the satisfaction of obligations secured by the security interest or other lien; and

(3) is not obligated to account to or pay the holder of the security interest or other lien for any surplus.

As amended in 2000.

§ 9–616.   Explanation of Calculation of Surplus or Deficiency.

(a) In this section:

(1) "Explanation" means1 a writing that:

(A) states the amount of the surplus or deficiency;

(B) provides an explanation in accordance with subsection (c) of how the secured party calculated the surplus or deficiency;

(C) states, if applicable, that future debits, credits, charges, including additional credit service charges or interest, rebates, and expenses may affect the amount of the surplus or deficiency; and

(D) provides a telephone number or mailing address from which additional information concerning the transaction is available.

(2) "Request" means a record:

(A) authenticated by a debtor or consumer obligor;

(B) requesting that the recipient provide an explanation; and

(C) sent after disposition of the collateral under Section 9–610.

(b) In a consumer-goods transaction in which the debtor is entitled to a surplus or a consumer obligor is liable for a deficiency under Section 9–615, the secured party shall:

(1) send an explanation to the debtor or consumer obligor, as applicable, after the disposition and:

(A) before or when the secured party accounts to the debtor and pays any surplus or first makes written demand on the consumer obligor after the disposition for payment of the deficiency; and

(B) within 14 days after receipt of a request; or

(2) in the case of a consumer obligor who is liable for a deficiency, within 14 days after receipt of a request, send to the consumer obligor a record waiving the secured party's right to a deficiency.

(c) To comply with subsection (a)(1)(B), a writing must provide the following information in the following order:

(1) the aggregate amount of obligations secured by the security interest under which the disposition was made, and, if the amount reflects a rebate of unearned interest or credit service charge, an indication of that fact, calculated as of a specified date:

(A) if the secured party takes or receives possession of the collateral after default, not more than 35 days before the secured party takes or receives possession; or

(B) if the secured party takes or receives possession of the collateral before default or does not take possession of the collateral, not more than 35 days before the disposition;

(2) the amount of proceeds of the disposition;

(3) the aggregate amount of the obligations after deducting the amount of proceeds;

(4) the amount, in the aggregate or by type, and types of expenses, including expenses of retaking, holding, preparing for disposition, processing, and disposing of the collateral, and attorney's fees secured by the collateral which are known to the secured party and relate to the current disposition;

(5) the amount, in the aggregate or by type, and types of credits, including rebates of interest or credit service charges, to which the obligor is known to be entitled and which are not reflected in the amount in paragraph (1); and

(6) the amount of the surplus or deficiency.

(d) A particular phrasing of the explanation is not required. An explanation complying substantially with the requirements of subsection (a) is sufficient, even if it includes minor errors that are not seriously misleading.

(e) A debtor or consumer obligor is entitled without charge to one response to a request under this section during any six-month period in which the secured party did not send to the debtor or consumer obligor an explanation pursuant to subsection (b)(1). The secured party may require payment of a charge not exceeding $25 for each additional response.

§ 9–617.   Rights of Transferee of Collateral.

(a) A secured party's disposition of collateral after default:

(1) transfers to a transferee for value all of the debtor's rights in the collateral;

(2) discharges the security interest under which the disposition is made; and

(3) discharges any subordinate security interest or other subordinate lien [other than liens created under [cite acts or statutes providing for liens, if any, that are not to be discharged]].

(b) A transferee that acts in good faith takes free of the rights and interests described in subsection (a), even if the secured party fails to comply with this article or the requirements of any judicial proceeding.

(c) If a transferee does not take free of the rights and interests described in subsection (a), the transferee takes the collateral subject to:

(1) the debtor's rights in the collateral;

(2) the security interest or agricultural lien under which the disposition is made; and

(3) any other security interest or other lien.

§ 9–618. Rights and Duties of Certain Secondary Obligors.

(a) A secondary obligor acquires the rights and becomes obligated to perform the duties of the secured party after the secondary obligor:

(1) receives an assignment of a secured obligation from the secured party;

(2) receives a transfer of collateral from the secured party and agrees to accept the rights and assume the duties of the secured party; or

(3) is subrogated to the rights of a secured party with respect to collateral.

(b) An assignment, transfer, or subrogation described in subsection (a):

(1) is not a disposition of collateral under Section 9–610; and

(2) relieves the secured party of further duties under this article.

§ 9–619. Transfer of Record or Legal Title.

(a) In this section, "transfer statement" means a record authenticated by a secured party stating:

(1) that the debtor has defaulted in connection with an obligation secured by specified collateral;

(2) that the secured party has exercised its post-default remedies with respect to the collateral;

(3) that, by reason of the exercise, a transferee has acquired the rights of the debtor in the collateral; and

(4) the name and mailing address of the secured party, debtor, and transferee.

(b) A transfer statement entitles the transferee to the transfer of record of all rights of the debtor in the collateral specified in the statement in any official filing, recording, registration, or certificate-of-title system covering the collateral. If a transfer statement is presented with the applicable fee and request form to the official or office responsible for maintaining the system, the official or office shall:

(1) accept the transfer statement;

(2) promptly amend its records to reflect the transfer; and

(3) if applicable, issue a new appropriate certificate of title in the name of the transferee.

(c) A transfer of the record or legal title to collateral to a secured party under subsection (b) or otherwise is not of itself a disposition of collateral under this article and does not of itself relieve the secured party of its duties under this article.

§ 9–620. Acceptance of Collateral in Full or Partial Satisfaction of Obligation; Compulsory Disposition of Collateral.

(a) Except as otherwise provided in subsection (g), a secured party may accept collateral in full or partial satisfaction of the obligation it secures only if:

(1) the debtor consents to the acceptance under subsection (c);

(2) the secured party does not receive, within the time set forth in subsection (d), a notification of objection to the proposal authenticated by:

(A) a person to which the secured party was required to send a proposal under Section 9–621; or

(B) any other person, other than the debtor, holding an interest in the collateral subordinate to the security interest that is the subject of the proposal;

(3) if the collateral is consumer goods, the collateral is not in the possession of the debtor when the debtor consents to the acceptance; and

(4) subsection (e) does not require the secured party to dispose of the collateral or the debtor waives the requirement pursuant to Section 9–624.

(b) A purported or apparent acceptance of collateral under this section is ineffective unless:

(1) the secured party consents to the acceptance in an authenticated record or sends a proposal to the debtor; and

(2) the conditions of subsection (a) are met.

(c) For purposes of this section:

(1) a debtor consents to an acceptance of collateral in partial satisfaction of the obligation it secures only if the debtor agrees to the terms of the acceptance in a record authenticated after default; and

(2) a debtor consents to an acceptance of collateral in full satisfaction of the obligation it secures only if the debtor agrees to the terms of the acceptance in a record authenticated after default or the secured party:

(A) sends to the debtor after default a proposal that is unconditional or subject only to a condition that collateral not in the possession of the secured party be preserved or maintained;

(B) in the proposal, proposes to accept collateral in full satisfaction of the obligation it secures; and

(C) does not receive a notification of objection authenticated by the debtor within 20 days after the proposal is sent.

(d) To be effective under subsection (a)(2), a notification of objection must be received by the secured party:

(1) in the case of a person to which the proposal was sent pursuant to Section 9–621, within 20 days after notification was sent to that person; and

(2) in other cases:

(A) within 20 days after the last notification was sent pursuant to Section 9–621; or

(B) if a notification was not sent, before the debtor consents to the acceptance under subsection (c).

(e) A secured party that has taken possession of collateral shall dispose of the collateral pursuant to Section 9–610 within the time specified in subsection (f) if:

(1) 60 percent of the cash price has been paid in the case of a purchase-money security interest in consumer goods; or

(2) 60 percent of the principal amount of the obligation secured has been paid in the case of a non-purchase-money security interest in consumer goods.

(f) To comply with subsection (e), the secured party shall dispose of the collateral:

(1) within 90 days after taking possession; or

(2) within any longer period to which the debtor and all secondary obligors have agreed in an agreement to that effect entered into and authenticated after default.

(g) In a consumer transaction, a secured party may not accept collateral in partial satisfaction of the obligation it secures.

§ 9–621.   Notification of Proposal to Accept Collateral.

(a) A secured party that desires to accept collateral in full or partial satisfaction of the obligation it secures shall send its proposal to:

(1) any person from which the secured party has received, before the debtor consented to the acceptance, an authenticated notification of a claim of an interest in the collateral;

(2) any other secured party or lienholder that, 10 days before the debtor consented to the acceptance, held a security interest in or other lien on the collateral perfected by the filing of a financing statement that:

(A) identified the collateral;

(B) was indexed under the debtor's name as of that date; and

(C) was filed in the office or offices in which to file a financing statement against the debtor covering the collateral as of that date; and

(3) any other secured party that, 10 days before the debtor consented to the acceptance, held a security interest in the collateral perfected by compliance with a statute, regulation, or treaty described in Section 9–311(a).

(b) A secured party that desires to accept collateral in partial satisfaction of the obligation it secures shall send its proposal to any secondary obligor in addition to the persons described in subsection (a).

§ 9–622.   Effect of Acceptance of Collateral.

(a) A secured party's acceptance of collateral in full or partial satisfaction of the obligation it secures:

(1) discharges the obligation to the extent consented to by the debtor;

(2) transfers to the secured party all of a debtor's rights in the collateral;

(3) discharges the security interest or agricultural lien that is the subject of the debtor's consent and any subordinate security interest or other subordinate lien; and

(4) terminates any other subordinate interest.

(b) A subordinate interest is discharged or terminated under subsection (a), even if the secured party fails to comply with this article.

§ 9–623.   Right to Redeem Collateral.

(a) A debtor, any secondary obligor, or any other secured party or lienholder may redeem collateral.

(b) To redeem collateral, a person shall tender:

(1) fulfillment of all obligations secured by the collateral; and

(2) the reasonable expenses and attorney's fees described in Section 9–615(a)(1).

(c) A redemption may occur at any time before a secured party:

(1) has collected collateral under Section 9–607;

(2) has disposed of collateral or entered into a contract for its disposition under Section 9–610; or

(3) has accepted collateral in full or partial satisfaction of the obligation it secures under Section 9–622.

§ 9–624.   Waiver.

(a) A debtor or secondary obligor may waive the right to notification of disposition of collateral under Section 9–611 only by an agreement to that effect entered into and authenticated after default.

(b) A debtor may waive the right to require disposition of collateral under Section 9–620(e) only by an agreement to that effect entered into and authenticated after default.

(c) Except in a consumer-goods transaction, a debtor or secondary obligor may waive the right to redeem collateral under Section 9–623 only by an agreement to that effect entered into and authenticated after default.

[Subpart 2. Noncompliance with Article]

§ 9–625.   Remedies for Secured Party's Failure to Comply with Article.

(a) If it is established that a secured party is not proceeding in accordance with this article, a court may order or restrain collection, enforcement, or disposition of collateral on appropriate terms and conditions.

(b) Subject to subsections (c), (d), and (f), a person is liable for damages in the amount of any loss caused by a failure to comply with this article. Loss caused by a failure to comply may include loss resulting from the debtor's inability to obtain, or increased costs of, alternative financing.

(c) Except as otherwise provided in Section 9–628:

(1) a person that, at the time of the failure, was a debtor, was an obligor, or held a security interest in or other lien on the collateral may recover damages under subsection (b) for its loss; and

(2) if the collateral is consumer goods, a person that was a debtor or a secondary obligor at the time a secured party failed to comply with this part may recover for that failure in any event an amount not less than the credit service charge plus 10 percent of the principal amount of the obligation or the time-price differential plus 10 percent of the cash price.

(d) A debtor whose deficiency is eliminated under Section 9–626 may recover damages for the loss of any surplus. However, a debtor or secondary obligor whose deficiency is eliminated or reduced under Section 9–626 may not otherwise recover under subsection (b) for noncompliance with the provisions of this part relating to collection, enforcement, disposition, or acceptance.

(e) In addition to any damages recoverable under subsection (b), the debtor, consumer obligor, or person named as a debtor in a filed record, as applicable, may recover $500 in each case from a person that:

(1) fails to comply with Section 9–208;

(2) fails to comply with Section 9–209;

(3) files a record that the person is not entitled to file under Section 9–509(a);

(4) fails to cause the secured party of record to file or send a termination statement as required by Section 9–513(a) or (c);

(5) fails to comply with Section 9–616(b)(1) and whose failure is part of a pattern, or consistent with a practice, of noncompliance; or

(6) fails to comply with Section 9–616(b)(2).

(f) A debtor or consumer obligor may recover damages under subsection (b) and, in addition, $500 in each case from a person that, without reasonable cause, fails to comply with a request under Section 9–210. A recipient of a request under Section 9–210 which never claimed an interest in the collateral or obligations that are the subject of a request under that section has a reasonable excuse for failure to comply with the request within the meaning of this subsection.

(g) If a secured party fails to comply with a request regarding a list of collateral or a statement of account under Section 9–210, the secured party may claim a security interest only as shown in the list or statement included in the request as against a person that is reasonably misled by the failure.

As amended in 2000.

§ 9–626.   Action in Which Deficiency or Surplus Is in Issue.

(a) In an action arising from a transaction, other than a consumer transaction, in which the amount of a deficiency or surplus is in issue, the following rules apply:

(1) A secured party need not prove compliance with the provisions of this part relating to collection, enforcement, disposition, or acceptance unless the debtor or a secondary obligor places the secured party's compliance in issue.

(2) If the secured party's compliance is placed in issue, the secured party has the burden of establishing that the collection, enforcement, disposition, or acceptance was conducted in accordance with this part.

(3) Except as otherwise provided in Section 9–628, if a secured party fails to prove that the collection, enforcement, disposition, or acceptance was conducted in accordance with the provisions of this part relating to collection, enforcement, disposition, or acceptance, the liability of a debtor or a secondary obligor for a deficiency is limited to an amount by which the sum of the secured obligation, expenses, and attorney's fees exceeds the greater of:

(A) the proceeds of the collection, enforcement, disposition, or acceptance; or

(B) the amount of proceeds that would have been realized had the noncomplying secured party proceeded in accordance with the provisions of this part relating to collection, enforcement, disposition, or acceptance.

(4) For purposes of paragraph (3)(B), the amount of proceeds that would have been realized is equal to the sum of the secured obligation, expenses, and attorney's fees unless the secured party proves that the amount is less than that sum.

(5) If a deficiency or surplus is calculated under Section 9–615(f), the debtor or obligor has the burden of establishing that the amount of proceeds of the disposition is significantly below the range of prices that a complying disposition to a person other than the secured party, a person related to the secured party, or a secondary obligor would have brought.

(b) The limitation of the rules in subsection (a) to transactions other than consumer transactions is intended to leave to the court the determination of the proper rules in consumer transactions. The court may not infer from that limitation the nature of the proper rule in consumer transactions and may continue to apply established approaches.

§ 9–627.   Determination of Whether Conduct Was Commercially Reasonable.

(a) The fact that a greater amount could have been obtained by a collection, enforcement, disposition, or acceptance at a different time or in a different method from that selected by the secured party is not of itself sufficient to preclude the secured party from establishing that the collection, enforcement, disposition, or acceptance was made in a commercially reasonable manner.

(b) A disposition of collateral is made in a commercially reasonable manner if the disposition is made:

(1) in the usual manner on any recognized market;

(2) at the price current in any recognized market at the time of the disposition; or

(3) otherwise in conformity with reasonable commercial practices among dealers in the type of property that was the subject of the disposition.

(c) A collection, enforcement, disposition, or acceptance is commercially reasonable if it has been approved:

(1) in a judicial proceeding;

(2) by a bona fide creditors' committee;

(3) by a representative of creditors; or

(4) by an assignee for the benefit of creditors.

(d) Approval under subsection (c) need not be obtained, and lack of approval does not mean that the collection, enforcement, disposition, or acceptance is not commercially reasonable.

§ 9–628.   Nonliability and Limitation on Liability of Secured Party; Liability of Secondary Obligor.

(a) Unless a secured party knows that a person is a debtor or obligor, knows the identity of the person, and knows how to communicate with the person:

(1) the secured party is not liable to the person, or to a secured party or lienholder that has filed a financing statement against the person, for failure to comply with this article; and

(2) the secured party's failure to comply with this article does not affect the liability of the person for a deficiency.

(b) A secured party is not liable because of its status as secured party:

(1) to a person that is a debtor or obligor, unless the secured party knows:

(A) that the person is a debtor or obligor;

(B) the identity of the person; and

(C) how to communicate with the person; or

(2) to a secured party or lienholder that has filed a financing statement against a person, unless the secured party knows:

(A) that the person is a debtor; and

(B) the identity of the person.

(c) A secured party is not liable to any person, and a person's liability for a deficiency is not affected, because of any act or omission arising out of the secured party's reasonable belief that a transaction is not a consumer-goods transaction or a consumer transaction or that goods are not consumer goods, if the secured party's belief is based on its reasonable reliance on:

(1) a debtor's representation concerning the purpose for which collateral was to be used, acquired, or held; or

(2) an obligor's representation concerning the purpose for which a secured obligation was incurred.

(d) A secured party is not liable to any person under Section 9–625(c)(2) for its failure to comply with Section 9–616.

(e) A secured party is not liable under Section 9–625(c)(2) more than once with respect to any one secured obligation.

PART 7   Transition

§ 9–701.   Effective Date.

This [Act] takes effect on July 1, 2001.

§ 9–702.   Savings Clause.

(a) Except as otherwise provided in this part, this [Act] applies to a transaction or lien within its scope, even if the transaction or lien was entered into or created before this [Act] takes effect.

(b) Except as otherwise provided in subsection (c) and Sections 9–703 through 9–709:

(1) transactions and liens that were not governed by [former Article 9], were validly entered into or created before this [Act] takes effect, and would be subject to this [Act] if they had been entered into or created after this [Act] takes effect, and the rights, duties, and interests flowing from those transactions and liens remain valid after this [Act] takes effect; and

(2) the transactions and liens may be terminated, completed, consummated, and enforced as required or permitted by this [Act] or by the law that otherwise would apply if this [Act] had not taken effect.

(c) This [Act] does not affect an action, case, or proceeding commenced before this [Act] takes effect.

As amended in 2000.

§ 9–703.   Security Interest Perfected before Effective Date.

(a) A security interest that is enforceable immediately before this [Act] takes effect and would have priority over the rights of a person that becomes a lien creditor at that time is a perfected security interest under this [Act] if, when this [Act] takes effect, the applicable requirements for enforceability and perfection under this [Act] are satisfied without further action.

(b) Except as otherwise provided in Section 9–705, if, immediately before this [Act] takes effect, a security interest is enforceable and would have priority over the rights of a person that becomes a lien creditor at that time, but the applicable requirements for enforceability or perfection under this [Act] are not satisfied when this [Act] takes effect, the security interest:

(1) is a perfected security interest for one year after this [Act] takes effect;

(2) remains enforceable thereafter only if the security interest becomes enforceable under Section 9–203 before the year expires; and

(3) remains perfected thereafter only if the applicable requirements for perfection under this [Act] are satisfied before the year expires.

§ 9–704.   Security Interest Unperfected before Effective Date.

A security interest that is enforceable immediately before this [Act] takes effect but which would be subordinate to the rights of a person that becomes a lien creditor at that time:

(1) remains an enforceable security interest for one year after this [Act] takes effect;

(2) remains enforceable thereafter if the security interest becomes enforceable under Section 9–203 when this [Act] takes effect or within one year thereafter; and

(3) becomes perfected:

(A) without further action, when this [Act] takes effect if the applicable requirements for perfection under this [Act] are satisfied before or at that time; or

(B) when the applicable requirements for perfection are satisfied if the requirements are satisfied after that time.

§ 9–705.   Effectiveness of Action Taken before Effective Date.

(a) If action, other than the filing of a financing statement, is taken before this [Act] takes effect and the action would have resulted in priority of a security interest over the rights of a person that becomes a lien creditor had the security interest become enforceable before this [Act] takes effect, the action is effective to perfect a security interest that attaches under this [Act] within one year after this [Act] takes effect. An attached security interest becomes unperfected one year after this [Act] takes effect unless the security interest becomes a perfected security interest under this [Act] before the expiration of that period.

(b) The filing of a financing statement before this [Act] takes effect is effective to perfect a security interest to the extent the filing would satisfy the applicable requirements for perfection under this [Act].

(c) This [Act] does not render ineffective an effective financing statement that, before this [Act] takes effect, is filed and satisfies the applicable requirements for perfection under the law of the jurisdiction governing perfection as provided in [former Section 9–103]. However, except as otherwise provided in subsections (d) and (e) and Section 9–706, the financing statement ceases to be effective at the earlier of:

(1) the time the financing statement would have ceased to be effective under the law of the jurisdiction in which it is filed; or

(2) June 30, 2006.

(d) The filing of a continuation statement after this [Act] takes effect does not continue the effectiveness of the financing statement filed before this [Act] takes effect. However, upon the timely filing of a continuation statement after this [Act] takes effect and in accordance with the law of the jurisdiction governing perfection as provided in Part 3, the effectiveness of a financing statement filed in the same office in that jurisdiction before this [Act] takes effect continues for the period provided by the law of that jurisdiction.

(e) Subsection (c)(2) applies to a financing statement that, before this [Act] takes effect, is filed against a transmitting utility and satisfies the applicable requirements for perfection under the law of the jurisdiction governing perfection as provided in [former Section 9–103] only to the extent that Part 3 provides that the law of a jurisdiction other than the jurisdiction in which the financing statement is filed governs perfection of a security interest in collateral covered by the financing statement.

(f) A financing statement that includes a financing statement filed before this [Act] takes effect and a continuation statement filed after this [Act] takes effect is effective only to the extent that it satisfies the requirements of Part 5 for an initial financing statement.

§ 9–706.   When Initial Financing Statement Suffices to Continue Effectiveness of Financing Statement.

(a) The filing of an initial financing statement in the office specified in Section 9–501 continues the effectiveness of a financing statement filed before this [Act] takes effect if:

(1) the filing of an initial financing statement in that office would be effective to perfect a security interest under this [Act];

(2) the pre-effective-date financing statement was filed in an office in another State or another office in this State; and

(3) the initial financing statement satisfies subsection (c).

(b) The filing of an initial financing statement under subsection (a) continues the effectiveness of the pre-effective-date financing statement:

(1) if the initial financing statement is filed before this [Act] takes effect, for the period provided in [former Section 9–403] with respect to a financing statement; and

(2) if the initial financing statement is filed after this [Act] takes effect, for the period provided in Section 9–515 with respect to an initial financing statement.

(c) To be effective for purposes of subsection (a), an initial financing statement must:

(1) satisfy the requirements of Part 5 for an initial financing statement;

(2) identify the pre-effective-date financing statement by indicating the office in which the financing statement was filed and providing the dates of filing and file numbers, if any, of the financing statement and of the most recent continuation statement filed with respect to the financing statement; and

(3) indicate that the pre-effective-date financing statement remains effective.

§ 9–707.   Amendment of Pre-Effective-Date Financing Statement.

(a) In this section, "Pre-effective-date financing statement" means a financing statement filed before this [Act] takes effect.

(b) After this [Act] takes effect, a person may add or delete collateral covered by, continue or terminate the effectiveness of, or otherwise amend the information provided in, a pre-effective-date financing statement only in accordance with the law of the jurisdiction governing perfection as provided in Part 3. However, the effectiveness of a pre-effective-date financing statement also may be terminated in accordance with the law of the jurisdiction in which the financing statement is filed.

(c) Except as otherwise provided in subsection (d), if the law of this State governs perfection of a security interest, the information in a pre-effective-date financing statement may be amended after this [Act] takes effect only if:

(1) the pre-effective-date financing statement and an amendment are filed in the office specified in Section 9–501;

(2) an amendment is filed in the office specified in Section 9–501 concurrently with, or after the filing in that office of, an initial financing statement that satisfies Section 9–706(c); or

(3) an initial financing statement that provides the information as amended and satisfies Section 9–706(c) is filed in the office specified in Section 9–501.

(d) If the law of this State governs perfection of a security interest, the effectiveness of a pre-effective-date financing statement may be continued only under Section 9–705(d) and (f) or 9–706.

(e) Whether or not the law of this State governs perfection of a security interest, the effectiveness of a pre-effective-date financing statement filed in this State may be terminated after this [Act] takes effect by filing a termination statement in the office in which the pre-effective-date financing statement is filed, unless an initial financing statement that satisfies Section 9–706(c) has been filed in the office specified by the law of the jurisdiction governing perfection as provided in Part 3 as the office in which to file a financing statement.

As amended in 2000.

§ 9–708.   Persons Entitled to File Initial Financing Statement or Continuation Statement.

A person may file an initial financing statement or a continuation statement under this part if:

(1) the secured party of record authorizes the filing; and

(2) the filing is necessary under this part:

(A) to continue the effectiveness of a financing statement filed before this [Act] takes effect; or

(B) to perfect or continue the perfection of a security interest.

As amended in 2000.

§ 9–709.   Priority.

(a) This [Act] determines the priority of conflicting claims to collateral. However, if the relative priorities of the claims were established before this [Act] takes effect, [former Article 9] determines priority.

(b) For purposes of Section 9–322(a), the priority of a security interest that becomes enforceable under Section 9–203 of this [Act] dates from the time this [Act] takes effect if the security interest is perfected under this [Act] by the filing of a financing statement before this [Act] takes effect which would not have been effective to perfect the security interest under [former Article 9]. This subsection does not apply to conflicting security interests each of which is perfected by the filing of such a financing statement.

Glossary

A

Accepted check A check that the drawee bank has signed. This signature is a promise that the bank will pay the check out of its own funds. (Chapter 24)

Accession The use of labor and/or materials to add value to the personal property of another. (Chapter 46)

Accommodation party Someone who does not benefit from an instrument but agrees to guarantee its payment. (Chapter 24)

Accord and satisfaction An agreement to settle a debt for less than the sum claimed. (Chapter 12)

Accounts Any right to receive payment for goods sold or leased, other than rights covered by chattel paper or instruments. (Chapter 26)

Accredited investor Under the Securities Act of 1933, an accredited investor is an institution (such as a bank or insurance company) or any individual with a net worth of more than $1 million or an annual income of more than $200,000. (Chapter 37)

Acquit To find the defendant not guilty of the crime for which he was tried. (Chapter 8)

Act of State doctrine A rule requiring American courts to abstain from cases if a court order would interfere with the ability of the President or Congress to conduct foreign policy. (Chapter 9)

Actus reus The guilty act. The prosecution must show that a criminal defendant committed some proscribed act. In a murder prosecution, taking another person's life is the *actus reus*. (Chapter 8)

Adhesion contract A standard form contract prepared by one party and presented to the other on a "take it or leave it" basis. (Chapter 13)

Adjudicate To hold a formal hearing in a disputed matter and issue an official decision. (Chapter 4)

Administrative law Concerns all agencies, boards, commissions, and other entities created by a federal or state legislature and charged with investigating, regulating, and adjudicating a particular industry or issue. (Chapter 1)

Administrator A person appointed by the court to oversee the probate process for someone who has died intestate (that is, without a will). (Chapter 47)

Administratrix A female administrator. (Chapter 47)

Adverse possession A means of gaining ownership of land belonging to another by entering upon the property, openly and notoriously, and claiming exclusive use of it for a period of years. (Chapter 44)

Affidavit A written statement signed under oath. (Chapter 8)

Affirm A decision by an appellate court to uphold the judgment of a lower court. (Chapter 1)

Affirmative action A plan introduced in a workplace for the purpose of either remedying the effects of past discrimination or achieving equitable representation of minorities and women. (Chapter 30)

After-acquired property Items that a debtor obtains after making a security agreement with the secured party. (Chapter 26)

Agent A person who acts for a principal. (Chapter 8)

Alternative dispute resolution Any method of resolving a legal conflict other than litigation, such as: negotiation, arbitration, mediation, mini-trials, and summary jury trials. (Chapter 3)

Amendment Any addition to a legal document. The constitutional amendments, the first ten of which are known collectively as the Bill of Rights, secure numerous liberties and protections directly for the people. (Chapter 1)

Annual report Each year, public companies must send their shareholders an annual report that contains detailed financial data. (Chapter 36)

Answer The pleading, filed by the defendant in court and served on the plaintiff, which responds to each allegation in the plaintiff's complaint. (Chapter 3)

Apparent authority A situation in which conduct of a principal causes a third party to believe that the principal consents to have an act done on his behalf by a person purporting to act for him when, in fact, that person is not acting for the principal. (Chapter 29)

Appellant The party who appeals a lower court decision to a higher court. (Chapter 3)

Appellate court Any court in a state or federal system that reviews cases that have already been tried. (Chapter 3)

Appellee The party opposing an appeal from a lower court to a higher court. (Chapter 3)

Arbitration A form of alternative dispute resolution in which the parties hire a neutral third party to hear their respective arguments, receive evidence, and then make a binding decision. (Chapter 3)

Arson Malicious use of fire or explosives to damage or destroy real estate or personal property. (Chapter 8)

Assault An intentional act that causes the plaintiff to fear an imminent battery. (Chapter 6)

Assignee The party who receives an assignment of contract rights from a party to the contract. (Chapter 16)

Assignment The act by which a party transfers contract rights to a third person. (Chapter 16)

Assignor The party who assigns contract rights to a third person. (Chapter 16)

Attachment A court order seizing property of a party to a civil action, so that there will be sufficient assets available to pay the judgment. (Chapter 5)

Authorized and unissued stock Stock that has been approved by the corporation's charter, but has not yet been sold. (Chapter 34)

Authorized and issued stock Stock that has been approved by the corporation's charter and subsequently sold. (Chapter 34)

B

Bailee A person who rightfully possesses goods belonging to another. (Chapter 13)

Bailment Giving possession and control of personal property to another person. (Chapter 13)

Bailor One who creates a bailment by delivering goods to another. (Chapter 13)

Battery The intentional touching of another person in a way that is unwanted or offensive. (Chapter 6)

Bearer paper An instrument payable "to bearer." Any holder in due course can demand payment. (Chapter 23)

Bilateral contract A binding agreement in which each party has made a promise to the other. (Chapter 10)

Bill of lading A receipt for goods, given by a carrier such as a ship, that minutely describes the merchandise being shipped. A **negotiable** bill of lading may be transferred to other parties, and entitles any holder to collect the goods. (Chapter 9)

Bill of Rights The first ten amendments to the Constitution. (Chapter 5)

Bill A proposed statute that has been submitted for consideration to Congress or a state legislature. (Chapter 4)

Blue sky laws State securities laws. (Chapter 37)

Bona fide occupational qualification A job requirement that would otherwise be discriminatory is permitted in situations in which it is *essential* to the position in question. (Chapter 30)

Bona fide purchaser Someone who buys goods in good faith, for value, typically from a seller who has merely voidable title. (Chapter 20)

Bonds Long-term debt secured by some of the issuing company's assets. (Chapter 34)

Brief The written legal argument that an attorney files with an appeal court. (Chapter 3)

Bulk sale A transfer of most or all of a merchant's assets. (Chapter 20)

Burden of proof The allocation of which party must prove its case. In a civil case, the plaintiff has the burden of proof to persuade the factfinder of every element of her case. In a criminal case, the government has the burden of proof. (Chapter 3)

Business judgment rule A common law rule that protects managers from liability if they are acting without a conflict of interest, and make informed decisions that have a rational business purpose. (Chapter 35)

Buyer in ordinary course of business Someone who buys goods in good faith from a seller who routinely deals in such goods. (Chapter 26)

Bylaws A document that specifies the organizational rules of a corporation or other organization, such as the date of the annual meeting and the required number of directors. (Chapter 34)

C

Capacity The legal ability to enter into a contract. (Chapter 10)

Certificate of deposit An instrument issued by a bank which promises to repay a deposit, with interest, on a specified date. (Chapter 23)

Certified check A check that the drawee bank has signed. This signature is a promise that the bank will pay the check out of its own funds. (Chapter 24)

***Certiorari,* writ of** Formal notice from the United States Supreme Court that it will accept a case for review. (Chapter 3)

Challenge for cause An attorney's request, during *voir dire*, to excuse a prospective juror because of apparent bias. (Chapter 3)

Chancery, court of In medieval England, the court originally operated by the Chancellor. (Chapter 1)

Charging order A court order granting the creditor of a partner the right to receive that partner's share of partnership profits. (Chapter 33)

Chattel paper Any writing that indicates two things: (1) a debtor owes money and (2) a secured party has a security interest in specific goods. The most common chattel paper is a document indicating a consumer sale on credit. (Chapter 26)

Check An instrument in which the drawer orders the drawee bank to pay money to the payee. (Chapter 23)

Chicago School A theory of antitrust law first developed at the University of Chicago. Adherents to this theory believe that antitrust enforcement should focus on promoting efficiency and should not generally be concerned about the size or number of competitors in any market. (Chapter 39)

CISG See Convention on Contracts for the International Sale of Goods. (Chapter 9)

Civil law The large body of law concerning the rights and duties between parties. It is distinguished from criminal law, which concerns behavior outlawed by a government. (Chapter 1)

Class action A method of litigating a civil lawsuit in which one or more plaintiffs (or occasionally defendants) seek to represent an entire group of people with similar claims against a common opponent. (Chapter 3)

Classification The process by which the Customs Service decides what label to attach to imported merchandise, and therefore what level of tariff to impose. (Chapter 9)

Close corporation A corporation with a small number of shareholders. Its stock is not publicly traded. (Chapter 32)

Codicil An amendment to a will. (Chapter 47)

Collateral The property subject to a security interest. (Chapter 26)

Collateral promises A promise to pay the debt of another person, as a favor to the debtor. (Chapter 15)

Collective bargaining Contract negotiations between an employer and a union. (Chapter 31)

Collective bargaining unit The precisely defined group of employees who are represented by a particular union. (Chapter 31)

Comity A doctrine that requires a court to abstain from hearing a case out of respect for another court that also has jurisdiction. **International comity** demands that an American court refuse to hear a case in which a foreign court shares jurisdiction if there is a conflict between the laws and if it is more logical for the foreign court to take the case. (Chapter 9)

Commerce clause One of the powers granted by Article I, §8 of the Constitution, it gives Congress exclusive power to regulate international commerce and concurrent power with the states to regulate domestic commerce. (Chapter 5)

Commercial impracticability After the creation of a contract, an entirely unforeseen event occurs which makes enforcement of the contract extraordinarily unfair. (Chapter 17)

Commercial paper Instruments such as checks and promissory notes that contain a promise to pay money. Commercial paper includes both negotiable and non-negotiable instruments. (Chapter 23)

Commercial speech Communication, such as television advertisements, that has the dominant theme of proposing a commercial transaction. (Chapter 5)

Common carrier A transportation company that makes its services available on a regular basis to the general public. (Chapter 46)

Common law Judge-made law, that is, the body of all decisions made by appellate courts over the years. (Chapter 1)

Common stock Certificates that reflect ownership in a corporation. Owners of this equity security are last in line for corporate pay-outs such as dividends and liquidation proceeds. (Chapter 34)

Comparative negligence A rule of tort law that permits a plaintiff to recover even when the defendant can show that the plaintiff's own conduct contributed in some way to her harm. (Chapter 7)

Compensatory damages Those that flow directly from the contract. (Chapter 18)

Complaint A pleading, filed by the plaintiff, providing a short statement of the claim. (Chapter 3)

Concerted action Tactics, such as a strike, used by a union to gain a bargaining advantage. (Chapter 31)

Condition A condition is an event that must occur in order for a party to be obligated under a contract. (Chapter 17)

Condition precedent A condition that must occur before a particular contract duty arises. (Chapter 17)

Condition subsequent A condition that must occur after a particular contract duty arises, or the duty will be discharged. (Chapter 17)

Confiscation Expropriation without adequate compensation of property owned by foreigners. (Chapter 9)

Conforming goods Items that satisfy the contract terms. If a contract calls for blue sailboats, then green sailboats are non-conforming. (Chapter 22)

Consent order An agreement entered into by a wrongdoer and an administrative agency (such as the Securities and Exchange Commission or the Federal Trade Commission) in which the wrongdoer agrees not to violate the law in the future. (Chapter 40)

Consequential damages Those resulting from the unique circumstances of *this injured party*. (Chapter 18)

Consideration In contract law, something of legal value that has been bargained for and given in exchange by the parties. (Chapter 12)

Constitution The supreme law of a political entity. The United States Constitution is the highest law in the country. (Chapter 1)

Contract A legally enforceable promise or set of promises. (Chapter 10)

Contract carrier A transportation company that does not make its services available to the general public but engages in continuing agreements with particular customers. (Chapter 46)

Contributory negligence A rule of tort law that permits a negligent defendant to escape liability if she can demonstrate that the plaintiff's own conduct contributed in any way to the plaintiff's harm. (Chapter 7)

Control security Stock owned by any officer or director of the issuer, or by any shareholder who holds more than 10 percent of a class of stock of the issuer. (Chapter 37)

Convention on Contracts for the International Sale of Goods A United Nations sponsored agreement that creates a neutral body of law for sale of goods contracts between companies from different countries. (Chapter 9)

Conversion A tort committed by taking or using someone else's personal property without his permission. (Chapter 6)

Cookie A small computer file that identifies the user of a computer. Internet sites typically place cookies on a computer's hard drive to track visitors to their site. (Chapter 42)

Copyright Under federal law, the holder of a copyright owns a particular expression of an idea, but not the idea itself. This ownership right applies to creative activities such as literature, music, drama, and software. (Chapter 43)

Corporation by estoppel Even if a corporation has not actually been formed, courts will sometimes enforce contracts entered into in the belief that the corporation did indeed exist. (Chapter 34)

Counter-claim A claim made by the defendant against the plaintiff. (Chapter 3)

Cover The buyer's right to obtain substitute goods when a seller has breached a contract. (Chapter 18)

Creditor beneficiary When one party to a contract intends to benefit a third party to whom he owes a debt, that third party is referred to as a creditor beneficiary. (Chapter 16)

Criminal law Rules that permit a government to punish certain behavior by fine or imprisonment. (Chapter 1)

Cross-examination During a hearing, for a lawyer to question an opposing witness. (Chapter 3)

Cure The seller's right to respond to a buyer's rejection of non-conforming goods; the seller accomplishes this by delivering conforming goods before the contract deadline. (Chapter 22)

D

Damages (1) The harm that a plaintiff complains of at trial, such as an injury to her person, or money lost because of a contract breach. (2) Money awarded by a trial court for injury suffered. (Chapter 6)

***De facto* corporation** Occurs when a promoter makes a good faith effort to incorporate (although fails to complete the process entirely) and uses the corporation to conduct business. The state can challenge the validity of the corporation, but a third party cannot. (Chapter 34)

De jure corporation The promoter of the corporation has substantially complied with the requirements for incorporation, but has made some minor error. No one has the right to challenge the validity of the corporation. (Chapter 34)

De novo The power of an appellate court or appellate agency to make a new decision in a matter under appeal, entirely ignoring the findings and conclusions of the lower court or agency official. (Chapter 4)

Debentures Long-term, unsecured debt, typically issued by a corporation. (Chapter 34)

Debtor A person who owes money or some other obligation to another party. (Chapter 26)

Decedent A person who has died. (Chapter 47)

Defamation The act of injuring someone's reputation by stating something false about her to a third person. *Libel* is defamation done either in writing or by broadcast. *Slander* is defamation done orally. (Chapter 6)

Default The failure to perform an obligation, such as the failure to pay money when due. (Chapter 26)

Default judgment Court order awarding one party everything it requested because the opposing party failed to respond in time. (Chapter 3)

Default rules Under the Uniform Partnership Act, these rules govern the relationship among the partners unless the partners explicitly make a different agreement. (Chapter 33)

Definiteness A doctrine holding that a contract will only be enforced if its terms are sufficiently precise that a court can determine what the parties meant. (Chapter 11)

Delegation The act by which a party to a contract transfers duties to a third person who is not a party to the contract. (Chapter 16)

Deponent The person being questioned in a deposition. (Chapter 3)

Deposition A form of discovery in which a party's attorney has the right to ask oral questions of the other party or of a witness. Answers are given under oath. (Chapter 3)

Derivative action A lawsuit brought by shareholders in the name of the corporation to enforce a right of the corporation. (Chapter 36)

Deterrence Using punishment, such as imprisonment, to discourage criminal behavior. (Chapter 8)

Devisee Someone who inherits under a will. (Chapter 47)

Direct examination During a hearing, for a lawyer to question his own witness. (Chapter 3)

Directed verdict The decision by a court to instruct a jury that it must find in favor of a particular party because, in the judge's opinion, no reasonable person could disagree on the outcome. (Chapter 3)

Disaffirmance The act of notifying the other party to a contract that the party giving the notice refuses to be bound by the agreement. (Chapter 14)

Discharge (1) A party to a contract has no more duties. (2) A party to an instrument is released from liability. (Chapter 17)

Disclaimer A statement that a particular warranty does not apply. (Chapter 21)

Discovery A stage in litigation, after all pleadings have been served, in which each party seeks as much relevant information as possible about the opposing party's case. (Chapter 3)

Dishonor An obligor refuses to pay an instrument that is due. (Chapter 24)

Dismiss To terminate a lawsuit, often on procedural grounds, without reaching the merits of the case. (Chapter 3)

Dissociation A dissociation occurs when a partner leaves a partnership. (Chapter 33)

Diversity jurisdiction One of the two main types of civil cases that a United States district court has the power to hear. It involves a lawsuit between citizens of different states, in which at least one party makes a claim for more than $75,000. (Chapter 3)

Domestic corporation A corporation is a domestic corporation in the state in which it was formed. (Chapter 34)

Donee A person who receives a gift. (Chapter 46)

Donee beneficiary When one party to a contract intends to make a gift to a third party, that third party is referred to as a donee beneficiary. (Chapter 16)

Donor A person who makes a gift to another. (Chapter 46)

Draft The drawer of this instrument orders someone else to pay money. Checks are the most common form of draft. The drawer of a check orders a bank to pay money. (Chapter 23)

Drawee The person who pays a draft. In the case of a check, the bank is the drawee. (Chapter 23)

Drawer The person who issues a draft. (Chapter 23)

Due Process Clause Part of the Fifth Amendment. *Procedural due process* ensures that before depriving anyone of liberty or property, the government must go through procedures which ensure that the deprivation is fair. *Substantive due process* holds that certain rights, such as privacy, are so fundamental that the government may not eliminate them. (Chapter 5)

Dumping Selling merchandise at one price in the domestic market and at a cheaper, unfair price in an international market. (Chapter 9)

Durable power of attorney An instrument that permits an attorney-in-fact to act for a principal. A durable power is effective until the principal revokes it or dies. It continues in effect even if the principal becomes incapacitated. (Chapter 47)

Duress (1) A criminal defense in which the defendant shows that she committed the wrongful act because a third person threatened her with imminent physical harm. (2) An improper threat made to force another party to enter into a contract. (Chapter 8)

Duty A tax imposed on imported items. (Chapter 9)

E

Easement The right to enter land belonging to another and make a limited use of it, without taking anything away. (Chapter 44)

Economic loss doctrine A common law rule holding that when an injury is purely economic, and arises from a contract made between two businesses, the injured party may only sue under the UCC. (Chapter 21)

Element A fact that a party to a lawsuit must prove in order to prevail. (Chapter 6)

Embezzlement Fraudulent conversion of property already in the defendant's possession. (Chapter 8)

Eminent domain The power of the government to take private property for public use. (Chapter 5)

Employee at will A worker whose job does not have a specified duration. (Chapter 30)

Enabling legislation A statute authorizing the creation of a new administrative agency and specifying its powers and duties. (Chapter 4)

Entrapment A criminal defense in which the defendant demonstrates that the government induced him to break the law. (Chapter 8)

Equal Protection Clause Part of the Fourteenth Amendment, it generally requires the government to treat equally situated people the same. (Chapter 5)

Equity The broad powers of a court to fashion a remedy where justice demands it and no common law remedy exists. An injunction is an example of an equitable remedy. (Chapter 1)

Error of law A mistake made by a trial judge that concerns a legal issue as opposed to a factual matter. Permitting too many leading questions is a legal error; choosing to believe one witness rather than another is a factual matter. (Chapter 3)

Estate The legal entity that holds title to assets after the owner dies and before the property is distributed. (Chapter 47)

Estoppel Out of fairness, a person is denied the right to assert a claim. (Chapter 29)

Evidence, rules of Law governing the proof offered during a trial or formal hearing. These rules limit the questions that may be asked of witnesses and the introduction of physical objects. (Chapter 3)

Exclusionary rule In a criminal trial, a ban on the use of evidence obtained in violation of the Constitution. (Chapter 8)

Exclusive dealing agreement A potential violation of §1 of the Sherman Act, in which a distributor or retailer agrees with a supplier not to carry the products of any other supplier. (Chapter 39)

Exculpatory clause A contract provision that attempts to release one party from liability in the event the other party is injured. (Chapter 13)

Executed contract A binding agreement in which all parties have fulfilled all obligations. (Chapter 10)

Executive agency An administrative agency within the executive branch of government. (Chapter 4)

Executive order An order by a president or governor, having the full force of law. (Chapter 1)

Executor A person chosen by the decedent to oversee the probate process. (Chapter 15)

Executory contract A binding agreement in which one or more of the parties has not fulfilled its obligations. (Chapter 10)

Executrix A female executor. (Chapter 47)

Exhaustion of remedies A principle of administrative law that no party may appeal an agency action to a court until she has utilized all available appeals within the agency itself. (Chapter 4)

Expectation interest A remedy in a contract case that puts the injured party in the position he would have been in had both sides fully performed. (Chapter 18)

Expert witness A witness in a court case who has special training or qualifications to discuss a specific issue, and who is generally permitted to state an opinion. (Chapter 3)

Export To transport goods or services out of a country. (Chapter 9)

Express authority Conduct of a principal that, reasonably interpreted, causes the agent to believe that the principal desires him to do a specific act. (Chapter 29)

Express contract A binding agreement in which the parties explicitly state all important terms. (Chapter 10)

Express warranty A guarantee, created by the words or actions of the seller, that goods will meet certain standards. (Chapter 21)

Expropriation A government's seizure of property or companies owned by foreigners. (Chapter 9)

F

Factfinder The one responsible, during a trial, for deciding what occurred, that is, who did what to whom, when, how, and why. It is either the jury or, in a jury-waived case, the judge. (Chapter 5)

Fair representation, duty of The union's obligation to act on behalf of all members impartially and in good faith. (Chapter 31)

False imprisonment The intentional restraint of another person without reasonable cause and without her consent. (Chapter 6)

Federal question jurisdiction One of the two main types of civil cases that a United States district court has the power to hear. It involves a federal statute or a constitutional provision. (Chapter 3)

Federalism A form of national government in which power is shared between one central authority and numerous local authorities. (Chapter 1)

Fee simple absolute The greatest possible ownership right in real property, including the right to possess, use, and dispose of the property in any lawful manner. (Chapter 44)

Fee simple defeasible Ownership interest in real property that may terminate upon the occurrence of some limiting event. (Chapter 44)

Felony The most serious crimes, typically those for which the defendant could be imprisoned for more than a year. (Chapter 8)

Fiduciary duty An obligation to behave in a trustworthy and confidential fashion toward the object of that duty. (Chapter 28)

Financing statement A document that a secured party files to give the general public notice that the secured party has a secured interest in the collateral. (Chapter 26)

Firm offer A contract offer that cannot be withdrawn during a stated period. (Chapter 11)

Fixtures Goods that are attached to real estate. (Chapter 26)

Foreign corporation A corporation formed in another state. (Chapter 34)

Foreign Sovereign Immunity Act A federal statute that protects other nations from suit in courts of the United States, except under specified circumstances. (Chapter 9)

Formal rulemaking The process whereby an administrative agency notifies the public of a proposed new rule and then permits a formal hearing, with opportunity for evidence and cross-examination, before promulgating the final rule. (Chapter 4)

Founding Fathers The authors of the United States Constitution, who participated in the Constitutional Convention in Philadelphia in 1787. (Chapter 1)

Framers *See* Founding Fathers. (Chapter 5)

Franchise An arrangement in which the franchisee buys from a franchiser the right to establish a business using the franchiser's trade name and selling the franchiser's products. Typically the franchiser also trains the franchisee in the proper operation of the business. (Chapter 32)

Fraud Deception of another person to obtain money or property from her. (Chapter 6)

Freedom of Information Act (FOIA) A federal statute giving private citizens and corporations access to many of the documents possessed by an administrative agency. (Chapter 4)

Freehold estate The present right to possess property and to use it in any lawful manner. (Chapter 44)

Frustration of purpose After the creation of a contract, an entirely unforeseen event occurs that eliminates the value of the contract for one of the parties. (Chapter 17)

Fully disclosed principal   If the third party in an agency relationship knows the identity of the principal, that principal is fully disclosed. (Chapter 29)

Fundamental rights   In constitutional law, those rights that are so basic that any governmental interference with them is suspect and likely to be unconstitutional. (Chapter 5)

G

GAAP   Generally accepted accounting principles. Rules set by the Financial Accounting Standards Board to be used in preparing financial statements. (Chapter 38)

GAAS   Generally accepted auditing standards. Rules set by the American Institute of Certified Public Accountants (AICPA) to be used in conducting audits. (Chapter 38)

GATT   *See* General Agreement on Tariffs and Trade. (Chapter 9)

General Agreement on Tariffs and Trade (GATT)   A massive international treaty, negotiated in stages between the 1940s and 1994 and signed by over 130 nations. (Chapter 9)

General deterrence   *See* Deterrence. (Chapter 8)

General intangibles   Potential sources of income such as copyrights, patents, trademarks, goodwill and certain other rights to payment. (Chapter 26)

Gift   A voluntary transfer of property from one person to another without consideration. (Chapter 46)

Gift *causa mortis*   A gift made in contemplation of approaching death. (Chapter 46)

Goods   Anything movable, except for money, securities, and certain legal rights. (Chapter 26)

Grantee   The person who receives property, or some interest in it, from the owner. (Chapter 44)

Grantor   (1) An owner who conveys property, or some interest in it. (2) Someone who creates a trust. (Chapter 44)

Greenmail   If a company is threatened with a hostile takeover, its board of directors may offer to buy the stock of the attacker at an above-market price with the hope that the attacker will take her profits and leave the company alone. (Chapter 35)

H

Hacking   Gaining unauthorized access to a computer system. (Chapter 42)

Harmless error   A ruling made by a trial court which an appeals court determines was legally wrong but not fatal to the decision. (Chapter 3)

Heir   Someone who inherits from a decedent who died intestate (that is, without a will). (Chapter 47)

Holder in due course   Someone who has given value for an instrument, in good faith, without notice of outstanding claims or other defenses. (Chapter 23)

Holographic will   A handwritten will that has not been witnessed. (Chapter 47)

Horizontal agreement or merger   An agreement or merger between two potential competitors. (Chapter 39)

Hybrid rulemaking   A method of administrative agency procedure incorporating some elements of formal and some elements of informal rulemaking, typically involving a limited public hearing with restricted rights of testimony and cross-examination. (Chapter 4)

I

Identify   In sales law, to designate the specific goods that are the subject of a contract. (Chapter 22)

Illegal contract   An agreement that is void because it violates a statute or public policy. (Chapter 13)

Illusory promise   An apparent promise that is unenforceable because the promisor makes no firm commitment. (Chapter 12)

Implied authority   When a principal directs an agent to undertake a transaction, the agent has the right to do acts that are incidental to it, usually accompany it, or are reasonably necessary to accomplish it. (Chapter 29)

Implied contract   A binding agreement created not by explicit language but by the informal words and conduct of the parties. (Chapter 10)

Implied warranty   Guarantees created by the Uniform Commercial Code and imposed on the seller of goods. (Chapter 21)

Implied warranty of habitability   A landlord must meet all standards set by the local building code, or otherwise ensure that the premises are fit for human habitation. (Chapter 44)

Import   To transport goods or services into a country. (Chapter 9)

In camera   "In the judge's chambers," meaning that the judge does something out of view of the jury and the public. (Chapter 3)

Incidental damages   The relatively minor costs, such as storage and advertising, that the injured party suffered when responding to a contract breach. (Chapter 18)

Incorporator   The person who signs a corporate charter. (Chapter 34)

Indemnification   A promise to pay someone else's obligations. (Chapter 28)

Independent agency   An administrative agency outside the executive branch of government, such as the Interstate Commerce Commission. (Chapter 4)

Independent contractor   Someone who undertakes tasks for others and whose work is not closely controlled. (Chapter 29)

Indictment   The government's formal charge that a defendant has committed a crime. (Chapter 8)

Indorser   Anyone, other than the issuer or acceptor, who signs an instrument. (Chapter 24)

Infliction of emotional distress   A tort. It can be the *intentional infliction of emotional distress*, meaning that the defendant behaved outrageously and deliberately caused the plaintiff severe psychological injury, or it can be the *negligent infliction of emotional distress*, meaning that the defendant's conduct violated the rules of negligence. (Chapter 6)

Informal rulemaking   The process whereby an administrative agency notifies the public of a proposed new rule and permits comment but is then free to promulgate the final rule without a public hearing. (Chapter 4)

Initial public offering (IPO)   A company's first public sale of securities. (Chapter 37)

Injunction   A court order that a person either do or stop doing something. (Chapter 1)

Instructions or charge   The explanation given by a judge to a jury, outlining the jury's task in deciding a lawsuit and the underlying rules of law the jury should use in reaching its decision. (Chapter 3)

Instruments   Drafts, checks, certificates of deposit and notes. (Chapter 26)

Insurable interest   A person has an insurable interest if she would be harmed by the danger that she has insured against. (Chapter 13)

Insured   A person whose loss is the subject of an insurance policy. (Chapter 47)

Insurer   The person who issues an insurance policy. (Chapter 47)

Integrated contract   A writing that the parties intend as the complete and final expression of their agreement. (Chapter 15)

Intentional tort   An act deliberately performed that violates a legally imposed duty and injures someone. (Chapter 6)

Inter vivos **gift**   A gift made "during life," that is, when the donor is not under any fear of impending death. (Chapter 46)

Inter vivos **trust**   A trust established while the grantor is still living. (Chapter 47)

Interest   A legal right in something, such as ownership or a mortgage or a tenancy. (Chapter 47)

Interference with a contract   *See* Tortious interference with a contract. (Chapter 6)

Interference with a prospective advantage   *See* Tortious interference with a prospective advantage. (Chapter 6)

Internet   An international computer network that connects smaller groups of linked computer networks. (Chapter 42)

Interpretive rules   A formal statement by an administrative agency expressing its view of what existing statutes or regulations mean. (Chapter 4)

Interrogatory   A form of discovery in which one party sends to an opposing party written questions that must be answered under oath. (Chapter 3)

Intestate   Without a will. (Chapter 47)

Inventory   Goods that the seller is holding for sale or lease in the ordinary course of its business. (Chapter 26)

Invitee   Someone who has the right to be on property, such as a customer in a shop. (Chapter 7)

Issue   All direct descendants such as children, grandchildren, and so on. (Chapter 1)

Issuer   The maker of a promissory note or the drawer of a draft. (Chapter 23)

J

Joint and several liability   All members of a group are liable. They can be sued as a group, or any one of them can be sued individually for the full amount owing. (Chapter 33)

Joint liability All members of a group are liable and must be sued together. (Chapter 33)

Joint venture A partnership for a limited purpose. (Chapter 32)

Judgment *non obstante veredicto* (n.o.v.) "Judgment notwithstanding the verdict." A trial judge overturns the verdict of the jury and enters a judgment in favor of the opposing party. (Chapter 3)

Judicial activism The willingness shown by certain courts (and not by others) to decide issues of public policy, such as constitutional questions (free speech, equal protection, etc.) and matters of contract fairness (promissory estoppel, unconscionability, etc.). (Chapter 5)

Judicial restraint A court's preference to abstain from adjudicating major social issues and to leave such matters to legislatures. (Chapter 5)

Judicial review The power of the judicial system to examine, interpret, and even nullify actions taken by another branch of government. (Chapter 4)

Jurisdiction The power of a court to hear a particular dispute, civil or criminal, and to make a binding decision. (Chapter 3)

Jurisprudence The study of the purposes and philosophies of the law, as opposed to particular provisions of the law. (Chapter 1)

Justification A criminal defense in which the defendant establishes that he broke the law to avoid a greater harm. (Chapter 8)

L

Larceny Taking personal property with the intention of preventing the owner from ever using it. (Chapter 8)

Law merchant The body of rules and customs developed by traders and businesspersons throughout Europe from roughly the fifteenth to the eighteenth century. (Chapter 19)

Lease A contract creating a landlord-tenant relationship. (Chapter 45)

Legal positivism The legal philosophy holding that law is what the sovereign says it is, regardless of its moral content. (Chapter 1)

Legal realism The legal philosophy holding that what really influences law is who makes and enforces it, not what is put in writing. (Chapter 1)

Legal remedy Generally, money damages. It is distinguished from equitable remedy, which includes injunctions and other non-monetary relief. (Chapter 18)

Legislative history Used by courts to interpret the meaning of a statute, this is the record of hearings, speeches, and explanations that accompanied a statute as it made its way from newly proposed bill to final law. (Chapter 4)

Legislative rules Regulations issued by an administrative agency. (Chapter 4)

Letter of credit A commercial device used to guarantee payment in international trade, usually between parties that have not previously worked together. (Chapter 9)

Libel *See* Defamation. (Chapter 6)

License To grant permission to another person (1) to make or sell something or (2) to enter on property. (Chapter 44)

Licensee A person who is on the property of another for her own purposes, but with the owner's permission. A social guest is a typical licensee. (Chapter 7)

Lien A security interest created by rule of law, often based on labor that the secured party has expended on the collateral. (Chapter 26)

Life estate An ownership interest in real property entitling the holder to use the property during his lifetime, but which terminates upon his death. (Chapter 44)

Limited liability company An organization that has the limited liability of a corporation but is not a taxable entity. (Chapter 32)

Limited liability limited partnership In a limited liability limited partnership, the general partner is not personally liable for the debts of the partnership. (Chapter 32)

Limited partnership A partnership with two types of partners: (1) limited partners who have no personal liability for the debts of the enterprise nor any right to manage the business, and (2) general partners who are responsible for management and personally liable for all debts. (Chapter 32)

Liquidated damages A contract clause specifying how much a party must pay upon breach. (Chapter 18)

Liquidated debt The amount of the indebtedness is not in dispute. (Chapter 12)

Litigation The process of resolving disputes through formal court proceedings. (Chapter 3)

Living trust A trust established while the grantor is alive. *See inter vivos* trust. (Chapter 47)

Living will An instrument that permits adults to refuse medical treatment. It can also appoint a health care proxy to make medical decisions for a person who has become incompetent. (Chapter 47)

Lockout A management tactic, designed to gain a bargaining advantage, in which the company refuses to allow union members to work (and hence deprives them of their pay). (Chapter 31)

M

Mailbox rule A contract doctrine holding that acceptance is effective upon dispatch, that is, when it is mailed or otherwise taken out of the control of the offeree. (Chapter 11)

Maker The issuer of a promissory note. (Chapter 23)

Material Important or significant. Information that would affect a person's decision if he knew it. (Chapter 14)

Mediation The process of using a neutral person to aid in the settlement of a legal dispute. A mediator's decision is non-binding. (Chapter 3)

Mens rea Guilty state of mind. (Chapter 8)

Merger An acquisition of one company by another. (Chapter 36)

Minor A person under the age of 18. (Chapter 14)

Minority shareholders Shareholders who do not own enough stock to control their corporation. (Chapter 36)

Minute book Records of shareholder meetings and directors' meetings are kept in the corporation's minute book. (Chapter 34)

Mirror image rule A contract doctrine that requires acceptance to be on exactly the same terms as the offer. (Chapter 11)

Misdemeanor A less serious crime, typically one for which the maximum penalty is incarceration for less than a year, often in a jail, as opposed to a prison. (Chapter 8)

Misrepresentation A factually incorrect statement made during contract negotiations. (Chapter 14)

Mitigation One party acts to minimize its losses when the other party breaches a contract. (Chapter 18)

Modify An appellate court order changing a lower court ruling. (Chapter 3)

Money laundering Taking the profits of criminal acts and either (1) using the money to promote more crime or (2) attempting to conceal the money's source. (Chapter 8)

Monopolization A company acquires or maintains a monopoly through the commission of unacceptably aggressive acts. A violation of §2 of the Sherman Act. (Chapter 39)

Mortgage A security interest in real property. (Chapter 44)

Mortgagee A creditor who obtains a security interest in real property, typically in exchange for money given to the mortgagor to buy the property. (Chapter 44)

Mortgagor A debtor who gives a mortgage (security interest) in real property to a creditor, typically in exchange for money used to buy the property. (Chapter 44)

Motion A formal request that a court take some specified step during litigation. A motion to compel discovery is a request that a trial judge order the other party to respond to discovery. (Chapter 3)

Motion to suppress A request that the court exclude evidence because it was obtained in violation of the Constitution. (Chapter 8)

Multinational enterprise A corporation that is doing business in more than one country simultaneously. (Chapter 9)

N

NAFTA *See* North American Free Trade Agreement. (Chapter 9)

National Labor Relations Board (NLRB) The administrative agency charged with overseeing labor law. (Chapter 4)

Nationalization A government's seizure of property or companies. (Chapter 9)

Natural law The theory that an unjust law is no law at all, and that a rule is only legitimate if based on an immutable morality. (Chapter 1)

Negative or dormant aspect of the Commerce Clause The doctrine that prohibits a state from any action that interferes with or discriminates against interstate commerce. (Chapter 5)

Negligence per se Violation of a standard of care set by statute. Driving while intoxicated is illegal; thus, if a drunk driver injures a pedestrian, he has committed negligence per se. (Chapter 7)

Negotiable instrument A type of commercial paper that is freely transferable. (Chapter 23)

Negotiation The transfer of an instrument. To be negotiated, order paper must be indorsed and then delivered to the transferee. For bearer paper, no indorsement is required—it must simply be delivered to the transferee. (Chapter 23)

Nominal damages A token sum, such as one dollar, given to an injured plaintiff who cannot prove damages. (Chapter 18)

Noncompetition agreement A contract in which one party agrees not to compete with another in a stated type of business. (Chapter 10)

North American Free Trade Agreement A commercial association among Canada, the United States, and Mexico designed to eliminate almost all trade barriers. (Chapter 9)

Note An unconditional, written promise that the maker of the instrument will pay a specific amount of money on demand or at a definite time. When issued by a corporation, a note refers to short-term debt, typically payable within five years. (Chapter 23)

Novation If there is an existing contract between *A* and *B*, a novation occurs when *A* agrees to release *B* from all liability on the contract in return for *C*'s willingness to accept *B*'s liability. (Chapter 16)

Nuncupative will An oral will. (Chapter 47)

Obligee The party to a contract who is entitled to receive performance from the other party. (Chapter 16)

Obligor The party to a contract who is required to do something for the benefit of the other party. (Chapter 16)

Obscenity Constitutional law doctrine holding that some works will receive no First Amendment protection because a court determines they depict sexual matters in an offensive way. (Chapter 5)

Offer In contract law, an act or statement that proposes definite terms and permits the other party to create a contract by accepting those terms. (Chapter 11)

Offeree The party in contract negotiations who receives the first offer. (Chapter 11)

Offeror The party in contract negotiations who makes the first offer. (Chapter 11)

Order paper An instrument that includes the words "pay to the order of" or their equivalent. (Chapter 23)

Output contract An agreement that obligates the seller of goods to sell everything he produces during a stated period to a particular buyer. (Chapter 11)

Override The power of Congress or a state legislature to pass legislation despite a veto by a president or governor. A congressional override requires a two-thirds vote in each house. (Chapter 4)

P

Parol evidence Written or oral evidence, outside the language of a contract, offered by one party to clarify interpretation of the agreement. (Chapter 15)

Parol evidence rule In the case of an integrated contract, neither party may use evidence outside the writing to contradict, vary, or add to its terms. (Chapter 15)

Part performance An exception to the statute of frauds permitting a buyer of real estate to enforce an oral contract if she paid part of the price, entered the property, and made improvements, with the owner's knowledge. (Chapter 15)

Partially disclosed principal If the third party in an agency relationship knows that the agent is acting for a principal, but does not know the identity of the principal, that principal is partially disclosed. (Chapter 29)

Partnership An association of two or more persons to carry on as co-owners of a business for profit. (Chapter 33)

Partnership at will A partnership that has no fixed duration. A partner has the right to resign from the partnership at any time. (Chapter 33)

Partnership by estoppel If a person who is not a partner implies that he is a partner or does not object when other people imply it, he is liable as if he really were a partner. (Chapter 33)

Patent The right to the exclusive use of an invention for 20 years. (Chapter 43)

Payable on demand The holder of an instrument is entitled to be paid whenever she asks. (Chapter 23)

Payee Someone who is owed money under the terms of an instrument. (Chapter 23)

***Per se* violation of an antitrust law** An automatic breach. Courts will generally not consider mitigating factors. (Chapter 39)

Peremptory challenge During *voir dire*, a request by one attorney that a prospective juror be excused for an unstated reason. (Chapter 3)

Perfect tender rule A rule permitting the buyer to reject goods if they fail in any respect to conform to the contract. (Chapter 22)

Perfection A series of steps a secured party must take to protect its rights in collateral against people other than the debtor. (Chapter 26)

Personal property All property other than real property. (Chapter 46)

Plain meaning rule In statutory interpretation, the premise that words with an ordinary, everyday significance will be so interpreted, unless there is some apparent reason not to. (Chapter 4)

Pleadings The documents that begin a lawsuit: the complaint, the answer, the counter-claim and reply. (Chapter 3)

Positive aspect of the Commerce Clause The power granted to Congress to regulate commerce between the states. (Chapter 5)

Precedent An earlier case that decided the same legal issue as that presently in dispute, and which therefore will control the outcome of the current case. (Chapter 1)

Predatory pricing A violation of §2 of the Sherman Act in which a company lowers its prices below cost to drive competitors out of business. (Chapter 39)

Preemption The doctrine, based on the Supremacy Clause, by which any federal statute takes priority whenever (1) a state statute conflicts or (2) there is no conflict but Congress indicated an intention to control the issue involved. (Chapter 5)

Preferred stock Owners of preferred stock have a right to receive dividends and liquidation proceeds of the company before common shareholders. (Chapter 34)

Preponderance of the evidence The level of proof that a plaintiff must meet to prevail in a civil lawsuit. It means that the plaintiff must offer evidence that, in sum, is slightly more persuasive than the defendant's evidence. (Chapter 3)

Presentment A holder of an instrument makes a demand for payment. (Chapter 24)

Pretermitted child A child omitted from a parent's will. (Chapter 47)

Prima facie "At first sight." A fact or conclusion that is presumed to be true unless someone presents evidence to disprove it. (Chapter 30)

Principal In an agency relationship, the principal is the person for whom the agent is acting. (Chapter 28)

Privacy Act A federal statute prohibiting federal agencies from divulging to other agencies or organizations information about private citizens. (Chapter 4)

Privity The relationship that exists between two parties who make a contract, as opposed to a third party who, though affected by the contract, is not a party to it. (Chapter 21)

Probable cause In a search and seizure case, it means that the information available indicates that it is more likely than not that a search will uncover particular criminal evidence. (Chapter 8)

Probate The process of carrying out the terms of a will. (Chapter 47)

Procedural due process *See* Due Process Clause. (Chapter 5)

Procedural law The rules establishing how the legal system itself is to operate in a particular kind of case. (Chapter 1)

Proceeds Anything that a debtor obtains from the sale or disposition of collateral. Normally, proceeds refers to cash obtained from the sale of the secured property. (Chapter 26)

Production of documents and things A form of discovery in which one party demands that the other furnish original documents or physical things, relating to the suit, for inspection and copying. (Chapter 3)

Product liability The potential responsibility that a manufacturer or seller has for injuries caused by defective goods. (Chapter 21)

Professional corporation A form of organization that permits professionals (such as doctors, lawyers, and accountants) to incorporate. Shareholders are not personally liable for the torts of other shareholders, or for the contract debts of the organization. (Chapter 32)

Profit The right to enter land belonging to another and take something away, such as minerals or timber. (Chapter 44)

Promissory estoppel A doctrine in which a court may enforce a promise made by the defendant even when there is no contract, if the defendant knew that the plaintiff was likely to rely on the promise, the plaintiff did in fact rely, and enforcement of it is the only way to avoid injustice. (Chapter 10)

Promissory note The maker of the instrument promises to pay a specific amount of money. (Chapter 23)

Promoter The person who creates a corporation by raising capital and undertaking the legal steps necessary for formation. (Chapter 34)

Promulgate To issue a new rule. (Chapter 4)

Prosecution The government's attempt to convict a defendant of a crime by charging him, trying the case, and forcing him to defend himself. (Chapter 8)

Prospectus Under the Securities Act of 1933, an issuer must provide this document to anyone who purchases a security in a public transaction. The prospectus contains detailed information about the issuer and its business, a description of the stock, and audited financial statements. (Chapter 37)

Protective order A court order limiting one party's discovery. (Chapter 3)

Proxy (1) A person whom the shareholder designates to vote in his place. (2) The written form (typically a card) that the shareholder uses to appoint a designated voter. (Chapter 36)

Proxy statement When a public company seeks proxy votes from its shareholders, it must include a proxy statement. This statement contains information about the company, such as a detailed description of management compensation. (Chapter 36)

Publicly traded corporation A company that (1) has completed a public offering under the Securities Act of 1933, or (2) has securities traded on a national exchange, or (3) has 500 shareholders and $10 million in assets. (Chapter 35)

Punitive damages Money awarded at trial not to compensate the plaintiff for harm but to punish the defendant for conduct that the factfinder considers extreme and outrageous. (Chapter 6)

Purchase money security interest A security interest taken by the person who sells the collateral to the debtor, or by a person who advances money so that the debtor may buy the collateral. (Chapter 26)

Q

Quantum meruit "As much as she deserves." The damages awarded in a quasi-contract case. (Chapter 10)

Quasi-contract A legal fiction in which, to avoid injustice, the court awards damages as if a contract had existed, although one did not. (Chapter 10)

Quid pro quo A Latin phrase meaning "this for that." It refers to a form of sexual harassment in which some aspect of a job is made contingent upon sexual activity. (Chapter 30)

Quiet enjoyment A tenant's right to use property without the interference of the landlord. (Chapter 45)

Quorum The number of voters that must be present for a meeting to count. (Chapter 36)

R

Ratification When someone accepts the benefit of an unauthorized transaction or fails to repudiate it once he has learned of it, he is then bound by it. (Chapter 29)

Real property Land, together with certain things associated with it, such as buildings, subsurface rights, air rights, plant life and fixtures. (Chapter 44)

Reasonable doubt The level of proof that the government must meet to convict the defendant in a criminal case. The factfinder must be persuaded to a very high degree of certainty that the defendant did what the government alleges. (Chapter 3)

Reciprocal dealing agreement An agreement under which Company *A* will purchase from Company *B* only if Company *B* also buys from Company *A*. These agreements are rule of reason violations of the Sherman Act. (Chapter 39)

Record date To vote at a shareholders meeting, a shareholder must own stock on the record date. (Chapter 36)

Red herring A preliminary prospectus. (Chapter 37)

Reformation The process by which a court rewrites a contract to ensure its accuracy or viability. (Chapter 18)

Refusal to deal An agreement among competitors that they will not trade with a particular supplier or buyer. Such an agreement is a rule of reason violation of the Sherman Act. (Chapter 39)

Registration statement A document filed with the Securities and Exchange Commission under the Securities Act of 1933 by an issuer seeking to sell securities in a public transaction. (Chapter 37)

Reliance interest A remedy in a contract case that puts the injured party in the position he would have been in had the parties never entered into a contract. (Chapter 18)

Remand The power of an appellate court to return a case to a lower court for additional action. (Chapter 1)

Reply A pleading, filed by the plaintiff in response to a defendant's counter-claim. (Chapter 3)

Repossess A secured party takes collateral because the debtor has defaulted on payments. (Chapter 26)

Repudiation An indication made by one contracting party to the other that it will not perform. (Chapter 22)

Request for admission A form of discovery in which one party demands that the opposing party either admit or deny particular factual or legal allegations. (Chapter 3)

Requirements contract An agreement that obligates a buyer of specified goods to purchase all of the goods she needs during a stated period from a particular seller. (Chapter 11)

Res ipsa loquitur A doctrine of tort law holding that the facts may imply negligence when the defendant had exclusive control of the thing that caused the harm, the accident would not normally have occurred without negligence, and the plaintiff played no role in causing the injury. (Chapter 7)

Resale price maintenance A *per se* violation of the Sherman Act in which a manufacturer enters into an agreement with retailers about the prices they will charge. (Chapter 39)

Rescind To cancel a contract. (Chapter 12)

Respondeat superior A rule of agency law holding that a principal is liable when a servant acting within the scope of employment commits a tort that causes physical harm to a person or property. (Chapter 29)

Restitution Restoring an injured party to its original position. (Chapter 14)

Restitution interest A remedy in a contract case that returns to the injured party a benefit that he has conferred on the other party, which it would be unjust to leave with that person. (Chapter 18)

Restricted security Any stock purchased in a private offering (such as one under Regulation D). (Chapter 37)

Retribution Giving a criminal defendant the punishment he deserves. (Chapter 8)

Reverse The power of an appellate court to overrule a lower court and grant judgment for the party that had lost in the lower court. (Chapter 3)

Revocation The act of disavowing a contract offer, so that the offeree no longer has the power to accept. (Chapter 11)

Rule of reason violation An action that breaches the antitrust laws only if it has an anticompetitive impact. (Chapter 39)

Rulemaking The power of an administrative agency to issue regulations. (Chapter 4)

S

S corporation A corporation that is not a taxable entity. (Chapter 32)

Sale on approval A transfer in which a buyer takes goods intending to use them herself, but has the right to return the goods to the seller. (Chapter 20)

Sale or return A transfer in which the buyer takes the goods intending to resell them, but has the right to return the goods to the original owner. (Chapter 20)

Scienter In a case of securities fraud, the plaintiff must prove that the defendant acted willfully, knowingly, or recklessly. (Chapter 37)

Secondary boycott Picketing, directed by a union against a company, designed to force that company to stop doing business with the union's employer. (Chapter 31)

Security Any purchase in which the buyer invests money in a common enterprise and expects to earn a profit predominantly from the efforts of others. (Chapter 37)

Security agreement A contract in which the debtor gives a security interest to the secured party. (Chapter 26)

Security interest An interest in personal property or fixtures that secures the performance of some obligation. (Chapter 26)

Separation of powers The principle, established by the first three articles of the Constitution, that authority should be divided among the legislative, executive, and judicial branches. (Chapter 5)

Servant An agent whose work is closely controlled by the principal. (Chapter 29)

Service mark A type of trademark used to identify services, not products. (Chapter 43)

Settlor Someone who creates a trust. (Chapter 47)

Sexual harassment Unwanted sexual advances, comments or touching, sufficiently severe to violate Title VII of the 1964 Civil Rights Act. (Chapter 30)

Shilling A seller at auction either bids on his own goods or agrees to cross-bid with a group of other sellers. (Chapter 42)

Short-swing trading Under §16 of the Securities Exchange Act, insiders must turn over to the corporation any profits they make from the purchase and sale or sale and purchase of company securities in a six-month period. (Chapter 37)

Signatory A person, company, or nation that has signed a legal document, such as a contract, agreement, or treaty. (Chapter 9)

Single recovery principle A rule of tort litigation that requires a plaintiff to claim all damages, present and future, at the time of trial, not afterwards. (Chapter 6)

Slander *See* Defamation. (Chapter 6)

Sole proprietorship An unincorporated business owned by a single person. (Chapter 32)

Sovereign immunity The right of a national government to be free of lawsuits brought in foreign courts. (Chapter 9)

Spam Unsolicited commercial or bulk e-mail. ("To spam" is to send such e-mail.) (Chapter 42)

Specific deterrence *See* Deterrence. (Chapter 8)

Specific performance A contract remedy requiring the breaching party to perform the contract, by conveying land or some unique asset, rather than by paying money damages. (Chapter 18)

Stakeholders Anyone who is affected by the activities of a corporation, such as employees, customers, creditors, suppliers, shareholders, and neighbors. (Chapter 35)

Stale check A check presented more than six months after its due date. (Chapter 25)

Stare decisis "Let the decision stand." A basic principle of the common law, it means that precedent is usually binding. (Chapter 1)

Statute A law passed by a legislative body, such as Congress. (Chapter 1)

Statute of frauds This law provides that certain contracts are not enforceable unless in writing. (Chapter 15)

Statute of limitations A statute that determines the period within which a particular kind of lawsuit must be filed. (Chapter 17)

Statute of repose A law that places an absolute limit on when a lawsuit may be filed, regardless of when the defect was discovered. (Chapter 21)

Statutory interpretation A court's power to give meaning to new legislation by clarifying ambiguities, providing limits, and ultimately applying it to a specific fact pattern in litigation. (Chapter 4)

Strict liability A tort doctrine holding to a very high standard all those who engage in ultrahazardous activity (e.g., using explosives) or who manufacture certain products. (Chapter 7)

Strike The ultimate weapon of a labor union, it occurs when all or most employees of a particular plant or employer walk off the job and refuse to work. (Chapter 31)

Strike suit A lawsuit without merit that defendants sometimes settle simply to avoid the nuisance of litigation. (Chapter 36)

Subpoena An order to appear, issued by a court or government body. (Chapter 4)

Subpoena *duces tecum* An order to produce certain documents or things before a court or government body. (Chapter 4)

Substantial performance The promisor performs contract duties well enough to be entitled to his full contract price, minus the value of any defects. (Chapter 17)

Substantive due process *See* Due Process Clause. (Chapter 5)

Substantive law Rules that establish the rights of parties. For example, the prohibition against slander is substantive law, as opposed to procedural law. (Chapter 1)

Summary judgment The power of a trial court to terminate a lawsuit before a trial has begun, on the grounds that no essential facts are in dispute. (Chapter 3)

Supermajority voting Typically, shareholders can approve charter amendments by a majority vote. However, sometimes corporations require more than a majority of shareholders (e.g., 80 percent) to approve certain charter amendments, such as a merger. These provisions are designed to discourage hostile takeovers. (Chapter 35)

Superseding cause An event that interrupts the chain of causation and relieves a defendant from liability based on her own act. (Chapter 7)

Supremacy Clause From Article VI of the Constitution, it declares that federal statutes and treaties take priority over any state law, if there is a conflict between the two or, even absent a conflict, if Congress manifests an intent to preempt the field. (Chapter 5)

T

Takings Clause Part of the Fifth Amendment, it ensures that when any governmental unit takes private property for public use, it must compensate the owner. (Chapter 5)

Tariff A duty imposed on imported goods by the government of the importing nation. (Chapter 9)

Tenancy by the entirety A form of joint ownership available only to married couples. If one member of the couple dies, the property goes automatically to the survivor. Creditors cannot attach the property, nor can one owner sell the property without the other's permission. (Chapter 44)

Tender To make conforming goods available to the buyer. (Chapter 22)

Tender offer A public offer to buy a block of stock directly from shareholders. (Chapter 35)

Term partnership When the partners agree in advance on the duration of a partnership. (Chapter 33)

Testamentary trust A trust created by the grantor's will. (Chapter 47)

Testator Someone who dies having executed a will. (Chapter 47)

Testatrix A female testator. (Chapter 47)

Third party beneficiary Someone who stands to benefit from a contract to which she is not a party. An *intended* beneficiary may enforce such a contract; an *incidental* beneficiary may not. (Chapter 16)

Three-Fifths Clause A clause in Article 1, section 2 of the United States Constitution, now void and regarded as racist, which required that for purposes of taxation and representation, a slave should be counted as three-fifths of a person. (Chapter 5)

Tort A civil wrong, committed in violation of a duty that the law imposes. (Chapter 6)

Tortious interference with a contract A tort in which the defendant deliberately impedes an existing contract between the plaintiff and another. (Chapter 6)

Tortious interference with a prospective advantage A tort in which the defendant deliberately obstructs a developing venture or advantage that the plaintiff has created. (Chapter 6)

Trade acceptance A draft drawn by a seller of goods on the buyer and payable to the seller or some third party. (Chapter 23)

Trade secret A formula, device, process, method, or compilation of information that, when used in business, gives the owner an advantage over competitors who do not know it. (Chapter 43)

Trademark Any combination of words and symbols that a business uses to identify its products or services and that federal law will protect. (Chapter 43)

Treasury stock Stock that has been bought back by its issuing corporation. (Chapter 34)

Trespass A tort committed by intentionally entering land that belongs to someone else, or remaining on the land after being asked to leave. (Chapter 6)

Trial court Any court in a state or federal system that holds formal hearings to determine the facts in a civil or criminal case. (Chapter 3)

Trust An entity that separates legal and beneficial ownership. (Chapter 47)

Tying arrangement A violation of the Sherman and Clayton Acts in which a seller requires that two distinct products be purchased together. The seller uses its significant power in the market for the tying product to shut out a substantial part of the market for the tied product. (Chapter 39)

U

Ultra vires An activity that is not permitted by a corporation's charter. (Chapter 34)

Ultrahazardous activity Conduct that is lawful yet unusual and much more likely to cause injury than normal commercial activity. (Chapter 7)

Unconscionable contract An agreement that a court refuses to enforce because it is fundamentally unfair as a result of unequal bargaining power by one party. (Chapter 13)

Undisclosed principal If a third party in an agency relationship does not know that the agent is acting for a principal, that principal is undisclosed. (Chapter 29)

Undue influence One party so dominates the thinking of another party to a contract that the dominant party cannot truly consent to the agreement. (Chapter 14)

Unfair labor practice An act, committed by either a union or an employer, that violates the National Labor Relations Act, such as failing to bargain in good faith. (Chapter 31)

Unilateral contract A binding agreement in which one party has made an offer that the other can accept only by action, not words. (Chapter 10)

Unliquidated debt A claimed debt that is disputed, either because the parties disagree over whether there is in fact a debt or because they disagree over the amount. (Chapter 12)

Usury Charging interest at a rate that exceeds legal limits. (Chapter 13)

Valuation A process by which the Customs Service determines the fair value of goods being imported, for purposes of imposing a duty. (Chapter 9)

Verdict The decision of the factfinder in a case. (Chapter 3)

Vertical agreement or merger An agreement or merger between two companies at different stages of the production process, such as when a company acquires one of its suppliers or distributors. (Chapter 39)

Veto The power of the president to reject legislation passed by Congress, terminating the bill unless Congress votes by a $^2/_3$ majority to override. (Chapter 4)

Void agreement An agreement that neither party may legally enforce, usually because the purpose of the bargain was illegal or because one of the parties lacked capacity to make it. (Chapter 10)

Voidable contract An agreement that, because of some defect, may be terminated by one party, such as a minor, but not by both parties. (Chapter 10)

Voir dire The process of selecting a jury. Attorneys for the parties and the judge may inquire of prospective jurors whether they are biased or incapable of rendering a fair and impartial verdict. (Chapter 3)

Warranty A guarantee that goods will meet certain standards. (Chapter 21)

Warranty of fitness for a particular purpose An assurance under the Uniform Commercial Code that the goods are fit for the special purpose for which the buyer intends them and of which the seller is aware. (Chapter 21)

Warranty of merchantability An assurance under the Uniform Commercial Code that the goods are fit for their ordinary purpose. (Chapter 21)

Whistleblower Someone who discloses wrongful behavior. (Chapter 30)

Winding up The process whereby the assets of a partnership are sold and the proceeds distributed. (Chapter 33)

World Wide Web A decentralized collection of documents containing text, pictures and sound that is accessible from Internet sites. It is a sub-network of the Internet. (Chapter 42)

Writ An order from a government compelling someone to do a particular thing. (Chapter 1)

Table of Cases

Y

Z

Index

M